INTERNATIONAL LITERARY MARKET PLACE 1988–89

INTERNATIONAL LITERARY MARKET PLACE 1988–89

R. R. BOWKER COMPANY
New York & London, 1988

Published by R. R. Bowker Company,
245 West 17th Street,
New York, N.Y. 10011

Copyright © 1988 by Reed Publishing USA, a division of Reed
Holdings, Inc.
Published by R. R. Bowker Division of Reed Publishing, USA

All rights reserved.
Reproduction of this work, in whole or in part,
without written permission of the publisher is prohibited.

International Literary Market Place may not be copied, in whole
or in part, for use as a mailing list or for incorporation into
a list available for rent, exchange or sale to another. Reed Publishing
USA retains exclusive right to rent or exchange this list.

International Standard Book Number 0-8352-2469-4
International Standard Serial Number 0074-6827
Library of Congress Catalog Card Number 77-70295

Printed and bound in the United States of America

The publishers do not assume and hereby
disclaim any liability to any party for
any loss or damage caused by errors or
omissions in *International Literary
Market Place*, whether such errors or
omissions result from negligence,
accident or any other cause.

Computer typeset by Millford Reprographics International Ltd, Luton, England

Contents

The material for each country or territory is grouped under a series of sub-headings which appear always in the same order, and the omission of any of them from a particular country or territory implies that no information is available. The headings are as follows:

General Information (language, population, currency, etc)
Book Trade Organizations
Book Trade Reference Books and Journals
Publishers
Remainder Dealers
Literary Agents
Book Clubs
Major Booksellers
Major Libraries
Library Associations
Library Reference Books and Journals
Literary Associations and Societies
Literary Periodicals
Literary Prizes
Translation Agencies and Associations

Preface	vii
Abbreviations	viii
Afghanistan	1
Albania	1
Algeria	1
Angola	2
Argentina	2
Australia	9
Austria	25
Bahamas	34
Bahrain	34
Bangladesh	34
Barbados	35
Belgium	35
Belize	47
Benin	47
Bermuda	47
Bolivia	48
Botswana	49
Brazil	49
Brunei	60
Bulgaria	60
Burkina Faso	62
Burma	62
Burundi	63
United Republic of Cameroun	63
Central African Republic	64
Chad	65
Channel Islands	65
Chile	65
People's Republic of China	67
Colombia	69
Popular Republic of Congo	72
Costa Rica	72
Cuba	73
Cyprus	74
Czechoslovakia	75
Denmark	79
Dominican Republic	86
Ecuador	87
Egypt	88
El Salvador	90
Ethiopia	90
Fiji	91
Finland	92
France	96
French Guiana	122
French Polynesia	122
Republic of Gabon	122
The Gambia	122
German Democratic Republic	123
Federal Republic of Germany	128
Ghana	180
Gibraltar	182
Greece	182
Guatemala	185
Guinea	186
Guyana	186
Haiti	186
Honduras	187
Hong Kong	187
Hungary	190
Iceland	193
India	195
Indonesia	216
Iran	220
Iraq	220
Republic of Ireland	221
Isle of Man	225
Israel	225
Italy	232
Ivory Coast	253
Jamaica	254
Japan	255
Jordan	266
Kampuchea	266
Kenya	266
Democratic People's Republic of Korea	268
Republic of Korea	269
Kuwait	272
Laos	272
Lebanon	272
Lesotho	274
Liberia	274
Libya	274
Liechtenstein	275
Grandy Duchy of Luxembourg	275
Macau	276
Democratic Republic of Madagascar	276
Malawi	277
Malaysia	278
Mali	281
Malta	281
Martinique	282
Mauritania	282
Mauritius	282
Mexico	283
Monaco	289
Mongolian People's Republic	290
Montserrat	290
Morocco	290
Mozambique	291
Namibia	291
Nepal	292
Netherlands	292
Netherlands Antilles	306
New Caledonia	307
New Zealand	307
Nicaragua	313
Niger	314
Nigeria	314
Norway	320
Pakistan	324
Panama	328
Papua New Guinea	329
Paraguay	329
Peru	330
Philippines	331
Poland	334
Portugal	339
Puerto Rico	344
Qatar	345
Réunion	346
Romania	346
Rwanda	348
Saudi Arabia	348
Senegal	349
Seychelles	350
Sierra Leone	350
Republic of Singapore	350
Somalia	354
Republic of South Africa	354
Spain	362
Sri Lanka	378
Sudan	379
Suriname	380
Swaziland	380
Sweden	381
Switzerland	391
Syria	406
Taiwan	407
Tanzania	408
Thailand	410
Togo	412
Trinidad and Tobago	412
Tunisia	413
Turkey	414
Uganda	416
Union of Soviet Socialist Republics	417
United Arab Emirates	421
United Kingdom	421
Upper Volta	490
Uruguay	490
Vatican City State	492
Venezuela	492
Socialist Republic of Viet Nam	494
Western Samoa	495
People's Democratic Republic of the Yemen	495
Yemen Arab Republic	495
Yugoslavia	495
Zaire	501
Zambia	503
Zimbabwe	504
INTERNATIONAL SECTION	507
Copyright Conventions	507
International Organizations	507
International Bibliography	514
International Literary Prizes	517
The ISBN System	523
BOOK TRADE CALENDAR	528
INDEX	537

Preface

The western publishing world in 1987–88 continued the movement of the previous two years towards yet larger conglomerates. This naturally has led to massive reorganizations within expanded groups, although most imprints continue at least in name, many in function, and a large number with a high degree of autonomy. The enthusiasm which publishing generates has ensured that all this activity has not deterred, and in fact has often encouraged, the formation of new publishing companies — some starting from completely new bases, others with a nucleus of established authors showing their preferences. Concentration of ownership is also apparent amongst booksellers.

ILMP 1988–89 has recorded such activities until the time of going to press. Doubtless the coming year will produce changes within large groupings, but it would be hard to imagine the takeover momentum continuing at its recent rate.

All 11,860 entrants in *ILMP* are annually sent copy of their existing entries for amendment. Where replies are not received directly and follow-ups not answered, other sources are used to ascertain the continued existence of entrants. The responses and other gathered data for *ILMP 1988–89* have resulted in a 39 per cent update of the information contained in the previous edition, including the deletion of 208 organizations which had ceased operating; this was more than offset by the number of new entries included. General information regarding individual countries and in such as the ISBN section is also updated on a continuing basis.

ILMP entrants are thanked for their co-operation in replying to requests for information. For interpreting and formulating this information most grateful acknowledgement goes to the invaluable team of Pat Brown, Martha Gordon-Smith, Rosemary Harley, Brenda Lynch and Anne Marshall. Comments and suggestions from users of *ILMP* are always welcome and should be sent to the Editorial Department, R R Bowker, Borough Green, Sevenoaks, Kent TN15 8PH, UK.

LINDA REDMAN
Consultant Editor

Abbreviations

+	Publisher's indication of interest in buying/selling international rights or editions
*	questionnaire not returned for this edition
AB	aktiebolag (= limited company)
AE	anónymos etereía
AG	Aktiengesellschaft (= public limited company)
al	aleja
Apdo	apartado (= post-box)
ApS	anpartsselskab (= private limited company)
A/S	(Norwegian) aksjeselskap, (Swedish) aktieselskab, (= limited company)
AS	anonim sirketi
ASBL	association sans but lucratif (= non-profit-making society)
Ave	(English, French) avenue, (Portuguese, Spanish) avenida
Bldg	building
Blvd	(Bulgarian, Romanian) bulevard, (English, French) boulevard
BP	boîte postale (= post-box)
BV	besloten vennootschap (= private limited company)
C	compagnía (= company)
CA	compañía anónima (= public limited company)
CEDEX	Courrier d'entreprise à distribution exceptionnelle
CFA	Communauté financière africaine
CFP	comptoirs français du Pacifique
Cia	companhia (= company)
Cía	compañía (= company)
Cie	compagnie (= company)
Co	(English) company, county, (German) Kompanie
c/o	care of
CP	(Italian) casetta postale, (Portuguese) caixa postal, (= post-box)
CV	commanditaire vennootschap (= limited partnership)
Dept	department
Dir	director
EE	'eterórruthmos 'etaireía
eV	eingetragener Verein (= registered society)
ext	extension
GmbH	Gesellschaft mit beschränkter Haftung (= private limited company)
Inc	incorporated
ISBN	international standard book number
Jl	jalan (= street)
KG	Kommanditgesellschaft (= partnership)
KK	kabushiki kaisha (= public limited company)
Lda	limitida (= limited)
Ltd	limited
Ltda	limitada (= limited)
Man Dir	managing director
Nachf	Nachfolger(s) (= successor(s))
nám	náměstí (= square)
NV	naamloze vennootschap (= public limited company)
OE	'omórruthmos 'etaireía
of	oficina (= office)
Off	office
Oy	osakeyhitiö (= limited company)
pA	per Adresse (= care of)
Pl	(Bulgarian) ploshtad, (English, French) place, (Polish) plac, (Russian) ploshchad', (Spanish) plaza
PL	postilokero (= post-box)
PLC	public limited company
PMB	private mail bag
PO	Post Office
Pty	proprietary
PVBA	personenvennootschap met beperkte aansprakelijkheid (= private limited company)
Pvt	private
qqv	quae vide (= which see, plural)
qv	quod vide (= which see, singular)
Rd	road
SA	(French) société anonyme, (Portuguese) sociedade anônima, (Spanish) sociedad anónima (= public limited company)
Sàrl	société à responsabilité limitée (= private limited company)
SAS	società in accomandita semplice (= limited partnership)
SCA	sociedad en comandita por acciónes (= limited partnership)
S de RL	sociedad de responsabilidad limitada (= private limited company)
Sdn Bhd	sendirian berhad (= private limited company)
SL	sociedad de responsabilidad limitada (= private limited company)
SNC	società in nome collettivo (= partnership)
SpA	società per azioni (= public limited company)
SPRL	société de personnes à responsabilité (= private limited company)
SRL	(Italian) società à responsabilità limita, (Spanish) sociedad de responsabilidad limitada, (= private limited company)
St	Saint, street
STD	subscriber trunk dialling
Str	(Danish) straede, (Dutch) straat, (German) Strasse, (Icelandic) strǽti, (Italian) strada, (Romanian) stradä (= street)
Sq	square
Tel	telephone number
u	utca (= street)
UCC	Universal Copyright Convention
ul	(Bulgarian) ulitsa, (Czech) ulice, (Polish) ulica, (Romanian) uliță, (Russian) ulitsa, (Serbocroatian, Slovak, Slovene) ulica (= street)
VEB	volkseigener Betrieb (= people's enterprise)
VZW	vereniging zonder winstoogmerk (= non-profit-making society)

A limited company is a corporation owned by shareholders (or stockholders) who may contribute capital to the company but are not otherwise generally liable for its debts.

A public company may invite anyone to become a shareholder, and its shares (or stock) are usually traded on a stock exchange. A private, or proprietary, company has a restricted number of shareholders and its shares are not traded on a stock exchange.

The owners of a partnership are generally liable for its debts, but a limited partnership has some owners who only contribute capital and are not otherwise liable for debts.

Afghanistan

General Information

Note: No replies were received to questionnaires sent to Afghanistan for this edition of *International Literary Market Place*. The information given in the 1987-88 edition has been repeated here but should be treated with caution.

Language: Pushtu and Persian
Religion: Sunni Muslim with approximately 1 million Shiite Muslim
Population: 15.9 million
Bank Hours: 0800-1200, 1300-1600 Saturday-Wednesday; 0800-1300 Thursday
Shop Hours: 0800-about 1800 Saturday-Thursday
Currency: 100 puls = 1 afghani
Copyright: Florence (see International section)

Publishers

Book Publishing Institute*, Herat
Subjects: Fiction, History, Religion
Founded: 1970 (by cooperation of Government Press and citizens of Herat)

Franklin Book Programs Inc*, PO Box 332, Kabul

Government Press*, Kabul
Subjects: Afghan history & literature, Textbooks, Newspapers, Magazines, Journals
Founded: 1870
Miscellaneous: Under supervision of Ministry of Information and Culture

Historical Society of Afghanistan*, Kabul
Dir: M Yakub Wahidi
Founded: 1931
Subjects: Afghan History and Culture
Publications: Afghanistan (in English, French and German); *Aryana* (in Dari and Pushtu), both quarterly

Ministry of Culture and Information, Book Publishing Department*, Kabul

Ministry of Education, Department of Educational Publications*, Kabul
Subjects: Primary & Secondary Textbooks in Pushtu and Dari

Pushtu Toulana, Afghan Academy*, Kabul
Subjects: Pushtu Language

Major Booksellers

Behzad Bookshop*, Welayat Ave, Kabul

Behzad Bookstore*, Shop No 122, Chahra-hi-Malikasghar, Kabul

Royal Afghanistan Press Department*, Kabul

University of Kabul Bookstores*, Ali-Abad, Kabul

Major Libraries

Institute of Education Library, Kabul University*, Kabul

Ministry of Education Library*, Kabul

Library of the **National Bank***, Kabul

Library of the **Press Department***, Kabul

Public Library*, Kabul

Library of the **Royal Palace***, Kabul

University Library*, Kabul

Albania

General Information

Language: Albanian
Religion: Islamic, but religious observances are discouraged by the government
Population: 2.7 million
Currency: 100 qintars = 1 lek
Export/Import Information: Importation of books is through State Trading Organization, Nah Shperndarjes Të (or NST) Librit, Blvd e Pezës, Tirana. Correspondence should be in Italian or French. Copies of correspondence to Albanian Legation in Rome. Import licences and strict exchange controls

Book Trade Organizations

Drejtoria Quëndrore e Përhapjes dhe e Propagandimit të Librit*, Tirana
Central Administration for the Dissemination and Propagation of the Book

Union of Writers and Artists of Albania*, 37 Z Baboci St, Tirana
Chairman: Dritero Agolli
Publications: Nëntori (monthly); *Drita* (weekly); *Les Lettres Albanaises* (published in French, quarterly); *Kultura Popullore* (published in Albanian, twice a year; French, annually)

Book Trade Reference Journals

Bibliografia kombëtare e Republikës Popullore, Libri Shqipërisë, Botim i Bibliotekës Kombëtare, Tirana
Albanian National Bibliography of Books

Bibliografia kombëtare e Republikës Popullore, Periodiku Shqipërisë, Botim i Bibliotekës Kombëtare, Tirana
Albanian National Bibliography of Periodicals

Libri (The Book), Rruga Konferenca e Pezës, Tirana

Publishers

'8' Nentori Publishing House*, Tirana
Subjects: Albania, Albanian Party of Work publications

N I S H Shtypshkronjave 'Mihal Duri'*, Tirana
Subjects: Government Publications, Education, Politics, Law

Naim Frasheri*, Tirana
Subject: Books in foreign languages

Ndërmarrja e Botimeve Ushtarake*, Tirana
Subjects: Military, Technology

Major Booksellers

Nah Shperndarjes Të Librit (NST)*, Blvd e Pezës, Tirana
State trading organization controlling importation of books

Ndërmarrja e Përhapjes së Librit*, Konfercenca e Pezës, Tirana Tel: 3323
Cable Add: Ndlibri Tirana
Distributor of books, journals and newspapers published in Albania in Albanian and foreign languages

Major Libraries

Botim i **Bibliotekës Kombëtare**, Tirana
Tel: 5887
National Library
Dir: Valdete Sala
Publications: Bibliografia kombëtare e Republikës Popullore, Libri Shqipërisë (Albanian National Bibliography of Books); *Bibliografia kombëtare e Republikës Popullore, Periodiku Shqipërisë* (Albanian National Bibliography of Periodicals)

Biblioteka **Shkencore e Universitetit Shtetëror të Tiranës***, Tirana
Scientific Library of the State University of Tirana

Shkodër Public Library*, Shkodër

Library Association

Council of Libraries*, Rruga 'Abdi Toptani', No 3, Tirana Tel: 7984/7823
President: M Domi

Literary Periodicals

Drita (weekly), Union of Writers and Artists of Albania, 37 Z Baboci St, Tirana

Kultura Popullore, Union of Writers and Artists of Albania, 37 Z Baboci St, Tirana
Published in Albanian, twice a year; French, annually

Les Lettres Albanaises, Union of Writers and Artists of Albania, 37 Z Baboci St, Tirana
Published in French, quarterly

Nëntori (monthly), Union of Writers and Artists of Albania, 37 Z Baboci St, Tirana

Shejzat (Pleiades), Piazza della Balduina 59, I-00136 Rome, Italy
Albanian language and literature

Algeria

General Information

Language: Arabic. French is the language of business and administration
Religion: Islamic
Population: 18.9 million
Bank Hours: 0900-1500 or 1600 Saturday-Wednesday
Shop Hours: 0900-1200, 1500-1900 Monday-Saturday
Currency: 100 centimes = 1 Algerian dinar
Export/Import Information: Books may be imported or exported only by or with permission of SNED State Monopoly, 3 blvd Zirout Yousef, BP 49, Alger Strasbourg. There are also quota restrictions. Permission to import usually entitles holder to obtain necessary foreign exchange; strict controls are in effect. Documentation formalities are rigidly enforced
Copyright: UCC (see International section)

Publishers

Publishing in Algeria is carried out by the following State monopoly:

2 ALGERIA — ARGENTINA

Enterprise nationale du Livre (ENAL)+*,
3 blvd Zirout Youcef, BP 49, Algiers
Tel: 639712   Cable Add: Sneda Alger
Telex: 53845 Sneda
Dir-General: Seghir Benamar; *Editorial:*
Abdel Krim Saïghi, Abdel Kader M'Silti
Subjects: General Fiction, General Non-fiction, Belles Lettres, Poetry, Biography, History, Africana, Philosophy, Religion, Juveniles, Arabic language & literature, French language, Dictionaries, Paperbacks, General & Social Science, University & Secondary Textbooks, Scientific & Technical, Sport, Travel
Bookshops: Librairies ENAL (Enterprise nationale du Livre) (qv under Major Booksellers)
Founded: 1983 (SNED 1966)
Miscellaneous: Previously Société nationale d'Edition et de Diffusion (SNED)

Société nationale d'Edition et de Diffusion (SNED), now Enterprise nationale du Livre (ENAL) (qv)

Major Booksellers

Librairies **E N A L** (Enterprise nationale du Livre)*, 3 blvd Zirout Youcef, Algiers
Tel: 639643
32 bookshops throughout Algeria
Sole importer, exporter and distributor of books and periodicals
Owned by: Enterprise nationale du Livre (ENAL) (qv)

Librairie **'Maison des Livres'***, 12 rue Ali Boumendjel, Algiers   Tel: 630067
Manager: Mohamed Seghir Oustani

Librairie du **Tiers Monde***, pl Emir Abdelkader, Algiers

Major Libraries

Archives nationales*, Palais du Gouvernement, Esplanade d'Afrique, Algiers

Bibliothèque centrale municipale*, 12 rue du 24 Février, Algiers

Bibliothèque municipale de Constantine*, Hôtel de Ville, Constantine

Bibliothèque municipale d'Oran*, 24 rue Dorgham Adda, Oran

Bibliothèque nationale*, ave du Docteur Frantz Fanon, Algiers   Tel: 630632/631049
Dir: Mahmoud-Agha Bouayed
Publications include: Bibliographie de l'Algérie (published in Arabic and French, twice a year)

Centre culturel français de Constantine, Bibliothèque*, 1 blvd de l'Indépendance, Constantine   Tel: 933563   Telex: 92745 Cefco
Librarian: Louys Etienne
Publications include: L'Esthétique de Baudelaire; Antonin Artauol; Boris Vian et la chanson

Centre culturel français d'Oran, Bibliothèque*, 112 rue Larbi Ben M'Hidi, Oran   Tel: 392049/393568
Chief Librarian: Eric Besnier

Ecole nationale polytechnique, Bibliothèque*, ave Pasteur, El-Harrach, Algiers

Institut d'etudes politiques et de l'information, Bibliothèque*, 37 rue Larbi Ben M'Hidi, Algiers
Chief Librarian: Ms Z Lemkami

Institut national agronomique, Bibliothèque*, El-Harrach   Tel: 761353/761987
Chief Librarian: Rosa Issolah

Institut Pasteur d'Algérie, Bibliothèque*, rue du Dr Laveran, Algiers   Tel: 653496
Chief Librarian: Mrs F Rafat

Bibliothèque universitaire, **Université d'Alger***, 2 rue Didouche Mourad, Algiers
Tel: 640215   Telex: 5385
Librarian: Zoulikha Bekaddour

Bibliothèque de l'**Université de Constantine***, BP 325, Constantine (Located at: Route de Ain el Bey, Constantine)   Tel: 691125   Telex: 92436
Chief Librarian: Sari Mahmoud

Université d'Oran, Bibliothèque*, BP 16, Es Sahia, Oran

Library Association

Institut de Bibliothéconomie et des Sciences documentaires*, Université d'Alger, 2 rue Didouche Mourad, Algiers
Institute of Library Management and Documentary Science

Library Reference Journal

Bibliographie de l'Algërie, Bibliothèque nationale, ave du Docteur Frantz Fanon, Algiers
Published in Arabic and French, twice a year

Literary Associations and Societies

Union des Ecrivains algériens*, 12 rue Ali Boumendjel, Algiers
Union of Algerian Writers

Literary Prize

Union des Ecrivains algériens*,
Awards annual literary prize for fiction, 10,000 Algerian dinars. Enquiries to Union des Ecrivains algériens, 12 rue Ali Boumendjel, Algiers

Angola

General Information

Note: No replies were received to questionnaires sent to Angola for this edition of *International Literary Market Place*. The information given in the 1987-88 edition has been repeated here but should be treated with caution.

Language: Portuguese, Bantu languages
Religion: Christian, Animist
Population: 7.1 million
Currency: 100 centavos = 1 kwanza
Export/Import Information: No tariff on books and advertising. Very restricted issuance of import licences. Advertising matter is currently given considerably lower priority. Exchange controls

Book Trade Organization

União dos Escritores Angolanos*, CP 2767, Luanda   Tel: 22155
Union of Angolan Writers
Secretary-General: António Cardoso

Publishers

Nova Editorial **Angolana** SARL*, CP 1225, Luanda
Man Dir: Pombo Fernandes
Subjects: General Books, Educational Books
Founded: 1935

Lello & Cia Lda*, CP 1245, Luanda
Bookshop: See under Major Booksellers
Subjects: General Fiction & Non-fiction, Secondary & Primary Textbooks

Major Booksellers

Livraria **4 Fevereiro***, Largo D João IV, CP 1245, Luanda   Tel: 32678

Argente, Sentos & Cia Lda*, CP 1314, Luanda

Lello & Cia Lda*, CP 1300, Luanda
Also Publisher (qv)

Livraria **Magalhães** Sarl*, CP 70, Lobito
Tel: 2241   Cable Add: Aljoma   Telex: 8217 Aljoma
Manager: M Magalhães

Major Libraries

Biblioteca Municipal*, CP 1227, Luanda
Librarian: Alberto Serra

Biblioteca **Nacional** Central de Angola*, CP 2915, Luanda   Tel: 37317
Director: Maria Gabriela Cardoso da Silva Antunes
Publication: Novas (News)

Direccão dos Serviços de Geologia e Minas de Angola Biblioteca*, CP 3244, Luanda

Universidade de Luanda Biblioteca*, CP 815, Luanda   Tel: 764
Librarian: A C Ferraz Correia

Library Reference Journal

Novas (News), Biblioteca Nacional Central de Angola, CP 2915, Luanda

Argentina

General Information

Language: Spanish
Religion: Roman Catholic
Population: 27.1 million
Bank Hours: 1000-1600 Monday-Friday
Shop Hours: 0900-1900 Monday-Saturday
Currency: 1,000 pesos = 1 austral
Export/Import Information: Import licences required, to obtain which importers must make advance payment of the import duties that are assessed mainly ad valorem on the CIF value. However, no import duties on books or similar material
Copyright: UCC, Berne, Buenos Aires (see International section)

Book Trade Organizations

Cámara Argentina de Publicaciones*, Reconquista 1011 – 6° piso, 1003 Buenos Aires Tel: (01) 3116855
Argentine Publications Association
President: Agustin dos Santos; *Manager:* Luis Francisco Houlin

Cámara Argentina del Libro*, Ave Belgrano 1580 – 6° piso, 1093 Buenos Aires Tel: (01) 388383
Argentine Book Association
Secretary: Amadeo G Sisco

Federación Argentina de Librerías, Papelerías y Actividades Afines*, Balcarce 179-183, Rosario, 2000 Santa Fe
Argentine Federation of Bookstores, Stationers and Related Activities
President: Jesús Gonzalez

S A D E (Sociedad Argentina de Escritores)*, Uruguay 1371, 1016 Buenos Aires Tel: (01) 413520/420773
Association of Argentine Writers
Dir: Horatio E Tarri
Publication: Boletín de la SADE (twice a month)

Sociedad General de Autores de la Argentina*, Pacheco de Melo 1818-20, Buenos Aires Tel: (01) 421227
Argentine Society of Authors

Standard Book Numbering Agency*, Cámara Argentina del Libro, Ave Belgrano 1580 – 6° piso, 1093 Buenos Aires Tel: (01) 388383
ISBN Administrator: Amadeo G Sisco

Publishers

A Z Editora SA*, Paraguay 1536, 1057 Buenos Aires Tel: (01) 446832/410845
Man Dir: José Rodolfo Carozzo; *Production:* Aníbal Emrique Villalba
Subjects: Law, Economics, History, Psychology
Founded: 1976

Editorial **Abacacía** SRL*, Lavalle 1294, 1048 Buenos Aires Tel: (01) 354161
Cable Add: Abacacía
Man Dir: Alfonso Barrio; *Editorial:* Rosa Linda Denari; *Sales:* María Magdalena Campañaro; *Production:* Tristán Alfredo Torres; *Publicity:* María Teresa Barrio
Branch Off: San Isidro, Ave Libertador Gral San Martín 14 – 665 – local 8, Acassuso, 1640 Buenos Aires
Subjects: Law, Economics, Finance
Founded: 1979
ISBN Publisher's Prefix: 950-9148

Editorial **Abaco** de Rodolfo de Palma SRL*, Tucumán 1429 – 4°D, 1050 Buenos Aires Tel: (01) 401675
Man Dir & Editorial: Rodolfo Depalma; *Sales:* James Farbinger; *Production:* Marcos José Azubel; *Psychology Section:* Daniel P Gómez Dupertuis
Branch Off: Centenera 461, Buenos Aires
Subjects: Law, Economics, Sociology, Philosophy, History, Psychology
Founded: 1975

Editorial **Abeledo** Perrot SAE e I+*, Lavalle 1280/1328, 1048 Buenos Aires Tel: (01) 352848
Man Dirs: Juan Carlos Abeledo, Emilio José Perrot; *Sales Dir:* Carlos Alberto Pazos
Subject: Law
Bookshop: At above address
1985: 57 titles *Founded:* 1901
ISBN Publisher's Prefix: 950-20

Editorial **Abril** SA+, Ave Belgrano 1580 – 4°, 1093 Buenos Aires Tel: (01) 377355
Telex: 22630 Ryela
Man Dir, Editor, Sales, Publicity: Roberto M Ares; *Rights & Permissions:* Alberto Cervetto
Editorial Huemul SA is the division of the company producing secondary & primary school textbooks
Subjects: Fiction, Non-fiction, Children's, Textbooks (Huemul)
1986: 242 titles *Founded:* 1961
ISBN Publisher's Prefix: 950-10

Editorial **Acme** SA+*, Santa Magdalena 633, 1277 Buenos Aires Tel: (01) 282014
Man Dir: Emilio I González
Subjects: General Fiction, Belles Lettres, Biography, How-to, Juveniles, Paperbacks, Technical, University & Primary Textbooks
Founded: 1949

Aguilar SA*, Balcarce 363, 1064 Buenos Aires Tel: (01) 301197/309887
Man Dir: Manuel Rodríguez; *Sales Dir:* Rosa Elena Comes
Parent Company: Aguilar SA de Ediciones, Spain (qv)
Branch Off: 9 de Julio 231, Córdoba
Subjects: Philosophy, Literature, Art, Psychology, Economics, Technical, Juveniles, Maps and Cartographical Materials
Founded: 1946

Librería **Akadia** Editorial+, Paraguay 2078, 1121 Buenos Aires Tel: (01) 8218664/8541345
Man Dir: José F Patlallan
Subject: Medicine
Bookshop: At above address
Founded: 1967

Editorial **Albatros** SRL*, Lavalle 3975, 1190 Buenos Aires Tel: (01) 861215
Man Dir: Roberto R Canevaro
Subjects: Agriculture, Animal Care & Breeding, Technical, How-to, Social Sciences, Medicine, University Textbooks
Founded: 1967

Editorial **Alfa** Argentina SA*, Defensa 599 – 3° piso, 1065 Buenos Aires Tel: (01) 331199/341473
Man Dir: Leonardo Milla; *Manager:* Héctor Allegrini
Subjects: General Fiction, Literature, Philosophy, Psychology, University Textbooks
Founded: 1971

Editorial Rodolfo **Alonso**, Rosetti 2707 esq Ricardo Gutiérrez, 1636 Olivos Tel: 7976312
Man Dir: Rodolfo Alonso; *Sales Manager:* Raquel Rebaudi Basavilbaso
Subjects: General Fiction & Non-fiction
Founded: 1968

Editorial **Américalee** SRL+*, Andonaegui 1138, 1427 Buenos Aires Tel: (01) 511491/522167
Man Dir: Héctor E Landolfi; *Sales Dir:* Josefa A S de Landolfi
Subjects: Technical Sciences, Sports, Cooking
Founded: 1939

Editorial **Americana***, Brasil 675, 1154 Buenos Aires Tel: (01) 238862
Man Dir: Manuel Rey Tosar
Subjects: History, Politics, Social Sciences, Arts, Fiction

Amorrortu Editores SA+, Paraguay 1225 – 7° piso, 1057 Buenos Aires Tel: (01) 3938812/3938869
Man Dir: Horacio de Amorrortu
Subjects: Anthropology & Religion, Economy, Philosophy, Psychology, Psychoanalysis, Education, Sociology, Argentine current affairs
Founded: 1967

Ediciones **Andromeda***, Mexico 625 – 1° piso, 1097 Buenos Aires Tel: (01) 308280
Man Dir, Rights & Permissions: Carlos Samonta; *Editorial:* Jorge A Sanchez
Subjects: General Fiction, Literature
Founded: 1975

Arbó SAC e I+*, Ave Martín García 653, 1268 Buenos Aires Tel: (01) 3620643/3620747
Man Dir: Ariel Arbó; *Technical Dir:* J M Barcala; *Publicity:* Clotilde E H de Arbó
Subjects: Science & Technology, Electronics & Telecommunications
Founded: 1912
ISBN Publisher's Prefix: 950-9022

Asociación Bautista Argentina de Publicaciones*, Rivadavia 3464, 1203 Buenos Aires Tel: (01) 888938/888924
Man Dir: Hans Iver Jorgensen; *Assistant Manager:* Emanuel Benavídez; *Editorial Dir:* Arnoldo Canclini
Branch Offs: San Martín 1572, 2000 Rosario, Santa Fe; Tucumán 351, 5000 Córdoba; San Martín 2242, 5500 Mendoza
Subject: Religion
Founded: 1906

Asociación Educacionista Argentina, see Editorial Stella

Editorial **Astrea** de Alfredo y Ricardo Depalma SRL, Lavalle 1208, 1048 Buenos Aires Tel: (01) 351880/354203
Man Dir: Alfredo Depalma; *Sales Dir:* Ricardo Depalma
Associate Company: Ediciones La Bastilla (qv)
Subjects: Law, Sociology, Politics, History, Philosophy, Economics
Bookshop: Librería Astrea (at above address)
Founded: 1968

Editorial El **Ateneo** Pedro García SALEI, Patagones 2463, 1282 Buenos Aires Tel: (01) 9429002/9429152/9429052 Cable Add: Ateneo
Dirs: Pedro García, Eustasio A García
Subjects: Medicine, Agronomy, Veterinary Science, Economics, Technical, Education, Business, University Textbooks
Bookshop: El Ateneo (qv under Major Booksellers)
Founded: 1912

Editorial **Atlántida** SA+, Florida 643, 1005 Buenos Aires Tel: (01) 3115416
Cable Add: Ediatlán Telex: 21163
Man Dir: Alfredo J Vercelli; *Sales Dir:* Fernando A Parodi
Subjects: Children's, Juveniles, Textbooks, Fiction, Non-fiction, Belles Lettres, Dictionaries
Bookshop: At above address
Founded: 1918

Asociación Ediciones La **Aurora**+, Dean Funes 1823, 1244 Buenos Aires Tel: (01) 9418940
Dir: Dr Hugo O Ortega; *Sales Dir:* Lic Mario C Ale
Subjects: Religion, Bible, Theology, Sociology, Psychology, Linguistics, Philosophy, History, Literature
Bookshops: Librería La Aurora: At above address and Corrientes 728, 1043 Buenos Aires
Founded: 1926

Barry Editorial Com Ind SRL, Talcahuano 860, 1013 Buenos Aires Tel: (01) 447075
Subject: Music

ARGENTINA

Ediciones La **Bastilla***, Lavalle 1208, 1048 Buenos Aires Tel: (01) 351880
Man Dir: Alfredo Depalma; *Sales Dir:* Ricardo Depalma
Associate Company: Editorial Astrea de Alfredo y Ricardo Depalma SRL (qv)
Subjects: Politics, History
Founded: 1972

SA Editorial **Bell***, Otamendi 215-17, 1405 Buenos Aires Tel: (01) 901076 Cable Add: Edibell
Man Dir: Hugo O Varela; *Sales Dir:* C E Lippold; *Publicity Dir:* S Frasso; *Advertising Dir:* Susana Tubal; *Rights & Permissions:* Mario Martínez
Subjects: How-to, General Science, Technical, Sports
Founded: 1927

Editorial **Beta** SRL*, Ave Santa Fe 2669 – 2° D, 2669 Buenos Aires Tel: (01) 8267660
Man Dir: Miguel Angel Bini
Subjects: Medicine, Psychology, University Textbooks
Founded: 1948

Bias Editora*, Lavalle 1294, 1048 Buenos Aires Tel: (01) 354161 Cable Add: Biasedita
Man Dir: Ival Rocca; *Editorial:* Ignacio Javier Barrio; *Sales:* Gustavo Jorge Claret; *Production:* Francisco Spatafora; *Publicity:* Rodolfo Esteban Amigorena
Subjects: Law, Economics
Bookshop: Bias Editora (Libros Jurídicos) (qv under Major Booksellers)
Founded: 1966
ISBN Publisher's Prefix: 950-0013

Librería **Bonum** SACI*, Maipú 859, 1006 Buenos Aires Tel: (01) 3929763 Cable Add: Bonum
Man Dir & Sales: Antonio Gremmelspacher
Subjects: Religion, Textbooks, Music, Philosophy, Psychology
Founded: 1960

Ediciones **Botella** al Mar*, Viamonte 2754 – 1° 5, 1213 Buenos Aires Tel: (01) 898073

Editorial **Bruguera** Argentina SAFIC*, Avalos 365, 1427 Buenos Aires Tel: (01) 5532885
Man Dir: Jorge Merlini
Parent Company: Editorial Bruguera SA, Spain (qv)

Editorial **Calicanto***, Suipacha 831 – 3° C, 1008 Buenos Aires Tel: (01) 317028
Man Dir: Eduardo Irazabal
Subjects: Literature & Criticism
Founded: 1975

Editorial **Cangallo** SACI*, Ave Belgrano 609, 1092 Buenos Aires Tel: (01) 338848/330204/332453
Man Dir: Norberto del Hoyo
Subjects: Law, Economics, Business, University Textbooks
Bookshop: At above address
Founded: 1968
ISBN Publisher's Prefix: 950-543

Editorial **Caymi***, 15 de Noviembre 1149, 1130 Buenos Aires Tel: (01) 232474
Subjects: Popular Science & Medicine, Yoga, Judo & Karate, Occultism, Sexology, Science Fiction, Spanish & South American Classics

Editorial **Celcius** SA*, Deán Funes 472-476, 1214 Buenos Aires Tel: (01) 932469/939414 Telex: 18522 Cecba
Subject: Medicine
ISBN Publisher's Prefix: 950-0018

Centro Editor de America Latina SA*, Cangallo 1228 – 2° D, 1038 Buenos Aires Tel: (01) 359449/350142 Cable Add: Centroedit
Man Dir: José Boris Spivacow; *Sales Dir:* Aldo Antonio Sangoi
Subjects: Literature, Biography, History, Art, Psychology, How-to, Juveniles, General Science, Social Science, Educational Materials
Founded: 1966

El **Cid** Editor SRL*, Alsina 500, 1087 Buenos Aires Tel: (01) 330071/349267/383795
President: Dr Eduardo Varela-Cid; *General Manager:* Julio A Oliva; *Sales:* Alberto Geraldes; *Production:* Violeta Retzlaff
Subsidiary Companies: El Cid Editor CA, Apdo 60010, Caracas 1060, Venezuela; El Cid Editor SAE, Spain (qv)
Bookshop: Librería Ciudad Educativa SA (Antigua Librería del Colegio) (qv under Major Booksellers)

Editorial **Científica Argentina***, Paraguay 1300, Buenos Aires Tel: (01) 443562
Man Dir: Fernando Duelo Cavero
Subjects: Argentine history, Pedagogy, Various

Editorial **Ciordia** SRL*, Ave Belgrano 2271, 1094 Buenos Aires Tel: (01) 481681
Man Dir: Eduardo B Ciordia; *Sales Dirs:* Manuel Ciordia, Carlos Danzini
Subjects: Literature, Philosophy, Psychology, University & Secondary Textbooks
Founded: 1938

Ciudad Nueva, Lezica 4354, 1202 Buenos Aires Tel: (01) 9814885
Parent Company: Città Nuova Editrice, Italy (qv for associate companies)
ISBN Publisher's Prefix: 950-586

Editorial **Claretiana**+*, Lima 1360, 1408 Buenos Aires Tel: (01) 279250 Cable Add: Editorial Claretiana
Man Dir, Editorial, Rights & Permissions: P Andrés Berasain; *Editor:* Antonio Hernando; *Sales:* Eduardo Righetti; *Publicity:* José Luis Pérez
Subject: Religion
1985: 17 titles *Founded:* 1956

Editorial **Claridad** SA*, San José 1627, Buenos Aires Tel: (01) 235573 Cable Add: Claridad Baires
President: Dr Ana Maria Cabanellas; *Vice-President:* Guillermo Cabanellas
Subject: General Literature
Founded: 1922

Editora **Close Up** SA*, Thames 2450, 1425 Buenos Aires Tel: (01) 7742961

Club de Lectores, Ave de Mayo 624, 1084 Buenos Aires Tel: (01) 343955
Man Dir: Juan Manuel Fontenla; *Sales:* Carlos A Alvano, María Flora Fontenla; *Publicity:* María Inés Fontenla
Subjects: History, Philosophy, Religion, Psychology, Social Science, University Textbooks
Founded: 1938

Librería del **Colegio** SA, Humberto 545 – 1° piso, 1103 Buenos Aires Tel: (01) 3621222/3621332/3625995
Subjects: Educational, Textbooks

Colmegna SA*, San Martín 2546, 3000 Santa Fe Tel: (042) 23102
Man Dir, Editorial, Sales: Nestor Lammertyn
Subjects: Literature, History, Poetry
Bookshop: At above address
Founded: 1889
ISBN Publisher's Prefix: 950-535

Editorial **Columba** SA*, Sarmiento 1889 – 5°, 1044 Buenos Aires Tel: (01) 454297
Man Dir: Claudio A Columba
Subjects: Classics in translation, Twentieth-century themes
Founded: 1953

Compañia Impresora Argentina SA*, Alsina 2049, 1090 Buenos Aires Tel: (01) 472308

Editorial **Conjunta** SRL*, Fr J S M de Oro 2587, 1425 Buenos Aires Tel: (01) 7741734

Ediciones **Contabilidad** Moderna SACIC*, Dr Regimiento de Patricios 1937, 1225 Buenos Aires Tel: (01) 217808/218448/281745
Man Dir: Juan Carlos García Stella; *Sales Manager:* Alberto D Lopez
Subjects: Business, Administration, Taxes, Law, Accounting
Founded: 1943

Editorial **Contempora** SRL*, Sarmiento 643 – of 522, 1382 Buenos Aires Tel: (01) 451793/452575
Subjects: Architecture, Gardening

Ediciones **Corregidor** SAICI y E*, Casilla de Correo 1042, Buenos Aires (Located at: Corrientes 1583, Buenos Aires) Tel: (01) 466116
Dir: Manuel Pampín
Subject: General Literature
Founded: 1972

Cosmopolita SRL*, Piedras 744, 1070 Buenos Aires Tel: (01) 3618049
Man Dir: Eva Ruth F de Rapp
Subjects: Technical, Agriculture
Founded: 1940

Editorial **Crea** SA, now Editorial Abril SA (qv)

Editorial **Crespillo** SA*, Defensa 485, 1065 Buenos Aires Tel: (01) 347384
Subjects: History, Arts, Maps

Depalma SRL*, Talcahuano 494, 1013 Buenos Aires Tel: (01) 461815
Man Dir: Roque Depalma; *Sales Dir:* Alberto E Barón; *International Marketing Manager:* Nicolás von der Pahlen; *Production & Rights Dir:* Roberto Suardíaz
Subjects: Law, History, Social Science, Business, University Texts
Bookshop: At above address
Founded: 1944
ISBN Publisher's Prefix: 950-14

Editorial **Difusión** SA*, Sarandí 1063, Buenos Aires Tel: (01) 9410088
Man Dir, Sales Dir: Domingo Palombella
Subjects: Literature, Philosophy, Religion, Juveniles, Education, Textbooks
Founded: 1936

Distasa, Córdoba 2064, 1120 Buenos Aires Tel: (01) 457609/469059
General Manager: Lorenzo Mario Lugo
Associate Companies: See under Alianza Editorial SA, Spain

E C A (Ediciones Culturales Argentinas)*, Ave Alvear 1690, 1014 Buenos Aires Tel: (01) 444124
Man Dir: Juan Luis Gallardo
Subjects: Argentine Literature, Publications of the Ministry of Culture & Education
Founded: 1961

E U D E B A (Editorial Universitaria de Buenos Aires)*, Ave Rivadavia 1571-73, 1033 Buenos Aires Tel: (01) 372202/378025/385478
Executive Delegate: General Arturo A Corbetta; *General Manager:* Colonel Francisco Basaldua; *Editorial:* José

Rodolfo Carozzo; *Sales:* Enrique Ossuni
Subjects: Literature, History, Logic,
Philosophy, Theology, Art, Music, Dance,
Drama, Geography, Topography,
Architecture, Anthropology, Archaeology,
Paleontology, Astronomy, Meteorology,
Natural Sciences, Physics, Chemistry,
Plastics, Agronomy, Medicine, Psychiatry,
Psychology, Veterinary, Mathematics,
Accountancy, Economics, Law, Education
Bookshop: Pasaje El Fundador-Local, 9
Obispo Trejo, 29 Cordoba, 5000 Codigo
Founded: 1958

Edicient SAIC+*, Mario Bravo 465,
Avellaneda, 1870 Buenos Aires Tel: (01)
2087451
President: José S Coda; *Technical Dir:* Ing
Mario Carlos Ginzburg; *Sales Dir:* Carlos
Norberto Rojas; *Publicity:* Teresa de
Hermosilla
Subjects: Technical, Electronics

Editorial Universidad SRL*, Corrientes
1250 – 4° J, 1043 Buenos Aires Tel: (01)
356490/356850
Subject: Textbooks

Editorial Universitaria de Buenos Aires,
see EUDEBA

Emecé Editores SA, Carlos Pellegrini 1069
– 9° piso, 1009 Buenos Aires Tel: (01)
3114710/3114906/3117327 Cable Add:
Emece Baires Telex: 17736 Emece
President: Dr Bonifacio del Carril;
Administration: Marcos I Fantin; *Editorial:*
Jorge O Naveiro, Bonifacio P del Carril,
Eduardo García Belsunce, Juan Forn;
Sales Dirs: Eduardo Fantin, Carlos A
Bustillo (export); *Production:* Francisco F
del Carril; *Publicity Dir:* José A Mateo;
Rights & Permissions: Jorge O Naveiro,
Bonifacio P del Carril
Orders to: Alsina 2062, 1090 Buenos
Aires Tel: (01) 473051 Telex: 21945
Emece
Associate Company: Emecé Mexicana SA
de CV, Vito Alessio Robles 140, Col
Florida, 01030 México, DF, Mexico
Book Club: Club 'El Libro del Mes'
Subjects: General Fiction, Non-fiction,
Biography, Essays, Mystery, History, Art,
Poetry, Children's
1986: 101 titles *Founded:* 1939

Espacio Editora SA*, Malabia 615 – 1°
piso, 1414 Buenos Aires Tel: (01) 8559082
President: Guillermo Raúl Kliczkowski;
Editorial and Rights & Permissions: Silvia
Leonor Wladimirski; *Sales:* Maria Carmen
Rivera; *Production:* Mirta Adriana Kracoff;
Publicity: Hugo Alberto Kliczkowski
Associate Company: Sociedad Ambiente (at
above address)
Subjects: Architecture, Design, History,
Ecology, Urban Planning
Founded: 1977
ISBN Publisher's Prefix: 84-0116

Espasa-Calpe Argentina SA*, Tacuarí 328,
Buenos Aires
Head Office: Editorial Espasa-Calpe SA,
Spain (qv)

Angel **Estrada** y Cía SA, Bolivar 462-66,
1066 Buenos Aires Tel: (01) 3316521
Telex: 17990 Estra
General Manager: Oscar Domecq
Subjects: How-to, Primary & Secondary
Textbooks, Books for Infants, Teaching
Guides, Atlas
Founded: 1869

Fabril Editora SA, California 2098 – 3°
piso, 1289 Buenos Aires Tel: (01) 213601
Subjects: General Non-fiction, Textbooks,
Reference Books, Arts, Humanities

Ediciones Librerías **Fausto***, Ave
Corrientes 1316, 1043 Buenos Aires Tel:
(01) 453914/456266
Manager: Rafael Zorrilla
Bookshops: Librería Fausto, Librería
Martín Fierro (qqv under Major
Booksellers)

Ediciones de la **Flor** SRL+, Anchoris 27,
1280 Buenos Aires Tel: (01) 235529/
275713
Man Dir: Daniel Divinsky; *Sales Dir:*
Ana M Miler; *Publicity & Advertising Dir,
Rights & Permissions:* Daniel Link
Subjects: Fiction, Literature, History,
Psychology, Juveniles, Humour
1986: 60 titles *1987:* 70 titles *Founded:*
1967
ISBN Publisher's Prefix: 950-515

Editorial **Galerna** SA+, Charcas 3741,
1425 Buenos Aires Tel: (01) 711739
Cable Add: Galerna
Dirs: Julio Martín Alonso, Hugo B Levin
Subsidiary Company: Distribuidora Galerna
— Galerna SRL (country and foreign
sales)
Subjects: Literature, History, Social
Sciences, Paperbacks, Patagonia
Bookshops: Librerías Galerna: Tucumán
1425 and Ave de Mayo 1469 (both Buenos
Aires)
Founded: 1967

Librería y Papelería Casa **García** SA, C
Pellegrini 41, 3500 Resistencia Chaco Tel:
(0711) 25930
Man Dir: José García Pulido; *Sales Dir:*
Luis Aguirre
Subjects: Fiction, Poetry, General
Literature & Literary Criticism, History,
Geography, Politics
Bookshop: At above address
Founded: 1939

Editorial **Géminis** SRL*, Barcena 2105 –
8° B, 1431 Buenos Aires Tel: (01) 513491
Executive President: Leonor de Pirro de
Baran; *Editorial:* Walter J Baran; *Sales:*
Norma Richard; *Production:* Mario di
Bartolo

Ediciones G **Gili** SA, Cochabamba 156,
1064 Buenos Aires Tel: (01) 3619998
Cable Add: Edig
Associate Company: Editorial Gustavo Gili
SA, Spain (qv)

Editorial **Glem** SACIF*, Ave Caseros
2056, 1264 Buenos Aires Tel: (01) 266641
President: José Alfredo Tucci; *Vice-
President:* Héctor Oscar Tucci; *Dir:*
Eduardo Anibal Tucci
Subjects: Technical, Psychology
Founded: 1933

Editorial y Librería **Goncourt***, Ave
Callao 1519, 1024 Buenos Aires Tel: (01)
449743
Man Dir: Jaime Fariña
Subjects: Fiction & Non-fiction
Bookshop: At above address
Founded: 1952

Goyanarte Editor SA*, Esmeralda 923 – 3°
B, 1007 Buenos Aires Tel: (01) 320023/
328362
Man Dir: César Amadeo López; *Sales
Dir:* Hugo Hanuel Vázquez
Subject: Fiction
Founded: 1969 (as Juan Goyanarte
Editore)

Gram Editora*, Cochabamba 1652, 1148
Buenos Aires Tel: (01) 268397
Dir: Manuel Herrero Montes
Subjects: Educational Books, Religion
Founded: 1925

Editorial Juan Carlos **Granda***, Corrientes
1243, 1043 Buenos Aires Tel: (01) 356114

Grijalbo SA*, Belgrano 1256, 1093 Buenos
Aires
Parent Company: Ediciones Grijalbo SA,
Spain (qv)
Subjects: Fiction & Non-fiction

Editorial **Guadalupe**+*, Julián Alvarez
2215, 1425 Buenos Aires Tel: (01) 846066
Man Dir: Luis Liberti; *Sales Dir:* Alberto
Klein; *Publicity Dir:* Maria Alicia Brunero;
Production, Rights & Permissions: Susana
Corlatti
Subjects: Pedagogy, Social Sciences,
Religion, Literature
Bookshops: Librería Guadalupe, Mansilla
3865, 1425 Buenos Aires; Librería Verbo
Divino, Vélez Sarsfield 76, 5000 Córdoba
Founded: 1895

Librería **Hachette** SA+, Rivadavia 739,
1002 Buenos Aires Tel: (01) 348481
Cable Add: Aglibrairi Baires Telex: 17479
Hacba
President: Juan A Musset; *Vice-President:*
Serge Martiano
Subjects: History, Travel, Literature,
Philosophy
Bookshop: See under Major Booksellers

Editorial **Hemisferio** Sur SA+, Pasteur
743, 1028 Buenos Aires Tel: (01) 489825/
488454 Telex: 18522 Cecba Clave 081
Man Dirs: Juan Angel Peri, Adolfo Luis
Peña
Associate Companies: Librería
Agropecuaria SA (at above address);
Editorial Agropecuaria Hemisferio Sur
SRL, Alzaibar 1328, Montevideo, Uruguay
Subjects: Agriculture, Veterinary Science,
Natural Science, Food Technology
Founded: 1966

Editorial **Hobby***, Constitución 2348,
Buenos Aires Tel: (01) 9414255
Man Dir: Marcelo Oscar Castroman; *Sales
Manager:* Norberto Luis Carca
Subjects: Technical
Founded: 1936

Editorial **Huemul** SA, Textbook division of
Editorial Abril SA (qv)

Librería **Huemul** SA+, Ave Santa Fe
2237, 1123 Buenos Aires Tel: (01) 831666
Man Dir, Editorial: Antonio Rego; *Sales,
Publicity, Rights & Permissions:* Carlos L
Sánchez
Subjects: University, Secondary & Primary
Textbooks, Children's
Bookshop: See under Major Booksellers
Founded: 1941

Editorial **Humanitas**+, Carlos Calvo 644,
1102 Buenos Aires Tel: (01) 3620746
Dir: Sela Sierra de Villaverde; *Sales:*
Osvaldo R Dubini; *Publicity:* Mauricio
Faistman
Orders to: Tres Américas, Alsina 722,
1087 Buenos Aires
Subjects: Social Sciences, Psychology,
Education, Psychological Textbooks
1986: 44 titles *1987:* 50 titles *Founded:*
1955
ISBN Publisher's Prefix: 950-582

Instituto de Publicaciones Navales*,
Córdoba 354, 1054 Buenos Aires Tel:
(01) 3110042

Editorial **Inter-Médica** SAICI, Junín 917
– 1° piso, Casilla de Correo 4625, Buenos
Aires Tel: (01) 833234/833148/8255572
President: Jorge Modyeivsky; *Vice-
President:* Sonia M B de Modyeivsky;
General Managers: Deborah and Eduardo
Modyeivsky Bakenroth
Subjects: Medicine, Dentistry, General
Science, University Textbooks
Founded: 1959

6 ARGENTINA

Biblioteca Popular Judía, Casilla de Correo 20, Suc 53, 1453 Buenos Aires (Located at: Larrea 744, 1030 Buenos Aires) Tel: (01) 9614534/9625028 Cable Add: Worldgress Baires
Editorial: Roberto Brzostowski, Pedro Olschansky
Subjects: Jewish History & Biography, Jewish Latinamerican Conference publications

Ediciones y Librería Jurídica*, Calle 45, No 532, 1900 La Plata Tel: (021) 41427
Subject: Law

Editorial Juventud (Distribuidora Tres Américas SAC), Rivadavia 3152, 1203 Buenos Aires Tel: (01) 889114/864070 Telex: 18522 Cecba
Parent Company: Editorial Juventud SA, Spain (qv)
Subjects: History, Juveniles, Fiction, Maps

Editorial Kapelusz SA*, Moreno 372, 1091 Buenos Aires Tel: (01) 346451/3928905 Cable Add: Kapelusz Telex: 18342 Ekasa
Vice-President: Jorge Poppi; *Sales Manager:* Hernando S Ferreres; *Publicity:* Carlos O Otero
Subsidiary Companies: Editorial Kapelusz Colombiana SA, Colombia (qv); Editorial Kapelusz Mexicana SA, Morelas 64, Apdo 32-491, México 1, DF, Mexico; Editorial Cincel SA, Spain (qv); Editorial Kapelusz SA, Ave Uruguay 1331, Montevideo, Uruguay; Editorial Kapelusz Venezolana SA, Venezuela (qv)
Subjects: Primary, Secondary & University Textbooks, Psychology, Pedagogy, Juveniles
Bookshop: Corrientes 999, Buenos Aires
Founded: 1905
ISBN Publisher's Prefix: 950-13

Editorial Kier SACIFI, Ave Santa Fe 1260, 1059 Buenos Aires Tel: (01) 410507/418243/422668
President: Alfonso Florencio Pibernus; *Vice-President:* José Grigna; *Man Dir:* Héctor Pibernus; *Sales Dir:* Alberto Pibernus
Subjects: Eastern Religions, Astrology, Tarots, Occultism, Rosicrucianism, Medicine
Bookshop: Librería Kier (qv under Major Booksellers)
1985: 18 titles *1986:* 26 titles *Founded:* 1907

Ediciones Larousse Argentina SA*, Valentin Gómez 3530, 1191 Buenos Aires Tel: (01) 876671 Cable Add: Editlarousse Telex: 0121783
President: Georges Lucas
Subjects: Dictionaries, Encyclopaedias

Latina SA, now part of Ediciones Preescolar SA (qv)

Editorial Victor Lerú SA*, Casilla 2793, Correo central, 1000 Buenos Aires Tel: (01) 9816098/9816198/9818978
Man Dir: Victor Nep; *Sales Dir:* León Nep
Subjects: Art, Architecture, Technology, Primary, Secondary & University Textbooks, Music, Dictionaries, History
Founded: 1944
ISBN Publisher's Prefix: 950-8205

La Ley SA Editora e Impresora+*, Tucumán 1471, 1050 Buenos Aires Tel: (01) 495481 Telex: 17465 Laley
President: Dr Carlos A Vanasco; *Vice-President:* Dr Iván D Posse Molina; *General Manager:* Juan C Milberg; *General Dir:* Enrique J Algorta Gaona; *Commercial Manager:* Manuel E Schkolnik; *Production:* Roberto Pedretti
Branch Offs: In all Argentinian provinces and in Asunción (Paraguay)
Subjects: Law, Economics, Philosophy, History
Founded: 1935

Carlos Lohlé SA, Tacuarí 1516, Casilla de Correo 3097, 1000 Buenos Aires Tel: (01) 279969
President: Carlos F P Lohlé; *Man Dir:* Francisco M Lohlé
Subjects: Literature, Poetry, Philosophy, Religion, Psychology, Social Science
Founded: 1953
ISBN Publisher's Prefix: 360-539

López Libreros Editores*, Ave Córdoba 2370, 1120 Buenos Aires Tel: (01) 485939
Man Dirs: Dr Pablo A López, Josefina A Lopez
Subject: Medicine
Bookshop: At above address
Founded: 1927

Editorial Losada SA, Morena 3362, 1209 Buenos Aires Tel: (01) 863347/863751/888608 Cable Add: Edilosada
President: Gonzalo Pedro Losada; *Man Dir:* Carlo Alberto Aramburu; *Sales Dir:* Manuel Taboada
Subjects: Fiction & Non-fiction, Classics, Poetry, Literary Studies, Philosophy, Psychology, Biography, History, Pedagogy, Secondary Textbooks
Founded: 1938

Ediciones Macchi+, Alsina 1535 PB, 1088 Buenos Aires Tel: (01) 460594
Man Dir: Raúl Luis Macchi; *Sales Dir:* Mendonça Julio Alberto
Subjects: Economic Sciences
Bookshop: Córdoba 2015, 1120 Buenos Aires
Founded: 1947

Macondo Ediciones SRL*, Lavalle 1882 – 1° piso, 1051 Buenos Aires Tel: (01) 458535
Man Dir: Dr Samuel Tarnopolsky; *Editorial, Publicity, Rights & Permissions:* Haydée M Jofre Barroso; *Sales, Production:* José Antonio Serrano
Subjects: Belles Lettres, Science, Economics, Politics, Fiction, Science Fiction, Poetry
Founded: 1976
ISBN Publisher's Prefix: 950-89000

Marymar Ediciones SA+, Chile 1432, 1098 Buenos Airès Tel: (01) 380391 Telex: 24728 Tresa
President: Isay Klasse; *Man Dir, Production Dir:* Saúl Cherny
Subjects: Social, Political & General Science, Economics, Philosophy, Architecture, Technology, Music, Cinema, History, Teaching, Library Science, Ecology, Fiction & Classics, Psychology
Founded: 1960
ISBN Publisher's Prefix: 950-503

Librería y Editorial La Médica*, Córdoba 2901, 2000 Rosario Tel: (041) 397858
Man Dir: Cataline C de Radeff; *Sales Dir:* Ruben T Radeff, Ricardo A Radeff, Roberto A Radeff
Subject: Medicine
Miscellaneous: Major Distributor of Schoolbooks and General literature

Editorial Médica Panamericana SA, Junin 831, 1113 Buenos Aires Tel: (01) 838819
President: Roberto Brik; *Production:* Daniel Brik; *Foreign Rights and International Sales:* Hugo Brik
Branch Offs: Santa Isabel 267, São Paulo, Brazil; Marcoleta 328, Santiago de Chile, Chile; Apdo Aéreo 076037, Bogotá, Colombia; Herschel 153, México 5, DF, Mexico; Hilarión Eslava 55, 28015 Madrid, Spain; Apdo 52096, Caracas 1050-A, Venezuela
Subjects: Medicine, Dentistry, Rehabilitation, Nursing
Founded: 1953

Editorial Librería Mitre SRL, Bartólome Mitre 2032, 1039 Buenos Aires Tel: (01) 9535856
Man Dir: Rodolfo Amura
Subjects: Technical (especially Mechanics)
Founded: 1949

Editorial Mundi SAIC y F+*, Casilla de Correo 47, Suc 53, 1453 Capital Federal (Located at: Paraguay 2100, Capital Federal) Tel: (01) 839339/839663
Production, Publicity, Rights & Permissions: Elena Garcia Mila
Subject: Dentistry
Founded: 1939
ISBN Publisher's Prefix: 950-545

Editorial Mundo Técnico SRL*, Guanahaní 176, 1274 Buenos Aires Cable Add: Muntex
Man Dir: Gustavo A Marini; *Sales Dir:* Juan C García Venturini
Subjects: Technical, Engineering, Atlases, How-to, School Dictionaries & Textbooks
Founded: 1972

Librería y Editorial Nigar SRL*, Humberto 1° 667, 1103 Buenos Aires Tel: (01) 3621794

Editorial Norte SA, José Mármol 2131, 1255 Buenos Aires Tel: (01) 9211440
Director-General: Alejandro I Lamarque
Subjects: Educational, Juveniles
Founded: 1961
ISBN Publisher's Prefix: 950-27

Ediciones Nueva Visión SAIC*, Tucumán 3748, 1189 Buenos Aires Tel: (01) 895050
Man Dir: Jorge José Grisetti; *Sales Manager:* Anibal Victor Giacone
Subjects: Social Sciences, Psychology, Architecture, Art, Theatre
Founded: 1954

Editorial Paidós SAICF*, Defensa 599 – 1° piso, 1065 Buenos Aires Tel: (01) 332275
Man Dir, Rights & Permissions: Enrique Butelman
Subsidiary Company: Ediciones Paidós Ibérica SA, Spain (qv)
Subjects: Social Sciences, Psychology, Medicine, Philosophy, Religion, History, Biography, Literature, University Textbooks
Bookshop: Librería Paidós, Las Heras and Canning, Buenos Aires
Founded: 1945

Ediciones Pannedille*, Chacabuco 129, Buenos Aires Tel: (01) 354957
Man Dir: Oscar Buonano
Subjects: History, Law, Technical
Founded: 1970

Casa Pardo SAC*, Defensa 1170, 1065 Buenos Aires Tel: (01) 346676 Cable Add: Pardoroman
Dir: Roman José Pardo
Subjects: General Literature, Humanism
Founded: 1892

Editora Patria Grande*, Rivadavia 6251, 1406 Buenos Aires Tel: (01) 6324374/6323255
General Manager and Rights & Permissions: Washington Uranga; *Editorial:* Carlos J Durán; *Sales:* Elsa S de Férnandez; *Production:* Carlos D Arnedillo; *Publicity:* Duilio López
Branch Off: Casilla de Correo 5, Suc 8, 1408 Buenos Aires
Subjects: Religious, Poetry, Juvenile
Bookshops: Librería Patria Grande (at

above address); Librería Didajé, José Cubas 3543, Buenos Aires
Founded: 1974
ISBN Publisher's Prefix: 950-046

Ediciones **Paulinas**+, Nazca 4249, 1419 Buenos Aires Tel: (01) 5723926/5724810 Cable Add: Paulinas
Man Dir: Daniela Ibañez; *Editorial, Production, Rights & Permissions, Publicity:* Ana Maria Martinez; *Sales Dir:* Julia Veloteri
Branch Offs: Junin esq Salte, 3400 Corrientes; San Martin 980, 5500 Mendoza; Antártida Argentina 178, 3500 Resistencia; San Jerónimo 2136, 3000 Sante Fé; 24 de Setiembre 512, 4000 Tucumán
Subjects: Education, Religion
Founded: 1940
ISBN Publisher's Prefix: 950-09

A **Peña** Lillo SA*, H Yrigoyen 1394-1086, Buenos Aires Tel: (01) 370994
Man Dir: Arturo Peña Lillo; *Sales Dir:* María Luisa Comellí; *Production & Publicity:* Laura Peña
Orders to: Rivadavia 739, Buenos Aires (Librería Hachette SA)
Subjects: History, Political Science, Economics, Sociology, Literature
Founded: 1956
ISBN Publisher's Prefix: 950-8203

Ediciones **Periféria** SRL*, Cangallo 1730 – 6° piso of 68, 1037 Buenos Aires Tel: (01) 450574
Subjects: Social Sciences, University Textbooks
Founded: 1971

Editorial Argentina **Plaza y Janés** SA*, Lambaré 893, Buenos Aires Tel: (01) 866769/866785
Man Dir: Jorge Perez; *Sales Dir:* Ernesto Pena
Subjects: General Fiction & Non-fiction

Editorial **Pleamar***, Corrientes 1994 – 1° piso, Buenos Aires
Man Dir: Andrés Alfonso Bravo
Subjects: Political & Social Science
Founded: 1965

Editorial **Plus Ultra** SAI & C, Callao 575, 1022 Buenos Aires Tel: (01) 465092/ 462953/462973 Cable Add: Plusultra
Man Dirs: Rafael Román, Lorenzo Marengo; *Editorial:* Carlos Alberto Loprete, José Isaacson; *Sales:* Ricardo Errea; *Production:* Renato Gardoni; *Publicity:* Lily Sosa de Newton
Subjects: Literature, History, Law, Textbooks, Economics, Philosophy, Politics, Sociology, Psychology, Pedagogy, Children's
Bookshop: At above address
Founded: 1964

Ediciones **Preescolar** SA, Ave de Mayo 953 – 7° piso, 1084 Buenos Aires Tel: (01) 382669/387174
Editorial: Juan Carlos Orgueira
Subjects: Pre-school books, Juveniles
Founded: 1971/1984
Miscellaneous: Incorporating Latina SA
ISBN Publisher's Prefix: 950-9574

Prolam SRL (Ediciones Economia y Empresa)*, México 625, Buenos Aires Tel: (01) 308280
Man Dir: Beatriz E P de Lambruschini
Subjects: Economics, Business, Science & Technology
Founded: 1958

Ricordi Americana SAEC, Tte Gral Juan Domingo Perón 1558, 1037 Buenos Aires Tel: (01) 409841 Cable Add: Ricordamericana Telex: 1222580 for Ricordi
President, General Manager: Renzo Valcarenghi; *Dir, Deputy Manager:* Ernesto Larcade; *Marketing:* Claudio Firmenich
Associate Companies: Ricordi Brasileira S/A, Rua Conselheiro Nébias 1136, 01203 São Paulo SP, Brazil; G e C Ricordi SpA, Italy (qv); G Ricordi & Co, Paseo de la Reforma 481-A, 06500 México, DF, Mexico
Subjects: Music, Musical Teaching Methods
Founded: 1924

Librería **Rodriguez** SA+*, Sarmiento 835, Buenos Aires Tel: (01) 358126/351959
President: Ernesto J Rodríguez; *Dir:* Ernesto J Rodríguez Gerino; *General Manager:* Bautista L Tello
Subjects: Children's, English textbooks
Bookshop: See under Major Booksellers

Editorial **Ruy** Diaz SAEIC+, Irigoyen 453/ 455, 1407 Buenos Aires Tel: (01) 6827324/ 6837117 Cable Add: Ediruy
Man Dir: Rafael Zuccotti
Branch Off: Casilla de Correo 46, Suc 6, 1406 Buenos Aires
Subjects: Educational, Atlases, Dictionaries
Founded: 1966
ISBN Publisher's Prefix: 950-9023

Editorial **Santiago** Rueda SRL*, Sarmiento 680 – 1° piso, 1041 Buenos Aires Tel: (01) 491874/497860
Man Dir: Enrique S Rueda
Subject: Literature
Founded: 1940

Schapire Editor SRL*, Uruguay 1249, 1016 Buenos Aires Tel: (01) 440765
Man Dir: Miguel Schapire
Subjects: Literature, Biography, History, Art, Psychology, Social Science, Juveniles
Founded: 1935

Selcon SAEC & I (Selección Contable)*, Sarandí 1067, 1222 Buenos Aires Tel: (01) 9410118
Sales & Advertising Dir: Domingo Palombella
Subjects: Business, Economics
Founded: 1942

Santiago **Sentis** Melendo*, Rivadavia 4076, 1205 Buenos Aires

Ediciones **Siglo XX** SAC & I*, Maza 177, 1206 Buenos Aires Tel: (01) 882758 Cable Add: Sigloveinte
Man Dir: Isidoro Wainer; *Sales Dir:* Carlos Zorrilla
Subjects: General Fiction & Non-fiction
Bookshop: At above address
Founded: 1943

Editorial **Sigmar** SACI+, Belgrano 1580 – 7° piso, 1093 Buenos Aires Tel: (01) 373045/384474 Cable Add: Sigmar Telex: 9073 Sigmar
Man Dir: Sigfrido Chwat
Subjects: Juveniles, Children's
Founded: 1941
ISBN Publisher's Prefix: 950-11

Editorial **Sopena** Argentina SACI e I, Moreno 957 – 7° piso, Buenos Aires Tel: (01) 3347182
Executive President: Daniel Carlos Olsen; *Dirs:* Marta A J Sopena de Olsen, Leopoldo Costa Urruty; *Manager:* Hipólito O Dhers
Subjects: Dictionaries, Language & Linguistics, Literature & Criticism, Spanish & Hispano-American classics, Chess, Health & Beauty, Practical Guides, Contemporary Politics, History, Children's Anthologies, all mainly paperback

Editorial **Stella***, Viamonte 1984, 1056 Buenos Aires Tel: (01) 460346
Asociación Educacionista Argentina
Subjects: Non-fiction, Textbooks

Studia Croatica*, Carlos Pelegrini 743 – 3° piso, Buenos Aires Tel: (01) 3927254

Editorial **Sudamericana** SA, Humberto 531 – 1° piso, 1103 Buenos Aires Tel: (01) 3622128/3627364/3627496 Cable Add: Librecol Telex: 18096
President: Edith K de Lopez Llovet; *Man Dir:* Jaime Rodrigué; *Editorial:* Enrique Pezzoni; *Sales Dir:* Francisco La Falce; *Publicity Dir:* María Marta Chimondeguy; *Rights & Permissions:* Gloria Lopez de Rodrigué
Associate Companies: Sudamericana/Planeta SA (Editores), Argentina (qv); Editorial Hermes SA, Mexico (qv); EDHASA (Editora y Distribuidora Hispano-Americana SA), Spain (qv)
Subjects: General Fiction & Non-fiction, Literature, Biography, History, Philosophy, Psychology
Founded: 1939

Sudamericana/Planeta SA (Editores)*, Humberto 555 – 1° piso, 1103 Buenos Aires Tel: (01) 3621222/3621332/3625995 Telex: 18096 Edipla
Executive President: Jaime Rodrigue; *General Manager:* Julio Perez Vega; *Editorial:* Arturo Infante; *Sales Dir:* Francisco La Falce; *Publicity Dir:* Maria Marta Chimondeguy; *Rights & Permissions:* Gloria Lopez Llovet de Rodrigue
Associate Companies: Editorial Planeta Argentina SAIC, Dirección Viamonte 1451, Buenos Aires, Argentina; Editorial Sudamericana SA Argentina (qv); Editorial Planeta SA, Spain (qv)
Subjects: General Fiction & Non-fiction, Literature, Biography, History, Psychology
Founded: 1983
ISBN Publisher's Prefix: 950-37

Editorial **Sur** SA*, Bulnes 1730, 1425 Buenos Aires Tel: (01) 231689

T E A (Tipográfica Editora Argentina)*, Lavalle 1430, 1048 Buenos Aires Tel: (01) 405668
Man Dir: Pedro San Martín; *Sales Dir:* María Teresa San Martín
Subjects: History, Social Science, Law, Economics, Philosophy
Founded: 1946
ISBN Publisher's Prefix: 950-521

Instituto Torcuato di **Tella***, 11 de Septiembre 2139, 1428 Buenos Aires Tel: (01) 7848264/7815013 Cable Add: Instella Baires
President: Guido Di Tella
Subjects: Social Sciences, Economics, History, Political Science, Epistemology and Methodology of the Social Sciences
Founded: 1958

Ediciones **Theoria** SRL*, Rivadavia 1255 – 4° piso of 407, Casilla de Correo 5096, 1033 Buenos Aires Tel: (01) 380131
Man Dir: Jorge O Orús; *Sales Dir:* José Luis Menéndez
Subjects: Literature, Biography, History, Religion
Founded: 1954

Editorial **Tiempo Contemporaneo***, Viamonte 1453 – 10° piso of 66, 1055 Buenos Aires Tel: (01) 459640
Man Dir: Alberto Mario Serebresky; *Sales Dir:* José Fuster
Subjects: General Fiction, History, Philosophy, Psychology, Technical, Medicine, Social Sciences, University Textbooks
Founded: 1969

Ediciones **Tres Tiempos** SRL*, Ave Belgrano 225, 1092 Buenos Aires Tel: (01) 342913/347184/338785
Man Dirs: José C Orríes e Ibars, Canio Carmelo Cillo; *Assistant Manager:* José Di Marco; *Editor:* Susana Margulies; *Production Dir:* Ana Barkacs van Gyarmath; *Sales Dirs:* Bibiana Longhi de Chas, Raúl Villar; *Advertising & Promotion:* Florinda Mintz; *Rights & Permissions:* Teresa Cillo; *Imports/Exports:* Alejandro Luis Calegari
Branch Off: Moreno 3201, Buenos Aires
Subjects: Anthropology, Architecture and Urbanism, Arts, Cinematography and Theatre, Demography, Ecology, Economics, Education, Philosophy, Psychology, Management, Technology, Sciences, Social & Political Sciences, Novels, Fiction & Poetry
Founded: 1975

Editorial **Troquel** SA*, Juan de Garay 1454, 1076 Buenos Aires Tel: (01) 230771 Cable Add: Troquelsa
President: María A C de Ressia; *Sales Manager:* Domingo Angel Ongarato
Subjects: General Literature, Technology, Textbooks
Founded: 1954
ISBN Publisher's Prefix: 950-16

Turner Ediciones, Alsina 1535 – 8° piso of 803, 1088 Buenos Aires Tel: (01) 466477
Man Dir: Mary C Turner
Subjects: Reference, Bibliography

Javier **Vergara** Editor SA+, San Martin 969 – 6° piso, 1004 Buenos Aires Tel: (01) 3112890/3117335/3113248 Telex: 18352 Jvedi
President: Javier Vergara; *Publicity:* Trinidad Vergara; *Rights:* Gabriela Cruz de Vergara
Branch Offs: Aldunate 484, Santiago, Chile; Ave Cuauhtemoc 1100, México, DF, Mexico; Platerías 3, 28016 Madrid, Spain
Subjects: General Fiction, Non-fiction, Biography, History, Music, Self-help
1986: 72 titles *Founded:* 1975

Victor P de **Zavalía** SA*, Alberti 835, 1223 Buenos Aires Tel: (01) 9421274/9423046
Man Dir: Víctor H de Zavalía; *Sales Dir:* Ricardo L de Zavalía
Subject: Law
1985: 8 titles *Founded:* 1950
ISBN Publisher's Prefix: 950-572

Literary Agents

International Editors' Co*, Nicolás Costa, Cabildo 1156, Buenos Aires Tel: (01) 7844613 Cable Add: Lifeplay
Also office in Spain (qv)

Lawrence **Smith** Literary Agency (1938), Ave de los Incas 3110, 1426 Buenos Aires Tel: (01) 5525012 Cable Add: Litagent Baires
President: Lawrence Smith
Specializes in book, serial and performing rights in Spanish and Portuguese languages worldwide

Book Clubs

Círculo de Lectores SA*, Bmé Mitre 699 – 5° y 6° piso, 1357 Buenos Aires Tel: (01) 303501/305771 Telex: 18212 Cal
Owned by: Bertelsmann AG, Federal Republic of Germany (qv)
Founded: 1971

Club **'El Libro del Mes'**, Alsina 2041, 1090 Buenos Aires
Members: 25,000
Owned by: Emecé Editores SA (qv)
Founded: 1968

Major Booksellers

Librerías **A B C** SA, Ave Córdoba 685, 1054 Buenos Aires Tel: (01) 3927887 Cable Add: Molagent
Manager: Horst Stephan
Also: Avda Libertador 13777, Martinez, 1646 Buenos Aires

American Books*, Tucumán 994 – 1° piso, Buenos Aires Tel: (01) 353704

El **Ateneo**, Florida 340, 1005 Buenos Aires Tel: (01) 466801
Manager: Ing Jorge Letemendia
Owned by: Editorial El Ateneo Pedro García SALEI (qv)

Bias Editora (Libros Jurídicos)*, Lavalle 1294, 1048 Buenos Aires Tel: (01) 354161
Manager: Rodolfo Esteban Amigorena
Owned by: Bias Editora (qv)

Librería **Ciudad Educativa** SA (Antigua Librería del Colegio)*, Alsinan 500, 1087 Buenos Aires Tel: (01) 330071
Manager: Dr Eduardo Varela-Cid
Owned by: El Cid Editor SRL (qv)

Distribuidora **Cuspide**, Suipacha 764, 1008 Buenos Aires Tel: (01) 3921727/3928868/3927434 Telex: 25477 Dicus
Manager: Joaquín Gil Paricio
Branch Off: Suipacha 1045, 1008 Buenos Aires Tel: (01) 3130486/3139362

Librería **Española** SCA*, Florida 943, 1005 Buenos Aires Tel: (01) 3123214/3125850

Librerías **Fausto***, Ave Corrientes 1311, 1043 Buenos Aires Tel: (01) 401222
Manager: Rafael Pedro Zorrilla
Also: Ave Santa Fe 1715, 1060 Buenos Aires Tel: (01) 412708
Owned by: Ediciones Librerías Fausto (qv)

Librería 'Martín **Fierro'***, Ave Corrientes 1264, 1043 Buenos Aires Tel: (01) 350444
Owned by: Ediciones Librerías Fausto (qv)

Ediciones **Garriga** Argentinas SA, Ave del Libertador 948 – Gal Las Victorias – loc 10A, 1012 Buenos Aires Tel: (01) 3939251/3940642

Librería **Hachette** SA, Rivadavia 739, 1002 Buenos Aires Tel: (01) 348481 Cable Add: Aglibrairi Baires Telex: 17479 Haeba
Also Publisher (qv)

Carlos **Hirsch** SRL*, Florida 165, Galería Güemes – 4°. piso, 1333 Buenos Aires Tel: (01) 332391/331787/307122 Cable Add: Hirsch Baires Telex: 21112 Uape
Managers: Leandro Moreiras, Mónica Bustos

Librería **Huemul** SA, Ave Santa Fe 2237, 1123 Buenos Aires Tel: (01) 831666/8252290
Manager: Carlos L Sánchez
Also Publisher (qv)

Librería **Kier**, Ave Santa Fe 1260, 1059 Buenos Aires Tel: (01) 410507/418243
Owned by: Editorial Kier SACIFI (qv)

H F **Martínez** de Murguía SAC y E*, Ave Córdoba 2270, Buenos Aires Tel: (01) 486173
President: Agustín T Aparicio

Librería **Norte***, Las Heras 2225, Buenos Aires Tel: (01) 843944

Nueva Visión*, Viamonte 500, Buenos Aires Tel: (01) 326434

Librería General de Tomas **Pardo** SRL*, Maipú 618, 1006 Capital Federal Tel: (01) 3920496/3936759

Librería **Rodriguez** SA+*, Sarmiento 835, Buenos Aires Tel: (01) 358126/351959
General Manager: Bautista L Tello
Also Publisher (qv)

Librería **Ross***, Córdoba 1347, Rosario Tel: (041) 65378

Librería **Santa Fe***, Ave Santa Fe 2386, 1123 Buenos Aires Tel: (01) 835746
Also: Ave Santa Fe 2928, 1125 Buenos Aires Tel: (01) 8219442
Importer

Librería **Sarmiento***, Libertad 1214-20, 1012 Buenos Aires Tel: (01) 414792
Managers: Alejandro Orloff, Enrique Orloff

Distribuidora **Tres Américas** Libros SAC*, Ave Rivadavia 3152, 1203 Buenos Aires Tel: (01) 889114 Telex: 18522 Cecba
President: Isay Klasse
Export: Chile 1432, 1098 Buenos Aires Tel: (01) 379558 Telex: 24728 Tresa

Major Libraries

Biblioteca del **Banco** Central de la República Argentina*, Reconquista 266, Buenos Aires
Library of the Central Bank

Biblioteca **Nacional***, México 564, 1097 Buenos Aires Tel: (01) 3619476
Dir: Dardo Cúneo

Biblioteca Nacional de Maestros*, Pizzurno 935, 1020 Buenos Aires Tel: (01) 440031
National Teachers' Library
Publications: La Biblioteca (monthly); Historia de la Biblioteca Nacional de Maestros

Biblioteca Publica Central*, Calle 47 No 510, La Plata

Biblioteca del **Congreso** de la Nacíon*, Rivadavia 1830, 1033 Buenos Aires Tel: (01) 409991
National Library of Congress

Biblioteca Pública Gratuita de **'La Prensa'***, Rivadavia 552, Buenos Aires

Biblioteca **Lincoln***, Florida 935, Buenos Aires

Biblioteca de la **Universidad de Buenos Aires***, Casilla de Correo 901, 1000 Buenos Aires (Located at: Azcuénaga 280, Buenos Aires) Tel: (01) 473394 Telex: 18694 Abuba

Biblioteca Central, **Universidad del Salvador***, Hipolito Yrigoyen 2447, 1089 Buenos Aires
Dir: Prof Hector Daniel Fiotto

Biblioteca Mayor de la **Universidad Nacional de Córdoba***, Casilla de Correo 63, 5000 Córdoba (Located at: Calle Obispo Trejo y Sanabria 242, Córdoba) Tel: (051) 46323 Telex: 51822 Bjcor
Principal Library of the National University of Córdoba
Dir: Professor Joaquín García
Publications: Informativo (irregular),) Monographs

Biblioteca Pública de la **Universidad Nacional de La Plata**, Plaza Rocha 137, 1900 La Plata Tel: (021) 214109 Telex:

31151 Bulap
Dir: Carlos J Tejo
Publications: Bulletin *Informaciones*

Library Associations

A B G R A (Asociación de Bibliotecarios Graduados de la República Argentina), Montevideo 581 – 5° piso, 1019 Buenos Aires Tel: (01) 409728
Association of Graduate Librarians of Argentina
President: Alberto S Querejeta; *Executive Secretary:* Elida Susana Iriondo
Publications include: Bibliotecologia y Documentacion: Boletín Informativo

Asociación Argentina de Bibliotecas y Centros de Información Cientificos y Tecnicos*, Ave Santa Fe 1145, Buenos Aires Tel: (01) 411405
Executive Secretary: Olga E Veronelli

Asociación de Ex-Alumnos de la Escuela Nacional de Bibliotecarios*, c/o Biblioteca Nacional, México 564, Buenos Aires

Dirección de **Bibliotecas Públicas** Municipales*, Talcahuano 1261, Buenos Aires
Director-General: Eduardo Belgrano Rawson

Centro de Documentación Bibliotecológica, Universidad Nacional del Sur, Ave Alem 1253, Bahía Blanca
Centre for Library Science Documentation
Dir: Atilio Peralta
Publications: Bibliografía Bibliotecológica Argentina (Argentine Library Science Bibliography); *Quién es Quién en la Bibliotecología Argentina* (Who's Who in Argentine Library Science); *Guía de las Bibliotecas Universitarias Argentinas* (Guide to Argentine University Libraries); *Documentación Bibliotecológica*

Colegio de Bibliotecarios de la Provincia de Buenos Aires*, Calle 48 No 633 – 3° piso of 315, 1900 La Plata

Instituto de Bibliográfia del Ministerio de Educación de la Provincia de Buenos Aires*, Calle 47 No 510 – 6 piso, 1900 La Plata
Dir: María del Carmen Crespi de Bustos
Publications: Bibliografía Argentina de Historia; Boletín de Información Bibliográfica

Library Reference Books and Journals

Books

Bibliografía Bibliotecológica Argentina (Argentine Library Science Bibliography), Centro de Documentación Bibliotecológica, Universidad Nacional del Sur, Ave Alem 1253, Bahía Blanca

Guía de las Bibliotecas Universitarias Argentinas (Guide to Argentine University Libraries), Centro de Documentación Bibliotecológica, Universidad Nacional del Sur, Ave Alem 1253, Bahía Blanca

Journals

La Biblioteca (monthly), Biblioteca Nacional de Maestros, Pizzurno 935, 1020 Buenos Aires

Bibliotecologia y Documentacion: Boletín Informativo, ABGRA (Asociación de Bibliotecarios Graduados de la República Argentina), Montevideo 581 – 5° piso, 1019 Buenos Aires

Literary Associations and Societies

Academia Argentina de Letras*, Sánchez de Bustamante 2663, 1425 Buenos Aires Tel: (01) 8023814/8027509
Argentine Academy of Letters
Secretary: Juan Carlos Ghiano
Publication: Boletín de la Academia Argentina de Letras (quarterly)
Library Publications include: Serie de Clásicos Argentinos, Serie de Acuerdos acerca del Idioma, Boletín, Serie Estudios Lingüísticos y Filológicos

Club de Poetas*, Casilla de Correo 189, 1401 Buenos Aires
Dir: Juan Manuel Fontenla
Publications include: Antología de Poetas Contemporaneos

The **Dickens** Fellowship (Argentine Branch), Calle Basavilbaso 1396, 1006 Buenos Aires
Honorary Secretary: D Miguel Alfredo Olivera

Instituto de Literatura, Calle 47 No 625, La Plata
Dir: Arturo Cambours
Publications: Investigaciones, Boletín

P E N Club International de Argentina*, Diagonal R Sáenz Pena 570 – 10° piso, 1035 Buenos Aires
Secretaries: Norberto Silvetti Paz, Carlos Villafuerte
Publications: Boletín and books

Literary Periodicals

Boletín, Academia Argentina de Letras (quarterly), Sánchez de Bustamante 2663, 1425 Buenos Aires

Boletín (twice a month), SADE (Sociedad Argentina de Escritores), Uruguay 1371, 1016 Buenos Aires

Comentario, Tucuman 2137 y San Martin 663, Buenos Aires

Criterio, Alsina 840, Buenos Aires

Davar, Sociedad Hebraica Argentina, Sarmiento 2233, Buenos Aires

Histonium, Paraná 464, Buenos Aires

Igitur Revista Literaria, Republica de Israel 115, Córdoba

Sur, Viamonte 494 – 8° piso, Buenos Aires

Literary Prizes

Argentine National Prize for Literature*
For best works of prose and poetry. Awarded every three years. Enquiries to Argentinian Ministry of Education and Justice, Secretary of Culture, Ave Alvear 1690, Buenos Aires

Alfredo A **Bianchi** Essay Prize*
For the best scholarly essay on any subject. Awarded annually. Enquiries to SADE (Sociedad Argentina de Escritores), Uruguay 1371, 1016 Buenos Aires

Buenos Aires Literary Prizes*
For the best works written or published during the year in Buenos Aires. Awards are given for fiction; essay (including biography and literary criticism); poetry. Awarded annually. Enquiries to Buenos Aires Municipality, Secretariat of Culture and Social Activities, Ave de Mayo 525, Buenos Aires

Carlos **Casavalle** Prize*
Awarded in turn for the best book published in Argentina in the following categories: fiction; poetry and drama; essay, including scientific writing. Awarded annually. Enquiries to Cámara Argentina del Libro, Ave Belgrano 1580 – 6° piso, 1093 Buenos Aires

Premio **Emecé** Annual Prize*
Established 1954. For the best unpublished novel or book of short stories in the Spanish language. Enquiries to Emecé Editores SA, Carlos Pellegrini 1069 – 9° piso, 1009 Buenos Aires

First Book Prize*
For the first literary work written by an author under 30. Awarded annually. Enquiries to Cámara Argentina del Libro, Ave Belgrano 1580 – 6° piso, 1093 Buenos Aires

Premio de '**La Nación**' Prize*
Given by the newspaper 'La Nación' for different types of literature. Enquiries to 'La Nación', Florida 343/San Martín, Buenos Aires CF

Fernando **Moreno** Poetry Prize*
For outstanding work in Poetry. Enquiries to SADE (Sociedad Argentina de Escritores), Uruguay 1371, 1016 Buenos Aires

Pablo **Rojas** Paz Prize*
For the best unpublished biography. Enquiries to SADE (Sociedad Argentina de Escritores), Uruguay 1371, 1016 Buenos Aires

Ricardo **Rojas** Prize*
For prose work (imaginative writing, criticism, essay). Awarded biennially. Enquiries to Buenos Aires Municipality, Secretariat of Culture and Social Activities, Ave de Mayo 525, Buenos Aires

Medalla de Oro de la **S A D E** (Sociedad Argentina de Escritores)*
Annual prize for the total output of an author. Enquiries to SADE (Sociedad Argentina de Escritores), Uruguay 1371, 1016 Buenos Aires

Sarmiento Prize*
For the best book of prose written during the year. Awarded annually. Enquiries to SADE (Sociedad Argentina de Escritores), Uruguay 1371, 1016 Buenos Aires

Australia

General Information

Language: English
Religion: Predominantly Protestant
Population: 14.6 million
Bank Hours: 1000-1500 Monday-Thursday; 1000-1700 Friday
Shop Hours: 0900-1700 Monday-Friday; usually 0900-1200 Saturday
Currency: 100 cents = 1 Australian dollar
Export/Import Information: No tariffs on books. Most books, especially of literary or educational nature, free of sales tax. No import licences for books; no seditious literature permitted
Copyright: UCC, Berne (see International section)

Book Trade Organizations

The **Association of Antiquarian Booksellers***, PO Box 356, Prahran, Victoria 3182
President: Kenneth Hince

Association of Australian University Presses, c/o University of Western Australia Press, University of Western Australia, Nedlands, WA 6009 Tel: (092) 3803182
President: V S W Greaves
Incorporating Melbourne University Press, New South Wales University Press Ltd, Sydney University Press, University of Queensland Press, University of Western Australia Press (qqv under Publishers), Deakin University Press (associate member)

Australian Book Publishers' Association, 161 Clarence St, Sydney, NSW 2000 Tel: (02) 295422 Telex: 121822 Fax: (02) 2621631
Dir: Jan Noble
Publication: Directory of Members

Australian Booksellers Association Inc, PO Box 173, North Carlton, Victoria 3054 Tel: (03) 3875422
The ABA is a Federal Association with branches in every State and represents booksellers' interests to government bodies, publishers and other organizations
President: Jean Ferguson; *Executive Dir:* Jane Stephens

Australian Copyright Council, 22 Alfred St, Milsons Point, NSW 2061 Tel: (02) 9572941
Chairman: Peter Banki; *Executive Officer:* Susan Bridge

Australian Society of Indexers, GPO Box 1251L, Melbourne, Victoria 3001
Secretary: Karen Borchardt
Affiliated with The Society of Indexers, UK (qv)
Publications: Australian Society of Indexers' Newsletter (quarterly); *Indexers Available*

Australian Standard Book Numbering Agency, National Library of Australia, Canberra, ACT 2600 Tel: (062) 621431 Cable Add: Natlibaust Telex: 62100 Fax: (062) 571703

The **Book** Trade Group of Western Australia, c/o Bookland Pty Ltd, 287-295 Lord St, East Perth, WA 6000
President: George Hancock; *Secretary:* Mae Gregory

Christian Bookselling Association of Australia, PO Box 576, Caringbah, NSW 2229 (Located at: Suite 2, 7-9 President Ave, Caringbah) Tel: (02) 5243347
Secretary: John Manners

I B I S Information Services Ltd*, GPO Box 995, Sydney, NSW 2001 Tel: (02) 2902844 Telex: 27585
Secretary: John Goodman

Literary Arts Board of the Australia Council*, PO Box 302, 168 Walker St, North Sydney, NSW 2060 Tel: (02) 9233333 Telex: 26023
Director: Tom Shapcott

National Book Council, Level 5, 1 City Rd, South Melbourne, Victoria 3205 Tel: (03) 6145111
President: Thomas Keneally; *Chairman:* Michael Zifcak
Publication: Australian Book Review

New South Wales Booksellers' Association*, PO Box Q87, Sydney, NSW 2000 (Located at: 66 King St, Sydney) Tel: (02) 279471
Secretary: Sue Harvey

Public Lending Right Scheme, Department of the Arts, Sport, the Environment, Tourism and Territories, PO Box 812, North Sydney, NSW 2060 (Located at: 3rd Floor, Northside Gdns, 168 Walker St, North Sydney) Tel: (02) 9233379 Telex: 26023 Fax: (02) 9227650 c/o Australia Council
Administrator, PLR: A N Johnson

Society of Editors (Victoria), c/o PO Box 176, Carlton South, Victoria 3053
Secretary: Lisa Berryman
Publications: The Society of Editors Newsletter (monthly), *Register of Freelance Publishing Services* (annual)

Standard Book Numbering Agency, see Australian Standard Book Numbering Agency

Tasmanian Booksellers' Association*, GPO Box 170, Launceston, Tasmania 7250
President: R F Tilley; *Secretary:* Y G Tilley

United States Book Association*, PO Box 154, Artarmon, NSW 2064
Secretary: Ian C Swallow

Western Australian Booksellers' Association, now The Book Trade Group of Western Australia (qv)

Book Trade Reference Books and Journals

Books

Australian & New Zealand Booksellers, W Thorpe Pty Ltd, 20-24 Stokes St, Port Melbourne, Victoria 3207

Australian and Pacific Book Prices Current, OP Books Pty Ltd, PO Box 591, Brookvale, NSW 2100

Australian Books in Print, D W Thorpe Pty Ltd, 20-24 Stokes St, Port Melbourne, Victoria 3207

Australian Serials in Print, D W Thorpe Pty Ltd, 20-24 Stokes St, Port Melbourne, Victoria 3207

Books Australia, PO Box 41, Glebe, NSW 2037
Annual catalogue

Directory of Australian Booksellers, Australian Book Trade Advisory Committee, 163 Clarence St, Sydney, NSW

Journals

The Australian Author (quarterly), Australian Society of Authors Ltd, 22 Alfred St, Milsons Point, NSW 2061

Australian Books, National Library of Australia, Canberra, ACT 2600

Australian Bookseller & Publisher, D W Thorpe Pty Ltd, 20-24 Stokes St, Port Melbourne, Victoria 3207

Australian Government Publications (quarterly, with annual cumulation), National Library of Australia, Canberra, ACT 2600

Australian National Bibliography (monthly, every four months, with annual cumulations), Nationala Library of Australia, Canberra, ACT 2600

Australian Society of Indexers' Newsletter (quarterly), Australian Society of Indexers, GPO Box 1251L, Melbourne, Victoria 3001

The Indexer, c/o Hazel K Bell, 139 The Ryde, Hatfield, Herts AL9 5DP, UK
Journal of Australian, American and British Societies of Indexers

Victorian Government Publications (VGP) (monthly and annual), State Library of Victoria, 328 Swanston St, Melbourne, Victoria 3000

Weekly Book Newsletter, D W Thorpe Pty Ltd, 20-24 Stokes St, Port Melbourne, Victoria 3207

Publishers

A D I S Health Science Press, now incorporated in Williams & Wilkins and Associates ADIS Pty Ltd (qv)

A D I S Press Australasia Pty Ltd, PO Box 132, Balgowlah, NSW 2093 (Located at: 404 Sydney Road, Balgowlah) Tel: (02) 9492022 Cable Add: Adinfo Sydney Telex: 25868 Adis Fax: (02) 9495007
Chief Editorial Office: ADIS Press Ltd, New Zealand (qv)
Associate Companies: ADIS Press Publications Ltd, Hong Kong (qv); ADIS Press Ltd, UK (qv); ADIS Press International Inc, Oxford Court Business Centre, Suite B-30, 582 Middletown Blvd, Langhorne, PA 19047, USA
Subject: Medicine
Founded: 1960

A E Press, see Stanley Thornes & Hulton (Aust) Pty Ltd

A P C O L, an imprint of Alternative Publishing Co-operative Ltd (qv)

Access Books, an imprint of Artlook Books (qv)

Addison-Wesley Publishers (Pty) Ltd*, A1/6-8 Byfield St, North Ryde, NSW 2113 Tel: (02) 8882733 Cable Add: Adiwes Sydney Telex: 71919
General Manager, Editorial and Rights & Permissions: Derek Hall; *School Sales Manager:* John Munro (school, juveniles and general)
Parent Company: Addison-Wesley Publishing Company, Reading, MA, USA
Associate Company: Addison-Wesley Publishers Ltd, UK (qv for other associates)
Subjects: Educational Books, Scientific and Technical Books, Juveniles

Albatross Books+, PO Box 320, Sutherland, NSW 2232 (Located at: 55 East Parade, Sutherland, NSW 2232) Tel: (0612) 5214455 Telex: 170808 Numcon Fax: (0612) 5211515
Chief Executive: John Waterhouse; *Editor:* Ken Goodlet; *Sales Manager:* Kevin Goddard
Associate Companies: Lion Publishing PLC (qv); Marc Europe, Bromley, Kent (both UK)
Subject: Religion (Illustrated children's books, teenage and adult fiction, Bible reference books, general adult paperbacks)
1986: 60 titles *1987:* 70 titles *Founded:* 1980
ISBN Publisher's Prefix: 0-86760

Algona Publications Pty Ltd, 16 Charles St, Northcote, Victoria 3070 Tel: (03) 4813337
Chief Executives: John R Brownlie, Gloria E Harman
Subjects: Australian flora, history and landscape for travellers; Bushcraft, survival and first aid; Outdoor activity guide books and maps: Australia and overseas
Founded: 1970
ISBN Publisher's Prefix: 0-909594

Allara Publishing*, 47 Deakin St, East Bentleigh, Victoria 3165
ISBN Publisher's Prefix: 0-85887

Allen & Unwin Australia Pty Ltd, 8 Napier St, North Sydney, NSW 2060 Tel: (02) 9226399 Cable Add: Deucalion Sydney Telex: 24331 Gaua Fax: (02) 9224317
Man Dir: P A Gallagher; *Editorial:* John Iremonger; *Sales:* Roger Ward, Paul Donovan; *Production:* Rhonda Black; *Publicity:* Maggie Hamilton
Parent Company: Unwin Hyman Ltd, UK (qv)
Associate Companies: Allen & Unwin (with the Port Nicholson Press), New Zealand (qv); Allen & Unwin Inc, 8 Winchester Pl, Winchester, MA 01890, USA
Branch Off: 156 Collins St, Melbourne, Victoria 3000
Subjects: Academic, Social Science, General Fiction and Non-fiction
Founded: 1976
ISBN Publisher's Prefixes: 0-86861, 0-04

Alternative Publishing Co-operative Ltd*, 26 Atkinson St, Arncliffe, NSW 2205 Tel: (02) 2113837/591937
Chairman: Michael Law; *Editorial, Sales, Production, Publicity, Rights & Permissions:* D K Cleaver
Imprint: APCOL
Subjects: Reference, High-priced Paperbacks, Psychology, University & Secondary Textbooks, History, Political Science, Sociology, Economics
Founded: 1975

Angus & Robertson Publishers, PO Box 290, North Ryde, NSW 2113 (Located at: Unit 4, 31 Waterloo Rd, North Ryde) Tel: (02) 8884111 Cable Add: Fragment Sydney Telex: 26452 Fax: (02) 8889972
Chief Executive: Terry T Hughes; *Publisher:* Jennifer Rowe; *Publishing Manager:* Roz Gatwood; *Production Manager:* Savio Au; *Publicity Manager:* Deborah Wood; *Rights & Permissions Manager:* Jane Scurr
Associate Companies: Angus & Robertson (UK), UK (qv); Salem House Publishers, 462 Boston St, Topsfield, MA 01983, USA
Subjects: General, Children's, Paperbacks: bias Australian
Founded: 1886
Miscellaneous: Firm is a division of News Ltd
ISBN Publisher's Prefix: 0-207

Ansay Pty Ltd+, PO Box 90, Leichhardt, NSW 2040 (Located at: 19-25 Beeson St, Leichhardt 1) Tel: (02) 5602044 Cable Add: Cowboy Sydney
Man Dir: Philip Lindsay; *Editorial, Production:* H E Lindsay; *Sales, Rights & Permissions:* P S Lindsay; *Publicity:* N McIntyre
Parent Companies: A L Lindsay & Co Pty Ltd, Lindsays Leichhardt Pty Ltd
Imprint: Dollar Books
Subjects: Fiction, Educational
Founded: 1972
ISBN Publisher's Prefix: 0-909245

Argo Press, an imprint of Colporteur Press Pty Ltd (qv)

Edward **Arnold** (Australia) Pty Ltd+, PO Box 234, Caulfield East, Victoria 3145 (Located at: 80 Waverley Rd, Caulfield East) Tel: (03) 5722211 Cable Add: Edarnold Melbourne Vic Telex: 35974 Fax: (03) 5722095
Dir: Terry Coyle; *Publishing:* Marie Kelly; *Production:* Roger Seddon; *Promotions:* Kathryn O'Connor
Parent Company: Hodder & Stoughton Ltd, UK (qv)
Subject: Secondary Textbooks
Founded: 1966, changed name 1975
ISBN Publisher's Prefix: 0-7131

Artlook Books*, The Maltings, 37 Stuart St, North Perth, WA Tel: (09) 3289188 Telex: 92881
Man Dir, Editorial: Helen Weller; *Sales:* Guy Weller; *Production:* Anne McInerney; *Publicity:* H M E Weller; *Rights & Permissions:* John Harper-Nelson
Imprint: Access Books
Subjects: Biography, History, Poetry, Fiction, Children's, Australiana
Bookshop: 164 Beaufort St, Perth, WA
Founded: 1978
ISBN Publisher's Prefixes: 0-86445 (Artlook), 0-949795 (Access)

Ashton Scholastic, PO Box 579, Gosford, NSW 2250 Tel: (043) 283555 Cable Add: Tonash Sydney Telex: 24881
Man Dir: Ken A Jolly; *Publishing, Rights & Permissions:* David Harris; *Marketing Manager:* Leonie M Sweeney; *National Sales Co-ordinator:* Gavin S Shepherd
Shipping Add: Railway Crescent, Lisarow, via Gosford
Parent Company: Scholastic Inc, 730 Broadway, New York, NY 10003, USA
Imprints: Classroom Magazine, Four Winds Press, Microzine, Scholastic, Twistaplot, Vagabond, Wildfire, Windswept, Wizware
Branch Offs: 1091 Toorak Rd, Hartwell, Victoria 3124; 5th Floor, Teachers Bldg, 495 Boundary St, Spring Hill, Queensland 4000; 254 Halifax St, Adelaide, SA 5000; 2nd Floor, Teachers Union Bldg, 150-152 Adelaide Terrace, Perth, WA 6000
Subjects: Juveniles, Paperbacks, Secondary & Primary Textbooks, Educational Materials
Book Clubs: Arrow, Lucky, Star, Teachers Bookshelf, Teenage, Wombat
Bookshop: Oldmeadow Booksellers (Australia) Pty Ltd, 18 Helen St, West Heidelberg, Victoria 3081
Founded: 1968
ISBN Publisher's Prefix: 0-86896

Associated Book Publishers (Aust) Ltd, 44-50 Waterloo Rd, North Ryde, NSW 2113 Tel: (02) 8870177 Telex: 27995 Asbook Fax: (02) 8889706
Man Dir: W J Mackarell
Division: Methuen LBC Ltd (qv)
Parent Company: Associated Book Publishers PLC, UK (qv)
Subsidiary Company: Reed Methuen Publishers Ltd, New Zealand (qv)
Branch Off: 150 Burwood Rd, Hawthorn,n Victoria

Aurora Press, an imprint of Chatto, Bodley Head & Jonathan Cape Australia Pty Ltd (qv)

Australasian Educa Press Pty Ltd (AE Press), now Stanley Thornes & Hulton (Aust) Pty Ltd (qv)

Australasian Publishing Co Pty Ltd+, Cnr Bridge Rd and Jersey St, Hornsby, NSW 2077 Tel: (02) 4762000 Cable Add: Publishing Hornsby Telex: 23274
Chairman: G C Greene; *Man Dir:* G A Rutherford; *Sales Dir:* J E Bullivant; *Publicity Dir and Rights & Permissions:* John Cody; *Distribution Dir:* K A Harrap
Subsidiary Company: Chatto, Bodley Head & Jonathan Cape Australia Pty Ltd (qv)
Branch Offs: 83 Glen Eira Rd, Ripponlea, Victoria 3183; 6 Nurran St, Mt Gravatt, Queensland 4122; 33 Pirie St, Adelaide, South Australia 5000
Subjects: General Fiction, Belles Lettres, Juveniles, Education, General Science
ISBN Publisher's Prefix: 0-900882

Australia & New Zealand Book Co Pty Ltd*, PO Box 459, Brookvale, NSW 2100 (Located at: 10 Aquatic Drive, Frenchs Forest, NSW 2086) Tel: (0612) 4524411 Telex: 70727
Chief Executive, Sales, Rights & Permissions: G Ross King
Parent Company: Bardon Investments Pty Ltd
Subsidiary Company: Australia & New Zealand Book Co Pty Ltd (ANZ), New Zealand (qv)
Imprint: ANZ
Branch Off: 69 Rosslyn St, West Melbourne, Victoria 3003
Subjects: Science, Technics, Medicine, Computers
Founded: 1964
ISBN Publisher's Prefix: 0-85552

Australian Academy of Science, GPO Box 783, Canberra, ACT 2601 Tel: (062) 475341 Cable Add: Acscican Telex: 62406 Acsci Fax: (062) 480639
Executive Secretary: H A W Southon; *Publications Officer, Sales and Rights & Permissions:* D French
Branch Off: 191 Royal Parade, Parkville, Melbourne, Victoria 3000
Subjects: High-quality educational, academic and scholastic books on a wide range of disciplines
Founded: 1956
ISBN Publisher's Prefix: 0-85847

Australian Broadcasting Corporation (Enterprises)*, GPO Box 9994, Sydney, NSW 2001 Tel: (02) 4378188 Telex: 176860 Abcenp
Chief Executive and Rights & Permissions: Glenn Hamilton; *Editorial:* Stuart Neal; *Marketing:* Amanda Emmett; *Production:* Lindsay Somerville; *Publicity:* Kate Reid
Parent Company: Australian Broadcasting Corporation (at above address)
Subjects: Non-fiction (general interest)
Bookshops: ABC Shop: Mezzanine Level, Centrepoint, Sydney, NSW 2000; Galleria Level, State Bank Centre, Bourke St, Melbourne, Victoria 3000; Wintergarden-on-the-Mall, Queen St Level, Brisbane, Queensland; The Carillon Centre, Hay St Level, Perth, WA; Southern Cross Arcade, Adelaide, SA; Upper Level, Monaro Mall Civic Square, Canberra, ACT; 167 Liverpool St, Hobart, Tasmania; Cnr Cavenagh & Bennett Sts, Darwin, NT
ISBN Publisher's Prefix: 0-642

The **Australian Council** for Educational Research Ltd+, PO Box 210, Hawthorn, Victoria 3122 (Located at: Radford House, Frederick St, Hawthorn) Tel: (03) 8191400 Cable Add: Aceres Fax: (03) 8195502
Man Dir: Dr B McGaw; *Sales Dir:* A Wilkins; *Publicity:* P Jeffery; *Editorial, Production, Rights & Permissions:* M Schoo
Subjects: Education, Textbooks, Educational materials and tests, Software
Bookshop: At above address
Founded: 1930
ISBN Publisher's Prefix: 0-85563

Australian Encyclopaedia Pty Ltd, see The Grolier Society of Australia Pty Ltd

Australian Government Publishing Service, GPO Box 84, Canberra, ACT 2601 (Located at: AGPS Bldg, Wentworth Ave, Ilingston, ACT 2604) Tel: (062) 954411 Telex: 62013 Fax: (062) 954454
Chief Executive: J L Leonard; *Government Printer:* G R Dempster (acting); *Director, Publishing, Rights & Permissions:* F Thompson; *Editorial:* H McLintock; *Sales:* R Missingham; *Marketing:* Ken Blair
Subject: Australian Government Publications and Legislation
Bookshops: Commonwealth Government Bookshops (qv under Major Booksellers)
Founded: 1970

Miscellaneous: Sales agent for publications of New Zealand Government Printer
ISBN Publisher's Prefixes: 0-642, 0-644

Australian Institute of Aboriginal Studies+, GPO Box 553, Canberra, ACT 2601 Tel: (062) 461111 Cable Add: Abinst
Principal: Warwick Dix; *Managing Editor, Publications and Rights & Permissions:* David R Horton
Warehouse: Acton House, Acton, ACT 2601
Subjects: Aboriginal studies (Australia), Anthropology, Archaeology, Ethnology, Ethnomusicology, Linguistics, Human Biology, Prehistory, Material culture, Aboriginal art, Education
ISBN Publisher's Prefix: 0-85575

Australian Institute of Criminology*, PO Box 28, Woden, ACT 2606 (Located at: 10-18 Colbee Court, Phillip, ACT 2606) Tel: (062) 822111 Cable Add: Austcrim
Dir: Richard Harding; *Editorial:* Jack Sandry
Subject: Criminology
Founded: 1976
ISBN Publisher's Prefix: 0-642

Australian National Gallery+*, GPO Box 1150, Canberra, ACT 2601 Tel: (062) 712501 Cable Add: Ang Canberra Telex: 61500
Head of Publications and Rights & Permissions: Elizabeth Bilney; *Editorial:* Dana Rowan; *Sales:* Marian Vickery; *Production:* Suzanna Campbell
Subjects: Art (related to the collection of the Australian National Gallery)
Bookshop: The Gallery Shop (at above address)
1985: 7 titles *Founded:* 1982
ISBN Publisher's Prefix: 0-642

Australian National University Press, PO Box 544, Potts Point, NSW 2011 Tel: (02) 3315211 Cable Add: Pergapress Sydney Telex: 27458 Fax: (02) 3322304
Man Dir: Jerry Mayer; *Publicity, Advertising:* P Doust; *Editor:* A Pender; *Rights & Permissions:* B Oakley
Warehouse: 19A Boundary St, Rushcutters Bay, NSW 2011
Parent Company: Pergamon Press (Australia) Pty Ltd (qv)
Subjects: Belles Lettres, Poetry, Biography, Geography, History, Reference, Social Science, Earth Sciences, University Textbooks, High-priced Paperbacks
Founded: 1965
ISBN Publisher's Prefix: 0-08, (ANUP pre-1985 0-7081)

Australian Universities Press Pty Ltd*, Offset House, 169-171 Philip St, Waterloo, NSW 2017 Tel: (02) 695633
Man Dir: R G Hackett
Subjects: Cookery Books, Australiana, Children's Books
ISBN Publisher's Prefix: 0-7249

Author Press, an imprint of Kelly Books (qv)

S John **Bacon** Pty Ltd+, PO Box 223, Oakleigh, Victoria 3166 (Located at: 9 Kingston Town Close, Oakleigh Tel: (03) 5631044 Cable Add: Interbac Melbourne Telex: 151218 Bacaus Fax: (03) 5697211
Man Dir: Andrew Tostevin; *Dirs:* Mary Bacon, Rohan Bacon, John Morgan, Joan Diemar; *Sales & Marketing:* R Wilson
Subsidiary Company: Lantern House Pty Ltd
Imprints: Interbac, Lantern House
Subjects: Theology, Christian Education, Devotional Music, Primary and Secondary Educational Books and Aids, Children's Books

1986: 8 titles *Founded:* 1938
ISBN Publisher's Prefix: 0-85579

Bahloo Computers, an imprint of R J Cleary (qv)

Bahloo Publishers, an imprint of R J Cleary (qv)

Bandicoot Books, an imprint of Night Owl Publishers Pty Ltd (qv)

Bantam, an imprint of Transworld Publishers (Australia) Pty Ltd (qv)

Blackwell Scientific Publications (Australia) Pty Ltd, 107 Barry St, Carlton, Victoria 3053 Tel: (03) 3470300 Cable Add: Blackwell Melbourne
Chief Executive: M Robertson
Parent Company: Blackwell Scientific Publications Ltd, UK (qv)
Subjects: Medicine; Life, Earth and Computer Sciences
1985: 27 titles *Founded:* 1981
ISBN Publisher's Prefix: 0-86793

Boobook Publications, PO Box 238, Balgowlah, NSW 2093 Tel: (02) 9492136
Man Dirs: Ian Hoyle, Sally Hoyle
Subjects: General, Martial Arts
Founded: 1981

Bookwise International, PO Box 296, Welland, SA 5007 (Located at: 5 Jeanes St, Beverley, SA 5007) Tel: (08) 2688222 Telex: 88471
Man Dir: Rod Davis
Branch Offs: 62 Wellington Parade, East Melbourne, Victoria 3002; 161 Clarence St, Sydney, NSW 2000
Subjects: Art, Graphic Art, Oriental Arts, Architecture, Photography, Social Sciences, Languages, Cooking, Quality Non-fiction, Travel Guides
Founded: 1957
Miscellaneous: Firm is also a wholesale distributor
ISBN Publisher's Prefix: 0-908054

Boolarong Publications+, 12 Brookes St, Bowen Hills, Queensland 4006 Tel: (07) 8541920 Telex: 41462 Bestad
Man Dir, Sales, Publicity, Rights & Permissions: L T Padman; *Editorial:* Mrs E M Bagnall; *Production:* G A Peake
Parent Company: Artists Associated Pty Ltd
Subjects: Art, Historical, Biographies
1985: 20 titles *1986:* 19 titles *Founded:* 1977
ISBN Publisher's Prefixes: 0-908175, 0-86439

David **Boyce** Publishing & Associates*, PO Box Q187, Queen Victoria Bldg, Sydney, NSW 2000 (Located at: 44 Regent St, Sydney) Tel: (02) 2111096/2111962 Telex: 7110101
Man & Sales Dir: David Boyce; *Production:* Jan Kenyon
Subjects: Automotive Technical
Founded: 1975
ISBN Publisher's Prefix: 0-909682

Breakthroughs, an imprint of Pan Books (Australia) Pty Ltd (qv)

Brodie's Notes, an imprint of Pan Books (Australia) Pty Ltd (qv)

William **Brooks Queensland**, see Brooks Waterloo

Brooks Waterloo+, 36 Albert Rd, South Melbourne, Victoria 3205 Tel: (03) 6995000 Telex: 151018 Fax: (03) 6905099
Chief Executive: Geoff Wright; *Editorial Manager:* Keryn Wood; *Managers:* Leon Bedington (Queensland), Mark Childs (NSW); *Sales & Publicity Manager:* Paul Tuffin; *Rights & Permissions:* Jane Warne

Parent Company: McPherson's Ltd, Level 43, Rialto, 525 Collins St, Melbourne, Victoria 3001
Branch Offs: Unit 17, Argyle Pl, Argyle St, Albion, Queensland 4010 Tel: (07) 2625399; 6th Floor 3 Smail St, Broadway, NSW 2007 Tel: (02) 2114825
Subjects: Educational (Primary and Secondary), Professional, Reference
1985: 33 titles *1986:* 34 titles *Founded:* 1986 (William Brooks 1920)
Miscellaneous: Previously William Brooks Queensland and Waterloo Press
ISBN Publisher's Prefix: 0-86440

Butterworths Pty Ltd, 271-273 Lane Cove Rd, North Ryde, NSW 2113 Tel: (02) 8873444 Telex: 122033 Fax: (02) 8874251
Man Dir: D J Jackson; *Editorial Dir, Rights & Permissions:* J Broadfoot; *Marketing:* T Sleigh; *Production:* B Coats
Parent Company: Butterworth & Co (Publishers) Ltd, UK (qv)
Branch Offs: 233 Macquarie St, Sydney NSW 2000; 160 William St, Melbourne, Victoria 3000; Commonwealth Bank Bldg, King George Sq, Brisbane, Queensland 4000; 45 St George's Terrace, Perth, WA 6000; 1st Floor, Vanguard Insurance Bldg, 195 Victoria Square, Adelaide, SA 5000; 8th Floor, Canberra House, Canberra, ACT 2600; 161 Macquarie St, Hobart, Tasmania 7000
Subjects: Law, Commerce, Medicine, Science, Technology
Bookshops: At Branch Office addresses
Founded: 1910
ISBN Publisher's Prefix: 0-409

C S I R O (Commonwealth Scientific and Industrial Research Organization), 314 Albert St, PO Box 89, East Melbourne, Victoria 3002 Tel: (03) 4187333 Telex: 30236
Sales & Marketing: Jeff Prentice
Shipping Add: 19 Rokeby St, Collingwood, Victoria 3066
Subjects: Engineering, Science & Technology, Agriculture
Founded: 1926
ISBN Publisher's Prefix: 0-643

Cambridge University Press, 10 Stamford Rd, Oakleigh, Victoria 3166 Tel: (03) 5680322 Cable Add: Cantabaust
Dir: Kim Harris
Subjects: Education, University, Secondary & Primary Textbooks
Head Office: Cambridge University Press, UK (qv)
ISBN Publisher's Prefix: 0-521

Carroll's, see Horwitz Grahame Pty Ltd

Cavalier Press Pty Ltd*, PO Box 5, South Yarra, Victoria 3141 (Located at: 45 Richmond Terrace, Richmond 3121) Tel: (03) 4292280 Telex: 38225
Joint Executive Dirs: Josef Vondra, Geoffrey M Gold
Subjects: Australian History, Ethnic History, Multiculturalism, Multilingual books on Australiana, International Affairs
Founded: 1979
ISBN Publisher's Prefix: 0-949743

Centre Publications*, PO Box 114, Saint Kilda, Melbourne, Victoria 3182 (Located at: 25 Chapel St, Saint Kilda) Tel: (03) 510631
Man Dir: Paul Sumner
Parent Company: Yoco Pty Ltd (at above address)
Associate Companies: THE Foundation (qv); The Yoga Education Centre (at above address)
Subjects: Education, Health
Founded: 1974

Century Hutchinson Australia Pty Ltd, PO Box 496, Hawthorn, Victoria 3122 (Located at: 16-22 Church St, Hawthorn) Tel: (03) 8623311 Telex: 37972 Fax: (03) 8616885
Man Dir: Ernie Mason; *Managing Editor, Rights & Permissions:* Matthew Kelly; *Publicity Manager:* Anne Wray
Subsidiary Company: Hutchinson Distributors Pty Ltd (at above address)
Associate Company: Century Hutchinson Ltd, UK (qv)
Branch Offs: 89-91 Albion St, Surry Hills, NSW 2010; 236 Elizabeth St, Brisbane, Queensland 4000; 3 Norman Rd, Roleystone, WA
Subjects: Biography, History, Reference, Juveniles, Fiction, Humour, Sporting, General Non-fiction
ISBN Publisher's Prefix: 0-09

Challenge, an imprint of Sapphire Books Pty Ltd (qv)

Chatto, Bodley Head & Jonathan Cape Australia Pty Ltd*, c/o Australasian Publishing Co Pty Ltd, Cnr Bridge Rd and Jersey St, Hornsby, NSW 2077 Tel: (02) 4762000 Telex: 23274
Man Dir: John Cody
Orders to: Australasian Publishing Co Pty Ltd (at above address)
Parent Company: Australasian Publishing Co Pty Ltd (qv)
Imprint: Aurora Press
Subjects: Fiction, Non-fiction, Reference, History, Children's, Australiana
Founded: 1977

Cheshire, an imprint of Longman Cheshire Pty Ltd (qv)

Chi Rho, an imprint of Lutheran Publishing House (qv)

Childerset Pty Ltd+, PO Box 471, Norwood, SA 5067 (Located at: 72 Rundle St, Kent Town) Tel: (08) 428931 Telex: 88765
Man Dir: David Ridyard
Associate Company: Children's Bookshelf of Australia
Subjects: Children's Picture-books
Founded: 1970
ISBN Publisher's Prefix: 0-909404

Churchill Livingstone, an imprint of Longman Cheshire Pty Ltd (qv)

Circus Books, now Schwartz Publishing (Victoria) Pty Ltd (qv)

Classroom Magazine, an imprint of Ashton Scholastic (qv)

Clearway, an imprint of Sapphire Books Pty Ltd (qv)

R J Cleary, PO Box 939, Darlinghurst, NSW 2010 (Located at: 86-77 Riley St, East Sydney) Tel: (02) 3322437 Cable Add: Clearpub Sydney Telex: 121822 attn SY3099 Fax: (02) 3322684 attn Clearpub
Man Dir: R J Cleary
Imprints: Bahloo Computers, Bahloo Publishers, Real-Life Education, Rent-a-Lesson, Success Education
Subjects: Biography, History, How-to, Reference, Juveniles, High-priced Paperbacks, Australiana, Series Books, Part-Works, Primary and Secondary Textbooks, Educational Materials, Children's Activities, Audiovisual, video, computer software, Co-editions, Special Projects
Founded: 1969
ISBN Publisher's Prefix: 0-85567

Cole Publications, 3 Creswick St, Hawthorn, Victoria 3122 Tel: (03) 8185640
Man Dir: Cole Turnley

Parent Company: Alterns Pty Ltd (at above address)
Subjects: Juveniles, Technical, Humour
Founded: 1868
ISBN Publisher's Prefix: 0-909900

William **Collins** Pty Ltd+*, GPO Box 476, Sydney, NSW 2001 (Located at: 55 Clarence St, Sydney) Tel: (02) 2902066 Cable Add: Folio Sydney Telex: 26292 Folio
Chairman and Man Dir: Terry Kitson; *Deputy Man Dir:* A A Leutenegger; *Publisher:* Richard Smart; *Senior Editor and Rights & Permissions:* Margaret R Jones; *Children's Editor:* Anne Bower Ingram; *Production Coordinator:* Carmen Mamo; *Publicity & Advertising:* Jan Garvan (Collins), Roz McGregor (Fontana), Debbie McInnes (Granada)
Warehouse & Shipping Add: Yarrawa Rd, Moss Vale, NSW 2577
Parent Company: William Collins PLC, UK (qv)
Subsidiary Company: Collins Dove (qv)
Branch Offs: Garden Sq, 643 Kessels Rd, Upper Mt Gravatt, Queensland; 45 Whitehorse Rd, Deepdene, Victoria 3103; 7-9 Maple Ave, Forestville, SA 5035; 26 Boag Pl, Morley, WA 6062; 100 Harris St, Pyrmont, NSW 2009
Subjects: Fiction, Non-fiction, Sport, Biography, Politics, Humour, Photography, History, Australiana, Natural History, Sociology, Popular Health, Children's
1985: 50 titles *Founded:* 1872

Collins Dove+*, PO Box 316, Blackburn, Victoria 3130 (Located at: Suite 1, 60-64 Railway Rd, Blackburn) Tel: (03) 8771333 Cable Add: Dovcom
Man Dir: J Garry Eastman; *Editorial:* David C Lovell, Don Drummond; *Sales, Publicity:* Sheila Drummond
Parent Company: William Collins Pty Ltd (qv)
Associated imprints: Drummond, Primary Education
Subjects: Catholic Theology, Religion, Moral Philosophy, Education, Teacher Reference, Politics
1985: 42 titles *Founded:* 1972
ISBN Publisher's Prefix: 0-85924

Colporteur Press Pty Ltd*, 96 Beattie St, Balmain, Sydney, NSW 2041 Tel: (02) 8184955 Telex: 71698
Chairman: A R Grabrovaz; *Publisher:* K B Banerji; *Editorial, Rights & Permissions:* Ken Banerji; *Sales:* Tony Grabrovaz; *Production, Publicity:* Prue Bucknall
Associate Company: Marketing and Book Distribution Services Pty Ltd (at above address)
Imprint: Argo Press
Branch Offs: MBDS Pty Ltd, 7th Floor, 608 St Kilda Rd, Melbourne, Victoria 3004; MBDS London Ltd, 90B Randolph Ave, London W9, UK
Subjects: Illustrated Non-fiction, Leisure, Cookery, Reference, Health, Gardening, Australiana, Co-editions
Founded: 1981
ISBN Publisher's Prefix: 0-86399

Commemorative Editions Pty Ltd, now part of Visa Books (qv)

Corgi, an imprint of Transworld Publishers (Australia) Pty Ltd (qv)

Coronet, an imprint of Hodder & Stoughton (Australia) Pty Ltd (qv)

Currawong Press Pty Ltd*, PO Box 233, Milson's Point, NSW 2061 Tel: (02) 9698122
Chief Executive: Phillip Mathews
Subjects: Mainly Non-fiction

Founded: 1946
Miscellaneous: Publishers of *Australian Children's Dictionary*
ISBN Publisher's Prefix: 0-85041

Currency Press Pty Ltd, 330 Oxford St, Paddington, NSW 2021 Tel: (02) 3576401 Cable Add: Dramabooks Sydney Telex: 21822 Pubtlx SY1253
Managing Editor: Katharine Brisbane Parsons; *Manager:* Ian Murdoch; *Publishing Manager and Rights & Permissions:* Sandra Gorman
Orders to: PO Box 452, Paddington, NSW 2021
Subjects: Drama, Films & Television (history/criticism); Theatre (history/criticism)
1985: 22 titles *1986:* 14 titles *Founded:* 1971
ISBN Publisher's Prefix: 0-86819

Curriculum Development Centre, PO Box 34, Woden, ACT 2606 Tel: (062) 891333 Cable Add: Education Canberra
Dir: Brent Corish; *Publications Manager:* John Hutchins; *Editorial:* Terry Gilmore; *Rights & Permissions:* Chris Vening
Subjects: Educational
ISBN Publisher's Prefix: 0-642

Cygnet Books, an imprint of University of Western Australia Press (qv)

Darling Downs Institute Press, The Darling Downs Institute of Advanced Education, PO Darling Heights, Toowoomba, Queensland 4350 Tel: (076) 312100 Cable Add: Ddiae Toowoomba Telex: 40010 Fax: (076) 301540
Dir: Jocelyn K Thompson
Parent Company: The Darling Downs Institute of Advanced Education
Subjects: General, Scholarly, Regional History, Literature
1985: 8 titles *1986:* 6 titles *Founded:* 1975
ISBN Publisher's Prefixes: 0-909306, 0-909414

Deakin University Press+, Deakin University, Victoria 3217 Tel: (052) 471156 Telex: 35625
Chief Executive: Louise Moran; *Sales, Publicity:* Fay Warby; *Production and Rights & Permissions:* Dr Nicholas Flower
Parent Company: Durac Ltd (at above address)
Subjects: Tertiary scholarly material, including Education, Educational Administration, Language Education & Linguistics, Curriculum Journalism, History, Philosophy of Science, Social Sciences, Distance Education
Founded: 1979
ISBN Publisher's Prefix: 0-7300

Dell, an imprint of Transworld Publishers (Australia) Pty Ltd (qv)

J M Dent Pty Ltd+, PO Box 289, Ferntree Gully, Victoria 3156 (Located at: 34-36 Wadhurst Drive, Boronia, Victoria 3155) Tel: (03) 2217333 Cable Add: Malaby Melbourne Telex: 134858 Dentoz
Publishing Manager and Rights & Permissions: Ms J L Day; *Marketing Manager:* V Beasley; *Publicity Manager:* Ms P Sheldrake
Parent Company: J M Dent & Sons Ltd, UK (qv)
Branch Off: Suite 24, 67 Christie St, St Leonards, NSW 2065
Subjects: Children's, General, Fiction, Australiana, Health & Fitness, Cookery & Crafts
1985: 5 titles *Founded:* 1977
ISBN Publisher's Prefix: 0-86770

Dezsery Publications Pty Ltd+, GPO Box 1499, Adelaide, SA 5001 (Located at: 408

King William St, Adelaide, SA 5001) Tel: (08) 2312910
Chief Executive: Dr Andrew Steven Dezsery
Subjects: Writings in English and other languages by immigrant writers in Australia, of different ethnic backgrounds
1987: 24 titles *Founded:* 1975
ISBN Publisher's Prefixes: 0-908287, 0-9597437

Dollar Books, an imprint of Ansay Pty Ltd (qv)

Doubleday, an imprint of Transworld Publishers (Australia) Pty Ltd (qv)

Dove Communications Pty Ltd, now Collins Dove (qv)

Drummond, an associated imprint of Collins Dove (qv)

E A Books, Level 4, 2 Ernest St, Crows Nest, NSW 2065 Tel: (02) 4381533 Telex: 27640 Eameab Fax: (02) 4385934
General Manager: Justin Paine
Parent Company: Institution of Engineers Australia, 11 National Ct, Barton, ACT 2600
Associate Companies: Engineers Australia Magazine, Chemical Engineering in Australia Magazine
Imprint: I E Aust Publications
Subjects: Civil, Electrical, Mechanical and Chemical Engineering
1985: 18 titles *1986:* 15 titles *Founded:* 1919 (I E Aust), 1976 (E A Books)
ISBN Publisher's Prefix: 0-85825

Educational Material Aid+, 10 South St, Strathfield, NSW 2135 Tel: (02) 767962
Dir: Yvonne McBurney
Subjects: Australian History and Novels designed to improve reading skills; Australian History for general reading
Bookshop: At above address
1986: 1 title *1987:* 1 title *Founded:* 1976
ISBN Publisher's Prefix: 0-908053

David **Ell** Press Pty Ltd+, PO Box 168, Chippendale, NSW 2008 (Located at: 137-139 Regent St, Chippendale) Tel: (02) 3191155 Telex: 70041 Fax: (02) 6985925
Man Dir: David Ell; *Managing Editor:* Kathryn Lamberton; *Assistant Editor:* Anna MacLeod; *Marketing Manager:* Jane Curry
Subsidiary Company: Ellsyd Press Pty Ltd (at above address)
Imprint: Ellsyd Press (paperbacks)
Subjects: Children's & Adults' mass-market, Decorative Arts (Australian)
1986: 24 titles *1987:* 30 titles *Founded:* 1978
ISBN Publisher's Prefixes: 0-908197, 0-949290 (Ellsyd Press)

Ellsyd Press, an imprint of David Ell Press Pty Ltd (qv)

Elm Tree, an imprint of Penguin Books Australia Ltd (qv)

Encyclopaedia Britannica (Australia) Inc, 22 Lambs Rd, Artarmon, NSW 2064 Tel: (02) 4384544 Telex: 23044 Enbrit
President: H De Weese; *Vice-President, Sales Administration:* N Bechler
Parent Company: Encyclopaedia Britannica Inc, Britannica Centre, 310 South Michigan Ave, Chicago, IL 60604, USA
Associate Company: Encyclopaedia Britannica International Ltd, UK (qv for other associate companies)
Subjects: Educational Reference, Dictionaries, Geography, Biography, Art, Science (all suitable for levels from kindergarten to tertiary education), Audiovisual material and teaching aids
ISBN Publisher's Prefix: 0-909263

Era Publications+, 220-222 Grange Rd, Flinders Park, SA 5025 Tel: (08) 3524122 Telex: 88765 Telcom AD077 Fax: (08) 2340023
Chief Executives: Rodney David Martin, Sandra Dorothy Martin
Orders to: PO Box 231, Brooklyn Park, SA 5032
Parent Company: R D Martin Pty Ltd (at above address)
Imprints: Keystone Paperbacks, Keystone Picture Books, Magic Bean Shared-Readers, Play to Learn
Subjects: Children's Picture-books, Educational Aids
1987: 30 titles *Founded:* 1972
ISBN Publisher's Prefix: 0-908507

John **Ferguson** Pty Ltd, 100 Kippax St, Surry Hills, Sydney, NSW 2010 Tel: (02) 2122766
Man Dir: John R Ferguson; *Editorial:* Karen Eyre
Orders to: Angus & Robertson Publishers, Unit 4, 31 Waterloo Rd, North Ryde, NSW 2113
Subjects: Australian General & Historical, Children's
1985: 55 titles *Founded:* 1975
ISBN Publisher's Prefix: 0-949118

Fine Arts Press Pty Ltd, Suite 2, 653 Pacific Highway, Killara, NSW 2071 Tel: (02) 4984933 Cable Add: Imprint Sydney Fax: (02) 4982775
Publisher: Sam Ure Smith; *Editors:* Leon Paroissien, Jennifer Phipps; *Assistant Editor:* Annabel Davie
Subjects: Art, Fine Arts, Periodical
Miscellaneous: Company also produces books for other publishers
ISBN Publisher's Prefix: 0-86917

Four Winds Press, an imprint of Ashton Scholastic (qv)

G W P, an imprint of Great Western Press Pty Ltd (qv)

Golden Press Pty Ltd, PO Box 390, Drummoyne, NSW 2047 (Located at: 5-01 Henry Lawson Business Centre, Birkenhead Point, Drummoyne) Tel: (02) 8199111 Cable Add: Goldpress Telex: 26070 Gpress Fax: (02) 8197494
General Manager: Ross Alexander; *Publisher:* John Fenton-Smith
Parent Company: Gordon & Gotch Ltd, GPO Box 767G, Melbourne, Victoria 3001
Subsidiary Company: Shakespeare Head Press (qv)
Associated imprints include: Little Golden Books
Branch Offs: Golden Press Pty Ltd, New Zealand (qv) and all Australian States
Subjects: Biography, History, How-to, Juveniles, Secondary & Primary Textbooks, Australiana, Non-fiction
1985: 70 titles
ISBN Publisher's Prefixes: 0-85558, 0-7302

Grahame Book Co, see Horwitz Grahame Pty Ltd

Grass Roots, an imprint of Night Owl Publishers Pty Ltd (qv)

Great Western Press Pty Ltd*, 19-47 Neridah St, Chatswood, NSW 2067 Tel: (02) 4997929 Cable Add: Wespres Sydney Telex: 21822 Attn Sy 915
Man Dir, Editorial: John Isaacs; *Sales:* Anne Isaacs; *Rights & Permissions:* Robert Elliott
Associate Company: Special Book Services, 22 Ganmain Rd, Pymble, NSW 2073
Imprint: GWP
Subjects: Children's (educational & reference)
Founded: 1974
ISBN Publisher's Prefix: 0-86901

Greenhouse Publications Pty Ltd+, 385 Bridge Rd, Richmond, Victoria 3121 Tel: (03) 4292122 Telex: 151516
Man Dirs: Sally R Milner, Peter Steer; *Dirs:* Richard Walsh, Robert Henty, Chris Mackenzie; *Publisher:* Sally R Milner; *Managing Editor:* Sue Mackinnon; *Marketing Dir:* Peter Steer; *Promotions Manager:* Kate Murray
Parent Company: Australian Consolidated Press, 54 Park St, Sydney, NSW 2000
Subjects: Technical, Educational, Children's, Feminist, Cookery, Health, Fiction, Historical, General Adult
Founded: 1975

The **Grolier** Society of Australia Pty Ltd*, 14 Mars Rd, Lane Cove, NSW 2066 Tel: (02) 4283722 Cable Add: Grolier Sydney Telex: 26584
Man Dir: Sommers Botha; *General Manager, Editorial:* Edwyn Petty (Schools & Libraries)
Parent Company: Grolier Inc, Sherman Tpke, Danbury, CT 06816, USA
Associate Companies: Grolier Inc (Africa, Canada, Europe, Far East, Latin America, New Zealand, UK); Franklin Watts Inc, USA
Subsidiary Company: Australian Encyclopaedia Pty Ltd, Sydney
Subjects: Reference, Educational, Children
Founded: 1960

Hamish **Hamilton**, an imprint of Penguin Books Australia Ltd (qv)

Harcourt Brace Jovanovich Group (Australia) Pty Ltd, Locked Bag 16, Marrickville, NSW 2204 (Located at: 30-52 Smidmore St, Marrickville) Tel: (02) 5178999 Telex: 23394 Fax: (02) 5172249
Man Dir: Barry Dingley; *Marketing Dir:* Don Conson; *Publicity:* Janet Taylor
Parent Company: Harcourt Brace Jovanovich Inc, Orlando, FL 32887-0405, USA
Associate Companies: Academic Press Inc (London) Ltd, Harcourt Brace Jovanovich Ltd, Holt, Rinehart & Winston, W B Saunders & Co Ltd (all UK – qqv); Academic Press Inc, The Harcourt Brace Jovanovich Bldg, Orlando, FL 32887; Coronado Publishers Inc, 1250 Sixth Ave, San Diego, CA 92101; Grune & Stratton Inc, Orlando, FL 32819; Instructor Publications Inc, Instructor Park, Dansville, NY 14437; Johnson Reprint Corporation, 757 Third Ave, New York, NY 10017 (all USA)
Branch Offs: 7c/622 St Kilda Rd, Melbourne, Victoria 3004; 10 Moa St, Otahuhu, Auckland, New Zealand
Subjects: Educational, Science, Technical, Medicine, Reprints, Trade

AUSTRALIA 15

Hargreen Publishing Co, PO Box 256, Melbourne, Victoria 3051 (Located at: 144 Chetwynd St, North Melbourne, Victoria) Tel: (03) 3299714
Chief Executive: Michael Haratsis Snr; *Editorial, Production, Rights & Permissions:* Tim Morfesse; *Sales, Publicity:* Michael Haratsis Jnr
Parent Company: M and M A H Nominees Pty Ltd
Subjects: Educational, Reference, Non-fiction, History
1985-86: 10 titles *Founded:* 1972
ISBN Publisher's Prefix: 0-949905

Harper & Row (Australasia) Pty Ltd+, PO Box 226, Artarmon, NSW 2064 (Located at: Frederick St, Artarmon) Tel: (02) 4396155 Cable Add: Bookserv Telex: 72598 Fax: (02) 4382542
Man Dir and Rights & Permissions: B D Wilder; *Editorial:* Lynne Segal (Trade), Lawrie Grigg (College); *Publicity:* Linda Gray; *Marketing Dir:* Adrian McComb
Parent Company: Harper & Row Inc, 10 East 53rd St, New York, NY 10022, USA
Associate Companies: Editora Harper & Row do Brasil Ltda, Brazil (qv); Harper & Row Ltd, UK (qv); Harper & Row Latinoamericana-Harla SA de CV, Mexico (qv); Harper & Row Publishers, Asia, Pte Ltd, Republic of Singapore (qv)

Heartlines, an imprint of Pan Books (Australia) Pty Ltd (qv)

Heinemann Educational Australia, an imprint of Heinemann Publishers Australia Pty Ltd (qv)

Heinemann Publishers Australia Pty Ltd, 85 Abinger St, PO Box 133, Richmond, Victoria 3121 Tel: (03) 4293622 Cable Add: Hebooks Melb Telex: 35347 Heaust Fax: (03) 4295891
Man Dir: Sandy Grant; *Publishing Dir:* Ron Norman (Educational); *Publisher:* Theresa Pitt (General); *Managing Editor:* Jill Taylor; *Marketing Dir:* Terry Greenwood (General); *Sales:* Martin Spears (Educational); *Production:* Louise Laverack; *Publicity:* Carol Bennetto (General), Ann Chan (Educational); *Rights & Permissions:* Helen Camp
Parent Company: The Heinemann Group of Publishers Ltd, UK (qv). Ultimate Parent Company: Reed International PLC, Reed House, 83 Piccadilly, London W1A 1EJ, UK
Imprints include: William Heinemann Australia (General), Heinemann Educational Australia (School)
Branch Offs: PO Box 366, Brighton, SA 5048; 261 Pacific Highway, North Sydney, NSW; PO Box 299, Spring Hill, Queensland 4000; PO Box 546, Subiaco, WA 6008
Subjects: Educational (mainly Secondary, some Tertiary), Fiction, Biography, Art, Cookery, Sport, Children's, Business
Founded: 1967
ISBN Publisher's Prefixes: 0-85561 (William Heinemann Australia), 0-85859 (Heinemann Educational Australia)

Hill of Content Publishing Co Pty Ltd+, 86 Bourke St, Melbourne, Victoria 3000 Tel: (03) 6543144 Cable Add: Colbook Telex: 37396
Man Dir: M G Zifcak, OBE; *Publisher, Rights & Permissions:* M Anderson; *Editorial:* L Gregory
Associate Company: Collins Booksellers Pty Ltd (qv under Major Booksellers)
Subjects: Australiana, Australian Literature, Educational, Politics, Health
Founded: 1965
ISBN Publisher's Prefix: 0-85572

Hodder & Stoughton (Australia) Pty Ltd*, 2 Apollo Pl, Lane Cove, NSW 2066 Tel: (02) 4281022 Cable Add: Expositor Telex: 24858
Man Dir: Michael Duffett; *Publishing Director, Children's Editor:* Margaret Hamilton; *Sales & Marketing:* John Vermeer (National Sales Manager), John Marron (Hardback); *Production Manager:* Linda Williams; *Publicity:* Elsa Petersen-Schepelern; *Rights & Permissions:* Shirley Watkins
Parent Company: Hodder & Stoughton Ltd, UK (qv)
Imprints: Coronet, Hodder & Stoughton Christian Books, Knight, New English Library, Sceptre, Teach Yourself
Branch Offs: 215 Waverley Rd, East Malvern, Victoria 3145; 13 Byres St, Newstead, Queensland 4006; 63 Ferguson St, Maylands, WA 6051; 32b Dew St, Thebarton, SA 5031
Subjects: General, Fiction, Children's, History, Education, Dictionaries, Religion, General Science, Travel
1985: 108 titles
ISBN Publisher's Prefix: 0-340

Horwitz Grahame Pty Ltd+, Horwitz Cammeray Centre, 506 Miller St, PO Box 306, Cammeray, NSW 2062 Tel: (02) 9296144 Cable Add: Horbooks Sydney Telex: 127833 Horwtz Fax: (02) 9571814
General Manager: L J Moore; *Dirs:* Brian B Nash (Educational Division), R B Fuller (Non-fiction); *Managing Editor:* Susan E Horwitz; *Rights & Permissions:* Judith Wallace
Subjects: How-to, Humour, Business, Reference, Low- & High-priced Paperbacks, Biography, History, Secondary & Primary Textbooks, Educational Materials
Bookshops: Grahames Bookshop (qv under Major Booksellers)
Founded: 1921
Miscellaneous: The Horwitz Group includes Carroll's, Horwitz Publications, Grahame Book Co, Martin Educational, Scripts Publications (all at above main address)
ISBN Publisher's Prefixes: 0-7255 (Horwitz), 0-7253 (Martin Educational), 0-7252 (Scripts)

Hutchinson Publishing Group (Australia) Ltd, now incorporated in Century Hutchinson Group Australia Ltd (qv)

Hyland House Publishing Pty Ltd, 23 Bray St, South Yarra, Victoria 3141 Tel: (03) 2416336
Editorial, Rights & Permissions: Anne Godden; *Sales, Production, Publicity:* Al Knight
Subjects: General Australian
Founded: 1977
ISBN Publisher's Prefixes: 0-908090, 0-947062

I E Aust Publications, an imprint of E A Books (qv)

Inkata Press Pty Ltd+, 4 Longbourne Ave, North Clayton, Victoria 3168 Tel: (03) 5600272 Telex: 30625 attn ME3733 Fax: (03) 5601791
Man Dir: C H Jerram; *Editorial Dir:* Patricia Sellar
Subjects: Science, Technology, Natural History, Agriculture
Founded: 1968
ISBN Publisher's Prefix: 0-909605

Interbac, an imprint of S John Bacon Pty Ltd (qv)

Island Press, 1/218 Ben Boyd Rd, Neutral Bay, NSW 2089
Man Dir: Philip Hammial
Subject: Poetry
1985: 4 titles *Founded:* 1970
ISBN Publisher's Prefix: 0-909771

Jacaranda Wiley Ltd+, GPO Box 859, Brisbane, Queensland 4001 (Located at: 65 Park Rd, Milton, Queensland 4064) Tel: (07) 3699755 Cable Add: Japress Telex: 41845 Fax: (07) 3699139
Man Dir: John Collins; *General Managers:* Peter Donoughue (Jacaranda Press), Brian Brennan (John Wiley); *Export Manager:* Greg Browne; *Manufacturing:* Alan Robbie; *Advertising:* Clare Nolan; *Rights & Permissions:* Robyn Brand
Shipping Add: 172 Robinson Road, Geebung, Queensland 4034
Parent Company: John Wiley & Sons Inc, Publishers, 605 Third Avenue, New York, NY 10158, USA
Associate Companies: John Wiley & Sons Canada Ltd, Canada; Wiley Eastern Ltd, India (qv); John Wiley & Sons Ltd, UK (qv)
Subsidiary Companies: Jacaranda Wiley (Hong Kong) Ltd, 19D, 257 Gloucester Rd, Causeway Bay, Hong Kong; Niugini Press Pty Ltd, PO Box 15, Port Moresby, Papua New Guinea
Imprints: The Jacaranda Press, Niugini Press, John Wiley
Branch Offs: 140A Victoria Rd, Gladesville, NSW 2111; 90 Ormond Rd, Elwood, Victoria 3184 (all in Australia); 4 Kirk St, Grey Lynn, Auckland 2, New Zealand
Subjects: Pre-school, Primary, Secondary and Tertiary Textbooks, Atlases
Founded: 1954
ISBN Publisher's Prefixes: 0-7016 (The Jacaranda Press, Niugini Press), 0-471 (John Wiley)

The **Joint Board** of Christian Education of Australia and New Zealand*, 2nd Floor, 10 Queen St, Melbourne, Victoria 3000 Tel: (03) 6544988
Chief Executive and Editorial: Dr D R Merritt; *Sales:* Mary Denton; *Production:* Howard Weedon; *Marketing:* Max Chellew; *Rights & Permissions:* Mavis Grierson
Imprint: Uniting Church Press
Branch Off: 75 Taranaki St, Wellington 1, New Zealand
Subjects: Religious Education, Pastoral Care, Youth Work, Worship
Bookshop: Educational Resources Centre (at above Melbourne address)
Founded: 1914
ISBN Publisher's Prefix: 0-85819

Michael **Joseph**, an imprint of Penguin Books Australia Ltd (qv)

Kangaroo Press Pty Ltd, PO Box 75, Kenthurst, NSW 2156 (Located at: 3 Whitehall Rd, Kenthurst) Tel: (02) 6541502 Cable Add: Kangaroops Telex: 176432 Duroff Fax: (02) 6512118
Dirs: David and Priscilla Rosenberg
Subjects: Non-fiction, Natural History, History, Biography, Australiana, Crafts, Gardening, Children's Fiction
1985: 40 titles *1986:* 40 titles *Founded:* 1981
ISBN Publisher's Prefixes: 0-949924, 0-86417

Kelly Books*, 763 Glenhuntly Rd, South Caulfield, Victoria 3162 Tel: (03) 5239653
Chief Executive: R A Jones
Parent Company: Editcetera Pty Ltd (at above address)
Imprints: Author Press, Pentacle Press
Subjects: General, Mystical, Australiana
Founded: 1978
ISBN Publisher's Prefix: 0-86744

Keystone Paperbacks, an imprint of Era Publications (qv)

Keystone Picture Books, an imprint of Era Publications (qv)

Knight, an imprint of Hodder & Stoughton (Australia) Pty Ltd (qv)

Kookaburra Technical Publications Pty Ltd, PO Box 648, Dandenong, Victoria 3175 Tel: (03) 5600841
Man Dir, Production: Geoff Pentland; *Editorial:* Miss J Martin; *Sales:* F Parks
Subject: Aviation history
Founded: 1963
ISBN Publisher's Prefix: 0-85880

Lansdowne Editions, an imprint of Lansdowne Press (qv)

Lansdowne Press+, 372 Eastern Valley Way, Willoughby, NSW 2068 Tel: (02) 4069222 Telex: 121546 Fax: (02) 4066919
Chief Executive: Kevin Weldon; *Publishing:* Anne Wilson; *General Manager:* Graham Fill; *Marketing Manager:* Mike Gutzeit
Parent Company: RPLA Pty Ltd (at above address – a subsidiary of Weldon Hardie Pty Ltd (qv))
Imprints: Lansdowne Editions, Lansdowne Press, Rigby Publishers, Runaway, Ure Smith, Weldons
Branch Off: Lansdowne-Rigby, 59 View Rd, Glenfield, Auckland, New Zealand
Subjects: Most subjects, especially Cooking, Gardening, Children's, Australiana, Art, Craft, Nature, Budget Books, Literature, Sport, Limited Editions
ISBN Publisher's Prefixes: 0-7018 (Lansdowne), 0-85179 & 0-7270 (both Rigby) 0-7254 (Ure Smith)

Lantern House, an imprint of S John Bacon Pty Ltd (qv)

The **Law** Book Co Ltd, 44-50 Waterloo Rd, North Ryde, NSW 2113 Tel: (02) 8870177 Cable Add: Asbook Telex: 27995 Asbook
Man Dir, Rights & Permissions: D S Lees; *Sales:* C McMurray; *Marketing Manager:* J K Leonard; *Production:* P Finneran
Branch Offs: 389 Lonsdale St, Melbourne, Victoria 3000; 40 Queen St, Brisbane, Queensland 4000; 6 Sherwood Court, Perth, WA 6000
Subjects: Law, Accountancy, Commerce
Miscellaneous: A division of Methuen LBC Ltd (qv)
ISBN Publisher's Prefix: 0-455

Leisure Press, an imprint of D W Thorpe Pty Ltd (qv)

Libra Books Pty Ltd*, GPO Box 10, Hobart, Tasmania 7001 Tel: (002) 251479
Chief Executive: B M Wicks
Subjects: Horse racing and breeding
Founded: 1972
ISBN Publisher's Prefix: 0-909619

Little Golden Books, an associated imprint of Golden Press Pty Ltd (qv)

Little Hills Press+, Suite 11, Regent House, 37-43 Alexander St, Crows Nest, NSW 2065 Tel: (02) 4376995 Fax: (02) 4385762
Chief Executive and Sales: Charles C Burfitt
Branch Off: Shillington House, Old Post Office, Church St, Shillington, Hertfordshire SG5 3LJ, UK
Subjects: Non-fiction, Fiction
1985: 10 titles *1986:* 18 titles *Founded:* 1981
ISBN Publisher's Prefix: 0-949773

Lonely Planet Publications Pty Ltd+, PO Box 88, South Yarra, Victoria 3141 Tel: (03) 4295100 Telex: 151554 Loneplan Fax: (03) 4270603
Man Dir: Tony Wheeler; *Editorial:* Maureen Wheeler; *Sales:* Andy Neilson; *Production:* Jim Hart
Branch Off: Embarcadero West, 112 Linden St, Oakland, CA 94607, USA
Subjects: Travel guides, Phrase-books
1986: 15 titles *1987:* 20 titles *Founded:* 1973
ISBN Publisher's Prefixes: 0-86442, 0-908086

Longman Cheshire Pty Ltd+*, Longman Cheshire House, Kings Garden, 95 Coventry St, Melbourne, Victoria 3004 Tel: (03) 6970666 Cable Add: Miscellany Melbourne Telex: 33501 Fax: (03) 6992041
Man Dir: N J Ryan; *Sales Dir:* F R Priatel; *Rights & Permissions:* N J Ryan; *Production:* P H R Hylands; *Publicity:* Cynthia Smith
Orders to: Penguin Books Australia, 487 Maroondah Highway, Ringwood, Victoria 3134
Parent Company: Longman Group (UK) Ltd, UK (qv)
Associate Company: Penguin Books Australia Ltd (qv)
Imprints: Cheshire, Churchill Livingstone, Oliver & Boyd, Pitman Publishing, Sorrett
Branch Offs: 33 Cooper St, Surry Hills, NSW 2010; Paddington Market, Unit 17, 261-265 Given Terrace, Paddington, Brisbane, Queensland 4064; 105 Gouger St, Adelaide, SA 5000; CWA House, 1174 Hay St, West Perth, WA 6005
Subjects: Educational (Primary, Secondary, Tertiary, Medical, Professional Textbooks)
1985: 152 titles *Founded:* 1976 (formed by merger of Longman Australia Pty Ltd and Cheshire Publishing Pty Ltd)
ISBN Publisher's Prefixes: 0-582, 0-7015 (Longman Cheshire), 0-85896 (Pitman Publishing)

Lothian Publishing Co Pty Ltd, 11 Munro St, Port Melbourne, Victoria 3207 Tel: (03) 6451544 Telex: 39476 Tcloth Fax: (03) 6464882
Man Dir and Rights: Peter Lothian; *Publisher:* Elizabeth McDonald; *Publicity:* Ros Fyffe; *Marketing, Sales:* Robert Ashby
Associate Company: Thomas C Lothian Pty Ltd (at above address)
Branch Offs: Shop 192, 392 Jones St, Ultimo, NSW 2007; 9 Taralinga Drive, Park Ridge, Queensland 4125; 1 John St, Kingswood, SA 5002; 90 Hampden Rd, Battery Point, Tasmania 7001; 141 Roberts Rd, Subiaco, WA 6008 (all Australia); Thomas C Lothian Pty Ltd, New Zealand (qv)
Subjects: General, Adult, Non-fiction, Australiana
1987: 33 titles *Founded:* 1910
ISBN Publisher's Prefix: 0-85091

Lowden Publishing Co, Lowdens Rd, Kilmore, Victoria 3764 Tel: (057) 821118 Cable Add: Lowden Kilmore
Man Dir: Jim Lowden
Associate Company: The Rural Store (Agricultural Booksellers)
Subjects: Biography, History, Reference, Religion, Transport
1985: 3 titles *1986:* 2 titles *Founded:* 1969
ISBN Publisher's Prefix: 0-909706

Lutheran Publishing House+, GPO Box 1368, Adelaide, SA 5001 (Located at: 205 Halifax St, Adelaide, SA 5000) Tel: (08) 2235468 Fax: (08) 2234552
General Manager: Martin Hoopmann; *Editorial and Rights & Permissions:* Everard Leske; *Sales:* Warren Schirmer; *Production:* Eric Winter
Imprint: Chi Rho
Subjects: Religion, Social Questions, Children, Religious Education
Bookshops: The Open Book: 110 Gawler Pl, Adelaide, SA 5000; 61b Murray St, Tanunda, SA 5352; 20 McDougall St, Milton, Queensland 4064. Australia Arcade: Ruthven St, Toowoomba, Queensland 4350; 198 Gray St, Hamilton, Victoria 3300; 703 Station St, Box Hill, Victoria 3128; 538 David St, Albury, NSW 2640
Founded: 1913
ISBN Publisher's Prefix: 0-85910

McGraw-Hill Book Co Australia Pty Ltd, 4 Barcoo St, Roseville East, NSW 2069 Tel: (02) 4064288 Cable Add: McGrawhill Sydney Telex: 20849 Fax: (02) 4065687
Man Dir: D F Fourke; *General Manager Service:* J H Fowlstone; *Editorial, Production and Rights & Permissions:* G Teague; *Business & Professional:* D Scott; *Education:* K Preece
Parent Company: McGraw-Hill Inc, 1221 Ave of the Americas, New York, NY 10020, USA
Associate Companies: See McGraw-Hill Book Co (UK) Ltd, UK
Branch Off: Suite 301, 3rd Floor, Pran Central Shopping Centre, Prahan, Victoria 3181
Subjects: Science & Engineering, Computers, Management, Educational, Professional & Reference, General Interest, School Textbooks, Training Material
1985: 42 titles *1986:* 42 titles *Founded:* 1964
ISBN Publisher's Prefix: 0-07

The **Macmillan Co** of Australia Pty Ltd+, Locked Bag 12, South Melbourne, Victoria 3205 (Located at: 107 Moray St, South Melbourne) Tel: (03) 6998922 Cable Add: Scriniaire Melbourne Telex: 34454 Fax: (03) 6906938
Chairman: Brian Stonier; *Man Dir:* John Rolfe
Education Division: Marketing Dir: Marek Palka; *School Publishing Dir:* Brian McCurdy
General Division: Publisher: Richard Smart; *Marketing Dir:* Peter Phillips
Parent Company: Macmillan Publishers Ltd, UK (qv for associate companies)
Subsidiary Company: Sun Books Pty Ltd (qv)
Branch Offs: 6-8 Clarke St, Crows Nest, NSW; also in Adelaide, Brisbane, Perth
Subjects: General Fiction, Biography, History, Music, Art, Religion, Juveniles, Paperbacks, Engineering, General & Social Sciences, University, Secondary & Primary Textbooks
Founded: 1896
ISBN Publisher's Prefix: 0-333

McPhee Gribble Publishers Pty Ltd*, 66 Cecil St, Fitzroy, Victoria 3065 Tel: (03) 4199010 Telex: 31494 Mt 45
Principals: H J McPhee, D M Gribble
Subjects: Non-fiction Paperbacks, Children's Non-fiction, Australian Fiction
Founded: 1975
ISBN Publisher's Prefix: 0-86914

Magic Bean Shared-Readers, an imprint of Era Publications (qv)

Martin Educational, see Horwitz Grahame Pty Ltd

Mead & Beckett Publishing+, 139 Macquarie St, Sydney, NSW 2000 Tel: (02) 277251 Cable Add: Meadbeck Sydney Telex: 73517
Chief Executives: Barbara Beckett, Rod Mead (Rights)
Parent Company: Mead & Beckett Pty Ltd (at above address)
Subjects: History, Wine, Food, Natural History, Travel, Art (all illustrated)
1985: 9 titles *Founded:* 1978
Miscellaneous: Co-publishers and packagers
ISBN Publisher's Prefix: 0-949698

Megalong Books, an imprint of Second Back Row Press Pty Ltd (qv)

Melbourne House (Australia) Pty Ltd*, 96-100 Tope St, South Melbourne, Victoria 3205 Tel: (03) 6996155 Telex: 34785 Melpub Fax: (03) 6908337
Dir, Publisher: Alfred Milgrom; *Marketing Dir:* Naomi Besen
Associate Company: Melbourne House (Publishers) Ltd, UK (qv)
Subjects: Computers, Computer software

Melbourne University Press, PO Box 278, Carlton South, Victoria 3053 Tel: (03) 3473455 Cable Add: Mupress Telex: 35185 Unimel Fax: (03) 3445104
Dir: P A Ryan; *Sales:* Nick Walker; *Rights & Permissions:* Sue Hardiman
Shipping Add: 268 Drummond St, Carlton, Victoria 3053
Branch Off: Library of Australian History, 17 Mitchell St, North Sydney, NSW 2060
Subjects: Belles Lettres, Poetry, Biography, History, Music, Art, Philosophy, Reference, Paperbacks, Medicine, Psychology, Engineering, General & Social Sciences, University & Secondary Textbooks
Bookshop: University Bookroom, University of Melbourne, PO Box 278, Carlton South, Victoria 3053
Founded: 1922
ISBN Publisher's Prefix: 0-522

Methuen Australia Pty Ltd, a division of Methuen LBC Ltd (qv)

Methuen LBC Ltd, 44-50 Waterloo Rd, North Ryde, NSW 2113 Tel: (02) 8870177 Telex: 21206 Asbook Fax: (02) 8889706
Man Dir: W J Mackarell
Divisions: The Law Book Co Ltd (qv); Methuen Australia Pty Ltd
Parent Company: Associated Book Publishers PLC, UK (qv)
Subjects: General, Academic, Educational
ISBN Publisher's Prefix: 0-454
Miscellaneous: A division of Associated Book Publishers (Aust) Ltd (qv)

Microzine, an imprint of Ashton Scholastic (qv)

Minerva's Express*, PO Box 71, Beaconsfield, NSW 2014 Tel: (02) 6988013
Man Dir: D Hunter; *Editorial, Production:* N Williams; *Sales, Publicity, Rights & Permissions:* P Henderson
Subjects: Photographic Dictionary/Travel Aid in 12 languages, Australian Fiction
Founded: 1979

Modern Teaching Aids Pty Ltd*, 26-28 Chard Rd, PO Box 608, Brookvale, NSW 2100 Tel: (02) 9392355 Telex: 27109 Teaid
Branch Off: 14A Trent St, Moorabbin
Subject: Educational Books

Moving Into Maths Pty Ltd, 484 St Kilda Rd, Melbourne, Victoria 3004 Tel: (03) 2694743 Telex: 36521 Rigmel Fax: (03) 2676803
Man Dir: Sue Donovan

Associate Company: Rigby Education (qv)
Subjects: Secondary English and Social Studies, Primary and Secondary Mathematics, Primary Reading Scheme
Founded: 1980
ISBN Publisher's Prefix: 0-7312

National Library of Australia, Canberra, ACT 2600 Tel: (062) 621111 Cable Add: Natlibaust Canberra Telex: 62100 Fax: (062) 571703
Dir: G Barrow (acting); *Editor:* Merril Thompson; *Publications Officer:* David R Brown
Subjects: National bibliographical publications, publications based on materials in the Library's collections
1985: 53 titles *1986:* 35 titles *Founded:* 1960
ISBN Publisher's Prefix: 0-642

Thomas **Nelson Australia**+, 480 La Trobe St, Melbourne, Victoria 3000 Tel: (03) 3295199 Cable Add: Thonelson Melbourne Telex: 33088 Fax: (03) 3295199
Man Dir: B J Rivers; *Executive Dir, Marketing:* L Koch; *Production Dir:* B Handley; *Rights & Permissions:* J Burke
Company is organized in Divisions as follows:
Nelson Publishers: *Publishing Dir:* W Harvey; *Marketing Dir:* B Whiteside; *Promotions Manager:* W Fraser
Nelson Education (Primary & Secondary Schools): *Publishing Dir:* E Curtain; *Marketing Manager:* C Todd
Nelson Wadsworth (Vocational & Further Education): *Dir:* L Koch; (Business & College): *Dir:* T Day; *Publisher:* C Jevons
Parent Company: International Thomson Organisation Publishing/Information Group, 245 Park Ave, New York, NY 10167-0058, USA
Associate Companies: Thomas Nelson & Sons (Canada) Ltd, 1120 Birchmount Rd, Scarborough, Ontario M1K 5G4, Canada; Thomas Nelson & Sons Ltd, UK (qv)
Branch Offs: 7th Floor, Dunstan House, 236 Elizabeth St, Brisbane, Queensland 4000; 89-97 Jones St, Ultimo, NSW 2007. For all other States, please contact Head Office in Melbourne
Subjects: High-quality books and materials for educational, professional and specialized markets predominantly within Australia and New Zealand
1985: 148 titles *1986:* 119 titles
ISBN Publisher's Prefix: 0-17

Nelson Wadsworth, 480 La Trobe St, Melbourne, Victoria 3000 Tel: (03) 3295199 Telex: 33088 Nelson Fax: (03) 3291204
Personnel: See Thomas Nelson Australia
Subjects: Tertiary Education, Nursing, Educational Software
Miscellaneous: Firm is Tertiary Division of Thomas Nelson Australia (qv)

New American Library, an imprint of Penguin Books Australia Ltd (qv)

New English Library, an imprint of Hodder & Stoughton (Australia) Pty Ltd (qv)

New South Wales University Press Ltd+, PO Box 1, Kensington, NSW 2033 Tel: (02) 6973403 Telex: 26054
General Manager: D S Howie
Imprint: Tafe Educational Books
Subjects: Biography, History, How-to, Philosophy, Reference, Engineering, General & Social Science, University and College Textbooks
Bookshop: College Shop, George St, Sydney
1987: 20 titles *Founded:* 1961

ISBN Publisher's Prefixes: 0-86840, 0-908237

Night Owl Publishers Pty Ltd, PO Box 764, Shepparton, Victoria 3630 Tel: (057) 947256
Chief Executive and Rights & Permissions: David A Miller; *Production:* Meg Miller
Imprints: Bandicoot Books, Grass Roots
Subjects: Homesteading, Natural Animal Husbandry, Self-sufficiency, Alternative Lifestyles
1985: 5 titles *Founded:* 1973

Nimaroo Publishers, PO Box 2046, Wollongong 2500 Tel: (042) 292297
Manager & Publicity: Stephen Standish; *Editorial:* P Balnaves; *Sales:* T Balnaves; *Production:* M Standish; *Rights & Permissions:* N Standish
Branch Off: 11 Airds Rd, Lower Templestone, Victoria 3107
Subjects: Commercial, Scientific
Founded: 1978
ISBN Publisher's Prefix: 0-9596525

Niugini Press, an imprint of Jacaranda Wiley Ltd (qv)

Odana Editions Pty Ltd+*, 65 Edward St, North Sydney, NSW 2060 Tel: (02) 9295546
Chief Executive: Lin Bloomfield
Associate Company: The Bloomfield Galleries, 118 Sutherland St, Paddington, NSW 2021
Subject: Art
Founded: 1978
ISBN Publisher's Prefix: 0-908154

Anne **O'Donovan** Pty Ltd*, 2nd Floor, 56 Claremont St, South Yarra, Victoria 3141 Tel: (03) 2419901
Man Dir: Anne O'Donovan
Subject: Adult Non-fiction
1985: 3 titles *1986:* 6 titles *Founded:* 1978
ISBN Publisher's Prefix: 0-908476

Oliver & Boyd, an imprint of Longman Cheshire Pty Ltd (qv)

Omnibus, an imprint of Penguin Books Australia Ltd (qv)

Omnibus Books+, 9 Edward St, Adelaide, SA 5000 Tel: (08) 2127499 Telex: 88765 Ad 027
Chief Executive, Sales and Production Dir: Sue Williams; *Chief Executive, Editorial and Publicity Dir:* Jane Covernton; *Managing Editor:* Celia Jellett; *Rights & Permissions:* Rosemary Williams
Subjects: Children's Picture-books, Poetry, Fiction, Non-fiction
Founded: 1980
ISBN Publisher's Prefix: 0-949641

Lloyd **O'Neil** Pty Ltd, now incorporated in Penguin Books Australia Ltd (qv)

Outback Press Pty Ltd, now Schwartz Publishing (Victoria) Pty Ltd (qv)

Oxford University Press, GPO Box 2784Y, Melbourne, Victoria 3001 (Located at: 253 Normanby Rd, South Melbourne, Victoria 3205) Tel: (03) 6464200 Cable Add: Oxonian Melbourne Telex: 35330
Regional Manager: Sandra McComb; *Dir Academic & General Division:* Tim Mahar; *Dir Educational Division:* Denise Quinn; *Academic & General Editorial:* Judy Benson; *Production Manager:* Anita Karl
Head Office: Oxford University Press, UK (qv)
Subjects: Non-fiction, Juveniles, Reference
ISBN Publisher's Prefix: 0-19

Pacific Publications (Australia) Pty Ltd*, GPO Box 3408, Sydney, NSW 2001 (Located at: 76 Clarence St, Sydney, NSW 2000) Tel: (02) 20231 Cable Add:

Pacpub Telex: 21242
Manager: John Berry
Parent Company: The Herald and Weekly Times of Melbourne
Branch Off: Pacific Publications, Herald & Weekly Times Bldg, 61 Flinders Lane, Melbourne, Victoria
Subjects: Pacific Islands (general & reference), Australian Agricultural & Technical Handbooks, *Pacific Islands Yearbook*, *Papua New Guinea Handbook*
Founded: 1930
ISBN Publisher's Prefix: 0-85807

Pan Books (Australia) Pty Ltd, E 68 Moncur St, Woollahra, NSW 2025 Tel: (02) 329952 Telex: 70157 Fax: (02) 3275024
Chief Executive: Brian Davies; *Publishing Dir:* James Fraser; *National Sales Manager:* Murray Donaldson; *Product Manager:* Margaret Seale; *Publicity Manager:* Debbie McInnes
Parent Company: Pan Books Ltd, UK (qv)
Imprints: Breakthroughs, Brodie's Notes, Heartlines, Pan, Pan Horizons, Pavanne, Personal Computer News Library, Picador, Piccolo
Subjects: Fiction, General Literature, Children's, Reference, Educational, General Non-fiction
Founded: 1973
ISBN Publisher's Prefix: 0-330

Pan Horizons, an imprint of Pan Books (Australia) Pty Ltd (qv)

Panorama Books, an imprint of Saint George Books (qv)

Pavanne, an imprint of Pan Books (Australia) Pty Ltd (qv)

Pavilion, an imprint of Penguin Books Australia Ltd (qv)

Pelham, an imprint of Pengiun Books Australia Ltd (qv)

Pelican, an imprint of Penguin Books Australia Ltd (qv)

Penguin Books Australia Ltd+, 487 Maroondah Highway, PO Box 257, Ringwood, Victoria 3134 Tel: (03) 8712400 Cable Add: Penguinook Melbourne Telex: 32458 Fax: (03) 8706086
Man Dir: P Field; *Publishing Dir:* B Johns; *Sales Dir:* Monsignor T Moloney
Parent Company: Penguin Publishing Co Ltd, UK (qv)
Associate Companies: Longman Cheshire Pty Ltd, Australia (qv); Penguin Books Canada Ltd, 2801 John St, Markham, Ontario L3R 1B4, Canada; Penguin Books (NZ) Ltd, New Zealand (qv); Viking Penguin Inc, 40 West 23rd St, New York, NY 10010, USA
Imprints: Elm Tree, Hamish Hamilton, Michael Joseph, New American Library, Omnibus, Pavilion, Pelham, Pelican, Penguin, Puffin, Sphere, Viking, Viking Kestrel, Viking O'Neil, Frederick Warne
Subjects: Paperbacks and Hardbacks, Juveniles, Fiction and Non-fiction
1986: 150 titles *1987:* 220 titles *Founded:* 1946
ISBN Publisher's Prefixes: 0-241 (Hamish Hamilton, Elm Tree), 0-7181 (Michael Joseph), 0-451 & 0-452 (New American Library), 0-949 (Omnibus), 0-907516 (Pavilion), 0-7207 (Pelham), 0-14 (Penguin), 0-7221 & 0-351 (Sphere), 0-670 (Viking), 0-7232 (Frederick Warne)

Pentacle Press, an imprint of Kelly Books (qv)

Pergamon Press (Australia) Pty Ltd+, 19A Boundary St, Rushcutter's Bay, NSW 2011 Tel: (02) 3315211 Telex: 27458 Pergap Fax: (02) 3322304
Chairman: I R Maxwell; *Man Dir, Publisher:* Jerry Mayer; *Rights & Permissions:* Bobbie Oakley
Subsidary Company: Australian National University Press (qv)
Sales Offs: Melbourne, Sydney
Subjects: Reference, Medicine, Psychology, Engineering, General & Social Science, University, Secondary & Primary Textbooks, Educational Materials, General Literature, Strategic & Defence Studies
Founded: 1968
ISBN Publisher's Prefix: 0-80

Personal Computer News Library, an imprint of Pan Books (Australia) Pty Ltd (qv)

Picador, an imprint of Pan Books (Australia) Pty Ltd (qv)

Piccolo, an imprint of Pan Books (Australia) Pty Ltd (qv)

Pinchgut Press+, 6 Oaks Ave, Cremorne, NSW 2090 Tel: (02) 905548
Chief Executive: Marjorie Pizer
Subjects: Poetry, Fiction, Australian
Founded: 1947
ISBN Publisher's Prefixes: 0-9598913, 0-949625

Pioneer Design Studio Pty Ltd+, North Rd, Lilydale, Victoria 3140 Tel: (03) 7355505
Man Dir: Derrick I Stone; *General Manager:* Carolyn R Stone
Subjects: History, Nature, Gardening
ISBN Publisher's Prefix: 0-909674

Pitman Publishing, an imprint of Longman Cheshire Pty Ltd (qv)

Play to Learn, an imprint of Era Publications (qv)

Pluto Press Australia, PO Box 199, Leichhardt, NSW 2040 Tel: (02) 8183358
Man Dir: Ric Sissons
Orders to: Australasian Publishing Co Pty Ltd, Cnr Bridge Rd and Jersey St, Hornsby, NSW 2077 Tel: (02) 4762000
Associate Company: Pluto Press, UK (qv)
Subjects: Current Affairs, Politics, Feminism, Thrillers, Academic, Social Sciences
1985: 4 titles *1986:* 6 titles *Founded:* 1984
ISBN Publisher's Prefix: 0-949138

Poetry Australia (South Head Press), Market Place, Berrima, NSW 2577 Tel: (048) 771421
Man Dir: Grace Perry; *Sales & Publicity:* John Millett
Subjects: Poetry & Criticism
1985-86: 6 titles *Founded:* 1964
ISBN Publisher's Prefix: 0-909185

The **Polding** Press+, 343 Elizabeth St, Melbourne, Victoria 3000 Tel: (03) 671740/ 675157/672394
Chief Executive: John A Phillips SJ; *Publicity Manager:* Glenn Willetts
Subjects: Biography, History, Religion
Bookshop: Central Catholic Library Bookshop (at above address)
Founded: 1968

Prentice-Hall of Australia Pty Ltd+*, 7 Grosvenor Pl, Brookvale, NSW 2100 Tel: (02) 9391333 Cable Add: Prenhall Sydney Telex: 74010 Phasyd
Man Dir: Patrick F Gleeson; *Editorial:* Ruth Matheson; *General Book Marketing Manager:* Wendy Livingston; *Tertiary Sales Manager:* Patrick Walsh; *Rights & Permissions:* Ted Gannon
Associate Company: Prentice-Hall (Simon & Schuster International Group), UK (qv)
Branch Off: Suite 4, 6 Riddell Parade, Elsternwick, Victoria 3185
Subjects: Elementary, Secondary and University Textbooks, Trade, Professional Reference, Art, Technical, Management, Medicine, Business, Nursing, Computers
ISBN Publisher's Prefix: 0-7248

Primary Education, an associated imprint of Collins Dove (qv)

Prism Books (Poetry Society of Australia)*, PO Box N110, Grosvenor St, Sydney, NSW 2000 Tel: (02) 9602304
Business Manager: Robert Adamson
Subjects: Art, Poetry (commercial & collector's editions), Art, Music, Photography
Founded: 1952
ISBN Publisher's Prefix: 0-909081

Puffin, an imprint of Penguin Books Australia Ltd (qv)

R P L A Pty Ltd, member of Weldon Hardie group (see Weldon Hardie Pty Ltd)

Reader's Digest Services Pty Ltd, GPO Box 4353, Sydney, NSW 2001 (Located at: 26-32 Waterloo St, Surry Hills, NSW 2010) Tel: (02) 6990111 Cable Add: Readigest Sydney
Man Dir: M Maton; *Editorial:* Suzanne Wagner (Condensed Books), Iain Parsons (Other Books); *Product Manager:* David Knibbs
Subjects: Condensed books, Reference, Educational, General
Book Club: Reader's Digest Condensed Books
ISBN Publisher's Prefix: 0-909486

Real-Life Education, an imprint of R J Cleary (qv)

Reed Books Pty Ltd, 2 Aquatic Drive, Frenchs Forest, NSW 2086 Tel: (02) 4518122 Telex: 27212 Reedoz Fax: (02) 4522066
General Manager, Marketing & Sales: D Maclellan; *Publisher:* W Templeman
Associate Companies: Lilyfield Publishers, Australia; Times Books International, Republic of Singapore (qv)
Subjects: Australia, General Non-fiction, Children's
1986: 200 titles *Founded:* 1964
ISBN Publisher's Prefix: 0-7301

Rent-a-Lesson, an imprint of R J Cleary (qv)

Review Publications Pty Ltd*, 1 Sterling St, Dubbo, NSW 2830 Tel: (068) 823283
Man Dir: William Hornadge
Subjects: Philately, Australian history
1986: 4 titles *Founded:* 1947
ISBN Publisher's Prefix: 0-909895

Rigby Education, Head Office, PO Box 6443, St Kildas Rd Central, Melbourne, Victoria 3004 (Located at: 484 St Kilda Rd, Melbourne) Tel: (03) 2694760 Cable Add: Rigmel Telex: 36521 Fax: (03) 2676803
Chief Executive: John Gilder; *Managing Editor:* Kate Lovett
Parent Company: Weldon Hardie Pty Ltd (qv)
Associate Companies: Lansdowne-Rigby Pty Ltd, 372 Eastern Valley Way, Chatswood, NSW 2067; Moving Into Maths Pty Ltd (qv)
Branch Offs: 2/283B Grey St, South Brisbane, Queensland 4101; 69 Guthrie St, Osborne Park, WA 6017; 32 The Parade, Norwood, SA 5067; 484 St Kilda Rd, Melbourne, Victoria 3004; 372 Eastern Valley Way, Chatswood, NSW 2067 (all Australia); 454 Virginia St (Highway 14), Crystal Lake, IL 60014, USA

Bookshop. Rigby School Centre (qv under Major Booksellers)
1986: 15 titles *1987:* 32 titles *Founded:* 1982
ISBN Publisher's Prefix: 0-7312

Rigby Publishers, an imprint of Lansdowne Press (qv)

Robin Books*, PO Box 355, Wynyard, Tasmania 7321 Tel: (004) 422025
Man Dir, Editorial, Sales, Rights & Permissions: Barney Roberts; *Production, Publicity:* Bruce McM Roberts
Subjects: Poetry, Short Stories
Founded: 1976
ISBN Publisher's Prefix: 0-908030

Runaway, an imprint of Lansdowne Press (qv)

Saint George Books*, GPO Box D162, Perth, WA 6001 (Located at: 125 St Georges Terrace, Perth, WA 6000) Tel: (09) 3210161 Telex: 92109
Editor: Ross Haig; *Sales:* Mark Willey
Parent Company: West Australian Newspapers Ltd (at above address)
Imprint: Panorama Books
Subjects: General Non-fiction, specializing in Australiana
1985: 4 titles *Founded:* 1980
ISBN Publisher's Prefixes: 0-86778 (Saint George), 0-949864 (Panorama)

Sapphire Books Pty Ltd+*, PO Box 222, Strathfield, NSW 2135 (Located at: 22 Gould St, Enfield, NSW 2136) Tel: (02) 6428200
Man Dir: J Franklin
Imprints: Challenge, Clearway
Subjects: School textbooks, Study guides
Founded: 1971
ISBN Publisher's Prefixes: 0-909286, 0-85861

Sceptre, an imprint of Hodder & Stoughton (Australia) Pty Ltd (qv)

Scholastic, an imprint of Ashton Scholastic (qv)

Schwartz Publishing (Victoria) Pty Ltd, 45 Flinders Lane, Melbourne, Victoria 3000 Tel: (03) 6542000
Man Dir, Editor-in-Chief: Morry Schwartz
Subjects: Fiction, Non-fiction
Founded: 1979
ISBN Publisher's Prefix: 0-86753

Science Research Associates Pty Ltd*, 84 Waterloo Rd, North Ryde, NSW 2113 Tel: (02) 8887833 Cable Add: Sciresant North Ryde Telex: 70185
Man Dir, Rights & Permissions: R J Barton; *Editorial, Production:* A Wong
Associate Company: Science Research Associates Ltd, UK (qv for other associates)
Subjects: Primary, Secondary, Tertiary & Other Textbooks, Multimedia Learning Systems, Business tests, Computer Training Programs
ISBN Publisher's Prefix: 0-574

Scripts Publications, see Horwitz Grahame Pty Ltd

Second Back Row Press Pty Ltd+, PO Box 43, Leura, NSW 2780 Tel: (047) 823588
Man Dirs: Tom Whitton, Wendy Whitton
Imprints include: Megalong Books (regional interest titles)
Subjects: Alternative Lifestyles, Technology, Politics, Feminism, Food & Health, Juveniles
1985-86: 5 titles *Founded:* 1973
ISBN Publisher's Prefix: 0-909325

Shakespeare Head Press*, Building 7, Birkenhead Point Shopping Centre, Carey St, NSW 2047 Tel: (02) 890421 Cable Add: Goldpress Telex: 26070

Chief Executive: A Beale; *Publisher:* John Fenton-Smith
Parent Company: Golden Press Pty Ltd (qv)
Subjects: Secondary & Primary Textbooks
1985: 43 titles
ISBN Publisher's Prefixes: 0-85558, 0-7302

Sorrett, an imprint of Longman Cheshire Pty Ltd (qv)

South Head Press (Poetry Australia), now Poetry Australia (South Head Press) (qv)

Spectrum Publications Pty Ltd, PO Box 75, Richmond, Victoria 3121 (Located at: 61 Somerset St, Richmond) Tel: (03) 4291404
Man Dir: H Rohr; *Editorial:* Irene Aili; *Sales:* M Peters; *Publicity:* Henry Rohr; *Production Department:* 23 Waverely St, Richmond
Subjects: Religion, Australiana, Art
ISBN Publisher's Prefixes: 0-909837, 0-86786

Sphere, an imprint of Penguin Books Australia Ltd (qv)

Success Education, an imprint of R J Cleary (qv)

Sugar and Snails Press Co-op Ltd+*, PO Box 276, Hawthorn, Victoria 3122 (Located at: 37 William St, Hawthorn) Tel: (03) 8195922
Sales, Publicity Coordinator: Robyn Starkey
Subjects: Children's non-sexist, Fiction and Non-fiction
Founded: 1974
ISBN Publisher's Prefix: 0-908092

Sun Books Pty Ltd+, 107 Moray St, South Melbourne, Victoria 3205 Tel: (03) 6998922 Cable Add: Sunbooks Telex: 34454 Fax: (03) 6906938
Chairman: Brian Stonier; *Man Dir:* John Rolfe
Parent Company: The Macmillan Co of Australia Pty Ltd (qv)
Imprint: Sun Papermac (Non-fiction Trade)
Subjects: General Fiction, Non-fiction, Biography, History, Music, Philosophy, Reference, Low- & High-priced Paperbacks
ISBN Publisher's Prefix: 0-7251

Sun Papermac, an imprint of Sun Books Pty Ltd (qv)

Sydney University Press, Press Bldg, University of Sydney, NSW 2006 Tel: (02) 6604997 Cable Add: Sydpress
Dir: David New
Subjects: Scholarly Books, University Textbooks
1985: 10 titles *1986:* 6 titles *Founded:* 1964
ISBN Publisher's Prefix: 0-424

T H E Foundation+, PO Box 359, Warwick, Queensland 4370 (Located at: Freestone Rd, Kingsford Heights, Warwick) Tel: (076) 661547 Telex: 44815
Executive Dir: Kenneth J Ingbritsen
Associate Company: Centre Publications (qv)
Subjects: Education, Health
Founded: 1970
ISBN Publisher's Prefix: 0-909698

Tafe Educational Books, an imprint of New South Wales University Press Ltd (qv)

Teach Yourself, an imprint of Hodder & Stoughton (Australia) Pty Ltd (qv)

Stanley Thornes & Hulton (Aust) Pty Ltd (AE Press), PO Box 186, Blackburn, Victoria 3130 (Located at: 74 Railway Rd, Blackburn) Tel: (03) 8780466 Telex: 38598 Educap
Chairman, Man Dir & Publisher: Andrew Snoek; *Sales & Promotion:* Dianne Genat

Parent Company: Kluwer Group, Netherlands (qv)
Subjects: Secondary and Vocational Education, History
1985: 10 titles *1986:* 17 titles *Founded:* 1980
ISBN Publisher's Prefix: 0-86787

D W Thorpe Pty Ltd*, 20-24 Stokes St, Port Melbourne, Victoria 3207 Tel: (03) 6451511 Cable Add: Bookstat Melbourne Telex: 39476 Thorpe
Man Dir, Production, Rights & Permissions, Editorial: Michael Webster; *Sales & Advertising Manager:* Pat White
Imprints include: Leisure Press
Subject: Reference
Founded: 1921
ISBN Publisher's Prefix: 0-909532

Transworld Publishers (Australia) Pty Ltd+, 1st Floor, 20 Young St, Neutral Bay, NSW 2089 Tel: (02) 6017122 Cable Add: Transcable Telex: 71471 Trapub
The above is the address for the publishing and marketing offices; administration and distribution is carried out from 15-23 Helles Ave, Moorebank, NSW 2170
Man Dir: G S Rumpf; *Publishing Dir:* Judith Curr (Corgi & Bantam); *Publishing Manger:* Rex Finch (Doubleday); *Sales & Marketing Dir:* Neville James
Parent Company: Ultimate parent company Bertelsmann AG, Federal Republic of Germany (qv)
Associate Company: Transworld Publishers Ltd, UK (qv)
Imprints: Bantam, Corgi, Dell, Doubleday
Subjects: Paperbacks: General, Fiction, Educational, Juveniles; Hardbacks: Fiction, Non-fiction
Book Club: Doubleday Australia Pty Ltd, Book Club Division
Founded: 1981

Turton & Armstrong Publishers Pty Ltd, 21 Lister St, Wahroonga, NSW 2076 Tel: (02) 4896719
Publisher: Paul Armstrong
Subjects: Industrial Archaeology, Special Interest, Technical, Educational
1986: 7 titles *1987:* 9 titles *Founded:* 1977
ISBN Publisher's Prefix: 0-908031

Twistaplot, an imprint of Ashton Scholastic (qv)

Uniting Church Press, an imprint of The Joint Board of Christian Education of Australia and New Zealand (qv)

Universal Business Directories Pty Ltd, now Universal Press Pty Ltd (qv)

Universal Press Pty Ltd, PO Box 155, North Ryde, NSW 2113 (Located at: 64 Talavera Rd, North Ryde) Tel: (02) 8881877 Telex: 70274 Directory Fax: (02) 8889850
Chief Executive: I E Webster; *General Manager:* P J Coleman
Branch Offs: Melbourne, Brisbane, Adelaide, Perth
Subjects: Business Directories, Street Directories, Maps and Travel Guides
1986: 120 titles *Founded:* 1938
ISBN Publisher's Prefix: 0-7261

University of New South Wales, now New South Wales University Press Ltd (qv)

University of Queensland Press, PO Box 42, St Lucia, Queensland 4067 Tel: (072) 3772127 Telex: 40315 Uniqld Press
General Manager: Laurie Muller; *Editorial:* Craig Munro, D'Arcy Randall; *Sales, Marketing:* Robert Brown; *Overseas Rights:* D'Arcy Randall; *Publicity & Advertising:* Alison Cotes; *Permissions:* Sue Abbey; *Production:* Terry Farley
Branch Off: University of Queensland

Press, UK (qv)
Subjects: Literature, Poetry, Biography, History, Philosophy, Reference, Social Science, Natural History, University & Secondary Textbooks
Bookshop: University Bookshop (at above address)
Founded: 1948
ISBN Publisher's Prefix: 0-7022

University of Western Australia Press+, Nedlands, WA 6009 Tel: (092) 3803182 Cable Add: Uniwest Perth Telex: 92992 Uniwa
Manager, Editorial, Sales, Production, Promotion and Rights & Permissions: V S Greaves
Imprint: Cygnet Books
Subjects: Literary Criticism, Biological Sciences, Biography, History, Music, Art, Philosophy, Reference, Religion, Social Sciences, University & Secondary Textbooks, General Adult Non-fiction
1985: 10 titles *1986:* 10 titles *Founded:* 1954
ISBN Publisher's Prefix: 0-85564

Ure Smith, an imprint of Lansdowne Press (qv)

V C T A Publishing Pty Ltd*, 33-37 Hotham St, Collingwood, Victoria 3066 Tel: (03) 5293400
Dir: Robert Taylor; *Publishing Manager:* Garry Bell
Parent Company: Victorian Commercial Teachers' Association
Subjects: Educational textbooks and teacher guides in Accountancy, Economics, Legal Studies, Consumer Education, Secretarial Studies, General Business Education
Founded: 1953
ISBN Publisher's Prefix: 0-86859

Vagabond, an imprint of Ashton Scholastic (qv)

The Helen **Vale** Foundation, now THE Foundation (qv)

Viking, an imprint of Penguin Books Australia Ltd (qv)

Viking Kestrel, an imprint of Penguin Books Australia Ltd (qv)

Viking O'Neil, an imprint of Penguin Books Australia Ltd (qv)

Visa Books+*, PO Box 186, Glen Iris, Victoria 3146 (Located at: Communications House, 9 Paran Pl, Glen Iris) Tel: (03) 256456 Telex: 38225
Publisher: Geoffrey M Gold
Associate Company: General Magazine Co (Australia) Pty Ltd
Subjects: Politics, Sports, History, Biography, Media & Communications, Economics, Culture
Founded: 1977
Miscellaneous: Firm is a division of South Continent Corporation Pty Ltd
ISBN Publisher's Prefix: 0-949763

Wadsworth International, now merged with Thomas Nelson Australia, see Nelson Wadsworth

Frederick **Warne**, an imprint of Penguin Books Australia Ltd (qv)

Was Is Press*, PO Box 2, Moreland 3058 Tel: (03) 3863166
Proprietor: Yvonne Rousseau

Franklin **Watts** Australia, 14 Mars Rd, Lane Cove, NSW 2066 Tel: (02) 4283722 Cable Add: Grolier Telex: 26584
General Manager: Dave Knowles
Parent Company: Franklin Watts Ltd, UK (qv)

Subjects: Children's
ISBN Publisher's Prefix: 0-86415

Weldon Hardie Pty Ltd, 372 Eastern Valley Way, Willoughby, NSW 2068 Tel: (02) 4069222 Telex: 121546 Fax: (02) 4066919
Chief Executive: Kevin Weldon
Members of group include: Lansdowne Press (qv), Lansdowne-Rigby, RPLA Pty Ltd, Rigby Education (qv), Rigby Publishers

Weldons, an imprint of Lansdowne Press (qv)

Westbooks Pty Ltd*, 127 Burswood Rd, Victoria Park, WA 6100 Tel: (09) 3618288
Dirs: Rayma and David Turton (Westbooks), Paul Armstrong (Turton & Armstrong)
Subjects: Educational, Technical, Juvenile, Industrial Archaeology
Bookshops (specialist children's): At above address; 4/29 Bayview Terrace, Claremont, WA 6010; Rapid Creek Shopping Centre, Rapid Creek, NT

Wild & Woolley Pty Ltd+, PO Box 41, Glebe, NSW 2037 (Located at: 16 Darghan St, Glebe, NSW 2037) Tel: (02) 6920166
Chief Executive: Pat Woolley
Associate Company: Allbooks Distribution
Subjects: Fiction, Cartoons, Politics
Founded: 1974
ISBN Publisher's Prefix: 0-909331

Wildfire, an imprint of Ashton Scholastic (qv)

John **Wiley**, an imprint of Jacaranda Wiley Ltd (qv)

Williams & Wilkins and Associates Pty Ltd+, PO Box 431, Artarmon, NSW 2064 (Located at: 43 Herbert St, Artarmon) Tel: (02) 4383155 Telex: 178059 Fax: (02) 4383094
Man Dir and Rights & Permissions: Tom MacLennan; *Editorial Dir:* Pamela Petty; *Marketing Manager:* Shelley Evans
Subjects: Medical, Allied Health, Dental, Veterinary, Nursing
1984: 15 titles *1986:* 15 titles
ISBN Publisher's Prefix: 0-86433

Windswept, an imprint of Ashton Scholastic (qv)

Wizware, an imprint of Ashton Scholastic (qv)

Wobbledagger, now Boobook Publications (qv)

Women's Movement Children's Literature Co-op Ltd, now Sugar and Snails Press Co-op Ltd (qv)

Literary Agents

Curtis Brown (Australia) Pty Ltd, 27 Union St, Paddington, Sydney, NSW 2021 Tel: (02) 3315301/336161 Cable Add: Browncurt Sydney
Man Dir: Tim Curnow; *Dir:* Margaret Connolly

Jeffrey B **Prentice**, Literary Agent, 93 Severn St, Box Hill North, Victoria 3129 Tel: (03) 8904750

Book Clubs

Arrow, PO Box 579, Gosford, NSW 2250 Tel: (043) 283555 Telex: 24881
Owned by: Ashton Scholastic (qv)

Australian Reader's Choice, see Doubleday Australia Pty Ltd, Book Club Division

BookAustralia, see Doubleday Australia Pty Ltd, Book Club Division

Book-of-the-Month Club, see Doubleday Australia Pty Ltd, Book Club Division

Doubleday Australia Pty Ltd, Book Club Division*, 91 Mars Rd, Lane Cove, NSW 2066
Includes: Australian Reader's Choice, BookAustralia, Book-of-the-Month Club, Doubleday Book Club, Doubleday History Book Club, The Literary Guild, Military Book Club, Postmarket
Owned by: Transworld Publishers (Australia) Pty Ltd (qv)

Doubleday Book Club, see Doubleday Australia Pty Ltd, Book Club Division

Doubleday History Book Club, see Doubleday Australia Pty Ltd, Book Club Division

The **Literary Guild**, see Doubleday Australia Pty Ltd, Book Club Division

Lucky, PO Box 579, Gosford, NSW 2250 Tel: (043) 283555 Telex: 24881
Owned by: Ashton Scholastic (qv)

Military Book Club, see Doubleday Australia Pty Ltd, Book Club Division

Postmarket, see Doubleday Australia Pty Ltd, Book Club Division

Reader's Digest Condensed Books, GPO Box 4353, Sydney, NSW 2001
Editor: Suzanne Wagner
Owned by: Reader's Digest Services Pty Ltd (qv)

Star, PO Box 579, Gosford, NSW 2250 Tel: (043) 283555 Telex: 24881
Owned by: Ashton Scholastic (qv)

Teachers Bookshelf, PO Box 579, Gosford, NSW 2250 Tel: (043) 283555 Telex: 24881
Owned by: Ashton Scholastic (qv)

Teenage, PO Box 579, Gosford, NSW 2250 Tel: (043) 283555 Telex: 24881
Owned by: Ashton Scholastic (qv)

Wombat, PO Box 579, Gosford, NSW 2250 Tel: (043) 283555 Telex: 24881
Owned by: Ashton Scholastic (qv)

Major Booksellers

Abbey's Bookshop, 131 York St, Sydney, NSW 2000 Tel: (02) 2643111
Manager: Peter Milne

Angus & Robertson Bookshops, GPO Box 1516, Sydney, NSW 2000 (Located at: Imperial Arcade, Sydney) Tel: (02) 2351188 Telex: 26254
80 branches
Owned by: Gordon & Gotch Ltd, GPO Box 767G, Melbourne, Victoria 3001

Australian Government Publications, now Commonwealth Government Bookshops (qv)

A W **Birchall** & Sons Pty Ltd, 118-120 Brisbane St, PO Box 170, Launceston, Tasmania 7250 Tel: (003) 313011 Telex: 58816
Man Dir: Raymond F Tilley
Branches: Birchalls Hobart, 93 Harrington St, Hobart; University Bookshop, University of Tasmania, Student Union Bldg, Churchill Ave, Sandy Bay, Hobart; The Institute Bookshop, Tasmanian State Institute of Technology, Plumer St, Mowbray; Birchalls Tech College Bookshop, Bathurst St, Hobart (all in

Tasmania)
Australia's oldest (founded 1844) and Tasmania's largest bookseller

Collins Booksellers Pty Ltd, 86 Bourke St, Melbourne, Victoria 3000 Tel: (03) 6543144 Cable Add: Colbook Telex: 37396
Man Dir: M G Zifcak, OBE; *Dir & General Manager:* Peter Shaw
38 branches
Associate Company: Hill of Content Publishing Co Pty Ltd (qv)

Commonwealth Government Bookshops, Mt Newman House, 200 St George's Terrace, Perth, WA 6000 Tel: (093) 224737
Also: 12 Pirie St, Adelaide; 294 Adelaide St, Brisbane; 70 Alinga St, Canberra; 162 Macquarie St, Hobart; 347 Swanston St, Melbourne; 120 Clarence St, Sydney
See also Australian Government Publishing Service

Dymock's Pty Ltd*, 428 George St, Sydney, NSW 2000 Tel: (02) 2334111
Man Dir: J P C Forsyth
Several branches

Foreign Language Bookshop*, 94 Elizabeth St, Melbourne, Victoria 3000 Tel: (03) 6542883
Manager: A Monester

Grahames Bookshop, Corner Pitt and Hunter Sts, Sydney, NSW 2000 Tel: (02) 2321966
Branches: Bankstown Shopping Square, Bankstown, NSW 2200; Mid-City Centre, 197 Pitt St, Sydney, NSW 2000; City Tatts, 200 Pitt St, Sydney, NSW 2000; MLC Bldg, 105 Miller St, North Sydney, NSW 2060; Imperial Centre, Mann St, Gosford, NSW 2250
Division of Horwitz Grahame Pty Ltd (qv)

Language Book Centre, 137 York St, Sydney 2000 Tel: (02) 2671397
Manager: Hanni Baaske

Queensland Book Depot, GPO Box 342, Brisbane, Queensland 4000 Tel: (07) 2293144
18 branches

Rigby School Centre, 32 The Parade, Norwood, SA 5067 Tel: (08) 429952
Manager: Robert Brady
Owned by: Rigby Education (qv)

University Co-operative Bookshop Ltd, 80 Bay St, Broadway, NSW 2007 Tel: (02) 2122211 Telex: 121968
General Manager: J McLoone
36 branches

Major Libraries

Australian Archives, NSW Regional Office, PO Box C328, Clarence St, Sydney, NSW 2000 (Located at: Level 2, 24 Market St, Sydney) Tel: (02) 296352 Fax: (02) 293253
Publications: Inventories, Guides (irregular)

Australian National University Library, GPO Box 4, Canberra, ACT 2601 Tel: (062) 495111 Cable Add: Natuniv Telex: 62694
Librarian: C R Steele
Publications include: User response to URICA: a catalogue on line

The **Barr Smith** Library, The University of Adelaide, GPO Box 498, Adelaide, South Australia 5001 Tel: (08) 2285333 Telex: 89141 Univad Fax: (08) 2240464
University Librarian: E J Wainwright
Publications: Newsline, University of Adelaide Library News

C S I R O (Commonwealtht Scientific and Industrial Research Organization)*, Central Information, Library and Editorial Section, Bureau of Scientific Services, PO Box 89, East Melbourne, Victoria 3002 (Located at: 314 Albert St, East Melbourne) Tel: (03) 4187333 Telex: 30236
Officer-in-Charge: P J Judge; *Editor-in-Chief:* B J Walby; *Chief Librarian:* P H Dawe; *Manager, Information Service:* C Garrow
Publications include: CSIRO Index, Commonwealth Regional Renewable Energy Resources Index (microfiche), Scientific and Technical Research Centres in Australia (microfiche), CSIRO-SDI User Manuals, CILES Biennial Report

The **Library Board** of Western Australia, now State Library Service of Western Australia (qv)

National Library of Australia, Canberra, ACT 2600 Tel: (062) 621111 Cable Add: Natlibaust Canberra Telex: 62100
Director-General: W M Horton; *Director of Publications:* G Barrow (acting)
Publications include: Bibliography of Australia, 1784-1900; Australian National Bibliography (monthly, every four months, with annual cumulations); APAIS (monthly, with annual cumulation); Australian Government Publications (quarterly, with annual cumulation); Australian Books; Australian Maps (annual)

The **State Library of New South Wales**, Macquarie St, Sydney, NSW 2000 Tel: (02) 2301414 Telex: 121150 Fax: (02) 2324816
State Librarian: A Crook (acting)
Publications include: Annual Report; New South Wales Official Publications Received in the State Library; Public Libraries Division: Newsletter; Public Libraries Division Statistics; A Directory of Services for The Use of Librarians and Other Information Agents; Research Service Bibliographies; State Library of NSW Programme of Events

State Library of Queensland*, William St, Brisbane, Queensland 4000
Includes the Oxley Library
Librarian: S L Ryan
Publications include: Queensland Government Publications, 1977- (quarterly); Directory of State and Public Library Service in Queensland (annual); The Development of State Libraries and their effect on the Public Library Movement in Australia, 1809-1964; North Queensland Towns and Districts Bibliography, 1975; Annual Report of the Library Board of Queensland; Public Libraries in Queensland: Statistical Bulletin (annual)

State Library of South Australia, GPO Box 419, Adelaide, SA 5001 (Located at: North Terrace, Adelaide, SA 5000) Tel: (08) 2238911 Telex: 82074 Fax: (08) 223390
Formerly Public Library of South Australia
State Librarian: E M Miller
Publications: Pinpointer (every two months, with annual cumulation); Annual Report

State Library of Tasmania*, 91 Murray St, Hobart, Tasmania 7000 Tel: (002) 308033 Telex: 58222
Publication: Annual report

State Library of Victoria*, 328 Swanston St, Melbourne, Victoria 3000 Tel: (03) 6699888 Telex: 38104
State Librarian: Jane La Scala
Publications include: Annual report; La Trobe Library Journal (twice a year); Victorian Government Publications (VGP)

(monthly and annual); Annual Statistical Bulletin of Public Libraries in Victoria

State Library Service of Western Australia, Alexander Library Bldg, Perth Cultural Centre, Perth, WA 6000 Tel: (09) 4273111 Telex: 92231 Wainf Fax: (09) 4273256
State Librarian: Robert Sharman
Publications include: Library Service of WA Newsletter; Directory of public library services (annual)

University of Melbourne Library*, Parkville, Victoria 3052 Tel: (03) 3415378 Telex: 30815 Fax: (03) 3481142
University Librarian: W D Richardson

University of New South Wales Library, PO Box 1, Kensington, NSW 2033 Tel: (02) 6972222 Telex: 120467 Unitec
Librarian: A R Horton
Publications include: Annual Report, Staff Papers

University of Queensland Library, St Lucia, Queensland 4067 Tel: (07) 3772304 Cable Add: Brisbane University Telex: 40315 Univqld Fax: (07) 3715896
University Librarian: F D O Fielding
Publications include: Annual Report

University of Sydney Library, Sydney, NSW 2006 Tel: (02) 6922222 Telex: 20056
University Librarian: Dr Neil A Radford

University of Western Australia Library, Nedlands, WA 6009 Tel: (09) 3802344 Cable Add: Uniwest Telex: 92992 Uniwa Fax: (09) 3824071
Librarian: A Ellis

Library Associations

Australian Advisory Council on Bibliographical Services (AACOBS)*, National Library of Australia, Canberra, ACT 2600
Chairman: F D O Fielding
Publications include: Library Services for Australia: The Work of AACOBS; Current Australian Reference Books: a list for medium and small libraries; Joint-use Libraries in the Australian Community; 'Pinpointer' Popular Periodicals on Microfiche (annual); You name it! Helpful hints for editors and publishers of journals; DIALS: Developments in Australian Library Science (annual); Census of Australian Library Services

Australian Association for Health Literature and Information Services Inc, PO Box 760, Woden, ACT 2606
Convenor: Mrs P Woolcock

Australian Library Promotion Council, Executive Director, 328 Swanston St, Melbourne, Victoria 3000 Tel: (03) 6637194
President: John Ward; *Honorary Secretary:* Stewart Edwards
Publication: Australian Library News (eight times a year)

Australian Medical Librarians' Group, ACT Branch, now Australian Association for Health Literature and Information Services Inc (qv)

Australian School Library Association*, PO Box 287, Alderley, Queensland 4051 Tel: (07) 3551238
Executive Secretary: Dr Roy Lundin
Publications include: School Libraries in Australia (official quarterly journal)

Australian Society of Archivists Inc, PO Box 83, O'Connor, ACT 2601

22 AUSTRALIA

President: Peter Crush; *Secretary:* Nancy U'Ren (at above address)
Publications include: Archives and Manuscripts (twice a year); *Archives and Manuscripts*, Vols 1-10 (microfiche); *ASA Bulletin* (six times a year); *Our Heritage: A Directory to Archives and Manuscript Repositories in Australia; Keeping Archives*

International Association of Music Libraries, Archives and Documentation Centres, Australian Branch, c/o Laurel Garlick, Music Librarian, State Library of Queensland, William St, Brisbane, Queensland 4000
President: Mary O'Mara
Publication: Continuo

Lasie Australia Co Ltd*, PO Box 602, Lane Cove, NSW 2066 Tel: (02) 4987577 (The Library Automated Systems Information Exchange)
President: Dorothy G Peake; *Executive Officer:* Arne L Pedersen
Publication: LASIE (Information Bulletin)

Library Association of Australia*, 376 Jones St, Ultimo, NSW 2007 Tel: (02) 6929233
President: P H Dawe; *Executive Dir:* Mrs J Adams
Publications include: Australian Library Journal; Incite (Newsletter); *Handbook; Directory of Special Libraries in Australia; Australian Academic and Research Libraries; Australian Special Libraries News; Orana* (Children's Libraries Newsletter); *Cataloguing Australia; Conference Proceedings; Library Services in Distance Education; Periodicals for School Libraries; Teacher Librarians: the mid 80s and beyond; Australian Librarian's Manual* (Vols I, II & III); *Libraries of Sydney 1985*

The **Library Automated Systems** Information Exchange, see Lasie Australia Co Ltd

Public Lending Right Scheme, The Administrator PLR, PO Box 812, North Sydney, NSW 2060 Tel: (02) 9233379 Telex: 26013

State Librarians' Council, c/o State Library Service of Western Australia, Alexander Library Building, Cultural Centre, Perth, WA 6000 Tel: (09) 4273325 Telex: 92231
Chairman: R C Sharman

Library Reference Books and Journals

Books

Australian Librarian's Manual (Vols I, II & III), Library Association of Australia, 376 Jones St, Ultimo, NSW 2007

Census of Australian Library Services, Australian Advisory Council on Bibliographical Services (AACOBS), National Library of Australia, Canberra, ACT 2600

Current Australian Reference Books: a list for medium and small libraries, Australian Advisory Council on Bibliographical Services (AACOBS), National Library of Australia, Canberra, ACT 2600

A Directory of Services for the Use of Librarians and other Information Agents, The State Library of New South Wales, Macquarie St, Sydney, NSW 2000

Directory of Special Libraries in Australia, Library Association of Australia, 376 Jones St, Ultimo, NSW 2007

Keeping Archives, Ann Pederson (Editor), Australian Society of Archivists Inc, PO Box 83, O'Connor, ACT 2601

Library Association of Australia: Handbook, Library Association of Australia, 376 Jones St, Ultimo, NSW 2007

Our Heritage: A Directory to Archives and Manuscript Repositories in Australia, Australian Society of Archivists Inc, PO Box 83, O'Connor, ACT 2601

Journals

Archives and Manuscripts, A Lemon (Editor), 704 Toorak Rd, Malvern, Victoria 3144

Australian Academic and Research Libraries, Library Association of Australia, 376 Jones St, Ultimo, NSW 2007

Australian Library Journal, Library Association of Australia, 376 Jones St, Ultimo, NSW 2007

Australian Library News (eight times a year), Australian Library Promotion Council, 328 Swanston St, Melbourne, Victoria 3000

Australian School Librarian (quarterly), PO Box 280, East Melbourne, Victoria 3001

Australian Special Libraries News, Library Association of Australia, 376 Jones St, Ultimo, NSW 2007

Cataloguing Australia (quarterly), c/o School of Librarianship, University of New South Wales, Kensington, NSW 2033

Incite, Library Association of Australia, 376 Jones St, Ultimo, NSW 2007
Newsletter

La Trobe Library Journal (twice a year), State Library of Victoria, 328 Swanston St, Melbourne, Victoria 3000

Library Services for Australia: The Work of AACOBS, Australian Advisory Council on Bibliographical Services (AACOBS), National Library of Australia, Canberra, ACT 2600

Orana, Library Association of Australia, 376 Jones St, Ultimo, NSW 2007
Children's Libraries Newsletter

'Pinpointer' Popular Periodicals on Microfiche (annual), Australian Advisory Council on Bibliographical Services (AACOBS), National Library of Australia, Canberra, ACT 2600

School Libraries in Australia, Australian School Library Association, PO Box 287, Alderley, Queensland 4051
Official quarterly journal

School Library Bulletin (quarterly), Education Department, Library Branch, State Library of Victoria, 328 Swanston St, Melbourne, Victoria 3000

Teacher-Librarian (quarterly), PO Box 21, Waverley, NSW 2024

Literary Associations and Societies

Association for the Study of Australian Literature Ltd, c/o English Department, University of Western Australia, Nedlands, WA 6009
Secretary: Delys Bird
Publication: Notes & Furphies

Australian Literature Society, incorporated in 1982 within Association for the Study of Australian Literature Ltd (qv)

Australian Society of Authors Ltd, 22 Alfred St, Milsons Point, NSW 2061 Tel: (02) 927235
Executive Officer: Denise Yates
Publications: The Australian Author (quarterly); *Australian Book Contracts; The acquisition of film rights in literary properties*; other publications of professional/industrial interest to those who write for publication

Australian Writers' Guild Ltd, 171 New South Head, Edgecliff, Sydney, NSW 2027 Tel: (02) 3261900
Executive Officer: Angela Wales
Publications include: Copyright and Technology: a symposium; The Writers' Directory: writers for screen, stage, radio and television in Australia; Conference Proceedings

Bibliographical Society of Australia and New Zealand (BSANZ), c/o Secretary, 76 Warners Ave, Bondi Beach, NSW 2026
Secretary: Rose T Smith
Publications include: Bulletin (quarterly); *Broadsheet* (three times a year)

Book Collectors' Society of Australia, 64 Young St, Cremorne, NSW 2090 Tel: (02) 902184
President: John Fletcher, Department of German, University of Sydney, NSW 2006
Publication: Biblionews and Australian Notes and Queries (quarterly), plus *Index 1947-1979, Index 1979-1983*

Bread and Cheese Club*, 51 Elizabeth St, Newport, Victoria 3015 Tel: (03) 3913039
Secretary: Dr Cyril Goode

Children's Book Council of Australia*, PO Box 420, Dickson, ACT 2602
President: Laurie Copping; *Secretary:* Lynn Fletcher Tel: (062) 813292
Branches in New South Wales, Queensland, South Australia, Tasmania, Victoria, Western Australia, Australian Capital Territory
Publication: Reading Time (quarterly) (New South Wales Branch)

The **Dickens** Fellowship, 29 Henley Beach Rd, Henley Beach, Adelaide, SA 5022 Tel: (08) 3567117
Honorary Secretary: G J Rowe
Also at:
Brisbane: Unit No 3, 12 Sydney St, New Farm, Queensland 4005
Honorary Secretary: Mrs G M Taylor
Melbourne: Flat 143, 200 Dorcas St, South Melbourne, Victoria 3205
Honorary Secretary: Mrs Barbara Barrett
Publication: Geranium Leaves (every two months)

Fellowship of Australian Writers Federal Council. The Council is re-formed in a different State branch every two years

Fellowship of Australian Writers (NSW), GPO Box 3448, Sydney, NSW 2001
Secretary: Gaye Manley
Membership: 800
Publication: Bulletin (twice a month)
Twenty-one regional branches in suburbs of Sydney and country towns

Fellowship of Australian Writers, Victorian, see Victorian Fellowship of Australian Writers

Fellowship of Australian Writers (WA)*, Tom Collins House, 9 Servetus St, Swanbourne, WA 6010

International P E N (Melbourne Centre)*, President, 101 Edgevale Rd, Kew, Victoria 3101
President: Barbara Giles; *Secretary:* Anne Parratt

International **P E N** (Sydney Centre)*, PO Box 153, Woollahra, NSW 2025 Tel: (02) 3281079
President: Alec Sheppard; *Secretary:* Patricia Thompson
Publication: Newsletter (quarterly)

Poetry Society of Australia*, PO Box N110, Grosvenor St, Sydney, NSW 2000
Joint Secretaries: Robert and Debra Adamson
Publications: New Poetry (quarterly); also poems, articles, reviews, notes and comments, interviews

Society of Women Writers (Australia), 'Mirrabooka', 141A Fuller St, Narrabeen, NSW 2101
Federal President: Joy Lindrum-Gillan
The Society is served by a changing State Federal Committee which every two years is nominated by a State branch

Victorian Fellowship of Australian Writers, J Hamilton, 1-317 Barkers Rd, Kew, Victoria 3101
Membership: 2,200

Literary Periodicals

A U M L A, Australasian Universities Language and Literature Association, James Cook University of North Queensland, Townsville, Queensland 4811
Journal of literary criticism, philology and linguistics; published in English and French

Aspect (quarterly), PO Box 275, Newport, NSW 2106

The Australian Author (quarterly), Australian Society of Authors Ltd, 22 Alfred St, Milsons Point, NSW 2061

Australian Book Review, National Book Council, Level 5, 1 City Rd, South Melbourne, Victoria 3205

Australian Literary Studies (twice a year), English Department, University of Queensland, St Lucia, Queensland 4067

Australian Writers and Their Work, Oxford University Press, GPO Box 2784Y, Melbourne, Victoria 3001

Biblionews and Australian Notes and Queries (quarterly), Book Collectors' Society of Australia, 64 Young St, Cremorne, NSW 2090

Helix (quarterly), 199 Maltravers Rd, Ivanhoe, Victoria 3079

Island Magazine (quarterly), PO Box 207, Sandy Bay, Tasmania 7005

Luna (twice a year), 101 Edgevale Rd, Kew, Victoria 3101

Meanjin Quarterly, University of Melbourne, Parkville, Victoria 3052
Magazine of literature, art and discussion

New Poetry (quarterly), Poetry Society of Australia, PO Box N110, Grosvenor St, Sydney, NSW 2000

Overland (quarterly), PO Box 249, Mount Eliza, Victoria 3930

Poetry Australia, The Market Place, Berrima, NSW 2577

Quadrant (monthly), PO Box C344, Clarence St, Sydney, NSW 2000

Reading Time (quarterly), Children's Book Council of Australia (New South Wales Branch), PO Box 159, Curtin, ACT 2605

Southerly (quarterly), English Department, University of Sydney, Sydney, NSW 2006

Westerly (quarterly), English Department, University of Western Australia, Nedlands, WA 6009

Literary Prizes

'The **Age**' Book of the Year*
Prizes of $3,000 each will be awarded by 'The Age' to the two Australian books of outstanding literary merit which best express Australia's identity or character. One prize will be for a work of imaginative writing; the other for a non-fiction work. One will be named 'The Age' Book of the Year, the other the best work in its category. Enquiries to The Literary Editor 'The Age', 250 Spencer St, Melbourne, Victoria 3000

The **Alice** Literary Award
Presented by the Society of Women Writers (Australia) biennially for a distinguished and long-term contribution to literature by an Australian woman. First presented in 1978. Enquiries to Joy Lindrum-Gillan, Federal President, Society of Women Writers (Australia), 'Mirrabooka', 141A Fuller St, Narrabeen, NSW 2101

Angus & Robertson Writers' Fellowship
For a manuscript or book project of outstanding originality, preferably by a new author. Contract with advance of $2,500. Enquiries to The Publisher, Angus & Robertson Publishers, PO Box 290, North Ryde, NSW 2113

Angus & Robertson Writers for the Young Fellowship
Section A: for a manuscript (fiction or non-fiction) with strength, orginality and relevance for the age group for which it is intended, preferably by a new author. Contract with advance of $2,000. Section B: for a picture-book text, strongly appealing to children under eight years. Contract with advance of $1,000. Enquiries to The Publisher, Angus & Robertson Publishers, PO Box 290, North Ryde, NSW 2113

The Kitty **Archer-Burton** Award
Presented by the Society of Women Writers (Australia) biennially for verse by a youth of under 19 years of age. First presented in 1979. Enquiries to Joy Lindrum-Gillan, Federal President, Society of Women Writers (Australia), 'Mirrabooka', 141A Fuller St, Narrabeen, NSW 2101

Australian Awards for Young Writers
Awarded by sponsors, the State of Victoria and the Victorian FAW for poetry, short stories, scripts and collections; for young writers 15-22 years. Varying conditions. Administered by Victorian Fellowship of Australian Writers. Closing date 31 January. Enquiries to J Hamilton, 1/317 Barkers Rd, Kew, Victoria 3101

Australian Literature Society Gold Medal
Award originated by Colonel, the Honourable R A Crouch in 1899 and continued by the Australian Literature Society until 1983 when the ALS incorporated with the Association for the Study of Australian Literature. It is awarded annually for the most outstanding Australian literary work, or (occasionally), for outstanding services to Australian literature. 1987 award to Alan Wearne for *The Night Markets*. Enquiries to Delys Bird, Secretary, Association for the Study of Australian Literature Ltd, Arts Faculty, University of Western Australia, Nedlands, WA 6009

Australian Natives' Association Literature Award
Founded in 1978 as an award for a book on an Australian theme. Prize $500. Administered by Victorian Fellowship of Australian Writers. Closing date 31 December. Enquiries to J Hamilton, 1/317 Barkers Rd, Kew, Victoria 3101

Bookman of the Year Award, now NBC Medal (qv)

Christopher **Brennan** Award, see FAW Christopher Brennan Award

Bronze Swagman Award
Awarded annually for Bush Verse. Bronze statuette of The Swagman, sculpted by Daphne Mayo, valued at $600, and a Winton opal, valued at $150. Closes 31 May. Enquiries to Winton Tourist Promotion Association, PO Box 44, Winton, Queensland 4735

The '**Canberra Times**' and the Commonwealth Bank National Short Story of the Year*
Established in 1974 and awarded annually for a short story. Entries must not exceed 2,500 words. $3,000 to winner, $1,200 to runner-up. Enquiries to Alison Young, Community Projects Officer, The 'Canberra Times', GPO Box 443, Canberra, ACT 2601

Ronald **Carson-Gold** Memorial Short Story Competition*
Awarded annually. Closes 23 April. Short story by Australian with Australian setting. 1st Prize $600, 2nd Prize $300, 3rd Prize $100. Administered by the Union Fidelity Trust. Enquiries to Carson-Gold Short Story Competition, PO Box 339, Toowong, Brisbane, Queensland 4066

Children's Book of the Year Awards*
Awarded annually by the Children's Book Council of Australia. (1) Book of the Year, established 1946; (2) Junior Book of the Year, established 1982. The Literature Board of the Australia Council for the Arts awards $3,500 to be distributed amongst the winners and commended (possibility of three). (3) Picture-book of the Year, established 1952. The Visual Arts Board of the Australia Council for the Arts awards $2,500 to be distributed amongst the winner (and possibly three commended titles). Enquiries to The Secretary, Children's Book Council of Australia, PO Box 420, Dickson, ACT 2602
or Library Services, 35 Mitchell St, North Sydney, NSW 2060

Tom **Collins** Poetry Prize
First awarded in 1977. Administered by Western Australia FAW, and sponsored by J Furphy & Sons, Shepparton, Victoria, since 1984, for a poem of up to 60 lines. Two prizes: $400 open, the other $100 for the best entry by a member of FAW (WA); the same person not eligible for both prizes. Closing date 31 December. Enquiries to Competition Secretary, Fellowship of Australian Writers (WA), 6 Alexandra Ave, Claremont, WA 6010

James **Cook** Australian Literary Studies Award, now Townsville Foundation for Australian Literary Studies Award (qv)

C J Dennis Award
$1,000, for a book about any aspect of natural science. Award provided by Victorian Government and administered by Victorian Fellowship of Australian Writers. Closing date 31 December. Enquiries to J Hamilton, 1/317 Barkers Rd, Kew, Victoria 3101

24 AUSTRALIA

C J Dennis Prize for Poetry, see Victorian Premier's Literary Awards

Anne Elder Poetry Award
$900 for first books of poetry. Administered by Victorian Fellowship of Australian Writers. Closing date 31 December. Enquiries to J Hamilton, 1/317 Barkers Rd, Kew, Victoria 3101

F A W Alan Marshall Award
For the best unpublished manuscript of fiction (or narrative poetry) which contains a strong narrative element. Prize currently $500. Sponsored and administered by Victorian Fellowship of Australian Writers. Closing date 31 December. Enquiries to J Hamilton, 1/317 Barkers Rd, Kew, Victoria 3101

F A W Barbara Ramsden Award
Awarded by the Victorian Fellowship of Australian Writers to both the author and to the publisher's editor (the latter in symbolic recognition of the importance of the publishing process) of an outstanding work of quality writing published each year. It is the Fellowship's major national award for quality writing and was founded by public subscription to honour Barbara Ramsden, MBE, a publisher's editor of distinction. The winning author (judged on merit by literary standards) and editor are each presented with a plaque specially designed by sculptor Andor Meszaros, depicting the origin of art. More than one work may be submitted by any publisher, author or publisher's editor in Australia. The 'editor' is to be that person the publisher regards as responsible for editing the work. Closing date 31 December. Enquiries to J Hamilton, 1/317 Barkers Rd, Kew, Victoria 3101

F A W Christopher Brennan Award
A plaque designed by sculptor Michael Meszaros is awarded to a poet in Australia whose work, particularly if sustained, achieves distinction. Entries not required. The most recent award was made to Les A Murray. Administered by the Victorian Fellowship of Australian Writers. Enquiries to J Hamilton, 1/317 Barkers Rd, Kew, Victoria 3101

F A W John Shaw Neilson Poetry Award
Awarded by the Victorian Fellowship of Australian Writers. Any kind of poem is acceptable with a minimum of 14 lines. Merit will be the criterion. First prize at least $150. Closing date 31 December. Enquiries to J Hamilton, 1/317 Barkers Rd, Kew, Victoria 3101

F A W Local History Award
For a book of Australian local or regional history published during the year. Administered by Victorian Fellowship of Australian Writers. Closing date 31 December. Enquiries to J Hamilton, 1/317 Barkers Rd, Kew, Victoria 3101

F A W Regional Branch Awards
Various FAW regional branches such as Parramatta, Ballarat, Eastwood, Geelong, Latrobe Valley and North Central hold occasional or regular awards, usually in the area of stories and poetry, for small cash prizes and sometimes publication. They are sometimes open within the State or the Nation

The **Festival** Awards for Literature
The awards are offered biennially by the South Australian Government and announced during Writers' Week of the Adelaide Festival of Arts. They replaced the Government Biennial Literature Prize in 1986. In 1988 the awards will include (1) National Fiction Award for a published novel or a collection of short stories ($12,500), (2) National Poetry Award ($12,500), (3) National Children's Literature Award ($12,500), (4) South Australian Award for Non-fiction by a South Australian writer ($12,500, (5) Carclew Fellowship, a six-month fellowship at Carclew to encourage young writers ($12,000). Enquiries to Department for the Arts, GPO Box 2308, Adelaide, SA 5001

Miles **Franklin** Award*
Awarded annually for a published novel, play or short stories portraying Australian life in any of its phases. Entrants must submit one copy of the published work to each of the five judges, and also one copy to the Permanent Trustee Co Ltd, within two months of its publication. Closing date is 31 January. For 1986 the award was $7,000. Enquiries to Permanent Trustee Co Ltd, Box 4270, GPO Sydney, NSW 2001

Grenfell 'Henry Lawson' Festival of Arts Prizes
Awarded annually in June with engraved bronze statuettes created by Sydney sculptor Alan Ingham, and cash. Awards are made for prose (a short story up to 5,000 words), verse, art and the words and music of an Australian popular song; also a bush ballad. Enquiries to Honorary Secretary, Henry Lawson Festival of Arts, PO Box 77, Grenfell, NSW 2810

Lyndal **Hadow** Short Story Award
Administered by Western Australia FAW for a short story not exceeding 3,000 words. Two prizes: $400 open, the other $100 for the best entry by a member of FAW (WA); the same person not eligible for both prizes. Alternates (even years) with Donald Stuart Short Story Award (odd years) — qv. Closing date 30 June. Enquiries to Competition Secretary, Fellowship of Australian Writers (WA), 6 Alexandra Ave, Claremont, WA 6010

The Grace **Leven** Prize for Poetry
Instituted under the Will of William Baylebridge, the Australian poet, who died in 1942. This prize of $200 is offered annually for 'the best volume of poetry published during the twelve months immediately preceding the year in which the award is made'. Competitors must be either Australian born, and writing as Australians, or they must be naturalized in Australia and have lived in that country for at least ten years. The volume chosen may have been published in any country, but copies of it must be freely obtainable in Australia. Enquiries to Perpetual Trustee Co Ltd, 39 Hunter St, Sydney, NSW 2000

Jessie **Litchfield** Memorial Award*
A cash prize of $300 and a bronze plaque awarded annually by the Bread and Cheese Club, Melbourne, to encourage writers who, in the opinion of the Committee, may make a contribution to Australian literature. Entry forms available on request accompanied by return postage. Enquiries to Dr Cyril Goode, Bread and Cheese Club, 51 Elizabeth St, Newport, Victoria 3015

Literary Arts Board of the Australia Council
The Literature Board supports the writing of all forms of creative literature, including novels, short stories, poetry and plays. Aid is also given to some non-fiction (especially biography, autobiography, history and the humanities). All individual applicants must use the Literature Board's application form. Enquiries to Secretary, Literary Arts Board of the Australia Council, PO Box 302, North Sydney, NSW 2060

Local History Award, see FAW Local History Award

The Walter **McRae Russell** Award
Awarded annually for the best first work of literary scholarship on an Australian subject published during the previous calendar year. Originated in 1983. Enquiries to Delys Bird, Secretary, Association for the Study of Australian Literature Ltd, Faculty of Arts, University of Western Australia, Nedlands, WA 6009

Alan **Marshall** Award, see FAW Alan Marshall Award

The Charles **Meeking** Award
Presented by the Society of Women Writers (Australia) biennially for verse by an Australian woman. First presented in 1979. Enquiries to Joy Lindrum-Gillan, Federal President, Society of Women Writers (Australia), 'Mirrabooka', 141A Fuller St, Narrabeen, NSW 2101

N B C Medal*
Awarded by the National Book Council to a person who has made a substantial contribution to the promotion of books, but who might not necessarily be expected to be eligible for many of the other awards listed in this section. Enquiries to Executive Secretary, National Book Council, Level 5, 1 City Rd, South Melbourne, Victoria 3205*

National Book Council Awards
Awarded by the National Book Council, with the support of The Book Printer and Qantas. The Awards are open to a writer under 35 years of age for any published book, or to a writer of any age for a first published book. The NBC Gold Banjo Award of $10,000 is for a book of highest literary merit, and the NBC Silver Banjo Award of $7,500 for a book of highest literary merit in a category other than that of the winner. Qantas is sponsoring the NBC/Qantas New Writers Award with a return airfare to the Frankfurt Book Fair and assistance in promoting the winning book there. Enquiries to Awards Secretary, National Book Council, Level 5, 1 City Rd, South Melbourne, Victoria 3205

John Shaw **Neilson** Poetry Award, see FAW John Shaw Neilson Poetry Award

New South Wales Premier's Literary Awards
Inaugurated in 1979 by the New South Wales Government to honour distinguished achievement by Australian writers. Awards are offered for a work of fiction ($10,000), non-fiction ($10,000), poetry ($5,000), a children's book ($2,000) and a play ($5,000). Since 1984, awards have been offered for film writing ($5,000) and television writing ($5,000). The Ethnic Affairs Commission Award of $5,000 is offered for a work which reflects an aspect of Australia's multicultural society. In addition, the committee judging the book awards may propose that a special award, with or without prize money, be made for a work not readily covered by the existing categories, or in recognition of a writer's achievements generally. Winners in all categories also receive commemorative medallions. Enquiriese1 to The Director, Office of the Minister for the Arts, PO Box R105, Royal Exchange, Sydney, NSW 2000

New South Wales Writer's Fellowship
Awarded by the New South Wales Government in conjunction with the New South Wales Premier's Literary Awards, the Fellowship, valued at $10,000 in 1986, is normally awarded to supplement a writer's income during work on an approved project likely to result in literary work of significant quality, or be of lasting benefit to the applicant's experience and development as a writer or the advancement of Australian literature in

general. Applicants are required to have been resident three years prior to and at the time of application. Enquiries to The Director, Office of the Minister for the Arts, PO Box R105, Royal Exchange, Sydney, NSW 2000

Palmer Prizes, see Victorian Premier's Literary Awards

Barbara **Ramsden** Award, see FAW Barbara Ramsden Award

The Mary **Silmore** Award
Awarded annually for the best first book of poetry published in Australia during the previous calendar year. Originated in 1985. Enquiries to Delys Bird, Secretary, Association for the Study of Australian Literature Ltd, Faculty of Arts, University of Western Australia, Nedlands, WA 6009

South Australian Government Festival Awards for Literature, now The Festival Awards for Literature (qv)

State of Victoria Short Story Awards
(1) Awarded annually; prizes of $1,000, $400 and $250 to Australian writers for original short stories. There will also be other awards, e.g. of $50 each for unpublished writers. Stories should be unpublished and not exceed 4,000 words. More than one entry may be submitted in all sections. (2) Awarded annually; prizes of $200, $75 and $50 to young writers 15-22 years. Sponsored by the Victorian Ministry for the Arts and administered by Victorian Fellowship of Australian Writers. Closing date 31 December. Enquiries to J Hamilton, 1/317 Barkers Rd, Kew, Victoria 3101

Walter **Stone** Memorial Award*
For a monograph, biography or bibliography on some aspect of Australian literature. Biennial prize of $500 plus certificate. Enquiries to Walter Stone Memorial Award, Fellowship of Australian Writers (NSW), GPO Box 3448, Sydney, NSW 2001

Donald **Stuart** Short Story Award
Administered by Western Australia FAW for a short story not exceeding 3,000 words. Two prizes: $400 open, the other $100 for the best entry by a member of FAW (WA); the same person not eligible for both prizes. Alternates (odd years) with Lyndal Hadow Short Story Award (even years) — qv. Closing date 30 June. Enquiries to Competition Secretary, Fellowship of Australian Writers (WA), 6 Alexandra Ave, Claremont, WA 6010

Herb **Thomas** Award
Formerly known as Con Weickhardt Award: presented for a published work of biography, autobiography or a memoir. $400. Administered by the Victorian Fellowship of Australian Writers. Closing date 31 December. Enquiries to Secretariat, 1/317 Barkers Rd, Kew, Victoria 3101

Townsville Foundation for Australian Literary Studies Award
$1,500 from the Townsville Foundation for Australian Literary Studies at the James Cook University of North Queensland. The award is made to the author of the best book in any field of writing dealing with any aspect of Australian life. The book must have been published in Australia, even if printed elsewhere. Closing date is 28 February. Enquiries to Executive Director, Foundation for Australian Literary Studies, English Department, James Cook University of North Queensland, Townsville, Queensland 4811

Victorian Premier's Literary Awards
Founded in 1985 by the Victorian Ministry for the Arts on the occasion of the centenary of the births of Vance and Nettie Palmer. The annual awards are (1) The Vance Palmer Prize for a work of fiction ($15,000), (2) The Nettie Palmer Prize for a work of non-fiction ($15,000), (3) The Louis Essow Prize for Drama ($7,500), (4) The A A Phillips Prize for Australian Studies ($7,500), (5) The C J Dennis Prize for Poetry ($5,000). Enquiries to Caroline Baum, Executive Secretary, Premier's Literary Awards, Victorian Ministry for the Arts, 168 Exhibition St, Melbourne, Victoria 3000

Warana Writers' Awards*
Awarded annually by the Fellowship of Australian Writers (Queensland Branch) for poetry, feature article and short story. Closes 25 August. Enquiries to Mrs Jean Scott, PO Box 339, Toowong, Brisbane, Queensland 4066

Con **Weickhardt** Award, see Herb Thomas Award

Patricia **Weickhardt** Award
Cash prize to an aboriginal writer. Administered by Victorian Fellowship of Australian Writers. Closing date 31 December. Enquiries to J Hamilton, 1/317 Barkers Rd, Kew, Victoria 3101

Patrick **White** Literary Award
Patrick White has applied his Nobel Prize money to establish a trust to make grants to Australian writers who have been inadequately recognized. Submissions are not required. Enquiries to Perpetual Trustees Australia Ltd, 39 Hunter St, Sydney, NSW 2000

Wilke Literary Award
For a work of non-fiction, of literary merit, published and wholly manufactured in Australia. Administered by the Victorian Fellowship of Australian Writers. Closing date 31 December. Enquiries to J Hamilton, 1/317 Barkers Rd, Kew, Victoria 3101

Austria

General Information

Language: German. There are speakers of Slovene in Southern Carinthia, Hungarian and a Croatian dialect in Burgenland
Religion: Predominantly Roman Catholic
Population: 7.56 million
Bank Hours: 0800-1230, 1330-1500 Monday-Wednesday, Friday; 0800-1230, 1330-1730 Thursday
Shop Hours: 0800-1800 Monday-Friday; 0800-1200 or 1300 Saturday
Currency: 100 groschen = 1 schilling
Export/Import Information: Member of the European Free Trade Association. Import licences not required for books. No exchange controls.
Copyright: UCC, Berne, Florence (see International section)

Book Trade Organizations

Bundesgremium des Handels mit Büchern, Kunstblättern und Musikalien, Zeitungen und Zeitschriften, A-1045 Vienna, Wiedner-Hauptstr 63, Postfach 440 Tel: (0222) 65053209 Telex: 111871 Buka
Federal Group for Traders in Books, Prints and Sheet Music, Newspapers and Periodicals
Man Dir: Karl Hanzal

Hauptverband der graphischen Unternehmungen Österreichs*, A-1010 Vienna 1, Grünangergasse 4
Austrian Graphical Association

Hauptverband des österreichischen Buchhandels, A-1010 Vienna 1, Grünangergasse 4 Tel: (0222) 5121535
Cable Add: Buchverein Vienna
Austrian Publishers' and Booksellers' Association
President: Otto Hausa; *Secretary:* Dr Gerhard Prosser
Miscellaneous: A number of subsidiary organizations are administered from the same office: e.g. Verband der Antiquare Österreichs; Verband österreichischer Kommissionäre, Grossobuchhändler und Auslieferer; Verband der Österreichischen Zeitungs- und Zeitschriften-Grossisten und der Werbenden Zeitschriftenhändler; Österreichischer Verlegerverband; Österreichischer Buchhändlerverband; Standard Book Numbering Agency (qqv)
Publications include: Anzeiger des österreichischen Buchhandels (Austrian Book Trade Gazette) (twice a month); *Adressbuch des österreichischen Buchhandels* (Directory of Austrian Book Trade); *Das österreichische Buch* (catalogue) (annual); *Bücher: Das Lesemagazin für Sie* (catalogue) (annual); *Österreichische Bibliographie* (Austrian Bibliography)

Interessengemeinschaft österreichischer Autoren*, A-1010 Vienna, Bankgasse 8 Tel: (0222) 634459
Association of Austrian Authors
Dir: Prof Milo Dor
Publications include: Katalog lieferbarer Bücher österreichischer Klein- und Autorenverlage (Catalogue of Books available from small Austrian publishers or published by authors themselves); *Autorensolidarität* (Author Solidarity) (twice a year)

Landesgremium Kärnten des Handels mit Büchern, Kunstblättern, Musikalien, Zeitungen und Zeitschriften, A-9020 Klagenfurt, Bahnhofstr 42 Tel: (04222) 57555
Carinthian Regional Group of Traders in Books, Prints, Sheet Music, Periodicals and Newspapers

Landesgremium Niederösterreich des Handels mit Büchern, Kunstblättern, Musikalien, Zeitungen und Zeitschriften*, A-1014 Vienna, Herrengasse 10 Tel: (0222) 636691
Lower Austria Regional Group of Traders in Books, Prints, Sheet Music, Periodicals and Newspapers

Landesgremium Oberösterreich des Handels mit Büchern, Kunstblättern, Musikalien, Zeitungen und Zeitschriften, A-4010 Linz, Hessenpl 3 Tel: (0732) 2800/2328
Upper Austria Regional Trade Association of Traders in Books, Prints, Sheet Music, Periodicals and Newspapers
General Secretary: Dr Helmut Hagenauer

Landesgremium Salzburg des Handels mit Büchern, Kunstblättern, Musikalien, Zeitungen und Zeitschriften, A-5027 Salzburg, Julius-Raab-Platz 1 Tel: (0662) 71571/71251 Telex: 3633

Salzburg Regional Group of Traders in Books, Prints, Sheet Music, Periodicals and Newspapers
Secretary: Dr Helmut Maurer

Landesgremium Steiermark des Handels mit Büchern, Kunstblättern, Musikalien, Zeitungen und Zeitschriften*, A-8021 Graz, Körblergasse 111-113 Tel: (0316) 601571
Styrian Regional Group of Traders in Books, Prints, Sheet Music, Periodicals and Newspapers

Landesgremium Tirol des Handels mit Büchern, Kunstblättern, Musikalien, Zeitungen und Zeitschriften, A-6020 Innsbruck, Meinhardstr 14/IV Tel: (05222) 35651/35290
Tyrol Regional Group of Traders in Books, Prints, Sheet Music, Periodicals and Newspapers
Secretary: Dr Manfred Scherb

Landesgremium Vorarlberg des Handels mit Büchern und Musikalien, A-6800 Feldkirch, Wichnergasse 9 Tel: (05522) 22511 Telex: 052213
Vorarlberg Regional Group of Traders in Books and Sheet Music
Man Dir: Heribert Eggler; *Secretary:* Dr Matthias Ammann

Landesgremium Wien des Handels mit Büchern, Kunstblättern, Musikalien, Zeitungen und Zeitschriften, A-1041 Vienna, Schwarzenbergpl 14 Tel: (0222) 652174
Vienna Regional Group of Traders in Books, Prints, Sheet Music, Periodicals and Newspapers

Literar-Mechana, Wahrnehmungsgesellschaft für Urheberrechte GmbH, A-1060 Vienna VI, Linke Wienzeile 18 Tel: (0222) 5872161
Organization for Copyright Protection
Man Dir: Franz-Leo Popp

Musikverleger Union Österreich*, A-1030 Vienna, Baumannstr 8-10 Tel: (0222) 731555
President: Dr Johann Juranek
Union of Austrian Music Publishers

Österreichischer Buchhändlerverband, A-1010 Vienna 1, Grünangergasse 4 Tel: (0222) 5121535
Austrian Booksellers' Association
President: Dr Klaus Remmer; *Secretary:* Dr Gerhard Prosser

Österreichischer Verlegerverband, A-1010 Vienna 1, Grünangergasse 4 Tel: (0222) 5121535
Association of Austrian Publishers
President: Hans W Polak; *Secretary-General:* Dr Gerhard Prosser

Staatlich genehmigte Literarische Verwertungsgesellschaft (LVG) Reg Gen mbH, A-1060 Vienna VI, Linke Wienzeile 18 Tel: (0222) 5872161
National Licensing Society for Literary Exploitation
President: Prof Milo Dor; *Man Dir:* Franz-Leo Popp

Standard Book Numbering Agency, c/o H Walter Ess, Hauptverband des Österreichischen Buchhandels, A-1010 Vienna 1, Grünangergasse 4 Tel: (0222) 5121535

Verband der Antiquare Österreichs, A-1010 Vienna 1, Grünangergasse 4 Tel: (0222) 5121535
Austrian Antiquarian Booksellers' Association
President: Dr Hansjörg Krug; *Secretary-General:* Dr Gerhard Prosser
Publication: Anzeiger des Verbandes der Antiquare Österreichs (Austrian Antiquarian Booksellers' Association Gazette)

Verband der österreichischen Zeitungs- und Zeitschriften-Grossisten und der Werbenden Zeitschriftenhändler, A-1010 Vienna, Grünangergasse 4 Tel: (0222) 5121535
Association of Austrian Newspaper and Magazine Wholesalers and Advertising Journal Sellers
President: Gerhard Loidl; *Secretary:* Dr Gerhard Prosser

Verband österreichischer Kommissionäre, Grossobuchhändler und Auslieferer, A-1010 Vienna 1, Grünangergasse 4 Tel: (0222) 5121535
Association of Austrian Book Wholesalers and Distributors
President: Dr Peter Eisler; *Secretary-General:* Dr Gerhard Prosser

Vereinigung des katholischen Buchhandels in Österreich, A-5020 Salzburg, Rupertusbuchhandlung, Dreifaltigkeitsgasse 12 Tel: (0662) 787330
Chairman: Bernhard Weis

Book Trade Reference Books and Journals

Books

(See also reference books listed under Federal Republic of Germany)

Adressbuch des österreichischen Buchhandels, (Directory of Austrian Book Trade), Hauptverband des österreichischen Buchhandels, A-1010 Vienna 1, Grünangergasse 4

Katalog lieferbarer Bücher Österreichischer Klein- und Autorenverlage (Catalogue of Books available from small Austrian publishers or published by authors themselves), Interessengemeinschaft Österreichischer Autoren, A-1010 Vienna, Bankgasse 8

Journals

Anzeiger des österreichischen Buchhandels (Austrian Book Trade Gazette) (twice a month), Hauptverband des österreichischen Buchhandels, A-1010 Vienna 1, Grünangergasse 4

Anzeiger des Verbandes der Antiquare Österreichs (Austrian Antiquarian Booksellers' Association Gazette), Verband der Antiquare Österreichs, A-1010 Vienna 1, Grünangergasse 4

Neuer Bücherdienst (Book Information Magazine), I Mainz, A-1040 Vienna, Schwindgasse 9

Österreichische Bibliographie (Austrian Bibliography), Hauptverband des österreichischen Buchhandels, A-1010 Vienna 1, Grünangergasse 4

Wiener Bücherbriefe (Viennese Book Letters), Forum Verlag GmbH, A-1050 Vienna 5, Sonnenhofgasse 8

Zeit im Buch (Today in the Book), A-1010 Vienna, Stephans Platz 6

Publishers

Adyar-Verlag, A-8011 Graz, Wartingergasse 31, Postfach 655 Tel: (0316) 657055
Man Dir: Norbert Lauppert
Subjects: Specialist Publishing House for Theosophical Literature: The Occult, Mysticism, Yoga, Eastern Religions
1985: 3 titles *1986:* 2 titles *Founded:* 1947
ISBN Publisher's Prefix: 3-85005

Age d'Homme-Karolinger Verlag GmbH & Co KG, A-1170 Vienna, Ortliebgasse 2 Tel: (0222) 4302093
Man Dir, Sales: Jean-Jacques Langendorf; *Editorial:* Dr Peter Weiss; *Publicity:* Cornelia Langendorf; *Rights & Permissions:* Hans Hofinger
Subjects: German, French and Slav Literature and History, History of German Ideologies
Founded: 1980
ISBN Publisher's Prefix: 3-85418

Akademische Druck- und Verlagsanstalt+*, A-8011 Graz, Neufeldweg 75, Postfach 598 Tel: (0316) 41153 Cable Add: Adeva Graz Telex: 032234 Grade
Manager: Dr Manfred Kramer; *Editors:* Inge Schwarz, Dr Karl Gratzl, Gerhard Lechner
Subsidiary Company: Codices Selecti (at above address)
Subjects: Encyclopaedias, Philology, Linguistics, Dictionaries, Anthropology, Arms and Military History, Orientalistics, Numismatics, History of Art, Archaeology, Musicology, Facsimile Editions of Illuminated Manuscripts
Founded: 1949
ISBN Publisher's Prefix: 3-201

Amalthea-Verlag*, A-1030 Vienna 3, Am Heumarkt 19 Tel: (0222) 723560
Dir: Dr Herbert Fleissner
Subjects: Belles Lettres, Art, Music, Fiction
Founded: 1917
Miscellaneous: Firm is a member of Buchverlage Ullstein Langen Müller/Herbig, Federal Republic of Germany (qv)

Andreas und Andreas Verlagsbuchhandel+, A-5020 Salzburg, Hans-Seebachstr 10 Tel: (0662) 21318 Cable Add: Andreasverlag Salzburg Telex: 06632022
Publishers: Wolf-Dietrich Andreas, Ingrid Andreas; *Dir:* Franz Pemwieser
Branch Offs: Oskar Andreas Nachfolger Herzog & Co, Reise- und Versandbuchhandel, A-1170 Vienna, Parhamerpl 9; Andreas und Andreas Verlagsbuchhandel Zweigniederlassung, D-8228 Freilassing, Federal Republic of Germany; Andreas und Andreas Verlagsanstalt, FL-9490 Vaduz, Liechtenstein
Subjects: General Fiction
Founded: 1956
ISBN Publisher's Prefix: 3-85012

Ferdinand **Berger** und Söhne, A-3580 Horn, Wienerstr 21-23, Postfach 14 Tel: (02982) 23174 Cable Add: Berger Horn Telex: 78613 Fax: (02982) 4161 Klappe 268
Subjects: Folk History, Art History, Anthropology, Archaeology, Reference, Natural Sciences, Periodicals
Founded: 1868

Bergland Verlag*, A-1051 Vienna, Spengergasse 39 Tel: (0222) 555641
Man Dir: Friedrich Geyer

Verlag 'Das **Bergland-Buch**'+, A-5024 Salzburg, Innsbrucker Bundesstr 46 Tel: (0662) 39895 Cable Add: Berglandbuch Salzburg Telex: 633588
Man Dir: Alfred Schulz
Orders to: Morawa & Co, A-1140 Vienna, Hackingerstr 52
Subjects: General Fiction, History, General Science, *Tieck* books
1985: 10 titles *Founded:* 1929
ISBN Publisher's Prefix: 3-7023

Verlag Alexander **Bernhardt**, A-6134
Vomperberg Tel: (05242) 2131
Associate Company: Verlag der Stiftung
Gralsbotschaft GmbH, Federal Republic of
Germany (qv)
Subject: Philosophy
Founded: 1945

Annette **Betz** Verlag+, A-1091 Vienna,
Postfach 306 (Located at: Alserstr 24,
Vienna) Tel: (0222) 425684/481538 Telex:
114802
Man Dir: Dr Otto Mang
Parent Company: Verlag Carl Ueberreuter
(qv)
Subjects: Children's, Picture-books
Founded: 1962
ISBN Publisher's Prefix: 3-219

Bibliographisches Institut GmbH, Vienna,
see Bibliographisches Institut und F A
Brockhaus AG, Federal Republic of
Germany

Josef Gotthard **Bläschke**-Verlag*, A-9143
St Michael, Feistritz 31 Tel: (04235) 2152
Man Dir: J G Bläschke
Subjects: Literature, Poetry, Biography,
Memoirs
ISBN Publisher's Prefix: 3-7053

Böhlau Verlag GmbH, A-1010 Vienna, Dr
Karl Lueger-Ring 12 Tel: (0222) 638735
Man Dirs: Dr Peter Rauch, Rudolf Siegle;
Production and Rights & Permissions:
Dr Peter Rauch; *Publicity:* Erich Horvath
Associate Company: Minerva GmbH,
A-1010 Vienna, Schottengasse 7/5
Branch Off: Böhlau-Verlag GmbH & Cie,
Federal Republic of Germany (qv)
Subjects: Theatre, Biography, History,
Music, Art and the Arts generally,
Philosophy, Religion, Psychology, General
& Social Science, University Textbooks,
Economics, Education, Law, Linguistics,
Geography
Founded: 1683
ISBN Publisher's Prefix: 3-205

Bohmann Druck und Verlag GmbH & Co
KG, A-1110 Vienna, Leberstr 122
Tel: (0222) 741595 Telex: 132312 Fax:
(0222) 741595183
Dirs: Dr Rudolf Bohmann, Heinz Keller
Subjects: Business, Computers, Travel
Founded: 1936
ISBN Publisher's Prefix: 3-7002

Verlag Dr Gerda **Borotha-Schoeler***,
A-1190 Vienna, Glatzgasse 4 Tel: (0222)
3494382/3490365
Orders to: Lechner & Sohn, A-1010
Vienna, Seilerstätte 5
Subject: General Knowledge

Wilhelm **Braumüller** Universitätsverlag
GmbH, A-1092 Vienna, Servitengasse 5
Tel: (0222) 348124
Man Dir: Brigitte Kaltschmid; *Sales
Manager:* Renate Piffl
Subjects: History, Philosophy, Psychology,
General Non-fiction, Juveniles, Agriculture,
Literature, Education, Social Science,
Economics, Periodicals
Founded: 1783
ISBN Publisher's Prefix: 3-7003

Verlagsbuchhandlung Julius **Breitschopf**+*,
A-1170 Vienna, Bergsteiggasse 5 Tel:
(0222) 437203 Cable Add:
Breitschopfbuch Telex: 07114539
Associate Companies: Moderne Jugende
Heute GmbH, Austria (qv); Julius
Breitschopf KG, Verlagsbuchhandlung,
Federal Republic of Germany (qv)
Subjects: Picture Books, Juveniles
Bookshops: A-1090 Vienna 9,
Nussdorferstr 62; A-1170 Vienna 17,
Kalvarienborgstr 30

Founded: 1913
ISBN Publisher's Prefix: 3-7004

Verlag **Carinthia**, A-9010 Klagenfurt,
Völkermarkter Ring 25, Postfach 197 Tel:
(04222) 57377 Telex: 422204
Publicity: Anton Kreuzer
Subjects: Fiction, Art, Religion

Codices Selecti, subsidiary of Akademische
Druck- und Verlagsanstalt (qv)

Compass Verlagsgesellschaft Rudolf Hanel
und Sohn, A-1013 Vienna 1, Wipplingerstr
32, Postfach 29 Tel: (0222) 5336616 Cable
Add: Compass Vienna
Man Dir: Werner Futter
Subjects: Austrian Industrial, Financial &
Commercial Directories, Economics,
Reference, Business
1987-88: 5 titles *Founded:* 1867
ISBN Publisher's Prefix: 3-85041

Cura Verlag GmbH, A-1037 Vienna,
Beatrixgasse 32, Postfach 49 Tel: (0222)
7136480
Man Dir: Harald Podoschek; *Publicity
Manager:* Eva M Kittelmann
Subjects: Educational, Religious,
Reference, *Selbsthilfen* series
1986: 6 titles *1987:* 6 titles
ISBN Publisher's Prefix: 3-7027

Dachs-Verlag GmbH+, A-1020 Vienna,
Lassingleithnerpl 3 Tel: (0222) 2605689
Man Dir: Dr Hubert Hladej
Subjects: Children's, Juveniles, Picture-
books
1985: 8 titles *1986:* 6 titles
Founded: 1987
ISBN Publisher's Prefix: 3-900763

Denzel-Verlag Auto- und Wanderführer,
A-6020 Innsbruck, Maximilianstr 9
Tel: (05222) 26880
Subjects: Geography, Atlases, Travel,
Touring, Climbing
Founded: 1952
ISBN Publisher's Prefix: 3-85047

Franz **Deuticke** Verlagsges mbH+*, A-1011
Vienna 1, Helferstorferstr 4, Postfach 761
Tel: (0222) 634345/636429
Man Dir: Franz Scharetzer
Orders to: Österr Bundesverlag GmbH,
A-2351 Wiener Neudorf, Postfach
Subjects: Non-fiction, Technical,
Psychology, General Science, University &
Secondary Textbooks, Earth Sciences
(Geography, Cartography, Geology,
Environmental Protection), Law
Bookshops: Buchhandlung Franz Deuticke,
Antiquariat Franz Deuticke, A-1011
Vienna 1, Helferstorferstr 4
Founded: 1878
ISBN Publisher's Prefix: 3-7005

Ludwig **Doblinger** (Bernard Herzmansky)
Musikverlag, A-1010 Vienna 1,
Dorotheergasse 10, Postfach 882
Tel: (0222) 515030 Cable Add: Musicdob
Vienna Telex: 133008 Dobli
Man Dir: Helmuth Pany
Subject: Music
Founded: 1876
ISBN Publisher's Prefix: 3-90035

Wilhelm **Ennsthaler**+, A-4400 Steyr,
Stadtpl 26 Tel: (07252) 22053 Telex:
28309 Ennsb
Subjects: Belles Lettres, Poetry, Natural
Health, History
Bookshop: At above address
Founded: 1880
ISBN Publisher's Prefix: 3-85068

Europa Verlags-GmbH, A-1232 Vienna,
Altmannsdorferstr 154-156 Tel: (0222)
672622 Cable Add: Europaverlag
Telex: 131326
Editorial Dir, Sales, Publicity: Karin

Unger; *Production:* Helmut Dunkel; *Rights
& Permissions:* Elfriede Nussgruber
Subjects: Philosophy, Natural, Social &
Political Science, Current Events,
Literature, Economics, Law, Belles Lettres
Founded: 1946
ISBN Publisher's Prefix: 3-203

Evangelischer Pressverband in Österreich*,
A-1030 Vienna, Ungargasse 9 Tel: (0222)
725475/725461 Telex: 115551
Publicity Manager: Paul Weiland
Founded: 1925

Facultas Verlag*, A-1090 Vienna,
Berggasse 4 Tel: (0222) 315659/343685
Telex: 076529 Icpfa
Associate Company: Literas-Verlag GmbH
(qv)
Subject: Sciences
ISBN Publisher's Prefix: 3-85076

Forum Verlag GmbH, A-1050 Vienna 5,
Sonnenhofgasse 8 Tel: (0222) 526411
Man Dir: N Schnabl; *Publicity Dir:* Dr P
Wasservogel
Subjects: General Fiction, General Science,
Art, Juveniles
Founded: 1952
ISBN Publisher's Prefix: 3-7006

Freytag-Berndt und Artaria,
Kartographische Anstalt*, A-1071 Vienna
7, Schottenfeldgasse 62 Tel: (0222)
939501 Telex: 133526
Chairmen: Dr W R Petrowitz, Harald
Hochenegg; *Sales Manager:* Wolfgang
Kaiser
Bookshops: A-1010 Vienna, Kohlmarkt 9;
A-1070 Vienna, Schottenfeldgasse 62;
A-6020 Innsbruck, Wilhelm-Greil Str 15
Subjects: Geography, Atlases, Maps

Georg **Fromme** und Co*, A-1051
Vienna 5, Arbeitergasse 1-7 Tel: (0222)
555641 Telex: 111969
Man Dir: Friedrich Geyer
Subjects: Textbooks, General Science,
Technology
Founded: 1748
ISBN Publisher's Prefix: 3-85086

Dr Heinrich **Fuchs***, A-1180 Vienna,
Thimiggasse 82

Gerold & Co, A-1011 Vienna, Graben 31
Tel: (0222) 5335014 Cable Add:
Geroldbuch Vienna Telex: 847136157
Gerol
Man Dir: Hans Neusser
Subjects: Philosophy, Linguistics
Bookshop: See under Major Booksellers
ISBN Publisher's Prefix: 3-900190

Verlag für **Geschichte und Politik**, A-1030
Vienna, Neulinggasse 26/3 Tel: (0222)
726258/753106
Man Dir: Dr Karl Cornides; *Sales Dir:*
Gerda Adler; *Publicity & Advertising:* Dr
Erika Rüdegger, Dr Éva Pripfl
Associate Company: Verlag Oldenbourg
(qv)
Subjects: History, Sociology, Economics,
Political Science
Founded: 1947
ISBN Publisher's Prefix: 3-7028

'**Globus**' Zeitungs-, Druck- und
Verlagsanstalt GmbH*, A-1206 Vienna 20,
Höchstädtpl 3 Tel: (0222) 334501 Cable
Add: Globusbuch Vienna
General Manager: H Zaslawski
Subjects: Politics, Popular Sciences, Belles
Lettres, Sports, Fiction, Newspapers
Founded: 1945
Miscellaneous: Firm are also general
representatives and distributors

Alois **Göschl** & Co*, A-1190 Vienna 19,
Trummelhofgasse 12 Tel: (0222) 321180
Proprietor: Hiltraud Lechner

28 AUSTRIA

Subjects: Health, Veterinary, Domestic Science, Juveniles
Founded: 1949

Verlag Herder & Co+, A-1011 Vienna 1, Wollzeile 33, Postfach 248 Tel: (0222) 5121413 Cable Add: Herderbuch Vienna Telex: 11046
Man Dir: Erich M Wolf; *Editorial:* Dr Gottfried Hierzenberger; *Sales:* Klemens Huber; *Advertising, Rights:* Ursula Lachner
Associate Companies: Verlag Herder GmbH & Co KG, Verlag A G Ploetz GmbH & Co KG (qqv, both Federal Republic of Germany); Herder Editrice e Libreria, Italy (qv); Editorial Herder SA, Librería Herder (qqv, both Spain); Herder AG, Switzerland (qv)
Bookshop: Herder & Co (qv under Major Booksellers)
Founded: 1886
ISBN Publisher's Prefix: 3-210

Herold Druck- und Verlagsgesellschaft mbH+, A-1080 Vienna, Postfach 321 (Located at: Vienna, Strozzigasse 8) Tel: (0222) 431551 Telex: 133547 Wspro
Man Dir: Franz Hörmann
Associate Company: Herold Verlagsgesellschaft mbH, D-8000 Munich 95, Claude Lorrainstr 11, Federal Republic of Germany
Subjects: Art, History, Religion (Catholic)
Founded: 1893
ISBN Publisher's Prefix: 3-7008

Bernard **Herzmansky**, see Ludwig Doblinger

Johannes **Heyn***, A-9020 Klagenfurt, Krassniggstr 42 Tel: (04222) 57012 Cable Add: Heyn Klagenfurt Telex: 042401
Man Dir: Gerd Zechner
Subjects: General Fiction, Belles Lettres, Poetry, Biography, History, How-to, Music, Art, Reference, Juveniles, Low- & High-priced Paperbacks, General Science, University, Secondary & Primary Textbooks
Bookshop: Buchhandlung Johannes Heyn (qv under Major Booksellers)
Founded: 1868
ISBN Publisher's Prefix: 3-85366

Edition E **Hilger***, A-1010 Vienna, Dorotheergasse 5 Tel: (0222) 525315
Man Dir & Production: Ernst Hilger; *Sales & Publicity:* Monica Zimmermann
Subjects: Collectors' Books, Art, Limited editions of original graphics
Founded: 1973

Ferdinand **Hirt** mbH & Co KG*, A-1094 Vienna, Postfach 39 (Located at: Vienna, Widerhofergasse 8) Tel: (0222) 343558 Telex: 115014
Managers: Götz Hirt-Reger, Herwig Seebauer, Sabine Hirt-Reger
Orders to: A-1232 Vienna, Allmannsolorferstr 154/156
Subjects: Science, Education, Academic, Geographical, Teachers' Training, Serials
Founded: 1965
ISBN Publisher's Prefix: 3-7019

Verlag **Hölder-Pichler-Tempsky**, A-1096 Vienna, Frankgasse 4, Postfach 127 Tel: (0222) 438993 Cable Add: Hapeteverlag
Man Dir: Gustav Glöckler
Subject: School Textbooks
1987: 40 titles *Founded:* 1921
ISBN Publisher's Prefix: 3-209

Brüder **Hollinek** & Co GmbH+, A-1130 Vienna, Gallgasse 40A Tel: (0222) 845346
Man Dir: R Hollinek; *Sales Dir:* Dr P Schübert; *Advertising Dir, Rights & Permissions:* R Hollinek
Subsidiary Company: Druckerei Brüder Hollinek, A-2384 Breitenfurt-Wien

Subjects: Reference, Medicine, Law
Bookshop: A-1238 Vienna, Feldgasse 13
Founded: 1872

Inn-Verlag, A-6023 Innsbruck, Rossaugasse 5, Postfach 29 Tel: (05222) 45331 Cable Add: Innverlag Innsbruck Telex: 053617 Innvlg
Publisher: Käte Glotz-Hagleitner; *Sales:* Manfred Hagleitner; *Production:* Klaus Hagleitner
Subjects: Technics, History, Sport, School Textbooks, Politics, Educational Materials
Bookshop: Kommissions-Reise & Versandbuchhandlung (at above address)
1986: 40 titles *Founded:* 1947
ISBN Publisher's Prefix: 3-85123

Jugend und Volk Verlagsgesellschaft mbH, A-1153 Vienna, Anschützgasse 1, Postfach 80 Tel: (0222) 857508
Man Dir: Dr Otto Schimpf; *Rights and Permissions:* Friedrich Themel
Subsidiary Company: Jugend und Volk Verlag GmbH, Federal Republic of Germany (qv)
Subjects: Belles Lettres, Music, Art, Picture Books, Juveniles, High-priced Paperbacks, Psychology, Social Science, Education, Viennese Memorabilia, Secondary & Primary Textbooks, Educational Materials, Austrian post-war literature, Periodicals, Reprints
Bookshop: Buchhandlung Zentrum Simmering, A-1110 Vienna, Simmeringer-Hauptstr 96A, Ekazent
Founded: 1921
ISBN Publisher's Prefix: 3-224

Verlag **Jungbrunnen**+, A-1011 Vienna 1, Rauhensteingasse 5, Postfach 583 Tel: (0222) 521299
Man Dir, Editorial, Rights and Permissions: Dr Ellen Weigel
Subjects: Juveniles, Psychology, Education
Founded: 1923
ISBN Publisher's Prefix: 3-7026

Juridica-Verlag GmbH*, A-1070 Vienna, Wimbergergasse 33 Tel: (0222) 933292
Managers: Werner Sopper, Grete Grill

Verlag A F **Koska***, A-1060 Vienna, Esterhazygasse 35 Tel: (0222) 574344
Manager: Prof Alfred F Koska

Verlag **Kremayr und Scheriau**, A-1120 Vienna, Niederhofstr 37 Tel: (0222) 834501/871641 Telex: 131405 Fax: (0222) 834501-4/871641-4
Man Dir: Dr Rudolf Helwig
Orders to (Trade Dept): Zentralgesellschaft Dr Berger, A-1010 Vienna, Singerstr 12
Parent Company: Verlagsgruppe Bertelsmann GmbH, Federal Republic of Germany (qv)
Subjects: General Fiction, History, How-to, Music, Art, Juveniles
Book Club: Buchgemeinschaft Donauland Kremayr & Scheriau
Bookshop: Buchhandlung ünd Zeitschriftenvertrieb Kremayr und Scheriau, A-1121 Vienna, Niederhofstr 37
Founded: 1950
ISBN Publisher's Prefix: 3-218

Kümmerley und Frey Verlags GmbH*, A-1050 Vienna, Nikolsdorferstr 8
Associate Companies: J Fink-Kümmerly und Frey Verlag GmbH, Federal Republic of Germany (qv); Kümmerly und Frey (Geographischer Verlag), Switzerland (qv)
Subjects: Maps, Travel

Verlag Elisabeth **Lafite**, A-1010 Vienna 1, Hegelstrasse 13 Tel: (0222) 526869
Subjects: Music books & periodicals
Founded: 1962
ISBN Publisher's Prefix: 3-85151

Landesverlag Buchverlag+, A-4010 Linz, Hafenstr 1-3, Postfach 50 Tel: (0732) 276451
Man Dir: Friedrich Müller; *Editorial, Rights & Permissions:* Josef Preundler; *Sales, Publicity:* Dr Harald Knill
Subsidiary Company: Veritas-Verlag (qv)
Subjects: Biography, History, Art, Literature, Countryside, Cookery, Gift Books
Bookshops: At above address; A-4810 Gmunden, Rathauspl 1; A-4710 Grieskirchen, Stadtpl 42, Postfach 2; A-4910 Ried i Innkreis, Wohlmayrgasse 4, Postfach 209; A-4150 Rohrbach, Marktpl 9, Postfach 3; A-4690 Schwanenstadt, Stadtpl 45; A-4600 Wels, Bahnhofstr 16, Postfach 146; A-4820 Bad-Ischl, Pfarrgasse 11; A-4840 Vöcklabruck, Stadtpl; A-4470 Enns, Hauptpl 14
1985: 20 titles *Founded:* 1872
ISBN Publisher's Prefix: 3-85214

Langenscheidt-Verlag GmbH*, A-1010 Vienna, Singerstr 12
Parent Company: Langenscheidt KG, Federal Republic of Germany (qv)
Subject: Foreign Languages

Leykam Buchverlagsges mbH, A-8011 Graz, Stempfergasse 3, Postfach 424 Tel: (0316) 76676 Cable Add: Leykam Graz Telex: 032209
Man Dir: Klaus Brunner
Subjects: Art, General Fiction, Textbooks
1986: 20 titles *Founded:* 1585
ISBN Publisher's Prefix: 3-7011

Literas-Verlag GmbH*, A-1090 Vienna, Berggasse 4 Tel: (0222) 315659/343685 Telex: 076529 Icpfa
Associate Company: Facultas Verlag (qv)
Subjects: Psychology, Belles-Lettres
Founded: 1981
ISBN Publisher's Prefix: 3-85429

Löcker Verlag+, A-1010 Vienna, Annagasse 3A Tel: (0222) 520282
General Manager: Erhard Löcker; *Rights & Permissions:* Dr Claudia Mazanek
Subjects: Modern Austrian History, Austrian Literature, Architecture, Design, Art, Photography
Associated Bookshops: Antiquariat Löcker und Wögenstein, A-1010 Vienna, Annagasse 5; Löcker GmbH, A-1010 Vienna, Gluckgasse 3
Founded: 1974
ISBN Publisher's Prefix: 3-85409

Paul **Mangold** Verlag*, A-8042 Graz, Neue Welt Hohe 3 Tel: (0316) 45633 Cable Add: Mangoldverlag
Man Dir: Paul Mangold
Subject: Juveniles
Founded: 1977
ISBN Publisher's Prefix: 3-900301

Manz'sche Verlags- und Universitätsbuchhandlung, A-1014 Vienna, Kohlmarkt 16 Tel: (0222) 5331781
Man Dirs: Franz Stein, Dr Anton C Hilscher
Subjects: Law, Economics, Taxation, University Textbooks, Educational Materials
Bookshops: See under Major Booksellers; FRIC, Technische Fachbuchhandlung, A-1040 Vienna, Wiedner Hauptstr 13
Founded: 1849
ISBN Publisher's Prefix: 3-214

Verlag Wilhelm **Maudrich***, A-1097 Vienna 9, Lazarettg 1, Postfach 21 Tel: (0222) 425241 Cable Add: Maudrich Verlag Vienna Telex: 135177
Man Dir: Gerhard Grois
Subjects: How-to, Medicine, Psychology, University Textbooks

Bookshop: Buchhandlung Wilhelm Maudrich für medizinische Wissenschaften (qv under Major Booksellers)
Founded: 1909
ISBN Publisher's Prefix: 3-85175

Progress-Verlag Dr **Micolini's** Wtw*, A-8010 Graz, Glacisstr 57 Tel: (03162)2 79508 Cable Add: Micolini Graz
Founded: 1934

Moderne Jugende Heute GmbH+*, A-1170 Vienna, Bergsteiggasse 5 Tel: (0222) 437203 Cable Add: Breitschopfbuch Telex: 07114539
Man Dir: Julius P Breitschopf
Associate Company: Verlagsbuchhandlung Julius Breitschopf (qv)
Subjects: Theme Books for Children and Young People, Painting Books
Founded: 1975

Modulverlag GmbH+, A-1010 Vienna, Mahlerstr 3 Tel: (0222) 5129892 Telex: 112816 Aplan
Publicity Manager: Dr Berthold Schwanzer
Subjects: Architecture, Design, Architectural Marketing Research
Founded: 1973

Morawa & Co*, A-1041 Vienna 14, Hackingerstr 52
Associate Companies: Bayerische Verlagsanstalt Bamberg (BVB), Federal Republic of Germany (qv); Adolf Zwimpfer, Switzerland (qv)
Book Club: Welt im Heim Morawa & Co

Otto **Müller** Verlag KG, A-5021 Salzburg, Ernst-Thunstr 11, Postfach 167 Tel: (0662) 881974 Cable Add: Müller Verlag
Man Dir, Sales & Publicity: Arno Kleibel
Subjects: Belles Lettres, Poetry, History, Religion, Psychology
1986-87: 40 titles *Founded:* 1937
ISBN Publisher's Prefix: 3-7013

Mundus, Österreichische Verlagsgesellschaft mbH, see Paul Zsolnay Verlag GmbH

Paul **Neff** Verlag KG+*, A-1010 Vienna, Johannesgasse 12 Tel: (0222) 5131031 Cable Add: Neffverlag
Man Dir: Dagmar Stecher-Konsalik
Parent Company: Hestia-Verlag GmbH, Federal Republic of Germany (qv)
Subjects: General Fiction, Biography, Music, Art
Founded: 1829
ISBN Publisher's Prefix: 3-7014

Edition **Neue Mitte***, A-1033 Vienna, Postfach 12 (Located at: A-1030 Vienna, Landstrasser Hauptstrasse 13-43) Tel: (0222) 733703
Man Dir: Kurt Sattlberger
Subjects: Political/Social (especially, alternatives to Marxism, future political projections)
Founded: 1976
ISBN Publisher's Prefix: 3-85401

Verlag **Neue Stadt** GmbH*, A-2380 Perchtoldsdorf (Vienna), Brucknergasse 13
Parent Company: Città Nuova Editrice, Italy (qv for associate companies)

Neufeld-Verlag und Galerie*, A-6890 Lustenau, Schillerstr 7 Tel: (05577) 4657 Cable Add: Neufeld Telex: 59162
Editorial, Rights & Permissions: Ivo Löpfe
Parent Company: Löpfe KG (at above address)
Associate Company: Neufeld-Verlag und Galerie, Switzerland (qv)
Founded: 1962

Wolfgang **Neugebauer** Verlag GmbH, A-5020 Salzburg, Petersbrunnstr 12 Tel: (0662) 849655

Man Dir: Wolfgang Neugebauer
Subjects: Theology, History, German Literature
Bookshop: Buchandlung W Neugebauer (qv under Major Booksellers)
Founded: 1975
ISBN Publisher's Prefix: 3-85376

Verlag **Niederösterreichisches Pressehaus** mbH+, A-3100 St Pölten, Gutenbergstr 12 Tel: (02742) 61561 Telex: 015512
Man Dir, Sales & Editorial: Dr Ingeborg Ornazeder; *Publicity:* Franz Gloser
Orders to: R Lechner & Sohn, A-1232 Vienna, Heizwerkstr 10
Subjects: History, Literature, Architecture, Art
Bookshop: Hippolyt-Buchhandlung, A-3100 St Pölten, Linzerstr 4
Founded: 1889
ISBN Publisher's Prefix: 3-85326

Obelisk-Verlag*, A-6020 Innsbruck, Falkstr 1 Tel: (05222) 20733
Proprietor: Helga Buchroithner
Subject: Children's

Oberösterreichischer Landesverlag, now Landesverlag Buchverlag (qv)

Octopus Verlag, A-1010 Vienna, Fleischmarkt 16 Tel: (0222) 5127146
Man Dir: Erich Skrleta
Subjects: Buddhism & Oriental Philosophies, Vienna
Bookshop: A-1010 Vienna, Fleischmarkt 16
Founded: 1973
ISBN Publisher's Prefix: 3-900290

Verlag **Oldenbourg**, A-1030 Vienna, Neulinggasse 26/3 Tel: (0222) 726258/ 753106
Man Dir: Dr Karl Cornides; *Sales Dir:* Gerda Adler; *Publicity & Advertising:* Dr Erika Rüdegger, Dr Éva Pripfl
Parent Company: R Oldenbourg Verlag GmbH, Federal Republic of Germany (qv)
Associate Company: Verlag für Geschichte und Politik (qv)
Subjects: Philosophy, Engineering, General & Social Science, University & Secondary Textbooks
Founded: 1957
ISBN Publisher's Prefix: 3-7029

Verlag **Orac***, A-1014 Vienna, Graben 17, Postfach 56 Tel: (0222) 528552
Man Dir, Production, Rights & Permissions: Helmut Hanusch; *Sales, Marketing:* Gerhard Höller
Subjects: Economics, Jurisprudence, Management, Sport, General Non-fiction
Bookshop: At above address
Founded: 1946

Österreichische Verlagsanstalt GmbH*, A-1051 Vienna, Spengergasse 39 Tel: (0222) 555641
Man Dir: Friedrich Geyer

Verlag der **österreichischen Akademie der Wissenschaften**, A-1010 Vienna, Dr Ignaz Seipelpl 2 Tel: (0222) 51581 Telex: 0112628
Publishing House of the Austrian Academy of Sciences
Man Dir: Brigitta Nowotny
Subjects: Archaeology, Architecture, Art, Belles Lettres, Biography, Byzantine and Oriental Studies, English Language and Literature, History, Jurisprudence, Maps, Music, Numismatics, Philology & Dialect Studies, Philosophy, Psychology, Reference, Social Science, Theatre, Urbanism, Paperbacks
1985: 66 titles *1986:* 60 titles *Founded:* 1973
ISBN Publisher's Prefix: 3-7001

Verlag des **österreichischen Gewerkschaftsbundes** GmbH*, A-1232 Vienna 23, Altmannsdorfferstr 154-156 Tel: (0222) 672622
Man Dir: Friedrich Löw
Founded: 1947

Österreichischer Agrarverlag, Druck- und Verlags- GmbH, A-1014 Vienna, Bankgasse 1/3, Postfach 136 Tel: (0222) 5339676 Cable Add: Agrarverlag Telex: 114030 Fax: (0222) 5339676
Man Dir: Dr Wolfgang Brandstetter
Orders to: Ing H Fischer, A-1141 Vienna, Linzerstr 32
Subjects: Agriculture & Forestry, Fiction, Periodicals
1985: 39 titles *1986:* 48 titles *Founded:* 1945
ISBN Publisher's Prefix: 3-7040

Österreichischer Bundesverlag GmbH+*, A-1010 Vienna 1, Schwarzenbergstr 5 Tel: (0222) 522561 Cable Add: Bundesverlag Vienna
Man Dir: Dkfm Kurt Biak
Orders to: A-2351 Wiener Neudorf, Postfach
Subsidiary Company: Österreichischer Gewerbeverlag GmbH (qv)
Subjects: Belles Lettres, History, Military History, Juveniles, Textbooks, Reference, Educational Materials, Art, Music, General Fiction, General Science
Founded: 1772
ISBN Publisher's Prefix: 3-215

Österreichischer Gewerbeverlag GmbH*, A-1014 Vienna, Herrengasse 10, Postfach 182 Tel: (0222) 630768
Man Dir, Sales, Publicity: Franz Scharefzer; *Editorial, Rights & Permissions:* Dr Josef Peter Ortner; *Production:* Heinz Stuiber
Parent Company: Österreichischer Bundesverlag GmbH (qv)
Subjects: Textbooks (vocational & instructional)
Founded: 1945
ISBN Publisher's Prefix: 3-85207

Österreichisches Katholisches Bibelwerk*, A-3400 Klosterneuburg, Stiftspl 8, Postfach 48 Tel: (02243) 2938
Man Dir, Editorial, Rights & Permissions: Dr Norbert Höslinger; *Sales:* Gerlinde Bieder
Subjects: Bibles, Scriptural Texts & Studies
Bookshop: A-1010 Vienna, Singerstr 7
Founded: 1966
Miscellaneous: Company is a member of AMB (qv under Federal Republic of Germany) and WCBFA (World Catholic Federation for the Biblical Apostolate)
ISBN Publisher's Prefix: 3-85396

Perlinger-Verlag GmbH+, A-6300 Wörgl, Brixentalerstr 61 Tel: (05332) 4521 Cable Add: Perlinger Verlag Wörgl Telex: 051205 Teltaz
Man Dir: Engelbert Perlinger
Subjects: Picture-books, Ethnology, Spiritual, Natural Medicine
Founded: 1977
ISBN Publisher's Prefix: 3-85399

Pinguin-Verlag, Pawlowski KG+*, A-6021 Innsbruck, Lindenbühelweg 2 Tel: (05222) 81183/81587 Cable Add: Pinguinverlag Innsbruck Telex: 053173
Man Dirs: Olaf Pawlowski, Hella Pflanzer
Subjects: Art, Juveniles, Non-fiction, Reference, Calendars
Founded: 1945
ISBN Publisher's Prefix: 3-7016

Georg **Prachner** KG*, A-1010 Vienna, Kärntnerstr 30 Tel: (0222) 5128549
Man Dir: O G Prachner

Subjects: Architecture, Art, Belles Lettres, History, Fiction
Bookshop: See under Major Booksellers

Prugg Verlag*, A-7000 Eisenstadt, Haydngasse 10 Tel: (02682) 2114
ISBN Publisher's Prefix: 3-85238

Universitätsverlag Anton **Pustet**, A-5021 Salzburg, Bergstrasse 12, Postfach 144 Tel: (0662) 73507/76392 Cable Add: Pustet Salzburg
Branch Off: Anton Pustet, Federal Republic of Germany (qv)
Subjects: Philosophy, Religion, Psychology, Education, Political Science, Law, Poetry and Iconographs of the University of Salzburg, Music
Founded: 1598
ISBN Publisher's Prefix: 3-7025

Residenz Verlag GmbH+, A-5020 Salzburg, Gaisbergstr 6 Tel: (0662) 25771 Telex: 632887
Man Dir, Editorial: Dr Jochen Jung; *Sales Manager:* Christl Sennewald; *Production:* Friedel Schafleitner; *Publicity:* Dr Barbara Brunner; *Rights & Permissions:* Renate Buchmann, Dr Barbara Brunner
Subjects: Belles Lettres, Poetry, Music, Art, Architecture
Founded: 1956
ISBN Publisher's Prefix: 3-7017

Ritter Verlag+, A-9020 Klagenfurt, Alter Platz 25/II Tel: (04222) 55709
Subjects: Pictorial Art, Literature
Founded: 1980
ISBN Publisher's Prefix: 3-85415

S N-Verlag, Salzburger Nachrichten Verlags GmbH & Co KG*, A-5020 Salzburg, Bergstr 14, Postfach 154 Tel: (0662) 775910
Subjects: Regional (Salzburg), Architecture, History, Music, Theatre

Verlag der **Salzburger Druckerei**, A-5020 Salzburg, Bergstr 12, Postfach 144 Tel: (0662) 73507/76392
Subjects: Arts, Poetry, History and Chronicles of Salzburg
ISBN Publisher's Prefix: 3-85338

Verlag für **Sammler***, A-8011 Graz, Sankt Peter Hauptstr 35e, Postfach 54 Tel: (0316) 42230
Subjects: History of Art, Culture, Manners & Morals, Folklore, Early History
ISBN Publisher's Prefix: 3-85365

Verlag **Sankt Gabriel**, A-2340 Mödling Tel: (02236) 86351 Telex: 79357 Drstga
Man Dir: Mag P Hubert Winkler
Parent Company: Missionshaus Sankt Gabriel (at above address)
Subjects: Books for Children and Young People, Religious Knowledge, Practical Theology, Education
Bookshops: At above address and A-1010 Vienna
Founded: 1905
ISBN Publisher's Prefix: 3-85264

Verlag **Sankt Peter**, A-5010 Salzburg, Postfach 113 Tel: (0662) 84216682 Telex: 063094
Man Dir: Dr R Rinnerthaler
Subjects: Austrian Church Art, Austrian Guidebooks, Religion
Founded: 1946
ISBN Publisher's Prefix: 3-900173

Paul **Sappl**, Schulbuch- und Lehrmittelverlag*, A-6332 Kufstein, Kaiserbach 43 Tel: (05372) 4300 Telex: 5119115
Branch Off: A-1050 Vienna, Stolberggasse 31-33
Subjects: School Books, Driving School Textbooks
Founded: 1953

Dr A **Schendl** GmbH und Co KG, A-1041 Vienna, Karlsgasse 15, Postfach 29 Tel: (0222) 655593
Dirs: Dr Anna Schendl, Franz Ogg
Subjects: History, Ethnography, Geography, Folklore, Art, Literature, Music, Economy, Periodicals

Schönbrunn-Verlag GmbH*, A-1010 Vienna 1, Trattnerhof 1 Tel: (0222) 5335022 Telex: 111295
Subjects: Popular Science, Children's
Founded: 1946

Anton **Schroll** & Co+*, Buch und Kunstverlag, A-1051 Vienna 5, Spengergasse 39 Tel: (0222) 555641 Cable Add: Schrollverlag Vienna
Man Dir: Friedrich Geyer
Branch Off: Anton Schroll & Co GmbH, Federal Republic of Germany (qv)
Subjects: Belles Lettres, History, Art
Founded: 1884
ISBN Publisher's Prefix: 3-7031

Severin Presse*, A-2346 Suedstadt Vienna, Dobrastr 112, Postfach 15 Tel: (02236) 811744
Publisher: Peter Croy
Subject: Art (Original Engravings)

Verlag Josef Otto **Slezak**+, A-1040 Vienna, Wiedner Hauptstr 42 Tel: (0222) 5870259
Sales Manager: Ilse Slezak
Subjects: Transport, especially historical accounts of railways and tramways in Austria and Europe generally
1986: 6 titles *1987:* 4 titles

Springer-Verlag KG, A-1010 Vienna, Mölkerbastei 5, Postfach 367 Tel: (0222) 639614 Cable Add: Springerbuch Vienna Telex: 114506 Fax (0222) 638158
Man Dir and Rights & Permissions: Bruno Schweder; *Chief Editor:* Dr Sepp Weingärtner; *Sales Dir, Promotion:* Rudolf Siegle; *Production Dir:* Bruno Skuhra; *Advertising Manager:* Thomas Schmuttermeier
Associate Company: Springer-Verlag New York Inc, 175 Fifth Ave, New York, NY 10010, USA
Subjects: Medicine, Natural Sciences, Engineering, Fundamental Science, Law, University Textbooks
Bookshop: Minerva Wissenschaftliche Buchhandlung GmbH, A-1010 Vienna, Schottengasse 7
1985: 71 titles *Founded:* 1924
ISBN Publisher's Prefix: 3-211

Steiger Verlag+, A-6622 Berwang, Mitteregg 4 Tel: (05674) 8327 Telex: 53194 Stv
Man Dir: Johannes Steiger
Subjects: Sport, Leisure, Austria
Bookshop: A-6622 Berwang, HNr 68
Founded: 1980
ISBN Publisher's Prefix: 3-85423

Leopold **Stocker** Verlag+*, A-8011 Graz, Bürgergasse 11, Postfach 438 Tel: (0316) 71636 Cable Add: Stockerverlag Graz
Publisher: Dr Ilse Dvorak-Stocker; *Editorial Sales, Publicity, Rights & Permissions:* Dr Peter Strallhofer
Subjects: Belles Lettres, Contemporary History, Literature, Hunting, Nature and Mountain Books, Specialist Books, Agricultural Textbooks and School Books
Founded: 1917

Verlag **Styria**+, A-8010 Graz, Schönaugasse 64, Postfach 831 Tel: (0316) 70630 Cable Add: Styriaverlag Graz Telex: 031925 Kleine Zeitung
Man Dir, Editorial: Dr Gerhard Trenkler; *Sales:* Wolfgang Fath; *Production:* Hans Paar; *Publicity:* Peter Altenburg; *Rights &*

Permissions: Margarethe Katholnig
Parent Company: Katholischer Pressverein
Branch Offs: Verlag Styria Köln, D-5000 Cologne 51, Schillerstr 6, Postfach 511029, Federal Republic of Germany; Verlag Styria, Repräsentanz Wien, A-1070 Vienna, St-Ulrichspl 2/12
Subjects: Religion, History, Philosophy, Biography, Education, Belles Lettres, Reference, Current Affairs
Bookshops: Buchhandlung Styria (qv under Major Booksellers); Buchhandlung Ulrich Moser, A-8010 Graz, Herrengasse 23; Bücherbox, A-8010 Graz, Goethestr 42
1986: 48 titles *1987:* 50 titles *Founded:* 1869
ISBN Publisher's Prefix: 3-222

Rudolf **Trauner** Verlag*, A-4020 Linz, Baumbachstr 4a Tel: (0732) 78241
Man Dir: Rudolf Trauner
Branch Off: A-4020 Linz, Köglstr 14
Subjects: Gastronomy, Cookery, Textbooks, Science, Books of Illustrations, Popular Medicine
Founded: 1946
ISBN Publisher's Prefix: 3-85320

Edition **Tusch**, A-1160 Vienna, Heigerleinstr 36 Tel: (0222) 455334 Cable Add: Editusch Vienna Telex: 116262 Tusch
Man Dir: Anton Tusch; *Editorial:* Heinz Handsur
Subject: Art
Founded: 1972
ISBN Publisher's Prefix: 3-85063

Verlagsanstalt **Tyrolia**, A-6020 Innsbruck, Exlgasse 20, Postfach 220 Tel: (05222) 81541 Cable Add: Tyrolia Verlag Innsbruck Telex: 53620
Dir: Dr Schiemer
Subjects: Theology, School Books, Juveniles, Tour Guides, Illustrated Books, General Non-fiction
Bookshops: Tyrolia (qv under Major Booksellers)
Founded: 1888
ISBN Publisher's Prefix: 3-7022

Verlag Carl **Ueberreuter**+, A-1091 Vienna, Alserstr 24, Postfach 306 66 Tel: (0222) 425684/481538 Cable Add: Ueberreuter Vienna Telex: 114802
Man Dir: Dr Otto Mang; *Editorial:* Dr Marion Pongracz, Michael Grabner; *Sales, Publicity:* Thomas C Sacken
Subsidiary Company: Annette Betz Verlag (qv)
Subjects: Juveniles, Children's (fiction and non-fiction), Books for Young Adults, Secondary & Primary Textbooks, Educational Materials
Founded: 1548
ISBN Publisher's Prefix: 3-8000

Universal Edition AG*, A-1015 Vienna, Bösendorferstr 12, Postfach 3 Tel: (0222) 658695 Cable Add: Musikedition Vienna Telex: 11397
Dirs: Dr J Juranek, S Harpner, A Schlee, M Kalmus, P Jacobus
Subsidiary Company (jointly owned with B Schott's Söhne, Federal Republic of Germany, qv): Wiener Urtext Edition-Musikverlag GmbH & Co KG (qv)
Subjects: Music, Musicology
Founded: 1901

Urban und Schwarzenberg GmbH*, A-1096 Vienna 9, Frankgasse 4, Postfach 102 Tel: (0222) 422731
Man Dir: Gunter Royer
Associate Company: Urban und Schwarzenberg, Federal Republic of Germany (qv)
Subjects: Medicine, Psychology, Physics
Bookshop: See under Major Booksellers

Founded: 1866
ISBN Publisher's Prefix: 3-85327

V W G Ö, see Verband der wissenschaftlichen Gesellschaften Österreichs

Verband der wissenschaftlichen Gesellschaften Österreichs (VWGÖ), A-1070 Vienna, Lindengasse 37 Tel: (0222) 932166/934756
Man Dir: Dr Rainer Zitta
1985: 30 titles *1986:* 33 titles *Founded:* 1954
ISBN Publisher's Prefix: 3-85369

Veritas-Verlag+, A-4010 Linz, Hafenstr 1-3, Postfach 403 Tel: (0732) 276451/276231
Man Dir: Friedrich Müller; *Editorial, Rights & Permissions:* Josef Preundler; *Sales, Publicity:* Dr Harald Knill
Parent Company: Landesverlag Buchverlag (qv)
Branch Off: D-8390 Passau, Grabengasse 25a
Subjects: Religion, Belles Lettres, Health, Family, Education, School Textbooks
Bookshops: Buchhandlung Veritas (qv under Major Booksellers)
1985: 40 titles *Founded:* 1945
ISBN Publisher's Prefix: 3-85329

Vorarlberger Verlagsanstalt GmbH*, A-6850 Dornbirn, Schwefel 81 Tel: (05572) 646970 Telex: 059519
Subject: Literature

Universitätsverlag **Wagner** GmbH, A-6010 Innsbruck, Andreas-Hoferstr 13/1, Postfach 165 Tel: (05222) 27721 Cable Add: Universitätsverlag Wagner Innsbruck
Man Dir: Gottfried Grasl
Subjects: Scientific Works, Maps, Illustrated Motoring Guides, Literature, Colloquial Poetry
Founded: 1554
ISBN Publisher's Prefix: 3-7030

Weilburg-Verlag, A-2700 Wiener Neustadt, Pottendorferstr 162 Tel: (02622) 52538
Owner and Man Dir: Helmut Dresel; *Sales:* Alois Huemer
Subjects: Art Books, Lyrical Poetry, Numbered and Autographed Bibliophile Editions
1985: 10 titles

Verlag **Welsermühl**+, A-4600 Wels, Maria-Theresiastr 41 Tel: (07242) 6941 Cable Add: Welsermühldruck Wels Telex: 025586
Dir: Karl Pramendorfer
Head Office: Verlag Welsermühl, Federal Republic of Germany (qv)

Verlag Galerie **Welz** Salzburg, A-5020 Salzburg, Sigmund-Haffnergasse 16, Postfach 123 Tel: (0662) 841771
Publisher: Franz Eder; *Sales:* Hannes Lüftenegger
Subject: Art, Art Books and Prints

Wiener Dom-Verlag, A-1080 Vienna, Postfach 321 (Located at: Vienna, Strozzigasse 8)
General Manager: Franz Hörmann
Subject: Religion
Founded: 1946
ISBN Publisher's Prefix: 3-85351

Wiener Urtext Edition-Musikverlag GmbH & Co KG*, A-1010 Vienna, Bösendorferstr 12 Tel: (0222) 658695 (publication), 657651 (sales) Cable Add: Musikedition Telex: 1397
Man Dir: Stefan G Harpner; *Sales Dir:* Vladimir Prusa
Parent Companies: B Schott's Söhne, Federal Republic of Germany (qv) and Universal Edition AG (qv)

Subject: Music, especially original scores of Bach, Beethoven, Brahms, Chopin, Haydn, Mozart, Schubert, Schumann. All accompanying texts are in German and English
Founded: 1972

Kunstverlag **Wolfrum***, A-1010 Vienna 1, Augustinerstr 10 Tel: (0222) 525398/524178 Cable Add: Witwolf Vienna
Man Dir: Hubert Wolfrum
Subjects: Art, Art Reproductions
Bookshop: See under Major Booksellers
Founded: 1919
ISBN Publisher's Prefix: 3-900178

Wort und Welt Verlag+*, A-6020 Innsbruck, Heiliggeiststr 21 Tel: (05222) 25923 Cable Add: Wortwelt Innsbruck
Publisher: Professor Dr Walter Miess; *Editorial:* Günther Schick; *Publicity:* Ingrid Formentini
Orders to: Thaurdruck, A/6065 Thaur bei Innsbruck
Branch Off: D-8039 Puchheim, Munich, Postfach, Federal Republic of Germany
Subjects: Humour, Textbooks, Art, Belles Lettres, Factbooks
1985: 8 titles *1986:* 8 titles *Founded:* 1972
ISBN Publisher's Prefix: 3-85373

Paul **Zsolnay** Verlag GmbH+*, A-1041 Vienna, Prinz-Eugenstr 30 Tel: (0222) 657661/651816 Cable Add: Zsolnayverlag Vienna Telex: 131515
Dir: Hans W Polak; *Sales Manager:* Wolfgang Dechant; *Editor:* Maria Gridling; *Production:* Peter Baumgartner; *Public Relations:* Elisabeth Dreihann-Holenia; *Rights & Permissions:* Olga Kaindl
Subsidiary Company: Paul Zsolnay Verlag GmbH, Federal Republic of Germany (qv)
Associate Company: Mundus, Österreichische Verlagsgesellschaft mbH (at above address)
Subjects: General Fiction, Non-fiction, Belles Lettres, Poetry, Biography, History, How-to, Music, Juveniles, Social & Political Science, Art, Medicine, Sports
1986: 36 titles *Founded:* 1923
ISBN Publisher's Prefix: 3-552

Book Clubs

Deutsche Buch-Gemeinschaft C A Koch's Verlag Nachfolger+, Zweigniederlassung Wien, A-1210 Vienna, Berlagasse 7-11 Tel: (0222) 392635 Telex: 114971 Dbgw
Also: Deutsche Buch-Gemeinschaft C A Koch's Verlag Nachfolger, Federal Republic of Germany (qv)

Buchgemeinschaft **Donauland** Kremayr & Scheriau, A-1121 Vienna, Niederhofstr 37 Tel: (0222) 834501 Telex: 131405
Owned by: Verlag Kremayr und Scheriau (qv)

Jos A **Kienreich***, A-8011 Graz, Sackstr 6, Postfach 828

Osterreichischer Buchklub der Jugend*, A-1041 Vienna, Mayerhofgasse 6 Tel: (0222) 651754
Members: 500,000
Founded: 1947

Elisabeth **Reiter***, A-6600 Reutte, Attlmayrstr 10

Welt im Heim Morawa & Co*, A-1041 Vienna 14, Hackingerstr 52, Postfach 54 Tel: (0222) 947641
Owned by: Morawa & Co (qv)

Major Booksellers

Hans **Fürstelberger***, A-4010 Linz, Landstr 49 Tel: (0732) 273177

Gerold & Co, A-1011 Vienna, Graben 31 Tel: (0222) 5335014 Cable Add: Geroldbuch Vienna Telex: 847136157 Gerol
Man Dir: Hans Neusser
Subscription agents and library jobber for European books and periodicals; also Publisher (qv)

A L **Hasbach**, A-1010 Vienna, Wollzeile 9 Tel: (0222) 5128876/5128932
Manager: Dr Herbert Borufka

Leopold **Heidrich***, A-1011 Vienna, Plankengasse 7 Tel: (0222) 523701
Manager: Wolfgang Heidrich

Gebhard **Heinzle's** Erben, A-6700 Bludenz, Josef-Wolf-Platz 2 Tel: (05552) 62066
Export and library supplier

Herder & Co, A-1011 Vienna, Wollzeile 33 Tel: (0222) 5121413
Man Dir: Erich M Wolf
Owned by: Verlag Herder & Co (qv)

Buchhandlung Johannes **Heyn**, A-9010 Klagenfurt, Kramergasse 2-4 Tel: (04222) 54249 Telex: 422401
Owners: Volkmar Zechner, Gert Zechner
Export and library supplier
See also Johannes Heyn (Publisher)

Buchhandlung Karl **Hofbauer***, A-8430 Leibnitz, Hauptpl 31, Postfach 68 Tel: (03452) 2793/2177
Managers: Karl & Jutta Hofbauer
Also: A-8430 Leibnitz, Grazerg 73 Tel: (03452) 3166

Eduard **Höllrigl**, A-5020 Salzburg, Sigmund-Haffnergasse 10 Tel: (0662) 841146/842651
Manager: H Stierle
Export and library supplier

Jos A **Kienreich***, A-8011 Graz, Sackstrasse 6
Manager: Peter Schmelzer
Export and library supplier

Antiquariat Walter **Krieg** Verlag*, A-1010 Vienna, Kärntnerstr 4 Tel: (0222) 5121093
Export and library supplier

Franz **Leo** & Co KG*, Universitätsbuchhandlung, A-1010 Vienna, Lichtensteg 1 Tel: (0222) 631451
Export and library supplier

Manz'sche Verlags- und Universitätsbuchhandlung, A-1014 Vienna, Kohlmarkt 16 Tel: (0222) 5331781
Export and library supplier; also Publisher (qv)

Buchhandlung Wilhelm **Maudrich** für medizinische Wissenschaften*, A-1097 Vienna, Spitalg 21a Tel: (0222) 424712 Telex: 135177
Manager: Gerhard Grois
Export and library supplier
Owned by: Verlag Wilhelm Maudrich (qv)

Robert **Mohr***, A-1010 Vienna, Singerstr 12 Tel: (0222) 51576
Proprietor: Dr Gottfried Berger
Wholesaler

Buchhandlung W **Neugebauer**, A-5020 Salzburg, Petersbrunnstr 12 Tel: (0662) 849655
Export and library supplier
Owned by: Wolfgang Neugebauer Verlag GmbH (qv)

Max **Pock**, Universitätsbuchhandlung, A-8010 Graz, Hauptplatz 1 Tel: (03122) 75254/79042 Telex: 031873

Manager: Dr Maximilian Pock
Export and library supplier

Georg **Prachner** KG, A-1010 Vienna, Kärntnerstr 30 Tel: (0222) 5128549
Manager: O G Prachner
Also Publisher (qv)

Buchhandlung **Styria**, A-8010 Graz, Albrechtgasse 5 Tel: (0316) 79355
Branches: A-1010 Vienna, Opernring 15; A-8750 Judenburg, Hauptpl 15; A-8720 Knittelfeld, Kärntnerstr 2
Owned by: Verlag Styria (qv)

Tyrolia, A-6010 Innsbruck, Maria Theresienstr 15 Tel: (05222) 24944
Manager: Wilhelm Leifels
Branches: Ehrwald, Fulpmes, Imst, Landeck, Lienz, Mayrhofen, St Johann, Schwaz, Telfs, Vienna, Wattens
Owned by: Verlagsanstalt Tyrolia (qv)

Urban und Schwarzenberg GmbH*, A-1096 Vienna 9, Frankgasse 4, Postfach 102 Tel: (0222) 422731
Manager: Gunter Royer
Also Publisher (qv)

Buchhandlung **Veritas**, A-4010 Linz, Harrachstr 5 Tel: (0732) 276401
Manager: Andreas Mayer
Owned by: Veritas-Verlag (qv)

Wagner'sche Universitätsbuchhandlung*, A-6021 Innsbruck, Museumstr 4 Tel: (05222) 22316 Telex: 053793
Dir: Ernst Angerer
Export and library supplier

Rupertusbuchhandlung Augustin **Weis** und Söhne KG, A-5024 Salzburg, Dreifaltigkeitsg 12 Tel: (0662) 78733
Manager: Bernhard Weis
Export and library supplier

Fachbuchhandlung für **Wirtschaft und Recht***, A-1181 Vienna, Währingerstr 122 Tel: (0222) 348391
Proprietor: Eleonore Stropek
Export and library supplier

Kunstverlag **Wolfrum***, A-1010 Vienna 1, Augustinerstr 10 Tel: (0222) 524178/ 525398 Cable Add: Witwolf Vienna
Manager: Erich Pospisil
Export and library supplier of art books; also Publisher (qv)

Zentralgesellschaft für buchgewerbliche und graphische Betriebe*, A-1010 Vienna, Singerstr 12 Tel: (0222) 5216760
Proprietor: Dr Gottfried Berger
Wholesaler

Major Libraries

Bibliothek des **Benediktinerklosters** Melk in Niederösterreich, A-3390 Melk Tel: (02752) 2312342
Library of the Melk Benedictine Monastery in Lower Austria
Librarian: P Gottfried Glassner

Administrative Bibliothek und Österreichische Rechtsdokumentation im **Bundeskanzeramt** *, A-1010 Vienna, Herrengasse 23
Administrative Library and Law Documentation of the Chancellery

Bundesstaatliche Studienbibliothek Linz*, A-4020 Linz, Schillerpl 2 Tel: (0732) 664071
Reference Library

Bibliothek des **Kriegsarchivs Wien***, A-1070 Vienna, Stiftgasse 2
Library of the War Archives Dept of the Austrian State Archives
Librarian: Dr Edith Wohlgemuth

Österreichische Nationalbibliothek, A-1015 Vienna, Josefspl 1 Tel: (0222) 53410 Telex: 112624 Oenb
Austrian National Library
Dir-General: Dr Magda Strebl
Publications include: Informationsführer Bibliotheken und Dokumentations- stellen in Österreich (Information Guide to Libraries and Documentation Centres in Austria)

Bibliothek der **Österreichischen Akademie der Wissenschaften**, A-1010 Vienna, Dr Ignaz Seipelpl 2 Tel: (0222) 51581/51257 Telex: 12628
Library of the Austrian Academy of Science
Dir: Dr Klaus Wundsam

Bibliothek des **Österreichischen Patentamtes**, A-1014 Vienna, Kohlmarkt 8-10
Library of the Austrian Patent Office
Librarian: Dr Ingrid Weidinger
Publications: Österreichisches Patentblatt; Österreichischer Markenanzeiger; Patentschriften

Österreichisches Staatsarchiv, A-1030 Vienna 1, Nottendorfergasse 2
Austrian State Archives
Publication: Mitteilungen des Österreichischen Staatsarchivs

Universitätsbibliothek Graz, A-8010 Graz, Universitätspl 3 Tel: (0316) 3803101 Telex: 31662
Librarian: Dr Franz Kroller
Publications include: Jahresbericht; News (Informationsschrift der Universitätsbibliothek Graz), Heft 1 (1987)

Universitätsbibliothek Innsbruck*, A-6010 Innsbruck, Innrain 50 Tel: (05222) 7240 Telex: 533708

Universitätsbibliothek Wien*, A-1010 Vienna, Dr-Karl-Lueger-Ring 1 Tel: (0222) 43002371
Librarian: Dr Ferdinand Baümgartner

Vienna International Centre Library*, A-1400 Vienna, Postfach 100 Tel: (0222) 2360 ext 2620 Cable Add: Inatom Vienna Telex: 112645

Wiener Stadt- und Landesarchiv, Magistratsabteilung 8, A-1082 Vienna, 1 Rathaus
Vienna Municipal Archives

Wiener Stadt- und Landesbibliothek, A-1082 Vienna, Rathaus Tel: (0222) 42800/ 42771
Vienna Municipal and County Library
Dir: Hofrat Mag Dr Franz Patzer

Library Associations

Dokumentationsstelle für neuere österreichische Literatur, A-1060 Vienna, Gumpendorferstr 15/1/13 Tel: (0222) 5861249
Documentation Centre for Modern Austrian Literature
General Secretary: Dr Heinz Lunzer
Publication: Zirkular

Österreichische Gesellschaft für Dokumentation und Information, c/o Austrian Standards Institute, A-1021 Vienna, Heinestr 38, Postfach 130
Austrian Society for Documentation and Information
Executive Secretary: B Hofer
Publication: Fakten Daten Zitate

Österreichisches Institut für Bibliotheksforschung, Dokumentations- und Informationswesen*, A-1014 Vienna, Josefspl 1

Austrian Institute for Library Research, Documentation and Information
President: Prof Dr Josef Mayerhöfer;
Secretary-General: Dr Karl Megner
Publication: Biblos (published in English and German)

Verband österreichischer Archivare, c/o A-1010 Vienna, Minoritenpl 1
Association of Austrian Archivists
Publication: Scrinium (twice a year)

Verband österreichischer Volksbüchereien und Volksbibliothekare*, A-1080 Vienna, Langegasse 37 Tel: (0222) 439722
Association of Austrian Public Libraries
Managing Chairman: Dr F Pascher;
Secretary: Heinz Buchmüller

Vereinigung österreichischer Bibliothekare, A-1015 Vienna, Josefspl 1 (Österreichische National-Bibliothek) Tel: (0222) 521684 Telex: 12624
Association of Austrian Librarians
President: Dr Ferdinand Baumgartner;
Secretary: Ronald Zwanziger
Publication: Mitteilungen (Bulletin) (quarterly)

Library Reference Books and Journals

Books

Dokumentation und Information in Österreich (Documentation and Information in Austria), Brüder Hollinek & Co GmbH, A-1130 Vienna, Gallgasse 40A

Informationsführer Bibliotheken und Dokumentations- stellen in Österreich (Information Guide to Libraries and Documentation Centres in Austria), Österreichische Nationalbibliothek, A-1015 Vienna, Josefspl 1

Journals

Biblos, Österreichisches Institut für Bibliotheksforschung, Dokumentations- und Informationswesen, A-1014, Vienna, Josefspl 1
Austrian journal for book and library personnel, documentation, bibliography and bibliophily; published in English and German

Mitteilungen der Vereinigung österreichischer Bibliothekare (Bulletin of the Association of Austrian Librarians) (quarterly), Vereinigung österreichischer Bibliothekare, A-1015 Vienna, Josefspl 1

Scrinium (twice a year), Verband österreichischer Archivare, c/o A-1010 Vienna, Minoritenpl 1

Literary Associations and Societies

Literaturkreis der Autoren, A-2700 Wiener Neustadt, Herzog-Leopoldstr 21
Administrators: Dr Peter Schuster, Erich Sedlak, Peter Zumpf
Publication: Januskopf

Österreichische Exlibris-Gesellschaft*, A-1040 Vienna, Johann Straussgasse 28-18
Austrian Bookplate-collectors' Society
Secretary: Oj Slattner, A-1021 Vienna, Postfach 74
Publications: Jahrbuch, Mitteilungen, books on the art of the bookplate and on bookplate-collecting

Österreichische Gesellschaft für Literatur, A-1010 Vienna, Herrengasse 5 Tel: (0222)

AUSTRIA 33

638159/630864
Austrian Literary Society
President: Dr W Kraus

Österreichischer Schriftstellerverband*,
A-1050 Vienna V, Kettenbrückeng 11
Tel: (0222) 564151
Austrian Writers' Association
General Secretary: Wilhelm Meissel

Österreichischer **P E N-Club**, Concordia
Haus, A-1010 Vienna 1, Bankgasse 8 Tel:
(0222) 5334459
Secretary: Ingrid Weiser

Adalbert **Stifter**-Gesellschaft*, A-1060
Vienna, Gumpendorferstr 15 Tel: (0222)
374354
President: Richard Eybner

Wiener Goethe-Verein, A-1010 Vienna,
Stallburggasse 2
President: Dr Herbert Zeman; *Vice-
President:* Prof Dr Hans-Joachim Becker
Publication: Jahrbuch (yearbook)

Anton **Wildgans**-Gesellschaft*, A-2340
Mödling, Andergasse 3 Tel: (02236) 28334

Literary Periodicals

Autorensolidarität (Author Solidarity)
(twice a year), Interessengemeinschaft
österreichischer Autoren, A-1010 Vienna,
Bankgasse 8

Blätter für das Wort, A-4810 Gmunden,
Traungasse

Blätter für Volksliteratur (Popular
Literature Magazine), Verein der Freunde
der Volksliteratur, Graz, Naglergasse 22

Eröffnungen (Communications), Hubert
Fabian Kulterer, A-1120 Vienna, Unter-
Meidlinger Str 16-18
Magazine for literature and pictorial art;
text mainly in German, occasionally in
English or Slovene

Eselsohr, G Pilz, A-4320 Perg, Stifterstr 4a

Heimatland, Schriftum aus Österreich,
Heimatland Verlag, A-1050 Vienna,
Margaretenstr 114

Literatur und Kritik (Literature and
Criticism), Otto Müller Verlag KG,
A-5021 Salzburg, Ernst-Thunstr 11

Literaturspiegel (Mirror to Literature),
Vienna 4, Schleifmühlgasse 23-29

Manuskripte (Manuscripts), A-8010 Graz,
Forum Stadtpark 1
Journal for literature, art, criticism

Modern Austrian Literature, Arthur
Schnitzler International Research
Association, c/o Donald G Daviau, Editor,
Department of German, University of
California, Riverside, CA 92502, USA
Text and summaries in English and
German

Moderne Literatur (Modern Literature),
Zeitschriftenverlag, Vienna, Favoritenstr
235-26

Podium, A-1030 Vienna, Radetzkystr 4

Projectil, A-5020 Salzburg, Sudtirolerpl 4/4/
10

Das Pult (The Desk), Klaus Sandler,
A-3100 St Pölten, Schiessfach 12
Journal for literature, art, criticism

Die Rampe, A-4020 Linz, Koglstr 14

Schriftum aus Österreich, Heimatland
Verlag, A-1050 Vienna, Margaretenstr 114

Schrifttumsspiegel (Mirror to Literature),
Gesellschaft für Ganzhehsforschung,
A-1191 Vienna, Franz Klein Gasse 1

Sprachkunst (Art of Language), Verlag der
österreichischen Akademie der
Wissenschaften, A-1010 Vienna, Dr Ignaz
Seipelpl 2
Contributions to the study of literature;
text in English, French, German and
Russian

Literary Prizes

Austrian literary prizes are generally not
associated with a single work, and are not
often awarded in a lump sum, because of
the high taxes authors have to pay. In
addition to those cited below, each
province has its own prize

Austrian Children's and Young People's
Book Prizes*
There are six categories: for books for
children up to seven years, up to 10 years,
up to 13 years; an 'Austrian Young
People's Book Prize', an 'Austrian
Children's and Young People's Non-fiction
Book Prize', an 'Austrian Children's and
Young People's Translation Prize', for
Book Illustration. The total prize money
available for distribution in 1987 is 190,000
Schillings. Prizewinning books are
purchased by the Ministry of Education,
Arts and Sport to an overall value of
140,000 Schillings. Enquiries to
Bundesministerium für Unterricht, Kunst
und Sport, A-1014 Vienna, Postfach 65,
Sektion IV/Abteilung 6

Austrian State Prize for Literature for
Children and Young People, see
Würdigungspreis für Kinder- und
Jugendliteratur

'Encouragement Prize'*
50,000 Schillings, awarded by jury.
Submissions accepted. Enquiries to
Bundesministerium für Unterricht, Kunst
und Sport, A-1014 Vienna, Postfach 65,
Sektion IV/Abteilung 3

Great Austrian State Prize*
This prize alternates between literature,
music and the fine arts. 200,000 Schillings,
for life's work. Awarded by
Österreichischer Kunstsenat. No
applications. Enquiries to
Bundesministerium für Unterricht, Kunst
und Sport, A-1014 Vienna, Postfach 65,
Sektion V/Abteilung 3

Literature Prize of the Province of
Steiermark*
Annual prize of 50,000 Schillings for a
writer's entire literary output. Enquiries to
Amt der Steiermärkischen
Landesregierung, A-8011 Graz,
Rechtsabteilung 6, Karmeliterplatz 2

New Writers Stipendium for Literature*
Four given each year. 8,000 Schillings each
month for twelve months, awarded by
jury. Submissions accepted. Enquiries to
Bundesministerium für Unterricht, Kunst
und Sport, A-1014 Vienna, Postfach 65,
Sektion IV/Abteilung 3

Rauriser Encouragement Award
Annual literary award sponsored by the
Salzburg provincial government and the
village of Rauris. 30,000 Schillings awarded
for a specific topic, as decided by jury.
Enquiries to Salzburger Landesregierung,
Kulturabteilung, A-5010 Salzburg, Postfach
527

Rauriser Literature Prize
Annual award sponsored by the Salzburg
provincial government. 80,000 Schillings
awarded for an outstanding first
publication in prose, as decided by jury.
Enquiries to Salzburger Landesregierung,
Kulturabteilung, A-5010 Salzburg, Postfach
527

'Recognition Prize'*
75,000 Schillings. Awarded by jury. No
applications. Enquiries to
Bundesministerium für Unterricht, Kunst
und Sport, A-1014 Vienna, Postfach 65,
Sektion IV/Abteilung 3

State Stipendium for Literature*
Eight given each year. 8,000 Schillings
each month for twelve months, awarded by
jury. Submissions accepted. Enquiries to
Bundesministerium für Unterricht, Kunst
und Sport, A-1014 Vienna, Postfach 65,
Sektion IV/Abteilung 3

Georg **Trakl** Prize
An irregular award to a writer of lyric
poetry for his/her complete poetical works.
75,000 Schillings. Most recent award to
Prof Dr Alfred Kolleritsch. Enquiries to
Salzburger Landesregierung,
Kulturabteilung, A-5010 Salzburg, Postfach
527

City of **Vienna** Prize
Originally founded in 1947. An annual
award of 75,000 Schillings is made to an
author for total literary output. Enquiries
to Magistratsabteilung 7, A-1082 Vienna,
Friedrich Schmidtpl 5

City of **Vienna Prize for Books** for Children
and Young People
Awarded annually by the City of Vienna
for distinguished books for children and
young people, including illustration.
Enquiries to Kulturamt der Stadt Wien,
A-1082 Vienna, MA 7 Friedrich
Schmidtpl 5

Anton **Wildgans** Prize of Austrian
Industry*
Awarded annually, at the beginning of the
autumn, to an Austrian lyric poet,
dramatist, novelist or essayist, young or
middle aged. The author must be an
Austrian citizen, writing in German, who
lives either in Austria or abroad.
Maximum prize 100,000 Schillings.
Awarded by a committee. No applications.
Enquiries to Vereinigung österreichischer
Industrieller, A-1031 Vienna

Würdigungspreis für Kinder- und
Jugendliteratur*
Conferred on an author in appreciation of
his life's work. Presented in 1980 for the
first time in a three-yearly cycle. Prize
money in 1986 was 60,000 Schillings.
Enquiries to Bundesministerium für
Unterricht, Kunst und Sport, A-1014
Vienna, Postfach 65, Sektion
IV/Abteilung 6

Translation Agencies and Associations

Österreichischer Übersetzer- und
Dolmetscherverband Universitas*, A-1190
Vienna, Gymnasiumstr 50 Tel: (0222)
317273
Association of interpreters and translators
President: Annie Weich

Bahamas

General Information

Language: English
Religion: Largest of 12 denominations are Baptist, Roman Catholic and Anglican
Population: 237,000
Bank Hours: 0930-1500 Monday-Thursday; 0930-1700 Friday
Shop Hours: 0900-1700 Monday-Thursday and Saturday; 0900-1200 Friday
Currency: 100 cents = 1 Bahamian dollar
Export/Import Information: No tariffs on books and advertising matter. No import licences required
Copyright: Berne, UCC (see International section)

Publishers

Beverly A **Brice**, Publisher, PO Box N4181, Nassau Tel: (032) 24718 Cable Add: Bricead
Subject: Tourist Guidebooks

Etienne **Dupuch** Jnr Publications Ltd, PO Box N7513, Nassau
Subjects: Tourist Periodicals and Books, Business, Educational, Maps

Major Booksellers

Bahamas Anglo American Book Store*, PO Box N9046, 9 Nassau Arcade, Hoffer Bldg, Bay St, Nassau Tel: (032) 50388

Bahamas Book & Bible House*, PO Box N356, Nassau Tel: (032) 23032

Christian Book Shop, PO Box N4924, Rosetta St, Palmdale, Nassau Tel: (032) 23237/21306
Manager: Marilyn Johnson

The **Island** Shop*, PO Box N3947, Bay St, Nassau Tel: (032) 24183/21588

Lee's Book Centre*, Bank Lane, PO Box N-8196, Nassau Tel: (032) 22128
Manager: Maria Lee

Tryma Book Shop*, PO Box N1243, Independence Shopping Centre, Nassau Tel: (032) 57478

United Bookshop & Stationers Ltd*, PO Box SS6220, Nassau Tel: (032) 28770/37315 Cable Add: Fantasia
The above is the office and wholesale department; retail stores in Nassau are at Madeira St Shopping Centre; Oakes Field Shopping Centre; Prince Charles Shopping Centre, Bay St
President: Sigmund A Pritchard; *Man Dir:* Myles H A Pritchard

Major Libraries

Department of **Archives***, Public Records Office, Ministry of Education, PO Box SS6341, Nassau Tel: (032) 23045
Director of Archives: D Gail Saunders

College of the Bahamas Library, PO Box N4912, Nassau Tel: (032) 38550 ext 240
Director of Library Services: Vanrea Thomas Rolle
Publication: Bahamas Reference Collection: a Bibliography (1980, with annual supplements)

John **Harvard** Lending Library*, PO Box F40, Freeport, Grand Bahama

Nassau Public Library, PO Box N3210, Nassau Tel: (032) 24907
Dir: Vanrea Rolle; *Librarian:* Anthony J Kriz

Bahrain

General Information

Language: Arabic (English used commercially)
Religion: Islamic, officially
Population: 364,000
Bank Hours: 0730-1200 Saturday-Wednesday; 0730-1100 Thursday
Bazaar Hours: 0800-1200, 1530-1800 Saturday-Thursday (few shops open Friday morning)
Currency: 1000 fils = 1 Bahrain dinar
Export/Import Information: Generally books dutied at 10%, most schoolbooks free of duty; none on advertising matter. No import licence required but no obscene literature permitted and for books (not for advertising) a Chamber of Commerce certificate is mandatory. No exchange controls

Major Booksellers

Al-**Aadab** Bookshop*, PO Box 384, Manama

Bahrain Bookshop*, PO Box 443, Manama Tel: 54415

Family Bookshop (Bahrain) WLL*, PO Box 1, Manama (Located at main branch: 129 Essa Al Kabeer Ave, Manama) Tel: 254288/256059 Telex: 8444 Fambah
Manager: Leif Munksgaard
Parent Company: Family Bookshop Group

Islamic Cultural Bookshop*, PO Box 873, Manama

National Bookshop and Branches*, PO Box 594, Manama

Literary Associations and Societies

Bahrain Writers and Literators Association*, PO Box 1010, Manama
Secretary: Abdul Qadir Aqeel

Bangladesh

General Information

Language: Bengali (English widely used commercially)
Religion: Islamic
Population: 88.6 million
Bank Hours: 0930-1330 Monday-Thursday; 0900-1100 Friday and Saturday
Shop Hours: 1000-2030 Monday-Friday; 1000-1400 Saturday
Currency: 100 paise = 1 taka
Export/Import Information: No tariff on books and advertising matter. Import licences required for all imports
Copyright: UCC

Book Trade Organizations

Bangladesh Pustak Prokashak o Bikreta Samity*, c/o Rahman Brothers, 5/1 Gopinath Datta, Kabiraj St (Babu Bazar), Dacca Tel: 282633
Bangladesh Publishers' & Booksellers' Association
Secretary: Azhirul Islam Khan

National Book Centre of Bangladesh*, 67a Purana Paltan, Dacca 2
Publication: Boi (text in Bengali)

Book Trade Reference Journal

Boi, National Book Centre of Bangladesh, 67a Purana Paltan, Dacca 2
Text in Bengali

Publishers

Adeylebros & Co*, 60 Patuatuly, Dacca 1
Bookshop: Adeyle Brothers (qv under Major Booksellers)

Anwari Publications*, 5/1 Simson Rd, Dacca 1

Banga Sahitya Bhavan*, 144 Government New Market, Dacca

Bangladesh Books International Ltd*, GPO Box 377, Dacca 3 (Located at: 1 Hefaq Bhaban, 1 RK Mission Rd, Dacca) Tel: 256071 ext 19 Cable Add: Bhabooks Dacca
Chairman: Moinul Hosein; *Man Dir:* Anower Hossain; *Dir:* Abdul Hafiz
Subjects: Educational, Academic, Reference, Children
Bookshop: See under Major Booksellers
Founded: 1975

Biswakosh*, 316 Government New Market, Dacca

Boighar*, 149 Government New Market, Dacca

Chalantika*, 177 Government New Market, Dacca

Crescent Publishers*, 77 Patuatuly, Dacca 1

Lekha Prokashani*, 18 Pyaridas Rd, Dacca 1

Mullick Bros*, 3/1 Bangla Bazar, Dacca
Subjects: Education, Secondary & Primary Textbooks
Bookshop: See under Major Booksellers

Pak Kitab Ghar*, 39 Patuatuly, Dacca

Rahman Brothers*, Educational Publishers, 5/1 Gopinath Datta, Kabiraj St (Babu Bazar), Dacca Tel: 282633

University Press Ltd, PO Box 2611, Dacca 2 (Located at: Red Cross Bldg, 114 Motijheel CA, Dacca) Tel: 232950/255789 Cable Add: Dunipress
Man Dir, Chief Executive: Mohiuddin Ahmed; *Sales:* M A Halim; *Production:* M Hassan
Subjects: Academic and Scholarly, Art and Architecture, Educational and Textbooks (Primary, Secondary, Tertiary), Supplementary Books for Schools, Reference, Scientific and Technical, Journals
Founded: 1975

Major Booksellers

Adeyle Brothers*, 60 Patuatuly, Dacca
Owned by: Adeylebros & Co (qv)

Ali Publications*, 77 Patuatuly, Dacca

Bangladesh Books International Ltd*, GPO Box 377, Dacca (Located at: Sales Centre, 1 Hefaq Bhaban, I RK Mission Rd, Dacca)
Manager: Abdul Hafiz
Also Publisher (qv)

Dacca Book Mart*, 38 Banglabazar, Dacca

Golden Book House*, 38 Banglabazar, Dacca

Hakkim's Bookshop*, 33 Banglabazar, Dacca

Hamidia Library*, 65 Chawk Circular Rd, Dacca

Mohammadi Library*, Chawk Circular Rd, Dacca

Mullick Bros*, 3/1 Bangla Bazar, Dacca
Also Publisher (qv)

Provincial Book Depot*, Dacca Stadium, Dacca

Provincial Library, 109/A Sarat Gupta Rd, Narinda, Dacca

Puthigar Ltd*, 74 Farashgonj, Dacca 1
Manager: J L Saha

Major Libraries

Bangladesh Braille Library for the Blind International*, PO Box 1144, Dacca Sadar, Dacca 1 (Located at: 15 Razar Duri, Dacca Sadar, Dacca)

Bangladesh Institute of Development Studies Library, GPO Box 3854, Dacca 2 (Located at: E-17 West Agargaon, Sher-e-Bangla Nagar, Dacca 7) Tel: 257360/ 257364

British Council Library*, GPO Box 161, Dacca 2 (Located at: 5 Fuller Rd, Dacca) Tel: 500107 Telex: 642470 Bric
Librarian: N Lack

Dacca University Library*, Dacca 2

Central **Public Library**, Dacca*, Shahbagh, Dacca 2

University of Rajshahi Library*, Rajshahi

Library Associations

Bangladesh Granthagar Samity*, c/o Library Training Institute, Public Library Building, Shahbagh, Dacca 2 Tel: 504269
Library Association of Bangladesh
General Secretary: Sultan Uddin Ahmad
Publication: Eastern Librarian (twice a year)

Directorate of Archives and Libraries*, 106 Central Rd, Dacca 5
Director: Dr K M Karim
Publications: Bangladesh National Bibliography (annual), *Article index* published in the daily newspapers

Library Reference Journals

Bangladesh National Bibliography (annual), Directorate of Archives and Libraries, 106 Central Rd, Dacca 5

Eastern Librarian (text in English) (twice a year), Bangladesh Granthagar Samity, c/o Library Training Institute, Public Library Building, Shahbagh, Dacca 2

Literary Associations and Societies

Dacca Centre for International **P E N***, 62 Purana Paltan, Haroon Enterprises Bldg, 1st Floor, Dacca 2
Secretary: Fazal Shahabuddin

Society of Arts, Literature and Welfare*, Society Park, K C Dey Rd, Chittagong
General Secretary: Md Abdul Hakim

Literary Prizes

Bengali Academy Literary Awards*
For an overall contribution to Bengali literature in the following categories: novel, short story, children's literature, poetry, essay, drama, literary research. Awarded annually. Enquiries to Bengali Academy, Burdwan House, Dacca

Barbados

General Information

Language: English
Religion: Anglican
Population: 263,000
Bank Hours: 0800-1300 Monday-Thursday; 0800-1300, 1500-1750 Friday
Shop Hours: 0800-1600 Monday-Friday; 0800-1200 Saturday
Currency: 100 cents = 1 Barbados dollar
Export/Import Information: No tariff on books. Import licence covering exchange required; no obscene literature permitted
Copyright: Berne, UCC (see International section)

Book Trade Reference Book

National Bibliography of Barbados, National Library Service, Culloden Farm, St Michael

Publishers

P P C Ltd*, Eldino, Gills Rd, St Michael

Major Booksellers

Christian Literature Crusade, PO Box 1239, Bridgetown (Located at: St Michael Plaza, St Michael's Row, Bridgetown) Tel: 4295630
Manager: Romain Graham

Cloister Book Store Ltd, Hincks St, Bridgetown Tel: 4262662
Man Dir: A Musgrave

Roberts Stationery Ltd*, PO Box 224, Bridgetown (Located at: 9 High St, Bridgetown) Tel: 4265500/4297268 Cable Add: Robertsco Telex: 2213 Pubtlx
Manager: Mrs T A L Roberts

Wayfarer Book Store Ltd*, Sunset Crest, St James Tel: 4321099
Man Dir: Nigel Deane
Five branches

Major Libraries

National Library Service*, Culloden Farm, St Michael
Dir: Miss J Y Blackman
Also: Main Lending Library, Coleridge St, Bridgetown
Publications: National Bibliography of Barbados; West Indian Collection

Public Library, now National Library Service (qv)

University of the West Indies*, Main Library, Cave Hill Campus, PO Box 64, Bridgetown Tel: 4251310 ext 235 Cable Add: Univados Barbados Telex: 2257 Univados
Librarian: Michael Gill

Library Association

Library Association of Barbados, PO Box 827E, Bridgetown
Secretary: Angela Skeete
Publications: Bulletin (irregular); *Update* (occasional irregular newsletter)

Library Reference Journal

Bulletin of the Library Association of Barbados (irregular), PO Box 827E, Bridgetown

Belgium

General Information

Language: Dutch in the north, French in the south. Brussels is officially bilingual. German in eastern Belgium
Religion: Predominantly Roman Catholic
Population: 9.86 million
Bank Hours: Variable locally. Brussels: 0900-1300 Monday-Friday; 1400-1630 Monday and Friday; 1430-1530 Tuesday-Thursday. Antwerp: 0930-1500 Monday-Friday; 1630-1800 Friday
Shop Hours: Variable. Department stores: 0915-1800 Monday-Saturday; open until 2100 Friday
Currency: 100 centimes = 1 Belgian franc
Export/Import Information: Member of the European Economic Community. No import licence required, just Model A form of notice of declaration of payment. No exchange controls
Copyright: UCC, Berne, Florence (see International section)

Book Trade Organizations

Algemene Vlaamse Boekverkopersbond, Frankrijklei 93, B-2000 Antwerp
Flemish Booksellers' Association

Association des Editeurs belges, 111 ave du Parc, B-1060 Brussels Tel: (02) 5382167
Belgian Publishers' Association
Dir: B Gerard
Publications: Annuaire des Editeurs belges; Catalogue des Editeurs scientifiques de la Communauté française de Belgique — Statistiques de l'édition belge

Bond Alleenverkopers van Nederlandstalige Boeken (BANB)*, p/a Het Spectrum, Bijkhoevelaan 12, B-2110 Wijnegem

36 BELGIUM

Association of Wholesalers of Dutch Books in Belgium
President: M Kluwer

Cercle Belge de la Librairie*, 35 rue de la Chasse Royale, B-1160 Brussels Tel: (02) 6405241
Belgian Booksellers' Association
President: M Destrebelge; *Secretary-General:* M Jezierski; *Administration:* N Mertens
Publications: Journal de la Librairie (Book Trade Journal) (10 times a year); *Annuaire du CBL; Annuaire 1985*

Standard Book Numbering Agency: for publications in Dutch see Bureau ISBN, Netherlands; for publications in French see Agence francophone pour la Numérotation internationale du Livre, France

Union des Editeurs de Langue française (UELF), 111 ave du Parc, B-1060 Brussels
International Union of Publishers of French Language Books
Dir: B Gerard

Vereniging ter Bevordering van het Vlaamse Boekwezen, Frankrijklei 93, B-2000 Antwerp Tel: (03) 2324684
Association for the Promotion of Flemish Books
Publication: Tijdingen (News)

Vereniging van Uitgevers van Nederlandstalige Boeken, Frankrijklei 93, B-2000 Antwerp Tel: (03) 2324684
Association of Publishers of Dutch Language Books
Secretary: A Wouters
Publications: Lijstenbook (List of Booksellers); *Tijdingen* (News)

Book Trade Reference Books and Journals

Books

Annuaire des Editeurs belges (Belgian Publishers' Annual), Association des Editeurs belges, 111 ave du Parc, B-1060 Brussels

Annuaire du CBL (Belgian Booksellers' Association Annual), Cercle Belge de la Librairie, 35 rue de la Chasse Royale, B-1160 Brussels

Lijstenbook (List of Booksellers), Vereniging van Uitgevers van Nederlandstalige Boeken, Frankrijklei 93, B-2000 Antwerp

Liste des Sociétés savantes et littéraires de Belgique (List of Belgian Learned and Literary Societies), Service belge des Echanges Internationaux, 80-84 rue des Tanneurs, B-1000 Brussels

Journals

Belgica Selecta, Belgian Institute of Information, Montoyerstr 3, B-1040 Brussels
Lists new Belgian books

Belgische Bibliografie, Bibliothèque royale Albert Ier, 4 blvd de l'Empereur, B-1000 Brussels

Bibliographie de Belgique, see *Belgische Bibliografie*

Boekengids (Guide to Books), Katholiek Centrum voor Lectuurinformatie en Bibliotheekvoorziening, Raapstr 4, Antwerp

Bulletin (quarterly), Commission belge de Bibliographie, 80-84 rue des Tanneurs, B-1000 Brussels

Journal de la Librairie (Book Trade Journal) (10 times a year), Cercle Belge de la Librairie, 35 rue de la Chasse Royale, B-1160 Brussels

Le Livre et l'Estampe (The Book and the Print) (twice a year), Société royale des Bibliophiles et Iconophiles de Belgique, 4 blvd de l'Empereur, B-1000 Brussels

Tijdingen (News), Vereniging van Uitgevers van Nederlandstalige Boeken/ Vereniging ter Bevordering van het Vlaamse Boekwezen, Frankrijklei 93, B-2000 Antwerp

Publishers

3 Arches, see Trois Arches

Edition et Diffusion **Academia**, 42 Passage de l'Ergot, B-1348 Louvain-la-Neuve Tel: (010) 452395
Man Dir: Yves Wellemans
Subjects: Human Sciences, Philosophy, Economics
Founded: 1987
ISBN Publisher's Prefix: 2-87209

Acco SV+, Tiensestr 134-136, B-3000 Louvain Tel: (016) 221249/233520/237731 Telex: 62547
Dir: H Van Slambrouck
Orders to: Acco-Uitgeverij (at above address)
Subsidiary Company: Academische Uitgeverij Amersfoort BV, Koningin Wilhelminalaan 17, 3800 AJ Amersfoort, Netherlands
Imprint: De Horstink
Subjects: Classic Languages and Culture, Linguistics, Economics, Law, Social Sciences, Education, Pedagogy, Mathematics, General Science, History, Physiotherapy, Psychology, Medicine, Religion, Philosophy, Criminology, Ethics
1985: 173 titles *Founded:* 1960
ISBN Publisher's Prefix: 90-334

Acta Medica Belgica ASBL*, 43 rue des Champs Elysées, B-1050 Brussels Tel: (02) 6480468
Subject: Medicine
Founded: 1945

Actuaquarto*, 20 allée des Bouleaux, B-6280 Gerpinnes Tel: (071) 216153
Man Dir and Sales, Production, Publicity, Rights & Permissions: Michel Paunet; *Editorial:* Jean Delahaut
Subject: Press in Education
Founded: 1970

Altiora NV, Abdijstr 1, B-3281 Averbode Tel: (013) 771751 Telex: 39104 Fax: (013) 777243
Dirs: J Meers, T Secuianu; *Editor:* N C Vranckx; *Production:* I Willems
Subjects: Education, Juveniles, Religion, Periodicals
ISBN Publisher's Prefix: 90-317

SC des Editions Jacques **Antoine**+, 55-57 rue des Éperonniers, B-1000 Brussels Tel: (02) 5124337
Dirs: L Antoine, D Haeyere
Subjects: Literature, Arts, Theatre
Founded: 1968

Antwerpse Lloyd NV, see Lloyd Anversois SA

Editions **Arcade-Fonds** Mercator*, Meir 85, B-2000 Antwerp Tel: (03) 2313840 Telex: 71876
Man Dir: J Martens
Associate Company: Fonds Mercator SA (qv)
Subject: Art
Founded: 1952
ISBN Publisher's Prefix: 2-8005

SC **Artis-Historia**+, 1 rue Carli, Evere, B-1140 Brussels Tel: (02) 2422320 Telex: 64996 Fax: (02) 2421818
Chief Executive and Rights & Permissions: Christian Kremer; *Sales Manager:* José Guyaux; *Production Manager:* Marie-Christine Dury; *Publicity Manager:* Marc Chougol
Subjects: Geography, History, Nature, Arts, Music, Tourism, Cookery, Leisure
Bookshops: See under Major Booksellers
1985-86: 30 titles *Founded:* 1948, companies merged to form Artis-Historia in 1976
ISBN Publisher's Prefix: 2-0832

Assimil, Uitgaven Nelis PVBA, Steenstr 5-7, B-1000 Brussels Tel: (02) 5114502/5134674
Man Dirs: R Nelis, S Peters; *Editorial:* C Caljon; *Commercial Dir:* S Peters
Subject: Languages (Home Studying)
ISBN Publisher's Prefix: 90-70077

Association des Sociétés scientifiques médicales belges (ASBL)*, 43 rue des Champs Elysées, B-1050 Brussels Tel: (02) 6480468
Vereniging van de belgische medische wetenschappelijke genootschappen VZW
Subjects: Medicine, Journals
Founded: 1945

Audivox*, Rubenslei 23, B-2018 Antwerp Tel: (03) 2328465
Dir: W Gonnissen
Subject: School Textbooks
Bookshop: See under Major Booksellers
Founded: 1953

Aurelia Books PVBA*, Museumlaan 17, B-9831 Sint-Martens-Latem Tel: (091) 825582
Dir: A d'Oosterlynck; *Sales, Publicity:* L Bullaert
Subjects: Training of Nurses, School Books, Flemish Folklore, Popular Devotion
Founded: 1972

Maison d'Editions **Bahá'íes** ASBL, rue du Trône 205, 1050 Brussels Tel: (02) 6470749
Subject: Bahá'í Religion
Founded: 1970
ISBN Publisher's Prefix: 2-87203

Belgisch Instituut voor Voorlichting en Documentatie (INBEL), see Institut belge d'Information et de Documentation

Uitgeverij van **Belle** PVBA, Steenweg op Ninove 116, B-1080 Brussels Tel: (02) 5213417/5210221
Dir: R van Belle
Subjects: Geography, History, Ethnography, Travel, Juveniles, Sports
Founded: 1938

Editions Gérard **Blanchart** & Cie SA+, 15 ave Ernest Masoin, B-1090 Brussels Tel: (02) 4783706 Telex: 25985 c/o Halbart
Administrator, Editorial and Sales: Charles Blanchart; *Production:* Thérèse Chantrenne; *Rights & Permissions:* Charles Blanchart, Thérèse Chantrenne
Subjects: Religion, Art, Photography, Railways, Children's and Teenagers'
1987: 8 titles *Founded:* 1958
ISBN Publisher's Prefix: 2-0121

Maison d'Edition A de **Boeck** SA, now Editions De Boeck-Wesmael SA (qv)

Société **Bordas-Dunod** Bruxelles SA*, 44 rue Otlet, B-1070 Brussels Tel: (02) 5238133 Telex: 24899 Bordun
Parent Company: Editions Bordas, France (qv for associate companies)
Subject: Textbooks
Bookshop: Librairie Beranger, 48 rue Cathédrale, B-4000 Liège

Founded: 1969
Miscellaneous: Company's main function is as a distributor of French-language books

Bourdeaux-Capelle SA*, 32 rue Barré, B-5500 Dinant Tel: (082) 222283/222277
Dir: Michel Bourdeaux
Subjects: Bibliography, Languages, Journals
Founded: 1913

De **Branding** NV, Korte Winkelstr 15, B-2000 Antwerp Tel: (03) 2332739
Dir: J P Ottow
Subjects: Nautical
Bookshop: Belgisch Maritiem Centrum (at above address)
Founded: 1956

Brepols Publishers IGP*, Baron F du Fourstr 8, B-2300 Turnhout Tel: (014) 415466 Telex: 34182
Chairman: Baron de Cartier de Marchienne; *Man Dir:* M Rolin
Associate Company: Editions Brepols SA, France (qv)
Branch Off: Editions Brepols-Lidis, 265 ave de Teruuven, Brussels
Subjects: Religion (Patristics, Bibles, Prayerbooks), History
Founded: 1797
ISBN Publisher's Prefix: 2-503

Vanden **Broele** BVBA, Hogeweg 12, B-8200 Bruges Tel: (050) 323445
Dir: E de Jonghe
Subjects: Law, Political, Administrative & Social Sciences, Popular Medicine
1985: 39 titles *1986:* 39 titles
ISBN Publisher's Prefix: 90-6267

A W **Bruna** en Zoon NV, Antwerpsesteenweg 29a, B-2630 Aartselaar Tel: (03) 8874018 Telex: 73159
Dir: J Raedschelders
Head Office: A W Bruna en Zoon's Uitgeversmaatschappij BV, Netherlands (qv)
Subjects: Juveniles, Literature, Paperbacks
Founded: 1966

Etablissements Emile **Bruylant** SA, 67 rue de la Régence, B-1000 Brussels Tel: (02) 5129845
Administrative Director-General: Jean Vandeveld; *Director-General:* Angèle Van Sprengel
Subjects: Law, High-priced Paperbacks, General & Social Science, University Textbooks
Bookshop: At above address
1985: 24 titles *1986:* 21 titles *Founded:* 1838
ISBN Publisher's Prefix: 2-8027

C E **D**-Samsom*, Louizalaan 485, B-1050 Brussels Tel: (02) 7207180
Dir: O Chrispeels
Parent Company: Wolters Samsom België NV (qv)
Subjects: Tax, Employment Law, Accountancy, Insurance, Management, Health and Safety, Health Care Management, Import and Export, Transport
Founded: 1964

Editions **C E F A** (Centre d'Education à la Famille et à l'Amour)*, 58 rue de la Prévoyance, B-1000 Brussels Tel: (02) 5131749
Man Dir: Pierre de Locht; *Sales:* Josette Maufroy
Subjects: The Family, Sexual Education, Religion
Bookshop: Librairie Novissima, 33 rue de la Concorde, B-1050 Brussels
Founded: 1961

C F E Belgique*, 1033a chaussée d'Alsemberg Bte 28b, B-1180 Brussels Tel: (02) 3761167 Telex: 64797 Foblex
Parent Company: Les Cahiers Fiscaux Européens Sàrl, France (qv)
Associate Company: JURIF Belgique (qv)
Subjects: European Taxation, Fiscal Law

C I A C O Editeur, 9 ave Einstein, B-1348 Louvain-la-Neuve Tel: (010) 418524
Manager: Bernard Mathot
Subjects: Sciences, Humanities, University Textbooks
Bookshop: DUC (Diffusion Universitaire CIACO), 7 Grand Place, B-1348 Louvain-la-Neuve
1987: 100 titles *Founded:* 1970
ISBN Publisher's Prefix: 2-87085

Carto BVBA, Gaucheretstr 139, B-1210 Brussels Tel: (02) 2161545 Cable Add: Cartopress Fax: (02) 2163026
Man Dir: Michiel Plaizier
Subsidiary Companies: Carpress, International Press Agency; European Cartographic Institute; Cremers (Schoollandkaarten) PVBA (qv); Cremers Cartographic Institute
Subjects: Geography, History, Secondary & Primary Textbooks, Educational Materials (Transparencies), Maps, Travel
Founded: 1950

Editions **Casterman***, 28 rue des Soeurs noires, B-7500 Tournai Tel: (069) 224141 Cable Add: Casteredim Tournai Telex: 57328
Man Dir: Louis-Robert Casterman; *Sales Dir:* Jean-Jacques Dursin; *Rights & Permissions:* Pierre Servais, Ivan Noerdinger
Subsidiary Company: Editions Casterman, France (qv)
Branch Offs: 44 ave de Roodebeek, B-1040 Brussels; De Morinel 25-29, 8251 HT Dronten, Netherlands
Subjects: General Fiction, Belles Lettres, Poetry, Biography, History, Music, Art, Philosophy, Reference, Religion, Juveniles, High-priced Paperbacks, Psychology, General & Social Science, University & Secondary Textbooks, Languages, Law, Geography, Sports, Travel, Medicine
Founded: 1780
ISBN Publisher's Prefixes: 2-203 (French), 90-303 (Dutch)

Centre d'Education à la Famille et à l'Amour, see Editions CEFA

Centre international d'Etudes de la Formation religieuse Lumen Vitae ASBL, now Editions Lumen Vitae ASBL

Centre national de Recherches 'Primitifs Flamands' ASBL, 1 parc du Cinquantenaire, B-1040 Brussels Tel: (02) 7354160
President and Rights & Permissions: A Janssens de Bisthoven; *Scientific Editor and Sales:* M Comblen
Subjects: Arts
Founded: 1950
ISBN Publisher's Prefix: 2-87033

Chanlis, 52 rue de Lennery, B-6430 Walcourt Tel: (071) 326394/611770 Telex: 51832 Manodl
Man Dir: Pierre Magain; *Sales:* M Nowak
Subjects: Numismatics, Archaeology, Arts
Bookshop: route de Mons 25A, B-6000 Charleroi
Founded: 1968
ISBN Publisher's Prefix: 2-87039

Editions **Chantecler**, Cleydaellaan 8, B-2630 Aartselaar, Antwerp Tel: (03) 8878300 Telex: 31739 Zuidb
Man Dir: Jan Vande Velden; *Editorial:* Bart Clinckemalie; *Production:* Eric Feyten; *Rights & Permissions:* Wilfried Wuyts
Parent Company: Zuidnederlandse Uitgeverij NV (qv)
Imprint: Pre-Ecole
Subjects: Children's Fiction & Non-fiction
Founded: 1947
ISBN Publisher's Prefix: 2-8034

La **Charte** NV, Oude Gentweg 108, B-8000 Bruges Tel: (050) 331235
Dir: J P Steevens
Subjects: Bibliography, Languages, Textbooks, Law, Political, Administrative & Social Sciences, Primary & Secondary Textbooks
Founded: 1948

De **Clauwaert***, Koning Albertlaan 17, B-3040 Korbeek-Lo, Louvain Tel: (016) 462229
Man Dir: W Vanden Eynde; *Sales Dir:* J Raymaekers
Subjects: General Fiction, Belles Lettres, Secondary Textbooks
Book Club: Boekengilde de Clauwaert
Founded: 1948

Cogedi SA, galerie des Princes 2-4, B-1000 Brussels Tel: (02) 5132038
Dir: Pierre Mardaga; *Rights & Permissions:* Pierre Mardaga, Gigi Dony
Subjects: Education, Pedagogy, Psychology, Architecture, Music
Founded: 1938

Colibrant, an imprint of Orbis en Orion Uitgevers NV (qv)

Editions **Complexe** SPRL+, 24 rue de Bosnie, B-1060 Brussels Tel: (02) 5388845 Telex: 64507 Patica
Man Dir, Publicity: Danielle Vincken; *Man Dir, Editorial:* André Versaille
Associate Company: Nouvelle Diffusion SPRL DPI (at above address)
Subjects: History, Human Sciences
Founded: 1971
ISBN Publisher's Prefix: 2-87027

Contact NV*, Elsbos 33, B-2520 Edegem Tel: (031) 572024/573486
Dir: A J H Binneweg
Subjects: Arts, Textbooks, Education, Pedagogy, Sports, Games, Literature, Paperbacks
Founded: 1946
ISBN Publisher's Prefix: 90-254

Creadif*, 52 ave de Tervueren, B-1040 Brussels Tel: (02) 7360630
Dir: M Servais
Subjects: Geography, History, Ethnography, Travel, Economy, Commerce, Law
Founded: 1974

Crédit Communal de Belgique SA*, 44 blvd Pacheco, B-1000 Brussels Tel: (02) 2144111 Cable Add: Crédit Communal Brussels Telex: 26354 Cregem
Man Dir: F Narmon; *Sales:* I Schiltz
Subjects: History, Politics, Law, Music, Fine Arts
1985: 21 titles *Founded:* 1960
Miscellaneous: Incorporates Pro Civitate

Cremers (Schoollandkaarten) PVBA*, Gaucheretstr 139, B-1000 Brussels Tel: (02) 2161545 Cable Add: Cartopress
Dir: Michiel Plaizier
Parent Company: Carto PVBA (qv)
Subjects: Textbooks, Geography, History, Ethnography, Travel, Journals
Founded: 1950

Crisp*, 35 rue du Congrès, B-1000 Brussels Tel: (02) 2183226
Man Dir: J Gerard-Libois; *Editorial:* Xavier Mabille; *Management:* M Julin
Subjects: Political Science, Industry, Finance
Founded: 1958

BELGIUM

Editions **Culture et Civilisation***, 115 ave Gabriel Lebon, B-1160 Brussels Tel: (02) 7345005 Cable Add: Jadam
Man Dir: Jos Adam
Subsidiary Company: Imprimerie Jos Adam (at above address)
Subjects: Biography, History, Geography, Ethnography, Travel, Music, Art, Philosophy, Reference, Religion, Medicine, Psychology, University Textbooks, Bibliography, Languages, Law, Social & General Sciences, Literature
Founded: 1960

De **Dageraad** PVBA*, Perenstr 13-15, B-2008 Antwerp Tel: (03) 2356866
Dir: R van Hevel
Founded: 1971

Le **Daily-Bul***, 29 rue Daily-Bul, B-7100 La Louvière Tel: (064) 222973
Man Dir: André Balthazar
Subjects: Literature, Poetry, Arts
Founded: 1957

Uitgeverij **Dap-Reinart** SV*, Industriepark B4, B-9140 Zele Tel: (052) 445171
Dir: A van Acker
Subjects: Juveniles, Literature, Education, Law, Religion
Book Club: Dap-Reinart Uitgeven
Founded: 1946

Daphne Diffusion SA*, Poortakkerstr 29, B-9820 Gent Tel: (091) 214591 Telex: 11659
General Manager: F Dubrulle

Davidsfonds VZW+, Blijde Inkomststr 79, B-3000 Louvain Tel: (016) 221801
Dir: N D'Hulst; *Editorial:* L Peeraer
Subjects: Arts, Law, Political, Administrative & Social Sciences, Education, Pedagogy, Sports, Games, Juveniles, Religion, Philosophy, Literature, Journals
Founded: 1875
ISBN Publisher's Prefix: 90-6152

Editions **De Boeck-Wesmael** SA+*, 203 ave Louise Bte 1, B-1050 Brussels Tel: (02) 6407272 Telex: 65701 Dbwes
Man Dir, Editorial, Production: Christian de Boeck; *Sales:* Alain van Langhendonck; *University Publications:* Michel Jezierski; *Juvenile Publications:* Marie David; *Publicity:* Evelyne Stubbe; *Rights & Permissions:* Georges Hoyos
Subsidiary Company: Afrique-Editions, 606 rue Colonel Ebeya, BP 9986, Kinshasa 1, Zaire
Subjects: Children's, Juveniles, Primary & Secondary Textbooks, Higher education, University Courses, Didactics
1985: 110 titles *Founded:* 1883
ISBN Publisher's Prefix: 2-8041

Uitgeverij **De Garve***, Groene Poortdreef 27, B-8200 St-Michiels, Bruges Tel: (050) 383846/380707
Dir: G Barbiaux
Parent Company: Drukkerij PVBA G Barbiaux
Subjects: (All titles in Flemish only) Bibliography, Language, Textbooks, Law, Politics, Social Science, Mathematics, Physics, Technical, Music
Founded: 1909

De Horstink, an imprint of Acco SV (qv)

Maison d'Editions Cl **Dejaie**+*, 1208 chaussée de Dinant, B-5150 Wépion Namur Tel: (081) 460266
Dir: M Cl M Dejaie
Subjects: Bibliography, Languages, Law, Political, Administrative & Social Sciences, Religion, Philosophy, Literature, Belles Lettres, Art, Erudition
Founded: 1972
ISBN Publisher's Prefix: 2-87157

Editions **Delta** SA+, 92-94 sq Plasky, B-1040 Brussels Tel: (02) 7369060 Telex: 65968 Delta
Man Dir: Georges-Francis Seingry
Associate Company: Guides Delta (at above address)
Subjects: Reference books (Directories, Yearbooks, Who's Who, Guides, Monographs) regarding EEC and other European Organizations; Belgian Restaurant Guides, General Literature, Art Books
1985: 10 titles *1986:* 10 titles *Founded:* 1974
ISBN Publisher's Prefix: 2-8029

Deltas, an imprint of Zuidnederlandse Uitgeverij NV (qv)

Denis & Co PVBA*, Sterckshoflei 28-30, B-2100 Deurne-Antwerp Tel: (03) 3213299/3220804
Subjects: Art, Law, Education, History, Juveniles, Philosophy

Desclée, Editeurs, Zone Industrielle Tournai-Ouest, rue de la Terre à Briques, B-7713 Marquain Tel: (069) 233188 Cable Add: Desclée Marquain Telex: 57429 Arciel
Dir: F Parys; *Literary Dir:* A Paul
Parent Company: Gedit Editions SA (qv)
Associate Companies: Editions Gamma, Belgium (qv); Editions Desclée et Cie, France (qv); Editions Gamma, France (qv)
Subjects: Religion, Philosophy, Missals, Theology, Literature
Bookshop: At above address
Founded: 1872

H **Dessain** NV*, Regenboog 5-9, B-2800 Mechelen Tel: (015) 416986
Man Dir: Charles Dessain
Subjects: Juveniles, Medicine, Music, Religion, Reference, Geography, History, Ethnography, Travel
Founded: 1854

H **Dessain** SPRL+*, 7 rue Trappé, B-4000 Liège Tel: (041) 237883
Man Dir: André Mols
Subjects: Religion, Mathematics, Textbooks, Education, Pedagogy, Sports, Games, General Science, Geography, History, Ethnography, Travel
Founded: 1719

Diligentia-Uitgeverij*, Sint-Jozefstr 7, B-9040 Oostakker Tel: (091) 511281
Dir: Frank Vermeiren
Subject: Textbooks
Founded: 1908
ISBN Publisher's Prefix: 90-70978

Edition **Doepgen** Verlag*, BP 140, B-4700 Eupen (Located at: Gospertstr 7, Eupen) Tel: (087) 556042/556264
Chief Executive, Editorial, Publicity, Rights & Permissions: Wolfgang Trees; *Sales, Production:* Heinz Doepgen
Subjects: War and History (Aachen, Liège and Maastricht regions)
Bookshops: At above address; Malmedyerstr 19, B-4780 Sint Vith
Founded: 1978
Miscellaneous: Publishes in German language for German-speaking part of Belgium

Editions J **Duculot** SA+, rue de la Posterie, Parc industriel, B-5800 Gembloux Tel: (081) 610061 Telex: 59309 Duculo Fax: (081) 615294
Administrator: Jean Verougstraete; *Publishing Dir, Sales, Publicity:* Georges David; *Editorial, Rights & Permissions:* Emmanuel Brutsaert; *Production:* Jean Flament
Orders to: Presses de Belgique, rue Gray 96, B-1040 Brussels

Subsidiary Company: Editions J Duculot, 16 rue Séguier, F-75006 Paris, France
Subjects: Belles Lettres, General Literature, Art, Religion, Juveniles, Linguistics, General Science, University, Secondary & Primary Textbooks, Guides, Regional Literature
Founded: 1919
ISBN Publisher's Prefix: 2-8011

Editions Jean **Dupuis** SA*, 39 rue Destrée, B-6001 Marcinelle-Charleroi Tel: (071) 364080 Telex: 51370
Dirs: Charles Dupuis, Michel Dupuis, P E Matthews
Associate Companies: Maison d'Editions J Dupuis Fils et Cie SA, France (qv); Uitgeveriji Dupuis NV, Sittard, Netherlands
Branch Off: 13 ave des Arts, B-1040 Brussels
Subjects: Cinema, Juveniles, Comics, Periodicals
Bookshop: 84 blvd St Germain, Paris 8, France
Founded: 1898
ISBN Publisher's Prefix: 2-8001

E P O+*, Lange Pastoorstr 25, B-2600 Berchem Tel: (03) 2396874
Man Dir: Marie-Paule Doumen; *Publisher:* Peter Aerts; *Sales:* Patrick van Buyten
Subjects: Politics, Economics, Law, Philosophy, History, Literature
Bookshop: Groene Weterman, Wolstr 7, B-2000 Antwerp
Founded: 1978
ISBN Publisher's Prefix: 90-6445

Editeurs de Litterature Biblique*, ch de Tubize 479, B-1420 Braine-L'Alleud Tel: (02) 3845402
Man Dir: M Cl Kroeker
Subjects: Education, Juveniles, Philosophy, Religion, Music, Pocketbooks
Founded: 1959

Editions interuniversitaires*, 52 ave de Tervueren, B-1040 Brussels Tel: (02) 7360630
Dir: M Servais
Subjects: Geography, History, Ethnography, Travel
Founded: 1974

Editions techniques et scientifiques SPRL, 35-43 rue Borrens, B-1050 Brussels Tel: (02) 6401040
Man Dir: A Louis
Subjects: General Technology, Law, Mathematics, Science, Geography, History, Ethnography, Travel, General
Founded: 1919

Editions universitaires SA*, 25 rue du Sceptre, B-1040 Brussels Tel: (02) 6488026
Dir: L Honhon
Subjects: Textbooks, Law Political, Administrative & Social Sciences, Education, Pedagogy, Sports, Games, Mathematics, General Science, Geography, History, Ethnography, Travel, Religion, Philosophy, Literature, Languages, Journals
Founded: 1944

Elsevier Librico NV*, Leuvensesteenweg 325, B-1940 Woluwe Tel: (02) 7209090 Cable Add: Elsbook Brussels Telex: 21831 Elsbru
Man Dir, Rights & Permissions: Elie Berwaerts; *Editorial:* Ingrid Symons; *Sales:* Jacqy Vandenberghe, Lieven Struye; *Production:* Piet van Roemburg; *Publicity & Advertising:* Willy Declerck
Parent Company: Elsevier-NDU, Netherlands (qv)
Associate Company: Uitgeversmaatschappij A Manteau NV (qv)
Imprints: Prins, Winkler

Subjects: Biography, History, Literature, Reference, Juveniles, Art, Practical Guides, Nature, Documentaries, Children's Books, Travel
Founded: 1960
ISBN Publisher's Prefix: 90-10

Emmaus, an imprint of Orbis en Orion Uitgevers NV (qv)

Editions **Erasme** (Scriptoria NV)*, Belgiëlei 147a, B-2018 Antwerp Tel: (03) 2395900 Telex: 31421 Edista
Man Dir: J Bruins Slot
Parent Company: Buhrmann-Tetterode BV, Paalbergweg 2, 1105 AG Amsterdam, Netherlands
Associate Company: Standaard Uitgeverij (Scriptoria NV) (qv)
Subjects: Medicine, Science, Reference, Encyclopaedias, Arts, Textbooks, Juveniles, Comic Books
Founded: 1924
ISBN Publisher's Prefix: 90-02

Erel PVBA, St-Sebastiaanstr 16, B-8400 Ostend Tel: (059) 701308
Dir: R Lanoye; *Publicity:* Monique Lanoye
Subjects: Arts, Bibliography, Languages, Education, Pedagogy, Sports, Games, Geography, History, Ethnography, Travel, Literature, Journals
Bookshop: At above address
Founded: 1946

Editions **Est-Ouest***, 66 rue St Bernard, B-1060 Brussels Tel: (02) 5386177
Dir: C André
Subjects: Art, Travel, Belles Lettres, Bibliography, Languages
Founded: 1939

European Press Scientific Publisher*, Kortrijksesteenweg 154, B-9000 Ghent Tel: (091) 213000 Telex: 11008 Eupress
Man Dir: R Desmet; *Editorial, International Books Department:* M Guy
Branch Off: Citadellaan 36, B-9000 Ghent; Borluutstraat, B-9000 Ghent; Postbus Amsterdam, NL-3802 Amsterdam, Netherlands
Subjects: Science (especially Medicine and Pharmacology), Medical Periodicals, Scientific Translations

Familia et Patria PVBA*, Handzamestr 155, B-8120 Handzame Tel: (051) 567336/ 227288
Dir: D Vandecandelaere
Subjects: Bibliography, Languages, Law, Political, Administrative & Social Sciences, Geography, History, Ethnography, Travel, Literature
Founded: 1966

Maison d'Edition: **'Feuilles Familiales'** ASBL, 11 rue Royale, B-1000 Brussels Tel: (02) 2183482
Associate Companies: NFF (Nouvelles Feuilles Familiales); Mouvement pour le Couple et la Famille
Subjects: Marriage & Family Relations, Psychology, Educational, Religion
1985: 1 title *Founded:* 1937

Fonds Mercator SA+*, Meir 85, B-2000 Antwerp Tel: (03) 2313840 Telex: 71876 Mfnv
Publisher: Dr Jan Martens
Associate Company: Editions Arcade-Fonds Mercator (qv)
Subjects: Arts, Geography, History, Ethnography, Travel, Literature, Music
Founded: 1965

Editions de la **Francité** (Imprimeries Havaux)*, 37c rue A Levêque, B-1400 Nivelles Tel: (067) 226131
Dir: LL Havaux
Branch Off: 20 rue du Pouvre, F-75001 Paris, France
Subjects: Arts, Bibliography, Languages, Textbooks, Education, Pedagogy, Sports, Games, Geography, History, Ethnography, Travel, Medicine, Literature, Religion, Philosophy, Journals, Paperbacks

Editions **Gamma**, Zone Industrielle Tournai-Ouest, rue de la Terre à Briques, B-7713 Marquain Tel: (069) 233188 Cable Add: Editions Gamma Marquain Telex: 57429 Arciel
Dir: F Parys; *Production Manager:* R Selke
Parent Company: Gedit Editions SA (qv)
Associate Companies: Desclée, Editeurs, Belgium (qv); Desclée et Cie, France (qv); Editions Gamma, France (qv)
Subjects: Education, How-to, Science & Technology, Textbooks, Sports, Games, Mathematics, Juveniles
Founded: 1962

Gedit Editions SA*, 13 rue Barthélemy Frison, B-7500 Tournai Tel: (069) 226105 Cable Add: Gedit Tournai Telex: 57251 Gedit
Dir: J Desclée
Subsidiary Companies: Desclée, Editeurs (qv); Éditions Desclée et Cie, France (qv); Editions Gamma (qv); Editions Gamma, France (qv)
Subjects: General
Founded: 1872

Editions **Gérard** et Cie SPRL, see Les Nouvelles Editions Marabout SA

Girault **Gilbert** SPRL*, 50 rue de l'Association, B-1000 Brussels Tel: (02) 2171430
Subject: Cartography
Founded: 1928, Reconstituted: 1956

Hachette International*, 715 chaussée de Waterloo, B-1180 Brussels Tel: (02) 3435600 Telex: 25028 Hachette Bru
Man Dir: J Andrieu-Delille
Subject: General

Imprimeries **Havaux**, a division of Editions de la Francité (qv)

Imprimerie **Hayez** SPRL*, 4 rue Fin, B-1080 Brussels Tel: (02) 4240004 Telex: 63467 Hayez
Man Dir: Serge Hayez; *Sales Dir:* Frédéric Hayez
Subjects: Belles Lettres, Poetry, Philosophy, Religion, History, Medicine, General Science, Sport
Founded: 1780

Heideland NV (Heideland PVBA)*, Grote Markt 1, B-3500 Hasselt Tel: (011) 224505
Dirs: L Nagels, Dr Johan Ducheyne
Subjects: Arts, Bibliography, Languages, Textbooks, Education, Sport & Games, Juveniles, Philosophy, Literature, Linguistics, General, Religion, Paperbacks, Periodicals
Bookshop: Boekhandel Heideland (qv under Major Booksellers)
Founded: 1945
ISBN Publisher's Prefix: 90-6440

Heideland-Orbis (NV M en I)*, Torenplein 6, Bus 13, B-3500 Hasselt Tel: (011) 212112 Telex: 39920
Dir: Theo van Erp; *Editorial Manager:* R Fransen; *Production:* H Leduc; *Publicity:* Mia Voordeckers
Subject: Reference
Founded: 1969
Miscellaneous: Firm is a member of Kluwer Group, Netherlands (qv)
ISBN Publisher's Prefix: 90-291

Uitgeverij **Helios***, Kapelsestr 222, B-2080 Kapellen Tel: (03) 6645320 Telex: 32242 Anvers Dnb
Man Dir: J Pelckmans
Associate Company: Uitgeverij De Nederlandsche Boekhandel (qv)
Subjects: General
Founded: 1976
ISBN Publisher's Prefix: 90-333

Editions **Hemma** SPRL+, 106 rue de Chevron, BP 32, B-4081 Stoumont-Chevron Tel: (086) 433636 Cable Add: Hemma Telex: 41507
Dir: Albert Hemmerlin
Subsidiary Companies: Diffusion Hemma, 8 rue Florian, F-93500 Pantin, France; Hemma Holland, Savannahweg 68, 3542 AW Utrecht, Netherlands; Hemma Verlag, Rotter-Bruch 26a, Postfach 1758, D-5100 Aachen, Federal Republic of Germany; Hemma HE SA, Secundino Esnaola – 8°, San Sebastian/Guipuzcoa, Spain
Subjects: Juveniles, Educational Books and Materials
1985: 213 titles *1986:* 198 titles *Founded:* 1952
ISBN Publisher's Prefix: 2-8006

Hernieuwen-Uitgaven PVBA*, Noordstr 100, B-8800 Roeselare Tel: (051) 201541
Subjects: Juveniles, Religion, Philosophy

Drukkerij-Uitgeverij **Hertoghs***, Turnhoutsebaan 319, B-2110 Wijnegem Tel: (031) 536040
Dir: J Hertoghs
Subject: Textbooks
Founded: 1945

M van **Hove** DPN*, Dorpstr 11, B-2080 Kapellen, Antwerp Tel: (031) 642407
Dir: M van Hove
Subjects: Religion, Philosophy, General
Founded: 1966

I N B E L, see Institut belge d'Information et de Documentation

Uitgeverij J van **In**+, Grote Markt 39, B-2500 Lier Tel: (03) 4805511 Telex: 72343 Inboek
Man Dir and Rights & Permissions: Dr Laurent Woestenburg; *Editorial:* Ludo Camps; *Sales:* Jacques Van Hellemont; *Production:* Danielle Brabrants; *Publicity:* Fred Caluwé
Parent Company: VNU, Netherlands (qv)
Subjects: Juveniles, University, Secondary & Primary Textbooks, Educational Materials, Modern Languages, Law, Periodicals
Bookshop: At above address
Founded: 1833
ISBN Publisher's Prefix: 90-306

Infoboek*, Roosterputstr 34, B-3990 Meerhout Tel: (014) 300477
Dir: W Verhaert
Subjects: Textbooks, Education, Sport & Games, Juveniles, Religion, Philosophy, Literature, Linguistics, Music
Founded: 1971

Institut belge d'Information et de Documentation (INBEL)*, Montoyerstr 3, B-1200 Brussels Tel: (02) 5126688 Telex: 21716 Inbel Bru
Belgisch Institut voor Voorlichting en Documentatie
Dir: F Coppieters
Subjects: Art, Bibliography, Law, Social Sciences, Literature, Periodicals
Founded: 1962

Institut royal des Relations internationales, 88 ave de la Couronne, B-1050 Brussels Tel: (02) 6482000 Telex: 20000 Irikib
Koninklijk Instituut voor Internationale Betrekkingen
Man Dir: Dr E Coppieters

Subjects: Political Science, Law, Economics, International Relations, Periodical
Founded: 1947

Uitgaven van **Interbankendienst** NV, see Services interbancaires SA

Interbooks*, Holle Weg 70, B-2550 Kontich Tel: (03) 4570816/4571395 Telex: 35521 Inbook
Chief Executive: F Vermeulen; *Production:* H de Schrÿver
Founded: 1950

J U R I F Belgique*, 1033a chaussée d'Alsemberg Bte 28b, B-1180 Brussels Tel: (02) 3761167 Telex: 64797 Foblex
Belgian Branch of the Société d'Etudes Juridiques Internationales et Fiscales (JURIF)
Parent Company: Les Cahiers Fiscaux Européens Sàrl, France (qv)
Associate Company: CFE Belgique (qv)
Subject: European Tax Laws

J Janssens PVBA+, Kruikstr 14, B-2018 Antwerp Tel: (03) 2391220
Dir: J Janssens
Subject: Plays
Founded: 1876

Keesing — Internationale Drukkerij en Uitgeverij NV, Keesinglaan 2-20, B-2100 Deurne Tel: (03) 3243890 Cable Add: Systeka Telex: 32507
Man Dir: Steven van de Rijt; *Publications Managers:* Koen Goderis (Dutch editions), André Biot (French editions), Roger van Mieghem
Parent Company: Keesing Beheer BV, Nijenburg 75, 1081 GE Amsterdam, Netherlands
Subsidiary Companies: Internationale d'Impression et d'Edition Keesing, Paris, France; Keesing (UK) Ltd, London, UK
Subjects: Puzzle Books, Periodicals
Founded: 1912
ISBN Publisher's Prefix: 90-71461

Die **Keure** NV*, Oude Gentweg 108, B-8000 Bruges Tel: (050) 331235
Dir: J P Steevens
Subjects: Textbooks, Law, Political, Administrative & Social Sciences, Primary & Secondary Textbooks
Founded: 1948

NV Uitgeverij **Kluwer***, Santvoortbeeklaan 21/23, B-2100 Deurne Tel: (03) 3256880
Dirs: H Noté, P Stoffels, J Verheggen; B Houdmont
Subjects: Law & Taxation, Scientific, School Books, Literature, Technical Books & Periodicals, Encyclopaedias
Founded: 1954
Miscellaneous: Firm is a member of Kluwer Group, Netherlands (qv)

Maarten Kluwer's Internationale Uitgeversonderneming NV, now Maklu Uitgevers NV (qv)

Koninklijk Instituut voor Internationale Betrekkingen, see Institut royal des Relations internationales

Koninklijke Academie voor Wetenschappen, Letteren en Schone Kunsten van België, Hertogsstr 1, B-1000 Brussels Tel: (02) 5112623
Belgian Royal Academy of Sciences, Letters and Fine Arts
Permanent Secretary: Gerard Verbeke
Orders to: Brepols Publishers IGP, Baron F du Fourstr 8, B-2300 Turnhout
Subjects: Pure & Applied Sciences, Humanities, Fine Arts, Music
1985: 13 titles *1986:* 18 titles *Founded:* 1938
ISBN Publisher's Prefix: 90-6569

Kritak uitgeverij+, Andreas Vesaliusstraat 1, B-3000 Leuven Tel: (016) 230131
Man Dir: André Van Halewijck
Subjects: Politics, Social affairs, Literature, Comics
Founded: 1976
ISBN Publisher's Prefix: 90-6303

Editions **Labor-Nathan**, 156-158 chaussée de Haecht, B-1030 Brussels Tel: (02) 2168150 Telex: 25532 Labor
Man Dir: Th Vanderworst; *All other offices:* J Fauconnier
Subjects: Belles Lettres, Poetry, Biography, History, Philosophy, Reference, Psychology, General & Social Science, Primary, Secondary & University Textbooks, Pedagogy, Economics
Founded: 1927
ISBN Publisher's Prefix: 2-8040

Editions **Lampe** d'Or ASBL, 23 ave Giele, B-1090 Brussels Tel: (02) 4279277
Man Dir: F M Van Dÿk
Subjects: Religion, Juveniles
Founded: 1955
ISBN Publisher's Prefix: 2-87001

Uitgeverij **Lannoo**, Kasteelstr 97, B-8880 Tielt Tel: (051) 402551 Telex: 81555 Fax: (051) 401152
Man Dirs: Godfried Lannoo, Luc Demeester
Subjects: Art, Philosophy, Religion, Juveniles, Paperbacks, Psychology, Education, Sports, Games, Travel, Poetry
Founded: 1909
ISBN Publisher's Prefix: 90-209

Maison Ferdinand **Larcier** SA, 39 rue des Minimes, B-1000 Brussels Tel: (02) 5129679/5124712
Man Dir: Jean-Marie Ryckmans
Subjects: Law (Belgian and International), Social Science, Science & Technology, Periodicals
Founded: 1839

Latomus — Société d'Études Latines de Bruxelles ASBL, 18 ave Van Cutsem, B-7500 Tournai
Editorial: M Renard; *Sales, Production, Publicity, Rights & Permissions:* Mme J Dumortier-Bibauw
Subjects: Bibliography, Latin, Philology, Roman Literature, History, Archaeology
Founded: 1937
ISBN Publisher's Prefix: 2-87031

Edition **Le Cri**+*, 32 rue Veyot, B-1060 Brussels Tel: (02) 5382040
Man Dir, Sales, Rights & Permissions: Christian Lutz; *Editorial:* Arnaud de la Croix; *Production:* Francis Jacoby
Orders to: Vander SA, 321 ave des Volontaires, B-1150 Brussels Tel: (02) 7629804
Parent Company: Edition Le Cri ASBL (at main company address)
Subjects: Fiction, Theatre, Monographs
Founded: 1981
ISBN Publisher's Prefix: 2-87106

Uiteverij Leon **Lesoil** VZW*, Geuzenstrt 20, B-2000 Antwerp Tel: (03) 2375372
Man Dir: Monique Laenen
Subject: Politics
Founded: 1973

Leuven University Press, Krakenstr 3, B-3000 Leuven
Dir: Prof W Van Hoecke
Orders to: Editions Peeters PVBA, Bondgenotenlaan 153, B-3000 Leuven
Subjects: Theology, Psychology, Pedagogy, Economics, Sociology, Political Studies, Music, Mathematics, Medicine, Philosophy
1985: 27 titles *1986:* 30 titles *Founded:* 1971
ISBN Publisher's Prefix: 90-6186

Editions de la **Librairie encyclopédique***, 1593 chaussée de Waterloo, B-1180 Brussels Tel: (02) 5132467
Man Dir: A C Leyenberger
Subjects: History, Reference, Law, Economics, Political & Social Science
Bookshop: Librairie encyclopédique Exportation-Antiquariat (at above address)
Founded: 1939

Editeurs de **Littérature** biblique*, 479 chaussée de Tubize, B-1420 Braine-l'Alleud Tel: (02) 3845402
Biblical Publications
Dir: M Cl Kroeker
Subjects: Education, Pedagogy, Sport, Games, Juveniles, Religion, Philosophy, Music, Journals, Paperbacks
Founded: 1959

Lloyd Anversois SA (Antwerpse Lloyd NV), Eiermarkt 23, B-2000 Antwerp Tel: (03) 2340550 Telex: 31446
Man Dir: M R Jaumotte
Subjects: Transport, Law, Maritime, Languages
Founded: 1904

Les Editions du **Lombard** SA+, ave Paul-Henri Spaak 1-11, B-1070 Brussels Tel: (02) 5225600 Cable Add: Lombarbel Brussels Telex: 23097
Man Dir: L Lottefier; *Rights & Permissions:* Viviane Rousie
Branch Offs: Lombard France, 16 rue de la Sablière, F-75014 Paris, France Tel: (1) 15430897; Lombard Nederland, Postbus 341, 2100 AH Heemstede, Netherlands Tel: (023) 290190
Subjects: Juveniles, Games, Education, History, Religion
Founded: 1946

Uitgeverij **Lotus**/Editions Lotus*, Leopoldstr 43, B-2000 Antwerp Tel: (031) 327010/327001
Man Dir: Jean-Pierre Zinje
Orders to: (French language books) Garnier Frères, BP 168, 19 rue des plantes, F-75665 Paris; (Dutch language books, Belgium) Denis, Sterckshoflei 28-30, B-2100 Deurne; (Dutch language books, Netherlands) Centraal Boekhuis, Postbus 125, Erasmusweg 10, Culemborg
Subjects: Novels, Documentary Works, Juveniles
Founded: 1977
ISBN Publisher's Prefixes: 90-6290 (Dutch language books); 2-87053 (French language books)

Editions **Lumen** Vitae ASBL*, 184 rue Washington, B-1050 Brussels Tel: (02) 3441882
International Centre for Studies in Religious Education
Man Dir, Sales: Pierre Mourlon-Baernaert
Subjects: Religion, High-priced Paperbacks, Psychology, Secondary & Primary Textbooks, Educational Materials, Pastoral Studies
Founded: 1936

NV **M en I**, see Heideland-Orbis and E Story-Scientia

Magic-Strip SA+, 18 pl Rouppe, B-1000 Brussels Tel: (02) 5111831
Dirs: Daniel Pasamonik, Didier Pasamonik; *Rights & Permissions:* Daniel Pasamonik
Subjects: Juveniles, Comic Books, Art Books
Founded: 1979
ISBN Publisher's Prefix: 2-8035

Maklu Uitgevers NV, Somersstr 13-15, B-2018 Antwerp Tel: (03) 2312900
Dirs: M Kluwer, E Boerwinkel
Subsidiary Company: Maklu BV,

Koninginnelaan 96, 7315 EB Apeldoorn, Netherlands
Subjects: Textbooks, Law, Political & Social Science, Education, Technical, Periodicals
Founded: 1972 (as Maarten Kluwer's Internationale Uitgeversonderneming NV)
Miscellaneous: Wholesaler (Dutch books)
ISBN Publisher's Prefix: 90-6215

Uitgeversmaatschappij A **Manteau** NV, Beeldhouwersstr 12, B-2000 Antwerp   Tel: (03) 2371792   Telex: 21831
Man Dir: E Berwaerts; *Sales Dir:* W Declerck
Subsidiary Company: A Manteau NV
Subjects: General Fiction, Belles Lettres, Poetry, Biography, Secondary Textbooks, Literary Periodicals
Founded: 1932
ISBN Publisher's Prefix: 90-223

Les Nouvelles Editions **Marabout** SA*, 30 ave de L'Energie, B-4430 Alleur   Tel: (041) 611863
Man Dir: Serge Martiano; *Sales Dir:* Jean-Paul Michaud
Branch Offs: 81 ave de Tervueren, B-1040 Brussels; 8 rue de Neslé, F-75006 Paris, France
Subject: Paperbacks
Founded: 1977
Miscellaneous: Formerly Editions Gérard et Cie SPRL

Pierre **Mardaga** SA, 2-4 galerie des Princes, B-1000 Brussels   Tel: (02) 5132038
Man Dir: Pierre Mardaga; *Rights & Permissions:* Pierre Mardaga, Gigi Dony
Associate Company: Soledi (Imprimeur-Editeur) SA (qv)
Subjects: Psychology, Social Science, Architecture, Music
Founded: 1938
ISBN Publisher's Prefix: 2-87009

Maredsous ASBL*, 8 rue de Maredsous, B-5198 Denee   Tel: (082) 699155
Dir: Père Léon-Nicolas Dayez
Subjects: Geography, History, Religion, Philosophy, General, Ethnography, Travel
Bookshop: At above address
Founded: 1924

Editions **Marie-Médiatrice** ASBL*, 172 ave Gevaert, B-1320 Genval   Tel: (02) 6537613
Director-General: André Martin
Subjects: Juveniles, Religion, Paperbacks
Founded: 1941

Mercatorfonds SA, see Fonds Mercator SA

Mercatorfonds Arcade, see Editions Arcade-Fonds Mercator

Editeur Paul F **Merckx***, 145a ave des Statuaires, B-1180 Brussels   Tel: (02) 3744156/3745158
Subjects: Art, Geography, History, Touring in Belgium
Founded: 1958

Mercurius PVBA*, Rodestr 44, B-2000 Antwerp   Tel: (031) 333708/333762
Dir: K Schenck
Subjects: Geography, History, Ethnography, Travel
Founded: 1894

Michelin (Département Cartes & Guides) SA*, 33 quai de Willebroek, B-1020 Brussels   Tel: (02) 2186100 ext 238   Cable Add: Pneumiclin
Dir: R Cammaerts
Subjects: Travel Guides, Maps
Founded: 1913

Mouvement pour le Couple et la Famille, associate company of Maison d'Edition: 'Feuilles Familiales' ASBL (qv)

N F F (Nouvelles Feuilles Familiales), associate company of Maison d'Edition: 'Feuilles Familiales' ASBL (qv)

Nauwelaerts Edition SA*, Mechelsestr 148, B-3000 Louvain   Tel: (016) 229096
Man Dir: W Vandermeulen
Associate Company: Vander Publishing (qv)
Subjects: History, Philosophy, Theology, Medicine, Psychology, Social Science, Economics, University Textbooks, Educational Materials, Literature
Founded: 1934

Uitgeverij De **Nederlandsche Boekhandel***, Kapelsestr 222, B-2080 Kapellen   Tel: (03) 6645320   Telex: 32242 Anvers Dnb
Man Dirs: J Pelckmans, R Pelckmans
Associate Companies: Uitgeverij Helios (qv); Uitgeverij Patmos (qv); (Uitgeverij Opdebeek is now wholly incorporated in Uitgeverij De Nederlandsche Boekhandel)
Subjects: History, Philosophy, Religion, Juveniles, Social Science, University, Secondary & Primary Textbooks
Bookshop: Sint Jacobsmarkt 7, B-2000 Antwerp
Founded: 1892
ISBN Publisher's Prefix: 90-289

Nouvelle Diffusion SPRL DPI, see Editions Complexe SPRL

Les **Nouvelles Editions Marabout** SA, see Marabout

Nouvelles Feuilles Familiales, see NFF

Uitgeverij S V **Ontwikkeling***, Leeuwerikstr 41, B-2000 Antwerp
Tel: (031) 338659
Dir: R Binnemans
Subjects: Novels, Poetry, History, Textbooks
Bookshops: Boekhandel Ontwikkeling: Ommeganckstr 35-37, Antwerp; Dés Boucherystr 18-20, Mechelen; J Brochhovenstr 28, Deurne, Antwerp
Founded: 1923

Uitgeverij **Opdebeek**, now incorporated in Uitgeverij De Nederlandsche Boekhandel (qv)

Orbis en Orion Uitgevers NV*, Lieven Bauwenstr 19, Bruges
Administrative Delegate: A Goyvaerts
Imprints: Colibrant, Emmaus, Orion
Subjects: Encyclopaedias, Non-fiction, Belles-Lettres, School Textbooks, Religion, Philosophy, Journals, Paperbacks
Founded: 1979
ISBN Publisher's Prefix: 90-264

Uitgeverij **Orientaliste** PVBA, now Peeters Publishers (qv)

Orion, an imprint of Orbis en Orion Uitgevers NV (qv)

De **Oude** Linden NV*, Abdijstr 40, B-3180 Tongerlo-Westerlo   Tel: (014) 544206
Dir: C van Heijst o praem
Subjects: Juveniles, Religion, Philosophy
Founded: 1962

Parsifal Publishing Co*, Lange Elzenstr 59, B-2000 Antwerp   Tel: (031) 323378
Chief Executive and Rights & Permissions: Christian Vandekerkhove; *Production:* Erna Droesbeke
Associate Company: Editions Verrycken (qv)
Subjects: Occult, Mystic, Parapsychology, Philosophy
Bookshops (jointly owned with Editions Verrycken, qv): Librairie Verrycken, Wiegstr 30, B-2000 Antwerp; Occult Bookshop, Hoogstr 68, B-2000 Antwerp
Founded: 1979
ISBN Publisher's Prefix: 90-6458

Uitgeverij **Patmos***, Kapelsestr 222, B-2080 Kapellen   Tel: (03) 6645320   Telex: 32242 Anvers Dnb
Dirs: J Pelckmans, R Pelckmans
Associate Company: Uitgeverij De Nederlandsche Boekhandel (qv)
Subjects: Education, Juveniles, Religion
ISBN Publisher's Prefix: 90-292

Peeters Publishers, BP 41, B-3000 Leuven (Located at: Bondgenotenlaan 153, Leuven)   Tel: (016) 235170   Telex: 65981 Pulb
Man Dir: Mrs E Peeters
Subjects: History, Philosophy, Religion, Theology, University Textbooks
Miscellaneous: Publish Oriental and foreign-language books

Uitgeverij **Plantyn**, Santvoortbeeklaan 21-23, B-2100 Deurne, Antwerp   Tel: (03) 3247897
Dir: F Van Hoof
Subjects: Education (all levels)
Founded: 1950
Miscellaneous: Firm is a member of Kluwer Group, Netherlands (qv)

Pre-Ecole, an imprint of Editions Chantecler (qv)

Preschool, an imprint of Zuidnederlandse Uitgeverij NV (qv)

Presses agronomiques de Gembloux ASBL+, 2 passage des Déportés, B-5800 Gembloux   Tel: (081) 612958   Telex: 59482 Fsagx
Dir: M C Debouche
Subjects: Agriculture, Forestry, Botany, Chemistry, Mathematics, Physics, Technical
Founded: 1965
ISBN Publisher's Prefix: 2-87016

Presses universitaires de Bruxelles ASBL, 42 ave Paul Heger, B-1050 Brussels
Tel: (02) 6499780
President: Thierry Lambrecht; *Man Dir:* Annik Goudsmet; *Sales:* Henri de Smet
Subjects: University Textbooks, especially Philosophy, Medicine, Engineering, Economics, General Science, Architecture
Bookshop: Librairie des Presses universitaires de Bruxelles (qv under Major Booksellers)
Founded: 1958
ISBN Publisher's Prefix: 2-500

Presses universitaires de Liège ASBL, Domaine Universitaire, Sart-Tilman Bâtiment B7, B-4000 Liège 1   Tel: (041) 562218
Subjects: Law, Political & Social Sciences, Medicine, General
Founded: 1969

Presses universitaires de Namur+, 8 Rempart de la Vierge, B-5000 Namur
Tel: (081) 229061   Telex: 59222 Facnam
Dir: P Rummens
Subjects: Publications of Namur University faculties (especially History, Literature, Philosophy, Religion, Geography, Science, Social Sciences, Computer Science, Law, University Textbooks)
1987: 10 titles   *Founded:* 1977
ISBN Publisher's Prefix: 2-87037

Prins, an imprint of Elsevier Librico NV (qv)

Pro Civitate, now Crédit Communal de Belgique (qv)

SA **Procura**, 26 rue Emile Carpentier, B-1070 Brussels   Tel: (02) 5212350   Telex: 22733
Man Dir: F Vanes
Subjects: Travel, General & Political Science, Educational Materials
Founded: 1881

Prodim SPRL+, 184 blvd Général Jacques, B-1050 Brussels Tel: (02) 6405970
Production et Diffusion medico-techniques SPRL
Editorial Dir, Production, Rights & Permissions: P Nile
Subjects: Textbooks, Medicine, Fundamental Sciences of Medicine
Bookshop: At above address
Founded: 1968
ISBN Publisher's Prefix: 2-87017

Production et Diffusion medico-techniques SPRL, see Prodim SPRL

Henri **Proost** & Cie, Everdongenlaan 23, B-2300 Turnhout Tel: (014) 416911 Telex: 33185 Fax: (014) 416492
Man Dir: Jef Proost; *Sales Dir:* Jan Jacobs
Subsidiary Companies: Bedford Editions Ltd, Salamander Books Ltd (qqv, both UK)
Subjects: Religion, Juveniles, Cookery, Gardening, Travel, History

André De **Rache***, Editeur, 127 rue du Château d'Eau, B-1180 Brussels Tel: (02) 3743950
Man Dir: A De Rache
Subjects: Belles Lettres, Poetry, Biography, Art
Founded: 1954

Reader's Digest SA*, 12a Grande Place, B-1000 Brussels Tel: (02) 4287100 Telex: 21876
Man Dir: R Morley
Subjects: Education, Sport & Games, Geography, History, Travel
Founded: 1947

Reinart Uitgaven, now Uitgeverij Dap-Reinart SV (qv)

La **Renaissance** du Livre SA*, 12 pl du Petit-Sablon, B-1000 Brussels Tel: (02) 5119914/5134751
Man Dir: H Roland Bousson
Subjects: Belles Lettres, History, Art, Juveniles, Law, Business, Reference, Educational Materials
Founded: 1923

Fondation André **Renard**, 9-11 pl St Paul, B-4000 Liège Tel: (041) 206211
Dirs: R Gillon, G Vandersmissen

La **Revue** nouvelle ASBL, 26 rue Potagère, B-1030 Brussels Tel: (02) 2187818
Dir: Michel Molitor
Subjects: Languages, Law, Economics, Political & Social Sciences, Education, Religion, Philosophy, Literature, Linguistics, Bibliography
Founded: 1945

De **Roerdomp***, Vandereydtlaan 46, B-2160 Brecht Tel: (031) 138401
Dir: J Lombaerts
Subjects: Law, Political & Social Sciences, Literature, Linguistics
Founded: 1967

Rossel Edition SA*, 112 rue Royale, B-1000 Brussels Tel: (02) 2177750 Telex: 24298
Manager: J Gerlache; *Rights & Permissions:* André-Paul Duchâteau
Associate Company: Rossel Edition, 73 rue d'Anjou, F-75008 Paris, France
Subjects: Education, Sports and Games, Documentary Reports, Period History, Juveniles, Periodicals
Founded: 1972

Publications de **Saint-André***, 1 allée de Clerlande, B-1340 Ottignies Tel: (010) 417463
Subjects: Pastoral, Liturgical, Anthropology, Contemporary Architecture (all periodicals)

Publications des Facultés universitaires **Saint Louis**, 43 blvd du Jardin Botanique, B-1000 Brussels Tel: (02) 2117894
Man Dir: M van de Kerchove; *Sales, Publicity:* Mella Thoua
Subjects: Humanities, Philosophy, Psychology, Theology, History, Law, Economics, Statistics
Founded: 1973
ISBN Publisher's Prefix: 2-8028

Samsom (CED), see CED-Samsom

Sanderus PVBA*, Remparden 36, B-9700 Oudenaarde Tel: (055) 311130
Dir: M van den Abeele
Subject: Textbooks
Founded: 1959

Schaubroeck PVBA*, Drapstr 23, B-9730 Nazareth Tel: (091) 854227
Dir: J Schaubroeck
Subjects: Law, Political & Social Sciences
Founded: 1911

Schott Frères SPRL (Éditeurs de Musique)*, 30 rue St-Jean, B-1000 Brussels Tel: (02) 5123980
Man Dir: Jean-Jacques Junne
Associate Company: Schott Frères Sàrl, France (qv)
Subject: Music
Founded: 1823

Editions **Sciences et Lettres**, see Imprimerie Georges Thone SA

De **Seizoenen** PVBA*, Prins Leopoldlei 60, B-2510 Mortsel Tel: (031) 496034
Dir: P Vanhout
Subject: Juveniles
Founded: 1958

Editions **Service** SA, 232 blvd Em Bockstael, B-1020 Brussels Tel: (02) 4282627/4280520
Dir: M Geets
Subjects: Law, Technical, Periodicals
Founded: 1949

Services interbancaires SA, 52 ave de Tervueren, B-1040 Brussels Tel: (02) 7360507
Dir: L Dewincklear
Subjects: Law, Political & Social Sciences, Periodicals
Founded: 1968

Uitgeverij De **Sikkel** NV+*, Nijverheidsstr 8, B-2150 Malle Tel: (03) 3124761 Telex: 34641 Sikkel
Man Dir: Karel de Bock
Subjects: Educational Books, Sports, Music, Software, Periodicals
Founded: 1919
ISBN Publisher's Prefix: 90-260

Simon Stevin NV, Zennestr 37, B-1000 Brussels Tel: (02) 5121085/5138295 Telex: 23602 Boetis
Dirs: L Van Hoorick, J De Hertogh
Parent Company: N V Drukkerij De Bouwkroniek
Subjects: Building, Wood Science, Technical, Surveying, Architecture, Engineering Science, Periodicals
Founded: 1930

Sinite Parvulos VBVB, B-3590 Hamont-Achel Tel: (011) 641078
Dir: L van Gassel
Subjects: Devotional Literature and Miscellaneous

Sintal*, Dekenstr 28, B-3000 Louvain Tel: (016) 223470
Dir: J Devos
Subjects: Geography, History, Ethnography, Travel
Founded: 1928

Snoeck-Ducaju en Zoon NV*, Begijnhoflaan 464, B-9000 Ghent Tel: (091) 234897 Telex: 12765
Dir: S Snoeck
Subjects: Snoeck's Literary Yearbook, Snoeck's almanakken
Founded: 1782

Soethoudt & Co NV*, Olieweg 15, B-2020 Antwerp Tel: (03) 2385820
Dir: W Soethoudt
Subjects: Literature, Poetry, General, Linguistics, Juveniles, Paperbacks
Founded: 1964

Soledi (Imprimeur-Editeur) SA*, 37 rue de la Province, B-4020 Liège
Dir: P Mardaga; *Rights & Permissions:* P Mardaga, Gigi Dony
Associate Company: Pierre Mardaga SA (qv)
Subjects: Arts, Languages, Education, Philosophy, Architecture, Linguistics, General
Founded: 1919

Sonneville Press (Uitgeverij) VTW, Postbox 1, B-8000 Bruges 1 (Located at: Singel 5, B-8200 St-Andries, Bruges)
Dir: J Sonneville
Subjects: Arts, Law, Political & Social Sciences, Education, Sport & Games, Geography, History, Ethnography, Travel, Religion, Philosophy, Literature, Linguistics, Music, Periodicals, Paperbacks
Founded: 1987 (1966)

Het **Spectrum** (IUM NV)*, Bijkhoevelaan 12, B-2110 Wijnegem Tel: (03) 3539800 Telex: 33545 Spant Fax: (03) 3531187
Dir: M Cornu
Parent Companies: Jointly owned by VNU Book Group, Netherlands (qv) and Internationale Uitgevers Maatschappij NV, Van Schoonbekestr 34-38, B-2018 Antwerp
Subjects: Arts, Bibliography, Philology, Languages, Law, Political & Social Sciences, Education, Sport & Games, Mathematics, Physics, Technical, Geography, History, Ethnography, Travel, Medicine, Religion, Philosophy, Literature, Linguistics, Music, Periodicals, General, Comics
Founded: 1946

Le **Sphinx** SA*, 5 rue de Danemark, B-1060 Brussels Tel: (02) 5370437/5381044
Publisher: Marcel Leempoel
Subjects: General Fiction, Belles Lettres, General
Founded: 1951

Splichal SA*, Apostoliekenstr 103, B-2300 Turnhout Tel: (014) 422441
Man Dir: L Verwaest Snr; *Dir:* L Verwaest Jnr
Subject: Religion
Founded: 1856

Standaard Uitgeverij (Scriptoria NV)*, Belgiëlei 147a, B-2018 Antwerp Tel: (03) 2395900 Telex: 31421 Edista
Man Dir: A G H A Baart
Parent Company: Buhrmann-Tetterode BV, Paalbergweg 2, 1105 AG Amsterdam, Netherlands
Associate Company: Editions Erasme (Scriptoria NV) (qv)
Subjects: General Fiction, How-to, Politics, Economics, General Science, Textbooks, Encyclopaedias, Dictionaries, Comics, Juveniles
Founded: 1924
ISBN Publisher's Prefix: 90-02

Steppe*, Aalstersesteenweg 99-101, B-9400 Ninove Tel: (054) 332591 Cable Add: Steppe-Ninove
Subjects: Textbooks, Mathematics, Physics, Technical

E **Story-Scientia** (NV M en I), 34-35 de Jamblinne de Meuxplein, B-1040 Brussels Tel: (02) 7368980
Dir: B Houdmont
Subject: Law
Founded: 1960
Miscellaneous: Firm is a member of Kluwer Group, Netherlands (qv)

De **Techniek***, J De Bomstr 61, B-2000 Antwerp Tel: (031) 378567
Dir: J Roggen
Subjects: Textbooks, Mathematics, Physics, Technical
Founded: 1926

BVBA Uitgeverij De **Tempel**, Tempelhof 41, B-8000 Bruges Tel: (050) 315505
Man Dir: Jeanne Verbeke
Subjects: Philosophy, Social Science (especially European unification), Archaeology
1986: 2 titles *Founded:* 1985 (1905)

Imprimerie Georges **Thone** SA*, 11-19 rue de la Commune, B-4020 Liège Tel: (041) 426154
Man Dir: Louis Maraval; *Editorial, Sales, Production, Publicity, Rights & Permissions:* Irene Severyns
Subsidiary Company: Editions Sciences et Lettres (at above address)
Subject: School and University Textbooks
Founded: 1898

Toulon*, Sportstr 35, B-8400 Ostend Tel: (059) 800927
Dir: P A Toulon
Subjects: Educational, Technical

Trois Arches+, 3 rue d'Ostin, B-5842 La Bruyère Tel: (081) 512333
Also known as 3 Arches
Man Dir, Rights & Permissions: Hugues Boucher
Subjects: Literature, Fine Art, Architecture, Photography, Children's, Bibliography
Founded: 1978

Editions **U G A** (Uitgeverij), Stijn Streuvelslaan 73, B-8710 Kortrijk-Heule Tel: (056) 355881 Cable Add: Uga Telex: 85579
Dir: L Deschildre; *Editorial, Sales:* Patrick van Assche
Branch Offs: Résidence Leopold, rue Borgnet 14, B-5000 Namur; 19 rue Guimard Bte 2, B-1040 Brussels
Subjects: Administration, History, Europe, Social Science, Law, Language, Journals
Founded: 1948
ISBN Publisher's Prefix: 90-6768

U O P C, see Union et Orientation de Presse et de Culture SA

Union et Orientation de Presse et de Culture (UOPC) SA*, 216 chaussée de Wavre, B-1040 Brussels Tel: (02) 6489689
Dir: Mrs Lefebvre
Subjects: Religion, Philosophy
Bookshop: UOPC (qv under Major Booksellers)
Founded: 1923

Unistad VZW, J Moorkensstr 46, B-2600 Antwerp Tel: (03) 3225243
Dir: R Claes
Orders to: Volkaertslei 8, B-2220 Wommelgem, Belgium; Bergschot 200, 4817 PD Breda, Netherlands
Parent Company: Città Nuova Editrice, Italy (qv for associate companies)

Universa PVBA, Hoenderstr 24, B-9200 Wetteren Tel: (091) 691563
Man Dir: A De Meester
Subjects: Textbooks, Geography, History, Ethnography, Travel
Founded: 1958

Universitaire Pers Leuven, see Leuven University Press

Editions **universitaires** SA, see under Editions

Presses **universitaires** de Bruxelles, de Liège, de Namur, see under Presses

Publications des Facultés **universitaires** Saint Louis, see under Saint Louis

Editions de l'**Université** de Bruxelles, 26 ave Paul Héger, B-1050 Brussels Tel: (02) 6423799 Telex: 23069 Unilib
Man Dir: Mrs M Mat
Subjects: Humanities, Social Sciences, Science, Medicine, Periodicals
1985: 46 titles *1986:* 36 titles *Founded:* 1972
ISBN Publisher's Prefix: 2-8004

Vademecum de Pharmacie*, 3 pl Rotenberg, B-4700 Eupen Tel: (087) 553271
Man Dir: Paul Schiltz
Subjects: Reference, Medicine, Pharmacy
Founded: 1963
ISBN Publisher's Prefix: 2-87058

Imprimeur — Editeur **Vaillant-Carmanne** SA, BP 22, B-4000 Liège Tel: (041) 223361
Man Dir: G Dengis
Subjects: Science, Education, Political Science, Belles Lettres, Religion, Medicine, Law, History, Science, Technical
Founded: 1838

Vander Publishing*, 321 ave des Volontaires, B-1150 Brussels Tel: (02) 7629804
Man Dir: Willy Vandermeulen
Associate Company: Nauwelaerts Edition SA (qv)
Subjects: Psychology, General & Social Science, Law, Economics, Politics, Languages
Founded: 1880
ISBN Publisher's Prefix: 2-8008

Librairie **Vanderlinden** SA*, 17 rue des Grands-Carmes, B-1000 Brussels Tel: (02) 5116140
Man Dir: J Vanderlinden
Subjects: Art, General Fiction, Juveniles, Textbooks, Paperbacks, Science, Mathematics
Bookshop: See under Major Booksellers
Founded: 1897

L **Vanmelle** (Drukkerij) NV*, Lt Willemotlaan 80, B-9910 Mariakerke (Ghent) Tel: (091) 233586 Telex: 11850
Dir: L Vanmelle
Subjects: Textbooks, Juveniles

Vereniging van de belgische medische wetenschappelijke genootschappen VZW, see Association des Sociétés scientifiques médicales belges (ASBL)

Editions **Verrycken***, Wiegstr 30, B-2000 Antwerp Tel: (031) 323378
Man Dir, Editorial, Rights & Permissions: Christian Vandekerkhove; *Production:* E Droesbeke; *Sales, Publicity:* E Vandekerkhove
Orders to: Verrycken Booksellers (at above address)
Associate Company: Parsifal Publishing Co (qv)
Subjects: Philosophy, Medicine, Parapsychology, Occult
Bookshops (jointly owned with Parsifal Publishing Co, qv): Librarie Verrycken (at above address); Occult Bookshop, Hoogstr 68, B-2000 Antwerp
Founded: 1976
ISBN Publisher's Prefix: 90-70181

Les Editions **Vie** ouvrière ASBL*, 4 rue d'Anderlecht, B-1000 Brussels Tel: (02) 5125090
Chief Executive: André Samain
Subjects: Religion, Juveniles, Psychology, Social Science, University & Secondary Textbooks, History, Economics, Photography
Founded: 1958
ISBN Publisher's Prefix: 2-87003

Albert de **Visscher** Editeur*, 60 rue Veydt, B-1050 Brussels Tel: (02) 5373518
Man Dir: Albert de Visscher
Subjects: Music, Art, Medicine, General Science
Founded: 1944

Vlaams Ekonomisch Verbond VZW, Brouwersvliet 5 Bus 4, B-2000 Antwerp Tel: (03) 2311660
Man Dir: R de Feyter; *Publicity:* M Paeleman
Subjects: Economics, Statistics
Founded: 1926

Vlaamse Bijbelstichting*, St Michielsstr 2, B-3000 Louvain Tel: (016) 337468
Subjects: Religious Literature connected with Catholic Bible production in Belgium, the Netherlands, Austria, Switzerland and Federal Germany
Miscellaneous: Company is a member of AMB (qv under Federal Republic of Germany)

Vlaamse Toeristenbond — Vlaamse Automobilistenbond, Sint-Jacobsmarkt 45, B-2000 Antwerp Tel: (03) 2203414 Telex: 31679
Dir: G Cooreman; *Publicity Manager:* A Bundervoet
Subjects: Tourism, Gastronomy

Drukkerij Het **Volk** NV*, Forelstr 22, B-9000 Ghent Tel: (091) 255701 Telex: 11228
Man Dir: J van Haverbeke
Subject: Juveniles
Bookshop: Boekhandel Het Volk (qv under Major Booksellers)

C De **Vries** Brouwers PVBA*, Haantjeslei 80, B-2000 Antwerp Tel: (03) 2374180
Dir: I de Vries
Subjects: Juveniles, History
Founded: 1946

De **Vroente***, Bosakkersstr 14, B-2460 Kasterlee Tel: (014) 556160
Dir: S Debroey
Subjects: Arts, Textbooks, Education

PVBA Imprimerie-Editions **Vyncke***, Savaanstr 92, B-9000 Ghent Tel: (091) 253960
Dirs: H Vyncke, D Vyncke
Subjects: Textbooks (for technical schools), Periodicals
Founded: 1922

Eugène **Wahle***, Château de la Gotte, B-4150 Nandrin Tel: (041) 715236
Manager: Carole Wahle
Subjects: Literature, History, Art, Archaeology, Geography, History of Glass & Guns
1985: 4 titles *Founded:* 1952
ISBN Publisher's Prefix: 2-87011

Wereldbibliotheek NV*, Leeuwerikstr 23, B-2000 Antwerp Tel: (031) 323642
Dir: L Reinalda
Subjects: Education, Sport & Games, Juveniles, General
Founded: 1947
ISBN Publisher's Prefix: 90-284

Maison d'Editions Ad **Wesmael-Charlier** SA, now Editions De Boeck-Wesmael SA (qv)

44 BELGIUM

Winkler, an imprint of Elsevier Librico NV (qv)

J B Wolters Leuven NV, Blijde-Inkomststr 50, B-3000 Louvain Tel: (016) 233488 Telex: 24525
Man Dir: J Germonprez
Parent Company: Wolters Kluwer NV, Netherlands (qv)
Subjects: Instruction and Education, Secondary & Primary Textbooks, Educational Materials
Founded: 1959
ISBN Publisher's Prefix: 90-309

Wolters Samsom België NV*, Louizalaan 485, B-1050 Brussels Tel: (02) 6499026 Telex: 62067 Wosabe
Parent Company: Wolters Kluwer NV, Netherlands (qv)
Subsidiary Company: CED-Samsom (qv)
Subjects: Publishing, literature distribution, social and fiscal information

Zuidnederlandse Uitgeverij NV+, Cleydaellaan 8, B-2630 Aartselaar, Antwerp Tel: (03) 8878300 Telex: 31739 Zuidb
Man Dir: Jan Vande Velden; *Publisher:* Bart Clinckemalie; *Production:* Eric Feyten; *Rights & Permissions:* Wilfried Wuyts
Subsidiary Companies: Editions Chantecler, Belgium (qv); Editions Chantecler, France; Centrale Uitgeverij, Netherlands
Imprints: Deltas, Preschool
Subjects: General Fiction and Non-fiction, Children's
Founded: 1946
ISBN Publisher's Prefix: 90-243

Literary Agents

Firma **Denis** & Co PVBA*, Sterckshoflei 28-30, B-2100 Antwerp (Deurne) Tel: (03) 3213299

Toneelfonds J **Janssens** PVBA, Kruikstr 14, B-2018 Antwerp Tel: (03) 2391220
Dir: J Janssens
Specialization: Plays

Julien C **Raasveld***, Karel-Meyvisstr 29, B-2710 Hoboken Tel: (03) 8281853
General Manager: Julien C Raasveld
Represents authors, publishers and agencies in and for the Dutch and French territories
Specialization: Fantasy and Science Fiction; Anthologies. Only printed works (no manuscripts)

Book Clubs

Boekengilde de **Clauwaert***, Koning Albertlaan 17, B-3040 Korbeek-Lo, Louvain
Owned by: De Clauwaert (qv)

Dap-Reinart Uitgeven*, Industriepark B4, B-9140 Zele
Owned by: Uitgeverij Dap-Reinart SV (qv)

Major Booksellers

SC **Artis-Historia**, 1 rue Carli, Evere, B-1140 Brussels Tel: (02) 2422320
100 bookshops throughout Belgium
Also Publisher (qv)

Audivox, Rubenslei 23, B-2018 Antwerp Tel: (03) 2328465
Wholesaler of imported educational books
Also Publisher (qv)

Boekhandel **Belis-Vinck**, Lange Leemstr 41, B-2018 Antwerp Tel: (03) 2327448
Manager: R Belis

Librairie **Castaigne** SPRL*, 34 rue du Fosse-aux-Loups, B-1000 Brussels Tel: (02) 2170424
Manager: Alain Lonnoy

Boekhandel **Heideland***, Grote Markt 1, B-3500 Hasselt Tel: (011) 224505
Owned by: Heideland NV (Heideland PVBA) (qv)

Office international de Librairie*, 30 ave Marnix, B-1050 Brussels Tel: (02) 5136675

Librairie des **Presses universitaires de Bruxelles**, 42 ave Paul Heger, B-1050 Brussels Tel: (02) 6499780
Scientific books
Owned by: Presses universitaires de Bruxelles ASBL (qv)

J **Story-Scientia** PVBA*, Van Duyseplein 8, B-9000 Ghent Tel: (091) 255757
Manager: J Story
Importer

Libris **Toison** d'Or SA*, 29 ave de la Toison d'Or, B-1060 Brussels Tel: (02) 5116400 Telex: 24084
Manager: Paul Beauvois

U O P C*, 216 chaussée de Wavre, B-1040 Brussels Tel: (02) 6489689
Owned by: Union et Orientation de Presse et de Culture (UOPC) (qv)

Librairie **Vanderlinden** SA*, 17 rue des Grands-Carmes, B-1000 Brussels Tel: (02) 5116140
Also Publisher (qv)

Boekhandel Het **Volk**, Forelstr 22, B-9000 Ghent
Owned by: Drukkerij Het Volk NV (qv)

Major Libraries

Bibliothèque royale **Albert Ier**, 4 blvd de l'Empereur, B-1000 Brussels Tel: (02) 5195311 Telex: 21157
Koninklijke Bibliotheek Albert I
Head Librarian: Martin Wittek
Publications include: Belgische Bibliografie (Bibliographie de Belgique); Bulletin BR (quarterly)

Archives générales du Royaume*, 2-6 rue de Ruysbroeck, B-1000 Brussels
National Archives

Bibliothèque principale de Bruxelles 1, rue des Riches Claires 24, B-1000 Brussels Tel: (02) 5129569 Telex: 26224

Bibliothèque **Fonds** Quetelet*, 6 rue de l'Industrie, B-1040 Brussels Tel: (02) 5127950
Library of the Ministry of Economic Affairs
Librarian: G De Saedeleer
Publications: Accroissements de la Bibliothèque centrale (Fonds Quetelet) (monthly)

Goethe-Institut — Deutsche Bibliothek, 58 rue Belliard, B-1040 Brussels Tel: (02) 2303970
Librarian: Charlotte Ezold

Institut royal des Sciences naturelles de Belgique, Bibliothèque*, 29 rue Vautier, B-1040 Brussels

Katholieke Universiteit Leuven, Universiteitsbibliotheek, Mgr Ladeuzeplein 21, B-3000 Leuven Tel: (016) 284611 Telex: 25715 Kulbib
University Library of Louvain
Librarian: J Roegiers
Publication: Ex officina (Bulletin of the Friends of Louvain University Library)

Bibliothèque centrale du **Ministère de l'Education** nationale*, 27 rue de Louvain, B-1000 Brussels

Bibliothèque Universitaire **Moretus Plantin***, 19 rue Grandgagnage, B-5000 Namur Tel: (081) 229061 Telex: 59222 Facnam
Librarian: Prof J Denis

Bibliothèque du **Musée royal de Mariemont***, 100 chaussée de Mariemont, B-6510 Morlanwelz-Mariemont Tel: (064) 221243/226563/212193
Librarian: M-B Delattre

Bibliothèque du **Parlement***, 2 Palais de la Nation, pl de la Nation, Brussels

Museum **Plantin-Moretus**, Vrijdagmarkt 22, B-2000 Antwerp Tel: (03) 2322455/2330294
Dir: Dr Francine de Nave; *Librarian:* Liliane Peeters-Demaeyer
Publications on sale include: The Plantin Press (1555-1589): A Bibliography of Works printed and published by Christopher Plantin at Antwerp and Leiden, 6 vols; *The Golden Compasses: A history and evaluation of the printing and publishing*, 2 vols

Bibliotheek **Rijksuniversitair Centrum**, Middelheimlaan 1, B-2020 Antwerp Tel: (03) 2180790 Telex: 33362 Rucabi

Bibliotheek van de **Rijksuniversiteit te Gent**, Rozier 9, B-9000 Ghent Tel: (091) 257571 Telex: 11793 Ubgent

Stadsbibliotheek, Hendrik Conscienceplein 4, B-2000 Antwerp Tel: (03) 2323073/2339712 Telex: 33610 Stbianb
Municipal Library
Dir: R Rennenberg

Bibliothèque centrale de l'**Université Catholique de Louvain**, see Katholieke Universiteit Leuven

Bibliothèque générale de l'**Université de Liège***, 1 pl Cockerill, B-4000 Liège Tel: (041) 420080 Telex: 41456
Head Librarian: Paulette Guillitte
Publication: Bibliotheca Universitatis Leordiensis

Bibliothèques de l'**Université libre de Bruxelles***, 50 ave Franklin D Roosevelt, B-1050 Brussels Tel: (02) 6422380 Telex: 23654 Ulbipe
Librarian: André Uyttebrouck

Universiteit Antwerpen Bibliotheken, Prinsstr 9, B-2000 Antwerp Tel: (03) 2316660 Telex: 33599 Ufsia
Librarian: L Simons
Universiteit Antwerpen consists of Universitaire Faculteiten Sint-Ignatius (UFSIA), Universitaire Instelling Antwerpen (UIA), Rijksuniversitair Centrum Antwerpen (RUCA), each with its own library

Vlaamse Bibliotheek Centrale (VzW)/VBC*, Goudbloemstr 10-12, B-2000 Antwerp Tel: (03) 2324260/2324161
Flemish Central Library

Library Associations

Archief- en Bibliotheekwezen in België, Koninklijke Bibliotheek Albert I, Keizerslaan 4, B-1000 Brussels Tel: (02) 5195351 Telex: 21157
Belgian Association of Archivists and Librarians (Archives et Bibliothèques de Belgique)
General Secretary: Tony Verschaffel
Publication: Archives et Bibliothèques de Belgique

BELGIUM 45

Association belge de Documentation*, BP 110, B-1040 Brussels 26
Belgian Association for Documentation
President: L Van Simaeys; *Secretary:* D Forton
Publications: Cahiers de la Documentation (text in Dutch, English, French); *ABD Flash*

Association des Archivistes et Bibliothécaires, see Archief- en Bibliotheekwezen in België

Association des Bibliothécaires-Documentalistes de l'Institut d'Etudes sociales de l'Etat*, 24 rue de l'Abbaye, B-1050 Brussels Tel: (02) 6493443
Association of Librarians and Documentalists of the State Institute of Social Studies
Secretary: Claire Gerard
Publication: Flash

Association des Bibliothécaires et du Personnel des Bibliothèques des Ministères de Belgique*, Quartier Reine Elisabeth, rue d'Evere – bloc 6, B-1140 Brussels
Association of Librarians and Library Personnel in Belgian Government Departments
President: G Braive

Association nationale des Bibliothécaires d'Expression française*, c/o Bibliothèque centrale de la Ville de Bruxelles, 24 rue des Riches Claires, B-1000 Brussels Tel: (02) 5129569/5124012 Telex: 26224 Slpbrub
National Association of French-speaking Librarians
President: H Leveau; *Secretary:* M Dagneau
Publication: Le Bibliothécaire: Revue d'Information culturelle et bibliographique

Association professionnelle des Bibliothécaires et Documentalistes (APBD), BP 31, B-1070 Brussels
Secretary: Alain Leens
Publications: Bloc-notes; Un cadeau, un livre (annual selection of children's books)

Centre national de Documentation scientifique et technique, 4 blvd de l'Empereur, B-1000 Brussels Tel: (02) 5195661 Telex: 221157
National Centre for Scientific and Technical Documentation
Dir: Dr A Cockx
Publications: Catalogue collectif belge et luxembourgeois des Périodiques étrangers en cours de publication; Inventaire des Centres belges de Recherche disposant d'une Bibliothèque ou d'un Service de Documentation (Directory of Belgian Research Centres and Documentation Services); *Key to Belgian Science (KBS); Belgian Environmental Research Index; Translation Services and Translators' Index (CBT)*

Vereniging van Religieus-Wetenschappelijke Bibliothecarissen*, Minderbroederstr 5, B-3800 St Truiden
Association of Theological Librarians
Secretary: K Van de Casteele, Spoorweglaan 237, B-2610 Wilrijk Tel: (03) 2301890
Publication: VRB-Informatie (quarterly)

Vlaamse Vereniging voor Bibliotheek-, Archief en Documentatiewezen (VVBAD), Goudbloemstr 10-12, B-2008 Antwerp Tel: (03) 2318349
Flemish Association of Librarians, Archivists and Documentalists
General Secretary: L van den Bosch
Publication: Bibliotheek- en Archiefgids (Library Guide) (quarterly)

Library Reference Books and Journals

Book

Inventaire des Centres belges de Recherche disposant d'une Bibliothèque ou d'un Service de Documentation (Directory of Belgian Research Centres and Documentation Services), Centre National de Documentation scientifique et technique, 4 blvd de l'Empereur, B-1000 Brussels

Journals

Archives et Bibliothèques de Belgique, Archief- en Bibliotheekwezen in België, Koninklijke Bibliotheek Albert I, Keizerslaan 4, B-1000 Brussels
Text in Dutch, English, French, German, Italian, Latin and Spanish

Le Bibliothécaire: Revue d'Information culturelle et bibliographique, Association nationale des Bibliothécaires d'Expression française, c/o Bibliothèque centrale de la Ville de Bruxelles, 24 rue des Riches Claires, B-1000 Brussels

Bibliotheek- en Archiefgids (Library Guide) (quarterly), Vlaamse Vereniging voor Bibliotheek-, Archief en Documentatiewezen (VVBAD), Goudbloemstr 10-12, B-2008 Antwerp

Bulletin de Documentation, Ministère des Communications et des PTT, 62 rue de la Roi, B-1040 Brussels
Text in Dutch, English, French and German

Cahiers de la Documentation, Association belge de Documentation, BP 110, B-1040 Brussels 26
Text in Dutch, English, French

Literary Associations and Societies

Académie royale de Langue et de Littérature françaises*, Palais des Académies, 1 rue Ducale, B-1000 Brussels
Royal Academy of French Language and Literature
Permanent Secretary: Georges Sion
Publications: Bulletin, Annuaire, Mémoires

Académie royale des Sciences, des Lettres et des Beaux-Arts de Belgique *, Palais des Académies, 1 rue Ducale, B-1000 Brussels Tel: (02) 5112623
Belgian Royal Academy of Sciences, Letters and Fine Arts
Permanent Secretary: Maurice Leroy
Publications: Monthly Bulletin, Memoirs, Year Book

Antwerp Bibliophile Society, c/o Museum Plantin-Moretus, Vrijdagmarkt 22, B-2000 Antwerp
Publication: De Gulden Passer

Association des Ecrivains belges de Langue française, Maison Camille Lemonnier – Maison des Ecrivains, 150 chaussée de Wavre, B-1050 Brussels Tel: (02) 5122968/5122863
Association of Belgian Writers in the French Language
President: Roger Foulon; *Secretary-General:* Philippe Delaby
Publications include: Nos Lettres Informations (ten a year)

Commission belge de Bibliographie, 80-84 rue des Tanneurs, B-1000 Brussels
Belgian Commission of Bibliography

Chairman: R Brucher
Publications: Bulletin (quarterly); *Coll: Bibliographia Belgica*

Koninklijke Academie voor Nederlandse Taal- en Letterkunde*, Koningstr 18, B-9000 Ghent Tel: (091) 252774
Royal Academy of Dutch Language and Literature
Permanent Secretary: M Hoebeke

Koninklijke Academie voor Wetenschappen, Letteren en Schone Kunsten van België, Hertogsstr 1, B-1000 Brussels Tel: (02) 5112623
Belgian Royal Academy of Sciences, Letters and Fine Arts
Permanent Secretary: Gerard Verbeke
Publications include: Proceedings (Academiae Analecta); Memoirs; National Biography; Fontes Historiae Artis Neerlandicae; Year Book; Iuris Scripta Historica
See also under Publishers

International P E N Club, Belgian French-Speaking Centre, ave du 11 novembre 76, BP 7, B-1040 Brussels Tel: (02) 7360214
President: Georges Sion; *General Secretary:* Raymond Quinot

International P E N Club, Flemish-Speaking Centre*, Albert Heyrbautlaan 48, B-1710 Dilbeek
General Secretary: Willem M Roggeman
Publications: PEN-Club Tijdingen; Poetry in Flanders now; Ten Modern Poets from Flanders; Ten Modern Essays from Flanders

Société belge des Auteurs, Compositeurs et Editeurs (SABAM), 75-77 rue d'Arlon, B-1040 Brussels Tel: (02) 2302660 Telex: 65854
Belgian Society of Authors, Composers and Publishers
President: Vic Legley; *Man Dirs:* Joseph Dethier, Ernest van der Eyken
Publication: Bulletin (quarterly)

Société de Langue et de Littérature wallonnes ASBL, Université de Liège, 7 pl du XX août, B-4000 Liège Tel: (041) 231960
Secretary: Victor George
Library: Literary and Philological collections
Publications: Bulletin de la Société de Langue et de Littérature wallonnes, Dialectes de Wallonie (both periodically)

Société royale des Bibliophiles et Iconophiles de Belgique, 4 blvd de l'Empereur, B-1000 Brussels
Secretary: A Grisay
Publication: Le Livre et l'Estampe (The Book and the Print) (twice a year)

Vereeniging der Antwerpsche Bibliophielen, c/o Museum Plantin-Moretus, Vrijdagmarkt 22, B-2000 Antwerp Tel: (03) 2322455/2330294
Antwerp Bibliophile Society
Editorial Secretary: M Del Schepper
Publication: De Gulden Passer (annual)

Literary Periodicals

Dietsche Warande en Belfort, Standaard Uitgeverij (Scriptoria NV), Belgiëlei 147a, B-2018 Antwerp
Journal for literature, art and spiritual life

Flambeau, 75 ave Emile de Beco, Brussels 5
Belgian review of political and literary questions

De Gulden Passer, Antwerp Bibliophile Society, c/o Museum Plantin-Moretus, Vrijdagmarkt 22, B-2000 Antwerp

Livres et Disques (Books and Records), Centre d'Action culturelle de la Communauté d'Expression française, 12 rue Saintraint, B-5000 Namur

Mandragora, Acacalaan 58, B-9620 Zottegem
Journal for literature and art; text in Dutch

Marginales, Albert Ayguesparse, 118 rue Marconi, B-1180 Brussels
Review of ideas and letters

Nieuw Vlaams Tijdschrift (New Flemish Journal), Leeuwerikstr 41, Antwerp

Revue générale belge (General Belgian Review), 21 rue de la Limité, B-1030 Brussels

Revue nouvelle (New Review), 305 ave van Volxem, B-1190 Brussels

Ruimten, Antwerpsesteenweg 488, Hoboken, Antwerp
Text in Dutch and German

Scarabée, Centre européen de Diffusion de la Culture, 137 rue de Livourne, Brussels

Streven, Sanderusstr 5, B-2000 Antwerp

Trefpunt (Meeting-point), Blankenbergs Literair Archief Trefpunt, Kerkstr 41, Te Blankenberge

Literary Prizes

Goblet d'**Alviella** Prize*
For the best work of a strictly scientific and objective character relating to the history of religions, published by a Belgian author. 50,000 francs. Awarded every five years. Enquiries to Académie royale de Belgique, Palais des Académies, 1 rue Ducale, B-1000 Brussels

Lode **Baekelmans** Prize
For the best literary work in Dutch — novel, poetry, play, radio play, essay, etc — dealing with the sea, sailors, navigation, the harbour, inland navigation or related topics. A prize of 50,000 francs is awarded every three years: the recipients must be Belgian nationals. Enquiries to the Koninklijke Academie voor Nederlandse Taal- en Letterkunde, Koningstr 18, B-9000 Ghent

Beernaert Prize*
For the most outstanding work of a Belgian author written in French language. Awarded annually. Enquiries to Académie royale de Langue et de Littérature françaises, Palais des Académies, 1 rue Ducale, B-1000 Brussels

Belgian Government Prizes for Literature (Ministry of the Flemish Community)*
Triennial State Prizes for prose, poetry, drama, essay and youth and children's literature. A triennial Great State Prize for a Literary Career. A triennial State Prize for the best translation of a Flemish literary work. Each year two, and every three years three, of these prizes may be awarded. The ordinary prizes amount to 200,000 francs and the Great State Prize to 400,000 francs. In 1984 the Great State Prize was awarded to M Rosseels; the State Prize for prose to H Claus. Enquiries to Ministerie van de Vlaamse Gemeenschap, Koloniënstr 29-31, B-1000 Brussels

Belgian Government Prizes for Literature (Ministry of French Culture)*
An annual State Prize for Literature, in turn awarded for prose, drama and poetry. A quinquennial State Prize for Critique and Essay and a quinquennial State Prize for a Literary Career are also awarded. The annual State Prize amounts to 175,000 francs, the Prize for Critique and Essay to 225,000 francs, and the State Prize for a Literary Career to 300,000 francs. Enquiries to Exécutif de la Communauté française de Belgique, Palais des Beaux-Arts, 23 rue Raventein, B-1000 Brussels

Ernest **Bouvier-Parviliez** Prize*
For the entire work of a Belgian author written in French. Awarded every four years. Enquiries to Académie royale de Langue et de Littérature françaises, Palais des Académies, 1 rue Ducale, B-1000 Brussels

Felix **Denayer** Prize*
For a single work or the entire literary work of a Belgian written in French. Awarded annually. Enquiries to Académie royale de Langue et de Littérature françaises, Palais des Académies, 1 rue Ducale, B-1000 Brussels

Jules **Duculot** Prize*
For a work in print or manuscript form, written in French, dealing with the history of philosophy. Awarded only to Belgians, or to foreigners holding an academic grade granted by a Belgian university. Printed work must have been published in the five years prior to the end of the relevant period. The prize is awarded for what appears the most deserving work, irrespective of whether it has been submitted for entry or not. 90,000 francs. Awarded every five years. Enquiries to Académie royale de Belgique, Palais des Académies, 1 rue Ducale, B-1000 Brussels

Charles **Duvivier** Prize*
For the Belgian author of the best work on the history of Belgian or foreign law, or on the history of Belgian political, judicial or administrative institutions. 50,000 francs. Awarded every three years. Enquiries to Académie royale de Belgique, Palais des Académies, 1 rue Ducale, B-1000 Brussels

Joseph **Gantrelle** Prize*
For a work in classical philology. 60,000 francs. Awarded biennially to Belgian authors. Enquiries to Académie royale de Belgique, Palais des Académies, 1 rue Ducale, B-1000 Brussels

Grand Franco-Belgian Literary Prize, see French Literary Prizes

Tobie **Jonckheere** Prize*
For a work, in published or manuscript form, devoted to the educational sciences. 50,000 francs. Awarded every three years. Enquiries to Académie royale de Belgique, Palais des Académies, 1 rue Ducale, B-1000 Brussels

Hubert **Krains** Prize
Awarded biennially (alternately prose and poetry) for the unpublished work of a writer below the age of 40. 20,000 francs. Founded in 1950 by the Association of Belgian Writers in the French Language in memory of one of its presidents. Awarded in 1985 for prose to Françoise Leroy-Lison. Enquiries to Association des Ecrivains belges de Langue française, Maison Camille Lemonnier – Maison des Ecrivains, 150 chaussée de Wavre, B-1050 Brussels

Malpertuis Prize*
For an outstanding contribution to Belgian literature in the field of drama, poetry, short story or essay written in French. Awarded biennially. Enquiries to the Académie royale de Langue et de Littérature françaises, Palais des Académies, 1 rue Ducale, B-1000 Brussels

Joseph-Edmond **Marchal** Prize*
For the Belgian author of the best work, in print or in manuscript form, on national antiques or archaeology. 50,000 francs. Awarded every five years. Winner for thirteenth period (1978-1982), Raymond Brulet. Enquiries to Académie royale de Belgique, Palais des Académies, 1 rue Ducale, B-1000 Brussels

Albert **Mockel** Grand Prize for Poetry*
For the best Belgian poet writing in French. Awarded every five years. Enquiries to Académie royale de Langue et de Littérature françaises, Palais des Académies, 1 rue Ducale, B-1000 Brussels

Gilles **Nélod** Prize
Founded in 1984 by Gilles Nélod and administered by the Association of Belgian Writers in the French Language. Awarded biennially for a previously unpublished work of fiction. 10,000 francs. Awarded in 1986 to Robert Montal. Enquiries to Association des Ecrivains belges de Langue française, Maison Camille Lemonnier – Maison des Ecrivains, 150 chaussée de Wavre, B-1050 Brussels

Emil **Polak** Prize*
For a distinguished literary work written in French, preferably by a poet. Awarded biennially. Enquiries to Académie royale de Langue et de Littérature françaises, Palais des Académies, 1 rue Ducale, B-1000 Brussels

Victor **Rossel** Prize*
For the best novel, or collection of short stories published during the year, written in French by a Belgian author. 200,000 francs. Awarded annually. Enquiries to 'Le Soir', 21 pl de Louvain, B-1000 Brussels

Saint-Genois Prize*
For the author of the best historical or literary work written in Dutch. 50,000 francs. Awarded every five years. Enquiries to Académie royale de Belgique, Palais des Académies, 1 rue Ducale, B-1000 Brussels

Suzanne **Tassier** Prize*
For a Belgian woman who, following study at a Belgian university, has obtained at least a doctorate. The prize is awarded for a major scientific work, dealing with a subject from history, law, philology or the social sciences: failing a meritorious work from one of these branches, then for a subject from the natural sciences, medicine or mathematics. Preference will be given to a work of an historical nature, in its widest sense. 60,000 francs. Awarded every two years. Enquiries to Académie royale de Belgique, Palais des Académies, 1 rue Ducale, B-1000 Brussels

Auguste **Teirlinck** Prize*
For a contribution to Flemish literature. 50,000 francs. Awarded every five years. Enquiries to Académie royale de Belgique, Palais des Académies, 1 rue Ducale, B-1000 Brussels

Carton de **Wiart** Prize*
For a book in the field of literary history or on subjects which relate to Belgian life. Alternately awarded for a work in French and in Flemish. 10,000 francs. Awarded every five years. Enquiries to Belgian Ministry of National Education, 67 rue Royale, B-1000 Brussels

Translation Agencies and Associations

Centre belge de Traduction, 4 blvd de l'Empereur, B-1000 Brussels Tel: (02) 5195656 Telex: 21157 Fax: (02) 5195679
Dir: Mme I Clemens

Belize

General Information

Language: English (and Spanish)
Religion: Catholic and various Protestant denominations
Population: 166,000
Bank Hours: 0800-1300 Monday-Thursday; 0800-1200, 1500-1800 Friday
Shop Hours: 0730-1130, 1300-16000 Monday-Saturday (some open 1900-2100 evenings); generally early closing Wednesday
Currency: 100 cents = 1 Belize dollar
Export/Import Information: No tariff on books. General licence. Nominal exchange controls
Copyright: UCC (see International section)

Major Booksellers

Belize Book Shop (Anglican Diocese)*, PO Box 147, Belize City (Located at: Corner Regent St & Rectory Lane, Belize City) Tel: 2054 Cable Add: Literary Belize
Manager: Shirley Smiling

Beuhler's Shoppe*, Fort George Hotel Lobby, Belize City Tel: 3491

The **Book Centre***, 144 North Front St, PO Box 426, Belize City Tel: 7457
Manager: Thomas Donovan

Christian Literature*, Christian Literature Centre, PO Box 76, Belize City (Located at: 66 Cnr King St & Plues St, Belize City) Tel: 2993
Manager: Bernard W Hudson

The **Emporium***, 2 Bishop St, Belize City Tel: 2566

Major Library

National Library Service*, The Central Library, PO Box 287, Bliss Institute, Belize City Tel: 7267
Chief Librarian: L G Vernon

Library Association

Belize Library Association, Central Library, PO Box 287, Bliss Institute, Belize City Tel: 7267
Secretary: Robert Hulse
Publication: Belize Library Association Bulletin

Benin

General Information

Language: French
Religion: About 15% Christian (mostly Roman Catholic), 13% Islamic, remainder traditional beliefs
Population: 3.6 million
Bank Hours: 0800-1130, 1430-1530 Monday-Friday
Shop Hours: 0800-1200, 1430-1730 Monday-Saturday. Larger ones close Monday, some open for a few hours Sunday morning
Currency: franc CFA
Export/Import Information: Import licence required but issued automatically for imports from EEC countries. Exchange controls for non-franc zone
Copyright: Berne (see International section)

Publishers

Government Printer (Office nationale d'edition de presse et d'imprimerie)*, BP 1210, Porto Novo Tel: 314061

Maison d'Edition **A B M***, BP 889, Cotonou Tel: 330690
Bookshops: Librarie-Papeterie ABM (qv under Major Booksellers)

Major Booksellers

Librairie-Papeterie **A B M***, BP 9086, Cotonou Tel: 312819
Also: Porto Novo
Owned by: Maison d'Edition ABM (qv)

Centre de Littérature Chrétienne*, BP 34, Cotonou

Librairie **Drouot** (Ets Robert Drouot)*, BP 33, Cotonou Tel: 3451

La **Maison** du Livre*, BP 341, Cotonou

Librairie **Nationale** (Ministère Education National)*, Porto Novo

Librairie SA Gaston **Nègre***, BP 52, Cotonou

Librairie **Notre Dame***, Ave Clozel, BP 307, Cotonou Tel: 314094
Manager: Damienne Yayi

Librairie **Protestante***, Ave Proche, BP 34, Cotonou

Sonapal*, BP 1389, Cotonou

Major Libraries

Archives nationales du Benin*, BP 6, Porto Novo
Director: A S Tidjari

Bibliothèque nationale du Benin*, BP 401, Porto Novo Tel: 212585

Institut national pour la formation et la recherche en éducation (Centre de documentation et d'information pédagogique), BP 437, Porto Novo Tel: 213486
Chief Librarian: Euloge Aigbede

Service de la Documentation de la publication, d'information scientifique et technique, BP 437, Porto Novo
Dir: G Metinhoue
Publication: Courrier de la Recherche au Bénin

Bibliothèque **Universitaire centrale***, BP 526, Cotonou Tel: 360074/360126 Cable Add: Biblionationale
Chief Librarian: Valentine Quenum
Publications: Bibliographie nationale (in preparation)

Bermuda

General Information

Language: English
Religion: Anglican
Population: 56,000
Bank Hours: 0930-1500 Monday-Thursday; 0930-1500, 1630-1800 Friday
Shop Hours: 0900-1700 Monday-Saturday
Currency: 100 cents = 1 Bermuda dollar. US currency circulates
Export/Import Information: No tariff on books and advertising matter. No import licence. Exchange controls on imports valued over $100
Copyright: Berne, UCC (see International section)

Publishers

Bermuda Press Ltd*, Reid St, Hamilton
Subject: Literature

Bermudian Publishing Co*, PO Box 283, Hamilton 5
Editor: Dinah Darby
Subjects: Social, General Affairs, Sport

Royal Gazette Ltd*, PO Box 1025, Hamilton Tel: 55881
General Manager and Rights & Permissions: K R Jensen; *Editorial:* D L White; *Sales:* R E Osborne
Subject: Literature

Major Booksellers

Baxters Ltd*, PO Box 1009, Hamilton 5 (Located at: Burnaby St, Hamilton) Tel: 23292 Telex: 3246 Cwt Xagy
Manager: Jonathan Baxter

Bermuda Book Store Ltd, Queen St, Hamilton Tel: 53698

The **Bookmart***, In the Annex on Reid St, Hamilton 5 Tel: 51647
Manager: E Linda Young

Major Libraries

Bermuda Archives, Government Administration Building, Hamilton HM12 Tel: 55151
Publications include: A guide to the records of Bermuda (1980)

Bermuda Library, Par-la-Ville, Hamilton HM11 Tel: 52905 Telex: 3775 Modus
Librarian: Cyril O Packwood

Bolivia

General Information

Language: Spanish
Religion: Roman Catholic
Population: 5.6 million
Bank Hours: 0900-1200, 1400-1630 Monday-Friday
Shop Hours: 0900-1200, 1400-1800 Monday-Friday; 0900-1200 Saturday
Currency: 100 centavos = 1 peso Boliviano
Export/Import Information: Member of the Latin American Free Trade Association. No tariffs on books, except for 10% on luxury bindings. No import licences, except for textbooks, but no pornography allowed. No advertising that includes imitation money, stamps, etc allowed. No exchange controls
Copyright: Buenos Aires (see International section)

Book Trade Organization

Cámara Boliviana del Libro*, Casilla 682, La Paz (Located at: Ave 20 de Octubre 2005, Edf Las Palmas Planta Baja of 5, La Paz) Tel: (02) 327039
Bolivian Booksellers' Association
President: Javier Gisbert

Book Trade Reference Books and Journals

Book

Informativo Amigo literario, Editorial los Amigos del Libro, Casilla 450, Cochabamba

Journals

Bibliografía Boliviana, Editorial los Amigos del Libro, Casilla 450, Cochabamba

Boletin Bibliografico Boliviano, Ediciones ISLA, Casilla N4311, La Paz
Text in Spanish, summaries in English and Spanish

Publishers

Ediciones los **Amigos del Libro***, Calle Mercado 1315, Casilla 4415, La Paz Tel: (02) 360517 Cable Add: Amigol
Dir: Werner Guttentag; *Managers:* Jaime Flores, Rita Arze
Parent Company: Editorial los Amigos del Libro (qv)
Bookshops: Librería los Amigos del Libro (qv under Major Booksellers)
Founded: 1977

Editorial los **Amigos del Libro***, Casilla 450, Cochabamba Tel: (042) 2920 Cable Add: Amigol
Man Dir: Werner Guttentag; *Sales Dir:* Ingrid Guttentag; *Foreign Sales Manager:* Eva Guttentag; *Production:* Jaime Flores, Rita Arze
Subsidiary Company: Ediciones los Amigos del Libro (qv)
Associate Company: Grijalbo Boliviana Ltda (qv)
Subjects: Bolivia, South America
Bookshops: Librería los Amigos del Libro (qv under Major Booksellers)
Founded: 1945

Editorial **Difusión***, Casilla 1510, La Paz (Located at: Ave 16 de Julio 1601, La Paz) Tel: (02) 328126
Man Dir: Jorge F Catalano; *Publicity & Advertising:* Carmelo Andrade
Subjects: Bolivian literature & history, Politics, Social Studies
Bookshop: Librería Difusión (qv under Major Booksellers)
Founded: 1960

Editorial y Librería **Don Bosco***, Casilla 4458, La Paz (Located at: Ave 16 de Julio 1899, La Paz)
Associate Company: Editorial Don Bosco SA, Mexico (qv for other associate companies)

Universidad Boliviana Tomás **Frías**, Div de Extensión Universitaria*, Casilla 36, Potosí
Subjects: Literature, History

Gisbert y Cia SA*, Calle Comercio 1270, Casilla 195, La Paz Tel: (02) 356806
Cable Add: Gisbercia
President: José Gisbert; *Managers:* Javier Gisbert, Armando Pagano
Subjects: Belles Lettres, History, Law, Textbooks, Accounting, Fiction
Bookshop: See under Major Booksellers
Founded: 1907

Grijalbo Boliviana Ltda*, Apdo 4415, La Paz
Managers: Werner Guttentag, Nancy de Montoya
Parent Company: Ediciones Grijalbo SA, Spain (qv)
Associate Company: Editorial los Amigos del Libro (qv)

Librería y Editorial **Juventud***, Plaza Murillo 519, Casilla 1489, La Paz
Tel: (02) 341694 Cable Add: Juventud
Man Dir: Rafael Urquizo; *Assistant Dir, Publicity:* Gustavo Urquizo; *Production:* Rafael Urquizo Mendoza
Orders to: Casilla 1489, La Paz
Subsidiary Company: Empresa Editora Urquizo SA
Branch Off: Calle Puerto Rico 1135, La Paz
Subjects: Literature, History, Social Science, University, Secondary & Primary Textbooks; General Cultural Subjects
Bookshop: Librería Juventud (qv under Major Booksellers)
Founded: 1946

Libreria Editorial **Popular**+*, Casilla 4171, La Paz (Located at: Perez Velasco 787, La Paz) Tel: (02) 324258
Man Dir, Editorial: German Villamor; *Sales:* Fernando Iturri
Imprint: Propia
Subject: National themes
Founded: 1935

Propia, an imprint of Libreria Editorial Popular (qv)

La **Universal** SRL+*, Calle Jenaro Sanjines 538, Casilla 2888, La Paz Tel: (02) 342961 Cable Add: Universal
Man Dir: Rolando Condori Salinas; *Editorial:* Marina Condori de Valencia; *Sales:* Walter Condori Salinas; *Production:* Edgar Condori Salinas; *Publicity:* Carmen Cadima de Condori; *Rights & Permissions:* Eva Oviedo de Condori
Subjects: Literature, Philosophy, History, Novels, Poetry, Biography, Children's
Bookshops: Latina, Calle Comercio 927, La Paz; El Ateneo, Calle Ballivian 1281, La Paz; Dupsal, Calle México 1456, La Paz
Founded: 1958

Universidad Mayor de San Andres, Editorial Universitaria*, Casilla 6548, La Paz

Major Booksellers

Librería los **Amigos del Libro***, Calle Mercado 1315, Casilla 4415, La Paz Tel: (02) 22794
Managers: Werner Guttentag, Nancy de Montoya
Branches include: Calle Gral Acha ollo and Ave Heroinas esq España (both Cochabamba); Hotel Sheraton, Aerport El Alto, La Paz
Owned by: Werner Guttentag (Ediciones los Amigos del Libro, Editorial los Amigos del Libro — qqv)

Librería **Difusión***, Casilla 1510, La Paz (Located at: Ave 16 de Julio 1601, La Paz) Tel: (02) 28126
Owned by: Editorial Difusión (qv)

Gisbert y Cía SA*, Calle Comercio 1270, Casilla 195, La Paz Tel: (02) 356806
Managers: Javier Gisbert, Armando Pagano
Also Publisher (qv)

Librería **Icthus***, Ave 16 de Julio 1800, Casilla 8353, La Paz Tel: (02) 54007
Manager: Salvador de la Serna
Owned by: Methodist Evangelical Church in Bolivia

Librería **Juventud***, Plaza Murillo 519, Casilla 1489, La Paz Tel: (02) 341694
Manager: Rafael Urquizo
Owned by: Librería y Editorial Juventud (qv)

Librería **La Paz***, Colón 618, Casilla 539, La Paz Tel: (02) 353323/357109
Manager: Carlos Burgos

Librería **Selecciones** SRL*, Casilla 972, La Paz (Located at: Ave 6 de Agosto 2105, La Paz) Tel: (02) 324159/329480 Cable Add: Selecciones La Paz

Alfonso **Tejerina** Ltda*, Comercio 1073, Casilla 834, La Paz

Major Libraries

Biblioteca y Archivo Nacional de Bolivia*, Calle Bolívar, Sucre

Biblioteca del **Congreso** Nacional*, Palacio Legislativo, La Paz

Biblioteca de la **Dirección de Cultura***, Alcaldía Municipal, Casilla 1856, La Paz
Library of Cultural Affairs Administration

Biblioteca Universitaria, Departamento de Bibliotecas **Universidad Boliviana** Tomás Frías*, CP 54, Potosí
Dir: Adolfo Vera del Carpio
Publications: Boletin de la Biblioteca Universitaria and occasional papers

Biblioteca Central de la **Universidad Mayor de San Andrés***, Ave Villazón 1995, Casilla 6548, La Paz

Biblioteca Central de la **Universidad Mayor de San Francisco Xavier***, Plaza 25 de Mayo, Apdo 212, Sucre

Biblioteca Central **Universitaria 'José Antonio Arze'***, Universidad Mayor de San Simón, Oquendo esq Sucre, Casilla 992, Cochabamba Tel: (042) 25506
Dir: Dr Efraín Virreira Sánchez
Publications include: Boletín Bibliográfico

Library Associations

Asociación Boliviana de Bibliotecarios (ABB)*, Casilla 992, Cochabamba
Bolivian Library Association
President: Dr Efraín Virreira Sánchez

Centro Nacional de Documentación Científica y Tecnológica*, Casilla 3283, La Paz Tel: (02) 359586
National Scientific and Technological Documentation Centre
Dir: Joŝe-Roberto Arze
Publications include: Serie Bibliografica (3-5 a year); *Actualidades* (annual)

Centro Nacional de Documentación e Información Educativa*, c/o Ministerio de Educación y Cultura, La Paz
National Centre of Documentation and Education Information
Dir: Rosa Melgar de Ipiña

Literary Associations and Societies

P E N Club de Bolivia (Centro Internacional de Escritores)*, Calle Goitia 17, Casilla 149, La Paz
Secretary: Yolanda Bedregal de Cónitzer

Literary Periodicals

Cultura Boliviana, Universidad Tecnica de Oruro, Departamento de Extension Cultural, Oruro

Presencia Literaria, Casilla 1913, La Paz

Literary Prizes

Bolivian Grand Prize for Literature*
For an outstanding achievement in the field of literature. Enquiries to the Bolivian Government, La Paz

Hector **Cossio Salinas** National Biography Prize*
Biennial prize for a previously unpublished biography of one of a number of named people whose lives and works have been important in the development of Bolivia. The author must be a Bolivian national (wherever resident) or a foreign resident who has lived in Bolivia for at least the preceding five years. Prizes of US$2,000, US$750 and US$500. Enquiries to Werner Guttentag, Editorial los Amigos del Libro, Casilla 450, Cochabamba

Premio Nacional de **Cultura***
Enquiries to Ministerio de Educación, La Paz

Premio de Novela 'Erich **Guttentag**'*
'Erich Guttentag' biennial prize for a previously unpublished novel. Prizes of US$2,000, US$750 and US$500. Enquiries to Editorial los Amigos del Libro, Casilla 450, Cochabamba

Franz **Tamayo** Prize*
For outstanding literary work. Prizes of 25,000, 15,000 and 5,000 Bolivian pesos. Awarded annually. Enquiries to La Paz Municipal Mayor's Office, La Paz

Botswana

General Information

Language: Setswana and English
Religion: Traditional
Population: 819,000

Bank Hours: 0830-1300 Monday-Friday; 0830-1100 Saturday
Shop Hours: 0800-1300, 1400-1700 or 1800 Monday-Saturday
Currency: 100 thebe = 1 pula
Export/Import Information: No tariffs on books or advertising matter. No import licence required; no obscene literature. Exchange controls

Book Trade Reference Journal

The National Bibliography of Botswana, Botswana National Library Service, Private Bag 0036, Gaborone

Publishers

Government Printer+, Private Bag 0081, Gaborone Tel: (031) 353202 Telex: 2414

Longman Botswana (Pty) Ltd*, PO Box 1083, Gaborone Tel: (031) 313969
Subsidiary Company: Longman Group Ltd, UK (qv)

Major Booksellers

Botswana Book Centre, PO Box 91, Gaborone (Located at: The Mall, Gaborone) Tel: (031) 352931 Cable Add: Books Telex: 2327 Books
Manager: J D Jones

Major Libraries

Botswana National Archives*, PO Box 239, Gaborone Tel: (031) 355591 Cable Add: Homes
Dir: Mrs T M Lekaukau

Botswana National Library Service*, Private Bag 0036, Gaborone Tel: (031) 352397/352288 Cable Add: Bonalibs
Acting Director of Library Service: Basiamangn Garebakwena
Publication: The National Bibliography of Botswana

Geological Survey Department Library, Private Bag 14, Lobatse Tel: (033) 327 Cable Add: Rocks Lobatse Telex: 2293 Geo
Technical Information Specialist: M Molefe

Government Teacher Training College Library*, PO Box 96, Lobatse

The **National Institute** of Development Research and Documentation*, University of Botswana, Private Bag 0022, Gaborone
Librarian: Stella Bakwena

University of Botswana Library, Private Bag 0022, Gaborone Tel: (031) 351155 Telex: 2429
Librarian: Mrs H K Raseroka
Publications: Annual Report, Accessions List

Library Association

Botswana Library Association*, PO Box 1310, Gaborone
Chairman: II Kay Raseroka; *Secretary:* Duduzile M Mbaakangi
Publication: Botswana Library Association Journal

Library Reference Journal

Botswana Library Association Journal,

Botswana Library Association, PO Box 1310, Gaborone

Literary Periodical

Marang, Department of English, University of Botswana, Private Bag 0022, Gaborone

Brazil

General Information

Language: Portuguese (some English spoken)
Religion: Roman Catholic
Population: 141 million
Bank Hours: Generally 1000-1500 Monday-Friday
Shop Hours: 0900-1700 Monday-Friday (many open much later); 0900-1230 or 1300 Saturday
Currency: 100 centavos = 1 cruzeiro
Export/Import Information: Member of the Latin American Free Trade Association. No tariffs on books and advertising, but luxury bindings and children's picture-books are dutied. Import licences and deposits required; exchange controls operate
Copyright: UCC, Berne, Buenos Aires, Florence (see International section)

Book Trade Organizations

Agência Brasileira do ISBN, Seção de Contribuição Legal, Biblioteca Nacional, Ave Rio Branco 219/39 – 3° andar, 20042 Rio de Janeiro RJ Tel: (021) 2407729/2408579 Telex: 02122941 Bn Rj
ISBN Administrator: Selma Mendes Fontes Sodré

Associação Brasileira de Livreiros Antiquarios, Rua do Rosario 155, 20041 Rio de Janeiro RJ
Brazilian Association of Antiquarian Booksellers

Associação Brasileira do Livro*, Ave 13 de maio 23 – salas 1610-12 e 1619-20, 20031 Rio de Janeiro RJ Tel: (021) 2409115
Brazilian Booksellers' Association
President: Ernesto Zahar

Câmara Brasileira do Livro, Ave Ipiranga 1267 – 10° andar, 01039 São Paulo SP Tel: (011) 2297855
Brazilian Book Association
Superintendent: José Gorayeb

Instituto Nacional do Livro*, Edifício Venâncio V, Setor de Diversões Sul, 70000 Brasília DF Tel: (021) 235628
National Book Institute
Dir: María Alice Barroso

Sindicato Nacional dos Editores de Livros (SNEL)*, Ave Rio Branco 37 – 15° andar – salas 1503-6 e 1510-12, 20097 Rio de Janeiro RJ Tel: (021) 2336481/2335484
Cable Add: Sindelivros
Brazilian Publishers' Association
Publications: Jornal do SNEL (monthly); *Guia das Editoras Brasileiras*; *Guia das Livrarias Brasileiras*; *Resumo Bibliográfico*

Standard Book Numbering Agency, see Agência Brasileira do ISBN

50 BRAZIL

Book Trade Reference Books and Journals

Book

O Mundo do Edição Luso-Brasileira (The World of Publishing, Portugal and Brazil), Publicações Europa-America Lda, CP 8, Estrada Lisbon-Sintra Km 14, 2726 Mem Martins, Portugal

Journals

Bibliografia Brasileira, Biblioteca Nacional, Ave Rio Branco 219-239, 20042 Rio de Janeiro RJ

Bibliografia Classificada, Centro de Investigação e Documentação, CP 23, Petropolis, Rio de Janeiro RJ

Boletim Bibliográfico, Biblioteca Nacional, Ave Rio Branco 219-239, 20042 Rio de Janeiro RJ

Boletim Bibliográfico Brasileiro, Estante Publicações, Ave Rio Branco 138 – 11° andar, Rio de Janeiro RJ

O Editor do Livros, Revistas e Jornais (The Publisher of Books, Reviews and Journals), Editora Métodos Ltda, Rua da Lapa 180 – sala 607, CP 15085, Rio de Janeiro GB

El Libro (The Book), Equilar Editores, Castillan 5, São Paulo 17

Guia das Editoras Brasileiras, Sindicato Nacional dos Editores de Livros (SNEL), Ave Rio Branco 37 – 15° andar – salas 1503-6 e 1510-12, 20097 Rio de Janeiro RJ

Guia das Livrarias Brasileiras, Sindicato Nacional dos Editores de Livros (SNEL), Ave Rio Branco 37 – 15° andar – salas 1503-6 e 1510-12, 20097 Rio de Janeiro RJ

Livros Novos (New Books), Atlantis Livros Ltda, CP 3752, 01000 São Paulo SP
Text in English and Portuguese

Pregão de Livros, J C Amaral Guimarães, Rua Conde de Sarzedas 246, 01512 São Paulo SP

Resumo Bibliográfico, Sindicato Nacional dos Editores de Livros (SNEL), Ave Rio Branco 37 – 15° andar – salas 1503-6 e 1510-12, 20097 Rio de Janeiro RJ

Revisto do Livro (Review of Books), Ministerio da Educação e Cultura, Of 3068, Brasília DF
Text in Portuguese and Spanish

Publishers

A G I R (Artes Graficas Industrias Reunidas SA), CP 3291, 20001 Rio de Janeiro RJ (Located at: Rua dos Invalidos 198, 20231 Rio de Janeiro) Tel: (021) 2216424/2520410 Cable Add: Agirsa
Man Dir: Jorge Eduardo d'Almeida Castro Faveret; *Editorial:* Márcia Hardman
Branch Offs: São Paulo, Belo Horizonte
Subjects: Literature, Juveniles, Social Science, Religion
Bookshop: Livraria Agir (qv under Major Booksellers)
Founded: 1944

Abril SA Cultural e Industrial*, Rua Paes Leme 524 – 10° andar, São Paulo SP Tel: (011) 8154677 Telex: 112209 Absa
Vice-President: João Gomez; *Man Dirs:* José Eduardo P Martins (Books), Anselmo Pecci (Education), Roberto Silveira (Partworks); *Rights:* Shozi Ikeda, Renê C X Santos (Book Club)
Branch Offs: 380 Lexington Ave – 17th floor, New York, NY 10168, USA Tel: (212) 8838825; 79 Gloucester Ave, London NW1 8LB, UK Tel: (01) 586 5074
Subjects: Reference, General Encyclopaedias, Literature, Music, Science, Illustrated Trade Books; School & Textbooks
Book Club: Círculo do Livro SA (jointly owned with Verlagsgruppe Bertelsmann GmbH, Federal Republic of Germany (qv))
Founded: 1950

Agents Editores Ltda*, Rua Almirante Baltazar 349, São Cristovão, 20941 Rio de Janeiro RJ Tel: (021) 2845988/2649988 Cable Add: Agentsrio Telex: 30159 Agts
Superintendent-Director: Francisco da Gama Lima Netto; *Editorial:* João Sergio Rao, Gabriel de Almeida, Sivio Dantas
Subjects: Security in Technical and Scientific fields (including Security, Counter-surveillance, Criminal investigation, Intelligence)
Founded: 1977

Editora Nova **Aguilar** SA+, Rua Bambina 25, Botafogo, 22251 Rio de Janeiro RJ Tel: (021) 2867822 Cable Add: Aguilar
President: Wellington Moreira Franco; *Vice-President:* Sergio Lacerda; *Dir:* Sebastião Lacerda
Branch Off: Ave Pedro Bueno 1509-1511, Jabaquara, 04342 São Paulo SP
Subject: General Literature
Founded: 1958

Livraria Francisco **Alves** Editora SA+, Rua Sete de Setembro 177, Centro, 20050 Rio de Janeiro RJ Tel: (021) 2213198
Man Dir: Léo Magarinos de Souza Leão; *Editorial:* Sid Pinto de Carvalho; *Sales:* Louise Leal
Parent Companies: Companhia de Navegação Marítima Netumar, Ave Presidente Vargas 482-3 – 18 – 23 e 27 andares, 20071 Rio de Janeiro RJ; Netumar International Inc, 26 Broadway – 6th Floor, New York, NY 10004, USA
Branch Offs: Rua Dr Vieira de Carvalho 144, 01210 São Paulo SP; Rua da Bahia 1060, 30000 Belo Horizonte MG
Subjects: University, High School and Primary Textbooks, Science, Astronomy, Non-fiction, General Fiction, Crime, Science Fiction, Occultism, Literature
Bookshops: Rua da Bahia 1060, Belo Horizonte; Rua Farme de Amoedo 57, Ipanema; Rua Sete de Setembro 177, Centro, Rio de Janeiro; Rua Uruguaiana 98, Rio de Janeiro; Barão de Itapetininga 246, São Paulo; Rua Dr Vieira de Carvalho 144, São Paulo
Founded: 1854

Editora Das **Americas** SA Edameris*, Rua Santa Isabel 152, V Buarque, 01221 São Paulo SP Tel: (011) 2217573/2218482
Man Dir: Mário Fittipaldi
Subjects: Poetry, Fiction, Biography, Crime & Adventure

Organização **Andrei** Editora Ltda+*, Rua Conselheiro Nebias 1071, São Paulo SP Tel: (011) 2207246 Cable Add: Carolandre
Dir: Edmondo L Andrei; *Sales Dir:* Alberto Mayer
Subjects: Medicine, Pharmacy, Veterinary Medicine, Homoeopathy, Acupuncture
Founded: 1956

Antenna Edições Técnicas Ltda, Ave Mal Floriano 143, 20060 Rio de Janeiro RJ Tel: (021) 2232442 Cable Add: Antenna
Man Dir: Gilberto A Penna; *Publicity:* Helio N Santos
Associate Company: Seleções Eletrônicas Editora Ltda (qv)
Branch Off: Rua Vitoria 395, São Paulo SP
Subjects: Electronics, Telecommunications
Bookshops: Lojas do Livro Eletrônico: Ave Mal Floriano 143 – sobreloja, 20060 Rio de Janeiro RJ; Rua Vitória 379-383, 01210 São Paulo SP
1985: 5 titles *1986:* 6 titles *Founded:* 1926
ISBN Publisher's Prefix: 85-7036

Ao Livro Técnico SA Indústria a Comércio, Rua Sá Freire 36-40, São Cristóvão, 20930 Rio de Janeiro RJ Tel: (021) 5804868 Cable Add: Litecnico Telex: 2130472 Alte
Man Dir: Reynaldo Max Paul Bluhm; *Editorial, Production:* Gisela Bluhm; *Sales and Rights & Permissions:* José Candela Pagan; *Publicity:* Paulo E Bluhm
Subsidiary Companies: DISAL (Distribuidores Associados de Livros Ltda), Rua Vitória 486-496, São Paulo SP; SODILIVRO (Sociedade Distribuidora de Livros Ltda), Rua Bela 611, São Cristóvão, 20930 Rio de Janeiro RJ
Subjects: Technical, Scientific, Children's, Art, Language Textbooks, English Language Teaching, School-books
Bookshops: COLIVRO — Comércio e Distribuição de Livros Ltda (qv under Major Booksellers); A Nossa Livraria de Belo Horizonte, Rua Tupis 262, 30190 Belo Horizonte MG (Branch: Ave do Contorno 6283 – loja 2, 3000 Belo Horizonte); DISAL (Distribuidores Associados de Livros Ltda), Rua Maria Antonia 380, São Paulo SP
Founded: 1933

Aquarius Editora e Distribuidora de Livros Ltda*, Rua Olavo Egidio 242, Santana, 02037 São Paulo SP Tel: (011) 2676522
Man Dir: José Gândido da Silva Fonseca; *Sales:* Manuel Fonseca
Founded: 1976

Editora **Artenova** Ltda*, Rua Prefeito Olimpio de Mello 1774, Benfica, 20000 Rio de Janeiro RJ Tel: (021) 2649198/2340965 Cable Add: Artnova
Man Dir: Alvaro Pacheco; *Editorial, Rights & Permissions, Sales, Publicity:* Luzia Regina Alves
Associate Companies: Artenova Filmes Ltda; Studio Artenova de Publicidade Ltda
Branch Off: Ave Augusto Pinto 122, Perdizes, São Paulo SP
Subjects: Literature, Sociology, Psychology, Occultism, Health, Cinema, History
Founded: 1971

Livraria Editora **Artes** Medicas Ltda, Rua Dr Cesario Motta Jr 63, Vila Buorque, 01221 São Paulo SP Tel: (011) 2219033 Cable Add: Leam
Man Dir: Henrique Hecht; *Editorial, Production, Rights & Permissions:* M Hecht; *Sales:* C dos Santos; *Publicity:* J Hecht
Subsidiary Companies: Editora Artes Medicas Sul Ltda, Rua General Vitorino 277, 90000 Pôrto Alegre; Livraria Artes Medicas Norte Ltda, Recifé
Subjects: Medicine, Dentistry
Founded: 1964

Livraria **Atheneu** Ltda*, Rua Bambina 74 – lojas A/B, Botafogo, 22251 Rio de Janeiro RJ Tel: (021) 2661295/2264793 Cable Add: Zigadag
Man Dir: Paulo da Costa Rzezinski; *Editorial Dir, Rights & Permissions:* Teodoro Luiz Reinke; *Sales Dir:* Genoval Rabelo; *Production Dir:* Kátia Alves
Branch Offs: Rua Senador Dantas 56B, Rio de Janeiro RJ; Rua Jesuino Pascoal 30, Santa Cecilia, São Paulo SP
Subjects: Medicine, Nursing, Psychology, Psychoanalysis, Psychiatry

Bookshops: 25 outlets
Founded: 1928

Editora **Atica** SA, CP 8656, 01507 São Paulo SP (Located at: Rua Barão de Iguape 110, Liberdade, São Paulo) Tel: (011) 2789322 Cable Add: Bom Livro Telex: 32969 Edat
President: Anderson Fernandes Dias; *Marketing Dir:* Wander Soares
Branch Off: Rua Barão de Ubá 173, Estácio, 20260 Rio de Janeiro RJ
Subjects: University, Secondary & Primary Textbooks, Pre-school Books, Children's, Brazilian and African Literature

Editora **Atlas** SA, Rua Conselheiro Nebias 1384, 01203 São Paulo SP Tel: (011) 2219144 Cable Add: Atlasedita
Man Dir: Luiz Herrmann; *Editorial, Marketing, Rights & Permissions:* A B Brandão; *Sales & Promotion:* E Bruder; *Production:* P Gerencer
Branch Offs: Amazonas, Brazília, Ceará, Goías, Minas Gerais, Paraná, Rio de Janeiro, Rio Grande do Sul, Santa Catarina
Subjects: Administration, Economics, Financial, Social Sciences, Computers
Founded: 1944

Atual Editora Ltda*, Rua José Antonio Coelho 785, V Mariana, 04011 São Paulo SP Tel: (011) 5751544
Man Dir: Gelson Iezzi; *Editorial:* José Carlos Monteiro da Silva; *Sales:* Osvaldo Dolce; *Production:* Samuel Lincon Silvério; *Publicity, Rights & Permissions:* José Roberto Brauner
Associate Company: Rio Atual Distribuidora de Livros Ltda, Rua Barão de Mesquita 28a, Rio de Janeiro RJ
Branch Offs: Rua General Osório 1099, Ribeirão Preto SP; Rua Constituição 1-46, Bauru SP
Subjects: Didactics, Literature
Founded: 1973

Gráfica Editora **Aurora** Ltda*, CP 7041, 20211 Rio de Janeiro RJ (Located at: Rua Frei Caneca 19, Centro, Rio de Janeiro) Tel: (021) 2220654
Man Dir: Francesco Molinaro; *Sales Dir:* Natale A Molinaro; *Publicity Dir:* Solange de Paula; *Advertising Dir:* Socrates de Paula
Subjects: Secondary & Primary Textbooks, Literature, Pedagogy, How-to, Law, Business, Masonic themes
Founded: 1945
ISBN Publisher's Prefix: 85-30

Editora **Beta** Ltda*, Estrada do Gabinal 1521, Jacarepaguá, Rio de Janeiro RJ Tel: (021) 3421818
Man Dir: Jacob Horowicz
Subjects: Literature, Children's

Bloch Editores SA*, Rua do Russel 804, 22214 Rio de Janeiro RJ Tel: (021) 2652012 Telex: 02121525
Publicity: Paulo Maia Poucinha, Expedito Jośe Chaves Grossi
Subject: Textbooks

Editora Edgard **Blücher** Ltda*, Rua Pedros Alvarenga 1245 – 2° andar – conj 22, 01000 São Paulo SP Tel: (011) 648114/645613 Cable Add: Blucherlivro
Man Dir: Edgard Blücher
Subjects: Engineering, Science, Business, University Textbooks
Founded: 1966

Editora Bertrand **Brasil** SA, Rua Benjamin Constant 142, Glória, 20241 Rio de Janeiro RJ Tel: (021) 2211132 Telex: 32294 Dfel
Man Dir: José Elias Salomão; *Sales Dir:* Altair Ferreira Brasil; *Rights &

Permissions: Rosemary Alves
Subjects: Sociology, History, Geography, General Fiction, Physical Fitness, Arts, Economics, Philosophy, Psychology, Religion
Founded: 1951 (as Difusão Editorial SA (DIFEL))

Editora do **Brasil** SA*, CP 4986, 01203 São Paulo SP (Located at: Rua Conselheiro Nébias 887-889, Campos Elíseos, São Paulo) Tel: (011) 2211663/2220211/2220818 Cable Add: Editabras
Branch Off: Rua do Resende 89, Centro, 20231 Rio de Janeiro RJ
Subjects: Education, Reference, Juveniles, History, Psychology, Sociology

Editora **Brasil-América** (EBAL) SA*, Rua General Almério de Moura 302/320, São Cristóvão, 20921 Rio de Janeiro RJ Tel: (021) 5800303 Cable Add: Ebalitada
Man Dir: Adolfo Aizen; *Editorial:* Naumin Aizen; *Production:* Fernando Albagli
Subject: Children's
Founded: 1945

Brasilia Editora Ltda*, Rua Cinco 15, Jardim da Penha, 29000 Vitória ES Tel: (027) 2271962 Cable Add: Brasilivros
Subjects: Textbooks, Home Economics, Mathematics

Editora **Brasiliense** SA+, CP 30644, 01416 São Paulo SP (Located at: Rua da Consolação 2697, São Paulo) Tel: (011) 2801222 Cable Add: Edibrasa Telex: 33271 Dblm
Man Dir, Editorial, Rights & Permissions: Caio Graco Prado; *Sales:* C C Guerrato; *Production:* Antonio Orzari
Subjects: Social Sciences, Humanities, Literature, Education, Juveniles
Bookshop: Livraria Brasiliense Editora SA (qv under Major Booksellers) and seven others in São Paulo
Founded: 1943

Editora **Bruguera** do Brasil Ltda*, Rua Mato Grosso 456, Consolação, 01239 São Paulo SP
Publicity Manager: Jorge Alberto Beillard
Parent Co: Editorial Bruguera SA, Spain (qv)

Livraria e Editora Juridica José **Bushatsky** Ltda*, CP 2826, 01007 São Paulo SP (Located at: Riachuelo 195, São Paulo) Tel: (011) 344148 Cable Add: Bushatsky
Man Dir and Production: Anna Bushatsky
Subject: Law
Bookshop: At above address
Founded: 1953

C E P A — Centro Editor de Psicologia Aplicada Ltda*, CP 15131, 20031 Rio de Janeiro RJ (Located at: Rua Senador Dantas 118 – 9° andar, Centro, Rio de Janeiro) Tel: (021) 2205545/2207195 Cable Add: Edicepa
Man Dir: Antonio Rodrigues
Subject: Psychology Textbooks and Tests
Founded: 1952

Editora **Campus** Ltda, Rua Barão de Itapagipe 55, Rio Comprido, 20261 Rio de Janeiro RJ Tel: (021) 2848443
Man Dir, Editorial: Claudio M Rothmuller; *Production Dir:* Otavio Studart; *Rights & Permissions:* Emilia Fernandez
Parent Company: Elsevier, Netherlands (qv)
Subject: Textbooks (all fields, except Law and Medicine, particularly Computers and Electronics)
Founded: 1976

Livraria Editora **Cátedra** Ltda*, Rua Senador Dantas 20 – salas 806-7, Centro, 20031 Rio de Janeiro RJ Tel: (021)

2227593
Subjects: Cookery, History, Children's, Reference, Sociology

Cedibra Editora Brasileira Ltda*, Rua Leonidia 2, Olaria, 21071 Rio de Janeiro RJ Tel: (021) 2807272 Cable Add: Edibras
Man Dir: Jan Rais; *Editorial:* Dulcy Grisolia; *Marketing:* Paul Margittai
Parent Company: Maxwell Communication Corporation plc, UK (qv)
Subjects: Juveniles, Fiction, Paperbacks
Founded: 1952

Centro Editor de Psicologia Aplicada Ltda, see CEPA

Centro Editorial Latino Americano Ltda*, CP 45329, 04016 São Paulo SP (Located at: Rua Amâncio de Carvalho 82, V Mariana, São Paulo) Tel: (011) 5442917
Man Dir: Silvino Anastácio; *Editorial, Production, Publicity and Rights & Permissions:* José Carlos Rolo Venâncio; *Sales:* Luis Alves Jnr
Orders to: Rua Franca Pinto 836, 040016 São Paulo SP
Parent Company: Global Editora e Distribuidora Ltda (qv)
Associate Company: Editora Ground Ltda (qv)
Branch Off: Global Nordeste Representacões, Ave Dantas Barreto 564 – 11° andar – salas 1104-5, Recife PE
Subjects: History, Politics, Health
Bookshops: Livraria Ground, Rua Siqueira Campos 143 – sobreloja 56, Rio de Janeiro; Vida Natural, Rua Amâncio de Carvallio 51, São Paulo
Founded: 1979

Cidade Nova Editora+, Rua Cel Paulino Carlos 29, 04006 São Paulo SP Tel: (011) 8843700
Man Dir: Celso Frioli; *Editorial, Publicity:* João M Motta
Parent Company: Città Nuova Editrice, Italy (qv for associate companies)
Branch Offs: Ave Serzedelo Correa 388 – sobreloja, 66010 Belém PA; Rua Professor Morais 574 – sobreloja, 30150 Belo Horizonte MG; Rua Pará 1836, Portão, 80310 Curitiba PR; Rua Santa Terezinha 400, 90040 Pôrto Alegre RS; Rua Marechal Deodoro 311, 50030 Recife PE; Via Bandeirantes km 47, 06730 Vargem Grande Paulista SP
Subjects: Religion, Family, Society, Juveniles
1985-86: 19 titles *Founded:* 1960
ISBN Publisher's Prefix: 85-7112

Editora **Civilização** Brasileira SA+, Rua Benjamin Constant 142, Glória, 20241 Rio de Janeiro RJ Tel: (021) 2211132
Man Dirs: José Maria Raposo, Olavo Gióra; *Editorial Dir:* Enio Silveira
Subjects: General Fiction, Belles Lettres, Poetry, Social Science
Founded: 1932

Editora **Codecri** Ltda+, Rua Carioca 59, Centro, 20050 Rio de Janeiro RJ Tel: (021) 2626760/2625323
Man Dir: Sergio de Magalhães Gomes Jacuarire; *Editorial, Production:* Jeferson de Andrade
Subsidiary Company: Jornal Pasquim (at above address)
Subjects: Belles Lettres, Fiction, Dictionaries
Founded: 1976

Concordia Editora Ltda+*, CP 3230, 90230 Pôrto Alegre RS (Located at: Ave São Pedro 639, Pôrto Alegre) Tel:

52 BRAZIL

(0512) 422859/422699 Cable Add: Concordia
Man Dir: Johanes Gedradt; *Sales, Publicity:* Luiz Ricardo Böttcher
Parent Company: Igreja Evangèlica Luterana do Brasil
Subjects: Religion, Music
Founded: 1923
Miscellaneous: Company previously known as Concordia SA-Artes Gráficas e Embalagens

Confraria dos Amigos do Livro Ltda+, Rua Bambina 25, Botafogo, 22251 Rio de Janeiro RJ Tel: (021) 2867822 Cable Add: Neofront Telex: 34695 Enfs
Man Dir, Sales & Publicity: Elson Mancen; *Editorial:* Sebastião Lacerda
Parent Company: Editora Nova Fronteira SA (qv)
Subject: Art books in special editions
Founded: 1976

Conquista, Empresa de Publicações Ltda*, Ave 28 de Setembro 174, Vila Isabel, 20551 Rio de Janeiro RJ Tel: (021) 2285709/2286752
Dir: Nilde Hersen Aragão da Fonseca; *Sales Dir:* António da Silva Aragão da Fonseca
Subjects: Children's, Textbooks
1985: 50 titles *Founded:* 1951

Editora e Gráfica Miguel **Couto** SA*, Rua Capitão Carlos 68, Bonsucesso, 21040 Rio de Janeiro RJ Tel: (021) 2807699
Man Dir: Paulo Kobler Pinto Lopes Sampaio; *Editorial:* Octacilio Ribeiro Lessa; *Sales:* José Geraldo Verginelli; *Production:* Victor Mauricio Notrica; *Publicity:* Alcides Lourenco Gomes; *Rights & Permissions:* Antenor Romanholo
Associate Companies: Curso Miguel Couto SA, Somatório Administração SA, Curso MCB
Subject: Textbooks
Founded: 1969

Editora **Cultrix**+, Rua Mario Vicente 360, Ipiranga, 04270 São Paulo SP Tel: (011) 633141
Man Dir: Diaulas Riedel
Associate Company: Editora Pensamento (qv)
Subjects: General Literature, Social & General Science, Economics, Education, Philosophy, History, Children's, Psychology, Sociology
Founded: 1956

Editora **Cultura Médica** Ltda*, CP 24052, 20550 Rio de Janeiro RJ (Located at: Rua São Francisco Xavier 111, Rio de Janeiro) Tel: (021) 2349798/2484888
Man Dir: Ezequiel Feldman
Orders to: Rua Dr Salamini 75, Apto 501, Rio de Janeiro
Subject: Medicine
Founded: 1966

Difusão Editorial SA (DIFEL), now Editora Bertrand Brasil SA (qv)

Livraria **Duas Cidades** Ltda*, CP 433, 01220 São Paulo SP (Located at: Rua Bento Freitas 158, Vila Buarque, São Paulo) Tel: (011) 375257
Man Dir: José Petronillo de Santa Cruz; *Sales Dir:* Mitsuro Nagata; *Publicity Dir:* Mara Valles
Branch Off: Ave Rio Branco 9, Sala 116, Centro, 20090 Rio de Janeiro RJ
Subjects: Literature, Philosophy, Religion, Psychology, Social Science, University Textbooks
Bookshop: See under Major Booksellers
Founded: 1956

E B A L, see Editora Brasil-América SA

E P U, see Editora Pedagogica e Universitaria Ltda

Edameris, see Editora Das Americas SA Edameris

Edart São Paulo Livraria Editora Ltda*, Rua França Pinto 840, Vilamaliana, 04011 São Paulo Tel: (011) 5442418
Man Dirs: José Carlos Rolo Venáncio, Luis Alves Jnr; *Dir of Editions:* José Carlos Rolo Venáncio; *Sales Dir:* Luis Alves Jnr; *Publicity Dir:* Inácio Bueno
Associate Company: Centro Editorial Latino Americano Ltda (qv)
Subjects: Medicine, Science, Technology, Psychology, History, Law, Mathematics, How-to, Primary, Secondary & University Textbooks
Founded: 1964

Editora Interamericana Ltda*, Rua Evaristo da Veiga 55 – 20° andar, 20031 Rio de Janeiro RJ Tel: (021) 2403922 Cable Add: Edinter Telex: 2123036
Man Dir: Raul Vazquez; *Editorial, Sales and Publicity:* Rodolfo Berardinelli; *Production:* J Belmonte
Associate Company: CBS International Publishing (CIP), USA
Subjects: Medicine and Related Sciences, Psychology, Business, Chemistry, Physical Education, Biology
Founded: 1972

Editora Moderna Ltda+*, CP 45364, 04511 São Paulo SP (Located at: Rua Afonso Brás 431, 04511 São Paulo) Tel: (011) 5315099
Man Dir: Prof Ricardo Feltre
Branch Off: Rua Sen Furtado 31, 20270 Rio de Janeiro RJ
Subjects: Textbooks, Social Science, Literature
Founded: 1968

Cía **Editora Nacional***, CP 5312, 03016 São Paulo SP (Located at: Rua Joli 294, Brás, São Paulo) Tel: (011) 2912355 Cable Add: Editora
Man Dir, Rights & Permissions: Jorge Antonio Miguel Yunes; *Editorial:* Paulo Marti
Branch Offs: Edifício Venâncio VI – DS bloco 0 – lojas 13 e 17, Brasília; Ave Lôbo Júnior 1011, Bairro Penha, Rio de Janeiro
Also: Bauru, Belém, Belo Horizonte, Campo Grande, Caruaru, Cuiabá, Curitiba, Fortaleza, Goiânia, Manaus, Natal, Pôrto Alegre, Recife, Ribeirão Preto, Salvador, São José do Rio Preto, São Luis, Teresina
Subjects: Pedagogy, History, Philosophy, Psychology, Technical, General & Social Science, Textbooks, Business, Fiction
Founded: 1925

Editora Pedagogica e Universitaria Ltda (EPU)*, CP 7509, 01051 São Paulo SP (Located at: Praça Dom José Gaspar 106 – 3° andar – sobreloja 15, 01047 São Paulo)
Manager and Partner: Wolfgang Knapp
Subjects: Science, Technics, Didactics
Founded: 1952

Seleções **Eletrônicas Editora** Ltda, CP 771, 20001 Rio de Janeiro RJ (Located at: Rua Costa Ferreira 128, 20221 Rio de Janeiro) Tel: (021) 2539268
Man Dir: Maria B A Penna; *Editorial:* Gilberto A Penna Jnr; *Publicity:* Helio N Santos
Associate Company: Antenna Edições Técnicas Ltda (qv)
Subjects: Electronics, Radio and TV Technology, Electricity
1985: 5 titles *1986:* 5 titles *Founded:* 1960
ISBN Publisher's Prefix: 85-7037

Editora **Espiritualista***, CP 7041, 20211 Rio de Janeiro RJ (Located at: Rua Frei Caneca 19, Centro, Rio de Janeiro) Tel: (021) 2220654
Man Dir: Francesco Molinaro; *Sales Dir:* Natale A Molinaro; *Publicity & Advertising Dir:* Socrates de Paula
Subjects: Philosophy, Religion
Founded: 1945
ISBN Publisher's Prefix: 85-94

Exped-Expansaõ Editorial Ltda*, Estrada dos Bandeirantes 1/700, Jacarepaguá, 22700 Rio de Janeiro RJ Tel: (021) 3420669/3420333 Telex: 33280
Dir & Editor: Ferdinando Bastos de Souza; *Publisher:* Gilberto Huber; *Editorial Manager:* Ricardo Augusto Pamplona Vaz
Subjects: General Literature, Didactics, Reference
Founded: 1967

F A E — Fundação de Assistência ao Estudante*, Rua Miguel Angelo 96, Maria da Graça, Rio de Janeiro RJ Tel: (021) 2617750/2614140
Man Dir: Rubens José de Castro Albuquerque; *Editorial Dir:* Luiz Pasquale Filho; *Sales Dir:* Avari de Campos; *Production Manager:* Maria Aparecida de Oliveira; *Publicity Manager:* Geni Hirata; *Rights & Permissions:* José Ribeiro de Castro Neto
Subject: Textbooks
Bookshops: 276 outlets throughout Brazil
Founded: 1967

F E N A M E — Fundação Nacional de Material Escolar*, Rua Miguel Angelo 96, Maria da Graça, Rio de Janeiro RJ Tel: (021) 2617750/2614140
Man Dir: Milton Durço Pereira; *Editorial Dir:* Tania Jatobá de Matos Menezes; *Sales Dir:* Murilo Alves Nunes; *Production Dir:* Antonio José de Britto; *Publicity Dir:* Ivan Estelita Campos; *Rights & Permissions:* José Ribeiro de Castro Neto
Subject: Textbooks
Bookshops: About 250 outlets throughout Brazil
Founded: 1967

Editora **F T D** SA*, CP 30402, 01519 São Paulo SP (Located at: Rua do Lavapés 1023, Cambuci, São Paulo) Tel: (011) 2788264
President: João Tissi; *Man Dir:* Paulo Alves Ferraz
Branch Offs: Rua Agenor Meira 4/67, Bauru, São Paulo; Rua Lavras 235, Carmo Sion, Belo Horizonte MG; Rua Mal Deodoro 887, Curitiba PR; Ave Goiás 1146, Goiânia GO; Ave Rio Branco 185, Londrina PR; Ave Tiradentes 963, Maringa; Ave Joana Angélica 963, Salvador BA; Rua Prof Baltazar 12, Vitória ES; Rua André Cavalcanti 78, Rio de Janeiro GB; Rua Martins Junior 39, Recife PE; Ave do Imperador 1203, Fortaleza CE
Subject: Textbooks
Founded: 1897

Editora **Forense-Universitaria** Ltda*, CP 2284, 20020 Rio de Janeiro RJ (Located at: Ave Erasmo Braga 227 – 3° andar – grupo 309, Rio de Janeiro) Tel: (021) 2526244/2225106

Editora e Encadernadora **Formar** Ltda*, CP 13250, 03168 São Paulo SP (Located at: Rua dos Trilhos 1126, Mooca, São Paulo) Tel: (011) 935133 Cable Add: Formar
Subjects: Education, Scientific & Technical, Cookery, History, Geography, Children's, Reference

Livraria **Freitas** Bastos SA*, Rua 7 de Setembro 127-129, 20050 Rio de Janeiro RJ Tel: (021) 2220250/2427647/2523767 Cable Add: Etiel
Branch Offs: Rua Maria Freitas – loja 110 A e D, Madureira, Rio de Janeiro RJ; Rua Domingos de Morais 2414, Vila Mariana, São Paulo SP; Rua 15 de Novembro 62-66, São Paulo SP
Subject: Law
Bookshop: See under Major Booksellers

Fundação Instituto Brasileiro de Geografia e Estatística (IBGE — CDDI/GECOM), Ave Beira Mar 436, 20021 Rio de Janeiro RJ Tel: (021) 5333094 Telex: 2130939 Ibge
Subjects: Statistics, Geography, Socio-economic Indicators, Periodicals, Maps
Founded: 1936

Fundação Nacional de Material Escolar, see FENAME

Editora Gustavo **Gili** do Brasil SA*, Rua Araripe Júnior 45, Andaraí, 20540 Rio de Janeiro RJ Tel: (021) 2880881 Cable Add: Gustobras
Parent Company: Editorial Gustavo Gili SA, Spain (qv)
Subjects: Architecture, Engineering

Global Editora e Distribuidora Ltda, CP 45329, 04016 São Paulo SP (Located at: Rua França Pinto 836, São Paulo) Tel: (011) 5724473
Man Dir, Sales: Luis Alves Jnr; *Editorial, Production, Publicity, Rights & Permissions:* José Carlos Rolo Venancio
Subsidiary Company: Centro Editorial Latino Americano Ltda (qv)
Associate Company: Editora Ground Ltda (qv)
Imprints: Parma, Prol, São Paulo Editora
Subjects: Linguistics, Romance, Humour, UFOs, Politics, Economics, Poetry, History, Theatre, Health, Children
1986: 626 titles *Founded:* 1973

Editora **Globo** Ltda+, Rua Itapiru 1209 – 5° andar, Rio Comprido, 20251 Rio de Janeiro RJ Tel: (021) 2735522 Telex: 23365 Fax: (021) 2735522
General Dir: Oscar Destros Neves; *Editorial Dir:* Gabriel Tranjan; *Sales Dir:* Marcos March
Parent Company: Livraria do Globo SA (qv under Major Booksellers)
Branch Offs: Rua Pernambuco 1077 – 6° andar, 30000 Belo Horizonte MG; Rua Santa Efigênia 212, Blumenac SC; Ave Santos Dumond 3060 – sala 712, 60000 Fortaleza CE; Rua do Curtume 665 – bloco D 705, Lapa Baixa SP; Rua Florêncio Yagartu 1313 – sala 203, 90000 Pôrto Alegre RS; Rua Barão do Amazonas 1297, 14100 Ribeirão Preto SP
Subjects: Fiction and Non-fiction, Education, Engineering, Dictionaries, Rural, Children's, Juveniles, Periodicals
1985: 56 titles *1986:* 72 titles *Founded:* 1954

Edições **Graal** Ltda+, Rua do Triunfo 177, Santa Ifigênia, 01212 São Paulo SP Tel: (011) 236522
Managing, Editorial & Publicity Dir, and Rights & Permissions: Fernando Gasparian; *Sales & Production Dir:* Marcus F Gasparian
Associate Company: Editora Paz e Terra (qv)
Subjects: Social Sciences, Philosophy, Psychology, Social Medicine, Economics, History, Sociology, Education
1985: 36 titles *1986:* 11 titles *Founded:* 1977

Ordem do **Graal** na Terra, CP 128, Embu, 06800 São Paulo SP (Located at: Ave 7 de Setembro 29200, Embu, São Paulo)
Man Dir: Harry von Sass
Subjects: Religion, Philosophy, History
Founded: 1947

Editorial **Grijalbo** Ltda*, Rua 7 de Abril 264 – loja B-2, 01044 São Paulo SP Tel: (011) 369544
Man Dir: José Monfort
Parent Company: Editorial Grijalbo SA, Spain (qv)
Subjects: Law, Technical
Founded: 1958

Editora **Ground** Ltda*, Rua França Pinto 844, São Paulo SP Tel: (011) 5724473
Man Dir: Armandina Venâncio
Associate Companies: Centro Editorial Latino Americano Ltda (qv); Global Editora e Distribuidora Ltda (qv)
Subjects: Natural Foods and Medicines, Alternative Living, Acupuncture, Ecology, Oriental Philosophy, Occultism & Esoterism, Mysticism
Bookshop: At above address
Founded: 1973

Editora **Guanabara** Koogan SA*, Travessa do Ouvidor 11, 20040 Rio de Janeiro RJ Tel: (021) 2245877 Cable Add: Edigua
Man Dir: Joao Pedro Lorch; *Editorial:* Aluisio T Affonso; *Sales:* C A Barifouse; *Production:* Francisco P Portella; *Publicity:* Renate Scheele; *Rights & Permissions:* Christina Norén
Subjects: Medicine, Dentistry, Life Sciences

Livraria Pioneira Editora/Enio Matheus **Guazzelli** e Cia Ltd+, Praça Dirceu de Lima 313, Casa Verde, 02515 São Paulo SP Tel: (011) 8583199
Dir: Enio M Guazzelli; *Marketing:* Renato Guazzelli; *Rights & Permissions:* Ricardo Guazzelli
Subjects: Social Sciences, Business and Management, Linguistics, Brazilian Studies, Architecture and Urbanism, General Subjects, Children's
Bookshop: At above address
1985: 14 titles *1986:* 20 titles *Founded:* 1960

Harbra, an imprint of Editora Harper & Row do Brasil Ltda (qv)

Editora **Harper & Row** do Brasil Ltda+*, CP 45312, 01000 Vila Marilena, São Paulo SP Tel: (011) 5703572/5704891 Cable Add: Habra Sao Telex: 25631 Ehrb
Man Dir, Editorial, Rights & Permissions: Julio E Emöd; *Sales:* Jose M Braga; *Production:* Maria Pia Castiglia
Parent Company: Harper & Row Inc, 10 East 53rd St, New York, NY 10022, USA
Associate Companies: Harper & Row (Australasia) Pty Ltd, Australia (qv); Harper & Row Ltd, UK (qv); Basic Books Inc, T Y Crowell: both Harper & Row Publishers Inc, 10 East 53rd St, New York, NY 10022; J B Lippincott, East Washington Sq, Philadelphia PA 19150 (all USA)
Imprint: Harbra
Subjects: University and High School Textbooks in Science, Mathematics, Engineering, Social Science, Business, Medicine, General Interest
Founded: 1976

Hemus Editora Ltda*, CP 9686, 01510 São Paulo SP (Located at: Rua da Glória 312, São Paulo) Tel: (011) 2799911 Cable Add: Hetec Telex: 32005 Edil
President: Eli Behar; *Man Dir:* Maxim Bchar
Subjects: Technical & Engineering, Textbooks, Juveniles, Philosophy, Science Fiction, General Literature
Founded: 1965

I B A M, see Instituto Brasileiro de Administraçao Municipal

I B E P, see Instituto Brasileiro de Edições Pedagógicas

I B I C T, see Instituto Brasileiro de Informação em Ciência e Tecnologia

I B R A S A (Instituição Brasileira de Difusão Cultural Ltda)*, Rua 21 de Abril 97, Brás, São Paulo Tel: (011) 929639
Man Dir: Jorge Leite
Orders to: IBREX Ltda, Rua 21 de Abril 101, Brás, 03047 São Paulo
Subjects: IBRASA Encyclopaedia, General Medical, Health & Sexuality, Parapsychology, Social Sciences, Psychology & Education, Philosophy, Politics, Economics, History, Exploration & Discovery, Modern Literature & Science
Bookshop: IBREX — Distribuidora de Livros e Material de Escritório Ltda (qv under Major Booksellers)
Founded: 1958

I P E A (Instituto de Planejamento Econômico e Social) Servicio Editorial*, CP 2672, Rio de Janeiro RJ (Located at: Ave President Antonio Carlos 51 – 13° andar, Centro, Rio de Janeiro) Tel: (021) 2428098 Cable Add: Planipea Telex: 2123115
Man Dir, Editorial, Production: A F Vilar de Queiro; *Sales, Publicity:* Gilberto V de Carvalho
Subject: Economics
Founded: 1971

I S A E C, see Editora Sinodal

Livro **Ibero-Americano** Ltda, CP 816, 20241 Rio de Janeiro RJ (Located at: Rua Hermenegildo de Barros 40, Rio de Janeiro) Tel: (021) 2325248/2528814/2329048 Cable Add: Nebrija
Man Dir: Ramón Martín González
Branch Off: Rua Conselheiro Crispiniano 29 – 1° pav, São Paulo SP
Bookshop: See under Major Booksellers
Subjects: History, Philosophy, Reference, Religion, Agronomy, Philology, Arts, Psychology, Textbooks (all levels), Photography, Electronics
Founded: 1946

Instituição Brasileira de Difusão Cultural Ltda, see IBRASA

Instituto Brasileiro de Administraçao Municipal (IBAM), Largo do IBAM 1, 22282 Rio de Janeiro RJ Tel: (021) 2666622 Cable Add: Ibambras Telex: 22638 Inbm
Superintendent-General: Cleuler de Barros Loyola; *Editor:* Gleisi Heisler Neves
Subjects: Law, Municipal Administration, Planning, O & M, Systems Analysis, Public Finance, Urban Development, Periodicals
Bookshop: At above address
Founded: 1952

Instituto Brasileiro de Edições Pedagógicas (IBEP)*, CP 5312, 03016 São Paulo SP (Located at: Rua Joli 294, Brás, São Paulo) Tel: (011) 2912355
Branch Off: Ave Lôbo Júnior 1011, Penha, 21020 Rio de Janeiro RJ
Subjects: Textbooks, Reference

Fundação **Instituto Brasileiro de Geografia** e Estatística (IBGE — CDDI/GECOM), see under Fundação

Instituto Brasileiro de Informação em Ciência e Tecnologia (IBICT), SCN Quadra 2 – bloco K, 70710 Brasília DF Tel: (061) 2266074 Telex: 2481

54 BRAZIL

Brazilian Institute for Information in Science and Technology
Dir: Antonio Agenor Briguet de Lemos
Subjects: Scientific & Technological Information, Information Science, Librarianship, Periodical

Instituto Campineiro de Ensino Agrícola+*, CP 1148, 13100 Campinas SP (Located at: Rua Antonio Lapa 78, Campinas) Tel: (0192) 519499 Cable Add: Icampi
Man Dir: Gervásio Souza Cavalcanti; *Sales Dir:* Esmeralda B Cavalcanti
Subject: Agriculture
Founded: 1955

Instituto de Planejamento Econômico e Social, see IPEA Servicio Editorial

Livraria **Interciência** Ltda, CP 1825, 20077 Rio de Janeiro RJ (Located at: Ave Pres Vargas 435 – 18° andar, Rio de Janeiro) Tel: (021) 2216850/2210993
Man Dir and Rights & Permissions: Edson do Nascimento Pereira; *Publicity:* Nize Nascimento
Subject: Science in general
Bookshop: At above address
Founded: 1969 (1975 as publisher)

Junta de Educação Religiosa e Publicações da Convenção Batista Brasileira (JUERP)*, CP 320, 20001 Rio de Janeiro RJ Tel: (021) 2690772 Cable Add: Batistas
General-Superintendent: Prof Joaquim de Paula Rosa; *Editorial and Rights & Permissions:* Prof Josemar de Souza Pinto; *Marketing:* Prof Napolião José Vieira; *Production:* Elias Borges de Athayde
Subject: Religion
Bookshops: Rua do Rosário 141/216, Centro, 20041 Rio de Janeiro RJ; Rua Mariz e Barris 39, Praça da Bandeira, 20270 Rio de Janeiro RJ; Ave Nil Peçanha 411, 25000 Caxias RJ; Rua Otávio Tarquinio 178, 26000 Nova Iguaçu RJ; Rua XV de Novembro 49, 24000 Niterói RJ; Rua Cel Vicente 614, 90000 Pôrto Alegre RS; Ave Visconde de São Lourenço 6, 40000 Salvador BA; Ave São João 816/820, 01000 São Paulo SP; SDS B1 G – loja 17 – conj Baracat, 70302 Brasília DF; Rua Barão de Itapemirim 208, 29000 Vitória ES; Trav Padre Prudêncio 61, 66000 Belém PA; Rua do Hospício 187, 50000 Recife PE; Rua Bahia 360 – sobre loja, 30000 Belo Horizonte MG; Rua Treze de Maio 2659, 79100 Campo Grande MS
1985: 29 titles *Founded:* 1907

Livraria **Kosmos** Editora, CP 3481, 20041 Rio de Janeiro RJ (Located at: Rua do Rosario 155, Centro, Rio de Janeiro) Tel: (021) 2227771
Man Dirs: Walter and Stefan Geyerhahn, Luiz C Poppi
Subjects: Engineering, History, Linguistics, Music, Reference, Tourism
Bookshop: Livraria Kosmos (qv under Major Booksellers)
Founded: 1935

L I S A (Livros Irradiantes SA)*, Ave Presidente Vargas 446 – sala 1802,2 Centro, 20071 Rio de Janeiro RJ
Man Dir: Leonídio Balbino da Silva; *Sales Dir:* Francisco de Paula Oliveira Filho
Subjects: Textbooks, Reference, Education
Founded: 1965

L T C-Livros Técnicos e Científicos Editora SA, Rua Vieira Bueno 21, São Cristóvão, 20920 Rio de Janeiro RJ Tel: (021) 5806055 Telex: 36909 Ltce
Man Dir: Propicio Machado Alves;
Editorial Manager: Sérgio Martins de Oliveira; *Sales Manager, Publicity, Promotion:* Zenio Rimes de Almeida; *Production Manager:* Antônio Carlos de Oliveira; *Rights & Permissions:* Jorge Augusto Marinho Diniz
Parent Company: Phidias Administração e Participações Ltda, Ave Almirante Barroso 52 – 10° andar, 20031 Rio de Janeiro RJ
Branch Off: Rua Vitória 486 – andar sala 204, 01210 São Paulo SP
Subjects: Scientific and Technical
1986: 126 titles *Founded:* 1968
ISBN Publisher's Prefix: 85-216

L T r Editora Ltda*, Rua Jaguaribe 571-585, Vila Buarque, 01224 São Paulo SP Tel: (011) 660458
Man Dir: Armando C Costa; *Sales:* Armando C Costa Jnr; *Production:* Arnaldo C Costa
Branch Off: Rua Anfilófio de Carvalho 29 – salas 607/8, Castelo, 20030 Rio de Janeiro RJ
Subject: Law
Founded: 1937

Editorial **Labor** do Brasil SA*, Mal Floriano 13 – 7 andar - conj 71/73, Pôrto Alegre RS
Dirs: Paulo F de Carvalho, Osmar Nestor Gomes
Branch Off: Rua Aurora 858 – 2 conj 23, São Paulo
Subjects: Art, Medicine, Science, Engineering, Technology

Lex Editora SA*, CP 12888, 04106 São Paulo SP (Located at: Rua Machado de Assis 57, São Paulo) Tel: (011) 5490122
Man Dir: Affonso Vitale Sobrinho;
Editorial: Dra Dulce Eugênia de Oliveira, Prof Roberto Fiuza de Andrade; *Sales:* Oswaldo Messina Jnr
Branch Off: Rua Ubaldino do Amaral 40 – loja C, 20231 Rio de Janeiro
Subjects: Law, Jurisprudence
1985: 11 titles *1986:* 11 titles *Founded:* 1937

Editora **Liber Juris** Ltda*, Rua da Assembléia 36 – 2° andar, Rio de Janeiro RJ Tel: (021) 2228742/2216664/2216954
Man Dir, Editorial, Production: Djalma de Magalhães; *Sales, Publicity:* André Luis Braga de Oliveira; *Rights & Permissions:* Djalma de Magalhães, Joao Manuel de Almeida
Parent Company: Livraria Cultural da Guanabara Ltda, Rua da Assembléia 38 – loja, Rio de Janeiro
Subject: Law
Bookshop: Livraria Cultural da Guanabara Ltda, Rua da Assembléia 38 – loja, Rio de Janeiro
Founded: 1972

Editora **Lidador** Ltda, Rua Hilario Ribeiro 154, Praça da Bandeira, 20220 Rio de Janeiro RJ Tel: (021) 2667179/2664105/2867593
Publicity Manager: Ruy Carvalho
Subjects: Economics, Music, Occultism, Sociology, Public Relations, Human Resources

Waldyr **Lima** Editora*, Rua Dr Bulhões 947, 20730 Rio de Janeiro RJ Tel: (021) 2691332/2893995
Director-General, Rights & Permissions: Waldyr Lima; *Editorial, Research & Planning Dir:* Lilian Moreira Neves; *Sales, Production, Publicity Dir:* Richard Noel Taylor
Subjects: Didactics, English as a foreign language, Portuguese
Founded: 1967

Editora Max **Limonad** Ltda+*, Rua Quintino Bocaiuva 191 – 4° andar – sala 41, 01004 São Paulo SP Tel: (011) 357393
Man Dir, Editorial & Commercial Dir: Moisés Limonad
Subjects: Law, Literature
1985: 23 titles *Founded:* 1944

Livraria Editora Técnica Ltda (LITEC)*, CP 30869, São Paulo SP (Located at: Rua dos Timbiras 257, São Paulo) Tel: (011) 2208983
Man Dir: Adalbert Walter Miehe; *Sales Dir:* José Lopes
Subjects: Electronics, Technical
Bookshop: LITEC — Livraria Editora Técnica Ltda (qv under Major Booksellers)
Founded: 1971

Livros Irradiantes SA, see LISA

Editora **Logosófica***, Rua Coronel Oscar Porto 818, 04003 São Paulo SP Tel: (011) 5701476/5706574
Man Dir, Editorial: José Antonio6 Antonini; *Sales:* José Maria Martins da Cunha; *Production:* Alvaro Puga Paz
Orders to: Rua Luiz Machado Pedrosa 96, 01431 São Paulo SP
Subject: Logosophy
Bookshops: SHCG — Norte, Area de Escolas Q704, 70000 Brasília DF; Rua Piauí 742, 30000 Belo Horizonte MG; Rua Barão de Rio Branco 63 – sala 1902, 80000 Curitiba PR; Rua Nunes Machado 14 – sala 25, 88000 Florianópolis SC; Rua 17A, 959 Setor Aeroporto, 74000 Goiânia GO; Rua General Polidoro 36, 22280 Rio de Janeiro RJ; Rua Capitão Domingos 72, 38100 Uberaba MG; and others in Argentina, Mexico, Paraguay and Uruguay
Founded: 1964

Edições **Loyola** SA*, CP 42335, 04216 São Paulo SP (Located at: Rua 1822 No 347, Ipiranga, São Paulo) Tel: (011) 639695/2746028
Subjects: Law, Education, Literature, Cinema, Economics, Philosophy, Psychology, Religion, Textbooks

Edições **'Lumen Christi'***, CP 2666, 20001 Rio de Janeiro RJ (Located at: Rua Dom Gerardo 40, Rió de Janeiro) Tel: (021) 2917122 Cable Add: Mosteiro Sanbento
Man Dir, Production, Publicity: D Hildebrando P Martins OSB; *Sales:* Nicolau Mueller OSB
Subjects: Liturgy, Theology, Spiritualism, Art
Bookshop: At above address
Founded: 1935

Editora **McGraw-Hill** do Brasil Ltda*, CP 20689, Itaim Bibi, 04533 São Paulo SP (Located at: Rua Tabapuá 1105, Itaim Bibi)
Man Dir: Milton Mira de Assumpção Filho
Parent Company: McGraw-Hill Inc, 1221 Ave of the Americas, New York, NY 10020, USA
Associate Companies: See McGraw-Hill Book Co (UK) Ltd, UK
Branch Offs: Rio de Janeiro, Belo Horizonte, Recife, Pôrto Alegre, Fortaleza, Curitiba
Subjects: Science & Technology
Founded: 1970

Editora **Magic-Corte** S/A*, Rua Aurora 858 – 6° andar, São Paulo SP Tel: (011) 2212211
Subjects: Fashion & Design

Editora **Mandarino** Ltda+*, CP 11000, Rio de Janeiro RJ (Located at: Rua Marquês de Pombal 172, Rio de Janeiro) Tel:

(021) 2215016/2324681
Man Dir: Ernesto Emanuele Mandarino;
Editorial: Elisa Maria Bruno, Mauricio
Peixoto Mandarino; *Sales:* José
Gabrielesco; *Production:* Mauricio Peixoto
Mandarino; *Publicity:* Mário Diniz
Associate Company: Publieco Promoçoes
Ltda, Rua Marqués de Pombal 171, CP
11030, Rio de Janeiro
Subjects: Spiritualism, Magic, Afro-
Brazilian Cults, Freemasonry
Founded: 1970

Editora **Manole** Ltda*, CP 1489, 01327
São Paulo SP (Located at: Rua 13 de
Maio 1026, São Paulo) Tel: (011)
2870746
*Man Dir, Editorial, Production, Rights &
Permissions:* Dinu Octau Manole; *Sales:*
Carlos Telles; *Publicity:* Ilma Manole
Subjects: Physiotherapy, Medicine,
Veterinary Medicine, Science, Psychology,
Computers, Sport
Founded: 1969

Mapa Fiscal Editora Ltda*, CP 30027,
01540 São Paulo SP (Located at: Rua
Miguel Telles Jr 394, Cambucí, São
Paulo) Tel: (011) 2784011 Cable Add:
Mapa Fiscal Telex: 1130323 Mfel
Man Dir: Jayro Gonçalves; *Editorial,
Sales, Production, Publicity Dir:* Roberto
Mateus Ordine
Branch Off: Rua do Russel 680 terreo,
Praia do Russel, Rio de Janeiro
Subject: Tax laws
Bookshop: Rua Barão de Paranapiacaba
93 – 6° of 63, Rio de Janeiro
Founded: 1952

Livraria **Martins** Editora SA*, Rua Rocha
274, Bela Vista, 01330 São Paulo SP
Tel: (011) 2880667
Branch Off: Rua Evaristo da Veiga 47,
Rio de Janeiro GB
Subjects: Literature, Juveniles, Art, Social
Sciences, Law, Economics, Geography,
History

Editora **Masson** do Brasil Ltda, Rua Borges
Lagoa 1044, 04038, São Paulo SP
Associate Companies: Masson Editeur,
France (qv); Masson Italia, Italy (qv);
Masson Editores, Mexico (qv); DIDSA,
Spain
Subjects: Medicine, Nursing, Biological
Sciences
Founded: 1978
ISBN Publisher's Prefix: 85-85005

Editora **Meca** Ltda*, Rua Araújo 81, Vila
Buarque, São Paulo SP Tel: (011)
2599049/2599034/2575346
W *Man Dir, Editorial, Production:* Cosmo
Juvela; *Sales:* Anna Maria Santos Brasil;
Publicity: Eduardo Leonel; *Rights &
Permissions:* Guarany Gallo
Subjects: General
Founded: 1970

Companhia **Melhoramentos** de São Paulo,
CP 8120, 01000 São Paulo SP (Located
at: Rua Tito 479, 05051 São Paulo)
Tel: (011) 2626866 Cable Add:
Melhoraluz Telex: 1123151 Melp
General Manager: Dr Rainer F Oellers;
Editorial & Production Managers: Dr
Murilo Ribeiro de Araújo, Eduardo
Yasuda
Branch Off: Rua Santo Afonso 52, Tijuca,
20511 Rio de Janeiro RJ
Subjects: Children's, Dictionaries,
Reference, General Literature
Bookshop: Livroluz, Largo do Arouche
167, São Paulo SP
1985: 63 titles *1986:* 75 titles *Founded:*
1915

Mestre Jou SA, Rua João Batista Leme da
Silva 126, Jatai, 05449 São Paulo SP Tel:
(011) 2629155
Man Dir: Juan Ramón Mestre-Olasolo;
Dir: Blanca Alcorta Berasategui
Subjects: Literature, History, Philosophy,
Psychology, Medicine, Technical &
Engineering, Social Sciences
Bookshops: See under Major Booksellers
Founded: 1946

Editora **Moraes** Ltda+*, Rua Ministro
Godoy 1002, 05015 São Paulo SP Tel:
(011) 8647849/628987/8641298
Man Dir: Orozimbo José de Moraes
Subjects: Education, Philosophy,
Psychology, Social Service, Literature,
Communications
Bookshop: Rua Curt Nimuendajú 19,
05015 São Paulo SP
Founded: 1969

Livraria **Nobel** SA Editora+*, CP 2373,
02910 São Paulo SP (Located at: Rua da
Balsa 559, São Paulo) Tel: (011) 8579444
Publicity: Ary Kuflik Benclowicz
Subjects: Textbooks, Agronomy,
Mathematics, Statistics, Science,
Engineering, Management & Economics,
Public Relations, Dictionaries, Veterinary,
Husbandry, Gardening, Literature
Bookshops: Livraria Nobel (qv under
Major Booksellers)
Founded: 1943
Miscellaneous: Also distributor

Noblet Indústria Gráfica e Editora Ltda*,
CP 15181, 01530 São Paulo SP (Located
at: Rua Almeida Torres 119/163, São
Paulo) Tel: (011) 2786152/2794406 Cable
Add: Altesse
Man Dir: Joseph Bekhor Abourbih;
Editorial: Wanderley Felipe; *Production:*
Fausto Taoka; *Publicity:* Josette A H
Savatovsky
Subjects: Fiction, Periodicals
Founded: 1968

Editorial **Nórdica** Ltda+, Rua Oito
Dezembro 353, 20550 Rio de Janeiro RJ
Tel: (021) 2848848 Cable Add: Nórdica
Telex: 2131810 Noca
Chief Executive: Jaime Bernardes
Subjects: General, Juveniles, Humour,
Politics, Cinema, Cookery, Economics,
Sports, Occultism, Fiction
1985-86: 70 titles *Founded:* 1970
ISBN Publisher's Prefix: 85-7007

Editora **Nova Aguilar** SA, Rua Bambina
25, 22251 Rio de Janeiro RJ Tel: (021)
2867822 Cable Add: Aguilar Telex: 34695
Enfs
President: Wellington Moreira Franco; *Man
Dir:* Sérgio Lacerda; *Editorial Dir:*
Sebastião Lacerda; *Sales:* Elson M da
Rocha
Parent Company: Editora Nova Fronteira
SA (qv)
Branch Off: Ave Pedro Bueno 1509-1511,
Jabaquara, 04342 São Paulo SP
Subjects: Complete works of important
Brazilian, Portuguese and International
writers and poets in luxury editions
Founded: 1958

Nova Epoca Editorial Ltda*, Ave
Angélica 55, Santa Cecilia, 01228 São
Paulo SP Tel: (011) 8269300
Man Dir: Maria Dorell; *Sales Dir:* Dr
Mark A Dorell; *Advertising Dir and Rights
& Permissions:* Valconi Moura de Oliveira
Subjects: General Fiction, Biography,
History, Religion, Philosophy, Reference,
Occultism
Founded: 1971

Editora **Nova Fronteira** SA+, Rua
Bambina 25, 22251 Rio de Janeiro RJ
Tel: (021) 2867822 Cable Add: Neofront
Telex: 34695 Enfs
President: Sérgio C A Lacerda; *Vice-
President:* Sebastião Lacerda; *Sales:*
Elson M da Rocha
Subsidiary Companies: Editora Nova
Aguilar SA (qv); Confraria dos Amigos do
Livro Ltda (qv)
Branch Off: Ave Pedro Bueno 1509-1511,
Jabaquara, 04342 São Paulo SP
Subjects: Fiction, Literature, Biography,
Psychology, History, Brazilian Problems,
Dictionaries, Poetry, Books for Children
and Young Adults
Founded: 1965

Livraria José **Olympio** Editora SA*, CP
9018, 22251 Rio de Janeiro RJ (Located
at: Rua Marquês de Olinda 12, Botafogo,
Rio de Janeiro) Tel: (021) 5510642 Cable
Add: Jolympio Telex: 21327 Ljoe
President: José Olympio Pereira Filho;
Man Dir: Luiz Octávio do Espírito
Santo; *Editorial:* Daniel Pereira and Vera
Teixeira Soares (Brazilian titles and World
Literature in translation), Ana Elisa
Gregori and Maria Luiza de Queiroz
(Books for Children and Young People)
Subsidiary Companies: Didacta, Encine
(both at above address)
Branch Offs: Ave Paulista 807 – 7° andar -
conj 701/2/3, 01311 São Paulo SP; Rua
Carijós 244 – 9° andar, Edifício Walmap,
30000 Belo Horizonte MG
Subjects: Biography, Brazilian Problems,
History, Literature, Philosophy,
Psychology, Sociology, Textbooks, Books
for Children and Young People,
Paperbacks
Founded: 1931

Pallas Editora e Distribuidora Ltda+, CP
7001, 21050 Rio de Janeiro RJ (Located
at: Rua Frederico de Albuquerque 44,
Higienópolis, Rio de Janeiro) Tel: (021)
2700186
Man Dir: Antonio Carlos Fernandes;
Editorial, Rights & Permissions: Cristina
F F Fernandes Warth; *Sales:* Ivan Malgeri
Subjects: Fiction, Social Sciences, National
Literature, Economics, Law, Psychology,
Occultism
Founded: 1975

Parma, an imprint of Global Editora e
Distribuidora Ltda (qv)

Edições **Paulinas**, CP 12899, 04117 São
Paulo SP (Located at: Rua Dr Pinto
Ferraz 183, São Paulo) Tel: (011)
5722362 Cable Add: Paulinos Telex:
1130791 Ramc
Man Dir and Publicity: W P Bosio;
Editorial and Rights & Permissions:
Manoel Quinta; *Sales:* A C D'Elboux;
Production: Arno Brustolin
Subjects: Religion, Philosophy, Psychology,
Biography, Juveniles, Primary & Secondary
Textbooks, Theological, Biblical, Liturgical,
Sociology, Community Health
Bookshops: Praça da Sé 180, and three
more in São Paulo; Rua México 111-B
and one more in Rio de Janeiro; one each
in Belém, Belo Horizonte, Brasília,
Campinas, Campo Grande, Caxias do Sul,
Cuiabá, Curitiba, Fortaleza, Goiânia,
Itajaí, Juiz de Fora, Maringá, Niterói,
Pôrto Alegre, Recife, Ribeirão Preto,
Salvador, São Luís, Vitória
1985: 160 titles *Founded:* 1930

Editora **Paz e Terra**+, Rua do Triunfo
177, Santa Ifigênia, 01212 São Paulo SP
Tel: (011) 2236522
General Manager, Sales & Editorial:
Fernando Gasparian; *Production, Publicity
and Rights & Permissions:* Marcus F
Gasparian

Subjects: Brazilian Studies, Latin-American Studies, Social Sciences, Philosophy, Cinema, Theatre, Political Science, Literature & Literary Theory
Bookshops: Livraria Argumento: Rua Oscar Freire 608, São Paulo; Rua Dias Ferreira 199, Rio de Janeiro. Livraria e Editora Livre, Rua Armando Penteado 44, São Paulo
1985: 34 titles *1986:* 25 titles *Founded:* 1966

Editora **Pensamento**+, Rua Mário Vicente 360, Ipiranga, 04270 São Paulo SP Tel: (011) 633141
Man Dir: Diaulas Riedel
Associate Company: Editora Cultrix (qv)
Subjects: Occult, Astrology, Psychology, Esotericism, Philosophy, Parapsychology, Orientalism, Theosophy
Founded: 1907

Editora **Perspectiva**, Ave Brigadeiro Luís Antônio 3025, Jardim Paulista, 01401 São Paulo SP Tel: (011) 2888388/2886878
Man Dir: J Guinsburg
Subjects: Social Science, Humanities, Cinema, Economics, Education, History, Philosophy, Music, Psychology, Religion

Pool Editorial Ltda*, CP 650, 50000 Recife PE (Located at: Rua Manoel Caetano 135, Derby, Recife) Tel: (081) 2215096/2215179 Cable Add: Poolne Telex: 2273 Alpp
Man Dir, Editorial: Marco Aurélio de Alcântara; *Sales:* Maristela Oliveira; *Production:* Marcos Lyra; *Publicity:* Hilton Cunha
Parent Company: Alcântara Promoções e Publicidade Ltda (at above address)
Subsidiary Company: ANE — Agencia Nordestina de Notícias (at above address)
Branch Off: Ave Franklin Roosevelt 23 – sala 605, 20000 Rio de Janeiro RJ
Subjects: Politics, Economics, Poetry, Belles Lettres, History
Bookshop: Livraria do Estacionamento Periférico da Ilha Joana Bezerra, Recife

Casa Editora **Presbiteriana***, Rua Comendador Norberto Jorge 40, Brooklin Paulista, 04602 São Paulo SP Tel: (011) 5431061/2236479
Man Dir: Rev Atael Fernando Costa
Subjects: History, Religion
Bookshop: Ave São João 439 – lojas 201-3, São Paulo
Founded: 1942

Editora **Primor** Ltda+*, Ave Almirante Barroso 63 – sala 2716, 20031 Rio de Janeiro RJ Tel: (021) 2404425/3711385 Cable Add: Primor Telex: 22150
Subsidiary Company: Gráfica Editora Primor SA (qv)
Subjects: Children's, Humour, Tourism, Illustrated Fiction and Non-fiction; International Co-Productions

Gráfica Editora **Primor** Ltda+*, Ave Almirante Barroso 63 – sala 2716, 20031 Rio de Janeiro RJ Tel: (021) 3716622 Telex: 22150
Man Dirs: Sergio Jacques Waissman, Simão Waissman; *Editorial and Rights & Permissions:* Sergio Jacques Waissman; *Sales, Publicity:* Miguel Paixão; *Production:* Paulo Duante
Parent Company: Editora Primor Ltda (qv)
Subjects: Didactics, Pre-school & Juvenile Literature, Reference, Art, General Interest, Notebooks, Illustrated books
Founded: 1969

Prol, an imprint of Global Editora e Distribuidora Ltda (qv)

Proton Editora Ltda, Ave Rebouças 3115, 05401 São Paulo SP Tel: (011) 2103616/8147922/8159708
President: Norberto R Keppe; *Man Dir:* Cláudia S Pacheco
Subjects: Psychoanalysis, Psychology, Medicine, General Science
Founded: 1976

Editora de **Publicações Científicas** Ltda+, CP 1555, 20911 Rio de Janeiro RJ (Located at: Rua Major Suckow 30-36, Rocha, Rio de Janeiro) Tel: (021) 2013722
Man Dir: José Maria de Sousa e Melo; *Editorial:* Dr Ismar Chavés da Silveira; *Sales, Publicity:* Luiz Carlos Ávila de Souza; *Production:* Edson de Oliveira Vilar
Associate Company: Editora de Publicações Médicas Ltda (EPUME) (at above address)
Branch Off: Rua Borges Lagoa 426, São Paulo
Subject: General Medicine, Odontology
Book Club: Club do Livro Científico
Founded: 1959

Distribuidora **Record** de Serviços de Imprensa SA+*, CP 884, 20291 Rio de Janeiro RJ (Located at: Rua Argentina 171, São Cristovão, Rio de Janeiro) Tel: (021) 5803668 Cable Add: Recordist Telex: 30501 Book
President & General Manager: Alfredo C Machado; *Vice-President:* Sergio C Machado
Branch Offs: Rua José Antônio Coelho 801, São Paulo SP; Ave Augusto de Lima 233, Belo Horizonte MG
Subjects: General Fiction & Non-fiction, Biography, History, Philosophy, Juveniles, Primary Textbooks
1985: 534 titles *Founded:* 1942

Editora **Resenha** Tributaria Ltda*, Rua Cel Xavier de Toledo 210 – conj 74 – 7° andar, Centro, 01048 São Paulo SP Tel: (011) 354445
Man Dir: Vaner Bícego; *Editorial Dir:* Valdyr Rezende Xavier; *Commercial Dir:* José Figueira da Cruz
Subjects: Law, Education

Editora **Reverté** Ltda*, CP 23001, 20910 Rio de Janeiro RJ (Located at: Ave do Exército 49, São Cristovão, Rio de Janeiro) Tel: (021) 2845244
Man Dir: E Rosel Albero

Editora **Revista** dos Tribunais Ltda*, CP 8153, 01501 São Paulo SP (Located at: Rua Conde do Pinhai 78, Centro, São Paulo) Tel: (011) 378689/379772
Man Dir: Nelson Palma Travassos; *Sales Dir:* Alvaro Malheiros
Subjects: Law, Economics, Philosophy, History, Reference, Sociology
Founded: 1955

Editora **Rideel** Ltda+, CP 12152, 02450 São Paulo SP (Located at: Alameda Afonso Schmidt 877, Santa Terezinha, São Paulo) Tel: (011) 2678344
Man Dir, Editorial, Publicity and Rights & Permissions: Italo Amadio; *Production:* Deise Garcia
Subjects: Reference, Medicine, Philology, History, Cooking, Infant/Juvenile Books, Sexual Education, Religion
Founded: 1971

Editora **Rio** Gráfica, now incorporated in Editora Globo Ltda (qv)

Editora Ana **Rosa**, now Editora Magic-Corte S/A (qv)

São Paulo Editora, an imprint of Global Editora e Distribuidora Ltda (qv)

Saraiva SA, Livreiros Editores*, CP 2362, 01139 São Paulo SP (Located at: Ave Marquês de São Vicente 1697, Barra Funda, São Paulo) Tel: (011) 8268422 Cable Add: Academica
President: Paulino Saraiva; *Vice-President:* Jorge Eduardo Saraiva; *Man Dir:* Ruy Mendes Gonçalves; *Editorial Dirs:* Antonio Alexandre Faccioli (Education), Juarez de Oliveira (Law); *Sales Dirs:* Nilson Lepera (Education), Antonio Luiz de Toledo Pinto (Universities); *Production Dir:* Antonio Xavier Cardoso
Branch Offs: Ave Marechal Rondon 2231, Rio de Janeiro; Rua Célia de Souza 571, Belo Horizonte; Ave Chicago 307, Pôrto Alegre; Ave Princesa Isabel 1555, Curitiba
Subjects: Law, Education, Business Administration, Economics, Primary, Secondary and University Textbooks
Bookshops: 17 branches in São Paulo
Founded: 1914

Sarvier — Editora de Livros Medicos Ltda*, CP 12927, 04012 São Paulo SP (Located at: Rua Dr Amancio de Carvalho 459, Vila Mariana, São Paulo) Tel: (011) 713439
Man Dir: Cid A Balieiro
Subjects: Medicine, Dentistry
Founded: 1965

Seleções Eletrônicas Editora Ltda, see Eletrônicas Editora Ltda

Editora **Sinodal**+, CP 11, 93001 São Leopoldo RS (Located at: Rua Epifânio Fogaça 467, São Leopoldo) Tel: (0512) 926366 Cable Add: Sinodal Telex: 511219 Xpsl
Man Dir and Rights & Permissions: Johannes F Hasenack; *Editorial:* Ilson Kayser; *Sales:* Luiz A Eichholz; *Production:* Renato R Krohn; *Publicity:* Egon H Musskopf
Parent Company: Instituição Sinodal de Assistência, Educação e Cultura (ISAEC) (at above address)
Subsidiary Company: Escola Superior de Teologia, CP 14, 93001 São Leopoldo RS
Associate Company: Colégio Sinodal (at above address)
Subjects: Theology, Religion, Education, Humanities, Sociology, Ecumenicity, Children's, Music, Periodicals
Bookshops: Editora Sinodal-Livraria, Livraria Volante (both at above main address)
1985: 35 titles *1986:* 40 titles *Founded:* 1949
ISBN Publisher's Prefix: 85-233

Livraria **Sulina** Editora, CP 357, 90020 Pôrto Alegre RS (Located at: Ave Borges de Medeiros 1030-36, Pôrto Alegre) Tel: (0512) 254755 Cable Add: Zipasul
President: Leopoldo Bernardo Boeck Jnr; *Vice-President:* Vilson Nailor Noer
Parent Company: Organização Sulina de Representações SA, Rua Cel Genuino 290, Pôrto Alegre (Distributor)
Subjects: Science, Technical, Law, Textbooks, Psychology
Bookshops: Livraria Sulina (qv under Major Booksellers)
Founded: 1946

Edições **Tabajara***, CP 1918, 90000 Pôrto Alegre RS (Located at: Rua dos Andradas 1774, Pôrto Alegre) Tel: (0512) 241073/247724
Assistant Manager: Maria Azambuja
Branch Off: Rua Santa Ifigênia 72, São Paulo
Subjects: Linguistics, Social & General Science, Mathematics, Sociology, Dramatic Art, Education, Textbooks

Livros **Técnicos e Científicos** Editora SA, see LTC

BRAZIL 57

Editora **Tecnoprint** Ltda*, CP 1880, 21040 Rio de Janeiro RJ (Located at: Rua Nova Jerusalém 345, Bonsucesso, Rio de Janeiro) Tel: (021) 2606122/2804090 Cable Add: Ediouro
Subjects: Cookery, Textbooks, Sports, Children's, Reference, Paperbacks
Founded: 1939

Editora **Universidade de Brasília**+, CP 153001, 70910 Brasília DF (Located at: Campus Universitário, Asa Norte, Brasília) Tel: (061) 2740022 ext 2110 (Editorial, Rights, Production), 2731055 (Sales), 2740022 ext 2221 (Advertising) Cable Add: Univerbrasilia Editora Telex: 611083 Unbs
Chairman: Timothy Martin Mulholland; *Editorial Dir and Rights & Permissions:* Lourenço Cazarré; *Sales Dir:* Alexandre Lima; *Production:* Elmano Rodrigues Pinheiro; *Advertising Dir:* Humberto Mancuzo
Branch Offs: Escritório de Representação da Universidade de Brasília, Ave Presidente Vargas 542 – 1309, 20210 Rio de Janeiro RJ Tel: (021) 2636959; Rua João Adolfo 118 – 6° andar – sala 608, 01050 São Paulo SP Tel: (011) 321413
Subjects: Social, Political and Physical Sciences, Humanities
Book Club: Clube do Livro da Universidade de Brasília
1985: 60 titles *1986:* 80 titles *Founded:* 1962
ISBN Publisher's Prefix: 85-230

Editora da **Universidade de São Paulo***, CP 11465, 05499 São Paulo SP (Located at: Antigo Edificio da Reitoria – 6° andar, Cidade Universitária 'Armando de Salles Oliveira', Butantã, São Paulo) Tel: (011) 2116988 Cable Add: Ruspaulo Telex: 36950
President: José Carneiro
Subjects: Scholarly, General Non-fiction
Founded: 1964

Livraria e Editora **Universitária de Direito** Ltda*, Rua Benjamin Constant 171 – 1° andar – salas 1-5, 01005 São Paulo SP Tel: (011) 356374/340314
Man Dir, Production: Armando Luiz Almeida Martins; *Editorial Dir:* Pedro Gellindo Sommavilla; *Sales Dir:* Armando des Santos Mesquita Martins
Subject: Legal works
Founded: 1968

Fundação Getúlio **Vargas**, CP 9052, 22250 Rio de Janeiro RJ (Located at: Praia de Botafogo 188, Rio de Janeiro) Tel: (021) 5510698 Cable Add: Fugevar
Man Dir: Mauro Gama; *Sales Dir:* Jorge Rangel da Matta
Subjects: Administration, Economics, Business, Sociology, Psychology, Education, Marketing, Accounting, Periodicals

Editora **Vecchi** SA*, Rua do Resende 144, Centro, 20231 Rio de Janeiro RJ Tel: (021) 2210822 Cable Add: Vekieditora Telex: 32756
Director-Superintendent: Delman Bonatto
Subjects: Biography, Cookery, Philosophy, Reference, Occultism, Religion, Juveniles, Magazines
Founded: 1913

Editora **Verbo** Ltda, CP 8811, 01526 São Paulo SP (Located at: Rua Bueno de Andrade 327, Liberdade, São Paulo) Tel: (011) 2792776 Cable Add: Verbo
Subjects: Art, Social Science, Reference, Juveniles, Education, Geography, History, Psychology, Religion

Vertente Editora Ltda*, Rua General Jardim 570, 01223 São Paulo SP Tel: (011) 2555194
Man Dir: Wladyr Nader; *Production Dir:* Paulo Douglas Barsotti
Subjects: Literature, Humanities, Periodicals
Bookshop: Escrita (at above address)
Founded: 1968

Editora **Vigília** Ltda, CP 2468, 30180 Belo Horizonte MG (Located at: Rua Felipe dos Santos 508, Bairro de Lourdes, Belo Horizonte) Tel: (031) 3372744/3372363/3372834
Branch Off: Rua Pareto 23, Tijuca, 20550 Rio de Janeiro RJ
Subjects: Textbooks, Linguistics, Brazilian Literature
ISBN Publisher's Prefix: 85-259

Editora **Visão** Ltda*, Rua Afonso Celso 243, Vila Mariana, 04119 São Paulo SP Tel: (011) 5494344 Cable Add: Revista Visão Telex: 23552/30665 Sevl
Man Dir: Henry Maksoud; *Publisher:* Isaac Jardanovski; *Sales Dir and Rights & Permissions:* Ayrton Pedro de Oliveira; *Production Manager:* Antonio Lopes Colhado
Branch Offs: Rua 19 de Fevereiro 140 – sobreloja, Rio de Janeiro RJ; Edifício Araguaia – 1° andar, Setor Comercial Sul, Brasília DF
Subjects: Humanities, Economics, Finance, Agriculture, Cattle Breeding, Diet, Commerce, Hobbies, Tourism, Politics, Science, Technology
Founded: 1952

Vozes Editora Ltda*, CP 90023, 25600 Petrópolis RJ (Located at: Rua Frei Luís 100, Petrópolis, Rio de Janeiro) Tel: (021) 435112 Cable Add: Vozes
Man Dir: Miguel Mourão de Castro
Branch Offs: Rua Senador Dantas 118, Rio de Janeiro RJ; Rua Senador Feijó 168, São Paulo SP; Rua Tupis 85 – loja 10, Belo Horizonte MG; Rua Riachuelo 1280, Pôrto Alegre RS; CRL/Norte, Q704 Bloco A 15, Brasília DF; Rua Conselheiro Portela 354, Recife PE; Rua Alferes Poli 52, Curitiba PR; Ave Tristão Gonçalves 1158, Fortaleza CE
Subjects: Belles Lettres, Linguistics, Communications, Philosophy, Religion, Administration, Psychology, Sociology
Founded: 1901

Zahar Editores+*, Rua México 31, Rio de Janeiro Tel: (021) 2400226
General Manager: Jorge Zahar; *Editorial:* Ana Cristina Zahar; *Sales Dir:* Jorge Zahar Jnr
Subjects: Social Science, Psychology, Business & Economics
Founded: 1957

Zip Editora Ltda*, Rua Leonidia 2, Olaria, 21071 Rio de Janeiro RJ Tel: (021) 2807272
Man Dir: Jan Rais; *Marketing:* Paul Margittai
Subjects: Children's, Juveniles, Mass market
Founded: 1978

Literary Agents

Carmen **Balcells** Agencia Literaria, CP 33113, Rua João Lira 97 – sala 202, Leblon, 22430 Rio de Janeiro RJ Tel: (021) 2943248 Cable Add: Copyright Rio Telex: 33961 Alcp
Manager: Ana Maria Santeiro
Head Office: Spain (qv)

Rômulo **Paes Barreto***, CP 16083, Largo do Machado, 22221 Rio de Janeiro RJ Tel: (021) 2659478

Mrs Karin **Schindler** — Dr J E Bloch Literary Agency, CP 19051, 04599 São Paulo SP Tel: (011) 2419077/2419177 Cable Add: Copyright Sãopaulo

Book Clubs

Círculo do Livro SA*, CP 7413, São Paulo SP (Located at: Al Ministro Rocha Azevedo 346, São Paulo) Tel: (011) 8818644 Cable Add: Cirlivro Telex: 31747
Man Dir: René César Xavier dos Santos; *Editorial Dir:* Esníder Pizzo
Owned by: Bertelsmann AG, Federal Republic of Germany (qv); Abril SA Cultural e Industrial (qv)

Club do **Livro Científico**, Rua Major Suckow 30-36, Rocha, 20911 Rio de Janeiro RJ
Owned by: Editora de Publicações Científicas Ltda (qv)

Clube do Livro da **Universidade de Brasília**, CP 153001, 70910 Brasília DF (Located at: Campus Universitário, Asa Norte, Brasília) Tel: (061) 2731055/2740022 ext 2186 Cable Add: Univerbrasilia Editora Telex: 611083 Unbs
Owned by: Editora Universidade de Brasília (qv)

Major Booksellers

Livraria **Agir**, Rua dos Invalidos 198, 20231 Rio de Janeiro RJ Tel: (021) 2216424/2520410
Managers: Jorge Eduardo d'Almeida Castro Faveret, Orlando Pedrosa H Jnr
Owned by: AGIR (Artes Graficas Industrias Reunidas SA)

Ao Livro Técnico SA, now COLIVRO — Comércio e Distribuição de Livros Ltda (qv)

Livraria **Brasiliense** Editora SA, Rua Barão de Itapetininga 99, 01042 São Paulo SP Tel: (011) 2311344/2311574
Manager: Caio Graco Prado
Owned by: Editora Brasiliense SA (qv)

C O L I V R O — Comércio e Distribuição de Livros Ltda, Rua Miguel Couto 35 – loja. C, 20070 Rio de Janeiro RJ Tel: (021) 2243177/2326434/2422636
Manager: Paulo Cezar Peixoto
Branches: Belém, Belo Horizonte, Brasília, Curitiba, Pôrto Alegre, Recife, Rio de Janeiro, Salvador, São Paulo
Widespread wholesaler and distributor
Owned by: Ao Livro Técnico SA Indústria a Comércio (qv)

Livraria **Canuto** Ltda*, Rua da Consolação 348 – 2° andar, 01302 São Paulo SP Tel: (011) 2595477
Manager: Knut Schendel

Livraria **Científica Técnica***, Rua Riachuelo 453 – loja 4, 50000 Recife PE Tel: (081) 24933

Livraria **Duas Cidades** Ltda*, CP 433, 01220 São Paulo SP (Located at: Rua Bento Freitas 158, Vila Buarque, São Paulo) Tel: (011) 2204702
Also Publisher (qv)

A Casa do Livro **Eldorado** Ltda, Rua Visconde de Piraja 365 – loja 17, 22410 Rio de Janeiro RJ Tel: (021) 2872147
Manager: Decio de Abreu

Livraria **Freitas** Bastos SA*, Rua 7 de Setembro 127-129, 20050 Rio de Janeiro RJ Tel: (021) 2220250/2427647/2523767
Also Publisher (qv)

Livraria do **Globo** SA, Rua dos Andradas 1416, Pôrto Alegre RS Tel: (0512) 24811
Subsidiary Company: Editora Globo (qv under Publishers)

I B R E X — Distribuidora de Livros e Material de Escritório Ltda, Rua 21 de Abril 101, Brás, 03047 São Paulo SP Tel: (011) 9482888
Owned by: IBRASA (Instituição Brasileira de Difusão Cultural Ltda) (qv)

Livro **Ibero-Americano** Ltda, CP 816, 20241 Rio de Janeiro RJ (Located at: Rua Hermenegildo de Barros 40, Rio de Janeiro) Cable Add: Nebrija Tel: (021) 2212026
Manager: Ramón Martín Ferreira
Also: Rua Conselheiro Crispiniano 29 – 1° pav, São Paulo SP
Also Publisher (qv)

Livraria **Kosmos**, CP 3481, 20041 Rio de Janeiro RJ (Located at: Rua do Rosario 155, Centro, Rio de Janeiro) Tel: (021) 2227771
Owned by: Livraria Kosmos Editora (qv)

Livraria **L E R***, Praça da República 71, 01045 São Paulo SP Tel: (011) 2596233
Managers: Ernesto H Zahar, Ernesto Zahar
Also: Praça da República 71, 01045 São Paulo SP
Importer, exporter & distributor

L I T E C — Livraria Editora Técnica Ltda*, CP 30869, São Paulo SP (Located at: Rua dos Timbiras 257, São Paulo) Tel: (011) 2208983
Manager: A W Miehe
Owned by: Livraria Editora Técnica Ltda (qv)

Livraria D **Landy**, Rua 7 de Abril 252 – 5° andar, São Paulo SP Tel: (011) 2551953/2553272
Manager: Desiderio Landy

Nova Livraria **Leonardo da Vinci** Ltda*, Ave Rio Branco 185 – lojas 2 3 e 9, 20040 Rio de Janeiro RJ Tel: (021) 2527192/2241329
Manager: Vanna Piraccini

Mestre Jou SA, Rua João Batista Leme da Silva 126, Jatai, 15449 São Paulo SP Tel: (011) 2629155
Manager: Juan Ramón Mestre-Olasolo
Also: Rua Senador Dantas 19 – sala 206, Rio de Janeiro
Also Publisher (qv)

Livraria **Nobel***, Rua da Balsa 559, 02910 São Paulo SP Tel: (011) 8579444
Dir: Ary Kuflik Benclowicz
Also: Rua de Consolação 49 and Rua Maria Antonia 108, São Paulo SP
Distributor
Owned by: Livraria Nobel SA Editora (qv)

Livraria Científica Ernesto **Reichmann** Ltda, CP 3935, 01051 São Paulo SP (Located at: Rua Dom José de Barros 168 – 6° andar – conj 61-62, 01038 São Paulo) Tel: (011) 2557501/2551342
Manager: Ernesto Reichmann

Livraria **Sulina**, CP 357, 90020 Pôrto Alegre RS (Located at: Ave Borges de Medeiros 1030-36, Pôrto Alegre) Tel: (0512) 254755
Also: Ave 7 de Setembro 1169, L 12 Bagé; Rua 15 de Janeiro 481 – loja 207 e 208, Canoas; Rua Julio de Castilhos 1657, Caxias do Sul; Praça Nereu Ramos 364 – loja H; Rua Marechal Floriano 1000, C 63 Santa Maria; and nine other bookshops in Pôrto Alegre
Owned by: Organização Sulina de Representações SA (see Livraria Sulina Editora)

Livraria **Triangulo** Editora SA*, CP 30317, 01051 São Paulo SP (Located at: Rua Barão de Itapetininga 255 – loja 23-24, São Paulo) Tel: (011) 2310922

Major Libraries

Arquivo Nacional*, Praça da República 26, 20211 Rio de Janeiro RJ Tel: (021) 2522338 Telex: 2134103 Anmj
Librarian: María de la Encarnación de España Iglesias
Publication: Mensário

Biblioteca Estadual*, Ave Presidente Vargas 1261, Rio de Janeiro RJ
State Library
Dir: Heloisa de Carvalho Cabral Lopes

Biblioteca Múnicipal Mário de Andrade*, CP 8170, 01302 São Paulo SP (Located at: Rua da Consolação 94, São Paulo) Tel: (011) 2394384/2565777
Dir: Maria da Guia de Oliveira Santiago
Publication: Boletim Bibliográfico Biblioteca Mário de Andrade (quarterly)

Biblioteca Nacional, Ave Rio Branco 219-239, 20042 Rio de Janeiro RJ Tel: (021) 2409229 Telex: 02122941 Bn Rj
Dir: Maria Alice Barroso
Publications include: Bibliografia Brasileira; Anais; Boletim Bibliográfico; Coleção Rodolfo Garcia

Biblioteca Pública de Minas Gerais, Praça de Liberdade 21, 30000 Belo Horizonte, Minas Gerais MG

Biblioteca Pública do Estado do Rio de Janeiro*, Praça da República, Niterói, Rio de Janeiro RJ

Centro de Documentação e Informação da Câmara dos Deputados*, Coordenaçaõ de Publiçacoẽs, Palácio do Congresso Nacional, Praça dos Três Poderes, 70160 Brasília DF Tel: (061) 245669 Telex: 0611164
House of Representatives' Centre of Documentation & Information
Dir: Mário Teles de Oliveira

Biblioteca do **Ministério das Relações Exteriores***, Esplanada dos Ministérios, 70040 Brasília DF Tel: (061) 2264305
Dir: Lílian Thomé Andrade (Librarian)
Publications: Aquisiçoẽs (monthly), *Aquisiçoẽs Bibliográficas* (annual), *Referência de Periódicos* (monthly)

Biblioteca da **Sociedade Brasileira** de Cultura Inglesa, CP 821, Rio de Janeiro RJ (Located at: Ave Graça Aranha 327 – andar, Rio de Janeiro RJ
Librarian: Ilka Beauchamp
Publication: Library Bulletin

Universidade de Brasília, Biblioteca Central*, CP 152951, 70910 Brasília DF (Located at: Campus Universitário, Asa Norte, Brasília) Tel: (061) 2740022 Telex: 1083
Dir: Cybele Villares Coelho

Sistema de Bibliotecas da **Universidade de São Paulo** (SIBI), CP 8191, 05508 São Paulo SP (Located at: Cidade Universitária, Butantan, São Paulo) Tel: (011) 2117448 Telex: 22092
University of São Paulo Library System
Dir: Maria Luiza Rigo Pasquarelli
Publications include: SIBI Informa

Biblioteca Central da **Universidade Federal do Paraná**, CP 441, Curitiba, Paraná PR
Dir: Maria A de Castro Correia

Centro de Ciências da Saude da **Universidade Federal do Rio de Janeiro***, Biblioteca Central – bloco L, Cidade Universitária, Ilha do Fundão, 20000 Rio de Janeiro RJ
Medical School Library of the University of Rio de Janeiro

Universidade Federal do Rio Grande do Sul (UFRGS), Biblioteca Central, CP 2303, 90001 Pôrto Alegre RS (Located at: Ave Paulo Gama 110, Pôrto Alegre) Tel: (0512) 242431 Telex: 0511055
Librarian: Zita Prates de Oliveira

Library Associations

Associação Brasileira de Bibliotecários, now Associação Profissional de Bibliotecários do Estado do Rio de Janeiro (APBERJ) (qv)

Associação dos Arquivistas Brasileiros, Praia de Botafoga 186 – sala B-217, 22253 Rio de Janeiro RJ Tel: (021) 5510748
Association of Brazilian Archivists
President: Jaime Antunes da Silva;
Secretary: Rosely Cury Rondinelli
Publication: Arquivo e Administração (twice a year)

Associação Paulista de Bibliotecários*, Rua 13 de Maio 1100 – 3° andar – conj 32, 01327 São Paulo SP Tel: (011) 2853831
Library Association of São Paulo
Executive Secretary: Madalena Sofia Mitiko Wada
Publications include: Obras de Referência em Bibliotecas Públicas (1981) (Reference Works in Public Libraries); *Palavra Chave* (library review, published periodically)

Associação Profissional de Bibliotecários do Estado do Rio de Janeiro (APBERJ)*, Rua Martins Torres 99, Santa Rosa, Niterói, 24000 Rio de Janeiro RJ
Brazilian Library Association
Previously known as Associação Brasileira de Bibliotecários
Publication: Guia de Bibliografia Especializada (Guide to Specialist Libraries)

Associação Rio-Grandense de Bibliotecários*, CP 2344, Pôrto Alegre, 90020 Rio Grande do Sul RS (Located at: Rua Dr Flores 245 – 7° andar – conj 902, Pôrto Alegre) Tel: (0512) 258194
Library Association of the State of Rio Grande do Sul
President: Carlos Luiz da Silva; *Secretary-General:* Manoel Fröhlich Henrique
Publications include: ARB Noticias (quarterly); *Catálogo Coletivo de periódicos* (Catalogue of Periodicals); *Organização de materiais especiais em bibliotecas* (Organization of Specialist Materials in Libraries)

Centro de Investigação e Documentação*, CP 23, Petropolis, Rio de Janeiro RJ
Publication: Bibliografia Classificada

Conselho Federal de Biblioteconomia (CFB)*, SCLRN 712-713 – bloco A – entr 31 sobreloja – sala 02, 70760 Brasília DF
Federal Council of Librarianship
President: Maria Lucia Almeida

Federação Brasileira de Associações de Bibliotecários (FEBAB)*, Rua Avanhandava 40 – conj 110, 01306 São Paulo SP Tel: (011) 2579979

Brazilian Federation of Library
Associations
President: Antônio Gabriel; *Secretary-General:* Maria Angelica Carneiro Martorano; *Editor:* Francisco José de Castro Ferreira
Publications: Revista Brasileira de Biblioteconomia e Documentação (Brazilian Review of Librarianship and Documentation); *Boletim*

Federação Brasileira de Associações de Bibliotecários — Comissão Brasileira de Documentação Jurídica (FEBAB/CBDJ)*, Rua Prof Antônio Maria Teixeira 120 – apt 802, Leblon, 22430 Rio de Janeiro RJ Tel: (021) 2592763
Brazilian Federation of Library Associations — Brazilian Committee of Legal Documentation
President: Nylma Thereza de Salles Velloso Amarante; *Executive Secretaries:* Tania Cordeiro Alvarez, Sérgio da Costa Velho
Publications: Notícias (News); many publications dealing with legal and related matters

Instituto Brasileiro de Informação em Ciência e Tecnologia (IBICT), Ave W-3N, Quadra 511 – bloco A, Ed Bittar Lote 1, 70750 Brasília DF
Brazilian Institute for Information in Science and Technology
Dir: Yone S Chastinet
Publications: Bibliografia Brasileira de Ciência da Informação (Brazilian Bibliography of Information Science) (annual); *Ciência da Informação* (Information Science) (three times a year)
Miscellaneous: Amongst other functions, maintains Brazilian Union Catalogue of Serials in microform, runs information centre on information science

Library Reference Books and Journals

Books

Bibliografia Brasileira de Ciência da Informação (Brazilian Bibliography of Information Science) (annual), Instituto Brasileiro de Informação em Ciência e Tecnologia (IBICT), Ave W-3N, Quadra 511 – bloco A, Ed Bittar Lote 1, 70750 Brasília DF

Guia de Bibliografia Especializada (Guide to Specialist Libraries), Associação Profissional de Bibliotecários do Estado do Rio de Janeiro (APBERJ), Rua Martins Torres 99, Santa Rosa, Niterói, 24000 Rio de Janeiro RJ
Covers all Latin America

Journals

Ciência da Informação (Information Science) (three times a year), Instituto Brasileiro de Informação em Ciência e Tecnologia (IBICT), Ave W-3N, Quadra 511 – bloco A, Ed Bittar Lote 1, 70750 Brasília DF

Notícias (News), Federação Brasileira de Associações de Bibliotecários — Comissão Brasileira de Documentação Jurídica (FEBAB/CBDJ), Rua Prof Antônio Maria Teixeira 120 – apt 802, Leblon, 22430 Rio de Janeiro RJ

Palavra Chave, Assoçiacão Paulista de Bibliotecários, Rua 13 de Maio 1100 – 3° andar – conj 32, 01327 São Paulo SP
Library review, published periodically

Revista Brasileira de Bibliteconomia e Documentação (Brazilian Review of Librarianship and Documentation), Federação Brasileira de Associações de Bibliotecários (FEBAB), Rua Avanhandava 40 – conj 110, 01306 São Paulo SP

Literary Associations and Societies

Academia Amazonense de Letras*, Rua Ramos Ferreira 1009, Manaus, 69000 Amazonas AM
President: Dr Mario Y Monteiro; *Secretary:* Tânia Regina Mesquita
Publication: Revista

Academia Brasileira de Letras, Ave Presidente Wilson 203, 20030 Rio de Janeiro RJ
President: Austregésilo de Athayde
Publication: Revista

Academia Brasiliense de Letras, CP 07/245, 70000 Brasília DF
President: Domingos Carvalho da Silva

Academia Cachoeirense de Letras*, Praça Jerônimo Monteiro 105 – 2° andar, Cachoeiro de Itapemerim, 29300 Espírito Santo ES
President: Evandro Moreira

Academia Catarinense de Letras*, Rua Vidal Ramos, Edifício José Daux – 5° andar, Florianópolis, 88000 Santa Catarina SC
Secretary-General: Sylvia Amélia Carneiro da Cunha
Publication: Revista

Academia Cearense de Letras*, Palácio Senador Alencar, Rua São Paulo 51, 60000 Fortaleza CE Tel: (085) 2315699
Secretary-General: J Denizard Macedo de Alcantara
Publications: Revista da Academia Cearense de Letras, Colécáo Dolor Barreira, Colécáo Antonio Sales

Academia de Letras*, João Pessôa, Paraíba PB

Academia de Letras da Bahia*, CP 662, Salvador, 40000 Bahia BA (Located at: Praça 15 de Novembro 15A, Salvador, Bahia)
Secretary: Antônio Loureiro de Souza
Publication: Revista (every 6 months)

Academia de Letras de Piauí*, Teresina, 64000 Piauí PI
President: José de Arimathéa Tito Filho
Publication: Revista

Academia de Letras 'Humberto de Campos', Rua 23 de Maio s/n, Vila Velha, Espírito Santo ES

Academia Feminina Espírito Santense de Letras*, Rua Bernardo Horta 30 – apdo 1, Jucutuara, Vitória, Espírito Santo ES
Women's Academy of Letters

Academia Matogrossense de Letras*, Rua 13 de Junho 173, Cuiabá, Mato Grosso MT
President: José de Merquita
Publication: Revista

Academia Mineira de Letras*, Rua Carijos 150 – 6° andar, 30000 Belo Horizonte, Minas Gerais MG
President: Vivaldi Moreira

Academia Paraibana de Letras, CP 334, 58000 João Pessoa (Located at: Rua Duque de Caxias 25, João Pessoa)
President: Afonso Pereira da Silva
Publications include: Revista

Academia Paranaense de Letras*, CP 8610, Curitiba, 80000 Paraná PR
President: Vasco José Taborda
Publications: Revista, and books

Academia Paulista de Letras*, Largo do Arouche 312, 01219 São Paulo SP 6 Tel: (011) 220722
President: Francisco Marins
Publications: Revista da Academia Paulista de Letras, Biblioteca Academia Paulista de Letras

Academia Pernambucana de Letras*, CP 50000, Recife, 50000 Pernambuco PE (Located at: Ave Rui Barbosa 1596, Graças, Recife, Pernambuco)
President: Dr Mauro Mota; *Secretary:* Dr Andrade Lima Filho
Publication: Revista

Academia Riograndense de Letras*, Rua Cândido Silveira 43, Pôrto Alegre, Rio Grande do Sul RS
Publication: Revista

P E N Clube do Brasil (Associação Universal de Escritores)*, Praia do Flamengo 172 – 11° andar, Rio de Janeiro RJ
President: Prof Marcos Almir Madeira
Publications: Boletim, novels, poetry
Also: PEN Centre de São Paulo, c/o Instituto Historico e Geografico, Rua Benjamin Constant 157 – 7° andar, São Paulo SP
President: Dr João de Scantimburgo

Literary Periodicals

Escrita (Writing), Vertente Editora Ltda, Rua General Jardim 570, 01223 São Paulo SP

Jornal de Letras (Journal of Letters), Rua Barata Ribeiro 774 – sobreloja 101, Copacabana-Rio, Guanabara

Opinião (Opinion), Ramos 78, Jardim Botanico, Rio de Janeiro RJ

Verbum (The Word), Universidade Catolica, Rua Marques de São Vicente 209, Rio de Janeiro RJ

Veritas (The Truth), Pontificia Universidade Catolica do Rio Grande do Sul, Ave Iparanga 6681, Pôrto Alegre RS

Literary Prizes

Graca **Aranha** Prize*
For the best Brazilian novel. Enquiries to PEN Clube do Brasil, Praia do Flamengo 172 – 11° andar, Rio de Janeiro RJ

Afonso **Arinos** Prize*
For the best work of fiction published or written during the two years preceding the year of award. Awarded annually.
Enquiries to the Brazilian Academy, Ave Presidente Wilson 203, Rio de Janeiro RJ

Olavo **Bilac** Prize*
For the best book of poetry. Awarded annually. Enquiries to the Brazilian Academy, Ave Presidente Wilson 203, Rio de Janeiro RJ

Viriato **Correa** Prize*
To the author of the best unpublished book for children. Enquiries to Instituto Nacional do Livro, Edifício Venâncio V, Setor de Diversões Sul, 70000 Brasília DF

Monteiro **Lobato** Prize*
For children's literature. Awarded annually. Enquiries to Brazilian Academy, Ave Presidente Wilson 203, Rio de Janeiro RJ

Julia **Lopes** de Ameida Prize*
For the best unpublished or published literary work written by a woman, preferably for a novel or collection of short stories. Awarded annually. Enquiries to Brazilian Academy, Ave Presidente Wilson 203, Rio de Janeiro RJ

Machado de Assis Prize*
Founded in 1943, this award is to an outstanding Brazilian writer for the sum of his work. Awarded annually. One of Brazil's highest literary honours. Enquiries to Brazilian Academy, Ave Presidente Wilson 203, Rio de Janeiro RJ

Odorico **Mendes** Prize*
For the best translation from foreign literature into the Portuguese language. Awarded annually. Enquiries to Brazilian Academy, Ave Presidente Wilson 203, Rio de Janeiro RJ

National Book Institute Prizes*
For outstanding unpublished literary works of fiction, poetry, history and essays. In addition, one prize is awarded for the best unpublished work of children's literature and another for illustrations of books for children. Awarded annually. Enquiries to Instituto Nacional do Livro, Edifício Venâncio V, Setor de Diversões Sul, 70000 Brasília DF

Silvio Romero Prize*
For best works in literary criticism and history of literature. Awarded annually. Enquiries to the Brazilian Academy, Ave Presidente Wilson 203, Rio de Janeiro RJ

Luisa Claudio de **Sousa** Prize*
For the best book published in the previous year. Novels, plays, literary history and criticism works are considered. Awarded annually. Enquiries to PEN Clube do Brasil, Praia do Flamengo 172 – 11° andar, Rio de Janeiro RJ

José **Verissimo** Prize*
For the best essay and a work of scholarship. Awarded annually. Enquiries to Brazilian Academy, Ave Presidente Wilson 203, Rio de Janeiro RJ

Brunei

General Information

Language: Malay and Chinese
Religion: Predominantly Islamic
Population: 228,000
Bank Hours: 0900-1200, 1400-1500 Monday-Friday; 0900-1100 Saturday
Shop Hours: 0730-1930 or 2000 Monday-Saturday in Bandar Seri Begawan, Tuesday-Sunday in Seria, Wednesday-Monday in Kuala Belait
Currency: 100 cents = 1 Brunei dollar
Export/Import Information: No tariff on books. No obscene literature allowed. Import licences not required. No exchange controls

Publishers

Leong Brothers*, 52 Jalan Bunga Kuning, PO Box 164, Seria Tel: (03) 22381 Cable Add: Leong

The **Star** Press*, Bandar Seri Begawan
Manager: F W Zimmermann
Founded: 1963

Major Booksellers

The **Brunei** Press*, Jalan Sungai, Kuala Belait
Manager: Ian MacGregor
Stockists and dealers for books handled by the Strait Times Press, Singapore

Sharikat Toko Buku **Kwang Hwa***, PO Box 1211, Bandar Seri Begawan (Located at: 308A Kiaw Lian Bldg, Bandar Seri Begawan) Tel: (02) 24075
Manager: Frederick Yong

Rex Bookstore*, PO Box 500, Brunei Hotel, Jalan Chevalier Tel: 2060

Major Library

Perpustakaan Dewan Bahasa dan Pustaka Brunei, Kementerian Kebudayaan, Belia dan Sukan, Jalan Elizabeth Ke II, Bandar Seri Begawan 2064
National Language and Literature Bureau Library
Librarian: Nellie Haji Sunny

Library Association

Persatuan Perpustakaan Kebangsaan Negara Brunei Darussalam*, c/o Perpustakaan Dewan Bahasa dan Pustaka Kementerian Kebudayaan, Belia dan Sukan, Jalan Elizabeth Ke II, Bandar Seri Begawan Tel: (02) 43511
National Library Association of Brunei
Secretary: Mohd Yusoff Haji Murni

Literary Associations and Societies

Angkatan Sasterawan dan Sasterawani (Asterawani)*, PO Box 434, Bandar Seri Begawan
Literary Association of Brunei
Secretary: Haji Leman Ahmad

Bulgaria

General Information

Language: Bulgarian. Russian widely used (English becoming common foreign language)
Religion: About 27% Eastern Orthodox, about 7% Islamic
Population: 8.9 million
Bank Hours: 0830-1145 Monday-Friday; 0800-1100 Saturday
Shop Hours: 0800-1300, 1600-1900 Monday-Saturday
Currency: 100 stotinki = 1 lev
Export/Import Information: Foreign trade is a state monopoly and tariffs are paid by enterprise involved. Books imported by the foreign trade organization 'Hemus', pl Slavejkov 11, Sofia. Exchange controls
Copyright: UCC, Berne (see International section)

Book Trade Organization

Darzhavno sdruzhenie **'Bulgarska kniga'** i petchat*, pl Slavejkov 11, Sofia Tel: (02) 879111 Telex: 22927 Kpms

Bulgarian Book and Printing State Association

Book Trade Reference Books

Books

Bulgarian Academic Books, Bulgarian Academy of Sciences, blvd Vitosha 39, Sofia C
Catalogue of the books and periodicals of the Bulgarian Academy of Sciences and the Academy of Agricultural Sciences in Bulgaria

Bŭlgarska Nacionalna Bibliografija, Ser 1-8 (The National Bibliography), Cyril and Methodius National Library, blvd Tolbuhin 11, 1504 Sofia

Bŭlgarski Knigopis (Bulgarian Books), part of *Bŭlgarska Nacionalna Bibliografija* (qv)

Bŭlgarski periodičen Pečat (Bulgarian Periodicals), part of *Bŭlgarska Nacionalna Bibliografija* (qv)

Publishers

Knigoizdatelstvo 'Georgi **Bakalov**'*, blvd Hristo Botev 3, Varna Tel: (052) 25077
Subjects: Maritime, Economics

Izdatelstvo na **Bulgarskata Akademia** na Naukite, ul Academician G Bonchev Bl 6, 1113 Sofia Tel: (02) 704054 Telex: 23132 Izdban
Publishing House of the Bulgarian Academy of Sciences
Publicity Manager: Todor Gradev
Subject: Science

Izdatelstvo na **Bulgarskata Komunisticheska Partiya**+*, blvd Lenin 47, 1507 Sofia Tel: (02) 4631
Publishing House of the Bulgarian Communist Party
Subjects: Philosophy, Politics, Sociology, Political Economy, History, Memoirs, Documentary Biographies, Fiction
Imprint: Partizdat
Founded: 1944

Bulgarski Houdozhnik*, ul Moskovska 37, 1000 Sofia Tel: (02) 876657
Dir: Stefan Kourtev
Subjects: Art, Archaeology, Juveniles
Founded: 1952

Bulgarski Pissatel*, ul 6 Septemvri 35, Sofia Tel: (02) 884734
Publishing House of the Union of Bulgarian Writers
Dir: Simeon Sultanov
Subjects: General Fiction, Belles Lettres

Izdatelstvo na **Bulgarskiya** Zemedelski Naroden Suyuz*, ul Yanko Zabounov 1, Sofia Tel: (02) 881951
Subjects: Social & Popular Politics, Agriculture, Fiction

Darzhavno Izdatelstvo 'Christo G **Danov**'*, ul Petko Karavelov 17, 4001 Plovdiv Tel: (032) 25231/25264
Dir: Peter Anastassov: *Editorial:* Atanas Mossengov
Parent Company: TPO 'Bulgarcka Kniga', pl Slavejkov 11, Sofia 1000
Subjects: Agriculture, University Textbooks, Fiction translations, Bulgarian Fiction & Poetry
Founded: 1855

Meditsina i Fizkultura*, pl Slavejkov 11, 1000 Sofia Tel: (02) 879111
Subjects: Biology, Geography, Hygiene, Medicine, Sports

Narodna Kultura, ul Gavril Genov 4, 1000 Sofia Tel: (02) 878063
Dir: Vera Gancheva
Subject: Belles Lettres
Founded: 1944

Narodna Mladezh*, ul Kaloyan 10, Sofia Tel: (02) 8681
People's Youth Publishing House
Manager: Marko Nedyalkov
Subjects: Juveniles, Philosophy, Mathematics, General, Political & Social Science, Original and Translated Fiction

Darzhavno Izdatelstvo **'Narodna Prosveta'***, ul Vasil Drumev 37, Sofia Tel: (02) 442211
Dir: Paunka Gocheva
Subject: Educational

Izdatelstvo na **Natsionalniya Savet** na Otetchestveniya Front, now Izdatelstvo na Otechestvenija Front (qv)

Darzhavno Izdatelstvo **'Nauka i Izkustvo'***, blvd Rouski 6, 1080 Sofia Tel: (02) 875701
State Publishing House 'Science & Art'
Dir: Ganka Slavthceva
Subjects: History, Art, Law, Philosophy, General & Social Science, Economics, Business, Languages, Mathematics, Physics and Natural Sciences
Founded: 1949

Izdatelstvo na **Otechestvenija** Front*, Benkovskistr 14, Sofia Tel: (02) 878481/882991
Publishing House of the National Council of the Fatherland Front
Subjects: History, Politics, Popular Science, Belles Lettres

Partizdat, an imprint of Izdatelstvo na Bulgarskata Komunisticheska Partiya (qv)

Izdatelstvo **Profizdat***, blvd Dondukov 82, Sofia Tel: (02) 872501
Publishing House of the Central Council of Bulgarian Trade Unions
Manager: Ivan Daskalov
Subjects: General Fiction, Belles Lettres, Political Science, Philosophy, General & Social Science

Sinodalno Izdatelstvo*, ul Sveta Sofia 2, Sofia Tel: (02) 883313
Synodal Publishing House
Subject: Liturgical Books

Sofia Press Agency, ul Slavyanska 29, Sofia Tel: (02) 885831 Cable Add: Sofia Press Telex: 22622
General Dir: Stefan Petrov
Subjects: General Fiction, Belles Lettres, Poetry, Biography, History, Political Science, Music, Art, Philosophy, Reference, Guides
Bookshop: At above address
Founded: 1967

Technica, blvd Rouski 6, Sofia Tel: (02) 875701
Chief Executive: Pétrana Vargova; *Editorial Manager:* Rumjana Manova
Subjects: Science & Popular Science, Reference, Manuals, Technical Dictionaries, Textbooks
1985: 427 titles *1986:* 314 titles *Founded:* 1958

Voenno Izdatelstvo*, ul Ivan Vazov 12, Sofia Tel: (02) 878116
Subjects: History, Social Sciences, Military

Darzhavno Izdatelstvo **Zemizdat***, blvd Lenin 47, PB 422, 1504 Sofia Tel: (02) 4631
State Agricultural Publishing House
Dir: Petar Angelov
Subjects: General Science, Agriculture, Textbooks, Hobbies, Cookery, Ecology, Non-fiction
Founded: 1949

Literary Agents

Jusautor, blvd Ernst Thälmann 17, 1463 Sofia Tel: (02) 873740 Cable Add: Jusautor Sofia Telex: 23042
Director-General: Yana Markova
Copyright Agency
The agency is the exclusive representative of Bulgarian authors of literary, scientific and art works, and also acts as an intermediary between foreign authors, publishers and agencies and Bulgarian users of their works

Major Booksellers

'Hemus' Foreign Trade Organization*, blvd Roussky 6, Sofia Tel: (02) 870365 Telex: 22267 Hemkik

Major Libraries

Central Historical **Archives***, ul Zhdanov 5, Sofia

Central **Archives** of the People's Republic of Bulgaria*, ul Slavanjska 4, Sofia

Bulgarian Academy of Sciences, Central Library, 7 Noemvri 1, 1040 Sofia Tel: (02) 878966
Library Dir: Prof Elena Savova
Publications: Bulgarian Academic Books, Collected Papers (irregular)

Central Agricultural Library, National Agro-industrial Union, blvd Lenin 125 – blok 1, 1040 Sofia

Central Medical Library, blvd G Sofiiski 1, 1431 Sofia
Dir: Dr Victoria Pentcheva

Central Scientific Technical Library*, blvd G A Nasser 50, PO Box 559, 1040 Sofia

Centre for Pedagogical Information and Documentation*, Lenin 125, Sofia

Cyril and Methodius National Library*, blvd Tolbuhin 11, 1504 Sofia Tel: (02) 882811 Telex: 22432 Natlib
Dir: Peter Karaangov
Publications include: Bibliotekite v Bŭlgariya (Bulgarian Libraries); *Bibliotekoznanie, Bibliografiya, Knigoznanie, Nauchna Informatsiya* (Library Science, Bibliography, Scientific Information); *Bibliotekar* (The Librarian); *Bŭlgarska Nacionalna Bibliografija, Ser 1-8* (The National Bibliography); *Bŭlgarski Knigopis* (Bulgarian Books) and *Bŭlgarski periodičen Pečat* (Bulgarian Periodicals) — each part of The National Bibliography

Municipal Library*, ul Gurko 1, Sofia

National Library 'Ivan Vazov', Nikola Vaptzarov 17, 4000 Plovdiv Tel: (032) 222915
Dir: Johan Lautliev

Sofia City and District State Archives*, ul Vitosha 2, Sofia
There are 26 District State Archives

Sofiiski Universitet 'Kliment Ohridsky' Bibliotcka, blvd Rouski 15, Sofia
Dir: Stefan Kăncev
University of Sofia Library

Central Library of the Higher **Technical Institutes***, Dr Cankov 2, Sofia

University of Sofia Library, see Sofiiski Universitet 'Kliment Ohridsky' Biblioteka

Library Associations

Bulgarian Union of Public Libraries*, ul Alabin 31, Sofia

Sekciya na Bibliotechnite Rabotnitsi pri Centralniya Komitet na Profesionalniya Sŭyuz na Rabotnitsite ot **Poligraficheskata Promishlenost i Kulturnite Instituti**, c/o Cyril and Methodius National Library, blvd Tolbuhin 11, 1504 Sofia Tel: (02) 882811
Section of the Librarians at the Professional Organization of the Workers in Polygraphics and Culture
President: Stefan Kăncev
Publications: Issues annual reports, and occasional publications jointly with the National Library, eg on IBY

Library Reference Books

Bibliotekar (The Librarian), Cyril and Methodius National Library, blvd Tolbuhin 11, 1504 Sofia

Bibliotekite v Bŭlgariya (Bulgarian Libraries), Cyril and Methodius National Library, blvd Tolbuhin 11, 1504 Sofia

Bibliotekoznanie, Bibliografiya, Knigoznanie, Nauchna Informatsiya (Library Science, Bibliography, Scientific Information), Cyril and Methodius National Library, blvd Tolbuhin 11, 1504 Sofia

Literary Associations and Societies

Bulgarian Academy of Sciences, Institute of Literature*, blvd Vitosha 39, Sofia C
Publication: Literatourna Missul (Literary Thought)

Bulgarian **P E N** Centre*, angel Kanchev 5, 1040 Sofia
President: Liliana Stefanova

Bulgarian Writers' Union*, angel Kanchev 5, 1040 Sofia
President: M Lyubomir Levchev
Publications: Literaturen Front (weekly), *Septemvri* (monthly), *Plamak* (The Flame) (monthly), *Slaveiche* (monthly, for children), *Savremennik* (quarterly), *Obzor* (Survey) (quarterly)

Komitet za Izkoustvo i Koultoura*, blvd Stambolissky 18, Sofia
Committee for Arts and Culture

Literary Periodicals

Literaturen Front (weekly), Bulgarian Writers' Union, angel Kanchev 5, 104044 Sofia

Literatourna Missul (Literary Thought), Bulgarian Academy of Sciences, Institute of Literature, blvd Vitosha 39, Sofia C
Text in Bulgarian, contents page in English and French

Obzor (Survey), Bulgarian Writers' Union, Committee for Friendship and Cultural Relations with Foreign Countries, angel Kanchev 5, 1040 Sofia
Bulgarian quarterly review of literature and the arts; text in English, Spanish and French

Plamak (The Flame), Bulgarian Writers' Union, angel Kanchev 5, 1040 Sofia
Monthly review of literature, art, publicity

Savremennik (quarterly), Bulgarian Writers' Union, angel Kanchev 5, 1040 Sofia

Literary Prizes

A competition for the best Bulgarian book published abroad is held at the annual Sofia International Book Fair

Bulgarian Publishing Award*
For the best artistic and technical achievements in the art of book publishing. Awarded annually. Enquiries to Bulgarian Book and Printing State Association and the Union of Bulgarian Artists, pl Slavejkov 11, Sofia

Burkina Faso

previously named Upper Volta

General Information

Language: French, officially
Religion: About 1 million Islamic, 250,000 Roman Catholic; remainder traditional beliefs
Population: 6.9 million
Bank hours: 0800-1200 Monday-Friday
Shop Hours: 0800-1200, 1500-1800 Monday-Saturday
Currency: CFA franc
Export/Import Information: Member of West African Economic Community. No tariff on books except children's picture-books and atlases; single advertising catalogues sent as printed matter free but otherwise dutied. Statistical Tax and Customs Stamp Tax. No import licences required for imports from EEC or Franc Zone
Copyright: Berne (see International section)

Publishers

Government Printer, Imprimerie Nationale*, BP 7040, Ouagadougou

Les **Presses** Africaines*, BP 1471, Ouagadougou Tel: (03) 334307 Telex: 5344 Presaf
Subjects: General Fiction, Religion, Secondary & Primary Textbooks
Bookshop: Librairie Jeunesse d'Afrique (qv under Major Booksellers)

Major Booksellers

Librairie **Attié***, BP 64, Ouagadougou

Librairie **Evangélique***, BP 29, Ouagadougou

Librairie de **France***, BP 73, Ouagadougou

Librairie **Jeunesse d'Afrique***, BP 1471, Ouagadougou Tel: (03) 333625 Telex: 5344 Presaf
Owned by: Les Presses Africaines (qv)

Major Libraries

American Cultural Center Library*, BP 539, Ouagadougou

Archives nationales*, Ouagadougou

Bibliothèque universitaire*, Université de Ouagadougou, BP 7021, Ouagadougou Tel: (03) 32944 Telex: 5270 UV
Librarian: Boureima Zorome

Bibliothèque du **Grand** Seminaire de Koumi*, BP 149, Bobo Dioulasso Tel: (09) 99753
Librarian: C Jouneau

Library Association

Association voltaique pour le Développement des Bibliothèques, des Archives et de la Documentation (AVDBAD)*, BP 1140, Ouagadougou
Voltan Association for the Development of Libraries, Archives and Documentation
Executive Secretary: Louis Aristide Rouamba

Burma

General Information

Language: Burmese (English used for foreign correspondence)
Religion: Buddhism
Population: 35.3 million
Bank Hours: 1000-1400 Monday-Friday; 1000-1200 Saturday
Shop Hours: Generally 0800-1700 Monday-Saturday
Currency: 100 pyas = 1 kyat
Export/Import Information: Burma has own complex tariff system, but duties are paid by State Trading Corporation No 9, 550-552 Merchant St, Rangoon, and Printing and Publishing Corporation, 228 Theinbyu St, Rangoon, principally. No tariffs on advertising. Books exempt from sales tax. Import licence required. Exchange controls; priorities apply
Copyright: No copyright conventions signed

Book Trade Organization

Burmese Publishers' Union*, 146 Bogyoke Market, Rangoon

Publishers

Hanthawaddy Book House*, 157 Bo Aung Gyaw St, Rangoon
Subjects: Textbooks, Multilingual Dictionaries
Bookshop: Hanthawaddy Bookshop (qv under Major Booksellers)

Knowledge Printing & Publishing House*, 130 Bo Gyoke Aung San St, Yegyaw, Rangoon
Subjects: Art, Education, Politics, Religion, Sociology
Bookshop: Knowledge Book House (qv under Major Booksellers)

Kyi-Pwar-Ye Book House*, 84th St, Letsegan Mandalay
Subjects: Travel, Arts, Religion, Juveniles

Sarpay Beikman Board*, 529 Merchant St, Rangoon Tel: (01) 83611 Cable Add: Sarbeikman
Chairman: Aung Htay; *Secretary:* Lt-Col Mg MgLay; *Sales, Publicity & Advertising:* U Tin Gyi; *Editorial:* Myo Thant
Subjects: Encyclopaedia, General Information, Culture, History, Applied Science, Agriculture, Law, Literature, Biography, Children's Journal
Bookshop: Sarpay Beikman Bookshop (qv under Major Booksellers)
Book Club: Sarpay Beikman Book Club
Founded: 1947

Shumawa Publishing House*, 146 Bogyoke Aung San Market, Rangoon
Bookshop: Shumawa Book House (qv under Major Booksellers)
Subjects: Mechanical Engineering, Technical

Shwepyidan Printing & Publishing House*, 12(A) Hninban St, Yegwaw Quarter, Rangoon
Subjects: Politics, Law, Religion

Smart & Mookerdum*, 221 Sule Pagoda Rd, Rangoon
Subjects: Arts, Juveniles, Cookery, Popular Sciences

Thudhammawaddy Press*, 55-56 Moung Khine St, Rangoon
Subject: Religion

Universities Administration Office*, Prome Rd, University Post Office, Rangoon
Chief Editor, Translations and Publications Department: U Wun

Book Club

Sarpay Beikman Book Club*, 529 Merchant St, Rangoon
Owned by: Sarpay Beikman Board (qv)

Major Booksellers

Chindwin Book Distributors*, 180 47th St, Rangoon

Gondu*, 209 33rd St, Rangoon

Hanthawaddy Bookshop*, 357 Bo Aung Gyaw St, Rangoon
Owned by: Hanthawaddy Book House

Hna Lon Hla*, 5 100th St, PO Box 87, Kandawlay PO, Rangoon

Knowledge Book House*, 130 Bo Gyoke Aung San St, Rangoon
Owned by: Knowledge Printing & Publishing House (qv)

Pagan Publishing House*, 123 Myamagonyi St, Kandawlay, Rangoon

Sabe U*, 148-150 33rd St, Rangoon

Sarpay Beikman Bookshop*, 529 Merchant St, Rangoon
Manager: U Tin Gyi
Owned by: Sarpay Beikman Board (qv)

Sarpay Lawka*, 173 33rd St, Rangoon

Shumawa Book House*, 1 Sandwith Rd, Rangoon
Owned by: Shumawa Publishing House (qv)

Thwe Thauk*, 341 Bo Aung Gyaw St, Rangoon

Major Libraries

Institute of Economics Library*, University Estate, Rangoon

Institute of Education Library*, University Estate, Rangoon

Rangoon **Institute of Technology** Library*, Gyogon, Insein PO, Rangoon
Librarian: Daw Myint Myint Khyn

International Institute of Advanced Buddhistic Studies Library*, Kaba-aye Pagoda Compound, Rangoon

Magwe College Library*, Magwe

Mandalay University Library, University of Mandalay, University Campus, University PO, Mandalay Tel: (02) 21211
Librarian: U Myint Thein

National Library*, Town Hall, Rangoon

State Library*, Moulmein

Universities' Central Library*, University Estate, Rangoon

Library Associations

Burma Library Association*, c/o International Institute of Advanced Buddhistic Studies, Kaba Aya, Rangoon

Jubilee Library Association*, c/o Steel Road, Toungoo

Literary Associations and Societies

Department of Ancient Literature and Culture, Ministry of Culture*, 1 Church Rd, Rangoon

Literary Prizes

National Literary Awards*
When the Burma Translation Society (now renamed Sarpay Beikman Board) was founded in 1947 it established the Best-Published-Novel-of-the-Year Prize with prize money of K1,000. The awards were gradually increased and in 1962 Sarpay Beikman was offering nine awards.
When Sarpay Beikman was taken over by the Revolutionary Government in August 1963 the Awards were transformed into National Literary Awards. More literary awards were gradually added and there are now 13 awards for the best published novel of the year, the best collection of short stories, the best belles lettres, the best book of knowledge (arts), the best book of knowledge (science), the best book of poems, the best translation of a world classic, the best translation in the general knowledge field, the best published play, the best book for children, the best book for youth, the best book on Burmese culture and the best book on political affairs.
Each national literary award now draws prize money of K6,000. Enquiries to The Secretary, Sarpay Beikman Board, 529 Merchant St, Rangoon

Sarpay Beikman Best Manuscripts Awards*
In 1969 Sarpay Beikman Board established a competition for the Best-Manuscripts-of-the-Year-Awards in order to discover new writers and to enable promising manuscripts to be published. There are 11 prizes for the best manuscripts of the year: for novels, short stories, belles lettres, general knowledge (arts), general knowledge (science), plays, children's literature, literature for youth, Burmese cultural affairs, political affairs and translations of a prescribed literary material. There are first, second and third prizes for each award and prize moneys are K5,000, K3,000 and K2,000 respectively.
All prize-winning manuscripts are published by Sarpay Beikman with the exception of translations, where only the manuscript which wins the first prize is published by Sarpay Beikman.

Enquiries to The Secretary, Sarpay Beikman Board, 529 Merchant St, Rangoon

Burundi

General Information

Language: French and Kirundi (a Bantu language)
Religion: About half Roman Catholic; others follow traditional beliefs
Population: 4.3 million
Bank Hours: Normally closed for cash transactions in afternoon but open for all other business morning and afternoon
Shop Hours: 0800-1200, 1400-1630 Monday-Friday; 0800-1200 Saturday
Currency: Burundi franc
Export/Import Information: Import licence required over value of 20,000 Burundi francs

Publishers

Government Printer*, BP 1400, Bujumbura

Major Booksellers

Burundi Literature Center*, BP 18, Gitega Tel: 2266

Imparudi (Imprimerie et Papeterie du Burundi)*, BP 509, Bujumbura Tel: 3125

Librairie Evangélique du Burundi*, BP 630, Bujumbura

Librairie Saint Paul*, BP 1360, Bujumbura

Major Libraries

Bibliothèque publique*, BP 960, Bujumbura

Bibliothèque publique de Kitega*, Kitega

Ecole normale supérieure, Bibliothèque*, BP 1065, Bujumbura Tel: 3544
Librarian: Deogratias Ndayizeye
Publication: Pédagogie

Institut Murundi d'Information et de Documentation (IMIDOC)*, 7 ave Malfeyt, BP 902, Bujumbura

Bibliothèque de l'Université du Burundi*, BP 1320, Bujumbura Tel: 5196/5446
Cable Add: Univarwa
Librarian: H Mununi

Literary Associations and Societies

Centre culturel du Burundi*, BP 1582, Bujumbura

United Republic of Cameroun

General Information

Language: French and English (officially bilingual)
Religion: Christian, Islamic, traditional
Population: 9.6 million
Bank Hours: East: 0800-1130, 1430-1630 Monday-Friday; West: 0800-1330 Monday-Friday
Shop Hours: 0800-1200, 1430-1730 (earlier closing in West) Monday-Friday; 0800-1200 Saturday
Currency: CFA franc
Export/Import Information: Member of Customs and Economic Union of Central Africa. Import licence, entitling holder to provision for necessary foreign exchange, required if value of import is over 500,000 CFA francs
Copyright: UCC Berne, Florence (see International section)

Book Trade Reference Book

Cameroon Imprints, BP 338, Douala

Publishers

Editions Buma Kor*, BP 727, Yaoundé Tel: 221556 Telex: 8231 Kn
Man Dir and Rights & Permissions: B D Buma Kor; *Sales:* Arrey Martin Ebot
Parent Company: Buma Kor & Co (Sàrl)
Imprint: Chemin Facile
Subjects: General, Children's and Christian Literature; Educational
Bookshop: Librairie Bilingue/The Bilingual Bookshop (qv under Major Booksellers)
Founded: 1977

Editions C L E*, BP 1501, Yaoundé Tel: 223554 Cable: Cle Yaoundé Telex: 8438 Kn
General Manager: Jean Dihang; *Sales Manager:* Sindjui Etienne
Subjects: General Fiction & Non-fiction, Belles Lettres, Poetry, Biography, History/Africana, How-to, Study Guides, Philosophy, Religion, Juveniles, Paperbacks, Medicine, General & Social Science, University & Secondary Textbooks
Founded: 1963
ISBN Publisher's Prefix: 2-7235

Centre d'Edition et de Production pour l'Enseignement et la Recherche (CEPER)*, Elig-Essono, BP 808, Yaoundé
Tel: 221323 Cable Add: Cepmae Yaoundé Telex: 8338
Dir General: Michel Dzukou Tahouo; *Sales Manager:* Wilfred W Banmbuh; *Production Manager:* John Matute Ewoma-Esunge
Subjects: General Non-fiction, History/Africana, Paperbacks, Science & Technology, General & Social Science, University & Secondary Textbooks
Founded: 1967

Centre d'Edition et de Production de Manuels scolaires de l'UNESCO*, Yaoundé

Chemin Facile, an imprint of Editions Buma Kor (qv)

UNITED REPUBLIC OF CAMEROUN

Editions Le **Flambeau***, BP 113,
Yaoundé Tel: 223672
Man Dir: Joseph Ndzie; *Sales:* Thomas Etoundi; *Production:* Raphael Nkonda
Subjects: General
Bookshop: At above address
Founded: 1977

Government Printer*, BP 1091, Yaoundé

Librairie/Imprimerie **Saint Paul***, Ave Monseigneur Vogt, BP 763, Yaoundé
Subjects: Religion, Christian tracts, Paperbacks, Secondary & Primary Textbooks
Bookshop: Librairie Saint Paul (qv under Major Booksellers)

Editions **Semences** Africaines+*, BP 5329, Yaoundé Nlongkak
Man Dir, Production: Philippe-Louis Ombede; *Editorial, Rights & Permissions:* Martin King Mbida; *Sales:* Lea Ombede
Orders to: BP 5329, Yaoundé-Nlongkak
Subjects: General Fiction, History, Africana, Religion, Paperbacks, Secondary & Primary Textbooks (in French and English only), Poetry, Theatre
Bookshop: BP 5329, Yaoundé-Nlongkak
Founded: 1974

Société Kenkoson d'Etudes Africaines*, BP 4064, Yaoundé
Chief Executive: Marie Salomé
Subjects: Academic, Law
Founded: 1975

Book Club

Academic Book Club*, BP 345, Kumba, South West Province
Manager: M P Napong

Major Booksellers

Librairie **'Aux Frères Réunis'***, BP 5346, Douala

Cameroun Book Centre*, 2C Nambeke St, BP 123, Victoria Tel: 332255

Ebibi Book Centre*, BP 89, Mankon-Bamenda, North West Province Tel: 361123

Librairie **Bilingue**/The Bilingual Bookshop*, BP 727, Mvog-Ada, Yaoundé Tel: 221556 Telex: 8231
Owned by: Editions Buma Kor (qv)

Librairie-Papeterie **Moderne***, BP 495, Yaoundé

Librairie-Papeterie **Protestante** CEBEC*, BP 225, Douala

Librairie **Populaire***, BP 322, Bafoussam Tel: (044) 441105

Presbyterian Book Depot and Printing Press Ltd (PRESBOOK), BP 13, Victoria Tel: 332114 Telex: 5613
Manager: W Abange
Branches: Presbook Mankon, BP 39, Bamenda; Presbook Buea, BP 19, Buea; Presbook Kumba, BP 87, Kumba; Presbook Kumbo, BP 4, Kumbo; Presbook Mamfe, BP 114, Mamfe; Presbook Tilco, BP 28, Tilco

Librairie **Saint Paul***, BP 763, Yaoundé Tel: 223404
Owned by: Librairie/Imprimerie Saint Paul (qv)

Major Libraries

Archives nationales du Cameroun*, BP 1053, Yaoundé Tel: 220078

Bibliothèque nationale du Cameroun*, BP 1053, Yaoundé Tel: 220078

British Council Library*, BP 818, Yaoundé (Located at: Les Galéries, rue J F Kennedy, Yaoundé) Tel: 231696/223172

Centre culturel américain, Bibliothèque de Prêt*, American Embassy, BP 817, Yaoundé
This is a lending library
Librarian: Emile Mongo-Bebey
Publications include: Selected bibliographies

Centre culturel français, Bibliothèque*, BP 513, Yaoundé Tel: 220533
Chief Librarian: Anne-Marie Bot

Collège camerounais des Arts, des Sciences et de la Technologie, Bibliothèque*, Bamili, BP Bamenda

Ecole normale supérieure, Bibliothèque*, BP 47, Yaoundé Tel: 221215

Pan African Institute for Development, The Library, BP 133, Buea, South-West Province Tel: 322186 Cable Add: Paid Buea Telex: 5735
Librarian: Eugene O Nwanosike

Université de Yaoundé, Bibliothèque*, BP 1312, Yaoundé Tel: 220744
Librarian: Peter Nkangafaok Chateh
Publication: Discours de la Rentrée Solennelle de l'Université (annual)

Victoria Public Library*, BP 13, Victoria Tel: 336211
Chief Librarian: Albert Kalle

Library Association

Association des Bibliothécaires, Archivistes, Documentalistes et Muséographes du Cameroun (ABADCAM)*, c/o P N Chateh, President, ABADCAM, Bibliothèque Universitaire, BP 1312, Yaoundé Tel: 220744
Association of Librarians, Archivists, Documentalists and Museum Curators of Cameroun
Secretary-General: Th Eno Belinga
Publication: Newsletter

Library Reference Journal

Newsletter, Association des Bibliothécaires, Archivistes, Documentalistes et Muséographes du Cameroun (ABADCAM), c/o P N Chateh, President, ABADCAM, Bibliothèque Universitaire, BP 1312, Yaoundé

Literary Associations and Societies

Association nationale des Poètes et Ecrivains camerounais (APEC)*, BP 2180, Yaoundé-Messa
National Association of Cameroun Poets and Writers
Secretary-General: R Philombe
Publication: Cameroun littéraire

Forum littéraire camerounais*, BP 73, Yaoundé
Cameroun Literary Workshop
Publication: Ozila

Literary Periodicals

Abbia, BP 4048, Yaoundé
Literary and cultural magazine edited by Bernard Fonlon; articles in English and French

Cameroun littéraire (Literary Cameroun), Association nationale des Poètes et Ecrivains camerounais (APEC), BP 2180, Yaoundé-Messa
Text in English and French

Ozila, Cameroun Literary Workshop, BP 73, Yaoundé
A 'little magazine' edited by Jean-Pierre Togolo

Central African Republic

General Information

Language: French, Sangho
Religion: About half Christian, half traditional
Population: 2.3 million
Bank Hours: 0700-1200 Monday-Saturday
Shop Hours: 0700 or 0800-1200 or 1230, 1430 or 1500-1830 or 1900 Tuesday-Saturday, mostly
Currency: CFA franc
Export/Import Information: Member of Customs and Economic Union of Central Africa. Import licence required but granted automatically for imports from EEC countries. Imports subject to quotas. Exchange controls outside franc zone
Copyright: Berne (see International Section)

Publishers

Government Printer (Imprimerie Centrale d'Afrique)*, BP 329, Bangui

Major Booksellers

Au Messager*, BP 823, Bangui

Librairie centrafricaine*, BP 823, Bangui (Located at: Ave de l'Independence) Tel: 611466

Librairie évangélique*, BP 240, Bangui

Papeterie Centrale*, BP 1442, Bangui

'Papyrus'*, BP 920, Bangui

Major Libraries

Bibliothèque Universitaire de Bangui*, BP 1450, Bangui Tel: 612000
Dir: Thomas Poussoumandji

Centre culturel français, Bibliothèqueque*, BP 971, Bangui Tel: 2927

Ecole normale primaire et supérieure, Bibliothèque*, BP 858, Bangui

Bibliothèque de l'**Université Jean-Bédel Bokassa**, now Bibliothèque Universitaire de Bangui (qv)

Chad

General Information

Language: French
Religion: Islamic in north, traditional and some Christian in south
Population: 4.5 million
Bank Hours: 0700-1200 Monday-Saturday
Shop Hours: 0700 or 0800-1200 or 1230. 1600-1900 Monday-Saturday; some close Monday
Currency: CFA franc
Export/Import Information: No tariff on books. Consumption tax on children's picture-books and advertising. Import licences required except for imports from the EEC and the Franc Zone
Copyright: Berne (see International section)

Publishers

Government Printer*, BP 453, N'Djamena

Major Booksellers

Georges **Abtour** SA, Librairie-Papeterie*, BP 103, N'Djamena

Librairie **Billeret***, BP 463, N'Djamena

Librairie **évangélique***, BP 127, N'Djamena

Librairie **Notre Dame***, BP 7, N'Djamena Tel: 3330

Major Libraries

Bibliothèque paroissiale*, Cathédrale Notre-Dame, BP 456, N'Djamena Parochial Library

Centre culturel français, Bibliothèque*, BP 901, N'Djamena Tel: 2920

Centre de Documentation et des Statistiques UNESCO*, BP 731, N'Djamena Tel: 2968

Bibliothèque de l'**Université du Tchad**, BP 1117, N'Djamena Tel: 2176
Chief Librarian: Kougueram Betha

Channel Islands

General Information

Language: English. French widely known. Norman-French now spoken by only a few
Religion: Predominantly Protestant (Church of England)
Population: 131,000
Bank Hours: 0930-1530 Monday-Friday
Shop Hours: 0900-1730 Monday-Wednesday, Friday and Saturday; 0900-1300 Thursday
Currency: Guernsey: 100 pence = 1 Guernsey pound. Jersey: 100 pence = 1 Jersey pound. 1 Guernsey pound = 1 Jersey pound = £1 sterling. British currency circulates and Bank of England notes are legal tender. Guernsey currency circulates in Jersey and vice versa
Copyright: Berne in its original version (see International section), but not signatory to subsequent revisions

Publishers

The **Ampersand** Press (CI) Ltd, 39 Victoria St, Alderney Tel: (048182) 3462
Editorial, Sales: Paul Davies; *Production, Publicity:* Colin Partridge
Subjects: Channel Islands (General), Military History & Fortification
Bookshop: The Alderney Bookshop (at above address)
Founded: 1982
ISBN Publisher's Prefix: 0-946346

Ashton & Denton Publishing Co (CI) Ltd, 3 Burlington House, St Saviour's Rd, St Helier, Jersey Tel: (0534) 35461/75805
Man Dir & Sales: A D W Mackenzie; *Editorial, Publicity:* Mrs Y E Aston; *Production:* M Mackenzie
Subjects: Local History, Holiday Guides
Founded: 1957

Toucan Press, Saravia, Rue des Monts, St Sampson, Guernsey Tel: (0481) 45091
Man Dir: G Stevens Cox; *Editorial:* G and J Stevens Cox; *Sales:* J Stevens Cox
Subjects: Archaeology, History, Thomas Hardy, Somerset, Dorset, Hairdressing, Wigmaking, Channel Islands, Folklore
Bookshops: Coleridge Bookshop, Rue des Monts, St Sampson, Guernsey; Old Curiosity Shop, Commercial Rd, St Sampson, Guernsey
Founded: 1850
ISBN Publisher's Prefix: 0-85694

Chile

General Information

Language: Spanish
Religion: Roman Catholic
Population: 11.1 million
Bank Hours: 0900-1400 Monday-Friday
Shop Hours (Santiago): 1000-1900 Monday-Friday; 0900-1300 Saturday
Currency: 100 centavos = 1 peso
Export/Import Information: Member of Latin American Free Trade Association
Copyright: UCC, Berne, Buenos Aires (see International section)

Book Trade Organizations

Cámara Chilena del Libro AG, Casilla 13526, Correo 21, Santiago (Located at: Ahumada 312 – of 806, Santiago) Tel: (02) 6989519
Chilean Publishers' and Booksellers' Association
President: Rodrigo Castro Cuevas; *Manager:* Carlos Franz Thorud

Standard Book Numbering Agency, c/o Cámara Chilena del Libro AG, Casilla 13526, Santiago Tel: (02) 6989519
ISBN Administrator: Hector Velis Meza

Book Trade Reference Journal

Bibliografía chilena, Biblioteca Nacional de Chile de la Dirección de Bibliotecas, Archivos y Museos, Ave Bernardo O'Higgins 651, Santiago

Publishers

Aguilar Chilena de Ediciones, now Isla Negra SA (qv)

Editorial Andrés **Bello**/Editorial Jurídica de Chile+, Ave Ricardo Lyon 946, Casilla 4256, Providencia, Santiago Tel: (02) 44665 Cable Add: Edibel Telex: 240901 Edjur
General Manager: William Thayer Arteaga; *Editorial:* Mercedes Gaju
Subjects: Medicine, History, Education, Literature, Law, Arts
Book Clubs: Clubs de Lectores 'Andrés Bello'
Bookshop: Librería Andrés Bello (qv under Major Booksellers)
1985: 134 titles *1986:* 131 titles *Founded:* 1947

Editorial Gustavo **Gili** Ltda+*, Casilla 13769, Santiago (Located at: Vicuña Mackenna 462, Santiago) Tel: (02) 2224567 Cable Add: Gusto Santiago
General Manager: Joaquín Lucas C
Associate Company: Editorial Gustavo Gili SA, Spain (qv)

Grijalbo y Cía Ltda*, Almirante Barroso 27, Santiago Tel: (02) 723027 Cable Add: Grijalbo Telex: 340260 Pbvtr Ck Grijalbo
Parent Company: Ediciones Grijalbo SA, Spain (qv)

Isla Negra SA*, Gálvez 176-180, Casilla 10133, Santiago
Parent Company: Aguilar SA de Ediciones, Spain (qv)

Editorial **Jurídica** de Chile, see Editorial Andrés Bello

Editorial **Nascimento** SA*, Casilla 2298, Santiago Tel: (02) 5550254 Cable Add: Nascimento
Man Dir: Carlos George-Nascimento Marquez
Subjects: General Fiction & Non-fiction, Scholarly
Bookshop: Librería Nascimento, San Antonio 390, Santiago
Founded: 1898

Ediciones **Paulinas***, Vicuña Mackenna 10777, Casilla 3746, Santiago Tel: (02) 2212883/2216065
Orders to: Librería San Pablo, Casilla 3746, Santiago Tel: (02) 6989145
Branches and associated companies in 20 countries
Subjects: Catholic texts, Books for Youth and Mass-Media series
Bookshops: Librería San Pablo (qv under Major Booksellers)

Pehuén Editores Ltda+, Casilla 10460, Santiago (Located at: Maria Luisa Santander 537, Santiago) Tel: (02) 465540
Publisher: Jorge Barros T; *Manager:* Alicia Cerda Z
1987: 63 titles *Founded:* 1983

Pineda Libros*, Bandera 101, Casilla 13556, Santiago Tel: (02) 721807
Man Dir: A Gonzalo Pineda
Subjects: Literature, History, Juveniles, Paperbacks
Bookshops: Pergola del Libro: Merced 838; Bandera 101 (both in Santiago)
Founded: 1944

Editorial **Pomaire** Ltda*, Casilla 10460, Santiago (Located at: Ave Manuel Montt 2534, Santiago) Tel: (02) 43330
Manager: Jorge Barros T
Head Off: Editorial Pomaire SA, Spain (qv for other branches)

Editorial El **Sembrador***, Casilla 2037, Santiago (Located at: Sargento Aldea

1041, Santiago) Tel: (02) 569454
Dir, Editorial: Isaías Gutiérrez V
Bookshop: Librería El Sembrador (qv under Major Booksellers)

Ediciones **Universidad Católica de Chile**, Casilla 114D, Santiago (Located at: Ave Bernardo O'Higgins 340 – of 212, Santiago) Tel: (02) 2224516 ext 2417
Dir: Gabriela Echeverría Duco
Founded: 1978

Editorial **Universitaria***, Maria Luisa Santander 0447, Casilla 10220, Santiago Tel: (02) 234555 Cable Add: Edunsa
Man Dir: Gabriela Matte Alessandri
Subjects: General Literature, General & Social Science, Technical, Textbooks
Founded: 1947

Ediciones **Universitarias** de Valparaíso, Casilla 1415, Valparaíso (Located at: Dr Montt, Saavedra 44, Valparaíso) Tel: (031) 252900 Telex: 230389 Ucval
Manager: Karlheinz Laage Hidalgo; *Art Dir:* Allan Browne Escobar
Parent Organization: Universidad Católica de Valparaíso (at above address)
Branch Off: Moneda 673 – 8° piso, Santiago
Subjects: General Literature, Social Sciences, Engineering, Education, Music, Arts, Textbooks, Children's
Founded: 1970

Empresa Editora **Zig-Zag** SA*, Casilla 84-D, Santiago (Located at: Amapolas 2075, Santiago) Tel: (02) 2235766 Telex: 340455 Zz Ck
General Manager: Rodrigo Castro Cuevas

Book Clubs

Clubs de Lectores 'Andrés **Bello**', Lyon 946, Casilla 4256, Santiago
There are two clubs: one for children (membership 20,000), the other for adults (membership 25,000)
Owned by: Editorial Andrés Bello/ Editorial Juridíca de Chile (qv)
Founded: 1979

Major Booksellers

Librería Andrés **Bello**, Huérfanos 1158, Santiago Tel: (02) 722116
Manager: Francisco Hoyl Sotomayor
Owned by: Editorial Andrés Bello/ Editorial Juridíca de Chile (qv)

Feria Chilena del Libro Ltda*, Miraflores 354, Casilla 10225, Santiago Tel: (02) 36519/35244
Manager: Juan Aldea Perez

Librería Universitaria*, Alameda 1050, Santiago Tel: (02) 84135

Librería **Orellana***, Esmeralda 1148, Casilla 280, Valparaíso Tel: (031) 51281

Librería **Parera***, Condell 1202-1206, Valparaíso Tel: (031) 57162

Librería y Editorial **Pax-Chile** Ltda*, Casilla 1499, Santiago (Located at: Almirante Barroso 337, Santiago) Tel: (02) 727841
Manager: Rene Ramirez Ramirez
Also: Huérfanos 786 – local 1, Santiago Tel: (02) 393822

Librería **San Pablo***, Ave Bernardo O'Higgins 1626, Casilla 3746, Santiago Tel: (02) 89145/716884
Manager: Hermano Pablo Uriarte
Branches: Calle Manuel Matta 2588, Casilla 232, Antofagasta; Calle Barros Arana 540, Casilla 1921, Concepción; Calle Pedro Montt, Casilla 1892, Valparaíso; Centro Catequístico, Calle Cienfuegos 60, Casilla 3429, Santiago; Hijas de San Pablo, Ave Vicuña Mackenna 6299, Casilla 3429, Santiago
Owned by: Ediciones Paulinas (qv)

Librería El **Sembrador***, Pasaje Matte 342-344, Casilla 2037, Santiago Tel: (02) 396675/35295
Branches: two in Santiago, and one in Africa
Owned by: Editorial El Sembrador (qv)

Major Libraries

Biblioteca Nacional de Chile de la Dirección de Bibliotecas, Archivos y Museos, Ave Bernardo O'Higgins 651, Santiago Tel: (02) 383206/383373
National Library of the Office of Libraries, Archives & Museums
Dir: Mario Arnello Romo
Publications include: Bibliografía chilena (formerly *Anvario de la Prensa*); *Referencias Críticas sobre Autores Chilenos*

Biblioteca del **Congreso** Nacional*, Compãnia 1175 – 2° piso, Casilla 1199, Santiago Tel: (02) 715331
Library of Congress
Annex: Huérfanos 1117 – 2° piso Tel: 69062
Dir: Jorge Ivan Hübner Gallo; *Chief Librarian:* Jose Miguel Vicuña Lagarrigue
Publications include: Boletín bibliográfico; Efimeros; Bibliografías especializadas (periodical series)

Biblioteca del **Instituto** Chileno-Británico de Cultura*, Casilla 3900, Santiago Tel: (02) 382156

Sistema de Bibliotecas de la Pontificia **Universidad Católica de Chile**, Vicuña Mackenna 4860, Santiago Tel: (02) 5550058/5554616 Telex: 240395
Dir: María Luisa Arenas Franco
Publication: Bibliografía Eclesiástica Chilena: Presentación del trabajo escrito

Biblioteca de la **Universidad Católica de Valparaíso**, Casilla 4059, Valparaíso (Located at: Ave Brasil 2950, Valparaíso) Tel: (031) 251024 Telex: 230389 Ucv
Dir: Carlos Ciuffardi P

Biblioteca Central de la **Universidad de Chile***, Calle Arturo Prat 23, Santiago

Universidad de Concepción Direccion de Bibliotecas*, Casilla 1807, Concepción Tel: (042) 24985 ext 24031

Library Associations

Centro Nacional de Información y Documentación (CENID)*, Casilla 297-V, Correo 21, Santiago (Located at: Canada 308, Santiago)
National Centre of Information and Documentation
Publications include: Serie Bibliográfica; Serie Directorios; Serie Información y Documentación (all irregular)

Colegio de Bibliotecarios de Chile, Diagonal Paraguay 383, Torre II, Departamento 122, Casilla 3741, Santiago Tel: (02) 2225652
Chilean Library Association
President: Marcia Marinovic S; *Secretary:* Isabel Margarita Rojas
Publications: Indices de Publicaciones Periodicas en Bibliotecología (Catalogue of Periodical Publications on Librarianship); *Micronoticias*

Library Reference Journal

Indices de Publicaciones Periodicas en Bibliotecología (Catalogue of Periodical Publications on Librarianship), Colegio de Bibliotecarios de Chile, Diagonal Paraguay 383, Torre II, Departamento 122, Casilla 3741, Santiago

Literary Associations and Societies

Chilean **P E N** Centre*, Tomas Guevara 2985, Santiago
Secretary: Eliana Cerda de Jarnholt

Sociedad de Bibliófilos Chilenos*, Casilla 895, Santiago
Society of Chilean Bibliophiles
Secretary: Ramón Eyzaguirre
Publication: El Bibliófilo Chileno (annual)

Literary Periodicals

El Bibliófilo Chileno (annual), Sociedad de Bibliófilos Chilenos, Casilla 895, Santiago

Efimeros, Biblioteca del Congreso Nacional, Compañia 1175 – 2° piso, Casilla 1199, Santiago

Mapocho, Editorial Universitaria, Maria Luisa Santander 0447, Casilla 10220, Santiago

Revista Chilena de Literatura (Chilean Review of Literature), Editorial Universitaria, Maria Luisa Santander 0447, Casilla 10220, Santiago

Taller de Letras, Editorial Universidad Católica, Diagonal Oriente 3300, Santiago

Literary Prizes

Andrés **Bello** Prize
Founded to encourage Chilean authors. A prize of US$1,500, and publication of the novel, awarded every two years. Most recent winner (1986) was Paulina Matta for *Album de fotografías*. Enquiries to Editorial Andrés Bello, Ave Ricardo Lyon 946, Casilla 4256, Providencia, Santiago

María Luisa **Bombal** Prize
Organized jointly by Editorial Andrés Bello and the municipality of Viña del Mar and awarded annually. Established in 1984 to encourage Chilean authors to write in the short-story genre. Prize is publication by Editorial Andrés Bello and US$1,877. 1986 winner was Carlos Ruiz Tagle for *El cementerio de Lonco*. Enquiries to Editorial Andrés Bello, Ave Ricardo Lyon 946, Casilla 4256, Providencia, Santiago

National Prize for Literature
Founded in 1942 in recognition of an author's sum of work. A monetary prize is awarded biennially. Enquiries to Ministerio de Educación de Chile, Dirección de Bibliotecas, Archivos y Museos, Ave Bernardo O'Higgins 651, Santiago

People's Republic of China

General Information

Language: Chinese: a single written language is used by speakers of several diverse spoken dialects. The most important spoken form is Mandarin, known in the People's Republic as *Putonghua* (= generally understood speech), which has been adopted as the national language of China. Other important spoken forms are Wu, Fukienese, Cantonese, Hakka and Amoy-Swatow
Religion: Buddhist, Islamic, Protestant, Roman, Taoist
Population: 1,047 million
Shop Hours: Generally 0900-0900 every day
Currency: 10 fen = 1 jiao; 10 jiao = 1 yuan
Export/Import Information: Foreign trade is a state monopoly. The foreign distributor for Chinese publications is Guoji Shudian, PO Box 399, Beijing. The importing organization is Waiwen Shudian, PO Box 88, Beijing

Book Trade Organizations

China I S B N Agency, The Press and Publication Administration of the People's Republic of China, 85 Dongsi Nan Dajie, Beijing Tel: 551231 Telex: 22024 Cpmco
ISBN Administrator: Mrs Sha Hongye

China National Publications Import and Export Corporation (CNPIEC), PO Box 88, Beijing Cable Add: Publimex Telex: 22313 Cpc
Branch Offs: Haberstr 7, D-6900 Heidelberg 1, Federal Republic of Germany Tel: (06221) 304455; 335 City Rd, London EC1, UK Tel: (01) 278 1833

China National Publishing Industry Trading Corporation*, PO Box 782, Beijing (Located at: 504 An Hua Li, Outside of An Ding Men, Beijing) Tel: 466251 Cable Add: Cnpitc Telex: 22497 Npapc
Branch Offs: 27 De Gui Lane, Fuzhou, Fujian; Sima Rd, Dashatou, Guangzhou, Guangdong; 380 Bei Suzhou Rd, Shanghai; 94 Munan Rd, He Ping District, Tianjin

Publishers Association of China*, 85 Dongsi Nandajie, Beijing

Standard Book Numbering Agency, see China ISBN Agency

Book Trade Reference Journal

Quan guo xin shu mu bian ji bu (Chinese National Bibliography), Bei Zong Bu Hu Tong 33 Hao, Beijing

Publishers

China Engineering Industry Press (CEIP), 1 Nanli, Baiwanzhuang, Beijing 100037 Tel: 891971 Cable Add: 8283 Telex: 22342 Scomi Fax: 891858
Chief Executive: Li Yongxing; *Editorial:* Wu Zengping; *Sales:* Chen Guohua; *Production:* Jin Xiaoling; *Publicity:* Feng Xia; *Rights & Permissions:* Wang Yunkung, Liu Jian
Parent Company: Scientech Information & Publication for Engineering Industry, Scomi
Subsidiary Company: China Agriculture Machinery Press (at above address)
Associate Companies: China Engineering Industry Press Printing Factory, 4 Ganjiakou, Haidian District, Beijing; China Engineering Industry Press Jingfeng Printing Factory, 88 Liuzhuangzi, Fengtai District, Beijing
Subjects: Mechanical, Electrical, Instrumentation, Automotive & Management Engineering
Bookshop: China Engineering Industry Press Bookshop, Baiduizi, Haidian District, Beijing
1985: 460 titles *1986:* 449 titles *Founded:* 1952
ISBN Publisher's Prefix: 7-111 (China Engineering Industry Press), 7-80032 (China Agriculture Machinery Press)

China Meteorological Press+, 46 Baishigiao Rd, West Suburb, Beijing Tel: 8312277/ 8312251 Cable Add: 2894
Editor-in-Chief: Prof Ji Naijin; *Sales:* Lin Peifen; *Production:* Chen Shubiao; *Publicity:* Zhou Shigian; *Rights & Permissions:* Shi Xiuju
Subjects: Meteorology, Environmental Sciences, Space Sciences, Oceanography, Geophysics, Geography, Journal
1985-86: 24 titles *Founded:* 1978
ISBN Publisher's Prefix: 7-5029

China National Publishing Industry Trading Corp*, PO Box 614, Beijing Tel: 555005 Cable Add: Cnpitc Telex: 22497 Npapc
Subjects: All

China Ocean Press, 1 Fuxingmenwai St, Beijing 100860 Tel: 867608 Telex: 22536 Nbo
President: Yang Wenhe; *General Editor:* Wang Zhaochun; *Sales, Production:* Luan Haitang; *Publicity and Rights & Permissions:* Zhang Jixian
Subjects: Marine Science and Technology, Sea-related Social Science, Marine Reference, Popular Science, Journals

China Social Sciences Publishing House*, A 31 Dongdan Waijiaobu Jie, Beijing Tel: 554954
Subject: Social Sciences
Founded: 1978

China Youth Publishing House*, 21 Shiertiao Hutong, Dongsi Beidajie, Beijing Tel: 444761
Subjects: Literature, Journals
Founded: 1953

Chinese Philatelic Magazine Press, 27 Dong Chang An St, Beijing
Editor-in-Chief: Wang Yongsheng
Subject: Philatelic magazines and books

Commercial Press, 36 Wangfujing St, Beijing Tel: 552026
Subjects: Reference, Foreign translations
Founded: 1897

Dolphin Books+, 24 Baiwanzhuang Rd, Beijing 37 Tel: 890951 ext 465 Cable Add: Folapress Telex: 22496 Cibtc
Man Dir: Xiao Shiling; *Editorial Dir and Rights & Permissions:* Li Shufen; *Sales, Publicity:* He Zhangyun; *Production:* Fang Yongming
Orders to: China International Book Trading Corporation (Guoji Shudian), PO Box 399, Beijing
Subject: Children's Picture-books
Founded: 1986
ISBN Publisher's Prefix: 7-80051

Foreign Language Teaching & Research Press+, PO Box 2442, Beijing (Located at: 2 Xisanhuan Beilu, Beijing) Tel: 893712/ 890351 Telex: 222378 Bfsu
Dir: Duan Shizhen; *Vice-Dir:* Liang Derun; *Editorial Manager, Publicity and Rights & Permissions:* Zheng Jiande; *Publishing Manager:* Zhao Wenyan; *Sales Manager:* Zheng Hongyi
Subjects: Textbooks, Reading Materials, Reference (inc Dictionaries), Monographic Studies (in English, Russian, German, French, Japanese, Arabic, Chinese), Books for Foreign Students of Chinese
1985: 68 titles *1986:* 69 titles
Founded: 1979
ISBN Publisher's Prefix: 7-5600

Foreign Languages Press+*, 24 Baiwanzhuang Rd, Beijing 37 Tel: 893238/ 890951 Cable Add: Folapress Telex: 22496 Cibtc
Editor-in-Chief: Luo Liang; *Sales:* Xu Mingqiang; *Rights & Permissions:* Xiao Shiling
English Department:
Editorial: Liang Liangxing; *Production:* Sun Lijie; *Publicity:* Huang Youyi
Orders to: China International Book Trading Corporation (CIBTC) (Guoji Shudian), PO Box 399, Beijing
Subjects: Anthropology, Archaeology, Biography & Reminiscences, China Basic Knowledge, Economics, Geography, Health & Medicine, History, Language, Law, Literature & Literary Criticism, Performing Arts, Political Science, Science & Technology, Sport, Travel, Visual Arts
Published languages, additional to Chinese: English, French, Spanish, German, Japanese, Arabic, Korean, Thai, Hindi, Urdu, Bengali, Portuguese, Swahili, Russian, Indonesian, Burmese, Vietnamese
1985: 420 titles *Founded:* 1952
ISBN Publisher's Prefix: 7-119

Geological Publishing House+, 64 Yangshi Dajie, Xisi, Beijing Tel: 667783 Telex: 22531 Mgmrc
Man Dir: Yu Hongzhang; *Editor-in-Chief:* Shen Shurong; *Sales Manager:* Ren Zhongyuan; *Production Manager:* Zhang Ruihua; *Rights & Permissions:* Liu Zuequiong
Subject: Geological Sciences
Bookshop: Geological Bookshop (at above address)
1985: 271 titles *1986:* 217 titles *Founded:* 1954
ISBN Publisher's Prefix: 7-116

Lianoning People's Publishing House, 2 Lane 1 – Section 6 – Nanging St, Shenyang Tel: 33316 Cable Add: 3652
Chief Executive: Chen Zhi-Qiang; *Editorial:* Li Fan; *Sales:* Hong Jing-Fu
Subjects: Political Theory, Economics, Culture & History, Classics, Foreign Language
1985: 250 titles *1986:* 270 titles *Founded:* 1951
ISBN Publisher's Prefix: 7-205

National Minorities Publishing House*, Beijing
Subject: Books in languages spoken by minorities in China

People's Literature Publishing House*, 166 Chaoyangmen Nei St, Beijing Tel: 553177
Also: Shanghai
Subjects: Literature, Children's
Founded: 1951

People's Medical Publishing House (PMPH)+, 10 Tian Tan Xi Li, Beijing Tel: 755431 Cable Add: 0427 Fax: 755429
Division of Ministry of Public Health

President: Dong Mianguo; *Deputy Editor-in-Chief:* Zhang Yuankang; *Sales, Dir:* Fan Jiefei; *Production:* Wang Duzhong
Subjects: Medicine, Pharmacology, Dentistry, Nursing Textbooks, Traditional Chinese Medicine, Public Health
Bookshop: 92 Dongdan Beidajie, Beijing
1985: 251 titles *1986:* 248 titles *Founded:* 1953

People's Sports Publishing House+, 8 Tiynguan Rd, Beijing 100061 Tel: 754525/757161
Chief Executive: Liu Xiuzheng; *Rights & Permissions:* Zhao Zhenping
Subjects: Sports, Chess (and Chinese Chess), Wushu Fitness and Health, Picture-books
1985: 144 titles *1986:* 124 titles *Founded:* 1954
ISBN Publisher's Prefix: 7-5009

The **Publishing House** of Law, PO Box 111, 23 Tai Ping Lu, Hai Dian District, Beijing Tel: 815325
Executive Dir, Editorial: Lan Ming-Liang; *Sales:* Wang Jia-jing; *Production, Publicity:* Ling Yu-jie; *Rights & Permissions:* Fiang-Xue-Yang
Subject: Law (including codes, rules & regulations)
Founded: 1980

S D X (Shenghuo-Dushu-Xinzhi) Joint Publishing Co, 166 Chaonei Dajie St, Beijing Tel: 555159 Cable Add: 1003
President: Shen Changwen; *Vice-President:* Dong Xiuyu; *Rights & Permissions:* Ze Wei, Yang Jin
Subjects: Philosophy, Economics, Sociology, Politics, Psychology, Management, History, Literature, Biography
Founded: 1932

Science Press*, 137 Chaoyangmennei St, Beijing Tel: 445426 Telex: 22313 Cpc
Subject: Sciences

Shanghai Educational Publishing House, 123 Yong Fu Rd, Shanghai Tel: 377165 Cable Add: 3413
Chief Executive: Chen Y; *Editorial:* Qi Hua; *Production:* Liang Guo Shu
Subjects: Pre-school and School Textbooks
Bookshop: At above address
1985: 210 titles *1986:* 195 titles *Founded:* 1958
ISBN Publisher's Prefix: 7-5320

Shanghai Scientific & Technical Publishers, 450 Rui-jin Er Rd, Shanghai 200020 Tel: 370160 Telex: 33384 Cpts
Chief Executive: Xu Fu-sheng; *Editorial and Rights & Permissions:* Hu Da-wei; *Sales:* Wang Feng-ying; *Production:* Zhang Hui-long; *Publicity:* Wang Pei-lin
Subjects: Natural Science, Engineering, Medical Science, Agriculture, Popular Science
Bookshop: SSTP Bookshop (at above address)
1985: 250 titles *1986:* 250 titles *Founded:* 1956

Shanghai Scientific & Technological Literature Publishing House, 2 Wukang Rd, Shanghai Tel: 370782
Chief Executive: Wang Lin Zhen; *Editorial:* Fang Jin Shan, Chi Wen Jun; *Sales:* Zhao Yi Liang; *Production, Publicity:* Qu Cheng Qing; *Rights & Permissions:* Sun Jian Yue
Parent Organization: Science and Technology Commission of Shanghai Municipality, 30 Fu Zhou Rd, Shanghai
Subjects: Science, Engineering, Agriculture, Medicine
1985: 118 titles *1986:* 130 titles *Founded:* 1978
ISBN Publisher's Prefix: 77-80513

Sinolingua+, 24 Baiwanzhuang Rd, Beijing 37 Tel: 890951 ext 602 Cable Add: Fola Press Telex: 22496 Cibtc
Chief Executive, Editorial: Chen Xiaoming; *Sales:* Chen Yushi; *Production:* Chen Junran; *Publicity:* Chen Hualan; *Rights & Permissions:* An Zongguo
Orders to: China International Book Trading Corporation (Guoji Shudian), PO Box 399, Beijing
Subject: Chinese language textbooks
1985: 12 titles *Founded:* 1985
ISBN Publisher's Prefix: 7-80052

Writers' Publishing House*, Beijing
A state enterprise publishing reprints of Chinese literature

Xinhua Publishing House, 57 Xuanwumen Xi Dajie, Beijing Tel: 668521/663880 Cable Add: 1631 Telex: 22316 Xna Bj
Dir, Editor-in-Chief: Xu Bang; *Editorial:* Zhou Daorong, Yang Chunhua (Pictorial albums); Chen Lekai; *Production:* Liang Mingze
Subjects: Journalism, Economics, Biography, Annuals, Culture
Bookshop: At above address
1985: 133 titles *1986:* 129 titles *Founded:* 1979

Youth Publishing House*, Beijing

Zhong Hua Book Co*, 36 Wangfujing St, Beijing Tel: 554504
Subject: Chinese Classics
Founded: 1912

Major Booksellers

China International Book Trading Corporation (CIBTC) (Guoji Shudian), PO Box 399, Beijing (Located at: 21 Chegongzhuang Xilu) Tel: 8022023 Cable Add: Cibtc Beijing Telex: 22496 Cibtc
President: Wang Qingyun
Distributor abroad for Chinese publications, importer of books published abroad

Guoji Shudian, see China International Book Trading Corporation (CIBTC)

Waiwen Shudian*, PO Box 88, 38 Suchou Hutong, Beijing
Importer for foreign publications

Major Libraries

Beijing daxue tushuguan*, Beijing
Peking University Library
Dir: Zihuang Shoujing

Beijing tushuguan, National Library of Beijing, now incorporated in Zhong-guo guo jia tushuguan (qv)

Chongqing Library*, Chongqing

Liaoning Library*, Shenyang (Mukden)

Nanjing tushuguan*, Nanjing, Jiangsu
Nanking Library

National Library of China*, 7 Wen Jin St, Beijing Tel: 6331321
Zhong-guo guo jia tushuguan. Formerly National Library of Beijing
Deputy Dir: Xie Daoyuan
Publications include: Documentation (series); The National Catalogue of Foreign Periodicals; Chinese Classification — A System Used in Chinese Libraries

Qinghua daxue tushuguan*, Beijing Tel: 282451 ext 2305
Qinghua University Library (formerly Tsing Hua University)

Shanghai tushuguan, 325 Nanjing Rd (W), Shanghai Tel: 563176
Shanghai Library
Hon Dir: Gu Ting-long

Yunnan Provincial Library*, Kunming
Dir: Mo Tien-chuang

Zhejiang tushuguan*, Hangzhou
Chekiang Library, Hangchow

Zhong-guo guo jia tushuguan, see National Library of China

Zhong-guo ke xue yuan tushuguan, 27 Wangfujing Dajie, Beijing Tel: 550017
Library of Academic Science
Dir: Shi Jian
Publication: Library Information

Zhongshan Library of Guangdong Province*, 62 Wende Rd, Guangzhou (Canton) Tel: 33306
Dir: Mrs Wang Zhi-Hua

Library Association

China Society of Library Science, 7 Wen Jin St, Beijing 7 Tel: 666331 ext 312 Telex: 222211 Nlc
Publication: Library News

Library Reference Books and Journals

Book

Chinese Classification — A System Used in Chinese Libraries, National Library of China, 7 Wen Jin St, Beijing

Journals

Library Information, Zhong-guo ke xue yuan tushuguan, 271 Wanfu Dajie, Beijing

Library News, China Society of Library Science, 7 Wen Jin St, Beijing

Literary Associations and Societies

China P E N Centre, 2 Shatan Beijie, Beijing
President: Ba Jin; *Secretary:* Bi Shuowang

Guangzhou Chinese P E N Centre*, 1/69 Wende Lu, Guangzhou
Secretary: Miss Huang Qingyun

Chinese Shanghai P E N Centre, 675 Julu Lu, Shanghai
Secretary: Mr Luo Luo

Literary Periodicals

China Books, China International Book Trading Corporation (CIBTC) (Guoji Shudian), PO Box 399, Beijing
Organ of the Corporation; English edition

Chinese Literature, Foreign Languages Press, 24 Baiwanzhuang, Beijing 37
Subscriptions to China International Book Trading Corporation (CIBTC) (Guoji Shudian), PO Box 399, Beijing; English and French editions

COLOMBIA 69

Colombia

General Information

Language: Spanish (English widely used in business)
Religion: Roman Catholic
Population: 29 million
Bank Hours: 0900-1500 Monday-Friday
Shop Hours: 0900-1230, 1430-1830 Monday-Saturday
Currency: 100 centavos = 1 peso
Export/Import Information: Member of Latin American Free Trade Association. Value added taxes on all imports; no sales tax on books. Ad valorem: none generally on books except on books bound in leather or similar materials, on photonovels of thrillers, detective stories etc, on horoscopes, on children's picture books, on atlases and on advertising catalogues. No import licence for books. Exchange licence from Banco de la Republica required
Copyright: UCC, Buenos Aires (see International section)

Book Trade Organizations

Camara Colombiana de la Industria Editorial, Apdo 8998, Bogotá (Located at: Carrera 7A No 17-51 of 409 y 410) Tel: (01) 821117/861805
Colombian Publishers' Association
Executive Dir: Juan Luis Mejia Arango
Publication: Libros Colombianos

Cámara Colombiana del Libro*, Carrera 54 No 52-15P3, Medellín Tel: (04) 457778
Colombian Book Association

Standard Book Numbering Agency, Cámara Colombiana de la Industria Editorial, Apdo Aéreo 8998, Bogotá (Located at: Carrera 7a No 17-51 of 409 y 410) Tel: (01) 2821117/2861805
ISBN Administrator: Juan Luis Mejia Arango

Book Trade Reference Books and Journals

Book

Guia de Editoriales, Distribuidores y Librerias de Bogotá, Centro Régional para el Fomento del Libro en América Latina y el Caribe (CERLAL), Calle 70 No 9-52, Apdo Aéreo 17438, Bogotá

Journals

Anuario Bibliográfico Colombiano 'Rubén Pérez Ortiz' (Colombian Bibliographical Annual), Instituto Caro y Cuervo, Apdo Aéreo 51502, Bogotá

Bibliografia Oficial Colombiana (Official Colombian Bibliography), Escuela Interamericana de Bibliotecología, Universidad de Antioquia, Apdo Aéreo 1226, Medellín

Libros Colombianos, Cámara Colombiana de la Industria Editorial, Apdo 8998, Bogotá

Publishers

A C P O, see Accion Cultural Popular ACPO — Editorial Andes

Accion Cultural Popular ACPO — Editorial Andes*, Apdo Aéreo 20037, Bogotá (Located at: Carrera 39A No 15-81, Bogotá) Tel: (01) 2699698/2684800 ext 240 Cable Add: Radiofonicas Bogota Telex: 45623 Accpo
Man Dir: Hernando Bernal A; *Editorial:* Javier Martinez Naranjo; *Sales and Rights & Permissions:* Luis Felipe Delgado, Manuel Hoyos
Subjects: Art, Colombia, Social Sciences, Literature
Founded: 1947 (ACPO — Editôra Dosmil 1964)
Miscellaneous: Formerly Accion Cultural Popular ACPO — Editora Dosmil
ISBN Publisher's Prefix: 84-8275

El **Ancora** Editores Ltda, Apdo 56882, Bogotá (Located at: Carrera 6a No 35-29, Bogotá) Tel: (01) 2877788/2882691
Man Dir: Patricia Hoher; *Editorial, Rights & Permissions:* Felipe Escobar; *Sales:* León Bedoya; *Production, Publicity:* Mónica Hoher
Subjects: History, Economics, Literature (Colombian & Latin American)
Bookshop: At above address
Founded: 1980
ISBN Publisher's Prefix: 84-89209

Editorial **Andes**, see Accion Cultural Popular ACPO

Editorial **Bedout** SA*, Apdo Aéreo 760, Medellín (Located at: Calle 61 No 51-04, Medellín) Tel: (04) 316900 Cable Add: Bedout
President: Elías Vélez; *Manager:* Libardo Statizábal C
Branch Offs: Calle 45 No 36-50, Apdo Aéreo 2845, Barranquilla; Calle 39 No 22-53, Apdo Aéro 12050, Bogotá; Calle 10 No 5-23 of 404, Cali; Plaza Fernández Madrid No 7-26 of 301, Apdo Aéreo 524, Cartagena; Apdo Aéreo 1283, Ibagué; Carrera 29 No 25-29 of 214, Manizales; Apdo Aéreo 1100, Montería; Calle 24 No 6-02, Apdo Aéreo 2649, Pereira
Subjects: Literature, Social Science, Didactics, Textbooks, Juveniles
Founded: 1889

Editorial **Bruguera** Colombiana Ltda*, Calle 20 No 42-C-43, Bogotá Tel: (01) 2682563
Man Dir: Antonio Mourin
Parent Company: Editorial Bruguera SA, Spain (qv)

C E D E (Centro de Estudios sobre Desarrollo Económico)+*, Universidad de los Andes, Apdo Aéreo 4976, Bogotá Tel: (01) 2824066 ext 189/2430295 ext 68
Dir: Augusto Cano
Subjects: Economics, Social Sciences
Founded: 1958

Instituto **Caro y Cuervo**, Apdo Aéreo 51502, Bogotá Tel: (01) 2557753
Man Dir: Ignacio Chaves Cuevas
Subjects: Belles Lettres, Linguistics, Philology, Reference
Bookshops: Librería Yerbabuena, Carrera 11 No 64-37, Bogotá; Librería Cuervo, Calle 10 No 4-69, Bogotá
Founded: 1942

Carvajal SA*, Apdo Aéreo 46, Cali Tel: (03) 681111 Cable Add: Carvajales Cali Telex: 055555/055650
Subsidiary Company: Editorial Norma SA (qv)
Subjects: Children's Pop-ups, Juveniles, Textbooks, Magazines, Atlases

Fundación **Centro** de Investigación y Educación Popular (CINEP), Carrera 5 No 33A-08, Apdo Aéreo 25916, Bogotá Tel: (01) 2324440/2871284
Man Dir and Rights & Permissions: Francisco de Roux; *Production, Publicity and Publications Manager:* Elena Gardeazábal
Subjects: Colombian Politics & Economics, Sociology
Founded: 1959

Ciudad Nueva*, Carrera 4A No 58-90, Bogotá 2
Parent Company: Città Nuova Editrice, Italy (qv for associate companies)

Colombiana de Ediciones SA **Colediciones***, Calle 48 No 67-152, Bogotá
Man Dir, Editorial, Rights & Permissions: Carlos Senior Pava; *Sales:* Harold Valencia Salinas; *Production:* Guillermo Cajale Santacoloma
Subsidiary Companies: Arte Libros Editores (at above address); Servicio de Documentacion (SD), Ave 22 No 37-90, Apdo 101, Bogotá
Associate Company: Librerías Unidas Ltda, Ave 22 No 37-90, Apdo 101, Bogotá
Subjects: The Family, Spiritualism, Sociology
Bookshop: Librería Ancora, Ave 22 No 37-90, Apdo 101, Bogotá
Founded: 1978

Cultural Colombiana Ltda, Calle 72 No 16-15/21, Apdo Aéreo 6307, Bogotá Tel: (01) 2355494/2176569/2176471 Cable Add: Culbiana
Man Dir: José Porto; *Editorial:* José Porto Vazquez; *Sales Dirs:* Hernando Salazar; *Production:* Maximilian Nicolás
Subjects: Primary & Secondary Textbooks
Bookshop: Librería Cultural Colombiana (qv under Major Booksellers)
Founded: 1951
ISBN Publisher's Prefix: 958-9013

Fondo Educativo Interamericano SA*, Apdo Aéreo 29696, Bogotá (Located at: Calle 36 No 22-33, Bogotá) Tel: (01) 2459279/2852773/2852542 Cable Add: Adiwes Bogota Telex: 45581
Man Dir: Alvaro Toledo Montes
Parent Company: Addison-Wesley Publishing Co Inc, Reading, MA 01867, USA
Associate Companies: See Addison-Wesley Iberoamericana, Mexico
Subjects: University Textbooks, School Texts, Trade Books
Founded: 1970

Editora **Guadalupe** Ltda, Apdo Aéreo 029765, Bogotá 1 (Located at: Carrera 42 No 10-57, Bogotá) Tel: (01) 2690788
Man Dir and Editorial: Marco A Moreno Hernandez; *Sales:* Mario E Joya Hernandez; *Production:* José Adel Lopez Q
Subjects: Sciences, Technology, Literature
Founded: 1969
ISBN Publisher's Prefix: 958-608

Inversiones Editoriales La Carreta*, Apdo 9026, Bogotá (Located at: Calle 17 No 4-95 of 205, Bogotá) Tel: (01) 2431249
Man Dir, Editorial: Mario Arrubla; *Sales:* Catalina Arrubla; *Production:* César Hurtado
Subsidiary Company: Distribuidora Letras, Carrera 50 No 52-8 of 407, Medellín
Subjects: History, Economics, Politics (generally on Colombia)
Bookshop: Librería Letras, Carrera 5A No 8-12, Cali
Founded: 1975

J R Editores, now RAM Editores (qv)

Editorial **Juventud** Ltda*, Apdo Aéreo 53694, Bogotá 2 (Located at: Calle 58 No 19-41, Bogotá) Tel: (01) 2557485/2557416
Man Dir: Santiago Preckler
Parent Company: Editorial Juventud SA, Spain (qv)

COLOMBIA

Editorial **Kapelusz** Colombiana SA+*, Apdo Aéreo 54926, Bogotá (Located at: Calle8 70A No 11-10, Bogotá) Tel: (01) 2112712/2492488 Cable Add: Kapelusz
Man Dir, Sales and Rights & Permissions: Diego Tenorio
Parent Company: Editorial Kapelusz SA, Argentina (qv)
Subjects: Pre-school, Primary, Secondary & University Textbooks, Pedagogy, Psychology, Physics
Bookshop: At above address
Founded: 1964

L E G I S — Legislación Económica Ltda+, Apdo Aéreo 98888, Bogotá (Located at: Ave Eldorado 8110, Bogotá) Tel: (01) 2634100 Cable Add: Legislación Telex: 43300 Legis
Man Dir: Miguel Enrique Caldas Caldas
Subsidiary Company: Legislación Económica Srl, URB Industrial la Urbina, Calle 8, Edifico Lec, Caracas, Venezuela
Subjects: Economics, Law, Commerce
Founded: 1952

Editorial **Labor** SAColombiana Ltda*, Carrera 16 No 30-25, Bogotá Tel: (01) 698301
Man Dir: Enrique Fajardo
Parent Company: Editorial Labor SA, Spain, (qv)

Ediciones **Larousse** Colombiana Ltda*, Apdo Aéreo 75548, Bogotá (Located at: Calle 65 No 5-50, Bogotá) Tel: (01) 2495475
Man Dir: Juan Carlos Sierra
Parent Company: Librairie Larousse, France (qv)
Subjects: Dictionaries, Encyclopaedias
Founded: 1983
ISBN Publisher's Prefix: 958-95024

Legislación Económica Ltda, see LEGIS

Ediciones **Lerner** Ltda+*, Apdo Aéreo 8304, Bogotá (Located at: Calle 8A No 64A-41, Bogotá) Tel: (01) 2628200 Cable Add: Edilerner Telex: 43195
Man Dir: Jack A Grimberg Possin;
Editorial: Juan Francisco di Doménico;
Sales: Isaac Steinvortz
Subjects: Literature, History, Medicine, Printing & Binding
Bookshop: Librería Lerner (qv under Major Booksellers)
Founded: 1959

Lito Technion Ltda*, Apdo Aéreo 80085, Bogotá (Located at: Calle 21 No 43A-23, Bogotá) Tel: (01) 2443502/2443177/2441538 Telex: 41456 Trnf
Man Dir: Benjamin Bursztyn V; *Editorial:* Samuel Bursztyn V; *Sales:* Ricardo Herrera G; *Production:* German Arias G; *Publicity:* Yonatan Bursztyn V
Subjects: Children's Fiction, Pre-school
Founded: 1980
ISBN Publisher's Prefix: 958-9007

Editorial **McGraw-Hill** Latinoamericana SA*, Transversal 42 B No 19-77, Apdo Aéreo 81078, Bogotá Tel: (01) 2682700/2688828 Telex: 43306
Man Dir, Editorial: Moisés Pérez Zavala;
Sales: Carlos Marquez; *Promotion:* Hermencia Morales
Orders to: Apdo Postal 2036, Colon, Panamá
Parent Company: McGraw-Hill de España SA, Spain (qv)
Associate Companies: See McGraw-Hill Book Co (UK) Ltd, UK
Subjects: Engineering, Technology, Biology, Physics, Chemistry, Mathematics, Psychology, Sociology, Textbooks, Business Administration, Economics, Accounting
Founded: 1969
ISBN Publisher's Prefix: 958-451

Editorial **Marca** Ltda*, Calle 39A No 22-43 – 1° piso, Bogotá Tel: (01) 2445116
Man Dir: Constanza Galvis; *Sales:* Ana Maria de Galvis; *Production:* Maria Teresa de Leal
Subjects: Scholarly, Cultural, Periodicals
Founded: 1977

Ediciones **Monserrate** Ltda*, Apdo Aéreo 100127, Bogotá (Located at: Calle(117 No 11A-65, Bogotá) Tel: (01) 2139398/2132041/2142417
Man Dir and Editorial: P Enrique Fajardo Villarraga; *Sales:* Maria Gladys de Diaz
Subjects: Technical, Scientific, Law, Dictionaries, Encyclopaedias, Odontology
Founded: 1977

Editorial **Norma** SA, Apdo Aéreo 46, Cali (Located at: Calle 29 Norte No 6A-40, Cali) Tel: (03) 675011/671712 Cable Add: Edinorma Telex: 55555 Fax: (03) 616581
President: Francisco Piedrahíta: *General Manager:* Fernando Gómez; *Editorial Dirs:* María del Mar Ravassa (Trade Division), Bernardo Peña (Textbook Division), María C Posada (Periodicals Division), Gustavo Adolfo Carvajal (International Division)
Parent Company: Carvajal SA (qv)
Branch Offs: Barranquilla, Bogotá, Bucaramanga, Cartagena, Cúcuta, Ibaqué, Manizales, Medellín, Neiva
Subjects: Textbooks, Children's, Juveniles, General Interest, Periodicals

Editorial La **Oveja** Negra Ltda, Apdo 075761, Bogotá DE (Located at: Carrera 14 No 79-17, Bogotá) Tel: (01) 2577900/2368198 Telex: 45369 Oveja Co/42580 Negra Fax: 2184695
Man Dir: José Vicente Kataraín Velez: *General Manager:* Alfredo Martínez; *Sales Dir:* Orlando Pardo; *Production Dir:* Jimena Lemoine; *Publicity Dir:* Allan Obando; *Rights & Permissions:* Ricardo Arango Dávila
Branch Offs: Transversal 93 No 62-46 Interior 16, Bogotá; also in Caracas, La Paz Lima, Quito
Subjects: Works of Gabriel García Márquez, Latin-American Literature, Social Sciences, Politics, History, Education, Children's, Biographies, Strip Cartoon Books
Bookshops: Calle 18 No 6-08, Bogotá Tel: (01) 2844832; 34 others throughout Colombia
Founded: 1977

Papusa Ltda*, Calle 26 No 13A-23 – 7° piso, Bogotá Tel: (01) 2825692 Telex: 0441302
Man Dir: Jaime Muñoz Polit; *Editorial:* Amanda Quijano, Ignacio Montealegre
Parent Company: Ediciones Libra SA, Matias Romero 1221, México 12, DF, Mexico
Subsidiary Companies: Dinalpusa, Janibi Editores (both at parent company address)
Associate Companies: Munoz Hnos SA, General Aguirre 166 y 10 de Agosto, Quito, Ecuador; Distribuidora Inca SA, Emilio Altahus, Lima, Peru
Subject: Teaching of Music
Book Club: Guitarra Facil
Founded: 1977

Ediciones **Paulinas**, Apdo Aéreo 100383, Bogotá (Located at: Transversal 40A No 43-43, Bogotá) Tel: (01) 2212620
Subjects: Religious, Social, Juveniles

Editorial **Pluma** Ltda*, Apdo Aéreo 345, Bogotá (Located at: Carrera 20 No 39B-50, Bogotá) Tel: (01) 2871412/2871432 Telex: 45101 Ntctv
Man Dir: Ernesto Gamboa Morales; *Sales:* Federico Rivas Franco; *Production:* Pilar Mahecha; *Publicity:* Carlos José Herrera;
Rights & Permissions: Deborah Dixon
Associate Company: Indice Ltda (at above address)
Subjects: Psychology, Sexology, Economics, Politics, Literature
Founded: 1976

Editorial **Presencia** Ltda+*, Calle 23 No 24-20, Bogotá Tel: (01) 2681634/2681817/2682241
Man Dir, Sales, Publicity: Alberto Umaña Carrizosa; *Editorial:* M C Jimero; *Production:* José B Restreps; *Rights & Permissions:* Alberto Umaña

Procultura SA*, Apdo Aéreo 044700, Bogotá (Located at: Calle 25C No 4-27, Bogotá) Tel: (01) 2820835/2820875
Manager: Gloria Zea; *Editorial:* Santiago Mutis; *Sales:* Magdalena de Trujillo; *Production:* Ana Maria Sierra; *Rights & Permissions:* Rafael Jimenez
Subjects: History, Literature, Poetry, Economics, Series *Nueva Biblioteca Colombiana de Cultura*
Founded: 1980

R A M Editores, Calle 20 Sur No 60-24, Interior 1-102, Apdo 21548, Bogotá DE Tel: (01) 2623067
Man Dir: Jaime Ramirez Palmar; *Sales:* Luz Helena S de Ramírez; *Production:* Bernarda Sabogal Rodríguez
Subjects: General Interest
1985: 2 titles *1986:* 5 titles *Founded:* 1983
ISBN Publisher's Prefix: 958-9063

Editorial La **Rosa**, Apdo Aéreo 11435, Bogotá (Located at: Carrera 6a No 35-29, Bogotá) Tel: 2877788/2872134 Telex: 45101

Siglo XXI Editores de Colombia Ltda*, Apdo Aéreo 19434, Bogotá
Man Dir: Santiago Pombo Vejarano
Parent Company: Siglo XXI de Espāna Editores SA, Spain (qv)
Associate Company: Siglo XXI Editores SA de CV, Mexico (qv)
Subjects: Anthropology, Sociology, Psychology, History, Fiction, Linguistics, Art, Architecture, Politics, Philosophy
Founded: 1976

Editorial **Temis** SA+, Calle 13 No 6-45, Apdos 5941 y 12008, Bogotá 1 Tel: (01) 2694721/2699235/2445297 Cable Add: Editemis
Man Dir: Jorge Guerrero; *Sales Dir:* Erwin Guerrero Pinzon
Subject: Law
Bookshop: Librería Temis Ltda (qv under Major Booksellers)
Founded: 1951
ISBN Publisher's Prefix: 84-8272

Ediciones **Tercer** Mundo Ltda*, Carrera 30 No 42-32, Apdo Aéreo 4817, Bogotá Tel: (01) 695129/695149 Cable Add: Tercer Mundo
Man Dir: Luis Carlos Ibáñez
Subjects: General Literature, Social Science
Bookshop: Librería Tercer Mundo (qv under Major Booksellers)
Founded: 1961

Universidad de Antioquia, Departamento de Publicaciones*, Apdo Aéreo 1226, Medellín Tel: (04) 2630011 ext 509
Dir: Luis Fernando Calderón
1985: 10 titles *Founded:* 1984

Carlos **Valencia** Editores SA+, Calle 71 No 1-50, Apdo Aéreo 22197, Bogotá Tel: (01) 2114928/2491825
General Manager: Margarita Valencia Vargas; *Editorial Manager, Sales, Publicity and Rights & Permissions:* Carlos Valencia Vargas
Subjects: Art, Children's Literature, Economics, Politics, Sociology, Colombian subjects and authors

Founded: 1976
ISBN Publisher's Prefix: 958-9044

Vértice Ltda*, Apdo Aéreo 41137, Bogotá DE1 (Located at: Calle 110 No 15-15, Bogotá) Tel: (01) 2143521
General Manager: Jesús Antonio Villa Posse
Founded: 1980

Voluntad Editores Ltda y Cía SCA*, Calle 37 No 7-43 – 2° piso, Apdo Aéreo 4692, Bogotá Tel: (01) 2858711 Cable Add: Voluntad
Man Dir: Samuel de Bedout Tamayo; *Editorial Dir and Rights & Permissions:* Gastón de Bedout Arbeláez; *Sales and Publicity Dir:* Gabriel Gil
Branch Offs: Barranquilla, Bogotá, Bucaramanga, Cali, Cartagena, Cúcuta, Ibague, Medellín, Montería, Pereira, Santa Marta
Subjects: Kindergarten, Primary and Secondary Textbooks
Bookshop: Ave 19 No 3-16 – 2° piso, Bogotá
Founded: 1930
ISBN Publisher's Prefix: 84-8270

Book Clubs

Círculo de Lectores SA*, Apdo Aéreo 52111, Bogotá (Located at: Calle 57 No 6-35 – 6° piso, Bogotá) Tel: (01) 2123211/2118525 Telex: 41255
Members: 910,000
Owned by: Bertelsmann AG, Federal Republic of Germany (qv)
Founded: 1970

Guitarra Facil*, Calle 26 No 13A-23 – 7° piso, Bogotá Tel: (01) 2825692
Owned by: Papusa Ltda (qv)

Major Booksellers

Librería **Aguirre**, Calle 53 No 49-123, Medellín Tel: (04) 2424268 Cable Add: Laguirre
Manager: Aura López Posada

Librería **América***, Calle 51 No 49-58, Apdo 11-92, Medellín Tel: (04) 419195 Cable Add: Janavar
Manager: Jaime Navarro

Librería **Buchholz***, Ave. Jiménez 8-40, Bogotá Tel: (01) 341309/415896/426350

Librería **Casa del Libro**, H Rajul & Cia Ltda*, Apdo Aéreo 5010, Bogotá (Located at: Calle 18 No 6-43, Bogotá) Tel: (01) 432668

Círculo de Lectores SA*, Apdo Aéreo 52111, Bogotá (Located at: Calle 57 No 6-35 – 6° piso, Bogotá)
Branches: Barranquilla, Bogotá (four), Cali (three), Cartagena, Manizales, Medellín, Pereira, Tunja

Librería **Cultural** Colombiana, Calle 72 No 16-15, Bogotá Tel: (01) 2176569/2176471/2176529
Manager: José Porto
Owned by: Cultural Colombiana Ltda (qv)

Librería **La Gran Colombia***, Calle 18 No 6-30, Bogotá Tel: (01) 421359/411755

Librería **del Ingeniero***, Ave Jiménez 7-45, Apdo Aéreo 14825, Bogotá Tel: (01) 2412507/2823610/2343260
Manager: Gladys de Pinzon

Librería **Lerner***, Ave Jiménez 4-35, Bogotá Tel: (01) 347826/430567
Manager: Luis A Burgos H
Owned by: Ediciones Lerner Ltda (qv)

Librería **Continental**, Carrera 50 No 52-06, Medellín Tel: (04) 2414948
Manager: Fernando Vega Bravo

Librería **Nacional** Ltda, Carrera 5 No 11-50, Apdo Aéreo 8092, Cali Tel: (03) 731250 Cable Add: Linalco AA Cali Telex: 55472
Manager: Hernando Ordoñez
Also: Unicentro Local No 1-146, Apdo Aéreo 100778, Bogotá Telex: 45310

Librería **San Pablo***, Carrera 9 No 15-01, Bogotá Tel: (01) 2433653/2345036
Manager: P Alirio Cepeda
Branches: Barranquilla (two), Bogotá, Cali, Cucuta, Manizales, Medellín (two)

Librería **del Seminario**, Apdo Aéreo 4567, Medellín, Antioquia (Located at: Calle 57 No 49-44 of 220, Centro Comercial Villanueva) Tel: (04) 2513622/2518142 Telex: 66922
Dir: Lorenzo Salazar Hoyos; *Sales Manager:* Hernando Neira
Distributor

Librería **Temis** Ltda, Calle 13 No 6-45, Bogotá Tel: (01) 423035/413325
Owned by: Editorial Temis SA (qv)

Librería **Tercer** Mundo*, Carrera 7A No 16-91, Bogotá Tel: (01) 695129/695149
Owned by: Ediciones Tercer Mundo Ltda (qv)

Librería **Uniandes***, Apdo Aéreo 4976, Bogotá (Located at: Carrera l No 18A-82, Bogotá) Tel: (01) 2824066 ext 139 & 144 Cable Add: Uniandes
General Manager: Arcesio Rodríguez P; *Marketing and Sales Manager:* César Augusto Peña; *International Trade:* David A Romero
Spanish and Latin American trade books; importers and subscription agents of academic and scientific publications
Parent Company: Bibliográfica Rodríguez y Peña Ltda

Major Libraries

Biblioteca **Agropecuaria** de Colombia (BAC)*, Apdo Aéreo 151123, El Dorado, Bogotá
Farming and Livestock Library of Colombia
Dir: Francisco Salazar Alonso
Publications include: Novedades BAC (BAC News)

Biblioteca **Luis-Angel Arango***, Banco de la República, Apdo Aéreo 12362, Bogotá (Located at: Calle 11 No 4-14, Bogotá) Tel: (01) 2439100/2827840 Cable Add: Redesbanco Biblioteca
Dir: Lina Espitaleta de Villegas
Publications include: Boletín Cultural y Bibliográfico; Estudios sobre Politica Economica

Archivo Nacional de Colombia, Biblioteca Nacional, Calle 24 No 5-60 – 4° piso, Bogotá
Dir: Pilar Moreno de Angel

Biblioteca **Nacional** de Colombia, Calle 24 No 5-60, Apdo Aéreo 27600, Bogotá
Tel: (01) 414029
Librarian: Conrado Zuluaga

British Council Library*, Apdo Aéreo 089231, Bogotá (Located at: Calle 87 No 12-79, Bogotá) Tel: (01) 2363882/2579632/2363976 Telex: 45715 Bcoun
Librarian: Maria Clemencia de Bohórquez

Centro de Estudios sobre Desarrollo Económico CEDE, Universidad de los Andes, Apdo Aéreo 4976, Bogotá Tel:

(01) 2430295 ext 68/2824066 ext 189 Telex: 42343 Unand
Centre for Studies on Economic Development

Universidad de Antioquia, Departamento de Bibliotecas, Apdo Aéreo 1226, Medellín
Publication: Bibliografía Bibliotecológica, Bibliográfica y de Obras de Referencia Colombianas (Bibliography of Library Science, Bibliography and Colombian Works of Reference)

Universidad de los Andes, Biblioteca General, Desarrollo de Colecciones, Apdo Aéreo 4976, Bogotá (Located at: Carrera 1E No 18A-10, Bogotá) Tel: (01) 2815824
Librarian: Balbina Ch de Montañes

Universidad de los Andes, Centro de Estudios sobre Desarrollo Económico (CEDE), see Centro de Estudios sobre Desarrollo Económico CEDE

Universidad Nacional de Colombia, Biblioteca Central*, c/o Dilia Elena Tuta de López, Apdo Aéreo 14490, Bogotá

Library Association

Asociación Colombiana de Bibliotecarios*, Calle 10 No 3-16, Apdo Aéreo 30883, Bogotá DE Tel: (01) 2694219
Colombian Library Association
Executive Secretary: Ms B N Cardona de Gil
Publication: Boletín

Library Reference Books and Journals

Book

Bibliografía Bibliotecológica, Bibliográfica y de Obras de Referencia Colombianas (Bibliography of Library Science, Bibliography and Colombian Works of Reference), Universidad de Antioquia, Departamento de Bibliotecas, Apdo Aéreo 1226, Medellín

Journals

Boletín, Asociación Colombiana de Bibliotecarios, Calle 10 No 3-16, Apdo Aéreo 30883, Bogotá

Boletín Cultural y Bibliográfico, Biblioteca Luis-Angel Arango, Banco de la República, Apdo Aéreo 12362, Bogotá

Boletín Informativo y Bibliográfico, Universidad de Narino, Biblioteca Central, Apdo Aéreo 505, Nacional 75, Narino

Literary Associations and Societies

Centro Filosófico-Literario*, Apdo Nacional 298, Manizales

P E N Internacional de Escritores de Colombia, Apdo Aéreo 51748, Bogotá
PEN International of Colombian Writers
President: David Mejía Velilla; *Secretary:* Maruja Vieirar

Literary Periodicals

Letras Nacionales, Calle 17 No 7-71 of 401, Bogotá

Razón y Fábula (Reason and Fiction), Universidad de los Andes, Apdo Aéreo 4976, Bogotá

Literary Prizes

'Revista Vivencias' and the Instituto Colombiano de Cultura have annual prizes

Cordoba Stories Prizes*
For stimulating and developing literary tastes. Diploma plus three prizes of 5,000, 3,000 and 2,000 Colombian pesos. Awarded annually. Enquiries to Cordoba Department, Secretary of Education, Montaria

Pamplona and its Culture Prize*
For stimulating a liking for reading in children. Awarded annually. Enquiries to Pedro de Orsua Public Library, Pamplona

José Ma **Vergara y Vergara** Prize*
For Colombian authors, to promote literary development. Diploma plus 10,000 Colombian pesos. Awarded annually. Enquiries to Colombian Ministry of National Education, Centro Administrativo Nacional (CAN), Bogotá

Popular Republic of Congo

General Information

Language: French
Religion: Traditional animist religions, Roman Catholicism
Population: 1.54 million
Bank Hours: 0630-1100 Monday-Saturday
Shop Hours: 0700 or 0800-1200 or 1300, 1500-1700 or 1730 Tuesday-Friday; 0700 or 0800-1200 or 1300 Saturday
Currency: CFA franc
Export/Import Information: Member of Customs and Economic Union of Central Africa. Goods for schools, the army, the police and health authorities are exempt from VAT. Import licences required for all goods. Favourable terms for imports from EEC countries
Copyright: Berne (see International section)

Publishers

Government Printer*, BP 58, Brazzaville

Société congolaise **Hachette***, BP 919, Brazzaville
Subjects: General Fiction, Belles Lettres, Education, Juveniles, Textbooks

Major Booksellers

Librairie **Hachette***, BP 2150, Brazzaville Tel: 2302

Librairie **Populaire***, BP 2212, Brazzaville

Maison de la Presse, Société congolaise Hachette*, BP 2150, Brazzaville

Office national des Librairies Populaires (ONLP)*, BP 577, Brazzaville Tel: 811582 Cable Add: Lipolaire Brazzaville
Director-General: Jean-Marie Niabia

Major Libraries

Bibliothèque nationale du Congo, Direction des Services de Bibliothèques, d'Archives et de Documentation*, BP 1489, Brazzaville Tel: 810853

Bibliothèque nationale populaire*, BP 114, Brazzaville Tel: 811287
Librarian: Francis Abaraka

Centre culturel français, Bibliothèque*, BP 2141, Brazzaville Tel: 812566
Les cahiers du cercle littéraire de Brazzaville

Centre Orstom de Brazzaville, Bibliothèque*, BP 165, Brazzaville Tel: 812680
Librarian: B Boccas

Ecole normale supérieure de l'Afrique centrale, Bibliothèque*, BP 237, Brazzaville Tel: 4454

Institut supérieur des sciences de l'éducation, Bibliothèque*, BP 1090, Brazzaville Tel: 813950
Librarian: Hildebert Banda

Bibliothèque universitaire, **Université Marien Ngouabi***, BP 2025, Brazzaville Tel: 811430
Dir: François Wellot-Samba
Publications: Dimi; *Annales*; *Repertoire d'auteurs congolais*; *Revue d'histoire anthropologie*. Also other lists and catalogues

Library Association

Direction générale des **Services** de Bibliothèques, Archives et Documentation*, BP 114, Brazzaville
General Management of Library, Archives and Documentation Services

Literary Periodical

Les cahiers du cercle littéraire de Brazzaville, Centre culturel français, Bibliothèque, BP 2141, Brazzaville

Costa Rica

General Information

Language: Spanish
Religion: Roman Catholic
Population: 2.25 million
Bank Hours: 0900-1500 Monday-Friday
Shop Hours: 0800-1200, 1400-1800 Monday-Saturday (some close Saturday afternoon)
Currency: 100 centimos = 1 colon
Export/Import Information: No import licences, but statistical recording prior to importation necessary. Imports over a certain value must be registered with Banco Central to be eligible for foreign exchange allocation
Copyright: Berne, UCC, Buenos Aires (see International section)

Book Trade Organizations

Instituto del Libro*, Ministerio de Cultura, Juventud y Deportes, Apdo 10227, San José
Dir: Juan Frutos Verdesia

Standard Book Numbering Agency*, Biblioteca Nacional, Apdo 10008, San José
ISBN Administrator: Efrain Picado

Book Trade Reference Journal

Anuario bibliográfico costarricense, Asociación Costarricense de Bibliotecarios, Apdo 3308, San José

Publishers

Editorial **Costa Rica**, Apdo 10010, San José Tel: 234875/239303
General Manager: Gérman Hernández Valle; *Sales:* Ivette Hernández; *Production:* Dennis Mesén Segura; *Publicity Manager:* Víctor Hugo Fernández
Subject: Literature of Costa Rica
Founded: 1959
ISBN Publisher's Prefix: 84-23

Dirección de Publicaciones*, Apdo 10227, San José Tel: 230797
Dir: Roberto Corella Furntes; *Editor:* Juan Frutos Verdesia
Subject: Literature in general

Editorial Universitaria Centroamericana (EDUCA)*, Apdo 64, Ciudad Universitaria 'Rodrigo Facio', 2060 San José (Located at San Pedro de Montes de Oca, San José) Tel: 258740/243727 Cable Add: Cosuca Telex: 3011 Cosuca
Dir: Carmen Maranjo; *Sales:* Zaida Ureña; *Production:* Alfredo Aguilar
Subjects: Science, Art, Philosophy
Founded: 1969
ISBN Publisher's Prefix: 84-8360

Imediex SA+*, Apdo 67, 1000 San José (Located at: San Miguel de Desamparados, San José) Tel: 277727/277827 Cable Add: Elecalvo Telex: 2610 Calvo
Man Dir, Rights & Permissions: Luis Fernando Calvo Fallas; *Production:* Olga Marta Segura Abarca
Parent Company: La Casa de las Revistas SA (at above address)
Subsidiary Companies: Servicios Litográficos Ltda; Metropolitana de Publicaciones (each at above address)
Subjects: Dictionaries (English & Spanish), Children's, Fiction, Literature, Cookery, Songbooks
Bookshops: Casa de las Revistas: Calle 5, Ave 0 y 2; Calle 0, Ave 0 y 1; Centro Comercial San José 2000; Calle 9, Ave 10 y 12; Calle 0, Ave 4 y 6 (all in San José)
1985: 13 titles *Founded:* 1982
ISBN Publisher's Prefix: 9977-943

Instituto Centro Americano de Administración Pública (ICAP)*, Dpto de Publicaciones, Apdo 10025, San José Tel: 223133 Cable Add; Icap Telex: 2180 Icap
Dir: Carlos Cordero d'Aubuisson
Subject: Technical
Founded: 1954

Instituto Interamericano de Cooperación para la Agricultura (IICA), Servicio Editorial, Apdo 55, 2200 Coronado Tel: 290222 Cable Add: Iicasanjose Telex: 2144 Iica
Editors: J André Ovellette (Institutional relations), Michael J Snarskis (General publishing); *Publicity, Production, Rights & Permissions:* Michael J Snarskis
Branch Offs: In every South American country, Canada and USA
Subjects: Agricultural Sciences &

Technology, Rural Development
1985: 14 titles *Founded:* 1942
ISBN Publisher's Prefix: 92-9039

Librería Imprenta y Litografía **Lehmann** SA*, Ave Central, Apdo 10011, San José Tel: 231212 Telex: 2540 Lill Eh
Man Dir: Antonio Lehmann Struve; *Publicity:* Orlando Mora
Subjects: General Fiction & Non-fiction
Bookshop: See under Major Booksellers
Founded: 1894

Universal **Librería**, Imprenta y Fotolitografia (Carlos Federspiel & Co) SA*, Ave Fernández Guell 42-E, Apdo 1532, San José Tel: 222222
Subject: Textbooks

Editorial de la **Universidad de Costa Rica**+, Apdo 75, Ciudad Universitaria Rodrigo Facio, 2060 San José Tel: 247957/ 253133 Telex: 2544 Unicori
President (Editorial Commission): Mario Murillo Rodríguez; *Dir:* Gilbert Carazo Gutiérrez
Subjects: University Textbooks, Technical, Social Science, Art, Music, Poetry, General
1985-86: 36 titles *Founded:* 1975
ISBN Publisher's Prefix: 9977-67

Editorial **Universidad Estatal** a Distancia (EUNED)*, Apdo 2, Plaza Gonzalez Viquez, San José Tel: 235430 Cable Add: Uned Telex: 3003
President, Rights & Permissions: Carlos Luis Fallas; *Editorial Dir:* Carlos A Arce Alfaro; *Sales Dir:* Hernan Mora Gonzalez; *Production:* Arnoldo Bermudez; *Publicity:* Enrique Villalobos
Subjects: University Textbooks, Politics, Economics, History, Philosophy, Farming, Education, Nursing
Bookshops: Libreria UNED: At above address; Calle 11, Ave 12-14, San José
Founded: 1977
ISBN Publisher's Prefix: 9977-64

Editorial **Universitaria Centroamericana** (EDUCA), see under Editorial Universitaria

Major Booksellers

Librería Universal Carlos **Federspiel***, Ave Fernández Guell 42-E, Apdo 1532, San José Tel: 222222

Librería Imprenta y Litografía **Lehmann** SA*, Ave Central, Apdo 10011, San José Tel: 231212
Also Publisher (qv)

Librería **Trejos** SA, Calle 11-13, Ave Fernández Guell, Apdo 1313, San José Tel: 217055 Telex: 2858 Ltsa
Manager: A Trejos

Major Libraries

Biblioteca Nacional*, Apdo 10008, San José (Located at: Calle 15 y 17, Ave 3 y 3, San José)
Director-General: Lic Efraín Picado Azofeifa

Biblioteca del **Centro** Cultural Costarricense-Norteamericano*, Apdo 1489, San José
International Communication Agency Library

Biblioteca de la **Universidad de Costa Rica***, Ciudad Universitaria Rodrigo Facio, 2060 San José Tel: 257372
Publications include: San Pedro de Montes de Oca

Library Association

Asociación Costarricense de Bibliotecarios*, Apdo 3308, San José
Costa Rican Association of Librarians
Secretary-General: Nelly Kopper
Publications: Anuario bibliográfico costarricense; Boletín

Library Reference Journal

Boletín, Asociación Costarricense de Bibliotecarios, Apdo 3308, San José

Literary Prizes

Editorial **Costa Rica** Literary Prize
Founded in 1973, this annual award is to encourage creative writing generally. The prize is 'rotated' in order to be open to all genres — fiction, stories, theatre, essays, short stories, poetry, biography, history. The most recent winner was Eduardo Oconitrillo. Enquiries to Editorial Costa Rica, Apdo 10010, San José

Aquileo J **Echeverría** Prize*
For Costa Rican citizens who have excelled in the fields of literature (novel, short story, poetry, essay, scientific literature); history; theatre; music; fine arts. 40,000 colones divided between the selected works. Total sum of awards cannot exceed 8,000,000 colones. Awarded annually. Enquiries to Costa Rican Ministry of Culture, Youth and Sport, General Directorate of Arts and Literature, Apdo 10227, San José

'**Joven** Creacion' Literary Prize
Formed in 1976 in collaboration with the Asociación de Autores, with the aim of stimulating young writing in the fields of poetry and narrative/stories. Enquiries to Editorial Costa Rica, Apdo 10010, San José

Carmen **Lyra** Literary Prize
Founded in 1974 in honour of the writer María Isabel Carvajal (pseudonym Carmen Lyra), this annual award is to encourage the writing of literature intended for children and young people. Enquiries to Editorial Costa Rica, Apdo 10010, San José

Cuba

General Information

Language: Spanish
Religion: Roman Catholic predominantly
Population: 9.83 million
Bank Hours: 0800-1200, 1415-1615 Monday-Friday; 0800-1200 Saturday
Currency: 100 centavos = 1 peso
Export/Import Information: Control of all import and export by Ministry of Foreign Trade; books imported and exported by Ediciones Cubanas, Apdo 605, Havana. No commercial advertising permitted in Cuba; brochures etc must be sent to the appropriate foreign trade organization. Exchange controlled by National Bank of Cuba
Copyright: UCC, Florence (see International section)

Book Trade Organization

Unión de Escritores y Artistas de Cuba*, Calle 17 No 351, Vedado, Havana Tel: (07) 324551
Union of Writers and Artists of Cuba
Administrative Secretary: William Mafud
Publications include: Unión, La Nueva Gaceta

Book Trade Reference Journal

Revolutionary Cuba, University of Miami Press, Coral Gables, FL, USA
Annual bibliographical guide

Publishers

Casa de las Américas*, Tercera y G, Vedado 4, Havana
Dir: Roberto Fernández Retamar
Subject: Latin American Literature
Founded: 1960

Editorial de **Ciencias Sociales***, Calle 14 No 4104e 41 y 43, Playa, Havana Tel: (07) 24801/23959
Dir: Ricardo Garcia Pampin
Subject: Social Sciences

Editorial **Científico** Técnica*, Calle 2 No 58e 3 y 5, Vedado, Havana
Dir: Jorge Luis Victorero Gonta
Subjects: Science, Engineering

Empresa Editoriales de **Cultura y Ciencia***, Palacio del Segundo Cabo, Calle O'Reilly No 4 esq a Tacón, Havana Tel: (07) 619700
Dir: Elenia Rodríguez Oliva
Imprint: Editorial Gente Nueva
Subject: Juvenile Literature

Editora Política*, Departamento de Orientación Revolucionaria del Comité Central del Partido Comunista de Cuba, Plaza de la Revolución, Havana
Subjects: Politics

Editorial **Gente Nueva**, an imprint of Empresa Editoriales de Cultura y Ciencia (qv)

Ministerio de Cultura*, Calle 15 No 602 esq C, Vedado, Havana Tel: (07) 310741/329526 Telex: 511400
Dir: Modesto González
Founded: 1976

Editorial **Oriente***, José Antonio Saco 356, Apdo 263, Santiago Tel: 8096 Telex: 061170
Dir: Reinaldo Cuesta Reina

Ediciones **Unión***, Calle 17 No 351, Vedado, Havana Tel: (07) 328114
Dir: Joaquín G Santana; *Production:* Juan Coury Giat; *Publicity:* Adolfo Martí Fuentes; *Rights & Permissions:* Centro Nacional de Derechos de Autor, Línea y G, Vedado
Subjects: Literature, Art

Universidad Central de la Villas, Carretera de Camajuani*, Km 10, Santa Clara
Subjects: Academic

Universidad de la Habana*, Apdo 3060, Havana 3 Tel: (07) 325238/328815
Subjects: Academic
Founded: 1934

Major Booksellers

Ediciones **Cubanas***, Apdo 605, Havana (Located at: Obispo 461, Havana)
This is part of Empresa de Comercio Exterior de Publicaciones

Manager: José Manuel Castro
Wholesale importer and exporter of books, periodicals and printing material

Major Libraries

Academia de Ciencias de la República de Cuba*, Biblioteca Central, Capitolio Nacional, Havana

Archivo Histórico de la Provincia Ciudad de la Habana*, Palacio de los Capitanes Generales, Plaza de Armas, Havana 1

Biblioteca Histórica Cubana y Americana*, Ciudad de la Habana, Oficina del Historiador de la Ciudad, Plaza de Armas, Havana 1

Biblioteca Nacional José Martí, Plaza de la Revolución, Apdo Oficial 3, Havana Tel: (07) 73613 Telex: 511963 Bnjm
National Library
Publications include: Guía de Bibliotecas y Centros de Documentación de la República de Cuba; Revista de la Biblioteca Nacional José Martí; Bibliografía Cubana; Indice General de Publicaciones Periódicas Cubanas; Boletínes Bibliograficas e Información Señal; Bibliografías Especializadas; Ediciones Especializadas sobre la Cultura y el Arte; Documentos Extranjeros Adquiridos; Guía de Bibliotecas y Centros de Documentación de la República de Cuba

Casa de las Américas, see Echeverría

Biblioteca 'José Antonio **Echeverría**'*, Casa de las Américas, Tercera y G, Vedado, Havana
Dir: Dr Marta Terry
Specialize in Latin-American Literature, History and Sociology

Biblioteca del **Instituto de Literatura** y Linguistica*, Salvador Allende 710, Havana

Biblioteca del **Instituto Pre-universitario** de la Habana*, Zulueta y San José, Havana
Library of the Pre-University Institute of Education

Biblioteca del **Museo de Zoologia***, 42 No 3307, Marianao 13, Havana
Dir: Dr Miguel L Jaume

Biblioteca 'Manuel **Sanguily**'*, Ministerio de Relaciones Exteriores, Calzada y G, Vedado, Havana

Biblioteca General de la **Universidad Central** de las Villas*, Santa Clara, Las Villas

Universidad de la Habana, Direccion de Informacion Cientifica, Dpto de Selección y Adquisición, Sección de Selección y Canje, Havana Tel: (07) 5573 Telex: 512210 Dict Uh

Biblioteca Central de la **Universidad de Oriente***, Apdo 5015, Santiago (Located at: Ave Patricio Lumumba s/n, Santiago)

Library Association

Library Association of Cuba*, c/o Dirección de Bibliotecas, Calle 15 y F, Vedado, Havana

Library Reference Books and Journals

Book
Guía de Bibliotecas y Centros de Documentación de la República de Cuba, Biblioteca Nacional José Martí, Plaza de la Revolución, Apdo Oficial 3, Havana

Journal
Revista de la Biblioteca Nacional José Martí, Biblioteca Nacional José Martí, Plaza de la Revolución, Apdo Oficial 3, Havana

Literary Periodicals

Taller Literario (Literary Workshop), Biblioteca Central de la Universidad de Oriente, Escuela de Letras, Apdo 5015, Santiago

Unión, Unión de Escritores y Artistas de Cuba, Calle 17 No 351, Vedado, Havana

Literary Prizes

David Prize*
An annual award of $500 is made to a writer whose work has not previously been published. Enquiries to Unión de Escritores y Artistas de Cuba, Calle 17 No 351, Vedado, Havana

U N E A C Prize
Established 1962. An annual award of $1,000 is made to a writer or writers for work in differing genres. Enquiries to Unión de Escritores y Artistas de Cuba, Calle 17 No 351, Vedado, Havana

Cyprus

General Information

Language: Greek and Turkish (English widely spoken)
Religion: Greek Orthodox and Islamic (among Turks)
Population: 629,000
Bank Hours: 0830-1200 Monday-Saturday
Shop Hours: Winter: 0800-1300, 1430-1730 Monday-Wednesday and Friday; 0800-1300 Thursday and Saturday. Summer 0730-1300, 1600-1900 Monday-Wednesday and Friday; 0730-1300 Thursday and Saturday
Currency: 1000 mils = 1 Cyprus pound. 50 mils is known as a shilling. Turkish currency circulates in area under Turkish control
Export/Import Information: No tariffs on books or advertising matter. No import licence specially required. Exchange control administered by Central Bank of Cyprus
Copyright: Berne, Florence (see International section)

Book Trade Organizations

Cyprus Booksellers Association*, Hatzisavva Bldg, Evagora Ave, Box 1455, Nicosia Tel: (02) 49500/62312
Secretary: Panikos Michaelides

Standard Book Numbering Agency, c/o Cyprus Centre for Registration of Books & Serials, Ministry of Education Cultural Service, Attn Inspector of Libraries, Nicosia Tel: (02) 403337 Cable Add: 5760 Mineduc
ISBN Administrator: Savvas L Petrides

Book Trade Reference Journal

O Kosmos Tou Kypriakou Vivliou (The World of Cypriot Books), MAM, PO Box 1722, Nicosia
Text in Greek

Publishers

M A M (The House of the Cyprus Publications)*, PO Box 1722, Nicosia Tel: (02) 472744
Subjects: Various, specializing in publications about Cyprus and works by Cypriot authors
Bookshop: See under Major Booksellers
Miscellaneous: Authorized distributors of Cyprus Government publications and works about Cyprus, and of publications by United Nations agencies and major international organizations

Major Booksellers

Hellenic Distribution Agency (Cyprus) Ltd*, Chr Sozou 2E, Nicosia Tel: (02) 44488/73664 Telex: 2616

A **Joannides** & Co, 30-32 Athens St, PO Box 141, Limassol Tel: (051) 62204
Telex: 5137 Ajoco
Manager: A Joannides
Also: Archbishop Makarios III Ave 147, Limassol

K P **Kyriakou** (Books — Stationery) Ltd, PO Box 159, Limassol (Located at: 3 Grivasa Digenis Ave, Panagides Bldg, Limassol) Tel: (051) 68508 Cable Add: Cybooks Telex: 2836 Cybooks
Man Dir: Kyriakos P Kyriakou

M A M (The House of the Cyprus Publications)*, PO Box 1722, Nicosia (Located at: Laiki Yitonia, Nicosia) Tel: (02) 472744
Manager: Th M Michaelidou
Also: Phaneromeni Library Building, Nicosia
Specializes in publications about Cyprus and works by Cypriot authors, also academic books. Authorized distributors of Cyprus Government publications and of publications of international organizations.
Also Publisher (qv)

K **Rustem** & Bro*, PO Box 239, Lefkoşa, Mersin 10, Turkey (Located at: 24 Kyrenia St, Nicosia Tel: (02) 2681 Cable Add: Rustem Br 4)

Iakovou **Yiannakis***, 22 Greg Xenopoulous St, Nicosia Tel: (02) 52197 Cable Add: Vivliopolis

Major Libraries

The Library of the **Archbishop Macarios III Foundation***, PO Box 1269, Nicosia
Librarian: Dr P J Stylianou

Library of the **Archbishopric**, PO Box 1130, Nicosia
Librarian: Dr Andreas N Mitsides

British Council Library*, PO Box 1995, Nicosia (Located at: 3 Museum St, Nicosia) Tel: (02) 42152

Library of the **Cyprus Museum**, PO Box 2024, Nicosia

Ministry of Education Library, Central PO, Eleftheria Sq, Nicosia Tel: (02) 403180
Librarian: Andreas G Thomas

Municipal Library*, PO Box 41, Famagusta

Municipal Library*, Limassol

Library of the **Paedagogiki Academia** (College of Education), Nicosia
Librarian: Frederiki Shiamma

Library of **Phaneromeni**, now part of The Library of the Archbishop Macarios III Foundation (qv)

Sultan's Library*, Evcaf, Nicosia

Turkish Public Library*, 49 Mecediye St, Nicosia

Library Association

Library Association of Cyprus*, c/o Pedagogical Academy, PO Box 1039, Nicosia Tel: (02) 402310
Secretary: Paris G Rossos
Publication: Deltion Vivliothikarion (Library Bulletin)

Library Reference Journal

Deltion Vivliothikarion (Library Bulletin), Library Association of Cyprus, c/o Pedagogical Academy, PO Box 1039, Nicosia

Literary Associations and Societies

Cyprus **P E N***, PO Box 3836, Nicosia
President: Panos Ioannides; *Vice-President, Secretary:* Dr Klitos Ioannides

Czechoslovakia

General Information

Language: Czech in Bohemia and Moravia, Slovak and Hungarian in Slovakia. Russian is common second language
Religion: Roman Catholic and Protestant
Population: 15.3 million
Bank Hours: 0800-1400 Monday-Friday
Shop Hours: 0900-1800 Monday-Friday (some shops until 2000 on Thursdays); most open half day Saturdays
Currency: 100 haler = 1 koruna
Export/Import Information: Import policy administered by Federal Ministry of Foreign Trade. Appropriate corporations for book importation are Artia, 11127 Prague 1, Ve Smečkách 30, or Slovart, Bratislava, Gorkého 17. Exchange control administered by State Bank
Copyright: UCC, Berne (see International section)

Book Trade Organizations

Výtvarná služba **Českého fondu** výtvarných umělcu, sekce krásné knihy a grafiky*, Prague 1, Nové Město, třída Politických vězňu 7
Creative service of the Czech Fund for Creative Artists, Section for the Well-designed book and Prints

Ministerstvo kultury CSR, Odbor knižní kultury, Prague 1, Staré Město, Na Perštýně 1
Czechoslovak Ministry of Culture, Department for Publishing and Book Trade
Publication: Books in Czechoslovakia

Slovenské ústredie knižnej kultúry, 81336 Bratislava, nám SNP 12
Slovak Centre for Publishing and Book Trade

Společnost pro krásné písmo a typografii*, Prague 1, Malá Strana, Říční 5
Association of Design and Typography

Svaz československých spisovatelu*, 11147 Prague 1, Národní třída 11
Union of Czechoslovak Writers
Chairman: Jan Kozák

Svaz českých spisovatelu*, 11147 Prague 1, Národní třída 11
Union of Czech Writers
Chairman: Ivan Skále
Publication: Literární měsíčník (Literary Monthly)

Zväz slovenských spisovateľov, 81508 Bratislava, Obrancov mieru 14
Union of Slovak Writers
Chairman: Ján Solovič; *Secretary-General:* Ladislav Ballek
Publications: Meridians 12-23; Slovenské Pomlady (monthly); *Romboid* (monthly); *Literárny Týženník*

Book Trade Reference Books and Journals

Book

Books in Czechoslovakia, Ministerstvo kuttury CSR, Prague 1, Staré Město, Na Perštýně 1
Survey of Czech and Slovak publishers, book-museums and important libraries

Journals

Bibliografický katalog CSSR (Czech National Bibliography), consisting of: *České knihy* (Czech Books) (weekly), Státní knihovna České socialistické republiky, 11001 Prague 1, Klementinum 190; *Slovenská národná bibliografia* (Slovak National Bibliography), (monthly), Matica slovenská, 03652 Martin, Novomeského 32; *České hudebniny* (Czech Music) (quarterly), Státní knihovna české socialistické republiky, 11001 Prague 1, Klementinum 190; *Slovenské hudebniny* (Slovak Music) (annual), Státní knihovna České socialistické republiky, 11001 Prague 1, Klementinum 190

Czech Books in Print, Artia, 11127 Prague 1, Ve Smečkách 30, PO Box 790

Nové knihy (New Books), Prague 1, Vězeňská 5

Slovak Books in Print, Slovart Ltd, Foreign Trade Company, Bratislava, Gorkého 17

Slovenské Pomlady, Zväz slovenských spisovateľov, 81508 Bratislava, Obrancov mieru 14
Monthly bulletin of Slovak literature in English, Russian, German, French and Spanish

Věda a knihy (Science and Books), Academia, 11229 Prague 1, Vodičkova 40

Publishers

Academia, 11229 Prague 1, Vodičkova 40 Tel: (02) 246241 Cable Add: Academybooks Prague
Publishing House of the Czechoslovak Academy of Sciences
Man Dir: Dr Radoslav Švec; *Editor-in-Chief:* Dr K Cerný; *Export Manager:* V Zilka; *Publicity & Advertising:* Mrs J Klášterská
Subjects: History, Philosophy, Psychology, Economy, Archaeology, Linguistics, Mathematics, Physics, Chemistry, Engineering, Geology, Encyclopaedias, Monographs, University Textbooks
Bookshop: 11229 Prague 1, Václavské nám 34
Founded: 1953

Albatros, 11001 Prague 1, Na Perštýně 1 Tel: (02) 2362565 Telex: 121605 Alba
Man Dir: Václav Mikeš; *Sales, Publicity & Advertising:* Jiří Lapáček
Subject: Books for Children and Young People
Book Club: KMČ (Young Readers' Club)
Founded: 1949

Alfa — Vydavateľstvo technickej a ekonomickej literatúry*, 81589 Bratislava, Hurbanovo nám 3 Tel: (07) 331441
Cable Add: Alfa Bratislava
Dir: Pavol Holéczy; *Sales Dir:* Jozef Bednárik
Subjects: Engineering, General, Special Dictionaries, University & Secondary Textbooks
Bookshop: Bratislava, Palackého ul 1
Founded: 1952
Miscellaneous: Sole importers of scientific and technical books from Western countries in Slovakia

Artia, 11127 Prague 1, Ve Smečkách 30, PO Box 790 Tel: (02) 2358565 Cable Add: Artiapublish Telex: 121065
Foreign language publishers
Man Dir: Miroslav Novák; *Sales Dir:* Peter Lančarič
Subjects: Art Books, Nature, Children's
Bookshop: See under Major Booksellers
Founded: 1953

Avicenum, zdravotnické nakladatelství, 11802 Prague 1, Malostranské nám 28 Tel: (02) 536601
Czechoslovak Medical Press
Subject: Medicine
Founded: 1953

Nakladatelství **Blok**, 65700 Brno, Rooseveltova 4 Tel: (05) 27244
Dir: Ivo Odehnal
Subjects: Fiction, Poetry, Regional Studies/History, Ethnography, Art/Literary Theory, Children's

Československý spisovatel, 11147 Prague 1, Národní 9 Tel: (02) 2320924 Cable Add: Spisovatel Prague
Dir: Dr Jan Pilař
Subjects: General Fiction, Belles Lettres, Poetry, Biography, Philosophy, Juveniles
Book Club: Klub přátel poezie (Club of the Friends of Poetry)
Bookshops: At above address; Brno, Česká 7
Founded: 1949

Nakladatelství **Dopravy** a spoju, 11578 Prague 1, Hybernská ul 5, Nové Město
Publishing House of the Ministry of Transport and Communications
Dir: Dr Vinter
Subjects: Science & Technology, Transport

Geodetický a kartografický podnik v Praze NP*, 17030 Prague 7, Kostelní 42
Cable Add: Geokart
Geodetic and Cartographic Enterprise in Prague
Man Dir: Dimitrij Gebauer; *Editor-in-Chief:* Aleš Hašek
Orders to: Artia, Foreign Trade Corporation, 11127 Prague 1,

CZECHOSLOVAKIA

Ve Smečkách 30
Subject: Cartography
Founded: 1954

Kruh*, 50021 Hradec Králové, Klicperova 197 Tel: (049) 22076/225458
Eastern Bohemian Regional Publishing House
Dir: Dr Josef Kubíček
Subjects: General Fiction, Biography, History, Music, Art, Low- & High-priced Paperbacks, Regional Literature
Founded: 1966

Landwirtschaftlicher Staatsverlag (Agricultural Publishing House), see Státní zemědělské nakladatelství

Lidové nakladatelství, 11000 Prague 1, Václavské nám 36 Tel: (02) 226383 Cable Add: Lidové nakladatelství Prague
Publishing House of the Union of Czechoslovak-Soviet Friendship
Editor-in-Chief: Magda Hajkora
Subjects: General Fiction, Belles Lettres, Poetry, Non-fiction, Juveniles, Low-priced Paperbacks, Social Science
Founded: 1948 (formerly Svět Sovětu)

Madáh*, Bratislava, Martarovicova 10
Publishing House for Books and Journals in the Hungarian Language
Subject: Books in Hungarian

Matica slovenská, 03652 Martin, Mudroňova 35
Publicity Manager: Dr Ondrej Kučera
Subjects: Bibliography, Museum Science, Information Sciences, Biography, History of Slovak Emigration

Melantrich, 11212 Prague 1, Václavské nám 36 Tel: (02) 260341 Cable Add: Melantrich Telex: 121422
Publishing House of the Czechoslovak Socialist Party
Man Dir: Jiří Krátký; *Sales Dir:* K Voleský; *Editorial:* Dr K Houba; *Production:* M Nevole
Subjects: Belles Lettres, Poetry, Biography, Philosophy, High-priced Paperbacks, Textbooks
Bookshops: Prague 1, Na příkopě 3; Prague 1, Jílská 9
Founded: 1898

Mladá fronta*, 11222 Prague 1, Panská 8 Tel: (02) 224141 Telex: 00245
Publishing House of the Czechoslovak Union of Youth
Dir: Dr Kornel Vavrinčík
Subjects: General Fiction, Belles Lettres, Poetry, Biography, History, Handbooks, Art, Philosophy, Juveniles, Low-priced Paperbacks
Founded: 1945

Mladé letá*, 89426 Bratislava, nám SNP 12 Tel: (07) 58241 Telex: 93421
Young Years: Slovak Publishing House of Children's Literature
Man Dir: Rudo Moric; *Editorial:* Dr Juraj Klaučo; *Sales Dir:* Gabriela Belopotocká; *Production:* Peter Turdoň; *Publicity:* Eva Hornišová
Subjects: Juveniles, Reference
Book Club: Club of Young Readers
Bookshop: Detská Kniha (The Child's Book), Bratislava, Hurbanovo nám 7
Founded: 1950

Naše vojsko, nakladatelství a distribuce knih NP, 12812 Prague 2, Na Děkance 3 Tel: (02) 299451
Publishing and Distribution House of Czechoslovak Army
Dir: Dr Stanislav Mistr; *Editorial:* Dr Vít Příkaský; *Sales:* Dr Stanislav Konopásek; *Rights & Permissions:* Dr Ludmila Hrdinová
Subjects: General Fiction, Medicine, Technical, Paperbacks, Juveniles, Military, Military Science, Psychology, History, Aviation
1985: 143 titles *1986:* 101 titles *Founded:* 1945

Nakladatelství **Obelisk***, Prague 1, Mikulandská 10
Publishing House of Czechoslovak Artists
Man Dir: Jiří Dvořák
Subject: Art

Vydavateľstvo **Obzor** NP, 81585 Bratislava, ul Československej armády 35 Tel: (07) 57251 Cable Add: Vydavateľstvo Obzor Bratislava
Horizon: Slovak Book & Periodical Publishing House for People's Education
Dir: Ján Princ (acting)
Subjects: Non-fiction, Encyclopaedias, Law, General Science, Textbooks, Paperbacks, Adults' Educational
Founded: 1953

Odeon, nakladatelství krásné literatury a umění, 11587 Prague 1, Národní 36 Tel: (02) 2366885 Cable Add: Odeon Praha Telex: 123055 Odeo
Publishing House of Literature and Art
Dir: Josef Kulíček; *Assistant Dir:* Dr Edvard Vonka; *Editorial:* Josef Šimon; *Sales, Publicity:* Dr M Burkon; *Production:* M Filipová; *Rights & Permissions:* Dr V Vocetková
Subjects: General Fiction, Belles Lettres, Poetry, Biography, Art, Reproductions
Book Club: Odeon Book Club (Klub čtenářů)
Bookshop: 11586 Prague 1, Na Florenci 3
1985: 139 titles *1986:* 135 titles *Founded:* 1953

Nakladatelství **Olympia***, 11588 Prague 1, Klimentská 1 Tel: (02) 2310924 Cable Add: Olympia Prague
Publishing House of Sports and Tourism
Man Dir: Karel Zelniček; *Sales Dir:* M Karas; *Publicity & Advertising:* V Urban
Subjects: Sports, Travel, Juveniles, Albums
Bookshop: Prague 1, Hybernská 34
Founded: 1954
Miscellaneous: Formerly Sportovní a turistické nakladatelství

Opus Records and Publishing House+, 82715 Bratislava, Mlynské nivy 73 Tel: (07) 235783/61783/69091 Telex: 92219
Man Dir: Dr Ivan Stanislav; *Commercial Dir:* Dr Ervín Pauliak; *Editorial:* Dr Marta Földešová; *Publicity:* Dr Pavol Fellegi; *Rights & Permissions:* Dr Zlatica Môciková; *International Dept (Licensing):* Rudolf Homer
Subject: Music
1985: 39 titles *1986:* 41 titles (each including sheet music) *Founded:* 1971

Nakladatelství **Orbis**, dissolved in 1977, part of activity taken over by Nakladatelství a vydavatelství Panorama (qv); name Orbis now attached to Press Agency

Osveta, 03654 Martin, Osloboditelov 21
Dir: Imrich Halda
Orders to: Slovart, Aussenhandels AG, 81764 Bratislava, Gottwaldovo nám 6
Subjects: Education, Popular Sciences, Tourism, Medicine
1985: 112 titles *Founded:* 1953

Vydavateľstvo SFVU **Pallas***, 88209 Bratislava, Štúrova 1/b
Publishing House of the Slovak Fund of Fine Arts
Subjects: Art, Literature, Biography

Nakladatelství a vydavatelství **Panorama**, 12072 Prague 2, Hálkova 1, PO Box 75 Tel: (02) 245449 Cable Add: Panorama Prague 2 Telex: 122657
Man Dir: Dr František Hanzlík
Subjects: Popular Science, Local History, Picture-books, Art, Law, Concise Encyclopaedias, Travels, Juveniles, Periodicals, Applied Arts
Founded: 1978
Miscellaneous: Formerly Nakladatelství Orbis

Panton, 11839 Prague 1, Říční 12 Tel: (02) 538151 Cable Add: Panton
Publishers of the Czech Music Fund — Prague
Man Dir: Jaroslav Hraba
Subjects: Music (Instruction, Works, Biography, General), Juveniles, Educational Materials
Bookshops: Prague 1, Jungmanova 30; Brno, Ceská 14; Bratislava, Sedlářská 10
Founded: 1958

Peace and Socialism International Publishers, 16616 Prague 6, Thakurova 3 Tel: (02) 325731/335111 Cable Add: Cssr Prag Srozt Telex: 123542 Wmr
Subjects: International Communist and Working-Class Movement. Periodicals include *World Marxist Review* (in 40 languages), *Information Bulletin* (in English, French, German, Spanish, Italian, Greek, Arabic, Portuguese)

Vydavateľstvo ROH **'Práca'**, 81271 Bratislava, Obrancov mieru 19 Tel: (07) 330838/333779/332347 Telex: 93283
Publishing House of the Revolutionary Trade Union Movement
Dir: Ján Duži
Subjects: Trade Unions (history and contemporary studies), Labour Problems, Social Security, Economics, Ergonomics, Labour and Management Rationalization, Labour Sociology and Psychology, Labour Law, Work Safety, Needlework Handbooks
Bookshop: Knižná predajn Práca, 81271 Bratislava, nám SNP 20
1985: 64 titles *1986:* 62 titles *Founded:* 1946

Práce*, 11258 Prague 1, Václavské nám 17, Nové Město
Publishing House of the Czech Trade Union Movement
Dir: Juraj Himal
Subjects: Belles Lettres, How-to, General, Political Science, Juveniles, Law, Engineering, Fiction, Non-fiction
Book Clubs: ERB, Kamarád
Founded: 1945

Nakladatelstvo **Pravda***, CS-81306 Bratislava, Gunduličova ul 12 Tel: (07) 335574
Dir: Viliam Kačer
Subjects: Fiction, Biography, History, Political Science, Philosophy, Social Science, Law, Economics
Book Club: ČKP (Členská knižnica Pravdy)
Miscellaneous: Firm is the publishing house of the Central Committee of the Communist Party of Slovakia

Príroda, vydavateľstvo kníh a časopisov*, 81534 Bratislava, Križkova 9 Tel: (07) 47241
Dir: Vincent Šugár; *Editorial:* Ján Braun
Subjects: Agriculture, Veterinary Science, Biology, Husbandry, Forestry, Nature Protection, Phytopathology, Beekeeping, Mechanisation of Agriculture, Horticulture, Specialized Multilingual Dictionaries, Encyclopaedias
Founded: 1949

Nakladatelství **Profil***, 70100 Ostrava 1, Cihlářská 51 Tel: (069) 53559/55129

CZECHOSLOVAKIA 77

Northern Moravian Publishing House
Dir: František Cečetka
Subjects: General Fiction, Belles Lettres, Poetry, Biography, History, Music, Art, Reference, Juveniles, Social Science, Psychology
Founded: 1957

Nakladatelství **Ruže***, 37196 Ceské Budějovice, Zižkovo nám 5 Tel: (038) 2250/5620/7693
Southern Bohemian Publishing House
Dir: František Podlaha
Subjects: General Fiction, Belles Lettres, History, Juveniles, Low-priced Paperbacks, Regional Literature
Founded: 1960

S N T L — Nakladatelství technické literatury+, 11302 Prague 1, Spálená 51 Tel: (02) 203774
Man Dir: Stanislav Kánský; Editorial: Dr V Šesták; Rights & Permissions: Dr A Vacek
Subjects: Engineering and Applied Technology, Science, Economics, Dictionaries, Reference, Periodicals
Book Club: Klub čtenár technické literatury (Club for Readers of Technical Literature)
Bookshop: Středisko technické literatury (Centre of Technical Literature) (at above address)
Founded: 1895

Severočeské nakladatelství*, 40021 Ústí nad Labem, Velká Hradební 33 Tel: (047) 28581
North Bohemian Publishing House
Dir: Jiří Švejda; Editor-in-Chief: Dr Václav Houžvička; Sales: Jiřina Kusová
Subjects: General Fiction, Belles Lettres, Poetry, Biography, History, Music, Art, Philosophy, Juveniles, General Science, Low-priced Paperbacks, Regional Literature
Founded: 1971

Slovenská kartografia NP, 83407 Bratislava-Krasňany, Pekná cesta 17 Tel: (07) 282001/282020 Cable Add: Kartografia Bratislava Telex: 92132 Karto
Slovak Cartographic Publishing House
Dir: P Kmeťko; Editorial: Zd Matula, Vertrieb Š Nemec
Orders to: Slovart AG, 81764 Bratislava, Gottwaldovo nám 6
Subject: Maps & Atlases
Bookshop: Slovenská kniha NP, 81106 Bratislava, Knihkupeotvo, Obchodná 9
1985-86: 26 titles Founded: 1957

Slovenské pedagogické nakladateľstvo*, Bratislava, Sasinkova 5 Tel: (07) 64551 Cable Add: Spn Bratislava
Slovak Publishing House for Educational Literature
Man Dir: Sergej Troščák
Subjects: History, Music, Art, Psychology, General Science, University, Secondary & Primary Textbooks, Education, Reference, Dictionaries
Founded: 1920

Vydavateľstvo **Slovenskej akadémie vied**, see VEDA

Slovenský spisovateľ*, 81367 Bratislava, Leningradská 2 Tel: (07) 333903
Publishing House of the Slovak Literary Fund
Man Dir: Vladimír Dudás Editorial: Štefan Strážay; Sales, Production: Rudolf Pernica; Publicity: Anna Sigmundová; Rights & Permissions: Ol'ga Pet'ková
Subjects: General Fiction, Belles Lettres, Poetry, Literary Theory and Criticism
Book Clubs: KMP (Kruh milovníkov poézie); NST (Nová sovietska tvorba);

SPKK (Spoločnosť priateľov krásnych kníh); Vavrín
Bookshop: Dom knihy (at above address)
Founded: 1950

Smena, 81284 Bratislava, Pražská 11 Tel: (07) 48539/48541 Cable Add: Bratislava Smena Telex: 09341
Publishing House of Slovak Central Committee of Socialist Youth Union
Dir: Rudolf Belan
Subjects: General Fiction, Belles Lettres, Poetry, Biography, History, Philosophy, Low- & High-priced Paperbacks, Psychology, Social Science, Juveniles, Hobbies
Book Club: Máj
Founded: 1949

Sport, 83258 Bratislava, Vajnorská 100
Dir: Július Chvalný
Subject: Sport
Miscellaneous: Firm is the publishing house of the Slovak Central Committee of the Czechoslovak Physical Culture Organization

Statisticke a evidencni vydavatelství tiskopisu*, 11000 Prague 1, Malá strana, Trziste 9
Publishing House of Statistics and Data
Subject: Reference

Státní pedagogické nakladatelství, 11301 Prague 1, Nové Město, Ostrovní 30 Tel: (02) 203787 Cable Add: Stapena Prague
State Publishing House for Educational Literature
Man Dir: Josef Papež
Subjects: History, Juveniles, Medicine, Psychology, Engineering, Social Science, Primary, Secondary & University Textbooks, Pedagogical Journals, Reference
Founded: 1775

Státní zemědělské nakladatelství, 11311 Prague 1, Nové Město, Václavské náměstí 47 Tel: (02) 226641
Agricultural Publishing House
Man Dir: Karel Koukal
Subjects: Agriculture, Forestry, Veterinary Science, Agronomy, Hobbies

Středočeské nakladatelství knihkupectví*, 11000 Prague 1, U Prašné brány 3
Central Bohemian Publishing House & Bookshop
Dir: František Pěkný
Subjects: Regional Literature, Fiction, General, Belles Lettres

Supraphon, Prague 1, Palackého ul 1 Tel: (02) 268141 Cable Add: Supraphon Praha Telex: 121218 Sunp
Publishing House of Music, Recordings, Sheet Music and Musicological Literature. Rental library of orchestral materials
Man Dir: Jan Kvídera; Foreign Connections, Rights & Permissions: Dr Pavel Smola; Editorial: Karel Vacek; Commercial Dir: Karel Arbes
Subject: Music
Bookshops: 150 branches
Founded: 1946

Svepomoc*, 11000 Prague 1, Gorkého nám 10, Nové Město
Publishing House of the Central Cooperative Council

Svoboda, 11303 Prague 1, Revoluční 15 Tel: (02) 2313562
Dir: Dr Stanislav Mareš
Subjects: History, Philosophy, Economics, Politics, Belles Lettres
Book Clubs: Friends of Antiquity, Readers Club of Svoboda
Miscellaneous: Firm is the publishing house

of the Central Committee of the Communist Party of Czechoslovakia

Tatran, 89134 Bratislava, Michalská 9 Tel: (07) 330141
Slovak Publishing House of Belles Lettres
Man Dir: Dr Anton Markuš; Sales: Dr Vladimír Sojak; Publicity & Advertising: Dr Tomás Oravec; Rights & Permissions: LITA, Slovak Literary Agency, 81530 Bratislava, Zámočnícka 9
Subjects: Belles Lettres, Poetry, Art
Book Club: Hviezdoslavova knižnica
Bookshop: At above address
1985: 112 titles Founded: 1947

V E D A, Vydavateľstvo Slovenskej akadémie vied*, 81430 Bratislava, Klemensová 19 Tel: (07) 50355 Cable Add: Veda Bratislava
Publishing House of the Slovak Academy of Sciences
Man Dir: Miroslav Murín; Editorial: Dr Ján Jankovič; Publicity Manager: Nina Hečková
Subjects: Technical Sciences, Natural Sciences, Linguistics, History, Archaeology, Philosophy, Psychology, Encyclopaedias, Dictionaries
Bookshop: Kníhkupectvo SAV, 81430 Bratislava, Dunajská 5
Founded: 1953

Východoslovenské vydavateľstvo NP, 04011 Košice, Alejová 3 Tel: (095) 65204
Slovak Publishing House
Man Dir: Mikuláš Jáger; Chief Editor: Stanislav Brnoliak
Subjects: Belles Lettres, History, Political Science, Juveniles, Regional Literature
1985: 46 titles 1986: 36 titles Founded: 1960

Vyšehrad*, Prague 2, Karlovo náměstí 5
Publishing House of the Czechoslovak People's Party
Subjects: Works of Contemporary Czech and World Writers, Popular Science, Contemporary Politics

Západočeské nakladatelství*, 30100 Plzeň, Moskevská 36
Western Bohemian Regional Publishing House
Dir: Václav Brašna
Subjects: General Fiction, Belles Lettres, History, Regional Literature, Juveniles

Literary Agents

D I L I A, 12824 Prague 2, Vyšehradská 28, Post Box 34 Tel: (02) 296651 Cable Add: Dilia Prag Telex: 121367 Dili
Theatrical and Literary Agency
Contact: Dr Robert Jurák

L I T A, 81530 Bratislava, ul Zámočnícka 9 Tel: (07) 334801/334806 Cable Add: Lita Bratislava
Slovak Literary Agency: the exclusive copyright organization representing Slovak authors in foreign transactions and foreign authors on the territory of Slovakia
Contact: Judr Matej Andráś

Book Clubs

Č K P (Členská knižnica Pravdy)*, 88205 Bratislava, Gunduličova ul 12
Members: 43,500
Owned by: Nakladatelstvo Pravda (qv)
Founded: 1958

Club of Young Readers*, 81519 Bratislava, nám SNP 12
Owned by: Mladé letá (qv)

78 CZECHOSLOVAKIA

E R B*, 11258 Prague 1, Václavské nám 17, Nové Město
Owned by: Práce (qv)

Friends of Antiquity, 11303 Prague 1, Revoluční 15 Tel: (02) 2313562
Owned by: Svoboda (qv)

Hviezdoslavova knižnica, 89134 Bratislava, Michalská 9
Owned by: Tatran (qv)

K M Č, Prague 1, Na Perštýně 1
Young Readers' Club
Owned by: Albatros (qv)

K M P (Kruh milovníkov poézie)*, 81367 Bratislava, Leningradská 2
Club for Poetry Lovers
Owned by: Slovenský spisovateľ (qv)

Kamarad*, 11258 Prague 1, Václavské nám 17, Nové Město
Owned by: Práce (qv)

Klub čtenářů technické literatury, 11302 Prague 1, Spálená 51
Club for Readers of Technical Literature
Members: 45,000
Supervised by: SNTL — Nakladatelství technické literatury (qv)
Subjects: Engineering and Applied Technology, Science, Dictionaries, Applied Economics
Founded: 1958

Klub přátel poezie, 11147 Prague 1, Národní 9
Club of the Friends of Poetry
Owned by: Československý spisovatel (qv)

Máj, 81284 Bratislava, Pražská 11
Owned by: Smena (qv)

N S T (Nová sovietska tvorba)*, 81367 Bratislava, Leningradská 2
Owned by: Slovenský spisovateľ (qv)

Odeon Book Club (Klub čtenářů), 11697 Prague 1, Celetna 11
Members: 250,000
Owned by: Odeon nakladatelství krásné literatury a umění (qv)
Subjects: Fiction, Art

Readers Club of Svoboda, 11303 Prague 1, Revoluční 15 Tel: (02) 2313562
Owned by: Svoboda (qv)

S P K K (Spoločnosť priateľov krásnych kníh)*, 81367 Bratislava, Leningradská 2
Society of Friends of Beautiful Books
Owned by: Slovenský spisovateľ (qv)

Vavrín*, 81367 Bratislava, Leningradská 2
Owned by: Slovenský spisovateľ (qv)

Major Booksellers

Artia, 11127 Prague 1, Ve Smečkách 30, PO Box 790 Tel: (02) 2358565
Import/export organization
Also Publisher (qv)

Kniha*, Prague 2, Nové Město, 8 Zitna
Dir: Miloslav Jeřábek
The central purchasing place for single bookselling businesses in Prague

Slovart Co Ltd, 81764 Bratislava, Gottwaldovo nám 6
Import/export organization

Major Libraries

Státní knihovna České socialistické republiky*, 11001 Prague 1, Klementinum 190 Tel: (Main switchboard) (02) 266541/267241; (Dir) 225192 Telex: 121207
State Library of the Czech Socialist Republic
Publications: České knihy (Czech Books) (weekly); *Ceské hudebniny* (Czech Music) (quarterly); *Slovenské hudebniny* (Slovak Music) (annual); *Novinky literatury* (Literary News)

Knihovna Národního muzea, 11579 Prague 1, tř Vítězného února 74 Tel: (02) 269451
National Museum Library
Dir: Dr Jaroslav Vrchotka
Publication: Sborník Národního muzea v Praze, řada C: literární historie (Magazine of the National Museum, Prague, Series C: Literary History) (quarterly)

Matica slovenská, 03652 Martin, Novomeského 32 Tel: 31371/31492/34035 Telex: 075331
Slovak National Library
Dir: Dr Viliam Mruškovič; *Librarian:* Dr Miroslav Bielik
Publications include: Slovenská národná bibliografia (Slovak National Bibliography) (monthly); *Čitadel* (The Reader) (monthly); *Slovensko* (Slovakia) (monthly); *Knižnice a vedecké informácie* (Libraries and scientific information) (every two months); *Kniha* (The Book); *Literárny archív* (Literary Archive); *Hudobný archív* (Music Archive); *archív* (Music Archive); *Literárnomuzejný letopis* (Literary Museum Annals); *Slováci v zahraničí* (The Slovaks abroad) (annually)

Městská knihovna v Praze, 11572 Prague 1, nám primátora Dr V Vacka 1
The City Library in Prague

Památník národního pisemnictví, Strahovská knihovna*, 11838 Prague 1, Strahovské nádvoří 132 Tel: (02) 538841
Museum of National Literature, Strahov Library

Slovenská technická knižnica*, 81223 Bratislava, Gottwaldovo nám 19
Slovak Technical Library

Ustredná knižnica **Slovenskej akadémie** vied, 81467 Bratislava, Klemensova 19 Tel: (07) 56321/51733 Telex: 93464 Uksav
Central Library of the Slovak Academy of Sciences

Státní technická knihovna, 11307 Prague 1, nám primátora Dr V Vacka 5
State Technical Library
Dir: Dr Eva Sošková
Periodicals include: Technická Knihovna (Technical Library); Czechoslovak scientific and technical periodicals contents

Státní vědecká knihovna, 60187 Brno, Leninova 5-7 Tel: (05) 747500 Telex: 62299
State Research Library
Chief Librarian: Dr Jaromír Kubíček

Státní vědecká knihovna, 77177 Olomouc, Bezručova 2 Tel: (068) 23441
State Scientific Library

Státní vědecká knihovna odbor technické literatury*, 66231 Brno, Veveří 95
State Technical Library in Brno

Univerzitná knižnica, 81417 Bratislava, Michalská 1 Tel: (07) 331151/333247 Telex: 93255 Uknz
University Library
Dir: Dr Marcel Kollár

Knihovny fakult a ústavu **University Karlovy***, Prague Libraries of Faculties and Institutes of Charles University

Library Associations

Slovenská knižničná RADA*, Ministerstvo kultúry SSR, 81331 Bratislava, Suvorovová 12
Slovak Library Council
Chairman: Dr S Pasiar

Ústřední knihovnická rada ČSR, Prague 1, Valdštejnské nám 4
Central Library Council of the Czech Socialist Republic
President: Prof Dr Jiří Kábrt

Zväz slovenskych knihovníkov a informatikov, 81417 Bratislava, Michalská 1 Tel: (07) 330557 Telex: 093255
Association of Slovak Librarians and Information Workers
Executive Secretary: Dr Elena Saka'lová
Publication: Zväzový bulletin (INFOS)

Library Reference Journals

Čitatel (The Reader), Matica slovenská, 03652 Martin, Novomeského 32
Text in Slovak, summaries in German and Russian

Knižnice a vedecké informácie (Libraries and scientific information) (every two months), Matica slovenská, 03652 Martin, Novomeského 32

Zväzový bulletin (INFOS), Zväz slovenskych knihovníkov a informatikov, 81417 Bratislava, Michalská 1

Literary Associations and Societies

Kruh priateľov detskej knihy na Slovensku*, 81519 Bratislava, nám SNP 12 Tel: 50539/58241
Circle of Friends of Children's Books in Slovakia

Literature Institute*, Slovak Academy of Sciences, Bratislava, Konventuá 13 Tel: (07) 313391
Publication: Slovenská literatúra (Slovak Literature)

Matice moravská*, Brno, Gorkého 14
Moravian Society of History and Literature
Secretary: Dr Jiří Malíř
Publication: Časopis Matice moravské (quarterly)

Czechoslovakian **P E N** Centre, 1180 Prague 1, Hradčanské nám 11
Secretary: Marta Kadlečikova

Společnost přátel knihy pro mládež*, 11001 Prague 1, Na Perštýně 1 Tel: 248851/245151
Association of Friends of Children's Books
Chairman: Bohumil Riha
Publications include: Bulletin (irregular); annual Bibliography

Index-**Společnost pro Československou literaturu** v zahraničí*, Postfach 410511, D-5000 Cologne 41, Federal Republic of Germany
Society for the Promotion of Czechoslovak Literature Abroad

Spolek Českých bibliofilu*, Prague, Nové Město, Václavské nám 39
Association of Czech Bibliophiles

Literary Periodicals

Červený Květ, Ostrava 1, Tyrsová 9
Literature and art

Česká literatura, Academia, 11229 Prague 1, Vodičkova 40
Text in Czech, summaries in English, French, German and Russian

Kniha (The Book), Matica slovenská, 03652 Martin, Novomeského 32

Literární měsíčník (Literary Monthly), Svaz českých spisovatelu, 11147 Prague 1, Národní třída 11

Meridians 12-23, Zväz slovenských spisovatel'ov, 81508 Bratislava, Obrancov mieru 14

Novinky literatury (Literary News), Státní knihovna České socialistické republiky, 11001 Prague 1, Klementinum 190

Sborník Národního muzea v Praže, řada C: literární historie (Magazine of the National Museum, Prague, Series C: Literary History) (quarterly), Knihovna Národniho muzea, 11579 Prague 1, tr Vítězného února 74
Quarterly; title also in Latin, summaries in English, French, German and Russian

Slovenská literatúra (Slovak Literature), Literature Institute, Slovak Academy of Sciences, Bratislava, Konventuá 13
Contents page and summaries in German and Russian

Slovenské pohlady na literatúru a umĕnie (Slovak View on Literature and Art), Slovenský spisovatel', 81367 Bratislava, Leningradská 2

Slowakei (Slovakia), Matus-Cernak-Institut, Kulturelles Zentrum der Slowaken in Deutschland, D-5000 Cologne 1, Postfach 100924, Federal Republic of Germany
Literary, scientific and political review

Svědectví, 6 rue du Pont de Lodi, Paris 6e, France, and Vienna V, Margaretenpl 7, Austria
Czech literary journal published abroad

Svetova literatura, Odeon, 11587 Prague 1, Národní 36
Review of foreign literature

Literary Prizes

Bratislava Town Prize
Awarded annually for outstanding work in fields including literature relating to the town of Bratislava. Enquiries to Zväz slovenských spisovatel'ov, 81508 Bratislava, Obrancov mieru 14

Brno Literary Prize*
For the best book written and published in Brno. Awarded annually. Enquiries to Svaz českých spisovatelu, 11147 Prague 1, Národní třída 11

Jan **Holly** Prize
Awarded annually by the Slovak Literary Fund for the best literary translations. Enquiries to Zväz slovenských spisovatel'ov, 81508 Bratislava, Obrancov mieru 14

Fraňo **Kráľ** Prize
For existing works or for outstanding achievements in the field of juvenile literature. The executive body of Fraňo Kráľ Prize is the Slovak Literary Fund, the Circle of Friends of Juvenile Literature and publishing house Mladé letá. The prize is awarded annually. Enquiries to Zväz slovenských spisovatel'ov, 81508 Bratislava, Obrancov mieru 14

Marie **Majerove** Prize*
The highest award for a life's work in the fields of Czech literature and art for children and young people. Awarded every other year. Enquiries to Svaz českých spisovatelu, 11147 Prague 1, Národní třída 11

Mladá fronta Award*
Awarded annually by the publishing house Mladá fronta (Young Front) for literary works of prose, poetry, journalism, popular science, also translations, published by them during the preceding year. Enquiries to Svaz českých spisovatelu, 11147 Prague 1, Národní třída 11

Mladé letá Prize
Awarded annually by the publishing house Mladé letá (Young Years) for outstanding books by Slovak writers published by them during the preceding year. Enquiries to Zväz slovenských spisovatel'ov, 81508 Bratislava, Obrancov mieru 14

Naše vojsko Prizes*
For a political book, a book on military theory and a book of fiction. Monetary prize is divided between the winners in each category. Enquiries to Svaz českých spisovatelu, 11147 Prague 1, Národní třída 11

Prague Literary Prize*
For the best creative work which has enriched human knowledge, contributed to the construction of socialism and furthered the development of culture in the City of Prague. Awarded annually. Enquiries to Svaz českých spisovatelu, 11147 Prague 1, Národní třída 11

Slovenský spisovatel' Prize
Awarded annually by the publishing house Slovak Writer for outstanding books by Slovak writers published by them during the preceding year. Enquiries to Zväz slovenských spisovatel'ov, 81508 Bratislava, Obrancov mieru 14

Smena Prize
Awarded annually by the publishing house Smena for outstanding books by Slovak writers published by them during the preceding year. Enquiries to Zväz slovenských spisovatel'ov, 81508 Bratislava, Obrancov mieru 14

Zväz slovenských spisovatel'ov Prize
Awarded annually by the Union of Slovak Writers for outstanding works of original Slovak poetry, prose, literary science and literature for children. Enquiries to Zväz slovenských spisovatel'ov, 81508 Bratislava, Obrancov mieru 14

Denmark

General Information

Language: Danish (English and German widely spoken). Faeroese in the Faroes. Greenlandic in Greenland
Religion: Lutheran
Population: 5.1 million
Bank Hours: 0930-1600 Monday-Friday; open until 1800 Thursday
Shop Hours: 0800 or 0900-1700 or 1730 Monday-Thursday; open until 1900 or 2000 Friday; open until 1200 or 1400 Saturday
Currency: 100 øre = 1 krone
Export/Import Information: Denmark is member of European Economic Community, Faroes and Greenland are not. No tariff on books except children's picture-books from non-EEC. No import licences required. Importers must be longest of alternative credit terms in contract, otherwise no exchange controls
Copyright: UCC, Berne, Florence (see International section)

Book Trade Organizations

D B K — Bookdistribution*, Siljangade 6, DK-2300 Copenhagen
Danish Booksellers Clearing House
Man Dir: Bjarne Pedersen

Danish ISBN Agency, Dansk bogfortegnelse, Bibliotekscentralen, Tempovej 7-11, DK-2750 Ballerup Tel: (02) 974000 Cable Add: Danliber Telex: 35370
ISBN Administrator: Morten Garde

Dansk Forfatterforening*, Tordenskjolds Gård, Strandgade 6, DK-1401 Copenhagen K Tel: (01) 955100
Danish Writers' Union
Chairman: Hans Hansen; *General Secretary:* Svend Erichsen
Publication: Forfatteren (8 a year)

Danske Antikvarboghandlerforening, Postboks 2184, DK-1017 Copenhagen K
Danish Antiquarian Booksellers' Association

Danske Boghandleres Kommissionsanstalt (DBK), now DBK — Bookdistribution (qv)

Den **Danske Boghandlerforening**, Boghandlernes Hus, Siljangade 6, DK-2300 Copenhagen S
Danish Booksellers' Association
Secretary: Elisabeth Brodersen
Publication: Det Danske Bogmarked (The Danish Book Market) (with Danske Forlaeggerforening)

Den **Danske Forlaeggerforening***, Købmagergade 11, DK-1150 Copenhagen K Tel: (01) 156688
Danish Publishers' Association
Dir: Erik V Krustrup
Publications: Det Danske Bogmarked (with Danske Boghandlerforening); *Fortegnelse over Samhandels-Berettigede Boghandlere MV* (Register of Licensed Booksellers etc)

Faellesekspeditionen*, Njalsgade 19, DK-2300 Copenhagen S Tel: (01) 541333
Joint Trade Counter

Forening for Boghaandvaerk*, Nørregade 26, DK-1165 Copenhagen K Tel: (01) 117812
Danish Book-craft Association
Publication: Bogvennen (The Book Lover) (yearbook)

Forening for Forlagsfolk, Anette Wad, c/o Forlaget Komma A/S, Frederiksborggade 26A, DK-1360 Copenhagen K Tel: (01) 229725
Association of Young Publishers

Standard Book Numbering Agency, see Danish ISBN Agency

Book Trade Reference Books and Journals

Book

Fortegnelse over Samhandels-Berettigede Boghandlere MV (Register of Licensed Booksellers etc), Den Danske Forlaeggerforening, Købmagergade 11, DK-1150 Copenhagen K

Journals

Bogormen (The Bookworm), Danish Book Trade Employees' Association,

80 DENMARK

Boghandlernes Hus, Siljangade 6, DK-2300 Copenhagen S
Journal for book trade employees

Bogvennen (The Book Lover), Brolaeggerstr 4, DK-1211 Copenhagen K or Forening for Boghaandvaerk, Nørregade 26, DK-1165 Copenhagen K

Dansk Bogfortegnelse (The Danish National Bibliography, Books), Bibliotekscentralen, Tempovej 7-11, DK-2750 Ballerup

Dansk Periodicafortegnelse (The Danish National Bibliography, Serials), Bibliotekscentralen, Tempovej 7-11, DK-2750 Ballerup

Det Danske Bogmarked (The Danish Book Market), Den Danske Boghandlerforening, Boghandlernes Hus, Siljangade 6, DK-2300 Copenhagen S

Publishers

Agertofts Forlag*, Købmagergade 50, DK-1150 Copenhagen K   Tel: (01) 154466
Man Dir: Ejnar Agertoft
Subject: Children's
Bookshop: The Children's Bookshop (at above address)
Founded: 1986
ISBN Publisher's Prefix: 87-88014

Akademisk Forlag, Postboks 54, DK-1002 Copenhagen K (Located at: Store Kannikestr 6-8, Copenhagen)   Tel: (01) 119826
Man Dir: Per Holm Rasmussen
Subjects: History, International History, Linguistics, Philosophy, Psychology, Law, Social Science, Economics, Engineering, General Science, Computer Science, University Textbooks, High-priced Paperbacks, Educational Materials
Founded: 1962
ISBN Publisher's Prefix: 87-500

Alma+, Kaalundsvej 13, DK-3400 Hillerød   Tel: (02) 255441
Chief Executive: Susanne Vebel
Subjects: Children & Young Adults (Fiction and Non-fiction)
1985: 26 titles   *1986:* 25 titles   *Founded:* 1984
ISBN Publisher's Prefix: 87-7243

Amadeus Forlag ApS, Trekronergade 15, DK-2500 Valby   Tel: (01) 303660   Fax: (01) 308080
Man Dir: Flemming Ettrup;   *Editor:* Carsten Berthelsen
Parent Company: Danmarks Biblioteksforening Forlag ApS (qv)
1986: 6 titles   *Founded:* 1986
ISBN Publisher's Prefix: 87-89028

Forlaget **Apostrof** ApS+*, Postboks 2580, Berggreensgade 24, DK-2100 Copenhagen Ø   Tel: (01) 208420   Cable Add: Miaetole
Publishers: Ole Thestrup, Mia Timm
Subjects: High-quality Children's Picturebooks, Fiction, Non-fiction, Mass-market Humour, Post-Freud Psychology, Literature
Founded: 1980
ISBN Publisher's Prefixes: 87-591, 87-88002

Arnkrone Forlaget A/S*, Fuglebækvej 4, DK-2770 Kastrup   Tel: (01) 507000
Man Dir: J Juul Rasmussen
Subjects: Art, Cultural History, Popular Medicine
Founded: 1941
ISBN Publisher's Prefix: 87-87007

Aschehoug Dansk Forlag A/S+, Klosterrisvej 7, DK-2100 Copenhagen Ø   Tel: (01) 294422   Cable Add: Asdanfo

Telex: 16987 Ash   Fax: (01) 271010
Man Dir: Erik Ipsen;   *Marketing Manager:* Jan B Thomsen
Subsidiary Companies: J Fr Clausens Forlag (qv); Grafisk Forlag (qv); H Hagerups Forlag (qv); H Hirschsprungs Forlag (qv)
Subject: Textbooks
Founded: 1914
ISBN Publisher's Prefix: 87-11

H M Bergs Forlag ApS*, Peder Skrams Gade 5, DK-1054 Copenhagen K   Tel: (01) 135480
Man Dir: H M Berg
Subject: Art
Founded: 1965
ISBN Publisher's Prefix: 87-7228

Bibliotekscentralens Forlag*, Tempovej 7-11, DK-2750 Ballerup   Tel: (02) 974000   Cable Add: Danliber   Telex: 35370   Fax: (02) 655310
Man Dir: Asger Hansen
Subjects: Bibliographies, Catalogues, Classification and cataloguing rules. Publish Danish National Bibliography
1985: 116 titles   *Founded:* 1939
ISBN Publisher's Prefix: 87-552

Bierman og Bierman A/S, Vestergade 120, DK-7200 Grindsted   Tel: (05) 320288/ 320481   Fax: (05) 321548
Man Dirs: Bo Lorentzen, Tom Selmer-Petersen
Holding Company: Bo Lorentzen ApS
Subjects: Management & Organization, Children's
Founded: 1968

Bogans Forlag A/S*, Kastaniebakken 8, DK-3540 Lynge   Tel: (02) 188055
Owner: Evan Bogan
Subjects: Quality Paperbacks (factual, general), Popular Science, Occult

Bonniers Specialmagasiner A/S, Nørre Farimagsgade 49, DK-1375 Copenhagen K   Tel: (01) 126612   Telex: 15712 Fogtdl
Publisher, Man Dir: Erik Skipper Larsen;
Publishing Dirs: Steen Hau, Lars Horve;
Book Publishing Manager: Jette Juliusson
Subsidiary Companies: Bonnier System A/S, Bjerringbrovej 116, DK-2610 Rødovre, Denmark; Selektiv Reklame A/S (at above address); Suomen Fogtdal Oy, Ohrahuhdantie 2, SF-00680 Helsinki, Finland; Editions Fogtdal, 51-57 rue Jules Ferry, F-93178 Bagnolet Cedex, France; Norsk Fogtdal A/S, Sagveien 17, N-0458 Oslo 4, Norway
Branch Off: Fogtdals Förlag, Ängelholmsgatan 1-3, S-214 22 Malmö, Sweden
Subjects: Home Decoration, DIY, Cooking, Gardening, Motoring, Boating, Science, Fashion, Needlework
Founded: 1959

Borgens Forlag A/S+, Valbygård, Valbygårdsvej 33, DK-2500 Valby   Tel: (01) 462100   Cable Add: Borgenbooks
Man Dirs and Editorial: Jarl Borgen, Niels Borgen;   *Sales:* Jacob Mahler;   *Production:* Erik Crillesen;   *Publicity:* Egon Dinesen;
Rights & Permissions: Mette Nymark
Orders to: DBK-bogdistribution, Siljangade 2-8, DK-2300 Copenhagen S
Subjects: General Fiction and Non-fiction, Art, Children's, Educational, Textbooks, Religion, Craft and Leisure, Practical Handbooks, Health & Social Science, Computers
1985: 347 titles   *1986:* 306 titles   *Founded:* 1948
ISBN Publisher's Prefix: 87-418

Børsens Forlag*, Postboks 2103, DK-1014 Copenhagen K (Located at: Møntergade

19, DK-1116 Copenhagen)   Tel: (01) 157250
Publishing Manager, Editorial: Flemming Cumberland;   *Sales Manager:* Bjarne Birch;
Production: Svend Erik Larsen
Subject: Management
ISBN Publisher's Prefix: 87-7553

Nyt Nordisk Forlag Arnold **Busck** A/S, see Nyt

Carit Andersens Forlag A/S, Malmøgade 3, DK-2100 Copenhagen Ø   Tel: (01) 260621   Telex: 16121
Publicity Manager: Erik Albrechtsen
Parent Company: Paul Klinge A/S
Subjects: Fiction, Non-fiction, Travel, Limited Editions, Illustrated books
1986: 15 titles   *1987:* 20 titles
ISBN Publisher's Prefix: 87-424

Carlsen if International Publishers, now Semic Forlagene A/S (qv)

J Fr **Clausens** Forlag+, Klosterrisvej 7, DK-2100 Copenhagen Ø   Tel: (01) 294422   Cable Add: Asdanfo   Telex: 16987 Ash   Fax: (01) 271010
Man Dir: Erik Ipsen;   *Marketing Manager:* Jan B Thomsen;   *Rights & Permissions:* Kaj Påskesen
Parent Company: Aschehoug Dansk Forlag A/S (qv)
Subject: Practical Handbooks
ISBN Publisher's Prefix: 87-11

Forlaget **Danmark** A/S, now incorporated in Lademann Ltd, Publishers (qv)

Danmarks Biblioteksforening Forlag ApS+, Trekronergade 15, DK-2500 Valby   Tel: (01) 308682   Fax: (01) 308080
Man Dir: Flemming Ettrup
Subsidiary Company: Amadeus Forlag ApS (qv)
Subjects: Libraries, General culture
Founded: 1982
ISBN Publisher's Prefix: 87-87244

Dansk Historisk Haandbogsforlag Ltd+, Klintevej 25, DK-2800 Lyngby   Tel: (02) 807200
Owner, Man Dir: Henning Jensen
Subjects: Genealogy, Heraldry, Culture, Local History
1986: 35 titles   *Founded:* 1976
ISBN Publisher's Prefixes: 87-85207, 87-88742

Christian **Ejlers'** Forlag, Postboks 2228, DK-1018 Copenhagen K (Located at: Brolaeggerstr 4, Copenhagen K)   Tel: (01) 122114
Man Dir: Christian Ejlers
Subjects: Educational & Academic, Art
Founded: 1967
ISBN Publisher's Prefix: 87-7241

Chr **Erichsens** Forlag A/S*, Kronprinsensgade 1, DK-1114 Copenhagen K   Tel: (01) 159595   Cable Add: Bogerich
Man Dir: Mr Kay Holkenfeldt
Subjects: Fiction, Mysteries, How-to, Juveniles, Handbooks
Founded: 1902
ISBN Publisher's Prefix: 87-555

F A D L's Forlag A/S (Foreningen af danske Laegestuderendes Forlag), Prinsesse-Charlottes-Gade 29, DK-2200 Copenhagen K   Tel: (01) 356287   Telex: 16698 Unbog
Man Dir: Hans Jespersen
Subjects: Medicine, Biology
Founded: 1962
ISBN Publisher's Prefix: 87-7437

Forlaget for **Faglitteratur** A/S, Vandkunsten 6, DK-1467 Copenhagen K   Tel: (01) 137900
Subjects: Medicine, Technology
ISBN Publisher's Prefix: 87-573

Fogtdals Blade A/S, now Bonniers Specialmagasiner A/S (qv)

Forlaget **Forum** A/S*, Snaregade 4, DK-1205 Copenhagen K Tel: (01) 147714 Cable Add: Forumbooks
Man Dir: Claus Brøndsted
Parent Company: Gyldendalske Boghandel — Nordisk Forlag A/S (qv)
Subjects: Fiction, General, Juveniles, Mysteries, High-priced Paperbacks
1985: 76 titles *Founded:* 1940
ISBN Publisher's Prefix: 87-553

Fremad A/S, Kronprinsengade 1, DK-1019 Copenhagen K Tel: (01) 934340 Cable Add: Bogfremad
Man Dir: Peter Johansen
Subjects: General Fiction, Juveniles, Textbooks, Periodicals
Bookshop: Boghandelen Fremad Frederikssundsvej 168, Brønshøj, DK-2700 Copenhagen
Founded: 1912
ISBN Publisher's Prefix: 87-557

J **Frimodts** Forlag, Korskaervej 25, DK-7000 Fredericia Tel: (05) 934455
Man Dir: Curt Graven Nielsen
Associate Company: Lohses Forlag (qv)
Subjects: Religion, Fiction
ISBN Publisher's Prefix: 87-7446

Forlaget **G M T**+, Meilgaard, DK-8585 Glaesborg Tel: (06) 317511
Publishers: Hans Jørn Christensen, Erik Bjørn Olsen
Subjects: History, Aesthetics, Politics, Philosophy, Psychology, Sociology, General Fiction, Textbooks, Educational Materials
Founded: 1971
ISBN Publisher's Prefix: 87-7330

Hans **Gades** Harbour Pilots Succ A/S, Malmøgade 3, DK-2100 Copenhagen Ø Tel: (01) 260621 Cable Add: Gadepilot Telex: 16121
Chief Executive, Sales, Publicity and Rights & Permissions: Erik Albrechtsen; *Editorial Manager:* Helge Nagel; *Production Manager:* Lisbet Albrechtsen
Parent Company: Paul Klinge A/S
Associate Company: Forlaget Mercantila A/S (qv)
Subject: Harbour Pilots (guides to ports)
1987: 1 title *Founded:* 1912
ISBN Publisher's Prefix: 87-9802

G E C **Gads** Forlag, Vimmelskaftet 32, DK-1161 Copenhagen K Tel: (01) 150558 Cable Add: Boggad
Man Dir: Kaj Lynnerup
Subsidiary Company: Gjellerup og Gad Forlagsaktieselskab (qv)
Subjects: Religion, Psychology, General Science, Education, Textbooks, Art, Reference, Law, Management
Bookshops: G E C Gad Dansk og Udenlandsk Boghandel A/S; Harck og Gjellerup Booksellers Ltd (qqv under Major Booksellers)
Founded: 1855
ISBN Publisher's Prefix: 87-12

Gjellerup og Gad Forlagsaktieselskab, Vimmelskaftet 32, DK-1161 Copenhagen K Tel: (01) 150558 Cable Add: Boggad
Managers: Harlad Bertelsen, Grethe Bryner
Parent Company: G E C Gads Forlag (qv)
Subjects: Reference, Primary, Secondary & Tertiary Textbooks, Educational Material
Founded: 1884
ISBN Publisher's Prefix: 87-13

Grafisk Forlag, Klosterrisvej 7, DK-2100 Copenhagen Ø Tel: (01) 294422 Cable Add: Asdanfo Telex: 16987 Ash Fax: (01) 271010

Man Dir: Erik Ipsen; *Marketing Manager:* Jan B Thomsen
Parent Company: Aschehoug Dansk Forlag A/S (qv)
Subjects: Textbooks, Easy Readers, Children's
ISBN Publisher's Prefix: 87-11

Grevas Forlag*, Luise Pihl, Auningvej 33, Sdr Kastrup, DK-8544 Marke
Man Dir: Eva Hemmer Hansen; *Sales Dir:* Luise Pihl
Subjects: General Fiction, Belles Lettres, Poetry, Biography, Art, Juveniles
Founded: 1966
ISBN Publisher's Prefix: 87-7235

Det **Grønlandske** Forlag*, Postboks 1009, DK-3900 Godthåb, Greenland (Located at: Hans Egedesvej 21, DK-3900 Godthåb) Tel: 22122 Cable Add: Groefobo Telex: 90638
The Greenlandic Publishing House
Man Dir: Repse Thaarup Høegh
Subjects: Children's, Juveniles, Fiction, Poetry
Bookshop: Atuagkat Bookstore (at above address)
Founded: 1956
ISBN Publisher's Prefix: 87-558

Guinness, an imprint of Forlaget Komma A/S (qv)

Gutenberghus Publishing Service A/S, Vognmagergade 11, DK-1148 Copenhagen K Tel: (01) 151925 Cable Add: Gpspubl Telex: 21143 Fax: (01) 141991
Dir: John Vilsøe; *Editorial:* Jørgen Hendel, Jorgen Fogedby
Parent Company: Gutenberghus Group, Copenhagen
Associate Companies: Egmont Verlag GmbH, Austria; A/S Serieforlaget, Denmark; Ehapa-Verlag GmbH, Federal Republic of Germany; Hjemmet A/S, Norway (qv); Hemmets Journal AB, Richters Förlag AB, Sweden (qqv); Egmont Verlag AG, Switzerland; London Editions, UK (qv)
Subjects: Juveniles, Periodicals

Gyldendalske Boghandel — Nordisk Forlag A/S, Klareboderne 3, DK-1001 Copenhagen K Tel: (01) 110775 Cable Add: Gyldendalske Copenhagen Telex: 15887 Gyldaldk
Dirs: Kurt Fromberg, Niels Agner; *Editorial:* Klaus Rifbjerg (Literary Dir), Vagn Grosen (General Trade), Karen Margrethe Henriksen (Juveniles), Peter Holst (Non-fiction reference books), Ole Norling-Christensen (Dictionaries), Egon Schmidt (Audiovisual Dir); *Sales Manager:* Poul Ringhof; *Rights & Permissions:* Per Finn Jacobsen; *Co-productions Manager:* Eyvind Thorsen
Subsidiary Companies: Forlaget Forum A/S; Samlerens Forlag A/S (qqv)
Subjects: General Fiction, Belles Lettres, Poetry, Biography, History, How-to, Music, Art, Philosophy, Reference, Juveniles, Low- & High-priced Paperbacks, Medicine, Psychology, General & Social Science, University, Secondary & Primary Textbooks, Educational Materials, Audiovisual Software
Book Clubs: Conamore (Gyldendals underholdningsbogklub); Gyldendals Bogklub; Gyldendals Børnebogkclub; Samlerens Bogklub
Founded: 1770
ISBN Publisher's Prefix: 87-01

P **Haase** & Søns Forlag A/S, Løvstr 8, DK-1152 Copenhagen K Tel: (01) 115999 Cable Add: Boghaase
Man Dir: Niels Jørgen Haase; *Editorial Manager:* Knud Andersen; *Foreign Rights:* Nina Jensen
Subsidiary Company: N J Haases Bookimport ApS
Imprints: Natur og Harmoni, Rasmus Navers
Subjects: Fiction, Non-fiction, Children's, Educational, Audiovisual Aids, Poetry, Humour, Alternative Health
Bookshop: P Haase & Søns Boghandel A/S (at above address)
Founded: 1877
ISBN Publisher's Prefix: 87-559

H **Hagerups** Forlag, Klosterrisvej 7, DK-2100 Copenhagen Ø Tel: (01) 294422 Cable Add: Asdanfo Telex: 16987 Ash Fax: (01) 271010
Man Dir: Erik Ipsen; *Marketing Manager:* Jan B Thomsen
Parent Company: Aschehoug Dansk Forlag A/S (qv)
Subjects: Juveniles, Secondary & Primary Textbooks
ISBN Publisher's Prefix: 87-11

Forlaget **Hamlet**, an imprint of Lademann Ltd, Publishers (qv)

Edition Wilhelm **Hansen** AS, Gothersgade 9-11, DK-1123 Copenhagen K Tel: (01) 117888 Cable Add: Musikhansen Telex: 19912 Fax: (01) 148178
Owners: Hanne and Lone Wilhelm Hansen, Tine Birger Christensen
Subsidiary Companies: Edition Wilhelm Hansen, Postfach 2684, D-6000 Frankfurt am Main, Federal Republic of Germany; Norsk Musikforlag A/S, Postboks 1499, Vika, N-Oslo 1, Norway; AB Nordiska Musikförlaget/Edition Wilhelm Hansen Stockholm, Sweden (qv); J & W Chester/ Edition Wilhelm Hansen London Ltd, Eagle Court, London EC1M 5QD, UK; Edition Wilhelm Hansen/Chester Music NY Inc, The Beaumont, Apt 12B, 30 West 61 St, New York, NY 10023, USA
Subjects: Music, Musicology, Art, Educational Materials
Founded: 1857
ISBN Publisher's Prefix: 87-7455

Hekla Forlag+, Postboks 9011, DK-1022 Copenhagen K (Located at: Store Kongensgade 61a-b, Copenhagen) Tel: (01) 911933 Cable Add: Heklapress
Owner & Man Dir, Editorial and Publicity: Helga W Lindhardt; *Sales and Rights & Permissions:* Lisbeth Møller-Madsen
Imprint: Vulkan
Subjects: General Trade, Fiction and Non-fiction, Paperbacks
1985: 29 titles *1986:* 25 titles *Founded:* 1979
ISBN Publisher's Prefix: 87-7474

Hernovs Forlag, Bredgade 14-16, DK-1260 Copenhagen K Tel: (01) 110775 Cable Add: Gyldendalske Copenhagen Telex: 15887 Gyldaldk
Subsidiary Company: Johs G Hernov, Vinimport ApS
Subjects: General Fiction, Non-fiction, Juveniles
Book Club: Hernovs Book Club
Founded: 1941
ISBN Publisher's Prefixes: 87-7215, 87-590

H **Hirschsprungs** Forlag, Klosterrisvej 7, DK-2100 Copenhagen Ø Tel: (01) 294422 Cable Add: Asdanfo Telex: 16987 Ash Fax: (01) 271010
Man Dir: Erik Ipsen; *Marketing Manager:* Jan B Thomsen
Parent Company: Aschehoug Dansk Forlag A/S (qv)
Subject: Textbooks
ISBN Publisher's Prefix: 87-11

82 DENMARK

Høst & Søns Forlag, Postboks 9019, DK-1022 Copenhagen K (Located at: Dronningens Tvaergade 5, DK-1302 Copenhagen K) Tel: (01) 155051/153031 Cable Add: Bookhøst
Man Dir: Erik C Lindgren
Subjects: Hobbies & Crafts, Languages, Books on Denmark, Juveniles, Reference
Founded: 1836
ISBN Publisher's Prefix: 87-14

Birgitte **Høvring's** Icelandic World Literature, Postboks 53, DK-3050 Humlebaek (Located at: Teglgårdsvej 531, DK-3050 Humlebaek) Tel: (02) 190926
Owner: Thorsteinn Stefánsson

Ibis, Skindergade 3B, DK-1159 Copenhagen K Tel: (01) 114255 Telex: 19921 Ibstcg Fax: (01) 911167
Editorial Dir, Rights & Permissions: Virginia Allen Jensen
Parent Company: International Children's Book Service (qv under Literary Agents)
Subjects: Books for Handicapped Children, Slides and filmstrips based on children's literature, supplementary enrichment materials
ISBN Publisher's Prefix: 87-980471

Informations Forlag ApS+*, St Kongensgade 40, DK-1264 Copenhagen K Tel: (01) 141426 Telex: 22658
Parent Company: 'Information' Daily Newspaper
Subjects: Non-fiction informative books on current issues, Politics, Fiction
Founded: 1975
ISBN Publisher's Prefix: 87-7514

A/S **Interpresse**, Postboks 11, DK-2880 Bagsvaerd (Located at: 32 Krogshoejvej, Bagsvaerd) Tel: (02) 443233 Cable Add: Stonepress Telex: 37416 Semic
Man Dir: Kurt Dahlgaard
Parent Company: Semic International AB, Sweden (qv)
Subjects: Juveniles, Comics
Founded: 1954
ISBN Publisher's Prefix: 87-456

Jespersen og Pios Forlag, now part of Lindhardt og Ringhof (qv)

Forlaget **Komma** A/S+, Postboks 2163, DK-1016 Copenhagen K (Located at: Frederiksborggade 26, Copenhagen) Tel: (01) 145583 Telex: 19149 Ladpub
Man Dir, Rights & Permissions: Lisbeth Andersen Skov; *Production:* Jørn Ekstrøm; *Publicity:* Bente Reinvaldt
Parent Company: Lademann Ltd, Publishers (qv)
Imprints: Guinness, Kommas Dyrebøger, Komma Helse, Komma Maritim, Komma Sport
Subjects: Popular Reference, Cookery, Maritime, How-to, Health
1986: 35 titles *1987:* 43 titles *Founded:* 1977
ISBN Publisher's Prefix: 87-7512

Kraks Forlag A/S, Nytorv 17, DK-1450 Copenhagen K Tel: (01) 120308
Chief Executive and Rights & Permissions: Ib Topholm; *Editorial:* Henning Terndrup; *Sales, Publicity, Production:* Jørgen Pedersen
Subjects: Trade and Export Directories, Danish *Who is Who*, Mapbooks of Danish towns
1986: 17 titles *Founded:* 1770
ISBN Publisher's Prefix: 87-7225

Lademann Ltd, Publishers, Linnesgade 25, DK-1361 Copenhagen K Tel: (01) 131650 Cable Add: Boglademann Telex: 19149
Publisher: J Lademann; *Dirs:* Eigil Winther, Jorgen Lundo; *Rights & Permissions:* Kirsten Jacobsen
Subsidiary Companies: Albatros Ltd; Forlaget Komma A/S (qv); Sesam Ltd. Forlaget Danmark A/S is now incorporated in Lademann Ltd, Publishers
Imprint: Forlaget Hamlet
Subjects: General
Book Clubs: Union Book Clubs
1985: 200 titles *1986:* 210 titles *Founded:* 1954
ISBN Publisher's Prefix: 87-15

Lindhardt og Ringhof+, Studiestr 14, DK-1455 Copenhagen Tel: (01) 111955 Cable Add: Eleteredit
Owners: Otto B Lindhardt, Gert Ringhof
Subjects: General Fiction and Non-fiction, Paperbacks
1985: 61 titles *1986:* 71 titles *Founded:* 1971
ISBN Publisher's Prefix: 87-7560

Lohses Forlag, Korskaervej 25, DK-7000 Fredericia Tel: (05) 934455
Man Dir: Curt Graven Nielsen
Associate Company: J Frimodts Forlag (qv)
Subjects: Religion, Juveniles
Founded: 1868
ISBN Publisher's Prefix: 87-564

Mallings ApS*, Gammel Kongevej 3-5, DK-1610 Copenhagen V Tel: (01) 243555 Cable Add: Mallingbook Telex: 15817 Jmco
Man Dir, Editorial, Rights & Permissions: Joachim Malling; *Sales:* Hannah Malling; *Production:* Michael Malling; *Publicity:* Dorthe Malling
Subjects: Juveniles, Educational, Picture-books
Founded: 1975
ISBN Publisher's Prefix: 87-7333

Martins Forlag A/S*, Postboks 5, DK-Gilleleje (Located at: Lille Fjellenstrupvej 25, Gilleleje)
Owner: Jens E Halkier
Subjects: General Fiction, Non-fiction, Juveniles
ISBN Publisher's Prefix: 87-566

Forlaget **Mercantila** A/S, Malmøgade 3, DK-2100 Copenhagen Ø Tel: (01) 260621 Telex: 16121
Publicity Manager: Erik Albrechtsen
Parent Company: Paul Klinge A/S
Associate Company: Hans Gades Harbour Pilots Succ A/S (qv)
Subject: Business Literature
1985: 1 title *1986:* 5 titles
ISBN Publisher's Prefix: 87-89010

Forlaget **Modtryk** AMBA+*, Anholtsgade 4-6, DK-8000 Aarhus C Tel: (0045) 6127912/6137674 Telex: 4556785 Mod
Man Dir: Anne Staeger; *Editorial:* Preben Bach, Ilse Noer (Textbooks); *Sales:* Niels Jørgen Jensen; *Production:* Jørgen Eie Christensen; *Rights & Permissions:* Preben Bach
Parent Company: Vaertshuset Aesken, Anholtsgade 8, DK-8000 Aarhus C
Subjects: Political Writings and Essays (especially in the field of the 'New Left' movement), Children's, School Books, Fiction, Thrillers
1985: 25 titles *Founded:* 1972
ISBN Publisher's Prefixes: 87-458, 87-620, 87-817, 87-881

Munksgaard, International Booksellers & Publishers Ltd, Nørresøgade 35, DK-1370 Copenhagen K Tel: (01) 127030 Cable Add: Bogotto Telex: 19431 Munks Fax: (01) 129387
Chairman of the Board: Per Saugman; *Man Dir:* Joachim Malling; *Editorial:* Peter Hartmann, Sven Erik Olsen
Parent Company: Blackwell Scientific Publications Ltd, UK (qv)
Subjects: Medicine, Nursing, Dentistry, Social Sciences, Psychology, School-books, Children's, Scientific Journals, Software
Bookshop: Munksgaard Book & Subscription Service (qv under Major Booksellers)
Founded: 1917
ISBN Publisher's Prefix: 87-16

Natur og Harmoni, an imprint of P Haase & Søns Forlag A/S (qv)

Rasmus Navers, an imprint of P Haase & Søns Forlag A/S (qv)

New Era Publications International ApS*, Store Kongensgade 55, DK-1264 Copenhagen K Tel: (01) 145128 Telex: 16828 Nwera
Man Dir: Lena Moatty; *Sales Manager:* Michel Moatty; *Production Dir:* Neil Lumsden; *Publicity Dir:* Laura Joffrey; *Foreign Rights Dir:* Worthington M Adams
Branch Offs: NE Publications Australia Pty Ltd, PO Box 23, Railway Sq, Sydney, NSW 2000; New Era Publications GmbH, Otto-Hahnstr 25, D-6072 Dreieich 1, Federal Republic of Germany; New Era Israel, 53 Shalom Aleichem St, Tel Aviv, Israel; New Era Italia, viale Monza 48, I-20127 Milan, Italy; New Era España, Luis Velez de Guevara 8 – of D, Madrid, Spain; NE Publications UK Ltd, Dowgate, Douglas Rd, Tonbridge, Kent TN9 2TS, UK
Subjects: Philosophy, Religion, Science Fiction, Management, Education, Self-Help, Self-Improvement
Founded: 1969
Miscellaneous: Formerly Scientology Publications Organization ApS
ISBN Publisher's Prefix: 87-7336

Nyt Nordisk Forlag Arnold Busck A/S, Købmagergade 49, DK-1150 Copenhagen K Tel: (01) 111103 Cable Add: Bookbusck
Man Dir: Ole Arnold Busck
Subsidiary Company: Det Schoenbergske Forlag A/S (qv)
Subjects: General Fiction, Biography, History, How-to, Music, Art, Philosophy, Reference, Religion, High-priced Paperbacks, Medicine, Psychology, General & Social Science, University, Secondary & Primary Textbooks
Bookshops: Arnold Busck International Boghandel A/S, Nordisk Boghandel A/S (qqv under Major Booksellers); Birkerød Boghandel, Arnold Busck A/S, Hovedgaden 37, DK-3460 Birkerød; Arnold Busck Antiquarians, Fiolstr 24, DK-1171 Copenhagen K
Founded: 1896
ISBN Publisher's Prefix: 87-17

Odense University Press, 36 Pjentedamsgade, DK-5000 Odense C Tel: (09) 141611
Man Dir: Jørgen Thomsen
Subjects: History, Literature, Philosophy, Medicine, Technology, Periodicals
Founded: 1970
ISBN Publisher's Prefix: 87-7492

Jörgen **Paludans** Forlag ApS*, Fiolstr 16, DK-1171 Copenhagen K Tel: (01) 15075 ext 45 & (01) 118203
Man Dir: Jörgen Paludan
Subjects: Non-fiction, Psychology, Education, History, Political Science, Economics, Reference, High-priced Paperbacks
ISBN Publisher's Prefix: 87-7230

Politikens Forlag A/S, Vestergade 26, DK-1456 Copenhagen K Tel: (01) 112122 Cable Add: Polbooks
Man Dir: Johannes Ravn; *Dir:* Henrik Reinvaldt

Subjects: General Non-fiction: Nature Study, History and Documentary, Sports, Games, Hobbies, Children's Folklore, Art, Literature, Music, Maps and Atlases, Travel, How-to
Founded: 1946
ISBN Publisher's Prefix: 87-567

C A Reitzel A/S*, Nørregade 20, DK-1165 Copenhagen K Tel: (01) 122400
Man Dir: Svend Olufsen
Subjects: General Science, Humanities, Non-fiction, Textbooks
Bookshop: See under Major Booksellers
Founded: 1819
ISBN Publisher's Prefix: 87-7421

Hans Reitzels Forlag A/S, Dronningens Tvaergade 5, DK-1302 Copenhagen K Tel: (01) 140451 Cable Add: Reitzelbooks
Man Dir: Erik C Lindgren; *Editorial, Rights & Permissions:* Beate Nellemann, Ole Gammeltoft
Subjects: Psychology, General & Social Science, University Textbooks, Philosophy, Reference, Hans Christian Andersen, High-priced Paperbacks
Founded: 1949
ISBN Publisher's Prefix: 87-412

Rhodos, International Science and Art Publishers*, Niels Brocks Gård, Strandgade 36, DK-1401 Copenhagen K Tel: (01) 543020 Cable Add: Sciencebooks Telex: 31502
Man Dir: Niels Blaedel
Subjects: Art, Nature, Fiction, High-priced Paperbacks, General & Social Science, Handbooks, Encyclopaedias
Founded: 1959
ISBN Publisher's Prefix: 87-7245

Rosenkilde og Bagger, Postboks 2184, DK-1017 Copenhagen K (Located at: Kron-Prinsens-Gade 3, Copenhagen) Tel: (01) 157044 Cable Add: Bogkunst
Man Dir: Hans Bagger
Subjects: Reprints, Facsimile Editions, High-priced Paperbacks, General Science
Founded: 1941
ISBN Publisher's Prefix: 87-423
Miscellaneous: Rare book department at above address

Rosinante+, Postboks 5, DK-2920 Charlottenlund (Located at: Kirkevej Independent, Charlottenlund) Tel: (01) 633999
Publisher: Merete Ries
Subjects: General Trade Books, Fiction (Danish & translated), Non-fiction, Immigrants, Politics, Economics, Ideas, Cookery
1985: 21 titles *1986:* 25 titles *Founded:* 1982
ISBN Publisher's Prefix: 87-7357

Samfundslitteratur+, Rosenoern Allé 9, DK-1970 Frederiksberg C Tel: (01) 356366
Publishers at Copenhagen School of Economics and Business Administration
Publisher, Editorial Dir: Mogens Eliasson; *Sales and Publicity Manager, Rights & Permissions:* Wilfried Roloff; *Production Manager:* Per Kjaempe
Subjects: Business and Economics textbooks
Bookshops: At above address; Fabrikvej 7, DK-2000 Copenhagen F
Founded: 1967

Samlerens Forlag A/S+, Snaregade 4, DK-1205 Copenhagen K Tel: (01) 131023
Man Dir: Johannes Riis
Parent Company: Gyldendalske Boghandel — Nordisk Forlag A/S (qv)
Subjects: General Fiction, Contemporary History & Politics, Psychology, Biographies, Humour
1985: 50 titles *1986:* 35 titles *Founded:* 1942
ISBN Publisher's Prefix: 87-568

Scandinavia Publishing House+*, Nørregade 32, DK-1165 Copenhagen K Tel: (01) 140091 Cable Add: Scandico Telex: 19449 Scanco
Man Dir: Jørgen Vium Olesen; *Production Manager:* Per Nielsen
Subjects: Juveniles, Educational, Religious (Christian) (all in Danish and other languages); Periodical
Book Club: Den Kristne Bogklub
Founded: 1979
ISBN Publisher's Prefix: 87-732

Det Schoenbergske Forlag A/S, Landemaerket 5, DK-1119 Copenhagen K Tel: (01) 113066 Cable Add: Schoenbook
Dirs: Ole Thestrup, Ole Stender; *Sales Manager:* Max-Erik Reinhold
Parent Company: Nyt Nordisk Forlag Arnold Busck A/S (qv)
Subjects: General Fiction, Belles Lettres, Poetry, Biography, History, Art, Philosophy, Reference, Travel, Low- & High-priced Paperbacks, Psychology, Trade Books, University, Commercial School, Secondary & Primary Textbooks
Founded: 1857
ISBN Publisher's Prefix: 87-570

A/S J H Schultz Forlag+, Møntergården, Møntergade 21, DK-1116 Copenhagen K Tel: (01) 121195 Cable Add: Bogschultz Fax: (01) 155772
Manager: Jens-Otto Nielsen
Subjects: Non-fiction, Law, EEC publications
Founded: 1661
ISBN Publisher's Prefix: 87-569

Scientology Publications Organization ApS, now New Era Publications International ApS (qv)

Semic Forlagene A/S*, Krogshojvej 32, DK-2880 Bagsvaerd Tel: (02) 443233 Telex: 22426 Carl
Man Dir: Niels Kølle
Parent Company: Semic International AB, Sweden (qv)
Associate Companies: Carlsen Verlag GmbH, Federal Republic of Germany (qv); Carlsen/if AB, Sweden (qv)
Subjects: Children's Picture-books, Educational, Comic Books

Skarv Publications ApS+*, Kongevejen 45B, DK-2840 Holte Tel: (02) 424745
Man Dir: Soren Koustrup
Subjects: Nature & Wildlife Books, Angling, Modern Biology, Geography, Animal Behaviour, Ecology, Ornithology, Hobbies, Sport
Founded: 1976
ISBN Publisher's Prefixes: 87-87581, 87-7545

A/S Skattekartoteket*, Palaegade 4, DK-1261 Copenhagen K Tel: (01) 117874
Man Dir: Peter Taarnhøj
Subject: Taxation (national and international)

Sommer og Sörensen Forlag ApS*, Mynstersvej 19, DK-1827 Frederiksberg C Tel: (01) 232555
Dirs: Erik Sommer, Aage Börglum Sörensen

Strandbergs Forlag, Vedboek Strandvej 475, DK-2950 Vedboek Tel: (02) 894760
Owner: Hans Jörgen Strandberg
Subjects: Cultural History, Computer Science, Humour

Finn Suenson Forlag*, Baekkebrovej 42, Tibitke, D-3220 Tistilde Tel: (01) 350025
Man Dir: Finn Suenson
Subjects: Handbooks, Museums
Founded: 1971
ISBN Publisher's Prefix: 87-201

Teknisk Forlag A/S*, Skelbaekgade 4, DK-1717 Copenhagen V Tel: (01) 216801 Cable Add: Technipress Telex: 16368 Tefko
Man Dir: Peter Müller; *Editor-in-Chief:* Henrik Reinvaldt
Subjects: Engineering, Computers, Business, Manuals, Directories, Guides
Founded: 1948
ISBN Publisher's Prefix: 87-571

Teknologisk Instituts Forlag, Postboks 141, DK-2630 Taastrup Tel: (02) 996611 Cable Add: Teknologisk Telex: 33416 Ti
Subjects: Technical, Special Literature and Handbooks for Crafts and Industries
ISBN Publisher's Prefix: 87-7511

Thaning og Appels Forlag*, H C Oerstedsvej 7b, DK-1879 Kastrup V Tel: (01) 224511
Man Dir: Absel Pedersen
Subjects: General Fiction, Belles Lettres, Art, History, Philosophy, Science & Technical Education, Psychology, How-to, Paperbacks
Founded: 1866
ISBN Publisher's Prefix: 87-413

Tiderne Skifter, Sankt Pedersstr 28 B2, DK-1453 Copenhagen K Tel: (01) 124284
Chief Executive, Editorial and Production: Claus Clausen; *Sales, Publicity and Rights & Permissions:* Bolette Bramsen
Orders to: Politikens Forlag A/S, Vestergade 26, DK-1456 Copenhagen K
Subjects: Fiction, Sexual and Cultural Politics, Criticism
Founded: 1979
ISBN Publisher's Prefix: 87-7445

Unitas Forlag, Valby Langgade 19, D-2500 Valby Tel: (01) 166033
Manager: Lorens Hedelund; *Editor:* Bo Torp Pedersen; *Publicity:* Inge Madsen
Parent Company: YMCA/YWCA
Subjects: Religion, Biography, Education, Fiction, Song & Music
1985: 4 titles *1986:* 8 titles *Founded:* 1914
ISBN Publisher's Prefix: 87-7517

Forlaget Vindrose A/S, Nybrogade 24, DK-1203 Copenhagen K Tel: (01) 135000
Man Dir: Erik Vagn Jensen; *Editorial and Rights & Permissions:* Line Schmidt-Madsen; *Production:* Susanne Hejlesen
Subjects: General Fiction, Belles Lettres, Poetry, Science, Social Science, High-priced Paperbacks
Founded: 1980
ISBN Publisher's Prefix: 87-7456

Vintens Forlag Ltd*, Njalsgade 19, DK-2300 Copenhagen S Tel: (01) 122121 Cable Add: Boglademann Telex: 19149
Publisher: Ludvig E Bramsen
Subjects: General Fiction, Belles Lettres, Philosophy, Low- & High-priced Paperbacks
Founded: 1950
ISBN Publisher's Prefix: 87-414

Vulkan, an imprint of Hekla Forlag (qv)

Wangels Forlag A/S*, Gammeltorv 8, DK-1457 Copenhagen K Tel: (01) 156111 Telex: 19387
Man Dir: Benny Frederiksen
Associate Company: Hjemmets Bokforlag A/S, Norway (qv)
Subject: General Fiction
Book Clubs: Childrens' Bookclubs, Danske Bogsamleres Klub

84 DENMARK

Founded: 1946
Miscellaneous: Firm is member of Gutenberghus Group
ISBN Publisher's Prefix: 87-7220

Winthers Forlag ApS, Gerdasgade 37, DK-2500 Valby Tel: (01) 441120
Man Dir: Benny Frederiksen; *Rights & Permissions:* Jesper Lund
Subsidiary Companies: Winthers, Finland; Winthers, Norway; Winthers, Sweden
Subjects: General Fiction, Low-priced Paperbacks
Founded: 1945
ISBN Publisher's Prefix: 87-18

Forlaget **Wøldike** K/S+, Stægers Allé 13, D-2000 Frederiksberg Tel: (01) 863954
Owner & Publisher: Ove Mølbeck
Subjects: Fiction & Non-fiction (all types of books for the general trade market)
Founded: 1969

Literary Agents

A/S **Bookman**, Fiolstr 12, DK-1171 Copenhagen K Tel: (01) 145720 Cable Add: Bookman Fax: (01) 120007
Miscellaneous: This company also acts as a Literary Agent in Sweden, Norway, Finland and Iceland for foreign authors

International Children's Book Service, Skindergade 3B, DK-1159 Copenhagen K Tel: (01) 114255 Telex: 19921 Ibstcg Fax: (01) 911167
Contact: Virginia Allen Jensen
Subsidiary Company: Ibis (qv under Publishers)

Leonhardt Literary Agency ApS, Studiestraede 35, DK-1455 Copenhagen K Tel: (01) 132523 Cable Add: Leolitag

Licht og Licht, Maglemosevej 46, DK-2920 Charlottenlund Tel: (01) 610908 Cable Add: Literagent Copenhagen Telex: 21131 Licht
Chief Executives: Ole Licht, Agnes Licht

Svend **Mondrup** International Literary Agency*, Tranegårdsvej 27, DK-2900 Hellerup Tel: (01) 627230 Telex: 16600 Fotex attn Interlitagent Copenhagen
Chief Executive: Svend Mondrup

Book Clubs

Children's Bookclubs*, Gammeltorv 8, DK-1457 Copenhagen K Tel: (01) 156111 Telex: 19387
Owned by: Wangels Forlag A/S (qv)

Conamore (Gyldendals underholdningsbogklub), Pilestr 51, DK-1001 Copenhagen K Cable Add: Gyldendalske Telex: 15887 Gyldal
Owned by: Gyldendalske Boghandel — Nordisk Forlag A/S (qv)
Subject: Entertainment
Founded: 1978

Danske Bogsamleres Klub*, Gammeltorv 8, DK-1457 Copenhagen K
Owned by: Wangels Forlag A/S (qv)

Gyldendals Bogklub, Pilestr 51, DK-1001 Copenhagen K Cable Add: Gyldendalske Telex: 15887 Gyldal
Owned by: Gyldendalske Boghandel — Nordisk Forlag A/S (qv)
Subjects: Fiction and General Non-fiction

Gyldendals Børnebogklub, Pilestr 51, DK-1001 Copenhagen K Cable Add: Gyldendalske Telex: 15887 Gyldal
Owned by: Gyldendalske Boghandel — Nordisk Forlag A/S (qv)

Hernovs Book Club, Bredgade 14-16, DK-1260 Copenhagen K
Owned by: Hernovs Forlag (qv)

Den **Kristne Bogklub**, Nørregade 32, DK-1165 Copenhagen K Tel: (01) 140091 Cable Add: Scandico Telex: 19449 Scanco
Members: 2,300
Owned by: Scandinavia Publishing House (qv)
Founded: 1980

Samlerens Bogklub, Pilestr 51, DK-1001 Copenhagen K Cable Add: Gyldendalske Telex: 15887 Gyldal
Owned by: Gyldendalske Boghandel — Nordisk Forlag A/S (qv)
Subjects: Fiction, Non-fiction, Political

Union Book Clubs, Linnesgade 25, DK-1361 Copenhagen K Tel: (01) 131650 Cable Add: Boglademann Telex: 19149
Owned by: Lademann Ltd, Publishers (qv)
Subjects: Fiction, Illustrated Non-fiction
Founded: 1959

Walt Disney Wonderful World of Reading*, Gammeltorv 8, DK-1457 Copenhagen K
Owned by: Walt Disney Productions A/S

Major Booksellers

Akademisk Boghandel, Universitetsparken, DK-8000 Aarhus C Tel: (06) 128844
Manager: Flemming Johansen

Biblioteksboghandelen ApS, Kultorvet 2, DK-1175 Copenhagen K
Manager: Nina E Jakobsen

Arnold **Busck** International Boghandel A/S, Købmagergade 49, DK-1150 Copenhagen K Tel: (01) 122453 Cable Add: Bookbusck
Manager: Troels Bek
Export Division is at above address
See also: Nyt Nordisk Forlag Arnold Busck A/S, Publishers

G E C **Gad** Dansk og Udenlandsk Boghandel A/S, Vimmelskaftet 32, DK-1161 Copenhagen K Tel: (01) 150558 G E C Gad Danish and Foreign Bookshop
Owned by: G E C Gads Forlag (qv)

Harck og Gjellerup Booksellers Ltd, G E C Gad Nørreport, Fiolstr 31-33, DK-1171 Copenhagen K Tel: (01) 129148/ 137233 Telex: 19110 Gjbook
Managers: Frederik Christiansen, Joergen F Lauridsen
Owned by: G E C Gads Forlag (qv)

Magasin du Nord A/S*, Book Department, The English Bookshop, Kongens Nytorv 13, DK-1095 Copenhagen K Tel: (451) 114433 Cable Add: Magdunord Telex 15975

Munksgaard Book & Subscription Service, Postboks 2148, DK-1016 Copenhagen K (Located at: Nørresøgade 35, Copenhagen) Tel: (01) 128570 Telex: 19431 Munks
Manager: J Vagn Jensen
Agent for UN, UNESCO, FAO, WHO, ILO, Council of Europe, OECD and IMF
Owned by: Munksgaard, International Booksellers & Publishers Ltd (qv)

Nordisk Boghandel A/S*, Østergade 16, DK-1100 Copenhagen K Tel: (01) 147007
Owned by: Nyt Nordisk Forlag Arnold Busck A/S (qv)

Polyteknisk Boghandel og Forlag, Anker Engelundsvej 1, DK-2800 Lyngby Tel: (02) 881488
Manager: Erling Sieverts

C A **Reitzel** A/S*, Nørregade 20, DK-1165 Copenhagen K Tel: (01) 122400
Man Dir: Svend Olufsen
Importer and exporter. Supplies universities, scientific libraries and institutions worldwide; also Publisher (qv)

Universitetsbogladen (Panumbogladen/ Naturfagsbogladen)*, Blegdamsvej 3, DK-2200 Copenhagen N Tel: (01) 351643 Telex: 16698 Unbog
Manager: Hans Jespersen
Branches: Panumbogladen (Medical bookshop), Blegdamsvej 3, DK-2200 Copenhagen N; Naturfagsbogladen (Natural Science bookshop), Universitetsparken 13, DK-2100 Copenhagen Ø

Major Libraries

Aalborg Universitetsbibliotek, Postboks 8200, DK-9220 Aalborg Ø Tel: (08) 159111 Telex: 69790 Aub

Århus Kommunes Biblioteker*, Mølleparken, DK-8000 Århus C Tel: (06) 136622 Telex: 64580 Arhubi
Århus Public Library

Danmarks Pædagogiske Bibliotek*, Lersø Parkallé 101, DK-2100 Copenhagen Ø Tel: (01) 298211
The National Library of Education

Danmarks Statistik Biblioteket, Sejrøgade 11, DK-2100 Copenhagen Ø
National Statistical Library

Danmarks Tekniske Bibliotek (DTB)*, Anker Engelunds Vej 1, DK-2800 Lyngby Tel: (02) 883088 Telex: 37148 Dtbc Fax: (02) 883040
National Technological Library of Denmark

Gentofte Kommunebibliotek, Ahlmanns Allé 6, Hellerup, DK-2900 Copenhagen Tel: (01) 627500 Telex: 19887
Gentofte Municipal Library
Chief Librarian: Helge Stenkilde

Institut Danois des Echanges Internationaux de Publications (IDE)*, Amaliegade 38, DK-1256 Copenhagen K Tel: (01) 156521
Danish Institute for International Exchange of Publications
Librarian: Ulla Højsgaard Jensen
Publication: Bibliografi over Danmarks offentlige publikationer (Annual bibliography, part of the Danish national bibliography)

Københavns Kommunes Biblioteker, Kultorvet 2, DK-1175 Copenhagen K Tel: (01) 136070 Telex: 16648 Kkbhb
Copenhagen Municipal Libraries
Librarian: Børge Sørensen

Københavns Stadsarkiv, Rådhuset, DK-1599 Copenhagen V
Copenhagen City Archives
Head Archivist: Helle Linde
Publication: Historiske Meddelelser om København (Historical Yearbook)

Det **Kongelige Bibliotek**, Christians Brygge 8, DK-1219 Copenhagen K Tel: (01) 930111 Telex: 15009
The Royal Library
National Librarian: Erland Kolding Nielsen
Publications include: Contributions to the H C Andersen Bibliography; Bibliography of Old Norse-Icelandic Studies; Catalogue of Oriental Manuscripts, Xylographs, etc in Danish Collections; Fund og Forskning i Det Kongelige Biblioteks Samlinger (Discovery and Research in the Collections in the Royal Library); *Magasin fra Det kongelige Bibliotek og Universitetsbiblioteket I*

Det **Nordjyske Landsbibliotek**, Postboks 839, Nytorv 26, DK-9100 Ålborg Tel: (08) 162544 Telex: 69605 Aalbib Fax: (08) 116622 (local 4800)
Central Library for the County of North Jutland
Librarian: Kr Lindbo-Larsen

Odense Centralbibliotek, Ørbaekvej 95, DK-5220 Odense
Odense County Library

Odense Universitetsbibliotek*, Campusvej 55, DK-5230 Odense M Tel: (09) 158600
Odense University Library

Rigsarkivet, Rigsdagsgården 9, DK-1218 Copenhagen K
National Record Office
Dir: Vagn Dybdahl

Roskilde University Library, Postboks 258, DK-4000 Roskilde Tel: (02) 757711 Telex: 43158

Statsbiblioteket*, Universitetsparken, DK-8000 Århus C Tel: (06) 122022 Telex: 64515
State and University Library
Librarian: Karl V Thomsen
Publications include: Statsbibliotekets løbende udenlandske tidsskrifter

Odense **Universitetsbibliotek**, see Odense

Universitetsbiblioteket 1*, Postboks 2201, Fiolstr 1, DK-1018 Copenhagen K Tel: (01) 130875
University Library: Humanities (Amager Branch: Njalsgade 80, DK-2300 Copenhagen S Tel: (01) 542211)
Librarian: Torben Nielsen

Universitetsbiblioteket 2: Danmarks natur- og laagevidenskabelige Bibliotek, Nørre Allé 49, DK-2200 Copenhagen N Tel: (01) 396523 Telex: 15097 Ubiskh
University Library: The National Scientific and Medical Library of Denmark
Chief Librarian: Kell Prehn
Publications include: Acta historica scientiarum naturalium et medicinalium

Library Associations

Arkivforeningen, Rigsarkivet, Rigsdagsgården 9, DK-1218 Copenhagen K Tel: (01) 923310
Archives Society
Secretary: Poul Olsen

Bibliotekarforbundet, Jagtvej 111, DK-2200 Copenhagen N Tel: (01) 852822
Union of Librarians
Secretary: Steen Stegeager Hansen
Publication: Bibliotek 70

Bibliotekscentralen, Tempovej 7-11, DK-2750 Ballerup Tel: (02) 974000 Cable Add: Danliber Telex: 35370
Danish Library Bureau
Man Dir: Asger Hansen; *Editor:* Jørgen Kjeldsen
Publications include: Dansk Artikelindeks; Aviser og Tidsskrifter (Danish Index of Articles, Periodicals and Newspapers); *Dansk billedfortegnelse* (The Danish National Bibliography, Visual records); *Dansk Bogfortegnelse* (The Danish National Bibliography, Books); *Dansk Lydfortegnelse* (The Danish National Bibliography, Sound recordings); *Dansk Periodicafortegnelse* (The Danish National Bibliography, Serials); *Dansk musikfortegnelse* (The Danish National Bibliography, Music); *Udenlandsk Bibliotekslitteratur i Danske Biblioteker* (Foreign Library Literature in Danish Libraries)

Danmarks Biblioteksforening, Trekronergade 15, DK-2500 Copenhagen Valby Tel: (01) 308682 Fax: (01) 308080
Danish Library Association
Dir: F Ettrup
Publications: Bogens Verden (Library Journal). *Biblioteksvejviser* (Library Guide) and *Biblioteksårbog* (Library Yearbook) published by Danmarks Biblioteksforening Forlag ApS

Danmarks Forskningsbiblioteksforening, Statsbiblioteket, Universitetsparken, DK-8000 Aarhus C Tel: (06) 125759
Danish Research Library Association: Section 1 Research Libraries; Section 2 Staff members of Danish Research Libraries
President: Mette Stockmarr; *Secretary:* Mogens Sandfær
Publication: DF-Revy

Danmarks Skolebibliotekarforening, Mariavej 1, Sdr Bjert, DK-6091 Bjert Tel: (05) 577101
Association of Danish School Librarians
Publication: Skole Biblioteket (The School Library), Kongshvilebakken 10-12, DK-2800 Lyngby

Danmarks Skolebiblioteksforening, Nørrebrogade 159, DK-2200 Copenhagen N Tel: (01) 811666
Association of Danish School Libraries
Chief Executive: Ib Juul; *Manager:* Ove Frank
Publication: Børn og Bøger (Children and Books); also books dealing with school libraries, youth culture, English summary

Dansk Musikbiblioteksforening, Sekretariatet, Duevej 14-6, DK-2000 Copenhagen F
Association of Danish Music Libraries (Danish section of AIBM/IAML)

Dansk Teknisk Litteraturselskab — DTL, Danmarks Tekniske Bibliotek, Anker Engelunds Vej 1, DK-2800 Lyngby Tel: (02) 883088
Danish Society for scientific and technological information and documentation

Foreningen af Medarbejdere ved Danmarks Forskningsbiblioteker, Statsbiblioteket, Universitetsparken, DK-8000 Aarhus C Tel: (06) 125759 Telex: 64515
Association of Staff Members of Danish Research Libraries (section 2 of the Danish Research Library Association)
President: Niels-Henrik Gylstorff; *Secretary:* Grethe Lillelund

Sammenslutningem af Danmarks Forskningsbiblioteker, Statsbiblioteket Universitetsparken, DK-8000 Aarhus C
Association of Danish Research Libraries (section 1 of the Danish Research Library Association)
President: Mette Stockmarr; *Secretary:* Mogens Sandfaer

Library Reference Books and Journals

Books

Biblioteksårbog (Library Yearbook), Danmarks Biblioteksforening, Trekronergade 15, DK-2500 Copenhagen Valby

Biblioteksvejviser (Library Guide), Danmarks Biblioteksforening, Trekronergade 15, DK-2500 Copenhagen Valby

Public Libraries in Denmark, Det Danske Selskab, Kulturvet 2, DK-1175 Copenhagen K

Udenlandsk Bibliotekslitteratur i Danske Biblioteker (Foreign Library Literature in Danish Libraries), Bibliotekscentralen, Tempovej 7-11, DK-2750 Ballerup

Journals

Bibliotek 70, Bibliotekarforbundet, Jagtvej 111, DK-2200 Copenhagen N

Biblioteken, Biblioteksskole, Birketinget 6, DK-2300 Copenhagen S

Bogens Verden (Library Journal), Danmarks Biblioteksforening, Trekronergade 15, DK-2500 Copenhagen Valby
Magazine for Danish library employees

DF-Revy, Danmarks Forskningsbiblioteksforening, Statsbiblioteket, Universitetsparken, DK-8000 Aarhus C

Restaurator, Restaurator Press, PO Box 96, DK-1004 Copenhagen K
International journal for the preservation of library and archival material; text in English, French, German and Russian

Skole Biblioteket (The School Librarian), Kongshvilebakken 10-12, DK-2800 Lyngby

Literary Associations and Societies

Dansk Exlibris Selskab, PO Box 1519, DK-2700 Copenhagen Brh
Danish Bookplate Society
Chairman: Leif Holmberg
Publications: Exlibris-Nyt (for Society members only); *Nordisk Exlibris Tidsskrift* (Scandinavian Bookplate Periodical)

Nyt **Dansk Litteraturselskab**, Bibliotekscentralen, Tempovej 7-11, DK-2750 Ballerup Tel: (02) 974000
New Danish Society for Literature
Manager: Jørgen Rishøj
Aims: Publication/Republication of books in short supply in libraries
Special activity: Magnaprint (large print books for partially-sighted)
Members: Public libraries only

Danske Sprog-og Litterurselskab, Frederiksholms Kanal 18A, DK-1220 Copenhagen Tel: (01) 130660
Danish Society of Language and Literature
Administrator: Dr Erik Dal
Publications include: Standard editions of literary, linguistic and historical texts, including diaries and correspondence: e.g. Hans Christian Andersen's Diaries (in Danish), a new series of annotated classical novels, *Danske Klassikere*

Kongelige Danske Videnskabernes Selskab, H C Andersens Boulevard 35, DK-1553 Copenhagen V Tel: (01) 113240
Royal Danish Academy of Sciences and Letters
President: Jens Lindhard; *Secretary:* Thor A Bak; *Editor:* Erik Dal
Publications: Oversigt (annual); four-monograph series: *Historisk-filosofiske Meddelelser, Historisk-filosofiske Skrifter, Biologiske Skrifter, Matematisk-fysiske Meddelelser*; and occasional publications

Danish **P E N** Centre, Samlerens Forlag A/S, Snaregarde 4, DK-1205 Copenhagen K
Secretary: Johannes Riis

Samfund til Udgivelse af Gammel Nordisk Litteratur*, Kjaerstrupvej 33, DK-2500

86 DENMARK — DOMINICAN REPUBLIC

Copenhagen Valby
Society for the Publication of Old Norse Literature
Secretary: Agnete Loth

Literary Periodicals

Bog-anmelderen (The Book Review), Bog-Anmelderens Tidsskrifter, Gammel Torv 16, DK-1457 Copenhagen

Børn og Bøger (Children and Books), Danmarks Skolebiblioteksforening, Nørrebrogade 159, DK-2200 Copenhagen N

Hvedekorn (Wheat Grain), Borgens Forlag A/S, Valbygård, Valbygårdsvej 33, DK-2500 Valby

Language and Literature, Copenhagen University, English Institute, Lille Kirkestr 1, DK-1072 Copenhagen K
Text in English

Nordisk Exlibris Tidsskrift (Scandinavian Bookplate Periodical), Dansk Exlibris Selskab, PO Box 1519, DK-2700 Copenhagen Brh

Orbis Litterarum, Munksgaard, International Booksellers & Publishers Ltd, Nørresøgade 35, DK-1370 Copenhagen K
International review of literary studies; text mainly in English, occasionally in French and German

Literary Prizes

Emil **Aarestrup** Prize
For outstanding poetry. DKr 4,000 and a medal. Awarded annually. Enquiries to Dansk Forfatterforening, Tordenskjolds Gård, Strandgade 6, DK-1401 Copenhagen K

The H C **Andersen** Prize
For scientists and writers connected with H C Andersen, for outstanding contributions to Danish literature. DKr 25,000. Awarded annually. Enquiries to Dansk Forfatterforening, Tordenskjolds Gård, Strandgade 6, DK-1401 Copenhagen K

Hans Christian **Andersen** Prize
For the best Danish book for children. Established in 1955 to commemorate the 150th anniversary of the birth of Andersen. Awarded annually. Enquiries to Nyt Nordisk Forlag Arnold Busck A/S, Købmagergade 49, DK-1150 Copenhagen K

Herman **Bang** Memorial Prize
For works of prose. DKr 4,000. Awarded annually. Enquiries to Dansk Forfatterforening, Tordenskjolds Gård, Strandgade 6, DK-1401 Copenhagen K

Danish Academy Prize for Literature
For an outstanding work of literature. DKr 100,000. Awarded bi-annually. Enquiries to The Danish Academy, Rungstedlund, 109 Rungsted Strandvej, DK-2960 Rungsted Kyst

Danish Critics Literary Prize, now known as Literaturkritikernes Laug (qv)

Danish Prize for Children's Literature
For the best Danish books for children and teenagers. Established 1954. DKr 20,000. Awarded annually. Enquiries to Danish Ministry of Cultural Affairs, Nybrogade 2, Copenhagen K

Johannes **Ewald** Prize
For prose, poetry and dramatic works. DKr 5,000. Awarded annually. Enquiries to Dansk Forfatterforening, Tordenskjolds Gård, Strandgade 6, DK-1401 Copenhagen K

Søren **Gyldendal** Prize
For Danish authors from any field whose work is of great literary value. DKr 30,000. Awarded annually. Enquiries to Gyldendalske Boghandel — Nordisk Forlag A/S, Klareboderne 3, DK-1001 Copenhagen K

Holberg Medal
For outstanding contributions to Danish literature. DKr 20,000 and a medal. Awarded annually. Enquiries to Dansk Forfatterforening, Tordenskjolds Gård, Strandgade 6, DK-1401 Copenhagen K

Literary Translation Prize
DKr 20,000. Awarded annually. Enquiries to Dansk Forfatterforening, Tordenskjolds Gård, Strandgade 6, DK-1401 Copenhagen K

Literaturkritikernes Laug (Critics Literary Prize)*
For literary and art criticism. DKr 5,000. Awarded annually. Enquiries to Literaturkritikernes Laug, c/o Hans Andersen, Jyllands-Posten, DK-8260 Viby Jylland

Martin Andersen **Nexø** Prize
DKr 5,000. Awarded annually. Enquiries to Dansk Forfatterforening, Tordenskjolds Gård, Strandgade 6, DK-1401 Copenhagen K

Adam Gottlob **Oehlenschläger** Prize
For prose works and poetry. DKr 5,000. Awarded annually. Enquiries to Dansk Forfatterforening, Tordenskjolds Gård, Strandgade 6, DK-1401 Copenhagen K

Henrik **Pontoppidan** Memorial Prize
For outstanding contributions to Danish literature. DKr 10,000. Awarded annually. Enquiries to Dansk Forfatterforening, Tordenskjolds Gård, Strandgade 6, DK-1401 Copenhagen K

Popular Science Prize
DKr 20,000. Awarded annually. Enquiries to Dansk Forfatterforening, Tordenskjolds Gård, Strandgade 6, DK-1401 Copenhagen K

Translation Agencies and Associations

Danish Translations Centre (DTC), Danish Centre for Documentation, c/o Danmarks Tekniske Bibliotek, Anker Engelunds Vej 1, DK-2800 Lyngby

Translatørforeningen, Bornholmsgade 1, DK-1266 Copenhagen K Tel: (01) 126044
Association of Danish Sworn Translators

Dominican Republic

General Information

Language: Spanish
Religion: Roman Catholic
Population: 5.43 million
Bank Hours: 0830-1230 Monday-Friday; some open 0830-1130 Saturday
Shop Hours: 0800-1200, 1400 or 1500-1800 Monday-Friday; some open Saturday
Currency: 100 centavos = 1 peso oro (= $US1). US currency is widely used
Export/Import Information: No import licences required for books. Exchange licence and approval from Central Bank required
Copyright: Berne, Buenos Aires (see International section)

Publishers

Publicaciones **Ahora** C por A*, Ave San Martin 236, Apdo 1402, Santo Domingo Tel: 5655581 Cable Add: Ahora Telex: 326438
Editorial: R Molina Morillo; *Sales:* Luis R Cordero; *Production:* José R Grau; *Publicity:* Manuel Fco Santana

Juan Max **Alemany***, E Henriquez 12, Santo Domingo

Editora **Alfa y Omega***, M Cabral 11, Santo Domingo

Editora El **Caribe***, Autop Duarte Km 7 1/2, Santo Domingo

Impresora **Carolina** C or A, Yolanda Guzmán 105, Santo Domingo
President: Mariano A Martinez Guzman

Editora **Colonial***, Moca 27-B, Santo Domingo Tel: 5657841/5671773

Rafael **Corporan** de los Santos*, S Valverde 44, Santo Domingo

Editora **Cosmos***, Calle N No 13, Feria, Santo Domingo

Dominican Books — Distribution Inc, now Sociedad Editorial — Dominicana SA (qv)

Editora **Cultural Dominicana***, San Martín 236, Santo Domingo

Editorama SA, Ave Tiradentes 56, Santo Domingo
Dir: Juan R Quiñones
Subject: Large-print books (Literature and Art)

Editorial Librería Dominicana*, Mercedes 45-49, Santo Domingo Tel: 96293/23893 Cable Add: Sirviendo
Dir: Julio Postigo
Subjects: General Literature, Religion, Law, Textbooks
Founded: 1937

Editora **Enriquillo***, I la Catolica 41, Santo Domingo

P A **Gómez***, E Tejera 15, Santo Domingo

Editora **Horizontes** de América*, A Fleming 2, Santo Domingo

La **Información***, M Gómez 16, Santiago

Editora **Listín** Diario, Paseo de los Periodistas 52, Santo Domingo

Editorial **Padilla***, San Fco Macorís 14, Santo Domingo
Bookshops: See under Major Booksellers

Editora Colegial **Quisqueyana** SA, Ave Tiradentes, Centro Comercial Naco, Apdo 905, Santo Domingo Tel: 5623247/5623363/ 5627091 Telex: 4318 Libros
Subjects: Pre-school, Primary & Secondary Textbooks and Educational Materials
Bookshop: See under Major Booksellers

Editora La **Razon***, J Verne 14, Santo Domingo

Sociedad Editorial — Dominicana SA+, Apdo 559, Santo Domingo Tel: 6875775/ 6889378 Cable Add: Franklin Franco

Telex: 4124/4699 Agemir
President: Luis Franco; *Editorial Dir:* F Franco; *Rights & Permissions:* F José Franco-Pte
Parent Company: Credilibros, Ramon Santana 2B, Santo Domingo
Subjects: History, Social Science, Law, Philosophy, Economics, Literature, Reference
1987: 20 titles *Founded:* 1975

Ultima Hora, Paseo de los Periodistas 12, Santo Domingo

Universidad Autónoma de Santo Domingo, Ciudad Universitaria*, Apdo 1355, Santo Domingo Tel: 5332011   Cable Add: 3460182 Uniausd
Subjects: Academic

Universidad Católica Madre y Maestra*, Departamento de Publicaciones, Autopista Duarte, Santiago de los Caballeros Tel: 5825105
Editorial Dir: Félix Fernández
Subjects: General
Founded: 1967

Major Booksellers

Caribe Grolier Inc*, L de Castro 203, Santo Domingo Tel: 6897373
Also: Hostos 208, Santo Domingo Tel: 6888544

Ediciones **Coquito***, E Tejera 19, Santo Domingo Tel: 6883021

Casa **Cuello**, El Conde 201, Apdo 98 – Zona 1, Santo Domingo Tel: 6896226/ 6874242
Manager: José del C Cuello

Disesa*, Hostos 202, Santo Domingo Tel: 6897644/6823533
Also: S Larga, Santo Domingo Tel: 6882163

Distribuidora Escolar SA (DISESA)*, Ave Abraham Lincoln-Pedro H Ureña, Santo Domingo Tel: 5654554
Also: Sabana Larga, Santo Domingo Tel: 5941780; El Sol, Santiago Tel: 5826006

Papelería **Fersobe** Hnos*, Ave Duarte 16-A, Santo Domingo Tel: 6894744
Also: Ave Mella 156, Santo Domingo Tel: 6881848

Casa **Herrera***, Mercedes 125, Santo Domingo Tel: 97568

Febio **Herrera***, Bolivar 40, Santo Domingo Tel: 6878677
Importer

Librería y Papelería **Lope de Vega***, L de Vega 55, Santo Domingo Tel: 5658066

Mella*, Ave Duarte 27, Santo Domingo Tel: 6886539

Niove*, 16 de Agosto 47, Santo Domingo Tel: 6894088

Editorial **Padilla***, El Conde 511, Santo Domingo Tel: 6820111/6880303
Branches: San Fco Macoris 14, Santo Domingo Tel: 6823101; El Conde 109, Santo Domingo Tel: 6880303
Also Publisher (qv)

Editora Colegial **Quisqueyana** SA, Ave Tiradentes, Centro Comercial Naco, Apdo 905, Santo Domingo Tel: 5623247/5623363
Also Publisher (qv)

Major Libraries

Archivo General de la Nación, Calle M E Diaz, Santo Domingo Tel: 5331608
National Archives

Biblioteca Dominicana*, Santo Domingo

Biblioteca Nacional*, César Nicolás Penson 91, Plaza de la Cultura, Santot Domingo
National Library

Biblioteca de la **Cámara Oficial** de Comercio, Agricultura e Industria del Distrito Nacional *, Apdo 815, Santo Domingo (Located at: Arzobispo Nouel 206, Altos, Santo Domingo)
Library of the Chamber of Commerce, Agriculture and Industry

Biblioteca Municipal de **Santo Domingo***, Padre Billini 18, Santo Domingo

Biblioteca de la **Secretaría de Estado de Relaciones Exteriores***, Estancia Ramfis, Santo Domingo
Library of the Secretariat of Foreign Affairs

Biblioteca de la **Universidad Autónoma** de Santo Domingo*, Ciudad Universitaria, Apdo 1355, Santo Domingo

Library Associations

Asociación Dominicana de Bibliotecarios (ASODOBI)*, c/o Biblioteca Nacional, Plaza de la Cultura, Santo Domingo Tel: 6884086
Dominican Association of Librarians
President: Prospero J Mella-Chavier; *Secretary-General:* Ms V Regús
Publication: El Papiro

Departamento de Documentación y Bibliotecas, Secretaria de Educación, Bellas Artes y Cultos, Santo Domingo
Library and Documentation Service

Grupo Bibliografico Nacional de la Republica Dominicana*, c/o Emilio Rodriguez de Morizi, Director, Archivo General de la Nacion, Calle Chiclana de la Frontera, Santo Domingo

Ecuador

General Information

Language: Spanish
Religion: Predominantly Roman Catholic
Population: 8.5 million
Bank Hours: 0900-1330 Monday-Friday
Shop Hours: 0930-1300, 1500-1900 Monday-Friday; 0930-1300 Saturday
Currency: 100 centavos = 1 sucre
Export/Import Information: Member of the Latin American Free Trade Association. Books and most advertising catalogues not dutiable. No import licences or exchange controls for books
Copyright: UCC, Buenos Aires (see International section)

Book Trade Organizations

Cámara Ecuatoriana del Libro*, Casilla 3329, Quito (Located at: Núcleo de Pichincha, Guayaquil 1629 – 4° piso, Quito) Tel: (02) 212226

President: Luis Aulestia Buttiononi; *Secretary:* Carlos Wong

Standard Book Numbering Agency, Cámara Ecuatoriana del Libro, Casilla 3329, Quito (Located at: Núcleo de Pichincha, Guayaquil 1629 – 4° piso, Quito)
ISBN Administrator: Luis Aulestia Buttioni

Publishers

Editorial **Bruguera** Ecuatoriana SA*, Casilla 9001, Agencia 7, Ave de la República 17-25 y Azuay, Quito
Parent Company: Editorial Bruguera SA, Spain (qv)

C I E S P A L (Centro Internacional de Estudios Superiores de Comunicación para América Latina), Departamento de Publicaciones, CP 584, Quito (Located at: Ave Diego de Almagro 2155 y Andrade Marín, Quito) Tel: (02) 544624/545831 Cable Add: Ciespal Telex: 2474 Ciespl
Dirs: Dr Luis E Proaño; Jorge Mantilla Jarrín (Orders)
Subjects: Social Communication, Development Planning, Research and Documentation, Periodicals
Founded: 1959

Cromograf SA*, Coronel 2207, PPB 4285, Guayaquil Tel: (04) 346400 Cable Add: Cromograf Telex: 3387 Ariel
Subjects: Juvenile/Children's, Paperbacks, Art Productions

Casa de la **Cultura** Ecuatoriana*, Ave 6 de Diciembre 794, Apdo 67, Quito Tel: (02) 230260 Cable Add: Casacultura
President: Edmundo Ribadeneira M
Branch Offs: Núcleo del Azuay, Apdo 4907, Cuenca; Núcleo del Guayas, Guayaquil
Subjects: General Fiction & Non-fiction, General Science (Ecuadorian authors only)
Founded: 1944

Editorial Interamericana del Ecuador CA*, Ave America 542, Quito
Manager: Manuel de Castillo

Grijalbo Ecuatoriana Ltda*, Casilla 9139, Suc 7, General Salazar 1116 y José Luís Tamayo, Quito Tel: (02) 230890/548306 Cable Add: Grijalbo Quito
Parent Company: Ediciones Grijalbo SA, Spain (qv)

Pontificia **Universidad Católica** de Ecuador*, 12 de Octobre 1076 y Carrion, Apdo 2184, Quito Tel: (02) 529240
Subjects: Literature, Art, Natural Sciences, Law, Anthropology, Sociology, Politics, Economics, Theology, Philosophy, History, Archaeology

Universidad Central del Ecuador, Dpto de Publicaciones*, Servicio de Almacén Universitario, Ciudad Universitaria, Quito

Universidad de Guayaquil, Dpto de Publicaciones*, Biblioteca Gral, Apdo 3834, Guayaquil Tel: (04) 392430
Man Dir: Leonor Villao de Santander
Subjects: General Literature, History, Philosophy, Fiction
Bookshop: Librería Universitaria (at above address)
Founded: 1930

Major Booksellers

Librería **Cervantes***, Vélez 416, Guayaquil Tel: (04) 15573

Librería **Cima**, Casilla 1242, Quito (Located at: Mañosca 200, Quito) Tel: (02) 571218/571318 Cable Add: Cimale
Manager: Edgar Freire Rubio
Also exporter

Librería **Científica** SA*, Venezuela y Pasaje Drouet Pérez, Quito Tel: (02) 12556
Also: Luque 223, Guayaquil (Tel: (04) 14555) and two other branches

Librería **Española***, Venezuela 961 y Mejía, Casilla 356, Quito
Tel: (02) 212060 Telex: 2503 Libre
Also: Librería Española Cía Ltda, Ave 10 de Agosto 1233, Casilla 356, Quito
Tel: (02) 543460

Librería **Universitaria**, García Moreno 739, Apdo 2982, Quito Tel: (02) 212521
Dir: Ing Carlos E Wong Flores
Importer/Exporter

Librería **Selecciones***, 9 de Octubre 735, Guayaquil
Also: Calle Benalcázar 543, Quito

Su Librería*, Apdo 2556, Quito Tel: (02) 210225
Manager: Carlos G Liebmann

Major Libraries

Archivo Nacional de Historia*, Ave 6 de Diciembre 332, Apdo 67, Quito
National Historical Archives

Biblioteca Ecuatoriana 'Aurelio Espinosa Pólit'*, Apdo 160, Quito Tel: (02) 530420
Librarian: Julián G Bravo

Biblioteca Nacional del Ecuador*, García Moreno y Sucre, Quito
National Library

Biblioteca de la **Casa de la Cultura Ecuatoriana**, see Biblioteca Nacional Eugenio Espejo de la Casa de la Cultura Ecuatoriana Benjamín Carrión

Biblioteca Nacional **Eugenio Espejo** de la Casa de la Cultura Ecuatoriana Benjamín Carrión, Apdo 67, Quito (Located at: Ave 12 de Octubre 555, Quito) Tel: (02) 230260
Library of Ecuadorian Culture

Museo y Biblioteca Municipal*, Ave 10 de Agosto y Calle Pedro Carbo, Guayaquil

Biblioteca de la **Universidad Central de Ecuador***, Ciudad Universitaria, Quito

Biblioteca General, **Universidad de Guayaquil***, Apdo 3834, Guayaquil

Library Association

Asociación Ecuatoriana de Bibliotecarios (AEB)*, Casa de la Cultura Ecuatoriana, Casilla 87, Quito Tel: (02) 528840/
Headquarters: (02) 263474
Ecuadorian Library Association
Executive Secretary: Elizabeth Carrion
Publications: Unidad Bibliotecaria

Library Reference Journal

Unidad Bibliotecaria, Asociacón Ecuatoriana de Bibliotecarios (AEB), Casa de la Cultura Ecuatoriana, Casilla 87, Quito

Egypt

General Information

Language: Arabic (English and French widely used)
Religion: Islamic
Population: 50.5 million
Bank Hours: Generally 0830-1230 Monday-Thursday; 1000-1200 Saturday
Shop Hours: 0830-1330, 1630-1900 Monday-Saturday
Currency: 100 piastres (1000 milliemes) = 1 Egyptian pound
Export/Import Information: No tariff on books. No import licences. Exchange control by Supreme Committee set up by Ministry of Finance, Economy and Foreign Trade. Banks authorized to execute foreign-exchange transactions. No longer government monopoly but some book importing done by Foreign Trade Company, Misr Import & Export Co, 6 Adly St, Cairo
Copyright: Berne, Florence (see International section)

Book Trade Organizations

Permanent Bureau of **Afro-Asian Writers***, 104 Kasr el-Aini St, Cairo

General Egyptian Book Organization*, Corniche el Nil, Boulac, Cairo Tel: (02) 775000/775109 Cable Add: Gebo Telex: 93932 Book
Chairman: Dr Ezz El Dine Ismail
Also Publisher (qv)

The **Public Organization** for Books and Scientific Appliances*, Cairo University, Orman, Ghiza, Cairo
Chairman: Kamil Seddik

Standard Book Numbering Agency*, c/o Dr Ezz El Dine Ismail, General Egyptian Book Organization, Corniche el Nil, Boulac, Cairo Tel: (02) 775371/775649 Telex: 93932 Booko

Publishers

Al **Ahram** Establishment*, Al-Galaa St, Cairo Tel: (02) 758333/745666/755500 Cable Add: Al Ahram Cairo Telex: 92001
Chairman, Editor-in-Chief: Ibrahim Nafei; *Sales:* Hany Tolba; *Production:* Fathi Al Charkawi; *Rights & Permissions:* Mrs Nawal El Mahallawi
Subsidiary Companies: Al Ahram Center for Strategic & Political Studies, Al Ahram Center for Scientific Translation, Al Ahram Center for Microfilm & Organization, Al Ahram Center for Computer & Management
Associate Companies: Al Ahram Commercial Press, Al Ahram Agency for Distribution
Branch Offs: In all main cities in Egypt
Subjects: Sciences and Humanities
Book Club: Al Ahram Book Club
Bookshops: Al Ahram Bookshop (qv under Major Booksellers)
Founded: 1875
Miscellaneous: Also translation agency, printer, distributor, importer, exporter

The **American University** in Cairo Press+, 113 Sharia Kasr el Aini, PO Box 2511, Cairo Tel: (02) 3542964 Cable Add: Victorious Telex: 92224 Aucai
Dir: Arnold Tovell; *Asst Dir:* Aleya Serour; *Managing Editor:* Neil Hewison; *Marketing Manager:* Cassandra Vivian; *Distribution Supervisor:* Tahang Shamaa
Subjects: Literature, Art, History, Egyptology, Africana, Anthropology, Arabic Language, Architecture, Coptology, Social Science, Textbooks, Guidebooks, Egypt and the Arab World, Religion, Natural Sciences, Reference, Periodicals
Bookshop: The AUC Bookstore (at above address)
1986: 25 titles *Founded:* 1960
ISBN Publisher's Prefix: 977-424

Al **Arab Publishing** House, PO Box 32, Faggalah, Cairo (Located at: 28 Faggalah St, Cairo) Tel: (02) 908025 Cable Add: Arabukshop Cairo
Man Dir: Prof Dr Saladin Boustany; *Sales Manager:* George G Eddé
Subjects: General Fiction, Belles Lettres, Poetry, Biography, History, Africana, Philosophy, Reference, Religion, Arabic Language & Literature, Arabic Manuscripts, Paperbacks, Social Science, University & Secondary Textbooks
Bookshop: Al Arab Bookshop (qv under Major Booksellers)
Founded: 1900

Cairo University Press*, Guiza-Orman, Giza, Cairo Tel: (02) 846144
Subject: University Textbooks

E S D U C K, see The Egyptian Society for the Dissemination of Universal Culture and Knowledge

Les **Editions universitaires** d'Egypte*, 41 Sharia Sherif Pasha, Cairo
Subject: University Textbooks

The **Egyptian Society** for the Dissemination of Universal Culture and Knowledge (ESDUCK)*, PO Box 21, Cairo (Located at: 1081 Corniche el Nil St, Garden City, Cairo) Tel: (02) 20295/25079 Cable Add: Esduck
Executive Manager: Dr Sayed R Haddara; *Editorial:* Inas Effat; *Production:* Faiza Hakim; *Rights & Permissions:* Khadiga Safwat
Subjects: Trade Books, Textbooks, Children's, Reference
Founded: 1953
Miscellaneous: Co-publisher with local and American firms. Translation agency

General Egyptian Book Organization*, Corniche el Nil, Boulac, Cairo Tel: (02) 775000/775109 Cable Add: Gebo Telex: 93932 Book
Chairman: Dr Ezz El Dine Ismail
Foreign Distribution Centre: Samady & Salha Bldg, Syria St, Beyrouth, Lebanon
Subjects: Arab classic and modern books in all fields
Bookshops: International Book Centre, Cairo, 21 branches throughout Egypt
Founded: 1961
ISBN Publisher's Prefix: 977-201

The **General Organization** for Government Press Affairs*, 22 Al Nil St, Imbaba, Guiza, Cairo
Government Printer

Government Printer, see The General Organization for Government Press Affairs

Dar Al **Hilal** Publishing Institution*, 16 Sharia Mohammed Ezz El Arab, Cairo
Tel: (02) 540610 Cable Add: Al Mussawar Cairo Telex: 92703 Hilal
Chief Executive: Makram Mohamed Ahmed
Subjects: Fiction, Non-fiction, Periodicals

Dar Al **Maaref**, 1119 Corniche el Nil St, Cairo Tel: (02) 777077 Cable Add:

EGYPT 89

Damaref Telex: 92199 Maaref
Chairman & Man Dir: Salah Montasser
Subsidiary Company: Dar Al-Maaref Liban Sàrl, Lebanon (qv)
Subjects: Academic, Scientific, General Islamic, School-books, Children's (in Arabic), University Textbooks (in English)
Bookshops: Alexandria, El Arish, Assiut, Asswan, Cairo, Esmaillia, El-Kom, Mansora, Qena, Shebin, Sohage, Tanta
Founded: 1890
ISBN Publisher's Prefix: 977-247

Dar Al-**Kitab** Al-Masri*, PO Box 156, Cairo Tel: (02) 742168/744657/754301 Cable Add: Kitamisr Telex: 22481/21581 attn 134 Ktm Cairo
President, Man Dir: El-Zein Hassan
Parent Company: Dar Al-Kitab Al-Alami (at above address)
Associate Company: Dar Al-Kitab Allubnani, Lebanon (qv)
Branch Offs: Beirut, Cairo, Casablanca, Geneva, Madrid, Paris
Subjects: Islamic, Turath, School and General Educational Textbooks (in Arabic, English, French, German, Spanish), Children's
Founded: 1929
Miscellaneous: Also distributor and printer

Middle East Book Centre*, 45 Sharia Kasr el-Nil, Cairo Tel: (02) 910980
Man Dir: Dr A M Mosharrafa; *Sales Manager:* A Ismail
Subjects: General Fiction, Belles Lettres, Poetry, Biography, History, Africana, Philosophy, Religion, Arabic Language & Literature, Paperbacks, General & Social Science, University & Secondary Textbooks
Founded: 1954

Dar al-**Nahda** al Arabia*, 32 Sharia Abdel-Khalek Sharwat St, Cairo
Subjects: Arabic Language & Literature
Bookshop: At above address

Editions le **Progrès***, 6 Sharia Sherif Pasha, Cairo
Man Dir: Wedi Choukri

The **Public Organization** for Books and Scientific Appliances*, Cairo University, Orman, Ghiza, Cairo
Chairman: Kamil Seddik
Subject: University Textbooks
Founded: 1965

Senouhy Publishers*, 54 Sharia Abdel-Khalek, Sarwat, Cairo
Man Dir: Leila A Fadel
Subjects: General Non-fiction, Belles Lettres, Poetry, History, Africana, Religion
Founded: 1956

Dar El **Shorouk**, 16 Gawad Husni St, Cairo Tel: (02) 774814/774578 Telex: 93091 Shrok
Chief Executive, Editorial and Rights & Permissions: Ibrahim El Moallem; *Sales:* Galal Ali; *Production:* Ahmed El Zayadi; *Publicity:* Ibrahim El Moallem, Helmi El Touni
Subjects: Political, Islamic, Literature, Children's
Bookshops: 2 Al Bursa St, Kasr El Nil; 1 Soliman Pasha Sq (both Cairo)
1985: 200 titles *1986:* 150 titles *Founded:* 1976

The **Sphinx***, Bookshop and Publishing House, 3 Shawarby St (Kasr El Nil) – 3rd Floor – apartment 305, Cairo Tel: (02) 744616 Cable Add: Bulhall Cairo Telex: 93927 Sfinx
Man Dir: Abd-el-Salam Hassan Sharara
Subjects: Educational and Academic Books
Founded: 1958

Literary Agents

The **Egyptian Society** for the Dissemination of Universal Culture and Knowledge (ESDUCK)*, PO Box 21, Cairo (Located at: 1081 Corniche el Nil St, Garden City, Cairo) Tel: (02) 20295/25079 Cable Add: Esduck
Executive Manager: Dr Sayed R Haddara

Book Club

Al **Ahram** Book Club*, Al-Galaa St, Cairo Tel: (02) 748080/755500/758203 Telex: 92001
Owned by: Al Ahram Establishment (qv under Publishers)

Major Booksellers

Al **Ahd** Al Gadeed Bookstore*, Farouk Zaky & Co, 4-5 Kamel Sidky St, Cairo Tel: (02) 900290/905296

Al **Ahram** Bookshops*, 165 Mohamed Farid St, Cairo Tel: (02) 924499 Telex: 92001
20 bookshops throughout Egypt
Owned by: Al Ahram Establishment (qv)

The **Anglo American** Bookshop*, 55 Algomhouria St, Cairo Tel: (02) 905262

The **Anglo Egyptian** Bookshop*, 165 Mohamed Farid St, Cairo Tel: (02) 914337
Proprietor: Sobhy Grais

Al **Arab** Bookshop, PO Box 32, Faggalah, Cairo (Located at: 28 Faggalah St, Cairo) Tel: (02) 908025 Cable Add: Arabukshop Cairo
Manager: Prof Dr Saladin Boustany
Agent of the Library of Congress PL 480
Owned by: Al Arab Publishing House (qv)

Librairie **Hachette***, 45 bis rue Champolion, Cairo

Al **Ittihad** Bookstore*, Mohamed Abdel Mouty Ismail, 3 Kamel Sidky St, Al Ezbekia, Cairo Tel: (02) 916403

Dar Al **Kutab** Al Hadeetha*, Tewfik Afeeti Amer & Co, 14 Al Goumhouria St, Abdeen, Cairo Tel: (02) 916107

Lehnert & Landrock*, 44 Sherif St, PO Box 1013, Cairo
Manager: K Lambelet
Owned by: Kurt & Edouard Lambelet Succ

Livres de France*, Immeuble Immobilia, rue Kasr el nil, Cairo Tel: (02) 51512

Misr Bookshop, PO Box 16, Faggalah, Cairo (Located at: 3 Kamel Sidki St, Faggalah, Cairo) Tel: (02) 908920 Cable Add: Damiltibaa Cairo
Manager: Amir Saïd El-Sahhar

Misr Import & Export Co*, 6 Adly St, Cairo
Importer/Exporter

Modern Cairo Bookshop*, 169 Tahreer St, Cairo

Saladdine Publications & Distributors Inc*, 28 Talaat Harb St, Abu Regela Building, Cairo Tel: (02) 758542

Ahmed **Shaker** Al Ansary*, Midan Birkit Al Ratly, Sikit Al Ratly No 3, Bab Al Sharea, Cairo Tel: (02) 932895

Major Libraries

Ain Shams University Library*, Kasr-el-Zaafran, Abbasiyah, Cairo

Alexandria Municipal Library*, 18 Sharia Menasce Moharrem Bey, Alexandria

American University in Cairo Library, 113 Sharia Kasr El-Aini, Cairo Tel: (02) 3542964
Librarian: Smith W Richardson

Al-Azhar University Library*, Al-Azhar St, Cairo Tel: (02) 904051

Dar-ul-Kutub*, Kurnish Al-Nil St, Cairo Egyptian National Library

Institute of Arab Research & Studies Library, 1 Tolombat St, Cairo Cable Add: Irealea Cairo
President: Prof Dr M S Abulezz

Ministry of Education Library*, 16 Sharia El-Falaki, Cairo

Ministry of Justice Library*, Midan Lazoghli, Abassia, Cairo Tel: (02) 831546
Librarian: Fekry Abou-El-Kheir

National Archives*, Citadel, nr Military Museum, Cairo Tel: (02) 921534

National Assembly Library*, Palace of the National Assembly, Cairo

National Information and Documentation Centre*, Al-Tahrir St, Dokki, Cairo
Publication: Directory of Scientific and Technical Libraries

University of Ain Shams Library, see Ain Shams University Library

University of Alexandria Library*, Ahmed Hassanein St, Shatby, Alexandria Tel: (03) 71675

University of Cairo Library*, Orman, Ghiza, Cairo Tel: (02) 845186

Library Associations

Algamiia Almasriia Lilmaktabat Almadrasiia*, 35 Algalaa St, Cairo
Egyptian School Library Association
Publication: Sahifat al-Maktabát (Egyptian Library Journal)

Egyptian Association for Archives and Librarianship*, c/o Library of Fine Arts, 24 El Matbâa Al-Ahlia, Boulac, Cairo
Executive Secretary: Ahmed M Mansour
Publication: Alam al-Maktabát (Library World)

National Information and Documentation Centre*, Al-Tahrir St, Dokki, Cairo
Publication: Directory of Scientific and Technical Libraries

Library Reference Books and Journals

Book

Directory of Scientific and Technical Libraries, National Information and Documentation Centre, Al-Tahrir St, Dokki, Cairo

Journals

Alam al-Maktabát (Library World), Egyptian Association for Archives and Librarianship, c/o Library of Fine Arts, 24 El Matbâa Al-Ahlia, Boulac, Cairo

Sahifat al-Maktabát (Egyptian Library Journal), Algamiia Almasriia Lilmaktabat Almadrasiia, 35 Algalaa St, Cairo

EGYPT — ETHIOPIA

Literary Associations and Societies

Atelier*, 1 Sharia St, Saba, Alexandria
Society of Artists and Writers
Secretary-General: L Hergenstein

High Council of Arts & Literature*, 9 Sharia Hassan Sabri, Zamalek, Cairo
Secretary: Youssef Al Sibai

Egyptian **P E N** Centre*, 34 Baghat Aly St, Zamalek, Cairo
Secretary: Dr Mursi Saad el Din

Literary Periodical

Lotus; Afro-Asian Writings, 104 Kasr el-Aini St, Cairo
Important quarterly review published for the Permanent Bureau of Afro-Asian Writers

Translation Agencies and Associations

Al **Ahram***, Al-Galaa St, Cairo Tel: (02) 755500/745666/758333 Cable Add: Pyramidad Telex: 92001/92544 Ahram

The **Egyptian Society** for the Dissemination of Universal Culture and Knowledge (ESDUCK)*, PO Box 21, Cairo (Located at: 1081 Corniche el Nil St, Cairo) Tel: (02) 20295/25079

El Salvador

General Information

Language: Spanish
Religion: Roman Catholic
Population: 5 million
Bank Hours: 0900-1200, 1345-1530 Monday-Friday
Shop Hours: 0800-1200, 1400-1800 Monday-Friday; 0800-1200 Saturday
Currency: 100 centavos = 1 colon
Export/Import Information: Member of the Central American Common Market. No import licences but exchange licence from Exchange Control Department of Central Reserve Bank required, if goods coming from outside Central America. Commercial banks authorize certain import payments
Copyright: UCC, Buenos Aires, Florence (see International section)

Publishers

Editorial Universitaria de la Universidad de El Salvador*, Apdo Postal 1703, San Salvador (Located at: Ciudad Universitaria, San Salvador) Tel: 256604
Dir: Armando Herrara
Subjects: Scholarly, Textbooks, General Literature
Founded: 1923

Ministerio de Educación del Gobierno de El Salvador*, Dirección General de Publicaciones, Pasaje Contreras 145, San Salvador Tel: 254605/259092
Man Dir, Rights & Permissions: Rafael Ruiz Blanco; *Editorial:* Mirna Priscila Gámez Sol; *Sales:* Raúl Vicente Parada; *Production:* Elmer Aristides Machuca; *Publicity:* Jorge Ortíz Espinosa
Orders to: Gerencia de Distribución, 9a Calle Oriente 104 y Ave España, San Salvador
Subjects: Literature, Art, Sociology, History, General Textbooks
Bookshop: 9a Calle Oriente 104 y Ave España, San Salvador
Founded: 1953

U C A Editores+, Apdo Postal 01-575, San Salvador (Located at: Universidad Centroamericana José Simeón Cañas, Autopista Sur, Jardines de Guadalupe, San Salvador) Tel: 234491
Dir: Rodolfo Cardenal SJ; *Editorial:* Ignacio Martín-Baró, Rafael Rodriguez, Jon Sobrino; *Production:* Rogelio Pedraz
Orders to: Distribuidora de Publicaciones de la Universidad Centroamericana José Simeón Cañas, Apdo 668, San Salvador Tel: 240011
Subjects: El Salvador (history, politics, literature), Social Science, Religion, Theology, Economy, Secondary & University Textbooks
Bookshop: Librería UCA (qv under Major Booksellers)
Founded: 1975
ISBN Publisher's Prefix: 84-8405

Major Booksellers

Librería Claudio **Bernard***, Calle Los Cedros 53, 100 metros al sur del IVU, San Salvador Tel: 256719

Clasicos Roxsil*, 6a Ave Sur 1-6, Santa Tecla Tel: 281212
Manager: Rosa Victoria Serrano de López

Librería **Cultural** Salvadoreña SA de CV*, Apdo Postal 2296, San Salvador (Located at: 7a Ave Norte 121, San Salvador) Tel: 712136/712090

Dissal SA de CV*, 9a Ave Norte 422, San Salvador Tel: 226983
Distribuidora Salvadoreña Le Revistas y Libros SA Le CU
Manager: Antonio Alas

Librería e Importadora **Neruda***, 29 Calle Poniente 222, Local No 6, San Salvador Tel: 251566
Manager: José Reynaldo Echeverría O

Librería **Renacimiento** SA de CV*, Apdo Postal 852, San Salvador (Located at: Final Pasaje 5 No 126 y 2a diagonal, Urbanización La Esperanza, San Salvador) Tel: 254541/263198

Distribuidora **Salvadoreña** de Revistas y Libros SA de CV, see Dissal SA de CV

Librería **U C A***, Apdo Postal 168, San Salvador (Located at: Universidad Centroamericana José Simeón Cañas, Autopista Sur, Jardines de Guadalupe, San Salvador) Tel: 240011 ext 193/234491

Librería **Universitaria** de la Universidad de El Salvador*, Apdo Postal 2028, San Salvador (Located at: Ciudad Universitaria, San Salvador) Tel: 258607/258022 ext 132

Major Libraries

Biblioteca Nacional*, 8a Ave Norte y Calle Delgado, San Salvador Tel: 213249

Biblioteca de la **Universidad Centroamericana** José Simeón Cañas*, Apdo Postal 168, San Salvador (Located at: Autopista Sur, Jardines de Guadalupe, San Salvador) Tel: 240011
Dir: Mélida Arteaga

Biblioteca Central de la **Universidad de El Salvador***, Ciudad Universitaria, San Salvador Tel: 258022 ext 115
Dir: Ana Aurora de Kapsalis
Publications: Boletín (monthly); *Lista de Adquisiciones Recientes* (monthly)

Library Associations

Asociación de Bibliotecarios de El Salvador*, Urbanización Gerardo Barrios Polígono, 'B' No 5, San Salvador Tel: 220409/253471
El Salvador Library Association
Secretary-General: Edgar Antonio Pérez Borja
Publication: Informa (Newsletter) (monthly)

Asociación General de Archivistas de El Salvador*, Edificio Sede 8, Calle Oriente 314, San Salvador
Association of Archivists of El Salvador

Library Reference Journal

Informa (Newsletter) (monthly), Asociación de Bibliotecarios de El Salvador, Urbanización Gerardo Barrios Polígono, 'B' No 5, San Salvador

Literary Periodical

Guíon Literario (Literary Summary), Ministerio de Educación del Gobierno de El Salvador, Dirección General de Publicaciones, Pasaje Contreras 145, San Salvador

Literary Prize

U C A Editores Literary Prize*
Founded 1980. Awarded each year for a work in a specified literary area. The prize is 3,000 colones and publication of the work. The most recent winner was Mariano Castro Moran for *Función política del ejército salvadoreño en el presente siglo*. Enquiries to UCA Editores, Apdo Postal 668, San Salvador

Ethiopia

General Information

Language: Amharic (English, French and Italian spoken)
Religion: Ethiopian Orthodox (allied to Coptic Church)
Population: 31.1 million
Bank Hours: 0830-1230, 1430-1730 Monday-Friday; 0830-1230 Saturday
Shop Hours: Addis Ababa: 0900-1300, 1500-2000 Monday-Saturday. Asmara: 0800-1300, 1600-2000 Monday-Friday
Currency: 100 cents = 1 birr
Export/Import Information: No tariff on books, but additional taxes. Advertising subject to customs and same taxes. No import licence required but Exchange Payment Licence necessary
Copyright: No copyright conventions signed

Book Trade Reference Books and Journals

Book

List of Ethiopian Authors, Addis Ababa University Library, PO Box 1176, Addis Ababa

Journal

Ethiopian Publications, Institute of Ethiopian Studies Library, Addis Ababa University, PO Box 1176, Addis Ababa
Ethiopian National Bibliography, irregular

Publishers

Addis Ababa University Press, PO Box 1176, Addis Ababa Tel: (01) 119148 Cable Add: AA Univ
Editor: Innes Marshall
Subjects: Public Health, Hydrology, Climatology, Botany, Ornithology, Conservation, Geology, Philosophy, University Textbooks, Reference, Works in English language
Founded: 1968

The **Bible** Churchmen's Missionary Society*, PO Box 864, Asmara Tel: (04) 114267
Dir: John Coracher
Subjects: General Fiction, Belles Lettres, Poetry, Biography, History, Africana, Religion, Juveniles, Amharic Language & Literature
Bookshop: PO Box 864, Asmara

Government Printer*, Government Printing Press, PO Box 1241, Addis Ababa

Major Booksellers

Asmara Bookshop*, 92 Victory Ave, Asmara Tel: (04) 110511
Manager: Keshi Gebremedhin T/Micael

Berhan Bookshop and Stationery*, PO Box 302, Addis Ababa

The **City** Bookshop*, PO Box 864, Asmara

E C A Bookshop Co-op Society*, PO Box 60100, Addis Ababa

Major Libraries

Addis Ababa University Library*, PO Box 1176, Addis Ababa Tel: (01) 115673
Librarian: Getachew Birru
Publication: List of Ethiopian Authors

Agricultural Institute Library, PO Box 307, Jimma, Keffa (Located at: Jimma Junior College of Agriculture, Jimma)
Librarian: Goitom Ghebru

Alemaya University of Agriculture Library, PO Box 138, Dire Dawa
Assistant Librarian: Asheber Haile

Asmara Public Library*, PO Box 259, Asmara (Located at: 82 Ras Alula St, Asmara) Tel: (04) 117044

Asmara University Library, PO Box 1220, Asmara Tel: (04) 113600 Cable Add: Asmuniv Telex: 42091
Deputy Librarian: Abdulkader Zekaria

British Council Library*, PO Box 1043, Addis Ababa (Located at: Artistic Bldg, Adua Ave, Addis Ababa) Tel: (01) 110022 Cable Add: Britcoun
Librarian: A M Hunde

Ethiopian Manuscript Microfilm Library*, PO Box 30274, Addis Ababa
Publication: Bulletin (quarterly)

Institute of Ethiopian Studies Library, Addis Ababa University, PO Box 1176, Addis Ababa Tel: (01) 115772 Cable Add: AA Univ
Librarian: Degife Gabre-Tsadik
Publications include: Ethiopian Publications (irregular); *List of Current Periodical Publications* (twice a year)

National Library and Archives of Ethiopia*, PO Box 717, Addis Ababa Tel: (01) 442241
Librarian: Arefaine Belay

Organization for African Unity Library*, PO Box 3243, Addis Ababa Tel: (01) 157700 Cable Add: Oau Telex: 21046
Chief Librarian: Mrs J C Ranairo Ravelo

Faculty of **Technology** Library, PO Box 385, Addis Ababa

United Nations Economic Commission for Africa Library, PO Box 3001, Addis Ababa Tel: (01) 447200 Cable Add: Eca Addis Ababa Telex: 21029
Librarian: Abdel-Rahman M Tahir
Publications include: Africa Index: Selected articles on socio-economic development (quarterly)

Library Association

Ethiopian Library Association*, PO Box 30530, Addis Ababa Tel: (01) 110844 ext 353
Publications: Bulletin; *Directory of Ethiopian Libraries*

Library Reference Books and Journals

Book

Directory of Ethiopian Libraries, Ethiopian Library Association, PO Box 30530, Addis Ababa

Journals

Bulletin, Ethiopian Library Association, PO Box 30530, Addis Ababa

Bulletin (quarterly), Ethiopian Manuscript Microfilm Library, PO Box 30274, Addis Ababa

List of Current Periodical Publications (twice a year), Institute of Ethiopian Studies Library, Addis Ababa University, PO Box 1176, Addis Ababa

Fiji

General Information

Language: English, Fijian, Hindi and Cantonese
Religion: Predominantly Protestant, with large minority of Hindus
Population: 677,500
Bank Hours: 1000-1500 Monday-Thursday; 1000-1600 Friday
Shop Hours: 0800-1630 or later Monday-Friday; early closing Wednesday or Saturday
Currency: 100 cents = 1 Fiji dollar

Export/Import Information: No tariffs on books and advertising. No import licences. Exchange control by central monetary authority; no specific exchange licence required and authorized banks perform transaction upon application
Copyright: Berne, UCC (see International section)

Book Trade Organization

Regional ISBN Agency, Pacific Information Centre, The University of the South Pacific Library, PO Box 1168, Suva Tel: 313900 ext 283 Telex: 2276
ISBN Administrator: Mrs Esther Williams

Standard Book Numbering Agency, see Regional ISBN Agency

Book Trade Reference Journal

Publications Bulletin, Government Printing and Stationery Department, Suva

Publishers

Indian Printing and Publishing Co*, PO Box 151, Suva
Man Dir: S M Bidesi Jnr
Subjects: Law, Administration, Business Management

Lotu Pasifika Productions*, PO Box 208, Suva Tel: 24314 Cable Add: Lotupak
Manager: Seru L Verebalavu
Subjects: Education, Religion, Poetry, Cookery

Oceania Printers Ltd*, PO Box 597, Suva Tel: 313044/313224
Subject: Literature

Sangam Sarada Printing Press*, PO Box 9, Nadi
Subjects: Literature, History, Geography

Tara Press*, Kings Rd, PO Box 923, Nasinu, Suva
Subjects: Literature, Music

Major Booksellers

Desai Bookshops, PO Box 160, Suva (Located at: 271 Victoria Parade, Suva) Tel: 314088 Cable Add: Desai Suva Telex: 2480 Mag
General Manager: David Mackie
10 branches throughout Fiji
Owned by: Magazines South Pacific Ltd, PO Box 160, Suva

Suva Book Shop, Greig St, PO Box 153, Suva Tel: 311355
Manager: Harinivas Singh

Major Libraries

Library Service of Fiji, PO Box 2526, Government Buildings, Suva Tel: 315303/311224

National Archives of Fiji*, PO Box 2125, Government Buildings, Suva Tel: 24031 Cable Add: Archivist

Suva City Library*, Victoria Arcade, Suva

University of the South Pacific Library, PO Box 1168, Suva Cable Add: University Suva Tel: 313900 Telex: 2276 Fax: 314305
Librarian: Mrs E W Williams
Publications include: South Pacific Research

92 FIJI — FINLAND

Register (annual); *South Pacific Bibliography* (annual); *South Pacific Periodicals Index*

Western Regional Library*, PO Box 150, Lautoka Tel: 60091

Library Association

Fiji Library Association (FLA)*, c/o Secretary, PO Box 2292, Government Bldgs, Suva
Publications: Newsletter; Journal

Library Reference Journals

Journal and *Newsletter*, Fiji Library Association (FLA), c/o Secretary, PO Box 2292, Government Bldgs, Suva

Finland

General Information

Language: Finnish and Swedish (officially bilingual); English and German spoken widely
Religion: Lutheran
Population: 4.8 million
Bank Hours: 0915-1615 Monday-Friday
Shop Hours: 0900-1700 or later Monday-Friday; 0900-1600 (1400 in summer) Saturday
Currency: 100 pennia = 1 markka
Export/Import Information: Member of European Free Trade Association. Free trade agreed with European Economic Community. No tariff on books or advertising. No import licences required on books
Copyright: UCC, Berne, Florence (see International section)

Book Trade Organizations

Kirja-ja Paperikauppojen Liitto ry*, PO Box 17, Martinkyläntie 45, SF-01721 Vantaa Tel: (90) 840866 Telex: 121394 Tltx attn Booksellers Helsinki
Finnish Booksellers' Association
Chief Executive: Olli Eräkivi

Standard Book Numbering Agency, Bibliographic Dept, Helsinki University Library, PL 312, SF-00171 Helsinki Tel: (90) 410566/410359 Telex: 122785 Tsk
This Agency is also a national ISDS Centre
ISBN Administrator: Dr Thea Aulo

Suomen Antikvariaattiyhdistys-Finska Antikvariatföreningen*, P Makasiininkatu 6, Magasinsgatan 6, SF-00130 Helsinki Tel: (90) 626352
Finnish Antiquarian Booksellers' Association

Suomen Kirjailijaliitto, Runeberginkatu 32 C 28, SF-00100 Helsinki Tel: (90) 445392/492278
Association of Finnish Authors
Executive Secretary: Päivi Liedes
Publications: Suomen Runotar; Suomalaisetkertojat

Suomen Kustannusyhdistys, Merimiehenkatu 12 A 6, SF-00150 Helsinki Tel: (90) 179185

Finnish Book Publishers' Association
Secretary-General: U Lappi
Publications: Kirjakauppalehti (Book Trade Journal); *Suomessa Ilmestyneen Kirjallisuuden Luettelo (Katalog över i Finland Utkommen Litteratur* (List of Books Published in Finland)

Suomen Nuortenkirjaneuvosto, Kankurink 7 B 34, SF-00150 Helsinki
Finnish Section of the International Board on Books for Young People (IBBY)
President: Vuokko Blinnikka; *Secretary:* Cita Reuter

Book Trade Reference Books and Journals

Books

The Finnish National Bibliography, Helsingin Yliopiston Kirjasto, Unioninkatu 36, PO Box 312, SF-00171 Helsinki
Also on microfiche

Suomessa Ilmestyneen Kirjallisuuden Luettelo (Katalog över i Finland Utkommen Litteratur) (List of Books Published in Finland), Suomen Kustannusyhdistys, Merimiehenkatu 12 A 6, SF-00150 Helsinki

Journals

Books from Finland, Helsingin Yliopiston Kirjasto, Unioninkatu 36, PO Box 312, SF-00171 Helsinki
Containing articles mostly in English, but also in French and German, quarterly

Kirjakauppalehti (Book Trade Journal), Suomen Kustannusyhdistys, Merimiehenkatu 12 A 6, SF-00150 Helsinki

Libristi (Journal for Booksellers' Assistants), PO Box 10242, Helsinki

Publishers

Akateeminen Kustannusliike Oy*, Mikonk 20 B 12, SF-00100 Helsinki Tel: (90) 174002
Manager: M O Mattila; *Sales:* Riitta Mattila
Subjects: Matriculation books, Religion, Fiction
Founded: 1927
ISBN Publisher's Prefix: 951-9023

Ekenäs Tryckeri AB*, PO Box 36, SF-10600 Ekenäs (Located at: Stationsvägen 1, Ekenäs) Tel: (911) 12800 Telex: 13150 Vne
Man Dir: Sven Sundström
Subjects: History, Politics
Founded: 1881
ISBN Publisher's Prefix: 951-9000

Etelä-Suomen Kustannus Oy*, PO Box 15, Huoltomiehentie 1, SF-21420 Lieto Tel: (921) 777502
Subjects: War, Reference, Science Fiction Paperbacks, Comics
ISBN Publisher's Prefixes: 951-9064, 951-9001

Edition **Fazer**+, PO Box 69, SF-00381 Helsinki (Located at: Takomotie 3, SF-00380 Helsinki) Tel: (90) 56011 Cable Add: Musikfazer Telex: 121738 Mufa
Man Dir (of Parent Company): John-Eric Westö; *Publishing Manager:* Jukka Kankainen; *Rights & Permissions:* Virpi Forsberg
Parent Company: Fazer Music Inc (at above address)
Subjects: Music, Music Education
Bookshop: Aleksanterink 11, SF-00100 Helsinki
1985: 50 titles *1986:* 50 titles *Founded:* 1897
ISBN Publisher's Prefix: 951-757

Forsamlingsforbundets Forlags AB, PO Box 285, SF-00121 Helsinki (Located at: Bangatan 29 A 1, SF-00120 Helsinki) Tel: (90) 647722
Man Dir and Production: Stig Frisk; *Sales:* Aili Hellström
Associate Company: Ab Fram (printing house), Vasaesplanaden 24, SF-65100 Vasa
Subject: Religion
Bookshop: Ab Gamlakarleby Bokhandel, Strandgatan 13, SF-67100 Karleby
Founded: 1920
ISBN Publisher's Prefix: 951-550

Government Printing Centre+, PO Box 516, SF-00101 Helsinki (Located at: Hakuninmaantie 2, Helsinki) Tel: (90) 56601 Telex: 123458 Vapk
Director-General: Olavi Perilä; *Director of Publication:* Mikko Iskala; *Editorial Manager:* Yrjö Hyötyniemi; *Marketing Manager:* Leo Eskola; *Rights & Permissions:* Mikko Iskala, Leo Eskola
Bookshops: Annankatu 44, 00100 Helsinki; Eteläesplanadi 4, 00130 Helsinki
1985: 302 titles *1986:* 398 titles *Founded:* 1959
ISBN Publisher's Prefixes: 951-859, 951-860

Gummerus Publishers, PO Box 479, SF-00101, Helsinki (Located at: Mannerheimintie 6A, Helsinki) Tel: (90) 644301 Telex: 123727 Fax: (90) 604998
Man Dir: Risto Lehmusoksa; *Publisher:* Pekka Salojärvi; *Editorial:* Risto Väisänen (Non-fiction), Kaarina Kolu (Children's & Juveniles); *Sales Dir:* Mikko Meronen; *Rights & Permissions:* Anna Thorwell
Subjects: General Fiction, Non-fiction, Children's, Juveniles, Reference, Encyclopaedias
Book Clubs: Book of the Month Ltd Finland, Koko Kansan Kirjakerho Oy (KKK Book Clubs Ltd) (both jointly owned)
Bookshops: Jyväskylä, Mänttä, Seinäjoki
Founded: 1872
ISBN Publisher's Prefix: 951-20

Hengellinen Laukibeirja, an imprint of Ristin Voitto ry (qv)

Karas-Sana Oy*, PO Box 48, Vivamo, SF-08101 Lohja Tel: (912) 87755
Man Dir: Toivo Saarinen; *Editorial and Rights & Permissions:* Eva Mesiäinen; *Production Manager:* Meeri Tolvanen
Parent Company: Kansan Raamattuseuran Säätio (at above address)
Subject: Christian Religion
1985: 28 titles *Founded:* 1974
ISBN Publisher's Prefix: 951-655

Karisto Oy, PO Box 102, SF-13101 Hämeenlinna (Located at: Paroistentie 2, Hämeenlinna) Tel: (917) 161551 Cable Add: Karisto Telex: 2348 Gold Fax: (917) 161555
Man Dir: Simo Moisio; *Literary Dir:* Ilmari Lehmusvaara; *Editorial and Foreign Rights:* Pirkko Mikkola
Branch Off: Kaisaniemenkatu 10, Helsinki
Subjects: General Fiction and Non-fiction, Juvenile Fiction
Founded: 1900
ISBN Publisher's Prefix: 951-23

Kustannusliike **Kirjaneliö**+, Töölönkatu 55, SF-00250 Helsinki Tel: (90) 440561
Orders to: Raamattutalo, PO Box 21, SF-76101 Pieksämäki
Subjects: Religion, Fiction, Juveniles

1985: 22 titles *1986:* 29 titles *Founded:* 1905
ISBN Publisher's Prefix: 951-600

Kirjatoimi omi Suomen Adrenttikirkko, PO Box 94, SF-33101 Tampere Tel: (931) 600000 Cable Add: Kirjatoimi Fax: (931) 600454
Man Dir and Rights & Permissions: Anna-Liisa Halonen; *Editor:* Matti J Lahti; *Sales & Publicity Manger:* Kalervo Aromäki; *Production Manager:* Jouko Kuiristo
Parent Organization: Seventh-day Adventist Church in Finland
Subjects: Spiritual, Health
1985: 5 titles *1986:* 6 titles
Founded: 1897
ISBN Publisher's Prefix: 951-629

Kirjayhtymä Oy, Eerikinkatu 28, SF-00180 Helsinki Tel: (90) 6944522 Cable Add: Kirjayhtymä
Man Dir: Martti Huhtamäki; *Publishing Dir:* Keijo Immonen; *Marketing Dir:* Heikki Rönnqvist; *Rights & Permissions:* Ritva Mäkelä, Aila Järvenpää (Geography & Biology)
Subjects: Fiction, Non-fiction, Textbooks
Founded: 1958
ISBN Publisher's Prefix: 951-26

Lasten Keskus Oy+, Särkiniementie 7, SF-00210 Helsinki Tel: (90) 6926344 Cable Add: Lasten Keskus
Man Dir: Pertti Rosenholm; *Editorial Dir, Production and Rights & Permissions:* Kalevi Virtanen
Subjects: Juveniles, Books for Parents and Teachers, Religion (Lutheran)
Bookshop: Lasten Kirjakauppa (Children's Bookstore), Fredrikinkatu 61, SF-00100 Helsinki
Founded: 1974
ISBN Publisher's Prefix: 951-626

National Board of Survey, Publications Division, PO Box 85, SF-00521 Helsinki Tel: (90) 1543137 Telex: 125254 Map Fax: (90) 147289
Chief Executive: Samppa Lukkarinen; *Editorial Manager:* Hannu Virolainen; *Sales Manager:* Päivikki Autio; *Production Dir:* Erkki-Sakari Harju; *Publicity Dir:* Hannu Sauliala
Subjects: Maps, Atlases, Nautical Charts
Bookshops: Karttakeskus Pasila (at above address); Karttakeskus Espa, Eteläesplanadi 4, SF-00130 Helsinki
Founded: 1919

Otava Kustannusosakeyhtiö, PO Box 134, SF-00121 Helsinki (Located at: Uudenmaankatu 8-12, Helsinki) Tel: (90) 19961 Cable Add: Otava Helsinki Telex: 124560
Chairman: Heikki A Reenpää; *Man Dir:* Olli Reenpää; *Vice Man Dir, Schools Dept Dir:* Dr Manu Renko; *Literary Dir:* Dr Jukka Tarkka; *Deputy Export Dir:* Matti Käki; *Production Dir:* Lauri Veijola
Subjects: General Fiction, Belles Lettres, Biography, History, How-to, Music, Art, Philosophy, Reference, Religion, Juveniles, Low- & High-priced Paperbacks, Textbooks, Educational Materials
Book Club: Suuri Suomalainen Kirjakerho Oy (jointly owned)
Bookshops: Kirja-Otava Oy (qv under Major Booksellers)
1985: 862 titles *1986:* 865 titles *Founded:* 1890
ISBN Publisher's Prefix: 951-1

Raamatun Tietokirja, an imprint of Ristin Voitto ry (qv)

Rakennuskirja Oy, Runeberginkatu 5, SF-00100 Helsinki Tel: (90) 6944911
Man Dir: Timo Olkkonen; *Deputy Man Dir:* Martti Tiula
Parent Company: Rakennustietosäätiö (Building Information Institute) (at above address)
Subject: Building
1985: 14 titles *1986:* 17 titles *Founded:* 1974
ISBN Publisher's Prefix: 951-682

Ristin Voitto ry+, PO Box 75, SF-01301 Vantaa Tel: (90) 826377
Man Dir: Valtter Luoto; *Publishing Manager:* Tytti Träff
Imprints: Hengellinen Lankibeirja, Raamatun Tietokirja
Book Club: Hyvän Sanoman Kirjat (Christian Book Club)
Subjects: Religion, Periodicals
1985: 52 titles *1986:* 50 titles *Founded:* 1926
ISBN Publisher's Prefixes: 951-605, 951-606

Holger **Schildts** Förlagsaktiebolag, Annegatan 16, SF-00120 Helsinki Tel: (90) 604892 Cable Add: Bokschildt
Man Dir: Stig-Björn Nyberg; *Rights & Permissions:* Helen Svensson
Subjects: General Fiction, Belles Lettres, Poetry, Biography, History, Music, Art, Philosophy, University Textbooks, Reference, Juveniles, High-priced Paperbacks
Founded: 1913
ISBN Publisher's Prefix: 951-50

Semic-Book, PO Box 317, SF-33101 Tempere Tel: (931) 111400 Telex: 22353 Semic Fax: (931) 111387
Chief Executive: Allan Tokoi; *Editorial, Production:* Marjaana Tulosmaa; *Sales:* Kurt-Erik Suvanto; *Publicity:* Pentti Molander; *Rights & Permissions:* Seija Kastari
Subject: Children's
1986: 50 titles *Founded:* 1986
Miscellaneous: Semic-Book is a division of Kustannus Oy Semic (at above address), which itself is a subsidiary company of Semic International AB, Sweden (qv)
ISBN Publisher's Prefixes: 951-9112, 951-876

Söderström et Co Förlagsaktiebolag, Wavulinsvägen 4, SF-00210 Helsinki Tel: (90) 6923681 Cable Add: Söderströms
Man Dir: Carl Appelberg
Subjects: General Fiction, Belles Lettres, Poetry, Biography, History, How-to, Art, Philosophy, Reference, Religion, Juveniles, Psychology, General Science, University, Secondary & Primary Textbooks
1985: 196 titles *1986:* 228 titles *Founded:* 1891
ISBN Publisher's Prefix: 951-52

Suomalaisen Kirjallisuuden Seura, PO Box 259, SF-00171 Helsinki (Located at: Hallituskatu 1, Helsinki) Tel: (90) 171229 Finnish Literature Society
Secretary-General/Director: Urpo Vento
Subjects: Folklore, Ethnology, Literary History, Linguistics
Founded: 1831
ISBN Publisher's Prefix: 951-717

Tammi Kustannusosakeyhtiö, Eerikinkatu 28, SF-00180 Helsinki Tel: (90) 6942700 Cable Add: Tammi Telex: 125482 Tammi Fax: (90) 6942700
Man Dir: Olli Arrakoski; *Marketing Dir:* Sakari Lahtinen; *Rights & Permissions:* Martina Sunell
Subjects: General Fiction, Belles Lettres, Poetry, Biography, History, How-to, Music, Art, Reference, Juveniles, Paperbacks, Psychology, Engineering, Social Science, University Textbooks
Book Clubs: Suuri Suomalainen Kirjakerho Oy, Uudet Kirjat (both associate partners)
1985: 232 titles *1986:* 249 titles *Founded:* 1943
ISBN Publisher's Prefix: 951-30

Tietoteos Publishing Co*, PO Box 40, SF-02211 Espoo (Located at: Yläportti 1 A, Espoo) Tel: (90) 881133
Man Dir: Jyrki K Talvitie
Associate Company: Multilibro Ltd, Ilmarinkatu 8, SF-00101 Helsinki
Subjects: Technical Dictionaries, Travel Guides, Finnish Air Force History series, Stock Market Manual, General Technical
Founded: 1948
ISBN Publisher's Prefix: 951-9035

Kustannus Oy **Uusi Tie***, PO Box 54, SF-00601 Helsinki (Located at: Oulunkyläntie 5, SF-00600 Helsinki) Tel: (90) 799244
Man Dir: Seppo Väisänen; *Sales:* Olavi Maijala
Subjects: Christian Religion, Theology, Children
Founded: 1964
ISBN Publisher's Prefix: 951-619

Amer-yhtymä Oy **Weilin ja Göös**+, PO Box 389, SF-00101 Helsinki (Located at: Ahertajantie 5, SF-02100 Espoo) Tel: (90) 43771 Cable Add: Weilingöös Telex: 122597 Weigs Fax: (90) 4377260
The above is the main address; the department of general literature is at Annankatu 31-33c, SF-00100 Helsinki Tel: (90) 6941566 Fax: (90) 6948615
President: Olle Koskinen; *Publisher:* Juha Vuori-Karvia; *Publishing Dirs:* Jaakko Manninen (Encyclopaedias and Reference), Eero Syrjänen (Educational); *Publishing Manager:* Leena Tarkka; *Editorial Managers:* Juhani Salokannel (Fiction), Liisa Steffa (General Non-fiction), Terttu Toiviainen (Children's); *Foreign Rights:* Kerstin Kvint, Box 45164, S-104 30 Stockholm, Sweden (Children's)
Subjects: Fiction & General Non-fiction, Biography, Business Management, Reference, Juveniles, Children's, Textbooks, Educational Materials
Book Clubs: Book of the Month Ltd Finland, Lasten parhaat kirjat (both jointly owned)
Bookshop: Kirjakievari, Mannerheimintie 40, SF-00100 Helsinki
Founded: 1872
ISBN Publisher's Prefix: 951-35

Werner Söderström Osakeyhtiö (WSOY), PO Box 222, SF-00121 Helsinki (Located at: Bulevardi 12, Helsinki) Tel: (90) 61681 Cable Add: Wsoy Helsinki Telex: 122644 Wsoy Fax: (90) 6168369
Man Dir: Antero Siljola; *Publishing Dir:* Keijo Ahti (Non-fiction, Encyclopaedias); *Assistant Literary Dir:* Matti Snell (Foreign Relations, Fiction and Non-fiction); *Managers:* Simo Mäenpää (Foreign Fiction and Non-fiction), Kaarina Joutsenniemi (How-to and Reference Books), Asko Rysa (Juveniles); *Educational Dir:* Heikki Kokkonen; *Rights & Permissions:* Satu Suomala
Subsidiary Company: Yliopistokirjakauppa Oy (qv under Major Booksellers)
Subjects: General Fiction, Non-fiction, Juveniles, Textbooks, Encyclopaedias, Audiovisual Materials, Micro Software, Educational Materials
Book Clubs: Suuri Suomalainen Kirjakerho Oy (jointly owned), Uudet Kirjat
Founded: 1878
ISBN Publisher's Prefix: 951-0

Yritystieto Oy — Foretagsdata AB*, PO Box 148, SF-00181 Helsinki (Located at: Kalevankatu 45 A 1, Helsinki) Tel: (90) 648292 Cable Add: Hibernia Telex: 121394 Tltx for Hibernia
Publisher: Börje Thilman
Subjects: Business, Directories, Reference
Founded: 1972
ISBN Publisher's Prefix: 951-9102

Literary Agents

A/S **Bookman**, Fiolstr 12, DK-1171 Copenhagen K, Denmark Tel: Copenhagen 145720 Cable Add: Bookman Copenhagen Fax: 451 120007 (Denmark)
This Danish-based company handles rights in Finland for foreign authors

Werner Söderström Osakeyhtiö (WSOY), PO Box 222, SF-00121 Helsinki (Located at: Bulevardi 12, Helsinki) Tel: (90) 61681 Cable Add: Wsoy Helsinki Telex: 122644 Wsoy Fax: (90) 6168369
Also Publisher (qv)

Book Clubs

Book of the Month Ltd Finland, PO Box 47, SF-00421 Helsinki
Owned by: Gummerus Publishers, Amer-yhtymä Oy Weilin ja Göös (qqv)
Subjects: Bestselling Novels, General Nonfiction

Hyvän Sanoman Kirjat, PO Box 75, SF-01301 Vantaa Tel: (90) 826377
Christian Book Club
Members: 7,500
Owned by: Ristin Voitto ry (qv)
Founded: 1969

Koko Kansan Kirjakerho Oy (KKK Book Clubs Ltd), Turunlinnantie 12A, SF-00930 Helsinki Tel: (90) 3432055
Owned by: Gummerus Publishers, Finland (qv); Bokförlaget Bra Böcker AB, Sweden (qv)
Founded: 1983

Lasten parhaat kirjat, PO Box 389, SF-00101 Helsinki Tel: (90) 43771
Children's Book Club
Owned by: Amer-yhtymä Oy Weilin ja Göös (qv), Oy Satusiivet – Sagovingar AB

Suuri Suomalainen Kirjakerho Oy, Köydenpunojankatu 2, SF-00180 Helsinki Tel: (90) 601466 Telex: 121394 Tltx Kirjakerho Fax: (90) 641157
The Great Finnish Book Club Ltd
Man Dir: Ari Ahola
Owned by: Werner Söderström Osakeyhtiö (WSOY), Otava Kustannusosakeyhtiö (qqv), Yhtyneet Kuvalehdet Oy. Tammi Kustannusosakeyhtiö (qv) is an associate partner

Bokklubben **Tre Böcker***, SF-02510 Oitbacka
Subjects: Classics, Current Affairs, Dictionaries, Encyclopaedias, Detective fiction, Periodicals

Uudet Kirjat, PO Box 222, SF-00121 Helsinki (Located at: Bulevardi 12, SF-00120 Helsinki) Tel: (90) 61681 Telex: 122644 Wsoy
The New Books
Members: 140,000
Contact: Kyösti Nuotio
Owned by: Werner Söderström Osakeyhtiö (WSOY), Tammi Kustannusosakeyhtiö (associate partner) (qqv)
Founded: 1980

Uusi Kirjakerho Oy, now Book of the Month Ltd Finland (qv)

Major Booksellers

Akateeminen Kirjakauppa, Keskuskatu 1, SF-00100 Helsinki Tel: (90) 12141 Cable Add: Akateeminen Telex: 125080 Akahe Fax: (90) 1214441
Chief Executive: Jorma Kaimio
Branches: Jyväskylä, Lappeenranta, Oulu, Tampere, Turku

Gummeruksen Kirjakauppa*, Kauppakatu 16, Asemaku, SF-40100 Jyväskylä Tel: (941) 10760 Telex: 28289 Kjgoy
Manager: Tellervo Salo

Kirja-Otava Oy, Tulliportinkatu 33, SF-70100 Kuopio Tel: (971) 116611
Overseas Marketing Manager: Heikki Pykäläinen
Branches: Iisalmi, Joensuu, Jyväskylä, Tampere
Owned by: Otava Kustannusosakeyhtiö (qv)

Lappeenrannan Kirjakauppa Oy*, Valtakatu 36, SF-53100 Lappeenranta Tel: (953) 15117

Pohjalainen Kirjakauppa Oy, Kirkkokatu 17, SF-90100 Oulu Tel: (981) 224133

Suomalainen Kirjakauppa Oy, Koivuvaarankuja 2, SF-01640 Vantaa
Manager: Antti Remes
Branches: Helsinki (six), Espoo, Hämeenlinna, Joensuu, Kouvola, Kuopio, Lahti, Mikkeli, Pori, Raahe, Tampere, Vaasa, Vantaa

Tampereen Kirjakauppa Oy*, Hämeenkatu 27, SF-33200 Tampere Tel: (931) 128380
Manager: Martti Helminen

Turun Kansallinen Kirjakauppa Oy, PO Box 135, SF-20101 Turku Tel: (921) 502444
Manager: Eero O Korte

Yliopistokirjakauppa Oy, Lönnrotinkatu 11, SF-00120 Helsinki Tel: (90) 649421 Telex: 125501 Yki
Manager: Marja Viita
Parent Company: Werner Söderström Osakeyhtiö (WSOY) (qv)

Major Libraries

Library of the **Central Statistical** Office of Finland, PO Box 504, SF-00101 Helsinki (Located at: Annankatu 44 – 2nd Floor, Helsinki) Telex: 1002111 Tilasto Fax: (90) 1734279
Chief Librarian: Heli Myllys
Publications include: Government Statistics (annual and monthly – mainly in Finnish and Swedish)

Eduskunnan Kirjasto, SF-00102 Helsinki Tel: (90) 4321 Telex: 121464 Ekirj
Library of Parliament
Chief Librarian: Eeva-Maija Tammekann
Publications include: Valtion virallisjulkaisut (Government publications in Finland annual bibliography); *Eduskunnan kirjaston julkaisuja* (Library of Parliament publications); *Bibliographia iuridica Fennica* (Legal Literature in Finland: annual bibliography)

Helsingin Kaupunginkirjasto — Valtakunnallinen yleisten kirjastojen keskuskirjasto*, Rikhardinkatu 3, SF-00130 Helsinki Tel: (90) 35801661 (central), 1662814 (information) Telex: 124794 Hkk
Helsinki City Library — National Central Library for Public Libraries
Chief Librarian: Prof Sven Hirn

Helsingin Yliopiston Kirjasto, Unioninkatu 36, PO Box 312, SF-00171 Helsinki Tel: (90) 1912740 Telex: 121538 Hyk
Helsinki University Library (National Library of Finland)
Librarian: Prof Esko Häkli
Branches: Slavonic Library, Neitsytpolku 1 B, PO Box 313, SF-00171 Helsinki Tel: (90) 661791; Science Library, Teollisuuskatu 23-25, SF-00510 Helsinki; Undergraduate Library, Leppäsuonkatu 7-9, SF-00100 Helsinki Tel: (90) 4027380
Publications include: Books from Finland (quarterly); *The Finnish National Bibliography* (also on microfiche); *Publications of the University Library at Helsinki*; *Opusculum* (quarterly); *Finuc-S* (Union catalogue of foreign serials in Finnish research libraries, microfiche edition)

Jyväskylän Yliopiston Kirjasto*, Seminaarinkatu 15, SF-0100 Jyväskylä Tel: (941) 291500 Telex: 28219
Jyväskylä University Library

Lääketieteellinen Keskuskirjasto*, Haartmanink 4, SF-00290 Helsinki Tel: (90) 418544 Telex: 121498 Lkk
Central Medical Library
Librarian: Ritva Sievänen-Allen

Oulun Yliopiston Kirjasto*, PO Box 186, SF-90101 Oulu (Located at: Kasarmintie 7, SF-90100 Oulu) Tel: (981) 223455 Telex: 32256 Oyk
Oulu University Library

Sibelius-Akatemian Kirjasto*, Töölönkatu 28, SF-00260 Helsinki Tel: (90) 408166
Sibelius Academy Library

Statistics Library, see under Library of the Central Statistical Office of Finland

Tampereen Yliopiston Kirjasto*, PO Box 617, SF-33100 Tampere (Located at: Tammelan Puistokatu 38, Tampere) Tel: (931) 156111 Telex: 22263 Tayk
Library of the University of Tampere

Teknillisen Korkeakoulun Kirjasto, Otaniementie 9, SF-02150 Espoo Tel: (90) 4512812 Telex: 121591 Fax: (90) 4512832
Helsinki University of Technology Library (National Library for Technology in Finland)
Librarian: Prof Elin Törnudd

Turun Yliopiston Kirjasto, SF-20500 Turku Telex: 62123 Tyk
Turku University Library
Librarian: H Eskelinen

University Libraries, see under town names

Valtionarkisto, PO Box 258, SF-00171 Helsinki
National Archives of Finland

Library Associations

Arkistoyhdistys ry*, Rauhankatu 17, SF-00170 Helsinki Tel: (90) 176911
Archival Association
Secretary-Treasurer: Lisa Salasmaa
Publications include: Arkisto (Archives) (in Finnish, summary in Swedish)

Kirjastonhoitajaliitto — Bibliotekarieförbundet ry, Rautatieläisenkatu 6, SF-00520 Helsinki Tel: (90) 15021
Finnish Librarians' Association
Executive Secretary: Jouko Lieko

Publication: Bulletin: Kirjastonhoitaja — Bibliotekarien

Kirjastonhoitajat ja informaatikot — Bibliotekarier och informatiker ry, Rautatieläisenkatu 6, SF-00520 Helsinki Tel: (90) 1502475
Association of Research and University Librarians
Executive Secretary: Marketta Honkanen
Publications: Issues newsletter to members

Kirjaston Hoitajien Liitd*, Akaua-Ialo, Rautatieläisenkatu 6, SF-00520 Helsinki
Central Federation of Librarians
Executive Secretary: Anna-Maija Hintikka
Publication: Kirjastolehti (Library Journal) — jointly with Suomen Kirjastoseura (qv)

Kirjastovirkailijat-Biblioteksanstallda ry*, c/o Helsinki University Library, PO Box 312, SF-00171 Helsinki (Located at: Unioninkatu 36, Helsinki) Tel: (90) 1912737
Association for Non-Professional Staff of Public and Research Libraries
Headquarters: Vipusentie 8, Helsinki
Tel: (90) 794276
Executive Secretary: Kirsti Tuominen
Publication: Volyymi (The Volume)

Suomen Kirjallisuuspalvelun Seura*, c/o Helsinki University of Technology Library, Otaniementie 9, SF-02150 Espoo
Finnish Association for Documentation
Publication: Suomen Erikoiskirjastojen Luettelo (Directory of Special Libraries in Finland)

Suomen Kirjastoseura, Museokatu 18 A 5, SF-00100 Helsinki Tel: (90) 492632
Finnish Library Association
Secretary-General: Tuula Haavisto
Publications include: Kirjastokalenteri (Library Calendar); *Kirjastolehti* (Library Journal) — jointly with Kirjastonhoitajien Keskusliitto-Bibliotekariernas Centralforbund ry (qv))

Suomen Tieteellinen Kirjastoseura, PO Box 217, SF-00171 Helsinki Tel: (90) 1912722
Finnish Research Library Association
Secretary: Annikki Hokynar
Publications: Signum; Guide to research libraries and information services in Finland

Tieteellisen Informoinnin Neuvosto, c/o Ministry of Education, PO Box 293, SF-00171 Helsinki Tel: (90) 134171 Telex: 122079 Mined
Finnish Council for Scientific Information and Research Libraries
Secretary-General: Hellevi Yrjölä

Tieteellisten Kirjastojen Virkailijat — Vetenskapliga Bibliotekens Tjänstemannaförening ry, now Kirjastonhoitajat ja informaatikot — Bibliotekarier och informatiker ry (qv)

Library Reference Books and Journals

Books

Guide to research libraries and information services in Finland, Suomen Tieteellinen Kirjastoseura, PO Box 217, SF-00171 Helsinki

Suomen Erikoiskirjastojen Luettelo (Directory of Special Libraries in Finland), Suomen Kirjallisuuspalvelun Seura, c/o Helsinki University of Technology Library, Otaniementie 9, SF-02150 Espoo

Journals

Bulletin: Kirjastonhoitaja — Bibliotekarien, Kirjastonhoitajaliitto — Bibliotekarieförbundet ry, Rautatieläisenkatu 6, SF-00520 Helsinki

Kirjastokalenteri (Library Calendar), Suomen Kirjastoseura, Museokatu 18 A 5, SF-001000 Helsinki

Kirjastolehti (Library Journal), Suomen Kirjastoseura, Museokatu 18 A 5, SF-00100 Helsinki
Jointly with Kirjastonhoitajien Keskusliitto-Bibliotekariernas Centralforbund ry (qv)

Signum, Suomen Tieteellinen Kirjastoseura, PO Box 217, SF-00171 Helsinki
Text in Finnish and Swedish; summaries in English

Volyymi (The Volume), Kirjastovirkailijat-Bibliotteksanstallda ry, c/o Helsinki University Library, Unioninkatu 36, PO Box 312, SF-00171 Helsinki

Literary Associations and Societies

Bibliofiilien Seura*, Lauttasaarentie 5 C 29, SF-00200 Helsinki
President: Onni M Turtiainen
Society of Bibliophiles

Finlands Svenska Författareförening, Runebergsgatan 32 C 27, SF-00100 Helsinki Tel: (90) 446266
Association of Swedish-language Authors in Finland
Secretary: Mette Jensen Sundholm

Kirjallisuudentutkijain Seura, Koskentie 11, SF-10470 Fiskars
The Literary Research Society
Secretary: Mervi Kantokorpi
Publication: Kirjallisuudentutkijain Seuran Vuosikirja (The Yearbook of the Literary Research Society)

Finnish P E N Center, PO Box 85, SF-00131, Helsinki
Secretary: Ann-Christine Salonen

Suomalainen Tiedeakatemia, Snellmaninkatu 9-11, SF-00170 Helsinki Tel: (90) 636800
Finnish Academy of Science and Letters
Secretary-General: Aarne Nyyssönen
Publications: Annales Academiae Scientiarum Fennicae; F F Communications; Documenta Historica; Vuosikirja (Yearbook)

Suomalaisen Kirjallisuuden Seura, PO Box 259, SF-00171 Helsinki (Located at: Hallituskatu 1, Helsinki) Tel: (90) 171229
Finnish Literature Society
Secretary-General/Director, Publications Dept: Urpo Vento; *Librarian:* Henni Ilomäki; *Director, Folklore Archive:* Pekka Laaksonen; *Director, Literature Archive:* Kaarina Sala; *Secretary-General, Finnish Literature Information Centre:* Marja-Leena Rautalin
Publications: Studia Fennica; Suomi; Tietolipas; Toimituksia; (irregular)

Suomen Arvostelijain Liitto, Bulevardi 3 B 19, SF-00120 Helsinki Tel: (90) 644463
Union of the Finnish Critics
Secretary: Tarja Lehto

Suomen Nuorisokirjailijat ry*, Aurorankatu 5 A 8, SF-00100 Helsinki
The Association of Finnish Writers for Children and Youth

Svenska Litteratursällskapet i Finland, Snellmaninkatu 9-11, SF-00170 Helsinki
Tel: (90) 636738
Swedish Literary Society in Finland
Publication: Skrifter (Writings)

Svenska Österbottens Litteraturförening, Auroravägen 10, SF-65610 Smedsby
Swedish Östrobotnian Literary Association in Finland
Secretary: Yvonne Hoffman
Publications: +21 (anthology of Östrobotnian prose); *Österbottnisk dikt — Runo Pohjanmaalla* (anthology of Swedish and Finnish poetry); *Inslag* (prose and poetry); *Horisont* (literary magazine)

Literary Periodicals

Horisont, Svenska österbottens Litteraturförening, Auroravägen 10, SF-65610 Smedsby
Literary magazine

Inslag, Svenska österbottens Litteraturförening, Auroravägen 10, SF-65610 Smedsby
Prose and poetry

Katsaus (Review), Kulttuurikeskus Kriittisen Korkeakoulun Kannatusyhdistys ry, Lehtikuusentie 6, SF-00270 Helsinki
Text mainly in Finnish, occasionally in Swedish

Parnasso, Hietalahdenranta 13, SF-00180 Helsinki

Skrifter (Writings), Svenska Litteratursällskapet i Finland, Snellmaninkatu 9-11, SF-00170 Helsinki

Virittäjä (The Kindler), Society for the Study of the Mother Tongue, Fabianink 33, SF-00170 Helsinki
Summaries in English, French, or German

Literary Prizes

Helsinki Prize*
Awarded annually by the City of Helsinki to an author (or artist) living in Helsinki. Enquiries to Helsingin Kaupungintalo, Pohjoisesplanadi 11-13, SF-00170 Helsinki

Tauno Karilas Prize*
For the writer of the year's best Finnish book for children. Awarded annually. Enquiries to Suomen Nuorisokirjailijat ry, Aurorankatu 5 A 8, SF-00100 Helsinki

Rudolf Koivu Prize*
For the best illustrated children's book. Organized by Suomen Nuorisokirjailijat ry and Grafia ry and awarded annually. Enquiries to Grafia ry, Jääkärinkatu 7, SF-00150 Helsinki

Arvid Lydecken Prize*
For the writer of the year's best Finnish book for children. Awarded annually. Enquiries to Suomen Nuorisokirjailijat ry, Aurorankatu 5 A 8, SF-00100 Helsinki

State Prizes for Literature*
Prizes for the best literary works. Awarded annually. Enquiries to State Committee for Literature, Ministry of Education, Rauhankatu 4, SF-00170 Helsinki

Anni Swan Medal
For the best children's and/or young adults' book of the previous three years. Awarded every three years. Enquiries to Suomen Nuortenkirjaneuvosto Kankurink 7 B 34, SF-00150 Helsinki

Tampere Prize*
For the best authors connected with the city of Tampere. Awarded annually. Enquiries to Tampere City Government, Tampere

Topelius Prize*
For the writer of the year's best Finnish textbook for children and young adults.

Organized by Suomen Nuorisokirjailijat ry and Grafia ry and awarded annually. Enquiries to Suomen Nuorisokirjailijat ry, Aurorankatu 5 A 8, SF-00100 Helsinki

France

General Information

Language: French. Basque in the Basque country of the southwest, Breton in Brittany, Catalan in Roussillon, Corsican in Corsica, Dutch along parts of border with Belgium, German in Alsace, Occitan in south; most people in these minority linguistic groups also speak French
Religion: Roman Catholic predominantly
Population: 53.7 million
Bank Hours: 0900-1600 Monday-Friday
Shop Hours: 0900-1200, 1400-1800 Tuesday-Saturday
Department Stores: 0930-1830 Tuesday-Saturday; open Monday in Paris
Currency: 100 centimes = 1 franc
Export/Import Information: Member of the European Economic Community. No tariff on books, except children's picture books from non-EEC. Import licences not required. Nominal exchange controls over a certain value. For imports over 50,000 francs, documents must be 'domiciliated' before any other transaction occurs. There is control of the book trade based on a number of legal and regulating provisions applying to the import of pirated publications, articles and writings that offend against morality, publications harmful to youth, writings forbidden by the Minister for the Interior; the customs official must submit articles subject to control for examination by the General Information Service of the Ministry of the Interior
Copyright: UCC, Berne, Buenos Aires, Florence (see International section)

Book Trade Organizations

A T C, see Syndicat Professionel Annuaire, Télématique et Communication

Agence francophone pour la Numérotation internationale du Livre (AFNIL-ISBN), Cercle de la Librairie, 35 rue Grégoire de Tours, F-75279 Paris cedex 06 Tel: (1) 43292101 ext 402 Telex: Lifran 270838 F
ISBN Administrator: Nathalie Bréaud

Association des Libraires spécialisés pour la Jeunesse, 48 rue Colbert, F-37000 Tours Tel: 47669590
President: Nathalie Beau; *Secretary:* Alain Fiévez

C E L F, see Centre d'Exportation du Livre Français

Centre d'Exportation du Livre Français, 9 rue de Toul, F-75012 Paris Tel: (1) 43473003 Telex: 215598 F
Dir: Hervé Gruenais

Cercle de la Librairie*, 35 rue Grégoire de Tours, F-75006 Paris cedex 06 Tel: (1) 43292101 Telex: Lifran 270838 F
Booksellers' Circle (Association of Book Trades and Industries)
The association covers all aspects of the book trade, producing publications and offering services through its subsidiary organizations: Editions Professionnelles du Livres, 30 rue Dauphine, F-75006 Paris; Editions du Cercle de la Librairie (qv); Promodis-Editions du Cercle de la Librairie; SBD (Société de banque de données bibliographiques du Cercle de la Librairie), 30 rue Dauphine, F-75006 Paris. The Electre bibliography database service is available through SBD
Secretary General: Marc Friedel
Publications include: La Bibliographie de la France – Biblio; Notices établies par le Dépôt Légal (Copyright Depositions); Les Livres Disponibles (French Books in Print); Le Répertoire International des Editeurs et Diffuseurs de Langue Française (International List of French Language Publishers and Distributors); Répertoire international des Librairies de Langue française (International List of French Language Bookshops); Répertoire des Livres au Format de Poche (List of Paperback (or Pocket Edition) Books); Études et Statistiques sur le Livre français (Statistics and Research on French Books); Catalogue général des ouvrages parus en langue française (General Catalogue of Works which have appeared in the French Language)

Chambre syndicale des Editeurs d'Annuaires et de Publications similaires, now incorporated in Syndicat Professionel Annuaire, Télématique et Communication (ATC) (qv)

F F I I G, see Fédération française de l'Imprimerie et des Industries Graphiques

Fédération française de l'Imprimerie et des Industries Graphiques, 115 blvd St-Germain, F-75006 Paris Tel: (1) 46342115
Secretary: Etienne Havet

Fédération française des Syndicats de Libraires*, 259 rue St-Honoré, F-75001 Paris Tel: (1) 42609793
The French Booksellers' Association
General Secretary: Louis Dubois
Publications: Lettre du Libraire; Libraires de France — L'Officiel de la Librairie

Office de Promotion de L'Edition Française, 35 rue Grégoire de Tours, F-75279 Paris cedex 06 Tel: (1) 43266166 Telex: Lifran 270838 F
French Publishing Promotion Bureau
Dir: Pierre-Dominique Parent; *General Secretary:* Marc Franconie
Miscellaneous: Function of the office is to organize the national stands of all French publishing companies at international book fairs as well as specific exhibitions throughout the world. It represents all French publishing houses

S E L E C, c/o L'Ecole des Loisirs, 11 rue de Sèvres, F-75006 Paris Tel: (1) 42229410
Association for the promotion and export of children's and teaching books
Dir: Jean Delas

S L A M, see Syndicat national de la Librarie Ancienne et Moderne

S L C F, see Sydicat des Libraires Classiques de France

S L L R, see Syndicat des Libraires de Littérature Religieuses

S L U T, see Syndicat des Libraires Universitaires et Techniques

Sacem (Société des Auteurs Compositeurs et Editeurs de Musique), 225 ave Charles-de-Gaulle, F-92521 Neuilly-sur-Seine cedex Tel: 47475650
Dir: Jean-Loup Tournier

Speld (Société de promotion à l'étranger du livre de droit, science économiques, sociales et humaines), 6 rue Victor-Cousin, F-75005 Paris Tel: (1) 46336910
General Secretary: Guy Hamonic

Standard Book Numbering Agency, see Agence francophone pour la Numérotation internationale du Livre

Syndicat des Conseils littéraires français*, c/o Agence Littéraire Michelle Lapautre, 6 rue Jean Carriès, F-75005 Paris Tel: (1) 47348241
Association of French Literary Agents
President: Michelle Lapautre

Syndicat des Libraires Classiques de France, 1 place Graslin, F-44000 Nantes Tel: 40897753
General Secretary: Jacques Vaudelin

Syndicat des Libraires de Littérature Religieuse, 35 rue Grégoire de Tours, F-75006 Paris
Secretary: Anne-Marie Martin

Syndicat des Libraires Universitaires et Techniques, 13 rue Basse-du-Rempart, F-86200 Loudun Tel: 49981996
Secretary: Michel Bisey

Syndicat national de la Librairie Ancienne et Moderne (SLAM), 4 rue Gît-le-Coeur, F-75006 Paris Tel: (1) 43294638/43540128
National Association of Antiquarian and Modern Booksellers
President: Jeanne Laffitte
Publication: Bulletin

Syndicat national de l'Edition*, 35 rue Grégoire de Tours, F-75006 Paris cedex 06 Tel: (1) 43292101 Telex: Lifran 270838 F
National Union of Publishers. Member of the Cercle de la Librairie (qv)
Secretary: Pierre Fredet

Syndicat national des Importateurs et Exportateurs de Livres, 35 rue Grégoire de Tours, F-75279 Paris cedex 06 Tel: (1) 43292101 ext 468
National Federation of Book Importers and Exporters
Secretary-General: M D Doumenc

Syndicat professionel Annuaire, Télématique et Communication (ATC)*, 35 rue Grégoire de Tours, F-75006 Paris Tel: (1) 43292101

U D E F Export, see Union des Editeurs Français en Sciences Humaines

U S L F, see Union Syndicale des Libraires de France

Union des Editeurs Français en Sciences Humaines, 35 rue Mazarine, F-75006 Paris Tel: (1) 43546746 Telex: 205434 F
Dir: François Chagneau
Union of French Social Science Publishers
Publications: Occasional bibliographies, available free on written request
Founded: 1963

Union Syndicale des Libraires de France, 40 rue Grégoire de Tours, F-75006 Paris Tel: (1) 46347420

Book Trade Reference Books and Journals

Books

Catalogue de l'Edition française (Catalogue of French Language Publishing), 22 rue de Condé, F-75006 Paris

Etudes et Statistiques sur le Livre français (Studies and Statistics on the French Book), Cercle de la Librairie, 35 rue Grégoire de Tours, F-75279 Paris cedex 06

Guide du Livre Ancien et du Livre d'Occasion (Antiquarian and second-hand book guide), Cercle de la Librairie, 35 rue Grégoire de Tours, F-75279 Paris cedex 06

Les Livres Disponibles (French Books in Print), Cercle de la Librairie, 35 rue Grégoire de Tours, F-75279 Paris cedex 06
Also available on microfiche and from database (Electre)

Répertoire des Livres au Format de Poche (Catalogue of Paperback Books), Cercle de la Librairie, 35 rue Grégoire de Tours, F-75279 Paris cedex 06

Le Répertoire international des Editeurs et Diffuseurs de Langue française (International List of French Language Publishers and Distributors), Cercle de la Librairie, 35 rue Grégoire de Tours, F-75279 Paris cedex 06

Répertoire international des Librairies de Langue française (International List of French Language Bookshops), Cercle de la Librairie, 117 blvd St-Germain, F-75279 Paris cedex 06

Journals

Art et Métiers du Livre (Art and Crafts of the Book), Cercle de la Librairie, 35 rue Grégoire de Tours, F-75279 Paris cedex 06

La Bibliographie de la France — Biblio (French National Bibliography), Cercle de la Librairie, 35 rue Grégoire de Tours, F-75279 Paris cedex 06

Book Promotion News (French edition), Unesco, 7 pl de Fontenoy, F-75700 Paris

Bulletin, Syndicat national de la Librairie Ancienne et Moderne, (SLAM), 4 rue Gît-le-Coeur, F-75006 Paris

Bulletin critique du Livre français (Critical Report on French Books), Association pour la Diffusion de la Pensée française, 21 bis rue la Perouse, F-75116 Paris
Text in English and Spanish

Bulletin du Livre (Book Report), 30 rue Dauphine, F-75006 Paris

Connaissance et Formation (Knowledge and Training), France Expansion, 336-340 rue St-Honoré, F-75001 Paris
Trade journal for the educational market

La Documentation française; 'Bibliographie sélective' des Publications officielles françaises (French Documentation, 'Selective Bibliography' of French Official Publications), Secrétariat général du Gouvernement, Paris

Documentation — technique, scientifique et commerciale (Documentation — Technical, Scientific and Commercial), Librairie Lavoisier, 11 rue Lavoisier, F-75384 Paris cedex 08
Text and summaries in English, French and German

Hebdo, see *Livres Hebdo*

Lettre du Libraire (The Bookseller's Letter), Fédération française des Syndicats de Libraires, 259 rue St-Honoré, F-75001 Paris

Libraires de France — l'Officiel de la Librairie (Official Gazette of the Book Trade), Fédération française des Syndicats de Libraires, 259 rue St-Honoré, F-75001 Paris

Liens, Editions du Cap, Palais de la Scala, Monte Carlo, Monaco

Livres (Books), Institut national de Recherches et de la Documentation pédagogique, 29 rue d'Ulm, F-75230 Paris

Livres de France, des Editions Professionnelles du Livre, 30 rue Dauphine, F-75006 Paris
Monthly guide to forthcoming books

Livres Hebdo, 30 rue Dauphine, F-75006 Paris
Weekly guide to new books

New French Books, Association pour la Diffusion de la Pensée française, 21 bis rue la Perouse, F-75116 Paris
English extracts from *Bulletin Critique du Livre français*

Prefaces, 30 rue Dauphine, F-75006 Paris
Presents new books in social and exact sciences, history and biology; published every two months

Publishers

Edition No **1**, 4 rue de Galliera, F-75116 Paris Tel: (1) 47230026 Telex: 630747
Man Dir: Philippe Scali; *Rights & Permissions:* Antoine Silly
Parent Company: Librairie Hachette (qv)
Subjects: Fiction, Children's, Sport
Founded: 1977
ISBN Publisher's Prefix: 2-86391

A B C Editions, 310 blvd de la Boissière, F-93100 Montreuil Tel: (1) 48548680
Man Dir: Jean-Michel Zunquin; *Sales:* Alain Hapiot
Associate Company: Breal (qv)
Subjects: Secondary School Textbooks
Bookshop: Etudiants Services, 34 rue Serpente, F-75006 Paris
Founded: 1982
ISBN Publisher's Prefix: 2-86769

A C L A, see EPLS — ACLA

A C R Edition Internationale+, 20 ter rue de Bezons, F-92400 Courbevoie/Paris Tel: (1) 47881492/43332001
Man Dir, Sales, Production, Publicity, Rights & Permissions: A Rafif; *Editorial:* Mrs M P Kerbrat
Subject: Art
1985: 7 titles *1986:* 6 titles *Founded:* 1983
ISBN Publisher's Prefix: 2-86770

Editions **A l'Ecart**+, 82 rue Dr Thomas, F-51100 Reims Tel: 26405444
Man Dir: William Thery
Subjects: Literary History, Writers' Letters, Women's Literature, Periodicals
1987: 45 titles *Founded:* 1979
ISBN Publisher's Prefix: 2-86924

A M P SA, 31 rue de l'Université, F-75007 Paris Tel: (1) 42220061 Telex: 201444 Amps
Man Dir, Rights & Permissions: Alexander Mosley; *Editorial, Production:* Charlotte Mosley; *Sales:* Jean Gadiot
Subjects: Science Fiction, Graphics
1985: 3 titles *Founded:* 1977
ISBN Publisher's Prefix: 2-86338

Academy Editions*, 5 rue d'Artois, F-75008 Paris
Publisher: Dr Andreas Papadakis
Orders to: Diffedit, 96 blvd du Montparnasse, F-75680 Paris cedex 14 Tel: (1) 43354700
Parent Company: Academy Editions, UK (qv)
Subjects: Art, Architecture
1985: 15 titles *Founded:* 1978

Editions **Acropole**+, 216 blvd St-Germain, F-75007 Paris Tel: (1) 45443823 Telex: 260717 Orem 309
Chairman: Franca Belfond; *General Manager, Editorial:* Gerard de Cortanze; *Rights & Permissions:* Véronique Garrigues
Parent Company: Editions Pierre Belfond (qv)
Subjects: General Fiction and Non-fiction, Belles Lettres
ISBN Publisher's Prefixes: 2-7144, 2-7357

Editions **Actes** Sud+, Passage du Mejan, F-13200 Arles Tel: 90498691
Man Dir: Françoise Nyssen; *Editorial:* Hubert Nyssen; *Production:* Bertrand Py; *Rights & Permissions:* Anne Wyvekens; *Publicity:* 18 rue de Savoie, F-75006 Paris
Orders to: PUF, 14 ave du Bois de l'Epine, F-91003 Evry cedex
Subjects: Literature, Essays, Biography, Theatre, Poetry
1985: 51 titles *Founded:* 1978
ISBN Publisher's Prefix: 2-86869

l'**Adret** éditions+, Route de Soueich, Encausse-les-Thermes, F-31160 Aspet
Man Dir: Jean Mandion
Subjects: Regional, History, General
1986: 14 titles *Founded:* 1983
ISBN Publisher's Prefix: 2-904458

Editions **Al Liamm**, 2 Venelle Poulbriquen, F-29200 Brest Tel: 98021084
Man Dir: Ronan Huon
Orders to: (non-French) above address; (French) Mlle Queille, 47 rue Notre-Dame, F-22200 Guingamp
Parent Company: Association Al Liamm (at above address)
Subjects: (in the Breton language) Educational, Fiction, Poetry, Plays
Founded: 1949
Miscellaneous: This is a non-commercial organization
ISBN Publisher's Prefix: 2-7368

Editions **Albatros**, see Copernic

Editions **Albin** Michel Bandes dessinées+, 22 rue Huyghens, F-75680 Paris cedex 14 Tel: (1) 43201220 Telex: 203379 Amichel f
Man Dir: Thierry Souccar; *Editorial Dirs:* Hervé Desinge, Marc Voline; *Public Relations:* Fabienne Chambaud; *Rights & Permissions:* Pierre Alain Szigeti, Claire Martineau
Subject: Adult comic strip books
Founded: 1982
ISBN Publisher's Prefix: 2-226

Editions **Allos**+, BP 127, F-77315 Marne la Vallée cedex 2 Tel: (01) 60175780 Telex: 693223 F Fax: (01) 60175052
Man Dir, Rights & Permissions: Louis Mercier; *Editorial:* Francis James; *Sales:* Verena Godefroy; *Production:* Hervé Sztang; *Publicity:* Geneviève Dalbard
Branch Offs: Nice, Monaco
Subjects: Economics, Management, Travel, Sports, Leisure
Bookshop: Allos International Bookstore (at above address)
1986: 23 titles *Founded:* 1986
ISBN Publisher's Prefix: 2-904631

Editions **Alpina**, 60 rue Mazarine, F-75006 Paris Tel: (1) 43298740 Telex: 204926 F
Man Dir: Alain Gründ
Associate Company: Librairie Gründ (qv)
Subjects: Guide Books
Founded: 1928
ISBN Publisher's Prefix: 2-7000

Alsatia SA, 29 rue Kléber, BP 9, F-68001, Colmar cedex Tel: 89411450
Man Dir: Eric de Valence; *Sales, Publicity, Advertising, Rights & Permissions:* Annie Christner
Subjects: Belles Lettres, Poetry, Biography, History, How-to, Religion, Low-priced Paperbacks, Medicine, Primary Textbooks, Educational Materials
Bookshops: Librairie Alsatia, 31 pl de la Cathédrale, F-67000 Strasbourg; Librairie Union, 4 pl de la Réunion, F-68100

Mulhouse; Librairie Union, 28 rue des Têtes, F-68000 Colmar; Librairie Union, 26 rue Charles de Gaulle, F-68130 Altkirch; Librairie Alsatia, 108 rue de la République, F-68500 Guebwiller
Founded: 1896
ISBN Publisher's Prefix: 2-7032

Editions d'**Amérique** et d'Orient, Adrien Maisonneuve, 11 rue St-Sulpice, F-75006 Paris Tel: (1) 43268635
Man Dir: Jean Maisonneuve
Subjects: Orientalia (History, Philosophy, Religion, Art, Social Science, Economics)
Founded: 1926
ISBN Publisher's Prefix: 2-7200

Editions de l'**Amitié**, G-T Rageot, 21 rue Cassette, F-75006 Paris Tel: (1) 45480731
Man Dir: Michel Foulon; *All other offices:* Mrs C Scob
Orders to: Librairie Hatier SA, 8 rue d'Assas, F-75006 Paris
Subjects: Juveniles, Documentary, Practical, Sport
1985: 23 titles *Founded:* 1941
Miscellaneous: Editions de l'Amitié is an imprint of Librairie Hatier (qv)
ISBN Publisher's Prefix: 2-7002

L'**Amitié par le Livre**, BP 2085, F-25051 Besançon cedex
Dir General: Henri Frossard
Subjects: Prose fiction, Poetry, Philosophy, Belles Lettres
Book Club: L'Amitié par le Livre
Founded: 1930
ISBN Publisher's Prefix: 2-7121

Editions **Amphora** SA+*, 14 rue de l'Odéon, F-75006 Paris Tel: (1) 43261087
Administration and Accounts: 51 blvd St-Michel, F-75005 Paris Tel: (1) 43253461
Man Dir: Roland Antoine; *Editorial, Publicity:* Françoise Antoine; *Sales, Production:* Michel Vaultier
Subjects: Sports and Leisure Activities
Founded: 1954
ISBN Publisher's Prefix: 2-85180

Edition **Anthèse**, 30 ave Jean Jaurès, F-94110 Arcueil Tel: (1) 46560667 Telex: 202382 F
Man Dir: Claude Draeger; *Sales:* Colette Gagey
Subjects: Art, Architecture, Biography, Illustrated books
Founded: 1983
ISBN Publisher's Prefix: 2-904420

Editions **Anthropos** Sàrl+, 96 blvd Auguste Blanqui, F-75013 Paris Tel: (1) 43378989
Man Dir: Maurice Guini; *Manager:* Pierre Guini
Orders to: Editions Anthropos, Librairie des Sciences de l'Homme, 15 rue Lacépède, F-75005 Paris Tel: (1) 45352247
Subjects: History, Philosophy, Social Sciences, Anthropology, Economy, Politics, Military
Bookshop: Editions Anthropos, Librairie des Sciences de l'Homme, 15 rue Lacépède, F-75005 Paris Tel: (1) 45352247
Founded: 1964
ISBN Publisher's Prefix: 2-7157

L'**Arbalète***, Marc Barbezat, 8 rue Paul-Bert, F-69150 Décines Tel: 78419313
Subjects: Literature, Art

Editions **Arcam**, 40 rue de Bretagne, F-75003 Paris Tel: (1) 42729312
Man Dir: Mrs Maïté Barrois; *Editorial, Sales, Production, Publicity:* Gérard Murail
Subjects: Poetry, Literature, Art
1985: 24 titles *1986:* 23 titles *Founded:* 1971
ISBN Publisher's Prefix: 2-86476

Publications **Aredit**+*, 357 blvd Gambetta, F-59200 Tourcoing Tel: 20267981 Telex: 130372 F
Editor: Emile Keirsbilk; *Editorial, Publicity:* Yves Catteloin
Subjects: Picture-Strip Books in instalments on War, Adventure, Westerns, Romance, Schoolgirl interests, Science Fiction

Arted (Editions d'Art)*, 6 ave du Coq, F-75009 Paris Tel: (1) 48747184
Publicity: Christian Hinard
Subjects: Fine Arts (especially Sculpture, Modern Painting)
Imprints: Editions d'Art, Septimus Editions
ISBN Publisher's Prefix: 2-85067

Editions **Arthaud** SA*, 20 rue Monsieur le Prince, F-75006 Paris Tel: (1) 43291220 Telex: Flamedi 205641 F
President: Charles-Henri Flammarion; *Dir:* R de Ayala; *Rights & Permissions:* as for Flammarion (qv)
Parent Company: Flammarion et Cie (qv)
Subjects: Literature, Arts, History, Travel Books, Sailing, Mountaineering, Sports
Founded: 1890
ISBN Publisher's Prefix: 2-7003

Arts et Métiers Graphiques*, 26 rue Racine, F-75006 Paris Tel: (1) 43291220 Telex: 205641
Man Dir: Adam Biro
Parent Company: Flammarion et Cie (qv)
Subject: Art
Founded: 1927
ISBN Publisher's Prefix: 2-7004

Compagnie Française des **Arts Graphiques** SA, 18 rue de l'Arcade, F-75008 Paris Tel: (1) 42654925
President: V P Victor-Michel
Subject: Art
Founded: 1939
ISBN Publisher's Prefix: 2-85001

L'**Asiathèque**+, 6 rue Christine, F-75006 Paris Tel: (1) 43253457
Dir: Isabelle Delloye; *Editorial Dir:* Christianne Thiollier
Subject: Asia
Bookshop: At above address
Founded: 1973

Editions **Assimil** SA, 13 rue Gay-Lussac, PO Box 25, F-94430 Chennevières sur Marne Tel: (1) 45768737 Telex: 232775 Assimil
Dir: J L Cherel; *Editorial:* J L Cherel; *Sales, Advertising:* Th. Vialatoux; *Production:* A Blanquet
Subjects: Self-instruction in Languages (textbooks, cassettes, records)
Bookshop: 11 rue des Pyramides, F-75001 Paris
Founded: 1929
ISBN Publisher's Prefix: 2-7005

L'**Astrolabe**, La Librairie du Voyageur, 46 rue de Provence, F-75009 Paris Tel: (1) 42854295
Man Dir: Jacques P Nobecourt; *Editorial:* Raymond M Chabaud; *Sales:* Odile Nobecourt
Orders to: ETAT, 20–22 rue de la Saussière, F-9200 Boulogne
Subjects: Travel, Geography, Cartography
1987: 8 titles *Founded:* 1974
ISBN Publisher's Prefix: 2-86230

Aubanel SA+*, 7 pl St-Pierre, F-84057 Avignon cedex Tel: 90824626
Man Dir: Laurent Theodore-Aubanel
Subjects: General Fiction, Psychology, Secondary Textbooks, Latin, Regional History, Tourist Guides, Provençal interest
Founded: 1744
ISBN Publisher's Prefix: 2-7006

Editions **Aubepine**, 56 bis rue du Louvre, F-75002 Paris Tel: (1) 42616579/42616589 Telex: 212859 F
Man Dir: Guy Humbert; *Editorial, Rights & Permissions:* F Thiery
Subsidiary Companies: Collection Feuille-Poche, Collection Kraft, Collection Nervure, Collection Petale, Collection Sepale (all at above address)
Subjects: Juveniles, Fiction, Literature, Art
1986: 4 titles *1987:* 4 titles *Founded:* 1981
ISBN Publisher's Prefix: 2-86675

Editions **Aubier-Montaigne** SA, 13 quai Conti, F-75006 Paris Tel: (1) 43265559
Man Dir: Mrs M Aubier-Gabail; *Sales Manager, Rights & Permissions:* Patrice Mentha
Parent Company: Flammarion et Cie (qv)
Subjects: Belles Lettres, Poetry, History, Philosophy, Reference, Religion, Psychology, University Textbooks, Pedagogy, Sociology, Languages
Founded: 1924

Etudes **Augustiniennes**, see under Etudes

Editions d'**Aujourd'hui** ('Les Introuvables'), F-83120 Plan de La Tour Tel: 94437079
Man Dir: Odette Charrière
Subjects: Literature, Music, Drama, Cinema, Poetry, Fiction, Human Sciences, Folklore, Esoteric
Founded: 1974
ISBN Publisher's Prefix: 2-7307

Les **Auteurs** Associés, member of CEA (qv)

Editions Philippe **Auzou**, see Editions Michel de Lile

Editions l'**Avant-Scène**, 16 rue des quatre Vents, F-75006 Paris
Man Dir: Jacques Leclére
Subjects: Theatre, Cinema, Opera, Ballet, Dance, Periodicals
Founded: 1949

Editions **B R G M**, see Bureau de Recherches Géologiques et Minières

Editions J-B **Baillière***, 10 rue Thénard, F-75005 Paris Tel: (1) 46342110 Telex: Livrcom 201326 F
Man Dir: M Roux Dessarps
Subjects: Medicine, Dentistry, Surgery, Agriculture and Horticulture, Technology and Industry
Founded: 1802
ISBN Publisher's Prefix: 2-7008

André **Balland**+, 33 rue St-André-des-Arts, F-75006 Paris Tel: (1) 43257440
Publisher: André Balland; *Sales:* Jean-Pierre Métais; *Rights & Permissions:* Sabine Balland
Subjects: Fiction, Documentaries, Humour, Biography
Founded: 1966
ISBN Publisher's Prefix: 2-7158

Baschet et Cie, Editeurs, an imprint of Editions de l'Illustration (qv)

Bayard-Presse SA, Editions du Centurion+*, 17 rue de Babylone, F-75007 Paris Tel: (1) 42229315 Telex: Edicent 201637
President: Bernard Porte; *Dir:* Nicolas Bardinet
Orders to: Sofedis, 29 rue St-Sulpice, F-75006 Paris
Associate Company: Editions du Centurion (qv)
Subjects: Juveniles, Religion, Literature
Founded: 1873
ISBN Publisher's Prefix: 2-7009

Editions **Beauchesne**, 72 rue des Sts-Pères, F-75007 Paris 6 Tel: (1) 45488028
Dir: Miss M Cadic

Subjects: Religion and Theology, Social and Political Science, Humanities, Reference, Current Affairs, Spirituality, The Church Today, Holy Scripture, Biography, History, Literature, Essays
Founded: 1851
ISBN Publisher's Prefix: 2-7010

Editions Pierre **Belfond**, 216 blvd St-Germain, F-75007 Paris Tel: (1) 45443823 Telex: 260717 F
Chairmen: Pierre Belfond, Franca Belfond; *Rights & Permissions:* Véronique Garrigues
Subsidiary Companies: Editions Acropole (qv); Sylvie Messinger Editrice (qv); Editions du Pré aux Clercs; Presses de la Renaissance (qv)
Subjects: General Fiction, Belles Lettres, Bibliophily, Poetry, Biography, History, Music, Art
Founded: 1963

Editions **Belin**+*, 8 rue Férou, F-75278 Paris cedex 06 Tel: (1) 46342142 Telex: Libelin 202978 F
Man Dir & Chairman: Max Brossollet; *Editorial:* Marie-Claude Brossollet; *Documentation:* Soraya Eghbal-Dupouey; *Marketing:* Henri Gibelin; *Rights & Permissions:* Françoise Fougeron
Subjects: Secondary & Primary Textbooks, Educational Material, Literary & Scientific Magazines, Juveniles, General Science
Founded: 1777
ISBN Publisher's Prefix: 2-7011

Société d'Edition 'Les **Belles Lettres**', 95 blvd Raspail, F-75006 Paris Tel: (1) 45487055/45445189 Telex: 641155 elita E 55
President, Man Dir: Pierre de Mijolla; *Commercial Dir, Editorial, Production:* Jean Malye
Subjects: Poetry, History, Philosophy, Literature, Religion, Scholarly, University Textbooks, Ancient History, Classical Philology
Bookshop: Librairie Guillaume Budé, 95 blvd Raspail, F-75006 Paris
1985: 40 titles *Founded:* 1919
Miscellaneous: This Société now incorporates the formerly independent firm Cathasia
ISBN Publisher's Prefix: 2-251

Berg International Editeurs+*, 129 blvd St-Michel, F-75005 Paris Tel: (1) 43267273 Cable Add: Bergedit Paris
Man Dir: Monique Gougaud
Subjects: Art, History, Anthropology, General, Reference, Religions
ISBN Publisher's Prefix: 2-900269

Berger-Levrault SA*, 229 blvd St-Germain, F-75007 Paris Tel: (1) 47055614 Telex: 270797 F
Above address is the Publishing Department of Company. The Trade Offices in Paris are at 5 rue Auguste-Comte
Man Dir: Jacques Lallemand; *Editorial:* Fréderic Toncieu; *Production:* Christine Frohly; *Rights & Permissions:* Cécile Gateff
Parent Company: Berger-Levrault Imprimerie, 18 rue des Glacis, F-54000 Nancy (Head Office and Printing Works)
Branch Off: 23 pl Broglie, F-67000 Strasbourg
Subjects: Co-editions in: Architecture (world and French regional), Ethnology, History, Juvenile, Human Sciences, Art, Third World and Administration, Paperbacks
Bookshop: Librairie Berger-Levrault, 23 pl Broglie, F-67000 Strasbourg
Founded: 1676
ISBN Publisher's Prefix: 2-7013

Société Internationale des Ecoles **Berlitz** SA*, 31 blvd des Italiens, F-75002 Paris Tel: (1) 47420509 Cable Add: Berliscool Paris
Subjects: Education, Textbooks
Founded: 1907
ISBN Publisher's Prefix: 2-7014

Editions **Bertrand-Lacoste**, 36 rue St-Germain-l'Auxerrois, F-75001 Paris Tel: (1) 42338200
Editorial: Jean Delogis; *Production:* Maud Auger; *Publicity:* Marie-Laurence Deslogis; *Rights & Permissions:* Jean-Pierre Arditty
Orders to: 36 rue St-Germain-l'Auxerrois
Subjects: Accountancy, Economics, Law, Computers
1987: 220 titles *Founded:* 1981
ISBN Publisher's Prefix: 2-7352

Bibliothèque nationale, 58 rue Richelieu, F-75084 Paris cedex 02 6 Tel: (1) 47038898
Man Dir: André Miquel
Subjects: History of books, Library Management, History, Literature
Bookshop: 71 rue Richelieu, F-75002 Paris
ISBN Publisher's Prefix: 2-7177

Société **Biblique** Française*, 30 ave Lénine, BP 31, F-93380 Pierrefitte Tel: (1) 48223896 Telex: ubssbf 610948 F
Man Dir: Jean-P Boyer; *Editorial:* Sylvia Barbu; *Sales, Production:* Dominique Donzelot
Subject: Bibles
ISBN Publisher's Prefix: 2-85300

Blondel La Rougery SA, 7 rue St-Lazare, F-75009 Paris Tel: (1) 48789554
Chairman: J Barbotte
Subjects: Maps and Charts, Commercial and Administrative
Founded: 1902
ISBN Publisher's Prefix: 2-7016

Editions Relais du **Bois** l'Abbé, member of CEA (qv)

Boosey & Hawkes Sagem, 7 rue Boutard, F-92200 Neuilly-sur-Seine Tel: (1) 47478992 Cable Add: Sonorous, Neuilly-sur-Seine
Subject: Music

Editions **Bordas**+, 17 rue Rémy-Dumoncel, BP 50, F-75661 Paris cedex 14 Tel: (1) 43201550 Telex: 260776 Fax: (1) 43228518
President, General Manager: Jean-Manuel Bourgois; *General Manager:* Jean Lissarrague; *Man Dirs:* Jacques Patry, Dominique Desmottes; *Editorial:* Philippe Fournier-Bourdier (Trade), Laurent Heilmann (Scientific/Technical), Alain Cardona (School); *Scientific Journals* (Gauthier-Villars): Anne-Marie Ruch; *Sales:* Jean-Michel Angenault (Bookshops), Alain Guilermin (Export), Catherine de Langhe (Mail Order); *Production:* Jean-Marc Gaultier; *Publicity:* Christine Gouffier (Trade), Dominique de Romanet (Scientific/Technical), Roland Castiglia (School); *Rights & Permissions:* Mireille Debenne (Trade/School), Maryvonne Vitry (Scientific/Technical)
Orders to: 11 rue Gossin, F-92543 Montrouge cedex Tel: (1) 46565266 Telex: 270004 Fax: (1) 47468121
Subsidiary Companies: Imprimerie Gauthier-Villars, 1 blvd Ney, F-75018 Paris; Editions MDI (qv); Société Bordas-Dunod Bruxelles SA (qv); SAVED, Immeuble Olf, 101 route de Villars, 1701 Fribourg, Switzerland
Imprints: Bordas, Dunod, Gauthier-Villars, Pédagogie Moderne, Garnier, Technique et Vulgarisation
Subjects: Educational (elementary to higher levels), General Non-fiction, Scientific, Technical, Reference (especially dictionaries and encyclopaedias)

Bookshops: Librairie Dunod, 30 rue Saint-Sulpice, F-75006 Paris and pl du Marechal de Lattre de Tassigny, F-75016 Paris; Librairie Beranger, 48 rue de la Cathédrale, B-4000 Liège, Belgium; Librairie des Sciences, Coudenberg 76, B-1000 Bruxelles, Belgium
1986: 260 titles *1987:* 339 titles *Founded:* 1946
ISBN Publisher's Prefixes: 2-04 (Bordas, Dunod, Gauthier-Villars), 2-7294 (Pédagogie Moderne), 2-7370 (Garnier), 2-7109 (Technique et Vulgarisation)

Pierre **Bordas et Fils***, BP 7, F-77630 Barbizon
Branch Off: 7 rue Princesse, F-75006 Paris Tel: (1) 43250451 Telex: 201167 F
Man Dir: Nicole Bordas; *Editorial, Rights & Permissions:* Pierre Bordas
Subjects: Leisure Pursuits, Tourism, Gastronomy, Guide Books, Photo Books, Juvenile, Educational, Literature, Poetry
Founded: 1978
ISBN Publisher's Prefix: 2-86311

Editions **Bornemann***, 15 rue de Tournon, F-75006 Paris Tel: (1) 43260588
Manager: Pierre C Lahaye
Subjects: Art, How-to, Sports, Nature, Pets
Founded: 1829
ISBN Publisher's Prefix: 2-85182

Société Nouvelle Editions N **Boubée**+, 9 rue de Savoie, F-75006 Paris Tel: (1) 46330030
Subjects: Biology, Archaeology, Entomology
Founded: 1941
ISBN Publisher's Prefix: 2-85004

Christian **Bourgois***, Editeur, 8 rue Garancière, F-75285 Paris Tel: (1) 46341280 Telex: Preci 204807 F
Editorial Dir: Ivan Nabokov
Subject: Literature, University and Political series
Miscellaneous: Member of the Presses de la Cité group (qv)
ISBN Publisher's Prefix: 2-267

Editions Colin **Bourrelier**, see Armand Colin

Bréal, 310 blvd de la Boissière, F-93100 Montreuil Tel: (1) 48548680
Man Dir: Jean-Michel Zunquin; *Sales:* Alain Hapiot
Associate Company: ABC Editions (qv)
Subjects: University Textbooks
Bookshop: Etudiants Services, 34 rue Serpente, F-75006 Paris
Founded: 1969
ISBN Publisher's Prefix: 2-85394

Emgleo **Breiz**, 40 rue de la République, F-29200 Brest Tel: 98448942
Man Dir, Rights & Permissions: M le Mercier; *Sales:* Miss Allain; *Production:* M le Gall; *Publicity:* M Keravel
Subjects: (in the Breton language) General
1986: 102 titles *Founded:* 1954
ISBN Publisher's Prefix: 2-900828

Editions **Brepols** SA*, 23 rue des Grands Augustins, F-75006 Paris Tel: (1) 46342188
Associate Company: Brepols Publishers IGP, Belgium (qv)
Subjects: Religion, General Literature
ISBN Publisher's Prefix: 2-85006

Michèle **Broutta** Oeuvres Graphiques Contemporaines*, 31 rue des Bergers, F-75015 Paris Tel: (1) 45779371
Man Dir: Michèle Broutta
Subjects: Art, Bibliophilism
Founded: 1970
ISBN Publisher's Prefix: 2-900332

Editions **Buchet/Chastel***, 18 rue de Condé, F-75006 Paris Tel: (1) 43260620/ 43269200 (Sales) Cable Add: Buchet/ Chastel Paris
Rights & Permissions: Guy Buchet; *Editorial Dir:* Edmond Buchet; *Sales Dir:* M Maron
Subjects: General Fiction, Belles Lettres, Biography, History, Philosophy, Music, Religion, Social Science, Medicine
Founded: 1930
ISBN Publisher's Prefix: 2-7020

Bureau de Recherches Géologiques et Minières (BRGM), BP 6009, F-45060 Orléans cedex (Located at: ave de Concyr, Orléans) Tel: 38643028 Telex: brgm a 780258 F
The above is the address of the Editorial and Sales offices. Administrative offices are at Tour Mirabeau 39-43, quai André Citroën, F-75739 Paris cedex 15
BRGM is the Office of Geological and Mineral Research in France (National Geological Department)
Subjects: Earth Sciences: texts connected with mineralogical and geological research (principally in France and Francophone areas of world); Specialized Maps and Charts
ISBN Publisher's Prefix: 2-7159

C D P — Julien Prélat SA*, 17 rue du Petit-Pont, F-75005 Paris Tel: (1) 46338761
Subjects: Odontology, Stomatology, (textbooks and special interest books), General Dentistry, Medicine, Alternative Medicine, Periodicals
Bookshop: Librairie Odonto Stomatologie (at above address)
Founded: 1946
ISBN Publisher's Prefix: 2-85039

C D U, see Centre de Documentation Universitaire

C E A (Collectif des Editeurs Associés), 129 rue de Crimée, F-75019 Paris Tel: (1) 42090764
Man Dir, Publicity: Serge Livrozet; *Editorial, Sales:* Bernard Chatron; *Production:* Pierre Ciron; *Rights & Permissions:* Jacques Darcanges
Orders to: Chiron-Diffusion, 40 rue de Seine, F-75006 Paris
Group Members: Les Auteurs Associés, Les Lettres Libres, both at 129 rue de Crimée, F-75019 Paris; les Editions Elise Gautier, BP 144, F-13675 Aubagne; les Editions Futur Antérieur, BP 26, F-91330 Yerres; Editions du Parhélion, 18 rue Abbé-Vallée, F-22000 St Brieuc Tel: 96335576; Editions Relais du Bois l'Abbé, 459 ave Pasteur, F-49000 Angers; La Septième Aurore, 50 rue Richer, F-75009 Paris Tel: (1) 42465986
Subjects: Fiction, Poetry, Human Sciences, History, Reportage
Bookshop: Les Lettres Libres, 129 rue de Crimée, F-75019 Paris
1985: 40 titles *Founded:* 1983 (CEA)
ISBN Publisher's Prefixes: 2-867751, 2-904140 (Auteurs Associés), 2-86768 (Parhélie)

C E L, see Coopérative de L'Enseignement Laïc

C E L S E (Compagnie d'Editions Libres, Sociales et Economiques SA)*, 68 rue Cardinet, F-75017 Paris Tel: (1) 42674123
Subjects: Road Transport (Vocational Training, Economics, Administration, Management, Social Science, Vocabulary of International Transport), Railway Systems world-wide
ISBN Publisher's Prefix: 2-85009

C E P Editions*, 20 ave Hoche, F-75008 Paris Tel: (1) 42250598 Telex: 680876 Upress
Also: rue d'Uzès, F-75002 Paris Tel: (1) 42961550
President: Christian Brégou
Subsidiary Companies: Librairie Larousse, Fernand Nathan (qqv)
Associate Company: Editions du Moniteur (qv)
Subjects: Architecture, Building, Town Planning, Technology

C E P A D, see Cepadues Editions SA

C E P L (Centre d'Etude et de Promotion de la Lecture)*, 2 rue du Roule, F-75001 Paris Tel: (1) 42338962
Subjects: Education, Popular Reference Works

C I L F, 103 rue de Lille, F-75007 Paris Tel: (1) 47050793
Secretary-General: Hubert Joly
Subjects: French Language, Dictionaries, Linguistics, Tropical Agriculture, Construction, Town Planning
Bookshop: 9bis rue des blancs-Manteaux, F-75004 Paris

C L D*, BP 203, 42 ave des Platanes, F-37172 Chambray-Les-Tours cedex Tel: 47282068
Man Dir, Editorial: Jean-Pierre Normand; *Sales and Rights & Permissions:* Jack Normand; *Production:* Pierre Proust; *Publicity:* Michel Jacquet
Subjects: Regional Interest, Folklore, History, Architecture, Religion, Tourism, Hunting
Founded: 1960

C L E T (Centre de Librairie et d'Editions Techniques)*, 27 blvd de Port-Royal, F-75013 Paris Tel: (1) 47071748
Man Dir: Gérard de Nussac; *Editorial, Sales:* Philippe Gualino
Subjects: Finance, Accountancy, Business Management, Law, Economics, Banking
Bookshop: Librairie CLET (at above address)
Founded: 1975
ISBN Publisher's Prefix: 2-85356

Editions du **C N R S** (Centre national de la recherche scientifique), 295 rue St Jacques, F-75005 Paris Tel: (1) 43265611 Telex: 260034
Man Dir: Gérard Lilamand; *Publicity & Advertising:* Liliane Bruneau, Presses du CNRS, 20–22 rue St Amand, F-75015 Paris Tel: (1) 45331600
Orders to: Presses du CNRS, 20–22 rue St Amand, F-75015 Paris
Parent Company: Centre national de la recherche scientifique
Associate Company: CNRS Laboratoire Intergeo (qv)
Bookshop: Librairie des Editions du CNRS (at above address)
Subjects: History, Geography, Literature, Linguistics, Music, Art, Philosophy, Reference, Religion, Psychology, Social Sciences, Education, Science & Technology, Law, Economics, Mathematics, Information Sciences, Electronics, Mechanics, Energy, Chemistry and Physics, Geology, Biology, Astronomy, Archaeology, Ecology, Ethnology
1986: 170 titles *Founded:* 1939
ISBN Publisher's Prefix: 2-222

C R E R, see Coopérative Régionale de l'Enseignement Religieux

Editions **Cahiers d'Art**, 14 rue du Dragon, F-75006 Paris Tel: (1) 45487673
Man Dir: Yves de Fontbrune
Subject: Art
Founded: 1926
ISBN Publisher's Prefix: 2-85117

Les **Cahiers Fiscaux** Européens Sàrl+, 51 ave Reine Victoria, F-06000 Nice Tel: 93810326
Man Dir: Simone Branca
Parent Company: Société d'Etudes Juridiques Internationales et Fiscales (JURIF) (at above address)
Subsidiary Companies: CFE Belgique, JURIF Belgique (both Belgium — qqv)
Subjects: European Taxation Systems and Fiscal Law (loose-leaf)
Founded: 1968

Editions **Calmann-Lévy** SA, 3 rue Auber, F-75009 Paris Tel: (1) 47423833 Cable Add: Caledit Telex: 290993 F
Man Dirs: Jean-Etienne Cohen-Séat, Alain Oulman; *Sales Dir:* Pascal Martin; *Rights & Permissions:* Alain Oulman, Thérèse Scaroni
Subjects: General Fiction, Science Fiction, History, Biography, Philosophy, Psychology, Social Sciences, Economics, Practical, Memoirs, Humour, Sport
Founded: 1836
ISBN Publisher's Prefix: 2-7021

Editions **Casteilla**, BP 301, F-78054 St Quentin en Yvelines Tel: 30454647 Telex: 699496 F
Commercial Manager: Robert Casalis; *Publicity:* Rinus Visser
Subjects: Textbooks for Technical, Commercial and Secondary Education; Economy, Legislation, Technical Drawing
Founded: 1950
Miscellaneous: Firm is a member of the Kluwer Group, Netherlands (qv)
ISBN Publisher's Prefix: 2-7135

Editions **Casterman**, 66 rue Bonaparte, F-75006 Paris Tel: (1) 43252005 Telex: 200001 F Edicast
President: Etienne Pollet; *Dirs:* A Boulanger, H Deswelle; *Sales Dir:* Daniel Robinshon; *Publicity, Advertising Dir:* Louis Gérard; *Rights & Permissions:* Pierre Servais, Ivan Noerdinger, Didier Platteau
Parent Company: Editions Casterman, Belgium (qv)
Branch Off: De Morinel 25-29, NL-8251 HT Dronten, Netherlands
Subjects: Children's Books and Albums, Picture Strips, Religion, Economics, Politics, Practical Living, Urban questions, Architecture, Painting, Photography, Cinema, Music, Poetry, Fiction, Records, Diaries
Founded: Tournai, 1780; Paris, 1857
ISBN Publisher's Prefix: 2-203

Cathasia, see Société d'Edition 'Les Belles Lettres'

Editions **Cedic**, 6, 10 blvd Jourdan, F-75014 Paris Tel: (1) 45650606
Man Dirs: Serge Pouts-Lajus, Michel Bussac; *Publicity, Advertising, Rights & Permissions:* Claire Touchard
Subjects: Educational Software
Founded: 1971
ISBN Publisher's Prefix: 2-7124

Centre d'Etude et de Promotion de la Lecture, see C E P L

Centre de Documentation Universitaire et Société d'Edition d'Enseignement Supérieur Réunis (CDU & SEDES)*, 88 blvd St-Germain, F-75005 Paris Tel: (1) 43252323 Telex: 206701 F
Manager: Pierre Constans
Subjects: History, Philosophy, Social Science, Economics, Education, School Books, Literature
Founded: 1933
ISBN Publisher's Prefix: 2-7181

Centre de Librairie et d'Editions Techniques, see CLET

Centre national de la recherche scientifique, see Editions du CNRS

Editions du **Centurion**, 17 rue de Babylone, F-75007 Paris Tel: (1) 42229315
Editorial: Bruno Chenu, Claude Naudin, Pierre Talec, Daniele Guilbert, Jacqueline Kergueno; *Publicity, Advertising:* Daniele Guilbert; *Rights & Permissions:* Magdeleine Leblanc, Sylvie Collombat
Orders to: Sofedis, 29 rue Saint Sulpice, F-75006 Paris
Associate Company: Bayard-Presse (qv)
Subjects: Religion, Juveniles, Social Sciences, General & Social Science, How-to, Education
Founded: 1870
ISBN Publisher's Prefix: 2-227

Cepadues Editions (CEPAD) SA+, 111 rue Nicolas Vauquelin, F-31100 Toulouse Tel: 61405736 Telex: message 520987 F
Man Dir: Jean Claude Joly
Subjects: Scientific, Advanced Technology, Data Processing, Teaching, Aviation, Space Research
Founded: 1969
ISBN Publisher's Prefix: 2-85428

Editions **Cercle d'Art** SA+, 90 rue du Bac, F-75007 Paris Tel: (1) 45442890 Telex: Publi Paris 250303 F
Man Dir: Philippe Monsel
Subject: Art
Founded: 1950
ISBN Publisher's Prefix: 2-7022

Editions du **Cercle de la Librairie***, 35 rue Grégoire de Tours, F-75279 Paris cedex 06 Tel: (1) 43292101 Telex: Lifran 270838 F
Man Dir: Pierre Frédet; *Editorial, Production:* Philippe Garnier; *Sales, Publicity:* Michel Bony
Parent Organization: Cercle de la Librairie (qv under Book Trade Organizations)
Subjects: Bibliographies, Library Science
Founded: 1983
ISBN Publisher's Prefix: 2-7654

Editions le **Cercle d'Or**, 12 rue du Moulin-La Chaume, F-85100 Les Sables d'Olonne Tel: 51957041
Man Dir: Jean-Luc Le Bihan; *Rights & Permissions:* Thierry Retureau
Subjects: Regional, Linguistics, History, Art, Maritime
Bookshop: 3 quai Rousseau-Mechin-La Chaume, F-85100 Les Sables d'Olonne
1987: 210 titles *Founded:* 1971
ISBN Publisher's Prefix: 2-7188

Editions du **Cerf**, 29 blvd La Tour Maubourg, F-75340 Paris cedex 07 Tel: (1) 45503407 Telex: 200684 Edicerf F
General Dir: P Moity; *Editorial Dirs:* D Barrios-Delgado, F D Boespflug, B Lauret, N J Sed; *Sales Dir, Publicity & Advertising:* J Mignon; *Rights & Permissions:* Mrs F de Chassey
Subjects: Bibles, Liturgy, Theology, History of Religion, Social Science, Children's, Paperbacks
Founded: 1929
ISBN Publisher's Prefix: 2-204

Chadwyck-Healey France, 3 rue de Marivaux, F-75002 Paris Tel: (01) 42868020
Man Dir: Donald Goldman
Associate Company: Chadwyck-Healey Ltd, UK (qv)
Subject: Bibliography
1985-86: 5 titles *Founded:* 1985
ISBN Publisher's Prefix: 2-86976

Editions du **Chalet**+, 77 rue de Vaugirard, F-75006 Paris Tel: (1) 45487860 Telex: 202036 F (Begedis SA)
Orders to: (France) Begedis (at above address); (Forcign) Arc-en-Ciel International, ZI Tournai Ouest, B-7713 Marquain, Belgium Telex: 57429 B
Associate Companies: Editions Desclée et Cie, Editions Gamma, Nouvelles Editions Mame, Editions Universitaires (qqv)
Subjects: Scripture, Spirituality, Theology, Roman Catholic Liturgy, Catechism, Oecumenicity
1987: 12 titles *Founded:* 1946
ISBN Publisher's Prefix: 2-7023

Editions **Champ Libre**, see Lebovici (Editions Gérard Lebovici/Champ Libre)

Librairie des **Champs-Elysées** SA, 79 blvd St-Germain, F-75006 Paris Tel: (1) 46348896
Man Dir: Michel Averlant
Imprints: Le Masque, Club des Masques
Subjects: Crime and Police
Founded: 1927
ISBN Publisher's Prefix: 2-7024

Chancerel Editions SA*, 4 rue Aumont Thièville, F-75017 Paris Tel: (1) 47660302 Telex: 640093 Chanced F
Chairman: Philippe Chancerel
Associate Company: Chancerel Publishers Ltd, UK (qv)
Subjects: Educational strip cartoons, Sport, Hobbies, Homecraft (in French and other European languages)
Founded: 1960
ISBN Publishers' Prefix: 2-85429

Editions **Charles-Lavauzelle** SA, BP 8, F-87350 Panazol Tel: 55312626
Man Dir: Jean Claude Mazaud; *Publishing Dir:* Guy Devatour; *Sales:* Vero Conrad; *Publicity:* Geneviève Giry; *Production:* Henri Chabrier
Branch Off: 20 rue de Léningrad, F-75008 Paris cedex Tel: (1) 43874230
Subjects: Military History, Law, Equestrian
Founded: 1831
ISBN Publisher's Prefix: 2-7025

Editions du **Chat** Perché, an imprint of Flammarion et Cie (qv)

Editions du **Chêne**+*, 79 blvd St-Germain, F-75288 Paris cedex 06 Tel: (1) 46348634 Telex: 206764 Chene Publ bti Paris
Man Dir, Editorial, Rights & Permissions: Hervé de La Martinière; *Editorial Assistant:* Joëlle De Vrin
Orders to: Groupe International Hachette (at above address)
Parent Company: Librairie Hachette (qv)
Subjects: Ancient, Graphic and Contemporary Art, Architecture, Photography, Cinema, Documentaries, Sport
Founded: 1939
ISBN Publisher's Prefix: 2-85108

Le **Cherche-Midi**, Éditeur+, 68 rue du Cherche-Midi, F-75006 Paris Tel: (1) 42227120
Man Dir: Jean Orizet
Subjects: Poetry, Humour
Founded: 1977

Editions du **Chiendent** Sàrl*, Marcevol Vinça F-66320 (Eastern Pyrenees) Tel: 68961130
Man Dir: Xavier d'Arthuys; *Production:* Dominique Poilpré
Orders to: Distique, 9 rue Edouard Jacques, F-75014 Paris
Subjects: General Literature, Eastern Pyrenees
Founded: 1977
ISBN Publisher's Prefix: 2-85999001

Editions **Chiron***, 40 rue de Seine, F-75006 Paris Tel: (1) 46331893 Telex: 200233 F
Chairman: Denys Ferrando-Dufort; *Promotion & Marketing:* Liliane Bertrand
Subjects: Education, Juveniles, Sports, Scientific, Technical, Leisure Pursuits, Health
Founded: 1906
ISBN Publisher's Prefix: 2-7027

Chotard et Associés, Editeurs, 68 rue Jean-Jacques Rousseau, F-75001 Paris Tel: (1) 42332519 Telex: 680126 Chotar
Man Dir: Yvon Chotard; *Sales Dir:* Jacques Chapellon; *Rights & Permissions:* Anne Chotard
Orders to: Sofedis, 29 rue St Sulpice, F-75006 Paris
Parent Company: Editions France Empire (qv)
Subjects: Psychology, Engineering, Technical, Economics, Marketing, Management, Social Science, University Textbooks
1985: 18 titles *1986:* 34 titles *Founded:* 1969
ISBN Publisher's Prefix: 2-7127

Clé International, 79 ave Denfert-Rochereau, F-75014 Paris Tel: (1) 43293399 Telex: 202846 F
Man Dir, Sales, Rights & Permissions: Michel Gudimard; *Editorial, Production:* Beatriz Job
Subjects: Books for the foreign market, especially teaching French as a foreign language
1985: 20 titles *1986:* 40 titles *Founded:* 1973

Club des Masques, an imprint of Librairie des Champs-Elysées SA (qv)

Armand **Colin**, Editeur, 103 blvd St-Michel, F-75005 Paris Tel: (1) 46341219 Telex: Acolin 201269 F
Man Dir: Jean-Max Leclerc; *Sales Dir:* Rémy Bourrelier; *Publicity & Advertising:* Yvette Dardenne; *Rights & Permissions:* Anne Nesteroff
Orders to: Armand Colin, BP 107, F-75663 Paris cedex 14
Subjects: History, Philosophy, Psychology, Pedagogy, Geography, General Literature, General & Social Science, University, Secondary & Primary Textbooks, Educational Materials
Founded: 1870
Miscellaneous: Incorporates publications of former separate Company, Editions Armand Colin Bourrelier
ISBN Publisher's Prefix: 2-200

Collectif des Editeurs Associés, see CEA

Compagnie d'Editions Libres, Sociales et Economiques, see CELSE

Compagnie Européenne de Fournitures et de Services Informatiques*, 9-13 rue Séguier, F-75006 Paris Tel: (1) 43256170 European Company for Data Processing Supplies and Services
Man Dir: Serge Ciregna
Subject: Bibliography of current titles of Data Processing Companies

Compagnie Européenne de Publication, see CEP Editions

Coopérative de l'Enseignement Laïc (CEL) SA*, BP 109, F-06322 Cannes La Bocca cedex (Located at: 189 ave Francis-Tonner, Cannes La Bocca) Tel: 93479611
Man Dir: Daniel le Blay; *Editorial:* Georges Delobbe
Subjects: Educational, Pedagogic, Periodicals
Book Club: Publications de l'Ecole Moderne Française (PEMF)
Bookshop: Librairie CEL, Alpha du Marais, 13 rue du Temple, Paris 4ème
Founded: 1928
ISBN Publisher's Prefix: 2-85311

Coopérative Régionale de l'Enseignement Religieux (CRER)*, 7 rue du Parvis St-Maurice, BP 2316, F-49023 Angers cedex Tel: 41884695
Man Dir: Michel Pourrias
Subject: Religion

Copernic*, 21 rue Cassette, F-75006 Paris Tel: (1) 42227700
Man Dir: Bertrand Sorlot; *Sales, Production, Rights & Permissions, Publicity:* Jeanne Bordeau
Associate Companies: Editions Albatross, Publeditec
Subjects: History, Documentary, Modern Thought, Philosophy/Religion, Myth and Fantasy
Founded: 1976
ISBN Publisher's Prefix: 2-85984

Librairie José **Corti**, 11 rue de Medicis, F-75006 Paris Tel: (1) 43266300
Man Dir, Editorial: Bertrand Fillaudeau; *Publicity, Rights & Permissions:* Isabelle Dibie
Subjects: Criticism, Essays
1985: 43 titles *Founded:* 1925
ISBN Publisher's Prefix: 2-7143

Courrier du Livre Sàrl*, 21 rue de Seine, F-75006 Paris Tel: (1) 43541891
Subjects: Philosophy, Religion, Ecology, Health and Nutrition, Organic Gardening, Yoga
ISBN Publisher's Prefix: 2-7029

Editeurs **Crépin-Leblond** et Cie SA*, 12 rue Duguay-Trouin, F-75006 Paris Tel: (1) 45489350
Man Dir: Mrs A R Henry; *Publicity:* Patrick Barraud
Subjects: Hunting, Shooting, Arms, Dogs, Horse-Riding, Nature
Founded: 1952
ISBN Publisher's Prefix: 2-7030

Editions **Cujas***, 4, 6 & 8 rue de la Maison Blanche, F-75013 Paris Tel: (1) 45889657/45888436
Man Dir: Pierre Joly; *Publicity Dir:* Jacqueline Joly
Subjects: Politics, Economics, Education, Social Sciences
Bookshops: Librairie J Joly, 19 rue Cujas, F-75005 Paris; Cujas Librairie, 2 rue de Rouen, F-92000 Nanterre
Founded: 1946
ISBN Publisher's Prefix: 2-254

D A F S A*, 125 rue Montmartre, F-75002 Paris Tel: (1) 42332123 Telex: 640472 Daf Doc
Chairman: Pierre Cabon; *Man Dir:* Yves Wilmors
Subjects: Economics, Finance, Industrial Information, On-line Information

Les Editions Roger **Dacosta***, 19 blvd Raspail, F-75007 Paris Tel: (1) 45441491
Man Dir: Jean Dacosta; *Sales Dir:* Carole Dacosta
Subjects: Medicine, Medical History, Dentistry
ISBN Publisher's Prefix: 2-85128

Jurisprudence Générale **Dalloz**, 11 rue Soufflot, F-75240 Paris cedex 05 Tel: (1) 43295080 Telex: 206446 F
Administration Office: 35 rue Tournefort, F-75240 Paris cedex 05 Tel: (1) 43310485
President, General Manager: Patrice Vergé; *Man Dir, Rights & Permissions:* G de Nussac; *Sales, Publicity Dir:* Ph Nani
Subjects: Law, Political Science, Reference, Business, Economics, Philosophy
Bookshop: Dalloz, 14 rue Soufflot, F-75240 Paris cedex 05
Founded: 1845
ISBN Publisher's Prefix: 2-247

Editions **Dangles** SA*, 18 rue Lavoisier, BP 36, F-45802 St Jean-de-Braye cedex Tel: (1) 438864180
Man Dir, Editorial, Production, Publicity, Rights & Permissions: J-Y Anstet Dangles; *Sales:* Alain Queant
Subjects: Naturopathy, Esotericism and Spirit Life, Psychology, Physical Culture, Ecology
1985: 20 titles *Founded:* 1926
ISBN Publisher's Prefix: 2-7033

Editions **Dardelet** SA*, 22 rue René-Thomas, F-38000 Grenoble Tel: 76961681
Subjects: Regional topics

Dargaud Editeur, 12 Blaise Pascal, BP 155, F-92201 Neuilly-sur-Seine Tel: (1) 47471133 Cable Add: Editfranc Neuilly Telex: 620631
Editorial: Patrick Verdin, Guy Vidal, Claude Moliterni
Publisher: Georges Dargaud; *Rights & Permissions:* Anthea Shackleton, Michel Lieuré, Michèle Vaudry
Subjects: Juveniles, Strip Cartoons, Magazines
ISBN Publisher's Prefix: 2-205

Editions du **Dauphin**, 43-45 rue de la Tombe-Issoire, F-75014 Paris Tel: (1) 43277900
Publishing Manager: Anne Tromelin
Subjects: General Fiction, Poetry, Social Science, How-to, Dictionaries, Documentaries, Regional Studies
Founded: 1936
ISBN Publisher's Prefix: 2-7163

De Boccard Edition-Diffusion, 11 rue de Médicis, F-75006 Paris Tel: (1) 43260037
Man Dir: Dominique Chaulet; *Manager:* Jean-Bernard Chaulet
Subjects: Archaeology, History, Ancient History, Religion, Orientalism, Belles Lettres, Art
ISBN Publisher's Prefix: 2-7018

Nouvelles Editions **Debresse***, 17 rue Duguay-Trouin, F-75006 Paris cedex 6 Tel: (1) 45481047
Man Dir: Pierre Moulin; *Editorial:* Paul Poncelet; *Sales:* Vincent Moulin; *Production, Publicity:* Josiane Muller
Subjects: General Fiction, Poetry, History, Social Science
Founded: 1933

La **Découverte**, 1 pl Paul-Painlevé, F-75005 Paris Tel: (1) 46334116
Man Dir: François Geze
Subjects: History, Philosophy, Sociology, Political Economy, Belles Lettres, Poetry, Low- & High-priced Paperbacks, Science Fiction
1985-86: 154 titles *Founded:* 1959
ISBN Publisher's Prefix: 2-7071

Delachaux Niestlé France SA*, 4 rue Laferrière, F-75009 Paris
Orders to: 6 rue du Mail, F-75002 Paris (for French publications); 79 route d'Oron, CH-1000 Lausanne 21, Switzerland (for international publications)
Parent Company: Editions Delachaux et Niestlé, Switzerland (qv)
Subjects: Medicine, Psychology, Education, Social & Natural History, Science, Juveniles, Technical, Mathematics, Architecture, Sports
Founded: 1860
ISBN Publisher's Prefix: 2-603

Librairie **Delagrave** Sàrl*, 15 rue Soufflot, F-75240 Paris cedex 05 Tel: (1) 43258866 Cable Add: Delagrave Paris Telex: Limodel 204252 F
Manager: Fabrice Delagrave; *Sales Dir:* J Roustan; *Publicity:* L Leiglon; *Rights & Permissions:* Y Blaise
Subjects: Juveniles, General Science, University, Technical, Secondary & Primary Textbooks, Educational Materials, Languages
Founded: 1865
ISBN Publisher's Prefix: 2-206

Editions J **Delmas** et Cie*, 4 rue de la Sorbonne, F-75005 Paris Tel: (1) 43256070
Man Dir, Sales, Rights & Permissions: Jacques Delmas; *Publicity:* Evelyne Alaux
Subjects: Accountancy, Law, Finance, Management, Insurance, Data Processing, Social and Factory Legislation, Dictionaries
Founded: 1947
ISBN Publisher's Prefix: 7034

Editions **Delville**, 40 rue du Four, F-75006 Paris Tel: (1) 42227290
Man Dir: Jean-Pierre Delville
Subjects: Cars, Music, Food, DIY, Practical, History
1986: 50 titles *Founded:* 1976
ISBN Publisher's Prefix: 2-85922

Editions **Denoël** Sàrl+*, 19 rue de l'Université, F-75007 Paris Tel: (1) 42615085 Cable Add: Edepege
Man Dir: Gérard Bourgadier; *Rights & Permissions:* Thérèse Mairesse
Parent Company: Editions Gallimard (qv)
Associate Company: Mercure de France (qv)
Subjects: General and Science Fiction, Art, Reference, Sports, Documents, History, Political Science, Economics, Philosophy, Psychology, Thrillers, De Luxe Editions
ISBN Publisher's Prefix: 2-207

Desclée de Brouwer SA+, 76 bis rue des Sts-Pères, F-75007 Paris Tel: (1) 45440763 Telex: 202098 F
Man Dir, Publicity: André Bourgeois; *Editorial:* Jacques Deschanel, Charles Ehlinger, Charles Chauvin; *Sales, Rights & Permissions:* Anna-Marie Coquier
Division: (Social Sciences) Epi (qv)
Subjects: Religion, Theology, Essays, History, Juveniles, Social Sciences, Psychiatry
1985: 45 titles *1986:* 46 titles *Founded:* 1875
ISBN Publisher's Prefix: 2-220

Editions **Desclée** et Cie*, 77 rue de Vaugirard, F-75006 Paris Tel: (1) 45487860 Telex: 202036 F (Begedis SA)
Orders to: (France) Begedis (at above address); (Foreign) Arc-en-Ciel International, ZI Tournai Ouest, B-7713 Marquain, Belgium Telex: 57429 B
Parent Company: Gedit SA, Belgium (qv)
Associate Companies: Desclée, Editeurs; Editions Gamma (qqv, both Belgium); Editions du Chalet; Editions Gamma; Nouvelles Editions Mame; Editions Universitaires (qqv)
Subjects: History, Philosophy, Religion, Social Science
Founded: 1872
ISBN Publisher's Prefix: 2-7189

Librairie **Desforges***, 29 quai des Grands-Augustins, F-75006 Paris Tel: (1) 43546054
Subjects: Technology, Building, Electro-technology, Esoteric, Naturopathy, Craft work, Technical Textbooks, Computers

Dessain et Tolra SA, 10 rue Cassette, F-75006 Paris Tel: (1) 42229020 Telex: elita 641155 ref d 32
Man Dir: Philippe Chopin; *General Manager:* Jean-Paul Biron; *Publicity:* Bernadette Py; *Rights & Permissions:* Catherine Marre
Subjects: Children's, Young Adults', Handicrafts, How-to, Art
Founded: 1964
ISBN Publisher's Prefix: 2-249

Editions **Desvigne**, 53-54 Quai Pierre Scize, F-69321 Lyon cedex 5 Tel: 782863
President: Anna Touzé
Branch Off: 30 rue des Favorits, F-75015 Paris Tel: 48285757
Subjects: Textbooks, Higher Grade

Education
Bookshop: Librairie Desvigne, 17 rue Republique, F-69002 Lyon Tel: 78270424
ISBN Publisher's Prefix: 2-7037

Les Editions des **Deux Coqs d'Or**, 28 rue de la Boétie, F-75008 Paris Tel: (1) 45621052 Cable Add: Deucodo Paris Telex: 650780 Fax: (1) 45619154
Man Dir: Jean-Michel Azzi; *Publishing and Art Dir:* François Martineau; *Publicity & Advertising:* Claude Gille; *Rights & Permissions:* Rictor Norton, Monique Lantelre
Parent Company: Western Publishing Co Inc, 1220 Mound Ave, Racine, WI 53404, USA
Subjects: Juveniles, Reference
Book Club: Education et Culture
Founded: 1948
ISBN Publisher's Prefix: 2-7192

La Maison du **Dictionnaire**, see Maison

Dictionnaires Le Robert, 107 ave Parmentier, F-75011 Paris Tel: (1) 43577313 Telex: Dicorob 240763 F
President, Man Dir: Charles-Albert de Waziers; *Publicity:* Denis A Fasse; *Technical Manager:* Jacques Pierre; *Export Manager:* Michel Terrier
Subject: Dictionaries
1987: 37 titles *Founded:* 1951
ISBN Publisher's Prefix: 2-85036

John **Didier Editions***, 1 rue des Chailles, F-92500 Rueil Malmaison Tel: (1) 47084545 Cable Add: Didier 92500 Rueil-Malmaison Telex: 25303 Service Didier 7084545
Man Dir, Editor: John Didier; *Assistant Editor:* Barbara Lyon; *Sales Dir:* C Perrin; *Advertising Dir:* R Mercier; *Publicity Dir:* L Meynier; *Rights & Permissions:* Miss R Camus
Subjects: Fiction, Non-fiction, General Trade, Belles Lettres, Biography, History, Theses, How-to, Art, Philosophy, Religion, Juveniles
Bookshop: The American Bookshop (at above address)
Founded: 1962

Société Nouvelle **Didier Erudition***, 6 rue de la Sorbonne, F-75005 Paris Tel: (1) 43544757
Man Dir, Editorial, Production: Mrs Jean Didier; *Sales, Rights & Permissions:* Mr Jean Didier
Subjects: Linguistics, Humanities, Periodicals
1985: 44 book titles/40 titles microform
Founded: 1978
ISBN Publisher's Prefix: 2-86460

Société **Didot-Bottin** SA, 28 rue du Dr-Finlay, F-75738 Paris cedex 15 Tel: (1) 45786166 Telex: 204286 F
Subjects: Encyclopaedias and Annuals concerning Business, Trades, International Commerce, Tourism, French Administration, Transport, Motor Cycling
Bookshop: At above address
Founded: 1796
ISBN Publisher's Prefix: 2-7039

Société de **Documentation** et d'Analyses Financières, see DAFSA

La **Documentation Française**+, 29-31 quai Voltaire, F-75340 Paris cedex 07 Tel: (1) 40157000 Telex: 204826 Docfran Paris
Publications of the General Secretary's Office of the French Government
Man Dir: Françoise Gallouedec-Genuys; *Sales, Promotion:* Alain-Marie Bassy, Xavier Turion; *Publicity:* Laura Esterházy; *Foreign Rights:* Celina Kader
Mail Order and Documentation requests to: 124 rue Henri Barbusse, F-93308 Aubervilliers cedex
Subjects: French and Foreign Politics, Economics, Regional Administration, Environment, Social Problems, Science and Technology, Law, the Arts, Audio visual; 40 Periodicals
Bookshops: 29-31 quai Voltaire, F-75007 Paris; 165 rue Garibaldi, F-69401 Lyon cedex 03; 124 rue Henri Barbusse, F-93308 Aubervilliers cedex
Founded: 1945
ISBN Publisher's Prefix: 2-11001

Doin Editeurs, 8 pl de l'Odéon, F-75006 Paris Tel: (1) 43253402 Telex: 203640
Man Dir: M Abadie
Subjects: Medicine, Life and Earth Sciences, Psychology, University Textbooks, Periodicals
Founded: 1874
ISBN Publisher's Prefix: 2-7040

Draeger Editeur, now incorporated in Edition Anthese (qv)

Droguet et Ardant*, 41 rue Henri Giffard, BP 1010, F-87004 Limoges 57 cedex Tel: 55374306 Telex: 580934
Man Dir: Robert Ardant; *Publicity Dir:* Suzanne Ardant
Subjects: Roman Catholic Devotional
ISBN Publisher's Prefix: 2-7041

Librairie Générale de **Droit et de Jurisprudence***, 20 rue Soufflot, F-75005 Paris Tel: (1) 43540719 Telex: 210023 Ogtel 741
Man Dirs: Françoise Marty, Jacqueline Hebert; *Sales Manager, Rights & Permissions:* Vincent Marty
Subjects: Social Science, Law, University Textbooks, Jurisprudence
Bookshop: LGDJ, 20 rue Soufflot, Paris
Founded: 1836
ISBN Publisher's Prefix: 2-275

Dunod, an imprint of Editions Bordas (qv)

Maison d'Editions J **Dupuis** Fils et Cie SA*, 8 rue Bellini, F-75782 Paris cedex 16 Tel: (1) 47277280
Associate Company: Editions Jean Dupuis SA, Belgium (qv)
Subjects: Juveniles, Literature

E A C, an imprint of Editions des Archives Contemporaines (qv)

E D H I S, see Histoire Sociale

E P A SA, 83 rue de Rennes, F-75006 Paris Tel: (1) 46090005 Telex: 202891 F
Man Dir, Editorial, Rights & Permissions: Arnauld de Fouchier; *Managing Editor:* Antoine Prunet; *Sales:* Thierry Quentin; *Production:* Gilles Blanchet; *Publicity, Mail Order, Press Agent:* Rosine Bertrand
Orders to: E P A, 18 rue d'Issy, F-92100 Boulogne Billancourt
Subjects: Aviation, Automobile, Railways, Military, Marine Interest, Photographic, Historical
Bookshops: 83 rue de Rennes, 75006 Paris; 92 rue Saint Lazare, 75009 Paris; 192 ave Victor Hugo, F-75116 Paris; 18 rue de l'Ancienne Préfecture, 69002 Lyon; 6 rue du Sec Arembault, 59800 Lille; 6A cours Lieutaud, F-13001 Marseille; 17 rue Croix Baragnon, F-31000 Toulouse
1985: 220 titles *Founded:* 1953
ISBN Publisher's Prefix: 2-85120

E P L S — A C L A+, 4 rue Chaptal, F-92300 Levallais Tel: (1) 47572500 Telex: 613814
Man Dir: Thierry Schimpff
Subject: Sport
Founded: 1980
ISBN Publisher's Prefix: 2-86519

Editions **E S F** (Editions Sociales Françaises), 17 rue Viète, F-75854 Paris cedex 17 Tel: (1) 47636876
President: Gérard Didier; *Man Dir:* Claude Chichet
Subsidiary Company: Entreprise Moderne d'Edition (qv)
Subjects: Education, Re-education, Pedagogy, Problems of Handicapped Children, Psychology, Social Problems and Legislation, Health and Nutrition
Founded: 1928
ISBN Publisher's Prefix: 2-7101

E T S F, see Editions Techniques et Scientifiques Françaises

Editions de l'**Ecole des Hautes Etudes en Sciences Sociales**, 131 blvd St-Michel, F-75005 Paris
Man Dir: Marie-Louise Dufour
Orders to: CID (at above address)
Subjects: Social and Human Sciences
1985: 16 titles *1986:* 20 titles
Founded: 1959
ISBN Publisher's Prefix: 2-7132

L'**Ecole**/L'Ecole des Loisirs Sàrl+*, 11 rue de Sèvres, F-75006 Paris Tel: (1) 42229410 Cable Add: Librecole Telex: Ecolois 205735 F
Man Dir: Jean Fabre; *Export Sales Manager, Rights & Permissions:* S Sevray; *Publicity and Advertising:* Jean Delas
Subjects: Juveniles, High-priced Paperbacks, University, Secondary & Primary Textbooks, Educational Materials
ISBN Publisher's Prefix: 2-211

Presses de l'**Ecole** Normale Supérieure, 45 rue d'Ulm, F-75230 Paris cedex 05 Tel: (1) 43291225
Man Dir: Georges Poitou; *Editorial:* Jean-Louis Fabiani; *Sales:* Jean-Claude Olivier; *Production:* Pascale Lehec
Subjects: University Textbooks
1987: 6 titles *Founded:* 1975
ISBN Publisher's Prefix: 2-7288

Edisud, La Calade, RN 7, F-13090 Aix-en-Provence Tel: 42216144 Telex: Bscedisud 30551 F
Man Dir, Sales, Production: Charles-Yves Chaudoreille; *Publicity, Rights & Permissions:* Anne-Marie Lapillonne
Subjects: Ecology, Energy, Agriculture, History, Geography, Music, Ethnology, Regional Interest (Provence), Mediterranean World, Berberian World, Mountaineering, General Topics
1985: 33 titles *1986:* 48 titles *Founded:* 1971
ISBN Publisher's Prefix: 2-85744

Société **Editart** Quatre Chemins, 3 pl St-Sulpice, F-75006 Paris Tel: (1) 43544073
Dir: François Heim
Subject: Art
Bookshop: Librairie des Quatre Chemins Editart (at above address)
Founded: 1924

Les **Editeurs Réunis***, 11 rue de la Montagne-Ste-Geneviève, F-75005 Paris Tel: (1) 43547446/43544381
Subjects: The company acts as sole agent for YMCA Press (qv) in publishing a very comprehensive list of Russian books in the original Russian
Founded: 1932

Edition No 1, see No 1

Les **Editions de Physique**, BP 112, F-91944 Les Ulis cedex (Located at: Zl de Courtaboeuf) Tel: (01) 69073688 Telex: Editphy 692321 F
Man Dir: J des Cloizeaux; *Publications Manager, Production:* Mrs J Berger; *Sales:* Brigitte Sors; *Publicity:* Susan Mackie;

Rights & Permissions: Corinne Coulamy
Subjects: Physics (research level); Periodicals
1985: 17 titles *1986:* 25 titles *Founded:* 1872
ISBN Publisher's Prefix: 2-86883

Editions des Archives Contemporaines, BP 398, F-75233 Paris cedex 05 Tel: (1) 43362404 Telex: 201307 Sienpub F
Man Dir: Françoise Chantrel-Riols
Orders to: 58 rue Lhomond, F-75005 Paris
Imprint: EAC
Subjects: History, Anthropology, Philosophy, Social and Political Sciences, Reprints
Founded: 1981
ISBN Publisher's Prefix: 2-903928

Editions Juridiques et Techniques, see Lamy SA

Editions Maritimes et d'Outre-Mer SA, 17 rue Jacob, F-75006 Paris Tel: (1) 46340310 Telex: 205652 JCLates
Managing Editor: Pierre Gutelle; *Rights & Permissions:* Emilie Levi
Parent Company: Editions Jean-Claude Lattès (qv)
Subjects: Sailing, Maritime History, Navigation, Reference
Founded: 1839
ISBN Publisher's Prefix: 2-7070

Editions Modernes Média*, 21 rue du Cardinal-Lemoine, F-75005 Paris Tel: (1) 43268384
Subjects: Philosophy, Linguistics, School Books, Pedagogy, Literature
ISBN Publisher's Prefix: 2-83398

Les **Editions Sociales-Messidor***, 146 rue du Faubourg-Poissonnière, F-75010 Paris Tel: (1) 42819103 Telex: 226 Sogedil
Man Dir: Claude Mazauric; *Publicity:* Katia Favard
Imprint: Messidor
Subjects: Philosophy, Social Science, Politics, Literature, Education, Languages, Economics, Marxism
Book Club: Livre Club Diderot
Bookshop: Librairie Racine, 24 rue Racine, F-75006 Paris
Founded: 1920
Miscellaneous: see also Editions La Farandole/Messidor
ISBN Publisher's Prefix: 2-209

Editions Sociales Françaises, see ESF

Editions Techniques SA*, 123 rue d'Alésia, F-75678 Paris cedex 14 Tel: (1) 45392291 Telex: Editec 270737 F
Also: 18 rue Séguier, F-75006 Paris Tel: (1) 43292130
Man Dir: Philippe Durieux; *Assistant Dir:* Robert Turberg; *Export Sales Dir:* J P Chamoux
Subjects: Law, Medicine, Engineering, University Textbooks, Encyclopaedias
Founded: 1907
ISBN Publisher's Prefix: 2-7110

Editions Techniques et Scientifiques Françaises*, 2-12 rue de Bellevue, F-75940 Paris cedex 19 Tel: (1) 42003305 Telex: PGV 230472 F
Man Dir: Jean-Pierre Ventillard; *Editorial, Sales, Production, Publicity:* Christian Cheneau
Subjects: Technical (radio, television, electronics, information science and associated themes), Periodicals

Ellipses — Edition Marketing Sàrl*, 32 rue Bargue, F-75015 Paris Tel: (1) 45677419
Man Dir: Jean-Pierre Benezet; *General Manager:* Marc Jammet
Subjects: Science, Technical, Medicine

1985: 53 titles *Founded:* 1973
ISBN Publisher's Prefix: 2-7298

Encyclopaedia Universalis France SA+*, 10 rue Vercingétorix, F-75014 Paris Tel: (1) 45394539/45396114 Cable Add: Encyversal Telex: 220064 F code 3121
President, Man Dir: Mr Baumberger; *Editorial:* Mr Bersani; *Production:* Mr Schweizer; *Marketing:* Mr Alba
Subjects: Encyclopaedias, Atlases
Founded: 1967
ISBN Publisher's Prefix: 2-85229

Coopérative de l'**Enseignement laïc**, see Coopérative

Editions **Entente**, 12 rue Honoré-Chevalier, F-75006 Paris Tel: (1) 42228070
Man Dir: Edouard Esmerian
Subjects: Ecology, Economics, Third World, Essays, Monographs on Minorities, Minority Languages, Documentary Accounts, International Relations, Historical Travel, Novels, Cookery
Bookshop: Librairie Entente (at above address)
1987: 77 titles *Founded:* 1975
ISBN Publisher's Prefix: 2-7266

Entreprise Moderne d'Edition, 17 rue Viète, F-75854 Paris cedex 17 Tel: (1) 49246876
President: Gérard Didier; *Man Dir:* Claude Chichet
Parent Company: Editions E S F (qv)
Subjects: Business Management, Personnel Training and Management, Data Processing, Technology, Periodicals
Founded: 1947
ISBN Publisher's Prefix: 2-7101

Les Editions de l'**Epargne**, 174 blvd St-Germain, F-75297 Paris cedex 06 Tel: (1) 45482452 Telex: 270833
Man Dir: Dominique Therond
Subjects: Investment, Economy and Finance, Family Budgets, aspects of Law
Founded: 1957
ISBN Publisher's Prefix: 2-85015

Epi+, 76 bis rue des Sts-Pères, F-75007 Paris Tel: (1) 45440763 Telex: 202098 F
Editorial: Charles Ehlinger; *Rights & Permissions:* Anna-Marie Coquier
Subjects: Social Sciences, Education, Group Therapy, Psychoanalysis, Yoga, Health Guides, Medical, Periodicals
Founded: 1947
Miscellaneous: the Social Sciences Division of Desclée de Brouwer SA (qv)
ISBN Publisher's Prefix: 2-220

Publications **Estoup et Roy** Sàrl*, 47 rue du Château-des-Rentiers, F-75013 Paris Tel: (1) 45838550
Subject: Education
ISBN Publisher's Prefix: 2-85016

Etudes Augustiniennes, 3 rue de l'Abbaye, F-75006 Paris Tel: (1) 43548025
Man Dir: Georges Folliet
Subjects: Theology and Church History (especially in relation to Saint Augustine)
1986: 8 titles *Founded:* 1954
ISBN Publisher's Prefix: 2-85121

L'**Expansion** Scientifique Française*, 15 rue St-Benoît, F-75278 Paris cedex 06 Tel: (1) 45484260
Man Dir: Pierre Bergeaud
Subject: Medicine
Bookshop: Librairie des Facultés de Médecine et de Pharmacie, 174 blvd St-Germain, F-75297 Paris cedex 06
Founded: 1925
ISBN Publisher's Prefix: 2-7046

Editions **Eyrolles**+, 61 blvd St-Germain, F-75240 Paris cedex 05 Tel: (1) 46342199 Telex: Eyrotp 203385 F

Man Dir: Claude Schoedler; *Editorial:* Jean Pierre Tissier
Subjects: Physical & Earth Sciences, Electricity, Mechanics, Data Processing, Electronics, Building and Architecture, Management, Hobbies
Bookshop: Librairie Eyrolles (at above address)
Founded: 1918
ISBN Publisher's Prefix: 2-212

Editions La **Farandole/Messidor***, 146 rue du Faubourg Poissonnière, F-75010 Paris Tel: (1) 42819103
Man Dir: Henri Siino; *Publicity:* Katia Favard
Subject: Juveniles
Founded: 1955
Miscellaneous: See also Les Editions Sociales/Messidor
ISBN Publisher's Prefix: 2-7047

Librairie Arthème **Fayard***, 75 rue des Sts-Pères, F-75006 Paris Tel: (1) 45443845 Telex: 240918 Trace F ext 645
Man Dir: Claude Durand; *Publicity:* Jean-Claude Berline; *Advertising Dir:* Claude Danis; *Rights & Permissions:* Marie-Annick Thabaud
Parent Company: Hachette (qv)
Subsidiary Company: Editions Le Sarment (qv)
Subjects: General Fiction, Biography, History, Religion, Music, Spirituality, Human and Social Science, Science, Technology, Atlases, Reference
Founded: 1854
ISBN Publisher's Prefix: 2-213

Des **Femmes**+, 6 rue de Mézières, F-75006 Paris Tel: (1) 42226074 Telex: Quotfem 202397 F
Proprietor, Man Dir: Antoinette Fourque; *General Manager:* Marie-Claude Grumbach
Subjects: General Fiction, Essays, Documents, History, Poetry, Biography, Art, Photography, Theatre, Juveniles, Low-priced Paperbacks, Cassettes
Bookshops: Librairie 'Des Femmes', 2 pl des Célestins, Lyon 2; Librairie 'Des Femmes', 35 rue Pavillon, F-13001 Marseille; Librairie 'Des Femmes', 74 rue de Seine, F-75006 Paris
Founded: 1974
ISBN Publisher's Prefix: 2-7210

Femme d'aujourd'hui, 34 rue Eugène-Flachat, F-75017 Paris Tel: (1) 42274949 Cable Add: Parisgraph Telex: 649964 Edifap

Editions du **Feu** Nouveau, 8 ave César-Caire, F-75008 Paris Tel: (1) 45224638
The above address is the Editorial Management office. Administration is at 5 rue Bayard, F-75393 Paris cedex 08 Tel: (1) 45625151 ext 4636
Man Dir: Odile Gaudin
Subjects: Religion, Literature
Founded: 1946
ISBN Publisher's Prefix: 2-85017

Editions **Filipacchi***, 63 Champs Elysées, F-75008 Paris Tel: (1) 42567272 Cable Add: JazMag Telex: UEM 290294
Manager and Editorial, Publicity, Rights & Permissions: Chantal Charpentier
Subjects: Modern Art, Photo-books and Photo-journalism, Sex, Jazz, Monographs of Star Personalities
Founded: 1970
ISBN Publisher's Prefix: 2-85018

First, Inc, 11 villa Thoréton, F-75015 Paris Tel: (1) 40609049
Man Dir: Thierry Souccar; *Editorial Dirs:* Fershid Bharucha, Robin Lent; *Public Relations:* Frédérique Ludier
Subjects: Business, Non-fiction

Founded: 1985
ISBN Publisher's Prefix: 2-87691

Librairie **Fischbacher**, International Art Book Distribution (import-export)*, 33 rue de Seine, F-75006 Paris Tel: (1) 43268487
Man Dir, Production, Publicity, Rights and Permissions: H Earle-Fischbacher; *Editorial:* M C Galand; *Sales:* P Diani
Parent Company: Librairie Fischbacher SA
Subsidiary Companies: International Art Books Distribution; Office de Documentation Bibliographique et de Diffusion
Subjects: Art, Primitive Art, Architecture, Belles Lettres, Musicology, Philosophy, History, Education, Religion, Juveniles
Bookshop: At above address
Founded: 1850
ISBN Publisher's Prefix: 2-7179

Flammarion et Cie*, 26 rue Racine, F-75278 Paris cedex 06 Tel: (1) 43291220 Cable Add: Flamedit Telex: flamedi 205641 F
Chairman: Charles-Henri Flammarion; *Man Dir:* Pascal Forbin; *Sales Manager:* Alain Flammarion; *Publicity, Advertising:* Catherine Bachelez; *Rights & Permissions:* Anne-Solange Noble
Orders to: Flammarion, 106-110 rue du Petit Leroy, BP 403, F-94152 Rungis cedex
Subsidiary Companies: Editions Arthaud SA, Editions Aubier-Montaigne SA, La Maison Rustique SA, J'ai Lu, Arts et Métiers Graphiques (qqv)
Imprints: Père Castor, Editions du Chat Perché
Subjects: General Fiction, Belles Lettres, Poetry, History, How-to, Photography, Art, Philosophy, Reference, Juveniles, Low- & High-priced Paperbacks, Economics, General & Social Science, University
Bookshops: See under Major Booksellers
Founded: 1875
ISBN Publisher's Prefix: 2-08

Editions **Fleurus** SA+*, 11 rue Duguay-Trouin, F-75006 Paris Tel: (1) 45443834 Telex: 201650 F
Man Dir: Jean Li Sen Lié; *Editorial:* Ms M C Charbonnier, René Berthier; *Sales Dir:* Guy Martignon; *Production:* Yves Jolly, Alberic de Palmaert; *Publicity:* Marie Fr Daru; *Rights & Permissions:* Roselyne des Gayets
Subjects: Religion, Psycho-Sociological, Illustrated Children's Albums, Picture strip stories, Technical Manuals
Founded: 1944
ISBN Publisher's Prefix: 2-215

Editions **Fleuve** Noir+*, 6 rue Garancière, F-75278 Paris cedex 06 Tel: (1) 46342161 Telex: Flenoir 204870 F
Man Dir: Patrick Siry; *Sales Dir:* Jean Marc de Caro; *Publicity Dir:* Jacques Dartus; *Rights & Permissions:* Jean-Marie Carpentier
Subjects: General Fiction (especially Crime and Science Fiction), Low-priced Paperbacks
Founded: 1949
Miscellaneous: Firm is a member of the Presses de La Cité group (qv)
ISBN Publisher's Prefix: 2-265

Les Editions **Foucher***, 128 rue de Rivoli, F-75038 Paris Tel: (1) 42363890
Founder-President: Ms Burgod-Foucher; *General Manager:* Bernard Foulon; *Publishing Manager:* A Tavard
Subjects: Education, Medicine, Economics, General & Social Science
Founded: 1934
ISBN Publisher's Prefix: 2-216

France-Caraïbes, an imprint of Editions Louis Soulanges 'Le Livre Ouvert' (qv)

Editions **France Empire***, 68 rue Jean-Jacques Rousseau, F-75001 Paris Tel: (1) 42332519 Telex: 680126
President, Man Dir: Yvon Chotard; *Sales Dir:* Jacques Chapellon; *Production:* Pierre Pousset; *Publicity:* Christine Colinet; *Rights & Permissions:* Anne Chotard, Dominique de Saint-Ours
Orders to: Stendhal Diffusion, 74 rue Stendhal, F-75020 Paris
Subsidiary Company: Chotard et Associés, Editeurs (qv)
Branch Off: 13 rue des Lombards, F-27000 Evreux
Subjects: Biography, History, Documentary, Religion, Reference, Novels, Aviation, Marine Interest, How-to, General Literature, Cinema, Theatre
Founded: 1945

France-Loisirs*, 123 blvd de Grenelle, F-75015 Paris Tel: (1) 45673565
Publicity: A Cinar
Subjects: Juveniles, Literature, Art

Les Editions **Franciscaines** SA*, 9 rue Marie-Rose, F-75014 Paris Tel: (1) 45407351
Imprint: Editions Franciscaines La Cordelle
Subjects: Saint Francis and the Franciscans (history and spirituality)
ISBN Publisher's Prefix: 2-85020

Henri **Frossard**, see L'Amitié par le Livre

J **Gabalda** et Cie (Librairie Lecoffre) SA*, 90 rue Bonaparte, F-75006 Paris Tel: (1) 43265355
Proprietor: J Gabalda
Subject: Religion, especially Biblical Studies and Archaeology
Founded: 1845
ISBN Publisher's Prefix: 2-85021

Editions **Galilée***, 9 rue Linné, F-75005 Paris Tel: (1) 43312384
Man Dir: Michel Delorme
Orders to: Sodis, BP 142, F-77403 Lagny sur Marne Tel: (1) 45311606/45335447
Subjects: History, Philosophy, Art, Social Science, Belles Lettres, Poetry, University Textbooks
Founded: 1971
ISBN Publisher's Prefix: 2-7186

Editions **Gallimard***, 5 rue Sébastien-Bottin, F-75007 Paris Tel: (1) 45443919 Cable Add: Enerefene Paris 044 Telex: 204121 Gallim
Man Dir: Claude Gallimard; *Editorial:* François Erval, Pierre Marchand; *Rights & Permissions:* Ania Chevallier, Hedwige Pasquet
Subsidiary Companies: Editions Denoël (qv); Mercure de France (qv)
Subjects: General Fiction, Belles Lettres, Poetry, Biography, History, Music, Art, Philosophy, Juveniles
Bookshop: Librairie Gallimard, 15 blvd Raspail, F-75007 Paris
Founded: 1911
ISBN Publisher's Prefix: 2-07

Editions **Gamma***, 77 rue de Vaugirard, F-75006 Paris Tel: (1) 45487860 Telex: 202036 (Begedis SA)
Orders to: (France) Begedis (at above address); (Foreign) Arc-en-Ciel International, 2 I Tournai Ouest, B-7713 Marquain, Belgium Telex: 57429 B
Parent Company: Gedit SA Tournai, Belgium (qv)
Associate Companies: Editions Desclée et Cie, Editions du Chalet, Nouvelles Editions Mame, Editions Universitaires (qqv); Desclée Editeurs, Editions Gamma (qqv, both Belgium)
Subjects: Social Science, Juveniles, School Books

FRANCE 105

Founded: 1963
ISBN Publisher's Prefix: 2-7130

Imprimerie Librairie **Gardet***, 16 rue du Pâquier, F-74000 Annecy Tel: 50454437 Telex: 310543 Gardet
Man Dirs: Clément Gardet, Jean-Baptiste Meylan
Subjects: Arts, Crafts, Hobbies, Educational
Founded: 1836
ISBN Publisher's Prefix: 2-7049

Editions **Garnier***, 8 rue Garancière, F-75285 Paris cedex 06 Tel: (1) 46341280 Telex: 204807 preci f
Subjects: Classics, Practical

Imprimerie **Gauthier-Villars***, 70 rue de Saint-Mandé, F-93100 Montreuil
An imprint of Editions Bordas (qv)

Les Editions **Gautier-Languereau** SA+, 18 rue Jacob, F-75278 Paris cedex 06 Tel: (1) 43250751 Telex: Gaulang 204020 F
Man Dir & Sales: Bernard Moreau
Subjects: General Fiction, How-to, Juveniles
Founded: 1885
ISBN Publisher's Prefix: 2-217

Editions M Th **Genin**, see LITEC

Librairie Orientaliste Paul **Geuthner** SA, 12 rue Vavin, F-75006 Paris Tel: (1) 46347130 Cable Add: Liborient Paris
Man Dir: Marc F Seidl-Geuthner
Subjects: Archaeology, Assyriology, Islam, Near & Far East, General Orientalia, Linguistics, Numismatics, Religion
Founded: 1901
ISBN Publisher's Prefix: 2-7053

Gibert Jeune SNC*, 27 quai St-Michel, F-75005 Paris Tel: (1) 43545732
Subject: Education
ISBN Publisher's Prefix: 2-900002

Editions De **Gigord***, 15 rue Cassette, F-75006 Paris Tel: (1) 45485521
Subjects: General Fiction, Belles Lettres, Education, Religion, University & Secondary Textbooks
Founded: 1830
ISBN Publisher's Prefix: 2-7054

Editions **J Glenat** SA+, BP 177, F-38008 Grenoble cedex (Located at: 6 rue Lieutenant Chanaron) Tel: 76873758 Telex: 320030 F
President, Joint Man Dir: Jacques Glénat; *Joint Man Dir:* Mr Vrac; *Editorial:* Stan Barets; *Sales:* Christine Glenat (Export); *Production:* Francis Bernard; *Publicity:* Regie 20, 130 rue de Rivoli, F-75001 Paris Tel: (1) 42961471; *Rights & Permissions:* Patricia Berlioz
Orders to: 17 rue Brézin, F-75014 Paris; (Export) BP 177, F-38008 Grenoble cedex
Branch Off: 17 rue Brézin, F-75014 Paris
Subsidiary Companies: Glenat-Concept, BP 177, F-38008 Grenoble cedex; Glénat-Images, BP 177, F-38008 Grenoble cedex; Glenat-Benelux, 10 ave L Gribaumont, B-1150 Brussels, Belgium; Glenat-Italia, via Ariberto 24, I-20123 Milan, Italy
Subjects: Humour, Adventure, Thrillers, Science Fiction, Erotica, Children's (all in strip cartoon form); Travel, Sport, Cookery, Tourism
Bookshop: Glenat-Librairie, 16 rue Lafayette, F-75009 Paris Tel: (1) 42469881
1987: 200 titles *Founded:* 1974
ISBN Publisher's Prefix: 2-27234

Jacques **Grancher**, Editeur*, 98 rue de Vaugirard, F-75006 Paris Tel: (1) 42226480 Cable Add: Sce de Vente/Librairies 5480317, 14 rue Littre, F-75006 Paris
Man Dir: Jacques Grancher

Subjects: Military Series (Uniforms, Arms), Memoirs (Art World), Health, Diet, Cookery Series, General Adult Non-fiction
Founded: 1952
ISBN Publisher's Prefix: 2-7146

Société des Editions **Grasset et Fasquelle**, 61 rue des Sts-Pères, F-75006 Paris Tel: (1) 45443814
Chairman: Jean-Claude Fasquelle; *Man Dirs:* Yves Berger, Bernard-Henri Lévy, Jean-Paul Enthoven; *Sales:* Jean-Pierre Pigeald; *Publicity and Advertising:* Monique Mayaud; *Production:* Jean-Pierre Decaens; *Administrative Dir:* Jean-Pierre Duflot; *Rights & Permissions:* Marie-Hélène d'Ovidio; *Public Relations:* Claude Dalla-Torre, Claudine Lemaire
Subjects: General Fiction and Non-fiction, Belles Lettres, Philosophy, Juveniles
Founded: 1907
ISBN Publisher's Prefix: 2-246

Jean **Grassin** Editeur, 50 rue Rodier, F-75009 Paris
Man Dir: Jean Grassin
Orders to: BP 75, F-56340 Carnac Plage
Subjects: Literature, Poetry, History, Bibliophily
Book Club: Poètes Présents
Bookshop: Pl de Port-en-Dro, F-56340 Carnac Plage Tel: 97529363
1985: 15 titles *Founded:* 1957
ISBN Publisher's Prefix: 2-7055

Groupe Expansion, 67 ave de Wagram, BP 570, F-75017 Paris cedex 17 Tel: (1) 47631211 Telex: 650242 manxpan
President and Man Dir: Jean-Louis Servan-Schreiber; *General Manager:* Hubert Zieseniss; *Publicity, International Advertising Dirs:* Jacques Louvet, Bruno Collentier (International)
Subjects: Economics, Politics, Social Sciences, Education, Literature, Law, Architecture, Scientific and Technical

Librairie **Gründ**, 60 rue Mazarine, F-75006 Paris 6 Tel: (1) 43298740 Cable Add: Gründ Paris Telex: 204926 F
President: Michel Gründ; *Man Dir:* Alain Gründ; *Rights & Permissions, Advertising:* P A Touttain
Associate Companies: Editions Alpina (qv); Editions Guy Le Prat
Subjects: Nature, Animals, Travel, Arts, How-to, Juvenile, Art Reference, Gift Books
Founded: 1880
ISBN Publisher's Prefixes: 2-7000, 2-85205

Librairie **Guénégaud** Sàrl, 10 rue de l'Odéon, F-75006 Paris Tel: (1) 43260791
Man Dir: Mr Huret
Subjects: History, Topography (France)
Founded: 1947
ISBN Publisher's Prefix: 2-85023

Editions d'Art Albert **Guillot***, 4 rue de Sèze, F-69006 Lyon Tel: 78521026
Subject: Art
ISBN Publisher's Prefix: 2-85096

Hachette*, 79 blvd St-Germain, F-75288 Paris cedex 06 Tel: (1) 43291224 Cable Add: Hachechi Paris 25 Telex: Hacsieg Paris 204434
Branch Off: Hachette Inc, 2 Park Ave, New York, NY 10016
Subsidiary Companies: Hachette/ Enseignement (qv); Hachette Guides Bleus (qv); Hachette-Jeunesse (qv); Hachette Littérature Générale (qv); Hachette Pratique (qv); Hachette-Sciences Humaines; Edition No 1 (qv); Editions du Chêne (qv); Editions Fayard (qv); Editions Grasset; Editions Jean-Claude Lattès (qv); Editions Mazarine (qv); Pluriel (qv); Editions Stock (qv) (all in France); Sociedad General Española de Librería SA, Spain (qv)
Subjects: General Fiction, Non-fiction, History, How-to, Philosophy, Art, Travel, Reference, Education, Juveniles, Science, Paperbacks, Textbooks, Architecture, Bibliography, Engineering, Music, Politics, Social Science, Games, Sport, Languages, Economics
Bookshops: Bookshops throughout the world
Founded: 1826
ISBN Publisher's Prefix: 2-01

Hachette/Enseignement (Hachette Educational)*, 79 blvd St-Germain, F-75288 Paris cedex 06 Tel: (1) 43291224 Cable Add: Hacheci-Paris 25 Telex: 204145 Haclass
Dirs: Marc Moingeon, Jacques Berthelot, Mireille Maurin; *Foreign Rights:* Françoise Laurent
Parent Company: Hachette (qv)
Subjects: Pedagogic and para-pedagogic books on every subject and for every level from Nursery School to University

Hachette Export Livre*, 79 blvd St-Germain, F-75288 Paris cedex 06 Tel: (1) 43291224 Telex: Hacoliv 203822 F
Subjects: General Fiction, Art Books, Classics, Juveniles, History, Educational Materials

Hachette Guides Bleus, 79 blvd St-Germain, F-75288 Paris cedex 06 Telex: (1) 46348634
Dir: Adelaïde Barbey; *Editorial:* Yann Delalande, Marie-Pierre Levallois
Parent Company: Hachette (qv)
Subjects: Tourism, Leisure
1986: 50 titles

Hachette-Jeunesse, 79 blvd St-Germain, F-75288 Paris cedex 06 Tel: (1) 46348634 Cable Add: Hacheci-Paris 25 Telex: 205133 F
Executive: Bertil Hessel; *Rights & Permissions:* Françoise Laurent
Parent Company: Hachette (qv)
Subjects: Illustrated Children's Books, Reference and educational series, How-to, Novels for the Young

Hachette-Littérature Générale, 79 blvd St-Germain, F-75288 Paris cedex 06 Tel: (1) 46348634 Telex: Halitg 205685
Dir: Adélaïde Barbey; *Editorial:* Françoise Cibiel; *Marketing:* Laurence Martin; *Publicity:* Claude Danis; *Foreign Rights:* David Campbell, Jacqueline Roblot
Parent Company: Hachette (qv)
Subjects: Reference Works, Science, Technical, History, Economics
1986: 60 titles *Founded:* 1970

Hachette Pratique, 79 blvd St-Germain, F-75288 Paris cedex 06 Tel: (1) 46348634
Dir: Adélaïde Barbey; *Editorial:* Sylvie Diarté
Parent Company: Hachette (qv)
Subjects: How-to, Games, Sport, Cookery, Fashion, Illustrated Books, Handicraft Manuals, Health, Leisure
1986: 20 titles

Le **Hameau**, Editeur+*, 15 rue Servandoni, F-75006 Paris Tel: (1) 43290550
Man Dir, Rights & Permissions: Paule Truchaud; *Publicity:* A R L, 17 rue St-Séverin, F-75006 Paris
Orders to: Le Hameau Diffusion (at above address)
Subjects: Psychology, Medicine, Essays
Bookshop: At above address
Founded: 1973
ISBN Publisher's Prefix: 2-7203

Harrap France SA*, 177 rue St-Honoré, F-75001 Paris
Dirs: Nicholas Berry, Daniel Segala
Parent Company: Harrap Ltd, UK (qv)
Subjects: Dictionaries, Languages

Librairie **Hatier** SA, 8 rue d'Assas, F-75006 Paris Tel: (1) 45443838 Cable Add: Libhatier Paris Telex: 202732 F
Man Dir: Bernard Foulon; *Sales Dir:* André Cazaux; *Rights & Permissions:* Gerard Campagnac
Imprint: Editions de l'Amitié (qv)
Subjects: Children's Fiction, Nature, Tour Guides, Chess, Sport, Educational, Language Teaching, Illustrated books, Computer Software
Bookshop: 59 blvd Raspail, F-75006 Paris
Founded: 1880
ISBN Publisher's Prefix: 2-218

Pierre **Hautot** SA*, 36 rue du Bac, F-75007 Paris Tel: (1) 42611015 Telex: Hautot 214293 F
Subject: Art
Founded: 1952

Fernand **Hazan** Editeur SA, 35-37 rue de Seine, F-75006 Paris Tel: (1) 43546872
Chairman: Eric Hazan; *Man Dir:* Dominique Carré
Subjects: Art, Architecture, Reference, Paperbacks
Founded: 1945
Bookshop: Editions Fernand Hazan (at above address)

Hermann (Editeurs des Sciences et des Arts) SA, 293 rue Lecourbe, F-75015 Paris Tel: (1) 45574540 Cable Add: Piby Paris Telex: Hermann Paris 200595
Man Dir: Pierre Berès
Subjects: Science, Art, Medical and Technical, Textbooks, Reference, Paperbacks
Bookshop: 6 rue de la Sorbonne, F-75005, Paris
Founded: 1870
ISBN Publisher's Prefix: 2-7056

Editions **Hermes**+, 51 rue Rennequin, F-75017 Paris Tel: (01) 43809571
Man Dir: M Menasce
Branch Offs: London, Lausanne
Subjects: Robotics, CAD/CFAO, Artificial Intelligence
1985: 17 titles *1986:* 18 titles *Founded:* 1981
ISBN Publisher's Prefix: 2-86601

Editions de l'**Herne**, 41 rue de Verneuil, F-75007 Paris Tel: (1) 42612506/42601000
Chairman, Man Dir, Rights & Permissions: Constantin Tacou; *Editorial, Press Agent:* Alexandre Tacou; *Sales:* Sodis
Subjects: Belles Lettres, Poetry, Philosophy, Social Science, Politics, Art, Novels, Strategy, Monograph Series (Cahiers) on major literary figures/ movements
Founded: 1964
ISBN Publisher's Prefix: 2-85197

Editions d'Art Les **Heures Claires** SA*, 19 rue Bonaparte, F-75006 Paris Tel: (1) 43293750
Owner: Jean Estrade
Subject: Art
Founded: 1945
ISBN Publisher's Prefix: 2-85026

Editions d'**Histoire Sociale** (EDHIS), 23 rue de Valois, F-75001 Paris Tel: (1) 42614778
Man Dir: Léon Centner
Subjects: Social and Economic History, Revolutions in France, Historical Documents, Periodicals
Bookshops: 23 rue de Valois, Paris; 144 Galerie de Valois, Paris 1er
1987: 237 titles *Founded:* 1967

Editions **Hommes et Techniques**+*, 5 rue Rousselet, F-75007 Paris Tel: (1) 45671840
Man Dir: D Bidart
Parent Company: Les Editions d'Organisation (qv)
Subjects: Business Management, Organizational Development
Founded: 1945
ISBN Publisher's Prefix: 2-7057

Pierre **Horay** Editeur, 22 bis passage Dauphine, F-75006 Paris Tel: (1) 43545390
Man Dir: Sophie Horay; *Editorial:* Jean-Jacques Lévêque; *Production:* Jean Paoli; *Rights & Permissions:* Colette Haro
Orders to: Flammarion, 26 rue Racine, F-75006 Paris
Subjects: General Fiction, Belles Lettres, Poetry, Biography, History, How-to, Music, Art, Juveniles, High-priced Paperbacks
1986: 12 titles *Founded:* 1946
ISBN Publisher's Prefix: 2-7058

Les **Humanoïdes** Associés, see SENHA

I G N (Institut Géographique National)*, 107 rue La Boëtie, F-75008 Paris Tel: (1) 42258790 Telex: Ign lb 660320 F
Man Dir: C Martinand; *Editorial:* M Osché; *Sales:* D Wintrebert; *Production:* L Massiani; *Publicity:* J Monteil; *Rights & Permissions:* Fr Chemouilli
Subject: Maps
Bookshop: At above address
Founded: 1940

Editions **I N S E R M**, 101 rue de Tolbiac, F-75654 Paris cedex 13 Tel: (01) 45841441 Telex: 270532 F
Man Dir, Editorial, Rights & Permissions: Suzy Mouchet; *Editorial, Production:* Claudine Geynet; *Sales:* Serge Hysenj; *Publicity:* France Bordes
Parent Organization: Institut National de la Santé et de la Recherche Médicale (at above address)
Subjects: Health, Medical and Scientific Research
Book Club: Centre de Documentation de l'INSERM (at above address)
1985: 15 titles *Founded:* 1970
ISBN Publisher's Prefix: 2-85598

Editions de l'**Illustration**+, 13 rue St-Georges, F-75009 Paris 9 Tel: (1) 42806118
Man Dir: Roger Allegret
Imprint: Baschet et Cie, Editeurs
Subjects: History, Art, How-to, Encyclopaedias, Travel, Science, Geography
Founded: 1843
ISBN Publisher's Prefix: 2-7059

A l'**Imprimerie** Quotidienne, 10 rue St-Germain, F-94120 Fontenay sous Bois Tel: (1) 48753797
Man Dir: Yfic Lunel; *Editorial:* Jean Pierre Burgart; *Production:* Odile Zimmerman
Subjects: Cookery, Theatre, Poetry, Encyclopaedias
1986: 24 titles *Founded:* 1978
ISBN Publisher's Prefix: 2-901167

Editions l'**Instant** Durable (Soprep), 5 rue de la Treille, F-63000 Clermont-Ferrand Tel: 73920789 Telex: 990174
General Manager: Alain de Bussac
Subjects: Architecture, Geography
1985-86: 14 titles
ISBN Publisher's Prefix: 2-86404

Institut d'Etudes Slaves, 9 rue Michelet, F-75006 Paris Tel: (1) 43265089
President: Yves Millet; *Sales, Publicity:* Jean-Marc Levent; *Production, Rights & Permissions:* Serge Aslanoff
Subjects: (Slavonic) Language, Literature, History, Sociology
1986: 10 titles *Founded:* 1920
ISBN Publisher's Prefix: 2-7204

Institut Géographique National, see IGN

Institut national de la Langue française, BP 3310, 44 ave de la Libération, F-54014 Nancy cedex Tel: 83962176
Dir: Bernard Quemada; *Deputy Dir:* Gerard Gorcy; *Secretary-General:* Nicole Nicoli
Subject: French language
1985: approx 18 titles *Founded:* 1977
ISBN Publisher's Prefix: 2-86484

Institut national de Recherche Pedagogique*, 29 rue d'Ulm, F-75230 Paris cedex 05 Tel: (1) 46349000 Cable Add: Inatrep
Dir: Francine Best; *Publications:* Janick Gazio
Parent Organization: Ministère de l'Education Nationale, 110 rue de Frenelle, F-75357 Paris
Subjects: Educational Science, Pedagogical Research
1986: 141 titles *Founded:* 1879
ISBN Publisher's Prefix: 2-7342

InterEditions Paris, 87 ave du Maine, F-75014 Paris Tel: (1) 43277450 Telex: 210311 Publi 147
Man Dir: Geoffrey M Staines; *Production, Rights & Permissions:* Monika Neumann; *Publicity:* Véronique Buret
Orders to: Bordas SA, 11 rue Gossin, F-92543 Montrouge cedex
Subjects: Biology, Chemistry, Physics, Mathematics, Computer Science, Business and Professional Subjects, Psychology
1985: 20 titles *1986:* 24 titles *Founded:* 1976
ISBN Publisher's Prefix: 2-7296

CNRS Laboratoire **Intergéo**, 191 rue St-Jacques, F-75005 Paris Tel: (1) 46337431
Man Dir: Paoló Pirazzoli
Parent Company: Centre national de la recherche scientifique (CNRS)
Subjects: Geography, Documentation, Periodicals
1985: 1 title *1986:* 1 title *Founded:* 1947
ISBN Publisher's Prefix: 2-901560

International Book Promotion, 79 blvd St-Germain, F-75288 Paris cedex 06 Tel: (1) 46348634 Telex: Edidir 204990 F
Man Dir: David Campbell; *Rights & Permissions:* Colette Veron
Orders to: Hachette SA, 12 rue François 1er, F-75008 Paris
Subjects: Fiction, Non-fiction, Medicine, Social Sciences, Practical
Founded: 1983

Les Editions du **Jaguar***, 3 rue Roquépine, F-75008 Paris Tel: (1) 42656930 Telex: Difcom 641654 F
General Manager, Foreign Rights: Danielle Ben Yahmed; *Publicity:* Jany Lecreux-Cournot; *Press:* C Eyquem
Subjects: History, Geography, Tourism, Human Sciences, Fine Arts
Founded: 1985
Miscellaneous: Formerly Editions Jeune Afrique
ISBN Publisher's Prefix: 2-86950

Editions **J'ai Lu**, 27 rue Cassette, F-75006 Paris Tel: (1) 45443876 Telex: Jailu 202765
Parent Company: Flammarion et Cie (qv)
Subjects: General Fiction, Belles Lettres, Science Fiction, Thrillers, Low-priced Paperbacks
Founded: 1958

Editions **Jeune Afrique**, see Les Editions du Jaguar

Journal des Notaires et des Avocats SA*, 6 rue de Mézières, F-75006 Paris Tel: (1) 45481210
Subject: Law
ISBN Publisher's Prefix: 2-85028

Editions René **Julliard***, 8 rue Garancière, F-75008 Paris Tel: (1) 46341280 Cable Add: Edijulliard Paris 110 Telex: 204807
Man Dir: Bernard de Fallois; *Rights & Permissions:* Josiane Bontron
Subjects: General Fiction, Belles Lettres, History, Political Science, Biography
Founded: 1931
Miscellaneous: Firm is a member of the Presses de la Cité group (qv)
ISBN Publisher's Prefix: 2-260

Editions **Juridiques et Techniques**, see Lamy SA

Jurif (Société d'Etudes Juridiques Internationales et Fiscales), see Les Cahiers Fiscaux Européens Sàrl

Karthala Editions+, 22-24 blvd Arago, F-75013 Paris Tel: (1) 43311559
Man Dir, Editorial, Rights & Permissions: Robert Ageneau; *Production:* Robert Ageneau
Subjects: Current Affairs, Third World, Africa
1985: 35 titles *1986:* 30 titles *Founded:* 1980
ISBN Publisher's Prefix: 2-86537

Editions **Klincksieck***, 11 rue de Lille, F-75007 Paris Tel: (1) 42603825
Joint Man Dir: Andrée Laurent-Klincksieck; *Joint Man Dir, Rights & Permissions:* Michel Pierre; *Publicity:* Sylvette Gassan
Subjects: Social Sciences, Philology, Linguistics, Archaeology, History, Belles Lettres, Aesthetics, Reference, General & Social Science
Founded: 1842
ISBN Publisher's Prefixes: 2-252, 2-86563

L I C E T, see Librairie Commerciale et Technique Sàrl

L I T E C, Librairies Techniques SA, 27 pl Dauphine, F-75001 Paris Tel: (1) 43266090 Management and Production offices are at 6 rue Victor-Cousin, F-75005 Paris Tel: (1) 46332237
Dir: Mrs Durieux
Parent Company: Editions Techniques, 18 rue Séguier, F-75006 Paris
Branch Off: 26 rue Soufflot, F-75005 Paris Tel: (1) 43290771
Subjects: Politics, Law, Commerce
1987: 61 titles
Miscellaneous: Firm incorporates Editions M Th Genin
ISBN Publisher's Prefix: 2-7111

L T Editions, see J Lanore

Editions Robert **Laffont**, 6 pl St-Sulpice, F-75279 Paris cedex 06 Tel: (1) 43291233 Cable Add: Edilaf Paris 110 Telex: 270607
Man Dir: Robert Laffont; *Rights & Permissions:* Zéline Guéna, Olga Begin, Béatrix Vernet
Associate Company: Les Editions Seghers (qv)
Subjects: General Fiction, History, Documentary, Philosophy, Religion, Art, Music, Biography, Medicine, General & Social Science, Psychology, High-priced Paperbacks, Textbooks, Translations
Founded: 1941
ISBN Publisher's Prefix: 2-221

Librairie Léonce Laget, 75 rue de Rennes, F-75006 Paris Tel: (1) 45489018 Cable Add: Liblaget Paris 110
Man Dir: Véronique Delvaux
Subjects: Art, History, Trades and Crafts, Architecture
Founded: 1955
ISBN Publisher's Prefix: 2-85204

Editions **Lahumière**, 88 blvd de Courcelles, F-75017 Paris Tel: (1) 47630395
Publisher: Anne Lahumière
Subject: Twentieth Century Art

Editions **Lamarre-Poinat** SA, 47 rue St André-des-Arts, F-75006 Paris Tel: (1) 43265838
Man Dir: Thierry Verret
Subjects: Medicine, Paramedical, Nursing
1986: 4 titles *1987:* 9 titles *Founded:* 1957
ISBN Publisher's Prefix: 2-85030

Lamy SA, Editions Juridiques et Techniques*, 155 rue Legendre, F-75850 Paris cedex 17 Tel: (1) 46272890 Telex: 650790
President: Gérard Lamy; *Sales:* Mr Casanova, Mr Dovat; *Publicity:* Mr Levy
Subjects: Law (Social, Fiscal, Company, Commercial, Transport and Transport Methods)
Founded: 1949

Editions Fernand **Lanore** Sàrl*, 1 rue Palatine, F-75006 Paris Tel: (1) 43256661
Dir: François Sorlot
Subjects: Belles Lettres, History, Philosophy, Secondary Textbooks, Education, Religion, Languages, Touring, Mountaineering
Founded: 1920

LT Editions-J **Lanore**-H Laurens+, 131 rue P V Couturier, F-92240 Malakoff Tel: (1) 46542707 Telex: Lanata 202 330
Associate Companies: Librairie-Editions J Lanore, 12 rue Dudinot, F-75007 Paris (Tel: (1) 47340288); Librairie LT, 4 rue de Tournon, F-75006 Paris (Tel: (1) 43294350)
Subjects: Pedagogy and Teaching Texts on Cookery and Catering, Dressmaking, Home Economy, Law, Technology, Careers, Art, Tourism, Architecture

Librairie **Larousse**+, 17 rue du Montparnasse, F-76006 Paris Tel: (1) 45443817 Cable Add: Liblarous 43 Paris Telex: 250828
Chairman and Man Dir: Christian Bregou; *Foreign Trade Dir:* Gilbert F Mitry; *Rights & Permissions:* H Deveaux
Parent Company: CEP Editions (qv, major shareholder)
Subsidiary & Affiliated Companies: Ediciones Larousse Argentina SA, Valentin Gomez 3530, Buenos Aires 1191, Argentina; Larousse-Belgique, 25-27 rue Godefroid Kurth, B-1140 Brussels, Belgium; Editora Larousse do Brasil, Av Almte Barrosa, 63s-2609, Rio de Janeiro, Brazil; Editions Françaises Inc, 1411 rue Ampere, Boucherville, QC J4B 5BO, Canada; Ediciones Larousse Colombiana Ltda, Colombia (qv); Ediciones Larousse SA, Marsella 53, Col Juarez, Delegacion cuautemoc, 06600 México City, Mexico; Larousse (Suisse) SA, Switzerland (qv)
Subjects: Dictionaries, Encyclopaedias, Reference, Textbooks, Juveniles, Paperbacks, Technical, General & Social Science, Linguistics
Founded: 1852
ISBN Publisher's Prefix: 2-03

Editions Jean-Claude **Lattès**, 17 rue Jacob, F-75006 Paris Tel: (1) 46340310 Telex: 205652
Man Dir: Nicole Lattès; *Editorial:* Malcy Ozannat, Odile Cail, Hubert Comte, Pierre Ripert, Jacques Baudoin; *Foreign Rights:* Emilie Levi
Parent Company: Hachette (qv)
Subsidiary Companies: Editions Maritimes, Editions de Trévise (qqv)
Subjects: General Fiction & Non-fiction, Biography, Documents, Music, How-to
1986: 90 titles *Founded:* 1968

Editions Henri **Laurens** Successeurs Sàrl, see Editions J Lanore

Editions Charles-**Lavauzelle** SA, see Charles

Editions Guy **Le Prat**, now part of Librairie Gründ (qv)

Editions Gérard **Lebovici**/Champ Libre*, 27 rue St-Sulpice, F-75006 Paris
Subjects: Classics, History, Social Science, Literature, Modern Theory
Founded: 1970
ISBN Publisher's Prefix: 2-85184

Editions **Lechevalier** Sàrl*, 120 blvd St Germain, F-75006 Paris Tel: (1) 46342160
Man Dir: Jacques Lechevalier
Subjects: Natural Sciences, Natural History, Biology, Entomology, Mycology, Ornithology, Silviculture, Botany, Zoology, Periodicals
Founded: 1875
ISBN Publisher's Prefix: 2-7205

Librairie **Lecoffre**, see J Gabalda et Cie

Editions Francis **Lefebvre**+, 5 rue Jacques Bingen, F-75854 Paris cedex 17 Tel: (1) 47631260
Dirs: J Icart, O Masson
Subject: Business Law
Bookshop: At above address
ISBN Publisher's Prefix: 2-85115

Daniel **Lelong** Editeur, 13 rue de Téhéran, F-75008 Paris Tel: (1) 45631319 Cable Add: Galmaeght Paris 037 Telex: 280660
Dir: Daniel Lelong
Subject: Art
ISBN Publisher's Prefix: 2-85087

Editions Dominique **Leroy**+, 61 rue Monsieur le Prince, F-75006 Paris Tel: (1) 43297233 Telex: Edl 202987 F
Man Dir: Dominique Leroy
Subjects: Adult Strip Cartoons, Erotic Fiction, Paperbacks
Imprints: Scarabée d'Or, Vertiges Bulles
Bookshop: At above address
Founded: 1970
ISBN Publisher's Prefix: 2-86688

Société Nouvelle des Editions **Letouzey** et Ané Sàrl, 87 blvd Raspail, F-75006 Paris Tel: (1) 45488014
Dirs: J Letouzey, F Dumont
Subjects: Dictionaries, Religion, History, Francophilism
Founded: 1885
ISBN Publisher's Prefix: 2-7063

Les **Lettres Libres**, member of CEA (qv)

Lettres Modernes Minard, see Minard

Editions Liana **Levi** Sàrl, 31 rue de l'Abbé Grégoire, F-75006 Paris Tel: (01) 42227510
Man Dir: Liana Levi; *Rights & Permissions:* Catherine Alicot
Orders to: Hachette Distribution
Subjects: Fiction, Non-fiction
1985: 6 titles *1986:* 7 titles *Founded:* 1983
ISBN Publisher's Prefix: 2-86746

Librairie Commerciale et Technique (Licet) Sàrl*, 110 rue de Rivoli, F-75001 Paris Tel: (1) 42332261
Man Dir: Bernard Grout; *All other offices:* J P Arditty *Subjects:* Accountancy, Typewriting, Business Techniques, Economics, Law, English, Statistics, Data Processing
Founded: 1963
ISBN Publisher's Prefix: 2-85232

Librairie Générale de Droit et de Jurisprudence, see Droit et Jurisprudence

Librairie Générale Française SA*, 79 blvd St-Germain, F-75006 Paris Tel: (1) 43265393
The above is the Head Office. Editorial and Production are run from Le Livre de Poche (qv)

Librairies Techniques SA, see LITEC

Licet, see Librairie Commerciale et Technique

Editions **Lidis** SA*, 37 rue du Four, F-75006 Paris Tel: (1) 45490950 Cable Add: Elidis Paris Telex: Elidis 270900 F
Man Dir, Rights & Permissions: Philippe Auzou
Subjects: Encyclopaedias, Human Sciences, Religion
Founded: 1955
ISBN Publisher's Prefix: 2-85032

Editions Michel de **Lile** et Philippe Auzou, 74 rue Stendhal, F-75020 Paris Tel: (1) 45421877 Telex: Lile-Auzou Sofadif 220686 F
Man Dir: Michel de Lile
Subjects: Art Editions, Facsimile Reproductions
Founded: 1978

Office Central de **Lisieux** SA, see under Office Central

Editions **Lito**, 41 rue de Verdun, BP 63, F-94503 Champigny-sur-Marne Tel: (1) 48821538 Telex: Edlit 680284
Man Dir, Rights & Permissions: Lennart Rosdahl; *Editorial:* Pierre Rosdahl; *Publicity:* Janine Ancelet
Orders to: Interco Diffusion (at above address)
Subsidiary Companies: Jesco, 35 rue H Barbusse, F-91380 Chilly Mazarin, France; Lito Editrice, Via Passo di Brizio 8, I-20148 Milan, Italy; Bokborgen AB, Karl Johans gata 2, S-252 22 Helsingborg, Sweden
Subjects: Children's Books, Puzzles, Teaching Aids, Paperbacks
Founded: 1958
ISBN Publisher's Prefix: 2-244

Le **Livre de Paris** Hachette, 3-5 ave de Garlande, F-92221 Bagneux Tel: (1) 46571140 Telex: Livpari 250026
Man Dir: E Vendroux; *Editorial:* J P Croset
Subjects: Dictionaries, Encyclopaedias, Art, How-to, Juveniles
ISBN Publisher's Prefix: 2-245

Le **Livre de Poche**, 79 blvd St-Germain, F-75006 Paris Tel: (1) 46348634
Man Dir, Rights & Permissions: Dominique Goust
Parent Company: Librairie Générale Française (qv)
Subjects: Fiction, Drama, Poetry, Classics (all both French and translated foreign); History, Biography, Current Affairs, Reference, Nature, Puzzles (all paperbacks)
Founded: 1953

Lumiere Biblique, an imprint of Les Editions de la Source Sàrl (qv)

Editions **M D I** (La Maison des Instituteurs), Parc des 10 Arpents, Dept 113, BP 69, F-78630 Orgeval Tel: 39756381 Telex: MDI Edit 698094 F
Man Dir: Jean Yves Priest; *Export Dir:*

Daniel Beaudat
Subjects: Juveniles, History, Geography, General Science, Secondary and Primary Textbooks, Educational Materials, Wall Maps, Audiovisual
Founded: 1954
ISBN Publisher's Prefix: 2-223

M E D S I (Médecine et Sciences Internationales)+*, 6 ave Daniel Lesueur, F-75007 Paris Tel: (1) 42732990 Telex: 205795
Man Dir: Timothy Hailstone; *Dir:* Mariette Guena; *Marketing Dir:* John Flavel; *Editorial:* Michelle Pradel; *Publicity:* Odile Pons
Subjects: Medical and Scientific
1985: 20 titles *Founded:* 1979
ISBN Publisher's Prefix: 2-86439

McGraw-Hill Inc, 28 rue Beaunier, F-75014 Paris Tel: (1) 45409438 Telex: 203009
Man Dir: Lidy Arslan
Parent Company: McGraw-Hill International, 1221 Ave of the Americas, New York, NY 10020, USA
Associate Companies: See McGraw-Hill Book Co (UK) Ltd, UK
Subjects: General Science, Technology, Economics, Finance, Computer Science
1986: 20 titles *Founded:* 1967
ISBN Publisher's Prefix: 2-7042

Les Editions **Magnard** Sàrl, 122 blvd St-Germain, F-75006 Paris cedex 06 Tel: (1) 43293952
Man Dir, Sales: Louis Magnard; *Literary Dir:* Thérèse Roche-Magnard; *Educational Dir:* Isabelle Magnard; *Foreign Rights:* Armandine Do Rosario
Subjects: Juveniles, University, Secondary & Primary Textbooks, Educational Materials, Pedagogy, International Series of Works in Basic French
Bookshop: Librairie de France (at above Paris address)
Founded: 1933
ISBN Publisher's Prefix: 2-210

La **Maison des Instituteurs**, see MDI

Editions de la **Maison des Sciences de l'Homme***, 54 blvd Raspail, F-75270 Paris cedex 06 Tel: (1) 42220294 Telex: 203104 F
Assistant Dir and Publicity: A C Heller; *Sales:* CID, 131 blvd St-Michel, F-75005 Paris; *Production:* R Hubshmit, M Meyer
Orders to: CID, 131 blvd St-Michel, F-75005 Paris
Subjects: Archaeology, Anthropology, History, Sociology, Psychology
Founded: 1977
ISBN Publisher's Prefixes: 2-7351, 2-901725

La **Maison du Dictionnaire**, 98 blvd du Montparnasse, F-75014 Paris Tel: (1) 43221293 Telex: 270105 ref 355 txfra b rungi
Man Dirs: Michel Feutry
Subject: Dictionaries (technical, specialized, general in many languages)
Founded: 1976
ISBN Publisher's Prefix: 2-85608

La **Maison** Rustique SA, 26 rue Racine, F-75006 Paris 6 Tel: (1) 43291220 Telex: Flamedi 205641 F Fax: (1) 43292148
Editor: Jean-Marie Pruvost-Beaurain
Parent Company: Flammarion et Cie (qv)
Subjects: Natural Science, Horticulture, Agriculture, Forestry
Founded: 1836
ISBN Publisher's Prefix: 2-7066

Adrien **Maisonneuve**, see Editions d'Amérique et d'Orient

Editions G P **Maisonneuve et Larose**, 15 rue Victor-Cousin, F-75005 Paris Tel: (1) 43543270 Telex: 270412 F Mledit

Man Dir: J-P Pinardon
Subjects: Orient, Africa, Middle East, Mythology, Languages, Bibliographies
Founded: 1835 and 1860 respectively, merged 1961
ISBN Publisher's Prefix: 2-7068

Maisonneuve SA, Editeur, 386 route de Verdun, BP 39, F-57160 Moulins les Metz Tel: 87601180
Man Dir: André-G Maisonneuve
Subjects: Acupuncture and Auriculotherapy, French and European Pharmacopoeia, Homoeopathy, Therapeutics
Founded: 1959
ISBN Publisher's Prefix: 2-7160

Editions **Maloine**+, 27 rue de l'École-de-Médecine, F-75006 Paris Tel: (1) 43256045 Telex: 203215 F
President, Man Dir, Rights & Permissions: Antonin Philippart; *Dir:* François Guérin; *Editorial:* Dr A Blacque Belair; *Sales:* Nathalie Moury; *Production, Publicity & Advertising:* Jean Phillipart
Subjects: Medicine, Veterinary, Science, Technical Reference
Bookshop: At above address
Founded: 1881
ISBN Publisher's Prefix: 2-224

Nouvelles Editions **Mame**, 77 rue de Vaugirard, F-75006 Paris Tel: (1) 45487860 Telex: 202036 F
Man Dir: Marcel Vervaet; *Editorial, Production:* Suzel Vervaet
Orders to: (France) Begedis (at above address); (Foreign) Arc-en-Ciel International, ZI Tournai Ouest, B-7713 Marquain, Belgium Telex: 57429 B
Associate Companies: Editions du Chalet, Editions Desclée et Cie, Editions Gamma, Editions Universitaires (qqv)
Subjects: The Bible, Religious Literature, Catechism, Liturgy, Juveniles
ISBN Publisher's Prefix: 2-7289

Editions **Marcus***, 15 rue Faraday, F-75017 Paris Tel: (1) 47632084 Telex: 643841
Man Dir: Patrick Arfi; *Sales:* Mrs Gaubert
Subjects: Tourist Guides, Maps
Founded: 1963
ISBN Publisher's Prefix: 2-7131

Editions **Maritimes et d'Outre-Mer** SA, see Editions

Le **Masque**, an imprint of Librairie des Champs-Elysées SA (qv)

Editions Charles **Massin** et Cie, 2 rue de l'Echelle, F-75039 Paris cedex 01 Tel: (1) 42603005 Telex: 240918 Trace
Subjects: Architecture, Interior Decoration, Arts
Founded: 1910
ISBN Publisher's Prefix: 2-7072

Masson Editeur*, 120 blvd St-Germain, F-75280 Paris cedex 06 Tel: (1) 46342160 Cable Add: Gemas Paris 025 Telex: Massoned 260946
Dir: Dr Jérôme Talamon; *Man Dir:* P Lahaye; *Sales Dir:* A Hapiot; *Rights & Permissions:* Françoise Han
Orders to: CCLS, 69 rue Barrault, F-75013 Paris
Subsidiary Company: Masson Italia Editori SpA, Italy (qv)
Associate Companies: Editora Masson do Brasil, Ltda, Brazil (qv); Masson Editores, Mexico (qv); Masson SA, Spain (qv); Masson Publishing USA Inc, 133 East 58th St, New York, NY 10022, USA
Subjects: Medicine, Scientific, Technical, Social Science, Law, Economics
Founded: 1804
ISBN Publisher's Prefix: 2-225

Editions **Mayer**, 45 rue Broca, F-75005 Paris Tel: (1) 45350293
Man Dir: F van Wilder
Subsidiary Company: Editions Publisol, 235 East 85th St (PO Box 39), New York, NY 10028, USA
Subjects: The Arts
Founded: 1962

Editions **Mazarine**, 75 rue des Sts-Pères, F-75006 Paris Tel: (1) 45443845
President, Man Dir: Claude Durand; *Editorial, Rights & Permissions:* Marie-Annick Thabaud
Parent Company: Hachette (qv)
Subjects: General Literature, Biographies, Science Reports
Founded: 1979
ISBN Publisher's Prefix: 2-86374

Editions **Mazenod-Editio** SA, 33 rue de Naples, F-75008 Paris Tel: (1) 45222366 Cable Add: Edimaz Telex: 281478 F
Man Dir: Anne de Margerie
Subjects: History, Art, Architecture
ISBN Publisher's Prefix: 2-85088

Médecines et Sciences Internationales, see MEDSI

Editions **Médiaspaul**+, 8 rue Madame, F-75006 Paris Tel: (1) 45446402 Telex: Edipaul 205794 F
Editorial: Mr Brondino
Parent Company: Siège Social, Chateau de Chanteloup, F-91290 Arpajon Tel: 64900772
Subjects: Religion, Biblical Documents, Spirituality, Liturgy, Lives of the Saints, Illustrated, Children's
Bookshop: 8 rue Madame, F-75006 Paris
Founded: 1982
ISBN Publisher's Prefix: 2-7122

Société des Editions **Mengès***, 6 rue Galilée, F-75016 Paris Tel: (1) 47235452 Telex: Cflglm 630385
Man Dir: Gérard Mareuil; *General Manager:* Jean Paul Mengès; *Production:* Michel Geneau; *Marketing:* Laurence Martin
Subjects: Gardening, Cookery, Beauty, Sport, Health, Illustrated Books
Founded: 1975
ISBN Publisher's Prefix: 2-85620

Mercure de France SA*, 26 rue de Condé, F-75006 Paris Tel: (1) 43292113
Man Dir: Simone Gallimard; *Production Dir:* Yves-Marie Maquet; *Rights & Permissions:* Nicole Boyer
Parent Company: Editions Gallimard (qv)
Associate Company: Editions Denoël Sàrl (qv)
Subjects: General Fiction, Belles Lettres, Poetry, History, Philosophy, Social Science, Psychology
Founded: 1891
ISBN Publisher's Prefix: 2-7152

Messidor, an imprint of Les Editions Sociales-Messidor (qv)

Sylvie **Messinger**, Editrice+, 24 rue de l'Abbé Grégoire, F-75006 Paris Tel: (1) 42227667
Man Dir: Sylvie Messinger; *Literary Dir:* Antonio Ramos; *Foreign Rights:* Véronique Garrigues
Orders to: (France) Hachette Distribution, ave Gutemberg, F-78316 Maurepas cedex; (Belgium) Presse de Belgique, 96 rue Gray, B-1040 Brussels; (Switzerland) Diffulivre, Jordils 41, CH-1025 Saintsulpice; (Canada) Edipresse, 5198 rue St-Hubert, Montreal, Quebec H2T 2Y3
Parent Company: Editions Pierre Belfond (qv)
Subjects: General Literature
1986: 21 titles *Founded:* 1981
ISBN Publisher's Prefix: 2-86583

Editions A M **Métailié**, 5 rue de Savoie, F-75006 Paris Tel: (1) 43266010
Man Dir: Anne Marie Métailié; *Literary Dirs:* M Carelli, P Dibie
Orders to: Presses Universitaires de France, 14 ave du Bois de l'Epine, F-91003 Evry cédex
Subjects: Foreign Literature, Ethnology, Sociology
1987: 50 titles *Founded:* 1979
ISBN Publisher's Prefix: 2-86424

Editions Albin **Michel**, see under Albin

Michelin et Cie (Services de Tourisme)*, 46 ave de Breteuil, F-75341 Paris cedex 07 Tel: (1) 45392500
Associate Company: Michelin Tyre PLC, UK (qv)
Subjects: Travel and Tourist Guides in several languages, Maps

Lettres Modernes **Minard***, 73 rue du Cardinal Lemoine, F-75005 Paris Tel: (1) 43544609
Man Dir, Production: Michel J Minard; *Sales:* Librairie Minard Diffusion; *Rights & Permissions:* Danièle Morgat
Associate Company: Librairie Minard (qv)
Subjects: General Literature, University Studies and Theses, Critical Studies
Founded: 1954
ISBN Publisher's Prefix: 2-256

Librairie **Minard***, 73 rue du Cardinal Lemoine, F-75005 Paris Tel: (1) 43544609
Man Dir: Michel J Minard; *Sales:* Librairie Minard Diffusion
Associate Company: Lettres Modernes Minard (qv)
Subjects: University Studies and Theses
ISBN Publisher's Prefix: 2-85210

Les Editions de **Minuit** SA+, 7 rue Bernard-Palissy, F-75006 Paris Tel: (1) 42223794
Man Dir: Jérôme Lindon
Orders to: Le Seuil, 27 rue Jacob, F-75006 Paris
Subjects: General Fiction, Philosophy, Social Science, Literary Works
Bookshops: Librairie Autrement Dit, 73 blvd St-Michel, F-75005 Paris; Librairie Compagnie, 58 rue des Ecoles, F-75005 Paris
Founded: 1942
ISBN Publisher's Prefix: 2-7073

Miroir Sprint Publications, see Les Editions Vaillant

Gérard **Monfort**, Saint-Pierre de Salerne, F-27800 Brionne Tel: 32448741
Man Dir: Gérard Monfort
Subjects: Literature, History, Art, Law, Archaeology, Ethnology
1985: 11 titles *1986:* 12 titles *Founded:* 1960

Editions du **Moniteur** et de l'Usine Nouvelle, 17 rue d'Uzès, F-75002 Paris Tel: (1) 42961550 Telex: 680876 F
President: Marc N Vigier; *Man Dir:* Guy de Dampierre; *Sales:* Y-L Walle
Associate Company: C E P Edition (qv)
Subjects: Architecture, Building Construction, Public Works, Home Economics, Laws and Regulations, Technical
Bookshops: Librairies du Moniteur, 15 rue d'Uzès, F-75002 Paris; 7 pl de l'Odéon, F-75006 Paris
ISBN Publisher's Prefix: 2-281

Editions **Montchrestien** SA, 26 rue Vercingétorix, F-75014 Paris Tel: (1) 43350167
Man Dir: Nathalie Jouven
Subjects: Law, Economic and Political Science, Current Events
ISBN Publisher's Prefix: 2-7076

Editions Paul **Montel***, 17 rue d'Uzés, F-75002 Paris Tel: (1) 42961550
Man Dir: Marc Vigier; *Dir:* Guy de Dampierre; *Sales:* Yves-Louis Walle
Subjects: Technical and Practical Aspects of Photography, Cinematography and Videography
ISBN Publisher's Prefix: 2-7075

Editions Albert **Morancé***, 1 rue Palatine, F-75006 Paris Tel: (1) 46332455
Dir: Jean Sorlot
Subjects: Fine Arts, Architecture
Book Club: Club du Livre d'Art
Founded: 1781
ISBN Publisher's Prefix: 2-85307

Editions Alain **Moreau***, 5 rue Eginhard, F-75004 Paris Tel: (1) 42725151
Editorial, Rights & Permissions, Sales: Alain Moreau
Orders to: Diffédit, 96 blvd Montparnasse, F-75014 Paris
Subjects: Social, Economic & Political Sciences, Social History
Founded: 1972
ISBN Publisher's Prefix: 2-85209

Morel Editeurs*, Les Imberts, F-84220 Gordes Tel: 90719175/90718180
Dir: Robert Morel
Associate Companies: Editions 'R' (qv); Editions 'Pratique'; Le 'A' (Periodical); Minimos; Boîtes pleines de Zodiaque, Beauté, Santé, Tourisme
Subjects: Belles Lettres, Poetry, Music, Art, Religion, Paperbacks, Architecture, Gastronomy, Folklore, Juvenile, Humour
Bookshops: La Fête (at above address); Chuion Diffusion, 40 rue de Seine, Paris 6; Payot Diffusion, Lausanne, Switzerland (qv under Major Booksellers); Nord-Sud, 74 rue Lesbroussart, B-1050 Brussels, Belgium
Founded: 1961

Editions de la Réunion des **Musées** Nationaux, 10 rue de l'Abbaye, F-75006 Paris Tel: (1) 43292145
Subjects: Archeology, Architecture, Fine Arts, Exhibition Catalogues, Dictionaries, Encyclopaedias, Ethnology, History, Painting, Sculpture
Founded: 1931
ISBN Publisher's Prefix: 2-7118

Editions du **Muséum National** d'Histoire naturelle*, 38 rue Geoffroy-St-Hilaire, F-75005 Paris Tel: (1) 43317124
Subject: Natural History
1985: 7 titles

N O E, see Nouvel Office d'Edition

Fernand **Nathan***, 9 rue Méchain, F-75014 Paris Tel: (1) 45875000 Cable Add: Nathaned Paris Telex: Natened 204525 F
Chairman: Jean-Jacques Nathan; *Executive Vice-President:* Jean-Paul Baudouin
Company operates divisions as follows:
Educational: *Dirs:* Jean-Jacques Nathan, Jean-Paul Gisserot; *Man Dir:* Philippe Clémençot; *Sales Dir:* Patrick de Porcaro; *Rights & Permissions:* Evelyne Mathiaud
Subjects: Textbooks, Reference, Dictionaries, Para-pedagogic
General Literature: *Editorial Dir:* Philippe Schuwer; *Sales Dir:* Jean-Jacques Rabilloud; *Rights & Permissions:* Evelyne Mathiaud
Subjects: Reference, Art, Guides, Nature, History, Atlases, How-to, Games, Sport, Juvenile, Children's
International: *Sales Dir:* Jean-Claude Richard; *Editorial Dir:* Françoise Juhel
Subjects: Books for French-speaking countries
Parent Company: CEP Editions (qv)
Subsidiary Companies: CEDIC, CLE, La Nouvelle Librairie, VIFI

Subjects: Reference, Dictionaries, Art, Philosophy, Textbooks, Psychology, General & Social Sciences, Guides, Nature, History, Education, Juvenile paperbacks
1985: 650 titles *Founded:* 1881
ISBN Publisher's Prefix: 2-09

Librairie A-G **Nizet** Sàrl*, 3 bis pl de la Sorbonne, F-75005 Paris Tel: (1) 43547976
Man Dir: A G Nizet
Subjects: Belles Lettres, University Textbooks, Literary
Founded: 1922
ISBN Publisher's Prefix: 2-7078

F De **Nobèle***, 35 rue Bonaparte, F-75006 Paris Tel: (1) 43260862 Cable Add: Denobelef Paris 110
Man Dir: F de Nobèle
Subjects: History of Art, Bibliography
Founded: 1885
ISBN Publisher's Prefix: 2-85189

Nouvel Office d'Edition, now part of Editions Pierre Belfond (qv)

Nouvelle Cité+*, 131 rue Castagnary, F-75015 Paris Tel: (1) 48281894
Man Dir, Rights & Permissions: Jean-Michel Merlin; *Editorial, Production, Publicity:* Jean-Pierre Rosa; *Sales:* Bernard Meunier
Parent Company: Città Nuova Editrice, Italy (qv for associate companies)
Subjects: Spiritual themes, Testimonies, Essays
1985: 25 titles *Founded:* 1963
ISBN Publisher's Prefix: 2-85313

Nouvelles Editions Françaises, 13 rue St-Georges, F-75009 Paris Tel: (1) 48785319
Dir: Eliane Allegret; *Man Dir:* Denis Baschet; *Sales Dir:* Roger Allegret
Subject: Art
Founded: 1946
ISBN Publisher's Prefix: 2-7079

Nouvelles Editions Latines*, 1 rue Palatine, F-75006 Paris Tel: (1) 43547742
Man Dir: Jean Sorlot
Subjects: General Fiction, Belles Lettres, Poetry, History, Travel and Tourism, Religion
Founded: 1928
ISBN Publisher's Prefix: 2-7233

Nouvelles Editions Rationalistes SA*, 14 rue de l'Ecole-Polytechnique, F-75005 Paris Tel: (1) 46330350
Subjects: Philosophy, Religion, History of Ideas, Rationalist Themes

O R S T O M, Institut Français de Recherche Scientifique pour le Développement en Coopération, 213 rue La Fayette, F-75480 Paris cedex 10 Tel: (1) 48037777 Cable Add: Orstom Paris Telex: 640295 F
Man Dir: Philippe Tenneson
Publishing Department and Orders to: Editions de l'ORSTOM, 70-74 route d'Aulnay, F-93140 Bondy Tel: 48473195 Telex: 215203 F
Subjects: Scientific and Technical Texts, Social Sciences connected with the Tropical and Mediterranean Areas of the World
Founded: 1943
ISBN Publisher's Prefix: 2-7099

Office Central de Lisieux SA*, 51 rue du Carmel, F-14100 Lisieux Tel: (031) 620188
Subject: Religion

Office de Documentation Bibliographique et de Diffusion, subsidiary of Librairie Fischbacher (qv)

Office de la Recherche Scientifique et Technique Outre Mer, see ORSTOM

Editions **Ophrys**, 6 ave J Jaurès, F-05002 Gap Tel: 92538572
Man Dir, Publicity & Advertising: Mrs B Monnier
Subjects: Linguistics, Belles Lettres, History, Philosophy, Education, Economics, Sociology
Bookshop: Editions Ophrys, succursale de Paris, 10 rue de Nesle, F-75006 Paris Tel: (1) 43268204 Telex: 203487 F
Founded: 1934
ISBN Publisher's Prefix: 2-7080

Editions de l'**Orante**, 6 rue du Général-Bertrand, F-75007 Paris Tel: (1) 45660016
Man Dir: Roselyne Lafarge
Subjects: Belles Lettres, Poetry, History, Philosophy, Religion
Founded: 1940
ISBN Publisher's Prefix: 2-7031

Editions Olivier **Orban**, 14 rue Duphot, F-75001 Paris Tel: (1) 42603696
Man Dir: Olivier Orban; *Editorial:* Catherine Blanchard; *Rights & Permissions:* Nicole Rollier
Subjects: General Fiction and Non-fiction
Founded: 1974
ISBN Publisher's Prefix: 2-85565

Les Editions d'**Organisation***, 5 rue Rousselet, F-75007 Paris 7 Tel: (1) 45671840
Dir: Dominique Bidart
Parent Company: Ecole Speciale des Travaux Publics
Subsidiary Company: Editions Hommes et Techniques (qv)
Subjects: Business Management & Organization generally (especially Data Processing, Personnel Training, Sociology, Industrial Law)
Bookshops: 7 rue de la Bourse, F-75002 Paris Tel: (1) 42974409; 97 blvd de la Liberté, F-59000 Lille Tel: 20543324; CESA-CFC, 1 rue de la Libération, F-78350 Joug en Josas Tel: (1) 6192624; ESSEC, ave de la Grande Ecole, F-95000 Cergy-Pontoise Tel: 30381452; Sur de Co, 79 rue de la République, F-75011 Paris Tel: (1) 43382671
Founded: 1953
ISBN Publisher's Prefix: 2-7081

Librairie **Orientaliste**, see Paul Geuthner SA

Michel de l'**Ormeraie***, 4 rue Labrouste, F-75725 Paris cedex 15 Tel: (1) 48284070
Man Dir and other offices: Michel de l'Ormeraie
Subjects: Exact Facsimiles (text and binding) of famous illustrated editions of French and other Literary Classics
Founded: 1970
ISBN Publisher's Prefix: 2-85135

Les Editions **Ouvrières** SA*, 12 ave Soeur-Rosalie, F-75013 Paris Tel: (1) 43379385
Subjects: History, Religion, How-to, Education, Juveniles, Political & Social Science, Economics
Founded: 1939
ISBN Publisher's Prefix: 2-7082

Editions **P A C** (Presse-Auto-Conseil)*, 3 rue Saint Roch, F-75001 Paris Tel: (1) 42615017
Subjects: Sport, Cinema, Crime Novels, Commentaries and Documentaries, Adventure Reports
Founded: 1975
ISBN Publisher's Prefix: 2-85336

P O F, see Publications Orientalistes de France

P U F, see Presses Universitaires de France

P U L, see Presses Universitaires de Lille

P Y C Edition+, 254 rue de Vaugirard, F-75740 Paris cedex 15 Tel: (1) 45322719 Telex: 202639 F
Man Dir: Pierre Benichou
Subjects: Mechanical Engineering, Heating, Air Conditioning, Solar Energy, Refrigeration, Metallurgy, Welding
Founded: 1934
ISBN Publisher's Prefix: 2-85330

Les Editions du **Pacifique**, see Société Nouvelle des Editions du Pacifique, French Polynesia

Editions du **Parhélie**, member of CEA (qv)

Paris-Caraïbes*, 34 rue Scheffer, F-75116 Paris Tel: (1) 45240609
Man Dir, Editorial: Louis Drout Soulanges
Associate Company: Editions Louis Soulanges (qv)
Subjects: Current literary, tourist, artistic, economic and social affairs in the Antilles

Jean-Jacques **Pauvert** Editeur*, Bénard 2bis, F-75014 Paris Tel: (1) 45413646
Dir: Jean-Jacques Pauvert
Orders to: Distribution Sodis, 128 ave de Mal de Lattre, F-77400 Lagny
Subjects: Fiction, Belles Lettres, Art, History, Reference, Social Science, Paperbacks, Poetry, Philosophy, Juveniles
Founded: 1945
ISBN Publisher's Prefix: 2-85092

Editions **Payot**+, 106 blvd St-Germain, F-75006 Paris 6 Tel: (1) 43297410 Telex: 203246 F
Man Dir: Jean-Luc Pidoux-Payot; *Sales Dir:* Pierre Stockman; *Editorial:* Marylène Daudier; *Publicity:* Anne Guillard
Subjects: Biography, History, Philosophy, Reference, Religion, Ethnology, Anthropology, Low-priced Paperbacks, Education, General Science, Humanities, Psychology and Psychoanalysis, Linguistics, Literature
Founded: 1912
ISBN Publisher's Prefix: 2-228

Pédagogie Moderne, an imprint of Editions Bordas (qv)

Editions **Pédone**+*, 13 rue Soufflot, F-75005 Paris Tel: (1) 43540597
Man Dir: Denis Pédone
Subjects: Law, Engineering, Agriculture, Mining, Management, Economics, Book Industry
1985: 16 titles *Founded:* 1837
ISBN Publisher's Prefix: 2-233

Père Castor, an imprint of Flammarion et Cie (qv)

Librairie Académique **Perrin***, 8 rue Garancière, F-75006 Paris Tel: (1) 46341280
Chairman: Claude Nielsen; *Foreign Rights:* Josiane Bontron
Subjects: Belles Lettres, History, Reference, Scholarly, Bibliography, Fiction, Arts, Religion
Founded: 1827
Miscellaneous: Member of Presses de la Cité group (qv)
ISBN Publisher's Prefix: 2-262

Editions **Phébus**, 17 rue Pierre Lescot, F-75001 Paris Tel: (1) 402602394
Man Dir: Jean-Pierre Sicre
Orders to: Inter-Forum, 13 rue de la Glacière, F-75013 Paris
Subjects: General Literature, Oriental (Eastern) Literature, Literary Criticism, Fine Arts

Editions A et J **Picard** SA+, 82 rue Bonaparte, F-75006 Paris Tel: (1) 43269673/43294489

Man Dir: Chantal Pasini-Picard
Subjects: General, Art, Fine Arts, Religious, Literary and Local History; Archaeology, Architecture, Reference, Education, Bibliography, Folklore, Philology, Textbooks, Musicology, Antiquarian Books
1985: 19 titles *1986:* 13 titles *Founded:* 1869
ISBN Publisher's Prefix: 2-7084

Editions Jean **Picollec**+, 47 rue Auguste Lançon, F-75013 Paris Tel: (1) 45897304
Man Dir: Jean Picollec
Orders to: CDE Sodis, 17 rue de Tournon, F-75006 Paris
Subjects: Literature, Fiction, Belles Lettres, Political History, Reportage
1985: 12 titles *1986:* 12 titles *Founded:* 1979
ISBN Publisher's Prefix: 2-86477

Editions **Pierron**+, 4 rue Gutenberg, F-57206 Sarreguemines Tel: 87951431 Telex: 860495 F
Dir: Jeannie Jung
Subjects: Education, History
ISBN Publisher's Prefix: 2-7085

Librairie **Plon** SA, 8 rue Garancière, F-75006 Paris Tel: (1) 46341280 Cable Add: Ploédit Paris 110 Telex: 204807
Chairman: Bruno Rohmer; *Foreign Rights:* Josiane Bontron
Subjects: General Fiction, History, Belles Lettres, Philosophy, How-to, Religion, Reference, Economics, Social Science, Scholarly, Arts, Maps, Travel, Anthropology, Trade Books
Founded: 1844
Miscellaneous: Member of Presses de la Cité group (qv)
ISBN Publisher's Prefix: 2-259

Pluriel, 79 blvd St-Germain, F-75288 Paris cedex 06 Tel: (1) 46348634 Telex: Halitg 205685
Dir: Adélaïde Barbey; *Editorial:* Georges Liébert
Parent Company: Hachette (qv)
Subjects: Documentary, Social Science, History
1986: 20 titles

Presses **Pocket***, 8 rue Garancière, F-75006 Paris Tel: (1) 46341280 Telex: Precite 204807 F
Subjects: Novels, Memoirs, War, Documentary, Science Fiction (all paperback)
Miscellaneous: Member of Presses de la Cité group (qv)

Editions du Centre Georges **Pompidou**+, F-75191 Paris cedex 04 Tel: (1) 42771233 Telex: cnac gp 212276
President: Jean Maheu; *Commercial, Rights:* Sabine Sautter, Clair Morizet
Orders to: Service Commercial (at above address)
Subjects: Art, Industrial Design, Architecture, Environment, Urbanism, Music, Acoustic Research, Various
1985-86: 70 titles *Founded:* 1977
ISBN Publisher's Prefix: 2-85850

Julian **Prélat**, see CDP — Julien Prélat

Société Nouvelle **Présence Africaine**+, 25 bis rue des Ecoles, F-75005 Paris Tel: (1) 43541374 Cable Add: Presafric Paris Telex: 200891 F
Man Dir: Mrs Alioune Diop; *Publicity, Rights & Permissions:* Geoffrey Jones
Subjects: General Fiction, Belles Lettres, Poetry, History, Philosophy, Reference, Religion, Low-priced Paperbacks, Primary Textbooks, Politics (all subjects pertain to Africa)

FRANCE

Bookshop: At above address
Founded: 1947
ISBN Publisher's Prefix: 2-7087

Presse-Auto-Conseil, see PAC

Les **Presses d'Ile-de-France** Sàrl*, 23 rue de Ligner, F-75020 Paris Tel: (1) 43679821
Man Dir: Gilles Le Grontec; *Manager:* François Ardonceau
Orders to: Sofedis, 29 rue St-Sulpice, F-75007 Paris
Subject: Juveniles
ISBN Publisher's Prefix: 2-7088

Les **Presses de la Cité***, 8 rue Garancière, F-75006 Paris Tel: (1) 43291280 Cable Add: Svennil Paris
President and Distribution Dir: Claude Nielsen; *Publicity and Advertising:* Nadia Leser; *Rights & Permissions:* Josiane Bontron
Subjects: General Fiction, History, How-to, Low- & High-priced Paperbacks
Founded: 1947
Presses de la Cité group: Christian Bourgois (qv); Editions Fleuve Noir (qv); Editions René Julliard (qv); Messageries Centrales du Livre (at above address); Librairie Académique Perrin (qv); Librairie Plon (qv); Presses Pocket (qv); le Rocher; G P Rouge et Or (qv); Solar (qv); UGE 10/18 (qv)
ISBN Publisher's Prefix: 2-258

Presses de la Fondation Nationale des Sciences Politiques, 27 rue St-Guillaume, F-75341 Paris cedex 07 Tel: (1) 45495050/45495021
Man Dir, Sales: Louis Bodin; *Editorial, Rights & Permissions:* Mireille Perche; *Production:* Josée Cabillon; *Public Relations:* Bernard Condominas
Subjects: Social Sciences, especially Political, Historical, Sociological, Economics
Founded: 1975
ISBN Publisher's Prefix: 2-7246

Presses de la Renaissance+, 37 rue du Four, F-75007 Paris Tel: (1) 45485982 Telex: 260717 orem 158
Man Dir: Fabienne Delmote; *Editorial:* Tony Cartano; *Rights & Permissions:* Françoise Triffaux
Parent Company: Pierre Belfond (qv)
Subjects: General Fiction and Non-fiction, Biography, History, Ethnology
Founded: 1971
ISBN Publisher's Prefix: 2-85616

Presses Universitaires de France (PUF), 108 blvd St-Germain, F-75279 Paris cedex 06 Tel: (1) 46341201
The above is the address of the Administration and Editorial offices; Public Relations and Publicity departments are at 90 blvd St-Germain, F-75005 Paris
President: Pierre Angoulvent; *Dirs:* Robert Ruelle, Pierre Wittmann; *Sales Dir:* Jean-Pierre Giband; *Editorial:* Michel Prigent; *Publicity, Advertising:* Gabrielle Hayat-Gelber; *Rights & Permissions:* Françoise Laye
Orders to: 14 ave du Bois de L'Epine, BP 90, F-91003 Evry cedex Tel: 60778205 Telex: PUF 600474 F
Subjects: Human Sciences, Biography, History, Geography, Music, Art, Philosophy, Reference, Religion, Engineering, Low- & High-priced Paperbacks, Psychology, Psychiatry, Medicine, General, Social & Political Science, University Textbooks
Bookshops: Librairie générale des PUF (qv under Major Booksellers); La Pochotheque, 17 rue Soufflot, F-75005 Paris
Founded: 1921

Presses Universitaires de Grenoble+, Domaine Universitaire, BP 47X, F-38040 St Martin d'Hères Tel: 76444378 Telex: Unisog 980910
Manager: Christian Auguste; *Commercial Manager:* Pierre Croce
Orders to: Distique, 9 rue E Jacques, F-75014 Paris
Subjects: Architecture, Anthropology, Sociology, Law, Economics, Management, History, Statistics, Literature, Medicine, Data Processing, Physics, Politics
1986: 35 titles *1987:* 38 titles
ISBN Publisher's Prefix: 2-7061

Presses Universitaires de Lille (PUL), BP 199, F-59654 Villeneuve d'Ascq cedex (Located at: rue du Barreau, F-59000 Lille) Tel: 20916535/20916824
Man Dir: University President; *Editorial, Production:* Daniel Beauvois; *Sales, Publicity, Rights & Permissions:* Jean-Gabriel Caby
Subjects: Social Sciences and Humanities, French and Foreign Literature, History, Philosophy, Law, Philology, Psychology
1985: 20 titles *Founded:* 1972
ISBN Publisher's Prefix: 2-85939

Presses Universitaires de Lyon+, 86 rue Pasteur, F-69007 Lyon Tel: 78692048
Man Dir: Joël Saugnieux; *General Manager:* Sylvette Salvit
Subjects: History, Economics, Management, Law, Political Science, Linguistics, Languages, Literature, Human Sciences, Multidisciplinary works
1986: 25 titles *Founded:* 1976
ISBN Publisher's Prefix: 2-7297

Presses Universitaires de Nancy+, 25 rue Baron Louis, BP 454, F-54001 Nancy cedex Tel: 83373765/83371297
Chairman: Jean-Marie Bonnet; *General Manager:* Jeanne Weill; *Editorial Manager:* Danièle Silvy-Leligois; *Sales:* Roger Mossovic; *Production:* Thérèse Rambaut; *Publicity, Rights & Permissions:* Danièle Silvy-Leligois
Subjects: History, Geography, Literature and Linguistics, Philosophy, Psychology, Sociology, Jurisprudence, Economic and Political Bibliography Teaching, Works and Theses of the Nancy II University, the European University Centre, European Conferences, Periodicals
1986: 35 titles *Founded:* 1976
ISBN Publisher's Prefix: 2-86480

Editions Edouard **Privat** SA, 14 rue des Arts, F-31068 Toulouse cedex Tel: 61230926 Telex: 521001 F
Man Dir: Yves Suaudeau; *Literary, Production:* Dominique Autié; *Sales Dir, Publicity:* Liliane Gestermann; *Press Relations:* Jacqueline Thomas; *Rights & Permissions:* Noëlle Lever
Subjects: French regional history and culture; Education, Psychology, Sociology, Philosophy, Pedagogy
Bookshop: At above address
1986: 45 titles *1987:* 50 titles *Founded:* 1839
ISBN Publisher's Prefix: 2-7089

Publi-Union*, 17 ave Niel, F-75017 Paris Tel: (1) 47668664
Man Dir: Michel Weulersse
Subjects: Law, Economics, Social Science, Education, Science & Technical
ISBN Publisher's Prefix: 2-85200

Publications Filmées d'Art et d'Histoire, 21 rue Médéric, F-92250 La Garenne-Colombes Tel: (1) 47803743
Man Dir: Françoise Goddet; *Sales:* Viviane Mella
Subjects: Books illustrated by slides on Art, History, Space Exploration, World Events

ISBN Publisher's Prefix: 2-85228

Publications Orientalistes de France (POF), 2 rue de Lille, F-75007 Paris Tel: (1) 42606705 Telex: 30311405 F
Dir: Simone Sieffert
Orders to: Distique, 17 rue Hoche, F-92240 Malakoff
Subjects: Eastern Europe and the Middle and Far East (all aspects, especially literature, bibliographies, vocabularies)
1986: 18 titles *Founded:* 1973
ISBN Publisher's Prefix: 2-7169

Editions **Pygmalion** — Gérard Watelet+, 70 Ave de Breteuil, F-75007 Paris Tel: (1) 45674077
Man Dir, Editorial: Gérard Watelet; *Sales, Rights & Permissions:* Luce Watelet
Subjects: General Literature, History, Biographies, Archaeology, Art, Fiction, Cinema
Founded: 1977
ISBN Publisher's Prefix: 2-85704

Société **Quatre Chemins**, see Editart

Editions **'R'**, Société Civile Typo, Graphique et Littéraire*, Les Imberts, F-84220 Gordes Tel: 90718180/90719175
Man Dir, Editorial, Rights & Permissions: Robert Morel; *Production, Publicity:* François Morel
Associate Company: Morel Editeurs (qv)
Subjects: Rites, Myths and Symbols, Sorcery, Encylopaedia of Tarot, Alternative Medicine, Fiction, Practical Living, Vocabulary Traditions and Images, Popular Literature, Tourism, Art, Gastronomy, Working Classes
Founded: 1977

R E C T A Foldex, BP 94, F-92303 Levallois-Perret (Located at: 27 rue Trebois, Levallois-Perret) Tel: (1) 42701203 Telex: 270105 F txfra 691
Man Dir: M Frey
Subject: Maps, Charts
Miscellaneous: RECTA = Réalisations, Études Cartographiques Touristiques et Administratives (Cartographic design and production in the touring and administrative fields)

R E M I, see Réalisations pour l'Enseignement Multilingue International

Société des Editions **Radio**, see SECF — Editions Radio

G-T **Rageot**, see Editions de l'Amitié

Editions **Ramsay**, 9 rue du Cherche-Midi, F-75006 Paris Tel: (1) 45445505
Man Dir: Paul Fournel; *Editorial:* Sabine Delattre; *Publicity:* Jean-Claude Gawséwitch; *Rights & Permissions:* Sabine Delattre
Subjects: Novels, Documentary Books, Fine Editions, Essays, History, Cinema
Bookshop: At above address
1986: 80 titles *Founded:* 1976
ISBN Publisher's Prefix: 2-85956

Sélection du **Reader's Digest** SA*, 212 blvd St-Germain, F-75007 Paris Tel: (1) 45480426 Cable Add: Readigest Paris
The above is the address of the Head Office; General Management is at 1-7 ave Louis Pasteur, BP 101, F-92223 Bagneux Tel: 6641616 Telex: Selread 200882 F
Man Dir: Henri Capdeville; *Marketing Dir:* Daniele Franck; *Editorial:* Denise Freidin; *Publicity:* Daniel Hubert
Subjects: General Fiction, History, How-to, Juveniles, Medicine, Science & Technology, Reference, Art, Architecture, Social Science, Economics, Travel, Nature, Tourism, Atlases
1985: 5 titles *Founded:* 1947
ISBN Publisher's Prefix: 2-7098

Réalisations pour l'Enseignement Multilingue International (REMI), 70 rue du Théâtre, F-75015 Paris Tel: (1) 45757849
Man Dir: Mrs D Holtzer
Subjects: Foreign language courses for Nursery and Primary schools (French, German, English)
Founded: 1966
ISBN Publisher's Prefix: 2-85134

Les Editions Albert **René**+*, 81 ave Marceau, F-75116 Paris Tel: (1) 47205521 Telex: 613160 F
Man Dir: Christian Philippsen
Orders to: Les Presses de la Cité, 8 rue Garancière, F-75006 Paris
Subject: Asterix Cartoons
1985: 1 title *Founded:* 1979
ISBN Publisher's Prefix: 2-86497

Yves **Rivière**, Editeur, 117 rue Vieille-du-Temple, F-75003 Paris Tel: (1) 42747784
Publisher, Man Dir: Yves Rivière
Subjects: Complete Lists of Artists' Works (Oeuvres Catalogues), Artist-illustrated books, Prints
Founded: 1971
ISBN Publisher's Prefix: 2-85666

Editions E **Robert**, L'Ecole et la Famille*, BP 4384, F-69242 Lyon cedex 04 (Located at: 28 rue du Bon-Pasteur, F-69001 Lyon) Tel: 78284899
Man Dir: Armand Rouveyrol
Subjects: Primary Textbooks, Educational Materials, Periodical
Founded: 1873
ISBN Publisher's Prefix: 2-7093

Dictionnaire Le **Robert**, see under Dictionnaires

Editions **Rombaldi** SA*, 15-17 rue de Rome, F-75008 Paris Tel: (1) 42942727 Telex: rombald 641854 F
President: Michel Leroux; *Commercial Dirs:* Henri Kaufman, Francis Petit; *Production Manager:* Henri Kaufman
Subjects: Cartoon Comics, General Books, Cards (Cookery, Knitting, DIY, Beauty, Disney)
Founded: 1920
ISBN Publisher's Prefix: 2-231

Guide **Rosenwald**, 10 rue Vineuse, F-75116 Paris Tel: (1) 45209336
Subject: Annuals

Editions **Roudil**, 53 rue St-Jacques, F-75005 Paris Tel: (1) 40334797
Man Dir: Henry Roudil
Subjects: History, Philosophy, University & Secondary Textbooks, Fiction
Founded: 1954
ISBN Publisher's Prefix: 2-85044

Editions **Rouff** SA*, 36 rue du Vieux-Pont-de-Sèvres, F-92100 Boulogne-Billancourt Tel: 6090140
Subjects: Humour, Shooting, Periodicals
ISBN Publisher's Prefix: 2-85045

G P **Rouge et Or**, 8 rue Garancière, F-75006 Paris Tel: (1) 46341280 Telex: Preci 204807 F
Subjects: Children's Literature
Miscellaneous: Firm is a member of the Presses de la Cité group (qv)

La **Rougery**, see Blondel La Rougery SA

Publications **Roy**, now incorporated in Publications Estoup et Roy (qv)

S E C A Codes Rousseau*, Ziat les Plesses, Chateau d' Olonne, F-85100 Les Sables d'Olonne Tel: 51211731 Telex: 711921 F
Subjects: Education, Juveniles, Audio Visual & Electronic Media
ISBN Publisher's Prefix: 2-7095

S E C F — Editions Radio*, 9 rue Jacob, F-75006 Paris Tel: (1) 43296370
Subjects: Engineering, Mass Media
Founded: 1934
ISBN Publisher's Prefix: 2-7091

S E D E S, see Centre de Documentation Universitaire

S E N H A, Société d'Exploitation des Nouveaux Humanoïdes Associés+*, 17 rue Monsigny, F-75002 Paris Tel: (1) 47424610 Telex: 213913
Also known as Les Humanoïdes Associés
Man Dir: Pascal Bourguignon; *Publishing Dir:* Jean-Pierre Dionnet
Subjects: Adult adventure and strip cartoons
Founded: 1975
ISBN Publisher's Prefix: 2-7316

S I M E P SA, 130 blvd St-Germain, F-75006 Paris
Name denotes Société d'Information medicale et d'Enseignement post-universitaire (Medical Information and Post-University Teaching Company)
Chairman: Bernard Duportet
Subject: Medicine
Founded: 1965
ISBN Publisher's Prefix: 2-85334

S N L, now Dictionnaires Le Robert (qv)

Editions **S O S** (Editions du Secours Catholique)*, 106 rue de Bac, F-75007 Paris Tel: (1) 45486066
Man Dir: Maurice Herr; *Publicity & Advertising:* Georges Fanucchi
Subjects: History, Philosophy, Religion, Social Science
Founded: 1949
ISBN Publisher's Prefix: 2-7185

S P E L D, 6 rue Victor-Cousin, F-75005 Paris Tel: (1) 46336910
A group of French publishers specializing in Law, Economics, Politics

S U D, 62 rue Sainte, F-13001 Marseille Tel: 91336068
Man Dir: Yves Broussard
Orders to: Ramsay CDE, 9 rue du Cherche Midi, F-75006 Paris
Subjects: Symposia, Foreign Property, Poetry, Literature, Periodicals
Founded: 1970
ISBN Publisher's Prefix: 2-86446

S U D E L (Société Universitaire d'Editions et de Librairie)*, 20 rue Corvisart, F-75640 Paris cedex 13 Tel: (1) 45354846
Subject: Education
ISBN Publisher's Prefix: 2-7162

Les Editions du **Sagittaire**, 61 rue des Sts-Pères, F-75006 Paris Tel: (1) 42229976
Dirs: Jean-Claude Fasquelle
Subjects: Fiction, Biography, History, General Literature
Founded: 1929

Editions **Saint-Germain-des-Prés** SA+*, 68 rue du Cherche-Midi, F-75006 Paris Tel: (1) 42227120
Editorial: Jean Breton; *Publicity:* Philippe Héraclès
Subject: Poetry
Founded: 1969

Editions **Saint-Paul** SA, 6 rue Cassette, F-75006 Paris Tel: (1) 46422980 (Issy-les-Moulineaux)
Man Dir: M Lerozier
Subsidiary Company: Editions Saint-Paul SA, Dept des Classiques Africains (at Branch Office address)
Branch Off: 184 ave de Verdun, F-92130 Issy-les-Moulineaux
Subjects: Religion, Religious History, Biography, Africana
Bookshop: Librairie Saint-Paul, 6 rue Cassette, F-75006 Paris
Founded: 1873
ISBN Publisher's Prefix: 2-85049

Editions **Salvator** Sàrl, BP 1175, F-68053 Mulhouse cedex (Located at: 9 Pont d'Altkirch) Tel: 89451430
Subject: Religion
Founded: 1924
ISBN Publisher's Prefix: 2-7067

Editions **Sand et Tchou** SA, 6 rue du Mail, F-75002 Paris Tel: (1) 42961693 Telex: 213464 F
Man Dir: Carl van Eiszner; *Rights & Permissions:* Agnès de Gorter
Subjects: General Fiction, Belles Lettres, Biography, How-to, Music, Reference, Paperbacks, Social Science, Psychology, Parapsychology, Esoterism, Astrology, Health
Founded: 1979
ISBN Publisher's Prefix: 2-7107

Editions Le **Sarment**+*, 75 rue des Sts-Pères, F-75006 Paris Tel: (1) 45443845
Man Dir: Jean-Claude Didelot; *Foreign Rights:* Marie-Annick Thabaud
Parent Company: Librairie Arthème Fayard (qv)
Subjects: Religious Works
Founded: 1980

K G **Saur** Editeur, 6 rue de la Sorbonne, F-75005 Paris Tel: (1) 43544754 Telex: Iso bur 630144
Parent Company: K G Saur Verlag, Federal Republic of Germany (qv)

Editions du **Scarabée***, 3 rue de la Montagne-Ste-Geneviève, F-75005 Paris Tel: (1) 43262394
Man Dir, Editorial, Production, Publicity, Rights & Permissions: Jacqueline Copfermann; *Sales:* Claudine Alexandre
Subjects: Psychology, Pedagogy, Physical Education
Book Club: Amis du Scarabée
Bookshop: Librairie du Scarabée (at above address)
1985: 6 titles *Founded:* 1945
ISBN Publisher's Prefix: 2-5112007

Scarabée d'Or, an imprint of Editions Dominique Leroy (qv)

Schott Frères Sàrl*, 35 rue Jean Moulin, F-94300 Vincennes Tel: 3743095
Associate Company: Schott Frères SPRL, Belgium (qv)
Subject: Music

Scolavox, 203 rue de Gençay, BP 429, F-86011 Poitiers Tel: 49462766
Man Dir: Claude Moreau; *Sales Dir:* Albert Combe
Subjects: Poetry, Primary Textbooks, Educational Materials
1987: 128 titles *Founded:* 1959
ISBN Publisher's Prefix: 2-85052

Editions du **Secours** Catholique, see SOS

La Société **Sécuritas** SA*, 2 rue de Châteaudun, F-75009 Paris Tel: (1) 48787206
Subjects: Technical, Law, Economics, Finance
ISBN Publisher's Prefix: 2-7097

Seditas (Société d'Editions et de Diffusion Tambourinaire-Sofradel)*, 186 rue du Faubourg-St-Honoré, F-75008 Paris Tel: (1) 45619600
Orders to: 41 rue Washington, F-75008 Paris
Subjects: Management, Scientific, Technical, Electronics
ISBN Publisher's Prefix: 2-85179

114 FRANCE

Les Editions **Seghers** SA*, 6 pl St-Sulpice, F-75006 Paris Tel: (1) 43291233
Telex: Edilaf 270607
President, Man Dir: Robert Laffont;
Literary Manager: Bernard Delvaille;
Rights & Permissions: Béatrix Vernet
Orders to: Inter Forum, 13 rue de la Glacière, F-75013 Paris Telex: 250055
Associate Company: Editions Robert Laffont (qv)
Subjects: Belles Lettres, Poetry, Biography, Memoirs, Art, Paperbacks
Founded: 1944
ISBN Publisher's Prefix: 2-232

Editions **Sélection** J Jacobs SA+*, 66 rue Falguière, F-75015 Paris Tel: (1) 43203188
Subjects: Technology, Fine Arts, How-to series
ISBN Publisher's Prefix: 2-7174

La **Septième** Aurore, member of CEA (qv)

Septimus Editions, an imprint of Arted (Editions d'Art) (qv)

Service Technique pour l'Education*, 19 blvd Poissonnière, F-75002 Paris Tel: (1) 35084756
Man Dir: Mrs Gradvohl
Subjects: General Fiction, Belles Lettres, Poetry, Biography, History, Music, Art, Philosophy, Reference, Religion, Juveniles, Educational Materials, Judaica
Bookshop: At above address
Founded: 1962

Editions du **Seuil**, 27 rue Jacob, F-75261 Paris cedex 06 Tel: (1) 43291215 Cable Add: Ediseuil Telex: 270024 F
President, Man Dir: Michel Chodkiewicz;
Editorial: Anne Fréyer, Denis Roche, François Wahl, Bruno Flamand, Jean-Claude Guillebaud, Jean Marc Roberts, Olivier Betourné; *Production:* Anne Poulain; *Marketing:* Jean Bussy; *Publicity:* Françoise Peyrot; *Rights & Permissions:* Prune Berge
Subsidiary Companies: Société d'Editions Scientifiques, Dimedia, (Montreal) Seuil-Diffusion
Subjects: General Fiction, Literature, Poetry, Biography, History, How-to, Music, Art, Philosophy, Reference, Religion, Low- & High-priced Paperbacks, Psychology, General & Social Science, University Textbooks, Politics
Founded: 1935
ISBN Publisher's Prefix: 2-02

Editions **Siloé** Sàrl*, 8 pl St-Sulpice, F-75006 Paris Tel: (1) 43260057
Subject: Religion, Art books
ISBN Publisher's Prefix: 2-85054

Editions André **Silvaire** Sàrl+, 20 rue Domat, F-75005 Paris Tel: (1) 43267234
Subjects: General Fiction, Belles Lettres, Poetry, Theatre, Philosophy, Social Sciences, Paperbacks
Founded: 1944
ISBN Publisher's Prefix: 2-85055

Sindbad+, 1 et 3 rue Feutrier, F-75018 Paris Tel: (1) 42553523
Man Dir: Pierre Bernard; *Publicity, Advertising:* Fattouma Haniche; *Rights & Permissions:* Claudine Rulleau
Subjects: General Fiction, Belles Lettres, Poetry, History, Art, Philosophy, Reference, Religion, Social and Political Science connected with the Arabic, Persian and general Muslim worlds
1985: 120 titles *Founded:* 1972
ISBN Publisher's Prefix: 2-7274

Editions **Sirey**, Diffusion Dalloz, 11 rue Soufflot, F-75240 Paris cedex 05 Tel: (1) 43295080 Telex: 206446 F
Administration Office: 35 rue Tournefort, F-75240 Paris cedex 05 Tel: (1) 43310485
Dir: Patrice Vergé; *Dir:* Gérard de Nussac; *Sales:* Philippe Nani; *Publicity:* Mrs A Stein
Subjects: History, Philosophy, Social Science, Law, Business, University & Secondary Textbooks, Economics
Founded: 1791
ISBN Publisher's Prefix: 2-248

Société d'Edition d'Enseignement Supérieur, see Centre de Documentation Universitaire

Société d'Editions Scientifiques, Dimedia, subsidiary company of Editions du Seuil (qv)

Société d'Etudes Juridiques Internationales et Fiscales, see Les Cahiers Fiscaux Européens Sàrl

Société d'Exploitation des Nouveaux Humanoïdes Associés, see SENHA

Société d'Exploitation et de Diffusion des Codes Rousseau, see SECA

Société d'Information médicale. et d'enseignement post-universitaire, see SIMEP

Société du Nouveau Littré, now Dictionnaires Le Robert (qv)

Société Française des Imprimeries Administratives Centrales, see Sofiac

Société Universitaire d'Editions et de Librairie, see SUDEL

Sodel (Editeur) SA*, 336-340 rue St-Honoré, F-75001 Paris Tel: (1) 42603180
Subjects: Science, Technical
ISBN Publisher's Prefix: 2-7102

Sofiac (Société Française des Imprimeries Administratives Centrales)*, 8 rue de Furstenberg, F-75006 Paris Tel: (1) 46342020
President: Pierre de Clerck; *General Manager:* Jean-Claude Goulon
Subjects: Economics, Social Science, Business Administration, Legal and Judicial, Accountancy

Sofradel-Seditas, see Seditas

Sofradif Editions Philippe Auzou+, 74 rue Stendhal, F-75020 Paris Tel: (1) 47972709
Publisher: Philippe Auzou; *Sales Manager:* Fred Frangeul
Subjects: Medicine, Law, Scientific and Technical Encyclopaedia in comic strip form

Solar*, 8 rue Garancière, F-75006 Paris Tel: (1) 4329180 Telex: Precite 204807
Subjects: Practical Books, Cookery, Sport, Nature
Miscellaneous: Firm is a member of the Presses de la Cité group (qv)

Editions d'Art Aimery **Somogy**+, 20 ave Rapp, F-75007 Paris Tel: (1) 45555874
Telex: 204473
Man Dir: Aimery Somogy
Subject: Art
Founded: 1937
ISBN Publisher's Prefix: 2-85056

Soprep, see Editions de l'Instant Durable

Editions Louis **Soulanges** 'Le Livrer Ouvert'*, 34 rue Scheffer, F-75116 Paris Tel: (1) 45538499
Man Dir, Sales Dir, Publicity: Louis Drouot Soulanges
Associate Company: Paris-Caraïbes
Imprint: France-Caraïbes
Branch Off: 5-7 rue Abel Ferry, F-75016 Paris Tel: (01) 5240609
Subjects: General Fiction, Philosophy, Reference, Religion, Juveniles
Founded: 1960

Les Editions de la **Source** Sàrl*, 5 rue de la Source, F-75016 Paris Tel: (1) 45253007
Man Dir: Rev Father Dom André Gozier;
All Other Offices: Rev Father Dom Norbert Balladur
Orders to: Office Général du Livre, 14 bis rue Jean-Ferrandi, F-75006 Paris Tel: (1) 45483828
Imprints: Lumière Biblique series
Subjects: Religion; Doctrine, Theology, Spirituality, Holy Scripture, Monastics and Benedictine History
Bookshop: Librairie Sainte Marie, 5 rue de la Source, F-75016 Paris
Founded: 1927
ISBN Publisher's Prefix: 2-900005

Editions **Stock**, 103 blvd St-Michel, F-75005 Paris Tel: (1) 46348936
President: Jean Rosenthal; *Editor in Chief:* Marie-Pierre Bay; *Sales:* Claude Denet;
Publicity, Rights & Permissions: Janine Noël
Parent Company: Librairie Hachette (qv)
Subjects: French and Foreign Literature, Human Sciences, Medicine, Juveniles, Cinema, Paperbacks
Founded: 1780
ISBN Publisher's Prefix: 2-234

Editions **Studia** SA*, 40 bis rue Maurice-Arnoux, F-92120 Montrouge Tel: 2533811
Subject: Education
ISBN Publisher's Prefix: 2-7104

Les Editions de la **Table** Ronde, 40 rue du Bac, F-75007 Paris Tel: (1) 42222891
President, Dir-General: Gwenn-Aël Bollore; *Man Dir:* Catherine du Vivier;
Publisher: Jean Picollec; *Editor:* Pierre-Guillaume de Roux; *Rights & Permissions:* Mahaut Pascalis
Subjects: General Fiction and Non-fiction, Belles Lettres, Biography, History, Religion, Psychology, Social Science
Founded: 1944
ISBN Publisher's Prefix: 2-7103

Les Presses de **Taizé**, Taizé-Communauté, F-71250 Cluny
Tel: 85501414 Telex: Cotaize 800753 F
Orders to: Editions du Seuil, 27 rue Jacob, F-75261 Paris cedex 06
Subject: Religious works
Founded: 1959

Editions **Tallandier***, 61 rue de la Tombe-Issoire, F-75677 Paris cedex 14 Tel: (1) 43201433
President, Director-General: Jacques Jourquin
Subjects: General Fiction (especially Romantic), Art, Belles Lettres, Reference, History, Geography, Paperbacks
Founded: 1865
Miscellaneous: Formerly Librairie Jules Tallandier
ISBN Publisher's Prefix: 2-235

Editions **Tardy** SA, 89 rue de Seine, F-75006 Paris Tel: 43260058 Telex: 205781
Man Dir, Rights & Permissions: Pierre Penet; *Dir:* Jacques Berne
Subjects: Religion, Catechisms, Parish Manuals, Religious Pedagogy
Founded: 1938
ISBN Publisher's Prefix: 2-7105

Editions **Taride** Sàrl, 2 bis pl du Puits de l'Ermite, F-75005 Paris Tel: (1) 43364040
Man Dir: Pierre-Alain Imhof; *General Manager:* Frédérique Imhof
Subjects: Geography, Travel, Cookery
Founded: 1852
ISBN Publisher's Prefix: 2-7106

Société d'Exploitation de **Tchou** Editeur Sàrl, now Editions Sand et Tchou (qv)

Société des Éditions **Technip**+, 27 rue Ginoux, F-75737 Paris cedex 15 Tel: (1) 45771108 Telex: 200375 Editecp F
Dir: Jacques Ledésert; *Assistant Dir:* Anna Béraud
Parent Company: Institut Français du Petrole
Subjects: Petroleum Science & Technology
Bookshop: At above address
1986-87: 40 titles *Founded:* 1956
ISBN Publisher's Prefix: 2-7108

Technique et Documentation (Librairie Lavoisier)+*, 11 rue Lavoisier, F-75384 Paris cedex 08 Tel: (1) 42653995 Telex: Lavoisi 649404 F
Publishers: Alain Deubel, Pierre Fenouil; *Publicity:* Cécile Prat
Subjects: Engineering, Industrial Safety, Environment, Metallurgy, Hydraulics, Chemistry, Electro-Technology, Biology, Food Industry and Technology, Agriculture, Civil Engineering, Oceanography, Reference
ISBN Publisher's Prefix: 2-85206

Technique et Vulgarisation SA, an imprint of Editions Bordas (qv)

Techniques de l'Ingénieur Sàrl*, 21 rue Cassette, F-75006 Paris Tel: (1) 42223550 The above is the address of the Editorial office, the Commercial office is at 8 pl de l'Odeon, F-75006 Paris Tel: (1) 46342240
Man Dir: Jacques Debaene; *Editorial:* Jean-Jacques Baron; *Publicity:* Gérard Delepoulle (at Commercial Office address)
Subjects: Scientific, Technical
ISBN Publisher's Prefix: 2-85059

Editions **Temps** Futurs Sàrl*, 102 ave Denfert Rochereau, F-75014 Paris Tel: (1) 43225014
Man Dir, Sales, Production, Publicity, Rights & Permissions: Sophie Barets; *Editorial:* Stan Barets
Subjects: Science Fiction, Cartoons
Bookshop: Librairie Temps Futurs, 8 rue Dante, F-75005 Paris
Founded: 1981
ISBN Publisher's Prefix: 2-86607

Librairie Pierre **Téqui** et Editions Téqui, 82 rue Bonaparte, F-75006 Paris Tel: (1) 43260458
Head Office: Le Roc St Michel, F-53150 St-Cénéré Tel: 43010181
General Manager: Pierre Lemaire; *Literary Manager:* G Cerbelaud Salagnac
Subjects: Education, Juveniles, Philosophy, Theology, Hagiography, Catechism, Sociology
ISBN Publisher's Prefix: 2-85244

Editions **Tests***, 41 rue de la Grange-aux-Belles, F-75483 Paris cedex 10 Tel: (1) 42022910
Subjects: Science, Technical, Audio-Visual, Electronic Media

Transédition, 41 rue de la Gaité, F-75014 Paris Tel: (1) 43215942
Man Dir, Editorial: Marc Dachy; *Sales:* Anne Barrès; *Production:* Paule Pousseele; *Publicity:* James Ravel; *Rights & Permissions:* Jacques Bekaert
Orders to: Distique, 17 rue Hoche, F-92240 Malakoff Tel: 46554214
Subsidiary Company: Editions Luna-Park
Associate Company: Montfaucon Research Center (at above address)
Subjects: Art, History of Art, Contemporary Literature, Avant-garde
Founded: 1972
ISBN Publisher's Prefix: 2-8025

Editions de **Trévise** BFB, 17 rue Jacob, F-75006 Paris Tel: (1) 46340310
Man Dir: Nicole Lattès; *Literary Dirs:* Pierre Ripert, Jacques Baudouin
Parent Company: Editions Jean-Claude Lattès (qv)
Subjects: Fiction, How-to
Founded: 1956
ISBN Publisher's Prefix: 2-86552

U G E 10/18*, 8 rue Garancière, F-75006 Paris Tel: (1) 46341280 Telex: Preci 204807 F
Subjects: University and Political series, Literature
Miscellaneous: Member of the Presses de la Cité group (qv)
ISBN Publisher's Prefix: 2-264

Editions **Universitaires***, 77 rue de Vaugirard, F-75006 Paris Tel: (1) 45487860 Telex: 202036 F (Begedis SA)
Orders to: (France) Diff-Edit, 96 blvd du Montparnasse, F-75014 Paris Tel: (1) 43354700 Telex: 201332 F; (Foreign) Arc-en-Ciel International, ZI Tournai-Ouest, B-7713 Marquain, Belgium Telex: 57429 B
Associate Companies: Editions du Chalet, Editions Desclée et Cie, Editions Gamma, Nouvelles Editions Mame (qqv)
Subjects: General Non-fiction, Popular Reference, Juveniles, Reportage, Literature, History, Biography, Philosophy, Education, Sociology, Astrology, Paperbacks
Founded: 1942
ISBN Publisher's Prefix: 2-7113

Presses **Universitaires** de France, de Grenoble, de Lille, de Lyon, de Nancy, see Presses

Editions de l'**Usine** Nouvelle, see Editions du Moniteur

Les Editions **Vaillant/Miroir** Sprint Publications*, 126 rue Lafayette, F-75461 Paris Tel: (1) 442469225 Telex: Edipif 640067
International Sales Manager: Alain Lesaint
Subjects: Juveniles, Comic books, Sport

Editions **Van de Velde**, La Petite Plaine, BP 22, Fondettes, F-37230 Luynes Tel: 47420623; Sales Office at 12 rue Jacob, F-75006 Paris Tel: (1) 43259343 Telex: 750882 F
Man Dir, Sales: Jean-Michel Cocoual; *Editorial, Production:* Francis Van de Velde; *Publicity:* Edith Frilet; *Rights & Permissions:* Dominique Picard
Subject: Music and Musical Instruction
Founded: 1898
ISBN Publisher's Prefix: 2-85868

Editions Francis **Van de Velde**, 12 rue Jacob, F-75006 Paris Tel: (1) 43259343 Telex: 750882 F
Man Dir, Editorial: Francis Van de Velde; *Sales, Rights and Permissions:* Dominique Picard
Subjects: Music, Musicology, Music Education

Editions de **Vergeures**, 23 ave Villemain, F-75014 Paris Tel: (1) 45392244 Telex: Incoser 206726 F
President: Jacques Dodeman; *Man Dir, Rights & Permissions:* Annie Weber
Subjects: Popular Encyclopaedias, Practical and How-to, Art Series
Founded: 1979
ISBN Publisher's Prefix: 2-7309

Vertiges+, 6 rue Pierre Lescot, F-75001 Paris Tel: (1) 4298214 Telex: 214889 F
Man Dir: Eugene Simion; *Production:* Djamila Hichour, Ranko Tolic; *Rights & Permissions:* Dominique Faber
Orders to: Carrere Distribution, 35-37 rue Gabriele Péri, F-92330 Issy-les-Moulineaux
Associate Company: Carrere Editions 13, 27 rue de Surène, F-75008 Paris
Subjects: Fiction, Biography, Politics
1985: 30 titles *Founded:* 1985
ISBN Publisher's Prefix: 2-86957

Vertiges Bulles, an imprint of Editions Dominique Leroy (qv)

Veyrier*, 12 rue de Nesle, F-75006 Paris Tel: (1) 46332018
Man Dir, Editorial: Henri Veyrier; *Sales:* Philippe Lefranc
Orders to: Anagramme (at above address)
Parent Company: Anagramme (at above address)
Subjects: Illustrated Books on Art, Cinema, Paris, Fiction
Bookshops: 17 ter ave de Clichy, F-75018 Paris; 20 rue J H Fabre, Saint Ouen
Founded: 1973

Editions **Vigot** Frères*, 23 rue de l'Ecole-de-Médecine, F-75006 Paris Tel: (1) 43295450 Telex: 201708 F
Man Dir: Daniel Vigot
Subjects: Medicine, Pharmacy, Nursing, Sports, Veterinary
Bookshop: Librairie Vigot (at above address)
Founded: 1890
ISBN Publisher's Prefix: 2-7114

Editions **Vilo** SA, 25 rue Ginoux, F-75015 Paris Tel: (1) 45770805 Cable Add: Edivilo Paris Telex: 200305 F
Man Dir: Mme Larfillon
Subjects: Art, History, Religion, Architecture, Reference, Maps, Literature, Non-fiction, Sports, Languages, Tourism, Automobiles
ISBN Publisher's Prefix: 2-7191

Librairie Philosophique J **Vrin**, 6 pl de la Sorbonne, F-75005 Paris 5 Tel: (1) 43540347
Man Dir: Gérard Paulhac
Subjects: Philosophy, Reference, Religion, Psychology, University Textbooks, History
Bookshops (new and secondhand books): Philosophy, Law, Religion at 6 pl de la Sorbonne, Paris; Literature, Art, History at 71 rue St Jacques, Paris
1986: 60 titles *Founded:* 1920
ISBN Publisher's Prefix: 2-7116

Librairie **Vuibert** SA*, 63 blvd St-Germain, F-75005 Paris Tel: (1) 43256100 Cable Add: Vuibert Paris Telex: 201005 F Vuibpar
President: Jean Adam; *Editorial:* Monique Griboval
Subjects: Mathematics, Physics, Chemistry, Biology, Earth Sciences, Schoolbooks, Children's Literature, Economics, Law
Founded: 1877
ISBN Publisher's Prefix: 2-7117

Gerard **Watelet**, see Editions Pygmalion

Editions et Librairie **Weber***, 24-28 rue du Moulinet, F-75013 Paris Tel: (1) 47885034 Cable Add: Webart-Paris
Subjects: Art, Architecture, Social Science, Juveniles, Reference
Founded: 1967
ISBN Publisher's Prefix: 2-7190

Galerie Lucie **Weill***, Au Pont des Arts, 6 rue Bonaparte, F-75006 Paris Tel: (1) 43547195
President: Lucie Weill
Subjects: Books with illustrations by famous artists
Book Club: Nouveau Cercle Parisien du Livre
Founded: 1930

116 FRANCE

Editions **Weka***, 12 cour St Eloi, F-75012 Paris Tel: (1) 43076050 Telex: 210504
General Manager: M von Oertzen;
Editorial: Philippe Chabaud, Laurence Martin, Laurence Regnault; *Production:* Olivier Dasson Ville, Marie-Françoise Zeitouni
Parent Company: Weka-Verlag, Postfach 1180, D-8901 Kissing, Federal Republic of Germany
Subjects: Law, Economics, Tax Law, Social Sciences, Management
Founded: 1979
ISBN Publisher's Prefix: 2-7337

Y M C A-Press*, 11 rue de la Montagne Ste-Geneviève, F-75005 Paris Tel: (1) 43547446
Subjects: Religion, Literature, Russian books (in Russian)
1985: 20 titles
Miscellaneous: See also Les Editeurs Réunis
ISBN Publisher's Prefix: 2-85065

Editions Philateliques **Yvert et Tellier***, 35 bis rue de Provence, F-75009 Paris Tel: (1) 47706298
Subjects: General, Encyclopaedias, Sports

Zodiaque+, la Pierre-qui-Vire, F-89830 St-Léger-Vauban Tel: 86322123 Cable Add: Zodiaque-89830 St Léger
Man Dir: José Surchamp
Distribution in France: Payot-Weber, 106 blvd St-Germain, F-75006 Paris
Distribution outside France: Marcel Weber, 13 rue de Monthoux, CH-1211 Geneva 2, Switzerland
Subjects: Ancient and Modern Art, Music
Founded: 1951
ISBN Publisher's Prefix: 2-7369

Literary Agents

Jean-Pierre **Boscq***, 65 rue du Faubourg St-Honoré, F-75008 Paris Tel: (1) 42666200

Agence Littéraire Alexandra **Chapman**, 27 rue Claude Bernard, F-75005 Paris Tel: (1) 45350429 Telex: Publi Bit 250302 F
Contact: Alexandra Chapman
Specialization: Represents American and European agents and publishers for French translation rights. Illustrated books, co-editions

D M Agence Littéraire*, 12 rue du Regard, F-75006 Paris Tel: (1) 45484503/ 42224233
Formerly McKee et Mouche
Dir: Donine Mouche

E A I S, 10 rue de l'Abreuvoir, F-92400 Courbevoie Tel: (1) 47880840 Telex: Chanced 640093 F Fax: (1) 47550943
Contact: Vera le Marié
Also: European American Information Services Inc, 110 East 59th St, 36th Floor, New York, NY 10022, USA Tel: (212) 308 7760 Telex: 6973186

Françoise **Germain**, 8 rue de la Paix, F-75002 Paris Tel: (1) 42616814

Agence **Hoffman***, 77 blvd St-Michel, F-75005 Paris Tel: (1) 43265694 Cable Add: Aghoff Paris Telex: 203605 F
Contacts: Boris or Georges Hoffman, Ursula Veit
There is a branch of this Agency in Munich, Federal Republic of Germany (qv)

Michelle **Lapautre**, 6 rue Jean Carriès, F-75007 Paris Tel: (1) 47348241 Cable Add: Milalit Paris Telex: 205247

Anne **Lenclud**, Pierre Lenclud, Agence Renault-Lenclud, 18 rue Blanche, F-75009 Paris Tel: (1) 45262679

McKee et Mouche, see DM Agence Littéraire

Matthias-Estienne, 27 rue du Dragon, F-75006 Paris Tel: (1) 42222912

La **Nouvelle Agence**, 7 rue Corneille, F-75006 Paris Tel: (1) 43258560 Telex: 250303 F (Paris Bourse)
Contact: Mary Kling

Frédérique **Porretta**, 28 rue de l'Université, F-75007 Paris Tel: (1) 47039448
Also: Barcelona, Spain (qv)

Promotion Littéraire, 26 rue Chalgrin, F-75116 Paris Tel: (1) 45004210 Cable Add: Promolit Paris
Dir: Mariella Giannetti

Bureau littéraire international Marguerite **Scialtiel**, 14 rue Chanoinesse, F-75004 Paris Tel: (1) 43547116
Contact: Geneviève Ulmann

Greta **Strassova**, 4 rue Gît-Le-Coeur, F-75006 Paris Tel: (1) 46333457
Formerly Héléna Strassova

Elise **Wandel Cruse**, 17 rue du Vieux-Colombier, F-75006 Paris Tel: (1) 45490356 Telex: 642138 Selex F – 221

Ellen **Wright**, 20 rue Jacob, F-75006 Paris 6 Tel: (1) 43542378

Book Clubs

L'**Amitié par le Livre**, Henri Frossard, BP 2085, F-25051 Besançon cedex
First book club founded in France (in 1930, by teaching profession), it is non-profitmaking and run by voluntary effort
Owned by: L'Amitié par le Livre (qv)

Club du Livre d'Art*, 1 rue Palatine, F-75006 Paris
Owned by: Editions Albert Morancé (qv)

Club du Livre SA*, 28 rue Fortuny, F-75017 Paris Tel: (1) 47638055
Man Dir: Philippe Lebaud
Subjects: Art, De Luxe Editions

Club Français du Livre*, 6 rue Galilée, F-75116 Paris

Livre Club **Diderot***, 146 rue du Faubourg-Poissonnière, F-75010 Paris
Owned by: Les Editions Sociales-Messidor (qv)
Subjects: Political and Economic Science, History, Poetry, Literature

Education et Culture, 28 rue de la Boétie, F-75008 Paris
Owned by: Les Editions des Deux Coqs d'Or (qv)

Nouveau Cercle Parisien du Livre*, 6 rue Bonaparte, F-75006 Paris
President: Daniel S Sickles
Subjects: Illustrated Books
Club is associated with publisher Galerie Lucie Weill (qv)

Poètes Présents, BP 75, F-56340 Carnac-Plage
Owned by: Jean Grassin Editeur (qv)
Founded: 1957
Subject: Poetry

Publications de l'Ecole Moderne Française (PEMF)*, 189 blvd F Tonner, BP 109, F-06322 Cannes la Bocca cedex Tel: 93479611 Cable Add: Pemf
This company runs five book clubs supplying series of books for children: aged 8-12 (BTJ), aged 10-15 (BT), aged over 15 (BT2); for teachers (L'Educateur), and for audiovisual supplies (BT Son)
Owned by: Coopérative de l'Enseignement Laïc (qv)

Amis du **Scarabée***, 3 rue de la Montagne-Ste-Geneviève, F-75005 Paris Tel: (1) 43262394
Owned by: Editions du Scarabée (qv)

Major Booksellers

Brentano's*, 37 ave de l'Opéra, F-75002 Paris Tel: (1) 42615250 Telex: Brentan 216781 F

F N A C, 136 rue de Rennes, F-75006 Paris Tel: (1) 45443912
Manager: Simone Mussard

Flammarion, 19 pl Bellecour, F-69002 Lyon Tel: 78380157 Telex: Flamlyo 300460 F
Manager: Jean-Noël Flammarion
Branches: One in Bordeaux; one in Dijon; two in Grenoble; three in Lyon; one in Marseilles; 12 in Paris. Also six in Montreal, Canada
Also Publisher (qv)

Librairie Joseph **Gibert***, 26 blvd St-Michel, F-75006 Paris Tel: (1) 43292141 Telex: gibliv 270162 F

Librairie La **Hune**, 170 blvd St-Germain, F-75006 Paris Tel: (1) 45483585
Man Dir: Georges Dupré
Owned by: Flammarion (qv)

Librairie **Mollat***, 11-15 rue Vital-Carles, F-33080 Bordeaux cedex Tel: 56448487 Telex: 541542 F
Also: 83-91 rue Porte-Dijeaux, F-33080 Bordeaux cedex

Librairie générale des P U F, 49 blvd St-Michel, F-75005 Paris Tel: (1) 43258340
Owned by: Presses Universitaires de France (qv)

Librairie de **Provence**, 31 cours Mirabeau, F-13100 Aix en Provence
Manager: M J Apprin

Librairie **Sauramps**, Le Triangle, pl de la Comédie, BP 9551, F-34045 Montpellier cedex Tel: 67588515 Telex: 480728
Manager: P Torreilles

Sodexport, 35 rue Grégoire de Tours, F-75006 Paris Tel: (1) 43259130 Telex: Lifran 270838 F
Association française pour la Diffusion du Livre Scientifique, Technique et Medical (French Society for the Distribution of Scientific, Technical and Medical books)

Librairie de l'**Université***, 17 rue de la Liberté, F-21025 Dijon cedex Tel: 80305117

Major Libraries

Archives nationales, 60 rue des Francs-Bourgeois, F-75141 Paris cedex 03 Tel: (1) 42771130
Publications: National Archive documents, which are sold and distributed by La Documentation Française (qv under Publishers)

Bibliothèque de l'**Arsenal***, 1 rue de Sully, F-75004 Paris Tel: (1) 42774421
Chief Librarian: Jean-Claude Garreta
Publication: Trésors de la Bibliothèque de l'Arsenal (exhibition, 1980)

Bibliothèque d'**Art et d'Archéologie** (Fondation Jacques Doucet), 3 rue

Michelet, F-75272 Paris cedex 06 Tel: (1) 43543527
Dir: Denise Gazier
This is a Paris University library

Bibliothèque mazarine, 23 Quai Conti, F-75006 Paris Tel: (1) 43548948
Chief Curator: Pierre Gasnault

Bibliothèque municipale de Besançon, 1 rue de la Bibliothèque, F-25044 Besançonó cedex Tel: 81812089
Librarian: Jacques Mironneau

Bibliothèque municipale de Grenoble, blvd Maréchal Lyautey, BP 1095, RP, F-38021 Grenoble cedex Tel: 76460156
Librarian: M Merland
Publications include: Bibliothèque municipale de Grenoble, Catalogue général auteurs des livres imprimés jusqu'à 1900, 1980, 12 vols (available from K G Saur, Federal Republic of Germany, qv)

Bibliothèque municipale de la Ville de Lyon*, 30 blvd Vivier-Merle, F-69431 Lyon cedex 03 Tel: 78628520
Librarian: Jean-Louis Rocher

Bibliothèque nationale, 58 rue de Richelieu, F-75002 Paris cedex 2 Tel: (1) 47038126
National Library
General Administrator: André Miquel
Publication: Revue de la Bibliothèque Nationale

Bibliothèque nationale et universitaire de Strasbourg, 5 rue du Maréchal Joffre, BP 1029/F, F-67070 Strasbourg cedex Tel: 88360068 (main address and Management and Legal Section); 6 place de la République, BP 1029/F, F-67070 Strasbourg cedex Tel: 88360068 (Literature and Human Sciences Section); 3 bis rue du Maréchal Joffre, BP 1029/F, F-67070 Strasbourg cedex Tel: 88360068 (Section dealing with Alsace region affairs); 4 rue Kirschleger, F-67085 Strasbourg cedex Tel: 88362323 (Medical Section); 72 route du Rhin, F-67400 Illkirch-Graffenstaden Tel: 88669077 (Pharmaceutical Annex); 34 blvd de la Victoire, BP 1037/F, F-67070 Strasbourg cedex Tel: 88613323 (Scientific and Technical Section)
Dir: Lily Greiner
Publications include: Bibliographie alsacienne; Catalogue critique des manuscrits persans; Papyrus grecs de la BNUS

Bibliothèque de Documentation Internationale Contemporaine, Campus Universitaire, F-92001 Nanterre cedex Tel: (1) 47214022
This is a Paris University library

Bibliothèque littéraire Jacques Doucet, 10 pl du Panthéon, F-75005 Paris Tel: (1) 43296100 (ext 22, 56, 72)
Librarian: François Chapon

Bibliothèque de l'Ecole des Langues orientales, 4 rue de Lille, F-75007 Paris Tel: (1) 42613790/42616203
Dir: Mrs M Debout

Bibliothèque de Géographie, 191 rue St-Jacques, F-75005 Paris Tel: (1) 43290147
This is a Paris University library

Bibliotheque de l'Institut de France, 23 quai de Conti, F-75006 Paris Tel: (1) 43268540
Librarian: Françoise Dumas

Bibliothèque Interuniversitaire de Médecine, 12 rue de l'Ecole de Médecine, F-75270 Paris cedex 6 Tel: (1) 43541675/43292177 ext 237/239
Dir and Chief Curator: Ms Y Gueniot
Publications include: Catalogue des Périodiques de la Bibliothèque (1976-1981); Bibliothèque de l'ancienne Faculté de Médecine de Paris: Catalogue des Livres du XVIe siècle extrait du catalogue général du fond ancien
This is a Paris University library

Bibliothèque du **Musée de l'Homme**, Palais de Chaillot, pl du Trocadéro, F-75116 Paris Tel: (1) 47045394
Dir: Jacqueline Dubois

Bibliothèque centrale du **Muséum national** d'Histoire naturelle, 38 rue Geoffroy St-Hilaire, F-75005 Paris Tel: (1) 43317124
Dir: Yves Laissus

Bibliothèque Interuniversitaire de **Pharmacie**, 4 ave de l'Observatoire, F-75270 Paris cedex 6 Tel: (1) 43291208 ext 416, 421, 415
Librarian: Marie-Edmée Michel
This is a Paris University library

Bibliothèque **Sainte-Geneviève**, 10 pl du Panthéon, F-75005 Paris Tel: (1) 43296100
Librarian: Geneviève Boisard
This is a Paris University library

Bibliothèque de la **Sorbonne**, 47 rue des Ecoles, F-75230 Paris cedex 5 Tel: (1) 40462211/43262194
Chief Librarian: Claude Jolly
Publications include: Mélanges de la Bibliothèque de la Sorbonne
This is a Paris University library

Bibliothèque de l'**Université de Strasbourg**, see Bibliothèque nationale et universitaire de Strasbourg

Bibliothèques des **Universités de Paris**
The following are Paris University Libraries (for further details please see individual listings in alphabetical order in this section):
Bibliothèque d'Art et d'Archéologie (Fondation Jacques Doucet); Bibliothèque de Documentation Internationale Contemporaine; Bibliothèque de Géographie; Bibliothèque Interuniversitaire de Médecine; Bibliothèque Interuniversitaire de Pharmacie; Bibliothèque Sainte-Geneviève; Bibliothèque de la Sorbonne

Service des Travaux Historiques de la **Ville de Paris** et Bibliothèque historique de la Ville de Paris, 24 rue Pavée, F-75004 Paris Tel: (1) 42744444
Librarian: Jean Derens

Library Associations

A B E F, see Association des Bibliothèques ecclésiastiques de France

A D B S, see Association des Bibliothécaires et Documentalistes Spécialisés

A M P, see Association pour la Médiathèque Publique

Association de l'Ecole nationale supérieure de Bibliothécaires, 17-21 blvd du 11 Novembre 1918, F-69100 Villeurbanne Tel: 78896445
Association of the National School of Librarianship
Chairman: Arlette Pailley-Katz; *General Secretary:* Christiane Baryla
Founded: 1967
Publication: Annuaire de l'Association de l'Ecole nationale supérieure de Bibliothécaires

Association des Archivistes français, 60 rue des Francs-Bourgeois, F-75141 Paris cedex 3 Tel: (1) 42771130
Association of French Archivists
President: Miss R Cleyet-Michaud; *Secretaries:* Miss M P Arnauld, Miss E Gautier-Desuaux
Publication: La Gazette des Archives (quarterly)

Association des Bibliothécaires et Documentalistes Spécialisés, 5 ave Franco-Russe, F-75005 Paris Tel: (1) 45510504

Association des Bibliothécaires français, 65 rue de Richelieu, F-75002 Paris Tel: (1) 42975767
Association of French Librarians
President: Jacqueline Gascuel; *Executive Secretary:* Anne-Françoise Bonnardel; *Permanent Secretary:* Monique Baptiste
Founded: 1906
Publication: Bulletin d'Information

Association des Bibliothèques ecclésiastiques de France (ABEF)*, 6 rue du Regard, F-75006 Paris
Association of Ecclesiastical Libraries in France
Executive Secretary: Jean-Marie Barbier
Publication: Bulletin de Liaison de l'ABEF

Association des Diplômés de l'Ecole de Bibliothécaires-Documentalistes*, Bibliothèque du Saulchoir, 43 bis rue la Glacière, F-75013 Paris Tel: (1) 45870533
Association of Graduates of the School of Librarians and Documentalists
Executive Secretary: Miss A Salavert
Publication: Bulletin d'Information (annual)

Association française des Documentalistes et Bibliothécaires spécialisés*, 5 ave Franco-Russe, F-75007 Paris Tel: (1) 45555516
French Association of Information Scientists and Special Librarians
Publication: Documentaliste — Science de l'Information

Association nationale des Bibliothécaires Municipaux*, c/o Ms Pintaparis, Hôtel de Coulanges, 37 rue des Francs-Bourgeois, F-75004 Paris
National Association of Municipal Librarians

Association pour la Médiathèque Publique (AMP)*, Bibliothèque municipale, 37 rue St-Georges, F-59400 Cambrai Tel: 27813520
Publication: Médiathèques Publiques (Quarterly Review)

D B M I S T, see Direction des Bibliothèques, des Musées et de l'Information Scientifique et Technique

Direction des Bibliothèques, des Musées et de l'Information Scientifique et Technique, 3-5 blvd Pasteur, F-75015 Paris Tel: (1) 45392575
A library administration department of the Ministère de l'Education Nationale
Dir: Denis Varloot
Publication: Bulletin des Bibliothèques de France

Fédération des Associations de Documentalistes et Bibliothécaires de l'Education nationale*, 29 rue d'Ulm, F-75007 Paris
Federation of Associations of National Educational Record Clerks and Librarians
President: Frànçoise Chapron, 25 rue F Berat, F-76140 Petit Quevilly

118 FRANCE

Library Reference Books and Journals

Books

Les Bibliothèques (The Libraries), Presses Universitaires de France, 108 blvd St-Germain, F-75279 Paris cedex 06

Les Bibliothèques publiques en France, ENSB-Presses, 17-21 blvd du 11 novembre 1918, F-69100 Villeurbanne

Journals

Bulletin de Liaison de l'ABEF, Association des Bibliothèques ecclésiastiques de France, 6 rue du Regard, F-75006 Paris

Bulletin d'Information (Information Bulletin), Association des Bibliothécaires français, 65 rue de Richelieu, F-75002 Paris

Bulletin des Bibliothèques de France (French Libraries' Report), Direction des Bibliothèques des Musées et de l'Information Scientifique et Technique, 3-5 blvd Pasteur, F-75015 Paris

Documentaliste — Science de l'Information (Custodian of Records), Association française des Documentalistes et Bibliothécaires specialisés, 5 ave Franco-Russe, F-75007 Paris
Review of documentary information and techniques; published five times a year

La Gazette des Archives (Archives Gazette), Association des Archivistes français, 60 rue des Francs-Bourgeois, F-75141 Paris cedex 3

Informatique (Data Processing), Editions d'Informatique, 82 rue Lauriston, F-75116 Paris

Inter-CDI, centre d'Etude de la Documentation et de l'Information Scolaires, 7 Résidence de Guinette, F-91150 Etampes
Journal for specialist librarians, published every two months

Revue de la Bibliothèque nationale, Bibliothèque nationale, 58 rue Richelieu, F-75084 Paris

Scribeco, bulletin bibliographique, Institut national de la Statistique et des Etudes économiques (INSEE), Division Documentation, 18 blvd Adolphe-Pinard, F-75675 Paris cedex 14

Literary Associations and Societies

Académie des Lettres et des Arts, see Société du Vieux Montmartre

Académie Goncourt, Salons Drouant, pl Gaillon, F-75001 Paris
President: Hervé Bazin

Les **Amis** de Milosz, 6 rue José-Maria-de-Heredia, F-75007 Paris Tel: (1) 43267234
Dir: Jean Audard

Centre national des Lettres, 53 rue de Verneuil, F-75007 Paris Tel: (1) 45493140
National Literary Centre
Secretary-General: Veronique Chatenay-Dolto

The **Dickens** Fellowship, 29 blvd Mariette, F-62200 Boulogne sur Mer
Honorary Secretary: Madeleine Petit

La **Joie** par les Livres, 8 rue Saint-Bon, F-75004 Paris Tel: (1) 48876195
Joy through Books — an experimental library and a documentation centre on children's literature
Dir: Geneviève Patte
Publications: La Revue des Livres pour Enfants and other special selections

Maison des Ecrivains, 53 rue de Verneuil, F-75007 Paris Tel: 45493140
Dir: Hughes de Kerret

P E N Club français, 6 rue François-Miron, F-75004 Paris Tel: (1) 42773787
President: René Tavernier; *Secretary:* Jean Orizet
Publication: News Bulletins to members (six per year)

S E L F, see Sydicat des Ecrivains de Langue Française

S N A C, see Syndicat National des Auteurs et Compositeurs

Scam (Société Civile des Auteurs Multimédias), Hôtel de Massa, 38 rue du Faubourg-St-Jacques, F-75014 Paris Tel: (1) 43541866
President: Charles Brabant

Société d'Etudes dantesques*, Centre universitaire méditerranéen, 65 promenade des Anglais, F-06100 Nice Tel: 93868156
President: Louis Gautier-Vignal (of The Society for Dantesque Studies)

Société d'Histoire littéraire de la France, 112 rue Mouge, F-75005 Paris
French Literary History Association
President: R Pomeau
Publications: Revue d'Histoire littéraire de la France (alternate months)

Société des Gens de Lettres*, Hôtel de Massa, 38 rue du Faubourg St Jacques, F-75014 Paris Tel: (1) 43541866
Society of Men and Women of Letters
General Secretary: Michèle Kahn
Publications: Revue des Lettres et de l'Audiovisual; Journal des Lettres et de l'Audiovisual

Société des Poètes Français, Hôtel de Massa, 38 rue du Faubourg St Jacques, F-75014 Paris
President: Jacques Raphael-Leygues; *Secretary-General:* Thérèse Mercier, 3 rue de l'Abreuvoir, F-78630 Orgeval
Publication: Bulletin Trimestriel

Société du Vieux Montmartre, c/o Musée de Montmartre, 12 rue Cortot, F-75018 Paris Tel: (1) 46066111
Formerly known as Académie des Lettres et des Arts
President: Claude Charpentier

Syndicat des Critiques littéraires*, 58 rue Claude Bernard, F-75005 Paris
Society of Literary Critics
Secretary: R André
Publication: Bulletin du Syndicat (quarterly)

Syndicat des Ecrivains de Langue Française, 1 rue de Courcelles, F-75008 Paris Tel: (1) 45637246

Syndicat National des Auteurs et Compositeurs, 80 rue Taitbout, F-75442 Paris cedex 09 Tel: (1) 48749630
President: Jean Drejac

Literary Periodicals

Bulletin critique du livre français, Association pour la Diffusion de la Pensée Française, 9 rue Anatole de la Forge, F-75017 Paris

Bulletin des Lettres (Literary Report), Librairie Lardanchet, 10 rue de Président-Carnot, F-69002 Lyon
Review of criticism and of literary and bibliophilic information

Critique, Les Editions de Minuit, 7 rue Bernard-Palissy, F-75006 Paris
General review of publications in France and abroad

Ecrit du Temps, Les Editions de Minuit SA, 7 rue Bernard-Palissy, F-75006 Paris

Figaro littéraire, 14 Rond-Point des Champs-Elysées, Paris 8e

Information littéraire, Editions J-B Baillière, 10 rue Thénard, F-75005 Paris

Lecture et Tradition (Reading and Tradition), Association pour la Diffusion de la Pensée Française, 9 rue Anatole de la Forge, F-75017 Paris

Lettres françaises (French Literature), 5 rue du Faubourg Poissonnière, Paris 9e

Lettres nouvelles (New Literature), 19 rue Aurélie, F-75007 Paris

Lire (monthly), 61 ave Hoche, F-75382 Paris cedex 08

Littérature, Larousse, 17 rue du Montparnasse, F-75298 Paris cedex 6

Lu (monthly), 37 rue de l'Arcade, F-75008 Paris

Magazine littéraire, Magazine-Expansion, 40 rue des Sts-Pères, Paris 7e

Le Monde des Livres (weekly), 5 rue des Italiennes, F-75008 Paris

La Nouvelle Revue française (monthly), 5 rue Sébastien-Bottin, F-75341 Paris cedex 07

Nouvelles littéraires, Arts, Sciences, Spectacles (News of Literature, the Arts, Sciences, Entertainments), 146 rue Montmartre, Paris 2e

Parler, Galerie 'Parti-Pris', 4 rue Alexandre 1er du Yougoslavie, Grenoble
Literary review

Passerelle, Pierre Béarn, 60 rue Monsieur le Prince, F-75006 Paris
Literary review

Quinzaine littéraire (Literary Fortnightly), 43 rue du Temple, F-75004 Paris 4

Revue de Littérature comparée (Review of Comparative Literature), Librairie Marcel Didier SA, 15 rue Cujas, F-75005 Paris
Text in English, French, German, Italian and Spanish

La Revue des Livres pour Enfants (Children's Books Review), La Joie par les Livres, 8 rue St-Bon, F-75004 Paris

Strophes, Jean Fremon, 9 rue de Belfort, F-9200 Asnières
Literary review

SUD, 62 rue Sainte, F-13001 Marseille
Literary review, quarterly

Trousse-livres, Ligue de l'Enseignement, 3 rue Récamier, F-75341 Paris cedex 7
Review of books for Juveniles, ten issues per year

Literary Prizes

Academy of Thirteen Prize*
Known as 'Prix le Boisson' and given for a work of prose or poetry. Sixteen bottles of famous wine. Awarded annually. Enquiries to Academy of Thirteen, 166 rue de la Burgonce, Niort, Deux-Sèvres

François-Joseph Audiffred Prize
For a published work best qualified to inspire love of ethics and virtue, and to discourage egoism and envy; or to stimulate knowledge and appreciation of the Country of France. Awarded annually. Enquiries to Académie des Sciences Morales et Politiques, Institut de France, 23 quai de Conti, F-75006 Paris

Aujourd'hui Prize
For a historical or political work relating to the contemporary period. 5,000 francs awarded annually. Enquiries to Secrétariat, 12 rue du Quatre Septembre, F-75002 Paris

Joseph Autran Prize
Awarded annually to a poet for the whole of his work. Enquiries to Société des Poètes Français, 38 rue du Faubourg St Jacques, F-75014 Paris

René Bardet Prize
For a poetic work. Awarded every two years. Enquiries to Académie Française, Institut de France, 23 quai de Conti, F-75006 Paris

André Barre Prize
For a work of the most original thought and clearest style by a non-cleric. Enquiries to Académie Française, Institut de France, 23 quai de Conti, F-75006 Paris

Alice Louis Barthou Prize
To a woman of letters. For one work or all of her work. Awarded annually. Enquiries to Académie Française, Institut de France, 23 quai de Conti, F-75006 Paris

Louis Barthou Prize
To a writer whose work or life has served the best interests of France. Awarded annually. Enquiries to Académie Française, Institut de France, 23 quai de Conti, F-75006 Paris

Max Barthou Prize
To a writer under 30 years of age whose talent has been proven or who has shown great promise. Awarded annually. Enquiries to Académie Française, Institut de France, 23 quai de Conti, F-75006 Paris

Charles Blanc Prize
For a written work, preferably treating issues in art. Awarded annually. Enquiries to Académie Française, Institut de France, 23 quai de Conti, F-75006 Paris

Pascal Bonetti Grand Prize
Annual award of 1,000 francs for the entire work of a poet. Enquiries to Société des Poètes Français, 38 rue du Faubourg St Jacques, F-75014 Paris

Bordin Prize
To encourage high quality literature. Awarded annually. Enquiries to Académie Française, Institut de France, 23 quai de Conti, F-75006 Paris

Jean Bouscatel Foundation Prize
Awarded every three years for a book of verse; failing this, for a book on poetry or on a poet or poets. Next award in 1990. Enquiries to Académie Française, Institut de France, 23 quai de Conti, F-75006 Paris

Broquette-Gonin Grand Prize
To the author of a philosophical, political or literary work, inspiring the love of truth, beauty and goodness. Awarded annually. Enquiries to Académie Française, Institut de France, 23 quai de Conti, F-75006 Paris

Louis Castex Prize
For a literary work celebrating a major voyage of exploration or archaeological or ethnological discovery. Fictional romance excluded. Awarded annually. Enquiries to Académie Française, Institut de France, 23 quai de Conti, F-75006 Paris

Hercule Catenacci Prize
To encourage the publication of de luxe illustrated books of poetry, literature, history, archaeology or music. Awarded annually. Enquiries to Académie Française, Institut de France, 23 quai de Conti, F-75006 Paris

Chateauneuf-du-Pape Grand Prize
Instituted by the town of Chateauneuf-du-Pape and other cities in the same area. Awarded every two years for a poetic work (unpublished, or published in previous five years) which, irrespective of subject, appears most deserving for its formal purity and lofty sentiments. 1,000 francs. Awarded preferably to a young poet. Enquiries to Société des Poètes Français, 38 rue du Faubourg St Jacques, F-75014 Paris

Honoré Chavée Prize*
To encourage work in linguistics and, in particular, research on romance languages. Awarded biennially. Enquiries to Académie des Inscriptions et Belles-Lettres, Institut de France, 23 quai de Conti, F-75270 Paris

François Coppée Prize
For the work of a poet, preferably just beginning his career. Awarded every two years. Enquiries to Académie Française, Institut de France, 23 quai de Conti, F-75006 Paris

Albert Dauzat Prize
Awarded annually for a poetic work in praise of animals. Enquiries to Société des Poètes Français, 38 rue du Faubourg St Jacques, F-75014 Paris

Eve Delacroix Prize
For a literary work, essay or novel combining literary quality, a sense of human dignity and the responsibilities of authorship. 5,000 francs. Awarded annually. Enquiries to Académie Française, Institut de France, 23 quai de Conti, F-75006 Paris

Deldebat de Gonzalva Foundation Prize
Founded in 1941, a medal is awarded every two years for a small body of poems classical in form and noble in inspiration. Enquiries to Société des Poètes Français, 38 rue du Faubourg St Jacques, F-75014 Paris

Marceline Desbordes-Valmore Prize
Founded 1937. Awarded annually to a female member of the Poetry Society, with a recognized talent at the height of its development. Enquiries to Société des Poètes Français, 38 rue du Faubourg St Jacques, F-75014 Paris

Deux Magots Prize*
Founded in 1933. For an avant-garde book by a young writer. Awarded annually. Enquiries to Café des Deux Magots, pl St-Germain-des-Prés, Paris

Dumas-Millier Prize
To a French writer over 45 whose work will be a credit to the French language and to the dissemination of French thought. Enquiries to Académie Française, Institut de France, 23 quai de Conti, F-75006 Paris

Alfred Dutens Prize*
For the most useful work on linguistics. Awarded every ten years. Enquiries to Académie des Inscriptions et Belles Lettres, Institut de France, 23 quai de Conti, F-75270 Paris

Erlanger Foundation Prize
Founded in 1921, a medal awarded every five years for a poem, 150 lines maximum, written by someone who has served in front line of combat. Next award in 1990. Enquiries to Société des Poètes Français, 38 rue du Faubourg St Jacques, F-75014 Paris

Fantasia Prize, see Jeune France Prize

Jules Favre Prize
For a literary work by a woman, poetry or prose, dealing with moral, educational, philological or historical questions. Awarded every two years. Enquiries to Académie Française, Institut de France, 23 quai de Conti, F-75006 Paris

Fémina Prize
Founded in 1904 by review 'Femina' to encourage writing and draw women of letters closer together. A jury of women of letters meets in Paris each December to select a literary work of imagination written in French, by man or woman, prose or poetry. 5,000 francs. Awarded annually. Awarded in 1986 to René Belletto for *L'Enfer* (POL). Enquiries to Secretary-General, 79 blvd St-Germain, F-75006 Paris

Jean Finot Prize
For a work of a humanitarian social trend. Awarded every two years. Enquiries to Académie des Sciences Morales et Politiques, Institut de France, 23 quai de Conti, F-75006 Paris

Paul Flat Prize
For the best critical work and the best novel published by a young writer (between 30 and 40 years of age). Awarded annually. Enquiries to Académie Française, Institut de France, 23 quai de Conti, F-75006 Paris

Ernest Fleury Prize
Instituted by Marthe-Claire Fleury in memory of her father, the poet Ernest Fleury. It is awarded annually for the whole of a poet's work (classical poetry, published or not). Enquiries to Société des Poètes Français, 38 rue du Faubourg St Jacques, F-75014 Paris

Marshal Foch Prize
For a book on the future of the nation's defence by a French officer, engineer, scholar or philosopher. Awarded every two years. Enquiries to Académie Française, Institut de France, 23 quai de Conti, F-75006 Paris

Pascal Fortuny Prize
To the author of a poem of 200 lines or less, preferably written in the classical form. Awarded annually. Enquiries to Académie Française, Institut de France, 23 quai de Conti, F-75006 Paris

Fouraignan Foundation Prize
Founded in 1914, a medal awarded every five years for a collection of poems in 18th century French style, inspired by current events. Next award in 1991. Enquiries to Société des Poètes Français, 38 rue du Faubourg St Jacques, F-75014 Paris

Gegner Prize
To a philosopher-writer whose works contribute to the progress of philosophic science. Awarded annually. Enquiries to Académie des Sciences Morales et Politiques, Institut de France, 23 quai de Conti, F-75006 Paris

Giles Prize*
For a work on China, Japan or the Far East. Awarded every two years to a French national only. Enquiries to

Académie des Inscriptions et Belles Lettres, Institut de France, 23 quai de Conti, F-75270 Paris

Goncourt Prize*
Founded by J and E de Goncourt, 21 December 1903, the annual prize honours a prose work by a younger writer with originality of spirit and form. The novel is the preferred medium. The award is the same as when the prize was originated, 50 francs. Awarded in 1986 to Michel Host for *Valet de Nuit*. The Academy also awards each year, in various French towns, prizes for short story, biography, historical novel and poetry. These awards range from 10,000 to 50,000 francs. Enquiries to Académie Goncourt, c/o Drouant, pl Gaillon, F-75001 Paris

Grand Franco-Belgian Literary Prize*
Established 1956. For the sum of work of a Belgian author written in the French language, free from any political, religious or philosophical bias. Monetary prize of 2,000 French francs. Awarded annually. Enquiries to Association des Ecrivains de Langue française (Mer et Outre-Mer), 38 rue du Faubourg St Jacques, F-75014 Paris, France

Grand Prize for Literature
To a prose-writer or poet for one or more works noteworthy in form and inspiration 10,000 francs. Awarded every two years. Enquiries to Académie Française, Institut de France, 23 quai de Conti, F-75006 Paris

Grand Prize for Poetry Criticism
Awarded every two years for a work or body of work of poetic criticism or exegesis. Enquiries to Société des Poètes Français, 38 rue du Faubourg St Jacques, F-75014 Paris

Grand Prize of French Poets
Awarded annually since 1936, for the whole body of a poet's work, as decided by the Committee of the Société des Poètes (no applications allowed). Enquiries to Société des Poètes Français, 38 rue du Faubourg St Jacques, F-75014 Paris

Cardinal Grente Foundation Prize
Awarded biennially for the entire works of a regular or secular member of the Roman Catholic clergy. Enquiries to Académie Française, Institut de France, 23 quai de Conti, F-75006 Paris

Edmond Haraucourt Prize
Replaces the J-M Renaitour Prize. Awarded annually to a member of the Société des Poètes for the whole body of his work (no applications allowed). Enquiries to Société des Poètes Français, 38 rue du Faubourg St Jacques, F-75014 Paris

Marie Havez-Planque Prize
One year for a collection of stories or for a psychological novel, in fine prose; the following year for a collection of classical poetry. Preferably to a previously unpublished author. Awarded annually. Enquiries to Académie Française, Institut de France, 23 quai de Conti, F-75006 Paris

Emile Hinzelin Foundation Prize
For a volume of verse or a play in verse following the rules of French prosody, and showing the author's love for France. Awarded every five years: next award in 1990. Enquiries to Société des Poètes Français, 38 rue du Faubourg St Jacques, F-75014 Paris

Clovis Hugues Prize
Awarded annually to a poet whose work is inspired by the same sentiments of social brotherhood as moved Clovis Hugues. Enquiries to Société des Poètes Français, 38 rue du Faubourg St Jacques, F-75014 Paris

Institut de France
The various Académies of the Institut award, in addition to those listed in this section, a large number of national and international prizes covering more specialized interests and disciplines

Interallié Prize
Awarded since 1930 for a high quality novel, preferably written by a journalist. Awarded annually. The winner for 1986 was Philippe Cabro for *Etudiant étranger* (Editions Gallimard). Enquiries to Roger Giron (General Secretary), 72 blvd de La Tour-Maubourg, F-75007 Paris

Jules Janin Prize
Awarded every three years for the best translation of a Greek or Latin work published during the period. Next award in 1989. Enquiries to Académie Française, Institut de France, 23 quai de Conti, F-75006 Paris

Jean-Christophe Prizes
Offered by Mrs Alice Cluchier in memory of the young tragedian, her son. These prizes are awarded every two years to two young poets for a manuscript each of minimum ten poems, one in classical form, the other in free verse. Enquiries to Société des Poètes Français, 38 rue du Faubourg St Jacques F-75014 Paris

Jeune France Prize
For the best unpublished book for young people. The book can cover any field. Awarded every two years. Enquiries to Les Editions Magnard Sàrl, 122 blvd St-Germain, F-75279 Paris cedex 6

Jouy Prize
Awarded biennially for a work published during the period designed as a study of modern-day behaviour, from an imaginative, critical or observationary viewpoint. Enquiries to Académie Française, Institut de France, 23 quai de Conti, F-75006 Paris

Labbé-Vauquelin Foundation Prize
Founded in 1924, a medal awarded every five years for a collection of reflective poetry regionally inspired. Next award in 1989. Enquiries to Société des Poètes Français, 38 rue du Faubourg St Jacques, F-75014 Paris

Georges Lafenestre Foundation Prize
Founded in 1938 by the family of Georges Lafenestre on the occasion of the poet's centenary, a medal is given for an unpublished poem of high inspiration and classical form, 150 lines maximum. Awarded every five years: next award in 1991. Enquiries to Société des Poètes Français, 38 rue du Faubourg St Jacques, F-75014 Paris

Lafontaine Prize
Awarded biennially for a work of popular morality. Enquiries to Académie Française, Institut de France, 23 quai de Conti, F-75006 Paris

Lambert Prize
To men of letters (or their widows) deserving of public recognition. Awarded annually. Enquiries to Académie Française, Institut de France, 23 quai de Conti, F-75006 Paris

Langlois Prize
For the best translation in verse or prose of a Greek, Latin or other foreign work into the French language. Awarded annually. Enquiries to Académie Française, Institut de France, 23 quai de Conti, F-75006 Paris

Eugène Le Mouël Foundation Prize
Founded in 1936, this is a medal awarded every five years for a poem in any genre, but preferably inspired by Eugène Le Mouël. Next award in 1990. Enquiries to Société des Poètes Français, 38 rue de Faubourg St Jacques, F-75014 Paris

Sébastien-Charles Leconte Foundation Prize
Founded in 1935 by Jean-Michel Renaitour, and awarded biennially in honour of a volume of classical poetry published in the preceding two years. Enquiries to Société des Poètes Français, 38 rue du Faubourg St Jacques, F-75014 Paris

Paul Lofler Foundation Prize
Awarded every two years for the best sonnet submitted for competition to the Société des Poètes. Enquiries to Société des Poètes Français, 38 rue du Faubourg St Jacques, F-75014 Paris

Jean Mace Prize*
For works of fiction or non-fiction either as published books or as manuscripts for readers aged 15-18. Awarded annually. Enquiries to General Secretary Jean-Louis Rollot, Ligue Française de l'Enseignement et de l'Education Permanente, Service Culturel, 3 rue Récamier, F-75007 Paris

Maille-Latour-Landry Prize
To a young, talented writer deserving encouragement to follow a literary career. Awarded biennially. Enquiries to Académie Française, Institut de France, 23 quai de Conti, F-75006 Paris

Médicis Prize
Awarded to an avant-garde novel, story or collection whose publication has not been accompanied by the celebrity or fame the author's talent deserves. Founded in 1958. Awarded in 1986 to Pierre Combescot for *Les Funérailles de la Sardine* (Grasset). Enquiries to 20 rue Cortot, F-75108 Paris

Narcisse Michaut Prize
For the best work of French literature. Awarded every two years. Enquiries to Académie Française, Institut de France, 23 quai de Conti, F-75006 Paris

Louis P Miller Prize
For works furthering the love of moral virtue, in particular remembrance and gratitude. Awarded annually. Enquiries to Académie Française, Institut de France, 23 quai de Conti, F-75006 Paris

Marcelle Millier Prize
To a female writer aged 45 or more, the entirety of whose work will do honour to French literature. Enquiries to Académie Française, Institut de France, 23 quai de Conti, F-75006 Paris

Montyon Prize
For any work published by a French author showing qualities of practical idealism. Awarded annually. Enquiries to Académie Française, Institut de France, 23 quai de Conti, F-75006 Paris

National Grand Prize for Literature
Established in 1950. To the writer who has contributed most to French literature. 50,000 francs. Awarded annually. Enquiries to French Ministry of Cultural Affairs, Direction du livre et de la lecture, 27 ave de l'Opéra, F-75001 Paris

National Grand Prize for Poetry
Established in 1981. To the poet who has contributed most to French poetry. 50,000

francs. Awarded annually. Enquiries to French Ministry of Cultural Affairs, Direction du livre et de la lecture, 27 ave de l'Opéra, F-75001 Paris

National Grand Prize for Translation
Established in 1985. To the translator who has contributed most to the standard of literary translation into the French language. 30,000 francs. Awarded annually. Enquiries to French Ministry of Cultural Affairs, Direction du livre et de la lecture, 27 ave de l'Opéra, F-75001 Paris

Alfred **Née** Prize
For a work showing originality of thought and style. Awarded annually. Enquiries to Académie Française, Institut de France, 23 quai de Conti, F-75006 Paris

Novel Prize
To a young prose-writer for a fictional work of high imaginative power. 20,000 francs. Awarded annually. Enquiries to Académie Française, Institut de France, 23 quai de Conti, F-75006 Paris

Paris Grand Prize for Literature*
For different forms of literature such as novel, poetry, criticism, essay, history, philosophy. Awarded annually (each year for a different form). Enquiries to Directeur des Affaires Culturelles, 17 Blvd Roland, F-75004 Paris

Paris Prize*
For a novel. Awarded annually. Enquiries to Academy of Letters and Arts, c/o Musée de Montmartre, 12 rue Cortot, F-75018 Paris

De **Pimodan** Foundation Prize
Founded in 1926, a medal is awarded every five years to a regional poet celebrating his land. Next award in 1992. Enquiries to Société des Poètes Français, 38 rue du Faubourg St Jacques, F-75014 Paris

Charles **Pitou** Foundation Prize
Founded 1928, a medal is awarded every five years for a poem in strictly classical form celebrating a French province, preferably Normandy. Next award in 1992. Enquiries to Société des Poètes Français, 38 rue du Faubourg St Jacques, F-75014 Paris

Raymond **Poincaré** Prize*
For a literary work which promotes a favourable view of the defence forces. Awarded to French citizens, or to foreigners who have served in a French military unit. 2,000 francs. Awarded annually. Enquiries to National Union of Reserve Officers, 17 ave de l'Opéra, F-75001 Paris

Hélène **Porgès** Prize
Awarded every four years for a nature book which will encourage in schoolchildren a love of their country. Enquiries to Académie Française, Institut de France, 23 quai de Conti, F-75006 Paris

Prose Poétique Prize
Awarded every five years at discretion of Committee of Société des Poètes for a work of poetry which ignores classical prosody but is essentially poetic in spirit. Next award in 1988. Enquiries to Société des Poètes Français, 38 rue du Faubourg St Jacques, F-75014 Paris

R T L (Radio Télé Luxembourg)/Poésie 1 Prize
Given annually, this award aims to focus public attention on a poet of merit. Enquiries to Secrétariat du Grand Prix RTL/Poésie 1, 68 rue du Cherche-Midi, F-75006 Paris

J-M **Renaitour** Prize, replaced by Edmond Haraucourt Prize (qv)

Théophraste **Renaudot** Prize*
Founded in 1926 by Gaston Picard and a group of journalists to honour Théophraste Renaudot, founder of the first French newspaper. It is awarded annually for a novel, and presented on the same day and in the same place as the Prix Goncourt. The prize carries no monetary award but is held in high esteem. Awarded in 1987 to René-Jean Clot for *L'Enfant halluciné* (Grasset).

Jean **Reynaud** Prize
Awarded every five years for the most meritorious work produced in the period (the work always to be of an original, innovative and imaginative character). Next award due in 1989, but if no work considered worthy, money is otherwise disposed of. Enquiries to Académie Française, Institut de France, 23 quai de Conti, F-75006 Paris

Roberge Prizes
One year to a young poet who has published no more than two volumes of verse. The following year to a young author who has published no more than two novels. Enquiries to Académie Française, Institut de France, 23 quai de Conti, F-75006 Paris

Albéric **Rocheron** Foundation Prize
Awarded for the critical, literary or historical study which best illustrates the relationship between the character of a period and its literature. Enquiries to Académie Française, Institut de France, 23 quai de Conti, F-75006 Paris

Duchess of **Rohan** Foundation Prize
Medal awarded every five years to a poet, preferably young, who submits work of maximum 200 lines in competition. Next award in 1988. Enquiries to Société des Poètes Français, 38 rue du Faubourg St Jacques, F-75014 Paris

Roucoules Foundation Grand Prize for Poetry
100,000 francs. Awarded annually. Enquiries to Académie Française, Institut de France, 23 quai de Conti, F-75006 Paris

Saint-Cricq-Theis Prize
Awarded every three years for a poetic work of a spiritualistic, ethical, dramatic, patriotic nature. Enquiries to Académie Française, Institut de France, 23 quai de Conti, F-75006 Paris

Saintour Prize
For works (lexicons, grammars, critical studies, commentaries, etc) on the study of the French language, in particular from the 16th century to the present. Awarded annually. Enquiries to Académie Française, Institut de France, 23 quai de Conti, F-75006 Paris

Short Story Prize
Awarded annually for a collection of short stories. Enquiries to Académie Française, Institut de France, 23 quai de Conti, F-75006 Paris

Sobrier-Arnould Prize
To the authors of the two best works which are both ethical and instructive to youth. Awarded annually. Enquiries to Académie Française, Institut de France, 23 quai de Conti, F-75006 Paris

Paul **Teissonnière** Prize
For the best published work of a liberal tendency on moral or religious philosophy. Enquiries to Académie Française, Institut de France, 23 quai de Conti, F-75006 Paris

Thiers Prize
For the encouragement of literature and historical research. Awarded every three years for the best historical work published since the previous prize. Next award in 1988. Enquiries to Académie Française, Institut de France, 23 quai de Conti, F-75006 Paris

Lucien **Tisserand** Prize
To a French novelist, aged between 40 and 50, with proven talent and an expected long future. Awarded annually. Enquiries to Académie Française, Institut de France, 23 quai de Conti, F-75006 Paris

Maurice **Trubert** Prize
For a prose or verse work of any kind, but which respects classical traditions and a Catholic moral outlook. Author must be French-born and under 30. Awarded biennially. Enquiries to Académie Française, Institut de France, 23 quai de Conti, F-75006 Paris

Antony **Valabrègue** Prize
To encourage a young poet who has published one volume of verse. Awarded biennially. Enquiries to Académie Française, Institut de France, 23 quai de Conti, F-75006 Paris

Valentine Abraham **Verlain** Prize
To a woman of letters or for a needy female artist. Awarded annually. Enquiries to Académie Française, Institut de France, 23 quai de Conti, F-75006 Paris

Verlaine Prize
Contest for all types of poetry except dramatic. Awarded every three years: next award in 1990. Enquiries to Académie Française, Institut de France, 23 quai de Conti, F-75006 Paris

Claire **Virenque** Prize
To young authors. One year for a collection of poems, the next for a novel or biography showing Christian or high ethical inspiration. Enquiries to Académie Française, Institut de France, 23 quai de Conti, F-75006 Paris

Volney Prize
For a work in comparative philology. Enquiries to Institut de France, 23 quai de Conti, F-75006 Paris

J J **Weiss** Prize
For a prose work in the purest classic style on travel, literature, literary or dramatic criticism or politics. Awarded every two years. Enquiries to Académie Française, Institut de France, 23 quai de Conti, F-75006 Paris*

Valentine de **Wolmar** Prize
For the finest novel or collection of poetry published during the year. Awarded annually. Enquiries to Académie Française, Institut de France, 23 quai de Conti, F-75006 Paris

Translation Agencies and Associations

A T L F, see Association des Traducteurs Littéraires de France

Association des Traducteurs Littéraires de France, 99 rue de Vaugirard, F-75006 Paris Tel: (1) 45491895
President: Françoise Cartano; *General Secretary:* Jacqueline Carnaud

Société Française des Traducteurs, 11 rue de Navarin, F-75009 Paris Tel: (1) 48784332
French Union of Translators

Transcom — General Translation and Communication Co Ltd, 96 blvd Auguste

Blanqui, F-75013 Paris Tel: (1) 43378989
Translation and typesetting of books in all languages

French Guiana

General Information

Language: French
Religion: Roman Catholic
Population: 66,000
Bank Hours: 0700-1130, 1400-1600 Monday-Friday
Shop Hours: 0800-1300, 1500-1800 Monday-Friday
Currency: French currency
Export/Import Information: Overseas department of France, which is a member of the European Economic Community. Tariff as for France. See France for domiciliation of documents. No import licences required. Same exchange restrictions as France.
Copyright: Berne, UCC (see International Section)

Major Booksellers

Mme **Beaufort***, 16 rue du Lieutenant-Brassé, BP 505, Cayenne Tel: 98

La **Boutique** Bleue*, ave Pasteur, BP 243, Cayenne

Emilio **Gratien***, 25 ave du Général de Gaulle, Cayenne Tel: 280

Librairie-Papeterie Universelle*, 26 rue Lallouette, Cayenne Tel: 240

Major Libraries

Bibliothèque Franconie*, Préfecture de la Guyane, BP 303, 97300 Cayenne

Institut français de Recherche Scientifique pour le Developpement en Cooperation, Centre ORSTOM de Cayenne, Bibliothèque, BP 165, 97323 Cayenne cedex Tel: 302785 Telex: 910608 FG
Office of Scientific and Technical Research Overseas

Literary Associations and Societies

Association des Amis du Livre*, Préfecture de la Guyane, BP 303, 97300 Cayenne
Association of Book Lovers

French Polynesia

General Information

Language: French, Tahitian, English
Religion: Roman Catholic
Population: 147,000
Bank Hours: 0730-1530 Monday-Friday; some 0730-1130 Saturday
Shop Hours: 0730-1100, 1400-1700 Monday-Friday; 0730-1130 Saturday
Currency: 100 centimes = 1 franc CFP
Export/Import Information: No tariff on books other than children's picture books; advertising matter subject to customs duty, import duty, although catalogues generally considered printed books. Advertising subject to Statistical Tax. Miscellaneous tax of 2% of customs value on books and advertising. No import licence required. Exchange controls

Publishers

Haere Po No Tahiti+, BP 1958, Papeete, Tahiti
Man Dir: L Shan
Subjects: Polynesia, Voyages and Exploration, Botany, History, Children's, Textbooks, Folk Tales and Legends, Linguistics
1985: 2 titles *1986:* 3 titles *Founded:* 1981
ISBN Publisher's Prefix: 2-904171

Société Nouvelle des Editions du **Pacifique**, see Times Editions/Editions du Pacifique, Republic of Singapore

Major Booksellers

Librairie **Au Ping-Pong***, 6 rue du Commandant-Destremeau, Papeete, Tahiti Tel: 133

Librairie **Hachette Pacifique** SA*, Fare Ute, BP 334, Papeete, Tahiti Tel: 425610 Telex: Hachpac 293 FP
General Manager: Daniel Hottin
Parent Company: NMPP (Nouvelles Messageries de la Presse Parisienne)
The following bookshops in French Polynesia are now under the management of Librairie Hachette Pacifique SA:
Hachette Pacifique Bruat, Hachette Vaïma, Kiosque Vaïma, Librairie Interpresse

Librairie R **Klima**, La Boutique, BP 31, pl Notre-Dame, Papeete, Tahiti Tel: 20063
Manager: Manuella Luciani

Republic of Gabon

General Information

Language: French
Religion: About half Roman Catholic and half animist
Population: 1.3 million
Bank Hours: 0700-1115, 1430-1615 Monday-Friday
Shop Hours: 0700 or 0800-1200 or 1230, 1430 or 1500-1830 or 1900 Monday-Saturday. Some close Monday
Currency: CFA franc
Export/Import Information: Member of the Customs and Economic Union of Central Africa. No tariff on books. Import licence required for all imports valued above a certain amount
Copyright: Berne (see International Section)

Publishers

Government Printer (Imprimerie Centrale d'Afrique)*, BP 154, Libreville

Editions du **Lion***, BP 754, Libreville
ISBN Publisher's Prefix: 2-901350

Saint-Joseph*, BP 58, Libreville

Major Booksellers

Centre de **Littérature** Evangélique*, BP 206, Oyem

Librairie **Nouvelle***, BP 612, Libreville Tel: 721616

Librairie **Sogalivre***, BP 50, Port-Gentil Tel: 52319

Sogapresse*, BP 121 Libreville Tel: 733131 Telex: 5418 go
Manager: Jacques Petit

Major Libraries

Archives et bibliothèque nationale*, BP 1188, Libreville Tel: 732543
Librarian: Gaston Rapontchombo

Centre Bibliothèque d'Information*, BP 3127, Libreville Tel: 21115

Centre culturel américain, Bibliothèque, BP 2237, Libreville Tel: 721558/722161
Librarian: Daniel Koumavor

Centre culturel français St-Exupéry Bibliothèque*, BP 2103, Libreville Tel: 721120

Collège Jésus Marie Bibliothèque*, BP 120, Bitam Tel: 277

Ecole normale supérieure Bibliothèque*, BP 16030, Libreville
Teachers' Training College Library
Librarian: Miss M E Bouscarle

Institut polytechnique de l'Afrique centrale Bibliothèque*, BP 1158, Libreville

Bibliothèque de l'**Université Omar Bongo***, BP 17013, Libreville Tel: 732956/732581 Telex: 32506
Dir: Jean Grégoire Aboghe-Obyan
Publications: Liste des nouvelles acquisitions (quarterly); Liste des périodiques en cours (annual); Inventaire du fonds documentaire, par discipline (annual)

The Gambia

General Information

Language: English
Religion: Islamic
Population: 601,000
Bank Hours: 0800-1300 Monday-Thursday; 0800-1100 Friday and Saturday
Shop Hours: 0800 or 0900-1200, 1400-1700 Monday-Thursday; 0800 or 0900-1200, 1500-1700 Friday; 0800 or 0900-1200 Saturday
Currency: 100 butut = 1 dalasi
Export/Import Information: No tariff on books. Import Tax on all. No import licence required. National Trading Corporation has no monopoly. Exchange controls

Book Trade Organization

Standard Book Numbering Agency*, National Library, PO Box 552, Banjul
ISBN Administrator: Sally N'Jie

Book Trade Reference Book

National Bibliography of the Gambia, Gambia National Library, PMB 552, Banjul

Publishers

The **Government Press***, Banjul Tel: 399 Telex: 2204

Major Booksellers

The **Gambia** Methodist Bookshop Ltd*, PO Box 203, Banjul Tel: 8179

Jeng's Bookshop*, PO Box 234, Banjul

Major Libraries

Gambia College Library*, Gambia College, Yundum Campus, Yundum Tel: (092) 811
Librarian: Rosanna A Ndaw

Gambia National Library*, Ministry of Education, Youth, Sports and Culture, PO Box 552, Banjul Tel: 8312
Chief Librarian: Sally P C N'Jie
Publications include: National Bibliography of the Gambia

Yundum College Library, see Gambia College Library

German Democratic Republic

General Information

Language: German. About 70,000 in Lusatia speak Serb but also speak German
Religion: About 60% Protestant, 8% Roman Catholic
Population: 16.7 million
Bank Hours: Generally 0800-1600 Monday-Friday; open Saturday morning
Shop Hours: Vary. Generally 0900 or 1000-1800 or 1900 Monday-Friday; open part day Saturday
Currency: 100 Pfennige = 1 Mark der DDR
Export/Import Information: Foreign trade is a state monopoly; books imported and exported by Buchexport, Leninstr 16, Postfach 160, DDR-7010 Leipzig. Import licences required and Foreign Trade Bank handles all payments. No advertising materials to be sent to private individuals; for preparation of advertising, contact Interwerbung GmbH, Berlin
Copyright: UCC, Berne (see International section)

Book Trade Organizations

Börsenverein der Deutschen Buchhändler zu Leipzig, Gerichtsweg 26, DDR-7010 Leipzig Tel: (041) 293851 Cable Add: Buchbörse
Association of German Democratic Republic Publishers and Booksellers in Leipzig
Publication: Börsenblatt für den Deutschen Buchhandel

Buchexport — Volkseigener Aussenhandelsbetrieb der Deutschen Demokratischen Republik, Leninstr 16, Postfach 160, DDR-7010 Leipzig Tel: (041) 71370 Telex: 051678
GDR Foreign Trade Enterprise
Publications: Nova; Wissen und Können; Buch der Zeit; Land und Leute; DDR-Gesamtkatalog; DDR-Periodica (trade journal catalogue)
The state organization for foreign trade. These catalogues contain particulars of the entire range of GDR publications

Deutsche Bücherei Abteilung Erwerbung ISBN-Agentur der DDR, Deutscher Platz 1, DDR-7010 Leipzig Tel: (041) 8812494 Telex: 51562 dbuech dd
ISBN Administrator: Klaus-Dieter Wilke

Ministerrat der Deutschen Demokratischen Republik, Ministerium für Kultur, Hauptverwaltung Verlage und Buchhandel, DDR-1080 Berlin, Clara-Zetkin-Str 90
Council of Ministers of the German Democratic Republic, Ministry of Culture, Main Department — Publishing and Bookselling

Standard Book Numbering Agency, see Deutsche Bücherei Abteilung Erwerbung ISBN-Agentur der DDR

Book Trade Reference Books and Journals

Books

Adressbuch des Volksbuchhandels der Deutschen Demokratischen Republik (Directory of the People's Book Trade of the GDR), Volksbuchhandel der DDR, Zentrale Zeitung, Friedrich-Ebert-Str 25, DDR-7010 Leipzig

Deutsches Bücherverzeichnis (German Book List, every five years), Deutsche Bücherei, Deutscher Pl, DDR-7010 Leipzig

Titel-Information (Title-Information), Leipziger Komissions- und Grossbuchhandel, Leninstr 16, DDR-7010 Leipzig

Journals

Beiträge zur Literaturkunde (Contributions to Literary Knowledge), VEB Bibliographisches Institut, Gerichtsweg 26, DDR-7010 Leipzig
Bibliography of selected newspaper and periodical contributions

Bibliographie der Bibliographien (Bibliography of Bibliographies), Deutsche Bücherei, Deutscher Pl, DDR-7010 Leipzig

Bibliographie der Übersetzungen deutschsprachiger Werke (Bibliography of Translations of German Language Works), Deutsche Bücherei, Deutscher Pl, DDR-7010 Leipzig

Bibliographie fremdsprachiger Germanica (Bibliography of Germanics in Foreign Languages), Deutsche Bücherei, Deutscher Pl, DDR-7010 Leipzig

Börsenblatt für den deutschen Buchhandel (German Book Trade Journal), Börsenverein der Deutschen Buchhändler zu Leipzig, Gerichtsweg 26, DDR-7010 Leipzig

Buch der Zeit (Books of the Day), Buchexport, Leninstr 16, DDR-7010 Leipzig
Text in English and German

DDR Gesamtkatalog (German Democratic Republic Complete Catalogue), Buchexport, Leninstr 16, DDR-7010 Leipzig
Annual catalogue in two volumes covering all titles published in preceding year

DDR Periodica, Buchexport, Leninstr 16, DDR-7010 Leipzig
Trade journal catalogue

Deutsche Nationalbibliographie und Bibliographie des im Ausland erschienenen deutschsprachigen Schrifttums (German National Bibliography and Bibliography of German Language Literature Published Abroad), Deutsche Bücherei, Deutscher Pl, DDR-7010 Leipzig

Jahresverzeichnis der Verlagsschriften (Annual List of Publications), Deutsche Bücherei, Deutscher Pl, DDR-7010 Leipzig

Nova, Buchexport, Leninstr 16, DDR-7010 Leipzig
Forthcoming books (table of contents and subtitles in English, German and Russian), two issues per month

Wissen und Können (Theory and Practice), Buchexport, Leninstr 16, DDR-7010 Leipzig
A series of 26 Catalogues covering every branch of knowledge under the headings: I — Social Sciences; II — Art and Literature; III — Natural Sciences; IV — Technical Science/Engineering; V — Agriculture and Forestry, Veterinary Science; VI — Medicine. The Catalogues list all books under the particular subject selected which are available for sale, in print or in course of preparation. Publication of each list is annual

Publishers

Akademie-Verlag Berlin+, Leipziger Str 3-4, Postfach 1233, DDR-1086 Berlin Tel: (02) 22360 Cable Add: Akademie-Verlag Berlin Telex: 114420 averl dd
Dir: Prof Dr Lothar Berthold
Affiliated Branch: Hermann Böhlaus Nachfolger (qv)
Subjects: History, Economics, Economic History, Philosophy, Literature, History of Art, History of Sciences, Archaeology, Ethnography, Oriental, Biology, Geology, Mathematics, Physics, Engineering, Chemistry, Medicine, Languages, Linguistics, Periodicals
1986: 300 titles *Founded:* 1946
Miscellaneous: Publishers of the Academy of Sciences of the GDR
ISBN Publisher's Prefix: 3-05

Altberliner Verlag+, Neue Schoenhauser Str 8, Postfach 44, DDR-1020 Berlin Tel: (02) 2806634
Dir: Dr Gerhard Dahne
Subject: Children's Books
Founded: 1945
ISBN Publisher's Prefix: 3-357

Aufbau-Verlag Berlin und Weimar, Französische Str 32, Postfach 1217, DDR-1080 Berlin Tel: (02) 2202421 Cable Add: Aufbauverlag Berlin Telex: Berlin 114739 aurul dd

Associate Company: Verlag Rütten und Loening, Berlin, German Democratic Republic
Subjects: General Fiction, Library of World Literature, Belles Lettres, Literary Criticism, Paperbacks, Periodicals
Founded: 1945

Johann Ambrosius **Barth** Verlagsbuchhandlung+, Salomonstr 18b, Postfach 109, DDR-7010 Leipzig Tel: (041) 70131 Cable Add: Barth Leipzig
Man Dir: Klaus Wiecke
Orders to; Buchexport, Postfach 160, DDR-7010 Leipzig
Subjects: Medicine, Dentistry, Stomatology, Psychology, Natural Science, Chemistry, Astronomy, Physics; Periodicals, Publications of the German Academy of Naturalists
Founded: 1780

VEB Verlag für **Bauwesen**+, Französische Str 13-14, Postfach 1232, DDR-1086 Berlin Tel: (02) 20410 Cable Add: Bauwesenverlag Berlin Telex: 112229 Trave
The Building Industry Publishing House
Man Dir: Siegfried Seeliger; *Editorial:* Siegfried Schikora; *Sales:* Franz Rautenstrauch; *Publicity:* Beate Hilke; *Production:* Günter Langer
Subjects: Civil Engineering, Architecture and Building Construction, Materials and Mechanics, Periodicals
Founded: 1960
ISBN Publisher's Prefix: 3-345

VEB **Bibliographisches Institut**, Leipzig, Gerichtsweg 26, Postfach 130, DDR-7010 Leipzig Tel: (041) 7801 Cable Add: Biblio Leipzig Telex: 512773
Man Dir: Helmut Bähring
Associate Company: VEB Verlag Enzyklopädiei Leipzig (qv)
Subjects: General Dictionaries, Reference, Biography, Bibliographies, German Language, Library Science, Literature, Periodicals
Miscellaneous: This organization has now taken over the titles of the former VEB Verlag für Buch- und Bibliothekswesen (dissolved)
Founded: 1826
ISBN Publisher's Prefix: 3-323

Hermann **Böhlaus** Nachfolger, Meyerstr 50a, DDR-5300 Weimar Tel: 2071 Cable Add: Böhlauverlag DDR-5300 Weimar
Dir: Prof Lothar Berthold; *Man Dir:* Stephan Ploog
Subjects: History of Law, Literature & Art, Critical Editions & Yearbooks, Mediaeval History
Founded: 1624
Miscellaneous: An affiliated branch of Akademie-Verlag Berlin (qv)
ISBN Publisher's Prefix: 3-7400

VEB **Breitkopf und Härtel** Musikverlag+, Karlstr 10, Postfach 147, DDR-7010 Leipzig Tel: (041) 7351 Cable Add: Breitkopfs
Man Dir: Dr Gunter Hempel; *Editorial:* Dr Eva Maria Hillmann; *Production:* Wolfgang Quinque; *Sales Dir:* Werner Hennig; *Advertising:* Ameli Möbius; *Rights & Permissions:* Thomas Nemson
Subjects: Music: Vocal and Instrumental, Biographies, Reference, Musicology
1985: 3 titles *1986:* 3 titles *Founded:* 1719
ISBN Publisher's Prefix: 3-7330

VEB F A **Brockhaus** Verlag Leipzig, Salomonstr 17, DDR-7010 Leipzig Tel: (041) 7846
Subjects: Picture and Travel books, Popular Science, Reportage, Encyclopaedias, Reference
Founded: 1805

VEB **Deutscher Landwirtschaftsverlag**, Reinhardtstr 14, DDR-1040 Berlin Tel: (02) 28930 Cable Add: Bauernbuch Berlin
Dir: Günter Holle; *Editorial:* Hein von Münster
Subjects: Agriculture, Horticulture, Forestry
1986: 52 titles *1987:* 55 titles *Founded:* 1960
ISBN Publisher's Prefix: 3-331

VEB **Deutscher Verlag der Wissenschaften***, Johannes-Dieckmann-Str 10, Postfach 1216, DDR-1080 Berlin Tel: (02) 22900 Cable Add: Devauwe Berlin Telex: 114390 dvw dd
Subjects: History, Philosophy, Psychology; General, Natural & Social Sciences; Physics, Chemistry, Mathematics
Founded: 1954

VEB **Deutscher Verlag für Grundstoffindustrie**, Karl-Heine-Str 27, DDR-7031 Leipzig Tel: (041) 474441 Cable Add: Grundstoffverlag Leipzig Telex: 051451 Grundstoffverlag
Subjects: Geological Sciences, Coal, Energy, Mining of Ores, Metallurgy, Potash, Chemistry and Chemical Process Technology, Popular Scientific Literature, Periodicals
Founded: 1960

VEB **Deutscher Verlag für Musik**+, Karlstr 10, Postfach 147, DDR-7010 Leipzig Tel: (041) 7351 Cable Add: Demusica Leipzig
Man Dir: Dr Gunter Hempel; *Editorial:* Dr Eva Maria Hillmann; *Production:* Wolfgang Quinque; *Sales Dir:* Werner Hennig; *Advertising:* Ameli Möbius; *Rights & Permissions:* Thomas Nemson
Subjects: Music: Vocal and Instrumental, Reference, Biographies, Children's and Young Peoples' Books on Music, Musicology, Facsimilies, Musical Belles Lettres
1985: 12 titles *1986:* 21 titles *Founded:* 1954
ISBN Publisher's Prefix: 3-370

Dieterich'sche Verlagsbuchhandlung, Mottelerstr 8, Postfach 88, DDR-7022 Leipzig Tel: (041) 58726
Associate Companies: Insel-Verlag (qv); Gustav Kiepenhauer Verlag (qv); Paul List Verlag (qv)
Subjects: World literature in translation
Founded: 1766
ISBN Publisher's Prefix: 3-7350

Dietz Verlag Berlin, Wallstr 76-79, Postfach 273, DDR-1020 Berlin Tel: (02) 27030 Cable Add: Dietzverlag Berlin Telex: 114741
Subjects: Social Science, Economics, Philosophy, Politics, History, Memoirs, Periodicals
Founded: 1945

VEB **Domowina** Verlag, Tüchmacherstr 27, DDR-8600 Bautzen Tel: 511316 Telex: 287220
Man Dir: Martin Benad; *Editorial:* Dr P Völkel
Subjects: Serbian: Literature, Popular Sciences, History, Culture, Periodicals (in Serbian and German languages)
Founded: 1958

VEB Verlag **Enzyklopädie** Leipzig, Gerichtsweg 26, Postfach 130, DDR-7010 Leipzig Tel: (041) 7801 Cable Add: Biblio Leipzig Telex: 512773
Man Dir: Helmut Bähring
Associate Company: VEB Bibliographisches Institut (qv)
Subjects: Languages, Dictionaries, Foreign Language Textbooks
Founded: 1956
ISBN Publisher's Prefix: 3-324

Eulenspiegel Verlag für Satire und Humor*, Kronenstr 73-74, Postfach 1239, DDR-1080 Berlin Tel: (02) 2202126 Cable Add: Eulenspiegelverlag Berlin
Associate Company: Verlag Das Neue Berlin (qv)
Subjects: Humour: Satire, Caricature, Cartoons
Founded: 1954

Evangelische Verlagsanstalt GmbH, Ziegelstr 30-31, Postfach 212, DDR-1040 Berlin Tel: (02) 2700521 Cable Add: Evaverlag Berlin
Dirs: Dr Forck, Dr Petzold
Subjects: Christian History, Devotional, Biblical Exegesis, Christian Fiction and Poetry, Biography, Art Books, Music, Periodicals
1986: 162 titles *Founded:* 1946
ISBN Publisher's Prefix: 3-374

VEB **Fachbuchverlag**, Karl-Heine-Str 16, Postfach 67, DDR-7031 Leipzig Tel: (041) 49500 Cable Add: Fachbuch Leipzig Telex: 51451 fachb dd
Man Dir: Dr Erhard Walter
Subjects: General Knowledge, Popular Science, Basic Technologies, Industries, Periodicals
1986: 168 titles *1987:* 169 titles *Founded:* 1949
ISBN Publisher's Prefix: 3-343

VEB Gustav **Fischer** Verlag, Jena, Villengang 2, Postfach 176, DDR-6900 Jena Tel: (078) 27332 Cable Add: Fischerbuch Telex: 05886176
Publicity Manager: Mr Kramer
Parent Companies: Volkseigene Verlage für Medizin und Biologie (qv)
Associate Companies: VEB Georg Thieme (qv); VEB Verlag Volk und Gesundheit (qv)
Subjects: Medicine, Veterinary, Biology, Periodicals
Founded: 1878

VEB **Fotokinoverlag**, Karl-Heine-Str 16, Postfach 67, DDR-7031 Leipzig Tel: (041) 49500 Cable Add: Fachbuch Leipzig Telex: 51451 fachb dd
Man Dir: Dr Erhard Walter
Subjects: Photography, Film, Periodicals
1986: 12 titles *1987:* 12 titles *Founded:* 1957
ISBN Publisher's Prefix: 3-7411

Verlag für die **Frau**, Friedrich-Ebert-Str 76-78, Postfach 1005/1025, DDR-7010 Leipzig Tel: (041) 71790 Telex: 512733
Subjects: Fashion, Family, Domestic Science, Periodicals
Founded: 1946

Akademische Verlagsgesellschaft **Geest und Portig** KG, Sternwarten Str 8, Postfach 106, DDR-7010 Leipzig Tel: (041) 293158/282545 Cable Add: Akabuch Leipzig Telex: 512381 avg uber eplei dd
Man Dir: Ing Heinz Kratz
Associate Company: BSB B G Teubner Verlagsgesellschaft (qv)
Subjects: Chemistry, Physics, Mathematics, History of Science, Periodicals
Founded: 1906

Greifenverlag zu Rudolstadt, Heidecksburg, Postfach 142, DDR-6820 Rudolstadt Tel: 2085
Subjects: Belles Lettres, Town and Countryside Books
Founded: 1919

GERMAN DEMOCRATIC REPUBLIC 125

VEB Hermann **Haack** Geographisch-Kartographische Anstalt Gotha, Justus-Perthes-Str 3-9, Postfach 274, DDR-5800 Gotha Tel: (0622) 3872 Cable Add: Geokart Gotha Telex: 615333 hago dd
Imprint: Haack Gotha
Subjects: Maps, Atlases, Geographic and Cartographic Publications, Periodicals
Founded: 1785
ISBN Publisher's Prefix: 3-7301

VEB **Harth** Musik Verlag, Karl-Liebknecht-Str 12, Postfach 467, DDR-7010 Leipzig Tel: (041) 312612 Cable Add: Musica Leipzig
Subjects: Music for Dance and Entertainment
Founded: 1946

Henschelverlag Kunst und Gesellschaft*, Oranienburger Str 67-68, Postfach 220, DDR-1040 Berlin Tel: (02) 28790 Cable Add: Henschelverlag Berlin
Dir: K Mittelstädt
Subjects: General Fiction, Film, Theatre, Music, Art, Architecture, Periodicals
Founded: 1945

VEB **Hinstorff** Verlag+, Kröpeliner Str 25, Postfach 1011, DDR-2500 Rostock Tel: (081) 34441 Cable Add: Hinstorff Verlag Rostock
Subjects: Contemporary Literature of the GDR, German Language Literature in Series, Scandinavian Literature in Translation, Literature in Low German, Homeland Literature and Studies, Maritime Literature
1985: 40 titles *1986:* 37 titles *Founded:* 1831
ISBN Publisher's Prefix: 3-356

S **Hirzel** Verlag, Sternwartenstr 8, Postfach 506, DDR-7010 Leipzig Tel: (041) 282263 Telex: 512381 shv eplei dd
Dir: Heinz Kratz
Subjects: Medicine, Veterinary Medicine, Agriculture, Natural Sciences, Dictionaries
1985: 5 titles *1986:* 10 titles *Founded:* 1853
ISBN Publisher's Prefix: 3-7401

VEB Friedrich **Hofmeister** Musikverlag+, Karlstr 10, Postfach 147, DDR-7010 Leipzig Tel: (041) 7351 Cable Add: Hofmeister Leipzig
Man Dir: Dr Gunter Hempel; *Editorial:* Dr Eva Maria Hillmann; *Production:* Wolfgang Quinque; *Sales Dir:* Werner Hennig; *Advertising:* Ameli Möbius; *Rights & Permissions:* Thomas Nemson
Subjects: Vocal and Instrumental Music, Song Books, Bibliographies, Yearbooks
1985: 1 titles *1986:* 2 titles *Founded:* 1807
ISBN Publisher's Prefix: 3-7331

Insel-Verlag Anton Kippenberg, Mottelerstr 8, Postfach 88, DDR-7022 Leipzig Tel: (041) 58726
Associate Companies: Insel-Verlag issues a common catalogue with: Gustav Kiepenheuer Verlag (qv); Dieterich'sche Verlagsbuchhandlung (qv); Paul List Verlag (qv)
Subjects: Literature, Art, Facsimile Editions, Classics of World Literature in Translation
Founded: 1899
ISBN Publisher's Prefix: 3-7351

Verlag **Junge Welt***, Postfach 43, DDR-1026 Berlin (Located at: Mauerstr 39-40, DDR-1080 Berlin) Tel: (02) 22330 Telex: 114483
Man Dir: Manfred Rucht
Subjects: Juvenile, Education, Science, Technical, Periodicals
Founded: 1951

Gustav **Kiepenheuer** Verlag, Mottelerstr 8, Postfach 88, DDR-7022 Leipzig Tel: (041) 58726
Associate Companies: Dieterich'sche Verlagsbuchhandlung (qv); Insel-Verlag (qv); Paul List Verlag (qv)
Subjects: Foreign Classics in Translation, Foreign Folklore, Far Eastern Studies, Quality German Literature
Founded: 1909
ISBN Publisher's Prefix: 3-378

Der **Kinderbuchverlag** Berlin, Behrenstr 40-41, Postfach 1225, DDR-1080 Berlin Tel: (02) 20933200 Cable Add: Kinderbuch Berlin
Subject: Children's Books
Founded: 1949

Koehler und Amelang, Hainstr 2, DDR-7010 Leipzig Tel: (041) 282379
Also: Charlottenstr 79, DDR-1080 Berlin Tel: (02) 2202711
Dir: Prof Dr Hubert Faensen
Associate Company: Union Verlag Berlin (VOB) (qv)
Branch Off: Talstr 3, DDR-7010 Leipzig Tel: 209519
Subjects: Cultural History, Art History, Biographical
Founded: 1789/1925
ISBN Publisher's Prefix: 3-7338

VEB Verlag der **Kunst**, Spenerstr 21, DDR-8019 Dresden Tel: (051) 34486 Cable Add: Kunstverlag Dresden
Subjects: Fine Arts, Reproductions
Founded: 1952

VEB Edition **Leipzig**+, Verlag für Kunst und Wissenschaft, Karl-Liebknecht-Str 77, Postfach 340, DDR-7010 Leipzig Tel: (041) 312612 Cable Add: Edileip Telex: 512918 edit dd
Man Dir: Dr Dieter Nadolski; *Sales Dir:* Monika Kollmus
Subjects: Art, History of Civilization, Nature Study, Hobbies, Scientific & Bibliophile Reprints (Publications are in numerous languages)
Founded: 1960
ISBN Publisher's Prefix: 3-361

VEB **Lied** der Zeit Musikverlag, Rosa-Luxembourg-Str 41, Postfach 10, DDR-1020 Berlin Tel: (02) 2805113
Subject: Music
Founded: 1954

Paul **List** Verlag, Mottelerstr 8, Postfach 88, DDR-7022 Leipzig Tel: (041) 58726
Associate Companies: Dieterich'sche Verlagsbuchhandlung (qv); Insel-Verlag (qv); Gustav Kiepenheuer Verlag (qv)
Subjects: Foreign Literature in translation
Founded: 1894

Militärverlag der DDR (VEB), Storkower Str 158, Postfach 46551, DDR-1055 Berlin Tel: (02) 4300618 Telex: 112673 mv
Man Dir: Dr Butter
Subjects: Military, Popular Science, Fiction, Periodicals
Founded: 1956

Mitteldeutscher Verlag Halle-Leipzig+, Thälmannpl 2, Postfach 295, DDR-4020 Halle/Saale Tel: (046) 8730
Man Dir: Dr Eberhard Günther; *Publishing Manager:* Karin Röntsch
Subjects: General Fiction & Non-fiction, Collected Works, Poetry, Essays, Literary Criticism, Belles Lettres, Biography, Novels
Founded: 1946

Buchverlag Der **Morgen***, Seelenbinderstr 152, DDR-1170 Berlin Tel: (02) 6504151 Cable Add: Buchmorgen Berlin Telex: 0112704

Man Dir: Dr Wolfgang Tenzler
Subjects: General Fiction, Belles Lettres, Poetry, Biography, Political Monographs
Founded: 1958

Verlag der **Nation***, Friedrichstr 113, Postfach 74, DDR-1040 Berlin Tel: (02) 28390
Dir: Hans-Otto Lecht
Subjects: Publications of the National Democratic Party of Germany, Current Politics, Biographical, Illustrated Texts, Historical Fiction, Belles Lettres, Cultural; Paperback Series
Founded: 1948

Verlag Das **Neue Berlin***, Kronenstr 73-74, Postfach 1239, DDR-1080 Berlin Tel: (02) 2202126 Cable Add: Neuesberlinbuch Berlin
Associate Company: Eulenspiegel Verlag (qv)
Subjects: Crime, Adventure, Science Fiction
Founded: 1946

Verlag **Neue Musik***, Leipziger Str 26, Postfach 1306, DDR-1086 Berlin Tel: (02) 2202051
Dir: Ferdinand Hirsch
Subjects: Music, Music Literature, Bibliographies, Periodicals
Founded: 1957
ISBN Publisher's Prefix: 3-7333

Verlag **Neues Leben**, Behrenstr 40-41, Postfach 1223, DDR-1080 Berlin Tel: (02) 20933200 Cable Add: Neuesleben Berlin Telex: 114781 nlkbv dd
Man Dir: Rudolf Chowanetz
Subjects: General Fiction and Non-fiction, Juveniles, Science Fiction, Paperbacks
1985: 283 titles *1986:* 294 titles *Founded:* 1946
ISBN Publisher's Prefix: 3-355

Neumann Verlag*, Salomonstr 26-28, Postfach 969, DDR-7010 Leipzig Tel: (041) 7426
Subjects: Leisure Gardening, Animals, Plants, Aquariums, Ornithology, Biology
Founded: 1947

VEB Edition **Peters** Musikverlag+, Talstr 10, Postfach 746, DDR-7010 Leipzig Tel: (041) 7721
Subjects: Music, Textbooks, Facsimile editions
Founded: 1800

Prisma-Verlag Zenner und Gürchott, Leibnizstr 10, Postfach 1461, DDR-7010 Leipzig Tel: (041) 281411
Man Dir: Klaus Zenner; *Publicity Dir:* Fritz Gürchott
Subjects: Archaeology, Art and Cultural History, Fine Illustrated Editions, Historical Novels (many non-fiction books have texts in German, English and Russian)
1985: 9 titles *1986:* 7 titles *Founded:* 1957
ISBN Publisher's Prefix: 3-7354

Pro Musica Verlag, Karl-Liebknecht-Str 12, Postfach 467, DDR-7010 Leipzig Tel: (041) 312612 Cable Add: Musica Leipzig
Subject: Music (school and student editions)
Founded: 1946

Verlag Philipp **Reclam** Jnr*, Nonnenstr 38, DDR-7031 Leipzig Tel: (041) 44501 Cable Add: Reclam Leipzig
Man Dir: Hans Marquardt; *Sales Dir:* Gottfried Berthold; *Publicity:* Susanna Seufert; *Advertising Dir:* Werner Th Otto
Branch Office: Margaretenstr 6, DDR-7050 Leipzig Tel: (041) 64151
Subjects: Reclam's Universal Library (a paperback series covering Belles Lettres,

Philosophy, History, Aesthetics, Music, Biography), Literature, Original Graphics (woodcuts, etchings, lithographs)
Founded: 1828
ISBN Publisher's Prefix: 3-379

Verlag **Rütten und Loening** Berlin, see Aufbau Verlag

Sankt-Benno Verlag GmbH, Verlag für katholisches Schrifttum, Thüringer Str 1-3, Postfach 98 and 112, DDR-7033 Leipzig Tel: (041) 474161 Cable Add: Bennoverlag Leipzig
Catholic Literature Publishing House
General Managers: Christoph Bockisch, Franz J Cordier
Subjects: Religion, Philosophy, Music, Catholic Literature in German and Latin Languages, Periodicals
Founded: 1951

VEB E A **Seemann** Buch- und Kunstverlag, Jacobstr 6, Postfach 846, DDR-7010 Leipzig Tel: (041) 7736 Cable Add: Kunstsemann
Subjects: Art, Reference, Encyclopaedias
Founded: 1858

Seven Seas Publishers, Glinkastr 13-15, DDR-1086 Berlin Tel: (02) 2202851 Cable Add: Sevenseasberlin
Subjects: General Fiction, Poetry, Biography, History, High-quality Paperbacks (in English)
Founded: 1957

Sportverlag+, Neustädtische Kirchstr 15, Postfach 1218, DDR-1086 Berlin Tel: (02) 22120 Cable Add: Sportverlag Berlin/DDR Telex: 112853 spov dd
Subjects: Physical Education, Sport, How-to, Chess, Angling
Founded: 1947

Staatsverlag der Deutschen Demokratischen Republik, Otto-Grotewohl-Str 17, DDR-1086 Berlin Tel: (02) 2336359 (export)/ 2331973 (publicity)/2331990 (sales) Cable Add: Staatsverlag Berlin Telex: 1152344 dd
The official State Publishing Company of the German Democratic Republic
Subjects: History, Social & Political Theory, Economics, Law, International Relations, Government Publications; Periodicals
Founded: 1963
ISBN Publisher's Prefix: 3-329

VEB Verlag **Technik**, Oranienburger Str 13-14, Postfach 201, DDR-1020 Berlin Tel: (02) 28700 Cable Add: Technikverlag Berlin Telex: Berlin 0112228 techn dd
Subjects: Science, Mechanical, Electrical and Electronics Engineering, Control Engineering and Automation, Cybernetics, Technical Dictionaries in numerous languages, Reference, University Textbooks, Periodicals
1985: 80 titles *1986:* 60 titles *Founded:* 1946
ISBN Publisher's Prefix: 3-341

BSB B G **Teubner** Verlagsgesellschaft, Sternwartenstr 8, Postfach 930, DDR-7010 Leipzig Tel: (041) 293158/282545 Cable Add: Teubnerianum Leipzig
Man Dir: Ing Heinz Kratz
Associate Company: Akademische Verlagsgesellschaft Geest und Portig KG (qv)
Subjects: Mathematics, Physics, Electronics, Optics, History of Science, General Technology, Data Processing, Architecture and Building, Classics
Founded: 1811

VEB Georg **Thieme**, Leipzig, Verlag für Medizin und Naturwissenschaften, Hainstr 17-19, Postfach 946, DDR-7010 Leipzig Tel: (041) 291656 Cable Add: Buchthieme Telex: 051533
Trade Department: VEB Gustav Fischer Verlag, Villengang 2, DDR-6900 Jena
Parent Company: Volkseigene Verlage für Medizin und Biologie (qv)
Associate Companies: VEB Gustav Fischer Verlag (qv); VEB Verlag Volk und Gesundheit (qv)
Subjects: Medicine, Bio-Science, Periodicals
Founded: 1886

VEB **Tourist** Verlag, Neue Grünstr 17, DDR-1020 Berlin Tel: (02) 2071018 Telex: c/o Volk und Gesundheit 114488 vogu dd
Man Dir: Dr Reginald Pustkowski;
Editorial: (Books, Guides) Mr Hofmann, (Maps, Atlases) Dr Gaebler; *Sales:* Mr Kaiser; *Production:* Mr Till; *Publicity:* Mr Dornburg
Orders to: VEB Tourist Verlag, Grosse HamburgerStr 32, DDR-1020 Berlin
Subject: Tourism (books, maps, guides, atlases)
1985-86: 20 titles *Founded:* 1977
ISBN Publisher's Prefix: 3-350

Transpress, VEB Verlag für Verkehrswesen, Französische Str 13-14, Postfach 1235, DDR-1086 Berlin Tel: (02) 20410 Cable Add: transpress Berlin Telex: 112229 travedd
Man Dir: Dr Harald Böttcher
Subjects: Transport and Traffic (Railways, Shipping, Motor Traffic, Aviation), Post and Telecommunications, Philately, Numismatics, Popular Science, Periodicals
1985: 102 titles *1986:* 106 titles *Founded:* 1960
ISBN Publisher's Prefix: 3-344

Tribüne Verlag und Druckereien des FDGB, Am Treptower Park 28-30, DDR-1193 Berlin Tel: (02) 27100 Cable Add: Bundesverlag Berlin Telex: Tribüne 0112611
Subjects: Trade Unionism, Belles Lettres
Founded: 1945

Union Verlag Berlin VOB, Charlottenstr 79, DDR-1080 Berlin Tel: (02) 2202711 Cable Add: Unionverlag Berlin
Dir: Klaus-Peter Gerhardt
Associate Company: Koehler und Amelang (qv)
Branch Off: Talstr 3, DDR-7010 Leipzig
Subjects: Political Science, Christian Literature, Belles Lettres, Christian Art, History of Philosophy and Religion
Founded: 1951
ISBN Publisher's Prefix: 3-372

Urania-Verlag (für populärwissenschaftliche Literatur)+, Salomonstr 26-28, Postfach 969, DDR-7010 Leipzig Tel: (041) 7426 Cable Add: Urania Leipzig
Subsidiary Companies: Neumann Verlag, Salomonstr 26-28, Postfach 969, DDR-7010 Leipzig; A Ziemsen Verlag, Lucas-Cranach-Str 21, Postfach 22, DDR-4600 Wittenberg Lutherstadt
Branch Offs: Jena, Leipzig, Berlin
Subjects: Popular Science, Cultural History, Hobbies, Periodicals
1987: 180 titles *Founded:* 1924

VEB Verlag **Volk und Gesundheit**, Neue Grünstr 18, Postfach 53, DDR-1020 Berlin Tel: (02) 2000621 Cable Add: Volksgesundheit Telex: 0114488
Trade Department: Villengang 2, DDR-6900 Jena
Parent Company: Volkseigene Verlage für Medizin und Biologie (qv)
Associate Companies: VEB Gustav Fischer Verlag (qv); VEB Georg Thieme (qv)
Subjects: Scholarship, Medicine, Biology, Veterinary
Founded: 1952

Verlag **Volk und Welt** (Verlag für internationale Literatur)+, Glinkastr 13-15, DDR-1086 Berlin Tel: (02) 2202851 Cable Add: Volkwelt Berlin
Dir: Jürgen Gruner
Subjects: General Fiction and Non-fiction (international) in German translation; Poetry, Reportage, Periodicals
Book Club: Buchklub 65
Founded: 1947

Volk und Wissen Volkseigener Verlag Berlin, Krausenstr 50, Am Spittelmarkt, DDR-1086 Berlin Tel: (02) 20430 Cable Add: Volkwissen Berlin Telex: 112181 vowiv dd
Dir: Mr Weber
Subjects: Schoolbooks, Pedagogy, Illustrated Instructional Material, Literary History, Sports Training, Periodicals
Founded: 1945

Volkseigene Verlage für Medizin und Biologie, Postfach 53, Neue Grünstr 18, DDR-1020 Berlin
Dir: Dr Künzel
Group Members: VEB Gustav Fischer Verlag, VEB Georg Thieme, VEB Verlag Volk und Gesundheit (qqv)

Verlag Die **Wirtschaft**+, Am Friedrichshain 22, DDR-1055 Berlin Tel: (02) 43870 Cable Add: wirtschaftsplan Berlin Telex: Berlin 114566
Subjects: Management, Economics, Mathematics, Statistics, Electronic Data Processing, Periodicals
Founded: 1946
ISBN Publisher's Prefix: 3-349

Z A Reprints, see Zentralantiquariat der DDR

Verlag **Zeit** im Bild*, Julian-Grimau-Allee 10, DDR-8010 Dresden Tel: (051) 48640 Telex: 2291
Manager: H Zumpe
Subjects: Politics, Foreign Languages, Economics, Periodicals
Founded: 1946

Zentralantiquariat der DDR — Reprintabteilung (ZA Reprints), Talstr 29, Postfach 1080, DDR-7010 Leipzig Tel: (041) 293641/295808 Cable Add: Zentralanti Leipzig Telex: 0512684
The Reprint Department of the Central Antiquarian and Second Hand Book Dealers' Office of the German Democratic Republic
Subjects: Special Editions, Reprints of specialized texts, especially of History, Sociology, History of Civilization, Medicine, Natural Sciences, Philosophy and Religion, Law, Economics, the Arts, Linguistics, German Literature, Ancient History (Classical, Oriental, African), Periodicals
Founded: 1964

A **Ziemsen** Verlag, Postfach 22, DDR-4600 Wittenberg Lutherstadt Tel: (0451) 2528
Subjects: Natural Sciences, Biology, Zoology, Botany, Palaeontology
Book Club: Die Neue Brehm-Bücherei
1985: 24 titles *Founded:* 1902

Literary Agents

Büro für Urheberrechte (BfU), Clara-Zetkin-Str 105, Postfach 1325 DDR-1086 Berlin Tel: (02) 2202931 Cable Add: Urbüro Berlin Telex: 112058 autor d
The Copyright Office attends to the copyright protection of scientific and

literary works, plays, works of fine arts and of photography in foreign countries as well as of the use of foreign authors' works inside the German Democratic Republic, and mediates contracts for use

Book Clubs

Buchclub 65, Glinkastr 13-15, DDR-1080 Berlin Tel: (02) 2202851
Owned by: Verlag Volk und Welt (qv)
Founded: 1965

Die **Neue Brehm-Bücherei**, Postfach 22, DDR-4600 Wittenberg Lutherstadt Tel: (0451) 2528
Owned by: A Ziemsen Verlag (qv)

Major Booksellers

Volksbuchhandlung **Haus** des Buches*, Ernst-Thälmann-Str 29, DDR-8010 Dresden

Volksbuchhandlung Edwin **Hoernle***, Ernst-Thälmann-Str 13, DDR-2000 Neubrandenburg

Volksbuchhandlung Alexander von **Humboldt**, Am Platz der Einheit, DDR-1560 Potsdam Tel: (033) 22539/23574
Manager: Friedrich Richter

Humboldt-Buchhandlung*, Bahnhofstr 1, DDR-9001 Karl-Marx-Stadt

Ulrich v **Hutten** Volksbuchhandlung*, Karl-Marx Str 184, DDR-12 Frankfurt an der Oder

Keysersche Buchhandlung*, Anger 11, DDR-5000 Erfurt

Volksbuchhandlung Robert **Koch**, Universitätsring 7 und 10, DDR-4000 Halle Tel: (046) 28397/23563

L K G (Leipziger Kommissions- und Grossbuchhandel), Leninstr 16, DDR-7010 Leipzig Tel: (041) 71370
Leipzig Wholesale Booksellers and Distributors
Dir: Jürgen Petry

Leibniz-Volksbuchhandlung*, Postfach 135, DDR-2751 Schwerin (Located at: Otto-Grotewohl-Str 3)

Leipziger Kommissions- und Grossbuchhandel, see LKG

Volksbuchhandlung Thomas **Mann***, Schiller Str 8, DDR-6900 Jena

Buchhandlung für **Medizin***, Friedrichstr 128, DDR-1040 Berlin

Universitätsbuchhandlung*, Str der Freundschaft 77, DDR-2200 Greifswald

Universitätsbuchhandlung, Grimmaische Str 30, DDR-7010 Leipzig

Universitätsbuchhandlung*, Kröpeliner Str 15, DDR-2500 Rostock

Erich-**Weinert**-Buchhandlung*, Wilhelm-Pieck-Allee 23-27, DDR-3010 Magdeburg Tel: (091) 3086416

Major Libraries

Ernst-Moritz-**Arndt**-Universität Universitätsbibliothek, Rubenowstr 4, DDR-2200 Greifswald

Berliner Stadtbibliothek*, Breitestr 37, Berlin C2

Deutsche Bücherei, Deutscher Pl, DDR-7010 Leipzig Tel: (041) 88120 Telex: 051562 dbuech dd
The German Library
Dir: Prof Dr Helmut Rötzsch
Publications: Deutsche Nationalbibliographie und Bibliographie des im Ausland erschienenen deutschsprachigen Schrifttums, Reihe A, B, (German National Bibliography and Bibliography of German Language Literature appearing abroad, Series A, B, C); *Deutsches Bücherverzeichnis* (German Book List, every five years); *Bibliographie der Übersetzungen deutschsprachiger Werke* (quarterly: Bibliography of Translations of German Language Works); *Bibliographie fremdsprachiger Germanica* (quarterly: Bibliography of Germanica in foreign languages); *Bibliographie der Bibliographien* (monthly: Bibliography of Bibliographies); *Jahresverzeichnis der Hochschulschriften der DDR, der BRD und von Berlin (West)* (Annual List of Academy Texts appearing in the GDR, the FRG, and in Berlin (West)); *Deutsche Musikbibliographie* (monthly: German Bibliography of Music); *Jahresverzeichnis der Musikalien und Musikschriften* (Annual List of Musical Scores and Texts); *Jahrbuch der Deutschen Bücherei* (German Library Yearbook); *Die Deutsche Bücherei im Bild* (The German Library in Pictures); *Wissenwertes über die Deutsche Bücherei* (Facts about the German Library); also other regularly-appearing Bibliographies and Directories

Deutsche Staatsbibliothek, Unter den Linden 8, Postfach 1312, DDR-1086 Berlin Tel: (02) 20780 Cable Add: Stabi Berlin Telex: 0112757
German State Library
Man Dir: Prof Dr Friedhilde Krause
Publications include: Berliner Titeldrucke, Jahreskatalog (Annual List of Berlin Title Impressions); *Zentralkatalog der DDR, Zeitschriften und Serien des Auslandes* (GDR Union Catalogue of Foreign Series and Periodicals); *Bibliographische Mitteilungen* (Bibliographical News); *Handschriften-Inventare* (Inventory of Manuscripts); *Kartographische Bestandsverzeichnisse* (Cartographical Stock Lists); *Gesamtkatalog der Wiegendrucke* (Union Catalogue of Incunabula); *Beiträge zur Inkunabelkunde* (Contributions to Incunabulogy); *Bibliothek seltener Bücher* (Library of Rare Books); *Sigel-Liste der Bibliotheken der Deutschen Demokratischen Republik* (Classification List of Libraries of the DDR); *Fontane-Blätter* (Fontane Folios); *Studien zum Buch- und Bibliothekswesen* (Studies on Book and Library Systems)

Humboldt Universität zu Berlin, Universitätsbibliothek, Clara-Zetkin-Str 27, DDR-1086 Berlin Tel: (02) 2078356
Librarian: Prof Dr Waltraud Irmscher

Karl-Marx-Universität, Universitätsbibliothek, Beethovenstr 6, DDR-7010 Leipzig Tel: (041) 3913310

Landwirtschaftliche Zentralbibliothek, Krausenstr 38-39, Postfach 1295, DDR-1086 Berlin
Central Agricultural Library

Nationale Forschungs- und Gedenkstätten der klassischen deutschen Literatur — Zentralbibliothek der deutschen Klassik, Platz der Demokratie 1, DDR-5300 Weimar Tel: 3552 Telex: 618975 nfg dd
National Research and Memorial Foundation of Classical German Literature — Central Library of German Classicism

Wilhelm-Pieck-Universität **Rostock** Universitätsbibliothek, Universitätsplatz 5, DDR-2500 Rostock
Dir: Karl-Heinz Jügelt

Sächsische Landesbibliothek, Marienallee 12, Postfach 467-468, DDR-8060 Dresden Tel: (051) 52677/576097 Telex: 2368
Dir: Prof Dr sc Burghard Burgemeister
Publications: Sächsische Bibliographiei (Saxony Bibliography); *Bibliographie Bildende Kunst* (Bibliography of Fine Arts); *Bibliographie Illustrierter Bücher der DDR* (Bibliography of Illustrated Books in the GDR); *Bibliographie Geschichte der Technik* (Bibliography of the History of Technology — in German language literature world-wide); *Bibliographie Musik* (Musical Bibliography) — covering both DDR publications on Music and foreign publications concerning the music of the German Democratic Republic); *Zeitgenössisches Musikschaffen in der Deutschen Demokratischen Republik* (Contemporary Musical Production in the GDR) — all annual

Zentrales **Staatsarchiv**, Berliner Str 98-101, DDR-1500 Potsdam
The National Archives of the German Democratic Republic

Stadt- und Bezirksbibliothek Leipzig, Mozartstr 1, Postfach 45, DDR-7010 Leipzig Tel: (041) 3913712
Dir: Reinhard Stridde

Universitäts- und Landesbibliothek Sachsen-Anhalt, August-Bebel-Str 13, DDR-4010 Halle/Saale Tel: (046) 8950 Telex: 4252 ulb hal dd

Universitätsbibliothek*, Goetheallee 6, DDR-6900 Jena Tel: (078) 8222239
Telex: 0588634
Dir: Prof Dr Lothar Bohmüller
Publications: Various bibliographical works

Universitätsbibliothek/Technische Zentralbibliothek der DDR, Technische Universität Dresden, Mommsenstr 13, DDR-8027 Dresden
Dir: Prof Dr Arndt Pflug

Zentralbibliothek der deutschen Klassik, see Nationale Forschungs- und Gedenkstätten der klassischen deutschen Literatur

Zentralinstitut für Information und Dokumentation der Deutschen Demokratischen Republik, Köpenicker Str 80-82, DDR-1020 Berlin Tel: (02) 2391280 Telex: 114690 ZIID dd Cable Add: Zeniid Berlin
Central Institute for Information and Documentation of the German Democratic Republic
Director: Mr Och
Publications include: Informatik (periodical on information science and technology, six per year); *Informationsdienst Übersetzungen* (translations of scientific and technological literature, on microfiche, irregular)

Library Association

Bibliotheksverband der Deutschen Demokratischen Republik, Hermann-Matern-Str 57, DDR-1040 Berlin Tel: (02) 2362845 Telex: 115147 zib dd
The Library Association of the German Democratic Republic
President: Gotthard Rückl; *Executive Dir:* Klaus Plötz
Publications include: Bibliotheksverband aktuell (Conference Reports, Publications relating to Librarianship — six times per year), *Das Bibliothekswesen in der Deutschen Demokratischen Republik — Jahresbericht* (Librarianship in the German

Democratic Republic — Annual Report)
Founded: 1964

Library Reference Books and Journals

Books

Die Deutsche Bücherei im Bild (The German Library in Pictures), Deutsche Bücherei, Deutscher Pl, DDR-7010 Leipzig

Jahrbuch der Bibliotheken, Archive und Informationsstellen der Deutschen Demokratischen Republik (Yearbook of the Libraries, Archives and Information Offices of the DDR), VEB Bibliographisches Institut, Gerichtsweg 26, Postfach 130, DDR-7010 Leipzig

Jahrbuch der Deutschen Bücherei (German Library Yearbook), Deutsche Bücherei, Deutscher Pl, DDR-7010 Leipzig

Sigel-Liste der Bibliotheken der Deutschen Demokratischen Republik (Classification List of Libraries of the DDR), Deutsche Staatsbibliothek, Unter den Linden 8, DDR-1080 Berlin

Wissenwertes über die Deutsche Bücherei (Facts About the German Library), Deutsche Bücherei, Deutscher Platz, DDR-7010 Leipzig

Journals

Das Bibliothekswesen in der Deutschen Demokratischen Republik — Jahresbericht (Librarianship in the German Democratic Republic — Annual Report), Bibliotheksverband der Deutschen Demokratischen Republik, Hermann-Matern-Str 57, DDR-1040 Berlin

Informatik, Zentralinstitut für Information und Dokumentation der Deutschen Demokratischen Republik, Köpenicker Str 80-82, DDR-1020 Berlin
Periodical on information science and technology

Zentralblatt für Das Bibliothekswesen (Central Journal for Library Science), VEB Bibliographisches Institut, Gerichtsweg 26, Postfach 130, DDR-7010 Leipzig
Text in German; contents page in English, French, German and Russian

Literary Associations and Societies

Institut für Literatur Johannes R **Becher***, Karl-Tauchnitz-Str 8, DDR-7010 Leipzig
Dir: Prof Hans Pfeiffer

Deutsche Schiller-Stiftung, Schillerstr/Schillerhaus, DDR-5300 Weimar Tel: 3552
President: Dr Hans Henning; *General Secretary:* Dr Siegfried Seidel
German Schiller Foundation
Publication: Aus dem Archiv der Deutschen Schiller-Stiftung

Deutsche Shakespeare-Gesellschaft, Platz der Demokratie 1, DDR-5300 Weimar Tel: 4076
President: Prof Dr Robert Weimann
German Shakespeare Society
Publication: Shakespeare-Jahrbuch

P E N Zentrum Deutsche Demokratische Republik, Friedrichstr 194-199, DDR-1080 Berlin Tel: (02) 2292688
President: Prof Heinz Kamnitzer; *Secretary:* Walter Kaufmann

Literary Periodicals

Bücherkarren, Verlag Volk und Welt, Glinkastr 13-15, DDR-1086 Berlin

Deutsche Literaturzeitung (German Literature Newspaper), Akademie-Verlag, Leipziger Str 3-4, DDR-1080 Berlin

Fontane-Blätter (Fontane Folios), Deutsche Staatsbibliothek, Unter den Linden 8, DDR-1086 Berlin

Ich Schreibe (I Write), VEB Friedrich Hofmeister Musikverlag, Karlstr 10, Postfach 147, DDR-7010 Leipzig

Literatur und Gesellschaft (Literature and Society), Buchexport, Leninstr 16, Postfach 160, DDR-7010 Leipzig

Marginalien, Aufbau-Verlag Berlin und Weimar, Französische Str 32, Postfach 1217, DDR-1080 Berlin
Journal for the art of the book and bibliophily

Neue deutsche Literatur (New German Literature), Aufbau-Verlag Berlin und Weimar, Französische Str 32, Postfach 1217, DDR-1080 Berlin

Sinn und Form, Deutsche Akademie der Künste, Rütten und Loening, Französische Str 32, Postfach 1217, DDR-1080 Berlin
Contributions to literature

Weimarer Beträge (Weimar Contributions), Aufbau-Verlag Berlin und Weimar, Französische Str 32, Postfach 1217, DDR-1080 Berlin
Journal for literature, aesthetics and culture

Literary Prizes

Johannes R **Becher** Prize
For lyrical poetry, awarded every other year. Enquiries to Minister für Kultur der Deutschen Demokratischen Republik, Molkenmarkt 1-3, DDR-1102 Berlin

Beginners' Prize*
Founded 1966. Awarded annually to beginners ('Debutanten') in the fields of prose, lyrical poetry and essay writing by the Institut für Literatur Johannes R Becher and the Mitteldeutscher Verlag. Enquiries to Institut für Literatur Johannes R Becher, Karl Tauchnitz-Str 8, DDR-7010 Leipzig

Debutantenpreis, see Beginners' Prize

Förder Prize*
Founded in 1966. Awarded annually to young authors of poetry or prose whose first book has been published by Mitteldeutscher Verlag. A fixed sum goes with the prize. Enquiries to Mitteldeutscher Verlag Halle Leipzig, Thälmannpl 2, Postfach 295, DDR-4020 Halle/Saale

Federal Republic of Germany

General Information

Language: German. Danish spoken by a Danish minority in South Schleswig, North Frisian in North Frisian Islands
Religion: Protestant and Roman Catholic
Population: 61 million
Bank Hours: Vary. 0800 or 0830 or 0900-1400, or 0900-1200, 1400-1530 Monday-Friday; open until 1800 Thursday
Shop Hours: 0800 or 0900-1830 Monday-Friday; 0800 or 0900-1400 Saturday (but 1800 on first Saturday of each month)
Currency: 100 Pfennige = 1 Deutsche Mark
Export/Import Information: Member of the European Economic Community. No tariff on books except children's picture books from non-EEC. None on advertising to be distributed free, if exporter's country grants reciprocal treatment, otherwise charged. Import Turnover Tax on books and advertising. No import licence required. No exchange controls
Copyright: UCC, Berne, Florence (see International section)

Book Trade Organizations

A G A V (Arbeitsgemeinschaft alternativer Autoren und Verlage), Postfach 3565, D-5500 Trier Tel: (06501) 3183 Telex: 4725916 suv d
Organization of Authors and Publishers

Adressbuchausschuss der Deutschen Wirtschaft, Adenauerallee 148, D-5300 Bonn 1 Tel: (0228) 104502 Telex: 886805 diht d Fax: (0228) 104158
German Trade Directory Committee

Arbeitsgemeinschaft Buchgemeinschaften im Börsenverein des Deutschen Buchhandels; Brahmsallee 9, D-2000 Hamburg 13 Tel: (040) 4106111 Telex: 2174871
Alliance of Book Clubs/Societies and related concerns in the German Publishers' and Booksellers' Association

Arbeitsgemeinschaft der Punktschrift-Drükerein, pA Deutsche Blindenstudienanstalt eV, Postfach 1160, D-3550 Marburg an der Lahn Tel: (06421) 606100 Telex: 4821106 Fax: (06421) 606229
Association of Braille Publishing Houses
Secretary: Rainer F V Witte

Arbeitsgemeinschaft der Vertriebsfachverbände, pA Verband Deutscher Buch- Zeitungs- und Zeitschriften-Grossisten eV, Postfach 410965, D-5000 Cologne 41 Tel: (0221) 401081
Alliance of the Distributive Trades Associations

Arbeitsgemeinschaft literarische und Sachbuchverlage, Charlottenstr 21c, D-7000 Stuttgart 1 Tel: (0711) 245272
Dir: Prof Dr Ferdinand Sieger
Joint Association of Literary and Non-fiction Publishers

Arbeitsgemeinschaft rechts- und staatswissenschaftlicher Verleger, Unter den Ulmen 96-98, D-5000 Cologne 51 Tel: (0221) 373021 Telex: 8883381

FEDERAL REPUBLIC OF GERMANY

Jurisprudence and Political Science Publishers' Alliance

Arbeitsgemeinschaft von Jugendbuchverlegern in der Bundesrepublik Deutschland eV, Deutscher Taschenbuch Verlag dtv junior, Postfach 400422, D-8000 Munich 40 Tel: (089) 398752
The Alliance of Publishers of Children's Books in the Federal Republic of Germany
Chairman: Maria Friedrich

Arbeitsgemeinschaft wissenschaftliche Literatur eV, Postfach 100133, D-6000 Frankfurt am Main 1
Joint Association for Scientific Literature
Director: Peter Czerwonka

Arbeitskreis für Jugendliteratur eV, Elisabethstr 15, D-8000 Munich 40
Youth Literature Committee (Section of IBBY)
Man Dir: F Meyer

Aussenhandels-Ausschuss, Foreign Trade Committee of Börsenverein des Deutschen Buchhandels eV (qv)

B A G Buchhändler-Abrechnungs-Gesellschaft mbH, Toengesgasse 4, Postfach 100322, D-6000 Frankfurt am Main 1 Tel: (069) 285535
Booksellers' Clearing-House Company
Managers: Heinz Günter Schmitz, Hubert Kauker

Berliner Verleger- und Buchhändlervereinigung eV*, Lützowstr 105, D-1000 Berlin 30 Tel: (030) 2621040
Berlin Publishers' and Booksellers' Association

Börsenverein des Deutschen Buchhandels eV, Großer Hirschgraben 17-21, Postfach 100442, D-6000 Frankfurt am Main 1 Tel: (069) 13060 Cable Add: Börsenblatt Telex: 413573 buchv d
German Publishers' and Booksellers' Association (Press and Information Dept); also has a Foreign Trade Committee (Aussenhandels-Ausschuss)
General Secretary: Dr Hans-Karl von Kupsch
Publications include: Börsenblatt für den Deutschen Buchhandel (German Book Trade Journal); Adressbuch für den deutschsprachigen Buchhandel (German-Speaking Book Trade Directory); *Deutsche Bibliographie* (German Bibliography); *Neuerscheinungs-Sofortdienst (CIP)* (New Titles Express Service (CIP)); *Archiv für Geschichte des Buchwesens* (Book History Archives); *Buch und Buchhandel in Zahlen* (Books and the Book Trade in Figures); *Die schönsten Bücher der Bundesrepublik Deutschland* (The Finest German Books); *Verzeichnis lieferbarer Bücher* (Catalogue of Available Books); *BuchJournal* (a general magazine for booksellers' customers); *How to obtain German books and periodicals*; *English Language Titles from German Publishers*

Buchhändler-Abrechnungs — Gesellschaft mbH, see BAG

Buchhändler-Vereinigung GmbH, Abteilung Dokumentation und Datenverarbeitung, Grosser Hirschgraben 17-21, Postfach 100442, D-6000 Frankfurt am Main 1 Tel: (069) 1306282 Telex: 413573 buchv d
The Booksellers' Association, Documentation and Data Processing Department (Standard Book Numbering Agency)
Dir: Wilfried H Schinzel

Bundesverband der deutschen Versandbuchhändler eV, An der Ringkirche 6, D-6200 Wiesbaden Tel: (06121) 449091
National Federation of German Mail-order Booksellers
Managers: Dr Stefan Rutkowsky, Kornelia Wahl

Deutscher Autoren Verband eV, Sophienstr 2, D-3000 Hannover 1 Tel: (0511) 322068
German Authors Association
Chairman: Detkef M Plaisier

Deutsches Jugendschriftenwerk eV, Raimundistr 2, D-6500 Mainz 1 Tel: (06131) 672085
German Young People's Writing

Europäische Verlagsgemeinschaft 'Ost'*, Bernadottestr 66, D-6000 Frankfurt am Main Tel: (069) 575391
Chief Executive: Stefan Filippi (East European languages)
Also: Bernauer Str 7, D-6457 Maintal 3 Tel: (06181) 47602
Chief Executive: Adolf Schröder (German, English, French languages)
The above Assocation is part of Deutsch-Ungarische Gesellschaft Frankfurt am Main 1970 eV (German-Hungarian Society) and comprises 25 publishing houses of similar interests

O Gracklauer Verlag und Bibliographische Agentur, Reuterpfad 6-8, D-1000 Berlin 33 Tel: (030) 8258139
Suppliers of bibliographic information and research into rights concerning deceased authors and extinct publishing companies
Proprietor: Rose M Meerwein

Hessischer Verleger- und Buchhändler-Verband eV, Grosser Hirschgraben 17-19, D-6000 Frankfurt am Main 1 Tel: (069) 282643
Hessen Publishers' and Booksellers' Federation
Chairman: Reiner Moog; *Managers:* Lisabeth Schubert, Gerhard Fastje

Informations-Zentrum Buch, Book Information Centre: an Association of prominent publishers who share information about their varied publishing programmes. Information can be obtained from any of the participating companies: Artemis und Winkler, Bouvier, Carl, Deutscher Taschenbuch Verlag, Duncker und Humblot, Ehrenwirth, W Fink, Frommann, Hanser, Herder, Hiersemann, Kiepenheuer und Witsch, Kindler, Klett, Klinkhardt und Biermann, W Kohlhammer, Kösel, Metzlersche Verlagsbuchhandlung, M Niemeyer, Nymphenburger, Piper, Quelle und Meyer, Reclam, E Schmidt (qqv)

Landesverband der Buchhändler und Verleger in Niedersachsen eV, Arndtstr 5, D-3000 Hanover 1 Tel: (0511) 14745
Provincial Federation of Booksellers and Publishers in Lower Saxony
Man Dir: Wolfgang Grimpe

Landesverband der Verleger und Buchhändler Bremen-Unterweser eV, Hinter dem Schütting 8, D-2800 Bremen 1 Tel: (0421) 326949
Bremen (Lower Weser) Provincial Federation of Publishers and Booksellers

Landesverband der Verleger und Buchhändler Rheinland-Pfalz eV, Schönbornstr 3, D-6500 Mainz 1 Tel: (06131) 234035
Rhineland-Palatinate Provincial Federation of Publishers and Booksellers

Landesverband der Verleger und Buchhändler Saar eV (LVBS), Eisenbahnstr 68, D-6600 Saarbrücken Tel: (0681) 55050
Saar Provincial Federation of Publishers and Booksellers

Landesverband des werbenden Buch- und Zeitschriftenhandels von Südwestdeutschland eV*, Strohberg 38, D-7000 Stuttgart 1 Tel: (0711) 602088/ 604056
Provincial Federation of the Book and Periodical Trade of South-west Germany

Munchner Arbeitsgemeinschaft der Verlagshersteller, Bahnhofstr 103/II, D-8032 Gräfelfing Tel: 852238
Munich Association of Publishers' Production Assistants

Norddeutscher Verleger- und Buchhändler-Verband eV, Brahmsallee 24, D-2000 Hamburg 13 Tel: (040) 4103161
North German Publishers' and Booksellers' Federation

Presse-Grosso, see Verband deutscher Buch-, Zeitungs- und Zeitschriften-Grossisten eV

Standard Book Numbering Agency, see Buchhändler-Vereinigung GmbH

Verband bayerischer Verlage und Buchhandlungen eV*, Enzenspergerstr 9, Postfach 800949, D-8000 Munich 80 Tel: (089) 484141
Bavarian Publishers' and Booksellers' Federation

Verband der Schulbuchverlage eV, Institut für Bildungsmedien, Zeppelinallee 33, Postfach 900540, D-6000 Frankfurt am Main 1 Tel: (069) 709046
Association of Publishers of Schoolbooks
Chief Executives: Hans-Peter Vonhoff, Andreas Baer

Verband der Verlage und Buchhandlungen in Baden-Württemberg eV, Paulinenstr 53, D-7000 Stuttgart 1 Tel: (0711) 625085 Telex: 721529 Vvb
Federation of Publishers and Booksellers in Baden-Württemberg
Man Dir: Johannes Scherer

Verband der Verlage und Buchhandlungen in Nordrhein-Westfalen eV, Marienstr 41, D-4000 Düsseldorf 1 Tel: (0211) 320951
Federation of Publishers and Booksellers in North Rhine-Westphalia
Secretary: Rudolf Hörmandinger

Verband deutscher Adressbuchverleger eV, Ritterstr 17-19, D-4000 Düsseldorf Tel: (0211) 320909 Telex: 8587075
Association of German Directory Publishers

Verband deutscher Antiquare eV, Braubachstr 34, D-6000 Frankfurt am Main 1 Tel: (069) 287263
German Antiquarian Booksellers' Association
President: Godebert M Reiss

Verband deutscher Bahnhofsbuchhändler*, Grosser Hirschgraben 19H, D-6000 Frankfurt am Main 1
Federation of German Railway Station Booksellers

Verband Deutscher Buch-, Zeitungs- und Zeitschriften-Grossisten eV, Classen-Kappelmann-Str 24, D-5000 Cologne 41 Tel: (0221) 401081
Federation of German Wholesalers of Books, Newspapers and Periodicals (also known as Presse-Grosso)
Chairman: Dr Eberhard Nolte; *Manager:* Gerd Kapp

Verband deutscher Bühnenverleger eV*, Bismarckstr 17, D-1000 Berlin 12 Tel: (030) 3416086
Federation of German Play Agencies and Stage Publishers

Verband deutscher Schriftsteller*, Ferdinandstor 1a, im Keller der alten

FEDERAL REPUBLIC OF GERMANY

Kunsthalle, D-2000 Hamburg 1
Association of German Writers
Chairman: Norbert Ney
Bavarian office: Schwanthalerstr 64, D-8000 Munich 2

Verband deutscher Schulbuchhändler eV*, Marienstr 41, D-4000 Düsseldorf Tel: (0211) 320951
Federation of German School Book Dealers

Verband katholischer Verleger und Buchhändler eV, Lehenstr 31, D-7000 Stuttgart 1 Tel: (0711) 6402061
Federation of Catholic Publishers and Booksellers
Manager: Wolfgang Grossmann

Verband norddeutscher Buch- und Zeitschriftenhändler eV*, An Der Rehbocksweide 22-24, D-3150 Hannoversch-Münden Tel: 4084
Federation of North German Booksellers and Newsagents

Verein für Verkehrsordnung im Buchhandel eV*, Postfach 2404, D-6000 Frankfurt am Main 1
Association for the Regulation of Dealing in the Book Trade

Vereinigung evangelischer Buchhändler, Lehenstr 31, D-7000 Stuttgart 1 Tel: (0711) 6401066
Association of Protestant Booksellers
Chairman: Manfred Siegel

Vereinigung selbständiger Verlagsvertreter, Schatten 6 Gewand, D-7000 Stuttgart (Büsnau) 80 Tel: (0711) 681457
Association of Independent Publishers' Representatives

Verlegervereinigung Rechtsinformatik eV, Verlag Neue Wirtschafts-Briefe GmbH, Eschstr 16-22, D-4690 Herne 1 Tel: (02323) 141201 Telex: 8229870
Association of Publishers of Legal Documentation
Chairman: Dr Karl-Friedrich Peter

Verwertungsgesellschaft Wort, Goethestr 49, D-8000 Munich 2 Tel: (089) 514120
Copyright Association
Chairman: Dr Maria Müller-Sommer; *General Manager:* Dr Ferdinand Melichar

Book Trade Reference Books and Journals

Books

Adressbuch für den deutschsprachigen Buchhandel (Directory of German-speaking Book Trade), Börsenverein des Deutschen Buchhandels eV, Grosser Hirschgraben 17-21, D-6000 Frankfurt am Main 1
Includes Austria, Switzerland, and German-speaking publishers and booksellers in other countries

Anschriften deutscher Buchhandlungen (Addresses of German Booksellers), Verlag der Schillerbuchhandlung Hans Banger, Mainzer Str 24, D-7142 Marbach 9

Anschriften deutscher Verlage und ausländischer Verlage mit deutschen Auslieferungen (Addressese of German Publishers and Foreign Publishers with German Distribution), Verlag der Schillerbuchhandlung Hans Banger, Mainzer Str 24, D-7142 Marbach 9

Die Begegnung (The Meeting), Elwert und Meurer, Hauptstr 101, D-1000 Berlin 62

Bestseller-Almanach, Dr Lothar Rossipaul Verlagsgesellschaft mbH, Bavariaring 24, D-8000 Munich 2
Bibliography containing 3,000 entries

Bibliographie des Buchhandels (Bibliography of the Book Trade), K G Saur KG, Pössenbacherstr 2, D-8000 Munich 71

Buch und Buchhandel in Zahlen (Books and the Book Trade in Figures), Börsenverein des deutschen Buchhandels eV, Grosser Hirschgraben 17-21, D-6000 Frankfurt am Main 1

Buchhändler Kalender (Booksellers' Calendar), Bibliographisches Institut AG, Dudenstr 6, Postfach 311, D-6800 Mannheim

Deutsches Verlagsregister (German Publishers' List), Stamm-Verlag GmbH, Goldammerweg 16, D-4300 Essen 1

Esoterik-Almanach, Dr Lothar Rossipaul Verlagsgesellschaft mbH, Bavariaring 24, D-8000 Munich 2
Bibliography containing 5,000 entries

Freude mit Büchern (Joy with Books), Verlag Bücherschiff Walter Reutin, Rheinstr 122, Postfach 210947, D-7500 Karlsruhe
German Book Catalogue

German Language Books Backlist, Mäander Verlag GmbH, Hundingstr 9, D-8000 Munich 19

Gesamtverzeichnis aller Taschenbücher, Dr Lothar Rossipaul Verlagsgesellschaft mbH, Bavariaring 24, D-8000 Munich 2
Bibliography listing 35,000 pocket-books

Handbuch des Buchhandels (Handbook of the Book Trade), Verlag für Buchmarktforschung, Beim Strohhause 34, D-2000 Hamburg 2

How to Obtain German Books and Periodicals, Börsenverein des deutschen Buchhandels eV, Postfach 100442, D-6000 Frankfurt am Main 1

Psychologie-Almanach, Dr Lothar Rossipaul Verlagsgesellschaft mbH, Bavariaring 24, D-8000 Munich 2
Bibliography containing 6,000 entries

Journals

AGB-Titeldienst (AGB-Title Service), Amerika-Gedenk-Bibliothek, Arbeitsstelle für das Bibliothekswesen, Fehrbelliner Pl 3, D-1000 Berlin 31
Recently published German-language books

Börsenblatt für den Deutschen Buchhandel (German Book Trade Journal), Börsenverein des deutschen Buchhandels eV, Grosser Hirschgraben 17-21, D-6000 Frankfurt am Main 1

Buch Aktuell (Contemporary Books), Westfalendamm 57, Postfach 1305, D-4600 Dortmund

Buchhändler heute (The Bookseller Today, monthly), Triltsch Druck und Verlag GmbH & Co KG, Herzogstr 53, D-4000 Düsseldorf 1

BuchJournal, Börsenverein des Deutschen Buchhandels eV, Grosser Hirschgraben 17-21, Postfach 100442, D-6000 Frankfurt am Main 1
Bi-monthly general magazine for booksellers' customers

Buchmarkt (Book Market), Rochusstr 34, Postfach 320545, D-4000 Düsseldorf 32
The largest independent journal for the book trade in German-speaking areas

Buchreport (Book Report, weekly), Westfalendamm 57, Postfach 1305, D-4600 Dortmund

Deutsche Bibliographie (German National Bibliography), Börsenverein des deutschen Buchhandels eV, Grosser Hirschgraben 17-21, D-6000 Frankfurt am Main 1

Dokumentation deutschsprachiger Verlage (Documentation of German-speaking Publishers), Günter Olzog Verlag, Thierschstr 11, D-8000 Munich 22

Goldmann's Mitteilungen für den Buchhandel (Goldmann's Communications for the Book Trade), Wilhelm Goldmann Verlag GmbH, Neumarkterstr 18, Postfach 800709, D-8000 Munich 80

Mitteilungsblatt für Dolmetscher und Übersetzer (Interpreters' and Translators' News Sheet, six per year), Bundesverband der Dolmetscher und Übersetzer eV (BDÜ), Rüdigerstr 79a, D-5300 Bonn 2

Die Neuen Bücher (New Books, three times a year), Dr Lothar Rossipaul Verlagsgesellschaft mbH, Bavariaring 24, D-8000 Munich 2

Philobiblon, Dr Ernst Hauswedell & Co Verlag, Magdalenenstr 8, D-2000 Hamburg 13
Quarterly journal for book and graphic art collectors

Taschenbücher, Halbjähriges Verzeichnis (Paperbacks, Half-yearly List), Verlag der Schillerbuchhandlung Hans Banger, Mainzer Str 24, D-7142 Marbach 9

Der Übersetzer (The Translator), Verband deutschsprachiger Übersetzer literarischer und wissenschaftlicher Werke eV (VDU), Kuhstr 11, D-4172 Straelen

Verzeichnis lieferbarer Bücher (German Books in Print), Börsenverein des deutschen Buchhandels eV, Grosser Hirschgraben 17-21, D-6000 Frankfurt am Main 1

Welt der Bücher — Der werbende Buch- und Zeitschriftenhandel (The World of Books — The Promotional Book and Periodical Trade), Bundesverband des werbenden Buch- und Zeitschriftenhandels eV, Brusseler Str 96, D-5000 Cologne 1

WerWasWo im Taschenbuch, Dr Lothar Rossipaul Verlagsgesellschaft mbH, Bavariaring 24, D-8000 Munich 2
Bibliography of new pocket-books; published twice a year

Publishers

A D A C Verlag GmbH, Am Westpark 8, Postfach 700126, D-8000 Munich 70 Tel: (089) 76760 Cable Add: Adacverlag Telex: 528404
Man Dir, Rights & Permissions:, Manfred M Angele; *Editorial:* Michael Dultz; *Sales:* Klaus Dehn; Promotion: Helmut Engerer; *Production:* Uto Rogner; *Advertising:* Horst Nitschke
Subjects: Travel Guides, Maps, Atlases, Handbooks (cars, motorcycles, motor-assisted cycles), Sport, Motoring Law, Periodicals
1986: 62 titles *Founded:* 1958
ISBN Publisher's Prefix: 3-87003

A D L A F, see Arbeitsgemeinschaft Deutsche Lateinamerika-Forschung

A M B (Arbeitsgemeinschaft mitteleuropäischer Bibelwerke) Association of Mid-European Biblical Presses, comprising Verlag Schweizerisches katholisches Bibelwerk, Switzerland (qv), Vlaamse Bijbelstichting, Belgium (qv), Österreichisches Katholisches Bibelwerk, Austria (qv), and Verlag Katholisches

Bibelwerk GmbH, Federal Republic of Germany (qv)

Aar-Verlag*, pA Archibook, Westendallee 97F, D-1000 Berlin 19
Orders to: Archibook, Westendallee 97F, D-1000 Berlin 19
Imprints: Abakon; Edition Lichterfelde; Life Sciences Research Reports
Subjects: Science (in English language), Architecture, Art
Founded: 1975
ISBN Publisher's Prefix: 3-8200

Abakus Schallplatten und Ulmtal Musikverlag Barbara Fietz, Haversbach 1, D-6349 Greifenstein 2, OT Allendorf Tel: (06478) 2250
Man Dirs: B and S Fietz; *Editorial, Sales, Publicity:* B Fietz; *Production:* S Fietz
Associate Company: Melos Musikverlag, Munich
Subjects: Song Books, Musical Scores, Musical Instructional Books (all with Christian religious emphasis)
Founded: 1974

Accidentia und Zester Druck- und Verlagsgesellschaft mbH*, Aachener Str 71, D-4000 Düsseldorf 1 Tel: (0211) 347042 Telex: 8584284
Man Dir: Horst W Zester
Subject: Photography
Founded: 1959
ISBN Publisher's Prefix: 3-920005

F A **Ackermanns** Kunstverlag, Wienerplatz 7-8, D-8000 Munich 80 Tel: (089) 488046 Cable Add: Kunstackermann Munich
Man Dir: Hubertus Weinert
Subjects: Art, Photographic
Founded: 1874
ISBN Publisher's Prefix: 3-8173

Agis Verlag GmbH, Ooser Luisenstr 23, Postfach 2220, D-7570 Baden Baden Tel: (07221) 64024/(07222) 48321 Cable Add: Agis Baden Baden
Man Dirs: Karl G Fischer, Karin Grochowiak
Subjects: Aesthetics, Cybernetics, Information Theory, Human and Natural Sciences, Philosophy
ISBN Publisher's Prefix: 3-87007

Agora-Verlag+, Hanseatenweg 10, Postfach 210533, D-1000 Berlin 21 Tel: (030) 3913775/3424824 Cable Add: Agora
Man Dir, Production: Manfred Schlösser; *Sales & Publicity:* Monika Schlösser-Fischer
Subsidiary Company: Erato-Presse
Branch Off: Lucasweg 17, D-6100 Darmstadt
Subjects: Literary Criticism, Belles Lettres, Poetry, Juveniles, Children's, Music, Theatre, Literature by exiles
Founded: 1960
ISBN Publisher's Prefix: 3-87008

L B **Ahnert**-Verlag, Markt 9, Postfach 314, D-6360 Friedberg 3 Tel: (06031) 3131 Cable Add: Ahnert-Verlag 6360 Friedberg 3 Telex: 415961 pvlg d
Man Dir: Rainer Ahnert; *Editorial, Publicity Manager:* Beate Danker
Subjects: Equestrian
ISBN Publisher's Prefix: 3-921142

Michael **Akselrad**, see Kübler und Akselrad KG

Alba Fachverlag GmbH und Co KG*, Römerstr 9, Postfach 320108, D-4000 Düsseldorf 30 Tel: (0211) 482068 Telex: 8585536
Man Dir, Rights & Permissions: Alf Teloeken; *Sales, Publicity:* D Wiesent; *Production:* K Hartung

Associate Company: Alba Publikation Alf Teloeken GmbH und Co KG (qv)
Subjects: Public Transport, Tunnelling
Founded: 1951
ISBN Publisher's Prefix: 3-87094

Alba Publikation Alf Teloeken GmbH und Co KG*, Römerstr 9, Postfach 320109, D-400006 Düsseldorf 30 Tel: (0211) 482069 Telex: 8585536
Man Dir, Rights & Permissions: Alf Teloeken; *Sales, Publicity:* D Wiesent; *Production:* K Hartung
Associate Company: Alba Fachverlag GmbH und Co KG (qv)
Subjects: Model Railways, Public Transport, Modelling, Periodicals
ISBN Publisher's Prefix: 3-87094

Verlag Karl **Albér** GmbH*, Hermann-Herder-Str 4, D-7800 Freiburg im Breisgau Tel: (0761) 273495 Telex: 07721440 vh d
Man Dir: Dr Meinolf Wewel
Orders to: Auslieferungsgemeinschaft Herder, Postfach, D-7800 Freiburg im Breisgau Tel: (0761) 27171
Parent Company: Verlag Herder (qv)
Subjects: Logic, History & Theory of Science, Philosophy, Psychology, Pedagogy, History, Law, Sociology, Political Science
Founded: 1939
ISBN Publisher's Prefix: 3-495

Alpha Literatur Verlag, August-Siebert-Str 9, D-6000 Frankfurt am Main 1 Tel: (069) 555325 Telex: 414890
Man Dir: Dr G Philipps
Subjects: Poetry, Belles Lettres, Theatre

Alternative Verlag GmbH*, Postfach 150230, D-1000 Berlin 15 (Located at: Konstanzer Str 11, D-1000 Berlin 31) Tel: (030) 8811970/8811570
Man Dir: H Brenner
Subjects: Literature, Social and Political Sciences, Philosophy, Theatre, Art
Founded: 1958

Anneliese **Althoff**, see Asso Verlag

Ambro Lacus, Buch- und Bildverlag W Kremnitz, see Lacus

Anabas-Verlag Günter Kämpf KG, Unterer Hardthof 25, D-6300 Giessen an der Lahn 1 Tel: (0641) 63455
Man Dir: Günter Kämpf
Orders to: Sova Verlagsauslieferung, 44 Franziusstraße, D-6000 Frankfurt am Main; West Berlin: Buchvertrieb Petra Lang, Lützowstr 105-106, D-1000 Berlin 30
Subjects: Belles Lettres, Poetry, History, Art, High-priced Paperbacks, Educational Materials
Founded: 1966
ISBN Publisher's Prefix: 3-87038

Anrich Verlag GmbH+, Hooge Weg 71, D-4178 Kevelaer 1 Tel: (02832) 3661
Man Dir: Gerold Anrich
Subjects: Juvenile and Children's
Founded: 1970
ISBN Publisher's Prefixes: 3-920110, 3-89106

Aquamarin-Verlag*, Voglherd 1, D-8018 Grafing Tel: (08092) 9444
Man Dir: Dr Peter Michel
Subjects: Mysticism, Spiritual Art
1986: 53 titles *Founded:* 1980
ISBN Publisher's Prefix: 3-922936

Arani-Verlag GmbH, Kurfürstendamm 126, Postfach 310829, D-1000 Berlin 31 Tel: (030) 8911008
Publisher: Horst Meyer; *Rights & Permissions:* Katharina Janike
Orders to: Libri VA, Postfach 3584, D-6000 Frankfurt am Main 3
Subjects: Belles Lettres, Poetry, History,

Berlin
1985: 11 titles *Founded:* 1947
ISBN Publisher's Prefix: 3-7605

Ararat Verlag GmbH, Bergmannstr 99a, D-1000 Berlin 61 Tel: (030) 6935080
Man Dir: Dr A I Dogan; *Marketing Manager:* Peter T Kampmann
Subjects: Turkish Literature in German translation, German-Turkish Twin-Language books, Turkish Schoolbooks (Readers), Turkish Literature Information Periodical
1985: 8 titles *1986:* 4 titles *Founded:* 1977
ISBN Publisher's Prefix: 3-921889

Verlag **Arbeiterbewegung und Gesellschaftswissenschaft***, Rosenstr 12-13, Postfach 510, D-3550 Marburg an der Lahn Tel: (06421) 63666
Workers' Movement and Sociology Publishing Co
Man Dir: Reinhold Jäger; *Editors:* Wolfgang Abendroth, Frank Deppe, Georg Fülberth, Gerd Hardach
Orders to: Buchvertrieb Grimmstrasse, Grimmstr 27, D-1000 Berlin 61
Subjects: Workers' Rights, Trade Unions, Social History
1985: 10 titles *Founded:* 1976
ISBN Publisher's Prefix: 3-921630

Arbeitsgemeinschaft Deutsche Lateinamerika-Forschung (ADLAF), pA Institut für Genossenschaftswesen, Abt Lateinamerika Universität, Am Stadtgraben 9, D-4400 Münster Tel: (0251) 832895 Telex: 892529 Unims d
German Association for Research on Latin America
Subjects: Embracing the work of more than 25 Member Institutes and more than 200 individual members in research areas of Archaeology, Ethnology, History, Literature, the Geo-Sciences, Economic and Social Sciences, Librarianship; also publish Periodicals and Bibliographies

Arbeitsgemeinschaft mitteleuropäischer Bibelwerke, see AMB

Verlag Die **Arbeitswelt** GmbH*, Grimmstr 27, D-1000 Berlin 61 Tel: (030) 6931073
Dirs: Dr Ulrich Laube
Subject: Politics (especially trade union studies), Social Science

Verlag für **Architektur**, Martiusstr 8, Postfach 440254, D-8000 Munich 44 Tel: (089) 348074 Telex: 5215517
Branch Off: Limmatquai 18, CH-8024 Zurich, Switzerland
Associate Companies: Artemis und Winkler Verlag (qv); Druckenmüller Verlag, (qv); Artemis Verlags AG, Switzerland (qv)
Subjects: Collected Works of Leading World Architects, Studio Paperback Series, Town Planning, Pre-Fabrication

Arena-Verlag Georg Popp AG & Co, Benziger Edition im Arena-Verlag, Rottendorfer Str 16, Postfach 5169, D-8700 Würzburg 1 Tel: (0931) 75011 Telex: 68833
Man Dir, Publicity: Hans-Georg Noack; *Rights & Permissions:* Barbara Küper; *Sales Dir:* Manfred Endres; *Production:* Winfried Popp
Subjects: General Non-fiction, Juvenile, Young Adults, Children's, Paperbacks
Founded: 1949
ISBN Publisher's Prefix: 3-401

Argos Press, Oberbuschweg, Postfach 1940, D-5000 Cologne 50 Tel: (0221) 39070 Telex: 888 3508
Man Dir: Robert Pütz; *Production and other offices:* Brigitte Klatt
Associate Companies: Druckerei Robert Pütz, Werbeagentur Robert Pütz,

FEDERAL REPUBLIC OF GERMANY

Fotostudio Robinson
Subjects: Illustrated books, Humour
Founded: 1978
ISBN Publisher's Prefix: 3-88420

Arkana-Verlag*, Fritz-Frey Str 21, Postfach 105767, D-6900 Heidelberg 1 Tel: (06221) 49974 Cable Add: arkanaverlag Telex: 46183 hvvfmd
Man Dir: Dr Ewald Fischer
Associate Companies: Karl F Haug Verlag GmbH & Co (qv); Verlag für Medizin Dr E Fischer GmbH (qv)
Subjects: Fringe Medicine, Occult, the Arts
ISBN Publisher's Prefix: 3-920042

Ars Edition GmbH, Friedrichstr 9, Postfach 430360, D-8000 Munich 40 Tel: (089) 393045 Telex: 5213554 Fax: (089) 336243
Man Dir: Marcel Nauer; *Sales:* Wolf-R Braun; *Production:* Gregor Schulze
Branch Off: Ars Edition, Switzerland (qv)
Subjects: Gift Books, Children's
1986: 306 titles *Founded:* 1896
ISBN Publisher's Prefix: 3-7607

Das **Arsenal**, Verlag für Kultur und Politik GmbH+, Tegeler Weg 5, D-1000 Berlin 10 Tel: (030) 3441827
The above is the editorial office; administration is c/o Buchvertrieb Grimmstrasse, Grimmstr 27, D-1000 Berlin 61 Tel: (030) 6933069
Man Dir: Dr Peter Moses-Krause
Subjects: Politics, Biography, Oral History, Publicity, Art, Film, Linguistics, Ethnology
Founded: 1977
ISBN Publisher's Prefix: 3-921810

Art Address Verlag Müller GmbH und Co KG, Grosse Eschenheimer Str 16, D-6000 Frankfurt am Main 1 Tel: (069) 295091 Telex: 411699 omf d
Publishers: Joachim Müller, Erwin Kohl; *Man Dir:* Michael Zils
Subject: Art
Founded: 1949

Artbook International, an imprint of Berghaus Verlag (qv)

Artemis und Winkler Verlag, Martiusstr 8, Postfach 444254, D-8000 Munich 44 Tel: (089) 348074 Cable Add: arte d Telex: 5215517
Man Dir: Franz Ebner; *Publicity Dir:* Anita Donat; *Advertising Dir:* Sunhild Gohle; *Rights & Permissions:* Birgit Endres
Associate Companies: Verlag für Architektur, Alfred Druckenmüller Verlag, (qqv, Federal Republic of Germany); Artemis Verlags AG, Verlag für Architektur (qqv, Switzerland)
Subsidiary Company: Winkler-Verlag (qv)
Subjects: (Artemis Verlag) Belles Lettres, The Humanities, Children's, Illustrated Books, History of Antiquity, Collected Works, Classics, Goethe, Oriental Studies; (Winkler Verlag) India Paper Editions and Special Editions of World Literature, Special series of Classics, Works of Zola, Germanistics
ISBN Publisher's Prefix: 3-7608

Aschendorffsche Verlagsbuchhandlung, Soesterstr 13, Postfach 1124, D-4400 Münster Tel: (0251) 6900 Cable Add: Verlag Aschendorff Münster
Telex: 0892830 wn ms d
Man Dirs: Anton Wilhelm Hueffer, Maxfritz Hueffer
Subjects: History, Philosophy, Religion, Psychology, Education, Law, Folklore, Philology, Textbooks, Foreign Languages, Periodicals
Founded: 1720
Miscellaneous: Firm is a member of vgs — Verlagsgesellschaft mbH & Co KG (qv)
ISBN Publisher's Prefix: 3-402

Assimil-Verlag KG, now incorporated in Pädagogischer Verlag Schwann/Bagel (qv)

Asso Verlag, Martin-Heix-Platz 3, D-4200 Oberhausen Tel: (0208) 802356
Orders to: VVA (Vereinigte Verlagsauslieferung GmbH), Postfach 7777, D-4830 Gütersloh 1; West Berlin: Verlag und Vertrieb Rotation, Mehringdamstr 51, D-1000 Berlin 61
Subjects: Contemporary Political Literature in prose, poetry, songs, graphics; Miners' Solidarity, Social History

Ästhetik und Kommunikation Verlags-GmbH, Tempelhofer Ufer 22, D-1000 Berlin 61 Tel: (030) 8028789
Man Dir, Editorial: Eberhard Knödler-Bunte; *Sales:* Waldemar Krause; *Production, Publicity:* Gisela Kayser
Subjects: Contemporary Issues, Political Culture, Aesthetics, Art, Literature, Periodicals
1987: 1 title *Founded:* 1969
ISBN Publisher's Prefix: 3-88245

Verlag **Atelier im Bauernhaus***, in der Bredenau 5, D-2802 Fischerhude Tel: (04293) 671
Subjects: Regional Books, Prose and Poetry in Bibliophile Editions, Novels, Graphics, Songbooks, Art Books

Atelier Verlag Andernach (AVA), Antel 74, D-547 Andernach Tel: (02632) 44432
Man Dir & Rights & Permissions: Rosa Werf; *Publicity Dir:* Frederik Marhofen
Subjects: Belles Lettres, Poetry, Art
Founded: 1966
ISBN Publisher's Prefix: 3-921042

Athenäum Verlag GmbH, Savignystr 53, Postfach 170101, D-6000 Frankfurt am Main 1 Tel: (069) 7560950 Telex: 414531
Publisher: Axel Rütters
Subsidiary Companies: Peter Hanstein Verlag GmbH (qv), Jüdischer Verlag, Syndikat und Europaische Verlagsanstalt, Verlag Anton Hain Meisenheim GmbH (qv) is a subsidiary of this group of companies. All companies are located at above address
Subjects: Philosophy, History, Textbooks, Paperbacks, Linguistics, Pedagogy, Politics, Psychology, Social Science, Literary Criticism, Languages, Economics, General Non-fiction
Founded: 1973
ISBN Publisher's Prefixes: 3-7610, 3-610

Atlantis-Verlag GmbH & Co KG*, Gachenaustr 31, D-8036 Herrsching
Head Off: Atlantis Verlag AG, Switzerland (qv)
Subjects: Art, Literature, History, Pictorial Geography, Travel
Founded: 1930
ISBN Publisher's Prefix: 3-7611

Ludwig **Auer** GmbH, Heilig-Kreuz-Str 12, Postfach 1152, D-8850 Donauwörth Tel: (0906) 731 Cable Add: Auer Donauwörth Telex: 051845
Subjects: History, Religion, Education, Textbooks, Juveniles
Founded: 1875
Miscellaneous: Firm is a member of TR-Verlagsunion GmbH (qv)
ISBN Publisher's Prefix: 3-403

Aulis Verlag Deubner & Co KG, Antwerpener Str 6-12, D-5000 Cologne 1 Tel: (0221) 518051 Telex: 8883068 avd d
Publishers: Karl-August Deubner, Wolfgang Deubner
Subjects: Non-fiction, (Natural Sciences), especially Biology, Chemistry, Mathematics, Physics, Geography
ISBN Publisher's Prefix: 3-7614

Aurum Verlag GmbH & Co KG, Franziskanerstr 9, Postfach 5204, D-7800 Freiburg im Breisgau Tel: (0761) 36409
Publisher: Günther Berkau; *Editorial:* Dr Elisabeth Sicard
Orders to: VSB-Verlagsservice GmbH, Georg-Westermann-Allee 66, Postfach 3320, D-3300 Brunswick Tel: (0531) 708277
Subjects: Psychology, Mysticism, Religion, Yoga, Meditation, Para-Medicine
1987: 200 titles *Founded:* 1974
ISBN Publisher's Prefix: 3-591

Aussaat-und-Schriftenmissions-Verlag GmbH*, Humboldtstr 15, Postfach 548, D-4390 Gladbeck Tel: (02043) 28028
Dirs: Thomas S von Puskás, Volker Stork; *Sales, Advertising:* Michael Lippkau; *Production:* Liesel Rennscheidt
Subjects: Evangelical and Scriptural Texts, Religion, Education, Juveniles, Paperbacks
Bookshop: At above address
Founded: 1978
ISBN Publisher's Prefixes: 3-7615 (Aussaat, Wuppertal); 3-7958 (Schriftenmissions, Gladbeck)

Verlag der **Autoren** GmbH & Co KG, Savignystr 63, Postfach 170509, D-6000 Frankfurt am Main Tel: (069) 742567 Cable Add: Autorenverlag Frankfurt
Dirs: Dr Karlheinz Braun, Peter Urban
Subjects: Texts for Theatre series *Theaterbibliothek*

Syndikat **Autoren- und Verlagsgesellschaft***, Savignystr 53, Postfach 174003, D-6000 Frankfurt am Main Tel: (069) 742567 Telex: 4185532
Author/Publisher Syndicate Company
Man Dir, Sales, Publicity: Axel Rütters; *Rights & Permissions:* Irmela Rütters
Orders to: VVA (Vereinigte Verlagsauslieferung GmbH), Postfach 7777, D-4830 Gütersloh 1; (West Berlin): Hans Schultz, Lützowstr 105-106, D-1000 Berlin 30
Subjects: Literary Criticism, Art Theory, Psychology, Psycho-analysis, Ethnology, Social Theory and Social History, Political Economy
Founded: 1976
ISBN Publisher's Prefix: 3-8108

Axel-Juncker Verlag Jacobi KG, see Juncker

B K V-Brasilienkunde Verlag GmbH+, Postfach 1220, D-4532 Mettingen (Located at: Sunderstr 15, Mettingen)
Man Dir: Dr Hubertus Rescher
Subjects: Brazil and Latin America (Problems, Documentary)
1985: 4 titles *1986:* 6 titles *Founded:* 1979
ISBN Publisher's Prefix: 3-88559

B L V Verlagsgesellschaft mbH, Lothstr 29, Postfach 400320, D-8000 Munich 40 Tel: (089) 127050 Cable Add: BLV Verlag Telex: 5215087/5212630
Man Dir: Dr D Ippen; *Publishing Dir:* Dr Rudolf Schneider; *Editorial:* Wilhelm Eisenreich, Jürgen Kemmler, Inken Kloppenburg; *International Relations Dir:* Curt Ablassmayer; *Rights & Permissions:* Ursula Holkko, Hannelore König
Subjects: Nature and Field Guides, Gardening and Indoor Plants, Household, Cookery and Crafts, Sports, Hobbies and Recreation, Alpinism and Mountain Climbing, Horses, Hunting and Fishing, Motor Cars and Motorcycles, Technical books on Agriculture, Forestry, Environment, Biology, Nutrition, Education, School Textbooks on Agriculture and Household
Founded: 1946
ISBN Publisher's Prefix: 3-405

B S-Verlag Manfred Kerler*, Marbacher Str 8, Postfach 450, D-7057 Winnenden-Stuttgart Tel: (07195) 8012
Subject: Transport

B V B, see Bayerische Verlagsanstalt Bamberg

J P **Bachem** Verlag GmbH, Ursulaplatz 1, D-5000 Cologne 1 Tel: (0221) 16190 Cable Add: Bachemhaus Cologne
Dirs: Dr Peter Bachem, Gerd Horbach
Subjects: Books on Cologne and the Rhenish lands, Economics, Social Science, Religion
Founded: 1818
ISBN Publisher's Prefix: 3-7616

Karl **Baedeker** GmbH, part of the Langenscheidt Group (qv)

Baedekers Autoführer-Verlag GmbH*, Marco-Polo-Zentrum, Zeppelinstr 44-I, Postfach 3162, D-7302 Ostfildern 4 (Kemnat) bei Stuttgart Tel: (0711) 4502262 Cable Add: Baedeker Stuttgart Telex: 721796 mair d
Man Dir: Dr Volkmar Mair; *Editorial:* Dr Peter Baumgarten
Subject: Travel Guides, Motoring Guides
Founded: 1951 (Stuttgart: originally 1827 Koblenz)
ISBN Publisher's Prefix: 3-87036

Hans A **Baensch**, see Mergus Verlag

Bahá'í Verlag GmbH, Eppsteiner Str 89, D-6238 Hofheim-Langenhain Tel: (06192) 22921
Subject: The Bahá'í Religion
ISBN Publisher's Prefix: 3-87037

Friedrich **Bahn** Verlag GmbH+, Zasiusstr 8, Postfach 1186, D-7550 Konstanz Tel: (07531) 23054
Man Dir: Herbert Denecke; *Manager, Rights & Permissions:* Herbert Denecke
Parent Company: Christliche Verlagsanstalt GmbH (qv)
Associate Company: Sonnenweg-Verlag (qv)
Subjects: Children's Books, Christian Instruction, Christianity
Founded: 1891
ISBN Publisher's Prefix: 3-7621

Bärenreiter-Verlag, Heinrich-Schütz-Allee 35-37, D-3500 Kassel-Wilhelmshöhe Tel: (0561) 31050 Cable Add: Bärenreiter, Kassel Telex: 992376
Management: Barbara Scheuch-Vötterle, Leonhard Scheuch, Dr Wolfram Göbel
Imprints include: Edition Bosse, Edition Hinnenthal, Edition Nagel
Branch Offs: Basle, Switzerland; London, UK; New York, USA
Subjects: Music, Reproductions of Ancient Topographical Maps, Periodicals
Founded: 1923
ISBN Publisher's Prefix: 3-7618

Verlag **Bartels und Wernitz** KG*, Reinickendorfer Str 113, Postfach 650380, D-1000 Berlin 65 Tel: (030) 4611011 Cable Add: Bartelswernitz Westberlin Telex: 181331 bawer d
Man Dir, Editorial, Sales and Advertising: Monika Schuchardt-Bartels
Orders to: Georg Lingenbrink, Postfach 3584, D-6000 Frankfurt am Main
Subjects: Sport (including training and history)
Founded: 1926
ISBN Publisher's Prefix: 3-87039

Otto Wilhelm **Barth**-Verlag KG, Stievestr 9, D-8000 Munich 19 Tel: (089) 172237 Telex: 5215282 d
Man Dir: Rudolf Streit-Scherz; *Editor:* Stephan Schuhmacher; *Sales:* Wolfgang Radaj, Alfred Vallotton; *Rights & Permissions:* Ursula Griessel
Parent Company: Scherz Verlag AG, Switzerland (qv)
Associate Company: Scherz Verlag GmbH, Munich (qv)
Subjects: Philosophy and Religions of the East, Mysticism
1986: 20 titles *Founded:* 1924
ISBN Publisher's Prefix: 3-502

Barudio und Hess Verlag*, Cornelius Str 19, D-6000 Frankfurt am Main Tel: (069) 745324
Man Dirs, Editorial: Dr Gunter Barudio, Dr Stephan Hess; *Sales, Production, Publicity, Rights & Permissions:* Stephan Hess
Subjects: Literature, Politics, Art, History, Economics
Founded: 1978
ISBN Publisher's Prefix: 3-922182

Basis-Verlag, Postfach 645, D-1000 Berlin 15 (Located at: Mariannenplatz 23, D-1000 Berlin 36) Tel: (030) 3239018
Subjects: Juveniles, Comics, Education, Documentary
ISBN Publisher's Prefix: 3-88025

Friedrich **Bassermann'sche** Verlagsbuchhandlung im Falken-Verlag GmbH, Schöne Aussicht 21, Postfach 1120, D-6272 Niedernhausen/Ts Tel: (06127) 7020 Telex: 4186585 fves d
Parent Company: Falken-Verlag GmbH (qv)
Subjects: Wilhelm-Busch-Edition
ISBN Publisher's Prefix: 3-87043

Bastei-Verlag Gustav H Lübbe, Scheidtbachstr 23-31, Postfach 200180, D-5070 Bergisch Gladbach 3 Tel: (02202) 1210 Cable Add: Scheidtbachstr 23-31 Telex: 887922
Man Dir: Gustav Lübbe; *Editorial:* Rolf Schmitz; *Sales:* H-J Karl; *Production:* D Deichmann (Fiction); N Anton (Juveniles); *Publicity:* L Becker-Voss, B Naporowski, P Breuer; *Rights & Permissions:* M Koelzer
Associate Company: Gustav Lübbe Verlag (qv)
Subjects: Paperbacks
Founded: 1953
ISBN Publisher's Prefix: 3-404

Ernst **Battenberg** Verlag, Prinzregentenstr 79, Postfach 800349, D-8000 Munich 80 Tel: (089) 4702066 Telex: 5216134 batt d
Man Dir, Editorial, Sales, Rights & Permissions: Ernst Battenberg
Subjects: Art and Antiques, Numismatics, Heraldry, Orders and Decorations, Old Maps, Facsimile Editions
Founded: 1956
ISBN Publisher's Prefix: 3-87045

Hermann **Bauer** Verlag KG+, Kronenstr 2, Postfach 167, D-7800 Freiburg Tel: (0761) 70820 Telex: 772821
Man Dir: Friedrich Kirner; *Editorial, Publicity, Rights & Permissions:* Gabriele Wälder; *Sales Manager:* Brigitte Kopp
Subjects: Astrology, Philosophy, Parapsychology, Yoga, Esoterica
ISBN Publisher's Prefix: 3-7626

Bauverlag GmbH, Wittelsbacherstr 10, Postfach 1460, D-6200 Wiesbaden 1 Tel: (06121) 7910 Cable Add: Bauverlag Wiesbaden Telex: 4186792 bvw d
Dirs: Michael Schirmer, Andreas Schirmer, Eberhard Blottner, Wolfgang Emmes; *Rights & Permissions:* Manfred Braun; *Sales:* Karlheinz Gross; *Publicity & Advertising:* Hans-Joachim Kopp
Subsidiary Companies: Verlag für Aufbereitung Schirmer und Zeh GmbH; Mauritius-Verlags-Messe-& Werbegesellschaft GmbH (both in Wiesbaden); Udo Pfriemer Buchverlag (qv)
Branch Off: Nikolsburger Str 11, D-1000 Berlin 31
Subjects: Civil Engineering, Architecture, Environment, Energy, Surveying, Town Planning, Building Materials, Drawing, Industrial Arts, Dictionaries, Books and Periodicals in both German and English languages
Founded: 1929
ISBN Publisher's Prefix: 3-7625

Bayerische Verlagsanstalt Bamberg (B V B), Laubanger 23, D-8600 Bamberg Tel: (0951) 79020
Man Dir: Kurt Kiening; *Other Offices:* Norbert Goebel
Associate Companies: Morawa & Co, Austria (qv); Adolf Zwimpfer, Switzerland (qv)
Subsidiary Company: Sankt Otto-Verlag GmbH (qv)
Subjects: Classics, World Literature Series, Poetry, Juveniles, Regional Literature
Bookshop: Goerres Buchhandlung, Lange Str 24, D-8600 Bamberg
Founded: 1949
ISBN Publisher's Prefix: 3-87052

Bayerischer Schulbuch-Verlag, Hubertusstr 4, Postfach 190253, D-8000 Munich 19 Tel: (089) 174067
Dir: Heinz Klüter; *Sales Manager:* Hartmut Köppelmann
Branch Offs: Ohmstr 10, D-8047 Karlsfeld; Friedrichstr 26, D-4000 Düsseldorf
Subjects: School textbooks, Educational Materials
ISBN Publisher's Prefix: 3-7627

Bechtle, Thomas-Wimmer-Ring 11, D-8000 Munich 22 Tel: (089) 2350080 Cable Add: Langenmüller Telex: 05215045
Dirs: Dr Herbert Fleissner, Otto Wolfgang Bechtle, Dr Friedrich Bechtle; *Man Dir:* Dr Konrad Dietzfelbinger
Orders to: VVA (Vereinigte Verlagsauslieferung GmbH), Postfach 7777, D-4830 Gütersloh 1 Tel: (05241) 801; West Berlin: BS Buch-Service GmbH Berlin, Kurfürstenstr 72-74, D-1000 Berlin 30 Tel: (030) 2695232
Subjects: Biography, History, Politics, Series Bechtle Anekdoten
Founded: 1868 (Book Department, 1949)
Miscellaneous: Firm is a cooperative member of Buchverlage Ullstein Langen Müller-Herbig (qv)
ISBN Publisher's Prefix: 3-7628

Verlag C H **Beck***, Wilhelmstr 9, Postfach 400340, D-8000 Munich 40 Tel: (089) 381891 Telex: 05215085 beck d
Dirs: Dr Hans D Beck, Wolfgang Beck
Associate Companies: Franz Vahlen GmbH (qv); Biederstein Verlag (qv)
Branch Off: Palmengartenstr 14, D-6000 Frankfurt am Main 1
Subjects: Ancient and Modern History, Archaeology, Literary History, Linguistics, Social Sciences, Anthropology, Theology, Philosophy, Economics, Law, Popular Non-fiction, Music, Art, Illustrated Books, Textbooks, Classics, Periodicals
Founded: 1763
ISBN Publisher's Prefix: 3-406

Edition Monika **Beck**, Am Römermuseum, D-6650 Homburg-Schwarzenacker/Saar Tel: (06848) 554
Man Dir/Proprietor: Monika Beck; *Editorial, Publicity Dir:* Bernhard Beck
Subjects: Bibliophile portfolios, First editions, Monograph portfolios
Book Club: Graphik-Klub
1985: 10 titles *Founded:* 1967

M P **Belaieff**, an imprint of C F Peters Musikverlag GmbH und Co KG (qv)

134 FEDERAL REPUBLIC OF GERMANY

Chr **Belser** AG für Verlagsgeschäfte und Co KG, Falkertstr 73, Postfach 1002, D-7000 Stuttgart 1 Tel: (0711) 2279922 Cable Add: Belserverlag Telex: 0722334 belag d
Publishers: Hans Weitpert, Hilde Weitpert-Vogt; *General Manager, Rights & Permissions:* Bernd Friedrich; *Sales Manager:* Herbert Lindauer; *Publicity:* Hubertus Wolf
Subjects: Art, Quality Reproductions, Facsimiles, Architecture, Music, Non-fiction, Travel, Book/Record combinations, Periodicals, Microfiche editions, Laser Vision editions (interactive)
Founded: 1835
ISBN Publisher's Prefix: 3-7630

Beltz Verlag*, Am Hauptbahnhof 10a Werderstr, Postfach 1120, D-6940 Weinheim Tel: (06201) 63071 Telex: 465500
Man Dir: Dr Manfred Beltz-Ruebelmann; *Sales, Publicity:* Eckhard Mueller
Subjects: Juveniles, Psychology, Social Science, Primary & University Textbooks
Founded: 1841
Miscellaneous: Firm is a member of vgs — Verlagsgesellschaft mbH & Co KG (qv)
ISBN Publisher's Prefix: 3-407

Benziger Verlag*, Kölnerstr 248, D-5000 Cologne 90 Tel: (02203) 100226 Telex: 8874591
Head Off: Benziger AG, Switzerland (qv)
Subjects: General Fiction and Non-fiction, Juveniles, Religion
ISBN Publisher's Prefix: 3-545

Edition Sven Erik **Bergh**, formerly of Tübingen, see Edition Sven Erik Bergh im Europabuch AG, Switzerland

Berghaus Verlag, Ramerding 18, D-8347 Kirchdorf/Inn Tel: (08571) 2042
Man Dir: Ursel Bader
Imprints: Artbook International, Berghaus International
Subject: Art
1987: 15 titles *Founded:* 1973
ISBN Publisher's Prefix: 3-7635

J F **Bergmann***, Agnes-Bernauer-Platz 8, D-8000 Munich 21 Tel: (089) 5803023 Cable Add: Bergmannverlag Munich Telex: 529029
General Managers: Dr Heinz Goetze, Dr Konrad F Springer, Claus Michaletz; *Editorial:* Prof Dr Hans J Clemens
Orders to: Springer Verlag, Heidelberger Pl 3, D-1000 Berlin 33
Parent Company: Springer-Verlag Berlin — Heidelberg — New York — Tokyo GmbH & Co KG (qv)
Subject: Medicine
Founded: 1878
ISBN Publisher's Prefix: 3-8070

Bergverlag Rudolf Rother GmbH*, Landshuter Allee 49, Postfach 67, D-8000 Munich 19 Tel: (089) 160081
Publisher: Rudolf Rother
Subjects: Mountaineering and Skiing
Founded: 1920
ISBN Publisher's Prefix: 3-7633

Berlin Verlag Arno Spitz+, Pacelli Allee 5, D-1000 Berlin 33 Tel: (030) 8326232
Proprietor, Publicity Manager: Arno Spitz
Subjects: International and Comparative Law, Politics, Philosophy, Bibliographies, Bibliographic Guides to Literature on various Sciences, Studies on Berlin, East European Studies, Periodicals
1985: 22 titles *1986:* 21 titles *Founded:* 1962
ISBN Publisher's Prefix: 3-87061

Berliner Handpresse Wolfgang Joerg und Erich Schoenig, Kohlfurter Str 35, D-1000 Berlin 36 Tel: (030) 6148728/6142605
Publisher: Wolfgang Joerg

Subjects: General Fiction, Arts, First Editions, Children's Books
Founded: 1961

Berliner Union GmbH, now absorbed by Verlag W Kohlhammer (qv)

Bernard und Graefe Verlag, Carl-Mand-Str 2, D-5400 Koblenz Tel: (0261) 807060 Telex: 862662 sps d Fax: (0261) 85169
Subjects: Military, History, Politics, Technology, Textbooks
Founded: 1918
ISBN Publisher's Prefix: 3-7637

Bertelsmann AG, Carl-Bertelsmann-Str 270, D-4830 Gütersloh 1 Tel: (05241) 801 Cable Add: Bertelsmann Gütersloh Telex: 933646
President, Chief Executive Officer: Dr Mark Wössner; *Vice-Chairman and Chief Executive Officer of Gruner + Jahr AG:* Gerd Schulte-Hillen; *Central Corporate Development:* Dr Michael Dornemann; *Division Presidents:* Dr Walter Gerstgrasser (Book & Record Clubs), Manfred Lahnstein (Electronic Media), Egmont Lueftner (Music & Video)
Subsidiary and Associate Companies include: Verlagsgruppe Bertelsmann GmbH (The Bertelsmann Publishing Group), Federal Republic of Germany (qv); Gruner + Jahr, Austria, France, Federal Republic of Germany, Spain, Switzerland, UK, USA *Book Clubs:* Bertelsmann Club Vetrieb; Bertelsmann Lesering; EBG Verlags; Europaring der Buch- und Schallplattenfreunde (all Federal Republic of Germany); Círculo de Lectores, Argentina (qv), Colombia, Ecuador, Spain, Venezuela; Buchgemeinschaft Donauland, Kremayr und Scheriau, Austria (qv); Doubleday, Australia (qv), Canada, New Zealand, USA; France Loisirs, Belgium, France, Switzerland; Circulo do Livro SA, Brazil (qv, jointly owned); Bertelsmann de Mexico, Mexico; ECI voor Boeken en Platen; Nederlandse Boekenclub; Nederlandse Lezerskring Boek en Plaat (qqv, all Netherlands); Circulo de Leitores, Portugal; Buch- und Schallplattenfreunde, Switzerland; Book Club Associates; The Leisure Circle (qqv, both UK)

Verlagsgruppe **Bertelsmann** GmbH, Neumarkterstr 18, Postfach 800360, D-8000 Munich 80 Tel: (089) 43189 Cable Add: Bertelsmann München Telex: 523259
The Bertelsmann Publishing Group
Chairmen: Dr Ulrich Wechsler, Dr Horst Benzing, Bernhard von Minckwitz, Olaf Paeschke, Klaus Porada
Parent Company: Bertelsmann AG (qv)
Member Companies: C Bertelsmann GmbH (qv); Bertelsmann Fachzeitschiften GmbH; Blanvalet Verlag GmbH (qv); Verlag Buch und Wissen; Verlag für Buchmarkt- und Medien-Forschung (qv); Central Versand; Fuchsbriefe Dr Hans Fuchs; Betriebswirt Verlag Dr Theodor Gabler GmbH (qv); Wilhelm Goldmann Verlag GmbH (qv); Guetersloher Verlagshaus Gerd Mohn (qv); Heinze; ILS Institut für Lernsysteme GmbH; Kartographisches Institut Bertelsmann (qv); Albrecht Knaus Verlag (qv); Lexikothek Verlag GmbH (qv); MMV — Medizin Verlag GmbH; Mosaik Verlag GmbH (qv); Prisma Verlag GmbH (qv); RV Reise- und Verkehrsverlag (qv); Friedr Vieweg und Sohn GmbH (qv); Verlag Heinrich Vogel Fachverlag GmbH; Westdeutscher Verlag GmbH (qv) (all Federal Republic of Germany); Transworld Publishers (Australia) Pty Ltd, Australia (qv); Plaza y Janés SA, Spain (qv); Transworld Publishers Ltd, UK (qv); Bantam Books Inc; Bertelsmann Publishing Group; Dell Publishing Co Inc; Doubleday & Co Inc; Laidlaw Brothers (all USA)
Founded: 1835
ISBN Publisher's Prefix: 3-570

Bertelsmann Lexikothek Verlag GmbH+, Carl-Bertelsmann-Str 270, D-4830 Gütersloh 1 Tel: (05241) 801 Telex: 933646
Dir: Dr Günther Hadding; *Rights & Permissions:* Ulrich K Dreikandt
Parent Company: Verlagsgruppe Bertelsmann GmbH (qv for associate companies)
Subjects: Encyclopaedias, Dictionaries, Reference

C **Bertelsmann Verlag** GmbH, Neumarkterstr 18, Postfach 800360, D-8000 Munich 80 Tel: (089) 431890 Cable Add: Bertelsmann München Telex: 523259
Dir: Jürgen Kreuzhage
Parent Company: Verlagsgruppe Bertelsmann GmbH (qv)
Associate Companies: See Verlagsgruppe Bertelsmann GmbH
Subjects: General Fiction & Non-fiction, Juveniles, Arts, Biography, Current Events, Foreign Works in Translation
Founded: 1835
Miscellaneous: Firm is a member of TR-Verlagsunion GmbH (qv)
ISBN Publisher's Prefix: 3-570

Verlag Das **Beste** GmbH*, Augustenstr 1, Postfach 178, D-7000 Stuttgart 1 Tel: (0711) 66020 Cable Add: Readigest Stuttgart Telex: 0723539
Man Dir: Werner Weidmann
Parent Company: The Reader's Digest Association, Inc, PO Box 235, Pleasantville, NY 10570, USA
Subsidiary Companies: Pegasus Buch- und Zeischriften-Vertriebs-GmbH, Plieninger Str 100, D-7000 Stuttgart 80; Medit Verlag GmbH, Werinherstr 71, D-8000 Munich 90
Subjects: General
Founded: 1952

Beton-Verlag GmbH*, Düsseldorfer Str 8, Postfach 110134, D-4000 Düsseldorf 11 Tel: (0211) 571068
General Manager: Emil Fuchs; *Editorial:* Dieter Bausch; *Publicity and Marketing:* Peter Fischer
Orders to: Abteilung Fachbuch (at above address)
Subjects: Structural Engineering, Technology and Architecture
Founded: 1958
ISBN Publisher's Prefix: 3-7640

Annette **Betz** Verlag, formerly of Munich, removed to Austria (qv)

Elke **Betzel** Verlag*, Bertha von Suttner Ring 5a, D-6000 Frankfurt am Main 78 Tel: (069) 682600
Subjects: Artistic Philosophy, Author/Artist Co-operation, Poetry, Drama
Miscellaneous: Formerly Gruppe Hinterhaus
ISBN Publisher's Prefix: 3-921818

Beuroner Kunstverlag GmbH, D-7792 Beuron 1 Tel: (07466) 264 Cable Add: Beuroner Kunstverlag
Dir: Gabriel Gawletta; *Publicity Manager:* Siegfried Studer
Subjects: Arts, Religion, Periodicals
Founded: 1898
ISBN Publisher's Prefix: 3-87071

Beuth Verlag GmbH, Burggrafenstr 6, D-1000 Berlin 30 Tel: (030) 26011 Telex: 183622 bvb d-185730 bvb d
Man Dirs: Hans Hermann Plischke, Dr-Ing Helmut Reihlen, Reinhold Welina; *Sales Dir:* Klaus-Peter Kendzia; *Publicity Dir:* Albrecht Geuther; *Advertising Dir:* Ulrich Block
Branch Off: Kamekestr 2-8, D-5000 Cologne Tel: (0221) 57131 Telex: 8881848 dim d
Subjects: Science, Technical
Founded: 1924
ISBN Publisher's Prefix: 3-410

Bibellesebund eV, Industriestr 2, Postfach 1129, D-5277 Marienheide 1 Tel: (02264) 7045
Scripture Union of Germany
Man Dir: Karl Schäfer; *General Manager:* Helmut Klein
Associate Company: Verlag Bibellesebund, Switzerland (qv)
Subjects: Christian Literature for Children and Teenagers
Founded: 1950
ISBN Publisher's Prefix: 3-87982

Bibliographisches Institut und F A Brockhaus AG+*, Dudenstr 6, Postfach 311, D-6800 Mannheim 1 Tel: (0621) 390101 Cable Add: Bifab Telex: 04-62107 bifab d
Man Dirs: Hubertus Brockhaus, Karl Felder, Claus Greuner, Ulrich Porak, Dr Michael Wegner; *Sales:* Rosita Throm; *Sales Dir, Rights & Permissions:* Claus Greuner
Subsidiary Companies: F A Brockhaus GmbH (qv); Mannheimer Verlagsauslieferung für Bücher GmbH, Mannheim; Südbuch Vertriebs GmbH, Mannheim (all Federal Republic of Germany); Bibliographisches Institut GmbH, Vienna, Austria; Bibliographisches Institut und F A Brockhaus AG, Switzerland (qv)
Subjects: Technology, Arts and Sciences, German Language, General Knowledge, Juveniles, General Science, University Textbooks, Encyclopaedias, Geography
Founded: 1826 (Bibliographisches Institut)
Miscellaneous: Publishers of the Duden series of Dictionaries, Brockhaus und Meyer series of Encyclopaedias
ISBN Publisher's Prefix: 3-411

Bibliomed — Medizinische Verlagsgesellschaft mbH, Nuernberger Str 10, Postfach 150, D-3508 Melsungen Tel: (05661) 6001
Man Dir: Hans-Martin Horn; *Editorial:* Helga Juckel; *Sales, Production, Publicity, Rights & Permissions:* Dr Claus Wagner
Subjects: Medicine, Nursing
1986: 39 titles *Founded:* 1976
ISBN Publisher's Prefix: 3-921958

Biederstein Verlag, Wilhelmstr 9, D-8000 Munich 40 Tel: (089) 381891 Telex: 05-215085 beck d
Man Dir: Wolfgang Beck
Associate Companies: Verlag C H Beck (qv); Franz Vahlen GmbH (qv)
Subjects: General Fiction, Popular Non-fiction
Founded: 1945
ISBN Publisher's Prefix: 3-7642

Georg **Bitter** Verlag+*, Herner Str 62, Postfach 100265, D-4350 Recklinghausen Tel: (02361) 25888/21400
Man Dir, Sales: Dr Georg Bitter; *Editorial:* Hans-Sigismund von Buch; *Publicity, Advertising:* Walter Stolzenberg; *Rights & Permissions:* Dr Georg Bitter, Marion R Liebchen
Subjects: Literature for Juveniles, Young Adults
Founded: 1968
ISBN Publisher's Prefix: 3-7903

Blanvalet Verlag, Neumarkterstr 18, Postfach 800360, D-8000 Munich 80 Tel: (089) 431890 Cable Add: Bertelsmann München Telex: 523259
Parent Company: Verlagsgruppe Bertelsmann GmbH (qv for associate companies)
Subjects: Belle Lettres, Juveniles, Biographies
Founded: 1935
ISBN Publisher's Prefix: 3-7645

Blaukreuz-Verlag Wuppertal+, Freiligrathstr 27, Postfach 201610 D-5600 Wuppertal 2 Tel: (0202) 621098
Publisher: Hans-Jürgen Weidtke
Parent Company: Blaues Kreuz in Deutschland eV, Wuppertal
Subjects: Alcoholism, Christian Books and Texts
1986: 90 titles *1987:* 95 titles
Miscellaneous: Firm is a contributor to the Telos (qv) series of evangelical paperbacks. See also Blaukreuz-Verlag Berne, Switzerland
ISBN Publisher's Prefixes: 3-920106, 3-89175

Bleicher Verlag*, Holderäcker Str 14, Postfach 100123, D-7016 Gerlingen Tel: (07156) 21033 Cable Add: Bleicherverlag
Publisher, Editorial, Rights & Permissions: Heinz M Bleicher; *Sales, Publicity:* Thomas Bleicher; *Production:* Rainer Abel
Subjects: General Fiction, Picture Books, Poster Books, Comic Verse, Periodicals
Founded: 1968
ISBN Publisher's Prefixes: 3-921097, 3-88350

Deutsche **Blindenstudienanstalt** eV, see under Deutsche

Bock und Herchen Verlag, Reichenbergstr 11e, Postfach 1145, D-5340 Bad Honnef 1 Tel: (02224) 5443
Man Dirs: Karl Heinrich Bock, Hans-Alfred Herchen
Subjects: Scientific Papers, Librarianship
Founded: 1977
ISBN Publisher's Prefix: 3-88347

Böhlau-Verlag GmbH & Cie*, Niehler Str 272-274, Postfach 600180, D-5000 Cologne 60 Tel: (0221) 765368 Cable Add: Böhlau, Cologne 60
Man Dir: Dr Günter J Henz
Head Off: Böhlau Verlag GmbH, Austria (qv)
Subjects: History, Music, Art, Philosophy, Modern Philology, Theology, General & Social Science
Founded: 1951

Boje-Verlag GmbH, Am Pestalozziring 14, Postfach 2829, D-8520 Erlangen Tel: (09131) 60600/606074 (Foreign Rights) Cable Add: Pestalozzi Erlangen Telex: 629766 pevau d Fax: (09131) 606078
Editorial: Herbert Günther; *Sales:* Dieter Wohlfahrt; *Production:* Dieter Mögel; *Publicity:* Monika Eisele; *Foreign Rights:* Marianne Vittinghoff
Subject: Juveniles
Founded: 1947
ISBN Publisher's Prefix: 3-414

Harald **Boldt** Verlag GmbH, Postfach 1110, D-5407 Boppard am Rhein 1 Tel: (06742) 2511
Man Dir, Publicity: Harald Boldt; *Sales Dir:* Heidrun Jansen; *Production, Rights & Permissions:* Peter Boldt
Associate Company: Boldt Druck Boppard GmbH
Subjects: Social, Political and Military History of Germany
Founded: 1951
ISBN Publisher's Prefix: 3-7646

Bollmann-Bildkarten-Verlag GmbH & Co KG, Lilienthalplatz 1, Postfach 1526, D-3300 Braunschweig Tel: (0531) 332069 Telex: 952546
Dir: Friedrich Bollmann
Subject: Maps
1986: 6 titles *1987:* 5 titles

Dr **Bolte** KG, see Polyglott-Verlag

Verlag Aurel **Bongers**+, Dortmunder Str 67, Postfach 100264, D-4350 Recklinghausen Tel: (02361) 41001 Cable Add: Bongers Recklinghausen
Proprietor, Publishing Dir, Rights & Permissions: Aurel Bongers Jnr; *Sales Dir:* Helmut Exner
Subjects: Art (Modern and Classical Painting and Sculpture, Eastern Church Art), Archaeology
1986: 10 titles *1987:* 8 titles *Founded:* 1931
ISBN Publisher's Prefix: 3-7647

Bonn Aktuell GmbH+, Pforzheimer Str 381, Postfach 310807, D-7000 Stuttgart 31 Tel: (0711) 881149
Publisher: Dr Horst Poller
Subjects: Politics, Current Affairs, Economics
ISBN Publisher's Prefix: 3-87959

Gebrüder **Borntraeger** Verlagsbuchhandlung+, Johannesstr 3A, D-7000 Stuttgart 1 Tel: (0711) 625001 Telex: 723363 schb d
Man Dirs: Dr Erhard Naegele (Production), Klaus Obermiller (Sales)
Associate Company: E Schweizerbart'sche Verlagsbuchhandlung (qv)
Subjects: Geology, Geomorphology, Geography, Geophysics, Meteorology, Metallography, Botany (including 'Cramer' publications), Biology, Oceanography, General Science
Founded: 1790
ISBN Publisher's Prefix: 3-443

C **Bösendahl**, Klosterstr 32-33, Postfach 1240, D-3260 Rinteln 1 Tel: (05751) 4511
Also: Obernstr 28, D-3060 Stadthagen Tel: (05721) 75700
Man Dir: Uwe Spengler
Subjects: Light Fiction, Local Interest
Founded: 1621
ISBN Publisher's Prefix: 3-87085

Editions **Bosse**, an imprint of Bärenreiter-Verlag (qv)

Gustav **Bosse** Verlag GmbH & Co KG, Von-der-Tann-Str 38, D-8400 Regensburg 1 Tel: (0941) 794091 Cable Add: Bosse Regensburg
Subjects: Musicology, Musical Pedagogy, Periodicals, Music Paperbacks

Oscar **Brandstetter** Verlag GmbH & Co KG, Stiftstr 30, Postfach 1708, D-6200 Wiesbaden Tel: (06121) 521002 Telex: 4186486 obra d
Man Dir: Günther H Fröhlen; *Editorial:* Dr Antonin Kucera
Subjects: Language & Technical Dictionaries
Founded: 1862
ISBN Publisher's Prefix: 3-87097

Brasilienkunde Verlag GmbH, see BKV

Bratt Institut für Neues Lernen GmbH+, Hervorsterstr 267, D-4180 Goch 5 Tel: (02823) 29094 Cable Add: Bratt Institut Fax: (02823) 4896
Man Dir: Bertil Bratt; *Editorial, Rights & Permissions, Sales, Production, Publicity:* Joachim C Duderstadt
Orders to: Hervorsterstr 267, D-4180 Goch 5
Parent Company: Studentlitteratur Utbildningshuset AB, Sweden (qv)
Associate Company: Chartwell-Bratt Ltd, UK (qv)
Subjects: Psychology, Textbooks, Science, Computer Studies
Founded: 1979
ISBN Publisher's Prefix: 3-88598

Verlag G **Braun** GmbH+, Karl-Friedrich-Str 14-18, Postfach 1709, D-7500 Karlsruhe Tel: (0721) 1651 Cable Add: Braunverlag Telex: 07826904
Man Dir: Dr Eberhard Knittel; *Dirs:* Karl Breh, Rolf Feez
Subjects: General Science, Medicine, Secondary Textbooks, Paperbacks, Periodicals
ISBN Publisher's Prefix: 3-7650

Verlag **Braun und Schneider***, Maximiliansplatz 9, D-8000 Munich 2 Tel: (089) 555580
Dirs: Dr Julius Schneider, Friedrich Schneider

136 FEDERAL REPUBLIC OF GERMANY

Subjects: Juveniles, Paperbacks, Illustrated Books
Founded: 1843
ISBN Publisher's Prefix: 3-87099

Umschau Verlag **Breidenstein** GmbH, see Umschau

Breitkopf und Härtel, Walkmühl-Str 52, Postfach 1707, D-6200 Wiesbaden 1 Tel: (06121) 402031 Cable Add: Breitkopfs Wiesbaden Telex: 4182647 eb d
Man Dirs: Lieselotte Sievers, Gottfried Möckel
Subjects: Music, Books on Music, Education
Founded: 1719
ISBN Publisher's Prefix: 3-7651

Julius **Breitschopf** KG*, Verlagsbuchhandlung, Schleissheimerstr 371B, D-8000 Munich 45 Tel: (089) 3514747
Associate Company: Verlagsbuchhandlung Julius Breitschopf, Austria (qv)
Subjects: Juveniles, Television Tie-in Books
ISBN Publishers' Prefix: 3-87254

Breklumer Verlag, Bundesstr 5-Kirchenstr, Postfach Bredstedt 1220, D-2257 Breklum Tel: (04671) 2028 Cable Add: Breklumer Verlag Breklum
Publisher: Manfred Siegel
Subject: Religion
ISBN Publisher's Prefix: 3-7793

Brendow-Verlag, Gutenbergstr 1, Postfach 1280, D-4130 Moers 1 Tel: (02841) 41036 Telex: 172841314 brend d
Dir: Hans Steinacker; *Sales:* Thomas Rickert; *Publicity, Rights & Permissions:* Hildegard Bernert
Subjects: Evangelical Religious Literature
1985-86: 35 titles *Founded:* 1849
Miscellaneous: Firm is a member of the Telos (qv) group of evangelical paperback publishers
ISBN Publisher's Prefix: 3-87067

Brigg Verlag GmbH+, Zusamstr 9, D-8900 Augsburg 1 Tel: (0821) 711347
Man Dir: Franz-Josef Büchler
Subjects: Illustrated and Bibliophile Books, Travel, Children's Regional Books, Belles Lettres, Poetry
Founded: 1950
Miscellaneous: Formerly Verlag die Brigg
ISBN Publisher's Prefix: 3-87101

F A **Brockhaus** GmbH+*, Dudenstr 6, D-6800 Mannheim 1 Tel: (0621) 39010 Cable Add: Brockhausverlag Telex: 462107 bifab d
Dirs: Ulrich Porak, Hubertus Brockhaus, Dr Michael Wegner; *Sales:* Elke Gerhard (Tel: (0621) 371066); *Publicity:* Peter Braun
Orders to: (Federal Republic of Germany) Mannheimer Verlagsauslieferung, Postfach 311, D-6800 Mannheim 1; (Berlin) Helga Hartwich, Lützowstr 105-106, D-1000 Berlin; (Austria) Zentralgesellschaft, Singerstr 12, A-1010 Vienna 1; (Switzerland) Schweizer Buchzentrum, POB, CH-4601 Olten
Parent Company: Bibliographisches Institut und F A Brockhaus AG (qv)
Subjects: Encyclopaedias, Language and other Dictionaries, Biography, History, General Science, Travel, Music, Schopenhauer, Nature, Animals, Fiction
1985: 10 titles *Founded:* 1805
ISBN Publisher's Prefix: 3-7653

R **Brockhaus** Verlag, Postfach 110152, D-5600 Wuppertal 11 (Located at: Champagne 7, D-5657 Haan) Tel: (02104) 69110
Publisher: Dr Ulrich Brockhaus; *Editorial:* Elisabeth Wetter, Günter Balders; *Sales:* Raimond Schmidt, Karl-Heinz Eisner
Associate Company: Oncken Verlag KG (qv)
Subjects: Popular Christian Literature, Theology, Biographies, Fiction, Juveniles, Song Books, Bibles and Bible Study
Founded: 1853
ISBN Publisher's Prefix: 3-417

Brönner Verlag Breidenstein GmbH, Stuttgarter Str 18-24, D-6000 Frankfurt am Main 1 Tel: (069) 26001 Telex: 0411964 Fax: (069) 2600223
Dirs: Klaus Breidenstein, Hans-Jürgen Breidenstein; *Editorial:* Eberhard Urban; *Sales Manager:* Hans-J Lesch
Associate Company: Umschau Verlag Breidenstein GmbH (qv for other Associate Companies)
Subject: Art
ISBN Publisher's Prefix: 3-599

Broschek Druck GmbH & Co KG*, Bargkoppelweg 61, D-2000 Hamburg 73
Publisher: Dr A Schneckenburger-Broschek
Subjects: Juveniles, Art History, Illustrated books
Founded: 1913
ISBN Publisher's Prefix: 3-87102

Broschek Verlag*, Bargkoppelweg 61, D-2000 Hamburg 73 Tel: (040) 67961 Cable Add: Christians Druck
Orders to: Hans Christians Druckerei & Verlag (qv)
Associate Company: Hans Christians Druckerei und Verlag (qv)
Subjects: Hamburg regional literature

Studio **Bruckmann** Kunst im Druck GmbH, Nymphenburger Str 84, Postfach 27, D-8000 Munich 20 Tel: (089) 125701 Cable Add: Bruckmannkoge Telex: 523739
Editor: Erhardt D Stiebner; *Sales:* Paul Rossnagl; *Publicity:* Fritz Scheuer; *Production:* Knut Liese
Associate Company: Verlag Bruckmann München (qv)
Subjects: Art, Special Editions
Founded: 1972
ISBN Publisher's Prefix: 3-7854

Verlag **Bruckmann** München, Nymphenburger Str 86, Postfach 27, D-8000 Munich 20 Tel: (089) 125701 Cable Add: Bruckmannkoge Munich Telex: 523739
Editor: Erhardt D Stiebner; *Publishing Manager:* Dr Jörg D Stiebner; *Sales:* Paul Rossnagl; *Publicity:* Fritz Scheuer; *Production:* Knut Liese
Associate Company: Studio Bruckmann Kunst im Druck (qv)
Subjects: Art, Special Editions, Illustrated Books on Landscape and Travel, Handbooks on European Arts and Crafts, Reference Books on Graphic Art/Design/Type/Printing, History, Mountaineering, Bavaria, Commemoration Volumes, Yearbooks, Exhibition Catalogues, Periodicals
Founded: 1858
Miscellaneous: Firm is a member of TR-Verlagsunion GmbH (qv)
ISBN Publisher's Prefix: 3-7654

Brunnen-Verlag GmbH*, Gottlieb-Daimlerstr 22, Postfach 5205, D-6300 Giessen Tel: (0641) 65088
Man Dir: Wilfried Jerke; *Editorial:* Helmut Jablonski; *Rights & Permissions:* Eva Büscher; *Sales Manager:* Andreas Walter
Branch Off: Brunnen-Verlag, Switzerland (qv)
Subjects: Religion, Juveniles
Founded: 1919
ISBN Publisher's Prefix: 3-7655

Brunnquell-Verlag der Bibel-und Missions-Stiftung Metzingen*, Karlstr 4, Postfach 1155, D-7430 Metzingen Tel: (07123) 2280
Man Dir: Thomas Weber
Subject: Religion
Founded: 1945
ISBN Publisher's Prefix: 3-7656

Verlag C J **Bucher** GmbH*, Ortlerstr 8, D-8000 Munich 70 Tel: (089) 769920 Telex: 522720 rin d
Publishing Dir, Editorial, Rights & Permissions: Axel Schenck; *Sales, Publicity:* Eduard Gogel; *Production:* Johannes Eikel
Subjects: Natural History, Animals, Cities and Countries, Art, Cultural History, Photography, Reference, Film Book series, General Non-fiction
1985: 30 titles *Founded:* 1926
ISBN Publisher's Prefix: 3-7658

Verlag für **Buchmarkt- und Medien-Forschung***, Carl-Bertelsmann-Str 270, Postfach 5555, D-4830 Gütersloh Tel: (05241) 802580 Telex: 933868/933646
Dir: Manfred Harnischfeger
Parent Company: Verlagsgruppe Bertelsmann GmbH (qv for associate companies)
Subjects: Book Trade, Bibliographies, Periodicals
Founded: 1962

Verlag **Büchse** der Pandora GmbH*, Postfach 2820, D-6330 Wetzlar (Located at: Alte Chaussee 4, D-6334 Asslar-Werdorf) Tel: (6443) 3361 Cable Add: 6334 Asslar-Werdorf
Man Dir: Peter Grosshaus, Stefan Blankertz
Subjects: 20th century Literature, Pedagogy, Philosophy, Art, Architecture, Anarchy
Bookshop (Associated): Buchladen Galerie/Werkstatt, Obertorstr 22-24, D-6330 Wetzler
Founded: 1977
ISBN Publisher's Prefix: 3-88178

Bund-Verlag GmbH*, Hansestr 63a, Postfach 900840, D-5000 Cologne 90 Tel: (02203) 30030 Telex: 08873362
Man Dir: Tomas Kosta; *Sales:* Karl-Heinz Antoni; *Production:* Heinz Biermann; *Publicity:* Waldemar Block; *Rights & Permissions:* Gunther Heyder, Inge Stalker
Subjects: Trade Union Policy, Industrial Law, Social Law and Studies, Legal Texts and Commentaries, Economics, Politics, Taxation and Finance, WSI Studies (Industrial Series), Periodicals connected with Social Services and Workers' Rights, Fiction, Poetry, Juvenile
Bookshops: Bund-Verlag GmbH Buchhandlung (at above address); Bund-Verlag Buchhandlung, Wilhelm-Leuschner Str 64, D-6000 Frankfurt am Main; Bund-Verlag GmbH Buchhandlung, Schwanthalerstr 64, D-8000 Munich 2
Founded: 1947
ISBN Publisher's Prefix: 3-7663

Bundes-Verlag GmbH+, Goltenkamp 4, Postfach 4065, D-5810 Witten Tel: (02302) 39940
Man Dir, Rights & Permissions: Erhard Diehl
Subjects: Current Christian topics, Aids to Everyday Living, Scriptural
Founded: 1887
ISBN Publisher's Prefix: 3-8137

Burckhardthaus-Laetare Verlag GmbH*, Schumannstr 161, D-6050 Offenbach am Main Tel: (069) 840003 Cable Add: Burckhardthaus
Dir: Karl-Heinz Reus
Subjects: Humanities, Arts, Textbooks,

Multimedia, Music, Education, Pedagogy, Psychology, Religion, Social Science, Games
ISBN Publisher's Prefix: 3-7664

Verlag Aenne **Burda** GmbH & Co KG, Am Kestendamm 2, Postfach 1160, D-7600 Offenburg Tel: (0781) 8402 Cable Add: burdamoden offenburg Telex: 752804
Subjects: Hobbies, Cookery, Handicrafts, Periodicals
ISBN Publisher's Prefix: 3-920158

Kartographischer Verlag **Busche** GmbH*, Kaiserstr 129, Postfach 114, D-4600 Dortmund 1 Tel: (0231) 597088
Man Dir: Günter Schiffmann; *Editorial:* Alfred Heinemann; *Publicity & Advertising Dir:* Jürgen Klaffka; *Rights & Permissions:* Günter Schiffmann, Jürgen Klaffka
Subjects: Street Maps, Atlases
Founded: 1972
ISBN Publisher's Prefixes: 3-921143, 3-88584

Helmut **Buske** Verlag, Schlüterstr 14, Postfach 132255, D-2000 Hamburg 13 Tel: (040) 452522
Man Dir: Helmut Buske
Subjects: Linguistics, Phonetics, Slav, Romance, Germanic and Oriental Studies, Philosophy, History, Minor Languages
Founded: 1959
ISBN Publisher's Prefix: 3-87118

Verlag **Busse und Seewald** GmbH*, Ahmserstr 190, Postfach 1344, D-4900 Herford Tel: (05221) 7750 Cable Add: Westverlag Herford Telex: 934717
Manager: Helmut Russ
Associate Companies: Westdeutsche Verlagsanstalt GmbH, Buchdruckerei und Verlag Busse (both at above address)
Subjects: Travel, Boating, Oriental Carpets, Interior Decor, Wine, Politics, Economics, History
Founded: 1947
ISBN Publisher's Prefix: 3-512

Verlag **Butzon und Bercker** GmbH, Postfach 215, D-4178 Kevelaer 1 (Located at: Hoogeweg 71, Kevelaer 1) Tel: (02832) 2906 Cable Add: Butzonbercker Telex: 812207 bbkev
Dirs: Edmund Bercker, Dr Edmund Bercker Jnr, Klaus Bercker; *Editorial:* Maria Groothusen; *Sales:* Klaus Behnke; *Production:* Otto Paustian; *Publicity:* Elisabeth von der Heiden; *Rights & Permissions:* Anne Moore
Subjects: Catholic Religion and Theology, Prayer and Meditation, Liturgy, Religious Teaching Books for Children
Founded: 1870
ISBN Publisher's Prefix: 3-7666

C I S – Verlag (Christlich-Islamisches Schriftum)*, Postfach 1145, D-4417 Altenberge Tel: (02505) 3534/3247
Man Dir: Prof Dr Adel Th Khoury; *Sales:* M S Abdullah
Orders to: Postfach 2309, D-4770 Soest Tel: (02921) 14116
Subjects: Christian-Islamic Writing, Theology, Philosophy, Culture, Literature, Periodicals
1985-86: 14 titles *Founded:* 1981
ISBN Publisher's Prefix: 3-88733

Caann Verlag GmbH+, von-Kleist-Weg 11, D-8037 Olching Tel: (08142) 14154
Man Dir: Klaus Wagner
Subjects: Fiction, Non-fiction
Founded: 1969
ISBN Publisher's Prefix: 3-87121

Verlag Georg D W **Callwey** GmbH & Co+, Streitfeldstr 35, Postfach 800409, D-8000 Munich 80 Tel: (089) 433096 Cable Add: Callweyverlag Telex: 5216752 cal v
Man Dir: Helmuth Baur-Callwey; *Editorial:* Roland Thomas, Dr Paulhans Peters; *Sales:* Traute Geier; *Production:* Christian Pfeiffer-Belli; *Publicity:* Ludger Marquardt
Subjects: Biography, History, Architecture, History of Art, Handicrafts, Landscape Architecture, Painting and Restoration, Stonemasonry, Horology, Periodicals
Founded: 1884
ISBN Publisher's Prefix: 3-7667

Calwer Verlag, Scharnhauser Str 44, D-7000 Stuttgart 70 Tel: (0711) 452019
Dir: Detlef Hellweg; *Sales, Publicity, Rights & Permissions:* Sibylle Fritz-Munz
Subjects: Reference, Encyclopaedias, Dictionaries, Education, Audiovisual/Visual Media, Religion, Periodicals
Founded: 1836
ISBN Publisher's Prefix: 3-7668

Campus Verlag GmbH+, Myliusstr 15, D-6000 Frankfurt am Main Tel: (069) 7259558 Fax: (069) 725078
Man Dir, Rights & Permissions: Frank Schwoerer; *Editors:* Klaus Gabbert, Benedikt Burkard, Thomas Schwoerer, Adalbert Hepp, Beate Koglin; *Sales Dir:* Jochen Woerner; *Production:* Klaus Schoeffner; *Advertising:* Norbert Friederich; *Publicity:* Benedikt Burkard
Subjects: Social Sciences, Psychology, Economics, Politics, History, Philosophy, Ethnology, University Textbooks
1985: 160 titles *1986:* 160 titles *Founded:* 1975
ISBN Publisher's Prefix: 3-593

Editio **Cantor**, Verlag für Medizin und Naturwissenschaften, Zollenreuterstr 11, Postfach 1255, D-7960 Aulendorf Tel: (07525) 431 Cable Add: Cantor Aulendorfwürtt Telex: 0732225 vebu d Fax: (07525) 2433
Man Dir: Rolf Halt
Subjects: Medicine, Pharmacy, Periodicals
Founded: 1947
ISBN Publisher's Prefix: 3-87193

Verlag Hans **Carl** GmbH & Co KG, Postfach 9110, D-8500 Nuremberg 11 (Located at: Breite Gasse 58-60, Nuremberg 1) Tel: (0911) 238338 Cable Add: Carlverlag Telex: 623081 brauw d
Man Dir, Editorial, Publicity Dir: Günter Schmiedel; *Sales, Production:* Raimund Schmitt; *Advertising Dir:* Doris Ammersdörfer
Subjects: General Fiction, Belles Lettres, Poetry, History (especially of Nuremberg), Art, Philosophy, General Science, Biochemistry, University Textbooks, Literature and Periodicals for the Brewing and Beverage Industries
Bookshop: Fachbuchhandlung Hans Carl (at above address)
1985: 9 titles *Founded:* 1861
ISBN Publisher's Prefix: 3-418

Carlsen Verlag GmbH, Postfach 1169, D-2057 Reinbek bei Hamburg (Located at: Dieselstr 6, D-2057 Reinbek bei Hamburg) Tel: (040) 7224051 Telex: 217879 carl d Fax: (040) 7224035
Joint Man Dirs: Carl-Johan Bonnier, Viktor Niemann
Parent Company: Semic International AB, Sweden (qv)
Subsidiary Company: Semic Verlag GmbH, Dieselstr 6, D-2057 Reinbek
Associate Companies: Semic Forlagene A/S, Denmark (qv); Carlsen if AB, Sweden (qv)
Subjects: Juveniles, Comics
Founded: 1953
ISBN Publisher's Prefix: 3-551

Ceres-Verlag Rudolf-August Oetker KG*, Oldentruper Str 131, Postfach Bielefeld 85, D-4800 Bielefeld 1 Tel: (0521) 2993126 Cable Add: Ceres Telex: 0932324
Man Dirs: Ernst A Kobusch, Peter Ruhl; *Editorial:* Gisela Knutzen; *Sales:* Konstantin Knust
Parent Company: August Oetker, Bielefeld
Subjects: Cookery, Wines, Bakery
Founded: 1951
ISBN Publisher's Prefix: 3-7670

Verlag **Chemie** GmbH, see VCH Verlagsgesellschaft mbH

Christian Verlag GmbH*, Akademiestr 7, D-8000 Munich 40 Tel: (089) 3818030
Joint Man Dirs: Gerhard Jestädt, Joseph T Ward
Parent Company: Time-Life Books BV, Netherlands (qv)
Subjects: Reference: Cultural History, Nature, Photography, Fine Arts, Music, Sports, Cooking, Illustrated Non-fiction
Founded: 1949
ISBN Publisher's Prefix: 3-88472

Hans **Christians** Druckerei und Verlag, Kleine Theaterstr 9-10, Postfach 301021, D-2000 Hamburg 36 Tel: (040) 35600635 Cable Add: Christians Druck
General Manager: Jens Christians
Associate Company: Broschek Verlag (qv)
Subjects: Art, Social History of Hamburg area, North German Topography and Dialect ('Op Platt'), Judaica, Folklore
Founded: 1740
ISBN Publisher's Prefix: 3-7672

Christliche Verlagsanstalt GmbH+, Zasiusstr 8, Postfach 1186, D-7750 Konstanz Tel: (07531) 23054
Man Dir, Manager, Rights & Permissions: Herbert Denecke
Subsidiary Companies: Friedrich Bahn Verlag (qv), Sonnenweg-Verlag, (qv)
Subjects: Novels, Biography, Religion, Juveniles, Low- & High-priced Paperbacks, Educational Materials
Bookshop: Buchhandlung der Christlichen Verlagsanstalt (at above address)
Founded: 1892
ISBN Publisher's Prefix: 3-7673

Christliche Verlagsgesellschaft mbH, Moltkestr 1, Postfach 1251, D-6340 Dillenburg 1 Tel: (02771) 34021 Cable Add: Christlicher Verlag Dillenburg
Man Dirs; Dieter Boddenberg, Günther Kausemann; *Editorial, Publicity, Production:* Dieter Boddenberg; *Sales:* Dieter Braas; *Rights & Permissions:* Günther Kausemann
Subsidiary Company: Christliche Bücherstuben (at above address)
Associate Company: Emmaus-Fernbibelschule Deutschland (at above address)
Subjects: Working Texts for Scriptural Instruction, Evangelical Non-fiction
Bookshops: At above address, and Marburger Tor 22, D-5900 Siegen 1; Alte Linner Str 124, D-4150 Krefeld 1; Münsterstr 27, D-4670 Lünen; Lindauerstr 8, D-8940 Memmingen; Im Kobbenrod 3, D-5970 Plettenberg; Harschbacherstr 12, D-5419 Raubach; Poststr 24, D-4780 Lippstadt; Am Königshof 43, D-4020 Mettmann; Neustadtstr 12, D-5980 Werdohl; Lennestr 25, D-5990 Altena; Kirchstr 19, D-5132 Übach-Palenberg; Königstr 20, D-2370 Rendsburg; Friedrichstr 10, D-4000 Düsseldorf
1986: 5 titles *1987:* 7 titles *Founded:* 1957
ISBN Publisher's Prefix: 3-921292

Christliches Verlagshaus GmbH, Motorstr 36, D-7000 Stuttgart 31 Tel: (0711) 830000

FEDERAL REPUBLIC OF GERMANY 137

Man Dir: Walter A Siering
Subjects: Religion (Juvenile & Young Adult); Paperbacks, Periodicals
Founded: 1872
ISBN Publisher's Prefix: 3-7675

Christophorus-Verlag GmbH, Hermann-Herder-Str 4, D-7800 Freiburg im Breisgau Tel: (0761) 27171 Telex: 07721440
Man Dir: Benno Baldes
Parent Company: Verlag Herder GmbH & Co KG (qv)
Subjects: Christian Religious for all ages, Leisure Crafts, Sheet Music
1987: 85 titles *Founded:* 1935
ISBN Publisher's Prefix: 3-419

Verlag Gisela **Chur**, Bronsfeld 51, Postfach 2114, D-5372 Schleiden Tel: (02445) 7112
Man Dir: Gisela Chur
Subject: Children's picture books
1986: 4 titles *Founded:* 1982
ISBN Publisher's Prefix: 3-924695

Cicero International Art GmbH*, Tierbergstr 6, D-7000 Stuttgart 30 Tel: (0711) 850829 Telex: 7252147 ciro d
Man Dir, Editorial, Sales, Rights & Permissions: F K Rothenbacher; *Production, Publicity:* Rolf Marxen, Waltraud Broghammer
Subject: Art
Founded: 1970
ISBN Publisher's Prefix: 3-921165

Claassen-Verlag GmbH*, Grupellostr 28, Postfach 9229, D-4000 Düsseldorf 1 Tel: (0211) 169060 Cable Add: Claassen-Verlag Telex: 8587327
Publisher: Helmut Friehlinghaus; *Sales, Publicity Manager:* Peter Schaper
Subjects: General Fiction, Literary Criticism, Linguistics, Languages, Biography
Miscellaneous: Firm is a member of Econ Verlagsgruppe (qv)
ISBN Publisher's Prefix: 3-546

Claudius Verlag GmbH+, Birkerstr 22, D-8000 Munich 19 Tel: (089) 1269000 Telex: 523718 epdm d
Dir: Paul Rieger; *Publicity:* Karl-Eberhard Beck
Parent Company: Evangelischer Presseverband für Bayern eV (qv)
Subjects: Religion, Paperbacks, University Textbooks, Educational Materials
1987: 12 titles *Founded:* 1954
ISBN Publisher's Prefix: 3-532

Colloquium Verlag GmbH+, Unter den Eichen 93, D-1000 Berlin 45 Tel: (030) 8328085
Partners: Anja Hess, Otto H Hess, Stefan Hess; *Senior Man Dir:* Otto H Hess; *Man Dir, Public Relations, Rights & Permissions:* Stefan Hess
Orders to: Koch, Neff, Oetinger & Co, Abt Verlagsauslieferung, Am Wallgraben 110, D-7000 Stuttgart-Vaihingen
Subjects: Current Affairs, Latin-American Studies, History, Pedagogy, Biography, School TV, Research and General Knowledge, Politics
1985: 23 titles *1986:* 15 titles *Founded:* 1948
ISBN Publisher's Prefix: 3-7678

Columbus Verlag Paul Oestergaard GmbH, Columbus Haus, Postfach 1180, D-7056 Weinstadt-Beutelsbach Tel: (07151) 68011 Cable Add: Columbus-verlag Telex: 0724382
Publishers: Peter Oestergaard, Rudi Heubach; *Sales:* Gerhard Reuschle
Subjects: Cartography, Reference
Founded: 1909
ISBN Publisher's Prefix: 3-87129

Verlag F **Coppenrath***, Martinistr 2, Postfach 3820, D-4400 Münster Tel: (0251) 42225 Cable Add: Martinistr 2 Telex: 891566 hoeco d
Man Dir: Wolfgang Hölker; *Sales:* Manfred Goldschmidt; *Production:* Joerg Rinow; *Publicity:* Gertrud Posch
Subsidiary Company: Verlag Wolfgang Hölker (qv)
Subjects: Arts and Design, General Non-fiction, Juvenile
1986: 120 titles *Founded:* 1768
ISBN Publisher's Prefix: 3-88547

Copress-Verlag, Schellingstr 39-43, Postfach 401280, D-8000 Munich 40 Tel: (089) 282423 Cable Add: Copress München Telex: 524368
Man Dir: Jens-Juergen Ventzki
Subject: Sport
ISBN Publisher's Prefix: 3-7679

Corian-Verlag Heinrich Wimmer*, Bernhard-Monath-Str 24a, Postfach 1169, D-8901 Meitingen Tel: (08271) 5951
Man Dir: Heinrich Wimmer
Subjects: Science Fiction, Fantasy
Founded: 1983
ISBN Publisher's Prefix: 3-89048

Cornelsen und Oxford University Press GmbH, Mecklenburgische Str 53, D-1000 Berlin 33 Tel: (030) 829960 Telex: 184968 cvk b
Man Dirs: Fritz von Bernuth, Simon Murison-Bowie
Orders to: Cornelsen Verlagsgesellschaft mbH & Co KG, Kammerratsheide 66, D-4800 Bielefeld 1
Parent Companies: Cornelsen Verlag GmbH & Co (qv); Oxford University Press, UK (qv)
Subjects: English Language Teaching (school and adult education textbooks)
Founded: 1971
ISBN Publisher's Prefix: 3-8109

Cornelsen und Schroedel GmbH & Co Geographische Verlagsgesellschaft KG, Mecklenburgische Str 53, Postfach 330109, D-1000 Berlin 33 Tel: (030) 82996263
Man Dirs: Otto Berger, Anton Kemper, Manfred Lösing
Parent Companies: Cornelsen Verlag GmbH & Co (qv), Schroedel Schulbuchverlag GmbH (qv)
Subjects: Secondary & Primary Textbooks on Geography, Atlases
1985: 20 titles *1986:* 24 titles *Founded:* 1963
ISBN Publisher's Prefix: 3-7680

Cornelsen Verlag GmbH & Co, Mecklenburgische Str 53, D-1000 Berlin 33 Tel: (030) 829960 Cable Add: Cevaukamedien Telex: 184968
Man Dirs: Franz Cornelsen, Hans-H Kannegiesser, Manfred Lösing; *Deputy Man Dirs:* Fritz von Bernuth, Werner Thiele
Orders to: Cornelsen Verlagsgesellschaft mbH & Co KG, Kammerratsheide 66, D-4800 Bielefeld 1
Associate Company: Cornelsen Verlagsgesellschaft mbH & Co KG (qv)
Subsidiary Companies: Cornelsen und Oxford University Press GmbH (qv); Cornelsen und Schroedel GmbH & Co Geographische Verlagsgesellschaft KG (qv); Cornelsen und Schroedel GmbH, Geographisch-Kartographische Anstalt, Düppelstr 21, D-4800 Bielefeld; Cornelsen Verlag Schumann-Girardet GmbH & Co KG, Am Wehrbahn 100, D-4000 Düsseldorf; Hirschgraben Verlag (qv); Velhagen und Klasing GmbH & Co (qv)
Subjects: Textbooks, Audiovisual aids for all student levels and adults

Founded: 1968
Miscellaneous: Firm is a member of vgs — Verlagsgesellschaft mbH & Co KG (qv)
ISBN Publisher's Prefix: 3-464

Cornelsen Verlagsgesellschaft mbH & Co KG, Kammerratsheide 66, Postfach 8729, D-4800 Bielefeld 1 Tel: (0521) 78720
Associate Company: Cornelsen Verlag GmbH & Co (qv)
Subjects: Mainly Teaching Aids in Natural Sciences, Languages, History, Geography, Social Studies, Sex Education

Corona Verlag KG, see Dipa-Verlag und Druck

Corvus Verlag*, Kurfürstendamm 157, Postfach 311120, D-1000 Berlin Tel: (030) 8854041 Telex: 0184212
Subjects: Popular Non-fiction, Lexicons, Co-productions

Verlag J G **Cotta'sche Buchhandlung**, now incorporated in Ernst Klett Verlag (qv)

J **Cramer**, see Gebrüder Borntraeger

D E B Verlag (das europäische Buch Literaturvertrieb GmbH), Thielallee 34, D-1000 Berlin 33 Tel: (030) 8324051
Orders to: VVA (Vereinigte Verlagsauslieferung GmbH), Postfach 7777, D-4830 Gütersloh 1
Dir: Tell Schwandt
Subjects: History, Philosophy, Politics, Economics, Marxism, Fine Arts, Theatre
ISBN Publisher's Prefixes: 3-920303, 3-88436

D J I, see Deutsches Jugendinstitut

D T V, see Deutscher Taschenbuch Verlag

D V A, see Deutsche Verlags-Anstalt GmbH

Damnitz Verlag*, Hohenzollernstr 146, D-8000 Munich 40 Tel: (089) 301015
Man Dir, Advertising, Rights & Permissions: Hermann Kopp; *Publicity Dir:* Liesl Neumann
Subjects: General Fiction, Belles Lettres, Poetry, Biography, How-to, Music, Art, Low-priced Paperbacks, Social Science
Founded: 1965

Verlag **Darmstädter Blätter** Schwarz und Co*, Haubachweg 5, D-6100 Darmstadt Tel: (06151) 48196
Man Dir: Dr Günther Schwarz
Subjects: Semantics, Languages, Dictionaries, Philosophy, Reference, Psychology, Social Science, University, Secondary & Primary Textbooks, Judaica, Cosmology
Founded: 1967
ISBN Publisher's Prefix: 3-87139

Verlag **Das Beste**, see Beste

Werner **Dausien**+, Postfach 1355, D-6450 Hanau am Main (Located at: Frankfurter Landstr 32, Hanau) Tel: (06181) 259052/82353 Telex: 4184879
Man Dir: Werner Dausien; *Editorial:* Eva Lobin
Orders to: Burgallee 67, D-6450 Hanau am Main Tel: (06181) 259052
Associate Company: Verlag Müller und Kiepenheuer (qv)
Subjects: How-to, Music, Art, Reference, Juveniles, University Textbooks
Founded: 1949
Bookshop: Salzstr 18, D-6450 Hanau am Main
ISBN Publisher's Prefix: 3-7684

R v **Decker's** Verlag G Schenck GmbH, im Weiher 10, Postfach 102640, D-6900 Heidelberg Tel: (06221) 489250 Telex: 0461727 hueh d
Dir: Dr Hans Windsheimer

Associate Companies: Kriminalistik Verlag (qv); C F Müller Jüristischer Verlag GmbH (qv)
Subjects: Law, Economy, Administration, Post and Telecommunications, Defence, Automation, Data Processing, Periodicals

Delius, Klasing und Co, Siekerwall 21, Postfach 4809, D-4800 Bielefeld 1, Tel: (0521) 5590 Cable Add: Buchklasing Telex: 0932934
Dirs: Konrad-Wilhelm Delius, Kurt Delius; *Production:* Leo Siebzehnrübl; *Publicity:* Wilhelm Meyerhenke; *Rights & Permissions:* Ilsemarie Steinbrinker
Subsidiary Company: Klasing und Co GmbH (qv)
Subjects: Yachting, Motor Boats, Seafaring and Navigation, Model Boat Building, Motor Cars, Surfing
Founded: 1911
ISBN Publisher's Prefix: 3-7688

Delphin Verlag GmbH*, Reichenbachstr 3a, D-8000 Munich 5 Tel: (089) 557641 Cable Add: Delphinverlag Telex: 522522
Man Dir: Martin Greil
Parent Company: Maxwell Communication Corporation plc, UK (qv)
Subsidiary Company: Delphin Verlag, Switzerland (qv)
Founded: 1963
ISBN Publisher's Prefix: 3-7735

Delp'sche Verlagsbuchhandlung, St Blasienstr 5, D-8000 Munich 13 Tel: (089) 358498 Telex: 61524
Man Dir: Heinrich Delp
Orders to: Delp, Kegetstr 11, D-8532 Bad Windesheim
Subjects: Folklore, Art
1986: 8 titles *Founded:* 1961
ISBN Publisher's Prefix: 3-7689

Desire und Gegenrealismus*, Verlag für Gegenrealismus, Lilienthalstr 8a, D-8460 Schwandorf 1 Tel: (09431) 60564
Man Dir, Rights & Permissions: Günther Dienelt; *Editorial, Production, Publicity:* Günther Dienelt, Swinda von Asgard; *Sales:* Günther Dienelt, Swinda von Asgard, Désirée de Llys-Dana
Associate Company: Eliwagar-Edition (at above address)
Subjects: Modern Art, Science-Fiction, Fantasy, Literature, Strip Cartoons
Founded: 1977
ISBN Publisher's Prefix: 3-88397

Engelbert **Dessart** Verlag KG, see Siebert und Engelbert Dessart Verlag GmbH

Dr Peter **Deubner** Verlag GmbH*, Fürst-Pückler-Str 30, Postfach 410268, D-5000 Cologne 41 Tel: (0221) 403028
Publisher: Dr Peter Deubner
Associate Companies: Deubner und Lange Verlag GmbH (at above address); Deubner und Wagner GmbH, Keigener Str 1, D-5000 Cologne 41
Subject: Jurisprudence (especially Fiscal Law)
Founded: 1974

Verlag für **Deutsch**, Max-Hueber-Str 8, D-8045 Ismaning/Munich Tel: (089) 9602325 Telex: 5213212 vfdf d
Man Dir: Dr Roland Schäpers; *Editorial:* Renate Luscher; *Production:* Dieter Rauschmayer
Subjects: Textbooks, Education
1986: 150 titles *Founded:* 1979
ISBN Publisher's Prefix: 3-88532

Verlag Harri **Deutsch**+, Gräfstr 47, D-6000 Frankfurt am Main 90 Tel: (069) 775021 Telex: 4189561 deut d
Publisher: Harri Deutsch; *Man Dir:* Dr Anton Reiter
Subsidiary Company: Verlag Harri Deutsch, Switzerland (qv)
Subjects: Natural Sciences, Technical, Textbooks, Reference, Mathematics, Economics, Foreign Languages, Multilingual Dictionaries, Agriculture, Paperbacks
Bookshop: Naturwissenschaftliche Fachbuchhandlung Harri Deutsch (at above address)
Founded: 1960
ISBN Publisher's Prefixes: 3-87144, 3-8171

Deutsche Bibelgesellschaft, Balinger Str 31, D-7000 Stuttgart 80 Tel: (0711) 71810 Cable Add: Bibelhaus Stuttgart Telex: 7255299 Bibl d
German Bible Society
Dirs: Dr Gernot Winter, Rev Dr Siegfried Meurer
Subjects: Bibles and New Testaments (readings, scholarly editions)
Founded: 1812/1981
ISBN Publisher's Prefix: 3-4380

Deutsche Blindenstudienanstalt eV, Postfach 1160, D-3550 Marburg an der Lahn (Located at: Am Schlag 8, Marburg) Tel: (06421) 606100 Telex: 4821106 Fax: (06421) 606229
German Institute for the Blind
Man Dir: Jürgen Hertlein; *Deputy Dir and Publishing Manager:* Rainer F V Witte
Subjects: Braille Production, Talking Books, Tactile Maps, Library Services for the Blind

Deutsche Jugend-Presse-Agentur KG, see Dipa-Verlag und Druck

Deutsche Verlags-Anstalt GmbH (DVA)+, Neckarstr 121, Postfach 209, D-7000 Stuttgart 1 Tel: (0711) 26310 Cable Add: deva Stuttgart Telex: 0722503
Publisher: Ulrich Frank-Planitz; *Editorial Dir:* Dr Reinhard Lebe; *Production:* Rudolf Wolf; *Publicity:* Barbara Hackländer; *Sales:* Isolde Kuhn; *Marketing:* Renate Wachsmann; *Subsidiary Rights:* Ingrid Zacke; *Foreign Rights:* Heide Radkowitz
Subsidiary Companies: Manesse Verlag, Switzerland (qv); Engelhorn Verlag (qv)
Subjects: Belles Lettres, Poetry, Biography, Politics, History, Philosophy, Psychology, General Science, Architecture, Music
Bookshop: Buchversand Herbert Krebs GmbH (at above address)
1985: 66 titles *1986:* 64 titles *Founded:* 1831
ISBN Publisher's Prefix: 3-421

Deutscher Adressbuch-Verlag für Wirtschaft und Verkehr GmbH, Holzhofallee 38, Postfach 110452, D-6100 Darmstadt Tel: (06151) 3910 Cable Add: Teladress Darmstadt Telex: 419548 dav d Fax: (06151) 391200
The German Directory Publishing Company for Industry and Commerce
Man Dirs: Günter M Hulwa (Publisher), Klaus Boller; *Editorial:* Claus Wonneberger; *Production:* Horst Becker; *Publicity:* Rudolf Diehl
Subjects: Business Reference Works (available on diskettes and magnetic tape)
1985-86: 5 titles (revised annually)
Founded: 1923
ISBN Publisher's Prefix: 3-87148

Deutscher Apotheker Verlag Dr Roland Schmiedel GmbH und Co, Birkenwaldstr 44, Postfach 40, D-7000 Stuttgart 1 Tel: (0711) 25820 Telex: 723636 daz d
Man Dirs: Hans Rotta, R Hack, V Sieveking
Associate Companies: S Hirzel Verlag GmbH & Co (qv); Franz Steiner Verlag Wiesbaden GmbH (qv); Wissenschaftliche Verlagsgesellschaft mbH (qv)
Subjects: Pharmacy, Periodicals
Bookshop: Deutscher Apotheker Verlag, Sortiments-Abteilung (at above address)
Founded: 1861
ISBN Publisher's Prefix: 3-7692

Deutscher Betriebswirte-Verlag GmbH+*, Bleichstr 20-22, Postfach 1332, D-7562 Gernsbach 1 Tel: (07224) 3091 Cable Add: dbv Gernsbach Telex: 78915 dbv d
Man Dirs: Dr Casimir Katz, Christel Katz
Subjects: Business Administration (management, marketing, company organization, accounting, personnel), Forestry & Timber Industries
Founded: 1926
ISBN Publisher's Prefixes: 3-921099, 3-88640

Deutscher Eichverlag*, Hopfengarten 21, Postfach 2903, D-3300 Brunswick Tel: (0531) 796030
Parent Company: Friedr Vieweg und Sohn GmbH (qv)

Deutscher Fachschriften-Verlag Braun GmbH & Co KG, Felsenstr 23, Postfach 2120, D-6200 Wiesbaden-Dotzheim 1 Tel: (06121) 4278588
Publisher: Erika Braun; *Publicity Manager, Rights & Permissions:* Friedrich Vohl
Subjects: Public Health, Law, Official Reports
Founded: 1954
ISBN Publisher's Prefix: 3-8078

Deutscher Fachverlag GmbH, Schumannstr 27, Postfach 100606, D-6000 Frankfurt am Main Tel: (069) 7433448 Telex: 0411862
Man Dirs: Eva Lorch, Klaus Kottmeier, Peter Russ; *Publishing Manager:* Frank Sellien
Associate Companies: Lorch-Verlag, Verlag Alfred Strothe (at above address)
Subjects: Handbooks, Trade Books (textiles, meat processing), Management, Specialized Law
Founded: 1950
ISBN Publisher's Prefix: 3-87150

Deutscher Gemeindeverlag GmbH*, Max-Planck-Str 12, Postfach 400263, D-5000 Cologne 40 Tel: (02234) 1060 Telex: dgv köln 08882662
The German Municipality Publishing Company
Parent Company: Verlag W Kohlhammer GmbH (qv)
Branch Offs (each responsible for own region): Hessbrühlstr 69, Postfach 800430, D-7000 Stuttgart 80; Alexanderstr 3, Postfach 1465, D-3000 Hanover Tel: (0511) 328721 Jägersberg 17, Postfach 1865, D-2300 Kiel 1 Tel: (0431) 554857; Philipp-Reis-Str 3, Postfach 421049, D-6500 Mainz 42 Tel: (06131) 59031-32; Theresienstr 124-1, Postfach 200625, D-8000 Munich 2 Tel: (089) 521359
Subjects: Local Government (legislation, environmental protection, social services), Periodicals
ISBN Publisher's Prefix: 3-555

Deutscher Instituts-Verlag GmbH, Gustav-Heinemann Ufer 84-88, Postfach 510670, D-5000 Cologne 51 Tel: (0221) 370801 Cable Add: Deutstitut Telex: 8882768
Man Dir, Rights & Permissions: Horst Schlechter; *Sales:* Norbert Anselm; *Production:* Wilhelm Fischer; *Publicity:* Horst Schlechte
Parent Company: Institut der Deutschen Wirtschaft, Cologne (German Economics Institute)
Subsidiary Companies: Librex – Buchvertrieb der Deutschen Wirtschaft GmbH; Edition Agrippa GmbH
Subjects: Economic, Company and Educational Policy; Literature

140 FEDERAL REPUBLIC OF GERMANY

Founded: 1951
ISBN Publisher's Prefix: 3-602

Deutscher Kunstverlag GmbH, Vohburger Str 1, D-8000 Munich 21 Tel: (089) 568145
Man Dirs: Dr Michael Meier, Helmut Kaufmann
Orders to: Koch, Neff, Oetinger & Co, Postfach 800620, Schockenriedstr 39, D-7000 Stuttgart 80
Subjects: Art History, Pictorial Guidebooks, Regional Art Books, Guides to Artistic Monuments, Egypotology, Catalogues, Yearbooks, Periodicals
Founded: 1921
ISBN Publisher's Prefix: 3-422

Deutscher Literatur-Verlag, Mühlenstieg 16-22, Postfach 701009, D-2000 Hamburg 70 Tel: (040) 682476 Telex: 213126
Man Dirs: Gerhard Melchert, Otto Melchert
Associate Companies: Martin Kelter Verlag GmbH & Co, Mero-Druck GmbH & Co KG
Subjects: Light literature, Humour
Founded: 1905
ISBN Publisher's Prefix: 3-87152

D T V-Deutscher Taschenbuch Verlag GmbH & Co KG*, Postfach 400422, D-8000 Munich 40 (Located at: Friedrichstr 1a, D-8000 Munich 40) Tel: (089) 3817060 Telex: 05215396
Man Dir: Heinz Friedrich; *Assistant Man Dir:* Dr Wolfram Göbel; *Editorial:* Ulrike Buergel-Goodwin, Maria Friedrich, Winfried Groth, Dr Walter Kumpmann, Maria Schedl-Jokl, Dr Lutz-Werner Wolff; *Sales Dir:* Ole Schultheis; *Advertising:* Klaus Bäulke; *Rights & Permissions:* Lore Cortis
Parent Company: Carl Hanser Verlag (part owner) (qv)
Subjects: General Fiction, Belles Lettres, Poetry, Biography, History, Music, Art, Cartoons, Postcard Books, Philosophy, Reference, Religion, Juveniles, Medicine, Psychology, General and Social Science, Secondary & Primary Textbooks, Classical Literature, Travel Guides, Maps, Two-language editions (all in paperback format)
Founded: 1961
ISBN Publisher's Prefix: 3-423

Deutscher Verlag für Kunstwissenschaft GmbH, Lindenstr 76, D-1000 Berlin 61 Tel: (030) 25913864 Telex: 183723
Man Dirs: Klaus Müller-Crepon, Prof Dr Peter Bloch, Prof Dr Henning Bock
Associate Company: Gebr Mann Verlag (qv)
Subject: Art in Germany, Periodicals
Founded: 1964
ISBN Publisher's Prefix: 3-87157

Deutscher Wirtschaftsdienst John von Freyend GmbH*, Fachverlag für Wirtschaft und Aussenhandel, Marienburger Str 22, D-5000 Cologne 51 Tel: (0221) 376950
Sales, Rights & Permissions Dir: Peter John von Freyend; *Editorial:* Dr Wilfried Naujoks, Edelgard Reiche; *Production:* Edelgard Reiche; *Publicity:* Karl Ludwig Ostermann, Udo Witych
Subjects: International Economics (loose-leaf); Chamber of Commerce publications; Finance, Commercial Law, Management, Environment Policy
1986: 50 titles
ISBN Publisher's Prefix: 3-87156

Deutsches Jugendinstitut (DJI), Freibadstr 30, D-8000 Munich 2 Tel: (089) 623060
Man Dir: Prof Dr Hans Bertram;
Editorial, Publicity, Rights & Permissions: Hans-Hermann Schwarzer; *Sales,*
Production: Hans-Hermann Schwarzer, Katharina Spoerl
Associate Company: Juventa Verlag GmbH (qv)
Subjects: Sociology, Social pedagogy
Founded: 1975
ISBN Publisher's Prefix: 3-87966

Dianus-Trikont Buchverlag GmbH+*, Tuerkenstr 55, D-8000 Munich 40 Tel: (089) 2714400/2719848
Publisher: Herbert Röttgen; *Rights & Permissions:* Doris Schottenloher
Subjects: General Fiction, Politics, Social Science, Economics, Biography, Mythology
ISBN Publisher's Prefixes: 3-920385, 3-88167

Eugen **Diederichs** Verlag GmbH & Co KG+, Merlosstr 8, Postfach 140171, D-5000 Cologne 1 Tel: (0221) 720672
Man Dirs: Ulf Diederichs, Klaus Diederichs; *Editorial:* Christa Hinze, Ruth Keen; *Sales Dirs:* Christine Quirmbach, Maryon Hoegen; *Production:* Roland Poferl, Martina Resch; *Advertising & Publicity Dirs:* Klaus Diederichs, Eberhart May; *Rights & Permissions:* Christa Hinze
Orders to: Koch, Neff und Oetinger & Co, Schockenriedstr 39, D-7000 Stuttgart 80; (West Berlin) Bernhard A Claudius, Schillerstr 13, D-1000 Berlin 12
Subjects: Belles Lettres, Biography, History, Philosophy, Eastern Religion and Literature, Sociology, Illustrated collections of Folk and Fairy Tales from all countries
Founded: 1896
ISBN Publisher's Prefix: 3-424

Verlag Moritz **Diesterweg**/Otto Salle Verlag, Hochstr 29-31, Postfach 110651, D-6000 Frankfurt am Main 1 Tel: (069) 13010 Telex: 413234 md d
Orders to: Koch, Neff und Oetinger & Co, Postfach 800620, D-7000 Stuttgart 80
Man Dir: Dietrich Herbst; *Rights & Permissions:* Mrs Gerber
Subjects: Educational; Psychology, Social Science, University, Secondary & Primary Textbooks, Educational Materials
Founded: 1860
ISBN Publisher's Prefixes: 3-425 (Diesterweg), 3-7935 (Salle)

Maximilian **Dietrich** Verlag, Weberstr 36, Postfach 1636, D-8940 Memmingen Tel: (08331) 2853
Man Dir: Curt Visel
Subsidiary Company: Edition Curt Visel (qv)
Subjects: Belles Lettres, Literature (illustrated)
1987: 2 titles *Founded:* 1946
ISBN Publisher's Prefix: 3-87164

Verlag J H W **Dietz** Nachf GmbH, Postfach 207352, D-5300 Bonn 2 Tel: (0228) 238083
Dir: Dr Heiner Lindner; *Editorial:* Martin Rethmeier; *Sales:* Peter Marold
Orders to: Verlagsauslieferung Georg Lingenbrink, Postfach 3584, D-6000 Frankfurt am Main 1
Associate Company: Verlag Neue Gesellschaft GmbH (qv)
Subjects: History, Politics, Sociology, Economics, Legal, Reprints
ISBN Publisher's Prefix: 3-8012

Dipa-Verlag und Druck GmbH & Co, Deutsche Jugend-Presse-Agentur KG, Nassauer Str 1-3, D-6000 Frankfurt am Main 50 Tel: (069) 586910
Man Dir: Gerd Hofmann
Subsidiary Company: Corona Verlag KG
Subjects: Biography, History, How-to, Psychology, Social Science, University Textbooks and Studies, Third World Problems, Studies on Children's Literature

Founded: 1948
ISBN Publisher's Prefix: 3-7638

Verlag **Dokumentation** Saur KG, see K G Saur Verlag KG

Don Bosco Verlag der Gesellschaft der Salesianer, Sieboldstr 11, D-8000 Munich 80 Tel: (089) 4138349
Dir: August Brecheisen; *Man Dir:* Johann Ernstberger; *Editorial:* Reinhold Storkenmaier; *Sales:* Johann Windmayer
Subjects: Education, How-to, Religion, Textbooks
Bookshop: At above address
Founded: 1948
ISBN Publisher's Prefix: 3-7698

Dreisam-Verlag+, Luisenstr 7, D-7800 Freiburg im Breisgau Tel: (0761) 36033
Man Dir: G Erler; *Manager:* C Lehr
Subjects: Campaign literature to combat nuclear plants, military drafting; Civil Rights and student advice on dealing with authorities; Ecology, Socio-political, Literary Works (Prose and Poetry)
1985: 16 titles *1986:* 15 titles *Founded:* 1975
ISBN Publisher's Prefixes: 3-921472, 3-89125

Cecilie **Dressler** Verlag, Poppenbütteler Chaussee 55, Postfach 230, D-2000 Hamburg 65 Tel: (040) 6070484 Telex: 02174230
Man Dirs: Thomas Huggle, Uwe Weitendorf; *Editorial:* Angelika Kutsch; *Sales:* Thomas Huggle; *Publicity:* Anke Lüdtke; *Rights & Permissions:* Uwe Weitendorf
Associate Company: Verlag Friedrich Oetinger (qv)
Subjects: Fiction, Juveniles, Paperbacks
Founded: 1928

Droemersche Verlagsanstalt Th Knaur Nachf, Rauchstr 9-11, Postfach 800480, D-8000 Munich 80 Tel: (089) 92710 Cable Add: Droemerverlag Telex: 522707
Man Dirs: Dr Karl Blessing, Rüdiger Hildebrandt; *Editorial:* Dr Rolf Cyriax, Ewald Dede, Hanna Kobbe, Franz Mehling, Dr Herbert Neumaier; *Production:* Dieter Klee; *Publicity Manager:* Ulrike Netenjakob; *Foreign Rights:* Alice Meyer
Parent Company: Verlagsgruppe Georg V, Holtzbrinck GmbH, Gänsheidestr 26, Stuttgart
Subjects: General Fiction, Non-fiction, Dictionaries, Reference, Current Events, Popular Science, How-to, Self-Help, Juvenile, Atlases, Paperbacks
Founded: 1901
Miscellaneous: Also known as Droemer Knaur Verlag
ISBN Publisher's Prefix: 3-426

Droste Verlag GmbH, Postfach 1135, D-4000 Düsseldorf 1 (Located at: Druckzentrum Düsseldorf, Zülpicher Str 10, D-4000 Düsseldorf 11) Tel: (0211) 5050 Cable Add: Drosteverlag Düsseldorf Telex: 8582495
Chairman and Man Dir: Dr Joseph Schaffrath; *Man Dirs:* Werner Gutzki, Dr Hans-Dieter Baumgart; *Publishing Dir:* Dr Manfred Lotsch; *Editorial:* Heidemarie Alertz; *Sales:* Thomas Borgartz; *Production, Publicity:* Helmut Schwanen
Subsidiary Company: Wilhelm Knapp Verlag (qv)
Subjects: History, Current Affairs, Politics, Economics, Social Sciences, Art, Belles Lettres, Humour and Satire, Picture Books, Düsseldorf
Founded: 1711
ISBN Publisher's Prefix: 3-7700

Druckenmüller Verlag, Martiusstr 8, Postfach 440254, D-8000 Munich 44 Tel: (089) 348074 Telex: 5215517
Associate Companies: Artemis und Winkler Verlag, Munich (qv); Verlag für Architektur, Munich (qv); Artemis Verlags AG, Verlag für Architektur (both in Switzerland, qqv)
Subjects: Encyclopaedia of Classical Antiquity, Classical Works, European Ancient History

Druffel-Verlag, Kreuzauger 8, D-8137 Berg 3 am Starnbergersee Tel: (08151) 50024
Dir: Dr Gert Sudholt; *Publisher:* Ursula Sündermann;
Subjects: Popular German History (especially relative to World War II), German Politics, Controversial Reportage
ISBN Publisher's Prefix: 3-8061

Drumlin Verlag GmbH+, Wolfegger Str 92, D-7987 Weingarten Tel: (0751) 46750
Man Dir: Stefan Keller; *Editorial:* Peter Benz, Stefan Keller; *Sales:* Elisabeth Benz; *Production:* Stefan Keller; *Publicity, Rights & Permissions:* Elisabeth Benz, Stefan Keller
Subjects: Fiction, Non-fiction
1985: 10 titles *1986:* 12 titles *Founded:* 1983
ISBN Publisher's Prefix: 3-924027

Monika **Dülk** Verlag*, Kirchhainer Damm 11, Postfach 490132, D-1000 Berlin 49 Tel: (030) 7444040
Subjects: City maps, Travel Guides

Horst-Werner **Dumjahn** Verlag+, Immenhof 12, Postfach 1746, D-6500 Mainz 1 Tel: (06131) 35600
Man Dir and Other Offices: Horst-Werner Dumjahn
Orders to: VVA (Vereinigte Verlagsauslieferung GmbH), Postfach 7777, D-4830 Gütersloh 1
Subjects: Railways and Railway History (Federal German and other countries)
Bookshop: Versandbuchhandlung und Antiquariat Horst-Werner Dumjahn (at above address)
1986: 37 titles *Founded:* 1974
ISBN Publisher's Prefixes: 3-921426, 3-88992

Ferd **Dümmlers** Verlag*, Kaiserstr 31-37, Postfach 1480, D-5300 Bonn 1 Tel: (0228) 223031 Cable Add: Dümmlerbuch
Man Dir: Helmut Lehmann
Subjects: Textbooks and Pedagogic books in Natural Sciences, Arts, Linguistics for Schools of all levels; Sports, Hobbies, History, Politics, Periodicals
Founded: 1808
Miscellaneous: Firm is a member of vgs — Verlagsgesellschaft mbH & Co KG (qv)
ISBN Publisher's Prefix: 3-427

DuMont Buchverlag GmbH & Co KG, Mittelstr 12-14, Postfach 100468, D-5000 Cologne 1 Tel: (0221) 20531 Telex: 8882 975 dbe b d
Publishers: Ernst Brücher, Daniel Brücher
Subjects: Archaeology, Art, Travel, Guidebooks, Games, Illustrated Books, Pocket Books
Founded: 1956
ISBN Publisher's Prefix: 3-7701

Duncker und Humblot GmbH, Dietrich-Schäfer-Weg 9, Postfach 410329, D-1000 Berlin 41 Tel: (030) 7912026
Subjects: History, Philosophy, General & Social Science, Law, University Textbooks
1985: 202 titles *1986:* 186 titles *Founded:* 1798
ISBN Publisher's Prefix: 3-428

Dustri-Verlag Dr Karl Feistle, Bahnhofstr 9, Postfach 49, D-8024 Deisenhofen-Munich Tel: (089) 6135041
Dirs: Dr Karl Feistle, Hans-Peter Eckardt
Subjects: Medicine, Paperbacks, Reference, Periodicals

E O S Verlag, Erzabtei Sankt Ottilien, D-8917 Sankt Ottilien Tel: (08193) 71261
Man Dir: Dr P Bernhard Sirch
Subjects: Religious (especially concerning Benedictine Order), Biblical and Doctrinal Studies
Bookshop: Klosterladen (at above address)
1985: 26 titles *Founded:* 1885
ISBN Publisher's Prefixes: 3-88096, 3-920289

Echter Würzburg Fränkische Gesellschafts-Druckerei, see Würzburg

Econ-Verlag GmbH*, Grupellostr 28, Postfach 9229, D-4000 Düsseldorf 1 Tel: (0211) 169060 Cable Add: Econ-Verlag Telex: 8587327
Publisher: Dr Franz-Lothar Hinz; *Sales, Marketing:* Peter Schaper
Subjects: Biography, History, Politics, Music, Art, Travel, Reference, Religion, Archaeology, Medicine, Psychology, General & Social Science, Audio-visual Teaching Aids, General Fiction
Miscellaneous: Firm is a member of Econ Verlagsgruppe (qv)
ISBN Publisher's Prefix: 3-430

Econ Verlagsgruppe*, Grupellostr 28, Postfach 9229, D-4000 Düsseldorf 1 Tel: (0211) 169060 Telex: 8587327
Publishing group comprising Claassen Verlag GmbH, Econ Verlag GmbH, Marion von Schroeder Verlag GmbH (qqv); Econ Taschenbuch Verlag GmbH. The group forms part of the newspaper publishing concern Rheinisch-Westfälische Verlagsgesellschaft mbH, Pressehaus NRZ, Sachsenstr 30, D-4300 Essen

Ehrenwirth Verlag GmbH, Postfach. 860348, D-8000 Munich 86 (Located at: Vilshofenerstr 8) Tel: (089) 989025 Telex: 0529667
Publisher: Martin Ehrenwirth; *Man Dir, Rights & Permissions:* Manfred Glück; *Sales, Publicity & Advertising Dir:* Gebhard von Doering; *Editorial:* Manfred Glück, Dr Ursula Ehrenwirth, Reinhard Stachwitz
Distribution: Verlegerdienst München, Postfach 1280, D-8031 Gilching
Subjects: General Fiction, Poetry, History, Biography, How-to, Natural Healing, Beekeeping, Fishing, Reference, High-priced Paperbacks, Psychology, Social Science, University, Secondary and Primary Textbooks, Educational Materials, Periodicals
Founded: 1945
Miscellaneous: Firm is a member of TR-Verlagsunion GmbH (qv)
ISBN Publisher's Prefix: 3-431

Eichborn Verlag+, Sachsenhäuser Landwehrweg 293, D-6000 Frankfurt am Main 70 Tel: (069) 681079/681070
Man Dir, Editorial, Rights & Permissions: Vito von Eichborn; *Sales, Publicity:* Bodo Horn; *Production:* Uwe Gruhle
Associate Company: Fuldaer Verlagsanstalt, Rangstr 3-7, D-6400 Fulda
Subjects: Literature, Photography, Politics, Cartoons, Periodical
1985: 85 titles *1986:* 120 titles *Founded:* 1980
ISBN Publisher's Prefix: 3-8218

Verlag **Eisenbahn**, Wallstr 7, D-7820 Waldshut
Subsidiary Company: Verlag Eisenbahn, Switzerland (qv)

Eisenbahn-Kurier Verlag, Mercystr 15, Postfach 5560, D-7800 Freiburg-im-Breisgau Tel: (0761) 75033 Telex: 7721698 ekv d
Man Dirs: Rudolf Wesemann, Wolfgang Schumacher; *Editorial:* Martin Weltner, Claus-Michael Peters; *Sales:* Karin Klemm; *Production:* Wolfgang Schumacher; *Publicity:* Christel Cerajewski; *Rights & Permissions:* Hansjürgen Wenzel
Subject: Railways worldwide
1985-86: 75 titles *Founded:* 1966
ISBN Publisher's Prefix: 3-88255

Ellenberg Verlag GmbH+*, Postfach 100705, D-5000 Cologne 1 (Located at: Am Urbacher Wall 35, D-5000 Cologne 90) Tel: (02203) 22675 Telex: 887115 ell d
Man Dir: Dr Eduard Ellenberg; *Publicity:* Gisela Ellenberg
Subsidiary Companies: Theaterverlag Ellenberg; Diplomatic Observer Verlag
Subjects: Belles Lettres, Anthologies, Documentaries, Politics, Theology, History, Philosophy, Economics, Art, Science, Poetry, Novels, Theatre, Literature, other areas of Scholarship, Periodicals
Founded: 1974
ISBN Publisher's Prefixes: 3-921369, 3-88577

Verlag Heinrich **Ellermann** GmbH & Co KG+, Romanstr 16, D-8000 Munich 19 Tel: (089) 133737 Cable Add: Ellerbuch, Munich
Man Dir: Christa Spangenberg
Orders to: Koch, Neff und Oetinger, Schockenriedstr 39, D-7000 Stuttgart 80 Tel: (0711) 78601
Imprints: Edition Spangenberg
Subjects: Belles Lettres, Juveniles
Founded: 1934
ISBN Publisher's Prefix: 3-7707

Elpis Verlag GmbH+*, Rohrbacherstr 20, D-6900 Heidelberg Tel: (06221) 15789
Dirs: Julian Köpke, Frank Seifert, Dr Manfred Thiel
Subjects: Philosophy, Encyclopaedias, Music, Poetry
1986: 2 titles *Founded:* 1977

Elwert und Meurer GmbH, Hauptstr 101, D-1000 Berlin 62 Tel: (030) 784003
Associate Company: Werbegemeinschaft Elwert und Meurer
Subjects: Psychology, Philosophy, Law, Sociology, Politics
ISBN Publisher's Prefix: 3-7669

N G **Elwert** Verlag, Postfach 1128, D-3550 Marburg an der Lahn (Offices at Reitgasse 7-9 and Pilgrimstein 30) Tel: (06421) 2502325 Cable Add: Elwert Marburg
Man Dir: Dr W Braun-Elwert
Subjects: History, Religion, Law, German Language & Literary History, Social Science
Founded: 1726
ISBN Publisher's Prefix: 3-7708

Monika **Emmerich** Amazonen Frauenverlag, Fidicinstr 28, D-1000 Berlin 61
Manager: Monika Emmerich
Subjects: Women's Cultural and Historical, Female Homosexual Themes, Lesbians in the Women's Movement

Encyclopaedia Britannica*, Berliner Allee 47, Postfach 200209, D-4000 Düsseldorf Tel: (0211) 324945 Telex: 8586933 Eb D
Manager: Rolf J Ellmers
Miscellaneous: Firm is an associate company of Encyclopaedia Britannica International Ltd, USA (see UK entry for other associates)

Friedemann von Engel Verlag*,
Friedbergstr 5, D-1000 Berlin 19 Tel: (030)
3233145
Man Dir: F V Engel
Subsidiary Company: Globetrotter-Verlag
(at above address)
Imprint: Tips für Trips
Subject: Travel Handbooks

Engelbert-Verlag GmbH & Co KG*,
Postfach 360, D-5893 Balve/Sauerland
Tel: (02375) 3099 Cable Add: Ever Balve
Telex: 827755 gezi d
Publisher: Helmut Levermann; *Production:*
Heinz Droste; *Sales Manager:* Helmut
Levermann
Subjects: Juveniles, Popular Science,
Information Books, General Fiction and
Non-fiction
Founded: 1930
ISBN Publisher's Prefix: 3-536

Engelhorn Verlag, Neckarstr 121, Postfach
209, D-7000 Stuttgart 1 Tel: (0711) 26310
Publisher: Ulrich Frank-Planitz
Parent Company: Deutsche Verlags-Anstalt
GmbH (qv)
Subjects: Belles Lettres, Biography,
Reprints, Facsimile
1985: 5 titles *1986:* 12 titles *Founded:*
1860

Carl **Engels** Musikverlag, see P J Tonger

F **Englisch** Verlag GmbH+, Webergasse
12, Postfach 2309, D-6200 Wiesbaden Tel:
(06121) 39478 Telex: 4186741
Man Dir: F-I Englisch
Orders to: VVA (Vereinigte
Verlagsauslieferung GmbH), Postfach 7777,
D-4830 Gütersloh 1
Subjects: General Non-fiction
1986: 138 titles *Founded:* 1973
ISBN Publisher's Prefix: 3-88140

Ferdinand **Enke** Verlag+, Postfach 1304,
D-7000 Stuttgart 1 (Located at: Rüdigerstr
14, D-7000 Stuttgart 330U) Tel: (0711)
89310 Cable Add: Enkebuch
Telex: 7252275 gtv d
Man Dirs: Dr Günther Hauff, Dr Jur
Albrecht Greuner, Frau Dr M Kuhlmann;
Sales Dir, Rights & Permissions: Joachim
Niendorf; *Publicity:* Elke Uhl
Associate Company: Georg Thieme Verlag
(qv)
Subjects: Medicine, Psychology, Social
Science, Veterinary, Geology, University
Textbooks, Scientific Journals
Founded: 1837
ISBN Publisher's Prefix: 3-432

Ensslin Jugendbuchverlag, see Ensslin und
Laiblin

Ensslin und Laiblin Verlag GmbH & Co
KG, Harretstr 6, Postfach 1532, D-7412
Eningen Tel: (07121) 8471 Cable Add:
Buchhaus Reutlingen Telex: 0729733
Man Dir: Joachim Ulrich Hebsaker;
Editorial: Grit Hebsaker, Elke Schäle;
Sales: Ariane Hebsaker-Schräpler;
Production: Christine Schmid; *Rights &
Permissions:* Joachim Ulrich Hebsaker,
Grit Hebsaker
Subjects: Children's Books, Non-fiction,
Science Fiction, Education
Founded: 1818
ISBN Publisher's Prefix: 3-7709

Hans P **Eppinger***, Brenzstr 16, D-7170
Schwäbisch Hall Tel: (0791) 53061 Cable
Add: Eppinger-Verlag Schwäbisch Hall
Man Dir: Hans Paul Eppinger
Subjects: Belles Lettres, Picture Books,
History, Anthropology, Juveniles
Founded: 1970
ISBN Publisher's Prefix: 3-87176

Verlag Peter **Erd** GmbH*,
Gaissacherstr 18, Postfach 750980, D-8000
Munich 75 Tel: (089) 7250126
Man Dir and other offices: Peter Erd
Subjects: Parapsychology, Aids to Living
Founded: 1975
ISBN Publisher's Prefix: 3-8138

Edition **Erdmann**, an imprint of
K Thienemanns Verlag (qv)

Horst **Erdmann** Verlag für Internationalen
Kulturaustausch*, Hartmayerstr 117,
Postfach 1380, D-7400 Tübingen 1
Tel: (07071) 62061 Cable Add:
Erdmannverlag Tübingen Telex: 7262741
erdm
Publicity & Sales Department: Milanweg 1,
D-7400 Tübingen Tel: (07071) 64409
Man Dir, Editorial, Production: Horst J
Erdmann; *Sales, Publicity, Rights &
Permissions:* Rosemarie Erdmann
Orders to: VA Koch, Neff und Oetinger,
Postfach 800620, D-7000 Stuttgart 80
Branch Off: Horst Erdmann Verlag & Co,
Bachofenstr 10, CH-4000 Basle,
Switzerland
Subjects: General Fiction, Belles Lettres,
Poetry, Biography, History, How-to,
Reference, Educational Materials
Founded: 1956
ISBN Publisher's Prefix: 3-7711

Eremiten-Presse und Verlag GmbH,
Fortunastr 11, Postfach 170143, D-4000
Düsseldorf 1 Tel: (0211) 660590
Joint Man Dirs: Friedolin Reske, Jens
D Olsson
Subjects: General Fiction, Belles Lettres,
Poetry, Art, High- & Low-priced
Paperbacks
Founded: 1949
ISBN Publisher's Prefix: 3-87365

Edition **Eres** Horst Schubert Musikverlag,
Hauptstr 35, Postfach 1220, D-2804
Lilienthal-Bremen Tel: (04298) 1676
Man Dir: Horst Schubert
Subjects: Music, Art, High-priced
Paperbacks, University, Secondary &
Primary Textbooks, Educational Materials
Founded: 1946
ISBN Publisher's Prefix: 3-87204

Wilhelm **Ernst** und Sohn Verlag für
Architektur und technische Wissenschaft,
Hohenzollerndamm 170, D-1000 Berlin 31
Tel: (030) 860003 Cable Add: Ernstsohn
Berlin Telex: 184143
Dir: Ernst Karl Schneider; *Editorial, Rights
& Permissions:* I Otto, A Menges; *Sales:* H-
J Winterstein; *Production:* Siegmar Hiller;
Publicity: Helga Hardegen
Parent Company: VCH Verlagsgesellschaft
mbH (qv)
Subjects: Technical, Architecture
Bookshop: Gropius'sche Buch- und
Kunsthandlung (at above address)
Founded: 1851
ISBN Publisher's Prefix: 3-433

Eulenhof-Verlag Ehrhardt Heinold, D-2351
Hardebek Post Brokstedt Tel: (04324) 502
Man Dir: Ehrhardt Heinold
Associate Company: Heinold Personal- und
Unternehmensberatung BDU (at above
address)
Subject: Information Media on the Book
Market
1986: 2 titles *1987:* 2 titles *Founded:* 1980
ISBN Publisher's Prefix: 3-88710

Euphorion Verlag Hans Imhoff, Wilhelm-
Busch-Str 41, D-6000 Frankfurt am
Main 50 Tel: (069) 523357 Cable Add:
Euphorion Frankfurt
Man Dir: H Imhoff; *Publicity Dir:* Benja
Bardé; *Rights & Permissions:* Ulrich
Raschke

Subjects: Belles Lettres, Poetry, Philosophy
Book Club: Freundesksreis des Euphorion
Verlages
Founded: 1963

Verlag **Europa-Lehrmittel**, Nourney,
Vollmer GmbH & Co, Postfach 201815,
D-5600 Wuppertal 2 (Located at: Kleiner
Werth 50) Tel: (0202) 554004
General Manager, Rights & Permissions:
Joachim Nourney; *Editor:* Armin
Steinmüller; *Sales:* Reinhard Lieber
Subjects: School and Professional
Textbooks (Metallurgy, Automobile,
Electrical, Electronics, Physics, Building,
Timber, Economics)
Founded: 1947
ISBN Publisher's Prefix: 3-8085

Das **Europäische Buch**, see DEB Verlag

Europäische Verlagsanstalt GmbH*,
Savignystr 53, Postfach 170101, D-6000
Frankfurt am Main 1 Tel: (069) 742567
Man Dir, Sales, Publicity: Axel Rütters;
Rights & Permissions: Irmela Rütters
Subjects: History, Philosophy, Psychology,
Social Science, Judaica, Political Science,
Economics, Trade Unions
Founded: 1946
ISBN Publisher's Prefix: 3-434

Europrisma-Verlag*, Auf dem Gelling 7,
D-5800 Hagen Tel: (02331) 46655
Dir: Stephan Ramrath

Verlag der **Evangelisch Lutherischen
Mission***, Schenkstr 69, D-8520 Erlangen
Tel: (09131) 33064
Publisher: Christoph Jahn; *Sales Manager:*
Eva Mueller
Subjects: Juveniles, Religion, Social
Science, Paperbacks
ISBN Publisher's Prefix: 3-87214

Verlag und Schriftenmission der
Evangelischen Gesellschaft für Deutschland
GmbH, Kaiserstr 78, D-5600 Wuppertal 11
Tel: (0202) 784018
Publishing House and Scriptural Mission of
the German Evangelical Society
Man Dir: Hans Mohr; *Sales, Production,
Publicity:* Herbert Becker
Subjects: Religious Literature; Telos and
Junior Telos texts (see Miscellaneous)
Founded: 1954
Miscellaneous: Firm is a member of the
Telos group (qv) publishing evangelical
paperbacks
ISBN Publisher's Prefix: 3-87857

Evangelischer Missionsverlag*, Postfach
1380, D-7015 Korntal-Münchingen 1
Tel: (0711) 831083
Man Dir: Erwin Scherer
Subjects: Religion, Juveniles, Educational
Materials
Bookshop: Buchhandlung des
Evangelischen Missionsverlag (at above
address)
Founded: 1920
ISBN Publisher's Prefix: 3-7714

Evangelischer Presseverband für
Bayern eV, Birkerstr 22, D-8000 Munich
19 Tel: (089) 1269000 Telex: 523718
Bavarian Evangelical Press Union
Dir: Paul Rieger; *Publicity Manager:* Karl-
Eberhard Beck
Subsidiary Company: Claudius Verlag
GmbH (qv)
Subjects: Evangelical Press Service, School
Books, Song Books, Periodicals
Founded: 1932
ISBN Publisher's Prefix: 3-583

Evangelisches Verlagswerk GmbH, now
part of Walter de Gruyter (qv)

Expert Verlag GmbH+*, Postfach 505,
D-7032 Sindelfingen Tel: (07031) 84071

Telex: 7265481 expe d
Publisher: Dipl-Ing Elmar Wippler; *Reader:* Dr Arnulf Krais; *Sales, Publicity, Rights & Permissions:* Dagmar Keller; *Production:* Jörg Hänsler
Subjects: Occupational/Professional Instruction Manuals (Technologies, Commerce, Business Law, Management, Energy), Technical
1985: 400 titles *Founded:* 1979
ISBN Publisher's Prefixes: 3-88508, 3-8169

Express Edition GmbH, Ritterstr 60B, Postfach 110263, D-1000 Berlin 61 Tel: (030) 2511136
Man Dir: Horst Herkner; *Editorial, Sales:* Gisela Aglaster-Herkner; *Rights & Permissions:* Horst Herkner
Subjects: Immigration themes, Migrant Homelands, Third World and South-East Asia, Social History, International Literature, Travel Guides
Bookshop: At above address
Founded: 1979
ISBN Publisher's Prefix: 3-88548

Extrabuch Verlag in der pädex-Verlags-GmbH+*, Fichardstr 38, D-6000 Frankfurt am Main Tel: (069) 591853
Parent Company: Pädex Verlags GmbH (at above address)
Subjects: Pedagogy, Social Sciences, Literature
Founded: 1976
ISBN Publisher's Prefixes: 3-921450, 3-88704

Fackelträger-Verlag GmbH, Goseriede 10-12, Postfach 1923, D-3000 Hanover 1 Tel: (0511) 14648
Man Dirs: Alois Hüser, Hans-Reinhard Kaeller; *Editorial Dir:* Peter Seifried; *Sales:* Siegfried Liebrecht
Parent Company: Zeitungsverlag Neue Westfälische GmbH & Co Kg, Niedernstr 23-27, Postfach 26, D-3000 Bielefeld 1
Subjects: Modern History, Humour, Cartoons
1985: 15 titles *1986:* 15 titles *Founded:* 1949
ISBN Publisher's Prefix: 3-7716

Fackelverlag G Bowitz GmbH, Herdweg 31, D-7000 Stuttgart 1 Tel: (0711) 290931 Cable Add: Fackelverlag Stuttgart Telex: 07255271
Subjects: General Fiction, History, How-to, Reference, Dictionaries, Low-priced Paperbacks
Founded: 1919
ISBN Publisher's Prefix: 3-87220

Falk-Verlag für Landkarten und Stadtpläne Gerhard Falk GmbH, Burchardstr 8, Postfach 102122, D-2000 Hamburg 1 Tel: (040) 3029000 Cable Add: falkverlag Telex: 02162175
Man Dir: Dr Helge Lintzhöft, Handelsregister AG Hamburg HRB 23204
Subjects: Maps, Guidebooks, Phrasebooks
1986: 12 titles *1987:* 23 titles *Founded:* 1945
ISBN Publisher's Prefixes: 3-920317, 3-88445

Falken-Verlag GmbH+, Schöne Aussicht 21, Postfach 1120, D-6272 Niedernhausen-Ts Tel: (06127) 7020 Telex: 4186585 fves d
Man Dirs: Frank Sicker, Dietrich John; *Publishing Manager:* Manfred Abrahamsberg; *Production:* Horst Gemmerich; *Publicity:* Barbara Aschenberner; *Rights & Permissions:* Doris Fürbeth
Subsidiary Company: Friedrich Bassermann'sche Verlagsbuchhandlung (qv)
Subjects: Natural foods and cookery, Herbalism, Popular Health, Natural History, Gardening, How-to, Sports and Pastimes, Motorcycling, Photography, Humour, Popular Computing, Further Education
1987: 126 titles *Founded:* 1923
ISBN Publisher's Prefix: 3-8068

Favorit-Verlag Huntemann und Markus & Co GmbH+, Stettiner Str 16, Postfach 1645, D-7550 Rastatt Tel: (07222) 22254 Cable Add: favoritverlag Telex: 786630
Subject: Children's Books

Willy F P **Fehling** GmbH, Spicherstr 22-26, Postfach 1960, D-3000 Hanover Tel: (0511) 33920 Cable Add: Fehlingwerk Hannover Telex: 0922758
Publisher: Werner von Holtzendorff-Fehling; *Man Dir, Editorial, Production:* Gerd Gehrold
Subject: Horticulture
Founded: 1912

Dr Karl **Feistle**, see Dustri-Verlag

Wolfgang **Fietkau** Verlag*, Potsdamer Chaussee 16, D-1000 Berlin 37 Tel: (030) 8025493
Publisher: Wolfgang Fietkau
Founded: 1959
Subject: Poetry, Belles Lettres
ISBN Publisher's Prefix: 3-87352

Barbara **Fietz**, see Abakus Schallplatten

Fikentscher und Co, see Technik Tabellen Verlag

Wilhelm **Fink** GmbH & Co Verlags KG, Ohmstr 5, D-8000 Munich 40 Tel: (089) 348017 Cable Add: Fink München
Man Dir: Axel Kortendieck
Orders to: Ferdinand Schöningh Verlag, Jühlenplatz am Rathaus, Postfach 2540, D-4790 Paderborn
Subjects: History, Literature, Law Study, Art, Criticism, Philosophy, Linguistics, Languages, Music, Classical Archaeology, Sociology, Psychology
1986: 160 titles *Founded:* 1962
ISBN Publisher's Prefix: 3-7705

J **Fink — Kümmerly und Frey** Verlag GmbH*, Zeppelinstr 29-31, D-7302 Ostfildern 4 Tel: (0711) 45060 Cable Add: Buch-Fink Telex: 723737 fkf d
Dir and Public Relations: Bodo Neiss
Subjects: Touring and walking guides (Germany and Europe) and related Non-fiction
Miscellaneous: Firm has developed from an association between the German company J Fink (founded 1894) and the Swiss cartographic company Kümmerly und Frey (founded 1852). The latter firm also continues as an independent company in Switzerland (qv)
ISBN Publisher's Prefix: 3-7718

Emil **Fink** Verlag*, Heidehofstr 15, D-7000 Stuttgart 1 Tel: (0711) 465330
Publisher: Richard Scheibel
Subjects: Arts, Maps
ISBN Publisher's Prefix: 3-7717

Finken-Verlag, now Neuer Finken-Verlag (qv)

Verlag für Medizin Dr Ewald **Fischer**, see Medizin

Fischer Taschenbuch Verlag GmbH*, Geleitsstr 25, Postfach 700480, D-6000 Frankfurt am Main 70 Tel: (069) 60620 Telex: 412410
Man Dirs: Monika Schoeller, Karl-Michael Mehnert, Dr Emmanuel A Wiemer; *Editorial:* Wolfgang Balk; *Sales, Publicity:* Ulrich Fritz, Frank Scheffter; *Production:* Wilfried Meiner
Parent Company: S Fischer Verlag GmbH (qv)
Subjects: Entertainment, Reference, Science, Literature, Encyclopaedias, Textbooks
Founded: 1952
ISBN Publisher's Prefix: 3-596

Gustav **Fischer** Verlag GmbH & Co KG+, Wollgrasweg 49, Postfach 720143, D-7000 Stuttgart 70 (Hohenheim) Tel: (0711) 455038 Cable Add: Fischerbuch
Man Dirs: Bernd von Breitenbuch, Dr W D von Lucius; *Sales, Advertising & Publicity Dir:* Gerhard Weber; *Rights & Permissions:* Dr W D von Lucius
Subjects: Medicine, Biology, Physical Anthropology, Psychology, Social Sciences, Economics, Information Science, Paperbacks, University Textbooks, Scientific Periodicals
1985: 150 titles *1986:* 154 titles *Founded:* 1878
ISBN Publisher's Prefix: 3-437

Rita G **Fischer** Verlag, Wilhelmshöher Str 39, D-6000 Frankfurt am Main 60 Tel: (069) 476282 Telex: 4189936 fivg d
Man Dir: Rita G Fischer
Subjects: Medicine, Politics, Psychology, Engineering, General and Social Science, How-to, University Textbooks, Quality Paperbacks
1985: 90 titles *Founded:* 1977
ISBN Publisher's Prefix: 3-88323

S **Fischer** Verlag GmbH, Geleitsstr 25, Postfach 700480, D-6000 Frankfurt am Main 70 Tel: (069) 60621 Cable Add: Buchfischer Telex: 0412410
Dirs: Monika Schoeller, Karl-Michael Mehnert, Dr Emmanuel D und Arnolf Conrad; *Sales:* Ulrich Fritz; *Production:* Wilfried Meiner; *Publicity:* Martina Gollhardt; *Rights:* Wolfgang Mertz
Subsidiary Companies: Fischer Taschenbuch Verlag GmbH (qv); Wolfgang Krüger Verlag GmbH (qv); Goverts im S Fischer Verlag
Subjects: General Fiction and Non-fiction, Belles Lettres, Poetry, Biography, History, Philosophy, Low- & High-priced Paperbacks, Psychology, Social Science, Music, Art, Reference for the layman
Founded: 1886
ISBN Publisher's Prefix: 3-10

W **Fischer** Verlag und Vertriebs GmbH, Valentinsbreite 59, Postfach 1817, D-3400 Göttingen Tel: (0551) 34560 Telex: 96746
Dir: Jutta Fischer
Subject: Juvenile Fiction and Non-fiction
Founded: 1985
ISBN Publisher's Prefix: 3-439

Verlag Johannes **Fix**, Postfach 1221, D-7060 Schorndorf (Located at: Im Rank 7, D-7067 Plüderhausen) Tel: (07181) 83674 Cable Add: Fix-Verlag Schorndorf
Man Dir: Johannes Fix
Subjects: Religion, Juveniles, Children's Picture Books
ISBN Publisher's Prefix: 3-87228

Fleischhauer und Spohn Verlag*, Maybachstr 18, Postfach 301160, D-7000 Stuttgart 30 Tel: (0711) 89340 Telex: 723113 umco d
Owned by: Dr Max Bez, Thomas Bez, Ursula Roth
Associate Company: Barsortiment G Umbreit GmbH und Co, Maybachstr 18, D-7000 Stuttgart 30 (Book Wholesaler)
Subjects: Belles Lettres, Travel Literature, Regional Literature, History
Founded: 1830
ISBN Publisher's Prefix: 3-87230

Verlag V **Florentz** GmbH, Postfach 340163, D-8000 Munich 34 (Located at: Gabelsbergerstr 15, D-8000 Munich 2) Tel:

144 FEDERAL REPUBLIC OF GERMANY

(089) 285503
Manager: Franz Frank; *Rights & Permissions:* Hans Traub
Associate Company: Tuduv Verlagsgesellschaft mbH (qv)
Subjects: Industrial Management, Political Economy, Jurisprudence, Regional Research, Periodicals
Founded: 1975
ISBN Publisher's Prefixes: 3-88259, 3-921491

Focus-Verlag*, Grünbergerstr 16, Postfach 110328, D-6300 Giessen Tel: (0641) 34760
Man Dir, Sales, Rights & Permissions: Mr Schmid; *Publicity, Advertising Dir:* Mr Neuhofer
Subjects: History, Reference, High-priced Paperbacks, Psychology, Social Science, University Textbooks
Founded: 1970
ISBN Publisher's Prefixes: 3-920352, 3-88349

Alfred **Förg** GmbH & Co KG, see Rosenheimer Verlagshaus

Forkel-Verlag GmbH, Felsenstr 23, Postfach 2120, D-6200 Wiesbaden-Dotzheim Tel: (06121) 4278588
Man Dir: Erika Braun; *Sales & Advertising Dir, Publicity, Rights & Permissions:* Friedrich Vohl
Subjects: Business Administration, Business Law, Promotion & Marketing, Data Processing
1985: 10 titles *Founded:* 1919
ISBN Publisher's Prefix: 3-7719

Rat für **Formgebung**, Eugen-Bracht-Weg 6, D-6100 Darmstadt Tel: (06151) 44051
Design Council of the Federal Republic of Germany (Publishing Department)
Design Dir: Ulrich Kern; *Manager:* Ernst Jörg Kruttschnitt
Subjects: Industrial, Graphic and Environmental Design, Ergonomics

Fortschritt für alle-Verlag, Schlossweg 2, D-8501 Feucht Tel: (09128) 3126 Cable Add: Fortschrit
Man Dir: Erika Herbst
Orders to: Auslieferung-Lebenskunde Vertrieb, Jägerstr 4, D-4000 Düsseldorf 1
Subjects: Popular Explanation of Scientific Advances
Founded: 1974
ISBN Publisher's Prefix: 3-920304

Verlag der **Francke** Buchhandlung GmbH*, Am Schwanhof 19, Postfach 640, D-3550 Marburg an der Lahn Tel: (06421) 25036
Man Dir, Editorial, Production, Publicity: Gerhard Kuhlmann; *Sales:* Liselotte Kerste
Subjects: Evangelical Theology, Biblical Studies, Christian Books for Children
Bookshops: Marburg, Hebronberg, Gunzenhausen, Velbert, Lemförde, Oberursel
Founded: 1950
Miscellaneous: Firm is contributor to the Telos series of evangelical paperbacks (qv)
ISBN Publisher's Prefix: 3-88224

Franckh'sche Verlagshandlung W Keller & Co, Pfizerstr 5-7, Postfach 640, D-7000 Stuttgart 1 Tel: (0711) 21910 Cable Add: Kosmosverlag Stuttgart Telex: 721669 kosm d Fax: (0711) 2191360
Dirs: Claus Keller, Euchar Nehmann; *Editorial:* Claus Keller; *Production:* Hansjörg-Staelin; *Publicity Dir:* Dr Juan-Hartwig Wulff; *Advertising Manager:* Jürgen Ritter; *Rights & Permissions:* Brigitta Ehrler
Subsidiary Companies: Franz Mittelbach-Verlag, Verlag Der Neue Schulmann (both at above address); W Spemann Verlag (qv)
Subjects: Natural Sciences, Technology, Sports and Hobbies, Railways, Military, Gardening, Fiction, Chess, Reference
Book Club: Kosmos-Gesellschaft der Naturfreunde
Founded: 1822
ISBN Publisher's Prefix: 3-440

Verlag **Frankfurter Bücher**, an imprint of Societäts-Verlag (qv)

Frankfurter Fachverlag Michael Kohl GmbH & Co KG*, Emil Sulzbach Str 12, Postfach 970115, D-6000 Frankfurt am Main 97 Tel: (069) 778410/776513
Associate Company: Kohl's Technischer Verlag Erwin Kohl GmbH & Co KG (qv)
Subjects: Electrical Engineering, Electronics, Industries, Crafts, Textbooks
ISBN Publisher's Prefix: 3-87234

Fränkische Gesellschafts-Druckerei Würzburg/Echter Verlag, see under Würzburg

Frankonius Verlag in Pallottinerdruck und Lahn-Verlag GmbH, Wiesbadener Str 1, Postfach 1461, D-6250 Limburg 1 Tel: (06431) 40030 Telex: 0484764 palan d
Man Dir: Engelbert Tauscher; *Publicity:* Werner Krämer; *Editorial:* Ursula Mock
Subjects: Textbooks (History, Languages, Social Sciences, Pedagogy and Training, Sports, Needlework)
Founded: 1976
ISBN Publisher's Prefix: 3-87962

Ernst **Franz** und Sternberg-Verlag+*, Max-Planck-Str 25, Postfach 1262, D-7430 Metzingen/Württemberg Tel: (07123) 6237 Telex: 07245334
Publisher: Gerhard Heinzelmann
Subject: Religion
ISBN Publisher's Prefix: 3-7722

Franzis-Verlag GmbH, Postfach 370120, D-8000 Munich 37 (Located at: Karlstr 37-41, D-8000 Munich 2) Tel: (089) 5117 Telex: 522301
Dir: Peter G E Mayer; *Editorial Dir:* Michael Heysinger; *Sales, Publicity Manager:* Peter Habersetzer; *Rights & Permissions:* Georg Geschke
Founded: 1924
ISBN Publisher's Prefix: 3-7723

Frauenbuchverlag+, Georgenstr 123, D-8000 Munich 40 Tel: (089) 183008/183013
Parent Company: Weismann Verlag – Frauenbuchverlag GmbH (qv)
Subjects: Woman's Literature, Non-fiction, Essays, Novels, Cartoons, Illustrated Books

Verlag **Frauenoffensive**, Kellerstr 39, D-8000 Munich 80 Tel: (089) 485102
Dirs: J Jakob, S Kohlstadt, G Kowitzke, H Schlaeger; *Editorial:* H Schlaeger, G Kowitzke; *Sales:* S Kohlstadt; *Production, Publicity:* G Kowitzke
Subjects: Feminist
Founded: 1974
ISBN Publisher's Prefix: 3-88104

Frech-Verlag GmbH und Co Druck KG*, Turbinenstr 7, Postfach 310902, D-7000 Stuttgart 31 (Weilimdorf) Tel: (0711) 832061 Telex: 7252156 fr d
Man Dir, Sales, Advertising: E A Krauss; *Publicity Dir, Rights & Permissions:* Mrs I Euler
Subjects: Crafts, Hobbies, Popular Electronics, Health (*Topp* series)
Founded: 1954
ISBN Publisher's Prefix: 3-7724

Verlag **freies Geistesleben***, Haussmann Str 76, D-7000 Stuttgart Tel: (0711) 283255
Man Dir: Dr W Niehaus; *Sales:* Heinrich Didwiszus
Subjects: Biography, History, How-to, Music, Art, Philosophy, Juveniles, High-priced Paperbacks, Medicine, Psychology, General & Social Science, Educational Materials
Founded: 1947

Verlag Dieter **Fricke** GmbH+*, Humboldtstr 67, D-6000 Frankfurt am Main 1 Tel: (069) 285139
Man Dir: Dieter Fricke
Subjects: Photography, Fine Arts, Ballet, Architecture, Design
Founded: 1976
ISBN Publisher's Prefix: 3-88184

Erhard **Friedrich** Verlag, Im Brande 15, D-3016 Seelze 6 Tel: (0511) 400040 Cable Add: Friedrich Telex: 0922923
Subjects: Theatre, Opera, Education, Arts
Founded: 1960
ISBN Publisher's Prefix: 3-617

Frisia-Verlag GmbH*, Mainzlarer Str 11, D-6301 Staufenberg 1 Tel: (06406) 3319
General Manager: Werner Struep; *Partner:* Gisela Struep
Subjects: North Sea Literature, Island Guides, Travel Guides, Maps
Founded: 1975
ISBN Publisher's Prefix: 3-88111

Verlag A **Fromm** GmbH & Co, Postfach 1948, D-4500 Osnabrück (Located at: Breiter Gang 11-14) Tel: (0541) 3100 Telex: 94916 fromm d
Publisher: Leo V Fromm; *Vice-President:* Annette Harms-Hunold; *Sales Manager:* Annegret Busch; *Public Relations:* Ursula Malzahn
Associate Companies: Edition Interfrom, Switzerland (qv); Fromm International Publishing Corp, 560 Lexington Ave at 50th Street, New York, NY 10022, USA
Subjects: Scientific texts by German-Speaking Authors on Politics, Economics, Society, Culture and Education, Nature, the Environment; Periodicals
ISBN Publisher's Prefix: 3-7729

Friedrich **Frommann** Verlag, Günther Holzboog GmbH & Co, König-Karl-Str 27, Postfach 500460, D-7000 Stuttgart 50 Tel: (0711) 569039 Telex: 7254754 frho d
Man Dir & Editorial: Günther Holzboog, Eva-Maria Holzboog; *Sales Dir:* H Gündert; *Publicity & Advertising Dir:* H Kruschwitz; *Rights & Permissions:* Günther Holzboog
Subjects: History, Philosophy, Political Science, Reference, Religion, Psychology, Psychoanalysis, Social Science, Pedagogy, History of Science, University Textbooks, Philosophical Journal
Founded: 1727
ISBN Publisher's Prefix: 3-7728

G D Bücherei, an imprint of Jan Tholenaar Verlag GmbH (qv)

G T B Siebenstern, an imprint of Gütersloher Verlagshaus Gerd Mohn (qv)

Franz-J **Gaber**, see Verlagsbuchhandlung Megapress

Betriebswirtschaftlicher Verlag Dr Th **Gabler** GmbH, Taunusstr 54, Postfach 1546, D-6200 Wiesbaden 1 Tel: (06121) 5340 Cable Add: Gablerverlag Telex: 4186567
General Managers: Dr Frank Lube, Dr Hans-Dieter Haenel; *Marketing:* Sepp Nagl
Parent Company: Verlagsgruppe Bertelsmann GmbH (qv)
Subjects: Business Administration, Personnel Management, Accounting, Insurance, Banking, Periodicals
Founded: 1929
ISBN Publisher's Prefix: 3-409

FEDERAL REPUBLIC OF GERMANY 145

Verlag für **Gegenrealismus**, see Desire und Gegenrealismus

GeoCenter Verlagsvertrieb GmbH, Neumarkter Str 18, D-8000 Munich 80 Tel: (089) 431890 Telex: 523259
Man Dir: Wolfgang Kunth; *Sales Manager:* Wolfgang Völcker
Parent Company: Internationales Landkartenhaus GeoCenter GmbH (qv)
Subjects: Maps, Atlases, Travel
ISBN Publisher's Prefix: 3-921435

Kunstverlag Dr Rudolf **Georgi**, Woldemar Klein*, Theaterstr 77, Postfach 407, D-5100 Aachen Tel: (0241) 477910 Telex: 832337
Man Dirs: Werner and Manfred Georgi
Subsidiary Company: Georgi Publishers, 35 West 38th St, New York, NY 10018, USA Tel: (212) 7300518
Subjects: History, How-to, Music, Art, General Science
Bookshops: Fachbuchhandlung Dr Rudolf Georgi, Theaterstr 77, Aachen
Founded: 1928
ISBN Publisher's Prefix: 3-87248

Carl **Gerber** Verlag, see Schwaneberger Verlag GmbH

Gerhardt Verlag, Jenaer Str 7, D-1000 Berlin 31 Tel: (030) 8543009
Man Dir: Renate Gerhardt
Subjects: Belles Lettres, Poetry, Art, Feminism, Quality Paperbacks, Music
Founded: 1962
ISBN Publisher's Prefix: 3-920372

Gerstenberg Verlag+, Postfach 100555, D-3200 Hildesheim (Located at: Rathausstr 20) Tel: (05121) 1060 Telex: 927108 gberg
Man Dir: Dr Viktor Christen; *Editorial:* Elmar Kreihe; *Sales, Publicity:* W J Dietrich; *Production:* Reinhard Fabian; *Rights & Permissions:* Gǔudrǔun Bilges
Subjects: Nature, Culture, Humour, Children's Books
Founded: 1796
ISBN Publisher's Prefix: 3-8067

Musikverlag Klaus **Gerth**, see Turmberg

Verlag Ernst und Werner **Gieseking***, Deckertstr 30, Postfach 130120, D-4800 Bielefeld 13 Tel: (0521) 14674 Telex: 932240
Publisher: Werner Gieseking
Associate Company: Deubner und Lange Verlag GmbH
Subjects: Law, Music
ISBN Publisher's Prefix: 3-7694

Gilles und Francke Verlag, Blumenstr 67-69, Postfach 100538, D-4100 Duisburg 1 Tel: (0203) 355097
Publisher, Proprietor: Werner Francke; *Sales:* Barbara Francke; *Publicity:* Ralf Gruna
Subjects: Leisure Activities, Poetry, Anthologies, Music, Fiction, Essays, Periodicals
Bookshop: G & F Buch und Zeitschriftenhandlung (at above address)
Founded: 1900
ISBN Publisher's Prefixes: 3-921104, 3-925348

W **Girardet** Buchverlag GmbH*, Am Wehrhahn 100, Postfach 7640, D-4000 Düsseldorf 1 Tel: (0211) 360301 Cable Add: Girardet Düsseldorf Telex: ueber 8581345 paed d
Dirs: Dr Hans Weymar, Franz Ehret
Associate Company: Pädagogischer Verlag Schwann/Bagel GmbH (qv)
Subjects: Electro-Technology, Engineering, Basic Sciences, Business Administration, Languages

Founded: 1865
ISBN Publisher's Prefix: 3-7736

Globetrotter-Verlag, see Friedemann von Engel Verlag

Glock und Lutz Verlag Heroldsberg, now Regio Verlag (qv)

Verlagsgesellschaft R **Glöss** und Co, Mörkenstr 7, Postfach 500344, D-2000 Hamburg 50 Tel: (040) 388573 Telex: 215667 vlg d Fax: (040) 386993
Publisher: Wolfgang Glöss
Subjects: Periodicals, Politics, Biography, Belles Lettres
ISBN Publisher's Prefix: 3-87261

Verlag **Glückauf** GmbH*, Postfach 103945, D-4300 Essen 1 Tel: (0201) 1059545 Telex: 8579545 gauf d
Man Dir, Editorial, Rights & Permissions: Dr-Ing R H Bachstroem; *Sales, Publicity:* H Schwab
Parent Company: Verein für die bergbaulichen Interessen, Friedrichstr 1, D-4300 Essen 1
Subject: Mining, Tunnelling
Bookshop: Günther und Schwan Sortiments- und Verlagsbuchhandlung GmbH, Hachestr 5, D-4300 Essen 1
Founded: 1912
ISBN Publisher's Prefix: 3-7739

Bruno **Gmünder** Verlag+, Lützowstr 105/VI, Postfach 301345, D-1000 Berlin 30 Tel: (030) 2611646
Man Dirs: B Gmünder, C von Maltzahn; *Rights & Permissions:* C von Maltzahn
Subjects: Literature for Homosexuals
1986: 8 titles *1987:* 12 titles *Founded:* 1981
ISBN Publisher's Prefixes: 3-924163, 3-9800578

Wilhelm **Goldmann** Verlag GmbH, Neumarkter Str 18, Postfach 800709, D-8000 Munich 80 Tel: (089) 431890 Cable Add: Goldmannverlag Munich
Man Dir: Jürgen Kreuzhage; *Editorial:* Klaus Eck; *Sales:* Volker Neumann; *Publicity:* Brigitte Nunner
Parent Company: Verlagsgruppe Bertelsmann GmbH (qv for associate companies)
Subjects: General Fiction, Crime, Science Fiction, Poetry, Biography, History, How-to, Art, Classics, Religion, Law, Medicine, Psychology & Education, General & Social Science, Cinema, Astrology
ISBN Publisher's Prefix: 3-442

Goldstadtverlag, see Karl A Schäfer Buch- und Offsetdruckerei Goldstadtverlag

Gondrom Verlag GmbH & Co Kg*, Bühlstr 4, Postfach 1, D-8589 Bindlach Tel: (09208) 510
Man Dir: Volker Gondrom; *Editorial, Production, Rights & Permissions:* Jürgen Berger
Subjects: Art, History, Juveniles, Literature
Founded: 1974
ISBN Publisher's Prefix: 3-8112

V **Gorachek** KG, see Possev-Verlag

Grabert-Verlag+, Am Apfelberg 18-20, Postfach 1629, D-7400 Tübingen 1 Tel: (07071) 68011 Cable Add: Grabert-Tübingen Telex: 07262863 grav d
Man Dir and Owner: Wigbert Grabert
Subjects: Belles Lettres, Biography, Arts, History (also pre-History and Contemporary History), Quality Paperbacks
Book Club: Deutscher Buchkreis (qv)
1985: 10 titles *Founded:* 1953
ISBN Publisher's Prefix: 3-87847

Gräfe und Unzer GmbH+, Isabellastr 32, Postfach 400709, D-8000 Munich 40 Tel: (089) 272720 Telex: 5216929 gu d
Man Dirs: Kurt Prelinger, Christian Strasser, Dieter Banzhaf; *Editorial:* Nina Andres (Cookery), Hans Scherz (Natural History), Doris Schimmelpfennig-Funke (Health); *Sales:* Claudia Reitter; *Rights & Permissions:* Ursula Feuerbacher
Orders to: Verlegerdienst München, Gutenbergstr, 8031 Gilching
Subjects: Cookery, Health, Natural History
Founded: 1722
ISBN Publisher's Prefix: 3-7742

Verlag der Stiftung **Gralsbotschaft** GmbH*, Lenzhalde 15, D-7000 Stuttgart 1 Tel: (0711) 294355
Associate Company: Verlag Alexander Bernhardt, Austria (qv)
Subjects: Philosophy, Religion

Greven Verlag Köln GmbH, Neue Weyerstr 1-3, D-5000 Cologne 1 Tel: (0221) 20330 Cable Add: Grevenverlag Köln Telex: 8882249 Fax: (0221) 2033218
Man Dir: Irene Greven; *Publishing Managers:* Dr Diethelm Schmidt, Manfred vom Stein
Subjects: Cologne and Region (Fine Art editions)
1985: 4 titles *1986:* 4 titles *Founded:* 1827
ISBN Publisher's Prefix: 3-7743

Julius **Groos** Verlag KG, Hertzstr 6, Postfach 102423, D-6900 Heidelberg 1 Tel: (06221) 303621 Cable Add: Groos Heidelberg
Man Dir: Dieter Wolff; *Sales Dir:* Renate Wolff
Subjects: Linguistics, Textbooks on Modern Languages, Educational Materials, Periodicals
1986: 21 titles *1987:* 38 titles *Founded:* 1804
ISBN Publisher's Prefix: 3-87276

Grote'sche Verlagsbuch-handlung KG*, Max-Planck-Str 12, Postfach 400263, D-5000 Cologne 40 Tel: (02234) 106 Cable Add: Groteverlag Telex: dgv Köln 08882662
Dir: Friedrich Plagge
Parent Company: Unternehmensgruppe Verlag W Kohlhammer GmbH (qv)
Subjects: History, Law, Literature, Economics, Administration, Social & Political Science, Periodicals
Founded: 1661
ISBN Publisher's Prefix: 3-7745

Verlag **Grundlagen** und Praxis GmbH & Co, Wissenschaftlicher Autorenverlag KG, Bergmannstr 40, Postfach 1507, D-2950 Leer Tel: (0491) 61886
Man Dir: Mrs M Harms
Subjects: Homoeopathy, Graphology, Philology
Founded: 1972

Matthias-**Grünewald**-Verlag+, Max Hufschmidt-Str 4a, Postfach 3080, D-6500 Mainz Tel: (06131) 839055
Publisher: Dr Jakob Laubach; *Editorial:* Hiltraud Laubach; *Sales Dir:* Ludwig Hahn; *Production:* Mr Wagner; *Publicity:* Brigitte Goerigk
Subjects: Religion, Biography, History, Juveniles
Founded: 1918
ISBN Publisher's Prefix: 3-7867

Walter de **Gruyter** & Co, Genthiner Str 13, D-1000 Berlin 30 Tel: (030) 260050 Cable Add: Wissenschaft Berlin 0184027 Telex: 184027 Fax: (030) 26005251
Man Dirs: Dr Kurt-Georg Cram, Dr Kurt Lubasch, Dr Hellnig Hassenpflug; *Sales:*

146 FEDERAL REPUBLIC OF GERMANY

Dietrich Rackow; *Publicity:* Joachim Oest
Subsidiary Companies: Aldine de Gruyter, Mouton de Gruyter, Walter de Gruyter Inc, all at 200 Saw Mill River Road, Hawthorne, NY 10532, USA
Branch Offs: Mouton de Gruyter, Amsterdam, Berlin
Subjects: Law, History, Linguistics, Philosophy, Theology, Classical Studies, Anthropology, Natural Sciences, Literary Criticism, Commerce, Technology, Social Sciences, Medicine; Works in German, English, French
ISBN Publisher's Prefixes: 3-11 (de Gruyter, Mouton), 0-202 (Aldine)

Verlag Klaus **Guhl***, Königin-Elizabethstr 8, D-1000 Berlin 19 Tel: 3213062
Man Dir: Dr Klaus-Dieter Guhl; *Editorial:* Fabian Carlos Guhl; *Sales:* Florian Robert Guhl; *Production:* Hans Paul Guhl; *Publicity:* Dr Kurt Kreiler; *Rights & Permissions:* Dr Thomas Bark
Orders to: Knobelsdorffstr 8, D-1000 Berlin 19
Subsidiary Companies: Fanel GmbH; Buchladen Bunter Bär GmbH
Branch Off: Knobelsdorffstr 8, D-1000 Berlin 19
Subjects: Politics, Literature, Art, Erotica
Bookshop: Bunter Bär-Guhl, Knobelsdorffstr 8, D-1000 Berlin 19
Founded: 1974
ISBN Publisher's Prefix: 3-88220

D **Gundert** Verlag*, Wildstr 7, Postfach 1240, D-8202 Bad Aibling Tel: (08061) 4046
Subjects: Juveniles, Young Adult
Founded: 1878
ISBN Publisher's Prefix: 3-87279

Verlag August **Güse** GmbH*, Hauptstr 103, D-6367 Karben 3 Tel: (06039) 480120 Telex: 415505 Guese
Subjects: Horticulture, Floriculture
Founded: 1954
ISBN Publisher's Prefix: 3-87278

Gutenberg-Gesellschaft, Liebfrauenpl 5, D-6500 Mainz Tel: (06131) 226420
President: Hermann-Hartmut Weyel; *Secretary General:* Gertraude Benöhr; *Editorial:* Prof Dr H-J Koppitz
Subjects: Printing, Library Science, *Gutenberg Yearbook*
Founded: 1901

Büchergilde **Gutenberg Verlagsgesellschaft** mbH, Untermainkai 66, Postfach 160165, D-6000 Frankfurt am Main 16 Tel: (069) 230115 Telex: 176999 buegi d
Man Dirs: Erhard Schumacher, Dr Wolf-Dieter Klingelhöfer; *Editorial, Rights & Permissions:* Edgar Pässler; *Sales:* Rolf Backhaus; *Production:* Grit Fischer; *Publicity:* Karin Hirschfeld
Parent Company: BGAG, Theaterplatz 2, D-6000 Frankfurt am Main 1
Subjects: Literary Works, Light Reading, Politics, History, Art, Children's, Juvenile
Book Clubs: Büchergilde Gutenberg (Federal Republic of Germany and Switzerland)
Founded: 1924
Miscellaneous: Primarily a Book Club, but also a publisher
ISBN Publisher's Prefix: 3-7632

Gütersloher Verlagshaus Gerd Mohn, Königstr 23, Postfach 1343, D-4830 Gütersloh Tel: (05241) 8620 Cable Add: Gütersloher Verlagshaus Telex: 0933868
Man Dir, Rights & Permissions: Hansjürgen Meurer; *Sales Dir, Publicity:* Otfrid Seippel
Subjects: Religion, Philosophy, Politics, Juveniles, Paperbacks

Imprint: GTB Siebenstern
Founded: 1835/1959
ISBN Publisher's Prefix: 3-579

H V A — Edition Schindele, Hugo-Stotz-Str 14, D-6900 Heidelberg Tel: (06221) 770227
Man Dir: Eilert Erfling
Subjects: Pedagogy, Psychology, Sociology, Rehabilitation, Special Teaching, Social Instruction
Founded: 1969

Haag und Herchen Verlag, Fichardstr 30, D-6000 Frankfurt am Main 1 Tel: (069) 550911 Telex: 414838 huh d
Man Dir: Hans-Alfred Herchen
Subjects: How-to, High-priced Paperbacks, Medicine, Politics, Psychology, Engineering, General & Social Science, University Textbooks
1985: 130 titles *1986:* 124 titles *Founded:* 1975
ISBN Publisher's Prefix: 3-88129

Dr Rudolf **Habelt** GmbH, Abt Verlag, Am Buchenhang 1, Postfach 150104, D-5300 Bonn 1 Tel: (0228) 232015 Cable Add: Buchhabelt Bonn
Man Dir: Wolfgang Habelt; *Editorial, Production:* Renate Schreiber
Subjects: Pre-History, Archaeology, Ancient History, Regional, Folklore
Bookshop: (Antiquarian) at above address

Walter **Hädecke** Verlag+, Postfach 1203, D-7252 Weil der Stadt Tel: (07033) 2264
Man Dir, Sales, Advertising, Rights & Permissions: Joachim Graff
Subjects: Reference, High-priced Paperbacks, Cook Books, Food and Drink, Public Health, Natural Medicine
Founded: 1919
ISBN Publisher's Prefix: 3-7750

Lehrmittelverlag Wilhelm **Hagemann** GmbH, Karlstr 20, Postfach 5129, D-4000 Düsseldorf Tel: (0211) 353811 Cable Add: Hagemannverlag Telex: 8587623 hage d
General Manager: Maria Schütte-Hagemann; *Sales:* Walter Kils-Hütten; *Production, Rights & Permissions:* Heinz W Schmidt
Subjects: Textbooks (biology, public health), Software, Wall charts
Miscellaneous: Firm is a member of vgs — Verlagsgesellschaft mbH & Co KG (qv)
ISBN Publisher's Prefix: 3-544

Mary **Hahn's** Kochbuchverlag, Thomas-Wimmer Ring 11, D-8000 Munich 22 Tel: (089) 2350080 Telex: 5215045
Publicity Manager: Gerhard Koralus
Subjects: Cookery, Home Economics
Miscellaneous: Firm is a member of Buchverlage Ullstein Langen-Müller/Herbig (qv)
ISBN Publisher's Prefix: 3-87287

Verlag Anton **Hain**, see Meisenheim

Hallwag Verlagsgesellschaft mbH, Marco-Polo-Str 1, D-7302 Ostfildern 4 bei Stuttgart Tel: (0711) 4502266 Telex: 721796 mair d
Dir: Ulrich Mailänder
Subjects: Maps, Town Plans, Travel and Touring Guides and Books; Pocket Information series on General Knowledge; Reference
Head Office: Hallwag Verlag AG, Switzerland (qv)
ISBN Publisher's Prefix: 3-444

Hamburger Lesehefte Verlag Iselt & Co Nfl mbH, Nordbahnhofstr 2, Postfach 1480, D-2250 Husum Tel: (04841) 6081 Telex: 28567 husum v d
Man Dir, Editorial, Rights & Permissions: Ingwert Paulsen Jnr; *Sales:* Alfred Lorenzen; *Production:* Ingwert Paulsen Snr
Parent Company: Husum Druck- und Verlagsgesellschaft mbH & Co KG (qv)
Associate Companies: Hansa Verlag Ingwert Paulsen Jnr (qv); Matthiesen Verlag Ingwert Paulsen Jnr (qv)
Subjects: Textbooks
Founded: 1953
ISBN Publisher's Prefix: 3-87291

Peter **Hammer** Verlag GmbH, Foehrenstr 33-35, Postfach 200415, D-5600 Wuppertal 2 Tel: (0202) 505066
Dir: Hermann Schulz
Associate Company: Jugenddienst Verlag (at above address)
Subjects: Latin America, African Literature, The Third World, Literature, Current Affairs, Meditation, Christian Action
ISBN Publisher's Prefix: 3-87294

Hansa Verlag Ingwert Paulsen Jnr, Nordbahnhofstr 2, Postfach 1480, D-2250 Husum Tel: (04841) 6081 Telex: 28567 husumv d
Associate Companies: Hamburger Lesehefte Verlag Iselt & Co Nfl mbH (qv); Husum Druck- und Verlagsgesellschaft mbH & Co KG (qv); Matthiesen Verlag Ingwert Paulsen Jnr (qv)
Subjects: Belles Lettres, Literary Criticism
ISBN Publisher's Prefix: 3-920421

Carl **Hanser** Verlag, Kolbergerstr 22, Postfach 860420, D-8000 Munich 86 Tel: (089) 926940 Telex: 0522837
Presidents: Joachim Spencker (Publisher), Franz-Joachim Klock (Finance); *Publisher:* Michael Krüger (Fiction); *Editorial:* Christoph Buchwald, Eginhard Hora, Kristian Wachinger (Fiction, Non-fiction), Dr Wolfgang Glenz (Plastics), Hans Joachim Niclas (Technical, Science); *Production Dir:* Klaus Weberbeck; *Sales Dirs:* Felicitas Feilhauer, Christoph Sickel; *Advertising Dir:* Günther Steidl; *Publicity:* Tatjana Michaelis, Christoph Sickel
Subsidiary Companies: Part-owner of Verlegerdienst München, Gutenbergstr, D-8031 Gilching and Deutscher Taschenbuchverlag (qv)
Subjects: General Fiction, Belles Lettres, Poetry, Biography, History, Philosophy, High-priced Paperbacks, Engineering, General Science, Macromolecular Chemistry, Plastics Engineering and Polymer Science, Business & Management, Computers Science, Dentistry, Periodicals
Founded: 1928
ISBN Publisher's Prefix: 3-446

Hänssler-Verlag, Friedrich Hänssler KG, Bismarckstr 4, Postfach 1220, D-7303 Neuhausen-Stuttgart Tel: (07158) 1770
Man Dir: Friedrich Hänssler; *Rights & Permissions:* Dieter Allgöwer
Subjects: Music, Art, Religion, Low-priced Paperbacks
Bookshop: Laudate GmbH, Versandbuchhandlung Friedrich Hänssler (at above address)
Founded: 1919
Miscellanous: Firm is a member of the Telos (qv) series publishing group; it also publishes all publications of the American Institute of Musicology
ISBN Publisher's Prefix: 3-7751

Peter **Hanstein** Verlag GmbH*, Savignystr 53, Postfach 170101, D-6000 Frankfurt am Main Tel: (069) 7560950 Telex: 414531
Publisher: Axel Rütters
Parent Company; Athenäum Verlag GmbH (qv)
Associate Companies: Jüdischer Verlag,

Syndikat und Europäische Verlagsanstalt; Verlag Anton Hain Meisenheim GmbH (qv) is a subsidiary company of this Group
Subject: Theology
Founded: 1878
ISBN Publisher's Prefix: 3-7756

Harlekin-Presse, see Hertenstein

Harrach Verlag*, Wöllsteiner Str 8, Postfach 745, D-6550 Bad Kreuznach Tel: (0671) 67073 Telex: 042815
Associate Company: Inter-Kunst und Buch GmbH (qv)
Subjects: Children's Books, Poetry

Verlag Otto **Harrassowitz**, Taunusstr 14, Postfach 2929, D-6200 Wiesbaden 1 Tel: (06121) 521046 Cable Add: Otto Harrassowitz Wiesbaden Telex: 4186135
Man Dir: Dr Helmut Petzolt; *Sales & Publicity Dir:* Albrecht Weddigen
Subjects: Book Trade and Library Science, Bibliographies, Cultural History, Orientalia and associated Eastern linguistic and religious studies, East European History and associated Slavic Language and Educational Studies, Middle East studies
Bookshop: See under Major Booksellers
1985: 95 titles *1986:* 93 titles *Founded:* 1872
ISBN Publisher's Prefix: 3-447

Litteraturverlag Karlheinz **Hartmann***, Rodheimer Str 17, D-6382 Friedrichsdorf im Taunus Tel: (06007) 7622
Man Dir: Karlheinz Hartmann; *Editorial:* Monica Herber
Branch Off: Kaulbachstr 18, D-6000 Frankfurt am Main 70 Tel: (069) 625511/632345
Subjects: Contemporary Literature, Reprints, Literary Criticism, Scenarios and Film Scripts, Modern Poetry, Horror
Founded: 1976
ISBN Publisher's Prefix: 3-87293

Verlag Gerd **Hatje**+*, Wildunger Str 83, Postfach 500468, D-7000 Stuttgart 50 Tel: (0711) 561109
Man Dir: Gerd Hatje
Subjects: Architecture, Interior Decoration, Art (especially Modern Art)
Founded: 1945
ISBN Publisher's Prefix: 3-7757

Haude und Spener Verlag, Postfach 3046, D-1000 Berlin 30 (Located at: Potsdamer Str 199) Tel: (030) 2165061
General Manager: Volker Spiess
Associate Company: Verlag Volker Spiess (qv)
Subjects: Literary History, Bibliographies, Collected Works, History, Cultural History, Reminiscences of Berlin
Founded: 1614
ISBN Publisher's Prefix: 3-7759

Rudolf **Haufe** Verlag GmbH & Co KG+, Hindenburgstr 64, Postfach 740, D-7800 Freiburg im Breisgau Tel: (0761) 36830 Cable Add: Haufeverlag Telex: 772442 haufe d Fax: (0761) 3683236 Btx 33933
Man Dirs: Dr G Friedrich, Dr M Jahrmarkt, G Osswald; *Editorial:* Dr G Friedrich, Dr M Jahrmarkt; *Sales, Production:* Dr M Jahrmarkt *Rights & Permissions:* Dr G Friedrich
Subsidiary Companies: WRS-Verlag (Wirtschaft, Recht, Steuern) GmbH & Co (qv); Information Verlags-GmbH & Co KG, Hindenburgstr 64, Postfach 740, D-7800 Freiburg im Breisgau
Subjects: Business and Law, Financial, Management, Social Science, University Textbooks
Founded: 1934
ISBN Publisher's Prefix: 3-448

Karl F **Haug** Verlag GmbH & Co, Postfach 102840, D-6900 Heidelberg 1 (Located at: Fritz-Frey-Str 21) Tel: (06221) 49974 Cable Add: haugverlag Telex: 481683 huufm d Fax: (06221) 400727
Man Dir: Dr E Fischer; *Production:* Dietmar Sieber; *Advertising:* Krisztina Fruh; *Sales:* Rolf Lenzen
Associate Companies: Arkana Verlag (qv); Verlag für Medizin Dr Ewald Fischer GmbH (qv)
Branch Off: Bergheimer Str 102, D-6900 Heidelberg
Subjects: Naturopathic, Homoeopathic, Fringe and Auxiliary Medical, Acupuncture, Health and Preventive Medicine, Periodicals
Bookshop: Haug & Cie Nachf GmbH, Med Wiss Buchhandlung und Antiquariat (Medical science books, new and second-hand/antiquarian)
Founded: 1903
ISBN Publisher's Prefix: 3-7760

Verlag H M **Hauschild** GmbH, Rigaer Str 3, D-2800 Bremen Tel: (0421) 392039 Telex: 244333 hwb d
Dirs: Friedrich Steinmeyer, Andreas Nagel
Parent Company: Werbedruck Bremen Grafischer Betrieb GmbH
Subjects: Art, Reference, Bremen Regional
Founded: 1854
ISBN Publisher's Prefix: 3-920699

Dr Ernst **Hauswedell** und Co Verlag, Rosenbergstr 113, Postfach 723, D-7000 Stuttgart 1 Tel: (0711) 638264
Joint Man Dirs: Gerd Hiersemann, Dr Reimar W Fuchs
Subjects: Reference Works for Book and Print Collectors, Bibliographies, Illustrated Books
Founded: 1927
ISBN Publisher's Prefix: 3-7762

Hayit Verlag GmbH+*, Hansaring 84-86, D-5000 Cologne 1 Tel: (0221) 123088 Telex: 8883390 have d
Man Dir, Publicity, Rights & Permissions: Ertay Hayit; *Editorial:* Ute Hayit; *Sales:* Mirza Hayit; *Production:* Beate Hayit
Associate Company: Hayit Druck GmbH (at above address)
Subjects: Guides (travel, student's), Turkestan
1986: 60 titles *Founded:* 1978
ISBN Publisher's Prefixes: 3-89210, 3-922145

Heckners Verlag, Postfach 1363, D-3340 Wolfenbüttel Tel: (05331) 5166
Subjects: Vocational (Business), Economics
Founded: 1895
Miscellaneous: Firm is a member of vgs — Verlagsgesellschaft mbH & Co KG (qv)

H **Heenemann** Verlagsgesellschaft mbH*, Bessemerstr 83-91, Postfach 420342, D-1000 Berlin 42 Tel: (030) 7537051 Telex: 183 796 hekg d
Subjects: Fishery and Fishing, Sociology and Popular Science, Enamels and Coatings
ISBN Publisher's Prefix: 3-87903

Heidmük-Verlag Günther U Müller*, Am schwarzen Meer 7, D-2800 Bremen 1 Tel: (0421) 492899
Man Dir: Günther U Müller
Subjects: Juveniles, Games

Verlag Egon **Heinemann***, Kösliner Weg 16, D-2000 Norderstedt 3 Tel: (040) 5232368/5239023
Publisher: Egon Heinemann
Subjects: Sailing, Sailing Ships, Nautical Literature, Yachting Charts
ISBN Publisher's Prefix: 3-87321

Ehrhardt **Heinold**, see Eulenhof-Verlag

Heinrichshofen's Verlag+*, Liebigstr 16, Postfach 620, D-2940 Wilhelmshaven Tel: (04421) 202004 Cable Add: Heinrichshofen Wilhelmshaven
President: Otto Heinrich Noetzel; *Man Dir:* Dr Viktor Kreiner; *Production:* Rolf Schneeberg
Associate Companies: Otto Heinrich Noetzel Verlag; Arthur Türk KG; Heinrichshofen Edition New York
Subject: Music
Founded: 1797

Verlag Georg **Heintz**, Wasserturmstr 7, D-6520 Worms Cable Add: Heintz
Subjects: Bibliography, German Exile Literature (from 1933), History and Documentation of Anti-Semitism, Fiction and Drama on related themes

G **Henle** Verlag, Postfach 710466, D-8000 Munich 71 (Located at: Forstenrieder Allee 122) Tel: (089) 754096 Telex: 05216392
Subsidiary Company: G Henle USA Inc, 2446 Centerline Industrial Dr, PO Box 1753 St Louis, MO 63043 (Tel: (314) 9910487)
Subject: Music, Original and Facsimile Editions, Reference Books (Music)
ISBN Publisher's Prefix: 3-87328

Henssel Verlag+*, Glinicker Str 12, D-1000 Berlin 39 Tel: (030) 8051493 Cable Add: Hensselverlag Berlin
Man Dir: Karl-Heinz Henssel; *Editorial:* Philipp Wendland
Subjects: General Fiction, Humour, Travel, Literary Theory, Poetry, Biography, Quality Paperbacks
Founded: 1938
ISBN Publisher's Prefix: 3-87329

F A **Herbig** Verlagsbuchhandlung, Thomas-Wimmer-Ring 11, D-8000 Munich 22 Tel: (089) 2350080 Cable Add: Langenmüller Telex: 05215045
Man Dir: Dr Herbert Fleissner; *Editorial:* Dr Bernhard Strückmeÿer; *Sales:* Gisela Weichert; *Publicity:* Dr Brigitte Sinhuber-Erbacher; *Rights & Permissions:* Dorothea Estermann
Orders to: VVA (Vereinigte Verlagsauslieferung GmbH), Postfach 7777, D-4830 Gütersloh 1
Subjects: Novels, Belles Lettres, Poetry, History, Art, Hobbies, Gift Books
Founded: 1821
Miscellaneous: Firm is a member of Buchverlage Ullstein Langen-Müller/Herbig (qv)
ISBN Publisher's Prefix: 3-7766

Herchen, see Bock und Herchen

Verlag **Herder** GmbH & Co KG*, Hermann-Herder-Str 4, Postfach, D-7800 Freiburg im Breisgau Tel: (0761) 27171 Cable Add: Herder Freiburgbreisgau Telex: 07721440 vhd
Man Dir: Dr Hermann Herder; *Sales Dir:* Franz Grossmann; *Publicity Manager:* Dr Ludwig Muth; *Rights & Permissions:* Alfred Zimmermann
Subsidiary Companies: Verlag Karl Albér GmbH, Christophorus-Verlag Herder GmbH, Verlag A G Ploetz GmbH & Co KG (qqv)
Associate Companies: Verlag Herder & Co, Austria (qv); Herder Editrice e Libreria, Italy (qv); Editorial Herder SA, Librería Herder (both in Spain, qqv); Herder AG, Switzerland (qv); Herder und Herder GmbH, Federal Republic of Germany (qv)
Subjects: General Fiction, Belles Lettres, Poetry, Biography, History, Art, Philosophy, Reference, Religion, Juveniles,

148 FEDERAL REPUBLIC OF GERMANY

Low- and High-priced Paperbacks, Psychology, Social Science, University, Secondary & Primary Textbooks, Educational Materials, Atlases, Encyclopaedias
Book Club: Herder Buchgemeinde
Bookshops: Located in major cities throughout Federal Republic of Germany
Founded: 1801
ISBN Publisher's Prefix: 3-451

Herder und Herder GmbH*, Verlag für Wirtschaft und Gesellschaft, Gärtnerweg 38, D-6000 Frankfurt am Main 1
Associate Companies: Verlag Herder GmbH & Co KG, Verlag A G Ploetz GmbH & Co KG (both in Federal Republic of Germany, qqv); Herder Editrice e Libreria, Italy (qv); Editorial Herder SA, Spain (qv); Herder AG, Switzerland (qv)
Subjects: Politics, Social Sciences, Economics
ISBN Publisher's Prefix: 3-585

Herold Verlag Brück KG+, Friedrichstr 16-20, Postfach 1940, D-7012 Fellbach 4 Tel: (0711) 513004
Dir: Peter Schwend; *Editorial:* Ulrich Höfker; *Marketing:* Harald Zillner
Subject: Juveniles
Founded: 1871
ISBN Publisher's Prefix: 3-7767

Hertenstein-Presse, Mathystr 36, D-7530 Pforzheim Tel: (07231) 27084
Publicity Manager: Ulrike Strauss
Subject: Verse and other texts, with original illustrations
Founded: 1967
Miscellaneous: Formerly known as Harlekin-Presse

Hestia-Verlag GmbH+, Egerländer Str 28, D-8580 Bayreuth Tel: (0921) 21007 Fax: (0921) 81925
Dirs: Heinz G Konsalik, Dagmar Stecher-Konsalik
Subsidiary Companies: Paul Neff Verlag KG, Austria (qv); Diana Verlag AG, Switzerland (qv)
Subjects: General Fiction and Non-fiction, History, Biography
1985-86: 40 titles *Founded:* 1954
ISBN Publisher's Prefix: 3-7770

Carl **Heymanns** Verlag KG, Luxemburger Str 449, D-5000 Cologne 41 Tel: (0221) 460100 Cable Add: Rechtsverlag Köln Telex: 8881888 chv d Fax: (0221) 4601069
Man Dir: Bertram Gallus; *Editorial:* H E Wohlfarth, K W Frohn, K Pompe, G Wertmüller, H Ivers; *Production:* C Free; *Publicity:* K Holtschneider; *Sales:* E Polscher
Subsidiary Companies: Gallus Druckerei KG, Berlin; Albert Nauck & Co, Cologne and Berlin; Euroliber Verlags- und Vertriebs-GmbH, Cologne
Branch Offs: Adalbert-Stifter-Str 15, D-5300 Bonn 1 Tel: (0228) 234550 Cable Add: Rechtsverlag Bonn; Postfach 26, D-8000 Munich 26 (Located at: Steinsdorfstr 10, D-8000 Munich 22) Tel: (089) 224811 Cable Add: Rechtsverlag München Telex: 524058 chvm d; Gutenbergstr 3-4, D-1000 Berlin 10 Tel: (030) 3914081/3922237 Cable Add: Rechtsverlag Berlin Telex: 181811 chvb b Fax: (030) 3912861
Subjects: Law, Human Rights, Taxation, Criminology, Political Science, Management Science and Training
Founded: 1815
ISBN Publisher's Prefix: 3-452

Wilhelm **Heyne** Verlag, Türkenstr 5-7, Postfach 201204, D-8000 Munich 2 Tel: (089) 288211 Cable Add: Heyneverlag München Telex: 0524218 Fax: (089) 2800943
Publisher: Rolf Heyne; *Editorial Dir:* Dr Hans-Peter Übleis; *Editorial:* Roswitha Heyne, Dr Günther Fetzer, Wolfgang Jeschke, Bernhard Matt, Werner Morawetz; *Sales Manager:* Friedhelm Koch; *Advertising Manager:* Horst Mikkat; *Rights & Permissions:* Traudel Eckardt
Subjects: (mainly paperbacks) General Fiction, Poetry, Biography, History, How-to, Cookery, Mystery, Romances, Occult, Films, Psychology, Science Fiction and Westerns, Cartoons
Founded: 1934
ISBN Publisher's Prefix: 3-453

Anton **Hiersemann** Verlag+, Rosenbergstr 113, Postfach 723, D-7000 Stuttgart 1 Tel: (0711) 638264
Man Dir, Rights & Permissions: Karl G Hiersemann
Subjects: Bibliography, Reference, History, Art, Humanities, Germanic Literature, Theatre, Classical Studies, Religion, Theology
1985: 50 titles *Founded:* 1884
ISBN Publisher's Prefix: 3-7772

Verlag **Hinder und Deelmann**, Postfach 1206, D-3554 Gladenbach (Hessen) Tel: (06462) 1301
Publishers: Johannes Deelmann, Rolf Hinder
Subjects: Philosophy, Religion, Social Science
ISBN Publisher's Prefix: 3-87348

Edition **Hinnenthal**, an imprint of Bärenreiter Verlag (qv)

Hippokrates-Verlag GmbH+, Postfach 593, D-7000 Stuttgart 1 (Located at: Rüdigerstr 14, D-7000 Stuttgart 30) Tel: (0711) 89310 Cable Add: Hippokratesverlag
Dir: Albrecht Hauff; *Publicity:* H-G Zimnik; *Sales:* Winfried Schmitt
Orders to: Koch, Neff und Oetinger & Co, Verlagsauslieferung Hippokrates, Postfach 210, D-7000 Stuttgart 1
Parent Company: Georg Thieme Verlag KG (qv)
Subjects: Medicine, Natural Sciences, Psychology, University and Secondary Textbooks
Founded: 1925
ISBN Publisher's Prefix: 3-7773

Hirmer Verlag+, Maréesstrasse 15, D-8000 Munich 19 Tel: (089) 1781011
Man Dirs: Aenne Hirmer, Albert Hirmer; *Editorial:* Albert Hirmer
Subjects: Quality illustrated Works on Archaeology, History of Art, Modern Art, German and other Art and Picture Galleries
Founded: 1948
ISBN Publisher's Prefix: 3-7774

Hirschgraben-Verlag GmbH, Fürstenberger Str 223, Postfach 180245, D-6000 Frankfurt am Main Tel: (069) 550491 Telex: 176117604 hgv ffm
Dirs: Dr F Löffelholz, Werner Thiele; *Editorial, Rights & Permissions:* Dr F Löffelholz; *Production:* Herbert Ludwig; *Publicity:* Hans-Albrecht Koeppel
Orders to: Cornelsen Verlagsgesellschaft mbH & Co KG, Postfach 8729, D-4800 Bielefeld 1
Parent Company: Cornelsen Verlag GmbH & Co (qv)
Subjects: School Textbooks, Education, German as a Foreign Language, Linguistics
1987: 86 titles *Founded:* 1946
ISBN Publisher's Prefix: 3-454

S **Hirzel** Verlag GmbH und Co, Birkenwaldstr 44, Postfach 347, D-7000 Stuttgart 1 Tel: (0711) 25820 Cable Add: Hirzelverlag, Stuttgart Telex: 723636 daz d
Man Dirs: R Hack, V Sieveking, Dr W Wessinger; *Manager:* K Hübler
Associate Companies: Deutscher Apotheker Verlag Dr Roland Schmiedel (qv); Franz Steiner Verlag Wiesbaden GmbH (qv); Wissenschaftliche Verlagsgesellschaft mbH (qv)
Subjects: Philosophy, Psychology, Engineering, General Science, Periodicals
Founded: 1853
ISBN Publisher's Prefix: 3-7776

Hobbit Presse, an imprint of Klett-Cotta Verlag (qv)

Hoch-Verlag, Kronprinzenstr 27, D-4000 Düsseldorf 1 Tel: (0211) 307001 Cable Add: Hochverlag Fax: (0211) 5182127
Man Dirs: Joachim Hoch, Eric Zinth de Kentzingen, Ursula Schareina; *Sales, Publicity and Advertising Dir:* Joachim Hoch; *Rights & Permissions:* Eric Zinth de Kenzingen
Subject: Juveniles
Founded: 1949
ISBN Publisher's Prefix: 3-7779

Ing W **Hofacker** GmbH Verlag, Tegernseerstr 18, D-8150 Holzkirchen/Obb Tel: (08024) 7331 Telex: 526973
Man Dir, Rights & Permissions, Editorial, Publicity: J Maier; *Production:* W Hofacker
Subjects: Electronics, Micro-Computers, Micro-Processing
Founded: 1968
ISBN Publisher's Prefixes: 3-921682, 3-88963

Dieter **Hoffmann** Verlag, Senefelderstr 75, D-6500 Mainz 41 Tel: (06136) 4116 Telex: 4187213
Dir: Dieter Hoffman
Subjects: History of German Aviation (in German and English texts), Aircraft Modelling, Hunting and Shooting Handbooks
Founded: 1960
ISBN Publisher's Prefix: 3-87341

Julius **Hoffmann** Verlag+, Pfizerstr 5-7, Postfach 788, D-7000 Stuttgart 1 Tel: (0711) 2191320
Man Dir: Kurt Hoffmann
Subjects: Building and Architecture, History of Art (many texts in English and French)
Founded: 1827
ISBN Publisher's Prefix: 3-87346

Hoffmann und Campe Verlag, Harvestehuder Weg 45, D-2000 Hamburg 13 Tel: (040) 441881 Cable Add: Hoca Telex: 0214259
Man Dirs: Lothar Menne, Karl-Udo Wrede; *Editorial:* Dr Anneliese Schumacher, Hubertus Rabe, Dr Helmut Wiemken, Dr Jutta Siegmund-Schultze; *Sales Dir:* Ulrich Meier; *Production:* Roland Kraft; *Publicity and Advertising Dir:* Frank Scheffter; *Rights & Permissions:* Helga Eberhard, Sibylle Meyer-Chory
Subjects: General Fiction and Non-fiction, Belles Lettres, Poetry, Biography, History, Music, Art, Philosophy, Psychology, General & Social Science, Marine History, Illustrated Books
Founded: 1781
ISBN Publisher's Prefix: 3-455

Verlag Karl **Hofmann** GmbH & Co, Steinwasenstr 6-8, Postfach 1360, D-7060 Schorndorf bei Stuttgart Tel: (07181) 7811 Fax: (07181) 7814
Man Dir: Ottmar Hecht; *Sales, Publicity:*

Thomas Hecht
Subjects: Sports, Technical Literature on glass utilization, Periodicals
1986: 37 titles *Founded:* 1904
ISBN Publisher's Prefix: 3-7780

Verlag für Psychologie, Dr C J **Hogrefe**, see Psychologie

Hohenloher Druck- und Verlagshaus, Verlag Hohenloher Tagblatt, Blaufelderstr 44, Postfach 80, D-7182 Gerabronn Tel: (07952) 6020 Cable Add: HDV-Gerabronn Telex: 74334
Publisher: Rolf Wankmüller
Subjects: Fiction, Poetry, Biography, Juvenilcs
ISBN Publisher's Prefix: 3-87354

Hohenrain-Verlag GmbH, Am Apfelberg 18, Postfach 1611, D-7400 Tübingen 1 Tel: (07071) 68012 Telex: 7262863
Man Dir: Wigbert Grabert
Subjects: Belles Lettres, Biography, History, Politics, Art, Fiction, Quality Paperbacks
1985: 8 titles *1986:* 6 titles *Founded:* 1985

Hohenstaufen Verlag Schumann KG, Freseniusstr 59, D-8000 Munich 60
Dir: Karl-Heinz Biebl
Subjects: Belles Lettres, Memoirs, Contemporary History

Verlag Wolfgang **Hölker**, Martinistr 2, Postfach 3820, D-4400 Munster Tel: (0251) 42225 Cable Add: Martinistrasse 2 Telex: 891566 hoeco d
Man Dir: Wolfgang Hölker; *Sales:* Manfred Goldschmidt; *Production:* Joerg Rinow; *Publicity:* Gertrud Posch
Parent Company: F Coppenrath Verlag (qv)
Subject: Cookery
1986: 150 titles *Founded:* 1973
ISBN Publisher's Prefix: 3-88117

Holle Verlag GmbH*, Friedhofstr 25, Postfach 320, D-7570 Baden Baden Tel: (07221) 23591 Telex: 0781108
Man Dir: G Du Ry van Beest Holle
Subjects: History, Art, Encyclopaedias
Founded: 1933
ISBN Publisher's Prefix: 3-87355

Verlags-GmbH **Höller und Zwick**+, Homburgstr 11, D-3300 Brunswick Tel: (0531) 502754
Man Dir: Klaus Holler
Subjects: Geography, History, Politics
1985: 3 titles *1986:* 8 titles *Founded:* 1983
ISBN Publisher's Prefix: 3-89057

Holsten Verlag Wolf Schenke KG, Am Damm 15a, D-2000 Hamburg 71 Tel: (040) 6402839
Man Dir: Wolf E Schenke
Subjects: History, Political Science
Founded: 1955

Verlag Gebr **Holzapfel**, Kienhorststr 61, D-1000 Berlin 51 Tel: (030) 4133098
Publisher: Klaus-J Holzapfel
Subject: Politics
ISBN Publisher's Prefix: 3-921226

Gunther **Holzboog** GmbH & Co, see Friedrich Frommann Verlag

Hans **Holzmann** Verlag GmbH und Co KG+, Gewerbestr 2, Postfach 1342, D-8939 Bad Wörishofen Tel: (08247) 3540 Cable Add: Holzmann Verlag Telex: 539331
Man Dir: Peter Holzmann; *Sales Dir:* Alfred Stempfle
Subjects: Business and Legal Advisory, Inventions and Patenting, Butchery and Meat Trade
Bookshop: Versandbuchhandlung Hans Holzmann, Postfach 1342, D-8939 Bad Wörishofen

Founded: 1936
ISBN Publisher's Prefix: 3-7783

Werner **Hörnemann** Verlag*, Merler Allee 128, Postfach 130109, D-5300 Bonn 1 Tel: (0228) 251376
Subjects: Hobbies, Cookery, Pottery and Ceramics
ISBN Publisher's Prefix: 3-87384

Horst-Werner Dumjahn Verlag, see Dumjahn

Humboldt-Taschenbuchverlag Jacobi KG, Neusser Str 3, Postfach 401120, D-8000 Munich 40 Tel: (089) 360960 Cable Add: Langenscheidt Munich Telex: 5215379 lkgm d Fax: (089) 36096258
Man Dirs: Karl Ernst Tielebier-Langenscheidt, Dr Florian Langenscheidt; *Editorial, Rights & Permissions:* Manfred Überall; *Sales Dir:* Peter Haering; *Advertising Dir:* Klaus Ferber; *Sales, Promotion:* through Langenscheidt KG (qv)
Subjects: Non-fiction Paperbacks, Practical Guides
Founded: 1953
Miscellaneous: Firm is a member of the Langenscheidt Group (qv)
ISBN Publisher's Prefix: 3-581

Edition **Hundertmark**, Brüsseler Str 29, D-5000 Cologne 1 Tel: (0221) 237944
Man Dir: Armin Hundertmark
Subjects: Contemporary Art Books, Literature, Periodicals
Founded: 1970

Husum Druck- und Verlagsgesellschaft mbH & Co KG, Nordbahnhofstr 2, Postfach 1480, D-2250 Husum Tel: (04841) 6081 Telex: 28567 husum v d
Man Dir, Editorial, Rights & Permissions: Ingwert Paulsen Jnr; *Sales:* Alfred Lorenzen; *Production:* Ingwert Paulsen Snr
Subsidiary Company: Hamburger Lesehefte Verlag Iselt & Co Nfl mbH (qv)
Associate Companies: Hansa Verlag Ingwert Paulsen Jnr (qv); Matthiesen Verlag Ingwert Paulsen Jnr (qv)
Subjects: Belles Lettres, Regional Interest
Founded: 1973
ISBN Publisher's Prefix: 3-88042

Dr Alfred **Hüthig** Verlag GmbH, Postfach 102869, D-6900 Heidelberg (Located at: Im Weiher 10) Tel: (06221) 4890 Cable Add: Hüthigverlag Heidelberg Telex: 0461727
Production: Willi Mayer; *Publicity:* Reinhard Janz; *Foreign Rights:* Jochen Schmitt
Subsidiary Companies: Hüthig und Pflaum Verlag GmbH & Co KG (qv); Philips Fachbücher (qv)
Associate Company: Hüthig und Wepf Verlag, Switzerland (qv)
Subjects: Chemistry, Chemical Engineering, Metallurgy, Dentistry, Cosmetics, Electronics, Computer Dictionaries, Periodicals
1985: 90 titles *1986:* approx 100 titles
Founded: 1925
ISBN Publisher's Prefix: 3-7785

Hüthig und Pflaum Verlag GmbH & Co KG, Postfach 190737, D-8000 Munich 19 (Located at: Lazarettstr 4, D-8000 Munich 19) Tel: (089) 126070 Telex: 0529408
Branch Off: Im Weiher 10, D-6900 Heidelberg 1
Parent Companies: Dr Alfred Hüthig Verlag GmbH and Richard Pflaum Verlag KG (qqv)
Subsidiary Companies: Helios Buchhandlung und Antiquariat GmbH, Helios Literatur-Vertrieb GmbH,

Eichborndamm 141-167, D-1000 Berlin 51 Tel: (030) 4116033 Telex: 0181632; Helios Literatur-Vertrieb GesmbH & Co KG, Industriestr B13, A-2345 Brunn, Austria Tel: (02236) 82420 Telex: 79299
Subject: Electrical Engineering
ISBN Publisher's Prefix: 3-8101

I D W-Verlag GmbH, Tersteegenstr 14, Postfach 320580, D-4000 Düsseldorf 30 Tel: (0211) 45610 Cable Add: ideweverlag Telex: 8584270
Subject: Business Administration, Tax Law, Finance, Auditing
1986: 30 titles
ISBN Publisher's Prefix: 3-8021

I L S (Institut für Lernsysteme) GmbH, member of Verlagsgruppe Bertelsmann GmbH (qv)

I M S F, see Institut für Marxistische Studien und Forschungen eV

I S P-Verlag (Internationale Sozialistische Publikationen)*, Mainzer Landstr 147, Postfach 111017, D-6000 Frankfurt am Main 2 Tel: (069) 736797
Subject: Politics

Idea Verlag GmbH+, Krautgartenweg 6, Postfach 1361, D-8039 Puchheim bei München Tel: (089) 803265
Also: Bruckerstr 46, D-8031 Gilching Tel: (08105) 19124
Man Dir, Editorial, Production, Rights & Permissions: Dr Uwe K Paschke; *Sales, Publicity:* Hariet Paschke
Branch Off: PEGA Verlag, Brucker Str 46, D-8031 Gilching Tel: (08105) 9124
Subjects: Technical and Scientific Texts, History, Literature, Hobbies, Games, Recreation, Sport
Founded: 1980
ISBN Publisher's Prefix: 3-88793

Hans **Imhoff**, see Euphorion-Verlag

Index eV*, Überlinger Str 13, Postfach 410511, D-5000 Cologne 41 Tel: (0221) 436939/372043
Publisher: Adolf Müller
Subjects: Belles Lettres, Poetry, Politics, Czech and Slovak Literature

Insel Verlag, Postfach 101130, D-6000 Frankfurt am Main (Located at: Suhrkamp House, Lindenstr 29-35) Tel: (069) 756010 Cable Add: Inselverlag Telex: 413972
Publisher: Dr Siegfried Unseld; *Man Dirs:* Dr Heribert Marré, Dr Gottfried Honnefelder, Dr Joachim Unseld; *Publicity:* Dr Christoph Groffy; *Advertising:* Clause Carlé; *Rights & Permissions:* Helene Ritzerfeld
Associate Companies: Deutscher Klassiker Verlag, Nomos Verlagsgesellschaft mbH & Co KG (qv), Suhrkamp Verlag (qv) (all Federal Republic of Germany); Suhrkamp Verlag AG, Zeltweg 25, CH-8032 Zurich, Switzerland; Suhrkamp Publishers New York, Inc, 175 Fifth Ave, New York, NY 10010, USA
Subjects: Classic German Literature (especially Goethe), Classic foreign authors in translation, Modern Classics, Cultural History, Bibliophilia, Books on Great Artists
Founded: 1899
ISBN Publisher's Prefix: 3-458

Institut für Lernsysteme (ILS), member of Verlagsgruppe Bertelsmann GmbH (qv)

Institut für Marxistische Studien und Forschungen eV (IMSF)*, Oberlindau 15, D-6000 Frankfurt am Main Tel: (069) 724914
Man Dir: Dr Heinz Jung; *All other offices:* J D Schmidt
Subjects: Publication of results of studies,

research etc, commentary on current political, economic and social questions; Periodicals
Founded: 1968
ISBN Publisher's Prefix: 3-88807

Inter-Kunst und Buch GmbH, Wöllsteinerstr 8, D-6550 Bad Kreuznach Tel: (0671) 67073 Telex: 042815
Associate Company: Harrach Verlag (qv)
Subjects: Graphics

Verlag **Internationale Solidarität** Verlagsgesellschaft mbH*, Zugweg 10, D-5000 Cologne Tel: (0221) 327817 Cable Add: Zugweg 10
Sales, Production: Ole Callsen
Subject: Politics

Internationales Landkartenhaus, Geo Center GmbH, Schockenriedstr 40A, D-7000 Stuttgart 80 Tel: (0711) 7889340 Telex: 7255508 ilh
Man Dir: Wolfgang Kunth; *Sales Manager:* Herbert Leuser
Subsidiary Company: GeoCenter Verlagsvertrieb GmbH (qv)
Subject: Maps, Geoscientific, Guides

Iselt und Co Nfl mbH, see Hamburger Lesehefte Verlag

J R O-Kartografische Verlagsgesellschaft mbH*, Kirschstr 12-16, Postfach 500370, D-8000 Munich 50 Tel: (089) 81081 Telex: 524123
General Manager: Klaus Wagner
Parent Company: Süddeutscher Verlag GmbH, Sendlinger Str 80, Postfach 202220, D-8000 Munich 2
Associate Company: Karl Wenschow GmbH (at above main address)
Subjects: Maps, Cartography, Organizational charts
Founded: 1922
ISBN Publisher's Prefix: 3-87378

Verlag **Jacobi** KG, see Axel Juncker

Jaeger und Waldmann, see Telex-Verlag

Jahreszeitenverlag+*, Poßmoorweg 5, Postfach 601220, D-2000 Hamburg 60 Tel: (040) 27171 Cable Add: Jalag Telex: 0213214
Subjects: Belles Lettres, Periodicals

Verlag Eduard **Jakobsohn***, Glogauer Str 22, D-1000 Berlin 36 Tel: (030) 6181258
Orders to: Pro Media Literaturvertrieb GmbH, Werner Voss Damm 54, D-1000 Berlin 42
Subjects: Alternative Living, Communes, Spanish Civil War, Witch-hunting, Red Indians, Literature

Stern-Verlag **Janssen** und Co, see Stern-Verlag

Wolfgang **Joerg** und Erich Schoenig, see Berliner Handpresse

Jüdischer Verlag, subsidiary of Athenäum Verlag GmbH (qv)

Jugend und Volk Verlag GmbH*, Claude-Lorrainstr, D-8000 Munich 40 Tel: (089) 374560
Man Dir: Mag Dr Otto Schimpf;
Production: Ludwig Ondrej; *Sales:* Werner Brunner; *Publicity:* Dr Renate Wagner;
Rights: Friedrich Themel
Orders to: Hauptstr 96a, D-1110 Ekazent Simmering
Parent Company: Jugend und Volk Verlagsgesellschaft mbH, Austria (qv)
Subject: Juveniles
1985: 308 titles *Founded:* 1921
ISBN Publisher's Prefix: 3-8113

Jugenddienst-Verlag, see Peter Hammer Verlag

Axel **Juncker**-Verlag Jacobi KG, Neusserstr 3, D-8000 Munich 40 Tel: (089) 360960 Fax: (089) 36096258
Man Dirs: Karl Ernst Tielebier-Langenscheidt, Dr Florian Langenscheidt;
Sales Dir: Peter Haering; *Sales, Promotion:* through Langenscheidt KG (qv); *Rights & Permissions:* Manfred Überall
Subjects: Reference, Dictionaries
Founded: 1902
Miscellaneous: Firm is a member of the Langenscheidt Group (qv)
ISBN Publisher's Prefix: 3-558

Junior International, Postfach 285, D-7300 Esslingen (Located at: Liebigstr 1-11, D-7301 Deizisau) Tel: (07153) 22011 Cable Add: Verlag Schreiber Telex: 7266880 jfs d
Associate Company: Verlag J F Schreiber GmbH (qv)

Jungjohann Verlagsgesellschaft mbH+*, Breslauerstr 5, D-7107 Neckarsulm Tel: (07132) 8013
Man Dir: Dr med Hartmut Jungjohann
Orders to: Lingenbrink, August-Schanz-Str, D-6000 Frankfurt am Main
Subjects: Medicine, Pharmacology, Natural Healing Practices, Cartoons
1985: 93 titles *Founded:* 1965
ISBN Publisher's Prefixes: 3-88454, 3-921689

Junius Verlag GmbH, Postfach 500745, D-2000 Hamburg 50 (Located at: Stresemannstr 375) Tel: (040) 892599
Man Dir: Rolf Wichmann
Subjects: German and International Politics, History, Social Sciences, the Workers' Movement, Trade Unions, East Europe and the USSR, Periodical
1987-88: 25 titles *Founded:* 1979
ISBN Publisher's Prefix: 3-88506

Juventa Verlag GmbH, Ehretstr 3, D-6940 Weinheim Tel: (06201) 17373
Man Dir: Lothar Schweim; *Publicity:* Margarethe Gräber
Associate Company: Deutsches Jugendinstitut (qv)
Subjects: Social Science, Education, Psychology, History
1986: 30 titles *Founded:* 1953
ISBN Publisher's Prefix: 3-7799

K L V, see Konkret Literatur Verlag GmbH

Ernst **Kabel** Verlag GmbH+, Postfach 605320, D-2000 Hamburg 60 (Located at: Sierichstr 21)
Man Dirs, Editorial: Joachim Jessen, Detlef Lerch; *Sales:* Heike Latendorf; *Production, Publicity:* Detlef Lerch; *Rights & Permissions:* Joachim Jessen
Subjects: Non-fiction History, Current Events, Documentary, Biography, Psychology, Maritime, Fiction
Founded: 1977
ISBN Publisher's Prefix: 3-8225

Verlagsgesellschaft Gerhard **Kaffke** mbH*, Postfach 371, D-8750 Aschaffenburg Tel: (06021) 28794
Man Dir: Bernhard Gregor
Subjects: Theology, Religion, Paperbacks
Founded: 1955
ISBN Publisher's Prefix: 3-87391

Chr **Kaiser** Verlag GmbH, Lilienstr 70, D-8000 Munich 80 Tel: (089) 483014
Dir: Manfred Weber
Subjects: Theology, Religion
Founded: 1845
ISBN Publisher's Prefix: 3-459

Verlag Ferdinand **Kamp** GmbH & Co KG*, Postfach 101309, D-4630 Bochum 1 (Located at: Widumestr 6, Bochum)

Tel: (0234) 15071
Subjects: Textbooks, Reference, Dictionaries, Education, Non-fiction, Paperbacks, Periodicals
Miscellaneous: Firm is a member of vgs — Verlagsgesellschaft mbH & Co KG (qv)
ISBN Publisher's Prefix: 3-592

S **Karger** GmbH Verlag für Medizin und Naturwissenschaften*, Angerhofstr 9, Postfach 1724, D-8034 Germering, Munich Tel: (089) 844021 Cable Add: Kargermedbooks Telex: 524865
Man Dir: W Kunz
Parent Company: S Karger AG, Switzerland (qv)
Subjects: Medicine, Psychology, Natural Science
Bookshop: Karger-Buchhandlung Ausstellung und Vertrieb internationaler medizinischer Fachliteratur (at above address)

Karl-May-Verlag, Joachim Schmid & Co*, Karl-May-Str 8, D-8600 Bamberg Tel: (0951) 54051
Main Publicity Dir: Joachim Schmid; *Sales Dir:* Lothar Schmid; *Production Dir:* Roland Schmid; *Rights & Permissions:* Joachim, Lothar and Roland Schmid
Subject: Children's Fiction
Founded: 1913
ISBN Publisher's Prefix: 3-7802

Karo-Bücher, an imprint of A Weichert Verlag (qv)

Kartographischer Verlag Wagner & Co KG, see Wagner

Kartographisches Institut Bertelsmann, Postfach 5555, D-4830 Gütersloh 1 (Located at Carl Bertelsmannstr 161, Gütersloh) Tel: (05241) 801 Telex: 933832
Dir: Karlheinz Thieme
Parent Company: Verlagsgruppe Bertelsmann GmbH (qv for associate companies)
Subject: Atlases

Verlag **Katholisches Bibelwerk** GmbH*, Silberburgstr 121A, D-7000 Stuttgart Tel: (0711) 626003
Dir: Martin Günther
Subject: Religious literature on practical aspects of Catholic Bible work in Federal Republic of Germany, Austria and Switzerland
Miscellaneous: Company is a member of AMB (qv)
ISBN Publisher's Prefix: 3-460

Katzmann-Verlag KG, Postfach 1827, D-7400 Tübingen 1 (Located at: Im Kaeppele 17, D-7408 Kusterdingen) Tel: (07071) 34858 Cable Add: Katzmann Verlag
Man Dir, Production, Publicity, Rights & Permissions: Dr Volker Katzmann; *Sales Dir:* Sibylle Katzmann
Associate Company: Heliopolis-Verlag Ewald Katzmann (at above address)
Subjects: Social Pedagogics, Social Work, Youth Work, Adult Education, Marriage and Family Counselling, Theology, Art, Religion, Periodical
Founded: 1945
ISBN Publisher's Prefix: 3-7805

Verlag Ernst **Kaufmann** GmbH+, Alleestr 2, Postfach 2208, D-7630 Lahr/Schwarzwald Tel: (07821) 26083 Telex: 0754973
Man Dir: Heinz Kaufmann; *Chief Editor:* Renate Schupp; *Public Relations, Distribution:* Michael Jacob
Subjects: Religious Education (books, materials), Children's
Founded: 1816

Miscellaneous: Member of Verlagsring Religionsunterricht (VRU = Religious Instruction Publishing Circle)
ISBN Publisher's Prefix: 3-7806

Kaynar GmbH*, Hansastr 86, D-4100 Duisburg 1 Tel: (0203) 331795
Publicity, Rights & Permissions: C Fuat Hendek; *Editorial:* Serap Sekercioğlu, Brigitte Spelliken
Subjects: Belles Lettres, Children's, Encyclopaedias, Schoolbooks in German and Turkish
Bookshop: At above address
1985: 23 titles *Founded:* 1973
ISBN Publisher's Prefix: 3-88689

Antiquariat und Verlag **Keip** GmbH, Hainer Weg 46-48, D-6000 Frankfurt am Main 70 Tel: (069) 614011 Telex: 411893 keip d Fax: (069) 627548
Publisher: Ulrich Keip; *Manager and Office Chief:* Johann Holler
Subjects: Law, Economics, Social Sciences, History
Founded: 1967
Miscellaneous: Also antiquarian bookseller

Franckh'sche Verlagshandlung, W **Keller** & Co, see Franckh'sche

Kessler Verlag für Sprachmethodik+, Plittersdorfer Str 91, Postfach 201351, D-5300 Bonn 2 Tel: (0228) 363004
Publisher: Hans-Peter Dürr-Auster
Subjects: Primary, Secondary and University Textbooks, Educational Materials, Languages
Founded: 1953
ISBN Publisher's Prefix: 3-8018

Keysersche Verlagsbuchhandlung GmbH, Rosenheimer Str 12, D-8000 Munich 80 Tel: (089) 4160090
Publishers: Heinz Friedrich Bläsing, Hermann Farnung, Klaus Rudloff; *Advertising:* Maria-Luise Hopp
Subject: Art
Founded: 1777
ISBN Publisher's Prefix: 3-87405

Kibu-Verlag GmbH*, Gerhart-Hauptmann-Str 12a, D-5750 Menden 2 Tel: (02373) 84588 Telex: 8202855
Dirs: Kunibert Birnkraut, Erhard Tamm
Subjects: Children's, Juveniles, Special Editions

Johannes **Kiefel** Verlag*, Linderhauser Str 60, D-5600 Wuppertal 2 Tel: (0202) 642084 Cable Add: Kiefel, Wuppertal-2
Dir: Ingeborg Kiefel
Subjects: Religion, Juveniles, Textbooks
Founded: 1920
ISBN Publisher's Prefix: 3-7811

Friedrich **Kiehl** Verlag GmbH, Pfaustr 13, Postfach 210747, D-6700 Ludwigshafen Tel: (0621) 695041 Telex: 0464810
Dir: Ernst-Otto Kleyboldt; *Sales Manager:* Regina König
Parent Company: Verlag Neue Wirtschafts-Briefe GmbH (qv)
Subjects: Law, Economics, Commerce, Banking
ISBN Publisher's Prefix: 3-470

Verlag **Kiepenheuer** und Witsch+, Rondorfer Str 5, D-5000 Köln-Marienburg Tel: (0221) 376850 Cable Add: Kiepenbücher Cologne Telex: 8881142 kiwi
Man Dir: Dr Reinhold Neven Du Mont; *Editorial:* Bärbel Flad, Erika Stegmann, Renate Matthaei, Helge Malchow; *Sales:* Heinz Biehn; *Foreign Rights & Permissions:* Traudel Jansen
Subjects: General Fiction, Belles Lettres, Biography, History, Social Science, Self-help

1985: 60 titles *1986:* 65 titles *Founded:* 1948
ISBN Publisher's Prefix: 3-462

Kilda Verlag*, Münsterstr 71, D-4402 Greven/Westfalen Tel: (0251) 36229 Cable Add: Kildagreven
Man Dir: Mr Pölking

Kindler Verlag GmbH, Rauchstr 9-11, D-8000 Munich 80 Tel: (089) 92710 Telex: 522707
Man Dirs: Dr Karl Blessing, Rüdiger Hildebrandt; *Editorial:* Hanna Kobbe, Dr Rolf Cyriax; *Foreign Rights:* Alice Meyer; *Publicity Manager:* Ulrike Netenjakob
Parent Company: Verlagsgruppe Georg von Holtzbrinck, Gänsheidestr 26, D-7000 Stuttgart 1
Subjects: Biography, History, Politics, Reference, Religion, Low- & High-priced Paperbacks, Psychology, General & Social Science, Encyclopaedias
Founded: 1951
ISBN Publisher's Prefix: 3-463

Klartext Verlagsgesellschaft mbH, Viehofer Pl 1, D-4300 Essen 1 Tel: (0201) 234538
Man Dirs: Ulrich Homann Ludger Classen, Kristiane Kremme; *Editorial:* Ludger Classen, Ulrich Homann; *Sales, Publicity:* Barbara Kirfel, Tina Bensch; *Production:* Frank Münschke, Kristiane Kremmer; *Rights & Permissions:* Ludger Classen
Subjects: History, Literature of the Ruhr, Social Politics, Self-help, New German Writing
1985: 15 titles *1986:* 24 titles *Founded:* 1982
ISBN Publisher's Prefix: 3-88474

Klasing und Co GmbH, Siekerwall 21, Postfach 4809, D-4800 Bielefeld 1 Tel: (0521) 5590 Cable Add: Buchklasing Bielefeld Telex: 932934 Dekla
Publishers: Konrad-Wilhelm Delius, Kurt Delius; *Sales & Publicity Manager:* Wilhelm Meyerhenke; *Rights & Permissions:* Ilsemarie Steinbrinker
Parent Company: Delius, Klasing & Co (qv)
Subjects: Yachting, Motor Boats
Bookshop: At above address
ISBN Publisher's Prefix: 3-87412

Kunstverlag Dr Rudolf Georgi, Waldemar **Klein**, see Georgi

Klens-Verlag GmbH, Prinz-Georg-Str 44, Postfach 320620, D-4000 Düsseldorf 30 Tel: (0211) 4499250
Publisher: Viktor Nolden
Subjects: Popular Christian Aids, Juveniles, and Youth Training
1986: 8 titles
ISBN Publisher's Prefix: 3-87309

Ernst **Klett** Verlag*, Rotebühlstr 77, Postfach 809, D-7000 Stuttgart 1 Tel: (0711) 66720 Telex: 722225 klet d Fax: (0711) 628053
Publisher: Michael Klett; *Publicity Manager:* Egon Schramm; *Foreign Relations:* Jürgen Meissner; *Rights and Export Sales:* Joachim Lange
Orders to: Stuttgarter Verlagskontor, Rotebühlstr 77, Postfach 809, D-7000 Stuttgart 1
Associate Companies: Klett-Cotta Verlag (qv), Stuttgarter Verlagskontor (both in Federal Republic of Germany); ÖBV — Klett-Cotta Verlagsgesellschaft mbH, Austria; Verlag Klett und Balmer & Co, Switzerland (qv)
Subjects: Textbooks and Educational Materials for all school subjects from Primary to College level, German as a foreign language, Pedagogics, Didactics
Founded: 1844

Miscellaneous: Klett is a member of TR-Verlagsunion GmbH (qv)
ISBN Publisher's Prefix: 3-12

Klett-Cotta Verlag*, Rotebühlstr 77, Postfach 809, D-7000 Stuttgart 1 Tel: (0711) 66720 Telex: 722225 klet d Fax: (0711) 628053
Man Dir: Michael Klett; *Editorial:* Dr Arbogast; *Foreign Relations:* Jürgen Meissner; *Rights:* Roland Knappe; *Export Sales:* Joachim Lange
Orders to: Stuttgarter Verlagskontor, Rotebühlstr 77, Postfach 809, D-7000 Stuttgart 1
Associate Companies: Ernst Klett (qv), Stuttgarter Verlags Kontor (both in Federal Republic of Germany); ÖBV — Klett-Cotta Verlagsgesellschaft mbH, Austria; Verlag Klett und Balmer & Co, Switzerland (qv)
Imprints: Hobbit Presse, Konzepte der Humanwissenschaften
Subjects: Fiction, Art, Linguistics, Psychoanalysis, Psychotherapy, Psychology, Education, Philosophy, Mythology, Ecology, History, Politics, Sociology
1985: 120 titles *Founded:* 1977
Miscellaneous: Company now incorporates Verlag Helmut Küpper and Verlag J G Cotta'sche Buchhandlung
ISBN Publisher's Prefixes: 3-12, 3-608

Klinkhardt und Biermann Verlagsbuchhandlung GmbH+, Rosenheimer Str 12, D-8000 Munich 80 Tel: (089) 4160090
Managers: Heinz Friedrich Bläsing, Hermann Farnung; *Trade Manager:* Maria-Luise Hopp
Subjects: Art, Antiques, Numismatics
Founded: 1907
ISBN Publisher's Prefix: 3-7814

v **Kloeden** KG+*, Wielandstr 24, D-1000 Berlin 15 Tel: (030) 8819617
Man Dir, Rights & Permissions: Friedrich v Kloeden; *Editorial:* Uta Grabe v Kloeden
Subjects: Children's, Educational, Reference
Bookshops: Schlüterstr 49, Berlin 12; Lindenstr 5, Peine; Wilhelmstr, Lüdenscheid; also in Cologne, Hamburg, Krefeld
Founded: 1967
ISBN Publisher's Prefix: 3-920564

Erika **Klopp** Verlag GmbH, Kurfürstendamm 126, Postfach 310829, D-1000 Berlin 31 Tel: (030) 8911008
Publisher: Horst Meyer; *Rights & Permissions:* Katharina Janike
Subject: Juveniles
1985: 13 titles *Founded:* 1925
ISBN Publisher's Prefix: 3-7817

Vittorio **Klostermann** GmbH, Frauenlobstr 22, Postfach 900601, D-6000 Frankfurt am Main 90 Tel: (069) 774011
Man Dirs: Michael Klostermann, Vittorio E Klostermann
Subjects: Philosophy, Bibliography, Romanistics, University Textbooks, General Science, History, Art, High-priced Paperbacks
Founded: 1930
ISBN Publisher's Prefix: 3-465

Ehrenfried **Klotz** Verlag, now incorporated in Vandenhoeck und Ruprecht (qv)

Fritz **Knapp** Verlag GmbH+, Junghofstr 16, Postfach 111151, D-6000 Frankfurt am Main 11 Tel: (069) 280151 Cable Add: Schauinsland Telex: 411397
Man Dirs: Alfons Binz, Peter Muthesius; *Editorial:* Peter Muthesius; *Marketing, Sales, Publicity:* Werner Scholz;

Production, Rights & Permissions: Alfons Binz
Associate Company: Verlag Helmut Richardi GmbH
Subjects: Finance, Economics, Economic Science, Reference, High-priced Paperbacks, Specialist Dictionaries, German Law in English/French Translation
Founded: 1949
ISBN Publisher's Prefix: 3-7819

Wilhelm **Knapp** Verlag*, Postfach 1135, D-4000 Düsseldorf 1 (Located at: Druckzentrum Düsseldorf, Zülpicher Str 10, D-4000 Düsseldorf 11) Tel: (0211) 5050 Telex: 8582495
Chairman and Man Dir: Dr Joseph Schaffrath; *Man Dirs:* Werner Gutzki, Dr Hans-Dieter Baumgart; *Publishing Dir:* Dr Manfred Lotsch; *Production, Promotion:* Helmut Schwanen
Parent Company: Droste Verlag GmbH (qv)
Subjects: Photography, Cinematography, Video
Founded: 1838
ISBN Publisher's Prefix: 3-87420

Droemer **Knaur** Verlag, see Droemersche Verlagsanstalt

Albrecht **Knaus** Verlag+, Neumarkterstr 18, D-8000 Munich 80 Tel: (089) 431890 Cable Add: Knausbooks München Telex: 523259
Man Partners: Dr Albrecht Knaus, Jürgen Kreuzhage; *Production:* Peter Sturm; *Sales:* Verlagsgruppe Bertelsmann GmbH (qv); *Publicity:* Gudrun Rohe
Orders to: VVA (Vereinigte Verlagsauslieferung GmbH), Postfach 7777, D-4830 Gütersloh 1
Parent Company: Verlagsgruppe Bertelsmann GmbH (qv)
Subjects: Fiction, Memoirs, History, Art
Founded: 1978
ISBN Publisher's Prefix: 3-8135

Verlag Josef **Knecht**-Carolusdruckerei GmbH, Liebfrauenberg 37, D-6000 Frankfurt am Main 1 Tel: (069) 281767
Dirs: Dr H Herder, Dr Marianne Regnier
Subjects: General Fiction, Paperbacks, Religion, Social Science, Philosophy, Non-fiction
Founded: 1946
ISBN Publisher's Prefix: 3-7820

Knorr und Hirth Verlag GmbH, D-3167 Ahrbeck vor Hannover Tel: (05136) 5501 Cable Add: Knorrhirth Ahrbeck
Man Dir: Berthold Fricke
Subjects: Art, Geography, Travel Guides, Almanacs (editions also in English, French, Dutch, Italian, Spanish and Japanese — several bilingual editions)
Founded: 1894
ISBN Publisher's Prefix: 3-7821

Verlagsanstalt Alexander **Koch** GmbH*, Postfach 3081, D-7000 Stuttgart 1 (Located at: Fasanenweg 18, D-7022 Leinfelden-Echterdingen 1) Tel: (0711) 75911 Telex: 7-255609 drw d
Man Dirs: Karl-Heinz Weinbrenner, L Drabarczyk; *Manager, Rights & Permissions:* Dr Erwin Schmid; *Editorial:* Eberhard Höhn, Rolf Sellin
Subjects: Architecture, Interior Decoration, Building Technology, Periodicals
Founded: 1890
ISBN Publisher's Prefix: 3-87422

K F **Koehler** Verlag*, Postfach 800620, D-7000 Stuttgart 80 (Located at: Schockenriedstr 39) Tel: (0711) 78601 Telex: 7255684 knov d
Dir: Till Grupp
Subjects: Humanities, History, Politics, Law, Social Science, Geography
Founded: 1789
ISBN Publisher's Prefix: 3-87425

Koehlers Verlagsgesellschaft+, Steintorwall 17, Postfach 2352, D-4900 Herford Tel: (05221) 59910 Cable Add: Koehlers Vlg D-4900 Herford Telex: 0934801 maxvg d
Publisher: Gerhard Bollmann; *Production:* Heinz Kameier; *Sales:* Hans-Focko Koehler; *Publicity:* Lütz Baukert
Associate Companies: Maximilian-Verlag, E S Mittler und Sohn GmbH, Verlag Offene Worte (all members of Maximilian-Verlagsgruppe — qv); Verlag Europäische Wehrkunde
Subjects: Fiction and Non-fiction, Shipping, Shipbuilding, Maritime and Offshore, Periodicals
ISBN Publisher's Prefix: 3-7822

Verlag Valentin **Koerner** GmbH, Hermann-Sielcken-Str 36, Postfach 304, D-7570 Baden Baden Tel: (07221) 22423
Publisher: Valentin Koerner
ISBN Publisher's Prefix: 3-87320

Verlag W **Kohlhammer** GmbH+*, Hessbrühlstr 69, Postfach 800430, D-7000 Stuttgart 80 Tel: (0711) 78631 Cable Add: Kohlhammer Stuttgart Telex: 07255820
Man Dirs: Dr Jürgen Gutbrod, Günter Haberland, Hans-Joachim Nagel; *Sales Dir:* Gerd W Ludwig; *Editorial Dir, Rights & Permissions:* Dr Alexander Schweickert
Subsidiary Companies: Deutscher Gemeindeverlag GmbH (qv); Grote'sche Verlagsbuch-handlung KG (qv); Kohlhammer und Wallishauser GmbH, Hechingen; W Kohlhammer Druckerei GmbH & Co, Stuttgart
Branch Offs: Berlin, Cologne, Mainz
Subjects: History, Art, Philosophy, Humanities, Religion, Theology, Law, Public Administration, Linguistics, Literary History, Economics, Natural Sciences, Medicine, Engineering, Electronics, Architecture, Travel
1985: approx 400 titles *Founded:* 1866
ISBN Publisher's Prefix: 3-17

Kohl's Technischer Verlag Erwin Kohl GmbH & Co KG*, Emil-Sulzbach-Str 12, Postfach 970115, D-6000 Frankfurt am Main 97 Tel: (069) 778410/776513
Associate Company: Frankfurter Fachverlag Michael Kohl GmbH & Co KG (qv)
Subjects: Civil & Mechanical Engineering
ISBN Publisher's Prefix: 3-87430

Komar, Oberaustr 1, Postfach 1132, D-8200 Rosenheim Tel: (08031) 17011 Telex: 0525793
Subjects: Juveniles, Psychology, Sports

Verlag **Kommentator**, Zeppelinallee 43, Postfach 970148, D-6000 Frankfurt am Main Tel: (069) 7930090
Man Dir: Dr Clemens J B Sandmann; *Editorial:* Gunter Herz; *Sales, Publicity:* Friedrich-Wilhelm Bremer
Associate Company: Alfred Metzner (qv)
Subjects: Law, Taxation
Miscellaneous: Firm is a member of the Kluwer Group, Netherlands (qv)
ISBN Publisher's Prefix: 3-7824

Verlag **Königshausen und Neumann**, Leistenstr 3, Postfach 6007, D-8700 Würzburg Tel: (0931) 76401
Man Dirs: Dr Johannes Königshausen, Dr Thomas Neumann
Subjects: Philosophy, Literary Science, Pedagogy, Sociology, Psychology, Economics, Archaeology, Law
1985: 46 titles *Founded:* 1979
ISBN Publisher's Prefix: 3-88479

Konkordia Verlag GmbH, Eisenbahnstr 31-33, Postfach 1240, D-7580 Bühl/Baden Tel: (07223) 28040 Telex: 78733 Fax: (07223) 280445
Subject: Textbooks
ISBN Publisher's Prefix: 3-7826

KLV **Konkret** Literatur Verlag GmbH*, Osterstr 124, D-2000 Hamburg 19 Tel: (040) 4910041 Telex: 2164613 konk d
Man Dir: Dr Dorothee Gremliza
Subjects: Politics, Alternative Medicine, Feminism, Current Affairs, Third World
Founded: 1978
ISBN Publisher's Prefix: 3-922144

Anton H **Konrad** Verlag*, Schulstr 5, Postfach 1206, D-7912 Weissenhorn Tel: (07309) 2657
Subjects: Arts, History
ISBN Publisher's Prefix: 3-87437

Konzepte der Humanwissenschaften, an imprint of Klett-Cotta Verlag (qv)

Bergstadtverlag Wilhelm Gottlieb **Korn** GmbH, an associate company of Jan Thorbecke Verlag GmbH & Co (qv)

Kösel-Verlag GmbH & Co+, Flüggenstr 2, D-8000 Munich 19 Tel: (089) 1790080 Cable Add: Köselverlag Munich Telex: 5215492 kvmu d
Man Dir: Dr Christoph Wild; *Production:* Friedhelm Jochems; *Sales:* Dieter Amman; *Rights & Permissions, Public Relations:* Ingrid Fink; *Advertising:* Marianne Schmid-Reichel
Subjects: Pedagogy, Philosophy, Religion, Educational Materials, Psychology, Textbooks, Social Science
Founded: 1593
Miscellaneous: Firm is member of TR-Verlagsunion GmbH (qv)
ISBN Publisher's Prefix: 3-466

Karin **Kramer** Verlag+, Postfach 440417, D-1000 Berlin-Neukölln 44 (Located at: Braunschweiger Str 26) Tel: (030) 6845055/6842598
Editorial and Publicity: Bernd Kramer
Subjects: Politics, Art, Literature, Education, Psychology, Anarchist Literature
Founded: 1970
ISBN Publisher's Prefix: 3-87956

Karl **Krämer** Verlag GmbH und Co+, Schulze-Delitzsch-Str 15, Postfach 800650, D-7000 Stuttgart 80 Tel: (0711) 620893 Cable Add: Fachbuchkraemer Stuttgart Telex: 722203 kkbau d
Man Dir, Rights & Permissions: Karl H Krämer; *Production, Publicity:* Gudrun Zimmerle
Associate Company: Verlag Karl Krämer & Co, Switzerland (qv)
Subjects: Town Planning, Architecture, Building Construction, Sociology
Bookshop: Fachbuchhandlung Karl Krämer, Rotebühlstr 40, Postfach 808, D-7000 Stuttgart 1
1986: 16 titles *Founded:* 1930
ISBN Publisher's Prefix: 3-7828

Dr Waldemar **Kramer** Verlagsbuchhandlung+, Bornheimer Landwehr 57a, Postfach 600445, D-6000 Frankfurt am Main 60 Tel: (069) 449045
Publishers: Dr Waldemar Kramer, Dr Henriette Kramer
Subjects: Science and Natural History, Biology, History, Art Education, Psychology, Geography, Nature Study, Environment, Periodicals
1985: 20 titles *1986:* 20 titles *Founded:* 1939
ISBN Publisher's Prefix: 3-7829

FEDERAL REPUBLIC OF GERMANY 153

Vereinigte Fachverlage **Krausskopf** Ingenieur Digest GmbH, Lessingstr 12, Postfach 2760, D-6500 Mainz Tel: (06131) 6090 Cable Add: Ver Fachverlage Telex: 4187752 Fax: (06131) 609100
Dir: Manfred Grunenberg
Parent Company: P P Cahensly, Limburg
Subjects: Technical Books, Periodicals
Founded: 1937
ISBN Publisher's Prefix: 3-7830

Buch- und Bildverlag W **Kremnitz**, see Lacus

Kreuz Verlag+*, Breitwiesenstr 30, Postfach 800669, D-7000 Stuttgart 80 Tel: (0711) 7800281
Man Dir: Dieter Breitsohl; *Editorial:* Johannes Thiele, Hildegunde Wöller; *Rights & Permissions:* Barbara Dressler; *Production:* Brigitte Gnieser; *Publicity:* Christa Altmann; *Sales:* Klaus Vahlbruch
Subjects: Reference, Religion, Education, Juveniles, Psychology, Social Science, Periodicals
1985: 33 titles *Founded:* 1945
ISBN Publisher's Prefix: 3-7831

Kriminalistik Verlag GmbH, Postfach 102640, D-6900 Heidelberg (Located at: im Weiher 10) Tel: (06621) 489250 Telex: 04-61727 huedh
Associate Companies: R v Decker's Verlag G Schenck GmbH (qv); C F Müller Juristischer Verlag GmbH (qv)
Subject: Criminology, Periodical

Alfred **Kröner** Verlag, Reinsburgstr 56, Postfach 1109, D-7000 Stuttgart 1 Tel: (0711) 620221
Man Dirs: Arno Klemm, Walter Kohrs
Subjects: Philosophy, Religion, Culture, Psychology, Pedagogy, Sociology, Economics, Law, Politics, History, Literature, Linguistics, Art, Music, Theatre, Reference (especially Dictionaries, Lexicons)
Founded: 1904
ISBN Publisher's Prefix: 3-520

Wolfgang **Kruger** Verlag*, Geleitsstr 25, Postfach 700480, D-6000 Frankfurt am Main 70 Tel: (069) 60620 Telex: 0412410
Man Dirs: Monika Schoeller, Karl-Michael Mehnert, Dr Emmanuel A Wiemer; *Sales, Publicity:* Ulrich Fritz, Frank Scheffter; *Production:* Wilfried Meiner
Parent Company: S Fischer Verlag GmbH (qv)
Subjects: General Fiction and Non-fiction
ISBN Publisher's Prefix: 3-8105

Kübler und Akselrad Verlag+, Hauptstr 190, D-6900 Heidelberg Tel: (06221) 13030
Dir: Michael Akselrad
Orders to: VVA (Vereinigte Verlagsauslieferung GmbH), Postfach 7777, D-4830 Gütersloh 1
Subjects: Literature, Non-fiction
1985: 10 titles *Founded:* 1972
ISBN Publisher's Prefix: 3-921265

Kubon und Sagner, see Verlag Otto Sagner

Wilhelm **Kumm** Verlag, Tulpenhofstr 45, D-6050 Offenbach am Main Tel: (0611) 884349 Cable Add: Kummverlag
Proprietor, Man Dir: Wilhelm Kumm
Subjects: Belles Lettres, Poetry
Founded: 1967
ISBN Publisher's Prefix: 3-7836

Kümmerley und Frey, see J Fink — Kummerley und Frey

Kunst und Wissen Erich Bieber OHG, Wilhelmstr 4, Postfach 102844, D-7000 Stuttgart 10, Tel: (0711) 241152 Cable Add: Kunstwissen Telex: 721929
Publishers: Erich, Jürgen and Wolfgang Bieber
Subjects: Technical Textbooks
ISBN Publisher's Prefix: 3-87953

Kunst und Wohnen Verlag, see Dr Wolfgang Schwarze Verlag

Deutscher Verlag für **Kunstwissenschaft**, see Deutscher Verlag

Verlag Helmut **Küpper**, now incorporated in Klett-Cotta Verlag (qv)

Kyrios-Verlag GmbH*, Luckengasse 8, Postfach 1740, D-8050 Freising Tel: (08161) 5527
Dir: Ursula Blum; *Sales Manager:* Eveline Kamm
Subjects: Religion, Social Work, Periodicals
Bookshop: Kyrios Buch-Kunst, Untere Hauptstr 33, D-8050 Freising
1985: 13 titles *Founded:* 1916
ISBN Publisher's Prefix: 3-7838

L N-Verlag Lübeck, Lübecker Nachrichten GmbH+, Königstr 53-57, Postfach 2238, D-2400 Lübeck 1 Tel: (0451) 1441 Telex: 026801
Man Dir: Charles Coleman; *Sales Dir:* Elmar Bruns
Subjects: Guidebooks
1986: 7 titles *1987:* 7 titles
ISBN Publisher's Prefix: 3-87498

Ambro **Lacus**, Buch- und Bildverlag W Kremnitz*, Frieding-Hurten-Str 25, D-8138 Andechs Tel: (08152) 1332 Cable Add: Kremnitz-Frieding
Man Dir: Walter Kremnitz
Subjects: Illustrated foreign travel books, Folk Stories and Legends, Legal and Historical Reference, Botany
Founded: 1974
ISBN Publisher's Prefix: 3-921445

Laetare, see Burckhardthaus-Laetare Verlag GmbH

Lahn-Verlag, Wiesbadener Str 1, Postfach 1461, D-6250 Limburg an der Lahn 1 Tel: (06431) 40030 Telex: 0484764 palan d
Publisher: Engelbert Tauscher; *Editorial:* Ursula Mock; *Publicity Manager:* Werner Krämer
Subjects: Religion, Philosophy, Education
Founded: 1900
ISBN Publisher's Prefix: 3-7840

Lambertus Verlag GmbH, Wölflinstr 4, Postfach 1026, D-7800 Freiburg im Breisgau Tel: (0761) 31566
Man Dirs: Gerhild Neugart, Fritz Boll
Subjects: Social Work, Social Security
Bookshop: Freiburger Bücherdienst (at above address)
1985: 24 titles *Founded:* 1898
ISBN Publisher's Prefix: 3-7841

Lamuv Verlag GmbH+, Martin Str 5, D-5303 Bornheim 3 Tel: (02227) 2111 Fax: (02227) 6885
Man Dir, Rights & Permissions: René Böll; *Editorial:* Karl-Klaus Rabe; *Sales:* Peter Flier
Subjects: Literature, Third World, Near East, Politics
Founded: 1976
ISBN Publisher's Prefixes: 3-921521, 3-88977

Landbuch-Verlag GmbH*, Kabelkamp 6, Postfach 160, D-3000 Hanover Tel: (0511) 678060 Cable Add: Landbuch Hanover Telex: 921169
Man Dir, Production, Rights & Permissions: Friedrich Butenholz; *Sales, Publicity:* Willi Ludwig Kröck
Subjects: Arts, Agriculture, Animal Breeding, Forestry, Sports, Nature, Hunting, Wildlife, Periodicals
Founded: 1945
ISBN Publisher's Prefix: 3-7842

Landsberger Verlagsanstalt Martin Neumeyer, Museumstr 14, Postfach 1452, D-8910 Landsberg Tel: (08191) 4055 Fax: (08191) 4055
Subjects: History, Hobbies, Mass Media, How-to, Regional Interest
ISBN Publisher's Prefix: 3-920216

Verlag Peter **Lang** GmbH, Eschborner Landstr 42–50, D-6000 Frankfurt am Main 90 Tel: (069) 7893041 Telex: 4189343 lang d
Man Dirs: Peter Lang, Rainer Jurischka
Parent Company: Verlag Peter Lang AG, Switzerland (qv)
Subjects: Arts, Sciences
1985: 744 titles *1986:* 859 titles *Founded:* 1970
ISBN Publisher's Prefix: 3-8204

Albert **Langen-Georg Müller Verlag**, Thomas-Wimmer-Ring 11, D-8000 Munich 22 Tel: (089) 2350080 Telex: 05215045
Man Dir: Dr Herbert Fleissner; *Editorial:* Dr Bernhard Struckmeyer; *Sales:* Gisela Weichert; *Publicity:* Dr Brigitte Sinhuber; *Rights & Permissions:* Dorothea Estermann
Subjects: General Fiction, Theatre, Reportage, Humour, Current Affairs
Founded: 1897
Miscellaneous: Firm is a member of Buckverlage Ullstein Langen-Müller/Herbig (qv)
ISBN Publisher's Prefix: 3-7844

Langenscheidt KG, Neusser Str 3, Postfach 401120, D-8000 Munich 40 Tel: (089) 360960 Cable Add: Langenscheidt Munich Telex: Munich 5215379 lkgm d Fax: (089) 36096258
Also: An der Langenscheidtbrücke, D-1000 Berlin 62
Man Dirs: Karl Ernst Tielebier-Langenscheidt, Andreas Langenscheidt, Dr Florian Langenscheidt; *Editorial:* Dr Walter Voigt, Dr Wolfgang Wieter, Dr Paul Rühl, Detlev Wagner; *Production:* Helmut Wahl; *Sales Dir:* Peter Haering; *Advertising Dir:* Klaus Ferber; *Export Dir:* Uwe Cordts; *Rights & Permissions:* Manfred Überall
Subsidiary Companies: Langenscheidt-Verlag, Austria (qv); Langenscheidt AG, Switzerland (qv); Langenscheidt Publishers Inc, 46-35 54 Rd, Maspeth, New York, NY 11378, USA
Subjects: Foreign Languages, German for Foreigners, Language Guides, Dictionaries, Textbooks, Audiovisual Materials
Founded: 1856
Miscellaneous: Firm is a member of the Langenscheidt Group and a member of TR- Verlagsunion GmbH (qqv for associate companies)
ISBN Publisher's Prefix: 3-468

The **Langenscheidt Group**, Neusser Str 3, Postfach 401120, D-8000 Munich 40 Tel: (089) 360960 Fax: (089) 36096258
The Group consists of: Langenscheidt KG (qv); Langenscheidt-Longman GmbH (qv); Langenscheidt-Hachette GmbH (qv); Polyglott-Verlag Dr Bolte KG (qv); Humboldt-Taschenbuchverlag Jacobi KG (qv); Mentor-Verlag Dr Ramdohr KG (qv); Axel Juncker-Verlag Jacobi KG (qv); Karl Baedeker GmbH (all in Federal Republic of Germany); Langenscheidt Publishers Inc, American Map Corp, Hagstrom Map Inc (all at 46-35 54 Rd, Maspeth, NY 11378, USA); Creative Sales Corp, 762 West Algonquin Rd, Arlington Heights, IL 6005, USA

Langenscheidt-Hachette GmbH, Neusser Str 3, Postfach 401120, D-8000 Munich 40 Tel: (089) 360960 Cable Add: Langenscheidt Munich Telex: 5215379 lkgm d Fax: (089) 36096258
Man Dirs: Karl Ernst Tielebier-Langenscheidt, Marc Moingeon; *Editorial:* Brigitte Peters; *Sales & Promotion:* Through Langenscheidt KG (qv)
Associate Companies: See entry for The Langenscheidt Group, also for Hachette SA, France
Subjects: French for German-speaking people
Founded: 1977
Miscellaneous: Firm is a member of the Langenscheidt Group (qv)
ISBN Publisher's Prefix: 3-595

Langenscheidt-Longman GmbH, Neusser Str 3, Postfach 401120, D-8000 Munich 40 Tel: (089) 360960 Cable Add: Langenscheidt Munich Telex: 5215379 lkgm d Fax: (089) 36096258
Man Dirs: Karl Ernst Tielebier-Langenscheidt, Paula Kahn; *Publishing Executive:* Uwe Mäder; *Sales & Promotion:* through Langenscheidt KG
Associate Companies: See entry for The Langenscheidt Group, also for the Longman Group UK Ltd, UK
Subjects: English Language Teaching
Founded: 1972
Miscellaneous: Firm is a member of the Langenscheidt Group (qv)
ISBN Publisher's Prefix: 3-526

Karl Robert **Langewiesche** Nachfolger Hans Koester KG+, Grüner Weg 6, Postfach 1327, D-6240 Königstein 1 Tel: (06174) 7333 Cable Add: Langewiesche Königsteintaunus
Man Dir, Production, Sales and Publicity, Rights & Permissions: Hans-Curt Koester; *Editorial:* Hans-Curt Koester
Subjects: Art, History, How-to, Music, University Textbooks, Architecture
Founded: 1902
ISBN Publisher's Prefix: 03-7845

Verlag **Langewiesche-Brandt** KG, Lechnerstr 27, D-8026 Ebenhausen bei München Tel: (08178) 4857
Man Dir: Kristof Wachinger
Subjects: Belles Lettres, Art Books, Autobiographical, Poetry, Quality Paperbacks, Posters
Founded: 1906
ISBN Publisher's Prefix: 3-7846

Verlag **Laterna magica** Joachim F Richter+, Stridbeckstr 48, D-8000 Munich 71 Tel: (089) 799011 Telex: 5214503
Publisher: Joachim F Richter; *All other offices:* Rudolf Majonica
Subjects: Photography, Books for Collectors
Founded: 1966
ISBN Publisher's Prefix: 3-87467

August **Lax**+*, Postfach, Kreuzstr 21, D-3200 Hildesheim Tel: (05121) 38013
Man Dir, Editorial, Rights & Permissions: Lorenz Lax
Associate Company: Filmsatz Gesellschaft (at above address)
Subjects: Archaeology, History, Pre-history, Folklore, Art History, Literature, Limericks, Lower Saxony Historical
Bookshop: Buchhandlung August Lax, Annenstr 36, D-3200 Hildesheim
Founded: 1849
ISBN Publisher's Prefix: 3-7848

Verlag Hermann **Leins**, see Rainer Wunderlich Verlag Hermann Leins

Leitfadenverlag Dieter Sudholt*, D-8131 Berg 3 (Assenhausen) Tel: (08151) 5342
Publisher: Volker Sudholt
Subjects: Tax Directories, Business, Law, Economics
ISBN Publisher's Prefix: 3-543

Verlag Otto **Lembeck**, Leerbachstr 42, D-6000 Frankfurt am Main 1 Tel: (06171) 53708 Cable Add: Lembeckdruck Frankfurtmain
Subjects: Religion, Ecumenical Studies, Africa
Founded: 1945
ISBN Publisher's Prefix: 3-87476

Verlag Lambert **Lensing** GmbH+, Westenhellweg 67, Postfach 875, D-4600 Dortmund 1 Tel: (0231) 147008 Cable Add: Lensingbuch Telex: 0822106
Man Dirs: N Theissen, K-J Biele; *Sales:* R Schnelle; *Publicity:* N Theissen; *Production:* G Marx
Subjects: Modern Languages, Modern Language Teaching, Educational Materials
Bookshop: Westenhellweg 86-88, Postfach 875, D-4600 Dortmund 1
Founded: 1870
ISBN Publisher's Prefix: 3-559

Georg **Lentz** Verlag, Thomas-Wimmer-Ring 11, D-8000 Munich 22 Tel: (089) 2350080 Telex: 5215045 nyvm d
Man Dir: Brigitte Fleissner-Mikorey
Subjects: Fiction and Non-fiction for Juveniles
Miscellaneous: Firm is a member of Buchverlage Ullstein Langen-Müller/Herbig (qv)
ISBN Publisher's Prefix: 3-88010

Leske Verlag und Budrich GmbH+*, Gerhart-Hauptmann-Str 27, Postfach 300406, D-5090 Leverkusen 3 Tel: (02171) 2079
Man Dir: Edmund Budrich
Subjects: Social Science, Sexology, Psychology, Philosophy, Middle East, University, Secondary and Primary Textbooks, Educational Materials, Periodicals
Founded: 1974
ISBN Publisher's Prefix: 3-8100

Leuchter-Verlag EG+, Industriestr 6-8, Postfach 1161, D-6106 Erzhausen Tel: (06150) 7565
Man Dir, Sales: Karl-Heinz Neumann
Subject: Religion
Founded: 1946

Liber Verlag GmbH, Hegelstr 45, Postfach 2946, D-6500 Mainz 1
Man Dir, Editorial: Tomo Matasić
Subjects: Literature, Literary Criticism, Linguistics, Foreign Language Teaching, Theses on Slavistics, History, Politics
1985-86: 4 titles *Founded:* 1977
ISBN Publisher's Prefix: 3-83111

Edition **Lichterfelde**, an imprint of Abakon Verlagsgesellschaft mbH (qv)

Verlag der **Liebenzeller Mission**, Liobastr 21, Postfach 1265, D-7263 Bad Liebenzell 1 Tel: (07052) 17131
Publishing Dir: Arthur Klenk
Subjects: Mission Reports, Theology, Methodology, also Fiction, Biographies and Devotional
Founded: 1906
Miscellaneous: Member of the Telos (qv) paperback series publishing group
ISBN Publisher's Prefix: 3-88002

Edition/Galerie **Lietzow**, Knesebeckstr 32, D-1000 Berlin 12 Tel: (030) 8812895
Man Dir: Godehard Lietzow, Karl-Horst Hartmann
Subjects: Biography, Art, Reference
1985: 4 titles *Founded:* 1970

Life Sciences Research Reports, an imprint of Abakon Verlagsgesellschaft mbH (qv)

Limes Verlag, Thomas-Wimmer-Ring 11, D-8000 Munich 22 Tel: (089) 2350080 Telex: 5215045
Man Dir: Marguerite Schlüter; *Sales:* Ingeborg Castell
Subjects: General Fiction, Belles Lettres, Poetry, History, Music, Art
Founded: 1945
Miscellaneous: Firm is a member of Buchverlage Ullstein Langen-Müller/Herbig (qv)
ISBN Publisher's Prefix: 3-8090

Limpert Verlag+*, Kaiser-Friedrich-Promenade 87, Postfach 1951, D-6380 Bad Homburg vdH 1 Tel: (06172) 6038 Telex: 0418135 limp
Man Dir, Rights & Permissions: Hermann Farnung; *Sales, Publicity:* Ruprecht Sickel
Subjects: Sport, Recreation
Founded: 1921

Lingen Verlag*, Marienburger Str 17, Postfach 510729, D-5000 Cologne Tel: (0221) 380066 Telex: 8882138
Man Dir: Helmut Lingen
Subjects: Atlases, Language, Cookery, Popular Non-fiction

Paul **List** Verlag KG, Goethestr 43, D-8000 Munich 2 Tel: (089) 51480 Telex: 0522405
Editorial: Dr Hansjörg Graf; *Sales:* Norbert Jennen; *Publicity:* Barbara Ziegler; *Advertising:* Herbert Wiesensarter
Associate Companies: Südwest Verlag GmbH & Co KG (qv); Süddeutscher Verlag Buchverlag (qv). See also Schroedel Schulbuchverlag GmbH
Subjects: General Fiction, Belles Lettres, Poetry, Biography, History, Music, Art, Philosophy, Reference, Religion, Psychology, General & Social Science, Secondary & Primary Textbooks
Founded: 1894
Miscellaneous: Firm is member of TR-Verlagsunion GmbH (qv)
ISBN Publisher's Prefix: 3-471

Paul **List Verlag und Schroedel** Schulbuchverlag, Goethestr 43, D-8000 Munich 2 Tel: (089) 51480 Telex: 522405
Man Dirs: Anton Kemper, Dr Wolfgang Reister; *Editorial, Production, Rights & Permissions:* Michael Ziegenbein
Orders to: Schroedel Schulbuchverlag GmbH, Postfach 810555, D-3000 Hannover 81
Parent Company: Schroedel Schulbuchverlag (qv)
Subjects: Atlases, School Textbooks
1985: 26 titles *1986:* 12 titles *Founded:* 1985
ISBN Publisher's Prefix: 3-626

Lit Verlag+, Dieckstr 56, D-4400 Munster Tel: (0251) 231972
Man Dir: Dr Wilhelm Hopf
Subjects: Science
1985: 50 titles *1986:* 50 titles *Founded:* 1981
ISBN Publisher's Prefix: 3-88660

Henry **Litolff's** Verlag, an imprint of C F Peters Musikverlag GmbH & Co KG (qv)

von **Loeper** Verlag GmbH+*, Kiefernweg 13, Postfach 311205, D-7500 Karlsruhe 31 Tel: (0721) 706567
Man Dir, Editorial, Rights & Permissions: Dankwart von Loeper; *Sales, Promotion:* Wolfgang Matthiessen
Subjects: Modern Literature, Fantasy, Gift Books, Poetry, Indian Foreign Language Texts
Bookshops: Buchhandlung von Loeper,

Bärenweg 35, D-7500 Karlsruhe 31; Universitätsbuchhandlung von Loeper, Kaiserstr 69, D-7500 Karlsruhe 1; Buchhandlung von Loeper, Gymnasiumstr 6, D-7500 Karlsruhe 41
Founded: 1979
ISBN Publisher's Prefix: 3-88652

Loewes Verlag KG, Bühlstr 4, Postfach 1, D-8589 Bindlach Tel: (092089) 510
Man Dir: Volker Gondrom; *Editorial:* Jürgen Weidenbach; *Publicity, Sales Dir, Rights & Permissions:* Tamara Hasselblatt
Subject: Juveniles
Founded: 1863
ISBN Publisher's Prefix: 3-7855

Lorber-Verlag, Hindenburgstr 3, Postfach 229, D-7120 Bietigheim Tel: (07142) 41081 Cable Add: Lorber, Bietigheim
Associate Company: Turm-Verlag (qv)
Subject: Religion
ISBN Publisher's Prefix: 3-87495

Lorch-Verlag GmbH, see Deutscher Fachverlag

R **Löwit** GmbH, see Vollmer/Löwit Verlagsgruppe

Gustav **Lübbe** Verlag GmbH, Scheidtbachstr 25, Postfach 200127, D-5060 Bergisch Gladbach 2 Tel: (02202) 1210 Telex: 887922
Man Dirs: Walter Fritzsche, Dr Peter Roggen; *Rights & Permissions:* Peter Molden; *Editorial:* Christiane Landgrebe, Elmar Klupsch, Anja Kleinlein (Pocket Books); *Sales:* Hans-Jochen Mundt; *Advertising:* Peter Breuer; *Press and Publicity:* Bärbel Naporowski
Associate Company: Bastei-Verlag Gustav H Lübbe (qv)
Subjects: General Fiction and Non-fiction, Biography, Archaeology, Modern History, History, Thrillers, Fantasy, How-to
Founded: 1964
ISBN Publisher's Prefix: 3-7857

Hermann **Luchterhand** Verlag GmbH & Co KG, Neuwied und Darmstadt+*, Zweigniederlassung Darmstadt, Donnersbergring 18a, Postfach 4250, D-6100 Darmstadt Tel: (06151) 33521 Telex: 0419310 Dvg
Man Dir: Dr Hans Altenhein; *Rights & Permissions:* Hannelore Kirchem
Orders to: Hermann Luchterhand Verlag, Postfach 1780, D-5450 Neuwied 1
Parent Company: Hermann Luchterhand Verlag, Heddesdorfer Str 31, Postfach 1780, D-5450 Neuwied. Ultimate parent company Wolters Kluwer NV, Netherlands (qv)
Imprint: Sammlung Luchterhand
Subjects: Fiction, Non-fiction
Founded: 1924
Miscellaneous: Luchterhand Literaturverlag GmbH is at above Darmstadt address and owned by Arche Verlag AG, Raabe und Vitali, Switzerland (qv)
ISBN Publisher's Prefix: 3-472

W **Ludwig** Verlag, Türltorstr 14, Postfach 1444, D-8068 Pfaffenhofen/Ilm 1 Tel: (08441) 5051 Telex: 55540
Man Dir: Angelika Ludwig-Smith; *Rights & Permissions:* Wolfgang Grünewald; *Sales:* Rosemarie Lüdwig; *Production:* Siegfried Rist
Subsidiary Companies: Afrika Verlag; Bayerland Press
Subjects: Popular Science, Current Affairs, Belles Lettres, Poetry, History
Founded: 1950
ISBN Publisher's Prefix: 3-7787

Luther-Verlag GmbH, Postfach 140380, D-4800 Bielefeld 14 Tel: (0521) 44860 Telex: 0937385 epwl d

Dir: Dr Gerhard E Stoll
Subject: Religion
Founded: 1911
ISBN Publisher's Prefix: 3-7858

Lutherisches Verlagshaus GmbH*, Knochenhauerstr 38-40, D-3000 Hanover 1 Tel: (0511) 1241739 Telex: 922686 epd h
Man Dir, Production, Publicity, Rights & Permissions: Klaus Wöhleke; *Editorial:* Dr Hans Weissgerber; *Sales:* Rainer Jörren
Parent Company: Lutherhaus Verlag GmbH (at above address)
Subjects: Theology, Liturgical works and practical aids, the Church today, General Religious Literature

Verlag Waldemar **Lutz**, Basler Str 130, D-7850 Lörrach Tel: (07621) 88812
Man Dir: Waldemar Lutz
Subjects: Regional Literature, Children's, School Books
Founded: 1978
ISBN Publisher's Prefix: 3-922107

M F B — Produktion (Phono- und Schriftenmission des Missionswerkes Frohe Botschaft eV)*, Nordstr 15, Postfach 1180, D-3432 Grossalmerode bei Kassel Tel: (05604) 6361/5120
The Record and Text Mission of the 'Good News' Mission Team
Man Dir, Rights & Permissions: Rev W Heiner
Subjects: Christian Evangelical, Juvenile Interest, How-to, Paperbacks, Texts in English, Periodicals

M V G, see Moderne Verlags GmbH

Mäander Verlag GmbH+, Schackstr 1, D-8000 Munich 22 Tel: (089) 1665259
Man Dir: Prof Dr Friedrich Piel
Orders to: Koch, Neff und Oetinger & Co GmbH, Schockenriedstr 39, D-7000 Stuttgart 80
Subjects: Art, Archaeology, Aesthetics, Philosophy, Reference
Founded: 1977
ISBN Publisher's Prefix: 3-88219

McGraw-Hill Book Co GmbH, Lademannbogen 136, D-2000 Hamburg 63 Tel: (040) 5382081 Telex: 2164048
Man Dir: Rolf Pakendorf; *Sales:* Gunter Hack, Curt Landau
Subjects: Medicine, Psychology, Engineering, General & Social Science, University & Secondary Textbooks, Educational Materials
Founded: 1969
Miscellaneous: Firm is an associate company of McGraw-Hill International Book Co New York (see UK entry for other associate companies). The Hamburg branch is the one from which all McGraw-Hill publications in English, German and Italian may be ordered from any point in Europe except Spain, Portugal and France
ISBN Publisher's Prefix: 0-07

Magnus Verlag+*, im Teelbruch 60-62, Postfach 185528, D-4300 Essen 18 Tel: (02054) 7077
Man Dir: Walter Stender
Subjects: Reference Books, Dictionaries

Otto **Meier** Verlag, see Ravensburger Buchverlag

Mairs Geographischer Verlag*, Marco-Polo-Str 1, D-7302 Ostfildern 4 (Kemnat) Tel: (0711) 454055 Cable Add: Mairverlag Telex: 721796
Man Dir: Dr Volkmar Mair; *Sales Dir:* Claus Benath
Subjects: Road Maps, Atlases
Founded: 1948
ISBN Publisher's Prefix: 3-87504

Mai's Reiseführer Verlag+, Im Finkenschlag 22, D-6072 Dreieich-Buchschlag Tel: (06103) 62933

Man & Sales Dirs: Ingo and Marie-Luise Schmidt di Simoni
Subjects: Travel Guides, especially to non-European countries
1986: 7 titles *Founded:* 1951
ISBN Publisher's Prefix: 3-87936

Gebr **Mann** Verlag GmbH & Co, Lindenstr 76, Postfach 110303, D-1000 Berlin 61 Tel: (030) 25913864 Telex: 183723
Man Dir: Klaus Müller-Crepon
Associate Company: Deutscher Verlag für Kunstwissenschaft (qv)
Subjects: Archaeology, History of Art
Founded: 1917
ISBN Publisher's Prefix: 3-7861

Manz Verlag, Anzinger Str 1, D-8000 Munich 80 Tel: (089) 4130010 Cable Add: Manzverlag Telex: 522504
Publisher: Eduard Niedernhuber; *Editorial:* Dr Karl Geisendörfer; *Sales, Publicity:* Ursel Wunder
Subsidiary Companies: Verlag J Pfeiffer (qv); Erich Wewel Verlag (qv)
Subjects: Educational Materials
Founded: 1830
ISBN Publisher's Prefix: 3-7863

Tibor **Marczell***, Nederlinger Str 93, D-8000 Munich 19 Tel: (089) 155985
Man Dir: Tibor Marczell
Subjects: Medical (including history, herbal, fringe)
Founded: 1964
ISBN Publisher's Prefix: 3-88015

Carl **Marhold** Verlagsbuchhandlung*, Hessenallee 12, Postfach 191409, D-1000 Berlin 19 Tel: (030) 3043732/3049032 Cable Add: Marholdverlag Berlin
Man Dir: Thomas W Jaeh
Subjects: Special Healing Pedagogy, Nursing Technologies, Teaching of Handicapped Children
Founded: 1891
ISBN Publisher's Prefix: 3-7864

Edition **Maritim**+, Stubbenhuk 10, D-2000 Hamburg 11 Tel: (040) 364048
Dir: Frank Grube
Subjects: Yachting, Nautical
ISBN Publisher's Prefixes: 3-922117, 3-89225

Maro Verlag, Riedingerstr 24, D-8900 Augsburg 1 Tel: (0821) 416033
Dir: B Kaesmayr
Subjects: Modern Poetry and Fiction
Founded: 1969
ISBN Publisher's Prefix: 3-87512

Verlag **Marxistische Blätter** GmbH*, Heddernheimer Landstr 78a, D-6000 Frankfurt am Main 50 Tel: (069) 571051
Publisher: Albert Maag; *Dir:* Jan Wienecke
Subjects: Politics, Marxist Literature, Periodical
Founded: 1969
ISBN Publisher's Prefix: 3-88012

März Verlag GmbH+*, Altenschlirferstr 33, D-6422 Herbstein 1 Tel: (06647) 1211
Man Dir: Jörg Schröder
Orders to: SOVA (Sozialistische Verlagsauslieferung GmbH, Franziusstr 44, D-6000 Frankfurt am Main 1)
Imprint: Ravenna Presse
Subjects: Fiction, Avant-garde, Politics
1985: 10 titles *Founded:* 1969
ISBN Publisher's Prefix: 3-88880

Hugo **Matthaes** Druckerei und Verlag GmbH & Co KG, Olgastr 87, Postfach 622, D-7000 Stuttgart 1 Tel: (0711) 21331 Cable Add: Matthaesverlag Telex: 721802
Subjects: Food Trade, Gastronomy

Matthes und Seitz Verlag GmbH*, Postfach 860528, D-8000 Munich 86 (Located at: Mauerkircherstr 10)

156 FEDERAL REPUBLIC OF GERMANY

Man Dir: Axel Matthes
Subjects: Literature, Arts, Fiction, Memoirs
Founded: 1977
ISBN Publisher's Prefix: 3-88221

Matthias-Grünewald-Verlag, see Grünewald

Matthiesen Verlag Ingwert Paulsen Jnr, Nordbahnhofstr 2, Postfach 1480, D-2250 Husum Tel: (04841) 6081 Telex: 28567 husumv d
Man Dir, Editorial, Rights & Permissions: Ingwert Paulsen Jnr; *Sales:* Alfred Lorenzen
Associate Companies: Hamburger Lesehefte Verlag Iselt & Co Nfl mbH (qv); Hansa Verlag Ingwert Paulsen Jnr (qv); Husum Druck- und Verlagsgesellschaft mbH & Co KG (qv)
Subjects: Textbooks, Science, Reference
Founded: 1892
ISBN Publisher's Prefix: 3-7868

Maximilian-Verlag, Steintorwall 17, Postfach 2352, D-4900 Herford Tel: (05221) 50001 Cable Add: Maximilian, Herford/Westf Telex: 0934801 maxvg d
Publisher: Gerhard Bollmann; *Production:* Heinz Kameier; *Sales:* Hans-Focko Koehler; *Publicity:* Lütz Baukert
Associate Companies: Koehlers Verlagsgesellschaft, E S Mittler und Sohn GmbH, Verlag Offene Worte; Verlag Europäische Wehrkunde; all members of Maximilian-Verlagsgruppe (qv)
Subjects: Philosophy, Law, Administration, History, Social Sciences; Periodicals
ISBN Publisher's Prefix: 3-7869

Maximilian-Verlagsgruppe, Steintorwall 17, Postfach 2352, D-4900 Herford Tel: (05221) 59910 Telex: 0934801 maxgv d
Group Members: Verlag E S Mittler und Sohn GmbH (qv), Maximilian-Verlag (qv), Koehlers Verlagsgesellschaft mbH (qv), Verlag Offene Worte (qv), Verlag Europäische Wehrkunde
Branch Off (for all members of group): Austr 19, D-5300 Bonn 2 Tel: (0228) 340884

Karl-**May**-Verlag, see Karl

Edition Hansjörg **Mayer**, Engelhornweg 11, D-7000 Stuttgart 1 Tel: (0711) 282036
Man Dir: Hansjörg Mayer
Branch Off: London
Subjects: Belles Lettres, Poetry, Music, Art, Ethnology, High-priced Paperbacks
Founded: 1964

J A **Mayer'sche** Buchhandlung, Ursulinerstr 17-19, Postfach 467, D-5100 Aachen Tel: (0241) 47770 Cable Add: Mayer Aachen Telex: 832768 Fax: (0241) 1660669
Man Dir, Publicity: Helmut Falter
Branch Off: Templergraben 44, D-5100 Aachen
Bookshops: At company and branch office addresses
ISBN Publisher's Prefix: 3-87519

Medea Frauenverlag*, Schopenhauerstr 11, D-6000 Frankfurt am Main 1 Tel: (069) 442363
Man Dirs: Eve Cronberger, Angelika Eberlein; *Editorial:* Marockh Lautenschlag; *Publicity:* Gitta Mohrdieck; *Rights & Permissions:* A Eberlein
Orders to: Frauenliteraturvertrieb (FLV), Schloßstr 94, D-6000 Frankfurt am Main 90
Subjects: Women's Literature, Science Fiction Fantasy
Founded: 1980
ISBN Publisher's Prefix: 3-922764

Verlag für **Medizin** Dr Ewald Fischer GmbH*, Fritz-Frey-Str 21, Postfach 105767, D-6900 Heidelberg 1 Tel: (06221) 49974 Cable Add: Verlagfürmedizin Telex: 461683 hvvfm d
Man Dir: Dr E Fischer; *Production:* Dietmar Sieber; *Advertising:* Krisztina Fruh
Associate Companies: Arkana Verlag (qv); Karl F Haug Verlag GmbH & Co (qv)
Branch Off: Bergheimer Str 102, D-6900 Heidelberg
Subjects: Medical (neglected/little-recognized fields, Chinese diagnosis), Periodicals
Bookshop: As for Karl F Haug Verlag & Co KG (qv)
Founded: 1967
ISBN Publisher's Prefixes: 3-921003, 3-88463

Medizinisch-Literarische Verlagsgesellschaft mbH, Postfach 120/140, D-3110 Uelzen Tel: (0581) 8080 Cable Add: ML-Verlag 3110 Uelzen 1 Telex: 091326
Man Dir, Rights & Permissions: E J Wenske; *Sales:* B Burandt; *Production:* G Grätz; *Publicity:* M Jess
Parent Company: C Beckers Buchdruckerei, 3110 Uelzen 1
Subjects: Medical, Acupuncture, Orthopaedics, Electro-Acupuncture texts in English; Periodicals
Founded: 1957
ISBN Publisher's Prefix: 3-88136

Verlagsbuchhandlung **Megapress**, Franz-J Gaber und W Poth GbR, Frankfurter Str 39, D-6078 Neu Isenburg Tel: (06102) 25951/23817
Publisher: F J Gaber
Subjects: Politics, Periodical
ISBN Publisher's Prefix: 3-87979

Felix **Meiner** Verlag GmbH, Richardstr 47, D-2000 Hamburg 76 Tel: (040) 294870
Man Dirs: Richard Meiner, Manfred Meiner
Subject: Philosophy, Periodicals
1985: 40 titles *Founded:* 1911
ISBN Publisher's Prefix: 3-7873

Verlag Anton Hain **Meisenheim** GmbH*, Savignystr 53, Postfach 170101, D-6000 Frankfurt am Main Tel: (069) 7560950 Telex: 414531
Man Dirs, Rights & Permissions: Axel Rütters, Dieter Hain
Parent Company: Publishing group Athenäum/Hanstein/Jüdischer (qv under Athenäum Verlag GmbH); Syndikat und Europäische Verlagsanstalt
Subjects: Philosophy, Economics, Sociology, Psychology, Pedagogy, German Literature, Classical Philology, Scientific Periodicals
Founded: 1946
ISBN Publisher's Prefix: 3-445

Otto **Meissner** Verlag, Binger Str 29, D-1000 Berlin 33 Tel: (030) 8237007
Dir: Dieter Beuermann
Subjects: General Non-fiction, Hobbies, Humanities
Founded: 1848
ISBN Publisher's Prefix: 3-87527

J Ch **Mellinger** Verlag GmbH*, 55 Büssenstr, Postfach 131164, D-7000 Stuttgart 1 Tel: (0711) 463565/246401
Managers: Wolfgang Militz, Elisabeth Militz
Subjects: Anthroposophy, Education, Literature, Juveniles, Games
Founded: 1926
ISBN Publisher's Prefix: 3-88069

Verlag Abi **Melzer** GmbH*, Wildscheuerweg 1, Postfach 301117, D-6072 Dreieich-Buchschlag Tel: (06103) 63061

Telex: 4185381 amp
General Manager: Abraham Melzer
Orders to: VVA (Vereinigte Verlagsauslieferung GmbH), Postfach 7777, D-4830 Gütersloh 1
Subjects: Picture Strips, Graphics, Comics, Children's Books, General Literature
Founded: 1975
ISBN Publisher's Prefix: 3-8201

Melzer Verlag KG, Wildscheuerweg 1, D-6072 Buchschlag
Man Dir: Horst Göhde; *Sales Dir:* Horst Beitlich
Subjects: Comics, Art, Juveniles
Founded: 1972
ISBN Publisher's Prefix: 3-7874

Verlag **Mensch und Arbeit** Robert Pfützner GmbH, Sandstr 3, D-8000 Munich 2 Tel: (089) 5515010 Cable Add: Pronto Munich
Man Dir: Robert Pfützner; *Rights & Permissions:* Wilhelm Höfelmaier
Subjects: How-to, Art, Social Science, Professional, Technical
Founded: 1957

Mentor-Verlag Dr Ramdohr KG, Neusser Str 3, Postfach 401120, D-8000 Munich 40 Tel: (089) 360960 Cable Add: Langenscheidt Munich Telex: 5215379 lkgm d Fax: (089) 36096258
Man Dirs: Karl Ernst Tielebier-Langenscheidt, Dr Florian Langenscheidt; *Editorial:* Inka S Wallgrün; *Sales Dir:* Peter Haering; *Advertising Dir:* Klaus Ferber; *Sales, Promotion:* through Langenscheidt KG (qv); *Rights & Permissions:* Manfred Überall
Subjects: Reference, Low-priced Paperbacks, Textbooks
Founded: 1904
Miscellaneous: Firm is a member of the Langenscheidt Group (qv)
ISBN Publisher's Prefix: 3-580

Mergus Verlag Hans A Baensch, Postfach 86, D-4520 Melle 1 Tel: (05422) 3636 Cable Add: Mergus Melle
Man Dir: Hans A Baensch
Subjects: Natural History, Care of Pets
Founded: 1977
ISBN Publisher's Prefix: 3-88244

Merlin Verlag Andreas Meyer Verlags GmbH und Co KG+, Gifkendorf 3, D-2121 Vastorf Tel: (04137) 7207
Publisher: Andreas J Meyer; *Sales Manager:* Ilse Meyer
Subjects: Arts, Literature, History
1985: 9 titles *Founded:* 1957
ISBN Publisher's Prefix: 3-87536

Verlag Wolf **Mersch**+, Günterstalstr 18, D-7800 Freiburg Tel: (0761) 702288
Man Dir: Wolf Mersch
Subjects: Fiction, Poetry, Social History, Literature of South Asia
1985: 30 titles *Founded:* 1979
ISBN Publisher's Prefix: 3-922156

Merve Verlag*, Crelle Str 22, D-1000 Berlin 62 Tel: (030) 7848433
Man Dirs: Hans-Peter Gente, Heidi Paris
Founded: 1970

Verlag für **Messepublikationen**, see Thomas Neureuter KG

J B **Metzlersche** Verlagsbuchhandlung, Kernerstr 43, Postfach 529, D-7000 Stuttgart 1 Tel: (0711) 223067 Cable Add: Metzlerverlag Stuttgart Telex: 7262891 Mepo d
Publisher: Günther Schweizer; *Sales Dir, Rights & Permissions:* Dieter Naveau; *Advertising Dir:* Ms Tenholt
Orders to: Hermann Leins Verlagsauslieferung, Holzwiesenstr 2,

FEDERAL REPUBLIC OF GERMANY 157

D-7408 Kusterdingen; (Berlin) VAB Verlagsauslieferungen M Jager KG, Lützow Str 105/bbz, D-1000 Berlin 30
Associate Company: C E Poeschel Verlag (qv)
Subjects: Philology, Human Sciences, Geodesy, Pedagogics, School Books
Founded: 1682
ISBN Publisher's Prefix: 3-476

Alfred **Metzner** Verlag, Zeppelinallee 43, Postfach 970148, D-6000 Frankfurt am Main Tel: (069) 7930090 Telex: 4189621 kome d
Dir: Dr Clemens J B Sandmann; *Editorial:* Marigret Meyer-Tabellion; *Sales:* Ernst Grundl; *Publicity:* Friedrich-Wilhelm Bremer
Associate Company: Verlag Kommentator (qv)
Subjects: Law, University Textbooks, International Finance Management
Founded: 1909
Miscellaneous: Firm is a member of the Kluwer Group, Netherlands (qv)
ISBN Publisher's Prefix: 3-7875

Gertraud **Middelhauve** Verlag, Wiener Platz 2, D-5000 Cologne 80 (Mülheim) Tel: (0221) 614982/612707
Man Dir, Editorial: Gertraud Middelhauve; *Publicity:* H Helmut Lotz; *Rights & Permissions:* Anne Schieckel
Orders to: VVA (Vereinigte Verlagsauslieferung GmbH), Postfach 7777, D-4830 Gütersloh 1
Subject: Juveniles
Founded: 1947
ISBN Publisher's Prefix: 3-7876

Wolfgang **Militz** und Co KG, see J Ch Mellinger Verlag

Minerva Publikation Saur GmbH, Heilmannstr 17, Postfach 710640, D-8000 Munich 71 Tel: (089) 791040 Cable Add: saur d Telex: 05212067 saur d
Man Dir: Klaus G Saur; *Editorial, Production, Publicity:* Elisabeth Gruber; *Sales:* Paul Fertl
Parent Company: Butterworth & Co (Publishers) Ltd, UK (qv)
Subjects: Economics, Sociology, Jurisprudence, Political Science, Liberal Arts, Pedagogy, Psychology, Technology, Physical Sciences, Medicine, Art, Theology
1985: 60 titles *1986:* 60 titles *Founded:* 1977
ISBN Publisher's Prefix: 3-597

Missio aktuell Verlag GmbH, Bergdriesch 27, Postfach 1170, D-5100 Aachen Tel: (0241) 30556 Telex: 832719 mira d
Man Dir: Ludwig Hahn
Subjects: Missionary Work, Third World
1985: 90 titles *Founded:* 1970
ISBN Publisher's Prefix: 3-921626

Missionswerkes Frohe Botschaft, see MFB

E S **Mittler** und Sohn GmbH+, Steintorwall 17, Postfach 2352, D-4900 Herford Tel: (05221) 59910 Cable Add: Mittler & Sohn, Herford/Westf Telex: 0934801 maxvg d
Publisher: Gerhard Bollmann; *Sales:* Hans-Focko Koehler; *Publicity:* Lütz Baukert; *Production:* Heinz Kameier
Associate Companies: Koehlers Verlagsgesellschaft, Maximilian-Verlag, Verlag Offene Worte, Verlag Europäische Wehrkunde (all members of Maximilian-Verlagsgruppe, qv)
Subjects: Military, Aviation, Maritime, Political, NATO Affairs, Periodicals
Founded: 1789
ISBN Publisher's Prefixes: 3-87547, 3-8132

Verlag **Moderne Industrie** AG & Co, Buchverlag*, Justus-von-Liebig-Str 1, Postfach 1761, D-8910 Landsberg am Lech Tel: (08191) 1251 Telex: 527114 moin d
President: Dr Reinhard Möstl; *Man Dir:* Erwin Huvart; *Sales:* Ingrid Spitz
Associate Company: Moderne Verlags GmbH (qv)
Subjects: Management (Personnel, Sales), Advertising, Data Processing, Marketing, Textbooks
1985: 70 titles *Founded:* 1952
ISBN Publisher's Prefix: 3-478

Moderne Verlagsgesellschaft mbH (MVG)*, Justus-von-Liebig-Str 1, Postfach 1761, D-8910 Landsberg am Lech Tel: (08191) 125 Telex: 527114
President: Dr Reinhard Möstl; *Man Dir:* Bernhard Roloff
Associate Company: Verlag Moderne Industrie (qv)
Subjects: How-to, Cookery, Hobbies, Popular Science
ISBN Publisher's Prefix: 3-478

Gütersloher Verlagshaus Gerd **Mohn**, see Gütersloher

J C B **Mohr** (Paul Siebeck), Wilhelmstr 18, Postfach 2040, D-7400 Tübingen Tel: (07071) 26064 Cable Add: Siebeck Tübingen Telex: 7262872 mohr d
Man Dir: Georg Siebeck; *Sales, Publicity:* Johannes Krämer; *Production:* Rudolf Pflug; *Rights & Permissions:* Jill Sopper
Subjects: History, Philosophy, Religion, General & Social Science, Economics, Law, University Textbooks
1985: 80 titles *1986:* 92 titles *Founded:* 1801
ISBN Publisher's Prefix: 3-16

Verlag **Molden** — S Seewald GmbH*, Stievestr 9, D-8000 Munich 19 Tel: (089) 176071 Telex: 529993
Publishers, Man Dirs: Sixt A Seewald, Dr Hansgeorg Kanno; *Editorial:* Sixt A Seewald; *Sales:* Dr Hansgeorg Kanno
Subjects: Non-fiction
Miscellaneous: Firm is a member of Buchverlage Ullstein Langen-Müller/Herbig (qv)
Founded: 1982

Mönch-Verlag GmbH & Co*, Heilsbacherstr 26, D-5300 Bonn 1 Tel: (0228) 64830 Telex: 8869429 mvkb d
Man Dir: Manfred Sadlowski; *Sales Dir, Rights & Permissions:* Jochen Essfeld; *Publicity Dir:* Harald Helex; *Advertising Dir:* Hansjochen Keilholz
Branch Off: Mönch-Verlag, Hübingerweg 33, D-5401 Waldesch
Subjects: History, How-to, Engineering, General Science, High-priced Paperbacks

Verlag **Moos** und Partner KG, Rottenbucher Str 30, D-8032 Gräfelfing vor München Tel: (089) 851311 Cable Add: MoosPartner
Man Dir: Detlev Moos
Subjects: Fringe Areas of Science and Art, Natural Sciences, German-American and International Relations
Founded: 1984
ISBN Publisher's Prefix: 3-89164

Morsak Verlag*, Kröllstr 5, Postfach 5, D-8352 Grafenau Tel: (08552) 1015 Telex: 57431
Man Dir, Production, Rights & Permissions: Erich Stecher; *Sales:* Rosa Zarham
Subjects: Bavaria, Textbooks
Founded: 1884
ISBN Publisher's Prefix: 3-87553

Morus-Verlag*, Grunewaldstr 24, D-1000 Berlin 41 Tel: (030) 8234081
Dir: Elmar Bachmann
Subject: Religion
Founded: 1945
ISBN Publisher's Prefix: 3-87554

Mosaik Verlag, Neumarkter Str 18, Postfach 800360, D-8000 Munich 80 Tel: (089) 431890 Cable Add: Bertelsmann München Telex: 523259
Man Dir: Wolfgang Kunth; *Publicity:* Helga Mahmoud-Treimer; *Rights & Permissions:* Angelika Strauss-Fischer
Parent Company: Verlagsgruppe Bertelsmann GmbH (qv for associate companies)
Subjects: How-to, Cookery, Health & Medicine, Gardening, Furnishing, Crafts, Hobbies, Field Guides, Sport, Reference
ISBN Publisher's Prefix: 3-570

Motorbuch-Verlag, Böblinger Str 18, Postfach 1370, D-7000 Stuttgart 1 Tel: (0711) 6402031 Cable Add: pico d Telex: 0722662
Man Dir: Dr Patricia Schotten; *Marketing Dir:* Jörg Ebert; *Sales:* Thomas Günther, Kurt Wölfle; *Rights & Permissions:* Brigitte Weller
Subjects: How-to, Reference, Engineering
Founded: 1962
Miscellaneous: Firm is a division of Buch- & Verlagshaus Paul Pietsch GmbH & Co KG (at above address)
ISBN Publisher's Prefixes: 3-87943, 3-613

Mouton de Gruyter, Genthiner Str 13, D-1000 Berlin 30 Tel: (030) 26005235/26005185 Telex: 0184027 Fax: (030) 26005251
Man Dirs: Dr Kurt-Georg Cram, Dr Kurt Lubasch, Dr Helwig Hassenpflug; *Chief Editor:* Dr Liebe-Harkort; *Publicity:* Joachim Oest
Parent Company: (since 1977) Walter de Gruyter and Co (qv)
Branch Offs: Mouton de Gruyter, Walter de Gruyter Inc, 200 Saw Mill River Rd, Hawthorne, NY 10532, USA; Mouton de Gruyter, Rivierstaete, Amsteldijk 166, 1079 LH Amsterdam, Netherlands
Subjects: Anthropology, Education, History, Linguistics, Philosophy, Psychology, Religion, Social Science
Founded: 1954
ISBN Publisher's Prefix: 3-11

Verlag C F **Müller**+, Amalienstr 29, Postfach 4320, D-7500 Karlsruhe 1 Tel: (0721) 20909 Telex: 7825909
Man Dir, Rights & Permissions: Dr Christof Müller-Wirth; *Sales:* Andreas Diecke; *Publicity:* Ulrike Wesollek-Rottmann
Subjects: Earth Sciences, Energy and Solar Technology, Ecology, Architecture, Periodicals
Founded: 1797
ISBN Publisher's Prefix: 3-7880

Verlagsgesellschaft Rudolf **Müller** GmbH*, Stolberger Str 84, Postfach 410949, D-5000 Cologne 41 Tel: (0221) 54970 Telex: 8881256
Publisher: Dr Walther Müller; *Dir:* Helmut Evers; *Sales Manager:* Peter von Klaudy; *Publicity Manager:* Ulrich Rausch
Branch Off: Johnsallee 53, D-2000 Hamburg 13
Subjects: Architecture, Construction, Engineering, Data Processing, Education, Do-it-yourself, Pets
Miscellaneous: Firm is a member of vgs — Verlagsgesellschaft mbH & Co KG (qv)
ISBN Publisher's Prefix: 3-481

Buchverlag Ullstein Langen-**Müller/Herbig**, see Ullstein

C F **Müller Juristischer** Verlag GmbH, Postfach 102640, D-6900 Heidelberg

(Located at: im Weiher 10) Tel: (06221) 489250 Telex: 0461727 hueh d
Associate Companies: Kriminalistik Verlag GmbH (qv); R v Decker's Verlag G Schenck GmbH (qv)
Subjects: Jurisprudence Textbooks, Commentaries and Law Practice, Academic Series

Verlag **Müller und Kiepenheuer**, Frankfurter Landstr 32, Postfach 1355, D-6450 Hanau am Main Tel: (06181) 259052/82353 Telex: 4184879
Publisher: Werner Dausien
Associate Company: Werner Dausien (qv)
Subjects: General Fiction, Arts, Maps
Founded: 1919
ISBN Publisher's Prefix: 3-7833

Müller und Steinicke Verlag, Lindwurmstr 21, D-8000 Munich 2 Tel: (089) 265881
Publisher: Werner Gissler
Subjects: Medicine and associated fields

Albert Langen-Georg **Müller** Verlag, see Langen

Munin Verlag GmbH, Postfach 3023, D-4500 Osnabruck Tel: (0541) 572278
Subject: War Histories of Waffen SS units
1985: 2 titles *1986:* 3 titles *Founded:* 1955
ISBN Publisher's Prefix: 3-921242

Muster-Schmidt Verlag, Grünberger Weg 6, Postfach 2741, D-3400 Göttingen Tel: (0551) 71741 Cable Add: Musterschmidt Telex: 96704 gofafi
Dirs: Hans Hansen-Schmidt, Eva Maria Gerhardy-Löcken
Branch Off: Vogelsangstr 7, CH-8033 Zurich, Switzerland
Subjects: Biography, History, Anthropology, Theory of Art and Design
Founded: 1905
ISBN Publisher's Prefix: 3-7881

N D V (Neue Darmstädter Verlagsanstalt), Postfach 1544, D-5340 Bad Honnef 1 (Located at: Hauptstr 74, D-5342 Rheinbreitbach) Tel: (02224) 3232/4353
Publisher: Klaus-J Holzapfel
Subject: Politics
ISBN Publisher's Prefix: 3-87576

Nachrichten-Verlags-GmbH*, Kurfürstenstr 18, Postfach 900749, D-6000 Frankfurt am Main 90 Tel: (069) 778079
Man Dir: Dr Werner Petschick; *Sales Dir:* Elfriede Krüger; *Publicity and Advertising Dir:* Gisela Mayer; *Rights & Permissions:* Ruth Malkomes
Subjects: Political aspects of Trade Unionism, Economics, Social Sciences
Founded: 1969
ISBN Publisher's Prefix: 3-88367

Edition **Nagel**, an imprint of Bärenreiter-Verlag (qv)

Gunter **Narr** Verlag, Postfach 2567, D-7400 Tübingen 1 (Located at: Dischingerweg 5) Tel: (07071) 78091
Manager, Sales Dir and Rights & Permissions: Gunter Narr; *Publicity Dir:* Brigitte Narr; *Advertising Dir:* Horst Schmid
Subjects: Linguistic studies (especially German, English and French), Literary Criticism, Romanesque Studies
Founded: 1969
ISBN Publisher's Prefix: 3-87808

Nelles Verlag GmbH*, Schleissheimer Str 371b, D-8000 Munich 45 Tel: (089) 3515084
Man Dir: G Nelles
Subjects: Guides, Maps
1986: 55 titles
ISBN Publisher's Prefix: 3-88618

Verlag Günther **Neske***, Kloster, Postfach 7240, D-7417 Pfullingen Tel: (07121) 71339 Cable Add: Neske-Verlag Pfullingen Telex: 0729790 neflu d
Publisher: Günther Neske; *Editorial, Publicity:* Brigitte Neske
Subjects: General Fiction, Humanities, Literary Criticism, Philosophy, Politics, Poetry, Psychiatry, Theology, Swiridoff Picture Books
Founded: 1951
ISBN Publisher's Prefix: 3-7885

Neue Darmstädter Verlagsanstalt, see NDV

Verlag **Neue Gesellschaft** GmbH, Postfach 201352, D-5300 Bonn 2 Tel: (0228) 238083
Dir: Dr Heiner Lindner; *Editorial:* Martin Rethmeier; *Sales:* Peter Marold
Orders to: Verlagsauslieferung Georg Lingenbrink, Postfach 3584, D-6000 Frankfurt am Main 1
Associate Company: Verlag J H W Dietz Nachf GmbH (qv)
Subjects: Politics, Legal, History, Sociology, Economics, Periodicals
ISBN Publisher's Prefix: 3-87831

Verlag **Neue Kritik** KG+, Kettenhofweg 53, D-6000 Frankfurt am Main Tel: (069) 727576
Orders to: Sozialistische Verlagsauslieferung GmbH, Franziusstr 44, D-6000 Frankfurt am Main
Subjects: Socialism, Art, Feminism
Founded: 1965
ISBN Publisher's Prefix: 3-8015

Verlag der **Neue Schulmann**, see Franckh'sche Verlagshandlung

Verlag **Neue Stadt** GmbH+, Gleissner Str 87, D-8000 Munich 83 Tel: (089) 405081 Cable Add: Neue Stadt
Man Dir: Wolfgang Bader; *Sales, Publicity and Advertising:* Gabriele Hartl; *Rights:* Wolfgang Bader
Parent Company: Città Nuova Editrice, Italy (qv for associate companies)
Branch Offs: Trostr 116, A-1100 Vienna, Austria; Seestr 426, Postfach 435, CH-8038 Zurich, Switzerland
Subjects: Music, Religion, Juveniles, Periodicals
1985–86: 22 titles *Founded:* 1965
ISBN Publisher's Prefix: 3-87996

Verlag **Neue Wirtschafts-Briefe** GmbH & Co, Eschstr 22, D-4690 Herne 1 Tel: (02323) 1410 Telex: 08229870 Cable Add: Steuerbriefe Herne
Man Dir: E-O Kleyboldt; *Sales and Advertising Dir:* J Müller-Grote
Subsidiary Company: Friedrich Kiehl Verlag GmbH (qv)
Subjects: Tax and Company Law, Accountancy, Industrial Management, Political Economics, Vocational Training, Periodicals
Founded: 1947
ISBN Publisher's Prefix: 3-482

Neuer Finken-Verlag*, Lindenstr 16, Postfach 1546, D-6370 Oberursel/Ts Tel: 53073 Cable Add: Neuer Finkenverlag Oberursel
Dir: Manfred Krick
Subjects: Children's, Juveniles, Textbooks, Education, Games
ISBN Publisher's Prefix: 3-8084

Neuer Jugendschriften-Verlag, see A Weichert Verlag

Verlag **Neuer Weg** GmbH*, Heusteigstr 88a, D-7000 Stuttgart 1, Postfach 3080 Tel: (0711) 6405894
Subjects: Marxist-Leninist Theory and Politics (including publications of the Marxist-Leninist Party of Germany (MLPD)), Novels, Proletarian Literature
Founded: 1971
ISBN Publisher's Prefix: 3-88021

Neukirchener Verlag des Erziehungvereins GmbH*, Andreas-Braem-Str 18-20, Postfach 1161, D-4133 Neukirchen-Vluyn 1 Tel: (02845) 392222 Cable Add: Verlagshaus neukirchenvluyn
Man Dirs: Jochen Böckler, Dr Christian Bartsch; *Editorial:* Dr Christian Bartsch
Subsidiary Company: Kalender-Verlag des Erziehungs-Vereins (at above address)
Subjects: Evangelical Christianity, Catholic and Reformed; Biblical Studies, Bible Archaeology, Belles Lettres
Bookshop: Neukirchener Buchhandlung (at above address)
Founded: 1888
ISBN Publisher's Prefix: 3-7887

Verlag Dr Thomas **Neumann**, see Königshausen und Neumann

Verlag J **Neumann-Neudamm** KG, Muhlenstr 9, Postfach 320, D-3508 Melsungen Tel: (05661) 2374/6374
Dir: Walter Schwartz
Subjects: Agriculture, Horticulture, Forestry, Hunting, Fishing, Natural Science, Aquarian Science
ISBN Publisher's Prefix: 3-7888

Martin **Neumeyer**, see Landsberger Verlagsanstalt

Verlag für Messepublikationen Thomas **Neureuter** KG, Pettenkoferstr 7, Postfach 482, D-8000 Munich 2 Tel: (089) 597186 Telex: 522918 mesu d Fax: (089) 554936
Publisher: Thomas Neureuter
Founded: 1948

Nicolaische Verlagsbuchhandlung Beuermann GmbH, Binger Str 29, D-1000 Berlin 33 Tel: (030) 8237007
General Manager: Dieter Beuermann
Subjects: Berlin, Politics, European Art and Photography
ISBN Publisher's Prefix: 3-87584

Verlag C W **Niemeyer**+, Osterstr 19, Postfach 101301, D-3250 Hameln 1 Tel: (05151) 200310 Cable Add: Dewezet Telex: 92859
Dir: Hans Freiwald
Orders to: VVA (Vereinigte Verlagsauslieferung GmbH), Postfach 7777, D-4830 Gütersloh 1
Associate Company: Adolf Sponholtz Verlag (qv)
Subjects: Scenic Picture Books (Germany), Quality Illustrated Books, Art and Architecture, Humour
Founded: 1797
ISBN Publisher's Prefix: 3-87585

Max **Niemeyer** Verlag, Pfrondorfer Str 4, Postfach 2140, D-7400 Tübingen Tel: (07071) 81104 Cable Add: Niemeyer Tübingen
Man Dir: Robert Harsch-Niemeyer; *Publicity and Marketing:* Manfred Korn
Subjects: General Literary Criticism; German, English & Romance Philology; Linguistics, Philosophy, History
1986: 106 titles *Founded:* 1870
ISBN Publisher's Prefix: 3-484

Nomos Verlagsgesellschaft mbH und Co KG*, Waldseestr 3-5, Postfach 610, D-7570 Baden Baden Tel: (07221) 21040 Telex: 0781201
Man Dir: Volker Schwarz; *Publicity:* Annette Saeger
Associate Companies: Insel Verlag (qv); Suhrkamp Verlag (qv)
Subjects: Jurisprudence, Economics, European Economy, Business Sciences,

FEDERAL REPUBLIC OF GERMANY 159

Political Science, International Co-operation, Periodicals
Founded: 1936
ISBN Publisher's Prefix: 3-7890

Verlag Wissenschaft und Politik, Berend von **Nottbeck**+, Salierring 14-16, D-5000 Cologne 1 Tel: (0221) 312878/315787 Cable Add: Politikbuch 5 Köln 1
Man Dir: C P von Nottbeck; *Sales & Advertising Dir:* Siegmund Mindt
Branch Off: Redaktion 'Deutschland Archiv', Goltsteinstr 185, D-5000 Cologne 51
Subjects: Political Science (especially in context of East-West relations), International Law and Problems, Dialogue with the German Democratic Republic
Founded: 1960
ISBN Publisher's Prefix: 3-8046

Verlag Monika **Nüchtern***, Breisacherstr 14, D-8000 Munich 80 Tel: (089) 481230
Man Dir: Monika Nüchtern
Subject: Films
Founded: 1976

Nusser Verlag+, Kaufbeurerstr 3, Postfach 500411, D-8000 Munich 50 Tel: (089) 146788
Man Dir: Dr Horst Nusser; *Sales:* Sibylle Nusser-Festner
Subjects: History, Geography, Popular Science, Art, Culture, Asiatic Topics, Audiovisual, Educational
Founded: 1972
ISBN Publisher's Prefix: 3-88091

Nymphenburger Verlagshandlung GmbH, Thomas-Wimmer-Ring 11, D-8000 Munich 22 Tel: (089) 2350080 Telex: 5215045
Man Dir: Dr Herbert Fleissner; *Sales, Publicity:* Ingeborg Castell; *Rights & Permissions:* Dorothea Estermann
Subjects: General Fiction, Belles Lettres, Biography, History, How-to, Philosophy, Sports, Hobbies, Mountaineering, General and Social Science
Founded: 1946
Miscellaneous: Firm is a member of Buchverlage Ullstein Langen-Müller/Herbig (qv)
ISBN Publisher's Prefix: 3-485

Oberbaumverlag, Pannierstr 54, D-1000 Berlin 44 Tel: (030) 6246921
Man Dir: Siegfried Heinrichs; *Publicity & Advertising Dir:* Walter Thümler
Subjects: Left-wing Political, German History, German and International Literature, General Culture
Founded: 1966

Oekumenischer Verlag Dr R-F Edel, Horringhausen 15, D-5880 Lüdenscheid Tel: (02351) 12449
Publicity Manager: Dr Reiner-Friedemann Edel
Orders to: Verlagsauslieferung H W Stier, Werdohlerstr 11, D-5880 Lüdenscheid
Subject: Christian Evangelical and Devotional, Ecumenical Theology and History, Cultural, Philosophical, Art

Paul **Oestergaard** GmbH, see Columbus Verlag

Verlag Friedrich **Oetinger**, Poppenbütteler Chaussee 55, Postfach 220, D-2000 Hamburg 65 Tel: (040) 6070055 Cable Add: Oetingerbuch Telex: 02174230
Man Dirs: Heidi Oetinger, Thomas Huggle, Uwe Weitendorf; *Editorial:* Else Marie Bonnet; *Sales:* Thomas Huggle; *Publicity:* Anke Lüdtke; *Rights & Permissions:* Uwe Weitendorf
Associate Company: Cecilie Dressler Verlag (qv)

Subjects: Juveniles, Illustrated Books
ISBN Publisher's Prefix: 3-7891

August **Oetker**, see Ceres-Verlag

Verlag **Offene Worte**, Steintorwall 17, Postfach 2352, D-4900 Herford Tel: (05221) 59910 Cable Add: Vlg Offene Worte, Herford/W Telex: 0934801 maxvg d
Publisher: Gerhard Bollmann; *Production:* Heinz Kameier; *Sales:* Hans-Focko Koehler; *Publicity:* Lütz Baukert
Associate Companies: Koehlers Verlagsgesellschaft, Maximilian-Verlag, E S Mittler und Sohn GmbH, Verlag Europäische Wehrkunde (all members of Maximilian-Verlagsgruppe, qv)
Subjects: Military, Politics, Periodicals
ISBN Publisher's Prefix: 3-87599

R **Oldenbourg** Verlag GmbH, Rosenheimer Str 145, Postfach 801360, D-8000 Munich 80 Tel: (089) 41120 Cable Add: Rograph München Telex: 0529296 Fax: (089) 4112207
Dirs: Dr Thomas von Cornides, Wolfgang Dick, Götz Ohmeyer, Johannes Oldenbourg
Orders to: Verlegerdienst München, Auslieferung R Oldenbourg Verlag, Gutenbergstr 1, Postfach 1280, D-8031 Gilching Tel: (08105) 21101
Subsidiary Companies: Verlag Oldenbourg, Austria (qv); Michael Prögel Verlag; VaW Verlag für angewandte Wissenschaften, Munich
Subjects: Modern Science and Technology, History and the Liberal Arts, Social Sciences, Psychology, Pedagogics and School Textbooks, Reference Works, Periodicals
Founded: 1858
Miscellaneous: Firm is a member of TR-Verlagsunion GmbH (qv)
ISBN Publisher's Prefix: 3-486 (Munich)

Verlag **Olle und Wolter** GmbH*, Postfach 4310, D-1000 Berlin 30 (Located at: Paul Lincke Ufer 44a, D-1000 Berlin 36) Tel: (030) 6125060
General Manager, Editorial: Ulf Wolter; *Sales and Publicity:* Maria Sata; *Rights & Permissions:* Orla Pass
Subjects: Politics, Economics, Philosophy, Literature, Scientific and Science Fiction, Ecology, Biography, Crime Fiction, Periodical
Founded: 1972
ISBN Publisher's Prefixes: 3-921241, 3-88395

Georg **Olms** Verlag AG, Hagentorwall 7, D-3200 Hildesheim Tel: (05121) 37007 Cable Add: Bookolms Hildesheim Telex: 927454 olms d
Publishers: W Georg Olms, Dr E Mertens; *Editorial:* Dr Peter Guyot, Doris Wendt; *Sales:* Edith Olms; *Production:* J-P Pracht; *Publicity:* Beathe Meyer; *Rights & Permissions:* K Burbach
Subsidiary Company: Edition Olms AG, Switzerland (qv)
Associate Company: Weidmannsche Verlagsbuchhandlung (at above address)
Branch Off: Georg Olms Verlag, c/o 111 West 57 St, New York, NY 10019, USA
Bookshop: Georg Olms, Verlagsbuchhandlung, Hagentorwall 7, D-3200 Hildesheim
Subjects: Languages and Language History, Books in foreign languages, History, Geography, Travel, Literature, Arts, Judaica, Science, Technology, Orientalia, Folklore, Theology, Law, Politics, Economics, Sociology, Psychology, Pedagogy, Philosophy, Classical Antiquities, Romance Studies, Reference, Paperbacks

Founded: 1945
ISBN Publisher's Prefix: 3-487

Verlag **Ölschläger** GmbH, Georgenstr 112, D-8000 Munich 40 Tel: (089) 2716451
Man Dir: Christina Ölschläger
Subjects; Communications, Journalism, Audiovisual
Founded: 1977
ISBN Publisher's Prefix: 3-88295

Verlag für Wirtschaftsskripten, Dipl Kfm C **Ölschläger** GmbH, see Wirtschaftsskripten

Günter **Olzog** Verlag GmbH+*, Thierschstr 11, D-8000 Munich 22 Tel: (089) 293272
Man Dir, Rights & Permissions: Dr Günter Olzog; *Sales, Publicity & Advertising Dir:* Johann Hacker
Subjects: History, Social Science, Educational Materials, Politics, East European Economics
Founded: 1949
Miscellaneous: Firm is a member of TR-Verlagsunion GmbH (qv)
ISBN Publisher's Prefix: 3-7892

Oncken Verlag KG, Postfach 110152, D-5600 Wuppertal 11 (Located at: Champagne 7, D-5657 Haen) Tel: (02104) 69110
Publisher: Dr Ulrich Brockhaus; *Editor and Publicity Manager:* Günter Balders; *Sales Manager:* Raimond Schmidt
Associate Company: R Brockhaus Verlag (qv)
Subject: Popular Religion, Juvenile, Fiction
ISBN Publisher's Prefix: 3-7893

Orangerie Galerie und Verlag, Gerhard F Reinz*, Helenenstr 2, D-5000 Cologne 1 Tel: (0221) 234684 Cable Add: Orangerie Telex: 8882939
Subject: Art

Orell Füssli und Parabel Verlag GmbH, Gaabstr 6, Postfach 4564, D-6200 Wiesbaden Tel: (06121) 401062 Telex: 4064160 orel d
Man Dir: Renate Schulze; *Sales:* Karin Schröter; *Production:* P Schnyder; *Publicity:* Eva Tobler; *Rights & Permissions:* Mrs Frey
Parent Company: Orell Füssli Verlag, Switzerland (qv)
Subjects: Reference, Railway, Illustrated (Orell Füssli), Children's Picture Books (Parabel)
ISBN Publisher's Prefixes: 3-2800 (Orell Füssli), 3-7898 (Parabel)

Orion-Heimreiter Verlag, Postfach 3667, D-2300 Kiel Tel: (0431) 553446 Cable Add: Orionheimreiter
Publisher: Dietmar Münier
Subjects: Prehistory, History, Human Sciences, Belles Lettres
Founded: 1983
ISBN Publisher's Prefix: 3-87588

Orlanda Frauenverlag, Pohlstr 64, D-1000 Berlin 30 Tel: (030) 2618049
Publicity: R Burgard, Dr D Schultz
Subjects: Literature by and about women (Pedagogy, Psychology, Medicine, History, Poetry, Sexuality, Belles Lettres)

Verlag **Osterrieth**, an imprint of Societäts-Verlag (qv)

P I A G, see Verlag Presse Informations Agentur GmbH

P R Verlag Wiesbaden, H G Schwieger*, Glückstr 12, D-6200 Wiesbaden Tel: (06121) 520030 Cable Add: PR Verlag, Wiesbaden
Man Dir: H G Schwieger

160 FEDERAL REPUBLIC OF GERMANY

Subjects: Belles Lettres, Poetry, Educational Materials
Founded: 1974
ISBN Publisher's Prefix: 3-921261

Päd extra buchverlag in der pädex Verlags GmbH, now Extrabuch Verlag in der pädex Verlags GmbH (qv)

Pädagogischer Verlag Schwann/Bagel GmbH*, Am Wehrhahn 100, Postfach 7640, D-4000 Düsseldorf 1 Tel: (0211) 360301 Cable Add: Schwannverlag Düsseldorf Telex: paed d 858 1345
Dirs: Dr Hans Weymar, Franz Ehret
Associate Company: W Girardet Buchverlag GmbH (qv)
Subjects: University, Secondary and Primary Textbooks, Educational Materials, History, Arts, Linguistics, Children's Books, Records
Founded: 1821
Miscellaneous: Now incorporates Assimil-Verlag KG
ISBN Publisher's Prefixes: 3-589, 3-590

Pahl-Rugenstein Verlag GmbH*, Gottesweg 54, D-5000 Cologne 51 Tel: (0221) 364051
Dir: Paul Neuhöffer; *Editorial:* Jürgen Hartmann, Dr Jürgen Harrer, Dr Christa Thoma-Herterich; *Sales, Publicity Manager:* Hajo Leib
Subjects: History, Politics, Literary Criticism, Education, Philosophy, Psychology, Social Science, Paperbacks, Economics, Periodicals, Sports
ISBN Publisher's Prefix: 3-7609

Paladin Verlag GmbH+, now owned by Franz Schneider Verlag GmbH (qv)

Papilio Print, an imprint of Peter Rump Verlag (qv)

Verlag Paul **Parey**+*, Spitalerstr 12, Postfach 106304, D-2000 Hamburg 1 Tel: (040) 339690 Cable Add: Pareyverlag Hamburg Telex: 2161391 parv d
Also: Lindenstr 44-47, D-1000 Berlin 61 Tel: (030) 2599040 Cable Add: Pareyverlag Berlin Telex: 184777 parv d
Man Dirs: Dr Friedrich Georgi, Dr Rudolf Georgi; *Publicity, Sales:* Dieter Both, Karlheinz Römer; *Rights & Permissions:* Dr Horst-Christian Etmer
Subjects: Biology, Veterinary Medicine, Foodstuffs, Agriculture, Forestry, Horticulture, Plant Medicine and Protection; Environment Protection, Hydro- and Cultural Technologies, Hunting, Sporting and Professional Fishing, Riding and Horses, Technical and Scientific Journals
1985: 30 titles *Founded:* 1848
ISBN Publisher's Prefixes: 3-490 (Hamburg), 3-489 (Berlin)

Parkland Verlag GmbH*, Schwabstr 189, Postfach 229, D-7000 Stuttgart 1 Tel: (0711) 298805 Telex: 721907
Man Dirs: Gerd Seibert, Dr Erhard Wendelberger; *Sales Dir:* Martina Deissner
Subjects: Non-fiction, Belles Lettres, Art
Founded: 1974

Verlag **Passavia**, Postfach 2147, D-8390 Passau 1 Tel: (0851) 700225 Cable Add: Passavia Telex: 57837
Publishing Dir, Rights & Permissions: M Teschendorff; *Sales:* Katharina Moritz
Subjects: Bavarian Topics, Folklore, Humour, Homecare, Belles Lettres, Fiction
1985: 7 titles *Founded:* 1888
ISBN Publisher's Prefix: 3-87616

Passavia Universitätsverlag und -Druck GmbH, Postfach 2147, D-8390 Passau 1 Tel: (0851) 700225 Telex: 57837 passav d
Publishing Dir, Rights & Permissions: Martin Teschendorff
Subjects: Sciences
1985: 18 titles
ISBN Publisher's Prefix: 3-922016

Galerie **Patio** Verlag*, Waldstr 115, D-6078 Neu-Isenburg
Man Dir: Walter Zimbrich; *Editorial:* Volker Müller; *Sales:* Franz Gaber, Renate Kafitz-Pfeuffer; *Production:* Manfred Linke, Yves Daniel Zimbrich; *Publicity:* Klaus Münschschwander; *Rights & Permissions:* David Ward, Regine Behrends
Subjects: Young Authors, New Editions of Older Texts, Handmade Books, the *Parabü* series of new, experimental texts (Patio's Book Rarity Library)
Founded: 1964

Patmos Verlag GmbH, Am Wehrhahn 100, Postfach 6213, D-4000 Düsseldorf 1 Tel: (0211) 167950 Cable Add: Patmos Verlag Telex: 8581345 paed d Fax: (0211) 1679575
Dirs: Dr Tullio Aurelio, Franz Ehret; *Sales, Publicity:* Klaus Opitz
Subjects: Roman Catholic Theology, Religion, Education, Juveniles, Textbooks
Founded: 1910
ISBN Publisher's Prefix: 3-491

Paul **Pattloch** im Weltbild Verlag GmbH+, Steinerne Furt 70, D-8900 Augsburg Tel: (0821) 70040 Cable Add: Weltbild Augsburg Telex: 17-82183791
Man Dir, Sales: Clemens Pattloch
Orders to: VVA (Vereinigte Verlagsauslieferung GmbH), an der Autobahn, Postfach 7777, D-4830 Gütersloh 1
Subjects: Religion, Bibles
Founded: 1827
ISBN Publisher's Prefix: 3-629

Paulinus Verlag, Fleischstr 62-65, Postfach 3040, D-5500 Trier Tel: (0651) 46040 Telex: 04727315
Publisher: Siegfried Fäth
Parent Company: Paulinus Druckerei GmbH (at above address)
Associate Company: Spee Buchverlag GmbH (qv)
Subjects: Religion, Theology
ISBN Publisher's Prefix: 3-7902

Ingwert **Paulsen** Jnr, see Hansa Verlag and Matthieson Verlag

Pawel Pan Presse*, zum Seemenbach 1, D-6470 Büdingen 2 Tel: (06041) 5821
Man Dir, Production: Sascha Juritz
Subjects: Contemporary Literature, Educative Art, Poetry, First Publications in Bibliophile Editions
Founded: 1972
ISBN Publisher's Prefix: 3-921454

Manfred **Pawlak** Grossantiquariat und Verlagsgesellschaft mbH*, Postfach 1149, D-8036 Herrsching (Located at: Gachenau Str 13) Tel: (08152) 1067 Telex: 0527724 mph d
Proprietor, Man Dir: Manfred Pawlak
Subjects: Biography, History, Art
Founded: 1949
Miscellaneous: The Company is a wholesale antiquarian and second-hand book dealer as well as a Publishing House

Agentur für wissenschaftliche Literatur Ulf **Pedersen** GmbH+*, Steinweg 5, D-3300 Brunswick Tel: (0531) 40294
Man Dir: Ulf Pedersen
Orders to: Cornelsen Verlagsgesellschaft mbH & Co Kg, Postfach 8729, D-4800 Bielefeld 1
Subject: Social Sciences
Founded: 1979
ISBN Publisher's Prefix: 3-88657

Pendragon Verlag+, Postfach 140251, D-4800 Bielefeld 14 Tel: (0521) 410280/499230
Man Dir, Sales, Rights & Permissions: Günther Butkus; *Editorial:* Hellmuth Opitz; *Production:* Udo Hellweg; *Publicity:* Susanne Bornemann
Subjects: Poetry, Fiction, Theatre, Bibliophilism, Special Editions, Essays, History, Reference
1985: 7 titles *1986:* 9 titles *Founded:* 1981
ISBN Publisher's Prefix: 3-923306

Perimed Fachbuch-Verlagsgesellschaft mbH+, Vogelherd 35, Postfach 3740, D-8520 Erlangen Tel: (09131) 6090 Telex: 629851
Publisher: Dr med Dietmar Straube; *Dir:* Hartmut Fandrey; *Production:* Norbert Wohlers; *Publicity:* Ilse Rottner; *Rights & Permissions:* Ilse Rottner
Subject: Medicine
Founded: 1969
ISBN Publisher's Prefixes: 3-88429, 3-921222

Pestalozzi-Verlag graphische Gesellschaft mbH, Am Pestalozziring 14, Postfach 2829, D-8520 Erlangen Tel: (09131) 60600 Cable Add: Pestalozzi Erlangen Telex: 629766 Pevau Fax: (09131) 606078
Man Dirs: Dr Reinhold Weigand, Norbert Franke; *Editorial:* Wolfgang Kaiser
Subjects: Children's Books
Founded: 1844
ISBN Publisher's Prefix: 3-614

Verlag J P **Peter**, Gebr Holstein GmbH & Co KG, Taubertalweg 42-Wildbad, Postfach 1262, D-8803 Rothenburg Tel: (09861) 5028
Man Dir, Sales, Publicity: Dr Gerhard Prinz
Subjects: Poetry, Religion, Educational Materials, Periodicals
Founded: 1884
ISBN Publisher's Prefix: 3-87625

C F **Peters** Musikverlag GmbH & Co KG, Kennedyallee 101, Postfach 700851, D-6000 Frankfurt am Main 70 Tel: (069) 6313066 Cable Add: Petersedit Telex: 411686 edpe d
Managing Partner: Dr Johannes Petschull
Associate Companies: C F Peters Corporation, New York, USA; Hinrichsen Edition Ltd, London, UK
Imprints: Edition Peters, Henry Litolff's Verlag, Edition Schwann, MP Belaieff
Subjects: Musical scores, Books on Music (all areas of Classical and Contemporary Music)
Founded: 1800
ISBN Publisher's Prefix: 3-87626

Dr Hans **Peters** Verlag+, Salisweg 56, Postfach 2012, D-6450 Hanau 1 Tel: (06181) 21632
Man Dir: Wolfgang A Nagel; *Sales:* Barbara Nagel; *Production:* Rainer G Tripp
Subjects: Art Books, Pictorial Books, Picture Books for Children
Founded: 1952
ISBN Publisher's Prefix: 3-87627

Fachbuchverlag Dr **Pfanneberg** & Co+, Postfach 110910, D-6300 Giessen 11 (Located at: Westanlage 36) Tel: (0641) 74034
Man Dirs, Rights & Permissions: Dr Günther Pfanneberg, Gero Pfanneberg; *Editorial:* Gero Pfanneberg; *Sales:* Christa Horn; *Production:* Gerhard Duske
Subjects: Hotels and Catering Trade Textbooks, Bakery and Confectionery, Technologies, Commerce, Trade Schools Textbooks
Founded: 1949
ISBN Publisher's Prefix: 3-8057

FEDERAL REPUBLIC OF GERMANY 161

Verlag J **Pfeiffer**+, Anzinger Str 1, D-8000 Munich 80 Tel: (089) 4130010
Publisher: Eduard Niedernhuber; *Editorial:* Dr Karl Geisendörfer; *Sales, Publicity:* U Wunder; *Production:* S Seitz
Parent Company: Manz Verlag (qv)
Subjects: How-to, Philosophy, Psychology, Religion, Juveniles, High-priced Paperbacks, Social Science, Educational Materials
Founded: 1882
ISBN Publisher's Prefix: 3-7904

Richard **Pflaum** Verlag KG*, Postfach 180737, D-8000 Munich 18 (Located at: Lazarettstr 4, D-8000 Munich 19) Tel: (089) 126070 Cable Add: Pflaumverlag Telex: 529408
Head of Book Department: Helmut Brackebusch
Subsidiary Company: Hüthig und Pflaum Verlag GmbH & Co KG (qv)
Subjects: Electrical Engineering, Electronics, Hobbies, Medicine, Periodicals
ISBN Publisher's Prefix: 3-7905

Udo **Pfriemer** Verlag GmbH*, Landwehrstr 68, Postfach 201940, D-8000 Munich 2 Tel: (089) 531604 Telex: 0523398
Parent Company: Bauverlag GmbH (qv)
Subjects: Energy, Alternative Energies, Maintenance Technology in Water, Gas, Helio systems; Sanitary, Health, Heating, Sewage Technology, History of Culture and Technology

Robert **Pfützner** GmbH, see Verlag Mensch und Arbeit

Philips Fachbücher, Dr Alfred Hüthig Verlag GmbH, Im Weiher 10, Postfach 102869, D-6900 Heidelberg Tel: (06221) 4890 Telex: 461727 Fax: (06221) 489279
Man Dir: Jochen Schmitt
Parent Company: Dr Alfred Hüthig Verlag GmbH (qv)
Subjects: Electronics, Electrical Engineering, Radio & Television
ISBN Publisher's Prefix: 3-7785

Philosophia Verlag GmbH+, Oettingenstr 25, Postfach 466, D-8000 Munich 22 Tel: (089) 221391 Telex: 0529070 iuskmd
Publisher: Ulrich Staudinger; *Editorial Board:* Hans Burkhardt, Albert H Zlabinger, Barry Smith; *Man Dir, Sales, Production, Rights & Permissions:* Hilla Hueber
Subjects: Philosophy, National Economy (in English and German)
Bookshop: Philosophia Book Service, Josephsburgstr 85, D-8000 Munich 80 Tel: (089) 434824
Founded: 1978 (originally 1966)
ISBN Publisher's Prefix: 3-88405

Physica-Verlag GmbH & Co, Tiergartenstr 17, Postfach 105280, D-6900 Heidelberg 1 Tel: (06221) 4870 Telex: 461723 sphdb d
Man Dir, Rights & Permissions: Dr Werner A Müller
Orders to: Springer GmbH & Co, Auslieferungs-Gesellschaft, Auftragsbearbeitung Herr R Egner, Haberstr 7, D-6900 Heidelberg-Rohrbach Tel: (06221) 304486
Parent Company: Springer-Verlag Berlin — Heidelberg — New York — Tokyo GmbH & Co KG (qv)
Subjects: Statistics, Economics, Business Administration, University Textbooks, Scientific Journals
Founded: 1952
ISBN Publisher's Prefix: 3-7908

Physik-Verlag GmbH+, Postfach 1260-80, D-6940 Weinheim Tel: (06201) 6020 Telex: 465516 vchwh d Fax: (06201) 602328
Man Dirs: Prof Helmut Grünewald, Hans Dirk Köhler; *Editorial:* Dr Hans Friedrich Ebel, Walter Greulich; *Sales:* Helmut Schmitzer; *Advertising:* Rainer Roth; *Production:* Maximilian Montkowski; *Rights & Permissions:* Dr Dietmar Schallwich
Parent Company: VCH Verlagsgesellschaft mbH (qv)
Subjects: Monographs, Textbooks, Periodicals
1986: 3 titles *Founded:* 1947
ISBN Publisher's Prefix: 3-87664

R **Piper** GmbH & Co KG, Verlag+, Georgenstr 4, Postfach 430120, D-8000 Munich 40 Tel: (089) 3818010 Cable Add: Piperverlag Munich Telex: 5215385
Orders to: Koch, Neff und Oetinger & Co, Am Wallgraben 110, D-7000 Stuttgart 80
Man Dirs: Dr hc Klaus Piper, Dr Ernst Reinhard Piper; *Editorial:* Dr Uwe Heldt, Patricia Reimann, Dr Klaus Stadler, Renate Dörner, Ulrich Wank; *Sales Manager:* Klaus-Michael Buck; *Rights & Permissions:* Dorothee Grisebach
Branch Off: R Piper & Co Verlag GmbH, Switzerland (qv)
Subjects: Literary Fiction, Biography, Sociology, Natural Sciences, Philosophy, Theology, Psychology, Music, Quality Paperbacks
1987: 220 titles *Founded:* 1904
ISBN Publisher's Prefix: 3-492

Plambeck & Co, Druck und Verlag GmbH+*, Xantener Str 7, Postfach 101053, D-4040 Neuss Tel: (02101) 59030 Telex: 8517506 and 8517530 plad d
Publicity Manager: Herbert Dege
Subjects: Paperbacks, Pocket Books, Periodicals

Verlag A G **Ploetz** GmbH & Co KG*, Habsburgerstr 116, D-7800 Freiburg im Breisgau Tel: (0761) 2717387
Man Dir: Hermann Scharnagl; *Editorial:* Falk Redecker; *Advertising/Public Relations:* Dr Joseph Nietfeld
Orders to: Verlag Herder, Hermann-Herder-Str 4, D-7800 Freiburg im Breisgau
Parent Company: Verlag Herder GmbH & Co KG (qv)
Associate Companies: Herder und Herder GmbH (qv); Verlag Herder & Co, Austria (qv); Herder Editrice e Libreria, Italy (qv); Herder AG, Switzerland (qv)
Subjects: Illustrated Popular Reference Works on Historical, Biographical, Geographical Themes; School Books, Sociology, Linguistics
Founded: 1880
ISBN Publisher's Prefix: 3-87640

Podzun-Pallas Verlag GmbH, Markt 9, Postfach 314, D-6360 Friedberg 3-Dorheim Tel: (06031) 3131 Cable Add: Podzun, Friedberg Telex: 415961 pvlg
Man Dir, Production, Rights & Permissions: Rainer Ahnert; *Editorial:* Mrs Danker; *Sales:* Mrs Neisel
Subjects: History, Illustrated Books, Periodicals
1987-88: 15 titles
ISBN Publisher's Prefix: 3-7909

C E **Poeschel** Verlag, Kernerstr 43, Postfach 529, D-7000 Stuttgart 1 Tel: (0711) 223067
Publisher: Mr Schweizer; *Sales Dir, Rights & Permissions:* Mr Naveau; *Advertising Dir:* Mr Kegler
Orders to: (Federal Republic of Germany): Verlagsauslieferung Hermann Leins GmbH & Co Verlags-KG, Postfach 7, D-7408 Kusterdingen; (in Berlin) VAB Verlagsauslieferungen M Jager KG, Lützowstr 105/bbz, D-1000 Berlin 30
Associate Company: J B Metzlersche Verlagsbuchhandlung (qv)
Subject: Economics
Founded: 1902
ISBN Publisher's Prefix: 3-7910

Pohl Druckerei und Verlagsanstalt Otto Pohl+, Herzog-Ernst-Ring 1, Postfach 103, D-3100 Celle Tel: (05141) 27081 Cable Add: Pohl, Celle
Dir: Manfred Senftleben
Subjects: Physical Education, Games, Sports, Gymnastics, Keep Fit
ISBN Publisher's Prefix: 3-7911

Verlag für **polizeiliches** Fachschrifttum, see Georg Schmidt-Römhild

Polyglott-Verlag Dr Bolte KG, Neusser Str 3, Postfach 401120, D-8000 Munich 40 Tel: (089) 360960 Cable Add: Langenscheidt Munich Telex: 5215379 lkgm d Fax: (089) 36096258
Man Dirs: Karl Ernst Tielebier-Langenscheidt, Dr Florian Langenscheidt; *Editor:* Dr Wilhelm Trappl; *Sales Dir:* Peter Haering; *Export Dir:* Uwe Cordts; *Advertising Dir:* Klaus Ferber; *Rights & Permissions:* Manfred Überall
Subjects: Travel Guides, Menu Guides, Phrasebooks, Dictionaries
Founded: 1902
Miscellaneous: Firm is a member of the Langenscheidt Group (qv)
ISBN Publisher's Prefix: 3-493

Polygraph Verlag GmbH+, Schaumainkai 85, Postfach 700854, D-6000 Frankfurt am Main 70 Tel: (069) 639066 Cable Add: Polygraphverlag Frankfurt Main Telex: 413562 Fax: (069) 6313502
Man Dir: H J Teichmann; *Sales Dir:* Peter Rüster; *Publicity Dir:* R Kreis; *Rights & Permissions:* Ulrike Schulz
Subjects: Textbooks and Reference Works for the Printing Industry and Allied Trades, Periodicals
Founded: 1947

Edition Georg **Popp** GmbH & Co, see Arena-Verlag Georg Popp GmbH & Co

Possev-Verlag V Gorachek KG, Flurscheideweg 15, D-6230 Frankfurt am Main 80 Tel: (069) 341265
All Offices: N B Jdanoff
Subjects: Contemporary Russian authors in the original Russian, Periodicals in Russian
Founded: 1945
Miscellaneous: The Company also runs a translation agency (qv under Gorachek)

W **Poth** GbR, see Verlagsbuchhandlung Megapress

Praesentverlag Heinz Peter*, Kleiststr 15, Postfach 2657, D-4830 Gütersloh Tel: (05241) 3188 Telex: 933831
Publisher: Heinz Peter
Subjects: General Fiction, Hobbies, Reference Books, Travel, Cookery
ISBN Publisher's Prefix: 3-87644

Präsenz-Verlag der Jesus-Bruderschaft+, Gnadenthal, D-6257 Hünfelden Tel: (06438) 8181
Dir: Brother Christian H Lüling
Subject: Religion
Founded: 1962
ISBN Publisher's Prefix: 3-87630

Verlag **Presse** Informations Agentur GmbH (PIAG), Stefanienstr 4, D-7570 Baden Baden Tel: (07221) 28994/25348 Cable Add: PIAG Baden Baden Telex: 781217 piag d
Man Dir: Dieter Brinzer; *Publicity & Advertising Dir:* Thea Gutzeit; *Sales Dir:* Klaus Pittner
Subject: Photography
Founded: 1963

162 FEDERAL REPUBLIC OF GERMANY

Guido **Pressler** Verlag+, Auf dem Strifft, D-5165 Hürtgenwald Tel: (02429) 1385
Subjects: Art, History, Literature, Bibliographies, History of Sciences
ISBN Publisher's Prefix: 3-87646

Prestel Verlag, Mandlstr 26, D-8000 Munich 40 Tel: (089) 3817090 Cable Add: Prestelverlag Telex: 5216366 Fax: (089) 38170935
Man Dir: Jürgen Tesch; *Sales Dir:* Gerda Behmenburg; *Advertising & Publicity Dir:* Grete Momsen; *Rights & Permissions:* Sieglinde van den Brandt
Subjects: General Non-fiction, Art, Reference, History
1986: 40 titles *Founded:* 1924
ISBN Publisher's Prefix: 3-7913

Helmut **Preussler** Verlag*, Rothenburger Str 25, D-8500 Nuremberg 70 Tel: (0911) 262323/267124 Cable Add: Preussler-Verlag
Man Dir, Editorial: Helmut Preussler; *Sales, Publicity:* Maria Pfann; *Production:* Werner Eckstein
Bookshop: Ernst Gebhard, Rothenburger Str 23-25, D-8500 Nuremberg
Founded: 1973
ISBN Publisher's Prefix: 3-921332

Prisma Verlag GmbH, Ringstr 16, D-4840 Rheda Tel: (05242) 415695 Telex: 931149
Dir: Aloys Hellmold
Parent Company: Verlagsgruppe Bertelsmann GmbH (qv for associate companies)
Subjects: Reprints, Special Editions, Encyclopaedias, Mail Order Series

Albert **Pröpster***, Schillerstr 46, Postfach 2149, D-8960 Kempten Tel: (0831) 22797
Subjects: Cookery Books, Specialist Gastronomy Books, Picture Books, Roman Catholic Interest Books

Propyläen Verlag, Lindenstr 76, D-1000 Berlin 61 Tel: (030) 2590 Cable Add: Ullsteinbuch Berlin Telex: 183723 vlgul d Fax: (030) 25913523
Dir: Dr Herbert Fleissner; *Publicity:* Helmut Krüger
Parent Company: Verlag Ullstein GmbH (qv)
Subjects: Arts, History, Literature
ISBN Publisher's Prefix: 3-549

Verlag für **Psychologie**, Dr C J Hogrefe, Rohnsweg 25, Postfach 3751, D-3400 Göttingen Tel: (0551) 54044
Proprietor: Dr C J Hogrefe; *Man Dir:* Dr H Lundberg; *Sales Dir:* Jürgen Grapentin; *Production:* B Otto; *Promotion:* J A Smith
Branch Offs: C J Hogrefe Inc, 12 Bruce Park Ave, Toronto, Ontario M4P 2S3, Canada; Verlag für Psychologie, Dr C J Hogrefe, Switzerland (qv)
Subjects: Psychology, Textbooks, Handbooks, Conference Reports, Yearbooks
Bookshop: Hogrefe International, Daimlerstr 40, D-7000 Stuttgart 50
Founded: 1949
ISBN Publisher's Prefix: 3-8017

Anton **Pustet**, Postfach 1421, D-8228 Freilassing
Head Office: Universitätsverlag Anton Pustet, Austria (qv)
Subjects: Philosophy, Religion, Psychology, Social Science, Music
Founded: 1598
ISBN Publisher's Prefix: 3-7916

Verlag Friedrich **Pustet***, Gutenbergstr 8, Postfach 110441, D-8400 Regensburg 11 Tel: (0941) 96044 Cable Add: Pustet Telex: 65672
Man Dir: Dr Friedrich Pustet; *Editorial:* Dr Gerd J Maurer; *Sales & Advertising Dir, Rights & Permissions, Production:* Karl Wittman
Subjects: Christian Religion, Art, Monographs, Biography, Folklore, Bavaria
Bookshops: Buchhandlung Friedrich Pustet, Regensburg, Gesandtenstr 6; Kleiner Exerzierplatz 4, Passau; Grottenau 4, Augsburg
Founded: 1826
ISBN Publisher's Prefix: 3-7917

Quell-Verlag, Furtbachstr 12A, Postfach 897, D-7000 Stuttgart 1 Tel: (0711) 601000
Dir: Walter Waldbauer; *Editorial, Rights & Permissions:* Dr Renate Sälter; *Publicity, Sales Manager:* Klaus Ruder
Subjects: General Fiction, Biography, History, Philosophy, Religion
Bookshops: Buchhandlung der Evangelischen Gesellschaft in Heidenheim, Ludwigsburg, Schäbisch Hall, Stuttgart, Ulm
1985: 40 titles *Founded:* 1830
ISBN Publisher's Prefix: 3-7918

Quelle und Meyer Verlag GmbH & Co+, Luisenpl 2, Postfach 4747, D-6200 Wiesbaden Tel: (06121) 373071
Man Dirs: Günther Fertig, Gerhard Stahl
Orders to: VVA (Vereinigte Verlagsauslieferung GmbH), Postfach 7777, D-4830 Gütersloh 1
Subjects: Philosophy, Religion, Psychology, Chemistry, Biology, Science, Social Science, Education, Languages, Literature, History, University, Secondary & Primary Textbooks
Founded: 1906
ISBN Publisher's Prefix: 3-494

R K W, see Rationalisierungs-Kuratorium

R V, see Reise- und Verkehrsverlag

Musikverlag Gerhard **Rabe** GmbH, subsidiary company of P J Tonger Musikverlag GmbH & Co (qv)

Radius-Verlag GmbH+, Kniebisstr 29, D-7000 Stuttgart 1 Tel: (0711) 283091
Man Dir: Wolfgang Erk
Subjects: General Fiction, Philosophy, Religion, Paperbacks, Psychology, Periodical
1986: 17 titles *1987:* 18 titles *Founded:* 1962
ISBN Publisher's Prefix: 3-87173

Rainer Verlag GmbH, Koertestr 10, D-1000 Berlin 61 Tel: (030) 6916536
Man Dir and Advertising: Rainer Pretzell; *Sales Dir:* Agnes Pretzell
Subjects: Belles Lettres, Poetry, Art, Quality Paperbacks
Founded: 1966

Dr **Ramdohr** KG, see Mentor-Verlag

Dokument und Analyse Verlag Bogislaw von **Randow**, Barer Str 43, D-8000 Munich 40 Tel: (089) 2720100
Publisher: Bogislaw von Randow; *General Manager:* Gerhard Fassmann; *Marketing Manager:* Regina Reiser; *Marketing Publicity:* Astrid Schneider
Subjects: Politics, Economics, Law, Sociology, Science, Culture, Periodical
Founded: 1972

Rationalisierungs-Kuratorium der Deutschen Wirtschaft eV (RKW), Düsseldorfer Str 40, Postfach 5867, D-6236 Eschborn Tel: (06196) 4951 Cable Add: Erkawe Telex: 4072755 rkw d
Registered Society of the German Industrial Rationalization Board
Managers: H Borns, Dr H Müller; *Publicity Manager:* H Degenhard
Branch Offs: In all areas of the Federal Republic of Germany
Subjects: Business Operation and Management, Labour and Social Economics, Engineering/Technology Interchange, Construction, Packaging, Consultancy, Further Training
Founded: 1921

Walter **Rau** Verlag, Benderstr 168a, Postfach 120407, D-4000 Düsseldorf 12 Tel: (0211) 283095 Telex: 08586682
Dirs: Gisela W Rau, Beatrix M Rau
Subjects: Arts, Education, Non-fiction, Social Science, Literature, Translations, Chess
Founded: 1930
ISBN Publisher's Prefix: 3-7919

Karl **Rauch** Verlag KG*, Grafenberger Alle 100, D-4000 Düsseldorf 1
Man Dir: Harald Ebner
Subjects: Documentation, History, Fiction, Book Industry, Translations
Founded: 1923
ISBN Publisher's Prefix: 3-7920

Agentur des **Rauhen Hauses** Hamburg GmbH, Beim Brüderhof 8, D-2000 Norderstedt 1 Tel: (040) 5260080
Dirs: Max Lenz, Willi Kohlmann
Subjects: Religion, Belles Lettres, Fiction, Juveniles, Art, Paperbacks
Founded: 1842
ISBN Publisher's Prefix: 3-7600

Gerhard **Rautenberg** Druckerei und Verlag GmbH & Co KG+*, Blinke 8, Postfach 1909, D-2950 Leer/Ostfriesland Tel: (0491) 4288 Cable Add: Rautenberg Leer
Dirs: Gerhard Rautenberg, Carl-Ludwig Rautenberg; *Editorial:* Gerhard Rautenberg
Branch Off: Druckerei und Verlag Gerhard Rautenberg GmbH & Co KG, Königstr 41, D-2208 Glückstadt
Subjects: Regional Guides within Germany, Humour, Popular Historical, General Fiction, Show Business
Bookshop: Rautenbergsche Buchhandlung, Postfach 1909, D-2950 Leer
Founded: 1825
ISBN Publisher's Prefix: 3-7921

Ravenna Presse, an imprint of März Verlag (qv)

Ravensburger Buchverlag Otto Maier GmbH+, Marktstr 22-26 und Robert Bosch Str 1, Postfach 1860, D-7980 Ravensburg Tel: (0751) 861 Cable Add: Maierverlag Telex: 0732926/0732921 Fax: (0751) 862289
Presidents: Otto J Maier, Dorothee Hess-Maier; *Man Dir:* Claus Runge; *Editorial:* Lothar Beyer, Michael Kohlhammer, Christian Stottele; *Production:* Rudolf Goeggerle; *Sales:* G R Niess; *Publicity:* Michael Pfleiderer; *Rights & Permissions:* Frank Jacoby-Nelson
Subsidiary Companies: Ravensburger Film und TV GmbH, Ravensburger Verlag GmbH (both Federal Republic of Germany); Ravensburger Spiele GmbH, Vienna, Austria; Editions Ravensburger SA, Attenschwiller, France; Ravensburger Italia, Milan, Italy; Otto Maier Benelux BV, Netherlands (qv); Carlit und Ravensburger AG, Switzerland
Subjects: Children's and Juvenile Fiction and Non-fiction, Adult Craft and Hobby, Art, Educational (Art, Pre- and Elementary School Materials), Paperbacks
Founded: 1883
ISBN Publisher's Prefix: 3-473

Ravenstein Verlag GmbH*, Auf der Krautweide 24, D-6232 Bad Soden/Ts Tel: (069) 590722 Cable Add: Ravensteinverlag
Man Dirs: Helga Ravenstein, Rüdiger Bosse

Subjects: National and International Road Maps, Country and Regional Touring and Walking Maps, Town Maps and Guides
Founded: 1830
ISBN Publisher's Prefix: 3-87660

Verlag **Recht und Wirtschaft** GmbH+, Häusserstr 14, Postfach 105960, D-6900 Heidelberg Tel: (06221) 9061 Cable Add: Rechtwirtschaft Heidelberg Telex: 461665 Fax: (06221) 906259
Associate Company: I H Sauer Verlag GmbH, Heidelberg (qv)
Subjects: Law and Economics, Tax, Social and Industrial Questions, Periodicals

Philipp **Reclam** Jun Verlag GmbH, Postfach 1349, D-7257 Ditzingen (Located at: Siemensstr 32, Ditzingen) Tel: (07156) 1630 Cable Add: Reclam Ditzingen Telex: 7266704 recl d
Publisher: Dr Dietrich Bode; *Publicity Dir:* Christoph Wilhelmi; *Sales Manager:* Jürgen Bernardi; *Rights & Permissions:* Dr Stephan Koranyi
Subjects: General Fiction, Belles Lettres, Poetry, Music, Art, Philosophy, Reference, Religion, Low-priced Paperbacks, University, Secondary & Primary Textbooks
Founded: 1828
ISBN Publisher's Prefix: 3-15

Regio Verlag, Kappenbühlstr 16, D-7485 Sigmaringendorf Tel: (07571) 3534
Publisher: Dr Lothar Johannes
Subjects: Regional Guides, Biography, History, Art
Founded: 1923
Miscellaneous: Formerly Glock und Lutz Verlag Heroldsberg
ISBN Publisher's Prefix: 3-8235

Dr Ludwig **Reichert** Verlag+, Tauernstr 11, D-6200 Wiesbaden Tel: (06121) 461851
Publisher: Dr Ludwig Reichert
Subjects: Facsimile Reprints, Art, Books and Libraries, Orientalia, Linguistics
Founded: 1970
ISBN Publisher's Prefixes: 3-920153, 3-88226

Otto **Reichl** Verlag+, 'Der Leuchter', Auf dem Hähnchen, D-5401 St Joar Tel: (02226) 5468
Man Dir: Matthias Draeger
Subjects: Philosophy, Religion, Parapsychology, Mysticism, Supernatural
1985-86: 5 titles *Founded:* 1909
ISBN Publisher's Prefix: 3-87667

Verlag Knut **Reim**, Dammtorstr 30, Postfach 302824, D-2000 Hamburg 36 Tel: (040) 342641
General Managers: Jens Christians, Knut Reim
Subjects: Juvenilia, Jurisprudence, Economics
Founded: 1958

Dietrich **Reimer** Verlag, Unter den Eichen 57, D-1000 Berlin 45 Tel: (030) 8314081
Publisher, Rights & Permissions: Dr Friedrich Kaufmann; *Editorial:* Andreas Müller; *Sales, Publicity:* Nina Hess; *Production:* Gudrun Jurrat, Jörg Hellwig
Orders to: Koch, Neff und Oetinger & Co Verlagsauslieferung GmbH, Schockenriedstr 39, D-7000 Stuttgart 80
Subjects: Ethnology, Archaeology, Art, Earth Sciences
Bookshops: Nautische Buchhandlung, Dietrich Reimer Fachbuchhandlung (both at above address)
1985: 70 titles *1986:* 70 titles *Founded:* 1846
ISBN Publisher's Prefix: 3-496

Ernst **Reinhardt** GmbH & Co Verlag+, Kemnatenstr 46, D-8000 Munich 19 Tel: (089) 1783005
Man Dir, Production: Karl Münster
Orders to: Postfach 380280, D-8000 Munich 38
Subjects: Psychology, Pedagogy, Education, Special Education, Medicine, Psychotherapy, Social Sciences, Philosophy, Divinity, Music
Founded: 1899
ISBN Publisher's Prefix: 3-497

Reise- und Verkehrsverlag GmbH (RV), Neumarkterstr 18, Postfach 800360, D-8000 Munich 80 Tel: (089) 431890 Telex: 523259 Fax: (089) 4312837
Man Dir: Dr Rainer Cordes; *Editorial:* Dieter Meinhardt; *Sales Manager:* Wolfgang Völcker; *Foreign Rights:* Gisela Goedecke
Parent Company: Verlagsgruppe Bertelsmann GmbH (qv for associate companies)
Subjects: Maps, Atlases, Guides
Founded: 1927

Rembrandt Verlag GmbH, Schaperstr 35, D-1000 Berlin 15 Tel: (030) 2135003
Man Dir: Dr Klaus J Lemmer
Subjects: Biography, History, Music, Art
Founded: 1923
ISBN Publisher's Prefix: 3-7925

Verlag Klaus G **Renner**, Adelheidstr 26, D-8000 Munich 40 Tel: (089) 2715495
Man Dir: Klaus Renner
Subjects: Belles Lettres, Poetry, Limited Editions
Founded 1973
ISBN Publisher's Prefix: 3-921499

Verlag Norman **Rentrop**+, Theodor Heuss Str 4, D-5300 Bonn 2 Tel: (0228) 364055 Telex: 17228309 ttx d attn rentrop Fax: (0228) 364411
Man Dir: Norman Rentrop; *Editorial, Publicity:* Michael Rieck; *Sales:* Mandy Prolze; *Production:* Monika Graf; *Rights & Permissions:* Reinhard Fey
Branch Offs: Pausinger Str 7B, A-5020 Salzburg, Austria; 1 Place du Lycée, F-68005 Colmar, France; Löwenstr 16, CH-8021 Zurich, Switzerland; 27A Old Gloucester St, London WC1N 3XX, UK; 323 South Franklin Bldg, Suite R-246, Chicago, IL 60606-7096, USA
Subject: Business Management
1986: 30 titles *Founded:* 1975
ISBN Publisher's Prefix: 3-8125

Rheingauer Verlagsgesellschaft mbH, Postfach 90, D-6228 Eltville am Rhein (Located at: Rheingauer Str 54) Tel: (06123) 2312 Telex: 04182921 rvg d
Man Dir, Rights & Permissions: Bernd Ley, Peter Halfar; *Sales:* Mr Mätzel, Mr Hülzer, Mr Stärk; *Production:* Bernd Ley; *Publicity:* Ingrid Bader
Orders to: Unipart-Verlag GmbH, Hofener Weg 33a, D-7148 Remseck-Aldingen
Subjects: Quality Illustrated Works, Low-priced Foreign Classics in Translation, Saga and Legend, Juvenile, General Non-fiction
Founded: 1975
ISBN Publisher's Prefix: 3-17319

Rheinland-Verlag GmbH, Abtei Brauweiler, D-5024 Pulheim 2 Tel: (02234) 8051
Orders to: Dr Rudolf Habelt GmbH, Abt Verlag (qv)
Branch Off: Postfach 150104, D-5300 Bonn
Subjects: Rhineland excavations, Regional Knowledge, Folklore, Care of Art and Monuments

Dr **Riederer** Verlag GmbH+, Gutbrodstr 9, Postfach 447, D-7000 Stuttgart 1 Tel: (0711) 639797
Man Dir: H Schneider
Subjects: Science, Engineering, Metallography, Materials Science
Founded: 1945
ISBN Publisher's Prefix: 3-87675

Rimbaud Verlagsgesellschaft mbH+, Viktoriaallee 24, Postfach 86, D-5100 Aachen Tel: (0241) 509172/542532 Telex: 832366 attn Kennwort Rimbaud Presse
Man Dir, Sales, Publicity: Walter Hoerner; *Editorial:* Reinhard Kiefer; *Production:* Bernard Albers
Subjects: Essays, Music, Poetry, Photography
Founded: 1983
ISBN Publisher's Prefix: 3-89086

Ringier-Verlag GmbH*, Ortlerstr 8, Postfach 700840, D-8000 Munich 70 Tel: (089) 769920 Telex: 522720
Man Dir: Wolf Prüter
Subjects: Photography, Mountaineering, Nature Study, Sports Periodicals
Founded: 1932
ISBN Publisher's Prefix: 3-7763

Ritzau KG Verlag Zeit und Eisenbahn, Landsberger Str 24, D-8911 Pürgen Tel: (08196) 252
Subjects: History of German Transport and Railways (including old timetables)
1985: 3 titles *1986:* 4 titles *Founded:* 1968
ISBN Publisher's Prefix: 3-921304

Robinson Verlag*, Wilhelm-Leuschner-Str 13, Postfach 16646, D-Frankfurt am Main Tel: (069) 232828
Man Dir, Rights & Permissions: Frank Brunner
Subjects: Contemporary Literature, Fantasy, Adventure, Social Problems, Giftbook series
Founded: 1981
ISBN Publisher's Prefix: 3-88592

Röderberg-Verlag GmbH*, Schumannstr 56, Postfach 101848, D-6000 Frankfurt am Main 1 Tel: (069) 751046 Telex: 414721
Manager: Johannes Bär; *Editorial, Production:* Peter Altmann; *Sales:* Horst Foerster
Subject: Politics
ISBN Publisher's Prefix: 3-87682

Rogner und Bernhard GmbH & Co Verlags KG, Reichenbachstr 33, Postfach 140480, D-8000 Munich 5 Tel: (089) 2014336 Telex: 05215482 buch d
Dir: Antje Ellermann
Subjects: General Fiction, Belles Lettres, Art, Photography
ISBN Publisher's Prefix: 3-8077

Lev **Roitman** Verlag+, Potsdamerstr 9, D-8000 Munich 40 Tel: (089) 349858/2102622
Publisher, Rights & Permissions: Lev Roitman
Orders to: Buchhandel-service, Schleissheimerstr 401, D-8000 Munich 45
Subjects: Fiction, Non-fiction, Biographies
1985: 6 titles *Founded:* 1982
ISBN Publisher's Prefix: 3-923510

Rombach Verlagshaus KG*, Lörracher Str 3, Postfach 1349, D-7800 Freiburg im Breisgau Tel: (0761) 49091 Telex: 772728 romba d
Man Dir (Rombach & Co GmbH): Dr Fritz Hodeige; *Dir:* (Rombach Verlagshaus KG): Christian H Hodeige
Parent Company: Rombach & Co GmbH (at above address)
Associate Companies: Rombach Druckhaus KG, Rombach Handelshaus KG, Rombach Medienhaus KG, Rombach Input Data KG (all at above address)

Subjects: History, Art, Social & Political Science, Black Music, Regional Topics, University Textbooks
Bookshop: Rombach-Center, Bertoldstr 10, D-7800 Freiburg
Founded: 1936
ISBN Publisher's Prefix: 3-7930

Rose-Verlag und Edition Rose-Verlag*, Seestr 12, D-8221 Seebruck Chiemsee Tel: (08667) 420 Cable Add: Rose-Verlag 8221 Seebruck Telex: 0526144 M Piepenstock
Man Dir, Rights & Permissions: Marianne Piepenstock; *Editorial, Sales, Production:* Michael Piepenstock
Subjects: Education and Upbringing, Health, Food, Religion
Founded: 1955
ISBN Publisher's Prefix: 3-920803

Rosenheimer Verlagshaus Alfred Förg GmbH & Co KG+, Am Stocket 12, D-8200 Rosenheim 2 Tel: (08031) 81081 Cable Add: Rosenheimer Verlagshaus Rosenheim Telex: 525732 rosen d
Man Dir: Alfred Förg; *Dir:* Berthold Rech; *Sales:* Alf Jungermann; *Rights & Permissions:* Hansjörg Decker
Subjects: Art, Folk Art, History, Needlecraft, General Fiction, Bavarica, Cartoons
Founded: 1968
ISBN Publisher's Prefix: 3-475

Rotbuch Verlag GmbH, Potsdamer Str 98, D-1000 Berlin 30 Tel: (030) 2611196
Man Dirs: Sigrid Ruschmeier, Angelika Areudt; *Editorial:* Gabriele Dietze, Dr Otto Kallscheuer; *Production:* Stefan Wantzeu; *Sales, Advertising:* Walter Hellmann, Sigrid Ruschmeier, Hannes Sieg, Angelika Areudt; *Publicity, Rights & Permissions:* Holger Behm
Orders to: Koch, Neff und Oetinger & Co, Postfach 800620, D-7000 Stuttgart 80
Subjects: Belles Lettres, Poetry, History, Social Science
ISBN Publisher's Prefix: 3-88022

Verlag **Roter Morgen***, Wellinghoferstr 103, Postfach 300526, D-4600 Dortmund-Hörde (30) Tel: (0231) 433691
Subjects: Speeches and Writings of Stalin and Enver Hoxha, Communism, Publications of the Communist Party of Germany (Marxist-Leninist), Periodical
Founded: 1977
ISBN Publisher's Prefix: 3-88196

Verlag **Roter Stern**, Holzhausenstr 4, Postfach 180147, D-6000 Frankfurt am Main Tel: (069) 599999
Publisher: K D Wolff
Associate Company: Stroemfeld Verlag AG, Switzerland (qv)
Subjects: Textbooks, Philosophy, Periodicals
ISBN Publisher's Prefix: 3-87877

Erich **Röth**-Verlag, Kassel, Korbacher Str 235, D-3500 Kassel-Nordshausen Tel: (0561) 401206 Cable Add: Röthverlag
Subjects: Folk tales and Folklore, Hungary, Translations from Hungarian, Music, Art
Founded: 1921
ISBN Publisher's Prefix: 3-87680

Bergverlag Rudolf **Rother**, see Bergverlag

Rowohlt Taschenbuch Verlag GmbH+, Hamburger Str 17, Postfach 1349, D-2057 Reinbek bei Hamburg Tel: (040) 72721 Cable Add: Rowohltverlag Reinbek Telex: 0217854
Dirs: Dr Helmut Dähne, Dr Michael Naumann, Erwin Steen, Horst Varrelmann; *Editorial:* Dr Michael Naumann; *Sales:* Lutz Kettmann; *Production:* Erwin Steen; *Publicity:* Asma Semler; *Rights &*

Permissions: Marianne Sparr
Parent Company: Rowohlt Verlag GmbH (at above address)
Subjects: Fiction and Non-fiction Paperbacks, especially, popular works on Life Sciences, History and Archaeology, Art, Politics, Psychology, Education, Philosophy, Religion, Social Sciences, Sports and Games, Juvenile, Foreign Literature in Translation
Founded: 1953
ISBN Publisher's Prefix: 3-499

Ruhland Verlag*, Goethestr 27, D-6000 Frankfurt am Main 1 Tel: (069) 285604
Publisher: Erich Ruhland; *Publicity, Rights & Permissions:* Dietrich Luhrs
Subject: Instruction courses and texts on Secretarial Work, Commerce, Business Management
Founded: 1968
ISBN Publisher's Prefixes: 3-88509, 3-920793

Peter **Rump** Verlag+, Buddestr 15, D-4800 Bielefeld 1 Tel: (0521) 179815
Man Dir: Peter Rump
Orders to: Prolit GmbH, Postfach 111008, D-6300 Giessen
Imprint: Papilio Print
Subjects: Travel Guides, Languages, Art
1986: 15 titles *Founded:* 1981
ISBN Publisher's Prefix: 3-922376

VWK **Ryborsch** GmbH, see VWK

S A S S-Verlagsgesellschaft mbH und Co KG*, Postfach 249, D-6440 Bebra (Located at: Nürnberger Str) Tel: (06622) 2005 Telex: 493412

S D V Saarbrücker Druckerei und Verlag GmbH+, Halbergstr 3, Postfach 442, D-6600 Saarbrücken Tel: (0681) 64941 Telex: 4421533 sdv d
Man Dir, Editorial: Peter Neumann; *Sales Manager:* Hannelore Rüppert
Parent Company: Paulinus-Druckerei GmbH, D-5500 Trier
Subjects: Folk Lore, Regional Lore, History, Art, Architecture, Language and Literature
1986: 10 titles *Founded:* 1922
ISBN Publisher's Prefix: 3-921646

Saatkorn-Verlag GmbH, Postfach 132215, Grindelberg 13-17, D-2000 Hamburg 13 Tel: (040) 4418710 Telex: 2166396 sav d
Man Dir: Reinhard Rupp; *Editorial:* Horst Zschunke; *Sales:* Rolf Naggatis; *Production:* Peter Streit; *Publicity:* Claus F Weidmüller; *Rights & Permissions:* Elke Englund
Subsidiary Company: Grindeldruck GmbH (at above address)
Associate Company: ESTEA Einkaufsagentur fur Bedarfsgüter, (at above address)
Subjects: Health, Theology, Juvenile, Childrens
Bookshop: Primavita-Laden, Helene-Lange-Str 1, D-2000 Hamburg 13
1985: 9 titles *1986:* 14 titles *Founded:* 1895
ISBN Publisher's Prefix: 3-8150

Verlag Otto **Sagner**, Heßstr 39-41, Postfach 340108, D-8000 Munich 34 Tel: (089) 522027 Cable Add: buchsagner München Telex: 5216711 kusa d
Publisher: Otto Sagner; *Editorial:* Prof Dr Peter Rehder
Orders to: Kubon und Sagner (at above address)
Parent Company: Kubon und Sagner (at above address)
Subject: Slavistics (Language and Literature)
Founded: 1959
ISBN Publisher's Prefix: 3-87690

Otto **Salle** Verlag, see Verlag Moritz Diesterweg/Otto Salle Verlag

Salvator Verlag GmbH*, Hermann-Josef-Str 4, Postfach 220, D-5370 Kall Tel: (02441) 5047
Dir: Andreas Münck
Subject: Religion

Eugen **Salzer**-Verlag GmbH & Co KG, Titotstr 5, Postfach 3048, D-7100 Heilbronn 1 Tel: (07131) 68294
Man Dirs: Hartmut Salzer, Barbara Salzer; *Sales Dir:* J Glage
Subjects: Fiction, Belles Lettres, How-to, Reference, Juveniles
Founded: 1891
ISBN Publisher's Prefix: 3-7936

Sammlung Luchterhand, an imprint of Hermann Luchterhand Verlag GmbH & Co KG (qv)

Verlag der **Sankt-Johannis-Druckerei** C Schweickhardt*, Heiligenstr 24, Postfach 5, D-7630 Lahr 12 Tel: (07821) 5810 Cable Add: Veritas Lahrschwarzwäld
Man Dir: Walter Guthmann; *Editorial, Publicity, Rights & Permissions:* Karl-Heinz Kern; *Sales:* Johannes Walter; *Production:* Helmut Schlegel
Subjects: Christian Devotional: stories, commentaries, travel books for young people and adults
Founded: 1896
Miscellaneous: Member of the Telos (qv) group publishing evangelical paperbacks
ISBN Publisher's Prefix: 3-501

Sankt Otto Verlag GmbH, Laubanger 23, D-8600 Bamberg Tel: (0951) 79020
Joint Man Dirs: Kurt Kiening, Helmut Treml; *Other Offices:* Norbert Göbel
Parent Company: Bayerische Verlagsanstalt Bamberg (qv)
Associate Companies: Morawa und Co, Austria (qv); Adolf Zwimpfer, Switzerland (qv)
Subjects: Catholic Religious Literature, Hymn Books, Devotional
Bookshop: Goerres Buchhandlung, Lange Str 24, D-8600 Bamberg
Founded: 1922
ISBN Publisher's Prefix: 3-87693

Sassafras Verlag, Bismarckplatz 43, D-4150 Krefeld Tel: (02151) 599555
Subject: Contemporary Writing
ISBN Publisher's Prefix: 3-922690

Satire Verlag GmbH*, Auerstr 1, D-5000 Cologne 60 Tel: (0221) 735929
Man Dir: Saskia E Wollschon; *Editorial:* Reinhard Hippen, Gerd Wollschon
Subject: Satire
Founded: 1977
ISBN Publisher's Prefix: 3-88268

I H **Sauer** Verlag GmbH+, Häusserstr 14, Postfach 105960, D-6900 Heidelberg Tel: (06221) 9061 Telex: 461665 Fax: (06221) 906259
Associate Company: Verlag Recht und Wirtschaft GmbH (qv)
Subjects: Industrial Management, Economics, Organization, Data Processing, Personnel Management, Rhetoric, Publicity, Series of Paperbacks for Industry

Verlag **Sauerländer** GmbH, Meisengasse 15, D-6000 Frankfurt am Main 1 Tel: (069) 284953
Publisher: Hans C Sauerländer
Parent Company: Sauerländer AG, Switzerland (qv)
Associate Company: Verlag Sauerländer, A-5020 Salzburg, Münzgasse 1, Austria
Subjects: Juveniles, Fiction, Sciences
ISBN Publisher's Prefix: 3-7941

J D **Sauerländer's** Verlag, Finkenhofstr 21, D-6000 Frankfurt am Main 1 Tel: (069) 555217
Publisher: Helmut A Baetz
Subjects: Forestry and Agricultural Sciences, Classical Philology
1986: 10 titles *Founded:* 1613/1816
ISBN Publisher's Prefix: 3-7939

K G **Saur** Verlag GmbH & Co KG, Heilmannstr 17, Postfach 711009, D-8000 Munich 71 Tel: (089) 791040 Cable Add: saur Telex: 5212067 Saur d Fax: (089) 7910499
Man Dir: Dr Klaus G Saur; *Sales:* Paul Fertl; *Promotion:* Ursela A Geisler; *Production:* Manfred Link; *Rights & Permissions:* Dr Vladimir Prusa
Parent Company: Butterworth & Co (Publishers) Ltd, UK (qv)
Subsidiary Companies: Minerva Publikation (qv); K G Saur Editeur France (qv);
Subjects: Reference, Social Science, Library Management, Documentation and Information Science, Data Processing, Microforms, CD-ROM
Founded: 1948
Miscellaneous: Formerly known as Verlag Dokumentation Saur KG, Munich
ISBN Publisher's Prefix: 3-598

Karl A **Schäfer** Buch-und Offsetdruckerei-Goldstadtverlag+, Finkensteinstr 6, D-7530 Pforzheim Tel: (07231) 42095 Cable Add: Goldstadtverlag
Publisher: Günter Schäfer
Orders to: Geo-Center, Neumarkter Str 18, D-8000 Munich 80
Subject: Travel Guides
Founded: 1956
ISBN Publisher's Prefix: 3-87269

Hermann **Schaffstein** Verlag*, pA Schroedel-Verlagsauslieferung, Postfach 810620, D-3000 Hanover
Sales: Paul Lazar
Orders to: Schroedel-Verlagsauslieferung, Postfach 810620, D-3000 Hanover
Subjects: Juveniles, High-priced Paperbacks
ISBN Publisher's Prefix: 3-588

Edition **Schangrila**, Wengenerstr 8, D-8961 Haldenwang Tel: (08374) 9790
Subjects: Alternative Medicine, Natural Food Cookery, Occult, Eastern Philosophy
Founded: 1984

F K **Schattauer** Verlag GmbH+, Lenzhalde 3, Postfach 2945, D-7000 Stuttgart 1 Tel: (0711) 221733 Telex: 177111402 Fax: (0711) 221735
Publishers: Dieter Bergemann, Prof Dr Dr Paul Matis; *Sales Manager:* Jochen Hintermeier
Subject: Medicine (all aspects) and related sciences
ISBN Publisher's Prefix: 3-7945

Moritz **Schauenburg** Verlag GmbH und Co KG, Schillerstr 13, Postfach 2120, D-7630 Lahr 1 Tel: (07821) 27830 Cable Add: Schauenburg Lahrschwarzwald Telex: 754943
Dir: Jörg Schauenburg
Subjects: General Fiction, Dialect texts, Music, Literature
Founded: 1794
ISBN Publisher's Prefix: 3-7946

Verlag Heinrich **Scheffler**, an imprint of Societäts-Verlag (qv)

G **Schenck**, see R v Decker's Verlag GmbH

Scherpe Verlag, Glockenspitz 140, Postfach 2630, D-4150 Krefeld Tel: (02151) 590111 Telex: 853892
Subjects: General Fiction, Juveniles, Arts, Education, Illustrated Books, Belles Lettres, Politics
ISBN Publisher's Prefix: 3-7948

Scherz Verlag GmbH, Stievestr 9, D-8000 Munich 19 Tel: (089) 172237 Telex: 5215282 sherz d
Man Dir: Rudolf Streit-Scherz; *Editorial Dir:* Gert Woerner; *Sales Dir:* Wolfgang Radaj; O W Barth-Verlag: Stephan Schuhmacher
Associate Company: Otto Wilhelm Barth-Verlag KG (qv)
Head Off: Scherz Verlag AG, Switzerland (qv)
Subjects: General Fiction, History, Politics, Belles Lettres, Documentary Works
Founded: 1957
ISBN Publisher's Prefix: 3-502

Gertrud E **Scheuerer** Verlag*, Hartmannsreit 44, D-8351 Schönberg Tel: (08554) 697
Man Dir: Gertrud Scheuerer; *Production:* Otto Scheuerer
Subject: Art
Founded: 1975

Fachverlag **Schiele und Schön** GmbH, Markgrafenstr 11, D-1000 Berlin 61 Tel: (030) 2516029 Cable Add: Schieleschön Berlin Telex: 181470 sunds d
Man Dir: Peter Schön
Subjects: Engineering, Electronics, Industry, Reference, Medicine, Hobbies, Periodicals
Founded: 1946

Kurt **Schilling**, see Scientia Verlag

Verlag Karl **Schillinger** KG, Wallstr 14, Postfach 1502, D-7800 Freiburg im Breisgau Tel: (0761) 33233/22891
Man Dir: Wolfgang Schillinger
Subjects: Nature Studies, Regional Literature
Founded: 1899
ISBN Publisher's Prefix: 3-921340

G **Schindele** Verlag, see HVA — Edition Schindele

Schirmer/Mosel Verlag GmbH, Franz-Joseph-Str 9, Postfach 401723, D-8000 Munich 40 Tel: (089) 393037 Telex: 5213687
Man Dirs: Lothar Schirmer, Erik Mosel; *Sales, Publicity, Rights & Permissions:* Lothar Schirmer; *Production:* Roland Hepp
Subjects: Art Books, Art History, Photo-Art
Founded: 1975
ISBN Publisher's Prefix: 3-88814

Verlag Bert **Schlender**+*, Alte Schmiede Lippoldsberg, Mühlenstr 6, D-3417 Wahlsburg 1 Tel: (05572) 4448
Man Dir: Bert Schlender
Subjects: General Fiction, Belles Lettres, Poetry, Art, Low- & High-priced Paperbacks
Bookshop: Versandbuchhandlung Bert Schlender (at above address)
Founded: 1973

Joachim **Schmid** & Co, see Karl-May-Verlag

Erich **Schmidt** Verlag GmbH*, Genthiner Str 30G, D-1000 Berlin 30 Tel: (030) 2611741 Telex: 183 671 esbve d Cable Add: ESVerlag Berlin
Branch Offs: Viktoriastr 44a, Postfach 7330, D-4800 Bielefeld Tel: (0521) 66061; Paosostr 7, D-8000 Munich 60
Subjects: Law, Economics, Management, Linguistics, Philology, Literature, Religion, Social Studies
Founded: 1924
ISBN Publisher's Prefix: 3-503

Verlag Dr Otto **Schmidt** KG, Unter den Ulmen 96-98, D-5000 Cologne 51
Tel: (0221) 373021 Telex: 8883381
Man Dir: Dr H M Schmidt; *Editorial:* Lopau Mechthild, Dr Katherine Knauth; *Sales, Publicity & Advertising Dir:* Edmund Arand
Subjects: University Textbooks, Jurisprudence, Tax Law
Bookshops: Buchhandlung Hermann Sack, Klosterstr 22, D-4000 Düsseldorf 1; Justiz Zentrum 3, D-5000 Cologne 1; Buchhandlung Hermann Sack, Mercatorstr 27, D-6000 Frankfurt am Main
Founded: 1905
ISBN Publisher's Prefix: 3-504

Verlag für polizeiliches Fachschrifttum Georg **Schmidt-Römhild**, Mengstr 16, Postfach 2051, D-2400 Lübeck 1 Tel: (0451) 160050 Telex: 26536 msr d Fax: (0451) 1600553
Publisher: Norbert Beleke; *Man Dir:* Hans-Jürgen Sperling
Associate Company: Max Schmidt-Römhild Verlag (qv)
Subjects: Psychology, Reference (criminology, legal and for public authorities)
Founded: 1892
ISBN Publisher's Prefix: 3-8016

Max **Schmidt-Römhild**, Verlag+, Mengstr 16, Postfach 2051, D-2400 Lübeck 1 Tel: (0451) 160050 Telex: 26536 msr d Fax: (0451) 1600553
Publisher: Norbert Beleke; *Man Dir:* Hans-Jürgen Sperling
Associate Company: Verlag für polizeiliches Fachschrifttum Georg Schmidt-Römhild (qv)
Subjects: History, Medicine, General & Social Science, Reference (criminology, forensic, legal, medical and for public authorities)
1985: 10 titles *1986:* 11 titles *Founded:* 1579
ISBN Publisher's Prefix: 3-7950

Dr Roland **Schmiedel**, see Deutscher Apotheker-Verlag

Wilhelm **Schmitz** Verlag*, Auf der Heide 5, D-6301 Wettenberg 2 (Wissmar) Tel: (06406) 2324
Dir: S Schmitz
Subjects: Art, Languages, German Studies, Slav Studies, East European Studies, Folklore
Founded: 1847

Galerie **Schmücking** Verlag*, Lessingplatz 12, D-3300 Brunswick Tel: (0531) 44960
Branch Offs: Bobtäärp 17, D-2286 Archsum/Sylt, Federal Republic of Germany; Galerie Schmücking, Sattelgasse 2, CH-4000 Basle, Switzerland
Subject: Art

Franz **Schneekluth** Verlag+, Postfach 221451, D-8000 Munich 22 (Located at: Widenmayer Str 34) Tel: (089) 221391 Telex: 0529070
Man Dir: Ulrich Staudinger; *Editorial:* Hans Christian Rohr, Eva Schuster; *Sales:* Peter Zebold; *Production:* Johanna Wolter; *Publicity and Public Relations:* Eva Schuster; *Rights & Permissions:* Renate Abrasch
Orders to: Verlegerdienst Munich GmbH & Co KG, Postfach 1280, D-8031 Gilching
Subject: Belles Lettres
1986: 34 titles *1987:* 28 titles *Founded:* 1949
ISBN Publisher's Prefix: 3-7951

Musikantiquariat und Verlag Dr Hans **Schneider**, Mozartstr 6, D-8132 Tutzing Tel: (08158) 3050
Proprietor: Dr Hans Schneider
Subject: Music
1985: 25 titles *Founded:* 1949
ISBN Publisher's Prefix: 3-7952

Verlag Lambert **Schneider** GmbH+, Hausackerweg 16, Postfach 105802, D-6900 Heidelberg 1 Tel: (06221) 21354
Publisher: Lothar Stiehm
Subsidiary Company: Lothar Stiehm Verlag (qv)
Subjects: Belles Lettres, Poetry, Biography, Literature, Humanities, History, Music, Art, Judaica, Philosophy, Reference, Religion, University & Secondary Textbooks
Founded: 1925
ISBN Publisher's Prefix: 3-7953

Rudolf **Schneider** Verlag+, Freseniusstr 59, D-8000 Munich 60 Tel: (089) 8113466 Cable Add: Schneider Verlag Munich 60
Publisher and Man Dir: Karl-Heinz Biebl
Subjects: Gift volumes, Artist-illustrated books, Children's
Founded: 1980
ISBN Publisher's Prefix: 3-7955

Franz **Schneider** Verlag GmbH+*, Frankfurter Ring 150, D-8000 Munich 46 Tel: (089) 381911 Telex: 05215804
Publisher: Franz Schneider; *Editorial, Foreign Rights:* Ulrich Störiko-Blume; *Sales:* Günter Reich; *Production:* Josef Loher; *Publicity:* Christiane Leithardt
Subject: Juveniles
Founded: 1913
ISBN Publisher's Prefix: 3-505

Verlag **Schnell und Steiner** GmbH und Co, Postfach 112, D-8000 Munich 65 (Located at: Paganinistr 92, Munich 60) Tel: (089) 8112015 Cable Add: Schnellsteiner München
Man Dir, Rights and Permissions: Karl A Stich; *Editorial:* Dr P Mai; *Sales:* Josef Fink; *Production:* Rudolf Winterstein
Branch Off: Schnell und Steiner, CH-8260 Stein am Rhein, Switzerland
Subjects: Biography, Art, History of Art, Art Guides, Catalogues, Religion, Travel Literature
Founded: 1934
ISBN Publisher's Prefix: 3-7954

Verlag die **Schönen Bücher**, see Dr Wolf Strache

Verlag Hans **Schöner**+, Friedrich-Ebert-Str 7-9, D-7535 Königsbach-Stein 1 Tel: (07232) 1023 Telex: 783760 whs
Man Dir, Rights & Permissions: Hans Schöner; *Editorial:* Evelyne Dingler, Wilfried Morlock; *Sales:* Heinz Mössner; *Production, Publicity:* Elke Schöner
Subsidiary Company: Werbeagentur Hans Schöner (at above address)
Subjects: Fashion Design and Photography, Music, Jewellery, Sculpture
Bookshop: At above address
1985: 3 titles *Founded:* 1971
ISBN Publisher's Prefix: 3-923765

Ferdinand **Schöningh** Verlag*, Jühenplatz am Rathaus, Postfach 2540, D-4790 Paderborn Tel: (05251) 29010 Cable Add: Schönbuch Paderborn Telex: 936929 fspb
Subjects: Educational Publishers for Schools and Colleges, Earth Sciences, History, Literary Criticism, Mathematics, Education, Philosophy, Physics, Politics, Psychology, Law, Religion, Social Science, Linguistics, Languages, Reference, Paperbacks
ISBN Publisher's Prefix: 3-506

B **Schott's** Söhne, Musikverlag*, Weihergarten, Postfach 3640, D-6500 Mainz 1 Tel: (06131) 2460 Cable Add: Scotson Telex: 4187821 scot d
Man Dirs: Dr Peter Hanser-Strecker, Ludolf Frhr von Canstein, Jürgen M Luczak; *Sales, Export Dir:* Jürgen M Luczak; *Editorial:* Brigitte Franken, Friedrich Wanek, Lothar Friedrich, Hilger Schallehn, Dr Wolf Kalipp, Mike Schoenmehl; *Sales:* Helmut Fischer; *Production, Publicity:* Dr Hanser-Strecker; *Rights & Permissions:* Volker Landtag
Orders to: Carl-Zeiss Str 1, PO Box 3640, D-6500 Mainz-Hechtsheim Tel: (06131) 5050
Associate Companies: Wega Verlag GmbH, Mainz; Ars-Viva-Verlag GmbH, Mainz; Eruzt Eulenburg & Co GmbH, Zurich, Switzerland; Fürstner Musikverlag GmbH, Mainz
Subsidiary Company (jointly owned with Universal Edition AG, Austria — qv): Wiener Urtext Edition-Musikverlag GmbH & Co KG, Austria (qv)
Branch Offs: European American Music Distributors Corp, Valley Forge, USA; Schott Japan Co Ltd, Tokyo, Japan; Schott & Co Ltd, 48 Great Marlborough St, London W1V 2BN, UK
Subjects: Music and Music Reference, High-priced Paperbacks, Journals, University, Secondary & Primary Textbooks, Educational Materials, Sheet Music
Founded: 1770
ISBN Publisher's Prefix: 3-7957

Verlag J F **Schreiber** GmbH+, Postfach 285, D-7300 Esslingen (Located at: Liebigstr 1-11, D-7301 Deizisau) Tel: (07153) 22011 Telex: 7266880 jfs d
Man Dir, Editorial: Gerhard Schreiber; *Production:* Rolf Bianchi; *Publicity:* Achim Hutt; *Rights & Permissions:* Elisabeth von Zobel
Associate Company: Junior International (qv)
Subjects: Children's and Juvenile, Painting Books, Nature Guides
Founded: 1831
ISBN Publisher's Prefix: 3-480

Verlag und **Schriftenmission** der Ev Ges für Deutschland GmbH*, see Evangelischen Gesellschaft

Schroedel Schulbuchverlag GmbH, Hildesheimer Str 202-206, Postfach 810760, D-3000 Hanover 81 Tel: (0511) 83881 Telex: 923527 hsvha d
Man Dirs: Dipl-Kfm Anton Kemper, Dr Werner Kugel
Orders to: Breslauer Str 60, D-32039 Sarstedt
Subsidiary Companies: Cornelsen und Schroedel GmbH & Co Geographische Verlagsgesellschaft KG (qv); Paul List Verlag und Schroedel Schlachtbuchverlag (qv)
Branch Offs: Lützowstr 105-106, D-1000 Berlin 30; Graf-Adolf-Pl 6, D-4000 Düsseldorf 1; Marsstr 4, D-8000 Munich 2; Adolfsallee 43, D-6200 Wiesbaden 1; Eberhardstr 1, D-7000 Stuttgart 1; Stiftstr 1, CH-6000 Lucerne 6, Switzerland
Subject: School Textbooks
Founded: 1982
Miscellaneous: Formerly Hermann-Schroedel Verlag KG
ISBN Publisher's Prefix: 3-507

Kurt **Schroeder** Verlag, Am weissen Stein 48, D-5653 Leichlingen 1
Tel: (02175) 3355
Man Dir: Hannsgeorg Schroeder
Subject: Travel Guides, Plant Guides
Founded: 1919
ISBN Publisher's Prefix: 3-87722

Marion von **Schroeder** Verlag GmbH*, Grupellostr 28, Postfach 9229, D-4000 Düsseldorf 1 Tel: (0211) 169060 Telex: 8587327
Publishers: Dr Hero Kind, Peter Schaper; *Sales Manager:* Herbert Borgartz; *Publicity Manager:* Achim Wendland
Subjects: Belles Lettres, Fiction, Foreign Literature, Biography, Fantastica
Founded: 1935
Miscellaneous: Firm is a member of Econ Verlagsgruppe (qv)
ISBN Publisher's Prefix: 3-547

Anton **Schroll** & Co GmbH*, Boosstr 15, D-8000 Munich 95 Tel: (089) 653590
Man Dir: Friedrich Geyer
Head Off: Anton Schroll & Co, Austria (qv)
Subjects: Art, Travel
Founded: 1953

Ferdinand **Schroll**, see Titania-Verlag

Verlag **Schule und Elternhaus**, Werner-Heisenberg-Str 7, Postfach 310130, D-3500 Kassel-Waldau Tel: (0561) 584061 Cable Add: Schule und Elternhaus
Telex: 0992450
Editorial: Wolfgang Steinmeier
Associate Company: Thiele und Schwarz Verlagshaus GmbH (qv)
Subjects: Education, Vocabularies, Series by Young Writers
ISBN Publisher's Prefix: 3-88056

Schuler Verlagsgesellschaft mbH*, Schloss Mühlfeld, D-8036 Herrsching Tel: (08152) 1087 Telex: 526493
Dirs: Anton Bolza, Rudolf Blanckenstein
Subjects: Art, Juveniles, Reference
Founded: 1946
ISBN Publisher's Prefix: 3-7796

v g s — Verlagsgesellschaft **Schulfernsehen** mbH & Co KG, now vgs Verlagsgesellschaft mbH & Co KG (qv)

Verlag **Schulte** und Gerth GmbH & Co KG*, Postfach 1148, D-6334 Asslar Tel: (06441) 8461 Telex: 483794
Publisher: Klaus Gerth
Subsidiary Company: Turmberg Verlag (Musikverlag Klaus Gerth) (qv)
Subjects: Music, Religion, Biography, Juveniles, General Non-fiction

Verlag R S **Schulz***, Berger Str 8-10, Seehang 4, D-8136 Percha-Kempfenhausen Tel: (08151) 149 Telex: 0526427
Publisher: Dr Rolf Simon Schulz
Subjects: Fiction, Architecture, Public Health, Law, Social Science, Veterinary Science, Periodicals
ISBN Publisher's Prefix: 3-7962

Hohenstaufen Verlag **Schumann** KG, see Hohenstaufen

Carl Ed **Schünemann** KG, Zweite Schlachtpforte 7, Postfach 106067, D-2800 Bremen 1 Tel: (0421) 369030 Telex: 244397
Man Dir: Klaus Kirchner; *Sales & Publicity Dir:* Herbert Kuhangel
Subjects: Belles Lettres, Art
Founded: 1810
ISBN Publisher's Prefix: 3-7961

Verlag K W **Schütz**, Mindener Str 34, Postfach 1180, D-4994 Preußisch Oldendorf Tel: (05742) 2073
Man Dir: Erwin Höke
Subjects: History, Juveniles
Bookshop: Versandbuchdienst Göttingen (at above address)
Founded: 1948
ISBN Publisher's Prefix: 3-87725

Schwabenverlag AG*, Senefelderstr 12, Postfach 4280, D-7302 Ostfildern 1 Tel:

(0711) 44060 Telex: 0723556
Man Dirs: Dieter Hirsmüller, Norbert Krippner, Bürkhard Dähnert (Book department)
Subsidiary Company: Süddeutsche Verlagsgesellschaft mbH (qv)
Subjects: Religion, Theology, Swabian Regional Interest, Fiction
Bookshops: Schwabenverlag Buchhandlung, Bahnhofstr 21, D-7090 Aalen; Spitalstr 17, D-7030 Ellwangen
Founded: 1848
ISBN Publisher's Prefix: 3-7966

Schwaneberger Verlag GmbH, Muthmannstr 4, D-8000 Munich 45 Tel: (089) 32393208 Cable Add: Schwanverlag München Telex: 5215342 gerb d
Man Dir, Rights & Permissions: Hans Hohenester; *Editorial:* Gerhard Webersinke; *Sales:* Karl-Heinz Nuss; *Publicity:* Horst Rogg
Associate Company: Carl Gerber Verlag GmbH
Subject: Philately
Founded: 1910
ISBN Publisher's Prefix: 3-87858

Edition **Schwann**, an imprint of C F Peters Musikverlag GmbH und Co KG (qv)

Pädagogischer Verlag **Schwann/Bagel** GmbH, see Pädagogischer

Otto **Schwartz** & Co*, Verlag und Buchdruckerei, Annastr 7, D-3400 Göttingen Tel: (0551) 31051
Man Dir: Dr Herbert Weisser, Konrad Weisser
Subjects: Social Science, Jurisprudence, University Textbooks, Educational Materials
Bookshop: Fachbuchhandlung Otto Schwartz & Co (at above address)
Founded: 1871
ISBN Publisher's Prefix: 3-509

Verlag **Schwarz** GmbH, Am Altenberg 7, D-7570 Baden Baden 23 Tel: (07223) 6923
Man Dir: Elke Schwarz-Fritz
Subjects: Belles Lettres, Poetry, Children's, Historical Novels
Founded: 1980 (as GmbH)
ISBN Publisher's Prefix: 3-15859

Dr Wolfgang **Schwarze** Verlag+, Heckinghauser Str 65, Postfach 202015, D-5600 Wuppertal 2 Tel: (0202) 622005
Man Dir, Rights & Permissions: Dr Wolfgang Schwarze; *Sales, Office Chief:* Ursula Rumker-Schulze
Subsidiary Company: Kunst und Wohnen Verlag GmbH (at above address)
Subjects: Art books on Antiquities, Illustrated books on the Home and Interior Architecture, Facsimile Engravings
Founded: 1968
ISBN Publisher's Prefix: 3-87741

Verlag der Sankt-Johannis-Druckerei C **Schweickhardt**, see Sankt-Johannis

J **Schweitzer** Verlag, Zeppelinallee 43, Postfach 970148, D-6000 Frankfurt am Main 1 Tel: (069) 30090
Man Dir: Marigret Meyer-Tabellion
Subjects: Jurisprudence, Legal Information
Miscellaneous: Firm is a member of the Kluwer Group, Netherlands (qv)

E **Schweizerbart'sche** Verlagsbuchhandlung, Johannesstr 3A, D-7000 Stuttgart 1 Tel: (0711) 625001 Cable Add: Schweizerbartverlag Stuttgart Telex: 723363 schb d
Man Dirs: Dr Erhard Naegele (Production), Klaus Obermiller (Sales)
Associate Company: Gebrüder Borntraeger Verlagsbuchhandlung (qv)
Subjects: Geology, Palaeontology, Mineralogy, Limnology, Botany, Fishery, Hydrobiology, Zoology, Anthropology, Periodicals
Founded: 1826
ISBN Publisher's Prefix: 3-510

H G **Schwieger**, see PR Verlag

Verlag Junge Gemeinde E **Schwinghammer** KG, Fangelsbachstr 11, Postfach 979, D-7000 Stuttgart 1 Tel: (0711) 643015 Cable Add: Jungegemeindeverlag
Dir: Siegfried Krumrey
Subjects: Religion, Educational Materials, Periodicals
1986: 4 titles *1987:* 5 titles *Founded:* 1928
ISBN Publisher's Prefix: 3-7797

Scientia Verlag und Antiquariat Kurt Schilling, Adlerstr 65, Postfach 1660, D-7080 Aalen 1 Tel: (07361) 41700 Cable Add: Scientia Aalenwuertt
Man Dir: Günter Schilling
Subjects: Reprints in History, Education, Philosophy, Law, Social Science, Economics, Theology
Founded: 1953
ISBN Publisher's Prefix: 3-511

Scriptor Verlag GmbH, c/o Hirschgraben Verlag, Fürstenbergerstr 223, D-6000 Frankfurt am Main 1 Tel: (069) 550491 Telex: 176997604 hgvffm d
Publishers: Dr Franz Löffelholz, Werner Thiele
Subjects: Linguistics, Communications, Literature, Sociology, Education
1987: 15 titles *Founded:* 1973
ISBN Publisher's Prefix: 3-589

E A **Seemann** Verlag, Nassestr 14, D-5000 Cologne 41 Tel: (0221) 461915
Man Dir: Elert A Seemann
Subjects: Art Books and Colour Reproductions, Art Reference
Founded: 1858

S **Seewald**, see Verlag Molden

Seewald Verlag GmbH & Co, see Verlag Busse und Seewald

Seibt Verlag, Leopoldstr 208, D-8000 Munich 40 Tel: (089) 36306769 Telex: 5214853 seib d
Man Dir: Roland Hoppenstedt
Subjects: Trade Directories in several languages
ISBN Publisher's Prefix: 3-922948

Sellier Verlag GmbH, Erfurter Str 4, D-8057 Eching bei München Tel: (089) 3192048
Man Dir: Kurt Sellier; *Editorial:* Marieta Hegewisch; *Sales Dir:* Friedrich Otto
Subjects: Juveniles, Secondary & Primary Textbooks, Educational Materials
Founded: 1702
ISBN Publisher's Prefix: 3-87137

Sendler Verlag, Mainzer Landstr 147, Postfach 111162, D-6000 Frankfurt am Main Tel: (069) 730234
Manager: Bernd Wagner
Subjects: Literature, Philosophy, Social Science
1985: 8 titles *1986:* 9 titles *Founded:* 1981
ISBN Publisher's Prefix: 3-88048

Paul **Siebeck**, see J C B Mohr

Siebert Verlag GmbH, see Siebert und Engelbert Dessart Verlag GmbH

Siebert und Engelbert Dessart Verlag GmbH*, Wildstr 7, Postfach 1240, D-8202 Bad Aibling Tel: (08061) 4045 Telex: 525957
Subjects: Children's Books, Puzzles and Games
Founded: 1967

ISBN Publisher's Prefixes: 3-8089 (Siebert), 3-920215 (Dessart)

J **Siegler**, see Symposion Verlag

Siemens AG — ZVW 5, Verlag*, Postfach 3240, D-8520 Erlangen Tel: (09131) 76566 Cable Add: Siemens erlangen Telex: 62921-320 si d
Publicity: W Blaudszun
Subjects: Electronics, Electro-technology (especially Textbooks, Instructional Material), Technical Periodicals
Founded: 1963
ISBN Publisher's Prefix: 3-8009

Signal-Verlag Hans Frevert*, Balger Hauptstr 8, Postfach 813, D-7570 Baden Baden Tel: (07221) 61817 Cable Add: Signal-Verlag Baden Baden
Publisher: Hans Frevert
Subjects: Juveniles, Reference, Encyclopaedias, Dictionaries, Politics
ISBN Publisher's Prefix: 3-7971

Verlag Ludwig **Simon***, Mozartstr 15, Postfach 247, D-8023 Munich-Pullach Tel: (089) 7930332
Subject: Illustrated Works
ISBN Publisher's Prefix: 3-7972

Verlag **Simon und Magiera** KG+, Nymphenburgerstr 166, D-8000 Munich 19 Tel: (089) 1689014
Man Dirs: Claudia Magiera, Gerd Simon
Subject: Far East
1986: 30 titles *Founded:* 1979
ISBN Publisher's Prefix: 3-88676

Societäts-Verlag, Frankenallee 71-81, Postfach 100801, D-6000 Frankfurt am Main 1 Tel: (069) 75011 Cable Add: Zeitung Frankfurtmain Telex: 0411655
Publisher: Dietrich Rusche; *Sales Manager:* Jörg Emich
Imprints: Verlag Frankfurter Bücher, Verlag Heinrich Scheffler, Verlag Osterrieth
Subjects: History, Business, Literature, Art, Economics
Founded: 1921
ISBN Publisher's Prefix: 3-7973

Sonnenweg-Verlag, Raitenaugasse 11, Postfach 1186, D-7750 Konstanz Tel: (07531) 23054
Man Dir, Rights & Permissions: Herbert Denecke
Parent Company: Christliche Verlagsanstalt GmbH (qv)
Associate Company: Friedrich Bahn Verlag (qv)
Subjects: General Fiction, Religious Guides, Introductory Readers
Founded: 1922
ISBN Publisher's Prefix: 3-7975

Spangenberg, an imprint of Verlag Heinrich Ellermann (qv)

Spectrum Verlag Stuttgart GmbH, Friedrichstr 16-20, Postfach 1940, D-7012 Fellbach 4 Tel: (0711) 513004 Cable Add: Spectrumverlag Telex: 07254675
Man Dir: Peter Schwend; *Sales, Publicity, Advertising Dir, Rights & Permissions:* Ulrich Höfker; *Marketing:* Harald Zillner
Subjects: How-to, Reference, Juveniles, Natural Science, Textbooks
Founded: 1963
ISBN Publisher's Prefix: 3-7976

Spee Buchverlag GmbH, Fleischstr 62-65, Postfach 3040, D-5500 Trier Tel: (0651) 46040 Telex: 0472735
Publisher: Siegfried Fäth
Parent Company: Paulinus Druckerei GmbH (at above address)
Associate Company: Paulinus Verlag (qv)
Subjects: History, Religion, Picture books
ISBN Publisher's Prefix: 3-87760

FEDERAL REPUBLIC OF GERMANY

W **Spemann** Verlag, Pfizerstr 5-7, Postfach 640, D-7000 Stuttgart 1 Tel: (0711) 21910 Cable Add: Kosmosverlag Stuttgart 6 Telex: 721669 kosm d Fax: (0711) 2191360
Dirs: Claus Keller, R Keller, E Nehmann
Parent Company: Franckh'sche Verlagshandlung W Keller & Co (qv)
Subjects: History, Culture, Art
Founded: 1873
ISBN Publisher's Prefix: 3-87762

Musikverlag Fritz **Spies** GmbH, subsidiary company of P J Tonger Musikverlag GmbH & Co (qv)

Verlag Volker **Spiess**, Potsdamerstr 199, Postfach 3046, D-1000 Berlin 30 Tel: (030) 2165061
Publisher, Editorial: Volker Spiess
Associate Company: Haude & Spener (qv)
Subjects: Library Science, Publishing, Literary Criticism, Mass Media, Education, Social Science, Linguistics, Languages, Periodicals
Founded: 1967
ISBN Publisher's Prefixes: 3-920889, 3-88435

Arno **Spitz**, see Berlin Verlag

Adolf **Sponholtz** Verlag+, Osterstr 19, Postfach 101301, D-3250 Hameln 1 Tel: (05151) 200310 Cable Add: Dewezet Telex: 92859
Dir: Hans Freiwald
Associate Company: Verlag C W Niemeyer (qv)
Orders to: VVA (Vereinigte Verlagsauslieferung GmbH), Postfach 7777, D-4830 Gütersloh 1
Subjects: General Fiction and Non-fiction, Juveniles, Literature, Animal stories, Hunting, Environment, Energy
Founded: 1894
ISBN Publisher's Prefix: 3-87766

Verlag für **Sprachmethodik**, see Kessler

Springer-Verlag Berlin — Heidelberg — New York — Tokyo GmbH & Co KG*, Tiergartenstr 17, D-6900 Heidelberg Tel: (06221) 4870 Telex: 461723
Also: Heidelberger Pl 3, D-1000 Berlin Tel: (030) 82071 Telex: 183319
Managing Partners: Dr Heinz Götze, Dr Konrad Springer, Claus Michaletz; *Man Dirs:* Prof Dietrich Götze (Editorial/Production), Jolanda L von Hagen (Marketing/Sales); *Editorial:* Karl Hauck; *Production Dir:* Heinz Sarkowski; *Sales Dir:* Peter Porhansl; *Marketing Dir:* Arnoud de Kemp; *Advertising Dir:* Lothar Siegel; *Distribution Dir:* Horst Drescher
Parent Company: Springer Verwaltungs GmbH, Berlin
Associate Companies: J F Bergmann, Federal Republic of Germany (qv); Springer-Verlag France, Paris, France; Springer-Verlag Hong Kong Ltd, Hong Kong; Springer Books (India) Pvt Ltd, India (qv); Eastern Book Service Inc, Springer-Verlag Tokyo Inc (both in Japan); Springer-Verlag (London) Ltd, London, UK; Springer-Verlag New York Inc, 175 Fifth Ave, New York, NY 10010, USA
Subsidiary Companies: Physica-Verlag GmbH & Co (qv); Dr Dietrich Steinkopff Verlag (qv); Birkhäuser Verlag AG, Switzerland (qv)
Subjects: Scientific and Technical: especially Medicine, Psychology, Biology; Earth Sciences, Mathematics, Physics, Chemistry, Computers; Engineering, Economics, Philosophy, Law; Reference Books, Paperbacks, Scientific Journals in German and English
Bookshops: Bookselling group comprises: Firma Dr Ludwig Häntzschel Internationale Buchhandlung GmbH, Göttingen; Lange und Springer Antiquariat, Berlin; Lange und Springer Wissenschaftliche Buchhandlung, Berlin; Freihofer AG, Zürich, Switzerland; Minerva Wissenschaftliche Buchhandlung GmbH, Vienna, Austria
Founded: 1842
ISBN Publisher's Prefix: 3-540

L **Staackmann** Verlag KG*, Leopoldstr 116, D-8000 Munich 40 Tel: (08027) 337/(089) 342248
Man Dir: Dr Friedrich Vogel
Subjects: General Fiction, Historical Novels, Folk Stories, Illustrated Primers on Curiosities and Folklore Objects
Founded: 1869

Städte-Verlag, E v Wagner und J Mitterhuber, Steinbeisstr 9, Postfach 2080, D-7012 Fellbach bei Stuttgart Tel: (0711) 576201 Cable Add: staedteverlag
Man Dir: J Mitterhuber; *Publicity Dir:* U H Moeller; *Rights Dir:* U Groh
Subjects: Maps, District and Town plans for the Federal Republic of Germany and Austria; Federal Republic of Germany Town Directories
Annually 400 new titles
Founded: 1951
ISBN Publisher's Prefix: 3-8164

Stähle und Friedel Verlagsgesellschaft mbH und Co, Neue Weinsteige 36, Postfach 492, D-7000 Stuttgart 1 Tel: (0711) 60446465 Cable Add: Stählefriedel Telex: 721550
Man Dir: Willy Klahm
Subject: Travel
ISBN Publisher's Prefix: 3-8116

Verlag **Stahleisen** mbH+, Sohnstr 65, D-4000 Düsseldorf 1 Tel: (0211) 67070 Cable Add: Stahleisen Düsseldorf Telex: 8582512
Man Dirs: Dr Dirk Springorum, Rainer Schellen, Wilfried Wendt; *Sales Manager:* Günter Hecker
Associate Company: Giesserei-Verlag GmbH
Subjects: Iron and steel
1986: 11 titles *Founded:* 1908
ISBN Publisher's Prefix: 3-514

Stapp Verlag Wolfgang Stapp, Marschnerstr 12, D-1000 Berlin 33 Tel: (030) 8349977
Publisher: Wolfgang Stapp
Subjects: Illustrated Books, Areas of the German Democratic Republic, Monographs on Artists, Prussian History
1987: 17 titles
ISBN Publisher's Prefix: 3-87776

Hanns-Joachim **Starczewski** Verlag/Künstlerhof-Galerie*, Im Silbertal 4a, Postfach 137, D-5410 Hohr-Grenzhausen Tel: (02624) 2052
Man Dir, Editorial: H-J Starczewski
Subjects: Painting, Sculpture
Founded: 1964
ISBN Publisher's Prefixes: 3-7981, 3-925612

Johannes **Stauda** Verlag, now part of Lutherisches Verlagshaus GmbH (qv)

Franz **Steiner** Verlag Wiesbaden GmbH, Birkenwaldstr 44, Postfach 347, D-7000 Stuttgart 1 Tel: (0711) 25820 Telex: 0723636 daz d
Man Dirs: Vincent Sieveking, Dr Wolfgang Wessinger, Reinhold Hack; *Production:* Gregor Hoppen; *Publicity:* Brunhild Engling
Orders to: Birkenwaldstr 44, Postfach 347, D-7000 Stuttgart 1 Tel: (0711) 25820 Telex: 0723636 daz d
Associate Companies: Wissenschaftliche Verlagsgesellschaft mbH (qv); S Hirzel Verlag GmbH & Co (qv); Deutscher Apotheker-Verlag Dr Roland Schmiedel GmbH & Co (qv)
Subjects: Literary Criticism, Archaeology, Art, Music, History, Religion, Classical and Modern Philology, Oriental Studies, Ethnology, Philosophy, Geography, History of Medicine and Science, Sciences, Periodicals
1985: 160 titles *Founded:* 1949
ISBN Publisher's Prefix: 3-515

Steinheim Verlag und Vertrieb GmbH*, Neuhauser Str 4, D-8000 Munich 2 Tel: (089) 268144/268253
Man Dirs: Werner Tiltz, Heino Siefert
Orders to: VSB Verlagsservice Braunschweig, Georg-Westermann-Allee 66, D-3300 Brunswick
Parent Company: Georg Westermann Verlag, Druckerei und Kartographische Anstalt GmbH & Co (Printing and Publishing Management Company), Georg-Westermann-Allee 66, D-3300 Brunswick
Subjects: Leisure, Travel, Medicine, Psychology
Founded: 1982
ISBN Publisher's Prefix: 3-88952

J F **Steinkopf** Verlag GmbH, Hackländerstr 33, Postfach 849, D-7000 Stuttgart 1 Tel: (0711) 245866 Cable Add: Steinkopf Stuttgart
Man Dir: Friedrich B Holst
Subjects: General Fiction & Non-fiction, Paperbacks, How-to, Religion, Social Science, Swabian Literature, Cities (history and development)
1985: 25 titles *1986:* 25 titles *Founded:* 1792
ISBN Publisher's Prefix: 3-7984

Dr Dietrich **Steinkopff** Verlag, Saalbaustr 12, Postfach 111442, D-6100 Darmstadt 11 Tel: (06151) 26538 Cable Add: Steinkopff Fax: (06151) 20849
Man Dir, Sales, Publicity, Rights & Permissions: Bernhard Lewerich;
Advertising: Springer-Verlag, Berlin — Heidelberg — New York — Tokyo
Parent Company: Springer-Verlag Berlin — Heidelberg — New York — Tokyo GmbH & Co KG (qv)
Subjects: Reference, Low- & High-priced Paperbacks, Medicine, Chemistry, Nutritional Science, University & Secondary Textbooks, Periodicals
Founded: 1948
ISBN Publisher's Prefix: 3-7985

Steintor Verlag, Rudolf Jüdes, Postfach 100549, D-3167 Burgdorf (Located at: Arndtstr 9c) Tel: (05136) 84954
Subject: Art
Bookshop: Gallerie Meiborssen, D-3453 Meiborssen Tel: (05535) 8851
1985: 23 titles *Founded:* 1969

Stephanus Edition Verlags GmbH+*, Tüfinger Str 3-5, Postfach 1160, D-7772 Uhldingen 1 Tel: (07556) 6509
Man Dir: Ursula Braun; *Editorial:* Hans Braun
Parent Company: Stephanus Edition Verlags AG, Switzerland (qv)
Subject: Christian persecution in Communist countries
Founded: 1978
ISBN Publisher's Prefix: 3-921213

Carl **Stephenson** Verlag GmbH & Co, Schaeferweg 14, Postfach 2755, D-2390 Flensburg Tel: (0461) 25800 Telex: 022710
Sales Manager: Dirk Rotermund
Subjects: Popular and Erotic Literature, Belles Lettres

Stern-Verlag Janssen & Co, Friedrichstr 24-26, Postfach 7820, D-4000 Düsseldorf 1 Tel: (0211) 38810

FEDERAL REPUBLIC OF GERMANY 169

Managing Partners: Horst and Klaus Janssen; *Production and Sales:* Oswald Sckaer
Subjects: Philosophy, Philology (especially of English)
Bookshop: At above address
Founded: 1900
ISBN Publisher's Prefix: 3-87784

Sternberg-Verlag, see Ernst Franz

Steyler Verlag, Bahnhofstr 9, Postfach 2460, D-4054 Nettetal 2 Tel: (02157) 120220
Subjects: Roman Catholic Theology, Novels, Juvenile, Meditations, Scientific Series, Bibles
ISBN Publisher's Prefix: 3-87787

Lothar **Stiehm** Verlag GmbH+, Hausackerweg 16, Postfach 105802, D-6900 Heidelberg 1 Tel: (06221) 21354
Publisher: Lothar Stiehm
Parent Company: Lambert Schneider Verlag GmbH (qv)
Subjects: Classical Philology, German Language & Literature, Bibliography, Literary Criticism
ISBN Publisher's Prefix: 3-7988

Stollfuss Verlag Bonn GmbH & Co KG, Dechenstr 7-11, Postfach 2428, D-5300 Bonn 1 Tel: (0228) 7240 Cable Add: Stollfussverlag Telex: 8869477 stvd
Man Dir: Wolfgang Stollfuss; *Editorial:* Alfred Mertens; *Sales:* Herbert Rolfsmeyer; *Production:* Reinhard Just; *Publicity:* Ernst-Wolfgang Buecken
Subjects: Official Publications of German Finance Ministry, Reference Works, Fiscal Law, Administration, Economics, Investment, Taxes, Legal Studies
ISBN Publisher's Prefix: 3-08

Verlag Dr Wolf **Strache** GmbH & Co KG, Friedhofstr 11, Postfach 101154, D-7000 Stuttgart Tel: (0711) 2576010 Cable Add: Schönbücher Telex: dbv c 723240
Subjects: Arts, Mass Media, Education
Miscellaneous: Formerly Verläg die Schönen Bücher
ISBN Publisher's Prefix: 3-7956

Verlag für das **Studium** der Arbeiterbewegung GmbH, see VSA

Stürtz Verlag*, Beethovenstr 5, D-8700 Würzburg Tel: (0931) 385235 Telex: 068798
Publisher: Walter Thierfelder
Subjects: Art, Wine, History of Travel, Guidebooks, Photographic Art, Scenic photo books, Hobbies, Sports, Meditation

Südbuch Vertriebsgesellschaft mbH, see Bibliographisches Institut AG

Süddeutsche Verlagsgesellschaft Ulm*, Sedelhofgasse 19-21, D-7900 Ulm Tel: (0731) 62047
Man Dir: Udo Vogt
Parent Company: Schwabenverlag AG (qv)
Subjects: Christian Devotion and Meditation, Theology, Preparation for Sacraments, Juvenile, Religious, Liturgical, Pedagogy, Psychology, Social Problems, Current Affairs
Founded: 1898
ISBN Publisher's Prefix: 3-88294

Süddeutscher Verlag Buchverlag, Goethestr 43, Postfach 780, D-8000 Munich Tel: (089) 51480 Telex: 0522405
Editorial: Dr H-P Rasp; *Sales:* Norbert Jennen; *Publicity:* Barbara Ziegler; *Advertising:* Herbert Wiesensarter
Associate Companies: Paul List Verlag KG (qv); Südwest Verlag GmbH & Co KG (qv)
Subjects: History, How-to, Art, Fiction, Reference, Religion, Non-fiction

Founded: 1945
ISBN Publisher's Prefix: 3-7991

Südwest Verlag GmbH und Co KG, Goethestr 43, D-8000 Munich 2 Tel: (089) 51480 Telex: 0522405
Sales: Norbert Jennen; *Production:* Roger Seitz; *Publicity:* Barbara Ziegler; *Advertising:* Herbert Wiesensarter
Associate Companies: Paul List Verlag KG (qv); Süddeutscher Verlag Buchverlag (qv)
Subjects: History, How-to, Art, Children's, Cookery, Sport
Founded: 1950
ISBN Publisher's Prefix: 3-517

Suhrkamp Verlag, Lindenstr 29-35, Postfach 101945, D-6000 Frankfurt am Main Tel: (069) 756010 Cable Add: Suhrkampverlag Telex: 413972
Publisher: Dr Siegfried Unseld; *Man Dirs:* Dr Heribert Marré, Dr Gottfried Honnefelder, Dr Joachim Unseld; *Advertising:* Claus Carlé; *Publicity:* Dr Christoph Groffy; *Rights & Permissions:* Helene Ritzerfeld
Associate Companies: Deutscher Klassiker Verlag, Insel Verlag (qv), Nomos Verlagsgesellschaft mbH & Co KG (qv) (all Federal Republic of Germany); Suhrkamp Verlag AG, Zeitweg 25, CH-8032 Zurich, Switzerland; Suhrkamp Publishers New York, Inc, 175 Fifth Ave, New York, NY 10010, USA
Imprints: Suhrkamp Taschenbuchverlag, Suhrkamp Verlag Wissenschaft
Subjects: General Fiction, Belles Lettres, Poetry, Biography, Philosophy, German-Jewish Writing in general, General Science, High- & Low-priced Paperbacks, Juveniles, Education, Psychology
Founded: 1950
ISBN Publisher's Prefix: 3-518

Sybex Verlag GmbH, Vogelsanger Weg 111, Postfach 300961, D-4000 Düsseldorf 30 Tel: (0211) 618020 Telex: 8588163 sybx d
Man Dirs: Alexander Schleber, Rodnay Zaks; *Sales:* Harald Kreutzberger
Associate Companies: Sybex Inc, 2021 Challenger Dr, NBR 100, Alameda, CA 94501, USA Tel: (415) 5238233; Sybex Paris, 6-8 Impasse du Cure, F-75018 Paris Tel: (01) 2039595 Telex: 211801
Subjects: Micro-computer technology and programming
Founded: 1981
ISBN Publisher's Prefix: 3-88745

Symposion-Verlag, J Siegler, Wagnerstr 12, Postfach 33, D-7300 Esslingen-N Tel: (0711) 350001 Cable Add: Symposion, Esslingen
General Manager: H A Siegler
Subjects: Equestrian Interest, Pets, International Model Railways Guide, Periodicals
Founded: 1964
ISBN Publisher's Prefix: 3-920877

Syndikat Autoren- und Verlagsgesellschaft, see Autoren- und Verlagsgesellschaft

T R- Verlagsunion GmbH, Thierschstr 11, Postfach 260202, D-8000 Munich 26 Tel: (089) 225431 Telex: 0522371 trd d
Man Dir: Andreas Keiser; *Editorial:* Beate Fischer, Gabriele Rieth, Gertrud Schwärzler; *Publicity:* Cornelia Wiedemann; *Sales:* Imogen Fries
Subjects: Educational Study Material for State examinations, Professional, Technical, Language Courses; Leisure Pursuit Study Companions. The Union publishes and distributes books, audio- and videocassettes sets of lessons etc, to link up with TV and radio programmes

Founded: 1968
Miscellaneous: The TR (Television and Radio) Publishing Union comprises two broadcasting companies (Bayerischer Rundfunk and Südwestfunk) and publishing companies: Ludwig Auer GmbH, C Bertelsmann Verlag GmbH, Verlag Bruckmann München, Ehrenwirth Verlag GmbH, Ernst Klett Verlag, Kösel-Verlag GmbH & Co, Langenscheidt KG, Paul List Verlag KG, R Oldenbourg Verlag GmbH, Günter Olzog Verlag GmbH (qqv) and is also associated with publishers Gräfe und Unzer, Franz Schneider, B Schott's Söhne (qqv), and Franckh'sche Verlagsbuchhandlung, Verlagsanstalt 'Bayerland'
ISBN Publisher's Prefix: 3-8058

Verlag **T Ü V** Rheinland GmbH, Sicherheitstechnik, Energie und Umweltschutz, Am Grauen Stein, Postfach 101750, D-5000 Cologne 91 Tel: (0221) 8393 2852 Telex: 8873659
Man Dir: Dr D Hohm; *Editorial:* J Fahrbach, H Niederheide; *Sales, Publicity:* Wolfgang Kierdorf; *Production:* Mr Braatz
Subjects: Safety Technology, Energy, Environmental Protection
Founded: 1972
ISBN Publisher's Prefix: 3-88585

Taylorix Fachverlag Stiegler und Co*, Mönchstr 29, Postfach 829, D-7000 Stuttgart 1 Tel: (0711) 2503202 Telex: 0723810
Dir: Dipl-Volkswirt Walter Alt
Subjects: Economics, Business, Law, Data Processing
ISBN Publisher's Prefix: 3-7992

Technik Tabellen Verlag Fikentscher und Co*, Eschollbrücker Str 39, Postfach 4135, D-6100 Darmstadt Tel: (06151) 61025 Cable Add: Fikentscher Telex: 419460
Publisher: Christoph Kässner; *Editorial:* Dr Thomas Krist
Subjects: Civil & Mechanical Engineering, Textbooks
ISBN Publisher's Prefix: 3-87807

Telex-Verlag Jaeger und Waldmann GmbH, Holzhofallee 38, Postfach 111060, D-6100 Darmstadt 11 Tel: (06151) 33020 Telex: 419389, 419253 jwtlx d Fax: (06151) 330250
Man Dir: Wolfgang Lich; *Foreign Manager, Editor:* Willi Lucius; *Advertising Manager:* Ludwig Nicolay
Subjects: International Telex, Teletex, Telefax and Tourism Directories
Founded: 1953
ISBN Publisher's Prefix: 3-87810

Alf **Teloeken** Verlag KG, see Alba Publikation

Telos series of Paperbacks. This is a series of Bible-based evangelical paperbacks (including works for children), each contributed by one of the following publishers:
Blaukreuz-Verlag Wuppertal (qv), Brendow-Verlag (qv), Verlag der Evangelischer Buchhandlung (qv), Hänssler-Verlag (qv), Verlag der Liebenzeller Mission (qv), Verlag der Sankt-Johannis-Druckerei C Schweickhardt (qv) (all in Federal Republic of Germany); Verlag der Schweizerischen Schallplattenmission (Swiss gramophone record mission), Schwengeler-Verlag (qv), Trachsel-Verlag (all in Switzerland)

Tende Verlag GmbH, Neustr 28, D-4408 Dülmen 3 Tel: (069) 771891

Man Dir: Annette Viktoria Uhlending; *Editorial:* J Monika Walther; *Production:* Claus Seitz; *Publicity:* Dr Vibeke Peusch; *Rights & Permissions:* A Uhlendung
Orders to: Sova, Franziusstr 44, D-6000 Frankfurt am Main 1
Subjects: Belles Lettres, Art, Film, Women's Interests
1985: 8 titles *1986:* 8 titles *Founded:* 1980
ISBN Publisher's Prefix: 3-88633

B G Teubner GmbH, Industriestr 15, Postfach 801069, D-7000 Stuttgart 80 Tel: (0711) 789010
Man Dir: Heinrich Krämer; *Sales, Publicity & Advertising Dir:* Walter Hirtz; *Rights & Permissions:* Sophie Penner
Subjects: History, Classical Philology, Reference, High-priced Paperbacks, Mathematics, Computer Science, Physics, Biology, Geography, Engineering, General & Social Science, Secondary & University Textbooks
Founded: 1811
ISBN Publisher's Prefix: 3-519

Edition **Text und Kritik** GmbH*, Levelingstr 6a, Postfach 800529, D-8000 Munich 80 Tel: (089) 432929
Man Dir: Dr Berndt Oesterhelt
Subjects: Contemporary Literature and Criticism, Reference Works, Musical Studies
ISBN Publisher's Prefixes: 3-921402, 3-88377

Konrad **Theiss** Verlag GmbH, Villastr 11, Postfach 730, D-7000 Stuttgart 1 Tel: (0711) 2686101 Cable Add: Theissverlag Stuttgart
Dir: Hans Schleuning; *Publicity, Sales:* Bernhard Driehaus; *Production:* Rolf Bisterfeld
Subjects: History, Arts, Non-fiction
1986: 35 titles *1987:* 39 titles
ISBN Publisher's Prefix: 3-8062

Thesen Verlag Vowinckel und Co, Kittlerstr 34, D-6100 Darmstadt Tel: (06151) 713326
Man Dirs: Heinrich Schirmer, Dr Ilse Shirmer-Vowinckel
Subjects: Literary Criticism, Linguistics, Social Science, Periodical
1986: 7 titles *Founded:* 1970
ISBN Publisher's Prefix: 3-7677

Thiele und Schwarz Verlagshaus GmbH, Werner-Heisenberg-Str 7, Postfach 310130, D-3500 Kassel-Waldau Tel: (0561) 584061 Cable Add: Thiele & Schwarz Kassel-Waldeau Telex: 0992450
Proprietor: Rolf Schwarz; *Editorial:* Wolfgang Steinmeier
Associate Company: Verlag Schule und Elternhaus (qv)
Subjects: General Fiction, Juveniles, Reprints
ISBN Publisher's Prefix: 3-87816

Georg **Thieme** Verlag+, PO Box 732, D-7000 Stuttgart 1 (Located at: Rüdigerstr 14, Stuttgart 30) Tel: (0711) 89310 Cable Add: Thiemebuch Telex: 7252275
Publishers: Dr Günther Hauff, Dr Albrecht Greuner; *Man Dir:* Achim Menge; *Sales:* Joachim Hillig; *Publicity:* Malik Lechelt, Ursula Polaczek; *Foreign Rights:* Märit Schütt
Subsidiary Companies: Hippokrates Verlag GmbH (qv); Thieme Medical Publishers Inc, New York, USA
Associate Companies: Ferdinand Enke Verlag (qv); Phil-Lip Verlag, Munich
Subjects: Medicine, Dentistry, Bioscience, Pharmacy, Chemistry, Veterinary, Earth Sciences, Social Sciences, Reference, Periodicals (many works in English)
Founded: 1886
ISBN Publisher's Prefix: 3-13

Karl **Thiemig** AG München*, Pilgersheimer Str 38, Postfach 900749, D-8000 Munich 90 Tel: (089) 62480 Cable Add: Thiemigdruck
Man Dir: Fritz Dittmar; *Advertising Dir:* Peter Schlaus
Subjects: Art, Travel, Natural Science, Technical, Management
Founded: 1950
ISBN Publisher's Prefix: 3-521

K **Thienemanns** Verlag, Blumenstr 36, D-7000 Stuttgart 1 Tel: (0711) 210550 Telex: 723933 thie d
Dirs: Hansjoerg Weitbrecht, Gunter Ehni
Imprints: Edition Erdmann, Edition Weitbrecht
Subjects: Fiction, Non-fiction, Juveniles, Children's Picture Books, Dietetics
Founded: 1849
ISBN Publisher's Prefix: 3-522

Jan **Tholenaar** Verlag GmbH, G D Bücherei*, Solseifen Nr 5, D-5222 Morsbach Tel: (02294) 6336
Man Dirs: Jan Tholenaar, Lilly Tholenaar; *All other offices:* Uwe Nersberg
Imprint: G D Bücherei (Large Print Library)
Subjects: Large Print: General Fiction (including English in translation), some Non-fiction
Founded: 1979
ISBN Publisher's Prefix: 3-88621

Jan **Thorbecke** Verlag GmbH & Co+*, Karlstr 10, Postfach 546, D-7480 Sigmaringen Tel: (07571) 3016 Cable Add: Thorbecke Telex: 732534
Dir, Editorial, Rights & Permissions: Georg Bensch; *Production:* Ulrich Ulrichs; *Publishing, Publicity and Sales Dir:* Dr Lothar Johannes
Associate Company: Bergstadtverlag Wilhelm Gottlieb Korn GmbH, Würzburg (Correspondence and Distribution: Karlstr 10, Postfach 546, D-7480 Sigmaringen)
Subjects: Historical, Geographical, Cultural Accounts of various European Regions, especially in Germany and Switzerland; Art History, Literature, Children's, European History
1985: 50 titles *Founded:* 1946
ISBN Publisher's Prefix: 3-7995

Tips für Trips, an imprint of Friedemann von Engel Verlag (qv)

Titania-Verlag Ferdinand Schroll+, Forststr 104B, Postfach 1352, D-7000 Stuttgart 1 Tel: (0711) 638125 Cable Add: Titaniaverlag Stuttgart
Publishers: Wolfgang Schroll, Gerdi Schroll
Subjects: General Fiction, Children's Story Books
ISBN Publisher's Prefix: 3-7996

S **Toeche-Mittler** Verlag*, Hindenburgstr 33, D-6100 Darmstadt Tel: (06151) 311551
Subjects: Non-fiction, Law, Sports, Economics
Miscellaneous: Firm was formerly Mittler & Sohn, Berlin
Founded: 1789
ISBN Publisher's Prefix: 3-87820

Tomus Verlag GmbH+, Prinzenstr 7, D-8000 Munich 19 Tel: (089) 132001 Telex: 5215528 Fax: (089) 1678071
General Manager: Claus-Jürgen Frank; *Assistant General Manager, Rights & Permissions:* Oliver A Frank
Associate Company: Telelit Verlag AG
Branch Off: Dr Wernerstr 5, D-8038 Gröbenzell
Subjects: Nature, Science, Animals, Hobbies, Travel, Cookery, Exclusive Art Editions, Humour, Reference
Founded: 1962
ISBN Publisher's Prefix: 3-8231

P J **Tonger** Musikverlag GmbH & Co*, Auf dem Brand 3, D-5000 Cologne 50 Tel: (0221) 392998
Man Dir: P J Tonger; *Sales Dir:* Hans Paul Zimmer; *Publicity Dir:* Hildegard Tonger; *Advertising Dir:* Peter Tonger
Subsidiary Companies: Carl Engels Musikverlag, Musikverlag Gerhard Rabe GmbH, Musikverlag Fritz Spies GmbH
Subjects: Music, Art
Founded: 1822

Touropa-Urlaubsberater, now part of Verlag Mensch und Arbeit Robert Pfützner GmbH (qv)

Trautvetter und Fischer Nachf, Gladenbacher Weg 57, Postfach 546, D-3550 Marburg Tel: (06421) 33309
Owned by: Dr Wilhelm A Eckhardt
Subjects: Local History and Guidebooks, Church Histories (Protestant)
1987: 2 titles *Founded:* 1941
ISBN Publisher's Prefix: 3-87822

Editions **Trèves**+*, Postfach 1401, D-1550 Trier 1 Tel: (06501) 3183
Man Dirs: Rainer Breuer, Uschi Dahm; *Chief Reader:* Bernhard Hoffmann
Branch Off: Editions Trèves Luxembourg, BP 57, L-6701 Grevenmacher, Luxembourg
Subjects: Music Books, Belles Lettres, Young Literature, Lyrical Poetry, Theatre, Art, Literary Periodicals, Politics, Satire, Science
Founded: 1974
ISBN Publisher's Prefix: 3-88081

Trikont-Dianus, see Dianus Trikont

Editions **Trobisch** GmbH, Postfach 2048, D-7640 Kehl am Rhein 1 Tel: (07851) 4551
Man Dir: Volker Gscheidle
Subjects: Christian practice and devotions, sex and marriage counselling etc, in German, French and English
Founded: 1972
ISBN Publisher's Prefix: 3-87827

Tübinger Vereinigung für Volkskunde eV*, Schloss, D-7400 Tübingen Tel: (07071) 294971
Man Dir: Georgis Eder; *Editorial, Production, Sales:* Prof H Bausinger, U Jeggle, G Korff, M Scharfe, B J Warneken
Subjects: Paperbacks, Reference (Humanities), History, Social Science, University Textbooks
Founded: 1963
ISBN Publisher's Prefix: 3-925340

Tuduv Verlagsgesellschaft mbH+, Postfach 340163, D-8000 Munich 34 (Located at: Gabelsbergstr 15, Munich 2) Tel: (089) 2809095
Manager: Franz Frank; *Copyright, Publications:* Hans Frank
Associate Company: Verlag V Florentz GmbH (qv)
Subjects: Biography, Communications, Cultural Science, Ethnology, History, History of Art, Linguistics, Literary Criticism, Politics, Political Science, Social Science, Speech Impediment, Healing Science, Theology, Textbooks
1985: 143 titles *Founded:* 1974
ISBN Publisher's Prefix: 3-88073

Turm-Verlag, Hindenburgstr 3, Postfach 229, D-7120 Bietigheim Tel: (07142) 41081 Cable Add: Turm, Bietigheim
Associate Company: Lorber-Verlag (qv)
Subjects: Health, Religion
ISBN Publisher's Prefix: 3-7999

FEDERAL REPUBLIC OF GERMANY 171

Turmberg-Verlag (Musikverlag Klaus Gerth)*, Emmeliusstr 31, Postfach 1148, D-6334 Asslar Tel: (06441) 8461 Telex: 483794
Parent Company: Verlag Schulte und Gerth (qv)
Subject: Music

Verlag **Tüv Rheinland** GmbH, see TÜV

U T B, see Uni-Taschenbücher GmbH

Verlag Dr Alfons **Uhl***, Mittlere Gerbergasse 1, D-8860 Nördlingen
Subjects: Architectural and Art History, Graphics and Book Illustration, Art Portfolios, Old Topographical Books

Verlag **Ullstein** GmbH*, PO Box 110303, D-1000 Berlin 11 (Located at: Lindenstr 76, D-1000 Berlin 61) Tel: (030) 25911 Cable Add: Ullsteinbuch berlin Telex: 183723 vlgul d
Man Dir: Viktor Niemann; *Marketing and Sales Dir:* Peter Wagner; *Publicity:* Till Waltz; *Chief Editor:* Adreas Catsch (Paperbacks)
Subsidiary Companies: Propyläen Verlag (qv), Ullstein Taschenbuchverlag
Subjects: Belles Lettres, Poetry, Biography, History, How-to, Music, Art, Travel, Geography, Ethnology, Popular Science, Social Sciences, Low- & High-priced Paperbacks, Educational Materials, Fiction, Military, Politics
Founded: 1903
Miscellaneous: Firm is a member of Buchverlage Ullstein Langen-Müller/Herbig (qv)
ISBN Publisher's Prefix: 3-550

Buchverlage **Ullstein Langen-Müller/Herbig**, Thomas-Wimmer-Ring 11, D-8000 Munich 22 Tel: (089) 2350080 Telex: 05215045
Man Dir: Dr Herbert Fleissner
Members of the Group: Bechtle Verlag (qv); Mary Hahn's Kochbuchverlag (qv); F A Herbig Verlagsbuchhandlung (qv); Albert Langen-Georg Müller Verlag (qv); Georg Lentz Verlag (qv); Limes Verlag (qv); Edition Meyster; Verlag Molden — S Seewald GmbH (qv) Nymphenburger Verlagshandlung (qv); Edition Thiemig; Verlag Ullstein GmbH (qv); Universitas Verlag (qv); Wirtschaftsverlag (qv) (all in Federal Republic of Germany); Amalthea-Verlag, Austria (qv)

Verlag Eugen **Ulmer** GmbH & Co, Wollgrasweg 41, Postfach 700561, D-7000 Stuttgart 70 (Hohenheim) Tel: (0711) 45070 Telex: 723634
Man Dir: Roland Ulmer; *Deputy Dir:* Alexander Hunn; *Production:* Dieter Kleinschrot; *Reader:* Dr Steffen Volk; *Sales Dir:* Gerhard Rentschler; *Publicity Dir:* Frank Wildhirt
Subjects: How-to, Reference, General Science, University Textbooks, Agriculture, Horticulture, Veterinary Science, Gardening, Animals, Periodicals, Paperbacks
Founded: 1868
Miscellaneous: Firm is a member of vgs — Verlagsgesellschaft mbH & Co KG (qv)
ISBN Publisher's Prefix: 3-8001

Umschau Verlag Breidenstein GmbH, Stuttgarter Str 18-24, D-6000 Frankfurt am Main 1 Tel: (069) 26001 Cable Add: Umschau Frankfurtmain Telex: 0411964
Man Dir: Hans-Jürgen Breidenstein; *Editorial Dir:* Bruno Back; *Sales:* Peter Schumacher
Associate Companies: Brönner Verlag Breidenstein GmbH (qv), Brönners Druckerei Breidenstein GmbH, Sigma Studio Breidenstein GmbH, Dateam Vertriebsgesellschaft mbH & Co KG (all at above address); Andres Verlag GmbH, Lenaustr 2, Hamburg
Subjects: Non-fiction, especially Photographic Travel Books, Art, General Science, Low- & High-priced Paperbacks, Periodicals
Founded: 1850
ISBN Publisher's Prefix: 3-524

Ungarischer Kultureller und Sozialer Fonds eV in der BRD*, Zweibrückenstr 2/IV, D-8000 Munich 2 Tel: (089) 294376
Hungarian Social and Cultural Foundation in the Federal Republic of Germany
Man Dir: András Piffkó; *Editorial:* János Röczey; *Rights & Permissions:* János Popovits
Parent Company: Zentralverband Ungarischer Organisationen in der BRD eV, at above address (Central Association of Hungarian Organisations in the Federal Republic of Germany)
Subjects: Works by Hungarian authors
Bookshops: Ungarischer Kultureller und Sozialer Fond in der BRD eV at above address
Founded: 1971

Uni-Taschenbücher (UTB) GmbH, Breitwiesenstr 9, Postfach 801124, D-7000 Stuttgart 80 Tel: (0711) 7801826
Dir: Volkmar Kalki
Orders to: Brockhaus Commission, Am Wallgraben 127-129, Postfach 800205, D-7000 Stuttgart 80
Subjects: Library Science, Biology, Chemistry, Electrical Engineering, Electronics, Humanities, History, Public Health, Business, Informatics, Data Processing, Engineering, Agriculture, Literary Criticism, Mathematics, Medicine, Education, Philosophy, Physics, Politics, Psychology, Religion, Social Science, Linguistics, Languages, Veterinary Science, Economics (all in paperback)
Miscellaneous: The company represents a group of 17 publishers producing paperbacks of a general academic/technical/scientific nature

Union Verlag Stuttgart*, Alexanderstr 51, D-7000 Stuttgart 1 Tel: (0711) 240996
Cable Add: Unionverlag
Man Dirs: Dr Heinz Winners, Ulrich Commerell
Parent Company: Otto Maier Verlag (qv)
Subject: Juveniles
Founded: 1890
ISBN Publisher's Prefix: 3-8002

Universitas Verlag, Thomas-Wimmer-Ring 11, D-8000 Munich 22 Tel: (089) 2350080
Publicity Manager: Gerhard Koralus
Subjects: General Fiction, Biography, History
Founded: 1922
Miscellaneous: Firm is a member of Buchverlage Ullstein Langen-Müller/Herbig (qv)
ISBN Publisher's Prefix: 3-8004

Verlag **Urachhaus** Johannes M Mayer GmbH, Urachstr 41, Postfach 131053, D-7000 Stuttgart 1 Tel: (0711) 260589/265939
Dir: Johannes Mayer; *Readers:* Marie-Luise Zeuch, Dr Wolfgang Huber, Roswitha von dem Borne; *Publicity & Marketing:* Winfried Altmann
Orders to: Koch, Neff und Oetinger & Co, Verlagsauslieferung, Schockenried Str 39, D-7000 Stuttgart 80
Subjects: History, Literary Criticism, Philosophy, Religion, Anthroposophy, Occultism, Children's Books, Art Books, History of Art
1985: 64 titles *Founded:* 1924
ISBN Publisher's Prefix: 3-87838

Urban und Schwarzenberg GmbH, Verlag für Medizin+, Pettenkoferstr 18, Postfach 202440, D-8000 Munich 2 Tel: (089) 53830 Telex: 523864
Man Dir: Michael Urban; *Marketing, Sales:* Daniel von Zastrow; *Rights & Permissions:* Susanne Engelhardt
Associate Companies: Urban und Schwarzenberg GmbH, Austria (qv); Urban & Schwarzenberg Inc, 7 East Redwood St, Baltimore, Md 21202, USA
Branch Off: Urban & Schwarzenberg, Austria (qv)
Subjects: Medicine, University Textbooks
Bookshop: Oscar Rothacker Verlagsbuchhandlung GmbH, Landwehrstr 38, D-8000 Munich 2
1985: 100 titles *Founded:* 1866
ISBN Publisher's Prefix: 3-541

V C H Verlagsgesellschaft mbH+, Postfach 1260-1280, D-6940 Weinheim Tel: (06201) 6020 Telex: 465516 vchwh d Fax: (06201) 602328
Man Dirs: Prof Helmut Grünewald, Hans Dirk Köhler; *Editorial:* Dr Hans Friedrich Ebel (Natural Sciences), Dr Gerd Giesler (Humanities), Sylvia Osteen (Medicine); *Production:* Maximilian Montkowski; *Sales:* Helmut Schmitzer; *Advertising:* Rainer Roth; *Rights & Permissions:* Dr Dietmar Schallwich
Subsidiary Companies: Wilhelm Ernst und Sohn Verlag für Architektur und technische Wissenschaft (qv); Physik-Verlag GmbH (qv); W und P Buchversand für Wissenschaft und Praxis, Boschstr 12, Postfach 1808, D-6940 Weinheim; Gropius'sche Buch- und Kunsthandlung GmbH, Berlin; VCH-Verlags AG, Switzerland (qv); VCH Publishers (UK) Ltd, 8 Wellington Court, Wellington St, Cambridge CB1 1HW, UK; VCH Publishers, Inc, Suite 909, 220 East 23rd St, New York, NY 10010-4606, and 303 NW 12th Ave, Deerfield Beach, FL 33442-1788, USA
Branch Office: Scientific Software, Dr Wolfgang Schmidt, Schmülingstr 4-6, D-4400 Münster
Subjects: Chemistry, Physics, Medicine, Biomedicine, Pharmacy, Computer Science, Biotechnology, Industrial Property Law, History, Philosophy, Art, Architecture, Civil Engineering, Food Sciences, University Textbooks, Monographs, Periodicals
1986: 220 titles *Founded:* 1921
Miscellaneous: Formerly Verlag Chemie GmbH
ISBN Publisher's Prefix: 3-527

V D E-Verlag GmbH (Verband Deutscher Elektrotechniker)+, Bismarckstr 33, D-1000 Berlin 12 Tel: (030) 3480010 Telex: 181683 vde d
Manager: Dr-Ing A Grütz, Merianstr 29, D-6050 Offenbach
Subjects: Electrical Engineering, Electronics, VDE- Specifications (many specifications may be bought in English), Communications Technology
Founded: 1929
ISBN Publisher's Prefix: 3-8007

V D I-Verlag GmbH (Verlag des Vereins Deutscher Ingenieure), Heinrichstr 24, Postfach 8228, D-4000 Düsseldorf 1 Tel: (0211) 61880 Cable Add: Ingenieurverlag Düsseldorf Telex: 08587743 Fax: (0211) 6188112
Man Dir: Dr Harald Wiebking; *Publishing Manager:* Peter Hohmann; *Sales, Rights & Permissions:* Siegfried Binder
Subjects: Engineering, Technology,

Scientific Reports, Proceedings, VDI Guidelines, Paperbacks, Serial Publications
1986: 29 titles *Founded:* 1923
ISBN Publisher's Prefix: 3-18

V-Dia-Verlag GmbH*, Heinrich-Fuchs-Str 95-97, Postfach 105980, D-6900 Heidelberg 1 Tel: (06221) 374041 Cable Add: Vaudia Heidelberg Telex: 0461781
Subjects: Audiovisual Aids, Geography, Astronomy, Biology, Medicine, History
Founded: 1953

V F M, see Verlag für Medizin Dr Ewald Fischer GmbH

v g s — Verlagsgesellschaft mbH & Co KG*, Postfach 180269, D-5000 Cologne 1 (Located at: Breite Str 118-120, Cologne) Tel: (0221) 219641
Man Dir: Dr Heinz Gollhardt
Associated Partners: Aschendorffsche Verlagsbuchhandlung (qv); Beltz Verlag (qv); C C Buchners Verlag, Bamberg; Cornelsen-Velhagen und Klasing GmbH & Co Verlag für Lehrmedien KG (qv); Ferd Dümmlers Verlag (qv); Lehrmittelverlag Wilhelm Hagemann (qv); Verlag Handwerk und Technik, Hamburg; Heckners Verlag (qv); Verlag Max Hueber; Verlag Ferdinand Kamp (qv); Verlagsgesellschaft Rudolf Müller GmbH (qv); Verlag Eugen Ulmer GmbH & Co (qv)
Subjects: Books for TV programmes (educational, juvenile, hobby, natural sciences), Periodicals, Audiovisual Materials, Training Systems, Microcomputer Technology and Programming
Founded: 1970
ISBN Publisher's Prefix: 3-8025

V M B, see Verlag Marxistische Blätter

V S A (Verlag für das Studium der Arbeiterbewegung GmbH), Stresemannstr 384a, D-2000 Hamburg 50 Tel: (040) 894069
Manager, Rights & Permissions: Gerd Siebecke; *Sales:* Brigitte Dudek
Orders to: VVA (Vereinigte Verlagsauslieferung GmbH), Postfach 7777, D-4830 Gütersloh 1
Subjects: Political and Social Science, Political and Social Movements, Periodical
ISBN Publisher's Prefix: 3-87975

V W K (Verlag für Wirtschafts-und-Kartographie Publikationen) Ryborsch GmbH+, Laubenstr 3, Postfach 2105, D-6053 Obertshausen 2 bei Frankfurt Tel: (06104) 7839 Telex: 4170606 rvwk d
Dir: Reinhard Ryborsch
Subjects: Economics, Aviation, Geography, Travel, City and Road Maps, Aeronautical Charts and Maps
1986: 6 titles *1987:* 5 titles *Founded:* 1975
ISBN Publisher's Prefix: 3-920339

Franz **Vahlen** GmbH*, Wilhelmstr 9, D-8000 Munich 40 Tel: (089) 381891
Dir: Dr Hans D Beck
Associate Companies: Verlag C H Beck (qv), Biederstein Verlag (qv)
Subjects: Law, Economics, Social Sciences, University Textbooks
Founded: 1870
ISBN Publisher's Prefix: 3-8006

Vandenhoeck und Ruprecht+, Theaterstr 13, Postfach 3753, D-3400 Göttingen Tel: (0551) 54031 Telex: 965226 van d
Dirs: Dr Arndt Ruprecht, Dr Dietrich Ruprecht; *Editorial:* Dr Winfried Hellmann; *Sales and Publicity:* Ursula Nahrgang
Subsidiary Company: Druckerei Hubert & Co, Robert-Bosch-Breite 6, D-3400 Göttingen
Branch Off: Vandenhoeck und Ruprecht, c/o Evang Verlags-Auslieferungen, Alinadier Str 11, CH-8302 Klotew 12, Switzerland
Subjects: University Textbooks, Research Monographs and Handbooks, Religion, Philology, History, Economics, Mathematics, Medical Psychology, Philosophy, Archaeology, German Philology, Periodicals
Bookshop: Deuerlich'sche Buchhandlung, Weender Str 33, D-3400 Göttingen
1985: 222 titles *1986:* 265 titles *Founded:* 1735
ISBN Publisher's Prefix: 3-525

Velhagen und Klasing GmbH & Co, Mecklenburgische Str 54, D-1000 Berlin 33
Man Dir: Franz Cornelsen
Subjects: Textbooks, Educational, Cartography
Miscellaneous: Part of Cornelsen GmbH & Co (qv)
Founded: 1835

Verlag für Deutsch, see Deutsch

Klaus Dieter **Vervuert** Buchhandel und Verlag, Wielandstr 40, D-6000 Frankfurt am Main 1 Tel: (069) 599615
Subjects: Specialist in books about Latin America, Spain and Portugal
1986: 16 titles
ISBN Publisher's Prefix: 3-921600

Friedr **Vieweg & Sohn** Verlagsgesellschaft mbH+, Faulbrunnenstr 13, Postfach 5829, D-6200 Wiesbaden 1 Tel: (06121) 160249 Telex: 4186928 vw v d
Orders to: VVA (Vereinigte Verlagsauslieferung GmbH), Postfach 7777, D-4830 Gütersloh 1
Man Dir: Dr Frank Lube; *Editorial:* Michael Langfeld; *Sales Manager:* Heinz Detering; *Publicity, Rights & Permissions:* Angelika Bolisega
Parent Company: Verlagsgruppe Bertelsmann GmbH (qv for associate companies)
Subsidiary Company: Deutscher Eichverlag (qv)
Subjects: Textbooks in Mathematics, Natural Sciences, Technology, Architecture, Monographs, School Books, Teaching Programmes, Microcomputer Books and Software, Periodicals
1985: 120 titles *1986:* 135 titles *Founded:* 1786
ISBN Publisher's Prefix: 3-528

Curt R **Vincentz** Verlag*, Schiffgraben 41-43, Postfach 6247, D-3000 Hanover 1 Tel: (0511) 3499944 Telex: 923846
Man Dir: Dr L Vincentz; *Sales:* Dr F Vincentz
Subjects: General Science, Paint Technology, Business, Nursing
Founded: 1893
ISBN Publisher's Prefix: 3-87870

Edition Curt **Visel**, Weberstr 36, Postfach 1636, D-8940 Memmingen Tel: (08331) 2853
Man Dir, Editorial, Production, Publicity, Rights & Permissions: Curt Visel; *Sales:* Hildegard Naegele
Parent Company: Maximilian Dietrich Verlag (qv)
Subjects: Books with Original Illustrations, Maps, Monographs on Artists, Periodicals
1987: 3 titles *Founded:* 1963
ISBN Publisher's Prefix: 3-922406

Vogel-Verlag KG, Max-Planck-Str 7-9, Postfach 6740, D-8700 Würzburg 1 Tel: (0931) 41021 Cable Add: Vogelverlag Würzburg Telex: 179318154 Fax: (0931) 44053
Man Dirs: Dr Kurt Eckernkamp, Wolfgang Lüdicke
Subjects: Agricultural, Automotive, Consulting, Electrical, Mechanical Engineering, Electronics, Metalworking, Management, Scientific and Technical Text Books, Foreign Language Publications (in 14 languages), Periodicals
Founded: 1891
ISBN Publisher's Prefix: 3-8023

Emil **Vollmer** Verlag, see Vollmer/Löwit Verlagsgruppe

Vollmer/Löwit Verlagsgruppe*, Gustav-Stresemann-Ring 12-16, Postfach 4060, D-6200 Wiesbaden Tel: (06121) 39331 Telex: 4186294
Dir: Sylvia Vollmer
Subjects: Art and Artists, Collectors' Books, Mythology, Natural History, Religions, History, Fiction, Belles Lettres, Juveniles, Popular Editions of Classics
Miscellaneous: This is a merger of R Löwit GmbH, Wiesbaden and Emil Vollmer Verlag GmbH, Wiesbaden

Thesen Verlag **Vowinckel** und Co, see Thesen

Kurt **Vowinckel** Verlag, Kreuzanger 8, D-8137 Berg am See Tel: (08151) 50025
Dir: Dr Gert Sudholt
Subjects: Current Affairs, Politics, Military
ISBN Publisher's Prefix: 3-87879

W R S-Verlag (Wirtschaft, Recht und Steuern) GmbH & Co, Fraunhoferstr 5, Postfach 1363, D-8033 Planegg/Munich Tel: (089) 8577944 Fax: (089) 8577990
Dirs: Dr Guenther Friedrich, Dr Manfred Jahrmarkt
Parent Company: Rudolf Haufe Verlag (qv)
Subjects: Economics, Law, Taxation

Karl **Wachholtz** Verlag, Rungestr 4, Postfach 2769, D-2350 Neumünster Tel: (04321) 56720 Cable Add: courier Telex: 299618
Dir: Walter Kardel; *Advertising, Sales:* Erich Gockel; *Production:* Norbert Brey
Subjects: Humanities, History, Arts, Reference, Encyclopaedias, Dictionaries, Literature, Reprints, Linguistics, Languages, Periodicals
1985: 65 titles *1986:* 51 titles *Founded:* 1924
ISBN Publisher's Prefix: 3-529

Verlag Klaus **Wagenbach** GmbH, Ahornstr 4, Postfach 1409, D-1000 Berlin 30 Tel: (030) 2115060
Man Dir, Editorial: Dr Klaus Wagenbach; *Sales:* Galina Rave; *Production:* Rainer Groothuis; *Publicity, Rights & Permissions:* Barbara Herzbruch
Subjects: General Fiction, Belles Lettres, Poetry, Low- and High-priced Paperbacks, Political and Social Science, Periodical
Founded: 1964
ISBN Publisher's Prefix: 3-8031

Kartographischer Verlag **Wagner** & Co KG*, Burgemeisterstr 32, D-1000 Berlin 42 Tel: (030) 7514051
Man Dir, Publicity: Andreas Lenz
Parent Company: Kartographische Anstalt Dr K H Wagner
Subjects: Maps, Cartography
Founded: 1981
ISBN Publisher's Prefix: 3-88825

Walter-Verlag GmbH Freiburg+, Grissheimer Weg 36, D-7843 Heitersheim Tel: (07634) 40340 Telex: 772961
Dirs: Hermann Maschkowitz, Dr Hans Richenberger; *Sales:* Richard Urbahn; *Publicity:* Karin Wagner

Parent Company: Walter Verlag AG, Switzerland (qv)
Subjects: Religion, Psychology, Travel Guides, Literature, Cultural History
Founded: 1924
ISBN Publisher's Prefix: 3-530

Ernst **Wasmuth** Verlag GmbH & Co+*, Fürststr 133, Postfach 2728, D-7400 Tübingen Tel: (07071) 33658
Man Dir: Dr Veronika Birbaumer; *Sales Dir:* Karl-Heinz Schattner; *Production:* Manfred Heinrich
Subjects: Architecture, Archaeology, History of Art, Applied Art
Bookshop: Wasmuth Buchhandlung & Antiquariat, Hardenbergstr 9A, D-1000 Berlin 12
Founded: 1872
ISBN Publisher's Prefix: 3-8030

Wehr und Wissen Verlagsgesellschaft mbH*, Heilsbachstr 26, D-5300 Bonn 1 (Duisdorf) Tel: (02221) 643066 Telex: 8869429 mvkb d
Man Dir: Manfred Sadlowski; *Sales Dir, Rights & Permissions:* Joachim Latka; *Publicity Dir:* Heinz-Jürgen Witzke; *Advertising Dir:* Peter Konietschke
Subjects: History, How-to, Quality Paperbacks, Military Manuals, Yearbooks

A **Weichert** Verlag, Tiestestr 14, D-3000 Hanover Tel: (0511) 813068 Telex: 923872 awv
Man Dir: Alfred Trippo; *Sales:* Hans H Droste
Associate Company: Neuer Jugendschriften-Verlag (at above address)
Imprint: Karo-Bücher
Branch Off: Hans Feulner, Lindenallee 25, D-1000 Berlin 19
Subject: Juvenile Fiction
Founded: 1872
ISBN Publisher's Prefix: 3-483

Wolfgang **Weidlich** Verlag, Beethovenstr 5, D-8700 Würzburg
Publisher, Rights & Permissions: Walter Thierfelder; *Editorial:* Wolfgang Weidlich; *Sales:* Irmgard Dürr; *Production:* Jürgen Roth; *Publicity:* Renate Morgenstern
Subjects: Architecture, General Fiction, History, Maps, Non-fiction
ISBN Publisher's Prefix: 3-8035

Weidmannsche Verlagsbuchhandlung, see Georg Olms Verlag AG

Verlag **Weinmann**+, Beckerstr 7, D-1000 Berlin 41 Tel: (030) 8554895
Man Dir: Dr Weinmann
Subject: Sport (especially the martial arts), Instruction books, Fitness Training, Sports Humour
1985-86: 10 titles *Founded:* 1961
ISBN Publisher's Prefix: 3-87892

Weismann Verlag-Frauenbuchverlag GmbH+, Georgenstr 12333, D-8000 Munich 40 Tel: (089) 183008
Man Dirs: Wolfgang Gartmann, Antje Kunstmann; *Editorial:* Antje Kunstmann, Nikolaus Hansen
Orders to: Verlagsauslieferung: mi, Justus-von-Liebigstr 1, D-8910 Landsberg
Subsidiary Company: Frauenbuchverlag (qv)
Subjects: Literature, Non-fiction, Theatrical texts for juveniles, Politics, Current Affairs, Novels, Cartoons
Founded: 1970
ISBN Publisher's Prefix: 3-921040

Gebrüder **Weiss** Verlag*, Hewaldstr 9, D-1000 Berlin 62 Tel: (030) 7817725
Owner: Richard Weiss
Subjects: General Fiction, Juveniles, Popular Science, Non-fiction, Paperbacks
Founded: 1945
ISBN Publisher's Prefix: 3-8036

Edition **Weitbrecht**, an imprint of K Thienemanns Verlag (qv)

Verlag **Welsermühl**+, Kufsteiner Str 8, D-8000 Munich 80 Tel: (089) 982031 Cable Add: welsermuhldruck Telex: 5216349
Dir, Editorial, Rights & Permissions: Karl Prämendorfer; *Sales:* Friederike Weiss-Füreder; *Production:* Friedrich Spendou; *Publicity:* K Füreder
Subsidiary Company: Zweimühlen Verlag GmbH (at above address)
Branch Off: Verlag Welsermühl, Austria (qv)
Subjects: General Non-fiction, Travel, Illustrated Books, Current Events
Founded: 1928
ISBN Publisher's Prefix: 3-85339

Weltforum Verlag GmbH*, Marienburgerstr 22, D-5000 Cologne 51 Tel: (0221) 37695
Dir: Sales, Rights & Permissions: Peter John von Freyend; *Editorial, Production:* Mrs Edelgard Reiche; *Publicity:* Karl Ludwig Ostermann, Udo Witych
Subjects: Political, Economic and Technological aspects of the Developing Nations
ISBN Publisher's Prefix: 3-8039

Weltkreis-Verlags-GmbH+*, Postfach 789, D-4600 Dortmund 1 Tel: (0231) 838010 Telex: 822292 plaen
Man Dir: Klaus Dietrich; *Editorial:* Wolfgang Elsner; *Publicity:* Berthold Besler; *Advertising Dir, Sales, Rights & Permissions:* Martin Strubelt
Orders to: (Federal Republic of Germany): Brücken Verlag, Postfach 1928, D-4000 Düsseldorf; (West Berlin): Rotation, Mehringdamm 51, D-1000 Berlin 61
Subjects: Belles Lettres, Poetry, Biography, How-to, Juveniles, Low-priced Paperbacks
Founded: 1958
ISBN Publisher's Prefix: 3-88142

Karl **Wenschow** GmbH, an associate company of JRO-Kartographische Verlagsgesellschaft mbH (qv)

Werner Verlag GmbH*, Berliner Allee 11a, Postfach 8529, D-4000 Düsseldorf 1 Tel: (0211) 320988 Cable Add: Wernerverlag Telex: 8587828
Man Dir: Klaus Werner; *Publicity Dir:* E Dickert
Subjects: University Textbooks, Reference, Engineering, Educational Materials, Law, Social Science, Economics
Founded: 1945
ISBN Publisher's Prefix: 3-8041

Westdeutscher Verlag GmbH+, Faulbrunnenstr 13, Postfach 5829, D-6200 Wiesbaden Tel: (06121) 160249 Telex: 4186928 vwvd
Man Dir: Dr Frank Lube; *Editorial:* Manfred Müller; *Sales:* Heinz Detering; *Rights & Permissions:* Angelika Bolisega
Orders to: VVA (Vereinigte Verlagsauslieferung), Postfach 7777, D-4830 Gütersloh 1
Parent Company: Verlagsgruppe Bertelsmann GmbH (qv for associate companies)
Branch Off: Reuschenberger Str 55, D-5090 Leverkusen 3
Subjects: History, Literature, Social Science, University Textbooks, Periodicals
1985: 50 titles *1986:* 65 titles *Founded:* 1947
ISBN Publisher's Prefix: 3-531

Westermann Schulbuchverlag GmbH, Georg-Westermann-Allee 66, Postfach 5520, D-3300 Brunswick Tel: (0531) 7080 Cable Add: Gewebuch Telex: 0952841 wbuch d
Editorial, Production, Rights & Permissions: Dr Carl-August Schröder; *Sales, Publicity:* Dr Peter Wille
Parent Company: Georg Westermann Verlag, Druckerei und Kartographische Anstalt GmbH & Co (Printing and Publishing Management Company), Brunswick
Subjects: History, Education, University/Secondary/Primary Textbooks, Educational Materials, Atlases, Maps
ISBN Publisher's Prefix: 3-14

Georg **Westermann** Verlag GmbH+, Georg-Westermann-Allee 66, Postfach 5529, D-3300 Brunswick Tel: (0531) 7080 Cable Add: Gewebuch Telex: 0952841 wbuch d
Man Dir: Dr Carl August Schröder; *Editorial, Production, Rights & Permissions, Sales, Publicity:* Dr Peter Wille
Parent Company: Georg Westermann Verlag, Druckerei und Kartographische Anstalt GmbH & Co (Printing and Publishing Management Company), Brunswick
Subjects: Non-fiction, Paperbacks, Periodicals
Founded: 1838
ISBN Publisher's Prefix: 3-07

Erich **Wewel** Verlag, Anzinger Str 1, D-8000 Munich 80 Tel: (089) 4130010 Telex: 522504
Publisher: Eduard Niedernhuber; *Editorial:* Dr Karl Geisendörfer; *Sales, Publicity:* Ursel Wunder
Parent Company: Manz Verlag (qv)
Subjects: Philosophy, Religion
1985-86: 20 titles *Founded:* 1936
ISBN Publisher's Prefix: 3-87904

Who's Who — the International Red Series Verlag GmbH*, Brunnenstr 61-65, D-4300 Essen 1 Tel: (0201) 63101 Telex: 857396 who rh d
President: H F Sutter; *Man Dir, Production, Rights & Permissions:* Jürgen Schmalenbach; *Sales:* Ulrich Gilsebach; *Publicity:* Armin Haffner
Parent Company: A Sutter GmbH, Brunnenstr 61-65, D-4300 Essen 1
Subsidiary Company: Who's Who in Italy SRL, CP 61, Via Roma 16, I-20091 Bresso Milano, Italy
Subjects: English Language Encyclopaedias (comprising Biographies of prominent living personalities in Arts, Literature, Medicine, Technology, Fashion), *International Red Series* of 'Who's Who' in Europe and European Organizations
Founded: 1972
ISBN Publisher's Prefix: 3-921220

Herbert **Wichmann** Verlag GmbH+, Amalienstr 29, Postfach 4320, D-7500 Karlsruhe 1 Tel: (0721) 20909 Telex: 7825909
Man Dir, Production, Rights & Permissions: Dr Christof Müller-Wirth; *Sales, Publicity:* Bernhard Krebs
Subjects: Geodesy, Photogrammetry, Land Registration, Cartography, Estate Evaluation, Periodicals
Founded: 1889
ISBN Publisher's Prefix: 3-87907

Winkler-Verlag, Martiusstr 8, Postfach 440254, D-8000 Munich 44 Tel: (089) 348074 Telex: 5215517
Man Dir: Franz Ebner
Parent Company: Artemis Verlag, see Artemis und Winkler
Associate Companies: Verlag für Architektur, Artemis Verlags AG (both in Switzerland, qqv)
Subjects: Biography, Literature

Founded: 1945
ISBN Publisher's Prefix: 3-538

Carl **Winter** Universitätsverlag GmbH, Lutherstr 59, Postfach 106140, D-6900 Heidelberg 1 Tel: (06221) 49111 Telex: 0461660
Publisher: Dr Carl Winter; *Sales:* Ruth Wutke
Subject: University Books
1985: 90 titles *1986:* 80 titles *Founded:* 1822
ISBN Publisher's Prefix: 3-533

Wirtschaft, Recht, Steuern, see WRS-Verlag

Verlag für **Wirtschafts-** und Kartographie-Publikationen, Ryborsch, see VWK

Verlag für **Wirtschaftsskripten**, Dipl-Kfm C Ölschläger GmbH, Brabanter Str 16, Postfach 401424, D-8000 Munich 40 Tel: (089) 363257
Man Dir: Claus Ölschläger
Subjects: Economics, Business, Management, Law
Founded: 1974
ISBN Publisher's Prefix: 3-921636

Wirtschaftsverlag, Thomas-Wimmer-Ring 11, D-8000 Munich 22 Tel: (089) 2350080 Telex: 215045
Publicity Manager: Gerhard Koralus
Subjects: Business Economics, Work Study and Allied Subjects
Miscellaneous: Firm is a member of Buchverlage Ullstein Langen-Müller/Herbig (qv)

Wison Verlag GmbH*, Weyertal 59, Postfach 410948, D-5000 Cologne 41 Tel: (0221) 443031
Publicity: Michael Wienand
Subjects: Economic Sciences, Data Processing, Research Reports

Wissen Verlag GmbH*, Schloss Mühlfeld, D-8036 Herrsching Tel: (08152) 1087 Telex: 526493
Dirs: Anton Bolza, Rudolf Blanckenstein
Subjects: Reference, Encyclopaedias, Dictionaries
ISBN Publisher's Prefix: 3-8075

Verlag **Wissenschaft** und Politik, see von Nottbeck

Verlag für **Wissenschaft**, Wirtschaft und Technik GmbH und Co KG+*, Amsbergstr 22, D-3388 Bad Harzburg 1 Tel: (05322) 73333 Telex: 957623 dvg
Man Dir: Barbara Schumacher; *Dirs:* Gisela Böhme, Reinhard Höhn
Subjects: Management, Sociology, Social Science, Primary and Secondary Textbooks, Economics, Rhetoric
Founded: 1960
ISBN Publisher's Prefix: 3-8020

Wissenschaftliche Buchgesellschaft*, Hindenburgstr 40, Postfach 111129, D-6100 Darmstadt 11 Tel: (06151) 33080
Man Dir: Werner Merkle; *Chief Reader:* Dr Ingold Dutz; *Rights & Permissions:* Christa Pantos
Subjects: History, Music, Art, Philosophy, Religion, Medicine, Psychology, General & Social Science, Classics, Literature, Language, Education, Mathematics, Archaeology, Jurisprudence, Economics
Book Club: Wissenschaftliche Buchgesellschaft
Founded: 1949
ISBN Publisher's Prefix: 3-534

Wissenschaftliche Verlagsgesellschaft mbH, Birkenwaldstr 44, Postfach 40, D-7000 Stuttgart 1 Tel: (0711) 25820 Telex: 723636 daz d
Man Dirs: Dr W Wessinger, V Sieveking, R Hack
Associate Companies: Deutscher Apotheker Verlag Dr Roland Schmiedel GmbH & Co (qv); S Hirzel Verlag GmbH & Co (qv); Franz Steiner Verlag Wiesbaden GmbH (qv)
Subjects: Medicine, Pharmacy, Biology, Chemistry, Physics, Periodicals
Founded: 1921
ISBN Publisher's Prefix: 3-8047

Wissenschaftlicher Autoren Verlag, see Verlag Grundlagen und Praxis GmbH & Co

Friedrich **Wittig** Verlag, In der Masch 6, D-2000 Hamburg 61 Tel: (040) 580358 Cable Add: Wittigverlag
Man Dir, Sales: Friedrich B Holst; *Editorial:* Friedrich Wittig, Henning Wendland; *Production:* Henning Wendland
Associate Company: Gerold und Appel Verlag (at above address)
Subjects: Religion, Arts, History, Bibliophily, Children's
Founded: 1946
ISBN Publisher's Prefix: 3-8048

Verlag Konrad **Wittwer** GmbH+, Nordbahnhofstr 16, Postfach 147, D-7000 Stuttgart 1 Tel: (0711) 25070 Telex: 723751
Man Dir: Konrad Wittwer; *Editorial, Sales, Publicity:* Mr Hasler
Subjects: Mathematics, Geodesy, General Literature, School Textbooks
Bookshop: Königstr 30, D-7000 Stuttgart 1
1986: 100 titles *Founded:* 1867
ISBN Publisher's Prefix: 3-87919

The **World of Books** Ltd+, Friedrich-Ebert-Str 80, D-6520 Worms Tel: (06241) 51425
Man Dirs: W P Smith, J M Ortez, R Becker
Head Office: 788-789 Finchley Rd, London, UK
Subjects: Current Events, Belles Lettres, Juvenile, Specialist Computer Operating Literature
1986-87: 100 titles *Founded:* 1981
ISBN Publisher's Prefix: 3-88325

Rainer **Wunderlich** Verlag Hermann Leins*, Hamburger Str 17, Postfach 1349, D-2057 Reinbek bei Hamburg Cable Add: Wunderlichverlag Telex: 7262891 mepo d
Man Dir: Günther Schweizer; *Sales & Publicity Manager:* Michael Hennig; *Rights & Permissions:* Kurt Neff
Parent Company: Rowohlt Verlag GmbH, (at above address)
Subjects: Belles Lettres, Poetry, Biography, History, Music, Art, Politics
Founded: 1926
ISBN Publisher's Prefix: 3-8052

Echter **Würzburg**, Fränkische Gesellschaftsdruckerei und Verlag GmbH, Juliuspromenade 64, Postfach 5560, D-8700 Würzburg Tel: (0931) 30910 Telex: 068862 Cable Add: Echterverlag
Dirs: Elmar Wegner, Heinz Otrauba
Subjects: Religion, Art, Fiction, Youth, Periodicals
Founded: 1900
ISBN Publisher's Prefix: 3-429

Xenos Verlagsgesellschaft mbH+, Am Hehsel 42, D-2000 Hamburg 63 Tel: (040) 5381909 Telex: 2174727 bix d
Man Dirs: Erwin Heimberger, H Kaiser; *Publicity:* Mrs Kuzeck; *Rights & Permissions:* Inge Modigell
Associate Company: Frankfurter Allgemeine Zeitung, Frankfurt am Main
Subjects: Juveniles, Non-fiction, Belles Lettres, Paperbacks
1986: 61 titles *1987:* 58 titles *Founded:* 1975
ISBN Publisher's Prefix: 3-8212

Z V W 5, see Siemens AG

Verlag Philipp von **Zabern***, Welschnonnengasse 13A, Postfach 4065, D-6500 Mainz Tel: (06131) 232214 Telex: 04187463 dwk
Man Dir: Franz Rutzen; *Sales:* Hermann Conrad
Subjects: Egyptology, Archaeology, Pre-history, Monographs, Periodicals
1985: 55 titles *Founded:* 1802
ISBN Publisher's Prefix: 3-8053

Dr **Zambon**, Leipziger Str 24, D-6000 Frankfurt am Main 90 Tel: (069) 779223
Publisher: Dr Giuseppe Zambon; *Sales:* Ulrich Karthaus
Subjects: Juveniles, Foreign-language Teaching, Reprints (bilingual titles German/Spanish)

Zechner und Hüthig Verlag GmbH, Daimlerstr 9, Postfach 2080, D-6720 Speyer am Rhein Tel: (06232) 33076 Cable Add: Zechner Verlag Speyer
Publisher: Rudolf Zechner
Subject: General Science
ISBN Publisher's Prefix: 3-87927

Verlag C **Zerling**+, Graefestr 26a, D-1000 Berlin 61 Tel: (030) 6929278
Also: Mehringdamm 51, D-1000 Berlin 61 Tel: (030) 6930550
Man Dir, Editorial, Production, Rights & Permissions: Clemens Zerling; *Sales:* Helmut Ahrens; *Publicity:* Sybille Zerling
Associate Company: Edition Ahrens, Fidicinstr 44, D-1000 Berlin 61
Subjects: Ethnology, Ethnic Medicine, Mysticism, Esoteric Fiction
1985: 7 titles *1986:* 7 titles *Founded:* 1979
ISBN Publisher's Prefix: 3-88468

Zero Verlag, Vierbaumer Heide 82A, D-4134 Rheinberg 4 Tel: (02843) 2769 Fax: (02843) 3668
Man Dir, Production, Rights & Permissions: Carl-Heinz Urselmann; *Editorial, Publicity:* Helmuth H Pohl; *Sales:* Frauke Urselmann, Helmuth H Pohl
Subjects: Philosophy and Literature (avante-garde), Wholefood Cookery
Founded: 1978
ISBN Publisher's Prefix: 3-922253

Zester Druck- und Verlagsgesellschaft mbH, see Accidentia

Verlag Andreas **Zettner** KG, Hofweg 12, Postfach 13, D-8707 Würzburg-Veitshöchheim Tel: (0931) 91970 Cable Add: Zettner Würzburg
Man Dir: Andreas Zettner
Subject: General Fiction
Book Club: Buchclub 69
Founded: 1955

Verlag Wolfgang **Zimmer**, Haunstetter Str 18, D-8900 Augsburg 1 Tel: (0821) 554135
Publisher: Wolfgang Zimmer
Subjects: Hobbies, Transport, Reference
ISBN Publisher's Prefixes: 3-87987, 3-87679

Paul **Zsolnay** Verlag GmbH*, Stresemannstr 300, D-2000 Hamburg 50 Tel: (040) 85431
Dirs: Kurt Lingenbrink, Hans Polak
Parent Company: Paul Zsolnay Verlag GmbH, Austria (qv)
Subjects: General Fiction, Poetry, Non-fiction
Founded: 1948
ISBN Publisher's Prefix: 3-552

Zweipunkt Verlag KG, Wilhelm-Leuschner-Str 1, D-6078 Neu Isenburg Tel: (06102) 27247
Subjects: Picture Books, Activity Books, Puzzles

Literary Agents

Brigitte **Axster**, Am Fronhof 3, D-4005 Meerbusch 1 Tel: (02105) 10096
Specialization: Representation of English authors, agents and publishers in Germany and the Netherlands

Balkan-Press, Schmied-Kochel-Str 20, D-8000 Munich 70 Tel: (089) 3204450

David **Carr** Literary Agency, Dahlmannstr 58, D-6000 Frankfurt 60 Tel: (069) 4960893

Agentur **Cobra***, Neuhaussstr 11, D-6000 Frankfurt am Main Tel: (069) 5602662
Contacts: Anna-Maria Krause-Poth, Joachim Schäfer, Heinz-Peter Weiss

Mo **Cohen**, Wentzelstr 15, D-2000 Hamburg 60 Tel: (040) 273814
Specializes in rights between publishers in Federal Republic of Germany, UK and USA

Dr rer pol Dr Julius **Démuth**, Krautgartenweg 22, D-6000 Frankfurt am Main 50 Tel: (069) 571970

Eulama SA*, Franziskanerstr 18, D-8000 Munich 80 Tel: (089) 489670
Specializations: Social Sciences, Politics, Psychology, Education, Philosophy, Religion, Linguistics, Literature, Mass Media, Architecture, Urban Studies, Latin American Literature, Books for Young Readers, Technology, Computer Science
Also: Eulama SRL, Italy (qv)

Fralit-F K Albrecht, Brahmsallee 29/1, D-2000 Hamburg 13 Tel: (040) 456073
Cable Add: Fralitagentur
Specializations: Tipposcripts for Publishers, Press, Broadcasting, Film and Theatre besides those which are strictly specialized for Medicine, Technology, Economics and related subjects
Also acts as Translation Supply Agency

G P A (Gerd Plessl Agentur und Verlags GmbH), Linprunstr 38, D-8000 Munich 2 Tel: (089) 554084 Telex: 5218062 gpa d
Specialization: Selling rights to German, South and East European publishers

Geisenheyner und Crone, Gymnasiumstr 31B, D-7000 Stuttgart 1 Tel: (0711) 293738 Cable Add: Gecelit Telex: 722664
Proprietor: Ernst W Geisenheyner
An international agency

Hans-Peter **Glückler** Literary Agency*, Buss-str 5, D-7800 Freiburg im Breisgau Tel: (0761) 77692

Hans Hermann **Hagedorn***, Erikastr 142, D-2000 Hamburg 20 Tel: (040) 4603232

Agence **Hoffman***, Seestr 6, D-8000 Munich 40 Tel: (089) 396402 Cable Add: Aghoff München
Contact: Frau Dagmar Henne
There is a branch of this Agency in Paris, France (qv)

Rose M **Meerwein**, Reuterpfad 6-8, D-1000 Berlin 33 Tel: (030) 8262039
Literary scout; no authors' representation

Dr Ray-Güde **Mertin**, Literarische Agentur, Friedrichstr 1, D-6380 Bad Homburg Tel: (06172) 29842
Head Off: Thomas Colchie Associates Inc, 700 Fort Washington Ave, New York, NY 10040, USA Tel: (212) 927 6993
Specialization: Representation of authors from Brazil, Portugal, Portuguese Africa, Spanish America, Spain

Gerd **Plessl** Agentur, see GPA

Quelle Press*, Postfach 1314, D-7800 Freiburg im Breisgau Tel: (07664) 7016
Cable Add: Quellepress Freiburg
Dir: Friedrich-Wilhelm König
Specializations: Romance, Gothic, Science Fiction, Fantasy, Western, Comics

Thomas **Schlueck***, Hinter der Worth 12, D-3008 Garbsen 9 Tel: (05131) 93053 Telex: 923419 litag d
Specialization: Full representation to Anglo-American authors, agents and publishers in German language areas

Skandinavia Verlag*, Ithweg 31, D-1000 Berlin 37 Tel: (030) 8137006/8616074
Contacts: Marianne Weno, Michael Günther
Specialization: Scandinavian Stage, Radio and TV plays

Corry **Theegarten-Schlotterer**, Kulmer Str 3, D-8000 Munich 81 Tel: (089) 932566 Cable Add: Cothee

Book Clubs

Bertelsmann Lesering*, Carl-Bertelsmannstr 270, Postfach 555, D-4830 Gütersloh
Members: 3 million
Owned by: Bertelsmann Club GmbH, Gütersloh
Founded: 1950

Verlag **Bibliotheca** Christiana, see Bonner Buchgemeinde

Bonner Buchgemeinde (BBG), Bertha-von-Suttner-Pl 21, D-5300 Bonn
Includes: Verlag Bibliotheca Christiana

Buchclub 69 GmbH, Hofweg 12, Postfach 13, D-8707 Würzburg-Veitshöchheim
Owned by: Verlag Andreas Zettner KG (qv)

Christlicher Bildungskreis Verlags GmbH*, Stuttgarter Str 161, Postfach 1440, D-7014 Kornwestheim

Deutsche Buch-Gemeinschaft C A Koch's Verlag Nachfolger*, Berliner Allee 6, Postfach 4131, D-6100 Darmstadt Tel: (06151) 3961 Cable Add: Lesestunde
Also: Deutsche Buch-Gemeinschaft C A Koch's Verlag Nachfolger, Austria (qv)

Deutscher Bücherbund GmbH & Co, Wolframstr 36, D-7000 Stuttgart 1 Tel: (0711) 25800 Telex: 0723829
Owned by: Verlagsgruppe Georg von Holtzbrinck GmbH, Gänsheidestr 26, D-7000 Stuttgart 1

Deutscher Buchkreis, Postfach 1629, D-7400 Tübingen Tel: (07071) 68011 Telex: 07262863 grav d
Owned by: Grabert-Verlag (qv)

E B G Verlags GmbH*, Stuttgarter Str 161, Postfach 1440, D-7014 Kornwestheim Tel: (07154) 1340 Telex: 715410 ebege d
Members: 1,300,000
Owned by: Bertelsmann Club GmbH, Gütersloh
Founded: 1950

Freundeskreis des **Euphorion** Verlags, Wilhelm-Busch-Str 41, D-6000 Frankfurt am Main 50
Owned by: Euphorion Verlag (qv)
Founded: 1976

Europäische Bildungsgemeinschaft Verlags GmbH, see EBG Verlags GmbH

Europaring der Buch- und Schallplattenfreunde, Carl-Bertelsmann-Str 270, D-4830 Gütersloh
Owned by: Bertelsmann Club GmbH, Gütersloh

Graphik Klub, Am Römermuseum, D-6650 Homburg-Schwarzenacker/Saar
Owned by: Edition Monika Beck (qv)

Büchergilde **Gutenberg**, Untermainkai 66, Postfach 160165, D-6000 Frankfurt am Main 16
Owned by: Büchergilde Gutenberg Verlagsgesellschaft mbH (qv)

Herder-Buchgemeinde, Hermann-Herder-Str 4, D-7800 Freiburg im Breisgau
Owned by: Verlag Herder GmbH & Co KG (qv)
Founded: 1952

Kosmos Gesellschaft, Pfizerstr 5-7, Postfach 640, D-7000 Stuttgart 1
Owned by: Franckh'sche Verlagshandlung W Keller & Co (qv)

Wissenschaftliche Buchgesellschaft*, Hindenburgstr 40, Postfach 111129, D-6100 Darmstadt 11
Scientific Book Society
Owned by: Wissenschaftliche Buchgesellschaft (qv)

Major Booksellers

Artibus et Literis, Friedrichstr 26, D-4000 Düsseldorf 1
Managing Partners: Horst and Klaus Janssen
Worldwide export and import of books and journals

Buchhandlung G D **Baedeker***, Kettwiger Str 33-35, Postfach 100345, D-4300 Essen 1 Tel: (02141) 221381

Blazek und Bergmann, Inhaber Dr Hans Bergmann, Universitätsbuchhandlung, Goethestr 1, D-6000 Frankfurt am Main 1 Tel: (069) 288648

Universitätsbuchhandlung **Bouvier** GmbH, Am Hof 32, D-5300 Bonn 1 Tel: (0228) 729010
Manager: Thomas Grundmann

Buchhandlung **Elwert und Meurer GmbH**, Hauptstr 101, D-1000 Berlin 62 Tel: (030) 784001

F B V Frauenbuchvertrieb GmbH*, Mehringdamm 32-34, D-1000 Berlin 61 Tel: (030) 2511666
Managers: R Krause, E Schoenkerl
Books written by women for women and published by women; subjects relating to women's movements

Buchhandlung Heinrich **Gonski** GmbH & Co*, Neumarkt 24, D-5000 Cologne 1 Tel: (0221) 210528
Manager: Ulrike Kok

Grossohaus Wegner und Co, Postfach 102540, D-2000 Hamburg 1 (Located at: Conventstr 12-14, D-2000 Hamburg 76) Tel: (040) 25760 Cable Add: Grossohaus Hamburg Telex: (02) 15096 Fax: (040) 2576250
Wholesaler and exporter of German books, including those in the English language published in German-speaking countries

Otto **Harrassowitz**, Taunusstr 5, Postfach 2929, D-6200 Wiesbaden Tel: (06121) 521046
Library Service Department: Dr Knut Dorn, Detlef Dorn; *Asia Department:* F O Weigel
See also Verlag Otto Harrassowitz

Heinrich **Hugendubel**, Salvatorplatz 2, D-8000 Munich 2 Tel: (089) 23891 Cable Add: Hugendubel Munich Telex: 0529651
Also: Marienplatz 22

Internationale Presse, Import- und Export GmbH, Borsigallee 17, D-6000 Frankfurt am Main 60 Tel: (069) 419198 Cable Add: Airedition Frankfurt Telex: 4189645 ip d Fax: (069) 425476
Man Dir: Claus-Michael Müller
Book and periodical wholesaler representing companies in France, Italy, Spain, United Kingdom, United States

Koch, Neff und Oetinger & Co*, Schockenriedstr 39, Postfach 800620, D-7000 Stuttgart 80 Tel: (0711) 78603325 Telex: 07255684 knov d stgt
Wholesaler

Barsortiment Georg Lingenbrink*, Stresemannstr 300, Postfach 500925, D-2000 Hamburg 50 Tel: (040) 853980 Telex: 214900 and 214673
Proprietor: Kurt Lingenbrink
Also: D-6000 Frankfurt-Preungesheim Tel: (069) 15260 Telex: 414606; D-5000 Cologne; D-8047 Munich-Karlsfeld; Nüremberg; Stuttgart

J A Mayersche Buchhandlung*, Ursulinerstr 17-19, D-5100 Aachen Tel: (0241) 48142 Cable Add: Mayer Aachen Telex: 832768
Manager: Helmut Falter

Vereinigte Verlagsauslieferung R Mohn HG, see VVA

Buchhandlung Wendelin Niedlich KG*, Schmale Str 9, D-7000 Stuttgart 1 Tel: (0711) 223287
Manager: W Niedlich

Hans Heinrich Petersen Buchimport GmbH, Lederstr 21, Postfach 540804, D-2000 Hamburg 54 Tel: (040) 5400810 Cable Add: buchpetersen hamburg Telex: 211401 hhp d
Man Dir: Johann Christian Petersen
Importer of books, audiovisual material from throughout world (but especially UK, USA, Netherlands)

Pro Media Literaturvertrieb GmbH*, Werner Voss Damm 54, D-1000 Berlin 42 Tel: (030) 7855971
Manager: Ruth Westerwelle
Wholesale marketing organization representing small publishing houses dealing with the alternative society

Stern-Verlag Janssen & Co, Friedrichstr 24-26, Postfach 7820, D-4000 Düsseldorf 1 Tel: (0211) 38810
Managing Partners: Horst and Klaus Janssen
New and antiquarian/second-hand books; worldwide export and import of books and journals

V V A (Vereinigte Verlagsauslieferung GmbH), an der Autobahn, Postfach 7777, D-4830 Gütersloh 1 Tel: (05241) 803574 Telex: 933827
Man Dir: Detthold Aden
Wholesale book supplier and publishers' delivery service

Buchhandlung Konrad Wittwer GmbH*, Königstr 30, PO Box 147, D-7000 Stuttgart 1 Tel: (0711) 25070 Telex: 723751

Major Libraries

Bayerische Staatsbibliothek, Ludwigstr 16, Postfach 340150, D-8000 Munich 34 Tel: (089) 21981
Bavarian State Library
Librarian: Dr F G Kaltwasser

Bibliothek für Zeitgeschichte, Konrad-Adenauer-Str 8, Postfach 769, D-7000 Stuttgart 1 Tel: (0711) 244117
Library for contemporary history. This library is housed in same building as the Württembergische Landesbibliothek (qv) but has separate administration
Dir: Prof Dr Jürgen Rohwer
Publications: Jahresbibliographie; Schriften der Bibliothek für Zeitgeschichte; Dokumentationene der B fZ; Wehrtechnik im Bild

Stiftung Centralbibliothek für **Blinde***, Adolfstr 44-46, D-2000 Hamburg 76 Tel: (040) 2206886
Central Library of the Institute for the Blind
Dir: Dr Friedrich Andrae

Bundesarchiv, Potsdamer Str 1, Postfach 320, D-5400 Koblenz-Karthause Tel: (0261) 5050 Telex: 261852 barchko d
Federal Archives. Publishing is undertaken by Harald Boldt Verlag (qv) and R Oldenbourg Verlag (qv)
President: Prof Dr Hans Booms

Deutsche Bibliothek, Zeppelinallee 4-8, D-6000 Frankfurt am Main 1 Tel: (069) 75661 Telex: 416643 deubi
National Library
Librarian: Prof Dr Günther Pflug

Deutsches Bucharchiv München, Institut für Buchwissenschaften, Erhardtstr 8, D-8000 Munich 5 Tel: (089) 2016064 Telex: 529813 debig d
German Bibliological Archives, Institute for Book Research
Dir: Dr Ludwig Delp; *Librarian:* Ursula Frank

Herzog August Bibliothek, Lessingplatz 1, Postfach 1364, D-3340 Wolfenbüttel Tel: (05331) 8080
Dir: Prof Dr Paul Raabe

Hessische Landes- und Hoch-schulbibliothek Darmstadt*, Schloss, D-6100 Darmstadt Tel: (06151) 125420
The Hesse Regional and University Library

Ibero-Amerikanisches Institut Preussischer Kulturbesitz, Potsdamer Str 37, D-1000 Berlin 30 Tel: (030) 2662500
Dir: Prof Dr Dietrich Briesemeister

Bibliothek des Instituts für Weltwirtschaft — Zentralbibliothek der Wirtschaftswissenschaften, Postfach 4309, D-2300 Kiel 1 (Located at: Düsternbrooker Weg 120, D-2300 Kiel 1) Tel: (0431) 8841 Telex: 0292479
Library of the Institute for World Economics — National Library of Economics

Niedersächsische Staats- und Universitätsbiliothek Göttingen, Prinzenstr 1, Postfach 2932, D-3400 Göttingen Tel: (0551) 395212 (Secretariat)
Librarian: Dir Helmut Vogt

Staats- und Universitätsbibliothek, Von-Melle Park 3, D-2000 Hamburg 13 Tel: (040) 41232213
Dir: Prof Dr Horst Gronemeyer

Staatsbibliothek Bamberg, Neue Residenz, Domplatz 8, D-8600 Bamberg Tel: (0951) 54014
Chief Librarian: Dr Bernhard Schemmel

Staatsbibliothek Preussischer Kulturbesitz, Potsdamer Str 33, Postfach 1407, D-1000 Berlin 30 Tel: (030) 2661 Telex 183160 staab d
State Library of the Prussian Cultural Foundation
Dir: Dr Richard Landwehrmeyer
Publications: Jahresbericht (annual); *Mitteilungen* (three times a year); *Sigelverzeichnis für die Bibliotheken der Bundesrepublik Deutschland einschl Berlin (West)* (Classification List for the Libraries of the Federal Republic of Germany including West Berlin), *Zeitschriften-Datenbank* (semi-annual), both produced in association with Deutsches Bibliotheksinstitut (qv)

Stadt- und Universitätsbibliothek, Bockenheimer Landstr 134-138, D-6000 Frankfurt am Main 1 Tel: (069) 79071 Telex: 414024 stub d
Dir: Mr Lehmann

Universitäts- und Stadtbibliothek, Universitätsstr 33, D-5000 Cologne 41 Tel: (0221) 4702260/4702214

Universitätsbibliothek*, Werthmannpl 2, Postfach 1629, D-7800 Freiburg im Breisgau Tel: (0761) 2033901 (management); 2034000 (enquiries); 2033940 (main reading room) Telex: 77274050 uf d
Dir: Prof Dr Wolfgang Kehr

Universitätsbibliothek der Eberhard-Karls-Universität, Wilhelmstr 32, Postfach 2620, D-7400 Tübingen 1 Tel: (07071) 292577

Universitätsbibliothek Erlangen-Nürnberg, Universitätsstr 4/Schuhstr 1a, D-8520 Erlangen Tel: (09131) 852151
Dir: Dr Konrad Wickert

Universitätsbibliothek Heidelberg*, Plöck 107-109, Postfach 105749, D-6900 Heidelberg 1 Tel: (06221) 542380
Library Dir: Prof Dr E Mittler
Publications include: Neuerwerbungslisten der Sondersammelgebiete Ägyptologie, Klassische Archäologie, Mittlere und Neuere Kunstgeschichte; Bibliothek-Forschung und Praxis; Bibliothek und Wissenschaft; Zeitschriftenverzeichnis Ägyptologie, Klassische Archäologie und Mittlere und Neuere Kunstgeschichte

Württembergische Landesbibliothek, Konrad-Adenauer-Str 8, Postfach 769, D-7000 Stuttgart 1 Tel: (0711) 2125424
Württemberg State Library
Dir: Dr Hans-Peter Geh
Miscellaneous: The Bibliothek für Zeitgeschichte is housed in same building, but has separate administration

Library Associations

A Sp B, see Arbeitsgemeinschaft der Spezialbibliotheken eV

Arbeitsgemeinschaft der Archive und Bibliotheken in der evangelischen Kirche, Veilhofstr 28, D-8500 Nuremberg 20
Joint Association of Archives and Libraries in the Evangelical Church
President: Dr Helmut Baier
Publications: Mitteilungen der AABevK (AABevK News Bulletin); *Veröffentlichungen der AABevK* (Publications of the AABevK)

Arbeitsgemeinschaft der kirchlichen Büchereiverbände Deutschlands, Wittelsbacherring 9, D-5300 Bonn Tel: (0228) 631055
Joint Association of Library Associations of the Churches in Germany
Executive Secretary: Erich Hodick

Arbeitsgemeinschaft der Kunstbibliotheken, pA Kunstbibliothek Staatliche Museen Preussischer Kulturbesitz, Jebensstr 2, D-1000 Berlin 12
Joint Association of Art Libraries

Arbeitsgemeinschaft der Parlaments- und Behördenbibliotheken, pA Bibliothek des Deutschen Patentamts, Zweibrückenstr 12, D-8000 Munich 2 Tel: (089) 2195/2606
Joint Association of Parliamentary and Administration Libraries
Chairman: Dr Eckhard Derday; *Executive Secretary:* Hubert Rothe
Publications: Arbeitshefte (Selected titles concerned with parliamentary and administrtive library topics) and *Mitteilungen* (News Bulletin)

Arbeitsgemeinschaft der Regionalbibliotheken, Badische Landesbibliothek, Erbprinzenstr 15, Postfach 1451, D-7500 Karlsruhe 1
Joint Association of Regional Libraries
President: Dr Gerhard Römer

Arbeitsgemeinschaft der Spezialbibliotheken eV (ASpB), Kekulé-Bibliothek, Bayer AG, D-5090 Leverkusen-Bayerwerk
Association of Special Libraries
Chairman: Dr Walter Manz; *Secretariat Dir:* Dr Marianne Schwarzer
Publication: Bericht über die Tagung (Conference Report; every 2 years)

Arbeitsgemeinschaft für juristisches Bibliotheks- und Dokumentationswesen, (Teilbibliothek Recht der Universitätsbibliothek), Eichleitnerstr 30, D-8900 Augsburg
Joint Association for Law Libraries and Legal Documentation
Chairman: Dr Hans-Burkard Meyer; *Editor:* Werner von Schaper
Publications: Mitteilungen der Arbeitsgemeinschaft für juristisches Bibliotheks- und Dokumentationswesen (three times yearly) and *Arbeitshefte* (irregularly)

Arbeitsgemeinschaft für medizinisches Bibliothekswesen, pA Robert Koch-Institut des Bundesgesundheitsamtes Bibliothek, Nordufer 20, D-1000 Berlin 65 Tel: (030) 4503328 Telex: 8579573 klies d
Joint Association for Medical Libraries
President: K Gerber

Arbeitsgemeinschaft katholischtheologischer Bibliotheken*, pA Studien- und Zentralbibliothek der Franziskaner, Hörsterpl 5, D-4400 Münster
Joint Association of Catholic Theological Libraries
Dir: P Heribald Wenke
Publications: Mitteilungsblatt (News Letter); *Veröffentlichungen der Arbeitsgemeinschaft katholischtheologischer Bibliotheken* (Publications of the Association — Nos 1-3 available); *Handbuch der kirchlichen katholisch-theologischen Bibliotheken in der Bundesrepublik Deutschland und in West-Berlin*

Bundesarbeitsgemeinschaft der katholisch-kirchlichen Büchereiarbeit, Wittelsbacherring 9, D-5300 Bonn Tel: (0228) 631055
National Joint Association of Library work in the Catholic Church
Executive Secretary: Erich Hodick

Deutsche Gesellschaft für Dokumentation eV, Westendstr 19, D-6000 Frankfurt am Main 1 Tel: (069) 747761
German Society for Documentation
President: Prof P Canisius
Publications include: Nachrichten für Dokumentation (Documentation News — 6 per year); *Internationale Aufgaben der DGD — Mitteilungen und Berichte* (Newsletter — 8 per year)

Deutscher Bibliotheksverband eV*, Bundesallee 184-185, D-1000 Berlin 31 Tel: (030) 8505274
Association of German Libraries
Chairman: Helmut Sontag

Deutscher Verband evangelischer Büchereien eV, Bürgerstr 2, D-3400 Göttingen Tel: (0551) 74917
German Association of Protestant Libraries
Chairman: Dr Hans Wulf; *Manager:* Christine Razum
Publications: Der EV Buchberater (quarterly); *Buchauswahl für EV Büchereien* (annual); *Handwörterbuch der evangelischen Büchereiarbeit 1980*

Deutsches Bibliotheksinstitut, Bundesallee 184-185, D-1000 Berlin 31 Tel: (030) 85050
German Library Institute
Dir: Prof Günter Beyersdorff
Publications: Bibliotheksdienst (monthly); *Forum Musikbibliothek* (quarterly); *Schulbibliothek aktuell* (quarterly), also several reference books, monographs, bibliographical and statistical services

Gesellschaft für Bibliothekswesen und Dokumentation des Landbaues (GBDL), Paracelsusstr 2, D-7000 Stuttgart 70 Tel: (0711) 459/2111
Society for Librarianship and Documentation in Agriculture
Publication: Mitteilungen der Gesellschaft für Bibliothekswesen und Dokumentation des Landbaues

Gesellschaft für Information und Dokumentation mbH (GID)*, GID-Informationszentrum (GID-IZ), Lyoner Str 44-48, Postfach 710363, D-6000 Frankfurt am Main 71 Tel: (069) 66871 Telex: 414351
Documentation and Information Society
Dir: Dr Peter Budinger
Publications: Verzeichnis Deutscher Informations- und Dokumentationsstellen Bundesrepublik Deutschland und Berlin (West); Verzeichnis laufend gehaltener Zeitschriften im GID-IZ; Forschungs- und Entwicklungsprojekte in Informationswissenschaft und -praxis; Internationale IuD-Gremien mit Beteiligung aus der Bundesrepublik Deutschland und Berlin (West); Verzeichnis Deutscher Datenbanken, Datenbankbetreiber und Informationsvermittlungsstellen; Thesaurus Guide, Analytical Directory of Thesauri

Internationale Vereinigung der Musikbibliotheken, pA Musikarchive und Musikdokumentationszentren, Gruppe Bundesrepublik Deutschland, Fachhochschule für Bibliothekswesen, Wolframstr 32, D-7000 Stuttgart 1
German Section of the International Association of Music Libraries
President: Prof Dr Wolfgang Krüger

V D D, Berufsverband Dokumentation, Information, Kommunikation eV*, Postfach 2509, D-5300 Bonn 1
Association of German Documentalists
Chairman: Dr Schmitz-Esser, Hamburg; *Vice-Chairman:* Dr Bernd Habel, Königswinter 21
Publications: Nachrichten für Dokumentation, Westendstr 19, D-6000 Frankfurt am Main 1; *VDD Schriftenreihe* (irregular)

Verband der Bibliotheken des Landes Nordrhein-Westfalen eV, Maischützenstr 57, D-4630 Bochum 1 Tel: (0234) 234582
Association of Libraries of North Rhine-Westphalia
President: H Lohse; *Secretary:* R Scheuerpflug
Publication: Mitteilungsblatt (News Sheet)

Verband deutscher Werkbibliotheken eV*, c/o BASF Aktiengesellschaft, Werkbücherei, Carl-Bosch Str, D-6700 Ludwigshafen Tel: (0621) 603689
Association of Industrial Libraries of the Federal Republic of Germany
President: Christiane Lüderssen

Verein Angehörige des mittleren und nichtdiplomierten Bibliotheksdienstes eV*, Klattenweg 59, Bremen
Association of Non-professional Librarians
Secretary: Melitta Thomas

Verein der Bibliothekare an öffentlichen Bibliotheken eV*, Stadtbibliothek, Rathaus Passage, D-6200 Wiesbaden Tel: (06121) 312266
Association of Public Librarians
President: Dipl-Bibl Karl-Heinz Pröve; *Secretary:* M Rothe
Publication: Buch und Bibliothek (from: Postfach 327, D-7410 Reutlingen)

Verein der Diplom-Bibliothekare an wissenschaftlichen Bibliotheken eV, pA Deutsches Bibliotheksinstitut, Bundesallee 184-185, D-1000 Berlin 31 Tel: (030) 8505122
Association of Certified Librarians at Academic Libraries
Chairman: Helga Schwarz
Publications include: Rundschreiben; Auswirkungen neuer Technologien auf Bibliotheken und Bibliothekare, 1984; Ausgewählte Literatur zu neuen Technologien, 1986; Ausbildung im Wandel, 1986

Verein deutscher Archivare (VdA), pA Generaldirektion der Staatlichen Archive Bayerns, Postfach 220240, D-8000 Munich 22 Tel: (089) 2198484
Association of German Archivists
Chairman: Dr Hermann Rumschöttel
Publication: Archive und Archivare (Register of Archives and Archivists) — at irregular intervals of several years

Verein deutscher Bibliothekare eV, Universitätsbibliothek, Olshäusenstr 29, D-2300 Kiel Tel: (0431) 8802700
Association of German Librarians
President: Dr Günther Wiegand; *Secretary:* Dr Else Wischermann
Publications: Zeitschrift für Bibliothekswesen und Bibliographie (Journal of Library Science and Bibliography); *Jahrbuch der deutschen Bibliotheken* (Yearbook of German Libraries)

Verein Deutscher Dokumentare eV, see VDD

Württembergische Bibliotheksgesellschaft, Postfach 769, D-7000 Stuttgart 1 (Located at: Konrad-Adenauer Str 8)
Society of Friends of the Württemberg State Library
Secretary: Dr Ursula Degenhard

Zentralstelle für maschinelle Dokumentation, see Gesellschaft für Information und Dokumentation

Library Reference Books and Journals

Books

Bibliothekswesen in Deutschland (Library Science in Germany), Börsenverein des deutschen Buchhandels eV, Grosser Hirschgraben 17-21, D-6000 Frankfurt 1

FEDERAL REPUBLIC OF GERMANY

Handbuch des Büchereiwesens (Handbook of Library Science), Verlag Otto Harrassowitz, Taunusstr 14, Postfach 2929, D-6200 Wiesbaden

Jahrbuch der Deutschen Bibliotheken (Yearbook of German Libraries), Verein Deutscher Bibliothekare eV, Universitätsbibliothek, Olshäusenstr 29, D-2300 Kiel

Libraries in the Federal Republic of Germany, Verlag Otto Harrassowitz, Taunusstr 14, Postfach 2929, D-6200 Wiesbaden 1

Sigelverzeichnis für die Bibliotheken der Bundesrepublik Deutschland einschl Berlin (West) (Classification List for the Libraries of the Federal Republic of Germany including West Berlin), Staatsbibliothek Preussicher Kulturbesitz, Potsdamer Str 33, Postfach 1407, D-1000 Berlin 30

Journals

Bibliotheksdienst (Library Service), Deutsches Bibliotheksinstitut, Bundesallee 184-185, D-1000 Berlin 31

Buch und Bibliothek (Book and Library), K G Saur KG, Pössenbacherstr 2, D-8000 Munich 71

Dokumentation, Fachbibliothek, Werksbücherei (DFW) Zeitschrift für Allgemein- und Spezial-bibliotheken, Büchereien und Dokumentationsstellen (Documentation, Technical Libraries' and Works Libraries' Journal for General and Special Libraries and Documentation Centres), Nordwestverlag Stephanie Schräpel, Güntherstr 21, D-3000 Hanover-Waldhausen

Nachrichten für Dokumentation (Documentation News), Deutsche Gesellschaft für Dokumentation eV, Westendstr 19, D-6000 Frankfurt am Main 1

Das Neue Buch, Borromäusverein, Wittelsbacherring 9, D-5300 Bonn; St Michaelsbund, Herzog-Wilhelmstr 5, D-8000 Munich 2
Book profile for Catholic library work

Die Neue Bücherei (Öffentlich Bucherein in Bayern — Bavarian Public Libraries magazine), Ludwigstr 16, D-8000 Munich 34

Schulbibliothek aktuell (School Library Today), Deutsches Bibliotheksinstitut, Bundesallee 184-185, D-1000 Berlin 31

Zeitschrift für Bibliothekswesen und Bibliographie (Journal of Library Science and Bibliography), Verein Deutscher Bibliothekare eV, Universitätsbibliothek, Olshäusenstr 29, D-2300 Kiel

Literary Associations and Societies

Arbeitskreis für Deutsche Dichtung eV*, Am Dorfe 115, D-3350 Ahlshausen Tel: (05553) 1053
German Poetry Committee
Chairman: Hans-Joachim Sander

Arbeitskreis für Jugendliteratur eV, Elisabethstr 15, D-8000 Munich 40
Youth Literature Committee — Section of the International Board on Books for Young People
Man Dir: Franz Meyer

Bundesverband deutscher Autoren eV*, Schlüterstr 39, Zimmer 109, D-1000 Berlin 12 Tel: (030) 8821050 Telex: 8821050/3915933
Association of German Authors
Acting Chairman: Rosemarie Fiedler-Winter; *Manager:* Siegfried Heinrichs

Deutsche Akademie für Sprache und Dichtung, Glückert-Haus, Alexandraweg 23, D-6100 Darmstadt Tel: (06151) 44823
German Academy of Language and Poetry
President: Prof Dr Herbert Heckmann; *Secretary-General:* Dr Gerhard Dette

Deutsche Dante-Gesellschaft eV, Servatiusstr 1, D-5340 Bad Honnef 6 Tel: (02224) 80198
President: Prof Dr August Buck
Publication: Deutsches Dante-Jahrbuch

Deutsche Freidrich-Schiller Stiftung eV*, Hauptverwaltung, Berliner Allee 6, D-6100 Darmstadt Tel: (06151) 866261

Deutsche Schillergesellschaft eV, Schillerhöhe 8-10, D-7142 Marbach am Neckar Tel: (07144) 6061
President: Dr Martin Cremer

Deutsche Shakespeare-Gesellschaft West eV, Rathaus, D-4630 Bochum
West German Shakespeare Society
President: Prof Dr Habick
Publications: Shakespeare Jahrbuch

Deutsche Thomas-Mann-Gesellschaft Sitz Lübeck, Königstr 67a, D-2400 Lübeck Tel: (0451) 160060
Chairman: Prof Dr Eckhard Heftrich

Europäische Märchengesellschaft eV*, Postfach 3265, D-4400 Münster Tel: (0251) 33632
Association for legends and folkstories
President: Dr Wolfdietrich Siegmund

Free German Authors' Association*, Pacelli-Str 8, D-8000 Munich 2 Tel: (089) 224452

Gutenberg-Gesellschaft, Liebfrauenplatz 5, D-6500 Mainz Tel: (06131) 226420
Gutenberg Society
President: Herman-Hartmut Weyel; *Secretary-General:* Gertraude Benöhr
Publications: Gutenberg-Jahrbuch, Kleine Drucke, Veröffentlichungen

Verein für **Hamburgische Geschichte**, ABC-Strasse 19A, D-2000 Hamburg 36 Tel: (040) 344848
The Hamburg Historical Society

Literarischer Verein in Stuttgart eV, Rosenbergstr 113, Postfach 723, D-7000 Stuttgart 1 Tel: (0711) 638264
Stuttgart Literary Society
President: Karl G Hiersemann
Publication: Bibliothek des Literarischen Vereins in Stuttgart Vol 1 (1842) — Vol 311 (1987)
The aim of the Society (founded in 1839) is to publish the texts of valuable unpublished manuscripts and old printed texts in a new form — especially with regard to old German literature

Maximilian-Gesellschaft eV, Rosenbergstr 113, Postfach 723, D-7000 Stuttgart 1
Book Collectors Society

P E N Zentrum Bundesrepublik Deutschland, Sandstr 10, D-6100 Darmstadt Tel: (06151) 23120
President: Martin Gregor-Dellin; *Secretary-General:* Prof Hanns Werner Schwarze

Adalbert **Stifter** Verein eV, Hochstr 8, D-8000 Munich 80
Chairman: Prof Otto Herbert Hajek

Carl **Zuckmayer** Gesellschaft eV*, Postfach 33, D-6506 Nackenheim Tel: (06135) 5625
Dir: Günter Ollig
Publication: Newsletter (quarterly)

Literary Periodicals

Alternative, Zeitschrift fur Literatur/Theorie, Alternative Verlag, Konstanzer Str 11, D-1000 Berlin 31

Akzente Carl Hanser Verlag, Kolberger Str 22, Postfach 860420, D-8000 Munich 80

Arcadia, Verlag Walter de Gruyter & Co, Genthiner Str 13, D-1000 Berlin 30

Basis, Suhrkamp Verlag, Lindenstr 29, D-6000 Frankfurt am Main

Die Begegnung, Autor, Verleger, Buchhändler, Leser, Buchhandlung Elwert und Meurer GmbH, Hauptstr 101, D-1000 Berlin 62

Besprechungen und Annotationen, Einkaufszentrale für offentlich Bibliotheken GmbH, Postfach 96, D-7410 Reutlingen

Buch aktuell, Harenberg Kommunikation, Westfalendamm 57, Postfach 1305, D-4600 Dortmund

Bücherkommentare (Book Commentaries), Rombach & Co GmbH, Lörracher Str 3, Postfach 1349, D-7800 Freiburg im Breisgau

Bücherschiff, Verlag Bücherschiff Walter Reutin, Rheinstr 122, Postfach 210947, D-7500 Karlsruhe 21

BuchJournal, Börsenverein des Deutschen Buchhandels eV, Grosser Hirschgraben 17-21, D-6000 Frankfurt am Main
Magazine for book-lovers

Bulletin Jugend und Literatur (Youth and Literature Bulletin), Lesen Verlag GmbH, Friedrichstr 13, D-8000 Munich

Der Bund, Schillderbund, deutscher Kulturverband eV, Lessingstr 6, D-6140 Bensheim

Bunte Blätter, Literarische Union eV, Schulstr 8, D-6645 Beckingen 1

Epitaph, Belgradstr 24, D-8000 Munich 40

Federlese, Georgenstr 43, D-8000 Munich 40

Formation, Zur Halle 5, D-6751 Sulybachtal 1, Kaiserlauten-Land

Hebbeljahrbuch, Westholstenische Verlagsanstalt Boyens & Co, Am Wulf-Isebrand-Pl, D-2240 Heide/Holstein

Imprimatur, Gesellschaft dem Bibliophilen eV, Postfach 160127, D-5400 Koblenz 16

Imprint, Lesen Verlag GmbH, Friedrichstr 13, D-8000 Munich
Literary journal for German-language literature

Kraus-Hefte, Levelinstr 6a, D-8000 Munich 80

Kritikon Litterarum, Thesen Verlag Vowinckel und Co, Kittlerstr 34, D-6100 Darmstadt

Kürbiskern, Damnitz Verlag GmbH, Hohensollernstr 144, D-8000 Munich 40

Lektüre, Lektüre Verlagsgesellschaft mbH, Bavariaring 24, D-8000 Munich 2

Literarische Blätter, Dietrich Str 26, D-4040 Neuss 1

Literarische Hefte (Literary Notes), Raith Verlag, Herzog Heinrich Str 21, D-8000 Munich 2

Literarische Umschau (Literary Review), Verlag Marie Hemmerle, Pullacherstr 1, D-8000 Munich 70

Literaturdienst, B Behrs Verlag GmbH, Auerhoffstr 10, D-2000 Hamburg

Literaturmagazin, Rowolt Verlag GmbH, Postfach 1349, D-2057 Reinbek

Litfass, Grainauer Str 11, D-1000 Berlin 30

Neue Rundschau (New Review), S Fischer Verlag, Geleitsstr 25, D-6000 Frankfurt am Main 70

Quickborn, Deichstr 48-50, D-2000 Hamburg 11
Magazine for literature and poetry in the low German dialects

Text und Kritik (Text and Criticism), Edition Text und Kritik, Levelingstr 6a, D-8000 Munich 80

Wolfenbütteler Notizen zur Buchgeschichte (Wolfenbütteler Notes on the History of Books), Pöseldorfer Weg 1, D-2000 Hamburg 13

Literary Prizes

Georg **Büchner** Prize
Founded in 1923 by Volksstaat Hessen, it has been given since 1951 by the Academy to writers who have been especially noteworthy through their work and have contributed to the current cultural scene in Germany. 30,000 DM. Awarded annually. Enquiries to Deutsche Akademie für Sprache und Dichtung, Glückert-Haus, Alexandraweg 23, D-6100 Darmstadt

Deutscher Jugendbuchpreis, see International Literary Prizes (The German Youth Book Award)

Alfred-**Döblin** Prize
Inaugurated in 1983, this award will generally be made every one or two years for unpublished work of an epic nature (including poetry). The amount awarded will be up to 20,000 DM. Enquiries to Akademie der Künste, Abteilung Literatur, Hanseatenweg 10, D-1000 Berlin 21

Konrad **Duden** Prize
For special achievement in the German language (co-sponsored by the Bibliographical Institute). 15,000 DM. Awarded every two years. Applications are not invited. Enquiries to Stadt Mannheim, Oberbürgermeister Abt Repräsentation, Rathaus E5, Postfach 2203, D-6800 Mannheim 1

Theodor **Fontane** Prize
Founded in 1948, this is the name for the major literary award given, either for a single work or for a body of work, by the Akademie der Künste (Academy of Arts). The award is 30,000 DM and is made once every six years (a similar award being made in other disciplines in the intervening five years). In addition, 'encouragement' prizes of 10,000 DM are given annually by the Akademie in each of the six disciplines — this includes one for literature and one for film/TV/radio work (which may be for writing). Enquiries to Akademie der Künste, Hanseatenweg 10, D-1000 Berlin 21

Sigmund **Freud** Prize
For a scientific presentation in prose. 10,000 DM. Awarded annually. Enquiries to Deutsche Akademie für Sprache und Dichtung, Glückert-Haus, Alexandraweg 23, D-6100 Darmstadt

German Youth Book Award, see International Literary Prizes

Goethe Prize
Founded in 1927 for work showing the value of, or respect for Goethe's ideals and thoughts. 50,000 DM awarded every three years. Enquiries to Amt für Wissenschaft und Kunst, Brückenstr 3-7, D-6000 Frankfurt am Main 70

Friedrich **Gundolf** Prize for Germanistics abroad
For essays in German. 10,000 DM. Awarded annually. Enquiries to Deutsche Akademie für Sprache und Dichtung, Glückert-Haus, Alexandraweg 23, D-6100 Darmstadt

The Alfred **Kerr** Prize for Literary Criticism*
Founded in 1976/77 by the Börsenblatt für den deutschen Buchhandel (German Book Trade Gazette). 5,000 DM plus a Certificate and the reimbursement of expenses incurred by the Presentation Ceremony. Awarded annually. For outstanding continuing literary criticism in a German-language newspaper, magazine, or TV or radio programme. Enquiries to Redaktion Börsenblatt, Chefredakteur Hanns Lothar Schütz, Grosser Hirschgraben 17-21, D-6000 Frankfurt am Main

Konsalik Novel Prize
Founded in 1982 jointly by Publishers Gustav Lübbe Verlag (qv), Wilhelm Goldmann Verlag GmbH, Munich (qv), and Wilhelm Heyne Verlag, Munich (qv). 40,000 DM, to be awarded annually, for a novel of contemporary life by a German author which also demonstrates national trends for an international readership. Enquiries to Verlag Wilhelm Goldmann, Neumarkter-Str 18, D-8000 Munich 80

Lessing Prize der Freien und Hansestadt Hamburg
To poets, writers, scholars in German cultural fields who are able to meet the challenge represented by the name of Lessing. 30,000 DM (less 10,000 DM for foundation fees). Awarded every four years. Enquiries to Kulturbehörde der Freien und Hansestadt Hamburg, Hamburgerstr 45, D-2000 Hamburg 76

Literature Prize*
To a poet or writer for his whole work. A monetary prize awarded annually. Enquiries to Bayerische Akademie der Schönen Künste, Max Joseph Platz 3, D-8000 Munich 22

Thomas **Mann** Prize
Founded in 1975 in honour of Thomas Mann, to celebrate the 100th anniversary of his birth. The prize will be awarded to personalities who have, through their literary work, shown the humanitarian spirit set out in the work of Thomas Mann. 15,000 DM. Awarded every three years. Enquiries to Der Senat der Hansestadt Lübeck, Amt für Kultur, Rathaushof, Postfach, D-2400 Lübeck 1

Johann Heinrich **Merck** Prize
For literary criticism. 10,000 DM. Awarded annually. Enquiries to Deutsche Akademie für Sprache und Dichtung, Glückert-Haus, Alexandraweg 23, D-6100 Darmstadt

Rheinland-Palatinate Prize
Founded in 1956 for a single work or body of work in literature (as well as fine art and music). Winner should be closely related to the area. 10,000 DM. Last awarded in 1985 to Ulf Hoelscher.

Enquiries to Rheinland-Palatinate Ministry of Culture, Mittlere Bleiche 61, D-6500 Mainz 1

Nelly **Sachs** Prize
The cultural prize of Dortmund City, instituted by the Dortmund City Council in 1961. Awarded every two years to personalities who have produced outstanding creative work in the art or cultural field. Current value 20,000 DM. Last awarded to Nadine Gordimer. Enquiries to Kulturamt der Stadt Dortmund, Südwall 2-4, D-4600 Dortmund 1

Schiller Prize
For outstanding achievements in the cultural field. 25,000 DM. Awarded every four years; applications are not invited. Enquiries to Stadt Mannheim, Oberbürgermeister Abt Repräsentation, Rathaus E5, Postfach 2203, D-6800 Mannheim 1

Johann Heinrich **Voss** Translation Prize
For a single work or life's work in translation. 10,000 DM. Awarded annually. Enquiries to Deutsche Akademie für Sprache und Dichtung, Glückert-Haus, Alexandraweg 23, D-6100 Darmstadt

Carl **Zuckmayer** Medal
Instituted 1978 by the Minister President of Rheinland-Pfalz (Rhineland Palatinate). The award is for those whose services to the German language make them worthy of honour in memory of Carl Zuckmayer, the noted German dramatist and poet. Awarded in 1987 to Tankred Dorst. Enquiries to Rheinland-Pfalz Kulturministerium, Mittlere Bleiche 61, D-6500 Mainz 1

Translation Agencies and Associations

Bundesverband der Dolmetscher und Übersetzer eV (BDÜ), Rüdigerstr 79a, D-5300 Bonn 2 Tel: (0228) 345000
Federal German Association of Interpreters and Translators
President: Hans Thomas Schwarz; *Secretary-General:* Georg Frantz
Publication: Mitteilungsblatt für Dolmetscher und Übersetzer (Interpreters' and Translators' News Sheet), six times per year

V **Gorachek** KG, Flurscheideweg 15, D-6230 Frankfurt am Main 80 Tel: (069) 341265
German-Russian-German Technical Translation Bureau
Chief Executive: N B Jdanoff
Owned by: Possev-Verlag V Gorachek KG (qv)

Verband deutschsprachiger Übersetzer literarischer und wissenschaftlicher Werke eV (VDÜ)*, Soatspad 18, D-4172 Straelen 6W Tel: (02834) 2510
Association of German-speaking translators of Literary and Scientific Works
Dir: Ursula Brackmann, Wilhelmskirch 204, D-7981 Horgenzell
Publication: Der Übersetzer (The Translator) (monthly)

Ghana

General Information

Language: English
Religion: About 40 per cent Christian, remainder follow traditional beliefs
Population: 11.45 million
Bank Hours: 0830-1400 Monday-Thursday; 0830-1500 Friday
Shop Hours: 0830-1230, 1330-1730 Monday, Tuesday, Thursday, Friday; 0830-1330 Wednesday and Saturday
Currency: 100 pesawas = 1 cedi
Export/Import Information: No tariffs on books; advertising matter over 1 kg gross weight 50%. Import licence required, but single copies of books under Open General Licence. Levy charged on import licences required. Credit terms not permitted
Copyright: UCC, Florence (see International section)

Book Trade Organizations

Ghana Association of Writers*, PO Box 2738, Accra
Publications: Okyeame; Takra

Ghana Book Development Council, PO Box M430, Ministry Branch PO, Accra Tel: 229178 Cable Add: Ghanabook
An agency of the Ministry of Education, GBDC co-ordinates and promotes creation, production and distribution of books, but does not itself publish
Deputy Executive Dir: Annor Nimako
Publications: Ghana Book World

Ghana Book Publishers' Association, c/o Ghana Universities Press, PO Box 4219, Accra
Secretary: W A Dekutsey

Ghana Booksellers' Association*, PO Box 7869, Accra Tel: 21551 Cable Add: Book supply
Secretary: F J Reimmer

Standard Book Numbering Agency, Ghana Library Board, Research Library on African Affairs, PO Box 2970, Accra Tel: 23526
Administrator: Christina D T Kwei

Book Trade Reference Journals

Ghana Book World (bi-annual), Ghana Book Development Council, Education Loop, PO Box M430, Accra

Ghana National Bibliography, c/o Research Library on African Affairs, PO Box 2970, Accra

Publishers

Advance Publishing Co Ltd*, New Town Rd, PO Box 2317, Accra New Town Tel: 21577
Man Dir: A O Mills
Subjects: General Non-fiction, Paperbacks

Adwinsa Publications (Ghana) Ltd*, PO Box 92, Legon (via Accra) (Located at: 3rd Floor, Advance Press Building, School Rd, Accra New Town) Tel: Accra 21577
Man Dir, Rights & Permissions: Kwabena Amponsah; *Editorial and General Manager:* Kwasi Asamoah; *Production:* Baffour Opoku Kontor; *Publicity:* Agyemang-Badu Patrick; *Sales:* Grace Amponsah
Orders to: Adwinsa Distribution Agency Ltd (at above address)
Subsidiary Company: Adwinsa Distribution Agency (at above address)
Associate Company: Adwinsa Publications (Sierra Leone), 31 Yiks Rd, Makeni, Sierra Leone
Branch Off: Adwinsa Bookstand (Eredec Hotel), PO Box 845, Koforidua
Subjects: General Subjects, Educational from Primary to University Level
Bookshops: Adwinsa Distribution Agency Ltd, Adwinsa House, A/Mdn/947, Madina-Accra; PO Box 92, Legon
Founded: 1977
ISBN Publisher's Prefix: 9964-955

Afram Publications (Ghana) Ltd*, 72 Ring Road East, PO Box M18, Accra
Tel: 74248 Cable Add: Aframbooks
Telex: 2171 SIC Accra
Man Dir, Rights & Permissions: Kwesi Sam-Woode; *Editorial:* Eric Ofei; *Marketing Manager:* Emmanuel A Manful
Subjects: General Fiction, Belles Lettres, Poetry, Biography, History, Africana, How-to Study Guides, Religion, General and Social Science, Paperbacks, Secondary and Primary Schools Textbooks
Founded: 1974
Miscellaneous: The Company is partly owned by the State Insurance Corporation of Ghana
ISBN Publisher's Prefix: 9964-70

Africa Christian Press+, PO Box 30, Achimota Tel: 225554
General Manager: Richard Crabbe; *Editorial:* R Mills-Tetteh; *Sales Manager:* Mrs E Dordoe
Subjects: Christian Fiction & Non-fiction, Biography, Paperbacks and Booklets (priority is given to African writers)
1985: 4 titles *Founded:* 1964
ISBN Publisher's Prefix: 9964-85352

Anowuo Educational Publications*, 2R McCarthy Hill, PO Box 3918, Accra
Tel: 24910
Also: PO Box 1, Asamang Ashanti Region Tel: 004
Publisher: S A Konadu; *Sales Manager:* I Oteng Konadu
Subjects: Africana, How-to, Study Guides, Reference, Juveniles, Books in Ghanaian Languages, Paperbacks, General Science, Secondary Textbooks, General Fiction, Belles Lettres, Poetry, History
Founded: 1966

Asempa Publishers+, PO Box 919, Accra
Tel: 221706
Manager: Rev Emmanuel Bortey; *Editorial:* Rev Jackson Yenn-Batah; *Production:* Sarah Ababio; *Sales:* J Ebo Whyte
Parent Company: Christian Council of Ghana (at above address)
Imprints: Asempa, IBRA (Ghana)
Subjects: Religion, Social Questions, African Music, Fiction
1986: 21 titles *Founded:* 1973
ISBN Publisher's Prefix: 9964-78

Benibengor Book Agency*, PO Box 40, Aboso
Man Dir: J Benibengor Blay
Subjects: General Fiction, Belles Lettres, Poetry, Biography, Juveniles, Paperbacks

Black Mask Ltd+, PO Box 252, FNT Kumasi Tel: 6454 Cable Add: BML
Man Dir: Yaw Owusu Asante; *Publicity:* Kwagi Asante; *Rights & Permissions:* Opia-Mensah Kumah
Branch Offs: Accra, Ghana; Freetown, Sierra Leone
Subjects: Educational Textbooks, Plays, Novels
1985-86: 2 titles *Founded:* 1979
ISBN Publisher's Prefix: 9964-960

Bureau of Ghana Languages*, PO Box 1851, Accra Tel: 64130/65194/65461 ext 513 Cable Add: Velbo, Accra, Ghana
Dir, Rights & Permissions: D E K Krampah; *Deputy Dir:* W K Adi; *Sales Manager:* J Gyekye-Aboagye
Branch Off: PO Box 177, Tamale, Northern Region, Ghana
Subjects: Fiction, Drama, Poetry, Biography, Science, School Textbooks, Dictionaries, Bibliographies, Material for New Literates. Books are published in 11 Ghanaian languages
Founded: 1951
Miscellaneous: Also acts as a Translation Agency/Association

Editorial and Publishing Services*, PO Box 5743, Accra
Man Dir: M Danquah
Subjects: General, Reference

Emmanuel Publishing Services+, PO Box 5282, Accra Tel: 25238 Cable Add: Emmapus Accra
Dir: Emmanuel K Nsiah
Subjects: Educational, Children's
Bookshops: Mayan Book Centre, PO Box 6173, Accra
Founded: 1978
Miscellaneous: Company has reprint arrangements in Ghana for Oxford University Press publications
ISBN Publisher's Prefix: 9964-73

Frank Publishing Ltd+*, PO Box M414, Ministry Branch Post Office, Accra
Tel: 29510 Cable Add: Knowledge
Man Dir, Editorial, Production: Francis K Dzokoto; *Sales, Public Relations:* Moses K Dzokoto
Subjects: Secondary School Textbooks
Founded: 1976
ISBN Publisher's Prefix: 9964-959

Ghana Publishing Corporation*, Publishing Division, PMB, Tema Tel: 4166/2521 (Tema); 66349 (Accra) Cable Add/Telex: Publishing Tema
Man Dir: F K Nyarko; *General Manager (Publishing Division):* K B Arkorful; *Editor-in-Chief:* J K Fuachie-Sobreh; *Rights & Permissions:* Miss O Agbenyega; *Sales Manager:* W D Opare; *Production:* Fred Odametey; *Publicity:* Fidelis D Adzakey
Parent Company: Ghana Publishing Corporation, Head Office, PO Box 4348, Accra
Sales & Distribution Division: PO Box 3632, Accra
Branch Offs: Accra, Cape Coast, Ho, Tamale, Koforidua, Hohoe, Sunyani, Bolgatanga, Kumasi, Wa, Swedru
Subjects: General Fiction & Non-fiction, Belles Lettres, Poetry, Biography, History, Africana, Languages, Reference, Juveniles, Books in Various Ghanaian languages, Paperbacks, Science & Technology, Social Science; University, Secondary and Primary Textbooks
Bookshops: See under Major Booksellers
Founded: 1965
ISBN Publisher's Prefix: 9964-1

Ghana Universities Press, PO Box 4219, Accra Tel: 225032 Cable Add/Telex: Univpress Accra
Dir: A S K Atsu; *Senior Editor:* W A Dekutsey
Subjects: General Non-fiction, Belles Lettres, Poetry, Biography, History, Africana, Philosophy, Religion, Law, Medicine, Psychology, Science & Technology, Social Science, University Textbooks
1986: 6 titles *Founded:* 1962
ISBN Publisher's Prefix: 9964-3

The **Government Printer** (Ghana Publishing Corporation, Printing Division)*, PO Box 124, Accra

I B R A, an imprint of Asempa Publishers (qv)

Moxon Paperbacks*, Barnes Rd, PO Box M 160, Accra Tel: 65397
Man Dir: James Moxon
Subjects: General Fiction & Non-fiction, Belles Lettres, Poetry, History, Africana, Reference, Juveniles, Guidebooks, Paperbacks
Bookshop: The Atlas Bookshop (qv under Major Booksellers)
Founded: 1967
ISBN Publisher's Prefix: 9964-954

Presbyterian Book Depot Ltd, see main entry under Major Booksellers and range of publications under Waterville Publishing House below

Sedco Publishing Ltd, PO Box 2051, Accra (Located at: Sedco House, Tabon St, North Ridge) Tel: 221332 Cable Add: Sedco Telex: 2456
Man Dir: Courage Kwami Segbawu; *Manager:* Adams Ahima
Subjects: Science, Law, History, Archaeology, Education, Business, Health, Social Studies, Vocational, Poetry, Fiction
Bookshop: At above address
Founded: 1975
ISBN Publisher's Prefix: 9964-72

Unilit Publishing Co*, PO Box 4432, Accra Tel: 22689
Publisher: Ronald Mensah
Subsidiary Company: Ghana Bible Research Centre (at above address)
Associate Company: Romans Book Company (at above address)
Subjects: Religion, Politics, Economics, Science, Fiction
Bookshop: Romans Book Shop (at above address)
Founded: 1970

Waterville Publishing House+, PO Box 195, Accra Tel: 663124/662415 Cable Add: Books Accra
Acting Man Dir: W O Boafo; *Publications Manager:* M O Sackey
Parent Company: Presbyterian Book Depot Ltd (qv under Major Booksellers)
Subjects: General Fiction & Non-fiction, Belles Lettres, Poetry, Biography, History, Africana, Religion, Juveniles, Paperbacks, General & Social Science, Secondary & Primary Textbooks (in local languages and English)
Founded: 1963

Book Club

Academic Book Club*, GPO Box 441, Takoradi
Manager: Muhammed Kamal

Major Booksellers

Astab Books Ltd*, Osu R E, PO Box 346, Accra Tel: 76766

The **Atlas** Bookshop*, Ambassador Hotel Gardens, PO Box M 160, Accra Tel: 65397
Manager: James Moxon
Parent Company: Moxon Paperbacks (qv)

Cape Coast University Bookshop*, PMB, Cape Coast Tel: 24409

E P Book Depot*, PO Box 42, Ho

Ghana Publishing Corporation, Distribution and Sales Division*, PO Box 124, Accra
Branches throughout Ghana

Kingsway Stores, Books and Periodicals Department, PO Box 1638, Accra

Methodist Book Depot Ltd, Atlantis House, Commercial St, PO Box 100, Cape Coast Tel: 2133/2326
Man Dir: Samuel Markin Yankah
Branches: Accra, Berekum, Kumasi, Swedru, Takoradi, Tarkwa, Tema

Presbyterian Book Depot Ltd*, Thorpe Rd, PO Box 195, Accra Tel: 63124/62415
Cable Add: Books Accra
Man Dir: C A Aboagye
Branches: Accra, Ada, Akim Oda, Koforidua, Kumasi, Nkawkaw, Odumase, Tamale, Tudu
Founded: 1910
Miscellaneous: The organization comprises bookselling, stationery supply, printing and publishing activities (see Waterville Publishing House)

Queensway Bookshop and Stores Ltd*, Bank Lane, PO Box 4276, Accra Tel: 62707 (Accra) Cable Add: Success Accra
Branch Off: Bank St, PO Box 20, Kumasi Tel: 4047 Cable Add: Success Kumasi
Manager: Kwaku Mensah
Suppliers of Educational, Library and HMSO Publications

University Bookshop*, University of Science and Technology, University Post Office, Kumasi Tel: 5351 ext 398/308 Cable Add: Kumasitech Kumasi
Manager: Joseph A Clifford-Wirrom

University Bookshop, University of Ghana, PO Box 1, Legon, Accra Tel: 75381 ext 8227/8827
Manager: S O Cofie

Major Libraries

Armed Forces Library Service*, Ministry of Defence, Burma Camp, Accra Tel: 76111 ext 2769
Librarian: Daniel Mensah-Adrah
Publication: Armed Forces Library Bulletin

Balme Library, see University of Ghana

British Council Library, Liberia Road, PO Box 771, Accra Tel: 221766 Telex: 2369 GH
Librarian: Peter Cox
Also: Claude St, PO Box 1996, Kumasi Tel: 3462

C S I R Central Reference and Research Library*, PO Box M 32, Accra Tel: 77651, extensions 32, 58
Council for Scientific and Industrial Research Library
Librarian: J A Villars
Publications include: Directory of Special and Research Libraries in Ghana; Union List of Scientific Serials in Ghanaian Libraries (1976); CSIR Recorder; Directory of Research Projects (Science & Technology) in Ghana (1978)

Central Bureau of Statistics, Economic Library*, PO Box 1098, Accra Tel: 66512
Cable Add: Ghanastats
Librarian: Francis K Dzokoto

Geological Survey Department Reference Library*, PO Box M80, Accra Tel: 28093
Librarian: E Oko Oddoye

Ghana Institute of Management and Public Administration, Library and Documentation Centre*, Greenhill, PO Box 50, Achimota Tel: 777625 Cable Add: Gimpa Achimota
Librarian: Teresa Cryedu

Ghana Library Board*, Thorpe Rd, PO Box 663, Accra Tel: 62795/65083/66337
Cable Add: Ghanlib Accra
Librarian: D Cornelius
Publications include: Ghana National Bibliography, A Guide to Creative Writing by Africans in English, Annual Reports

Institute of African Studies Library*, University of Ghana, PO Box 73, Legon Tel: 75381 ext 9348
Librarian: Olive Akpebu

Research Library on African Affairs, PO Box 2970, Accra Tel: 23526/28402
Librarian: Christina D T Kwei
Publications: Ghana National Bibliography (annual); *Current Ghana Bibliography* (every two months)

School of Administration Library*, University of Ghana, PO Box 78, Legon
Librarian: Mrs C H K Agama

University of Cape Coast Library*, PMB, Cape Coast Tel: 24409 ext 370
Librarian: E K Koranteng
Publication: Bulletin

University of Ghana Library, Balme Library, PO Box 24, Legon Tel: 75381 ext 410 Cable Add: University Legon
Librarian: J K T Kafe
Publications: Annual Report; Bulletin

University of Science and Technology Library*, Private Bag, Kumasi Tel: 5351 ext 235
Librarian: S A Afre

Library Association

Ghana Library Association*, PO Box 4105, Accra
Secretary: D B Addo
Publication: Ghana Library Journal (irregular)

Library Reference Books and Journals

Books

Directory of Libraries in Ghana, Department of Library and Archival Studies, University of Ghana, Legon

Directory of Special and Research Libraries in Ghana, CSIR Library, PO Box M 32, Accra

Journal

Ghana Library Journal (bi-annual), Ghana Library Association, PO Box 4105, Accra

Literary Periodicals

Asemka, c/o French Department, University of Cape Coast, Cape Coast

Okyeame, Ghana Association of Writers, PO Box 2738, Accra
This journal has been defunct for some time now, but there are plans to recommence publication shortly. The Association also publishes a newsletter entitled *Takra*

Translation Agencies and Associations

Bureau of Ghana Languages*, PO Box 1851, Accra
Also Publisher (qv)

Gibraltar

General Information

Language: English (both English and Spanish used commercially)
Religion: Christian (mainly Roman Catholic) and Jewish predominantly
Population: 29,000
Bank Hours: Mostly 0900-1530 Monday-Friday, plus 1630-1800 Friday
Shop Hours: 0900-1300, 1500-1930 Monday-Friday; 0900-1300 Saturday (Jewish shops closed Saturday)
Currency: 100 pence = £1 Gibraltar pound = £1 sterling. British coins are legal tender and Bank of England notes are widely used
Export/Import Information: No tariff on books or advertising matter. No import licence. Exchange controls except for transactions with the UK
Copyright: Berne, UCC see International section

Major Booksellers

The **Book Centre***, 219 Main St, PO Box 248
Manager: Mabel Pizarro

Francis **Caruana***, 249 Main St

Gibraltar Bookshop, 300 Main St Tel: 71894
Manager: A Benady

Gibraltar Junior Bookshop*, 1 Governor's Parade Tel: 75554
Manager: Anne Benady
Junior literature

Imperial News Agency and Bookshop*, 291-93 Main St Tel: 76964
Managers: Joseph Hosken, Emily Olivero
Junior and adult literature, especially paperbacks

Major Libraries

Gibraltar Garrison Library, Library Gardens, Governor's Parade Tel: 77418
Librarian: Mrs L M Huart
Secretary: J M Searle
Local and military history. Lending service for subscribing members

Gibraltar Library Service, see John Mackintosh Hall Library*

John **Mackintosh Hall** Library, John Mackintosh Hall, Main St Tel: 78000
Librarian: Ronald J Miel
Free lending library set up under will of late John Mackintosh, mainly adult fiction. Now incorporating the Gibraltar Library Service

Greece

General Information

Language: Greek
Religion: Greek Orthodox
Population: 9.6 million
Bank Hours: 0800-1300, 1730-1930 Monday-Saturday. Some open 0800-2200 daily
Shop Hours: Vary. Generally 0800-1500 Monday, Wednesday, Saturday; 0800-1330 Tuesday, Thursday, Friday; 1630-2000 Monday-Saturday
Currency: 100 lepta = 1 drachma
Export/Import Information: Member of the European Economic Community. No tariff on non-Greek books except children's picture books (free from EEC). Foreign-language advertising catalogues and other advertising matter free from EEC. Children's picture books and advertising matter subject to stamp duty, and books and advertising subject to small additional taxes, University Tax and Bank Fee, Contribution for Farmer's Social Assistance. Only books printed in Greek need import licence; all advertising matter other than price lists require licence. No special exchange controls
Copyright: UCC, Berne, Florence (see International section)

Book Trade Organizations

Etairia Ellinon Logotechnon*, Gennadiou 6, Athens 126
Society of Greek Writers
Secretary: Vassilis Messologhitis

Fédération panhellénique des Editeurs et Libraires, see Panhellenic Federation

Panhellenic Federation of Publishers and Booksellers (PFPB)*, Arahovis 61, GR-10681 Athens Tel: (01) 3625458
President: S Halkiadakis
General Secretary: George Dardanos
Publications: Emis Ke To Vivlio (monthly); *Bibliographical Bulletin* (bi-monthly)

Standard Book Numbering Agency*, Information and Library Services Books' Distribution Organization, Doxapatri 18, GR-11473 Athens
ISBN Administrator: Ms A L Martin-Papazoglou

Syllogos Ekdoton Bibliopolon Athinon*, Themistocleus 54, GR-10681 Athens Tel: (01) 3630029
Publishers and Booksellers Association of Athens
President: D Pandeleskos
Secretary: S Patakis

Book Trade Reference Books and Journals

Book

Greek Bibliography, Ministry to the Prime Minister's Office, General Direction of Press, Research and Cultural Relations Division, Athens

Journals

Bulletin analytique de Bibliographie hellénique (Analytical Bulletin of Hellenic Bibliography), Institut Français d'Athènes, 29-31 Odos Sina, Athens 144

Emis Ke To Vivlio, Panhellenic Federation of Publishers and Booksellers (PFPB), Arahovis 61, Athens 145

New Books, I D Kollaros & Co Corporation, Solonos 60, Athens 135
Bibliographic quarterly bulletin

Publishers

Angyra Publishing House, D A Papadimitriou SA+*, Kifison 85, Egaleo, Athens 101 Tel: (01) 3455276/3456734
Man Dir: Dimitrios Papadimitriou
Subsidiary Company: Harmi-Press Publications, Haroula Papadimitriou (qv)
Subjects: General Fiction, Belles Lettres, Poetry, History, Religion, Juveniles, Children's Low-priced Paperbacks, Psychology
Bookshop: Bookstore Angyra, Piraeus 18, GR-10431 Athens
Founded: 1932 (as Angyra Ekdotikos Oikos)

Apostoliki Diakonia of the Church of Greece, Iassiou 1, GR-11521 Athens Tel: (01) 7248681
Chief Executive: Bishop Anastasios Yannoulatos; *Editorial, Rights & Permissions:* Evangelos Lekkos; *Production:* John Michael
Subjects: Liturgical, Religious, Children's, Patrology
Bookshop: Dragatsaniou 2, GR-10559 Athens
Founded: 1936

Arlekin, an imprint of Harlenic Hellas AE (qv)

John **Arsenides** Ekdotis*, Akadimias 57, Athens 143 Tel: (01) 618707/629538
Man Dir: John Arsenides
Subjects: Biography, History, Philosophy, Social Science

Aspioti-Elka SA*, Vouliagmenis 276, Athens 459 Tel: (01) 9711021 Cable Add: Elkasp Telex: 215519 Gon gr
Subjects: History, Archaeology, Folklore

Assimakopouli, 45 Harilaou Trikoupi St, Athens Tel: (01) 3611720/3619082

Astir*, Papadimitriou, Alexandros, Lycourgou 10, Athens
Subjects: Religion, especially referring to Greek Orthodox Church; Children's and Juveniles

Ekdotike **Athenon** SA+, Vissarionos 1, GR-10672 Athens Tel: (01) 3608911
Man Dirs: George A Christopoulos, John C Bastias
Associate Company: Ekdotike Hellados SA, Philadelphias 8, Athens (Printer)
Subjects: History, Archaeology, Art, High-priced Paperbacks
Bookshop: Ekdotike Athenon, Omirou 11, GR-10672 Athens
1986: 64 titles *Founded:* 1961

Atlantis M Pechlivanides & Co SA+*, Leontiou 23, GR-11745 Athens Tel: (01) 9220071/3231624
Subjects: General Fiction, Non-fiction, Education, Art, Children's
Bookshop: Korai 8, GR-10564 Athens Tel: (01) 3231624
Founded: 1927

Atlas-Diagoras*, Ch Trikoupi 13, Athens 142 Tel: (01) 627342

Bell Best Sellers, an imprint of Harlenic Hellas AE (qv)

Bergadi Editions*, Michel Bergadis, Mavromichali 4, Athens TT 143 Tel: (01) 3614263
Also: Doryleou 22, Athens 602 Tel: 3614263
Subjects: History, Sociology, Belles Lettres, Juveniles

Boukoumanis' Editions+, Elias Boukoumanis, Mavromichali 1, GR-10679 Athens Tel: (01) 3618502 Cable Add: 214422 RC GR
Man Dir: Elias Boukoumanis; *Rights & Permissions:* Mrs Trisevgeni Vourgarides
Subjects: History, Sociology, Belles Lettres, Children's, Psychology, Education, Politics, Ecology, Philosophy
Founded: 1968

GREECE 183

Chrissi Penna — Les Editions de la Plume d'Or, Argentinis Dimokratias Sq 6, GR-11472 Athens Tel: (01) 6461238
Man Dir: K Papachrysanthou
Parent Company: Papachrysanthou Chryss SA (qv)
Associate Company: Oscar Press (qv)
Subjects: Juvenile, Educational, Non-fiction
1985: 6 titles *1986:* 6 titles *Founded:* 1964

Chryssos Typos, Z Pigis 7, GR-10678 Athens Tel: (01) 3619977
Subjects: Medicine, Science, History, Art, Photography, Children's Fiction

G **Dardanos** — H Karakatsanis-C Dardanos & Co Ltd — Gutenberg, Solonos 103, Athens Tel: (01) 3600127/3626684/3624606
Also: Didotou 55-57, Athens
Man Dir, Editorial, Publicity, Rights & Permissions: George Dardanos; *Sales:* Christos Dardanos; *Production:* Haralambos Karakatsanis
Orders to: Didotou 55-57, Athens
Subjects: Art, Education, Literature, Sociology, Philosophy, History, Politics, Economics, Children's Books
Bookshop: Solonos 103, Athens
Founded: 1963

Difros*, Giannis Goudelis, Akademias 57, Athens
Subjects: Modern Greek Literature

Dodoni*, Asklipiou 3, Athens 143
Subjects: Fiction, Non-fiction, Juveniles, Encyclopaedias, History, Maps

Ekdoseis **Domi** AE, Pokratous 67, GR-10680 Athens Tel: (01) 3612056
Subject: Encyclopaedias

Dorikos Publishing House+, Mavromichali 64, GR-10680 Athens Tel: (01) 3629675
Man Dir, Rights & Permissions: Aristides Klados; *Editor:* Roussos Vranas
Associate Company: Apospreritis Editions, Eressou 9, GR-10680 Athens Tel: (01) 3604161
Subjects: Biography, Memoirs, Children's, Classics, Fiction, History, Philosophy, Poetry, Psychology, Politics, Theatre, Chess
1985-86: 40 titles *Founded:* 1958

Ecole française d'Athènes+, Didotou 6, GR-10680 Athens Tel: (01) 3612518
Cable Add: Ecofrance
Man Dir, Editorial: O Picard
Orders to: Diffusion de Boccard, 11 rue de Medicis, F-75005 Paris, France
Subjects: Greek Archaeology & History
1985: 10 titles *Founded:* 1846
ISBN Publisher's Prefix: 960-86958

P **Efstathiadis** & Sons SA, Valtetsiou 14, PO Box 8102, GR-10680 Athens Tel: (01) 3600495/3615011 Cable Add: Efbook Athens Telex: 216176
Branch Off: Olympou-Diikitiriou 34, Salonika Tel: 511781
Subjects: English language teaching books and courses for Greek students; miscellaneous books connected with English (and some other languages)

G C **Eleftheroudakis** SA*, Constitution Square, Nikis 4, GR-10563 Athens Tel: (01) 3222255 Cable Add: Elefbooks Telex: 0219410 Elef GR
Man Dir: Virginia Eleftheroudakis-Gregos
Branch Off: Sinopis 2, Tower of Athens
Subjects: Greece, Dictionaries, Fiction, Juvenile, Texts in Greek, English
Bookshop: See under Major Booksellers
Founded: 1915

Eteria Ellinikon Ekdoseon*, Akadimias 84, Athens 142 Tel: (01) 3630282/3631724/3607343
Man Dir: Stavros Tavoularis; *Editorial:* by Committee; *Sales:* Dr Caounis; *Production:* Rodakis Pericles; *Publicity:* Karayannis Nicolaos
Subjects: General Fiction, Belles Lettres, Poetry, History, Philosophy, Primary Textbooks, Educational Materials
Bookshop: Etairia Ellinikon Ekdoseon, Ermou 44, Salonika
Founded: 1958

Ekdoseis **Filon***, Panepistimiou 10, GR-10671 Athens Tel: (01) 3618705
Subjects: Literature, Philosophy, Juveniles

Giovanis, Zoodochou Pigis 7, GR-10678 Athens Tel: (01) 638572
Subjects: General Science, Reference, Maps, Geography, History, Religion, Photography, Medicine, Children's, Art

Dardanos **Gutenberg**, see Dardanos

Harlenic Hellas AE*, Hippocratous 57, GR-10680 Athens Tel: (01) 3629723/3628127/3609438 Telex: 221702 Arlk Gr
Man Dir, Rights & Permissions: Idris Thomas; *Editorial:* Omiros Avramides; *Marketing, Sales Manager:* Elias Ordolis
Parent Company: Harlequin Enterprises Ltd, 225 Duncan Mill Rd, Don Mills, Ontario M3B 3K9, Canada
Imprints: Arlekin, Bell Best Sellers
Subjects: Adventure, Romance, Thrillers
Founded: 1979

Harmi-Press Publications, Haroula Papadimitriou+*, 85 Kifisou Ave, Egaleo, Athens Tel: (01) 3455276/3471503 Telex: 210804 aste gr
Man Dir: Haroula Papadimitriou; *Editorial Dir:* Anastasia Papadimitriou
Parent Company: Angyra Publishing House (qv)
Subjects: Children's, Periodicals

Denise **Harvey** & Co+, Lambrou Fotiadi 6, Mets, GR-11636 Athens Tel: (01) 9233547
Man Dir: Denise Harvey; *General Manager:* Doreen Raptaki; *Editorial:* Philip Sherrard
Imprint: Romiosyni (series)
Subjects: (English) Modern Greek Culture, Belles Lettres, Poetry, Music, Biography, (Greek) Belles Lettres, Poetry, Translations, Religious and Philosophical Studies

Ikaros Ekdotiki*, Voulis 4, Athens Tel: (01) 3225152/3235262
Subject: Literature

Irini Publishing House — Vassilis G Katsikeas Ltd, Asklipiou 36, GR-10679 Athens Tel: (01) 3639259/3610465 Cable Add: Catgroup Athens Telex: 223639 Kats gr
President, Rights & Permissions: Vassilis G Katsikeas; *Editorial:* Vicky Pantazopoulou; *Sales:* Alkis Michailidis; *Production:* Vassiliki Valimiri; *Publicity:* Ourania Katsikea
Subsidiary Companies: Eudotiki Irini Ltd, Society Irini (both at above address)
Associate Company: K and K Ltd, Asklipiou 45, GR-10680 Athens Tel: 3609489 Telex: 223639 Kats gr
Branch Off: Aristotelous 7, GR-54624 Salonika Tel: (031) 261069
Subjects: Politics, Sociology, Economics, Fiction, Poetry, History, Biography
1985: 30 titles *1986:* 40 titles Founded: 1973

Kastaniotis Editions+, Zoodochou Pigis 3, GR-10678 Athens Tel: (01) 3603234/3601331/3638967
Man Dir, Editorial: Athanasios Kastaniotis; *Editorial:* Anna Stamatopoulou; *Sales:* Kostas Lambakis; *Production:* Alkis Tsakopiakos; *Publicity, Rights &
Permissions:* George Papakyriakis
Subsidiary Company: Chronos Editions (at above address)
Subjects: Psychology, Psychoanalysis, Philosophy, Pedagogy, Greek and Foreign Literature, Cinema, Essays, Juvenile, Children's, Dictionaries
Founded: 1969

Kedros*, G Gennadiou 6, GR-10678 Athens Tel: (01) 3615783/3603572
Subjects: Literature, Philosophy, Juveniles
Founded: 1954

I D **Kollaros** & Co Corporation, Solonos 60, GR-10672 Athens Tel: (01) 3635970
Publicity Manager: Evangelos Daskalou
Subjects: Modern Greek Literature, Fiction, History, Juveniles
Bookshop: Hestia Bookstore, 60 Solonos St, Athens
1985: 50 titles *Founded:* 1885

Koymantereas*, Mavromihali 83, Athens Tel: (021) 3246188

Leon Editions, an imprint of Costas Spanos (qv)

Melissa Publishing House*, Navarinou 10, GR-10680 Athens Tel: (01) 3611692
Man Dir: George Rayias; *Sales Dir:* Chrys Rayias
Branch Off: Tsimiski 41, Salonika
Subjects: History, Art
Founded: 1954

Minoas*, Androu 6, Athens 801 Tel: (01) 8231669
Man Dir: Elias Konstantazopoulos
Subjects: General Fiction, Belles Lettres, Poetry, Biography, History, Music, Art, Reference, Juveniles, High-priced Paperbacks
Bookshop: Patission 126, Athens
Founded: 1948

Editions **Moressopulos**, Cherefontos 2, Plaka, PO Box 30564, GR-10033 Athens Tel: (01) 3234217 Telex: 216465 Mas Gr
Chief Executive: Stavros Moressopulos; *Man Dir, Editorial:* Yannis Pikramentos; *Sales:* Maria Remi; *Production:* Nickos Ballis; *Publicity:* Yanna Remi; *Rights & Permissions:* Voula Moressopulos
Subsidiary Companies: Editions Photografia, Editions Canal, Photografia Magazine, Camera International Magazine, Sport and Hobbies Magazine, Hellenic Photography (all at above address)
Associate Companies: Photopia Ltd, Hellenic Centre of Photography (non-profit making) (both at above address)
Branch Off: Vass Georgiou Ave 21, PO Box 10710, GR-54110 Salonika Tel: (031) 819624
Subjects: Photography, Cinematography, Video, Computing, Crafts & Hobbies, Sports, Literature, Juveniles, Non-fiction, Current Affairs
Book Club: Photographia Book Club (at above address)
Bookshop: Photographia Bookshop (at above address)
1985-86: 20 titles *Founded:* 1977
ISBN Publisher's Prefix: 960-366

Multieditions Ltd+*, Ippokratous 88, Athens Tel: (01) 3642911 Telex: 223185 Mult Gr
Man Dirs: Tilemachos Kanakis, Seraphim Tsakanikas
Subjects: Fiction, Non-fiction, Comics
Founded: 1976

Nikas, Solonos 102 and Mavromihali 16, GR-10680 Athens Tel: (01) 3634686

Oscar Press, Anthemion and Pigon, N Kifissia, GR-14564 Athens Tel: (01) 8070825

Man Dir: Kir Papachrysanthou;
Production: Konst Mastrantonis
Parent Company: Papachrysanthou Chryss SA (qv)
Associate Company: Chrissi Penna SA (qv)
Subjects: Paperbacks, Juvenile, Periodicals
1986: 14 titles *1985:* 70 titles *Founded:* 1979

Papachrysanthou Chryss SA, Graphic Arts, Anthemion and Pigon, N Kifissia, GR-14564 Athens Tel: (01) 8070803/8071150
Man Dir: K Papachrysanthou
Subsidiary Companies: Chrissi Penna (qv), Oscar Press (qv)
Subjects: General, Juvenile, Tourist Guides, Paperbacks
1986: 62 titles *1985:* 85 titles *Founded:* 1888

D A **Papadimitriou**, see Angyra Publishing House

Haroula **Papadimitriou**, see Harmi-Press

Kyr I **Papadopoulos** E E+, G Papandreou 118, Metamorfosi-Attikis Tel: (01) 2817127 Telex: 225176 Book Gr
Man Dir: Kyr Papadopoulos; *Sales:* P Hatjibodojis; *Production:* S T Giafalias; *Rights & Permissions:* R Papadopoulou
Subjects: Various, for children aged 2-14
Founded: 1953

Papaioannou*, Venizelou 34, Athens Tel: (01) 618139
Associate Company: Educational Company

Papazissis Publishers SA*, Nikitara 2, GR-10678 Athens Tel: (01) 3622496/3609150/3638020 Telex: 219807 Itec
Man Dir: Victor Papazissis; *Sales, Advertising:* Pericles Lytras; *Rights & Permissions:* Stefanos Vlachos
Parent Company: Corais Ltd (at above address)
Subjects: Economics, Sociology, Philosophy, Politics, Law, Education, Environment, Greek Recent History, University Handbooks (especially on Economics), Textbooks
Bookshop: Papazissis Bookshop (at above address)
Founded: 1929

Papyros Press*, Voulis 17, Athens Tel: (01) 3220013

Patakis Publications, Nikitara 3, GR-10678 Athens Tel: (01) 3638362/3645236
Man Dir: Stefanos Patakis; *Editorial:* Konstantinos Petropoulous, Christina Jatzogloy, Konstantinos Stamatis; *Sales:* Melpomeni Pataki; *Production:* Fotis Violatzis; *Publicity:* Philippos Drakontaidis; *Rights & Permissions:* Andreas Darzentas
Subjects: Educational, Children's, Literary, Criticism
1985: 20 *1986:* 50 titles *Founded:* 1974
ISBN Publisher's Prefix: 960-293

Pergamini Editions, an imprint of Costas Spanos (qv)

M **Psaropoulos** & Co EE, Kriezotou 3, GR-10671 Athens Tel: (01) 3607307/3609345/3606807 Telex: 8008 Psar gr
Man Dir: Tassos Psaropoulos; *Editorial:* Thalia Iacovidis; *Sales:* A Sofocleous; *Production:* D Marcomatis; *Publicity:* P Pissanos; *Rights & Permissions:* M Psaropoulos
Subsidiary Companies: Anglohellenic Printing, Tatoiou 118, Varybobi, Attiki; Finedawn Publishers, 25 Nottingham Pl, London W1M 3FF, UK
Subjects: Medical, Fiction, Children's Books, Periodicals
Founded: 1962

G **Rayas**, Nayarinou 10, Athens Tel: (01) 3611692

Romiosyni, an imprint of Denise Harvey & Co (qv)

Siamandas*, Akadimias 61, Athens Tel: (01) 615777/627164
Subjects: General Fiction & Non-fiction, History, Juveniles

J **Sideris** OE Ekdoseis*, Stadiou 44, Athens Tel: (01) 3229638
Subjects: Literature, Science, Linguistics, Juvenile

Costas **Spanos***, Mayromihali 7, GR-10679 Athens Tel: (01) 3614332 Cable Add: Bibliospan
Man Dir, Editorial: C Spanos; *Sales:* John Papadakis; *Publicity:* Sophia Tjimoianni
Imprints: Leon, Pergamini
Subjects: Rare Books, Limited Editions, Byzantine and Post-Byzantine
Bookshop: At above address

Technical Chamber of Greece*, Kar Servias 4, GR-10562 Athens Tel: (01) 3254591
General Director: V Torolopoulos
Subjects: Science, Technology, Periodicals
Founded: 1923
Miscellaneous: The Technical Chamber of Greece (TEE) is a corporate body, under public law, supervised by the Ministry of Public Works

Tegopoulos*, Panepistimiou 57, Athens

Travintal Ltd, PO Box 17092, Kolonaki, GR-10024 Athens Tel: (01) 2822418/6713803 Telex: 21 4716 elbr for travintal
Man Dir, Rights & Permissions: Nina Moselund; *Editorial:* Nina Casimaty; *Sales:* Nicolas Stavridis; *Production:* George Mansolas; *Publicity:* Niels G Moselund
Parent Company: Travintal Ltd, PO Box 9150, GPO Hong Kong
Subjects: Travel and Business Handbooks
Founded: 1975

Tria Phylla Editions+, Dedalou 20, GR-10558 Athens Tel: (01) 3236062/3230183
Man Dir, Rights & Permissions: Dr Emmanuela de Nora Cantoni; *Editorial:* Kostis Vrettakos; *Sales:* Mata Loupassi; *Production:* Jenny Papadimitriou
Parent Company: LDT, PO Box 7798, FDR Station, New York, NY 10022, USA
Subjects: Photography, Architecture, Art, Design, Limited Editions of Prints and Portfolios, Greek Contemporary Poetry and Literature (in Greek, English, German, French)
1985: 8 titles *1986:* 10 titles *Founded:* 1978

Typos*, Londou 8, Athens Tel: (01) 619084

D & J **Vardikos***, A Metaxa 2, Exarchia, Athens TT 145 Tel: (01) 3631146/3602150
Man Dir: Dimitrios Vardikos
Parent Company: Vivliotechnica Hellas (at above address)
Subsidiary Company: Bookbinding Industry (at above address)
Branch Off: Davaki 34, Kallithea, Athens
Subjects: Aviation Encyclopaedia and Dictionary, Attika Juvenile Books and Children's Encyclopaedia (all cassette-assisted)
Bookshop: Inter-Attica, Davaki 34, Kallithea, Athens
Founded: 1978

J **Vasiliou** Bibliopoleion*, Ippocratous 15, GR-10679 Athens Tel: (01) 3623382/3623480
Subjects: Fiction, History, Philosophy, Dictionaries

Frères **Vlasis***, Londou 2, Athens Tel: (01) 639128
Subjects: History, Reference, General Science

Z O E, Karytsi 14, Athens 124 Tel: (01) 3223560
Man Dir: G Karadzas
Subject: Religion
Bookshops: At above address and St Sophia 41, Salonika; also in three other Greek cities
Founded: 1907

Har **Zolindakis***, Panepistimiou 65, Athens Tel: (01) 314546/316504
Subject: History

Literary Agents

Anglo-Hellenic Agency, Kriezotou 3, Syntagma, GR-10671 Athens Tel: (01) 3606808/3607307 Telex: 8008 Psar
Specializations: Translations, Medical, Cartoons, Comics, Periodicals

Educational Materials Enterprises SA*, PO Box 3580, GR-10210 Athens (Located at: Solonos 10) Tel: (01) 3633617 Cable Add: Kingsyn Telex: 214226 Eme Gr
Contacts: Alkaios Angelopoulos, Setis Heretis, Jonathan Webber
Representing overseas publishers and literary agencies for the Greek market

Book Clubs

Photographia Book Club, Cherefontos 2, Plaka, PO Box 30564, GR-10033 Athens Tel: (01) 3234217 Telex: 216465 Mas Gr
Owned by: Editions Moressopulos (qv)

Vivliofilia, Mavromichali 7, GR-10679 Athens Tel: (01) 3614332
Owned by: Costa Spano
Founded: 1929

Major Booksellers

American Bookstore*, Amerikis 23, Athens Tel: (01) 3624151
See also A Samouhos Bookstore

Librairie **Cacoulides** (T Cacoulides & Co), blvd Panepistimiou 25-29, GR-10564 Athens Tel: (01) 3229560
Manager: Thomas Cacoulides

P **Efstathiadis** & Sons SA*, Valtetsiou 14, Athens TT 144 Tel: (01) 615011/3600495
Importers and exporters

G C **Eleftheroudakis** Co Ltd*, International Bookstore, Constitution Sq, Nikis 4, Athens 126 Tel: (01) 3222255
Man Dir: Virginia Eleftheroudakis-Gregou
Also Publisher (qv)

Hestia Bookstore, Solonos 60, GR-10672 Athens Tel: (01) 3635970
Owned by: I D Kollaros & Co Corporation (qv)
Manager: Marina Karaitidis

C **Kakoulides**, now Librairie Cacoulides (qv)

Gr **Kaloudis***, Filonos 31, Piraeus Tel: (01) 479027

Kaufmann*, Stadiou 28, Athens Tel: (01) 3222160

John **Mihalopoulos** & Son SA*, PO Box 10073, GR-54110 Salonika (Located at: Hermou 75) Tel: (031) 279695/263786 Telex: 418562
Manager: C Mihalopoulos

GREECE — GUATEMALA 185

Minoas*, Patission 126, Athens Tel: (01) 815664

Molho's International Bookshop*, Tsimiski 10, GR-54624 Salonika Tel: (031) 275271 Telex: 412885 limo gr

John **Pantelides**, Amerikis 11, GR-10672 Athens Tel: (01) 3623673 Telex: 224609 Paza gr

A **Samouhos** Bookstore*, Kassaveti 4, Kifisia, Athens
Under same management as American Bookstore (qv)

Major Libraries

Athens Academy Library*, 28 Odos Venizelou, Athens

Athens College Library*, Athens College, PO Box 5, Psychico, Athens Tel: (01) 6714621

British Council Library*, PO Box 3488, GR-10210 Athens Tel: (01) 3633211
Librarian: Julie Carpenter

Eugenides Foundation Technical Library, Syngrou Ave 387, GR-17564 Palaio Phaliro
Librarian: Fotini-Claire Lendaris

Gennadius Library, American School of Classical Studies at Athens, Souidias 61, GR-10676 Athens Tel: (01) 7210536
Librarian: S Papageorgiou

National Library of Greece*, Panepistemiou 32, GR-10679 Athens Tel: (01) 3614413 (Secretary)/3608495 (Director)
Dir: Dr Panayotis G Nicolopoulos

Library of the **National Technological University** of Athens*, Odos 28, Octovriou 42, Athens

Pan Library ('Circle of the Friends of Progress')*, Odos Giorgios 43, Tripolis, Arcadia

Parliament Library*, Palaia Anactora, Athens Tel: (01) 3235030
Librarian: Maria Anastassopoulou
Publications include: Incunabula and Editions of the 15th and 16th Centuries

Library of the **Technical Chamber** of Greece*, Lekka 23-25, Athens Tel: (01) 3254590

Library of the **Three Hierarchs***, Odos Demetriados-Ogl, Volos

Library of the **University of Salonika**, Salonika Tel: (031) 991618
Librarian: D Dimitriou

Library Association

Enossis Ellenon Bibliothakarion, Skouleniou 4, GR-10561 Athens Tel: (01) 3226625
Greek Library Association
Secretaries: Sofia Palamiotou, Niko Contopoulou
Publication: Bulletin

Library Reference Books and Journals

Book

Guide to Greek Libraries and Cultural Organizations, National Printing Office, Athens

Journal

Greek Library Association Bulletin, Skouleniou 4, Athens TT 124

Literary Associations and Societies

Association of Arts and Letters*, c/o Mitropoleos 38, Athens Tel: (01) 3233033
General Secretary: S Xefloudas

The **Circle** of Greek Children's Books*, Zalongou 7, GR-10678 Athens Tel: (01) 3602990
Greek National Section of the International Board on Books for Young People (IBBY)
Secretary: Mrs Loty Petrovits-Andrutsopulu
Publications include: Deltio (annual newsletter); two anthologies

Kentron Ekdoseos Ellinon Syngrafeon*, Academy of Athens, Anaguostopoulou 14, Athens 136
Centre for the Publication of Ancient Greek Authors
Dir: Ch Floratos

P E N Centre, Skoufa 60a, Athens 144
President: Jean P Coutsocheras; *Secretary:* Yannis Manglis

Women's Literary Society*, Evrou 4, Athens 611

Literary Periodicals

Aiolika Grammatia (Aeolian Letters), Hodos Nircos 41, Palaion Phaliron, Athens

Diaghonios (Diagonal), Dinos Christianopoulous, Franklin Roosevelt, Salonika 4

Nea Hestia, G C Eleftheroudakis SA, Nikis 4, GR-10563 Athens
Text in Greek

Literary Prizes

Circle of the Greek Children's Book IBBY (Greek Section) Prizes*
Inaugurated in 1970. Awarded annually for various types of children's literature. Prizes range from 20,000 to 80,000 drachmas. Last awarded to Vasilis Hatzivasiliou for *Meres tis Almyras* (Days of Salinity). Enquiries to General Secretary, Circle of the Greek Children's Book IBBY (Greek Section), Zalongou 7, GR-10678 Athens

King Paul National Foundation Prize*
For an essay on community development written by an adolescent. Awarded annually. Enquiries to King Paul National Foundation, Philellinon 9, Athens 118

Tsakalos Prize*
For prose work, poetry and criticism, published by the members of the Society. 50,000 drachmas. Awarded annually. Enquiries to Society of Greek Writers, Mitropoleos 38, Athens 126

Women's Literary Society Prizes*
Each year the Society awards prizes for the following works for children: historical novel on a subject from Greek history; poems for very young children; poems for older children; a book of short stories; a theatrical play for older children; journeys and excursions within Greece. Enquiries to Women's Literary Society, Evrou 4, Athens 611

Guatemala

General Information

Language: Spanish
Religion: Roman Catholic
Population: 7.26 million
Bank Hours: 0900-1500 Monday-Friday
Shop Hours: 0800-1200, 1400-1800 Monday-Friday; 0800-1200 Saturday
Currency: 100 centavos = 1 quetzal
Export/Import Information: Member of the Central American Common Market. Duty on catalogues is Q 0.03 per gross kilo. No import licences, no exchange control
Copyright: UCC, Buenos Aires, Florence (see International section)

Book Trade Organization

Gremial de Libreros de Guatemala*, Ave Reforma 13-70, Zona 9, Edificio Real Reforma Interior 13N, Guatemala City Tel: (02) 313326/27505/26478
Association of Booksellers of Guatemala
President: Victor Hugo Granados Gonzalez

Publishers

Editorial del **Ministerio de Educacion** 'Jose de Pineda Ibarra'*, 15° Ave 3-22, Zona 1, Guatemala City

Piedra Santa+, 7a Ave 4-45, Zona 1, Guatemala City Tel: (02) 21867/510231/28603 Telex: 9225
Man Dir: Oralia Díaz de Piedra Santa; *Sales:* Ruby González; *Production, Rights & Permissions:* Irene Piedra Santa
Subjects: Pre-Primary, Primary & Secondary Schoolbooks, University Textbooks, Further Education, Literature, Science & Technology, Social Sciences, Tourism, Pedagogy, Psychology, Philosophy, Belles Lettres, Accountancy, Engineering, Sports, Health
Bookshops: See under Major Booksellers
Founded: 1947
ISBN Publisher's Prefix: 84-8377

Seminario de Integración Social Guatemalteca, 11 Calle No 4-31, Zona 1, Guatemala City Tel: (02) 29754
Subjects: Sociological, Ecological, Educational, Anthropological texts connected with Guatemala
Founded: 1956

Universidad de San Carlos de Guatemala, Editorial Universitaria*, Ciudad Universitaria, Zona 12, Guatemala City
Subjects: Technical & Scientific University Textbooks

Book Club

Libroclub de Guatemala, Ave Elena 'B' 2-25 Zona 2, El Sauce, Guatemala City Tel: (02) 313326
Man Dir: Victor Hugo Granados Gonzalez
See also Librería Cervantes (Bookseller)

Major Booksellers

Librería **'13 Calle** El Tecolote'*, 13 Calle 8-61, Zona 1, Guatemala City Tel: (02) 81055
Manager: Mrs Consuelo Martínez

Librería **Acrópolis***, 9 Ave 13-20, Zona 1, Guatemala City Tel: (02) 80819

Librería **C E E S**, Apdo postal 652, Guatemala City Tel: (02) 323883

Librería **Cervantes** — Libroclub de Guatemala*, Ave Reforma 13-70, Zona 9, Edificio Real Reforma Interior 13N, Guatemala City Tel: (02) 313326
Manager: Victor Hugo Granados Gonzalez
Direct importers and distributors of books in Spanish, English, German and French

Distribuidora de Libros, Rodrigo Galindo, 11 Calle 4-15, Zona 1, Guatemala City Tel: (02) 28746

Edelcid Libros Científicos*, 11 Calle 8-66, Zona 1, Guatemala City Tel: (02) 20934

Distribuidora Cultural **I G A** Bookstore, Ruta 1, 4-05, Zona 4, Apdo Postal 691, Guatemala City Tel: (02) 67064/310022/310218
Manager: Ricardo Sosa

Librería Universal, 13 Calle 4-16, Zona 1, Guatemala City
Manager: Olga A de Manrique
Owned by: Distribuidora General Universal

Piedra Santa, 7a Ave 4-45, Zona 1, Guatemala City Tel: (02) 510231/21867/23051
Branches: 6a Calle 9-68, Zona 1, Guatemala City Tel: (02) 84832; 11 Calle 6-50, Zona 1, Guatemala City Tel: (02) 85087; Trébol, Autovía Mixco 1-96, Zona 7, Guatemala City Tel: (02) 715044; Géminis, 12 Calle 1-25, Zona 10, Edificio Geminis 10, Guatemala City Tel: (02) 311309/311302; Obelisco, Ave Las Américas 15-89, Zona 13, (Edificio Obelisco), Guatemala City Tel: (02) 62702
Also Publisher (qv)

El **Tecolote**, see 13 Calle

Librería **Tuncho** Granados G*, 10 Calle 6-56, Zona 1, Apdo Postal 13, Guatemala City, CA Tel: (02) 24736/27269
Also: La Plaza del Sol, Calle Montúfar y 2 Ave, Zona 9, Guatemala City CA

Major Libraries

Archivo General de Centro*, América, 4a Ave, 7a-8a Calles, Zona 1, Guatemala City

Biblioteca Nacional de Guatemala (National Library)*, 5a Ave 7-26, Zona 1, Guatemala City
Librarian: Eva Evans

Biblioteca Central de la **Universidad de San Carlos**, Ciudad Universitaria, Zona 12, Guatemala City Tel: (02) 760790 ext 284/285
Publications: Boletín Bibliográfico; Boletín Contenidos

Library Association

Asociación Bibliotecologica Guatemalteca*, c/o The Director, Biblioteca Nacional de Guatemala, 5a Avenida 7-26, Zona 1, Guatemala, CA
Library Association of Guatemala

Literary Periodical

Alero (Eaves), Universidad de San Carlos, Confederacions Universitaria Centroamericana, Guatemala City

Guinea

General Information

Language: French
Religion: Islamic predominantly
Population: 4.5 million
Bank Hours: 0800-1300 Monday-Saturday
Shop Hours: 0730-1230, 1430-1830 Monday-Saturday
Currency: 100 cauris = 1 syli
Export/Import Information: Books imported by State Trading Corporation: Libraport, BP 270, Conakry. Tariffs listed as free for books except children's picture books. Import licences
Copyright: Berne, UCC (see International section)

Publishers

Editions du **Ministère de l'Education Nationale***, Secrétariat à la Recherche Scientifique, BP 561, Conakry
Subjects: General, Educational

Major Booksellers

Libraport*, BP 270, Conakry
State Trading Corporation

Major Libraries

Bibliothèque nationale*, BP 561, Conakry
Librarian: M K Keita

Direction de la Bibliothèque nationale*, BP 561, Conakry Tel: 41420
Librarian: Lansana Sylla

Institut polytechnique de Conakry Bibliothèque*, BP 1147, Conakry

Library Association

Direction de la Recherche scientifique et technique*, BP 561, Conakry Bibliothèque nationale Tel: 461010
National Research and Documentation Institute
Dir: Lansana Sylla

Guyana

General Information

Language: English. Creolese is widely used, and Amerindian dialects
Religion: Hindu, Islamic, Christian
Population: 848,800
Bank Hours: 0800-1230 Monday-Thursday; 0800-1230 and 1500-1700 Friday
Shop Hours: 0800-1130, 1300-1600 Monday-Friday; 0800-1130 Saturday
Currency: 100 cents = 1 Guyana dollar
Export/Import Information: No tariff on books. Only advertising of commercial value, subject to duty. Guyana National Trading Corporation, 45-47 Water St, Georgetown is sole importer of books. Import licence required. Nominal exchange controls

Book Trade Organization

Regional ISBN Agency (CARICOM)*, Caribbean Community Secretariat, PO Box 10827, Georgetown Tel: (02) 69281
Telex: 2263 Carisec Gy
ISBN Administrator: Carol Collins

Standard Book Numbering Agency, see Regional ISBN Agency (CARICOM)

Book Trade Reference Book

Guyanese National Bibliography, National Library, PO Box 10240, Georgetown

Publishers

Guyana National Printers Ltd*, 1 Public Rd, La Pénitence, Georgetown
Dir: Novear de Freiyas

Major Booksellers

Guyana National Trading Corporation (GNTC)*, PO Box 10480, 231 Camp St and South Rd, Georgetown Tel: (02) 71543/72379
Manager: L F Austin
Sole importer of books

Major Libraries

Guyana Medical Science Library*, Georgetown Hospital Compound, Georgetown

National Library*, PO Box 10240, Georgetown Tel: (02) 62690/62699
Chief Librarian: Joan L Christiani
Publication: Guyanese National Bibliography

Library Association

Guyana Library Association*, 76-77 Main St, PO Box 10240, Georgetown Tel: (02) 62690
Secretary: Wenda Stephenson
Publication: Bulletin

Library Reference Journal

Bulletin, Guyana Library Association, 76-77 Main St, PO Box 10240, Georgetown

Literary Periodical

University of Guyana Language Forum, University of Guyana, PO Box 841, Georgetown
Review of literary, linguistic and educational studies (text in English)

Haiti

General Information

Language: French and Creole
Religion: Roman Catholic
Population: 5 million
Bank Hours: 0900-1300 Monday-Friday

Business Hours: Winter: 0800-1700; Summer: 0700-1600
Currency: 100 centimes = 1 gourde = $US0.20. US currency is widely used
Export/Import Information: Books charged ad valorem, children's picture books per kilo net. Advertising matter under 1 kilo gross weight duty-free. No import licences or exchange controls, other than occasional exchange rationing, leading to delays
Copyright: UCC (see International section)

Publishers

Editions **Caraïbes***, Lalue, PO Box 2013, Port-au-Prince Tel: 2-3179 Telex: ITT 2030198

Maison Henri **Deschamps**+*, Grand' Rue, PO Box 164, Port-au-Prince
Man Dir: Jacques Deschamps; *Editorial Dir:* Maël Fouchard; *Production Dirs:* Wilhelm Frisch Jnr, Henri R Deschamps; *Sales Dirs:* Jacques Deschamps Jnr, Peter J Frisch, Claude Deschamps
Subjects: History, Religion, Literature, Education, Fiction

Editions du **Soleil***, BP 2471, rue du Centre, Port-au-Prince Tel: (01) 23147 Telex: Ppbooth 2030001 attn Lisocial
Subject: Education

Theodor*, Imprimerie, rue Dantes Destouches, Port-au-Prince
Subjects: History, Literature, Fiction

Major Libraries

Bibliothèque du petit Séminaire*, Port-au-Prince

Bibliothèque nationale d'Haiti (National Library)*, 193 rue du Centre, Port-au-Prince Tel: (01) 20236

Bibliothèque **Saint Louis de Gonzague***, Port-au-Prince
Librarian: Frère Constant

Literary Associations and Societies

Le **Bibliophile** (The Book Lover)*, Cap Haïtien
Secretary: Louis Toussaint
Publications: La Citadelle (weekly); Stella (monthly)

Literary Periodicals

La Citadelle, Le Bibliophile, Cap Haïtien

Stella, Le Bibliophile, Cap Haïtien

Literary Prize

Prix littéraire Henri **Deschamps**
Inaugurated in 1975 and awarded annually. Open to unpublished Haitian writers, on any subject. Awarded in 1987 to Dr Jacques Godard for his novel *Pourquoi les Campêches seignent ils?* Enquiries to Maison Henri Deschamps, Grand' Rue, PO Box 164, Port-au-Prince

Honduras

General Information

Language: Spanish (English on northern coast)
Religion: Roman Catholic
Population: 3.7 million
Bank Hours: 0830-1200, 1400-1630 Monday-Friday
Shop Hours: Tegucigalpa: 0800-1200, 1330-1800 Monday-Friday; 0800-1200 Saturday; San Pedro Sula: 0730-1100, 1330-1800 Monday-Friday; 0800-1200 Saturday
Currency: 100 centavos = 1 lempira = $US0.50
Export/Import Information: Member of the Central American Common Market but has applied tariffs to imports from other CACM countries since December 1970. No tariff on books. Duty on catalogues is per kilo. No import licences. No exchange controls
Copyright: Buenos Aires (see International section)

Book Trade Reference Journal

Bibliografía hondureña (Honduras Bibliography), Banco Central de Honduras, PO Box C-58, 1A Calle, Tegucigalpa

Publishers

Editorial Universitaria*, Universidad de Honduras, Tegucigalpa

Industria Editorial **Lypsa***, Apdo Postal 167-C, Tegucigalpa Tel: 229775
Manager: José Bennaton
Bookshop: Librería Lypsa (qv under Major Booksellers)

Editorial **Nuevo** Continente*, Ave Cervantes, Tegucigalpa Tel: 225073

Major Booksellers

Librería **Lypsa***, Apdo Postal 167-C, Tegucigalpa Tel: 226824
Manager: J A Bennaton
Owned by: Industria Editorial Lypsa (qv)

Ney's Libros and Revistas*, Apdo 609, Tegucigalpa Tel: 23865

Librería Universitaria Jose T **Reyes***, Universidad Nacional Autónoma de Honduras, Tegucigalpa DC

University Library, see Reyes

Major Libraries

Biblioteca Nacional de Honduras*, 6a Ave Salvador Mendieta, Tegucigalpa

Sistema Bibliotecario*, Ciudad Universitaria, Carretera Suyapa, Tegucigalpa Tel: 322204/325804 Telex: 1289 Unah Ho
Dir: Orfylia Pinel S
Publication: Boletín del Sistema Bibliotecario

Library Association

Asociación de Bibliotecarios y Archiveros de Honduras*, 3 Avenidas, 4 y 5 Calles, No 416 Comayagüela, DC, Tegucigalpa Association of Librarians and Archivists of Honduras
Secretary-General: Juan Angel Ayes R
Publication: Catálogo de Préstamo

Library Reference Journal

Catálogo de Préstamo, Asociación de Bibliotecarios y Archiveros de Honduras, 3 Avenidas, 4 y 5 Calles, No 416 Comayagüela, DC, Tegucigalpa

Hong Kong

General Information

Language: English and Cantonese
Religion: Traditional Chinese beliefs, especially Buddhist
Population: 5.5 million
Bank Hours: 0900-1640 Monday-Friday; 0900-1200 Saturday
Department stores: 1000-2000 Monday-Saturday
Currency: 100 cents = 1 Hong Kong dollar
Export/Import Information: No tariffs on books and advertising. No import licences required. No exchange controls
Copyright: Berne, UCC (see International Section)

Book Trade Organizations

Anglo-Chinese Textbook Publishers Organization Ltd*, PO Box 223, Quarry Bay (Located at: Cornwall House, 18th Floor, Tong Chong St, Quarry Bay) Tel: (05) 648475
Chairman: William Shen; *Secretary:* Lawrence Pang

Books Registration Office MSB*, 2201 Park-In Commercial Centre, Dundas St, Mongkok, Kowloon Tel: (03) 316660 Telex: 73380 Govhk Hx
ISBN Administrator: Edward W S Tse

Hong Kong Booksellers' & Stationers' Association*, Man Wah House, Kowloon Tel: (03) 3882356

Hong Kong Educational Publishers Association Ltd*, 1105 Yau Yue Bldg, 127-131 Des Voeux Rd C
President: Au Bak Ling

Hong Kong Publishers' & Distributors' Association*, National Bldg, 4th Floor, 240-246 Nathan Rd, Kowloon

Standard Book Numbering Agency, see Books Registration Office MSB

Publishers

A D I S Press Publications Ltd*, 1802-3 Tung Sun Commercial Centre, 194-200 Lockhart Rd, Wanchai
Publicity Manager: Mrs Lina Cheung
Associate Company: ADIS Press Australasia Pty Ltd, Australia (qv)

The **Art** Publisher*, 166 Java Rd, 2/F, North Point
Subjects: Art, Textbooks

Book Marketing Ltd, North Point Industrial Building, Flat A, 17F, 499 King's Rd, Hong Kong Tel: (05) 5620121 Cable Add: Marketbook Telex: bmark 72216 hx
Man Dir: Bernard Chiu King Sum
Associate Companies: Kelly and Walsh Ltd, GPO Box 96, Hong Kong; Swindon Book Co (qv)
Subjects: Educational books and periodicals
Founded: 1973
ISBN Publisher's Prefix: 0-962211

C B S Publishing Asia Ltd*, 1002 Inter-Continental Plaza, Tsim Sha Tsui East, Kowloon Tel: (03) 7241799 Telex: 50871 Holts Hx
Man Dir: Alan Taylor; *Marketing Dir:* Ted Shore
Parent Company: CBS International Publishing (CIP), (a division of Columbia Broadcasting System Inc), 383 Madison Ave, New York, NY 10017, USA

HONG KONG

Associate Company: CBS Publishing Pty Ltd, Australia (qv)
Branch Offices: Bangalore, Bombay, New Delhi, Singapore
Subjects: Medicine, Engineering, Natural Sciences, Social Sciences, Humanities, Behavioural Sciences (Professional, Reference, Textbooks)
Founded: 1983

C F W Publications Ltd+, 1602 Alliance Bldg, 130 Connaught Rd Central, Hong Kong   Tel: (05) 430004   Fax: (05) 438007
Man Dir: Allan Amsel
Subjects: Travel and Travel Guides, Oriental Cookery and General Themes, Children's
Founded: 1979
ISBN Publisher's Prefix: 962-7031

China Cultural Corporation*, 345 Des Voeux Rd West, 5th Floor, Hong Kong   Cable Add: Chinacult Hong Kong   Telex: 76759 cctrw hx
Manager: Richard L C Wong
Associate Company: Shanghai Book Co Ltd (qv)
Subjects: Business Reference, Chinese Culture, Periodicals (in English and Chinese)

The **Chinese University Press**, The Chinese University of Hong Kong, Shatin, New Territories, Hong Kong   Tel: (00) 6952508   Cable Add: sinoversity   Telex: 50301 cuhk hx   Fax: (00) 6954234
Dir: T L Tsim; *Editorial:* William C Ho, Y C Wei, C P Tsang; *Sales, Rights & Permissions:* Patrick T H Kwong; *Production:* Kingsley Ma
Subjects: Chinese and South-East Asian Studies, Books on Hong Kong, Dictionaries, Books in Chinese and English on Business, the Arts, Sciences, Literature, Linguistics, History, Geography, Philosophy, Psychology, Journalism, Reprints of Rare Books, Periodicals
1985: 35 titles   *1986:* 30 titles   *Founded:* 1977
ISBN Publisher's Prefix: 962-201

Chopsticks Publications Ltd+*, Kowloon Central PO Box 73515, Kowloon (Located at: 116D Waterloo Rd, Ground Floor, Kowloon)   Tel: (03) 7115989/7115911   Cable Add: Chopcuisin, Hong Kong
Dir, Rights & Permissions: Cecilia J Au-Yeung; *Sales, Production, Publicity:* Wilson Au-Yeung
Subjects: Chinese Cuisine, Gourmet trips in Hong Kong and China
1985: 3 titles   *1986:* 4 titles   *Founded:* 1975
ISBN Publisher's Prefix: 962-7018

Commercial Press Ltd (Hong Kong Branch)+, 4th Floor, Kiu Ying Bldg, 2D Finnie St, Quarry Bay   Tel: (05) 651371   Cable Add: Compress   Telex: 86564 Cmprs HX
Man Dir: Cho Jat Lee; *Editorial:* Man Hung Chan; *Sales:* Tai Tseng Kwok; *Production:* Ms Pik Shan Yau; *General Manager:* Chi Hong Lo; *Rights & Permissions:* Wai Ming Choi
Orders to: 2nd Floor, Block B, Merit Industrial Bldg, 94 Tokwawan Rd, Kowloon
Parent Company: Commercial Press, People's Republic of China (qv)
Subsidiary Company: Hong Kong Educational Company, 5th Floor, Kiu Ying Bldg, 2D Finnie St, Quarry Bay
Associate Company: The Joint Publishingn Company, 10 Queen Victoria St, Hong Kong
Branch Offs: Commercial Press, Malaysia; Commercial Press, Republic of Singapore
Subjects: General trade books, Dictionaries, Textbooks, Academic, Chinese Classics, Art & Culture, Bilingual readers, Translations, Western/Traditional Chinese medicine
Bookshops: Book Centre, Yee Wo St, Causeway Bay; North Point Sub-branch, 395 King's Rd, Hong Kong; Mongkok Sub-branch, 608 Nathan Rd, Kowloon
1985: 70 titles   *Founded:* 1897
ISBN Publisher's Prefix: 962-07

Dawn Books, member of Ling Kee Group (qv)

The **Educational** Publishing House Ltd*, 14th Floor, Tsuen Wan Industrial Centre, TWTL, 24 Texaco Rd, Tsuen Wan, New Territories, Hong Kong   Tel: (00) 289081/289932   Telex: 35330 eph hx
Associate Companies: Fook Hing Offset Printing Co Ltd, The World Publishing Co, Kam Pui Enterprises Ltd, The Seashore Publishing Co, Harris Book Co Ltd, Hong Kong Housing Projects Corp Ltd, Pan-Lloyds (HK) Ltd

F E P International (HK) Ltd*, Unit 2A, 5th Floor, Whampoa Terminal Bldg, Wan Hoi St, Hung Hom, Kowloon
Head Off: FEP International Private Ltd, Republic of Singapore (qv)
Subject: Textbooks

Federal Publications (HK) Ltd*, Units 903-905 Tower B, 9th Floor, Hunghom Commercial Centre, 37 Ma Tau Wai Rd, Kowloon
Man Dir: Tom Y L Ng
Associate Companies: Federal Publications Sdn Bhd, Malaysia (qv); Federal Publications (S) Pte Ltd, Times Books International (qqv, both Republic of Singapore)
Subjects: Textbooks, General Subjects, Periodicals

Good Earth Publishing Co*, c/o Everyman Book Co Ltd, 71A Prince Edward Rd, Chit King Industrial Bldg, 10th Floor, San Po Kong, Kowloon
Subject: Textbooks

Greenwood Press*, 47 Pokfulam Road, G/F
Subject: Textbooks

H K Health Knowledge Publication*, Flat A, 1st floor, 7 Gough St
Subject: Textbooks

Hong Kong Cultural Press Ltd*, 8/F Lee Sum Factory Bldg, 23 Sze Mei St, San Po Kong, Kowloon
Subject: Textbooks

Hong Kong Publishing Co Ltd*, 307 Yu Yuet Lai Bldg, 43-55 Wyndham St, Central, Hong Kong   Tel: (05) 259053   Cable Add: Hkpublish   Telex: 78018 stkhx hx
Man Dir: Dean Barrett; *Editor:* Julia Birch
Subjects: Guidebooks, Photo-books and Fiction about Asia, especially Thailand
1986: 14 titles   *Founded:* 1975
ISBN Publisher's Prefix: 962-7035

Hong Kong University Press+, University of Hong Kong, 'Bethanie', 139 Pokfulam Rd   Tel: (05) 502703 (Sales)/502791 (Editorial)/507871 (Publisher)   Cable Add: University   Telex: 71919 cereb hx
Publisher, Rights & Permissions: Leon Comber; *Editor:* Y K Fung; *Sales:* Pekie Tang; *Production:* Ada Wan, Grace Fung
Subjects: Archaeology, History, Anatomy, Life Sciences, Physical Sciences, Social Sciences, Economics, Languages (especially Chinese), Literature, Asian Studies, Fine Arts, Geography, Law, Medicine, Philosophy, Seamanship, General Non-fiction, Paperbacks, Micro-prints, Classics Reprints, Educational (in English and Chinese)
1986-87: 20 titles   *Founded:* 1956
ISBN Publisher's Prefix: 962-209

Hung Fung Book Co*, 18 Tsat Tse Mui Rd, G/F
Subject: Textbooks

Jing Kung Educational Press*, 53 Hollywood Rd
Subject: Textbooks

King Shing Publishing Co*, 89 Sai Yee St, G/F, Kowloon
Subject: Textbooks

T H Lee & Co Ltd*, 1-15 Electric St, Upper Ground Floor, Wanchai
Subject: Textbooks

Ling Kee Group+, Zung Fu Industrial Bldg, 1067 King's Rd, Quarry Bay   Tel: (05) 616151   Telex: 62733 lkpc hx   Fax: (05) 8450980
Founder-owner, Chairman, Chief Executive: Au Bak Ling; *Chief Operating Officer:* Albert Au
Group Members:
Ling Kee Group (at above address), comprising Ling Kee Publishing Co Ltd (qv); Ling Kee Book Store Ltd, Hong Kong; Ling Kee Publishing Co (S) Pte Ltd, Republic of Singapore; Ling Kee Publishing Co Ltd, Taiwan; Ling Kee Publishing Co Inc, New York, USA. Unicorn Publishing Group, Yau Yue Bldg, 7/F, 127-131 Des Voeux Rd, Central, Hong Kong, comprising Unicorn Books Ltd (qv); Dawn Books, Hong Kong; Unicorn Books (S) Ltd, Republic of Singapore; Unicorn Publications Inc, New York, USA.
Ling Kee (UK) Ltd, UK (qv)

Ling Kee Publishing Co Ltd+, Zung Fu Industrial Bldg, 1067 King's Rd, Quarry Bay   Tel: (05) 616151   Cable Add: Bookland   Telex: 62733 lkpc hx
Chairman, Chief Executive: Au Bak Ling; *Chief Operating Officer:* Albert Au
Subjects: Reference, University, Secondary & Primary Textbooks, Educational Materials
Bookshops: Ling Kee Book Store Ltd, Yau Yue Building, 127-131 Des Voeux Rd, Central, Hong Kong   Tel: (05) 435383; 678 Nathan Rd, Mongkok, Kowloon   Tel: (03) 941800
Founded: 1949
Miscellaneous: Firm is a member of Ling Kee Group (qv)

Longman Group (Far East) Ltd, Cornwall House, 18th Floor, Tong Chong St, Quarry Bay   Tel: (05) 618171   Telex: 73051 lghk hx   Fax: (05) 657440 G 2 and 3
Man Dir: William Shen; *Publicity Manager:* Lesley Pausey
Subjects: Primary and Secondary Textbooks, Professional, Chinese Trade, Business
Miscellaneous: Firm is a member of the Longman Group UK Ltd, UK (qv)

Macmillan Publishers (China) Ltd, 19th Floor, Warwick House, Taikoo Trading Estate, 28 Tong Chong St, Quarry Bay   Tel: (05) 636206/620101/643115   Cable Add: Macpublish, Hong Kong   Telex: 85969 Penhk Hx
Man Dir: Yiu Hei Kan (Hong Kong and China Divisions)
Parent Company: Macmillan Publishers, UK (qv)
Subjects: Secondary Textbooks, China
Founded: 1969

HONG KONG 189

Oxford University Press, 18th Floor, Warwick House, Taikoo Trading Estate, 28 Tong Chong St, Quarry Bay Tel: (05) 610221 Cable Add: Oxonian Hong Kong Telex: 65522 hx Fax: (05) 658491
General Manager: A F D Scott; *Editorial:* Mrs F D Lauder (Educational), Mrs S Faircloth (Academic), Wong Wai-man (Chinese); *Marketing:* P Tam (Educational), Rebecca Ng (Academic & General); *Production:* P Ling
Parent Company: Oxford University Press, UK (qv)
Subsidiary Company: Keys Publishing Co Ltd
Subjects: School textbooks/supplementary books in English, Chinese; Bi-Lingual Reference; Academic and General Works relating to Hong Kong and China
1985: 108 titles *1986:* 124 titles *Founded:* 1961
ISBN Publisher's Prefix: 0-19 (OUP UK)

Perfecting Press*, 233 Lockhart Rd, 20th Floor, Flat A
Publicity Manager: Fung Pui Ming
Subject: Textbooks

Shanghai Book Co Ltd, 179 Connaught Rd West, 5th Floor, Flat A, Hong Kong Tel: (05) 486160/489889 Cable Add: Shoobook, Hong Kong
Man Dir: Lapshan Wong
Associate Companies: Shanghai Book Co (Pte) Ltd, Singapore (qv); Shanghai Book Co, (KL) Sdn Bhd, Malaysia; China Cultural Corporation, Hong Kong (qv)
Imprint: The Won Yit Book Co
Subjects: Textbooks and General, in Chinese and English
Founded: 1946
ISBN Publisher's Prefix: 962-239

South China Morning Post Ltd+*, Publications Division, PO Box 47, Morning Post Bldg, Tong Chong St, Hong Kong Tel: (05) 622271 Cable Add: Postscript Hong Kong Telex: hx 86008
Editorial: Howard Coats; *Advertising, Sales Manager:* Hilary Davies; *Production:* Edgar Chiu
Subjects: Television, Entertainment, Hong Kong
Bookshops: SCM Post Family Bookshops in Star Ferry, Furama Hotel, Ocean Centre — on Hong Kong Island and Kowloon
Founded: 1976

Sun Ya Publications (HK) Ltd+, 659 King's Rd, 4/F, Flat D, North Point Tel: (05) 647587 Cable Add: 6386 Telex: 85849 Clwso Hx Fax: (05) 659951
Man Dir, Editorial, Rights & Permissions: Miss Wai Wai-Ying; *Sales:* Chan Yiu Tong, Chan Chung-Chiu; *Production:* Miss Tsang Suet-Ying; *Publicity:* Miss Cheung Pui-Ling
Subjects: Children's and Juvenile Picture Books, Fiction and Non-fiction
Founded: 1961
ISBN Publisher's Prefix: 962-08

Times Educational Co Ltd, A 7/F Melbourne Industrial Bldg, 16 Westlands Road, Quarry Bay Telex: 63321 Timbk Hx
Subsidiary Company: Times Educational Co Sdn Bhd, Malaysia (qv)
Subjects: Educational, General Works, Trade Books

Travel Publishing Asia Ltd+, 1801 World Trade Centre, Causeway Bay, Hong Kong Tel: (05) 8903067 Cable Add: Trvpubasia Telex: 76591 Tpal Hx
Man Dir, Editorial: Roy Howard; *Sales, Publicity Manager:* Cynthia Caldwell; *Production Manager:* Anthony Ng

Subjects: Travel, Thailand, Advertising
1987: 10 titles *Founded:* 1983
ISBN Publisher's Prefix: 962-7088

Unicorn Books Ltd+, Yau Yue Bldg, 7/F, 127-131 Des Voeux Rd, Central, Hong Kong Tel: (05) 411205 Telex: 66236 ublp hx
Chief Operating Officer: Albert K W Au
Subjects: Quality books in Chinese and other Asian languages for direct mailing
Miscellaneous: Firm is a member of the Ling Kee Group, Hong Kong (qv)

Union Press Ltd*, 9 College Rd, Kowloon
Subject: Textbooks

Witman Publishing Co (HK) Ltd, 9-11 Tsat Tse Mui Rd, Ground Floor, North Point Tel: (05) 626279/631973
Manager: Ms S C Yau
Subjects: Textbooks, Languages (English and Chinese), Juvenile Fiction
Founded: 1978
ISBN Publisher's Prefix: 962-7044

The **Won Yit** Book Co, an imprint of Shanghai Book Co Ltd (qv)

Major Booksellers

East Asia Book Co*, 39 Shu Kuk St, North Point

Eastern Book Service Ltd*, 11-C Majestic Bldg, 80 Nathan Rd, Kowloon Tel: (03) 685645 Cable Add: Bookseast HK Telex: 41255 ebs hx
Man Dir: Jack R Sherman
Publishers' Agents and Stockists. Associated with Eastern Book Service offices in Singapore, the Philippines and Malaysia (qqv)

Far East Publications Ltd*, Unit D, 2nd Floor, Freder Centre, 68 Sung Wong Toi Rd, Tokwawan, Kowloon Tel: (03) 656234/658862
General Manager: Tom Ng
Miscellaneous: Also major distributor of books, from Mok Chong St, Kowloon City Rd

Hong Kong Book Centre Ltd*, On Lok Yuen Bldg, 25 Des Voeux Rd, Central, Hong Kong
Manager: M T Li
Associate Company: Swindon Book Co (qv)

Howard Book Co*, 74 Argyle St, Kowloon

Jing Kung Book Store*, 53 Hollywood Rd

Kwong Hin Bookstore*, 75 Hollywood Rd

Swindon Book Co, 13-15 Lock Rd, Kowloon Cable Add: Swindon Telex: 50441 swin hx
Managers: Rupert S C Li, Daisy K Y Li
Associate Companies: Book Marketing Ltd (qv); Hong Kong Book Centre Ltd (qv); Kelly and Walsh Ltd, GPO Box 96, Hong Kong
Branch: University Book Store (qv)

Tai Kuen Book Store, Ground Floor, 315 Queen's Rd West

Times Book Centre*, Lower Ground Floor 23, Houston Centre, 63 Mody Rd, Tsim Sha Tsui East, Kowloon Tel: (03) 7226583
Manager: Daisy Chan
Also: G31 Hutchison House, 10 Harcourt Rd, Central, Hong Kong Tel: (05) 259727; C and E, Milton Mansion, 96 Nathan Rd, Kowloon Tel: (03) 7217138; Polytechnic Bookstore, 2nd Floor, Amenities Bldg, Hong Kong Polytechnic, Kowloon Tel: (03) 654807

University Book Store, Ground Floor, Run Run Shaw Bldg, University of Hong Kong, Pokfulam Rd Tel: (05) 468412/8592107
Manager: Susan Kuyper
A branch of Swindon Book Co (qv)

Major Libraries

British Council Library, Easey Commercial Bldg 1/F, 255 Hennessy Rd, Wanchai Tel: (05) 756501 Telex: 74141 bcoun hx

Chinese University of Hong Kong Library System, Shatin, New Territories
University Librarian: Dr David S Yen
Publications include: University Library Bibliographical Series: no 1 — *Union Catalogue of Serials;* no 2 — *Union Catalogue of Audio-Visual Materials;* no 3 — *An Annotated Guide to Serial Publications of Hong Kong Government;* no 4 — *Serials of Hong Kong 1845-1979;* no 5 — *Newspapers of Hong Kong 1841-1979;* no 6 — *History of Medicine: an Annotated Bibliography of Titles at The Chinese University of Hong Kong;* no 7 — *Union Catalogue of Asian Fine Arts Collection;* no 8 — *Catalogue of the Chinese Rare Books in the Libraries of The Chinese University of Hong Kong*

Hong Kong Junior Chamber of Commerce Libraries*, 272 Queen's Rd Central, 15/F, Flat C Tel: (05) 543 8913
Contact: Peony Kwok (Chamber of Commerce Assistant National Secretary-General)

Hong Kong Polytechnic Library, Hung Hom, Kowloon Tel: (03) 638344 Cable Add: Polyteched Telex: 38964 polyx hx
Librarian: Barry L Burton
Publication: Hongkongiana: an index to selected Hong Kong periodicals

Sun Yat-Sen Library*, 172-174 Boundary St, Kowloon

University of Hong Kong Libraries, University of Hong Kong, Pokfulam Rd Tel: (05) 8592203

Urban Council Public Libraries, 6th Floor, High Block, City Hall, Edinburgh Pl, Hong Kong Tel: (05) 233688 Telex: 60645 ucusd hx
Chief Librarian: Barbara Luk

Library Association

Hong Kong Library Association, PO Box 10095, General Post Office, Hong Kong
Publication: Journal of the Hong Kong Library Association (irregular)

Library Reference Journal

Journal of the Hong Kong Library Association, Hong Kong Library Association, PO Box 10095, General Post Office, Hong Kong
Text in English and Chinese

Literary Associations and Societies

Chinese Language and Literature Association*, Block A1, Fa Po Villa, 1st Floor, Fa Po St, Yau Yat Chuen, Kowloon
Secretary: Leung Nga Mei

Hong Kong Chinese P E N Centre, Victoria Park Mansion, 15th Floor, Flat A, Paterson St

President: Prof Chi-tai Chu; *Secretary:* William Hsu
Publication: PEN News (weekly in Chinese)

Hong Kong English **P E N** Centre, 10 Phoenix Court, Block D, DF 7th Floor, Marconi Rd, Kowloon Tong, Kowloon
President: Dr Owen H H Wong; *Secretary:* Miss Lee Wai-ling

Literary Periodicals

Eastern Horizon, Lee Tsung-ying, 472 Hennessy Rd, 3rd Floor
Text in English

PEN News, Hong Kong Chinese PEN Centre, Victoria Park Mansion, 15th Floor, Flat A, Paterson St
Text in Chinese

Shui Hsing Cha Chi (Mercury Magazine), Louise Bao, GPO Box 13154
Text in Chinese, title in Chinese and English

Wu Hsia Shih Chieh, 7-13 Hsin Chieh, 2nd Floor

Hungary

General Information

Language: Hungarian (German widely known)
Religion: Predominantly Roman Catholic
Population: 10.7 million
Bank Hours: 0830-1700 Monday-Friday; 0830-1330 Saturday
Shop Hours: 1000-1800 Monday-Friday; 1000-1500 Saturday
Currency: 100 fillér = 1 forint
Export/Import Information: Trade is carried out by about 400 companies which are authorized by the Ministry of Foreign Trade. Exchange controls. Book importing and exporting is through Kultura – Hungarian Foreign Trading Co, H-1389 Budapest 62, Postafiók 149; atlases through Cartographia, H-1443 Budapest, Postafiók 132. Magyar Hirdeto, Budapest, is a full service advertising agency
Copyright: UCC, Berne (see International section)

Book Trade Organizations

Magyar Írók Szövetsége, Budapest VI, Bajza u 18
Union of Hungarian Writers
President: Tibor Cseres; *General Secretary:* Miklós Veress

Magyar Könyvkiadók és Könyvterjesztök Egyesülése, H-1367 Budapest, Postafiók 130 (Located at: H-1051 Budapest V, Vörösmarty tér 1 X) Tel: (01) 184758
Association of Hungarian Publishers and Booksellers
President: András Petró; *Secretary General:* Ferenc Zöld
Founded: 1878
Publications: Könyvvilag; Hungarian Book Review (also published in French and German); A Könyv (Books)

Országos Széchényi Könyvtár Magyar ISBN Iroda*, H-1827 Budapest Pollack Mihálytér 10 Telex: biblnathung 224226
ISBN Administrator: Dr Susánszky Zoltánné

Standard Book Numbering Agency, see Országos Széchényi Könyvtar Magyar ISBN Iroda

Book Trade Reference Journals

Hungarian Book Review, Kultura, H-1389 Budapest, Postafiók 149
Text in English, French and German

Könyv és nevelés (Books and Education), Orszagos pedagógiai könyvtár és múzeum, Budapest V, Honvéd u 19, Postafiók 49

Könyvvilag (Book World), Magyar Könyvkiadók és Könyvterjesztök Egyesülése, H-1367 Budapest, Postafiók 130

Magyar könyvszemle (Hungarian Bibliographical Journal), Akadémiai Kiadó, Publishing House of the Hungarian Academy of Sciences, H-1363 Budapest, Postafiók 24
Review of the history of books, bibliography and documentation (summaries in English, French, German or Russian)

Magyar nemzeti bibliográfia: Könyvek bibliográfiája (Hungarian National Bibliography: Bibliography of books), Országos Széchényi Könyvtár, H-1827 Budapest, Múzeum körút 14-16

Uj könyvek (New Books), Konyvtártudományi és módszertani központ, H-1827 Budapest, Buduvári Palota F épület

Publishers

Akadémiai Kiadó, H-1363 Budapest, Postafiók 24 Tel: (01) 111010 Cable Add: Akadémiai Kiadó Budapest Telex: 226228 Ak Nyo H
Publishing House of the Hungarian Academy of Sciences
President: György Hazai; *Sales, Promotion:* András Tasnádi (Home), Gèza Takács (International)
Subjects: Belles Lettres, General & Social Science, Medicine, Biology, Earth Sciences, Engineering, University Textbooks, Archaeology, Book Industry, History, Arts, Reference, Literature, Music, Philosophy, Psychology, Politics, Law, Languages, Veterinary Science, Economics
Bookshop: Stúdium Akadémiai Könyvesbolt, H-1052 Budapest V, Váci u 22
Founded: 1828
ISBN Publisher's Prefix: 963-05

Cartographia, H-1443 Budapest XIV, Bosnyák tér 5, Postafiók 132 Tel: (01) 634639 Cable Add: Cartographia Telex: 226218
Subjects: Maps, Atlases

Corvina Press, H-1364 Budapest 4, Vörösmarty tér 1, Postafiók 108 Tel: (01) 176222 Cable Add: Corvina Budapest Telex: 224440
Dir: István Bart; *Production Manager:* János Szilassy; *Sales, Advertising & Publicity Dir:* Gábor Ila; *Editorial Dir:* Béla Reviczky
Orders to: Kultura, H-1389 Budapest 62, Postafiók 149
Subjects: Books in Hungarian & foreign languages, Art, Music, Fiction, Juveniles, Tourist Guides, General Information, Cookery Books, Sport
Founded: 1955
ISBN Publisher's Prefix: 963-13

Európa Könyvkiadó, H-1363 Budapest V, Kossuth Lajos tér 13-15, Postafiók 65 Tel: (01) 312700 Cable Add: Euroliber Telex: 225645
Man Dir: János Domokos; *Editorial Manager:* Dr Zs Gereniséf; *Sales, Rights & Permissions:* Dr L Sármány; *Production:* I Miklósi; *Publicity:* L Horváth
Subjects: General Fiction, Belles Lettres, Poetry, Biography, Philosophy, Bibliophile interest
Founded: 1945
ISBN Publisher's Prefixes: 963-07, 963-207

Gondolat Könyvkiadó, H-1088 Budapest, Bródy Sándor u 16 Tel: (01) 343380
Man Dir: Dr Margit Siklós
Subjects: Reference, Art, General & Social Science
Founded: 1957
ISBN Publisher's Prefix: 963-281

Helikon Kiadó+, H-1053 Budapest, Eötvös L u 8 Tel: (01) 174765 Telex: 227100
Man Dir: Magda Molnár
Subjects: Belles Lettres, Art, History
Bookshop: Helikon Bookshop, H-1052 Budapest, Sütö u 2
1985: 35 titles *1986:* 37 titles *Founded:* 1982
ISBN Publisher's Prefix: 963-207

Képzömüvészeti Alap Kiadóvállalata*, H-1051 Budapest V, Vörösmarty tér 1 Tel: (01) 184981
Publishing House of the Fine Arts Foundation
Manager: Dr László Seres; *Editorial:* Teréz Horváth; *Sales:* János Pintér; *Production:* György Szedlák; *Publicity:* Tibor Geröly
Subject: Fine Arts
Bookshop: Képesbolt, Budapest VI, Deák tér 6
Founded: 1954

Kossuth Könyvkiadó, H-1366 Budapest, Steindl u 6, Postafiók 127 Tel: (01) 117440
Publishing House of Political Literature
Man Dir: György Nonn; *Deputy Man Dir:* József Nyirö; *Sales Dir:* Sándor Méth; *Rights & Permissions:* Artisjus (qv under Literary Agents)
Subjects: History, Philosophy, Belles Lettres, Social and Political Sciences, Psychology, Business, Periodicals
1986: 180 titles *Founded:* 1944
ISBN Publisher's Prefix: 963-09

Közgazdasági és Jogi Könyvkiadó, H-1374 Budapest V, Nagy Sándor u 6, Postafiók 578 Tel: (01) 126430/312327 Telex: 226511
Man Dir: V Dalos; *Editorial, Publicity:* Dr F Böszörmenyi; *Sales:* L Szigeti; *Rights & Permissions:* Artisjus (qv under Literary Agents)
Distribution: Artisjus, Budapest
Subjects: Economics, Law, Sociology, Education, Children's Literature
Founded: 1955
ISBN Publisher's Prefixes: 963-220, 963-221 (Közgazdasági és Jogi Könyvkiadó), 963-223 (Minerva)

Magvetö Könyvkiadó*, H-1051 Budapest V, Vörösmarty tér 1 Tel: (01) 176222
Man Dir: Miklós Jovánovics; *Sales, Publicity:* I Matolcsy; *Managing Editors:*

M Hegedös, M Ferch; *Rights & Permissions:* Artisjus (qv under Literary Agents)
Subjects: General Fiction, Belles Lettres, Poetry, History, Music, Art, Aesthetics, Philosophy, Low-priced Paperbacks
1985: 227 titles *Founded:* 1955
ISBN Publisher's Prefix: 963-14

Medicina Könyvkiadó*, H-1361 Budapest, Postafiók 9 (Located at: H-1054 Budapest, Beloiannisz u 8)
Publishing House of Medical Literature
Man Dir: Prof Dr István Árky; *Editors:* Dr Erzsébet Krudy, Dr Mihály Berend, Dr Bulcsu Buda; *Production:* Márton Orlai; *Rights & Permissions:* Artisjus (qv under Literary Agents)
Subjects: Medicine, Travel, Sports
Founded: 1957
ISBN Publisher's Prefixes: 963-240 (Medical), 963-243 (Travel), 963-253 (Sports)

Mezögazdasági Könyvkiadó Vállalat+*, Budapest V, Báthory u 10 Tel: (01) 116650/318397
Agricultural Publishing House
Manager: Dr Pál Sárkány
Subjects: Agriculture, Reference, General Science, Textbooks
Bookshop: Agricultural Bookstore, Budapest V, Vécsei u 5
1985: 95 titles *Founded:* 1950
ISBN Publisher's Prefixes: 963-230, 963-231, 963-232

Móra Ferenc Ifjúsági Könyvkiadó, H-1146 Budapest XIV, Május 1 út 57-59 Tel: (01) 212390 Telex: 227027 morak h
Man Dir: János Sziládi
Subjects: Juveniles, Science Fiction
Founded: 1950
ISBN Publisher's Prefix: 963-11

Editio **Musica Budapest**, H-1370 Budapest, Postafiók 322 (Located at: Budapest V, Vörösmarty tér 1) Tel: (01) 184228
Cable Add: Editiomusica Telex: 225500 embh
Man Dir: István Homolya
Subject: Sheet Music, Books on Music
Founded: 1950

Müszaki Könyvkiadó*, H-1014 Budapest 1, Szentháromság tér 1 Tel: (01) 160860 Cable Add: Editechn Telex: 226490 mkh
Publishing House of Technical Literature
Man Dir: Herbert Fischer; *Editorial:* András Kelen
Subjects: Science, Technical, Textbooks, Yearbooks, Catalogues
Bookshops: 100 in Budapest, 154 elsewhere throughout country
Founded: 1949
ISBN Publisher's Prefix: 963-10

Statisztikai Kiadó Vállalat+, H-1300 Budapest, Postafiók 99 (Located at: H-1033 Budapest 3, Kaszásdülö u 2) Tel: (01) 688635/803311 Telex: 226699 skv h
Statistical Publishing House
Man Dir: József Kecskés; *Sales Dir:* Dr László Oláh; *Publicity and Advertising Dir:* Piroska Gerely; *Rights & Permissions:* Artisjus (qv under Literary Agents)
Parent Organization: Central Statistical Office, H-1024 Budapest, Keleti Károly u 5-7
Subjects: Statistics, Computing, Economics, Social Science
Bookshop: Statistical and Computing Bookshop, Budapest II, Keleti Károly u 10 Tel: (01) 158018
1985-86: 186 titles *Founded:* 1954
ISBN Publisher's Prefix: 963-40

Szépirodalmi Kiadó, H-1073 Budapest, Lenin Körút 9-11, Postafiók 58 Tel: (01) 221285
Man Dir: Márton Tarnóc; *Rights & Permissions:* Ministry of Culture
Subjects: General Fiction, Belles Lettres, Poetry, Low- & High-priced Paperbacks, Educational Materials
Founded: 1950
ISBN Publisher's Prefix: 963-15

Táncsics Szakszervezeti Kiadó*, H-1139 Budapest, Váci u 69-79 Tel: (01) 141479/335790
Manager: István Kádár
Subjects: Technical, Non-fiction, Reference, Periodicals

Tankönyvkiadó Vállalat*, H-1055 Budapest V, Szalay u 10-14, Póstafiók 20 Tel: (01) 324915
Textbook Publishing House
Man Dir: András Petró; *Editorial:* Sándor Hinora; *Sales:* Hugó Dobos; *Production:* Lajos Lojd; *Rights & Permissions:* Artisjus (qv under Literary Agents)
Subjects: Textbooks, Educational Literature, Language Books, Periodicals
Founded: 1949
ISBN Publisher's Prefix: 963-17

Zrinyi Katonai Kiadó*, H-1087 Budapest VIII, Kerepesi u 29/b
Publishing House of the Hungarian Army
Manager: László Bedó
Subjects: Military & Popular Science

Literary Agents

Artisjus*, H-1364 Budapest, Vörösmarty tér 1, Postafiók 67 Tel: (01) 184704
Cable Add: Artisjus Telex: 226527 Arjus H
Agency for Literature, Theatre and Music of the Hungarian Bureau for Copyright Protection
Contact: Vera Acs

Major Booksellers

Állami könyvterjesztö vállalat*, H-1052 Budapest V, Deák Ferenc u 15
Hungarian State Book-Distributing Enterprise. It distributes books to its 112 bookshops

Állami könyvterjesztö vállalat országos antikvár*, Budapest V, Múzeum körút 21
Hungarian State Book-Distributing Enterprise, Department for Antiquarian Books

Könyvértékesitö Vállalat*, H-1391 Budapest, Postafiók 204 Tel: (01) 297649 Telex: 226772
Hungarian Wholesale Book Trading Enterprise
This organization holds stocks and despatches all editions from Hungarian publishers, and handles imported books for the retail trade. It also sells books directly for bookshops owned by co-operatives, and has a Library Service department which supplies the entire Hungarian Library network

Kultura, H-1389 Budapest 62, Postafiók 149 Tel: (01) 359370 Cable Add: Kulturpress Telex: 22-4441
Dir: J Szabó
Hungarian Foreign Trading Co — the export-import organization, representing the publications of different Hungarian publishers

Müvelt Nép Könyvterjesztö Vállalat, H-1370 Budapest 5, Postafiók 370 (Located at: H-1061 Budapest 6, Népköztársaság u 21) Tel: (01) 429760 Telex: 224914
Dir: Sándor Preszter

Major Libraries

Budapesti Müszaki Egyetem Központi Könyvtára*, Budapest IIII, Budafoki u 4-6
Budapest Technical University Central Library

Eötvös Loránd Tudományegyetem Egyetemi Könyvtár*, H-1372 Budapest, Károlyi Mihály u 10, Postafiók 483 Tel: (01) 185866
Central Library of Loránd Eötvös University

Föapátsági Könyvtar*, H-9090 Pannonhalma Tel: Pannonhalma 7022
Library of the Archabbacy (Benedictine)
Librarian: Szabo Floris

Föszékesegyházi Könyvtár, H-2500 Esztergom, Bajcsy Zsilinszky u 28 Tel: Esztergom 527
Cathedral Library
Dir: Dr Mathias Érdös

József Attila Tudományegyetem Központi Könyvtára, H-6701 Szeged, Dugonics tér 13 Tel: (062) 24022 Telex: 82605 jatek h
Central Library of the Attila József University
Chief Librarian: Dr Béla Karácsonyi
Publications: Dissertationes ex Bibliotheca Universitatis de Attila József Nominatae; Acta Universitatis Szegediensis de Attila József Nominatae; Acta Bibliothecaria (all irregular); Könyvtártörténeti Füzetek (History of Libraries series, with German summaries, four vols published out of projected ten)

Kossuth Lajos Tudományegyetem Egyetemi Könyvtár, H-4010 Debrecen Tel: 5216835 Telex: 72200
Lajos Kossuth University Library
Chief Librarian: Dr Olga Gomba
Publication: Könyv és Könyvtár

Könyvtártudományi és módszertani központ, H-1827 Budapest, Budavári Palota F épület
Centre for Library Science and Methodology
Dir: Ferenc Szente
Publications: Uj könyvek; Könyvtári figyelo; Magyar könyvtári szakrodalom bibliográfiája; Hungarian Library and Information Science Abstracts; Könyvtári és Dokumentációs Szakirodalom, Referálo Lap; Vengerskaá literatura po bibliotekovedeniú i informatike, Referativnyj Zurnal

Központi statisztikai hivatal könyvtár és dokumentációs szolgálat, H-1525 Budapest II, Keleti Károly u 5, Postafiók 10
Library and Documentation Service of the Central Statistical Office
Dir-General: Dr István Csahók
Publications include: Statisztikai módszerek-Témadokumentáció (Statistical Methods Surveys of Literature on Various Subjects); Történeti statisztikai tanulmányok (Studies on Historical Statistics); Történeti statisztikai füzetek (Papers on Historical Statistics)

Uj **Magyar Központi** Levéltár*, H-1014 Budapest, Hess András tér 4
New Central Archives of Hungary

HUNGARY

Magyar Országos Levéltár, H-1250
Budapest I, Bécsikapu tér 4, Postafiók 3
Tel: (01) 1565811
National Archives of Hungary
Publications include: Levéltári Közlemények; Magyar Országos Levéltár Kiadványai

Magyar Tudományos Akadémia Könyvtára, H-1361 Budapest V, Akadémia u 2, Postafiók 7 Tel: (01) 382344 Telex: 224132 aktar h
Library of the Hungarian Academy of Sciences
Librarian: Dr György Rózsa
Publications: Publicationes Bibliothecae Academiae Scientiarum Hungaricae; Catalogi Collectionis Manuscriptorum Bibliothecae Academiae Scientiarum Hungaricae; Oriental Studies; Budapest Oriental Reprints; Informatics and Scientometrics

Országos Müszaki, Információs Központ és Könyvtár*, H-1428 Budapest, Múzeum u 17, Postafiók 12 Tel: (01) 336309 Telex: 224944 Omikk h
National Technical Information Centre and Library
Director-General: Mihály Ágoston;
Librarian: Tibor Futala
Publications: Many journals, abstracts, conference reports on technological subjects, often in translation, including: Hungarian R and D Abstracts Science and Technology; *Uj Kutatási és Müszaki Fejlesztési Jelentések az Országos Müszaki Könyvtárban* (New Research and Development Reports in the Holdings of the Central Technical Library); *Tudományos és Müszaki Tájékoztatás* (Scientific and Technical Information); *Audiovizuális Közlemények, Oktatástechnikai, Szervezéstechnikai és Tájékoztatástechnikai Szakfolyóirat* (Audiovisual Review, Journal for Education Technology, Organization- and Information Technology)
Miscellaneous: Technoinform, the Library's Foreign Trade Department, offers translation from Hungarian and other languages

Országos Széchényi Könyvtár, H-1827 Budapest I, Budavári Palota F épület
Tel: (01) 556167 Telex: biblnathung 224226 (Information Dept: Tel: 558857)
National Széchényi Library
Dir: Prof Gyula Juhász
Publications include: Magyar nemzeti bibliográfia: Könyvek bibliográfiája (Hungarian National Bibliography: Bibliography of Books); *Magyar nemzeti bibliográfia: Zenemüvek bibliográfiája* (Hungarian National Bibliography: Bibliography of Musical Works); *Magyar nemzeti bibliográfia: Idöszaki kiadványok repertóriuma* (Hungarian National Bibliography: Repertory of Periodical Publications); *Magyar nemzeti bibliográfia: Idöszaki kiadványok bibliográfiája* (Hungarian National Bibliography: Bibliography of Periodical Publications); *Az Országos Széchényi Könyvtár évekönyve* (National Széchényi Library Year Book); *A magyar irodalom és irodalomtudomány bibliográfiája* (Bibliography of Hungarian Literature and Literary Studies); *Külföldi magyar nyelvü kiadványok* (Foreign Hungarian-language Publications); *Hungarika irodalmi szemle* (Hungarika: a Literary Review); *Kurrens külföldi idöszaki kiadványok a magyar könyvtárakban* (Current Foreign Periodical Publications in Hungarian Libraries); *Mikrofilmek címjegyzéke* (List of Microfilm Titles): *Idöszaki kiadványok* (Periodical Publications), *Modern nyomtatványok* (Modern Printed Matter), *Színes grafikus plakátok* (Coloured Graphic Posters), *Zenemütári gyüjtemény* (Collection of Musical Works); *Az Országos Széchényi Könyvtár kiadványai* (1984) (The National Széchényi Library Publications (1984)); *Az Országos Széchényi Könyvtár mikrofilm jegyzékel: Uj sorozat* (Lists of the National Széchényi Library Microfilms: New Series)
Also a National Centre for Library Science and Methodology and a Hungarian national ISBN, ISSN, ISDS centre

Fövárosi Szabó Ervin Könyvtár, H-1371 Budapest, Szabó Ervin tér 1, Postafiók 487 Tel: (01) 330580 (Information Service: 343581)
Ervin Szabó Municipal Library
Publications: Selected bibliographies of Hungarian sociological and music literature; yearbook; publications on local history

Tiszáninneni Református Egyházkerület Nagykönyvtára, H-3950 Sárospatak, Rákóczy út 1 Tel: Sárospatak 11057
Library of the Cistibiscan Reformed Church District

University of Loránd Eötvös Central Library, see Eötvös Loránd Tudományegyetem Egyetemi Könyvtár

Library Associations

Magyar Könyvtárosok Egyesülete*, H-1014 Budapest I Uri u 54-56
Association of Hungarian Librarians
President: Mrs Ibolya Billédi; *Secretary:* Dezsö Kovács

MTESZ Tájékoztatási Tudományos Tanács, H-1055 Budapest, Kossuth tér 6-8 Tel: (0361) 533333 Telex: 225792 Mtesz h
Information Science Council of the Federation of Technical and Scientific Societies
President: Dr Pál Gágyor; *Secretary:* György Reich

Library Reference Books and Journals

Books

Könyvtártörténeti Füzetek (History of Libraries series), József Attila Tudományegyetem Központi Könyvtára, H-6701 Szeged, Dugonics tér 13
With German summaries; four vols published out of projected ten

Journals

Hungarian Library and Information Science Abstracts, Könyvtártudományi és módszertani központ, H-1827 Budapest, Budavári Palota F épület
Text in English and Russian

Könyvtári figyelo (Library Review), Könyvtártudományi és módszertani központ, H-1827 Budapest, Budavári Palota F épület
Summaries in English, German and Russian

Magyar könyvtári szakirodalom bibliográfiája (Hungarian Library Literature), Könyvtártudományi és módszertani központ, H-1827 Budapest, Budavári Palota F épület
Text in Hungarian, titles and summaries in English

Literary Associations and Societies

Magyar Bibliofil társaság*, Budapest VIII, Brody Sándor u 16
Hungarian Society of Bibliophiles

Magyar Irodalomtörténeti Társaság*, Budapest 1052, Pesti Barnabás u 1
Society of Hungarian Literary History
President: Gabor Tolnai
Publications: Irodalomtörténet

Magyar Tudományos Akadémia Irodalomtudományi Intézete, H-1118 Budapest XI, Ménesi u 11-13
Institute of Literary Studies of the Hungarian Academy of Sciences
Dir: Prof Tibor Klaniczay
Publications: Irodalomtörténeti Közlemények (quarterly); *Helikon* (quarterly); *Literatura* (quarterly); *Irodalomtörténeti Könyvtár* (monographs); *Irodalomtörténeti Füzetek* (papers); *Neo-Helikon* (quarterly)

Magyar P E N Club, H-1051 Budapest V, Vörösmarty tér 1 Tel: (01) 184143
President: Dr Iván Boldizsár; *Secretary:* István Bart
Publications: The Hungarian PEN, Le PEN hongrois (yearly bulletin)

Literary Periodicals

Hungarika (a Literary Review), Országos Széchényi Könyvtár, H-1827 Budapest I, Budavári Palota F épület

Kortárs (Contemporary), Kultura, H-1389 Budapest, Postafiók 149

Kritica (Critic), Kultura, H-1389 Budapest, Postafiók 149
Summaries in French, German and Russian

Literatura, Magyar Tudományos Akadémia Irodalomtudományi Intézete, H-1118 Budapest XI, Ménesi u 11-13

Magyar muhely (Hungarian Workshop), Paul Nagy, 139 ave Jean-Jaurès, F-92120 Montrouge, France
Literary and artistic review (text in Hungarian)

New Hungarian Quarterly, H-1088 Budapest 8, Rákóczi u 17
Text in English

Literary Prizes

József **Attila** Prize
For highly significant work in prose or poetry. Given to writers, poets and critics. Since 1950 awarded to 8-10 people a year. Enquiries to Ministry of Culture of the Hungarian People's Republic, Budapest

S Z O T Prizes
Awarded annually. Established in 1958 by the Central Council of Hungarian Trade Unions, prizes are awarded to artists, scientists, educators, as well as for literary works. Nominees are people who excel in improving worker-artist contacts and in disseminating knowledge. Selection is by public opinion poll. SZOT is the Central Council of Hungarian Trade Unions. Enquiries to Szakszervezetek Országos Tanácsa DIJ, H-1415 Budapest 6, Dózsa György ut 84/B

Translation Agencies and Associations

Magyar Írok Szövetsége*, Budapest VI, Bajza u 18 Tel: (01) 228840
Hungarian Writers' Union
Has a section of literary translators

Iceland

General Information

Language: Icelandic (widespread knowledge of Danish and English)
Religion: Lutheran
Population: 228,000
Bank Hours: 0930-1530 Monday-Friday
Shop Hours: 0900-1800 Monday-Friday; open until 2200 Thursday or Friday, open until noon Saturday
Currency: 100 aurar (singular: eyrir) = 1 króna (plural: krónur)
Export/Import Information: Member of the European Free Trade Association. No tariff on books. Sales Tax. No import licences required. No exchange controls for books but they may not be imported on credit
Copyright: UCC, Berne, Florence (see International section)

Book Trade Organizations

Félag Islenzkra Bókaútgefenda, Laufásvegi 12, 101 Reykjavik Tel: (01) 27820
Icelandic Publishers' Association
Chairman: Eyjólfur Sigurdsson; *General Manager:* B Gíslason

Félag Islenzkra Bókaverzlana*, Skólavödustig 2, Reykjavik
Icelandic Booksellers' Association
Publication: Bóksalafélag Islands Sjötíu og Fimm Ára

Innkaupasamband Bóksala HF*, Sundaborg 9, Reykjavik Tel: (01) 85088 Telex: 2210 heild is
Booksellers' Import Association
Man Dir: Haukur H Gröndal

Rithöfundasamband Islands, PO Box 949, 121 Reykjavik Tel: (01) 13190
Writers' Union of Iceland
Chairman: Sigurdur Pálsson; *Man Dir:* Rannveig G Ágústsdóttir

Book Trade Reference Books and Journals

Book

Bóksalafélag Islands Sjötíu og Fimm Ára (75 years of the Icelandic Booksellers' Association), Félag Islenzkra Bókaverzlana, Skólavödustig 2, Reykjavik
Contains addresses of publishers and booksellers

Journals

Bókalisti (Booklist), Borgarbókasafn, Thingholtsstr 29A, Reykjavik

Íslensk bókaskrá (The Icelandic National Bibliography), Landsbókasafn Íslands, Reykjavik

Landsbókasafn Íslands, Árbok (Year Book), Landsbókasafn Islands, Reykjavik
Contains an annual list of Icelandic publications

Publishers

Almenna Bókafélagid+, Austurstr 18, PO Box 9, 101 Reykjavik Tel: (01) 25544 Cable Add: Bókafélagid Telex: 2046
Man Dir: Kristján Jóhannsson; *Editorial:* Eirikur H Finnbogason; *Sales Dir:* Anton Örn Kaernested; *Production:* Kristinn Dagsson; *Rights & Permissions:* Stefania Pétursdóttir
Subjects: General Fiction, Non-fiction, Belles Lettres, Poetry, Biography, History, Secondary Textbooks, Juvenile, Children's
Bookshop: Bókaverzlun Sigfúsar Eymundssonar (BSE), Reykjavik
Book Clubs: The AB Book Club (BAB); The MAB Cookery Book Club
Founded: 1955

Bókaútgáfa Thórhalls **Bjarnarsonar***, Skemmuvegi 4, 200 Kopavogi

Bókaútgáfan **Björk***, Háholti 7, 300 Akranes

Bokaforlag Odds **Björnssonar**, Tryggvabraut 18-20, PO Box 558, 602 Akureyri Tel: (09) 622500 Cable Add: Prentverk
Man Dir: Geir S Björnsson; *Advertising Dir:* Kirstjan Kristjansson
Subjects: General Fiction, Belles Lettres, Poetry, Biography, History, How-to, Music, Art, Philosophy, Reference, Religion, Juveniles, Educational Materials
Book Club: Heima er Bezt Book Club
1985: 14 titles *1986:* 12 titles *Founded:* 1897

Bokas hf*, Adalstr 35, 400 Isafirdi

Bókaverslun Sigfusar **Eymundssonar**, Austurstr 18, 101 Reykjavik
Subject: Educational Books
Bookshop: At above address

Forlagid+, Frakkastíg 6A, PO Box 786, 121 Reykjavik Tel: (01) 25188 Telex: Forfrakk 3000 Simtex Is
Man Dir: Jóhann Páll Valdimarsson; *Editorial Dir:* Thorvaldur Kristinsson
Subjects: General, Juveniles, Educational
1986: 26 titles *Founded:* 1984

Fjolvi*, Klapparstig 16, PO Box 624, 101 Reykjavik Tel: (01) 26659 Telex: 2159 Rethor
Man Dir: Sturla Eiriksson; *Editorial:* Thorsteinn Thorarensen
Subjects: History, Natural History, Sciences, Fiction, Poetry
Book Clubs: Bokaklubbur Fjolva; Particip 'Verold'
Founded: 1966

Bókaútgáfa Gudjóns Ó **Gudjónssonar***, Thverholti 13, Reykjavik Tel: (01) 27233

Heimskringla*, PO Box 392, 121 Reykjavik (Located at: Laugavegi 18, Reykjavik) Tel: (01) 15199
Publications Editor: Halldor Gudmundsson; *General Manager:* Arni Einarsson
Parent Company: Mál og menning (qv)

Bókaútgáfan **Helgafell***, Veghúsastíg 7, 101 Reykjavik Tel: (01) 16837

Bókaútgáfan **Hildur***, Skemmuvegi 36, 200 Kópavogi Tel: (01) 76700

Hladbúd hf, subsidiary of Idunn (qv)

Bókaútgáfan **Hlidskjálf***, Ingólfsstr 22, 101 Reykjavik Tel: (01) 17520

Iceland Review*, PO Box 8576, 121 Reykjavik (Located at: Höfdabakki 9) Tel: (01) 84966 Telex: 2121
Man Dir: Haraldur J Hamar
Subjects: Iceland (all aspects, series in English), Icelandic Literature in foreign translation
1985: 50 titles *Founded:* 1963

Icelandic Cultural Fund, Publishing Department, PO Box 1398, 101 Reykjavik (Located at: Menningargódur, Skalholtsstig 7) Tel: (01) 621822
Man Dir: Hrólfur Halldórsson
Parent Organization: Icelandic Cultural Ministry, Hverfisgata 6, 101 Reykjavik
Subjects: Icelandic History and Literature, also selected Classics in translation
Bookshop: Skalholsstig 7, 101 Reykjavik
Founded: 1928

Idunn, Braedraborgarstíg 16, PO Box 294, 121 Reykjavik Tel: (01) 28555 Cable Add: Publishers, Reykjavik Telex: 2308 publis is
Owner: Valdimar Jóhannsson; *Man Dir:* Jon Karlsson
Subsidiary Company: Hladbud (University Textbooks)
Subjects: General Fiction, Juveniles, Educational, Poetry, Law, Psychology, Philology, History, Natural Sciences, Philosophy, Management, Social Sciences, Art
Founded: 1945

Ísafoldarprentsmidja hf, Thingholtsstr 5, 101 Reykjavik Tel: (01) 17165

Hid **Íslenzka Bókmenntafélag**, Thingholtsstr 3, PO Box 1252, 121 Reykjavik Tel: (01) 21960
President: Sigurdur Líndal; *Chief Executive:* Sverrir Kristinsson
Subjects: History, Art History, Law, Linguistics, Literature, Philosophy, Politics, Psychology, Social Science, Natural Science
Founded: 1816

Snaebjörn **Jonsson** & Co hf (The English Bookshop)*, PO Box 1131, 101 Reykjavik (Located at: Hafnarstr 4) Tel: (01) 13133 Cable Add: Books Reykjavik
Man Dir: Benedikt Kristjánsson
Subjects: All Subjects
Bookshops: The English Bookshop (qv under Major Booksellers); Bókaverzlun Snaebjarnar, Hafnarstr 4, Reykjavik
Founded: 1927

Leiftur hf*, Höfdatúní 12, 105 Reykjavik Tel: (01) 17554

Bókagerdin **Lilja***, Amtmannsstíg 2b, 101 Reykjavik

Mál og menning+*, PO Box 392, 121 Reykjavik (Located at: Laugavegi 18, Reykjavik) Tel: (01) 15199
Man Dir: Arni Einarsson; *Editorial:* Halldor Gudmundsson, Silja Adalsteinsdottir
Subsidiary Company: Heimskringla (qv)
Book Clubs: Mál og menning, Uglan
Bookshop: Bókabúd Mals og menningar (qv under Major Booksellers)
Founded: 1937

Bókaútgáfa **Menningarsjóds** og **Pjódvinafélagsins**, Skálholtsstígur 7, 101 Reykjavik Tel: (01) 621822
Manager: Hrólfur Halldórsson

Námsgagnastofnun, PO Box 5192, 125 Reykjavik (Located at: Lawgavegur 166) Tel: (01) 28088 Cable Add: Edice Telex: 3000 Simtext Is-Edice
National Centre for Educational Materials
Dir: Ásgeir Gudmundsson; *Editorial:* Sigurdur Pálsson; *Production:* Bogi Indridason; *Rights & Permissions:* Eiríkur

Grímsson; *Publicity, Sales, Distribution:* Haukur Viggósson
Subjects: School Textbooks, Educational Materials
Bookshop: At above address
1985: 111 titles *1986:* 72 titles *Founded:* 1937

Bókaútgafan **Örn og Örlyguru** hf+, Sídumúli 11, 108 Reykjavik Tel: (01) 84866 Cable Add: Örn og Örlygur
Telex: 2197 Ornice
Owner and Man Dir: Örlygur Hálfdanarson
Subjects: General Fiction, Belles Lettres, Poetry, Biography, History, How-to, Dictionaries, Reference, Religion, Juveniles, Low- & High-priced Paperbacks, Social Science
Book Club: Bókaklúbbur Arnar og Örlygs (qv)
Founded: 1966

Ríkisútgáfa Námsbóka, see Námsgagnastofnun

Rökkur, bókaútgáfan*, Flókagötu 15, Reykjavik Tel: (01) 18768

Saga Publishing Co*, PO Box 93, 121 Reykjavik (Located at: Höfdabakki 9) Tel: (01) 84966 Telex: 2121
Man Dir: Haraldur J Hamar
Subjects: General (Adults and Juveniles)
Founded: 1971

Setberg*, Freyjugötu 14, PO Box 619, 121 Reykjavik Tel: (01) 17667 Cable Add: Setbergpublish
Subjects: History, Juveniles, General Non-fiction, Fiction, Illustrated Juvenile

Bókaútgáfan **Skjaldborg** sf*, Hafnarstr 67, 600 Akureyri Tel: (06) 11024

Skuggsjá bókaforlag, Strandgötu 31, 220 Hafnarfjördur Tel: (01) 50045
Subject: General Fiction

Bókaútgáfan **Snaefell***, Alfaskeidi 58, 220 Hafnarfirdi

Stofnun Árna Magnússonar á Íslandi, Árnagardi vid Sudurgötu, IS-101 Reykjavík Tel: (01) 25540
Man Dir, Editorial: Prof Jónas Kristjánsson; *Sales, Production:* Sigurgeir Steingrímsson
Subjects: Old Icelandic Literature and Icelandic Studies (to 1850)
1985: 1 title *Founded:* 1962

Bókaútgáfan **Sudri***, PO Box 1214, Kleppsvegi 2, 105 Reykjavik Tel: (01) 36384

Svart á hvítu*, Borgartún 29, 105 Reykjavik Tel: (01) 18860/22229
Man Dir, Editorial, Rights & Permissions: Björn Jónasson; *Sales, Production, Publicity:* Gudmundur Thorsteinsson
Subjects: General Fiction, Non-fiction
Book Club: Svart á hvítu Bókafélag
Founded: 1981

Bókaútgáfan **Thjódsaga***, Thingholtsstr 27, 101 Reykjavik Tel: (01) 13510
Subjects: Icelandic Folklore, General Fiction, Travel, General Science, Juveniles

Literary Agents

A/S **Bookman**, Fiolstr 12, DK-1171 Copenhagen K Tel: Copenhagen 145720 Cable Add: Bookman, Copenhagen Fax: 451 120007 (Denmark)
This Danish-based company handles rights in Iceland for foreign authors

Book Clubs

The **A B** Book Club (BAB), PO Box 9, 121 Reykjavik (Located at: Austurstr 18) Tel: (01) 25544
Members: 16,400
Owned by: Almenna Bókafélagid (qv)
Founded: 1974

Bókaklúbbur **Arnar og Örlygs**, Sídumúli 11, 108 Reykjavik Tel: (01) 83999 Telex: 2197
Man Dir: Örlygur Hálfdanarson
Owned by: Örn og Örlygur hf (qv)
Miscellaneous: Incorporates activities of former Hraundragni Club

B A B, see AB Book Club

Bókaklúbber **Fjolva***, Klapparstig 16, 101 Reykjavik Tel: (01) 26659
Owned by: Fjolvi (qv)

Heima er Bezt Book Club, PO Box 558, 602 Akureyri (Located at: Tryggvabraut 18-20)
Owned by: Bokaforlag Odds Björnssonar (qv)

Hraundragni Book Club, see Arnar og Örlygs

The **Icelandic Libertarians'** Book Club*, PO Box 1334, 121 Reykjavik (Located at: Haga v/Hofsvallagoetu, 107 Reykjavik) Tel: (01) 27866
Members: 395
Owned by: The Freedom Association (see also the Icelandic Libertarians' Bookshop, under Major Booksellers)
Specialization: Economics, History, Philosophy, Political Science, Libertarianism
Founded: 1979

The **M A B** Cookery Book Club, PO Box 9, 121 Reykjavik (Located at: Austurstr 18) Tel: (01) 25125
Members: 11,500
Owned by: Almenna Bókafélagid (qv)
Founded: 1984

Mal og menning*, Laugavegi 18, 121 Reykjavik Tel: (01) 15199
Owned by: Mal og menning, Publisher (qv)

Svart á hvítu Bókafélag*, Borgartún 29, 105 Reykjavik Tel: (01) 18860
Owned by: Svart á hvítu (qv)

Uglan*, Laugavegi 18, 121 Reykjavik Tel: (01) 15199
Paperback Book Club
Owned by: Mal og menning, Publisher (qv)

Particip **'Verold'***, Bradraborgarstig 7, 101 Reykjavik
Owned by: Fjolvi (qv)

Major Booksellers

The **English Bookshop***, PO Box 1131, Reykjavik (Located at: Hafnerstr 4) Tel: (01) 13133/14281 Cable Add: Books Reykjavik
Manager: Benedikt Kristjánsson
Owned by: Snaebjörn Jónsson & Co hf (qv)

Bókábudin **Helgafell***, Laugavegur 100, Reykjavik

The **Icelandic Libertarians'** Bookshop*, PO Box 1334, 121 Reykjavik (Located at: Haga v/Hofsvallagoetu, 107 Reykjavik) Tel: (01) 27866 Telex: 2231 toggur is Specializing in History, Politics, Economics, Philosophy, with special emphasis on the ideology of Libertarianism
Manager: Skafti Hardarson
Owned by: The Freedom Association (see also the Icelandic Libertarians' Book Club)

The **International Bookshop**, Bókaverzlun Sigfúsar Eymundssonar, Austurstr 18, Reykjavik Tel: (01) 19707/16997/32620

Bókaverzlun **Ísafoldar***, Austurstr 10, Reykjavik

Bókabúd **Máls og menningar***, Laugavegi 18, 101 Reykjavik Tel: (01) 24242 Telex: 2265 istrav att mm
Manager: Arni Einarsson
Importers and Exporters
Owned by: Mál og menning (qv)

Major Libraries

Borgarbókasafn Reykjavíkur*, Thingholtsstr 27 & 29A, 101 Reykjavik Tel: (01) 27155
City Library of Reykjavik
City Librarian: Thórdís Thorvaldsdóttir
Publication: Bókalisti

Háskólabókasafn, 101 Reykjavik Tel: (01) 694300 Telex: 2307 ísinfo
University Library
Head Librarian: Einar Sigurdsson
Publication: Annual Report

Landsbókasafn Íslands, Reykjavik Tel: (01) 13375 (Director)/16864 (Staff)
National Library of Iceland
Librarian: Dr Finnbogi Gudmundsson
Publications: Landsbókasafn Íslands, Arbók (Yearbook); Íslensk bókaskrá (Icelandic National Bibliography); Handritasafn Landsbókasafns (Catalogue of Manuscripts)

Thjodskjalasafn (National Archives)*, Safnahús, Reykjavik

University Library, see Háskólabókasafn

Library Associations

Bókavardafélag Islands, Box 7050, 127 Reykjavik
Icelandic Library Association
President: Thórdís Thorvaldsdóttir
Secretary: Asdís Egilsdóttir
Publications: Fregnir (Newsletter) and Bókasafnid (The Library)

Felag bokavarda i islenskum rannsoknarbokasofnum, Nattúrufraedistofnun Íslands, PO Box 5320, 125 Reykjavik Tel: (01) 29822
Society of Librarians in Icelandic Research Libraries
Executive Secretary Reference: Palína Hédinsdóttir

Library Reference Journal

Fregnir (Newsletter), Bókavardafélag Islands, Box 7050, 127 Reykjavik

Literary Associations and Societies

Hid Íslenzka bókmenntafélag, Thingholtsstr 3, PO Box 1252, 121 Reykjavik
Icelandic Literary Society
President: Sigurdur Lindal
Publication: Annual Journal, Skírnir (twice a year)

International **P E N** Centre, Hagamel 17, PO Box 7103, R-7 Reykjavik
President: Thor Vilhjálmsson; *Secretary:* Hrafn Gunnlaugsson

Literary Periodical

Skirnir, Hid Íslenszka bókmenntafélag, Thingholtsstr 3, PO Box 1252, 121 Reykjavik

India

General Information

Language: Hindi and English are used for official purposes. Fourteen other languages are accorded recognition by the constitution, including Sanskrit which is not now spoken. Generally each administrative state includes speakers of a particular major language. In all, over 1500 languages and dialects are spoken in India
Religion: Predominantly Hindu
Population: 684 million
Bank Hours: 1000-1400 (1100-1500 Bombay) Monday-Friday; 1000-1200 Saturday (1100-1300 Bombay)
Shop Hours: Delhi: 0930-1930; Calcutta and Bombay: 1000-1830; Madras: 0900-1930. All effective Monday-Saturday, some open Sunday. Many close 2 hours for lunch
Currency: 100 paise = 1 rupee
Export/Import Information: No tariff on books but advertising matter is dutied. Import licences required. Educational books may be imported by booksellers under open general licence. Exchange transactions restricted.
Copyright: UCC, Berne, Buenos Aires (see International section)

Book Trade Organizations

Ahmedabad Publishers' & Booksellers' Association*, 47 Gandhi Rd, Ahmedabad 380001 Tel: (0272) 366917
President: C J Modi

Akhil Bhartiya Hindi Prakashak Sangh*, A2/1 Krishan Nagar, Delhi 110051
President: Arvind Kumar; *General Secretary:* Mishrilal Sharma

All India Booksellers' & Publishers' Association*, 17-L Connaught Circus, PO Box 328, New Delhi 110001 Tel: (011) 42166
President: A N Varma

Assam Publishers' & Booksellers' Association, Lawyers Book Stall, Gauhati

Authors' Guild of India, F/12 Jangpura Extension, New Delhi 110014
Secretary General: Rajendra Awasthy
Publication: The Indian Author

Bihar Rajya Pustak Vyayasayee Sangh, PO Box 27, Patna 800004 (Located at: Tara Bhawan, Ashok Raj Path, Patna)
President: N K Singh; *General Secretary:* N K Jha

Bombay Booksellers' and Publishers' Association, 25 6th Floor Bldg No 3, Navjivan Co-op Housing Society Ltd, Dr Bhadkamkar Marg, Bombay 400008 Tel: (022) 398691
Executive Secretary: U S Manikeri;
Honorary Secretary: C P Gupta
Publication: BBPA News

Booksellers' and Publishers' Association of South India, PO Box 1056, Kilpauk, Madras 600010 Tel: (044) 664998

Capexil Book Division*, 8 Shaheed Bhagat Singh Marg, New Delhi 110001 Tel: (011) 310346 Cable Add: Capexil Telex: 0312237
A national agency to promote Indian books and publications abroad

Chandigarh Booksellers' Association*, SCO No 3 Sector 17-E, Chandigarh Tel: (0172) 23594
President: V S Puri

Delhi State Booksellers' and Publishers' Association, c/o The Students' Stores, Kashmere Gate, PO Box 1511, Delhi 110006 Tel: (011) 231867/2515726
President: Devendra Sharma; *Honorary Secretary:* Bhupinder Chowdhri

Educational Publishers' Association*, 2607 Amir Chand Marg, New Delhi 110006

Federation of Indian Publishers, Federation House, 18-I-C Institutional Area, JNU Rd, New Delhi 110067 Tel: (011) 654847
President: S K Sachdeva; *Honorary General Secretary:* S K Bhatia

Federation of Publishers and Booksellers Associations in India, 1st Floor, 4833/24 Govind Lane, Ansari Rd, New Delhi 110002 Tel: (011) 272845
President: Sunil Sachdev; *Honorary Secretary:* Devendra Sharma
Publications include: Recent Indian Books; FPBA Newsletter; Directory of Members; Book Industry in India Problems & Prospects (1980); Publishing as a Medium of Communication with the Third World by Tarzie Vittachie (UNICEF) (1982)

Gujarat State English Language Booksellers' Association, Academic Book Centre, 10 Walkeshwar, Ambawadi, Ahmedabad 380015 Tel: (0272) 837883
President: R N Shah

The **Gujarat Textbook** Publishers' Association*, Balgovind Kuberdas & Co, Gandhi Rd, Ahmedabad

Himachal Publishers' & Booksellers' Association*, Goel Book Depot, Palampur Tel: 43151
President: H K S Goel

Karnataka Publishers' and Booksellers' Association*, 504 Avenue Rd, Bangalore 560002

Kerala Publishers & Booksellers Association*, Paico Bldgs, Jew St, Ernakulam, Cochin 682031 Tel: (0484) 360068
President: D C Kizhakemuri, D C Books, Kottayam 686001 Tel: (0481) 3114/8214/3226; *Secretary:* S V Pai, Pai & Co, Paico Bldgs, Jew St, Ernakulam, Cochin 682031 Tel: (0484) 360068/367515/360412

Lanka Booksellers' Association*, Kohinoor Bldgs, University Rd, Varanasi Tel: (0542) 62771
President: Lalchand Mankhand

Meerut Publishers' Association*, c/o Rastogi Publications, Shivaji Rd, Meerut 250002, Uttar Pradesh

National Agency for ISBN*, Raja Rammohun Roy National Educational Resources Centre, Ministry of Human Resource Development, 1-W-3 Curzon Road Barracks, Kasturba Gandhi Marg, New Delhi 110001 Tel: (011) 381739/382549 Cable Add: Educind
ISBN Administrator: Vijai Govind (Chief Documentation Officer)

Poona Booksellers' & Publishers' Association*, Hindustan Sahitya, 309 Shaniwar Peth, Poona 30

Publishers' & Booksellers' Association of Andhra Pradesh*, Sree Venkateswara Book Depot, Main Rd, Guntur 522003
Secretary: P Narasimha Rao

Publishers' and Booksellers' Association of Bengal*, 93 Mahatma Gandhi Rd, Calcutta 700007
Publication: Granthajagat

Publishers' and Booksellers' Guild, PO Box 12341, Calcutta 700073 (Located at: 5-A Bhawani Dutta Lane, Calcutta) Tel: (033) 311541 Cable Add: Acabooks
President: Debajyoti Datta; *Honorary General Secretary:* Suprokash Basu
Publication: Calcutta Book Fair Directory (annual)

Publishers' Association of South India*, 1 Sunkurama Chetty St, Madras 600001 Tel: (044) 29402
President: T V S Mani

Rajasthan Pustak Vyavasayee Sangh*, SMS Highway, Jaipur 302003
President: R S Bhatt; *General Secretary:* H V Jain

Standard Book Numbering Agency, see National Agency for ISBN

Book Trade Reference Books and Journals

Books

American Book Trade in India, Asian Bookmarket Information Service, 73-47-255th St, Glen Oaks, New York 11004, USA
A directory of wholesale and retail booksellers

Bookdealers in India, Sheppard Press Ltd, PO Box 42, Russell Chambers, Covent Garden, London WC2E 8AX, UK
A directory of antiquarian booksellers in Bangladesh, Bhutan, India, Nepal, Pakistan and Sri Lanka

Directory of Book Trade in India, National Guide Books Syndicate, 5c-54 Rohtak Rd, New Delhi 110005

Directory of Foreign Book Trade in India, Lord International, 19 Netaji Subhash Marg, Daryaganj, New Delhi 110002

Indian Books, Indian Bibliographic Centre, 236 Kot Kishan Chand, Jullundur 4, Punjab
Annual directory of books in English

Indian Books, Researchco, 1865 Trinagar, Delhi 110035
Annual bibliography of books in English

Indian Books in Print, Indian Bibliographies Bureau, 2153/2 Fountain, Delhi 6

Indian Publishers' Directory, Mukherjee & Co Pvt Ltd, 2 Bankim Chatterjee St, Calcutta 700073

Journals

American and British Book News, Kunnuparampil P Punnoose, 6/77 WEA Karol Bagh, New Delhi 110005

Asian Literary Market Review, Kunnuparampil Bldgs, Kurichy 686549, Kottayam District, Kerala
English bi-monthly

BEPI, DKF Trust, 74-D Anandnagar, Delhi 110035
Annual bibliography of English publications in India

Book Review Supplement, Delhi Library Association, PO Box 1270, c/o Hardayal (Hardinge) Public Library, Queen's Garden, Delhi 110006

Book Reviews in Public Administration, Indian Institute of Public Administration, Indraprastha Estate, Ring Rd, New Delhi 110001

Current Bulletin, Current Books, PO Box 212, Kottayam 686001

Directory of Members, Federation of Publishers and Booksellers Associations in India, 1st Floor, 4833/24 Govind Lane, Ansari Rd, New Delhi 110002

FPBA Newsletter, Federation of Publishers and Booksellers Associations in India, 1st Floor, 4833/24 Govind Lane, Ansari Rd, New Delhi 110002

Granthajagat, Publishers' and Booksellers' Association of Bengal, 93 Mahatma Gandhi Rd, Calcutta 700007

Indian Book Chronicle, Vivek Trust, G-11 Hauz Khas Market, New Delhi 110016 Fortnightly book news and reviews

Indian Book Industry, Sterling Publishers Pvt Ltd, L-10 Green Park Extension, New Delhi 110016

Indian Books, Mukherjee Library, 1 Gopi Mohan Dutta Lane, Calcutta 700003 Information leaflet

Indian National Bibliography, Central Reference Library, c/o National Library, Belvedere, Calcutta 700027

Indian Publisher and Bookseller, Popular Book Depot, Dr Bhadkamkar Rd, Bombay 400007

Kerala Publisher, Kunnuparampil Bldgs, Kurichy 686549, Kottayam District, Kerala Bilingual bi-monthly

Paperbound Books (quarterly), 6/77 WEA Karol Bagh, New Delhi 110005

Publishing News, D K Agencies (P) Ltd, H-12 Bali Nagar, New Delhi 110015

Pustak Parichaya, 2/35 Ansari Rd, Daryaganj, Delhi 6
Text in Hindi

Recent Indian Books, Federation of Publishers and Booksellers Associations in India, 1st Floor, 4833/24 Govind Lane, Ansari Rd, New Delhi 110002

Publishers

A S Prakashan*, 37/2 New Prabhat Nagar, Quilla Parikshit Garh Rd, Meerut Tel: (0121) 75246 Cable Add: Publication
Man Dir, Sales Dir: K K Mittal; *Publicity, Advertising Dir:* A K Mittal
Subjects: Physics, Chemistry, Mathematics, General & Social Sciences, University Textbooks, Commerce, Management
Bookshop: At above address
Founded: 1955
Miscellaneous: Also remainder dealer (qv)

A U Press & Publications+*, Andhra University, Visakhapatnam 530003 Tel: (0891) 64871 ext 227
Registrar, Rights & Permissions: A U Waltair
Subjects: Languages, Literature, Humanities, Sciences
Founded: 1926

Aadiesh Book Depot, 7A-29 WEA Karol Bagh, New Delhi 110005 Tel: (011) 5724103/2915325
Chief Executive: Aadiesh Kumar Jain
Imprint: Nalanda Books
Subject: Dictionaries
Bookshop: 4123 Nai Sarak, Delhi 110006

Abhinav Publications*, E-37 Hauz Khas, New Delhi 110016
Dir: Shakti Malik
Subjects: Indian Art & Archaeology, Indology, Humanities, Literature, Social Sciences, Criminology, Politics
Founded: 1972

Abhishek Publications*, SCO 57-58-59, Sector 17-C, Chandigarh 160017
Chief Executive, Production, Publicity: S L M Prachand; *Editorial:* Mrs Geeta Mehndiratta; *Sales, Rights & Permissions:* Bharat Bhushan
Associate Company: Nirjhar Prakashan, 3625 Sector 23-D, Chandigarh 160023
Subjects: History, Politics, Philosophy, General
Founded: 1977

The **Academic Press**, Old Subzi Mandi, Gurgaon, Haryana 122001 Tel: 22005
Editorial: Satya Prakash; *Sales:* Kapil Jain; *Publicity:* Pankaj Jain; *Production, Rights & Permissions:* Sanjeev Jain
Subjects: Social Sciences, Humanities
Founded: 1968

Academic Publishers, PO Box 12341, Calcutta 700073 (Located at: 12/1A Bankim Chatterjee St, Calcutta) Tel: (033) 323547/324697 Cable Add: Acabooks
Man Dir: Bimal Kumar Dhur; *Sales Dir:* B L Dutta
Branch Off: Shantimohun House, I-1/16 Ansari Rd, New Delhi 110002 Cable Add: Bookworld
Subjects: Accountancy, Commerce, Management, Medicine, Research, University Textbooks
Founded: 1958

Academy of Comparative Philosophy & Religion+*, Guruder Mandir, Hindwadi, Belgaum 590011 Tel: (0831) 22231
Chief Executive, Production, Publicity: J V Parulekar; *Editorial:* P K Bhagoji; *Sales:* G V Dharwadkar
Subjects: Philosophy, Religion, Mysticism, Morals
Founded: 1967

Academy of Islamic Research & Publications*, PO Box 119, Lucknow 226007 (Located at: Nadwatul Ulama, Lucknow) Tel: (0522) 42948 Cable Add: Nadwi
President, Rights & Permissions: S Abdul Hasan Ali Nadwi; *Chief Executive, Editorial:* S Mohammad Rabey Nadwi; *Manager, Production:* Mohammad Ghiyathuddin Nadwi; *Sales:* Zakiuddin Nadwi; *Publicity:* S M Ghutran Nadwi
Branch Off: Karachi, Pakistan
Subjects: Islamic Literature, History, Current Affairs, Hadith and Quran
Founded: 1959

Directorate of **Adult** Education*, 34 Community Centre, Basant Lok, Vasant Vihar, New Delhi 110057 Tel: (011) 671890/674860 Cable Add: Adultedu
Chief Executive: Miss H K Singh
Subject: Adult Education
Founded: 1978

Advaita Ashrama, 5 Dehi Entally Rd, Calcutta 700014 Tel: (033) 290898 Cable Add: Vedanta
President, Editor: Swami Ananyananda; *Manager:* Swami Kamalananda
Subjects: Religion, Philosophy, Yoga, Vedanta, Indian Culture, Education
1985: 5 titles *1986:* 31 titles *Founded:* 1899

Affiliated East West Press Pvt Ltd*, 104 Nirmal Tower, 26 Barakhamba Rd, New Delhi 110001 Tel: (011) 44398 Cable Add: Bookmail
Man Dir: K S Padmanabhan; *Editorial Dir:* Kamal Malik
Subjects: Science, Engineering, Technology, Humanities, Social Sciences, Low-priced Reprintst of US and British Textbooks
Founded: 1962

Agam Kala Prakashan*, 34 Community Centre, Ashok Vihar, Delhi 110052 Tel: (011) 713395
Editorial, Sales, Publicity, Rights & Permissions: Agam Prasad; *Production:* A K Bhargava
Associate Company: Agam Prakashan
Subjects: Indian Art, Archaeology, Culture
Founded: 1977

Agricole Publishing Academy+, 208 Defence Colony Flyover, New Delhi 110024 Tel: (011) 692703/694825
Partners: Mrs L Jain, S C Jain; *Chief Development Officer:* T C Jain
Subjects: Agricultural Sciences, Technology, Engineering, Energy, Behavioural Sciences, Economics, Industry, Rural Development, Sociology
Bookshop: At above address
1985: 46 titles *1986:* 55 titles *Founded:* 1978

Ahlvwalia Book Depot, PO Box 2507, New Delhi 110005 (Located at: 9988 New Rohtak Rd, New Delhi)
Partners: J N Ahlvwalia, R K Ahlvwalia
Subject: Urdu Literature (Fiction and Non-fiction)
Founded: 1954

Ajanta Publications (India), 1 UB Jawahar Nagar, Delhi 110007 Tel: (011) 2926182
Chief Executive: K Jasbir
Orders to: Ajanta Books International (at above address)
Subjects: Indology, Indian Literature, Philosophy, Hinduism, Archaeology, Art, Religion, Management, Public Administration, Sociology, Political Science, Anthropology, Linguistics, English Language and Literature
Bookshop: Ajanta Books International (at above address)
1985: 50 titles *1986:* 50 titles *Founded:* 1975

Akhila Bharaliya Sanskrit Parishad*, Mahatma Gandhi Marg, Hazratganj, Lucknow 226001 Tel: (0522) 43962
Subjects: Sanskrit and Indology, based on Sanskrit, Pali and Psakrita
Founded: 1951

Alekh Prakashan*, V-8 Navin Shahdara, Delhi 110032 Tel: (011) 204331
Chief Executive: Umesh Chand
Subjects: Literature, Journalism, Linguistics (all in Hindi & English), General Science, Psychology, Social Science, Botany, Wildlife, Yoga
Founded: 1976

Allied Publishers Private Ltd*, 15 J N Heredia Marg, Ballard Estate, Bombay 400038 Tel: (022) 261959/261950 Cable Add: Folio Telex: 0112090 Appl In
Man Dir: R N Sachdev; *Editorial, Rights & Permissions:* Sunil Sachdev; *Sales Manager:* S Subramanyam; *Production:* Ravi Sachdev; *Publicity:* S Banerjee
Branch Offs: Prarthana Flats, opposite Thakor Baug, Navrangpura, Ahmedabad 380009; Jayadeva Hostel Bldg, 5th Main Rd, Gandhinagar, Bangalore 500009; 17 Chittaranjan Ave, Calcutta 700072; 3-5-1129 Kachiguda Cross Rd, Hyderabad

500027; 150 B-6 Mount Rd, Madras 600002; 13-14 Asaf Ali Rd, New Delhi 110002
Subjects: General Fiction, Belles Lettres, Art, History, Philosophy, Education, How-to, Psychology, Law, Social Science, Political Science, General Science, Technology
Founded: 1934

Amar Prakashan+, A1/139-B Lawrence Rd, Delhi 110035 Tel: (011) 7113182
Cable Add: Amarpra
Chief Executive: H S Juneja; *Editorial:* Surjeet Anand; *Sales:* Hardeep Singh; *Publicity:* Miss Sutinder Kaur; *Production:* Maheep Singh; *Rights & Permissions:* Miss Sukhwinder
Subjects: Sociology, History, Economics, Management, Political Science, Indology
1986: 10 titles *1987:* 12 titles *Founded:* 1977
ISBN Publisher's Prefix: 81-85061

Amarko Book Agency, E-79 Amar Colony, Lajpat Nagar, New Delhi 110024
Man Dir, Production, Publicity, Rights & Permissions: V N Bhardwaj
Subjects: History, Philosophy, Religion
Founded: 1973

Ambika Publications*, B-1/598 Janak Puri, New Delhi 110058 Tel: (011) 591072
Cable Add: Ambika
Man Dir, Editorial, Rights & Permissions: P P Anand; *Sales:* Ms Manmeet Maini; *Production:* Suhas Nimbalkar; *Publicity:* Ms Nirdosh Anand
Associate Companies: Arpan International (at above address); Tagore Trading Co, ED 54 Tagore Gardens, New Delhi 110027
Branch Off: The Mall, Solan 173212, Western Himalayas
Subjects: Sociology, Politics, Anthropology, Ancient and Mediaeval History, Art, Religion, Buddhism, Tibetan Studies, Management
Bookshop: Himachal Book House, Mayur Complex, The Mall, Solan 173212, Western Himalayas Tel: 736
Founded: 1977

Amerind Publishing Co (P) Ltd, subsidiary of Oxford & IBH Publishing Co Pvt Ltd (qv)

Amina Book Stall*, Post Office Rd, Trichur 680001 Tel: (0487) 23387/23254/25290
Chief Executive: Haji K B Aboobacker
Associate Company: Amina Printers (at above address)
Subjects: Humanities, Social Science, Fiction, Islamic Literature in Malayalam
Founded: 1948

Amudha Nilayam Ltd*, PO Box 674, Madras 600014 (Located at: 46 Royapettah High Rd, Madras) Tel: (044) 841343
Man Dir: K V Jagannathan
Subjects: Tamil Classics, Literature, Fiction, Criticism
Bookshop: At above address
Founded: 1949

Anand Paperbacks, an imprint of Orient Paperbacks (qv)

Ananda Ashram, see Satya Press

Ankur Publishing House, Uphaar Cinema Bldg, Green Park Extension, New Delhi 110016 Tel: (011) 664611
Man Dir: Mrs Seema Mukerjee
Associate Company: Sanjay Composers and Printers (at above address)
Subjects: Politics, Science, Literature
Founded: 1976

Antiquarian Book House*, 7 Malka Ganj, Delhi 110007 Tel: (011) 236080
Proprietor, Man Dir: Gajendra Singh
Parent Company: Bharatiya Publishing House (qv)
Subjects: Antiquarian, Indian History, Art, Architecture, Archaeology, Religion and Philosophy, Travel, Linguistics, Reference, Social Sciences
Founded: 1982

Archaeological Survey of India*, Janpath, New Delhi 110001 Tel: (011) 382121
Cable Add: Archaeology
Editorial: H Sarkar; *Sales:* S R Varma
Subjects: Archaeology, Epigraphy

Arnold Publishers (India) Pvt Ltd*, AB-9 Safdarjang Enclave, New Delhi 110029 Tel: (011) 670806 Cable Add: Heinemann
Man Dir: G A Vazirani; *Editorial, Rights & Permissions:* Ms Rashmi Bhushan; *Production:* Mukesh Vazirani; *Publicity:* Ms Rani Roy; *Sales:* R K Rana
Associate Company: Edward Arnold (Publishers) Ltd, UK (qv)
Imprints: Mayfair Paperbacks, Sanskriti, Zebra Books for Children
Subjects: Art, General Fiction, Belles Lettres, Poetry, Philosophy, Religion, Reference, Literary Criticism, Medicine, Engineering, Social Science, Political Science, University, Secondary & Primary Textbooks, Low-priced Paperbacks
Founded: 1969

Ashish Publishing House, 8-81 Punjabi Bagh, New Delhi 110026 Tel: (011) 500581/5410924
Editorial: S B Nangia; *Sales:* Gopal Sharma
Subjects: History, Political Science, Economics, Education, Biography, Public Administration, Sociology, Rural Development
ISBN Publisher's Prefix: 81-7024

Asia Publishing Co*, A-132 College St Market, Calcutta 700007 Tel: (033) 342386
Editorial: Gita Dutta; *Sales:* Ashim Mukherjee
Subject: Fiction
Founded: 1954

Asian Educational Services, PO Box 4534, New Delhi 110016 (Located at: C-2/15 SDA, New Delhi) Tel: (011) 660841
Cable Add: Asiabooks New Delhi
Publisher: Jagdish Jetley; *Chief Executive:* J N Kapoor; *Publicity, Rights & Permissions:* Mrs Saroj Jetley
Service Centres: 31 Hauzkhas Village Rd, New Delhi 110016 Tel: (011) 660187; PO Box 680, Madras 600014 (Located at: 5 Sripuram First St, Madras) Tel: (044) 845040 Cable Add: Asiabooks Madras
Subjects: South Indian and Sri Lankan Studies, Religion, Philosophy, History, Art, Archaeology, Literature, Indian Language Dictionaries and Grammars
1985: 50 titles *1986:* 43 titles *Founded:* 1973
ISBN Publisher's Prefix: 81-206

Asian Publishers, PO Box 205, Muzaffarnagar, Uttar Pradesh 251001 (Located at: 85-C New Mandi, Muzaffarnagar) Tel: 3775
Man Dir, Publicity: Mittal Ved Prakash; *Sales:* Mittal Satya Prakash; *Production:* Mittal Dinesh Kumar
Subsidiary Company: Kalanidhi Printing Press (at above address)
Subjects: Technical, Scientific, Agricultural
Bookshop: Mittal & Company (at above address)
Founded: 1971

Asian Trading Corporation+, PO Box 2587, Bangalore 560025 (Located at: St Thomas Bldg, 150 Brigade Rd, Bangalore) Tel: (0812) 51807 Cable Add: Paspin
Chief Executive: F M Pais; *Sales:* P Travers
Associate Company: Jyothi Book House, 156 Brigade Rd, Bangalore 560025
Subjects: Religion especially Catholicism, Theology, Philosophy, Counselling, Sociology, Psychology, Mass Media Communication, Indology
1985-86: 45 titles *Founded:* 1946
ISBN Publisher's Prefix: 81-7086
Miscellaneous: Also exporters, importers and booksellers

Associated Publishing House+, E-22 Preet Vihar, Vikas Marg, New Delhi 110092 Tel: (011) 5723069
Man Dir, Sales: Ravinder K Paul; *Editorial, Production Dir:* Ashok K Paul; *Publicity Dir, Rights & Permissions:* Sharda Paul
Subjects: General, Philosophy, Religion, Belles Lettres, Poetry, History, Art, Reference, Social Science, Business, Public Administration, Economics, Planning, Reprints
1985: 19 titles *1986:* 9 titles *Founded:* 1966
ISBN Publisher's Prefix: 81-7045

Atma Ram & Sons+*, PO Box 1429, Delhi 110006 (Located at: Kashmere Gate, Delhi) Tel: (011) 2523082/2518159 Cable Add: Books Delhi
Man Dir, Publicity, Rights & Permissions: Ish Kumar Puri; *Editorial, Production:* Sushil Kumar Puri; *Sales:* Ashutosh Pury
Branch Off: 17 Ashok Marg, Lucknow
Subjects: Belles Lettres, Art, History, Philosophy, Religion, Education, Reference, How-to, Juveniles, Medicine, Engineering, Social Science, Science & Technology, Paperbacks, Textbooks
Bookshop: See under Major Booksellers
Founded: 1909

Sri **Aurobindo** Books Distribution Agency (SABDA), Sri Aurobindo Ashram, Pondicherry 605002 Tel: (0413) 4980 Cable Add: Sabda Telex: 0469221 Sas In
Man Dir: B Poddar; *Sales:* Mrs Sunanda Poddar; *Rights & Permissions:* Sri Harikant Patel
Branch Off: 'Sahakar' B Rd, Bombay 400020
Subjects: Yoga, Philosophy, Religion, Education, History, Social & Political Science (English, French, German, Sanskrit)
Bookshops: 9B rue de la Marine; 2 rue de la Caserne (both in Pondicherry)
1985: 40 titles *1986:* 50 titles *Founded:* 1952
ISBN Publisher's Prefix: 81-7058

Avinash Reference Publications+, 14 Rukmini Nagar, Kolhapur 416005
Chief Editor: Dr J A Naik; *Manager:* Mrs Sunanda Naik
Associate Company: Dr Naik Co (at above address)
Subjects: Research Documents and Directories on Foreign Policy, Foreign Trade, International Defence, Indian Economics, Sociology and Agriculture
Founded: 1978
ISBN Publisher's Prefix: 81-85175

B I G Database Publishing Pvt Ltd, 36C Connaught Pl, New Delhi 110001 Tel: (011) 326717/352081
Man Dir, Publicity: Kapil Malhotra; *Editorial:* Arun Coyal; *Sales:* S Khanna; *Production:* K D Sharma
Associate Companies: Orient Paperbacks (qv); Vision Books Pvt Ltd (qv)
Subjects: Economic Reference
1985: 3 titles *1986:* 1 title *Founded:* 1984
ISBN Publisher's Prefix: 81-85166

B P B Publications+*, 376 Old Lajpat Rai Market, Delhi 110006 Tel: (011) 237147/231747/267741 Cable Add: Radiocraft
President: G C Jain
Branch Offs: 4-3-269 Giriraj Lane, Bank St, Hyderabad 500001; 8/1 Ritchie St, Mount Rd, Madras 600002
Subjects: Electronics and Computers (in English)
Bookshop: Radio & Craft Publications, 4794 Bharat Ram Rd, 23 Daryaganj, New Delhi 110002
Founded: 1958

B R Publishing Corporation*, 461 Vivekananda Nagar, Delhi 110035 Tel: (011) 278368 Cable Add: Deekay Pub
Chief Executive, Editorial, Production: I C Mittal; *Sales, Rights & Permissions:* S K Bhatia; *Publicity:* Praveen Mitaal
Orders to: D K Publishers' Distributors, 1 Ansari Rd, New Delhi 110002
Parent Company: D K Publishers' Distributors (qv under Major Booksellers)
Associate Companies: D K Publications (qv); Neeraj Publishing House (qv)
Subjects: Art, Archaeology, History, Social Sciences, Anthropology
Founded: 1974

K P Bagchi & Co+, 286 B B Ganguli St, Calcutta 700012 Tel: (033) 267474/269496
Editorial, Chief Executive, Publicity, Rights & Permissions: P K Bagchi; *Editorial, Sales, Production:* K K Bagchi
Branch Off: I-1698 C R Park, New Delhi 110019 Tel: (011) 6430068
Subjects: Anthropology, History, Economics, Political Science, Indology, Sociology, Language and Literature
Founded: 1972

Bahá'í Publishing Trust*, PO Box 19, New Delhi 110001 (Located at: Bahá'í House, 6 Canning Rd, New Delhi) Tel: (011) 389326/387004/389664 Cable Add: Bahaifaith Telex: 0314881 Nsa In
Man Dir, Production, Rights & Permissions: D Vahedi; *Editorial, Sales, Publicity:* N Sabet
Parent Company: National Spiritual Assembly of the Bahá'ís of India (at above address)
Subject: Bahá'í Religion
1985: 16 titles *Founded:* 1954

The **Bangalore** Printing & Publishing Co Ltd*, PO Box 1807, Bangalore 560018, Karnataka (Located at: 88 Mysore Rd, Bangalore) Tel: (0812) 601638/601027 Cable Add: Mudrashala
Man Dir: H C Ramanna
Branch Off: The Bangalore Press, Statue Sq, Mysore
Subjects: Biography, Philosophy, Religion, Psychology, Social Science, University, Secondary & Primary Textbooks, Agriculture, Nutrition, Fiction (in English and Kannada languages)
Bookshop: Bangalore Press Agencies, Avenue Rd, Bangalore 2
Founded: 1916

Bani Mandir, New Market, Dibrugarh, Assam 786001 Tel: 21255 Cable Add: Bani Mandir
Chief Executive: Chandra Kanta Hazarika; *Editorial, Rights & Permissions:* Surjya Kanta Hazarika; *Sales:* Ujjal Kumar Hazarika; *Publicity:* Utpal Kumar Hazarika
Subjects: Fiction, Criticism, School and College Textbooks, Reference Books
Founded: 1949

Bani Publications*, 30 Pataldanga St, Calcutta 700009 Tel: (033) 352901
Chief Executive: Sakti Sadan Bhattacharyya; *Editorial:* Sivasadhan Bhattacharyya; *Sales:* S R Mukherjee
Subject: Oriental & Indological Studies

Bansal & Co*, K-16 Naveen Shahdara, Delhi 110032 Tel: (011) 204292
Chief Executive: R S Bansal; *Editorial, Sales, Production, Publicity, Rights & Permissions:* Arun Bansal
Subjects: Bibliography, Indology, Hindi Literature in English (Series of 15 volumes, *Contours and Landmarks in Hindi Literature*)
Founded: 1959

Better Yourself Books*, 28-B Chatham Lines, Allahabad 211002, Uttar Pradesh Tel: (0532) 53728
Man Dir: Fr Abraham Nedumpuram; *Publicity:* Arnold K
Parent Company: Saint Paul Publications (qv)
Subjects: Home Life, Self-improvement, Biography, Moral Science, Indology, Fiction, Practical Psychology, Sex Education, Media Education
Founded: 1954

Bhaimi Prakashan*, 537 Lajpat Rai Market, Delhi 110006 Tel: (011) 269032
Editorial: P K Bhatia; *Sales:* Bhimsen Shastri
Subject: Sanskrit Language and Literature

Bhaktivedanta Book Trust*, Hare Krishna Land, Juhu, Bombay 400049 Tel: (022) 626860 Cable Add: Iskcon
Chief Executive: Bhima Das; *Editorial:* Nivas Acarya Das
Subject: Vedic Culture

Bharat-Bharati*, B-28-15 Durgakund, Varanasi 5
Owner: Suresh Pandey; *Man Dir:* Ganga Nath Pandey
Subjects: Poetry, History, Music, Art, Philosophy, Religion, Oriental & Indian Studies
Founded: 1968

Bharat Law House*, J-10/13 Rajouri Garden, New Delhi 110027 Tel: (011) 5438066
Chief Executive, Production: D C Puliani; *Sales:* Ashok Puliani; *Editorial:* Ravi Puliani; *Publicity:* Mahesh Puliani
Associate Company: Bharat Publishing House (at above address)
Branch Off: 15 Mahatma Gandi Marg, Allahabad 211001
Subject: Law
1985: 12 titles *Founded:* 1957

Bharati Sahitya Sadan Sales*, 30-90 Connaught Circus, New Delhi 110001 Tel: (011) 343557
Editorial: Padmesh Datt; *Sales:* Yogendra Datt
Subject: Hindi Literature
Founded: 1946

Bharatiya Jnanpith, see Jnanpith

Bharatiya Publishing House*, 42-43 UB Jawaharnagar, Delhi 110007 Tel: (011) 236080/220274
Chief Executive, Production, Publicity: Gajendra Singh; *Sales:* Digvijay Singh
Subsidiary Company: Antiquarian Book House (qv)
Branch Off: B-9/45 Pilkhana, Sonarpura, Varanasi
Subjects: Ancient Indian History, Art, Architecture, Archaeology, Religion, Philosophy, Jainism, Yoga, Sanskrit
Founded: 1960

Bharatiya Vidya Bhavan, Kulapati KM Munshi Marg, Bombay 400007 Tel: (022) 8118261/4 Cable Add: Bhavidya Bombay Girgaon
Executive Secretary, Editorial, Rights & Permissions: S Ramakrishnan
Branch Offs: Ahmedabad, Bangalore, Baroda, Belgaum, Bharwari, Bharuch, Bhatpara, Bhimavaram, Bhopal, Bhubaneswar, Calcutta, Calicut, Cannanore, Chandigarh, Coimbatore, Dakor, Delhi, Ernakulam, Guntur, Hyderabad, Jaipur, Jammu, Jamnagar, Jodhpur, Kakinada, Kannyakumari, Kanpur, Kodaikanal, Kurkunta, Lucknow, Madras, Mangalore, Mukundgarh, Nagpur, New Delhi, Palghat, Patna, Pune, Ramachandrapuram, Ratangarh, Renukoot, Rourkela, Serampur, Tadapalligudam, Trichur, Trivandrum, Varanasi, Visakhapatnam (all in India); 4a Castle Town Rd, London W14 9HQ, UK Tel: (01) 381 3086/381 4608; 79 Milk St, Boston, MA 02109, USA Tel: (617) 4264525; 65-09 Queens Blvd, Woodside, NY 11377, USA Tel: (212) 4247878/7793613
Subjects: History, Philosophy, Religion, Art, Literature, Culture, Biography, Gita, Vedas, Upanishads, Sanskrit Studies, Gandhiana, Mythology, Fiction, Sociology, Periodicals (in English, Hindi, Gujarati, Sanskrit)
Founded: 1938

Bihar Hindi Granth Akademi*, Premchand Marg, Rajendra Nagar, Patna 800016 Tel: (0612) 51432
Chairman: Lokesh Nath Jha; *Dir, Rights & Permissions:* Dr B N Thakur; *Editorial:* Yoganand Jha; *Sales, Production, Publicity:* Ramchandra Singh
Subjects: Science and Humanities at University level (in Hindi)
Founded: 1970

The **Bihar State** Textbook Publishing Corporation Ltd*, Budh Marg, Patna 800001 Tel: (0612) 21975
Chief Executive: D P Chaudhary; *Editorial:* D N Jha; *Production:* Devabrat Sarkar
Subject: Academic
Founded: 1966

Book Field Centre, an imprint of Era Book Enterprises (qv)

Book Mark*, 6 Bankim Chatterjee St, Calcutta 700073
Chief Executive: Pradip Bose
Subject: Literature
Founded: 1974

Booklinks Corporation, 3-4-423/5 & 6 Narayanaguda, Hyderabad 500029 Tel: (0842) 65021/62282/65550 Cable Add: Booklinks
Chief Executive, Editorial: K B Satyanarayana; *Sales, Production, Publicity:* K Ramakrishna
Subject: Social Sciences
Bookshop: At above address
Founded: 1965

Bookventure*, 14 Thaninabhalam Chetty Rd, Madras 600017 Tel: (044) 441970
Proprietor: Lakshmi Krushnamurti
Subjects: General Fiction, Belles Lettres, Poetry, Biography, History, Music, Art, Philosophy, General Science
Founded: 1965

Bright Careers Institute, 1525 Nai Sarak, Delhi 110006 Tel: (011) 269227/268661/276554 Telex: ND 03162887
Chief Executive, Sales: P S Bright; *Editorial:* D Sarna; *Production, Publicity:* T S Banga
Associate Company: C R Competition Refresher (Private) Ltd (at above address)
Branch Offs: 1747-A Sector 23-B, Chandigarh; Adda Tanda, Jullundur
Subjects: General Knowledge, English Language, Essays, Competition Books, History, Science, Mathematics, Management, Business, Humour,

Periodicals
Founded: 1968

Business Information Group, see BIG Database Publishing Pvt Ltd

Capital Book House*, 26 U B Jawahar Nagar, Delhi 110007 Tel: (011) 220226
Chief Executive: R S Verma; *Editorial:* S Verma; *Sales:* Ajay Dev; *Production:* Rajiv
Subjects: Economics, History, Commerce
Founded: 1964

Central Book Depot (Publishers)*, 44 Johnstonganj, Allahabad Tel: (0532) 2408/2130/53727
Man Dirs: K L Bhargava, M L Bhargava; *Sales Dir:* H S Banerji
Subsidiary Company: Indian University Press, 18-C Queens Rd, Allahabad
Branch Off: 13 University Rd, Allahabad
Subjects: History, Philosophy, Medicine, Psychology, Engineering, General & Social Science, University & Secondary Textbooks
Founded: 1880

Central Hindi Directorate*, Ministry of Education, Government of India, West Block VII, RK Puram, New Delhi 110066 Tel: (011) 699511 Cable Add: Rajbhasha
Dir: Dr R C Rangra; *Deputy Dir (Publishing):* R M Jain; *Sales:* Dr B L Srivastava
Subjects: Scientific and Technical, Dictionaries and Reference in Hindi
Founded: 1960

Central Institute of Indian Languages*, Manasagangotri, Mysore 570006 Tel: (0821) 23820/23558 Cable Add: Bharati
Chief Executive: D P Pattanayak
Subjects: Linguistics, Language Teaching
Founded: 1969

Central Tibetan Secretariat, Information Office of His Holiness The Dalai Lama, Gangchen Kyishong, Dharamsala 176215, Himachal Pradesh Tel: 2457
General Secretary: Sonam Topgyal; *Sales Manager:* Pasang Tsering; *Production, Publicity, Rights & Permissions:* Lodi G Gyari
Subsidiary Companies: Sheja Press, McLeod Ganj, Dharamsala Cantt, Himachal Pradesh; Tibetan Bulletin (at above address); Tibetan Freedom Press, Toon Soong, Tenzin Norgay Rd, Darjeeling, West Bengal
Subjects: Tibetan History, Religion, Culture, Current Events
Founded: 1961

Chanakya Publications+, F10/14 Model Town, Delhi 110009 Tel: (011) 7111976 Cable Add: Chanakya
Man Dir: Akhileshwar Jha; *Sales:* C K Jha; *Production:* S Jha, R P Maurya; *Editorial, Publicity, Rights & Permissions:* R Jha
Subjects: Indian Studies, Humanities, Social Sciences (especially relating to modern India), Indian Literature (in English)
1985: 11 titles *1986:* 12 titles *Founded:* 1980
ISBN Publisher's Prefix: 81-7001

S Chand & Co Ltd+, PO Box 5733, New Delhi 110055 (Located at: Ravindra Mansion, Ram Nagar, New Delhi) Tel: (011) 772080 Cable Add: Eschand, New Delhi Telex: 0312185
Man Dir: S L Gupta; *Editorial, Publicity:* Ms Shashi Kanta; *Sales:* R K Seth; *Exports:* P S Bhatti; *Rights & Permissions:* R K Gupta
Subsidiary Company: Eurasia Publishing House Pvt Ltd (qv)
Associate Companies: Blackie & Son (Calcutta) Pvt Ltd; Rajendra Ravindra Printers Pvt Ltd, New Delhi; Shyamlal Charitable Trust (Publications), New Delhi
Branch Offs: Bangalore, Bombay, Calcutta, Cochin, Guwahati, Hyderabad, Jalandhar, Lucknow, Madras, Nagpur, Patna
Subjects: Arts, Philosophy, Economics, Commerce, Social & Political Science, Science and Technology, Medicine, English and Hindi Literature
Bookshop: 4/16-B Asaf Ali Rd, New Delhi 110002
Founded: 1917
ISBN Publisher's Prefix: 81-219

Charotar Publishing House*, opposite Amul Dairy, Civil Court Rd, Anand 388001 Tel: 3582
Chief Executive, Editorial, Production, Publicity, Rights & Permissions: Ramanbhai C Patel; *Sales:* Bhavin R Patel
Subsidiary Company: Charotar Books Distributors (at above address)
Branch Offs: nr Post Office, Vallabh Vidyanagar, Via Anand; Amul Dairy Rd, Anand
Subject: Engineering Textbooks
Founded: 1944

Chaukhambha Orientalia, PO Box 1032, Varanasi 221001 (UP) (Located at: Gokul Bhawan K-37/109, Gopal Mandir Lane, Varanasi) Tel: (0542) 63354/65889 Cable Add: Gokulotsav
Managing Partner: Braj Bhavan Das Gupta
Branch Off: Bungalow Rd, 9 U B Jawahar Nagar, Delhi 110007
Subjects: Indian Classical Literature, Oriental Art, Science, Ayurved (Indian Medicine) (in Sanskrit, Hindi, English)
Founded: 1974

Chetana Pvt Ltd*, 34 Rampart Row, Bombay 400023 Tel: (022) 244968 Cable Add: Indology
Man Dir: Sudhakar S Dikshit; *Publicity:* K T Vaidya
Subjects: Philosophy, Religion
Founded: 1946

Children Book House*, PO Box 3854, New Delhi 110049 (Located at: A-4 Ring Rd, NDSE 1, New Delhi) Tel: (011) 692003 Cable Add: Bookheaven
Sales: Rakesh Gupta; *Production:* R S Gupta
Subject: Children's Books

Children's Book Trust, Nehru House, 4 Bahadur Shah Zafar Marg, New Delhi 110002 Tel: (011) 3316970 Cable Add: Childtrust
Chief Executive: K Shankar Pillai; *General Manager, Rights & Permissions:* Ravi Shankar; *Editorial:* C G R Kurup; *Sales, Publicity:* H R Khurana
Subjects: Children's Books
Founded: 1957
ISBN Publisher's Prefix: 81-7011

Chowkhamba Sanskrit Series Office, PO Box 1008, Varanasi 221001 (UP) (Located at: K-37/99 Gopal Mandir Lane, Varanasi) Tel: (0542) 63145 Cable Add: Chowkhamba Series, Varanasi
Man Dir, Publicity, Rights & Permissions: Bithal Das Gupta; *Editorial:* Pandit Ramchandra Jha; *Sales, Production:* Brij Mohan Das Gupta
Associate Company: Krishnadas Academy, PO Box 1118, K-37/118 Gopal Mandir Lane, Varanasi 221001
Subjects: Juveniles, Educational Materials, Primary, Secondary & University Textbooks, Poetry, Biography, History, Music, Art, Philosophy, Reference, Religion, Oriental, Indology
Bookshops: At above address; Chowk, Chitra Cinema Bldg, Varanasi 221001
Founded: 1892

The **Christian** Literature Society*, PO Box 501, Park Town, Madras 600003 Tel: (044) 39296/7 Cable Add: Vedic
General Secretary, Editorial, Rights & Permissions: Dr T Dayanandan Francis
Branch Off: The Diocesan Press, PO Box 455, Madras 600007
Subjects: Religion, Textbooks, General, Children's Books
Bookshops: CLS in Bangalore, Cochin, Coimbatore, Hyderabad, Madras, Madurai, Tiruvalla, Trivandrum
Founded: 1857

Chugh Publications*, PO Box 101, Allahabad (Located at: 2 Strachey Rd, Allahabad) Tel: (0532) 3177
Chief Executive, Production, Publicity, Rights & Permissions: Ramesh Chugh; *Sales:* Suman Chugh
Associate Company: R S Publishing House, 20 Mahatma Gandhi Marg, Allahabad
Subjects: Humanities, Social Sciences
Bookshop: Universal Book Shop (qv under Major Booksellers)
Founded: 1975

Classical Publishing Co, 28 Shopping Centre, Karampura, New Delhi 110015 Tel: (011) 5723689
Man Dir, Editorial: Bal Krishan Taneja; *Marketing:* Miss Suman Sharma; *Production:* Nirmal Rani; *Publicity:* R P Singh
Subjects: Social Sciences
1985: 23 titles *1986:* 24 titles *Founded:* 1976
ISBN Publisher's Prefix: 81-7074

College Book House+*, PO Box 103, Trivandrum 695001 (Located at: Industrial Estate, Pappanamcode, Trivandrum) Tel: (0471) 2214
Man Dir, Editorial, Production, Rights & Permissions: M Easwaran; *Sales:* M Girija; *Publicity:* M Easwaran
Subjects: Indian Studies, Religion, Philosophy, Education, Economics, Sociology, History, Kerala (South India)
Bookshop: College Book House, Library Division (at above address)
Founded: 1973

Concept Publishing Co*, H-13 Bali Nagar, New Delhi 110015 Tel: (011) 503967
Chief Executive: Naurang Rai; *Editorial:* Anees Chishti; *Sales, Publicity:* Ashok Kumar
Parent Company: D K Agencies (P) Ltd (qv under Major Booksellers)
Subjects: Indology, Anthropology, Art, Sociology, Philosophy, Economics, Public Administration, Geography, Bibliography, History, Political Science, Management, Agricultural Sciences
1985: approx 60 titles *Founded:* 1975

Crescent Publishing Co*, 2035 Qasimjan St, Ballimaran, Delhi 110006 Tel: (011) 262545/262521/273946 Cable Add: Newerabuks Telex: 03161988 Hpit In
Man Dir, Publicity, Rights & Permissions: Mohammad Khalid; *Editorial:* Dr S Q R Ilyas; *Sales:* Mohammad Suhaib Abbasi
Subjects: Islam, Academic
Founded: 1976

Current Books*, PO Box 212, Kottayam 686001 (Located at: VIII/493 Railway Station Rd, Kottayam) Tel: (0481) 3114/3226/5018 Cable Add: Current Books
Chief Executive: D C Kizhakemuri; *Editorial:* M S Chandrasekhara Warrier; *Sales:* P K Jayapalan; *Production, Publicity:* V R Radhakrishnan Nair; *Rights & Permissions:* Ponnamma Deecee
Associate Companies: D C Books (qv); Kairali Children's Book Trust (qv); Kairali Mudralayam (qv)

Branch Offs and Bookshops: Alleppey Tel: (0477) 4197; Ernakulam Tel: (0484) 351590; Kottayam Tel: (0481) 5342; Kozhikode Tel: (0495) 76362; Tellicherry Tel: 668; Trichur Tel: (0487) 20660; Trivandrum Tel: (0471) 77693
Subjects: Fiction, Non-fiction
Founded: 1952

D C Books+*, PO Box 214, Kottayam 686001 (Located at: Good Shepherd St, Kottayam) Tel: (0481) 3114/3226/8214 Cable Add: Deecibooks
Chief Executive, Rights & Permissions: D C Kizhakemuri; *Editorial:* M S Chandrasekhara Warrier; *Sales:* T K Murukesan; *Production, Publicity:* D Sreekumar
Associate Companies: Current Books (qv); Kairali Children's Book Trust (qv); Kairali Mudralayam (qv)
Subjects: Fiction, Poetry, Literature, Children's Books, Reference Books
Book Clubs: Classics Club, D C Book Club
Founded: 1974

D C Press, an imprint of Kairali Children's Book Trust (qv)

D K Publications*, 29/10 Shakti Nagar, Delhi 110007 Tel: (011) 710169 Cable Add: Deekaypub
Proprietor, Publicity: Praveen Mittal; *Editorial, Production:* I C Mittal; *Sales, Rights & Permissions:* S K Bhatia
Associate Companies: BR Publishing Corporation (qv); D K Publishers' Distributors (qv under Major Booksellers); Neeraj Publishing House (qv)
Branch Off: T C 789 Devivilas Compound, Chenthittal, Trivandrum 23
Subjects: Humanities and Social Sciences
Founded: 1974

D K F Trust*, 74-D Anandnagar, Delhi 110035 Tel: (011) 504418 Cable Add: Dikaybook
Chief Executive: Sh Khazan Chand; *Editorial, Sales, Production, Publicity, Rights & Permissions:* Naurang Rai
Subject: Directories
Founded: 1977

Darsan Books Private Ltd*, VJT Hall Rd, Palayam, Trivandrum 695034, Kerala State Tel: (04826) 470 Cable Add: Darsanbooks
Man Dir, Production: Sebastian Mathew; *Editorial:* Kunnuparambil P Punnoose; *Sales:* Dominic Mathew, Sebastian Mathew; *Publicity:* Dominic Mathew; *Rights & Permissions:* Kunnuparambil P Punnoose, Sebastian Mathew
Subjects: Humanities, Social Science, Fiction, Religion, Science, Technology
Book Club: Darsan International Bestsellers Book Club
Bookshop: Darsan Bookshop (at above address)
Founded: 1983
Miscellaneous: Also remainder dealer (qv)

Dastane Ramchandra & Co+, 830 Sadashiv Peth, Chitrashala Chowk, Poona 411030 Tel: (0212) 448193/54681
Man Dir: R D Dastane; *Editorial, Production:* S R Dastane; *Sales, Publicity, Rights & Permissions:* Vishwas Dastane
Associate Company: Abhang Stores, Printers & Stationers (at above address)
Subjects: Chemistry, Geology, Geography, Botany, Sociology, Economics, Literature, Archaeology
Bookshop: 456 Raviwar Peth, Poona 411002
Founded: 1960
ISBN Publisher's Prefix: 81-85080

Daystar Publications*, B-2/48A Lawrence Rd, Keshavpuram, New Delhi 110035 Tel: (011) 7113017
Chief Executive: Mrs Indu Lekha; *Editorial, Sales, Production, Publicity, Rights & Permissions:* Dr G R Garg, Dr V P Garg
Subject: Book Trade
Bookshop: See under Major Booksellers
Founded: 1978

Deep & Deep Publications*, D-1/24 Rajouri Garden, New Delhi 110027 Tel: (011) 504498
Chief Executive, Rights & Permissions: K D Singh; *General Manager, Sales, Publicity:* G D Singh; *Editorial:* H S Bhatia; *Production:* G S Bhatia
Subjects: Politics, Military Affairs, Law
Founded: 1974
Miscellaneous: Also booksellers and exporters

Dev Sahitya Kutir (P) Ltd+*, 21 Jhamapukur Lane, Calcutta 700009 Tel: (033) 354294/5
Editorial: A C Mazumdar; *Sales:* Barun Chandra Mazumdar; *Production:* P K Mazumdar
Subject: Children's Books

Dhanpat Rai & Sons*, 1683 Nai Sarak, Delhi 110006 Tel: (011) 265367
Partners: O P Kapur, J C Kapur, K K Kapur
Branch Offs: Delhi, Jullundur
Subjects: Engineering, Education, Commerce
Founded: 1929

Diamond Comics (P) Ltd*, 2715 Daryaganj, New Delhi 110002 Tel: (011) 266317/273493
Man Dir: Narender Kumar Verma; *Editorial:* Gulshan Rai Verma
Associate Companies: Diamond Books International, Diamond Pocket Books (both at above address); Punjabi Pustak Bhandar (qv)
Subject: Juveniles (in Hindi and English)

Dini Book Depot*, 4160 Urdu Bazar, Jamamasjid, Delhi 110006 Tel: (011) 268632/274855 Cable Add: Dini Book
Managing Partner, Sales, Production: Arshad Saeed; *Editorial:* Rashid Saeed; *Publicity:* Shahid Saeed
Subsidiary Company: Saeed International (Regd), 2112 Nahar Khan St, Daryaganj, New Delhi 2
Subjects: Islamic Studies, Textbooks
Founded: 1945
Miscellaneous: Also importers, exporters and suppliers

Disha Publications, 3/5 Model Town, Delhi 110009
Man Dir, Publicity: B R Chawla
Parent Company: Heritage Publishers (qv)
Associate Companies: Intellectuals' Rendezvous, Aggarwal Bhawan, 4C Ansari Rd, New Delhi 110002; Pankaj Publications International (qv)
Subjects: Biography, History, Bibliography, Literature, Reference, Religion, Economics, Language, Social Science, Philosophy
Founded: 1973

Doaba House*, 1688 Nai Sarak, Delhi 110006 Tel: (011) 274669
Chief Executive, Editorial, Sales, Rights & Permissions: S N Malhotra; *Production, Publicity:* A C Seth
Bookshop: At above address
Subjects: Literary Criticism, Books and Periodical (in English)
Founded: 1924

E B C Publishing Pvt Ltd, 348 Lalbagh, Lucknow 226001 Tel: (0522) 44328 Cable Add: Lawbook
Chief Executive, Rights & Permissions: P L Malik; *Publishing Dir:* Surendra Malik; *Sales, Marketing and Publicity Dir:* Vijay Malik; *Production Dir:* K K Malik
Associate Company: Eastern Book Co (qv)
Subject: Law

Eastern Book Co+, 34 Lalbagh, Lucknow 226001 Tel: (0522) 43171/44328/46517 Cable Add: Lawbook Telex: 535436 Fast In attn EBC
Chief Executive: C L Malik; *Editorial:* Surendra Malik; *Sales, Rights & Permissions:* P L Malik; *Production:* Kamal Malik; *Publicity, Exports:* Vijay Malik
Associate Companies: EBC Publishing Pvt Ltd (qv); Law Times Press, 56-C Singarnagar, Lucknow 226005; Manav Law House, 2-A Strachey Rd, Civil Lines, Allahabad; Eastern Book Co (Sales), Kashmere Gate, Delhi 110006; Eastern Book Publishing Co, 34-A Lalbagh, Lucknow 226001
Subject: Law
1985: 133 titles *1986:* 146 titles *Founded:* 1947
ISBN Publisher's Prefix: 81-7012

Eastern Law House Pvt Ltd+, 54 Ganesh Chunder Ave, Calcutta 700013 Tel: (033) 274989/272301 Cable Add: Lauriports, Calcutta
Man Dir, Editorial, Production, Publicity, Rights & Permissions: Asok De
Branch Off: 36 Netaji Subhas Marg, Daryaganj, New Delhi 110002
Subjects: Law, Accounting, Political & Social Science
Bookshops: 54 Ganesh Chunder Ave, Calcutta 700013; 36 Netaji Subhas Marg, Daryaganj, New Delhi 110002
Founded: 1918

Educational Enterprises*, 5/1 Ramnath Mazumdar St, Calcutta 700009 Tel: (033) 340101/424880
Chief Executive: S Ghosh; *Editorial:* Dr Arun Ghosh
Subjects: Education, Psychology

Era Book Enterprises*, 14 Mohan Nivas, Chandavarkar Rd, Bombay 400019 Tel: (022) 8828293 Cable Add: Goldenhill
Chief Executive, Rights & Permissions: Eranna R Jinde; *Editorial:* C V Bhimasankaram; *Sales:* V R Jinde; *Production:* B Ramakumar; *Publicity:* J E Rao
Subsidiary Company: Book Field Centre, 316/3 Sir Balchandra Rd, Bombay 400019
Imprint: Book Field Centre
Branch Off: 2/30 Khariboudi St, Adoni 518301
Subjects: Mathematics, Education
Founded: 1979

Ess Ess Publications, 4837/24 Daryaganj, Ansari Rd, New Delhi 110002 Tel: (011) 260807 Cable Add: Ess Ess Publications
Man Dir, Publicity, Rights & Permissions: Mrs Sheel Sethi; *Editorial, Sales, Production:* S K Sethi
Orders to: Ess Ess Publishers' Distributors, KD-6A Ashok Vihar, Delhi 110052 Tel: (011) 7117308
Parent Company: Ess Ess Publishers' Distributors, KD-6A Ashok Vihar, Delhi 110052 Tel: (011) 7117308
Subsidiary Company: Sumit Publications, KD-6A Ashok Vihar, Delhi 110052 Tel: (011) 7117308
Subjects: Humanities, Social Sciences, Library and Information Science
1985: 15 titles *1986:* 16 titles *Founded:* 1974
ISBN Publisher's Prefix: 81-7000

Eurasia Publishing House Pvt Ltd*, Ravindra Mansion, Ram Nagar, New Delhi 110055 Tel: (011) 772080/528684 Cable Add: Eschand Telex: 0312185
Man Dir: S L Gupta; *Editorial, Publicity:* R C Kumar; *Sales Dir, Rights & Permissions:* R K Gupta
Parent Company: S Chand & Co Ltd (qv)
Subjects: Low-priced reprints of American educational books, Psychology, Engineering, General & Social Sciences, University Textbooks
Founded: 1960

Firma KLM Private Ltd (Incorporating Firma KL Mukhopadhyay)*, 257B BB Ganguly St, Calcutta 700012 Tel: (033) 274391 Cable Add: Indology (Calcutta)
Man Dir, Rights & Permissions: K L Mukhopadhyay; *Editorial, Production:* S P Ghosh; *Sales, Publicity:* R N Mukherji
Associate Company: Firma Mukhopadhyay, 2/1 Dr Aksay Pal Rd, Calcutta 700034
Subjects: Humanities, Social Sciences
Founded: 1950

Frank Brothers & Co (Publishers) Pvt Ltd, 4675-A Ansari Rd, 21 Daryaganj, New Delhi 110002 Tel: (011) 263393/279936 Telex: 0313265 Fran In
Man Dir: Suresh C Govil
Bookshop: IV/85 Chandni Chowk, Delhi 110006 Tel: (011) 276791/268884

G D K Publications*, 3623 Chawri Bazar, Delhi 110006 Tel: (011) 266901/2 Cable Add: Gursons Delhi
Chief Executive: D P Chopra
Subjects: Indology, Social Sciences, History, Philosophy, Politics
Founded: 1978

Galgotia Booksource, PO Box 688, New Delhi 110001 (Located at: 17-B Connaught Place, New Delhi) Tel: (011) 321844 Telex: 312879 Star In
Publisher: Neeraj Galgotia; *Editorial:* S Rajan
Bookshop: E D Galgotia & Sons (qv under Major Booksellers)
1986: 35 titles *1987:* 50 titles *Founded:* 1982

Galgotia Publications Pvt Ltd+, PO Box 7221, New Delhi 110002 (Located at: 5 Ansari Rd, Daryaganj, New Delhi) Tel: (011) 272006 Telex: 0312879 Star In
Chief Executive, Editorial: Suneel Galgotia; *Sales:* Vinod Behl; *Production:* Jayanthi; *Publicity:* Gautam Rawat
Subjects: Technical, Engineering, Management, General Paperbacks
Bookshop: E D Galgotia & Sons (qv under Major Booksellers)
1986-87: 32 titles *Founded:* 1972

Ganesh & Co, 41 Pondy Bazar, Madras 600017 Tel: (044) 441006
Partners: S Ganesh Prasad, S Ranganathan
Subjects: Philosophy, Religion
Founded: 1910

Gaurav Publishing House, an imprint of Sterling Publishers Pvt Ltd (qv)

Geetha Book House*, K R Circle, Mysore 570001 Tel: (0821) 33589 Cable Add: Books
General Manager: M Gopalakrishna; *Sales Manager:* M Gururaja Rao; *Rights & Permissions:* M Sathyanarayana Rao
Subjects: Belles Lettres, Poetry, Biography, History, Philosophy, Reference, Religion, Low- & High-priced Paperbacks, General & Social Science, University Textbooks
Bookshop: At above address

Geological Survey of India*, 27 Jawaharlal Nehru Rd, Calcutta 700016 Tel: (033) 232314 Cable Add: Geosurvey

Director-General: S K Mukherjee
Subject: Geology

CM **Ghosh** Publishers Pvt Ltd+, 22/1 Bidhan Sarani, Calcutta 700006 Tel: (033) 311471
Sales Manager: D K Bose; *Production, Rights & Permissions Dir:* T K Bhar; *Publicity Dir:* A Das
Subsidiary Company: Indian Publishing House (qv)
Subjects: Nursery and primary level children's books
Bookshop: At above address
1986: 3 titles *1987:* 1 title *Founded:* 1986

Gitanjali Publishing House, Lajpat Nagar 4, New Delhi 110024 Tel: (011) 6430991
Subjects: Economics, Social Science, History, Politics, Humanities
Bookshop: Indian Book Service (at above address)
Founded: 1962

Goel Publishing House*, Subhash Bazar, Meerut 250002 Tel: (0121) 72843/76189
Man Dir, Editorial: B D Rastogi; *Sales:* Atul Krishna; *Production:* K Krishna; *Publicity & Advertising Dir:* Kamalni Rastogi
Subsidiary Company: Krishna Prakashan Mandir, 119 Krishna Vihar, Shivaji Road, Meerut 250001
Bookshop: Goel Publishing, Krishna Prakashan Mandir, Subhash Bazar, Meerut 250002 UP
Subjects: Mathematics, Chemistry, History, Art, Political Science, Economics, University & College textbooks
Founded: 1948

Good Companions, Ushakirai Bldg, Raopura, Baroda Tel: (0265) 55433
Chief Executive: N K Kate; *Editorial, Sales, Production, Publicity:* Girish N Kate
Subjects: Economics, Social Science, Technical, General
Founded: 1945

Directorate of **Government** Publications*, Netaji Subhash Marg, Bombay 400004 Tel: (022) 355181 Cable Add: Diprintery
Chief Executive: V K Vispute
Subject: General

Gyan Bharati*, 4-14 Roop Nagar, Delhi 7 An imprint of National Publishing House (qv)

Hans Prakashan, 18 Nyaya Marg, Allahabad Tel: (0532) 3077
Chief Executive: Mahendra Pal Jha; *Production:* Amrit Rai
Subject: Fiction
Founded: 1949

Hans Publishers, Kamani Chambers, Ballard Estate, Bombay 400038 Tel: (022) 263516 Cable Add: Bukmel
Chief Executive: Miss M Pereira
Parent Company: Myna Press (qv)
Subjects: Great works of the present century and reprints of outstanding books
Founded: 1963

Harjeet & Co, PO Box 5752, New Delhi 110055 (Located at: 1920 Street 10th, Chuna Mandi, New Delhi) Tel: (011) 770572/770430 Cable Add: Book Centre ND Telex: 03165938
Chief Executive, Production: Dr P N Jain; *Editorial, Rights & Permissions:* Ashok Jain; *Sales, Publicity:* Kuldeepe Jain
Associate Companies: B Jain Publishers (P) Ltd; Jain Publishing Co; World Homoeopathic Links (qqv)
Subjects: Homoeopathy, Biochemistry, Magnetotherapy, Acupuncture, Allied Medical Topics
Founded: 1972

Hemkunt Press, A-78 Naraina Industrial Area Phase I, New Delhi 110028 Tel: (011) 505079 Cable Add: Hembooks
Man Dir, Rights & Permissions: G P Singh
Subjects: Religion, Juveniles, Secondary & Primary Textbooks
Founded: 1948

Heritage Publishers+, 4348 Madan Mohan St, 4C Ansari Rd, Daryaganj, New Delhi 110002 Tel: (011) 266258 Cable Add: Heripub
Man Dir, Publicity: B R Chawla
Subsidiary Companies: Disha Publications (qv); Intellectuals' Rendezvous, Aggarwal Bhawan, 4C Ansari Rd, New Delhi 110002; Pankaj Publications International (qv)
Subjects: Biography, History, Bibliography, Literature, Reference, Religion, Economics, Language, Social Science, Philosophy
Founded: 1973

Himalaya Publishing House*, 4A-16 Sangeeta, 71 Juhu Rd, Santa Cruz West, Bombay 400054 Tel: (022) 351186/355798
Chief Executive, Editorial, Sales, Publicity: D P Pandey; *Production:* Kooverjibhai; *Rights & Permissions:* Mrs Meena Pandey
Show Room: 'Ramdoot', Dr Bhalerao Marg (Kelewadi), Girgaum, Bombay 400004 Tel: (022) 360170/355798
Subjects: Arts, Commerce, Science, Management, Law
Founded: 1976

Himalayan Books*, 17-L Connaught Pl, New Delhi 110001 Tel: (011) 352126/351731 Cable Add: Himalayan Books
Man Dir, Editorial: Ms Pawan Chowdhri; *Sales, Production, Publicity, Rights & Permissions:* Ms V Chowdhri
Associate Company: English Book Store (qv under Major Booksellers)
Subjects: Architecture, Himalayas, Tourism, Religion, Culture, Nursing, Military Science, Aviation
Founded: 1981

Hind Pocket Books Private Ltd*, GT Rd, Shahdara, Delhi 110032 Tel: (011) 202046/202332 Cable Add: Pocketbook Delhi
Man Dir: Dina N Malhotra; *Marketing, Rights & Permissions:* Shekhar Malhotra
Associate Companies: Indian Book Company, Clarion Books, Saraswati Vihar (all at above address)
Subjects: General, Fiction, Non-fiction, Self Improvement, Do-It-Yourself, Biography
Book Clubs: Gharelu Library Yojna, Clarion Book Club
Founded: 1958

Hindi Pracharak Sansthan*, PO Box 106, Pishachmochan, Varanasi 221001 Tel: (0542) 62867/62114/52965 Cable Add: Prakashak
Editorial: K C Beri, V P Beri, R P Beri, A K Beri; *Sales:* Vivek Beri
Branch Offs: 23 Kabir Rd, Calcutta 700026; Adhyapak Prakashan Sansthan, 19 Garbarjhala Park, Lucknow 226001 Tel: (0522) 46323; Sahitya Bharti, 263 Rabindra Sarani, Calcutta 700007
Subject: Hindi Literature, Periodical
Book Club: Pracharak Book Club
Founded: 1905

Hindustan Publishing Corporation (India)*, 6 U B Jawahar Nagar, Delhi 110007 Tel: (011) 2915059
Man Dir: S K Jain; *Editorial, Rights & Permissions:* J K Jain; *Sales:* P C Kumar; *Production:* B B Jain
Subsidiary Company: Hindustan Book Agency, 17 U B, Jawahar Nagar, Delhi 110007
Subjects: Archaeology, Bibliography and

Information Science, Mathematics, Statistics, Physics, Chemistry, Earth Sciences, Life Sciences, Social Sciences
Founded: 1960

I B D, see International Book Distributors

I B H, see India Book House Pvt Ltd

I S P C K, see Indian Society for Promoting Christian Knowledge

Idarah Fikre Jadeed, 922 Kucha Rohella Khan, 1st floor, Daryaganj, New Delhi 110002 Tel: (011) 270284
Chief Executive: Ajay Didden; *Sales:* Rakesh K; *Production:* S Kumar
Subjects: Fiction, Criticism, History, Library Science, General (in Urdu)
Founded: 1985
Miscellaneous: Also distributor and publisher of Urdu books

Idarah-I-Adabiyat-I-Delli*, 2009 Qasimjan St, Delhi 110006 Tel: (011) 513550
Editorial: Muhammad Ahmed; *Sales:* Lachhman Das
Subjects: Islamic Studies
Founded: 1972

Inba Nilayam*, 95 Kutchery Rd, Mylapore, Madras 600004 Tel: (044) 72547
Chief Executive: Soma Swaminathan; *All other offices:* Ramanathan S
Associate Company: Vellayan Pathippagam (at above address)
Subjects: Politics, Philosophy, History, Novels, Juveniles
Founded: 1947

India Book House Pvt Ltd, Eruchshaw Bldg, 3rd floor, 249 Dr DN Rd, Bombay 400001 Tel: (022) 264364/5
Dirs: G L Mirchandani, H G Mirchandani, D G Mirchandani; *Editorial:* P C Manaktala (Adult books), Anant Pai (Children's)
Associate Companies: IBH Export Division, IBH Subscription Agency (both at Fleet Fasteners Bldg, MV Rd, Marol Naka, Andheri (East), Bombay 400059; IBH Magazine Services (at above address); IBH Publishers Pvt Ltd, Mahalaxmi Chambers, 5th floor, 22 Bhulabhai Desai Rd, Bombay 400026
Subjects: Management, Health, Cookery, Humour, Biography, Indian Culture and Tradition, Children's
Bookshop: India Book House (qv under Major Booksellers)

Indian Books Centre*, 40/5 Shakti Nagar, Delhi 110007 Tel: (011) 7126497
Man Dir, Rights & Permissions: Naresh Gupta; *Export Dir:* Sunil Gupta; *Sales:* Anil Gupta; *Publicity:* Virender Gupta
Subsidiary Company: Sri Satguru Publications (qv)
Associate Companies: Bibliotheca Indo-Buddhica Series, Sri Garib Dass Oriental Series (both at above address)
Subjects: Art, Archaeology, Religion and Philosophy (especially Buddhism), Languages, Literature, Linguistics, Numismatics, Sanskrit, Reference, Sociology
Bookshop: At above address
Founded: 1976

Indian Council for Cultural Relations*, Azad Bhavan, Indraprastha Estate, New Delhi 110002 Tel: (011) 272114/262052/262053 Cable Add: Culture Telex: 0314904
Branch Offs: Bangalore, Bombay, Calcutta, Chandigarh, Madras, Varanasi
Subjects: Literature, Culture, Cultural Relations, Performing and Fine Arts
Founded: 1950

Indian Council of Agricultural Research, Krishi Bhavan, Dr Rajendra Prasad Rd, New Delhi 110001 Tel: (011) 388991 Cable Add: Agrisec Telex: 03162249 Icar In
Dir: Dr V S Bhatt (Publication and Information); *Business, Advertising:* M Prasad; *Publicity and Public Relations:* S K Sharma
Subjects: Agriculture, Animal Husbandry, General, Textbooks, Periodicals, Handbooks, Monographs and Bulletins

Indian Council of Medical Research*, PO Box 4508, New Delhi 110029 (Located at: Ansari Nagar, New Delhi) Tel: (011) 653980/652794 Cable Add: Scientific Telex: 3163067 Icmr In
Chief Executive: V Ramalingaswami; *Editorial, Sales, Publicity, Rights & Permissions:* G V Satyavati; *Production:* K Satyanarayana
Subject: Biomedical Research
Founded: 1911

Indian Council of Social Science Research (ICSSR), 35 Ferozeshah Rd, New Delhi 110001 Tel: (011) 385959 Cable Add: Icsores Telex: 3161083 Issr In
Chief Executive, Editorial, Production: Iqbal Narain; *Sales, Publicity:* S P Agrawal; *Rights & Permissions:* D D Narula
Subjects: Social Sciences, Abstracts and reviews of research, Periodicals
Founded: 1969

Indian Documentation Service, Gurgaon, Haryana 122001 Tel: 22005
Editorial, Production, Rights & Permissions: Satyaprakash; *Sales:* Pankaj Kumar, Sanjeev Kumar; *Publicity:* Pankaj Kumar
Subject: Bibliography
1985: 5 titles 1986: 2 titles *Founded:* 1970

Indian Folklore Society, 3 Abdul Hamid (British Indian) St, Calcutta 700069 Tel: (033) 236334
President: Sophia Wadia; *Honorary Dir of Research, General Secretary, Editorial, Rights & Permissions, Publicity:* Sankar Sen Gupta
Orders to: Indian Publications (at above address)
Subjects: Folklore, Anthropology, Archaeology, Ethno-Musicology, Ethno-Botany, Psychology, Tribal Studies, Geography, Folk Performing Arts, Periodical
Founded: 1957

Indian Institute of Advanced Study*, Rashtrapathi Nivas, Simla 171005 Tel: (0177) 2227 Cable Add: Institute
Publication Officer: S K Sharma; *Sales:* B B Lal
Subject: Scholarly

Indian Institute of World Culture*, PO Box 402, Basavangudi, Bangalore 560004 (Located at: 6 Shri B P Wadia Rd, Basavangudi, Bangalore) Tel: (0812) 602581
Honorary Secretary: Anand R Kundaji
Subject: East-West Culture

Indian Museum, 27 Jawaharlal Nehru Rd, Calcutta 700016 Tel: (033) 299902/299979 Cable Add: Imbot
Dir: Dr R C Sharma
Subjects: Arts, Archaeology, Anthropology, Botany, Geology, Zoology, Periodical
Founded: 1814

Indian Press (Publications) Pvt Ltd*, 36 Pannalal Rd, Allahabad, Uttar Pradesh Tel: (0532) 53190 Cable Add: Publikason
Man Dir: D P Ghosh; *Sales, Production, Publicity, Rights & Permissions:* N G Bagchi
Associate Company: Indian Publishing House (qv)
Subject: Textbooks in Hindi, Bengali & English (also publishes in Gurmukhi, Urdu, Marathi & Nepali languages)
Founded: 1884

Indian Publications, 3 Abdul Hamid (British Indian) St, Calcutta 700069 Tel: (033) 236334/325080
Man Dir, Sales: C R Sen; *Editorial, Production, Rights & Permissions:* Sankar Sen Gupta; *Publicity:* C R Sen, D Bhowmick
Subsidiary Company: Kalyani Prakashani (at above address)
Branch Off: 74 Mahatma Gandhi Rd, Calcutta 700009
Subjects: Social Science, Humanities, with special reference to Folklore, Anthropology, Archaeology, Ancient History, Bengali Literature, Mass Communication and Traditional Culture (in English and Bengali only)
Founded: 1956

Indian Publishing House*, 22/1 Bidhan Saranee, Calcutta 700006 Tel: (033) 347398
Manager, Sales: D K Bose; *Production:* Supratik Ghosh, Dipankar Ghosh
Parent Company: C M Ghosh Publishers Pvt Ltd (qv)
Associate Company: Indian Press (Publications) Pvt Ltd (qv)
Subjects: Political Science, Philosophy, History, Economics, Science, Engineering, Children's
Founded: 1908

Indian Society for Promoting Christian Knowledge (ISPCK), PO Box 1585, Kashmere Gate, Delhi 110006 Tel: (011) 2517353 Cable Add: Lithouse Delhi
General Secretary: Rev James Massey; *Editor:* Lanita Charles; *Assistant Dir, Marketing Manager:* Ashish Amos
Subjects: Biblical, Biography, Church and Church History, Christian Life and Education, Comparative Religions, Devotional, Liturgy, Theology, Social, Political
Bookshops: 51 Chowringhee Rd, Calcutta 700071; opp Liberty Cinema, Residency Rd, Sadar, Nagpur 440001
Founded: 1711 (as autonomous body 1958)

Institute for Christian Publishing & Communications Research+*, Kunnuparampil Bldgs, Kurichy 686549, Kottayam, Kerala State Tel: (04826) 470
Man Dir: K P Punnoose; *Editorial, Publicity:* Santhamma Punnoose
Parent Company: K P Punnoose Communications Co (qv for associate companies)
Subject: Christian Literature
Founded: 1982

Intellectual Publishing House, 23 Daryaganj, Pratap Gali, New Delhi 2 Tel: (011) 279911
Associate Company: Intellectual Book Corner
Subjects: History, Politics, Sociology, Philosophy, Religion, Art, Archaeology
Founded: 1974

Inter-India Publications*, D-17 Raja Garden Extension, New Delhi 110015 Tel: (011) 504418
Chief Executive, Editorial, Rights & Permissions: M C Mittal; *Sales:* Praveen Mittal
Parent Company: DK Publishers' Distributors (qv under Major Booksellers)
Subjects: Indology, Geography, Art, Anthropology, Sociology, Archaeology,

Philosophy, Religion, Economics, History, Agriculture, Political Science, Numismatics
Founded: 1977

International Book Distributors*, 1st floor, 9/3 Rajpur Rd, Dehra Dun 248001   Tel: 27497   Telex: 595280
Man Dir & other offices: R P Singh Gahlot
Subjects: Agriculture, Botany, Zoology and Wildlife, Forestry
Founded: 1976

Interprint, Mehta House, 16-A Naraina II, New Delhi 110028   Tel: (011) 5724234/584450   Cable Add: Calmaker   Telex: 314918 Meta In/3165187 Fash In
Man Dir, Editorial, Production, Rights & Permissions: S N Mehta; *Sales, Publicity:* V V R Murty
Orders to: Calendar Makers Corporation (at above address)
Parent Company: Mehta Offset Works (at above address)
Subjects: Medicine, Life Sciences, Computers, Educational Software, Oriental Studies, General
1985: 8 titles   *1986:* 10 titles   *Founded:* 1971
ISBN Publisher's Prefix: 81-85017

Intertrade Publications (India) Pvt Ltd, subsidiary of KK Roy (Pvt) Ltd (qv)

Jaico Publishing House*, 125 Mahatma Gandhi Rd, Bombay 400023   Tel: (022) 270621/270746/270760   Cable Add: Jaicobooks
Man Dir: Jaman H Shah; *Editorial, Production, Sales, Publicity, Rights & Permissions:* Ashwin J Shah
Subsidiary Company: Jaico Press Pvt Ltd
Branch Offs: Jaico Book House, 14-1 1st Main Rd, 6th Cross, Gandhi Nagar, Bangalore 560009; Jaico Book Enterprises, 3 Orient Row, Park Circus, Calcutta 700017; Jaico Book House, 5-9-24/71 Lake Hills Rd, Basheer Bagh, Hyderabad 500483; Jaico Book Distributors, G-2, 16 Ansari Rd, Daryaganj, New Delhi 110002
Subjects: Oriental and Western Classics, Indian and Western Fiction, Palmistry, Astrology, Philosophy, Religion, Biography, Autobiography, Reference, Language, Sex, Marriage, Love, Health, Yoga, Management, Economics, Humour, History, Politics, Cookery, Law, Crime, Psychology, Self-improvement
Bookshop: Jaicos (qv under Major Booksellers)
Founded: 1947

B **Jain Publishers** (P) Ltd, PO Box 5775, New Delhi 110055 (Located at: 1921 Chuna Mandi St 10th, New Delhi)   Tel: (011) 770572/242967   Telex: 03165938 Jain In
Man Dir: Dr Premnath Jain; *Sales, Production, Publicity:* Kuldeep Jain; *Editorial, Rights & Permissions:* Ashok Jain
Associate Company: Harjeet & Co (qv)
Subjects: Homoeopathy, Magnetotherapy, Acupuncture, Nature Cure
Founded: 1967

Jain Publishing Co*, 2798 Rajguru Rd, New Delhi 110055   Tel: (011) 770430
Chief Executive, Production: Dr P N Jain; *Editorial, Sales, Publicity, Rights & Permissions:* Ashok Jain
Orders to: PO Box 5752, New Delhi 110055
Associate Company: Harjeet & Co (qv)
Subjects: Homoeopathy, Allied Medical Books
Founded: 1972

Jaipur Publishing House*, Chaura Rasta, Jaipur 302003   Tel: (0141) 62257
Manager: Rajesh Agarwal; *Production:* R C Agarwal; *Sales:* Dhoop Chand Jain
Subject: Academic
Founded: 1960

Jaisingh & Mehta Publishers Pvt Ltd, 18/20 K Dubash Marg, Bombay 400023   Tel: (022) 225353/225425   Telex: 1171665 Quip In
Man Dir, Rights & Permissions: Ananda Jaisingh; *Editorial:* H J Vakeel; *Sales:* B N Chatterjee
Branch Off: New Delhi
Subjects: General, Art, Indology, Sanskrit and Vedantic Studies, Archaeology, University Textbooks, Periodical
Founded: 1942
ISBN Publisher's Prefix: 0-210

Jaypee Brothers Medical Publishers+*, PO Box 7193, New Delhi 110002 (Located at: G-16 EMCA House, 23B Ansari Rd, New Delhi)
Editorial: Jitendar Vij; *Sales:* Pawaninder Vij
Subject: Medical Sciences

Jnanada Prakashan+*, Govind Mitra Rd, Patna 800004   Tel: (0612) 50331
Editorial: T Chowdhary; *Sales:* R Chowdhary; *Production, Publicity, Rights & Permissions:* S B Chowdhary
Subsidiary Company: Hastamalak Prakashan (at above address)
Branch Offs: Gurudwara Rd, Bhagalpur Tel: 898; Ashok Market, Motijhil, Muzaffarpur; 24 Daryaganj, New Delhi Tel: (011) 272047; S N Gangully Rd, Ranchi Tel: (0651) 20769
Subjects: Accountancy, Commerce, Management, Secretarial, Vocational, Hobbies, Physics, Chemistry, Botany, Zoology, Mathematics, Statistics, Economics, Political Science, Philosophy, Psychology, Logic, Sociology, History, Languages
Founded: 1949

Bharatiya **Jnanpith***, B-45/47 Connaught Pl, New Delhi 110001   Tel: (011) 322294   Cable Add: Jnanpith
Dir, Rights & Permissions: Lakshmi Chandra Jain; *Sales, Production:* B S Rahi; *Publicity:* Dr Gulab Chandra Jain
Subjects: Indology (rare and previously unpublished texts in Sanskrit, Pali, Prakrit, Apbhramsha, Kannada and Tamil, with translations), Hindi Literature (in original, and translation from Indian languages)
Founded: 1944

Kairali Children's Book Trust*, PO Box 624, Kottayam, Kerala State 686001   Tel: (0481) 3114
Chief Executive, Rights & Permissions: D C Kizhakemuri; *Editorial:* Dr K Velayudhan Nair; *Sales:* Current Books; *Production:* V P Sreedharan Nayanar; *Publicity:* G Sreekumar
Orders to: Current Books, VIII/493 Railway Station Rd, Kottayam 686001
Associate Companies: Current Books (qv); DC Books (qv); Kairali Mudralayam (qv)
Imprint: D C Press
Subjects: Biographies, Indian history, Mythology
Book Club: Kairali Club
Founded: 1980

Kairali Mudralayam*, Moolepparambil Bldgs, opp R M S Office, Kottayam 686001   Tel: (0481) 5018/5342
Managing Partner: D C Kizhakemuri; *Editorial:* M S Chandrasekhara Warrier; *Sales:* D C Ponnamma; *Production, Publicity, Rights & Permissions:* Mary John
Associate Companies: Current Books (qv); D C Books (qv); Kairali Children's Book Trust (qv)
Subjects: Fiction, Biography, Humour, Crime Thrillers (especially Sherlock Holmes)
Founded: 1978

Kalyani Publishers+*, 1/1 Rajinder Nagar, Ludhiana (Punjab)
Man Dir: Raj Kumar
Branch Off: 4863/2 Bharat Ram Rd, 24 Daryaganj, New Delhi 110002
Subject: Educational
Bookshop: Lyall Book Depot, Chaura Bazar, Ludhiana

Karnataka Cooperative Publishing House Ltd*, 164 1st Main Rd, Chamarajpet, Bangalore 560018

B D **Kataria** & Sons*, opp Clock Tower, Ludhiana   Tel: (0161) 21107
Chief Executive: Verinder Kataria
Subjects: Engineering, Technology

Kendriya Hindi Sansthan, Agra 282005   Tel: (0562) 76758/72352   Cable Add: Shikshan Agra
Chief Executive, Editorial, Rights & Permissions: Prof Bal Govind Misra; *Sales, Production, Publicity:* Dr Devendra Kumar Sharma
Branch Offs: Delhi, Gauhati, Hyderabad, Mysore, Shillong
Subjects: Linguistics, Language, Language Teaching, Lexicography
Founded: 1961
Miscellaneous: Autonomous body fully financed by Ministry of Education, Government of India

Kerala Sahitya Akademi, PO Box 501, Trichur 680020 (Located at: Town Hall Rd, Trichur)   Tel: (0487) 23569
Secretary: M K Madhavan Nayar; *Publications Officer:* C K Anandan Pillai
Subjects: Literary
Founded: 1956

Kerala University, Department of Publications*, Trivandrum 695034   Tel: (0471) 60692
Chief Executive: Chemmanam Chacko; *Production, Sales:* S Krishna Iyer
Subjects: Scholarly
Founded: 1939

Khanna Publishers, 2-B Nath Market, Nai Sarak, Delhi 110006   Tel: (011) 2912380
Subjects: Engineering, Technical

Kitab Ghar*, Main Bazar, Gandhi Nagar, New Delhi 110031   Tel: (011) 213206
Chief Executive, Rights & Permissions: Satya Brat Sharma; *Editorial, Production:* Jagat Ram Sharma; *Sales, Publicity:* Dev Datt
Subjects: Social and General Sciences, Novels, Poetry, Drama, Biography (in Hindi)
Founded: 1970

Kitabastan*, 30 Chak, Allahabad 211003   Tel: (0532) 51885   Cable Add: Kitabastan
Chief Executive: Anwar Ullah Khan
Subjects: General (in English, Urdu, Persian, Arabic)
Founded: 1932

Konkani Bhasha Mandal*, 49-B Erasmo Carvalho St, Margao, Goa 403601   Tel: 2331
Editorial: Udai L Bhembro; *Sales:* M R Borkar
Subject: Konkani Literature

Kosi Books, an imprint of Vidyarthi Mithram Press (qv)

Kothari Publications+, Jute House, 12 India Exchange Pl, Calcutta 700001

Tel: (033) 209563/206572 Cable Add: Zeitgeist
Man Dir: H Kothari
Parent Company: Kothari Organisation (at above address)
Associate Companies: India-International News Service; Kothari Consultants (both at above address)
Subjects: Technical, Reference, Management
Founded: 1961
Miscellaneous: Publisher of *Who's Who* series in India

Krishna Brothers, PO Box 97, Ajmer 305001 (Located at: Mahatma Gandhi Marg, Ajmer) Tel: 20935
Editorial, Publicity: J K Agarwal; *Sales:* Om Prakash Singodia
Subjects: Hindi and English literature, Textbooks
1986: 7 titles *Founded:* 1939

Krishna Prakashan Mandir, subsidiary of Goel Publishing House (qv)

Kundalini Research and Publication Trust*, D-291 Sarvodaya Enclave, New Delhi Tel: (011) 653864 Cable Add: Innerlight
Subjects: Yoga, Philosophy, Religion
Founded: 1977

Kutub Khana Ishayat-ul-Islam, 3755 Churiwalan, Delhi 110006 Tel: (011) 263567/265854 Cable Add : Kutubiexpo Telex: 4898 Kutub In
Editorial, Sales: V K Sachdeva
Subject: Islamic Books (in Arabic and English)

Lakshmi Narain Agarwal*, Hospital Rd, Agra 3 Tel: (0562) 73160
Man Dir: P N Agarwal
Subjects: Education, Textbooks
Founded: 1916

Lalit Kala Akademi (National Academy of Art)*, Rabindra Bhavan, New Delhi 110001 Tel: (011) 387241 Cable Add: Artakademi
Chairman: Prof Sankho Chaudhuri; *Acting Secretary:* M Rajaram; *Sales:* Kewal Krishan
Subject: Indian Art
Founded: 1954

Lalvani Brothers*, PO Box 545, Bombay 400001 (Located at: Taj Bldg, 210 Dr Dadabhoy Naoroji Rd, Bombay) Tel: (022) 266811/2 Cable Add: Lalbrother Bombay Telex: 0116529 Nrvo In
Man Dirs, Editorial, Sales, Production, Publicity, Rights & Permissions: S P Lalvani, Mrs P K Sitlani
Associate Companies: Indian Lead, Rampart House, Rampart Row, Bombay; Lalvani Publishing House, 210 Dr DN Rd, Bombay 400001
Branch Offs: 4 Daryaganj, Ansari Rd, Delhi 110006; 8 State Bank Lane, Mount Rd, Madras 2; Globe Bldg, 7-E Lindsey St, Calcutta 16
Subjects: Juvenile, Art, Technical, Educational
Founded: 1922
ISBN Publisher's Prefix: 81-112

Law Books in Hindi Publishers*, Vidhi Sahitya Prakashan, Ministry of Law, Justice and Company Affairs, Indian Law Institute Bldg, Bhagwan Das Rd, New Delhi 110001 Tel: (011) 389001 Cable Add: Patrika
Sales Manager: C B Deogam
Subject: Law

Law Publishers, PO Box 1077, Allahabad 1 (Located at: Sardar Patel Marg, Allahabad) Tel: (0532) 4198/3427 Cable Add: Publishers Allahabad

Chief Executive: Subhash Sagar
Associate Company: Delhi Law House, 77 Gokhale Market, Delhi 6
Subject: Law
Founded: 1961

Lipi Prakashan*, 1 Ansari Rd, Daryaganj, New Delhi 110002 Tel: (011) 273729
Editorial, Production, Publicity, Rights & Permissions: J S Vyas; *Sales:* M L Sharma
Subjects: Novels, Short Stories, Biographies, Literary Criticism, Linguistics, Philology, Education, Politics, Political Science, Dictionaries, Children's Literature (in Hindi and English)
Founded: 1970

The **Little Flower** Co, 43 Ranganathan St, T Nagar, Madras 600017 Tel: (044) 441538 Cable Add: Lifco
Senior Partner: T N C Varadan
Branch Off: Lifco Sales Dept, 17/1 Nandi Koil St, Teppakulam, Tiruchirapalli 620002
Subjects: General Fiction, History, How-to, Music, Art, Philosophy, Reference, Religion, Low-priced Paperbacks, Medicine, General Science, University, Secondary & Primary Textbooks
Founded: 1929

Little Swan, an imprint of Orient Longman Ltd (qv)

Lok Vangmaya Griha Ltd*, Bhupesh Gupta Bhavan, 85 Sayani Rd, Prabhadevi, Bombay 400025 Tel: (022) 4228222/ 4226468
General Manager: S K Kulkarni; *Sales:* K K Parvatkar
Branch Offs: Red Flag Bldg, Bindu Chowk, Kolhapur; 5-22-32 Tilak Path, Aurangabad; 562 Sadashiv Peth, Poona 411030
Subjects: General, Humanities
Bookshops: PPH Book Stall, S V P Rd, Bombay 400004; People's Book House, Fort, Bombay 400001
Founded: 1973

Lord International*, 19 Netaji Subhash Marg, Daryaganj, New Delhi 110002 Tel: (011) 272375
Chief Executive, Editorial, Sales, Rights & Permissions: Sunil Chaudhry; *Production:* Ramesh Chaudhry; *Publicity:* Rajesh Chaudhry
Subjects: Book Trade, Mailing Lists
Founded: 1971
Miscellaneous: Also Distributors and Publishers' Representatives

M P Text Book Corporation*, M S Mandal Campus, Bhopal Tel: (0755) 62135/63059
Publisher: O V Nagar
Subject: Academic
Founded: 1968

Tata **McGraw-Hill** Publishing Co Ltd, 4/12 Asaf Ali Rd (3rd Floor), New Delhi 110002 Tel: (011) 273105/271303 Cable Add: Corinthian Telex: 2257 Tmhd
Dir: Balan Subramanian; *General Manager:* Dr N Subrahmanyam; *Publicity:* N S Nagan
Parent Company: McGraw-Hill Book Co, 1221 Ave of the Americas, New York, NY 10020, USA
Associate Companies: See McGraw-Hill Book Co (UK) Ltd, UK
Subjects: Philosophy, Low- & High-priced Paperbacks, Medicine, Psychology, Engineering, General & Social Science, University Textbooks, Educational Materials, Agriculture, Biological Sciences, Management and Economics, Mathematics, Technology
Founded: 1970

Macmillan India Ltd, 2/10 Ansari Rd, Daryaganj, New Delhi 110002 Tel: (011) 273814/273624/272993 Cable Add: Publishco Telex: 3162718 Mild In
Man Dir: S G Wasani; *Editorial, Rights & Permissions:* Rajiv Beri
Head Off: 50/4 Palace Rd, Bangalore 560052
Branch Offs: Mercantile House, Magazine St, Reay Rd (East), Bombay 400010; 3-4-424 Narayanaguda, Hyderabad 500029; Kala Bhawan, 6 Naval Kishore Rd, Hazratganj, Lucknow 226001; 21 Patullos Rd, Madras 600002; Sinha Kothi, Sinha Library Rd, Patna 800001; Gandhari Bldg, Gandhari Amman Koil St, Trivandrum 695001
Subjects: History, Philosophy, Biology, Chemistry, Medicine, Psychology, Engineering, Computing, Mathematics, General & Social Sciences, University, Secondary & Primary Textbooks, Economics, Management, Political Science, Reference, Fiction, Dictionaries
Founded: 1903
Miscellaneous: Firm is 40 per cent owned by Macmillan Publishers Ltd, UK (qv)
ISBN Publisher's Prefix: 81-3390

Madhyo Pradesh Hindi Granth Academy*, Shivajj Nagar, Bhopal 462011 Tel: (0755) 62084 Cable Add: Academy
Dir: Prof S D Misra; *Editorial:* Navin Sagar; *Sales:* Brij Bihari Dixit; *Production, Publicity:* Dr Shiv Kumar, Ram Prakash
Subjects: University Textbooks, Humanities, Science, Agriculture, Engineering, Medical Sciences

Mahajan Brothers+*, Super Market Basement, Ashram Rd, nr Natraj Cinema, Ahmedabad 380009 Tel: (0272) 408537 Cable Add: Periodical
Man Dir: Dinker Mahajan
Subject: Textiles
Founded: 1953

Manohar Publications, 1 Ansari Rd, Daryaganj, New Delhi 110002 Tel: (011) 262796/275162
Man Dir, Rights & Permissions: Ramesh Jain; *Editorial:* N K Jain; *Sales, Production, Publicity:* K K Saxema
Subjects: History, Sociology, Politics, Indology
Founded: 1969

Munshiram **Manoharlal** Publishers Pvt Ltd, PO Box 5715, New Delhi 110055 (Located at: 54 Rani Jhansi Rd, New Delhi) Tel: (011) 771668/773650/512745 Cable Add: Litereture New Delhi Telex: 3165233 Jnir In
Chief Executive: Manoharlal Jain; *Editorial Dir:* Devendra Jain; *Sales Dir:* Ashok Jain
Associate Companies: Indian Book Import Co, 11-B Court Rd, Delhi 110054; Oriental Books Reprint Corporation, PO Box 5715, 54 Rani Jhansi Rd, New Delhi 110055
Subjects: Art, Architecture, Religion, Philosophy, History, Politics, Linguistics, Languages, Encyclopaedias, Music, Dance, Drama, Theatre, Anthropology, Sociology
Bookshop: 4416 Nai Sarak (Amir Chand Marg), Delhi 110006
1985: 58 titles *1986:* 70 titles *Founded:* 1952
ISBN Publisher's Prefix: 81-215

Manosabdam Books, an imprint of Vidyarthi Mithram Press (qv)

Marg Publications, 3rd floor, Army and Navy Bldg, 148 Mahatma Gandhi Rd, Bombay 400023 Tel: (022) 242520
Chief Executive: J J Bhabha; *Editorial:* Dr Saryu Doshi; *Sales, Publicity:* A D Katrak; *Production:* B J Bilimoria; *Rights & Permissions:* Mrs R S Sabavala
Parent Company: Tata Sons Ltd

Subject: Art
Founded: 1947

Markazi Maktaba Islami*, 1353 Chitli Qabar, Delhi 110006 Tel: (011) 262862 Cable Add: Markaz
Sales: Firasat Ali
Subject: Islamic Literature

Marwah Publications+*, H-39 Green Park Extension, New Delhi 110016 Tel: (011) 664296
Proprietor: Jaspal Singh; *Editorial:* Anees Chishti; *Sales:* Aman Preet Singh
Subjects: Humanities, Social Sciences
Founded: 1975

Mayfair Paperbacks, an imprint of Arnold Publishers (India) Pvt Ltd (qv)

Mayoor Paperbacks, an imprint of National Publishing House (qv)

Meenakshi Prakashan*, Begum Bridge, Meerut 250002 Tel: (0121) 74133/75062/72001
Chief Executive: Shri Chandra Prakash; *Editorial:* Ashok Gupta; *Sales:* S Sudhakar; *Production:* Ashok Kumar; *Publicity:* M C Gupta; *Rights & Permissions:* T C Sharma
Branch Off: 4 Ansari Rd, Daryaganj, New Delhi 110002
Subjects: Economics, Education, Commerce, Psychology, Hindi Literature, Physical and Biological Sciences, History, Management, Political Science, Sociology
Founded: 1964

Milind Publications Pvt Ltd*, 6-E Rani Jhansi Rd, New Delhi 110055 Tel: (011) 520838
Man Dir, Sales, Rights & Permissions: Rajiv K Aggarwal; *Editorial, Production:* K R Seshagiri Rao
Subjects: Belles Lettres, Fiction, History, Law, Philosophy, Psychology, Politics, Social and General Science
Founded: 1980

Minerva Associates (Publications) Pvt Ltd, 7-B Lake Pl, Calcutta 700029 Tel: (033) 423783
Chairman, Man Dir, Production, Publicity, Rights & Permissions: Sushil Mukherjea; *Editorial Dir:* O K Ghosh; *Sales:* T K Mukherjee
Subjects: Political Science, History, Social Science, Economics, Psychology, Education, Belles Lettres, Literary Criticism, Philosophy
Founded: 1973

The **Minerva Publishing** House*, 51 Sait Colony II St, Egmore, Madras 8

Ministry of Information & Broadcasting*, Publications Division, Government of India, Patiala House, New Delhi 110001 Tel: (011) 386942 Cable Add: Exinfor
Dirs: Dr S S Shashi, A A Shiromany
Branch Offs: Commerce House, Currimbhoy Rd, Ballard Pier, Bombay; 8 Esplanade East, Calcutta; State Archaeological Museum Bldg, Public Garden, Hyderabad; 10-B Station Rd, Lucknow; LL Auditorium, Anna Salai, Madras; Super Bazar (2nd floor), Connaught Circus, New Delhi; Bihar State Co-operative Bank Bldg, Ashoka Rajpath, Patna; nr Government Press, Press Rd, Trivandrum
Subjects: Art & Culture, History, Speeches & Writings, Land & People, Flora & Fauna, Biographies, Reference, Juveniles, General & Social Science

Mitra & Ghosh Publishers Pvt Ltd*, 10 Shyama Charan De St, Calcutta 73 Tel: (033) 343492/348791 Cable Add: Mitra & Ghosh, Calcutta
Chief Executive, Production: Sabitendra Nath Roy; *Editorial:* G K Mitra; *Sales:* M C Chakravarty; *Publicity:* P K Bose; *Rights & Permissions:* P K Pal
Branch Off: 86/1 Mahatma Gandhi Rd, Calcutta 700009
Subjects: Novels, Fiction, Travel, Essays, Juvenile, Periodical
Bookshops: At both above addresses
1985: 60 titles *Founded:* 1934

Modern Book Agency Pvt Ltd, 10 Bankim Chatterjee St, Calcutta 700073 Tel: (033) 321066/321113 Cable Add: Bibliophil
Man Dir, Rights & Permissions: Rabindranarayan Bhattacharya; *Sales:* Nisith Kumar Bose; *Production:* Debnarayan Bhattacharya
Associate Company: B B Brothers & Co, 16/1 Shyamacharandey St, Calcutta 700073
Subjects: School and College Textbooks, Reference, Children's Literature (in English and Bengali)
Bookshop: At above address
Founded: 1928

Motilal Banarsidass+, Bungalow Rd, Jawahar Nagar, Delhi 110007 Tel: (011) 2911985/2918335 Cable Add: Gloryindia Telex: 03166053 Enky In/03165367 Kkrc In
Managing Partner: Shantilal Jain; *Editorial:* N P Jain; *Publishing:* J P Jain; *Sales:* Rajiv P Jain; *Export:* R P Jain
Branch Offs: 24 Racecourse Rd, Bangalore (Karnataka); 120 Royapettah High Rd, Mylapore, Madras 600004; Ashok Rajpath, opposite Patna College, Patna 800004 (Bihar) Tel: (0612) 51442; PO Box 75, Chowk, Varanasi 221001 (UP) Tel: (0542) 62898
Subjects: Religion, Philosophy, History, Linguistics, Sanskrit, Arts, Literature, Medicine
Bookshop: See under Major Booksellers
1985: 24 titles *1986:* 30 titles *Founded:* 1903
ISBN Publisher's Prefix: 81-208

Mouj Prakashan Griha*, Khatau Wadi Girgaum, Bombay 400004, Maharashtra

Mudra Prakashan, 4858/24A Daryaganj, New Delhi 110002 Tel: (011) 277230
Man Dir, Production, Publicity, Rights & Permissions: Hemant Gupta; *Editorial:* Shekhar Mehra; *Sales:* Ashok Sharma
Subjects: Textbooks and Educational Materials
Founded: 1986

A **Mukherjee** & Co Pvt Ltd, 2 Bankim Chatterjee St, Calcutta 700073 Tel: (033) 341606/341499
Dir: Rajeev Neogi
Subjects: Educational Materials, Non-fiction, Religion, Politics, Travel, Children's
Founded: 1940

Mukherji Book House*, PO Box 11492, Calcutta 700006 (Located at: 8A Duff Lane, Calcutta)
Subjects: Reference, Bibliography
Founded: 1963

Myna Press*, PO Box 1526, Bombay 400038 (Located at: 32 R Kamani Marg, Bombay) Tel: (022) 261347 Cable Add: Bukmel
Chief Executive: Mohan Panjabi
Subsidiary Company: Hans Publishers (qv)
Subject: Juveniles
Founded: 1970

Nalanda Books, an imprint of Aadiesh Book Depot (qv)

Narosa Publishing House, 6 Community Centre, Panchsheel Park, New Delhi 110017 Tel: (011) 6433992/6433818 Cable Add: Narosa New Delhi Telex: 3161661 Nar In
Man Dir: N K Mehra
Associate Companies: Narosa Book Distributors (at above address); Springer Books (India) Pvt Ltd (qv)
Branch Offs: 35-36 Greams Rd, Thousand Lights, Madras 600006 Tel: (044) 475362/475372 Cable Add: Spriverlag Madras; 306 Shiv Centre, D B C Sector 17 PO KU Bazar, New Bombay 400705 Tel: (02154) 683646/670056 Cable Add: Narosa Vasihi New Bombay
Subjects: Pure and Applied Science, Medicine
1986: 14 titles *1987:* 10 titles *Founded:* 1977

National Book Agency (P) Ltd, 12 Bankim Chatterjee St, Calcutta 700073 Tel: (033) 311432/324576 Cable Add: Marxslist
Man Dir: Salil Kumar Ganguli
Subject: Marxist-Leninist Literature
Founded: 1939

National Book Trust India*, A-5 Green Park, New Delhi 110016 Tel: (011) 664667/664540/664020 Cable Add: Nabotrust Telex: 03161634
Chairman: Krishna Kripalani; *Dir:* Dr Syed Asad Ali; *Joint Dirs:* H N Sinha (Administration & Finance), U Prabhakar Rao (Development); *Deputy Dirs:* Jyotish Datta Gupta (Arts), M L Munshi (Exhibitions), C L Nagpal (Subsidies), D Das Gupta (Information & Publicity), Dhruv Bhargava (Production)
Book Centres: Government Higher Secondary School, Amritsar; II floor Eastern Wing, Jayanagar Shopping Complex, Bangalore; CIDCO Bldg, Sector 1, 2nd floor, Vashi, Bombay; 67/2 Mahatma Gandhi Rd, Calcutta; City Central Library Bldg, Ashok Nagar, Hyderabad; University Library Bldg, Manasgangotri, Mysore; A-4 Green Park, New Delhi; University Library, Visvabharati University
Subjects: Covering all aspects of human endeavour with particular reference to India; meant for a general readership
Founded: 1957

National Council of Applied Economic Research, Publications Division*, Parisila Bhavan, 11 Indraprastha Estate, New Delhi 110002 Tel: (011) 3317860 Cable Add: Arthsandan Telex: 316580 Ncar In
Director-General: I Z Bhatty
Subject: Economics and allied subjects
1985-86: 3 titles *Founded:* 1956

National Council of Educational Research & Training, Publication Department*, Sri Aurobindo Marg, New Delhi 110016 Tel: (011) 663983/662707/662708 Cable Add: Edusearch
Head of Publications: Jaipal Nangia; *Chief Production Officer:* C N Rao; *Chief Editor:* Prabhakar Dwivedi
Subjects: Secondary & Primary Textbooks, Educational Materials
Founded: 1962

National Museum*, Janpath, New Delhi 110011 Tel: (011) 383459/389368
Editorial: C B Pandey; *Sales:* V P Dwivedi; *Production:* N R Banerjee
Subjects: Indian Art and Museology

National Publishing House*, 23 Daryaganj, New Delhi 110002 Tel: (011) 274161/275267
Man Dir: K L Malik; *Editorial, Production, Rights & Permissions:* S K Malik; *Sales:* M K Malik; *Sales Promotion:* A-95 Sector 5, Noida 201301 (UP) Tel: 3683/4507
Parent Company: K L Malik & Sons Pvt Ltd (at above address)

Imprints: Mayoor Paperbacks, Gyan Bharati (qv)
Branch Offs: K L Malik & Sons Pvt Ltd, 34 Netaji Subhash Marg, Allahabad 3; Malik & Co, Chaura Rasta, Jaipur 302003
Subjects: Humanities, Social Science, Hindi Literature
Bookshops: At company and branch office addresses
Founded: 1950
ISBN Publisher's Prefix: 81-214

Navajivan Trust, Post Navajivan, Ahmedabad 380014 Tel: (0272) 447329
Man Dir, Rights & Permissions: Jitendra T Desai; *Editorial:* Balmukund Dave; *Sales, Publicity:* Pushpa Hathi
Branch Off: 130 Princess St, Bombay 2
Subjects: Biography, History, Philosophy, Reference, Religion, Books about and by Mahatma Gandhi
1985: 18 titles *1986:* 10 titles *Founded:* 1919

Navrang+, RB-7 Inderpuri, New Delhi 110012 Tel: (011) 589914 Cable Add: Vedanta Telex: 0315417 East In
Man Dir & other offices: Sushil Singal
Subject: Humanities
Founded: 1968

Navyug Publishers*, 9-B Pleasure Garden Market, Chandni Chowk, Delhi 110006 Tel: (011) 278370
Editorial: Pritam Singh; *Sales:* Gurbachan Singh
Subject: Punjabi Literature
Founded: 1949

Naya Prokash, PO Box 11468, Calcutta 700006 (Located at: 206 Bidhan Sarani, Calcutta) Tel: (033) 349566 Cable Add: Napkas
Production, Rights & Permissions, Editorial: B Mitra; *Partner, Sales, Publicity:* P S Basu
Subsidiary Companies: Arunima Printing Works; Darbari Udjog
Subjects: Indology, Social Science, Management, History, Economics, Politics, Military Studies, Linguistics, Botany, Medical Science, Horticulture
Bookshop: At above address
1985: 1 title *1986:* 5 titles *Founded:* 1962

Neeraj Publishing House*, B-3/94 Ashok Vihar, Phase II, Delhi 110052
Chief Executive, Publicity: Praveen Mittal; *Editorial, Production:* I C Mittal; *Sales, Rights & Permissions:* S K Bhatia
Orders to: DK Publishers' Distributors, 1 Ansari Rd, New Delhi 110002
Parent Company: DK Publishers' Distributors (qv under Major Booksellers)
Associate Companies: BR Publishing Corporation (qv); DK Publications (qv)
Subjects: Art, Archaeology, History
Founded: 1981

Neeta Prakashan+, PO Box 3853, New Delhi 110049 (Located at: A-4 Ring Rd, South Extension Part I, New Delhi) Tel: (011) 692013/5 Cable Add: Loveneeta
Managing Proprietor: Shanti Devi; *Sales, Production, Publicity, Rights & Permissions Executive:* Rakesh Gupta
Subjects: Educational books (in Hindi, English, Sanskrit)
1985: 20 titles *1986:* 15 titles *Founded:* 1960

Nem Chand & Brothers, Civil Lines, Roorkee 247667 Tel: 2258/2752 Cable Add: Enginjour
Warehouse: Opposite Old Dy S P Office, Roorkee 247667
Man Dir, Rights & Permissions: N C Jain; *Editorial Dir:* Dr Ashok K Jain; *Sales Dir:* Anil Jain; *Production Dir:* P K Jain; *Publicity, Advertising Dir:* T K Jain
Subsidiary Company: Roorkee Press, Roorkee
Subject: Engineering
Founded: 1951

Nettikadan Corporation (Books Unit), Nettikadan Bldg, Karakkat Rd, Ernakulam South 682016, Kerala
Managing Partner: Andrew Nettikadan; *Publishing Manager:* Miss Livi Andrew Nettikadan; *Manager:* T M Antony; *Publicity Manager:* Tom Thomas
Associate Company: Joseph Thomasons & Co (qv)
Subjects: Educational (in English and Malayalam)
Founded: 1978

New Book Centre*, PO Box 10815, Calcutta 700009 (Located at: 14 Ramanath Majumdar St, Calcutta)
Manager, Sales: A K Das; *Editorial:* K Sen; *Production:* Suren Dutt
Subject: Reference

New Light Publishers*, B-9 Rattan Jyoti, 18 Rajendra Pl, New Delhi 110008 Tel: (011) 5712137
Managing Partner: A S Chowdhry; *Editorial:* Prof R P Chopra; *Publicity, Advertising:* R K Chowdhry
Subjects: Self-Improvement, English Language, General Knowledge, Books for Competitive Examinations
Founded: 1964

The **New Order** Book Co*, Ellis Bridge, Ahmedabad 380006 Tel: (0272) 79065/445409 Cable Add: Nyuorder
Proprietor: D V Trivedi
Subjects: Humanities, Indology, Antiquarian, Arts, Reprints
Founded: 1939

Nirmal Book Agency*, 89 Mahatma Gandhi Rd, Calcutta 700007 Tel: (033) 348405
Editorial: Biswanath De; *Sales:* Nirmal Kumar Saha
Subject: Children's Books

Orient Longman Ltd, 5-9-41/1 Basheer Bagh, Hyderabad 500029 Tel: (0842) 230343/237936 Telex: 1556803 Olex In
Chairman: J Rameshwar Rao; *Editorial:* Sujit Mukherjee; *Sales:* E Raghavan; *Rights & Permissions:* N R Arur
Subsidiary Company: Sangam Books Ltd, UK (qv)
Associate Company: Longman Group UK Ltd, UK (qv)
Imprints: Sangam Books, Swan, Little Swan
Branch Offs: 80/1 Mahatma Gandhi Rd, Bangalore 560001; Kamani Marg, Ballard Estate, Bombay 400038; 17 Chittaranjan Ave, Calcutta 700072; 5-9-41/1 Bashir Bagh, Hyderabad 500029; 160 Anna Salai, Madras 600002; 1/24 Asaf Ali Rd, New Delhi 110002; Jamal Rd, Patna 800001
Subjects: General Non-fiction, Biography, History, Philosophy, Reference, Juveniles, Low- & High-priced Paperbacks, Medicine, Psychology, Engineering, General & Social Science, Technology, University, Secondary & Primary Textbooks, Educational Materials
Bookshops: The Bookpoint (India) Pvt Ltd, R Kamani Marg, Ballard Estate, Bombay 400038; 3-5-820 Hyderguda, Hyderabad 500029
Founded: 1948

Orient Paperbacks+, 36-C Connaught Pl, New Delhi 110001 Tel: (011) 352081/312978 Cable Add: Visionbook
A division of Vision Books
Man Dir: Vishwanath; *Editorial, Production:* Kapil Malhotra; *Sales, Publicity, Rights & Permissions:* Sudhir Malhotra
Orders to: Sales Office, Madrassa Rd, Kashmere Gate, Delhi 110006 Tel: (011) 2517001/2514274/2512267
Parent Company: Vision Books Pvt Ltd (qv)
Associate Companies: BIG Database Publishing Pvt Ltd (qv); Rajpal & Sons (qv); Ravindra Printing Press; Shiksha Bharati (qv); Shiksha Bharati Press, G T Rd, Shadara, Delhi 32
Imprints: Anand Paperbacks, Vision Books
Branch Off: Vasant, Ground Floor, 3-B Pedder Rd, Bombay 400026 Tel: (022) 4929343
Book Club: Orient Book Club
Subjects: International Bestseller Reprints, General Non-fiction, Self-tuition Series, Indo Anglian Fiction, Indian Culture and Thought, Poetry, Drama, Occult, Palmistry, Astrology, Sports, Adventure, Yoga, Health, Alternative Medicine, Reference
1985: 60 titles *1986:* 60 titles *Founded:* 1967

Oxford & I B H Publishing Co Pvt Ltd, 66 Janpath, New Delhi 110001 Tel: (011) 321035/320518 Cable Add: Indamer Telex: 315261 Am In
Dirs: Gulab Primlani, Mohan Primlani; *Editorial:* Mrs I V Ramchandani; *Sales, Publicity:* Raju Primlani; *Production Manager:* A P Gopalakrishnan
Subsidiary Companies: Amerind Publishing Co (P) Ltd (at above address); Oxonian Press (P) Ltd (qv)
Branch Offs: 22 Park Mansion, Park St, Calcutta 700016; N-56 Connaught Circus, New Delhi 110001
Subjects: Reference, Medicine, Psychology, Engineering, University Textbooks
Bookshops: Oxford Book & Stationery Co (qv under Major Booksellers)
Founded: 1962

Oxford University Press+, PO Box 43, New Delhi 110001 (Located at: YMCA Library Bldg, Jai Singh Rd, New Delhi) Tel: (011) 321190/321322/322769 Cable Add: Oxorient Telex: 61108 Oxon
General Manager: S K Mookerjee; *Deputy General Manager:* N A O'Brien; *Publicity:* R K Jain
Parent Company: Oxford University Press, UK (qv)
Branch Offs: Faraday House, P-17 Mission Row Extension, GPO Box 530, Calcutta 700013; Oxford House, Anna Salai, PO Box 1079, Madras 600006; 2/11 Ansari Rd, Daryaganj, PO Box 7035, New Delhi 110002; Oxford House, Apollo Bunder, PO Box 31, Bombay 400039
Subjects: Academic & General books for all levels (school, college, university and research), Languages (Arabic, Assamese, Bengali, English, French, Garo, Gujarati, Hindi, Kannada, Khasi, Malayalam, Marathi, Oriya, Punjabi, Sanskrit, Tamil, Telugu, Urdu)
Founded: 1912
ISBN Publisher's Prefix: 0-19

Oxonian Press (P) Ltd*, N-56 Connaught Circus, New Delhi 110001 Tel: (011) 3314957 Cable Add: Indamer
Dir, Rights & Permissions: Gulab Primlani; *Sales Dir:* Dr A M Primlani; *Publicity Manager:* Ms Vinita Naharwar
Parent Company: Oxford & IBH Publishing Co Pvt Ltd (qv)
Branch Offs: 29 Wodehouse Rd, Bombay; 17 Park St, Calcutta 700016; 165 Golf Links, New Delhi 110003
Subjects: Reference, Medicine,

Engineering, General Science, University Textbooks
Bookshop: See Oxford & IBH Publishing Co

Paico Publishing House*, M G Rd, Ernakulam, Cochin 682035 Tel: (0484) 355835 Cable Add: Paico
Man Dir: Kenchana V Pai
Associate Company: Pai & Co, Broadway, Ernakulam, Cochin 682031
Subjects: General Fiction, History, General Science, University, Secondary & Primary Textbooks, Childrens Books
Bookshop: Paico Books & Arts, M G Rd, Cochin 682011
Founded: 1955

M/s Bishan Singh Mahendra **Pal Singh**, PO Box 137, Dehra Dun 24048 (Located at: A-23 Connaught Pl, Dehra Dun) Tel: 24048
Man Dir, Sales: Gajendra Pal Singhg Gahlot; *Editorial, Publicity, Rights & Permissions:* R G S Gahlot; *Production:* Srimati Jaswanti Devi
Subjects: Agriculture, Biology, Botany, Ecology, Entomology, Forestry, Microbiology, Natural History
Bookshop: At above address
Founded: 1957

Panchasheel Prakashan, Film Colony, Chaura Rasta, Jaipur 302003 Tel: (0141) 65072
Editorial: M C Gupta; *Sales:* O P Agarwal
Subjects: Academic, Fiction
Founded: 1968

Panjab University Publication Bureau, Chandigarh 160014 Tel: (0172) 22782
Secretary: R K Malhotra
Subjects: Belles Lettres, Poetry, Biography, History, Philosophy, Reference, Religion, Social Science, University Textbooks
Bookshop: At above address
Founded: 1948

Pankaj Publications International, 73D Kishanganj Market, Delhi 110007
Man Dir, Publicity: Kawaljit Arora
Parent Company: Heritage Publishers (qv)
Associate Companies: Disha Publications (qv); Intellectual's Rendezvous, Aggarwal Bhawan, 4C Ansari Rd, New Delhi 110002
Subjects: Biography, History, Bibliography, Literature, Reference, Religion, Economics, Language, Social Science, Philosophy
Founded: 1973

Parimal Prakashan+*, 'Parimal', Khadkeshwar, Aurangabad 431001 Tel: 4556
Man Dir, Production: A B Dashrathe; *Sales:* S D Shinde
Branch Offs: 4th floor Shivganga Chambers, Bajirao Rd, Pune; 31-A Saifee Manzil, Kennedy Bridge, Bombay
Subjects: Social Sciences, Humanities, Marathi Literature, Archaeology, Medical Science, English Literature
Bookshop: Marathwada Book Distributors (at above address)
Founded: 1974

Parkash Brothers*, 546 Books Market, Ludhiana 141008 Tel: (0161) 37258 Cable Add: Parkash Books
Chief Executive, Editorial: R P Tandon; *Sales, Production, Publicity:* K L Tandon; *Rights & Permissions:* Vijay Tandon, Vinod Tandon
Associate Company: Vijaya Publications (at above address)
Branch Off: Mai Hiran Gate, Jullundur
Subjects: Education, Physics, Engineering
Bookshop: At above address
Founded: 1948-9

Path Publishers*, 305A Hans Bhavan, Bahadur Shah Zafar Marg, New Delhi 110002 Tel: (011) 272539/622120
Chief Executive, Editorial, Publicity, Rights & Permissions: P J Koshy; *Sales:* Mohan Eapen; *Production:* S K Bhatnagar
Subjects: Law, Commerce
Founded: 1979

Pearl Publishers*, 206 Bidhan Saranee, Calcutta 700006
Proprietor: M Bhattacharjee; *Editorial:* S Roy; *Sales:* T Roy
Subjects: Political Science, Economics
Founded: 1977

People's Publishing House (P) Ltd, 5-E Rani Jhansi Rd, New Delhi 110055 Tel: (011) 523349/521724 Cable Add: Quamikitab
Chairman: T Madhavan; *General Manager:* P P C Joshi
Subjects: Belles Lettres, Poetry, Biography, History, Philosophy, Juveniles, Low- & High-priced Paperbacks, Engineering, Social Science, University Textbooks
Bookshop: 2 Marina Arcade, Connaught Pl, New Delhi 110001 Tel: (011) 344064
Founded: 1942

Pilgrim Publishers*, 56 Jatin Das Rd, Calcutta 700029, West Bengal Tel: (033) 464323
Man Dir: S De; *Editorial:* Mrs R Mukherjee; *Sales:* F C Dutta; *Production, Publicity:* T K Mukherjee
Parent Company: Traco, India
Subjects: Literature, History, Art, Archaeology
Bookshop: 18B/1B Tamer Lane, Calcutta 700009
Founded: 1966

Pitambar Publishing Co, 888 East Park Rd, Karol Bagh, New Delhi 110005 Tel: (011) 770067/776058/5721321 Cable Add: Pitambar New Delhi Telex: 0315579 Ptbr In
Man Dirs: Ved Bhushan, Anand Bhushan, Sushil Bhushan; *Sales:* R G Sharma; *Publicity:* Anand Bhushan; *Editorial:* B N Ahuja; *Production, Rights & Permissions:* Ved Bhushan
Associate Companies: Ambar Prakashan; Bharat Enterprises, Delhi; Computel Systems & Services; Parijat Enterprises, New Delhi; Piyush Printers Publishers Pvt Ltd, New Delhi; Reliant Microsystems Pvt Ltd
Subjects: General Fiction, Reference, University, Secondary & Primary Textbooks
Bookshop: At above address
1985: 150 titles *1986:* 200 titles *Founded:* 1947

Popular Prakashan Pvt Ltd, 35C Pandit Madan Mohan Malaviya Marg, Popular Press Bldg, opposite Roche, Tardeo, Bombay 400034 Tel: (022) 4941656/4945294/4944295 Cable Add: Nandibook
Man Dir: Ramdas Ganesh Bhatkal; *Joint Dir:* Sadanand Ganesh Bhatkal
Parent Company: Popular Book Depot (qv under Major Booksellers)
Branch Off: 4648/1 Ansari Rd, 21 Daryaganj, New Delhi 110002
Subjects: Anthropology, Sociology, Arts, Crafts, Music, Biography, Economics, Education, History, Literature, Law, Philosophy, Religion, Politics, Administration, Physics, Mathematics, Chemistry, Medicine
Founded: 1924

Prabhat Prakashan*, 205 Chawri Bazar, Delhi 110006 Tel: (011) 264676
Chief Executive: Shyam Sunder; *Editorial:* Shyam Bahadur Verma; *Sales:* Raghuvir Verma; *Production:* Dharam Vir
Branch Off: Mathura
Subjects: Miscellaneous
1985: 95 titles *Founded:* 1952

Prachi Prakashan, PO Box 3537, New Delhi 110024 (Located at: L-3 Lajpatnagar III, New Delhi) Tel: (011) 6836175
Proprietor: A K Dash
Subject: Anthropology, Social Sciences, Literature
Founded: 1976

Prakash Prakashan*, 8 Ram Nagar Colony, Agra 2, Uttar Pradesh

Prakasham Publications*, Alleppey 688003, Kerala State Tel: (0477) 2771/2181
Chief Executive: Vithuvattickal Lucas; *Editorial:* Hormice C Perumali; *Sales:* J Chirayail
Subjects: General, Fiction
Founded: 1967

Prayer Books*, 43-B Nandaram Sen St, Calcutta 700005 Tel: (033) 542306
Chief Executive, Sales, Production: Subrata Saha; *Editorial:* Subhas Saha; *Publicity, Rights & Permissions:* Mrs Papiya Saha
Subject: Literature (in Bengali and English)
Founded: 1978

Prentice-Hall of India Pvt Ltd*, M-97 Connaught Circus, New Delhi 110001 Tel: (011) 352590/351779 Cable Add: Prenhall New Delhi Telex: 3161808 Ph In
Chairman, Man Dir: Asoke K Ghosh
Associate Companies: Prentice-Hall (Simon & Schuster International Group), UK (qv); Prentice-Hall Inc, Englewood Cliffs, NJ 07632, USA
Subject: Textbooks
Founded: 1963

Printox*, E-210 Pragati Vihar, Lodhi Rd, New Delhi 110003 Tel: (011) 693097
Proprietor: S G Nene
Branch Off: 1557 Sadashiv Peth, Poona 411030 Tel: (0212) 442960; K-15/7 Bibihatia, Varanasi 211001
Subjects: Politics, Social Science, Literary Criticism, Philosophy, Ancient Indian Literature, Art

Progressive Corporation Pvt Ltd, 3rd floor, Jehangir Wadia Bldg, 51 Mahatma Gandhi Rd, Flora Fountain, Fort Bombay 400023 Tel: (022) 2044813/2041634 Cable Add: Progcorp
Man Dir: Mrs D R Davar; *Sales Dirs:* Dr Rustom S Davar, Nanabhoy S Davar
Branch Off: 305 Triplicane High Rd, Madras 600005
Subjects: Management & Commerce, Accountancy, Business Law, Banking, Computers, Economics, Statistics, Marketing, Salesmanship, Advertising
Founded: 1932

Promilla and Co, Sonali, C-127 Sarvodaya Enclave, New Delhi 110017 Tel: (011) 668720
President and Editor: Prof D H Butani; *Editorial, Production, Rights & Permissions Dir:* Ashok Butani; *Sales Manager:* M M Khanna; *Publicity Manager:* Nirmala Butani
Subjects: History, Reference, Religion, Arts, Economics, Politics, Sociology
1985: 2 titles *1986:* 4 titles *Founded:* 1970
ISBN Publisher's Prefix: 81-85002

Publication Board of Assam*, Bamunimaidan, Gauhati 781021

Publications & Information Directorate*, Hillside Rd, New Delhi 110012 Tel: (011) 586301 Cable Add: Publiform
Editorial: Y R Chadha; *Sales:* Kishan Singh
Subject: Scientific

Punjab State University Textbook Board*, S C O 2935-36, Sector 22-C, Chandigarh 160022 Tel: (0172) 28983
Editorial: Prithipal Singh Kapur; *Production, Sales:* M Singh Rattan
Subject: Academic

Punjabi Pustak Bhandar*, Dariba, Delhi 110006 Tel: (011) 266232
Managing Partner: Gulshan Rai Verma
Associate Companies: Diamond Books International, Diamond Pocket Books, Diamond Comics (P) Ltd (qv) (all at 2715 Daryaganj, New Delhi 110002)

K P **Punnoose** Communications Co+*, Kunnuparampil Bldgs, Kurichy 686549, Kottayam District, Kerala Tel: (04826) 470
Man Dir, Editorial, Sales, Production, Rights & Permissions: K P Punnoose; *Publicity:* Jaffe Punnoose
Subsidiary Companies: Institute for Christian Publishing & Communications Research (qv); Jaffe Books (qv under Remainder Dealers); Jaffe Publishing Management Service (qv under Literary Agents)
Subjects: Book Trade, Publishing, Communications
Founded: 1975

Radha Krishna Prakashan*, 2 Ansari Rd, Daryaganj, New Delhi 110002 Tel: (011) 275851 Cable Add: Lokpriya Delhi
Man Dir: Om Prakash
Subjects: General Fiction, Belles Lettres, Poetry, Biography, Juveniles, High-priced Paperbacks, University Textbooks
Founded: 1965

Radha Soami Satsang Beas, PO Dera Baba Jaimal Singh, Distt Amritsar 143204 Tel: Rayya 50, Dhilwan 40 Cable Add: Radhasoami Satsang Beas
Man Dir, Production, Publicity: K S Narang; *Secretary, Rights & Permissions:* S L Sondhi; *Sales:* J C Moorgai (Home), Krishin Babani (Abroad)
Parent Company: Charitable & Religious Society, Radhasoami Satsang Beas
Subjects: Religion, Philosophy
Founded: 1957

Radiant Publishers+*, E-155 Kalkaji, New Delhi 110019 Tel: (011) 635477
Man Dir, Sales, Rights & Permissions, Production, Publicity: V K Jain; *Editorial:* Sunita Jain
Subjects: Politics, International Affairs, Economics, Sociology, History
Founded: 1973

Rajasthan Hindi Granth Academy*, A-26/2 Vidyalaya Marg, Tilak Nagar, Jaipur 302004 Tel: (0141) 46210
Chief Executive: Dr Raghava Prakash; *Editorial:* Dr M P Dadhich; *Sales, Publicity:* K N Agrawal; *Production:* Mahesh Jain
Subjects: Social Science, Science, Humanities (in Hindi)
Founded: 1969

Rajesh Publications*, 1 Ansari Rd, Daryaganj, New Delhi 110002 Tel: (011) 274550
Man Dir: Gupta Mohan Lal
Subjects: History, Geography, Religion, Philosophy, Economics, General
Founded: 1970

Rajhans Prakashan Mandir*, Dharma Alok, Ram Nagar, Meerut, Uttar Pradesh

Rajkamal Prakashan Pvt Ltd*, 8 Netaji Subhash Marg, New Delhi 110002
Subjects: Juveniles, Education, Paperbacks

Rajneesh Foundation*, Shree Rajneesh Ashram, 17 Koregaon Park, Poona 411001 Tel: (0212) 28127/20981/20982 Cable Add: Tathata Telex: 0145421 Tao
Man Dir, Sales, Rights & Permissions: Ma Yoga Laxmi; *Publicity:* Swami Krishna Prem
Subjects: Religion, Philosophy, Psychology; the teachings of Bhagwan Shree Rajneesh (English and Hindi)
Bookshop: At above address
Founded: 1969

Rajpal & Sons, PO Box 1064, Delhi 110006 (Located at: Kashmere Gate, Delhi) Tel: (011) 2519104/2523904 Cable Add: Rajpalsons Delhi
Man Dir: Mr Vishwanath; *Sales:* Ishwar Chandra; *Editorial:* Mahendra Kulshreshtna; *Publicity, Rights & Permissions:* Kapil Malhotra
Associate Companies: Orient Paperbacks (qv); Shiksha Bharati (qv); Vision Books Pvt Ltd (qv)
Subjects: General Fiction, Literary Criticism, Humanities, Science, Textbooks, Juveniles
Bookshop: At above address
Founded: 1891

Ram Prasad & Sons*, Hospital Rd, Agra 282003 Tel: (0562) 72935 Cable Add: Modern
Man Dir: H N Agarwala; *Sales Dir:* R N Agarwala; *Publicity & Advertising:* B N Agarwala
Subsidiary Companies: Modern Printers, 1153 Bagh Muzaffar Khan, Agra 2; Sanchi Prakashan, Bhopal 1
Subjects: Agriculture & Veterinary Science, Commerce & Economics, Education & Psychology, Engineering & Technology, Geography, Mathematics & Statistics, Physics, Political Science, Sociology, Social Work, Criminology, University, Secondary & Primary Textbooks
Bookshops: Modern Book Depot, Hospital Rd, Agra 3; Bal Vihar, Hamidia Rd, Bhopal 1
Founded: 1905

Sri **Ramakrishna** Math*, PO Box 635, Mylapore, Madras 600004 (Located at: 16 Sri Ramakrishna Math Rd, Mylapore, Madras) Tel: (044) 71231
President: Sri Ramakrishna Math
Subjects: Religion, Culture, Philosophy
Bookshops: 16 Ramakrishna Math Rd, Mylapore, Madras 4; South Mada St, Mylapore, Madras 4
Founded: 1897

Rastogi Publications*, Shivaji Rd, Meerut 250002 Tel: (0121) 73698/73132 Cable Add: Rastogico
Editorial: Mrs Prakash Wati; *Sales, Publicity:* H K Rastogi; *Production, Rights & Permissions:* R K Rastogi
Associate Company: Rastogi Associates (at above address)
Subsidiary Companies: Pioneer Printers, Rastogi & Co (both at above address)
Subjects: University Textbooks in Botany, Political Science, Zoology and Education
Founded: 1966

Ratnabharati, PO Box 486, Bombay 400001 (Located at: Ilaco House, Sir Pherozeshah Mehta Rd, Bombay) Tel: (022) 2860739 Cable Add: Pustaken
Editorial, Production: Punit Batra; *Sales, Publicity, Rights & Permissions:* Ranjit Batra
Subjects: Children's (illustrated)
Founded: 1965

Rekha Prakashan+, 16 Daryaganj, New Delhi 110002 Tel: (011) 279907
Chief Executive, Rights & Permissions: K C Aryan; *Editorial:* S Aryan; *Sales:* B N Aryan; *Production, Publicity:* G D Aryan
Subjects: Art, Indology
Founded: 1973

Reliance Publishing House+, 3026/7H Shiv Chowk, Ranjit Nagar, New Delhi 110008 Tel: (011) 5722605/586889
Man Dir, Editorial, Production, Rights & Permissions: S K Bhatia; *Sales:* M K Bhatia; *Publicity:* Gita Bhatia
Parent Company: Gita Enterprises (at above address)
Subsidiary Company: Linguaphone Distributors (at above address)
Subjects: Humanities, Social Sciences, Agriculture, Library Science, Reference
1986: 13 titles *1987:* 15 titles *Founded:* 1985
ISBN Publisher's Prefix: 88-85047

Researchco, 1865 Trinagar, Delhi 110035 Tel: (011) 7128547 Cable Add: Searchbook Telex: 3162205 Srch In
Manager: O P Vaish; *Sales:* Anil Jain
Subsidiary Company: Researchco Reprints (at above address)
Branch Off: A T Rd, Tarajan, Jorhat 785001
Subjects: Scientific, Technical
Founded: 1969

Roli Books International, 5 Ansari Rd, Daryaganj, New Delhi 110002 Tel: (011) 276325/276277 Cable Add: Rolipub Telex: 66184 Roli In
Publisher, Rights & Permissions: Pramod Kapoor; *Editorial:* Manjulika Dubey; *Sales, Publicity:* Sanjeev Ohri
Associate Companies: Lustre Press Pvt Ltd (at above address); Lustre Print Media Pvt Ltd (at above address)
Subjects: Travel, Architecture, Sculpture, Painting, Dance (illustrated)
Founded: 1979

Roorkee Press, see Nem Chand & Brothers (qv)

K K **Roy** (Pvt) Ltd, PO Box 10210, Calcutta 700019 (Located at: 55 Gariahat Rd, Calcutta) Tel: (033) 474872 Cable Add: Helbell
Man Dir, Rights & Permissions: Dr K K Roy; *Sales Dir:* S Paul; *Publicity Dir:* Renu Kochhar; *Advertising Dir:* G Govindan
Subsidiary Company: Intertrade Publications (India) Pvt Ltd (at above address)
Subjects: Belles Lettres, Poetry, Biography, History, Philosophy, Reference, Religion, Medicine, University Textbooks
Founded: 1954

Rupa & Co*, PO Box 12333, Calcutta 700073 (Located at: 15 Bankim Chatterjee St, Calcutta) Tel: (033) 344821/346305 Cable Add: Rupanco
Man Dir, Editorial, Rights & Permissions: D Mehra; *Sales:* R N Barman; *Production:* N D Mehra, R K Mehra; *Publicity:* S K Mehra, C K Mehra
Branch Offs: 94 South Malaka, Allahabad 211001; 102 Prasad Chambers, Swadeshi Mills Compound, Opera House, Bombay 400004; 3831 Pataudi House Rd, Daryaganj, New Delhi 110002
Subjects: Art, Education, History, Literature, Fiction, Philosophy, Religion, Sport, Pastimes
Bookshop: See under Major Booksellers
Founded: 1936

S B D Enterprises+, PO Box 1061, Delhi 110006 (Located at: 4422-23 Nai Sarak, Delhi) Tel: (011) 2911823/2923105/2913081
Managing Partner: Kanwaljit Singh
Subjects: Literature, Social Sciences
1986: 50 titles *Founded:* 1978
Miscellaneous: Also booksellers and distributors

Sage Publications India Pvt Ltd+, 2nd floor, 32 M-block Market, Greater Kailash-I, New Delhi 110048 Tel: (011) 6419884 Cable Add: Sagepub New Delhi 110024
Man Dir: Tejeshwar Singh; *Editorial:* Payal Mehta; *Sales:* Rakesh Datta; *Marketing:* Sunanda Ghosh
Associate Companies: Sage Publications Ltd, UK (qv); Sage Publications Inc, 275 South Beverly Drive, Beverly Hills, CA 90212, USA
Subject: Social Sciences
1986: 18 titles *1987:* 28 titles *Founded:* 1981
ISBN Publisher's Prefix: 81-7036

Sahitya Akademi*, Rabindra Bhavan, 35 Ferozeshah Rd, New Delhi 110001 Tel: (011) 388667 Cable Add: Sahityakar National Academy of Letters
Subject: Indian Literature

Sahitya Bhawan Pvt Ltd*, 93 KP Kakkar Rd, Allahabad 211003 Tel: (0532) 51077
Man Dir, Rights & Permissions: Girish Tandon; *Editorial:* Onkar Sharad; *Sales:* Ram Chandra Sharma; *Production:* P K Singh; *Publicity:* Ram Nath
Associate Company: Vivek Prakishthan (at above address)
Subjects: Hindi Literature and University Textbooks
Bookshop: At above address
Founded: 1917

Sahitya Pravarthaka Co-operative Society Ltd*, PO Box 94, Kottayam 686001, Kerala Tel: (0481) 4111/4112/4114 Cable Add: Sahithyam
Secretary: K P Sreemandiram; *Sales:* K S Pillai; *Production:* P Gopinath
Orders to: Sales Manager, National Book Stall, Kottayam
Subjects: Literature, Art, Science
Bookshops: National Book Stall, PO Box 40, Kottayam 686001 (and branches throughout Kerala)
Founded: 1945

Sahitya Samsad, an imprint of Shishu Sahitya Samsad Pvt Ltd (qv)

Saint Paul Publications*, 28-B Chatham Lines, Allahabad 211002 Tel: (0532) 53728
Chief Executive: Fr Anselm Poovathanikunnel; *Editorial, Rights & Permissions:* Fr Joe Narivelil; *Sales:* Br Ignatius T; *Production:* Br Vincent C; *Publicity:* Fr George Chathanatt
Imprint: Better Yourself Books (qv)
Branch Offs: Bangalore 73; Bombay 50; Cochin 11; New Delhi 1; Madras 1
Subjects: Practical Psychology, Self-improvement, Fiction, Biography, Spiritual
Bookshops: Examiner Press Bookshop, 35 Dalal St, Bombay 400023; St Paul Book Centre, Broadway, Cochin 31, Kerala; Good Pastor International Book Centre, 63 Armenian St, Madras 600001; Saint Paul International Book Centre, H-30 Connaught Circus, New Delhi 110001
Founded: 1952

Sanchi Prakashan, subsidiary of Ram Prasad & Sons (qv)

Sangam Books, an imprint of Orient Longman Ltd (qv)

Sanskrit Pustak Bhandar*, 38 Bidhan Sarani, Calcutta 700006 Tel: (033) 341208
Chief Executive: Shyama Pada Bhattacharya
Subjects: Indology, Reference
Founded: 1932
Miscellaneous: Also book dealers

Sanskriti, an imprint of Arnold Publishers (India) Pvt Ltd (qv)

Rashtriya Sanskrit **Sansthan***, 2-A Ramkishor Rd, Civil Lines, Delhi 54 Tel: (011) 222545/6 Cable Add: Sansthan
Chief Executive: Dr R K Sharma; *Editorial, Sales, Production, Publicity:* A Sampathnarayanan
Founded: 1970

Saraswat Library, 206 Bidhan Sarani, Calcutta 700006 Tel: (033) 316345
Managing Partner: B Bhattacharyya
Subjects: Poetry, History, Music, Art, Philosophy, Reference, Religion, Juveniles, General & Social Science, University, Secondary Textbooks
Bookshop: At above address
Founded: 1914

Sarita Prakashan+*, 175 Nauchandi Grounds, Meerut City Tel: (0121) 73515/ 75075 Cable Add: Prabhatpress Telex: 0594215
Man Dir, Publicity, Rights & Permissions: K A Rastogi; *Editorial:* Rahul Rastogi; *Sales:* Atul Rastogi; *Production:* Abhay Rastogi
Subsidiary Companies: Prabhat Offset Printers Pvt Ltd; Prabhat Press
Branch Off: Netaji Subhash Marg, Daryaganj, New Delhi Tel: (011) 276292
Subjects: Engineering, Botany, Literature, Reference
Founded: 1963

M C **Sarkar** & Sons (P) Ltd*, 14 Bankim Chatterjee St, Calcutta 700073

Sasta Sahitya Mandal, N-77 Connaught Circus, New Delhi 110001 Tel: (011) 3310505 Cable Add: Satsahitya
President: Lakshminiwas Birla; *Secretary:* Yashpal Jain
Branch Off: Zero Rd, Allahabad Tel: (0532) 50034
Subjects: History, Agriculture, Textbooks, Literature, Education, Philosophy, Psychology, Languages, Paperbacks, Economics
Founded: 1925

Sri **Satguru** Publications*, 1st floor, 40/5 Shakti Nagar, Delhi 110007 Tel: (011) 7126497
Man Dir, Rights & Permissions: Anil Kumar Gupta; *Export, Sales:* Sunil Gupta; *Publicity:* Virender Gupta
Parent Company: Indian Books Centre (qv)
Associate Companies: Bibliotheca Indo-Buddhica Series; Sri Garib Dass Oriental Series (both at above address)
Subjects: Religion, Philosophy, History, Linguistics, Sanskrit, Arts, Literature, Indian Medicine
Founded: 1980
ISBN Publisher's Prefix: 81-7030

Satya Press*, c/o Ananda Ashram, Thattanchavady, Pondicherry 605009 Tel: 2403 Cable Add: Yoga Life
Chief Executive: Dr Swami Gitananda; *Editorial:* Meenakshi Devi
Imprint: Yoga Life
Subjects: Yoga, Indian Philosophy (in English only)
Bookshop: Ananda Book Shop (at above address)
Founded: 1969

Sawan Kirpal Publications*, 2 Canal Rd, Vijay Nagar, Delhi 110009 Tel: (011) 7110757
Man Dir: S Darshan Singh; *Editorial:* Dr Vinod Sena; *Sales:* Rajesh Seth; *Production:* Jay Linksman; *Publicity:* Chris McCluney
Parent Company: Sawan Kirpal Publications Spiritual Society, H-11 Vijay Nagar, Delhi 110009

Branch Off: Rt 1, PO Box 24, Bowling Green, Virginia 22427, USA
Subject: Religion
Founded: 1977

Scientific Book Agency, PO Box 239, Calcutta 700001 Tel: (033) 295885/292915/ 229405 Cable Add: Pentacle Telex: Argosy 0212846
Man Dir: J Sinha; *Editorial:* P Sinha; *Science Editors:* Atish Sinha, Soumendra Sinha, Snehamoy Sinha; *Market Development Manager:* Miss Meenakshi Sinha; *Sales Dir:* S P Sinha; *Production:* S Sinha; *Publicity & Advertising:* Snehamoy Sinha; *Rights & Permissions:* Swapan Mitra
Branch Offs: 79/2 Mahatma Gandhi Rd, Calcutta 700009; 56-D Mirza Ghalib St, Calcutta 700016
Subjects: History, Medicine, Economics, Politics, Physics, Chemistry, Biological Sciences, Veterinary, Engineering
Founded: 1954

Scientific Publishers, opp Police Lines, Maan Bhawan 1st floor, Ratanada Rd, Jodhpur 342001 Tel: 24154 Cable Add: Scientific
Man Dir, Editorial: Pawan Kumar; *Sales:* Mohan Lal
Parent Company: United Book Traders (at above address)
Subsidiary Company: Sharda Publishing House, Sharda Sadan Subhas Colony, Defence Lab Rd, Jodhpur 342003
Subjects: Biology, Social Sciences
1985: 15 titles *1986:* 25 titles *Founded:* 1976

Seemant Prakashan, 922 Kucha Rohella Khan, Daryaganj, New Delhi 110002 Tel: (011) 270284
Chief Executive: Narinder Nath Soz; *Sales:* Rajesh Didden; *Production:* Ajay Didden
Subjects: General (Hindi and Urdu)
Founded: 1976

Selina Publishers, 4725/21A Dayanand Marg, Daryaganj, New Delhi 110002 Tel: (011) 277230/277375
Man Dir, Publicity, Rights & Permissions: H L Gupta; *Editorial:* Preeti Mehra; *Production:* Subhash Arora; *Sales:* V Kohli
Subsidiary Company: Sanket Paperbacks
Associate Company: Granth Bharati (Printing Press)
Branch Off: 48 Daryaganj, New Delhi 110002
Subjects: Textbooks, Educational Materials
Book Club: Sanket Library Yojna
Founded: 1975

Shakti Books, an imprint of Vikas Publishing House Pvt Ltd (qv)

Sharda Prakashan, Mehrauli, New Delhi 110030 Tel: (011) 653982
Chief Executive, Production, Rights & Permissions: Vijay Dev Jhari; *Editorial, Publicity:* Ravinder Jhari; *Sales:* R D Jhari
Subsidiary Company: Nalanda Prakashan, 33/1 Mehrauli, New Delhi 110030
Associate Companies: Itihas Shodh Sansthan, 33/1 Mehrauli, New Delhi 110030; Jharison, Bhullehullian Rd, Mehrauli, New Delhi 110030
Subjects: Literary Criticism, Fiction, Drama, Memoirs, Children's Literature, General
Bookshop: 16-F3 Ansari Rd, Daryaganj, New Delhi 110002 Tel: (011) 279853
Founded: 1971

R R **Sheth** & Co*, PO Box 2517, Bombay 400002 (Located at: 110/112 S Gandhi Marg, Bombay) Tel: (022) 313441 Cable Add: Literature Bombay
Man Dir: Bhagatbhai Bhuralal Sheth
Associate Company: Lokpriya Prakashan (at above address)

Branch Off: Opp Phuvara, Gandhi Rd, Ahmedabad 380001 Tel: (0272) 380573
Subjects: Gujarati literature
Bookshops: See under Major Booksellers
Founded: 1926

Shiksha Bharati, Madarsa Rd, Kashmere Gate, Delhi 110006 Tel: (011) 2523904
Man Dir, Rights & Permissions: Sudhir Malhotra; *Editorial:* Meera Johri; *Sales, Publicity:* Mrs Parveen Malhotra; *Production:* Indu Malhotra
Associate Companies: Orient Paperbacks (qv); Rajpal & Sons (qv); Vision Books Pvt Ltd (qv)
Subsidiary Company: Shiksha Bharati Press, 18 G T Rd, Shahdara, Delhi 110032
Subjects: Juveniles, Educational
Founded: 1959

Shishu Sahitya Samsad Pvt Ltd*, 32-A Acharya Prafulla Chandra Rd, Calcutta 700009 Tel: (033) 357669 Cable Add: Qualibooks
Man Dir: Mohendranath Dutt; *Editorial Manager, Publicity Manager:* Golokendu Ghosh; *Sales, Production, Rights & Permissions Dir:* Debajyoti Dutt
Imprint: Sahitya Samsad
Subjects: Juvenile Literature, Lexicons, Classics, Art
Founded: 1951

Shree Mahavir Book Depot (Publishers)*, 2603 Nai Sarak, Delhi 110006 Tel: (011) 262993/7110823/2910242
Chief Executive: Ram Kanwar; *Editorial:* Prem Chandra; *Sales, Rights & Permissions:* Hem Chandra; *Production:* Ram Chandra; *Publicity:* Harish Chandra
Subjects: Commerce, Accountancy, Management, Law, Economics, Political Science, History, Geography, Physics, Chemistry, Biology, Mathematics, Music, Domestic Science
Founded: 1948

Shree Saraswati Sadan*, A-I/32 Safdarjang Enclave, New Delhi 110029 Tel: (011) 661539
Chief Executive, Sales, Production, Rights & Permissions: Amitabh Ranjan; *Editorial, Publicity:* Mrs Abha Ranjan
Branch Off: Mussoorie (UP)
Subjects: History, Politics, Sociology, Historical Fiction (in English and Hindi)
Founded: 1972

Shri Ram Centre for Industrial Relations and Human Resources*, 5 Sadhu Vaswani Marg, New Delhi 110005 Tel: (011) 585134 Cable Add: Sricir
Man Dir, Editorial, Rights & Permissions: Arun Joshi; *Sales, Production, Publicity:* K K Bhargava
Subject: Indian Journal of Industrial Relations
Founded: 1963

Skyline Publishing House*, 28/2 St No 3, Friends Colony, Shahdara, Delhi 110032 Tel: (011) 203346
Chief Executive: Surjeet Gupta; *Editorial, Rights & Permissions:* S N Sarkar; *Sales:* Nawab Singh; *Production, Publicity:* Chandrasekhar
Subjects: Current Affairs, Economics, Self-improvement, Yoga, Cookery, Beauty Culture
Founded: 1979

Smriti Prakashan*, 124 Shah Rara Bagh, Allahabad 211003 Tel: (0532) 54589
Chief Executive, Editorial, Production: Bal Krishna Tripathi; *Sales:* Niraj Kumar Tripathi; *Publicity:* Deepak
Subjects: General
Bookshop: At above address
Founded: 1969

Somaiya Publications Pvt Ltd+, 172 Mumbai Marathi Grantha Sangrahalaya Marg, Dadar, Bombay 400014 Tel: (022) 4130230 Cable Add: Bookmark, Bombay
Bombay Executive: K S Hattangadi; *Delhi Executive:* T V Kunhi Krishnan
Parent Company: The Godavari Sugar Mills Ltd, Fazalbhoy Bldg, Mahatma Gandhi Rd, Bombay 400001
Associate Companies: The Book Centre Ltd (Book Sales Division), Ranade Rd, Dadar, Bombay 400028; The Book Centre Ltd (Printing Press Division), Plot No 103, 6th Rd, Sion, Bombay 400022
Branch Off: F-6 Bank of Baroda Bldg, Parliament St, New Delhi 110001
Subjects: Architecture, Commerce, Education, Engineering, History, Political Science, Religion and Philosophy, Language, Literature, Management, Mathematics, Physics, Chemistry
Founded: 1967

South Asian Publishers Pvt Ltd, 36 Netaji Subhash Marg, Daryaganj, New Delhi 110002 Tel: (011) 276292
Chief Executive, Editorial, Rights & Permissions: Vinod Kumar; *Production, Publicity:* K A Rastogi
Branch Off: 177 Avvai Shanmugham Salai, Madras 600086
Subjects: Academic Works in Science, Technology, Social Sciences
Founded: 1980

Spectrum Publications+, PO Box 45, Guwahati 781001, Assam (Located at: Pan Bazar, Guwahati) Tel: (0361) 24791 Cable Add: Spectrum, Guwahati
Publisher: Krishan Kumar; *Editorial:* A K Hazarika; *Sales:* Shekhar Kar; *Publicity:* Ranjit Brahma
Subjects: Tourism, Reference, Anthropology, Sociology, Annual Yearbooks and Directories, Children's Books, Journals
Bookshop: United Publishers (qv under Major Booksellers)
Founded: 1976

Springer Books (India) Pvt Ltd, 6 Community Centre, Panchsheel Park, New Delhi 110017 Tel: (011) 6433992/6433818 Cable Add: Narosa Telex: 3161661 Nar In
Man Dir: N K Mehra
Associate Companies: Springer-Verlag Berlin — Heidelberg — New York — Tokyo GmbH & Co KG, Federal Republic of Germany (qv); Narosa Publishing House (qv); Narosa Book Distributors (at above address)
Branch Offs: 306 Shiv Centre, DBC Sector 17, PO KU Bazar, New Bombay 400705 Tel: (02154) 683646/670056 Cable Add: Spriverlag Vashi New Bombay; 35-36 Greams Rd, Thousand Lights, Madras 600006 Tel: (044) 475362 Cable Add: Spriverlag Madras
Subjects: Pure and Applied Science, Medicine
Founded: 1980

Sree Rama Publishers*, 4000 Market St, Secunderabad 500025 Tel: 73128 Cable Add: Books, Secunderabad
Man Dir: Shiva Ramaiah Pabba; *Editorial:* Sreenivas Prabhu Pabba; *Sales:* Subash Chandra Sekhar Pabba; *Production:* Shivaramaiah Pabba; *Publicity, Rights & Permissions:* Shivarajaiah Pabba
Orders to: 113 Sarojini Devi Rd, Secunderabad 500003
Parent Company: Sree Rama Book Depot, Market St, Secunderabad
Associate Companies: Popular Book House, Pan Bazaar, Secunderabad; Sree Sita Rama Book Depot, Siddiamber Bazar, Hyderabad
Subjects: Primary & Secondary Textbooks, Theology in local language and English
Bookshops: Sree Rama Book Depot, Gunfoundry, Hyderabad 500001; Sree Rama Book Depot, Siddiamber Bazar, Hyderabad
Founded: 1916

The **Standard** Book Depot*, Avenue Rd, Bangalore 560002 Tel: (0812) 26535/72625 Cable Add: Stanbook
Man Dir, Rights & Permissions: B Rajashekar; *Editorial:* B Gurunath; *Sales:* B Ananth; *Production:* R L Narasimhiah; *Publicity:* S Sudhindra
Subjects: Fiction, General Literature, Popular Science, Juveniles
Bookshop: At above address
Founded: 1935

Star Publications (Pvt) Ltd*, 4/5B Asaf Ali Rd, New Delhi 110002 Tel: (011) 273335/274874/265135 Cable Add: Starpublis Telex: 315328 Star In
Man Dir, Sales, Production, Publicity: Amar Nath
Associate Company: Star Book Centre, Delhi 110006
Subsidiary Company: Publications India, New Delhi 110001
Subjects: Paperbacks in Urdu and Hindi
Book Club: Star Book Bank
Bookshop: See under Major Booksellers
Founded: 1969

State Institute of Languages*, Kerala, 'Nalanda', Trivandrum 695003 Tel: (0471) 61306
Dir, Production, Publicity, Rights & Permissions: Dr A N P Ummerkutty; *Assistant Dirs:* Dr K Velayudhan Nair, N Ramesan; *Editorial:* N Vigayan (Social Sciences), Dr C G Kartha (Physical Sciences), K N Sreenivasan (Natural Sciences), K K Krishna Kumar (Technical Sciences), P Balan (Languages); *Sales:* N Velappan Nair
Subjects: University Level Textbooks in Regional Languages, Malayalam
Founded: 1968

Sterling Publishers Pvt Ltd+*, L-10 Green Park Extension, New Delhi 110016 Tel: (011) 669560/660904 Cable Add: Paperbacks Telex: 03161443 Rgnt In
Chairman, Rights & Permissions: O P Ghai; *Man Dir:* S K Ghai; *Editorial:* R K Kakar; *Sales:* S Jana; *Production:* Gulab Pratihar; *Publicity:* Anita Bhasin
Associate Companies: Oriental University Press, 2 Salisbury Mansion, St. Ann's Rd, Harringay, London N15 3JP, UK; Envoy Press, 141 East 44th St, Suite 511, New York, NY 11017, USA
Imprint: Gaurav Publishing House
Branch Off: 24 Race Course Rd, Madhav Nagar, Bangalore 560001
Subjects: History, Philosophy, Economics, Reference, Low-priced Paperbacks, Social Science, University Textbooks, Political Science, Agriculture, Art, Autobiography, Education, Fiction, International Relations, Library Science, Management and Administration, Religion, Sociology, Science and Technology, Medicine
Book Club: Book Lovers Club
1985: 150 titles *Founded:* 1965
ISBN Publisher's Prefixes: 81-207 (Sterling), 81-85006 (Gaurav)

The **Students'** Book Co*, SMS Highway, Jaipur 302003 Tel: (0141) 72455 (shop), 74087 (res)
Proprietor, Rights & Permissions: Tara Chand Verma; *Man Dir:* J D Verma; *Editorial, Sales, Production:* Subhash Chandra Verma; *Publicity:* Satish Chandra Verma

Subsidiary Company; United Printers, Radha Damoderji Ki Gali, Chaura Rasta, Jaipur 302003
Subjects: Science, Commerce, Arts, Sanskrit, Hindi, English, Rajasthani
Bookshops: Chinmaya Prakashan, Chaura Rasta, Jaipur 302003; Vaner Prakashan, Chaura Rasta, Jaipur 302003
Founded: 1939

Subodh Pocket Books*, 2/4240A Ansari Rd, New Delhi 110002 Tel: (011) 274513/ 278858
Chief Executive, Rights & Permissions: Vijay Kumar; *Sales, Production:* Anil Kumar Arya
Subsidiary Companies: Govindram Hasanand, 4408 Nai Sarak, Delhi 110006; Subodh Publications, 2/3B Ansari Rd, New Delhi 110002
Subjects: Fiction, Non-fiction, Vedic literature
Founded: 1965

Sudha Publications Pvt Ltd*, B-5 Prabhat Kiran, Rajendra Pl, New Delhi 110008 Tel: (011) 5718495
Man Dir, Rights & Permissions: S K Sachdeva; *Publicity & Advertising Dir:* Vijay Lakshmi
Founded: 1960

Sultan Chand & Sons+, 4792-23 Daryaganj, New Delhi 110002 Tel: (011) 278659/ 277843/279080
Man Dir: Prakash Chand; *Editorial, Production:* S Chand; *Sales, Publicity, Rights & Permissions:* Manohar Pant
Associate Companies: Sultan Chand & Sons Pvt Ltd, 24 Daryaganj, New Delhi 110002; Sultan Chand Publishing House Pvt Ltd, 23 Daryaganj, New Delhi 110002
Subjects: Management, Business, Accounting, Law, Commerce, Economics, Biology, Chemistry, Physics, Maths, Statistics, Political Science, Public Administration
Bookshop: Premier Book Co (at above main address)
1985: 30 titles *1986:* 33 titles *Founded:* 1950

Suman Prakashan Pvt Ltd, 24-B/9 Desh Bandhu Gupta Rd, Dev Nagar, New Delhi 110005 Tel: (011) 5710759/5729106/5710772
Dir: R N Malhotra

Surjeet Book Depot (Regd)+, PO Box 1425, Delhi 110006 (Located at: 4074-75 Nai Sarak, Delhi) Tel: (011) 2913081/ 2915967
Managing Partner: Harnam Singh
Subjects: Literature, Social Science
1986: 215 titles *Founded:* 1950
Miscellaneous: Also bookseller, distributor and remainder dealer (qv)

Swan, an imprint of Orient Longman Ltd (qv)

Tamil Puthakalayam*, 58 T P Koil St, Triplicane, Madras 600005 Tel: (044) 843226
Chief Executive: K N Muthiah; *All other offices:* K N Muthiah, A Kannan
Subjects: Fiction, Drama, Literary Criticism, Religion, Medicine, General
Founded: 1946

Taraporevala (DB) Sons & Co Pvt Ltd, 210 Dr Dadabhai Naoroji Rd, Bombay 400001 Tel: (022) 2041433/2049782 Cable Add: Bookshop, Bombay
Chief Executive: Prof Russi J Taraporevala; *Dirs:* Mrs Manekbai J Taraporevala, Miss Sooni J Taraporevala
Subjects: Indian Art, Culture, History, Sociology, Secondary & University Textbooks, Reprints of scientific and technical titles
Founded: 1864

Taraporevala Publishing Industries Pvt Ltd, 'Woodlands', 67 Dr G Deshmukh Marg, Bombay 400026 Tel: (022) 4923341 Cable Add: Tarabook, Bombay
Subjects: Management, Computer Technology, Social Science, Chemical Engineering, Natural Sciences, Technology, Reprints

Tata McGraw-Hill Publishing Co Ltd, see under McGraw-Hill

Thacker & Co Ltd*, 18-20 Kaikhushroo Dubash Marg, Bombay 400023 Tel: (022) 242745/242683/242667 Cable Add: Booknotes
Dir: J M Chudasama; *Chief Executive:* Anil Laud
Subjects: History, Political & Social Science, Law, Business, University Textbooks
Bookshop: At above address

The **Theosophical Publishing** House, Adyar, Madras 600020 Tel: (044) 412904 Cable Add: Theotheca
Sales, Operations, Publicity Manager: R Gopalaratnam; *Editorial, Rights & Permissions:* John Clarke
Associate Companies: The Theosophical Publishing House, 306 W Geneva Rd, PO Box 270, Wheaton, IL 60189, USA; The Theosophical Publishing House Ltd, 12 Bury Pl, London WC1A 2LE, UK
Subjects: Philosophy, Religion, Universal Brotherhood, Occultism, Theosophy
Founded: 1913
ISBN Publisher's Prefix: 0-8356

Joseph **Thomasons** & Co, 7 Anand Bazar, Ernakulam, Kerala State 682016 Tel: (0484) 35235 Cable Add: Jetco
Chief Executive: Andrew Nettikadan; *Publicity:* Tom Thomas
Associate Company: Nettikadan Corporation (Books Unit) (qv)
Subjects: General
Founded: 1958

Thomson Press (India) Ltd*, PO Box 314, New Delhi 110001 (Located at: K Block Connaught Circus, New Delhi) Tel: (011) 353808/350225/352724 Cable Add: Thompress Telex: ND 2651
Man Dir: Aroon Purie; *Marketing Services Manager:* Rusi Brij; *General Manager:* Chander Rai
Associate Company: Living Media India Ltd, F-40 Connaught Pl, New Delhi 110001
Branch Off: 28 A&B Jolly Maker Chambers II, Nariman Point, Bombay 400021
Subject: Children's Books

Central **Tibetan** Secretariat, see Central

Today & Tomorrow's Printers & Publishers*, 24-B/5 Desh Bandhu Gupta Rd, New Delhi 110005 Tel: (011) 5721928/ 5727770
Man Dir, Editorial, Rights & Permissions: Rajendra Kumar Jain; *Sales, Publicity, Production:* R P Tiwari
Subjects: Indian Studies, Agriculture, Natural History, Science, Textbooks, Reference
Bookshop: At above address
Founded: 1967

Travancore Law House, M G Rd, Cochin 682011 Tel: 353766
Chief Executive: S Joseph
Subjects: Law, Commerce, Management
Founded: 1934

Trimurti Publications Pvt Ltd+*, W-152 Greater Kailash-I, New Delhi 110048 Tel: (011) 6416317
Man Dir, Sales, Rights & Permissions: S P Kumria; *Publicity Dir:* Sudarshan Kumria
Subjects: History, Political Science, Economics, Religion, Philosophy, Reference, Social Science, University Textbooks
Founded: 1972

N M **Tripathi** Pvt Ltd*, 164 Shamaldas Gandhi Marg, Bombay 400002
Man Dir: Arvind S Pandya; *Executive Manager:* Virendra Majmudar
Subjects: Law, Commerce, Gujarati
Bookshop: See under Major Booksellers
Founded: 1888

University Publishers, Railway Rd, Jullundur City 144001 Tel: (0181) 2645 Cable Add: Best Books
Dirs: A N Chopra, R K Chopra; *Sales Dir:* O P Sharma; *Publicity Dir:* Rajinder Pal; *Advertising Dir:* Budhi Ram
Subjects: Fiction, History, Political Science, Technology, Educational Materials
Founded: 1947

Upkar Prakashan, 2/11A Swadeshi Bima Nagar, Agra 282002 Tel: (0562) 65110/ 61802 Cable Add: Competion
Chief Executive, Publicity, Rights & Permissions: M S Jain; *Sales, Production:* N S Jain
Associate Company: Pratiyogita Darpan (at above address)
Subjects: General Knowledge, Competition Books, General
Bookshop: Vijaysing Jain, Bookseller, Hospital Rd, Agra
Founded: 1973

The **Upper India** Publishing House Pvt Ltd*, Aminabad, Lucknow UP 226018 Tel: (0522) 42711 Cable Add: Balance
Man Dir: S Bhargava
Subjects: History, Reference, General & Social Science, Secondary & University Textbooks (in Hindi & English)
Founded: 1921

Vakils Feffer & Simons Ltd+*, 9 Sprott Rd, Ballard Estate, Bombay 400038 Tel: (022) 261221 Cable Add: Fleetbooks
Man Dir: Mrs A F Shaikh
Subjects: Educational, College Textbooks, Cookery, Art, Religion

Vani Prakashan*, 4697/5, 21-A Daryaganj, New Delhi 110002 Tel: (011) 276379
Chief Executive, Editorial, Production, Publicity: Ashok Kumar Maheshwari; *Sales:* Arun Kumar Maheshwari
Associate Companies: Konarka Prakashan, 61-F Kamla Nagar, Delhi 110007; Ankur Prakashan, Maheshwari Publications, both at 1/3017 Ramnagar, Mandali Rd, Shadhara, Delhi 32
Subjects: Hindi Fiction, Poetry, Criticism, History
Founded: 1968

Venus Press & Book Depot*, Konni, Kerala Tel: 16
Editorial: E K Sekhar; *Sales:* P Viswaswaran Pillay
Subjects: Novels, Short Stories, Humour
Bookshop: Venus Book Depot (at above address)
Founded: 1946

Vidhi Sahitya Prakashan, see Law Books in Hindi Publishers

Vidyapuri*, Balubazar, Cuttack 753002, Orissa Tel: (0671) 23637 Cable Add: Vidyapuri
Managing Partner, Editorial, Production, Publicity, Rights & Permissions: Pitamber Mishra; *Partner:* Ramananda Mishra; *Sales:* S K Sarangi
Associate Companies: Goswami Press (at above address); Graftek Pvt Ltd,

Bhubaneswar 751002; Rainbow Offset (P) Ltd, Bhubaneswar 751002
Subjects: College Textbooks, General Literature, Children's Literature
Bookshop: At above address
Founded: 1961

Vidyarthi Mithram Press+*, PO Box 81, Kottayam 686001, Kerala State (Located at: Baker Rd, Kottayam) Tel: (0481) 3281/3282/4713 (after office hours 2616) Cable Add: Vidyarthi
Man Dir: Koshy P John
Associate Companies: Auroville Publishers, Kottayam; John Samuel Bros, Main Rd, Trivandrum
Imprints: Kosi Books, Manosabdam Books
Subjects: Fiction, Textbooks, Children's Books
Book Club: Vidyarthi Mithram Novel Club
Bookshop: Vidyarthi Mithram Book Depot (qv under Major Booksellers)
Founded: 1928

Vikas Publishing House Pvt Ltd+*, 5 Ansari Rd, New Delhi 110002 Cable Add: Vikasbooks Telex: 592252 Viph/In
Man Dir: Narendra Kumar
Imprint: Shakti Books
Subjects: Adventure, Mountaineering, Agriculture, Animal Husbandry, Art, Architecture, Travel, Biography, Memoirs, Botany, Chemistry, Cookery, Demography, Economics, Education, Engineering, Fiction, Futurology, Geography, Geology, History, Culture, Library Science, Literature, Management, Commerce, Mass Media, Mathematics, Medicine, Military Affairs, Philosophy, Religion, Physics, Politics, Current Affairs, Psychology, Public Administration, Science, Sociology, Anthropology, Sports, Games, Zoology, Children's Books
Founded: 1969

Vishal Publications*, Adda Hoshiarpur, Jullundur City 144001 Tel: (0181) 5177/5388
Man Dir: Pardeep Jain; *Sales Dir:* Rajinder K Jain; *Publicity & Advertising:* Sunil Jain
Branch Offs: Vishal Publications, 6 U B Bungalow Rd, Delhi 110007
Founded: 1973

Vision Books Pvt Ltd+, Madarsa Rd, Kashmere Gate, Delhi 110006 Tel: (011) 2517001/2512267/352081 Cable Add: Visionbook
Chairman: Vishwa Nath; *Man Dir, Rights & Permissions, Publicity, Sales:* Sudhir Malhotra; *Publishing Dir:* Kapil Malhotra; *Editor:* Swapan Mukerjee
Subsidiary Companies: Anand Paperbacks; Orient Paperbacks (qv)
Associate Companies: BIG Database Publishing Pvt Ltd (qv); Rajpal & Sons (qv); Ravindra Printing Press; Shiksha Bharati (qv)
Branch Off: 3-B Peddar Rd, 'Vasant' Ground Floor, Bombay
Subjects: General Fiction, Military Science and History, Sciences, Current Affairs, Indology, Management, Religion, Anthropology, Education, International Relations, Medicine, Mountaineering, Travel, Health, Do-it-Yourself
Book Clubs: Anand Book Club, Orient Book Club
1985: 100 titles *1986:* 100 titles *Founded:* 1975

Voluntary Health Association of India, 40 Institutional Area, South of IIT, New Delhi 110016 Tel: (011) 668071/2 Cable Add: Volhealth
Editorial: Alok Mukhopadhyay; *Rights & Permissions:* Dr James S Tong; *Sales, Production, Publicity:* N M Mathew
Subjects: Health, Nutrition, Management
Founded: 1973

Vora & Co Publishers Pvt Ltd, 3 Round Bldg, Kalbadevi Rd, Bombay 400002
Man Dir: K K Vora; *Publicity:* A M Vora
Subjects: Education, Textbooks, Law, Economics, Banking, Literature, History

A H Wheeler & Co (P) Ltd*, 23 Lal Bahadur Marg, Allahabad 211001

Wilco Publishing House*, 33 Ropewalk Lane, Rampart Row, Fort Bombay 400001 Tel: (022) 242574 Cable Add: Wilbook
Man Dir: Jaisukh H Shah
Subjects: Fiction, Reference, Philosophy, Psychology, Business, Management, Inspirational, Self-help
Founded: 1958

Wiley Eastern Ltd+*, 4835/24 Ansari Rd, Daryaganj, New Delhi 110002 Tel: (011) 276802/267996 Cable Add: Wileyeast
Dir: Anand R Kundaji; *Chief Executive:* Asanga Machwe; *Marketing Manager:* K K Gulati; *Editorial:* H S Poplai; *Production:* M S Sejwal
Associate Company: John Wiley & Sons Ltd, UK (qv for other associates)
Subjects: Psychology, Engineering, Social Science, University Textbooks, Indian Art, Science, Humanities
Bookshops: The Wiley Eastern Book Shop, 4654/21 Daryaganj, New Delhi 110002; John Wiley Bookshop, Abid House, Dr Bhadkamkar Marg, Bombay 400007; Wiley Eastern Bookshop, 40/8 Ballygunje Circular Rd, Calcutta 700019; The Wiley Bookshop, 6 Shri BP Wadia Rd, Basavangudi, Bangalore 560004
Founded: 1966
ISBN Publisher's Prefix: 0-85226

World Homoeopathic Links*, PO Box 5775, New Delhi 110055 (Located at: 1910 St 11, Chuna Mandi, New Delhi) Tel: (011) 770430
Chief Executive: Dr P N Jain; *Editorial, Publicity, Rights & Permissions:* Ashok Jain; *Sales, Production:* Pradeep Jain
Associate Company: Harjeet & Co (qv)
Subjects: Homoeopathy, Medical Reference
Founded: 1979

The **World Press** Pvt Ltd, 37-A College St, Calcutta 700073 Tel: (033) 311074/325141/323332 Cable Add: Takshasila Calcutta
Chairman: J Sinha; *Man Dir, Sales, Editorial, Administration:* S Bhattacharyya; *Production:* S K Bhattacharji; *Publicity, Advertising, Rights & Permissions:* L Bhattacharjee
Subjects: Economics, History, Political & Social Science, Business, Law, Mathematics, Geology, Botany, Statistics, Library Science, Reference
Bookshop: At above address
Founded: 1947

Writers Workshop*, 162/92 Lake Gardens, Calcutta 700045 Tel: (033) 468325
Man Dir, Publicity: P Lal
Subjects: General Fiction, Belles Lettres, Poetry, Philosophy, Reference, Religion, Low- & High-priced Paperbacks
Founded: 1958

Yoga Life, an imprint of Satya Press (qv)

Zebra Books for Children, an imprint of Arnold Publishers (India) Pvt Ltd (qv)

Remainder Dealers

A S Prakashan*, 37/2 New Prabhat Nagar, Quilla Parikshit Garh Rd, Meerut Tel: (0121) 75246
Chief Executive: Sanjay Mittal
Also publisher (qv)

Books Bargain*, 4-C Ansari Rd, Daryaganj, New Delhi 110002 Tel: (011) 266258
Man Dir: Mrs L V Kalra
Also wholesaler

Darsan Books Private Ltd*, V J T Hall Rd, Palayam, Trivandrum 695034
Man Dir: Sebastian Mathew
Also publisher (qv) and bookseller

Gangarams Book Bureau, 72 Mahatma Gandhi Rd, Bangalore 560001 Tel: (0812) 570277/565189
Manager: N Gangaram
All subjects. Main enterprise is as retail bookseller

Jaffe Books*, Aymanathuparampil House, Kurichy 686549, Kerala State
Proprietor: Santhamma Punnoose
Parent Company: K P Punnoose Communications Co, Publisher (qv for associate companies)
Non-fiction books from the USA and UK

Koshal Book Depot*, 3611/5 Nowrang Colony, Trinagar, Delhi 110035
Partner: Rishi Pal Sharma
All subjects

Surjeet Book Depot (Regd), PO Box 1425, Delhi 110006 (Located at: 4074-75 Nai Sarak, Delhi) Tel: (011) 2913081/2915967
Managing Partner: Harnam Singh
Specialization: Literature, Social Science, Mathematics, Management and Commerce
Also publisher (qv)

Literary Agents

Ajanta Books International, 1 U B Jawahar Nagar, Bungalow Rd, Delhi 110007 Tel: (011) 2926182
Contact: S Balwant (proprietor)
Specialization: Social sciences and humanities

Jaffe Publishing Management Service*, Kunnuparampil Bldgs, Kurichy 686549, Kottayam District, Kerala State Tel: (04826) 470
Man Dir: K P Punnoose
Specialization: Original and reprint rights in academic books and general adult trade books. Sheet deals and translation rights
Parent Company: K P Punnoose Communications Co, Publisher (qv for associate companies)

Book Clubs

Anand Book Club, Madarsa Rd, Kashmere Gate, Delhi 110006
Owned by: Vision Books Pvt Ltd (qv)

Book Lovers Club, Sterling House, L-10 Green Park Extension, New Delhi 110016
Owned by: Sterling Publishers Pvt Ltd (qv)

Clarion Book Club*, G T Rd, Shahdara, Delhi 110032
Owned by: Hind Pocket Books Private Ltd (qv)

Classics Club*, D C Books, PO Box 214, Kottayam 686001
Members: 4,500
Owned by: D C Books (qv)
Founded: 1982

D C Book Club*, D C Books, PO Box 214, Kottayam 686001
Members: 2,500
Owned by: D C Books (qv)
Founded: 1975

Darsan International Bestsellers Book Club*, V J T Hall Rd, Palayam, Trivandrum 695034 Tel: (04826) 470 Cable Add: Darsanbooks
Owned by: Darsan Books Private Ltd (qv)

E M E S C O Book Club*, 3237 R P Rd, Secunderabad 500003
Members: 3,700
Owned by: Andhra Pradesh Book Distributors
Founded: 1977

Gharelu Library Yojna*, G T Rd, Shahdara, Delhi 110032
Owned by: Hind Pocket Books Private Ltd (qv)

Home Library Plan*, 3237 R P Rd, Secunderabad 500003
Members: 3,000
Owned by: Andhra Pradesh Book Distributors
Founded: 1960

Kairali Club*, Current Books, VIII/493 Railway Station Rd, Kottayam 686001
Owned by: Kairali Children's Book Trust (qv)

Orient Book Club, Madarsa Rd, Kashmere Gate, Delhi 110006 Tel: (011) 2517001/ 2514274
Members: 35,000
Owned by: Vision Books Pvt Ltd (qv)

Pracharak Book Club*, PO Box 106, Pishachmochan, Varanasi 221001
Members: 3,978
Owned by: Hindi Pracharak Sansthan (qv)
Founded: 1976

Radical Book Club*, 6 Bankim Chatterjee St, Calcutta 12

Sanket Library Yojna, 4725/21A Dayanand Marg, Daryaganj, New Delhi 110002
Owned by: Selina Publishers (qv)

Star Book Bank*, 4/5B Asaf Ali Rd, New Delhi 110002
Members: 15,000
Owned by: Star Publications (Pvt) Ltd (qv)
Subject: Books in Hindi

Vidyarthi Mithram Novel Club*, PO Box 81, Baker Rd, Kottayam 686001, Kerala State
Owned by: Vidyarthi Mithram Press (qv)

Major Booksellers

Al Book Co (Pvt) Ltd*, 210 D N Rd, Bombay 400001 Tel: (022) 260019 Cable Add: Arabian Telex: 116683 Arabian
Man Dir: J K Kapur
Importer of children's books

Atma Ram & Sons*, Kashmere Gate, Delhi 110006 Tel: (011) 2523082/2518159 Cable Add: Books
Manager: Ish Kumar Puri
Importer — all subjects; also Publisher (qv)

Bangalore Book Bureau, 2nd floor, 72 Mahatma Gandhi Rd, Bangalore 560001 Tel: (0812) 575715/579778/570277
Manager: G C Bhuj
Importer — all subjects

Biblia Impex Pvt Ltd, 2/18 Ansari Rd, New Delhi 110002 Tel: (011) 278034/278870 Cable Add: Elysium
International bookseller and subscription agent

Current Technical Literature Co (Pvt) Ltd, Malhotra House, PO Box 1374, Bombay 400001 Tel: (022) 261045 Cable Add: Cutelico
Man Dir: R K Murti

Also: Calcutta, Hyderabad, Madras, New Delhi
Scientific, technical and medical books

D K Agencies (P) Ltd, H-12 Bali Nagar, New Delhi 110015 Tel: (011) 504418/ 5413463 Cable Add: Dikaybook New Delhi Telex: 3166778 Dk In
International bookseller and subscription agent

D K Publishers' Distributors*, 1 Ansari Rd, Daryaganj, New Delhi 110002 Tel: (011) 278368 Cable Add: Deekaypub
Partners: I C Mittal, Praveen Mittal, Parmil Mittal
The largest wholesale house for Indian books, stockist of the publications of more than 600 Indian publishers

Daystar Publications*, B-2/48A Lawrence Rd, Keshavpuram, New Delhi 110035 Tel: (011) 7113017
Manager: Mrs Indu Lekha Garg
Importer and exporter of books and journals; also Publisher (qv)

English Book Store*, 17-L Connaught Circus, New Delhi 110001 Tel: (011) 352126/351731
Partners: S D Chowdhri, Bhupinder Chowdhri
Associate Company: Himalayan Books (qv)
Importer — military science, aviation, nursing, foreign languages, travel, religion

E D Galgotia & Sons, PO Box 688, New Delhi 110001 (Located at: 17-B Connaught Pl, New Delhi) Tel: (011) 321844 Telex: 312879 Star In
Dirs: Suneel Galgotia, Neeraj Galgotia; *Manager:* S D Vashisht
Importer, wholesaler and retail bookseller of technical, scientific, medical and management books
See also publishers Galgotia Booksource and Galgotia Publications Pvt Ltd (qqv)

Higginbothams Ltd*, PO Box 311, Madras 600002 (Located at: 814 Anna Salai, Madras) 6 Tel: (044) 811841 Cable Add: Booklover
Man Dir: V Balaraman
Importer — all subjects

Hindi Book Centre, 4/5-B Asaf Ali Rd, New Delhi 110002 Tel: (011) 274874/ 273335/268651 Cable Add: Starpublis Telex: 0315328
Specialization: General books in Hindi

India Book House, Mahalaxmi Chambers, 22 Bhulabhai Desai Rd, Bombay 400026 Tel: (022) 367049/388088
Import, Sales Dir: Deepak G Mirchandani; *Manager:* Lal Vaswani
Publishers' representative and wholesale distributor
Owned by: India Book House Pvt Ltd (qv)

International Book House Pvt Ltd*, Indian Mercantile Mansions (Extn), Madame Cama Rd, Bombay 400039 Tel: (022) 2021634/2021795 Cable Add: Interbook
General Manager: C V Thambi; *Manager:* N Vijayaraghavan
Branches: 97 Residency Rd, Bangalore 560025 Tel: (0812) 560193; 30 Homi Mody St, Bombay 400023 Tel: (022) 2044859
Importer — adult trade books

International Book Traders, A-85 Derawal Nagar, opp Model Town II, Delhi 110009 Tel: (011) 741817/7122527
Man Dir: D S Chaudhary
Publisher, importer and distributor of scientific and technical books

J K Export House*, 2944 Kucha Mai Das, Bazar Sita Ram, Delhi 110006
Proprietor: K Jitendra
Exporter of any books published in India

Jaicos, 127 Mahatma Gandhi Rd, Bombay 400023 Tel: (022) 273787 Cable Add: Jaicobooks
Manager: Razak Bijliwala
Importer
Owned by: Jaico Publishing House (qv)

Motilal Banarsidass, 41 U A Bungalow Rd, Jawahar Nagar, Delhi 110007 Tel: (011) 2911985/2918335 Cable Add: Gloryindia
Managing Partner: N P Jain
Importer and exporter of Indological books; also Publisher (qv)

Oxford Book & Stationery Co, Scindia House, New Delhi 110001 Tel: (011) 3314957 Cable Add: Indamer Telex: 315261 Am In
Man Dir: Gulab Primlani
Also: 17 Park St, Calcutta 700016
Importer
Owned by: Oxford & IBH Publishing Co Pvt Ltd (qv)

Popular Book Depot*, Dr Bhadkamkar Marg, Bombay 400007 Tel: (022) 359401 Cable Add: Quixote
Importer

Rupa & Co*, 15 Bankim Chatterjee St, Calcutta 700073 Tel: (033) 344821
Dir: D Mehra
Also: 94 South Malaka, Allahabad 211001; 102 Prasad Chambers, Opera House, Bombay 400004; 3831 Pataudi House Rd, Daryaganj, New Delhi 110002
Importer — all subjects; also Publisher (qv)

R R Sheth & Co*, 110-112 Princess St, Keshavbag, Bombay 400002 Tel: (022) 313441 Cable Add: Literature Bombay
Also: opp Phuvara, Gandhi Marg, Ahmedabad 380001 Tel: (0272) 380573
Largest wholesaler of Gujarati and Hindi books; also Publisher (qv)

Star Publications (Pvt) Ltd*, 4/5B Asaf Ali Rd, New Delhi 110002 Tel: (011) 273335/ 274874/265135 Cable Add: Starpublis Telex: 315328
Also: Export Division, 50 Kalu Sarai, Hauz Khas, New Delhi 110016
Exporter of Indian books to world libraries and booksellers; also Publisher (qv)

N M Tripathi Pvt Ltd, 164 Shamaldas Gandhi Marg, Bombay 400002 Tel: (022) 313651/294048
Manager: V J Majmudar
Importer of law books; also Publisher (qv)

U B S Publishers' Distributors Ltd, PO Box 7015, New Delhi 110002 (Located at: 5 Ansari Rd, New Delhi) Tel: (011) 273601 Cable Add: Allbooks Telex: 3165106/ 3165321 Ubs In
Importer

United Book Traders, PO Box 91, Jodhpur 342001 (Located at: Ratanada Rd, opposite Police Lines, Jodhpur) Tel: (0986) 24154
Man Dir: P R Sharma
Importer of scientific & technical books and periodicals, exporter of Indian books

United Publishers, PO Box 82, Guwahati 781001 (Located at: Panbazar Main Rd, Guwahati) Tel: (0361) 26381 Cable Add: Unipub Guwahati Telex: 0235219 Unit In
Man Dir: Krishan Kumar
Owned by: Spectrum Publications (qv)
Wholesale and export booksellers in English and all Indian languages

Universal Book Distributors*, 117/H-1/294-B Model Town, Pandu Nagar, Kanpur 208025 Tel: (0512) 81300 Cable Add: Worldmags
Managing Partner: A K Chawla
Importer and subscription agent

Universal Book Shop*, 20 Mahatma Gandhi Marg, Allahabad Tel: (0532) 3177
Partner: Ramesh Chugh
Owned by: Chugh Publications (qv)

Vidyarthi Mithram Book Depot, Baker Rd, Kottayam 686001, Kerala Tel: (0481) 3281/3282/2616 Cable Add: Vidyarthi
Manager: Koshy P John
Branches: Calicut, Ernakulam, Kottayam, Palghat, Quilon, Thiruvalla, Trichur, Trivandrum
Owned by: Vidyarthi Mithram Press (qv)

Major Libraries

American Center Library, 24 Kasturba Gandhi Marg, New Delhi 110001
Libraries and Books Services Officer: Ann D Lee
Branches: 4 New Marine Lines, Bombay 400020; 7 Jawaharlal Nehru Rd, Calcutta 700013; 1 Bidhan Sarani, Calcutta 700073; Gemini Circle, Madras 600006

Asiatic Society Library*, Town Hall, Bombay 400023, Maharashtra

Bombay University Library*, Bombay University, Karmaveer Bhaurao Patil Marg, Fort, Bombay 32 Tel: (022) 273621

British Council Library*, AIFACS Bldg, Rafi Marg, New Delhi 110001 Tel: (011) 381401 Telex: 4370
Southern India: 737 Anna Salai, Madras 600002 Tel: (044) 86151; *Eastern India:* 5 Shakespeare Sarani, Calcutta 700071 Tel: (033) 445378 Telex: 3131 Bcca In; *Western and Central India:* 178 Backbay Reclamation, Bombay 40021 Tel: (022) 223480/223560/223484

The **British Library***, Lal Darwaja, Ahmedabad 380001
Librarian: V W Karnick
Branches: 29 St Mark's Rd, Bangalore 560001; New Shopping Centre, Roshanpura Naka, Bhopal 462003; 5-9-20/A Secretariat Rd, Hyderabad 500004; Mayfair Bldg, Hazratganj, Lucknow 226001; Bank Rd, Patna 800001; 917/1 Ferugusson College Rd, Shivaji Nagar, Pune 411004; Club Rd, Ranchi; YMCA Bldg, Trivandrum 695001

Central Library*, nr Mandvi Bank Rd, Baroda, Gujarat State Tel: (0265) 540133
Librarian: N C Pandya

Central Library*, Town Hall, Bombay 400023, Maharashtra

Central Secretariat Library*, G Block, Shastri Bhavan, New Delhi 110001

Connemara (State Central) Public Library*, Egmore, Madras 600008

Delhi Public Library*, S P Mukerji Marg, Delhi 110006 Tel: (011) 2512382 (Director)
Dir: G M Ahuja

Delhi University Library System*, University of Delhi, Delhi 110007 Tel: (011) 2518848/2521521 ext 371
University Librarian: Prof A P Srivastava

Gujarat Vidyapith Granthalaya, Ahmedabad 380014 Tel: (0272) 446148 (Combined university, state central and public library)
Librarian: K L Shah
Publications: Tapas Nibandh Suchi (Gujarati) (Bibliography of Dissertations); *Gujarati Samayik Lekh Suchi* (Gujarati) (Indexing of Articles from Selected Gujarati Journals)

Indian Council of World Affairs Library*, Sapru House, Barakhamba Rd, New Delhi 110001
Librarian: Ashok Jambhekar
Publication: Documentation on Asia (annually)

Indian Institute of Technology Central Library, Madras 600036 Tel: (044) 415342 ext 207 Cable Add: Technology Telex: 417362 Iitm In
Librarian: V S Nazir Ahmed

Inter Library Resources Centre, 35 Ferozeshah Rd, New Delhi 110001 Tel: (011) 381571/624155 Cable Add: Icsores Telex: 3161083 Issr In
Dir: S P Agrawal

Madras Literary Society Library*, College Rd, Madras 600006

National Archives of India, Janpath, New Delhi 110001
Librarian: R C Puri

The **National Library**, Government of India, Belvedere, Calcutta 700027 Tel: (033) 455381 Cable Add: Librarian Telex: Ca 7935
Dir: Prof Ashin Das Gupta; *Librarian:* Ms Kalpana Das Gupta
Publications include: India's National Library; India's National Library: Systematisation and Modernisation; The National Library and Public Libraries in India; Newsletter (quarterly)

National Museum Library*, Janpath, New Delhi 110001

Nehru Memorial Museum and Library*, Teen Murti House, New Delhi 110011
Dir: Prof Ravinder Kumar

Sahitya Akademi Library, Rabindra Bhavan, 35 Ferozeshah Rd, New Delhi 110001 Tel: (011) 388667 Cable Add: Sahityakar
Librarian: K C Dutt
Literature in 22 Indian languages and English

State Central Library*, Hyderabad 12, Andhra Pradesh

Library Associations

Delhi Library Association*, PO Box 1270, Delhi 110006 (Located at: c/o Hardayal (Hardinge) Public Library, Queen's Garden, Delhi)
Publications: Book Review Supplement (quarterly), *Library Herald* (quarterly), *Indian Press Index* (monthly)

Documentation Research and Training Centre*, Indian Statistical Institute, 31 Church St, Bangalore 560001 Tel: (0812) 579656 Cable Add: Statistica
Head: Dr G Bhattacharyya
Publications: Annual Seminar, DRTC (annual), *Refresher Seminar, DRTC* (annual)

Federation of Indian Library Associations*, Misri Bazar, Patiala, Punjab
President: Prof P N Kaula

Government of India Librarians Association*, c/o Planning Commission Library, Yojana Bhavan, Sansad Marg, New Delhi 110001 Tel: (011) 381365
President: M K Jain; *Secretary:* O S Sachdeva
Publications include: Directory of Government of India Libraries in Delhi (2 parts); *GILA Bulletin* (quarterly)

Indian Association of Academic Librarians*, c/o Dr Zakir Husein Library, Jamia Milia Islamia University, Jamia Milia, Okhla, New Delhi 110025 Tel: (011) 632360
Secretary: M M Kashyap
Publication: Newsletter

Indian Association of Special Libraries and Information Centres*, P 291 CIT Scheme No 6M, PO Kankurgachi, Calcutta 700054 Tel: (033) 359651
General Secretary: S K Kapoor
Publications include: Bulletin (4 a year), *Newsletter* (12 a year), *Indian Library Science Abstracts* (4 a year)

Indian College Library Association, 66 Ranjan Colony, Hyderabad 500253 Tel: (0842) 525282
President: A P Jain

Indian Library Association, A/40-41, Flat 201, Ansal Bldgs, Dr Mukerjee Nagar, Delhi 110009
President: T S Rajagopalan; *General Secretary:* C P Vashishth
Publications include: Bulletin; Newsletter

Library Reference Books and Journals

Books

Directory of Government of India Libraries in Delhi (2 parts), Government of India Librarians Association, c/o Planning Commission Library, Yojana Bhavan, Sansad Marg, New Delhi 110001

The National Library and Public Libraries in India, The National Library, Government of India, Belvedere, Calcutta 700027

University Libraries in India: A guide for direct mail promotion, Asian Bookmarket Information Service, 73-47-255th St, Glen Oaks, New York 11004, USA

Journals

Annals of Library Science and Documentation, Indian National Scientific Documentation Centre, Hillside Rd, New Delhi 110012

Bulletin, Indian Association of Special Libraries and Information Centres, P 291 CIT Scheme No 6M, PO Kankurgachi, Calcutta 700054

Bulletin, Indian Library Association, A/40-41, Flat 201, Ansal Bldgs, Dr Mukerjee Nagar, Delhi 110009

GILA Bulletin (quarterly), Government of India Librarians Association, c/o Planning Commission Library, Yojana Bhavan, Sansad Marg, New Delhi 110001

Herald of Library Science, Banaras Hindu University, c/o Editor P N Kaula, C-1, Varanasi 221005

Indian Librarian, 233 Model Town, Jullundur 3, Punjab

Indian Library Movement, 148 Allenby Lines, Ambala Cantt

Indian Library Science Abstracts, Indian Association of Special Libraries and Information Centres, P 291 CIT Scheme No 6M, PO Kankurgachi, Calcutta 700054

Journal of Indexing and Reference Work, Mukherjee Library, 1 Gopi Mohan Dutta Lane, Calcutta 3

Journal of Library and Information Science, Department of Library Science, University of Delhi, Delhi 110007

Journal of Library Science, Nagpur University, Nagpur, Maharashtra

Journal of Library Service, Ravikrupa Trust, 1760 Gandhi Rd, Ahmedabad 1

Karnatak Granthalaya, S R Gunjal, Granthalaya Vijnana Prakashana, Saptapur,

Dharwar, Karnatak State
Text in Kannada, contents page in English and Kannada

Liblit, Library Literacy Circle, Kurukshetra, Haryana

Library Herald, Delhi Library Association, PO Box 1270, c/o Hardayal (Hardinge) Public Library, Queen's Garden, Delhi 110006

Pustakalaya, Gujarat Pustakalaya Sahayak Sahkari Mandal Ltd, PO Box 10, Raopura, Baroda
Text in Gujarati

Literary Associations and Societies

Indian Folklore Society, 3 Abdul Hamid (British Indian) St, Calcutta 700069 Tel: (033) 236334
General Secretary: Sankar Sen Gupta
Also: 74 Mahatma Gandhi Rd, Calcutta 700069
Publications: Folklore (monthly); *Lokabnitha* (in Hindi, every two months)

Madras Literary Society and Auxiliary of the Royal Asiatic Society*, College Rd, Madras 600006
Honorary Secretary: U Ramesh Rao

National Academy of Letters, see Sahitya Akademi

All-India P E N Centre, Theosophy Hall, 40 New Marine Lines, Bombay 400020 Tel: (022) 292175 Cable Add: Care Aryahata, Bombay
Founder-Organizer: Sophia Wadia;
Secretary-Treasurer: Prof Nissim Ezekiel
Publications: The Indian PEN (quarterly), PEN series on Indian literatures, *PEN Conference Proceedings*

Sahitya Akademi, Rabindrar Bhavan, 35 Ferozeshah Rd, New Delhi 110001 Tel: (011) 388667 Cable Add: Sahityakar
National Academy of Letters; regional offices in Bombay, Calcutta and Madras
Secretary: Prof Indra Nath Choudhuri
Publications: Indian Literature (English, bi-monthly), *Samkaleen Bharateeya Sahitya* (Hindi, quarterly), *Samskrita Pratibha* (Sanskrit, twice a year)

Literary Periodicals

Art & Poetry Today, Samkaleen Prakashan, 2762 Rajguru Marg, New Delhi 110055

Bengali Literature, 53 Bidhan Palli, Jadavpur, Calcutta 32

Contemporary Indian Literature, H-328 Narayana, New Delhi 28
Text in English

Cultural News from India, Indian Council for Cultural Relations, Azad Bhavan, Indraprastha Estate, New Delhi 110002

Dhara, Dhara Publications, 37 D Gupta Colony, Delhi 110009
Monthly review of Indian literature

Indian Author, C-44 Gulmohar Park, New Delhi 110049

Indian Horizons, Indian Council for Cultural Relations, Azad Bhavan, Indraprastha Estate, New Delhi 110002

Indian Literary Review, Chetna Publications, 4837/24 Ansari Rd, New Delhi 110002

Indian Literature, National Academy of Letters, Rabindra Bhavan, 35 Ferozeshah Rd, New Delhi 110001
English bi-monthly

The Indian PEN (quarterly), All-India PEN Centre, Theosophy Hall, 40 New Marine Lines, Bombay 400020
Text in English

Indian Writing Today, Nirmala-Sadanand Publishers, 35c Tardeo Rd, Bombay 400034

Katha-Sahitya (monthly), Mitra & Ghosh Publishers Pvt Ltd, 10 Shyama Charan De St, Calcutta 73

Lalit Kala, Lalit Kala Akademi, Rabindra Bhavan, New Delhi 110001

Language Forum, Bahri Publications (Pvt) Ltd, 57 Sant Nagar, New Delhi 110065

Literary Criterion, Popular Prakashan Pvt Ltd, 35C Pandit Madan Mohan Malaviya Marg, Popular Press Bldg, opposite Roche, Tardeo, Bombay 400034

Literary Half-Yearly, Literary Press, H H A Gowda, Mysore 9

Literary Studies, Razdan House, Sirhindi Darwaza, Patiala, Panjab
Quarterly review of literature and criticism from the Panjab

Marg, Army & Navy Bldg, M G Rd, Bombay 400001

Miscellany, Writers Workshop, 162-92 Lake Gardens, Calcutta 700045

Opinion Literary Quarterly, 40-C Ridge Rd, Bombay 400006

Poet, 3 Venkatesan St, Madras 600017

Samkaleen Bharateeya Sahitya, National Academy of Letters, Rabindra Bhavan, 35 Ferozeshah Rd, New Delhi 110001
Quarterly journal in Hindi

Samskrita Pratibha, National Academy of Letters, Rabindra Bhavan, 35 Ferozeshah Rd, New Delhi 110001
Twice yearly journal of creative writing in Sanskrit

Triveni, Machilipatnam 521001

Vagartha, Joshi Foundation, N-3 Panchsheel Park, New Delhi 110017
Critical quarterly of Indian literature

Literary Prizes

Andhra Pradesh Sahitya Akademi Awards*
For best literary works in Telugu. Two prizes of 3,500 Indian rupees each and seven prizes of 2,500 Indian rupees each. Awarded annually. Enquiries to The Secretary, A P Sahitya Akademi, Saifabad, Hyderabad 500004

Bhai Santokh Singh Prize
Awarded annually to an Indian national domiciled in Haryana State for substantial contribution towards Punjabi literature. 3,100 Indian rupees. Enquiries to The Director, Haryana Sahitya Akademi, Chandigarh 160018

Books for Neoliterates Prizes*
For manuscripts in Indian languages by Indian nationals. 1,000 Indian rupees for each book. Awarded annually. Enquiries to Director, Directorate of Adult Education, 34 Community Centre, Vasant Vihar, New Delhi

Central Hindi Directorate Awards*
For non-Hindi speaking authors, 16 prizes of 2,500 Indian rupees each, awarded annually. Enquiries to the Director, Central Hindi Directorate, West Block VII, RK Puram, New Delhi 110066

Certificate of Honour*
To Arabic, Persian and Sanskrit scholars who have made outstanding contributions to Arabic, Persian and Sanskrit study. 5,000 Indian rupees. Awarded annually by the President. Enquiries to Office of the President, Government of India, New Delhi

I C Chacko Award
For the best book published in Malayalam during the preceding three years in the fields of science and linguistics. 1,000 Indian rupees awarded annually. Enquiries to Kerala Sahitya Akademi, PO Box 501, Town Hall Rd, Trichur 680020, Kerala State

Escorts Book Award
Instituted by Escorts Ltd in 1965 and administered by Delhi Management Association. For original books on management principles and practices by Indian writers. 5,000 and 3,000 Indian rupees each. Awarded annually. Enquiries to Executive Director, Delhi Management Association, 1/21 Asaf Ali Rd, New Delhi 110002

Geeta Prize
Awarded annually to an Indian national domiciled in Haryana State for substantial contribution towards Sanskrit literature. 3,100 Indian rupees. Enquiries to The Director, Haryana Sahitya Akademi, Chandigarh 160018

Hali Prize
Awarded annually to an Indian national domiciled in Haryana State for substantial contribution towards Urdu literature. 3,100 Indian rupees. Enquiries to The Director, Haryana Sahitya Akademi, Chandigarh 160018

Haryana Sahitya Prize
Awarded annually to an Indian national for outstanding work on literature, art, history and culture of Haryana. 3,100 Indian rupees. Enquiries to The Director, Haryana Sahitya Akademi, Chandigarh 160018

Indian Books Centre Oriental Studies Award*
For the best work in Oriental Studies, published in Sanskrit, English, Tibetan or Hindi. 1,100 Indian rupees, a shawl and a citation are awarded on a regular basis. Enquiries to the Director, Indian Books Centre Oriental Studies Award, 40/5 Shakti Nagar, Delhi 110007

Indian National Academy of Letters Awards, see Sahitya Akademi Awards

Jnanpith Literary Award*
For the best literary work in any Indian language by an Indian national. 150,000 Indian rupees awarded annually. Enquiries to Bharatiya Jnanpith, B/45-47 2nd Floor, Connaught Pl, New Delhi 110001

Sumnesh Joshi Award*
For an outstanding first literary publication in Hindi. 750 Indian rupees awarded annually. Enquiries to The Secretary, Rajasthan Sahitya Akademi, Udaipur, Rajasthan

Kerala Sahitya Akademi Awards
For literary works in Malayalam published during the preceding three years, in the following categories: fiction; drama; poetry; short stories; criticism; biography. 5,000 Indian rupees each awarded annually. Enquiries to The Secretary, Kerala Sahitya Akademi, PO Box 501, Town Hall Rd, Trichur 680020, Kerala State

Kesari Award*
Best unpublished novel in Malayalam, 3,000 Indian rupees. Awarded annually. Enquiries to The Manager, D C Books, PO Box 214, Kottayam 686001, Kerala State

C B Kumar Award
For best collection of essays in Malayalam. 1,500 Indian rupees awarded annually. Enquiries to The Secretary, Kerala Sahitya Akademi, PO Box 501, Town Hall Rd, Trichur 680020, Kerala State

Kunkumam Award*
Established by the late R Krishna Swami Reddiar in 1971 for best unpublished novel in Malayalam. 11,111 and 5,001 Indian rupees awarded for first and second prize respectively. The most recent winners were P L Antony for *The Black Cat in the Dark Room* and Sri Perunna PR for *The Temple Bull*. Enquiries to The Editor, Kunkumam Weekly, Thevally, Quilon 691009, Kerala State

Kuttippuzha Award
For the best book of criticism published in Malayalam during the preceding three years. 2,000 Indian rupees awarded once every two years. Enquiries to Kerala Sahitya Akademi, PO Box 501, Town Hall Rd, Trichur 680020, Kerala State

Law Books in Hindi Prize
Awarded annually for law books/manuscripts in Hindi. The first prize is 10,000 Indian rupees and prizes up to 100,000 Indian rupees may be awarded. Enquiries to Vidhi Sahitya Prakashan, Ministry of Law and Justice, Govt of India, Indian Law Institute Bldgs, Bhagwandas Rd, New Delhi 110001

Meera Memorial Award*
Founded 1959. For best literary work in Hindi. 9,000 Indian rupees awarded annually. Enquiries to The Secretary, Rajasthan Sahitya Akademi, Udaipur, Rajasthan

K R Namboodiri Award
For best work on Vedic literature in Malayalam. 1,000 Indian rupees awarded annually. Enquiries to The Secretary, Kerala Sahitya Akademi, PO Box 501, Town Hall Rd, Trichur 680020, Kerala State

Orissa Sahitya Akademi Award*
Founded in 1960 for best literary works in regional language published during a particular period of three years in six different categories of books: (1) novel and short stories; (2) poetry and Kavya; (3) drama, including one-act plays; (4) essay and literary criticism; (5) travelogue, biography, scientific literature; (6) children's literature. 1,000 Indian rupees awarded annually. Enquiries to Orissa Sahitya Akademi, Museum Bldgs, Bhubaneswar 751014, Orissa

M P Paul Award*
For best unpublished fiction in Malayalam. 3,0000 Indian rupees awarded annually. Enquiries to The Manager, D C Books, PO Box 214, Kottayam 686001, Kerala State

M P Paul Prize*
For best published fiction in Malayalam. 1,000 Indian rupees awarded annually. Enquiries to The Secretary, Sahitya Pravarthaka Cooperative Society Ltd, PO Box 94, Kottayam 1, Kerala State

Prithviraj Memorial Award*
For the best literary work in Rajasthani. 7,000 Indian rupees awarded annually. Enquiries to The Secretary, Rajasthan Sahitya Akademi, Udaipur, Rajasthan

Ranghey Raghav Award*
For Hindi fiction. 2,000 Indian rupees awarded annually. Enquiries to The Secretary, Rajasthan Sahitya Akademi, Udaipur, Rajasthan

Rajasthan Sahitya Akademi Awards*
For the best literary works in Hindi, Rajasthani and Sanskrit. Eight prizes of 2,000 Indian rupees each awarded annually. Enquiries to The Secretary, Rajasthan Sahitya Akademi, Udaipur, Rajasthan

Kanhaiyalal Sahal Award*
For best work of Hindi prose. 2,000 Indian rupees awarded annually. Enquiries to The Secretary, Rajasthan Sahitya Akademi, Udaipur, Rajasthan

Sahitya Akademi Awards*
For outstanding literary works written in each of the 22 languages of India recognized by the Indian National Academy of Letters (Sahitya Akademi). 10,000 Indian rupees each. Awarded annually to Indian nationals only. Enquiries to The Secretary, Sahitya Akademi, Rabindra Bhavan, 35 Ferozeshah Rd, New Delhi 110001

Sahitya Pravarthaka Benefit Fund Awards*
For best works in Malayalam. Five prizes of 2,000 Indian rupees each awarded annually. Enquiries to The Secretary, Sahitya Pravarthaka Co-operative Society Ltd, PO Box 94, Kottayam 1, Kerala State

Sidhawat Award*
For children's literature in Hindi. 1,100 rupees awarded annually. Enquiries to The Secretary, Rajasthan Sahitya Akademi, Udaipur, Rajasthan

Soviet Land Nehru Awards
For Indian nationals. For literary works, journalistic works in Indian languages and in English and meritorious work done in creative, cultural and public fields for promoting Indo-Soviet friendship, world peace and international amity. Three prizes of 20,000 Indian rupees with a fortnight's trip to USSR and three prizes of 10,000 Indian rupees with a fortnight's trip to USSR. Two prizes of 8,000 Indian rupees with a fortnight's trip to USSR. Ten prizes of 5,000 Indian rupees each. Five awards for children 10-13 age group for painting competition — a month's holiday at the Artek Young Pioneers Camp, Black Sea Coast, Crimea. Awarded annually. Enquiries to Soviet Land, Embassy of the USSR in India, 25 Barakhamba Rd, New Delhi 1

Sudhindra Award*
For Hindi poetry. 2,000 Indian rupees awarded annually. Enquiries to The Secretary, Rajasthan Sahitya Akademi, Udaipur, Rajasthan

Sur Prize
Awarded annually to an Indian national domiciled in Haryana State for outstanding contribution towards Hindi literature. 5,100 Indian rupees. Enquiries to Director, Haryana Sahitya Akademi, Chandigarh 160018

Sree Padmanabha Swami Prize
For the best children's literature published in Malayalam during the preceding three years. 1,000 Indian rupees awarded annually. Enquiries to Kerala Sahitya Akademi, PO Box 501, Town Hall Rd, Trichur 680020, Kerala State

Tagore Award*
For the best unpublished novel in Malayalam, 7,500 Indian rupees awarded annually. Enquiries to The Manager, D C Books, PO Box 214, Kottayam 686001, Kerala State

Urdu Akademy Awards*
Awarded annually to Indian nationals for Urdu literature. Enquiries to U P Urdu Akademy, 11 Hazratganj, Lucknow

Major Tek Singh **Virdi** Literary Prizes*
Awarded annually to children under 15 years for short stories, essays and dramas in Punjabi. Three prizes of 100, 75 and 50 Indian rupees. Enquiries to Modern Sahit Academy, 'Gulfashan', East Mohan Nagar, Link Rd, Amritsar

Translation Agencies and Associations

Amerind Publishing Co (P) Ltd, N-56 Connaught Circus, New Delhi 110001 Tel: (011) 3314957 Cable: Indamer Telex: 315261 Am In
Dir: Gulab Primlani
Translating Russian, German, Japanese, Hindi

Indian National Scientific Documentation Centre*, 14 Satsang Vihar Marg, off SJS Sansanwal Marg, Special Institutional Area, New Delhi 110067 Tel: (011) 665837 Cable Add: Insdoc Telex: 2499
Translating European and Asian languages into English

National Social Science Documentation Centre, 35 Ferozeshah Rd, New Delhi 110001 Tel: (011) 385959 Cable Add: Icsores Telex: 3161083 Issr In
Chief Executive: S P Agrawal
Publications: Research Information Series
Translation facility for European and Asian languages into English (and vice versa) is available on request

Indonesia

General Information

Language: Bahasa Indonesia (a form of Malay) is official language. English is common second language. About 250 other languages are spoken in Indonesia
Religion: About 85% Islamic, 5% Hindu (principally on Bali), 5% Christian
Population: 170 million
Bank Hours: Generally 0800-1400 Monday-Thursday; 0800-1500 Friday; 0800-1300 Saturday
Currency: Rupiah
Export/Import Information: Books subject to tariff and import sales tax, but on recommendation of Minister of Basic Education and Culture, partial or total exemption may be granted. Advertising dutied and taxed. All imports subject to margin of Profit Tax. Exchange control. Books and printed matter using Indonesian languages prohibited. Imports require no licence but are categorized into four groups for credit arrangement controls
Copyright: No copyright conventions signed

Book Trade Organizations

Ikatan Penerbit Indonesia (IKAPI), Jl Kalipasir 32, Jakarta Pusat 10330 Tel: (021) 321907

Association of Indonesian Book Publishers
President: Dr Azmi Syahbuddin; *Secretary General:* Dr Arselan Harahap
Publication: Bulletin, Books in General

Indonesian ISBN Agency, Perpustakaan Nasional, The National Library of Indonesia, Department of Education and Culture, PO Box 3624, Jakarta 10002 (Located at: Jl Imam Bonjol 1, Jakarta)
ISBN Administrator: Dr Nurhadi

Book Trade Reference Journals

Berita Bibliografi (Indonesian Book News), Yayasan Idayu, Jl Dr Abdulrachman Salch 26, Jakarta
Text in Indonesian

Bibliografi Nasional Indonesia Kumulasi (Cumulative Bibliography of Indonesia), Indonesian Center for Scientific Documentation and Information, PO Box 3065/JKT, Jakarta 10002

Bulletin, Association of Indonesian Book Publishers, Jl Kalipasir 32, Jakarta Pusat 10330

Publishers

Akadoma*, Jl Proklamasi No 61, Jakarta Tel: (021) 882328

Alma'Arif*, Jl Tamblong No 48-50, Bandung Tel: (022) 50708

Alumni Press, PO Box 272, Bandung (Located at: Jl Dr Djundjunan 190, Bandung) Tel: (022) 87672 Telex: 28460 Alumni IA
Man Dir, Rights & Permissions: Eddy Damian; *Editorial:* Ani, Yayat Ruchiyat; *Sales:* Punomo; *Production Manager:* Philips
Branch Offs: Jl Jend A Yani 206E, Banjarmasin; Wisma Sawah Besar, 8th Floor, Jl Sukarjo Wiryopranoto 30, Jakarta Tel: (021) 372730 Telex: 46810 Alumni Ia; Putri Hijaubaru 37, Medan Tel: (061) 510615; Jl Kartini 22B, Tanjungkarang Tel: (0721) 53135
Subjects: Law, Economics, Social Sciences, Medicine, Psychology
Bookshop: H Juanda St 54, Bandung Tel: (022) 58290
Founded: 1966

CV Angkasa (Publishers)+*, PO Box 354/Bd, Bandung (Located at: Jl Merdeka 6, Bandung) Tel: (022) 58330/51795 Telex: 28530 Angkasa Bandung
Chief Executive: Dr Fachri Said; *Editorial Manager:* Djajoesman; *Sales Manager:* Greg Nobel; *Production Manager:* Ir Pandit Parma; *Rights & Permissions:* Dadi Pakar
Associate Company: PT Mutiara Sumber Widya (qv)
Subjects: Children's Fiction and Non-fiction, Religion, Textbooks, Academic, Reference, Trade Books
Bookshop: Balai Buku Angkasa (at above address)
Founded: 1967

Pustaka **Antara***, Jl Majapahit No 28, Jakarta Tel: (021) 341321
Man Dir: H M Joesoef Ahmad
Subjects: School Textbooks, Children's books, Politics, Religion, General
Founded: 1952

CV Antarkarya, Jl Maluku 35, Jakarta Pusat Tel: (021) 324189
Dir: Hassan Shadily

Aries Lima, see PT New Aqua Press

Asia Afrika*, Jl Paneleh No 18, Surabaya Tel: (031) 278175

Perum **Balai** Pustaka+, Jl D Wahidin No 1, Jakarta Pusat Tel: (021) 374711/362981/365994 Cable Add: Perum Balai Pustaka Telex: 45905 Pnbp Jkt
President, Dir: Dr Zakaria Idris; *Editorial, Production Dir:* Kuntjono Sastrodarmodjo; *Sales, Publicity Dir:* Dr Chasan Mintara; *Rights & Permissions Dir:* Ismu Amran
Branch Offs: Jl Pulogadung Kav No Jl5, Pulogadung, Jakarta Timur; Jl Rawagatel No 17, Pulogadung, Jakarta Timur
Subjects: General, Education, Culture, Textbooks, Children's
Book Club: KPI (Klub Perpustakaan Indonesia)
1985-86: 200 titles *Founded:* 1917
ISBN Publisher's Prefix: 979-407

Bale Bandung — Sumur Bandung*, Jl Asia Afrika 82, Bandung Tel: (022) 59137/52156
Manager: H Moh Koerdi
Subject: Textbooks

PT Bhakti Centra Baru*, Jl Jend Akhmad Yani No 15, Ujung Pandang Tel: (0411) 5192 Cable Add: Bhakti Baru Telex: 71156 Hakalla UP
Man Dir: Drs H M Jusuf Kalla; *Publicity Manager:* Alwi Hamu
Branch Off: Jl Lembang 9, Jakarta Tel: (021) 336364
Subjects: Religion, General, Textbooks
Founded: 1972

PT Bhratara Karya Aksara+, Jl Rawabali II/5, Kawasan Industri Pulogadung, Jakarta Tel: (021) 4890280/8191818 Telex: 49283 brabook ia
Man Dir: Ahmad Jayusman; *General Manager:* Adit Jayusman; *Production:* Robinson Rusdi
Orders to: Bhratara Bookshop, Jl Otista III/29, Jakarta Timur Tel: (021) 8191858
Associate Company: Verbo bv, Amsterdam, Netherlands
Branch Offs: Jogja, Malang, Medan, Surabaya
Subjects: History, Technical, Applied Technology, Sociology, Agriculture, Education, Economics, Health, Languages, General
Bookshop: Bhratara Bookshop, Jl Otista III/29, Jakarta Timur Tel: (021) 8191858 Telex: 49283 Brabook Ia
1985-86: 160 titles *Founded:* 1958
Miscellaneous: Also printer and book importer/exporter
ISBN Publisher's Prefix: 979-410

Bina Ilmu*, Jl Tunjungan No 53E, Surabaya Tel: (031) 472214

Binacipta*, Jl Ganesya 4, Bandung Tel: (022) 84319
Dir: O Bardin

PT Bulan Bintang, Penerbit dan Penyebar Buku-buku+, Jl Kramat Kwitang I/8, Jakarta 10420 Tel: (021) 342883/346247
President: Amran Zamzami; *Vice President, Editor-in-Chief:* Fauzi Amelz
Subjects: Art, Social Science, Philosophy, Psychology, Literature, Law, Business, Economics, Finance, Education, Fiction, Engineering, General Non-fiction, History, Political Science, Juveniles, Science, Technology, Sports
1985-86: 20 titles *Founded:* 1954
ISBN Publisher's Prefix: 979-418

Bumi Restu*, PO Box 404, Jakarta (Located at: Jl Letjen Haryono MT Persil 23, Jakarta) Tel: (021) 882746

Cerdas*, Jl Palasari No 125, Bandung

Dian Rakyat*, PO Box 51, Jakarta (Located at: Jl Rawa Gelam I No 4, Jakarta) Tel: (021) 481809/482459

C V **Diponegoro** Penerbit, 44-46 Mohd Toha, Bandung 471215 Tel: (022) 40252 Cable Add: C V Diponegoro Bandung
Man Dir: A A Dahlan; *Editorial, Sales, Production, Publicity:* Dr Anisah Dahlan
Subjects: Religion, University Textbooks
Founded: 1963

PT Djambatan Penerbit NV*, Tromolpos 116, Jakarta Tel: (021) 345131/341678
Manager: Roswitha Pamoentjak
Subjects: Art, Literature, Juveniles, Textbooks, Religion, Philosophy, Sociology, Maps
Founded: 1958

PT Dunia Pustaka Jaya, Jl Kramat Raya 5K, Jakarta Pusat 10450 Tel: (021) 367339 Cable Add: Depeje
Dirs: Yus Rusamsi, Sumaryoto; *Editors:* Sugiarta Sriwibawa, Rukasah S W, Rohimah
Subjects: General, Fiction, Poetry, Art, Essays, Drama, Culture, Islam, Philosophy, Children's Books
Founded: 1971

Eresco PT*, Jl Hasanudin No 9, Bandung Tel: (022) 82311 Cable Add: Erescopete Bandung
Man Dir: Mrs H P Rochmat Soemitro; *Editorial:* Prof Dr H Rochmat Soemitro; *Sales:* Mr Amun, Mr Harsono
Branch Off: Jl Perapatan 22 Pav Jakarta Tel: (021) 368000
Subjects: Law, Economics, Philosophy, Psychology, Taxation
Book Club: Himpunan Masyarakat Pencinta Buku (HMPB)
Bookshops: Jl Hasanudin 9, Bandung; Jl Perapatan 22 Pav Jakarta Tel: (021) 368000
Founded: 1956

Erlangga*, Jl Kramat IV (Kernolong) No 11, Jakarta 10420 Tel: (021) 356593/3803508
Dir: M Hutauruk S H

PT Gaya Favorit Press, Book Division+, Jl Rasuna Said, Blok B, Kav 32-33, Jakarta Selatan Tel: (021) 513816 Telex: 62338 Fega IA
Man Dir: Sofjan Alisjahbana; *Editorial:* Christine Pangemanan, Soekanto SA; *Sales:* Irwan SLT; *Production, Publicity, Rights & Permissions:* Christine Pangemanan
Parent Company: PT Gaya Favorit Press (at above address)
Subjects: Juvenile Fiction, Adult Fiction, Homecraft, other Non-fiction
Founded: 1972

PT Gramedia*, PO Box 615, Dak Jakarta Pusat (Located at: Palmerah Selatan 22 lantai 4) Tel: (021) 543008 Cable Add: Kompas Jakarta Telex: Kompas JKT 46327
General Manager: J Adisubrata; *Editorial:* A Haryono (Fiction), G Sugijanto (General, Non-fiction); *Sales:* A M Sutartono; *Production:* A Harijadi; *Publicity:* G Aris Buntarman; *Rights & Permissions:* Nora Sutadi
Subjects: Children's, General, Fiction and Non-fiction
Bookshops: Gramedia Bookshop (qv under Major Booksellers)
Founded: 1973

PT Grip*, Jl Kawung No 2, Surabaya, Jawa Timur Tel: (031) 22564
Man Dir, Editorial: Suripto; *Sales:* F D Praseno; *Production:* S Sawitri; *Publicity:* Satriyo Purwanto
Branch Off: Jl Kembung 22, Jakarta

INDONESIA

Subjects: Textbooks, Politics, Social Science
Founded: 1957

Penerbit PT BPK Gunung Mulia+*, Jl Kwitang 22, Jakarta Pusat Tel: (021) 372208
Dir: Liem Kie Djian
Subjects: Primary and Secondary Textbooks, Trade and Professional Books, Religion
Bookshop: Toko Buku PT BPK Gunung Mulia (qv under Major Booksellers)
Founded: 1950

Firma **Harris***, Jl Veteran Gedung Olahraga No 6, Medan Tel: (061) 22272

Hidakarya Agung*, Jl Kebon Kosong F-74, Jakarta Tel: (021) 351074

Ichtiar Baru — van Hoeve*, Cideng Barat 62, Jakarta Tel: (021) 341226/41551
Subjects: Textbooks, Reference, Law, Social Sciences, Economics

PD & I **Ikhwan***, Jl Bujana Dalam No 10, Blok G, Kebayoran Baru, Jakarta Tel: (021) 772679

PT **Indira***, Jl Borobudur No 20, Jakarta Pusat Tel: (021) 882754/882250/881018 Cable Add: Indira Jakarta Telex: 48211 Indira Ia
Man Dir: Djojoadinoto Wahyudi
Bookshops: See under Major Booksellers
Subjects: Education, Technical, General
Founded: 1950

Indrajaya*, Jl Jatibaru No 20, Jakarta Tel: (021) 364372

Institut Dagang Muchtar*, Jl Embong Wungu 8, Surabaya Tel: (031) 42973

Islamiyah*, Jl Sutomo P 328/329, Kotakpos 11, Medan Tel: (061) 25421

Yayasan **Jaya Baya**, PO Box 250, Surabaya 60275 (Located at: Jl Embong Malang 69-H, Surabaya) Tel: (031) 41169

Kanisius*, Jl P Senopati 24, Jogjakarta Tel: (0274) 2309 Telex: 25143
Subjects: Textbooks, Religion, Engineering, Juveniles, Arts, Education, Economics

Karunia*, Jl Paneleh 18-A, Surabaya Tel: (031) 44120

Katalis PT Bina Mitra Plaosan+, Jl Pratama III/18, Jakarta 13220 Tel: (021) 4880082
Publisher, Rights & Permissions: Elisabeth Soeprapto-Hastrich; *Senior Editor:* Ms Rasfiati Iskarno; *Marketing Supervisor:* Gertrud Moeljono; *Business Manager, Production:* Kisbandi Soeprapto; *Editorial Assistant, Publicity:* Gabriella Martiyah
Imprint: Siemens-Penuntun Berencana
Subjects: Vocational Training, Trade, How-to, Popular Science, Non-fiction for Adults and Children, Modern Literature, Academic
1986: 9 titles *Founded:* 1986
ISBN Publisher's Prefix: 979-8060

Yayasan **Kawanku**, Jl Daan Mogot KM 13 Cengkareng, Jakarta 11730 Tel: (021) 613432

Kinta*, Jl Chik Di Tiro No 54-A, Jakarta Tel: (021) 351394

Kurnia Esa*, Jl Jend Sudirman Kav 36A, Blok B4, Bendungan Hilir, Jakarta Tel: (021) 350043/5/6 Telex: 44328

L P3 E S (Lembaga Penelitian, Pendidikan Dan Penerangan Ekonomi Dan Sosial), PO Box 493 Jkt, Jakarta 10002 (Located at: Jl Letjen S Parman 81, Slipi, Jakarta 11420) Tel: (021) 597211
The Institute for Economics and Social Research, Education and Information

Dir: Aswab Mahasin; *Editorial Manager:* Imam Ahmad; *Business, Publicity Manager:* Maruto
Subjects: Academic, Popular Science
Founded: 1971
ISBN Publisher's Prefix: 979-8015

Madju*, Jl Sutomo No P 341-342, Medan Tel: (061) 25428

Marfiah*, Jl Kalibutuh No 131, Surabaya

CV Haji **Masagung***, PO Box 145, Jakarta (Located at: Jl Kwitang 8, Jakarta) Tel: (021) 362909 Cable Add: Gunungagung Telex: 01144359 Jkt
President: Mr Masagung; *Manager:* Ali Amran
Subsidiary Company: Masagung Books Pte Ltd, Singapore (qv)
Subjects: Librarianship, Juveniles, Textbooks, Science, Biography, Language, Literature
Bookshops: PT Gunung Agung; Toko Buku Sari Agung (qqv under Major Booksellers)
Founded: 1953

PT **Mutiara** Sumber Widya+, Jl Pulokambing 9, Industrial Estate Pulogadung, Jakarta Timur Tel: (021) 483810/483335/481005 Telex: 46709 Mutiara Ia
Chief Executive: H Firdaus Oemar; *Dir:* Fahmi Oemar
Subsidiary Companies: CV Mutiara Bhakti, Jln Praban 7, Surabaya; Mutiara Permata Widya, Jln Singosari 31, Semarang
Associate Company: CV Angkasa (Publishers) (qv)
Subjects: Juveniles, Maps, Mathematics, Music, Education, Physics, Religion, Economics

PT **New Aqua** Press/Aries Lima*, Jl Rawa Gelam II/4, Jakarta Timur Tel: (021) 482163

Penerbit **Nusa** Indah, Jl Katedral 5, Ende 86312 Flores/NTT Tel: 251 Cable Add: Arnoldus Ende
Dir: Henri Daros; *Managing Editor:* Lucas Lege; *Marketing Manager:* Frans Ndoi; *Production, Design:* Eman Diaz
1985: 45 titles *1986:* 30 titles *Founded:* 1970
ISBN Publisher's Prefix: 979-429

P A T C O*, Jl Sawahan Sarimulyo 14, Surabaya Tel: (031) 310021
Man Dir: Adolf Pattyranie
Subjects: Local Interest, Maps and Guides
Bookshop: TB Puncak Agung, Pasar Tambahrejo Blok A 21A, Jl Kapas Krampung, Surabaya
Founded: 1972

Pelajar*, Jl Palasari 83-85, Bandung Tel: (022) 57559

Pelita Masa*, Jl Lodaya No 25, Bandung Tel: (022) 50823

Pembangunan*, Jl Grinting I/15, Blok A, Kebayoran Baru, Jakarta Tel: (021) 342469
Managers: Mr Sumantri, Mr Soewando
Branch Offs: Bandung, Jogjakarta, Madiun and Surabaya
Subjects: Textbooks, Juveniles, Sciences
Founded: 1953

Pembimbing Masa*, PO Box 3281, Jakarta (Located at: Pusat Perdagangan Senen, Blok I, Lantai IV/2, Jakarta) Tel: (021) 367645/366042
Bookshop: PT Pembimbing Masa (qv under Major Booksellers)

Pradnya Paramita, PO Box 146/Jkt, Jakarta 10002 (Located at: Jl Otto Iskandarinata Raya 115, Jakarta 13330)

Tel: (021) 8199774/8199777/8199778 Cable Add: Pradnya Jkt
President, Dir: Soenarto Sindoepranoto; *Production Dir:* Dr Mimien Saleh; *Sales Dir:* Soelistihardjo; *Sales Executive:* J Josojuwono; *Editorial:* A F Julianto
Subjects: General, Primary, Secondary & University Textbooks
Bookshops: See under Major Booksellers
Founded: 1973

Remaja Karya*, Jl Ciateul No 34-36, kotakpos 284, Bandung Tel: (022) 58226

Rosda*, Jl Raya Cimahi, Padalarang Km 12.5 No 858, Bandung Tel: (022) 56627; Jl Kramat Kwitang II No 4, Jakarta Tel: (021) 354920

Sastra Hudaya*, Jl Proklamasi No 61, Jakarta Tel: (021) 882328

Siemens-Penuntun Berencana, an imprint of Katalis PT Bina Mitra Plaosan (qv)

A B **Sitti** Syamsiyah*, Jl Secoyudan No 28, Sala/Surakarta Tel: 4721

Pustaka **Star***, Jl Moh Toha No 58, Bandung Tel: (022) 58710

Sumatera*, Jl R Dewi Sartika I No 1, Bandung

Sumur Bandung*, Jl Asia Afrika 82, Bandung Tel: (022) 59137

Tarate*, Jl Sumatera No 26-30, kotakpos 243, Bandung Tel: (022) 51067

Tintamas Indonesia PT, Jl Kramat Raya 60, Jakarta Pusat 10420 Tel: (021) 346186
Dir: Miss Marhamah Djambek
Subjects: Biography, History, Philosophy, Reference, Religion, Law, High-priced Paperbacks
Bookshop: At above address
Founded: 1947

U P Indonesia*, Jl Jend A Yani No 19, Jogjakarta

Warga*, Jl Karangmenjangan 61, Surabaya Tel: (031) 472160/472872

Widjaja*, Jl Pecenongan No 48-C, Jakarta Tel: (021) 363446

C V **Yasaguna***, Jl Dr Saharjo 50, Jakarta Selatan Tel: (021) 824528
Manager: Hilman Madewa
Subjects: Agriculture, Popular Manuals for Professional Vocations

Book Clubs

Himpunan Masyarakat Pencinta Buku*, PO Box 354 KBY, Jakarta, Selatan (Located at: Jl Tebet Raya 69, Jakarta, Selatan) Tel: (021) 821573
The Association of Bibliophiles
Members: 14,300
Owned by: Eresco PT (qv)
Founded: 1979

K P I, Jl Dr Wahidin No 1, Jakarta Pusat
Klub Perpustakaan Indonesia
Owned by: Perum Balai Pustaka (qv)

Major Booksellers

Effendi Harahap Bookstore*, Jl Abimanyu Raya 17, Semarang

Gramedia Bookshop*, 109 Jl Gajahmada, Jakarta Tel: (021) 627809
General Manager: Indra Gunawan
Also: Jl Merdeka 43, Bandung; Jl Melawai IV/13, Jakarta; Jl Pintu Air 72, Jakarta; Jl Jendral Sudirman 56, Jogjakarta; Jl Basuki Rachmat 95, Surabaya
Owned by: PT Gramedia (qv)

PT **Gunung Agung***, Jl Irian 5, Jayapura
Also: Jl Kwitang 8, Jakarta
Owned by: CV Haji Masagung (qv)

Toko Buku PT BPK **Gunung Mulia***, Jl Kwitang 22, Jakarta Pusat Tel: (021) 372208
Dirs: Liem Kie Djian, Tony Karnadi, T O Hutabarat
Branches: Medan, Surabaya, Ujung Pandang
Owned by: Penerbit PT BPK Gunung Mulia (qv)

PT **Indira***, Jl Braga No 10, Bandung
Also: Jl Jendral Sudirman 62, Jogjakarta; Jl Sam Ratulangi 37, Jakarta Pusat; Jl Gajah Mada 3-5, Duta Merlin Shopping Arcade, Jakarta Pusat; Pusat Perdagangan Senen Blok I Lantai IV 32-34, Jakarta Pusat; Jl Melawai V No 6, Jakarta Selatan; Jl Braga 111, Bandung; Jl Tunjungan 71, Surabaya; Jl Veteran 3394A, Palembang; Jl Sumatra 37, Den Pasar, Bali
Importers of General/Trade books and Educational/Scientific/Technical books and textbooks. Library suppliers to foreign libraries of Indonesian printed books; also Publisher (qv)

Toko Buku **Malabar***, 347 Oto Iskandarinata Bandung

Toko Buku **Melawai***, Jakarta

Toko Buku **Merbabu***, Semarang

Toko Buku Pustaka **Mimbar***, Medan

PT **Pembimbing** Masa*, Pusat Perdagangan Senen, Blok 1, Lantai IV No 2, PO Box 3281 Jkt, Jakarta Pusat Tel: (021) 367645/366042
Also: Jl Raya Pajajaran 7, Bogor
Importer, bookshop, subscription agency
Owned by: Pembimbing Masa (qv)

Pradnya Paramita, PO Box 146/Jkt, Jakarta 10002 Tel: (021) 360411
Manager: Waslan Soeriapranata
Also: Jl Kebon Sirih 46, Jakarta Pusat; Jl Kiai Maja 2A, Kebayoran Baru, Jakarta Selatan 12120
Also Publisher (qv)

Toko Buku **Sari Agung***, Tunjungan 5, Surabaya
Manager: J I Adipradja
Owned by: CV Haji Masagung (qv)

CV Toko Buku **Tropen**, Tromolpos 3604, Jakarta 10002 Tel: (021) 362695/363543 Cable Add: Tropen Telex: 49524 Tropen IA Fax: (021) 3800566
Manager: Yohan Slamet
Also: 113 Jl Pasar Baru, Jakarta 10710

Major Libraries

Arsip Nasional Republik Indonesia*, Jl Ampera Raya, Cilandak III, Jakarta Selatan Tel: (021) 781851
National Archives

Bidang Bibliografi dan Deposit, Pusat Pembinaan Perpustakaan*, Departemen P dan K, Jl Medan Merdeka Selatan 11, Jakarta Tel: (021) 360136
National Bibliographic and Deposit Centre, Centre for Library Development
Librarian: Paul Permadi
Publication: Bibliografi Nasional Indonesia (quarterly)

Perpustakaan **Biro** Pusat Statistik*, Jl Dr Sutomo 8, Jakarta
Library of Central Bureau of Statistics

British Council Library*, S Widjojo Centre, Jl Jenderal Sudirman 71, Jakarta Tel: (021) 587411/587731 Telex: 45246 Bricon Jkt
Information and Libraries Officer: Flavia McCarney
Also: Jl Lembong 4A-6, Bandung Tel: (022) 50788; Jl A Yani 2, Medan Tel: (061) 325735

Perpustakaan **Dewan** Perwakilan Rakyat — RI*, Jln Jenderal Gatot Subroto, Senayan, Jakarta Pusat
Library of Indonesian Parliament

Pusat **Dokumentasi dan Informasi Ilmiah**, PO Box 3065/JKT, Jakarta 10002 (Located at: Jl Jenderal Gatot Subroto, Jakarta) Tel: (021) 583465/510719/511063 Telex: 45875 IA
Indonesian Centre for Scientific Documentation and Information
Publications include: Direktori Perpustakaan Khusus dan Sumber Informasi di Indonesia (Directory of Special Libraries and Information Sources in Indonesia) (irregular); *Indeks Majalah Ilmiah Indonesia* (Index of Indonesian Learned Periodicals) (semi-annual); *Baca* (Read) (bi-monthly); *Bibliografi Khusus* (Special Bibliographies) (irregular); *Indeks Laporan Penelitian dan Survei* (Index of Research and Survey Report) (annual); and lists of acquisitions (books and microfiches)

Library of **Hasanuddin** University*, Perpustakaan Pusat, Universitas Hasanuddin, Kampus Baraya, Ujung Pandang Tel: (0411) 3029 Telex: 71179

Perpustakaan Jajasan **Hatta***, Malioboro 85, Jogjakarta
Hatta Foundation Library

Perpustakaan Pusat **Institut** Teknologi Bandung*, Jl Ganesya 10, Bandung 40132 Tel: (022) 83814 Telex: ITB BD 28324
Central Library, Bandung Institute of Technology
Chief Librarian: Dr Ai Andaniah Setiadi
Publications include: Proceedings Institut Teknologi Bandung

Perpustakaan **Islam***, Jl P Mangkubumi 38, Jogjakarta Tel: (0274) 2078
Islamic Library

Perpustakaan **Museum** Nasional, Departemen Pendidikan dan Kebudayaan*, Merdeka Barat 12, Jakarta Tel: (021) 360551
Library of the National Museum, Ministry of Education and Culture
Librarian: Miss M H Prakoso
Publications: Library Guide, Newspaper catalogue and other subject catalogues

Perpustakaan **Nasional**, PO Box 3624, Jakarta 10002 (Located at: Jl Imam Bonjol 1, Jakarta) Tel: (021) 342529
National Library of Indonesia

National Library for Agricultural Sciences, Jl Ir Haji Juanda 20, Bogor Tel: (0251) 21746 Cable Add: Pustaka

National Library of Indonesia, see Perpustakaan Nasional

Perpustakaan **Negara***, Malioboro 175, Jogjakarta
State Library

Pusat **Pembinaan** Perpustakaan, Departemen P dan K Bidang, Bibliografi dan Deposit *, Medan Merdeka Selatan 11, Tromolpos 274, Jakarta-Pusat Tel: (021) 360136
Centre for Library Development, Department of Education and Culture, Deposit Library
Publication: Berita Bulanan, checklist of Serials in the Libraries of Indonesia

Library of **Political and Social History***, Medan Merdeka Selatan 11, Jakarta Tel: (021) 360136
Librarian: Mrs Sayangbati-Dengah, WW
Publications: Press index; Index Artikel Tentang Negara (Index of Official Publications); *Index Pemilu* (Index of General Elections)

Library Association

Ikatan Pustakawan Indonesia*, c/o National Library, Jl Imam Bonjol 1, Jakarta 10002 Tel: (021) 342529
Indonesian Library Association
President: Ms Mastini Hardjo Prakoso
Publication: Majalah Ikatan Pustakawan Indonesia

Library Reference Books and Journals

Book

Direktori Perpustakaan Khusus dan Sumber Informasi di Indonesia (Directory of Special Libraries and Information Sources in Indonesia), Indonesian Centre for Scientific Documentation and Information, PO Box 3065/JKT, Jakarta 10002

Journals

Baca (Read) (quarterly), PO Box 3065, Jakarta

Berita Bulanan (Bulletin), Centre for Library Development, Department of Education and Culture, Deposit Library, Medan Merdeka Selatan 11, Jakarta

Berita Idayu (Idayu News), Yayasan Idayu, Jl Dr Abdulrachman Saleh 26, Jakarta

Checklist of Serials in the Libraries of Indonesia, Centre for Library Development, Department of Education and Culture, Deposit Library, Medan Merdeka, Selatan 11, Jakarta

Diurnal Perpustakaan (Library Journal), Perpustakaan Umum Makassar, Jl Kajaolalidjo 16, PO Box 16, Ujung Pandang
Text in Indonesian or English

Index Artikel Tentang Negara (Index of Official Publications), Library of Political and Social History, Medan Merdeka Selatan 11, Jakarta

Majalah Ikatan Pustakawan Indonesia (Indonesian Library Association Journal), Indonesian Library Association, c/o National Library, Jl Imam Bonjol 1, Jakarta 10002

Literary Associations and Societies

P E N Centre*, c/o Jl Cemara 6, Jakarta Pusat
Secretary: Dr Toeti Heraty Noerhadi

Iran

General Information

Language: Persian (Farsi), Turkish and Armenian in Northwest, Arabic in Southwest, Kurdish in Kurdistan (English or French also)
Religion: Islamic (Shi'a sect)
Population: 37.4 million
Bank Hours: Generally Winter: 0800-1300 Saturday-Thursday; 1600-1800 Saturday-Wednesday; Summer: 0730-1300, 1700-1900 Saturday-Wednesday, 0730-1130 Thursday
Shop Hours: Generally Winter: 0800-2000 Saturday-Thursday; 0800-1200 Friday; Summer: 0800-1300, 1700-2100 Saturday-Thursday, 0800-1200 Friday
Currency: rial
Export/Import Information: No tariff on books and advertising but catalogues subject to VAT. Import licences required. Publications offending public order, official religion or morality prohibited. Exchange controls, with new regulations issued each March
Copyright: No copyright conventions signed

Book Trade Reference Books and Journals

Books

A Directory of Iranian Periodicals, The National Library of Iran, 30 Tir St, Tehran 11364

The Iranian National Bibliography, The National Library of Iran, 30 Tir St, Tehran 11364

Rules and Standards for Publishing Books, The National Library of Iran, 30 Tir St, Tehran 11364

Journal

Bibliography of Persia (annual), Book Society of Islamic Republic of Iran, PO Box 1936, Tehran

Publishers

Amir Kabir Book Publishing Co, Esteghlal Sq, Tehran Tel: (021) 316935/390751
Dir: Ali Motalleb
Parent Company: Sasman-e Tablighat-e Eslami
Subsidiary Company: Shokufeh Books
Subjects: Textbooks, General
Founded: 1948

Eghbal Publishing Organisation+*, Shahabad Ave, Tehran Tel: (021) 318701
Man Dir: J Eghbal; *Publications Dir:* S Eghbal; *Production Dir:* M Eghbal
Branch Off: 155 Jomhoori Ave, Tehran
Subjects: Juveniles, Fiction
Bookshop: 273 Dr Shariati Ave, Tehran
Founded: 1903

Majlis Press*, Baharistan Ave, Tehran
Subjects: Juveniles, Fiction

Scientific and Cultural Publications Center*, Ministry of Culture and Higher Education, PO Box 1936, Tehran Tel: (021) 686320
President: F A Larijani
Subjects: Science, Culture

University of Tehran Publication & Printing Organization*, Kargar shomali Ave, Tehran Tel: (021) 632062/632063
Man Dir: Dr Firuz Harirchi; *Sales, Publicity:* Hassan Sanaie; *Rights &*
Permissions: J Qajarieh
Subjects: University Textbooks
Bookshops: Ave 16 Azar, Tehran; Enqelab Ave, Tehran; Amirabad shomali Ave 16, Tehran
Founded: 1944

Major Booksellers

Daneshdjou Bookstore*, 222 Shah Reza St, Tehran Tel: (021) 48365

Major Libraries

Astaneh Qods Central Library*, Mashhad Tel: (051) 20845
Publications include: Meshkat (quarterly catalogue of manuscripts)

Iranian Documentation Centre (IRANDOC), Ad 1188, Enqelab Ave, Tehran Tel: (021) 662223/662140 Cable Add: Asnad Telex: 212889 TN
Dir: Mohammad Naghi Mahdavi

The **National Library** of Iran, 30 Tir St, Tehran 11364 Tel: (021) 673315/673564
Dir: S Hasan Shahrestani
Publications include: (Texts all in Persian) *A Directory of Iranian Periodicals*; *The Iranian National Bibliography*; *List of Persian Subject Headings*; *The Name Authority List of Authors and Famous People*; *National Library of Iran*; *Rules and Standards for Publishing Books*

Parliament Library, No 1 (Ketab-Khaneh Majles-e Showraye Eslami, no 1)*, Baharestan Sq, Tehran Tel: (021) 393257/310001
Dir: A Haeri

Parliament Library, No 2 (Ketab-Khaneh Majles-e Showraye Eslami, no 2)*, Emam Khomeyni Ave, Tehran Tel: (021) 662906
Dir: A Haeri

T E B R O C (Tehran Book Processing Centre), now part of the National Library of Iran (qv)

University of Ferdowsi Library*, PO Box 331, Mashhad Tel: (021) 33075
Librarian: A J Darbandi

University of Isfahan Library, Isfahan

Central Library, **University of Tabriz**, Tabriz
Dir: Mrs F Ghoreishy

Central Library and Documentation Centre of **University of Tehran***, Shahreza Ave, Tehran

Library Association

Association of Registered Archivists of Iran Secretariat*, Lalezar Ave, Passage Afrashteh, 1st floor, Tehran

Library Reference Book

List of Persian Subject Headings, The National Library of Iran, 30 Tir St, Tehran 11364

Literary Associations and Societies

Book Society of Islamic Republic of Iran*, PO Box 1936, Tehran Tel: (021) 220326
Secretary: Fazel A Larijani
Publication: Bibliography of Persia

Iraq

General Information

Language: Arabic, Kurdish (English is the principal foreign language in Baghdad)
Religion: Islamic
Population: 12.8 million
Bank Hours: Winter: 0900-1300 Saturday-Wednesday; 0900-1200 Thursday; Summer: 0800-1200 Saturday-Wednesday, 0800-1100 Thursday
Shop Hours: Winter: 0830-1430, 1700-1900 Saturday-Wednesday, 0830-1330 Thursday; Summer: 0800-1400, 1700-1900 Saturday-Wednesday, 0800-1300 Thursday
Currency: 1,000 fils = 1 Iraqi dinar
Export/Import Information: No tariffs on books and advertising. Import licences required. Exchange control, influenced by annual foreign exchange budget. Importation by state trading company or established importer. The state trading company is the National House for Publishing, Distributing and Advertising, Aljamhuria St, PO Box 624, Baghdad
Copyright: No copyright conventions signed

Book Trade Reference Journal

Iraqi Bulletin for Publications, National Library, al-Jumhuriya St, Baghdad

Publishers

Al **Ma'arif** Ltd*, Mutanabi St, Baghdad
Subjects: Books in several Middle-Eastern languages, French and English, Fiction, Politics
Founded: 1929

National House for Publishing, Distributing and Advertising*, PO Box 624, Baghdad (Located at: Aljamhuria St, Baghdad)
Tel: (01) 68391 Cable Add: Donta
Telex: 2392
Subjects: Politics, Economics, Education, Agriculture, Sociology, Commerce, General Science, Books in Arabic and other Middle-Eastern languages (also distributor)
Founded: 1972
Miscellaneous: Firm is attached to the Ministry of Information and is the sole importer and distributor of newspapers, magazines, periodicals and books

Major Booksellers

The export of Iraqi books is handled by the National House for Publishing, Distributing and Advertising (qv under Publishers)

Major Libraries

Al-Awqaf*, PO Box 14146, Baghdad Tel: (01) 4166104/4169361/4158041
Library of Waqfs
Librarian: Jassim Al-Juboori
Branches at: Al-Qazzaza Library, Baghdad; Munier Al-Qadhi Library, Baghdad; Adhamiya, Mosul; Main Mosque, Anbar; Amarah; Nasiriyah; Sulaymaniyah; Kerkuk; Diala

College of Agriculture Library, University of Baghdad*, Abu Ghraib

The **Diwan** Library, Ministry of Education, Baghdad

Library of the **Iraq Museum***, Baghdad

Library of the **Iraq Natural History**
Research Centre and Museum*, University
of Baghdad, Bab Al-Muadham, Baghdad
Tel: (01) 68361/65790
Publications include: Bulletin, Publication

Library of the **Mosul Museum***, Mosul

Mosul Public Library*, Mosul

National Centre of Archives*, PO Box
594, Baghdad (Located at: The Building of
the National Library, 2nd floor, Baghdad)
Cable Add: Centarchiv
Director-General: Salim Al-Alousi

National Library*, al-Jumhuriya St,
Baghdad
Dir: Fouad Y M Qazanchi
Publications: Iraqi National Bibliography (3
times yearly); *Accumulation List* (annual);
al-Maktaba al-Arabia Journal

Scientific Documentation Centre, Scientific
Research Council, PO Box 2441, Jadiriya,
Baghdad Tel: (01) 7765116/7764689 Telex:
2187 Bathilmi IK

Central Library of the **University of
Baghdad***, PO Box 12, Baghdad (Located
at: Safi El-Din Ali-Hilli St, Baghdad) Tel:
(01) 64742

Library Associations

Arab Archivists Institute*, c/o National
Centre of Archives, PO Box 594, Baghdad

Iraq Library Association*, PO Box 4081,
Baghdad-Adhamya Tel: (01) 27077
Secretary: N Kamalal-Deen

Library Reference Journals

Arab Archives Journal, National Centre of
Archives, PO Box 594, Baghdad

The Library, Al-Muthanna Library,
Al-Mutanabbi St, Baghdad

Republic of Ireland

General Information

Language: English and Irish
Religion: Roman Catholic
Population: 3.5 million
Bank Hours: 1000-1230, 1330-1500 Monday-
Friday. Most open until 1700 Thursday
Shop Hours: 0900 or 0930-1730 Monday-
Saturday
Currency: 100 pence = 1 Irish pound
Export/Import Information: Member of the
European Economic Community. No tariff
on books except on prayer and similar
books from non-UK and children's picture
books from non-EEC. Pamphlets dutied
from non-EEC. VAT is charged. No
import licences. Exchange controls
Copyright: UCC, Berne (see International
section)

Book Trade Organizations

B H I, see Book House Ireland

Book House Ireland, 65 Middle Abbey St,
Dublin 1 Tel: (01) 730108

Administrator: Clara Clark
Publication: Book House Ireland News
(quarterly)

**Booksellers Association of Great Britain and
Ireland (Irish Branch)**, Book House
Ireland, 65 Middle Abbey St, Dublin 1
Tel: (01) 730108
Contact: Clara Clark

C L É: The Irish Book Publishers'
Association, Book House Ireland, 65
Middle Abbey St, Dublin 1 Tel: (01)
730108
Contact: Clara Clark
*Publication: The CLÉ Directory of the
Irish Book World*

Cumann Leabharfhoilsitheoirí Éireann,
see CLÉ

Irish Books Marketing Group, Book House
Ireland, 65 Middle Abbey St, Dublin 1
Tel: (01) 730108
Chairman: Michael Gill
*Publication: The Market for Books in the
Republic of Ireland*

Irish Educational Publishers' Association,
c/o Gill & Macmillan Ltd, Goldenbridge
Industrial Estate, Inchicore, Dublin 8
Tel: (01) 531005 Telex: 92197 Fax: (01)
531005 ext 125
Secretary: Hubert Mahony

National Federation of Retail Newsagents*,
Republic of Ireland District Council, 63
Middle Abbey St, Dublin 1
Tel: (01) 730408/730985
District Secretary: M J Gaynor

Book Trade Reference Books and Journals

Books

*The CLÉ Directory of the Irish Book
World*, CLÉ: The Irish Book Publishers'
Association, Book House Ireland, 65
Middle Abbey St, Dublin 1

Irish Books in Print, S J Cleary Publishers,
Ballymerrigan House, Wicklow, Co
Wicklow

*The Market for Books in the Republic of
Ireland*, Irish Books Marketing Group,
Book House Ireland, 65 Middle Abbey St,
Dublin 1

Journals

Book House Ireland News (quarterly),
Book House Ireland, 65 Middle Abbey St,
Dublin 1

Books Ireland, Goslingstown, Kilkenny
The trade journal and review medium of
the Irish publishing industry; published 10
times a year

Irish Publishing Record, School of
Librarianship, University College, Belfield,
Dublin 4

Leabharagan An Aosa Dig (Primary
Bookshelf), Nessa Ni Mhurchu, 45 St
Brendan's Ave, Malahide Rd, Dublin 5
Text in English and Gaelic

Publishers

Academy Microfilms (Dublin), see The
University Press of Ireland

The **Academy** Press, now part of The
University Press of Ireland (qv)

Acorn Books, an imprint of The Children's
Press (qv)

Anvil Books Ltd, 90 Lower Baggot St,
Dublin 2 Tel: (01) 762359 Cable Add:
Anvil
*Man Dir, Sales, Production, Publicity,
Rights & Permissions:* Rena Dardis;
Editorial: Dan Nolan
Associate Company: The Children's Press
(qv)
Subjects: Biography, Irish History,
Folklore, Sociology
1985: 1 title *1986:* 3 titles *Founded:* 1964
ISBN Publisher's Prefixes: 0-900068,
0-947962

Arlen House Ltd+*, Kinnear Court, 16-20
South Cumberland St, Dublin 2 Tel: (01)
717383 Telex: 92343
Chief Executive: Catherine Rose
Associate Company: Women's Education
Bureau
Imprint: The Women's Press
Subjects: Women's Studies, Feminist
Literature, History, Biography, Poetry,
Contemporary Fiction, Classics
Founded: 1975
ISBN Publisher's Prefixes: 0-905223,
0-185132

Attic Press+, 44 East Essex St, Dublin 2
Tel: (01) 716367
Coordinators, Production: Roisin Conroy,
Mary Paul Keane; *Editorial, Rights &
Permissions:* Mary Paul Keane; *Sales:*
Bridie Murray; *Publicity:* Roisin Conroy
Orders to: Turnaround Distribution, 27
Horsell Rd, London N5, UK
Parent Company: Irish Feminist
Information Publications (IFI) (at above
address)
Subjects: Feminism and Women's Interest,
Social Comment, Literature
1985: 8 titles *1986:* 10 titles *Founded:*
1984
ISBN Publisher's Prefix: 0-946211

Bluett & Co Ltd+, 95 Lower Baggot St,
Dublin 2 Tel: (01) 762639
Chief Executive and all other offices: Syd
Bluett
Subjects: Literature, Art, Humour
1985: 6 titles *Founded:* 1980
ISBN Publisher's Prefix: 0-907899

Boethius Press Ltd*, Clarabricken, Clifden,
Co Kilkenny Tel: (056) 29746
Man Dir, Editorial: L J Hewitt
Subsidiary Company: Boethius Design and
Typeset (at above address)
Subjects: Early Music, Biography, Botany
and Gardens, Irish Studies (History and
Archaeology), Plate Books and
Topography, Facsimiles
1985: 9 titles *Founded:* 1973
ISBN Publisher's Prefixes: 0-904263,
0-86314

Boole Press Ltd, PO Box 5, Dun
Laoghaire, Co Dublin (Located at: 51
Sandycove Rd, Dun Laoghaire) Tel: (01)
808025 Telex: 30547 Shcn Ei ref Boole
Fax: (01) 805990 ref Boole
Man Dir: M O'Reilly; *General Manager:*
M McGlynn; *Senior Editor:* J J H Miller
Subjects: Scientific, Technical, Medical,
Scholarly
1985: 6 titles *1986:* 5 titles *Founded:* 1979
ISBN Publisher's Prefix: 0-906783

Brandon Book Publishers Ltd+, Dingle,
Co Kerry Tel: (066) 51463
Man Dir, Editorial: Steve MacDonogh;
Production: Bernard Goggin
Imprint: Peninsula Press
Subjects: Fiction, Biography, History,
Politics, Sport, Literary Studies, Folklore,
Social Studies, General
1985: 10 titles *1986:* 7 titles *Founded:*
1982
ISBN Publisher's Prefix: 0-86322

Brogeen Books, an imprint of The Dolmen
Press Ltd (qv)

Brophy Educational Books Ltd+, 108 Sundrive Rd, Dublin 12 Tel: (01) 973061/971617
Publisher, Editorial, Production, Publicity, Rights & Permissions: Kevin T Brophy; *Sales:* A O'Reilly
Associate Company: Brophy International Publishing Ltd (at above address)
Imprints: Brophy Books, Canavaun Books
Subjects: Educational, General Non-fiction, Sports, Cookery, Politics, Biography, Autobiography, Irish Interest, Humour, Verse, Quiz Books
1985: 10 titles *1986:* 10 titles *Founded:* 1977
ISBN Publisher's Prefix: 0-907960

Canavaun Books, an imprint of Brophy Educational Books Ltd (qv)

Careers & Educational Publishers Ltd+*, 193 Ard Easmuinn, Dundalk, Co Louth Tel: (042) 35705
Man Dir, Editorial, Publicity, Rights & Permissions: Eamonn Patrick O'Boyle; *Sales:* Christina O'Boyle; *Production:* William J O'Keeffe
Imprint: Heritage Books
Branch Off: Lower James St, Claremorris, Co Mayo Tel: (094) 71093
Subjects: Educational Directories, Careers, Cookery, Quizzes, Hobbies
Bookshops: Eamonn P O'Boyle's Book Sales (at above address); Kilcolman Press Bookshop, Convent Rd, Claremorris, Co Mayo
Founded: 1976
ISBN Publisher's Prefix: 0-906121

The **Children's** Press+, 90 Lower Baggot St, Dublin 2 Tel: (01) 762359 Cable Add: Children's Press Dublin
Man Dir, Editorial, Sales, Production, Publicity, Rights & Permissions: Rena Dardis
Associate Company: Anvil Books Ltd (qv)
Imprints: Acorn Books, Hawthorn Books
Subject: Children's
1985: 4 titles *1986:* 4 titles *Founded:* 1981
ISBN Publisher's Prefixes: 0-900068, 0-947962

An **Clóchomhar** ITA*, 13 Gleann Carraig, Dublin 13 Tel: (01) 324906
Subjects: Books in Irish language

Clódhanna Teo*, c/o 6 Harcourt St, Dublin 2 Tel: (01) 757401
Publicity Manager: Donnchadh Ó Laodha

The **Columba** Press+, 8 Lower Kilmacud Rd, Blackrock, Co Dublin Tel: (01) 832954
Chief Executive, Editorial: Seán O Boyle; *Sales, Publicity, Rights & Permissions:* Cecilia West; *Production:* John McCurrie
Subsidiary Company: Columba Bookservice (at above address)
Subjects: Religion, Theology, Catechetics
1985: 18 titles *1986:* 24 titles *Founded:* 1985
ISBN Publisher's Prefix: 0-948183

Cork University Press, University College, Cork Tel: (021) 276871 ext 2163
Executive Secretary: D J Counihan; *Sales:* Anne Lee (ext 2348)
Subjects: Biography, History, Music, Art, Philosophy, Literature, Reference, Religion, Medicine, Psychology, Engineering, General & Social Science, University Textbooks
Bookshop: Cork University Press (Retail Sales), University College, Cork
Founded: 1925
ISBN Publisher's Prefix: 0-902561

The **Dolmen** Press Ltd+*, The Lodge, Mountrath, Portlaoise Tel: (0502) 32213
Man Dir: Liam Miller; *Sales, Publicity, Rights & Permissions:* Maire Block
Imprints: Brogeen Books, Five Lamps Press
Subjects: Art and Architecture, Belles Lettres, Drama, Poetry, Fiction, Travel and Topography, Young Readers
Founded: 1951
ISBN Publisher's Prefix: 0-85105

Dominican Publications, 69 Upper O'Connell St, Dublin 1 Tel: (01) 731355/731760
Chief Executive, Editorial, Sales: Austin Flannery; *Advertising, Production:* Bernard Treacy
Branch Off: Saint Saviour's, Granby Lane, Dublin 1 Tel: (01) 721611
Subject: Religion
Book Clubs: Doctrine and Life Book Club, Religious Life Review Book Club, Scripture in Church Book Club
Bookshops: At above addresses
Founded: 1897
ISBN Publisher's Prefixes: 0-9504797, 0-907271

Dublin Institute for Advanced Studies, 10 Burlington Rd, Dublin 4 Tel: (01) 680748 Telex: 31687 Dias Ei
Subjects: Celtic Studies, Physics

Eason & Son Ltd, 66 Middle Abbey St, Dublin 1 Tel: (01) 733811 Telex: 32566 Fax: (01) 730477
Man Dir: S D Carpenter; *Editorial, Sales, Production, Publicity, Rights & Permissions:* Harold Clarke
Subsidiary Companies: Eason & Son (NI) Ltd, Boucher Rd, Belfast; Eason Advertising (at above address); Irish Representation Ltd, 52 Corporation St, Dublin 1
Imprint: Irish Heritage Series
Subjects: Irish interest, Non-fiction
Bookshops: See under Major Booksellers
1985: 7 titles *1986:* 6 titles *Founded:* 1886
ISBN Publisher's Prefix: 0-900346

Ecclesia Press, an imprint of Irish Academic Press (qv)

The **Economic & Social** Research Institute, 4 Burlington Rd, Dublin 4 Tel: (01) 760115
Man Dir, Editorial: Prof Kieran A Kennedy; *Sales, Production, Publicity, Rights & Permissions:* John Roughan
Subjects: Economic and social research
1985: 11 titles *1986:* 14 titles *Founded:* 1960
ISBN Publisher's Prefix: 0-7070

The **Educational Company** of Ireland, PO Box 43A, Dublin 12 (Located at: Ballymount Rd, Walkinstown, Dublin) Tel: (01) 500611
Chief Executive: Frank Maguire; *Executive Dirs:* S O'Neill, Ursula Daly, P McCann, R McLoughlin
Branch Off: 20-1 Talbot St, Dublin 1
Subjects: History, Religion, Irish, English, Geography, French, Technical, Domestic Science, Computer Studies, Career Guidance, Mathematics, Commerce
Founded: 1877
Miscellaneous: Firm is a trading unit of Smurfit Ireland Ltd
ISBN Publisher's Prefix: 0-901802

C J Fallon, PO Box 1054, Dublin 20 (Located at: Lucan Rd, Palmerstown, Dublin) Tel: (01) 265777
Man Dir: H McNicholas; *Editorial:* N White; *Secretary:* P Tolan
Subjects: Secondary & Primary Textbooks, Business
Founded: 1927
ISBN Publisher's Prefix: 0-7144

Five Lamps Press, an imprint of The Dolmen Press Ltd (qv)

Foilseacháin Náisiúnta Tta*, 29 Sraid Ui Chonaill Iocht, Ath Cliath 1 Tel: (01) 745314
General Manager: Séames Ó Cathaseigh

Folens and Co Ltd*, Airton Rd, Tallaght, Dublin 24 Tel: 515311
Man Dir: D Folens
Subject: Educational
ISBN Publisher's Prefix: 0-86121

An **Foras** Forbartha*, St Martin's House, Waterloo Rd, Ballsbridge, Dublin 4 Tel: (01) 602511 Cable Add: Foras Dublin Telex: 30846
National Institute for Physical Planning and Construction Research
Chief Executive Officer: L M McCumiskey; *Information and Training:* S Smyth
Subject: Environmental Research
Founded: 1964
ISBN Publisher's Prefix: 0-906120

Four Courts Press Ltd+, Kill Lane, Blackrock, Co Dublin Tel: (01) 892922
Man Dir: Michael Adams
Subjects: Philosophy, Theology
1985: 5 titles *1986:* 6 titles *Founded:* 1969
ISBN Publisher's Prefix: 0-906127

The **Gallery** Press, 19 Oakdown Rd, Dublin 14 Tel: (01) 985161
Chief Executive, Editorial: Peter Fallon; *Sales:* Jean Barry
Associate Company: Deerfield Publications Inc, Deerfield, MA 01342, USA
Subjects: Poetry, Plays, Prose
1985: 10 titles *1986:* 9 titles *Founded:* 1970
ISBN Publisher's Prefixes: 0-902996, 0-904011, 1-85235

Gill & Macmillan Ltd, Goldenbridge Industrial Estate, Inchicore, Dublin 8 Tel: (01) 531005 Cable Add: Gillmac Dublin Telex: 92197 Fax: (01) 541688
Man Dir: M H Gill; *Editorial Dir:* H Mahoney; *Sales Dir:* Peter Thew; *Publicity:* Eveleen Coyle; *Production Manager:* Mairead Peters; *Rights & Permissions:* D Rennison
Associate Company: Macmillan Publishers Ltd, UK (qv)
Subjects: Belles Lettres, Biography, History, Philosophy, Religion, Paperbacks, University, Secondary & Primary Textbooks
Founded: 1968 (formerly Gill & Son)
ISBN Publisher's Prefix: 0-7171

The **Glendale** Press Ltd+, 18 Sharavogue, Glenageary Rd Upper, Dun Laoghaire, Co Dublin Tel: (01) 800854
Man Dir, Editorial, Rights & Permissions: Thomas F Turley; *Sales:* Fergus Corcoran; *Production:* Paul Bray
Subjects: Academic, Irish Interest, Maritime, Biography, Children's
1985: 5 titles *1986:* 6 titles *Founded:* 1981
ISBN Publisher's Prefix: 0-907606

Golden Eagle Books Ltd, subsidiary of The Mercier Press Ltd (qv)

The **Goldsmith** Press Ltd, Newbridge, Co Kildare Tel: (045) 33613
Publicity Manager: Peter Mulreid; *Business Manager:* V M Abbott
Subjects: Literature, Fiction, Poetry, Art, Cookery, Irish Interest
1986: 6 titles *1987:* 9 titles
ISBN Publisher's Prefix: 0-904984

An **Gúm**+, 44 Sr Uí Chonaill, Dublin 1 Tel: (01) 717101 Telex: 31136 Fax: (01) 725993
Senior Editor: Caoimhín ó Marcaigh; *Editorial:* Dónall ó Cuill, Máire Nic Mhaolaín; *Sales:* Séamus ó Súilleabháin; *Production:* John Dixon;

Publicity: Séamus ó Murchír
Orders to: An Áis, 31 Sr na bhFíníní, Dublin 2
Parent Organization: The Department of Education, Dublin 2
Imprint: Oifig an tSoláthair
Subjects: Lexicography, Textbooks, Children's, General, Music, Drama
Bookshop: Oifig Dhíolta Foilseacháin Rialtais, Sr Theach Laighean, Dublin 2
1985: 40 titles *1986:* 35 titles *Founded:* 1928

Hawthorn Books, an imprint of The Children's Press (qv)

Heritage Books, an imprint of Careers & Educational Publishers Ltd (qv)

Institute of Public Administration*, 59 Lansdowne Rd, Dublin 4 Tel: (01) 697011 Cable Add: Admin Dublin
Dir (Publications): James D O'Donnell; *Manager:* Iain MacAulay; *Sales:* James Moraghan
Subjects: Irish Government, Economics, Law, Social Policy and Administrative History, Periodicals
1985: 5 titles *Founded:* 1957
ISBN Publisher's Prefixes: 0-902173, 0-906980

Irish Academic Press+, Kill Lane, Blackrock, Co Dublin Tel: (01) 892922
Man Dir: Michael Adams; *Sales:* J G O'Connor
Associate Company: The Round Hall Press (at above address)
Imprints: Irish University Press, Ecclesia Press
Subjects: History, Government Documents, Irish Studies
1985: 7 titles *1986:* 9 titles *Founded:* 1974
ISBN Publisher's Prefix: 0-7165

Irish Heritage Series, an imprint of Eason & Son Ltd (qv)

Irish Management Institute+, Sandyford Rd, Dublin 16 Tel: (01) 983911 Telex: 30325 Fax: (01) 955147
Chief Executive: Maurice O'Grady; *Book Publishing and Distribution Manager:* Alex Miller
Subjects: Management Practice, Economics, Research Reports
1985: 28 titles *Founded:* 1952
ISBN Publisher's Prefix: 0-903352

The **Irish Times** Ltd, General Services Dept, 11-15 D'Olier St, Dublin 2 Tel: (01) 792022 Telex: 93639 Fax: (01) 793910
Subjects: Reprints, Political, Satirical, Educational, Literary, Twentieth Century Chronology, Modern Irish Short Stories, Microfilm (1859 to present of 'The Irish Times'), Microfiche (Sinn Fein Rebellion Handbook 1916)
ISBN Publisher's Prefix: 0-907011

Irish University Press, an imprint of Irish Academic Press (qv)

Kerryman Ltd, Clash Industrial Estate, Tralee, Co Kerry Tel: (066) 21666 Telex: 28100
Man Dir: Bryan G Cunningham; *Editorial:* Seamus McConville; *Sales, Production:* Bernard O'Keeffe
Parent Company: Independent Newspapers Ltd, Middle Abbey St, Dublin 1
Subjects: Children's, Religious, Historical
Founded: 1970
ISBN Publisher's Prefix: 0-946277

The **Lilliput** Press Ltd, Gigginstown, Mullingar, Co Westmeath Tel: (044) 72112
Man Dir: Antony Taylor Farrell
Orders to: Gill & Macmillan Ltd, Goldenbridge Industrial Estate, Inchicore, Dublin 8
Subjects: Irish Literature (autobiography, reference), History
1985: 5 titles *1986:* 6 titles *Founded:* 1984
ISBN Publisher's Prefix: 0-946640

The **Mercier** Press Ltd+, 4 Bridge St, Cork Tel: (021) 504022 Telex: 75463
Man Dir, Rights & Permissions: J F Spillane; *Editorial:* M Feehan
Subsidiary Companies: C K Distributors Ltd, 14 Templeshannon, Enniscorthy, Co Wexford; Mercier Distributors Ltd; Golden Eagle Books Ltd (both at above address)
Branch Off: 24 Lower Abbey St, Dublin Tel: (01) 744141
Subjects: Irish Literature, History, Politics, Biography, Folklore, Travel, Humour, Theology, Philosophy, Religion, Music, Art, Reference, High-priced Paperbacks
Bookshops: The Mercier Bookshop Ltd (qv under Major Booksellers)
Founded: 1946
ISBN Publisher's Prefix: 0-85342

Morrigan Book Co+, Killala, Co Mayo
Publishers: G Kennedy, H Kennedy
Subjects: Specialist Guides, General Non-fiction, Periodical
1987: 10 titles *Founded:* 1982
ISBN Publisher's Prefix: 0-907677

National Gallery of Ireland, Merrion Sq West, Dublin 2 Tel: (01) 615133 Fax: (01) 608397
Chief Executive: Homan Potterton; *Editorial:* Elizabeth Mayes; *Sales:* Mary Lynagh; *Rights & Permissions:* Frances Gillespie
Subject: Art
1985: 6 titles *1986:* 5 titles *Founded:* 1975
ISBN Publisher's Prefix: 0-903162

New Writers' Press*, 61 Clarence Mangan Rd, Dublin 8
Man Dir: Michael Smith
Subjects: Poetry, Criticism, Hardbacks and Paperbacks
Founded: 1967

O'Brien Educational, 20 Victoria Rd, Rathgar, Dublin 6 Tel: (01) 979598
Editorial, Rights & Permissions: Seamus Cashman; *Sales, Production:* Michael O'Brien
Associate Companies: The O'Brien Press (qv)
Subjects: Science, Art, Humanities, English, History, Celtic Studies, Contrast Studies, Teachers' Handbooks and Aids, Career Guidance, Business Studies, Environmental Studies, Urban Studies
Miscellaneous: Publishers to the Curriculum Development Unit, Trinity College, Dublin 2, and to other educational institutions in Ireland and the EEC
ISBN Publisher's Prefixes: 0-905140, 0-86278

The **O'Brien** Press, 20 Victoria Rd, Rathgar, Dublin 6 Tel: (01) 979598
Man Dir, Rights & Permissions: Michael O'Brien; *Editorial:* Íde ní Laoghaire
Orders to: Gill & Macmillan Ltd, Goldenbridge Industrial Estate, Inchicore, Dublin 8
Subjects: General Fiction, Biography, History, Architecture/Planning, Anthropology, Quality Paperbacks, Natural History, Illustrated Books, Folklore, Children's Books, Food and Drink, Language, Medicine, Music, Politics, Sociology, Topography
Founded: 1974
ISBN Publisher's Prefixes: 0-905140, 0-86278

Oifig an tSoláthair, an imprint of An Gúm (qv)

Peninsula Press, an imprint of Brandon Book Publishers Ltd (qv)

Poolbeg Press Ltd*, Knocksedan House, Forrest Great, Swords, Co Dublin Tel: (01) 401133 Telex: 24639
Man Dirs: Philip MacDermott, Hilary O'Donoghue; *Editorial:* Hilary O'Donoghue, Sean McMahon; *Sales:* Philip MacDermott Ltd; *Publicity:* Margaret Daly
Parent Company: Philip MacDermott Ltd
Subjects: General
Founded: 1976

Publishers Group South West (Ireland)+, Allihies, Bantry, Co Cork Tel: (027) 73025
President: Tony Lowes; *Vice-President:* Peter Haston
Associate Company: FOMT Releasing & Distributing, 151 Balleybooley Rd, Larne, Co Antrim BT40 2SY, UK
Imprint: Christa-Jo Utley
Subjects: Contemporary Fiction, Philosophy, Children's
1985: 5 titles *1986:* 7 titles *Founded:* 1984
ISBN Publisher's Prefix: 1-870618

Royal Dublin Society, Science Section, Ballsbridge, Dublin 4 Tel: (01) 680645 Cable Add: Society Dublin Telex: 90352 Rds Ei
Subjects: Botany, History of Science, General Science
1987: 3 titles *Founded:* 1731
ISBN Publisher's Prefix: 0-86027

Runa Press*, 2 Belgrave Terrace, Monkstown, Dublin Tel: (01) 801869
Subjects: Poetry, Philosophy

Stationery Office (Oifig an tSolathair), Bishop St, Dublin 8 Tel: (01) 781666 Cable Add: Enactments
Sales, Publicity: Leo Ginnetty
Bookshop: Government Publications Sales Office, Sun Alliance House, Molesworth St, Dublin 2
Founded: 1922

Tansy Books*, Knocktree Cottage, Enniskerry, Co Wicklow Tel: 868514
Dir: John Feeney
Subjects: Fiction, Psychology, Essays, History
Founded: 1976

Turoe Press Ltd+*, 69 Jones Rd, Dublin 3 Tel: (01) 786913
Chief Executive: Michael F Roberts
Subjects: Social Questions, Sociology, Social History, Reference, Practical
Founded: 1980
ISBN Publisher's Prefix: 0-905223

The **University Press** of Ireland*, 17 Brighton Square, Rathgar, Dublin 6 Tel: (01) 962946
Publisher: Sean I Browne; *Editorial:* Catherine Osborn
Associate Company: Academy Microfilms (Dublin) (at above address)
Subjects: History, Biography, Scholarly Monographs, Literature, Literary Criticism, Photography
Founded: 1976
ISBN Publisher's Prefix: 0-906187

Christa-Jo Utley, an imprint of Publishers Group South West (Ireland) (qv)

Veritas Publications+, Veritas House, 7-8 Lower Abbey St, Dublin 1 Tel: (01) 788177
Dir: Father Martin Tierney; *Editorial:* Fiona Biggs; *Commercial Manager:* Tom Griffin; *Marketing, Publicity:* Myra Delaney
Parent Company: The Catholic Communications Institute of Ireland

Subjects: Religion, Catechism, Low- & High-priced Paperbacks, University, Secondary & Primary Textbooks, Educational Materials
Bookshops: Veritas & Co Ltd (qv under Major Booksellers)
Founded: 1900
Miscellaneous: Veritas Publications is the publishing division of the Catholic Communications Institute of Ireland Inc
ISBN Publisher's Prefixes: 0-905092, 0-86217

Ward River Press*, Knocksedan House, Forrest Great, Swords, Co Dublin Tel: 401133 Telex: 24639
Man Dirs: Philip MacDermott, Bernadette MacDermott, David Marcus; *Editorial, Rights & Permissions:* Hilary O'Donoghue; *Sales:* Philip MacDermott Ltd; *Publicity:* Margaret Daly
Subjects: General Interest
Founded: 1980

Wolfhound Press+, 68 Mountjoy Square, Dublin 1 Tel: (01) 740354
Publisher: Seamus Cashman; *Publicity, Rights & Permissions:* Siobhan Campbell
Orders to: Gill & Macmillan Ltd, Goldenbridge Industrial Estate, Inchicore, Dublin 8 Tel: (01) 531005
Subjects: Belles Lettres, Art, Biography, History, Juveniles, Fiction, Literary Studies, Law
1986: 18 titles *Founded:* 1974
ISBN Publisher's Prefixes: 0-9503454, 0-905473, 0-86327

The **Women's** Press, an imprint of Arlen House Ltd (qv)

Book Clubs

Doctrine and Life Book Club, 69 Upper O'Connell St, Dublin 1 Tel: (01) 721611
Members: 4,000
Owned by: Dominican Publications (qv)

Religious Life Review Book Club, 69 Upper O'Connell St, Dublin 1 Tel: (01) 731760
Members: 4,000
Owned by: Dominican Publications (qv)

Scripture in Church Book Club, 69 Upper O'Connell St, Dublin 1 Tel: (01) 731760
Members: 6,000
Owned by: Dominican Publications (qv)

Major Booksellers

Book Stop, Dun Laoghaire Shopping Centre, Dun Laoghaire, Co Dublin
Manager: John Davey
Also: Blackrock Shopping Centre, Blackrock, Co Dublin

The **Bray** Bookshop, 15 Quinsboro Rd, Bray, Co Wicklow
Manager: Helen Clear

The **Dundrum** Bookshop, 14 Main St, Dundrum, Dublin 14
Manager: Josie Corcoran

Eason & Son Ltd, 40-41 Lower O'Connell St, Dublin 1 Tel: (01) 733811
Head Off: 80 Middle Abbey St, Dublin 1 Tel: (01) 733811 Telex: 32566 Fax: (01) 730477
Also: Antrim, Athlone, Ballymena, Belfast, Coleraine, Cork, Craigavon, Dun Laoghaire, Limerick, Lisburn, Newtownards
Also Publisher (qv)

Egans Bookshop, 114 Oliver Plunkett St, Cork Tel: (021) 272929

Greene & Co, 16 Clare St, Dublin 2 Tel: (01) 762554
Manager: E J Pembrey

Fred **Hanna** Ltd, 27-29 Nassau St, Dublin 2 Tel: (01) 771255/720797

Hodges Figgis & Co Ltd, 56 Dawson St, Dublin 2 Tel: (01) 774754
Manager: Walter Pohli
Bookstall: National Institute of Higher Education, Dublin 9
Owned by: Pentos Retailing Group Ltd (qv under Major Booksellers, UK)

The **Library** Shop, Trinity College, College St, Dublin 2 Tel: (01) 772941
Manager: J G Duffy

The **Mercier** Bookshop Ltd, 4 Bridge St, Cork Tel: (021) 504022 Telex: 75463 Mrcr Ei
Manager: Ms M L McNamara
Also: The Mercier University Bookshop, Boole Library, University College, Cork Tel: (021) 504022; Mercier Library Suppliers, 24 Lower Abbey St, Dublin 1 Tel: (01) 788259
Owned by: The Mercier Press Ltd (qv)

O'Gorman Ltd, Printing House, Galway
Manager: Ronnie O'Gorman

O'Mahony & Co Ltd, 120 O'Connell St, Limerick Tel: (061) 48155/48302
School Booksellers Department at 40 Thomas St, Limerick Tel: (061) 49322
Man Dir: Frank O'Mahony
Also: 9 Lower Castle St, Tralee, Co Kerry

Paperback Centre*, Stillorgan, Co Dublin Tel: (01) 886341

Veritas & Co Ltd, Veritas House, 7-8 Lower Abbey St, Dublin 1 Tel: (01) 788177
Manager: Robert Farquharson
Also: Veritas & Co, 14-15 Bridge St, Cork; Veritas Family Bookshop, 4 Dublin Rd, Stillorgan, Co Dublin; The Mater Dei Institute, Clonliffe Rd, Dublin 3; Veritas, Adelaide St, Sligo
Owned by: Veritas Publications (qv)

Major Libraries

The Chester **Beatty** Library, 20 Shrewsbury Rd, Dublin 4 Tel: (01) 692386
Among items on display at the Library is material showing the development of the written word from 2700 BC (the date of the Library's earliest clay tablet) down to modern times
Librarian: W Lockwood

Boole Library, see University College Cork

Central **Catholic** Library, 74 Merrion Sq South, Dublin 2
Librarian: Maurice Curtis

Dublin Public Libraries*, Cumberland House, Fenian St, Dublin 2 Tel: (01) 687333
City and County Librarian: Deirdre Ellis-King

James **Hardiman** Library, see University College Galway

National Library of Ireland, Kildare St, Dublin 2 Tel: (01) 765521
Dir: Michael Hewson
Publications: The Irish Face (1987); *The National Library of Ireland* (1984)

Oireachtas Library, Leinster House, Dublin 2 Tel: (01) 789911
Librarian: Maura Corcoran
(Selective works of parliamentary interest)

Public Record Office of Ireland, Four Courts, Dublin 7 Tel: (01) 733833

Representative Church Body Library, Braemor Park, Rathgar, Dublin 14 Tel: (01) 979979
Librarian, Archivist: Dr R Refaussé

Royal College of Surgeons in Ireland Library, St Stephen's Green, Dublin 2 Tel: (01) 780200 Ex 248 Telex: 30795 Rcsi Ei Fax: (01) 780934
Librarian: Miss B M Doran
Publication: Journal of the Irish Colleges of Physicians and Surgeons

Royal Dublin Society Library, Ballsbridge, Dublin 4 Tel: (01) 680645 Cable Add: Society, Dublin Telex: 90352 Rds Ei
Librarian: M Kelleher

Trinity College Library*, College St, Dublin 2 Tel: (01) 772941 Telex: 25442

University College Cork, Boole Library*, Cork Tel: (021) 276871 Telex: 6050

University College Dublin Library, Belfield, Dublin 4 Tel: (01) 693244 Telex: 93207 Ei
Librarian: S Phillips
Publication: Irish Publishing Record

University College Galway, James Hardiman Library, Galway

Library Associations

Central **Catholic Library** Association Inc*, 74 Merrion Sq South, Dublin 2

An **Chomhairle** Leabharlanna, 53/54 Upper Mount St, Dublin 2 Tel: (01) 761167/761963 Telex: 93904 Icls Ei
Library Council. This is the development agency for public libraries in Ireland
Dir: T Armitage
Publications: Annual Report; Irish Library News; Serial Holdings in Irish Libraries; Serials Information News and TIPS

Cumann Leabharlann na h-Éireann, 53 Upper Mount St, Dublin 2
Library Association of Ireland
Honorary Secretary: W P Smith
Publication: An Leabharlann (The Irish Library) (published jointly with the Northern Ireland Branch, The Library Association) (4 per year)

Cumann Leabharlannaithe Scoile (CLS)*, Irish Schools Library Association, Loreto College, Foxrock, Co Dublin
Irish Association of School Librarians
Executive Secretary: Sister Monaghan

Irish Society for Archives, Dublin Diocesan Archives, Archbishop's House, Drumcondra, Dublin 9 Tel: (01) 379253
Secretary: David C Sheehy
Publication: Irish Archives Bulletin

National Library of Ireland Society*, Kildare St, Dublin 2 Tel: (01) 765521
Secretary: D O'Luanaigh

Library Reference Journals

An Leabharlann (The Irish Library), Library Association of Ireland, 53 Upper Mount St, Dublin 2
Published jointly with Northern Ireland Branch

Irish Library News, An Chomhairle Leabharlanna, 53/54 Upper Mount St, Dublin 2
Monthly newsheet issued free to libraries

Long Room, Trinity College, Friends of the Library, College St, Dublin 2

Serial Holdings in Irish Libraries, An Chomhairle Leabharlanna, 53/54 Upper Mount St, Dublin 2

REPUBLIC OF IRELAND — ISRAEL 225

Literary Associations and Societies

Irish Academy of Letters*, 4 Ailesbury Grove, Dundrum, Dublin 14
Secretary: Evan Boland

Irish P E N*, 26 Rosslyn, Killarney Rd, Bray, Co Wicklow
President: Francis Stuart; *Secretary:* Arthur Flynn

Literary Periodicals

Comhar (Cooperation), 37 Sraid na Bhfinini, Dublin
Text in Irish

Dublin Magazine, Irish Academy of Letters, 4 Ailesbury Grove, Dundrum, Dublin 14

Journal of Irish Literature, Proscenium Press, PO Box 361, Newark, DE 19711, USA

Literary Prizes

Denis **Devlin** Memorial Award for Poetry
Given for the finest collection of poetry in the English language by an Irish citizen published in the previous three years. Next awarded 1989. Value IR £1,100. Enquiries to The Arts Council/An Chomhairle Ealaíon, 70 Merrion Sq, Dublin 2

Gregory Medal*
For distinction in letters or outstanding literary work in Irish. Awarded periodically. Enquiries to Irish Academy of Letters, 4 Ailesbury Grove, Dundrum, Dublin 14

Macaulay Fellowship
Awarded in literature every three years to young Irish writers, usually under 30 years of age. Value IR £3,500. Next awarded 1990. Enquiries to The Arts Council/An Chomhairle Ealaíon, 70 Merrion Sq, Dublin 2

National Poetry Competition, see under UK Literary Prizes

Novel Prize*
For the best novel written in Irish. Awarded annually. Enquiries to Irish Academy of Letters, 4 Ailesbury Grove, Dundrum, Dublin 14

Prize for Poetry in Irish, see International Literary Prizes

Rooney Prize
Annual award for Irish literature of IR £2,500, given as an incentive to a young Irish writer. Enquiries to Jim Sherwin, RTE, Dublin 4

Ryman New Writers Awards, see under UK Literary Prizes

Marten **Toonder** Award
Awarded in literature every three years. Value IR £3,000. Next award in 1989. Enquiries to Literature Officer, The Arts Council/An Chomhairle Ealaíon, 70 Merrion Sq, Dublin 2

Whitbread Literary Awards, see Literary Prizes, UK

Isle of Man

General Information

Language: English. Manx is spoken as a second language by about 500 people
Religion: Predominantly Protestant
Population: 64,000
Bank Hours: 0930-1530 Monday to Friday
Shop Hours: 0900-1730
Currency: 100 pence = 1 Isle of Man pound = 1 sterling. British coins and banknotes are legal tender
Export/Import Information: In customs union with UK. No tariff or VAT on books
Copyright: Berne, UCC (see International section)

Publishers

The **Mansk** Svenska Publishing Co Ltd+, 17 North View, Peel Tel: Peel 2855 (STD code 062484)
Man Dir: G V C Young, OBE
Branch Off: Spellinge Gard, S-590 20 Mantord, Sweden
Subjects: History, Historical Novels, Children's, Dictionaries, Biographies
Founded: 1980

Norris Press*, Victoria St, Douglas

Shearwater Press Ltd*, 4 Auckland Terrace, Ramsey Tel: Ramsey 812114 (STD code 0624) Telex: 629824 Bell
Man Dir, Editorial: Peter Crellin
Subjects: History, Local History, Topography, Fine Art, Fiction, Isle of Man
Founded: 1973
ISBN Publisher's Prefix: 0-904980

Major Booksellers

Bridge Bookshop Ltd, Shore Rd, Port Erin Tel: Douglas 833376 (STD code 0624)
Manager: Joan Hook

The **Lexicon** Bookshop, 63 Strand St, Douglas Tel: Douglas 73004 (STD code 0624)
Proprietor: M H Castle

St Paul's Bookshop*, Church Walk, St Paul's Sq, Ramsey

Major Libraries

The **Douglas** Public Library*, Ridgeway St, Douglas Tel: Douglas 23021 (STD code 0624)
Librarian: J R Bowring

Ramsey Library*, The Town Hall, Parliament Sq, Ramsey Tel: Ramsey 812228 (STD code 0624)
Librarian: Miss A V McGeagh

The **Rural** Library*, Lord St, Douglas

Israel

General Information

Language: Hebrew and Arabic (English and German widely known)
Religion: Predominantly Jewish
Population: 3.9 million
Bank Hours: 0830-1230 Sunday-Thursday; also 1600-1700 Sunday-Tuesday and Thursday
Shop Hours: Usually Sunday 0800-1300, 1600-1800; weekdays 0800-1300, 1600-1900; many close Friday afternoon
Currency: 100 agorot (singular: agora) = 1 Israeli shekel
Export/Import Information: Books (except for children's picture books) and advertising duty-free. Books exempt from most additional taxes. No import licence required for books but must apply for importing number; exchange granted automatically
Copyright: UCC, Berne, Florence (see International section)

Book Trade Organizations

Association of Hebrew Writers*, PO Box 7111, Tel Aviv
Chairwoman: Shulamit Lapid
Publication: Moznayim (monthly)

Book and Printing Center — Israel Export Institute, PO Box 50084, Tel Aviv (Located at: 29 Hamered St, Tel Aviv) Tel: (03) 630830 Cable Add: Memex Telex: 35613
Dir: Tova Krim
Division of the Israel Export Institute. Organizes and promotes activities relating to the export of Israeli books, publishing and printing services
Publications: Israel Book News (quarterly); *Israel Book Trade Directory* (biennially); *Israeli Books in Print in Languages other than Hebrew* (1986; irregular); *Publishers and Printers of Israel*

Book Publishers' Association of Israel, PO Box 20123, Tel Aviv 67132 (Located at: 29 Carlebach St, Tel Aviv) Tel: (03) 284191 Telex: 341118 Bxtvil ext 5089
The Association administers two subsidiary co-operative associations and two joint publishing companies — Ma'alot and Yachdav (qqv)
Man Dir: Arie Friedler

The **Institute** for the Translation of Hebrew Literature, PO Box 4140, Ramat Gan 61041 (Located at: 31 Jabotinsky Rd, Sifri Bldg, Ramat Gan) Tel: (03) 7524420 Cable Add: Targum Telaviv Telex: 341118 Bxtv Il ext 1272
Man Dir: Mrs Nilli Cohen
Activities of the Institute include promotion of modern Hebrew literature in translation and co-publishing projects, subsidies to authors and publishers for translations of Hebrew literary works and their publication abroad
Publications: Modern Hebrew Literature (quarterly, incorporating *Hebrew Book Review*); *Bibliography of Modern Hebrew Literature in Translation* (biannually)

Israel I S B N Group Agency, c/o Centre for Public Libraries, PO Box 242, Jerusalem 91002 Tel: (02) 247392
ISBN Administrator: Gad Rosenblatt

Standard Book Numbering Agency, see Israel ISBN Group Agency

Book Trade Reference Books and Journals

Books

Israel Book Trade Directory (biennially), Book and Printing Center — Israel Export Institute, PO Box 50084, Tel Aviv

Israeli Books in Print in Languages other than Hebrew (irregular), Book and Printing Center — Israel Export Institute, PO Box 50084, Tel Aviv

Publishers and Printers of Israel, Book and Printing Center — Israel Export Institute, PO Box 50084, Tel Aviv

Journals

Annual Index to Hebrew Periodicals, University of Haifa Library, Mount Carmel, Haifa 31999

Bibliography of Modern Hebrew Literature in Translation (biannually), The Institute for the Translation of Hebrew Literature, PO Box 4140, Ramat Gan 61041

Hadashot al Pirsuma Ha-memshala (News about Government Publications), Israel Government Printer, Jerusalem

Israel Book News (quarterly), Book and Printing Center — Israel Export Institute, PO Box 50084, Tel Aviv

Kirjath Sepher (City of the Book), Jewish National and University Library, PO Box 503, Jerusalem 91004
Bibliographical quarterly; text in Hebrew

Publishers

'A' Publishing Institute*, PO Box 894, Jersualem
Manager: A Chitov
Subjects: Orthodox Textbooks, Religion

Academon (The Hebrew University Students' Printing and Publishing House), The Hebrew University Campus, PO Box 41, Jerusalem Tel: (02) 636253/882163 Telex: 26458 Scopm Il
Man Dir: Yitzhak Tzur
Bookshops: Academon, at the four Hebrew University campuses, Jerusalem & Rehovot
Subjects: Academic
Founded: 1952

Academy of the Hebrew Language+*, Giv'at Ram, PO Box 3449, Jerusalem 91034 Tel: (02) 632242
President: Prof Joshua Blau; *Man Dir:* Nathan Efrati
Subjects: Hebrew: Linguistics, Dictionaries, Terminology, Periodicals, Concordances

Achiasaf Publishing House Ltd*, PO Box 4810, Tel Aviv (Located at: 13 Joseph Hanassi St, Tel Aviv) Tel: (03) 283339
Man Dir: Schachna Achiasaf
Subjects: General Non-fiction, Reference, Juveniles, Popular Science, Textbooks, Fiction, Dictionaries
Founded: 1933

Achiever, 22 Hahistadrut St, Jerusalem Tel: (02) 225740
Managers: D Kessler, S Atzmon
Subject: General

Adam Publishers+*, PO Box 33390, Tel Aviv (Located at: 34 Yitzhak Sadeh St, Tel Aviv) Tel: (03) 336332/339821 Cable Add: Inba Telex: 341187
Man Dirs: Yehuda Melzer, Aryeh Mor; *Editorial:* Muli Melzer; *Sales, Rights & Permissions:* Yael Azulai
Associate Company: Adama Books, 306 West 38th St, New York, NY 10018, USA
Subjects: Belles Lettres, Juveniles, University Textbooks, Biography, Politics, Philosophy, General, Reference, Cookery
Founded: 1978

Agudat Harashash*, 7 Bezalel St, Jerusalem Tel: (02) 226904
Manager: I Hasid
Subjects: Orthodox Textbooks, Religion

Aleph Publishers Ltd*, 49 Nachmani St, Tel Aviv Tel: (03) 612003
Man Dir: B Feldenkreis
Subjects: Art, Science, History of Israel, Textbooks, Belles Lettres, Poetry, Juveniles, Reference
Founded: 1962

Am Hasefer*, 9 Bialik St, PO Box 4055, Tel Aviv Tel: (03) 53040
Man Dir: D Lipetz
Subjects: Belles Lettres, Biography, History, Art, Political Science, Periodicals, Numismatics
Founded: 1955

Am Oved Publishers Ltd, PO Box 470, Tel Aviv (Located at: 22 Maze St, Tel Aviv) Tel: (03) 291526 Cable Add: Amoved, Telaviv Telex: 1568
Man Dir: Aharon Kraus
Orders to: Distributor's Centre for Israeli Books Ltd, 22 Nachmani St, PO Box 2811, Tel Aviv
Subjects: General Fiction, Belles Lettres, Poetry, Biography, History, Philosophy, Reference, Juveniles, Low-priced Paperbacks, Psychology, Social Science, University, Secondary & Primary Textbooks
Founded: 1942

Amichai Publishing House Ltd*, 5 Joseph Hanassi St, Tel Aviv Tel: (03) 284990
Man Dir: Yitzhak Oron
Subjects: Reference, General Fiction, Juveniles, Popular Science, Textbooks, Languages
Founded: 1948

Amikam, 33 Frishman St, Tel Aviv 63561 Tel: (03) 228957

Amir Publishing Co Ltd*, 38 Reines St, Giv'atayim Tel: (03) 322027
Man Dir: Avraham Amir; *Editorial:* Immanuel Blauschild
Subjects: Cartography, Guide Books, Historical and Biblical Subjects, Judaica
Founded: 1965

Ariel Publishing House*, PO Box 3328, Jerusalem 91033 (Located at: 23 Hechalutz St, Jerusalem) Tel: (02) 524414
Chief Executive: Schiller Ely
Subjects: History, Religion, Historical Geography, Old photographs and art, concerning Jerusalem and the Holy Land
Founded: 1976

Armon Publishing House Ltd*, 36 Beit Vegan St, Jerusalem Tel: (02) 533991
Subjects: General Fiction, Languages
Founded: 1965

Arrow Co*, PO Box 8022, Jerusalem (Located at: 6 Wedgwood St, Jerusalem) Tel: (02) 633830

Arsan Publishing House Ltd, see Kivunim

Atheret Publishing House+*, PO Box 5380, Herzeliya 46101 (Located at: 12 Malchey Yehuda St, Herzeliya 46348) Tel: (052) 88205 Telex: 341730 Speed Il att Atherpub
Man Dir, Editorial: Dorit Tsuriel; *Sales, Production:* Z Jacob
Subjects: Business Management, Periodicals
1985: 2 titles *Founded:* 1977

Bar Ilan University Press, Bara Ilan University, Ramat Gan 52100 Tel: (03) 718401
Chairman: Prof Daniel Sperber; *General Manager:* Miriam Drori
Subjects: Judaica, Biblical Studies, Talmud and Rabbinic Literature, Jewish and General History, Philosophy, Psychology, Law, Literature, Linguistics, Education
1987: 23 titles *Founded:* 1958

Bar Urian Publishing House*, Bar Ilan University, Ramat Gan Tel: (03) 756012
Man Dir: M Wiesel
Subject: University Textbooks
Bookshop: Bar Ilan University
Founded: 1965

Barlevi*, PO Box 21557, Tel Aviv Tel: (03) 822030
Manager: Mr Barlevi
Subjects: Juveniles, Hobbies, Games, Sports

Beit Lochamei Hagetha'ot, Kibbutz Lochamei Hagetha'ot Tel: (04) 920412
Manager: B Anolik
Branch Off: 102 Arlosoroff St, Tel Aviv
Subjects: Holocaust, World War II, Jewish Resistance against Nazism
Founded: 1950

Ben-Zvi Institute, PO Box 7504, Jerusalem 91076 Tel: (02) 639204; Yad Ben-Zvi Tel: (02) 639201
Dir: Prof Nehemia Levtzion; *Editorial Secretary:* Michael Glatzer
Subjects: History and culture of Jewish Communities in the East, Periodicals
1985: 7 titles *1986:* 7 titles *Founded:* 1948
ISBN Publisher's Prefix: 965-235

The **Bialik** Institute, PO Box 92, Jerusalem 91920 (Located at: 37 Pierre Koenig St, Jerusalem) Tel: (02) 710502
Dir General: Y J Taub
Subjects: Philosophy, Hebrew and Yiddish Literature, Belles Lettres, Poetry, Palestinology, Biblical Encyclopaedia, Archaeology, Jewish Studies, History, Arts
Founded: 1935

Bitan*, 31 Szold, Ramat Hasharon Tel: (03) 480792
Manager: A Bitan
Associate Company: Zmora Bitan-Publishing House (qv)
Subjects: General

Boostan Publishing House*, PO Box 2811, Tel Aviv Tel: (03) 382926 Cable Add: Boostanmod Telaviv
Man Dir: Mordechai Sheingarten; *Sales Dir:* Roni Birkenfield; *Publicity Dir:* Riva Almagor; *Advertising Dir:* Sara Wohlfeiler; *Rights & Permissions:* Dalia Sheingarten
Subsidiary Company: Distributors' Centre for Israeli Books Ltd (address as above)
Subjects: General Fiction, Belles Lettres, Poetry, Biography, History, How-to, Juveniles, High-priced Paperbacks, Medicine, Psychology, Educational Materials
Founded: 1969

Bronfman's Agency Ltd*, PO Box 1109, Tel Aviv 61010 (Located at: 82 Levinsky St, Tel Aviv) Tel: (03) 375284 Cable Add: Bronagency Telex: 341165 Il
Dir General: Nir Baruch; *Dir:* C Aronson
Subject: Textbooks
Bookshop: See under Major Booksellers

Cana Publishing House Ltd, PO Box 1199, Jerusalem 91010 (Located at: Merkaz Sapir, Givat Shaul, Jerusalem) Tel: (02) 528407 Telex: 26587 Carta Il
President, Editor-in-Chief: Eviatar Nur; *Publisher:* Shay Hausman
Subjects: Archaeology, Botany, History,

Fiction
Founded: 1981
ISBN Publisher's Prefix: 965-264

Carta, The Israel Map and Publishing Co Ltd+, PO Box 2500, Jerusalem 91024 (Located at: Yad Harutzim St, Jerusalem) Tel: (02) 713536 Cable Add: Carmap Telex: 26587 Carta Il
President: Emanuel Hausman; *Executive Vice-President:* Shay Hausman; *Editor-in-Chief:* Baruch Sarel; *Judaica Editor:* Moshe Kohn; *Editorial:* Lorraine Kessel, Sara Postavski, Pirchia Cohen, Barbara Ball; *Art Dir:* Eli Kellerman
Orders to: 13 Bezalel Jaffe St, Tel Aviv 65796 Tel: (03) 624842/611779
Imprint: Nitzanim
Subjects: Cartography, Educational Materials, History, Reference (in Hebrew and English), General, Juveniles
Founded: 1958
ISBN Publisher's Prefix: 965-220

Chatam Sofer Institute*, PO Box 836, Jerusalem Tel: (02) 638175
Manager: Mr Leible
Subject: Religion

Gaalyah **Cornfeld**+*, 185 Hayarkon St, Tel Aviv 63453 Tel: (03) 221737 Cable Add: Cornfeld Hayarkon 185
Chief Executive, Editorial: G Cornfeld
Subjects: Bibles, Archaeology, Palestine, Jewish History, Early Christianity, Ancient Jerusalem, Photography, General
Founded: 1957

Culture and Education Enterprises Ltd, see Mifalei Tarbut Vehinuch

Davar*, 45 Sheinkin St, Tel Aviv Tel: (03) 286141
Manager: R Mali

The **Domino** Press Ltd+, PO Box 4143, Jerusalem 91041 Tel: (02) 660868/662580 Telex: 265871/451 Monref G (Prefix: AUR 411)
Dirs: Dalia Dovrat, Deborah Harris, Beth Elon
Subjects: Belles Lettres, General Non-fiction, Juvenile, Art and Architecture
1986: 50 titles *1987:* 60 titles *Founded:* 1981

Dvir Publishing House, PO Box 149, Tel Aviv 61001 (Located at: 58 Maze St, Tel Aviv) Tel: (03) 622991 Telex: 341118 Bxtvil 5326
Man Dirs: Ohad Zemora, Asher Bitan; *Editorial, Rights & Permissions:* Ohad Zmora; *Sales:* Shachar Zmora; *Production:* Maya Dvash; *Publicity:* Asher Bitan
Parent Company: Zmora Bitan-Publishing House (qv)
Subsidiary Companies: Dvir Distribution; Karni Publishers Ltd (qv); Megiddo Publishing Co Ltd
Subjects: Judaism, Classic and Modern Hebrew Literature, Dictionaries, Textbooks, Illustrated Children's Books, Juveniles, Poetry
1985: 21 titles *1986:* 14 titles *Founded:* 1924

E S H (English for Speakers of Hebrew), an imprint of University Publishing Co (qv)

Edanim Publishers, c/o Yediot Aharonot, 138 Petah Tikva Rd, Tel Aviv 61000 Tel: (03) 212212 Telex: 33847
Publisher: Asher Weill; *Man Dir:* Didi Menusy
Parent Companies: Weill Publishers (qv) and Yediot Aharonot Newspaper
Subjects: Contemporary Events, Biography, History (especially Israeli), Reference
1985: 10 titles *1986:* 16 titles *Founded:* 1975

Eked Publishing House, PO Box 11138, Tel Aviv (Located at: 29 Bar-Kochba St, Tel Aviv) Tel: (03) 283648
Man Dir: Maritza Rosman
Associate Company: Traklin Ltd (qv)
Subjects: Belles Lettres, Poetry, Fiction
Founded: 1959

El-Am Publishing (Israel) Ltd*, PO Box 16495, Tel Aviv Tel: (03) 228964/442918 Cable Add: Elampub, Telaviv
Man Dirs: Eliyahu Amiqam, Moshe Segalovitz; *Editorial:* Rabbi Dr A Zvi Ehrman
Subject: Judaica
Founded: 1966

Encyclopaedia Judaica, Givat Shaul B, PO Box 7145, Jerusalem Tel: (02) 521201 Telex: 25-275
Man Dir: Yaacov Pachter; *Sales Dir:* Jorge Zafran
Parent Company: Keter Publishing House Jerusalem Ltd (qv)
Subject: Reference

Eshkol-Jerusalem*, PO Box 5202, Jerusalem Tel: (02) 285351
Manager: S Weinfeld
Subject: Judaica

Feldheim Publishers Ltd*, PO Box 6525, Jerusalem Tel: (02) 533947/8/9
Man Dir: Yaakov Feldheim; *Sales Dir:* Chaim Vomberg
Branch Off: P Feldheim, 96 East Broadway, New York, NY
Subjects: Biography, History, Philosophy, Reference, Religion, Juveniles
Founded: 1939
ISBN Publisher's Prefix: 0-87306

H **Fisher***, PO Box 1951, Tel Aviv Tel: (03) 744892
Manager: H Fisher
Subject: Juveniles

Franciscan Printing Press, PO Box 14064, Jerusalem Tel: (02) 286594 Cable Add: Terrasanta Jerusalem
Man Dir: Fausto Celli (Father Beniamino)
Subjects: Religion, Theology, Archaeology, Guide Books, Periodicals
1985: 19 titles *1986:* 18 titles *Founded:* 1847

Freund Publishing House Ltd+*, PO Box 35010, Tel Aviv (Located at: 61 Nachmani St, Tel Aviv) Tel: (03) 615335
Chief Executive Officer: H E Freund; *Editor, Medical Journals:* Dr J Backon; *Production Manager:* Ann Dvorin
Branch Off: Suite 500, Chesham House, 150 Regent St, London W1R 5FA, UK
Subjects: Chemistry, Medicine and Technology, Educational Games, Children's, Co-productions
1985: 15 titles *Founded:* 1968
Miscellaneous: Also Translation Agency (qv)
ISBN Publisher's Prefix: 965-294

S **Friedman** Publishing House Ltd*, PO Box 4337, Tel Aviv 61042 (Located at: 27 Gruzenberg St, Tel Aviv) Tel: (03) 656091/659756
General Manager: Shmuel Friedman
Subjects: General

Ghetto Fighters' House Publishers, see Beit Lochamei Hagetha'ot

Hadar*, PO Box 17061, Tel Aviv (Located at: 50 Reiness Street, Tel Aviv) Tel: (03) 237082/417971
Manager: I Amrami
Subjects: General
Founded: 1950

Hakibbutz Hameuchad Publishing House Ltd*, 3 Taas, Ramat Gan Tel: (03) 7514938

Man Dir: A Avishai; *Sales Manager:* Moshe Ne'eman
Subjects: General Fiction, Belles Lettres, Poetry, Biography, History, How-to, Music, Art, Philosophy, Reference, Religion, General & Social Science, University, Secondary & Primary Textbooks, Educational Materials, Agriculture, Psychology
Founded: 1940

The **Historical Society** of Israel, an imprint and associate company of The Zalman Shazar Centre (qv)

Holy Land Map Co Ltd, now Terra Sancta Arts (qv)

Inbal Travel Information (1983) Ltd, PO Box 39090, Tel Aviv 64071 (Located at: 2 Chen Blvd, Tel Aviv) Tel: (03) 285621 Telex: 358556 Danel Il attn Inbal
President: Michael Shichor
Subject: Travel Guides
1985: 2 titles *1986:* 2 titles *Founded:* 1983
ISBN Publisher's Prefix: 965-288

Institute for Publishing Hebrew Books*, PO Box 18, Zichron Yaakov (Located at: 9 Hazayit St, Zichron Yaakov) Tel: (063) 99540 Telex: 35770 Coin Il
Chief Executive: Rabbi S M Jungerman
Subject: The Talmud
Founded: 1973

Institute for the Talmudic Encyclopaedia and Complete Israeli Talmud*, Zichron Yaakov Tel: (06) 399540
Dir: I Jungerman

The **Institute for the Translation** of Hebrew Literature+, PO Box 4140, Ramat Gan 61041 (Located at: 31 Jabotinsky Rd, Sifri Bldg, Ramat Gan) Tel: (03) 7524420 Cable Add: Targum Telaviv Telex: 341118 Bxtv Il ext 1272
Dir: Mrs Nilli Cohen
Subject: Modern Hebrew Literature in Translation
1985: 6 titles *1986:* 5 titles *Founded:* 1962
ISBN Publisher's Prefix: 965-255

International Science Services*, PO Box 2039, Rehovot 76120 Tel: (08) 476216 Telex: 341167 Coin Il ext MIB
Dir: Miriam Balaban
Branch Offs: Boston University, Center for Philosophy and History of Science, Boston, MA 02115, USA; Couwenhoven 62-49, 3703 HN Zeist, Netherlands
Subjects: Science, Technology, Medicine, Education, Philosophy, Communications
Founded: 1968
ISBN Publisher's Prefix: 0-86689

The **Israel Academy** of Sciences & Humanities, PO Box 4040, Jerusalem 91040 (Located at: 43 Jabotinsky Rd, Jerusalem) Tel: (02) 636211
Man Dir: Dr Shimeon Amir; *Dir of Publications:* Shmuel Reem
Subjects: Archaeology, History, Philosophy, Religion, Botany, Zoology, Scholarly Publications in Sciences, Humanities, Judaica
Bookshop: At above address
1985: 12 titles *1986:* 14 titles *Founded:* 1959
ISBN Publisher's Prefix: 965-208

Israel Exploration Society, PO Box 7041, Jerusalem (Located at: 5 Avida St, Jerusalem) Tel: (02) 227991
Man Dir: J Aviram
Subjects: Archaeology, Biblical and Ancient History, Geography, Periodicals
Founded: 1913

Israel Program for Scientific Translations, a subsidiary of Keter Publishing House Jerusalem Ltd (qv)

Israel Universities Press, Givat Shaul B, PO Box 7145, Jerusalem Tel: (02) 521201 Telex: 25275
Man Dir: Yaacov Pachter
Parent Company: Keter Publishing House Jerusalem Ltd (qv)
Subjects: General & Social Science, Reference, Middle East Studies, University Textbooks, Politics

Israel Yearbook Publications Ltd, PO Box 17130, Tel Aviv 61171 (Located at: 13 Blum St, Tel Aviv
Managing Editor: Menachem Kna'an

Israeli Music Publications Ltd*, PO Box 7681, Jerusalem 91076 (Located at: 25 Keren Hayesod St, Jerusalem 94188) Tel: (02) 241377
Dir: Stanley Simmonds
Subject: Music
Founded: 1949

Izreel Publishing House Ltd*, 76 Dizengoff St, Tel Aviv Tel: (03) 285350
Man Dir: Alexander Izrael
Subjects: General Fiction, Belles Lettres, Poetry, Biography, History, Reference, Psychology, Juveniles, University, Secondary & Primary Textbooks, Educational Materials
Founded: 1933

Jerusalem Publishing House Ltd+, PO Box 7147, Jerusalem 91071 (Located at: 39 Tchernechovski St, Jerusalem) Tel: (02) 667744/636511 Telex: 26456 Jepub Fax: (02) 634266
Man Dir: Shlomo S Gafni; *Editorial Manager:* Rachel Gilon
Subjects: Illustrated Encyclopaedias, History, Archaeology, Reference, Illustrated Guides, Economics, Politics, Art, The Bible
1985: 14 titles *1986:* 15 titles *Founded:* 1967

Karni Publishers Ltd, PO Box 149, Tel Aviv 61001 (Located at: 58 Mazeh St, Tel Aviv) Tel: (03) 622991
Man Dirs: Ohad Zmora, Asher Bitan
Parent Company: Dvir Publishing House (qv)
Subsidiary Company: Megiddo Publishing Co (at above address)
Subjects: General Fiction, Belles Lettres, Poetry, Biography, How-to, Juveniles, Secondary & Primary Textbooks, Reference
Founded: 1951

Kernerman Publishing Ltd+, 27 Reading St, Ramat Aviv, Tel Aviv 69024 Tel: (03) 419061 Telex: 342184 Csmc Il attn Kernerman Fax: (03) 334794 attn Kernerman
Chief Executive: Ari Kernerman; *Production Manager:* Esther Havatzelet
Orders to: Lonnie Kahn Ltd, 77 Yehudah Halevy St, Tel Aviv
Subsidiary Companies: Kernerman Publishing Inc and Lexicon Software, 100 Canyon Ave, Suite 301, Downsview, Ontario M3H 5T9, Canada
Subjects: English Language and Literature Textbooks, Dictionaries
1985-86: 10 titles *Founded:* 1965
ISBN Publisher's Prefix: 965-307

Keter Publishing House Jerusalem Ltd, PO Box 7145, Jerusalem 91071 (Located at: Givat Shaul B, Jerusalem) Tel: (02) 521201 Telex: 25275
Man Dir: Yaacov Pachter; *Chief Editor:* Jon Feder; *Sales Dir:* Jorge Safran; *Production Manager:* Yaacov Zoreff
Subsidiary Companies: Encyclopaedia Judaica (qv); Israel Program for Scientific Translations; Israel Universities Press (qv); Keter Inc, New York, USA; Keter Marketing Services Ltd; Keterpress Enterprises; Rolnick-Keter; Shikmona Publishing Co Ltd (qv)
Subjects: Judaica, Religion, Philosophy, Reference, Fiction, Juveniles, Medicine, Psychology, Engineering, Social Sciences, Guides, Art
Founded: 1959

Kiryat Sefer Ltd*, PO Box 370, Jerusalem (Located at: 15 Arlosoroff St, Jerusalem) Tel: (02) 521141
Man Dir: Avraham Sivan
Subjects: Poetry, Juveniles, Atlases, Dictionaries, Secondary & Primary Textbooks, Fiction, Religion
Founded: 1933

Kivunim Publishing House Ltd*, PO Box 37517, Tel Aviv 61374 Tel: (08) 456234/455132
Man Dir: Arieh Sandler
Branch Off: 3 Achim Trebes St, Rehovot 76488
Subjects: Politics, Management, Administration, Sport, Humour, How-to, General
Founded: 1980
ISBN Publisher's Prefix: 965-276

Koren Publishers, PO Box 4044, Jerusalem 91040 (Located at: 33 Herzog St, Jerusalem) Tel: (02) 660188
Man Dirs: Eliahu Koren, Eli Kahn; *Publicity:* Eli Kahn
Associate Company: Maron Publishing Co Ltd
Subjects: Bibles, Religion
1985-86: 14 titles *Founded:* 1962
ISBN Publisher's Prefix: 965-301

Ledori+*, 10 Trumpeldor St, Tel Aviv Tel: (03) 658655
Manager: B Gefner
Subjects: General Books

Lewin-Epstein Ltd, PO Box 1020, Jerusalem (Located at: Romema, 7 Harikma St, Jerusalem) Tel: (02) 531929
Dirs: M Weksler, A Friedman
Subjects: Judaica

A **Lewin-Epstein-Modan** Ltd*, 26 Homa Vemigdal, Tel Aviv Tel: (03) 330067 Cable Add: Offset
Man Dir: C Modan; *Sales Dir:* Eliezer Ben-Ami
Subjects: General Fiction, Belles Lettres, Poetry, History, How-to, Music, Art, Reference, Juveniles, High-priced Paperbacks, Education, Science
Founded: 1930

M O D, an imprint of Ministry of Defence Publishing House (qv)

Ma'alot, 29 Carlebach St, Tel Aviv Tel: (03) 284191 Telex: 341118 Bxtv Il ext 5089
Dir: Arie Friedler
Subjects: Secondary & Primary Textbooks
Founded: 1969
Miscellaneous: Established by the Book Publishers' Association of Israel as a jointly-owned publishing house in which most of the members of the Association are shareholders

Ma'ariv Book Guild (Sifriat Ma'ariv)*, PO Box 20208, Tel Aviv (Located at: 72A Dereh Petah Tikva Rd, Tel Aviv) Tel: (03) 332212/338386 Cable Add: Ma'ariv Telaviv Telex: 033735
Publisher and Editor-in-Chief: Aryeh Nir; *Man Dir:* Yzack Yachin
Subjects: Biography, Reference, Education, History, Juveniles, Travel, Politics, Religion, Popular Science, Geography, Children, Encyclopaedias
Book Club: Ma'ariv Book Club
Founded: 1954

Machbarot Lesifrut*, PO Box 22383, Tel Aviv (Located at: 32 Schocken St, Tel Aviv)
Publisher: Ohad Zmora
Associate Company: Zmora Bitan-Publishing House (qv)
Subjects: Fiction, History, Juveniles, Literature (especially of Middle Ages), Politics, Linguistics

The **Magnes** Press*, Hebrew University, Jerusalem Tel: (02) 660341
Man Dir: B Yehoshua
Subjects: Biography, History, Music, Art, Philosophy, Psychology, Archaeology, Oriental Studies, Law, Sciences, Bibliography, University Textbooks
Founded: 1929

Makor Publishing Ltd, PO Box 7383, Jerusalem Tel: (02) 717257/717258/711573
Man Dir: I Ravitzki
Subjects: Judaica, Reprints
Founded: 1969

S J Mansour*, 1 Meyouhas St, Mahane Yehuda, Jerusalem Tel: (02) 221650
Manager: S J Mansour
Subject: Judaica

Y Marcus & Co Ltd+*, 6 Ben Yehuda St, Jerusalem Tel: (02) 228281
Manager: S Eilam
Subjects: General
Bookshop: At above address Tel: (02) 228281

Rubin Mass Ltd, PO Box 990, Jerusalem 91009 (Located at: 11 David Marcus St, Jerusalem) Tel: (02) 632565 Cable Add: Rubin Mass Jerusalem Telex: 26144 attn Mass 7790 Fax: (02) 233693 attn Mass 7790
Man Dir: Oren Mass; *Sales:* Aharon Bier
Subjects: Religion, Jewish Studies, Medicine, Secondary Textbooks, Educational Materials, Politics, Philosophy, Psychology, Biography
Bookshop: At above address
1986-87: 40 titles *Founded:* 1927
ISBN Publisher's Prefix: 965-09

Massada Press Ltd, PO Box 1232, Jerusalem 92141 (Located at: 29 Yabotinsky St, Jerusalem) Tel: (02) 632310 Cable Add: Encyclomas Telex: 26144 Bxjm Il ext 7067
Board Chairman, Chief Executive: Alexander Peli; *Man Dir:* Nathan Regev; *Rights & Permissions:* David Peli
Subjects: Belles Lettres, Biography, History, How-to, Cookery, Music, Art, Philosophy, Encyclopaedias, Judaica, Reference, Religion, Juveniles, High-priced Paperbacks, Psychology, General and Social Science, Educational Materials
Book Club: Massada Press Ltd
Founded: 1932

Massada Publishers Ltd, PO Box 842, Givatayim 53583 (Located at: 13 Tfutsot Israel St, Givatayim) Tel: (03) 771121 Cable Add: Peliprint Telex: 361211 Mape Il
Man Dir: Yoav Barash
Associate Companies: Peli Printing Works Ltd; Reprocolor Ltd
Subjects: History, Art, Juveniles, Cookery, General Fiction, Reference, How-to, Textbooks
Founded: 1932
ISBN Publisher's Prefix: 965-10

Megiddo Publishing Co, a subsidiary of Karni Publishers Ltd (qv)

Merkaz Le-Chinuch Torani*, PO Box 18, Zichron Yaakov Tel: (063) 99540 Telex:

35770 Coin Il
Man Dir: Rabbi Shalom Meir Jungerman
Subject: Orthodox Textbooks

Michaelmark Books, 254 Hayarkon St, Tel Aviv 63504 Tel: (03) 5460714 Telex: 341667 Att MIC
Publisher: Myrna Pollak
Subjects: Fiction, Popular Non-fiction
Founded: 1976

Microshur Ltd*, PO Box 6838, Jerusalem 91067 Tel: (02) 232713 Telex: 26244 Raveh Il Microshur
Manager: Menachem Shalev; *Editorial:* Dr Gabriella Shalev
Subsidiary Company: Shure Publications Ltd
Subject: Legal
Founded: 1978
ISBN Publisher's Prefix: 965-215

Mifalei Tarbut Vehinuch*, 53 Weizmann St, Tel Aviv 62091 Tel: (03) 219181
Culture and Education Enterprises Ltd
Manager: Y Cohen
Subjects: Music, Textbooks, Pedagogy

Ministry of Defence Publishing House*, 27 David Elazar St, Hakiriya, Tel Aviv Tel: (03) 205605/217940
Dir: Shalom Seri; *Deputy Dir:* Joseph Perlovitch; *Production:* Izack Kempler
Imprint: MOD
Subjects: Military Science & History, Israeli Geography & History
Founded: 1939

M **Mizrahi** Publishing House*, 106 Allenby St, Tel Aviv Tel: (03) 621492 Cable Add: Mizedition, Telaviv
Man Dirs: Meir Mizrahi, Israel Mizrahi
Branch Off: 33 Hagivea St, Savyon Tel: 344661
Subjects: History, Medicine, Science, Juveniles, Encyclopaedias, Fiction
Founded: 1960

M C **Mor-Carmi** Ltd, 2 Nordau St, Herzlia 46541 Tel: (052) 78311/3 Fax: (052) 570570
Man Dir, Sales, Rights & Permissions: Uri Mor; *Editorial, Production, Publicity:* Yoram Shavit
Subsidiary Company: High Tech Publications Inc, 8 Sheffield Rd, Great Neck, NY 11021, USA
Subjects: Technical, Scientific
Founded: 1968

Moreshet*, 166 Ibn Gavirol St, Tel Aviv

Mossad Harav Kook, see Rav Kook Institute

Nateev-Printing and Publishing Enterprises Ltd*, by Reading Bridge, PO Box 6048, Tel Aviv Tel: (03) 454135 Cable Add: Nateevpub, Telaviv Telex: 03-2470 Att Nateev
Man Dir: Mordecai Ra'anan
Imprint: Otpaz
Subjects: Religion, Juveniles, General
Founded: 1971

Netzach*, PO Box 164, Bnei Brak Tel: (03) 796413
Manager: Mr Rootenberg
Subject: Judaica

M **Newman***, 12 Hasharon St, Tel Aviv Tel: (03) 30621
Manager: B Tcherikover
Subjects: Judaica, Bible Studies, Fiction, Juveniles, Education

Nitzanim, an imprint of Carta, The Israel Map and Publishing Co Ltd (qv)

Ofer Publishing House*, 7 Shvil Aco, Tel Aviv Tel: (03) 625487
Manager: S Aluf

Subject: Juveniles
Founded: 1958

Otpaz, an imprint of Nateev-Printing and Publishing Enterprises Ltd (qv)

Otzar Hamoreh*, Israel Teachers' Union, PO Box 303, Tel Aviv (Located at: 8 Ben Saruk St, Tel Aviv) Tel: (03) 260211
Manager: P Hagin
Subjects: Education, Pedagogy, Textbooks, Mathematics, Psychology, Didactic Games
Founded: 1951

Papyrus, PO Box 39287, Tel Aviv 61392 (Located at: Tel Aviv University, Tel Aviv) Tel: (03) 420672/420578
Editorial: Itzchak Tamir
Parent Company: Dyonon Mifal Hashichpul (qv under Major Booksellers)
Subjects: History, Medicine, Psychology, Philosophy, Literature, Law
Bookshop: Dyonon Mifal Hashichpul (qv under Major Booksellers)
ISBN Publisher's Prefix: 965-306

Alexander **Peli** Ltd, PO Box 1232, Jerusalem 92141 (Located at: 29 Yabotinsky St, Jerusalem) Tel: (02) 719441 Telex: 26144 Bxjm Il ext 7067
Chairman: Alexander Peli; *Man Dir:* Nathan Regev; *Publicity Manager:* David Peli
Subsidiary Companies: Alumoth Company Ltd; Encyclopedia Publishing Company; Jewish History Publications 1961 Ltd
Subjects: General, Judaica, Encyclopaedias, Belle Lettres, Poetry, Biography, History, How-to, Music, Art, Philosophy, Reference, Religion, Juveniles, High-priced Paperbacks, Psychology, General and Social Science, Secondary and Primary Textbooks, Educational Materials, Facsimiles

Dahlia **Pelled** Publishers Ltd+, PO Box 33325, Tel Aviv 61332 (Located at: 64 Pinsker St, Tel Aviv) Tel: (03) 295148/287560/280640
Man Dir, Publicity, Rights & Permissions: Dahlia Pelled; *Editorial:* Israel Pelled; *Sales:* Raanan Rogel; *Production:* Ruti Bar-Lev
Subsidiary Company: People and Computers (at above address)
Subjects: Juvenile, Comics, Magic, Computer
Founded: 1980

Y L **Peretz** Publishing Co*, 14 Brenner St, Tel Aviv 65246 Tel: (03) 281751
Man Dir: S Schweitzer
Subjects: Poetry, Essays, History, Judaica, Belles Lettres, Philosophy, Sociology, Art (all in Yiddish, also some in Hebrew)
Founded: 1956

Ramdor Publishing Co Ltd*, 23 Levanda St, Tel Aviv Tel: (03) 373705
Man Dir: Uri Shalgi
Founded: 1960
Subject: Mass-market paperbacks

Rav Kook Institute+, PO Box 642, Jerusalem Tel: (02) 526231
Dir: Rabbi M Katzenelenbogen
Subjects: Jewish Studies, History, Philosophy, Midrashic & Halachic Law, Theology
1985: 21 titles *1986:* 21 titles *Founded:* 1937
Miscellaneous: A non-profit-making public corporation supported by the Jewish Agency, Ministry of Education & Culture and Ministry of Religious Affairs. Also provides financial support for works in above subjects

E **Rubinstein***, PO Box 7026, Jerusalem (Located at: 1 King David St, Jerusalem)

Tel: (02) 521623
Manager: E Rubinstein
Subject: Textbooks

Sadan Publishing House Ltd+*, PO Box 16096, Tel Aviv 64953 (Located at: 1 King David Blvd, Tel Aviv) Tel: (03) 267543 Cable Add: Sadanbooks Telex: 35770 Coin Il Sadan
President: David Sadan; *Managing Editor:* Ronny Stein
Subsidiary Company: Sadan Publication International Inc, New York, NY, USA
Subjects: Reference, Geography, Natural History, Archaeology, Guides, Folklore, Bible Studies, Religion, Law
Founded: 1962
Miscellaneous: Firm is also an international co-publisher and packager
ISBN Publisher's Prefix: 965-234

Schocken Publishing House Ltd+, PO Box 2316, Tel Aviv 61022 (Located at: 3 Nafcha St, Tel Aviv 65231) Cable Add: Schockenis Telex: 342449 Drcs
Publisher: Racheli Edelman
Subjects: General Fiction and Non-fiction, Literature, Judaism, Poetry, Philosophy, Social Sciences, Politics, Law, Children's, Juvenile
Founded: 1938

Shikmona Publishing Co Ltd*, PO Box 4044, Jerusalem 91040 (Located at: 33 Herzog St, Jerusalem) Tel: (02) 660188
Man Dirs: Eli Kahn, Eliyahu Korén
Parent Company: Keter Publishing House Jerusalem Ltd (qv)
Subjects: History, Archaeology, Art, Politics, Zionism, Textbooks
Founded: 1965

Shmulik*, 18 Shivtei Yisrael St, Ramat Hasharon

Sifriat Poalim Ltd*, 2 Homa Vemigdal, Tel Aviv 67771 Tel: (03) 378945/376845
Dir: Nathan Shaham; *Management:* Amram Gordon; *Sales:* Lipa Weiss; *Production:* Yaakov Karayu; *Rights & Permissions:* Yehudit Kandel
Subjects: Labour Zionist Movement, General Fiction, Belles Lettres, Art, Juveniles, History, Philosophy, Social Science, Paperbacks
Bookshop: See under Major Booksellers
Founded: 1939

Samuel **Simson** Ltd*, PO Box 14227, Tel Aviv (Located at: 100 Yehuda Halevi St, Tel Aviv) Tel: (03) 280456
Man Dir: Samuel Simson
Subject: Juveniles
Founded: 1954

Sinai Publishing Co*, 72 Allenby St, Tel Aviv Tel: (03) 623622
Man Dir: Akiva Schlesinger; *Editorial, Rights & Permissions:* Moshe Schlesinger
Subsidiary Company: Sinai Export Co Ltd, 15 Balfour St, Tel Aviv
Subject: Judaica
Bookshop: Sinai Bookstore, 72 Allenby St, Tel Aviv
Founded: 1853

R **Sirkis** Publishers Ltd+, PO Box 22027, Tel Aviv 61220 (Located at: 131 Bialik St, Ramat Gan) Tel: (03) 7510792 Cable Add: Electisco Telex: 341249 Elcts Il Fax: (03) 7511628
Chairman: Rafael Sirkis; *President, Chief Editor:* Ruth Sirkis; *General Manager:* Eliav Cohen
Subjects: Cooking, How-to, Children, Self-help, Parenting
1985: 9 titles *1986:* 14 titles *Founded:* 1983

J **Sreberk**+, 16 Balfour St, Tel Aviv 65211 Tel: (03) 293343
Manager: Z Namir; *Production Manager:* Y Namir
Subjects: Textbooks, Juveniles, Literature
Founded: 1951

Steimatzky Ltd, PO Box 628, Tel Aviv 61006 (Located at: Citrus House, 22 Harakevet St, Tel Aviv) Tel: (03) 622536 Cable Add: Steimatzky Beithadar Telaviv Telex: 361430 Steim Il Fax: (03) 615359
Chairman: Eri M Steimatzky; *Man Dir:* Yehoshua Masliah
Subjects: General Fiction, Music, Art, Juveniles, Children's, Pictorial Albums, Biography, Reference, Social Science, Judaica, Maps, University, Secondary & Primary Textbooks, Low-priced Paperbacks
Bookshops: See under Major Booksellers
Founded: 1925

Talmudic Encyclopaedia Publications*, Yad Harav Herzog, Beit Vegan, Jerusalem Tel: (02) 423242

Tarbut Vehinuch*, 53 Weizmann St, Tel Aviv Tel: (03) 254867

Tcherikover Publishers Ltd*, 12 Hasharon St, Tel Aviv 66185 Tel: (03) 370621
Manager, Editorial: B Tcherikover
Subjects: Textbooks, Education, Handbooks, Psychology, Economics, Literature, History, Art, Languages, Geography, Criminology, Management
1985: 13 titles

Teachers' Union, see Otzar Hamoreh

Tel Aviv University, Publications Sales Division, now incorporated in Dyonon Mifal Hashichpul group: please see Papyrus

Terra Sancta Arts*, PO Box 10009, Zahala, Tel Aviv 61100 (Located at: 31 Ehud St) Tel: (03) 473597/289630 Telex: 35770 Coin Il
Man Dir: Nachman Ran
Branch Off: Disengof Center, Tel Aviv Tel: (03) 289630
Subjects: Maps, Books on the Holy Land, the Bible, Facsimile editions
Founded: 1972
Miscellaneous: Formerly Holy Land Map Co Ltd

Traklin Ltd, PO Box 11138, Tel Aviv 61111 Tel: (03) 283648
Associate Company: Eked Publishing House (qv)
1985-86: 72 titles

University Publishing Co, 28 Hanatziv St, Tel Aviv Tel: (03) 259057
Dirs: Mordechai Mass, Natan Eden
Imprint: ESH (English for Speakers of Hebrew)
Subjects: School Texts, Belles Lettres, Academic
Founded: 1971

Vaad Hayeshivot Be'eretz Israel*, 4 Havatzelet St, Jerusalem Tel: (02) 225042
Man Dir: A Halevi Sher
Subject: Judaica

The **Van Leer** Jerusalem Institute*, PO Box 4070, Jerusalem 91040 (Located at: Einstein Sq, Jerusalem) Tel: (02) 667141
Executive Editor: Esther Shashar
Subjects: Philosophy, History and Philosophy of Science, Sociology, Arab-Israel Relations, Contemporary Israel
1985: 1 title *1986:* 1 title
ISBN Publisher's Prefix: 965-271

Weill Publishers, PO Box 7705, Jerusalem 91076 Tel: (02) 342018
Man Dir: Asher Weill
Subsidiary Company: Edanim

Publishers (qv)
Subjects: General
Founded: 1975
Miscellaneous: Firm also offers publishers' editorial and production services

The **Weizmann** Science Press of Israel*, PO Box 801, Jerusalem 91007 (Located at: Horkania 8a, Jerusalem) Tel: (02) 663203 Telex: 26144 Bx Jm attn Wspi ext 7086
Man Dir: Fabian Nachman; *Publicity Manager:* Mrs Hava Aspler
Subjects: General Science, General Technology, Periodicals
Founded: 1951

Yachdav, United Publishers Co Ltd, PO Box 20123, Tel Aviv (Located at: 29 Carlebach St, Tel Aviv) Tel: (03) 284191 Telex: 341118 Bxtv Il ext 5089
Man Dir: Arie Friedler
Subjects: Philosophy, Psychology, Social Science, Administration
Founded: 1960
Miscellaneous: Established by the Book Publishers' Association of Israel as a jointly-owned publishing house in which most of the members of the Association are shareholders

Yad Eliahu Chitov*, PO Box 894, Jerusalem Tel: (02) 285617
Man Dir: H Ben-Arza
Subject: Orthodox Textbooks

Yad Vashem — the Holocaust Martyrs' and Heroes' Remembrance Authority*, PO Box 3477, Jerusalem 91034 Tel: (02) 531202 Cable Add: YadVashem Jerusalem
Chairman: Dr Yitzhak Arad; *Editorial:* Dr Aharon Weiss, Prof Yisrael Gutman; *Sales:* Josef Dolev; *Production:* Prof Y Gutman; *Secretary-General:* Shimshon Eden
Branch Off: Heychal Wolyn, 10 Korazin St, PO Box 803, Givatayim, near Tel Aviv
Subject: Holocaust
Founded: 1953

Yavneh Ltd+, 4 Mazeh St, Tel Aviv 65213 Tel: (03) 297856
Man Dir: Avshalom Orenstein
Subjects: General Fiction, Music, Religion, General Science, Juveniles, Textbooks, Atlases
Founded: 1932

Yediot Ahronoth Enterprises (Book Dept)*, PO Box 37744, Tel Aviv 61376 (Located at: 12 Mikveh Yisrael St, Tel Aviv) Tel: (03) 621065 Telex: 33847
Manager: Moshe Bamberger
Parent Company: Yedioth Ahronoth (The Evening Newspaper of Israel)
Subjects: Non-fiction, Judaica, Health, Songs and Lyrics
Founded: 1952

Yeshurun*, 12 Gesher Hahayim, Jerusalem Tel: (02) 522556
Dir: Mr Pardes
Subject: Orthodox Textbooks

Yesod*, 16 Maze St, Tel Aviv Tel: (03) 291180
Manager: Y Wachtel
Subject: Textbooks

Yuval*, 13a Yeffe Nof St, Haifa Tel: (04) 330724
Manager: I Blachman
Subject: Textbooks

S **Zak** & Co*, 2 King George St, Jerusalem Tel: (02) 227819/227236
Man Dir: M Zak
Subjects: Science, Fiction, Philosophy, Reference, Religion, Children's, Juveniles, University, Secondary & Primary Textbooks, Educational Materials
Bookshops: At above address, and 7 Ezrat Israel St, Jerusalem
Founded: 1930

The **Zalman Shazar** Centre+, PO Box 4179, Jerusalem 91041 (Located at: 22 Rashba St, Jerusalem) Tel: (02) 637171
Chairmen and Editorial: Prof Menahem Stern (Hebrew), Dr Shmuel Almog (English); *Dir, Rights & Permissions:* Zvi Yekutiel; *Production Manager:* Yitzchak Cohen
Associate Company and Imprint: The Historical Society of Israel (at above address)
Subject: Jewish history
Founded: 1973
ISBN Publisher's Prefix: 965-227

Zelkowitz*, 6 Maze St, Tel Aviv Tel: (03) 296648
Manager: A Zelkowitz
Subject: Juveniles

Zmora Bitan-Publishing House, PO Box 22383, Tel Aviv 66556 (Located at: 32 Schocken St, Tel Aviv) Tel: (03) 812244 Telex: 341118 Bxtvil 5326
Publishers: Ohad Zmora, Asher Bitan; *Editorial, Rights & Permissions:* Ohad Zmora; *Sales:* Eran Zmora; *Production:* Daniella De-Nur; *Publicity:* Asher Bitan
Associate Companies: Bitan (qv); Machbarot Lesifrut (qv)
Subsidiary Companies: Dvir Publishing House (qv); Erez Books (at above address); Metziuth Books (at above address); Mrganit Books (at above address)
Subjects: Fiction, Non-fiction, Children's, Classics, Biography, Politics, Economics, Anthropology, History, Cookery, Self-help
Bookshops: Muza I, 54 Pinsker St, Tel Aviv; Muza II, 99 Ibn Gvirol St, Tel Aviv; Muza III, Aharoni Centre, Kfar-Saba
1985: 98 titles *1986:* 140 titles *Founded:* 1973
ISBN Publisher's Prefix: 965-325

Literary Agents

Bar-David Literary Agency*, 1 Hashahar St, PO Box 1104, Tel Aviv Tel: (03) 656814/5/6 Cable Add: Davidbarco Telex: 33721 Brvid Il
Contact: Mrs Varda Mor

The **Book Publishers'** Association of Israel, International Promotion and Literary Rights Department, PO Box 20123, Tel Aviv 67132 (Located at: 29 Carlebach St, Tel Aviv) Tel: (03) 284191 Telex: 341118 Bxtvil ext 5089
Contact: Lorna Soifer

Moadim*, 144 Hayarkon St, Tel Aviv 63451 Tel: (03) 444829
Play Publishers and Literary Agents
Contact: Maya Tavi

Rogan-Pikarski Literary Agency, PO Box 4006, Tel Aviv 61040 (Located at: 200 HaYarkon St, Tel Aviv) Tel: (03) 231880 Cable Add: Overworked Tel Aviv
Dirs: Barbara Rogan (New York), Ilana Pikarski (Tel Aviv)

Shalom **Sella***, PO Box 1154, Jerusalem (Located at: 9 Heleni Hamalka St, Jerusalem) Tel: (02) 242881/242882/243962 Cable Add: Scitrans Telex: 26140

Book Clubs

Ma'ariv Book Club*, 72A Dereh Petah Tikva Rd, Tel Aviv Tel: (03) 332212/338386

Owned by: Ma'ariv Book Guild (qv)
Founded: 1979

Massada Press Ltd, PO Box 1232, Jerusalem 92141 (Located at: 29 Yabotinsky St, Jerusalem)
Owned by: Massada Press Ltd, Publisher (qv)

Major Booksellers

Librairie Française **Alcheh***, 55 Nachlat Benyamin St, Tel Aviv Tel: (03) 614173/624817
Manager: Yohanan Djerassi
Largest importer of French books in Israel; also importer of English and Spanish books

Bronfman's Agency Ltd*, PO Box 1109, Tel Aviv 61010 (Located at: 82 Levinsky St, Tel Aviv) Tel: (03) 375286 Cable Add: Bronagency Telex: 341165 Il
Manager: Nir Baruch
Also exporter, and Publisher (qv)

Emanuel **Brown***, PO Box 10217, Tel Aviv 61101 (Located at: 214 Dizengoff Rd, Tel Aviv) Tel: (03) 225728
Proprietor: Emanuel Brown
Specializes in general books and remainders

Distributors' Centre for Israeli Books Ltd*, 22 Nachmani St, PO Box 2811, Tel Aviv

Dyonon Mifal Hashichpul, PO Box 39287, Tel Aviv 61392 (Located at : Tel Aviv University, Tel Aviv) Tel: (03) 420672 (head office)/420413 (import office) Telex: 342171 Versy Il attn Dyonon
General Manager: Eli Granit; *Import Manager:* Rouven Ziv
Also: Bar-Ilan University
Importer, exporter, wholesaler; see also publisher, Papyrus (qv)

Educational Book Centre*, PO Box 202, Ramallah Tel: 952122/954574/954570 Telex: 25281
Managers: G Soudah, J Soudah

Mifal **Hashichpul**, now incorporated in Dyonon Mifal Hashichpul (qv)

Heiliger & Co Ltd*, 3 Nathan Strauss St, Jerusalem 94227 Tel: (02) 225036 Telex: 26144 Bxjmil 7154
Managers: Ruth Ratzkowski, Hugo H Mendelsohn, Eitan Kahan
Also: 19 Balfour St, Tel Aviv 65211 Tel: (03) 285397; 25 Nordau St, Haifa 33122 Tel: (04) 664165
Exporter, Importer and Distributor, Subscription Centre, specializing in Scientific and Medical books

Israbook, PO Box 17130, Tel Aviv 61171 (Located at: 13 Blum St, Ramat Aviv) Tel: (03) 416881
Man Dir: Menachem Kna'an
Exporters and suppliers of books and journals in all languages originating with all publishers and learned institutions in Israel

Lonnie **Kahn** & Co Ltd, PO Box 37613, Tel Aviv 61375 (Located at: 77 Jehuda Halevi St, Tel Aviv) Tel: (03) 623693/624138
Also importer and distributor

Ludwig **Mayer** Ltd, PO Box 1174, Jerusalem 91000 (Located at: 4 Shlomzion Hamalka St, Jerusalem) Tel: (02) 222628 Telex: 26144 Bxjm Il 7014

J **Robinson** & Co, PO Box 4308, Tel Aviv 61040 (Located at: 31 Nachlat Benyamin St, Tel Aviv) Tel: (03) 615461
Also exporter and antiquarian bookseller

Sharbain's Bookshop*, PO Box 19903, Jerusalem (Located at: Salah Eddin St, Jerusalem) Tel: (02) 286775
Manager: Jiryes I Sharbain

Sifriat Poalim Ltd*, PO Box 526, Tel Aviv (Located at: 73 Allenby St, Tel Aviv) Tel: (03) 291431
Also Publisher (qv)

Steimatzky Ltd, PO Box 628, Tel Aviv 61006 (Located at: Citrus House, 22 Harakevet St, Tel Aviv) Tel: (03) 622536 Cable Add: Steimatzky Beithadar Tel Aviv Telex: 361430 Steim Il Fax: (03) 615359
40 bookshops and 30 franchises throughout Israel
Importer, exporter, wholesaler and publishers' representative; also Publisher (qv)

Universal Library*, Salah-e-Din St, East Jerusalem Tel: (02) 82624
Specializes in books on the Middle East and religious books

Major Libraries

Central Library of **Agricultural Science***, PO Box 12, Rehovot 76100

The Central **Archives** for the History of the Jewish People*, PO Box 1149, Jerusalem 91010 (Located at: Sprinzak Bldg, Jerusalem University Campus, Jerusalem) Tel: (02) 635716
Formerly Jewish Historical General Archives
Dir: Dr Daniel J Cohen

Bar Ilan University Library*, Ramat Gan 52100 Tel: (03) 718486 Telex: 342290 Il
Administrative Dir: Ya'akov Aronson

Ben-Gurion University of the Negev Library*, PO Box 653, Beersheva 84105 Tel: (057) 664422

'Dvir Bialik' Municipal Central Public Library*, Hibat-Zion St 14, Ramat Gan
Librarian: Ora Nebenzahl

Israel State Archives*, Prime Minister's Office, Jerusalem 91919 Tel: (02) 639231
Publications: Documents on the Foreign Policy of Israel (series); *Israel Government Publications* (annual)

Jerusalem City (Public) Library, PO Box 775, Jerusalem (Located at: Betzalel St 11, Jerusalem) Tel: (02) 224156/226785
Dir: A Vilner

Jewish National and University Library, PO Box 503, Jerusalem 91004 Tel: (02) 585039 Telex: 25367
Dir: Prof M Beit-Arié
Publications include: *Index of Articles on Jewish Studies; Kiryat Sefer* (bibliographical quarterly)

Knesset Library*, Hakirya, Jerusalem 91999 Tel: (02) 554245
Librarian: Dr Camillo Dresner

Municipal Library*, PO Box 32, Tel Aviv (Located at: 25 King Saul Blvd, Tel Aviv)

Pevsner Public Library, PO Box 5345, Haifa 31053 (Located at: 54 Pevsner St, Haifa) Tel: (04) 667766

Technion — Israel Institute of Technology Libraries, Haifa 32000 Tel: (04) 292507 (Elyachar Central Library) Telex: 46650
Dir: Nurit Roitberg

Tel Aviv University Library*, PO Box 39038, Ramat Aviv, Tel Aviv Tel: (03) 420745/420883

University of Haifa Library*, Mount Carmel, Haifa 31999 Tel: (04) 240289/246650/240497 Telex: 4046660
Dir: Prof Shmuel Sever
Publication: Index to Hebrew Periodicals (annually)

Weizmann Institute of Science Libraries*, Rehovot 76100 Tel: (08) 483298 (WIX Central Library)/(08) 482111 (Weizmann Institute) Cable Add: Weizinst Telex: 361934
Chief Librarian: Ilana Pollack

Library Associations

Centre for Public Libraries, PO Box 242, Jerusalem 91002
Publications: Leket (reviews of books); *Yad-la-Koré* (The Reader's Aid) (library quarterly), and library monographs

Information Processing Association of Israel*, PO Box 13009, Jerusalem
Secretary: Tuvia Saks
Publication: Ma'ase Cho-shev (6 a year)

Israel Library Association*, PO Box 303, Tel Aviv Tel: (03) 261111
Executive Secretary: Ruth Porath

Israel Society of Special Libraries and Information Centres (ISLIC)*, PO Box 20125, Tel Aviv 61200 Tel: (03) 297781
Honorary Secretary: S Langermann
Publications: Bulletin (2 times a year), *Contributions to Information Science* (irregular)

Library Reference Journals

Bibliography of Modern Hebrew Literature in Translation (biannual), The Institute for the Translation of Hebrew Literature Ltd, PO Box 4140, Ramat Gan 61041

Bulletin, Israel Society of Special Libraries and Information Centres, PO Box 20125, Tel Aviv 61200

Index to Hebrew Periodicals (annual), University of Haifa Library, Mount Carmel, Haifa 31999

Kethavim Benossey Med'a (Contributions to Information Science), Israel Society of Special Libraries and Information Centres, PO Box 20125, Tel Aviv 61200

Kiryat Sefer, Jewish National and University Library, PO Box 503, Jerusalem 91004
Bibliographical quarterly

Leket (Gleaning), Centre for Public Libraries, PO Box 242, Jerusalem 91002

Ma'ase Cho-shev (Action and Thought), Information Processing Association of Israel, PO Box 13009, Jerusalem

Yad-la-Koré (The Reader's Aid), Centre for Public Libraries, PO Box 242, Jerusalem 91002

Literary Associations and Societies

Acum Ltd (Society of Authors, Composers and Music Publishers in Israel), PO Box 14220, Tel Aviv 61140 (Located at: 118 Rothschild Blvd, Tel Aviv) Tel: (03) 240115 Telex: 35770 Coin Il/35771 Coin Il
Dir-General: R Kedar

Mekise Nirdamin Society*, PO Box 4344, Jerusalem
Secretary: Dr I Ta-Shma

Publishes Hebrew works of the older classical Jewish literature

Israeli P E N Centre*, 19 Shmaryahu Lewine St, Jerusalem 96664
President: Aharon Megged; *Secretary:* Haim Toren

Literary Periodicals

Caiet Pentru Literatura Si Istoriografie (Journal of Literature and Historiography), Cenaclul Literar 'Menora', PO Box 763, Jerusalem
Text in Hebrew, Romanian and Yiddish

HSL (Hebrew University Studies in Literature), The Hebrew University of Jerusalem, Institute of Languages and Literatures, Jerusalem
Text in English and French

Ha-Sifrut (Literature), Tel Aviv University, Ramat Aviv, Tel Aviv
Hebrew and comparative literature, literary theory and poetics; text in Hebrew with summaries in English

Image, The Hebrew University of Jerusalem, Jerusalem
Text in English

Modern Hebrew Literature, The Institute for the Translation of Hebrew Literature, PO Box 4140, Ramat Gan 61041
Quarterly; incorporating Hebrew Book Review

Siidemot, Ichud Hakvutzot and Hakibbutzim, Youth Division, 10 Dubnov St, Tel Aviv
Literary digest of the kibbutz movement; text in English

Literary Prizes

Bialik Prize for Literature*
The highest literary award of the Tel-Aviv-Yafo Municipality, awarded in two categories: belles-lettres and Jewish studies. 80,000 shekels. Awarded annually. Enquiries to Tel-Aviv-Yafo Municipality, Tel Aviv

Brenner Prize*
In recognition of outstanding literary works. 12,000 shekels. Awarded annually. Enquiries to Hebrew Writers' Association, PO Box 7111, Tel Aviv

Holon Literary Prize*
To encourage literary talent in Israel. 50,000 shekels. Awarded every year. Enquiries to Holon Municipality, Holon

Israeli Prize in Humanities and Social Sciences*
For the most original, outstanding contribution to the humanities and social sciences. 110,000 shekels. Awarded annually in each one of the following areas: (1) Judaica, Modern Hebrew Literature and Education; (2) the Humanities and the Social Sciences; (3) the Arts; (4) Science and Technology; (5) outstanding life-long service to the welfare of Israeli society. Enquiries to Dr Moshe Gilboa, Israeli Ministry of Education and Culture, 20 Mamila St, Jerusalem 91911

Israeli Prize in Jewish Studies, Hebrew Literature and Education, see Israeli Prize in Humanities and Social Sciences

Israeli Prize in the Arts, see Israeli Prize in Humanities and Social Sciences

Shazar Prize*
Awarded to immigrant writers, young authors and writers dealing with the Holocaust. 5,000/12,000 shekels to each author. Awarded annually. Enquiries to Israeli Ministry of Education and Culture, 34 Shivtei Israel St, Jerusalem 95105

Tchernichowsky Prize*
For outstanding translations into Hebrew. 60,000 shekels divided between two translators: one of belles-lettres and one of scientific material. Awarded biennially. Enquiries to Tel-Aviv-Yafo Municipality, Tel Aviv

Translation Agencies and Associations

Freund Publishing House Ltd*, PO Box 35010, Tel Aviv (Located at: 61 Nachmani St, Tel Aviv) Tel: (03) 615335
Chief Executive Officer: H E Freund
Specializing in Russian, French, German and Flemish; also Publisher (qv)

The **Institute** for the Translation of Hebrew Literature, PO Box 4140, Ramat Gan 61041 (Located at: 31 Jabotinsky Rd, Sifri Bldg, Ramat Gan) Tel: (03) 7524420 Cable Add: Targum Telaviv Telex: 341118 Bxtv Il ext 1272

Scientific Translations International Ltd*, PO Box 1154, Jerusalem (Located at: 9 Heleni Hamalka St, Jerusalem) Tel: (02) 242881/242882/243962 Cable Add: Scitrans Telex: 26140

Italy

General Information

Language: Italian. German and Ladin are officially recognized in Trentino-Alto Adige; Slovene in Trieste
Religion: Roman Catholic
Population: 57 million
Bank Hours: 0830-1330, 1500-1600 Monday-Friday
Shop Hours: 0900-1230, 1500-1900 Monday-Saturday; many close Monday morning
Currency: Lira
Export/Import Information: Member of the European Economic Community. No tariff on books except children's picture books from non-EEC; advertising matter other than single copies is dutied. VAT on books and advertising matter. No import licence required.
Copyright: UCC, Berne, Florence (see International section)

Book Trade Organizations

Agenzia per l'Area di Lingua Italiana ISBN, Editrice Bibliografica SRL, Viale Vittorio Veneto 24, I-20124 Milan Tel: (02) 6597950/6597246
ISBN Administrator: Michele Costa

Associazione Italiana Editori, Via delle Erbe 2, I-20121 Milan Tel: (02) 8059244/8057058
Rome office: Via Crescenzio 19, I-00193 Rome Tel: (06) 6540298/6548450
Italian Publishers' Association
Secretary-General: A Ormezzano
Publications: Catalogo dei Libri Italiani in Commèrcio; Giornale della Libreria

Associazione Librai Antiquari d'Italia, Via Jacopo Nardi 6, I-50132 Florence Tel: (055) 243253
Antiquarian Booksellers' Association of Italy
President: Dr Vittorio Soave, Libreria Antiquaria Soave, Via Po 48, I-10123 Turin

Associazione Librai Italiani*, Piazza G G Belli 2, I-00153 Rome Tel: (06) 5803844
Italian Booksellers' Association
Publication: Libreria

I P L (Istituto Propaganda Libraria)*, Via Mercalli 23, Milan
Institute of Bookshop Advertising

Standard Book Numbering Agency, see Agenzia per l'Area di Lingua Italiana ISBN

Book Trade Reference Books and Journals

Books

Gli Editori Italiani, Editrice Bibliografica SRL, Viale Vittorio Veneto 24, I-20124 Milan
Listing over 2,000 Italian publishers

Italian Books in Print, Editrice Bibliografica SRL, Viale Vittorio Veneto 24, I-20124 Milan

Italian Periodicals in Print, Editrice Bibliografica SRL, Viale Vittorio Veneto 24, I-20124 Milan

Le Librerie Italiane (Italian Booksellers), Editrice Bibliografica SRL, Viale Vittorio Veneto 24, I-20124 Milan

Journals

Bibliografia Nazionale Italiana (Italian National Bibliography), Central Institute of the Union Catalogue of Italian Libraries and Bibliographical Information, Viale Castro Pretorio 105, I-00185 Rome

Bollettino (Bulletin, monthly), Ufficio della Proprietà Letteraria, Artistica e Scientifica, Rome

Bollettino bibliografico, Libreria Internazionale Seeber, Via dei Tornabuoni 68R, I-50123 Florence

Catalogo dei Libri Italiani in Commèrcio (Italian Books in Print), Italian Publishers' Association, Via delle Erbe 2, I-20121 Milan

Il Compratore (The Buyer), Editoriale A-Z, Via P Kolbe 8, I-20317 Milan

Gazzettino Librario (Book Trade Gazette), Piazza Lotario 6, Rome
Advertises book wants and offers

Giornale della Libreria (Book Trade Journal), Italian Publishers' Association, Via delle Erbe 2, I-20121 Milan

Libreria (The Book Trade), Italian Booksellers' Association, Piazza G G Belli 2, I-00153 Rome

Libri e Riviste d'Italia (Italian Books and Periodicals), Via Boncompagni 15, I-00187 Rome
Available in Italian edition and international edition in English, French, German and Spanish

Libro Cattòlico (The Catholic Book), Union of Italian Catholic Publishers, Via Domenico Silveri 9, I-00165 Rome

Mundus, CP 2236, Rome

Ragguaglio Librario (Book Report), Institute of Bookshop Advertising, Via Mercalli 23, Milan

Publishers

A M Z Editrice SpA, Via Cortina d'Ampezzo 17, I-20139 Milan Tel: (02) 5396846 Cable Add: Editamz Telex: 310607 Amzed I
Man Dir, Editorial: Mario Abriani; *Rights & Permissions:* Lucia Calza
Subjects: Children's, Juveniles, Fiction, Non-fiction
1985: 51 titles *1986:* 70 titles *Founded:* 1955

A P E, Bologna, see Ape

Edizioni **A P E** SpA, Via Boscovich 44, I-20124 Milan Tel: (02) 209341 Telex: 325294 Mursia I
Man Dir: Dr Piero Bajetta
Parent Company: Ugo Mursia Editore SpA (qv)
Subjects: Textbooks
Founded: 1974

Edizioni **A R E S***, Via Stradivari 7, I-20131 Milan Tel: (02) 209202
Dir: Dr Cesare Cavalleri
Subjects: Philosophy, Theology, Architecture, Psychology
Founded: 1957

Edizioni Gruppo **Abele**+*, Via Giolitti 21, I-10123 Turin Tel: (011) 8395444
Man Dir: Antonio Monaco; *Editorial:* Pierangelo Bassignana; *Production:* Sergio Serra; *Publicity:* Graziella Ricupero; *Rights & Permissions:* Claire-Lise Vuadens
Orders to: Libreria Edizioni Gruppo Abele, Via dei Mercanti 6, I-10122 Turin
Parent Company: CSC (Cooperativa Servizi Culturali) (at above address)
Subjects: Education, Minority Groups, Adolescence, Drug and Alcohol Abuse, Ecology, Peace and Nonviolence, Disarmament, Communications
Bookshop: Libreria Edizioni Gruppo Abele, Via dei Mercanti 6, I-10122 Turin Tel: (011) 518427
1985: 23 titles *Founded:* 1983
ISBN Publisher's Prefix: 88-7670

Edizioni **Abete**, Via Tiburtina 655, I-00159 Rome Tel: (06) 430056/435225/4385591
Chief Executive: Dr Luigi Abete; *Editorial:* Dr Mauro Miccio; *Sales:* Dr Nicola Fusca, Dr Francesco Matassi, Franco Morbiducci
Parent Company: A Be T E SpA — Azienda Beneventana Tipografica Editoriale
Subjects: Literature, Theatre, Philosophy, Economics, Business, Law
Founded: 1946
ISBN Publisher's Prefix: 88-7047

Accademia (Milano)*, Via Columella 36, I-20128 Milan Tel: (02) 2552593
Subject: General Literature
Founded: 1967

Accademia Naz dei Lincei*, Via della Lungara 10, I-00165 Rome Tel: (06) 650831
Subjects: Art, Archaeology, Biology, Economics, Management, Mathematics, History
Founded: 1847
ISBN Publisher's Prefix: 88-218

Edizioni **Accordo** SRL, Galleria del Corso 4, I-20122 Milan Tel: (02) 794746 Cable Add: Curcimusic Telex: 332683 Curci I
Chief Executive: Dr Giuseppe Gramitto Ricci
Associate Company: Edizioni Curci SRL (qv)
Subject: Music
1985: 3 titles *1986:* 1 title *Founded:* 1948

Mario **Adda** Editore SNC, Via Tanzi 59, I-70121 Bari Tel: (080) 339502
Man Dir and other offices: Mario Adda
Subjects: History, Art, Literature, Local Interest
1985: 7 titles *Founded:* 1964

Adelphi Edizioni SpA, Via S Giovanni sul Muro 14, I-20121 Milan Tel: (02) 871266/866177/8058945
Man Dir: Luciano Foà; *Editorial Dir:* Roberto Calasso; *Publicity:* Emanuela Canali; *Production:* Piero Bertolucci
Orders to: Edizioni Adelphi, Servizio Vendita Libri, c/o Fratelli Fabbri Editori, Via Mecenate 91, I-20138 Milan Tel: (02) 50951
Subjects: General Fiction, Belles Lettres, Biography, Music, Art, Philosophy, Religion, Psychology, General Science
1985: 39 titles *1986:* 44 titles *Founded:* 1962

Giacomo **Agnelli** Editore, see Giunti Publishing Group

Ermanno **Albertelli** Editore, Via S Sonnino 34, I-43100 Parma Tel: (0521) 94702 Cable Add: Albertelli Parma Telex: 532271 Edialb I
Chief Executive, Production: Ermanno Albertelli; *Sales:* Viviana De Luca
Subsidiary Company: Tuttostoria (Azienda di distribuzione) (at above address)
Subjects: Military Modelling, Military History, War Games, Arms, Railways
Founded: 1968

Libreria **Alfani** Editrice SRL*, Via degli Alfani 88, I-50121 Florence Tel: (055) 284397/298800
Chief Executive: Umberto Panerai
Subjects: University Publications
Bookshops: Libreria Alfani, Via degli Alfani 84/86 R, I-50121 Florence; Libreria Ateneo, Piazza San Marco 3/R, Florence
Founded: 1968

Alfieri Edizioni d'Arte*, San Marco 1991, I-30124 Venice Tel: (041) 23323
Dirs: Giorgio Fantoni, Massimo Vitta Zelman; *Editorial:* Carlo Pirovano; *Rights & Permissions:* Marisa Inzaghi, Mirella Tenderini
Parent Company: Electa Editrice (qv)
Subjects: Modern Art, Venetian Art, Architecture, Periodicals, Numbered Editions
Founded: 1939

Alinari Fratelli SpA Istituto di Edizioni Artistiche, Largo Fratelli Alinari 15, I-50123 Florence Tel: (055) 217842 Cable Add: Idea
Man Dir: Claudio de Polo Saibanti
Bookshops: Fratelli Alinari, Via Vigna Nuova 48r, Florence; Fratelli Alinari, Via Alibert 16, Rome
Subjects: Art, Educational Materials, Photography
Founded: 1854
ISBN Publisher's Prefix: 88-7292

Edizioni **All'Insegna** del Veltro, Viale Osacca 13, I-43100 Parma Tel: (0521) 31587
Chief Executive: Claudio Mutti
Subjects: Esoterica, History of Religion, Mediaeval Studies, Oriental Studies, Islamic Studies, Greek Philosophy
Founded: 1977

Editrice **Ancora**, Via GB Niccolini 8, I-20154 Milan Tel: (02) 3189941
Man Dir: Medici Severino; *Editorial Dir:* Zini Vigilio; *Sales Dir:* Giordani Saverio
Subjects: Religion, Juveniles, Social Science
Founded: 1934
ISBN Publisher's Prefix: 88-7610

Franco **Angeli** Libri SRL, CP 17130, I-20127 Milan (Located at: Viale Monza 106, Milan) Tel: (02) 2827651
Man Dir: Dr Franco Angeli; *Sales:* Dr Stefano Angeli; *Production:* Odoardo Merlin
Subjects: Anthropology, Architecture, Law of Employment and Labour Relations, Economics, Teaching and Education, Geography, History, Politics, Psychology, Finance, Sociology, Urban and Regional Studies, Physics, Electrical Engineering, Electronics, Data Processing, Mathematics, Science, Management, Marketing, Publicity, Public Relations, Essays
Founded: 1955
ISBN Publisher's Prefix: 88-204

Coop Editrice **Antigruppo Siciliano**, Via Argenteria km 4, I-91100 Trapani, Sicily Tel: (0923) 38681
Man Dir, Rights & Permissions: Nina Di Giorgio; *Editorial:* Nat Scammacca; *Sales:* Stanley H Barkan; *Production:* Ignazio Navara; *Publicity:* Nat Scammacca, Stanley H Barkan
Associate Company: Cross-Cultural Communications, Stanley H Barkan, 239 Wynsum Ave, Merrick, Long Island, NY 11566, USA
Subjects: Poetry, Prose
1985: 10 titles *Founded:* 1980
ISBN Publisher's Prefix: 0-89304

Editrice **Antroposofica** SRL*, Viale Majno 17, I-20122 Milan Tel: (02) 799059
Man Dir: Dr Iberto Bavastro
Parent Company: Rudolf Steiner Verlag, Switzerland (qv)
Subjects: Anthroposophy, Works of Rudolf Steiner
1985: 14 titles *Founded:* 1959

Organizzazione Didattica Editoriale **Ape**+, Via Augusto Murri 56, I-40137 Bologna Tel: (051) 392670 Cable Add: Ape Murri 565 Bologna
Chief Executive, Editorial, Production, Rights & Permissions: Gina Cesari; *Sales:* Giorgio Ognibene
Subjects: Civics Textbooks for Children, Fiction, Local History
1985-86: 3 titles *Founded:* 1964

Ape, Milan, see A P E

Ruggero **Aprile***, Via Vittime di Bologna 14, I-10156 Turin Tel: (011) 240124 Telex: 213211
Man Dir: Ruggero Aprile; *Sales:* Valerio Aprile
Subjects: Fiction, History, Juveniles, Art
Founded: 1973
Miscellaneous: Also known as PEA — Produzioni Editoriale Aprile

Edizioni L'**Arciere** SRL+*, Via Roma 8, I-12100 Cuneo Tel: (0171) 3174 Cable Add: Arciere Edizioni Cuneo
Chief Executive, Sales, Rights & Permissions: Aldo Sacchetti; *Editorial, Production, Publicity:* Mario Donadei
Subjects: Local History, Art and Culture, History of the Resistance, Essays, Poetry, Fiction, Memoirs, Mountains, Touring
Founded: 1973

Argalia Editore delle Arti Grafiche Editoriali SRL, CP 150, I-61029 Urbino (Located at: Via S Donato 148C, Urbino) Tel: (0722) 328756
Subjects: Philosophy, History, Literature, Criticism, Education, Science, Fiction, Poetry, Classical Drama, Economics
1987: 3 titles *Founded:* 1942

234 ITALY

Aristea Editrice SpA*, Via Cesare Saldini 25, I-20133 Milan Tel: (02) 730103/730003
Subjects: Language, Dictionaries, Encyclopaedias, Children's, Textbooks
Founded: 1953

Savitri SRL — Edizioni **Arka**+*, Via don Minzoni 20, I-20090 Vimodrone (MI) Tel: (02) 2503396
Man Dir: Umberto Costanzia; *Editorial:* Ginevra Viscardi
Subjects: Oriental Philosophy, Illustrated books for children
1985: 15 titles *Founded:* 1984
ISBN Publisher's Prefix: 88-85762

Editore Armando **Armando** SRL+, Piazza Sidney Sonnino 13, I-00153 Rome Tel: (06) 5894525/5817245/5806420
Man Dir: Enrico Jacometti
Subjects: Psychology, Philosophy, Social Sciences, Politics, Textbooks, Education, Linguistics, Languages, Children's, Sociology, Nursing
1985: 78 titles *Founded:* 1963

Armenia Editore SpA, Viale Cà Granda 2, I-20162 Milan Tel: (02) 6438766
Chief Executive: Dr Giovanni Armenia; *Rights & Permissions:* Patrizia Michellini
Subjects: Paranormal, Astrology, Alternative Medicine, Hobbies, Sports, Fitness, Biography, Management
Founded: 1972
ISBN Publisher's Prefix: 88-344

Arnaud Editrice SRL+*, Via XXVII Aprile 13, I-50129 Florence Tel: (055) 496333
Chief Executive: Alfredo Meletti
Also: Via J Nardi 27, I-50132 Florence
Subjects: Art, History, Politics
Founded: 1944

Arsenale Editrice SRL+, CP 341, I-30123 Venice (Located at: San Marco 4708, Venice) Tel: (041) 5205903/5221579
Telex: 480481 Apivers I sub 128 Fax: (041) 5221579
Man Dir, Rights & Permissions: Andrea Grandese; *Editorial:* Maddalena Redolfi; *Sales:* Giorgio Tamaro; *Production:* Luigi Ciscato
Associate Company: Editoriale Bortolazzi — Stei SRL, Via Monte Comun 30, I-37057 San Giovanni Lupatoto (VR)
Subjects: Art, Architecture, History, Philosophy
Bookshop: San Croce 29, I-30125 Venice
1985: 20 titles *1986:* 20 titles *Founded:* 1984
ISBN Publisher's Prefix: 88-7743

Casa Editrice **Astrolabio-Ubaldini** Editore*, Via Guido d'Arezzo 16, I-00198 Rome Tel: (06) 862131
Chief Executive: Francesco Gana; *Editorial:* Francesco Cardelli; *Sales, Production:* Fiorenzo Bertillo
Subjects: Psychoanalysis, Psychology, Psychiatry, Oriental Philosophy, Epistemology, Parapsychology, Sociology
Founded: 1946

Editrice **Atanor** SRL+, Via Salaria 416, I-00199 Rome Tel: (06) 8313907
Man Dir: Anna Maria Papini; *Editorial:* Francesco Albanese
Subjects: Esoterica, Magic, Alchemy, Masonry, Orientalia
1985: 15 titles *Founded:* 1912

Edizioni Dell'**Ateneo** SpA*, CP 7216, I-00192 Rome (Located at: Via Boezio 6, Rome) Tel: (06) 7593456
Man Dir: Franco Volta; *Sales:* Bruno Volta; *Production:* Sergio Petrelli
Orders to: Via Ruggero Bonghi 11/B, I-00184 Rome
Subjects: Belles Lettres, Poetry, Biography, History, Music, Art, Philosophy, Classical Philology, Cinema, Reference, Religion, High-priced Paperbacks, Psychology, Engineering, General & Social Science, Secondary and University Textbooks, Economics, Medicine, Aeronautics, Navy, Army
Founded: 1946

Verlagsanstalt **Athesia**+, Postfach 417, I-39100 Bolzano-Bozen (Located at: Lauben 41, Bolzano-Bozen) Tel: (0471) 932000 Cable Add: Athesia Verlag, Bozen Telex: 400161
Man Dir, Production: Peter Plattner; *Sales Manager:* Richard Fieg; *Publicity Manager:* Gustav Theiner
Subjects: Art, Travel, Guidebooks, Periodicals, History, Maps, Textbooks, Poetry, Mountaineering (in German and Italian)
Bookshops: Bozen, Brixen, Bruneck, Meran, Schlanders, Sterzing
1985: approx 30 titles *1986:* approx 45 titles *Founded:* 1907
ISBN Publisher's Prefix: 88-7014

Atlantica Editrice SARL*, Via Gramsci 11a, I-71043 Manfredonia (Foggia)
Branch Off: CP 38, I-71043 Manfredonia
Subjects: Classical Languages, Linguistics, General Science, Regional Culture
Founded: 1974
ISBN Publisher's Prefix: 88-7085

Edizioni **Augustinus**+, Via Salita del Convento 55, I-90132 Palermo-Rocca Tel: (091) 420861
Man Dir, Editorial, Sales, Production, Publicity: Anna Maria Firmano' Simoncini; *Rights & Permissions:* Eulama SRL (qv under Literary Agents)
Subjects: Philosophy, Theology, History, Humanities
1986: 8 titles *1987:* 3 titles *Founded:* 1983

M d'**Auria** Editore della 'EST — Editoriale Studi e Testi — SNC'+, Calata Trinità Maggiore 52, I-80134 Naples Tel: (081) 5518963
Dir: Gianni Macchiavelli; *Publicity:* Paola Raeli; *Bookshop Dir:* Gabriele Iaccarino
Subjects: Religion, History, Classical Literature
Bookshop: Libreria Internazionale— International Book Center M d'Auria, Calata Trinità Maggiore 53, I-80134 Naples
1986: 48 titles *Founded:* 1887

Automobilia*, Viale Monte Santo 2, I-20124 Milan Tel: (02) 651229/651279
Man Dir: Bruno Alfieri; *Editorial:* Bettina Cristiani; *Sales:* Luisa Alfieri; *Production:* Massimo Fabbri
Subjects: Automobiles, Boating
1985: 16 titles *Founded:* 1979
ISBN Publisher's Prefix: 88-85058

Edizioni delle **Autonomie** SRL, Via Cesare Balbo 35, I-00184 Rome Tel: (06) 4751307/4751906
Chief Executive: Stelvio Minelli; *Production:* Bruno Puglielli
Parent Company: Lega per le Autonomie e i Poteri Locali, Via Cesare Balbo 43, I-00184 Rome
Branch Offs: 22 throughout Italy
Subjects: Local Government, Planning, Health
Founded: 1977

Giunti **Barbera** Editore, see Giunti Publishing Group

Editoriale **Bari**, see Editorialebari

Edizioni Oreste **Barjes**, see Giunti Publishing Group

Bastogi*, Viale Ofanto 142g, I-71100 Foggia Tel: (0881) 25070
Subjects: General Literature, Scholarly, Religion, Essays, History
Founded: 1979

Casa Editrice Luigi **Battei**, Str Cavour 5/C, I-43100 Parma Tel: (0521) 33733/283077
Chief Executive: Antonio Battei; *Editorial:* Binno Moguaru
Subjects: Local History, Art, Architecture, Literature, Poetry, Essays
Founded: 1872

Edizioni d'Arte di Carlo E **Bestetti** & C SAS+*, Via di San Giacomo 18, I-00187 Rome Tel: (06) 6790174
Man Dir: Carlo Bestetti
Subjects: Art, Architecture, Industry
Founded: 1947

Del **Bianco** Editore, CP 40, I-33100 Udine (Located at: Via S Daniele 11, Udine) Tel: (0432) 501134 Cable Add: Del Bianco Udine
Subjects: Engineering, General Science, University & Secondary Textbooks, Art, History
Founded: 1933

Biblical Institute Press, see Pontificio Istituto Biblico

Bibliopolis—Edizioni di Filosofia e Scienze SpA+*, Via Arangio Ruiz 83, I-80122 Naples Tel: (081) 664606
Man Dir: Dr Francesco del Franco
Subjects: Science and Philosophy
Founded: 1976
ISBN Publisher's Prefix: 88-7088

B **Boggero** Editore, see Giunti Publishing Group

Bollati Boringhieri Editore SpA, Corso Vittorio Emanuele 86, I-10121 Turin Tel: (011) 541371 Cable Add: Edibor
Man Dir: Giulio Bollati; *Editorial Manager:* Filippo Macaluso; *Sales:* Alessandro Rangaioli; *Public Relations:* Roberto Gilodi; *Foreign Rights:* Agnese Incisa
Subjects: Philosophy, Science, Psychology, Economics, Social Sciences, History, Classics, Fiction, University Textbooks
Founded: 1957
ISBN Publisher's Prefix: 88-339

Bompiani, Via Mecenate 91, I-20138 Milan Tel: (02) 50951 Cable Add: Librifabbri Milano Telex: 311321 Fabbri I
Dir: Mario Andreose; *Rights & Permissions:* Carla Tanzi
Subjects: Fiction, Non-fiction, Theatre, Science, Art, Juveniles, Dictionaries, Encyclopaedias
Founded: 1929
Miscellaneous: Member of Gruppo Editoriale Fabbri, Bompiani, Sonzogno, Etas SpA

Bonacci-Libreria Editrice, Via Paolo Mercuri 23, I-00193 Rome Tel: (06) 6565995
Man Dir: Giorgio Bonacci
Subjects: Belles Lettres, History, Secondary Textbooks
Bookshop: At above address
1985: 19 titles *1986:* 21 titles *Founded:* 1942
ISBN Publisher's Prefix: 88-7573

Giuseppe **Bonanno** Editore, Via Vittorio Emanuele 188, I-95024 Acireale Tel: (095) 601984
Chief Executive: Prof Pina Strano; *Editorial:* Giuseppe Bonanno; *Dir:* Mauro Bonanno
Subjects: Il Risorgimento, Ancient History, Philosophy, Folklore, Modern Culture
Bookshop: Libreria Bonanno (at above

address)
Founded: 1966

Casa Editrice **Bonechi**+, Via dei Cairoli
18b, I-50131 Florence Tel: (055) 576841/2
Telex: 571323 CEB
Man Dir: Giampaolo Bonechi; *Editorial:*
Giovanna Magi, Marco Banti
Subjects: Art, Travel
Founded: 1973
ISBN Publisher's Prefix: 88-7009

Ditta F **Bongiovanni** SAS, Via Rizzoli 28E,
I-40125 Bologna Tel: (051) 225722
Man Dir: Giancarlo Bongiovanni;
Editorial: Barbara Bongiovanni;
Production: Andrea Bongiovanni
Subjects: Music, Musicology
1985: 5 titles *1986:* 4 titles *Founded:* 1905

Edizioni **Bora** SNC di E Brandani & C*,
Via Jacopo di Paolo 42, I-40128 Bologna
Tel: (051) 356133/374394
Subject: Contemporary Art (Books and
Periodicals)
Founded: 1971
ISBN Publisher's Prefix: 88-85638

Edizioni **Borla** SRL*, Via delle Fornaci 50,
I-00165 Rome Tel: (06) 6381618
Man Dir: Dr Vincenzo D'Agostino
Subjects: Philosophy, Psychology,
Sociology, Anthropology, Education,
History, Religion, Politics, Juveniles,
Periodicals
Founded: 1863
ISBN Publisher's Prefix: 88-263

Bottega d'Erasmo*, Via G Ferrari 9,
I-10124 Turin Tel: (011) 830331/831264
Cable Add: Erasmus Turin
Subjects: Religion, Philosophy, Mediaeval,
Art, Literature, Philology, History, Law
Founded: 1948

Bovolenta*, Via Belletti 14, I-44100
Ferrara Tel: (0532) 26614
Subjects: Literary Criticism, Philosophy,
Children's, Scholarly, History
Founded: 1975
ISBN Publisher's Prefix: 88-369

Bracciodieta Editore+*, Via Principe
Amedeo 25, I-70121 Bari Tel: (080)
212959/219274
Man Dir: Dr Giuseppe Bracciodieta;
Editorial: Domenico Bracciodieta; *Sales:*
Rete Concessionari; *Publicity:* G S P SAS
Subsidiary Company: Editorialebari (qv)
Subjects: Fiction, Culture, Scholarly
Founded: 1979

Bramante Editrice SpA, Via Generale
Biancardi 1 bis, I-21052 Busto Arsizio
Tel: (0331) 620324
Man Dir: Dr Guido Ceriotti
Subjects: History, Music, Art, General
Science, Military, Architecture
Founded: 1958

Edizioni **Brenner**+*, Via Idria 6, I-87100
Cosenza Tel: (0984) 74537
Man Dir, Editorial, Production: Walter
Brenner; *Sales:* Franco De Buono;
Publicity: Lucia D'Amato; *Rights &
Permissions:* Iaconianni Enrico
Subjects: Ethnology, Local History,
Medical Rehabilitation
Bookshop: Casa del Libro, Piazza dei
Bruzi 18, I-87100 Cosenza
Founded: 1959

Bresci Editore*, Via A Lamarmora 37,
I-10128 Turin Tel: (011) 585214
Dir: Count Bernardino del Boca di
Villaregia
Imprint: Edizioni L'Età dell'Acquario
Subjects: Alternative Movements,
Theosophy, Anthropology, New Age
Founded: 1971

Edizioni **Bresciane**+, Via Pila 19, I-25100
Brescia San Eufemia Tel: (030) 361204
Man Dir, Editorial, Sales, Production:
Bruno Enzo
Subjects: Poetry, Fiction, Philosophy,
Education, Criticism, Essays, General
1985: 7 titles *Founded:* 1980

L'Erma di **Bretschneider** SRL, CP 6192,
I-00193 Rome (Located at: Via Cassiodoro
19, Rome) Tel: (06) 6874127/6874129
Chief Executive, Editorial: Dr Roberto
Marcucci
Subjects: Archaeology, Classical Philology,
Ancient History, Architecture
Bookshop: Libreria L'Erma (at above
address)
Founded: 1946
ISBN Publisher's Prefix: 88-7062

Dr Giorgio **Bretschneider**, Via Crescenzio
43, I-00193 Rome Tel: (06) 659361 Cable
Add: Giobrerom
Man Dir: Giorgio Bretschneider
Subjects: Classical Antiquity, Archaeology,
Ancient History
Bookshop: At above address
Founded: 1974
ISBN Publisher's Prefix: 88-7689

Edizioni **Bucalo** SMC*, CP 51, I-04100
Latina Tel: (0773) 413226
Chief Executive: Adriana Boccio; *All other
offices:* Dr Salvatore Bucalo
Parent Company: C Sopra
Branch Off: Viale Regina Margherita 176,
I-00198 Rome Tel: (06) 857837
Subjects: Law, Scholarly, Fiction,
Encyclopaedias, Law Periodicals
Founded: 1965
ISBN Publisher's Prefix: 88-7456

Buffetti*, Via Sud Africa 29, I-00144
Rome Tel: (06) 5920993
Subjects: Law, Economics, Management
Founded: 1973
ISBN Publisher's Prefix: 88-19

Bulzoni Editore SRL (Le Edizioni
Universitarie d'Italia)+, Via Dei
Liburni 14, I-00185 Rome Tel: (06)
4955207
Man Dir, Editorial: Mario Bulzoni; *Sales:*
Ivana Capitani; *Production:* Paola Bulzoni;
Publicity: Anna Catarinozzi
Subjects: Law, Sociology, Science, Fiction,
Engineering, Arts, Literature, Philosophy,
Linguistics, University Textbooks, Theatre,
Cinema, Essays
Bookshop: Libreria Ricerche, Via Liburni
10/12, I-00185 Rome
1985: 190 titles *Founded:* 1969

C E A — Casa Editrice Ambrosiana, Via
Frua 6, I-20146 Milan Tel: (02) 4691583
Subjects: Biology, Chemistry, Physics,
Engineering, Medicine
Founded: 1940
ISBN Publisher's Prefix: 88-267

C E D A M (Casa Editrice Dr A Milani)*,
Via Jappelli 5/6, I-35121 Padua Tel: (049)
656677
Dirs: Antonio Milani, Carlo Porta
Subjects: Belles Lettres, Philosophy,
General & Social Science, Textbooks,
Book Industry, Engineering, Arts,
Literature, Languages, Fiction, Economics,
Politics, Medicine, Law
Founded: 1902
ISBN Publisher's Prefix: 88-13

C E D I S SRL*, Via Francesco Denza 52,
I-00197 Rome Tel: (06) 878052
Chief Executive: Dr Marco Massacesi
Founded: 1973
ISBN Publisher's Prefix: 88-85018

C E L U P SRL*, Via G Carducci 1/d,
I-90141 Palermo Tel: (091) 586673

Chief Executive: Dr Lillo Buttige'
Bookshop: At above address
Founded: 1958

C E M, see Casa Editrice Maccari and
Casa Editrice Marietti SpA

Edizioni **C E P I M**, Via Buonarroti 38,
I-20145 Milan Tel: (02) 4982129/4694778
Telex: 335025 Dipres I
Man Dir: Sergio Bonelli; *Editorial:* Decio
Canzio; *Sales:* Liliana Gentini; *Production:*
Luigi Corteggi
Subsidiary Companies: Araldo; Edizioni
Daim Press; Edizioni L'Isola Trovata; all
in Milan
Subjects: Comic Strip Books, Far West
Stories, Adventure Tales, Stories of
Exploration and Travel
Founded: 1968

C E T E M (Casa Editrice Testi Elementari
Milano) SRL*, Via Paolo Lomazzo 58,
I-20154 Milan Tel: (02) 315904/315918
Man Dir: Carlo Solaro
Subjects: Textbooks
1985: 12 titles *Founded:* 1954

C L E U P — Cooperativa Libraria Editrice
dell'Università di Padova, Via G Prati 19,
I-35100 Padua Tel: (049) 650261
Chief Executives: Antonio Modesti, Gian
Paolo Domeneghini, Sandro Carpanese;
Editorial: Antonio Modesti; *Sales:* Gian
Paolo Domeneghini; *Rights & Permissions:*
Sandro Carpanese
Orders to: Libreria CLEUP, Via San
Francesco 64, I-35100 Padua Tel: (049)
39557
Subjects: University Textbooks,
Engineering, Agriculture, Architecture,
Linguistics, Philosophy, Science, Local
Culture, Mathematics, Statistics,
Psychology, Psychoanalysis, Political
Science, Sociology, Medicine, Surgery,
Acupuncture, Cinema, Law, Economics
Bookshop: Libreria CLEUP, Via San
Francesco 64, I-35100 Padua Tel: (049)
39557
Founded: 1962

Editrice **C L U E B**+*, Via Marsala 24,
I-40126 Bologna Tel: (051) 224780/237758/
220736
Cooperativa Libraria Universitaria Editrice
Bologna
Man Dir: Antonio Mandelli
Orders to: CLUEB, Piazza G Verdi 2/A,
I-40126 Bologna Tel: (051) 275797
Subjects: Education, University Textbooks,
Agriculture, Botany, Architecture,
Psychology, Music, Humanities, Art,
Language
1985: 40 titles *Founded:* 1959

C L U E D — Cooperativa Libraria
Universitaria Editrice Democratica*, Via
Celoria 20, I-20133 Milan Tel: (02) 230668
Subjects: Scholarly, Essays, Science
Founded: 1972
ISBN Publisher's Prefix: 88-7059

C L U P — Cooperativa Libraria
Universitaria del Politecnico, Piazza
Leonardo da Vinci 32, I-20133 Milan Tel:
(02) 235320
Subjects: Architecture, Urban Studies,
Engineering, Science, Technology, Tourism
Founded: 1969
ISBN Publisher's Prefix: 88-7005

C L U T Editrice+, Corso Duca degli
Abruzzi 24, I-10129 Turin Tel: (011)
542192/888908
Cooperativa Libraria Universitaria Torinese
Man Dir: Michele Ruffino; *Editorial:*
Daniela Martino; *Sales:* Luciana Re
Parent Company: Cooperativa Libraria
Universitaria Torinese Scrl, Via S Ottavio
24, I-10124 Turin
Subjects: Scientific and Technical,

Humanities, Textbooks
Bookshops: Corso Duca degli Abruzzi 24, I-10129 Turin; Via S Ottavio 20, I-10124 Turin
1985: 12 titles *Founded:* 1960

C P E — Centro Programmazione Editoriale*, Via Canaletto 20b, I-41030 San Prospero (Modena) Tel: (059) 908065
Subjects: Scholarly, Mathematics, Education, Psychology
Founded: 1973

Cadmo Editore SRL+*, CP 6225, I-00100 Rome (Located at: Largo Olgiata 15, I-00123 Rome) Tel: (06) 3788350
Man Dir, Sales: Prof Milena Di Marco; *Editorial:* Prof Lido Giuseppe Chiusano
Subjects: Philosophy, History, Social Science, Philology, Linguistics, Politics, General
1985: 6 titles *Founded:* 1975

Edizioni **Calderini**+, Emilia Lev 31, I-40139 Bologna Tel: (051) 492211 Cable Add: Calderini Telex: 214821 Calboz
Man Dir: S Perdisa; *Rights & Permissions:* Luisa Manzoni Balboni; *Publicity:* Massimo Manzoni
Parent Company: Calderini SRL (at above address)
Associate Companies: Edagricole-Edizioni Agricole (qv); Edagricole Periodici SpA (at above address); Officine Grafiche Calderini, 14 Emilia, I-40126 Ozzano
Branch Offs: Via Bronzino 14, Milan; Via Puglie 3, Rome
Subjects: Art, Sport, Hobbies, Electronics, Mechanics, Electrical Engineering, University & Secondary Textbooks, Architecture, Natural Sciences, Travel Guides
Bookshops: Via Zamboni 18, Bologna; Via Bronzino 10, Milan; Via Roma 67, Padua; Via Boncompagni 73, Rome
1985: 75 titles *1986:* 52 titles *Founded:* 1952
ISBN Publisher's Prefix: 88-7019

Camera dei Deputati Ufficio Stampa e Pubblicazioni+, Piazza Montecitorio, I-00186 Rome Tel: (06) 6760 Telex: 612523
Chief Executive: Dr Umberto Coldagelli; *Editorial Coordinator:* Dr Stefano Rizzo (Tel: 67179328); *Sales:* Anna Maria Muscillo
Subjects: Law, Legislation, Economics, History, Bibliography
Bookshop: Libreria della Camera dei Deputati, Via Uffici del Vicario 17, Rome
1985: 19 titles *Founded:* 1848

Canova SRL+*, CP 252, I-31100 Treviso (Located at: Via Calmaggiore 31, Treviso) Tel: (0422) 382383
Man Dir, Editorial, Rights & Permissions: Fausto Zoppelli; *Sales:* Luigi Facchini; *Production, Publicity:* Ennio Zoppelli
Subsidiary Company: Grafiche Zoppelli SpA, Viale della Liberazione 40, Dosson di Casier (TV)
Subjects: Textbooks, Art, History of Art
Bookshops: Corso Mazzini 7, Conegliano; Via Calmaggiore 31, Treviso
1985: 7 titles *Founded:* 1945
ISBN Publisher's Prefix: 88-85066

Edizioni **Cantagalli**, CP 155, I-53100 Siena (Located at: Via Camporegio 33, Siena) Tel: (0577) 42102
Chief Executive: Pietro Cantagalli
Subjects: Patristics, Hagiography, Local History and Customs
1985: 18 titles *Founded:* 1927

Capitol Editrice Dischi CEB*, Via Minghetti 17/19, I-40057 Cadriano di Granarolo Emilia (Bologna) Tel: (051) 766612/766421/2 Cable Add: Edicapitol Bologna Telex: 511039 Edcapi I
Man Dir: Maurizio Malipiero; *Rights & Permissions:* Raffaele Malipiero; *Production Manager:* Guiseppe Parini
Subjects: General Fiction, Art, Biography, Reference, Medicine, Juveniles, Secondary & Primary Textbooks, Educational Materials, Audiovisual
Founded: 1956

Capone Editore SRL*, Via Caprarica 35, I-73020 Cavallino di Lecce Tel: (0832) 611877
Editorial: Lorenzo Capone
Subjects: Local History, Poetry, Essays, Contemporary Art, Ethnography
Founded: 1980

Nuova Casa Editrice Licinio **Cappelli** SpA*, Via Marsili 9, I-40124 Bologna Tel: (051) 330411 Cable Add: Cappelli Editore Bologna *Man Dir:* Mario Musso; *Editorial:* Dr Umberto Magrini
Subjects: General Fiction, Belles Lettres, Poetry, Biography, History, Art, Philosophy, Reference, Religion, Juveniles, Low-priced Paperbacks, Medicine, Psychology, General & Social Science, Primary, Secondary and University Textbooks, Filmscripts, Drama, Music, Politics
1985: 135 titles *Founded:* 1851

Casa Musicale Edizioni **Carrara** SRL*, CP 158, I-24100 Bergamo (Located at: Via A da Calepio 4, Bergamo) Tel: (035) 243618 Cable Add: Carrara Musica Bergamo
Editorial, Production: Vinicio Carrara; *Sales, Publicity, Rights & Permissions:* Roberto Mazzoleni
Subjects: Musical Theory and Education, Sheet Music
Founded: 1912

Edizioni **Carroccio***, Via Terraglione 22, I-35010 Vigodarzere (PD) Tel: (049) 700568
Man Dir: Luciano Lincetto
Subjects: Catholicism, History of Religion
1985: 14 titles *Founded:* 1947

Casa del Libro Editrice, now Gangemi Editore e Casa del Libro (qv)

Casalini Libri+*, Via B da Maiano 3, I-50014 Fiesole (Florence) Tel: (055) 599941 Cable Add: Casalini Fiesole
Man Dirs: Mario Casalini, Barbara Casalini, Michele Casalini
Subjects: History, Philosophy, Sociology
Founded: 1968
Miscellaneous: Firm's main function is as a book exporter (see under Major Booksellers)

Edistudio di Brunetto **Casini**+*, CP 213, I-56100 Pisa (Located at: Via Giordano Bruno 6/8, Pisa) Tel: (050) 48670 Cable Add: Edistudio CP 213 Pisa
Chief Executive: Brunetto Casini
Subsidiary Company: Composit (Fotocomposizione elaborazione grafica) (at above address)
Subjects: Esperanto (theory, history and teaching), Music, Local Culture and History
1985: 5 titles *1986:* 6 titles *Founded:* 1978
ISBN Publisher's Prefix: 88-7036

Edizioni **Castello di Antonio Careddu**, CP 27 bis, I-09134 Cagliari/Pirri (Located at: Via Campania 27, I-09121 Cagliari) Tel: (070) 290552/562296
Man Dir: Antonio Careddu; *Editorial:* Dr Piero Pischedda; *Sales:* Dr Stefano Picciau
Subjects: Fiction, Children's, Philosophy, Poetry, Tourism, Art
Book Club: Sardegna Cinque (at above address)
1985: 11 titles *Founded:* 1982

Il **Castello-Collane** Tecniche*, Via Carlo Ravizza 16, I-20149 Milan Tel: (02) 462010
Chief Executive, Editorial: Mosé Menotti; *Sales:* Paola Alloni; *Production, Rights & Permissions:* Paolo Lazzarin
Subjects: Handbooks on Photography, Cinema, Leisure Activities, Sports, Cookery, Painting, Origami
Founded: 1955

Celuc Libri*, Via Santa Valeria 5, I-20123 Milan Tel: (02) 806976/800113
Man Dir: Giovanni Barbatiello
Subjects: Philosophy, Literary Criticism, History, Economics, Law, Political and Social Science, Mathematics, Statistics, Information Science, Religion, University Textbooks
Bookshop: Libreria Celuc Libri (at above address)
Founded: 1969 (as CELUC), 1974 (as Celuc Libri SRL)

Centro Diature*, Costa Scarpuccia 1, I-50125 Florence Tel: (055) 282729 Cable Add: Centrodi Florence
Man Dir: Alessandra Marchi
Subjects: Art, Reference
Bookshop: At above address
Founded: 1968
ISBN Publisher's Prefix: 88-7038

Centro Documentazione Alpina*, Via della Rocca 29, I-10123 Turin Tel: (011) 835123/8397759
Editorial: Giorgio Daidola, Roberto Mantovani
Subject: Mountains
1985: 10 titles *Founded:* 1970
ISBN Publisher's Prefix: 88-85504

Centro Internazionale del Libro SpA, see Nardini

Centro Studi Terzo Mondo+, Via GB Morgagni 39, I-20129 Milan Tel: (02) 29409041
Chief Executive: Prof Umberto Melotti; *Editorial, Rights & Permissions:* Elena Sala
Subjects: Problems of the Third World, Sociology, Anthropology, History, Economics, Geography, Political Science, Literature, Poetry
Founded: 1964

Cesco **Ciapanna** Editore SpA+*, Via Lipari 8, I-00141 Rome Tel: (06) 897441 Telex: 613429 Fograf I
Chief Executive: Cesco Ciapanna; *Rights & Permissions:* Carla Alberti
Subjects: Photography, Hi-Fi, Solar Energy, Drugs, Science
Founded: 1967

Ciarrapico Editore+*, Via G Sgambati 1, I-00197 Rome Tel: (06) 803380
Publisher: Giuseppe Ciarrapico; *Editorial, Rights & Permissions:* Marcello Veneziani; *Sales:* Dr Giuseppe Paolillo; *Publicity Manager:* Rosella Giraldi
Associate Companies: Acta Medica (at above address); La Fenice SRL (qv); Field Educational Italia, Piazza Montegrappa 4, I-00195 Rome
Subjects: Politics, History, Science, Law, Philology, Philosophy
Founded: 1972
ISBN Publisher's Prefix: 88-7518

Ciba — Geigy Edizioni+, CP 88, I-21047 Saronno (VA) (Located at: Str Statale 233 (Varesina) km 20.5, I-21040 Origgio) Tel: (02) 96541/96542746 Cable Add: Cibageigy Saronno Telex: 332407/332470 Cigy
Man Dir, Production, Publicity: Dr Giovanni Bravi; *Editorial:* Dr Leone Halfer; *Sales:* Maria Guzzetti
Subjects: Medicine, Botany, Science
1985: 13 titles *Founded:* 1981
ISBN Publisher's Prefix: 88-7645

Edizioni **Cinque** Lune+, Piazza delle Cinque Lune 113, I-00186 Rome Tel: (06) 65151 Telex: 613276 Fax: (06) 6568181
Chief Executive: Dr Carlo Ragni; *Editorial:* Dr Gian Paolo Cresci
Subjects: History, Sociology, Economics, Politics
Bookshop: Libreria Internazionale Paesi Nuovi, Piazza Montecitorio 59/A, Rome
1986: 18 titles *1987:* 20 titles *Founded:* 1954

Ciranna e Ferrara*, Via Pacini 42, I-20038 Seregno (Milan) Tel: (0362) 230849
Subjects: Scholarly
Founded: 1976

Editrice **Ciranna — Roma**, Via Capograssa 115, I-04010 Borgo S Michele (Latina) Tel: (0773) 250746
Chief Executive, Rights & Permissions: Dr Lidia Fabiano
Subjects: Textbooks on Language, Literature, History, Geography, Mathematics, Science, Philosophy, Education, Psychology, Art, Technology, Commerce, Law, Public Services
Founded: 1953

Cisalpino — La Goliardica*, Via Bassini 17/2, I-20133 Milan Tel: (02) 293907
Subjects: Literary Criticism, Linguistics, Law, Economics, Management, History
Founded: 1946
ISBN Publisher's Prefix: 88-205

Città Nuova Editrice+, Via degli Scipioni 265, I-00192 Rome Tel: (06) 3595212/310955/383062
Man Dirs: Vittorio Fasciotti, Dr Giovanni Battista Dadda
Subsidiary Companies: Ciudad Nueva, Argentina (qv); Verlag Neue Stadt GmbH, Austria (qv); Unistad VZW, Belgium (qv); Cidade Nova Editora, Brazil (qv); Ciudad Nueva, Colombia (qv); Nouvelle Cité, France (qv); Verlag Neue Stadt GmbH, Federal Republic of Germany (qv); Nieuwe Stad, Netherlands (qv); New City, Philippines (qv); Cidade Nova, Portugal (qv); Editorial Ciudad Nueva, Spain (qv); Verlag Neue Stadt, Switzerland (qv); New City, UK (qv); New City Press, 206 Skillman Ave, Brooklyn, New York, NY 11211, USA
Subjects: Religion, Philosophy, Psychology, Reference, Juveniles, Pedagogy, Educational, Secondary Textbooks, Patristics, Theology, Sociology
1985: 118 titles *1986:* 121 titles *Founded:* 1959
ISBN Publisher's Prefix: 88-311

Cittadèlla Editrice*, CP 46, I-06081 Assisi (Located at: Via Ancaiani 3, Assisi) Tel: (075) 813595 Cable Add: Cittadella Editrice
All offices: Nello Giostra, Gabriella Persico, Giuseppina Pompei
Subjects: Biography, Religion, Psychology, Social Science, Social Problems, Theology
Founded: 1945

Claudiana Editrice, Via Principe Tommaso 1, I-10125 Turin Tel: (011) 689804
President: Pastore Ermanno Genre; *Editorial:* Dr Carlo Papini; *Sales, Rights & Permissions:* Dr Dario Gardiol
Subjects: History of Religion, Theology, Bible Studies, Ethics, Political Issues
Bookshops: Libreria Claudiana, Via Francesco Sforza 12A, I-20122 Milan; Libreria Claudiana, Piazza Libertà, I-10066 Torre Pellice (Turin); Via Pr Tommaso 1, I-10125 Turin; Libreria di Cultura Religiosa, Piazza Cavour 32, I-00193 Rome
Founded: 1855
ISBN Publisher's Prefix: 88-7016

La **Coccinella** Editrice SRL, Via Crispi 77/79, I-21100 Varese Tel: (0332) 224690 Telex: 326169 per La Coccinella
Editorial Dirs: Giorgio Vanetti, Loredana Farina; *Sales, Rights & Permissions:* Giuliana Crespi; *Production Dir:* Domenico Caputo
Subjects: Pre-school, Educational, Activity Books
Founded: 1977
ISBN Publisher's Prefix: 88-7703

Compograf Edizioni La Salamandra*, Via S Valeria 5, I-20123 Milan Tel: (02) 806976
Man Dir, Editorial, all other offices: Giovanni Barbatiello
Imprint: La Salamandra
Subjects: Feminism, Critiques of society, Libertarian thought, Critical Marxism, Sexual freedom, Psychoanalysis, Biography, Autobiography, Oriental Studies
Founded: 1975

Edizioni di **Comunità** SpA*, Largo Augusto 1, I-20122 Milan Tel: (02) 790957
Man Dir: Ernesto Ferrero; *Sales Dir:* Ezio Cagnola
Associate Company: Arnoldo Mondadori Editore SpA (qv)
Subjects: Architecture, Art, Design, Sociology, Politics, History, Economics, Law, Science, Computer Science
Founded: 1946
ISBN Publisher's Prefix: 88-245

Fratelli **Conte** Editore SRL+, Via Andrea d'Isernia 59, I-80122 Naples Tel: (081) 683667/669771
Man Dirs: Ferdinando Conte, Mario Conte
Subjects: School Textbooks, Fiction
Founded: 1967

Continental SRL Editrice*, Via Gianforte Suardi 7, I-24100 Bergamo Tel: (035) 237088
Man Dir, Rights & Permissions: Luigi Maria Facheris; *Editorial:* Ornella Crispiatico; *Sales, Publicity:* Paola Sala; *Production:* Roberto Poli
Subjects: Education, Children's
1985: 3 titles *Founded:* 1974

Cooperativa Libraria Editrice dell'Università di Padova, see CLEUP

Cooperativa Libraria Universitaria Editrice Bologna, see CLUEB

Cooperativa Libraria Universitaria Torinese, see CLUT Editrice

Edizioni Libreria **Cortina** Verona SRL+, Via Carlo Cattaneo 8, I-37121 Verona Tel: (045) 594177 Telex: 431107 Cortin I Fax: (045) 597551
Chief Executive, Editorial: Alfredo Sarcullo; *Publicity:* Elena Mauri
Associate Companies: Edizioni Libreria Cortina Milan, Largo Richini 1, I-20100 Milan; Edizioni Libreria Cortina Padua, Via Marzolo 2, I-35100 Padua; Libreria Scientifica Cortina (qv); Cortina International-Verona (at above address); Cortina Reviews (at above address)
Subjects: Medicine, Science, Law, Engineering, Architecture, Mathematics
Bookshops: Libreria Cortina (at above address); Palazzetto d'Ingresso, Policlinico Borgo Roma, Via delle Menegone, I-37134 Verona
1985: 15 titles *1986:* 40 titles *Founded:* 1971
ISBN Publisher's Prefixes: 88-85037, 88-7749

Costa e Nolan SpA+, Via Peschiera 21, I-16122 Genoa Tel: (010) 873888
Man Dir, Rights & Permissions: Carla Costa; *Editorial:* Eugenio Buonaccorsi; *Sales, Publicity:* Stefano Tettamanti
Subjects: Art, Theatre, Italian Literature, Fiction, Essays, Economics
1985: 12 titles *Founded:* 1982
ISBN Publisher's Prefix: 88-7648

Edizioni **Cremonese** SpA+, Borgo Santa Croce 17, I-50122 Florence Tel: (055) 2476371 Cable Add: Edizioni Cremonese
Man Dir: Alberto Stianti
Subjects: History, Reference, Engineering, General Science, University & Secondary Textbooks, Architecture, Mathematics, Aviation
Founded: 1930
ISBN Publisher's Prefix: 88-7083

La **Culturale**+, Via GB Morgagni 39, I-20129 Milan Tel: (02) 29409041
Chief Executive: Prof Umberto Melotti; *Editorial, Rights & Permissions:* Elena Sala
Subjects: Sociology, Economics, Politics, History, Philosophy, Marxism
Founded: 1964

Edizioni **Curci** SRL, Galleria del Corso 4, I-20122 Milan Tel: (02) 794746 Cable Add: Curcimusic Telex: 332683 Curci I
President, General Manager: Giuseppe Gramitto Ricci
Associate Company: Edizioni Accordo SRL (qv)
Subjects: Music, Arts, Textbooks
1985: 21 titles *1986:* 26 titles *Founded:* 1860

Armando **Curcio** Editore SpA+, Via Arno 64, I-00198 Rome Tel: (06) 84871 Cable Add: Curcioroma Telex: 614666 Curcio I
Chairman: Dr Aldo Stacchi; *Man Dir:* Dr Silvio Rotunno
Subjects: Art, Reference, Geography, History, Travel, Encyclopaedias
Founded: 1928
ISBN Publisher's Prefix: 88-7555

Edizioni **D E I** Roma*, Via Nomentana 12, I-00161 Rome Tel: (06) 859075/862730
Man Dir, Production: Carlo Bartoli; *Editorial, Publicity:* Giuseppe Rufo; *Sales:* Grazia Jacomelli
Subjects: Textbooks, Civil Engineering, Law
Bookshop: Edizioni DEI Roma — Tipografia del Genio Civile (at above address)
1985: 10 titles *Founded:* 1860
ISBN Publisher's Prefix: 88-7722

Edizioni **Dalla Parte** delle Bambine, Via Turati 38, I-20121 Milan Tel: (02) 6595406
Subject: Illustrated, feminist books for infants, children and women
Founded: 1975

Dall'Oglio Editore SRL*, Via Santa Croce 20-2, I-20122 Milan Tel: (02) 8351575
President: Andrea dall'Oglio; *Man Dir:* Bruno Romano
Subjects: General Fiction, Belles Lettres, Poetry, Biography, History, Low-priced Paperbacks
Founded: 1925
ISBN Publisher's Prefix: 88-7718

Dami Editore SRL*, Via Gesù 10, I-20121 Milan Tel: (02) 705497/705527 Telex: 311499 Eurdam I
Subjects: Fiction, Illustrated Children's Books, Animals
Founded: 1972

Casa Editrice G **D'Anna**+*, Via dei Della Robbia 26, I-50132 Florence Tel: (055) 242800/242801 Cable Add: D'Anna Florence
Man Dir, Sales, Publicity, Rights & Permissions: Giuseppe D'Anna; *Editorial, Production:* Guido D'Anna
Subjects: Scholarly, Cultural
1985: 36 titles *Founded:* 1926

G De Bono Editore+*, Via Masaccio 220, I-50132 Florence Tel: (055) 576022
Chief Executive: Giuseppe De Bono; *Editorial:* Dr Franca Barbiera
Subjects: Textbooks, Education, Philosophy, Fiction, Children's
Founded: 1958

Giovanni De Vecchi Editore SpA+, Via Vittor Pisani 16, I-20124 Milan Tel: (02) 6554851 Telex: 331081 Deved I
Subjects: Business Administration, Legal, Sports, Hunting and Fishing, Domestic Animals, Humour, Occult Sciences, Gardening and Agriculture, Medicinal Herbs, Medical, Yoga
Founded: 1973

Edizioni Dedalo SpA+, CP 362, I-70123 Bari (Located at: Traversa de Blasio, Zona Industriale, Bari) Tel: (080) 371555/371025/371008
Man Dir: Raimondo Coga
Subjects: Politics, History, Art, Cinema, Architecture, Urban Studies, Philosophy, Psychology, Science
1985: 46 titles *1986:* 27 titles *Founded:* 1965
ISBN Publisher's Prefix: 88-220

Edizioni Dehoniane+, Via Marechiaro 38-42-46, I-80123 Naples Tel: (081) 7694856 Cable Add: Edizioni Dehoniane Napoli
Chief Executive: Vitantonio Giampietro; *Editorial:* Luigi Cortese; *Sales, Publicity, Rights & Permissions:* Angelo Veneziani; *Production:* Pala Giusto, Giuseppe Catani
Parent Company: Congregazio Ne Dei Sacerdoti Del S Cuore IM (at above address)
Subjects: Philosophy, Ethics, Education, Psychology, Religion, Sociology
Bookshop: Libreria Dehoniana, Via Depretis 60, I-80133 Naples
Founded: 1964

Edizioni Dehoniane Bologna (EDB)*, Via Nosadella 6, I-40123 Bologna Tel: (051) 306811
Shipping Add: Via Dal Ferro 4, I-40138 Bologna
Man Dir: Andrea Tessarolo; *Sales Dir, Rights & Permissions:* Giuseppe Albiero; *Publicity Dir:* Sancini Vittorio
Subjects: Philosophy, Religion, Juveniles, Secondary & Primary Textbooks, Educational Materials
Bookshop: Libreria Presbyterium, Padua
Founded: 1965
ISBN Publisher's Prefix: 88-10

Edizioni dell'Orso SAS+, Via Piacenza 66, I-15100 Alessandria Tel: (0131) 42349
Man Dir: Gian Paolo Calligaris; *Editorial:* Lorenzo Massobrio
Subjects: Language, History, Poetry, Local Interest
1985: 11 titles *Founded:* 1979
ISBN Publisher's Prefix: 88-7694

Di Baio Editore SpA+, Via Settembrini 11, I-20124 Milan Tel: (02) 6692254/6692255/6694465
Subjects: Design, Architecture, Construction, the Home, Cookery
Founded: 1973
ISBN Publisher's Prefix: 88-7080

Dimensione Umana, an imprint of Gruppo Editoriale Le Stelle SpA (qv)

Domus Editoriale, Via Achille Grandi 5/7, I-20089 Rozzano (Milan) Tel: (02) 824721 Telex: 313589 Edidom I
Subjects: Art, Motorcars, Cooking, Tourism, Architecture, Periodicals
Founded: 1929
ISBN Publisher's Prefix: 88-7212

Edizioni E — Elle SRL, Via San Francesco 62, I-34133 Trieste Tel: (040) 772376 Telex: 460628 Edilib I
Man Dir: Giancarlo Stavro Santarosa; *Editorial:* Orietta Fatucci Stock; *Rights & Permissions:* Sandra Goruppi
Orders to: Editrice Piccoli, Via San Sofia 10, I-20100 Milan
Subject: Children's
1985: 30 titles *1986:* 40 titles *Founded:* 1984
ISBN Publisher's Prefixes: 88-85012, 88-7068

Edizioni E B E*, Via dei Prefetti 17, I-00186 Rome Tel: (06) 6794144
Chief Executive: Giovanni Di Capua; *Sales:* Norma Merli
Orders to: Via FS Nitti 12, I-00191 Rome Tel: (06) 3272972
Subjects: Politics, Modern History, Children's
Founded: 1973

E C I G — Edizioni Culturali Internazionali Genova, Via Caffaro 19/10, I-16124 Genoa Tel: (010) 208800/208664
Man Dir: Dr Gian Luigi Blengino
Subjects: University Textbooks, Esoterica, Science and Technology, Linguistics
1984: 35 titles *1985:* 38 titles *Founded:* 1971
ISBN Publisher's Prefix: 88-7545

E D B, see Edizioni Dehoniane Bologna

E D T/Musica+, Via Alfieri 19, I-10121 Turin Tel: (011) 515917/511496
Chief Executive: Enzo Peruccio
Subject: Musicology
1985: 6 titles *1986:* 6 titles *Founded:* 1976
ISBN Publisher's Prefix: 88-7063

E M I, see Editrice Missionaria Italiana

E M P, also known as Messaggero di San Antonio (qv)

Edizioni E/O+, Via Camozzi 1, I-00195 Rome Tel: (06) 352829
Man Dir, Rights & Permissions: Sandro Ferri; *Editorial:* Sandra Ozzola; *Sales:* Tom Joannucci; *Production:* Alfredo Lavarini; *Publicity:* Sergio Vezzali
Subjects: Fiction
1985: 12 titles *Founded:* 1979
ISBN Publisher's Prefix: 88-7641

E R G A SNC di Carla Ottino Merli & C (Edizioni Realizzazioni Grafiche — Artigiana)*, Via Francesco Montebruno 7N, I-16139 Genoa Tel: (010) 891833
Chief Executive: Marcello Merli; *Editorial:* Marco Merli
Subjects: Science, Literature, History, Religion, Sport, Folklore, Cookery, Local Interest
Founded: 1966

E R I — Edizioni R A I Radiotelevisione Italiana SpA+*, Via Arsenale 41, I-10121 Turin Tel: (011) 57101 Cable Add: Edrad Turin
Man Dir: Dr Alberto Luna
Orders to: Via del Babuino 51, I-00187 Rome
Parent Company: RAI Radiotelevisione It, Viale Mazzini 14, Rome
Associate Companies: Sacis, Via Tomacelli 139, Rome; Sipra, Via Bertola 34, Turin; Fonit Cetra, Via Meda 45, Milan; Telespazio, Via Alberto Bergamini 50, Rome
Subjects: Art and Collector's editions, Literature and Civilization, Essays, General Culture, Sociology, Classics in Translation, Home and Garden, Children's books, Language courses, Communications, Cinema, Public opinion polls, Music
Bookshop: At above address
Founded: 1949

E S I, see Edizioni Scientifiche Italiane

Ecole Francaise de Rome*, Piazza Navona 62, I-00186 Rome Tel: (06) 6569629
Subjects: Art, Archaeology, Law, History
Founded: 1881

Edagricole-Edizioni Agricole+, CP 2202, I-40139 Bologna (Located at: Emilia Lev 31, Bologna) Tel: (051) 492211 Cable Add: Edagri Telex: 510336
Man Dir: Sergio Perdisa; *Editorial:* Luisa Manzoni Balboni; *Sales:* Luigi Perdisa Jnr; *Publicity:* Massimo Manzoni
Associate Companies: Calderini Industrie Grafiche ed Editoriali SRL; Edizioni Calderini (qv); Edagricole Periodici SpA
Branch Offs and Bookshops: Via Zamboni 18, Bologna; Via Bronzino 14, Milan; Via Roma 67, Padua; Via Boncompagni 73, Rome
Subjects: Agriculture, Veterinary Science, Gardening, Nutrition, Applied Biology, Natural Science, Directories
1985: 136 titles *1986:* 68 titles *Founded:* 1936
ISBN Publisher's Prefix: 88-206

Editalia (Edizioni d'Italia)*, Via di Pallacorda 7, I-00186 Rome Tel: (06) 6569537/6541592
Man Dir: Lidio Bozzini; *Rights & Permissions:* Arrigo Pecchioli
Subjects: History, Art, Customs
Founded: 1952
ISBN Publisher's Prefix: 88-7060

Editorialebari+*, Via Principe Amedeo 25, I-70121 Bari Tel: (080) 212959/219274
Sales: Rete Concessionari
Parent Company: Bracciodieta Editore (qv)
Subjects: Fiction, Philosophy, Education
Founded: 1965

Editrice Bibliografica SRL+, Viale Vittorio Veneto 24, I-20124 Milan Tel: (02) 6597950/6597246
Subjects: Bibliographies and Reference Publications for the Book Trade, Library Science
1985: 14 titles *1986:* 18 titles *Founded:* 1974
ISBN Publisher's Prefix: 88-7075

Editrice Cooperativa*, Via Tagliamento 25, I-00198 Rome Tel: (06) 8444942/8441888
Chief Executive: Roberto Bigi
Founded: 1950
ISBN Publisher's Prefix: 88-7361

L'**Editrice Scientifica**, see Guadagni

Edizioni del Centro*, I-25044 Capo di Ponte (BS) Tel: (0364) 42091 Cable Add: Centrostudi Capodiponte Telex: 301504 Archeo I
Chief Executive: Prof Emmanuel Anati; *Production:* Ariela Fradkin
Parent Company: Centro Camuno di Studi Preistorici (at above address)
Subjects: Prehistoric and Primitive Art, Archaeology, Anthropology, History of Religions, Museums, Cultural Heritage, Art History
Founded: 1964

SAS Editrice Effelle di Marino Fabbri+, Via Guglielmo Saliceto 2, I-00161 Rome Tel: (06) 869050/8441953
Man Dir, Sales, Rights & Permissions: Marino Fabbri; *Editorial:* Petracchi Giovacchino; *Production, Publicity:* Leonardi Afra Fabbri
Subjects: School Textbooks, Education, Psychology, Children's, Fiction
1985: 11 titles

Giulio Einaudi Editore SpA*, CP 245, I-10121 Turin (Located at: Via Umberto Biancamano, Turin) Tel: (011) 533653/545384 Telex: 220344

Subjects: General Fiction, Belles Lettres, Poetry, History, Music, Art, Philosophy, Juveniles, Low- & High-priced Paperbacks, Psychology, Social Science, University Textbooks
Founded: 1933

Electa Editrice*, Via Trentacoste 7, I-20134 Milan   Tel: (02) 215631   Telex: Tradex 313123
Dirs: Giorgio Fantoni, Massimo Vitta Zelman; *Editorial:* Carlo Pirovano; *Rights & Permissions:* Marisa Inzaghi, Mirella Tenderini
Subsidiary Companies: Alfieri Edizioni d'Arte (qv); Arcadia Electa, Milan; Electa Firenze, Florence; Electa Moniteur, Paris; Electa Promotion, Venice; Fantonigrafica, Venice
Subjects: Modern Art, Visual Art, Architecture, Photographic, Catalogues of major exhibitions
Founded: 1948
ISBN Publisher's Prefix: 88-435

Edizioni dell'**Elefante**, Piazza dei Caprettari 70, I-00186 Rome   Tel: (06) 6543710
Chief Executive: Dr Enzo Crea; *Editorial:* Benedetta Origo Crea
Subjects: History of Art, Classical and Rare Texts, Exhibition Catalogues, Essays, Miscellaneous
1985: 2 titles   *Founded:* 1964

Emme Edizioni*, Via San Maurilio 13, I-20123 Milan   Tel: (02) 865951
Man Dir, Editorial: Rosellina Archinto Marconi; *Rights & Permissions:* Renata Discacciati
Subjects: How-to, Juveniles, High-priced Paperbacks, Educational Materials
Founded: 1966
ISBN Publisher's Prefix: 88-294

Edizioni **Equestri** SRL*, Viale Bianca Maria 19, I-20122 Milan   Tel: (02) 705093/ 783905/791474   Telex: 351115 Ediber I   Fax: (02) 780904
Man Dir: Giorgio Bernardini de Pace; *Editorial:* Elena Quarestani; *Publicity:* Anna Venturi
Associate Company: Studio Editoriale SRL
Subjects: Horses, Equitation
1985: 6 titles   *Founded:* 1983

L'**Erma** di Bretschneider SRL, see Bretschneider

Edi **Ermes** SRL+, Via Timavo 12, I-20124 Milan   Tel: (02) 6073892
Chief Executive: Dr Italo Grandi
Subjects: Medicine and Surgery, Veterinary Science, Biology, Economics, Arts, Textbooks
1985: 12 titles   *1986:* 16 titles   *Founded:* 1973
ISBN Publisher's Prefixes: 88-85019, 88-7051

Edizioni L'**Età** dell'Acquario, an imprint of Bresci Editore (qv)

Etas Libri, Via Mecenate 91, I-20138 Milan   Tel: (02) 50951   Cable Add: Librifabbri Milan   Telex: 311321 Fabbri I
Dir: Filippo Ambrosini; *Rights & Permissions:* Carla Tanzi
Subjects: Reference, Law, General & Social Science, Economics, Business Administration, Technical
Founded: 1963
Miscellaneous: Member of Gruppo Editoriale Fabbri, Bompiani, Sonzogno, Etas SpA

Edizioni **Europa**, Via G B Martini 6, I-00198 Rome   Tel: (06) 8449124
Subjects: Art, Music, History, Politics, Economics
Founded: 1944

Gruppo Editoriale **Fabbri, Bompiani**, Sonzogno, Etas SpA, see individual entries Bompiani, Etas Libri, Gruppo Editoriale Fabbri SpA, Sonzogno

Gruppo Editoriale **Fabbri** SpA+, Via Mecenate 91, I-20138 Milan   Tel: (02) 50951   Cable Add: Librifabbri Milan   Telex: 311321 Fabbri I
Man Dir: Mario Speranza; *International Department Dir:* Armando Peres
Subjects: Music, Art, Juveniles, Reference, Medicine, Secondary & Primary Textbooks, Leisure Books, General Encyclopaedias, Science, History, Nature
Founded: 1945
Miscellaneous: Other members of the group are Bompiani, Etas Libri and Sonzogno (qqv)

Faenza Editrice SpA, CP 68, I-48018 Faenza (Located at: Via Pier De Crescenzi 44, Faenza)   Tel: (0546) 663488   Telex: 550387 Editfa I
Man Dir: Prof Goffredo Gaeta; *Editorial, Sales, Publicity:* Franco Rossi
Subjects: Architecture, Science, Technology, Electronics, Industries, Crafts, Arts, Ceramics, Frames, Bathrooms & Fittings
Founded: 1965

Giangiacomo **Feltrinelli** SpA*, Via Andegari 6, I-20121 Milan   Tel: (02) 808346/7   Cable Add: Fedit Milan
Subjects: General Fiction, Belles Lettres, Poetry, Art, Music, History, General Science, Reference, Paperbacks, University Textbooks, Philosophy, Juveniles
Founded: 1954
ISBN Publisher's Prefix: 88-07

La **Fenice** SRL*, Via G Sgambati 1, I-00198 Rome   Tel: (06) 862973   Telex: 680285 Fielde I
Editorial: Dr Marcello Veneziani; *Sales:* Dr Giuseppe Paolillo; *Publicity:* Rossella Giraldi
Parent Company: Gruppo Italfin '80, Via Pinciana 25, I-00197 Rome
Subsidiary Company: SPC (Stabilimenti Poligrafici Cassino), Villa Santa Lucia, Cassino
Associate Companies: Casa Editrice Acta Medica (at above address); Ciarrapico Editore (qv); Casa Editrice Field Educational Italia, Piazza Montegrappa 4, I-00195 Rome
Subjects: History, Military History, Philosophy
Founded: 1951
ISBN Publisher's Prefix: 88-7518

Edizioni **Ferro** SpA*, Via Cusani 5, I-20121 Milan   Tel: (02) 866272
Man Dir: Pia Ferro
Subjects: Medicine, Pedagogy, Sociology
Founded: 1963
ISBN Publisher's Prefix: 88-7010

Libreria Editrice **Fiorentina** di Vittorio e C SAS*, Via Giambologna 5, I-50132 Florence   Tel: (055) 579921
Editorial: Vittorio Zani
Subjects: Religion, Social Problems, Education, Local Interest, Ecology, Alternative Culture
Founded: 1902

S F **Flaccovio** Editore*, Via Ruggiero Settimo 37, I-90139 Palermo   Tel: (091) 589442/334249/584268
Subjects: General Science, History, Art, Folk Art, Archaeology, Local Interest
Bookshops: Libreria SF Flaccovio (qv under Major Booksellers)
Founded: 1939

Fògola Editore in Torino*, Piazza Carlo Felice 19, I-10123 Turin   Tel: (011) 535897/ 531570
Subjects: History, Fiction, Essays, Limited Editions of Classics
Bookshop: Libreria Dante Alighieri (at above address)
Founded: 1965

Arnaldo **Forni** Editore SRL, Via Gramsci 164, I-40010 Sala Bolognese (Bologna)   Tel: (051) 954142/954198
Man Dir: Giuseppina Forni
Subjects: Mainly reprints covering Masonry, Medicine, Middle Ages, Military, Minerology, Music, Theatre, Dance, Numismatology, Occultism, Ornithology, Renaissance, Science, History, Classics, Religion; Periodicals
Founded: 1973

Aldo **Francisci** Editore+, Via Puccini 27, I-35031 Abano Terme (PD)   Tel: (049) 810956
Chief Executive: Aldo Francisci
Subjects: Literature, Philosophy, Psychiatry, Sociology, Archaeology, Poetry, Local Guides, Politics, History, Economics, Education, Library Science, Health, Art, Periodicals
1986: 120 titles   *1987:* 150 titles   *Founded:* 1977

Edizioni **Frassinelli** SRL, Via Monte di Pietà 24, I-20121 Milan   Tel: (02) 806066   Telex: 325481 Sperli I
President, Publisher: Dr Tiziano M Barbieri; *Man Dir:* Donatella M Barbieri; *Sales:* Ornella Robbiati; *Editorial, Rights Dir:* Rosaria Carpinelli; *Rights & Permissions:* Marica Fioroni
Parent Company: Sperling e Kupfer Editori SpA (qv)
Subjects: Literary Fiction, General Non-fiction, Biography, Illustrated, Art
1985: 30 titles   *Founded:* 1932
ISBN Publisher's Prefix: 88-7684

Edizioni **Futuro**, Via Caprera 6, I-37126 Verona   Tel: (045) 45955/915622   Telex: 480833
Chief Executive: Vinicio de Lorentiis; *Editorial:* Marco Monico; *Sales:* P Luigi Riphetti; *Production:* Giorgio Bonuzzi; *Publicity:* Moreno Adami; *Rights & Permissions:* Anna Negri
Subsidiary Companies: Edizioni V de Lorentis; Moderna International (both at above address)
Subjects: Illustrated Biographies, Guides, Art, Nature
Founded: 1979
ISBN Publisher's Prefix: 88-7650

Aulo **Gaggi** Editore*, Via Andrea Costa 131-5, I-40134 Bologna   Tel: (051) 410696
Man Dir, Rights & Permissions: Aulo Gaggi; *Editorial, Publicity:* Giovanna Galotti; *Sales Manager:* Enzo Badiali
Subject: Medicine
Founded: 1965

Adriano **Gallina** Editore+*, Salita Tarsia 142, I-80135 Naples   Tel: (081) 349820
Man Dir, Editorial: Adriano Gallina; *Editorial:* Maria Gallina; *Sales:* Giuseppe Gallina
Subjects: Art, Archaeology, Poetry, Cookery, Local Interest
1985: 12 titles   *Founded:* 1969

Giuseppe **Galzerano** Editore+, I-84040 Casalvelino Scalo (Salerno)   Tel: (0974) 62028   Cable Add: Galzerano Casalvelino Scalo (sa)
Chief Executive and all other offices: Giuseppe Galzerano
Subjects: Politics, Anarchism, Society, Farming, Popular and Local History, Emigration, Fiction, Memoirs, Poetry
1985: 10 titles   *1986:* 9 titles   *Founded:* 1975

Editrice **Gammalibri**, an imprint of Kaos Edizioni (qv)

Gangemi, Via Giulia 95, I-00186 Rome Tel: (06) 6548792
Subjects: Architecture, Urban Studies, Cinema, Medicine, Essays, Local Interest
Founded: 1966
ISBN Publisher's Prefix: 88-7448

Gangemi Editore e Casa del Libro, Corso Garibaldi 168, I-89100 Reggio Calabria Tel: (0965) 94844
Chief Executive: Giuseppe Gangemi
Orders to: Licosa SpA (qv)
Branch Off: Via Giulia 95, I-00186 Rome Tel: (06) 6548792
Subjects: Art, Architecture, Urban Studies, Ancient History, Local History, Literature, Medicine
Bookshop: At above main address
Founded: 1970
Miscellaneous: Formerly Casa del Libro Editrice
ISBN Publisher's Prefix: 88-7448

Editrice **Garigliano** SRL+*, Via Di Biasio 10, I-03043 Cassino (Frosinone) Tel: (0776) 21869 Cable Add: Editrice Garigliano Cassino
Chief Executives: Marisa Canzano, Santina Vitale; *Editorial:* Rodolfo Vitale; *Sales:* Monaco Maria Rosaria; *Production:* Antonio Violo; *Publicity:* Giovanni Violo; *Rights & Permissions:* Elena Vettese
Subjects: Philosophy, Education, Psychology, Italian, French and English Literature
Bookshop: Libreria Universitaria (at above address)
Founded: 1968

Garzanti Editore+, Via Senato 25, I-20121 Milan Tel: (02) 77871 Cable Add: Garzantieditore Telex: 325218 Gared
Publisher: Dr Livio Garzanti; *Editorial:* Piero Gelli; *Sales Manager:* Francesco Rampini; *Rights & Permissions:* Franca De Dominicis
Associate Company: A Vallardi (at above address)
Subjects: General & Crime Fiction, Literature, Poetry, Art, Politics, Biography, History, Reference, Juveniles, Low- & High-priced Paperbacks, Secondary & Primary Textbooks, Encyclopaedias, Dictionaries
Bookshops: Libreria Garzanti, Galleria Vittorio Emanuele 66-68, I-20121 Milan; Libreria Garzanti, Palazzo Dell' Università, Pavia
1985: 70 titles *Founded:* 1861

Creazioni **Gensy**, see Giunti Publishing Group

Bruno **Ghigi** Editore+*, Via Poletti 6, I-47037 Rimini Tel: (0541) 24269
All offices: Bruno Ghigi
Subjects: History, Geography, Maps
Founded: 1955
ISBN Publisher's Prefix: 88-85640

Ghisetti e Corvi Editori SpA*, Corso Concordia 7, I-20129 Milan Tel: (02) 706232/706233/706234
Subjects: Primary and Secondary Textbooks
Founded: 1937
ISBN Publisher's Prefix: 88-85061

Edizioni **Giada**+, Piazza Principe di Camporeale 27, I-90134 Palermo Tel: (091) 574010
Man Dir: Maria Galioto; *All other offices:* Dr Luigi d'Agostino
Parent Company: Linee d'Arte Giada SRL (at above address)
Subjects: Art, History, Architecture, Gift Books
Bookshops: At above address

1985: 40 titles *Founded:* 1976
ISBN Publisher's Prefix: 88-7664

Editrice **Giannotta** di Sebastiano Pace Giannotta+, Viale Regina Margherita 2/e-2/f, I-95125 Catania Tel: (095) 447629 Cable Add: Editrice Giannotta
Man Dir, Editorial: Sebastiano Pace Giannotta
Subjects: Law, Literature, Philosophy, Sociology, Science, Sicilian Folklore and Dialect, University Textbooks, Cartography
Bookshop: Libreria Editrice Giannotta (at above address)
Founded: 1965

G **Giappichelli** Editore di Giorgio Giappichelli & C SAS*, Via Po 21, I-10124 Turin Tel: (011) 8397019/8397303
Subjects: University Publications, Economics, Law, Philosophy, Politics, Sociology, Classical and Modern Philology
Bookshop: Libreria Editrice Scientifica di G Giappichelli, Via Vasco 2, I-10124 Turin
Founded: 1921

Mario Lapucci — Edizioni del **Girasole**, Via Baccarini 80, I-48100 Ravenna Tel: (0544) 22830
Chief Executive: Mario Lapucci
Subjects: History, Art, Archaeology, Language and Folklore of Romagna, Poetry, Miscellaneous
Founded: 1966
ISBN Publisher's Prefix: 88-7567

A **Giuffrè** Editore SpA+, Via Busto Arsizio 40, I-20151 Milan Tel: (02) 3010106/3010136
Man Dir: Giuseppe Giuffrè; *Chief Editor:* Gaetano Giuffrè
Branch Off: Via V Colonna 40, I-00193 Rome Tel: (06) 659938/6569792
Subjects: History, Law, Social & Political Science, Economics
Founded: 1931
ISBN Publisher's Prefix: 88-14

Giunti Publishing Group+*, Via V Gioberti 34, I-50121 Florence Tel: (055) 670451/5 Cable Add: Marzolib Florence Telex: 571438 Giunti
Also: Via Scipione Ammirato 37, I-50136 Florence
Dir: Dr Sergio Giunti; *Rights & Permissions:* Roberto Borrani, Davide Mazzanti
Subjects: Art Books, Essays, Fiction, Psychology, Pedagogy, Mathematics, Chemistry, National Edition of Works of Leonardo da Vinci, Galileo Galilei, Italian publishers of National Geographic Society books, Linguistics, Dictionaries, School Textbooks, Juveniles, Popular Science, History, Guidebooks, Handbooks, Periodicals
Miscellaneous: Group comprises: Editrice Giunti Marzocco, Giunti Barbera Editore, Editrice Universitaria, Edizioni Ofiria, Giacomo Agnelli Editore, Giunti Martello Editore, Creazioni Gensy, Edizioni Oreste Barjes, ME/DI Sviluppo, OS (Organizzazioni Speciali SRL) (qv), B Boggero Editore, Lisciani e Giunti Editori, Edizioni Primavera

Società Editrice La **Goliardica** Pavese SRL+, Viale Taramelli 18, I-27100 Pavia Tel: (0382) 21101/29674
Chief Executive & other offices: Dario De Bona
Branch Off: Via Lombroso 21, Pavia Tel: (0382) 29674
Subjects: Scientific Textbooks for Universities
1986: 10 titles *Founded:* 1977

Grafica e Arte Bergamo*, Via Francesco Coghetti 108, I-24100 Bergamo

Tel: (035) 255014
Man Dirs and other offices: Emilio Agazzi, Luigi Agazzi
Subjects: Photography, Art, Local History
1985: 7 titles *Founded:* 1975

Grafis Edizioni, Via 2 Giugno 4, I-40033 Casalecchio di Reno (Bologna) Tel: (051) 758235
Man Dir: Franco Trippa; *Editorial:* Cristina Agostini, Maria Soglia
Orders to: Centro Di, Piazza de' Mozzi 1/R, I-50125 Florence
Subject: Art
1985: 21 titles *Founded:* 1965

Grafo Edizioni*, Via Agostino Bassi 20, I-25123 Brescia Tel: (030) 393221/308957
Chief Executive: Roberto Montagnoli; *Editorial:* Lucio Maninetti; *Sales:* Mauro Rota, Franco Agnelli; *Production:* Paola Pierattini
Subsidiary Companies: Cheiron; La Ricerca Folklorica (both at above address)
Subjects: History, Art, Popular Culture, Local Interest
Founded: 1974
ISBN Publisher's Prefix: 88-7385

Editoriale **Grasso** SRL+, Via E Collamarini 21, I-40138 Bologna Tel: (051) 534221
Chief Executive, Production: Domenico Grasso; *Editorial:* Serena Serafini; *Sales, Publicity, Rights & Permissions:* Domenico Grasso Jnr
Subjects: Medicine, Veterinary Science, Science
Bookshop: Libreria dello Studente, Via San Vitale 55/A, I-40125 Bologna
1985-86: 10 titles *Founded:* 1969
ISBN Publisher's Prefix: 88-7055

Gregorian University Press, see Pontificia Università Gregoriana

Libreria Editrice **Gregoriana**, Via Roma 82, I-35122 Padua Tel: (049) 661033 Fax: (049) 663640
Man Dir: Don Giancarlo Minozzi
Subjects: Religion, Philosophy, Sociology, Psychology
Bookshop: Libreria Gregoriana (qv under Major Booksellers)
Founded: 1922
ISBN Publisher's Prefix: 88-7706

Ernesto **Gremese** Editore SRL+*, Via Orazio 3, I-00192 Rome Tel: (06) 318136/386533
Chief Executive: Ernesto Gremese
Branch Off: Via Cola Di Rienzo 136, I-00192 Rome Tel: (06) 386533
Subjects: Literature, Textbooks
Bookshop: Libreria Internazionale Ernesto Gremese SNC, Via Cola di Rienzo 136, I-00192 Rome Tel: (06) 386533
Founded: 1954

Gremese Editore SRL+*, Via Virginia Agnelli 88, I-00151 Rome Tel: (06) 532092/5377600
Chief Executive: Dr Gianni Gremese
Subjects: Cinema, Theatre, Music, Photography, Dance, Art, Sport, Technical, Literature, Astrology, Computers, Cookery, Travel (all illustrated)
1985: 72 titles *Founded:* 1978
ISBN Publisher's Prefixes: 88-7605, 88-7742

Piero **Gribaudi** Editore, Corso Galileo Ferraris 67, I-10128 Turin Tel: (011) 500360
Publishers: Piero Gribaudi, Maria Luisa Gribaudi Monferrini
Subjects: Philosophy, Religion, Social Science
Founded: 1966

L'Editrice Scientifica SAS di L G
Guadagni*, Via Ariberto 20, I-20123
Milan   Tel: (02) 8390274
Dir: Dr Leonarda Guadagni
Subjects: Pharmaceuticals, Chemistry,
University Textbooks
Founded: 1940
ISBN Publisher's Prefix: 88-85010

Guanda*, Via Lentasio 9, I-20122 Milan
Tel: (02) 804916
Subjects: Fiction, Poetry, Essays
Founded: 1932
ISBN Publisher's Prefix: 88-235

Tipografia Editrice **Guerra***, Via S Andrea
delle Fratte, I-06080 Perugia   Tel: (075)
789090
Publicity Manager: Chellini Gastone
Orders to: RUX edel, Via E Fermi 26,
I-06100 Perugia   Tel: (075) 751324
Subjects: Educational, Italian Language
1985: 37 titles   *Founded:* 1883
ISBN Publisher's Prefix: 88-7715

Guida Editori SpA+*, Via D Morelli
16/B, I-80121 Naples   Tel: (081) 425404
(Administration)/425309 (Editorial)
Chairman: Prof Massimo Lo Cicero;
President: Prof Giuseppe Galasso; *Vice
President:* Dr Mario Guida; *Editorial Dir:*
Prof Clotilde Izzo; *Commercial Dir:* Dr
Roberto Coppola
Warehouse: Via Ventaglieri 83, I-80135
Naples   Tel: (081) 341843
Subjects: History, Philosophy, Essays, Art,
Quality Editions, Fiction
1985: 64 titles   *Founded:* 1973
ISBN Publisher's Prefix: 88-7042

Guidicini e Rosa Editori SNC, Via Pasubio
74, I-40133 Bologna   Tel: (051) 416933
Chief Executives: Gabriele Guidicini, Rino
Rosa
Subjects: Local Interest, History, Fiction,
Poetry
Founded: 1976
ISBN Publisher's Prefix: 88-85648

Herbita Editrice di Leonardo Palermo, Via
Vincenzo Errante 44, I-90127 Palermo
Tel: (091) 237716/6167716   Cable Add:
Herbita Palermo
Chief Executive: Leonardo Palermo
Subjects: Politics, Law, Literature, Classics,
Philosophy, Mathematics, Textbooks
Founded: 1973

Herder Editrice e Libreria, Piazza
Montecitorio 117-120, I-00186 Rome
Tel: (06) 6794628
Man Dir: Oriol Schaedel
Associate Companies: Verlag Herder &
Co, Austria (qv); Verlag Herder GmbH &
Co KG, Federal Republic of Germany
(qv); Herder und Herder GmbH, Federal
Republic of Germany (qv); Verlag A G
Ploetz GmbH & Co KG, Federal Republic
of Germany (qv); Editorial Herder SA,
Spain (qv); Herder AG, Switzerland (qv)
Subjects: Religion, History, Philosophy,
Archaeology, Oriental Studies, Philology
and Linguistics, Periodicals, Occasional
titles
Founded: 1955

Hermes Edizioni SRL+*, Via Flaminia
158, I-00196 Rome   Tel: (06) 3601656
General Manager: Giovanni Canonico;
Editorial: Romualdo d'Alessandro; *Sales:*
Graziella Torre; *Rights & Permissions:*
Luigi Coppe
Parent Company: Edizioni Mediterranee
SRL (qv)
Subjects: Alternative Medicine, Astrology,
Nature, Dietetics
Founded: 1979

Casa Editrice Libraria Ulrico **Hoepli**
SpA+*, Via Hoepli 5, I-20121 Milan
Tel: (02) 865446   Cable Add: Hoepli
Milan   Telex: 313395 Hoepli I
Shipping Add: Via Mameli 13, I-20129
Milan
Man Dirs: Dr Ulrico Hoepli, Gianni
Hoepli, Dr Ulrico Carlo Hoepli; *Sales Dir:*
Dr Ulrico Carlo Hoepli; *Rights &
Permissions:* Dr Susanna Schwarz Bellotti
Branch Off: Via Mameli 13, I-20129 Milan
Subjects: How-to, Art, Reference,
Dictionaries, Juveniles, Low- & High-
priced Paperbacks, Engineering, General &
Social Science, University & Secondary
Textbooks, Handbooks, Technology, Law
Bookshop: Ulrico Hoepli Libreria
Internazionale (qv under Major
Booksellers)
1985: 74 titles   *Founded:* 1870
ISBN Publisher's Prefix: 88-203

Idea Books*, Via Cappuccio 21, I-20123
Milan   Tel: (02) 860154/807997   Cable
Add: Ideabooks Milano   Telex: 323352
Ideabk I
Dirs: Filippo Passigli, Cinzia Bonfanti
Subjects: Visual Arts, Photography,
Architecture, Design
Bookshops: Florence; Milan
Founded: 1979
ISBN Publisher's Prefix: 88-7017

Casa Editrice Libraria **Idelson** di G
Gnocchi+, Via Alcide De Gasperi 55,
I-80133 Naples   Tel: (081) 324733/324317
Cable Add: Idelson Naples
Chief Executive: Guido Gnocchi
Subjects: Medicine, Biology
Founded: 1908
ISBN Publisher's Prefix: 88-7069

Edizioni **Il Cerchio**+, Via Cairoli 85,
I-47037 Rimini (FO)   Tel: (0541) 56008
*Man Dir, Production, Rights &
Permissions:* Dr Adolfo Morganti;
Editorial: Dr Maurizio Mecozzi; *Sales:*
Gloria Rubinato; *Publicity:* Dr Sergio de
Vita
Parent Company: Cooperativa Culturale Il
Cerchio (at above address)
Subjects: Anthropology, Philosophy,
History of Religion, History
Bookshop: Libreria Cooperativa Il Cerchio
(at above address)
1985: 8 titles   *1986:* 6 titles   *Founded:* 1979

Il Quadrante SRL, Via Lagrange 7,
I-10123 Turin   Tel: (011) 515072
Man Dir, Editorial: Ezio Quarantelli;
Sales: Franco Caldera; *Publicity:* Donata
Danna; *Rights & Permissions:* Enrico
Pasini
Subsidiary Company: Mostre e Musei SRL
Subjects: Fiction, Contemporary Art,
Memoirs, Essays
1985: 6 titles   *Founded:* 1980
ISBN Publisher's Prefix: 88-381

Ila — Palma*, Via La Lumia 5/7, I-90139
Palermo   Tel: (091) 332051
Subjects: Art, Archaeology, Economics,
Management, Philosophy, Essays, History
Founded: 1960
ISBN Publisher's Prefix: 88-7704

Editrice **Innocenti** SNC+, Via Zara 36,
I-38100 Trento   Tel: (0461) 36521   Cable
Add: Editrice Innocenti Trento
Chief Executive: Luciano Innocenti;
Publicity: Silvia Nones
Associate Company: Casa Editrice
Principato, Via Fauché 10, Milan
Subjects: Scholarly, Languages
1987: 6 titles   *Founded:* 1972

Editrice **Iskra**+*, Via Adige 3, I-20135
Milan   Tel: (02) 576866
Chief Executive, Publicity: Renato de Pra
Subjects: History of the Workers'
Movement, Politics, Economics, Philosophy
Founded: 1981

Isper SRL+, Corso Dante 124, I-10126
Turin   Tel: (011) 633950
Chief Executive: Dr Carlo Actis Grosso
Branch Offs: Via Lambro 4, I-20129 Milan;
Via G Paisiello 12, I-00198 Rome; Corso
del Popolo 46, I-30172 Venice
Subjects: Business Studies, Management
Book Club: Isper Club
Founded: 1965

Istituto Centrale di Statistica*, Via Cesare
Balbo 16, I-00184 Rome   Tel: (06) 471666
Cable Add: Istat Roma   Telex: Istat
610338
President: Prof Guido M Rey; *Dir
General:* Dr Luigi Pinto; *Dir of
Information:* Prof Vicenzo Siesto
Branch Offs: Viale Liegi 13, I-00198
Rome; Via A Rava 150, I-00142 Rome;
Via Tuscolana 1774, Rome
Subjects: Political Economy, Statistics,
Demography
Bookshop: Via A Depretis 82, I-00184
Rome   Tel: (06) 4751666
Founded: 1926

Istituto Centrale per il Catalogo Unico
delle Biblioteche Italiane e per le
Informazioni Bibliografiche*, Viale Castro
Pretorio 105, I-00185 Rome   Tel: (06)
4959217
Central Institute of the Union Catalogue
of Italian Libraries and Bibliographical
Information
Dir: Angela Vinay
Subjects: Bibliography, Library Science
Miscellaneous: See also under Library
Associations
ISBN Publisher's Prefix: 88-7107

Istituto della Enciclopedia Italiana+*,
Piazza Paganica 4, I-00186 Rome   Tel: (06)
67311   Cable Add: Enciclopedia
Subjects: Encyclopaedias, Dictionaries,
Reference, Art, Audiovisual Materials
ISBN Publisher's Prefix: 88-12

Casa Editrice **Istituto della Santa**, Via
Scavini 2, I-28100 Novara   Tel: (0321)
20660   Cable Add: Dellasanta Novara
Subjects: Textbooks for Secretarial,
Commercial and Business Studies
Founded: 1956

Istituto Geografico de Agostini SpA, Via
Giovanni da Verrazano 15, I-28100
Novara   Tel: (0321) 4241   Cable Add:
Geografico Novara   Telex: 200290
Edidea I   Fax: (0321) 471830
Branch Off: Via Mosè Bianchi 6, I-20149
Milan   Tel: (02) 4694451
Subjects: Belles Lettres, Art, Reference,
History, Religion, Juveniles, Textbooks,
Geography, Literature
Founded: 1901

Istituto Grafologico, see Girolamo Moretti

Istituto Idrografico della Marina, Passo
Osservatorio 4, I-16134 Genoa   Tel: (010)
265451/252631/252667   Cable Add:
Maridrografico   Telex: 270435/226521
Maridr I
Dir: C A Alfredo Civetta; *Vice Dir:* C V
Lanfranco Giuglietti; *Production:* C V
Francesco Spanio; *Public Relations:* C F
Antonio Cairo; *Map Division:* C F Sandro
Pancrazzi
Subjects: Nautical
1985: 17 titles   *Founded:* 1872

Istituto Nazionale di Studi Romani, Piazza
dei Cavalieri di Malta 2, I-00153 Rome
Tel: (06) 5743445/5743442
Dir: Dr Fernanda Roscetti
Subjects: History, Classical Literature,
Bibliographies, Architecture, Art
Founded: 1925

Casa Editrice **Istituto Padano** di Arti Grafiche*, Via delle Industrie 1, I-45100 Rovigo Tel: (0425) 28164 Cable Add: Ipag Rovigo
Man Dir: Dr Amleto Brigo; *Sales:* Dr Carlo Brigo; *Production:* Dr Alberto Brigo
Subjects: Theology, Religion, Science
Founded: 1946

Istituto per l'**Enciclopedia** del Friuli Venezia Giulia*, Via Marco Volpe 17/b, I-33100 Udine Tel: (0432) 208055
President: Romano Scarcia; *Chief Executive:* Cesare Russo; *Editorial:* Domenico Cerroni Cadoresi; *Sales:* Annamaria Toffolini
Subsidiary Company: Centro Diffusione, Via Marco Volpe 17/a, I-33100 Udine
Subjects: Encyclopaedias, Art, History, Guides, Linguistics, Essays, Fiction, Children's
Founded: 1969

Istituto Poligrafico e Zecca dello Stato, Piazza G Verdi 10, I-00198 Rome Tel: (06) 85081 Fax: (06) 85082517
Dir: Alfredo Maggi
Subjects: Law, Politics, Linguistics, Literature, Fiction, Arts, Stamps, Metal Coins
Founded: 1928
Miscellaneous: State Publishing House and Italian State Stationery Office

Istituto Storico Italiano per l'Età Moderna e Contemporanea, Via Michelangelo Caetani 32, I-00186 Rome Tel: (06) 6540922
Man Dir: Prof Armando Saitta; *Editorial:* Dr Marina Maura
Subjects: Italian and European History
1987: 6 titles *Founded:* 1934

Editrice **Italscambi***, Via Mazzini 30, I-10123 Turin Tel: (011) 238872 Cable Add: Italscambi CP 23 Turin
Chief Executive: Lorenzo Masetta
Subsidiary Company: 'Controcampo' (current events periodical, at above address)
Branch Off: Via Mazzini 30, I-10123 Turin
Subjects: Literature, Poetry, Fiction
Founded: 1972

Editoriale **Jaca** Book+*, Via Aurelio Saffi 19, I-20123 Milan Tel: (02) 4982341 Telex: 324267
Man Dir: Dr Sante Bagnoli; *Editorial Dir:* Dr Maretta Campi; *Editors:* Dr Elio Guerriero (Theology), Dr Massimo Guidetti (History); *Production:* Dr Guido Orsi; *Rights & Permissions:* Laura Geronazzo; *Co-editions:* Daniela Bernabò
Subjects: History, Philosophy, Religion, Psychology, Social & Political Science, Economics, Juveniles, Fiction, Literature, Art, Co-editions
Founded: 1966
ISBN Publisher's Prefix: 88-16

Gruppo Editoriale **Jackson** SpA+, Via Rosellini 12, I-20124 Milan Tel: (02) 6880951/5 Telex: 333436 Geijt I Fax: (02) 6880951/6948238
Man Dir: Giampietro Zanga; *Editorial:* Dr Daniele Comboni; *Sales, Production:* Maurizio Calvi, Gianluca Rivoli; *Publicity:* Filippo Canavese; *Rights & Permissions:* Roberto Pancaldi
Subsidiary Companies: Jackson Hispania SA, Plaza Republica del Ecuador 2, 28016 Madrid, Spain; GEJ Publishing Group Inc, 1143 Quince Ave, Sunnyvale, CA 94087, USA
Subjects: Information Science
1987: 300 titles *Founded:* 1974
ISBN Publisher's Prefix: 88-7056

Editrice **Janus** SpA+, Via dei Capodiferro 12, I-24100 Bergamo Tel: (035) 247180
Man Dir, Editorial: Alessandro Nicolini; *Sales, Production:* Marco Zingarelli
Subjects: Scholarly, Children's Fiction
1985: 10 titles *Founded:* 1956

L U **Japadre** Editore, CP 170, I-67100 L'Aquila (Located at: Piazza dell'Annunziata 6, L'Aquila) Tel: 25587/26025/26488
Man Dir and other offices: Leandro Ugo Japadre
Branch Off: Via Padova 94, I-00161 Rome Tel: (06) 429382
Subjects: Art, Literature, History, Philosophy, Science, Technology, Economics, Religion, Psychology, Sociology, Folklore, Fiction, Poetry, Linguistics
Bookshops: 2 Corso Federico II 49, L'Aquila; Piazza dell'Annunziata 6, L'Aquila
Founded: 1966
ISBN Publisher's Prefix: 88-7006

Casa Editrice Dr Eugenio **Jovene** SpA, Via Mezzocannone 109, I-80134 Naples Tel: (081) 206518/206575/206455 Cable Add: Jovene
Man Dir: Dr Alessandro Rossi
Subjects: Law, Economics
Founded: 1854

Kaos Edizioni+, Viale Abruzzi 58, I-20131 Milan Tel: (02) 228063
Man Dir: Domenico Nodari; *Publicity, Rights & Permissions:* Mauro Maggio
Imprint: Editrice Gammalibri
Subjects: Music, Sport, Politics, Cinema, Theatre, Literature, Cookery, Crafts, Practical
Founded: 1976

La Casa Verde Editrice SNC+, Via Ospedaletto 40, I-37066 Sommacampagna (Verona) Tel: (045) 510783
Man Dirs: Silvano Pizzighella, Maurizio Savi
Subjects: Agriculture, Biology, Nutrition
1985: 36 titles *Founded:* 1983

Edizioni **La Scala**, CP 156, I-70015 Noci (Located at: Monastero Padri Benedettini Madonna della Scala, Noci) Tel: (080) 737400 Cable Add: Benedettini Noci
Chief Executive, Editorial: Padre Giuseppe Quirino Poggi
Subjects: Religion, Liturgy, Sacred Music, Biography
1985: 6 titles *1986:* 12 titles *Founded:* 1947

La Tartaruga Edizioni, Via Turati 38, I-20121 Milan Tel: (02) 6555036
Subjects: Literature, Essays, Theatre
Founded: 1975
ISBN Publisher's Prefix: 88-7738

Antonio **Lalli** Editore+*, Via Fiume 60, I-53036 Poggibonsi (Siena) Tel: (0577) 933305 Cable Add: Lalliedit Poggibonsi
Chief Executive: Antonio Lalli; *Editorial:* Fioranna Casamenti; *Publicity:* Mida Ciappi
Subjects: Fiction, Poetry, Drama, Biography, Memoirs, Local Interest and Dialect, Juveniles, Thrillers and Detective Novels, Humour, Sociology, Philosophy, Education, Politics, Customs, Religion, Cinema, Science, Bibliography, Rare Books, Art, Current Events, Comics
Founded: 1965

Luciano **Landi** Editore SRL+*, CP 80, I-52027 San Giovanni Valdarno (FI) (Located at: Corso Italia 189, San Giovanni Valdarno) Tel: (055) 92112/93075 Cable Add: Landi Editore Sangiovanniarno

Man Dir, Editorial, Rights & Permissions: Landi Luciano; *Sales:* Alda Santini; *Publicity:* Stefano Artini
Branch Off: CP 606, I-50100 Florence
Subjects: Essays, Folklore, Local Interest, Art, Literature, History, Sport, Encyclopaedias
1985: 52 titles *Founded:* 1960

Mario **Lapucci**, see Edizioni del Girasole

Giuseppe **Laterza** e Figli SpA+*, Via di Villa Sacchetti 17, I-00197 Rome Tel: (06) 803693/878053
Shipping Add: Via F Zippitelli 3, Zona Industriale, I-70123 Bari
Man Dir: Vito Laterza (Rome); *Editorial Dir:* Enrico Mistretta (Rome); *Sales Dir:* Domenico Scoppio (Bari); *Production:* Pasquale Laterza; *Press, Publicity & Advertising:* Giuseppe Laterza (Rome); *Rights & Permissions:* Antonia Sollecito
Branch Off: Via D Alighieri 51, I-70121 Bari Tel: (081) 213413/214024/219452
Subjects: Belles Lettres, Biography, Art, Reference, Religion, Architecture, Classics, History, Archaeology, Science, Economics, Philosophy, Low- & High-priced Paperbacks, Psychology, Social Science, University & Secondary Textbooks
Bookshop: Libreria Internazionale Laterza, Via Sparano 134, I-70121 Bari
1985: 160 titles *Founded:* 1885
ISBN Publisher's Prefixes: 88-420, 88-421

Edizioni **Laurus** Robuffo*, Via della Macchiarella 146, I-00119 Rome Tel: (06) 5651492
Chief Executive: Mario Robuffo
Subject: Law
Founded: 1973

Il **Lavoro Editoriale**, CP 118, I-60121 Ancona (Located at: Via Volturno 2, Ancona) Tel: (071) 205355/50378
Man Dir, Sales: Ennio Montanari; *Editorial:* Giorgio Mangani; *Publicity:* Massimo Canalini
Branch Off: Via Santa Maria Maggiore 7, I-40121 Bologna Tel: (051) 267943
Subjects: Literature, History, Humanities, Medicine, Local Interest, Magazines
1987: 100 titles *Founded:* 1979
ISBN Publisher's Prefix: 88-7663

Edizioni **Lavoro** SRL*, Via Boncompagni 19, I-00187 Rome Tel: (06) 4746420/4951885
Man Dir, Rights & Permissions: Mario Bertin; *Editorial:* Gianni Bebardelli; *Sales:* Patrizia Ippoliti; *Publicity:* Gioacchino de Chirico
Subjects: Sociology, Politics, Philosophy, History, Fiction
Bookshop: Libreria EL, Via Rieti 11, I-00198 Rome Tel: (06) 863591
1985: 39 titles *Founded:* 1982
ISBN Publisher's Prefix: 88-7910

Casa Editrice **Le Lettere** SRL, Costa San Giorgio 28, I-50125 Florence Tel: (055) 215142
Chief Executive: Dr Giovanni Gentile; *Sales, Administration:* Carlo De Simone
Subjects: Facsimile Reprints of Rare Books, History, Philosophy, Language, Literature, Dictionaries, Encyclopaedias
Founded: 1956

Casa Editrice Felice **Le Monnier***, Via Antonio Meucci 2, I-50015 Grassina (Florence) Tel: (055) 6813801
Subjects: Belles Lettres, Biography, History, How-to, Art, Philosophy, Religion, Juveniles, Multilingual Dictionaries, Languages
Founded: 1836
ISBN Publisher's Prefix: 88-00

ITALY 243

Levrotto e Bella Libreria Editrice Universitaria SAS*, Corso Vittorio Emanuele II 26, I-10123 Turin Tel: (011) 832535
Man Dir, Editorial, Rights & Permissions: Terenzio Gualini; *Sales:* Carmela Bueti, Giampiero Garnero
Subjects: University Textbooks, Technology and Science
Bookshop: Libreria del Politecnico, Corso Einaudi 57, I-10129 Turin
1985: 22 titles *Founded:* 1942

Edizioni **Librex***, Via Bellezza 15, I-20136 Milan Tel: (02) 5456906 Cable Add: Librex Milan Telex: 320208
General Manager: Antonio Mancia; *Export:* M Luisa Franceschini; *Production:* Luciano Baroni
Subjects: Reference, Juveniles, International Co-productions, Encyclopaedias
Founded: 1966

Licosa SpA, CP 552, I-50121 Florence (Located at: Via Lamarmora 45, Florence) Tel: (055) 579751 Cable Add: Licosa Firenze Telex: 570466 Licosa I
Libreria Commissionaria Sansoni
Man Dir: Dr Giovanni Gentile
Branch Off: Via Bartolini 29, I-20155 Milan
Subjects: Philology, Linguistics, Literature, Archaeology, Art, Architecture
Bookshops: At above main and branch office addresses
Founded: 1951
ISBN Publisher's Prefix: 88-85828

Liguori Editore SRL+, Via Mezzocannone 19, I-80134 Naples Tel: (081) 206077 Cable Add: Liguori Napoli
Man Dir: Dr Rolando Liguori; *Editorial, Rights & Permissions:* Guido Liguori; *Sales:* Franco Liguori; *Publicity:* Maria Liguori
Orders to: Sales Department, Via Posillipo 394, I-80123 Naples Tel: (081) 669547
Subjects: Linguistics, Literary Criticism, Philosophy, History, Sociology, Anthropology, Law, Economics, Mathematics, Astronomy, Natural Sciences, Medicine, Technology, Periodical
Bookshop: Libreria Commissionaria Liguori SNC, Via Mezzocannone 21-23, I-80134 Naples Tel: (081) 206687
1985: 82 titles *1986:* 78 titles *Founded:* 1949
ISBN Publisher's Prefix: 88-207

Editrice **Liguria** SNC di Norberto Sabatelli & C, CP 181, I-17100 Savona (Located at: Via dei De Mari 4r, Savona) Tel: (019) 20917
Chief Executive: Norberto Sabatelli
Subjects: Fiction, Criticism, Theatre, Poetry, History, Art, Essays, Tourism, Gastronomy, Technical
Founded: 1934

Linea Verde, an imprint of Gruppo Editoriale Le Stelle SpA (qv)

Casa Editrice **Lint**, CP 501, I-34134 Trieste (Located at: Via di Romagna 30, Trieste) Tel: (040) 360396/360421
Man Dir: Maria Rosa Casagrande Maetzke; *Editorial, Sales, Production, Publicity:* Prof Riccardo Maetzke
Subjects: Science, Art, Scholarly
1985: 20 titles *Founded:* 1962

Lisciani e Giunti Editori, see Giunti Publishing Group

Liviana Editrice SpA+, Via Luigi Dottesio 1, I-35138 Padua Tel: (049) 8710099
Man Dir: Giorgio Raccis; *Editorial:* Francesco Cadoni; *Rights & Permissions:* Michela Melchiori
Subjects: School Textbooks
1985: 30 titles *1986:* 40 titles *Founded:* 1948
ISBN Publisher's Prefix: 88-7675

Vincenzo **Lo Faro** Editore*, Via San Giovanni Laterano 276, I-00184 Rome Tel: (06) 734518/737336
Chief Executive: Vincenzo Lo Faro; *Editorial:* Letizia Carile
Subjects: Drama, Poetry, Philosophy, Education, Medicine, Religion, Ecology, Sociology, Encyclopaedias, Dictionaries, Art, Law, Fiction, Children's
Bookshop: At above address
Founded: 1967

Editrice La **Locusta***, Via del Castello 20, I-36100 Vicenza Tel: (0444) 32604
Chief Executive: Rienzo Colla
Subjects: Essays, Religion, Poetry
Founded: 1954

Loescher Editore SpA, Via Vittorio Amedeo II 18, I-10121 Turin Tel: (011) 549333
Dirs: Maurizio Pavia, Gambaudo Luciano, Maria Laura Gardoncini, Carlo Cartiglia, Michele Lessona
Subjects: University & Secondary Textbooks
1985: 30 titles *Founded:* 1867
ISBN Publisher's Prefix: 88-201

Loffredo Editore Napoli SpA+*, Via Consalvo 99/H, Parco San Luigi, isol D, I-80126 Naples Tel: (081) 619073
Chief Executive: Mario Loffredo; *Editorial, Sales, Rights & Permissions:* Alfredo Loffredo; *Production:* Alfredo Loffredo Jnr; *Publicity:* Enzo Loffredo
Subjects: Textbooks in Philosophy, Religion, Literary Criticism, Essays, Literature, Language, History, Mathematics, Science
Bookshop: Libreria Luigi Loffredo, Via Kerbaker 19/21, I-80129 Naples
Founded: 1880

Longanesi & C*, Via Salvini 3, I-20122 Milan Tel: (02) 782551/5 Cable Add: Editlong Milan Telex: 310672 Messit I
President: Stefano Passigli; *Man Dir:* Mario Spagnol; *Editorial:* Lorenzo Pellizzari; *Sales:* Guglielmo Tognetti; *Production:* Pierangela Negri; *Publicity:* Luigi Brioschi; *Rights & Permissions:* Aleksandra Stefanovic
Subjects: General Fiction, Belles Lettres, Biography, History, How-to, Music, Art, Philosophy, Religion, Low-priced Paperbacks, Medicine, Psychology, General & Social Science
Founded: 1946
ISBN Publisher's Prefix: 88-304

Angelo **Longo** Editore, CP 431, I-48100 Ravenna (Located at: Via Paolo Costa 33, Ravenna) Tel: (0544) 27026
Editorial, Production, Sales: Alfio Longo
Subjects: Art, Archaeology, Bibliography, Philology, Italian Classics, Philosophy, Linguistics, Pedagogy, Critical Literature, Sociology, History, History of Art, Poetry, Fiction, Theatre, History of Masonry
Bookshop: Libreria Dante di A M Longo (qv under Major Booksellers)
1985: 55 titles *1986:* 70 titles *Founded:* 1962

Lucarini Editore SRL+, Viale Mazzini 146, I-00195 Rome Tel: (06) 334348/336217 Telex: 620238
Man Dir: Dr Luciano Lucarini; *Editorial:* Roberto Bonghio, Gabriella d'Anna; *Sales:* Massimo Mengucci; *Publicity:* Davra Marchi; *Rights & Permissions:* Pina Carzedda
Orders to: Via Trionfale 8406, I-00135 Rome
Subjects: Fiction, Classics, Philosophy, Sport, Encyclopaedias, Scholarly, Periodicals
1985: 40 titles *Founded:* 1976
ISBN Publisher's Prefix: 88-7033

Lusva Editrice*, Via Roncaglia 27, I-20146 Milan Tel: (02) 4985386
Chief Executive: Luca Maria Vizzotto
Subjects: Quality Books, Juveniles, Fiction, Poetry, Educational
Founded: 1977

Lyra Libri SAS, Via Volta 43, I-22100 Como Tel: (031) 279146
Chief Executive, Editorial: Maurizio Rosenberg Colorni
Subjects: General, Sexuality, Psychology, Health
1986: 8 titles *1987:* 12 titles *Founded:* 1986
ISBN Publisher's Prefix: 88-7733

Casa Editrice **M E B** SRL*, Via Makallè 73, I-35138 Padua Tel: (049) 661147/661873 Telex: 215669 Muzzio
Chief Executive: Dr Franco Muzzio; *Production:* Sergio Fardin; *Publicity:* Stella Longato Muzzio
Associate Company: Franco Muzzio & C Editore SpA (qv)
Subjects: Parapsychology, UFOs, Magic, Health, Sport, Manuals
Founded: 1956
ISBN Publisher's Prefix: 88-7669

M E/D I Sviluppo, see Giunti Publishing Group

Casa Editrice **Maccari** (C E M)+, CP 120, I-43100 Parma (Located at: Via Trento 53, Parma) Tel: (0521) 771268/73281 Cable Add: Cemparma Fax: (0521) 73281
Man Dir: Cesare Maccari Jnr; *Editorial:* Mariapia Luchini; *Production:* Alighiero Maccari
Subjects: Medicine, Surgery, Biology
1985: 13 titles *Founded:* 1946
ISBN Publisher's Prefix: 88-7532

Edizioni **Magistero**+*, CP 306, I-40100 Bologna (Located at: Str Maggiore 37, I-40125 Bologna) Tel: (051) 233980
Chief Executive: Giovanni Leonardi
Subject: Education
Founded: 1976

Magnus Edizioni SpA+, Via Spilimbergo 180, I-33034 Fagagna UD Tel: (0432) 800081 Telex: 460656 Lema I
Chief Executive, Editorial, Rights & Permissions: René Leonarduzzi; *Sales, Publicity:* Antonio Stella; *Production:* Enrico Mazzoli
Subjects: Photography, Art & Design
1985: 30 titles *1986:* 36 titles *Founded:* 1977
ISBN Publisher's Prefix: 88-7057

Malipiero SpA Editore*, Via Liguria 12-14, I-40064 Ozzano Emilia (Bologna) Tel: (051) 792111 Cable Add: Malipiero Telex: 510260 Matex I
Dirs: Dr Perpaolo Malipiero, Giuseppe Malipiero; *Editorial Dir:* Donata Malipiero
Subjects: Juveniles, Hobbies, Education
Founded: 1969

Umberto **Manfredi***, Via Principe Paternò 100/102, I-90144 Palermo Tel: (091) 254053/453046
Chief Executive: Umberto Manfredi
Subjects: Italian Literature, Literary Criticism, Law, History
Founded: 1973

Manfrini Editori*, CP 1, I-38060 Calliano (Trento) (Located at: Str Statale del Brennero) Tel: (0464) 84156 Cable Add: Grafiche Manfrini Telex: 400581 Manfri I

Man Dir: Edoardo Manfrini
Parent Company: R Manfrini SpA
Vallagarina Arti Grafiche (at above address)
Branch Off: Via Virgilio 6, I-39100 Bolzano
Subjects: Tourist Guides & Books, Natural Science, Art, Literature, History, other Non-fiction
Founded: 1919
ISBN Publisher's Prefix: 88-7024

Casa Editrice **Marietti Scuola** SpA, Via Adam 19, I-15033 Casale Monferrato Tel: (0142) 76311
Man Dir: Dr Federico Franchi
Associate Company: Casa Editrice Marietti SpA (qv)
Subject: School Textbooks

Pietro **Marietti** SpA, see Edizioni Piemme

Casa Editrice **Marietti** SpA+*, Via Palestro 10/7, I-16122 Genoa Tel: (010) 885826
Man Dir: Dr Silvio Riolfo
Associate Company: Casa Editrice Marietti Scuola SpA (qv)
Subjects: Religion, Secondary & Primary Textbooks, History, Philosophy, Essays, Fiction
Founded: 1820
ISBN Publisher's Prefix: 88-211

Aldo **Marino** Editore*, Piazza Trento 3/d, I-95128 Catania Tel: (095) 447971
Subjects: Literature, Literary Criticism, Science
Bookshop: Libreria Scientifica di Aldo Marino (at above address)
1985: 24 titles *Founded:* 1977

Alberto **Marotta** Editore SpA*, Via dei Mille 78/82, I-80121 Naples Tel: (081) 418881
Man Dir: Alberto Marotta; *Editorial:* Dott Giuseppe Maggi; *Sales:* Pasquale Marotta
Branch Offs: Via Monte di Pieta 1/A, I-20121 Milan; Via Nizza 45, I-00198 Rome
Subjects: General Fiction, Belles Lettres, Poetry, Biography, Music, Art, Social Science, Dictionaries, Encyclopaedias, History, Neapolitan Studies, Medicine, Science
Bookshops: Via dei Mille 78-80-82; Via Francesco Giordani 46; Via Giuseppe Verdi 46 (all in Naples)
Founded: 1959

Marsilio Editori SpA, Fondamenta S Chiara, S Croce 518a, I-30125 Venice Tel: (041) 707188/707641
Man Dir: Dr Paolo Lenarda; *Editorial, Production, Rights & Permissions:* Emanuela Bassetti; *Sales, Publicity:* Maria Concetta Fozzer
Associate Companies: Marsilio Periodici SRL (at above address); Cataloghi Marsilio SRL (at above address)
Subjects: General Fiction, Architecture, Social & Political Science, Economics, Psychology, Literature, Arts
Founded: 1961
ISBN Publisher's Prefix: 88-317

Editore **Martano***, Via Cesare Battisti 3, I-10123 Turin Tel: (011) 531758
Chief Executive: Liliana Dematteis
Subjects: Art, Cinema, Architecture, Music
Founded: 1968
ISBN Publisher's Prefix: 88-85636

Giunti **Martello** Editore, see Giunti Publishing Group

Martinucci Pubblicazioni Mediche SAS*, Via G Imperatrice 10, I-80131 Naples Tel: (081) 252717
Man Dir, Editorial: Luigi Martinucci; *Sales:* Flavia Panniello; *Production:* Promeco SRL; *Rights & Permissions:* Ivonne Carbonaro
Subjects: Medicine, Science
Bookshop: Libreria Scienze Mediche Martinucci, Via T de Amicis 60, I-80145 Naples
1985: 7 titles *Founded:* 1978

Editrice Giunti **Marzocco**, see Giunti Publishing Group

Marzorati Editore SRL+, Via Pordoi 8, I-20019 Settimo Milano Tel: (02) 3287409/ 3288230
Man Dir: Antonio Marzorati; *Editorial:* Romain Rainero; *Sales:* Carlo Marzorati; *Production:* Franco Faglioni; *Publicity:* Patrizia Fatigati; *Rights & Permissions:* Francesca Marzorati
Subjects: Literature, History, Philosophy, Geography
Founded: 1942
ISBN Publisher's Prefix: 88-280

Editrice **Massimo** SAS di Crespi Cesare e C+, Corso di Porta Romana 122, I-20122 Milan Tel: (02) 5454104/5453144/5460320
Man Dir: Dr Cesare Crespi
Subjects: General Fiction, Biography, History, Religion, Juveniles, Low- & High-priced Paperbacks, Psychology, General & Social Science, Secondary Textbooks, Philosophy
Bookshop: Agenzia Mescat (at above address)
1985: 21 titles *1986:* 26 titles *Founded:* 1951
ISBN Publisher's Prefix: 88-7030

Masson Italia Editori SpA+, CP 12118, I-20133 Milan (Located at: Via Statuto 2/4, Milan) Tel: (02) 6367 Telex: 335347 Etmi I
Man Dir: Dr Solly Cohen; *Editorial:* Lucia Pacini Panconesi (Medicine), Letizio Cacciabue (Computer Sciences); *Sales:* ETMI SRL, Via Basilicata, I-20098 San Giuliano (Milan); *Production:* Andretta Reati; *Publicity:* Gianluigi Cervi; *Rights & Permissions:* Lidia Lupi
Parent Company: Masson Editeur, France (qv)
Associate Companies: ETMI SRL (at above address); Il Giornale del Medico SRL (at above address); Il Polso SRL, Via Statuto 4, I-20121 Milan; Masson Italia Periodici SRL, Via Statuto 4, I-20121 Milan
Branch Off: Viale Regina Margherita 269, I-00198 Rome Tel: (06) 8441435/868331
Subjects: Medicine, Chemistry, Dentistry, Physics, Technology, Information Science, Textbooks
1985: 99 titles *Founded:* 1976
ISBN Publisher's Prefix: 88-214

Mastrogiacomo Editore*, Via delle Piazze 13, I-35100 Padua Tel: (049) 22707
Man Dir: Dr Gaetano Mastrogiacomo
Subsidiary Company: Galleria d'Arte Moderna 'Images 70' (at above address)
Subjects: Cinema, Arts, Politics and Current Events, Poetry, Magic, Historical Research, Cookery, Fiction, Customs
Founded: 1977

Franca **May** Edizioni SRL, Via dei Riari 79-80, I-00165 Rome Tel: (06) 6545656
Man Dir: Franca Fratini Gatto
Subject: Art
1985: 1 title *1986:* 1 title *Founded:* 1974

Nuove Edizioni Gabriele **Mazzotta** SRL*, Foro Buonaparte 52, I-20121 Milan Tel: (02) 8690050
Man Dir: Gabriele Mazzotta; *Sales Dir:* Alberto Bini; *Publicity Dir:* Nadine Bortolotti; *Rights & Permissions:* Maura Pizzorno
Subjects: History, Architecture, Art, Low- & High-priced Paperbacks, Psychology, Social Science, Photography
Founded: 1966
ISBN Publisher's Prefix: 88-202

Medical Media, an imprint of Multimedia SRL (qv)

Edizioni **Medicea** SRL*, Via Gordigiani 40e, I-50127 Florence Tel: (055) 363057
Subjects: Architecture, Radio and Television, Government, Urban Studies, Science
Founded: 1975

Edizioni **Mediche Italiane** di Giovanni Sartorio*, Viale Golgi 24, I-27100 Pavia Tel: (0382) 25106
Man Dir, Editorial: Giovanni Sartorio; *Sales:* Giacomo Giardino; *Publicity:* Chiara Vanelli
Subsidiary Company: Fotocomposizione Pavese
Associate Company: Edizioni Logos International SRL, Via Lombroso 10, Corso Garibaldi 6, I-27100 Pavia
Subject: Medical Textbooks
Bookshops: Libreria Ticinum, Corso Mazzini 2/c, Pavia; Libreria Il Torchio, Corso Garibaldi 4, Pavia; Libreria Universitaria (at above address)
1985: 18 titles *Founded:* 1977

Organizzazione Editoriale **Medico Farmaceutica** SRL*, CP 10434, I-20110 Milan (Located at: Via Edolo 42, I-20125 Milan) Tel: (02) 6688376/6884386 Telex: 323598 Oemfmi I
Dir: Lucio Marini
Subjects: Medicine, Pharmacy, Veterinary Science
Founded: 1940
ISBN Publisher's Prefix: 88-7076

Mediolanum Editori Associati SRL+*, Viale Pasubio 6, I-20154 Milan Tel: (02) 653451 Cable Add: Edifin Milano Telex: 351420 Edifin I
Man Dir: Dr Nicola Bovoli; *Editorial:* Giorgio Bombi; *Production:* Anna Schiavon; *Publicity:* Publisponsor; *Rights & Permissions:* Sonia Zucconi
Parent Company: Gruppo Edifin SpA (at above address)
Associate Companies: Bianca; Consuledis; Edifin; Edimail; Nuova Meeting; Pubblicitta'; Publisponsor; R P Studio; Solving
Subjects: Wine and Food, Tourism, Sport, Politics
1985: 4 titles *Founded:* 1984
ISBN Publisher's Prefix: 88-7712

Edizioni **Mediterranee** SRL+*, Via Flaminia 158, I-00196 Rome Tel: (06) 3601656
General Manager: Giovanni Canonico; *Editorial:* Romualdo D'Alessandro; *Sales:* Graziella Torre; *Rights & Permissions:* Luigi Coppe
Subsidiary Company: Hermes Edizioni SRL (qv)
Subjects: ESP, Parapsychology, Occult, Magic, Yoga, Zen, Meditation, UFOs, Astrology, Alternative Medicine, Philosophy, Psychology, Art, Archaeology, Sport
Founded: 1953

Memorie Domenicane, Piazza San Domenico 1, I-51100 Pistoia Tel: (0573) 25004
Editorial: Eugenio Marino, Armando F Verde
Parent Company: Centro Riviste della Provincia Romana dei Frati Predicatori (at above address)

Subjects: History, Theology
1986: 17 titles *Founded:* 1884

Casa Editrice **Menna** di Sinisgalli Menna Giuseppina*, CP 26, I-83100 Avellino (Located at: Via Vasto 15/19, Avellino)
Chief Executive: Nunzio Menna
Subjects: Poetry, Fiction, Theatre, History, Children's, Law
Bookshop: At above address
Founded: 1976

Messaggero di San Antonio+*, CP 1100-1103, I-35123 Padua (Located at: Via Orto Botanico 11, Padua) Tel: (049) 664322 Cable Add: Messaggero Padova Telex: 430855 Msa I
Chief Executive: P Luciano Marini; *Editorial:* P Giacomo Panteghini; *Sales, Production, Publicity, Rights & Permissions:* P Agostino Varotto
Subjects: Religion, History, Biography, Current Events, Children's
Bookshop: Libreria Messaggero, Piazza del Santo 17, I-35123 Padua
1985: 50 titles
ISBN Publisher's Prefix: 88-7026

Nicola **Milano Editore**+*, Via Marsili 9, I-40124 Bologna Tel: (051) 330483
Chief Executive: Mario Musso
Parent Company: Nicola Milano Editore, Corso Ferrero 5, I-12060 Farigliano (Cuneo)
Subsidiary Company: Milano Stampa, Corso Ferrero 5, I-12060 Farigliano (Cuneo)
Subjects: Textbooks for Children, Scholarly
Founded: 1969

Milano Libri*, Via A Rizzoli 2, I-20132 Milan Tel: (02) 2588
Associate Company: RCS Rizzoli Libri SpA (qv)
Subjects: Fiction, Juveniles, Essays, Manuals
ISBN Publisher's Prefix: 88-318

Milella Editore, CP 160, I-73100 Lecce Tel: (0832) 28885/28142
Subjects: Literary Essays, History, Philosophy, Education
Bookshops: Libreria Milella, Via Palmieri 30, I-73100 Lecce; Viale Taranto 1, I-73100 Lecce
Founded: 1945
ISBN Publisher's Prefix: 88-7048

Minerva Italica SpA*, CP 216, I-24100 Bergamo (Located at: Via Maglio del Rame 6, Bergamo) Tel: (035) 237331
Man Dir: Arnoldi Gianni
Branch Offs: Via Alfani 68, I-50121 Florence; Via S Sebastiano is 247a, I-98100 Messina; Via Petrella 6, I-20124 Milan; Via A Emo 162-168, I-00136 Rome; Via Lattanzio 90-94, I-70126 Bari
Subjects: General Fiction, Juveniles, Arts, University, Secondary & Primary Textbooks, Educational Materials
Founded: 1951
ISBN Publisher's Prefix: 88-298

Editrice **Missionaria** Italiana (E M I)+, Via Roncati 32, I-40134 Bologna Tel: (051) 434392
Man Dir, Editorial, Production: Francesco Grasselli; *Sales:* Father Noè Cereda; *Publicity:* Father Pino Mariani
Subjects: Religion, Missionary Work, Anthropology, Third World
1985: 41 titles *Founded:* 1977
ISBN Publisher's Prefix: 88-307

Edizioni **Moderne** SRL, Via Magnasco 1, I-35100 Padua Tel: (049) 611981/611630
Chief Executive, Sales: Vincenzo Amicucci; *Editorial:* Dr Andrea Colasio; *Production, Rights & Permissions:* Sonia Amicucci; *Publicity:* Laura Amicucci

Subjects: Scholarly, Education, Law, Economics
Founded: 1979

Monas Hierogliphica Centro Studi+, Via Borghetto 5, I-20122 Milan
Editorial: Nicolas Monti; *Publicity:* Elena Elli
Subjects: Art, Photography, Architecture, Design
Founded: 1978

Arnoldo **Mondadori** Editore SpA, CP 1772, I-20100 Milan (Located at: Via Arnoldo Mondadori, I-20090 Segrate, Milan)
Tel: (02) 75421 Cable Add: Mondadori Segrate (Mi) Telex: 320457 Mondmi I
Chairman, Chief Executive: Sergio Polillo; *Vice-President:* Leonardo Mondadori; *Man Dir:* Emilio Fossati; *General Managers:* Leonardo Mondadori (Books), Giampaolo Grandi (Magazines); *Editor-in-Chief:* Giordano Bruno Guerri; *Advertizing Manager:* Lorenzo Pellicioli; *Publicity Manager:* Carlo Sartori; *Direct Marketing General Manager:* Giampaolo Grandi
Associate Companies: Editrice Abitare Segesta; Edizioni di Comunità SpA (qv); Harlequin Mondadori; Il Saggiatore SpA (qv)
Branch Offs: Arnoldo Mondadori Editore, Via Sicilia 136-138, I-00100 Rome; Mondgraph, 9-11 Ave Franklin Roosevelt, Paris 75008, France; Mondadori Deutschland GmbH, Klenzestrasse 38, 8 Munich 5, Federal Republic of Germany; Mondadori Scandinavia AB, Kungsgatan 58, S-111 22 Stockholm, Sweden; A Mondadori Editore Co Ltd, 1-4 Argyll St, London W1 1AD, UK; AME Publishing Ltd, 740 Broadway, New York, NY, USA
Subjects: General Fiction, Classics, Romance, Detective Stories, Poetry, Biography, History, How-to, Music, Art, Philosophy, Reference, Religion, Juveniles, Low- & High-priced Paperbacks, Medicine, Psychology, General Science, Secondary Textbooks, Educational Materials, Printing Plants & Paper Mills
Book Club: CDE SpA Gruppo Mondadori
Bookshops: Branches throughout Italy
Founded: 1907
ISBN Publisher's Prefix: 88-04

Edizioni Scolastiche Bruno **Mondadori**+*, Via Archimede 23, I-20129 Milan Tel: (02) 5456036
Chairman: Roberta Mondadori; *Man Dir:* Roberto Gulli; *General Manager:* Mario Candiani
Subject: Textbooks
Founded: 1945

Mondadori Ragazzi, Via Rivoltana 8, I-20090 Segrete (Milano) Tel: (02) 75421 Telex: 320457 Mondmi I

Edizioni del **Mondo** Giudiziario*, Viale Angelico 90, I-00195 Rome Tel: (06) 351071
Man Dir: Augusto Brusca; *Editorial, Sales, Production, Publicity:* Anna Tabili Brusca
Subject: Law
Founded: 1946

Monduzzi Editore SpA+, Via Ferrarese 119/2, I-40128 Bologna Tel: (051) 370337 Telex: 226265 Mondbo I
Chief Executive: Dr Gianni Monduzzi; *Sales Manager:* Claudio Benedetti; *Marketing:* Dr Mauro Bettocchi
Subjects: Medicine, Chemistry, Physics, Biological Sciences, Nursing
1985: 34 titles *1986:* 35 titles *Founded:* 1978
ISBN Publisher's Prefix: 88-323

ITALY 245

Editrice **Morcelliana** SpA+, Via Gabriele Rosa 71, I-25121 Brescia Tel: (030) 46451
Man Dir: A W Stefano Minelli
Associate Company: Editrice La Scuola SpA (qv)
Subjects: History, Philosophy, Religion, Social Science
Founded: 1925
ISBN Publisher's Prefix: 88-372

Istituto Grafologico Girolamo **Moretti**, Scale San Francesco 8, I-60121 Ancona Tel: (071) 201759
Chief Executive, Editorial: P Fermino Giacometti; *Sales:* P Enrico Petrucci
Branch Off: Piazza San Francesco 7, I-61029 Urbino (Pesaro) Tel: (0722) 2639
Subject: Graphology
1985: 2 titles *1986:* 4 titles *Founded:* 1958

Federico **Motta** Editore SpA+, Via Branda Castiglioni 7, I-20156 Milan Tel: (02) 3272841 Telex: 350397 Motta I
Chief Executive, Rights & Permissions: J Federico Motta; *Editorial:* Ugo Lolli; *Sales:* Massimo Tunzio (Italy), Geraldo Saporta (International); *Production:* Italo di Giancamillo
Subjects: Encyclopaedias, Dictionaries, Classics, Art, Science
Founded: 1929

Mucchi Editore SRL, Via Emilia Est 1527, I-41100 Modena Tel: (059) 374094
Subjects: History, Philosophy, Science, Technical, Textbooks, Hobbies, Literature, Education, Law, Languages

Società Editrice Il **Mulino***, Via Santo Stefano 6, I-40125 Bologna Tel: (051) 233415/6
Man Dir: Giovanni Evangelisti; *Sales Dir:* Marcello Bolognini; *Publicity Dir:* Edmondo Berselli; *Rights & Permissions:* Luisa Pece
Subjects: History, Philosophy, Linguistics & Literary Criticism, Political Science, Law, Economics, Reference, Low-priced Paperbacks, Psychology, Social Science, University Textbooks, Journals
Founded: 1954
ISBN Publisher's Prefix: 88-15

Multigrafica Editrice SRL, Viale dei Quattro Venti 52/A, I-00152 Rome Tel: (06) 5892839/5891496
Chief Executive: Mario Bonsignori
Subjects: Art History, Architecture, History, Archaeology, Folklore, Law
Founded: 1970
ISBN Publisher's Prefix: 88-7597

Multimedia SRL*, Via Lardichella 17 (Camaldoli), I-80131 Naples Tel: (081) 252717
Man Dir: Luigi Martinucci; *Editorial:* Vittorio Taccani; *Sales:* Antonella Martinucci; *Production:* Giovanni Forlani; *Publicity:* Gianbattista Bilo; *Rights & Permissions:* Luigi Setaro
Imprint: Medical Media
Subject: Medicine
Founded: 1986

Ugo **Mursia** Editore SpA*, Via Tadino 29, I-20124 Milan Tel: (02) 209341 Cable Add: Umedizioni Milan Telex: 325294 Mursia I
Man Dir: Dr Giancarla Mursia; *Editorial:* Dr Roberto Tozzi; *Publicity:* Dr Floriana De Martino; *Sales:* Fiorenza Mursia; *Production:* Dario Maggi; *Rights & Permissions:* Dr Flavio Fagnani
Subsidiary Companies: Nautilus SRL; Edizioni APE SpA (qv)
Subjects: General Fiction, Belles Lettres, Poetry, Biography, History, Art, Philosophy, Reference, Religion, Juveniles, General & Social Science
Founded: 1922

Franco **Muzzio** & C Editore SpA*, Via Makallè 73, I-35138 Padua Tel: (049) 661147/661873/664757 Telex: 432005 Muzzio
Chief Executive: Franco Muzzio; *Editorial:* Odette Infanti; *Sales:* Ennio Pengo; *Production:* Sergio Fardin; *Publicity:* Paola Bianchini; *Rights & Permissions:* Stella Longato Muzzio
Associate Companies: Arcana Editrice SRL, Piazza Aspromonte 15a, I-20131 Milan; Casa Editrice MEB SRL (qv)
Subjects: Electronics, Computers and Computer Science, Alternative Sources of Energy, Natural Sciences, Music, Pocket Handbooks, General Non-fiction
Founded: 1973
ISBN Publisher's Prefix: 88-7021

Casa Editrice Roberto **Napoleone**+, Via Antonio Chinotto 16, I-00195 Rome Tel: (06) 3612691/3612693
Chief Executive: Roberto Napoleone
1985: 25 titles *1986:* 25 titles *Founded:* 1974

Nardini Editore — Centro Internazionale del Libro SpA, Via Scipione Ammirato 37, I-50136 Florence Tel: (055) 670330
Subjects: Juveniles, Philosophy, Religion, Esoteric Studies, Biography, Art, Essays, Poetry, Classics, Educational, Economics, Medical
Founded: 1956

New Interlitho SpA*, Via Curiel, I-20090 Trezzano S/N Tel: 4451926/4452753 Telex: 311140
Dir & Sales Manager: Renzo Aimini
Subjects: Juveniles, Encyclopaedias

Newton Compton Editori SRL, Via Germanico 197, I-00192 Rome Tel: (06) 3580205/316900
Subjects: General Fiction, Belles Lettres, Poetry, History, Philosophy, Social & General Science, Anthropology, Mathematics, Psychology, Political Science, Reference, How-to, Archaeology
Founded: 1969

Umberto **Nicoli** Editore*, Via Mistrali 7, I-43100 Parma Tel: (0521) 35959 Cable Add: Nicoli Editore Parma Telex: 530259 Cciaa Pr I
Chief Executive: Umberto Nicoli
Parent Company: Casa Editrice Nicoli, Via A Frank 4, I-43100 Parma
Subsidiary Company: Pubblitalia (at above address)
Subjects: Fiction, Essays, History, Poetry, Sport, Periodicals
Founded: 1976

Nistri — **Lischi** Editori, Piazza del Castelletto 7, I-56100 Pisa Tel: (050) 28031 Cable Add: Lischi Pisa
Man Dir: Luciano Lischi; *Sales:* Lucia Lischi
Subjects: Literary Criticism
1985: 10 titles *Founded:* 1780

Editrice **Nord** SRL, Via Rubens 25, I-20148 Milan Tel: (02) 405708/4042207
Man Dir: Gianfranco Viviani; *Editorial:* Sandro Pergameno, Alex Voglino, Piergiorgio Nicolazzini
Subjects: Fantasy and Science Fiction
Founded: 1964

Nuova Alfa Editoriale+, Via Leandro Alberti 95, I-40139 Bologna Tel: (051) 495162
Man Dir, Production: Maurizio Armaroli; *Editorial, Publicity:* Emanuela Spinsanti; *Sales:* Rosaria Alberico
Subjects: Art, Exhibition Catalogues, Essays
1985: 28 titles *Founded:* 1954
ISBN Publisher's Prefix: 88-7779

La **Nuova Italia** Editrice SpA*, Via Ernesto Codignola, I-50018 Casellina di Scandicci (Florence) Tel: (055) 27981
Man Dirs: Mario Casalini, Federico Codignola, Mario Ermini, Sergio Piccioni
Branch Offs: Via Panoramica 30, I-60123 Ancona; Via Dieta di Bari 38/c, I-70121 Bari; Via E Bernardi 14, I-40133, Bologna; Via D Cimarosa 14, I-09100 Cagliari; Corso Italia 158/D, I-87100 Cosenza; Via P Villari 33, I-50136 Florence; Via di Serretto 41/2, I-16131 Genoa; Via Negroli 12, I-20133 Milan; Via S Alfonso Maria de' Liguori 3, I-80141 Naples; Via Altichieri da Zevio 3, I-35100 Padua; Via Jolanola 15, I-90146 Palermo; Viale Carso 46, I-00195 Rome; Via Colli 24 (angolo Corso Montevecchio), I-10129 Turin; Via Adigetto 39, I-37100 Verona
Subjects: Biography, History, Art, Philosophy, Reference, Young Adult, Low- & High-priced Paperbacks, Psychology, Social Science, University & Secondary Textbooks
Founded: 1926
ISBN Publisher's Prefix: 88-221

Gruppo Editoriale **Nuova Vita** SpA, now Gruppo Editoriale Le Stelle SpA (qv)

Editrice **Nuovi Autori***, Via Gaudenzio Ferrari 14, I-20123 Milan Tel: (02) 8399338
Man Dir: Fulvio Aglieri; *Editorial:* Mariapia Baldaccini; *Sales:* Lella Giacomelli; *Publicity:* Alessandra Aglieri
Subjects: Poetry, Essays, Fiction
1985: 60 titles *Founded:* 1980

Nuovi Sentieri Editore*, Via Ripa 2, I-32100 Belluno Tel: (0437) 50308
Man Dir: Bepi Pellegrinon; *Editorial:* Loris Santomaso; *Sales:* Antonio Zullo
Subjects: Local History, Arts, Poetry, Literature, Photography
Founded: 1971
ISBN Publisher's Prefix: 88-85510

O E M F, see Medico Farmaceutica

O S (Organizzazioni Speciali SRL), Via Scipione Ammirato 37, I-50136 Florence Tel: (055) 672997/675446
Subject: Psychology
Miscellaneous: Member of Giunti Publishing Group
Founded: 1950

Officina Edizioni di Aldo Quinti, Via Virginia Agnelli 58, I-00151 Rome Tel: (06) 5313460
Chief Executive: Aldo Quinti; *Publicity:* Jolanda Ridolfi
Subjects: Architecture, Urban Studies, Art, Sociology, Ethnology, Linguistics, Theatre, Cinema
1985: 32 titles *Founded:* 1966

Edizioni **Ofiria**, see Giunti Publishing Group

Editoriale **Olimpia** SpA*, CP 258, I-50129 Florence (Located at: Viale Milton 7, Florence) Tel: (055) 489331/490750/473915 Telex: 573084 Edol I
Man Dir: Enrico Vallecchi; *Editorial, Rights & Permissions:* Attilio Vallecchi
Subjects: Hunting and Fishing, Sport, Technology, Science, General
1985: 22 titles *Founded:* 1939

Casa Editrice Leo S **Olschki***, Viuzzo del Pozzetto, I-50126 Florence Tel: (055) 687444/5
Man Dir: Alessandro Olschki
Subjects: Biography, History, Music, Art, Reference, Bibliography, Religion, Paperbacks, Medicine, Social Science, University Textbooks, General Humanities
Founded: 1886
ISBN Publisher's Prefix: 88-222

Olympia Press Italia*, Via Tunisia 41, I-20124 Milan Tel: (02) 6570569
Man Dir: Mario Carrillo
Subjects: General Fiction, General Science, Erotica
Founded: 1969

Nuove Edizioni **Operaie** SRL, now Sapere 2000 SRL

Organizzazioni Speciali SRL, see O S

Edizioni **Orientalia** Christiana, Piazza Santa Maria Maggiore 7, I-00185 Rome Tel: (06) 7312254
General Dir: James Lee Dugan SJ
Subjects: Eastern Christianity (History, Theology, Liturgy, Canon Law), Periodicals
Founded: 1923

P E A — Produzioni Editoriale Aprile, see Aprile

Paideia Editrice, Via Corsica 130, I-25125 Brescia Tel: (030) 222094
Man Dir: Prof Dr Giuseppe Scarpat; *Editorial:* Dr Marco Scarpat
Subjects: Belles Lettres, Poetry, Music, Art, Philosophy, Religion, University Textbooks
1986: 26 titles *Founded:* 1945

Palatina Editrice*, Borgo Giacomo Tommasini 9/A, I-43100 Parma
Chief Executives: Isabella Marchesi, Maria Casalinuovo; *Editorial:* Guglielmo Capacchi, Giancarlo Zarattini
Subjects: Local Interest, Art, History, Africana, Music, Literature, Travel, Language, Dictionaries, Folklore
Bookshop: Libreria Palatina Editrice (at above address)
Founded: 1965

Fratelli **Palombi** SRL*, Via dei Gracchi 181-85, I-00192 Rome Tel: (06) 354960
Man Dir: Dr Mario Palombi
Subsidiary Company: (Sales) Organizzazione Rab, Via del Crocifisso 51, I-00165 Rome
Subjects: Mainly concerning Rome (history, art)
Founded: 1914
ISBN Publisher's Prefix: 88-7621

G B **Palumbo** & C Editore SpA, Via B Ricasoli 59, I-90139 Palermo Tel: (091) 588850/334961
Manager: Giovan Battista Palumbo
Subjects: Literary Criticism, Linguistics, Scholarly, Essays
Founded: 1939

Edizioni **Panini** SpA+*, Viale Emilio Po 380, I-41100 Modena Tel: (059) 331133 Cable Add: Edipan Modena Italia Telex: 510650
Publisher: Franco Panini
Subjects: Educational, Sport, Card albums for children
Founded: 1963
ISBN Publisher's Prefix: 88-7686

Edizioni **Paoline** SRL+, Piazza Soncino 5, I-20092 Cinisello Balsamo (Milano) Tel: (02) 6600621 Telex: 325183 Epbook I
Man Dir, Sales: Emilio Bettati; *Editorial:* Antonio Tarzia; *Production:* Alessandro Marengo; *Publicity:* Fedele Molino
Orders to: CEP SRL, Corso Regina Margherita 2, I-10153 Turin Tel: (011) 836744
Parent Company: Società San Paolo, Rome
Subsidiary Company: CEP SRL, Corso Regina Margherita 2, I-10153 Turin
Associate Companies: Sampaolo Audiovisivi SRL, I-00148 Rome; SAIE Editrice SRL (qv); Società San Paolo Gruppo Periodici SRL, I-20145 Milan

Branch Offs: Via Soperga 45, I-20127 Milan Tel: (02) 2871581; Via Alessandro Severo 58, I-00145 Rome Tel: (06) 5424450
Subjects: Encyclopaedias, Dictionaries, General Fiction, Belles Lettres, Biography, History, How-to, Music, Art, Philosophy, Reference, Religion, Juveniles, Low- & High-priced Paperbacks, Medicine, Psychology
Bookshops: 98 bookshops throughout Italy
1985: 75 titles *1986:* 150 titles *Founded:* 1914
ISBN Publisher's Prefix: 88-215

Edizioni **Parallelo 38**+*, Via 3 Settembre 7, I-89100 Reggio Calabria Tel: (0965) 330300
Subjects: Art, Archaeology, Law, Economics, Poetry, History, Politics, Philosophy, Literature, Religion, Theatre, Fiction, Education, Psychology, Local Interest
Founded: 1970

G B **Paravia** & C SpA*, CP 485, I-10100 Turin Centro (Located at: Corso Racconigi 16, I-10139 Turin) Tel: (011) 7710166 Telex: 221652 Edito I
Editorial: Dr Guido Gay
Subjects: Scholarly
1985: 25 titles *Founded:* 1700

Passigli Editori di A Passigli & C SAS+, Via di Doccia 5, I-50135 Florence Tel: (055) 609428/697800 Telex: 575573 Amusic I
Man Dir: Prof Stefano Passigli; *Editorial:* Dr Luca Merlini; *Sales:* Dr Alvise Passigli; *Rights:* Domitilla Baldeschi
Subjects: Biography, Music, Letters, Literature, Politics, Current Events
1985: 18 titles *1986:* 22 titles *Founded:* 1981
ISBN Publisher's Prefix: 88-368

Pàtron Editore SRL+, Quarto Inferiore, Via Badini 12, I-40127 Bologna Tel: (051) 767003
General Dir: Riccardo Pàtron
Subjects: Literature, Linguistics, History, Philosophy, Psychology, Sociology, Art, Medicine, Engineering, Agriculture, Law
Bookshop: Libreria Internazionale Pàtron (qv under Major Booksellers)
1985: 40 titles *1986:* 42 titles *Founded:* 1920

Luigi **Pellegrini** Editore+, CP 158, I-87100 Cosenza (Located at: Via Roma 80/b, Cosenza) Tel: (0984) 21472/25245/25066 Cable Add: Pellegrini Editore Cosenza
Chief Executive, Rights & Permissions: Luigi Pellegrini; *Editorial, Sales:* Walter Pellegrini; *Publicity:* Erminia Petramala
Subjects: History, Fiction, Essays, Poetry, Theatre
Founded: 1952

Il **Pensiero** Scientifico Editore SRL+*, Via Panama 48, I-00198 Rome Tel: (06) 863633/859506/863349
President: Annamaria De Feo; *General Manager:* Francesco De Fiore; *Publicity Manager:* Michele Dalla; *Promotion Manager:* Luca De Fiore; *Foreign Rights, Production:* Gaetano Ruvolo
Subjects: Medicine, Health Education, Psychoanalysis
Founded: 1946
ISBN Publisher's Prefix: 88-7002

Piccin Nuova Libraria SpA*, Via Altinate 107, I-35121 Padua Tel: (049) 655566
Man Dir, Production, Rights & Permissions: Dr Massimo Piccin; *Editorial:* Lorenza Dainese; *Sales:* Dr Raffaello Steccanella
Associate Company: Piccin Editore SAS (periodical publisher)
Subjects: Medicine, Biology, Science, Literature, Law
Founded: 1980
ISBN Publisher's Prefix: 88-299

Cartiere Binda de Medici SpA Divisione Editoriale **Piccoli**, Via S Sofia 10, I-20122 Milan Tel: (02) 861847/808034 Cable Add: Lapiccoli Milano Telex: 332599 Genint I
Subject: Children's
1985: 161 titles *1986:* 188 titles *Founded:* 1943
ISBN Publisher's Prefix: 88-261

Edizioni **Piemme** di Pietro Marietti SpA+, Via del Carmine 5, I-15033 Casale Monferrato Tel: (0142) 70356
Man Dir: Pietro Marietti; *Editorial:* Luciano Pacomio; *Rights & Permissions:* Valeria Caprioglio
Subjects: Religion, Theology, Liturgy, Art, Scholarly
1985: 49 titles *Founded:* 1982
ISBN Publisher's Prefix: 88-384

La **Pietra***, Via Fulvio Testi 75, I-20126 Milan Tel: (02) 6428440
Man Dir: Enzo Nizza
Subjects: Politics, Anti-Fascism and Resistance, History, Art
1985: 10 titles *Founded:* 1962

La **Pilotta** Editrice Coop RL*, Via Garibaldi 21, I-43100 Parma Tel: (0521) 206904
President: Dr Gian Paolo Anghinetti; *Editorial:* Prof Antonio Martinelli
Subjects: Poetry, Fiction, Essays
Founded: 1978

Pirola*, Via Comelico 24, I-20135 Milan Tel: (02) 5488061
Subjects: Architecture, Urban Studies, Business, Law, Economics, Management, Engineering
Founded: 1781
ISBN Publisher's Prefix: 88-324

Pitagora SNC*, Via del Legatore 3, I-40138 Bologna Tel: (051) 534554
Chief Executive: Franco Stignani; *Editorial:* Mauro Bovini; *Sales:* Adolfo Francioni; *Publicity:* Angela Fabbri
Associate Company: Tecnoprint SNC (at above address)
Subjects: Technology, Engineering, Mathematics, Geology, Linguistics
Bookshops: Via Saragozza 112, Bologna; Via Zamboni 57, I-40126 Bologna
Founded: 1958
ISBN Publisher's Prefix: 88-371

Amilcare **Pizzi** SpA*, Via M de Vizzi 86, I-20092 Cinisello Balsamo (Milan) Tel: (02) 618361 Telex: 330006 Ampiz I
Chief Executive: Massimo Pizzi
Subsidiary Company: Silvana Editoriale SpA (qv)
Subjects: Art, Illustrated Books, Encyclopaedias, Paperbacks, Calendars, Catalogues
Founded: 1920

Studio Bibliografico Adelmo **Polla***, Via Prato 2, I-67044 Cerchio (Aq) Tel: (0863) 78522
Man Dir: Adelmo Polla; *Editorial:* Maria G Romanelli
Subjects: Literature, History (General & Local), Philology, Archaeology, Travel
1985: 26 titles *Founded:* 1974

Editrice **Pontificia** Università Gregoriana, Piazza della Pilotta 35, I-00187 Rome Tel: (06) 6781567
Gregorian University Press
Man Dir: Pasquale Puca
Associate Company: Editrice Pontificio Istituto Biblico (qv)
Subjects: Theology, Philosophy, Canon Law, Sociology, Psychology
Bookshop: Libreria Gregoriana, Piazza della Pilotta 4, I-00187 Rome
1985: 15 titles *Founded:* 1913
ISBN Publisher's Prefix: 88-7652

Editrice **Pontificio** Istituto Biblico, Piazza della Pilotta 35, I-00187 Rome Tel: (06) 6781567
Biblical Institute Press
Man Dir: Pasquale Puca
Associate Company: Editrice Pontificia Università Gregoriana (qv)
Subjects: Scientific Studies, Biblical Studies, Ancient Languages, Archaeology
Bookshop: Libreria Gregoriana, Piazza della Pilotta 4, I-00187 Rome
1985: 15 titles *Founded:* 1913
ISBN Publisher's Prefix: 88-7653

Casa Editrice Neri **Pozza**, CP 513, I-36100 Vicenza (Located at: Contra' Oratorio dei Servi 19-21, I-36100 Vicenza) Tel: (0444) 227228/236585 Cable Add: Edipozza
Man Dir: Neri Pozza
Subjects: Ancient and Modern Art, Literary Criticism and History, Politics, Local Interest
1985: 15 titles *Founded:* 1946

Edizioni Luigi **Pozzi** SRL+, Via Panama 68, I-00198 Rome Tel: (06) 863548
Chief Executive: Luigi Pozzi; *Editorial:* Maurizio Pozzi
Subject: Medicine
1985: 16 titles *Founded:* 1893
ISBN Publisher's Prefix: 88-7025

Pratiche Editrice+, Borgo delle Grazie 18, I-43100 Parma Tel: (0521) 285648
Chief Executive: Oreste Bergamaschi; *Editorial, Production, Publicity, Rights & Permissions:* Susanna Boschi; *Sales:* Sergio Marchioro
Parent Company: Societa' Produzioni Editoriali SRL (at above address)
Subjects: Literary Criticism, Psychoanalysis, Philosophy, History, Theatre, Cinema
1985: 15 titles *1986:* 8 titles *Founded:* 1976
ISBN Publisher's Prefix: 88-7380

Edizioni **Primavera** SRL+*, Via V Gioberti 32/E, I-50121 Florence Tel: (055) 675918
Orders to: Giunti Marzocco, Via V Gioberti 34, I-50121 Florence
Subjects: Children's, Tourism
Founded: 1981

Principato*, Via Fauché 10, I-20154 Milan Tel: (02) 312025
Subject: Scholarly
Founded: 1926

Priuli e Verlucca, Editori+, Stradale Torino 11, I-10018 Pavone Can (Torino) Tel: (0125) 239929 Cable Add: Priuli Verlucca Ivrea Telex: 210619 Univra I (049 Priver)
Chairman: Cesare Verlucca; *Production Dir:* Gherardo Priuli
Subjects: Life and Traditions of the Alpine Region, Nature, Photographic Studies of Regional Costume and Culture, Graphic Arts
Founded: 1971

Edizioni **Quasar** di Severino Tognon+, Via Quattro Novembre 152, I-00187 Rome Tel: (06) 6789888
Associate Companies: Edizioni Latium, Via Dino Frescobaldi 76, I-00137 Rome; Nuova Editrice Romana, Via Pompeo Magno 1, I-00192 Rome
Subjects: Archaeology, Art, Photography
Bookshop: Libreria Archeologica, Via

Palermo 23, I-00184 Rome
Founded: 1972
ISBN Publisher's Prefix: 88-85020

Edizioni **Quattro Venti**+, CP 156, I-61029 Urbino (Located at: Via Dini 16, Urbino) Tel: (0722) 2588
Man Dir, Editorial, Rights & Permissions: Anna Veronesi; *Sales, Production, Publicity:* Giorgio Balestrieri
Subjects: Philosophy, Literature, History, Art, Sport
1985: 30 titles *Founded:* 1981
ISBN Publisher's Prefix: 88-392

Editrice **Queriniana**, Via Piamarta 6, I-25187 Brescia Tel: (030) 294653
Man Dir: Gianfranco Ransenigo; *Sales:* Ettore Pelati; *Advertising:* Mario de Risio; *Rights & Permissions:* Rosino Gibellini
Branch Offs: Rome, Milan
Subjects: Philosophy, Religion, Theology
Founded: 1965

Aldo **Quinti**, see Officina Edizioni

Edizioni **R A I** Radiotelevisione Italiana SpA, see ERI

R C S Rizzoli Libri SpA, Via Angelo Scarsellini 17, I-20161 Milan Tel: (02) 2588 Cable Add: RCS Editori SpA, Milan Telex: Rizzoli 312119
Chairman: Dr Giorgio Fattori; *Man Dir:* Dr Marco Polillo; *Editorial:* Dr Gian Arturo Ferrari, Dr Paolo Settimio Cavalli; *Marketing:* Giuseppe Paschetto; *Rights & Permissions:* Dr Donatella Ciapessoni
Associate Companies: Milano Libri (qv); Sansoni Editore Nuova (qv)
Subsidiary Company: Rizzoli International Publications, New York, NY, USA
Subjects: General Fiction, Belles Lettres, Biography, History, Music, Hobbies, Medicine, Art, Religion, Juveniles, Low- & High-priced Paperbacks, Illustrated, Economics, Social Science, Reference, Textbooks
Bookshops: Libreria Rizzoli (qv under Major Booksellers)
Founded: 1909
Miscellaneous: Also Literary Agent (qv)
ISBN Publisher's Prefix: 88-17

Red/Studio Redazionale SRL+, Via Volta 43, I-22100 Como Tel: (031) 279146
Chief Executive, Editorial: Maurizio Rosenberg Colorni
Subjects: Alternative and Popular Medicine, Ecology, Soft Technologies, Natural Agriculture, Organic Nutrition, Psychology and Psychoanalysis, New Psychotherapies, Early Childhood
1986: 24 titles *1987:* 44 titles *Founded:* 1977
ISBN Publisher's Prefix: 88-7031

Franco Maria **Ricci** Editore*, Via Cino Del Duca 4/8, I-20122 Milan Tel: (02) 798444/793117 Telex: 313514 Fmri
Man Dir: Franco Maria Ricci
Associate Company: Leon Atayan, 6869 West Grand River Ave, Lansing, MI 48906, USA
Subjects: Art, Graphic Design, Reference, Periodicals, Limited editions
Bookshops: Librerie Ricci (qv under Major Booksellers)
Book Clubs: Club dei Bibliofili; Collectors Club of Franco Maria Ricci
Founded: 1965
ISBN Publisher's Prefix: 88-216

Riccardo **Ricciardi** Editore SpA, Via A Manzoni 10, I-20121 Milan Tel: (02) 875155/804248
President: Dr Maurizio Mattioli; *Man Dir:* Dr Vicenzo Caltabiano
Subjects: Italian Classics, History, Philology
1985: 3 titles *Founded:* 1907

Edizioni del **Riccio** SAS di G Bernardi+, Via Ugo Foscolo 41, I-50124 Florence Tel: (055) 2280286/2298420
Chief Executive: Giuliano Bernardi
Subjects: Cookery, Linguistics, Psychoanalysis, Alternative Medicine, Maps, Illustrated Books
1985: 7 titles *1986:* 9 titles *Founded:* 1977

G e C **Ricordi** SpA*, Via Berchet 2, I-20121 Milan Tel: (02) 8881 Telex: 310177 Ricor I
President: Gianni Babini; *Vice-President:* Eugenio Clausetti; *Man Dir:* Dr Guido Rignano
Subsidiary Companies: Ricordi Dischi SpA (at above address); Arti Grafiche Ricordi SpA, Via Cortina d'Ampezzo 10, I-20139 Milan; Gruppo Editoriale Musica Leggera Ricordi (at above address)
Associate Companies: Ricordi Americana SAEC, Argentina (qv); Ricordi Brasileira S/A, Rua Conselheiro Nébias 1136, 01203 Sao Paulo SP, Brazil; Ricordi Canada, Canada; Ricordi Londra, UK; G Ricordi & Co, Paseo de la Reforma 481-A, 06500 México, DF, Mexico; Ricordi Monaco, Monaco; Ricordi Parigi, France
Subjects: Scholarly, Music, Art
Founded: 1808
ISBN Publisher's Prefix: 88-7592

Edizioni **Ripostes**+, CP 135, I-84100 Salerno Tel: (089) 323896
Man Dir, Sales, Production, Rights & Permissions: Alessandro Tesauro; *Editorial:* Franz Theunis, Franco Xibilia, Rubina Giorgi; *Publicity:* Franco Xibilia
Branch Off: Borgo Pio 185, I-00193 Rome Tel: (06) 6568909
Subjects: Fiction, Philosophy, Poetry, Essays, Literature
1986: 25 titles *1987:* 20 titles *Founded:* 1981

Editori **Riuniti**, Via Serchio 9-11, I-00198 Rome Tel: (06) 866383
Man Dir: Bruno Peloso; *Sales Dir, Publicity:* Gina Bellot; *Rights & Permissions:* Ombretta Borgia
Subjects: History, Politics, Sociology, Philosophy, Economics, Law, Contemporary Fiction, Literature, Linguistics, Pedagogy, Science, Psychology, Visual Arts, Children's, Encyclopaedias, Reviews
Founded: 1953
ISBN Publisher's Prefix: 88-359

Rizzoli Editore SpA, now RCS Rizzoli Libri SpA (qv)

Libreria Editrice **Rogate**+, Via dei Rogazionisti 8, I-00182 Rome Tel: (06) 776430/7576115 Cable Add: Rogate Rogazionisti Rome
Editorial: Vito Magno; *Publicity:* Nunzio Spinelli
Subjects: Religion, Theology
1985: 50 titles *1986:* 50 titles *Founded:* 1976

Dott Prof Tommaso **Romano**, see Edizioni Thule

Rosenberg e Sellier Editori in Torino+, Via Andrea Doria 14, I-10123 Turin Tel: (011) 532150 Cable Add: Rosenberg Sellier
Man Dir and all other offices: Katie Roggero
Subjects: Philology, Social Sciences, Philosophy, Women's Studies
1985-86: 15 titles *Founded:* 1883
ISBN Publisher's Prefix: 88-7011

Rubbettino Editore+, Viale dei Pini 8, I-88049 Soveria Mannelli (CZ) Tel: (0968) 62034/62037 Cable Add: Rubbettino Soveria Mannelli Fax: (0968) 62035

Editorial Dir: Carlo Carlino; *Editorial:* Orazio Barrese; *Sales:* Mario Colistra
Subjects: Humanities, Essays, Current Events, Philosophy, Poetry, Fiction, Education, Periodicals
Founded: 1972

Rusconi Libri SpA+, Via Livraghi 1/B, I-20126 Milan Tel: (02) 2574141/2576417 Cables: Rusconi Editore Milano Telex: 312233
General Manager: Terruccio Viviani; *Editorial:* Luciano Beggiato; *Sales:* Alberto Nascimben; *Rights & Permissions:* Maura Bastiglia
Orders to: Eurolibri (at above address)
Parent Company: Rusconi Editore, Via Vitruvio 43, I-20124 Milan
Branch Offs: Rome, Paris and New York
Subjects: Fiction and Non-fiction, Literature, Biography, Music, History, Religion, Illustrated and Art
Bookshop: Libreria Internazionale Rusconi, Via Vitruvio 43, I-20124 Milan
1985: 80 titles *Founded:* 1968
ISBN Publisher's Prefix: 88-18

S A G E P, Piazza Merani 1, I-16145 Genoa Tel: (010) 313453 Telex: 281343 SAGEP I Fax: (010) 312618
Publisher: Eugenio de Andreis; *Sales Manager:* Carla Bisacchi
Subjects: Architecture, Art, Economy, Ethnography, History, Natural Sciences, Travel and Tourism
Founded: 1965
ISBN Publisher's Prefix: 88-7058

S A I E Editrice SRL, Corso Regina Margherita 2, I-10153 Turin Tel: (011) 871022
Publicity: Fedele Molino
Associate Company: Edizioni Paoline SRL (qv)
Subjects: Reference, Encyclopaedias, Dictionaries, Literary Criticism, Multimedia, Philosophy, Linguistics, Languages, Economics, Religion, Medicine, History, Earth Sciences, Philosophy, Education, Art, Juveniles
Founded: 1954

S E I (Società Editrice Internationale)+*, Corso Regina Margherita 176, I-10152 Turin Tel: (011) 5211441 Cable Add: SEI Turin Telex: 216216 Sei Toi
Man Dir: Gian Nicola Pivano; *Editorial:* Francesco Meotto; *Sales:* Paolo Bottazzi; *Production:* Enrico Paolucci Delle Roncole; *Rights & Permissions:* Giovanni Casse'
Branch Offs: Bari, Bologna, Cagliari, Catania, Florence, Genoa, Milan, Naples, Palermo, Padua, Pescara, Rome, Turin
Subjects: General Fiction, Belles Lettres, Biography, History, Art, Philosophy, Religion, Juveniles, Psychology, General & Social Science, Educational Materials, Textbooks, Paperbacks, Language Laboratories
1985: 48 titles *Founded:* 1908
ISBN Publisher's Prefix: 88-05

S I A D Edizioni SRL, now part of Armenia Editore SpA (qv)

Norberto **Sabatelli** & C, see Editrice Liguria

Il **Saggiatore** SpA+*, Via San Senatore 10, I-20122 Milan Tel: (02) 875119/875892
President, Man Dir: Maria Laura Boselli; *Editorial:* Glauco Arneri; *Rights & Permissions:* Renata Castellina
Associate Company: Arnoldo Mondadori Editore SpA (qv)
Subjects: History, Philosophy, Economics, Architecture, Mathematics, Social Sciences, Geography, Linguistics, Art, Music, Belles Lettres
Founded: 1958

La **Salamandra**, an imprint of Compograf Edizioni (qv)

Salerno Editrice SRL+, Via di Donna Olimpia 186, I-00152 Rome Tel: (06) 5315684/8
Chief Executive: Prof Enrico Malato
Subjects: Literature, Essays, Fiction, Music, Biography, Sociology, Classics, Criticism, Facsimiles
Founded: 1972
ISBN Publisher's Prefix: 88-85026

Collegio **San Bonaventura** di Grottaferrata, Collegio San Bonaventura, Via Vecchia di Marino 28, I-00046 Grottaferrata (Rome) Tel: (06) 9459248
Subjects: Religion, Theology, Franciscan history, Bibliography
Bookshop: At above address
1985: 3 titles *Founded:* 1877
ISBN Publisher's Prefix: 88-7013

Sansoni Editore Nuova, Via Varchi 47, I-50132 Florence Tel: (055) 243334
Associate Company: RCS Rizzoli Libri SpA (qv)
Subjects: Literary Criticism, Dictionaries, Scholarly, Essays
Founded: 1873
ISBN Publisher's Prefix: 88-383

Sapere 2000 SRL, Via F Turati 48, I-00185 Rome Tel: (06) 730776
Man Dir: Angelo Ruggieri
Subjects: Politics, Sociology, Religion, Culture
Founded: 1976
ISBN Publisher's Prefix: 88-7673

Fausto **Sardini** Editrice, Via Pace 37, I-25040 Bornato in Franciacorta (Brescia) Tel: (030) 725123 Cable Add: Fausto Sardini-Editore-Bornato Fax: (030) 7254348
Chief Executive: Fausto Sardini; *Editorial:* Meris Apolone
Subjects: History, Art, Religion, Science, Poetry, Fiction, Local Interest
Bookshop: At above address
1985: 6 titles *Founded:* 1969
ISBN Publisher's Prefix: 88-7506

Giovanni **Sartorio**, see Edizioni Mediche Italiane

Savitri SRL, see Edizioni Arka

Scala Istituto Fotografico Editoriale, Via Chiantigiana 62, I-50011 Antella (Florence) Tel: (055) 641541 Cable Add: Scalafoto Telex: Scalapub 58428
Subjects: Textbooks, Multimedia, Illustrated Art Books, Photography, Audiovisual Aids
Founded: 1953

Salvatore **Sciascia**, Corso Umberto 111, I-93100 Caltanissetta Tel: (0934) 21946 Cable Add: Sciascia Editore
Man Dir: Salvatore Sciascia
Subjects: History, Arts, Literature, Essays, Poetry, Literary Studies, Periodical
Founded: 1946

Libreria **Scientifica Cortina***, Corso Marconi 34/A, I-10125 Turin Tel: (011) 6507074/6508665
Chief Executive: Walter Barp
Parent Company: Edizioni Libreria Cortina Torino (at above address)
Associate Companies: Edizioni Libreria Cortina Milan, Largo Richini 1, I-20100 Milan; Edizioni Libreria Cortina Padua, Via Marzolo 2, I-35100 Padua; Edizioni Libreria Cortina Verona SRL (qv)
Subjects: University, School and Professional Textbooks on Medicine, Pharmacy, Veterinary Science, Nursing
Bookshop: At above address
1985: 8 titles

Edizioni **Scientifiche Italiane**+, Via dei Taurini 27, I-00185 Rome Tel: (06) 492664
President: Pietro Perlingieri; *Chairman:* Francesco De Simone; *Dir:* Giovanna Delfino
Subjects: General & Social Science, Economics, Geography, Architecture, History, Arts, Music, Cinema, Dance, Communications, Maps, Agriculture, Literature, Medicine, Philosophy, Law
Founded: 1945

Casa Editrice **Scode** SpA*, Corso Monforte 36, I-20122 Milan Tel: (02) 702026 Cable Add: Scode Milano
President: Carlo Gandini
Subjects: Architecture, History, Hobbies, Arts, Maps, Literary Criticism, Religion, Encyclopaedias, Linguistics, Educational
Founded: 1978

Editrice La **Scuola** SpA+, Via Cadorna 11, Brescia Tel: (030) 29931 Cable Add: Scuola Brescia Telex: 300836 Scuola Brescia
President: Dr Ing Luciano Silveri; *Man Dir:* Dr Ing Adolfo Lombardi; *General Manager:* Giuseppe Covone
Associate Companies: Editrice Morcelliana SpA (qv); Edizioni Studium SpA (qv)
Branch Offs: Bari, Bologna, Milan, Naples, Rome
Subjects: Philosophy, Religion, Juveniles, Psychology, Secondary & Primary Textbooks, Educational Materials
Founded: 1904
ISBN Publisher's Prefix: 88-350

Scuola Vita, an imprint of Gruppo Editoriale Le Stelle SpA (qv)

Sellerio Editore*, Via Siracusa 50, I-90141 Palermo Tel: (091) 6254194/6254258
Subjects: Literature, Popular Art, Anthropology, Archaeology, History, Photography, Semiotics, Sociology
1985: 41 titles *Founded:* 1969
ISBN Publisher's Prefix: 88-7581

Editrice **Sigla** Tre SNC*, CP 264, I-06100 Perugia (Located at: Via XIV Settembre 13, Perugia) Tel: (075) 61590
Editorial: Antonio Carlo Ponti; *Sales, Production, Publicity:* Giancleto Toschi
Subjects: Yearbooks, Guides, Medicine, Art, Poetry, Essays, Literature
Founded: 1981

Angelo **Signorelli** Editore SNC*, Via Paola Falconieri 84, I-00152 Rome Tel: (06) 539954/533827 Cable Add: Signorelli Editore Roma
Chief Executive: Oliviero Alpa; *Editorial:* Giorgia Signorelli, Gilberta Alpa
Subjects: Textbooks and Educational Materials
Founded: 1912

Silvana Editoriale SpA+*, Via M de Vizzi 86, I-20092 Cinisello Balsamo, Milan Tel: (02) 6172464
Chief Executive: Massimo Pizzi
Parent Company: Amilcare Pizzi SpA (qv)
Subjects: Art, Facsimile books, Photographs, Architecture, Illustrated books
Founded: 1953
ISBN Publisher's Prefix: 88-366

Società Storica Catanese*, Via Etnea 248, piano nobile, Catania
Man Dir: Dr Michele D'Agata; *Editorial:* Giuseppe Trovato Pennisi; *Sales:* Francesco Romeo Giuzzetta; *Production:* Giovanni Assaro; *Publicity:* Dr Davide D'Agata; *Rights & Permissions:* Prof Rita Siciliano
Subjects: History, Literature, Sociology, Law, Local Interest, Poetry, General
1985: 98 titles *Founded:* 1955

Libraria Editoriale **Sodalitas** SAS, Centro Internazionale Studi Rosminiani, Corso Umberto 15, I-28049 Stresa Tel: (0323) 31623/30091
Publicity: Vincenzo Sala
Subjects: Philosophy, Theology
Founded: 1925

Edizioni del **Sole** 24 Ore*, Via Lomazzo 52, I-20154 Milan Tel: (02) 313821/342088/344027 Telex: 331325 I 24 Ore
Dir General: Gianni Rizzoni; *Editorial:* Francesco Bogliari
Subjects: Economics, Management, Law
1985: 50 titles *Founded:* 1983

Sonzogno, Via Mecenate 91, I-20138 Milan Tel: (02) 50951 Cable Add: Librifabbri Milan Telex: 311321 Fabbri I
Dir: Mario Andreose; *Rights & Permissions:* Carla Tanzi
Subjects: Adventure, Romance, Mystery, General Non-fiction
Miscellaneous: Member of Gruppo Editoriale Fabbri, Bompiani, Sonzogno, Etas SpA
Founded: 1818

La **Sorgente** SRL+, Via Garofalo 44, I-20133 Milan Tel: (02) 230025/230720
Man Dir, Rights & Permissions: Dr Giorgio Vignati
Subject: Juveniles
Founded: 1936

Sperling e Kupfer Editori SpA, Via Monte di Pietà 24, I-20121 Milan Tel: (02) 876614 Cable Add: Kupferedit Milan Telex: 325481 Sperli I
President, Publisher: Tiziano M Barbieri; *Man Dir:* Donatella M Barbieri; *Editorial, Rights Dir:* Rosaria Carpinelli; *Sales:* Ornella Robbiati; *Rights & Permissions:* Marica Fioroni
Subsidiary Company: Edizioni Frassinelli SRL (qv)
Subjects: General Fiction & Non-fiction, Economics, Management, Biography, Health, Travel, Sports, How-to
1985: 90 titles *Founded:* 1889
ISBN Publisher's Prefix: 88-200

Spirali Edizioni*, Via Hugo 1, I-20123 Milan Tel: (02) 801331/801471
Man Dir: Cristina Frua De Angeli; *Editorial:* Annalisa Scallo
Subjects: Psychoanalysis, Art, Law, Philosophy, Literature, Music, Poetry
Founded: 1978

Stampa Alternativa Editrice*, CP 741, I-00100 Rome Tel: (06) 380711
Man Dir, Editorial: Marcello Baraghini; *Sales:* Angelo Leone
Orders to: Nuovi Equilibri, Via del Collegio 19, I-01100 Viterbo
Subjects: Art, Music, Nutrition, Medicine
1985: 12 titles *Founded:* 1971

Gruppo Editoriale Le **Stelle** SpA*, Via G Vasari 15, I-20135 Milan Tel: (02) 5455641
Imprints: Dimensione Umana, Linea Verde, Scuola Vita, Edizioni Le Stelle
Subjects: Fiction, Science, History, Geography, Religion, Music, Primary & Secondary Textbooks, Educational Materials, Pedagogy, Didactics, Picture Books
Founded: 1954

Edizioni di **Storia** e Letteratura, Via Lancellotti 18, I-00186 Rome Tel: (06) 6540556
Chief Executive: Maddalena De Luca
Subjects: Scholarly, History, Philosophy, Economics, Politics, Social Studies, Literature
Founded: 1943

Edizioni **Studium** SpA+, Via Cassiodoro 14, I-00193 Rome Tel: (06) 6565846/6875456 Cable Add: Studium Rome
Associate Company: Editrice La Scuola SpA (qv)
Subjects: Literature, History, Philosophy, Religion, General & Social Science, University Textbooks, Periodical
Founded: 1927
ISBN Publisher's Prefix: 88-382

Sugarco Edizioni SRL*, Viale Tunisia 41, I-20124 Milan Tel: (02) 652192/6570569
Man Dir: Dr Massimo Pini; *Editorial:* Donatella Cerutti; *Sales:* Vincenzo Nagari; *Production:* Gianni Bagetto
Subjects: General Fiction, Belles Lettres, Biography, History, Philosophy, Guides
Founded: 1956

Tecniche Nuove SRL, Via Moscova 46/9a, I-20121 Milan Tel: (02) 6590351 Telex: 334647 Techs I Fax: (02) 6571058
Man Dir: Giuseppe Nardella; *Editorial:* E Guaglione; *Publicity:* S Savona
Subsidiary Company: Grafica Quadrifoglio
Subjects: Information Science, Electronics, Energy, Oil, Plastics, Manufacturing, Business, Automation, Nutrition
Founded: 1960
ISBN Publisher's Prefix: 88-7081

Edizioni del **Teresianum***, Piazza San Pancrazio 5/A, I-00152 Rome Tel: (06) 582362/5810140
Chief Executive: Ildefonso Moriones; *Sales, Publicity:* Makoto Wada
Parent Company: Edizioni dei Padri Carmelitani Scalzi, Corso d'Italia 38, I-00198 Rome
Subjects: Theology, Bibliography
Founded: 1966

Casa Editrice **Testi** Elementari Milano SRL, see CETEM

Nicola **Teti** e C Editore SRL*, Via Enrico Nöe 23, I-20133 Milan Tel: (02) 2043597/2043539
Man Dir: Nicola Teti; *Editorial:* Piero Lavatelli; *Sales:* Vincenzo Fracchiolla; *Production:* Rita Vaccari, Vanna Guzzi; *Publicity:* Nino Oppo; *Rights & Permissions:* Rita Vaccari
Subjects: Textbooks, Encyclopaedias, Politics, Marxism, Social Science, Juveniles, Reprints of Socialist documents, Natural History, History, Pedagogy
Founded: 1971
ISBN Publisher's Prefix: 88-7039

Dott Prof Tommaso Romano — Edizioni **Thule**+, Via Ammiraglio Gravina 95, I-90139 Palermo Tel: (091) 323699
Chief Executive: Dr Tommaso Romano; *Publicity:* Studio Grafico FM-Arch Dely Anania; *Rights & Permissions:* Ignazio Romano
Subjects: Philosophy, Education, History, Theology, Fiction, Poetry, Sociology, Sport, Tourism, Criticism
Book Club: Edi Thule Club
Founded: 1971

Edizioni **Thyrus** SRL+, CP 41, I-05031 Arrone (TR) (Located at: Via della Rinascita 12, Arrone) Tel: (0744) 78422 Cable Add: Ufficio Postale Arrone
Man Dir, Production, Rights & Permissions: Dr Osvaldo Panfili; *Editorial:* Prof Lido Pirro; *Sales:* Nobili Nevia
Associate Company: Emmeci SNC, Via Curio Dentato, I-05100 Terni
Subjects: Fiction, History and Local History, Education, Psychology, Sociology, Humanities, Theology
Book Club: Circolo Astrolabio (qv)
Founded: 1956

Tilgher-Genova SAS*, Via Assarotti 52, I-16122 Genoa Tel: (010) 870653/891140
Chief Executive: Lucio Bozzi
Subjects: Literary Criticism, Philosophy, Humanities
Founded: 1971

Editrice **Tirrenia** Stampatori SAS*, Via G Ferrari 5, I-10124 Turin Tel: (011) 877010
Editorial, Sales, Production, Publicity: Andrea Ariozzi Masino, Anna Maria Bertolina
Orders to: Promeco SRL, Via Carlo Torre 29, I-20148 Milan
Subjects: General
1985: 12 titles *Founded:* 1977
ISBN Publisher's Prefix: 88-7763

Todariana Editrice*, Via Lazzaro Papi 15, I-20135 Milan Tel: (02) 5460353
Chief Executive, Editorial: Teodoro Giuttari
Subjects: Fiction, Poetry, Essays, Psychology, Sociology, Travel, Fantasy and Science Fiction, Dialect Studies
1985: 11 titles *Founded:* 1967
ISBN Publisher's Prefix: 88-7015

Edizioni della **Torre***, Via Toscana 70, I-09100 Cagliari Tel: (070) 490716/485770 Cable Add: Edizioni della Torre Cagliari
Chief Executive: Salvatore Fozzi
Subsidiary Company: Agenzia Libraria Fozzi, Via Toscana 72, I-09100 Cagliari
Subjects: History, Sociology, Literature, Linguistics, Local Interest
Founded: 1974

Casa Editrice Luigi **Trevisini**, Via Tito Livio 10, I-20137 Milan Tel: (02) 5450704/5452647 Cable Add: Trevisini Milano
Chief Executive: Luigi Trevisini; *Editorial:* Dr Giusi Trevisini
Subject: School Textbooks
Founded: 1849
ISBN Publisher's Prefix: 88-292

Edizioni Il **Tripode** SRL, Viale Gramsci 12, I-80122 Naples Tel: (081) 683086/681267
Man Dir: Dr Giuseppe Martano
Subject: Scholarly
Founded: 1972

U T E T (Unione Tipografico-Editrice Torinese), CP 1166 Ferrovia, I-10125 Turin (Located at: Corso Raffaello 28, Turin) Tel: (011) 65291 Cable Add: UTET Turin
President: Dr Gianni Merlini
Subjects: Belles Lettres, History, Art, Architecture, Music, Religion, Philosophy, Reference, Psychology, Law, Veterinary Science, General & Social Science, Juveniles, University Textbooks
Founded: 1791
ISBN Publisher's Prefix: 88-02

Ubulibri+, Via B Ramazzini 8, I-20129 Milan Tel: (02) 2715569
Man Dir, Editorial: Franco Quadri; *Sales, Publicity, Rights & Permissions:* Silvia Bergero; *Production:* Giulio Lupieri
Subjects: Cinema, Theatre
1985: 9 titles *1986:* 10 titles *Founded:* 1979

Editoriale **Umbra** SNC di Carnevali e Zanello+*, Via Pignattara 38, I-06034 Foligno-Perugia Tel: (0742) 53174 Cable Add: Editoriale Umbra Foligno
Man Dir, Editorial, Rights & Permissions: Mirko Zanello; *Sales:* Giovanni Carnevali; *Publicity:* Ida Saltarelli
Subjects: History of Art, Contemporary History, Essays
1985: 4 titles *Founded:* 1982
ISBN Publisher's Prefix: 88-85659

Umbria Editrice*, I-06070 San Mariano (PG) Tel: (075) 798020
Chief Executive: Antonio Carlo Ponti
Subjects: Poetry, Fiction, Art, Essays
Founded: 1971

Edizioni **Unicopli** Scrl+, Via Verona 9, I-20135 Milan Tel: (02) 8466502/8466950
Chief Executive, Editorial Dir, Rights & Permissions: Marilena Jerrobino; *Editorial:* Marilena Jerrobino (Economics, Sociology), Roberto Favaro (Music), Alessandra Facchi (Education, Linguistics, Geography, Philosophy, Literature), Stefano Nutini (Psychology, History, Law), Tiziano Cornegliani (Psychiatry, Medicine); *Production, Publicity:* Piera Aldeghi
Subjects: University Textbooks, Essays
1985: 100 titles *Founded:* 1980
ISBN Publisher's Prefixes: 88-7061, 88-400

Editrice **Universitaria**, see Giunti Publishing Group

Società Editrice **Universo***, Via G Battista Morgagni 1, I-00161 Rome Tel: (06) 859063/8445243
Subjects: Medicine, Physics, Chemistry, Engineering, Mathematics

Edizioni **Uomini** Nuovi*, I-21030 Marchirolo (Varese) Tel: (0332) 723007/723363
Chief Executive, Editorial: Dr Giuseppe E Laiso; *Sales:* Ruth Laiso; *Publicity:* Anna Rossinelli; *Rights & Permissions:* Giuseppe Piccolo
Subjects: Christian Inspiration, the Church, Stories for Infants and Children
Founded: 1964

Vallardi Industrie Grafiche+*, Via Trieste 20, I-20020 Lainate (Milan) Tel: (02) 9370284 Cable Add: Valgraf, Lainate Telex: 314523 Vallig I
Publisher: Giuseppe Vallardi; *Dir:* Victor Hayon; *Editorial:* Emanuela Vallardi
Subjects: Atlases, Juveniles
Founded: 1969

Vallecchi Editore SpA*, Viale Milton 7, I-50129 Florence Tel: (055) 473915 Telex: 573084 Edol I
Man Dir: Enrico Vallecchi
Subjects: Art, Fiction, Classics
Founded: 1982

Valmartina Editore SRL+, CP 1444, I-50122 Florence (Located at: Via Dei Servi 13, Florence) Tel: (055) 217874/5
President: Luigi Vecchia; *Editorial:* Carlo Pasquinelli; *Production:* Giorgio Raccis; *Rights & Permissions:* Michela Melchiori
Orders to: Via L Dottesio 1, I-35138 Padua Tel: (049) 8710099
Subjects: Language Instruction, Tourism, School Textbooks
1986: 15 titles *1987:* 20 titles *Founded:* 1951

Società Editrice **Vannini**, CP 68, I-25100 Brescia (Located at: Viale d'Italia 8b, Brescia) Tel: (030) 56272/57089 Cable Add: Vannini Brescia
Subjects: Scholastic, Reference, Law
1985: 4 titles *Founded:* 1950

Giovanni De **Vecchi** Editore SpA, see De Vecchi

Vita e Pensiero*, Largo Gemelli 1, I-20123 Milan Tel: (02) 8856
Subjects: Literary Criticism, Philosophy, Religion, Essays, History
Founded: 1918
ISBN Publisher's Prefix: 88-343

Voce della Bibbia, CP 90, I-41043 Formigine (Modena) (Located at: Via Cavallotti 14, Formigine) Tel: (059) 556303
General Dir: Ettore Calanchi
Parent Company: Back to the Bible

Broadcast, Box 82808, Lincoln, Nebraska 68501, USA
Subjects: Evangelism, Christian literature, Bible correspondence courses, Music
Founded: 1961

G **Zanibon** Edizioni Musicali*, Piazza dei Signori 44, I-35100 Padua Tel: (049) 30167 Cable Add: Zanibon Musica Padua
Chief Executive, Editorial: Dr Guglielmo Travaglia Zanibon; *Sales:* Ugo Armelin; *Rights & Permissions:* Tina Testa
Subsidiary Companies: Edizioni Drago; Edizioni Orfeo (both at above address)
Subjects: Instrumental and Chamber Music, Vocal Music, Educational, Musicology
Bookshop: At above address
Founded: 1908

Nicola **Zanichelli** SpA, Via Irnerio 34, I-40126 Bologna Tel: (051) 293111
Chairman: Giovanni Enriques; *Dir General:* Federico Enriques
Subjects: History, Philosophy, Reference, Dictionaries, Mathematics, Chemistry, Biology, Medicine, Pharmacology, Engineering, General Science, University & Secondary Textbooks, Law, Psychology, Visual Design, Architecture, Juveniles, Physics, Electronics, Linguistics, Literature, Geography, Earth Sciences, Paperbacks, Education
Bookshop: Libreria Zanichelli, Portici del Pavaglione, Piazza Galvani l/h, I-40126 Bologna
Founded: 1859
ISBN Publisher's Prefix: 88-08

Edizioni **Zara**, Via Portilia 6, I-43100 Parma Tel: (0521) 45945
Chief Executive: Isabella Marchesi; *Editorial:* Giancarlo Zarattini
Subject: University Textbooks
1985: 10 titles *1986:* 12 titles *Founded:* 1979

Literary Agents

Agenzia Letteraria Internazionale SRL, Via Manzoni 41, I-20121 Milan Tel: (02) 6572465/6572594/6572596 Telex: 323574 Linali I

Dais Literary Agency, Via di Santa Maria in Monticelli 67, I-00186 Rome Tel: (06) 655356

Eulama SRL, Via Torino 135, I-00184 Rome Tel: (06) 460636 Cable Add: Eularom Telex: 620086 Eulama I
President: Harald Kahnemann
Specializes in social sciences, politics, psychology, education, philosophy, religion, linguistics and literature, mass-media, technology, computer science, architecture, urban studies, Spanish and Latin-American literature and books for young readers, quality fiction
Branch Off: Eulama SA, Federal Republic of Germany (qv)
Also Translation Agency (qqv)

I L A (International Literary Agency), I-18010 Terzorio (IM) Tel: (0184) 484048 Cable Add: Friedmann Terzorio (IM)
An American agency headquartered in Europe (with representatives in Britain, Spain, Holland and Scandinavia), specializing in handling of foreign language translation rights to multi-volume book and magazine projects, children's books, encyclopaedias, bestsellers (in all European languages)

Agenzia di Rosemary Ann **Liedl** & Co, Via Ascanio Sforza 21, I-20136 Milan Tel: (02) 8323640
Contact: Rosemary Liedl

Living Literary Agency Elfriede Pexa, Via Villoresi 13, I-20143 Milan Tel: (02) 8325839 Telex: 335142 attn Living

Natoli and Stefan Literary Agency, Galleria Buenos Aires 14, I-20124 Milan
Manager: G Natoli
Also Translation Agency (qv)

Christa **Pucci***, Largo Generale Gonzaga del Vodice 2, I-00195 Rome Tel: (06) 3612471

Rizzoli Editore SpA*, Via Rizzoli 2, I-20132 Milan
Also Publisher and Major Bookseller (qqv)

Mirella Vescovi **Tenderini**, Corso Venezia 46, I-20121 Milan Tel: (02) 796806 Telex: 322298 Strain
Contact: Mirella Tenderini
Specializes in art, architecture, photography and illustrated books

Book Clubs

C D E SpA Gruppo Mondadori, Via Durazzo 4, I-20134 Milan Telex: 320457 Mondmi I
Owned by: Arnoldo Mondadori Editore SpA (qv)

Circolo Astrolabio, Via Pacinotti 20b, I-05100 Terni
Owned by: Edizioni Thyrus SRL (qv)

Club dei Bibliofili*, Via Cino del Duca 4-8, I-20122 Milan
Owned by: Franco Maria Ricci Editore (qv)
Also associated with Book Club, Les Amis de Franco Maria Ricci, France (qv)

Collectors Club of Franco Maria Ricci*, Via Cino del Duca 4-8, I-20122 Milan
Owned by: Franco Maria Ricci Editore (qv)

Isper Club, Corso Dante 124, I-10126 Turin Tel: (011) 633950
Owned by: Isper SRL (qv)

Sardegna Cinque, CP 27 bis, I-09134 Cagliari/Pirri (Located at: Via Campania 27, I-09121 Cagliari) Tel: (070) 290552/562296
Owned by: Edizioni Castello di Antonio Careddu (qv)

Edi **Thule** Club, Via Ammiraglio Gravina 95, I-90139 Palermo
Owned by: Edizioni Thule (qv)

Major Booksellers

Libreria all' **Accademia** SNC di Randi Pietro, CP 1003, I-35139 Padua (Located at: Via S Lucia 1, Padua)
The above is the head office address
Manager: Pietro Randi
Bookshops: Libreria Draghi-Randi, Via Cavour 17-19 (general bookshop, foreign department, subscriptions); Libreria Universitaria, Via 8 Febbraio 10 (law, literature, university textbooks); Libraria Accademia, Via Accademia 2 (humanities, classics, history, psychology); Libreria Nuova Moderna, Via Paolotti 5 (medicine, engineering, sciences) (all I-35139 Padua) Tel: (049) 35976/24525/26648

Casalini Libri*, Via B da Maiano 3, I-50014 Fiesole (Florence) Tel: (055) 599941 Cable Add: Casalini Fiesole
Man Dirs: Mario Casalini, Gerda Casalini von Grebmer, Barbara Casalini, Michele Casalini
General book exporter; also Publisher (qv)

Libreria Internazionale Fratelli **Cocco**, Largo C Felice 76, I-09100 Cagliari, Sardinia Tel: (070) 657785
Manager: Antonio Cocco
Also: Via Manno 9, I-09100 Cagliari, Sardinia Tel: (070) 668207

Libreria **Dante** di A M Longo, Via A Diaz 39, I-48100 Ravenna Tel: (0544) 33500
Owned by: Angelo Longo Editore (qv)

Libreria **Feltrinelli***, Via del Babuino 41, Rome Tel: (06) 6793360
Also: Via Carlo Alberto 2 and Piazza Castello 9, Turin; Piazza Porta Ravegnana 1, Bologna; Via Cavour 12-20, I-50129 Florence Tel: (055) 292196

Libreria SF **Flaccovio***, Via Ruggiero Settimo 37, I-90139 Palermo Tel: (091) 589442
Manager: Sergio Flaccovio
Also: Piazza Orlando 15, Palermo; Via E Basile 136, Palermo; Piazza Don Bosco 3, Palermo; Libreria Dante, Quattro Canti Citta, Palermo
Owned by: S F Flaccovio Editore (qv)

Libreria **Gregoriana**, Via Roma 37, I-35122 Padua
Also: Via Vescovado 33, I-35100 Padua; Piazza Duomo 5, Padua; Piazza Signori 44, Padua
Owned by: Libreria Editrice Gregoriana (qv)

Ulrico **Hoepli** Libreria Internazionale*, Via Hoepli 5, I-20121 Milan Tel: (02) 865446
Managers: Dr Ulrico Carlo Hoepli, Roberto Taneggi
Owned by: Casa Editrice Libraria Ulrico Hoepli SpA (qv)

Libreria **Liberma***, CP 492 (San Silvestro), Rome (Located at: Via di Saponara 20A, I-00125 Acilia-Roma)
Manager: Stefano Busetti

Libreria Internazionale Giuseppe **Luna***, Via Gramsci 41-43, I-06034 Foligno Tel: (0742) 52581

Libreria Editrice **Minerva**, Via Castiglione 13-15, Bologna

Libreria Commissionaria Internazionale di Raffaele **Pancaldi***, Via S Petronio Vecchio 3, I-40125 Bologna Tel: (051) 229466
Manager: Raffaele Pancaldi

Libreria Internazionale **Pàtron**, Via Zamboni 24, I-40126 Bologna Tel: (051) 275735
Owned by: Pàtron Editore SRL (qv)

Randi Pietro, see Accademia

Librerie **Ricci***, Via Durini 19, Milan Tel: (02) 7702
Also: Piazza Plebiscito 18/A, Ancona; Via Farini 27, Bologna; Contrada del Soncin Rotto 4, Brescia; Via delle Belle Donne 41/R, Florence; Via Torre 60, Modena; Via Siracusa 7/A, Palermo; Via Affò 1, Parma; Via dei Mille 13, Pisa; Via Borgognona 4/D, Rome (all Italy); 36 place du Grand Sablon, Brussels, Belgium; 12 rue des Beaux-Arts, Paris, France; 13 rue de Monthoux, Geneva, Switzerland
Owned by: Franco Maria Ricci Editore (qv)

Libreria **Rizzoli** della Rizzoli Editore SpA, Galleria Vittorio Emanuele II 79, I-20121 Milan
Manager: Aldo Allegri
Also: Libreria Internazionale Rizzoli SRL, Galleria Colonna, Largo Chigi 15, Rome Tel: (06) 6796641
Owned by: R C S Rizzoli Libri SpA (qv)

ITALY

Rosenberg e Sellier SpA, Via Andrea Doria 14, I-10123 Turin Tel: (011) 518388
Proprietors: Ugo Gianni Rosenberg, Elvi Rosenberg
International import-export bookseller and subscription agent

Libreria Internazionale **Seeber**, Via Tornabuoni 68 R, I-50123 Florence Tel: (055) 215697/282546
Manager: Carla Rossi

Libreria Internazionale **Sperling e Kupfer***, Via Cappellari 3, I-20123 Milan Tel: (02) 8051882
Manager: Onorato Ciriotti

Major Libraries

Biblioteca **Ambrosiana**, Piazza Pio XI 2, I-20123 Milan Tel: (02) 800146
Librarian: Enrico Galbiati

Biblioteca **Angelica***, Piazza S Agostino 8, I-00186 Rome Tel: (06) 6875874/6568041
Dir: Dr Silvana Verdini

Biblioteca Comunale dell' **Archiginnasio***, Piazza Galvani 1, I-40124 Bologna Tel: (051) 225509/279731
Dir: Valerio Montanard
Publication: L'Archiginnasio Bollettino della Biblioteca Comunale di Bologna

Archivio Centrale dello Stato, Piazzale degli Archivi, EUR, I-00144 Rome Tel: (06) 5920371
National Archives
Librarian: Eugenia Nieddu Orifici
Publications include: Biblioteca

Biblioteca dell' **Archivio Storico** Civico e Biblioteca Trivulziana*, Castello Sforzesco, I-20121 Milan Tel: (02) 6236, ext 3946/3960/3967
Librarian: Prof Dr Giulia Bologna

Biblioteca Nazionale **Braidense**, Palazzo di Brera, Via Brera 28, I-20121 Milan
Tel: (02) 872376/808345/8053360
Dir: Dr Carlo Carotti

Biblioteca Nazionale **Centrale***, Piazza Cavalleggeri 1, Florence Tel: (055) 244441/2/3
Dir: Dr Anna Lenzuni

Biblioteca Nazionale **Centrale** Vittorio Emanuele II*, Viale Castro Pretorio 105, I-00185 Rome Tel: (06) 4989
Dir: Dr Anna Maria Vichi Giorgetti
Publication: Bollettino delle opere moderne straniere acquisite dalle Biblioteche Pubbliche statali Italiane

Biblioteca Nazionale **Marciana**, Palazzi della Libreria Vecchia e della Zecca, San Marco 7, I-30124 Venice Tel: (041) 5208788
Dir: Dr Gian Albino Ravalli Modoni

Biblioteca Nazionale **Vittorio Emanuele III***, I-80132 Naples (Palazzo Reale) Tel: (081) 407921/402842/425093
Dir: Dr Maria Grazia Malatesta Pasqualitti

Biblioteca **Universitaria***, Largo Porta S Agostino 337, I-41100 Modena Tel: Central (059) 222248; Director 210530
Librarian: Dr Ernesto Milano

Biblioteca Musicale Governativa del **Conservatorio di Musica** S Cecilia*, Via dei Greci 18, Rome Tel: (06) 6784552/12
Librarian: Dr Domenico Carboni

Biblioteca **Estense***, Largo Porta San Agostino 337, I-41100 Modena Tel: Central (059) 222248; Director 230195
Dir: Dr Ernesto Milano

European University Institute Library*, Badia Fiesolana, Via dei Roccettini 5, I-50016 San Domenico di Fiesole, Florence Tel: (055) 477931 Cable Add: Univeur Telex: 571528 Iue
Librarian: Willy Dehennin

Biblioteca Medicea **Laurenziana***, Piazza S Lorenzo 9, I-50123 Florence Tel: (055) 210760/214443
Chief Librarian: Dr Antonietta Morandini

Biblioteca Comunale **Malatestiana***, Piazza Bufalini 1, I-47023 Cesena (Forlì) Tel: (0547) 21297
Librarian: Dr Antonio Brasini

Biblioteca **Riccardiana***, Via dei Ginori 10, I-50129 Florence Tel: (055) 212586/211379
Dir: Dr Maria Prunai Falciani

Università degli Studi di Firenze, Biblioteca della Facolta di Lettere e Filosofia*, Piazza Brunelleschi, I-50121 Florence Tel: (055) 264081
Dir: Dr Tomaso Urso

Library Associations

Associazione Italiana Biblioteche*, CP 2461, I-00100 Rome A-D
Italian Library Association
Chairman: Dr Luigi Crocetti; *Secretary:* Dr Giovanni Lazzari
Publications: Bollettino d'Informazioni; Quaderni del Bollettino d'Informazioni

Associazione Nazionale Archivistica Italiana*, Via di Ponziano 15, I-00152 Rome Tel: (06) 585067
National Association of Italian Archivists
Secretary: Antonio Dentoni-Litta
Publication: Archivi e Cultúra (two a year)

Istituto Centrale per il Catalogo Unico delle Biblioteche Italiane e per le Informazioni Bibliografiche*, Viale Castro Pretorio 105, I-00185 Rome Tel: (06) 4959217
Central Institute of the Union Catalogue of Italian Libraries and Bibliographical Information
Dir: Angela Vinay
Publications: Bibliografia Nazionale Italiana; Manuale di Catalogazione Musicale; Periodici Italiani 1886-1981; Quaderno RICA; Regole Italiane di Catalogazione per Autori; Soggettario per i Cataloghi delle Biblioteche Italiane; Le Edizioni Italiane del XVI sec, Guida alla Catalogazione per Autori delle Stampe, Inventari Non a Stampa de Manoscritti; Bibliografia di Inventari e Cataloghi a Stampa dei Manoscritti; I Emilia Romagna — Il Friuli Venezia Giulia

Istituto Centrale per la Patologia del Libro*, Via Milano 76, I-00184 Rome
Central Institute of Book Pathology
Dir: Dr Maria Di Franco
Publication: Bollettino

Società Italiana di Documentazionen e d'Informazione*, Via Vittoria Colunna 39, I-00139 Rome Tel: (06) 3604841
Italian Association of Documentation and Information
Vice President: Carlo Cya
Publications: Documentazione e Informazione (annual)

Library Reference Books and Journals

Books

Almanàcco dei Bibliotecari Italiani (Almanac of Italian Libraries), Fratelli Palombi SRL, Via del Gracchi 181-185, I-00192 Rome

Annuario Bibliografico per Le Biblioteche (Bibliographical Annual for Libraries), Federation of Italian Public Libraries, c/o La 'Società Umanitaria', Via Daverio 7, I-20122 Milan

Annuario delle Biblioteche Italiane (Italian Library Annual), Fratelli Palombi SRL, Via del Gracchi 181-185, I-00192 Rome

Periodici Italiani 1886-1981 (Italian Periodicals), Istituto Centrale per il Catalogo Unico delle Biblioteche Italiane e per le Informazioni Bibliografiche, Viale Castro Pretoria 105, I-00185 Rome

Regole Italiane di Catalogazione per Autori (Italian Rules of Cataloguing by Author), Istituto Centrale per il Catalogo Unico delle Biblioteche Italiane e per le Informazioni Bibliografiche, Viale Castro Pretorio 105, I-00185 Rome

Journals

Accademie e Biblioteche d'Italia (Academies and Libraries of Italy), Fratelli Palombi SRL, Via del Gracchi 181-185, I-00192 Rome

Archivi e Cultura (Archives and Culture), National Association of Italian Archivists, Via di Ponziano 15, I-00152 Rome

Bollettino d'Informazioni (Information Bulletin), Italian Library Association, CP 2461, I-00100 Rome A-D

Soggettario per i Cataloghi delle Biblioteche Italiane (Subject Collections in Italian Libraries), Istituto Centrale per il Catalogo Unico delle Biblioteche Italiane e per le Informazioni Bibliografiche, Viale Castro Pretorio 105, I-00185 Rome

Literary Associations and Societies

Accademia di Scienze, Lettere ed Arti*, Piazza Indipendenza 17, Palermo
Secretary: Professor Romualdo Giuffrida
Publications: Atti di Lettere e di Scienze; Bollettino Relativo Al Beni Culturali della Sicilia; Memoirs; Supplements

Accademia Ligure di Scienze e Lettere*, Via Balbi 10, I-16126 Genoa
Secretary-General: P Scotti

Accademia Nazionale di Scienze, Lettere ed Arti*, Palazzo Coccapani, Corso Vittorio Emanuele II 59, Modena
President: Professor Antonio Pignedoli
Publications: Atti e Memorie

Accademia Petrarca di Lettere, Arti e Scienze*, Via dell'Orto, Arezzo
Secretary: Dr Guido Goti
Publication: Atti e Memorie della Accademia, Studi Petrarcheschi

Accademia Virgiliana di Scienze, Lettere ed Arti di Mantova*, Via Accademia 47, I-46100 Mantua Tel: (0376) 320314
President: Prof Eros Benedini
Librarian: Mons Luigi Bosio
Secretary: Comm G Amadei
Publications: Atti di Convegni tenuti presso l'Accademia Virgiliana; Atti e Memorie NS (annual)

Cenacolo di Studi Storico, Artistico, Letterari, Via Ammiraglio Gravina 95, I-90139 Palermo
President: Dr Tommaso Romano; *Secretary:* Prof Gaetano Arnò
Publication: Quaderni

Empire International Club, Via Ammiraglio Gravina 95, I-90139 Palermo
Tel: (091) 323699

President: Prof Dr Salvatore Barberi;
Secretary-General: Prof Dr Tommaso Romano
Publication: Quaderni dell'Empire

Istituto Lombardo Accademia di Scienze e Lettere, Via Brera 28, I-20121 Milan
President: Prof G Bolognesi

Keats-Shelley Memorial Association, Piazza di Spagna 26, Rome
Dir: Sir Joseph Cheyne
Publications: Bulletin, Journal, A Room in Rome

P E N International Centre*, c/o Piazzo Belgiojoso 2, I-20123 Milan
President: Mario Soldati; *Secretary:* La Contessa Piovene

Società Dante Alighieri*, Palazzo di Firenze, Piazza Firenze 27, I-00186 Rome
Tel: (06) 6794638
Secretary-General: G Cota
Publication: Pagine della Dante (quarterly)
For the teaching and diffusion of Italian language and culture throughout the world

Società Dantesca Italiana, Via dell'Arte della Lana 1, I-50123 Florence
President: Prof Dr Francesco Mazzoni;
Librarian: Dr Gabriella Pomaro
Publications: Studi Danteschi, Quaderni degli Studi Danteschi, Edizione Nazionale delle Opere di Dante Alighieri
(Library open to public)

Literary Periodicals

Belfagor, Casa Editrice Leo S Olschki, Viuzzo del Pozzetto, I-50126 Florence

Bibliofilia (Bibliophily), Casa Editrice Leo S Olschki, Viuzzo del Pozzetto, I-50126 Florence
Text in English, French, German and Italian

Il giornale storico della letteratura italiana (Historical Journal of Italian Literature), Loescher Editore SpA, Via Vittorio Amedeo II 18, I-10121 Turin

Italia Che Scrive, Via dei Banchi Vecchi 61, Rome

Lettere Italiane (Italian Letters), Viuzzo del Pozzetto (Viale Europa), I-50126 Florence

Libri Paese Sera, Società Editrice 'Il Rinnovamento', Via dei Taurini 19, I-00185 Rome

Nuòva Corrènte (New Current), Via Lattuada 26, Milan
Text in several languages

Paideia, Via Corsica 58m, I-25100 Brescia
Literary review with bibliographical information; text in English, French, German and Italian

Penarete-Letture d'Italia (Readings from Italy), Via Beruto 7, I-20131 Milan

Pròve di Letteratura (Examinations of Literature), Nino Palumbo, Via Ai Castagneti 4, San Michele di Pagana, Rapallo

Rassegna della Letteratura Italiana (Review of Italian Literature), Sansoni Editore Nuova, Via Varchi 47, I-50132 Florence

Revue des Etudes italiennes, Librairie Marcel Didier SA, 15 rue Cujas, F-75005 Paris, France

Rivista di Letteratura Moderne e Comparate (Review of Modern and Comparative Literature), Sansoni Editore Nuova, Via Varchi 47, I-50132 Florence
Text in English, French and Italian

Uomini e libri (Men and Books), Emme Edizioni, Via San Maurilio 13, I-20123 Milan

Literary Prizes

Bagutta Prize*
Founded in 1927 for the best book of the year, given for several literary forms including the novel and poetry. 5,100,000 lire, awarded annually. Enquiries to Bagutta Restaurant, Via Bagutta 14, Milan

Campiello Prize
Instituted in 1963 and promoted by the seven industrial association founder members of Fondazione Campiello. For a previously unpublished work of fiction. Annual award of 16,000,000 lire. The winner in 1986 was Alberto Ongaro for *La partita* (Longanesi). Enquiries to Ca' Mocenigo Gambara, Secretariat of the Campiello Prize, Accademia 1056, Venice

Strega Award
Founded in 1947 by Maria Bellonci and Guido Alberti for a work of fiction. The winner in 1986 was Maria Bellonci for *Rinascimento privato* (Arnoldo Mondadori). Enquiries to Via Fratelli Ruspoli 2, Rome

Viareggio Prizes
Founded in 1929, since 1967 the annual award has been divided into three sections: fiction, non-fiction and poetry. Sometimes given to foreign writers and poets. 10,000,000 lire. In 1986 the winners were (fiction) Marisa Volpi for *Il maestro della betulla* (Vallecchi); (non-fiction) Giorgio Candeloro for *Storia dell'Italia Moderna* (Giangiacomo Feltrinelli); (poetry) Mario Socrate for *Il punto di vista* (Garzanti). Enquiries to Gabriella Sobrino, Premio Viareggio, Via Francesco Borgatti 25, I-00191 Rome

Olga **Visentini** Prize*
For the best book for young people. 1,500,000 lire. Awarded biennially. Enquiries to Olga Visentini Foundation, Cerea, Verona

Translation Agencies and Associations

A A B I T T I (Associazione Anna Bonanome Interpreti Traduttori Trascrittori Italiani)*, Via Acherusio 44, I-00199 Rome Tel: (06) 8389684/8393457
Italian Association of Translators and Interpreters
Secretary: Anna Bonanome-Via

A N I T I (Associazione Nazionale Italiana Traduttori ed Interpreti), Via Lambrate 10, I-20131 Milan Tel: (02) 2870336
National Association for Translators and Interpreters
Chairman: Bonda Ajmone; *Secretary General:* Prof Gustavo Dresbach

Eulama SRL, Via Torino 135, I-00184 Rome Tel: (06) 460636 Cable Add: Eularom Telex: 620086 Eulama I
Also Literary Agent (qqv)

Natoli and Stefan Literary Agency*, Galleria Buenos Aires 14, I-20124 Milan
Manager: G Natoli
Also Literary Agent (qv)

Ivory Coast

General Information

Language: French
Religion: 65% traditional, 23% Islamic, 12% Christian
Population: 10 million
Bank Hours: 0800-1200, 1500-1900 Monday-Friday
Shop Hours: 0800-1200, 1530-1830 or 1900 Monday-Friday; 0800-1200, 1430-1730 Saturday
Currency: CFA franc
Export/Import Information: Member of West African Economic Community. No tariff on books; single copies free but most advertising subject to customs duty, fiscal duty and VAT. No import licences required for imports from EEC or Franc Zone
Copyright: Berne, Florence (see International section)

Book Trade Reference Journal

Bibliographie de la Côte-d'Ivoire, Bibliothèque de l'Université nationale de Côte d'Ivoire, 08 BP 859, Abidjan 08
The national bibliography, published annually in two volumes since 1969

Publishers

Centre d'Edition et de Diffusion africaines (CEDA), 04 BP 541, Abidjan 04 Plateau Tel: 222055/228137/326002 Telex: 22451 Ceda Ci
Man Dir: Venance Kacou; *Editorial Dir:* Christian Lescure
Subjects: General Non-fiction, Biography, History, Africana, Philosophy, Reference, Religion, Juveniles, Law, Paperbacks, General & Social Science, Secondary & Primary Textbooks
Bookshop: See under Major Booksellers (qv)
Miscellaneous: Distributors on behalf of INADES, the National University of the Ivory Coast and the Bibliothèque nationale

Centre de Publications Evangeliques*, 08 BP 900, Abidjan 08 Tel: 444805
Dir: Marjorie Shelley; *Administrator, Sales:* Jacques Blocher; *Administrator, Publicity:* E S Emmett
Subjects: General Non-fiction, Religion, Christian Tracts, Paperbacks, Periodicals for adults and children
Founded: 1970

Government Printer*, Imprimerie nationale, BP V87, Abidjan

I N A D E S — Edition (Institut africain pour le développement économique et social), 08 BP 8, Abidjan 08 Tel: 441594
Man Dir, Editorial: Raymond Deniel; *Sales:* Pierre Bayala
Subjects: African studies, Philosophy, Religion, Economics, Agriculture, Sociology, Essays
Founded: 1975

Les **Nouvelles Editions Africaines**+*, 01 BP 3525, Abidjan 01 (Located at: 1 blvd de Marseille, Abidjan 01) Tel: 321251/321622 Telex: 22564 Nea CI
Dir General: Mrs K L Liguer-Laubhouet
Parent Company: Les Nouvelles Editions Africaines, Senegal (qv)
Associate Company: Les Nouvelles Editions Africaines, Togo (qv)

Subjects: Bibliography, Fiction, Poetry, Theatre, Religion, Art, Juveniles, History, Textbooks
Founded: 1972
ISBN Publisher's Prefix: 2-7236

Université d'Abidjan, see Université nationale de Côte d'Ivoire

Université nationale de Côte d'Ivoire*, Secretariat general aux Publications, 01 BP V34, Abidjan 01 Tel: (225) 440859/441285 Cable Add: Rectuniv Abidjan Telex: 26138 Rectu Ci
Publications Dir: Gilles Vilasco
Subjects: General Non-fiction, History, Africana, Reference, Law, Medicine, General & Social Science, Economics, Geography, Linguistics, Sociology, Periodicals
Founded: 1964
ISBN Publisher's Prefix: 2-7166

Major Booksellers

Librairie **Carrefour**, 08 BP 326, Abidjan 08 (Located at: 22 blvd de France, Abidjan) Tel: 442370 Telex: 28133
Manager: Monique Barnet

Centre d'Edition et de Diffusion africaines, 04 BP 541, Abidjan 04 Tel: 222055/228137/326002
Manager: Venance Kacou
Also Publisher (qv)

Librairie de **France**, Raoul Barnoin, ave Chardy, 01 BP 228, Abidjan Tel: 321518 Cable Add: Lfcessci Telex: 22323

Maison des Livres*, 23 blvd de la République, BP 4645, Abidjan Tel: 322887

Librairie **Villepastour**, 01 BP 2461, Abidjan 01 (Located at: Rue de la Paix Marcory, Abidjan) Tel: 353352/355117 Telex: 42454 Vip Ci
Manager: J Villepastour

Major Libraries

Archives Nationales de Côte d'Ivoire, BP V126, Abidjan Tel: 327578

Bibliothèque centrale de la Côte d'Ivoire*, BP 6243, Abidjan-Treichville Tel: 227536
Librarian: Michel Amoikoy

Bibliothèque municipale*, BP 24, Plateau, Abidjan

Bibliothèque nationale, BP V180, Abidjan Tel: 323872
Librarian: Odette Gnahore

Bibliothèque de l'Université nationale de Côte d'Ivoire*, 08 BP 859, Abidjan 08 Tel: 439000 ext 3393 Telex: 469 Rectuniv
Dir: Francoise N'Goran
Publications include: Annales de l'Université d'Abidjan; Bibliographie de la Côte d'Ivoire

Centre culturel américain, Bibliothèque*, 01 BP 1866, Abidjan 01

Centre culturel français, Bibliothèque*, 01 BP 3995, Abidjan 01 Tel: 321599 Telex: 23699 Am Fra

I N A D E S (Institut africain pour le Développement économique et social) Documentation*, 08 BP 8, Abidjan 08 Tel: 441594
Librarian: Yves Morel
Publications: Le Fichier-Afrique (bi-monthly); bibliographies

Library Associations

Association pour le Développement de la Documentation, des Bibliothèques et Archives de la Côte d'Ivoire (ADBACI)*, c/o Bibliothèque Nationale, BP V180, Abidjan
Secretary General: Cangah Guy

Literary Associations and Societies

Centre de **P E N** de Côte d'Ivoire*, 01 BP 1354, Abidjan 01
President: Le Gouverneur Guy Nairay;
Secretary: L M A Kanie

Literary Periodical

Revue de littérature de l'esthétique nègre-africaines, Les Nouvelles Editions Africaines, 01 BP 3525, Abidjan 01

Literary Prize

Prix Littéraire Mobil*
First sponsored 1980. A prize of CFA 250,000 for an outstanding book by an author from the Ivory Coast (unpublished manuscripts also considered). The sponsors undertake the publication of the prize-winning book in English translation. Enquiries to Mobil Oil Cote d'Ivoire, 13 Impasse Paris-Village, 01 BP 1777, Abidjan 01

Jamaica

General Information

Language: English
Religion: Predominantly Protestant
Population: 2.3 million
Bank Hours: 0900-1400 Monday-Thursday; 0900-1200, 1430-1700 Friday
Shop Hours: Downtown Kingston: 0900-1600 Monday and Tuesday, Thursday-Saturday; 0900-1200 Wednesday. Other areas: 0900-1700, with early closing Thursday
Currency: 100 cents = 1 Jamaican dollar
Export/Import Information: No tariff on books, but advertising matter dutied. No import licence required for books; no obscene literature permitted. Exchange restrictions
Copyright: No copyright conventions signed

Book Trade Organizations

Booksellers' Association of Jamaica*, c/o Sangster's Book Stores Ltd, 101 Water Lane, Kingston Tel: 9223640
Secretary: Keith Shervington

University of the West Indies Publishers Association*, c/o Mrs Margaret Mendes, PO Box 42, Kingston 7 Tel: 9271201

Book Trade Reference Books and Journals

Book

Book Production in Jamaica: A Select List of Jamaican Publications, Jamaica Library Service, PO Box 58, Kingston 5

Journal

Jamaican National Bibliography, National Library of Jamaica, PO Box 823, 12 East St, Kingston

Publishers

Caribbean Universities Press Jamaica Ltd*, PO Box 83, Kingston 7 (Located at: 18 Melmac Ave, Kingston 5) Tel: 9262628
Man Dir: Carmen Latty
Subjects: Academic, Education (Spanish and English)

Government Printing Office*, 77 Duke St, Kingston
Subject: Law

Heinemann Educational Books (Caribbean) Ltd+, 175 Mountain View Ave, Kingston 6 Tel: 9275659/9278317 Cable Add: Hebooks Kingston Telex: Jmtl Nkn 2441/2 Fax: 9274666
Chief Executive: Ian Randle; *Editorial:* Jennifer Anderson; *Sales:* Dianne Wedderburn
Parent Company: The Heinemann Group of Publishers Ltd, UK (qv)
Subjects: Educational, General
1985: 6 titles *Founded:* 1976
ISBN Publisher's Prefix: 976-605

Institute of Jamaica Publications*, 2a Suthermere Rd, Kingston 10 Tel: 9294785/6
Man Dir: Olive Senior
Subjects: Cultural, Historical, Scientific
Founded: 1967

Jamaica Publishing House Ltd, 97 Church St, Kingston Tel: 9221385/7 Cable Add: Japub
Chairman: Mrs Ellorine Walker; *Acting Manager:* Leo A Oakley
Parent Company: Jamaica Teachers' Association
Subjects: Educational, Biography, Business, English language and literature, Geography, Geology, History, Home Economics, Languages, Mathematics, Music, Psychology, Social Sciences
Founded: 1969

Kingston Publishers Ltd+, 1A Norwood Ave, Kingston 5 Tel: 9260042/9260091 Cable Add: Kingbooks Telex: Fitzgram 2293
Warehouse: 7 Norman Rd, Kingston Tel: 9284359
Chairman: L M J Henry
Founded: 1972

Longman Jamaica Ltd*, PO Box 489, Kingston 10 (Located at: 95 Newport Blvd, Newport West, Kingston) Tel: 9235193 Cable Add: Longjam Kingston
Man Dir: Shirley Y Carby; *Editor, Production:* Dorothy Noel; *Sales, Publicity:* Lancelot Henry; *Rights & Permissions:* Dorothy Noel, Shirley Carby
Parent Company: Longman Group Ltd, UK (qv)
Subjects: Primary and Secondary Textbooks, Caribbean Geography for Secondary and Tertiary levels
Founded: 1982
ISBN Publisher's Prefix: 976-8010

Major Booksellers

Bolivar Bookshop*, 1D Grove Rd, Kingston 10 Tel: 9268799
Owner: Hugh Dunphy

Henderson's Book Store*, 27 St James St, Montego Bay

Kingston Bookshop Ltd, 70b King St, Kingston Tel: 9224056 Cable Add: Futurity Jamaica
Manager: S A R Fuller

Literary Supplies*, 38 Mandeville Plaza, Mandeville

Novelty Trading Co*, 53 Hanover St, Kingston
Manager: Tony Bridge

Readers' Book Shop*, Liguanea Plaza, 134 Old Hope Rd, Kingston 6

Sangster's Book Stores Ltd, PO Box 366, Kingston (Located at: 101 Water Lane, Kingston) Tel: 9223640
Man Dir: S Kumaraswamy
Also: 97 Harbour St, Kingston
Owned by: Gleaner Co Ltd

Shadeed's Educational & General Supplies Ltd*, 14 French St, Spanish Town
Manager: Leonora Newman

Stationery & Educational Book Centre Ltd*, Silver Slipper Plaza, Kingston 5

Teachers' Book Centre Ltd*, 95 Church St, Kingston Tel: 924716/923843

Times Stores Ltd, 8 King St, Kingston
Manager: Lawrence Garvey

Major Libraries

Jamaica Archives*, Spanish Town

Jamaica Library Service*, PO Box 58, Kingston 5 (Located at: 2 Tom Redcam Dr, Kingston) Tel: 9263310
Dir: Sybil Iton
Publications include: Book production in Jamaica: a select list of Jamaican publications; Jamaica Poetry: a checklist, slavery to the present

National Library of Jamaica*, PO Box 823, Kingston (Located at: 12 East St, Kingston) Tel: 9220620 Cable Add: Nalijam
Dir: Stephney Ferguson
Publications: The Gleaner Index (quarterly index to the Daily Gleaner of Jamaica); Jamaican National Bibliography

University of the West Indies Library*, Mona, Kingston 7 Tel: Librarian 9276661 ext 294; Reference Desk 9276661 ext 296 or 9270923 Cable Add: Univers Telex: 2123
Librarian: Mrs A Jefferson

Library Association

Jamaica Library Association*, PO Box 58, Kingston 5
Honorary Secretary: Valda Adeyiga
Publications: Bulletin (annually), JLA News (quarterly)

Library Reference Journal

Bulletin, Jamaica Library Association, PO Box 58, Kingston 5

Literary Associations and Societies

P E N Club*, 1 Norbrook Rd, Apt 4, Kingston 8
Secretary: George Clough

Japan

General Information

Language: Japanese
Religion: Buddhist and Shinto
Population: 117 million
Bank Hours: 0900-1500 Monday-Friday; 0900-1200 Saturday
Shop Hours: No fixed weekly holiday; department stores usually close Wednesday or Thursday, others Sunday. Generally department store hours are 1000-1800
Currency: yen
Export/Import Information: No tariff on books and advertising matter. Only declaration by importer to a foreign exchange bank is required
Copyright: UCC, Berne, Florence (see International section)

Book Trade Organizations

Antiquarian Booksellers' Association of Japan, 29 San-Ei-Cho, Shinjuku-ku, Tokyo 160 Tel: (03) 3595519 Cable Add: Yushodo Tokyo Telex: 02324136
President: Kenichiro Nakao

Copyright Research Institute*, 2-12-8 Shimbashi, Minato-ku, Tokyo

Japan Book Importers Association, Room 612, Aizawa Bldg, 20-3 Nihonbashi 1-chome, Chuo-ku, Tokyo 103 Tel: (03) 2716901
Secretary: Mitsuo Shibata
Publication: JBIA Directory (annual)

Japan Book Publishers Association*, 6 Fukuro-machi, Shinjuku-ku, Tokyo 162 Tel: (03) 2681301 Cable Add: Shosekikyo Tokyo
President: Toshiyuki Hattori; *Executive Dir:* Sadaya Murayama; *Secretary:* Masaaki Shigehisa
Publications: Japanese Books in Print; The Catalogue of Books in the Near Future; Bulletin of the Japanese Book Publishers Association

Japan I S B N Agency*, Japan Publishers Bldg, 6 Fukuro-machi, Shinjuku-ku, Tokyo 162 Tel: (03) 2684494
Secretary-General: Naotoshi Matsudaira

Nihon Shoten Kumiai Rengokai, 1-2 Kanda Surugadai, Chiyoda-ku, Tokyo 101 Tel: (03) 2940388
Japan Booksellers' Federation
Publications: Kodomonohon Long-seller-list (Children's Books: A List of Best Sellers); Zenkoku Shoten Meibo (Address Book of Japan Booksellers); Zenkoku Shoten Shinbun (Newspaper for booksellers)

Publishers' Association for Cultural Exchange, 1-2-1 Sarugaku-cho, Chiyoda-ku, Tokyo 101 Tel: (03) 2915685 Cable Add: Publishersasso Fax: (03) 2333645
President: Tatsuro Matsumae; *Man Dir:* Shoichi Nakajima
European Representation: Euro-Japanische Gesellschaft eV, c/o Creative Reise GmbH, Rossmarkt 21, D-6000 Frankfurt, Federal Republic of Germany
Publications: Contemporary Japanese Books; Guide to Publishers and Related Industries in Japan; Guide to Foreign Publishers

Standard Book Numbering Agency, see Japan ISBN Agency

Textbook Publishers' Association of Japan (Kyokasho Kyokai)*, 20-2 Honshiocho Shinjuku-ku, Tokyo 160
Secretary: Masae Kusaka

Women Writers' Association*, 17 Yanaka-Shinizucho, Daito-ku, Tokyo

Book Trade Reference Books and Journals

Books

Contemporary Japanese Books, Publishers' Association for Cultural Exchange, 1-2-1 Sarugaku-cho, Chiyoda-ku, Tokyo 101

Directory of Japanese Publishing and Bookselling, British Book and Educational Display Centre, Iwanami Jimbo-Cho Bldg, 1 Jimbo 2 2-chome, Kanda, Chiyoda-ku, Tokyo 101

Guide to Foreign Publishers, Publishers' Association for Cultural Exchange, 1-2-1 Sarugaku-cho, Chiyoda-ku, Tokyo 101

Journals

Biblia, Tenri University Press, Tenri Central Library, Tenri City, Nara
Text in Japanese

Bulletin of the Japanese Book Publishers Association, 6 Fukuro-machi, Shinjuku-ku, Tokyo 162

The Catalogue of Books in the Near Future, Japan Book Publishers Association, 6 Fukuro-machi, Shinjuku-ku, Tokyo 162

A Comprehensive Bibliography of Japanese Periodicals, The Shuppan News Co Ltd, 3-2-4 Misaki-cho, Chiyoda-ku, Tokyo 101

A Comprehensive Catalogue of Collected Works, Publishers in Japan, The Shuppan News Co Ltd, 3-2-4 Misaki-cho, Chiyoda-ku, Tokyo 101

Guide to Publishers and Related Industries in Japan, Publishers' Association for Cultural Exchange, 1-2-1 Sarugaku-cho, Chiyoda-ku, Tokyo 101

Japan Book News, Publishing Research Associates, c/o Kyowa Book Co, Kanda, PO Box 173, Tokyo

Japanese Books in Print, Japan Book Publishers Association, 6 Fukuro-machi, Shinjuku-ku, Tokyo 162

Japanese National Bibliography, National Diet Library, 1-10-1 Nagata-cho, Chiyoda-ku, Tokyo 100
Weekly and quarterly index

Japanese Publications News and Reviews, 3-2-4 Misaki-cho, Chiyoda-ku, Tokyo

Newsletter, Tokyo Book Development Centre, 6 Fukuro-machi, Shinjuku-ku, Tokyo

Seihon Kai, Tokyodo Co Ltd, 3-5 Kanda-Nishiki-cho, Chiyoda-ku, Tokyo
Text in Japanese

Shinkan Nyusu (News of New Books), Tokyo Shuppan Hanbai Co Ltd, 53 Higashigoken-cho, Shinjuku-ku, Tokyo

256 JAPAN

Shuppan Nenkan, Shuppan Nyusu-sha, Tokyo
Annual information on publishing for the previous year

Shuppan Nyusu (Publishers' News) (three times a month), Shuppan Nyusu-sha, 2-4 Misaki-cho 3-chome, Chiyoda-ku, Tokyo 101

Zen Nihon Shuppanbutsu Somokuroku, see Japanese National Bibliography

Zenkoku Shoten Meibo (Address Book of Japanese Booksellers), Japan Booksellers' Federation, 1-2 Kanda Surugadai, Chiyoda-ku, Tokyo 101

Publishers

A D A Edita Tokyo Co Ltd, 3-12-14 Sendagaya, Shibuya-ku, Tokyo 151 Tel: (03) 4031581
Director: Yukio Futagawa; *Sales Manager:* Takato Kawahara
Subject: Architecture
Founded: 1972

Addison-Wesley Publishers Japan Ltd*, Nichibo Bldg, 1-2-2 Sarugaku-cho, Chiyoda-ku, Tokyo 101
Parent Company: Addison-Wesley Publishing Co Inc, Reading, MA 01867, USA
Associate Companies: Addison-Wesley (S) Pte Ltd, Singapore (qv); Addison-Wesley Publishers Ltd, UK (qv)

Akane Shobo Co Ltd*, 3-2-1 Nishikanda, Chiyoda-ku, Tokyo Tel: (03) 2630641
President: Mutsuto Okamoto; *Editor-in-Chief:* Yoshiaki Ushiro
Subjects: Juveniles, Science, Literature, Picture Books

Akita Shoten Publishing Co Ltd*, 10-8 Iidabashi 2-chome, Chiyoda-ku, Tokyo 102 Tel: (03) 2647011
President: Sadami Akita; *Editorial:* Nobumichi Akutsu, Taizo Kabemura; *Sales:* Toshimichi Okubo; *Foreign Rights:* Noriyoshi Oda
Subjects: General Subjects, Juveniles, History, Social Science, Literature, Magazines
Founded: 1948

Aoki Shoten Co Ltd*, 60 Kanda Jimbo-cho 1-chome, Chiyoda-ku, Tokyo 101 Tel: (03) 2920481
President: Noboru Yamane; *Foreign Trade:* Kiyoshi Furukawa; *Foreign Rights:* Toyoichi Eguchi
Subject: Social Science
Founded: 1947

Asakura Publishing Co Ltd, 6-29 Shin-Ogawa machi, Shinjuku-ku, Tokyo 162 Tel: (03) 2600141
President: Kunizo Asakura; *Foreign Trade:* Takaaki Yano; *Foreign Rights:* Yutaka Saito
Subjects: Medicine, Natural Science, Engineering, Industry, History, Geography, Pedagogy, Sociology
Founded: 1929

Baifukan Co Ltd, 3-12 Kudan-Minami 4-chome, Chiyoda-ku, Tokyo 102 Tel: (03) 2625256
Chairman: Kenji Yamamoto; *President, Sales, Publicity:* Itaru Yamamoto; *Editorial:* Itaru Yamamoto, Tsuyoshi Nohara, Masayuki Gotou; *Production:* Fumio Shigematu; *Rights & Permissions:* Tsuyoshi Nohara
Subjects: Mathematics, Statistics, Computer Science, Physics, Chemistry, Biology, Engineering, Psychology, Sociology

1985: 79 titles *Founded:* 1924
ISBN Publisher's Prefix: 4-563

Baseball Magazine-Sha Co Ltd*, 3-10-10 Misaki-cho, Chiyoda-ku, Tokyo 101 Tel: (03) 2380081 Telex: J29865 Bbm
President: Tsuneo Ikeda; *Vice-President:* Ikuo Ikeda
Branch Offs: Tokuma Bldg, 6-16 Nozaki-cho, Kita-ku, Osaka-shi, Osaka Tel: (06) 3156141/3156144; 15 rue des Abbesses, F-75018 Paris, France Tel: (1) 42523165
Subjects: Sports, Physical Education, Psychology, History, Fitness
Founded: 1946
ISBN Publisher's Prefix: 4-583

Bijutsu Shuppan-Sha, Inaoka Bldg, 2-36 Kanda, Jinbo-cho, Chiyoda-ku, Tokyo Tel: (03) 2342151 Cable Add: Fineart Book Tokyo
President: Atsushi Oshita; *Sales Manager:* Shonosuke Kaizu
Subsidiary Company: Bijutsu Shuppan Design Centre, 2-19 Ichigaya Honmura-cho, Shinjuku-ku, Tokyo 162
Subjects: Art, Architecture, Design
Founded: 1905

Bungeishunju Ltd*, 3-23 Kioi-cho, Chiyoda-ku, Tokyo 102 Tel: (03) 2651211
President: Goro Kanbayashi; *Foreign Trade:* Ikuo Sumi; *Foreign Rights:* Tatsuo Nishinaga
Subjects: General Fiction and Non-fiction, Philosophy, Religion, History, Geography, Social Science, Art, Economics, Politics, Natural Science, Industry, Language, Literature, High- and Low-priced Paperbacks
1985: 306 titles *Founded:* 1922

Business Center for Academic Societies Japan*, 16-3 Hongo 6-chome, Bunkyo-ku, Tokyo 113 Tel: (03) 8175811 Cable Add: Hongobucas Telex: 02722268 Bcjsp J
Also: 4-16 Yayoi 2-chome, Bunkyo-ku, Tokyo 113 Tel: (03) 8151903; 40-14 Hongo 2-chome, Bunkyo-ku, Tokyo 113 Tel: (03) 8175831
Director-General: J Kondo; *Man Dir, Rights & Permissions:* T Yamada; *Marketing Dir, Publicity:* M Ebihara; *Production:* B Todoroki
Associate Companies: Japan Scientific Societies Press, 2-10 Hongo 6-chome, Bunkyo-ku, Tokyo 113; Center for Academic Publications Japan (qv)
Subjects: Academic, all Sciences
1985: 120 titles (group) *Founded:* 1971
ISBN Publisher's Prefixes: 4-930813, 4-7622, 4-905648

Center for Academic Publications Japan*, 4-16 Yayoi 2-chome, Bunkyo-ku, Tokyo 113 Tel: (03) 8175821 Fax: (03) 8175820
Man Dir: T Ohmi
Orders to: Business Center for Academic Societies Japan (at above address)
Associate Company: Japan Scientific Societies Press, 2-10 Hongo 6-chome, Bunkyo-ku, Tokyo 113
Founded: 1972

Chikuma Shobo Publishing Co Ltd, 8 Kanda Ogawamachi 2-chome, Chiyoda-ku, Tokyo 101-91 Tel: (03) 2917651
Administrator: Hidesato Sekine; *Editorial, Rights & Permissions:* Masahiko Morimoto; *Sales, Publicity:* Akio Kikuchi; *Production:* Kazuyoshi Tsunoda
Subjects: General Fiction, Belles Lettres, Poetry, Biography, History, Religion, Music, Art, Philosophy, Juveniles, High-priced Paperbacks, Psychology, General & Social Science, Secondary Textbooks
Founded: 1940

Child Honsha Co Ltd+*, 24-21 Koishikawa 5-chome, Bunkyo-ku, Tokyo 112 Tel: (03) 8133781
President: Ikuzoh Shibasaki; *Editorial, Foreign Rights:* Yasuyuki Ouchi; *Sales, Publicity:* Hirosato Okada; *Foreign Trade:* Katsuharu Mibu; *Production:* Fumio Moromachi; *Rights & Permissions:* Kotaro Ohashi
Associate Company: Kyodo Printing Co Ltd
Subsidiary Companies: Basic Inc; Hisakata Child Co Ltd; Mikawa Child Co Ltd
Subjects: Juveniles, Education
Founded: 1930

Chuo-Tosho Co Ltd+, Motoseiganji-sagaru, Aburanokoji-dori, Kamigyo-ku, Kyoto 602 Tel: (075) 4412174
Chief Executive: Toshihiko Hirokou; *Editorial, Publicity, Rights & Permissions:* Takanori Ikeda; *Sales:* Tetsuo Hattori; *Production:* Tsuneo Takeuchi
Subjects: Secondary Textbooks, Japanese, English
Founded: 1950

Chuokoron-Sha Inc*, 2-8-7 Kyobashi, Chuo-ku, Tokyo 104 Tel: (03) 5631261 Cable Add: Chuokoron Tokyo Telex: J32505 Chuokor
President: Hoji Shimanaka; *Man Dir:* Shigeru Takanashi; *International Section Dir:* Yukio Shimanaka
Subjects: General Fiction, Belles Lettres, History, Art, Philosophy, Low-priced Paperbacks, Politics, Economics, Natural Science, Social Science, Religion, Periodicals
Founded: 1886

Corona Publishing Co Ltd*, 46-10 Sengoku 4-chome, Bunkyo-ku, Tokyo 112 Tel: (03) 9413131
President: Tatsumi Gorai; *Editorial Dirs:* Hiroshi Nakamata, Sumio Hatano
Subjects: Natural Science, Technology
1985: 60 titles *Founded:* 1927

Daiichi Shuppan Co Ltd*, 1-39 Kanda Jimbo-cho, Chiyoda-ku, Tokyo 101 Tel: (03) 2914576
President: Gen Kurita; *Foreign Trade and Foreign Rights Executive:* Yoshiya Takamatsu
Subjects: Medicine, Natural Science, Nutrition, Magazines
Founded: 1945

Diamond Inc*, 1-4-2 Kasumigaseki, Chiyoda-ku, Tokyo Tel: (03) 5046381 Cable Add: Keizaidia Tokyo
President: Yuzuru Kawashima; *Editorial:* Mineo Iwamochi; *Sales:* Kazuya Tsubaki; *Production:* Senji Nakajima; *Publicity:* Gunpei Sakai; *Rights & Permissions:* Katsuyoshi Saito
Subsidiary Companies: Diamond (weekly economics journal); Diamond Agency; Diamond Big; Diamond Fund; Diamond Graphics; Diamond Service; President K K
Branch Off: Osaka
Subjects: Non-fiction, Business, Economics, Management, Finance, Marketing
Founded: 1913

Elsevier Science Publishers (Japan), 28-1 Yushima 3-chome, Bunkyo-ku, Tokyo 113 Tel: (03) 8360810 Cable Add: Elsevier Telex: 02657617
Sales and editorial services office of Elsevier Science Publishers BV, Netherlands (qv)

Froebel-Kan Co Ltd*, 3-1 Kanda Ogawa-cho, Chiyoda-ku, Tokyo 101 Tel: (03) 2927781/9 Cable Add: Froebelkan Tokyo Telex: J24907
President: Yuji Okayasu; *International Division:* Harry H Idichi (General

Manager); Tony S Endo (Manager)
Associate Company: Toppan Co (S) Pte Ltd, Singapore (qv)
Subjects: Juveniles, Educational Materials
Founded: 1907

Fukuinkan Shoten Publishers Inc+*, 6-3 Honkomagome 6-chome, Bunkyo-ku, Tokyo 113 Tel: (03) 9420032 Cable Add: Fukuinkanshoten Tokyo Telex: J33597 Aab Forchild
Chairman: Tadashi Matsui; *President:* Katsumi Sato; *Editorial:* Ken Minakuchi; *Sales:* Toyoichiro Yonetani; *International Dept:* Tamotsu Hozumi
Subjects: Children's books
Book Club: Fukuinkan Ehon Library
1985: 120 titles *Founded:* 1952
ISBN Publisher's Prefix: 4-8340

Fuzambo Publishing Co*, 1-3 Kanda Jimbo-cho, Chiyoda-ku, Tokyo 101 Tel: (03) 2912171
President: Kiichi Sakamoto
Subjects: General Works, Philosophy & Religion, Social Sciences, History, Geography, Law, Literature, Language, Art, Juveniles, Dictionaries
Founded: 1886

Gakken Co Ltd+, 4-40-5 Kami-ikedai, Ohta-ku, Tokyo 145 Tel: (03) 7268111 Cable Add: Gakkencol Tokyo Telex: Gakkenco J26389
President: Hiroshi Furuoka; *Foreign Affairs Executive:* Ryu Tanaka; *Foreign Rights:* Yasushi Tochigi
Subjects: General Fiction, Fine Arts, Encyclopaedias, Dictionaries, Juveniles, Children's Picture Books, Illustrated Books, History, Natural and Social Science, Japanese, Languages, Music, Textbooks, Reference, Education, Educational Materials, Audiovisual Aids, Magazines, Sports, Hobbies
1985: 350 titles *1986:* 350 titles *Founded:* 1946

Gakuseisha Publishing Co Ltd*, 27-14 Shikahama 3-chome, Adachi-ku, Tokyo 123 Tel: (03) 8573031
President: Masami Tsuruoka; *Foreign Rights Executive:* Teruo Ohtsu
Subjects: Philosophy, Religion, Ancient History, Archaeology, Geography, Law, Sociology, Language, Literature, Juvenile, Reference
1985: 50 titles *Founded:* 1952

Hakusui-Sha Co Ltd*, 3-24 Kanda-Ogawa-machi, Chiyoda-ku, Tokyo 101 Tel: (03) 2917811 Cable Add: Hakusuisha Tokyo
President: Takashi Takahashi; *Foreign Trade Executive:* Souichi Kobayashi; *Foreign Rights Executive:* Kazuaki Fujiwara
Subjects: Dictionaries, Languages, Fiction, Non-fiction, Literature, Drama, Music, Art, Philosophy
Founded: 1915

Hakuyu-Sha*, 9 Ageba-cho, Shinjuku-ku, Tokyo 162 Tel: (03) 2688271
Man Dir: Eiji Takamori; *Foreign Trade Executive:* Montaro Ono; *Publicity & Advertising:* Kazuya Baba; *Foreign Rights:* Eiji Takamori
Subjects: Dictionaries, Natural Science, Industry
Founded: 1948

Hayakawa Publishing Inc*, 2-2 Kanda-Tacho, Chiyoda-ku, Tokyo 101 Tel: (03) 2523111 Cable Add: Hayakawa Tokyo Telex: 02222331 Books J Fax: (03) 2541550
President, Chief Executive Officer: Kiyoshi Hayakawa; *Executive Vice-President, Foreign Trade & Rights Executive:* Hiroshi Hayakawa
Subjects: General Fiction, Paperbacks, Foreign Fiction, Non-fiction, History, Biography, Autobiography, Philosophy & Religion, Art, Juveniles, Natural Social & Political Sciences, Literature, Magazines, Plays, Mysteries, Science Fiction, Fantasy
1985: 240 titles *Founded:* 1945

Heibonsha Ltd, Publishers, 5 Sanban-cho, Chiyoda-ku, Tokyo 102 Tel: (03) 2650451 Cable Add: Booksheibonsha
President: Naoya Shimonaka; *Foreign Rights Dir:* Hiroshi Shimonaka
Subjects: Encyclopaedias, Japanese & Chinese studies, General Non-fiction, Art, Reference, Education, History, Philosophy, Social Science, Periodical
Founded: 1914

Hikarinokuni Ltd*, 3-2 Uehon-machi, Tennoji-ku, Osaka 543 Tel: (06) 7681151
President: Yoshio Okamoto; *Man Dir:* Yotaro Matsumoto; *Editorial & Export Dir:* Masaaki Tsuchiya
Subjects: Juveniles, Education
1985: 600 titles *Founded:* 1945

Hirokawa Publishing Co, PO Box 38 Hongo, Bunkyo-ku, Tokyo 113-91 (Located at: 27-14 Hongo 3-chome, Bunkyo-ku, Tokyo 113) Tel: (03) 8153651 Cable Add: Higesehi Tokyo
President: Setsuo Hirokawa; *Vice-President:* Hideo Hirokawa
Subjects: Medicine, Pharmacy, Natural Sciences, Engineering
Founded: 1926

Hoikusha Publishing Co Ltd*, 17-13 Uemachi 1-chome, Higashi-ku, Osaka 540 Tel: (06) 7621731 Cable Add: Hoikusha
President: Tatsuo Imai; *Man Dir:* Osamu Yoshino; *Editorial:* Hiroshi Murakami
Branch Off: 1-1 Minami-Otsuka, Toshima-ku, Tokyo 170
Subjects: Natural History, Poetry, Biography, History, How-to, Music, Art, High-priced Hard cover books, General Science, Illustrated Nature & Craft Books in English & Japanese
Founded: 1947
ISBN Publisher's Prefix: 4-586

Hokuryukan Co Ltd, 3-21 Nishiki-cho, Kanda, Chiyoda-ku, Tokyo 101 Tel: (03) 2913854
President, Editorial: Motojiro Fukuda; *Foreign Department:* Hisako Fukuda
Subjects: Juveniles, General Science, Reference, Encyclopaedias, Textbooks
Founded: 1891
ISBN Publisher's Prefix: 4-89312

The **Hokuseido** Press, 46 Kanda Jinbo-cho 1-chome, Chiyoda-ku, Tokyo 101 Tel: (03) 2943301 Cable Add: Hoksedpres Tokyo Fax: (03) 2943305
Dir: Masazo Yamamoto; *Sales, Advertising:* Akira Ogura; *Rights & Permissions:* Yasuko Jujo
Subjects: Belles Lettres, Poetry, Biography, Philosophy, Religion, University Textbooks
Founded: 1914
ISBN Publisher's Prefix: 4-590

Holp Book Co Ltd*, 19-13 Shinjuku 2-chome, Shinjuku-ku, Tokyo 160 Tel: (03) 3566211 Cable Add: Holpbook Tokyo Telex: 2322421
President: Makito Nakamori; *Editorial:* Shinya Ato; *Rights & Permissions, International Trade:* Minoru Shibuya
Branch Offs: 180 throughout Japan
Subsidiary Company: Holp Shuppan, Publishers
Subjects: Art, Education, Geography, Juveniles, Literature, Mathematics, Reproductions, Science
Founded: 1964

Hyoronsha Publishing Co Ltd, 17 Tsukudohachiman-cho, Shinjuku-ku, Tokyo 162 Tel: (03) 2609401
President: Mrs Mina Takeshita; *Chief Editor:* Saburo Tsuyama; *Sales Manager:* Zenzo Uchida
Subjects: Philosophy & Religion, Education, History, Social Science, Industry, Language, Juveniles, Reference
Founded: 1948

Ie-No-Hikari Association+*, 11 Funagawara-cho, Ichigaya, Shinjuku-ku, Tokyo 162 Tel: (03) 2603151 Cable Add: Ienohikari Tokyo Telex: 2322367 Ienohi J
President: Mitsugu Horiuchi; *Man Dir:* Akira Suzuki; *Executive Dirs:* Hachiro Kanda, Syozo Nitta; *Book Publications:* Kunio Kuroki
Subjects: General, Social Science, Agriculture, Periodicals
1985: 37 titles *Founded:* 1925

Igaku-Shoin Ltd, PO Box 5063, Tokyo International (Located at: 5-24-3 Hongo, Bunkyo-ku, Tokyo 11391) Tel: (03) 8175600 Cable Add: Igakushoin Telex: 2723334 (Head Office and Publishing Departments), 2722738 (Foreign Book Department)
President: Yu Kanehara; *Vice-Presidents:* Naobumi Ando (Medical Publications), Noboru Nakajima (Nursing Publications), Osamu Nishikawa (Sales), Takayoshi Ishihara (Foreign Books); *Senior Editor:* Hideho Nakamura (International Publishing); *Managers:* Masayuki Nishizawa (Foreign Books and Journals), Shunzo Hata (Marketing and Book Imports)
Subsidiary Companies: Igaku-Shoin Medical Publishers Inc, 1140 Ave of the Americas, New York, NY 10036, USA; Medical Sciences International Ltd (qv)
Subjects: Medical and Dental Sciences, Nursing
Founded: 1944
ISBN Publisher's Prefixes: 4-260, 0-89640

The **International Nursing** Foundation of Japan+, 2-4 3-chome, Kudan-Kita, Chiyoda-ku, Tokyo 102 Tel: (03) 2646667 Cable Add: Infurse Tokyo
Man Dir: Dr Kazuharu Ogura; *Editorial:* Miss Chiyoe Shima, Tetsuro Nishizaki; *Rights & Permissions:* Ichiro Takeuchi; *Publicity & Advertising:* Miss Etsuko Toyoshima
Subjects: Nursing Science (National & International)
Founded: 1971

International Society for Educational Information Inc, Koryo Bldg, Wakaba 1-18, Shinjuku-ku, Tokyo 160 Tel: (03) 3581138/3581506
Executive Dir: Michiko Kaya
Subject: Japan

Ishiyaku Publishers Inc*, 7-10 Honkomagome 1-chome, Bunkyo-ku, Tokyo 113 Tel: (03) 9443131 Cable Add: Mepharma Tokyo Telex: 2723298 Mdp J Fax: (03) 9443140
Chairman: Dr Takashi Imada; *President and Dir of International Office:* Hiroshi Miura; *Publishers:* Yukuhide Yonekawa (Medical), Akio Fukushima (Medical), Takao Suda (Dental); *Marketing Dirs:* Yutaka Shimizu, Tai Watanabe
Orders to: Tokyo Mail Service Co Ltd, 23-5 Sugamo 4-chome, Toshima-ku, Tokyo 170
Branch Off: Kansai Branch, c/o Manden Bldg, 11-23 Nishi-Tenma 4-chome, Kita-ku, Osaka-shi 530
Subjects: Medicine, Dentistry, Pharmacology, Nutrition, Veterinary Medicine

258 JAPAN

Bookshops: Shigaku Shoten Ltd, 2-5 Inohana 2-chome, Chiba-shi 280; Shiensha Ltd, c/o Yamashita Bldg, 9-5 Misakicho 2-chome, Chiyoda-ku, Tokyo 101
1985: 160 titles *Founded:* 1921

Iwanami Shoten, Publishers, 2-5-5 Hitotsubashi, Chiyoda-ku, Tokyo 101 Tel: (03) 2654111 Cable Add: Iwanamipress Tokyo Telex: J29495 Iwanami Fax: (03) 2218998
Chairman: Yujiro Iwanami; *President:* Toru Midorikawa; *Senior Man Dir, Publicity:* Yoshikatsu Nakajima; *Dir, Chief Editor:* Ryosuke Yasue; *Foreign Rights:* Takao Hori, Takeko Tomita, Sachiko Kagaya
Subjects: Biography, Economics, History, Reference, Philosophy, Psychology, Art, Juveniles, Social & Natural Science, Paperbacks, University Textbooks, Dictionaries, Periodicals
Bookshop: Iwanami Book Center
1985: 484 titles *1986:* 474 titles *Founded:* 1913
ISBN Publisher's Prefix: 4-00

Iwasaki Publishing Co Ltd*, 9-2 Suido 1-chome, Bunkyo-ku, Tokyo 112 Tel: (03) 8129131
President: Matsutoshi Okawa; *Sales Manager:* Tutomu Yasuda; *Editorial:* Masayasu Konishi
Subjects: Juveniles, Art
Founded: 1934

Japan Broadcast Publishing Co Ltd*, 41-1 Udagawa-cho, Shibuya-ku, Tokyo 150 Tel: (03) 4647311 Cable Add: Nhpublishco Tokyo
President: Kazuo Fujinei; *Man Dir:* Tsutomu Takeda; *Foreign Trade Executive:* Michio Okubo; *Foreign Rights Executive:* Ayao Kanno
Subjects: Radio, Television, Philosophy, Religion, History, Geography, Social & Natural Sciences, Politics, Law, Economics, Engineering, Medicine, Technology, Industry, Art, Language, Juveniles, Literature, Reference, Textbooks
1985: 252 titles *Founded:* 1931

Japan Publications Inc, PO Box 5030 Tokyo International, Tokyo 100-31 (Located at: 1-2-1 Sarugaku-cho, Chiyoda-ku, Tokyo 101) Tel: (03) 2958411 Cable Add: Nichiboshuppan Tokyo Telex: J27161 Fax: (03) 2958416
President: Iwao Yoshizaki; *Vice-President:* Yoshiro Fujiwara; *Executive Dir:* Soshichi Toyoshima; *Editor-in-Chief:* Richard L Gage; *Sales Dir:* Yukishige Takahashi; *Rights & Permissions:* Masatoshi Sato
Parent Company: Japan Publications Trading Co Ltd (Import and Export) (qv under Major Booksellers)
Subsidiary Company: Japan Publications (USA) Inc, 45 Hawthorn Pl, Briarcliff Manor, NY 10510, USA
Subjects: History, How-to, Reference, Juveniles, Health, Macrobiotics, Hobbies, High-priced Paperbacks
1985: 107 titles *Founded:* 1942

Japan Scientific Societies Press, see Business Center for Academic Societies Japan

The **Japan Times**, Publications Department, 5-4 Shibaura 4-chome, Minato-ku, Tokyo 108
Man Dir: Akio Ishizawa
Subjects: Non-fiction, Reference, Textbooks, Japan, Japanese Language
ISBN Publisher's Prefix: 4-7890

Japan Travel Bureau Inc*, Publishing Division, Oki Bldg, 3 Kanda Kaji-Cho 3-chome, Chiyoda-ku, Tokyo 101 Tel: (03) 2578390 Cable Add: Jtbbook Tokyo Telex: 2228020 Jtb Bok J
General Manager: Yukio Kinoshita; *Editor-in-Chief:* Teruo Saito (Books in English); *Foreign Trade Manager:* Kazuhiko Hamada
Subsidiary Companies: Densan Process Co; Kotsu Print Co; Kotsu Seihon Co; Toyo Books Co
Branch Offs: The International Bldg, 45 Rockfeller Plaza, New York, NY 10020, USA; 624 South Grand Ave, Suite 1410, Los Angeles, CA 90014, USA; 402 Qantas Bldg, Union Sq, 360 Post St, San Francisco, CA 94108, USA; The Royal Exchange Bldg, 56 Pitt St, Sydney, Australia; Waikiki Business Plaza, 2270 Kalakaua Avenue, Honolulu, Hawaii 96815; 20 rue Quentin Bauchart, Paris 75008, France; Room 2123, Hotel Miramar, Nathan Rd, Kowloon, Hong Kong; c/o Guam Hilton Hotel, Ipao Beach, Guam; Via Emilia 47, Rome, Italy; 5 Rue Chantepoulet, Geneva, Switzerland; 50-51 Russell Square, London WC1B 4JQ, UK
Subjects: General, Travel Guides, Maps, History, Geography, Language
Founded: 1912
ISBN Publisher's Prefix: 0-87040

K T K/Terra Scientific Publishing Co*, 307 Shibuyadai-haim, 4-17 Sakuragaoka-cho, Shibuya, Tokyo Tel: (03) 4968791
Publisher: Keiji Oshida

Kadokawa Shoten, 2-13-3 Fujimi-cho, Chiyoda-ku, Tokyo 102 Tel: (03) 2388451
Man Dir: Haruki Kadokawa; *Editorial:* Kichinosuke Sato; *Sales:* Tsugihiko Kadokawa; *Production:* Yukio Hashimoto; *Publicity:* Masatoshi Tojo; *Rights & Permissions:* Hiroshi Tagami
Subjects: General Fiction, Fine Arts, History, Religion, Literature, Dictionaries
Founded: 1945

Kaibundo Publishing Co Ltd*, 2-5-4 Suido, Bunkyo-ku, Tokyo 112 Tel: (03) 8153291 Fax: (03) 8153953
President: Yoshihiro Okada; *Editorial Dir:* Yuji Tamura; *Foreign Trade, Foreign Rights:* Shin-ichi Arihara
Subjects: Maritime Affairs, Ship-building, Safety Engineering, Insurance, Risk Management
Founded: 1914

Kairyudo Publishing Co*, 3-18 Kanda Nishiki-cho, Chiyoda-ku, Tokyo 101 Tel: (03) 2931811/9
President: Takahiro Nakamura; *Editorial, Foreign Trade, Foreign Rights:* Takao Iwase; *Sales:* Shoichi Akane; *Production, Publicity:* Mistunobu Okawa
Associate Company: Kairyukan Publishing Co Ltd
Branch Offs: Fukuoka, Nagoya, Osaka, Sapporo
Subjects: Textbooks, Natural Science, Art, Language, Reference, Teaching Aids
Founded: 1926

Kaisei-Sha Publishing Co Ltd+, 3-5 Ichigaya Sadohara-cho, Shinjuku-ku, Tokyo 162 Tel: (03) 2603221 Cable Add: Kaiseisha Telex: J32721 Kaiseico
President: Hiroshi Imamura; *Editorial Dir:* Mitsuo Takamori; *Sales Dir:* Rokuroh Isohata; *Editor, Foreign Rights:* Hiroshi Konno
Subject: Juveniles
1985: 146 titles *1986:* 188 titles *Founded:* 1936

Kaitaku-Sha*, 2-5 Kanda Jinbo-cho, Chiyoda-ku, Tokyo 101 Tel: (03) 2657641
President: Kunio Naganuma; *Foreign Trade:* Takehito Yamaguchi; *Foreign Rights:* Yasuhiko Yamamoto
Subjects: Reference, Education, Language, Literature
Founded: 1927

Kajima Institute Publishing Co Ltd*, 5-13 Akasaka 6-chome, Minato-ku, Tokyo 107 Tel: (03) 5822251 Telex: 02422467 Kajima J attn Kajima Inst Pub Co Fax: (03) 5892928
President: Keiji Matsumoto; *Foreign Trade:* Waichi Kawamura; *Foreign Rights:* Sachie Furuta
Subjects: Architecture, Urban Engineering, Civil Engineering
Bookshops: Kasumigaseki Bookstore, 3-2-5 Kasumigaseki, Chiyoda-ku, Tokyo; Shinjuku Mitsui Building Bookstore, 2-1 Nishishinjuku, Shinjuku-ku, Tokyo; Shibuya Tohoseimei Building Bookstore, 2-15 Shibuya, Shibuya-ku, Tokyo
Founded: 1963

Kanehara & Co Ltd*, 31-14 Yushima 2-chome, Bunkyo-ku, Tokyo 113-91 Tel: (03) 8117161 Cable Add: Kaneharaco Tokyo
President and General Manager: Hideo Kanehara; *Manager (Foreign Business):* Hiroshi Kohno
Subjects: Medicine, Technology, Industry
1985: 342 titles *Founded:* 1875

Kawade Shobo Shinsha, 2-32-2 Sendagaya, Shibuya-ku, Tokyo 151 Tel: (03) 4783251
President: Masaru Shimizu
Subjects: General Fiction and Non-fiction, Natural & Social Science, Art, History, Philosophy
Founded: 1886

Keigaku Publishing Co Ltd+, 1-46 Kanda Jimbo-cho, Chiyoda-ku, Tokyo 101 Tel: (03) 2333731 Fax: (03) 2333730
Publisher: Kazumi Mitsui; *Editorial Dir:* Yutaka Toida; *Sales Manager:* Toshihiko Kawamura; *Production Manager:* Hiroshi Oshikiri; *Foreign Rights:* Ms Tomoko Okuda
Associate Company: Yugaku-sha Ltd (qv)
Subjects: Computers, Communications, Electronics, Science
1985: 120 titles *1986:* 120 titles *Founded:* 1969
ISBN Publisher's Prefix: 4-7665

Kenkyusha Ltd, 9 Kanda Surugadai 2-chome, Chiyoda-ku, Tokyo 101 Tel: (03) 2912301 Fax: (03) 2931194
President: Shiro Nagai; *Foreign Trade Executive:* Hiroji Yamazaki; *Foreign Rights Executive:* Josuke Okada
Subjects: Reference, Languages, Dictionaries
1986: 47 titles *Founded:* 1907

Kinokuniya Co Ltd (Publishing Department), 17-7 Shinjuku 3-chome, Shinjuku-ku, Tokyo 160-91 Tel: (03) 3540131 Cable Add: Kinokuni Telex: J2424344 Kinoku
General Manager: Yoshibumi Araki; *Sales:* Takeo Sakuma
Associate Companies: Kinokuniya Book-Stores of America Co Ltd, 1581 Webster St, San Francisco, CA 94115, USA; 110 S Los Angeles St, Los Angeles, CA 90012, USA; Kinokuniya Publications Service of New York Co Ltd, 633 Third Ave, Suite 1925, New York, NY 10017, USA; Kinokuniya Publications Service of London Co, Radnor House, 93-97 Regent St, London W1, UK
Subjects: Biography, History, Music, Art, Philosophy, Politics, Medicine, Psychology, Engineering, General Science, Social Science, University Textbooks
Bookshops: See under Major Booksellers
Founded: 1926

Kodansha Ltd, 12-21 Otowa 2-chome, Bunkyo-ku, Tokyo 112 Tel: (03) 9451111 Cable Add: Kodanshapublish Tokyo Telex: J34509 Kodansha Fax: (03) 9466200
President: Sawako Noma; *Editorial:* Katsuhisa Kato; *Sales:* Yoshitaka Matsuba; *Rights & Permissions:* Toyo Yoshizaki
Subsidiary Companies: Kodansha International Ltd (qv); Kodansha Scientific Ltd (qv)
Branch Offs: Fukuoka, Hiroshima, Nagoya, Osaka, Sapporo, Sendai (all Japan); New York, USA
Subjects: General Fiction and Non-fiction, Religion, Philosophy, History, Geography, Art, Politics, Economics, Pedagogy, Sociology, Natural Science, Medicine, Language, Literature, Home, Juveniles, Reference Books, Periodicals, Comics
Book Club: Kodansha Disney Children's Book Club
Founded: 1909

Kodansha International Ltd, 2-2 Otowa 1-chome, Bunkyo-ku, Tokyo 112 Tel: (03) 9446491 Cable Add: Kodanshaint Tokyo Telex: J28750 Kodanint Fax: (03) 9441560
President: Toshiyuki Hattori; *Man Dir, Managing Editor:* Koki Mori; *Sales:* Keiji Suzuki; *Rights & Permissions:* Kent W Livingston; *Publicity:* Nobuki Abe; *Art Dir:* Shigeo Katakura
Parent Company: Kodansha Ltd (qv)
Branch Off: Kodansha International-USA Ltd, 10 East 53rd St, New York, NY 10022, USA
Subjects: Specializing in Japan and Asia: General Fiction, Belles Lettres, Art, How-to, History, Philosophy, Reference, Traditional Crafts, Martial Arts, Cooking
1985: 47 titles *1986:* 34 titles *Founded:* 1963
ISBN Publisher's Prefix: 0-87011

Kodansha Scientific Ltd*, Nisho Bldg 4F, 9-25 Shin-Ogawa-Cho, Shinjuku-ku, Tokyo 162 Tel: (03) 2353701
Parent Company: Kodansha Ltd (qv)
Subjects: Scientific Texts, Reference
Founded: 1970

Komine Shoten Publishing Co Ltd*, 6 Yotsuya Funa-machi, Shinjuku-ku, Tokyo
Man Dir: Hiroe Komine
Subjects: Education, Juveniles, Picture Books
Founded: 1946

Kosei Publishing Co, 2-7-1 Wada, Suginami-ku, Tokyo 166 Tel: (03) 3833151 Cable Add: Koseishuppansha Tokyo Fax: (03) 3847444
President: Tadashi Furukawa; *Foreign Trade, Foreign Rights Executive:* Hiroshi Nomura
Subjects: Religion, Juveniles, English Translations, Literature, Magazines
1985: 43 titles *1986:* 71 titles *Founded:* 1966

Koseisha-Koseikaku Co Ltd*, 8 San-ei-cho, Shinjuku-ku, Tokyo 160 Tel: (03) 3597371
President: Hisao Satake; *Editorial:* Fukase Simao; *Publishing:* Hajime Torizuka
Subjects: Philosophy, Sociology, Natural Sciences, Technology, Industry, Astronomy
Founded: 1922

Kyo Bun Kwan Inc, 4-5-1 Ginza, Chuo-ku, Tokyo 104 Tel: (03) 5618446 Cable Add: Kyobunkwan Tokyo Fax: (03) 5355033
Subject: Religion
Bookshop: At above address
Founded: 1885

Kyoritsu Shuppan Co Ltd, 6-19 Kobinata 4-chome, Bunkyo-ku, Tokyo 112 Tel: (03) 9472511
President: Masao Nanjo; *Editorial Dir:* Mitsuaki Nanjo; *Sales Dir:* Hiroshi Todoroki; *Rights & Permissions:* Keiko Goto
Subjects: Natural Science, Mathematics, Computers, Physics, Chemistry, Biology, Engineering, Medicine, Industry, Textbooks
1985: 128 titles *Founded:* 1926

M E D S I, an imprint of Medical Sciences International Ltd (qv)

McGraw-Hill Book Co Japan Ltd, 77 Bldg, 4-14-11 Ginza, Chuo-ku, Tokyo 104 Tel: (03) 5428821 Telex: J28372 Fax: (03) 5428826
Man Dir: Ryoichi Araki
Parent Company: McGraw Hill Inc, 1221 Ave of the Americas, New York, NY 10020, USA
Associate Companies: See McGraw Hill Book Co (UK) Ltd, UK

Maruzen Co Ltd*, PO Box 5050, Tokyo International 10031 (Located at: 3-10 Nihonbashi 2-chome, Chuo-ku, Tokyo 103) Tel: (03) 2727211 Cable Add: Maruya Tokyo Telex: J26516-26517
Chairman: Shingo Iizumi; *President:* Kumao Ebihara; *Dirs:* Junji Sekine (Publishing Division), Shozo Miyake (Export), Eiichi Kobayashi (Import Foreign Books & Subscriptions)
Subsidiary Companies: Maruzen Asia (Pte) Ltd, Singapore (qv); Maruzen International Co Ltd, New York, USA
Subjects: General Science, Physics, Chemistry, Chemical Engineering, Civil Engineering, Architecture, Machine and Electrical Engineering, Medicine, University Textbooks, Dictionaries, Medical Periodicals
Bookshops: See under Major Booksellers
Founded: 1869

Medical Friend Co Ltd+, 2-4 Kudan Kita 3-chome, Chiyoda-ku, Tokyo 102 Tel: (03) 2646611
President: Kazuharu Ogura; *Editorial, Publicity, Advertising, Sales, Rights & Permissions:* Yoshihiro Ogura
Subjects: Medical, Paramedical, Nursing Science & Arts, Specialist Publications, Textbooks and Periodicals
1985: 98 titles *Founded:* 1947

Medical Sciences International Ltd+*, Kida Bldg, 1-2-13 Yushima, Bunkyo-ku, Tokyo 113 Tel: (03) 2555681 Cable Add: Medsijapan Tokyo
President: Takahiko Shimoyama
Parent Companies: Igaku-Shoin Ltd (qv); Little, Brown & Co, 34 Beacon St, Boston, MA 02106, USA
Imprint: MEDSI
Subjects: Medicine, Nursing
1985: 14 titles *Founded:* 1979
ISBN Publisher's Prefix: 4-943921

Meiji Shoin Co Ltd, 1-16 Kanda Nishiki-cho, Chiyoda-ku, Tokyo 101 Tel: (03) 2923741 Fax: (03) 2924429
Man Dir: Akira Miki; *Editorial:* Kunio Kawami; *Sales:* Harunori Saito
Branch Offs: Fukuoka, Osaka
1985: 70 titles *1986:* 80 titles *Founded:* 1896
ISBN Publisher's Prefix: 4-625

Minerva Shobo Co Ltd, 1 Tsutsumidani-cho, Hinooka Yamashina, Yamashina-ku, Kyoto 607 Tel: (075) 5815191 Fax: (075) 5810589
President: Nobuo Sugita; *Editorial Dir:* Kiyoshi Igarashi; *Foreign Trade:* Keizo Sugita; *Foreign Rights:* Takeo Isozaki
Subjects: Philosophy & Religion, History, Social Welfare, Gerontology, Social Science, Literature, Reference
Founded: 1948

Misuzu Shobo Publishing Co Ltd*, 17-15 Hongo 3-chome, Bunkyo-ku, Tokyo 113 Tel: (03) 8159181
Foreign Trade, Foreign Rights: Toshito Obi; *Sales Dir:* Yoshio Aida
Subjects: Art, Literature, Psychiatry, Mathematics, Natural Sciences, Human and Social Sciences
Founded: 1946

Morikita Shuppan Co Ltd*, 4-11 Fujimi 1-chome, Chiyoda-ku, Tokyo 102 Tel: (03) 2658341 Fax: (03) 2658341
President: Hajime Morikita; *Foreign Trade Executive:* Kazuo Mori; *Foreign Rights Executive, Publicity:* Takeshi Watanabe
Subjects: Natural Science, Technology, College and University Textbooks
Founded: 1940 (as Morikita Shoten)

Nagai Shoten Co Ltd*, 21-15 Fukushima 8-chome, Fukushima-ku, Osaka 553 Tel: (06) 4521881
President, Man Dir, Editorial: Tadao Nagai
Subject: Medicine
1985: 6 titles *Founded:* 1946
ISBN Publisher's Prefix: 4-8159

Nankodo Co Ltd+*, 42-6 Hongo 3-chome, Bunkyo-ku, Tokyo 113 Tel: (03) 8117234 Cable Add: Booknankodo Telex: 2722203 Nankod J Fax: (03) 8115031
President: Takehiko Kodachi; *Dirs:* Koji Arai (Publications), Masao Takahashi (Foreign Division); *Sales Dir:* Shoji Sano; *Managers:* Takayuki Izumi (Planning, Publicity), Iwao Tojo (Imports)
Branch Off: Oike-minami Teramachi dori, Nakakyo-ku, Kyoto 604
Subjects: Medicine, Language, Natural Science, Technology
1985: 95 titles *Founded:* 1879

Nanzando Co Ltd*, 4-1-11 Yushima, Bunkyo-ku, Tokyo 113 Tel: (03) 8143681
Man Dir: Hajime Suzuki
Subjects: Reference, High-priced Paperbacks, Medicine, University Textbooks, Pharmacology
Founded: 1901

Nihon Bunka Kagakusha Co Ltd*, 15-17 Honkomagome 6-chome, Bunkyo-ku, Tokyo 113 Tel: (03) 9463131 Cable Add: Nihonbunkamm Tokyo
President, Foreign Rights: Mohachi Motegi; *Foreign Trade Executive:* Haruo Kurihara
Subjects: Education, Social Science, Medicine, Reference Books
1985: 18 titles *Founded:* 1948

Nihon Vogue Co Ltd*, 3-23 Ichigaya Honmura-cho, Shinjuku-ku, Tokyo 162 Tel: (03) 2697690 Telex: J2322931 Ysdtyo attn 6107
President: Tadanobu Seto; *Foreign Trade:* Nobuaki Seto
Subjects: Knitting, Crocheting, Embroidery, Handicrafts (in Paperback)
Founded: 1954

Nishimura Co Ltd+, 1-754-39 Asahimachi-dori, Niigata 951 Tel: (025) 2232388 Fax: (025) 2247165
President: Masanori Nishimura; *General Dir:* Masanobu Nishiyama; *International Division Manager, Rights & Permissions:* Dr Takashi Suzuki; *Sales Manager:* Masaru Gotoh; *Production Manager:* Kazuo Inomata; *Publicity Manager:* Tsutomu Maeda
Branch Offs: Akita, Tokyo
Subjects: Medical, Dental, Veterinary, Nursing & Health, Children's, Art
Bookshops: 68-2 Aza-Hasunuma, Hiroomote, Akita-shi 010; at above address
1985: 13 titles *1986:* 35 titles *Founded:* 1979
ISBN Publisher's Prefix: 4-89013

Obunsha Co Ltd, 55 Yokodera-cho, Shinjuku-ku, Tokyo 162 Tel: (03) 2666101 Cable Add: Obunsha Tokyo
Chief Executive Officer: Kazuo Akao; *Executive Vice-President:* Fumio Akao; *General Affairs Manager:* Hiromitsu Tsuboi; *Books Manager:* Masayoshi Arai; *Magazine Manager:* Takayuki Shirota; *Advertising Manager:* Masaru Wakabayashi; *Educational Projects, New Media Projects Manager:* Yukio Nakayama; *Sales Manager:* Tomio Inayoshi
Associate Companies: The Asahi National Broadcasting Co Ltd, 1-1-1 Roppongi, Minato-ku, Tokyo 106; English Educational Foundation of Japan, 55 Yokodera-cho, Shinjuku-ku, Tokyo 162; Japan LL Education Center, 3-14-16 Shimo-ochiai, Shinjuku-ku, Tokyo 161; Nippon Cultural Broadcasting Inc, 1-5 Wakabacho, Shinjuku-ku, Tokyo 160; Obunsha International Inc, 55 Yokodera-cho, Shinjuku-ku, Tokyo 162; Seeds Inc, Eimei Bldg 2F, 363-4 Yamabuki-cho, Shinjuku-ku, Tokyo 162; The Society for Testing English Proficiency, 1 Yarai-cho, Shinjuku-ku, Tokyo 162
Branch Offs: Fukuoka, Hiroshima, Nagoya, Osaka, Sapporo, Sendai
Subjects: Reference, Encyclopaedias, Dictionaries, Magazines, Newspapers, General Science, Textbooks, Translations, History, Picture Books, Children's and Juveniles, Sports, Computers
Founded: 1931

Ohmsha Ltd+, 1 Kanda Nishiki-cho 3-chome, Chiyoda-ku, Tokyo 101 Tel: (03) 2330641 Cable Add: Ohmsha Telex: 02223125 Ohmsha J
President: N Taneda; *Executive Dir:* Seiji Sato
Subjects: Science and Engineering, Periodicals
1985: 180 titles *1986:* 180 titles *Founded:* 1914

Ondori Sha Publishers Co Ltd, 32 Nishi Goken-cho, Shinjuku-ku, Tokyo 162 Tel: (03) 2683101
President: Toshizo Takeuchi; *Editor:* Takeo Sanada; *Sales:* Hideaki Takeuchi
Subjects: Knitting, Lacework, Embroidery, Handicrafts
1985: 52 titles *1986:* 54 titles *Founded:* 1945
ISBN Publisher's Prefix: 4-277

Ongaku No Tomo Sha Corporation, 6-30 Kagurazaka, Shinjuku-ku, Tokyo Tel: (03) 2352111 Cable Add: Ongakunotomo Tokyo Telex: J23718 Ontoa
President: Sunao Asaka; *Rights & Permissions:* Teruaki Kurata
Orders to: Tomo Music Enterprise Co, 6-30 Kagurazaka, Shinjuku-ku, Tokyo
Subsidiary Companies: TOA Music International Co, 6-32 Kagurazaka, Shinjuku-ku, Tokyo; Suiseisha Music Publishers, 3-3 Sanban-cho, Chiyoda-ku, Tokyo; Tomo Music Enterprise Co, 6-30 Kagurazaka, Shinjuku-ku, Tokyo; Musica Nova Co, 6-30 Kagurazaka, Shinjuku-ku, Tokyo
Subjects: Music, Music Scores and Textbooks, Educational, Periodicals
1985: 229 titles *Founded:* 1941

The **Oriental Economist**, see Toyo Keizai Shinposha Ltd

Otsuki Shoten Publishers*, 11-9 Hongo 2-chome, Bunkyo-ku, Tokyo 113 Tel: (03) 8134651 (Sales)/(03) 8142931 (Editorial)
President, Production: Tomotaka Taira; *Editorial:* Isao Saho; *Sales:* Atsuo Harada
Subjects: Economics, Philosophy, History, Socialism, General Arts
Founded: 1946

Oxford University Press KK, Enshu Bldg, 3-3 Otsuka 3-chome, Bunkyo-ku, Tokyo 112 Tel: (03) 9420101/9421101/9422101 Cable Add: Oxonian Tokyo Telex: 2723520 Ouptok J Fax: (03) 9422100
Manager: T Kawawaki
Parent Company: Oxford University Press, UK (qv)
Branch Off: 1-1-19-207 Nishi Midorigaoka, Toyonaka-shi, Osaka-fu 560 Tel: (06) 8562892

Pacifica Ltd, now incorporated in Seibu Time Co Ltd (qv)

Poplar Publishing Co Ltd+, 5 Suga-cho, Shinjuku-ku, Tokyo 160 Tel: (03) 3572211 Cable Add: Poplarpub Fax: (03) 3592359
President: Haruo Tanaka; *Foreign Rights Executive:* Tetsuo Kubota
Subjects: Juveniles, Fiction, Biography, History, Geography, Natural Sciences, Picture Books
1985: 227 titles *1986:* 273 titles *Founded:* 1947

Prentice-Hall of Japan Inc, Jochi Kojimachi Bldg 3F, 6-1-25 Kojimachi, Chiyoda-ku, Tokyo 102 Tel: (03) 2381050 Telex: 6502958590
President: Teruo Ono (Books & Rights Sales)
Subjects: Engineering, Technology, Sciences, Social Sciences, Business, Economics, Humanities, Medicine, Nursing, ESL, Children's, Audiovisual materials
Miscellaneous: Firm is an affiliate of Simon & Schuster International, Englewood Cliffs, NJ 07632, USA (see Prentice-Hall (Simon & Schuster International Group), UK for associate companies). The ultimate parent company is Simon & Schuster Inc, 1230 Ave of the Americas, New York, NY 10020, USA
Founded: 1961

The **Reader's Digest** of Japan Ltd*, 1-1 Hitotsubashi 1-chome, Chiyoda-ku, Tokyo 100 Tel: (03) 2844111 Cable Add: Readigest Tokyo Telex: J23941 Rdtyo
President: T D Wakefield; *Vice-President:* Shugi Fujimori; *Editor-in-Chief* (Magazine): Ko Shioya; *Editor* (Condensed Books): Yoshiko Tamura
Subjects: Geography, Education, Natural Science, Art, Language, Literature, Juveniles
Founded: 1946 (in Japan)

Risosha Ltd*, 46 Akagishita-machi, Shinjuku-ku, Tokyo 162 Tel: (03) 2681306
President: Tetsuo Shimomura; *Foreign Trade:* Tsugumoto Ishii; *Foreign Rights:* Kazumasa Doi
Subjects: Philosophy, Religion, Literature
Founded: 1927

Ryosho-Fukyu-Kai Co Ltd, 8-2 Kasuga 1-chome, Bunkyo-ku, Tokyo 112 Tel: (03) 8131251 Fax: (03) 8116490
President & Editor: Ichigaku Kawanaka; *Foreign Trade Executive:* Isao Hiramatsu; *Foreign Rights Executive:* Fumio Kimura; *Man Dir:* Kiyoshi Funakoshi
Subjects: Law, Social & Political Sciences, Public and Local Administration
Founded: 1914

Saera Shobo (Librairie Çà et Là), 1 Ichigaya-Sadoharacho 3-chome, Shinjuku-ku, Tokyo 162 Tel: (03) 2684261 Fax: (03) 2684262
Chief Executive: Toshiichi Uraki
Imprint: Toshiichi Uraki
Subject: Children's
1985: 22 titles *1986:* 17 titles *Founded:* 1948
ISBN Publisher's Prefix: 378

Sangyo-Tosho Publishing Co Ltd*, 11-3 Iidabashi 2-chome, Chiyoda-ku, Tokyo 102 Tel: (03) 2617821
President: Mrs Misako Iizuka; *Man Dir:* Katsuhisa Morita; *Editorial:* Takehiko Ezura; *Sales:* Eiji Horino
Subjects: Natural Science, Engineering, Technology, Industry, Philosophy
Founded: 1925

Sankei Shuppan Co*, 6-1-25 Kojimachi, Chiyoda-ku, Tokyo 102 Tel: (03) 2341341 Telex: J22235 Sankei Simbun
Man Dir: Mitsuo Kamiya; *Editorial:* Kohei Hattori; *Sales:* Koichi Ohta; *Rights & Permissions:* Chikayoshi Nakada
Parent Companies: The Sankei Shimbun (Newspaper), Fuji Telecasting Co, Nippon Broadcasting Co
Subjects: General Non-fiction, Mystery, History, Social & Political Sciences, Industry, Art, Literature, Juveniles, Journals
Founded: 1950

Sanseido Co Ltd, 2-22-14 Misaki-cho, Chiyoda-ku, Tokyo 101 Tel: (03) 2309411
Chairman: Hisanori Ueno; *Man Dir:* Masaaki Moriya; *Editorial, Publicity, Rights & Permissions:* Toshio Gomi; *Sales:* Kohji Suzuki; *Production:* Kohji Tomishima
Subjects: Dictionaries, Textbooks, Law, History, Reference, High-priced Paperbacks, General & Social Science, Natural Science, Educational Materials, Literature, Languages
Founded: 1881
ISBN Publisher's Prefix: 4-385

Sansyusya Publishing Co Ltd, 1-5-34 Shitaya, Taito-ku, Tokyo 110 Tel: (03) 8421711 Cable Add: Sansyusyapubl Tokyo Telex: Oisco J33380 Fax: (03) 8453965
President: Kanji Maeda; *Sales, Publicity, Advertising, Rights & Permissions Dir:* Shohei Ohara
Subjects: Language Textbooks, Dictionaries, Educational Materials, Scientific Linguistic Reprints
Founded: 1938

Sanyo Shuppan Boeki Co Inc, PO Box 5037, Tokyo International 100-31 Tel: (03) 6693761 Cable Add: Sanyobook Tokyo Telex: 2524435 Sanyob Fax: (03) 6693768
President, Editorial, Rights & Permissions: Toshiaki Ibe; *Foreign Trade:* Masahiro Takeda
Associate Company: Shinryo Bunko K K (medical bookstore)
Branch Offs: Niihama, Osaka, Tsukuba
Subjects: Food and Cookery, Science, Chemistry
Founded: 1956
Miscellaneous: Also importers

Seibu Time Co Ltd, Time Life Bldg, 3-6 Ohtemachi 2-chome, Chiyoda-ku, Tokyo Tel: (03) 2793400
Publisher: Sueaki Takaoka; *Editor-in-Chief:* Masatoshi Takeuchi
Parent Companies: Seibu Saison Group, Time Inc
Subjects: General Fiction and Non-fiction
Founded: 1983

Seibundo Shinkosha Publishing Co Ltd, 5 Nishikicho 1-chome, Kanda, Chiyoda-ku, Tokyo 101 Tel: (03) 2921211 Cable Add: Varipubco Tokyo
Man Dir, Sales: Shigeo Ogawa; *Editorial:* Hiroshi Irokawa; *Publicity:* Tetsuzo Tamura
Subjects: Commerce, Agriculture, Horticulture & Landscaping, Natural Science, Technology, Industry, Audio

Electronics, Hobbies, Games, Juvenile
1985: 428 titles *Founded:* 1912
ISBN Publisher's Prefix: 4-416

Seiwa Shoten Co Ltd*, 2-5 Kamitakaido 1-chome, Suginamiku, Tokyo 168 Tel: (03) 3290031 Cable Add: Seiwapublishers
President: Youji Ishizawa; *Editor-in-Chief:* Yoshinori Asanuma; *Sales Manager:* Masaharu Fujiwara; *System Manager:* Yukio Shimura; *Foreign Books Manager:* Yumi Matsuzawa
Subjects: Medicine, Psychiatry, Psychology, Language
Book Club: Bookclub Psyche
Bookshops: 1-11 Kamitakaido, 1-chome, Suginamiku, Tokyo 168; 2-5 Kamitakaido, 1-chome, Suginamiku, Tokyo 168
Founded: 1976

Seizando-Shoten Publishing Co Ltd, 4-51 Minami-motomachi, Shinjuku-ku, Tokyo 160 Tel: (03) 3575861 Fax: (03) 3575867
President: Minoru Ogawa; *Editorial:* Yoshihiro Munekata; *Sales:* Yoshio Kimura; *Production:* Yuhei Shibuya; *Publicity:* Masayuki Toyama; *Rights & Permissions:* Kokichi Shioji
Subjects: Maritime, Technology, Transport
Founded: 1953
ISBN Publisher's Prefix: 4-425

Sekai Bunka Publishing Inc*, 4-2-29 Kudan-kita, Chiyoda-ku, Tokyo 102 Tel: (03) 2625111 Cable Add: Sebunpub
President: Tsutomu Suzuki; *Foreign Trade & Rights:* Shuzo Aizawa
Branch Off: 501 Fifth Ave, Suite 2102, New York, NY 10017, USA
Subjects: Art, History, Geography, Juveniles, Educational Materials, Audiovisual
Founded: 1946

Shakai Shiso-Sha*, 25-21 Hongo 1-chome, Bunkyo-ku, Tokyo 113 Tel: (03) 8138101
President: Kazuki Komorida; *Editorial:* Hitoshi Tanaka; *Sales:* Tadashi Kamatsuka
Subjects: General Fiction, Fine Arts, Architecture, Poetry, Music, History, Travel, Social Science, Theatre
Founded: 1947

Shiko-Sha Co Ltd, 10-12 Hiroo 2-chome, Shibuya-ku, Tokyo 150 Tel: (03) 4007151/4 Cable Add: Lmdecw Tokyo Telex: J24903 Fax: (03) 4007294
Man Dir: Yasoo Takeichi
Subject: Juveniles
Founded: 1950

Shincho-Sha Co Ltd*, 71 Yarai-cho, Shinjuku-ku, Tokyo 162 Tel: (03) 2665411 Cable Add: Shinchosha Telex: J27433 Shincho
President: Ryoichi Sato; *Sales:* Shunichi Sato; *Publishing Department:* Hiroshi Nitta; *Foreign Rights:* Hideki Umezawa
Subjects: General Fiction, Fine Arts, History, Philosophy, Social Science, Reference, Literature, Periodicals
Founded: 1896

Shindan to Chiryo Co Ltd*, Room 406, Marunouchi Bldg, Marunouchi 2-4-1, Tokyo 100 Tel: (03) 2144957
President: Hiroshi Fujizane; *Editorial:* Takeshi Hisatsugi
Subject: Medicine
Founded: 1914

Shinkenchiku-Sha Co Ltd, 31-2 Yushima 2-chome, Bunkyo-ku, Tokyo 113 Tel: (03) 8117101 Cable Add: Japanarch Tokyo Fax: (03) 8162937
President: Yoshio Yoshida; *General Manager, Foreign Rights Executive:* Masao Nakamura
Subsidiary Company: The Japan Architect Co Ltd (at above address)
Subjects: Architecture, Periodicals
Founded: 1925

Shogakukan Inc*, 2-3-1 Hitotsubashi, Chiyoda-ku, Tokyo 101 Tel: (03) 2305211 Cable Add: Shogakukan Tokyo Telex: 2322191 Shogak J
President: Tetsuo Ohga; *Man Dir:* Tokio Ueno; *Editorial:* Shiro Hayashi; *Sales:* Masamichi Tsuge; *Production:* Iwajiro Hirotani; *Foreign Rights:* Shonosuke Kanehira
Associate Company: Shueisha Publishing Co Ltd (qv)
Subjects: Art, How-to, Juveniles, Dictionaries, Geography, History, Encyclopaedias, Travel, Literature, Non-fiction, Photography
1985: 1,089 titles *Founded:* 1922

Shokabo Publishing Co Ltd, 8-1 Yonban-cho, Chiyoda-ku, Tokyo 102 Tel: (03) 2629166
Man Dir: Tatsuji Yoshino; *Foreign Rights:* Keisaku Habu; *Foreign Trade:* Saneatsu Makiya
Subjects: Mathematics, Natural Science, Technology
Founded: 1897

Shokokusha Publishing Co Ltd*, 25 Saka-machi, Shinjuku-ku, Tokyo 160 Tel: (03) 3593231
President: Taishiro Yamamoto; *Sales Dir:* Kanji Morishita; *Editorial Dir:* Takeshi Goto
Subjects: Fine Arts, Technical, Architecture, Engineering, General Science, University Textbooks, Educational Materials
1985: 56 titles *Founded:* 1932

Shueisha Publishing Co Ltd*, 2-5-10 Hitotsubashi, Chiyoda-ku, Tokyo 101 Tel: (03) 2306111
President: Sueo Horiuchi; *Editorial:* Hiroshi Ohaka; *Sales:* Sunichi Kondou; *Foreign Trade:* Takeo Hasegawa; *Foreign Rights:* Sunao Okoda, Kei Shiozawa
Associate Company: Shogakukan Inc (qv)
Subjects: General Fiction, Non-fiction, Art, Language, Literature, Juveniles, Periodicals
Founded: 1926

Shufu-to-Seikatsu Sha Ltd*, 5-7 Kyobashi 3-chome, Chuo-ku, Tokyo 104 Tel: (03) 5635120
Man Dir: Tokumitsu Higuchi; *Editor-in-Chief:* Miss Miyako Kiyohara; *Publishing Department, Foreign Rights:* Shujiro Murakawa
Subjects: Philosophy & Religion, History, Medicine, Technology, Art, Literature, Juveniles
Founded: 1935

Shufunotomo Co Ltd+, 2-9 Kanda Surugadai, Chiyoda-ku, Tokyo 101 Tel: (03) 2941118 Cable Add: Shufunotomo Tokyo Telex: J26925 Shufutk Fax: (03) 2933926
President: Haruhiko Ishikawa; *Manager of International Department:* Kazuhiko Nagai
Subjects: Cookery, Flower Arrangement, Bonsai, Gardening, How-to, General Fiction
Founded: 1916

Shuppan News Co Ltd*, 3-2-4, Misaki-cho, Chiyoda-ku, Tokyo Tel: (03) 2622077
Editorial: Takeo Yoshizawa; *Sales:* Keiji Kinoshita; *Rights & Permissions:* Tetsuzo Suzuki
Founded: 1949
ISBN Publisher's Prefix: 4-7852

The **Simul** Press Inc, Kowa Bldg No 9, 1-8-10 Akasaka, Minato-ku, Tokyo 107 Tel: (03) 5824221 Cable Add: Simulshuppan Tokyo Fax: (03) 5824220
President and Editor-in-Chief: Katsuo Tamura; *Senior Man Dir:* Eiko Ikuta; *Dir, Overseas Affairs:* Masumi Muramatsu; *Senior Editor:* Daitaro Suwabe; *Marketing:* Takayuki Kawazoe; *Publicity:* Koichiro Watanabe
Associate Company: Simul International, Inc
Subjects: General, Philosophy and Religion, Social Sciences, History, Education, Business and Economics, Current Affairs, Language, Literature, English-language books on Japan and Asia
1985: 60 titles *1986:* 60 titles *Founded:* 1967

Sogensha Publishing Co Ltd*, 4-2 1-chome, Nishitenma, Kita-ku, Osaka 530 Tel: (06) 3632531
President: Bunji Yabe
Associate Company: Tokyo Sogensha Co Ltd (qv)
Subjects: Art, History, Philosophy, Religion, Low-priced Paperbacks, Medicine, Psychology, University Textbooks, Educational Materials
Founded: 1925

Syokabo Publishing Co Ltd, 8-1 Yombancho, Chiyoda-ku, Tokyo 102 Tel: (03) 2629166
President, Foreign Rights, Foreign Trade: Tatsuji Yoshino
Subjects: Mathematics, Natural Science and Engineering
Founded: 1715

Taishukan Publishing Co Ltd*, 3-24 Kanda-Nishiki-cho, Chiyoda-ku, Tokyo 101 Tel: (03) 2942221
Man Dir: Toshio Suzuki; *Sales, Publicity, Advertising:* Ninji Nakamura; *Rights & Permissions:* Toshio Saeki
Subjects: Reference, High-priced Paperbacks, Language & Linguistics, Sports, Social Science, University & Secondary Textbooks, Educational Materials, Dictionaries, Periodicals
1985: 70 titles *Founded:* 1918

Takahashi Shoten Co Ltd*, 22-13 Otowa 1-chome, Bunkyo-ku, Tokyo 112 Tel: (03) 9434525
President: Kyushiro Takahashi; *Foreign Trade Executive:* Yukihiko Takahashi
Subjects: Technology, Law Education, Medicine, Language, Juveniles
Founded: 1939 (as Kowado Co Ltd)

Tankosha Publishing Co Ltd*, Tanko Bldg, Horikawa Kuramaguchi-agaru, Kita-ku, Kyoto 603 Tel: (075) 4325151
President: Yoshiharu Naya; *Editorial Dir, Foreign Trade and Rights:* Shiro Usui
Subjects: Philosophy & Religion, History, Art, Japanese Culture
Founded: 1945

Teikoku-Shoin Co Ltd, 3-29 Kanda Jinbo-cho, Chiyoda-ku, Tokyo 101 Tel: (03) 2611584 Cable Add: Books Teikoku Telex: 2324921 Tekoku J
President: Takashi Goto; *Editorial, Foreign Rights:* Chozo Miyakawa; *Foreign Trade:* Toshio Soeda
Subjects: History, Geography, Maps, Atlases, Textbooks
Founded: 1926

Tokai University Press, Shinjuku Tokai Bldg, 3-27-4 Shinjuku, Shinjuku-ku, Tokyo 160 Tel: (03) 3561541
President: Tatsuro Matsumae; *Dir:* Wataru Yamada; *Editorial:* Yasunosuke Yamamoto; *Sales, Publicity:* Takao Nakajin; *Production:* Chimaju Kato

Orders to: Maruzen Co Ltd, PO Box 5050, Tokyo International 100-31
Subjects: Philosophy, Religion, History, Social & Natural Science, Biology, Oceanography, Technology, Art, Language, Literature
Founded: 1962
Miscellaneous: Tokai University European Centre is at Strandvej 476, DK-2950 Vedbæk, Denmark

Tokuma-Shoten, 4-10-1 Shinbashi, Minato-ku, Tokyo Tel: (03) 4336231
President: Yasuyoshi Tokuma; *Editor:* Minoru Hagiwara; *Foreign Trade:* Osamu Okamura
Subjects: General Fiction, Non-fiction, Belles Lettres, How-to, Social Science, Art, Games, Sports, Juveniles
Founded: 1954

Tokyo Kagaku Dozin Co Ltd*, 36-7 Sengoku 3-chome, Bunkyo-ku, Tokyo 112 Tel: (03) 9465311
President: Atsushi Ueki; *Editorial:* Minako Ozawa
Subjects: Natural Science, Medical Science, Chemistry
Founded: 1961

Tokyo News Service Ltd, Tsukiji Hamarikyu Bldg, 10th Floor, 3-3 Tsukiji 5-chome, Chuo-ku, Tokyo 104 Tel: (03) 5428521 Cable Add: Tradenews Tokyo Telex: 2523285 Stnews J
President: T Okuyama
Branch Off: Osaka Tel: (06) 2316051
Subjects: Shipping, Foreign Trade, Aviation, Television, Tourism
Founded: 1947

Tokyo Shoseki Co Ltd, 6-14-9 Honkomagome, Bunkyo-ku, Tokyo 113 Tel: (03) 9424132 Telex: J27317 Topbook Fax: (03) 9424119
President: Tamio Odaka; *Sales, Rights & Permissions:* Minoru Kiso
Parent Company: Toppan Printing Co Ltd, 1-5-1 Taito, Taito-ku, Tokyo 110
Subsidiary Company: Asutoro Publishing Co Ltd (at above address)
Associate Company: Toppan Co Ltd (qv)
Branch Offs: Chubu, Hokkaido, Kansai Chugoku, Kyushu, Tohoku
1985: 29 titles *1986:* 33 titles *Founded:* 1909

Tokyo Sogensha Co Ltd*, 1-5 Shin Ogawa-machi, Shinjuku-ku, Tokyo 162 Tel: (03) 2688201
Chairman: Takao Akiyama; *President:* Ichiro Hiramatsu; *Editorial:* Yasunobu Togawa; *Sales:* Haruo Hashimoto
Associate Company: Sogensha Publishing Co Ltd (qv)
Subjects: Detective Stories, Science Fiction, Social Science, Literature
1985: 70 titles *Founded:* 1925

Tokyo Tosho Co Ltd*, 2-5-22 Suido, Bunkyo-ku, Tokyo 112 Tel: (03) 8147818
President: Tsuyoshi Katayama; *Foreign Trade Executive:* Hiroyasu Katayama; *Foreign Rights:* Shizuo Stowe
Subjects: Natural Science, Popular Science, Engineering, Biographies
Founded: 1955

Toppan Co Ltd, Shufunotomo Bldg, 1-6 Kanda Surugadai, Chiyoda-ku, Tokyo 101 Tel: (03) 2953461 Cable Add: Toppan Book Tokyo Telex: J27317 Fax: (03) 2935963
Chief Executive: Shinji Komatsu; *Man Dir:* Moto Sekino; *Dir:* Naomi Yoshikawa
Subsidiary Company: Toppan Co (S) Pte Ltd, Singapore (qv)
Associate Company: Tokyo Shoseki Co Ltd (qv)

Subjects: Medicine, Psychology, Engineering, Social Science, Agriculture, Economics, Mathematics, Statistics, Zoology, Biology, Chemistry, Physics, Languages and Linguistics
Founded: 1963
ISBN Publisher's Prefix: 4-8101

Toyo Keizai Shinposha Ltd (The Oriental Economist)*, 4 Hongoku-cho 1-chome, Nihonbashi, Chuo-ku, Tokyo 103 Tel: (03) 2465403 Cable Add: Orinomist Tokyo
President: Hiromu Takayanagi; *Man Dir:* Motohiro Nakajima; *Foreign Trade:* Akio Kamio; *Foreign Rights:* Kunio Akagi
Subjects: Scholastic, Economics, General Non-fiction, Directories, Industry, Social Science
Founded: 1895

Charles E **Tuttle** Co Inc+, 2-6 Suido 1-chome, Bunkyo-ku, Tokyo 112 Tel: (03) 8117106/9 Telex: 2723170 Tutbks J Fax: (03) 8116953
President, Editorial, Publicity, Production: Nicholas Ingleton; *Sales:* Yutaka Watanabe; *Rights & Permissions:* Barbara Brackett
Branch Offs: 402 Seki, Tama-ku, Kawasaki-shi, Kanagawa 214; Wako Bldg, 7 Showa-cho 2-chome, Suita-shi, Osaka 564; PO Box 410, Rutland, VT 05701, USA
Subjects: Japanese & Asian Studies, Art, Hobbies and Crafts, Cookery, Fiction, Martial Arts, Poetry, Belles Lettres, Literature, Travel, Political & Social Science, Juveniles, Languages
Bookshop: Kanda Bookshop (qv under Major Booksellers)
Founded: 1948
ISBN Publisher's Prefix: 0-8048
Miscellaneous: Importer and wholesaler of books from the UK and USA

U N A C Tokyo*, 1-4-7 Azabu-da, Minato-ku, Tokyo 106 Tel: (03) 5857069/5853069 Cable Add: Unacprod
Publisher: Masaomi Unagami

University of Tokyo Press+, 7-3-1 Hongo, Bunkyo-ku, Tokyo 113 Tel: (03) 8110964 Cable Add: Universitypress Fax: (03) 8149458
Man Dir: Kazuo Ishii; *Associate Dirs:* Norihiro Sato, Tadashi Yamashita; *Marketing, Rights & Permissions:* Masami Yamaguchi
Subjects: History, Philosophy, Reference, Religion, Medicine, Psychology, Engineering, Natural & Social Sciences, University Textbooks
Bookshop: Yurinsha Ltd, PO Box 63, Hongo Post Office, Tokyo
1985: 159 titles *1986:* 151 titles *Founded:* 1951
ISBN Publisher's Prefixes: 0-86008, 4-13

Toshiichi **Uraki**, an imprint of Saera Shobo (Librairie Çà et Là) (qv)

John **Weatherhill**·Inc*, 7-6-13 Roppongi, Minato-ku, Tokyo Tel: (03) 4048871 Cable Add: Weatherhill Tokyo Telex: J26601
President: Yoshiharu Naya; *Vice President:* Takeshi Yamazaki; *Sales:* Yutaka Shimoji (Japan & Far East); *Rights & Permissions:* Miriam F Yamaguchi
Subjects: Belles Lettres, Poetry, Biography, History, How-to, Music, Art, Reference, Religion, Juveniles, High-priced Paperbacks (all on Asia)
Founded: 1962

Yama-Kei (Publishers) Co Ltd*, 1-1-33 Shiba-Daimon, Minato-ku, Tokyo 105 Tel: (03) 4364021
President: Yoshimitsu Kawasaki; *Foreign Trade:* Susumu Harada; *Foreign Rights:*

Yoshitake Murakami
Branch Off: 1-12-12 Esaka-cho, Fukita-Shi, Osaka
Subjects: Mountaineering, Ski-ing, Geography, Natural Science
Founded: 1930

Yohan Publications Inc+, 14-9 Okubo 3-chome, Shinjuku-ku, Tokyo 160 Tel: (03) 2041758 Cable Add: Bookyohan Telex: J2324818 Yohan Fax: (03) 2090288
President: Masahiro Watanabe
Parent Company: Yohan (Western Publications Distribution Agency) (qv under Major Booksellers)
Subjects: Fiction, Non-fiction, Illustrated Books, English and other language teaching books
1985-86: 20 titles *Founded:* 1963
ISBN Publisher's Prefix: 4-89684

Yokendo Ltd*, 30-15 Hongo 5-chome, Bunkyo-ku, Tokyo 113 Tel: (03) 8140911
President: Toshio Oikawa; *Foreign Rights:* Kiyoshi Oikawa
Subjects: Natural Science, Agriculture, Engineering
Founded: 1914

Yugaku-sha Ltd+, 1-46 Kanda Jimbo-cho, Chiyoda-ku, Tokyo 101 Tel: (03) 2333731 Fax: (03) 2333730
Publisher: Kazumi Mitsui; *Editorial, Sales Manager:* Yoshiaki Tokunaga; *Production Manager:* Hiroshi Oshikiri; *Foreign Rights:* Ms Tomoko Okuda
Associate Company: Keigaku Publishing Co Ltd (qv)
Subjects: Children's, General
1985: 60 titles *1986:* 60 titles
ISBN Publisher's Prefix: 4-8416

Yuhikaku Publishing Co Ltd*, 2-17 Kanda Jimbo-cho, Chiyoda-ku, Tokyo 101 Tel: (03) 2641311 Cable Add: Yuhikakubook
Chairman: Shiro Egusa; *President:* Tadataka Egusa; *Foreign Trade and Rights:* Amori Yamamoto
Subjects: Law, Economics, Sociology, Psychology, History, Education
1985: 212 titles *Founded:* 1877

Yushodo Co Ltd, 29 San-ei-cho, Shinjuku-ku, Tokyo 160 Tel: (03) 3571411 Cable Add: Yushodo Tokyo Telex: 02324136
President: Mitsuo Nitta; *Editorial:* Yoshito Yamada
Subsidiary Companies: Publishers International Corp; Yushodo Film Publications Ltd; Yushodo Publication Ltd
Branch Offs: Kansai, Kyoto; Annex Bldg, Ohtsuka, Tokyo
Subjects: Political Economics, Japanese Classical Literature

Zoshindo Juken-Kenkyusha, 19-15 2-chome Shinmachi, Nishi-ku, Osaka 550
President: Shigetoshi Okamoto
Subjects: Education, Juveniles
1986: 780 titles *Founded:* 1890

Literary Agents

Bureau des Copyrights Français, Nitta Bldg 2-1, Ginza 8-chome, Chuo-ku, Tokyo 104 Tel: (03) 5724080/5713404 Cable Add: Francoright Telex: J32429 Txbcf
Handling all copyrights, translation rights, foreign rights, co-productions
Founded: 1952

The **English Agency** (Japan), 305 Azabu Empire Mansion, 4-11-28 Nishi Azabu, Minato-ku, Tokyo Tel: (03) 4065385 Cable Add: Engagent Telex: J34843 Eajsok Fax: (03) 4065387
Dirs: Desmond Briggs, William Miller,

Peter Thompson; *Managers:* Junzo Sawa, Kimikazu Kiyota
London Representative: Eleanor Corey Tel: (01) 994 7670
New York Representative: Alison Bond Tel: (212) 3623350
Specialization: Sales of book and ancillary rights for translation both into and from Japanese; adviser for rights deals with the Republic of Korea; author's agent for books with international appeal

Japan Foreign Rights Centre (JFC), Akimoto Bldg, 1-38 Kanda Jimbo-cho, Chiyoda-ku, Tokyo 101 Tel: (03) 2918571 Cable Add: Rightcent Tokyo Telex: 236502972789 Mci Uw Fax: (03) 2918573
Man Dir: Akiko Kurita; *Dirs:* Hiroshi Imamura, Yoshitake Shinoto
Specialization: Japanese book rights, co-production, video and computer software

Japan U N I Agency Inc*, Naigai Bldg, 1-1 Kanda Jimbo-cho, Chiyoda-ku, Tokyo 101 Tel: (03) 2950301 Cable Add: Uniliterary Telex: J27260 Unilit
President: Noboru Miyata; *Dirs:* Yoshio Taketomi, Okimitsu Ohishi

Kurita Bando Literary Agency, now Japan Foreign Rights Centre (JFC) (qv)

Orion Press*, 1-55 Kanda Jimbo-cho, Chiyoda-ku, Tokyo 101 Tel: (03) 2951400 Cable Add: Orionagy Telex: J24408 Orionagy
Contact: T Sakai

Tuttle-Mori Agency Inc*, Fuji Bldg 8F, 2-15 Kanda-Jimbocho, Chiyoda-ku, Tokyo Tel: (03) 230 4081 Cable Add: Tuttmori Tokyo Telex: 02324915 Tutmor J
President: Tom Mori; *Editorial Dir:* Kiyoshi Asano; *Editorial Manager:* Yoshikazu Iwasaki; *Business Department Dir:* Sakae Mino; *Business Department Manager:* Yuji Takeda
Also: Sandford J Greenburger Associates Inc, 55 Fifth Ave, New York, NY 10003, USA Tel: (212) 2065600 Cable Add: Inlitbur Telex: 420633 *(Contacts:* Nikki Smith, Lucy Stille); 58D Clifton Gardens, London W9 1AU, UK Tel: (01) 286 8701 Telex: 28905 ref 2171 Monref G *(Contact:* Anne Martyn)
Dealing in book rights, serial rights, co-productions; motion picture, TV, radio and stage rights, merchandising rights

The **Yamami** Agency*, 2-6-46-501 Uenohara Higashi-Kurume-Shi, Tokyo 203 Tel: (0424) 720411/735366 Cable Add: Yamami Tanashi Telex: 02822323 Yamami J
President: Hideo Yamami; *Dir:* Hiroko Yamami
Specialization: Book rights (fiction, non-fiction, academic, juvenile, media book sales promotion), serial rights, motion picture rights, TV rights, radio rights, stage rights, merchandising rights

Book Clubs

Books-on-Japan-in-English Club*, Shin Nichibo Bldg, 2-1 Sarugaku-cho 1-chome, Chiyoda-ku, Tokyo 101
President: Iwao Yoshizaki; *Secretary-General:* Akio Takeuchi
Founded: 1955
Miscellaneous: Club consists of 41 leading publishers, bookstores, exporters, and printers of English-language books and periodicals dealing with Japan and Orient

Fukuinkan Ehon Library*, c/o Fukuinkan Shoten Publishers Inc, 6-6-3 Honkomagome, Bunkyo-ku, Tokyo 113
Owned by: Fukuinkan Shoten Publishers Inc (qv)
Subject: Children's Books

Kodansha Disney Children's Book Club, 12-21 Otowa 2-chome, Bunkyo-ku, Tokyo 112
Owned by: Kodansha Ltd (qv)
Subject: Children's Books

Bookclub **Psyche***, Seiwa Shoten Co Ltd, 2-5 Kamitakaido 1-chome, Suginamiku, Tokyo 168
Owned by: Seiwa Shoten Co Ltd (qv)
Subject: Psychiatry

Major Booksellers

Asahiya Shoten Ltd (Booksellers)*, Osaka-Fukoku-Seimei Bldg 3F, 2-4 Komatsubara-cho Kita-ku, Osaka 530 Tel: (06) 3150971 Foreign Books Department: c/o Asahi Bldg, 17-9 Toyosaki 3-chome, Ohyodo-ku, Osaka 531 Tel: (06) 3727251
President: Takeshi Hayashima
16 bookstores throughout the country

Goethe Book Dealers Inc*, Room 560, Marunouchi Bldg, Chiyoda-ku, Tokyo 100 Tel: (03) 2117839

Ikubundo Publishers Co*, 30-21 Hongo 5-chome, Bunkyo-ku, Tokyo 113 Tel: (03) 8145571/5

Japan Publications Trading Co Ltd (Import and Export), 2-1 Sarugaku-cho 1-chome, Chiyoda-ku, Tokyo 101 Tel: (03) 2923751 Cable Add: Shutsubo Tokyo Telex: J27161 Jptco Fax: (03) 2920410
Subsidiary Companies: Japan Publications Inc (qv); JP Trading Inc, Brisbane, CA 94005, USA

Kanda Bookshop, 3 Kanda Jimbo-cho 1-chome, Chiyoda-ku, Tokyo 101 Tel: (03) 2917071/2 Fax: (03) 2938005
Also: American Club Shop, 1-2 Azabu-dai 2-chome, Minato-ku, Tokyo 106 Tel: (03) 5838381; Okinawa Plaza Book Shop, 242 Yamazoto, Okinawa-shi, Okinawa 904 Tel: (0989) 333520
Owned by: Charles E Tuttle Co Inc (qv)

Kinokuniya Co Ltd, 17-7 Shinjuku 3-chome, Shinjuku-ku, Tokyo 160-91 Tel: (03) 3540131 Cable Add: Kinokuni Tokyo Telex: 02414344
59 branches throughout Japan
Also Publisher (qv)

Kurita Shuppan Hanbai Co Ltd*, 3-1 Higashisakashita 1-chome, Itabashi-ku, Tokyo 174 Tel: (03) 9652111
Distributor

Maruzen Co Ltd*, 3-10 Nihonbashi 2-chome, Chuo-ku, Tokyo 103 Tel: (03) 2727211 Cable Add: Maruya Tokyo Telex: J26516/J26517
Branches: Fukuoka, Hiroshima, Kanazawa, Kobe, Kyoto, Nagoya, Okayama, Osaka, Sapporo, Sendai, Tsukuba
Importer-Exporter; also Publisher (qv)

Nippon Shuppan Hanbai Inc*, 3 Kanda Surugadai 4-chome, Chiyoda-ku, Tokyo 101 Tel: (03) 2331111 Cable Add: Honnippan Tokyo Telex: J25627 Nippan Distributors

Tokyo Shuppan Hanbai Co Ltd (Distributors), 6-24 Higashigoken-cho, Shinjuku-ku, Tokyo 162 Tel: (03) 2696111 Cable Add: Hontohan Tokyo Telex: 2322141 Fax: (03) 2671085
Overseas Division Manager: Kainan Tanaka

United Publishers Services Ltd, Kenkyu-sha Bldg, 9 Kanda Surugadai 2-chome, Chiyoda-ku, Tokyo 101 Tel: (03) 2914541 Cable Add: Unitedbooks Tokyo Telex: J33331 Fax: (03) 2928610
The largest stock holding agent of overseas publishers in the Japanese foreign book market; a member of Times Publishing Group, Republic of Singapore

Yohan (Western Publications Distribution Agency), 14-9 Okubo 3-chome, Shinjuku-ku, Tokyo 160 Tel: (03) 2080181 Cable Add: Bookyohan Tokyo Telex: 2324818 Yohan J Fax: (03) 2090288
President: Masahiro Watanabe
Also: Fukuoka, Hiroshima, Nagoya, Okinawa, Osaka, Sapporo, Sendai, Yokohama, and 10 bookshops in Tokyo
Wholesale importers and distributors of books and magazines; stockists for publishers
Subsidiary Company: Yohan Publications Inc (qv)

Major Libraries

Hokkaido University Library, Kita-8, Nishi-5, Sapporo 060 Tel: (011) 7162111
Librarian: Kimio Ohno
Publication: Yuin (The Hokkaido University Library Bulletin, in Japanese, quarterly)

Kokuritsu Kobunshokan*, 3-2 Kitanomaru Park, Chiyoda-ku, Tokyo
National Archives

Kyoto Sangyo University Library*, Kamigamo, Kita-ku, Kyoto Tel: (075) 7012151

Kyushu University Library*, 6-10-1 Hakozaki-machi, Fukuoka City, Fukuoka Prefecture

School of **Library** and Information Science Library*, Keio University, Mita Minato-ku, Tokyo 108 Tel: (03) 4534511
Librarian: Motoko Sekiguchi

Nagoya University Library*, Furo-cho, Chikusa-ku, Nagoya

National Diet Library, 1-10-1 Nagata-cho, Chiyoda-ku, Tokyo 100 Tel: (03) 5812331/5812341
Librarian: Kiyohide Ibusuki
Publications include: Accession List – Foreign Language Publications (monthly); *Biblos* (monthly); *Catalog of Materials on Japan in Western Languages in the National Diet Library* (in English); *Directory of Japanese Scientific Periodicals* (in Japanese and English); *Directory of Special Collections in Japanese Libraries; Japanese National Bibliography* (weekly and quarterly index); *Japanese Periodicals Index* (quarterly); *Reference* (monthly); *Union List of Serial Publications in Public Libraries*

Osaka Gakuin University Library*, Kishibe, Suita City, Osaka

Osaka Prefectural Nakanoshima Library*, 1-2-10 Nakanoshima, Kita-ku, Osaka Tel: (06) 2030474

Tenri Central Library, Tenri University, Somanouchi-cho 1050, Tenri City, Nara 632 Tel: (07436) 31511 ext 6750
Chief Librarian: Hidetsugu Ueda

Tohoku University Library*, Kawauchi, Sendai City 980

Tokyo Metropolitan Central Library, 5-7-13 Minami-Azabu, Minato-ku, Tokyo 106 Tel: (03) 4428451
Dir: Yoichi Maeda

JAPAN

The **Toyo** Bunko*, Honkomagome 2-chome, 28-21, Bunkyo-ku, Tokyo 113 Tel: (03) 9420121
Publications: Memoirs of the Research Department of the Toyo Bunko
Also Centre of East Asian Cultural Studies for UNESCO, for which publications include various directories, bibliographies, textbooks

University Libraries, see under town names

University of Tokyo Library, Hongo 7-3-1, Bunkyo-ku, Tokyo 113 Tel: (03) 8122111

Waseda University Library*, 6-1 Nishiwaseda 1-chome, Shinjuku-ku, Tokyo 160 Tel: (03) 2034141 ext 5132
Librarian: Harukaze Furukawa

Library Associations

Gakujutsu Bunken Fukyu-Kai, c/o Tokyo Institute of Technology, 2-12-1 O-okayama, Meguro-ku, Tokyo 152
Association for Science Documents Information
President: Shu Kambara

Joho Kagaku Gijutsu Kyokai, Sasaki Bldg, 5-7 Koisikawa 2, Bunkyo-ku, Tokyo 112 Tel: (03) 8133791
Information Science and Technology Association (INFOSTA)
President: Y Nakamura
Publications: Informant (microfiche, twice yearly); *Journal of Information Science and Technology Association*

Joho Shori Gakkai, Hoshina Bldg, 2-4-2 Azabu-Dai, Minato-ku, Tokyo 106 Tel: (03) 5050505 Telex: 02425340 Ips J Fax: (03) 5847925
Information Processing Society of Japan
President: Prof Y Ohno
Publications: Journal of Information Processing (English, quarterly), *Joho-shori* (Journal of IPSJ, Japanese, monthly), *Transactions of IPSJ* (Japanese, monthly)

Mita Society for Library and Information Science, School of Library and Information Science, Keio University, Mita, Minatoku, Tokyo 108 Tel: (03) 4533920
Secretary: Shuichi Ueda
Publication: Library and Information Science (annual)

Nihon Toshokan Kyokai, 1-10, 1-chome, Taishido, Setagaya-ku, Tokyo 154 Tel: (03) 4106411
Japan Library Association
Secretary-General: Hitoshi Kurihara
Publications: Toshokan Zasshi (monthly), *Gendai no Toshokan* (quarterly), *Nippon no Sankotosho Shikiban* (quarterly), *Nippon no Toshokan* (annually), *Sentei Tosho Somokuroku* (annually), *Toshokan nenkan* (annually)

Nippon Igaku Toshokan Kyokai*, c/o Business Centre for Academic Societies, 4-16 Yayoi 2-chome, Bunkyo-ku, Tokyo 113
The Japan Medical Library Association
Secretary: Hiroko Shobuzawa
Publications: Igakuvtoshokan; *List of current periodicals acquired by the Japanese Medical, Dental and Pharmaceutical Libraries*; *Union Catalogue of Foreign Books in the Libraries of Japan Medical Schools*

Nippon Nogaku Toshokan Kyogikai (JAALD)*, Taiyo Seimei Bldg, 2-17-2 Shibuya, Shibuya-ku, Tokyo 150 Tel: (03) 4090722
Japan Association of Agricultural Librarians and Documentalists
Secretary: Mrs Shukuko Kamiya
Publications: Bulletin of JAALD (quarterly), *JAALD Series* (occasional)

Nippon Toshokan Gakkai, c/o Toyo Daigaku Shakaigakubu Toshokangaku Kenkyushitsu, 5-28-20 Hakusan, Bunkyo-ku, Tokyo 112
Japan Society of Library Science
Executive Secretary: Yasuo Iwabuchi
Publications: Bibliography on Library Science (annual), *Toshokangakkai Nempo* (Annals) (quarterly)

Nippon Yakugaku Toshokan Kyogikai*, c/o Library, Faculty of Pharmaceutical Sciences, University of Tokyo, Hongo 7-3-1, Bunkyo-ku, Tokyo 113
Japan Pharmaceutical Library Association
Publication: Yakugaku Toshokan (Pharmaceutical Library Bulletin)

Senmon Toshokan Kyogikai (SENTOKYO), c/o National Diet Library, 1-10-1 Nagata-cho, Chiyoda-ku, Tokyo 100 Tel: (03) 5811364
Japan Special Libraries Association
President: Noboru Goto; *Executive Dir:* Konosuke Hayasi
Publications: Bulletin (five times yearly), *Directory of Special Libraries*, 1985 (in Japanese); *Directory of Information Sources in Japan*, 1986 (in English)

Library Reference Books and Journals

Books

Directory of Information Sources in Japan, Japan Special Libraries Association, c/o National Diet Library, 1-10-1 Nagata-cho, Chiyoda-ku, Tokyo 100
In English

Directory of Special Collections in Japanese Libraries, National Diet Library, 1-10-1 Nagata-cho, Chiyoda-ku, Tokyo 100

Directory of Special Libraries, Japan Special Libraries Association, c/o National Diet Library, 1-10-1 Nagata-cho, Chiyoda-ku, Tokyo 100

Nippon no Toshokan (Library of Japan), Japan Library Association, 1-10, 1-chome, Taishido Setagaya-ku, Tokyo 154

A Survey of Special Collections in Japan, The Shuppan News Co Ltd, 3-2-4 Misaki-cho, Chiyoda-ku, Tokyo 101

Journals

Biblos (monthly), National Diet Library, 1-10-1 Nagata-cho, Chiyoda-ku, Tokyo 100

Bulletin, Japan Special Libraries Association, c/o National Diet Library, 1-10-1 Nagata-cho, Chiyoda-ku, Tokyo 100

Handbook, Japan Special Libraries Association, c/o National Diet Library, 1-10-1 Nagata-cho, Chiyoda-ku, Tokyo 100

Japanese Periodicals Index (quarterly), National Diet Library, 1-10-1 Nagata-cho, Chiyoda-ku, Tokyo 100

Journal of Information Science and Technology Association, Information Science and Technology Association, Sasaki Bldg, 5-7 Koisikawa 2, Bunkyo-ku, Tokyo 112

Library System, Medical Library and Information Centre, Keio University, 35 Shinanomachi, Shinjuku-ku, Tokyo
Text in Japanese

Nippon no Sakotosho Shikiban (Reference Library Quarterly of Japan), Japan Library Association, 1-10 Taishido 1-chome, Setagaya-ku, Tokyo

Reference (monthly), National Diet Library, 1-10-1 Nagata-cho, Chiyoda-ku, Tokyo 100

Sendai no Toshokan (Library of Today), Japan Library Association, 1-10 Taishido 1-chome, Setagaya-ku, Tokyo

Toshokan-Kai (Library World), Japan Institution for Library Science, Tenri University, Tenri, Nara
Text in Japanese, table of contents in English

Toshokan Zasshi (Library Journal), Japan Library Association, 1-10 Taishido 1-chome, Setagaya-ku, Tokyo

Literary Associations and Societies

The **Dickens** Fellowship*, Bungei-Gakubu, Seijo University 6-1-20, Seijo Setagaya, Tokyo
Honorary Secretary: Prof Koichi Miyazaki

Japan Essayists' Club*, c/o Yujiro Chiba, 1-1-1 Shimbashi, Minato-ku, Tokyo

Japan Poet Club*, c/o Showa Joshi University, 1-7 Taishido, Setagaya-ku, Tokyo

Japan Poets' Association*, c/o Seitaro Yarita, 401 4-chome Ikebukuro, Toshima-ku, Tokyo

Nihon Dokubungakkai, c/o Ikubundo, Hongo 5-30-21, Bunkyo-ku, Tokyo 113
Japanese Society of German Literature
President: Prof Yoshio Koshima
Publication: Doitsu Bungaku (German Literature) (twice yearly)

Nihon Eibungakkai*, 601 Kenkyusha Bldg, 9 Surugadai 2-chome, Kanda, Chiyoda-ku, Tokyo 101
English Literary Society of Japan
President: Yuichi Takamatsu
Publication: Studies in English Literature (three times yearly)

Nippon Bungaku Kyokai*, 2-17-10 Minami-otsuka, Toshima-ku, Tokyo Tel: (03) 9412740
Japanese Literature Association
President: Tamotsu Hirosue
Publication: Japanese Literature (monthly)

Nippon Furansu-go Furansu-bungaku Kai*, c/o La Maison franco-japonaise, 2-3 Kanda-Surugadai, Chiyoda-ku, Tokyo
Japanese Society of French Language and Literature
President: Hiroshi Tajima
Publication: Etudes de Langue et Littérature françaises (half-yearly)

Nippon Hikaku Bungakukai*, Aoyamagakuim University, Shibuya-ku, Tokyo
Comparative Literature Society of Japan
General-Secretary: Saburo Ota
Publications: Journal (annually), *Bulletin* (quarterly)

Nippon Romazikai*, Yosida Honmati 27, Kyoto
Japanese Society of Roman Letters
President: Ogata-Zyun'iti
Publication: Romazi Sekai (The World of Roman Letters)

Nippon Rosiya Bungakkai*, Faculty of Literature Waseda University, Toyama-cho, Shinjuku-ku, Tokyo
Russian Literary Society of Japan
Secretary-General: General K Nakano
Publication: Bulletin

Japan **P E N** Club*, Room 265, Syuwa Residential Hotel, 9-1-7 Akasaka, Minato-ku, Tokyo 107 Tel: (03) 4021171
President: Shusaku Endu; *Secretary:* Hotsuki Ozaki
Publications include: Japanese Literature Today (annually since 1976)

Society for the Promotion of Japanese Literature*, c/o Bungei Shunju Publishing Co Ltd, 3-23 Kioi-cho, Chiyoda-ku, Tokyo 102

Literary Periodicals

Doitsu Bungaku (German Literature), Nihon Dokubungakkai, Hongo 5-30-21, Bunkyo-ku, Tokyo 113

Doshisha Literature, Doshisha University, English Literature Society, Kyoto
Journal of English literature and philology; text in English

Doshisha Studies in Foreign Literature, Doshisha University, Foreign Literature Society, Kyoto
Text in Japanese, English, French or German

East-West Review, Doshisha University, Department of English, Kyoto
Essays and translations

Etudes de Langue et Littérature françaises (Studies in French Language and Literature), Nippon Furansu-go Furansu-bungaku Kai, c/o La Maison franco-japonaise, 2-3, Kanda-Surugadai Chiyoda-ku, Tokyo

Hon: a Book-bin for Scholars, Yushodo Booksellers Ltd, 29 Saneicho, Shinjuku-ku, Tokyo 160

Japan Quarterly, Asahi Shimbun-Sha, Tokyo

Japanese Literature, Nippon Bungaku Kyokai, 2-17-10 Minami-otsuka, Toshima-ku, Tokyo

Japanese Literature Today (1976-85) (annual), Japan P E N Club, Room 265, Syuwa Residential Hotel, 9-1-7 Akasaka, Minato-ku, Tokyo 107

Mototachi no Kagaribi, Kodansha International Ltd, 2-2 Otowa 1 chome, Bunkyo-ku, Tokyo 112

Outlook (Japan), Yoshidahon-machi, Sakyo-Ka, Kioto

The Sea, Chuokoron-Sha Inc, 2-8-7 Kyobashi, Chuo-ku, Tokyo 104

Studies in English Literature, Nihon Eibungakkai, 601 Kenkyusha Bldg, 9 Surugadai 2-chome, Kanda, Chiyoda-ku, Tokyo 101

Literary Prizes

Akutagawa Prize*
In memory of Ryunosuke Akutagawa for works written by previously unpublished authors. One of the most important literary prizes in Japan. 500,000 yen and a specially made watch. Awarded twice a year. Enquiries to The Society for the Promotion of Japanese Literature, c/o Bungei Shunju Publishing Co Ltd, 3-23 Kioi-cho, Chiyoda-ku, Tokyo 102

Culture Prize*
For outstanding achievement in the following areas: illustrations, photographs, book designs, juvenile cartoons and picture books: 300,000 yen. Non-fiction: 500,000 yen. Awarded annually to publishers in Japan. Enquiries to Kodansha Ltd, 2-12-21 Otowa, Bunkyo-ku, Tokyo 112

Japan Essayists' Club Prize*
For the best essays and criticism including those in book form, especially the work of new authors. 100,000 yen. Awarded annually. Enquiries to Japan Essayists' Club, c/o Yujiro Chiba, 1-1-1 Shimbashi, Minato-ku, Tokyo

Japan Poet Club Prize*
For an author who has contributed significantly to poetry. 50,000 yen. Awarded annually. Enquiries to Japan Poet Club, c/o Showa Joshi University, 1-7 Taishido, Setagaya-ku, Tokyo

Japan Translation Prize for Publisher*
For outstanding translations. Awarded annually. Enquiries to Japan Society of Translators, Rm 208, Shiba Mansion, 5-11-6 Toranomon, Minato-ku, Tokyo

Japan Woman Writer Prize*
For the best novel. 1,000,000 yen. Awarded annually. Enquiries to Chuokoron-Sha Inc, 2-8-7 Kyobashi, Chuo-ku, Tokyo 104

Japan Women Writers' Literary Prizes*
To encourage women novelists. Awarded annually. Enquiries to Women Writers' Association, 17 Yanaka-Shimizucho, Daito-ku, Tokyo

Kikuchi Prize*
In memory of Kan Kikuchi. 500,000 yen and a specially made clock. Awarded annually. This prize is given for significant achievement in Japanese literature, drama, cinema, newspaper, broadcasting, book or magazine publication. It can otherwise be given to the individual or group who showed the most creative achievement in the year in the introduction of Japanese literature to foreign countries. Enquiries to The Society for the Promotion of Japanese Literature, c/o Bungei Shunju Publishing Co Ltd, 3-23 Kioi-cho, Chiyoda-ku, Tokyo 102

Kishida Prize for Drama*
In commemoration of the playwright Kunio Kishida for an outstanding work by a new playwright. 200,000 yen. Awarded annually. Enquiries to Hakusui-Sha Co Ltd, 3-24 Kanda-Ogawa-machi, Chiyoda-ku, Tokyo 101

Mainichi Publishing Culture Prize*
To the authors and publishers of works contributing to human culture. 100,000 yen. Awarded annually. Enquiries to Mainichi Newspapers Publishing Co, 1-1, 1-chome, Hitotsubashi, Chiyoda-ku, Tokyo

Yukio **Mishima** Award
Established 1987. For a literary work (novel, criticism, poetry, drama) written by a new or moderately well-known writer and published during the preceding year. Annual award of commemorative plaque and 1,000,000 yen. Enquiries to Shincho-Sha Co Ltd, 71 Yarai-cho, Shinjuku-ku, Tokyo 162

Modern Poet Prize*
500,000 yen awarded annually for works by a leading poet. Enquiries to Japan Poets' Association, c/o Seitaro Yarita, 401 4-chome Ikebukuro, Toshima-ku, Tokyo

Mr H's Prize*
For works by a new poet. 500,000 yen and a table clock. Awarded annually. Enquiries to Japan Poets' Association, c/o Seitaro Yarita, 401 4-chome Ikebukuro, Toshima-ku, Tokyo

Naoki Prize*
In memory of Sanjugo Naoki, for the most promising writer of popular literature. 500,000 yen and a specially made watch. Awarded twice a year. Enquiries to The Society for the Promotion of Japanese Literature, c/o Bungei Shunju Publishing Co Ltd, 3-23 Kioi-cho, Chiyoda-ku, Tokyo 102

Noma Prize for Juvenile Novel*
For the best juvenile novel. 1,000,000 yen. Awarded annually. Enquiries to Kodansha Ltd, 2-12-21 Otowa, Bunkyo-ku, Tokyo 112

Noma Prize for Literature*
For the best Japanese novel of the year. 2,000,000 yen. Awarded annually. Enquiries to Kodansha Ltd, 2-12-21 Otowa, Bunkyo-ku, Tokyo 112

Oya Soichi Non-fiction Prize
To encourage new non-fiction writers. US$2,000, plus round-the-world air ticket, contributed by JAL Co Ltd. Awarded annually. Enquiries to Society for the Promotion of Japanese Literature, 3-23 Kioi-cho, Chiyoda-ku, Tokyo 102

The **Sankei** Award for Children's Books and Publications*
For authors of outstanding works published for children, in Japanese (including translations). First prize of 500,000 yen, five prizes of 100,000 yen and an Artistic Design Prize of 100,000 yen. Publishers of the works are also recognized. Awarded annually. Enquiries to Sankei Newspaper Co, 1-7-2 Otemachi, Chiyoda-ku, Tokyo

Shincho Gakugei-Sho
Established 1987. For a creative work of non-fiction contributing to Japanese art, literature or culture and published during the preceding year. Annual award of commemorative plaque and 1,000,000 yen. Enquiries to Shincho-Sha Co Ltd, 71 Yarai-cho, Shinjuku-ku, Tokyo 162

Shogakukan Literary Prize*
For the best novel, poem, drama and non-fiction for children published during the preceding year. 500,000 yen. Awarded annually. Enquiries to Shogakukan Inc, 2-3-1 Hitotsubashi, Chiyoda-ku, Tokyo 101

Tanizaki Junichiro Prize*
To recall the works by Tanizaki and to celebrate the publisher's birthday. 1,000,000 yen. Enquiries to Chuokoron-Sha Inc, 2-8-7 Kyobashi, Chuo-ku, Tokyo 104

Shugoro **Yamamoto** Award
Established 1987. For an outstanding novel written by a new or moderately well-known writer and published during the preceding year. Annual award of commemorative plaque and 1,000,000 yen. Enquiries to Shincho-Sha Co Ltd, 71 Yarai-cho, Shinjuku-ku, Tokyo 162

Yomiuri Literature Prize*
Established in 1950 for the best work in six categories: novel, essay and travels, drama, literary study and translation, poetry and haiku, critique and biography. 1,000,000 yen each, awarded annually. The latest prizewinners in each category were: Takako Takahashi for *Ikari no Ko* (Kodansha Ltd) and Hideo Takubo for *Kaizu* (Kodansha Ltd) (joint award, novel); Inako Sata for *Tsuki no En* (Kodansha Ltd) (essay and travels); Fumi Saito for *Hakadorikayukamu* (Fushiki Shoin Publishing Co) (poetry and haiku); Masaaki Kanno for *Stephane Mallarme* (Chuokoron-Sha Inc) and Chiaki Matsudaira for *Anabasis* (Chikuma Shobo Publishing Co Ltd) (joint award, literary study and translation). There were no awards in the categories of drama and

critique and biography. Enquiries to Yomiuri Newspapers Publishing Co, 1-7-1 Otemachi, Chiyoda-ku, Tokyo

Yoshikawa Prizes*
For the most popular novel: 2,000,000 yen. For a new novelist: 500,000 yen. Awarded annually. Enquiries to Kodansha Ltd, 2-12-21 Otowa, Bunkyo-ku, Tokyo 112

Translation Agencies and Associations

Japan Society of Translators*, Orion Press, 1-55 Kanda Jinbo-cho, Thiyoda-ku, Tokyo 101

Jordan

General Information

Language: Arabic. English widely used by business people
Religion: Islamic, large Christian minority
Population: 3.2 million
Bank Hours: 0830-1230 Saturday-Thursday
Shop Hours: 0900-1300, 1500-1900 Saturday-Thursday
Currency: 1000 fils = 1 dinar; 10 fils is known as a piastre
Export/Import Information: No tariffs on books and advertising matter, but tax applies. Import licences required but granted freely. Air freight must be by Jordanian national airline. Transportation insurance must be arranged in Jordan
Copyright: No copyright conventions signed

Book Trade Reference Books

Jordanian National Bibliography (annually), Jordan Library Association, PO Box 6289, Amman

Palestinian Bibliography: A List of Books Published by the Arabs in Palestine 1948-1980, Jordan Library Association, PO Box 6289, Amman

Palestinian-Jordanian Bibliography, Jordan Library Association, PO Box 6289, Amman

Publishers

Jordan Book Centre Co Ltd+, PO Box 301 Al-Jubeiha, Amman Tel: (06) 606882/676882 Cable Add: Jordan Book Centre Jubeiha, Jordan Telex: 21153 Fax: (06) 9626602016
Chief Executive: I Sharbain
Subjects: General Fiction & Non-fiction
Bookshop: See under Major Booksellers
1985: 3 titles *1986:* 6 titles *Founded:* 1982

Jordan Distribution Agency, PO Box 375, Amman Tel: (06) 30191 Cable Add: Jodistag Amman Telex: 22083 Distag Jo
Chairman, General Manager: Raja Elissa;
Deputy Chairman, Dir: Nadia Elissa
Subjects: Jordanian Tourism and History
Founded: 1951

Jordan House for Publication, PO Box 1121, Amman (Located at: Basman St, Amman) Tel: (06) 24224 Telex: 22056 Bestours Jo

Man Dir: Mursi Elashkar; *Editorial:* Dr Mohamad Takrouri
Subjects: Medical, Secondary & University Textbooks
Bookshops: 2 Basman St, Amman; Jabal Amman St, Amman
Founded: 1952

Major Booksellers

Jordan Book Centre Co Ltd, PO Box 301 Al-Jubeiha, Amman Tel: (06) 676882/606882 Telex: 21153 Fax: (06) 9626602016

Sharbain's Bookshop, PO Box 2427, Jebel Amman, Amman

University of Jordan Bookshop, University of Jordan, PO Box 13307, Amman

Yarmouk University Bookstore, Yarmouk University, Irbid Tel: (02) 71100 Cable Add: Yarmouk Jordan Telex: 51533 Jo

Major Libraries

American Center Library*, PO Box 676, Amman (Located at: 3rd Circle, Jebel Amman, Amman) Tel: (06) 41520/44371 ext 374
Librarian: Ms Jumana Esau

Amman Public Library*, c/o City Librarian, PO Box 182181, Amman Tel: (06) 27719/637111 Telex: 21969 Amcity Jo
City Librarian: Farouk Mo'az

British Council Library*, Amman Centre, Jebel Amman, Amman Tel: (06) 36147 Telex: 21823 Bcjor Jo

Public Library*, PO Box 348, Irbid

University of Jordan Library*, University of Jordan, Amman Tel: (06) 843555/843666 Telex: 21629 Unvj jo
Director: Dr Hani Al-Amad
Publications include: Al-Maktaba (monthly newsletter); *The Library Guide* (in English and Arabic); *Periodical Holdings* (in English and Arabic); *Arab References till 1980* (in Arabic); *Jordanian Publications in 1982*

Yarmouk University Library*, Yarmouk University, Irbid Tel: (02) 71100/71115 Cable Add: Yarmouk Jordan Telex: 51533 Yarmuk Jo
Dir: Dr F Mansour

Library Association

Jordan Library Association, PO Box 6289, Amman Tel: (06) 29412
President: Farouk Mo'az; *Vice-President:* Nayef A A Khalifeh; *Executive Secretary:* Adib Akel
Publications: Rissalat al-Maktaba (The Message of the Library) (quarterly); *Palestinian-Jordanian Bibliography 1900/1970 and 1971-1975*; *Directory of Libraries in Jordan 1976*; *Jordanian National Bibliography* (annually); *Introduction to Librarianship and Information Science* (in Arabic), *1982*; *The Palestinian Bibliography: a List of Books Published by the Arabs in Palestine 1948-1980*; *Directory of Jordanian Periodicals*, 1982; *Anglo-American Cataloguing Rules* (2nd Edition; in Arabic), 1983; *Directory of Libraries and Librarians in Jordan* (bilingual), 1984; *Technical Processing of Information* (in Arabic)

Library Reference Books and Journals

Books

Directory of Libraries and Librarians in Jordan, (bilingual) 1984, Jordan Library Association, PO Box 6289, Amman

Directory of Jordanian Periodicals, Jordan Library Association, PO Box 6289, Amman

Journal

Rissalat al-Maktaba (The Message of the Library), Jordan Library Association, PO Box 6289, Amman
Text in Arabic, summaries in English

Kampuchea

General Information

It has not been possible to obtain information on publishing and bookselling in Kampuchea for several years. In view of the changed circumstances of the country, information obtained in the past has been omitted from this edition of *International Literary Market Place*
Language: Khmer, French
Religion: Theravada Buddhist
Population: 6.7 million
Business Hours: 0700-1400 Monday-Saturday
Currency: riel
Export/Import Information: Little current information available; free foreign exchange market arrangements not operating
Copyright: UCC, Florence (see International section)

Kenya

General Information

Language: Swahili (also English)
Religion: About 30% Christian, 6% Islamic; remainder traditional beliefs
Population: 15.3 million
Bank Hours: 0900-1400 Monday-Friday; 0900-1100 first and last Saturday of each month (except on coast, where banks open and close half an hour earlier)
Shop Hours: 0830-1230, 1400-1630 Monday-Friday; 0830-1200 or 1230 Saturday
Currency: 100 cents = 1 Kenya shilling
Export/Import Information: No tariff on books or advertising matter. Import licences and exchange controls
Copyright: UCC (see International section)

Book Trade Organizations

Kenya Booksellers' and Stationers' Association*, PO Box 20373, Nairobi Tel: (02) 21031
Secretary: Adrian P Louis

Kenya Publishers' Association*, c/o PO Box 72532, Nairobi Tel: (02) 336377
Secretary: James Clarke

Standard Book Numbering Agency, Kenya National Library Services, PO Box 30573, Nairobi Tel: (02) 27871/29186
ISBN Administrator: Francis C Ochola

Book Trade Reference Books and Journals

Book

Kenya National Bibliography, Kenya National Library Service, Ngong Rd, PO Box 30573, Nairobi

Journal

Bookshop Bulletin, Textbook Centre, Kijabe St, PO Box 47540, Nairobi

Publishers

A F E R (African Ecclesial Review), an imprint of Gaba Publications (qv)

C P I, an imprint of Camerapix Publishers International Ltd (qv)

Camerapix Publishers International Ltd, PO Box 45048, Nairobi Tel: (02) 23511/334398 Cable Add: Movietone Nairobi Telex: 22576
Man Dir: Mohamed Amin; *Editorial:* Brian Tetley; *Sales:* Nazma Rawji; *Production:* Duncan Willetts
Imprint: CPI
Subjects: Illustrated books, especially on Africa, Middle East and Asia
Founded: 1960

Comb Books+*, PO Box 20019, Nairobi
Man Dir: David Maillu
Subjects: General Fiction, Social Anthropology, Sexual Problems, Educational
Founded: 1972

East African Directory Co*, PO Box 41237, Nairobi Tel: (02) 24151
Man Dir: T A Bhatt
Parent Company: United Africa Press Ltd (qv)
Subject: Reference
Founded: 1947

East African Literature Bureau, see Kenya Literature Bureau

East African Publishing House, Lusaka Close, PO Box 30571, Nairobi Tel: (02) 557417 Cable Add: Afrobooks Nairobi
Man Dir: E N Wainaina; *Chief Editor, Rights & Permissions:* Gacheche Waruingi; *Marketing, Publicity, Sales, Distribution:* James K Muraya; *Production:* John Mwazo
Parent Company: E A Cultural Trust
Associate Company: Afropress Ltd, PO Box 30502, Nairobi
Branch Off: PO Box 3209, Dar es Salaam, Tanzania
Subjects: General Fiction & Non-fiction, Belles Lettres, Poetry, Biography, History, Africana, How-to, Study Guides, Reference, Religion, Juveniles, Books in Kiswahili and other East African languages, Paperbacks, General & Social Science, University, Secondary & Primary Textbooks
Founded: 1965

Evangel Publishing House, PO Box 28963, Nairobi Tel: (02) 802033 Cable Add: Evangelit Nairobi
Man Dir, Editorial, Rights and Permissions: Rev B D Brand; *Sales, Publicity:* Rev Elkanah S Ayiga; *Production:* David Koop
Subjects: General Non-fiction, Reference, Religion, Christian Tracts, Paperbacks, Children's Books
Bookshop: At above address
ISBN Publisher's Prefix: 9966-850

Foundation Books, Kencom House, Moi Ave, PO Box 73435, Nairobi Tel: (02) 723876
Sub-regional Co-ordinator, Regional Centre for Book Promotion in Africa; Co-publishing programme Eastern Africa Region
Man Dir: F O Okwanya; *Editorial:* C O Ojienda; *Sales Promotion:* Moses Gondi; *Production:* Sophia Wanjiku Ojienda
Subjects: Belles Lettres, Poetry, Biography, History, Africana, Juveniles, Books in Kiswahili, Paperbacks, Social Science, Secondary & Primary Textbooks, Adult Education Primers, Mathematics
Founded: 1974

Gaba Publications, AMECEA Pastoral Institute, PO Box 4002, Eldoret Tel: (321) 32244
Dir, Editor: Fr Felician N Rwehikiza
Imprints: AFER (African Ecclesial Review), Spearhead (series)
Subjects: Religion, Anthropology, Scripture, Third World Theology, Religious Education
1985: 11 titles *Founded:* 1959

Government Printer*, Government Printing Press, PO Box 30128, Nairobi

Heinemann Kenya Ltd+, Kijabe St, PO Box 45314, Nairobi Tel: (02) 22057/28949/22144 Cable Add: Hebooks Nairobi
Man Dir, Rights and Permissions: Henry Chakava; *Editorial:* Paul N Njoroge, Mrs Nazi Kivutha, Jimmi Makotsi, Anne Wanjie; *Sales Dir:* Johnson K Mugweru; *Sales Manager:* John Mutuku; *Trade Manager:* Onyango Ogutu
Associate Company: The Heinemann Group of Publishers Ltd, UK (qv)
Subjects: General Fiction & Non-fiction, Belles Lettres, Poetry, Biography, History, Africana, Study Guides, Juveniles, Swahili Language & Literature, Paperbacks, General & Social Science, Business Education, University, Secondary & Primary Textbooks
1985: 41 titles *1986:* 44 titles *Founded:* 1967

Kenya Literature Bureau*, Ngong' Rd, PO Box 30022, Nairobi Tel: (02) 723450/722657 Cable Add: Literature Nairobi
Formerly East African Literature Bureau

The Jomo **Kenyatta** Foundation, PO Box 30533, Nairobi Tel: (02) 540291/557222 Cable Add: Foundation
Chief Executive: J K Arap Sang; *Publicity, Rights & Permissions:* A K N Mbuvi; *Chief Editor:* J Kariara; *Production Manager:* Ben Ole Mollel
Parent Organization: Ministry of Education, PO Box 30040, Nairobi
Subjects: Secondary and Primary Textbooks
Founded: 1966

Longman Kenya Ltd, Funzi Rd, PO Box 18033, Nairobi Tel: (02) 541345 Cable Add: Longman Nairobi Telex: 24101
Man Dir: Dr E M Mugiri; *Publishing Manager:* A S Yahya; *Marketing Manager:* F Njagi; *Distribution Manager:* T Kamuyu; *Rights & Permissions:* Longman Group (UK) Ltd, UK (qv)
Parent Company: Longman Group UK Ltd, UK (qv)
Subjects: General Fiction & Non-fiction, Belles Lettres, Poetry, Biography, History, Africana, Reference, Juveniles, Books in 14 Kenyan languages, Paperbacks, General & Social Science, Secondary & Primary Textbooks
Founded: 1965

Newspread International, PO Box 46854, Nairobi Tel: (02) 331402 Cable Add: Newspread Telex: 22143 Bureau
Executive Editor: Kul Bhushan; *Production Manager:* Benedict Mutisya Nzomo
Subjects: Reference
Founded: 1971

Njogu Gitene Publications, PO Box 72989, Nairobi
Publicity Manager: Jayne Ng'ang'a
Subjects: Belles Lettres, Poetry, Juveniles, Books in Kiswahili, Secondary & Primary Textbooks
Founded: 1970

Oxford University Press*, East and Central Africa, PO Box 72532, Nairobi (Located at: First Floor, Science House, Monrovia St, Nairobi) Tel: (02) 336377 Cable Add: Oxonian Nairobi Telex: 22574 Colybrand Nairobi (for OUP)
Regional Manager, Rights & Permissions: James Clarke; *Editor:* Brian Hocking; *Sales:* Abdallah Ismaily
Branch Offs: Dar es Salaam, Tanzania (qv); Harare, Zimbabwe (qv)
Subjects: General Literature, Africana, Reference, Academic and College, Secondary & Primary Textbooks, Books in Kiswahili
Founded: 1954
Miscellaneous: Firm is a branch of Oxford University Press, UK (qv)
ISBN Publisher's Prefix: 0-19

Salama Publications Ltd*, PO Box 48009, Nairobi
Subjects: How-to, Study Guides, Secondary Textbooks

Spearhead, an imprint of Gaba Publications (qv)

Success Publications*, PO Box 10893, Nairobi
Subjects: How-to, Study Guides

Text Book Centre Ltd, Kijabe St, PO Box 47540, Nairobi Tel: (02) 330340/330341
Man Dir: M J Rughani; *General Manager:* C D Shah
Subjects: Belles Lettres, Poetry, Juveniles, Books in Kiswahili, Paperbacks, Secondary & Primary Textbooks
Bookshops: See under Major Booksellers, also Westlands Sarit Centre, PO Box 47540, Nairobi

Transafrica Press*, Kenwood House, Kimathi St, PO Box 49421, Nairobi Tel: (02) 22245
Man Dir: John Nottingham
Subjects: General Fiction & Non-fiction, Belles Lettres, Poetry, Biography, History, Africana, How-to, Study Guides, Reference, Religion, Juveniles, Books in Kiswahili, Social Science, Secondary & Primary Textbooks, Paperbacks, Wall Maps
1985: 12 titles *Founded:* 1976

United Africa Press Ltd*, Victoria House, Victoria St, PO Box 41237, Nairobi Tel: (02) 24151
Man Dir: T A Bhatt
Subsidiary Company: East African Directory Co (qv)
Subjects: General, Educational, Reference, Animals
Founded: 1952

Uzima Press Ltd, PO Box 48127, Nairobi (Located at: St John's Gate) Tel: (02) 20239/335699
Man Dir: Rev Horace Etemesi
Subjects: Religion, Fiction, Social Sciences, Books for new literates, Children's Books
Founded: 1974

Vipopremo Agencies*, Koinange St, PO Box 47717, Nairobi Tel: (02) 27189
Subjects: How-to, Study Guides

Major Booksellers

The **Bookshop** Ltd*, Esso House, Kaunda St, PO Box 30247, Nairobi Tel: (02) 23364

The **Catholic Bookshop** Ltd*, Kaunda St, PO Box 30249, Nairobi Tel: (02) 25172/338514
Manager: Sr Giovanna

Dhanani's Ltd*, Kimasi St, Corner House, PO Box 72399, Nairobi Tel: (02) 27049

E S A Bookshop*, Church House, Government Rd, PO Box 30167, Nairobi Tel: (02) 20158

Keswick Book Society*, Portal House, Banda St, PO Box 10242, Nairobi Tel: (02) 26047
Manager: Miss M Håkanson

S J Moore Ltd*, Moi Ave, PO Box 30162, Nairobi Tel: (02) 22213
Manager: R M Rughani

Mount Kenya Bookshop Ltd*, PO Box 281, Nyeri Tel: (0171) 2513
Branches: PO Box 659, Nakuru Tel: (037) 2806; PO Box 10, Kakamega Tel: 20163; PO Box 29, Meru Tel: 20036
Man Dir: David M Mwangi

Patwa (Embakasi) Ltd*, PO Box 19200, Nairobi Airport, Embakasi, Nairobi

Prestige Booksellers*, Prudential Assurance Bldg, PO Box 45425, Nairobi Tel: (02) 23515

Text Book Centre Ltd, Kijabe St, PO Box 47540, Nairobi Tel: (02) 330340 Cable Add: Text books Telex: 23037 Sarit
Manager: C D Shah
Also Publisher (qv)

University of Nairobi Bookshop*, PO Box 30197, Nairobi Tel: (02) 334244 ext 2111, 2353 Cable Add: Varsity
Manager: Miss N N Kagondu

Wanyee Bookshop Ltd*, Aga Khan Walk, PO Box 46815, Nairobi Tel: (02) 331769
Manager: Mrs L W Wanyee

Major Libraries

Egerton College Library*, PO Njoro Tel: (02) 274447

Kabete Library*, University of Nairobi, PO Box 29053, Kabete

Kenya Agricultural Research Institute, PO Box 30148, Nairobi Tel: (02) 32880 Cable Add: Agfororg
Librarian: Daniel Njoroge Kaiyare

Kenya National Archives, PO Box 49210, Nairobi Tel: (02) 28959/26007/28020 Cable Add: Archives
Librarian: Nancy Kamau
Founded: 1946
Publications: Acquisitions guides (various)

Kenya National Library Service, Ngong' Rd, PO Box 30573, Nairobi Tel: (02) 725550/725569/725983
Dir: Apollo R Oluoch
Publications include: Kenya National Bibliography; Kenyan Periodicals Directory

Kenya Polytechnic Library*, PO Box 52428, Nairobi Tel: (02) 338231
Librarian: Cephas Dennis Odini

Kenya Technical Teachers' College Library*, PO Box 44600, Nairobi Tel: (02) 520211
Librarian: William G Kinyanjui
Publications include: Secondary School Library Facilities in Central Province, Kenya; The Problems of Providing Library Services to School Children in Developing Countries; Serials Literature, Exploitation and Use in Libraries; Mwalimu Kenya Education Supplement (monthly)

Kenyatta University Library, PO Box 43844, Nairobi Tel: (02817) 356-9; 247/421/459
Librarian: James Mwangi Nganga
Publications include: Directory of Research in the University; Annual Report; Education in Kenya since Independence: a bibliography, 1963-1983; Education in Kenya: an Index . . . — December 1984

McMillan Memorial Library*, Banda St, PO Box 40791, Nairobi Tel: (02) 21844
Chief Librarian: R G Opondo

Mines and Geological Department Library, Machakos Rd, PO Box 30009, Nairobi Tel: (02) 541040 Cable Add: Mineralogy

Ministry of Agriculture and Livestock Development Library, Kilimo House, PO Box 30028, Nairobi Tel: (02) 720030 ext 2504, 2505, 2519
Under the charge of The Library Services Co-ordinator
Publications include: Economic Review of Agriculture

University of Nairobi Libraries*, PO Box 30197, Nairobi Tel: (02) 334244 Cable Add: Varsity Nairobi
Branches: Chiromo, Kabete, Kikuyu

Library Association

Kenya Library Association, PO Box 46031, Nairobi
Secretary: Lily Nyariki
Publications: Maktaba; Kelias News (bi-monthly)

Library Reference Journal

Maktaba, Kenya Library Association, PO Box 46031, Nairobi
Biannual official journal of the Kenya Library Association

Literary Periodicals

Busara, Kenya Literature Bureau, PO Box 30022, Nairobi
Biannual literary magazine published under the auspices of the Department of Literature, University of Nairobi

Dhana, Kenya Literature Bureau, PO Box 30022, Nairobi
The Makerere University, Department of Literature, biannual journal of creative writing

Joe, Joe Publications Ltd, PO Box 30362, Nairobi
Monthly magazine with regular literary contributions, reviews of new books and plays, etc

Joliso, Kenya Literature Bureau, PO Box 30022, Nairobi
Biannual literary and cultural magazine

Umma, Kenya Literature Bureau, PO Box 30022, Nairobi
The University of Dar es Salaam, Department of Literature, biannual journal of creative writing

Democratic People's Republic of Korea

General Information

Language: Korean
Religion: Confucian, Buddhist
Population: 17.9 million
Currency: 100 jun = 1 won
Export/Import Information: No tariff information; all importation and exportation must go through Korea Publications Export & Import Corporation, Pyongyang

Book Trade Reference Journal

Catalogue of Korean Publications, Korea Publications Export & Import Corporation, Chulpanmul, Pyongyang
English listing of books published in various languages

Publishers

Academy of Sciences Publishing House*, Central District Nammundong, Pyongyang
Subjects: Science, Chemistry, Geology, Metallurgy, Physics, Biology, History, Maps, Mathematics, Meteorology, Education, Economics
Founded: 1953

Academy of Social Sciences Publishing House*, Pyongyang
Subject: Social Sciences

Agricultural Books Publishing House*, Pyongyang
President: Li Hyun U
Subjects: Agriculture, Industry

Educational Books Publishing House*, Pyongyang
Subject: Education, Textbooks

Foreign Languages Publishing House*, Pyongyang
President: L Ryang Hun
Subjects: Books on Korea, Foreign publications in translation, Periodicals (English language)

Higher Educational Books Publishing House*, Pyongyang
Acting President: Shin Jong Sung
Subjects: Education, Academic, Mathematics, Physics

Industrial Publishing House*, Pyongyang
Subjects: Trade, Industry

Kumsong Youth Publishing House*, Pyongyang
Subjects: Children's, Juveniles

Literature and Art Publishing House*, Pyongyang
Subjects: Fiction, Arts

Mass Culture Publishing House*, Pyongyang

Railway Publishing House*, Pyongyang
Subject: Railways

Science and Encyclopaedia Publishing House*, Pyongyang
Subjects: Science, Dictionaries

Workers' Party of Korea Publishing House*, Pyongyang
Subjects: Fiction, Politics

Major Booksellers

Korea Publications Export & Import Corporation*, Chulpanmul, Pyongyang
Cable Add: Chulpanmul, Pyongyang
Export Manager: Kim Myong Sob
The sole importing and exporting organization

Major Libraries

People's Grand Study Centre*, Pyongyang
State Central Library*, Pyongyang

Library Association

Library Association of the Democratic People's Republic of Korea*, State Central Library, Pyongyang Tel: 3-8741
Executive Secretary: Li Geug

Republic of Korea

General Information

Language: Korean (English also spoken in business)
Religion: Buddhist, Christian, Confucian
Population: 42 million
Bank Hours: 0930-1600 Monday-Friday; 0930-1300 Saturday
Shop Hours: 1000-1900 Monday-Saturday
Currency: won
Export/Import Information: No tariffs on books and advertising matter. Authorizations for import of books and publications are reviewed annually by the Korean government. Import licences are required. Exchange controls; prior deposits required at present
Copyright: UCC (see International section)

Book Trade Organization

Korean Publishers Association, 105-2 Sagan-dong, Chongno-ku, Seoul 110 Tel: (02) 7340790/7338402/7352701 Cable Add: Bookhouse Seoul
President: In-Kyu Lim; *Secretary-General:* Doo-Young Lee
Publications: K P A Journal (monthly, Korean); Korean Publication Yearbook (annual, Korean); Newsletter on New Books (monthly, Korean); Books from Korea (biennial, English)

Book Trade Reference Books and Journals

Books

Books from Korea (biennial), Korean Publishers Association, 105-2 Sagan-dong, Chongno-ku, Seoul 110
Text in English

Catalogue of Government Publications, National Assembly Library, Yoi-dong 1, Yeongdeungpo-gu, Seoul 150
Includes University publications

Korean Publication Yearbook, Korean Publishers Association, 105-2 Sagan-dong, Chongno-ku, Seoul 110

Journals

K P A Journal (monthly), Korean Publishers Association, 105-2 Sagan-dong, Chongno-ku, Seoul 110

Korean National Bibliography, Central National Library, 100-177 Hoehyun-dong 1-ka, Chung-ku, Seoul 100

Newsletter on New Books (monthly), Korean Publishers Association, 105-2 Sagan-dong, Chongno-ku, Seoul 110

Publishers

Baik Rog Publishing Co*, 130-2 Insa-dong, Chongno-ku, Seoul 110 Tel: (02) 7245240
President: Hi Kyung Kim
Subjects: Literature, Juvenile

Bak Yung Sa*, 219 Pyong-dong, Chongno-ku, Seoul 110 Tel: (02) 7336771
President: Jong-man Ahn
Subjects: Philosophy, Literature, Social Science, Linguistics, Science
Founded: 1952

Beupmun Sa Publishing Co*, 1-48 Cheung-dong, Chung-ku, Seoul 100 Tel: (02) 7356317
President and Publicity: Hyo Seon Bae; *Man Dir:* Chul Hwan Kim; *Dir:* Choong Young Jun; *Editorial:* Bok Hyun Choe
Subsidiary Company: Minjungseorim Publishing Co (qv)
Subjects: Law, Accountancy, Economics, Management, Politics, Public Administration, Education, Psychology, Sociology
Founded: 1952

Changjo Sa*, 92 Sinmun-ro 2-ka, Chongno-ku, Seoul 110
President: Deok Kyu Choi
Subjects: Literature, Linguistics, History
Founded: 1963

Dan Kook University Press*, 8 Hannam-dong, Yongsan-ku, Seoul 140 Tel: (02) 7935034
President: Choong Shik Chang
Subjects: Literature, History, School Reference

Daihak Publishing Co*, 125 4-ka, Myongryun-dong, Chongno-ku, Seoul 110 Tel: (02) 7642745
President: Jin Young Yoon
Subjects: Juvenile, Technology

Dong Hwa Publishing Co*, 130-4 Wonhyo-ro 1-ka, Yongsan-ku, Seoul 140 Tel: (02) 7135411
President: In-Kyu Lim; *Editorial Dir:* Kyoung-Sik Roh; *Sales Dir:* Byong-Don Ann; *Production Dir:* Chong-Choon Seo; *Publicity Dir:* Kun-Han Park
Subjects: Literature, Fine Arts, History, Philosophy, Children's Picture Books
Founded: 1968

Eulyoo Publishing Co Ltd, PO Box 362, Gwanghwa-Mun, 46-1 Susong-dong, Chongno-ku, Seoul 110 Tel: (02) 7334745/7338150 Cable Add: Eulyoo Seoul
President: Chin Sook Choung; *Man Dir:* Pil Young Choung; *Editorial, Production:* Il Joon Park; *Sales:* Nam Soo Lee
Subjects: Literature, Philosophy, Linguistics, History
Founded: 1945

Ewha Womans University Press*, 11-1 Daehyun-dong, Seodaemun-ku, Seoul 120 Tel: (02) 3626076
President: Eui Sook Cheung; *Dir:* Young-Il Kim
Subjects: Humanities, Social/Natural/Applied Sciences, Music, Fine Arts, Dance, Education, Philosophy, Religion, Linguistics
Founded: 1949

Gimm-Young Press*, 198-1 Kwanhun-dong, Chongno-ku, Seoul 110 Tel: (02) 3132331
President: Jung Sup Gimm
Subjects: Religion, Philosophy, Science

Han Jin Publishing Co*, 65-15 3-ka Pil-dong, Chung-ku, Seoul 100 Tel: (02) 2610184
President: Gab Jin Han
Subjects: Literature, Religion, Juvenile, Arts

Hak Won Publishing Co Ltd*, 44-37 Yeoido-dong, Yongdeungpo-ku, Seoul 150 Tel: (02) 7820181
President: Young-Su Kim
Subjects: Child care, Cookery, Fine Arts, Literature, Home Economics, Social Science, Periodicals
Founded: 1945

Hollym Corporation, Publishers, 14-5 Kwanchol-dong, Chongno-ku, Seoul 110 Tel: (02) 7357551/7355146
President: In-Soo Rhimm; *Man Dir:*, *Publicity Dir:* Shin-Won Chu; *Sales Dir:* Yong-Kwon Kim; *Advertising Dir:* Tae-Hong Jeong
Branch Off: Hollym International Corp, 18 Donald Place, Elizabeth, NJ 07208, USA
Subjects: English-language-only books on Korea comprising General Fiction, Belles Lettres, Poetry, Biography, History, Juveniles, High-priced Paperbacks
Book Club: Korea Book Club
Founded: 1963

Hwimoon Publishing Co*, 30 Kyunji-dong, Chongno-ku, Seoul 110 Tel: (02) 724897
Man Dir: Myong Hui Yi
Subjects: General Fiction, Belles Lettres, Poetry, Biography, History, Philosophy, Religion, Juveniles
Founded: 1961

Hyang Mun Publishing Co, 39-16 Kyonji-dong, Chongno-ku, Seoul 110 Tel: (02) 7324790/7350447
President: Joong Ryol Nah
Subjects: Agriculture, Science, History, Engineering, Home Economics
Founded: 1957

Hyun Am Publishing Co*, 627-5 Ahyun-dong, Mapo-ku, Seoul 121 Tel: (02) 3625022
Man Dir: Keun-Tae Cho; *Publicity:* Sang-Won Cho
Subjects: Philosophy, Literature, Religion
Founded: 1951

Il Cho Kak*, 9 Gongpyung-dong, Chongno-ku, Seoul 110 Tel: (02) 7335430 Cable Add: Ichopublico Seoul
Man Dir: Man-Nyun Han; *Sales Dir:* L J Kim; *Publicity Dir:* J Y Choi
Subjects: History, High-priced Paperbacks, Medicine, Psychology, Engineering, General & Social Science, Secondary & University Textbooks, Educational Materials, Law, Philosophy
Founded: 1953

Il Ji Sa Publishing Co*, 46-1 Chunghak-dong, Chongno-ku, Seoul 110 Tel: (02) 7323980
Man Dir: Sung Jae Kim; *Publicity Dirs:* Byungki Yoo, Donhong Cho
Subjects: General Fiction, Belles Lettres,

Poetry, History, Archaeology, Philosophy, Sociology, Linguistics, Children's Books
Founded: 1956

Jeongeumsa Publishing Co*, PO Box Central 7, 22-5 Chungmu-ro 5-ka, Chung-ku, Seoul 100 Tel: (02) 279580/255681 Cable Add: Jeongeumsa
President: Tong-Seek Chair; *Sales Dir:* Choong-tae Kim; *Publicity & Advertising:* Joo Park
Subjects: General Fiction, Belles Lettres, Philosophy, Social Science
Bookshop: 22-5, 5-ka, Chungmu-Ro, Jung-gu, Seoul
Founded: 1928

Junpa Kwahak Sa*, 156-10 Dongkyo-dong, Mapo-ku, Seoul 121 Tel: (02) 3224238
President: Yung Soo Shon
Subjects: Sciences, Engineering
Founded: 1956

Jungwoo Sa*, 432-12 Galhyun-dong, Eunpyung-ku, Seoul 122 Tel: (02) 3886137
President: Je Sook Seo
Subjects: Literature, Religion

Kam Sung Publishing Co Ltd+, 242-63 Gongdeog-dong, PO Box 92, Mapo-ku, Seoul 121 Tel: (02) 7139651/7179541 Fax: (02) 7179544
Representative Dir: Nak Joon Kim; *Executive Dir:* Sung-Chul Kang; *Man Dir:* Bo-Hwan Lee; *Manager:* Dae-Shik Kim; *Assistant Managers:* Chae-Hyung Lee, Gwang-So Lee
Subsidiary Company: Kum Sung Textbook Co Ltd (at above address)
Associate Companies: Shin Won Planning Co, 250-4 Towha-dong, Mapo-ku, Seoul; Kum Sung Art Production, 250-1 Towha-dong, Mapo-ku, Seoul
Branch Offs: 100 local branches; also Han Kang Buchhandlung, Kaiserstr 42, 6000 Frankfurt am Main, Federal Republic of Germany
Subjects: General, Children's
1985: 20 series *1986:* 23 series *Founded:* 1965

Kemongsa+, 12-23 Kwanchul-dong, Chongno-ku, Seoul 110 Tel: (02) 7347818/7322248 Telex: Kemsy K22642
President: Choon Sik Kim; *Editorial Dir:* Jin Joo Woo
Subjects: Juveniles, Education
Founded: 1950

Ko Mun Sa*, 617-8 Ahyun-dong, Mapo-ku, Seoul 121 Tel: (02) 3923831
President: Yun ki Baik
Subjects: Medicine, Pharmacy, Dictionaries

Korea Britannica Corporation*, CPO Box 690, Seoul 100 Tel: (02) 2752151/2757081/2664111 Cable Add: Britannica-Seoul Telex: Ebkorea K27286
Chief Executive: Yun Sang Rhee; *Publicity, Rights & Permissions:* Yong Namkung
Parent Company: Encyclopaedia Britannica Inc, Britannica Center, 310 South Michigan Ave, Chicago, IL 60604, USA
Subjects: General, Educational, Children's
Founded: 1968

Korea Directory Co, CPO Box 3955, Seoul 100 (Located at: 21-3 Mugyo-Dong, Chung-ku, Seoul 100) Tel: (02) 7761140/7761370/7571267
President: Sung Tae Kim; *Manager:* O R Kim
Subjects: Directories, Periodicals

Korea Textbook Co Ltd*, 62-7 1-ka Manri-dong, Chung-ku, Seoul 100 Tel: (02) 3925855
President: Hak Soo Lee
Parent Company: Kwangmyong Printing & Publishing Co Ltd (qv)
Subjects: Arts, Education, Politics

Korea University Press*, 1-2, Anam-dong 5-ka, Sungbuk-ku, Seoul 132 Tel: (02) 9236311/9221068
President: Joon Bum Lee; *Dir:* U-Chang Kim
Subjects: Philosophy, History, Literature, Sociology, Language, Education, Psychology, Social Science, Natural Science, Engineering, Agriculture
Founded: 1956

The **Korean Culture** and Arts Foundation*, 1-130 Dongsung-dong, Chongno-ku, Seoul 110 Tel: (02) 7625231
President: Chung Han-mo
Subjects: Literature, Culture and Arts

Kwang Jang Press*, 80 Sagan-dong, Chongno-ku, Seoul 110 Tel: (02) 7226704
President: Won Kim
Subjects: Arts, Engineering

Kwangmyong Printing & Publishing Co Ltd*, CPO Box 3785, Seoul (Located at: 62 Manri-dong 1-ka, Chung-ku, Seoul) Tel: (02) 7530671/7536584 Cable Add: Kwangmyong, Seoul Telex: K27229 Kortuna
President: Hak Soo Lee; *Dir:* Yun Bai Yoon
Subsidiary Companies: Korea Textbook Co (qv); Kwangmyong Toppan Moore Printing Co
Subject: Korean Art (ancient and contemporary)
Founded: 1951

Kyobo Publishing Inc, 1 1-ka Chongno, Chongno-ku, Seoul 110 Tel: (02) 7222455
Subjects: Literature, Politics, Law
Bookshop: Kyobo Book Centre Co Ltd (qv under Major Booksellers)

Kyohaksa Publishing Co Ltd+, 105-67 Kongdock-dong, Mapo-ku, Seoul Tel: (02) 7174473
President: Cheol-Woo Yang
Subjects: Primary, Secondary & University Textbooks, Children's Books, Dictionaries, Business, Non-fiction

Kyung Hee University Press*, 1 Hoegi-dong, Dongdaemun-ku, Seoul 131 Tel: (02) 9660061
President: Chi Yol An
Subjects: Language, History, Philosophy, Social Science

Kyung In Munwha Sa*, 86-2 Yunhee-dong, Seodaemun-ku, Seoul 120
President: Sang Ha Han
Subjects: General, History, Philosophy
Founded: 1969

Kyungnam University Press*, 449 Weolyoung-dong, Masan, Kyungsang Namdo
President: Tae Lim Yoon
Subjects: Social Science, Philosophy

Min Eum Sa*, 44-1 Kwanchul-dong, Chongno-ku, Seoul 110 Tel: (02) 7342000
President: Maeng-Ho Pak
Subjects: Literature, Philosophy, Engineering, Social Science, Linguistics, History, Science
Founded: 1966

Minjungseorim Publishing Co*, 1-48 Cheung-dong, Chung-ku, Seoul 100 Tel: (02) 7356317
President: Chul Hwan Kim; *Editorial:* Han Seong Yu
Parent Company: Beupmun Sa Publishing Co (qv)
Subjects: Dictionaries
Founded: 1979

Mun Woon Dang*, 45-3 Myongnyun-dong, Chongno-ku, Seoul Tel: (02) 7626010/7433504

President: Sung Bum Lee
Subjects: Engineering, Science
Founded: 1962

Omun Kak*, 696-31 Yogsam-dong, Kangnam-ku, Seoul 135 Tel: (02) 5572051
President: Yung Hwan Kim; *Editorial:* Kyun Hee Kim; *Publicity:* Jai Yung You; *Sales:* Jai Yong Kim; *Production:* In Soo Kim; *Rights & Permissions:* Kae Choong Chang
Associate Company: Yueil Publishing and Marketing Cooperation, Room 509, Jungeun Bldg, 22-5 Chungmu-ro 5th Avenue, Chung-ku, Seoul 100
Subjects: Literature, Korean Language, Social Science, Children's Books, School Textbooks, Picture Books
Founded: 1959

Pan Korea Book Corporation*, 134 1-ka Sinmunro, Chongno-ku, Seoul 110 Tel: (02) 7231421 Cable Add: Pankorbooks Seoul Telex: Pkbook K24149
President: Yoon-Sun Kim
Subjects: Language, Literature, Technology

Panmun Book Co Ltd*, CPO Box 1016, 40 Chongno 1-ka, Chongno-ku, Seoul 110 Tel: (02) 7338688/7325131 Cable Add: Panmuse Seoul Telex: K27546 Panmuse
Man Dir: I H Liu; *Sales Dir:* H B Choi
Subjects: Medicine, General & Social Science, University Textbooks
Bookshops: At above address, and 16 Kwangbok-dong 1-ka, Pusan
Founded: 1955

Po Chin Chai Co Ltd*, 8 Dangsan-dong 5-ka, Youngdeungpo-ku, Seoul 150 Tel: (02) 6792351/6795968 Telex: Pochcha K33448 Fax: (822) 6762821
President: Joon Ki Kim; *Chief Executive:* Dal-Hoon Lee; *Editorial:* Kang Hurh
Subjects: Technology, Fine Arts, Textbooks, History, Social Science
Founded: 1912

Sam Joong Dang Publishing Co*, 244-5 Huam-dong, Yongsan-ku, Seoul 140 Tel: (02) 7545919/7545401
President: Mi-Ryung Cho
Subjects: Literature, History, Philosophy, Social Science, Dictionaries, Encyclopaedias
Founded: 1931

Sam-seong Publishing Co Ltd, 340-2, 6 Ga, Dangsan-dong, Yeongdeungpo-gu, Seoul 150 Tel: (02) 6753561
President: Bong Kyu Kim
Subjects: Literature, Dictionaries, History, Children's Books, Art, Women's Books, Business Books
Founded: 1952

Samwha Publishing Co*, 15 Ulchiro 2-ka, Chung-ku, Seoul 100
President: Kon Su Yu
Subjects: Children's Books, Social Science, Linguistics, Fine Arts
Founded: 1962

Se Kwang Music Publishing Co*, 232-32 Seogye-dong, Yongsan-gu, Seoul 140 Tel: (02) 7140046 Fax: (02) 7192191
President: Shin-Joon Park; *Sales Dir:* Song Yeong Il; *Publicity Dir:* Ha Jung Hi
Subject: Music
Founded: 1953

Sejong Daewang Kinyom Saophoe*, 1-57 Chongryangli-dong, San, Dondaemun-ku, Seoul
President: Gwan Ku Yi
Subjects: Religion, Classical Literature, Modern History

Seoul Computer Press*, CPO Box 8850, Seoul 100 Tel: (02) 2756566
President: Jin-Wang Kim

Subjects: Language, Literature, Social Science

Seoul International Publishing House, Yongdong CPO Box 629, Seoul 135 Tel: (02) 5429308
President: Chung-Gil Shim
Orders to: European Book Service, Flevolaan 36-38, Postbus 124, 1380 AC Weesp, Netherlands (Europe); Charles E Tuttle Co Inc, PO Box 410, Rutland, VT 05701, USA
Subjects: Juvenile, Tourist Guides, Art, History, Cooking, Language, Photography, Specialized books on Korea in English
1985: 3 titles *Founded:* 1977
Miscellaneous: Formerly Seoul International Tourist Publishing Co

Seoul National University Press*, 56-1 Shinrim-dong, Kwanak-ku, Seoul 151 Tel: (02) 8790434/8790727
President: Bong-Sik Park; *Dir:* Jong-Chul Lim
Subjects: Language, Philosophy, General/Medical/Natural/Social Sciences, Art, History, Literature
Founded: 1961

Shin Jin Gak*, 1-67 Nogosan-dong, Mapo-ku, Seoul 121 Tel: (02) 7176272
President: Jae-Gul Kim
Subjects: Arts, Literature

Si-sa-yong-o-sa Publishers Inc*, 55-1 Chongno 2-ka, Chongno-ku, Seoul 110 Tel: (02) 2696621 Cable Add: English books, Seoul, Korea
President: Jae-Shik Min; *Vice-President:* Jae-shik Min; *Editorial Dir:* Chon-young Hwang; *Publicity Dir:* Chong-man Choi; *Sales Dir:* Kapchin Cho; *Production Dir:* Hyuk-hwan Kwon
Subjects: Linguistics, Language, Literature, Dictionary, Periodicals
Founded: 1959

Singu Munwha Sa*, 68-2 Susong-dong, Chongno-ku, Seoul
President: Yong Ik Yi
Subjects: Literature, History, Linguistics, Children's Books
Founded: 1952

Sogang University Press*, 1-1 Shinsu-dong, Mapo-ku, Seoul 121 Tel: (02) 7176041
President: In-Syek Sye; *Dir:* Jae-Son Lee
Subjects: History, Literature, Language, General and Social Science

Sung Eum Kak Seoul*, 35-104 Samchung-dong, Chongno-ku, Seoul 110 Tel: (02) 7230220
President: Dong-Min Ahn
Subjects: Philosophy, Religion

Tamgu Dang Publishing Co*, 101-1 Kyungwun-dong, Chongno-ku, Seoul 110 Tel: (02) 7308961
Shipping Add: PO Box 240, Kwang-hwa-mun, Seoul
President: Suk Woo Hong; *Sales Dir:* Jean Byong-hun; *Publicity Dir:* Kim Chang-su; *Advertising Dir:* Lee Chung-rim
Subjects: History, Classics, Art, Technology, Reference, Low- & High-priced Paperbacks, University & Secondary Textbooks
Founded: 1950

Universal Publications Agency Ltd*, 54 Kyonji-Dong, Chongno-ku, Seoul 110 Tel: (02) 7347611 Cable Add: Changhoshin Seoul Telex: K28504 Unipub
Manager: Il Chung Ha
Bookshop: See under Major Booksellers

Yonsei University Press*, 134 Shinchon-dong, Seodaemun-ku, Seoul 120 Tel: (02) 3926201

President: Se Hee Ahn; *Dir:* Hyan-Gang Ha
Subjects: General, Philosophy, Religion, Social Science, Natural Science, Literature, Art, Technical Science, Medicine, Pharmacology
Founded: 1955

Literary Agents

Mediabank, PO Box 530, Kwanghwamoon, Seoul 110 Tel: (02) 7420425 Telex: Joorog K26781
Chief Executive: Jay Sung Rhee
Specialization: Children's Books, El-Hi Reference Books, English Learning Material

Book Club

Korea Book Club, 14-5 Kwanchol-dong, Chongno-ku, Seoul
Members: 10,000
Owned by: Hollym Corporation, Publishers (qv)
Founded: 1973

Major Booksellers

Airport Bookshop*, Civil International Airport, Seoul

Kyobo Book Centre Co Ltd, PO Box 1658, Seoul (Located at: 1 1-ka Chongno, Chongnu-ku, Seoul) Tel: (02) 7307891 Cable Add: Kyobobook Seoul Telex: Kyobo K25081
President: Son-Suk-Ray; *Dirs:* Chin Chang-Kap, Son Jae-One; *Supervisor:* Shin Dong-Jae
Owned by: Daehan Education Insurance Co Ltd

Panmun Book Co Ltd*, CPO Box 1016, Seoul Tel: (02) 7338688
Also: 16 Kwangbok-dong 1-ka, Pusan

Science Publications Centre*, 21 Chongno 1-ka, Chongno-ku, Seoul 110 Tel: (02) 7336719/7350934

Seung mun Book Co, CPO Box 2485, 155-12 Kwanhun-dong, Chongno-ku, Seoul Tel: (02) 7336148

Universal Publications Agency Ltd*, 54 Kyonji-dong, Chongno-ku, Seoul 110 Tel: (02) 7358772 Cable Add: Changhoshin Seoul Telex: K28504 Unipub
Manager: Il Chung Ha
Also Publisher (qv) and distributor

Major Libraries

Dongguk University Central Library*, 26 3-ka, Pil-dong, Jung-gu, Seoul 100

Ewha Womans University Library, 11-1 Daehyun-dong, Sudaemun-ku, Seoul 120 Tel: (02) 3626151 ext 654
Librarian: Ock-Soon Noh

International Communication Agency Library*, 63 1-ka, Ulchiro, Chung-ku, Seoul

Korea Institute of Science and Technology Library*, PO Box 131, Dong Dae Mun, Seoul Tel: (02) 9678801/9678901 Telex: kistrok K27380

Korea University Library, 1 Anam-dong, Sungbook-ku, Seoul Tel: (02) 942641

Kyungpook National University Central Library*, 1370 Sankyuck-dong, Pukku, Taegu Tel: (02) 920268

National Assembly Library*, Yoi-dong 1, Yeongdeungpo-gu, Seoul 150 Tel: (02) 7882271
Publications: Review; Catalogue of Government Publications

Central **National Library***, 100-177 Hoehyun-dong 1-ka, Chung-ku, Seoul 100 Tel: (02) 7524152
Publication: Korean National Bibliography

Seoul National University Library*, 56-1 Shinrim-dong, Kwanak-ku, Seoul 151 Tel: (02) 8775690

Transport Library*, Seoul

United Nations Depository Library, Korea University Library, 1 Anam-dong, Sungbook-ku, Seoul
Chief Librarian: Kim Deouk Hoon

Yonsei University Library, Yonsei University, 134 Sinchon-dong, Sudaemoon-ku, Seoul 120

Library Associations

Hanguk Seoji Hakhoe*, c/o National Assembly Library, Yoi-dong 1, Yeongdeungpo-gu, Seoul
Korean Bibliographical Society

Hanguk Tosogwan Hakhoe*, c/o Department of Library Science, Sung Kyun Kwan University, 53 3-ka, Myonglyun-dong, Chongno-ku, Seoul 110
Korean Library Science Society
Publication: Tosogwan Hak (Journal of the Korean Library Science Society, Korean with English abstracts)

Korean Library Association*, 100-177, Hoehyun-dong 1-ka, Chung-ku, Seoul 100 Tel: (02) 7524864/7525613
Executive Director: Dae Kwon Park
Publications: KLA Bulletin (monthly); *Library Research* (bi-monthly); *Korean Decimal Classification; Korean Cataloguing Rules; Statistics on Libraries in Korea; The Patterns of Book Cover Design in Korea (1392-1945)*

Korean Micro-Library Association*, Central National Library Bldg, 100-177 Hoehyun-dong 1-ka, Chung-ku, Seoul 100
Publication: Micro-Library Bulletin

Library Reference Books and Journals

Books

Bibliography of Korean Bibliographies, Kyong'in Munwha Sa, 86-2 Yonhi-dong, Seodaemun-ku, Seoul

Korean Cataloguing Rules, Korean Library Association, 100-177 Hoehyun-dong 1-ka, Chung-ku, Seoul 100

Journals

KLA Bulletin (monthly), Korean Library Association, 100-177 Hoehyun-dong 1-ka, Chung-ku, Seoul 100

Library Research (bi-monthly), Korean Library Association, 100-177 Hoehyun-dong 1-ka, Chung-ku, Seoul 100

Micro-Library Bulletin, Korean Micro-Library Association, Central National Library Bldg, 100-177 Hoehyun-dong 1-ka, Chung-ku, Seoul 100

Review National Assembly Library, Processing and Reference Bureau, Yoi-dong 1, Yeongdeungpo-gu, Seoul 150

Statistics on Libraries in Korea, Korean Library Association, 100-177 Hoehyun-dong 1-ka, Chung-ku, Seoul 100

Tosogwan Hak, c/o Ewha Womans University Library, 11-1 Daehyun-dong, Sudaemun-ku, Seoul 120
Journal of the Korean Library Science Society, text in Korean with English abstracts

Literary Associations and Societies

Korean **P E N** Centre, 186-210 Janchung-dong 2-ka, Jung-gu, Seoul 100
President: Mrs Sook Hee Chun; *Secretary:* Prof Hyun Bok Lee
Publications: The Korean PEN; Asian Literature

Literary Periodical

Asian Literature, Korean PEN Centre, 186-210 Janchung-dong 2-ka, Jung-gu, Seoul 100

Literary Prize

Literary Prize*
In recognition of an outstanding literary work. $US 5,000. Awarded annually. 1986 winner in the field of juvenile literature was Hyo-sun Uh. Enquiries to Korean National Academy of Arts, 1 Seajong Ro, Chongno-ku, Seoul

Kuwait

General Information

Language: Arabic. English widely spoken
Religion: Islamic
Population: 1.4 million
Bank Hours: 0800-1200 (0830-1230 during Ramadan) Saturday-Thursday
Shop Hours: 0800-1200 or 1230, 1530 or 1600-2030 Saturday-Thursday; 0800-1200 Friday (markets and shopping centres also open 1530-2030); during Ramadan: 0830 or 0900-1230, 1930-0130 or 0200 Saturday-Thursday
Currency: 1000 fils = 1 Kuwaiti dinar
Export/Import Information: No tariffs on books or advertising in reasonable quantity; all immoral and seditious publications prohibited. Import licence required. No exchange permit required
Copyright: No copyright conventions signed

Publishers

Kuwait Publishing House*, PO Box 5209, Kuwait Tel: 510188

Ministry of Information*, PO Box 193, Kuwait Tel: 415301 Cable Add: Alirshad Telex: Mi 22030 Kt, Mi 46151 Kt
Subjects: Art, Geography, History, Physics, Sociology, Textbooks, Maps, Literature, Mathematics, Education, Linguistics

Press Agency*, PO Box 1019, Kuwait Tel: 432269/411495 Cable Add: Matboat Telex: Matboat 46046 Kt
Man Dir: Abdullah M N Harami;
Editorial: K A Harami, Ibrahim M Hadi
Subjects: General (in Arabic and English)
Bookshops: in Kuwait and Salmaiy
Founded: 1954

Wkallat Matbouat*, PO Box 1019, Kuwait
Subject: Travel, Maps

Major Booksellers

Gulf Union Co*, Al-Othman Bldg, Al Soor St, Apt 14, PO Box 2911, Safat Tel: 2411688 Cable Add: Florya Kuwait Telex: 23491 Florya Kt
Man Dir: Tahseen S Khayat

Major Libraries

Kuwait Central Library, PO Box 26182, 13122 Safat Kuwait Tel: 2415180/2415185 Cable Add: Thaquf Telex: 44554 Nccal Kt
Librarian: Mrs Wafa'a H Al-san'e

Kuwait University Central Library*, Kuwait University, Libraries Department, PO Box 17140, Khaldiya, Kuwait Tel: 813182 Telex: Kuniver 2616 Kt
Publication: The Library Bulletin

National Scientific and Technical Information Center (NSTIC), Kuwait Institute for Scientific Research, PO Box 24885, 13109 Safat Tel: 4816988/4816237 Cable Add: Science Kuwait Telex: Kisr Kt 22299
Dir: Mrs Ferial Al-Freih

Library Association

Kuwait University Libraries Department*, Chief Librarian's Office, PO Box 17140, Khaldiya, Kuwait
Publication: The University Library

Library Reference Journals

The Library Bulletin, Kuwait University Central Library, Kuwait University, Libraries Department, PO Box 17140, Khaldiya, Kuwait

The University Library, Kuwait University Libraries Department, PO Box 17140, Khaldiya, Kuwait

Laos

General Information

Note: No replies were received to questionnaires sent to Laos for this edition of *International Literary Market Place*. The information given in the 1987-88 edition has been repeated here but should be treated with caution.

Language: Lao
Religion: Theravada Buddhist
Population: 3.7 million
Bank Hours: 0800-1200, 1400-1700 Monday-Friday
Shop Hours: 0800-2200 Monday-Friday
Currency: kip
Export/Import Information: No tariff on books (except children's picture books), none on most advertising matter. No import licences required for books.
Exchange controls
Copyright: UCC (see International section)

Publishers

Lao-phanit*, Vientiane Ministère de l'Education nationale, Comité littéraire, Bureau des Manuels scolaires, Vientiane
Subjects: Education, Physics, Sociology, Economics, History, Cookery, Arts, Geography, Music, Fiction

Pakpassak Kanphin*, 9-11 quai Fa-Hguun, Vientiane

Major Libraries

Bibliothèque nationale*, BP 704, Vientiane

Bibliothèque de l'**Ecole** royale de Médecine*, BP 131, Vientiane

Library Association

Association des Bibliothécaires Laotiens*, c/o Direction de la Bibliothèque nationale, Ministry of Education, BP 704, Vientiane
Association of Laos Librarians

Lebanon

General Information

Language: Arabic (French and English also used)
Religion: 50% Christian (predominantly Maronite), 50% Muslim
Population: 2.7 million
Bank Hours: 0830-1230 Monday-Friday; 0830-1200 Saturday
Shop Hours: Vary. Generally 0900-1900 in winter, 0800-1500 in summer
Currency: 100 Lebanese piastres = 1 Lebanese pound
Copyright: UCC, Berne (see International section)

Publishers

Arab Institute for Research and Publishing, Sakiat-Al Janzeer, PO Box 11-5460, Beirut Tel: (01) 807900 Cable Add: Moukayali Telex: 40067
Subjects: Works in Arabic and English

Dar **Assayad***, PO Box 1038, Beirut Tel: (01) 452700 Telex: Sayad 44224 le
Man Dir: Bassam Freiha
Subjects: Politics, Periodicals
Founded: 1943

Les **Editions Arabes**, part of Naufal Group SRL, Lebanon (qv)

Geoprojects Sàrl*, PO Box 113, 5294 Beirut Tel: (01) 344346 Telex: 22661 Eltoup le
Man Dir: Tahseen Khayat
Subjects: Tourist Maps & Guides Series, Arabic books
Founded: 1978

Dar el-**Ilm** Lilmalayin*, PO Box 1085, Beirut (Located at: rue de Syrie, Beirut) Tel: (01) 304445/816639/224502 Cable Add: Malayin Telex: 23166 Mlayin
Man Dir: Taref Osman; *Editorial Dir:* Munir Balbaki; *Sales:* Ahmad Kanafani

Subsidiary Companies: Bardico Paper Co; Alulum Printers; Alharf Alelectroni Co; Dar Shehrazad Co
Subjects: Textbooks, Islamic Studies, Dictionaries, History, Mathematics, Physics, Law, Children, Health, Languages, Literature, Philosophy, Education, Psychology, Biographies
Founded: 1945

Institute for Palestine Studies, Publishing and Research Organization*, Anis Nsouli St – off Verdun, PO Box 11-7164, Beirut Tel: (01) 814174 Cable Add: Dirasat Telex: Madaf 23317 le
Dirs: Dr Philip Mattar, Mahmoud Soueid; *Executive Secretary:* Prof Walid Khalidi; *Editorial, Production:* Taan Saab, Mary Neznek; *Sales, Publicity:* Mrs Afaf Minkara Daouk, Julie Bourns
Branch Off: 3501 M Street NW, PO Box 25301, Georgetown Station, Washington, DC 20007, USA Tel: (202) 342 3990 Telex: 7108221166 Dirasat Wsh
Subjects: The Palestine Question and the Arab-Israeli conflict
1985: 27 titles *Founded:* 1963
ISBN Publisher's Prefix: 0-88728

The **International Documentary** Centre of Arab Manuscripts*, Darwish Bldg, rue de Syrie, PO Box 2668, Beirut
Proprietor: Zouhair Baalbaki
Subjects: Reprints, Facsimiles
Founded: 1965

Dar al **Kash'shaf***, Assad Malhamee St, PO Box 112091, Beirut Tel: (01) 815527/296805 Cable Add: Dakashaf Beirut
Proprietor: A M Fathallah
Subjects: Scouting, Atlases, Maps, Business
Founded: 1930

Khayat Book and Publishing Co Sàrl*, 90-94 rue Bliss, Beirut
Man Dir: Paul Khayat
Subjects: Fiction, History, Juveniles, Arts, Maps, Medicine, Education, Law, Religion, Social Sciences, Games, Sports, Economics, Books on the Middle East, Islam, Arabic, Reprints

Dar Al-**Kitab** Allubnani*, PO Box 3176, Beirut Tel: (01) 237537/254054 Cable Add: Kitaliban Telex: 22865 Ktl
Man Dir: El-Zein Hassan
Associate Company: Dar Al-Kitab Al-Masri, Egypt (qv)
Branch Offs: Paris, Geneva, Madrid, Casablanca
Subjects: Islamic, Turath, Textbooks (in Arabic, English, French)
Bookshop: Librairie de l'Ecole, PO Box 3176, Beirut
Founded: 1929

Librairie du Liban, Riad Al-Solh Sq, PO Box 11-945, Beirut Tel: (01) 258259/295735/862957 Cable Add: Librarie du Liban, Beirut Telex: 21037 Libsay le
Librairie du Liban Group head office is at Boutros Boustani St, Sayegh Bldg, Zokak el Blat, PO Box 11-945, Beirut
Man Dirs: Khalil and George Sayegh; *Editorial:* Ahmad Khatib; *Sales:* Suhail Berjawi; *Production:* Albert Mutlag; *Publicity:* George Sayegh; *Rights & Permissions:* Khalil Sayegh
Subjects: Academic & Technical Textbooks, Medical Reference & Textbooks, Fiction, Literature, Linguistics, Travel, Islam, Dictionaries, Children's Books, English Language Teaching Textbooks
Bookshops: Lebanon Bookshop, Librairie du Liban (qqv under Major Booksellers); Sayegh Bookshop, Diab Bldg, Al Tayef St, Bawabat Al Salhieh, PO Box 704, Damascus, Syria

Showrooms: Longman Arab World Centres at PO Box 11-954, Beirut, Lebanon; Amir Mohamed St, Al Houjairi Bldg, PO Box 6587, Amman, Jordan; 15th St, Central Khartoum, PO Box 1391, Sudan
Sphinx Publishing Co, Egypt (qv) is also a member of the Group
Founded: 1944

Dar Al-**Maaref** Liban Sàrl*, Esseily Bldg, sq Riad Al-Solh, PO Box 11-2320, Beirut Tel: (01) 223574/294064/383621 Cable Add: Damaref Beirut
Man Dir: Dr Fouad Ibrahim; *General Manager:* Joseph Nachou; *Sales:* Joseph Ibrahim
Parent Company: Dar Al Maaref, Egypt (qv)
Subjects: Juveniles, Textbooks in Arabic
Founded: 1959

Mac Purcell*, PO Box 1135294, Beirut

Macdonald Middle East Sàrl, see Naufal Group SRL

Darl el-**Machreq** Sàrl, c/o Librairie orientale, PO Box 946, Beirut Tel: (01) 326469 Cable Add: Cathopress Telex: Impcat 42733
Man Dir, Rights & Permissions: Paul Brouwers; *Publicity:* Michel Mourad
Orders to: Librairie orientale, PO Box 1986, Beirut
Subjects: Archaeology, Geography, Educational, History, Dictionaries, Religion, Art, Literature, Languages, Science, Philosophy, Periodicals
Founded: 1853
ISBN Publisher's Prefix: 2-7214

Naufal Group Sàrl+, PO Box 11-2161, Naufal Bldg, Mamari St, Beirut Tel: (01) 354394/354898 Telex: Naustn 22210 le
Man Dir, Rights & Permissions: Sami Naufal; *Editorial:* Kamal Khauli, Tony Naufal; *Sales, Production:* Ahmed Bahsoun
Subsidiary Companies: Macdonald Middle East Sàrl; Les Éditions Arabes
Imprints: Naufal, Macdonald, Editions Arabes
Branch Off: Naufal Group Europe Sarl, 116 Ave Champs Elysées, Paris, France Tel: (1) 45631727 Telex: 641605 F
Subjects: Encyclopaedias and General Knowledge, Fiction, Children's Books, History, Law, Literature
Bookshops: Librairies Antoine (three shops), Hamra, PO Box 656, Beirut
Founded: 1970

Dar Al **Raed** Al Lubnani, Hazmieh St, Kamel Al Assaad Bldgs, PO Box 93 Sammouri, Beirut Tel: (01) 450757/451581 Cable Add: Kassammoury Telex: 43499 le Raed
Chief Executive: Raed Sammouri; *Editorial:* Fadia Khoury; *Sales:* Ola Ramadan; *Production:* George Jabro; *Publicity:* Rima Khoury; *Rights & Permissions:* Hussein Ibrahim
Branch Off: Dar Al Raed Al Rabi, Rawchi Blvd, Al Istiklal
1985: 30 titles *1986:* 42 titles *Founded:* 1971

Major Booksellers

Librairies **Antoine***, rue Patriarche Hoyek, Beirut Tel: (01) 229745

Esquire*, rue Sidani, Beirut Tel: (01) 348074

Help Bookshop*, rue Jeanne d'Arc, Im Saghiri, Beirut Tel: (01) 341679

Tahseen S **Khayat***, Uncle Sam's Bookshop, PO Box 8375, Beirut Tel: (01) 344346
Also: Tahseen S Khayat, United Arab Emirates (qv)

Lebanon Bookshop, 42 Bliss St, Ras Beirut, Beirut Tel: (01) 344968
Owned by: Librairie du Liban (qv)

Librairie du Liban, Imm Esseily, pl Riad Solh, PO Box 11-945, Beirut Tel: (01) 252537/862957 Telex: 45297 Libsay
Marketing Manager: Jean A Doummar
Also: Lazarieh Bldg, Emir Bachir St, Beirut Tel: (01) 259744; Rubeiz Bldg, Hamra St, Beirut Tel: (01) 344070
Also publisher (qv)

Major Libraries

Libraries of **American University** of Beirut, Beirut Tel: (01) 340740/865250 ext 28005 Telex: amunob 20801 le
Acting University Librarian: Leila Freije
Incorporating as main library Nami C Jafet Memorial Library Tel: (01) 865250 ext 28005

Library of **Beirut Arab University***, PO Box 5020, Beirut

Bibliothèque nationale du Liban*, pl de l'Etoile, Imm du Parlement, Beirut Tel: (01) 256160/256161
Publication: Bulletin bibliographique

Bibliothèque orientale, rue de l'Université St Joseph, PO Box 166775, Achrafieh, Beirut
Dir: Martin J McDermott

Bibliothèque de l'**Ecole** supérieure des Lettres*, rue de Damas, Beirut

Library of the **Faculty of Engineering***, Université St Joseph, PO Box 1514, Beirut
Librarian: Henri Ketterer

Library of the **Faculty of Law***, Université St Joseph, PO Box 293, Beirut

Library of the **French Faculty of Medicine**, Pharmacy and Dentistry, Université St Joseph, PO Box 5076, Beirut

Bibliothèque de l'**Institut** Français d'Archéologie du Proche Orient*, rue Omar Daouk, PO Box 11-1424, Beirut
Dir: Georges Tate

Nami C **Jafet** Memorial Library, see Libraries of American University of Beirut

Library of the **Monastery of St-Saviour** (Basilian Missionary Order of St-Saviour)*, Saïda

Library of the **Near East School** of Theology*, PO Box 13-5780, Chouran, Beirut

Library of the **Syrian Patriarchal Seminary***, Seminary of Charfet, Daroon-Harissa Tel: (09) 903040
Secretary: Fr Joseph Melki

Library Association

The **Lebanese Library** Association*, c/o Bibliothèque nationale du Liban, pl de l'Etoile, Imm du Parlement, Beirut Tel: (01) 256160
Executive Secretary: Linda Sadaga
Publication: Newsletter

Library Reference Journals

Bulletin bibliographique, Bibliothèque nationale du Liban, pl de l'Etoile, Imm du Parlement, Beirut

Newsletter, The Lebanese Library Association, c/o Bibliothèque nationale du Liban, pl de l'Etoile, Imm du Parlement, Beirut

Literary Associations and Societies

Lebanese **P E N** Club, Camille Aboussouan, 102 quai Louis Bleriot, F-75116 Paris, France
President: Camille Aboussouan

Lesotho

General Information

Language: English, Sesotho (a Bantu language)
Religion: Roman Catholic and Protestant
Population: 1.3 million
Bank Hours: 0830-1300 Monday-Friday; 0830-1100 Saturday
Shop Hours: Winter: 0830-1630 Monday-Friday; 0830-1300 Saturday; Summer: 0800-1630 Monday-Friday; 0800-1300 Saturday. Usually closed weekdays 1300-1400
Currency: 100 lisente = 1 loti (plural: maloti). 1 loti = 1 rand. South African currency is also legal tender
Export/Import Information: No tariffs on books or advertising matter. No import licence required; no obscene literature permitted. Exchange controls being relaxed

Publishers

Government Printer*, Mazenod Printing Press, PO Mazenod, Maseru

Longman Lesotho (Pty) Ltd, PO Box 1174, Maseru 100 (Located at: 607 Cathedral Area, Mohlaka House, Maseru 100) Tel: 314254
Parent Company: Longman Group UK Ltd, UK (qv)

Mazenod Institute*, PO Box 18, Mazenod 160 (Railhead: Maseru Station) Tel: 62224 Telex: 271 Bb
Manager: Fr B Mohlalisi
Subjects: History, Africana, Religion, Sesotho Language & Literature, Secondary & Primary Textbooks
Founded: 1933

Morija Sesuto Book Depot*, PO Box 4, Morija
Subjects: Belles Lettres, Poetry, History, Africana, Religion, Juveniles, Southern Sesotho Language, Paperbacks, General Science, Secondary & Primary Textbooks
Founded: 1862

Saint Michael's Mission*, The Social Centre, PO Box 25, Roma
Man Dir: Rev Fr M Ferrange; *Production:* Peter Ntsaoana
Subjects: Biography, History, Africana, Religion, Social Science, Secondary & Primary Textbooks, Anthropology
Founded: 1968

Major Booksellers

Lesotho Book Centre*, PO Box MS 608, Maseru Tel: 3783

Mazenod Book Centre, PO Box 39, Mazenod 160 (Located at: Mazenod, Railhead: Maseru Station) Tel: 62224 Cable Add: Mazbooks Telex: 4271 Lo
Manager: Rev Fr M Gareau

Morija Sesuto Book Depot*, PO Box MJ 4, Morija Tel: 204

Major Libraries

British Council Educational Resource Centre*, PO Box 429, Maseru 100 Tel: 312601
Librarian: Rosina Mphethi

Lesotho National Library Service, PO Box 985, Maseru 100 Tel: 322592
Librarian: Ms Dikeledi J Setlogelo
Publication: Annual Report

National University of Lesotho Library*, PO Box 180, Roma Tel: 201 Cable Add: Uniter Telex: 303 BB
Librarian: Mrs M M Lebotsa

Library Association

Lesotho Library Association, Private Bag A26, Maseru 100 Cable Add: Lelia Maseru
Secretary: S M Mohai
Publications include: Lesotho Library Association Newsletter (annual)

Liberia

General Information

Language: English and a number of African languages
Religion: Islamic, Protestant; traditional beliefs followed by many
Population: 1.9 million
Bank Hours: 0800-1200 Monday-Thursday; 0800-1400 Friday
Shop Hours: 0800-1300, 1500-1800 or longer
Currency: 100 cents = 1 Liberian dollar
Export/Import Information: No tariff on books and advertising matter. Public Fund Levy. No import licence or exchange control
Copyright: UCC (see International section)

Publishers

Cole & Yancy*, PO Box 286, Monrovia
Man Dir: Henry B Cole
Subjects: General, Reference, Annuals, Paperbacks
Bookshop: See under Major Booksellers

Government Printer*, Government Printing Office, Department of State, Monrovia

Liberian Literary & Educational Publications*, PO Box 2387, Monrovia
Man Dir: S Henry Cordor
Subjects: General, Educational, Belles Lettres, Poetry

Major Booksellers

Wadih M **Captan** Bookstores*, Randall St, PO Box 414, Monrovia Tel: 21393

Cole & Yancy Bookshop Ltd*, PO Box 286, Monrovia
Also Publisher (qv)

Liberian Educational Materials Supply Corporation*, New Port St, PO Box 2088, Monrovia Tel: 22356
Manager: N Chandru

National Bookstore*, Carey St, PO Box 590, Monrovia Tel: 222096

University Bookstore*, University of Liberia, Monrovia Tel: 22515 ext 225

Major Libraries

College of Our Lady of Fatima Library*, Harper

Cuttington University College Library, PO Box 277, Monrovia Tel: 21065

Government Public Library*, Ashmun St, Monrovia

International Communication Agency Library*, Broad St, Monrovia

University of Liberia Libraries*, PO Box 9020, Monrovia Tel: 22537
Dir: Dr C Wesley Armstrong
Publication: Newsletter

Libya

General Information

Language: Arabic
Religion: Islamic
Population: 2.9 million
Bank Hours: Generally Winter: 0830-1230; Summer: 0800-1200 Saturday-Thursday
Shop Hours: Vary greatly. Friday is weekly holiday but some Christian shops closed Sunday. Many are open 0830-1230, 1500-1730 Saturday-Thursday (slightly earlier hours in summer months)
Currency: 1,000 dirhams = 1 Libyan dinar
Export/Import Information: No tariff on books; advertising dutied. Charity Tax and Municipal Tax levied on dutiable goods. Open General Licence for books. Exchange permit, liberally granted, required. Import and export of books is handled by the General Company for Publishing, Advertising and Distribution, Tripoli
Copyright: Berne (see International section)

Publishers

Al-**Fatah** University, General Administration of Libraries, Printing & Publications*, PO Box 13543, Tripoli Tel: (021) 621988 Telex: 20629 TP Univ Ly
Subjects: Academic
Bookshop: University Bookshop, PO Box 13113, Tripoli
Founded: 1955

General Press Corporation*, General Publication and Advertising Co, PO Box 959, Tripoli Tel: (021) 45773/45777/45537
Publicity: Moustafa A Elmasri
Subjects: General, Educational, Academic

Major Booksellers

General Company for Publishing, Advertising and Distribution*, Suf el Mahmudi, PO Box 959, Tripoli Tel: (021) 45773 Telex: 20235

Orient Bookshop*, PO Box 255, Tripoli

Major Libraries

Benghazi Public Library*, Shar'a 'Umar al-Mukhtar, Benghazi

Al-**Fateh** University, The Central Library*, PO Box 13104, Tripoli Tel: (021) 604000 ext 2466

Government Library*, 14 Shar'a al-Jazair, Tripoli

Institut Culturel Français Bibliothèque*, 15-17 Sciara Karachi, PO Box 683, Tripoli Tel: (021) 35567
Librarian: Mrs Girard Michèle
Publication: Bulletin (monthly)

National Archives*, Castello, Tripoli

National Library*, Secretariat of Information, PO Box 9127, Benghazi Tel: (061) 96379/97073/90509

Tripoli Public Library*, 14 Al-Jazair St, Tripoli

University of Garyounis Library*, PO Box 1308, Benghazi (Located at: University of Garyounis, Benghazi) Tel: (061) 29713 Telex: Unigar 40175, Unigar 40057
Librarian: Ahmed M Gallal

University of Libya Library, name changed to University of Garyounis Library (qv)

Liechtenstein

General Information

Language: German
Religion: Roman Catholic
Population: 26,000
Bank Hours: 0800-1230, 1330-1630 Monday-Friday
Shop Hours: 0800-1215, 1330-1830 Monday-Friday; 0800-1215, 1330-1600 or 1700 Saturday
Currency: Swiss franc
Export/Import Information: No tariff on books. Most books exempt from Turnover Tax. Advertising matter usually dutiable, some exempt from Turnover Tax. No import licences required. No exchange controls
Copyright: UCC, Berne, Florence (see International section)

Book Trade Organization

Syndicat de la Librairie ancienne et du Commerce de l'Estampe en Suisse (Vereinigung der Buchantiquare und Kupferstichhändler der Schweiz), Schloss Str 6, FL-9490 Vaduz
Association of Antiquarian Book and Print Sellers in Switzerland
President: Walter Alicke

Publishers

Buch und Verlagsdruckerei AG*, Im Städtle 32, FL-9490 Vaduz

Frank P van **Eck** Publishers+*, Im Quäderle 11, Postfach 816, FL-9490 Vaduz Tel: (075) 29557 Telex: 77030
Man Dir: Elisabeth Schaedler
Subjects: Golf, Art, Bibliography
Founded: 1982
ISBN Publisher's Prefix: 3-905501

A R **Gantner** Verlag KG*, Postfach 225, FL-9490 Vaduz (Located at: Beckagässle 4)
Subjects: Art, Literature, Botany

Liechtenstein Verlag AG, Schwefelstr 33, Postfach 133, FL-9490 Vaduz Tel: (075) 23925 Telex: 889326 esge fl Fax: (075) 24340
Man Dir: Albart Piet Schiks
Subjects: Belles Lettres, Poetry, History, Educational Materials
Founded: 1945
Miscellaneous: Also a literary agent (qv)

Literarische Agentur und Verlagsgesellschaft*, Litag Anstalt, Beckägässle 4, FL-9490 Vaduz
Dir: Mrs B Gantner

Sändig Reprint Verlag Hans R Wohlwend, Am Schrägen Weg 12, FL-9490 Vaduz
Dir: Hans R Wohlwend
Subjects: Natural Sciences, Linguistics, Fiction, Folklore, Music, History
ISBN Publisher's Prefix: 3-253

Topos Verlag AG, Industriestr 105, Postfach 156, FL-9491 Ruggell Tel: (075) 34757 Cable Add: Topos Telex: 889199
Man Dir: Graham A P Smith
Subjects: Law, Economics, Social Science, Periodicals
Founded: 1977
ISBN Publisher's Prefix: 3-289

Literary Agents

Liechtenstein Verlag AG, Schwefelstr 33, Postfach 133, FL-9490 Vaduz Tel: (075) 23925 Telex: 889326 esge fl Fax: (075) 24340
Firm is also a publisher (qv)

Major Booksellers

Siegfried **Feger***, Tanzpl 24, FL-9494 Schaan
Proprietor: Siegfried Feger

Major Library

Liechtensteinische Landesbibliothek, Oeffentliche Stiftung, Postfach 385, FL-9490 Vaduz Tel: (075) 66343
National Library
Director: Dr Alois Ospelt

Literary Associations and Societies

P E N Club Liechtenstein, Postfach 416, FL-9490 Vaduz Tel: (075) 27271
President: Dr Hans Hass; *Secretary:* Manfred Schlapp

Grand Duchy of Luxembourg

General Information

Language: French, German. Also Luxembourg dialect, Letzeburgesch
Religion: Roman Catholic
Population: 364,000
Bank Hours: 0900-1200, 1330-1630 Monday-Friday
Shop Hours: 0800-1200, 1400-1800 Monday-Saturday. Most close Monday morning
Currency: 100 centimes = 1 Luxembourg franc. Belgian currency also circulates. 1 Luxembourg franc = 1 Belgian franc
Export/Import Information: Member of the European Economic Community. In customs union with Belgium and Netherlands. No tariff on books except children's picture books from non-EEC; advertising other than single copies dutied. VAT on books and advertising. No import licence required. No exchange controls
Copyright: UCC, Berne, Florence (see International Section)

Book Trade Organizations

Fédération Luxembourgeoise des Editeurs de Livres, 23 allée Scheffer, L-2520 Luxembourg Tel: 473125/24971
Luxembourg Federation of Book Publishers
General Secretary: Guy Binsfeld
Miscellaneous: A Department of the Confédération du Commerce Luxembourgeois

Fédération luxembourgeoise des Travailleurs du Livre*, 38 rue Goethe, Luxembourg
Luxembourg Federation of Workers in the Book Trade
President: Henri Bauler
Secretary: Gusty Stefanetti

Book Trade Reference Journal

Bibliographie luxembourgeoise (Luxembourg Bibliography), Bibliothèque nationale du Grand-Duché de Luxembourg, 37 blvd F D Roosevelt, L-2450 Luxembourg

Publishers

Editions Guy **Binsfeld**+, 14 pl du Parc, L-2313 Luxembourg Tel: 496868
Man Dir, Production, Publicity, Rights & Permissions: Guy Binsfeld; *Editorial:* Pit Haerold; *Sales:* Constant Scholtes Jnr
Subjects: Belles Lettres, Non-fiction, Law, Photography, Tourist Guides, Art, New Music
1985: 20 titles *1986:* 22 titles *Founded:* 1980
ISBN Publisher's Prefix: 3-88957

Christian **Butterbach***, BP 516, Luxembourg Tel: 26926/26927/22022 Cable Add: Interferences
Owner and Manager: Christian Butterbach
Subjects: Literature, Periodical
Founded: 1959
ISBN Publisher's Prefix: 3-921400

Publisher **Krippler-Muller***, 1 rue Batti Weber, Bereldange

Man Dir: J-P Krippler
Subjects: Belles Lettres, History, Maps, Regional Literature, Law, Languages
Bookshop: At above address
Founded: 1949

Edouard **Kutter**, 17 rue des Bains, Luxembourg
Subjects: Art, Photography, Facsimile editions on Luxembourg

Imprimerie **Saint-Paul** SA, 2 rue Christophe-Plantin, L-2988 Luxembourg Tel: 49931 Telex: Wortlu 3471
Man Dir: André Heiderscheid; *Production:* Paul Thill; *Publicity:* Charles Jourdain
Subject: Literature

Verlag-Buchhandlung Joseph **Thielen**, 222 route de Thionville, L-2610 Howald
Owner and Manager: Joseph Thielen
Founded: 1950

Major Booksellers

Librairie **Bourbon**, 11 rue du Fort Bourbon, Luxembourg

Librairie De **Bourcy**, see Librairie du Centre

Librairie Paul **Bruck**, 22 Grand-rue, Luxembourg

Librairie du **Centre**, 49 blvd Royal, L-2449 Luxembourg Tel: 26613/27999
Independent Subscription Department: ABO-Service Centre SA, 49 blvd Royal, L-2449 Luxembourg
Proprietor: Lucien de Bourcy

Librairie R **Daman**, 4 rue de Brabant, Diekirch

Librairie **Diderich** Sàrl*, 2 rue Victor-Hugo, BP 70, Esch-sur-Alzette Tel: 554083
Manager: J-Cl Diderich

Librairie **Ernster**, 27 rue du Fossé, L-1536 Luxembourg Tel: 25077
Manager: Pierre Ernster

Librairie **Française**, 1 pl d'Armes, Luxembourg Tel: 20067

Messageries du Livre*, 18 rue Christophe Plantin, L-2339 Luxembourg-Gasperich Tel: 4998888 Telex: 2515

Librairie **Muller-Groff***, 4a ave Pasteur, Luxembourg

Librairie Armand **Peiffer***, ave Monterey, L-2163 Luxembourg Tel: 25444

Librairie **Promoculture**, BP 1142, 14 rue Duchscher, L-1011 Luxembourg Tel: 480691 Telex: 3112 Promo lu
Manager: Albert P Daming

Major Libraries

Archives de l'Etat, Plateau du St-Esprit, BP 6, L-2010 Luxembourg
National Archives

Bibliothèque de Gouvernement, 37 blvd F D Roosevelt, L-2450 Luxembourg

Bibliothèque de la Ville, 26 rue Emile Mayrisch, Esch-sur-Alzette
Librarian: Fernand Roeltgen

Bibliothèque nationale du Grand-Duché de Luxembourg, 37 blvd F D Roosevelt, L-2450 Luxembourg Tel: 26255
Publications: Bibliographie luxembourgeoise; Bibliographie d'histoire luxembourgeoise

Macau

General Information

Language: Portuguese, Cantonese (English used in business)
Religion: Chinese, the majority of population are Buddhist and Roman Catholic is religion of Europeans
Population: 287,000
Bank Hours: 0930-1700 Monday-Friday; 0930-1200 Saturday
Shop Hours: 0900-1730 Monday-Saturday
Currency: 100 avos = 1 pataca. Hong Kong currency is also widely used but there is no fixed exchange rate
Export/Import Information: Macau is a free port
Copyright: Berne, UCC (see International section)

Major Booksellers

The **World Book** Company, PO Box 201, 68 Rua Dos Mercadores Tel: 573591
Cable Add: Libiblioteca
Manager: V M Lam

Major Libraries

Biblioteca Nacional de Macau*, Edificio do Leal Senado

Biblioteca **Sir Robert Ho Tung***, Largo do Sto Agostinho

Democratic Republic of Madagascar

General Information

Language: French and Malagasy
Religion: About 40% Christian, 5% Islamic, remainder traditional beliefs
Population: 8.7 million
Bank Hours: 0800-1100, 1400-1600 Monday-Friday. Closed afternoon preceding a holiday
Shop Hours: 0800-1200, 1400-1800 Monday-Saturday
Currency: Malagasy franc
Export/Import Information: For books and advertising matter, customs and import duties, also unique tax. Import licence required
Copyright: Berne, Florence (see International Section)

Book Trade Organization

Office du Livre Malagasy (OLM)*, BP 617, Tananarive Tel: (02) 24449
Secretary-General: Juliette Ratsimandrava

Book Trade Reference Books

Books

Bibliographie annuelle de Madagascar, Bibliothèque universitaire, Campus universitaire, BP 906, Tananarive

Bibliographie nationale de Madagascar, Bibliothèque nationale, BP 257, Anosy, Tananarive

Publishers

Editions **Ambozontany***, BP 40, 301 Fianarantsoa Tel: (07) 50653
Man Dir: Justin Bethaz; *Editorial:* Nicola Giambrone; *Sales:* José Minien
Subjects: Scholarly, Cultural, Social, Historical, Religious
Bookshop: At above address
Founded: 1962

Maison d'Edition Protestante **'Antso'***, 19 Lalana Venance Manifatra, BP 660, Tananarive Tel: (02) 20886 Cable Add: Fijekrima Antso
Man Dir: Hans Andriamampianina; *Editor:* José Rambinintsoa
Subjects: Religion, Sociology, Politics, Economics, Children's, Juveniles, Practical, Journals
Bookshop: Bookshop Antso, Lot IIB 18, Totohabato Ranavalona 1, Tananarive
Founded: 1966

Government Printer*, Imprimerie nationale, BP 38, Tananarive

Madagascar Print & Press Co+, rue H Rabesahala, BP 953, Tananarive Tel: (02) 22536 Telex: Madprint c/o 22261 Hiltel Mg
Man Dir, Editorial: Georges Ranaivosoa; *Sales, Publicity:* CEMOI (see Subsidiary Company)
Subsidiary Company: Communication et Media — Ocean Indien (CEMOI), BP 46, Tananarive
Subjects: General, Literature, History, Technical
Founded: 1969

Société de Presse et d'Edition de Madagascar*, BP 1570, Tananarive
Man Dir: Mrs Rajaofera-Andriambelo
Subjects: General Non-fiction, Reference, General Science, University Textbooks

Société Malgache d'Edition, BP 659, Ankorondrano, Tananarive Tel: (02) 22635
Man Dir: Rahaga Ramaholimihaso; *Publicity:* Daniel Ramanandraibe
Subjects: University & Secondary Textbooks
Bookshop: See under Major Booksellers
Founded: 1959

Société Nouvelle de l'Imprimerie Centrale*, BP 1414, Tananarive
Man Dir: M Hantzberg
Subjects: Paperbacks, General Science, University, Secondary & Primary Textbooks
Founded: 1959

Imprimerie **Takariva***, 4 rue Radley, BP 1029, Antanimena, Tananarive
Tel: (02) 22128
Man Dir: Paul Rapatsalahy
Subjects: General Fiction, Malagasy Languages, Paperbacks, Secondary Textbooks
Founded: 1933

Trano Printy Loterana-Trano Printy Fiangonana Loterana Malagasy (TPFLM)-(Imprimerie Luthérienne)*, 9 ave Grandidier, BP 538, Antsahamanitra, Tananarive Tel: (02) 24569/23340

Man Dir: Abel Arnesa; *Editorial:* Pastor Mamy Andriamahenina
Subjects: General Fiction, Religion, Paperbacks, Secondary & Primary Textbooks
Bookshop: See under Major Booksellers
Founded: 1875

Major Booksellers

Bibliomad*, 11 rue Indira Ghandi, BP 602, Tananarive Tel: (02) 23280
Manager: Ramaromandray Amédée

Librairie de Madagascar*, 38 ave de l'Indépendance, BP 402, Tananarive Tel: (02) 22454
Manager: Yves Balanche

Librairie luthérienne*, ave Grandidier, BP 538, Tananarive Tel: (02) 23340/24569
Manager: Abel Arnesa

Librairie mixte Sàrl*, 37 bis ave du 26 Juin 1960, BP 3204, Analakely, Tananarive Tel: (02) 25130
Manager: Jean Razakasoa

Librairie universitaire*, 26 rue Amiral Pierre, Tananarive

Société Malgache d'Edition*, BP 659, Ankorondrano, Tananarive Tel: (02) 22635
Manager: Rahagar Ramaholimihaso
Also Publisher (qv)

Librairie **'Tout pour l'Ecole'***, Immeuble Vitasoa, rue de Nice, BP 1099, Tananarive Tel: (02) 23521

Trano Printy Loterana*, 9 ave Grandidier, BP 538, Antsahamanitra, Tananarive Tel: (02) 24569/23340
Also Publisher (qv)

Major Libraries

Archives nationales de Madagascar*, BP 3384, Tananarive
Dir: Mrs Razoharinoro

Bibliothèque municipale*, ave 18 Juin, BP 729, Tananarive Tel: (02) 21176

Bibliothèque nationale, BP 257, Anosy, Tananarive Tel: (02) 25872
Librarian: Louis Ralaisaholimanana
Publications include: Bibliographie nationale de Madagascar

Bibliothèque universitaire*, Campus universitaire, BP 906, Tananarive Tel: (02) 21103
Librarian: Miss de Nuce
Publication: Bibliographie annuelle de Madagascar

Bibliothèque du Centre culturel **'Albert Camus'***, 14 ave de l'Indépendance, BP 488, Tananarive Tel: (02) 21375/23647
Librarian: Dominique Seurin

Collège rural d'Ambatobe*, Bibliothèque, BP 1629, Tananarive

Direction Générale de la Banque des Données de l'Etat*, Publications and Documentation Section, BP 485, Tananarive Tel: (02) 20081
Director General: Armand Roger Randrianarivony; *Librarian:* Tantely Rabenjambalason

Institut national de la statistique et de la recherche économique, now Direction Générale de la Banque des Données de l'Etat

United States Information Agency Library, 4 rue Dr Razafindratandra, Ambohidahy, 101 Tananarive

Literary Periodical

Fanasina, BP 1574, Analakely, Tananarive
Literary and current affairs weekly

Literary Prize

Literature Prize*
For an outstanding novel. 130,000 Malagasy francs. Awarded every two years. Enquiries to Malagasy Ministry of Cultural Affairs, Anosy, Tananarive

Malawi

General Information

Language: English, Cinyanja and Citumbuku (Bantu languages) are official languages
Religion: About 35% Christian (Roman Catholic and Presbyterian); 10% Islamic, remainder traditional beliefs
Population: 5.9 million
Bank Hours: 0800-1230 Monday, Tuesday, Thursday, Friday; 0800-1130 Wednesday; 0800-1030 Saturday
Shop Hours: 0730 or 0800-1600 or 1700 Monday-Friday (with some closing for lunch); until midday Saturday
Currency: 100 tambala = 1 Malawi kwacha
Export/Import Information: No tariff on books; some advertising matter subject to duty. No import licence required.
Exchange controls
Copyright: UCC (see International section)

Book Trade Reference Journal

Malawi National Bibliography, c/o National Archives of Malawi, PO Box 62, Zomba

Publishers

Christian Literature Association in Malawi, PO Box 503, Blantyre (Located at: Glyn Jones Rd) Tel: 620839
Subjects: General Fiction, Poetry, Biography, History, Africana, Religion, Juveniles, Christian Tracts, Paperbacks
Bookshop: CLAIM (qv under Major Booksellers)
Founded: 1968

Government Printer (Imprimerie Nationale)*, Government Printing Department, Ministry of Finance, PO Box 37, Zomba Tel: 523155

Popular Publications, PO Box 5592, Limbe Tel: 651139/651833/651464 Telex: 4814 Montfort Ml
General Manager, Publisher, Rights & Permissions: Bro John Kleinpenning; *Editorial:* Allan E Ulanga; *Sales:* Paul Chitinga; *Production:* E R Sambani; *Publicity:* Bro M D Fesani
Parent Company: Montfort Press (at above address)
Subjects: Novels, Short Stories, Poetry, Plays, History, Religious
Bookshop: Moni Bookshop (at above address)
1985: 2 titles *1986:* 3 titles *1987:* 8 titles
Founded: 1976

Major Booksellers

C L A I M Bookshop, PO Box 503, Blantyre Tel: 620839
Manager: J T Matenje
Owned by: Christian Literature Association in Malawi (qv)

Central Bookshop Ltd*, PO Box 264, Blantyre Tel: 635447
Manager: A Hamid Sacranie
School suppliers

Malawi Book Service*, PO Box 30044, Chichiri, Blantyre 3 (Located at: Ginnery Corner, Kamuzu Highway) Tel: 670044/670416/670926 Cable Add: Literature Blantyre Telex: 4537 Mbs Ml
General Manager: M U K Mlambala
Branches: PO Box 225, Kasungu (Tel: 253237); Lilongwe City Centre Shop, PO Box 30502, Lilongwe 3 (Tel: 733931); Lilongwe Old Shop, PO Box 201, Lilongwe (Tel: 720068); PO Box 114, Mzuzu (Tel: 332232); University Bookshop, PO Box 344, Zomba (Tel: 522218); Zomba Town Bookshop, Private Bag 6, Zomba (Tel: 522659)

Times Bookshop Ltd*, Victoria Ave, Private Bag 39, Blantyre Tel: 636355 Telex: 4112 Blantyre
Manager: Shaibu Itimu
Parent Company: Blantyre Printing and Publishing Co

Major Libraries

British Council Library*, PO Box 30222, Plot No 13/20, Capital City, Lilongwe 3 Tel: 730484/730266 Telex: 4476 Bricoun Ml
Also: Victoria Ave, PO Box 456, Blantyre Tel: 620204

Bunda College of Agriculture Library, University of Malawi, PO Box 219, Lilongwe Tel: 721455 Cable Add: Bundagric
Librarian: Margaret E Ngwira

Malawi National Library Service, PO Box 30314, Lilongwe 3 Tel: 730626
Dir: R S Mabomba
Regional Library for the North at PO Box 227, Mzuzu (Tel: 332819); Regional Library for the South at PO Box 30074, Chichiri, Blantyre 3 (Tel: 671436); Lilongwe Branch Library, PO Box 341, Lilongwe (Tel: 720379); Limbe Branch Library, PO Box 5394, Limbe (Tel: 640457); Zomba Branch Library, PO Box 210, Zomba (Tel: 523260)

National Archives of Malawi, PO Box 62, Zomba Tel: 522922
Librarian: D D Najira
Publications include: Malawi National Bibliography

Regional Library for the North, see Malawi National Library

Regional Library for the South, see Malawi National Library

University of Malawi Libraries*, PO Box 280, Zomba Tel: 522222
Librarian: S Mwiyeriwa
Publications: Directory of Malawi Libraries; An Annotated Bibliography of Education in Malawi; Report on University Libraries; Library Bulletin

University of Malawi, Polytechnic Library, PMB 303, Chichiri, Blantyre 3 Tel: 670411 Telex: Polytechnic 4613 Polytec Ml
Librarian: Paul Kanthambi

Library Association

The **Malawi Library Association**, PO Box 429, Zomba Tel: 522222
Secretary: G B Shaba
Publications: MALA Bulletin; Libraries in Malawi: Textbook for Library Assistants; Manual for Small Libraries

Library Reference Books and Journals

Books

Directory of Malawi Libraries, University of Malawi Libraries, PO Box 280, Zomba

Manual for Small Libraries, Malawi Library Association, PO Box 429, Zomba

Journal

Mala, Malawi Library Association, PO Box 429, Zomba

Literary Associations and Societies

The **Writers'** Group*, PO Box 280, Zomba Tel: 522222 ext 267
Secretary: Dr A J M Nazombe
Publications: Odi; The Muse

Literary Periodicals

Odi, The Writers' Group, PO Box 280, Zomba

The Muse, The Writers' Group, PO Box 280, Zomba

Malaysia

General Information

Language: Bahasa Malaysia (Malay) is official language; English widely used; Chinese, Tamil and several local languages
Religion: Islam is the official religion and predominates, there is also a large Buddhist group
Population: 15.7 million
Bank Hours: West Malaysia (some states observe Muslim weekly holiday): 1000-1500 Monday-Friday; 0930-1130 Saturday. Sabah: 0800-1200, 1400-1500 Monday-Friday; 0900-1100 Saturday. Sarawak: 1000-1500 Monday-Friday; 0930-1130 Saturday
Shop Hours: West Malaysia varies; average 0830-1830 Monday-Saturday. Sabah: 0800-1830 Monday-Saturday. Sarawak: 0900-1800 Monday-Friday; 0900-1300 Saturday
Currency: 100 cents = 1 Malaysian dollar (or ringgit)
Export/Import Information: No tariff on books. Advertising matter dutied per lb, subject to CIF surtax. No obscene literature allowed. Import licences required only in Sabah, for books not having on first or last printed page the name and address of printer and publisher. No exchange controls
Copyright: Florence (see International section)

Book Trade Organizations

Malaysian Book Publishers' Association, PO Box 335, Kuala Lumpur (Located at: No 399A Jalan Tuanku Abdul Rahman, Kuala Lumpur) Tel: (03) 2925823 Telex: MA 28140 Antara
Honorary Secretary: Johnny Ong

Persatuan Pengimpot-Pengimpot Buku Malaysia*, 25 Lorong Rahim Kajai 13, Taman Tun Dr Ismail, 60000 Kuala Lumpur Tel: (03) 7193485
Malaysian Book Importers Association
Honorary Secretary: K Arul

Persatuan Penjual-Penjual Buku Malaysia*, 25 Lorong Rahim Kajai 13, Taman Tun Dr Ismail, 60000 Kuala Lumpur
Malaysian Booksellers Association
Honorary Secretary: K Arul

Standard Book Numbering Agency*, c/o National Library of Malaysia, Acquisition Division, 4th & 5th Floors, Wisma SYS, Jalan Raja Laut, 50572 Kuala Lumpur Tel: (03) 2912110/2912044 Cable Add: Natlib Kualalumpur Telex: Natlib Kuala Lumpur MA 30092
ISBN Administrator: Mrs Primalani Kukanesan

Book Trade Reference Journals

Berita Oxford, Oxford University Press, 7 Jalan Semangat, PO Box 523 Jalan Sultan, 46760 Petaling Jaya, Selangor
Text in English and Malay

Bibliografi Negara Malaysia (Malaysian National Bibliography) (quarterly, annually), National Library of Malaysia, 1st Floor, Wisma Thakurdas/Sachdev, Jalan Raja Laut, 50572 Kuala Lumpur

Publishers

Academia Publications P Ltd*, 10 Jalan 217, Petaling Jaya, Selangor

Pustaka **Aman** Press Sdn Bhd, 4200-A Simpang Tiga-Telipot, Jalan Pasir Puteh, Kota Bharu, Kelantan

Pustaka **Antara**, 399A Jalan Tuanku Abdul Rahman, 50100 Kuala Lumpur Tel: (03) 2980044/2980159/2980237 Cable Add: Antara Telex: MA 28140
Bookshop: At above address

Anthonian Store Sdn Bhd*, 235 Jalan Brickfields, Kuala Lumpur 09-08 Tel: (03) 441711
Man Dir: Anthony B C Soh; *Editorial, Production, Publicity, Rights & Permissions:* Francis C K Lee; *Sales:* Michael Julian
Associate Companies: Eastview Productions Sdn Bhd (qv); Anthonian (Pte) Ltd, Republic of Singapore; Pusat Bahan Sumber Sdn Bhd
Branch Offs: 70 Jalan Leech, Ipoh, Perak; 48 SS 2/67, Sungei Way, Subang, Selangor; Lot LG 02-07, Komplek Wilayah, Kuala Lumpur; 26 Lerong Taman Ipoh Satu, Ipoh Garden South, Ipoh, Perak
Subjects: Educational and General in English and Malay
Bookshops: See under Major Booksellers
Founded: 1949

Arenabuku Sdn Bhd+*, 25 Lorong Rahim Kajai Tigabelas, Taman Tun Dr Ismail, 60000 Kuala Lumpur Tel: (03) 7193485
Man Dir & other offices: K Arul
Subjects: Children's, General, Academic

Bookshop: At above address
1985: 19 titles *Founded:* 1981
ISBN Publisher's Prefix: 967-970

Berita Publishing Sdn Bhd, 22 Jalan Liku, 59100 Kuala Lumpur Tel: (03) 2744322 Telex: MA 30259
General Manager: Lo Cheng Choy; *Sales:* S Jeya Dev; *Production:* A Ravindranath; *Publicity:* Gerry Ho; *Rights & Permissions:* Gulrose Karim
Parent Company: The New Straits Times Press (Malaysia) Berhad Balai Berita, 31 Jalan Riong, Kuala Lumpur 22-03
Subsidiary Companies: Berita Book Centre Sdn Bhd; Berita Distributors Sdn Bhd (both at above address)
Subjects: Reference, Fiction, Workbooks, Cookery, Business, Periodicals, Juveniles, Educational
Founded: 1973
ISBN Publisher's Prefix: 967-969

Book Distributors Sdn Bhd*, 8-1/8-2 Jalan Batai, PO Box 944, Kuala Lumpur 01-02

The **Cultural Supplies** Co, see Syarikat Cultural Supplies Sdn Bhd

Dewan Bahasa dan Pustaka, PO Box 10803, 50926 Kuala Lumpur Tel: (03) 481011/481169/481240 Cable Add: Bahasa
Director General: Datuk Haji Hassan Ahmad; *Editorial:* Haji Syed Omar (Literature), Haji Khalid Haji Hussein (Language), Haji Ariffin Siri (Textbooks), Haji Salleh Daud (General), Hajah Hamsiah (Children's); *Sales Manager:* Haji Sha'ari Abdullah; *Production:* Rahmat Ramly; *Publicity:* A Rahim Esa; *Rights & Permissions:* Halim Abdullah
Branch Offs: Kota Kinabalu, Sabah; Kuching, Sarawak
Subjects: Textbooks in Malay, Literature, General Books, Children's Books, Higher Education, Magazines and Journals
Bookshop: At above address
Founded: 1956

Eastern Universities Press*, Lot 8238, Jalan 222, 46100 Petaling Jaya, Selangor Tel: (03) 7561066/7561119
Manager: Christine Chong
Parent Company: Hodder & Stoughton Ltd, UK (qv)
Subjects: Primary and Secondary Textbooks, Art, Archaeology, Architecture, Biography, Botany, Customs and Usage, Economics and Politics, Languages, Sociology, Religion, Travel, Topography

Eastview Productions Sdn Bhd*, 19-19A Jalan SS 5B/4, Kelana Jaya, Selangor Tel: (03) 762614/762669
Man Dir: Johnny Ong
Associate Companies: Anthonian Store Sdn Bhd (qv); Pacific Book Centre, Singapore (qv under Major Booksellers); Pan Pacific Book Distributors (S) Pte Ltd, Manhattan Press (Singapore) Pte Ltd (qqv, both Republic of Singapore)
Imprints: Eastview Malaysiana Library, Eastview Visual Library
Subjects: General, Children's, Dictionaries, Textbooks
Founded: 1980
ISBN Publisher's Prefix: 967-60

F E P International Sdn Bhd*, 8246 Jalan 225, PO Box 1091, Petaling Jaya, Selangor Tel: (03) 560877/560381 Cable Add: Bookmark
Man Dir: Lim Mok Hai
Head Off: FEP International Private Ltd, Republic of Singapore (qv)
Subjects: Reference, Children's General Non-fiction, Secondary & Primary Textbooks, Dictionaries
1985: 50 titles

MALAYSIA

Penerbit Fajar Bakti Sdn Bhd, 3 Jalan 13/3, PO Box 1050, Jalan Semangat, 46860 Petaling Jaya, Selangor Darul Ehsan Tel: (03) 7563111 Cable Add: Fajar Petaling Jaya Telex: 37578
Regional Manager: R E Brammah; *Man Dir:* M Sockalingam; *Editorial Managers:* A Fadzil Yassin, Edda De Silva; *Marketing:* Koh Seng Hwi; *Production:* Yap Kok Hoong; *Publicity:* Angela Low
Parent Company: Oxford University Press (qv)
Imprint: Penerbit Fajar Bakti
Subjects: Malay Language Teaching, Dictionaries, Reference, Secondary Textbooks, General (in Malay and English)
Bookshop: At above address
1986: 1674 titles *Founded:* 1969
ISBN Publisher's Prefix: 0-19

Federal Publications Sdn Bhd*, Lot 8238, Jalan 222, 46100 Petaling Jaya, Selangor Tel: (03) 7561066/7561119 Cable Add: Fedpubs Kuala Lumpur
Divisional General Manager: H H Chiam; *Assistant General Manager:* Jesse W van den Driesen
Associate Companies: Federal Publications (S) (Pte) Ltd, Singapore (qv); Federal Publications (HK) Ltd, Hong Kong (qv); Far East Publishers Ltd, General Books Division, 117/3 Soi Sama Han, Sukhumvit 4 (South Nana), Bangkok 10110, Thailand
Subjects: Education, General

Geetha Publishers Sdn Bhd*, 13A Jalan Kovil Hilir, Kuala Lumpur
Man Dir: Mr Sethu
Subjects: History, Education, How-to, Reference, Textbooks, Bibliography, Book Industry

International Book Service, 33 Jalan 20/16, 46300 Petaling Jaya, Selangor Tel: (03) 7760514/7751566
Man Dir, Production, Publicity, Rights & Permissions: M N Meera; *Editorial:* Maarof Saad; *Sales:* Mohamed Mustafa
Subsidiary Company: Palanduk Publications (M) Sdn Bhd, 23M Jalan SS2/67, 47300 Petaling Jaya, Selangor
Subjects: General, Vocational, Technical, Children's Books
Bookshop: At above address
1985: 34 titles *1986-87:* 23 titles *Founded:* 1982
ISBN Publisher's Prefix: 967-950

Jabatan Penerbitan Universiti Malaya, see under Universiti

Longman Malaysia Sdn Bhd*, No 3 Jalan Kilang A, off Jalan Penchala, Petaling Jaya, Selangor Tel: (03) 520466 Cable Add: Freegrove Kualalumpur
Man Dir: J B Ho
Parent Company: Longman Group (UK) Ltd, UK (qv)
Subjects: Educational Materials, Textbooks

Macmillan Publishers (M) Sdn Bhd, 126B Jalan SS 24/2, Taman Megah, 47301 Petaling Jaya, Selangor
Manager: Lim Kuan Seng
Parent Company: Macmillan Publishers Ltd, UK (qv)

Malaya Books Suppliers Co*, 183 Lebuh Carnarvon, Pulau Pinang

Malaya Educational Supplies Sdn Bhd*, 48 Jalan Raja Laut, Kuala Lumpur
Subject: Education

The **Malaya Press** Sdn Bhd*, 24B Jalan Bukit Bintang, Kuala Lumpur Tel: (03) 423053/425764
Man Dir: Lai Wing Chun; *Editorial:* Yiu Hong; *Sales:* Chong Tim Seng

Parent Company: Union Cultural Organization Sdn Bhd, 10 Jalan 217, Petaling Jaya, Malaysia
Associate Companies: Hong Kong Cultural Press Ltd, 9 College Rd, Kowloon, Hong Kong; Singapore Press (Pte) Ltd, 303 North Bridge Rd, Singapore 7, Republic of Singapore
Subject: School Textbooks
Bookshops: Ipoh Book Co, 75 Market St, Ipoh, Perak; Malaya Book Co, 22-24 Jalan Bukit Bintang, Kuala Lumpur
Founded: 1958

Malayan Law Journal (Pte) Ltd, 10th Floor, Wisma Hamzah Kwong Hing, No 1 Lbh Ampang, 50100 Kuala Lumpur Tel: (03) 2321218/2321375 Telex: MA 30216 Mljkl
Parent Company: Butterworth & Co (Publishers) Ltd, UK (qv)
Head Off: Malayan Law Journal (Pte) Ltd, Republic of Singapore (qv)
Subjects: Law, Accountancy, Tax
Bookshop: At above Malayan address
ISBN Publisher's Prefix: 967-962

Malaysian Law Publishers Sdn Bhd*, PO Box 12146, Kuala Lumpur (Located at: 19 Jalan Thamby Abdullah, Kuala Lumpur) Tel: (03) 2740605
Man Dir, Rights & Permissions: Hamid Ibrahim; *Editorial:* Maimoonah Hamid; *Sales:* Nassir Hamid; *Publicity:* Faridah Hamid
Associate Companies: Malaysian Current Law Journal Sdn Bhd; Malaysian Law Tutors Sdn Bhd
Subjects: Legal Profession Books, Directories, Forms, Industrial Law Reports, Legal and Business Diaries, Periodicals (including Malaysian Current Law Journal)
Bookshop: At above address
1986: 160 titles *Founded:* 1979

Marican & Sons (M) Sdn Bhd, PO Box 10958, Kuala Lumpur (Located at: 321 Jalan Tuanku Abdul Rahman, 50100 Kuala Lumpur) Tel: (03) 981133/981218 Cable Add: Maricanews Telex: MA 31697 Manews
Man Dir: S Y Syed Muhammed; *Editorial, Rights & Permissions:* Dr Y Mansoor Marican; *Sales Manager:* Mr Dorai; *Publicity Manager:* Mr Rasul
Subsidiary Company: Marican & Sons (M) Sdn Bhd, 171 Middle Rd, Singapore 0718, Republic of Singapore
Subjects: Children's, Politics, Statistics, Dictionaries
Bookshops: See under Major Booksellers
Founded: 1922
ISBN Publisher's Prefix: 0-9934

Pustaka **Melayu** Baru*, 1015 Selangor Mansion, Jalan Masjid India, Kuala Lumpur

Minerva Publications*, PO Box 191, Seremban, Negeri Sembilan Tel: (06) 714436
Man Dir: Tajudin Muhammed
Parent Company: News and Periodicals Store, 96 Jalan Birch, Seremban, Negeri Sembilan
Subsidiary Companies: Bahagia Books Centre, 2115 Malayan Mansion, Kuala Lumpur; Best Book Agency, 40 Lapangan Merdeka, Petaling Jaya
Subject: English Literature
Bookshop: 96 Jalan Birch, Seremban, Negeri Sembilan
Founded: 1964

Oxford University Press, 7 Jalan Semangat, PO Box 523 Jalan Sultan, 46760 Petaling Jaya, Selangor Tel: (03) 7551744 Cable Add: Oxonian Petaling Jaya Telex: MA 37283 Oupres Fax: (03) 7568119
Regional Manager: R E Brammah
Parent Company: Oxford University Press, UK (qv)
Subsidiary Company: Penerbit Fajar Bakti Sdn Bhd (qv)
Branch Off: Oxford University Press Pte Ltd, Unit 221, Ubi Avenue 4, Singapore 1440, Republic of Singapore
Subjects: Educational, English Language Teaching, General, Dictionaries, Reference, Malaysiana, Asian subjects
Founded: 1957
ISBN Publisher's Prefix: 0-19

Pan Malayan Publishing Co Sdn Bhd*, 211 Jalan Bandar, Kuala Lumpur 01-30

Panther Publishing*, 90A Jalan Berhala, Brickfields, Kuala Lumpur 09-02 Tel: (03) 442364/442841
Chief Executive, Publicity: R Vijesurier; *Editorial, Production:* Bella Mary Peters; *Sales:* Mary Rajam
Branch Off: Block 151, No 650-K, Lorong 4, Toa Payoh, Singapore 1231, Republic of Singapore
Subjects: School Textbooks, Revision Guides, Travel Books, Street Guides
Founded: 1972

Preston Corporation Sdn Bhd*, 18 Jalan 19/3, Petaling Jaya, Selangor Tel: (03) 7563734/5 Telex: Prest MA 37433
Associate Companies: Times Educational Co Sdn Bhd, Malaysia (qv); Vista Productions Ltd, A7/F Melbourne Industrial Bldg, 16 Westlands Rd, Quarry Bay, Hong Kong; Preston Corporation (Pte) Ltd, 9 Irving Place, Singapore 1336, Republic of Singapore (Telex: Presin rs 26690)
Subjects: School Books, General

Sino-Malay Publishing Co*, 183 Lebuh Carnarvon, Pulau Pinang

Pustaka **Sistem** Palajaran Sdn Bhd*, 255-B Jalan Perkasa Satu, Taman Maluri, Batu 3, Cheras, Kuala Lumpur
Man Dir: Michael Ong
Subjects: School Textbooks, Children's Books

Pustaka **Sri Jaya** Sdn Bhd*, 14 Jalan Kancil, off Jalan Pudu, 55100 Kuala Lumpur
Subjects: Juveniles, Textbooks

Syarikat Cultural Supplies Sdn Bhd*, 14 Lorong Brunei Dua, off Jalan Pudu, Kuala Lumpur 06-18 Tel: (03) 427228/412791
Dir: Kow Ching Chuan

Syarikat Dian Sdn Bhd*, 97A Jalan Raja Abdullah, Kampung Baru, Kuala Lumpur

Syarikat United Book Sdn Bhd*, 187-189 Lebuh Carnarvon, Pulau Pinang

Text Books Malaysia Sdn Bhd*, Peti Surat 30, Segamat, Johore (Located at: 39 Jalan Buloh Kasap, Segamat, Johore)

Times Books International, 8238 Jalan 222, Petaling Jaya 46100, Selangor
Head off: Times Books International, Republic of Singapore (qv)

Times Educational Co Sdn Bhd*, 22 Jalan 19/3, Petaling Jaya, Selangor Tel: (03) 7571766 Cable Add: Timesbooks Telex: Prest MA 37433
Orders to: Preston Corporation Sdn Bhd, 18 Jalan 19/3, Petaling Jaya, Selangor
Parent Company: Times Educational Co Ltd, Hong Kong (qv)
Associate Companies: Preston Corporation Sdn Bhd, Malaysia (qv); Preston-Times Printing & Publishing, Selangor, Malaysia; Preston Corporation (Private) Ltd, Republic of Singapore

MALAYSIA

Subjects: Primary & Secondary School Textbooks, Children's Books, Cookery, General

Uni-Text Book Company*, PO Box 1114, Jalan Semangat, Petaling Jaya, Selangor (Located at: 24 SS 24/13, Taman Megah, Petaling Jaya, Selangor) Tel: (03) 753907/754005
Man Dir: Bob E S Lim; *Editorial:* E S Lim; *Production:* E H Lim; *Sales:* Theresa Chung
Associate Company: Uni-Text Distributors Private Ltd (at above address)
Subjects: Malay History, Religion, Literature, Juvenile (local and regional culture), Educational
Bookshop: At above address

United Publishers Services (M) Sdn Bhd, Lot 8238, Jalan 222, Petaling Jaya 46100, Selangor
Man Dir, Editorial, Production, Rights & Permissions: Goh Kee Seah; *Sales, Publicity:* Liew Kon Fatt
Associate Companies: United Publishers Service Hong Kong Ltd, Hong Kong; United Publishers Services Tokyo Ltd, Japan (qv)
Branch Offs: No 8, 1st Floor, Leboh Naning, Penang; 106 Boon Keng Rd, 07-05 Singapore 1233, Republic of Singapore
Subjects: Educational, General, Paperbacks
Founded: 1968

University of Malaya, Department of Publications+, Pantai Valley, 59100 Kuala Lumpur Tel: (03) 7574361/7574473 Cable Add: Varsitipress Kuala Lumpur Telex: MA 39845
Head of Dept, Publicity, Rights & Permissions, Editorial: Abdul Manaf Saad
Subjects: General Fiction, Textbooks, Poetry, History, Politics, Economics, General & Social Science, Medicine, Bahasa Malaysia
Founded: 1954
ISBN Publisher's Prefix: 967-9940

Utusan Publications and Distributors Sdn Bhd+*, PO Box 12235, 46M Jalan Lima, off Jalan Chan Sow Lin, Kuala Lumpur
General Manager: Othman Karim

Major Booksellers

Anthonian Store Sdn Bhd*, 235 Jalan Brickfields, Kuala Lumpur 09-08 Tel: (03) 441711
Manager: Anthony B C Soh
Branch Offs: 70 Jalan Leech, Ipoh, Perak; 48 SS 2/67, Sungei Way, Subang, Selangor; 26 Lerong Taman Ipoh Satu, Ipoh Garden South, Ipoh, Perak; Lot LG 02-07, Komplek Wilayah, Jalan Dang Wangi, Kuala Lumpur; also in 110 schools
Also Publisher (qv)

Cosdel (Singapore) Pte Ltd*, PO Box 6073, Pudu, Kuala Lumpur 06-10 Tel: (03) 489772/489224 (Located at: 23-25 Jalan Jejaka 7, Taman Maluri; Batu 3, Jalan Cheras, Kuala Lumpur)
Manager: Robert Foo
Distributors

Eastern Book Service Sdn Bhd*, 10-A Jalan Telawi Empat, Bangsar Baru, Kuala Lumpur Tel: (03) 941229 Cable Add: Eastbook
General Manager: Encik Abdul Malik
Publishers' agents and stockists

Johore Central Store Sdn Bhd, 55-58 Jalan Ibrahim, 80000 Johor Bahru Tel: (07) 223637/221841

Kwang Hwa Bookstore Pte Ltd, 26 Carpenter St, PO Box 326, Kuching, Sarawak Tel: (082) 22968
Manager: Francis Hsu Cheng Loo

M P H Distributors Sdn Bhd, Lot 2, Jalan 241, PO Box 1076, Jalan Semangat, 46972 Petaling Jaya, Selangor Tel: (03) 7746166 Telex: Jcm MA 37402 Fax: (03) 7562359
Assistant General Manager: Patrick Goh Yong Meng; *Operations Manager:* Teh Choon Pong; *Sales Managers:* Steven Koo, Gary Loo
Owned by: Jack Chia Enterprises Malaysia Berhad

Marican Sdn Bhd, 321 Jalan Tuanku Abdul Rahman, 50100 Kuala Lumpur Tel: (03) 2981133/2981218 Cable Add: Maricanews Telex: MA 31697 Manews
General Manager: C C Lo
Also: 171 Middle Rd, Singapore 0718; 4th Floor, Ruby Warehouse Complex, 8 Kaki Bukit Rd 2, Singapore 1441 (both Republic of Singapore)
Major wholesaler; also Publisher (qv)

Nabco Pendidekan Sdn Bhd*, 24 Market St, PO Box 301, 30740 Ipoh, Perak Tel: (05) 548436/518439
Man Dir: Walter Chong

Parry's Book Center (Sri Abdul Wahab Sdn Bhd), PO Box 10960, 60 Jalan Negara, Taman Melawati, 53100 Kuala Lumpur Tel: (03) 4079180/4087235/4079176
Dir: Abdul Wahab
University and library suppliers

Rex Book Store*, 40-2 K L Arcade, Jalan Masjid India, Kuala Lumpur

Times Distributors Sdn Bhd*, 130-A Jalan Thamby Abdullah Brickfields, Kuala Lumpur
General Manager: Mike Sim; *Sales Manager:* Bernard Yeap
Also: 2 Jurong Port Rd, Singapore 2261, Republic of Singapore

University of Malaya Co-operative Bookshop Ltd, PO Box 1127, Jalan Pantai Baru, 59700 Kuala Lumpur Tel: (03) 7565000/7565425 Telex: Unimal MA 39845
General Manager: Khaeruddin Sudharmin

Major Libraries

Arkib Negara Malaysia, Malay name of National Archives of Malaysia (qv)

British Council Library*, PO Box 10539, Jalan Bukit Aman, Kuala Lumpur 01-02 Tel: (03) 987555/987690/987791 Cable Add: Britcoun Kualalumpur Telex: MA 31052
Branches: Penang (PO Box 595); Kota Kinabalu (PO Box 746); Kuching (PO Box 615)

Kuala Lumpur Public Library*, Sam Mansion, Jalan Tuba, Kuala Lumpur

Lincoln Resource Center*, USIS, US Embassy, 376 Jalan Tun Razak, 50700 Kuala Lumpur Tel: (03) 2420291/2425478/2484865
Chief Librarian: Sophia Lim Enghwa

Ministry of Agriculture Library, Jalan Mahameru, 50624 Kuala Lumpur Tel: (03) 2982011 Cable Add: Tani Kuala Lumpur
Librarian: Ms Norkhaton Yunus

National Archives of Malaysia*, Jalan Duta, 50568 Kuala Lumpur Tel: (03) 2543244/2543329 Cable Add: Arkib Kualalumpur
Publications include: Annual Report of the National Archives; Bulletins

National Library of Malaysia, 1st Floor, Wisma Thakurdas/Sachdev, Jalan Raja Laut, 50572 Kuala Lumpur Tel: (03) 2923144/2923270/2923348 Cable Add: Natlib Kuala Lumpur Telex: MA 30092
Acting Director General: Dr D E K Wijasuriya
Publications: Malaysian National Bibliography (quarterly, annually); *Malaysian Periodicals Index* (biannually); *Malaysian Newspaper Index* (quarterly); *Index to Malaysian Conferences* (annually); *Directory of Libraries in Malaysia; Current Malaysian Serials* (non-government); *Bibliography of books in Bahasa Malaysia; Directory of Librarians in Malaysia*

National University of Malaysia Library*, Bangi, Selangor Tel: (03) 350199 Telex: MA 31496
Acting Chief Librarian: Zainal Azman Rajuddin

Perpustakaan Negeri Sabah, Malay name of Sabah State Library (qv)

Rubber Research Institute of Malaysia Library*, PO Box 10150, Kuala Lumpur 16-03 Tel: (03) 467033 Cable Add: Searching Telex: Rrim MA 30369
Librarian: J S Soosai

Sabah State Library*, Kota Kinabalu, Sabah Tel: Pengarah 54064/Pejabat Am 54333/54243/54493 Telex: Saslib MA 80236
Dir: Mrs Adeline Leong

Sarawak State Library*, Jalan Jawa, Kuching Tel: (082) 22911
State Librarian: Johnny Kueh

Selangor Public Library, Persiaran Indah, 40572 Shah Alam, Selangor Tel: (03) 5597667
Librarian: Mrs Shahaneem Mustafa
Publications: Annual Report; Accession List

Tun Razak Library*, Jalan Club, Ipoh, Perak Tel: (05) 514979/514808
Librarian: Chang Sinn Nean
Publications: Malaysiana Collection (plus supplement); *Accession Lists* (in English, Malay, Chinese and Tamil)

Library Tun Seri Lanang, Universiti Kebangsaan Malaysia*, Bangi, Selangor

Universiti Kebangsaan, see Library Tun Seri

Universiti Teknologi Malaysia Library*, Jalan Gurney, 54100 Kuala Lumpur Tel: (03) 2929033 Telex: 30090 Utm
Chief Librarian: Che Sham Hj Mohd Darus

University Library, Universiti Sains Malaysia, 11800 Penang Tel: (04) 883822 Cable Add: Unisains Telex: MA 40254
Chief Librarian: Lim Huck Tee

University of Agriculture Malaysia Library*, Serdang, Selangor Tel: (03) 9486101 Cable Add: Unipertama Sungaibesi Telex: Uniper MA 37454
Chief Librarian: Tuan Syed Salim Agha

University of Malaya Library*, Pantai Valley, Kuala Lumpur 22-11 Tel: (03) 575887 Telex: MA 37453
Librarian: Mrs Khoo Siew Mun
Publications include: Kekal Abadi (quarterly newsletter)
Miscellaneous: Special collections in Medicine, Law, Malay Languages/Culture, Chinese, Tamil

University of Technology Malaysia Library, see Universiti Teknologi Malaysia Library

Library Association

Persatuan Perpustakaan Malaysia, PO Box 12545, Kuala Lumpur
Library Association of Malaysia
Honorary Secretary: Ahmad Ridzuan Wan Chik
Publications: Majallah Perpustakaan Malaysia (annually); *Berita PPM* (bi-monthly); *Sumber Pustaka* (official newsletter)

Library Reference Books and Journals

Books

Directory of Librarians in Malaysia, National Library of Malaysia, 1st Floor, Wisma Thakurdas/Sachdev, Jalan Raja Laut, 50572 Kuala Lumpur

Directory of Libraries in Malaysia, National Library of Malaysia, 1st Floor, Wisma Thakurdas/Sachdev, Jalan Raja Laut, 50572 Kuala Lumpur

Journals

Majallah Perpustakaan Malaysia (official journal), Persatuan Perpustakaan Malaysia, PO Box 12545, Kuala Lumpur
Text in English and Malay

Sumber Pustaka (official newsletter), Persatuan Perpustakaan Malaysia, PO Box 12545, Kuala Lumpur
Text in English and Malay

Literary Associations and Societies

Dewan Bahasa dan Pustaka, PO Box 10803, Jalan Lapangan Terbang, 50926 Kuala Lumpur Tel: (03) 2481011 Telex: MA 32683
Language and Literary Development Agency of the Ministry of Education
Dir General: Datuk Haji Hassan bin Ahmad
Publications: Dewan Bahasa; Dewan Masyarakat; Dewan Pelajar; Dewan Sastera (monthly); *Dewan Budaya; Dewan Siswa* (monthly); *Tenggara* (half-yearly)

Literary Periodical

Tenggara (half-yearly), Dewan Bahasa dan Pustaka, PO Box 10803, Jalan Lapangan Terbang, 50926 Kuala Lumpur
Text in English and Malay

Literary Prizes

Anugerah Sastera Negara Prize
National Literary Award. Founded 1980, the highest governmental award to an author writing in the national language, who has made a major contribution to the development of the country's literature. Award consists of M$30,000, publication facilities and other benefits. Enquiries to Dewan Bahasa dan Pustaka, PO Box 10803, 50926 Kuala Lumpur

Hadiah Sastera Malaysia Prize
Malaysian Literary Prize. Founded 1982, and awarded by the Malaysian Government biennially for creative writing in the national language, covering short story, novel, poetry and drama, and with the aim of encouraging new talent and enhancing the quality of the national literature. Enquiries to Dewan Bahasa dan Pustaka, PO Box 10803, 50926 Kuala Lumpur

Mali

General Information

Language: French
Religion: Islamic
Population: 6.9 million
Working Hours: 0730-1430 Monday-Thursday and Saturday; 0730-1230 Friday
Currency: Malian franc
Export/Import Information: Member of the West African Economic Community. No tariff on books but subject to VAT at varying rates. Advertising matter (more than single copy) subject to tariff, import tax and VAT. All goods subject to local tax of percentage of customs value. Import licence required. Importation is either by private importers or state enterprises. Exchange controls for non-franc zone
Copyright: Berne (see International section)

Publishers

Government Printer (Imprimerie Nationale)*, ave Kassé Keita, BP 21, Bamako

Editions Imprimeries du **Mali***, ave Kassé Keita, BP 21, Bamako Tel: 22041
Man Dir: Barthélémy Koné
Subsidiary Companies: Editions populaires; Imprimerie Kassé Keita; Imprimerie nationale
Subjects: General Fiction & Non-fiction, Belles Lettres, Poetry, Biography, History, Africana, Religion, Paperbacks, Social Science, University, Secondary & Primary Textbooks
Founded: 1972

Major Booksellers

Librairie **Deves et Chaumet***, BP 64, Bamako

Librairie populaire de Mali*, ave Kassé Keita, BP 28, Bamako Tel: 23403

Major Libraries

Bibliothèque municipale*, Bamako

Bibliothèque nationale*, ave Kassé Keita, BP 159, Bamako Tel: 224963
Director: Abdoul Aziz Diallo
Publication: Néant

Bibliothèque du **Centre culturel français** de Bamako, Ambassade de France, BP 1547, Bamako Tel: 224019/225828
Librarian: Anne-Marie Le Bot

Centre Djoliba recherche-formation pour le développement, Bibliothèque*, BP 298, Bamako Tel: 222527
Dir: Francis Verstraete

Centre français de Documentation, now Centre culturel français (qv)

Ecole normale supérieure*, Bibliothèque, BP 241, Bamako

Library Association

Inspection des **Archives**, Musées et Bibliothèques du Mali*, BP 241, Bamako
Inspectorate of Archives, Museums and Libraries of Mali

Malta

General Information

Language: Maltese (English second language)
Religion: Roman Catholic
Population: 364,000
Bank Hours: 0830-1230 Monday-Friday; 0830-1200 Saturday
Shop Hours: 0900-1300, 1530-1900 Monday-Saturday
Currency: 10 mils = 1 cent, 100 cents = 1 Maltese pound
Export/Import Information: No tariff on books or advertising. No import licence required. Exchange control by Central Bank
Copyright: Berne, UCC (see International section)

Book Trade Reference Book

Malta National Bibliography (annual), National Library of Malta, 36 Old Treasury St, Valletta

Publishers

A C **Aquilina** & Co*, 58D Republic St, Valletta Tel: 624774/626357 Cable Add: Aqlina Vallettamalta Telex: 1762 Aqlina
Publicity Manager: Josef Portelli
Subjects: Literature, History
Bookshop: See under Major Booksellers

Gulf Publishing Ltd, now Publishers' Enterprises Group (PEG) Ltd (qv)

Ideal, an imprint of A Vassallo and Sons Ltd (qv)

Lux Press*, St Joseph St, Hamrun
Publicity Manager: A Micallef
Subject: Literature

Mediterranean Publishing Co Ltd*, PO Box 546, Valletta (Located at: 34E Archbishop St, Valletta) Tel: 25820/620300/607981 Cable Add: Mepuco Mw Telex: Mw 532 Mepuco
Man Dir: Leo Brincat
Founded: 1976

P E G Ltd, see Publishers' Enterprises Group

Progress Press*, PO Box 328, Valletta (Located at: Strickland House, 341 St Paul St, Valletta) Tel: 24031 Cable Add: Progress Telex: Mw 341
Man Dir: W B Asciak
Parent Company: The Allied Newspapers Ltd
Subjects: Literature, Malta
Founded: 1957

Publishers' Enterprises Group (PEG) Ltd*, PEG Bldg, Herbert Ganado St, Hamrun Tel: 24186
Man Dir, Editorial, Rights & Permissions: Emanuel Debattista; *Sales:* Victor Mifsud; *Production, Publicity:* Gaetan Cilia

Subjects: Leisure, Educational, Children's, Cookery, Technical, Tourism
Founded: 1983

The **University of Malta** Publications Section, Administration Bldg, The University of Malta, Msida Tel: 36451 Cable Add: University Malta Telex: Mw 407 Hieduc
Subjects: Maltese Folklore & History, Maltese Legal History, Natural History, Linguistics
Founded: 1953

A **Vassallo** and Sons Ltd, PO Box 20, Main Gate St, Victoria, Gozo Tel: 553944
Imprint: Ideal
Subjects: School Textbooks, Maps, Guides, Religion
Bookshops: The Ideal Bookshop (qv under Major Booksellers); Il-Bxara T-Tajba, Charity St, Victoria, Gozo

Major Booksellers

A C **Aquilina** & Co*, 58D Republic St, Valletta Tel: 624774/ 626357 Cable Add: Aqlina Valletta Malta Telex: 1762 Aqlina
Also Publisher (qv)

The **Hamrun** Library*, 673 St Joseph Rd, Hamrun Tel: 28542

The **Ideal** Bookshop, Main Gate St, Victoria, Gozo Tel: 553944
Also: Il-Bxara T-Tajba (Christian Bookshop), Charity St, Victoria, Gozo Tel: 553944
Manager: A Vassallo
Owned by: A Vassallo and Sons Ltd (qv)

Merlin Library Ltd, Mountbatten St, Blata I-Bajda Tel: 221205 Telex: Mw 623 Mergru
Dir: A J Gruppetta
Branch Off: 57 Old Bakery St, Valletta Tel: 603112
Also Wholesalers and Remainder Dealers

Giov **Muscat** & Co Ltd, PO Box 348, Valletta (Located at: 213 St Ursola St, Valletta; 48 Merchants St, Valletta) Tel: 227668/233879/232923 Cable Add: Herald Malta Telex: Mw 727
Man Dir: S Magri

Sapienza's Library*, 26 Republic St, Valletta Tel: 625621
Manager: Louis Sapienza

Major Libraries

Gozo Public Library, Vajringa St, Victoria, Gozo Tel: 556200

National Library of Malta, 36 Old Treasury St, Valletta Tel: 226585
Librarian: John B Sultana
Publication: Malta National Bibliography

University of Malta Library, Msida Tel: 314306
Librarian: Paul Xuereb
Publications include: Malta, Official Statistical Publications, 2nd ed, 1981; Il-Poezija bil-Malti 1964-74; A Bibliography of Maltese Bibliographies 1978; Law: Select reference sources 1987

Library Association

Ghaqda Bibljotekarji/Library Association (Valletta)*, c/o Din l-Art Helwa, 133 Melita St, Valletta
Secretary: Anthony F Sapienza
Publications include: GhB/LA Newsletter; Bibliography of Children's Literature in Malta; Directory of Publishers, Printers, Book Designers and Book Dealers in Malta

Library Reference Books and Journals

Book

A Bibliography of Maltese Bibliographies, University of Malta Library, Msida

Journal

GhB/LA Newsletter, Ghaqda Bibljotekarji/Library Association (Valletta), c/o Din l/Art Helwa, 133 Melita St, Valletta

Martinique

General Information

Language: French
Population: 325,000
Currency: French Guiana, Guadeloupe and Martinique franc
Export/Import Information: Tariff same as France. Overseas tax and reduced VAT on books. Small quantity of advertising free. No import licences required. Exchange restrictions as in France
Copyright: Berne, UCC (see International section)

Publishers

Editions **Tygre***, BP 715, 97207 Fort-de-France, Cedex Martinique
Subject: Tourism

Major Booksellers

A **Jean-Charles***, 32 et 47 rue Schoelcher, Fort-de-France Tel: 4155
Branches: Four

Major Libraries

Direction des Services d'**Archives** de la Martinique*, Tartenson, route de la Clairière, BP 649, 97262 Fort-de-France
Director: Liliane Chauleau
Publications include: Inventaire analytique (1985)

Bibliothèque Victor **Schoelcher***, rue de la Liberté, 97200 Fort-de-France, Martinique
Librarian: Jacqueline Leger

Mauritania

General Information

Language: Arabic and French
Religion: Islamic
Population: 1.6 million
Bank Hours: 0800-1115, 1430-1630 Monday-Friday
Shop Hours: Vary. Generally 0800-1200, 1430-1800 Monday-Saturday. Some closed Monday morning, some open Sunday morning
Currency: ouguiya
Export/Import Information: Member of the West African Economic Community. No tariff on books. Advertising matter (other than single copies) subject to fiscal, customs duty and added tax. Import licences and exchange controls apply to imports outside of EEC and franc zone
Copyright: Berne (see International section)

Publishers

Government Printer (Imprimerie Nationale)*, BP 618, Nouakchott

Imprimerie Commerciale et Administrative de Mauritanie*, BP 164, Nouakchott
Subjects: Education, Textbooks

Major Libraries

Arab Library*, Chinguetti

Direction des **Archives nationales**, Bibliothèque publique et Centre du Documentation, BP 77, Nouakchott Tel: 52317 Telex: Prim 580 Mtn
Dir: Moktar Ould Hemeina

Bibliothèque nationale*, BP 20, Nouakchott Tel: 24-35 or 278

Centre culturel **Saint-Exupery**, Bibliothèque, BP 225, Nouakchott

Mauritius

General Information

Language: English and French
Population: 1,000,000
Bank Hours: 1000-1400 Monday-Friday, 0930-1130 Saturday
Shop Hours: 0800-1600 or later Monday-Saturday
Currency: 100 cents = 1 Mauritius rupee
Export/Import Information: No tariff on books and advertising but there is a special levy. No import licence required
Copyright: UCC (see International section)

Book Trade Reference Journal

Quarterly Memorandum of Books Printed in Mauritius and Registered in the Archives, Mauritius Archives, Development Bank of Mauritius Complex, Coromandel

Publishers

De l'édition **Bukié** Banané, 5 rue Edwin Ythier, Rose Hill Tel: 542327
Man Dir: Dev Virahsawmy
Orders to: Librairie le Cygne, Royal Rd, Rose Hill, Mauritius
Subjects: Creole Literature, Poetry, Drama
Founded: 1979

Government Printer (Imprimerie Nationale)*, Government Printing Office, Elizabeth II Ave, Port Louis

Major Booksellers

Librairie **Allot**, Botanical Gardens St, Curepipe Tel: 61253 Cable Add: Allot Mtius
Managers: Jean Desjardins, Guy Charoux

Librairie **Bonanza***, Corner of Virgile Naz and Monsignor Gonin Sts, Port Louis Tel: 5179

Librairie **Bourbon***, 28 Bourbon St, Port Louis Tel: 21467
Manager: Mrs M Allagapen

Librairie Le **Colibri***, St Jean Rd, Quatre Bornes Tel: 2445
Also: Arcades Atchia, Royal Rd, Rose Hill Tel: 1126

Librairie Le **Cygne***, Royal Rd, Rose Hill Tel: 2444

Librairie des **Mascareignes**, 5 Queen St, Rose Hill Tel: 42748 Cable Add: Manjoo Rose Hill
Manager: Farouk S Manjoo
Also: Quatre Bornes Book Centre, 77 route Saint Jean, Quatre Bornes

Nalanda Co Ltd*, 30 Bourbon St, Port Louis Tel: 0160

Quatre Bornes Book Centre, see Mascareignes

Librairie du **Trèfle***, Royal St, Port Louis Tel: 1106
Also: Les Arcades, Curepipe Tel: 25

Major Libraries

British Council Library, PO Box 111, Royal Rd, Rose Hill Tel: 42034

Carnegie Library*, Queen Elizabeth II Terrace, Curepipe Tel: 864041
Librarian: I Dassyne

City Library*, City Hall, Municipality of Port Louis, PO Box 422, Port Louis Tel: 20831 Cable Add: Cerne/Port Louis
Librarian: Gaetan Benoit
Publications include: Annual Report; Newspapers Index: Mauritius; Bibliography: Mauritiana in City Library; Literary Publishing and Bibliographical Control in Mauritius

Junior Library*, Moka Rd, Rose Hill Tel: 42003
Librarian: Abdul Soogali

Mauritius Archives, Development Bank of Mauritius Complex, Coromandel
Dir: Dr P H Sooprayen
Publications: Annual Report of the Archives Department (including a bibliographical supplement); *Quarterly Memorandum of Books Printed in Mauritius and Registered in the Archives*

Mauritius Institute Public Library, PO Box 54, Port Louis Tel: 20639
Head Librarian: Sewannah Ankiah

University of Mauritius Library, Reduit Tel: 541041/45420
Librarian: B R Goordyal
Publications include: University of Mauritius Report (Annual); *University of Mauritius Calendar; Journal of the University of Mauritius*

Library Association

Mauritius Library Association*, c/o The British Council, Royal Rd, Rose Hill
Secretary: N Ramboccus
Publication: Mauritius Library Association Newsletter (quarterly)

Library Reference Journal

Mauritius Library Association Newsletter (quarterly), Mauritius Library Association, c/o The British Council, Royal Rd, Rose Hill

Literary Associations and Societies

Académie mauricienne de Langue et de Littérature*, Curepipe
Secretary: C de Rauville
Publication: Oeuvres et Chroniques de l'Océan indien

Mexico

General Information

Language: Spanish
Religion: Roman Catholic
Population: 67.4 million
Bank Hours: 0900-1330 Monday-Friday
Shop Hours: 1000-1900 Monday, Tuesday, Thursday, Friday; 1100-2000 Wednesday and Saturday
Currency: 100 centavos = 1 peso
Export/Import Information: Member of the Latin American Free Trade Association. Foreign language books and textbooks generally dutied per kg legal weight, children's picture books ad valorem or per kg, whichever greater, and require import licence. Three copies of non-Spanish advertising catalogues free but all others require licence and dutied ad valorem. Customs request from Bank of Mexico all necessary information to decide cases of tariff
Copyright: UCC, Berne, Buenos Aires (see International section)

Book Trade Organizations

Cámara Nacional de Comercio, Sección de Librerías*, Paseo de la Reforma 42, Delegación Cuauhtémoc, 06048 México, DF Tel: (05) 5922677 Telex: 1777262 Cn Come
National Trade Association, Booksellers' Section

Cámara Nacional de la Industria Editorial, Holanda 13, Col San Diego, Churubusco, 04120 México 21, DF Tel: (05) 6882011/6882434 Telex: 1772969
Mexican Publishers' Association
Secretary General: R Servin Arroyo

Centro Mexicano de Escritores AC*, Luis G Inclán No 2709, Col Villa da Cortés, 03130 México 13, DF
Mexican Authors' Centre
Executive Secretary: Felipe García Beraza
Publication: Recent Books in Mexico

Centro Nacional de Información, Agencia Nacional I S B N, Dirección General del Derecho de Autor, Mariano-Escobedo 438, 5° piso, Col Verónica Anzures, 11590 México, DF Tel: (05) 2035254/5455868
ISBN Administrator: Alejandra Martínez Gamboa

Instituto Mexicano del Libro AC*, Paseo de la Reforma 95, Depto 603 México, DF Tel: (05) 5352061
Mexican Book Institute
Secretary-General: Isabel Ruiz González

Standard Book Numbering Agency, see Centro Nacional de Información, Agencia Nacional ISBN

Book Trade Reference Books and Journals

Books

Anuario Bibliográfico (Bibliographical Yearbook), Instituto de Investigaciones Bibliográficas, Biblioteca Nacional de México and Hemeroteca Nacional de México, Centro Cultural, Ciudad Universitaria, Delegación Coyoácan, 04510 México, DF

Bibliografía Mexicana (Mexican Bibliography), Instituto de Investigaciones Bibliográficas, Biblioteca Nacional de México and Hemeroteca Nacional de México, Centro Cultural, Ciudad Universitaria, Delegación Coyoácan, 04510 México, DF

Journals

Boletín Bibliográfico Mexicano (Mexican Bibliographical Bulletin), Editorial Porrúa SA, Argentina 15, 5° piso, México 1, DF

Fuente Editorial, Deduce SA, Apdo 27-030, 06760 México 7, DF
A directory of the Mexican publishing industry

Recent Books in Mexico, Centro Mexicano de Escritores AC, Luis G Inclán No 2709, Col Villa da Cortés, 03130 México 13, DF

Publishers

Aconcagua Ediciones y Publicaciones SA, Apdo 12-1141, 03020 México, DF (Located at: Xochicalco No 352, Col Narvarte, Deleg Benito Juarez, 03020 México, DF) Tel: (05) 5361292/5361660/5432280
Dir: Julio Sanz Crespo
Associate Companies: Editorial Siluetas, Bartolomé Mitre 3745-49, 1201 Buenos Aires, Argentina; Editorial Timun Mas SA, Spain (qv)
Head Off: Ediciones Ceac SA, Spain (qv)
Subjects: Literature, History, How-to, Religion, Technology, Juveniles, Low-priced Paperbacks, University Textbooks, Educational Materials

Addison-Wesley Iberoamericana SA*, Apdo 22-456, 14000 México, DF (Located at: San Marcos 102, Col Tlalpan, Delegación Tlalpan, CP 14000) Cable Add: Adiwes Telex: 01771410 Feime
President: Juan José Fernandez Gaos; *Vice-President:* Jonathan Rose; *Editorial, Rights & Permissions:* Laura Valencia; *Publicity:* Josefina Joveu
Parent Company: Addison-Wesley Publishing Co Inc, Reading, MA 01867, USA
Associate Companies: Fondo Educativo Interamericano in Colombia, Panama, Puerto Rico, Venezuela (qqv); Addison-Wesley Publishers Ltd, UK (qv for other associate companies)
Subjects: All Educational
Founded: 1972
ISBN Publisher's Prefix: 968-201

Aguilar SA+*, Ave Universidad 757, 03100 México, DF Tel: (05) 6886211 Cable Add: Guilarditor Telex: 1773621 Amedme

284 MEXICO

Man Dir, Editorial: Antonio Ruano Fernández; *Sales:* Enrique Morales Buenromero; *Publicity:* Aurelio Reyes Gil
Parent Company: Aguilar SA de Ediciones, Spain (qv)
Subjects: Arts, Literature, History, Economy, Philosophy, Children's, Maps
Founded: 1965
ISBN Publisher's Prefix: 968-19

Alianza Editorial Mexicana*, José Morán 93-1A, México 18, DF Tel: (05) 5159391/5167108
Man Dir: Alberto E Díaz
Associate Companies: See under Alianza Editorial SA, Spain

Arbol Editorial SA de CV*, Ave Cuauhtémoc 1430, Santa Cruz Atoyac, 03310 México, DF Tel: (05) 6883842
Man Dir, Rights & Permissions: Gerardo Gally; *Production:* Margara Clavé
Subjects: Health, Naturism, Oriental Philosophy, Rural Technology
Founded: 1979
ISBN Publisher's Prefix: 968-461

Ariel, member of Grupo Editorial Planeta (qv)

Editorial **Avante** SA, Luis Gonzalez Obregon no 9-altos, Apdo 45-796, 06020 México, DF Tel: (05) 5108804/5217563
Man Dir: Luis Quiros Presa; *Editorial, Rights & Permissions, Production:* Ana Luisa Quiros Esteban; *Sales, Publicity:* Mario Alberto Hinojosa Saenz
Imprints: Impresora Galve SA, Callejon de San Antonio Abad no 39, Col Transito, Mexico 8, DF; Impresora Multiple SA, Bolivia, Col Centro, Mexico 1, DF
Subjects: Kindergarten Textbooks, Pre-School and Primary Teaching Aids, Poetry, Drama, Biography, Miscellaneous Educational, Social Sciences, Linguistics, Maps
Founded: 1950

Editorial **Azteca** SA+, Calle La Luna 225-227, 06300 México, DF Tel: (05) 5261157 Cable Add: Edasa
Man Dir: Alfonso Alemón Jalomo; *Sales Dir:* Juan Alemón Jalomo
Subjects: General Literature, Technical, Popular Science
Founded: 1956

Editorial **Banca y Comercio** SA*, Reforma 202, 06600 México, DF Tel: (05) 5353587
Man Dir: Carlos Prieto Sierra; *Assistant Manager:* Martha C Gutiérrez
Subjects: Business & Administration, Mathematics, Law
Founded: 1934

Libreria y Ediciones **Botas** SA, Justo Sierra 52, Apdo 941, México 1, DF Tel: (05) 5223896/5224717
Man Dir: Andres Botas Arredondo; *Sales Dir:* Esperanza Delgado Zúñiga
Subjects: Art, History, Economics, General Fiction, Philosophy, Law, General Science, Medicine, Reference
Founded: 1910

Editorial **Bruguera** Mexicana SA*, Ave Popocatepetl 421-6, Col Gral Anaya, 03340 México, DF Tel: (05) 6889022/6889717
Telex: 01771264 Brugme
Dir: Pedro Lopez Lopez
Parent Company: Editorial Bruguera SA, Spain (qv)

Ediciones el **Caballito** SA*, Isabel la Catolica 922, Col Postal, Delegacion Benito Juarez, 03410 México, DF Tel: (05) 5903653/6963400
Man Dir, Editorial: Manuel Lopez Gallo; *Sales:* Alfonso Garcia Espino; *Production:* Teresa Dey; *Rights & Permissions:* Manuel Lopez Gallo, Teresa Dey
Subsidiary Company: Presencia Latinoamerica (at above address)
Associate Company: Impoli SA (at above address)
Subjects: Sociology, Mexican History and Economy, General Non-fiction
Bookshop: Libreria del Soltano SA, Ave Juarez 64, Sotano Centro, México 1, DF
Founded: 1967
ISBN Publisher's Prefix: 968-6011

Centro de Estudios Monetarios Latinoamericanos (CEMLA), Durango 54, México 7, DF Tel: (05) 5330300 Cable Add: Cemla, Mexico Telex: 1771229 cemlme
Man Dir: Jorge González del Valle; *Editorial, Rights & Permissions:* Juan Manuel Rodriguez; *Sales:* Claudio Antonovich; *Production:* Cristina Conde
Subjects: Economics, Finance, Periodicals
Founded: 1952

El **Colegio** de México AC+, Depto de Publicaciones, Camino al Ajusco 20, 10740 México, DF Tel: (05) 5682922/5686033 ext 388, 297 Cable Add: Colmex Telex: 1777585 Colme
Man Dir: José Antonio Valadez; *Promotion, Distribution:* Teresa Martínez López; *Production:* Joel Palazvelos
Subjects: Literature, Linguistics, Sociology, History, International Relations, Demography, Economy, Urbanistic Development, Asian and African Studies, Methodology, Political Science
Bookshop: Librería de El Colegio de México (at above address)
1985: 380 titles *Founded:* 1940

Compañía General de Ediciones SA de CV+, Mier y Pesado 130, Col del Valle, 03100 México, DF Tel: (05) 5437016/6874699 Cable Add: Sayrols Mexico Telex: 01771403 Dsayme
Man Dir: Gonzalo Araico Montes de Oca; *Marketing Director:* Eduardo Peña Alfaro; *Sales:* Eleazar Osorio
Subsidiary Company: Sayara Corporation, Vallarino Bldg, 11th Floor, Elvira Mendez and 52nd St, PO Box 9890, Panamá 4, Panama
Associate Companies: Libros y Revistas SA de CV (qv); Publicaciones Sayrols SA de CV (qv); Editorial Sayrols SA de CV
Subjects: Literature, Popular Science, General Interest, How-to
Bookshop: Librería Mexico Apatzingan, Heriberto Jara 31, Apatzingan, Michoacan
1985: 25 titles *1986:* 30 titles *Founded:* 1949
ISBN Publisher's Prefix: 968-403

Editorial **Concepto** SA*, Ave Cuauhtémoc 1430, Santa Cruz Atoyac, 03310 México, DF Tel: (05) 6883842
Man Dir, Rights & Permissions: Gerardo Gally; *Production:* Margara Clavé
Subjects: Architecture, Psychology, Pedagogy, Children's books, Alternative Technology, How-to
Founded: 1977
ISBN Publisher's Prefix: 968-405

Ediciones **Contables y Administrativas** SA*, Heriberto Frías 1451-101, Col del Valle, Delegacíon Benito Juárez, 03100 México, DF Tel: (05) 5590443
Man Dir: Pedro Gasca Rocha; *Sales Dir:* Gustavo Gasca Bretón
Branch Off: Zaragoza 39-106, Guadalajara, Jalisco, Mexico
Subjects: Technical, Accounting & Management
Founded: 1967

Cía Editorial **Continental** SA (CESCA), Calzada de Tlalpan 4620, Apdo 22022, México 22, DF Tel: (05) 5732300 Cable Add: Ediconti Telex: 1760261 Contme
Man Dir: Miguel León Garza; *Sales Manager:* Jorge Orozco Umaña
Subjects: Science & Technology, Textbooks
Founded: 1954

Ediciones **Copilco** SA, see La Prensa Medica Mexicana SA (qv)

Publicaciones **Cosmos***, España 396, Col Granjas Estrella, 09880 México, DF Tel: (05) 5829928
Man Dir: Catalina Ramirez de Arellano; *Editorial:* César Macazaga; *Sales, Publicity:* Raul Macazaga; *Production:* Carlos Macazaga
Subjects: Buyers' Directories (chemicals, rubber, plastics, equipment)
Founded: 1963
ISBN Publisher's Prefix: 968-7095

Publicaciones **Cultural** SA, see Publicaciones

Deduce SA*, Tuxpan 63 202A, Col Roma Sur, 07 México, DF Tel: (05) 5644398
Dir-General: Ramiro Lafuente López; *Sales:* Antonio López Ocampo; *Publicity:* Elia Torres Ortiz
Subjects: Bibliographies, Publishing, Teaching, Reference, Agriculture, Ecology (all in microfiche)

Editorial **Diana** SA+, Roberto Gayol 1219, Apdo 44-986, 03100 México, DF Tel: (05) 5750711 Cable Add: Edisa Telex: 1777618 Dimeme
President: José Luis Ramírez; *Corporate Dir:* Carlos Huerta; *General Manager:* Iván Garciá; *Sales:* Roberto Merino; *Editor:* Fausto Rosales
Subsidiary Companies: Editorial Universo SA (qv); Editorial Origen SA; Edivisión Cía Editorial SA
Subjects: Fiction, General Non-fiction, Technical, Juveniles
Bookshop: At above address
Founded: 1946

Editorial **Diogenes** SA, Apdo 82-016, Contadero Cuajimalpa, 05500 México, DF (Located at: Arteaga y Salazar 21, Contadero Cuajimalpa, México 18, DF)
Dir: Emmanuel Farballo
Subjects: Belles Lettres, History, Social & Political Science, Medicine
1985: 18 titles *1986:* 12 titles

Ediciones **Don Bosco***, Apdo 920-Centro, Delegación Cuauhtémoc, 06000 México, DF Tel: (05) 5121101
Dir: Alfonso Burciaga Saucedo; *Deputy Dir, Rights & Permissions:* Milagros Magaña del Campo; *Sales:* Jaime Padilla
Parent Company: Moneda, 24-Centro, Delegación Cuauhtémoc, 06000 México, DF
Associate Companies: Editorial y Librería Don Bosco, Ave 16 de Julio 1899, Casilla 4458, La Paz, Bolivia; Edebe, Spain (qv); Central Catequista Salesiana, Madrid Alcalá 164, Madrid, Spain
Subjects: Religious
Bookshops: Moneda: 24-Centro, 06000 México, DF; 5 de Mayo 23, 06000 México, DF; Colegio Salesiano No 35, Col Anáhuac, Delegación Miguel Hidalgo, 11320 México, DF
Founded: 1958
ISBN Publisher's Prefix: 968-6662

E D A M E X, see Editores Asociados Mexicanos SA

Editorial **Edicol** SA, Murcia 2, Col Mixcoac Ins, Apdo 19-376, 03920 México, DF Tel: (05) 5637900/5981512
Man Dir: Jorge Silva Escamilla
Subjects: Design, Communication,

Education, Sociology, Social Sciences, Languages and Literature, Reading Manuals
Founded: 1970
ISBN Publisher's Prefix: 968-408

Editora Nacional+*, Dr Erazo 42, PO Box 06720, México 7, DF Tel: (05) 5782354
Man Dir: Rubén Rendón Vargas; *Publicity:* Juan Carlos R Barceul
Subject: General Literature

Editores Asociados Mexicanos SA (EDAMEX), Heriberto Frías 1104, 03100 México, DF Tel: (05) 5757035/5591499/5591566
Man Dir: Manuel Colmenares G; *Editorial, Publicity, Rights & Permissions:* Octavio Colmenares V; *Sales:* Jorge Espinosa; *Production:* Sergio de Miguel
Associate Company: Editorial Meridiano SA
Subjects: Social Sciences, Economics, Politics, Literature, Communications, Recreation, Humour
Founded: 1963
ISBN Publisher's Prefix: 968-409

Emecé Mexicana SA de CV, see Emecé Editores SA, Argentina

Empresas Editoriales SA*, Praga 56, Apdo 6-791, México 6, DF Tel: (05) 5110162
Subject: General Fiction
Founded: 1944

Ediciones **Era** SA de CV*, Apdo 74-092, 09080 México, DF (Located at: Ave 102, Col Granjas Esmeralda, Delegación Iztapalapa, 09810 México, DF) Tel: (05) 5817744 Cable Add: Liberamex
Man Dir: Mrs Nieves Espresate Xirau
Branch Offs: Alemania 1266, Apdo 32-140, 44100 Guadalajara, Jal Tel: (036) 149048; Diego de Montemayor 635 Sur Centro, 64000 Montemayor, NL Tel: (0471) 420812
Subjects: General Fiction, Art, Belles Lettres, Social & Political Science, Economics, Quarterly Political Reviews
Founded: 1960

Editorial **Esfinge** SA*, Colima 220-503, 06790 México, DF Tel: (05) 5112771/5142823/5250774
Man Dir: Agustín Mateos Muñoz; *Sales Dir:* Eduardo Mateos Gay
Subjects: Literature, Law, Science, University, Secondary & Primary Textbooks
Founded: 1957
ISBN Publisher's Prefix: 968-412

Espasa-Calpe Mexicana SA*, Pitágoras 1139, México 12, DF
Head Office: Editorial Espasa-Calpe SA, Spain (qv)

Ediciones **Euroamericanas**, Apdo 24-434, 06700 México, DF (Located at: Textitlán 38, St Ursula Coapa, México) Tel: (05) 5250266
Man Dir: Klaus Thiele
Subjects: History and Anthropology of the Americas, Practical Technology, Languages
1987: 8 titles *Founded:* 1971
ISBN Publisher's Prefix: 968-414

Editorial **Extemporaneos** SA*, Poniente 126-A, No 400 Col Residencial Vallejo, Apdo 78-048, México 14, DF Tel: (05) 5875424/5878785 Cable Add: Ediextempo México
Dir General, Editorial: Lautaro Gondalez Porcel; *Sales, Publicity, Production:* Romeo Medina; *Rights & Permissions:* Eva Somlo
Subjects: Anthropology, Architecture, Art, Economics, Philosophy, Humour, Literature, Pedagogy, Politics, Sociology, Theatre

Book Club: Club de Lectores Extemporaneos
Bookshop: Librerías Extemporaneos SA, Hamburgo 260, México 6, DF
Founded: 1975
ISBN Publisher's Prefix: 968-415

Fernández Editores SA de CV+, Eje 1 Pte México Coyoacán 321, Col Xoco, 03330 México, DF Tel: (05) 6889855/6889317/6044833 Telex: 1773630 Fesame
President: Luis Fernández González; *Man Dir:* Luis Gerardo Fernández; *Production Manager:* Luis Benjamin Fernández; *Commercial Manager:* Luis Miguel Fernández
Subjects: Textbooks, Education, Technical Subjects, Children's Books
Founded: 1943

Fondo de Cultura Económica, Ave Universidad 975, Apdo 44975, 03100 México 12, DF Tel: (05) 6601461 Cable Add: Doraca Telex: 1775866 Foceme
Man Dir: Jaime García Terrés; *Senior Editor:* José C Vázquez; *Production:* Adolfo Castañón; *Sales:* José Luis Valdés; *Publicity:* Angelica de Icaza; *Rights & Permissions:* Alicia Hammer
Subsidiary Company: Fondo de Cultura Económica, Spain (qv)
Branch Offs: Suipacha 617, Buenos Aires, Argentina; Tarapacá 1224, Santiago de Chile, Chile; Carrera 18, No 33-46, Bogotá, Colombia; Berlín 238, Miraflores, Lima, Peru; Edif Centro Capriles, Local E-23, Plaza Venezuela, Caracas 1050, Venezuela
Subjects: Economics, Sociology, History, Philosophy, Politics, Law, Scientific and Technical Studies, Mexican Studies and Archival Documents, Art, UNESCO Publications
Bookshop: At above address
Founded: 1934

Fondo Educativo Interamericano de Mexico SA, now Addison-Wesley Iberoamericana SA (qv)

Impresora **Galve** SA, an imprint of Editorial Avante SA (qv)

Editorial Gustavo **Gili** de Mexico SA* Valle de Bravo 21, Naucalpan, 53050 México, DF Tel: (05) 5606011 Cable Add: Gusto México Telex: 1772918 Gilime
Associate Company: Editorial Gustavo Gili SA, Spain (qv)

Editorial **Grijalbo** SA*, Apdo 17-568, México 17, DF (Located at: Calz Sn Bartolo Navcalpan 282, Col Argentina Poniente, Del Miguel Hidalgo, 11230 México, DF) Tel: (05) 3584355 Cable Add: Grijalmex Telex: 1771415 Egsame
Editorial: Aldo Falabella Tucci, Rogelio Carvajal; *Sales:* Victor Lemus, José Fuster; *Publicity:* Enrique Aguilar, Alicia Velázquez
Parent Company: Ediciones Grijalbo SA, Spain (qv)
Subjects: General Fiction & Non-fiction
Founded: 1954

Harla SA de CV, see Harper & Row Latinoamericana

Harper & Row Latinoamericana-Harla SA de CV+, Antonio Caso 142, Apdo 30-546, México 4, DF Tel: (05) 5924277 Cable Add: Harpemex Telex: 1777235
Dir General: Jaime Arvizu; *Sales:* Ignacio Sanchez (Home), Roberto Alcalá (Export), Enrique Retis (English Division)
Parent Company: Harper & Row Publishers Inc, 10 East 53rd St, New York, NY 10022, USA
Associate Companies: Harper & Row (Australasia) Pty Ltd, Australia (qv);

MEXICO 285

Harper & Row Ltd (UK) (qv); Newbury House Publishers Inc, Cambridge, USA; Editorial Pedagogica Iberoamericana SA de CV (Episa Bookshop)
Subjects: University & Secondary Textbooks, Science & Technology, Medicine, Psychology, Engineering, English as a second language
Founded: 1970
ISBN Publisher's Prefix: 968-006

Editorial **Hermes** SA+, Calz Ermita Iztapalapa No 266, Col Sinatel, 09470 México, DF Tel: (05) 5810198/5811075/5820378 Cable Add: Editermes
Man Dir: Sergio Sánchez Dávila; *Sales:* Adolfo de la O Becerril; *Production, Rights & Permissions:* Virginia García Fiesco
Associate Companies: Editorial Sudamericana SA, Argentina; EDHASA, Spain (qqv)
Subjects: General Fiction, Belles Lettres, History, Art
1985: 40 titles *1986:* 16 titles *Founded:* 1944
ISBN Publisher's Prefix: 968-446

Editorial **Herrero** SA*, Río Amazonas 44, Apdo 2404, México 5, DF Tel: (05) 5664900
General Dir: Donato Elías Herrero; *Manager:* Ricardo Arancón L
Subjects: Art, Technical, Textbooks
Founded: 1945

Editorial **Innovacion** SA*, España 402-A, Col Granjas Estrella, 09880 México, DF Tel: (05) 6703485/5829928
Man Dir: Catalina Ramírez de Arellano
Subjects: Middle-American Archaeology, Náhuatl Culture
1985: 3 titles *Founded:* 1972

Instituto de Investigaciones Sociales — Universidad Nacional Autónoma de Mexico, Torre II de Humanidades, 7° piso, Ciudad Universitaria, 04510 México, DF Tel: (05) 5505215 ext 2945/2949
A Department of the Universidad Nacional Autónoma (qv)
Man Dir: Carlos Martínez Assad; *Sales Dir:* Armida Vázquez A
Subjects: Mexican and International Social Studies, Periodicals
Founded: 1939

Instituto Indigenista Interamericano*, Ave Insurgentes Sur No 1690, Col Florida, 01030 México, DF Tel: (05) 6600007/6600132 Cable Add: Indigeni
Man Dir, Rights & Permissions: Alejandro Camino; *Sales:* Marina Villalobos
Subjects: Social Studies, Anthropology, Latin America, Periodicals
Founded: 1940

Instituto Nacional de Antropologia e Historia*, Córdoba 47, México 7, DF Tel: (05) 5144222
Subjects: Mexican Archaeology & Anthropology, History
Founded: 1822

Instituto Nacional de Bellas Artes, Dirección de Literatura, Lázaro Cárdenas 2, 3° piso, Torre Latinoamericana, Centro de la Ciudad de México, 06007 México, DF
Subjects: Biography, Literature, Reference

Instituto Panamericano de Geografía e Historia*, Ex-Arzobispado 29, 11860 México, DF Tel: (05) 2775888/5151910 Cable Add: Ipaghis
Secretary General: Leopoldo Rodriguez; *Editorial Dir:* Lea Salinas
Subjects: Geography, Cartography, History, Anthropology, Geophysics, Folklore, Periodicals

Intersistemas SA de CV+, Fernando Alencastre 110, Delegación M Hidalgo, 11000 México, DF Tel: (05) 5400798 Telex: 01772931 Isme
Man Dir: Pedro Vera Cervera; *Editorial:* Joel Rodriguez S; *Sales:* Alfredo Rodriguez; *Rights & Permissions:* Marco Antonio Chávez
Associate Companies: Intermedica, Junin 917 1° A, Capital Federal Buenos Aires, Argentina; Gráficas Enar SA, Pedro Muguruza 3-1°, Madrid 16, Spain; Patient Care Communications Inc, 690 Kinderkamac Rd, Oradell, NJ 07649, USA
Subjects: Medical
Founded: 1970
ISBN Publisher's Prefix: 968-6166

Editorial **Iztaccihuatl** SA*, Miguel Schultz No 21, Apdo 2343, 06470 México, DF Tel: (05) 5352321 Cable Add: Eiztamexa
President: Orlando Vieyra Legorreta
Subject: General Literature
Founded: 1946

Editorial **Jus** SA de CV, Plaza de Abasolo 14, Col Guerrero, 06300 México, DF Tel: (05) 5260538/5260616/5260540
President: Juan Landerreche Obregón; *Man Dir:* Maricel Buiza Figueroa; *Sales Manager:* Dalila Farias Godinez
Subjects: Law, Textbooks, History, Political & Social Sciences
Bookshop: Librería Nave SA, Filomeno Mata 18G, Centro, Mexico, DF
Founded: 1941
ISBN Publisher's Prefix: 968-423

Lasser Press Mexicana SA*, Praga 56, Col Juárez, Apdo 6-791, 06600 México, DF Tel: (05) 5142215 Cable Add: Laspresa Telex: 1777529 Coseme
President: Guillermo Menéndez Castro; *Dir:* Guillermo Menéndez Valdés
Subjects: Non-fiction, Biographies, Contemporary International Literature (in Spanish)
Founded: 1972
ISBN Publisher's Prefix: 968-458

Libros y Revistas SA de CV*, Mier y Pesado 128, Col del Valle, 03100 México, DF Tel: (05) 6874699/6603535 Telex: 01771403 dsayme
General Dir, Editorial, Rights & Permissions: Marcial Frigolet Lerma; *General Manager, Commercial Dir:* Joaquin Roca Romero; *Production:* Miguel Montaño
Parent Company: Publicaciones Sayrols SA de CV (qv)
Associate Companies: Compania General de Ediciones SA de CV (qv); Metropolitana de Publicaciones SA
Subjects: Fashion, Handicrafts, Health & Beauty, Children's, Educational, Dictionaries, General Interest
Founded: 1925

Editorial **Limusa** SA*, Balderas 95, 1° piso, México 1, DF Tel: (05) 5853500 Cable Add: Elimusa Telex: 01772581 Expo me
Man Dir: Carlos Noriega Milera; *Executive Vice-President:* Francisco Trilles Mercader; *General Manager:* Carlos Noriega Arias
Subjects: Science & Technology, Social Science, History, Psychology, University & Secondary Textbooks, Children's, Law, Physics & Chemistry
Founded: 1962

Litoimpresores SA*, España 396, Col Granjas Estrella, 09880 México, DF Tel: (05) 5829928/6703485
Man Dir: César Macazaga Ordoño; *Publicity:* Catalina Castañeda
Subjects: Buyer's Guides
1985: 9 titles *Founded:* 1956

Logos Consorcio Editorial SA+*, General Molinos del Campo 64, Col San Miguel Chapultepec, 11850 México, DF Tel: (05) 5151633
Man Dir: Enrico Garcia Alonso S
Subject: General

Libros **McGraw-Hill** de Mexico SA de CV*, Apdo 5-237, México 5, DF (Located at: Atlacomulco 499-501, San Andrés Atoto, Naucalpan, 53500 Edo de México) Tel: (05) 5769044 Cable Add: Lmchme Telex: 01774284
Man Dir: Moisés Perez Zavala; *Publishers:* Carlos Ríos, José Ashuh, Enrique Pereda, Jorge Aguilar; *Rights & Permissions:* Ernesto Bañuelos
Parent Company: McGraw-Hill Inc, 1221 Ave of the Americas, New York, NY 10020, USA
Associate Companies: See McGraw-Hill Book Co (UK) Ltd, UK
Branch Offs: Monterrey, N L; Guadalajara, Jal
Subjects: Social Sciences, Business & Administration, Medicine, Computation, Textbooks
Founded: 1967

Editorial El **Manual** Moderno SA de CV, Ave Sonora 206, Col Hipódromo, 06100 México, DF Tel: (05) 5740333 Cable Add: Editma Telex: 1764241 Emamme
Chairman & President: Dr Gustavo Setzer; *Vice-President:* C P Héctor Morales; *Editorial:* Dr Jorge Orizaga; *Sales:* Fernando Carvajal (Home), José Pérez (Foreign); *Production:* Felipe Vázquez; *Rights & Permissions:* Maria del Carmen Pichardo
Subjects: Medicine, Psychology, Nursing, Veterinary Science, Dentistry, Psychological Tests
Founded: 1958
ISBN Publisher's Prefix: 968-426

Publicaciones **Marcombo** SA+, Apdo 61-197, 06600 México, DF (Located at: Roma 19 Mezzanine, Col Juárez, 06600 México) Tel: (05) 5926345/5661524
Man Dir: Enrique Reyes Mofín; *Production, Publicity:* Gonzalo Ferreyra Cortés; *Rights & Permissions:* Baltazar Feregrino Paredes
Parent Company: Marcombo SA de Boixareu Editores, Spain (qv)
Associate Company: Representaciones y Servicios de Ingeniería SA (qv)
Subjects: Engineering, Management, Electronics
Founded: 1980
ISBN Publisher's Prefix: 968-41

Masson Editores, Dakota 383, Colonia Nápoles, Apdo 18-848, 03810 México, DF Tel: (05) 6870933 Telex: 1777604
President: Dr Jérome Talamon; *Man Dir:* Bruno Vanneuville
Parent Company: Masson Editeur, France (qv)
Associate Companies: Editora Masson do Brasil Ltda, Brazil (qv); Masson italia editori — ETMI, via Pascoli 55, I-20133 Milan, Italy; Masson SA, Spain (qv); Masson Publishing USA Inc, 211 East 43rd St, Room 1306, New York, NY 10017, USA
Founded: 1978

Editores **Mexicanos Unidos** SA*, L González Obregón 5-B, Apdo 45-671, 06020 México, DF Tel: (05) 5128516/5218870
Man Dir, Editorial: Fidel Miro Solanes; *Dir:* Sonia Miro de Laclau; *Manager:* Roque Laclau Gaona
Subjects: General Fiction & Non-fiction

Bookshop: Libro-Mex Editores SRL, Argentina 23, México 1, DF
Founded: 1954
ISBN Publisher's Prefix: 968-15

Galeria de Arte **Misrachi** SA*, Génova 20, 06600 México, DF Tel: (05) 5334551
Manager: Enrique Beraha Misrachi; *Editorial, Sales, Production, Rights & Permissions:* Alberto J Misrachi; *Publicity:* Carlos Beraha Cohen
Subject: Art
Bookshops: At above address; also Central de Publicaciones SA (qv under Major Booksellers)
Founded: 1961
ISBN Publisher's Prefix: 968-7047

Editorial Joaquín **Mortiz** SA, Tabasco 106, Apdo 7-832, 06700 México 7, DF Tel: (05) 5331250 Cable Add: Morditor
Man Dir, Editorial: Joaquín Díez-Canedo; *Sales, Rights & Permissions:* Magdalena Blanco; *Production, Publicity:* Joaquín Díez-Canedo Flores
Associate Company: Editorial Planeta SA, Spain (qv)
Subjects: General Fiction & Non-fiction, History, Psychology, Social Science
Founded: 1962
Miscellaneous: Firm is a member of the Grupo Editorial Planeta (qv)
ISBN Publisher's Prefix: 968-27

Impresora **Multiple** SA, an imprint of Editorial Avante SA (qv)

Organización Editorial **Novaro** SA+*, Apdo 10500, México 1, DF Tel: (05) 5760155 Cable Add: Novaromex Telex: 01774419 Novame
Director General: Constantino Lacayo
Subjects: Juveniles, Popular Paperbacks
Founded: 1950

Editorial **Nuestro Tiempo** SA, Ave Universidad no 771 desps 103, 104, Col del Valle, Delegación Benito Juárez, 03100 México, DF Tel: (05) 6886564
Man Dir: Esperanza Nacif Barquet
Subsidiary Company: Editores Reunidos SA de CV, Diego de Montemayor 635 Sur Centro, 64000 Monterrey, NL
Branch Off: Agencia Guadalajara, Alemania 1266, Col Vallarta, 44100 Guadalajara, Jal Tel: (036) 149048
Subjects: Social Sciences
Founded: 1966
ISBN Publisher's Prefix: 968-427

Nueva Editorial Interamericana SA de CV*, Cedro 512, Apdo 26370, 06450 México, DF Tel: (05) 5413155 Cable Add: Tusmexa
President: Luis Castañeda M; *Commercial Dir:* Rafael Sáinz
Associate Companies: Emalsa SA, Spain (qv); CBS Publishing Group, 383 Madison Ave, New York, NY 10017, USA
Subjects: Medicine and Health Sciences, General Science and Technology, Textbooks
Founded: 1944

Editorial **Nueva Imagen** SA*, Apdo 600, México 1, DF (Located at: Escollo 316, México 20, DF) Tel: (05) 6802988 Telex: 1771427 Eni Me
Administrative Dir: Enrique Sealtiel Alatriste L; *Editorial Dir:* Guillermo J Schavelzon
Subjects: General Fiction, History, Economics, Art, Science, Social Science, Anthropology, Sociology, Humour, Linguistics, Public Health, Latin American problems
Founded: 1976
ISBN Publisher's Prefix: 968-429

Editorial **Orion**, Sierra Mojada 325, Lomas de Chapultepec, México 10, DF Tel: (05) 5200224
Man Dir: Silvia Hernandez Vda de Cárdenas; *Sales Dir, Rights & Permissions:* Laura Hernandez Baltazar; *Publicity Dir:* Silvia Hernandez Baltazar; *Advertising:* Mariaelena Molina
Subsidary Companies: Edit Vila; Edit Cuzamil SA
Subjects: Literature, Philosophy, Religion, Mysticism, Yoga, Astrology, Theosophy, Psychology & Parapsychology
Founded: 1942
ISBN Publisher's Prefix: 968-6053

Editorial **Patria** SA de CV*, Ave San Lorenzo 160, Del Iztapalapa, 09860 México, DF Tel: (05) 5127651/5184509/5486850
Man Dir: Lic René Solís; *Deputy Manager & Administrator:* Rafael Valdes; *Sales & Publicity Dir:* Jorge M Passano; *Rights & Permissions:* Isabel Lasa
Subjects: Literature, Biography, History, Philosophy, How-to, Secondary & Primary Textbooks, Pre-School Teaching Aids, Children's Books
Founded: 1933
ISBN Publisher's Prefixes: 968-6054, 968-39

Libreria **Patria** SA*, 5 de Mayo 43, Apdo 2055, México 1, DF Tel: (05) 5852099
Man Dir: Francisco Majewski M
Orders to: Belisario Dominguez 53, México 1, DF
Subsidiary Company: Samara, Cia Papelera SA, 5 de Mayo 29-C, México 1, DF
Subjects: Textbooks, Literature, General
Bookshops: See under Major Booksellers; also Belisario Dominguez 53, México 1, DF
Founded: 1940

Ediciones **Paulinas** SA*, Ave Taxqueña 1792, México 21, DF Tel: (05) 5491454
General Manager: Ricardo Rojas Sarmiento
Subjects: Religion, Education
Bookshop: Librería San Pablo, Ave Madero 61-A, México 1, DF
Founded: 1947

Grupo Editorial **Planeta***, Clavijero 70, 06840 México, DF Tel: (05) 5422659
Man Dir, Editorial: Joaquín Díez-Canedo; *Production, Rights & Permissions:* Francisco Campos
Parent Company: Difusión Editorial SA, part of Grupo Planeta – see Editorial Planeta SA, Spain
Group Members: Editoriales Ariel, Joaquin Mortiz (qv), Planeta, Seix Barral
Subjects: General Fiction & Non-fiction, History, Psychology, Social Science
Founded: 1977
ISBN Publisher's Prefix: 968-6640

Editorial **Porrúa** SA, Argentina 15, 5° piso, México 1, DF Tel: (05) 5228800
Cable Add: Porruas Mexico
Man Dir: José Antonio Pérez Porrúa
Subject: General Literature
Bookshop: Librería de Porrúa Hnos y Cía (qv under Major Booksellers)
Founded: 1900

La **Prensa Médica** Mexicana*, Apdo 20-413, San Angel, Alvaro Obregón, 01000 México, DF (Located at: Paseo de Las Facultades 26, Fraccionamiento Copilco-Universidad, Coyoacán, 04360 México, DF) Tel: (05) 5504500/5504690
Cable Add: Laprememex
Man Dir and Rights & Permissions: Carolina Amor de Fournier; *Administration:* Guadalupe Arias de Gutiérrez; *Production:* Dr Jorge Avendaño-Inestrillas; *Sales & Publicity*

Dir: Juan de Dios Díaz-Salgado
Associate Company: Ediciones Copilco SA, Ezequiel Ordoñez 73, Copilco el Alto, Coyoacán, 04360 México, DF
Subjects: Medicine, Social Science, Psychology, Biology, Veterinary
Bookshop: Librería de las Facultades, Paseo de las Facultades 26, Copilco-Universidad, Coyoácan, 04360 México, DF
Founded: 1945
ISBN Publisher's Prefix: 968-435

Editorial **Progreso** SA*, Apdo 26-372, 02860 México, DF Tel: (05) 5411189
Subjects: Secondary & Primary Textbooks

Publicaciones Cultural SA de CV+, Lago Mayor 186, Col Anáhuac, 11320 México, DF Tel: (05) 5456860/5310690 Telex: 1763159 Pucume
Man Dir: Carlos Frigolet Lerma; *Sales:* Victórico Albores Santiago; *Rights & Permissions:* Aurelio Xicoténcatl Hernández; *Production:* Mario Muñoz Rodríguez
Subjects: University, Secondary and Primary Textbooks, Educational Materials
Founded: 1965
ISBN Publisher's Prefix: 968-6058

Publicaciones Marcombo SA, see Marcombo

Representaciones y Servicios de Ingeniería SA+, Apdo 61-195, 06600 México, DF (Located at: Roma 19 Mezzanine, Col Juarez, 06600 México) Tel: (05) 5354143/5661524
Man Dir, Editorial: Enrique Reyes Morfín; *Production, Publicity:* Gonzalo Ferreyra Cortes; *Rights & Permissions:* Baltazar Feregrino Paredes
Associate Company: Publicaciones Marcombo SA (qv)
Subjects: Engineering, Management, Technology
Founded: 1965
ISBN Publisher's Prefix: 968-6062

Salvat Mexicana de Ediciones SA de CV, Presidente Masaryk 101, 5° piso, Col Chapultepec Morales, 11570 México, DF Tel: (05) 2506041 Telex: 1763096 Seiame
Man Dir: Leopoldo Escobar; *Editorial, Rights & Permissions:* Mari Carmen Tejero; *Sales:* Jorge Merino (Medicine), Francisco Paillés (Encyclopaedias); *Special Promotions:* Francisco Rivera; *Production:* Jaime Martí; *Publicity:* Francisco Paillés
Parent Company: Salvat Editores SA, Spain (qv)
Subsidiary Companies: Comercial Salvat de México SA de CV (at above address); Gráficas Monte Alban SA de CV, Fracc Agroindustrial La Cruz, Querétaro, Qro
Subjects: Dictionaries, History, Geography, Art, Fiction, Juveniles, Cooking, Language Courses, Medicine and Hospitals
Bookshops: Librería Mariano Escobedo, Mariano Escobedo 438, Col Polanco; Librería de Cd Universitaria, Odontología 69, Local 9; Librería Satelite, Plaza Satelite, Local D-155, Cd Satelite; Librería La Villa, Calzada de Guadalupe 192, Local 13 Vallejo (en Gigante); Librería de Morelia, Ave Francisco I Madero Pte 533, Centro, Morelia, Mich; Librería de Puebla, Ave 17 Ote, 424-2 Col El Carmen, Puebla
ISBN Publisher's Prefix: 968-32

Publicaciones **Sayrols** SA de CV*, Mier y Pesado 128, Col de Valle, 03100 México, DF Tel: (05) 6603535/6874699 Cable Add: Sayrols Mexico Telex: 01771403 dsayme
General Dir, Editorial, Rights & Permissions: Marcial Frigolet Lerma;

General Manager, Commercial Dir: Joaquin Roca Romero; *Production:* Miguel Montaño
Subsidiary Companies: Libros y Revistas SA de CV (qv); Metropolitana de Publicaciones SA (at above address)
Associate Company: Compania General de Ediciones SA de CV (qv)
Subjects: Fashion, Handicrafts, Health & Beauty, Children's, Educational, Dictionaries, General Interest
Founded: 1925

Seix Barral, member of Grupo Editorial Planeta (qv)

Siglo XXI Editores SA de CV, Apdo 20-626, Col San Angel, 01000 México, DF (Located at: Ave Cerro del Agua 248, Col Romero de Terreros, Del Coyoácan, 04310 México, DF) Tel: (05) 6587999 Cable Add: Sigloedit
Man Dir, Editorial: Arnaldo Orfila R; *General Manager:* Concepción Zea; *Sales:* Rafael Dávalos; *Production:* Martí Soler V; *Publicity:* Dolores de la Peña; *Rights & Permissions:* Guadalupe Ortiz
Branch Offs: Apdo 32-140, Guadalajara, Jal; Diego de Montemayor 635 Sur, 64000 Monterrey, NL
Parent Company: Siglo XXI de España Editores SA, Spain (qv)
Associate Company: Siglo XXI Editores de Colombia Ltda, Colombia (qv)
Subjects: History, Psychology, Economics, Arts, Literature, Health & Society, Education, Criminology & Law, Sociology, Anthropology, Architecture, Politics, Philosophy, Urban Studies, Linguistics, Latin-American Politics, Marxism
Founded: 1966
ISBN Publisher's Prefix: 968-23

Time-Life International de México SA*, Apdo 5-592, Leibnitz 13, México 5, DF (Located at: Reforma 195, 8° piso, México 5, DF) Tel: (05) 5469000 Cable Add: Tlimsa Telex: (017) 71358
General Manager: Koos H Siewers
Subject: Non-fiction
Founded: 1962

Editorial **Tradicion** SA, Sur 22 Número 14 (entre Oriente 259 y Canal de San Juan), Col Agrícola Oriental, Iztacalco, 08500 México, DF Tel: (05) 5582249
Man Dir: Jose Maria Abascal C; *Editorial:* Salvador Abascal
Subjects: History, Mexican History, Political Science, Theology, Religion, Philosophy
Founded: 1972

Editorial **Trillas** SA*, Ave Río Churubusco 385 Pte, 03340 México, DF Tel: (05) 6884233 Cable Add: Etrillasa
Man Dir: Francisco Trillas Mercader; *Editorial:* Carlos Trillas Salazar; *Sales:* Jesús Galera Lamadrid; *Production:* Alfonso Durán; *Publicity:* Sergio Shinji
Associate Companies: Cía Editorial Carmex SA, Venezuela 1962, Buenos Aires, Argentina; Cía Editorial Comex SA, Apdo aéreo 15-15, Bogotá, Colombia; Alamex SA, Brusi 18, Barcelona 6, Spain; Limex Venezolana CA, Ave Lima Quinta Lourdes, Los Caobos, Caracas, Venezuela
Branch Off: (Commercial Division), Calzada de la Viga 1132, Col Apatlaco, Deleg Iztapalapa, 09439 México, DF Tel: (05) 6579188
Subjects: Psychology, Education, Medicine, Veterinary, Mathematics, General & Social Science, Technical, Law, University & Secondary Textbooks, Schoolbooks, Pre-school, Children's, Business
Bookshop: Librería Studio (qv under

MEXICO

Major Booksellers)
1985: 460 titles *1986:* 1700 titles *Founded:* 1953
ISBN Publisher's Prefix: 968-24

Universidad Nacional Autónoma de México*, Distribuidora de Libros de la Unam, Porto Alegre 260, 09440 México, DF Tel: (05) 6742552/5395508
Subjects: General University Textbooks, Scholarly
Bookshops: Librería Insurgentes, Ave Insurgentes Sur 299, Col Hipódromo Condesa, 06170 México, DF Tel: (05) 5845512/5842497; Librería de Zona Comercial, Corredor de Zona Comercial, Ciudad Universitaria, 04510 México, DF Tel: (05) 5505215 ext 2278; Librería del Palacio de Minería, Tacuba 5, 06000 México, DF Tel: (05) 5181315
Founded: 1935

Editorial **Universo** SA de CV*, Cerezas No 89, Col del Valle, 03100 México, DF Tel: (05) 6706038
Man Dir, Rights & Permissions: Enrique Ivan García H; *Editorial:* Fausto Rosales; *Sales:* Manuel Valdez Islas; *Production:* Enrique Escamilla; *Publicity:* Maria del Refugio Salinas
Parent Company: Editorial Diana SA (qv)
Associate Companies: Editorial Origen SA; Edivision Cia Editorial SA
Branch Offs: Guadalajara, Monterrey; Buenos Aires, Argentina; Caracas, Venezuela
Subjects: General Interest, Fiction and Non-fiction
Founded: 1979
ISBN Publisher's Prefix: 968-35

Editorial **Varazen** SA*, Anaxagoras, 1400-Col, St Cruz, 08310 México, DF Tel: (05) 5335274/5146573
Man Dir: Luis Maria Molachino Agostena
Parent Company: Editorial Teide SA, Spain (qv)
Subjects: Cultural, Educational
Founded: 1968
ISBN Publisher's Prefix: 968-7128

Literary Agents

Passano editor, Ave Universidad 1815 C-106, Coyoacan, 04310 Mexico, DF Tel: (05) 5669211/5669451 Telex: Lireme 1761233

Book Clubs

Bertelsmann de Mexico SA*, Div Circulo Mexicano de Lectores, Ave la Paz No 26, Col San Angel, México 20, DF Telex: 1761195 Cileme
Members: 200,000
Owned by: Bertelsmann AG, Federal Republic of Germany (qv)

Círculo Mexicano de Lectores, see Bertelsmann de Mexico SA

Club de Lectores Extemporaneos*, Poniente 126-A, No 400 Col Residencial Vallejo, Apdo 78-048, México 14
Owned by: Editorial Extemporaneos SA (qv)

Major Booksellers

American Book Store SA de CV*, Ave Madero No 25, Apdo 79 Bis, Col Centro Delegación Cuauhtemoc, 06000 México, DF Tel: (05) 5127279/5127284/5120306
Branches: Circuito Médicos No 2, Ciudad Satélite, 53100 Edo de México Tel: (05) 3930682/3930843; Ave Revolución No 1570-A, Delegación Alvaro Obregon, 01020 México, DF Tel: (05) 5500162/5488901

Librería **Bellas Artes***, Ave Juárez No 18, México 1, DF Tel: (05) 5182917
Manager: Miguel Noriega

Central de Publicaciones SA*, Ave Juárez 4, Apdo 2430, México 1, DF Tel: (05) 5104331
Owned by: Galeria de Arte Misrachi SA (qv)

Cia Internacional de Publicaciones SA de CV*, (Libreria Anglo Americana), Serapio Rendon 125, Apdo 30-528, México 4, DF Tel: (05) 5666400 Cable Add: Mexbri Telex: Cxpme 01771743 Mex

Librería **Cosmos***, Ave Padre Mier 474 Oriente, 64000 Monterrey, NL Tel: (083) 435935/456935
Manager: José Luis Font Solana

Librerías de **Cristal**, see Ediapsa de CV/Librerías de Cristal

Ediapsa de CV/Librerías de Cristal*, Ave Alvaro Obregón 85, 06760 México, DF Tel: (05) 5116723 Cable Add: Ediapsa Telex: 01776359 Crisme
Manager: Ricardo Cruz López
Many branches in Mexico City and other cities

Librería **Font**, López Cotilla 440, Guadalajara, Jalisco Tel: (036) 140820

Librerías **Gonvill** SA de CV, 8 de Julio No 825, Guadalajara, 44100 Jalisco Tel: (036) 139019
Manager: Jorge E González Villalobos

Librería **Hamburgo** SA*, Insurgentes Sur No 58, México 6, DF Tel: (05) 5277316/5145086
Also: Ribera de San Cosme 133, México 4, DF Tel: (05) 5464736; Insurgentes Sur 317, México 11, DF Tel: (05) 5744015

Librería **Interacadémica** SA de CV*, Ave Sonora 206, Col Hipódromo, 06100 México, DF Tel: (05) 5842511 Cable Add: Libinter Telex: 1773596 Aldime
Administrative Manager: Lourdes Reyes

Librería **Letrán***, Ave San Juan de Letrán 5-C, México, DF Tel: (05) 5123232

Librería **Tecnológico** SA*, Ave E Garza Sada 2440, Col Tecnológico, Monterrey, 64810 Nuevo León Tel: (083) 583812
Manager: Carlos Amero Diaz

Librería **Universitaria***, Insurgentes Sur No 299, México, DF Tel: (05) 5646637 (and several branches)

Librolandia del Centro SA de CV, Matamoros 83, Hermosillo, Sonora Tel: (0621) 20634/23193 Telex: Olsame 058878
Dir: Nicolás Estrada F
60 bookshops located in 33 cities throughout México

Librería Editorial Gerardo **Mayela**, Emiliano Zapata 60-B, 06060 México, DF Tel: (05) 5225556
Manager: Manuel García Blanco

Editores **Mexicanos** Unidos*, Luis González Obregón 5-B, México, DF Tel: (05) 5217596

Librería **Patria***, Ave 5 de Mayo 43, México 1, DF Tel: (05) 5852099
Also Publisher (qv)

Librería de **Porrúa** Hnos y Cía, Apdo M-7990, Argentina 15, México 1, DF Tel: (05) 5228800 Cable Add: Porruas
Owned by: Editorial Porrúa SA (qv)

Librería **Studio** SA*, Jaime Balmes 11, Locales 35-C & 36-C, Col Chapultepec Morales, México, DF Tel: (05) 3587839
Owned by: Editorial Trillas SA (qv)

Major Libraries

Archivo General de la Nación*, Apdo 1999, México 1, DF (Located at: Eduardo Molina y Albañiles, Col Penitenciaria Amp, Deleg Venustiano Carranza, 15350 México, DF) Tel: (05) 7895915/7895296
Dir: Leonor Ortiz M Prieto
Publication: Boletín

Archivo Nacional, see Archivo General de la Nación

Archivos Históricos y Bibliotecas*, Instituto Nacional de Antropologia e Historia, Paseo de la Reforma y Gandhi, 11560 México, DF Tel: (05) 5536342/5536231

Biblioteca Central*, Ciudad Universitaria, Apdo 70219, 04510 México, DF Tel: (05) 5489780
Librarian: Adolfo Rodriguez Gallardo
Publications include: Directorio de Bibliotecas UNAM; Catálogo Colectivo de Publicaciones Periódicas

Biblioteca Central, Universidad Autónoma Chapingo, 56230 Chapingo, México
Incorporating previously named Escuela Nacional de Agricultura
Librarian: Rosa Maria Ojeda Trejo
Publications: Periodicals *Chapingo*, *Revista de Geografía Agrícola*, *Textual*

Biblioteca de México*, Plaza de la Ciudadela 6, 06040 México, DF Tel: (05) 5104644/5104945
Librarian: Carmen E de García Moreno

Biblioteca Nacional de Agricultura, now at Biblioteca Central, Chapingo (qv)

Biblioteca Nacional de Antropología e Historia, Paseo de la Reforma y Gandhi, 11560 México, DF Tel: (05) 5536231/5536342
Dir: Stella Ma Gonzales Cicero

Biblioteca Nacional de México, República del Salvador 70, Centro, 06000 México, DF Tel: (05) 5129316/5103161/5121771
Co-ordinator: Roberto Sánchez Rivera
Also: Centro Cultural Universitario, Insurgentes Sur s/n, Delegación Coyoacán, 04510 México, DF Tel: (05) 6550020/6551344 ext 2030
Co-ordinator: Jesús Márquez Narváez

Biblioteca del **Congreso de la Unión***, Tacuba 29, México, DF

Biblioteca 'Benjamin **Franklin**' (USIS)*, Calle Londres 16, 06600 México, DF Tel: (05) 5910244
Dir: Tom H Raymond
Publication: Boletín de Selección de Adquisiciones Recientes (quarterly)

Hemeroteca Nacional de México*, Centro Cultural, Ciudad Universitaria, Delegación Coyoacán, 04510 México, DF
National Periodicals Library

Biblioteca del **Instituto Anglo-Mexicano de Cultura**, Calle M Antonio Caso 127, Apdo 30-457, 06470 México, DF Tel: (05) 5355146/5666144/5664500 Telex: 01772938 Brcome
British Council Library

Biblioteca del **Instituto Panamericano de Geografía** e Historia*, Ex-Arzobispado 29, 11860 México, DF
Pan American Institute of Geography and History

Biblioteca del **Instituto Tecnológico** y de Estudios Superiores de Monterrey, Sucursal de Correos 'J', 64849 Monterrey, Nuevo León
Librarian: Lic Sergio Martinez F
Publications include: Cybertec (Computer Sciences); *Situacion* (Economics); *Tetla-ni* (monthly paper of the Institute)

Biblioteca de la **Universidad Iberoamericana**, Centro de Informacion Academica, Prolongación Reforma 880, Col Lomas Santa Fe, Delegación Alvaro Obregón, 01210 México, DF
Dir: Lic Ma Antonieta Graf G

Library Associations

Asociación de Bibliotecarios de Instituciones de Enseñanza Superior e Investigación (ABIESI)*, Apdo 5-611, 06500 México, DF
Association of Librarians of Higher Education and Research Institutions
President: Nahúm Pérez Paz
Publications: Cuadernos de Abiesi; Archivos de Abiesi; Boletín de Abiesi

Asociación Mexicana de Bibliotecarios AC (AMBAC)*, Apdo 27-651, Administración de Correos 27, 06760 México, DF Tel: (05) 5487472
Mexican Association of Librarians
President: Rosa Maria F de Zamora; *Secretary:* Rosalba Cruz
Publications: Noticiero (Bulletin); *Memorias de Jornadas*

Escuela Nacional de Biblioteconomía y Archivonomía*, Viaducto Miguel Alemán 155, 03400 México, DF
National School of Librarianship and Archives
Dir: Prof Eduardo Salas Estrada
Publication: Bibliotecas y Archivos

Instituto de Investigaciones Bibliográficas, Biblioteca Nacional de México and Hemeroteca Nacional de México, Centro Cultural, Ciudad Universitaria, Delegación Coyoacán, 04510 México, DF Tel: (05) 6550020
Institute of Bibliographic Research
Dir: María del Carmen Ruiz Castañeda; *Coordinator:* Jesús Márquez Narváez
Also: República del Salvador No 70, Centro, 06000 Mexico, DF Tel: (05) 5129316/5103161
Coordinator: Roberto Sánchez Rivera
Publications include: Boletín; Bibliografía Mexicana; Anuario Bibliográfico

Library Reference Books and Journals

Books

Anuario de Bibliotecología Archivología Informática (Annual of Library Science, Archives, and Information Science), Universidad Nacional Autónoma de México, Porto Alegre 260, 09440 México, DF

Directorio de Bibliotecas de la Ciudad México (Directory of Libraries of the City of Mexico), Universidad de las Américas, Biblioteca, 16 Carretera Mexico-Toluca, México 10, DF

Journals

Bibliotecas y Archivos (Libraries and Archives), Escuela Nacional de Biblioteconomía y Archivonomía, Viaducto Miguel Alemán 155, 03400 México, DF

Boletín, Archivo General de la Nación, Eduardo Molina y Albañiles, Col Penitenciaria Amp, Deleg Venustiano Carranza, 15350 México, DF

Boletín, Instituto de Investigaciones Bibliográficas, Biblioteca Nacional de México and Hemeroteca Nacional de México, Centro Cultural, Ciudad Universitaria, Delegación Coyoacán, 04510 México, DF

Noticiero (News), Asociación Mexicana de Bibliotecarios AC, Apdo 27-651, Administración de Correos 27, 06760 México, DF

Literary Associations and Societies

Mexican **P E N** Centre, Paseo de la Reforma 104-401, 06600 México, DF
President: Julieta Campos; *Secretary:* Gabriel Zaid
Publication: Boletín del PEN (quarterly)

San Miguel **P E N** Centre, Jesus 27, Apdo 368, San Miguel de Allende, Gto, 37700 México, DF Tel: (05) 46520435
President: Joseph Gottlieb; *Secretary:* Naomi Boulton

Literary Periodicals

Comunidad (Community), Universidad Iberoamericano, Cerro de las Torres 395, México 21, DF

Cuadernos Americanos (American Notebooks), Ave Coyocán 1035, Apdo 965, México, DF

El Cuento, Ave División del Norte 521-101, México 12, DF
Magazine of imagination

Lectura (Readings), Apdo 545, Bolivar 23-4, México, DF

Letras, Libreria y Ediciones Botas SA, Justo Sierra 52, Apdo 941, Mexico 1, DF
Literary and bibliographical publication

Mexico Quarterly Review, University of the Americas, 15 Sta Catavina Martir, via Puebla, Puebla, México
Text in English and Spanish

Plural, Cía Editorial Excelsior, SCL, Reforma 18, México, DF

Salamandra (Salamander), Editorial Alfonso Reyes, Adolfo Prieto 2407 Oriente, Monterrey, NL

Literary Prizes

National Prize for Literature*
For the best literary works in the fields of the novel, poetry, essay, biography, drama and motion picture scriptwriting. 100,000 Mexican pesos. Awarded annually. Enquiries to Mexican Ministry of Public Education, Brazil 21, México 1, DF

Xavier Villaurrutia Prize*
For poetry, prose, novel, short story, drama or essays by new or young authors. Prizes totalling 400,000 pesos are awarded annually. Enquiries to Sociedad Alfonsina Internacional, Ave Transmisiones 42, Lomas de San Angel Inn, 01790 México, DF

Monaco

General Information

Language: French
Religion: Roman Catholic
Population: 26,000
Bank Hours: 0830-1730 Monday-Friday
Shop Hours: 0830-1300, 1600-1930 Monday-Friday
Currency: French franc
Copyright: Berne, UCC (see International section)

Publishers

Académie Internationale de Tourisme*, 4 rue des Iris, Monte Carlo Tel: (93) 309768
President: Prof Mario Grego; *Editorial:* Paul Wagret
Subjects: Travel Literature, Dictionary of Tourism
Founded: 1951

Editions de l'**Oiseau-Lyre**, Les Remparts Tel: (93) 300944
Man Dir: Margarita M Hanson
Subject: Music

Editions **Regain***, Palais Miami, 10 blvd d'Italie, Monte Carlo Tel: (93) 506204
Subjects: Poetry, Anthologies, Literature
Founded: 1946

Les Editions du **Rocher**, 28 rue du Comte Félix Gastaldi, Monaco Tel: (93) 303341
Subject: General Literature

Editions André **Sauret** SA, 8 quai Antoine 1er, BP 448, MC 98011 Monaco Cedex Tel: (93) 506884
Subjects: Art, Fiction, Bibliophily
ISBN Publisher's Prefix: 2-85051

Major Booksellers

Les **Beaux Livres***, 4 rue des Iris, Monte Carlo Tel: (93) 307390
Manager: Claude Lepine

Quartier-Latin*, 26 blvd Princess-Charlotte, Monte Carlo Tel: (93) 302621

Sainte-Dévote*, 19 blvd Princess-Charlotte, Monte Carlo Tel: (93) 302279

Major Library

Bibliothèque Louis Notari, 8 rue Louis Notari, Monte Carlo Tel: (93) 309509
Director: Hervé Barral

Literary Associations and Societies

P E N Club*, c/o Directeur du Musée d'Anthropologie Préhistorique, blvd du Jardin Exotique, Monte Carlo 98000
President: Jean Lorenzi; *Secretary:* Louis Barral

Mongolian People's Republic

General Information

Note: No replies were received to questionnaires sent to the Mongolian People's Republic for this edition of *International Literary Market Place*. The information given in the 1987-88 edition has been repeated here but should be treated with caution.
Language: Mongolian
Religion: None (Tibetan Buddhist Lamaism suppressed in 1930's)
Population: 1.7 million
Bank Hours: Vary. 0800-1700 or 1800 with lunch closing
Shop Hours: Generally 0900-1500
Currency: 100 mongo = 1 tugrik

Publishers

Mongolgosknigotorg*, Ulan-Bator
Function: Distributor

State Press*, Ulan-Bator
Subjects: Geography, Politics, Law

Major Booksellers

State Book Trading Office*, Leniny gudamch 41, Ulan-Bator Tel: 22312
Cable Add: Mongolbook

Major Library

State Archives*, Ulan-Bator State Public Library of the Mongolian People's Republic, Lenin Prospekt, Ulan-Bator
Tel: 22396
Dir: M Bayaizul

Montserrat

General Information

Language: English
Religion: Anglican and other Protestant denominations and Roman Catholic
Population: 12,000
Bank Hours: 0800-1200 Monday-Thursday; 0800-1200, 1500-1700 Friday
Shop Hours: 0800-1200, 1300-1600 Monday-Thursday; 0800-1200, 1300-1700 Friday; 0800-1300 Saturday
Currency: 100 cents = 1 East Caribbean dollar
Export/Import Information: No tariffs on books and advertising catalogues. Parcel Tax on each postal parcel. No import licences required
Copyright: Berne, UCC (see International section)

Major Booksellers

Empire Shop*, George St, PO Box 210, Plymouth Tel: Montserrat 2400
Managers: Ernst and Edith Herman

Major Library

Montserrat Public Library*, Plymouth, Montserrat Tel: Montserrat 2444
Principal Librarian: V J Grell

Morocco

General Information

Language: Arabic, French, Spanish
Religion: Islamic
Population: 20 million
Bank Hours: Summer: 0830-1130; 1500-1700 Monday-Friday; rest of year: 0815-1130, 1415-1630 Monday-Friday
Shop Hours: Tangiers: 0900-1200, 1600-2000; rest: 0900-1200, 1500-1800 or 1900
Currency: 100 centimes = 1 dirham
Export/Import Information: No tariff on books; most advertising dutiable. Special Tax, and Stamp Duty of percentage of import duty. No import licences required. Exchange controls but permission liberally granted
Copyright: UCC, Berne (see International section)

Book Trade Organization

Syndicat des Librairies du Maroc*, 10 ave Dar el Maghzen, Rabat
Moroccan Booksellers' Association

Book Trade Reference Journal

Bibliographie nationale marocaine (National bibliography) (monthly), Bibliothèque générale et Archives du Maroc, ave Ibn Battouta, BP 1003, Rabat

Publishers

Government Printer (Imprimerie Officielle), ave Jean Mermoz, Rabat-Chellah, Chellah
Tel: 65024

Dar El **Kitab***, pl de la Mosqueé, Quartier des Habous, BP 4018, Casablanca Tel: 63381 Telex: 26630 Darki
Foreign Department: 18 rue Maréchal, Casablanca Tel: 241168/246326
President: Boutaleb Abdou Abdelhay; *Manager:* Mrs Soad Kadiri; *Publicity Manager:* Mounjedine Abdel-Ghani; *Production:* Ferhat Mohamed
Subjects: History, Africana, Philosophy, General & Social Science
Founded: 1948

Editions **La Porte**+, 281 ave Mohammed-V, Rabat Tel: (07) 69958
Man Dir: Mohamed Rafii Doukkali
Subsidiary Companies: Librairie aux Belles Images (Bookshop)
Subjects: Law, Economics, Ministry of Justice Publications (in French and Arabic), Morocco Tourist Guides, Arab and French Language Teaching, Religion (the Koran, Islam)
Bookshops: Librairie aux Belles Images (qv under Major Booksellers)

Les Editions **Maghrebines***, 5-13 rue Soldat Roch, Casablanca Tel: 245148 Telex: Edima 22994 M
Subjects: General Non-fiction, History, Africana, Reference, Law, Science & Technology, General Science, Medicine
Founded: 1962

Major Booksellers

Librairie **'Aux Belles Images'**, 281 ave Mohammed V, Rabat Tel: (07) 69958
Owned by: Editions La Porte (qv)

Librairie des **Colonnes**, 54 blvd Pasteur, BP 352, Tangier Tel: (09) 36955
Dir: Mrs R Muyal
Owned by: Nouvelle Société Kalila wa Dimna

Cultura-Maroc*, 10 rue Bendahan, Casablanca Tel: 275990

Librairie des **Ecoles***, 12 ave Hassan II, Casablanca Tel: 66741

Librairie **Farairre***, 43 rue de Foucauld, Casablanca Tel: 220388

Librairie de **France***, 4 rue Chenier, Casablanca Tel: 26534

Librairie **nationale***, 2 ave Mers Sultan, Casablanca Tel: 273678
Manager: Philippe Saint Martin Tillet
Wholesaler

Librairie **Livre-Service**, 46 ave Allal Ben Abdellah, Rabat Tel: (07) 24495 Telex: 32746 M Smer
Executive and General Manager: Abdellah Tahri
Owned by: SMER Diffusion (qv)

Maghreb Livres, 53 rue Oved Ziz, BP 725, Rabat Tel: (07) 71491

S M E R Diffusion*, 3 rue Ghazza, Rabat
Tel: (07) 23725/25960 Telex: 32746M
Dir: Youssef Slaoui
Branch Off: 73 rue Pierre Parent, Casablanca
Subjects: Human & Social Science
Bookshops: Librairie Livre-Service (français) (qv under Major Booksellers); Librairie Livre-Service (français – arabe), 11 rue Poincare, Casablanca; Librairie Livre-Service (arabe), 36 ave Allal Ben Abdellah, Rabat; Librairie de l'Agdal, angle ave de France, Agdal, Rabat

Major Libraries

Bibliothèque générale et Archives*, BP 41, Tetuan
Librarian: M M Dellero

Bibliothèque générale et Archives du Maroc*, ave Ibn Battouta, BP 1003, Rabat Tel: (07) 71890/72152
Librarian: Fassi Abderrahmane
Publication: Bibliographie nationale marocaine

Bibliothèque municipale*, 142 ave de l'Armeé Royale, Casablanca Tel: 274170/223798
Dir: Haj Mohamed Bouzid

Bibliothèque municipale (Meknès), Zankat Al-Wahda Al-Ifriquia, BP 47 (service), Meknès Tel: (05) 22881
Librarian: Mohammed Ajana

Centre culturel français, Bibliothèque, 121 blvd Zerktouni, Casablanca Telex: 21647
Fax: 256745
Dir: Bernard Schnerb; *Librarian:* Marie-Claude Warmé

Centre national de Documentation, Charii Maa El Ainaïn, Haut Agdal, BP 826, Rabat Tel: (07) 74944 Telex: CND 31052 M Rabat
Director: Ahmed Fassi Fihri

Ecole Mohammedia d'Ingénieurs*, Bibliothèque, BP 765, Rabat Tel: (07) 72647

Institut scientifique chérifien*, Bibliothèque, ave Moulay Chérif, Rabat
Publication: Travaux

Bibliothèque de l'**Université Al Quarawiyin***, BP 790, Fès

Bibliothèque de l'**Université Ben Youssef***, Cité Universitaire, BP 314, Marrakech Tel: (04) 25465
Librarian: Seddik Larbi

Bibliothèque de l'**Université Mohammed V***, ave Moulay Chérif, Rabat

Mozambique

General Information

Language: Portuguese in and near large towns; Bantu languages; English widely spoken in business circles
Religion: Mainly traditional beliefs; some Christian (mainly Roman Catholic), and Islamic (in north)
Population: 12 million
Bank Hours: 0800-1100 Monday, Tuesday, Thursday, Friday; 0800-1000 Wednesday and Saturday
Shop Hours: 0800-1130, 1400-1700 Monday-Friday; 0800-1200 Saturday
Currency: 100 centavos = 1 Mozambique escudo
Export/Import Information: Children's picture books dutied per kg net weight, otherwise books and advertising matter duty-free. No additional taxes apply. Import licences and strict exchange controls; authorities have classified books and advertising as List 3 in priorities

Book Trade Organization

Instituto Nacional do Livro e do Disco, CP 4030, Avda 24 de Julho 1921, Maputo Tel: 20839/20870 Telex: 6-288 Inld Mo
INLD is a state organization responsible for the importation, exportation and distribution of books (and records), and all printing and publishing activities
Director: Arménio Correia

Publishers

Empresa Moderna Lda*, 13 Ave da Republica, CP 473, Maputo
Man Dir: Louis Galloti
Subjects: General Fiction & Non-fiction, History, Africana, University & Secondary Textbooks
Founded: 1937

Government Printer (Impressa Nacional de Moçambique)*, CP 275, Maputo

Editora **Minerva** Central*, CP 212, Maputo Telex: 6-561 Miner Mo
Man Dir: J F Carvalho
Subsidiary Company: J A Carvalho & Co Ltd

Subjects: Medicine, General Science, University & Secondary Textbooks
Founded: 1908

Major Booksellers

Academica Lda*, 47 rua Joaquim Lapa, Maputo Tel: 3576

Armazens Distribuidores Lta*, CP 1215, Maputo

A W **Bayly** & Co Lda*, CP 185, Maputo

Cooperative das Casas*, 32 rua Major Araujo, Maputo

Minerva Central*, J A Carvalho & Co Lda, CP 212, Maputo

Major Libraries

Arquivo Historico de Moçambique*, CP 2033, Maputo
Librarian: Antonio Sopa

Biblioteca Municipal*, Maputo

Biblioteca Nacional de Moçambique*, CP 141, Maputo
Librarian: Joaquim Chigogoro Mussassa

Instituto nacional de Geologia (Centro de Documentação)*, CP 217, Maputo

Bibliotecas da **Universidade Eduardo Mondlane**, Divisão de Documentação, CP 1169, Maputo Tel: 743081
The University Eduardo Mondlane does not have a Central Library, but controls 15 departmental libraries. The Divisão de Documentação is the department responsible for all library and documentation services throughout the University.
Head of Services: Wanda Do Amaral

Namibia

General Information

Language: Afrikaans, German and English
Religion: About half of population Christian; rest follow traditional beliefs
Population: 1 million
Currency: South African
Copyright: Berne (see International section)

Book Trade Reference Book

Namibische National Bibliographie 1971-75, contact Nordiska Afrikaininstitutets Bibliotek, BP 2126, S-750 02 Uppsala, Sweden

Publishers

Bureau for Indigenous Languages*, Department of Bantu Education, PMB 13236, Windhoek 9100 Tel: (061) 24601 Cable Add: Imfundo Windhoek Telex: 3178
Head: W Zimmermann; *Rights & Permissions:* Department of Education and Training, Pretoria, South Africa
Subjects: Primary and Secondary School Textbooks in indigenous languages (Nama, Ndonga, Kwanyama, Kwangali, Mbukushu, Herero)
Founded: 1964
ISBN Publisher's Prefix: 0-621

Gamsberg Publishers (Pty) Ltd*, PO Box 22830, Windhoek 9000 (Located at: 396 Kaiser St, Windhoek) Tel: (061) 28714 Telex: 3108
Man Dir, Editorial, Rights & Permissions: Dr J J Viljoen; *Production:* Mrs H Fourie; *Sales, Publicity:* H van Wyk
Subjects: Educational (in nine indigenous languages of Namibia, English, Afrikaans and German), General Literature
Bookshop: Gamsberg Bookshop, 21 Post St, Windhoek
Founded: 1977
ISBN Publisher's Prefix: 0-86848

Major Booksellers

Bible Society of SWA/Namibia, 428 Kaiser St, Windhoek 9000
Regional office of The United Bible Societies

Central News Agency*, PO Box 2104, Windhoek

Edumeds Pty Ltd, PO Box 2961, Windhoek 9000 (Located at: 398 Kaiser St) Tel: (061) 26371
Man Dir: Dr J J Viljoen; *Manager:* A D Grové

Nasionale Boekhandel (SWA) (Pty) Ltd, PO Box 1099, Windhoek 9000 Tel: (061) 37406
Manager: J Lategan
Owned by: Nasionale Boekhandel Ltd, South Africa (qv)

Major Libraries

Administration Library, now Estorff Reference Library (qv)

Archives Service, Department of National Education, PB 13250, Windhoek 9000 Tel: (061) 293911 ext 385

Estorff Reference Library, Private Bag 13186, Windhoek 9000 (Located at: Peter Muller St, Windhoek 9000) Tel: (061) 229251 ext 633
Librarian: Mrs P B Pieterse

Technical High School Library*, PMB 12014, Windhoek 9111

Windhoek Public Library, Private Bag 13183, Windhoek 9000 Tel: (061) 224163 (counter), (061) 224899 (librarian)
Librarian: Miss G Kölling

Library Association

South African Institute for Librarianship and Information Science (South West Africa/Namibia Branch), c/o Department of National Education, Private Bag 13236, Windhoek 9000

Translation Agencies and Associations

Bureau for Indigenous Languages*, Private Bag 13236, Windhoek 9000

Nepal

General Information

Language: Nepali
Religion: Hindu, Tibetan Buddhist
Population: 15 million
Bank Hours: 1000-1700 Sunday-Friday
Shop Hours: 1000-1700 Sunday-Friday
Currency: 100 paise = 1 Nepalese rupee
Export/Import Information: No tariff on books and advertising. Import licences required. Exchange controls

Publishers

Department of Publicity*, Ministry of Communications, Katmandu

Educational Enterprise, Mahankalsthan, Katmandu Tel: 223749
Subject: Education

International Progressive Books and Periodicals*, 903 Ason Kamalakshee Tole, Pragatisheel Chowk Bhitra, Katmandu City 30 (Katmandu GPO 7101) Tel: 211938 Cable Add: Anterpragatisheelsaphoopasa Katmandu Nepal
Man Dir: Ganesh Lall Ranjitkar; *Editorial:* Ganesh Dass Yamy, Aneeta Shobha Tuladhar; *Sales:* Padma L Tuladhar, Suneeta D Tuladhar, Parbatee S Ranjitkar; *Production:* Shanta S Ranjitkar; *Publicity:* Chandrawatee S Ranjitkar; *Rights & Permissions:* Renooka S Tuladhar
Orders to: Nayan Baneshowre Marg, PO Box 3000, Katmandu City 33 (Katmandu GPO 44601)
Branch Offs: Throughout Nepal
Subjects: Politics, Economics, Philosophy, History, Literature, Social Science, Science, Technology, Educational Textbooks, Engineering, Biology, Business, Mathematics, Medicine, Biography, Juveniles, Periodicals
Bookshops: Janapriya Pustak Bhandar, Patan Dhoka, Lalitpur; Jagriti Books Centre, Itahary Sunsary, Koshee Zone; People's Books Centre, Chenpur, Sakhuwa Sabha, Koshee Zone; People's Books and Periodicals Centre, Datraya Square, Bhaktapur; Banepa Books Depot, Banepa Nayan Bazar, Kavrepalanchok Dist; People's Friendship Books and Periodicals Shop Dathwee Chhen Twa Gallee, Ranjit Books and Periodicals Shop Bhidyo Twa Gallee (both via Katmandu Mail Centre); Nepal Books and Periodicals House Maisthan Tole, Birganj
Founded: 1963

Lakoul Press*, Palpa-Tanben
Subjects: Education, Physical Sciences

Mahabir Singh Chiniya Main*, Makhan Tola, Katmandu

Mandas Sugatdas, now International Standards Books and Periodicals (P) Ltd (qv)

Nepal Academy*, Ganabahal Dharhara, Katmandu
Subjects: Science, Literature, History, Art, Social Science

Ratna Pustak Bhandar, Bhotahity, PO Box 98, Katmandu
Manager: G P Shrestha
Subjects: Textbooks, Nepalese Fiction
Founded: 1945

Sajha Prakashan, Co-operative Publishing Organization*, Pulchowk lalitpur, Katmandu Tel: 521023/521118 Cable Add: Sajha Prakashan Katmandu
Chairman: Shri Jivan Lal Satyal; *General Manager:* K C S Pradhan
Branch Offs: 40 branches and sub-offices throughout Nepal
Subjects: Literary, Educational Textbooks, General (published in English and Nepali)
Founded: 1966

Major Booksellers

Educational Enterprises (Pvt) Ltd, Kingsway, Kantipath, Katmandu Tel: 212508/223749

International Standards Books and Periodicals (P) Ltd, PO Box 3000, Katmandu 44601 (Located at: Kamabakshee Tole, Gha 3/333, Chowk Bhitra, 3rd Floor, Katmandu-3 City Katmandu 44601) Tel: 222110/223036/224005 Cable Add: Anterrashtriya Star Ko Saphoo Pasa Katmandu Telex: 3000 Isb-Ass/KTM-NP Fax: 223036ISB-ASS
Centre for central general selling, distribution and wholesale order supplies, subscription and publication
Chief Executive: Ganesh Lall Chhipa; *Senior Man Dir:* Suindra Lal Chhipa; *Editorial:* Dharma Ratna Ranjit, Miss Chandra Laxmee Ranjit; *Sales:* Miss Bigya Ranjit, Miss Bijaya Ranjit, Miss Beena Ranjit; *Production:* Miss Suneeta Ranjit, Miss Aneeta Shobha Ranjit; *Publicity:* Miss Sabitree Ranjit, Miss Laxmee Shobha Ranjit; *Rights & Permissions:* Dr Kedar Ranjit, Swoyambu Ranjit
Orders to: Bhotahity Tole, Cha 1/333, Chowk Bhitra, PO Box 3000, Katmandu-3 City, Katmandu GPO 44601
Branch Offs: Biratnagar; Rajbiraj; Janakpurdham Chowk; Hetaunda; Birgunj; Katmandu City Branch, Ason Kamabakshee Tole; Katmandu Valley Branch, Bhotahity Tole, Katmandu; Arniko Main Branch, Arniko Barbise 87 KM; Tibet Area: Khasa City Branch, Narayangadh, Mungling Centre; Pokhara City Branch; Butawal Area; Siddhartha Nagar (Bhairahawa) City Branch; Tansen-Palpa Area and Nepalgunj Area in Nepal
Subjects: Political Science, Geography, Education, Sociology, Law, Anthropology, Management and Business Studies, Psychology, Classical Studies, Archaeology, Art and Architecture, English Literature, Modern Languages and Literature, History, Philosophy, School Textbooks, Music, Nursing, Dentistry, History of Science and Technology, Economics, Earth Science, Soil Science, Agriculture and Forestry, Engineering, Physics, Mathematics, Chemistry, Life Science, Medicine, Humanities, Children's, Periodicals
Bookshops: National Book House, Butwal; Nepal Books Centre, Palpa, Tansen; Phokhara Bookshop, Mahendra Pool, Pokhara; Nepalgunj Books Store, Nepalgunj; Hetaunda Books Centre, Hetaunda
Founded: 1965

Januka Pustak Bhandar*, Budhhat Chowk, Biratnagar (Morang) Tel: 226 Cable Add: Januka Biratnagar

Nepal Booksellers*, 6/78 Dharmapath, Katmandu Tel: 14603
Manager: Pra Kash Shrestha

Ratna Pustak Bhandar, Bhotahity, Katmandu

Sahayogi Prakashan*, Tripureshwar, Katmandu

Major Libraries

American Library*, Katmandu
Bir Library*, Ranipolhari, Katmandu
British Council Library*, PO Box 640, Kanthi Path, Katmandu Tel: 11305
National Library*, Katmandu
Nepal-Bharat Sanskritik Kendra Pustakalaya*, (Indian Embassy), Ganga Path, Katmandu
Central Library, **Tribhuvan** University, Kirtipur, Katmandu Tel: 13277 ext 133
Chief Librarian: Mrs Shanti Mishra

Library Association

Nepal Library Association*, PO Box 207 GPO, Asan Tole, Katmandu

Netherlands

General Information

Language: Dutch; Frisian in Friesland (though all speakers of Frisian also speak Dutch). English is common second language
Religion: Mainly Roman Catholic and Protestant
Population: 14.6 million
Bank Hours: 0900-1600 Monday-Friday
Shop Hours: 0900-1730 or 1800 Monday-Saturday. Many close Monday morning
Currency: 100 cents = 1 Netherlands gulden = 1 Dutch florin
Export/Import Information: Member of the European Economic Community. No tariff on books except children's picture books from non-EEC; advertising other than single copies is dutied; VAT: normal rate 19%; special rate 5%, includes books and journals. Import licences required for certain countries (not USA or UK)
Copyright: UCC, Berne, Florence (see International section)

Book Trade Organizations

Centraal Boekhuis BV*, Erasmusweg 10, Postbus 125, 4100 AC Culemborg Tel: (03450) 75911 Telex: 40098 Cboek

Collectieve Propaganda van het Nederlandse Boek (CPNB), Postbus 10576, 1001 EN Amsterdam (Located at: Keizersgracht 391, 1016 EJ Amsterdam) Tel: (020) 264971
Foundation for the Collective Promotion of the Dutch Book
Dir: Henk Kraima
Publications: Premium Bookweek; Children's Bookweek: special publications (2); *Gids Boek en Jeugd* (yearly); *Literaire Boekengids* (half-yearly); *Kinderboekenmolen* (yearly)

Bureau I S B N*, Centraal Boekhuis, Postbus 125, 4100 AC Culemborg (Located at: Erasmusweg 10) Tel: (03450) 75314 Telex: 40098 Cboek
ISBN Administrator: Dick Denteneer; *Secretary:* Mrs M J Kersaan

Koninklijke Nederlandse Uitgeversbond*, Keizersgracht 391, 1016 EJ Amsterdam Tel: (020) 267736 Telex: 15541

Royal Dutch Publishers' Association
Secretary: R M Vrij
Founded: 1880

Nederlandsche Vereeniging van Antiquaren, Jansweg 39, Hofje van Staats, 2011 KM Haarlem Tel: (023) 323986
Netherlands Association of Antiquarian Booksellers
Secretary: Drs F W Kuyper

Nederlandsche Vereeniging voor Druk- en Boekkunst*, Bestevaerstr 10, Haarlem
Netherlands Society for the Art of Printing and Book Production
Secretary: F Mayer
Publications: Mededelingen (irregular) and books

Nederlandse Boekverkopersbond, Waalsdorperweg 119, 2597 HS The Hague Tel: (070) 244395
Dutch Booksellers Association
President: J v d Plas; *Executive Secretary:* A C Doeser
Publications include: Vademecum voor de Boekhandel (annual directory)

Standard Book Numbering Agency, see under ISBN

Stichting Speurwerk betreffende het Boek, Frederiksplein 1, 1017 XK Amsterdam Tel: (020) 254927
Book Research Foundation for the Netherlands
Dir: A A Herpers
Publications: Speurwerk Boeken Omnibus (The Dutch Book Market — quarterly); *Boekenvakboek 1986* (Publishing Industry Statistics); *Structural Analysis of the Book Market in Netherlands*

Vereeniging ter bevordering van de belangen des Boekhandels, Frederiksplein 1, Postbus 5475, 1007 AL Amsterdam Tel: (020) 240212
Association for the Promotion of the Interests of Booksellers and Publishers
Secretary: Mrs M van Vollenhoven-Nagel
Publications: Boekblad (weekly); *Lijstenboek* (annual)

Vereniging van Uitgeversvertegenwoordigers*, Westerstr 62, Wormerveer
Association of Publishers' Representatives
Publication: Vertegenwoordiger

Book Trade Reference Books and Journals

Books

Bibliografie van in Nederland verschenen Officiële en Semi-officiële Uitgaven (Bibliography of Official and Semi-official Publications), Royal Library, Prins Willem Alexanderhof 5, 2509 LK The Hague

Boekenvakboek, Stichting Speurwerk betreffende het Boek, Frederiksplein 1, 1017 XK Amsterdam
Publishing industry statistics

Lijstenboek (annual), Vereeniging ter bevordering van de belangen des Boekhandels, Postbus 5475, Frederiksplein 1, 1007 AL Amsterdam
A list of Dutch booksellers and publishers

Vademecum voor de Boekhandel (Booksellers Directory) (annual), Nederlandse Boekverkopersbond, Waalsdorperweg 119, 2597 HS The Hague

Journals

Boekblad (News-sheet for the Book Trade) (weekly), Vereeniging ter bevordering van de belangen des Boekhandels, Frederiksplein 1, Postbus 5475, 1007 AL Amsterdam

Boekenband (The Bond of Books), Christelijke Blindenbibliotheek, Putterweg 140, Ermelo

De Boekverkoper (The Bookseller), Nederlandse Boekverkopersbond, Waalsdorperweg 119, 2597 HS The Hague

Book Mill, Netherlands Graphic Export Centre, Prinsengracht 668, Amsterdam

Brinkman's Cumulatieve Catalogus (Brinkman's Cumulative Book Catalogue), Samsom Uitgeverij BV, Postbus 4, Alphen aan den Rijn

Buitenlandse Boek (The Foreign Book), Prinsengracht 1083, Amsterdam

Duitse Boek (The German Book), Editions Rodopi BV, Keizersgracht 302-304, 1016 EX Amsterdam
Text in Dutch and German

Gouden Uren (Golden Hours), Nederlandse Boekenclub, ECI voor Boeken en Platen BV, Postbus 400, 4130 EK Vianen

Nieuwe Pockets en Paperbacks (New Pocket-books and Paperbacks), Nederlandse Boek, Prinsengracht 1083, Amsterdam

Nijhoff Information, Martinus Nijhoff FB, Lange Voorhout 9-11, Postbus 269, The Hague
Books and periodicals from the Netherlands in foreign languages

Prisma, Protestantse Stichting tot Bevordering van het Bibliotheekwezen en de Lectuurvoorlichting in Nederland, Parkweg 20a, Voorburg
Book reviews for public libraries

Spectrum Boekengids, Uitgeverij Het Spectrum BV, Park Voorn 4, 3454 JR De Meern

Speurwerk Boeken Omnibus (The Dutch Book Market) (quarterly), Stichting Speurwerk betreffende het Boek, Frederiksplein 1, 1017 XK Amsterdam

Vertegenwoordiger (The Representative), Vereniging van Uitgeversvertegenwoordigers, Westerstr 62, Wormerveer

Publishers

A L F A, Postbus 26, 5360 AA Grave (Located at: Brugstr 5, 5361 GT Grave) Tel: (08860) 73966
Man Dir: Leo J H Kerssemakers
Parent Company: Alfa Antiquarian Booksellers (at above address)
Branch Off: Van Welderenstr 17, 6511 MB Nijmegen
Subjects: Mediaeval Literature and History
Bookshops: One at company, one at branch office address (above)
1987: 28 titles *Founded:* 1977
ISBN Publisher's Prefix: 90-70407

A O, an imprint of Stichting IVIO (qv)

A P A (Academic Publishers Associated), Postbus 1850, 1000 BW Amsterdam
Man Dir: G van Heusden
Orders to: Postbus 122, 3600 AC Maarssen Tel: (030) 436166
Subsidiary Companies: Fontes Pers (qv); Holland University Press BV (qv); Oriental Press BV (qv); Philo Press-Van Heusden-Hissink & Co CV (qv)
Subjects: Academic Books in the Arts, Humanities and Sciences
Founded: 1967
Miscellaneous: Formerly Associated Publishers Amsterdam
ISBN Publisher's Prefix: 90-6037

Academic Publishers Associated, see APA

Acco, an imprint of Academische Uitgeverij Amersfoort VB (qv)

Addison-Wesley Publishing Group, Postbus 5598, 1007 AN Amsterdam (Located at: de Lairessestr 90, 1071 PJ Amsterdam) Tel: (020) 764044/45 Cable Add: Adiwes Amsterdam Telex: 14046 wss nl
President: Frans Gianotten; *Rights & Permissions:* Allison Lobdell, Addison-Wesley, USA; *Vice-President Operations:* Jan Fleere
Parent Company: Addison-Wesley Publishing Co Inc, Reading, MA 01867, USA
Subsidiary Companies: Addison-Wesley Publishers BV; Addison-Wesley Europe BV
Associate Companies: Addison-Wesley Publishers Ltd, UK (qv for other associates)
Subjects: Computer Science, Reference, Juveniles, Technology, Economics, University, Secondary & Primary Textbooks, Educational Materials, General, EFL, Business, Management
Founded: 1942
ISBN Publisher's Prefixes: 0-201 (Addison-Wesley), 0-8053 (Benjamin), 90-6789

Agathon, an imprint of Unieboek BV (qv)

Uitgeverij **Ambo** BV+, Amalialaan 23, Postbus 308, 3740 AH Baarn Tel: (02154) 18441 Telex: 43272
Publisher: I Gay
Imprint: Libra
Subjects: Religion, Philosophy, Psychiatry, Sociology, Psychology, History, Literary Books
Miscellaneous: Firm is a member of the Combo Group, Netherlands (qv)
1985: 40 titles *1986:* 78 titles
ISBN Publisher's Prefix: 90-263

Academische Uitgeverij **Amersfoort** BV, Postbus 395, 3800 AJ Amersfoort (Located at: Koningin Wilhelminalaan 17, 3800 AJ Amersfoort) Tel: (033) 11523/17958
Editorial, Sales, Rights & Permissions: C H J Stavenuiter; *Production:* S de Kock; *Publicity:* C H J Stavenuiter, M Römer
Parent Company: Acco CV, Belgium (qv)
Imprints: Acco, De Horstink
Subjects: Science, Religion, Academic
1986: 30 titles *Founded:* 1986
ISBN Publishers Prefixes: 90-334 (Acco), 90-6184 (De Horstink)

Amsterdam Boek BV, now incorporated in Uitgeverij Het Spectrum BV (qv)

Ankh-Hermes BV, Postbus 125, 7400 AC Deventer (Located at: Smyrnastr 5, 7413 BA, Deventer) Tel: (05700) 33355
Man Dir, Rights & Permissions: Paul Kluwer
Subjects: Philosophy, Psychology, Astrology, Yoga, Alternative Medicine, Herbs, Eastern Religions
Founded: 1949
ISBN Publisher's Prefix: 90-202

Aramith Uitgevers, Postbus 7467, 1007 JL Amsterdam Tel: (020) 627189/623000 Telex: 26401 Intx
Chief Executive: Rene Boerdam; *Editorial:* Elisabeth Nijssen
Subjects: Art, Holography, Mathematics
1985: 10 titles *1986:* 10 titles *Founded:* 1984
ISBN Publisher's Prefix: 90-6834

BV Uitgeverij de **Arbeiderspers***, Postbus 3879, 1001 AR Amsterdam (Located at: Singel 262, 1016 AC Amsterdam) Tel: (020) 237195 Telex: 11556 Apqwu
Man Dir: Theo A Sontrop; *Editorial:* Martin Ros; *Publicity:* Gert Jan Hemmink
Associate Companies: Em Querido's

Uitgeverij BV (qv), Wetenschappelijke Uitgeverij BV
Subjects: General Fiction & Non-fiction, Paperbacks
ISBN Publisher's Prefix: 90-295

Ark Boeken Publishing House+, Donauweg 4, 1043 AJ Amsterdam Tel: (020) 114847
General Dir: J Ruijsink; *Publishing Dir:* B Hartman; *Production Manager:* A Rietveld
Subjects: Religious, Juveniles, Picture Books
Bookshop: BKV-Lektuurcentrum, Hoofstr 55, 3970 KB Driebergen
1986: 38 titles *1987:* 52 titles *Founded:* 1913
Miscellaneous: Ark Boeken Publishing House combines the activities of Vereeniging tot Verspreiding der Heilige Schrift (Association for Distribution of the Holy Scripture) and Bijbel Kiosk Vereniging (Bible Kiosk Society)
ISBN Publisher's Prefix: 90-338

Uitgeverij Jan van **Arkel**+, Alexander Numankade 17, 3572 KP Utrecht Tel: (030) 731840
Chief Executive: Jan van Arkel
Orders to: Ruward, Spuiblvd 231, 2501 CL The Hague
Subjects: Economics, State planning, Geography, Ecology
1985: 10 titles *1986:* 10 titles *Founded:* 1974
ISBN Publisher's Prefix: 90-6224

A **Asher** & Co, BV*, Keizersgracht 489-91, 1017 DM Amsterdam Tel: (020) 222255 Cable Add: Asherbooks Telex: 14070 ashni-nl
Man Dir: Nico Israel; *Sales Dir:* Julius W Steiner
Associate Companies: Nico Israel, Theatrum Orbis Terrarum (qqv)
Subjects: General & Natural Science, Reference
Founded: 1830

Associated Publishers Amsterdam, renamed APA (Academic Publishers Associated) (qv)

Atrium, an imprint of Icob cv Uitgeverij (qv)

Bert **Bakker** BV*, Herengracht 406, 1017 BX Amsterdam Tel: (020) 241934 Telex: 13340 BBNL
Man Dir: Bert Bakker; *Editorial:* Mai Spijkers
Subjects: Dutch and Foreign Literature, History, Psychology, Social Science, Family Interest, High Quality Children's
Founded: 1893
Miscellaneous: Firm is member of the Kluwer Group (qv)
ISBN Publisher's Prefixes: 90-6019, 90-315

Uitgeverij **Balans**+, Herengracht 164, 1016 BP Amsterdam Tel: (020) 268982
Orders to: Centraal Boekhuis, Postbus 100, 4100 BA Culemborg
Publisher: Jan G Gaarlandt; *Rights & Permissions:* Francoise Gaarlandt-Kist
Imprint: Balans
Subjects: Non-fiction, Autobiography, History, Politics, Sociology
1986: 10 titles *1987:* 20 titles *Founded:* 1986
ISBN Publisher's Prefix: 90-5018

A A **Balkema**, Postbus 1675, 3000 BR Rotterdam (Located at: Vijverweg 8, 3062 JP Rotterdam) Tel: (010) 4145822 Telex: 41605 tkom nl Fax: (02523) 74784
Man Dir: A T Balkema; *Rights & Permissions:* G Balkema-Pieterse
Branch Offs: A A Balkema Publishers, Republic of South Africa (qv); A A Balkema Publishers, Old Post Rd, Brookfield, VT 05036, USA
Subjects: English-language publications on African Studies, Palaeontology, Marine Biology, Aquaculture, Botany, Zoology, Soil and Rock Mechanics, Mining Engineering, History (especially South African), Hydraulic Research
1986: 70 titles *Founded:* 1932
ISBN Publisher's Prefix: 90-6191

H J W **Becht's** Uitgeversmij BV/Uitgeverij J H de Bussy BV, now incorporated in Uitgeverij J H Gottmer/H J W Becht BV (qv)

Uitgeverij **Bekadidact**, see Combo Uitgeversgroep

John **Benjamins** BV+, Postbus 52519, 1007 HA Amsterdam (Located at: Amsteldijk 44, Amsterdam) Tel: (020) 738156 Cable Add: Benper, Amsterdam Telex: 15789 jb
Man Dir: John L Benjamins (Amsterdam), Paul Peranteau (USA)
Branch Off: John Benjamins North America Inc, 1 Buttonwood Sq, Philadelphia, PA 19130, USA Tel: (215) 5646379 Telex: 7106701085
Subjects: History of Art, Linguistics, Literature, Philosophy, Philology, Reference, Semiotics, Cultural History, Social Science, Educational Materials, Reprints of backfile Periodicals
Founded: 1964
ISBN Publisher's Prefixes: 90-272 (European), 0-915027 (USA)

De **Bezige** Bij, Van Miereveldstr 1, Postbus 5184, 1071 DW Amsterdam Tel: (020) 735731 Cable Add: Beebook
Man Dir: A J R Hamming
Subjects: General Fiction, Belles Lettres, Poetry, Children's Books
Founded: 1945
ISBN Publisher's Prefix: 90-234

Uitgeverij **Bigot en Van Rossum** BV+, Nassaulaan 10, Postbus 108, 3740 AC Baarn Tel: (02154) 17241 Telex: 73250 line nl ref 588 Fax: 2159 32127
Dirs: Joop Verweij, Jan van Willegen; *Editorial, Rights & Permissions:* Jan van Willegen; *Sales:* Joop Verweij
Associate Companies: BV Uitgeverij De Kern, Uitgeverij Mingus BV (qqv, both at above address)
Subjects: General Fiction, Paperbacks, Popular Non-fiction
1985: 22 titles *1986:* 20 titles *Founded:* 1934
ISBN Publisher's Prefix: 90-6134

Erven J **Bijleveld**, Janskerkhof 7, 3512 BK Utrecht Tel: (030) 317008
Man Dir: J B Bommeljé Jnr
Subjects: Philosophy, Religion, Medicine, Psychology, Social Science, History
1986: approx 12 titles *Founded:* 1864

H W **Blok** Uitgeverij BV, Schiedamsevest 59, 3012 BD Rotterdam Tel: (010) 4137997
Subjects: Dutch for Spanish-speaking and Portuguese for Dutch-speaking persons
ISBN Publisher's Prefix: 90-70008

Boek Promotions BV*, Postbus 88, 1250 AB Laren NH (Located at: Hilversumseweg 16, 1251 EX Laren NH) Tel: (02153) 10154
Owner: Peter J Houbolt
Act mainly as packagers for sponsored books

Boekencentrum BV+, Scheveningseweg 72, Postbus 84176, 2508 AD The Hague Tel: (070) 512111
Dirs: L vd Herik, G J Bothof
Subjects: Education, Theology, Religion

De **Boekerij** BV+, Singel 466-468, 1017 AW Amsterdam Tel: (020) 261655 Telex: 13373 Boek nl Fax: (020) 237675
Man Dirs: Marijke Bartels, R C M Hogenes; *Editorial:* Marijke Bartels (Director), Henny Bodenkamp (Children's); Henk Figee (Fiction); Dr W Wybrands Marcussen (History); *Sales:* R C M Hogenes; *Production:* Piet Pors; *Publicity:* Ariane Verdenius; *Rights & Permissions:* Nel Drijvers-Dils
Parent Company: M & P Boeken BV, Schoutlaan 4, 6002 EA Weert
Imprints: Amber, Van Goor, De Bataafsche, Leeuw
Subjects: General & Literary Fiction, Children's, History
1986: 175 titles *Founded:* 1986 (1880)

de **Boer** Maritiem, an imprint of Unieboek BV (qv)

Bohn, Scheltema en Holkema*, Postbus 13079, 3507 LB Utrecht (Located at: Emmalaan 27, Utrecht) Tel: (030) 511274
Man Dir: Jan van Geelen
Subjects: University Textbooks (Medicine, Public Health)
Founded: 1752
Miscellaneous: Firm is a member of the Kluwer Group (qv)
ISBN Publisher's Prefix: 90-313

Boom-Pers Boeken- en Tijdschriftenuitg BV, Kromme Elleboog 2, Postbus 58, 7940 AB Meppel Tel: (05220) 54306 Telex: 42829
Editorial & Directors' Off: Keizersgracht 725, 1017 DX Amsterdam Tel: (020) 226107 Cable Add: Boompers
Man Dirs: H L Bouman, J H Boom
Subjects: Philosophy, Philosophy of Science, Psychology, General, Psychiatry, Social & Political Science, Paedagogy, Periodicals
Bookshops: Kamper Boekhandel, Oude Str 82, Kampen; De Brunte, Snijderstr 11, Lelystad; Boekhandel Boom, Winkelcentrum Gordiaan, Lelystad; Boekhandel v/h G Taconis, Hoofdstraat West 10, Wolvega (all in Netherlands)
Founded: 1842
ISBN Publisher's Prefix: 90-6009

Born NV Uitgeversmaatschappij*, Esstr 10, Postbus 22, Assen
Man Dir: H Born
Subjects: General Fiction, How-to, Philosophy, Textbooks, Reference, Juveniles, Medicine, Engineering, Social Science, Low- & High-priced Paperbacks
Founded: 1885
Miscellaneous: Firm is a member of the Kluwer Group (qv)
ISBN Publisher's Prefix: 90-283

Bosch en Keuning, Bremstr, Postbus 1, 3740 AA Baarn Tel: (02154) 18241 Telex: beka-43272
Man Dir: Robbert Ammerlaan
Subjects: Biography, History, Music, Art, Religion, Low- & High-priced Paperbacks, Medicine, Primary Textbooks, Educational Materials, Popular Science (Sesam Pocketbooks)
Founded: 1925
Miscellaneous: Firm is a member of the Combo Group (qv)
ISBN Publisher's Prefix: 90-246

E J **Brill**, Plantijnstr 2, 2321 JC Leiden Tel: (071) 312624 Cable Add: Brill Leiden Telex: 39296
Manager: Dr W Backhuys
Subsidiary Company: E J Brill/Scandinavian Science Press, Langase 4 Ganløse, 2760 Målov, Denmark
Editorial Off: D Ward, 209 Crofton Lane, Orpington, Kent BR6 0BL, UK
Branch Off: Orient Buchhandlung am

Friesenplatz, E J Brill GmbH, Antwerpener Str 6-12, D-5000 Cologne 1, Federal Republic of Germany
Subjects: Classical, Mediaeval and Renaissance Studies, Religion, Oriental & Islamic Studies, University Textbooks, Zoology, Botany, Geology, Palaeontology
Founded: 1683
ISBN Publisher's Prefix: 90-04

Educatieve Uitgeverij Ten **Brink**, now Educatieve Uitgeverij Edu'Actief (qv)

De **Brug**-Djambatan BV*, Postbus 8411, 3503 RK Utrecht (Located at: Reactorweg 160, 3542 RK Utrecht) Tel: (030) 430254 Telex: 70245 Awbru nl Cable Add: Djambatan Utrecht
Man Dir: M C Hopman
Associate Company: Bruna Pockethuis BV (qv)
Subjects: History, Reference, Geography, Cartography, Educational Materials (Atlases, Wall Maps)
Founded: 1949

A W **Bruna** en Zoon's Uitgeversmaatschappij BV+, Postbus 8411, 3503 RK Utrecht (Located at: Atoomweg 464, 3542 AD Utrecht) Tel: (030) 450411 Cable Add: Brunazoon Telex: 70245 Awbru nl Awbru nl
Dir: Cees de Bruin; *Publishers:* Marian van der Beek (Fiction), Bram Wolthoorn (Non-fiction)
Parent Company: BV Friese Pers, Leeuwarden
Associate Company: Bruna Pockethuis (qv)
Branch Off: A W Bruna en Zoon NV, Belgium (qv)
Subjects: General Fiction, Belles Lettres, History, Philosophy, Paperbacks, Psychology, General & Social Science, Computer Books
Founded: 1868
ISBN Publisher's Prefix: 90-229

Bruna Pockethuis BV+*, Postbus 8411, 3503 RK Utrecht (Located at: Reactorweg 160, 3542 AD Utrecht) Tel: (030) 430254 Cable Add: Brunazoon Telex: 70245 Awbru nl
Dir: Martin C Hopman; *Publisher (Non-fiction), Rights & Permissions:* Marian van der Beek
Parent Company: BV Friese Pers, Leeuwarden
Associate Companies: A W Bruna en Zoon's Uitgeversmaatschappij BV (qv); De Brug-Djambatan BV (qv)
Imprints: Brunette, Grote Beren, Pandora Pockets, Zwarte Beertjes
Branch Off: Antwerpsesteenweg 29A, B-2630 Aartselaar, Belgium
Subjects: Low-priced fiction and non-fiction paperbacks
Founded: 1955
ISBN Publisher's Prefix: 90-449

Brunette, an imprint of Bruna Pockethuis BV (qv)

Buijten en Schipperheijn BV Drukkerij en Uitg Mij v/h*, Valkenburgerstr 106, NL-1001 Amsterdam Tel: (020) 236612
Subject: Philosophy, Religion, History, Literature
Founded: 1902
ISBN Publisher's Prefix: 90-6064

J H de **Bussy** BV, see H J W Becht's Uitgeversmij bv

Uitgeverij G F **Callenbach** BV, Ambachtsstr 13c, 3861 RH Nijkerk Tel: (03494) 51241 Telex: beka-43722
Man Dir: G F Callenbach; *Rights & Permissions:* Mrs P van Elven-Scholtes
Subjects: General Fiction, Belles Lettres, Poetry, Religion, Juveniles, Low- & High-priced Paperbacks, Psychology, Psychiatry, Medicine, Sociology, Hobbies
Founded: 1854
Miscellaneous: Firm is a member of the Combo Group, Netherlands (qv)
ISBN Publisher's Prefix: 90-266

Uitgeverij **Cantecleer** BV, Postbus 24, 3730 AA De Bilt (Located at: Dorpsstr 74, 3732 HK De Bilt) Tel: (030) 764014 Telex: Maxel 47825
Man Dir: J A J Jungerhans; *Editors:* L de Jonge, S Ruhe
Subjects: Art, Juveniles, Handicrafts, Travel Guides, Paperbacks
Founded: 1949
Miscellaneous: Firm is a member of the Combo Group (qv)
ISBN Publisher's Prefix: 90-213

Castrum Peregrini Presse, Postbus 645, 1000 AP Amsterdam (Located at: Herengracht 401, 1017 BP Amsterdam) Tel: (020) 235287
Man Dir: M R Goldschmidt
Subjects: History of Literature, History of Art, Belles Lettres, Poetry, Biography, History, Archaeology, Philology, History of Ideas, Reference
1985: 5 titles *Founded:* 1951
ISBN Publisher's Prefix: 90-6034

De **Centaur**, an imprint of Omega Boek BV (qv)

Cicero, an imprint of Uit-Mij West-Friesland (qv)

Combo Uitgeversgroep*, Postbus 1, Bremstr 11, 3740 AA Baarn Tel: (02154) 18241
Members of the Combo Group in the Netherlands include: Uitgeverij Ambo BV (qv), Uitgeverij Bekadidact, Bosch en Keuning (qv), Uitgeverij Callenbach BV (qv), Uitgeverij Cantecleer BV (qv), Uitgeverij De Fontein BV (qv), Uitgeverij ten Have (qv), Uitgeverij Market Books BV, Uitgeverij 'In den Toren' (qv), Uitgeverij Van Walraven (qv)

Uitgeverij **Contact** BV, Keizersgracht 486, 1017 EH Amsterdam Tel: (020) 261771 Telex: 70694 Luve
Man Dir: Bert de Groot; *Editorial:* Harko Keijzer
Subjects: Dutch and translated literature, Psychology, Pregnancy and Childcare, New Science, History
Miscellaneous: Firm is a member of the Kluwer Group

Dick **Coutinho** BV+, Postbus 10, 1399 ZG Muiderberg (Located at: Badlaan 2, 1399 GN Muiderberg) Tel: (02942) 1888
Man Dir, Editorial: Dick Coutinho; *Sales:* Jeane Oosterbaan; *Production:* Marijke Faber; *Publicity, Rights & Permissions:* Marieke Tambach
Subjects: University textbooks
1985: 135 titles *Founded:* 1977
ISBN Publisher's Prefix: 90-6283

Van **Dale** Lexicografie*, Mariaplaats 21-C, Utrecht Tel: (030) 331484
Man Dir, Rights & Permissions: Prof Dr B P F Al; *Editorial:* Mrs T E Broersma, H A C Schutz, K Nieuwenburg; *Sales, Publicity:* W L Detiger; *Production:* S Bekkers, K Nieuwenburg
Subject: Dictionaries
Founded: 1976
Miscellaneous: Firm is a member of the Kluwer Group (qv)
ISBN Publisher's Prefix: 90-6648

Dekker en Van de Vegt+, Postbus 526, 6500 AM Nijmegen Tel: (080) 232765 Cable Add: Dekkervegt Nijmegen
Man Dir: K W J van Rossum
Parent Company: Van Gorcum BV (qv)
Subjects: High-priced Paperbacks, Medicine, Social Sciences, Psychology, Secondary Textbooks
1985: 16 titles *Founded:* 1856
ISBN Publisher's Prefix: 90-255

Delft University Press*, Civil Engineering Bldg, Stevinweg 1, Postbus 5048, 2628 CN Delft Tel: (015) 783254 Telex: 38151
Dir: Ir P A M Maas; *Editorial:* Lydia ter Horst-ten Wolde
1985: 97 titles *Founded:* 1972
ISBN Publisher's Prefix: 90-6275

Jacob **Dijkstra's** Uitgeversmaatschappij BV, a subsidiary of Wolters Kluwer NV (qv)

Diligentia BV, now VNU Business Publications (qv)

van **Dishoeck**, an imprint of Unieboek BV (qv)

van **Ditmar**, see Nijgh en van Ditmar

De Brug-**Djambatan** BV, see De Brug

Uitgeversmaatschappij Ad **Donker** BV, Koningin Emmaplein 1, 3016 AA Rotterdam Tel: (010) 4363009
Dir: Willem A Donker
Subjects: General Fiction, Biography, History, High-priced Paperbacks, Psychology, Sociology, Education
1985: 30 titles *Founded:* 1938
ISBN Publisher's Prefix: 90-6100

De **Driehoek** BV+, Keizersgracht 756, 1017 EZ Amsterdam Tel: (020) 246426
Director: H J Heule
Subjects: Medicine, Health, Yoga, Herbs, Nutrition, Vegetarianism, Mysticism, Buddhism, Astrology
1985-1986: 20-30 titles *Founded:* 1933
ISBN Publisher's Prefix: 90-6030

Uitgeverij **Dwarsstap**, an imprint of Uitgeverij SUN (qv)

E C I voor Boeken en Grammofoonplaten BV+, Postbus 400, 4130 EK Vianen (ZH) (Located at: Laanakkerweg 14-16, 4124 PB Vianen (ZH)) Tel: (03473) 79911 Telex: 47449
Man Dir: J A Lancée; *Editorial:* H Buth; *Rights & Permissions:* B Tromp
Parent Company: Bertelsmann AG, Federal Republic of Germany (qv)
Subjects: General Fiction and Non-fiction
Book Club: ECI voor Boeken en Platen BV
Founded: 1967
ISBN Publisher's Prefix: 90-70038

East-West Publications Fonds BV+, Anna Paulownastr 78, Postbus 85617, 2508 CH The Hague Tel: (070) 644590 Telex: 32412 Tesh
Chief Executive: L W Carp; *Sales:* W F Teunissen
Subjects: Sufism, Religions, Mysticism, Symbolism, Middle East Culture, Mediaeval Art & Iconography, Music, Children's
Founded: 1966
ISBN Publisher's Prefix: 90-70104

Educatieve Uitgeverij **Edu'Actief** BV+, Postbus 56, 7940 AB Meppel (Located at: Industrieweg 12, 7940 AD Meppel) Tel: (05220) 62222 Telex: c/o Drukkerij Ten Brink BV: 42469 Brink NL
Man Dir: Drs R Smit
Subject: Educational books for 6-18 year olds
Founded: 1848
ISBN Publisher's Prefix: 90-5117

Educa International, a member of the Kluwer Group (qv)

Educaboek BV+*, Industrieweg 1, Postbus 48, 4100 AA Culemborg Tel: (03450) 71911 Telex: 47306
Chairman: Dr M J van Dalen
Subjects: Textbooks, Secondary, General and Vocational Education, Technical, Educational Materials
Founded: 1970

296 NETHERLANDS

Miscellaneous: Firm is a member of the Kluwer Group, and controls the imprints Schoolpers (qv), Stam/Robijns, Stam Technische Boeken, Tjeenk Willink-Noorduijn
ISBN Publisher's Prefix: 90-11

Elmar BV, Delftweg 147, 2289 BD Rijswijk (Z.H) Tel: (015) 123623
Man Dirs: M Roodnat, H Masthoff
Subjects: Biography, History, How-to, Reference, Medicine & General Science, Science Fiction, Sport
Founded: 1961

Elsevier, Jan van Galenstr 335, 1061 AZ Amsterdam Tel: (020) 5159111 (Internal and External Relations Tel: (020) 5152341/ 5152289) Cable Add: Elsevier Telex: 16479 elsvi nl
President: Prof P J Vinken; *Deputy Chairman:* L van Vollenhoven; *Other members of Executive Board:* C B Alberti, O ter Haar, H B M Luykx
Dutch Subsidiaries: Elsevier Nederland BV, Elsevier Participaties BV, Elsevier Services BV (all at above address); Elsevier Science Publishers BV (qv); Elsevier Boeken BV (qv); Nederlandse Dagbladunie BV, Westblaak 180, 3012 KN Rotterdam; Dagblad van Rijn en Gouwe BV, P Doelmanstr 8, 2405 CE Alphen a/d Rijn; BV De Dordtenaar, Stationsweg 39, 3311 JW Dordrecht; Brabants Nieuwsblad BV, Molenstr 7, 4701 JK Roosendaal; Van Boekhoven-Bosch BV, Europalaan 12, 3526 KS Utrecht; Krips Repro BV, Kaapweg 6, 7944 HV Meppel; Misset Grafische Bedrijven, Mercuriusstr 35, 7006 RK Doetinchem; Periodieken Service Holland BV, Keppelseweg 15, 7001 CE Doetinchem; Uitgeversmaatschappij C Misset BV, Hanzestr 1, 7006 RH Doetinchem; Set and Match BV, BV Uitgeversmaatschappij Bonaventura, BV Uitgeversmaatschappij Annoventura, Folio Groep BV (all at Hoogoorddreef 60, 1101 BE Amsterdam); Elsevier Leersystemen BV, Koninklijke PBNA BV (both at Velperbuitensingel 6, 6828 CT Arnhem 1); Studiecentrum Bȳzondere Cursussen (SBC) BV, Westelijke Parallelweg 54, 3331 EW Zwijndrecht; Northprint BV, Industrieweg 1b, 7944 HS Meppel; Het Vrije Volk CV (50%), W de Withstraat 25, 3012 BL Rotterdam
Foreign Subsidiaries: Elsevier Librico NV, Pan European Publishing Company, International Equipment News Europe NV (50%) (all in Belgium); Editora Campus Ltda, Brazil (qv); Elsevier – Thomas Fachverlag GmbH (50%) (Federal Republic of Germany); Excerpta Medica Asia Ltd, Hong Kong; Elsevier Scientific Publishers (Ireland) Ltd, Irish Elsevier Printers Ltd (both in Republic of Ireland); Elsevier Science Publishers (Japan) (qv), Excerpta Medica KK, Tokyo (both in Japan); Elsevier SA, Elsevier Trading & Copyrights SA, Elslux Holding SA, Elsevier Sequoia SA, Excerpta Medica SA (all in Switzerland); Elsevier International Bulletins, Elsevier Editorial Services Ltd, Elsevier-IRCS Ltd, Elsevier Publications (Cambridge) (all in UK); Elsevier US Holdings Inc, Congressional Information Service Inc, Greenwood Press, Elsevier Science Publishing Company Inc, Excerpta Medica Inc, Medical Examination Publishing Company Inc, Praeger Publishing Division, Delta Communications, Gordon Publications (all in USA)
Subjects: Agricultural, Veterinary, Food and Environmental Sciences; Chemistry; Computer, Information and Communications Sciences; Earth and Planetary Sciences; Economics; Econometrics; History; Law; Life Sciences;
Linguistics; Literature; Mathematics; Logic; Mechanics; Operations Research; Statistics; Management; Systems and Control; Physics; Psychology; Psychiatry; Social, Political and Instructional Sciences; Technology; Engineering; Clinical Medicine; Multilingual Dictionaries; Reference Works; Handbooks; Paperbacks; Textbooks; Illustrated Books; Atlases; Periodicals; Educational Materials; Electronic Databases; Printing Industry
Founded: 1985 (NV Uitgeversmaatschappij Elsevier 1880)
Miscellaneous: Elsevier-NDU was a holding company formed in 1979 by a merger of NV Uitgeversmaatschappij Elsevier and Nederlandse Dagbladunie NV

Elsevier Biomedical Press, a division of Elsevier Science Publishers BV (qv)

Elsevier Boeken BV+, Postbus 879, 1000 AW Amsterdam (Located at: Jan van Galenstr 335, 1061 AZ Amsterdam) Tel: (020) 5159222 Cable Add: Elsbook Telex: 16479 Elsvi nl
Man Dir and Publicity: Drs N P van den Berg; *Publishers:* N F Kuipers (Arts, History, Popular Science), J N M Brugge (Reference, Dictionaries); *Sales:* Th Brandsen; *Rights:* M van Blijswijk
Parent Company: Elsevier Nederland BV, a subsidiary of Elsevier (qv)
Imprints: Elsevier, Kramers, Manteau (Antwerpen en Amsterdam), Winkler Prins
Subjects: Non-fiction, Reference, Dictionaries

Elsevier Science Publishers BV, Postbus 2400, 1000 CK Amsterdam (Located at: Sara Burgerhartstr 25, 1055 KV Amsterdam) Tel: (020) 5862911 Cable Add: Espom amsterdam Telex: 10704 espom nl
Man Dir: J J F Kels; *Dirs:* Dr Th van der Raadt, Dr M F J Pijnenborg
Divisions: Elsevier Biomedical Press, Molenwerf 1, 1014 AG Amsterdam; Excerpta Medica Medical Communications, Jan van Galenstr 335, 1061 AZ Amsterdam; Physical Science & Engineering Division (at above address)
Orders to: ESP Marketing Services, Postbus 211, 1000 AE Amsterdam Tel: (020) 5803911 Cable Add: Elspubco Telex: 18582 espa nl
Parent Company: Elsevier Nederland BV, a subsidiary of Elsevier (qv)
Associate Companies: Editora Campus, Brazil (qv); Elsevier Scientific Publishers (Ireland) Ltd, Republic of Ireland; Elsevier Sequoia SA, Switzerland; Elsevier Applied Science Publishers Ltd (qv), Elsevier Editorial Services Ltd (both UK); Elsevier Science Publishing Co Inc, Medical Examination Co Inc (both at 52 Vanderbilt Ave, New York, NY 10017, USA)
Subsidiary Company: Geo Abstracts Ltd, Regency House, 34 Duke St, Norwich NR3 3AP, UK
Imprints: Elsevier, North-Holland, Elsevier Applied Science, Excerpta Medica, Elsevier International Bulletins, Elsevier Sequoia; Cuadra/Elsevier
Branch Offs: Editions Scientifiques Elsevier, Paris, France; Elsevier Science Publishers (Japan), Japan (qv); Elsevier Science Publishers, CPO Box 1922, Seoul, Republic of Korea; Elsevier International Bulletins, Elsevier Publications (Cambridge) (both UK)
Subjects: Agricultural, Veterinary, Food and Environmental Sciences; Chemistry; Computer, Information and Communications Sciences; Earth and Planetary Sciences; Economics; Econometrics; History; Law; Life Sciences; Linguistics; Literature; Mathematics; Logic; Mechanics; Operations Research; Statistics;
Management; Systems and Control; Physics; Psychology; Psychiatry; Political and Instructional Sciences; Technology; Engineering; Clinical Medicine; Multilingual Dictionaries
Founded: 1946
ISBN Publisher's Prefix: 0-444

Elsevier's Wetenschappelijke Uitgeverij, a division of Elsevier Science Publishers BV (qv)

Uitgeverij Hans **Elzenga** BV, Postbus 517, 2100 AM Heemstede (Located at: Landszichtlaan 38, 2101 ZJ Heemstede) Tel: (023) 290044
Man Dir: Hans Elzenga
Subjects: Juvenile, General
1985: 10 titles *1986:* 12 titles *Founded:* 1982
ISBN Publisher's Prefix: 90-6692

Enschedé en Zonen, Klokhuisplein 5, Postbus 114, 2000 AC Haarlem Tel: (023) 184569 Telex: 41049 Fax: (023) 325550

Excerpta Medica, an imprint of Elsevier Science Publishers BV (qv)

Uitgeverij **F E D** BV, member of the Kluwer Group (qv)

Facsimile Uitgaven Nederland BV (FUN), subsidiary of Theatrum Orbis Terrarum (qv)

Falkplan/CIB, now Falkplan-Suurland BV (qv)

Falkplan-Suurland BV, Postbus 9510, 5602 LM Eindhoven (Located at: Baltesakker 17, 5625 TC Eindhoven) Tel: (040) 642111 Telex: 51874 svehv Fax: (040) 410955
Man Dirs: D R A Suurland, J A Suurland
Associate Company: Suurland Holding BV
Subject: Maps

Frank **Fehmers** Productions+, Singel 512, 1017 AX Amsterdam Tel: (020) 238766 Cable Add: Intpubcon Telex: 16740 fepro nl Fax: (020) 246262
Man Dir: Frank Fehmers; *International Co-productions:* Meghan Ferrill
Associate Companies: Frank Fehmers Productions Inc, 300 East 59th St, New York, NY 10022, USA; Frank Fehmers Productions Ltda, Estrada do Tombo 401, Bloco N Apt 102, 22450 Rio de Janeiro RJ, Brazil; Frank Fehmers Publishing BV, Groot Davelaarweg 20, Curaçao, Netherlands Antilles
Subjects: Juveniles, Television, Merchandising, Licensing, International Book and Film Co-productions
ISBN Publisher's Prefix: 90-6151

Feministische Uitgeverij Sara, see Sara

Uitgeverij De **Fontein** BV, Prinses Marielaan 8, Postbus 1, 3743 AH Baarn Tel: (02154) 22141 Telex: beka-43272
Man Dir: W Hazeu
Subjects: General Fiction & Non-fiction, Juveniles, High-priced Paperbacks
Founded: 1946
Miscellaneous: Firm is a member of the Combo Group (qv)
ISBN Publisher's Prefix: 90-261

Fontes Pers (APA), Postbus 1850, 1000 BW Amsterdam
Orders to: APA, Postbus 122, 3600 AC Maarssen
Parent Company: APA (Academic Publishers Associated) (qv)
Subjects: Maritime History, History of Law
ISBN Publisher's Prefixes: 90-302, 90-6039

Foris Publications Holland, Postbus 509, 3300 AM Dordrecht (Located at: Mijlweg 79, Dordrecht) Tel: (078) 510454 Cable Add: Intergraph Dordrecht Fax: (078) 510972
Man Dir: Henk J La Porte; *Assistant*

Manager: Mrs Bep IJsselstijn-Oosterling
Parent Company: Intercontinental Graphics Holland BV
Subsidiary Companies: ICG Printing BV; Foris Publications USA Inc, PO Box 5904, Providence, RI 02903, USA
Subjects: Languages, Linguistics, Anthropology, Latin American Studies, Indonesia, Development Studies
Bookshop: Postma Scientific BV, Postbus 3585, 1001 AJ Amsterdam
1985: 40 titles *1986:* 50 titles *1987:* 60 titles
Founded: 1978
Miscellaneous: Publishers for KITLV (Royal Institute of Linguistics and Anthropology), Leiden and CEDLA (Centre for Latin American Research and Documentation), Amsterdam
ISBN Publisher's Prefix: 90-6765

Free University Press, an imprint of VU Boekhandel/Uitgeverij BV (qv)

Uitgeverij W **Gaade** BV, Postbus 625, 3900 AP Veenendaal Tel: (08385) 28224
Man Dir: Yvonne van Oort
Subjects: Art, Cultural History, Nature, Instructional Art and Craft Books, International Co-productions
Founded: 1954
ISBN Publisher's Prefix: 90-6017

Gaberbocchus Press, a subsidiary of Uitgeverij De Harmonie (qv)

Gamma, an imprint of Infopers (qv)

Van **Gennep** Ltd+, Spuistr 283, 1012 VR Amsterdam Tel: (020) 247033
Man Dirs: R O van Gennep, J H Jansen; *Foreign Rights:* Annelies de Korver
Subjects: Belles Lettres, History, Political Science, Architecture, Art
Bookshops: Van Gennep Nieuwezijds, Nieuwe Zijds Voorburgwal 330, 1012 RW Amsterdam; Boekhandel Van Gennep, Oude Binnenweg 131b, 3012 JD Rotterdam
Founded: 1969
ISBN Publisher's Prefix: 90-6012

BV Uitgeversbedryf Het **Goede Boek***, Koningin Wilhelminastr 8, Postbus 122, 1270 AC Huizen Tel: (02152) 53508
Dir: W E J Rikmans; *Advertising Dir:* F Rikmans
Subjects: Children's Books, Computer Software Handbooks, Sport
1985: 16 titles *Founded:* 1932
ISBN Publisher's Prefix: 90-240

Van **Gorcum** BV+, Industrieweg 38, 9403 AB Assen Tel: (05920) 46846 Cable Add: Vangorcum
Man Dir: G Vlieghuis; *Dirs:* L Dijkema (General & Academic Books), K W J van Rossum (Dekker en Van de Vegt, Nijmegen), H L Leenen (Van Gorcum, Maastricht); *Sales:* J van Veen; *Rights & Permissions:* D Bakkes
Orders to: Van Gorcum, PO Box 43, 9400 AA Assen
Subsidiary Companies: Dekker en Van de Vegt (qv); Van Gorcum, Maastricht
Branch Off: Alexander Battalaan 95, 6221 CC Maastricht
Subjects: Social Science, Anthropology, Medicine, History, Language & Literature, Law, Philosophy, Psychology, Economics, Religion, Geography, Education, University Textbooks
1985: 85 titles *Founded:* 1800
ISBN Publisher's Prefix: 90-232

Uitgeverij J H **Gottmer**/H J W Becht BV, Postbus 160, 2060 A D Bloemendaal (Located at: Prof van Vlotenweg 1a, Bloemendaal) Tel: (023) 257150 Telex: 41856
Dirs: Mrs H V M Gottmer, C van Wijk, J Schilt
Subjects: General Fiction, Religion, Juveniles, General Non-fiction
Founded: 1937
ISBN Publisher's Prefix: 90-257

BV v/hB **Gottmer's** Uitgeversbedrijf*, Sint Annastr 167, Postbus 103, 6500 AC Nijmegen Tel: (080) 231098
Man Dir: B Gottmer
Subjects: Religion, Humour, Cartoons, Mysticism
Founded: 1950
ISBN Publisher's Prefix: 90-6075

Gouda Quint BV, Postbus 1148, 6801 MK Arnhem (Located at: Willemsplein 2, Arnhem) Tel: (085) 454762
Man Dir: K H Mulder
Subjects: Textbooks, Law, Taxation, Periodicals
Founded: 1739
Miscellaneous: Firm is a member of the Kluwer Group (qv)
ISBN Publisher's Prefix: 90-6000

De **Graaf** Publishers, Zuideinde 40, Postbus 6, 2420 AA Nieuwkoop Tel: (01725) 1461 Cable Add: Degraaf Nieuwkoop
Man Dir: Maria Emilie de Graaf
Subsidiary Company: Miland Publishers (qv)
Subjects: Reference, Religion, University Textbooks
Founded: 1959
ISBN Publisher's Prefix: 90-6004

Griffioen Paperbacks, an imprint of Em Querido's Uitgeverij BV (qv)

De **Groot** Goudriaan, a subsidiary of Uitgeversmaatschappij J H Kok BV (qv)

Grote Beren, an imprint of Bruna Pockethuis BV (qv)

B R **Grüner** BV, Nieuwe Herengracht 31, 1011 RM Amsterdam Tel: (020) 264371 Cable Add: Veriditas
Publisher: Bruno Roland Grüner
Subjects: Philosophy, Religion, Social Science, Periodicals, Poetry, Politics, Classical Antiquity, Ancient History
1985: 29 titles *Founded:* 1967
ISBN Publisher's Prefix: 90-6032

H E S Publishers+, Postbus 129, 3500 AC Utrecht (Located at: Oude Gracht 206, Utrecht) Tel: (030) 316977 Telex: 47352 Forum nl
Chief Executive: S S Hesselink; *Editorial:* Willemijn van Asbeck van Dorp; *Production:* Gemma Coumans; *Publicity:* Ans Bedaux
Subjects: Bibliography, Cartography, Linguistics, Literature, Classics, Ancient History, History, Art, Philosophy, Theology, Gastronomy
1985: 22 titles *1986:* 30 titles *Founded:* 1971
ISBN Publisher's Prefix: 90-6194

de **Haan**, an imprint of Unieboek BV (qv)

Ten **Hagen** BV*, Prinsessegr 21, Postbus 34, 2501 AG The Hague Tel: (070) 924311 Telex: 33079
Subjects: Publications for trade and industry, especially for the building trade and architecture
Miscellaneous: Firm is a member of the Kluwer Group, Netherlands (qv)

De **Harmonie**, Postbus 3547, 1001 AH Amsterdam (Located at: Singel 390, Amsterdam) Tel: (020) 245181
Man Dir: Jaco Groot; *Rights & Permissions:* Dieneke Corvers
Subsidiary Company: Gaberbocchus Press
Subjects: Modern Dutch and International Literature, Illustrated Books, Juveniles, Humour
Founded: 1972
ISBN Publisher's Prefix: 90-6169

Harper & Row, Publishers, Noorderweg 68, 1221 AB Hilversum Tel: (035) 830635 Telex: 73174 Harow NL Fax: (035) 851673
Head Off: Harper & Row Inc, 10 East 53rd St, New York, NY 10022, USA
Miscellaneous: Above is the Harper & Row marketing office for Continental Europe (see UK for associate companies)

Uitgeverij ten **Have** NV, Prinses Marielaan 8, Postbus 1, 3740 AA Baarn Tel: (02154) 22144 Telex: beka-43272
Man Dir: Ton van der Worp
Subject: Religion
Founded: 1831
Miscellaneous: Firm is a member of the Combo Group, Netherlands (qv)
ISBN Publisher's Prefix: 90-259

Helmond, Zuiddijk 2a, Postbus 23, 5705 CS Helmond Tel: (04920) 39784 Telex: 51337
Man Dir: Dr M H J Hendriks
Subjects: How-to, Juveniles, Low- & High-priced Paperbacks, Reference
Founded: 1913
ISBN Publisher's Prefix: 90-252

Uitgeverij **Heuff** Nieuwkoop*, Postbus 5347X, 1380 GH Weesp (Located at: Hoogstr 20, 1381 VS Weesp) Tel: (02940) 18900 Cable Add: Heuff/Nieuwkoop
Man Dir: H Heuff
Subjects: Music, Art, History, Illustrated Books, Juveniles, Fiction
Founded: 1970
ISBN Publisher's Prefix: 90-6141

Uitgeverij **Heureka***, Postbus 5347, 1380 GH Weesp (Located at: Hoogstr 20, 1381 VS Weesp) Tel: (02940) 17912
Man Dir: F H B Cladder
Subjects: History (Political, Social & Cultural)
Founded: 1976
ISBN Publisher's Prefix: 90-6262

Gérard Th Van **Heusden** (APA), see Philo Press-Van Heusden-Hissink & Co CV (APA)

G W **Hissink** & Co (APA), see Philo Press-Van Heusden-Hissink & Co CV (APA)

Van **Holkema** en Warendorf, an imprint of Unieboek BV (qv)

Holland*, Spaarne 110, 2011 CM Haarlem Tel: (023) 323061
Man Dir: Rolf van Ulzen; *Sales Dir, Permissions:* Ruurt van Ulzen
Subjects: General Fiction, Belles Lettres, Poetry, Reference, Juveniles, High-priced Paperbacks, General Science
Founded: 1921
ISBN Publisher's Prefix: 90-251

Holland University Press BV (APA), Postbus 1850, 1000 BW Amsterdam
Orders to: APA, Postbus 122, 3600 AC Maarssen
Parent Company: APA (Academic Publishers Associated) (qv)
Subjects: Academic Books on the Humanities, European Studies
ISBN Publisher's Prefixes: 90-302, 90-6039

Uitgeverij **Hollandia** BV, Postbus 70, 3740 AB Baarn (Located at: Beukenlaan 20, 3741 BP Baarn) Tel: (02154) 18941 Cable Add: Hollandia, Baarn Telex: 43776 incom attn Hollandia
Man Dir: Tonnis Muntinga
Subjects: General Fiction, History, Nautical, Gardening, Travel
Founded: 1899
ISBN Publisher's Prefix: 90-6045

De **Horstink**, an imprint of Academische Uitgeverij Amersfoort BV (qv)

NETHERLANDS

NV I C U (Informatie en Communicatie Unie NV), now Wolters Kluwer NV

Stichting I V I O+, Schans 18-02, Postbus 37, 8200 AA Lelystad Tel: (03200) 26514
Manager: A L Greiner
Imprints: IVIO, AO, Wereldschool
Subject: Educational
Founded: 1936
ISBN Publisher's Prefix: 90-6121

Icob cv+, Postbus 392, 2400 AJ Alphen aan den Rijn (Located at: Ondernemingsweg 60, Alphen aan den Rijn) Tel: (01720) 37231 Telex: 39700 icob nl
Man Dir: Hans Meijer; *Editorial, Publicity:* Peter Albarda
Imprint: Atrium
Subjects: Art, Natural History, Reference, Illustrated
1985: 36 titles *1986:* 39 titles *Founded:* 1969
Miscellaneous: Also remainder dealer
ISBN Publisher's Prefix: 90-6113

Uitgeverij In den Toren, Prinses Marielaan 8, Postbus 1, 3740 AA Baarn Tel: (02154) 18241 Telex: 43272
Man Dir: Wim Hazeu
Subjects: History, Social Sciences, Politics
Miscellaneous: Firm is a member of the Combo Group (qv)

Infopers*, PO Box 41, 7940 AA Meppel (Located at: Zuideinde 18, 7941 GH Meppel) Tel: (05220) 70559 Telex: 42685
Man Dir: J P Giehtoorn; *Editorial:* H G Andriese
Parent Company: Drukkerij Giethoorn BV (at above address)
Imprints: Gamma, Promoboek
Subjects: Psychology, Psychomedicine, Dancing, Business, Periodicals
Founded: 1978 (Gamma), 1982 (Infopers)
ISBN Publisher's Prefixes: 90-6380 (Gamma), 90-6639 (Infopers)

Intermedium, a subsidiary of Uitgeversmaatschappij J H Kok BV (qv)

B M Israel BV, NZ Voorburgwal 264, 1012 RS Amsterdam Tel: (020) 247040
Cable Add: Isrealbook
General Manager: M Israel
Subjects: Reference, History of Medicine, Sciences, Arts
Bookshop: Boekhandel en Antiquariaat B M Israel BV (at above address)
ISBN Publisher's Prefix: 90-6078

Nico Israel*, Keizersgracht 489-91, 1017 DM Amsterdam Tel: (020) 222255 Cable Add: Ennibook Telex: 14070 ashni nl
Man Dir: Nico Israel
Associate Companies: A Asher en Co BV, Theatrum Orbis Terrarum (qqv)
Subjects: History, Reference, University Textbooks, Geography, Cartography, Bibliography, Travel, Periodicals
Founded: 1950
ISBN Publisher's Prefix: 90-6072

Jeugd Salamander, an imprint of Em Querido's Uitgeverij BV (qv)

Stichting De Jonge Onderzoekers, see Federatie DJO

Dr W Junk Publishers, Postbus 163, 3300 AD Dordrecht (Located at: Spuiboulevard 50, 3311 GR Dordrecht) Tel: (078) 334922 Telex: 29245
Man Dir: A Visser; *Publisher:* Wil R Peters
Orders to: Kluwer Academic Publishers Group, Distribution Centre, Postbus 322, 3300 AH Dordrecht
Subject: Biology
Founded: 1899

Miscellaneous: See also Martinus Nijhoff/Dr W Junk Publishers
ISBN Publisher's Prefix: 90-6193

K A I B, an imprint of Kluwer Algemene Informatieve Boeken BV (qv)

K B S, see Katholieke Bijbelstichting

Uitgeverij Kadmos, Postbus 174, 3990 DD Houten Tel: (03403) 78364 Telex: 40468 Fax: (03403) 77600
Chief Executive: H Verschoor; *Editorial, Sales, Production, Rights & Permissions:* A Groendijk; *Publicity:* H Middelburg
Parent Company: M & P Books, Schoutlaan 4, 6002 EA Weert
Associate Companies: M & P Books, Weert; De Boekerij, Amsterdam; Unieboek (qv)
Subjects: Fiction, Non-fiction
1985: 42 titles *1986:* 48 titles *Founded:* 1983
ISBN Publisher's Prefix: 90-6790

Katholieke Bijbelstichting, Baroniestr 43, Postbus 27, 5280 AA Boxtel Tel: (04116) 73537
Manager: A E van Wensen
Subjects: Religious literature on practical aspects of Catholic Bible work in the Netherlands and Belgium
1985: 6 titles *1986:* 6 titles

Keesing Uitgeversmaatschappij BV, Postbus 1118, 1000 BC Amsterdam (Located at: Hogehilweg 13, Amsterdam) Tel: (020) 5641111 Telex: 14641 Fax: (020) 970305
Chief Executive: P T Both; *Editorial:* Drs R Bos, Drs H Ulrich; *Sales:* Mrs H Meijer, Mrs W Woutersen, N van Zaane; *Production:* J Haveman
Parent Company: The International Keesing Organization, Van Nijenrodeweg 879, 1081 BG Amsterdam
Subsidiary Companies: Keesing Belgium, Keesinglaan 2-20, B-2100 Deurne Antwerp, Belgium (qv); Keesing France, Société Française d'Impression et d'Edition, 49 rue de Lisbonne, 75008 Paris, France; Keesing England, Puzzle Corner Ltd, Somers House, Linkfield Corner, Redhill, Surrey RH1 1BB, UK
Subjects: Assimil linguistic courses, Educational, General Fiction & Non-fiction
Founded: 1911 (Keesing Organization), 1976 (Keesing Publishers)
ISBN Publisher's Prefix: 90-6083

BV Uitgeverij De Kern+, Nassaulaan 10, Postbus 108, 3740 AC Baarn Tel: (02154) 17241 Telex: 73250 line nl ref 588 Fax: 2159 32127
Dirs: Joop Verweij, Jan van Willegen; *Editorial, Rights & Permissions:* Jan Van Willegen; *Sales:* Joop Verweij
Associate Companies: Bigot en Van Rossum BV, Uitgeverij Mingus BV (qqv, both at above address)
Subjects: General Fiction, Popular Non-fiction
1985: 25 titles *1986:* 24 titles *Founded:* 1977
ISBN Publisher's Prefix: 90-325

Uitgeverij Kluitman Alkmaar BV, Postbus 231, 1700 AE Heerhugowaard (Located at: Kelvinstr 20, Heerhugowaard) Tel: (02207) 17326
Dirs: Drs P F A Stanco, Mrs H Stanco-Gerla
Subject: Juveniles
Founded: 1864
ISBN Publisher's Prefix: 90-206

Kluwer Algemene Boeken BV+, Postbus 235, 6710 BE Ede (Located at: Het Huis Kernhem, Kernhemseweg 7, 6718 ZB Ede) Tel: (08380) 19031 Cable Add: ZKede Telex: 37095 ZKede Fax: (08380) 19031
Man Dir: P I A P M Zwaga; *Sales:* J J J Schoen; *Chief Editor:* G L M Vlaskamp; *Permissions:* Judith Verberne
Subjects: How-to, General Science, Atlases, Reference
Founded: 1970
ISBN Publisher's Prefix: 90-6117

Kluwer Algemene Informatieve Boeken BV*, Postbus 449, 3500 AK Utrecht (Located at: Savannahweg 60, 3542 AW Utrecht) Tel: (030) 434944 Telex: 70729 Oency nl
General Manager: Dick Kok
Imprint: KAIB
Subjects: General Reference
Founded: 1981
Miscellaneous: Firm is a member of the Kluwer Group (qv)
ISBN Publisher's Prefixes: 90-6046, 90-6158

Kluwer Bedrijfswetenschappen, Postbus 23, 7400 GA Deventer Tel: (05700) 20577 Telex: 49774
Publisher: Albert Langevoort
Subjects: Business, Economics, Periodicals
Miscellaneous: Firm is a member of the Kluwer Group (qv)
ISBN Publisher's Prefix: 90-267

Kluwer Group, Postbus 23, 7400 GA Deventer (Located at: Binnensingel 3, Deventer) Tel: (05700) 48111 Telex: 49660
Man Dirs: J J C Alberdingk Thijm, P D Zuiderveld, J Somerwil, Drs R Pieterse
Divisional Dirs: F W B van Humalda van Eysinga (Academic), A Th A Drabbe (Business & Professional), M J van Dalen (Educational), C H van Kempen (Law & Taxation), J Bommer (Technical), A van Beck (Retail Bookselling), B Scheepmaker (Printing)
Associate Company: Wolters Kluwer NV (qv)
Members of the Kluwer Group in the Netherlands: Publishing Houses: Bert Bakker (qv); Bohn, Scheltema en Holkema (qv); Uitgeversmij Born (qv); Uitgeverij Contact (qv); Van Dale Lexicografie (qv); Educaboek (qv); Uitgeverij FED; Gouda Quint (qv); Ten Hagen (qv); Instituut voor Bedrijfswetenschappen; International Journals Group Holland; Kluwer Algemene Informatieve Boeken (qv); Kluwers Courantenbedrijf; Kluwer Law and Taxation Publishers (Kluwer Fiscaal-Juridisch) (qv); Kluwer Bedrijfswetenschappen (qv); Kluwer Technische Boeken (qv); Kluwer Technische Tijdschriften; Kluwerpers; Uitgeverij Kosmos (qv); Libresso; Van Loghum Slaterus (qv); Uitgeverij Luitingh (qv); NBD Product-Information Systems; Novapres; Martinus Nijhoff/Dr W Junk Publishers (qv); Novi; Oosthoek (qv); Uitgeverij Reidel (qv); De Ruiter-Gorinchem; Schoolpers (qv); Uitgeverij Skarabee; Stam/Robijns; Stam Technische Boeken; Stam Tijdschriften; H E Stenfert Kroese; W E J Tjeenk Willink (qv); Vastgoedmarkt; Uitgeverij Veen/Reflex & Uitgeverij L J Veen (qv); Zomer en Keuning Boeken (qv); Printers: Drukkerij De Lange an Leer; Drukkerij Salland; Drukkerij Tulp
Members outside the Netherlands: Australasian Educa Press Pty Ltd (AE Press), Australia (qv); Heideland-Orbis (NV M en I) (qv), NV Uitgeverij Kluwer (qv), Uitgeverij Plantyn (qv), E Story-Scientia (NV M en I) (qv), Wetenschappelijke Uitgevers Groep (all in Belgium); Editions André Casteilla SA (qv), Educalivre, Istra (all in France); Kommentator Verlag (qv), Hermann

Luchterhand Verlag (qv), Alfred Metzner Verlag (qv), J Schweitzer Verlag (qv), Verlag H Stam, Thalhammer Verlag GmbH (all in Federal Republic of Germany); Kluwer Curaçaó NV, De Curaçaosche Courant NV (both in Netherlands Antilles); Graham & Trotman Ltd (qv), Kluwer Publishing Ltd (qv), L Van Leer & Co Ltd, MTP Press (qv), Stanley Thornes & Hulton (Publishers) Ltd (qv), (all in UK); Kluwer Boston Inc, Kluwer Law Book Publishers Inc (New York), Kluwer USA Inc (Hingham, MA), Martinus Nijhoff (Boston), Martinus Nijhoff Booksellers and Subscription Agents (Boston), Josephson/Kluwer Legal Educational Centers (Los Angeles, CA), Services Rating Organization (Birmingham, MI), Accountline Financial Services (Philadelphia) (all in USA)
Subjects: Law and Taxation, Academic Publications in various fields, Educational, Technical, Encyclopaedias, Trade Books and Magazines, Graphic Industries, Newspapers and Periodicals
Bookshops: Boekhandel Broese Kemink, Utrecht; Dekker en Van de Vegt, Nijmegen; De Gelderse Boekhandel, Arnhem; Boekhandel Gianotten, Tilburg — Breda; Martinus Nijhoff, The Hague; Boekhandel Praamstra, Deventer; Scheltema Holkema Vermeulen, Amsterdam — Haarlem; Stamboekhandel, Eindhoven — Venlo; Studieboekencentrale, Ede/Zoetermeer Verwijs & Stam, The Hague; Wetenschappelijke Boekhandel Rotterdam, Rotterdam
Founded: 1889
ISBN Publisher's Prefixes: 90-6117 (Kluwer NV), 90-207 (Stenfert-Kroese) (prefixes for other Group members are given under individual entries)

Kluwer Law and Taxation Publishers, Staverenstr 15, Postbus 23, 7400 GA Deventer Tel: (05700) 91911 Telex: 49295
Publisher and Chief Executive: Daniel Bos; *Marketing Director:* Marcel Nieuwenhuis
Subjects: International Business Law and Taxation, Labour Law and Industrial Relations, Social Security, European Law, Real Estate Law, Maritime/Transport/Air Law
Branch Offs: Antwerp, Brussels, Frankfurt, London, Boston, New York
Miscellaneous: Firm is a member of the Kluwer Group (qv)
ISBN Publisher's Prefixes: 90-268, 90-200, 90-312, 90-654

Kluwer Technische Boeken BV*, Brink 25, Postbus 23, 7411 BS Deventer Tel: (05700) 91911 Telex: 49560 klutb nl
Man Dir: Noud H L van Herk; *Editorial:* Benno van Lochem; *Foreign Rights:* Oeble Hoekstra; *Sales:* Noud H L van Herk; *Production:* Dick Laus
Subsidiary Company: Kluwer Technische Boeken, Santvoortbeeklaan 21-23, Deurne, Belgium
Subjects: Electronics, Motor Engineering, Hobbies, Do-it-yourself, Engineering, Building, Dictionaries, Photography
Miscellaneous: Firm is a member of the Kluwer Group (qv)
ISBN Publisher's Prefix: 90-2010

Kluwerpers, a member of the Kluwer Group (qv)

F **Knuf** Publishers, Postbus 720, 4116 ZJ Buren Tel: (03447) 1691
Subjects: Musicology and Musical Theory, Biography and Musical History, Periodicals
ISBN Publisher's Prefix: 90-6027

Uitgeversmaatschappij J H **Kok** BV+, Gildestr 5, 8263 AH Kampen Tel: (05202) 92555 Cable Add: Kok Kampen Telex: 42721 jh kok nl
Man Dir: W E Steunenberg; *Assistant Man Dirs:* A C Van Dam, B A Endedijk; *Editorial:* E K Klement, J van Beusekom, J J Weggemans, A R T de Vos, R Posthuma, H Bouma; *Rights & Permissions:* G Brinkman; *Educational:* R H Ipenburg
Subsidiary Companies: De Groot Goudriaan, Kampen; Intermedium, Kampen; Kok Agora, Kampen; Uitgeverij Omniboek, The Hague; J N Voorhoeve, The Hague; La Rivière en Voorhoeve, Kampen
Subjects: General Fiction, Belles Lettres, Poetry, Biography, History, How-to, Art Philosophy, Religion, Textbooks, Educational Materials, Reference, Juveniles, Psychology, Sociology, General & Social Science, Low- & High-priced Paperbacks, Alternative Medicine, Nature, Hobbies & Crafts, Calendars
Book Club: VCL (series of novels)
1985: about 500 titles *1986:* about 520 titles *Founded:* 1894
ISBN Publisher's Prefixes: 90-242 (Kok), 90-6140 (De Groot), 90-6536 (Intermedium), 90-6207 (Omniboek), 90-297 (Voorhoeve), 90-6084 (La Rivière en Voorhoeve)

Kok Agora, a subsidiary of Uitgeversmaatschappij J H Kok BV (qv)

Kosmos BV, Oudegracht 134-136, Postbus 14095, 3508 SC Utrecht Tel: (030) 345211 Telex: 70684 Luve
Man Dir: Bert de Groot; *Editorial:* J Meerman
Subjects: Natural History, Pets, Travel, Sport, Health, Cookery, Occult, Reference
Miscellaneous: Children's books now with Bert Bakker BV (qv). Kosmos BV is a member of the Kluwer Group (qv)

Kramers, an imprint of Elsevier Boeken BV (qv)

Kugler Publications BV, Postbus 516, 1180 AM Amstelveen (Located at: Prinsengracht 573, Amsterdam) Tel: (03120) 278070 Telex: 18180 Simon nl Fax: (03120) 380524
Man Dir: Simon Kugler
Subjects: Medical, Criminology, Biology
ISBN Publisher's Prefix: 90-6299

La Rivière en Voorhoeve, a subsidiary of Uitgeversmaatschappij J H Kok BV (qv)

Boekhandel en Uitgeverij **Laetitia***, Postbus 81078, 3009 GB Rotterdam (Located at: Tjonger 13, Rotterdam, Zevenkamp) Tel: (010) 216231
Man Dir: Nettie Essed; *Sales:* Dr W R W Donner
Parent Company: Essed Enterprises, 36A Schietbaanlaan, Rotterdam
Subsidiary Company: Steven Press, Zoetermeer
Subjects: Fiction, Children's, College Textbooks, Third World Literature especially Suriname and Netherlands Antilles
Bookshop: At above address
Founded: 1976
ISBN Publisher's Prefix: 90-6543

Allert de **Lange** BV*, Damrak 62, 1012 LM Amsterdam Tel: (020) 227363
Publicity: R D de Ruiter

Uitgeverij **Lannoo***, Nieuwe 's-Gravelandseweg 17, Postbus 17, 1400 AA Bussum Tel: (02159) 34241 Telex: 43064
Subjects: Travel, Children's, Religious, Poetry, Art, Paperbacks, Education, Psychology, Sports, Games
ISBN Publisher's Prefix: 90-209

Leiden University Press, c/o Postbus 9000, 2300 PA Leiden (Located at: Plantijnstr 2, 2321 JC Leiden) Tel: (071) 312624 Telex: 39296 Cable Add: Brill Leiden
Subjects: History, Languages, Law, Social Sciences, Biology, Philosophy
ISBN Publisher's Prefix: 90-9004

Lemniscaat+, Vijverlaan 48, Postbus 4066, 3006 AB Rotterdam Tel: (010) 4141744 Cable Add: Lemniscaat Rotterdam
Dirs: J C Boele van Hensbroek, Dr Marijke Boele van Hensbroek-Reesink, Bob Markus; *Editor:* Engelien Scholtes; *Rights & Permissions:* Susanne Padberg
Subjects: Juveniles, Picture Books, Psychology, Social Science
1985: 23 titles *1986:* 28 titles *Founded:* 1963
ISBN Publisher's Prefix: 90-6069

Uitgeverij **Leopold** BV*, Badhuisweg 232, 2564 CD The Hague Tel: (070) 512711
Man Dir: Liesbeth ten Houten; *Permissions:* Jacolien Kingmans
Parent Company: Nijgh en Van Ditmar NV (qv)
Subjects: General Fiction, Juveniles, High-priced Paperbacks
Founded: 1923
ISBN Publisher's Prefix: 90-258

Libra, an imprint of Uitgeverij Ambo BV (qv)

Littera Scripta Manet, Rijsseltweg 10, 7211 EP Eefde (Gorssel) Tel: (05759) 1950
Man Dir: A Rutgers; *Editorial:* Mrs R L Rutgers-Schiff; *Other Offices:* A Rutgers
Subjects: General Science, Ornithology
Bookshop: International Hobby-Bookshop, Gorssel
Founded: 1947
ISBN Publisher's Prefix: 90-6036

Van **Loghum** Slaterus, Geert Grootestr 4, Postbus 23, 7400 GA Deventer Tel: (05700) 10811 Telex: 49295
Publisher: Drs J Mulder
Subjects: Humanities, Public Health, Education, Psychology, Social Science, Linguistics, Languages, Periodicals
Miscellaneous: Firm is a member of the Kluwer Group (qv)
1985: 45 titles *1986:* 40 titles
ISBN Publisher's Prefix: 90-6001

Luctor Publishing — Stadler en Sauerbier BV*, Weegbreestr 11, Postbus 33017, NL-3012 Rotterdam Tel: (010) 180081 Cable Add: Sensoffset Telex: 23411
Subjects: Juveniles, Educational

Uitgeverij **Luitingh** BV, Oudegracht 134-136, Postbus 14095, 3508 SC Utrecht Tel: (030) 349211 Telex: 70684 Luve
Man Dir: A de Groot
Subsidiary Companies: Novapres BV; Uitgeverij Skarabee BV
Subjects: General Fiction and Non-fiction, Low- & High-priced Paperbacks
Founded: 1946
Miscellaneous: Firm is a member of the Kluwer Group (qv)
ISBN Publisher's Prefixes: 90-245 (Luitingh), 90-6071 (Skarabee)

Otto **Maier** Benelux BV*, Heliumweg 16, Amersfoort Tel: (03490) 11445 Telex: 47991
Parent Company: Ravensburger Buchverlag, Otto Maier GmbH, Federal Republic of Germany (qv)
Subjects: Architecture, Hobbies, Juveniles, Non-fiction

L C G **Malmberg** BV, Leeghwaterlaan 16, 5233 BA 's-Hertogenbosch Tel: (073) 215565 Cable Add: Malmberg

's-Hertogenbosch Telex: 50058 Fax: (073) 210512
General Manager: K van der Pas; *Publisher:* Dr J V Velthoven
Subjects: Pre-school, Primary & Secondary Textbooks, Educational Materials, Educational Juveniles, Teaching Equipment for Physics, Chemistry and Biology, Educational Software and Hardware
Founded: 1885
Miscellaneous: Firm is a part of Educational Book Publishing division of VNU BV (qv)
ISBN Publisher's Prefix: 90-208

Manteau, an imprint of Elsevier Boeken BV (qv)

Meinema/Waltman*, Hippolytusbuurt 4, Postbus 3150, Delft Tel: (015) 125915
Subject: Textbooks

Meulenhoff Educatief BV+*, Postbus 100, 1000 AC Amsterdam (Located at: Herengracht 507, 1017 BV Amsterdam) Tel: (020) 235707 Cable Add: Manuscript Telex: 16234
Man Dirs: D van Foeken, Cl W Suermondt, AC van Hoek, M A Nouwen; *Editorial:* T A vd Veen, W ten Oever, T Scheffer
Parent Company: Meulenhoff en Co BV (at above address)
Associate Companies: Meulenhoff Informatief, Meulenhoff International, Meulenhoff Nederland BV (qqv), Meulenhoff/Landshoff, European Book Service
Subjects: Educational Materials, Textbooks
ISBN Publisher's Prefix: 90-280

Meulenhoff Informatief+*, Postbus 100, 1000 AC Amsterdam (Located at: Herengracht 507, 1017 BV Amsterdam) Tel: (020) 235707 Cable Add: Manuscript Telex: 16234
Editorial Dir: Mrs E van Unen
Parent Company: Meulenhoff en Co BV (at above address)
Associate Companies: Meulenhoff Educatief BV, Meulenhoff International, Meulenhoff Nederland BV (qqv)
Subjects: Informative Non-fiction, Reference, Children's
ISBN Publisher's Prefix: 90-290

Meulenhoff International*, Postbus 100, 1000 AC Amsterdam (Located at: Herengracht 507, 1017 BV Amsterdam) Tel: (020) 267555 Cable Add: Intart Telex: 16234
Man Dirs: L van Krevelen, A Voster; *Editors:* R van de Griend, A Snijder; *Production:* I Hillen
Parent Company: Meulenhoff en Co BV (at above address)
Associate Companies: Meulenhoff Educatief BV, Meulenhoff Informatief, Meulenhoff Nederland BV (qqv), Meulenhoff/Landshoff
Subjects: Co-productions, General Non-fiction, Art
Miscellaneous: Firm's main activity is selling co-productions internationally

Meulenhoff Nederland BV, Postbus 100, 1000 AC Amsterdam (Located at: Herengracht 507, 1017 BV Amsterdam) Tel: (020) 267555 Cable Add: Manuscript Telex: 16234
Man Dir: Laurens van Krevelen; *Editorial:* Maarten Asscher, Tilly Hermans, Wouter Donath Tieges; *Production:* Ineke Hillen; *Rights & Permissions:* Maarten Asscher
Parent Company: Meulenhoff en Co BV (at above address)
Associate Companies: Meulenhoff Educatief BV, Meulenhoff International, Meulenhoff Informatief (qqv), Meulenhoff/Landshoff

Subjects: Dutch and translated foreign literature, Science Fiction, Non-fiction
Founded: 1895
ISBN Publisher's Prefix: 90-290

Miland Publishers, Zuideinde 40, Postbus 6, 2420 AA Nieuwkoop
Parent Company: De Graaf Publishers (qv)
ISBN Publisher's Prefix: 90-6003

Uitgeverij **Mingus** BV+, Postbus 108, 3740 AC Baarn Tel: (02154) 17241 Telex: 73250 line nl ref 588 Fax: (02159) 32127
Chief Executives: Joop Verweij, Jan van Willegen; *Editorial:* Teus Verweij, Jan van Willegen; *Sales:* Joop Verweij; *Rights & Permissions:* Jan van Willegen
Associate Companies: BV Uitgeverij De Kern, Uitgeverij Bigot en Van Rossum BV (qqv, both at above address)
Subjects: General non-fiction
1985: 16 titles *1986:* 16 titles *Founded:* 1981
ISBN Publisher's Prefix: 90-6564

Mirananda Publishers BV+, Postbus 93157, 2509 AD The Hague (Located at: Laan van Nieuw Oost Indië 262, 2593 CE The Hague) Tel: (070) 835408
Man Dir: Manda Plettenburg
Orders to: Centraal Boekhuis, Erasmusweg 10, Culemborg
Subjects: Art (Western and Oriental), Religion, Mysticism, Yoga, Theosophy, Astrology, Popular Science, Psychology, Philosophy, Quality Paperbacks, Linguistics, Education, Literature
1985: 18 titles *Founded:* 1976
ISBN Publisher's Prefix: 90-6271

Mondria Publishers, Postbus 67, 2390 AB Hazerswoude-dorp Tel: 1728-8841 Telex: 26401 Intx NL att Mondria
Chief Executive, Sales, Publicity: Drs Henk R Mondria; *Editorial, Production, Rights & Permissions:* Mrs J Kieboom
Subjects: Humour, Cartoonbooks
1985: 25 titles *1986:* 36 titles *Founded:* 1980
ISBN Publisher's Prefix: 90-6555

Mouton Publishers, now in the Federal Republic of Germany (qv)

De **Muiderkring** BV, Hogeweyselaan 227, Postbus 370, 1380 AH Weesp Tel: (02159) 31851 Telex: 15171
Man Dir: C Both; *Sales:* B Hofman
Subjects: Electronics, Computers, Hobbies

Mulder Holland BV+, Postbus 8064, 1005 AB Amsterdam (Located at: Transformatorweg 35, 1014 AJ Amsterdam) Tel: (020) 824805 Cable Add: Emzet Amsterdam Telex: 14627 Fax: (020) 860177
Publisher: John Winkel
Parent Company: Internatio Müller
Subject: Juveniles

Uitgeverij Maarten **Muntinga**, Postbus 7262, Brahmsstr 24, 1007 JG Amsterdam Tel: (020) 719770/735160 Telex: 43776 Inco NL att 16509
Imprint: Rainbow Pocketboeken
ISBN Publisher's Prefix: 90-6766

Muusses, Van IJsendijkstr 154, Postbus 13, 1440 AA Purmerend Tel: (02990) 33151
Man Dirs: B Haisma, Drs D T Visser
Subjects: Primary, Secondary and Vocational Educational
Founded: 1872
ISBN Publisher's Prefixes: 90-231, 90-6970

Uitgeverij **N I B**, Postbus 144, 3700 AC Zeist (Located at: Wilhelminalaan 7, Zeist) Tel: (03404) 21624
Dir: Dr H C van Hummel; *Editorial:* A J W Boks; *Publicity:* A Meyer

Subjects: Secondary Textbooks (Chemistry, Biology, Modern Languages, History, Physics, Mathematics, Science Education, Computer Literacy, Educational Software)
ISBN Publisher's Prefix: 90-275

Nederlandsche Zondagsschool Vereeniging*, Bloemgracht 65, 1016 KG Amsterdam Tel: (020) 239121
Subjects: Religion, Juveniles, Games

Uitgeverij H **Nelissen** BV+*, Parkstr 47, 3743 ED Baarn Tel: (02154) 12386
Man Dir, Editorial, Permissions: R M M Nelissen; *Sales, Publicity, Production:* Dick Boer
Subjects: Religion, Sociology, Politics, Education, Philosophy, Social Sciences, Textbooks
1985: 31 titles *Founded:* 1922
ISBN Publisher's Prefix: 90-244

Nieuwe Stad*, St Stephanusstr 11, Nijmegen
Parent Company: Città Nuova Editrice, Italy (qv for associate companies)

Nieuwe Wieken, an imprint of Omega Boek BV (qv)

NV Uitgeverij **Nijgh en Van Ditmar***, Badhuisweg 232, 2564 CD The Hague Tel: (070) 512711
Man Dir: A J J Siebelink; *Editorial:* N D Dekker, A E Blatter, J D M Mulder; *Permissions:* Ms L ten Houten
Subsidiary Companies: Uitgeverij Leopold BV, Rotterdam University Press (qqv)
Subjects: General Fiction, Belles Lettres, Poetry, Biography, History, Juveniles, High-priced Paperbacks, Engineering, Secondary Textbooks, Home Economics
Founded: 1837
ISBN Publisher's Prefix: 90-236

Martinus **Nijhoff**/Dr W Junk Publishers, Spuiboulevard 50, 3311 GR Dordrecht Tel: (078) 334922 Telex: 29245 Fax: (078) 334254
Dir: A Visser; *Production:* Dieke van Wijnen
Orders to: Kluwer Academic Publishers Group, Distribution Centre, Postbus 322, 3300 AH Dordrecht
Branch Offs: MTP Press, UK (qv); Kluwer Academic Publishers, 101 Philip Drive, Assinipi Park, Norwell, MA 02061, USA
Subjects: Philosophy, Religion, Textbooks, Reference, Psychology, Social Science, Medicine, Applied Sciences, Veterinary Sciences, Agriculture, International Law/Relations/Politics, Economics, Forestry, Biology, Entomology, Ecology, Engineering, Biotechnology
Bookshop: See under Major Booksellers
Founded: 1853
Miscellaneous: Firm is a member of the Kluwer Group (qv). See also Dr W Junk, Publishers
ISBN Publisher's Prefix: 90-247

BV **Noord-Hollandsche** Uitgeversmaatschappij, a division of Elsevier Science Publishers BV (qv)

Noordhoff International Publishing, see Sijthoff en Noordhoff International Publishers

Noorduijn BV, Postbus 1148, 6801 MK Arnhem (Located at: Willemsplein 2, Arnhem) Tel: (085) 454762
Man Dir: K H Mulder
Subjects: Law and Taxation
Founded: 1819
ISBN Publisher's Prefix: 90-203

North Holland, an imprint of Elsevier Science Publishers BV (qv)

Novapres BV, a subsidiary of Uitgeverij Luitingh BV (qv)

Omega Boek BV*, Postbus 20072, 1000 HB Amsterdam (Located at: Sarphatistr 13, 1017 WS Amsterdam) Tel: (020) 231969/245284
Orders to: Centraal Boekhuis, Erasmusweg 10, Culemborg
Imprints: De Centaur, Nieuwe Wieken, Triton Pers, Omega Jeugdboekerij
Subjects: General Fiction and Non-fiction, War Stories, Thrillers, Art, Children's Books, Gift Books
Founded: 1968
ISBN Publisher's Prefixes: 90-6057, 90-6142

Uitgeverij **Omniboek**, a subsidiary of Uitgeversmaatschappij J H Kok BV (qv)

Oosthoek*, Savannahweg 60, Utrecht Tel: (030) 434944 Telex: 70729
Man Dir: F Mertens
Subjects: Encyclopaedias, Reference books
Miscellaneous: Firm is a member of the Kluwer Group (qv)
ISBN Publisher's Prefix: 90-6046

Orbit BV, a subsidiary of Theatrum Orbis Terrarum (qv)

Oriental Press BV (APA), Postbus 1850, 1000 BW Amsterdam
Orders to: APA, Postbus 122, 3600 AC Maarssen
Parent Company: APA (Academic Publishers Associated) (qv)
Subjects: Oriental Studies, Text editions
ISBN Publisher's Prefix: 90-6023

Pandora Pockets, an imprint of Bruna Pockethuis BV (qv)

Philo Press-Van Heusden-Hissink & Co CV (APA), Postbus 1850, 1000 BW Amsterdam
Orders to: APA, Postbus 122, 3600 AC Maarssen
Parent Company: APA (Academic Publishers Associated) (qv)
Subjects: Academic (Arts and Humanities, History of Sciences, Oriental Studies)
Miscellaneous: Firm incorporates Gérard Th Van Heusden (APA) and G W Hissink & Co (APA)
ISBN Publisher's Prefixes: 90-6022, 90-6024, 90-6025

Uitgeverij **Ploegsma***, Postbus 19857, 1000 GW Amsterdam (Located at: Keizersgracht 616, 1017 ER Amsterdam) Tel: (020) 262907
Man Dir: Paul Brinkman
Subjects: Children's books, Juveniles, How-to, Natural Science, Handicraft, Leisure
ISBN Publisher's Prefix: 90-216

Polak en Van Gennep Uitg Mij BV*, Reguliersgracht 50, 1017 LT Amsterdam Tel: (020) 226288
Man Dir: B M Hosman
Subjects: Scientific Literature, General Literature
Founded: 1964
ISBN Publisher's Prefix: 90-253

Promoboek, an imprint of Infopers (qv)

Pudoc, Centre for Agricultural Publishing and Documentation, Gen Foulkesweg 19, Postbus 4, 6700 AA Wageningen Tel: (08370) 89222 Telex: 45015
Man Dir: J M Schippers; *Sales Manager:* J Vermeulen
Subjects: Natural Science, Agriculture
Founded: 1957
ISBN Publisher's Prefix: 90-220

Em **Querido's** Uitgeverij BV, Singel 262, 1016 AC Amsterdam Tel: (020) 237195
Man Dir: Ary T Langbroek
Associate Company: Uitgeverij De Arbeiderspers BV (qv)
Imprints: Griffioen Paperbacks, Jeugd Salamander Paperbacks, Salamander Paperbacks, De Viergang
Subjects: General Fiction, Belles Lettres, Poetry, Biography, History, Music, Art, Juveniles, Low-priced Paperbacks
Founded: 1915
ISBN Publisher's Prefix: 90-214

Rainbow Pocketboeken, an imprint of Uitgeverij Maarten Muntinga (qv)

D **Reidel** Publishing Co, Postbus 17, Dordrecht (Located at: Spuiblvd 50, Dordrecht) Tel: (078) 334911 Cable Add: Reipubco Telex: 29245
Man Dir: J F Hattink; *Publishers:* D Larner (Mathematical Physical Sciences), Janjaar Blom (Chemical Sciences), Roger Cooper (Earth & Environmental Sciences), G Kier (Astronomy), M Scrivener (Humanities, Social Sciences), Derek Middleton (Computer Sciences); *Promotion Managers:* A van't Hart, M Siegan (Sciences), E van Steenderen (Humanities, Social Sciences), Bob Donegan (Humanities — North America), Christine Nagele (Sciences — North America); *Production:* R Doornebal; *Permissions:* N de Boer
Subsidiary Company: D Reidel, 101 Philip Drive, Assinippi Park, Norwell, MA 02061, USA
Branch Off (editorial): 307 Shibuyadai-haim, 4-17 Sakuragaoka-cho, Shibuya, Tokyo, Japan Tel: (03) 4968791
Subjects: Philosophy, Humanities, Linguistics, Mathematics, Astronomy, Chemistry, Environmental and Earth Sciences, Energy, Periodicals
1985: 180 titles *1986:* 200 titles *1987:* 215 titles
Miscellaneous: Firm is a member of the Kluwer Group (qv)
ISBN Publisher's Prefix: 90-277

Editions **Rodopi** BV, Keizersgracht 302-304, 1016 EX Amsterdam Tel: (020) 227507
Dir: Fred van der Zee
Subjects: History, Philosophy, Religion, Languages and Literature, Classical Antiquity, History of Medicine & Natural Sciences
Founded: 1966
ISBN Publisher's Prefix: 90-6203

Rostrum Publishing, Postbus 594, 2003 RN Haarlem Tel: (023) 315507 Telex: 71178 Fax: (023) 325749
Chief Executive: Robert Hofman; *Editorial:* Marja Geevers (Film); *Sales:* Laura Smith; *Production:* Ellen Pardede; *Publicity:* Eleonore Hofman; *Rights & Permissions:* Robert Hofman
Subjects: Film, Fitness, General Non-fiction
1985: 20 titles *1986:* 20 titles *Founded:* 1975
ISBN Publisher's Prefix: 90-328

Rotterdam University Press, Badhuisweg 232, 2597 JS The Hague Tel: (070) 512711 Telex: 31517 Nijgh nl
Man Dirs: N D Dekker, W J Oerlemans
Parent Company: BV Uitgeverij Nijgh en Van Ditmar (qv)
Subjects: Economics, Development Planning, Social Science, University Textbooks
Founded: 1964
ISBN Publisher's Prefix: 0-90237

S M D Educatieve Uitgevers (Spruyt, Van Mantgem en De Does), Postbus 63, 2300 AB Leiden (Located at: Langebrug 87, 2311 TJ Leiden) Tel: (071) 146541
Subjects: Medical, Educational, Technical
Founded: 1907
ISBN Publisher's Prefix: 90-238

Uitgeverij **S U N***, Bijleveldsingel 9, 6521 AM Nijmegen Tel: (080) 221700
Publicity, Permissions: Wilfried Uitterhoeve
Imprint: Uitgeverij Dwarsstap
Subjects: Culture, Philosophy, History, Architecture, Periodicals
Founded: 1969
ISBN Publisher's Prefix: 90-6168

Salamander Paperbacks, an imprint of Em Querido's Uitgeverij BV (qv)

Samsom Stafleu, Postbus 4, 2400 MA Alphen aan den Rijn (Located at: Stadhoudersplein 1, 2404 BE Alphen aan den Rijn) Tel: (01720) 62054 Cable Add: Stafleu Publishers Alphen aan den Rijn Telex: 39682
Publisher: H R Schlick
Subjects: Medicine, Nursing, Dental Science
Founded: 1947
Miscellaneous: Firm is an imprint of Samsom Uitgeverij BV (qv)
ISBN Publisher's Prefixes: 90-6016, 90-6065

Samsom Uitgeverij BV, Postbus 4, 2400 MA Alphen aan den Rijn (Located at: Stadhoudersplein 1, 2404 BE Alphen aan den Rijn) Tel: (01720) 62324 Cable Add: Samsom Alphenrijn Telex: 39682 Fax: (01720) 62044
Man Dir: P C Minderhout; *Dirs:* Dr A de Ruiter, H J Demoet, C J Steur; *Publishing Dirs:* C L Stafleu, W van Zanten; *Rights & Permissions:* C L Stafleu
Parent Company: Wolters Kluwer NV (qv for associate companies)
Imprints: Samsom Stafleu (qv), Samsom H D Tjeenk Willink
Subjects: Business, Fiscal Law, Management, Textbooks, Social Science, Finance, Computer Science, Administration, Public Health, Medical, Nursing, Sales Management, Dental, Sports, Informatics, Public Administration
Founded: 1882
ISBN Publisher's Prefixes: 90-14 (Samsom), 90-6092 (Samsom Tjeenk Willink)

Feministische Uitgeverij **Sara**, Keizersgracht 231, 1016 DV Amsterdam Tel: (020) 262520
Editorial: Mirre Bots; *Publicity, Rights & Permissions:* Connie Boekhout
Subjects: Feminism, Biography, History, Literature, Psychology, Education, Practical, Photobooks (all written, illustrated and published exclusively by women)
1985: 30 titles *Founded:* 1977
ISBN Publisher's Prefix: 90-6328

Schoolpers*, PO Box 48, 4100 AA Culemborg Tel: (03450) 71911
Chairman: P D Zuiderveld; *Man Dir:* J Th Timmer; *Production & Sales:* Educaboek BV (qv)
Subject: Textbooks
Miscellaneous: Firm is a member of the Kluwer Group (qv)

Schuyt en Co CV*, Postbus 563, 2003 RN Haarlem (Located at: Gedempte Oude Gracht 35, 2011 GL Haarlem) Tel: (023) 325440 Telex: 41532 sco nl
General Manager: K C Schuyt; *Sales:* W G Kok; *Publisher:* F Poiesz
Subsidiary Company: Schuyt en Co NV, Hansahuis, Suikerrui 5, 2000 Antwerp, Belgium
Subjects: Art, History, Railways, Geography, Business, Cooking
Founded: 1952
ISBN Publisher's Prefix: 90-6097

Uitgeverij Gary **Schwartz***, Herengracht 22, Postbus 162, 3600 AD

Maarssen Tel: (03465) 62778
Dir & other offices: Gary Schwartz
Subjects: Fine Art Books
1985: 4 titles *Founded:* 1972
ISBN Publisher's Prefix: 90-6179

Semic Juniorpress BV, Zwartweg 6, 1412 GD Naarden Telex: 4473114 cacjp nl
Man Dir: Guillermo Hierro
Parent Company: Semic International AB, Sweden (qv)
Subjects: Comic Magazines, Colouring Books, Albums, Pocketbooks

Septuaginta BV Uitgeverij, now known as Icob cv (qv)

Servire BV Uitgevers, Secr Varkevisserstr 52, 2225 LE Katwijk aan Zee Tel: (01718) 16741
Chief Executive: Felix Erkelens
Associate Company: Hunter House Inc, Publishers, 748 East Bonita Ave, Suite 105, Pomona, CA 91767, USA
Subjects: Books in Dutch, English on Human Endeavour and Creativity, Mysticism, Alternative Living, Education, Psychology
Founded: 1921
Miscellaneous: Also Literary Agent (qv)
ISBN Publisher's Prefixes: 90-6077, 90-6325

A W Sijthoff's Uitgeversmaatschappij BV, Postbus 5217, 1007 AE Amsterdam Tel: (020) 793227 Cable Add: Shoff Telex: 10493
Dir: Frans Pruyt; *Editor-in-chief:* Hanca Leppink
Parent Company: Wolters Kluwer NV (qv for associate companies)
Subjects: General Non-fiction and Fiction
Founded: 1851
ISBN Publisher's Prefix: 90-218

Uitgeverij **Skarabee** BV, a subsidiary of Uitgeverij Luitingh BV (qv)

Smeets Illustrated Projects*, Molenveldstr 90, Postbus 17, 6001 HL Weert Tel: (04950) 70911 Telex: 37550
Manager: V Pokorny
Parent Company: Royal Smeets Offset
Subjects: Art, Illustrated Books

Uitgeverij Het **Spectrum** BV, Park Voorn 4, 3454 JR De Meern Tel: (03406) 63737 Cable Add: Het Spectrum BV, De Meern Telex: 47677 Fax: (03406) 63965
Dirs: Joost C Bloemsma, R Emmelkamp, Jan van den Heuvel; *Editorial:* Martin Appelman, Amy Bais, Joke Meijer, George Pape, Bart Drubbel; *Sales:* Ivonne Koolen; *Production:* Ludger van Zwetszelaar; *Publicity:* Marianne Tielemann; *Rights & Permissions:* Jane Baird
Orders to: Postbus 2073, 3500 GB Utrecht
Associate Company: International Visual Resource BV (at above address)
Subjects: General Fiction, Encyclopaedias, Science & Technical, Textbooks, Paperbacks, Partworks, Pocket Editions
Founded: 1935
ISBN Publisher's Prefix: 90-274

Spruyt, van Mantgem en de Does BV, see SMD Educatieve Uitgevers

Staatsdrukkerij en Uitgeverijbedrijf*, Postbus 20014, 2500 EA The Hague (Located at: Chr Plantijnstr 1, The Hague) Tel: (070) 789911 Telex: 32486
Subjects: Government Publications
ISBN Publisher's Prefix: 90-9012

Stafleu's Wetenschappelijke Uitgeversmaatschappij BV, now Samsom Stafleu (qv)

Stam/Robijns, an imprint of Educaboek BV (qv), member of the Kluwer Group (qv)

Stam Technische Boeken, an imprint of Educaboek BV (qv), member of the Kluwer Group (qv)

De **Steenuil**, an imprint of Uit-Mij West-Friesland (qv)

Educational Publishers M **Stenvert** en Zoon BV, Postbus 70, 7300 AB Apeldoorn (Located at: Sutton 10, Apeldoorn) Tel: (055) 414644

A J G **Strengholt's** Boeken, Anno 1928, BV+, Hofstede 'Oud Bussem', Flevolaan 41, 1411 KC Naarden Tel: (02159) 58411 Cable Add: Editoras Telex: 43191 hobu nl Fax: (02159) 46173
Parent Company: Strengholt BV (at above address)
Orders to: Postbus 338, 1400 AH Bussum
Man Dirs: F E Breitenstein, G van Oorschot
Subjects: General Fiction, Belles Lettres, Biography, History, How-to, Music, Art, Textbooks, Reference, High-priced Paperbacks
Founded: 1928
ISBN Publisher's Prefix: 90-6010

Swets en Zeitlinger BV, Heereweg 347, 2161 CA Lisse Tel: (02521) 19113 Cable Add: Swezeit-Lisse Telex: 41325 szlis nl Fax: (02521) 15888
Dirs: A Swets, C Schuurman; *Editorial, Permissions:* K J Plasterk; *Sales, Production, Publicity:* J Lammerts
Subsidiary Companies: Swets (UK) Ltd, 32 Blacklands Way, Abingdon Business Park, Abingdon, Oxon OX14 1SX, UK; Swets North America Inc, PO Box 517, Berwyn, PA 19312, USA; Europériodiques SA, Parc Activites Pissaloup, BP 104, F-78191 Trappes Cedex, France; Swets-Servicos para Bibliotecas Ltda, Rua Anfilófio de Carvalho 29, Grupo 410 Castelo, 20030 Rio de Janeiro, RJ, Brazil; Swets & Zeitlinger GmbH, Bockenheimer Anlage 13, D-6000 Frankfurt am Main 1, Federal Republic of Germany; Nihon Swets Inc, Koshi-ichi Bldg 406, Jingumae 6-chome 19-16, Shibuyaku, Tokyo 150, Japan; Swets & Zeitlinger, Box 30297, 434 03 Kungsbacka, Sweden
Subjects: Music, Medicine, Psychology, Engineering, Life Sciences, Education, English Language, Psychological Tests
Founded: 1901
ISBN Publisher's Prefix: 90-265

Theatrum Orbis Terrarum, Keizersgracht 489-491, 1017 DM Amsterdam Tel: (020) 222255 Cable Add: Asherbooks Telex: 13185 Fax: (020) 270221
Publisher: Nico Israel
Subsidiary Companies: Orbit BV; Facsimile Uitgaven Nederland NV (FUN) (both at above address)
Associate Companies: A Asher & Co, Nico Israel (qqv)
Subjects: Biography, Bibliography, History, Cartography, Music, Art, Philosophy, Reference, Religion, High-priced Paperbacks, Medicine, General Science
Founded: 1963
ISBN Publisher's Prefix: 90-221

BV Uitgeverij en Boekhandel W J **Thieme** & Cie*, Industrieweg 85, Postbus 7, 7200 AA Zutphen Tel: (05750) 94911 Cable Add: Thieme Zutphen Telex: 49789 thizu
Dir: K Schillemans
Subjects: General Science, Biology, Schoolbooks
Founded: 1792
ISBN Publisher's Prefix: 90-03

Uitgeversmaatschappij de **Tijdstroom** BV*, Postbus 14, Noorderwal 38, Lochem Tel: (05730) 3651 Telex: 49642
Man Dir: B Mathis
Subjects: Art, Antiques, Medicine, Nursing, Hospital Sciences, Physiotherapy
Founded: 1924
ISBN Publisher's Prefix: 90-6087

Time-Life Books BV+, Ottho Heldringstr 5, 1066 AZ Amsterdam Tel: (020) 5104911 Cable Add: Time-Life Amsterdam Telex: 14288
Editorial: Kit van Tulleken (London); *Production:* Hartmut Belling (London); *Rights & Permissions:* Hans Bergmans (London)
Subsidiary Companies: Christian Verlag GmbH, Federal Republic of Germany (qv); Time-Life Books, UK (qv)
Branch Offs: ave Matignon 17, F-75008 Paris, France; Akademiestr 7, D-8000 Munich 40, Federal Republic of Germany; New Bond St, London W1Y 0AA, UK
Subjects: Art, Cookery, Gardening, General, Social & Political Science, History, How-to, Photography
ISBN Publisher's Prefix: 90-6182

H D **Tjeenk Willink** BV*, now Samsom H D Tjeenk Willink (qv under Samsom Uitgeverij BV)

W E J **Tjeenk Willink** BV, Koestr 8, Postbus 25, 8000 AA Zwolle
Man Dir: K E van der Linde; *Publicity:* W M de Wit
Subject: Law (textbooks, periodicals)
Miscellaneous: Firm is a member of the Kluwer Group (qv)
ISBN Publisher's Prefix: 90-271

Uitgeverij De **Toorts**, Nijverheidsweg 1, Postbus 9585, 2003 LN Haarlem Tel: (023) 319360 Cable Add: Gradus Haarlem Telex: 41494
Man Dir: J Hesseling; *Editorial, Publicity, Rights & Permissions:* Mrs M Klis; *Sales:* Mrs A Meyër; *Production:* C C Zwart
Subjects: General, Health, Humanities, Management, Medicine, Music, Psychology, Psychotherapy, Children's Books, Literature
Founded: 1936
ISBN Publisher's Prefix: 90-6020

Triton Pers, an imprint of Omega Boek BV (qv)

Unieboek BV, Postbus 97, 3990 DB Houten (Located at: Gebouw Spoorgaard, Onderdoor 7, 3995 DW Houten) Tel: (03403) 77660 Cable Add: Unieboek Telex: 40468 Uboek nl
Dir: A C Akveld; *Publicity Manager:* Mrs K Weaver
Associate Company: Uitgeverij Kadmos (qv)
Imprints: Agathon, de Boer Maritiem, van Dishoeck, de Haan, van Holkema en Warendorf, het Wereldvenster
Subjects: General Fiction & Non-fiction (including multi-volume reference), Maritime, Music, Art, Archaeology, Cookery, Politics, Literature, Juveniles (all ages), History, Thrillers
Founded: 1890
ISBN Publisher's Prefixes: 90-228, 90-269, 90-293

Uniepers BV+, Postbus 8082, 1005 AB Amsterdam Tel: (020) 112397/113589 Telex: Mayday 41275/41500 for Uniepers Fax: (02521) 17879 for Uniepers
Chief Executive and Sales: Marinus H van Raalte; *Editorial, Publicity, Rights & Permissions:* Marieke Bemelman; *Production:* Albert v d Klashorst
Subjects: History, Art, Music, Gardening, Wine & Cookery (all mainly co-editions)
1985: 37 titles *1986:* 50 titles *Founded:* 1961
ISBN Publisher's Prefix: 90-6825

Universitarie Pers Leiden, see Leiden University Press

Stichting **V A M**, Rouboslaan 30, Postbus 399, 2250 AJ Voorschoten Tel: (01717) 4141
Foundation for training employers and employees in the motor trade
Subjects: Technical and educational books for the motor trade
Founded: 1948
ISBN Publisher's Prefix: 90-405

V N U — Verenigde Nederlandse Uitgeversbedrijven BV, Postbus 4079, 2003 EB Haarlem (Located at: Ceylonpoort 5-25, 2037 AA Haarlem Schalkwijk) Tel: (023) 304304 Telex: 41549
Subsidiary Companies and Divisions: Educational Book Publishing (comprising L C G Malmberg BV (qv); Spectrum Boekhandel BV, De Meern; Plenary Publications International (Europe) BV, Amstelveen (all Netherlands); Uitgeverij Het Spectrum, Uitgeverij J van In (qqv, both Belgium); VNU Business Press Group BV (qv); VNU Magazine Group; VNU Sales Group; VNU Printing Group; VNU Newspaper Group (all Netherlands); VNU Amvest Inc, 3232 Ellicott St NW, Washington DC 20008, USA

V N U Business Press Group BV+, Rijnsburgstr 11, 1059 AT Amsterdam Tel: (020) 5102911 Telex: 10366
Man Dir: F X I Koot
Parent Company: VNU — Verenigde Nederlandse Uitgeversbedrijven BV (qv)
Subsidiary Companies: VNU Business Press Syndication International BV, Amsterdam, VNU Business Publications BV (qv) (both Netherlands); Business Press Group, Brussels, Belgium; VNU Business Publications BV London, UK; Hayden Publishing Co, New Jersey, USA
Subjects: Information Sciences, Business and Marketing, Computer Usage, Data Management, Career Guidance

V N U Business Publications BV*, Rijnsburgstr 11, 1059 AT Amsterdam Tel: (020) 5102911 Cable Add: Publipress Amsterdam Telex: 14407
Dir: R van den Bergh
Parent Company: VNU Business Press Group BV (qv)
Subject: Trade Publications

V U Boekhandel/Uitgeverij BV, PO Box 7161, 1007 MC Amsterdam (Located at: De Boelelaan 1105, 1081 HV Amsterdam) Tel: (020) 444355 Telex: 18191 Vuboe NL
Man Dir: P R Rienks; *Editorial:* F Grijzenhout; *Sales:* J Olivier
Imprints: V U Uitgeverij, Free University Press
Subjects: Academic level books on Philosophy, Theology, Medicine, History, Science, Politics, Sociology, Biology, Psychology, Economics, Law, Languages
Bookshop: At above address
1985: 83 titles *1986:* 99 titles *Founded:* 1980
ISBN Publisher's Prefix: 90-6256

Uitgeverij **Veen/Reflex & Uitgeverij LJ Veen** BV, Postbus 14095, Oudegracht 134-136, 3511 AX Utrecht Tel: (030) 349211 Telex: 70684 Luve
Man Dir: Bert de Groot; *Editorial:* Dick Gubbels (Senior editor, Dutch literature), Eva Cossee (Fiction), Christian van Gelderen (Non-fiction), André Swertz (Art); *Sales Manager:* Joop Boezeman; *Publicity:* Johanna Kroon; *Production:* John van Wijngaarden
Subjects: Literature, Business books, Popular Science, Art

Founded: 1887 (Veen)
Miscellaneous: Firm is a member of the Kluwer Group (qv)
ISBN Publisher's Prefixes: 90-204 (Veen), 90-6322 (Veen/Reflex)

Vereeniging tot Verspreiding der H Schrift, see Ark Boeken Publishing House

Versluys' Uitgeverij BV*, Postbus 1086, 1300 BB Almere (Located at: Randstad 21-25, 1314 BE Almere-stad) Tel: (03240) 37372
Man Dir: J W M Baron van Boetzelaer; *Sales Manager:* J H Goedheer; *Editor:* W L Miner
Subject: Textbooks
1985: 85 titles *Founded:* 1875
ISBN Publisher's Prefix: 90-249

De **Viergang**, an imprint of Em Querido's Uitgeverij BV (qv)

J N **Voorhoeve**, a subsidiary of Uitgeversmaatschappij J H Kok BV (qv)

De **Walburg** Pers*, Postbus 222, 7200 AE Zutphen (Located at: Zaadmarkt 84a-86, Zutphen) Tel: (05750) 10522
Man Dirs, Publicity, Rights & Permissions: Dr C F J Schriks, J van't Leven, J Smal
Subjects: History, Culture, Monuments, Architecture, Theatre
1985: 40 titles *Founded:* 1961
ISBN Publisher's Prefix: 90-6011

Uitgeverij Van **Walraven** BV*, Emmalaan 1, Apeldoorn Tel: (055) 218959
Miscellaneous: Firm is a member of the Combo Group (qv)
ISBN Publisher's Prefix: 90-6049

Uitgeverij **Waltman**, see Meinema Waltman

Wereldbibliotheek BV+, Nieuwezijds Voorburgwal 130, 1012 SH Amsterdam Tel: (020) 381899 Telex: 41695 Vribo Ref Wereldbibliotheek
Man Dir: J B I M Kat
Subjects: High quality Fiction and Non-fiction, Belles Lettres

Wereldschool, an imprint of Stichting IVIO (qv)

het **Wereldvenster**, an imprint of Unieboek BV (qv)

Uit-Mij **West-Friesland**+, Kleine Noord 7-9, 1621 JD Hoorn Tel: (02290) 18941 Cable Add: Westfriesland
Man Dir: F H Jonkers; *Editorial, Rights & Permissions:* A Feller; *Sales:* Mevr J Paulsen-Schönberger; *Publicity:* J van Hoorn; *Production:* L J Sweerts
Parent Company: West-Friesland Beheer BV (at above address)
Associate Company: Drukkerij West-Friesland/Boekprojectontwikkeling (qv)
Imprints: Cicero, De Steenuil, Witte Raven
Subjects: General Fiction, Juveniles, General Science, Low- & High-priced Paperbacks
1985: 75 titles *1986:* 70 titles *Founded:* 1944
ISBN Publisher's Prefix: 90-205

Drukkerij **West-Friesland/Boekproject-ontwikkeling**, Postbus 45 & 562, 1620 AA Hoorn (Located at: Kleine Noord 7-9, 1621 JD Hoorn) Tel: (02290) 18941/10529
Man Dir, Editorial, Publicity: L J Sweerts; *Sales:* Erik Sterken; *Rights & Permissions:* Ad P Feller
Parent Company: West-Friesland Beheer BV (at above address)
Associate Company: Uit-Mij West-Friesland (qv)
Subjects: Non-fiction, Short stories, Local history
1985: 4 titles *1986:* 2 titles *Founded:* 1918

Uitgeverij **Westers**, Hammarskjöldhof 7, 3527 HC Utrecht Tel: (030) 931043 Cable Add: Westers Utrecht
Man Dir and other offices: R J N M Westers Snr
Subjects: Children's Books, Novels
Bookshop: At above address
1985: 10 titles *Founded:* 1967
ISBN Publisher's Prefix: 90-6107

Uitgeverij T **Wever** BV, Postbus 59, 8800 AB Franeker (Located at: Zilverstr 4, Franeker) Tel: (05170) 3147
Subjects: History, Philosophy, Politics, Theology

Winkler Prins, an imprint of Elsevier Boeken BV (qv)

Witte Raven, an imprint of Uit-Mij West-Friesland (qv)

Wolters Kluwer NV, Meeuwenlaan 6, 8001 BC Zwolle Tel: (038) 272727 Telex: 42311
Chairman: M Ververs; *Vice-Chairman:* J Kist
Subsidiary Companies include: Jacob Dijkstra's Uitgeversmaatschappij BV, Postbus 284, 9700 AG Groningen; Samson Uitgeverij BV (qv), A W Sijthoff's Uitgeversmaatschappij BV (qv), Wolters-Noordhoff BV (qv) (all Netherlands); Wolters Samsom België NV, J B Wolters Leuven NV (qqv, both Belgium); Editorial Praxis SA, Spain; Croner Publications Ltd (qv), Eclipse Publications Ltd, Financial Training Publications Ltd (qv), Mary Glasgow Publications Ltd (qv), Wayland (Publishers) Ltd (all UK); Aspen Publishers Inc, Aspen Systems Corporation (both 1600 Research Blvd, Rockville MD 20850, USA); Panel Publishers Inc, 14 Plaza Rd, Greenvale, NY 11548, USA; Raven Press Ltd, 1185 Ave of the Americas, New York, NY 10036, USA
Associate Company: Kluwer Group (qv)

Wolters-Noordhoff BV, Damsport 157, Postbus 58, 9728 PS Groningen Tel: (050) 226922 Telex: 53443 Fax: (050) 264866
Man Dirs: Drs J G Felkman Rooda, Drs P W van Wel; *Rights & Permissions:* P G A Geenen
Orders to: Postbus 567, 9700 AN Groningen
Parent Company: Wolters Kluwer NV (qv for other associate companies)
Associate Company: Wolters-Noordhoff-Longman BV (qv)
Subjects: Secondary & Tertiary Textbooks, Educational Materials, Maps, Atlases
Founded: 1836, 1858
ISBN Publisher's Prefix: 90-01

Wolters-Noordhoff-Longman BV, Postbus 58, 9700 MB Groningen (Located at: Damsport 157, 9728 PS Groningen) Tel: (050) 226238 Telex: 53443/53529
General Executive: W Dannis
Associate Companies: Wolters-Noordhoff BV (qv); Longman Group UK Ltd, UK (qv)
Subjects: English Language Teaching

Zomer en Keuning Boeken BV+, Postbus 235, 6710 BE Ede (Located at: Het Huis Kernhem, Kernhemseweg 7, 6718 ZB Ede) Tel: (08380) 19031 Cable Add: ZKede Telex: 37095 ZKede Fax: (08380) 19031
Man Dir: P I A P M Zwaga; *Sales,Publicity:* J J Schoon; *Chief Editor:* G L M Vlaskamp; *Permissions:* Judith Verberne
Subjects: Nature, Gardening, Cookery, Handicrafts, Medicine, How-to, Reference, Religion (Protestant), Bibles

Book Club: Spiegelserie
Founded: 1919
Miscellaneous: Firm is a member of the Kluwer Group (qv)
ISBN Publisher's Prefix: 90-210

Zuid Boekprodukties BV, Postbus 50118, 1305 AC Almere-Haven Tel: (03240) 15505 Telex: 41804 Vnk nl
General Dir: W B J M de Koning
Imprint: Zuidboek
Subjects: Pets, Gardening, Plants and Flowers, Sports, Hobbies, Cookery
Founded: 1983
ISBN Publisher's Prefix: 90-6248

Zwarte Beertjes, an imprint of Bruna Pockethuis BV (qv)

Uitgeverij **Zwijsen** BV*, Gasthuisring 58, Postbus 805, 5000 AV Tilburg Tel: (013) 353635
Man Dirs: J N A Verwielen, G M Janssen; *Publicity Manager:* N J Filippo
Subjects: Juveniles, Primary Textbooks
Founded: 1846
ISBN Publisher's Prefix: 90-276

Remainder Dealers

Icob cv, Postbus 392, 2400 AJ Alphen aan den Rijn (Located at: Ondernemingsweg 60, Alphen aan den Rijn) Tel: (01720) 37231 Telex: 39700 icob nl
Man Dir: Hans Meijer
Also Publisher (qv)

Literary Agents

Auteursbureau Greta **Baars-Jelgersma**, Den Heuvel 73, 6881 VD Velp Tel: (085) 635017 Telex: Incom 43776/11000
Also: Bovensteweg 46, 6585 KD Mook Tel: (08896) 1470
Specialization: International co-printing of illustrated books; mediation of copyrights; translations from Scandinavian and German languages into Dutch

Gans en Rombach Auteursagenter, now Rombach & Partners (qv)

International Literatuur Bureau BV, Postbus 10014, 1201 DA Hilversum (Located at: Koninginneweg 2A, 1217 KW Hilversum) Tel: (035) 13500 Cable Add: ILB Telex: 73201 ILB
Contact: Menno Kohn

Maydo **Kooy** Literary Agency, Kerkstr 301, 1017 GZ Amsterdam Tel: (020) 268774 Telex: 26401
Contact: Maydo van Marwijk Kooy
Specialization: Translation rights

Prins en Prins*, De Lairessestr 6, Postbus 5400, 1007 AK Amsterdam Tel: (020) 761001 Cable Add: prinsrights
Chief Executive: Henk Prins

Rombach & Partners, Postbus 121, 2110 AC Aerdenhout (Located at: Bentveldsweg 100, 2111 ED Aerdenhout) Cable Add: Rombook Fax: (023) 247698
Contact: Coen J Rombach

Servire BV Uitgevers, Secr Varkevisserstr 52, 2225 LE Katwijk aan Zee Tel: (01718) 16741
Chief Executive: Felix Erkelens
Also Publisher (qv)

Book Clubs

E C I voor Boeken en Platen BV, Laanakkerweg 14-16, Industrieterrein Hagestein, 4124 PB Vianen ZH Tel: (03473) 79911 Telex: 47449
Book Clubs: Nederlandse Boekenclub, Nederlandse Lezerskring Boek en Plaat BV (qqv)
Owned by: ECI voor Boeken en Grammofoonplaten BV (qv)

English Book Club*, Postbus 24, 3417 ZG Montfoort
The above address is for Netherlands enquiries. Head office is Book Club Associates, UK (qv under UK Book Clubs)
Owned by: W H Smith & Son Ltd (London) and Doubleday & Co Inc (New York)

Nederlandse Boekenclub, ECI voor Boeken en Platen BV, Postbus 400, 4130 EK Vianen
Netherlands Book Club
Manager: A L P Bongaards
Branch Off: Nederlandse Boekenclub (Boek en Plaat), Belgium (qv)
Subjects: General Fiction and Non-fiction
Members: 350,000
Owned by: ECI voor Boeken en Platen BV (qv)

Nederlandse Lezerskring Boek en Plaat BV, Wildenborch 2, Diemen NH, Postbus 2201, 1000 EK Amsterdam
Members: 500,000
Owned by: ECI voor Boeken en Platen BV (qv)
Founded: 1966

Spiegelserie Boekenclub, Postbus 235, 6710 BE Ede (Located at: Het Huis Kernhem, Kernhemseweg 7, 6718 ZB Ede)
Owned by: Zomer en Keuning Boeken BV (qv)

V C L*, Gildestr 5, 8263 AH Kampen
Owned by: Uitgeversmaatschappij J H Kok BV (qv)

Major Booksellers

Athenaeum Boekhandel, Spuiblvd 14-16, Amsterdam Tel: (020) 233933
Manager: G Schut

Broese Kemink BV, Stadhuisbrug 5, Postbus 38, 3500 AA Utrecht Tel: (030) 313804
Man Dir: P P Hogervorst; *Manager:* J P Eenens
Service centre: Zandweg 69C, 3454 J W de Meern Tel: (03406) 64224 Telex: 40411 Boek
Owned by: Kluwer NV (qv)

Bruna BV, Meidoornkade 12, 3992 AE Houten Tel: (03403) 91911 Telex: 47518
President: B Hagens
Largest bookshop chain in Netherlands, operating 14 large bookshops (listed below) and over 450 other book, magazine and stationery retailers throughout country
Bookshops: A P-Standaard Boekhandel (Delft, Zaandam); Boekhandel Bergmans (Maastricht); Boekhandel H Coebergh (Haarlem); Boekhandel Hugo Jonkers (Eindhoven); Boekhandel Mensing en Visser (The Hague); Moderne Boekhandel (Amsterdam); Boekhandel Mosmans ('s-Hertogenbosch); Boekhandel Plantijn (The Hague); Boekhandel Revers en van Brummen (Dordrecht); Boekhandel F Schoth (Boxmeer); Ten Have en Hoofdstadboekhandel (Amsterdam); Boekhandel Van Broek (Zeist); Boekhandel Van Leeuwen (Roosendaal); Boekhandel Voorhoeve en Dietrich (Hilversum)
Owned by: Bührmann-Tetterode NV

Dekker en Nordemann BV, now Faxon Europe BV (qv)

Dekker v d Vegt, Plein 1944, No 129, 6500 GT Nijmegen Tel: (080) 221010 Telex: 9900-48202 deveg
Manager: P H M Hooghof
Branches: Th van Aquinostr 2A, 6525 GD Nijmegen Tel: (080) 551127; Brandstr 23, 6131 CS Sittard Tel: (04490) 28100
Owned by: Kluwer NV (qv)

Faxon Europe BV, Postbus 197, 1000 AD Amsterdam (Located at: Hogehilweg 10, 1101 CC Amsterdam) Tel: (020) 910591 Telex: 14651 Fax: (020) 911735
Manager: J Ch Germain
International bookseller and subscription agent
Owned by: Faxon Company, USA

Boekhandel **Gianotten** BV*, Heuvelpoort 359, 5038 DW Tilburg
Orders to: Beneluxlaan 59, 5042 WK Tilburg Tel: (013) 682991 Telex: 52460
Two branches in Tilburg and one in Breda
Manager: Theo P M van Meijel
Owned by: Kluwer NV (qv)

Ginsberg Univ Boekhandel*, Breestr 127-129, Postbus 9003, 2300 PA Leiden Tel: (071) 124642/141773
Manager: Mrs C Bos-Vink

Kooyker BV*, Nieuwe Rijn 15-16, Postbus 24, 2300 AA Leiden Tel: (071) 144146 Telex: 39434 Kooynl
Man Dir: Fj Arkenau

Rudolf **Müller** International Booksellers, Overtoom 487, Postbus 9016, 1006 AA Amsterdam Tel: (020) 165955 Telex: 12582 Rmbks nl
Managers: R Müller, Mrs C M Griffioen

Martinus **Nijhoff** BV, Postbus 269, 2501 AX The Hague (Located at: Noordwal 4, The Hague) Tel: (070) 469460 Cable Add: Bookshague Telex: 34164 nijbu nl Fax: (070) 654829
Manager: Th P M van Meijel
Also subscription agent
Part of the Kluwer Group (qv)

Scheltema Holkema Vermeulen BV*, Postbus 271, 1000 AG Amsterdam Tel: (020) 267212 Telex: 17193
Manager: R A Koops

BV Algemene Boekhandel en Antiquariaat H De **Vries** Boeken, Postbus 274, 2000 AG Haarlem (Located at: Ged Oude Gracht 21-27/Jacobynestr 3-7, Haarlem) Tel: (023) 319458 Telex: 41695 Vribo nl
Man Dir: R H C de Vries; *Managers:* Paula Goos (General bookshop); Alex Szirmai (Sports Literature Dept); C W van Beek (School Textbooks); Dik Ramkeme (Antiquarian Books)

Major Libraries

Bibliotheek van het **Centraal Bureau** voor de Statistiek, Prinses Beatrixlaan 428, Postbus 959, 2270 AZ Voorburg
Library of the Netherlands Central Bureau of Statistics
Librarian: Dr Th Vreugdenhil
Also: Kloosterweg 1, Postbus 4401, 6401 CZ Heerlen

Hoofdafdeling **Documentaire Research** en Informatieverstrekking van de Exportbevorderings- en Voorlichtingsdienst*, Bezuidenhoutseweg 151, 2594 AG The Hague Tel: (070) 797209 Telex: 31099 Ecza nl Cable Add: Econinf
Documentary Research and Information Department of the Netherlands Foreign

Trade Agency (formerly Economic
Information Service)
Head: J H Ypma
Miscellaneous: Producer of the Foreign
Trade and Econ Abstracts Database
(online through Dialog, Datastar and
Belindis)

Bibliotheek- en Documentatie-centrum van
de **Economische** Voorlichtingsdienst, now
Hoofdafdeling Documentaire Research en
Informatieverstrekking van de
Exportbevorderings- en Voorlichtingsdienst
(qv)

Gemeentebibliotheek Rotterdam, Hoogstr
110, 3011 PV Rotterdam Tel: (010)
4338911 Telex: 25221 gbr nl
Rotterdam Municipal Library
Librarian: P J Th Schoots

Bibliotheek van het **Internationaal Instituut**
voor Sociale Geschiedenis, Kabelweg 51,
1014 BA Amsterdam Tel: (020) 843695
Library of the International Institute of
Social History
Librarian: J Kloosterman

Koninklijke Bibliotheek, Postbus 90407,
2509 LK The Hague (Located at: Prins
Willem Alexanderhof 5, 2509 LK The
Hague) Tel: (070) 140911 Telex: 31500
Royal (National) Library
Publications include: (in co-operation with
others) *Dutch Bibliography — Brinkman's
Cumulatieve Catalogus*; *Centrale Catalogus
voor Periodieken* (Union Catalogue of
Periodicals, in book form); *Treasures of
the Royal Library* (illuminated mediaeval
manuscripts); *Bibliography of Translations*
(from the Dutch) *of North and South
Netherlandic Publications*; *Bibliography of
Cartographic Materials in the Netherlands*;
*Bibliografie van in Nederland verschenen
Officiële en Semi-officiële Uitgaven*
(Bibliography of Official and Semi-official
Publications)

Bibliotheek der **Koninklijke Nederlandse
Akademie** van Wetenschappen,
Kloveniersburgwal 29, 1011 JV
Amsterdam Tel: (020) 222902
Library of Royal Netherlands Academy of
Arts and Sciences
Dir: Dr J A W Brak

Bibliotheek der **Landbouwhogeschool**, now
Bibliotheek der Landbouwuniversiteit (qv)

Bibliotheek der **Landbouwuniversiteit**,
Postbus 9100, 6700 HA Wageningen Tel:
(08370) 84440 Telex: 45015
Library of the Agricultural University

Openbare Bibliotheek, Bilderdijkstr 1-3,
2513 CM The Hague Tel: (070) 469235
Public Library
Librarian: W M Renes

Rijksmuseum Meermanno-Westreenianum/
Museum van het Boek, Prinsessegracht 30,
2514 AP The Hague Tel: (070) 462700
National Book Museum
Keeper: Drs J Offerhaus

Bibliotheek der **Rijksuniversiteit**,
Wittevrouwenstr 7-11, Postbus 16007, 3500
DA Utrecht Tel: (030) 392500 Telex: NL
47103 ubutr Fax: (030) 328198
University Library, Utrecht
*Publications include: Handschriften en
Oude Drukken van de Utrechse
Universiteitsbibliotheek* (MSS and Old
Books of University Library, Utrecht:
Exhibition Catalogue 1984)

Bibliotheek der **Rijksuniversiteit te
Groningen**, Postbus 559, 9700 AN
Groningen (Located at: Broerstr 4, 9712
CP Groningen)

Bibliotheek der **Rijksuniversiteit te Leiden**,
Postbus 9501, 2300 RA Leiden (Located
at: Witte Singel 27, Leiden) Tel: (071)
272801 Telex: 39060
Librarian: J J M van Gent

Universiteitsbibliotheek*, Universiteit van
Amsterdam, Singel 425, 1012 WP
Amsterdam Tel: (020) 5259111
Librarian: Dr E Braches

Library Associations

Centrum voor Literatuuronderzoekers*,
Zonegge 1901, 6903 GW Zevenaar
Centre for Literary Research — a section
of the Dutch Librarians' Association

Convent van Universiteitsbibliothekarissen
in Nederland, Association of University
Librarians in the Netherlands — see UKB

Federatie van Organisaties van Bibliotheek-,
Informatie-, Dokumentatiewezen
(FOBID), Taco Scheltemastr 5, 2597 CP
The Hague Tel: (070) 141541
Federation of Library Information and
Documentation Organizations
Co-ordinating Officer: Mrs F Droogh
*Publications include: Library and
Documentation Guide*; *Library and
Documentation Centres in the Netherlands*;
Cataloguing Rules (parts 1-8)

**International Federation of Library
Associations** and Institutions (IFLA)*, The
Royal Library, Postbus 95312, 2509 CH
The Hague Tel: (070) 140884 Telex:
34402 kb nl
See also under International Organizations
section

Nederlands Bibliotheek en Lektuur Centrum
(NBLC), Taco Scheltemastr 5, Postbus
93054, 2509 AB The Hague Tel: (070)
141500 Telex: 32102 nblc nl
Dutch Centre for Public Libraries and
Literature
Executive Dir: D Reumer
Publications: Bibliotheek en Samenleving;
Open (published jointly)

**Nederlandse Vereniging van
Bibliothekarissen**, Documentalisten en
literatuuronderzoekers (NVB), pa Mrs H J
Krikke-Scholten, Nolweg 13D, 4209
AW Schelluinen Tel: (01830) 23386
Netherlands Librarians' Society
Secretary: G Koers
Publication: Open (published jointly)

Protestantse Stichting tot Bevordering van
het Bibliotheekwezen en de
Lectuurvoorlichting in Nederland, Parkweg
20a, Voorburg Tel: (070) 861779 Cable
Add: Adcel nl Telex: 33216
Protestant Foundation for the Promotion
of Librarianship and Reading Information
in the Netherlands
Publication: Prisma

Stichting Bibliotheek en
Documentatieacademies, Herengracht 330,
Postbus 10895, 1001 EW Amsterdam Tel:
(020) 265155
Foundation for Library and Information
Schools
Secretary: Ms J A Kaars

U K B (Samenwerkingsverband van de
Universiteitsbibliotheken, de Koninklijke
Bibliotheek en de Bibliotheek van de
Koninklijke Nederlandse Akademie van
Wetenschappen), c/o J L M van Dijk,
Librarian, Limburg University, Postbus
616, 6200 MD Maastricht Tel: (043)
888427 Telex: 56726
Association of the University Libraries, the
Royal Library and the Library of the
Royal Netherlands Academy of Arts and
Sciences
President: Dr R L Schuursma
Secretary: Dr J L M van Dijk

Vereniging van Archivarissen in Nederland,
Postbus 11645, 2502 AP The Hague
Association of Archivists in the
Netherlands
Executive Secretary: Y Bos-Rops
Publication: Nederlands Archievenblad

**Vereniging voor het Theologisch
Bibliothecariaat***, Postbus 289, 6500 AG
Nijmegen
Association for Theological Librarianship
(the above is the address of the
Secretariat)
Executive Secretary: R van Dijk
Publications: Mededelingen van de VTB;
Bibliografie Doctorale Scripties Theologie

Library Reference Books and Journals

Books

Bibliotheek- en Documentatiegids (Library
and Documentation Guide), NOBIN, Van
Karnebeeklaan 19, The Hague

Brinkman's Cumulatieve Catalogus (Dutch
Bibliography), Koninklijke Bibliotheek,
Postbus 90407, 2509 LK The Hague

Journals

Archievenblad (Archive News), Vereniging
van Archivarissen in Nederland, Postbus
11645, 2502 AP The Hague

Bibliotheek en Samenleving (Library and
Social Life), Nederlands Bibliotheek en
Lektuurcentrum (NBLC), Taco
Scheltemastr 5, Postbus 93054, 2509 AB
The Hague

Mededelingen van de VTB
(Communications), Vereniging voor het
Theologisch Bibliothecariaat, Postbus 289,
6500 AG Nijmegen

Open, Nederlandse Vereniging van
Bibliothekarissen, Documentalisten en
literatuuronderzoekers (NVB), pa Mrs H J
Krikke-Scholten, Nolweg 13D, 4209 AW
Schelluinen
Professional journal for librarians,
researchers, archivists and documentalists
(joint publication)

Literary Associations and Societies

The **Dickens** Fellowship*, 26-28 Marktstr,
1411 EA Naarden
Honorary Secretary: J C Van Kessel

Foundation for the Promotion of the
Translation of Dutch Literature, Singel
450, 1017 AV Amsterdam Tel: (020)
231056/257189
Dir: Joost de Wit
*Publication: Writing in Holland and
Flanders*

Maatschappij der Nederlandse
Letterkunde*, Universiteitsbibliotheek,
Postbus 9501, 2300 RA Leiden
Society of Netherlands Literature (the
above is the address of the Secretariat)
*Publications: Tijdschrift voor Nederlandse
Taal- en Letterkunde* (quarterly); *Jaarboek
der Maatschappij* (annually); *De negentiend
eeuw* (quarterly)

Friesian P E N Centre*, Wormerveerstr
126, 1013 SL Amsterdam
Secretary: Pier Boorsma

Netherlands Centre of the International **P E N**, Operalaan 39, 2907 KA Capelle, a/d IJssel
President: Joost de Wit; *Secretary:* Martin Mooij

Literary Periodicals

Amsterdamer Publikationen zur Sprache und Literatur (Amsterdam Publication on Language and Literature), Editions Rodopi NV, Keizersgracht 302-304, 1016 EX Amsterdam

Boeken-Zoekblad (Hard-to-Find Books), 'Stabo/All-Round' BV, Oosterweg 68, Groningen

Castrum Peregrini, Castrum Peregrini Presse, Herengracht 401, 1017 BP Amsterdam
Journal for literature and art; text in German

Forum der Letteren, Smits NV, Westeinde 135, 15 The Hague

Gids (Guide), Meulenhoff Nederland BV, Herengracht 507, 1017 BV Amsterdam

Hemelspleet, Bilderdijksstr 45a, Rotterdam

Hollands Maandblad (Holland Monthly), Drukkeij Trio, Nobelstr 27, The Hague

Kentering, NV Uitgeverij Nijgh & Van Ditmar, Badhuisweg 232, 2597 JS The Hague
Literary review

Lezen om te Leven (Reading as a Life Style), 'Stabo/All-Round' BV, Oosterweg 68, Groningen

De negentiend eeuw (The Nineteenth Century), Maatschappij der Nederlandse Letterkunde, Universiteitsbibliotheek, Postbus 9501, 2300 RA Leiden

Quaerendo, Theatrum Orbis Terrarum, Keizersgracht 489-491, 1017 DM Amsterdam
A quarterly journal from the Low Countries devoted to manuscripts and printed books; text mainly in English, occasionally in French and German

Revisor, Keizersgracht 608, Amsterdam

De Ronde Tafel, Madoerastr 10, 2585 VB The Hague
Cultural magazine; 6 per year

Trotwaer, Miedema Pers, Nieuweburen 97-103, Postbus 45, Leeuwarden
Text in Frisian

Writing in Holland and Flanders, Foundation for the Promotion of the Translation of Dutch Literature, Singel 450, 1017 AV Amsterdam
Text in English

Literary Prizes

A K O Literature Prize
Established 1986 and sponsored by AKO. Any literary work written originally in the Dutch language and published in The Netherlands or Belgium is eligible for nomination. Publishers may nominate a maximum of six or a minimum of three titles. Annual award of 50,000 Dutch florins. The first winner in 1987 was J Bernlef for *Publiek Geheim* (Em Querido's Uitgeverij BV, Amsterdam). Enquiries to Stichting AKO Literatuur Prijs, Sparrenlaan 37, 3742 WD Baarn

Amsterdam Prizes
For the best drama (Albert van Dalsum prize), prose (Multatuli prize), poetry (Herman Gorter prize) and essay (Busken Huet prize). Awarded annually, except the essay prize, which is given every other year. Enquiries to Amsterdam City Government, Stichting Amsterdams Fonds voor de Kunst, Town Hall, Kamer 4390, Amstel 1, 1011 PN Amsterdam

F **Bordewijk** Prize
For the best Dutch novel. 5,000 Dutch florins. Awarded annually. Enquiries to Jan Campertstichting, Burg de Monchyplein 9, The Hague

Jan **Campert** Prize
For outstanding Dutch poetry. 5,000 Dutch florins. Awarded annually. Enquiries to Jan Campertstichting, Burg De Monchyplein 9, The Hague

Albert van **Dalsum** Prize, see Amsterdam Prizes

Dutch Literature Prize
Established 1956. To the most outstanding prose writer, essay writer or poet in the Netherlands or in Belgium writing in Dutch. 18,000 Dutch florins. Awarded triennially. Enquiries to Nederlandse Taalunie, Stadhoudersplantsoen 2, 2517 JL The Hague

Dutch Prize for the Best Children's Book
For the best Dutch children's books — a Golden Slate Pencil and 3,000 Dutch florins. For Dutch or foreign, translated books — Silver Slate Pencils (maximum 10). Also a Golden Brush and 3,000 Dutch florins for the best Dutch illustrated children's book and two Silver Brushes for Dutch or foreign illustrated work. Awarded annually. Occasionally a Golden Key for a children's/young persons' book with new developments (technically or in subject matter) is awarded. Enquiries to the Foundation for the Collective Promotion of the Dutch Book, Keizersgracht 391, 1016 EJ Amsterdam

Herman **Gorter** Prize, see Amsterdam Prizes

The G H 's-**Gravesande** Prize
For special services to literature. 5,000 Dutch florins. Awarded irregularly. Enquiries to Jan Campertstichting, Burg De Monchyplein 9, The Hague

J **Greshoff** Prize
For the best Dutch essay. 5,000 Dutch florins. Awarded every two years. Enquiries to Jan Campertstichting, Burg de Monchyplein 9, The Hague

Nienke van **Hichtum** Prize
For the best Dutch children's book. 5,000 Dutch florins. Awarded every two years. Enquiries to Jan Campertstichting, Burg de Monchyplein 9, The Hague

Lucy B and C W van der **Hoogt** Prize*
To an outstanding Dutch writer. 5,000 Dutch florins and a medal. Awarded annually. Enquiries to Maatschappij der Nederlandse Letterkunde (Society of Netherlands Literature), c/o Postbus 9501, 2300 RA Leiden

Busken **Huet** Prize, see Amsterdam Prizes

Constantijn **Huygens** Prize
To a distinguished Dutch author for all his works. 10,000 Dutch florins. Awarded annually. Enquiries to Jan Campertstichting, Burg De Monchyplein 9, The Hague

Multatuli Prize, see Amsterdam Prizes

State Prize for Children's and Youth Literature*
For the best author's work for children and young people. 6,500 Dutch florins. Awarded triennially. Enquiries to Netherlands Ministry of Welfare, Health and Culture, Postbus 5406, 2280 HK Rijswijk

State Prize for Literature, the P C Hooft Prize*
For important and original literary works in Dutch. 10,000 Dutch florins. Awarded annually where possible: one year for poetry, the next year for prose, the next year for literary essay. Enquiries to Netherlands Ministry of Welfare, Health and Culture, Postbus 5406, 2280 HK Rijswijk

Vijverberg Prize, replaced by The G H 's-Gravesande Prize (qv)

West-Friesland Literary Prize
Founded in 1986 for publications in the Westfries language, a dialect of the Dutch language. Awarded every three years. Enquiries to Uit-Mij West-Friesland, Kleine Noord 7-9, Postbus 45, 1620 AA Hoorn

Translation Agencies and Associations

I P M C International, Heijerstr 1, 5563 BM Westerhoven Tel: (04902) 43501
Translation and setting into all commercial languages, including Arabic, Chinese, Japanese. Offices and associates in Bahrain, Germany, Hong Kong, Ireland, UK (qv), USA

Netherlands Antilles

General Information

Language: Dutch. English and Spanish widely spoken
Religion: Roman Catholic
Population: 256,000
Bank Hours: 0830-1130, 1400-1600 Monday-Friday. St Maarten: 0800-1300 Monday-Friday (also 1600-1700 on Friday)
Shop Hours: 0800-1200, 1400-1800 Monday-Saturday
Currency: 100 cents = 1 Netherlands Antilles gulden
Export/Import Information: No tariff on books or advertising. No import licences. No exchange controls
Copyright: Berne, UCC (see International section)

Publishers

Curaçaosche Drukkerij en Uitgevers Maatschappij*, c/o Beurs en Nieuwsberichten, PO Box 3011, Willemstad, Curaçao
Subjects: Geography, Travel

Van Dorp Aruba NV, Nassaustr 77, PO Box 596, Oranjestad, Aruba

Drukkerij de Stad NV*, Compagniestr 41, Willemstad, Curaçao
Dir: Ronald Yrausquin
Subject: Law

Ediciones Populares*, Compagniestr 41, Willemstad, Curaçao
Dir: Ronald Yrausquin
Subjects: Popular Sciences, Literature
Founded: 1929

Tipografia Nacional*, Bitterstr 3, Curaçao
Subject: Law

NETHERLANDS ANTILLES — NEW ZEALAND 307

De **Wit** Stores NV, VAD Bldg, PO Box 386, L G Smith Blvd 110, Oranjestad, Aruba Tel: (599-8) 23500 Cable Add: Dewitstores Telex: 5137 Vadws na
Man Dir: F Olmtak
Subjects: History of the Netherlands Antilles, Papiamentu Language Textbooks in English, Dutch and Spanish
Bookshops: Aruba Boekhandel (qv under Major Booksellers); Aruba Post; Boulevard Book and Drugstore

Major Booksellers

Aruba Boekhandel, Nassaustr 94, Oranjestad, Aruba Tel: (599-8) 23648 Cable Add: Dewitstores Telex: 5137 Vadws na
Buyer: Mrs E Kock
Owned by: De Wit Stores NV (qv)

Boekhandel **Augustinus***, Abraham de Veerstr 12, Curaçao Tel: (599-9) 612782 Telex: 1042 Augbk na
Manager: Marcel E Jansen

Van **Dorp-Eddine** NV, PO Box 3001, Willemstad, Curaçao Telex: 1041 Dorcu NA Fax: (599-9) 624867
Also: Schottegatweg Oost 185 Tel: (599-9) 616966; Roodeweg 13 Tel: (599-9) 626133/626139/626180; Breedestr Punda Tel: (599-9) 611502/612177; Promenade Winkel Centrum Tel: (599-9) 70544/70545; International Airport Tel: (599-9) 88425; drugstores in several hotels

Kantoor Boekhandel Salinja NV KBS*, Schottegatweg Oost 106, Curaçao Tel: (599-9) 37288

Mensing's Caminada*, Schottegatweg Oost, Curaçao Tel: (599-9) 70222
Manager: S Mensing

Novo Book and Gift Store*, PO Box 3652, Schottegatweg Oost 215D, Curaçao Tel: (599-9) 61646
Manager: George A Perry

Boekhandel **Salas** NV, PO Box 3044, Fokkerweg 50, Curaçao Tel: (599-9) 612303/612201/612564 Telex: 3457 Salas NA

Major Libraries

Openbare Leeszaal en Bibliotheek, Johan van Walbeeckplein 13, Willemstad, Curaçao Tel: (599-9) 611582/612840
Public Reading Room and Library
Librarian: Rose Marie de Paula

Openbare Leeszaal en Boekerij*, Eilandgebied, Aruba
Public Reading Room and Library
Librarian: Alice van Romondt

Universiteits-Bibliotheek, Universiteit van de Nederlandse Antillen, PO Box 3059, Jan Noorduynweg 111, Willemstad, Curaçao Tel: (599-9) 84422 Telex: 1411 Una na
Librarian: Stanley R Criens

Library Association

Asociacion di Biblioteka i Archivo di Korsow (Carbido)*, Stoppelweg 4, Willemstad, Curaçao Tel: (599-9) 623434
Association of Libraries and Archives
President: Maritza F Eustatia

New Caledonia

General Information

Language: French
Population: 142,000
Business Hours: 0730-1100, 1400-1800 Monday-Friday; 0730-1100 Saturday
Currency: CFP franc
Export/Import Information: No tariff on books except luxury bindings and children's picture books. Advertising matter generally dutiable. Special Tax on all. No import licences required

Publishers

Editions d'**Art Calédoniennes***, 40 rue de Paris, BP 1626, Val Plaisance, Nouméa Tel: 261184/278389 Telex: 048 nm
Subjects: Fine Editions, Reprints, Travel & Exploration

Hachette Calédonie*, 10 RT1 bis, Ducos BP E2, Nouméa cedex Tel: 282688 Telex: Hachcal 096 nm
Publisher and distributor
Man Dir: Edouard Terzian
Bookshop: See under Major Booksellers

Major Booksellers

Barrau*, 16 et 18 rue Anatole-France, Nouméa Tel: 3093

Hachette Calédonie*, 11 ave du Maréchal-Foch, BP E2 Nouméa cedex Tel: 272001 Telex: Hachcal 096 nm
Man Dir: Edouard Terzian
Also Publisher (qv)

J P L*, 32 rue de la République, Nouméa Tel: 286032
Dir: Jacques Leyraud

Montaigne*, 24 rue de Sébastopol, BP 267, Nouméa Tel: 3488

Pentecost*, 24 rue de l'Alma, Nouméa Tel: 2114
Importer/Exporter

Major Libraries

Bibliothèque **Bernheim**, Bibliothèque territoriale de la Nouvelle-Calédonie*, BP G1, Nouméa (Located at: no. 17, route 13, Nouméa) Tel: 272343
Librarian: Hélène Colombani
Publications include: Bulletin de liaison de la Bibliothèque Bernheim (quarterly)

South Pacific Commission Library*, South Pacific Commission, PO Box D5, Nouméa Cedex

New Zealand

General Information

Language: English
Religion: Predominantly Protestant
Population: 3.3 million
Bank Hours: 0930-1600 Monday-Friday
Shop Hours: 0900-1730 Monday-Friday (open until 2100 either Thursday or Friday). Some local shops open Saturday
Currency: 100 cents = 1 New Zealand dollar
Export/Import Information: No tariffs on books and advertising. No import licences, but literature 'indecent' or 'advocating violence, lawlessness, disorder or seditiousness' prohibited. No special exchange controls
Copyright: UCC, Berne, Florence (see International section)

Book Trade Organizations

Book Marketing Council Inc, PO Box 40086, Glenfield, Auckland
Chairman: Lance Earney
Publications: The Book Buyer & Book Buying Patterns in New Zealand

Book Publishers Association of New Zealand Inc, Box 44-146, Pt Chevalier, Auckland 2 (Located at: 12 Maranui Ave, Pt Chevalier, Auckland 2) Tel: (09) 892533
President: Rosemary Stagg; *Dir:* Gerard Reid
Publication: Publishing News (members only)

Booksellers Association of New Zealand (Inc), PO Box 11377, Wellington Tel: (04) 728678
President: Philip King; *Dir:* John Schiff

Christian Booksellers' Association (NZ Chapter), 12 Rangiatea Rd, Epsom, Auckland 3
Secretary: M J Frith

Copyright Council of New Zealand Inc, PO Box 9241, Wellington
Chairman: Bernard Darby; *Secretary:* Tony Chance

New Zealand Book Trade Organization Inc, now Book Marketing Council (qv)

Publishers' Promotional Fund Inc, PO Box 44146, Auckland 2 (Located at: 12 Maranui Ave, Pt Chevalier, Auckland 2) Tel: (09) 892533
Chairman: Graham Beattie; *Executive Dir:* Gerard Reid

Standard Book Numbering Agency, National Library of New Zealand, Private Bag, Wellington 1 Tel: (04) 743000 Telex: NZ 30076 Fax: (04) 743035
ISBN Administrator: K S Williams

Book Trade Reference Books and Journals

Book

New Zealand Books in Print, D W Thorpe Pty Ltd, 384 Spencer St, Melbourne, Victoria, Australia 3003

Journals

New Zealand Bookseller & Publisher, Stockton House (Publisher), PO Box 46, Albany, Auckland

New Zealand National Bibliography, National Library of New Zealand, PMB, Wellington 1

Spotlight; on the book, stationery, magazine, greeting cards, and toys trades in New Zealand, PO Box 3911, Auckland

Publishers

A B P (NZ) Ltd, see Associated Book Publishers (NZ) Ltd

NEW ZEALAND

A D I S Press Ltd, Centorian Dr, Mairangi Bay, Auckland 10 Tel: (09) 4038181 Telex: ADIS NZ 21334 Fax: (09) 4781418
President and Publisher: Graeme S Avery; *Editor-in-Chief:* Rennie C Heel
Associate Companies: ADIS Press Australasia Pty Ltd, Australia (qv); ADIS Press Publications Ltd, Hong Kong (qv); ADIS Press International Ltd, Suite 15c, Manchester International Office Centre, Styal Rd, Wythenshawe, Manchester M22 5WL, UK; ADIS Press International Inc, Suite 13-30, Oxford Court Business Center, 582 Middletown Blvd, Langhorne, PA 19047, USA
Subjects: Clinical Pharmacology, Therapeutics & Medicine
1985: 4 titles *1986:* 11 titles *Founded:* 1962
ISBN Publisher's Prefix: 0-86471

Action Publications, PO Box 5160, Christchurch (Located at: 49 Hudson St, Christchurch) Tel: (03) 516460
Man Dir: Desmond Sewell; *Sales:* Andrew Sewell
Subjects: Secondary Textbooks, Geography, Social Studies
Founded: 1971
ISBN Publisher's Prefix: 0-908586

Allen & Unwin (with the Port Nicholson Press)+*, Private Bag, Wellington (Located at: 60 Cambridge Terrace, Wellington) Tel: (04) 845969
New Zealand Publisher: Bridget Williams
Associate Company: George Allen & Unwin Australia Pty Ltd, Australia (qv)
Parent Company: Unwin Hyman Ltd, UK (qv)
Subjects: New Zealand Literature, History, Politics, Social Science, Natural History
1985: 11 titles *Founded:* 1981
ISBN Publisher's Prefix: 0-86861

Allied Press Ltd, 70 Lower High St, PO Box 517, Dunedin Tel: (024) 774760 Telex: Odt NZ 5692
Parent Company: Otago Press and Produce Ltd, Lower Stuart St, Dunedin
Subjects: General Non-fiction, especially concerning New Zealand
Bookshop: Star Shop, Lower Stuart St, Dunedin
Founded: 1863
ISBN Publisher's Prefix: 0-86466

Ashton Scholastic Ltd, Private Bag, Penrose, Auckland 6 (Located at: 165 Marua Rd, Panmure, Auckland 6) Tel: (09) 596089 Cable Add: Ashco Telex: NZ 21203 Fax: (09) 593860
Man Dir: Graham Beattie; *Marketing:* M Fitzgerald; *Sales:* B Denny; *Editorial:* L Handy
Parent Company: Scholastic Inc, 730 Broadway, New York, NY 10003, USA
Subsidiary Company: NZ School Book Fairs
Subjects: Educational, Children's, Periodicals, Teaching Aids, Computer Software
Book Clubs: Lucky, Arrow, Bofur, Teenage, Teachers' Bookshelf
1985-86: 6 titles *1986-87:* 19 titles
Founded: 1962
ISBN Publisher's Prefixes: 0-908643, 1-86943

Asia Pacific Books*, PO Box 3978, Wellington Tel: (04) 736363 Cable Add: Haaspress Telex: NZ 3588 Att Haaspress
Publisher: Anthony Haas; *Rights, Marketing:* Murray Humphries
Associate Companies: Asia Pacific Research Unit; Asia Pacific Economic News
Subjects: Economics, Geography, Politics, Social Change, Cookery, Management, How-to, Electronics (Data Bases)
Founded: 1970
ISBN Publisher's Prefix: 0-908583

Associated Book Publishers (NZ) Ltd, see Reed Methuen Publishers Ltd

Auckland University Press, University of Auckland, PMB, Auckland Tel: (09) 737654/737656
Managing Editor: Ms E P Caffin
Orders to: (in New Zealand) Pacific Publishers, PO Box 5844, Auckland; (outside New Zealand) nearest branch of Oxford University Press
Subjects: Demography, Ethnology, Geography, History, Biography, Language, Literature, Fiction, Poetry
1985: 5 titles *1986:* 11 titles *Founded:* 1966
ISBN Publisher's Prefix: 1-86940

Thomas Avery & Sons Ltd*, PO Box 442, New Plymouth, North Island Tel: (067) 85646 Cable Add: Avery New Plymouth
Man Dir: R Sutherland; *General Manager:* M H Cardale
Subjects: History, Secondary & Primary Textbooks
Bookshop: See under Major Booksellers
Founded: 1882

B C N Z Enterprises, an imprint of TVNZ Publishing (qv)

David **Bateman** Ltd+, PO Box 65062, Mairangi Bay, Auckland 10 Tel: (09) 4444680 Telex: NZ 63389 Batman Fax: (09) 4440389
Shipping Add: Golden Heights, 32-34 View Rd, Glenfield, Auckland 10
Man Dir, Editorial: David L Bateman; *Sales, Publicity:* Paul Parkinson; *Rights & Permissions:* Janet Bateman
Branch Offs: c/o Tony Tizzard, Fiesta Products, PO Box 4176, Christchurch; Paul Bird, PO Box 678, Wellington (both New Zealand); David Bateman Ltd, PO Box 257, Buderim 4556, Queensland, Australia; David Bateman Ltd, The Gables, Whitchurch, Hampshire, UK
Subjects: Natural History, Art, Travel, Reference, General Non-fiction, Juveniles, Business, Cookery, Encyclopaedias
1985: 14 titles *1986:* 20 titles *Founded:* 1979
ISBN Publisher's Prefix: 0-908610

Benton Ross Publishers Ltd+, Private Bag, Takapuna, Auckland 9 (Located at: 46 Parkway Drive, Glenfield, Auckland 9) Tel: (09) 4795230
Man Dir, Editorial, Production: Robert M Ross; *Sales, Publicity:* Helen E Benton
Subjects: History, Politics, New Zealand, Fiction
1985: 5 titles *1986:* 10 titles *Founded:* 1980
ISBN Publisher's Prefix: 0-908636

Brick Row Publishing Co Ltd+, PO Box 85-057, Auckland 10 Tel: (09) 4106993 Telex: Eclipse NZ 63019
Editorial and Sales Office: 11 Cockayne Crescent, Forrest Hill, Auckland 10 Tel: (09) 4106993
Man Dir, Editorial: Oswald L Kraus; *Sales, Publicity:* Ruth Kraus
Subjects: Crafts, Children's, General Non-fiction, Science
Founded: 1978
ISBN Publisher's Prefix: 0-908595

Brookfield Press+, PO Box 1201, Auckland (Located at: 87 Edmund St, Auckland 5) Tel: (09) 557637
Man Dir, Editorial, Production, Rights & Permissions: Richard Webster; *Sales, Publicity:* Don Wall
Parent Company: Brookings Bookshop (1971) Ltd (at above address)
Subsidiary Company: Brookings Agencies Ltd (at above address)
Subjects: New Zealand History, Philosophy, Astrology, Psychic Phenomena, Esoteric
Founded: 1971
ISBN Publisher's Prefix: 0-86467

Bush Press Communications Ltd, PO Box 33-029, Takapuna, Auckland 9
Man Dir: Gordon Ell
Subjects: Wildlife and Outdoor, Children's, Applied Arts, Hobbies, Archaeology, History, General New Zealand Non-fiction
1985: 6 titles *1986:* 8 titles *1987:* 8 titles
Founded: 1979
ISBN Publisher's Prefix: 0-908608

Butterworths of New Zealand Ltd, PO Box 472, Wellington (Located at: 205-207 Victoria St) Tel: (04) 851479 Cable Add: Butterwort Wellington Telex: 31306 Fax: (644) 851598
Man Dir: P G Kirk; *Publishing Dir:* P J Downey; *Marketing Dir:* N A Rossiter
Parent Company: Butterworth & Co (Publishers) Ltd, UK (qv)
Subjects: Legal, Medical, Scientific, Technical
Bookshop: Johns Bldg, 21-23 Chancery St, Auckland 1
1985: 11 titles *Founded:* 1914
ISBN Publisher's Prefix: 0-409

C B S Australia Publishing Pty Ltd, now incorporated in Harcourt Brace Jovanovich Group Australia Pty Ltd (qv)

Cape Catley Ltd, PO Box 199, Picton (Located at: Whatamongo Bay, Queen Charlotte Sounds) Tel: 37708 Picton
Man Dir: Christine C Catley
Orders to: Brick Row, PO Box 85-057, Auckland
Subjects: Fiction, Memoirs, Local History
1986: 2 titles
ISBN Publisher's Prefix: 0-908561

Capper Press Ltd+, PO Box 1388, Christchurch Tel: (03) 67170 Cable Add: Avonprint Christchurch
Publicity: Don Ellis
Associate Company: Avon Fine Prints Ltd
Subjects: Reprints of rare and out-of-print New Zealand, Australian and Pacific books

Caveman Publications Ltd, now Northcott Reeves, Publishers (qv)

The **Caxton** Press, 113 Victoria St, PO Box 25088, Christchurch Tel: (03) 68516 Cable Add: Imprint
Man Dir: E B Bascand
Subjects: Belles Lettres, Poetry, Biography, History, Music, Art, Education, Gardening
ISBN Publisher's Prefix: 0-908563

Centre for Resource Management, Lincoln College, PO Box 56 Lincoln College, Canterbury Tel: (03) 252811 ext 596 Telex: 4200 NZ
Dir, Rights & Permissions: Dr John Hayward; *All other offices:* Tracy Williams
Subject: Environmental Management
Founded: 1960

Century Hutchinson NZ Ltd+, PO Box 40086, Glenfield, Auckland 10 (Located at: 189 Archers Rd, Glenfield, Auckland 10) Tel: (09) 4447197/524 Telex: 60824 Hutpub
Man Dir: Lance Earney; *Publishing Dir:* David Ling
Associate Company: Century Hutchinson Ltd, UK (qv)
Subjects: General & Academic
1985: 9 titles *1986:* 4 titles *1987:* 15 titles
Founded: 1977
ISBN Publisher's Prefix: 0-09

Cicada Press+, PO Box 64-009, Birkenhead South, Auckland 10 Tel: (09) 4180890
Man Dir: R K St Cartmail
Subjects: Poetry, Fiction, Fine Arts, Religion
Founded: 1978
ISBN Publisher's Prefix: 0-908599

William **Collins** Publishers Ltd+, PO Box 1, Auckland (Located at: 31 View Rd, Glenfield, Auckland) Tel: (09) 4443740 Cable Add: Folio Telex: NZ 21685 Fax: (09) 4441086
Man Dir: Robert W Fisher; *National Sales Manager:* Anne Johnson; *Marketing Manager:* Tony Fisk; *Advertising, Publicity & Promotions Manager:* Catherine Larsen
Parent Company: William Collins PLC, UK (qv)
Subjects: Fiction, Natural History, Art, Cartography, Reference, Religion, Biographies, Children's, New Zealand, Liturgical, Dictionaries, Gardening, Sport, Travel
Founded: 1888

D S I R, an imprint of Science Information Publishing Centre (qv)

Dunmore Press Ltd+, PO Box 5115, Palmerston North (Located at: 109 Napier Rd, Palmerston North) Tel and Cable Add: (063) 79242 Telex: Dunmore NZ 3960
Dirs: Murray and Valerie Gatenby; *Editorial:* Murray Gatenby; *Marketing, Rights & Permissions:* Valerie Gatenby
Subjects: History, Fiction, General, Academic and University Textbooks
1985: 26 titles *Founded:* 1975
ISBN Publisher's Prefixes: 0-908564, 0-86469

Endeavour, an imprint of Pacific Publishers (qv)

Forum, an imprint of Viking Sevenseas Ltd (qv)

Fourth Estate Books Ltd*, PO Box 9344, Wellington Tel: (04) 859019 Cable Add: Natbus
Productions Manager: Caroline Mitchell
Parent Company: Fourth Estate Holdings
Subjects: Business, Law, Politics
Founded: 1976

Golden Press, Private Bag, Rosebank, Auckland 7 (Located at: 717 Rosebank Rd, Avondale, Auckland) Tel: (09) 884588/887763, also (03) 790307 (Christchurch), (04) 894189 (Wellington) Cable Add: Gold Press Auckland Telex: Gpnz 60926
General Manager: Alan Smith; *Marketing Services:* Philip Klink
Parent Companies: Western Publishing Co Inc, 1220 Mound Ave, Racine, WI 53404, USA; Gordon & Gotch, 114 William St, PO Box 767G, Melbourne, Australia
Imprints: Golden, Golden Press, Step Ahead, Whitman
Head Off: Golden Press Pty Ltd, Australia (qv)
Branch Offs: 102 Adelaide Rd, Newtown, Wellington; 293-307 Tuam St, Christchurch
Miscellaneous: Firm is a division of Gordon & Gotch (NZ) Ltd, 2 Carr Rd, Mt Roskill, Auckland 4

Halcyon Publishing Ltd+, CPO Box 360, Auckland 1 (Located at: Unit 14, 46 Ellice Rd, Glenfield) Tel: (09) 4445920 Telex: NZ 60642 Econz Att Halcyon
Man Dir, Sales, Rights & Permissions: Graham Gurr; *Editorial Consultant:* Antony Entwistle; *Publicity:* A M Tearle
Subsidiary Companies: The Halcyon Press; Halcyon Books; Hole in the Bank Books

Subjects: Outdoor Pursuits, Children's, Business
1985: 5 titles *Founded:* 1984
ISBN Publisher's Prefix: 0-908685

Harcourt Brace Jovanovich Group Australia Pty Ltd, PO Box 22-245, Auckland 6 Tel: (09) 2762087 Fax: (09) 2764676
Manager: Sue Barton

Heinemann Publishers (New Zealand) Ltd+, PO Box 36064, Northcote, Auckland 9 Tel: (09) 4190119 Cable Add: Hebooks Telex: NZ 61902 Hebooks
Warehouse: Cnr College Rd and Kilham Ave, Northcote, Auckland 9
Man Dir, Sales: D J Heap; *Publicity:* P Janssen; *Education Dir:* Graham McEwan
Parent Company: The Heinemann Group of Publishers Ltd, UK (qv for associate companies)
Subjects: University & School Textbooks, Fiction, Hobbies, Technical, Children's, General, Medical
1985: 23 titles *Founded:* 1969
ISBN Publisher's Prefix: 0-86863

Hodder & Stoughton Ltd+, PO Box 3858, Auckland 1 (Located at: 46 View Rd, Glenfield, Auckland 10) Tel: (09) 4443640 Cable Add: Expositor Auckland Telex: NZ 21422
Man Dir: Paul Sheldon; *Publishing Dir:* H Hingley
Parent Company: Hodder & Stoughton Ltd, UK (qv)
Subjects: Fiction, Non-fiction, Children's books
1985: 30 titles *Founded:* 1971
ISBN Publisher's Prefix: 0-340

Hole in the Bank Books, subsidiary company of Halcyon Publishing Ltd (qv)

Hutchinson Group (NZ) Ltd, now incorporated in Century Hutchinson Group NZ Ltd (qv)

Jacaranda Wiley Ltd, PO Box 2259, Auckland (Located at: 4 Kirk St, Grey Lynn, Auckland) Tel: (09) 764620 Cable Add: Japress
Miscellaneous: Firm is a branch of Jacaranda Wiley, Australia (qv)

The **Joint Board** of Christian Education of Australia and New Zealand, PO Box 6133, Te Aro, Wellington 1 (Located at: 75 Taranaki St, Wellington 1)
Head Off: 2nd Floor, 10 Queen St, Melbourne, Victoria 3000, Australia (qv)

Kiwi Tales Publications+, PO Box 25-114, St Heliers Bay, Auckland Tel: (09) 398030
Man Dirs: Angela Greenhalgh, Barry Greenhalgh; *Editorial:* Angela Greenhalgh; *Sales, Production, Publicity, Rights & Permissions:* Barry Greenhalgh
Subject: Children's Fiction
Founded: 1983
ISBN Publisher's Prefix: 0-908687

Lansdowne Press (NZ) Ltd, 59 View Rd, Glenfield, Auckland

Lindon Publishing+, PO Box 39225, Auckland West Tel: (09) 760647 Telex: Aknz 2553 CPO (Lindon)
Man Dir, Editorial, Publicity, Rights & Permissions, Sales: Michael Guy; *Production:* Laserlab
Subjects: Humour, Adventure, Cookery, General
Founded: 1981
ISBN Publisher's Prefix: 0-86470

Longman Paul Ltd+, Private Bag, Takapuna, Auckland 9 (Located at: 182-190 Wairau Rd, Takapuna, Auckland 9)

Tel: (09) 4444968 Telex: NZ 21041 Fax: (09) 4441470
Man Dir: Rosemary Stagg; *Editors:* Ken Harrop, Susan Davis; *Sales Dir:* Elizabeth Nelson
Parent Company: Longman Group UK Ltd, UK (qv)
Subjects: Primary, Secondary & Tertiary Textbooks
Founded: 1968
ISBN Publisher's Prefix: 0-582

Thomas C **Lothian** Pty Ltd, Private Bag, Takapuna, Auckland 9 (Located at: 3/3 Marken Place, Glenfield, Auckland 10) Tel: (09) 4441948 Cable Add: Lothwell Telex: NZ 60455
Manager: D M Forrester
Head Office: Lothian Publishing Co Pty Ltd, Australia (qv)
Subjects: General Non-fiction, Educational, Children's
Founded: 1954
ISBN Publisher's Prefix: 0-85091

McGraw-Hill Book Co, New Zealand Ltd, 5 Joval Pl, Manukau City, CPO Box 85, Auckland 1 Tel: (09) 2779891 Fax: (09) 2781523
Manager: Janet Powell
Parent Company: McGraw Hill Book Co, 1221 Ave of the Americas, New York, NY 10020, USA
Associate Companies: See McGraw-Hill Book Co (UK) Ltd, UK (qv)
Subjects: Educational
Founded: 1974
ISBN Publisher's Prefix: 0-07

John **McIndoe** Ltd, PO Box 694, Dunedin Tel: (024) 770355
Shipping Add: 51 Crawford St, Dunedin
Man Dir: M M McIndoe; *Managing Editor:* B Larson; *Editorial:* I Lonie; *Publicity:* C Froud
Subjects: General Fiction, Belles Lettres, Poetry, Biography, History, How-to, Music, Art, Reference, High-priced Paperbacks, Medicine, General Science, University Textbooks
Founded: 1893
ISBN Publisher's Prefixes: 0-908569, 0-86868

The **Macmillan Company** of New Zealand Ltd+, 48 Northcote Rd, Northcote, Auckland 1309 Tel: (09) 4191725 Cable Add: Macpublish Telex: Coatink NZ 21971 Fax: (09) 4191588
Man Dir: David Joel; *Editorial:* Bronwen Nicholson; *Sales Managers:* Sallie van Schreven (Educational), Bronwen Nicholson (Academic); *Publicity:* Carol Coffey
Parent Company: Macmillan Publishers Ltd, UK (qv)
Subjects: Secondary Textbooks, General Books, School Books, Tertiary Books
1985: 15 titles *1986:* 2 titles *Founded:* 1977
ISBN Publisher's Prefix: 0-333

Mallinson Rendel Publishers Ltd+, 5A Grass St, Oriental Bay, PO Box 9409, Wellington Tel: (04) 857340
Joint Man Dirs: E A Mallinson, D Rendel; *Publicity:* Ann Mallinson
Associate Company: David Rendel Associates Ltd, PO Box 10058, Wellington
Subjects: Children's Books, Historical, Social, Law, Aviation, Poetry
1985: 8 titles *1986:* 6 titles *Founded:* 1980
ISBN Publisher's Prefix: 0-908606

Methuen New Zealand, a subsidiary of Reed Methuen Publishers Ltd (qv)

Mills Publications Ltd+, PO Box 35175, Naenae, Lower Hutt (Located at; 69

Sydney St, Petone) Tel: (04) 687515
Telex: NZ 30630 Att Mills
Chief Executive and Rights & Permissions:
Harry Mills
Subject: Non-fiction
1986: 3 titles *Founded:* 1982
ISBN Publisher's Prefix: 0-908722

Millwood Press Ltd, 291b Tinakori Rd,
Wellington 1 Tel: (04) 735176 Cable Add:
Siersprod Telex: 31255 Jsp Wn
Dirs: Jim and Judy Siers
Subjects: New Zealand and Pacific
1985: 3 titles *1986:* 6 titles *1987:* 4 titles
Founded: 1972
ISBN Publisher's Prefix: 0-908582

Moa Publications Ltd, PO Box 26092,
Auckland (Located at: 23A Pah Rd,
Epsom, Auckland) Tel: (09) 655306 Fax:
(09) 656875
Man Dir: John G Blackwell; *Editor:* Janet
Blackwell
Imprint: Orakau House
Subjects: Sport, General
1986: 16 titles *Founded:* 1971
ISBN Publisher's Prefix: 0-908570

N Z Listener, an imprint of TVNZ
Publishing (qv)

New Women's Press Ltd+, PO Box
47-339, Auckland (Located at: 85
Richmond Rd, Auckland 2) Tel: (09)
784978
Man Dir: Wendy Harrex
Subjects: Books by, for, and about women
1985: 3 titles *1986:* 7 titles *Founded:* 1982
ISBN Publisher's Prefix: 0-908652

New Zealand Council for Educational
Research, PO Box 3237, Wellington
Tel: (04) 847939 Cable Add: Edsearch
Dir: Ian D Livingstone; *Publicity Dir,
Rights & Permissions:* Peter Ridder
Subjects: Educational Books & Materials
Founded: 1934
ISBN Publisher's Prefix: 0-908567

New Zealand Government Printing Office*,
Private Bag, Wellington Tel: (04) 737320
Telex: 31370 Govprnt
Bookshops: 25 Rutland St, Auckland; 159
Hereford St, Christchurch; 123 Princes St,
Dunedin; Kings Arcade, Hamilton;
Mulgrave St, Wellington; Cubacade,
Wellington
Subjects: Legislation, Education, Social,
New Zealand History and General,
Horticulture
Founded: 1862
ISBN Publisher's Prefix: 0-477

Newrick Associates Ltd+*, PO Box 820,
Wellington Tel: (04) 844095/851877 Cable
Add: Backgam Telex: 3909 Att Newrick
Man Dir: Henry P Newrick
Associate Companies: Multimedia
Associates Ltd; Professional Publications
(qv)
Subjects: Art, Antiques, Reference
Founded: 1967

Nexus Books*, PO Box 67-008, Mount
Eden, Auckland 3
Manager: A J C Begg
Subject: Mathematics
Founded: 1973
ISBN Publisher's Prefix: 0-85912

Northcott Reeves, Publishers, now Square
One Books (qv)

Nova Pacifica Publishing Co Ltd+*, PO
Box 11-106, Wellington (Located at: 2-14
Allen St, Wellington) Tel: (04) 849126
Telex: NZ 3588 Att Nova Pacifica
Man Dir, Editorial, Sales: Murray
Humphries; *Production:* Raymond Labone
Subjects: Natural History, History of
Science, New Zealand, General

Founded: 1979
ISBN Publisher's Prefix: 0-908603

Orakau House, an imprint of Moa
Publications Ltd (qv)

Otago Heritage Books, PO Box 5361,
Dunedin Tel: (024) 771500
Editorial: G J Griffiths; *Rights &
Permissions:* J A Cox
Subjects: Local History, Educational
Bookshop: 356 Moray Place East, Dunedin
1985: 7 titles *1986:* 3 titles *1987:* 3 titles
Founded: 1977

Outrigger Publishers & Rimu Publishing
Co Ltd, PO Box 13049, Hamilton
Man Dir, Editorial: Norman Simms; *Sales:*
Theola Wyllie; *Publicity:* Rae Marshall
USA Office: 814 Broadway, New York,
NY 10003, USA
Subjects: Literature, Criticism, Folklore,
Periodicals
ISBN Publisher's Prefixes: 0-908571
(Outrigger), 0-908703 (Rimu)

Oxford University Press, PO Box 11149,
Ellerslie, Auckland 5 (Located at:
5 Ramsgate St, Ellerslie, Auckland 5) Tel:
(09) 590460/596914 Cable Add: Oxonian,
Auckland Telex: NZ 60777 Fax: (09)
590941
Manager: Jeff Olson; *Managing Editor:*
Anne French
Subjects: History, Politics, Law, Literature,
Art, The Pacific, Children's Books
Founded: 1947
Miscellaneous: Branch of Oxford University
Press, UK (qv)
ISBN Publisher's Prefix: 0-19

Pacific Publishers+, PO Box 5844,
Auckland 1 (Located at: 95 Mt Eden Rd,
Mt Eden, Auckland) Tel: (09) 775196
Telex: NZ 60402 Fax: (09) 395503
*Publishing Manager and Rights &
Permissions:* Tony Izzard
Parent Company: Whitcoulls Ltd, Private
Bag, Auckland
Imprints: Endeavour, Pacific, Whitcoulls
Publishers
Subjects: General, Non-fiction, How-to,
New Zealand, Educational
Bookshops: Whitcoulls Ltd (qv under
Major Booksellers)
1985: 28 titles *1986:* 30 titles *Founded:*
1883
Miscellaneous: Formerly Whitcoulls
Publishers
ISBN Publisher's Prefixes: 0-7233
(Whitcoulls), 0-8647 (Pacific), 0-8648
(Endeavour)

Penguin Books (NZ) Ltd, Private Bag,
Takapuna, Auckland 9 (Located at: 182-
190 Wairau Rd, Auckland 10) Tel: (09)
4444965 Cable Add: Penguinook
Auckland Telex: 21041 Fax: (09) 444
1470
Managing Editor: Geoff Walker; *Sales:*
Colin Cox; *Marketing:* Karen Ferns
Parent Company: Penguin Publishing Co
Ltd, UK (qv)
Associate Company: Penguin Books
Australia Ltd, Australia (qv)
1986: 20 titles *1987:* 30 titles *Founded:*
1973
ISBN Publisher's Prefix: 0-14

Pilgrims South Press Ltd*, PO Box 5101,
Moray Pl, Dunedin (Located at: 371 York
Pl, Dunedin) Tel: (024) 778275 Telex:
Dn 5204
*Man Dir, Editorial, Production, Rights &
Permissions:* Stephen Higginson; *Sales,
Publicity:* Niki Stewart
Branch Off: PO Box 9612, Newmarket,
Auckland

Subjects: Art, Literature, Children's,
History, Sociology, Anthropology,
Cartoons
Founded: 1976

Pitman Publishing NZ Ltd*, PO Box
38688, Petone, Wellington Tel: (04)
683623 Telex: NZ 30253
Man Dir: Gil McGahey; *Publicity:* T Weir
Associate Company: Pitman Publishing Ltd,
UK (qv)
Branch Off: Box 2107, Auckland
ISBN Publisher's Prefixes: 0-85896,
0-908575

Port Nicholson Press Ltd, see Allen &
Unwin

Price Milburn & Co Ltd, Private Bag,
Petone (Located at: 1 Te Puni St, Petone)
Tel: (04) 687179 Cable Add: Mice
Wellington Telex: NZ 30656
General Manager: P Stewart; *Publishing
Manager:* Judith Holloway
Parent Company: Education House Ltd
Subjects: Juveniles, Social Science,
Secondary & Primary Textbooks,
particularly Junior Readers
Founded: 1957
Miscellaneous: Publishes for New Zealand
Educational Institute
ISBN Publisher's Prefix: 0-7055

Professional Publications*, PO Box 820,
Wellington Tel: (04) 844095/851877 Cable
Add: Backgam Telex: 3909 Att Newrick
Man Dir: Henry P Newrick
Associate Companies: Multimedia
Associates Ltd; Newrick Associates
Ltd (qv)
Subjects: Business, Economics, Taxation
Founded: 1979

A H & A W **Reed** Ltd, see Reed Methuen
Publishers Ltd

Reed Methuen Publishers Ltd+, Private
Bag, Birkenhead, Auckland 10 Tel: (09)
486039 Cable Add: Reedkiwi Telex: NZ
21944
Man Dir: Neil J Aston; *Publisher:* P M
Bradwell
Parent Company: Associated Book
Publishers (Aust) Ltd, Australia (qv)
Subsidiary Companies: Methuen New
Zealand, Sweet & Maxwell (NZ) Ltd
(both at above address)
Branch Off: 39 Rawene Rd, Birkenhead,
Auckland 10 Tel: (09) 486039
Subjects: General Fiction and Non-fiction,
Biography, History, How-to, Art,
Reference, Social Science, Politics,
Horticulture, Natural History, Outdoor
Pursuits, Sport, Cookery, Children's, Trade
Paperbacks
1985: 44 titles *Founded:* 1907
Miscellaneous: Company name covers
combined operations of Associated Book
Publishers (NZ) Ltd and A H & A W
Reed Ltd
ISBN Publisher's Prefixes: 0-589 (Reed
Methuen); 0-456, 0-457 (both ABP (NZ))

Ray **Richards** Publisher, PO Box 31240,
Milford, Auckland 9 (Located at:
49 Aberdeen Rd, Castor Bay, Auckland 9)
Tel: (09) 4105681
Man Dir: Ray Richards; *Editorial:* Barbara
Richards; *Production:* Nicki Richards
Associate Company: Richards Literary
Agency (qv)
Branch Off: 54 Ranui Terrace, Linden,
Wellington
Subjects: New Zealand Biography, History,
Agriculture, Horsemanship
1985: 4 titles *1986:* 4 titles *1987:* 4 titles
Founded: 1978
ISBN Publisher's Prefix: 0-908596

NEW ZEALAND 311

Rimu Publishing Co Ltd, see Outrigger Publishers & Rimu Publishing Co Ltd

Benton **Ross** Publishers Ltd, see Benton

S I P C, see Science Information Publishing Centre

Science Information Publishing Centre (SIPC), DSIR, PO Box 9741, Wellington (Located at: Science Information Publishing Centre, DSIR, 16 Kent Terrace, Wellington) Tel: (04) 858939 Cable Add: Sidsir Telex: Research NZ 3276
Man Dir and other offices: Dr Norman Hawcroft
Imprints: SIPC, DSIR
Subjects: Biological, Physical, Earth and Social Sciences, Industrial, Technology & Applied Science, Periodicals, Maps, Charts
1985: 20 titles *1986:* 14 titles
Miscellaneous: Publishers for the Department of Scientific and Industrial Research (New Zealand Government's largest research organization)
ISBN Publisher's Prefix: 0-477

Seto Publishing Ltd+, CPO Box 4028, Auckland (Located at: Apt D, 11 Whitaker Pl, Auckland) Tel: (09) 34486 Telex: NZ 63516
Man Dirs, Publicity, Rights & Permissions: Tom Hepburn, Selwyn Jacobson; *Editorial, Sales:* Tom Hepburn; *Production:* Selwyn Jacobson
Orders to: Reed Methuen Publishers Ltd, Private Bag, Birkenhead, Auckland 10
Subjects: Sport, Humour, Art, General
1985: 3 titles *1986:* 7 titles *Founded:* 1980
ISBN Publisher's Prefix: 0-908697

Sevenseas Publishing Pty Ltd, now Viking Sevenseas Ltd (qv)

Shortland Educational Publications*, PO Box 56133, Dominion Rd, Auckland 3 Tel: (09) 687128 Cable Add: Newspress
Managing Editor: Roger Gold
Parent Company: NZ Newspapers Ltd, PO Box 1409, Auckland
Branch Offs: Newspaper House, Wellington; Christchurch Star, Christchurch
Subjects: Gardening, Cookery, Sports, Children's Activities, General
Founded: 1977
ISBN Publisher's Prefix: 0-86867

Southern Press Ltd, PO Box 50-134, Porirua, Wellington Tel: (04) 331899
Man Dir, Editorial, Sales, Production, Rights & Permissions: R H Stott; *Publicity:* J Stott
Subsidiary Company: Rails Publishing Ltd (at above address)
Subjects: Transport, Technology, New Zealand History
Founded: 1971
ISBN Publisher's Prefix: 0-908616

Square One Books, PO Box 2143, Dunedin (Located at: 16 Atkinson St, Dunedin) Tel: (024) 53117
Publisher and Distribution: Trevor Reeves
Subjects: Literature, Non-fiction, Health, Welfare, Medical, Social, Politics, Humour, Women's Books, Science Speculation, Architecture
Founded: 1984
Miscellaneous: Formerly Northcott Reeves Publishers
ISBN Publisher's Prefix: 0-908562

Step Ahead, an imprint of Golden Press (qv)

Sweet & Maxwell (NZ) Ltd, a subsidiary of Reed Methuen Publishers Ltd (qv)

T V N Z Enterprises, an imprint of TVNZ Publishing (qv)

T V N Z Publishing, PO Box 3819, Auckland (Located at: 7 Elliott St, Auckland) Tel: (09) 391414 Cable Add: Teltwo Auckland Telex: NZ 60225 Telsale Fax: (09) 389347
Chief Executive: Maurice Smyth, Controller TVNZ International; *Acting Publishing Manager and all other offices:* Marian Harkness
Parent Company: Television New Zealand, Broadcasting Corporation of New Zealand
Associate Company: NZ Listener, Broadcasting Corporation of New Zealand, PO Box 3140, Wellington
Imprints: NZ Listener, BCNZ Enterprises, TVNZ Enterprises, TVNZ Publishing
Subjects: Mainly TV tie-ins
Bookshop: TVNZ Shop, PO Box 1514, Christchurch
1985: 7 titles *1986:* 12 titles
ISBN Publisher's Prefix: 0-908690

Alister **Taylor** Publishers*, The Mall, Russell, Bay of Islands Tel: Russell 37633 Cable Add: Taylor, Russell Telex: NZ 2583 Alister Taylor
Chief Executive: Alister Taylor; *Rights & Permissions:* Deborah Coddington
Subjects: Limited and Fine Editions, Fiction, Poetry, New Zealand, Art, Photography, Politics, General
Founded: 1971
ISBN Publisher's Prefix: 0-908578

University of Canterbury Publications Committee, PB, Christchurch Tel: (03) 482009 Cable Add: Canterbury University Telex: NZ 4144
Subjects: Fine Art, History, Literature, Physics, Chemistry, Social Sciences, Natural Science, Political Science, Engineering
1985: 1 title *1986:* 1 title *1987:* 2 titles
Founded: 1960
ISBN Publisher's Prefix: 0-900392

University of Otago Press, PO Box 56, Dunedin Tel: (024) 771640
Managing Editor: W S Sewell
Orders to: John McIndoe Ltd, PO Box 694, Dunedin
Subjects: Scholarly Monographs, Biography, Music, Poetry, Literature, History, Medicine, Anthropology, Dentistry
Founded: 1958
ISBN Publisher's Prefix: 0-908569

Victoria University Press, Victoria University of Wellington, Private Bag, Wellington Tel: (04) 721000
Business Manager: Byron Buick-Constable; *Editor:* Fergus Barrowman; *Sales:* Bruce McKenzie (Allen & Unwin)
Orders to: Allen & Unwin (NZ) Ltd, Private Bag, Wellington Tel: (04) 845969 Telex: NZ 30758
Subjects: General Academic, New Zealand Drama, Short Stories, History, Politics, Sociology, Anthropology, Language and Communications, Law, Religion, Psychology, Zoology, Botany, Economics, Architecture
1985: 12 titles *1986:* 6 titles *1987:* 7 titles
ISBN Publisher's Prefix: 0-86473

Viking Sevenseas Ltd, PO Box 152, Paraparaumu (Located at: 23B Ihakara St, Paraparaumu) Tel: (058) 71990 Cable Add: Vikseven
Man Dir and other offices: Murdoch Riley
Associate Companies: Viking Record Co Ltd; Classic Editions
Imprints: Forum, Viking Sevenseas Ltd
Subjects: New Zealand Non-fiction, Health, Nutrition
1986: 3 titles *Founded:* 1963
ISBN Publisher's Prefix: 0-85467

Whitcoulls Publishers, an imprint of Pacific Publishers (qv)

Whitman, an imprint of Golden Press (qv)

Wilson & Horton Ltd, PO Box 32, Auckland Tel: (09) 795050 Cable Add: Herald Telex: NZ 2325 Fax: (09) 8362, 8222
ISBN Publisher's Prefix: 0-86864

Literary Agents

Joseph **Lockhart** Associates Ltd*, 1-519 Richardson Rd, Mount Roskill, Auckland 4 Tel: (09) 694378

Richards Literary Agency, PO Box 31240, Milford, Auckland (Located at: 49 Aberdeen Rd, Castor Bay, Auckland 9 and 54 Ranui Terrace, Linden, Wellington) Tel: (09) 4105681
Contacts: Ray Richards, Barbara Richards, Nicki Richards
Specializations: General, Educational, Academic, Juvenile, Film, Television, Stage, Radio

Book Clubs

Arrow, Private Bag, Penrose, Auckland 6
Owned by: Ashton Scholastic Ltd (qv)

Bofur, Private Bag, Penrose, Auckland 6
Owned by: Ashton Scholastic Ltd (qv)

Book of the Month Club, see Doubleday New Zealand Ltd, Book Club Division

BookNewZealand, see Doubleday New Zealand Ltd, Book Club Division

Doubleday Book Club, see Doubleday New Zealand Ltd, Book Club Division

Doubleday History Book Club, see Doubleday New Zealand Ltd, Book Club Division

Doubleday Military Book Club, see Doubleday New Zealand Ltd, Book Club Division

Doubleday New Zealand Ltd, Book Club Division*, Private Bag, North Shore Centre, Auckland 9 (Located at: 1 Parkway Drive, Mairangi Bay Industrial Estate, Auckland 10)
Operated by Doubleday Australia Pty Ltd, Australia (qv)
Includes: Book of the Month Club, BookNewZealand, Doubleday Book Club, Doubleday History Book Club, Doubleday Military Book Club, The Literary Guild

The **Literary Guild**, see Doubleday New Zealand Ltd, Book Club Division

Lucky, Private Bag, Penrose, Auckland 6
Owned by: Ashton Scholastic Ltd (qv)

Teachers' Bookshelf, Private Bag, Penrose, Auckland 6
Owned by: Ashton Scholastic Ltd (qv)

Teenage, Private Bag, Penrose, Auckland 6
Owned by: Ashton Scholastic Ltd (qv)

Major Booksellers

Jill Anderson's **A B C** Bookshop*, 284 Trafalgar St, Nelson

Thomas **Avery** and Sons Ltd*, 79 Devon St, New Plymouth, North Island
Manager: Miles Cardale
Also Publisher (qv)

Beattie and Forbes*, PO Box 186, Napier
Managers: Catherine Robins, Janet Allan

G H **Bennett** & Co Ltd, 38-42 Broadway, PO Box 138, Palmerston North Tel: (063) 83009 Cable Add: Bennibooks Telex: NZ

3649 Benbook
Also: Bennetts Bookshop Ltd (at above address); Bennetts University Book Centre Ltd, Private Bag, Massey University Palmerston North Tel: (063) 66020 Telex: NZ 31607
Group General Manager: Trevor Day

Dorothy **Butler** Ltd, Fountain Court, The Three Lamps, Ponsonby, Auckland 2 Tel: (09) 767283
Specialist children's bookshop

Goddard's Bookshop Ltd, 21 Devonport Rd, PO Box 41, Tauranga Tel: (075) 87803
Man Dir: Ray Goddard

Hedley's Bookshop Ltd*, PO Box 746, Masterton Tel: (059) 82875
Manager: David Hedley
Branch Off: Hedley Australia, Box 1058 Ivanhoe, Victoria 3079, Australia
Also publisher and distributor

Horizon Bookshop Ltd, PO Box 30-240, Lower Hutt, Wellington (Located at: Cnr High St and Waterloo Rd, Lower Hutt, Wellington) Tel: (04) 698406/663256
Manager: Steven Sedley

London Bookshops Ltd, 10 Brandon St, PO Box 97, Wellington 1 Tel: (04) 731905 Telex: Att London Bookshops, c/o Wnpubtx No 3588
Dirs: D K Emanuel, P J Emanuel, R Rosenberg
Branches: St Luke's Shopping Centre, Mount Albert, Auckland; Shore City, Takapuna, Auckland; Glenfield Shopping Mall, Glenfield, Auckland; Downtown Mall, Queen St, Auckland; Lynmall City, New Lynn, Auckland; Henderson Square, Henderson, Auckland; Manukau City Shopping Centre, Manukau, Auckland; 99 Cashel St, Christchurch; 239 George St, Dunedin; 477 Victoria St, Hamilton; Hartham Pl, Porirua; Maidstone Mall, Upper Hutt; 190 High St, Lower Hutt; 326 Lambton Quay, Wellington; Kirkcaldie & Stains Ltd, Brandon St, Wellington; 106 Cuba St, Wellington; 39 Willis St, Wellington

Roy **Parsons***, Massey House, 126 Lambton Quay, Wellington 1

School Supplies Ltd, 9-11 Pollen St, Grey Lynn, PO Box 68443, Newton, Auckland Tel: (09) 789419 Telex: NZ 63426
Dir: David Simpson; *Manager:* Graham Wadams
Branches: 5 Wall Pl, Linden, Wellington; PO Box 50-384 Porirua; 50 Hannah St, PO Box 224, Whangarei; 363 Tuam St, PO Box 22-512, Christchurch; 68 Bridgman St, PO Box 2124, South Dunedin; 56 White St, PO Box 1981, Rotorua
Owned by: Whitcoulls Group Ltd

Unity Books Ltd, 119-125 Willis St, Wellington Tel: (04) 738438
Manager: A H Preston

University Book Shop (Auckland) Ltd, Student Union Bldg, 34 Princes St, Auckland 1 Tel: (09) 771869 Cable Add: Unibooks Fax: (09) 394278
Manager: Kitty Wishart

University Book Shop (Canterbury) Ltd*, University Drive, University of Canterbury, Christchurch Tel: (03) 488579 Cable Add: Unibooks
Manager: David Ault
Also: The Book Shop in the Arts Centre, Arts Centre, Christchurch Tel: (03) 60568

University Book Shop (Otago) Ltd, 378 Great King St, PO Box 6060, Dunedin North Tel: (024) 776976 Cable Add: Unibooks
Manager: Bill Noble

Whitcoulls Ltd, 95 Mt Eden Rd, Private Bag, Auckland Tel: (09) 392233 Telex: NZ 60402 Fax: (09) 395503
Chief Executive: R G Sutherland
Owned by: Pacific Publishers (qv)

Major Libraries

Auckland Public Library, Lorne St, PO Box 4138, Auckland 1 Tel: (09) 770209 Telex: NZ 2750 Fax: (09) 371558
Librarian: Helen M Tait

Canterbury Public Library, PO Box 1466, Christchurch Tel: (03) 796914 Telex: NZ 4620
Librarian: Dorothea Brown
Publication: Bookmark (monthly)

Canterbury University Library, Private Bag, Christchurch
Librarian: R W Hlavac

Dunedin Public Library, PO Box 5542, Moray Place, Dunedin Tel: (024) 743690
City Librarian: Norah Familton

General Assembly Library*, Parliament House, Wellington 1 Tel: (04) 749199

Manukau Public Libraries*, Manukau City Council, Private Bag, Manukau City Tel: (09) 2756065
City Librarian: Roy Carroll

National Archives*, Air New Zealand Bldg, 129-141 Vivian St, PO Box 6148, Te Aro, Wellington Tel: (04) 856109
Dir: R F Grover

National Library of New Zealand, Private Bag, Wellington 1 Tel: (04) 743000 Telex: NZ 30076 Fax: (04) 743107
Librarian: P G Scott
Publications include: New Zealand National Bibliography; *National Register of Archives and Manuscripts in New Zealand*

Palmerston North Public Library, PO Box 1948, Palmerston North Tel: (063) 83076
Librarian: I W Malcolm

Alexander **Turnbull** Library, National Library Bldg, Molesworth St, PO Box 12349, Wellington Tel: (04) 743000
Publications include: Turnbull Library Record (2 issues per annum)

University of Auckland Library, PB, Auckland Tel: (09) 737999 Telex: NZ 21480 Fax: (09) 33429
Librarian: P B Durey

University of Otago Library, PO Box 56, Dunedin Tel: (024) 771640
Librarian: M J Wooliscroft
Publication: Annual Report

Wellington Public Library, PO Box 1992, Wellington Tel: (04) 729529
Deputy City Librarian: J Hill; *Librarian:* B K McKeon

Library Associations

International Association of Music Libraries, New Zealand Branch, Inc, Canterbury Public Library, PO Box 1466, Christchurch Tel: (03) 796914
Secretary: Timothy Jones
Publications include: Crescendo; Orchestral Scores (Performing Editions list); *Sing!* (Choral Scores Catalogue); *Directory of New Zealand Musical Organizations; Bibliography of Writings about New Zealand Music Published to end of 1983*

New Zealand Library Association*, 20 Brandon St, PO Box 12212, Wellington 1 Tel: (04) 735834
Publications include: DISLIC (Directory of special libraries and information centres in New Zealand); *Public Libraries of New Zealand* (1985); *Standards for Special Libraries in New Zealand; Who's Who in New Zealand Libraries* (1986); *Library Life* (newsletter, 11 per year); *New Zealand Libraries* (quarterly)

Library Reference Books and Journals

Books

DISLIC (Directory of special libraries and information centres in New Zealand), New Zealand Library Association, 20 Brandon St, PO Box 12212, Wellington 1

Public Libraries of New Zealand, New Zealand Library Association, 20 Brandon St, PO Box 12212, Wellington 1

Who's Who in New Zealand Libraries, New Zealand Library Association, 20 Brandon St, PO Box 12212, Wellington 1

Journals

Library Life (11 times yearly), New Zealand Library Association, 20 Brandon St, PO Box 12212, Wellington 1

New Zealand Libraries (quarterly), New Zealand Library Association, 20 Brandon St, PO Box 12212, Wellington 1

Literary Associations and Societies

Bibliographical Society of Australia and New Zealand (BSANZ), c/o Secretary, 76 Warners Ave, Bondi Beach, NSW 2026, Australia
Secretary: Rose T Smith
Publications include: Bulletin (quarterly); *Broadsheet* (three times a year)

The Christchurch **Dickens** Fellowship, PO Box 6126, Christchurch Tel: (03) 486281
Honorary Secretary: Peter Oakley
Also: Dunedin, Wellington

The Dunedin **Dickens** Fellowship*, 18 Woodside Terrace, Andersons Bay, Dunedin
Secretary: Wyn A Comer
Also: Christchurch, Wellington

The Wellington **Dickens** Fellowship, Branch 121, 65 Mitchell St, Brooklyn, Wellington 2
Secretary: Maybelle Ryan
Also: Christchurch, Dunedin

International Writers Workshop New Zealand (Inc), 15 Killarney Ave, Torbay, Auckland 10

The **New Zealand Authors'** Fund, Department of Internal Affairs, Private Bag, Wellington Tel: (04) 738699 Cable Add: Internal Telex: Intafb NZ 31134, Intafl NZ 31098
Secretary: P Brewer

New Zealand Book Council, PO Box 11377, Wellington
Secretary: Jean Needham
Publications: Writers in Schools; Book Buyers in New Zealand; Books You Couldn't Buy (censorship in New Zealand)

New Zealand Maori Artists & Writers Society Inc, now Nga Puna Waihanga (qv)

New Zealand Women Writers' Society, 125 Marine Parade, Seatoun, Wellington 3
Secretary: Barbara Wilkinson

New Zealand Writers Guild*, PO Box 9116, Wellington Tel: (04) 849511
Chairman: John Smythe; *Secretary:* Bob Kerr

Nga Puna Waihanga, PO Box 1512, Rotorua (Located at: c/o Averill Herbert, 13 Branch Rd, Lake Okareka, Rotorua)
Founded: 1973
Formerly New Zealand Maori Artists & Writers Society Inc

P E N International New Zealand Centre, PO Box 2283, Postal Centre, Wellington
President: Louis Johnson; *Secretary:* Jean Needham
Publication: PEN Gazette (quarterly)

The Playwrights Association of New Zealand (Inc)*, PO Box 3578, Wellington

Literary Periodicals

Arena, Noel Farr Hoggard, PO Box 6188, Te Aro, Wellington
A literary magazine

English in New Zealand, Stockton House (Publisher), PO Box 46, Albany
A teachers' quarterly

Islands, Robin Dudding, 4 Scaly Rd, Torbay, Auckland 10
A New Zealand quarterly of arts and letters

Landfall, Caxton Press, 113 Victoria St, PO Box 25088, Christchurch

Mate, Wellesley St, PO Box 5670, Auckland
A magazine of New Zealand writing

New Quarterly Cave, Outrigger Publishers Ltd, PO Box 13049, Hamilton
An international magazine of arts and ideas

Northland, Northland Magazine Inc, PO Box 694, Whangarei

Literary Prizes

Award for Achievement
Founded in 1958 for a contribution to literature. NZ$1,000. Awarded annually. Awardee is nominated by the Literary Fund Advisory Committee: applications are not accepted. Enquiries to The Secretary, New Zealand Literary Fund, Department of Internal Affairs, Private Bag, Wellington

Bank of New Zealand Novice Writers' Award
To assist writers whose works have not previously been published. Awarded biennially. Award in 1987 NZ$1,000. Enquiries to New Zealand Women Writers' Society Inc, PO Box 11-352, Wellington

Bank of New Zealand Young Writers' Awards
For an unpublished short story written by a secondary-school pupil (over 13 years). Award in 1987 NZ$1,000. A grant of NZ$500 is given to the library of the secondary school attended by the winner. Awarded biennially. Enquiries to New Zealand Women Writers' Society Inc, PO Box 11-352, Wellington

Best First Book of Poetry Award
This prize incorporates the Jessie Mackay Award and is for the best first book of published poetry. NZ$1,000. Awarded annually. Enquiries to PEN International New Zealand Centre, PO Box 2283, Wellington

Best First Book of Prose Award
This prize incorporates the Hubert Church Award and is for the best first book of prose. NZ$1,000. Awarded annually. Enquiries to PEN International New Zealand Centre, PO Box 2283, Wellington

Buckland Award
Founded in 1966 by the late Freda M Buckland for the work of the highest literary merit by a New Zealand writer. Awarded annually. Enquiries to Buckland Award, Trustees Executors and Agency Company of New Zealand Ltd, 24 Water St, PO Box 760, Dunedin

Choysa Bursaries for Children's Book Writers and Illustrators
A bursary of NZ$10,000, established in 1979 to enable an author of imaginative work for children to work full-time for a period of up to one year on an approved project(s) which will reach book form. A new award of NZ$2,000 was made from 1987 to illustrators of children's picture books. Enquiries to The Secretary, New Zealand Literary Fund, Department of Internal Affairs, Private Bag, Wellington

Hubert Church Award, see Best First Book of Prose Award

Russell Clark Award*
For the most distinguished illustrations for a children's book. Illustrator must be a citizen or resident of New Zealand. Bronze medal and NZ$250. Awarded annually. Enquiries to New Zealand Library Association, 20 Brandon St, PO Box 12212, Wellington 1

Esther Glen Award*
For the best children's book by an author who is a citizen of, or resident in, New Zealand. Bronze medal and NZ$250. Awarded annually. Most recent winner was Margaret Mahy for *The Changeover* (Dent). Enquiries to New Zealand Library Association, 20 Brandon St, PO Box 12212, Wellington 1

Government Publishing Awards for the New Zealand Children's Books of the Year, see New Zealand Children's Books of the Year

I C I Writer's Bursary
Founded in 1978, this is an annual award of NZ$10,000, made to one or more writers (not necessarily of repute) with potential to work full-time for up to six months on an approved project. Enquiries to The Secretary, New Zealand Literary Fund, Department of Internal Affairs, Private Bag, Wellington

Literary Fund Writing Bursary
Award of NZ$10,000 to enable writers of creative literature in fictional prose, poetry or drama to work full-time on an approved programme for a period of up to six months. Enquiries to The Secretary, New Zealand Literary Fund, Department of Internal Affairs, Private Bag, Wellington

Jessie Mackay Award, see Best First Book of Poetry Award

Katherine Mansfield Memorial Award
For an unpublished short story. Sponsored by the Bank of New Zealand. First prize NZ$4,000, second prize NZ$1,500 in 1987. Awarded biennially. Enquiries to New Zealand Women Writers' Society Inc, PO Box 11-352, Wellington

New Zealand Book Awards
Annual awards of NZ$4,000 for the best New Zealand book by a New Zealand author published each year in the categories of poetry, fiction, non-fiction and book production. 1987 winners in the first three categories were Allen Curnow for *The Loop in the Lone Kauri Road* (Auckland University Press) and Elizabeth Nannestad for *Jump* (Auckland University Press); Patricia Grare for *Potiki* (Penguin Books (NZ) Ltd); Virginia Myers for *Head and Shoulders* (Penguin Books (NZ) Ltd). Enquiries to The Secretary, New Zealand Literary Fund, Department of Internal Affairs, Private Bag, Wellington

New Zealand Children's Books of the Year
Sponsored by the New Zealand Government Printer and awarded annually. The Awards aim to provide recognition and reward to New Zealand authors and illustrators of high-quality children's literature and are awarded in three categories: (1) NZ$1,500 to the author of the best children's story book; (2) NZ$1,500 to the author of the best non-fiction book; (3) NZ$1,000 each to the author and illustrator of the best picture story book (one award of NZ$1,500 where the author and illustrator are the same person). 1987 award winners were Robyn Kahukiwa for *Taniwha* (best picture story book) and Barry Faville for *The Keeper* (best story book). Enquiries to The Secretary, New Zealand Literary Fund, Department of Internal Affairs, Private Bag, Wellington

New Zealand Literary Fund
In addition to awards specifically mentioned, various grants are made from time to time by the above Fund to writers, publishers of creative literature and literary magazines. Enquiries to The Secretary, New Zealand Literary Fund, Department of Internal Affairs, Private Bag, Wellington

Wattie Book of the Year Award
Established 1967. For the book of the year based on: (1) quality of writing and illustrations; (2) quality of editing, design and production; (3) impact on the community. Open only to New Zealand book publishers. First prize NZ$15,000, second NZ$7,000, third NZ$3,000. The 1987 winner was Maurice Shadbold for *Season of the Jews* (Hodder & Stoughton Ltd). Enquiries to Book Publishers Association of New Zealand Inc, PO Box 44-146, Pt Chevalier, Auckland 2

Young Writers' Incentive Awards
For prose and poetry by New Zealanders under 20. NZ$250, NZ$125 and NZ$75. Enquiries to PEN International New Zealand Centre, PO Box 2283, Wellington

Nicaragua

General Information

Language: Spanish
Religion: Roman Catholic
Population: 3.3 million
Bank Hours: 0830-1500 Monday-Friday; 0830-1130 Saturday
Shop Hours: 0800-1200, 1430-1730 or longer Monday-Saturday
Currency: 100 centavos = 1 córdoba
Export/Import Information: Catalogues dutied per gross kilo. Compensatory Tax on advertising. No import licences or

exchange controls
Copyright: UCC, Buenos Aires, Florence (see International section)

Publishers

Academia Nicaragüense de la Lengua*, Biblioteca Nacional, Calle del Triunfo 302, Managua
Subject: Languages

Editorial **Nueva Nicaragua***, Apdo RP-073, Managua (Located at: Paseo Salvador Allende, Km 3-1/2 Carretera Sur, Managua) Tel: (02) 96317/96823 Telex: 1033 Enn nk
Executive Dir: Roberto Diaz Castillo; *Production Dir:* Irene Menocal Bravo; *Sales:* Betty Mejia Lopez
Orders to: Centro Comercial Linda Vista, Modulo E-11
Subjects: Literature, History (Nicaraguan), Politics, Religion, Social Sciences, Folklore, Fiction, Non-fiction, Poetry
1985: 40 titles *Founded:* 1981
Miscellaneous: Also co-productions

Editorial **San José***, Calle Central Este 607, Managua

Editorial **Unión***, Avda Central Norte, Managua
Subject: Travel

Universidad Nacional de Nicaragua, Librería y Editorial*, León
Subjects: Education, History, Mathematics, Law, Philology, Economics, Sciences, Politics, Literature

Major Booksellers

Librería **América***, Bosques de Altamira, Managua Tel: (02) 80895

Centro Cultural Bautista*, Apdo 5776, Cuidad Jardin No E5, Managua Tel: (02) 24714
Manager: Stanley D Stamps

Librería Recinto 'Ruben **Dario'***, Universidad Nacional Autonoma de Nicaragua, Apdo 663, Managua

Librería Cultural Nicaraguense*, Apdo 807, Managua Tel: (02) 6663

Librería Tecnológica Universitaria*, Universidad Centroamericana, Apdo 69, Managua Tel: (02) 80351

Librería **Universitaria***, Universidad Nacional Autónoma de Nicaragua, León Tel: (031) 2612

Librería **Recalde***, Apdo 666, Managua Tel: (02) 81156/61239

Major Libraries

Archivo Nacional*, Casa de Gobierno, Managua
Publication: Boletin Tecnico Informativo del Archivo Nacional

Biblioteca Nacional*, Calle del Triunfo 302, Managua

Biblioteca Central del **Universidad Nacional** de Nicaragua*, León

Library Associations

Asociación de Bibliotecas Universitarias y Especializadas de Nicaragua*, Apdo 68, León
Association of University and Special Libraries of Nicaragua
Publication: Boletín

Asociación Nicaraguense de Bibliotecarios (ASNIBI)*, Biblioteca Nacional, Ministerio de Educacion Publica, Barrio 'La Fuente', Managua
Nicaraguan Association of Librarians
Executive Secretary: Susana Morales Hernández

Library Reference Journal

Boletín (Bulletin), Asociación de Bibliotecas Universitarias y Especializadas de Nicaragua, Apdo 68, León

Literary Associations and Societies

Nicaraguan **P E N** Centre, PO Box 5867, Managua
Secretary: Noel Correa

Literary Periodical

Nicaráuac, Edificio de Patrimonio Cultural, Plaza de Comunicaciones, Apdo 3269, Managua
Ministry of Culture literary review

Niger

General Information

Language: French
Religion: 85% Islamic, remainder traditional beliefs
Population: 5.1 million
Bank Hours: 0800-1100, 1600-1700 (cool season 1530-1700) Monday-Friday
Business Hours: 0730-1230, 1600-1800 (cool season 1530-1730) Monday-Friday; 0730-1230 Saturday
Currency: CFA franc
Export/Import Information: Member of West African Economic Community. No tariff on books; advertising matter subject to Fiscal and Customs Duties (EEC members pay percentage of Customs Duty). Also Statistical Tax.
Copyright: Berne (see International section)

Publishers

Government Printer (Imprimerie Générale du Niger)*, BP 61, Niamey

Major Booksellers

Librairie **Fellicelli et Poli***, BP 331, Niamey

Librairie **Mauclert** et Cie*, BP 10778, Niamey Tel: 722778

Major Libraries

Bibliothèque de l'**Ambassade** de France*, BP 10660, Niamey

Archives nationales*, Présidence de la République, BP 550, Niamey

Centre de Documentation de l'Autorité du Bassin du Niger*, BP 933, Niamey Tel: 723964 Telex: 5256 Augani

Documentation Centre of the Niger Basin Authority
Dir: Josué Ebolo Ebolo
Parent Organization: Niger Basin Authority (Autorité du Bassin du Niger), at above address
Publications: Concerning development of the natural resources of the River Niger Basin
Founded: 1971

Centre d'Enseignement supérieur de Niamey*, Bibliothèque, BP 237, Niamey
University Education Centre

Bibliothèque l'**Ecole** nationale d'administration du Niger*, BP 542, Niamey Tel: 722853
Librarian: Elyane Maiga

Institut de recherche en Sciences humaines, BP 318, Niamey Tel: 735141/733955 Telex: Uninim
Librarian: Sai'dou Harouna
Publications: Etudes Nigériennes

Bibliothèque de l'**Université de Niamey***, BP 237, Niamey Tel: 732713

Nigeria

General Information

Language: English, Hausa
Religion: 45% Islamic (mainly in north), 35% Christian, remainder traditional beliefs
Population: 77.1 million
Bank Hours: 0800-1500 Monday; 0800-1300 Tuesday-Friday
Shop Hours: Vary locally. 0800-1230, 1400-1630 Monday-Friday; 0800-1230 Saturday
Currency: 100 kobo = 1 naira
Export/Import Information: No tariffs on books or advertising matter. Open general licence. Obscene literature prohibited. Exchange controls
Copyright: UCC, Florence (see International section)

Book Trade Organizations

Nigerian Book Development Council*, 6 Obanta Rd, Apapa, Lagos State Tel: (01) 874863
Secretary: Alhaja M M Musa

Nigerian Booksellers' Association, c/o Mr Bisi Aladejana, Bisi Books, 720 Oyo Rd, Mokola, Ibadan, Oyo State
Secretary: Bisi Aladejana

Nigerian I S B N Agency, The Director, National Library of Nigeria, 4 Wesley St, PMB 12626, Lagos Tel: (01) 634704/630053 Cable Add: Biblios Telex: 20117
Agency Head: S E A Sonaike
Publications: Nigerian ISBN Manual and Directory

Nigerian Publishers' Association, PO Box 2541, GPO Ibadan (Located at: Isolak Bldg, Queen Elizabeth Rd, Mokola) Tel: (022) 411557 Telex: 31113
President: F S Ogunniyi; *Executive Secretary:* Tope Popoola
Publication: The Publisher (bi-annual)

Standard Book Numbering Agency, see Nigerian ISBN Agency

University Booksellers Association of
Nigeria*, c/o Benin University Bookshop,
University of Benin, PMB 1154, Benin,
Bendel State Tel: (052) 243780
President: S O Ehiede

Book Trade Reference Books and Journals

Books

Publishing in Nigeria, Ethiope Publishing
Corporation, Ring Rd, PMB 1332, Benin
City

Serials in Print in Nigeria, National Library
of Nigeria, 4 Wesley St, PMB 12626,
Lagos

Journals

National Bibliography of Nigeria, National
Library of Nigeria, 4 Wesley St, PMB
12626, Lagos
Published annually since 1950; cumulations
before 1971 published by the Ibadan
University Press (also available as a weekly
service)

New Nigeriana, University Bookshop Ltd,
Obafemi Awolowo University, Ile-Ife
Biannual checklist, available free of charge
from the University Bookshop

Nigerian Books in Print, National Library
of Nigeria, 4 Wesley St, PMB 12626,
Lagos

Northern Nigerian Publications (annual),
Ahmadu Bello University Library, Samaru-
Zaria

Publishers

A B I C (Publishers)*, 9 Edozien St, Box
13740, Enugu, Anambra State Tel: (042)
331827
President: C N C Asomugha; *Marketing
Manager:* F Mgbajiaka
Subjects: Reference, School Textbooks,
Local History, Poetry, Trade Books,
Children's
Founded: 1978
ISBN Publisher's Prefix: 978-2269

Academy Press Ltd, subsidiary of West
African Book Publishers Ltd (qv)

Adebara Publishers Ltd*, PO Box 1970,
Ibadan Telex: 20311
Man Dir, Editorial: Dele Adebara; *Sales,
Publicity:* Bisi Oke; *Production:* Layi
Bankole; *Rights & Permissions:* Kayode
Ayeni
Imprints: Adebara, Awoko, Gangan,
Kakaki
Subjects: Africana, Educational, Business,
Professional, Children's, Reference,
Novels, Radical Views, Scholarly,
Research, Religion, Biography
Book Club: Amebo Book Club
Founded: 1979
ISBN Publisher's Prefix: 978-147

African Universities Press, Pilgrim Books
Ltd, PMB 5617, Ibadan (Located at: New
Oluyole Industrial Estate, Phase II Ibadan-
Lagos Expressway, Ibadan) Tel: (022)
317218 Cable Add: Pilgrim Ibadan Telex:
20311 Box 078
Man Dir: John E Leigh; *Executive Dir:* Dr
E A M Leigh
Parent Company: Pilgrim Books Ltd (at
above address)
Subjects: Primary, Secondary and Tertiary
Textbooks

Africana-FEP Publishers Ltd, 79 Awka Rd,
PMB 1639, Onitsha Tel: (046) 210669
Cable Add: Afribook, Onitsha, Nigeria
Man Dir: P N C Omabu; *Marketing:*
Ralph O Ekpeh
Branch Offs: 22-26 Park Rd, Zaria; 9 Old
Lagos Rd, PMB 5632, Ibadan
Subjects: How-to, Study Guides, General
Science, Secondary & Primary Textbooks,
At a Glance and *Made Easy* series;
University & College books on Education,
English, Management, Politics, Linguistics
Founded: 1971

Africana Publishers (Nig) Ltd, now
Africana-FEP Publishers Ltd (qv)

Ahmadu Bello University Press Ltd,
PMB 1094, Zaria Tel: (069) 50054 Cable
Add: Unibello Press Zaria Telex: 75241
Zarabu Ng
Man Dir, Editorial, Rights & Permissions:
Dr A Ghaji; *Editorial:* Yusuf Tanko;
Production: Mohammed Audi Abubakar
Subjects: History, Africana, Reference,
Social Sciences, Education, Veterinary
Medicine
Founded: 1974
ISBN Publisher's Prefix: 978-125

Albah Publishers+, PO Box 6177, Bompai,
Kano (Located at: 100 Kurawa, Kano
City) Cable Add: Albah Kano
Chairman, Editorial: Bashari F Roukbah;
Sales & Publicity Manager: Idris A
Muhammad; *Production:* Basiru Ahmad
Associate Company: Brunswick Publishing
Co, PO Box 555, Lawrenceville,
VA 23868, USA
Subjects: Scholarly, Africana, Islam,
Educational, Textbooks (in Hausa)
Bookshop: Baban Layi, Gyadi-Gyadi,
Zariya Rd, Kano
Founded: 1978
ISBN Publisher's Prefix: 978-2380

Alliance West African Publishers & Co,
Orindingbin Estate, New Aketan Layout,
PMB 1039, Oyo Tel: (038) 230798
Chairman, Man Dir: Chief M O
Ogunmola; *Sales:* L Oyeniji; *Publicity,
Permissions:* Kehinde Ogunmola
Subjects: Biography, History, Africana,
How-to, Study Guides, Nigerian
Languages, General Science, Secondary &
Primary School Textbooks
Founded: 1971

Aowa Press & Publications*, PO Box
3090, Ibadan
Subjects: How-to, Study Guides, Primary
& Secondary Textbooks

Aromolaran Publishing Co Ltd, PO Box
1800, Ibadan Tel: (022) 715980
Telex: 31158 Arbook Nigeria
Man Dir: Dr Adekunle Aromolaran; *Sales:*
Mrs V M Aromolaran
Subjects: Belles Lettres, Poetry, Biography,
How-to, Study Guides, Religion, Juveniles;
Arts, Science and General Books for
Primary and Secondary Schools and
Universities, Periodicals
Founded: 1970

Awoko, an imprint of Adebara Publishers
Ltd (qv)

Black Academy Press+*, PO Box 255,
Owerri, Imo State Tel: (083) 230606/
232606 Cable Add: Bapress
Man Dir: Dr S Okechukwu Mezu
Subjects: General Non-fiction, Belles
Lettres, Poetry, Biography, History,
Africana

C S S Bookshops, Agency and Publishing
Division*, Bookshop House, 50-52 Broad
St, PO Box 174, Lagos Tel: (01) 633010/
633081 Cable Add: Bookshops
Man Dir: Chief Ademola Adetutu
Subsidiary Company: CSS Bookshops, PO
Box 174, Lagos (and area offices at Benin,
Enugu, Ibadan, Port Harcourt, Zaria)
Subjects: General Non-fiction, Biography,
History, Africana, Religion, General
Science, Law, Medicine, Secondary &
Primary Textbooks

Challenge Publications, Publishing Division
of ECWA Productions Ltd (qv)

Conch Magazine Ltd, Publishers*, PO Box
573, Owerri, Imo State (Located at:
1 Lagos St, Owerri)
Man Dir: Sunday Anozie
Subsidiary Company: Conch Magazine Ltd,
102 Normal Ave, Buffalo, NY 14213, USA
Subjects: General Non-fiction, Belles
Lettres, Poetry, History, Africana,
Paperbacks, Social Science

Cross Continent Press Ltd+*, 226 Murtala
Muhammed Way, PO Box 282, Yaba,
Lagos State Tel: (01) 862437 Cable Add:
Croconpres Lagos
Man Dir: T C Nwosu; *Editorial, Publicity:*
Miss A C Ikeme; *Marketing:* Miss P N
Ikekwem
Subsidiary Company: Editorial Consultancy
& Agency Services (qv under Literary
Agents)
Branch Off: Kess Nwagwu, PO Box 2273,
Owerri, Imo State
Subjects: General Fiction & Non-fiction,
Belles Lettres, Poetry, Biography, How-to,
Study Guides, Juveniles, Paperbacks,
Primary, Secondary & Tertiary Textbooks
Founded: 1974
ISBN Publisher's Prefix: 978-134

Daily Times of Nigeria Ltd*, Publication
Division, New Isheri Rd, PMB 21340,
Ikeja, Lagos State Tel: (01) 900850 Cable
Add: Daily Times Lagos Telex: 21333
Times Ng
Chief Executive: Segun Osoba; *Editorial:*
Faruk Mohammed; *Sales:* Funsho
Akindele; *Production:* J M Teshola
Subsidiary Company: Times Press Ltd
Subjects: Reference, Nigerian *Who's Who*
Book Club: Times Book Club
Founded: 1925

Daystar Press (Publishers), Daystar House,
PO Box 1261, Ibadan Tel: (022) 23230
Man Dir, Editorial, Rights & Permissions:
Modupe Oduyoye; *Production:* Rachel
Alao; *Trade:* James Akimboye; *Publicity:*
A Osuji; *Marketing:* Sola Ladipo
Subjects: Christian Religion, Health, Home
& Family Life, Nigerian Culture
Founded: 1962
ISBN Publisher's Prefix: 978-122

Delta Publications (Nigeria) Ltd+, 172
Ogui Rd, PO Box 1172, Enugu, Anambra
State Tel: (042) 253215
Man Dir, Rights & Permissions: C D E
Onyeama; *Editorial Dir:* Mrs E O
Onyeama; *Sales:* Boniface Odiha;
Production, Publicity: Jane Anyabuine
Subjects: Biography, Memoirs, Fiction,
General
1985: 10 titles *Founded:* 1982
ISBN Publisher's Prefix: 978-2335

E C W A Productions Ltd, PMB 2010, Jos
Tel: (073) 52230/53897 Telex: 81120
Ecwap Ng
Man Dir: Dr Philip S Usman; *General
Manager:* Jonathan A Babstunde
(Publications)
Subjects: General, Educational, Religion
Bookshops: Challenge Bookshops (qv
under Major Booksellers)
Miscellaneous: Challenge Publications is
Publishing Division of ECWA Productions
Ltd

Educational Research Institute*, PO Box
277, Ibadan

316 NIGERIA

Man Dir: Areoye Oyebola
Subjects: General Non-fiction, Biography, History, Africana, How-to, Study Guides, Religion, General & Social Science, Secondary & Primary Textbooks
Founded: 1970

Elizabethan Publishing Co+*, 41 Ogunlana Drive, PO Box 3377, Surulere, Lagos Tel: (01) 835305
Chief Executive: Elizabeth Osisanya; *Dir:* Prof C A Kogbe
Subsidiary Company: Ogie Elegant-Twins, PO Box 3377, Surulere, Lagos Tel: (01) 832113
Subjects: Academic, Geology, Nigerian Culture
Founded: 1976

Emotan Publishing Co (Nigeria) Ltd*, 152nd Ire St, Benin City
Man Dir: P O Onaghise
Subjects: General Fiction, Belles Lettres, Poetry, Paperbacks

Ethiope Publishing Corporation*, Ring Rd, PMB 1332, Benin City, Bendel State Tel: (052) 243870 Cable Add: Ethiope Telex: 41110
General Manager: Sunday N Olaye
Subjects: General Fiction & Non-fiction, Belles Lettres, Poetry, Biography, History, Africana, How-to, Study Guides, Philosophy, Reference, Juveniles, Paperbacks, Science & Technology, General & Social Science, Law, University & Secondary Textbooks
Founded: 1970

Evans Brothers (Nigeria Publishers) Ltd, Jericho Rd, PMB 5164, Ibadan Tel: (022) 417570 Cable Add: Edbooks Ibadan Telex: 31104 Edbook
Man Dir: B O Bolodeoku; *Sales Dir:* S A Oke; *Managing Editor:* Mrs L I Durodola
Associate Company: Evans Brothers Ltd, UK (qv)
Branch Offs: Kaduna, Lagos and Owerri
Subjects: Educational, General Non-fiction, Belles Lettres, Poetry, Biography, History, Africana, Reference, Juveniles, Paperbacks, Science & Technology, General & Social Science, Secondary & Primary Textbooks
Founded: 1966
ISBN Publisher's Prefix: 978-167

Olaiya **Fagbamigbe** Ltd (Publishers)*, 11 Methodist Church Rd, PO Box 14, Akure Tel: (034) 2075 Cable Add: Fagbamigbe Akure
Man Dir: Mrs M E Fagbamigbe; *Editor:* Yinka Obatuyi; *Publicity:* Gbenga Fagbamigbe; *Rights & Permissions:* Yetunde Fagbamigbe
Branch Off: New Ife Rd, PO Box 1176, Agodi Gate, Ibadan
Subjects: Educational and General
Founded: 1976
ISBN Publisher's Prefix: 978-164

Fourth Dimension Publishing Co Ltd, Plot 64A, City Layout, New Haven, PMB 01164, Enugu Tel: (042) 339969 Telex: 51319 Fdpubs Ng
Chief Executive: V U Nwankwo; *Editorial, Production:* Franklin N Ejiofor; *Sales:* Don M Unonu; *Publicity:* Patrick Onwuasoanya; *Rights & Permissions:* Uche Ogakwu
Subsidiary Company: Fourth Dimension Book Centre
Subjects: Fiction, Educational
Bookshops: 17 Okpara Ave, PMB 01164, Enugu; 7 Wetheral Rd, Owerri
1985: 150 titles *1986:* 103 titles *Founded:* 1976
ISBN Publisher's Prefix: 978-156

Gangan, an imprint of Adebara Publishers Ltd (qv)

Gbabeks Publishers Ltd*, PO Box 584, Kaduna (Located at: L 16 Ibadan St, Kaduna) Tel: (062) 217976
Man Dir, Editorial, Production, Rights & Permissions: Tayo Ogunbekun; *Sales, Publicity:* Segun O Osazuwa
Subjects: Chemistry, Accountancy, Business Administration, Marketing, Engineering, Education, Research Development, English, Physics, Mathematics
1985: 2 titles *Founded:* 1982
ISBN Publisher's Prefix: 978-2416

Heinemann Educational Books (Nigeria) Ltd, 1 Ighodaro Rd, Jericho, PMB 5205, Ibadan Tel: (022) 417060/417061/410267 Cable Add: Hebooks Ibadan Telex: 31113 Hebook NG
Executive Chairman: Aigboje Higo; *Man Dir, Rights & Permissions:* Akin Thomas; *Editorial & Production Dir:* Ayo Ojeniyi; *Sales, Marketing & Publicity Dir:* Ezekiel M Ojo
Associate Company: The Heinemann Group of Publishers Ltd, UK (qv for associate companies)
Satellite Warehouses: Owerri Depot: 5 Orlu Rd, PO Box 2304, Owerri; Zaria Depot: No 4 Kantinkori, Kaduna Rd, PMB 1122, Zaria; Jos Depot: No BP 557 Jingiri Rd, Bukuru By-pass, PO Box 6989, Jos
Branch Offs: T5 Rafin Pa Laranto, PO Box Jos; PA 223, Zoo Rd, Phase II PO Box 10292, Kano; F7A, Fed Low Cost Housing Estate, PO Box 1727, Enugu; Flat 4, 14 Akanni Taiwo St, Oke-Efon, Abeokuta, Lagos; Flat 1, 38/40 Akowojo Rd, Egbeda, off Dopemu Rd, Agege, Lagos; House 224 behind Elephant House, Ahmadu Bello Way, PO Box 2071, Sokoto, Ondo State; 2 Alakure St, PO Box 532, Akure, Ondo State; PO Box 675 Benin City
Subjects: Educational (Primary, Post-Primary and Tertiary), Law, Medicine and General
1985-86: 50 titles *Founded:* 1960
ISBN Publisher's Prefix: 978-129

Heritage Books, 2/8 Calcutta Crescent, c/o Come-Chop, PO Box 610, Apapa, Lagos Tel: (01) 871333/875389
Man Dir: Naiwu Osahon; *Senior Editor, Rights & Permissions:* Bakin Kunama; *Publicity:* Edia Apolo
Subsidiary Company: Obobo Books (qv)
Subjects: General Fiction and Non-fiction, Belles Lettres, Poetry, Black Power, Paperbacks, Periodical
Bookshop: Heritage (The Bookshop), PO Box 930, Apapa, Lagos
Founded: 1971

I C I C (Directory Publishers) Ltd, PO Box 5736, Surulere, Lagos (Located at: Directory House, 6 Taoridi St, Animashaun Estate, opp Census Office, Surulere, Lagos) Tel: (01) 831909 Cable Add: ICIC Lagos
Dirs: Olu Adeyemi, Prof Akin L Mabogunje, Mrs Yinka Adeyemi; *Group Sales Manager:* D A Ajiboye
Subjects: General, Reference, Telephone and Business Directories
Founded: 1965

Ibadan University Press, University of Ibadan, Ibadan Tel: (022) 462550 ext 1244 Cable Add: Univpress Ibadan
Head of Marketing: Bisi Ogunleye
Subjects: History, Africana, Philosophy, Reference, Agriculture, Medicine, Psychology, Science & Technology, General & Social Science, Law, University Textbooks, Scholarly books
Founded: 1952
ISBN Publisher's Prefix: 978-121

Ilesanmi Press (Educational Publishers) Ltd*, Akure Rd, PO Box 204, Ilesha Tel: 2062/2017 Cable Add: Ilesanmi Press Ilesha
Man Dir, Rights & Permissions: G E Ilesanmi; *Publishing, Production Dir:* G O Ilesanmi; *Marketing Dir:* C A Ilesanmi; *Editorial:* C U Awioke
Branch Offs: Uyo, Kano, Ibadan, Lagos, Akure, Jos, Onitsha, Minna
Subjects: Biography, History, Africana, How-to, Study Guides, Books in Yoruba Language, Teacher Training Manuals, General & Social Science, Engineering, Music, Chemistry, Physics, Mathematics, Sciences, English, Igbo, Hausa
Bookshop: Faji, Ilesha
Founded: 1956
ISBN Publisher's Prefix: 978-157

Institute of African Studies*, Publications Section, University of Ibadan, Ibadan Tel: (022) 400550/400579
Dir, Editorial, Rights & Permissions: Prof Bolanle Awe; *Editorial, Sales, Production:* Mabel Segun
Subject: Africana
Founded: 1962

Islamic Publications Bureau, 136A Isolo Rd, Mushin, Lagos Tel: (01) 523221 Cable Add: Alislam
Man Dir: Ahmad Patel
Branch Offs: 40 Sultan Bello Rd, PO Box 5106, Kaduna Tel: (062) 217813; 453 Airport Rd, New Commercial Layout, PO Box 420, Kano
Subjects: Islamic Literature and Arabic Books
Founded: 1969

Kakaki, an imprint of Adebara Publishers Ltd (qv)

Kolasanya Publishing Enterprise*, 2 Epe Rd, Oke-Owa, PMB 2099, Ijebu-Ode, Ogun State
Man Dir: Kola Osunsanya
Subjects: General Non-fiction, How-to, Study Guides, General Science, Secondary & Primary Textbooks

Lagos University Press Ltd, Publication Division, University of Lagos Post Office 132, Akoka, Yaba, Lagos Tel: (01) 860695/800500 ext 409
Dir: Bodunde Bankole; *Sales:* Ade Ogidan; *Production:* A Balogun, S B Oyenuga
Subjects: Biography, Humanities, Africana, Law, Social Science, University Textbooks, Medicine, Education
Founded: 1980
ISBN Publisher's Prefix: 978-2264

Lantern Books, an imprint of Literamed Publications Nigeria Ltd (qv)

Literamed Publications Nigeria Ltd, PMB 21068, Ikeja, Lagos (Located at: Plot 45, Alausa Village, Oregun Industrial Estate) Tel: (01) 962512
Man Dir: O Lawal-Solarin; *Publishing Dir:* Dr Sola Solle
Imprint: Lantern Books
Branch Off: 18 Langsmead, Blindley Heath, Lingsfield, Surrey, UK
Subjects: Educational, Political, Social, Children's Literature, Periodicals
Founded: 1969
ISBN Publisher's Prefix: 978-2281

Longman Nigeria Ltd*, 52 Oba Akran Ave, PMB 21036, Ikeja, Lagos Tel: (01) 963007/963176 Cable Add: Longman Ikeja
Man Dir: Felix A Iwerebon; *Marketing Manager:* C O Ojiji; *Publishing Manager:*

O Agboola; *Production:* A W Amaeshi
Associate Company: Longman Group UK Ltd, UK (qv)
Subjects: General Fiction & Non-fiction, Belles Lettres, Poetry, Biography, History, Africana, Reference, Religion, Juveniles, Books in Nigerian Languages (various), Paperbacks, Psychology, Science & Technology, General & Social Science, University, Secondary & Primary Textbooks
Founded: 1961

Macmillan Nigeria Publishers Ltd*, Ibadan Lagos Expressway, Nr Methodist High School, PO Box 1463, Ibadan (Located at: Oluyole Industrial Estate, Scheme 2, Ibadan) Tel: (022) 316896 Cable Add: Macbook Ibadan Telex: Mabook 31141
Chairman, Man Dir: Olu Anulopo; *Deputy Man Dir:* I Ademokun; *Publishing:* B U Iwu; *Marketing:* E Ohuka, J S Oyalami; *Production:* A Adebusuyi; *Publicity:* D Obisesan
Orders to: PO Box 264, Yaba
Associate Company: Macmillan Publishers Ltd, UK (qv)
Branch Offs: PO Box 434, Akure; PMB 1286, Benin City; PO Box 766, Ilorin; PO Box 390, Onitsha; PO Box 476, Owerri; PO Box 192, Uyo; PO Box 264, Yaba; PO Box 1395, Zaria
Subjects: Biography, History, Africana, Religion, Juveniles, Books in various Nigerian Languages, Paperbacks, General & Social Science, University, Secondary, Primary and Nursery Textbooks, General Fiction
Founded: 1965
ISBN Publisher's Prefix: 978-132

Thomas Nelson (Nigeria) Ltd*, Nelson House, 8 Ilupeju By-Pass, PMB 1303, Ikeja, Lagos Tel: (01) 961452 Cable Add: Thonelson Ikeja
Executive Chairman: Prof C O Taiwo; *Man Dir:* S O Daramola; *Marketing Dir:* E B Iyekolo; *Advisory Dir:* G E Muller; *Publishing Manager:* S Mabogunje
Parent Company: Thomas Nelson International, Toronto, Canada
Associate Company: University Publishing Co, Nigeria (qv)
Subjects: General Fiction and Non-fiction, Africana, Books in various Nigerian Languages, General & Social Science, Textbooks

New Horn Press Ltd, PO Box 4138, University Post Office, Ibadan
Chairman: Dr Abiola Irele; *Senior Editor, Rights & Permissions:* Mrs Bassey Irele
Subjects: General Fiction & Non-fiction, Belles Lettres, Poetry, How-to, Study Guides, Paperbacks, Textbooks
Founded: 1974
ISBN Publisher's Prefix: 978-2266

Nigerian Institute of International Affairs, PO Box 1727, Lagos (Located at: 13 Kofo Abayomi Rd, Victoria Island, Lagos) Tel: (01) 615606/615610 Cable Add: Internations Lagos Telex: 22638
Chief Executive: Prof Gabriel O Olusanya; *Editorial:* Prof G O Olusanya, Prof R A Akindele, Dr Bassey Ate, Bukar Bukarambe; *Sales:* S E Bassey
Subjects: International Politics, Economics, Jurisprudence
Founded: 1961
ISBN Publisher's Prefix: 978-2276

Nigerian Trade Review*, PO Box 603, Marina, Lagos
Man Dir: Chief P A Dawodu
Subjects: General, Business Directories
Founded: 1958

Nok Publishers (Nigeria) Ltd*, PO Box 1005, Enugu, Anambra State (Located at: First Avenue, Independence Layout, Enugu) Tel: (042) 339014 (Enugu), (01) 632835 (Lagos) Telex: 21810 Gcwn Ng
Man Dir: Ahaji A C Ude; *Sales:* Jane Odenisbo; *Production:* Louis Umerah
Parent Company: Nok Publishers International, 150 5th Avenue, New York, NY 10011, USA
Subjects: Africana (Art & Culture, History, Politics, Philosophy, Sociology, Religions, Literature, Folklore, Poetry, Education, Law, Economics), African Bibliographic Series
Founded: 1973
ISBN Publisher's Prefix: 0-88357

Northern Nigerian Publishing Co Ltd+*, Gaskiya Bldg, PO Box 412, Zaria, Kaduna State Tel: (069) 32087 Cable Add: Gasmac Telex: 75243 Gasmac Nig
General Manager: Alhaji Husaini Hayat; *Managing Editor:* Moh-Tukur Garba; *Marketing Manager:* Alhaji Mamman Maina; *Sales Manager:* Sunny S Shirima
Associate Company: Macmillan Publishers Ltd, UK (qv)
Subjects: General Non-fiction, Belles Lettres, Poetry, Biography, History, Africana, Religion, Juveniles, Books in Hausa and other Nigerian Languages, Paperbacks, Secondary & Primary Textbooks

Nwamife Publishers Ltd, 10 Ibiam St, Uwani, PO Box 430, Enugu Tel: (042) 338254 Cable Add: Nwamife Enugu
Chairman: Dr Felix C Adi; *Sales, Production, Publicity:* Samuel Umesike; *Editorial, Rights & Permissions:* Dr Nina Mba
Subjects: General Fiction & Non-fiction, Belles Lettres, Poetry, Biography, History, Africana, How-to, Study Guides, Juveniles, Igbo Language & Literature, General Science, Law, University, Secondary & Primary Textbooks, Paperbacks
Founded: 1970
ISBN Publisher's Prefix: 978-124

Flora **Nwapa** & Co, see Tana Press Ltd

Obafemi Awolowo University Press Ltd, Ile-Ife, Oyo State Tel: (038) 2291 ext 2882 Cable Add: Press Awovarsity
General Manager: Akin Fatokun; *Senior Editor:* Adenike Adeyanju; *Publishing Manager:* Mrs Adenike Osadolor; *Production Manager:* Pius Ejiogu
Subjects: Biography, History, Africana, Philosophy, Reference, Religion, Law, Social Science, University Textbooks, Education
Founded: 1968

Obobo Books, 2/8 Calcutta Crescent, c/o Come-Chop, PO Box 610, Apapa, Lagos Tel: (01) 871333/875389
Chief Executive: Miss Obobo Osahon; *Editorial:* Bakin Kunama; *Sales, Publicity:* Edia Apolo; *Production:* Edun Osahon
Parent Company: Heritage Books (qv)
Subjects: Children's, Short Stories, Colouring Series, Adventure Series, Biographies
Bookshop: Heritage (The Bookshop), PO Box 930, Apapa, Lagos
Founded: 1981
ISBN Publisher's Prefix: 978-186

Ogunsanya Press, Publishers and Bookstores Ltd*, Orita Challenge, PO Box 95, Ibadan Tel: (022) 310924 Cable Add: Pombapress
Man Dir, Editorial, Rights & Permissions: Chief Lucas Justus Popo-Ola Ogunsanya; *Sales, Publicity:* E A Faleke; *Production:* A S Banjo

Branch Off: Popo-Ola Jubilee Lodge, Oke Imoru, PO Box 155, Ijebu Ode, Ogun State
Subjects: History, Geography, Mathematics, English, Science, Social Studies, Arabic
Bookshop: 64 Agbeni St (opp Foko Junction), Ibadan
Founded: 1970

Omoleye Publishing Co Ltd, PO Box 1265, Ibadan, Oyo State Tel: (022) 314766
Man Dir: Mike Omoleye
Subjects: General, Fiction, Yoruba Culture, Periodical

Onibonoje Press & Book Industries (Nigeria) Ltd, Felele Layout, PO Box 3109, Ibadan Tel: (022) 313956 Telex: 31657 Bonoje NG
Chairman: Gabriel Onibonoje; *Man Dir:* J Olu Onibonoje
Branch Offs: Benin City, Ikot Ekpene, Jos, Kano, Lagos, Onitsha, Sokoto, Zaria
Subjects: General Fiction & Non-fiction, Belles Lettres, Poetry, Biography, History, Africana, How-to, Study Guides, Religion, Juveniles, Yoruba Language & Literature, Paperbacks, General & Social Science, Primary, Secondary & Teacher Training College Textbooks
Book Club: Onibonoje Book Club
Bookshop and Showroom: SW8/77 Oke-Ado, Ibadan
Founded: 1958

Orisun Editions*, PO Box 3079, Ibadan
Man Dir: Bola Ige
Subjects: General, Belles Lettres, Poetry

People's Publishing Co Ltd*, PO Box 3121, Lagos
Subjects: General Non-fiction, Socialism

Pilgrim Books Ltd, see African Universities Press

Sketch Press Ltd*, Sketch Bldgs, New Court Rd, PMB 5067, Ibadan Tel: (022) 414851 Cable Add: Sketch Telex: 31591
Man Dir: Peter Ajayi; *Editorial:* Ademola Idowu
Subjects: General Books, Reference Books
Founded: 1964

Spectrum Books Ltd, Sunshine House, 2nd Commercial Rd, Oluyole Estate, PMB 5612, Ibadan Tel: (022) 3100588/311215 Cable Add: Specta Telex: 31588
Chief Executive: Joop Berkhout; *Editorial:* Chris Bankole; *Sales, Publicity:* Labi Olayinka; *Operations Manager:* 'Gbenro Adegbola
Associate Company: Safari Books (Export) Ltd, Compendium House, 32 Hue St, St Helier, Jersey, Channel Islands, UK
Subjects: Educational, Fiction
Founded: 1978
ISBN Publisher's Prefix: 978-2265

Tana Press Ltd and Flora Nwapa & Co+*, 2A Menkiti Lane, Ogui, Enugu, Anambra State Tel: (042) 338857 Cable Add: Tana Telex: 51164 Lake NG
Man Dir: Flora Nwakuche (née Nwapa); *Editorial:* Dr Nina Mba; *Sales, Publicity:* Nigerian Publishers Services Ltd (qv); *Production:* E N Benyeogo, M A Ubah; *Rights & Permissions:* Flora Nwapa & Co
Orders to: Nigerian Publishers Services Ltd, Trusthouse, PO Box 62, Ibadan; Third World Publications, 151 Stratford Rd, Birmingham B11 1RD, UK; Three Continents Press, 1346 Connecticut Ave NW, Washington, DC 20036, USA
Branch Off: PO Box 2, Oguta, Imo State
Subjects: Children's, Short Stories, Novels
Founded: 1979
ISBN Publisher's Prefix: 978-2272

Third World First Publications, now Heritage Books (qv)

NIGERIA

University of Ife Press, now Obafemi Awolowo University Press Ltd (qv)

University Press Ltd, Three Crowns Bldg, Jericho, PMB 5095, Ibadan Tel: (022) 411356/412313/412386 Cable Add: Oxonian Ibadan Telex: Ibadan 31121 Oxonia Ng
Man Dir: Michael O Akinleye;
Administration Manager: B O Adeleke;
Publishing Manager: S A Adewuyi;
Operations Manager: O Bankole
Warehouse: PMB 5142 Jericho, Ibadan Tel: (022) 413117
Associate Company: Oxford University Press, UK (qv)
Subjects: General Fiction & Non-fiction, Poetry, Biography, History, Africana, Reference, Religion, Juveniles, Books in various Nigerian Languages, Paperbacks, Medicine, Science & Technology, General & Social Science, University, Secondary & Primary Textbooks
Founded: 1949

University Publishing Co, 11 Central School Rd, PO Box 386, Onitsha Tel: (046) 223 Onitsha Cable Add: Varsity Box 386 Onitsha
Dirs: F C Ogbalu, W C Ifezue; *Editorial:* J Oranyeludike; *Sales:* D O Dandy; *Production:* I Nweke; *Publicity:* Christian Ogbalu; *Permissions:* Cecilia Ogbalu
Orders to: Varsity Bookshop, 64 New Market Rd, Onitsha
Associate Companies: Cynako International Press, Aba; Thomas Nelson (Nigeria) Ltd (qv); African Literature Bureau, Aba
Branch Offs: Azikiwe Rd, Aba; Eke-Amawbia, Awka; Oye Olisa Ogbunike, Onitsha-Enugu Rd, Awka; Varsity Bookshop/Press, Oye Agu Junction, Abagana, Njikoka LGA; 64 New Market Rd, Onitsha; Afor Igwe, Ogidi
Subjects: General Non-fiction, Belles Lettres, Poetry, Biography, History, Africana, Philosophy, Religion, Juveniles, Igbo Language & Literature, Quality Paperbacks, Primary & Secondary Textbooks, Periodicals, Books in Vernacular and Dialect
Bookshops: Varsity Bookshop/Press at: Oye-Agu, Abagana, Njikoka LGA; Eke-Amawbia, Amawbia, Awka LGA; Aba; Abiriba, Ohafia LGA
Founded: 1959
ISBN Publisher's Prefix: 978-160

Varsity Industrial Press, 11 Central School Rd, PO Box 386, Onitsha
Man Dir: E O Ugwuegbulem
Subjects: Igbo Language & English, Primary & Secondary Textbooks
Book Club: Varsity Book Club

John **West** Publications Ltd*, John West House, Plot A Block 2, Acme Rd, Ogba, PMB 21001, Ikeja — Lagos Cable Add: Jakpress Telex: 26446 Wes Pal
Executive Dir: Bayo Fadoju
Subjects: General Non-fiction, Biography, How-to, Study Guides, Reference, Annuals, Paperbacks
Founded: 1962

West African Book Publishers Ltd*, PO Box 3445, Ilupeju Industrial Estate, Lagos Tel: (01) 964555 Cable Add: Acadpress
Chairman: B A Idris Animashaun; *Dir:* Mrs A O Obadagbonyi; *Editor:* E Edu
Subjects: Reference, Paperbacks, Health, General Science, Educational, Children's General
Founded: 1967

Literary Agents

Editorial Consultancy & Agency Services*, PO Box 4573, Lagos (Located at: 226 Murtala Muhammed Way) Tel: (01) 862437 Cable Add: Edicanses Lagos
Authors' & Publishers' Agents & Consultants
Editorial Director: T C Nwosu; *Assistant Editor:* Miss A C Ikeme
Special Interests: Africana/Nigeriana, Fiction, Plays, Educational Books at all levels
Parent Company: Cross Continent Press Ltd (qv)

F C **Ogbalu***, PO Box 386, 11 Central School Rd, Onitsha

Book Clubs

Amebo Book Club*, PO Box 1970, Ibadan
Owned by: Adebara Publishers Ltd (qv)

Onibonoje Book Club, PO Box 3109, Ibadan
Owned by: Onibonoje Press & Book Industries (Nigeria) Ltd (qv)
Subjects: Fiction, Drama

Times Book Club*, 3-7 Kakawa St, PO Box 139, Lagos
Owned by: Daily Times of Nigeria (qv)

Varsity Book Club, PO Box 386, 11 Central School Rd, Onitsha
Owned by: Varsity Industrial Press (qv)

Major Booksellers

Ahmadu Bello University Bookshop Ltd, PMB 11, Samaru, Zaria
General Managers: K A Momott, Mrs Amnim

Benin University Bookshop*, University of Benin, PMB 1154, Benin City Tel: (052) 243780
Manager: S O Ehiede

Book Representation Co Ltd*, PMB 5349, E9/806B Ife Rd, Agodi Area, Ibadan Tel: (022) 716293

C S S (Nigeria) Bookshops Ltd*, Bookshop House, 50-52 Broad St, PO Box 174, Lagos Tel: (01) 633010/633081
Branches throughout the country
Also Publisher (qv)

Challenge Bookshops, Agege Motor Rd, PMB 12256, Lagos Tel: (01) 523890
General Manager: E M Gara
34 branches throughout the country, and several wholesale outlets
Owned by: ECWA Productions Ltd (qv)

Edekes Bookshop Stores Ltd, 2 Falolu Rd, PO Box 974, Surulere, Lagos

Hart Mossman & Co Ltd*, PMB 2283, Lagos

Kwaratech Bookshop*, Kwara State College of Technology, PMB 1375, Ilorin Tel: (031) 2440 ext 14

Mabrochi International Co Ltd, PO Box 1509, Surulere, Lagos
Manager: P I Igwe-Ofor
Head Office: 143 Apapa Rd, Ebute Metta, (West) Lagos State
Branches: Y11 Ibadan St, Kaduna, Kaduna State (General Books); W10 Ahmadu Bello Way, Kaduna (Law and Business books)
Specializes in mail order services.
Academic jobber for overseas universities and libraries

Morison Arnold Ltd*, 63 Hadejia Rd, PO Box 251, Kano

Niger (Acada) Bookshop Ltd*, 90 Ojuelegba Rd, PMB 3151, Surulere, Lagos Tel: (01) 834016

Nigerian Baptist Book Store Ltd*, PMB 5070, Oke Bola, Ibadan Tel: (022) 412841/412862 Cable Add: Baptistore Ibadan Telex: 20311 Box 148

Nigerian Book Suppliers Ltd, PO Box 4440, 28 Akinremi St, Ikeja, Lagos State Tel: (01) 932245 Telex: 20202 Tds Box 052 Ikeja
Man Dir: B Fatayi-Williams
Bookseller and library supplier specializing in professional books (especially legal, management, banking and accountancy), Africana, mass market paperback fiction, and library titles for tertiary level libraries
Associate Company: Universal Distributors Ltd (qv)

Nigerian Publishers' Services Ltd*, PO Box 62, Ibadan Tel: (022) 316008 Telex: 31478
Dir: T D Otesanya; *Marketing:* Dare Arokoyo
Branch Offs: 37A Omeagana St, off Modebe Ave, PO Box 4073, Onitsha; BB2 Old Jos Rd, PO Box 722, Zaria Tel: (069) 34170
Distributors

Odusote Bookstores Ltd, 68 Lagos By-Pass, PO Box 244, Ibadan Tel: (022) 316451 Cable Add: Odbook, Ibadan Telex: 31215 (Odbook NG)
Man Dir: Ola Odusote; *Manager:* Kolade Musuro
Also: 177 Herbert Macaulay St, Yaba, Lagos State Tel: (01) 861248

Rational Bookshops (Nigeria)*, Rational Bldgs, Oke-Bola, PO Box 3162, Ibadan

Universal Distributors Ltd*, PO Box 7036, 28 Akinremi St, Ikeja, Lagos Tel: (01) 932245
Man Dir: B Fatayi-Williams; *General Manager:* Mrs O Williams; *Bookshop Sales Manager:* Mrs V P Oseni
Also: 'Bestseller' – three bookshops at Falomo Shopping Centre, Ikoyi, Lagos; Durbar Hotel, Kaduna; 18 Mission Rd, Benin City
Associate Company: Nigerian Book Suppliers Ltd (qv)

University Bookshop Ltd, Obafemi Awolowo University, Ile-Ife Tel: (038) 2291 ext 2145 and 2146 Cable Add: Bookshop Ifevarsity
Man Dir: Oyeniyi Osundina
Branches: Lagere, Ondo, Ila-Orangun, Ado-Ekiti

University Bookshop (Nigeria) Ltd*, University of Ibadan, Ibadan Tel: (022) 62550 ext 1208
General Manager: Akin Aqbebi
Also: University College Hospital

University of Lagos Bookshop, Yaba, Lagos Tel: (01) 820279
Also: College of Medicine, University of Lagos, Idi-Araba, Surulere, Lagos

University of Nigeria Bookshop Ltd, Nsukka Tel: (042) 771939 ext 7
Manager: G I Uzuegbu

Major Libraries

Agricultural Library*, PMB 1044, Samaru-Zaria Tel: (069) 32571 ext 212
Librarian: Malam R Salami
Publications include: Library Accession List (monthly); *List of Current Serials in the*

Library (annually); *KWIC Index to the Abstracting & Indexing Publications currently being received by the IAR Library*, 2nd edition 1976

Ahmadu Bello University Library*, Samaru-Zaria Tel: (069) 32553 Telex: 75241 Zarabu Ng
Publication: Northern Nigerian Publications (annual)

Anambra State Central Library*, PMB 1026, Enugu, Anambra State Tel: (042) 254331/254339 Cable Add: Libraries
Librarian: M Okoye

Bendel State Library, PMB 1127, Benin City, Bendel State Tel: (052) 241457 Cable Add: Library Benin
Dir: D O Oboro
Publication: Bendel Library Journal
Bendel Library Bookshops are at the above address

Benin University Library*, PMB 1191, Benin City Tel: (052) 241675
University Librarian: O O Ogundipe
Publications include: Annual Report; Library News; List of Serials

Ibadan University Library*, Ibadan Tel: (022) 400550 ext 1424/26/1496 Telex: 31233 Iba Lib Ng
Librarian: T Olabisi Odeinde
Publications include: Library Record (monthly); *Annual Report, 1981/82*; Guides to reference sources in the Library

International Institute of Tropical Agriculture Library, PMB 5320, Ibadan Tel: (022) 413440 Cable Add: Tropfound Ikeja Telex: 31417 Tropib Ng; Tds Iba Ng 20311 (Box 015)
Librarian: Dr S M Lawani

Library Board of **Kaduna** State*, PMB 2061, Bida Rd, Kaduna Tel: (062) 242590/ 210322/214417
Dir: Shehu Ibrahim Shika
Publications: Annual Report; New Additions to Stock (monthly)

Kano State Library Board, PMB 3094, Kano Tel: (064) 625614
Director: Alhaji Shehu Mukhtar
Publications include: Newsletter; Bulletin; Library Guide

Lagos City Council Libraries*, 48 Broad St, PMB 2025, Lagos Tel: (01) 635287/ 635216

National Archives of Nigeria Library, PMB 4, University of Ibadan Post Office, Ibadan Tel: (022) 415000 Cable Add: Darchnes
Librarian: O A Momoh
Publications: Catalogues; Bibliographies; Handlists; Guides

National Library of Nigeria*, 4 Wesley St, PMB 12626, Lagos Tel: (01) 634704/ 656590/656591 Cable Add: Biblios Telex: 20117
Publications include: Libraries in Nigeria, a Directory; National Bibliography of Nigeria; Nigerian Books in Print; Nominal List of Practising Librarians in Nigeria; Serials in Print in Nigeria; Nigerbiblios (quarterly); *Afribiblios* (twice a year)

Nnamdi Azikiwe Library, University of Nigeria, Nsukka Tel: (042) 771444 Cable Add: Nigersity Library Telex: Ulions 51496
Librarian: S C Nwoye
Publications include: Nsukka Library Notes; UNLAN (University of Nigeria Library Accessions and News); *Readers' Guide; Annual Report*

Obafemi Awolowo University Library*, Ile-Ife, Oyo State Tel: (038) 2290

University of Lagos Library*, Akoka, Yaba, Lagos Tel: (01) 800502 ext 362, (01) 800504 ext 362

University of Nigeria Library, see Nnamdi Azikiwe

Library Associations

Anambra State School Libraries Association, c/o Enugu Campus Library, University of Nigeria, Enugu Tel: (042) 252080 Cable Add: Nigersity Enugu
Honorary Secretary: Dr Dorothy S Obi
Publications include: School Libraries Bulletin (3 times a year); *Manual for School Libraries on Small Budgets*

Nigerian Association of Agricultural Librarians and Documentalists (NAALD)*, c/o Library & Business Information Centre, Lagos Chamber of Commerce & Industry, Commerce House, 1 Idowu Taylor St, Victoria Island, Lagos Tel: (01) 613902/613906/613911
Secretary: S B Akande

Nigerian Library Association, PMB 99, Abuja Tel: (01) 630053
Secretary: L I Elizistor
Publications: Nigerian Libraries (three a year); *NLA Newsletter*
(There are also regional associations in the various states under the umbrella of the Nigerian Library Association)

Library Reference Books and Journals

Books

Directory of Lagos Libraries, Oceana Publications Inc, Dobbs Ferry, NY 10522, USA

Libraries in Nigeria. A Directory, National Library of Nigeria, 4 Wesley St, PMB 12626, Lagos

Nominal List of Practising Librarians in Nigeria (annually), National Library of Nigeria, 4 Wesley St, PMB 12626, Lagos
Names and addresses of practising librarians at 59 libraries in Nigeria

Journals

Afribiblios (twice a year), National Library of Nigeria, 4 Wesley St, PMB 12626, Lagos

Bendel Library Journal, Bendel State Library, PMB 1127, Benin City, Bendel State

ECS School Libraries Bulletin, East Central State School Libraries Association, c/o Enugu Campus Library, University of Nigeria, Enugu

Library Record (monthly), Ibadan University Library, Ibadan

NLA Newsletter, Nigerian Library Association, PMB 99, Abuja

Nigerbiblios (quarterly), National Library of Nigeria, 4 Wesley St, PMB 12626, Lagos

Nigerian Libraries (3 a year), Nigerian Library Association, PMB 99, Abuja
The official publication of the Nigerian Library Association; the Association also publishes a mimeographed newsletter

Nsukka Library Notes, Nnamdi Azikiwe Library, University of Nigeria, Nsukka, Anambra State

Literary Associations and Societies

Nigerian Writers' Club*, 76 St Finbarrs College Rd, Akoka, Yaba, Lagos State
Publication: Visions at Dawn

In addition to the above, small literary societies and writers' circles, etc, are attached to the English departments at the various universities

Literary Periodicals

Afriscope (monthly), Pan Afriscope (Nigeria) Ltd, 45 Saibu St, PMB 1119, Yaba, Lagos
Contains a regular 'Literary Scene' column which features book reviews and gives extensive coverage to cultural and literary events throughout Africa

The Benin Review, Ethiope Publishing Corporation, Ring Rd, PMB 1332, Benin City
The journal covers all the arts in Africa, both traditional and modern, and is also concerned with cultural life in the Black World generally

The Muse (irregular), A literary journal published by the English Association at Nsukka, University of Nigeria, Nsukka

Nigeria Magazine, Cultural Division, Federal Ministry of Information, PMB 12524, Lagos
Bi-monthly cultural and literary magazine published since 1932

Oduma, Rivers State Council for Arts and Culture, 74-76 Bonny St, PMB 5049, Port Harcourt

Visions at Dawn, Nigerian Writers' Club, 76 St Finbarrs College Rd, Akoka, Yaba, Lagos State

Note: There are several more 'little magazines', largely in mimeographed form, published by English departments and writers' groups at the various universities

Literary Prizes

Concord Press Award for Academic Publishing
Sponsored by M K O Abiola (founder and Chairman of the Concord Press of Nigeria Ltd). The principal aim of the Award is to encourage publication of works by Nigerian authors and scholars which are suitable as textbooks at University level. 3,000 naira awarded annually. Enquiries to The Secretary, Concord Press Award for Academic Publishing, c/o University Bookshop, Obafemi Awolowo University, Ile-Ife, Oyo State

Delta Fiction Award
For an unpublished novel on any subject, although theme should have an international flavour. 2,000 naira. Enquiries to Editor, Delta Fiction Award, Delta Publications (Nigeria) Ltd, 172 Ogui Rd, PO Box 1172, Enugu

Federal Radio Corporation of Nigeria*
Various literary and drama competitions are sponsored by the Federal Radio Corporation of Nigeria, Lagos, from time to time. Enquiries to Federal Radio Corporation of Nigeria, Broadcasting House, Ikoyi, Lagos

Ife Book Fair Prizes, see Concord Press Award for Academic Publishing

Nigerian Book Development Council Book Prize*
For the best book of social significance by a Nigerian author. 200 naira awarded annually. Enquiries to Nigerian Book Development Council, 6 Obanta Rd, Apapa, Lagos State

Nigerian Book Development Council Literary Prize*
For the best book written by a Nigerian and published in Nigeria (excluding children's books). 300 naira awarded annually. Enquiries to Nigerian Book Development Council, 6 Obanta Rd, Apapa, Lagos State

Translation Agencies and Associations

Igbo Language Translation Agency, c/o University Publishing Co Ltd, 11 Central School Rd, PO Box 386, Onitsha

The **Nigeria Educational Research Council***, PO Box 8058, Lagos (Located at: 3 Jibowu St, Yaba, Lagos) Tel: (01) 862272/862269 Cable Add: Edusearch, Lagos
The Research Council has a Translation Bureau attached to it

Norway

General Information

Language: Norwegian. There are two distinct forms: Bokmål (sometimes called Riksmål) and Nynorsk (formerly called Landsmål) whose relative importance has changed in recent years. About 90% of Norwegian books are now published in Bokmål and it is the medium of instruction in most schools. Danish and Swedish are usually intelligible to speakers of Norwegian
Religion: Lutheran
Population: 4.1 million
Bank Hours: 0845-1545 (1515 in summer) Monday-Wednesday and Friday; 0815-1800 (1700 in summer) Thursday
Shop Hours: 0830-1700 Monday-Friday; 0830-1400 Saturday
Currency: 100 øre = 1 Norwegian krone (plural: kroner)
Export/Import Information: Member of the European Free Trade Association. No tariff on books except children's picture books. Books exempt from VAT. No duty on advertising. No import licence required. Nominal exchange controls
Copyright: UCC, Berne, Florence (see International section)

Book Trade Organizations

Bok Og Papiransattes Forening, Ovre Vollgate 15, N-0158 Oslo 1
Norwegian Book Trade Employees' Association
Publications: Norsk Bokhandlermatrikkel; Norsk Boknøkkel

Norsk Antikvarbokhandlerforening, Universitetsgt 18, N-0164 Oslo 1
Norwegian Antiquarian Booksellers' Association

Norsk Bokhandler Medhjelper Forening, now Bok Og Papiransattes Forening (qv)

Norsk Bokhandlersamband, c/o Vestlandskes Bokhandel, Vetrlidsalm 1, N-5000 Bergen
Norwegian Christian Booksellers' Union
Chairman: Gottfred Eriksen; *Secretary:* Liv Ellinor Vik

Norsk Boknummerkontor, Universitetsbiblioteket i Oslo, Drammensvegen 42, N-0255 Oslo 2 Tel: (02) 553630 Telex: 76078 Ub N
ISBN Agency
Administrator: Tove Jareld

Norsk Forleggersamband, c/o Ansgar Forlag A/S, Møllergata 26, N-0179 Oslo 1
Norwegian Christian Publishers' Union
Chairman: Thorstein Lindhjem; *Secretary:* Eva Rise

Norsk Musikkforleggerforening*, Postboks 822 Sentrum, N-0104 Oslo 1
Norwegian Music Publishers' Association

Norske Bokhandlerforening*, Ovre Vollgate 15, Oslo 1 Tel: (02) 410760
Norwegian Booksellers' Association
Publication: Bok og Samfunn

Den Norske Forfatterforening, Rådhusgata 7, Postboks 327 Sentrum, Oslo 1 Tel: (02) 424077
Norwegian Authors' Association
Secretary-General: Lars Espen Bakke; *Manager:* Tordis Fjeldstad

Den Norske Forleggerforening, Ovre Vollgate 15, N-0158 Oslo 1 Tel: (02) 421355/422285
Norwegian Publishers' Association
Dir: Paul Martens Røthe

Norwegian Association of Children's and Young People's Authors*, Rådhusgata 7, Oslo 1

Sentral Bokhandel A/S, O H Bangsvei 51, Postboks 127, N-1322 Høvik Tel: (02) 532376
Dir: Oivind Sander

Standard Book Numbering Agency, see Norsk Boknummerkontor

Book Trade Reference Books

Bibliografi over Norges Offentlige Publikasjoner (Bibliography of Norwegian Government Publications), Universitetsbiblioteket i Oslo, Drammenesveien 42, N-1302 Oslo

Norsk Bokhandlermatrikkel (Norwegian Booksellers Membership List), Bok Og Papiransattes Forening, Ovre Vollgate 15, N-0158 Oslo 1

Publishers

Akademika, PO Box 84 Blindern, N-0314 Oslo 3 Tel: (02) 455055 Cable Add: Unibok Oslo Telex: 78610 Ubokn
Manager: Per Grönneberg Andresen

Ansgar Forlag A/S, Møllergate 26, N-0179 Oslo 1 Tel: (02) 362800 Telex: 19602 ansgr n Fax: 362000
Executive Dir, Publisher, Rights & Permissions: Svenn Otto Brechan
Subjects: General Fiction, Children's, Juveniles, Poetry, Religion, Art, Biography, Psychology, Paperbacks
1985: 35 titles *1986:* 45 titles *Founded:* 1934
ISBN Publishers' Prefix: 82-503

H Aschehoug & Co (W Nygaard) A/S, Sehestedsgate 3, Oslo 1 Tel: (02) 429490 Cable Add: Aco Oslo
Man Dir: William Nygaard; *Assistant Man Dir:* Ole Sagfossen; *Dir, School Book Department:* Kjell Hjertø; *Editorial:* Marit Notaker, Egil Kristoffersen, Irja Thorenfeldt, Ivar Havnevik; *Marketing:* Terje Fredriksen; *Rights & Permissions:* Marit Notaker
Subsidiary Companies: Kunnskapsforlaget I/S (qv) (jointly owned with Gyldendal Norsk Forlag qv); Olaf Norlis Bokhandel A/S (jointly owned with F Beyer, Bergen); Tano A/S Forlaget (qv); Yrkeskopplæring I/S (qv) (jointly owned)
Subjects: General Fiction and Non-fiction, Reference, Juveniles, Quality Paperbacks, General & Social Science, Secondary & Primary Textbooks, Computer Software
Book Club: Den Norske Bokklubben A/S (with three other Norwegian publishers)
Founded: 1872
ISBN Publisher's Prefix: 82-03

Aventura Forlag+, Arbiensgt 7, N-0253 Oslo 2 Tel: (02) 444045 Fax: (02) 552944
Man Dir: Øivind Arneberg; *Chief Editor:* Anton F Andresen; *Editorial:* Anne-Grethe Messel, Arve Torkelsen, Ellinor Prydz; *Sales:* Marit Hagen, Ellinor Prydz; *Publicity:* Øivind Arneberg, Arve Torkelsen; *Production:* Arne Olsen; *Rights & Permissions:* Anton F Andresen, Øivind Arneberg
Subjects: Fiction, Non-fiction, General
1985: 35 titles *1986:* 25 titles *Founded:* 1983
ISBN Publisher's Prefix: 82-588

Bergendal Forlag*, Postboks 1894 Vika, Oslo 1 Tel: (02) 244861 Cable Add: Bergendalbok
Man Dir: Pål H Christiansen
ISBN Publisher's Prefix: 82-90382

Bladkompaniet A/S+, Stålfjæra 5, N-0975 Oslo 9 Tel: (02) 257190
Man Dir, Rights & Permissions: Finn Arnesen; *Sales Dir:* Ole Waagenes; *Advertising:* Björg Vollan
Subjects: General Fiction, Paperbacks, Magazines
1985: 124 titles *1986:* 130 titles *Founded:* 1915
ISBN Publisher's Prefix: 82-509

F Bruns Bokhandels Forlag A/S, Kongensgate 10, Postboks 476, N-7001 Trondheim Tel: (07) 510022
Dir: Fridthjov Brun
Subjects: Science, Technology
Bookshop: At above address
Founded: 1873
ISBN Publisher's Prefix: 82-7028

J W Cappelens Forlag A/S+, Kirkegaten 15, N-0153 Oslo 1 Tel: (02) 429440 Cable Add: Cappelen
Chairman: Sigmund Strømme; *Man Dirs:* Jan Wiese, Anders Heger, Gro Stangeland; *Editorial:* Per Glad, Aase Gjerdrum, Svenn Fosseng, Ola Haugen; *Sales:* Kirsti Sögstad; *Production:* Kjell Nordahl; *Rights & Permissions:* Kirsten Lier
Parent Company: Albert Bonniers Förlag AB, Sweden (qv)
Subsidiary Companies: Bedriftsökonomens Forlag A/S; Boksenteret A/S; Forlaget Liv A/S; Yrkeskopplæring I/S (qv – jointly owned)
Subjects: General Fiction, Non-fiction, Textbooks, Reference, Maps, Religion, Juveniles, Low- & High-priced Paperbacks, Encyclopaedias
Book Club: Den Norske Bokklubben A/S (with three other Norwegian publishers)
1985: 254 titles *1986:* 347 titles *Founded:* 1829
ISBN Publisher's Prefix: 82-02

NORWAY 321

N W Damm og Søn A/S+, Tvetenveien 32, Postboks 6140 Etterstad, N-0620 Oslo 6 Tel: (02) 649210 Cable Add: Damson Telex: 72400 fotex n Fax: (02) 630557
Man Dir: Per Støkken
Parent Company: Gutenberghus, Copenhagen, Denmark
Associate Company: Hjemmet A/S (qv)
Subjects: How-to, Children's, Textbooks, Dictionaries, Guidebooks
1985: 45 titles *1986:* 42 titles *Founded:* 1843
ISBN Publisher's Prefix: 82-517

Dreyers Forlag A/S, Arbiensgate 7, N-0253 Oslo 2 Tel: (02) 443810 Cable Add: Dreyerbok Telex: 79621 drefo
Man Dir: Hans B Butenschön; *Editorial:* Øistein Parmann; *Sales, Publicity:* Bodil Kruse; *Production:* Bjørn Pedersen; *Rights & Permissions:* Tordis Boelgen, Astrid Borgen
Subjects: General Fiction, Non-fiction, Belles Lettres, Music, Art, Low- & High-priced Paperbacks
1985: 45 titles *Founded:* 1942
ISBN Publisher's Prefix: 82-09

J W Eides Forlag A/S, Nygårdsgate 3, Postboks 146, N-5001 Bergen Tel: (05) 214990
Man Dir: Trine Kolderup Flaten; *Editorial Manager:* Jan H Landro
Subjects: General Fiction, History, Music, Art, Media, University, Secondary & Primary Textbooks, Educational Materials, Juveniles
ISBN Publisher's Prefix: 82-514

Elingaard Forlag A/S, now Nå Forlag A/S (qv)

Ex Libris Forlag A/S+, Krumgata 7, Postboks 2715 St Hanshaugen, N-0131 Oslo 1 Tel: (02) 693208 Telex: 79225 exlib n Fax: 569740
Man Dir: Øyvind Hagen; *Editor-in-chief:* Aud Norlin
Subjects: Non-fiction, Bellestric, Thrillers, Biography, Philosophy, Art, Quality Paperbacks
1985: 18 titles *1986:* 23 titles *1987:* 39 titles *Founded:* 1982
ISBN Publisher's Prefix: 82-7384

Fabritius Forlag AS, Postboks 84 Grefsen, N-0409 Oslo 4 Tel: (02) 224041 Telex: 77013 Fax: (02) 157991
Man Dir: Bjørn Hagen
Subjects: Law, Database Information, Sponsored Books
1985: 6 titles *1986:* 8 titles *Founded:* 1844
ISBN Publisher's Prefixes: 82-90545, 82-07

Fonna Forlag L/L*, Postboks 6912 St Olavs Plass, N-0130 Oslo 1 Tel: (02) 201303/201201
Subjects: General Fiction, Poetry, Biography, Magazines, Juveniles
Founded: 1940
ISBN Publisher's Prefix: 82-513

Friundervisningens Forlag+, Sørkedalsveien 10B, N-0369 Oslo 3 Tel: (02) 694090
Man Dir, Rights & Permissions: Tove Andreassen; *Editorial:* Irene Solberg; *Sales:* Tove Engh Hansen; *Production:* Gerd Volder; *Publicity:* I Solberg, G Volder
Subjects: Adult Educational (especially languages), Educational Materials
Founded: 1948
ISBN Publisher's Prefix: 82-7020

John Griegs Forlag*, Postboks 248, N-5001 Bergen Tel: (05) 233900 Cable Add: Bokgrieg
Man Dir: Hermond J Berg Lindersen
Subjects: Non-fiction, Fiction for Children, Co-editions, Sports Periodical
Founded: 1721
ISBN Publisher's Prefix: 82-533

Grøndahl og Søn Forlag A/S, Postboks 2308 Solli, N-0210 Oslo 2 (Located at: Munkedamsveien 35, Oslo 2) Tel: (02) 419740 Cable Add: Bokgrøndahl Fax: (02) 412091
Man Dir: Finn P Nyquist; *Editor-in-chief:* Jan Ivar Haugen
Subjects: General Non-fiction, Nature & Cultural (illustrated), Fiction, Children's
Founded: 1812
ISBN Publisher's Prefix: 82-504

Gyldendal Norsk Forlag, Sehestedsgt 4, Postboks 6860 St Olavs Plass, N-0130 Oslo 1 Tel: (02) 200710 Cable Add: Gyldendal Telex: 72880 Gyldn N
Man Dir: Andreas Skartveit; *Assistant Man Dir:* Nils Kare Jacobsen; *Marketing Dir:* Sindre Guldvog; *Editorial Dirs:* Per Christian Øiestad (Educational Textbooks), Snorre Evensberget (Non-fiction); *Chief Editors:* Irene Engelstad (Norwegian Fiction), Gordon Hølmebakk (Translated Fiction), Harald Ursin-Holm (Translated Fiction, Paperbacks, Theological Literature), Øyunn Krokann (Children's); *Rights & Permissions:* Eva Lie-Nielsen
Subsidiary Companies: Kunnskapsforlaget I/S (qv) (jointly owned with H Aschehoug & Co A/S, qv); Yrkeskopplæring I/S (qv) (jointly owned)
Subjects: General Fiction, Science Fiction, Belles Lettres, Poetry, Art, Music, Biography, History, How-to, Politics, Philosophy, Psychology, Reference, Religion, Social Science, Secondary & Primary Textbooks, Children's books, *Easy Readers*, Encyclopaedias, Paperbacks, Periodicals
Book Club: Den Norske Bokklubben A/S (with three other Norwegian publishers)
Founded: 1925
ISBN Publisher's Prefix: 82-05

Henny's Forlag*, Postboks 1894 Vika, Oslo 1
Man Dir: M Andenäs; *Dirs:* P Christiansen, J Jansen
Subjects: General Fiction, Biography, History, How-to, Philosophy, Religion
Founded: 1962

Hjemmenes Forlag A/S*, Postboks 25 Holmenkollen, N-0324 Oslo 3 Tel: (02) 143151
Publisher: Yngve Woxholth
Subject: Cultural and Historical Books (mainly in colour)

Hjemmet A/S*, Kristian den IVs gate 13, Oslo 1 Tel: (02) 429470 Telex: 76677
Man Dir: Torstein Bore
Parent Company: Gutenberghus Group, Denmark
Associate Companies: N W Damm og Søn, Hjemmets Bokforlag A/S (qqv); Gutenberghus Publishing Service A/S, Denmark (qv)
Founded: 1911
ISBN Publisher's Prefix: 82-7315

Hjemmets Bokforlag A/S, Kristian Augusts gate 10, Oslo 1 Tel: (02) 429165 Telex: 77074 Novel
Man Dir: Arne Fr Mathisen; *Assistant Man Dir:* June Heggenhougen
Parent Company: Gutenberghus Group, Denmark
Associate Companies: Gutenberghus Publishing Service A/S and Wangels Forlag A/S, Denmark (qqv); Ehapa Verlag GmbH, Federal Republic of Germany; Hjemmet A/S, Norway (qv); Hemmets Journal AB, Sweden (qv)
Subjects: General Fiction, Non-fiction, Encyclopaedias, Reference, Juveniles, Quality Paperbacks
Book Clubs: Disney Junior Bokklub, Donald Ducks Bokklub, Bokklubben Feminina, Hjemmets Bokklubb, Hjemmets Kokebokklub, Bokklubben Ny Krim

Founded: 1969
ISBN Publisher's Prefix: 82-7001

Kunnskapsforlaget I/S, Sehestedsgt 4, Postboks 6736 St Olavs Plass, N-0130 Oslo 1 Tel: (02) 205215
Man Dir: Lars Bucher Johannessen; *Marketing Dir:* Ivar Nyfløt; *Chief Editor:* Egil Tveterås; *Production:* Rolf Andersson
Parent Companies: H Aschehoug & Co A/S, Gyldendal Norsk Forlag (qqv)
Subjects: Encyclopaedias, Dictionaries
Founded: 1975
ISBN Publisher's Prefix: 82-573

Lanser Forlag A/S*, Bernhard Getzgate 3C, N-0165 Oslo 1 Tel: (02) 204005
Man Dir, Sales, Production Publicity: Svein Lanser; *Editorial, Rights & Permissions:* Hans Erich Lampel
Subsidiary Company: Frilanser Printing Service
Subjects: Philosophy, Health, Science
Founded: 1977
ISBN Publisher's Prefixes: 82-7328, 82-90209

Lunde Forlag og Bokhandel A/S+, Grensen 19, N-0159 Oslo 1 Tel: (02) 429130 Cable Add: Norskluth
Editor: Torstein Lindhjem; *Production:* Paul Odland; *Rights & Permissions:* Jan Bøe
Subjects: Religion, Theology, Juveniles, Children's, General Fiction, Poetry, Biography, Educational Materials
Bookshop: Lunde Forlag og Bokhandel A/S, C Sundtgate 2, N-5000 Bergen
Founded: 1905
ISBN Publisher's Prefix: 82-520

Luther Forlag A/S*, St Halvardsgate 77, N-0657 Oslo 6 Tel: (02) 192780
Man Dir: Aage Ringerike
Subjects: General Fiction, Biography, History, Religion, Juveniles, Low- & High-priced Paperbacks, Dictionaries
1985: approx 50 titles
ISBN Publisher's Prefix: 82-531

Harald **Lyche** & Co A/S, now incorporated in Erik Sandberg A/S (qv)

Ernst G **Mortensens** Forlag A/S, Sørkedalsveien 10A, N-0369 Oslo 3 Tel: (02) 603090/691909 Cable Add: Pressmort Telex: 77626 Fax: (02) 692542
Man Dir: Terje Johansen; *Editorial:* Alv B Aronsen, Bjørn Glorvigen, Kari Syse Grøsland, Solveig Høysaeter, Jorn Pettersen, Stein Stør; *Sales:* Egil Storaas; *Information:* Knut-Jørgen Erichsen; *Advertising:* R Marthinsen; *Rights & Permissions:* Per R Mortensen Jnr
Subsidiary Companies: NPS (Norsk Presseservice A/S), Oslo; Forenede Trykkerier A/S, Oslo; Direct Mail A/S, Oslo
Subjects: General, Periodicals
Founded: 1933
ISBN Publisher's Prefix: 82-527

N K I-Forlaget*, Løxavn 15, Postboks 113, N-1351 Rud Tel: (02) 135790
Publisher: Jan Lien; *Editorial:* Sverre Harald Amundsen, Solvar Hofsøy; *Sales, Publicity:* Torgeir Oma
Subjects: Secondary Textbooks, Technical Textbooks
Founded: 1967
ISBN Publisher's Prefix: 82-562

N K S-Forlaget+, Postboks 5853, Hegdehaugen, N-0308 Oslo 3 (Located at: Industrigata 45, Oslo 3) Tel: (02) 568500
Man Dir: Hallstein Laupsa
Orders to: Forlagsentralem I/S, Postboks 1, Furuset, N-1001 Oslo 10
Subjects: Secondary School & College Textbooks, Handbooks, Reference Books

NORWAY

1985: 45 titles *Founded:* 1971
ISBN Publisher's Prefix: 82-508

Nå Forlag A/S*, Postboks 7058 H, Oslo 3
(Located at Oscarsgate 55, Oslo 2)
Tel: (02) 565070
Parent Company: Libertas, Oscarsgate 55,
Oslo 2
Subjects: Politics, Marketing, Economy
Formerly Elingaard Forlag A/S
ISBN Publisher's Prefix: 82-505

Noregs Boklag L/L, Trondheimsveien 15,
N-0560 Oslo 5 Tel: (02) 687600
Manager: Jan Kløvstad
Subjects: General Fiction, Plays, Poetry,
Biography, Music, Juveniles
Founded: 1923
ISBN Publisher's Prefix: 82-522

Norsk Kunstforlag A/S+*, Postboks 2559,
Solli, Oslo 2 Tel: (02) 414603
Man Dir: Ivar Grimsmo
Subjects: General, Art, Atlases
ISBN Publisher's Prefix: 82-90069

Det **Norske Samlaget**+, Postboks 4672
Sofienberg, N-0506 Oslo 5 (Located at:
Trondheimsvegen 15, Oslo 5) Tel: (02)
687600
Man Dir: Audun Heskestad; *Editorial,
Rights & Permissions:* Olav Hr Rue; *Sales:*
Jan Klövstad; *Production:* Asta Magni
Lykkjen
Subjects: General Fiction, Belles Lettres,
Poetry, Biography, History, Philosophy,
Religion, Textbooks, Reference, Juveniles,
High-priced Paperbacks, Periodicals
1985: 168 titles *1986:* 164 titles *Founded:*
1868
ISBN Publisher's Prefix: 82-521

Norwegian University Press, see
Universitetsforlaget

Novus Forlag A/S, Postboks 748 Sentrum,
N-0106 Oslo 1 Tel: (02) 698552
Publisher: Olav Røsset
Subjects: Education, General
1985: 8 titles *1986:* 10 titles *Founded:*
1972
ISBN Publisher's Prefix: 82-7099

Pax Forlag A/S, Postboks 2336 Solli,
N-0201 Oslo 2 Tel: (02) 557070
Man Dir: Paul Hedlund; *Editorial, Rights
& Permissions:* Birgit Bjerck;
Administration: Bjørn Smith-Simonsen
Subjects: Fiction, Political and Social
Science, Feminist Literature,
Encyclopaedias, Quality Paperbacks
1987: 20 titles *Founded:* 1964
ISBN Publisher's Prefix: 82-530

Pedagogisk Forlag A/S*,
Dronningensgaten 23, Oslo 1 Tel: (02)
414927
Subjects: Textbooks, Educational Materials

Rune Forlag*, Postboks 1202, N-7001
Trondheim Tel: (075) 32362
Publisher: Erling Skjølberg
Subject: General
ISBN Publisher's Prefix: 82-523

Erik **Sandberg** A/S+,
Nedre Vollgate 9, N-0158 Oslo 1 Tel:
(02) 110585 Telex: 17580
Chief Executive, Rights & Permissions:
Trond Wikborg; *Editorial:* Arild Rønsen,
Per Martinsen; *Sales:* Tor Nilsen;
Production: Iril Kolle; *Publicity:* Solveig
Thime
Subjects: Yearbooks (Pleasure Crafts,
Hi-fi), Norwegian Farms Series, General
Fiction, Non-fiction, Textbooks, Periodicals
Founded: 1973
ISBN Publisher's Prefix: 82-7316

Chr **Schibsteds** Forlag+, Kristian IV's
Gate 1, Postboks 1178 Sentrum, N-0107
Oslo 1
Tel: (02) 205060 Telex: 71230 aft n
General Manager, Rights & Permissions:
Per G Damsgaard; *Sales Dir:* Arne
Andreassen
Orders to: Forlagsentralen, Postboks 6005
Etterstad, Oslo 6
Parent Company: Schibsted, Postboks 1178
Sentrum, N-0107 Oslo 1
Subjects: How-to, Reference, Juveniles,
Nature, Biography
1985: 30 titles *1986:* 28 titles *Founded:*
1839
ISBN Publisher's Prefix: 82-516

Semic nordisk forlag A/S+, Postboks 6320
Etterstad, N-0604 Oslo 6 Tel: (02) 650090
Telex: Semic N
Man Dir: Terje Ruud Johnsen; *Publisher:*
Fred W Seierland
Parent Company: Semic International AB,
Sweden (qv)
Subjects: Romance, Novels, Crime, War,
Westerns
Founded: 1966
ISBN Publisher's Prefix: 82-535

Skolebokforlaget I/S
Undervisningslitteratur+*, Arbiensgate 7,
N-0253 Oslo 2 Tel: (02) 449892/443810/
924900 Cable Add: Edbooks Ytre
Enebakk Telex: 19125 mafco
Man Dir: Hans B Butenschøn; *Textbooks
Manager:* Anne-Lise Gjerdrum
Orders to: Cappelens Forlagsekspedisjon,
Risalleen 5, N-0374 Oslo 3
Subjects: Educational
1985: 19 titles *Founded:* 1979
ISBN Publisher's Prefix: 82-7317

Snøfugl Forlag, Postboks 95, N-7084
Melhus Tel: (07) 870055
Chief Executive, Editorial: Åsmund
Snøfugl; *Sales:* Audhild Øye
Associate Company: A/S Bygdetrykk,
N-7084 Melhus
Subjects: General
Founded: 1972
ISBN Publisher's Prefix: 82-7083

Solum Forlag A/S, Postboks 140 Skøyen,
N-0212 Oslo 2 Tel: (02) 500400
Man Dir: Knut Endre Solum; *Editorial:*
Tor Kaare Kvaal
Subjects: General Fiction & Non-fiction,
Science, Textbooks, Educational Materials,
Children's Books, Humanities
1986: 30 titles *1987:* 50 titles
ISBN Publisher's Prefix: 82-560

Stabenfeldt A/S, Haugesundsgate 43,
Postboks 1544 Kjelvene, N-4001 Stavanger
Tel: (04) 521553 Cable Add: Bokorm
Telex: 30761 Fax: (04) 526217
Man Dir: Tor Tjeldflåt
Subsidiary Company: SE-bladene
Subjects: General Fiction & Non-fiction
Founded: 1920
ISBN Publisher's Prefix: 82-532

P F **Steensballes** Forlag, Postboks 55,
N-2261 Kirkenaer Tel: (066) 47822
Publisher: Bjarne H Reenskaug
Subjects: Hunting, Fishing
ISBN Publisher's Prefix: 82-7004

Tano A/S Forlaget, Kr Augustgate 7A,
Oslo 1 Tel: (02) 110260 Cable Add:
Tanumlag
Publishing Dir: Tove Kolle; *Editorial:*
Vigdis Bunkholdt, Knut Fjerdingstad, Jon
Gisle
Parent Company: H Aschehoug & Co
(W Nygaard) A/S (qv)
Associate Company: Yrkeskopplæring I/S
(qv)
Subjects: General Non-fiction, Reference,
Textbooks, Education
ISBN Publisher's Prefix: 82-518

Tanum-Norli Forlaget A/S, now Tano A/S
Forlaget (qv)

Teknologisk Forlag*, Tvetenveien 152,
Oslo 6 Tel: (02) 261250
Man Dir, Rights & Permissions: Rudolf
Jenssen; *Assistant Dir:* Tom Harald
Jenssen; *Editorial Dir:* Tore Egeberg; *Sales
Dir:* Karl H Ormen
Subjects: How-to, Philosophy, Textbooks,
Reference, Engineering, General Science
Founded: 1958
ISBN Publisher's Prefix: 82-512

Tiden Norsk Forlag, Postboks 8324,
Hammersborg (Located at: Storgt 23D,
Oslo 1) Tel: (02) 429520 Cable Add:
Tiden
Man Dir: Trygve Johansen; *Editorial,
Rights & Permissions:* Sidsel Cornier;
Production: Karin Stok
Subjects: General Fiction & Non-fiction,
Textbooks, Reference, Paperbacks,
Juveniles
Book Club: Den Norske Bokklubben A/S
(with three other Norwegian publishers)
Bookshop: Arbeidernes Bok- og
Papirhandel, Youngstorget 4, Oslo 1
Founded: 1933
ISBN Publisher's Prefix: 82-10

I/S **Undervisningslitteratur**, now
Skolebokforlaget I/S Undervisningslitteratur
(qv)

Universitetsforlaget*, Postboks 2959,
Tøyen, N-0608 Oslo 6 (Located at:
Kolstadgt 1, Oslo 6) Tel: (02) 276060
Cable Add: Universitypress, Oslo Telex:
11896 Ufor N
Norwegian University Press
Man Dir: Trygve Ramberg; *Editorial:*
Fredrik Nissen, Randi Bauer, Terje Sørlie,
Marit Landsen Bernsten, Lars Lie, Johan
Hauknes, Marianne Egeland; *Marketing
Manager:* Anne Skranefjell (national);
Sales Manager: Sissel Henriksen; *Rights &
Permissions:* Elisabet Middelthon
Orders to: Postboks 2977, Tøyen, N-0608
Oslo 6
Subjects: Technical, Reference, Science,
Paperbacks, Textbooks, Higher-level
scientific & research publications in
English, Educational Materials, Periodicals
1985: 750 titles *Founded:* 1950
Miscellaneous: Publishers for the University
of Oslo, The University of Bergen, the
University of Tromsø, and other
institutions of higher learning
ISBN Publisher's Prefix: 82-00

Yrkeskopplæring I/S*, Postboks 6899
St Olavs Plass, N-0130 Oslo 1 Tel: (02)
205230
Publisher, Man Dir: Birger Mølbach
Parent Companies: H Aschehoug & Co
(W Nygaard) A/S (qv), J W Cappelens
Forlag A/S (qv), Gyldendal Norsk Forlag
(qv)
Associate Company: Tano A/S Forlaget
(qv)
Subjects: Secondary School Textbooks (for
handicraft and industry trade courses)
1985: 60 titles *Founded:* 1979
ISBN Publisher's Prefix: 82-585

Literary Agents

A/S **Bookman**, Fiolstr 12, DK-1171
Copenhagen K, Denmark (qv) Tel:
Copenhagen 145720 Cable Add:
Bookman, Copenhagen Fax: 451 120007
(Denmark)
This Danish-based company handles rights
in Norway for foreign authors

E M B L A, see Pat Shaw Associates

Ulla **Løhren** Literary Agency, Postboks 150 Tåsen, N-0801 Oslo 8 (Located at: Gjennomfaret 7, Oslo) Tel: (02) 230207 Cable Add: Ullabooks
Dir: Ulla Løhren

Suzanne **Palme** Literary Agency, Postboks 7112 Homansbyen, N-0307 Oslo 3 Tel: (02) 448174 Cable Add: Palmebook
Dir: Suzanne Palme

Pat **Shaw** Associates*, Fredbosvei 61, N-1370 Asker Tel: (02) 782829
Formerly EMBLA

Book Clubs

Bokklubbens **Barn**, see Den Norske Bokklubben A/S
Subject: Juveniles

Det **Beste** A/S*, Postboks 1160 Sentrum, Oslo 1

Disney Junior Bokklub, Kristian Augusts gate 10, Oslo 1 Tel: (02) 429165 Telex: 77074 Fax: (02) 114707
Owned by: Hjemmets Bokforlag A/S (qv)
Subject: Juvenile Fiction

Donald Ducks Bokklubb, Kristian Augusts gate 10, Oslo 1 Tel: (02) 429165 Telex: 77074
Owned by: Hjemmets Bokforlag A/S (qv)
Subject: Juvenile fiction

Bokklubbens **Ekstrabøker**, see Den Norske Bokklubben A/S

Bokklubben **Feminina**, Kristian Augusts gate 10, Oslo 1 Tel: (02) 429165 Telex: 77074
Owned by: Hjemmets Bokforlag A/S (qv)
Subject: Fiction

Hjemmets Bokklubb, Kristian Augusts gate 10, Oslo 1 Tel: (02) 429165 Telex: 77074
Owned by: Hjemmets Bokforlag A/S (qv)
Subjects: Fiction, Non-fiction

Hjemmets Kokebokklubb, Kristian Augusts gate 10, Oslo 1 Tel: (02) 429165 Telex: 77074
Owned by: Hjemmets Bokforlag A/S (qv)
Subject: Cookery

Bokklubbens **Lyrikkvaennene**, see Den Norske Bokklubben A/S
Subject: Poetry

Den **Norske** Bokklubben A/S, Postboks 150, Vollsveien 13, Lysaker, N-1321 Stabekk Tel: (02) 580050 Telex: 74213 Bokkl n
Includes: Den Norske Bokklubben, Bokklubbens Barn, Bokklubbens Ekstrabøker, Bokklubbens Lyrikkvaennene, Bokklubben Nye Bøker, Bokenes Verden
Members: 430,000
Owned by: H Aschehoug & Co (W Nygaard) A/S, J W Cappelens Forlag A/S, Gyldendal Norsk Forlag, Tiden Norsk Forlag (qqv)
Subjects: Fiction, Biography, Travel
Founded: 1961

Bokklubben **Ny Krim**, Kristian Augusts gate 10, Oslo 1 Tel: (02) 429165 Telex: 77074
Owned by: Hjemmets Bokforlag A/S (qv)
Subject: Crime Fiction

Bokklubben **Nye Bøker** (New Book Club), see Den Norske Bokklubben A/S

Bokenes **Verden**, see Den Norske Bokklubben A/S

Major Booksellers

F **Beyer** Bok-Og Papirhandel A/S*, Strandgaten 4, N-5000 Bergen Tel: (05) 321180 Cable Add: Bokbeyer, Bergen
Manager: Birger Knudsen

F **Bruns** Bokhandel*, Kongensgate 10, Postboks 476, N-7000 Trondheim

Gardum A/S*, Søregate 22, Postboks 242, N-4001 Stavanger Tel: (04) 520200/520400
Manager: Reider Gardum

Ed B **Giertsen** A/S*, Småstrandgate, Postboks 217, N-5001 Bergen Tel: (05) 219680

Johan **Grundt** Tanum A/S, now Tanum-Karl Johan A/S (qv)

Lyngs Bokhandel A/S, Postboks 328, N-7001 Trondheim (Located at: Olav Trygvasonsgate 26, N-7000 Trondheim) Tel: (07) 512544
Manager: Ragnvald C Knudsen

Olaf **Norlis** Bokhandel A/S, Universitetsgaten 24, N-0162 Oslo 1 Tel: (02) 429135 Telex: 79265 Norli N
Manager: Tom Vister
Specialization: Medicine, Education, Business, Computers, Travel, Scandinavian literature, Books in minority and immigrant languages
Library supplier, exporter
Owned by: H Aschehoug & Co (W Nygaard) A/S and F Beyer (qqv)

Norsk Bokimport A/S, Postboks 784, Ovre Vollgate 15, N-0106 Oslo 1 Tel: (02) 417050 Telex: 72068 Nobok
Manager: Einar Bruvik
Importer

Erik **Qvist** Bokhandel A/S, Drammensveien 16, N-0255 Oslo 2 Tel: (02) 445269
Manager: Erik Chr Qvist

Sellevolds Bokhandel A/S, Nedre Slottsgate 8, Oslo 1 Tel: (02) 425258/ 414150/421529
Manager: Arne Iversen

Sentral Bokhandel A/S*, Postboks 127, N-1322 Høvik Tel: (02) 532376

H **Sundems** Bokhandel A/S*, Storgate 12, N-8000 Bodø Tel: (081) 20154
Manager: Carl August Veigård

Tanum-Karl Johan A/S, Postboks 1177 Sentrum, N-0107 Oslo 1 Tel: (02) 429310 Cable Add: Tanumbok Telex: 72427 Tanum N Fax: (02) 806878
Dir: Petter A Knudsen; *Manager:* Bjørg Andreassen
Importer, exporter, wholesaler

Tapir*, University of Trondheim, N-7079 Flatasen
Manager: Hans G Auganaes

Universitetsbokhandeln, now Akademica (qv)

Major Libraries

Bergen offentlige Bibliotek Horda land Fylkesbibliotek*, Strömgt 6, N-5000 Bergen Tel: (05) 319750
Bergen Public Library

Deichmanske Bibliotek, Henrik Ibsens gate 1, Oslo 1 Tel: (02) 204335 Telex: 18337 deich n
City Library of Oslo
Chief Librarian: Liv Saeteren

Drammen Folkebibliotek, Gamle Kirkeplass 7, Postboks 1136, N-3001 Drammen Tel: (03) 832890 Telex: 78483 Fbdra N
Public Library of Drammen

Fellesbiblioteket for det Kongelige Norske Videnskabers Selskab, Museet og Norges Laererhøgskole, incorporated in Universitetsbiblioteket i Trondheim (qv)

Styret for det **Industrielle Rettsvern** Bibliotek, Middelthunsgate 15b, Postboks 8160 Dep, N-0033 Oslo 1 Tel: (02) 461900 Telex: 19152 nopat n Fax: (02) 609843
Library of the Norwegian Patent Office
Librarian: Ms Turi Stokke

Det **Kongelige** Norske Videnskabers Selskab, incorporated in Universitetsbiblioteket i Trondheim (qv)

Kristiansand Folkebibliotek, Postboks 476, N-4601 Kristiansand Tel: (042) 29165 Telex: 21149 Kribi n
Municipal Library

Norges **Landbrukshøgskoles** Bibliotek*, Postboks 12, N-1432 Ås-NLH Tel: (02) 949060 Telex: 77125 Nlhbi n
Library of the Agricultural University of Norway

Riksarkivet, Folke Bernadottes vei 21, N-0862 Oslo 8
National Archives of Norway

Statistisk Sentralbyras Bibliotek, Postboks 8131 Dep, N-0033 Oslo 1 Tel: (02) 413820 Cable Add: Statistikk
Library of the Central Bureau of Statistics
Librarian: Hilde Rødland

Stavanger Bibliotek*, Postboks 310-320, N-4001 Stavanger Tel: (04) 507464 Telex: 33181 fb sta n

The **Technical University** Library of Norway, Høgskoleringen 1, N-7034 Trondheim Tel: (07) 595110 Cable Add: NTHB Telex: 55186 nthhb n Fax: (07) 595103
Director: Mrs Randi Gjersvik
Publications include: Universitetet i Trondheim Norges tekniske høgskole Bilioteket Publikasjoner fra laerere og tjenestemenn ved NTH (Annual Bibliography)

Universitetsbiblioteket i Bergen, Möhlenprisbakken 1, N-5000 Bergen Tel: (05) 212500 Telex: 42690 ubb n
Librarian: Knut L Espelid
Publication: Bibliothek og Forskning

Universitetsbiblioteket i Oslo, Drammensveien 42, N-0255 Oslo 2 Tel: (02) 553630 Telex: 76078 ubn
The Royal University Library (National Library)
Librarian: Jan Erik Röed
Publications: Bibliografi over Norges Offentlige Publikasjoner; Norsk Bokfortegnelse; Norske Tidsskriftartikler

Universitetsbiblioteket i Trondheim*, Erling Skakkesgt 47C, N-7000 Trondheim Tel: (07) 592205 Telex: 55384 Bibl n
University Library of Trondheim. Incorporating libraries of the College of Arts and Sciences and of the Museum (formerly Library of the Royal Norwegian Society of Sciences and Letters, DKNVS)
Chief Librarian: Kari Christensen

The **University of Trondheim**, Norwegian Institute of Technology, now The Technical University Library of Norway (qv)

Videnskabers Selskab Biblioteket, incorporated in Universitetsbiblioteket i Trondheim (qv)

NORWAY — PAKISTAN

Library Associations

Arkivaforeningen, Postboks 10, Kringsjå, N-0807 Oslo 8
The Association of Archivists
Publication: Norsk arkivforum

Kommunale Bibliotekarbeideres Forening*, c/o Bjoern Bringsvaerd, Skien Bibliotek, Postboks 349, N-3700 Skien
The Association of Public Library Employees
Publication: Kontakten (six a year)

Norsk Bibliotekforening, Malerhaugveien 20, N-0661 Oslo 6 Tel: (02) 688576
Norwegian Library Association
Secretary-Treasurer: Gro Langeland

Norsk Dokumentasjonsgruppe, c/o Brodd, Dahlenenggt 26, Oslo 4
Norwegian Documentation Society
President: Siv Hunstad

Norsk Fagbibliotekforening, Universitetsbiblioteket i Oslo, Drammensveien 42, N-0255 Oslo 2 Tel: (02) 553630
Norwegian Association of Special Libraries
Chairman: Hans Martin Fagerli
Publications: NFF-informasjon (free to all members); *NFF skrifter* (occasionally)

Norske Bibliotekansattes Landsforbund, Postboks 9202 Vaterland, N-0134 Oslo 1
Norwegian Library Employees' Association
Publications: Meldinger (6-8 a year)

Norske Deitidsbibliotekarers Yrkeslag*, N-7100 Rissa
Chairman: Solfrid Rønning
Norwegian Association for Part-Time Librarians

Norske Forskningsbibliotekarers Forening, now Norsk Fagbibliotekforening (qv)

Riksbibliotektjenesten, Postboks 2439 Solli, N-0202 Oslo 2 (Located at: Drammensveien 42, N-0255 Oslo 2) Tel: (02) 430880 Telex: 76078 ub n
National Office for Research and Special Libraries
Director: Bendik Rugaas
Publications include: Handbook of Research and Special Libraries (irregular); *Synopsis* (6 per year); *Skrifter fra Riksbibliotektjenesten* (irregular)

Library Reference Books and Journals

Book

Bibliothek og Forskning (Library and Research), Universitetsbiblioteket i Bergen, Möhlenprisbakken 1, N-5000 Bergen

Journals

Bok og Bibliotek (Book and Library), Statens Bibliotektilsyn, Munkesdamsveien 62, N-1301 Oslo

Meldinger (Announcements), Norske Bibliotekansattes Landsforbund, Postboks 9202 Vaterland, N-0134 Oslo 1

Literary Associations and Societies

Information Office for Norwegian Literature Abroad, Postboks 239 Sentrum, N-0103 Oslo 1 Tel: (02) 411294
Manager: Kristin Brudevoll

Norske Akademi for Sprog og Litteratur, Oslo
Norwegian Academy for Language and Literature
Secretary: L R Langslet

Det Norske Videnskaps-Akademi*, Drammensveien 78, Oslo 2 Tel: (02) 444296 Cable Add: Norakad
The Norwegian Academy of Science and Letters
Secretary-General: Prof Dr A Semb-Johansson; *Executive Secretary:* Kjell Herlofsen
Publications: Skrifter; Avhandlinger; Årbok

Norwegian P E N Centre, c/o Ase-Marie Nesse, Fridtjof Nansensvei 24B, N-0369 Oslo 3
President: Per Egil Hegge; *Secretary:* Kristin Brudevoll

Literary Periodicals

Edda (Scandinavian), Universitetsforlaget, Postboks 2959 Tøyen, N-0608 Oslo 6
Literary research

Norseman, Nordmanns-Forbundet, Raadusgate 23b, Oslo

Samtiden (The Age), H Ascheoug & Co (W Nygaard) A/S, Sehestedsgate 3, Oslo 1
Journal for politics, literature and social questions

Syn og Segn (Vision and Tradition), Det Norske Samlaget, Trondheimsveien 15, Oslo 5

Vinduet (The Window), Gyldendal Norsk Forlag, Sehestedsgt 4, N-0130 Oslo 1

Literary Prizes

Bastian Prize
Awarded annually for an outstanding translation by one of the members of the Norwegian Association of Translators. Enquiries to Norwegian Association of Translators, Postboks 579 Sentrum, N-0105 Oslo 1

Children's Book Prize
For the best books for children by Norwegian authors, for illustrations by Norwegian artists in books for children, for picture-books, for translations and for comic strips. Awarded annually. Enquiries to Norwegian Directorate for Public and School Libraries, Postboks 8145 Dep, N-0033 Oslo 1

N W Damm Children's Book Prize
Founded in 1952, an award of 50,000 Norwegian kroner is made every second year. Enquiries to N W Damm og Søn A/S, Tvetenveinen 32, Postboks 6140, Etterstad, Oslo 6

Dobloug Prize
For outstanding literary work by two Norwegian and two Swedish writers. 40,000 Swedish crowns in each category awarded annually. This award cannot be applied for. Enquiries to Swedish Academy, Börshuset, Källargränd 4, S-111 29 Stockholm, Sweden

Translation Prize
Established 1968. For translations from foreign literature. 30,000 Norwegian kroner. Awarded annually. Enquiries to Norwegian Cultural Council, Grev Wedels plass, Postboks 101 Sentrum, N-0102 Oslo 1

Tarjei Vesaas Debutant Prize
To a writer under 30 for the best first book of prose or poetry. 8,000 Norwegian kroner. Awarded annually. Enquiries to Norwegian Authors' Association, Rådhusgata 7, Oslo 1

Translation Agencies and Associations

Norwegian Association of Translators, Postboks 579 Sentrum, N-0105 Oslo 1

Pakistan

General Information

Language: Urdu is national language but English is used commercially
Religion: Islamic
Population: 83.8 million
Bank Hours: 0900-1300 Saturday-Wednesday; 0900-1100 Thursday
Shop Hours: 0930-1300, 1500-2000 Saturday-Thursday
Currency: 100 paisa = 1 Pakistan rupee
Export/Import Information: No tariff on books, magazines and advertising matter. Import licence issued freely if required. Anti-Islamic and obscene literature prohibited. Exchange controls
Copyright: UCC, Berne, Buenos Aires, Florence (see International section)

Book Trade Organizations

National Book Council of Pakistan*, 14D Al-Markaz F-8, Ayub Market, PO Box 1610, Islamabad Tel: (051) 853581/850892 Cable Add: Bookouncil
Also: Theosophical Hall, M A Jinnah Rd, Karachi Tel: (021) 71385/74148 Cable Add: Bookouncil; 126 Riwaz Garden, Lahore Tel: (042) 68315 Cable Add: Bookouncil; 175 Block A, Unit 5, Latifahad, Hyderabad
Dir General: Dr M I Hussain; *Assistant Dir:* Ajaz Rahi
Publications include: Kitab (Urdu, monthly); *Books from Pakistan; Karachi Book Trade Directory*; also trade directories, manuals, bibliographies, survey reports

Pakistan Publishers' and Booksellers' Association*, YMCA Bldg, Shahra-e-Quaid-e-Azami, Lahore
Also: 3 Fatima Jinnah Rd, Karachi 4

Standard Book Numbering Agency, Government of Pakistan, Department of Libraries (Ministry of Education), House No 555, Street 83, G-6/4 Islamabad Tel: (051) 822449
ISBN Administrator: Abdul Hafeez Akhtar

Book Trade Reference Books and Journals

Books

Books from Pakistan, National Book Council of Pakistan, 14D Al-Markaz F-8, Ayub Market, PO Box 1610, Islamabad

Karachi Book Trade Directory, National Book Council of Pakistan, 14D Al-Markaz F-8, Ayub Market, PO Box 1610, Islamabad

Pakistan Book Trade Directory, Library Promotion Bureau, Karachi University Campus, PO Box 8421, Karachi-32

Journals

Kitab, National Book Council of Pakistan, 14D Al-Markaz F-8, Ayub Market, Islamabad
Text in Urdu

Pakistan National Bibliography (annual), Directorate of Libraries, National Bibliographical Unit, c/o Liaquat Library, Stadium Rd, Karachi

Publishers

Aane-Adab, Chowk Anarkali, Lahore Tel: (042) 54069
Proprietor: Sh Abdul Salam

Shaikh Muhammad **Ashraf**, 7 Aibak Rd, New Anarkali, Lahore Tel: (042) 53171/53489 Cable Add: Islamiclit Lahore
Publisher: Sh Muhammad Ashraf; *Man Dir:* Sh Shahzad Riaz; *Home Sales:* M D Khawaja; *Export Sales:* Khurshid Hussain; *Literary Adviser:* M Ashraf
Subjects: Books about Islam, Islamic History, Biography in English
Bookshop: At above address
1985: 22 titles *1986-87:* 24 titles *Founded:* 1923

Azim Publishing House+, Khyber Bazar, Peshawar Tel: (0521) 63313
Chief Executive: Azimullah Khan
Subjects: History, Literature, Islamiat, Technical, Scientific

Barque & Co*, Barque Chambers, Barque Sq, 87 Shahrah-e-Liaquat Ali Khan, PO Box 201, Lahore
Man Dir: A M Barque
Branch Off: Karachi
Subjects: Trade Directories, Journals, Who's Who
Founded: 1930

The **Book** House, PO Box 734, Lahore 2 (Located at: 8 Trust Bldg, Urdu Bazar, Lahore 2) Tel: (042) 61212 Cable Add: Bookhouse
Proprietor: Muhammad Saeed; *General Manager:* Muhammad Hamid Saeed
Subjects: Religion, Library, Textbooks
Founded: 1951
Miscellaneous: Exporters of English and Urdu books and Textbooks

Carvan Book House, Kutchery Rd, Lahore Tel: (042) 52296
Proprietor: Ch Abdul Hameed; *Managing Partner:* Ch Abdul Hamid
Subjects: General, Textbooks

Classic*, 42 Shahrah-e-Quaid-e-Azam, Lahore Tel: (042) 61830 Cable Add: Classic 42 Mall Lahore
Man Dir, Editorial, Production, Permissions: Agha A Hussain; *Sales, Publicity:* S Akbar Zaidi
Orders to: Classic, 42 The Mall, Lahore
Subsidiary Companies: Shish Mahal Kitab Ghar, Classic Bookshop (both in Lahore)
Associate Company: Menarva Publications, Lahore
Subjects: The Arts, National Topics, Fiction
Bookshop: 42 The Mall, Lahore
Founded: 1956

Malik **Din Mohammad** & Sons, see Malik

East and West Publishing Co+, 22 Corner Chambers, Chundrigar Rd, Karachi-0102 Tel: (021) 212036 Cable Add: Goodbooks
Publisher: Rafique Akhtar; *Man Dir:* Dr Nasir Rafique
Subjects: Pakistan, Research Material, Biographies, *Pakistan Year Book*
Founded: 1971

Economic and Industrial Publications, Al-Masiha, 47 Abdullah Haroon Rd, PO Box 7843, Karachi 3
Publicity: Saleem Haidari
Subjects: Economics, Industrial Development, Finance, Periodicals
Founded: 1965

Ferozsons (Private) Ltd*, 60 Shahrah-e-Quaid-e-Azam, Lahore Tel: (042) 301196 Cable Add: Ferozsons Telex: 44382 Feroz PK
Man Dir, Publicity: A Salam; *Editorial, Sales Dir:* Zaheer Salam
Branch Offs: 33/C-6, Pechs, Karachi 29; also 150 outlets throughout Pakistan
Subjects: Islamic, Regional, Juveniles, Dictionaries (native and foreign languages)
Bookshops: See under Major Booksellers
Founded: 1894

Frontier Publishing Co, 22 Urdu Bazar, Lahore Tel: (042) 55262
Proprietor: Muhammad Arif
Subsidiary Company: National Book Service, Urdu Bazar, Lahore

Sh **Ghulam** Ali & Sons (Pvt) Ltd, Adbi Market, Chowk Anarkali, PO Box No 528, Lahore Tel: (042) 52908/64065 Telex: 44422 Asia pk
Dirs: Sh Bashir Ahmad, Sh Niaz Ahmed, Arshad Niaz, Imran Ahmad
Branch Offs: M A Jinnah Rd, Karachi Tel: (021) 722254/723092/722784; Yadkar Line, Chotki Ghitti, Hyderabad Tel: (0221) 24431
Subjects: Islamic Studies, Holy Koran, Educational, Children's Books, General, Periodicals

Government Publications*, Manager of Publications, Federal Publications Branch, Government of Pakistan, Deputy Controller, Stationery and Forms Bldg, University Rd, Karachi 5

Hamdard Foundation, Nazimabad, Karachi 18
President: Hakim Mohammed Said
Subjects: Health, History of Traditional Medicine, History of Science and Islam

Idara-e-Faroghe-Undu, Aibak Rd, Lahore
Proprietor: Javed Tufail
Subjects: Literature, Education

Idara Siqafat-e-Islamia, Club Rd, Lahore 3

Ilmi Kitab Khana*, Urdu Bazar, Lahore Tel: (042) 62833
Proprietor: Ch Sardar Mohammad
Subjects: Textbooks, Educational

Islami Kitab Khana, Sadar Bazar, Mianwali, Punjab Tel: (0459) 2995
Subject: Law

Islamic Book Centre*, 25B Masson Rd, PO Box 1625, Lahore 3 Tel: (042) 66272/54205 Cable Add: Islamibook
Man Dir, Publicity Dir: Muhammad Sajid Saeed; *Sales Dir, Advertising Dir:* Muhammad Hamid Saeed
Branch Offs: J M Malik, 35 Cawdor Rd, Fallowsfields, Manchester M14 6LS, UK; 26 Paisa Akhbar (Anarkali), Lahore 2 Tel: (042) 60716; Malik, Jal al Bldg, Urdu Bazar, Lahore 2
Subjects: Religion, University, Secondary & Primary Textbooks

Institute of **Islamic Culture**, Club Rd, Lahore 3 Tel: (042) 53908 Cable Add: ICULT
Subject: Islam & Islamic ideology
Founded: 1950

Islamic Publications (Private) Ltd*, 13-E Shahalam Market, Lahore 8 Tel: (042) 325243 Cable Add: Alilm
Man Dir: Ashfaque Mirza; *General Manager:* Abdul Waheed Khan

PAKISTAN 325

Subjects: Standard Islamic literature on current topics
Founded: 1960

Islamic Research Institute*, PO Box 1035, Islamabad (Located at: Faisal Mosque Complex) Tel: (051) 850751 Cable Add: Islamserch
Director General: Dr S M Zaman; *Sales:* Mumtaz Liaqat
Subjects: History, Law, Religion, Periodicals (in English, Arabic and Urdu)
Founded: 1960
Miscellaneous: The Institute is a Faculty of the International Islamic University, Islamabad

Kazi Publications*, PO Box 1845, Lahore (Located at: 121 Zulqarnain Chambers, Ganpat Rd, Lahore) Tel: (042) 61893 (office), (042) 212386 (residence)
Man Dir, Editorial, Publicity, Rights & Permissions: Muhammad Ikram Siddiqi; *Sales:* Zubair Ahmad; *Production:* Muhammad Iqbal Siddiqi
Subjects: Islamic Religion, Holy Koran, Ahadith, Islamic History and Jurisprudence
Founded: 1978

Kitabi Dunya*, Mcleod Rd, Lahore
Proprietor: Ch Sultan Ahmed
Subject: Detective Fiction

Maktaba-i-Danial, an imprint of Pakistan Publishing House (qv)

Maktaba Jadeed*, PO Box 456, Lahore
Proprietor: Ch Rasheed Ahmed
Subject: Fiction

Maktaba Meri Library*, Chowk Urdu Bazar, Lahore 2
Proprietor: Basheer Ahmed
Subject: Paperbacks

Malik Din Mohammad & Sons*, Bull Rd, Lahore Tel: (042) 54315/52621
Proprietor: Malik Mohammad Arif
Branch Off: Chundrigar Rd, Karachi
Subject: Islamic Studies

Malik Sirajuddin & Sons, Kashmiri Bazar, Lahore 8 Tel: (042) 52169/311498/65539 Cable Add: Serajsons Telex: 52169
Man Dir: A R Malik; *Editorial, Production, Publicity & Permissions:* S A Malik; *Sales:* A A Malik
Subsidiary Companies: Siraj Mohammadi Press, 73 Circular Rd, Outside Akbari Gate, Lahore; Ayaz Book Binding Works, Bazar Tezabian, Kashmiri Bazar, Lahore 8
Associate Companies: Gul I Khandan, Urdu Monthly; Islamic Juntrri (both at Kashmiri Bazar, Lahore 8)
Branch Offs: Chowk Urdu Bazar, Lahore 2; 18-19 M J Hospital (WAQF), O/S Mori Gate, Circular Rd, Lahore
Subjects: Islamic religion and practices (in Arabic, English & other languages); Teach Yourself books, Biography, Psychology, Fiction, Children's
Bookshop: At above address
Founded: 1934

Maqbool Academy*, Adabi Market, Chowk Anarkali, Lahore Tel: (042) 64740
Proprietor: Maqbool Ahmed Malik
Subject: Fiction

Nafees Academy, PO Box 91, Karachi (Located at: Wazir Bldg, 1-Tirath Das Rd, Urdu Bazar, Karachi 1) Tel: (021) 737181/213303/735993
Proprietor: Tariq Iqbal Gahandri
Subjects: History, Educational, General

The **Oriental & Religious** Publishing Corp Ltd*, Rabwah
Subjects: The Holy Koran in Arabic and English, Commentaries on the Koran, Islam

Orientalia Publishers & Booksellers, 6 Habib Bank Bldg, Chowk Urdu Bazar, c/o PO Box 2387, Lahore 2 Tel: (042) 54205 Cable Add: Accubook
Subjects: Oriental, Persian, Urdu History, Arabic, Pakistan, specialist in Urdu books

Oxford University Press (Pakistan Branch), PO Box 13033, Karachi 8 (Located at: 5 Bangalore Town, Main Sharae Faisal, Karachi) Tel: (021) 440532/447793 Cable Add: Oxonian Karachi Pakistan Telex: c/o 25743 Taq Pk
General Manager: Zia Husain
Parent Company: Oxford University Press, UK (qv)
Showroom: Mian Chambers, 3 Temple Rd, Lahore Tel: (042) 305804
Subjects: School & College Textbooks, Reference, General, Pakistan, Islamic Studies, Oxford in Asia Historical Reprints *1985:* 9 titles *1986:* 10 titles *Founded:* 1952

P P H, an imprint of Pakistan Publishing House (qv)

Pak American Commercial Ltd*, PO Box 7359, Karachi 0301 (Located at: Zeb-un-nisa St, Saddar, Karachi) Tel: (021) 514713/511721 Cable Add: Pakacinc Karachi
Dir: Agha M Jaffri; *Editorial, Production:* M Younus Shaikh; *Sales, Publicity:* Ahsan Jaffri; *Rights & Permissions:* Abbas Jaffri
Branch Off: 53/2 Kashmir Rd, PO Box 294, Rawalpindi Tel: (051) 63709 Cable Add: Pakacinc
Subjects: History, Political Science
Bookshops: See under Major Booksellers
Founded: 1949

Pak Publishers*, Urdu Bazar, Lahore

Pakistan Law Times Publications*, Kabir St, Urdu Bazar, Lahore

Pakistan Publications*, Shahrah Iraq, PO Box 183, Karachi 1
Subjects: Books about Pakistan in Urdu, Arabic and English

Pakistan Publishing House, Victoria Chambers 2, 1st Floor, Abdullah Haroon Rd, Sadar, Karachi 3 Tel: (021) 511457 Cable Add: Prilect
Dir: M Noorani; *Editorial Dirs:* Ms Hoori Noorani, Kamran Noorani; *Sales Manager:* Matin M Khan; *Production Manager:* Mohammad Yusuf; *Rights & Permissions:* Mohammad Iqbal
Subsidiary Company: Maktaba-i-Danial (at above address)
Associate Company: Pakistan Law House, Pakistan Chowk, PO Box 90, Karachi 1
Imprints: PPH, Maktaba-i-Danial
Subjects: History, Law, Literature
Founded: 1966

People's Publishing House, PO Box 862, Lahore (Located at: 18-A Mozang Rd, Lahore) Tel: (042) 54512
Man Dir, Publication: Abdur Rauf Malik; *Sales:* A R Meerza; *Publicity:* M Siddique
Subject: Social Science
Founded: 1947

Premier Book House*, PO Box 1888, Lahore (Located at: Room 2, Shahin Market, Anarkali, Lahore) Tel: (042) 64385
Proprietor: Mohammad Khalil
Subject: Islamic Literature
Bookshop: At above address
Founded: 1950

Publishers International, PO Box 4259, Bandukwala Bldg 4, 1 1 Chundrigar Rd, Karachi Tel: (021) 237534
Man Dir: Kamaluddin Ahmad
Subjects: Advertising, Reference, Trade Directories, Science, Technical
Founded: 1948

Publishers United Ltd*, PO Box 1689, Lahore (Located at: 176 Anarkali, Lahore) Tel: (042) 52238 Cable Add: Pubun
Warehouse: 9 Rattigan Rd, Lahore Tel: (042) 53423
Man Dir: Mohammad Amin
Subjects: Religion, Economics, Technical, Reference
Founded: 1942

Qaumi Kutab Khana*, 19-Ferozepur Rd, Lahore Tel: (042) 413168
Proprietor: Mohammad Ahsan & Bros

Quaid-i-Azam University, Islamabad Tel: (051) 829328 Cable Add: Quaid-i-Azam University Islamabad
Manager: Rashid Ahmed Khan
Subjects: Social Sciences, Chemistry
Founded: 1973

'Rast Gufter' Press*, Bhawana Bazar, Lyallpur
Manager & Proprietor: Shamshar Ali Baskhshi
Founded: 1889

Royal Book Co, PO Box 7737, Karachi 3 (Located at: 232 Saddar Cooperative Market, Abdullah Haroon Rd, Karachi 3) Tel: (021) 514244
Proprietor: Jamshed Mirza
Branch Off: 402 Rehman Centre, Zaibunnisa St, Karachi
Subjects: Politics, Economics, Banking, General History, Asian Historical Reprints
Bookshop: At above address
Founded: 1963

H M Saeed Co*, Dr Ziauddin Ahmad Rd, Pakistan Chowk, Karachi
Proprietor: Mohammad Zaki
Subjects: Islamic Studies, Literature (in Arabic, Urdu, Persian)

Sang-e-Meel Publications, Chowk Urdu Bazar, Lahore Tel: (042) 65187
Proprietors: Niaz Ahmad, Ijaz Ahmad, Afzal Ahmad
Branch Off: 25 Lower Mall, Lahore Tel: (042) 212983
Subjects: History and Islamic Studies, Reference Books (especially Persian, Arabic, Urdu Dictionaries), Reprints of books on Afghanistan and Pakistan

Malik Sirajuddin & Sons, see Malik

Taj Co Ltd, Manghopir Rd, PO Box 530, Karachi Tel: (021) 294221/295459 Cable Add: Kalampak Telex: 24839 Tajco Pk
Man Dir: Amjad Hussain Khokhar
Branch Offs: Rawalpindi, Lahore
Subject: Religion
Bookshop: Sale Depot, Taj Co Ltd, M A Jinnah Rd, Karachi
Founded: 1929

Taxation*, 6 Liaquat Rd, Lahore 6

University Book Agency*, Khyber Bazar, Peshawar Tel: (0521) 62534
Subjects: General, Textbooks

Urdu Academy Sind*, Jinnah Rd, Karachi 2 Tel: (021) 213730 (Office), (021) 614289 (Residence) Cable Add: Literature
Proprietor: Ala-ud-Din Khalid
Branch Offs: Lahore, Hyderabad
Subjects: General, Textbooks, Reference
Founded: 1947

West-Pak Publishing Co (Pvt) Ltd, PO Box 374, Lahore 2 Tel: (042) 877709/52427 Cable Add: Wespublish Lahore
Chief Executive: Syed Mahmud Shah
Subjects: Textbooks and Holy Quran
Founded: 1932
Miscellaneous: Government Printers, Importer, Exporter

Major Booksellers

Bookrama, 56 New Urdu Bazar, Karachi Importer and library supplier, associated with S I Gillani, Bookseller (qv)
Manager: Shahzad Namjee

Ferozsons (Private) Ltd*, 60 Shahrah-e-Quaid-e-Azam, Lahore Tel: (042) 301196 Cable Add: Ferozsons Telex: 44382 Feroz PK
Also: 277 Peshawar Rd, Rawalpindi; 33/C-6, Pechs, Karachi 29
Managers: S M Khurshid, Aftab Awan, Ms Malik
Also Publisher (qv)

S I Gillani, Surriaya Mansion, PO Box 1463, 65 The Mall, Lahore Tel: (042) 322970 Cable Add: Longman Lahore
Office Manager: Sylvester Nicholas
See also Bookrama

Khyber Bookshop*, Peshawar University, Peshawar

Liberty Books (Pvt) Ltd, International Division, PO Box 7427, Karachi 03 Tel: (021) 513026/510798 Cable Add: Bookazine Telex: 23207 Libst pk
Managing Dir: A Hussein; *Sales Dir:* Saleem Hussein
Branches: Pearl Continental Hotel, Holiday Inn, Hotel Sheraton, Clifton (all Karachi); Distribution Division, 3 Rafiq Plaza, Inverarity Rd, Saddar, Karachi 03 Tel: (021) 513026/510798

S M Mir, 40 Chartered Bank Chambers, Talpur Rd, Karachi 2 Tel: (021) 237621
Also Publishers' Agent & Exporter

Mirza Book Agency, 65 Shahrah-e-Quaid-e-Azam, PO Box 729, Lahore 3 Tel: (042) 66839 Cable Add: Knowledge
Managing Partner: M H Mirza

N G M Communication, PO Box 2614, Karachi 19 Cable Add: Anjeeamcom Karachi
Manager: Nizam Nazim
Commercial and Government bookseller, library supplier and publishers' distributor, back-issue dealer, international subscription agent, exporter

Pak American Commercial Ltd, PO Box 7359, Karachi 0301 (Located at: Zeb-un-nisa St, Saddar, Karachi 3) Tel: (021) 514713/511721 Cable Add: Pakacinc Karachi
Dir: Ahsan Jaffri
Branches: 53/2 Kashmir Rd, PO Box 294, Rawalpindi Tel: (051) 63709; Pak American Commercial (Pvt) Ltd, 1st Floor, Pak Chamber, 5 Temple Rd, Lahore
Wholesale/retail bookseller and subscription agent; also publisher (qv)

Pak Book Corporation, Aziz Chambers, 21 Queen's Rd, Lahore Tel: (042) 55972/56366 Cable Add: Magbookco Telex: 44488 Mian Pk (call Pak Book)
Man Dir: M A Khan Akter; *Dir:* M Iqbal Cheema
Branch Offs: I & T Centre, G-6/1/1, Khayaban-e-suharwardy, Islamabad Tel: (051) 822456 Cable Add: Pakbookco; Star Centre, Main Tariq Rd, Pechs, Karachi 2913 Tel: (021) 449129

Paradise Book Stall*, Shambhu Nath Rd, off Shahrah-e-Iraq Saddar, Karachi 3 Tel: (021) 512704/528034 Cable Add: Magazines Telex: 23220 Pbsmg pk
Partner: Shaukat Ali

Paramount Books (Pvt) Ltd, 152/0, Block 2, Pechs, Karachi 29 Tel: (021) 441650/ 443264 Cable Add: Parabooks Karachi Telex: 25856 Pbl Pk
Dir: Iqbal S Mohammad
Branches: Lahore; Rawalpindi
Wholesale stockist and distributor

Petiwala Corporation*, Ismail Mansion, Strechen Rd, Pakistan Chowk, Karachi 1 Tel: (021) 218643

Royal Book Co*, PO Box 7737, 232 Saddar Cooperative Market, Abdullah Haroon Rd, Karachi 3 Tel: (021) 514244
Also: 402 Rehman Centre, Zaibunnisa St, Karachi

Major Libraries

Agriculture University Library, see under University

British Council Library*, 32 Mozang Rd, PO Box 88, Lahore Tel: (042) 54278
Also: 14 Civic Centre, Ramna 6, PO Box 1135, Islamabad Tel: (051) 22205 Telex: 5641; 20 Bleak House Rd, PO Box 10410, Karachi 0406 Tel: (021) 51236/38 Telex: 25570; 35 The Mall, PO Box 49, Peshawar Tel: (0521) 73278

Central Secretariat Library*, Government of Pakistan, Islamabad

Ewing Memorial Library*, Forman Christian College, Lahore 11

Government College Library*, Lahore

Dr Mahmud Husain Library, University of Karachi, Karachi 32 Tel: (021) 418227
Librarian: M K Alam
Publications include: Guide to Bibliographical Sources; Catalogue of rare books

Islamic Research Institute Library*, PO Box 1035, Islamabad

Khyber Medical College Library*, Peshawar, NWFP Tel: (0521) 40211/40226
Librarian: Sain Mohammad Malik

Liaquat Memorial Library*, Stadium Rd, Karachi 5

National Archives of Pakistan*, 14-P Markaz F/8, Islamabad
Branches: Quaid-e-Azam Papers Unit, Secretariat Block-D, Islamabad; SK Centre Bldg, 2nd Floor, nr Frere Market Rd, AM2, Karachi

National Library, Islamabad

Pakistan Forest Institute, Central Forest Library, PO Forest Institute, Peshawar, NWFP

Pakistan Institute of Nuclear Science & Technology Library*, PO Nilore, Rawalpindi

Pakistan Scientific and Technological Information Centre (PASTIC)*, Quaid-i-Azam University Campus, PO Box 1217, Islamabad
Dir: Dr Aejaz Ahmad Malik
Branches: This information service has sub-centres at Karachi, Lahore, Peshawar and Quetta
Publications include: Pakistan Science Abstracts (quarterly); *Directory of Scientific Periodicals of Pakistan* (annual)

Planning Commission Library*, Government of Pakistan, 'P' Block, Pakistan Secretariat, Islamabad

Punjab Public Library*, Lahore
Librarian: Mohammad Aslam

Punjab University Library*, 1 Al-Biruni Rd, Lahore 2/12 Tel: (042) 67962
Chief Librarian: M Anwar-ul-Haque
Publications include: Catalogues of manuscripts in various languages held by Library

Sind University Central Library*, University of Sind, New Campus, Jamshoro, Sind Tel: 71225
Librarian: Mohammad Ishaque Laghari

University of Agriculture Library, Faisalabad Tel: (0411) 25911 ext 328 Cable Add: Agrivarsity
Librarian: Najaf Ali Khan

University of Baluchistan Library, Quetta, Baluchistan

University of Engineering and Technology Library*, Lahore Tel: (042) 339243 Cable Add: Univengtech
Acting Librarian: Muhammad Ramzan

University of Karachi Library, see Dr Mahmud Husain Library

University of Peshawar Library*, Peshawar
Librarian: I U Khan

Library Associations

Government of Pakistan Department of Libraries, House No 555, Street 83, G-6/4, Islamabad Tel: (051) 822449/810212

Karachi University Library Science Alumni Association*, c/o Dept of Library Science, University of Karachi, Karachi 32
Secretary: S Zia Haider
Publication: Newsletter

Library Promotion Bureau, Karachi University Campus, PO Box 8421, Karachi-32
Secretary-General: Dr G A Sabzwari
Publications include: Secondary School Library Resources and Services in Pakistan; Bibliographical Services Throughout Pakistan, 2nd Edition; Documents Procurement Service; Libraries of Pakistan; Who's Who in Library and Information Science; University Librarianship in Pakistan; Pakistan Library Bulletin (quarterly); *Pakistan Book Trade Directory*

Pakistan Library Association*, Headquarters Office, Khyber Medical College, Peshawar
President: Arbab Mohammad Jehangir Khan; *Secretary-General:* Sain Mohammad Malik
Publications include: PLA Newsletter; Code of Ethics for Librarians; Public Libraries Facilities in Pakistan; Standards of College Libraries; Standards of Special Libraries; Standards of University Libraries

Society for the Promotion and Improvement of Libraries, Al-Majid, Hamdard Centre, Nazimabad, Karachi 18
President: Hakim Mohammed Said;
Secretary: M Asifuddin
Publications include: Plan for Development of Libraries in Pakistan; Islamic Studies

Library Reference Books and Journals

Books

Libraries of Pakistan, Library Promotion Bureau, Karachi University Campus, PO Box 8421, Karachi-32

Plan for Development of Libraries in Pakistan, Society for the Promotion and Improvement of Libraries, Al-Majid, Hamdard Centre, Nazimabad, Karachi 18

Public Libraries Facilities in Pakistan, Pakistan Library Association, Headquarters Office, Khyber Medical College, Peshawar

Who's Who in Library and Information Science, Library Promotion Bureau, Karachi University Campus, PO Box 8421, Karachi-32

Journal

Pakistan Library Bulletin (quarterly), Library Promotion Bureau, Karachi University Campus, PO Box 8421, Karachi-32

Literary Associations and Societies

Anjuman Taraqqi-e-Urdu Pakistan, Baba-e-Urdu Rd, Karachi 1
For the promotion of the Urdu language and literature
President: N H Jafri; *Secretary:* Jamiluddin A'Ali
Publications: Urdu (quarterly); *Qaumi Zaban* (monthly)

Pakistan Board for Advancement of Literature*, Narsing Das Garden, Club Rd, Lahore

Pakistan Writers' Guild, 1 Montgomery Rd, Lahore
Research Officer: Inamul Haq Javeid
Publication: Ham Qalam (monthly)

Punjab Textbook Board*, 21/E-11, Gulberg-111, Lahore
Similar Textbook Boards exist at Hyderabad, Peshawar, Quetta

Sindhi Adabi Board, Sind University Campus, Jamshoro, Hyderabad, Sind
To promote the language, literature and culture of the Sind region
Secretary: Mohammad Husain Turk

Literary Periodicals

Ham Qalam (monthly), Pakistan Writers' Guild, 1 Montgomery Rd, Lahore

Perspective, Pakistan Publications, Shahrah Iraq, PO Box 183, Karachi

Qaumi Zaban (monthly), Anjuman Taraqqi-e-Urdu Pakistan, Baba-e-Urdu Rd, Karachi 1
Survey of Urdu language and literature

Literary Prizes

Adamjee Prize
Founded in 1960 for the best book of creative and progressive poetry, novel, short story, drama, travelogue or biography. 20,000 rupees. Awarded annually. Administered by the Pakistan Writers' Guild in Karachi. Enquiries to Pakistan Writers' Guild, Central Office, PO Box 697, Saddar Rd, Peshawar

Dawood Prize for Literature
Founded in 1963 for the best books on literary research, literary history, literary criticism; for research works on the Pakistan movement; and for the best translation. 25,000 rupees. Sponsored by the Dawood Foundation. Awarded annually. Enquiries to the Pakistan Writers' Guild, Central Office, PO Box 697, Saddar Rd, Peshawar

Habib Bank Prize for Literature
Founded in 1968 for the best translation or adaptation of the year (into English or a Pakistani language) of a modern or

classical work in any Pakistani language, 25,000 rupees. Awarded annually. Enquiries to Pakistan Writers' Guild, Central Office, PO Box 697, Saddar Rd, Peshawar

National Bank of Pakistan Prize for Literature
Founded in 1964 for the best books on economics and scientific, technical and professional subjects. 25,000 rupees. Awarded annually. Enquiries to Pakistan Writers' Guild, Central Office, PO Box 697, Saddar Rd, Peshawar

Pakistan Board for Advancement of Literature Awards*
For academic works in Urdu, and for articles and poems published in Pakistan journals. Awarded annually. Enquiries to Pakistan Board for Advancement of Literature, Narsing Das Garden, Club Rd, Lahore

President's Award for Pride of Performance*
For notable achievements in literature. Awarded annually. Enquiries to Pakistan Ministry of Education, Islamabad

Prizes for Manuscripts for Juveniles
Six prizes for creative writing in the field of children's literature in the Urdu language. Awarded annually. Enquiries to Pakistan Writers' Guild, Central Office, PO Box 697, Saddar Rd, Peshawar

Regional Literature Awards
For the best literary works, including the novel, short story, drama, poetry, biography, travel, literary criticism or research work, in each of the four regional languages of Punjabi, Pushto, Sindhi and Gujrati. Awarded annually. Enquiries to Pakistan Writers' Guild, Central Office, PO Box 697, Saddar Rd, Peshawar

United Bank Prize for Literature
Founded in 1967 for books in Urdu and Bengali in the following categories: for children up to 15 years of age; and poetry or prose, fiction or non-fiction, for young children. 20,000 rupees. Awarded annually. Enquiries to Pakistan Writers' Guild, Central Office, PO Box 697, Saddar Rd, Peshawar

Panama

General Information

Language: Spanish (English widely used)
Religion: Roman Catholic
Population: 1.8 million
Bank Hours: 0800-1300 or 1330 Monday-Friday
Shop Hours: 0900-1800 Monday-Saturday
Currency: 100 centesimos = 1 balboa = $US 1. US currency is used
Export/Import Information: No tariffs on books and advertising matter. No import licences or exchange controls
Copyright: UCC, Buenos Aires (see International section)

Publishers

Editorial **Bruguera** Centroamericana y Panamá SA*, Apdo 358-9A, Panamá Tel: 692515 Cable Add: Brugcepa Telex: 2661 P Booth PG
Dir: Luis Eduardo Henao Yepes (for Central America and Panama)
Parent Company: Editorial Bruguera SA, Spain (qv)

Ediciones Librería **Cultural Panameña** SA*, Apdo 2018, Panamá 1 Tel: 235628/236267 Cable Add: Culpasa
Man Dir, Editorial: A J Fraguela R; *Sales:* F M Fraguela Ruiz; *Publicity:* Manuel A Fraguela R
Subjects: University, Secondary & Primary Textbooks, Antiquaria, Reference Works
Bookshop: Librería Cultural Panameña SA (qv under Major Booksellers)
Founded: 1955

Dirección de Estadística y Censo*, Contraloría General de la República, Apdo 5213, Panamá 5 Tel: 643734 Cable Add: Estadicen-Contraloría Panama
Man Dir: Francisco A Rodríguez P; *Editorial:* Amílcar Villarreal; *Sales, Production, Publicity:* Silvia de Ibarra
Subject: Panamanian Statistics (including National census)
1985: 40 titles *Founded:* 1941

Editorial **Universitaria***, Estafeta Universitaria, Universidad de Panamá Tel: 642087 Cable Add: Cuidad Universitaria
Man Dir, Editorial: Dr Carlos M Gasteazoro; *Sales:* Eduvigis Vergara; *Production:* Prof Carlos N Ho; *Publicity:* Mary R de Natera
Subjects: History, Philosophy, Geography, Sciences, Law, Literature, Art, Architecture, Social Sciences, Technical, Education
Bookshops: University Bookshop
Founded: 1969

Fondo Educativo Interamericano*, Ave Federico Boyd y Calle 51, Edificio Eastern – 6° piso, Panamá
Parent Company: Addison-Wesley Publishing Co Inc, Reading, MA 01867, USA
Associate Companies: See Addison-Wesley Iberoamericana SA, Mexico

Ediciones **Instituto Nacional** de Cultura*, Apdo 662, Panamá 1 Tel: 220880 Cable Add: Inac
President: Aristides Martínez Ortega; *Editorial, Sales:* Arysteides Turpana; *Production:* Pedro Montañez; *Publicity:* Norma de la Espada
Subjects: Literature in general, History, Anthropology, Archaeology, Folklore, Sociology
Founded: 1976

Editorial **McGraw-Hill** Latinoamericana SA*, Apdo 6-1064, Panamá Tel: 271911 Cable Add: Books-Panama Telex: 3682331 Mhla
Man Dir, Editorial, Permissions: Anibal Torres
Parent Company: McGraw-Hill Inc, 1221 Ave of the Americas, New York, NY 10020, USA
Associate Companies: See McGraw-Hill Book Co (UK) Ltd, UK
Branch Off: Editorial McGraw-Hill Latinoamericana SA, Puerto Rico (qv)
Subjects: Scholarly, Reference, University, Secondary & Primary Textbooks
Founded: 1966

Major Booksellers

Librería **Argosy***, Via Argentina y Via España, Apdo 6620, Panamá 5 Tel: 235344
Proprietor: Gerasimos Kanelopulos

Librería **Cultural Panameña** SA*, Via España 16, Apdo 2018, Panamá 1 Tel: 235628/237280 Cable Add: Culpasa
Manager: Amador J Fraguela R
Also: Four other branches

Librería **Menéndez**, Galerías Obarrio, Via Brasil, Panamá
Branches: Ave Justo Arosemena y Calle 36, Panamá; Librería Santa Ana, Plaza Santa Ana, Panamá; Librería Menéndez Paitilla, Panamá

Servicio Continental de Publicaciones*, Calle 29 Este 5-70, Apdo 1379, Panamá 1 Tel: 258133
Manager: Bertha G de Otero
Also: Two other branches

Servicio de Lewis*, Calle 26 y Ave Balboa, Apdo 1634, Panamá 1 Tel: 627000
Manager: Rodrigo A Burgos J
Branches: Gran Morrison Chain of Stores

Major Libraries

Biblioteca Nacional*, Calle 22 Este bis 1265, Apdo 2444, Zona 3, Panamá Tel: 624777/620393
Dir: Prof Algis Borrero E
Publications: Bibliografías nacionales

Biblioteca Bio-Médica del Laboratorio Conmemorativo **Gorgas**, Apdo 6991, Panamá 5 (Located at: Ave Justo Arosemena No 35-30, Panamá 5) Tel: 274111/256550 Cable Add: Gomela Telex: Gml pa 3480333
Also at Box 935, APO Miami, FL 34002, USA
Gorgas Memorial Laboratory, Bio-medical Research Library
Dir: Dr Rolando E Sáenz; *Librarians:* Lic Nora E Osses, Lic Gloria O de Cano

Universidad de Panama, Biblioteca Interamericana Simón Bolívar, Estafeta Universitaría, Panamá
Librarian: Nuria F de González
Publications include: Boletín Bibliográfico

Library Associations

Asociación de Bibliotecarios Graduados del Istmo de Panamá, c/o Director de la Biblioteca Bio-Médica del Laboratorio Conmemorativo Gorgas, Apdo 6991, Panamá 5 Tel: 274111
Association of Graduate Librarians of the Isthmus of Panama (AGLIP)
President: Prof Manuel Víctor De Las Casas; *Secretary:* Iris de Espinosa

Asociación Panameña de Bibliotecarios*, c/o Apdo 10808, Estafeta Universitaría, Panamá
Panama Library Association
President: Bexie Rodríguez de De León
Publication: Boletín

Library Reference Journal

Boletín (Bulletin), Asociación Panameña de Bibliotecarios, c/o Apdo 10808, Estafeta Universitaría, Panamá

Literary Prize

Literary Prize*
Founded in 1946 by Ricardo Miró to pay tribute to those who furthered the cause of learning, arts and sciences. Awarded annually. A prize of $2,000 is given in each of five sections: poetry, short story,

fiction, theatre, essay. Enquiries to 'Revista Nacional de Cultura', Instituto Nacional de Cultura, Apdo 662, Panamá 1

Papua New Guinea

General Information

Language: English is one of official languages, as is pidjin English or neo-Melanesian; also over 900 other distinct languages are in use
Religion: Majority follow traditional beliefs. Sizeable Anglican, Roman Catholic, United Church (Methodist) and Ecumenist congregations
Population: 3.5 million
Bank Hours: 0900-1400 Monday-Thursday; 0900-1700 Friday
Shop Hours: 0900-1800 Monday-Friday; 0900-1200 Saturday
Currency: 100 toea = 1 kina
Export/Import Information: No tariff on books and advertising but import tax on non-educational books. No import licence for books, but no obscene literature permitted

Book Trade Organization

Standard Book Numbering Agency, National Library Service, PO Box 5770, Boroko Tel: 256200 ext 36 Telex: NE 22234
ISBN Administrator: Fraiser McConnell

Book Trade Reference Journal

Papua New Guinea National Bibliography, National Library Service of Papua New Guinea, PO Box 5770, Boroko
Quarterly annual cumulation

Publishers

The **Christian Book** Centre*, PO Box 222, Madang
Subjects: Literature, Religion

Gordon and Gotch (PNG) Pty Ltd*, PO Box 1395, Port Moresby (Located at: Dogura Rd, 6 Mile, Saraga) Tel: 254551/254855 Cable Add: Gotchbooks Port Moresby Telex: Pngotch NE 22263
General Manager: B J Stephensen
Parent Company: Gordon and Gotch (Australia) Pty Ltd, 114 William St, Melbourne, Victoria 3001, Australia
Subsidiary Companies: New Guinea Book Depot; Taurama Newsagency
Subjects: Travel, Natural History, Languages, Cookery, New Guinea History, Art and Folklore, Juveniles
Bookshop: Papua New Guinea Book Depot (qv under Major Booksellers)
Founded: 1970
ISBN Publisher's Prefix: 0-909093

Major Booksellers

Burns Philp (NG) Ltd*, Kieta, Bougainville (and other branches)

Papua New Guinea Book Depot*, PO Box 1395, Port Moresby Tel: 254551 Cable Add: Gotchbooks Port Moresby Telex: Pngotch NE 22263
Manager: Don Smith
Owned by: Gordon and Gotch (PNG) Pty Ltd (qv)

Rabaul Newsagency, c/o Bali Merchants Pty Ltd, PO Box 390, Rabaul Telex: NE 92969 Fax: (675) 921146

Steamships Trading Co*, PO Box 30, Goroka

University Book Shop Inc, PO Box 114, University PO Tel: 245375 Telex: NE 22366
Manager: C Pearce

Major Libraries

Administrative College of Papua New Guinea Library*, PO Box 6177, Boroko Tel: Port Moresby 256133

National Library Service of Papua New Guinea, PO Box 5770, Boroko Tel: Port Moresby 256200 Cable Add: Png Lib Boroko Telex: NE 22234
National Librarian: Otto Kakaw
Publications include: Papua New Guinea National Bibliography; *National Union List of Serials*; *Selective Index to the Times of Papua New Guinea*

University of Papua New Guinea Library*, PO Box 319, University Post Office, Port Moresby Tel: Port Moresby 245280 Telex: 22366
Publications include: Guide to Manuscripts in the New Guinea Collection, by Nancy Lutton (1980); *New Guinea Periodical Index* (quarterly)

Library Association

Papua New Guinea Library Association*, PO Box 5368, Boroko Tel: 256200
President: Margaret J Obi
Publications include: Directory of Libraries in Papua New Guinea; *Library and Information Services for the Public*; *PNGLA Nius* (newsletter); *The Best of Tok Tok*; *Tok tok bilong haus buk* (journal of the PNGLA)

Library Reference Books

Directory of Libraries in Papua New Guinea, Papua New Guinea Library Association, PO Box 5368, Boroko

Guide to Manuscripts in the New Guinea Collection, by Nancy Lutton (1980), University of Papua New Guinea Library, PO Box 319, University Post Office, Port Moresby

National Union List of Serials, National Library Service of Papua New Guinea, PO Box 5770, Boroko

Literary Periodical

Bikmaus (quarterly), Institute of Papua New Guinea Studies, PO Box 1432, Boroko

Paraguay

General Information

Language: Spanish (Guarani, an aboriginal Indian tongue, is universally spoken)
Religion: Roman Catholic
Population: 3.2 million
Bank Hours: 0730-1100 Monday-Friday
Shop Hours: 0700 or 0730-1200, 1500-1800 Monday-Friday; open until noon Saturday
Currency: guarani
Export/Import Information: Member of Latin American Free Trade Association. Children's picture books and atlases are dutied, plus added tax and compensatory tax. Advertising catalogues subject to added tax and compensatory tax. Additional taxes on all goods; also Consular Fee. No import licences required. Exchange controls; foreign exchange surcharge
Copyright: UCC, Buenos Aires (see International section)

Book Trade Organization

Cámara Paraguaya del Libro*, Casilla de Correo 1705, Asunción
Paraguayan Publishers' Association
President: Lic don Rubén Lisboa;
Secretary: Lic Nidia Vera Radice

Publishers

Editorial **Comuneros***, Casilla de Correo 930, Asunción (Located at: Cerro Corá 289, Asunción) Tel: 46176/44667
Proprietor: Ricardo Rolon
Subjects: Social History, Poetry
Bookshop: Librería Comuneros (qv under Major Booksellers)
Founded: 1963

Ediciones **Diálogo***, Calle Brasil 1391, Asunción
Manager: Miguel Angel Fernández
Subjects: Fine Arts, Literature, Poetry, Criticism, History, Science
Founded: 1957

Ediciones **Nizza***, Casilla de Correo 2596, Asunción (Located at Eligio Ayala 1073, Asunción) Tel: 47160
President: Dr José Ferreira Martinez
Subject: Medicine
Bookshop: Agencia de Librerías Nizza SA (qv under Major Booksellers)

Major Booksellers

Librería El **Ateneo***, General Diaz 347, Asunción Tel: 43668

El **Colegio** SA*, Casilla de Correo 1449, Asunción
Importer/Exporter, Wholesaler

Librería **Comuneros***, Casilla de Correo 930, Asunción (Located at: Cerro Corá 289, Asunción) Tel: 46176/44667
Owned by: Editorial Comuneros (qv)

Librería La **Cultura***, Palma esq Montevideo, Asunción Tel: 45093

Librería **Internacional***, Casilla de Correo 991, Asunción (Located at: Estrella 721, Asunción) Tel: 41423
Manager: Adolfo N Buzó

Librería **Universal**, Casilla de Correo 432, Asunción (Located at: Mcal Estigarribia 430, Asunción) Tel: 90633
Manager: Klaus Henning

Agencia de Librerías **Nizza** SA*, Casilla de Correo 2596, Asunción (Located at: Eligio Ayala 1073, Asunción) Tel: 25440
Owned by: Ediciones Nizza (qv)

Selecciones SA Comercial*, Iturbe 436, Asunción Tel: 41588

Major Libraries

Biblioteca y Archivo Nacionales*, Mariscal Estigarriba 95, Asunción
National Library and Archives

Biblioteca de la **Sociedad Científica** del Paraguay*, Ave España 505, Asunción
Library of the Paraguayan Scientific Society

Library Associations

Asociación de Bibliotecarios del Paraguay*, Casilla de Correo 1505, Asunción
Association of Paraguayan Librarians
Secretary: Mafalda Cabrerar
Publication: Revista de Bibliotecologia y Documentación Paraguaya

Asociación de Bibliotecarios Graduados del Paraguay*, Ave España 1098, Casilla de Correo 2906, Asunción
President: Olga S de Machado; *Secretary:* Margarita Escobar de Morel
Publication: Abigrap Informaciones (Boletin informativo semestral)

Asociación de Bibliotecarios Universitarios del Paraguay*, c/o Prof Yoshiko M de Freundorfer, Head, Escuela de Bibliotecologia, Universidad Nacional de Asunción, Asunción
Paraguayan Association of University Librarians
President: Prof Gloria Ondina Ortiz C; *Secretary:* Celia Villamayor de Díaz

Comisión Paraguaya Documentación e Información*, c/o Instituto de Ciencias, Universidad Nacional, Ave España 1098, Asunción
Paraguayan Committee of Documentation and Information
Executive Secretary: Luis Fernando Meyer

Library Reference Journal

Revista de Bibliotecologia y Documentación Paraguaya (Review of Paraguay Library Science and Documentation), Asociación de Bibliotecarios del Paraguay, Casilla de Correo 1505, Asunción

Literary Associations and Societies

P E N Club del Paraguay, Casilla de Correo 487, Asunción
President: Dr José Antonio Bilbao; *Secretary:* William Baecker

Peru

General Information

Language: Spanish
Religion: Roman Catholic
Population: 17.8 million
Bank Hours: January-March: 0830-1130 Monday-Friday; April-December: 0845-1245 Monday-Friday
Shop Hours: January-March: 0930-1245, 1615-1900 Monday-Saturday; April-December: 0900-1245, 1515-1900 Monday-Saturday (some close Saturday afternoon)
Currency: 100 centavos = 1 inti
Export/Import Information: Member of Andean Group within the Latin American Free Trade Association. Children's picture books and advertising matter dutied per kg + VAT, sales tax applies on advertising matter. No freight tax on books but there is wholesalers' tax. Import licences required. Exchange controls
Copyright: UCC, Buenos Aires (see International section)

Book Trade Organizations

Asociación Nacional de Escritores y Artistas (ANEA), Jirón Puno 421, Apdo 4505, Lima Tel: 287074
National Association of Writers and Artists
President: Dr Luis Hernán Ramirez

Cámara Peruana del Libro, Jirón Washington 1206, Of 507-508, Apdo 10253, Lima 1 Tel: 325694
Peruvian Publishers' Association
President: César Oliver López

Book Trade Reference Journals

Anuario Bibliográfico Peruano (Peruvian National Bibliography), Biblioteca Nacional, Ave Abancay, Apdo 2335, Lima 1

Biliografía Nacional, Biblioteca Nacional, Ave Abancay, Apdo 2335, Lima 1
Peruvian monthly bibliographical information

Publishers

Librerías **A B C** SA, Sta Catalina 217, Apdo 53, Arequipa Tel: 422900 Cable Add: Molagent
Man Dir: Herbert H Moll
Associate Company: Cordoba 685, Buenos Aires, Argentina
Subjects: History, Peruvian Art & Archaeology
Bookshops: See under Major Booksellers
Founded: 1956

Asociación Editorial **Bruño**, Ave Arica 751, Breña, Apdo 1759, Lima Tel: 244134
Man Dir: Hno Francisco Alvarez Penelas
Subjects: University, Secondary & Primary Textbooks and Educational Materials
Founded: 1950

Editorial **Desarrollo** SA, Ica 242, 1° piso, Apdo 3824, Lima Tel: 285380/286628
Cable Add: Edidesa
Man Dir: Luis Sosa Núñez; *Assistant Manager:* Bertha de Berrospi
Bookshop: Librería de Editorial Desarrollo (at above address)
Subjects: Business, Accounting, General Reference, Industrial Engineering
Founded: 1965

Editorial **Ecoma** SA*, Ave Arequipa 4168 'B', Miraflores 18, Lima Tel: 473017
Cable Add: Ecoma
Man Dir: Eduardo Congrains Martin; *Sales Dir:* Ramón Lalupu Lazaro
Subjects: Paperbacks, Literature, Biography, History, Philosophy, Juveniles
Founded: 1970

Distribuidora exclusivo **Grijalbo** SA*, Apdo 4978, Lima
Parent Company: Ediciones Grijalbo SA, Spain (qv)

Editorial **Horizonte***, Nicolás de Piérola 995, Lima 1 Tel: 279364
Man Dir: Humberto Damonte Larraín; *Production Manager:* Eduardo Collazos Tuesta; *Sales Manager:* Juan Damonte Valencia
Subjects: Literature, Social and Economic Sciences, Anthropology, Education, History, Art, Linguistics, Philosophy
Bookshop: At above address
1985-1986: 14 titles *Founded:* 1968

Promotion Editorial **Inca** SA, now Ediciones Peisa (qv)

Instituto de Estudios Peruanos, Horacio Urteaga 694, Jesus Maria, Lima 11 Tel: 323070/244856 Cable Add: Ieperu
Man Dir: Efraín Gonzales de Olarte; *Sales Manager:* Lucía Cano
Subjects: Peruvian studies in Agriculture, Archaeology, Economics, History, Anthropology, Linguistics, Politics
1986: 6 titles *Founded:* 1964

Iris SA*, Jirón Junín 424, Lima 1
Parent Company: Editorial Bruguera SA, Spain (qv)

Librería-Editorial Juan **Mejía** Baca*, Jirón Azángaro 722, Lima Tel: 274067
Man Dir: Juan Mejía Baca
Subjects: Peruvian Literature and History
Founded: 1945

Mosca Azul Editores SRL+, Conquistadores 1130, Lima 27 Tel: 415988
Dirs: Mirko Lauer, Abelardo Oquendo
Subjects: Fiction & Non-fiction, Social Science, University Textbooks
Founded: 1972

Ediciones **Peisa** (Promoción Editorial Inca SA)+*, Apdo 11155, Lima (Located at: Emilio Althaus 460, Oficina 202, Lima 14) Tel: 718884 Telex: 20038 Dinsa Pe
Man Dir: Germán Coronado Vallenas; *Editor:* Martha Muñoz de Coronado
Subjects: Peruvian Literature and History, Juvenile, Children's Books

Editorial **Plata** SA*, Casilla 5595, Lima 100 Tel: 422900
Man Dir: Herbert H Moll
Subjects: South America — History, Art, Guidebooks, Juveniles, Maps
Founded: 1971 (in Venezuela)

Librería **Studium** SA+, P1 Francia 1164, Apdo 2139, Lima Tel: 326278 Cable Add: Studium
Man Dir: Andrés Carbone O; *Assistant Manager:* Andrés Carbone Montes; *Exports:* Enrique Marchena
Subjects: Textbooks and General Culture
Bookshops: See under Major Booksellers
Founded: 1936

Fondo Editorial de la **Universidad Católica***, Apdo 1761, Lima 100 (Located at: Fundo Pando, Pueblo Libre, Lima 21) Tel: 622540 ext 220
Man Dir: José E Aguero González
Subjects: Anthropology, Archaeology, Economics, Ethnology, Law, Sciences, Education, Philosophy, History, Linguistics, Literature, Logic, Sociology, Theology, Psychology
ISBN Publisher's Prefix: 84-89292

Universidad Nacional Mayor de San Marcos*, Apdo 454, Lima (Located at: Direccion Universitaria de Biblioteca y Publicaciones, Ave República de Chile

295, of 508, Lima) Tel: 319689
Man Dir: Juan de Dios Guevara, Rector de la Universidad
Subjects: Medicine, Law, Science, General Literature, Engineering, Textbooks
Founded: 1952

Editorial **Universo** SA, Ave Nicolás Arriola 2285, La Victoria, Apdo 241, Lima 13 Tel: 241639/233190
Man Dir: José Antonio Aquino Benavides; *Executive Manager:* Salvador Lau Barraza
Subjects: Social Science, Textbooks
Founded: 1967

Major Booksellers

Librarías **A B C** SA, Apdo 5595, Lima 100 (Located at: Ave Central 671, Of 604, San Isidro, Lima)
Man Dir: Herbert H Moll
Branches: Centro Comercial Todos, San Isidro; Edificio El Pacífico, Miraflores
Also Publisher (qv)

Librería **Arica***, Paseo de la República 3285, San Isidro, Lima 1 Tel: 401670

Editorial **Interamericana** SA*, Apdo 76, Lima 1 (Located at: Av 28 de Julio 787, Lima 1) Tel: 233471/241944/241845
General Manager: Dr José de la Riva-Agüero

Librería **Epoca***, Jirón Unión 1042, Apdo 4703, Lima Tel: 249545

Librería La **Familia** SA*, PSJ Peñaloza 112, Lima Tel: 243544/248031/325516
Telex: 20038 PE
Manager: Armando Benites O

Librería **Galería** Castro Soto, Miguel Dasso 200, San Isidro, Lima Tel: 401343

Librería **Internacional** del Perú*, Casilla 1417, Boza 892, 2° piso, Lima Tel: 288611

Librería Juan **Mejía** Baca*, Jirón Azángaro 722, Lima Tel: 274067

Nicolas **Ojeda** Fierro e Hijos, see Librería 'La Universidad'

Librería **Studium** SA, Pl Francia 1164, Apdo 2139, Lima Tel: 326278
Branches: Jirón de la Unión 560, Lima; Colmena 626, Lima; Ave Larco 720, Miraflores; Saenz Peña 625, Callao; Francisco Pizarro 533, Trujillo; Calle Moral 107A-107B, Arequipa; Elías Aguirre 251, Chiclayo; Calle Real 377, Huancayo; Calle Arequipa 110, Ayacucho; Tacna 216, Piura; Mesón de la Estrella 144, Cuzco; Tacna 145, Ica; Prospero 268-270, Iquitos
Also Publisher (qv)

Librería de la **Universidad Nacional Mayor de San Marcos***, Av Nicolás de Piérola 1282, Lima 1 Tel: 240876
Dir: Aída Ramírez Medina

Librería '**La Universidad**', Nicolas Ojeda Fierro e Hijos SRL Ltda, Ave Nicolás de Piérola 639, Lima Tel: 282461
Also: Ave Nicolás de Piérola 681, Lima Tel: 282036/282133

Major Libraries

Archivo General de la Nación del Peru*, Calle Manuel Cuadros s/n, Palacio de Justicia, Apdo 3124, Lima Tel: 275930/282829
Chief Librarian: Dr Luis Enrique Tord

Biblioteca Nacional*, Ave Abancay, Apdo 2335, Lima 1 Tel: 277331/287690

Dir: Franklin Pease García Yrigoyen
Publications: Anuario Bibliográfico Peruano (Bibliographical Annual of Peru); *Bibliografía Nacional* (Peruvian monthly bibliographical information); *Boletín de la Biblioteca Nacional* (Bulletin of the National Library); *Revista Fénix* (Phoenix Magazine); *Gaceta Bibliotecaria* (Library Gazette)

Biblioteca Central de la **Pontificia** Universidad Católica del Perú, Av Universitaria Cdra 18, San Miguel, Apdos 1761-5729, Lima

Biblioteca Central de la **Universidad Nacional de Cuzeco***, Apdo 167, Cuzco

Biblioteca Central de la **Universidad Nacional de San Agustín***, Apdo 23, Arequipa

Biblioteca Central de la **Universidad Nacional Mayor de San Marcos***, Apdo 454, Lima

Library Associations

Agrupación para la Integración de la Información Socio-Económica (ABIISE)*, Apdo 2874, Lima 100
Library Group for the Integration of Socio-economic Information
Dir: Betty Chiriboga de Cussato
Publications include: Directorio de Bibliotecas Especializadas del Perú

Asociación de Bibliotecas Agricolas*, c/o Library, Universidad Nacional Agraria, La Molina, Lima
Association of Agricultural Librarians

Asociación Peruana de Archiveros*, Jr Manuel Cuadros s/n, Palacio de Justicia, Apdo 3124, Lima Tel: 275930
Peruvian Association of Archivists

Asociación Peruana de Bibliotecas (APB)*, Bellavista 561, Lima 18 Tel: 474869
Peruvian Library Association
Secretary: Ms C Barrenechea de Castro

Library Reference Books and Journals

Book

Directorio de Bibliotecas Especializadas del Perú (Directory of Special Libraries of Peru), Agrupación para la Integración de la Información Socio-Económica (ABIISE), Apdo 2874, Lima 100

Journals

Boletín, Biblioteca Nacional, Ave Abancay, Apdo 2335, Lima 1

Boletín Bibliografico (Bibliographical Bulletin), Universidad Nacional Mayor de San Marcos, Ave República de Chile 295, Apdo 454, Lima

Fénix, Biblioteca Nacional, Ave Abancay, Apdo 2335, Lima 1
Review of Peruvian libraries

Gaceta Bibliotecaria (Library Gazette), Biblioteca Nacional, Ave Abancay, Apdo 2335, Lima 1

Literary Associations and Societies

Centro del **P E N** Internacional*, Santa Teresita 327, San Isidor, Lima
Secretary: Blanca Varela

Literary Periodicals

Después, Roca y Boloña 633, Lima 18

Revista Peruana de Cultura (Peruvian Review of Culture), Instituto Nacional de Cultura, Ancash 390, Lima 1

Textual, Instituto Nacional de Cultura, Ancash 390, Lima 1

Literary Prize

Premio **Universo***
For the best novel. Awarded every other year. Enquiries to Editorial Universo SA, Ave Nicolás Arriola 2285, La Victoria, Apdo 241, Lima 30

Philippines

General Information

Language: Pilipino (also called Tagalog) is official language. English widely used. Nine other major languages of the Malayo-Polynesian group, and about 60 other languages, are also spoken
Religion: Predominantly Roman Catholic; Islamic on Mindanao and the Sulu Archipelago
Population: 56 million
Bank Hours: 0900-1600 Monday-Friday
Shop Hours: Vary. Many open 0900-1200, 1400-1930 Monday-Saturday (some close 1730; some open Sunday)
Currency: 100 centavos = 1 peso
Export/Import Information: Duty on books except those which are philosophical, historical, economic, scientific, technical or vocational, approved by Department of Education for use of certain institutions (not exceeding 10 copies for an institution, or 2 for an individual) or for encouragement of sciences or fine arts; no tariffs on Bibles and similar religious books. No duty on advertising matter. No import licences, but no obscene or immoral literature permitted. Release certificate issued on behalf of Central Bank required to clear goods. Imports subject to sales tax. No formal exchange controls but most imports need Letter of Credit (over $100 in any month, for example)
Copyright: Berne, UCC, Buenos Aires, Florence (see International section)

Book Trade Organizations

Book Development Association of the Philippines (BDAP), 40 Valencia St, New Manila, Quezon City 3008 Tel: (02) 783976 Cable Add: Verareyes Manila
Telex: 63740 Vri PN
Organization of Philippine book publishers, booksellers, printers and designers
President: Louie O Reyes; *Corporate Secretary:* Esther M Pacheco

Philippine Book Dealers' Association*, MCC PO Box 1103, Makati Commercial Centre, Makati, Metro Manila
President: José Benedicto

Philippine Educational Publishers' Association, 927 Quezon Ave, Quezon City Tel: (02) 9213788/968316
President: Jesus Ernesto Sibal

Standard Book Numbering Agency, The
National Library of the Philippines, T M
Kalaw St, Manila Tel: (02) 501011 Telex:
40726 Nalib Pm
ISBN Administrator: Lily Orbase

Publishers

Abiva Publishing House Inc*, 851-881
G Araneta Blvd, Quezon City Tel: (02)
7120245
Man Dir: Luis Q Abiva Jnr; *Sales Dir:*
Alfredo de Guzman; *Publicity Dir:* Mila
S Precioso; *Advertising Dir:* Felicito
Q Abiva; *Rights & Permissions:* Milagros R
Arceo
Subsidiary Company: Hiyas Press Inc
Subjects: History, Reference, Religion,
General Science, Primary Textbooks,
Educational Materials
Founded: 1963

Addison-Wesley Publishing Co Inc*, 125
Don Manuel, Quezon City Tel: (02)
7124534 Cable Add: Adiwes
Consultant: Ricardo M Hizon
Miscellaneous: Firm is a branch of Addison-
Wesley Publishing Co Inc, USA

Alemar-Phoenix Publishing House Inc, now
Phoenix Publishing House Inc (qv)

Alip & Sons Publishing Inc*, 1306 Dos
Castillas St, Manila
Man Dir: Dr E M Alip; *Sales Dir:* Ella B
Ortega; *Publicity Dir:* Miss Bellen A Alip;
Advertising Dir: Rita A Aramil
Subjects: Textbooks, Reference
Founded: 1946

Associated Publishers Inc*, 459 Quezon
Ave, Quezon City, PO Box 449, Manila
President: Magdawgal B Elma
Subjects: Medicine, Education, Law
Founded: 1952

Ateneo de Manila University Press+, PO
Box 154, Manila (Located at: Bellarmine
Hall, Loyola Heights, Quezon City) Tel:
(02) 962526/998721/982541
Dir: Esther M Pacheco
Subjects: Philippine Literature, Textbooks,
Humanities & Social Sciences (with
reference to the Philippines)
Founded: 1972

Bookman Publishing House*, PO Box 709,
Manila (Located at: 373 Quezon Ave,
Quezon City) Tel: (02) 7124813/7124818/
7124860 Cable Add: Bookman
President: Ceferino M Picache; *Sales Dir:*
Soriano Seda; *Editorial Dir:* Mrs Patrocinio
S Picache
Subsidiary Companies: Bookman Printing
House, Mission Publishing Co (both at 373
Quezon Ave, Quezon City)
Subjects: Textbooks & Reference for
Elementary, Secondary & Collegiate
Schools, Educational Materials
Founded: 1945

Bustamente Press Inc*, 155 Panay Ave,
Quezon City
President: Pablo N Bustamente Jnr
Subjects: Textbooks on English, Sciences,
Mathematics
Founded: 1949

Capitol Publishing House Inc, 54 Don
Alejandro A Roces Ave, Quezon City

Communication Foundation for Asia*, PO
Box SM-434, Manila 2806 Cable Add:
Socomter Manila Telex: 27854 Cfa Ph
President: Antonio Tria Tirona; *Editorial,
Sales:* Belinda Tablante
Subjects: Religion, Textbooks,
Development Communication, Social
Philosophy, Children's
Founded: 1973

Erehwon Publishing House*, 569 Padre
Faura, Ermita, Manila
Subjects: General Fiction, Belles Lettres,
How-to
Bookshop: At above address

R M Garcia Publishing House*, 903
Quezon Ave, Quezon City Tel: (02)
999847/993286 Cable Add: Romgar Manila
Orders to: PO Box 1860, Manila
Man Dir, Sales, Publicity: Rolando M
Garcia; *Editorial:* Maridel Garcia
Parent Company: R P Garcia Publishing &
Printing Co Inc
Subjects: College Textbooks for Philippine
Schools, Filipiniana (historical), Education,
History & Government, Business
Founded: 1951
ISBN Publisher's Prefix: 971-1024

Heritage Publishing House*, PO Box 3667,
Manila (Located at: 6 St William cor
Lantana, Cubao, Quezon City)
President: Mario R Alcantara; *Man Dir:*
Ricardo S Sanchez
Subjects: Art, Anthropology, History,
Political Science
Bookshop: At above address
Miscellaneous: Previously MCS Enterprises
Inc

I R R I, see International Rice Research
Institute

Industry & Trade Publishers*, 5 Martelino
St, Quezon City
Subjects: Business, Industry

International Rice Research Institute
(IRRI), PO Box 933, Manila Tel: (02)
7420717/7420580 Cable Add: Ricefound
Manila Telex: 45365 Rice Inst PM
Man Dir: Dr Thomas R Hargrove
Imprint: IRRI
Subject: Rice production (all aspects)
Bookshops: Verlag Josef Margraf,
TRIOPS, Tropical Scientific Books,
Raiffeisenstr 24, D-6070 Langen, Federal
Republic of Germany; Oxford Book &
Stationery Co, Scindia House, New Delhi
110001, India; Publishers International
Corporation, 2nd Newfield Bldg, 42-3
Ohtsuka 3-Chome Bunkyo-ku, Tokyo 112,
Japan; Harvest Farm Magazine, 14
Wenchow St, Taipei, Taiwan;
Agribookstore, IADS Inc, 1611 North
Kent St, Arlington, VA 22209, USA
1985: 22 titles *1986:* 12 titles *Founded:*
1960
ISBN Publisher's Prefix: 971-104

Jonef Publications*, 1137 Looban, Paco,
Manila Tel: (02) 598910/502702/597647
Man Dir: J N Francisco
Subjects: Reference, Primary &
Intermediate Textbooks
Founded: 1950

Lawyers' Co-operative Publishing Co
(Philippines) Inc*, Quezon Blvd Extension
63, PO Box 449, Quezon City, Manila
President: Magdangal B Elma
Subjects: Law, Medicine, Dental, Nursing,
Technical
Founded: 1913
Miscellaneous: Firm is an affiliate of
Lawyers' Co-operative Publishing Co, New
York, NY 14603, USA

M C S Enterprises Inc, now Heritage
Publishing House (qv)

Mutual Books Inc, 425 Shaw Blvd,
Mandaluyong, Metro Manila Tel: (02)
797538/796050/7211114 Cable Add: Mubinc
Shipping Add: PO Box 245, Greenhills,
San Juan, Metro Manila
President: Alfredo S Nicdao Jnr
Associate Company: Alfredo S Nicdao Jnr
Inc
Subjects: Business, Economics,
Management, Accounting, Mathematics,
Secretarial, Computers
Founded: 1959

National Book Store, 701 Rizal Ave,
Manila Tel: (02) 494306 Cable Add:
Nabost Manila Telex: 27890 NBS-PH;
41144 NBS-PM
Man Dir: Benjamin C Ramos; *Sales Dir:*
Mitto Licauco; *Publicity & Advertising:*
Mrs Socorro C Ramos; *Rights &
Permissions:* Alfredo C Ramos
Subjects: General Fiction & Non-fiction,
How-to, Music, Art, Juveniles, Low-priced
Paperbacks, University, Secondary &
Primary Textbooks
Bookshops: See under Major Booksellers
Founded: 1945
Miscellaneous: Firm reprints over 300 titles
annually for foreign publishers

New City*, PO Box 332, Manila (Located
at: 1933 St Pasay City, Manila)
Parent Company: Città Nuova Editrice,
Italy (qv for associate companies)

Philippine Book Co*, 851 Orouieta St, Sta
Cruz, Manila Tel: (02) 274337
Subjects: General Fiction, Belles Lettres,
School texts
Bookshop: At above address

Philippine Education Co Inc*, PO Box
706, Makati Commercial Center, Manila
(Located at: Banawe St, corner Quezon
Ave, Quezon City) Tel: (02) 604666/
603041 Cable Add: Pecoi Manila Telex:
7222321
General Manager: Antero L Soriano
Subjects: General Fiction, Belles Lettres,
Art, Social Science, Textbooks,
Educational Materials
Bookshops: See under Major Booksellers

Phoenix Publishing House Inc, 927 Quezon
Ave, Quezon City 3008
Tel: (02) 9213788/962131/968316
President: Jesus Ernesto R Sibal; *Vice-
President, Operations:* Anita S
Mangalindan; *Editor-in-Chief:* Avelina
J Gil; *Sales:* Maria Victoria G Afable; *Art
Dir:* David S Cruz
Associate Companies: Central Lawbook
Publishing Co, Phoenix Press, Phoenix
Educational Systems Inc (all 927 Quezon
Ave, Quezon City); Central Book Supply,
769 Rizal Ave
Branch Off: Alemar's Bldg, Cnr P del
Rosario & Junquera Sts, Cebu City
Subjects: Sciences, Social Studies, Religion,
Languages, Literature, History, Sociology,
Communication Arts, Values Education
Bookshop: Alemars (qv under Major
Booksellers)
1985: 59 titles *Founded:* 1958
Miscellaneous: Formerly Alemar-Phoenix
Publishing House Inc
ISBN Publisher's Prefix: 971-06

Regal Publishing Co*, 1729 J P Laurel St,
San Miguel, Manila 2804 Tel: (02)
7415427/7410659/7410660 Cable Add:
Repress Manila
Man Dir, Editorial, Publicity: Corinna B
Mojica; *Sales:* L B Benipayo; *Production:*
J B Benipayo; *Permissions:* A B Benipayo
Associate Company: Benipayo Press Inc,
1131 Quezon Ave, Heroes Hills, Quezon
City 3008
Subjects: Philippine Writings, Philippine
and English Translations of German Books
Founded: 1958

Sinag-Tala Publishers Inc+, PO Box 536,
Greenhills Post Office, Rizal 3113 (Located
at: 4/F Regina Bldg, Aguirre St, Legaspi
Village, Makati, Metro Manila) Tel: (02)

8192681/8192586 Cable Add: Sinapub Manila
Man Dir, Rights & Permissions: L A Uson; *Editorial:* R Lardizabal; *Sales:* D Gonzalez
Subjects: Business, Economics, Educational Textbooks, Home and Family, Religion
Founded: 1969

Solidaridad Publishing House, 531 Padre Faura, Ermita, Manila Tel: (02) 586581/591241 Cable Add: Soldad
Man Dir: F Sionil Jose
Subjects: Biography, Fiction, History, Reference, Periodical
Bookshop: Solidaridad Bookshop (at above address)
Founded: 1965

University of the Philippines Press, E de los Santos St, Diliman, Quezon City 3004
Dir, Rights & Permissions, Editorial: Renato Correa; *Sales, Publicity:* Pilar E Tongson; *Production:* Francisco Felix
Subjects: General Fiction, Belles Lettres, Art, Music, Religion, Philosophy, How-to, Medicine, Business, Law, Psychology, Political & Social Science, Science & Technology, Educational Materials

University Publishing Co*, Central Office, 1128 Washington, Sampaloc, Manila
Dirs: Dr José M Aruego and Constancia E Aruego
Subjects: Business, Law, Educational Materials
Founded: 1936

Vera-Reyes Inc+, 40 Valencia St, New Manila, Quezon City 3008 Tel: (02) 783976 Cable Add: Verareyes Manila Telex: 63740 Vri pn Fax: (632) 8179742
Man Dir: L O Reyes; *Publishing Dir:* Gerardo P Legaspi
Subsidiary Company: International Typesetting Services
Subjects: Arts & Culture, Religion, Philosophy, History
Bookshop: Vera-Reyes Inc, Medical Books Division (at above address)
Founded: 1964
ISBN Publisher's Prefix: 971-151

Book Club

Alemar's Best Sellers Club*, 927 Quezon Ave, Quezon City
Members: 2,400
Owned by: Alemar's (see under Major Booksellers)
Founded: 1977

Major Booksellers

Alemar's, North Mall Bldg, Makati Commercial Center, Makati, Metro Manila Tel: (02) 856735/857140 Telex: 23312 Rhp ph bx 1102
Branches: 526 United Nations Ave, Manila; 927 Quezon Ave, Quezon City; Fiesta Carnival, Cubao, Quezon City; Holiday Plaza Libertad Cnr, F B Harrison St, Pasay City; CM Recto St, Davao City; 1428 Taft Ave, Manila; Pl del Rosario, cnr Junquera St, Cebu City; 769 Rizal Ave, Manila
Book Club: Alemar's Best Sellers Club
Owned by: Phoenix Publishing House Inc (qv)

Bookmark Inc, 264 E Vito Cruz Ext, Makati, Metro Manila Tel: (02) 872328/887022/8160744
Manager: José Maria Lorenzo Tan
Branches: 357 T Pinpin, Escolta, Manila Tel: (02) 481804 Cable Add: Bookmark Manila; Greenbelt, Makati, Metro Manila Tel: (02) 8151088; Casa Filipina Bldg, Alabang, Metro Manila Tel: (02) 8423187; Ermita, Manila Tel: (02) 584215; Timog Ave, cnr Quezon Blvd, Quezon City Tel: (02) 976349; Estrada and Taft Ave, Manila Tel: (02) 593359; Session Rd, Baguio City Tel: 4912; Maharlika Livelihood Center, Baguio City

Eastern Book Service Corp, No 3 Malamig, UPPO Box 10, Diliman, Quezon City 3004 Tel: (02) 9222512 Cable Add: Eastbook Manila
Manager: Linda F Sherman
Wholesaler and retailer

Goodwill Trading Co Inc, (Goodwill Book Store), PO Box 2942, Manila Tel: (02) 406711/405085/406114 Cable Add: Gotrade Manila Telex: 27302 Gtc Ph
President and General Manager: Manuel Cancio

G Miranda & Sons, 1887 C M Recto Ave, Manila Tel: (02) 7311516/7414382/7414917

National Book Store, 701 Rizal Ave, Manila Tel: (02) 494306 Cable Add: Nabost Manila Telex: 27890 Nbs-ph; 41144 Nbs-pm
General Manager: Ms Socorro C Ramos
Also: 14 branches in Manila, Metro Manila, Caloocan, Quezon City
Also Publisher (qv)

Philippine Book Co*, 851 Oroquieta St, Sta Cruz, Manila Tel: (02) 7115829

Philippine Education Co Inc*, 1104 Castillejos, Manila Tel: (02) 401370 Cable Add: Pecoi Manila Telex: 7222321
General Manager: Antero L Soriano
Branches: Araneta Center, Cubao, Quezon City; Makati Commercial Center, West Drive Arcade, Makati; Broadway Centrum, Doña Juana Rodriguez and Aurora Blvd, Quezon City
Also Publisher (qv)

Popular Book Store*, Mapua Institute Bldg, Manila Tel: (02) 7115184/7115189 Cable Add: Pobost
General Manager: Joaquin Po; *Manager:* Katherine Ann P Palomera
Owned by: Popular Trading Corporation

Major Libraries

Ateneo de Manila University Libraries*, PO Box 154, Manila

Ayala Museum Library & Iconographic Archives*, PO Box 259 MCC, Makati, Metro Manila 3116 Tel: (02) 899925
Head Librarian: Estrella P Tobilla
Publications: Catalog of Filipiniana Books and Bound Periodicals in the Ayala Museum Library and Iconographic Archives (1978); *A Collection of Maps in the Ayala Museum Library and Iconographic Archives* (1980); *A Checklist of Rare and Contemporary Filipiniana Serials in the Ayala Museum Library and Iconographic Archives* (1981)

Far Eastern University Library, PO Box 609, Manila 2806
Dir: Celedonio O Resurreccion
Publication: Far Eastern University Journal

Manila City Library*, Manila City Library, Room 372, 3rd Floor, City Hall, Manila 2801 Tel: (02) 408810

The **National Library** of the Philippines, T M Kalaw St, PO Box 2926, Ermita, Manila Tel: (02) 583258 (Filipiniana); (02) 582271 (Reference); (02) 582660 (Public Documents) Cable Add: Nalibphils Telex: 40726 Nalib

Philippine Normal College Library & Library Science Departments*, Taft Ave, Manila 2801 Tel: (02) 475314

Scientific Clearinghouse and Documentation Services Division, Science Promotion Institute, NSTA Bicutan, Taguig, PO Box 3596, Manila
Chief: Dr Irene D Amores
Publications include: R & D Philippines; Series of Philippine Scientific Bibliographies; Philippine Science & Technology Abstracts; SEA Abstracts; Union List of Serials of NSTA and its Agencies; Union Catalogue of NISST

Silliman University Library, Dumaguete City 6501
Librarian: Prof Eliseo P Bañas
Publication: Silliman University Library Occasional Bulletin

Ramona S **Tirona** Memorial Library*, The Philippine Women's University, Taft Ave, Manila 2801 Tel: (02) 503277
Librarian: Esperanza A Sta Cruz
Publications include: Philippine Educational Forum; Administrative Bulletin; PWU Bulletin/FTB Bulletin; The Alumni Link and Philippine Women's University Forum; The Link

University of Manila Central Library, 546 Dr M V de los Santos, Sampaloc, Manila

University of San Carlos Library System, P del Rosario St, Cebu City 6401 Tel: (032) 70874
Dir: Marilou P Tadlip

University of Santo Tomas Library*, España, Manila 2806 Tel: (02) 210081 (local 234)

University of the East Library, Claro M Recto Ave, Manila ZC 2806
Chief Librarian: Sarah C De Jesus

University of the Philippines Library*, Gonzalez Hall, Diliman, Quezon City 3004 Tel: (02) 976061/8 (local 284)
Publications include: Philippine Bibliography

Library Associations

Association of Special Libraries of the Philippines (ASLP)*, PO Box 4118, Manila
President: Jesusa C Manhit
Publications: ASLP Bulletin (annual); *Directory of Special Library Resources and Research Facilities in the Philippines*

Bibliographical Society of the Philippines*, c/o National Archives, National Library Bldg, T M Kalaw, Ermita, Manila
Secretary-Treasurer: Leticia R Maloles
Publication: Newsletter

National Institute of Science and Technology, Division of Documentation, see Scientific Clearinghouse and Documentation Services Division

Philippine Library Association, c/o National Library, T M Kalaw St, Ermita, Manila 2801 Tel: (02) 590177
Secretary: Carmencita A Sta Cruz
Publication: PLAI Bulletin (annual); *PLAI Newsletter* (half-yearly)

Library Reference Books and Journals

Books

Bibliography of Philippine Bibliographies, Ateneo de Manila University Press, PO Box 154, Manila

334 PHILIPPINES — POLAND

Directory of Special Library Resources and Research Facilities in the Philippines, Association of Special Libraries of the Philippines (ASLP), PO Box 4118, Manila

Philippine Bibliography, University of the Philippines Library, Gonzalez Hall, Diliman, Quezon City 3004

Journals

Bulletin (annually), Association of Special Libraries of the Philippines (ASLP), PO Box 4118, Manila

Bulletin (annually), Philippine Library Association, c/o National Library, T M Kalaw St, Ermita, Manila 2801

Journal of Philippine Librarianship, University of the Philippines, Institute of Library Science, Diliman, Quezon City
Text in English

Newsletter, Bibliographical Society of the Philippines, c/o National Archives, National Library Bldg, T M Kalaw St, Ermita, Manila

Newsletter, University of the Philippines, Institute of Library Science, Diliman, Quezon City

Literary Associations and Societies

Kawika*, 1655 Soler, Santa Cruz
Society of Tagalog Writers
Secretary: Gemiliane Pinade
Publication: Liwayway (weekly)

International **P E N** Centre, Solidaridad Publishing House, 531 Padre Faura, Ermita, Manila
President: Alejandro Roces; *Secretary:* F Sionil José

Literary Periodicals

Balthazar, Balthazar Publishing House, 1782 M Adriatico, Malate, Manila

Diliman Review, University of the Philippines, College of Arts and Sciences, Diliman, Quezon City D-505

Far Eastern University Journal, Far Eastern University, PO Box 609, Manila 2806

Manila Review, Bureau of National and Foreign Information, Department of Public Information, PO Box 3396, Manila
Text in English; Philippines journal of literature and the arts

Philippine Studies, Ateneo de Manila University Press, PO Box 154, Manila

Literary Prizes

Cultural Centre of the Philippines Literary Awards
Awarded annually for the best volume of verse and best play written in English and in Pilipino languages. Awards are also made every five years for fiction (novel), epic poetry, criticism and biography, marking the special inaugurations of the Centre. Open to Filipino citizens, resident or non-resident. Prizes 10,000 Philippine pesos in each category. Prizes also for 2nd and 3rd places. Winning works are published in the series *Ani*. Enquiries to Cultural Centre of the Philippines, Roxas Blvd, Manila

Don Carlos **Palanca** Memorial Awards for Literature Contest*
For novels, short stories, poetry, essays and plays written in English and in Pilipino languages. Annual awards are given in each of the language divisions for the best entries in the following six categories: novel — 25,000 Philippine pesos grand prize; short story, poetry, essay, one-act play — 7,000 Philippine pesos first prize; three-act play — 12,000 Philippine pesos first prize. Enquiries to Don Carlos Palanca Memorial Awards for Literature Contest, c/o La Tondeña Inc, 453 C Palanca St, Quiapo, Manila

Poland

General Information

Language: Polish (German and Russian used, English especially among young people)
Religion: Roman Catholic
Population: 35.6 million
Bank Hours: 0900-1300 Monday-Friday; 0800-1300 Saturday
Shop Hours: 1100-1900 Monday-Saturday
Currency: 100 groszy = 1 zloty
Export/Import Information: Book importation done by the Foreign Trade Enterprise Ars Polona, ul Krakowskie Przedmieście 7, PO Box 1001, 00-068 Warsaw, which pays any duties applicable. Advertising may be placed through AGPOL Foreign Trade Advertising agency, ul Kierbedzia 4, PO Box 7, 00-957 Warsaw. No import licences as such required. All overseas trade is conducted in foreign currency. Small quantities of advertising materials duty free
Copyright: Berne, UCC (see International section)

Book Trade Organizations

A G P O L (Przedsiebiorstwo Reklamy i Wydawnictw Handlu Zagranicznego)*, PO Box 7, 00-957 Warsaw (Located at: ul Kierbedzia 4, Warsaw) Tel: (022) 416061 Cable Add: Agpol Warszawa Telex: 813364 Agpol Pl
Foreign Trade Publicity and Publishing Enterprise
Dir: Mieczyslaw Kroker
Offers publicity services abroad for Polish foreign trade and in Poland for foreign companies
Founded: 1956

Ars Polona, see RSW (below) and Major Booksellers

Bioru Miedzynarodowego Numeru Ksiazki*, ul Mazowiecka 9, 00-052 Warsaw Tel: (022) 264431
ISBN Administrator: Mrs Halina Wylezinska

Polskie Towarzystwo Wydawców Ksiazek, ul Mazowiecka 2-4, 00-048 Warsaw Tel: (022) 260735
Polish Publishers' Association
President: Stanislaw Bebenek; *Deputy Presidents:* Zygmunt Gebethner, Andrzej Karpowicz, Andrzej Kurz
Publication: Przeglad Ksiegarski i Wydawniczy (jointly with Zrzeszenie Ksiegarstwa, qv under Major Booksellers)

R S W (Robotnicza Spóldzielnia Wydawnicza) 'Prasa-Ksiazka-Ruch'*, ul Bagatela 14, 00-950 Warsaw Tel: (022) 28851
Workers' Publishing Cooperative
Includes 'Ksiazka i Wiedza' (qv), Interpress (qv), Krajowa Agencja Wydawnicza (qv), RSW (Robotnicza Spóldzielnia Wydawnicza) 'Prasa-Ksiazka-Ruch' (qv), Agencja Wydawnicza (qv) and Wydawnictwo Artystyczno-Graficzne; also Ars Polona (qv under Major Booksellers)
Publications include: Literatura (Literature); Teksty (Texts)

Standard Book Numbering Agency, see Bioru Miedzynarodowego Numeru Ksiazki

Stowarzyszenie Autorów Zaiks, ul Hipoteczna 2, 00-092 Warsaw Tel: (022) 277577 Telex: 812470 Zaiks Pl
Society of Authors
President: Edmund Osmańczyk; *General Manager:* Witold Kolodziejski; *Foreign Dept Manager:* Wlodzimierz Lalak

Stowarzyszenie Ksiegarzy Polskich*, ul Mokotowska 4-6, 00-641 Warsaw Tel: (022) 252874
Association of Polish Booksellers (social organization for State book trade employees)
President: Tadeusz Hussak
Publication: Ksiegarz

Zjednoczenie Przedsiebiorstw Wydawniczych Naczelny Zarzad Wydawnictw*, ul Krakowskie Przedmieście 15-17, 00-071 Warsaw Tel: (022) 268830
United Publishers — Central Publishing Board

Zwiazek Literatów Poliskich*, Krakowskie Przedmieście 87-89, 00-079 Warsaw Tel: (022) 268421/260589
President: Wojczech Zukrowski
Union of Polish Writers

Book Trade Reference Books and Journals

Books

Polish Publishers and Booksellers, Państwowy Instytut Wydawniczy, PO Box 377, 00-950 Warsaw
Text in English

Ruch Wydawniczy w Liczbach (Polish Publishing in Figures), Instytut Bibliograficzny Biblioteki Narodowej, ul Hankiewicza 1, 00-973 Warsaw

Journals

Books in Polish or Relating to Poland, The Polish Library, 238 King St, London W6, UK

Ksiegarz (The Bookseller), Association of Polish Booksellers, ul Mokotowska 4-6, 00-641 Warsaw

New Books, Ossolineum, Rynek 9, PO Box 70, 50-106 Wroclaw
Editions in English and Polish

New Polish Publications, Ars Polona, PO Box 1001, 00-068 Warsaw
A monthly review of Polish books; editions in English, German and Russian

Przeglad Ksiegarski i Wydawniczy (Publishing and Bookselling Review), Zjednoczenie Ksiegarstwa, ul Jasna 26, 00-950 Warsaw
Published jointly with the Polish Publishers' Association

Rocznik Literacki (The Literary Yearbook), Państwowy Instytut Wydawniczy, PO Box 377, 00-950 Warsaw

Soon to Appear, Foreign Trade Publicity and Publishing Enterprise, ul Kierbedzia 4, PO Box 7, 00-957 Warsaw
French, German and Russian editions
Zapowiedzi Wydawnicze (Publishing Announcements), United Booksellers, ul Jasna 26, 00-950 Warsaw

Publishers

Agencja Autorska, ul Hipoteczna 2, 00-092 Warsaw Tel: (022) 278396
Authors' Agency
Associate Company: Polskie Wydawnictwo Muzyczne (qv)
Subjects: Contemporary Polish writers, Periodicals
Also Literary Agency (qv)

Wydawnictwa Normalizacyjne **'Alfa'**, PO Box 206, 00-950 Warsaw (Located at: ul Nowogrodzka 22, Warsaw) Tel: (022) 287261 Telex: 812374 Wuen Pl
Editor-in-Chief: Jerzy Wysokiński; *Production Dir:* Zdzislaw Adamski; *Sales Manager:* Malgorzata Lukaszczuk
Imprints: Wydawnictwa 'Alfa'; Wydawnictwa ALFA
Subjects: Standards and sets of standards, Periodicals, Fiction, Science Fiction, Children's, Popular Science, Manuals, Games
Bookshop: ul Sienna 63, Warsaw
1985: 39 titles *Founded:* 1956
ISBN Publisher's Prefix: 83-7001

Wydawnictwo **Arkady***, PO Box 169, 00-950 Warsaw (Located at: ul Sienkiewicza 15, Warsaw) Tel: (022) 269441
Dir, Editor-in-Chief: Eugeniusz Piliszek; *Deputy Editor:* Eugenia Krzemińska-Niemiec; *Production:* Jan Krajewski
Orders to: Ars Polona, PO Box 1001, 00-068 Warsaw
Subjects: Art, Architecture, Building
Founded: 1957
ISBN Publisher's Prefix: 83-213

Ars Christiana*, PO Box 471, 00-873 Warsaw (Located at: ul Ogrowdowa 37, Warsaw) Tel: (022) 204738
Subjects: Religion, Periodicals
Founded: 1951

Wydawnictwa **Artystyczne i Filmowe**, ul Pulawska 61, 02-595 Warsaw Tel: (022) 455301/455584
Man Dir: Jerzy Wittlin; *Editorial:* Edward Rylukowski; *Editorial, Publicity:* Andrzej Dulewicz
Orders to: Ars Polona (see Major Booksellers)
Subjects: Art, Film, Theatre, Reprints of old books and engravings
Founded: 1959

Instytut Wydawniczy **Centralnej Rady Związków Zawodowych***, ul W Spasowskiego 1-3, 00-389 Warsaw Tel: (022) 279011
Publishing House of Trade Unions
Dir: Tadeusz Lipski
Subjects: Health and Safety at Work, Workers' Education and Culture, Trade Union Movement, Living Conditions
Bookshop: Księgarnia Skladowa, Mariensztat 8, 00-302 Warsaw
Founded: 1950
ISBN Publisher's Prefix: 83-202

Spółdzielnia Wydawnicza **'Czytelnik'**+, ul Wiejska 12a, 00-490 Warsaw Tel: (022) 281441 Cable Add: Czytelnik Warsaw
Man Dir, Editor-in-Chief: Stanislaw Bebenek; *Foreign Dept:* Andrzej Mokrzewski
Subjects: General Fiction, Belles Lettres, Poetry, Juveniles, Low-priced Paperbacks, Social Science, Memoirs, Journalism
Founded: 1944

Drukarnia Narodowa, an imprint of Polskie Wydawnictwo Muzyczne (qv)

Państwowe Wydawnictwo **Ekonomiczne***, ul Niecala 4a, 00-098 Warsaw Tel: (022) 278001 Cable Add: Pewue
State Economic Publishers
Dir, Editor-in-Chief: Zbigniew Gajczyk; *Deputy Editor:* Teresa Zwierzyńska-Buballo
Imprint: PWE
Subjects: Scholarly, Reference, Economics, Social Science, Business
Bookshop: At above address
Founded: 1949

Wydawnictwo **'Epoka'***, PO Box 393, 00-018 Warsaw (Located at: ul W Hibnera 11, Warsaw) Tel: (022) 278081 Cable Add: Wydawnictwo Epoka Warszawa
Subjects: Publications of the Central Committee of the Democratic Party, Periodicals
Founded: 1957

Wydawnictwa **Geologiczne**, PO Box 72, 00-975 Warsaw (Located at: ul Rakowiecka 4, Warsaw) Tel: (022) 494927
Dir: Dr Marian Saldan
Subjects: Academic and professional books on Geology, Surveying
Founded: 1953
ISBN Publisher's Prefix: 83-220

Wydawnictwo Harcerskie **'Horyzonty'**, incorporated in new organization Mlodziezowa Agencja Wydawnicza (qv)

Państwowy **Instytut** Wydawniczy+, PO Box 377, 00-950 Warsaw (Located at: ul Foksal 17, Warsaw) Tel: (022) 260201/261536 Cable Add: Piw
State Publishing Institute
Man Dir: Michal Kabata; *Deputy Editors-in-Chief:* Teresa Jankowska, Leszek Kamiński; *Sales:* Barbara Mianowska; *Vice Dir, Production:* Stefan Michalski; *Publicity:* Danuta Naleszkiewicz; *Rights & Permissions:* Regina Malgorzata Greda
Subjects: General Fiction, Belles Lettres, Poetry, Biography, Theatre, Popular Science, History, History of Culture, Essays, Memoirs
Bookshop: At above address
1985: 110 titles *1986:* 117 titles *Founded:* 1946
ISBN Publisher's Prefix: 83-06

Wydawnictwo **'Interpress'***, PO Box 388, 00-585 Warsaw (Located at: ul Bagatela 12, Warsaw) Tel: (022) 219325 Cable Add: Interpress Warszawa Telex: 814481/814775 Pai Pl
Editor-in-Chief: Tadeusz Lon; *Editorial:* Maciej Bem; *Production, Sales:* Witold Bójski; *Publicity, Rights & Permissions:* Jerzy Guz
Branch Offs: Dechant Heimbachstr 19, Bad Godesberg, D-5300 Bonn 2, Federal Republic of Germany Tel: (228) 313440; Hagalundsgatan 10 1, 151, S-171 50 Solna, Stockholm, Sweden Tel: (8) 821065
Subjects: Contemporary and Historical Poland, Popular Science, Tourist Guides
Founded: 1967
Miscellaneous: Member of RSW (qv under Book Trade Organizations)
ISBN Publisher's Prefix: 83-223

Państwowe Wydawnictwo **'Iskry'**, PO Box 897, 00-375 Warsaw (Located at: ul Smolna 11-13, Warsaw) Tel: (022) 276001/3 (Central) 279415 (Director) Cable Add: Iskry
Dir, Editor-in-Chief: Lukasz Szymański; *Deputy Dir:* Józef Ferber; *Deputy Editor:* Maciej Krasicki
Subjects: General Fiction, Belles Lettres, Poetry, Biography, Travel & Adventure, How-to, Religion, Juveniles, Low- & High-priced Paperbacks, Social Science
Founded: 1952
ISBN Publisher's Prefix: 83-207

Państwowe Przedsiebiorstwo Wydawnictw **Kartograficznych**, ul Solec 18-20, 00-410 Warsaw Tel: (022) 283251 Cable Add: Pepewuka, Warszawa
Dir: Alina Meljon Tel: (022) 280236; *Editor:* Jerzy Ostrowski Tel: (022) 283251
Subjects: Geographical and Historical Maps and Atlases; Geodetic, Cartographic books
1985: 115 titles *1986:* 103 titles *Founded:* 1951

Wydawnictwa **Komunikacji i Lacznośći***, PO Box 71, 02-546 Warsaw (Located at: ul Kazimierzowska 52, Warsaw) Tel: (022) 492751 Telex: 812736 Pl
Transport and Communications Publishers
Dir, Editor-in-Chief: Wieslaw Jezewski; *Deputy Editors:* Maria Lopuszniak, Bogumil Zieliński, Ryszard Godlewski (Magazines); *Production:* Józef Grudziński
Subjects: Mechanical Engineering, Aeronautics, Electronics, Radio, Communications, Transport
Founded: 1949
ISBN Publisher's Prefix: 83-206

Krajowa Agencja Wydawnicza (KAW), PO Box 179, 00-679 Warsaw (Located at: ul Wilcza 46, Warsaw) Tel: (022) 286481/286485 Telex: 813487 Kaw Pl
Man Dir, Editor-in-Chief: Dobroslaw Kobielski; *Editorial:* Jedrzej Bednarowicz; *Deputy Editors:* Tadeusz Kaczmarek, Zbigniew Zlotnicki; *Production:* Wladyslaw Szeszko; *Sales:* Józef Maka
Branch Offs: Ul Podedwornego 12a, 15-269 Bialystok; ul Floriańska 33, 31-019 Cracow; ul św Ducha 111/113, 80-801 Gdańsk; ul 3 Maja 36, 40-097 Katowice; ul Sienkiewicza 3/5, 90-113 Łódź; ul Buczka 28, 20-076 Lublin; ul Slowackiego 22, 60-823 Poznań; ul Komunistów 10, 35-030 Rzeszów; ul Orla Bialego 5, 70-562 Szczecin; pl Solny 14, 50-062 Wroclaw
Subjects: Culture, Science, Educational material, Juveniles, Politics, Guides, Belles Lettres, Sport, Science and Detective Fiction
Founded: 1974
Miscellaneous: Member of RSW (qv under Book Trade Organizations)

Wydawnictwo **'Ksiazka i Wiedza'**, PO Box 476, 00-950 Warsaw (Located at: ul Smolna 13, Warsaw) Tel: (022) 275401 Cable Add: KiW Warszawa Telex: 817630 Kiw Pl
Dir, Editor-in-Chief: Witold Skrabalak; *Editors:* Ryszard Drzewiecki, Ignacy Gajewski, Jaroslaw Ladosz, Tadeusz Tarnogrodzki; *Production:* Andrzej Gierkowski
Subjects: History, Politics, Sociology, Philosophy, Belles Lettres
Founded: 1918
Miscellaneous: Member of RSW (qv under Book Trade Organizations)

Państwowy Zaklad Wydawnictw **Lekarskich**, PO Box 379, 00-950 Warsaw 1 (Located at: ul Dluga 38-40, Warsaw) Tel: (022) 314281 Cable Add: Wydlek Warszawa
Polish State Medical Publishers
Dir: Ignacy Nyka; *Editorial Secretary:* Alicja Mazur; *Editor-in-Chief:* Aleksander Tulczyński; *Deputy Editor-in-Chief:* Maria D Dziak

336 POLAND

Subjects: Medicine, Biology, Biochemistry, Pharmacy, Psychology, Textbooks, Monographs, Dictionaries, Periodicals, Audiovisual Materials
Founded: 1945

Wydawnictwo **Literackie**+*, ul Dluga 1, 31-147 Cracow Tel: (094) 224644/224761/224802
Dir: Andrzej Kurz Tel: (094) 225423; *Editorial:* Katarzyna Krzemuska Tel: (094) 228950, Krystyna Migdalska Tel: (094) 220514; *Production:* Jan Malik
Branch Off: Plac Solny 14a, 50-062 Wroclaw
Subjects: Classical and Contemporary Belles Lettres, Memoirs, History, Literature, Theatre, Film, Art, Translations
1985: 172 titles *Founded:* 1953

Wydawnictwo **Lodzkie**+*, PO Box 372, 90-447 Lodz (Located at: ul Piotrkowska 171-173, Lodz) Tel: (04) 360331/360376
Editorial Dir: Jacek Zaorski; *Sales & Publicity:* Janina Sobczak; *Production:* Grazyna Bis-Stepniak; *Rights & Permissions:* Alfreda Gorzkiewicz
Subjects: Polish Belles Lettres (mainly modern); Translations of literature from the Soviet Union and Yugoslavia, and from French, German and English; Socio-Scientific Literature; Humanities, Memoirs
Founded: 1957
ISBN Publisher's Prefix: 83-218

Wydawnictwo **Lubelskie**, ul Okopowa 7, 20-022 Lublin Tel: (028) 27344
Dir, Editor-in-Chief: Ireneusz Caban; *Deputy Editor:* Ludwik Zabielski
Subjects: Science, Social & Political Sciences, Humanities, Belles Lettres, Juveniles, Poetry, Translations from Ukrainian
Founded: 1957

Ludowa Spóldzielnia Wydawnicza, ul Grzybowska 4, 00-131 Warsaw Tel: (022) 200251 Cable Add: LSW, Warszawa
People's Publishing Cooperative
Chairman, Editor-in-Chief: Leon Janczak; *Deputy President:* Jerzy Wiśniewski; *Editorial:* Józef Aniol
Subjects: Polish Literature, History, The Peasant Movement, Agricultural Problems
Founded: 1946

Wydawnictwo **Ministerstwa Obrony Narodowej**, ul Grzybowska 77, 00-844 Warsaw Tel: (022) 201261/494705
Publishing House of the Ministry of National Defence
Dir: Franciszek Stepniowski; *Editor-in-Chief:* Jan Ignaczak; *Deputy Editors:* Kazimierz Madej, Mieczyslaw Mikrut; *Production:* Ewa Czarnecka-Napieraj
Subject: Military (History, Memoirs, Technical Literature)
Founded: 1947

Mlodziezowa Agencja Wydawnicza*, al Stanów Zjednoczonych 53, 04-028 Warsaw Tel: (022) 132041/9
Youth Publishing Agency and Publishing Co-operative
Agency Editor-in-Chief: Zygmunt Konopka; *Editorial:* Andrzej Murawski; *Sales:* Halina Popiolek; *Production:* Wieslaw Felczak
Subjects: Literature for children and young people; Instructions and Programmes of Polish Socialist Youth Organizations; Belles Lettres, Sociology, Politics, Popular Science; Handbooks
Founded: 1974
Miscellaneous: This organization replaces the former Wydawnictwo Harcerskie 'Horyzonty'. It is also a Workers' Publishing Co-operative, allied to RSW (qv under Book Trade Organizations). Mlodziezowa acts as both Agency and Publisher for Polish youth

Wydawnictwo **Morskie**, ul Szeroka 38-40, 80-835 Gdańsk Tel: (098) 311031/311035
Man Dir, Editorial: Jerzy Szulczewski; *Vice-Dir:* Wladyslaw Kawecki; *Sales, Publicity:* Waldemar Bozestowski; *Production:* Elzbieta Smolarz; *Rights & Permissions:* Zbigniew Semmerling
Subjects: Maritime, Technical, Economics, Popular Science, Belles Lettres, History
Book Club: Publisher's Club
Bookshop: Publisher's Bookshop (qv under Major Booksellers)
Founded: 1951
ISBN Publisher's Prefix: 83-215

Polskie Wydawnictwo **Muzyczne**, PO Box 115, 31-111 Cracow (Located at: al Krasińskiego 11a, Cracow) Tel: (094) 227044 Cable Add: PWM
Polish Music Publishers
Man Dir: Mieczyslaw Tomaszewski; *Editorial:* Stanislaw Haraschin; *Sales:* Wladyslaw Duda; *Production:* Stanislaw Blawacki; *Publicity:* Halina Czubińska; *Rights & Permissions:* Jan Paździora
Orders to: Ars Polona, PO Box 1001, 00-068 Warsaw
Associate Company: Agencja Autorska (qv)
Subsidiary Company: Centralna Biblioteka Muzyczna-Nutowa, ul Senatorska 13-15, 00-075 Warsaw
Imprint: Drukarnia Narodowa
Branch Off: 'Synkopa', ul Senatorska 13-15, 00-075 Warsaw
Subject: Music
Bookshop: Skladnica Ksiegarska, ul Smoleńsk 33, Cracow
1985: 226 titles *1986:* 209 titles *Founded:* 1945
ISBN Publisher's Prefix: 83-224

Instytut Wydawniczy **'Nasza Ksiegarnia'**, PO Box 380, 00-389 Warsaw (Located at: ul W Spasowskiego 4, Warsaw) Tel: (022) 262431 Cable Add: Nasza Ksiegarnia
Telex: 817823 Nk
Dir, Editor-in-Chief: Czeslaw Wiśniewski; *Deputy Editor:* Anna Wegrzyn; *Deputy Production Dir:* Zbigniew Antczak
Subjects: Fiction for children and juvenils, Popular Science, Education, Periodicals
1985: 205 titles *Founded:* 1921

Państwowe Wydawnictwo **Naukowe**, see PWN

Wydawnictwa **Naukowo-Techniczne**, PO Box 359, 00-950 Warsaw (Located at: ul Mazowiecka 2-4, Warsaw) Tel: (022) 267271 Cable Add: Ente Warszawa
Man Dir, Editor-in-Chief: Dr Zygmunt Kaczorowski; *Deputy Dir:* Adam Urbanicki; *Deputy Editors:* Henryk Najberg, Krzysztof Radziwill, Aniela Topulos
Subjects: Applied Mathematics & Physics, Computer Science, Electrical & Electronic Engineering, Chemistry, Automation, Machine Design & Technology, Foodstuffs Industry, Light Industry, Technical & Scientific Encyclopaedias, Dictionaries & Vocabularies at all levels
1985: 89 titles *1986:* 85 titles *Founded:* 1949
ISBN Publisher's Prefix: 83-204

Wydawnictwa **Normalizacyjne**, see 'Alfa'

Zaklad Narodowy im **Ossolińskich** Wydawnictwo Polskiej Akademii Nauk+, PO Box 911, 50-106 Wroclaw (Located at: ul Rynek 9, Wroclaw) Tel: (07) 38625
Cable Add: Ossolineum Wroclaw
Telex: 0712771
Ossolineum-Publishing House of the Polish Academy of Sciences
Man Dir: Eugeniusz Adamczak; *Editor-in-Chief:* Zdzislaw Kujawski; *Foreign Rights:* W Brodzki, B Kocowska
Orders to: Ars Polona, PO Box 1001, 00-068 Warsaw
Branch Offs: ul Manifestu Lipcowego 19a, 31-110 Cracow; ul Lagiewniki 56, 80-855 Gdansk; ul Moniuszki 5, 90-101 Lódź; ul Dluga 26, 00-238 Warsaw
Subjects: Bibliographies, History, Art, Philosophy, Psychology, Physical Sciences, Medicine, Earth Sciences, Law, Politics, Literature, Education, Sociology, Technology, Geography, Economics, Languages, Ethnology, University Textbooks, Educational Materials, Periodicals
1985: 550 titles *1986:* 606 titles *Founded:* 1817
ISBN Publisher's Prefix: 83-04

P W E (Państwowe Wydawnictwo Ekonomiczne), see Ekonomiczne

P W N (Państwowe Wydawnictwo Naukowe)*, PO Box 391, 00-251 Warsaw (Located at: ul Miodowa 10, Warsaw) Tel: (022) 262291 Cable Add: Pewuen Warszawa
Polish Scientific Publishers. Publish books in foreign languages and co-operate with foreign publishers
Dir, Editor-in-Chief: Rafal Lakowski; *Deputy Dirs:* Zygmunt Klos, Jerzy Kozlowski, Kazimierz Mliczewski; *Editors:* Stanislaw Piaścik (Humanities), Zygmunt Kaczorowski (Science), Ryszard Marcinkowski (Encyclopaedias and Dictionaries)
Branch Offs: ul Wieckowskiego 13, 90-721 Lódź; ul Slawkowska 14, 31-014 Cracow; ul Ratajczaka 35, 61-816 Poznań; ul Pretficza 9-11, 53-328 Wroclaw
Orders to: Ars Polona, PO Box 1001, 00-950 Warsaw; or to Orpan Export, Palac Kultury, 00-901 Warsaw
Subjects: All fields of learning (except medicine), Languages, Encyclopaedias, Dictionaries, University Textbooks, Co-editions, Periodicals
Founded: 1951

'Pallottinum' Wydawnictwo Stowarzyszenia Apostolstwa Katolickiego*, PO Box 1095, 60-959 Poznan (Located at: ul Przybyszewskiego 30, Poznan) Tel: (06) 47212
Publishers of the Catholic Apostolate Association
Dir: Stefan Dusza; *Deputy Dir:* Stanislaw Gawrylo; *Editorial:* Kazimierz Jacaszek
Subjects: Catholic Philosophy and Theology
Founded: 1948

Instytut Wydawniczy **Pax**, ul Chocimska 8-10, 00-791 Warsaw Tel: (022) 499517
Chief Editor: Józef Wolkowski; *Executive Editor, Secretary:* Krzysztof Doroszewski
Subjects: Contemporary Christian Theology, Church History, Cultural History, Modern History, Philosophy, Literature
Founded: 1949

Wydawnictwo Stowarzyszenia Spoleczno-Kulturalnego **'Pojezierze'**, al Zwyciestwa 32, 10-578 Olsztyn Tel: (027) 24088/24089
Dir, Editor-in-Chief: Andrzej Wakar; *Deputy Dirs:* Roman Marchwiński, Jerzy Adam Sokolowski
Subjects: Belles Lettres, Popular Science, Art
Founded: 1957
ISBN Publisher's Prefix: 83-7002

Polish Scientific Publishers, see PWN

Wydawnictwo **Poznańskie**, PO Box 63, 60-967 Poznań (Located at: ul A Fredry 8, Poznań) Tel: (061) 221901 Telex: 0413693

Dir, Editor-in-Chief: Dr Jerzy Ziolek; *Deputy Dir:* Milosz Glowacki; *Deputy Editor:* Zofia Szmajs
Subjects: Science, History of Poland and Polish culture, Modern Polish and Foreign Fiction, Children's, Science Fiction
Founded: 1956
Miscellaneous: Specializes in translations from the literature of Scandinavian and German-speaking countries
ISBN Publisher's Prefix: 83-210

Wydawnictwo **Prawnicze***, ul Wiśniowa 50, 02-520 Warsaw Tel: (022) 496151
Dir, Editor-in-Chief: Dr Stanislaw Ziembiński (Tel: 494705) *Deputy Editor:* Ryszard Chrzanowski (Tel: 499410)
Subjects: Law and Criminology
1985: 62 titles *Founded:* 1952
ISBN Publisher's Prefix: 83-219

R S W (Robotnicza Spóldzielnia Wydawnicza) 'Prasa-Ksiazka-Ruch', ul Jagiellońska 103, 85-027 Bydgoszcz Tel: (052) 411540 Telex: 0562845
Chief Executive: Zbigniew Cieśliński; *Editorial:* Dr Wieslaw Krzysztoszek; *Sales, Production, Publicity, Rights & Permissions:* Ewa Grinberg
Parent Company: RSW (Robotnicza Spóldzielnia Wydawnicza) 'Prasa-Ksiazka-Ruch' (qv under Book Trade Organizations)
Bookshop: Księgarnia Domu Ksiaźki, ul Marii Konopnickiej 30, 85-124 Bydgoszcz
1985: 27 titles *1986:* 31 titles *Founded:* 1982
ISBN Publisher's Prefix: 83-7003

Wydawnictwo **Radia i Telewizji***, ul Chelmska 9, 00-724 Warsaw Tel: (022) 412264
Dir, Editor-in-Chief: Teresa Bartoszek; *Production:* Maciej Pcion
Subjects: Radio and Television, Educational Aids, Fiction, Current Affairs, Popular Science, Periodicals
Founded: 1968

Państwowe Wydawnictwo **Rolnicze i Leśne**+, PO Box 374, 00-950 Warsaw (Located at: al Jerozolimskie 28, Warsaw) Tel: (022) 266451 Cable Add: Pewril Warszawa Telex: 817509 Pl Pwril
State Agricultural and Forestry Publishers
Dir, Chief Editor: Mr Marian Bajorek; *Deputy Editors:* Halina Gutowski, Jan Czajka (Periodicals); *Production:* Danuta Kozlowska
Branch Off: ul Ratajczaka 33, 61-816 Poznań
Subjects: Textbooks, Reference, Agriculture, Forestry, Food Science, Veterinary Science
Founded: 1947
ISBN Publisher's Prefix: 83-09

Wydawnictwo Spóldzielcze CZSR **'Samopomoc Chlopska'***, PO Box 38, 00-013 Warsaw (Located at: ul Jasna 1, Warsaw) Tel: (022) 271524 Cable Add: Zetwuceres Warszawa Telex: 813622
Cooperative Publishing House of the Central Union of Agricultural 'Peasant Self-Aid' Cooperatives
General Manager: Piotr Baryla
Subjects: Books and Periodicals for the Cooperatives
Founded: 1957

Wydawnictwo **'Slask'**, PO Box 36-67, 40-161 Katowice (Located at: ul Armii Czerwonej 51, Katowice) Tel: (032) 583221
'Silesia' Publishing House
Dir, Editor-in-Chief: Jeremi Gliszczyński; *Production:* Zygmunt Odrobny
Subjects: Mining and Metallurgy, Belles Lettres, Literature, Children's, Translations from Czech and Slovak, Social and Political Literature, Popular Science
1985: 71 titles *1986:* 62 titles *Founded:* 1954

Wydawnictwo **Sport i Turystyka***, ul H Rutkowskiego 7-9, 00-021 Warsaw Tel: (022) 262451
Sport and Tourism Publishers
Dir, Editor-in-Chief: Eugeniusz Skrzypek; *Deputy Editor:* Eugeniusz Gotowiec
Subjects: Sport, Travel, Tourism, Art
Founded: 1953

Zarzad Wydawnictw **Statystycznych i Drukarni**, al Niepodleglosci 208, 00-925 Warsaw Tel: (022) 259545/254886 Cable Add: Gus Telex: 814581
Statistical Publications and Printing Board of the Central Statistical Office
Man Dir: Jerzy Sufin-Suliga; *Editorial:* Christo Cwetkow
Subject: Statistics
Founded: 1966

Księgarnia **Świetego Wojciecha***, PO Box 288, 60-967 Poznan (Located at: pl Wolności 1, Poznan) Tel: (06) 59186/7 Cable Add: Albertinum Poznan Telex: 0414220 Kmp
St Adalbert's Bookshop
Man Dir: Dr Michal Maciolka
Branch Offs: ul Królewska 15, 20-109 Lublin; ul Freta 48, 00-227 Warsaw
Subjects: Biblical Texts, Theology, Catechism, Periodicals
Bookshops: At above main and branch offices addresses
Founded: 1895

Wydawnictwa **Szkolne i Pedagogiczne**, PO Box 480, 00-950 Warsaw (Located at: pl H Dabrowskiego 8, Warsaw) Tel: (022) 265451/55 Cable Add: Wuesipe Warszawa
Man Dir: Jerzy Loziński; *Rights & Permissions:* Piotr Ozieblo; *Advertising, Head of Foreign Dept:* Marek Nowakowski
Orders to: Ars Polona, PO Box 1001, 00-068 Warsaw
Branch Off: Delegatura WSiP, Basztowa 15, 31-143 Cracow
Subjects: Primary, Secondary and Vocational Textbooks, Education, Psychology, Periodicals
Founded: 1945

Towarzystwo Przyjaciól Ksiazki (TPK)*, ul Hipoteczna 2 ZAIKS, 00-092 Warsaw Tel: (022) 277304
Society of Friends of Books
Man Dir: Alexandre Bochenski
Branch Offs: Rynek Gl 35, 31-011 Cracow; Plac Wolnosci 12, 40-078 Katowice; uk św Jadwigi 3/4, 50-266 Wroclaw; ul Slowackiego 9, Rzeszów
Subject: Book Collecting
Founded: 1957

Wydawnictwo Kultura Zycia Codziennego **'Watra'***, al Jerozolimskie 87, 02-001 Warsaw Tel: (022) 212241
Dir, Editor-in-Chief: Miroslaw Brzostowski; *Deputy Editor:* Józef Unger; *Production:* Andrzej Torzewski
Subjects: Health, Domestic Science, Food, Sewing, Cosmetics, Periodicals
Founded: 1954

Wydawnictwa Przemyslu Maszynowego **'Wema'***, PO Box 90, 00-950 Warsaw (Located at: ul Danilowiczowska 18, Warsaw) Tel: (022) 275456
Chief Executive: Czeslaw Borski; *Editorial Dir:* Maria Hoffmannowa; *Production:* Jan Waszczatyński
Subject: Mechanical Engineering
Founded: 1967

'Wiedza Powszechna' Państwowe Wydawnictwo, PO Box 162, 00-054 Warsaw (Located at: ul Jasna 26, Warsaw) Tel: (022) 277651
Man Dir, Editor-in-Chief: Tadeusz Kosmala; *Editorial:* Józef Chlabicz; *Deputy Editorial:* Janina Wunderlich
Orders to: Ars Polona, PO Box 1001, 00-068 Warsaw
Subjects: Encyclopaedias, Dictionaries, Language Handbooks, Popular Science
Founded: 1952
ISBN Publisher's Prefix: 83-214

Wydawniczo Oświatowa Spóldzielnia Inwalidów **'Wspólna Sprawa'***, ul Zelazna 40, 00-832 Warsaw Tel: (022) 209071
Educational Publishing Co-operative of the Disabled
President: Leopold Baranowski; *Publishing Manager:* Hanna Sporczyk
Subjects: Graphic art textbooks for primary and nursery schools; Periodicals for foreign language sessions; Games
Founded: 1956

Wydawnictwo TPPR **'Wspólpraca'**, Marszalkowska 115, 00-932 Warsaw Tel: (022) 275509
Chief Executive: Ryszard Pogonowski; *Production:* Kazimierz Andruk
Subjects: USSR Classic and contemporary literature (including children's & juvenile) in translation, Polish-USSR relations
1985: 2 titles *1986:* 2 titles *Founded:* 1984
ISBN Publisher's Prefix: 83-7018

Spoleczny Instytut Wydawniczy **'Znak'**, ul Wiślna 12, 31-007 Cracow Tel: (012) 224548
Man Dir: Jacek Woźniakowski
Subjects: Religion, Philosophy, History, Belles Lettres
Founded: 1959

Literary Agents

Agencja Autorska, ul Hipoteczna 2, 00-950 Warsaw Tel: (022) 278396
Contact: Wladyslaw Jakubowski, Andrzej Mierzejewski
Also Publisher (qv)

Mlodziezowa Agencja Wydawnicza, Youth Publishing Agency – see main entry under Publishers

Book Clubs

Club of Twentieth Century Poetry*, Horizons of Technology Club of Popular Science Books, ul Nowolipie 4, 00-950 Warsaw

New Countryside Book Club*, ul Nowolipie 4, 00-950 Warsaw

Publisher's Club, ul Szeroka 38-40, 80-835 Gdańsk
Owned by: Wydawnictwo Morskie (qv)

Major Booksellers

Ars Polona*, PO Box 1001, 00-068 Warsaw (Located at: ul Krakowskie Przedmieście 7, Warsaw) Tel: (022) 261201 Cable Add: Ars Polona Warszawa Telex: 813498
Foreign Trade Enterprise. Book importation is through this organization, which pays any duties applicable
Chief Dir: Janusz Palacz
Miscellaneous: Member of RSW (see under Book Trade Organizations)

338 POLAND

Dom Ksiazki*, ul Jasna 26, 00-950 Warsaw Tel: (022) 277651 Telex: Nr 0325418 Deka Pl
Collective name for the State-owned Polish book-retailing enterprises. There are 18, each controlling 50-250 bookshops throughout Poland, subordinate to Zrzeszenie Ksiegarstwa (qv)

Orpan Export*, Palac Kultury, 00-901 Warsaw

Powszechna Ksiegarnia Wysylkowa*, ul Nowolipie 4, 00-950 Warsaw Tel: (022) 310021
Organization for mail order, subordinate to Zrzeszenie Ksiegarstwa (qv)

Publisher's Bookshop, ul Starowiejska 35, Gdynia
Owned by: Wydawnictwo Morskie, Publisher (qv)

Państwowe, Przedsiebiorstwo 'Skladnica Ksiegarska'*, ul Mazowiecka 9, 00-052 Warsaw Tel: (022) 264431
Dir: Bronislaw Palimaka
Organization for wholesale book trade, subordinate to Zrzeszenie Ksiegarstwa (qv)

Zrzeszenie Ksiegarstwa, PO Box 48, 00-950 Warsaw (Located at: ul Jasna 26) Tel: (022) 277651 Telex: 812448 Deka Pl
Dir: Jan Królik Tel: (022) 268393
National organization for the sale of books; subordinate to the Minister of Culture and Art and controlling Skladnica Ksiegarska (wholesale), Dom Ksiazki (retail), and Powszechna Ksiegarnia Wysylkowa (mail order) (qqv under 'Major Booksellers')
Publication: Przeglad Ksiegarski i Wydawniczy (jointly with the Polish Publishers' Association)

Major Libraries

Naczelna Dyrekcja **Archiwów Państwowych**, ul Dluga 6, 00-950 Warsaw
Main Directorate of the Polish State Archives

Archiwum Akt Nowych, al Niepodleglości 162, 02-554 Warsaw

Archiwum Glówne Akt Dawnych*, ul Dluga 7, 00-263 Warsaw Tel: (022) 311525
Central Archives for Historical Documents

Biblioteka Jagiellońska, Aleja Mickiewicza 22, 30-059 Cracow Tel: (094) 345579/345945/336377; Secretary 330903; Director 331971 Telex: 0325682 Bj Pl
Dir: Dr Jan Pirozynski
Publication: Biuletyn Biblioteki Jagiellońskiej (annually)

Biblioteka Narodowa, ul Hankiewicza 1, 00-973 Warsaw Tel: (022) 224621 (main bldg)/(022) 313241 (special collections)/ 257241 (new bldg) Telex: 813702 Bn Pl
The National Library. See also Instytut Bibliograficzny
Dir: Dr Stanislaw Czajka
Publications: Biuletyn Informacyjny Biblioteki Narodowej (The National Library Information Bulletin); *Rocznik Biblioteki Narodowej* (The National Library Yearbook); *Katalog Rekopisów* (Catalogue of Manuscripts); *Katalog Mikrofilmów* (Catalogue of Microfilms); *Centralny Katalog Zagranicznych Wydawnictw Ciaglych w Bibliotekach Polskich* (Union Catalogue of Current Foreign Periodicals in Polish Libraries); *Centralny Katalog Ksiazek Zagranicznych* (Union Catalogue of Foreign Books)

Biblioteka Publiczna m st Warszawy, ul Koszykowa 26, 00-553 Warsaw Tel: (022) 217852
Public Library of Warsaw
Librarian: Helena Zarachowicz
Publication: Prace Biblioteki Publicznej m st Warszawy

Centrum Informacji Naukowej, Technicznej i Ekonomicznej, Skrytka pocztowa 355, al Niepodleglości 186, 00-950 Warsaw
National Centre for Scientific, Technical and Economic Information
Publications: Aktualne Problemy Informacji i Dokumentacji (bimonthly); *Informator Nauki Polskiej* (Polish Research Guide)

Glówna Biblioteka Lekarska, ul Chocimska 22, 00-791 Warsaw Tel: (022) 491156/ 497851 Telex: 814820
Central Medical Library
Dir: Dr Janusz Kapuścik

Biblioteka **Glówna Politechniki** Warszawskiej*, plac Jedności Robotniczej 1, 00-661 Warsaw Telex: 816467 Bgpw Pl
Library of the Technical University of Warsaw

Instytut Bibliograficzny Biblioteki Narodowej, ul Hankiewicza 1, 00-973 Warsaw
Bibliographical Institute (a Division of the National Library – see Biblioteka Narodowa)
Librarian: Krystyna Ramlau-Klekowska
Publications: Bibliografia Wydawnictw Ciaglych (Bibliography of Serials); *Bibliografia Zawartości Czasopism* (Index to Periodicals); *Polonica Zagraniczne* (Foreign Polonica); *Przewodnik Bibliograficzny* (Bibliographical Guide); *Ruch Wydawniczy w Liczbach* (Polish Publishing in Figures)

Zaklad Narodowy im **Ossolińskich Biblioteka** Polskiej Akademii Nauk, ul Szewska 37, 50-139 Wroclaw Tel: (07) 444471/444472 (Library), (07) 34304 (Director) Telex: 0342787 Boss Pl
Library of the National Ossoliński Institute of the Polish Academy of Sciences
Dir: Janusz Albin
Publication: Ze Skarbca Kultury (twice yearly)

Biblioteka **Śląska**, ul Francuska 12, 40-956 Katowice Tel: (032) 516441/4 Telex: 0312534 Bsk Pl
Silesian Library
Dir: Dr Miroslaw Strzoda
Publication: Ksiaznica Śląska
Miscellaneous: Specializes in scientific publications, but has many special collections covering Literature, History, Law and Religion and especially Silesian Interest

Biblioteka **Uniwersytecka**, ul Ratajczaka 38-40, 60-816 Poznan Tel: (06) 57416

Biblioteka **Uniwersytecka w Warszawie**, Krakowskie Przedmieście 26-28 and 32, 00-927 Warsaw Tel: (022) 264155 (Chief Librarian), (022) 264047 (Department of Scientific Information) Telex: 817016 Buwar Pl
Library of the University of Warsaw
Librarian: Dr Jadwiga Krajewska
Publication: Prace Biblioteki Uniwersyteckiej w Warszawie (irregularly)

Biblioteka **Uniwersytecka we Wrocławiu**, ul Karola Szajnochy 10, 50-076 Wroclaw Tel: (071) 443432 Telex: 0712477 Buw Pl
University Library Wroclaw
Librarian: Dr Stefan Kubów

Biblioteka **Uniwersytetu Mikolaja Kopernika**, ul Gagarina 13, 87-100 Toruń Tel: (056) 14408/23352 Telex: 552382 But Pl
Library of the Mikolaj Kopernik University of Toruń
Librarian: Stefan Czaja

Library Associations

Polish Academy of Sciences, Scientific Information Centre*, ul Nowy Swiat 72, 00-330 Warsaw Tel: (022) 268410 Telex: 815414 Oinpan
Publications include: Informator o Wynikach Badań Naukowych (Polish agricultural research); *Katalog Mikrofilmów* (Catalogue of imported microfilms) (annual); *Przeglad Informacji o Naukoznawstwie* (Review of information on the science of science); *Przeglad Literatury Metodologicznej* (Review on methodological literature); *Zagadnienia Informacji Naukowej* (selected problems on scientific information)

Stowarzyszenie Bibliotekarzy Polskich, ul Konopczyńskiego 5-7, 00-953 Warsaw Tel: (022) 275296/270847
Polish Librarians' Association
Chairman: Stefan Kubów; *Secretary-General:* Andrzej Jopkiewicz
Publications: Przeglad Biblioteczny (Library Review); *Bibliotekarz* (The Librarian); *Poradnik Bibliotekarza* (The Librarian's Handbook); *Informator Bibliotekarza i Ksiegarza* (Guide for the Librarian and Bookseller)

Library Reference Books and Journals

Books

Bibliografia Wydawnictw Ciaglych (Bibliography of Serials), Instytut Bibliograficzny Biblioteki Narodowej, ul Hankiewicza 1, 00-973 Warsaw

Informator Bibliotekarza i Ksiegarza (Guide for the Librarian and Bookseller), Polish Librarians' Association, ul Konopczyńskiego 5-7, 00-953 Warsaw

Rocznik Biblioteki Narodowej (National Library Yearbook), National Library, ul Hankiewicza 1, 00-973 Warsaw
Covers scientific library science; text in Polish with English summaries

Journals

Aktualne Problemy Informacji i Dokumentacji (Current Problems in Information and Documentation), National Centre for Scientific, Technical and Economic Information, al Niepodleglości 186, 00-950 Warsaw
Summaries in English, French, Polish and Russian

Bibliografia Zawartości Czasopism (Index to Periodicals), Instytut Bibliograficzny Biblioteki Narodowej, ul Hankiewicza 1, 00-973 Warsaw

Bibliotekarz (The Librarian), Polish Librarians' Association, ul Konopczyńskiego 5-7, 00-953 Warsaw
Text in Polish, summaries in English and Russian

Poradnik Bibliotekarza (The Librarian's Handbook), Polish Librarians' Association, ul Konopczyńskiego 5-7, 00-953 Warsaw

Przeglad Biblioteczny (Library Review), Polish Librarians' Association, ul Konopczyńskiego 5-7, 00-953 Warsaw
Summaries in English

Studia o Ksiazce (Studies on the Book), Ossolineum, Rynek 9, PO Box 70, 50-106 Wroclaw

POLAND — PORTUGAL 339

Literary Associations and Societies

Instytut Badań Literackich, Nowy Świat 72, Palac Staszica, 00-330 Warsaw Tel: (022) 265231/269945
Institute of Literary Research of the Polish Academy of Sciences
Acting Dirs: Prof Witold Nawrocki, Dr Krystyna Sierocka
Publications: Pamietnik Literacki (Literary Journal, quarterly); *Biuletyn Polonistyczny* (Bulletin of Polish Literary Scholarship, quarterly); *Kwartalnik Historii Prasy Polskiej* (Quarterly of the History of the Polish Press); *Literary Studies in Poland* (semi-annual); and other Literary Study series

Polish **P E N** Centre*, Iwicka 8a, m-8, 00-735 Warsaw
President: Juliusz Zulawski; *Secretary:* Prof Wladyslaw Bartoszewski

Towarzystwo Literackie im Adama Mickiewicza, Nowy Świat 72, 00-330 Warsaw
Mickiewicz Literary Society
President: Prof Dr Zdzislaw Libera
Publication: Rocznik (Yearbook)

Towarzystwo Przyjaciól Ksiazki*, ul Hipoteczna 2, 00-092 Warsaw
Society of Friends of Books

Towarzystwo Przyjaciól Nauk w Przemyślu, ul Rynek 4, 37-700 Przemyśl
Society of Science and Letters of Przemyśl
Chairman: Mieczyslaw Mazurek; *Secretary:* Tadeusz Burzyński
Publications include: Rocznik Przemyski (23 vols); *Biblioteka Przemyska* (17 vols); *Rocznik Nauk Medycznych* (7 vols)

Literary Periodicals

Literatura (Literature), RSW, ul Bagatela 14, 00-950 Warsaw

Literatura na świecie (World Literature), Ars Polona, ul Krakowskie Przedmieście 7, PO Box 1001, 00-068 Warsaw

MKL (Miesiecznik Kulturalny Litery) (Monthly Journal of Literary Culture), Targ Drzewny 3-7, 80-886 Gdansk

Miesiecznik Literacki (Monthly Review of Literature), Ars Polona, ul Krakowskie Przedmieście 7, PO Box 1001, 00-068 Warsaw

Nowy Wyraz (New Expression), Ars Polona, ul Krakowskie Przedmieście 7, PO Box 1001, 00-068 Warsaw

Pamietnik Literacki (Literary Journal), Institute of Literary Research of the Polish Academy of Sciences, Nowy Świat 72, Palac Staszica, 00-330 Warsaw
Contents page in English, Polish and Russian; quarterly

Poezja (Poetry), Ars Polona, ul Krakowskie Przedmieście 7, PO Box 1001, 00-068 Warsaw

Polish Literature, Agencja Autorska, ul Hipoteczna 2, 00-092 Warsaw
Text in English and French

Ruch Literacki (The Literary Movement), Polish Academy of Sciences, Historico-Literary Commission, ul Slawkowska 17, Cracow

Teksty (Texts), RSW, ul Bagatela 14, 00-950 Warsaw

Twórczość (Literary monthly), Ars Polona, ul Krakowskie Przedmieście 7, PO Box 1001, 00-068 Warsaw

Zycie Literackie (Literary Life), ul Wislna 2, Cracow

Literary Prizes

Cracow City Literary Prize*
For the entire work of an author whose life and writings were connected with Cracow. Awarded annually. Enquiries to Cracow City Council and Cracow Section of the Union of Polish Writers, ul Kanonicza 7, Cracow

Polish Ministry of National Defence Prize
For the best book dealing with military history, strategy, tactics, techniques; documentary papers, memoirs and belles lettres. Awarded biennially. Enquiries to Polish Ministry of National Defence Publishing House, ul Grzybowska 77, 00-844 Warsaw

Polish Prime Minister Award for Literature for Children and Youth*
For the entire work of an author of books for children and young people. Awarded annually. Enquiries to Polish Prime Minister's Office, ul Ujazdowskie 113, Warsaw

Polish Union of Socialist Youth Prose Award*
For the best novel by an author under 30. Awarded annually. Enquiries to Polish Union of Socialist Youth and the Daily Paper 'Sztandar Mlodych', ul Wspolna 61, Warsaw

Warsaw City Prize*
For the entire work of a distinguished author writing for children and young people. Awarded annually. Enquiries to Warsaw Municipal Council, Department of Culture, pl Dzierzynskiego 3-5, Warsaw

Warsaw City Prize for Young Poets*
For best poetry written by a young author. Co-sponsored by the Warsaw Creative Youth Club of the Polish Union of Writers and the Students' Club 'Hybrydy'. Awarded annually. Enquiries to Warsaw Municipal Council, Department of Culture, pl Dzierzynskiego 3-5, Warsaw

Mariusz **Zaruski** Literary Prize*
For the authors of best books about the sea. Awarded annually. Enquiries to Marine Club of the League of the Friends of Soldiers, ul Chocimska 14, Warsaw

'Zycie Literackie' Prize*
For literary criticism, journalism and essays. Awarded annually. Enquiries to Zycie Literackie, ul Wislna 2, Cracow

Translation Agencies and Associations

Stowarzyszenie Tlumaczy Polskich, ul Marszalkowska 2, 00-581 Warsaw Telex: 816494 Pais Pl
Association of Polish Translators and Interpreters
President: Prof Jerzy Pieńkos

Portugal

General Information

Language: Portuguese
Religion: Roman Catholic
Population: 9.8 million
Bank Hours: 0830-1145, 1300-1445 Monday-Friday
Shop Hours: 0900-1300, 1500-1900 Monday-Friday (some do not close midday); 0900-1300 Saturday. Generally closed Monday morning October-November
Currency: 100 centavos = 1 Portuguese escudo
Export/Import Information: Member of European Economic Community. Foreign language books from most countries dutied per kg (free from UK and reduced from EEC); atlases and children's picture books have higher tariff rate and children's picture books have an import surcharge. Small quantity of advertising duty-free. No import licence required for goods not exceeding a certain value, otherwise licence including permission to transfer foreign exchange required
Copyright: UCC, Berne (see International section)

Book Trade Organizations

Associação Portuguesa dos Editores e Livreiros, Ave dos Estados Unidos da América 97 – 6° Esq, 1700 Lisbon Tel: (01) 889136 Cable Add: Apel
Portuguese Association of Publishers and Booksellers
President: Dr Francisco Espadinha; *Secretary-General:* Dr Jorge de Carvalho Sá Borges; *General Manager:* José Narciso Vieira
Branch Offs: Rua D Diogo de Sousa 133, 4700 Braga; Rua Ferreira Borges 103, 3000 Coimbra; R da Fábrica 33 – 4° Ap 42, 4000 Porto
Publications: Livros de Portugal, Boletim Bibliográfico (monthly); *Livros Disponiveis* (Portuguese Books in Print) (both available from Largo de Andaluz 16 – 1° Esq, 1000 Lisbon)

Instituto Português do Livro e da Leitura, Secretaria de Estado da Cultura, Ave de Berna 13 – 4°, 1000 Lisbon Tel: (01) 764047/764048/763039
President: José Afonso Furatdo

Standard Book Numbering Agency*, Associação Portuguesa dos Editores e Livreiros, Largo de Andaluz 16 – 1° Esq, 1000 Lisbon Tel: (01) 546182
ISBN Administrator: Isabel Carvalho

Book Trade Reference Books and Journals

Books

Livros Disponiveis (Portuguese Books in Print), Associação Portuguesa dos Editores e Livreiros, Ave dos Estados Unidos da América 97 – 6° Esq, 1700 Lisbon

O Mundo do Edição Luso-Brasileira (The World of Publishing, Portugal and Brazil), Publicações Europa-America Lda, CP 8, Estrada Lisbon-Sintra Km 14, 2726 Mem Martins

PORTUGAL

Journal

Livros de Portugal (Portuguese Books), Associação Portuguesa dos Editores e Livreiros, Ave dos Estados Unidos da América 97 – 6° Esq, 1700 Lisbon

Publishers

Edições **70** Lda, Ave Elias Garcia 81, 1000 Lisbon   Tel: (01) 761736/762854   Telex: 64489 Textos P
Man Dir: J J Soares da Costa; *Editorial Dir, Rights & Permissions:* Artur Lopes-Cardoso; *Production Dir:* Rui Oliveira; *Sales:* Luis Pereira dos Santos
Subjects: General Fiction, Literature, History, Philosophy, Economics, Educational, Occult, Leisure Pursuits, University Textbooks, Comics, Children's, Art, Architecture
Founded: 1970

A E I, CP 1865, 1018 Lisbon codex (Located at: Largo Prof Fernando Fonseca, lote 114-115, r/c – A, 2795 Linda-a-Velha)   Tel: (01) 4194802 ext 1
Agência Europeia de Imprensa
Founded: 1962
Miscellaneous: Firm is also a Literary Agency (qv)

Ediçoes **Afrontamento**, CP 1309, Oporto (Located at: Rua de Costa Cabral 859, Oporto)   Tel: (02) 489271
Man Dir, Editorial, Production: José Sousa Ribeiro; *Sales, Publicity:* Marcela Figueiredo Torres; *Rights & Permissions:* Arnaldo Fleming
Subjects: General Literature, Social Sciences, Urban Studies, Politics, Cinema
1985: 18 titles   *1986:* 24 titles   *Founded:* 1963

Livraria **Almedina**, Arco de Almedina 15, 3049 Coimbra codex   Tel: (039) 26980/26199
Man Dir and all other offices: Joaquim Machado
Associate Companies: Livraria Almedina/Porto Ltda, Rua de Ceuta 79, 4000 Oporto; Edições Globo Ltda, Rua S Filipe Nery 37A, 1200 Lisbon
Subjects: Law, Education, Textbooks
Bookshop: Arco de Almedina 15, Rua Ferreira Borges 121, 3049 Coimbra codex
Founded: 1955

Arménio **Amado** Editora de Simões, Beirão & Ca Lda+*, Ceira, 3000 Coimbra
Man Dir: Luis França
Subjects: Philosophy, Religion, Psychology, Social Science, Law, Architecture, History, Politics, Languages
Founded: 1929

Amigos do Livro*, Rua Fernão Mendes Pinto 42, 1400 Lisbon   Telex: 14295
Dirs: José Soares Marques Henriques, Carlos Henrique Silva Martins da Luz; *Sales Dir:* Fernando Rui da Costa Rodrigues; *Production Dir:* João José Quintas Poeiras; *Editorial & Publicity Dir:* Mário Correia
Subjects: Literature, Cartoon Strips, History, Science, Sport, Religion
Founded: 1971

Edições **Antígona**, CP 4192, 1504 Lisbon codex
Editorial, Sales, Production: Manuel Luís de Oliveira
Subjects: Essays, Literature, Fiction, History, Sociology, Politics
1985: 3 titles   *1986:* 3 titles   *Founded:* 1979

Apáginastantas - Cooperativa de Serviços Culturais, CP 4254, 1507 Lisbon codex
Tel: (01) 668987

Man Dir: Anabela Mendes; *Editorial:* João Barrento
Subjects: Literature, Literary Theory and Criticism, Human and Social Sciences
1987: 19 titles   *Founded:* 1982

Livraria **Apostolado** da Imprensa*, Rua da Boavista 591, Oporto   Tel: (02) 27875
Man Dir, Editorial: Manuel Morujão, Américo Nunes; *Publicity:* A Nunes da Rocha
Branch Off: Rua da Lapa 111, 1200 Lisbon   Tel: (01) 660214
Subjects: General Fiction, Belles Lettres, Poetry, Biography, Philosophy, Religion, Juveniles, Secondary Textbooks
Bookshop: At above address
Founded: 1922

Livraria **Arnado** Lda, CP 375, 3007 Coimbra codex (Located at: Rua Joao Machado 9-11, Coimbra)   Tel: (039) 27573
Man Dir: José Fernandes de Almeida
Parent Company: Porto Editora Lda (qv)
Subsidiary Company: Empresa Literária Fluminense Lda
Subjects: Scholarly, Scientific, Legal, Literary
Founded: 1966

Editorial **Aster***, Largo D Estefânia 8 – 1° Esq°, Lisbon 1   Tel: (01) 534611/532973
Man Dir, Sales, Publicity, Rights & Permissions: Fernando de Souza; *Editorial:* Dr H Barrilaro Ruas; *Production:* João Alves
Branch Offs: Praça Guilherme Gomes Fernandes 24 – 2° Esq°, Oporto; Rua de Santo André 7, 4700 Braga
Subjects: General Fiction, Belles Lettres, Poetry, Biography, History, Music, Art, Philosophy, Religion, Psychology, How-to, Juveniles, Paperbacks, Secondary and University Textbooks
Founded: 1954

Livraria Editora **Atlântida** Ltda*, Rua Ferreira Borges 103, Coimbra
Dir: Afonso Queiró
Subject: Law

Editorial **'Avante!'***, Ave Santos Dumont 57 – 3°, 1000 Lisbon
Man Dir: Francisco Melo
Orders to: C D L (Central Distribuidora Livreira) SARL, Ave Santos Dumont 57 – 3°, 1000 Lisbon
Subjects: Politics, Economics, Philosophy, General Fiction
Founded: 1974

B E, an imprint of Básica Editora (qv)

Básica Editora*, Rua de Entre Campos 36 – r/c Esq, 1700 Lisbon   Tel: (01) 779273/730056
Man Dir, Rights & Permissions: Francisco Prata Ginja; *Editorial:* Rui Ferreira Lopes da Costa; *Sales:* Platano Editora SARL (qv); *Production, Publicity:* Maria Jorge Lopes da Costa
Imprint: B E
Subjects: Textbooks, Pedagogy
Bookshop: Livraria Básica, Ave Elias Garcia 49-B, 1000 Lisbon
Founded: 1974

Livraria **Bertrand** SARL*, CP 37, 2701 Amadora codex   Tel: (01) 974571   Cable Add: Libertran   Telex: 12709
Man Dir: Amaro de Matos; *Editorial, Rights & Permissions:* Piedade Ferreira; *Sales:* Carlos Grade; *Production:* Pina Mendes; *Publicity:* Ferreira da Cruz
Subjects: General Portuguese and Foreign Literature, Social Sciences, Juveniles (all ages), Dictionaries, School Books, Cartoon Strips
Bookshops: See under Major Booksellers
Founded: 1732

Brasília Editora (J Carvalho Branco & Cia Lda)+*, CP 101, 4001 Oporto codex (Located at: Rua José Falcão 173, Oporto)   Tel: (02) 315854   Cable Add: Brasiliaeditora
Man Dir: J Carvalho Branco; *Editorial, Rights & Permissions:* Dr Zulmira C Branco; *Sales, Publicity:* Dr Isabel C Branco; *Production:* J Silva Couto
Associate Company: Livraria Leitura — Fernandes e Branco Lda, Rua de Ceuta 88, Oporto
Subsidiary Company: Livraria Boa Leitura, Ave Almirante Reis 256, Lisbon
Subjects: Portuguese and Foreign Literature, Belles Lettres, Fiction, Poetry, Biography, How-to, Philosophy, Religion, Psychology, Social Science, Politics, Yoga, Sex, Occult
Bookshops: Livraria Leitura, Ave Almirante Reis 256B, Lisbon; Rua de Ceuta 88, Oporto
Founded: 1961

Editorial **Caminho** SARL+*, Alameda de Santo António dos Capuchos 6B, 1100 Lisbon   Tel: (01) 542683/549381
Man Dir: Zeferino Antas de Sousa Coelho
Orders to: C D L, Ave Santos Dumont 57 – 2°, 1000 Lisbon
Subjects: General Fiction, Socio-Political, Juveniles
Founded: 1977

Centro do Livro Brasileiro Lda*, Rua Almirante Barroso 13 – 2°, 1000 Lisbon   Tel: (01) 560165/6/7
Man Dir, Editorial: Alvaro Conçalves Pereira
Associate Company: Editora Portuguesa de Livros Técnicos e Cientificos Lda (qv)
Subjects: Philosophy, Religion, Social Science, Philology, Pure and Applied Science, Art, History, Geography, General
Bookshop: Rua 31 de Janeiro 146, Oporto
Founded: 1963

Cidade Nova*, Rua Dr Camilo Dionízio Álvares 13, 2775 Parede
Parent Company: Città Nuova Editrice, Italy (qv for associate companies)

Publicações **Ciência e Vida** Lda+, Rua Vitor Cordon 24 – 1° Dto, 1200 Lisbon   Tel: (01) 320565
Man Dir, Editorial: Jerónimo Simões
Subjects: Medicine, Livestock, Cattle, Agriculture and Forestry
1985: 12 titles   *1986:* 8 titles   *Founded:* 1979

Livraria **Civilizacão** (Américo Fraga Lamares & Ca Lda)+, Rua Alberto Aires de Gouveia 27, Oporto 1   Tel: (02) 22286/22287/32382   Cable Add: Alamares
Man Dir: Arquitecto Moura Bessa; *Rights & Permissions:* Maria Alice Moura Bessa
Branch Off: Ave Almirante Reis 102 r/c-Dto, Lisbon 1   Tel: (01) 823389
Subjects: Social and Political Science, Economics, History, Art, Fiction, Juveniles
Founded: 1921

Coimbra Editora Lda+, CP 101, 3002 Coimbra codex (Located at: Rua do Arnado, 3000 Coimbra)   Tel: (039) 25459
Man Dir: António Frederico de Araujo Serpa
Subjects: Law, Literature, Education, Psychology, Linguistics, Scholarly
Bookshop: Rua Ferreira Borges 79, 3000 Coimbra
1985: 36 titles   *1986:* 37 titles   *Founded:* 1920

Editorial **Confluência** Lda, CP 2620, 1116 Lisbon codex (Located at: Rua Almeida e Sousa 23, Lisbon)   Tel: (01) 663853
Man Dir, Editorial: Rogério Mendes de

Moura; *Sales:* Rogério Moreira; *Production:* Paulo Caraças; *Publicity:* M Conceição Silva; *Rights & Permissions:* María Isabel Azevedo
Subject: Dictionaries
1986: 4 titles *Founded:* 1945

Edições **Cosmos**, Rua da Emenda 111 – 2°, 1200 Lisbon 2 Tel: (01) 322050 Cable Add: Cosmos Lisboa
Man Dir: Manuel R de Oliveira
Subjects: Music, Sociology, History
Founded: 1938

Sá da **Costa** Editora, see under Sá

D I F E L - Difusão Editorial Lda, Rua D Estefânia 46B, 1000 Lisbon Tel: (01) 537677/545839/545886 Telex: 64030 Difel P
Man Dir: Manuel Pedroso Marques; *Editorial:* Cristina Gaspar; *Sales:* Francisco Vicente
Subjects: Belles Lettres, Portuguese and foreign fiction, General Non-fiction
1985: 22 titles *1986:* 26 titles *Founded:* 1983

Distri Editora-Sociedade Editora Lda, Rua Vasco da Gama 4-4-A, 2685 Sacavem Tel: (01) 2525394/2525407 Cable Add: Distedit Telex: 16588
Man Dir, Editorial: Pedro de Vasconcelos; *Production, Publicity, Sales, Rights:* Carlos Quaresma
Parent Company: Electro Liber Lda (at above address)
Associate Company: Distri Cultural-Sociedade Difusora de Cultura (at above address)
Subjects: Fiction, Poetry, Essays, Children's, Tourism, Educational
Bookshops: International Press Center, Ave Liberdade 9, 1000 Lisbon; Lisbon and Faro Airports; several in the Algarve
1985: 40 titles *Founded:* 1977

Publicações **Dom Quixote** Lda+, Rua Luciano Cordeiro 119, 1098 Lisbon codex Tel: (01) 538079/538088 Cable Add: Quixote Telex: 14331 Quixot P
Man Dir: Nelson de Matos; *Editorial:* Manuel Alberto Valente; *Rights & Permissions:* João Carlos Alvim
Subjects: General Fiction, Belles Lettres, Poetry, History, Education, Philosophy, Science, Social Science, Reference, Children's Books, Cartoons, Humour
Founded: 1965

Editora Portuguesa de Livros Técnicos e Científicos Lda, see Livros Técnicos

Elo, an imprint of Perspectivas e Realidades (qv)

Editorial **Enciclopédia** Lda*, Rua António Maria Cardoso 33, 1200 Lisbon Tel: (01) 373047/373048/373049
Chief Executive: Dr Gomes Mota; *International Manager:* Dr Carlos Nogueira
Subjects: Encyclopaedias, Fiction, History, Art, Technical
1985: 2 titles *Founded:* 1934

Livraria **Escolar** Infante, Manuel Ferreira & Gomes Lda, Rua de Santa Teresa 20-22, 4000 Oporto Tel: (02) 26281/317098
Publicity Manager: Manuel Gomes; *Sales Manager:* Manuel Ferreira
Subjects: History, Religion, Juveniles, Paperbacks, General & Social Science, Secondary & Primary Textbooks, Educational Materials, Law
Bookshop: Livraria Escolar Infante (at above address)
Founded: 1962

Editorial **Estúdios** Cor Sarl*, Rua João Pereira da Rosa 20-A, 1200 Lisbon Tel: (01) 328889/362146 Telex: 16619 Luar P
Publicity: António Lousão
Subjects: Belles Lettres, Biography, History, Art, Philosophy, Politics, Juveniles, General Science, Translations, General Fiction, Paperbacks
Founded: 1949

Publicações **Europa-America** Lda, CP 8, Estrada Lisbon-Sintra Km 14, 2726 Mem Martins Tel: 9211461/2/3 Cable Add: Europamérica Telex: 42255 Pea P
Man Dir: Francisco Lyon de Castro; *Co-Manager:* Tito Lyon de Castro; *Editorial Dir:* José Moura Pimenta; *Sales Dir:* Eduardo Lyon de Castro
Subsidiary Companies: Editorial Inquérito Lda (qv); Grafica Europam Lda; Publicações Forum Lda, CP 50, 2726 Mem Martins codex; Publicações Trevo Lda (qv)
Branch Offs: Delegação de Lisbon, Rua das Flores 45 – 1°, Lisbon; Delegação do Pôrto, Rua 31 de Janeiro, 221 Oporto
Subjects: General Fiction, Biography, History, How-to, Music, Art, Philosophy, Reference, Medicine, Psychology, General & Social Science, Nursery books, Juveniles, Low- & High-priced Paperbacks, University Textbooks, Educational Materials, Belles Lettres, Poetry, Engineering, Technical
Bookshops: Lojas Europa-America, Ave Marquês de Tomar 1-B, Rua das Flores 45 – 1°, Lisbon; Ave António Enes 14-B, Ave Elias Garcia 104-B, Queluz; Ave 1 de Maio 61, Castelo Branco; Pr Ferreira de Almeida 21-22, Faro; Ave 25 de Abril 48, Almada; Rua José Relvas, 15 B-C, Parede; Arcadas do Parque, Estoril; (Centro Comercial Pão de Açúcar, Lojas 6 e 7) Estrada Nacional 6-50, Cascais
Founded: 1945

Europress Editores e Distribuidores de Publicaçoēs Lda+, CP 12, 2675 Odivelas (Located at: Praceta da Republica, Lote A-1, Loja A, Póvoa Sto Adriaõ, Odivelas) Tel: (01) 9876180/9870741
Man Dir, Publicity, Rights & Permissions: António Bento Vintém; *Editorial:* Eduardo Brum; *Sales:* António Serrão Ferreira; *Production:* Victor M Pinto Pedro
Subsidiary Company: Heuris, R D Luísa de Gusmão 6 – 1° Esq, 1600 Lisbon
Associate Companies: Pentaedro-Publicidade e Artes Gráficas Lda, Praceta da Republica, Lote A-1, Loja B, Póvoa Sto Adriaõ, 2675 Odivelas; Revista de Bioquímica Aplicada, Rua General Celestino da Silva 101 – 16° Dto, 1500 Lisbon
Subjects: Fiction, Essays, Poetry, History, Sport, Biochemistry, Science, Law, Children's, Cartoons, Comics, Paperbacks
Bookshops: Bolsonoite I-Livraria Bar Lda, Ave Rainha D Leonor 25-A, 1600 Lisbon; Bolsonoite II, Rua Agusto Gil 6A, 2675 Odivelas
1985: 122 titles *1986:* 150 titles *Founded:* 1982

Livraria Editora **Figueirinhas** Lda*, Praça da Liberdade 67, 4000 Oporto Tel: (02) 324935/324960/324985
Man Dir, Publicity: João Pimenta; *Editorial, Sales, Production, Rights & Permissions:* Mario Figueirinhas
Subjects: General Literature
Founded: 1944

Forja Editora Sarl*, Rua da Emenda 30 – 3° C, 1200 Lisbon Tel: (01) 322334 Cable Add: Ediforja
Man Dir, Editorial, Production, Publicity, Rights & Permissions: Anibal Telo; *Sales:* João Sá
Subjects: Fiction, Juveniles, Theatre, Cinema
Founded: 1974

Editorial **Franciscana***, Montariol, CP 17, 4701 Braga codex Tel: (053) 22490
Man Dir: António Pedro da Anunciação
Subjects: Biography, History, Music, Art, Philosophy, Religion, Juveniles, Theology
Bookshops: Livraria Editorial Franciscana, Rua de Cedofeita 350, Oporto; Montariol, Braga
Founded: 1922

Editorial **Futura**, Ave 5 de Outubro 317 – 1°, 1600 Lisbon Tel: (01) 779114
Man Dir: José Chaves Ferreira
Subjects: General Literature, Comics
Founded: 1970

G E C T I (Gabinete de Especialização e Cooperação Tecnica Internacional L)+*, CP 1918, 1004 Lisbon codex (Located at: Ave Republica 47-6D, Lisbon) Tel: (01) 768877/771940/772154
Man Dir, Editorial: A Almeida Teixeira
Subjects: Business, Administration, Marketing, Professional Training, Programmed Learning
Founded: 1963

Gabinete de Especialização e Cooperação Tecnica Internacional, see GECTI

Gradiva-Publicações Lda+, Rua Almeida e Sousa 21 – r/c Esq, 1300 Lisbon Tel: (01) 674067/8
Man Dirs: Fernando Silva, Luis Alves; *Editorial:* Guilherme de Carvalho Negrão Valente; *Sales, Publicity:* Luis Manuel Vaz Alves; *Production:* José Fernando Gonçalves da Silva; *Rights & Permissions:* Maria do Rosário Pedreira
Subjects: Science, History, Fiction, Science Fiction, Philosophy, Education
1986-87: 96 titles *Founded:* 1981

Livros **Horizonte** Lda, Rua das Chagas 17 – 1° Dto, 1121 Lisbon codex Tel: (01) 366917/368505 Cable Add: Livroshorizonte
Man Dir, Editorial: Rogério Mendes de Moura; *Sales:* Rogério Moreira; *Production:* Paulo Caraças; *Publicity:* M Conceição Silva; *Rights & Permissions:* María Isabel Azevedo
Subjects: Pedagogy, Psychology, Sociology, History, Physical Culture, University Textbooks, Arts, Children's and Juveniles
1985: 96 titles *1986:* 98 titles *Founded:* 1953

Edições **I T A U** (Instituto Tecnico de Alimentação Humana) Lda*, Ave da República 46-A r/c Esq, Lisbon 1 Tel: (01) 733307/733482/733245
Man Dir: Júlio Roberto; *Editorial, Sales, Production, Publicity:* José Maria Paula
Orders to: Ave Elias Garcia 87-A, Lisbon 1
Parent Company: Instituto Tecnico de Alimentação Humana Lda
Subjects: Human Nutrition, Pedagogy, Poetry, Literature, Sociology, Juvenile Literature
Founded: 1969

Imprensa Nacional-Casa da Moeda*, Rua D Francisco Manuel de Melo 5, Lisbon 1 Tel: (01) 685684 Cable Add: INCM
Man Dir, Editorial, Sales & Publicity: Dr Américo Farinha de Carvalho
Branch Offs: Four in Lisbon, one each in Oporto and Coimbra
Subjects: Political and Civil Administration, Archaeology, Arts, Economics, Ethnography, Ethnology, Pharmacy, Philology, Philosophy, History, Memoirs, Religion
Bookshops: Livraria Camões, Rua Bittencourt da Silva 12C, Rio de Janeiro, Brazil; Gabinete Portugues de Lectura, Rua do Imperador 290, Recife, Brazil
Founded: 1768

Editorial Inquérito Lda+, Travessa da Queimada 23 – 1° Dto, 1200 Lisbon Tel: (01) 328659 Telex: 42255 Pea P
Man Dir: Francisco Lyon de Castro
Orders to: Publicações Europa-America Lda, CP 8, 2726 Mem Martins codex
Parent Company: Publicações Europa-America Lda (qv)
Subjects: General Fiction, Belles Lettres, History, Philosophy, Juveniles, Social Science, Law, Economics
Founded: 1938

Instituto Tecnico de Alimentaçao Humana, see I T A U

Américo Fraga **Lamares** & Ca Lda, see Livraria Civilizaçao

Lello e Cia Lda*, Rua Conde de Vizela 12, Oporto 1 Tel: (02) 23209
Dir: J Pinto Mesquita Lello
Subjects: Fine Arts, Education, Textbooks

Lello e Irmão*, Rua das Carmelitas 144, 4000 Oporto Tel: (02) 22037/318170 Cable Add: Jolello
Man Dir: Edgar Pinto Da Silva Lello
Subjects: General Literature, Juveniles, History, Dictionaries
Founded: 1881

Editora **Livros** do Brasil Sarl, CP 2953, 1200 Lisbon (Located at: Rua dos Caetanos 22, Lisbon) Tel: (01) 362621/323170/326113 Cable Add: Librasil
Man Dir, Rights & Permissions: Antonio de Souza-Pinto; *Editorial, Publicity:* Joaõ Palma-Ferreira; *Sales:* José Manuel Lopes Filipe
Associate Company: Editores Associados Lda
Branch Off: Rua de Ceuta 80, Oporto
Subjects: General and Science Fiction, Politics, History, Biography, Philosophy, Scientific Research
Founded: 1944

Editora Portuguesa de **Livros Técnicos** e Científicos Lda*, Rua Almirante Barroso 13 – 1° Dto, 1000 Lisbon Tel: (01) 560168
Man Dir: Álvaro Gonçalves Pereira; *Editorial Manager:* Dr João Cabral Fernandes
Associate Company: Centro do Livro Brasileiro Lda (qv)
Subjects: Social Science, Psychology, Science, Medicine, Computers, General, Engineering, Nursing
Founded: 1981

Livraria **Lopes Da Silva**-Editora de M Moreira Soares Rocha Lda, Rua Chã 101-103, 4000 Oporto Tel: (02) 21678/26017
Man Dir: Mário Moreira Soares Da Rocha
Subjects: Medicine, Science, Technical
1986-87: 7 titles *Founded:* 1870

Livraria **Luzo-Espanhola** Lda*, Rua Nova do Almada 86-90, 1294 Lisbon codex Tel: (01) 324917/367667/327536 Cable Add: Livraluso
Man Dir: Inocencio Casimiro Araujo
Subjects: Medicine, Technical, Textbooks, Economics
Bookshops: Livraria Luzo-Espanhola e Brasileira Lda, Ave 13 Maio 23 – 4°, Rio de Janeiro, Brazil; Livraria Luzo-Espanhola Lda, Rua da Sofia 121 – 1°, Coimbra; Livraria Cientifico Médico do Pôrto, Rua do Carmo 14, Oporto
Founded: 1941

Editora **McGraw-Hill** de Portugal Lda*, Rua Rosa Damasceno 11 A-B, 1900 Lisbon Tel: (01) 577322 Telex: 14724 Mghill P
Manager: Francisco Paes Mamede

Parent Company: McGraw-Hill International Book Co, 1221 Ave of the Americas, New York, NY 10020, USA
Associate Companies: See McGraw-Hill Book Co (UK) Ltd, UK

Fernando **Machado** e Co Ltd, Rua das Carmelitas 15, 4000 Oporto Tel: (02) 25718
Man Dir: Manuel Correia Vieira
Branch Off: Rua dos Clérigos 23, 4000 Oporto
Bookshop: Livraria Fernando Machado (at above address)
Founded: 1922

Mafra, an imprint of Perspectivas e Realidades (qv)

Livraria Tavares **Martins**+*, Rua dos Clérigos 14, Oporto Tel: (02) 23459
Man Dir: Jorge de Amorim
Subjects: Drama, Poetry, Biography, History, Art, Philosophy, Religion, Law, Juveniles
Founded: 1911

Meribérica — Editorial e Comercialização de Direitos Lda*, Ave Alvares Cabral 84 – 1° Dto, 1296 Lisbon codex Tel: (01) 688912/3/4
Man Dirs: Adriano Eliseu, Telmo Protásio; *Editorial:* Adriano Eliseu; *Production:* Branca Protásio
Subjects: Children's Books
Book Club: Clube Walt Disney

Editorial **Minerva***, Rua Luz Soriano 31-33, 1200 Lisbon Tel: (01) 322535
Dir: Artur Augusto Campos
Subjects: General Fiction, Juveniles, Paperbacks, Reference
Founded: 1927

Moraes Editores SARL*, Rua do Século 34 – 2°, 1200 Lisbon Tel: (01) 325391/327717
Chairman: Dr Nuño de Carvalho; *Literary Dir:* Ivonne Cunha Rêgo; *Commercial Manager:* Rosa Marques
Subjects: General Fiction, Portuguese Literature, Politics, Sociology, Pedagogy, Human Sciences, Psychology, Law
Bookshop: Livraria Moraes, Largo do Picadeiro 11, 1200 Lisbon
Founded: 1955

Nova Renascença*, Rua Coutinho de Azevedo 214, 4000 Porto Tel: (02) 692284/569002
Subjects: Poetry, Art, Essays, Periodical
Founded: 1980

Livraria Editora **Pax** Lda*, Rua do Souto 73-77, 4700 Braga Tel: (053) 22604 Cable Add: Pax
Man Dir and other offices: José Moreira
Subjects: Fiction, Belles Lettres, Poetry, History, Ethnography, Travel, Spiritual Life, Theatre, Education

Parceria A M **Pereira** Lda*, Rua Augusta 44-54, Lisbon 2 Tel: (01) 361730/361710 Cable Add: Parcepereira
Subjects: General Fiction, Belles Lettres, Biography, History, How-to, Juveniles, Social Science, Technical, Primary Textbooks
Founded: 1848

Editorial **Perpétuo** Socorro*, Rua Dr Alves da Veiga 207, Oporto Tel: (02) 564251
Subjects: Religion, Education
Founded: 1946

Perspectivas e Realidades*, Rua Ruben Leitão 4 – 2° E, Lisbon Tel: (01) 371371/371372 Telex: 42458 Perspe P
Man Dir: João Soares; *Sales:* Maria do Carmo; *Publicity:* Rui Perdigão

Associate Company: Diglivro Ldá (qv under Major Booksellers)
Imprints: Elo; Mafra
Subjects: Literature, Politics, Children's, Scholarly
Founded: 1975

Platano Editora SARL, Ave de Berna 31 – 2° Esq, Lisbon 1 Tel: (01) 774250/779278
Editorial: Francisco Prata Ginja
Subsidiary Companies: Alicerce Editora Lda, Oporto; Paralelo Editora Lda, Lisbon
Subjects: Primary, Secondary and Technical School Books, Theatre, Poetry, Juveniles
Bookshop: Alicerce Editora Lda, Rua Guerra Junqueiro 456, Oporto

Editorial **Portico***, Rua Dr Julio Dantas 4, Lisbon 1

Porto Editora Lda, Rua da Restauração 365, 4099 Oporto codex Tel: (02) 25813 Telex: 27205 Ported P
Man Dirs: José A Teixeira, Vasco F Teixeira
Subsidiary Company: Livraria Arnado Lda (qv)
Associate Company: Empresa Literaria Fluminense Lda, Rua de S João Nepomuceno 8-A, 1200 Lisbon
Subjects: University, Secondary & Primary Textbooks, Educational Materials, Maps, Foreign Language Teaching and Dictionaries, Law, General Non-fiction, Children's
Bookshops: Rua da Fábrica 90, Oporto; Praça D Filipa de Lencastre 42, Oporto
1985: 118 titles *1986:* 120 titles *Founded:* 1944

Editorial **Presença**, Rua Augusto Gil 35-A, 1000 Lisbon Tel: (01) 734191 Cable Add: Presença Lisboa Telex: 62596 Epres P
Man Dir, Editorial: Francisco Espadinha; *Sales and Marketing:* Manuel Aquino; *Production:* Conceição Parente; *Rights & Permissions:* Manuela Cardoso
Subjects: Sociology, Politics, Philosophy, History, Children's Books, Hobbies, School Textbooks
Founded: 1960

Quatro Elementos Editores+, Rua Arneiros 54 (lote F) – 2° Fte, 1500 Lisbon Tel: (01) 703695
Subjects: Literature, Fiction, Poetry, Essays, Art, Photography
1985: 3 titles *1986:* 1 title *Founded:* 1978

Edicões António **Ramos***, Rua Padre Luís Aparício 9 – 1° F, 1100 Lisbon Tel: (01) 577205
Man Dir, Editorial: António Ramos; *Sales:* Maria Júlia Rodrigues; *Production:* Paulo Ramos; *Publicity:* Nuno Vasco
Orders to: Diglivro, Rua das Chagas 2, 1200 Lisbon
Subjects: General Fiction and Non-fiction
Founded: 1977

Realizações Artis Lda*, Rua das Taipas 12 – r/c Esq, 1200 Lisbon Tel: (01) 363796
Man Dirs: Rogério de Freitas, Ermelinda Penedo
Subjects: Belles Lettres, Poetry, Biography, Art
Founded: 1950

A **Regra** do Jogo+*, Rua Luz Soriano 19 – S/L Esq, 1200 Lisbon Tel: (01) 360113/373294
Man Dir, Rights & Permissions: José Leal de Loureiro; *Literary Dir:* Fernando Pereira Marques
Subjects: Fiction, Poetry, Music, History, Juveniles, Anthropology, Philosophy, Economy
1985: 160 titles *Founded:* 1974

PORTUGAL 343

M Moreira Soares **Rocha** Lda, see Livraria Lopes Da Silva

Edições **Rolim** Lda*, CP 3079, 1302 Lisbon (Located at: Rua Fialho de Almeida 38 – 2° Dto, 1000 Lisbon) Tel: (01) 553375
Man Dir: Maria Rolim Ramos
Subjects: Political Science, Sociology, Languages, History, Literature
Founded: 1976

Sá da Costa Editora, Praça Luís de Camões 22 4, Lisbon 1294 codex Tel: (01) 360721 Cable Add: Livrosacosta Telex: Sacost 15574 P
Subjects: Textbooks, History, Philosophy, Literature, Classics, Essays
Bookshop: Livraria Sá da Costa (qv under Major Booksellers)
Founded: 1913

Edições **Salesianas**+, Rua Dr Alves da Veiga 128, 4000 Oporto Tel: (02) 565750/ 563870
Man Dir: Lino Ferreira; *Editorial, Production, Publicity:* Manuel Filipe Lourenço
Branch Off: Rua Saraiva de Carvalho 275, 1300 Lisbon Tel: (01) 664142
Subjects: Biography, Religion, Juveniles, Comics, Paperbacks, Psychology, Technical, Educational Materials
Bookshops: Livraria Salesiana, Largo Luis de Camões 7-9, 7000 Evora Tel: (066) 24580; Rua Saraiva de Carvalho 275, 1300 Lisbon Tel: (01) 609065
Founded: 1947

A M **Teixeira** e Cia (Filhos) Lda (Livraria Classica Editora)*, Praça dos Restauradores 17, 1298 Lisbon codex Tel: (01) 321229/321391/321286 Cable Add: Classica
Editorial, Rights & Permissions: Francisco Paulo; *Production, Publicity:* José Ramos
Subjects: General Fiction, Belles Lettres, Poetry, History, Reference, Religion, Juveniles, General and Social Science, Psychology, University and Primary Textbooks, Agriculture, Philology, Electronics, Economics, Management
Founded: 1903

Texto Editora+, CP 4081, 1502 Lisbon (Located at: Estrada de Benfica 462, 1500 Lisbon) Tel: (01) 7145543
Man Dirs: Fernando Costa Marques, Manuel José Ferrão; *Editorial, Publicity:* Ana Maria Fontes de Melo; *Sales, Rights & Permissions:* Luís Carlos Veloso
Parent Company: Texto – Sociedade Editora e Distribuidora de Livros Lda
Subsidiary Company: Distexto – Sociedade Editora e Distribuidora de Publicações Lda, Estrada de Benfica 462-E, 1500 Lisbon
Associate Company: Publilivro – Editora e Distribuidora de Publicações Lda, Estrada de Benfica 462-C, 1500 Lisbon
Branch Off: Rua da Torrinha 228 loja E, 4000 Oporto
Subjects: Pre-School, Primary & Secondary Textbooks, Health, Education, Management, Cooking, Children's
Bookshops: Livraria Texto Editora, Estrada de Benfica 462-C, 1500 Lisbon; Rua da Torrinha 228 loja E, 4000 Oporto
1985: 96 titles *1986:* 130 titles *Founded:* 1977

João Romano **Torres** & Cia Lda*, Livraria Romano Torres, Largo de Sao Mamede 3-A, 1200 Lisbon Tel: (01) 601244
Man Dir: Amelia Lucas Torres Farinha; *Editorial, Publicity, Rights & Permissions:* Francisco de Noronha e Andrade; *Sales, Production:* Osorio Marques Martins
Subjects: Historical Works, World Classics, Romantic Fiction, Juvenile Adventure Stories
Founded: 1885

Publicações **Trevo** Lda, CP 50, 2726 Mem Martins codex Telex: 42255 Pea
Man Dir, Editorial: Tito Lyon de Castro; *Sales:* Eduardo Lyon de Castro
Parent Company: Publicações Europa-America Lda (qv)
Subject: Colouring Books
Founded: 1976

Editora **Ulisseia** Lda, Ave Visconde Valmor 47 – 1° Dto, 1000 Lisbon Tel: (01) 734300 Telex: 15177 Verbo P
Man Dir: Fernando Guedes; *Editorial, Production:* Martins de Oliveira; *Sales:* David Duarte; *Publicity:* C M Guedes
Orders to: Rua Carlos Testa 1 – 2°, 1000 Lisbon
Parent Company: Editorial Verbo SA (qv)
Subjects: Fiction, Contemporary Literature, Classics, General Interest
Founded: 1950

Editorial **Verbo** SA, Rua Carlos Testa 1, Lisbon Tel: (01) 562131 Cable Add: Verbo Telex: 15177 Verbo P
Man Dir: Fernando Guedes; *Sales Dir:* David Duarte
Subsidiary Companies: Editora Ulisseia Lda (qv); Verbo Publicações Periódicas
Subjects: Encyclopaedias, History, Juveniles, General Science, Educational Materials
1986: 125 titles *Founded:* 1959
Miscellaneous: Door-to-door sales by EDC-Empresa de Divulgaçao Cultural Sarl, Ave Duque de Avila 193, Lisbon; direct mail sales by Verbo Postal

Livraria **Verdade e Vida** Editora, Cava da Tria, Fatima Tel: (049) 51417
Subjects: Biography, History, Philosophy, Religion, Theology, Psychology, Juveniles, Fiction, Education
Bookshop: At above address
Founded: 1945

Literary Agents

A E I, CP 1865, 1018 Lisbon codex (Located at: Largo Prof Fernando Fonseca, lote 114-115, r/c – A, 2795 Linda-a-Velha) Tel: (01) 4194802 ext 1
Agência Europeia de Imprensa
Firm is also a Publisher (qv)

Ilidio da Fonseca Matos, Rua de S Bernardo 68-3, 1200 Lisbon Tel: (01) 669780 Cable Add: Ilphoto
Man Dir: Ilidio Matos

Book Clubs

Círculo de Leitores, Rua Eng Paulo de Barros 22, 1599 Lisbon codex Tel: (01) 709215/709221/709224 Telex: 18343 cilecl p Fax: (01) 707149
Man Dir: Manfred Grebe; *Editorial Dir:* António Mega Ferreira
Subjects: Fiction, Biography, Juvenile, Encyclopaedias, Scientific, Historical, General Non-fiction, Special Editions
Owned by: Bertelsmann AG, Federal Republic of Germany (qv)
Founded: 1971

Clube **Walt Disney***, Ave Alvares Cabral 84 – 1° Dto, 1296 Lisbon codex
Owned by: Meribérica-Editorial e Comercializaçao de Direitos Lda (qv)

Major Booksellers

Livraria **Bertrand***, Travessa Mário Sacramento 9, 3800 Aveiro Tel: (034) 22510 Telex: 37360 Litran
Manager: Antero Braga
Also: Ave Dr L Peixinho 87-B, Aveiro; Largo da Portagem 9, Coimbra; Rua D Francisco Gomes 27, Faro; Ave Roma 13-B, Lisbon; Rua Dr J Soares 4-A, Lisbon; Rua D Estefânea 46-C/D, Lisbon; Rua de Santo António 43, 45, 65, Shopping Center, Brasilia, Oporto; Rua Sacadura Cabral 32, Vian do Castelo
Also Publisher (qv)

Biblarte Lda*, Rua de Sao Pedro de Alcantara 71, 1200 Lisbon
Manager: Ernesto Martins

Livraria **Buchholz**, Rua Duque de Palmela 4, 1296 Lisbon codex Tel: (01) 547358/524859
Manager: K Sousa Ferreira

C D L (Central Distribuidora Livreira) Sarl*, Ave Santos Dumont 57 – 2°, 1000 Lisbon Tel: (01) 731752/769744/779825
Dir: Mario Lino
Company has 17 other bookshops, five in Lisbon and 12 in other cities

Livraria **Castro e Silva***, Rua da Rosa 29-31, 1200 Lisbon Tel: (01) 367380

Diglivro Ldá (Distribuidora de Informação Geral)*, Rua Vitor Cordon 45 (Páteo Bragança, porta B), 1200 Lisbon

Expresso Sarl*, CP 21, Buraca/Damaia, Lisbon

Livraria **Nunes***, Rua de S Domingos de Benfica 5-A, Lisbon 4

Livraria **Portugal**, Dias e Andrade Lda, CP 2681, Rua do Carmo 70-74, 1117 Lisbon codex

Livraria **Sá** da Costa, Rua Garrett 100-102, 1294 Lisbon codex
Manager: Manuel F da Costa
Owned by: Sá da Costa Editora (qv)

Editorial o **Século***, Rua do Século 73, Lisbon 2

Livraria **Sousa e Almeida** Lda, Rua da Fábrica 42, 4000 Oporto Tel: (02) 310073

Major Libraries

Biblioteca da **Academia** das Ciências de Lisboa, Rua da Academia das Ciências 19, 1200 Lisbon Tel: (01) 363866
Library of the Academy of Sciences

Biblioteca da **Ajuda**, Palacio da Ajuda, 1300 Lisbon Tel: (01) 638592
Dir: Melba Ferreira da Costa

Arquivo Nacional da Torre do Tombo, Palácio de S Bento, 1200 Lisbon Tel: (01) 664415/667680
National Archives of Torre do Tombo
Dir: José Pereira da Costa

Biblioteca Municipal Central*, Palácio Galveias, Largo do Campo Pequeno, Lisbon

Biblioteca Nacional*, Rua Ocidental do Campo Grande 83, 1751 Lisbon codex Tel: (01) 767786
Deputy Dir: Dr Maria Luisa Cabral
Publication: Boletim de Bibliografia Portuguesa (Portuguese Bibliographical Bulletin)

Biblioteca Popular de Lisboa*, Rua Ivens 35 and Rua de Academia das Ciências 19, Lisbon

344 PORTUGAL — PUERTO RICO

Librarian: Joaquim Daniel Ferreira das Neves

Biblioteca Pública de Braga*, Universidade do Minho, Praça do Municipio, 4700 Braga Tel: (053) 27021/3
Librarian: Henrique Barreto Nunes

Biblioteca Pública de Ponta Delgada*, The Azores

Biblioteca Pública e Arquivo Distrital de Évora, Largo do Conde de Vila Flor, Évora Tel: (066) 22369
Public Library and District Archives
Librarian: Isabel Cid

Biblioteca Pública Municipal do Porto, Passeio S Lázaro, 4099 Porto codex Tel: (02) 565361
Municipal Library of Oporto
Dir: L Cabral

Centro de Documentacão Científica e Técnica, Ave Prof Gama Pinto 2, 1699 Lisbon codex Tel: (01) 731300/731350 Telex: 62593 Iifm P
Centre of Scientific and Technical Information, a branch of the Instituto Nacional de Investigação Científica (National Scientific Research Institute)
Dir: Carlos Pulido

Biblioteca do **Palácio** Nacional de Mafra, Terreiro de João V, Mafra Tel: (061) 52332
Dir: Luis Filipe Marques da Gama

Biblioteca Geral da **Universidade de Coimbra**, 3049 Coimbra codex Tel: (039) 25541/25542
Dir: Prof Dr Aníbal Pinto de Castro
Publications include: Acta Universitatis Conimbrigensis; Boletim; Revista da Universidade; Sumários das Publicações Periódicas Portuguesas

Library Association

Associação Portuguesa de Bibliotecários, Arquivistas e Documentalistas, Edificio da Biblioteca Nacional, Campo Grande 83, 1751 Lisbon codex Tel: (01) 767862
Portuguese Association of Librarians, Archivists and Documentalists
President: Luis Filipe de Abreu Nunes;
Secretaries: João da Silva Gonçalves, Maria Isabel Carneiro
Publications: Cadernos de Biblioteconomia, Arquivística e Documentação (twice yearly); *Notícia BAD* (quarterly)

Library Reference Books and Journals

Book

Lista das Bibliotecas Portuguesas (List of Portuguese Libraries), Centre of Scientific Documentation, Campo dos Mártires da Pátria 130, Lisbon

Journals

Boletim Bibliográfico, Associação Portuguesa dos Editores e Livreiros, Ave dos Estados Unidos da América 97 – 6° Esq, 1700 Lisbon

Boletim de Bibliografia Portuguesa (Portuguese Bibliographical Bulletin), Biblioteca Nacional, Rua Ocidental do Campo Grande 83, 1751 Lisbon

Cadernos de Biblioteconomia, Arquivística e Documentação (Library Management, Archives and Documentation), Associação Portuguesa de Bibliotecários, Arquivistas e Documentalistas, Edificio da Biblioteca Nacional, Campo Grande 83, 1751 Lisbon codex
Twice yearly; summaries in English

Sumários das Publicações Periódicas Portuguesas, Biblioteca Geral da Universidade de Coimbra, 3049 Coimbra codex

Literary Associations and Societies

Instituto Português da Sociedade Científica de Goerres, c/o Universidade Católica Portuguesa, Palma de Cima, 1600 Lisbon Tel: (01) 7265554
Portuguese Institute of the Goerres Research Society
Researches into the language and literature of the 16th and 17th centuries
Publication: Portugiesische Forschungen (Researches in Portuguese)

Portuguese **P E N** Centre*, York House, Rua das Janelas Verdes 32, 1200 Lisbon
President: Almeida Faria; *Secretary:* Clara Rocha

Literary Periodicals

Coloquio-Letras (Dialogue-Literature), Empresa Nacional de Publicidade, Ave da Liberdade 266, Lisbon 2

Jornal de Letras e Artes (Journal of Letters and Arts), Rua Vitor Bastos 14A, Lisbon 1

Ocidente (The West), Antonio H de Azevedo Pinto and Amelia de Azevedo Pinto, Rua de S Felix 41D, Lisbon
Cultural review

Peninsula, Agencia Internacional de Livraria e Publicações Lda, R S Pedro de Alcantara, 63-1 D, Lisbon

Seara Nova (New Harvest), Empresa de Publicidade 'Seara Nova' Sarl, R Bernardo Lima 42 – r/c, 1191 Lisbon codex

Literary Prizes

Children's and Juvenile Literature Prize*
For the best book written for readers between four and sixteen. 15,000 escudos. Awarded annually. Enquiries to Portugal State Secretariat for Information and Tourism, Palacio Foz, Lisbon 2

Ricardo **Malheiros** Prize*
6,000 escudos awarded annually to an author for a work of imaginative literature. Enquiries to Academia das Ciências, rua Academia das Ciências 19, Lisbon 2

National Award for Poetry and the Novel*
Two prizes, one for the best book of poetry and the other for the best novel or book of short stories. 50,000 escudos each. Awarded annually. Enquiries to Portugal State Secretariat for Information and Tourism, Palacio Foz, Lisbon 2

National Essay Award*
For the best essay written by a Portuguese author and printed in Portuguese. 50,000 escudos. Awarded every other year. Enquiries to Portugal State Secretariat for Information and Tourism, Palacio Foz, Lisbon 2

Revelation Awards (Poetry and Prose)*
Four prizes, two given for the best unpublished manuscript of poetry and two for prose. 5,000 escudos. Awarded annually. Enquiries to Portugal State Secretariat for Information and Tourism, Palacio Foz, Lisbon 2

Puerto Rico

General Information

Language: Spanish and English
Religion: Roman Catholic
Population: 3.2 million
Bank Hours: 0900-1430 Monday-Friday
Shop Hours: 0900-1730 or 1800 Monday-Saturday
Currency: US currency
Export/Import Information: No tariff on books and advertising matter. No import licences required
Copyright: UCC (see International section)

Book Trade Organization

Sociedad Puertorriqueña de Escritores*, Apdo 4962, San Juan
Puerto Rican Society of Writers
President: Ernesto Juan Fonfrías

Book Trade Reference Journal

Anuario bibliográfico puertorriqueño (Puerto Rican Annual Bibliography), Estado Libre Asociado de Puerto Rico, Dept de Instrucción Pública, Río Piedras

Publishers

Editorial **Antillana**, an imprint of Editorial Cultural (qv)

Editorial **Club** de la Prensa*, Apdo 4692, San Juan, PR 00903
Subjects: Fiction, Maps, Folklore

Editorial **Cordillera** Inc, Calle O'Neill 157, Hato Rey, PR 00918 Tel: 7676188/7647635 Cable Add: Cordillera
Man Dir, Editorial, Production: Héctor E Serrano; *Sales, Publicity:* Isaac Serrano
Subjects: General Literature, Social Studies, Spanish
Founded: 1962
ISBN Publisher's Prefix: 0-88495

Editorial **Edil** Inc*, Apdo 23088, Universidad de Puerto Rico, Río Piedras, PR 00931 (Located at: Calle Julian Blanco, Esquina Ramírez Pabón, Río Piedras, PR 00925) Tel: (809) 7632958/7643740 Cable Add: Edil
Man Dir: Norberto Lugo Ramírez; *Sales Dir:* Eunice Lugo Frank; *General Manager, Publicity Dir:* Consuelo Andino
Subjects: General Literature (especially major Puerto Rican and South American authors), Social & Political Sciences, Economics, Law, Education, Life Sciences, History, Language, Poetry, Drama, Belles Lettres
Founded: 1967

Editorial **Cultural***, Apdo 21056, Río Piedras Station, PR 00928 Tel: 7659767
Man Dir: Francisco Vázques; *Sales Dir:* Aida Vázquez; *Publicity Dir:* F V Alamo
Imprint: Editorial Antillana
Branch Off: Editorial Antillana, Roble 51, Río Piedras, PR 00925
Subjects: Literature, Biography, History, University and Secondary Textbooks

Bookshop: Librería Cultural (qv under Major Booksellers)
Founded: 1949

Fondo Educativo Interamericano*, Apdo 29853, 65th Infantry Station, Río Piedras, PR 00929
Parent Company: Addison-Wesley Publishing Co Inc, Reading, MA 01867, USA
Associate Companies: See Addison-Wesley Iberoamericana SA, Mexico

Grijalbo Puerto Rico Inc, Apdo 23025 UPR, Río Piedras 00931 Tel: 7655065
President: Norberto Lugo Ramírez; *Sales, Publicity:* Reinaldo Ocasio
Parent Company: Ediciones Grijalbo SA, Spain (qv)

Instituto de Cultura Puertorriqueña*, Apdo 4184, San Juan, PR 00905 Tel: 7210563/ 7251988/7257515 Telex: 3859686
Dir: Prof Elías López Sobá; *Editorial Dir:* Marta Aponte Alsina; *Sales:* Ileana Colón de Barreto
Orders to: San Francisco 305, San Juan, PR 00901
Subjects: General Literature, History, Music, Poetry, Anthropology
Bookshop: Librería del Instituto de Cultura Puertorriqueña, San Francisco 305, San Juan, PR 00901
Founded: 1955

Editorial **McGraw-Hill** Latinoamericana SA*, Apdo 20712, Río Piedras, PR 00928
Regional Manager Caribbean: Herminio de Jesuí
Parent Company: McGraw-Hill International Book Co, 1221 Ave of the Americas, New York, NY 10020, USA
Subjects: Primary, Secondary & University Textbooks, Reference, Educational Materials
Miscellaneous: Branch office of Editorial McGraw-Hill Latinoamericana SA, Panama (qv)

Editorial y Librería La **Reforma**, Calle El Roble 54, Río Piedras, PR 00925 Tel: 7651635
Man Dir: Germán Stevenson
Parent Company: Fortress Church Supply Stores
Subject: Religion
Founded: 1954

University of Puerto Rico Press (EDUPR)+*, Apdo X, Estacion UPR, Río Piedras, PR 00931 Tel: 7630812 (editorial), 7518251 (sales) Cable Add: Edupr Telex: 9171
Acting Dir: Evaristo Díaz Velázquez; *Chief Editor:* Brunhilda M Rexach; *Assistant Marketing Manager:* José Ortiz; *Publicity:* María Teresa Flórez
Subjects: General Fiction, Belles Lettres, Poetry, History, Art, Philosophy, Reference, Low- & High-priced Paperbacks, Medicine, Psychology, Engineering, General & Social Science, University Textbooks, Educational Materials
Founded: 1932
ISBN Publisher's Prefix: 0-8477

Major Booksellers

Librería **Alma Mater** Inc*, 867 Cabrera St, Santa Rita, Río Piedras, PR 00925 Tel: 7646752/7646276
Manager: Elías Cruz

Librería **Escorial***, Recinto Sur 313, San Juan, PR 00901 Tel: 7250972

Librería **Hispanoamericana***, Apdo 20830, Río Piedras, PR 00928 (Located at: Ave Ponce de León 1013, Río Piedras) Tel: 7633415
Manager: Juan E Gallagher

Librería **Cultural***, Roble 51, Río Piedras, PR 00925 Tel: 7659767
Manager: Francisco Vazquez
Owned by: Editorial Cultural (qv)

Librería Cultural Puertorriqueña Inc*, Ave Fernandez Junco 1406 — Parada 20, Apdo 8863, Santurce, PR 00910

Librería Universitaria de Puerto Rico, Apdo B J Estación UPR, Río Piedras 00931

Librería La **Tertulia**, Amalia Marin esq Ave González, Río Piedras, PR 00925 Tel: 7651148

Librería **Thekes***, Plaza las Américas, San Juan Tel: 7651539

Major Libraries

Agricultural Experiment Station Library*, Box H, Río Piedras

Archivo General de Puerto Rico, Instituto de Cultura Puertorriqueña, Apdo 4184, San Juan, PR 00905 Tel: 7220331/7222113
National Archives of Puerto Rico
Dir: Miguel Angel Nieves

Biblioteca General de Puerto Rico (General Library), Instituto de Cultura Puertorriqueña, Apdo 4184, San Juan, PR 00905 Tel: 7242680/7230052
Dir: María de las M Aviles

Caribbean Regional Library, University Station, Apdo 21927, San Juan, PR 00931 Tel: (809) 7640000 ext 3319
Librarian: Almaluces Figueroa de Cruz
Publication: Bibliografía actual de Caribe (Current Caribbean Bibliography (irregular))

Inter American University of Puerto Rico Library*, San Germán

University of Puerto Rico, General Library, Mayaguez Campus*, Mayaguez

University of Puerto Rico, General Library, Río Piedras Campus*, Box C, UPR Station 00931 Tel: (809) 7640000/7514080
Acting Dir: Ms Noris J Vázquez

University of Puerto Rico, Medical Sciences Campus Library*, Apdo 5067, San Juan, PR 00936

Library Association

Sociedad de Bibliotecarios de Puerto Rico, Apdo 22898, Universidad de Puerto Rico, Río Piedras, PR 00931 Tel: 7640000 ext 2122
Society of Librarians of Puerto Rico
President: Sylvia M de Olmos; *Executive Secretary:* Manuelita Martínez
Publications: Boletín, Informa (Newsletter), *Cuadernos Bibliotecologicos, Cuadernos Bibliograficos*

Library Reference Journals

Boletín (Bulletin), Society of Librarians of Puerto Rico, Apdo 22898, Universidad de Puerto Rico, Río Piedras, PR 00931
Text in English and Spanish

Informa (Newsletter), Society of Librarians of Puerto Rico, Apdo 22898, Universidad de Puerto Rico, Río Piedras, PR 00931

Literary Associations and Societies

Congreso de Poesia de Puerto Rico (Puerto Rican Congress of Poetry)*, c/o Colegio de Agricultura y Artes Mecánicas, Mayaguez
President: Francisco Lluch Mora

P E N Club de Puerto Rico, Ave Ponce de León 900, Miramar 00907 Tel: 7240309
President: Dr Luis Nieves Falcón; *Secretary:* Wenceslaw Serra Deliz

Literary Periodicals

Asomante, Asociación de Graduadas de la Universidad de Puerto Rico, Apdo 1142, San Juan, PR 00902

Atenea, University of Puerto Rico at Mayaguez, College of Arts and Sciences, Mayaguez, PR 00708
Text in Spanish, English, French and Italian

Sin Nombre, Sin Nombre Inc, 55 Cordero St, Santurce, PR 00911

Zona Carga y Descarga, Apdo 3871, San Juan, PR 00903

Qatar

General Information

Language: Arabic (English used commercially)
Religion: Islamic (Wahabi sect)
Population: 237,000
Bank Hours: 0730-1130 Saturday-Thursday
Shop Hours: 0730-1200, 1430-1800 Saturday-Thursday (some open few hours Friday morning)
Currency: 100 dirhams = 1 Qatar riyal
Export/Import Information: No tariff on books or advertising matter. No import licence; no obscenity permitted

Major Booksellers

Abdulla **Abdulghani** & Sons Co*, PO Box 111, Doha

Codco Est*, PO Box 1990, Doha Tel: 26573/25867

Family Bookshop*, PO Box 5769, Doha Tel: 424148 Cable Add: Fambook Doha
Manager: Abdallah Ghousseini
Owned by: Family Bookshop Group Co, PO Box 1020, Limassol, Cyprus

Major Libraries

National Library*, PO Box 205, Doha Tel: 422842/321390/321391 Telex: 4743
Dir: Mohammed Hamad Al-Nassr

Réunion

General Information

Language: French
Religion: Predominantly Roman Catholic
Population: 491,000
Bank Hours: 0800-1500
Business Hours: Generally 0800-1200, 1400-1800
Currency: 100 centimes = 1 Réunion franc
Export/Import Information: No tariff on books and advertising. Books have reduced VAT. No import licence. Nominal exchange control over certain value
Copyright: Berne, UCC (see International section)

Major Booksellers

Librairie **Daude***, 97400 St-Denis

Firmin **Pause***, 2 rue Sadi-Carnot, Le Port

Librairie Universitaire de la Réunion*, 13 ave de la Victoire Tel: 210758
Manager: Apavou

Major Libraries

Archives départementales de la Réunion*, Le Chaudron, 97490 Sainte-Clotilde Tel: 280244
Librarian: Marie-Claude Buxtorf

Bibliothèque centrale de Prêt, 1 pl Joffre, 97488 St-Denis Cedex Tel: 210324
Librarian: Marie-Colette Maujean

Bibliothèque départementale, 52 rue Roland Garros, 97400 St-Denis Tel: 211396/211586
Librarian: Alain-M Vauthier

Bibliothèque municipale*, blvd Hubert-Delisle, 97410 St-Pierre Tel: 250824
Librarian: Jules Volia

Université de la Réunion, Bibliothèque Universitaire*, 97489 St-Denis Cedex Tel: 281873
Dir: Catherine Es-Salhi

Literary Periodical

Ti-Kabar, BP 213, 97420 Le Port

Romania

General Information

Language: Romanian. German and Hungarian in some areas
Religion: Romanian Orthodox
Population: 22.2 million
Bank Hours: 0900-1200, 1300-1500 Monday-Friday; 0900-1200 Saturday
Shop Hours: 0900-1900 Monday-Friday; early closing Saturday
Currency: 100 bani = 1 leu
Export/Import Information: Book import and export co-ordinated by Centrala Editoriala, Piata Scînteii 1, R-79715 Bucharest. The commercial operations are carried out by Artexim-Foreign Trade Co, PO Box 33-16, R-70055 Bucharest. Import licences required. Exchange controls: terms of payment established in the sales contract
Copyright: Berne (see International section)

Book Trade Organizations

Centrala Editoriala*, Piata Scînteii 1, R-79715 Bucharest Tel: (00) 181255
The state body which co-ordinates all book publishing and selling activity
General Dir: Gheorghe Trandafir
Publications: Carti în curs de aparitie (Books to be published); *Romanian Books*

Uniunea Scriitorilor din Republica Socialista România, Calea Victoriei 115, R-71102 Bucharest
Writers' Union of the Socialist Republic of Romania
President: Dumitru Radu Popescu
Publications: Convorbiri Literare (Literary Conversations); *Igaz Szo*; *Knijevni Jivot*; *Luceafarul*; *Neue Literatur*; *Orizont* (Horizon); *România Literara* (Literary Romania); *Secolul XX* (Twentieth Century); *Steaua* (The Star); *Utunk*; *Vatra*; *Viata Românească* (Romanian Life)

Book Trade Reference Journals

Bibliografia Republicii Populare Romîne (Romanian National Bibliography), Central State Library, Str Ion Ghica 4, R-70018 Bucharest

Carti în curs de aparitie (Books to be published, quarterly), Centrala Editoriala, Piata Scînteii 1, R-79715 Bucharest

Carti Noi (New Books), Book Centre, Str Biserica Amzei 5-7, Bucharest

Romanian Books, Centrala Editoriala, Foreign Relations Department, Piata Scînteii 1, R-79715 Bucharest
Quarterly bulletin; text in English or French

Romanian Books in Foreign Languages, Book Centre, Str Biserica Amzei 5-7, Bucharest

Publishers

Editura **Academiei** Republicii Socialiste România, Calea Victoriei 125, R-79717 Bucharest Tel: (00) 502130 Cable Add: Edacad
Publishing House of the Academy of the Socialist Republic of Romania
Man Dir: C Busuioceanu
Orders to: Rompresfilatelia, PO Box 12-201, R-78104 Bucharest
Subject: Science (in Romanian and other languages)
Founded: 1948

Editura **Albatros***, Piata Scînteii 1, R-79718 Bucharest Tel: (00) 180448
Man Dir: Mircea Sântimbreanu
Subject: Juveniles
Founded: 1969

Editura **Cartea Românească***, Str Nuferilor 41, R-79721 Bucharest Tel: (00) 149352
Dir: Marin Preda
Subjects: Contemporary Fiction, Poetry and Drama, Literary History and Criticism
Founded: 1969

Editura **Ceres***, Piata Scînteii 1, R-79722 Bucharest Tel: (00) 180174
Man Dir: Gabriel Manoliu
Subjects: Agriculture, Forestry, Animal Husbandry, Veterinary Medicine, Textbooks
Founded: 1953

Editure Ion **Creanga**, Piata Scînteii 1, R-71725 Bucharest Tel: (00) 182525
Man Dir: Viniciu Gafita; *Production, Publicity:* Eleonora Nitescu
Subjects: Poetry, Biography, History, Music, Art, Belles Lettres, Literature, Fiction — all for children
Founded: 1969

Editura **Dacia***, Str 1 Mai 23, R-3400 Cluj-Napoca Tel: (51) 18912
Dir: Alexandru Caprariu; *Production Dir:* Vasile Vancea; *Publicity, Public Relations:* Mrs Dana Prelipceanu; *Rights & Permissions:* Aurel Câmpeanu, Mrs Miess Emma
Subjects: Literature, Art, Science (in Romanian, Hungarian, German, Serbo-Croat)
Founded: 1969

Editura **Didactica si Pedagogica***, Str Spiru Haret 12, R-79724 Bucharest Tel: (00) 152455
Man Dir: Dr C I Floricel; *Editorial:* Pop Avram; *Sales, Publicity, Rights & Permissions:* Stelian Galos
Subjects: University, Secondary & Primary Textbooks, Maps and Atlases (in Romanian and other languages)
Founded: 1951

Editura **Eminescu***, Piata Scînteii 1, R-79731 Bucharest Tel: (00) 177380
Man Dir: Valeriu Rîpeanu
Subjects: Romanian Classical & Contemporary Literature, Poetry, History (all in various languages)

Editura **Facla***, Str Pestalozzi 14, R-1900 Timisoara Tel: (061) 14212/18218
Dir: Ion Marin Almajan
Subjects: Fiction, Science, Technology, Art (Romanian, Hungarian, German, Serbo-Croat)
Founded: 1972

Editura **Junimea***, 1 Blvd Gh Dimitrov, R-6600 Jassy Tel: (081) 17290
Dir: Mircea Radu Iacoban
Subjects: Original and Translated Works in Literary and Technical fields, Literary Theory and Criticism
Founded: 1969

Editura **Kriterion***, Piata Scînteii 1, R-79726 Bucharest Tel: (00) 174060
Dir: Géza Domokos
Subjects: Books in Hungarian, German, Serbo-Croat, Ukrainian, Yiddish and Romanian, Classical and Contemporary Literature, Science, Technology, Art
Founded: 1969

Litera Publishing House, Piata Scînteii 1, R-79727 Bucharest Tel: (00) 182471
Manager: Gheorghe Buzatu
Subject: Literature

Editura **Medicala***, Str Smîrdan 5, R-79728 Bucharest Tel: (00) 143252
Medical Publishing House
Man Dir: Dr Ion Teodorescu Exarcu
Subjects: Medical & Pharmaceutical Literature, Textbooks, Periodicals
Founded: 1954

Editura **Meridiane**, Piata Scînteii 1, R-79729 Bucharest Tel: (00) 181087
Man Dir: George Sorin Movileanu; *Editor-in-Chief:* Modest Morariu
Subjects: Fine Arts, Folk Art, Theatre, Cinema, Architecture
Founded: 1952

Editura **Militara***, 28A Cobalcescu,
R-79735 Bucharest   Tel: (00) 133601
Subjects: Military Science, History, Fiction
Bookshop: Libraria Militara (Military
Bookshop), Bd Gheorghe Gheorghiu-
Dej 2, N2 Sector 5, Bucharest
Founded: 1950

Editura **Minerva***, Piata Scînteii 1,
R-79732 Bucharest   Tel: (00) 184464
Manager: Aurel Martin
Subjects: Literary (especially Classical and
Foreign), Bilingual Editions, Poetry,
Folklore, Various Series
Founded: 1969

Editura **Muzicala***, Str Poiana Narciselor 6,
R-70718 Bucharest   Tel: (00) 138743
Man Dir: Aurel Popa
Subjects: Scores, Musicology
Founded: 1958

Editura **Politica***, Piata Scînteii 1, R-79734
Bucharest   Tel: (00) 172987
Man Dir: Dumitru Ghise
Subjects: Political & Social Sciences (in
Romanian, Hungarian, German and Serbo-
Croat)
Founded: 1945

Editura **'Scrisul Românesc'***, Str Mihai
Viteazul 4, R-1100 Craiova   Tel: (041)
13763
'Romanian Writing' Publishing House
Dir: Ilarie Hinoveanu
Subjects: Social & Political Science,
Literature, Technical
Founded: 1972

Editura **Sport-Turism***, Str Vasile Conta
16, R-79736 Bucharest   Tel: (00) 107480
Sports and Tourism Publishing House
Editor: Gheorghe Constantinescu
Subjects: Sports, Travel Guides
Founded: 1975

Editura **Stiintifică si Enciclopedică**, Piata
Scînteii 1, R-71341 Bucharest   Tel: (00)
175168
Scientific and Encyclopaedia Publishing
House
Man Dir: Dr Mircea Mâciu; *Production
Manager, Sales Dir:* Alexandru Banciu
Subjects: Encyclopaedias, Dictionaries,
Reference, Physical & Social Sciences,
World Literature, Romanian Language
Studies, Philology, Foreign Language
Reference
1986: 126 titles   *Founded:* 1975 (by
amalgamation of Romanian Encyclopaedic
Publishing House and Scientific Publishing
House)
Miscellaneous: The Foreign Encyclopaedias
Office supplies any encyclopaedic
materials, information, data, statistics,
maps and illustrations concerning Romania
required by foreign publishing houses

Editura **Tehnica**, Piata Scînteii 1, R-79738
Bucharest   Tel: (00) 180630
Man Dir: Ion Iliescu
Subjects: Engineering, General Science and
Technology, Dictionaries, Reference
1985: 174 titles   *1986:* 157 titles   *Founded:*
1950

Editura **Univers***, Piata Scînteii 1, R-79739
Bucharest   Tel: (00) 181762
Man Dir: Prof Dr Romul Munteanu;
Publicity, Advertising: N Alexe
Subjects: Translations of Fiction, Poetry,
Drama, Biography, Literary Criticism
Founded: 1961

Major Booksellers

Artexim — Foreign Trade Co*, PO Box
33-16, R-70055 Bucharest (Located at:
Piata Scînteii 1, Bucharest)   Tel: (00)
157672   Telex: 011191
Carries out all the commercial operations
connected with book import and export

Major Libraries

Academia de Studii Economice, Biblioteca
Centrala, Piata Romana 6, sector 1,
R-70167 Bucharest   Tel: (00) 110610
Telex: Asero 11863

Biblioteca **Academiei Republicii Socialiste
România***, Calea Victoriei 125, Bucharest
Tel: (00) 503043

Biblioteca Filialei Cluj a **Academiei
Republicii Socialiste România***, Str
Kogalniceanu 12-17, Cluj
The Library of the Cluj Branch of the
Academy of the RSR

Archivele Statului*, Bul Gheorghe,
Gheorghiu-Dej 29, Bucharest
National Archives

Biblioteca Centrala de Stat a Republicii
Socialiste România*, Str Ion Ghica 4,
R-70018 Bucharest   Tel: (00) 161260/507063/
140746
Central State Library

Biblioteca Centrala Universitara*, Str
Onesti 1, sector 1, Bucharest 1   Tel: (00)
132557
Dir: Dr Ion Stoica; *Deputy Dir:* Ivona
Dumitrescu
*Publications include: Literatura româna:
Ghid bibliografic*; *Repertoriul periodicelor
din principalele biblioteci din Bucuresti*

Biblioteca Centrala Universitara*, Str
Clinicilor 2, R-3400 Cluj-Napoca   Tel:
(051) 21092

**Biblioteca Centrala Universitara 'Mihail
Eminescu'***, Str Pacurari 4, Jassy   Tel:
(081) 40709

Biblioteca Judeteana Timis*, Piata
Libertatii 3, Timisoara

Biblioteca **Facultatii** de Medicina din
Bucuresti, renamed Institutul de medicina
si farmacie (qv)

I N I D, see Institutul National de
Informare si Documentare

Institutul de medicina si farmacie
Biblioteca Centrala, Blvd Dr Petru Groza
8, R-76241 Bucharest
Central Library of the Institute of
Medicine and Pharmacy (formerly
Biblioteca Facultatii de Medicina)
Dir: Silvica Petre

Institutul National de Informare si
Documentare (INID), Str Cosmonautilor
27-29, R-70141 Bucharest 1   Tel: (00)
134010   Telex: 11247
National Institute for Information and
Documentation
Dir: Gheorghe Anghel
*Publications: Abstracts of Romanian
Scientific and Technical Literature* (in
English, French, Russian and Romanian);
*Buletin de referate din literatura stiintifica si
tehnica româna*; *Information and
Documentation Problems/Probleme de
informare si documentare* (in English and
Romanian)

Biblioteca **Institutului Politehnic** Bucuresti,
Calea Grivitei 132, Bucharest
Librarian: Dr George Anca
Publication: Buletinul Institutului Politehnic

Biblioteca Municipala 'Mihail **Sadoveanu**'*,
Str Nikos Beloiannis 4, Bucharest

University Libraries, see Biblioteca

Library Association

Asociatia Bibliotecarilor din RSR*,
Biblioteca Centrala de Stat, Str Ion Ghica
4, R-70018 Bucharest   Tel: (00) 503765
Librarians' Association of Romania
Executive Secretary: St Gruia
Publication: Revista Bibliotecilor (Library
Review) (monthly)

Library Reference Books and Journals

Book

Ghidul Bibliotecilor din România (Guide
to Libraries in Romania), Editura
Enciclopedică Româna, Calea Victoriei
126, Bucharest

Journals

Buletinul de Informare în Bibliologie
(Librarianship Information Bulletin),
Central State Library, Str Ion Ghica 4,
R-70018 Bucharest

*Fise Signaletice ale Articolelor din
Domeniul Bibliologiei* (Indicative Cards for
Articles in the Field of Librarianship),
Central State Library, Str Ion Ghica 4,
R-70018 Bucharest

*Information and Documentation Problems/
Probleme de informare si documentare*,
National Institute for Information and
Documentation, Str Cosmonautilor 27-29,
R-70141 Bucharest
Text in English and Romanian

Revista Bibliotecilor (Library Review),
Librarians' Association of Romania,
Biblioteca Centrala de Stat, Str Ion Ghica
4, R-70018 Bucharest

Revista de Referate in Bibliologie
(Librarianship Abstracts Review), Central
State Library, Str Ion Ghica 4, R-70018
Bucharest

Literary Associations and Societies

Institutul de Istorie si Teorie Literara
'George **Calinescu**'*, Blvd Republicii 73,
Bucharest
Dir: Professor Dr Zoe Dumitrescu-
Busulenga
*Publication: Revista de Istorie si Teorie
Literara* (quarterly)

Centrul de Lingvistica Istorie Literara si
Folclor*, Aleea Mihail Sadoveanu 12,
Jassy
Dir: A Teodorescu
*Publication: Anuar de Linguisticasi Istorie
Literară*

Romanian **P E N Centre***, Casa Scriitorilor
Mihail Sadoveanu, Calea Victoriei 115,
Bucharest
Secretary: Geo Dumitrescu

Literary Periodicals

Cahiers roumains d'Etudes Littéraires
(Romanian Literary Studies), Editura
Univers, Piata Scînteii 1, R-79739
Bucharest
Text in French and English, occasionally in
German, Russian, Spanish and Italian

Convorbiri Literare (Literary
Conversations), Writers' Union of the
Socialist Republic of Romania (Jassy
branch), Palatul Culturii, Jassy

Manuscriptum (Manuscripts), Muzeul Literaturii Romane, Central State Library, Str Ion Ghica 4, R-70018 Bucharest

Orizont (Horizon), Writers' Union of the Socialist Republic of Romania (Timisoara branch), Pta Vasile Roaita 3, Timisoara

Revista de Istorie si Teorie Literara (Review of Literary History and Theory), Publishing House of the Academy of the Socialist Republic of Romania, Calea Victoriei 125, R-79717 Bucharest
Summaries in French and Russian

Romania Literara (Literary Romania), Writers' Union of the Socialist Republic of Romania, Calea Victoriei 115, R-71102 Bucharest

Romanian Review, Foreign Languages Press, Str Ion Ghica 5, Bucharest
Text in English, French, German and Russian

Secolul XX (Twentieth Century), Writers' Union of the Socialist Republic of Romania, Calea Victoriei 115, R-71102 Bucharest

Steaua (The Star), Writers' Union of the Socialist Republic of Romania, Calea Victoriei 115, R-71102 Bucharest

Viata Romineasca (Romanian Life), Writers' Union of the Socialist Republic of Romania, Calea Victoriei 115, R-71102, Bucharest

Literary Prizes

Literary Award*
Founded 1966 for literary (and artistic) works reflecting humanistic and democratic ideals. Awarded annually for social and political literature (one prize), reportage (two prizes), journalism (one prize), poetry (three prizes), debut in poetry (five prizes), prose (two prizes), debut in prose (one prize), literary history and criticism (two prizes), debut in literary history and criticism (two prizes), drama (one prize) and science fiction (one prize). Enquiries to Romanian Union of Communist Youth, Str Onesti 6-8, Bucharest

Writers' Union Prize*
For an outstanding contribution to Romanian literature in poetry, prose, drama, literary criticism, history of literature, literary reportage, literature for children and youth, translations from world literature, and for a promising new literary work by a young writer. Awarded annually. Enquiries to Writers' Union of the Socialist Republic of Romania, Calea Victoriei 115, R-71102 Bucharest
(Separate prizes are awarded by Bucharest, Cluj, Jassy, Timisoara, Craiova, Sibiu, Brasov and Tîrgu-Mures Writers' Associations. Awarded annually. For further information contact the appropriate Associations of the Writers' Union of the Socialist Republic of Romania)

Rwanda

General Information

Language: Kinyarwanda (a Bantu tongue) and French
Religion: About 50% traditional beliefs, majority of remainder Roman Catholic, some Islamic
Population: 5 million
Bank Hours: 0830-1130 Monday-Friday for cash transactions; other business 1400-1700 Monday-Friday
Shop Hours: Dawn to dusk
Currency: Rwanda franc
Export/Import Information: No tariff on books and advertising, but Statistical Tax. Import licence, for statistical purposes, and Foreign Exchange Licence required. Application to National Bank, through authorized bank
Copyright: Berne (see International section)

Publishers

Government Printer (Imprimerie National du Rwanda)*, BP 351, Kigali

Imprimerie de Kabgayi*, BP 66, Gitarama
Associate Companies: Diocèse de Kabgayi ASBL; Editions Bibliques et Liturgiques (both at above address)

Editions **Rwandaises***, Caritas Rwanda, BP 1078, Kigali Tel: 6503
Man Dir: Abbé Cyriaque Munyansanga; *Editorial:* Albert Nambaje
Subsidiary Company: Caritas Rwanda (at above address)
Subjects: Religion, Kinyarwanda language, General, Educational, Children's Paperbacks
Bookshop: Librairie Caritas (qv under Major Booksellers)

Major Booksellers

Librairie **Caritas***, BP 1078, Kigali Tel: 6503
Owned by: Editions Rwandaises (qv)

Librairie universitaire*, BP 125, Butare Tel: 325

Somec-Rwanda*, BP 628, Kigali Tel: 5378/5497

Major Libraries

Bibliothèque de l'**Institut national** de la recherche scientifique*, BP 218, Butare

Bibliothèque du **Service** geologique du Rwanda*, Ministère des Resources Naturelles, Mines et Carrières, BP 413, Kigali Tel: 6620

Bibliothèque de l'**Université Nationale du Rwanda***, BP 54, Butare Tel: 271
Dir: Claudien Ntarwanda

Saudi Arabia

General Information

Language: Arabic (English widely understood)
Religion: Islamic (officially)
Population: 9 million
Bank Hours: 0830-1200, 1700-1900 Saturday-Wednesday; 0830-1130 Thursday. During Ramadan: 1000-1330 Saturday-Thursday
Shop Hours: 0900-1200, 1600-2100 Saturday-Thursday. During Ramadan closed until sunset, then open until 0200
Currency: 100 halalahs = 1 Saudi riyal
Export/Import Information: No tariffs on books; advertising matter subject to ad valorem duty but if total duty on one consignment is less than 50 riyals, matter can enter free. Catalogues distributed gratis, usually admitted free. All printed matter except textbooks subject to censorship. No import licences required
Copyright: No copyright conventions signed

Publishers

Al **Jazirah** Organization for Press, Printing, Publishing*, PO Box 354, Riyadh (Located at: Al-Nassiriah St, Riyadh)
Dir-Gen: Saleh Al-Ajroush; *Editor-in-Chief:* Khalid el Malek
Subject: Politics, Law
Founded: 1964

Saudi Publishing and Distributing House*, PO Box 2043, Jeddah 21451 (Located at: Al-Jouhra Bldg, 2nd floor, Bughdadia) Tel: (02) 6424043/6432821/6224255 Cable Add: Nashradar Telex: 604351 Nashra SJ/602687 Fonoon SJ
Chairman: Mohammad Salahuddin; *Man Dir:* Mohammed Ali Al-Wazir
Subjects: Arabic and English publications
Miscellaneous: Also importers and distributors of English and Arabic books (academic and general)

Major Booksellers

Al-**Adab** Bookshop*, Riyadh Tel: (01) 27865

Dabbous Stores*, King St, Jeddah

Mohamed Noor Salah **Jamjoom & Bros***, PO Box 12, Jeddah

Riyadh Modern Bookshop*, PO Box 2010, Riyadh 11451 Tel: (01) 27993 Telex: 405629

Ali **Wahbah** Bookshop*, Riyadh Tel: (01) 67654

Major Libraries

Educational Library*, General Directorate of Broadcasting, Press and Publications, Jeddah

Institute of Public Administration Library*, PO Box 205, Riyadh 11141 Tel: (01) 4792366 Cable Add: Ipadmin Telex: 401160 SJ
Dir of Libraries: Mostafa M Sadhan

Islamic University Library*, PO Box 170, Al-Madinah Al-Monawwarah Tel: 8236803 Telex: 470022 Islami

King Abdulaziz University Library*, Deanship of Library Affairs, PO Box 3711, Jeddah 21481 Tel: (02) 6890256 Telex: 601141 Kauni SJ
A Central Library with 10 branches in various faculties
Dean: Dr Hisham A Abbas
Publications: Annual Index of Umm Al-Qura (Arabic); *Catalogue of MSS in the Central Library* (Arabic); *Dissertations on Saudi Arabia* (English)

Dar al **Kutub** al-Wataniya*, King Faisal St, Riyadh

The **Library** and Documentation Centre, see Institute of Public Administration Library

National Library*, King Faisal St, Riyadh
Publication: Bulletin

Iman M Ben **Saud** Islamic University, Deanery Libraries*, PO Box 4124, Riyadh Tel: (01) 30771/30661

Saudi Library*, Riyadh

University Libraries*, King Saud University, PO Box 22480, Riyadh 11495 Tel: (01) 4676148 Cable Add: University Telex: 401019 Ksu SJ
Dean: Dr S A Al-Rashid

Library Reference Journal

Bulletin, National Library, King Faisal St, Riyadh

Senegal

General Information

Language: French
Religion: About 80% Islamic, 10% Christian (mostly Roman Catholic)
Population: 5.7 million
Bank Hours: Generally 0800-1115, 1430-1630 Monday-Friday
Shop Hours: Vary, and some open Sunday morning, some close Monday morning. Generally are 0800-1200, 1430-1800 Monday-Saturday
Currency: CFA franc
Export/Import Information: Member of West African Economic Community. No tariff on books except atlases. Added taxes apply to atlases. Advertising matter (more than one copy) subject to fiscal and customs duty plus added taxes. Import licences and exchange controls apply for imports from outside EEC, Franc Zone, USA and Canada
Copyright: Berne, UCC (see International section)

Book Trade Reference Journal

Bibliographie du Sénégal, Archives du Sénégal, Immeuble administratif, ave Roume, Dakar

Publishers

Africa Editions, BP 1826, Dakar Tel: 210880
Man Dir: Joel Decupper
Subjects: General Literature, Reference Works, Annuals, Telephone Directory, Periodicals
Founded: 1958

Agence de Distribution de Presse*, BP 374, Dakar (Located at: 4 rue Carnot, Dakar) Tel: 23522
Man Dir: François Terrier
Subjects: General, Reference
Bookshop: See under Major Booksellers
Miscellaneous: Affiliated to NMPP, Paris

Centre Sénégalaise d'Editions et de Diffusion*, 31 rue Wagane Diouf, BP 1745, Dakar Tel: 26994
Man Dir: Jacques Coudon Jaefus
Subjects: General Fiction, Law, Medicine, Paperbacks, Secondary Textbooks
Founded: 1974

Codesria*, PO Box 3304, Dakar (Located at: Fann Residence, Dakar) Tel: 230211
Telex: 3339 Codes SG
Chief Executive: Abdallah S Bujra;
Editorial: Abdallah S Bujra, Thandika Mkandawire
Subject: Socio-Economic Development in Africa

Government Printer (Imprimerie du Gouvernement)*, BP 1, Dakar (Located at: rue Fisque, Dakar)

Les **Nouvelles** Editions Africaines+, BP 260, Dakar (Located at: 10 rue El Hadj Amadou Assane Ndoye, Dakar) Tel: 211381/221580
President, Dir General: Papa Guèye Ndiaye; *Commercial Dir:* Djibril Faye; *Education Dir:* Madiéyna Ndiaye; *Production Dir:* Abdoulaye Diouf
Subsidiary Companies: Les Nouvelles Editions Africaines, Ivory Coast (qv); Les Nouvelles Editions Africaines, Togo (qv)
Subjects: General Fiction & Non-fiction, Belles Lettres, Poetry, Biography, History, Africana, Philosophy, Religion, Juveniles, Paperbacks, Psychology, Education, Encyclopaedias, General & Social Science, University, Secondary and Primary Textbooks
Book Club: Club Afrique-Loisirs
Founded: 1972
ISBN Publisher's Prefix: 2-7236

Société Africaine d'Edition*, 16 bis rue de Thiong, BP 1877, Dakar Tel: 217977, 220284
Man Dir: Pierre Biarnes
Branch Off: 32 rue de l'Echiquier, F-75010 Paris, France Tel: 5230233
Subjects: African Politics and Economics
Founded: 1961

Société d'Edition d'Afrique Nouvelle, BP 283, Dakar (Located at: 9 rue Paul Holle, Dakar) Tel: 223825 Telex: 1403 Clairaf Dakar
Man Dir: Athanase Ndong; *Senior Editor, Rights & Permissions:* René Odou
Subjects: African affairs, Religion, Magazines

Editions des **Trois Fleuves***, 57 ave du Pdt Lamine Gueye, BP 123, Dakar Tel: 222077
Man Dir: Roland de Boistel, Bertrand de Boistel
Subjects: General Non-fiction, Luxury Editions
Founded: 1972

Book Club

Club **Afrique-Loisirs**, BP 260, Dakar (Located at: 10 rue El Hadj Amadou Assane Ndoye, Dakar)
Owned by: Les Nouvelles Editions Africaines (qv)

Major Booksellers

Agence de Distribution de Presse*, BP 374, Dakar (Located at: 4 rue Carnot, Dakar) Tel: 220251
Also Publisher (qv)

Librairie afrique*, BP 1240, Dakar (Located at: 58 ave William Ponty, Dakar) Tel: 214223
Manager: D Cabrita

Librairie clairafrique, BP 2005, Dakar (Located at: pl de l'Indépendance, Dakar) Tel: 222169/218409 Telex: 21403 Clairaf
Manager: Charles Friederich

Librairie nouvelle de l'Ouest Africain (LINOA)*, Bldg Maginot, 43 ave Maginot, BP 2039, Dakar Tel: 26450

Librairie universitaire et technique*, BP 396, Dakar Tel: 210208

Mamadou Traoré Ray Autra*, BP 2380, Dakar

Librairie du **Point d'Interrogation***, BP 437, Dakar

Librairie Editions PFD **Sankore***, 25 ave William Ponty, BP 7040, Dakar Tel: 22105

Major Libraries

L'**Alliance** française, Bibliothèque*, 10 rue Colbert, BP 1777, Dakar Tel: 20105

Archives du Sénégal*, Immeuble administratif, ave Roume, Dakar Tel: 215072
National Archives of Senegal
Dir: Saliou Mbaye
Publications include: Bibliographie du Sénégal; Rapport Annuel

Centre culturel français Gaston **Berger**, Bibliothèque*, BP 368, St-Louis

Centre culturel américain, Bibliothèque*, pl de l'Indépendance, BP 49, Dakar Tel: 225928/220124

Centre culturel français, Bibliothèque*, 96 rue Blanchot, BP 4003, Dakar Tel: 211821/216427

Centre culturel français Gaston Berger, see Berger

Centre de Recherches et de Documentation du Sénégal (CRDS)*, BP 382, St-Louis (Located at: rue Neuville, Pointe Sud, St-Louis) Tel: 611050
Librarian: Laurent Gomis

Bibliothèque de l'**Ecole** normale supérieure*, BP 5036, Dakar-Fann (Located at: blvd Bourguiba, Dakar-Fann) Tel: 212242
Librarian: Adama Dièye

Lycée de Jeunes Filles Ameth **Fall**, Bibliothèque*, BP 1, St-Louis Tel: 71000

I D E P, see Institut africain

Institut africain de Développement Economique et de Planification (IDEP), Bibliothèque*, BP 3186, Dakar (Located at: derrière Assemblée Nationale, Dakar) Tel: 214831 Telex: 579 Idep
Librarian: Samuel K Odoteye

Institut fondamental d'Afrique noire, Bibliothèque*, Université de Dakar, BP 206, Dakar-Fann Tel: 220090

Université de Dakar, Bibliothèque*, BP 2006, Dakar-Fann Tel: 216981

Library Associations

A N B A D S, see Association nationale des Bibliothécaires, Archivistes et Documentalistes sénégalais

Association nationale des Bibliothécaires, Archivistes et Documentalistes sénégalais (ANBADS)*, Ecole de Bibliothécaires, Archivistes et Documentalistes de Dakar (EBAD), BP 3252, Dakar Tel: 230739
Executive Secretary: Mamadou Lamine Ndoye

Commission des Bibliothèques de l'ASDBAM (Association Senegalaise pour le Développement de la Documentation, des Bibliothèques, des Archives et des Musées)*, BP 375, Dakar Tel: 34139
Commission of the Libraries of the Senegal Association for the Development of

Documentation, Libraries, Archives and Museums

Library Reference Book

Répertoire des Bibliothèques et Organismes de Documentation au Sénégal (Catalogue of the Libraries and Documentation Centres of Senegal), Ecole de Bibliothécaires, Archivistes, et Documentalistes, BP 3252, Dakar-Fann
Information on 124 libraries, archives and documentation centres throughout Senegal

Literary Associations and Societies

P E N Club du Senegal*, 127 ave du Président Lamine Gueye, Dakar
President: Ousmane Sembene

Literary Periodical

L'Afrique littéraire et artistique, Société Africaine d'Edition, BP 1877, Dakar

Seychelles

General Information

Language: English and French
Religion: Roman Catholic
Population: 63,000
Currency: 100 cents = 1 Seychelles rupee
Export/Import Information: No tariffs on books and advertising. Books on Open General Licence

Major Booksellers

Chez Nanon*, Royal St, Victoria
Newservice Ltd*, Seychelles News Service, PO Box 131, Kingsgate House, Mahe Tel: 22309 Cable Add: Legal Seychelles Telex: 231752 Legal
Man Dir: Jemy Wadia

Sierra Leone

General Information

Language: English
Religion: Mainly traditional beliefs but also Islamic and Christian
Population: 3.47 million
Bank Hours: 0800-1330 Monday-Thursday; 0800-1400 Friday
Shop Hours: 0800-1200 or 1230, 1400-1630 or 1700 Monday-Friday; 0800-1230 Saturday
Currency: 100 cents = 1 leone
Export/Import Information: No tariff on books except children's picture books and advertising matter. Open general licence. Exchange controls

Book Trade Reference Journal

Sierra Leone Publications, Sierra Leone Library Board, PO Box 326, Freetown
The national bibliography, published annually since 1962

Publishers

Njala Educational Services Centre*, Njala University, PMB, Freetown
Subjects: General, University and School Textbooks

Sierra Leone University Press*, PO Box 87, Freetown (Located at: Fourah Bay College, Freetown) Tel: 27300/23494/27399 Cable Add: Fourahbay
Chairman, Honorary Editor: Prof Eldred Jones; *Honorary Secretary, Rights & Permissions:* Prof W S Marcus Jones
Subjects: General Non-fiction, History, Africana, Religion, Social Science, University Textbooks
Founded: 1968

United Christian Council Literature Bureau*, Bunumbu Press, PO Box 28, Bo Tel: 462
Man Dir: Robert Sam-Kpakra
Subjects: Books in Mende, Temne, Susu

Major Booksellers

Fourah Bay College Bookshop Ltd*, University of Sierra Leone, Freetown Tel: 27351/25307

Njala University College Bookshop*, PMB, Freetown Tel: Njala exchange: ext 26, 71 Cable Add: Njalunbooks
Manager: Prof D R G Gwynne-Jones

The **Sierra Leone** Diocesan Bookshops Ltd, PO Box 104, Freetown Tel: 22302 Cable Add: Bookshop Freetown

Major Libraries

Public **Archives** of Sierra Leone*, c/o Institute of African Studies, PO Box 87, Freetown

British Council Library, PO Box 124, Freetown (Located at: Tower Hill, Freetown) Tel: 22227 Telex: 3453 Bricon SL

Fourah Bay College Library*, University of Sierra Leone, PO Box 87, Freetown Tel: 27337
Librarian: Gladys M Jusu-Sheriff
Publications include: Annual Report: List of New Accessions to the Sierra Leone Collection; Printed Catalogue of the Sierra Leone Collection; Report on Visit to Francophone University Libraries in West Africa

Milton **Margai** Teachers' College Library*, Goderich, PMB, Freetown Tel: 024305
Librarian: Mrs Abator M Thomas

Njala University College Library (University of Sierra Leone)*, Private Mail Bag, Freetown Tel: 00412
Librarian: Patrick W Saidu
Publications: Library Bulletin; Annual Report; Occasional papers

Sierra Leone Library Board, PO Box 326, Freetown Tel: 23848/26993
Chief Librarian: Mrs G E Dillsworth
Publications: Annual Report; Sierra Leone Publications (annual)

United States Information Service Library*, American Embassy, Walpole St, Freetown

University of Sierra Leone, see Njala

Library Association

Sierra Leone Library Association*, c/o Sierra Leone Library Board, PO Box 326, Freetown Tel: 23848
Secretary: Miss F Thorpe
Publications: Sierra Leone Library Journal (biannual), *Directory of Libraries and Information Services*

Library Reference Books and Journals

Book

Directory of Libraries and Information Services, Sierra Leone Library Association, PO Box 326, Freetown

Journal

Sierra Leone Library Journal, Sierra Leone Library Association, PO Box 326, Freetown

Republic of Singapore

General Information

Language: English
Religion: All major religions, especially Confucianism, Islam, Buddhism, Taoism
Population: 2.4 million
Bank Hours: 1000-1500 Monday-Friday; 0930-1130 Saturday
Shop Hours: 0900-1800 Monday-Saturday
Currency: 100 cents = 1 Singapore dollar
Export/Import Information: No tariffs on books and advertising. Import licences; no seditious publications permitted. Nominal exchange control
Copyright: Florence (see International section)

Book Trade Organizations

National Book Development Council of Singapore*, Bukit Merah Branch Library, Bukit Merah Central, Singapore 0315 Tel: 2732730
Honorary Secretary: R Ramachandran
Publications: NBDCS News (quarterly newsletter); *Singapore Book World*

Singapore Book Publishers' Association*, PO Box 846, Colombo Court Post Office, Singapore 0617
Honorary Secretary: Peh Chin Hua (Tel: 7601388)

Singapore Booksellers' Association*, 428-429 Katong Shopping Centre, Singapore 15 Tel: 401495
President: N T S Chopra

Standard Book Numbering Agency, National Library, Stamford Rd, Singapore 0617 Tel: 3309635 Cable Add: Natlib Singapore Telex: Rs 26620
ISBN Administrators: Mrs Chang Soh Choo, Miss Tok Sok Hoon

Book Trade Reference Books and Journals

Books

Books in Singapore, Chopmen Publishers, 865 Mountbatten Rd 05-28/29, Katong Shopping Centre, Singapore 1543
A survey of publishing, printing, bookselling and library activity

Singapore Periodicals Index (annually), National Library, Stamford Rd, Singapore 0617

Journals

The Memoranda of Books Registered in the 'Catalogue of Books Printed or Published in Singapore' under the Provisions of the Printers and Publishers Act, National Library, Stamford Rd, Singapore 0617

Singapore Book World, National Book Development Council of Singapore, Bukit Merah Branch Library, Bukit Merah Central, Singapore 0315

Singapore National Bibliography (SNB), National Library, Stamford Rd, Singapore 0617

Publishers

Addison-Wesley (S) Pte Ltd, 15 Beach Rd, 05-09/10 Beach Centre, Singapore 0718
Dir, General Manager (Asia): Paul Goulding; *Executive Editor:* Stephen Troth; *Sales:* Ooi Inng Huat; *Publicity:* Annie Mok
Parent Company: Addison-Wesley Publishing Co Inc, Reading, MA 01867, USA
Associate Companies: Addison-Wesley Publishers Japan Ltd, Japan (qv); Addison-Wesley Publishers Ltd, UK (qv)

K C Ang Publishing Pte Ltd, Kent Ridge PO Box 1005, Kent Ridge Post Office, Singapore 9111 Tel: 4741680 Telex: RS 55370 Skat
Man Dir: K C Ang
Imprint: Bunny Books
Subject: Children's
1985: 4 titles *1986:* 15 titles *Founded:* 1985
ISBN Publisher's Prefix: 9971-974

Apa Productions (Pte) Ltd+, 3 Gul Crescent, Singapore 2262 Tel: 8612755 Cable Add: Apaproduct Telex: Apasin rs 36201
Chairman, Publisher, Rights & Permissions: Hans Hoefer; *Editorial:* Vivien Kim; *Sales, Publicity:* Yinglock Chan; *Production:* Rafie Sain
Associate Company: Apa Productions (HK) Ltd, 5th Floor, The Chinese Club Bldg, 21-22 Connaught Rd, Central, Hong Kong
Imprints: Apa-Maps; The Insight Chronicles; Insight Guides
Subjects: Travel Guides, Maps, History
Founded: 1971
ISBN Publisher's Prefix: 9971-925

Book Emporium Singapore (Pte) Ltd, see Singapore Book Emporium

Graham Brash Pte Ltd+, Prinsep House, 36-C Prinsep St, Singapore 0718 Tel: 3382497/3383705 Cable Add: Bookscout Singapore Telex: rs 23718 Feenix GB
Man Dir: K C Campbell; *Sales Dir, Publicity:* C I Campbell
Subjects: General, Academic, Educational (in English, Chinese, Malay)
1986: 120 titles
ISBN Publisher's Prefix: 9971-947

Bunny Books, an imprint of K C Ang Publishing Pte Ltd (qv)

Butterworth & Co (Asia) Pte Ltd, 30 Robinson Rd 12-01, Tuan Sing Towers, Singapore 0104 Tel: 2241622 Telex: RS 42890 Bg Asia Fax: 2252939
Man Dir: Mike McKinley; *Sales:* Tony Poh; *Promotion:* Audrey Chiang; *Editorial:* Stephen J Stout
Parent Company: Butterworth & Co (Publishers) Ltd, UK (qv for associate companies)
Subjects: Textbooks, Reference, Law, Science, Medicine, Technical, Journals
1986-87: 17 titles *Founded:* 1982

Celebrity Educational Publishers, 85 Genting Lane 09-04B, Singapore 1334 Tel: 7446453 Fax: 7477536
Man Dir, Editorial: Christopher S C Tan; *Sales:* Henry K H Ng; *Production, Publicity:* Lily Tay
Subsidiary Company: Willet Children's Books Australia, PO Box 98, Walkerville 5081, South Australia, Australia
Subjects: English Language, Science, Children's Literature
1986: 2 titles *Founded:* 1983
ISBN Publisher's Prefix: 9971-44

Chopmen Publishers*, 865 Mountbatten Rd 05-28/29, Katong Shopping Centre, Singapore 1543 Tel: 3441495 Cable Add: Nirmalji Singapore
Man Dir: N T S Chopra
Subjects: Reference, Social & General Science, Fiction, General, Religion, Poetry, Asiatic Studies, University & Secondary Textbooks, Paperbacks, Educational Materials
Founded: 1966
Miscellaneous: Also Literary Agent (qv)
ISBN Publisher's Prefix: 9971-68

Dynasty Books, an imprint of Times Editions/Les Editions du Pacifique (qv)

Educational Publications Bureau Pte Ltd, Block 162, Bukit Merah Central 04-3545, Singapore 0315 Tel: 2780881 Telex: EPB RS 56289 Fax: 2782456
General Manager: Au Pui Chuan; *Senior Editor:* Paula Mary Grosse; *Marketing:* Benson Yow Choong Kwong; *Production:* Steven Tan Cheng Huat
Parent Company: Singapore National Printers Ltd, 303 Upper Serangoon Rd, Singapore 1334
Subject: Educational
Bookshops: EPB Bedok, 204 Bedok North Street 1, 01-423, Singapore 1646 Tel: 4437980; EPB Bukit Merah, 161 Bukit Merah Central 01-3719, Singapore 0315 Tel: 2730092; EPB Clementi, 450 Clementi Ave 3, 01-297, Singapore 0512 Tel: 7770052; EPB Clementi West, 725 Clementi West St 2, 01-206, Singapore 0512 Tel: 2780881; EPB Outram Park, 20 Outram Park 02-187/213, Singapore 0316 Tel: 2202377
1985: 331 titles *1986:* 198 titles *Founded:* 1980

F E P International Private Ltd*, 348 Jalan Boon Lay, Jurong, Singapore 2261 Tel: 2650311 Cable Add: Bookmark Telex: Fep rs 25601
General Manager: Richard Toh; *Publishing Manager, Rights & Permissions:* Wong Sek Ohn; *Publishing:* Dr S Ramalingam (Science and Maths), Ms Goh Bee Choo (Language and Arts)
Branch Offs: Australia, Egypt, Ghana, Hong Kong, India, Jamaica, Kenya, Lesotho, Malaysia, Nigeria, Pakistan, Philippines, Swaziland, Thailand, Trinidad, UK, Zimbabwe
Subjects: Textbooks, Children's, Reference, Dictionaries, Encyclopaedias (in English, Chinese, Malay, Arabic)

Founded: 1960
Miscellaneous: Firm is also a large offset printer specializing in colour work
ISBN Publisher's Prefix: 9971-1

Federal Publications (S) (Pte) Ltd+, Times Jurong, 2 Jurong Port Rd, Singapore 2261 Tel: 2658855 Cable Add: Fedpubs, Singapore Telex: rs 35846 Fax: 2685979
General Manager: Y H Mew; *Managing Editor:* Valerie Barth; *Marketing Manager:* T Y Cheong
Parent Company: Times Publishing Group, 1 New Industrial Rd, Singapore 1953
Associate Companies: Federal Publications (HK) Ltd, Hong Kong (qv); Federal Publications Sdn Bhd, Malaysia (qv); STP Distributors Sdn Bhd (qv under Major Booksellers); Times Books International (qv); Times Periodicals Pte Ltd
Subjects: Educational, Children's, General, Reference
1985: 241 titles *Founded:* 1957
ISBN Publisher's Prefix: 9971-4

Gunung Agung (S) Pte Ltd, now Masagung Books Pte Ltd (qv)

Harper & Row Publishers, Asia, Pte Ltd, 37 Jalan Pemimpin 02-01, Singapore 2057 Tel: 2583577/2581954 Cable Add: Harpernrow Telex: rs 28212 Harsin
Man Dir: Steven Goh Lai Hock; *Sales Executive:* Bernard Tang
Parent Company: Harper & Row Publishers Inc, 10 East 53rd St, New York, NY 10022, USA
Associate Company: Harper & Row Ltd, UK (qv for other Associate Companies)
Subjects: General, Social Sciences, Medicine, Humanities
Founded: 1984

Heinemann Educational Books (Asia) Ltd*, 41 Jalan Pemimpin 03-05, Singapore 2057 Tel: 2583255 Telex: rs 24299 Hebooks
Man Dir: Charles Cher; *Manager (Production):* Haji Basri Sumanee; *Marketing:* Andrew Yeo Siew Thong, Jimmy Quek
Parent Company: The Heinemann Group of Publishers Ltd, UK (qv)
Subjects: Educational, Textbooks, Fiction
ISBN Publisher's Prefix: 9971-64

The **Insight Chronicles**, an imprint of Apa Productions (Pte) Ltd (qv)

Insight Guides, an imprint of Apa Productions (Pte) Ltd (qv)

Institute of Southeast Asian Studies+, Heng Mui Keng Terrace, Pasir Panjang, Singapore 0511 Tel: 7780955 Cable Add: Iseas Telex: rs 37068 Iseas Fax: 7781735
Dir: Kernial S Sandhu; *Editorial, Sales, Production, Publicity, Rights & Permissions:* Triena Ong; *Librarian:* Mrs Lim Pui Huen
Subjects: Politics and Strategic Studies, Economics and Social Change in Southeast Asia
1985: 36 titles *1986:* 36 titles *Founded:* 1968
ISBN Publisher's Prefix: 9971-902

Longman Singapore (Pte) Ltd, 25 First Lok Yang Rd, Jurong Town, Singapore 2262 Tel: 2682666 Cable Add: Freegrove Singapore Telex: Lms rs 24268 Fax: 2641740
Man Dir: James B Ho; *Executive Dirs:* Lim Soo Heng, Robert Chan Siew Fun; *Editorial, Publicity, Rights & Permissions:* Michelle Lie (Educational), Sheila Murugasu (Professional); *Sales:* Daniel Chew (Educational), John Lim (Professional); *Production:* David Chng
Parent Company: Longman Group UK Ltd, UK (qv)

Subjects: Textbooks, Medicine, Science, Technology, Professional
1985: 119 titles *Founded:* 1982

McGraw-Hill International Book Co+*, 348 Jalan Boon Lay, Jurong, Singapore 2261 Tel: 2654633 Cable Add: McGrawbook Singapore Telex: rs 36791 McGraw Fax: 2652972
Man Dir: R Radhakrishnan
Parent Company: McGraw-Hill Inc, 1221 Ave of the Americas, New York, NY 10020, USA
Associate Companies: See McGraw-Hill Book Co (UK) Ltd, UK
Subject: Educational Materials
Founded: 1969

Macmillan Southeast Asia Pte Ltd*, 41 Jalan Pemimpin 03-04, Singapore 2057 Tel: 2521337 Cable Add: Publish Singapore Telex: rs 23196
Executive Dir: Loh Mun Wai
Parent Company: Macmillan Publishers Ltd, UK (qv)

Malayan Law Journal (Pte) Ltd, 3 Shenton Way 14-03, Shenton House, Singapore 0106 Tel: 2203684 Cable Add: Malool Telex: rs 28904 Mljlaw
Chairman, Chief Executive, Man Dir, Publicity: Amir Mallal; *Man Dir, Editorial, Production, Rights & Permissions:* Al-Mansor Adabi; *Sales:* Y Jamalluddin
Parent Company: Butterworth & Co (Publishers) Ltd, UK (qv)
Branch Off: Malayan Law Journal (Pte) Ltd, Malaysia (qv)
Subjects: Law, Accountancy, Tax
Bookshops: At above main and branch office addresses
1985-86: 11 titles *Founded:* 1932
ISBN Publisher's Prefix: 9971-70

Malaysia Press Sdn Bhd*, 745-747 North Bridge Rd, Singapore 0719 Tel: 2933454
Dir: Hassan Bin Omar; *Man Dir:* Abu Talib Bin Ally; *Publicity, Advertising:* Dawood Bin Omar, Salleh Bin Abu Talib
Subsidiary Company: Pustaka Melayu (at above address)
Subjects: School Textbooks, Educational Books in the Malay language
Founded: 1962

Manhattan Press (Singapore) Pte Ltd+*, Apt Blk 144 Viking Rd 01-91, Singapore 0315 Tel: 2788111 Cable Add: Pacolmac Telex: rs 36496 Pacman Fax: 2780303
Man Dir: Seow Kui Lim; *Assistant General Manager:* Catherine Ngien
Parent Company: Pan Pacific Book Distributors (S) Pte Ltd (qv)
Associate Companies: Eastview Productions Sdn Bhd, Malaysia (qv); Manhattan Press (HK) Ltd, Room 1006 Guardforce Centre, 3 Hok Yuen St East, Hung Hom, Kowloon, Hong Kong Tel: (03) 3638249/ 3638240
Subjects: Education, Textbooks, Children's, General, Reference
Bookshops: As under Pan Pacific Book Distributors (S) Pte Ltd (qv)
Founded: 1979

Maruzen Asia (Pte) Ltd*, Pasir Panjang PO Box 67, Singapore 9111 (Located at: 51 Ayer Rajah Crescent 07-05/17, Singapore 0513) Tel: 7759844 Telex: Mapore rs 26521 Cable Add: Maruzen Singapore
Man Dir, Editorial: Yuki Hatori; *Marketing:* David Tan
Parent Company: Maruzen Co Ltd, Japan (qv)
Associate Company: Maruzen International Co Ltd, New York, USA
Subjects: Technical, Social and Medical Sciences, Asian Studies
Founded: 1978

Masagung Books Pte Ltd, 140 Paya Lebar Rd, 02-03 A-Z Bldg, Singapore 1440 Tel: 7469291/7469298 Cable Add: Gasing Singapore Telex: rs 34500 A/B Gasing
Chairman: Haji Masagung; *Manager:* Tan Tho Quek
Parent Company: CV Haji Masagung
Subjects: Indonesia, South East Asia, Asia
Bookshop: See under Major Booksellers
Founded: 1980

Pustaka **Nasional** Pte Ltd*, Beach Rd 13-11, Shaw Towers, Singapore 0718 Tel: 2941917/8 Cable Add: Hudaya Telex: rs 25521 Smcc Pn
Subjects: Malay and Arabic books
ISBN Publisher's Prefix: 9971-77

Oxford University Press Pte Ltd, Unit 221, UBI Ave 4, Intrepid Warehouse Complex, Singapore 1440 Tel: 2853766 Cable Add: Oxonian Singapore Telex: rs 37960 Oxpres
Manager: Goh Teow Huat
Subjects: Educational, General, Academic
Miscellaneous: Firm is a branch of Oxford University Press, UK (qv)

P G Publishing Pte Ltd, Alexandra PO Box 318, Singapore 9115 Tel: 2357700/ 2350006 Cable Add: PG Pub Telex: rs 39967
Man Dir, Editorial: Ms P G Chan; *Sales, Rights & Permissions:* Ms Chiam Soo Lee; *Publicity:* George Tan
Subsidiary Company: P G Lim Pte Ltd, Suite 0609 Mount Elizabeth Medical Centre, Mount Elizabeth Rd, Singapore 0922
Imprints: PG Asian Economy Editions, PG Originals, PG-Positive Health Guide series
Subjects: Medical
Bookshop: PG Lucky Plaza Medical Books, 304 Orchard Rd, 04-22 Lucky Plaza, Singapore 0923
Founded: 1983
ISBN Publisher's Prefixes: 9971-909, 9971-973

Les Editions du **Pacifique**, an imprint of Times Editions (qv)

Pan Pacific Book Distributors (S) Pte Ltd+*, Apt Blk 144 Viking Rd 01-91, Singapore 0315 Tel: 2788111 Cable Add: Pacolmac Telex: rs 36496 Pacman Fax: 2780303
Man Dir: Seow Kui Lim; *Assistant General Manager:* Catherine Ngien; *Assistant Sales and Marketing Manager:* Lim Eng Wee
Subsidiary Company: Manhattan Press (Singapore) Pte Ltd (qv)
Associate Companies: Eastview Productions Sdn Bhd, Malaysia (qv); Manhattan Press (HK) Ltd, Room 1006 Guardforce Centre, 3 Hok Yuen St East, Hung Hom, Kowloon, Hong Kong Tel: 3638249/ 3638240
Subjects: Pre-school materials, Secondary and Primary Textbooks, Reference, General Literature
Bookshops: Anthonian Private Ltd, Apt Blk 231, 9 Bain St, Bras Basah Complex, Singapore 0718 Tel: 3373581/3363312; Pacific Book Centre (S) Pte Ltd (qv under Major Booksellers)
Founded: 1971
ISBN Publisher's Prefix: 9971-63

Select Books Pte Ltd, 19 Tanglin Rd 03-15, Tanglin Shopping Centre, Singapore 1024 Tel: 7321515 Cable Add: Selbooks Telex: RS 38419 Sm
Man Dir, Editorial, Production: Lena U Wen Lim; *Sales, Publicity:* Joyce Chia
Subjects: Urban Planning, Environment, Third World Development, Southeast Asia
Bookshop: See under Major Booksellers
1985: 1 title *1986:* 1 title *Founded:* 1976

Shing Lee Book Store+*, 120 Hillview Ave 05-06/07, Kewalram Hillview, Singapore 2366 Tel: 7601388 Cable Add: Shingbook Telex: rs 39255 Bai
General Manager: Peh Chin Hua; *Sales Manager:* Peh Chin Thye; *Publishing:* Ms Peh Soh Ngoh
Associate Company: Singapore Book Emporium (qv)
Branch Offs: Booklines Associated International (HK) Co, Hong Kong; Booklines Associated International (M) Sdn Bhd, Malaysia
Subjects: Textbooks, Children's, Reference, Dictionaries, Cookery, General (in English, Malay and Chinese)
Founded: 1935
ISBN Publisher's Prefix: 9971-66

Simon & Schuster (Asia) Pte Ltd, 24 Pasir Panjang Rd 04-31, PSA Multi Storey Complex, Singapore 0511 Tel: 2789611 Cable Add: Prenhall Singapore Telex: rs 37270 Phsea Fax: 2734400
Man Dir: Stephen M Smith; *Business Manager:* Peter Goh; *Regional Sales Manager:* Gunawan Hadi; *Trade Sales Manager:* P C Than; *Operations and Advertising Manager:* Iris Low
Parent Company: Simon and Schuster Inc, 1230 Ave of the Americas, New York, NY 10020, USA
Associate Company: Prentice-Hall (Simon & Schuster International Group), UK (qv for other associate companies)
Branch Off: Pacific Centre, 10th Floor, Bank of America Bldg, 1 Kowloon Park Drive, Tsim Sha Tsui, Kowloon, Hong Kong
Subjects: Belles Lettres, Poetry, History, How-to, Music, Art, Philosophy, Reference, Travel Guides, Religion, Medicine, Psychology, Engineering, Computer Textbooks, General and Social Science, University Textbooks, Management, English as a Second Language, Educational and Audio Materials
Founded: 1975
ISBN Publisher's Prefixes: 0-13 (Prentice-Hall and Parker), 0-668 (Arco), 0-89303 (Brady), 0-87624 (Institute of Business Planning), 0-87909/0-8359 (Reston), 0-8385 (Appleton-Lange), 0-87628 (Center for Applied Research in Education), 0-205 (Allyn and Bacon), 0-671 (Simon and Schuster)

Singapore Book Emporium+*, 120 Hillview Ave 05-06/07, Kewalram Hillview, Singapore 2366 Tel: 7601388 Cable Add: Shingbook Telex: rs 39255 Bai
Managing Chairman: Peh Boon Poh; *Deputy Chairman:* Mrs Peh Boon Poh; *Man Dir:* Peh Chin Hua; *Publishing Dir:* Peh Soh Ngoh
Associate Company: Shing Lee Book Store (qv)
Branch Offs: Booklines Associated International (HK) Co, Hong Kong; Booklines Associated International (M) Sdn Bhd, Malaysia
Subjects: Textbooks, Children's, Reference, Dictionaries, Cookery, General
Founded: 1961
ISBN Publisher's Prefix: 9971-61

Singapore University Press Pte Ltd, National University of Singapore, Kent Ridge, Singapore 0511 Tel: 7761148/ 7756666 ext 323 Cable Add: Singpress
Manager, Editor: Patricia Tay
Subjects: Scholarly studies in the Arts and Social Sciences with emphasis on Southeast Asia, Sciences, Medicine, Accountancy and Management Studies, Law, Pedagogy, Bibliographies, Periodicals

1986-87: 20 titles *Founded:* 1971
ISBN Publisher's Prefix: 9971-69

Southeast Asian Ministers of Education Organization (SEAMEO), Regional Language Centre (RELC), see International section (International Organizations)

Stamford College Publishers*, 218 Queen St, Singapore 0718 Tel: 3373144/8 Telex: rs 25596
Man Dir, Publicity: L P Nicol; *Editorial:* L Thomas; *Sales:* J Dennis; *Production:* Mr Arangasamy
Branch Off: Stamford Executive Bookshop, Petaling Jaya, Malaysia
Subjects: Educational Books
Bookshop: At above address
1985: 10 titles *Founded:* 1970
ISBN Publisher's Prefix: 9971-83

Times Books International+, Times Centre, 1 New Industrial Rd, Singapore 1953 Tel: 2848844 Cable Add: Times Telex: rs 25713 Fax: 2881186
Man Dir, Rights & Permissions: Shirley Hew; *Editorial:* Shova Loh; *Sales, Publicity:* Seah Tzi Yan; *Production:* Jenny Soh
Parent Company: Times Publishing Group (at above address)
Subsidiary Company: Straits Times Press Singapore
Associate Companies: Federal Publications (S) (Pte) Ltd (qv); Times The Bookshop (qv under Major Booksellers); Reed Books Pty Ltd, Australia (qv); Federal Publications Ltd, Hong Kong (qv); Times Publishing Bhd, Japan; Far East Publications, Thailand; Marshall Cavendish Books Ltd, UK (qv); Marshall Cavendish Corporation, 575 Lexington Ave, New York, NY 10022, USA
Branch Off: Times Books International, Malaysia (qv)
Subjects: Asian Cookery, Asian Customs and Traditions, Politics, Social Commentary, Tropical Gardening, Literature & Creative Writing
1985: 55 titles *1986:* 60 titles *Founded:* 1979
ISBN Publisher's Prefix: 9971-65

Times Editions/Les Editions du Pacifique+, 422 Thomson Rd, Singapore 1129 Tel: 2550011 Telex: rs 37908 Edtime Fax: 2532562
Man Dir: Didier Millet; *Editors:* Olivier Canaveso, Tan Kok Eng, Jean-Claude Le Cardinal, Angelina Philips, Gretchen Lin; *Marketing Manager:* Charles Orwin
Parent Company: Times Publishing Group, 1 New Industrial Rd, Singapore 1953
Imprints: Dynasty Books, Les Editions du Pacifique
Subjects: Travel, Natural Science, History, Non-fiction, Cookery, Aerial Photography, Illustrated, Gift books
1985: 36 titles *1986:* 40 titles *Founded:* 1984
ISBN Publisher's Prefixes: 2-85700, 9971-40

Toppan Co (S) Pte Ltd, PO Box 22, Jurong Town Post Office, Singapore 2262 (Located at: 38 Liu Fang Rd, Jurong, Singapore 2262) Tel: 2656666/2656105 Cable Add: Toppan Singapore Telex: rs 21596 Fax: 2658298
Man Dir: Chu Bong; *Project Dir:* Y Kawada
Parent Company: Toppan Co Ltd, Japan (qv)
Associate Company: Froebel-Kan Co Ltd, Japan (qv)
Subjects: Agriculture, Biochemistry, Biology, Botany, Chemistry, Civil, Electrical and Industrial Engineering, Earth Sciences, Economics, Mathematics, Mechanics, Medicine, Physiology, Physics, Statistics, Zoology

The **World Book** Co (Pte) Ltd*, Block 231 Bain St 04-57, Bras Basah Complex, Singapore 0718 Tel: 2225755 Telex: rs 36020
Publisher: Chou Cheng Chuen; *Man Dir:* C N Chou; *Publication Manager:* Tommy Chung; *Editor:* Loh Siew Tuck
Branch Offs: Brunei, Hong Kong, Malaysia
Subjects: Educational, General, Periodicals (English and Chinese)
Founded: 1930
ISBN Publisher's Prefix: 9971-3

World Scientific Publishing Co Pte Ltd+, PO Box 128, Singapore 9128 (Located at: Farrer Rd, Singapore) Tel: 2786188 Cable Add: Cospub Singapore Telex: RS 28561 Wspc
Man Dir: Ms D Liu; *Senior Scientific Editor:* Dr Jose C Martinez; *Editor:* Miss G K Tan; *Assistant Manager:* Miss Sherlyn Tan (Sales), Miss S W Chan (Marketing, Promotion)
Subjects: Physics, Mathematics, Biology, Medicine, Computer Science, Engineering
1985: 79 titles *Founded:* 1980
ISBN Publisher's Prefixes: 9971-83, 9971-966, 9971-950, 9971-978, 9971-50

Literary Agents

Chopmen Publishers*, 865 Mountbatten Rd 05-28/29, Katong Shopping Centre, Singapore 1543
Contact: N T S Chopra
Also Publisher (qv)

Major Booksellers

Asia Book Co, Block 52, Chin Swee Rd 03-71, Singapore 0316 Tel: 5343186/5343188/5343420
Manager: William Chong

East and West Centre Pte Ltd*, 124 First Floor, Bt Timah Plaza, Jalan Anak Bukit, Singapore 2158

Educational Aids Production Co Pte Ltd*, 33 Beo Crescent, Singapore 3

Educational Book Centre Pte Ltd*, 69 Stamford Rd, Singapore 0617 Tel: 3377731

Far East Book Co, now known as East and West Centre Pte Ltd (qv)

Hashim bin Haji Abdullah*, 134 Arab St, Singapore 0719 Tel: 2987196

M P H Bookstores (S) Pte Ltd, 71-77 Stamford Rd, Singapore 0617 Tel: 3363633/3361821 Cable Add: Empress Singapore Telex: RS 35853 Mphmag
Branches: MPH Parkway Parade Tel: 3481483; MPH Robinson Rd Tel: 2226423; MPH Centrepoint Basement Tel: 2356938; MPH Centrepoint Level 4 Tel: 7344010; MPH Changi Airport Tel: 5420744
Also Wholesalers, MPH Distributors (S) Pte Ltd, 601 Sims Drive 03-07/21, Pan-I Complex, Singapore 1438 Tel: 7471088

Masagung Books Pte Ltd, 140 Paya Lebar Rd, 02-03 A-Z Bldg, Singapore 1440 Tel: 7469298/7469291 Telex: rs 34500 A/B Gasing
Also Publisher (qv)

Modern Book Store*, 34 Bras Basah Rd, Singapore 7

Pacific Book Centre (S) Pte Ltd, Apt Blk 144 Viking Rd 01-91, Singapore 0315 Tel: 4736222 Cable Add: Pacolmac Telex: rs 36496 Pacman
Managing Dir: Low Tai Ee; *Manager:* Lawrence Tan
Also: Alexandra Branch, Apt Blk 136, 01-155 Alexandra Rd, Singapore 0315 Tel: 4740577; Bras Basah Branch, Bain St, 02-69 Block 231, Bras Basah Complex, Singapore 0718 Tel: 3381024; Havelock Branch, Apt Blk 22, 01-675 Havelock Rd, Singapore 0316 Tel: 2724326; Jurong East Branch, Block 130 01-221, Jurong East St 13, Singapore 2365 Tel: 5666153; Pasir Panjang Branch, 02-02 PSA Bldg, 460 Alexandra Rd, Singapore 0512 Tel: 2781090; Queenstown Branch, Apt Blk 6C, 01-48 Margaret Drive, Singapore 0314 Tel: 4745701
Owned by: Pan Pacific Book Distributors (S) Pte Ltd (qv)

S T P Distributors Sdn Bhd, Times Centre, 1 New Industrial Rd, Singapore 1953 Tel: 2848844/2872233 Cable Add: Stpsales Singapore Telex: rs 28068 STP Fax: 2881186
Divisional General Manager: Thomas Heng; *Assistant General Manager:* Andrew Chua Kim Poh
Owned by: Times Publishing Group

Select Books Pte Ltd, 19 Tanglin Rd 03-15, Tanglin Shopping Center, Singapore 1024 Tel: 7321515
Man Dir: Lena U Wen Lim
Also Publisher (qv)

Shanghai Book Co Pte Ltd, 81 Victoria St, Singapore 0718 Tel: 3360144 Cable Add: Shoobook Telex: Khnco RS 29297 Shoobook attn Mrs Tan
Manager: Wang Hung Jen

Times The Bookshop, Times Centre, 1 New Industrial Rd, Singapore 1953 Tel: 2848844 Cable Add: Times Singapore Telex: RS 25713 Fax: 2881186
Manager: Arthur Lee
Branches: 19 in Singapore
Owned by: Times Publishing Group

University Book Store, 160 Orchard Rd, 02-07 Orchard Point, Singapore 0923 Tel: 2354206

The **World Book** Co (Pte) Ltd, Block 231, Bain St, 04-57 Bras Basah Complex, Singapore 0718 Tel: 3382323 Telex: rs 36020 Wbksin Fax: 3371186
Manager: Tommy Chung

Major Libraries

American Library Resource Center*, American Embassy, 30 Hill St, Singapore 0617

Nanyang University Library, merged in 1980 with the former University of Singapore to form the National University of Singapore Library (see below)

National Archives, 140 Hill St Bldg, Hill St, Singapore 0617

National Library, Stamford Rd, Singapore 0617 Tel: 3377355 Cable Add: Natlib Singapore Telex: rs 26620 Fax: 3309611
Dir: Mrs Hedwig Anuar
Publications include: Accessions List (monthly); *Annual Report*; *Checklist of Current Serials*; *Government Services Directory* (second edition); *The Memoranda of Books Registered in the 'Catalogue of Books Printed or Published in Singapore' under the Provisions of the*

Printers and Publishers Act; *Singapore National Bibliography* (quarterly, with annual supplement); *Singapore Periodicals Index* (annual); *Union Catalogue of Scientific and Technical Serials*; *Masterlist of Southeast Asian Microforms Supplement*; Bibliographies, booklists, library guides (periodically)

National University of Singapore Library, Kent Ridge, Singapore 0511 Tel: 7722069
Telex: 51112 Nusbur Fax: 7773571
Chief Librarian: Peggy Wai Chee Hochstadt
Publications include: Catalogue of Singapore/Malaysia Collection and Supplements; Accessions List (monthly); *Catalogue of Audiovisual Resources*; *Index to Periodical Articles relating to Singapore, Malaysia, Brunei and ASEAN*; *Singapore Conference Index*; *Annual Report*; handbooks and guides to the various libraries of the National University of Singapore Library System

Library Association

Library Association of Singapore, c/o National Library, Stamford Rd, Singapore 0617
Honorary Secretary: Shirley See-Toh Wai Keong
Publications include: Directory of Libraries in Singapore (1983); *LAS Newsletter* (quarterly); *Singapore Libraries* (annual); *Standards for Bibliographical Compilations* (1980); *Universal Bibliografical Control in Southeast Asia: Conference Papers and Proceedings* (1976); *Who's Who in Singapore Librarianship* (1976)

Library Reference Books and Journals

Books

Directory of Libraries in Singapore, Library Association of Singapore, c/o National Library, Stamford Rd, Singapore 0617

Singapore Libraries (annual), Library Association of Singapore, c/o National Library, Stamford Rd, Singapore 0617

Journals

Checklist of Current Serials, National Library, Stamford Rd, Singapore 0617

LAS Newsletter (quarterly), Library Association of Singapore, Stamford Rd, Singapore 0617

Singapore Periodicals Index, National Library, Stamford Rd, Singapore 0617

Literary Associations and Societies

Chinese Language and Literary Society*, Jurong Rd, Singapore 22
Publication: Hsin Sheng

Literary Periodical

Hsin Sheng (New Life), Chinese Language and Literary Society, Jurong Rd, Singapore 22

Literary Prizes

National Book Development Council of Singapore Book Awards
First awarded in 1976 for outstanding works of creative and non-creative writing by local authors in any of the four official languages (Malay, English, Chinese, and Tamil). The awards are for fiction, poetry, drama, non-fiction, and children's and young people's books. Up to fifteen prizes of 500 to 1,000 Singapore dollars. Awarded every two years. Enquiries to National Book Development Council of Singapore, c/o Bukit Merah Branch Library, Bukit Merah Central, Singapore 0315

Somalia

General Information

Note: No replies were received to questionnaires sent to Somalia for this edition of *International Literary Market Place*. The information given in the 1987-88 edition has been repeated here but should be treated with caution.

Language: Somali is the national language; Arabic, Italian and English are official languages and widely spoken. Swahili in southern coastal towns
Religion: Islamic
Population: 4.6 million
Bank Hours: 0800-1130 Saturday-Thursday
Shop Hours: 0800-1230, 1630-1900 Saturday-Thursday
Currency: 100 cents = 1 Somali or Samli shilling
Export/Import Information: No tariff on books; advertising matter distributed gratis is not dutied, otherwise Revenue and Customs Duty charged. Also Administration and Wharfage Taxes. Exchange controls

Publishers

Government Printer*, Ministry of Information, Mogadishu

Somalia d'Oggi*, Piazzale della Garesa, PO Box 315, Mogadishu
Subjects: Law, Economics

Major Booksellers

Samater's Bookshop*, PO Box 936, Mogadishu

Major Libraries

Local Government Council Library*, Hargeisa

National Library of Higher Education and Culture*, Ministry of Higher Education and Culture, Mogadishu

Biblioteca dell' **Universita Nazionale** della Somalia*, PO Box 15, Mogadishu Tel: 2535

Republic of South Africa

General Information

Language: English and Afrikaans
Religion: Predominantly Protestant. Politically most important is the Dutch Reformed Church (about 3 million adherents). About 1.8 million Methodists, 1.5 million Anglicans, 1.2 million Roman Catholics. Most of the black population belongs to separatist churches, combining traditional and Christian beliefs
Population: 28.4 million
Bank Hours: 0900-1530 Monday-Friday; 0830-1100 Saturday
Shop Hours: Vary province to province. Often 0830-1700 Monday-Friday; 0830-1300 Saturday
Currency: 100 cents = 1 rand
Export/Import Information: No tariffs on books or advertising matter. No import licence required. No obscene literature permitted.
Copyright: Berne (see International section)

Book Trade Organizations

Associated Booksellers of Southern Africa Ltd*, PO Box 326, Howard Place 7450 Tel: (021) 538907
Secretary: P G van Rooyen

Book Trade Association of South Africa*, PO Box 326, Howard Place 7450 Tel: (021) 538907 Telex: 526713

Directorate of Publications*, Private Bag 9069, Cape Town 8000 Tel: (021) 456518
Telex: 5721667
Dir: Prof Dr A Coetzee
See also Publications Appeal Board below

Overseas Publishers' Representatives Association of Southern Africa, PO Box 371, Isando 1600 Tel: (011) 9741181
Secretary: J Savage

Publications Appeal Board*, Private Bag X114, Pretoria 001 Tel: (012) 36353
Telex: 53668
Appellate tribunal from the Directorate of Publications (qv)

South African Publishers' Association, PO Box 326, Howard Place 7450 Tel: (021) 538907
Secretary: P G van Rooyen

Standard Book Numbering Agency, State Library, PO Box 397, Pretoria 0001 Tel: (012) 218931 Telex: SA 322171
ISBN Administrator: Mrs B C Kellermann

Book Trade Reference Books and Journals

Books

Books in Print South Africa, Cedarwood Text, PO Box 51254, Randburg 2125

Catalogue of Books (English) Published in Southern Africa, Still in Print (1970), C Struik, Corner Wale and Loop Sts, PO Box 1144, Cape Town

Journals

Central News, Central News Agency Ltd, PO Box 10799, Johannesburg 2000
Trade organ published by CNA, the large

bookselling chain with branches throughout the country
Index to South African Periodicals, Johannesburg Public Library, Market Sq, Johannesburg 2001
South African National Bibliography, The State Library, Vermeulen St, PO Box 397, Pretoria 0001
Text in Afrikaans, Bantu languages and English, published since 1933; annual volume and quarterly cumulations; also available as a weekly card service

Publishers

Acacia Books, an imprint of Via Afrika Ltd (qv)

Africasouth Paperbacks, an imprint of David Philip Publisher (Pty) Ltd (qv)

B L A C Publishing House*, PO Box 17, Athlone, Cape Town
Man Dir: James Matthews
Subjects: General Fiction, Belles Lettres, Poetry, Paperbacks
Founded: 1974

A A **Balkema** Publishers*, PO Box 3117, Cape Town (Located at: 93 Keerom St, Cape Town) Tel: (021) 442866 Cable Add: Balkema Cape Town
Man Dir: A A Balkema
Head Office: A A Balkema, Netherlands (qv)
Subjects: African and Oriental Studies, Palaeontology, Archaeology, Botany, Zoology, Ecology, Agriculture, Soil Engineering, Mining
Founded: 1930
ISBN Publisher's Prefix: 0-86961

Jonathan **Ball** Publishers (Pty) Ltd*, PO Box 548, Bergvlei, Sandton 2012 Telex: 424235 SA
Man Dir, Rights & Permissions: Jonathan Augustus Ball; *Sales:* Nicholas Britt
Orders to: Hodder & Stoughton Southern Africa (at above address)
Branch Off: PO Box 435, Eppindust, Cape 7475
Subjects: South African History & Politics, African Interest, Fiction
Founded: 1977
ISBN Publisher's Prefix: 0-86850

Bible Society of South Africa, PO Box 6215, Roggebaai, Cape Town 8012 (Located at: 15 Anton Anreith Arcade, Roggebaai, Cape Town) Tel: (021) 212040 Cable Add: Testaments Cape Town Telex: 527964
Chief Executive, General Secretary, Rights & Permissions: Rev G E van der Merwe; *Sales, Production:* Rev A Stranex; *Publicity:* N Turley
Imprints: Bible Society, Bybelgenootskap
Branch Offs: Bloemfontein, Cape Town, Durban, Kempton Park, Kwazulu, Port Elizabeth, Soweto
Subjects: Bibles, Scriptural Selections, Bible Society historical research material, Bible translation and research aids
Bookshops: 65 Maitland St, Bloemfontein 9301; 15 Anton Anreith Arcade, Roggebaai, Cape Town 8001; 97 Russell St, Durban 4001; Bible House, 18 Central Ave, Kempton Park 1620; Bible House, 31 Cotswold Ave, Cotswold, Port Elizabeth 6045; Bible House, Stand 5080, Zone 5, Pimville, Soweto 1808
1985: 19 titles *1986:* 31 titles *Founded:* 1820 (as auxiliary of British & Foreign Bible Society), 1965 as autonomous body
ISBN Publisher's Prefix: 0-7982

Books of Africa (Pty) Ltd, PO Box 1516, Cape Town 8000 (Located at: 39 Atlantic Rd, Muizenberg 7951) Tel: (021) 888316
Man Dir, Rights & Permissions: T V Bulpin; *Sales:* M Bulpin; *Production, Art:* Solveig Stibbe
Subsidiary Company: T V Bulpin Publications
Subjects: Biography, History, Africana, Art
1986: 6 titles *Founded:* 1962
ISBN Publisher's Prefix: 0-949956

The **Brenthurst** Press (Pty) Ltd, PO Box 87184, Houghton 2041 (Located at: Federation Rd, Parktown, Johannesburg) Tel: (011) 6466024
Chief Executive: Cynthia Kemp
Subjects: Africana (fine editions of hitherto unpublished works from the private library of H F Oppenheimer of Johannesburg)
1986: 1 title *1987:* 1 title *Founded:* 1974
ISBN Publisher's Prefix: 0-909079

T V **Bulpin** Publications, a subsidiary of Books of Africa (Pty) Ltd (qv)

Butterworth Publishers (Pty) Ltd*, PO Box 792, Durban 4000 (Located at: 8 Walter Pl, Waterval Park, Mayville, Durban 4001) Tel: (031) 294247 Cable Add: Butterlaw Durban
Man Dir: Colin Chisholm
Subjects: Law, Medicine, Science & Technology, University Textbooks
1985: 260 titles Founded: 1935
ISBN Publisher's Prefix: 0-409

Bybelgenootskap, an imprint of Bible Society of South Africa (qv)

C M P Reprints, an imprint of Sasavona Publishers & Booksellers (qv)

C N A, see Central News Agency Ltd

C U M Books (Pty) Ltd, see Christian Publishing Co

Calvyn-Jubileumboekefonds, PO Box 20004, Noordbrug 2522 Tel: (01481) 23986
Associate Company: Interkerklike Uitgewerstrust (qv)

Killie **Campbell** Africana Library, an imprint of University of Natal Press (qv)

Centaur Publishers (Pty) Ltd, PO Box 1144, Cape Town 8000 Tel: (021) 216740 Cable Add: Dekena Telex: 526713 Fax: (021) 216744
Man Dir: G Struik; *Editorial Dir:* P Borchert; *Sales, Publicity, Rights & Permissions:* J D Wilkins; *Production Dir:* W Reinders
Parent Company: Struik Holdings (Pty) Ltd (at above address)
Associate Companies: Map Studio, PO Box 11204, Johannesburg 2000; Struik Book Distributors (Pty) Ltd; SA Readers Choice (Pty) Ltd; Struik Publishers (qv); Struik-Winchester
Subject: General
Founded: 1981

Central News Agency Ltd+*, PO Box 10799, Johannesburg 2000 (Located at: Laub St, New Centre, Johannesburg) Tel: (011) 8361711
Subjects: General, Paperbacks
Bookshops: See under Major Booksellers

Century Hutchinson SA Pty Ltd, PO Box 337, Bergvlei 2012 Tel: (011) 7862983 Cable Add: Hutchbooks Telex: 423981
Man Dir: Pieter Snyman
Associate Company: Century Hutchinson Ltd, UK (qv)

Subjects: General Fiction & Non-fiction, Belles Lettres, Poetry, University & Secondary Textbooks, Paperbacks, Juvenile
Founded: 1966

Christian Publishing Co — CUM Books (Pty) Ltd, PO Box 38, Roodepoort 1725 (Located at: Baanbreker Ave 2, Helderkruin, Roodepoort 1725) Tel: (011) 7642460 Cable Add: Chrispub Telex: 425847
Chairman: J J M Jacobs; *Publishers:* Freddie Crous, Koos van Niekerk
Imprints: CUM Books (Pty) Ltd, Digma Publications
Subjects: Religion, Law, General
Founded: 1939

Church Publishing Trust, see Interkerklike Uitgewerstrust

College of Careers (Pty) Ltd*, PO Box 2081, Cape Town 8000 (Located at: Print Centre, Wesley St, Cape Town 8001) Tel: (021) 452041/452051
Man Dir: Richard S Pooler; *Editorial:* C Ruse
Imprints: College of Careers Study Aids; College Tutorial Press; Faircape Books; Outlines
Subjects: Educational, General
Founded: 1946
ISBN Publisher's Prefixes: 0-7985 (Study Aids), 0-949945 (College Tutorial Press)

College Tutorial Press, an imprint of College of Careers (Pty) Ltd (qv)

Collins Publishers (SA) (Pty) Ltd, PO Box 61342, Marshalltown 2107 (Located at: 10-14 Watkins St, Denver Ext 4, Johannesburg 2094) Tel: (011) 6222900 Cable Add: Fontana Johannesburg Telex: 423702 SA Fax: (011) 6223553
Man Dir: Malcolm Edwards; *Sales and Marketing Dir:* Paul J Hardingham; *Publicity, Rights & Permissions:* Pamela S Wood
Parent Company: William Collins PLC, UK (qv)
Associate Company: William Collins (Africa) (Pty) Ltd (at above address)
Subjects: Southern Africa (wildlife, reference)
Founded: 1982
ISBN Publisher's Prefix: 0-0620

Countrywide Books, an imprint of David Philip Publisher (Pty) Ltd (qv)

Daan Retief Publishers, see HAUM-Daan Retief Publishers (Pty) Ltd

Delta Books (Pty) Ltd+, PO Box 41021, Craighall 2024 (Located at: Delta House, 111 Central St, Houghton, Johannesburg 2196) Tel: (011) 7287121 Cable Add: Reppub
Man Dir, Rights & Permissions: Adriaan Donker; *Deputy Man Dir:* Nicholas W Combrinck; *Sales, Publicity:* Karin Donker; *Editorial:* Murray Coombes
Associate Company: Ad Donker (Pty) Ltd (qv)
Subjects: Botany, Gardening, Sports, Health, How-to
1985: 10 titles *Founded:* 1980
ISBN Publisher's Prefixes: 0-908387, 0-86852

Digma Publications, an imprint of Christian Publishing Co — CUM Books (Pty) Ltd (qv)

Ad **Donker** (Pty) Ltd+, PO Box 41021, Craighall 2024 (Located at: Delta House, 111 Central St, Houghton, Johannesburg 2196) Tel: (011) 7287121 Cable Add: Reppub
Man Dir, Rights & Permissions: Adriaan Donker; *Deputy Man Dir:* Nicholas W Combrinck; *Sales, Publicity:* Karin Donker;

Editorial: Murray Coombes
Associate Companies: Delta Books (Pty) Ltd (qv); International Publishers' Representatives (SA) (Pty) Ltd; The Science Press (Pty) Ltd (at above address)
Subjects: General Fiction & Non-fiction, Poetry, Africana, Academic
1985: 35 titles *Founded:* 1973
ISBN Publisher's Prefixes: 0-908387, 0-86852

Drommedaris, an imprint of Struik Publishers (qv)

Dutch Reformed Church Publishers, PO Box 4539, Cape Town 8000 Tel: (021) 215540 Cable Add: D R C Publishers Telex: 76922
Man Dir: W J van Zijl; *Editorial, Rights & Permissions:* Mrs H Venter; *Sales, Publicity:* Mrs M Volschenk; *Production:* W Theron
Parent Company: N G Kerk-Uitgewers (at above address)
Subjects: Christian Literature (educational and general)
Bookshops: 28 bookshops throughout South Africa
Founded: 1818
ISBN Publisher's Prefix: 0-86991

E L D Trust, an imprint of The UCCSA Publications Department (qv)

The **Ecumenical Literature** Distribution Trust, now UCCSA Publications Department (qv)

Educum Uitgewers Beperk*, PO Box 9573, Johannesburg 2000

Erroll Marx Publishers, an imprint of HAUM-Daan Retief Publishers (Pty) Ltd (qv)

Erudita Publications (Pty) Ltd*, PO Box 29159, Melville 2109, Transvaal
Man Dir: Chris van Rensburg
Subjects: Reference, Directories

Faircape Books, an imprint of College of Careers (Pty) Ltd (qv)

Femina, an imprint of Juventus/Femina Publishers (qv)

Flesch Financial Publications (Pty) Ltd, PO Box 3473, Cape Town (Located at: 4 Gordon St, Gardens, Cape Town) Tel: (021) 467472 Cable Add: Fairlead Telex: 527826
Man Dir: S Flesch; *Editorial:* C G Thompson; *Sales Manager:* Derek Wood
Branch Off: 9th floor, Medical City, 106 Eloff St, PO Box 3473, Johannesburg
Subjects: Reference, Finance
1985: 4 titles *Founded:* 1966
ISBN Publisher's Prefix: 0-949989

Folio, an imprint of Juventus/Femina Publishers (qv)

Da **Gama** Publishers (Pty) Ltd, 4th floor Cavendish Chambers, 183 Jeppe St, Johannesburg 2000
Man Dir: Colleen Broadley
Subjects: General Non-fiction, Educational, Reference, Travel Books

Government Printer*, Bosman St, Pretoria

T W **Griggs** & Co (Pty) Ltd, PO Box 466, Durban 4000 (Located at: 341 West St, Durban 4001) Tel: (031) 3048571 Cable Add: Adamsco
Rights & Permissions: E G Rabjohn
Parent Company: Adams & Co Ltd (qv under Major Booksellers)
Subjects: Africana, Education, General

H & R Academica (Pty) Ltd*, PO Box 557, Pretoria 0001 (Located at: 607 Southern Life Bldg, 239 Pretorius St, Pretoria) Tel: (012) 218465 Cable Add: Hurou Pretoria
General Manager: J J Human; *Manager:* N Smith
Parent Company: Human & Rousseau (Pty) Ltd (qv)
Subjects: Secondary and University Textbooks
Founded: 1964
ISBN Publisher's Prefix: 0-86874

H A U M-Daan Retief Publishers (Pty) Ltd+, PO Box 12, Pretoria 0001 (Located at: DRU Bldg, 413 Hilda St, Hatfield, Pretoria) Tel: (012) 437731 Telex: 322436
Chairman: J C Oelofse; *Man Dir, Production:* M A C Jacklin; *Editorial, Sales, Publicity, Rights & Permissions:* Dr H J M Retief
Parent Company: HAUM (Hollandsch Afrikaansche Uitgevers Maatschappij) (qv)
Imprints: Daan Retief Publishers; Erroll Marx Publishers; Mustard Seed Christian Publishers; Scholastic Publishers
Subjects: Children's, Large Print, Textbooks, Educational, Religion, African Languages
Book Clubs: Kinderklub, Young People's Book Club
Founded: 1974
ISBN Publisher's Prefixes: 0-7959, 0-629 (Mustard Seed)

H A U M Educational Publishers*, PO Box 629, Pretoria 0001
Parent Company: HAUM (Hollandsch Afrikaansche Uitgevers Maatschappij) (qv)
Subject: Tertiary Textbooks

H A U M (Hollandsch Afrikaansche Uitgevers Maatschappij)+*, Prima Park 4 & 6, Cnr Klosser & King Edward Rd, Parow 7500 Tel: (021) 926123
Manager, Publisher: C J Hage
Subsidiary Companies: HAUM-Daan Retief Publishers (Pty) Ltd (qv); HAUM Educational Publishers (qv); De Jager-HAUM (qv); Juventus/Femina Publishers (qv)
Subjects: General Fiction & Non-fiction, Belles Lettres, Poetry, Biography, History, Juveniles, Books in Afrikaans, Science and Technology, General Science, University Textbooks
Bookshops: HAUM Academic Bookshop; HAUM Booksellers (qqv under Major Booksellers)
1985: 61 titles *Founded:* 1894
ISBN Publisher's Prefix: 0-7986

Heinemann Publishers Southern Africa Pty Ltd, PO Box 61581, Marshalltown, Johannesburg 2107 Tel: (011) 7287351 Cable Add: Shebooks Telex: 487187
Parent Company: The Heinemann Group of Publishers Ltd, UK (qv)

Human & Rousseau (Pty) Ltd+, PO Box 5050, Cape Town 8000 (Located at: State House, 3-9 Rose St, Cape Town)
Tel: (021) 251280 Cable Add: Persdiens Telex: 520294
Man Dir: J J Human; *Assistant General Manager:* H D Büttner; *Marketing Manager:* J J Labuschagne
Parent Company: Nasionale Boekhandel Ltd (qv)
Subsidiary Company: H & R Academica (Pty) Ltd (qv)
Branch Off: Atrium Bldg, 60 Glenwood Rd, PO Box 558, Lynnwood Glen, Pretoria Tel: (012) 477774 Cable Add: Hurou Pretoria
Subjects: General Fiction & Non-fiction, Cookery, Crafts, Belles Lettres, Poetry, Biography, History, Africana, Philosophy, Reference, Religion, Juveniles, General Science, University and Secondary Textbooks (in Afrikaans and English)
1986: 216 titles *1987:* 246 titles *Founded:* 1959
ISBN Publisher's Prefix: 0-7981

Hutchinson Group (SA) (Pty) Ltd, now incorporated in Century Hutchinson SA Pty Ltd (qv)

Institute for Reformational Studies, c/o Potchefstroom University for Christian Higher Education, Potchefstroom 2520 Tel: (01481) 23484 Cable Add: PUK Telex: 421363
Dir: Prof B J Van der Walt; *Sales:* Mrs G C Loots; *Publicity:* Mrs M C Swanepoel; *Rights & Permissions:* Mrs R E van Biljon
Parent Company: Potchefstroom University for Christian Higher Education
Subjects: Christianity, Christian Higher Education, Calvinism, The Reformation
Founded: 1966
ISBN Publisher's Prefix: 0-86990

Interkerklike Uitgewerstrust*, PO Box 2744, Pretoria 0001 Tel: (012) 215132
Inter-Church Publishing Trust
Chief Executive: B R Buys
Associate Companies: Calvyn-Jubileumboekefonds (qv); N G Kerk-Uitgewers
Subjects: Religious handbooks for Schools, Universities, Colleges and Churches; also Visual Aids
ISBN Publisher's Prefix: 0-620

De **Jager** — HAUM, PO Box 629, Pretoria 0001 (Located at: HAUM Bldg, 227 Minnaar St, Pretoria) Tel: (012) 3252200 Telex: 322228 RSA Fax: (012) 287309
Man Dir: Pret Scholtz; *Editorial, Production:* Lena Kohler; *Sales:* Hans Kirsten; *Promotion:* Suna de Beer; *Rights & Permissions:* C Richter
Parent Company: HAUM (Hollandsch Afrikaansche Uitgevers Maatschappij) (qv)
Subject: School Textbooks, Books in African languages
Founded: 1974

Juta & Co Ltd+, PO Box 123, Kenwyn 7790 (Located at: Mercury Crescent, Hillstar Industrial Township, Wetton, Cape Town) Tel: (021) 711181 Cable Add: Juta
Man Dir: J E Duncan; *Sales Manager:* L Massella; *Senior Editor, Rights & Permissions:* G Stanford
Branch Offs: Suite 5B Mangrove Beach Centre, Somtseu Rd, Durban 4001; PO Box 1010, Johannesburg 2000; PO Box 3176, Pietersburg 0700; Consultare Chambers, Hancock St, North End, Port Elizabeth 6001; 10th floor Merino Bldg, Bosman St, Pretoria 0002; PO Box 403, Umtata, Transkei
Subjects: Reference, Law, Medicine, Science and Technology; General School, University & Educational Textbooks
Bookshops: See under Major Booksellers
1985: 123 titles *Founded:* 1853
ISBN Publisher's Prefix: 0-7021

Juventus/Femina Publishers+*, PO Box 1151, Pretoria 0001 Tel: (012) 265681 Telex: 32228
Man Dir: Piet Scholtz; *Manager, Editorial:* Gert Basson; *Chief Publisher:* Kobie Gouws; *Sales:* Robbie Goossen; *Production:* Manus Oberholzer; *Publicity:* Sas Klopper; *Rights & Permissions:* Hettie Scholtz
Parent Company: HAUM (Hollandsch Afrikaansche Uitgevers Maatschappij) (qv)
Imprints: Femina, Folio, Juventus
Subjects: Fiction and Non-fiction, General, Juveniles, Women's, Family
Founded: 1980

Die **Kinderpers** Van SA*, PO Box 2652, Cape Town 8000
Subject: Children's Books

Lexicon Publishers (Pty) Ltd, PO Box 371, Isando 1600 (Located at: Hulley Rd, Isando) Tel: (011) 9741181 Telex: 429772 Fax: (011) 9744311
Man Dir, Editorial, Rights & Permissions: John A Savage; *Sales:* Sue McNally; *Publicity:* Vickie Jones
Subjects: General Non-fiction, Medicine, Science and Technology, General Science, School and University Textbooks, Training Materials
1985: 23 titles *1986:* 38 titles *Founded:* 1966
Miscellaneous: Formerly McGraw-Hill Book Co (South Africa) (Pty) Ltd
ISBN Publisher's Prefix: 1-86813

Longman Penguin Southern Africa (Pty) Ltd, now a subsidiary of Maskew Miller Longman (Pty) Ltd (qv)

Lovedale Press, Private Bag X1346, Alice Ciskei 5700 Tel: (0404) 31135/7
General Manager: B B Finca
Subjects: General Fiction and Non-fiction, Belles Lettres, Poetry, Biography, History, Africana, Books in various Southern African languages, Educational Books
Bookshops: Alice Bookshop, Main St, Alice Ciskei; 49 Madiera St, Umtata, Transkei
Founded: 1841

Lux Verbi (Pty) Ltd+, PO Box 1822, Cape Town 8000 (Located at: 30 Waterkant St, Cape Town) Tel: (021) 253505 Telex: 526922
Executive Chairman: W J van Zijl; *Publishing:* Hester Venter; *Marketing:* Maryna Volschenk
Subsidiary Company: Waterkant-Uitgewers (Edms) Bpk (qv)
Subject: Christian Literature, Theology
Book Club: New Day Readers Circle
Bookshops: 33 Waterkant St, Cape Town; Suite 402, 30 Waterkant St, Cape Town; Central Square 37, Union St, East London; OK Centre, Shop 404, Murchison St, Ladysmith; The Mall, c/o Malanand Sauer St, Vanderbijlpark
Founded: 1956
ISBN Publisher's Prefix: 0-86997

M P S A, an imprint of Macdonald Purnell (Pty) Ltd (qv)

Macdonald Purnell (Pty) Ltd, PO Box 1401, Randburg 2125 (Located at: 10 Burke St, Randburg) Tel: (011) 7875830 Cable Add: Purprint Johannesburg Telex: 424985 SA
Man Dir: Ethne Anderson
Parent Company: Maxwell Communication Corporation plc, UK (qv)
Associate Company: Macdonald & Co (Publishers) Ltd, UK (qv)
Imprint: MPSA
Subjects: Educational, Academic, Co-editions, General
Founded: 1948
ISBN Publisher's Prefix: 0-86843

McGraw-Hill Book Co (South Africa) (Pty) Ltd, now Lexicon Publishers (Pty) Ltd (qv)

Macmillan South Africa (Publishers) (Pty) Ltd, now Southern Book Publishers (Pty) Ltd (qv)

Map Studio, an associate company of Struik Publishers (qv)

Maskew Miller Longman (Pty) Ltd+*, PO Box 396, Cape Town 8000 (Located at: Howard Drive, Pinelands 7405) Tel: (021) 537750 Cable Add: Maskewmiller Capetown Telex: 5726053
Man Dir: M A Peacock; *Publishers:* K McCallum, M Kantey, D Paizee; *Sales:* G Visser; *Production:* A Visser; *Publicity:* M Markstein
Subsidiary Companies: Willem Gouws (Pty) Ltd; Longman Penguin Southern Africa (Pty) Ltd; Maskew Miller (Pty) Ltd; Maskew Miller (SWA) (Pty) Ltd, PO Box 9251, Eros, Namibia
Associate Company: Longman Group UK Ltd, UK (qv)
Branch Offs: 11B Brand St, Kimberley; Cnr Grace & Station Sts, Port Elizabeth; Milpark Galleries, Auckland Park, Johannesburg; Basement Shop 1, Norlaine Centre, Union Lane, Pinetown 3600
Subjects: Juveniles, Books in Afrikaans, English and African languages, Paperbacks, Primary and Secondary Textbooks, Educational
Bookshops: See under Major Booksellers
ISBN Publisher's Prefix: 0-636

The **Methodist** Publishing House and Book Depot, PO Box 708, Cape Town 8000 (Located at: 52 Burg St, Cape Town) Tel: (021) 231247 Cable Add: Methodist
Book Steward: M Fearns
Subjects: Religion, Books in Xhosa and Zulu
Bookshops: PO Box 1452, Benoni 1500; PO Box 708, Cape Town 8000; PO Box 108, Durban 4000; PO Box 8508, Johannesburg 2000; PO Box 1042, Kimberley 8300; PO Box 1233, Pietermaritzburg 3200; PO Box 666, Pinetown 3600; PO Box 17, Port Elizabeth 6000
Founded: 1894
ISBN Publisher's Prefix: 0-949942

Mustard Seed Christian Publishers, an imprint of HAUM-Daan Retief Publishers (Pty) Ltd (qv)

N G Kerk Jeugboekhandel*, PO Box 396, Bloemfontein 9300
Formerly Sondagskool Boekhandel
Bookshop: At above address

N G Kerkboekhandel Transvaal (DRC Publishers), PO Box 245, Pretoria 0001 (Located at: Visagiestraat 234, Pretoria) Tel: (012) 218401
General Manager: J Olivier; *Editorial:* Mrs I Hickey
Branch Offs: 16 branches in Transvaal and Natal
Subjects: Religion, Theology (in Afrikaans and English)
Bookshop: N G Kerkboekhandel Transvaal (qv under Major Booksellers)
1986: 30 titles *Founded:* 1947
ISBN Publisher's Prefix: 0-7987

Nasionale Boekhandel Ltd, PO Box 122, Parow 7500 (Located at: 386 Voortrekker Rd, Parow) Tel: (021) 5911131 Cable Add: Nasboek Telex: 526951 SA
Group Man Dir: P J Botha
Subsidiary and Associate Companies: Cape Booksellers Ltd; Human & Rousseau (Pty) Ltd (qv); Nasboek (Natal) Ltd; Nasionale Boekwinkels Bpk (qv under Major Booksellers); Nasou Ltd (qv); Natal Booksellers Ltd, Durban; Oudiovista Productions (Pty) Ltd (qv); J L van Schaik (Pty) Ltd (qv); Van Schaik's Bookstore (Pty) Ltd (qv under Major Booksellers); Tafelberg Publishers Ltd (qv); Via Afrika Ltd (qv); Via Afrika (Bophuthatswana) Ltd, Mafikeng; Via Afrika (Ciskei) Ltd, King Williamstown; Via Afrika (OFS) Ltd, Bloemfontein; Via Afrika (Transkei) Ltd, Umtata; Via Afrika (Lebowa) Ltd, Pietersburg; Rygill's Educational Suppliers, Durban; Heer Printers (Pty) Ltd, Pretoria (all in Republic of South Africa); Nasionale Boekhandel (SWA) (Pty) Ltd, Namibia (qv)
Subjects: General, Educational, Academic, Medicine
Book Club: Leserskring (Leisure Hour)
Founded: 1950

Nasou Ltd+, PO Box 105, Parow 7500 (Located at: 386 Voortrekker Rd, Goodwood, Parow) Tel: (021) 5911131 Cable Add: Nasou Cape Town Telex: 527751 Fax: (021) 5915800
Man Dir: W R van der Vyver; *Manager, Rights & Permissions:* L I Naude; *Publicity & Advertising:* F D Maree
Parent Company: Nasionale Boekhandel Ltd (qv for Associate Companies)
Branch Offs: PO Box 1058, Bloemfontein 9300; PO Box 279, East London 5200; PO Box 912, Kimberley; PO Box 556, Pinetown 3600; PO Box 95, Port Elizabeth 6000; PO Box 6135, Pretoria 0001
Subjects: Reference, University, Secondary & Primary Textbooks; Educational software for BBC, Commodore and IBM compatibles
Founded: 1963
ISBN Publisher's Prefix: 0-625

Rebecca **Ostrowiak** School of Reading, PO Box 4106, Germiston South 1411 Tel: 514262
Principal: Edna Freinkel
Parent Company: Readucate (Pty) Ltd (at above address)
Subjects: Remedial reading teaching for children and adults
Founded: 1969

Otter Books, an imprint of David Philip Publisher (Pty) Ltd (qv)

Oudiovista Productions (Pty) Ltd*, PO Box 150, Parow 7500 Tel: (021) 5911131 Cable Add: Oudiovista
Man Dir: G J J Rousseau; *Manager:* W R van der Vyver
Parent Company: Nasionale Boekhandel Ltd (qv)
Subjects: Educational, Audiovisual Aids
Founded: 1969
ISBN Publisher's Prefix: 0-620

Outlines, an imprint of College of Careers (Pty) Ltd (qv)

Oxford University Press Southern Africa*, PO Box 1141, Cape Town 8000 (Located at: Top Floor, Harrington House, 37 Barrack St, Cape Town) Tel: (021) 457266 Cable Add: Oxonian Capetown Fax: (021) 9550022
General Manager: N C Gracie; *Editorial:* Ms R Seagrief; *Academic Sales:* G Younge; *Trade Sales:* Peter Hyde; *Educational Publicity:* Jutta Geider; *Customer Services:* Alison Neish
Parent Company: Oxford University Press, UK (qv)
Branch Offs: PO Box 41390, Craighall, Johannesburg 2024; PO Box 37166, Overport 4067
Subjects: General Fiction and Non-fiction, Belles Lettres, Poetry, Biography, History, Africana, Juveniles; Books in Xhosa, Zulu, Sotho, Tswana, Shona and Afrikaans; General & Social Science, Educational, Textbooks, Music, Prayer Books; Paperbacks
1985: 18 titles *Founded:* 1915
ISBN Publisher's Prefix: 0-19

Perskor Books (Pty) Ltd, PO Box 845, Johannesburg 2000 (Located at: 28 Height St, Doornfontein, Johannesburg) Tel: (011) 285460 Cable Add: Vaderland Telex: 83561, 87483/4
Man Dir: F Wessels; *Editorial, Rights &*

Permissions: P V Heerden; *Sales:* S J Fourie; *Production:* A Bothma; *Publicity:* S Kloppers
Orders to: Perskor-Boekwinkel, PO Box, Maraisburg, 1700 (Located at: 4 Banfield Rd, Industria North, Maraisburg)
Subsidiary Company: Perskor Publishers (at above address)
Subjects: Education, Law, General
Book Clubs: Klub 707; Klub-Dagbreek; Klub Saffier
Bookshops: Johannesburgse Boekwinkel; Perskor Bookshop (qqv under Major Booksellers)
Founded: 1940
ISBN Publisher's Prefix: 0-628

David **Philip** Publisher (Pty) Ltd, PO Box 408, Claremont, Cape 7735 (Located at: 217 Werdmuller Centre, Claremont, Cape Province) Tel: (021) 644136 Cable Add: Philipub, Cape Town Telex: 527566 Philipub
Man Dir: David Philip; *Rights & Permissions Dir:* Marie Philip
Imprints: Africasouth Paperbacks; Countrywide Books; Otter Books
Branch Offs: 402 Hampstead House, 46 Biccard St, Braamfontein 2001 Tel: (011) 4031614; 81 Tatham Rd, Pietermaritzburg, Natal 3201 Tel: (0331) 54789
Subjects: General Fiction & Non-fiction, Belles Lettres, Poetry, Biography, History, Africana, Juveniles, Social Sciences, Politics, University Textbooks, Reference Books, Paperbacks
1985: 38 titles *1986:* 40 titles *Founded:* 1971
ISBN Publisher's Prefixes: 0-908396, 0-86486

Pretoria Boekhandel (Pty) Ltd+*, PO Box 23334, Innesdale 0031 Tel: (012) 761531
Man Dir: L S van der Walt
Subjects: Children's fiction in Afrikaans, Educational, Textbooks
Founded: 1971
ISBN Publisher's Prefix: 0-86880

Pro Rege Press Ltd*, PO Box 343, Potchefstroom 2520
Associate Companies: N G Kerkboekhandel Transvaal (qv); Interkerklike Uitgewerstrust (qv); N G Kerk-Uitgewers
Subjects: General Fiction & Non-fiction, Religion, Secondary Textbooks
ISBN Publisher's Prefix: 0-949988

Publitoria (Pty) Ltd+*, PO Box 23334, Innesdale 0031 Tel: (012) 761531
Man Dir: L S van der Walt
Subjects: Educational, Reference, School Textbooks
Founded: 1982
ISBN Publisher's Prefix: 0-86880

Pula Press, an imprint of The UCCSA Publications Department (qv)

Ravan Press (Pty) Ltd, PO Box 31134, Braamfontein, Johannesburg 2017 (Located at: 23 O'Reilly Rd, Berea, Johannesburg) Tel: (011) 6435552
Subjects: Specializes in Socio-Political studies of Southern Africa; also General Fiction & Non-fiction, Poetry, Drama, Biography, History, Africana, Religion, Children's, Paperbacks, Periodicals, Educational
Founded: 1973
ISBN Publisher's Prefix: 0-86975

Reader's Digest South Africa, Reader's Digest House, 130 Strand St, Cape Town 8001 Tel: (021) 254460 Cable Add: Readigest Cape Town Telex: 5720333
Man Dir: Nick McRae; *Editorial:* C J Walton (Books), Wendy Pankhurst (Magazine); *Sales, Publicity:* T C Wray; *Production:* Jack Nel; *Rights & Permissions:* Chris Walton
Parent Company: Reader's Digest Association, PO Box 235, Pleasantville, NY 10570, USA
Subjects: Local Interest, Wildlife, Food and Wine, Health

Readucate (Pty) Ltd, see Ostrowiak School of Reading

S A Cultural Holdings (Pty) Ltd*, PO Box 9019, Johannesburg 2000 Tel: (011) 4021400 Telex: J83031 Cable Add: Knowingly
Man Dir: Hilton W Payne
Parent Company: Sage Holdings (Pty) Ltd
Subsidiary Companies: Encyclopaedia Britannica (SA) (Pty) Ltd; Ensiklopedie Afrikana (Edms) Bpk; IQ Progressons (Pty) Ltd

S A Kultuurbeleggings, see S A Cultural Holdings (Pty) Ltd

Sable, an imprint of Struik Publishers (qv)

Sasavona Publishers & Booksellers, Private Bag X8, Braamfontein 2017 (Located at: 1st floor Celton House, 9 De Beer St, Braamfontein, Johannesburg 2001) Tel: (011) 4032502
Manager: M A Chapatte
Parent Company: Evangelical Presbyterian Church – Swiss Mission in SA (at above address)
Imprints: CMP Reprints, Sasavona Books, Swiss Mission Publications
Subjects: Religion, Education, Literature, General
Bookshop: At above address
1985: 7 titles *1986:* 4 titles *Founded:* 1974 (1875 as Swiss Mission Publishing)
ISBN Publisher's Prefix: 0-907985

J L van **Schaik** (Pty) Ltd+, PO Box 724, Pretoria 0001 (Located at: Libri Bldg, Church St, Pretoria) Tel: (012) 212441 Cable Add: Bookschaik Pretoria Telex: 322340 SA
General Manager: H G Raubenheimer
Parent Company: Nasionale Boekhandel Ltd (qv)
Subjects: General Fiction & Non-fiction, Belles Lettres, Poetry, Biography, History, Africana, How-to, Study Guides, Reference, Religion, Juveniles, Books in Afrikaans and Southern African languages, Psychology, General & Social Science, University & Secondary Textbooks
1985: 42 titles *Founded:* 1914
ISBN Publisher's Prefix: 0-627

Scholastic Publishers, an imprint of HAUM-Daan Retief Publishers (Pty) Ltd (qv)

The **Science** Press (Pty) Ltd, an associate company of Ad Donker (Pty) Ltd (qv)

Shuter & Shooter (Pty) Ltd, PO Box 109, Pietermaritzburg 3200, Natal (Located at: 230 Church St, Pietermaritzburg) Tel: (0331) 58151 Cable Add: Shushoo Telex: 643771 SA
Man Dir: M N Prozesky; *Editorial:* L van Heerden; *Sales:* D Ryder; *Publicity:* J A Wilken; *Production:* J Sharpe; *Rights & Permissions:* Jo-Anne Goodwill
Parent Company: The Natal Witness (Pty) Ltd
Associate Company: Kwa-Zulu Booksellers (Pty) Ltd, PO Box 362, Pietermaritzburg 3200
Subsidiary Company: Shuter & Shooter (Transkei) (Pty) Ltd, PO Box 648, Umtata, Transkei Tel: (0471) 2786
Branch Offs: PO Box 395, Claremont 7735 Tel: (021) 619003; 219 Werdmuller Centre, Newry St, Claremont 7700, Cape Town; 5th floor, Plein Centre, 100 Plein St, Johannesburg Tel: (011) 3373980; PO Box 214, Ladanna 0704 Tel: (01521) 73357; Shop 18b, 18 Witklip St, Annadale, Pietersburg 0700
Subjects: General Non-fiction, Biography, History, Africana, Science and Technology, General and Social Sciences, Primary and Secondary Textbooks, Books in Zulu, Xhosa, Northern and Southern Sotho, Siswati, Venda, Tswana and Tsonga
Bookshop: See under Major Booksellers
Founded: 1925
ISBN Publisher's Prefix: 0-86985

Sondagskool Boekhandel, now known as N G Kerk Jeugboekhandel (qv)

Southern Book Publishers (Pty) Ltd, PO Box 548, Bergvlei 2012 Tel: 7860001 Telex: 424235 SA
Man Dir: Mike Anderson
Subjects: General Non-fiction, Politics, History, Natural History, University and Technical Textbooks
Founded: 1987
ISBN Publisher's Prefix: 0-86812

Star Schools*, PO Box 31648, Braamfontein 2017 (Located at: 115 Everite House, 20 de Korte St, Braamfontein) Tel: 3396665
Man Dir: W M Smith
Subjects: Science & Maths, University & Secondary Textbooks
Founded: 1974
Miscellaneous: Affiliated with the Argus Group of Newspapers and Eastern Province Herald. Company previously known as Technitrain (Pty) Ltd

Struik Publishers+, PO Box 1144, Cape Town 8000 (Located at: Struik House, Oswald Pirow St, Cape Town 8001) Tel: (021) 216740 Cable Add: Dekena Capetown Telex: 526713 SA Fax: (021) 216744
Man Dir: Gerry Struik; *Editorial:* Peter Borchert; *Sales, Publicity, Rights & Permissions:* Dick Wilkins; *Production:* Wim Reinders
Parent Company: Struik Holdings (Pty) Ltd (at above address)
Subsidiary Companies: Struik-Winchester (at above address); Timmins Publishers (Pty) Ltd (qv)
Associate Companies: Centaur Publishers (Pty) Ltd (qv); Map Studio, PO Box 11204, Johannesburg 2000; SA Reader's Choice (Pty) Ltd; Struik Book Distributors
Imprints: Drommedaris; Sable
Branch Offs: Suite 6002, Overport City, Ridge Rd, Durban 4001; PO Box 11204, Johannesburg 2000
Subjects: Southern Africa, Wildlife, Cookery, Illustrated Books
1985: 23 titles *1986:* 46 titles *Founded:* 1962
ISBN Publisher's Prefix: 0-86977

Struik-Winchester, a subsidiary company of Struik Publishers (qv)

Swiss Mission Publications, an imprint of Sasavona Publishers & Booksellers (qv)

Tafelberg Publishers Ltd+, PO Box 879, Cape Town 8000 (Located at: 28 Wale St, Cape Town) Tel: (021) 241320 Cable Add: Boeknuus Cape Town Telex: 521473 SA
Man Dir: D J van Niekerk
Parent Company: Nasionale Boekhandel Ltd (qv)
Subjects: General Fiction & Non-fiction, Belles Lettres, Poetry, Biography, History, Africana, How-to, Study Guides, Reference, Religion, Juveniles, Books in Afrikaans, Paperbacks

1985: 92 titles *1986:* 70 titles *Founded:* 1950
ISBN Publisher's Prefix: 0-624

Target Publishers (Edms) Bpk*, PO Box 2688, Klerksdorp 2570

Taurus*, PO Box 85218, Emmarentia 2029 Tel: 7264059
Chief Executives: Ernst Lindenberg, John Miles, Ampie Coetzee
Parent Company: Licomil Co (Pty) Ltd (at above address)
Subject: South African Literature in English and Afrikaans
Founded: 1975

Technitrain (Pty) Ltd, now known as Star Schools (qv)

Thomson Publications SA (Pty) Ltd, PO Box 8308, Johannesburg 2000 (Located at: Thomson House, cnr Hendrik Verwoerd Drive and Will Scarlett Rd, Randburg) Tel: (011) 7892144/7892055 Telex: 422125
Man Dir: J Brady
Subjects: Reference, Annual/Biennial Buyers' Guides, Periodicals

Timmins Publishers (Pty) Ltd, PO Box 1144, Cape Town 8000 Tel: (021) 216740 Cable Add: Dekena Telex: 526713 Fax: (021) 216744
Man Dir: G Struik; *General Manager:* P Borchert; *Assistant General Manager:* P Martin; *Sales Dir:* J D Wilkins
Parent Company: Struik Publishers (qv)
Subjects: General
1985: 12 titles *Founded:* 1935
ISBN Publisher's Prefix: 0-86978

Treffer-Uitgewers (Edms) Ltd, PO Box 3599, Pretoria 0001

The **U C C S A** Publications Department, PO Box 31083, Braamfontein 2017 (Located at: 2nd floor Congregational Centre, 75 de Korte St, Braamfontein, Johannesburg 2001) Tel: (011) 3391261
The United Congregational Church of South Africa Publications Department
General Manager: W Westenborg
Imprints: ELD Trust, Pula Press
Subjects: Religious, Liturgical
Bookshop: At above address
Founded: 1986 (as UCCSA Publications Department; 1973 ELD Trust, 1970 CPSA, pre-1970 SPCK)
ISBN Publisher's Prefix: 0-86881

The **United Congregational** Church of South Africa Publications Department, see UCCSA

United Protestant Publishers (Pty) Ltd, see Lux Verbi (Pty) Ltd

University of Natal Press, PO Box 375, Pietermaritzburg 3200 Tel: (0331) 63320 Telex: 63719
Man Dir: Ms M P Moberly
Imprint: Killie Campbell Africana Library
Subjects: South African History, Politics, Ornithology, Botany, Natal and Zulu Studies, Africana, General Literature, Reprints
1985: 6 titles *1986:* 6 titles *Founded:* 1947
ISBN Publisher's Prefix: 0-86980

University of South Africa+, Department of Publishing Services, PO Box 392, Pretoria 0001 Tel: (012) 4401816 Cable Add: Unisa Telex: 350068
Publications Management: by Publications Committee
Subjects: General Non-fiction, Anthropology, Botany, Communications, Criminology, Economics, Education, Fine Arts, Poetry, Biography, History, Africana, Philosophy, Reference, Religion, Theology, Psychology, Science & Technology, Social Science, Geography, Academic Journals, Library Science, Linguistics, Literature, Law, Mathematics, Music, Politics, Statistics, University Textbooks
1985: 23 titles *1986:* 16 titles *Founded:* 1873
ISBN Publisher's Prefix: 0-86981

University Publishers & Booksellers (Pty) Ltd, PO Box 29, Stellenbosch 7600 (Located at: De Waal Centre, Andringa St, Stellenbosch) Tel: (02231) 70337/70397 Cable Add: Biblia Stellenbosch
Man Dir: B B Liebenberg
Subjects: General Non-fiction, Juveniles, University & Secondary Textbooks

Valiant Publishers (Pty) Ltd*, Sandton City, PO Box 78236, Sandton 2146 Tel: 7835012/5 Telex: 83023
Man Dir: F R Metrowich; *General Manager, Rights & Permissions:* A N Keevy
Subjects: General Non-fiction, History, Africana, Reference, Religion, TFH Pet Books
Founded: 1975

Via Afrika Ltd, PO Box 151, Pretoria 0001 Tel: (012) 261075 Cable Add: Via Afrika
Publisher: J S Verreynne; *Assistant Publisher:* I Keyser; *General Manager:* E R Arnold; *Production Manager:* E van der Merwe
Parent Company: Nasionale Boekhandel Ltd (qv)
Imprint: Acacia Books
Subjects: General Fiction, Belles Lettres, Poetry, Books in Zulu, Xhosa and other Southern African Languages, Science and Technology, General & Social Science, University, Secondary & Primary Textbooks
Bookshops: Via Afrika Book Store (qv under Major Booksellers)
1985: 74 titles *1986:* 72 titles *Founded:* 1970
ISBN Publisher's Prefixes: 0-7994, 0-86817 (Acacia)

J P van der Walt en Seun (Pty) Ltd+, PO Box 123, Pretoria 0001 (Located at: 380 Bosman St, Pretoria) Tel: (012) 3252100 Telex: 320691 SA
Man Dir: D H van der Walt; *Editorial:* R J J van Rensburg
Subjects: General Fiction & Non-fiction, Philosophy, Reference, Religion, Law, Juveniles, Books in Afrikaans, Paperbacks, University Textbooks
Book Clubs: Eike-Boekklub, Erina se Boekklub, Keurbiblioteek, Kinderkeur, Knutseltjie, Look and Cook Club, President Boekklub, Romankeur, Treffer-Boekklub
Founded: 1947
ISBN Publisher's Prefix: 0-7993

Waterkant-Uitgewers (Edms) Bpk, PO Box 4539, Cape Town 8000 Tel: (021) 215540
Man Dir: W J van Zijl; *Publicity:* Mrs E M Volschenk
Parent Company: Lux Verbi (Pty) Ltd (qv)
Associate Company: Waterkant Publishers
Subject: Christian Literature
Founded: 1980
ISBN Publisher's Prefix: 0-907992

Who's Who of Southern Africa, PO Box 81284, Parkhurst 2120 (Located at: 41 19th St, Parkhurst, Johannesburg) Tel: (011) 8802406/7888380
Managing Editor: K L M Essberger
Subjects: Reference, Annuals

Witwatersrand University Press*, 1 Jan Smuts Ave, Johannesburg 2001 Tel: (011) 7162023 Telex: 422460 SA
Chief Executive: Mrs N H Wilson
Subjects: General Non-fiction, Belles Lettres, Poetry, Biography, History, Philosophy, Reference, Religion, Medicine, Psychology, Science & Technology, Social Science, University and School Textbooks, Africana, Books in Zulu, Xhosa and other Southern African Languages
Bookshop: 36 Jorissen St, Johannesburg 2001
1985: 8 titles *Founded:* 1923
ISBN Publisher's Prefix: 0-85494

Literary Agents

The **International Press** Agency (Pty) Ltd, PO Box 67, Howard Place 7450 (Located at: 44 Howard Centre, Pinelands 7405, Cape Province) Tel: (021) 531926 Cable Add: Inpra Howard Place South Africa Telex: 526837 SA
Man Dir: Dr Ursula A Barnett

Book Clubs

Klub 707, PO Box 4892, Johannesburg 2000 Tel: (011) 7769111
Owned by: Perskor Books (Pty) Ltd (qv)
Subjects: Fiction: especially Suspense, Espionage, Detective, Thrillers (in Afrikaans)

Klub-Dagbreek, PO Box 4892, Johannesburg 2000
Owned by: Perskor Books (Pty) Ltd (qv)
Subject: Fiction

Eike-Boekklub, PO Box 123, Pretoria 0001 (Located at: 380 Bosman St, Pretoria) Tel: (012) 3252100 Telex: 320691 SA
Owned by: J P van der Walt en Seun (Pty) Ltd (qv)
Subject: Children's Books

Erina se Boekklub, PO Box 123, Pretoria 0001 (Located at: 380 Bosman St, Pretoria) Tel: (012) 3252100 Telex: 320691 SA
Owned by: J P van der Walt en Seun (Pty) Ltd (qv)

Keurbiblioteek, PO Box 123, Pretoria 0001 (Located at: 380 Bosman St, Pretoria) Tel: (012) 3252100 Telex: 320691 SA
Owned by: J P van der Walt en Seun (Pty) Ltd (qv)
Subject: Fiction

Kinderkeur*, PO Box 123, Pretoria 0001 (Located at: 380 Bosman St, Pretoria) Tel: (012) 3252100 Telex: 320691 SA
Owned by: J P van der Walt en Seun (Pty) Ltd (qv)

Kinderklub, PO Box 12, Pretoria 0001 Tel: (012) 437731 Telex: 322436
Specialization: Books in Afrikaans
Owned by: HAUM-Daan Retief Publishers (Pty) Ltd (qv)

Knutseltjie, PO Box 123, Pretoria 0001 (Located at: 380 Bosman St, Pretoria) Tel: (012) 3252100 Telex: 320691 SA
Owned by: J P van der Walt en Seun (Pty) Ltd (qv)

Leserskring, PO Box 6528, Roggebaai 8012 Tel: (021) 212251 Telex: 521875 Leisure Hour
Owned by: Nasionale Boekhandel Ltd (qv)
Members: 250,000

Look and Cook Club, PO Box 123, Pretoria 0001 (Located at: 380 Bosman St, Pretoria) Tel: (012) 3252100 Telex: 320691 SA
Owned by: J P van der Walt en Seun (Pty) Ltd (qv)

New Day Readers Circle, PO Box 1822, Cape Town 8000 (Located at: 30 Waterkant St, Cape Town) Tel: (021)

360 REPUBLIC OF SOUTH AFRICA

253505 Telex: 526922
Owned by: Lux Verbi (Pty) Ltd (qv)

President Boekklub, PO Box 123, Pretoria 0001 (Located at: 380 Bosman St, Pretoria) Tel: (012) 3252100 Telex: 320691 SA
Owned by: J P van der Walt en Seun (Pty) Ltd (qv)

Romankeur*, PO Box 123, Pretoria 0001 (Located at: 380 Bosman St, Pretoria)
Owned by: J P van der Walt en Seun (Pty) Ltd (qv)

Klub **Saffier**, PO Box 4892, Johannesburg 2000
Owned by: Perskor Books (Pty) Ltd (qv)
Subject: Fiction

Treffer-Boekklub*, PO Box 123, Pretoria 0001 (Located at: 380 Bosman St, Pretoria)
Owned by: J P van der Walt en Seun (Pty) Ltd (qv)
Subject: Fiction

Young People's Book Club, PO Box 12, Pretoria 0001 Tel: (012) 437731 Telex: 322436
Owned by: HAUM-Daan Retief Publishers (Pty) Ltd (qv)

Major Booksellers

Adams & Co Ltd, PO Box 466, Durban 4000 (Located at: 341 West St, Durban) Tel: (031) 3048571
Man Dir: P D Adams

Bookwise (Pty) Ltd*, PO Box 260865, Shakespeare House, Commissioner St, Johannesburg 2000
Branches: Bedfordview, Braamfontein, Roggebaai

Central News Agency Ltd*, PO Box 10799, Johannesburg 2000 Tel: (011) 8361711
Also: PO Box 9, Cape Town 8000 Tel: (021) 541261; PO Box 938, Durban 4000 Tel: (031) 451875 (and further 250 branches throughout the country)
Also Publisher (qv)

Exclusive Books (Pty) Ltd*, PO Box 17554, Hillbrow 2038, Transvaal (Located at: 48 Pretoria St, Hillbrow) Tel: (011) 6425068 (shop)/6438131 (office) Telex: 424094 SA
Man Dir: Jeremy Gordin
Also: PO Box 4628, Cape Town 8000 (Located at: Southern Life Arcade, 101 St Georges St, Cape Town 8000) Tel: (021) 226860 Telex: 5726078 SA
Owned by: Premier Group Ltd

Fogarty's Bookshop, PO Box 1881, Port Elizabeth 6000 (Located at: Main St at Market Sq, Port Elizabeth) Tel: (041) 21035/24655
Manager: Teresa Fogarty

H A U M Academic Bookshop, PO Box 343, Stellenbosch 7600 (Located at: Trust Bank Centre, Andringa St) Tel: (02231) 70385/70315
Manager: Mrs D C Mooi
Owned by: HAUM (qv)

H A U M Booksellers*, PO Box 460, Pretoria 0001 (Located at: Nedbank Forum, Festival St, Hatfield, Pretoria 0083) Tel: (012) 437051/772188/437371 Telex: 320962 SA
Manager: T Botha
Owned by: HAUM (qv)

Johannesburgse Boekwinkel, RAU-Campus, PO Box 91119, Aucklandpark 2006 Tel: 7266034/5 Telex: 425557 SA
Owned by: Perskor Books (Pty) Ltd (qv)

Juta & Co Ltd, PO Box 30, Cape Town 8000 (Located at: Regis House, Church St, Cape Town 8001) Tel: (021) 234320 Telex: 523072 SA
Also: African Life Centre, Commissioner & Eloff St, PO Box 1010, Johannesburg 2000 Tel: (011) 235521 Telex: 482436 SA; PO Box 123, Kenwyn 7790 Tel: (021) 711181 Fax: (021) 715010
Also Publisher (qv)

Literary Services (Pty) Ltd, PO Box 31361, Braamfontein 2017 Tel: 3391711 Telex: 425011 SA
Man Dir: C E L Wolf
Academic books

Logans University Bookshop (Pty) Ltd, 229 Francois Rd, Durban
Office & Warehouse: 622 Umbilo Rd, Durban 4001 Tel: (031) 253221
Also: Nedbank Plaza, Pietermaritzburg Tel: (0331) 41580; 660 Umbilo Rd, Durban (Medical Books); Moore Rd, Durban (General Books) Telex: 624583 Fax: (031) 256136

Maskew Miller Longman (Pty) Ltd, Howard Drive, Pinelands 7405 Tel: (021) 537750 Cable Add: Maskewmiller Telex: 526053
Branches: Basement Shop 1, Norlaine Centre, Union Lane, Pinetown, Durban 3600 Tel: (031) 28557; 87 Turffontein Rd, Stafford, Johannesburg 2001 Tel: (011) 6838325; 11B Brand St, Kimberley 8301 Tel: (0531) 33407; Cnr Grace and Station Sts, Port Elizabeth 6000 Tel: (041) 28557; Maskew Miller (SWA) Ltd, Eros Shopping Centre, Cnr Omuramba & Klein Windhoeks Rds, Windhoek 9103, Namibia Tel: (061) 32653
Also Publisher (qv)

N G Kerkboekhandel Transvaal, PO Box 245, Pretoria 0001 (Located at: Visagiestr 234, Pretoria) Tel: (012) 218401
Owned by: N G Kerkboekhandel Transvaal (DRC Publishers) (qv)

Nasionale Boekwinkels Bpk, PO Box 602, Parow 7500 Tel: (021) 5911131 Cable Add: Nasboek Cape Town Telex: 526951
General Manager: W F Struik
Branches: PO Box 119, Parow 7500; PO Box 912, Kimberley 8300; PO Box 2063, Cape Town 8000; PO Box 3626, Randburg 2125; PO Box 95, Port Elizabeth 6000; PO Box 1715, Port Elizabeth; PO Box 1058, Bloemfontein 9300; PO Box 1047, Bloemfontein 9300; PO Box 279, East London 5200; Griet se Akademiese Boekhandel, PO Box 2377, Stellenbosch 7600; Nasboek (Natal) (Pty) Ltd, PO Box 1702, Durban 4000; PO Box 760, Newcastle 2940; Rygills Educational Suppliers (Pty) Ltd, PO Box 1702, Durban 4000
Owned by: Nasionale Boekhandel Ltd (qv)

Perskor Bookshop, PO Box 845, Johannesburg 2000
Branches: PO Box 309, Kroonstad 9500; PO Box 133, Bellville 7530; PO Box 102, Maraisburg 1700; PO Box 15531, Lynn East 0039
Owned by: Perskor Books (Pty) Ltd (qv)

Pilgrims Booksellers (Pty), PO Box 3559, Cape Town Telex: 5724178
At Old Mutual Centre, Cavendish Sq and Main Rd, Sea Point (all Cape Town)
Manager: V Tarica

Van Schaik's Bookstore (Pty) Ltd*, PO Box 724, Pretoria 0001 (Located at: Libri Bldg, Church St, Pretoria) Tel: (012) 212441 Cable Add: Bookschaik Telex: 322340 SA
Manager: W P van der Merwe
Owned by: Nasionale Boekhandel Ltd (qv)

Shuter & Shooter (Pty), PO Box 109, Pietermaritzburg (Located at: 230 Church St, Pietermaritzburg) Tel: (0331) 58151 Telex: 643771 SA Fax: (0331) 943096
Also Publisher (qv)

United Book Distributors (Pty) Ltd*, PO Box 17294, Hillbrow 2038 (Located at: 1st Floor, Permad House, 28 Betty St, Jeppestown) Tel: 6146431 Cable Add: Unibooks Telex: 482991 SA
Manager: J Gordin
Wholesalers and Distributors

Universitas Books (Pty) Ltd, PO Box 1557, 0001 Pretoria Tel: (012) 212211 Cable Add: Africabook Telex: 322917 SA Fax: (012) 264649
Man Dir: P Z Groenewald
Owned by: C N A Gallo Ltd

Via Afrika Book Store, PO Box 4886, Randburg 2125 Tel: 7922213/7922223
Also: PO Box 248, Pietersburg; PO Box 380, Pietermaritzburg; PO Box 107, King William's Town; PO Box 259, Umtata
Owned by: Via Afrika Ltd (qv)

Major Libraries

Cape Provincial Library Service*, PO Box 2108, Cape Town 8000 (Located at: Hospital & Chiappini Sts, Cape Town) Tel: (021) 2582271

Cape Town City Libraries, PO Box 4728, Cape Town 8000 (Located at: Old Drill Hall, Parade St, Cape Town) Tel: (021) 2102036
Librarian: C H Vermeulen

Centre for Scientific and Technical Information of the National Institute for Informatics*, PO Box 395, Pretoria 0001 Tel: (012) 869211 Cable Add: Navorsinfo Telex: 321287 SA
Dir: V A Shaw
A department of the Council for Scientific and Industrial Research (CSIR), at the same address. Information services are provided to South African research and industrial establishments

Department of National Education Library, PB X122, Pretoria 0001 (Located at: Oranje-Nassau Bldg, Schoeman St, Pretoria) Tel: (012) 269971
Chief Librarian: A P B Wessels
Publication: Library News

Durban Municipal Library, PO Box 917, Durban 4000 Tel: (031) 3040111
Librarian: H I Moran
Publications include: Annual Report; Accessions Lists; Booklists; Bookworm (staff quarterly magazine)

Government Archives, Cape Archives Depot, Library, PB X9025, Cape Town 8000 (Located at: 62 Queen Victoria St, Cape Town) Tel: (021) 241340 (Branch of Department of National Education)
Archivist: Miss M George

Government Archives, Natal Archives Depot, Library, PB X9012, Pietermaritzburg 3200 (Located at: 231 Pietermaritz St, Pietermaritzburg) Tel: (0331) 24712
Chief Archivist: S J Ferreira

Government Archives, Orange Free State Archives Depot, Library*, PB X20504, Bloemfontein 9300 (Located at: 37 Elizabeth St, Bloemfontein) Tel: (051) 72840
Archivist: J W Cronje

Government Archives, Transvaal Archives Depot, Library, PB X236, Pretoria 0001

(Located at: Union Bldgs, Church St, Pretoria) Tel: (012) 24971
Archivist: Dr M H Buys

Johannesburg Public Library, Market Sq, Johannesburg 2001 Tel: (011) 8363787
City Librarian: Miss L Kennedy
Publications: Municipal Reference Library Bulletin (monthly); *Index to South African Periodicals* (annual)

Library of Parliament*, PO Box 18, Cape Town 8000 Tel: (021) 458165
Chief Librarian: G Swanepoel

Orange Free State Provincial Library*, Private Bag X20606, Bloemfontein 9300 Tel: (051) 70511 Cable Add: Oranvry Telex: 267056
Librarian: G L Nordier

Pretoria Public Library, PO Box 2673, Pretoria 0001 (Located at: 159 Andries St, Pretoria) Tel: (012) 216361
City Librarian: F R P de Bruyn

Royal Society of South Africa Library*, University of Cape Town Libraries, Rondebosch 7700 Tel: (021) 698531
Honorary Librarian: Prof W Gevers
Publications: Transactions of the Royal Society of South Africa (irregular)

South African Library*, PO Box 496, Cape Town 8000 Tel: (021) 246320 Telex: 522604 SA
Dir: P E Westra
Publications: Quarterly Bulletin; Grey Bibliographies; Reprint series; Cape Almanac (Reprint) Series; South African Newspapers on Microfilm

State Library, PO Box 397, Pretoria 0001 (Located at: Vermeulen St, Pretoria) Tel: (012) 218931 Telex: SA 322171
Dir: Prof R B Zaaiman
Publications: Contributions to Library Science; Directory of Southern African Libraries; Index to South African Periodicals (ISAP); Joint Catalogue of Monographs in Southern African Libraries (JC); Periodicals in Southern African Libraries (PISAL); South African National Bibliography; Reprint series; Micrographic series; Indexes; Bibliographic series

Transvaal Provincial Library and Museum Service*, PB X288, Pretoria 0001 Tel: (012) 2802442 Cable Add: Transator Telex: 30302
Publications: Overvaal Musea, Book parade

University of Cape Town Libraries*, Private Bag, Rondebosch 7700 Tel: (021) 698531 Telex: 5720327
Librarian: A S C Hooper
Publications: Bibliographical series (irregular); *Jagger Journal* (annually); *Varia series* (irregular)

University of Pretoria, Library Services*, Hillcrest, Pretoria 0002 Tel: (012) 4202241 Cable Add: Puniv Telex: 30160
Dir: Prof E D Gerryts
Publications include: Biblioteekdiens Verslagreeks (series of reports, published only in Afrikaans); *The library and the copyright law, act 98 of 1978 as amended, as well as applicable regulations*

University of South Africa Library*, PO Box 392, Pretoria 0001 Tel: (012) 4401904 Cable Add: Unisa Pretoria Telex: 3777
Dir: Prof J Willemse

University of the Witwatersrand Library*, Private Bag 31550, Braamfontein 2017 Tel: (011) 7161111/7162366 (Publications) Cable Add: Uniwits Telex: 450297 Juill
Librarian: Prof R Musiker
Publications include: Wits Journal of Librarianship and Information Science; Historical and Literary Papers: Inventories of Collections, Bibliographical Series, Occasional Publications Series, Official Publications Series; Africana, Annual Report

Library Associations

African Library Association of South Africa*, c/o Library, University of the North, Private Bag X5090, Pietersburg 0700 Tel: Sovenga 33 Cable Add: Unikol Telex: 30808
Secretary-Treasurer: Mrs A N Kambule
Publication: Newsletter (quarterly)

South African Institute for Librarianship and Information Science, PO Box 36575, Menlo Park, Pretoria 0102
Publications: South African Journal for Librarianship and Information Science, Newsletter

Library Reference Books and Journals

Book

Directory of Southern African Libraries, State Library, PO Box 397, Pretoria 0001

Journals

Bookworm, Durban Municipal Library, PO Box 917, Durban 4000

The Cape Librarian, Cape Provincial Library Service, PO Box 2108, Cape Town 8000
Text in Afrikaans and English

Free State Libraries, Orange Free State Provincial Library, Private Bag X20606, Bloemfontein 9300

Index to South African Periodicals (ISAP), State Library, PO Box 397, Pretoria 0001

Library News, Department of National Education Library, Oranje-Nassau Bldg, Schoeman St, PB X122, Pretoria 0001

Libri Natales, Natal Provincial Library, PB 9016, Pietermaritzburg 3200

Mousaion II, Department of Library Science, University of South Africa, PO Box 392, Pretoria

Municipal Reference Library Bulletin (monthly), Johannesburg Public Library, Market Sq, Johannesburg 2001

Newsletter, South African Institute for Librarianship and Information Science, PO Box 36575, Menlo Park, Pretoria 0102

Periodicals in Southern African Libraries (PISAL), State Library, PO Box 397, Pretoria 0001

Quarterly Bulletin of the South African Library, South African Library, PO Box 496, Cape Town 8000

Skoolbiblioteek/School Library, Transvaal Education Library Service, PB X290, Pretoria 0001

South African Journal for Librarianship and Information Science, South African Institute for Librarianship and Information Science, PO Box 36575, Menlo Park, Pretoria 0102
The official publication of the South African Institute of Librarianship and Information Science, published quarterly

Wits Journal of Librarianship and Information Science, University of the Witwatersrand Library, Private Bag 31550, Braamfontein 2017

Literary Associations and Societies

Artists' and Writers' Guild of South Africa*, 37-17th St, Parkhurst, Johannesburg 2001

P E N Club*, The Ridge, Clifton
President: Gerald Gordon

Literary Periodicals

Contrast, South African Literary Journal Ltd, 3 Scott Rd, PO Box 3841, Claremont, Cape Town
Text in English and Afrikaans

Dialogue, PO Box 102, Wynberg 7824
A literary annual for young writers

English in Africa, Institute for the Study of English in Africa, Rhodes University, Grahamstown 6140
Critical articles on all aspects of African literature written in English

Kwanza Journal, PO Box 41, Pretoria 0001
Literary reviews, poetry, creative writing

New Classic, Ravan Press (Pty) Ltd, PO Box 31134, Braamfontein, Johannesburg 2017
Quarterly literary and cultural magazine, originally published as *The Classic*

New Coin, Institute for the Study of English in Africa, Rhodes University, Grahamstown 6140
Previously unpublished poems by South African poets

Ophir, Ravan Press (Pty) Ltd, PO Box 31134, Braamfontein, Johannesburg 2017
Biannual poetry magazine

South African Literary Journal, PO Box 3841, Cape Town 8000

Unisa English Studies, University of South Africa, PO Box 392, Pretoria 0001
Literary articles and reviews

Literary Prizes

Stephen **Black** Prize for Drama, see Department of National Education Literary Prizes for South African Citizens

Jochem van **Bruggen** Prys vir Prosa, see Department of National Education Literary Prizes for South African Citizens

C N A Literary Award
Established in 1961 for the best original works, one in English and one in Afrikaans, published for the first time during the calendar year of the competition. 5,000 rand each plus a bronze plaque, with an additional prize of 2,000 rand for the best designed book. Awarded annually. Books must be in one of following categories: novel, short story, poetry, biography, drama, history, travel. Authors must be South African citizens or registered permanent residents of South Africa. The latest winners were, in English, Ellen Kuzwayd for *Call Me Woman* (Ravan Press) and, in Afrikaans, T T Cloete for *Allotroop* (Tafelberg). Enquiries to The Director, Book Trade Association of South Africa, PO Box 326, Howard Place 7450

Roy **Campbell** Prize for Poetry, see Department of National Education Literary Prizes for South African Citizens

Department of National Education Literary Prizes for South African Citizens*
Established 1957. In the English Section,

the names of the prizes awarded are as follows: Stephen Black Prize for Drama; Roy Campbell Prize for Poetry; Pauline Smith Prize for Prose.
In the Afrikaans Section, the names of the prizes are as follows: J W F Grosskopf Prys vir Drama; C Louis Leipoldt Prys vir Poesie; Jochem van Bruggen Prys vir Prosa.
Prizes of 1,250 rand are awarded in each of the two sections. Enquiries to Director-General for National Education, Private Bag X122, Pretoria 0001

English Association (South African Branch) Literary Prizes
For original unpublished manuscripts by residents of Southern Africa. Subject, literary form and amount of award vary from year to year. Three prizes are usually awarded annually according to the standard reached. Enquiries to English Association, PO Box 1180, Cape Town 8000

Percy **Fitzpatrick** Medal*
For outstanding books for children written in English. Awarded biennially. Enquiries to South African Institute for Library and Information Science, c/o Prof Carl Lohann, Institute for Research into Children's Literature, Potchefstroom University, Potchefstroom 2520

J W F **Grosskopf** Prys vir Drama, see Department of National Education Literary Prizes for South African Citizens

Katrine **Harries** Award*
For outstanding illustrations in South African children's books, regardless of language. Awarded biennially. Enquiries to South African Institute for Library and Information Science, c/o Prof Carl Lohann, Institute for Research into Children's Literature, Potchefstroom University, Potchefstroom 2520

Hertzog Prize
A prestige prize for Afrikaans literature. Prizes are awarded in rotation for poetry, drama and prose. 2,000 rand. Awarded annually. Enquiries to South African Academy of Science and Arts, PO Box 538, Pretoria 0001

W A **Hofmeyr** Prize
Awarded annually for the best literary work published by Tafelberg, Human & Rousseau, Nasou and Via Afrika; 2,000 rand and a Gold Medallion. Enquiries to Nasionale Boekhandel, PO Box 122, Parow 7500

Tienie **Holloway** Medal
Established in 1969 by Dr J E Holloway. A gold medal is awarded every three years to a writer who has produced the best work in Afrikaans literature for infants. Enquiries to South African Academy of Science and Arts, PO Box 538, Pretoria 0001

C P **Hoogenhout** Award*
To encourage the production of outstanding Afrikaans children's books. Awarded biennially. Enquiries to South African Institute for Library and Information Science, c/o Prof Carl Lohann, Institute for Research into Children's Literature, Potchefstroom University, Potchefstroom 2520

C J **Langenhoven** Prize
For outstanding work in field of Afrikaans linguistics. 500 rand. Awarded every three years. Enquiries to South African Academy of Science and Arts, PO Box 538, Pretoria 0001

C Louis **Leipoldt** Prys vir Poesie, see Department of National Education Literary Prizes for South African Citizens

M E R Prize
Awarded annually for the best children's book published by Tafelberg, Human & Rousseau, Nasou and Via Afrika. 2,000 rand and a gold medallion. Enquiries to Nasionale Boekhandel, PO Box 122, Parow 7500

H Recht **Malan** Prize
Awarded annually for the best non-fiction book published by Tafelberg, Human & Rousseau, Nasou and Via Afrika, 2,000 rand and a gold medallion. Enquiries to Nasionale Boekhandel, PO Box 122, Parow 7500

Eugène **Marais** Prize
For a first, or early, work of belles lettres in Afrikaans by a young writer. 250 rand. Awarded annually. Enquiries to South African Academy of Science and Arts, PO Box 538, Pretoria 0001

Mofolo-Plomer Prize
Initiated by Nadine Gordimer and Ravan Press and Ad Donker for a South African writer resident in Southern Africa or elsewhere. For a novel or a collection of short stories in English. Enquiries to Mofolo-Plomer Prize Committee, c/o Ravan Press (Pty) Ltd, PO Box 31134, Braamfontein 2017, Johannesburg

Perskor Prize for Light Reading
5,000 rand awarded every three years. Enquiries to Perskor Books (Pty) Ltd, PO Box 845, Johannesburg 2000

Perskor Prize for Literature
For the best literary work published in Afrikaans by Perskor. 5,000 rand awarded every three years. Enquiries to Perskor Books (Pty) Ltd, PO Box 845, Johannesburg 2000

Perskor Prize for Youth Literature
For the best youth work published in Afrikaans by Perskor. 5,000 rand awarded every three years. Enquiries to Perskor Books (Pty) Ltd, PO Box 845, Johannesburg 2000

Gustav **Preller** Prize
For literary science and literary criticism in Afrikaans. Awarded every 3 years. Enquiries to South African Academy of Science and Arts, PO Box 538, Pretoria 0001

Thomas **Pringle** Awards
Awarded every year in three of five categories, including play, book, film and television reviews in newspapers and periodicals; literary articles or substantial book reviews in academic and other journals, and in newspapers; articles on language and the teaching of English in academic, teachers' and other journals, and in newspapers; short stories and one-act plays in periodicals; and poetry in periodicals. 100 rand prize in each category. Enquiries to English Academy of Southern Africa, PO Box 124, Witwatersrand 2050

Scheepers Prize
For the best book written for children. 500 rand. Awarded every three years. Enquiries to South African Academy of Science and Arts, PO Box 538, Pretoria 0001

Olive **Schreiner** Prize for English Literature
For original literary work in English by a promising South African writer and published in South Africa. 500 rand. Awarded annually in one of the following categories: prose, poetry, drama. Enquiries to English Academy of Southern Africa, PO Box 124, Witwatersrand 2050

Pauline **Smith** Prize for Prose, see Department of National Education Literary Prizes for South African Citizens

South African Academy of Science and Arts Prizes
The Academy awards a number of prizes for works in Afrikaans; the following are noted in this section: Hertzog Prize; Tienie Holloway Medal; C J Langenhoven Prize; Eugène Marais Prize; Gustav Preller Prize; Scheepers Prize; Translation Prize. See individual entries for details. Enquiries to South African Academy of Science and Arts, PO Box 538, Pretoria 0001

Translation Prize
For translation of belles lettres from any language into Afrikaans. 250 rand awarded annually. Enquiries to South African Academy of Science and Arts, PO Box 538, Pretoria 0001

Translation Agencies and Associations

Torpis Publishing Co*, PO Box 1275, Bloemfontein Tel: (051) 71506
Man Dir: D Pistor
Afrikaans and German into English

Spain

General Information

Language: Castilian (the most widely used) is what foreigners know as Spanish; Basque in the north, Catalan in the east, Galician in the north-west. Most speakers of Basque, Catalan and Galician also speak Castilian
Religion: Roman Catholic
Population: 37.4 million
Bank Hours: Vary. Generally 0900-1300 or 0900-1600 Monday-Friday; half day Saturday
Shop Hours: Generally 0900-1300, 1700-2000 Monday-Saturday
Currency: 100 céntimos = 1 peseta
Export/Import Information: Member of European Economic Community. Varying tariffs on books, related to type, binding, language, etc; children's picture books dutied and taxed; compensatory tax on books in general. Most advertising matter is tariff-free but taxed. Import licence required; foreign books subject to censorship. Exchange controls
Copyright: UCC, Berne, Florence (see International section)

Book Trade Organizations

Agencia Española del ISBN*, Instituto Nacional del Libro Español, Calle Santiago Rusiñol 8, Madrid 3 Tel: (91) 2330802/2330902 Telex: 47891 fcli e
ISBN Administrator: Rafael Martínez Alés

Asociación de Escritores y Artistas Españoles*, Calle de Leganitos 10, Madrid 28013
Spanish Writers' and Artists' Association
Secretary: José G Manrique de Lara

Asociación Española de Editores de Musica (AEDEM)*, Carrera de San

Jeronimo, No 29 1°C, Madrid 14
Spanish Association of Music Publishers

Associació d'Editors en Llengua Catalana*, Valencia 279 – 1a planta, 08009 Barcelona Tel: (93) 2155091
Association of Publishers in Catalan

Federación de Asociaciones Nacionales de Distribuidores de Ediciones*, Reina Mercedes 18, Madrid 20
Federation of National Associations of Publications Distributors

Federación de Gremios de Editores de España, Calle Paseo de la Castellana 82 - 7°, 28046 Madrid Tel: (91) 4115795/4115713 Telex: 48457 Fgee E
Federation of Spanish Publishers' Associations
Secretary: Milagros del Corral

Gremi de Llibreters de Barcelona i Catalunya*, Calle Mallorca 272-276, 1a planta, 08037 Barcelona Tel: (93) 2154254
Booksellers' Association of Barcelona and Catalonia
Publication: Llibreria

Instituto Nacional del Libro Español*, Calle Santiago Rusiñol 8, Madrid 3 Tel: (91) 2330802/2330902/2334502
The National Institute of Spanish Books (which deals with the promotion of Spanish books)
Secretary: Eduardo Nolla López
Publications: El Libro Español (monthly); Guía de Editores de España; Guía de Libreros y Distribuidores de España; Libros Españoles ISBN (annual); Libros Infantiles y Juveniles

Publiexport SA, Calle Explanada 16, 28040 Madrid Tel: (91) 4427222 Telex: 49416 Publ E
Exporting and publishing consortium – a group of more than 200 companies comprising publishers, graphic art businesses and distributors
President: Raúl Rispa; *General Secretary:* Néstor García; *Sales and Marketing Dir:* Luis Izquierdo; *Promotion Manager:* Berta I Concha; *Special Services Manager (including Rights):* Louise Ciallella

Servei del Llibre de la Generalitat de Catalunya, Calle Mallorca 272-276, 08037 Barcelona Tel: (93) 2159004
Catalan Book Service of the Generalitat de Catalunya
Head of Dept: Segimon Borràs
Publication: Catàleg de Llibres en Català (Catalogue of books in Catalan)

Spanish Book Center*, Badajoz 171, 08018 Barcelona Tel: (93) 3003011 Telex: 98466 Sbcr e
Man Dir: Antonio Rodrigo
Export organization for all books published in Spain
Publication: New Books from Spain

Standard Book Numbering Agency, see Agencia Española del ISBN

Book Trade Reference Books and Journals

Books

Guía de Editores de España (Guide to the Publishers of Spain), Instituto Nacional del Libro Español, Calle Santiago Rusiñol 8, Madrid 3

Guía de Libreros y Distribuidores de España (Guide to the Booksellers and Distributors of Spain), Instituto Nacional del Libro Español, Calle Santiago Rusiñol 8, Madrid 3

Indice Cultural Español (Spanish Cultural Index), Dirección General de Relaciones Culturales, Ministerio de Asuntos Exteriores, Plaza de la Provincia 1, Madrid 12

Libros en Venta (Books for Sale), Turner Ediciones SRL, Alsina 1535, 8° piso, of 803, 1088 Buenos Aires, Argentina
Annual supplement covering Spanish language book production throughout the world

Libros Españoles ISBN (Spanish Books assigned ISBNs), Instituto Nacional del Libro Español, Calle Santiago Rusiñol 8, Madrid 3

Journals

Bibliografía Española (Spanish Bibliography), Instituto Bibliográfico Hispánico, Calle de Atocha 106, 28012 Madrid

Bibliografía Española: Suplemento de Publicaciones Periódicas (Periodical Publications Supplement to Spanish Bibliography), Instituto Bibliográfico Hispánico, Calle de Atocha 106, 28012 Madrid

Cuadernos de Bibliografía Española (Notebook of Spanish Bibliography), Instituto Bibliográfico Hispánico, Calle de Atocha 106, 28012 Madrid

El Libro Español (The Spanish Book), Instituto Nacional del Libro Español, Calle Santiago Rusiñol 8, Madrid 3

Llibreria (Bookselling), Gremi de Llibreters de Barcelona i Catalunya, Calle Mallorca 272-276, 1a planta, 08037 Barcelona

New Books from Spain, Spanish Book Center, Badajoz 171, 08018 Barcelona

Publishers

Ediciones **29**+*, Mandri 41, Barcelona 22 Tel: (93) 2123836
Man Dir: Alfredo Lloreme Diez
Subjects: Fiction, Literature, Poetry, General Non-fiction
Founded: 1968
ISBN Publisher's Prefix: 84-7175

Edicions **62** SA+, Provenza 278 – 1° 1a, 08008 Barcelona Tel: (93) 2160062
Man Dir: Ramon Bastardes i Porcel; *Editorial Dir:* Josep M Castellet; *Sales, Publicity:* Joaquim Sabria; *Rights & Permissions:* Josefina Revilla
Associate Company: Ediciones Peninsula (qv)
Subsidiary Company: Distribuciones de Enlace SA (Distributors), Bruc 49, 08009 Barcelona
Subjects: General (in Catalan)
1985: 127 titles *1986:* 118 titles *Founded:* 1963
ISBN Publisher's Prefix: 84-297

Editorial **A E D O S** SA+, Consejo de Ciento 391, 08009 Barcelona Tel: (93) 3170141/3012845
Man Dir: Juan Badosa
Subjects: Agriculture, Veterinary Science, Sports, How-to, Biography
1985: 5 titles *Founded:* 1939
ISBN Publisher's Prefix: 84-7003

Publicacions de l'**Abadia** de Montserrat, Abadia de Montserrat, Barcelona Tel: (93) 2450303
Shipping Add: Ausias March 92-98, 08013 Barcelona
Man Dir: Josep Massot Muntaner; *Sales, Advertising & Publicity:* Jordi Ubeda;

SPAIN 363

Rights & Permissions: Bernabé Dalmau
Subjects: Religion, History, Geography, Biography, Literature, Juveniles, Travel (mostly in Catalán)
1985: 74 titles *1986:* 73 titles *Founded:* 1915
ISBN Publisher's Prefix: 84-7202

Editorial **Acebo** SA+*, E Jardiel Poncela 4, 28016 Madrid Tel: (91) 2505310
Parent Company: Promoción Popular Cristiana (qv under PPC)
Subject: Education
ISBN Publisher's Prefix: 84-7103

Editorial **Acervo** SL*, Apdo 5319, 08006 Barcelona (Located at: Julio Verne 5-7, Barcelona) Tel: (93) 212264/2474425
Man Dir: Ana Perales
Subjects: General Literature, Science, Fiction, Law, History
Founded: 1954
ISBN Publisher's Prefix: 84-7002

Editorial **Acribia** SA+, Apdo 466, 50006 Zaragoza (Located at: Calle Royo 23, Zaragoza) Tel: (976) 232089
Man Dir: Pascual López Lorenzo; *Sales, Publicity, Advertising:* Mercedes Marcen
Subjects: Veterinary Science, Agriculture, General Science, Medicine, Nutrition, Oceanography, Marine Biology
Founded: 1957
ISBN Publisher's Prefix: 84-200

Aguilar SA de Ediciones+, Juan Bravo 38, 28006 Madrid Tel: (91) 2763800/4315422 Cable Add: Guilarditor Telex: 47137 Agata Fax: (91) 4316481
President: Jesús de Polanco Gutierrez; *Vice President:* Francisco Pérez González; *Dir General:* Ambrosio Maria Ochoa Vázquez; *Editorial Dirs:* Jaime Salinas Bonmatí, Mauricio Santos Arrabal; *Dir, Children's Books:* Miguel Azaola; *Sales Dir:* José Manuel López Bottiglieri
Branch Offs: Aguilar SA, Argentina (qv); Isla Negra SA, Chile (qv); Libreria Científica, Colombia; Edidac, Ecuador; Aguilar SA, Mexico (qv); La Familia y Studium, Peru; Itaca SA, Spain; Editemas y Dilae SA, Venezuela (qv)
Subjects: General Fiction & Non-fiction, Classics, History & Geography, Art, Philosophy & Religion, General & Social Sciences, Medicine, Reference, Cartography, Children's
ISBN Publisher's Prefix: 84-03

Editorial **'Alas'**, Apdo 36274, Barcelona 7 (Located at: Valencia 234, Barcelona) Tel: (93) 2537506
Subjects: Sports, How-to, Parapsychology, Crosswords, Martial Arts, Periodicals
ISBN Publisher's Prefix: 84-203

Alba SA+, Apdo 2494, Madrid 80 (Located at: Ave Navalafuente 1, Venturada (Madrid)) Tel: (91) 2336133
Man Dir and other offices: José Luis Inés
Subject: Literature
1986: 15 titles *1987:* 22 titles *Founded:* 1983
ISBN Publisher's Prefix: 84-7567

Ediciones **Alfaguara** SA+, Príncipe de Vergara 81 – 1°, Madrid 7 Tel: (91) 2619700 Cable Add: Guara Madrid Telex: 43879 Edea E
Man Dir: Ambrosio Ochoa; *Editor-in-Chief:* José María Guelbenzu; *Publicity, Promotion:* Angeles Martín; *Rights & Permissions:* Rosa Benavides
Subjects: General Fiction, Literature, Children's Books, Universal Classics
Founded: 1964
ISBN Publisher's Prefix: 84-204

Editorial **Alhambra** SA+, Apdo 40FD, 28001 Madrid (Located at: Claudio Coello

76, Madrid) Tel: (91) 4316460 Cable Add: Edimbrasa Telex: 47688 Wxyz E
President: Erich Ruiz Albrecht; *Editorial, Rights & Permissions:* Ramón Nieto Alvarez-Uría; *Sales:* Pedro Jarque de Leva (International), Fernando Ruiz (Spain), Javier Laría Quincoces (Spain); *Production:* Juan Moreno; *Publicity:* María Teresa Esteban
Branch Offs: Enrique Granados 61, 08008 Barcelona; Iruña 12, 48014 Bilbao; Plaza de las Descalzas 2, 18009 Granada; Pasadizo de Pernas 13, 15005 La Coruña; Tomas Morales 48, 38004 Las Palmas; Saturnino Calleja 1, 28002 Madrid; Reina Mercedes 35, 41012 Seville; General Porlier 14, 38004 Santa Cruz de Tenerife; Cabillers 5, 46003 Valencia; Julio Ruiz de Alda 12, 47013 Valladolid; Concepción Arenal 25, 50005 Zaragoza; Editorial Alhambra Mexicana SA de CV, Calle Amores 2027, Colonia del Valle, 03100 México DF, Mexico
Subjects: Medicine, General Science, Literature, History, Philology, Philosophy, Psychology, Art, Nursing, Reference, Children's, Pre-school, University, Secondary and Primary Textbooks, Audiovisual Aids, Languages
Bookshops: At above main and branch offices addresses
1985: 292 titles *1986:* 260 titles *Founded:* 1942
Miscellaneous: Incorporating Editorial Mezquita SA
ISBN Publisher's Prefix: 84-205

Alianza Editorial SA+, Apdo 9107, 28043 Madrid (Located at: Milán 38, Madrid) Tel: (91) 2000045 Telex: 45746
Man Dir: Diego Hidalgo; *Editorial:* Javier Pradera; *Sales & Marketing:* Faustino Linares; *Publicity:* Ezequiel Mendez; *Rights & Permissions:* Monica Acheroff
Associate Companies: Alianza Editorial Argentina, Córdoba 2064, Buenos Aires, Argentina; Distasa, Argentina (qv); Alianza Distribuidora de Colombia, Colombia; Alianza Editorial Mexicana, Mexico (qv); Revista de Occidente SA (qv)
Subjects: General Fiction, Belles Lettres, Poetry, History, Music, Art, Philosophy, Political and Social Science, High-priced Paperbacks, Mathematics, General Science
1985: 181 titles *Founded:* 1965 (as publishers)
ISBN Publisher's Prefix: 84-206

Ediciones El **Almendro**+, El Almendro 10, 14006 Cordoba Tel: (957) 274692
Man Dir, Editorial: Francisca Molina Cobo
Parent Company: Librería El Almendro
Subjects: History, Poetry, Law, General Non-fiction, Regional Fiction, Children's, History of Art, Andalusian Art, Hebrew Studies, Textbooks, Periodical
Founded: 1982

Ediciones **Altea** SA+, Príncipe de Vergara 84, Madrid 6 Tel: (91) 2625300 Cable Add: Edialtea Telex: 43879
Man Dir: Ambrosio Ochoa; *Editorial Dir:* Miguel Azaola; *Sales:* José Manuel Lopez Bottiglieri; *Promotion:* María Angeles Martín; *Co-productions:* Juan Ramón Azaola; *Rights & Permissions:* Rosa Benavides
Subjects: Activity, Children's and Picture Books
Founded: 1973
ISBN Publisher's Prefix: 84-372

Editorial **Anagrama**, Calle Pedró de la Creu 58 – 1°1a, 08034 Barcelona Tel: (93) 2037652 Telex: 98753 Agram E
Man Dir: Jorge de Herralde
Subjects: Literature, Philosophy, Psychology, Social Science, Anthropology
Founded: 1968
ISBN Publisher's Prefix: 84-339

Ediciones **Anaya** SA+, Josefa Valcárcel 27, 28027 Madrid Tel: (91) 7429111 Cable Add: Edinaya Telex: 22039 Anaya E
President: Germán Sánchez Ruipérez; *Vice President:* Juan José Losada; *Man Dir:* Enrique Coque; *Editorial, Rights & Permissions:* Ramiro Sánchez; *Sales:* Antonio Gutierrez
Parent Company: Grupo Anaya (at above address)
Associate Companies: Algaida Editores SA, Avda de San Francisco Javier s/n, Edificio Hermes, 41005 Seville; Ediciones Generales Anaya, Anaya Multimedia (both at above address); Editorial Barcanova SA (qv); Editorial Biblograf SA (qv); Ediciones Cátedra SA (qv); Credsa, Calabria 108, 08015 Barcelona; Ediciones Pirámide SA (qv); Editorial Tecnos SA (qv); Ediciones Versal SA (qv); Edicions Xerais de Galicia, Doctor Marañón 10, 36211 Vigo
Subjects: University, Secondary & Primary Textbooks, Educational Materials
Founded: 1959
ISBN Publisher's Prefix: 84-207

Editoriales **Andaluzas** Unidas SA, Calle Diego de Merlo 8 bajos a & b, 41003 Seville Tel: (954) 410604/410804
President: Manuel Angel Vázquez Medel; *Dir:* Manuel Barrera Blasco
Founded: 1984
ISBN Publisher's Prefix: 84-7587

Editorial **Aranzadi** SA*, Carlos III 34, Pamplona Tel: (948) 331212/249950
Man Dir: Estanislao de Aranzadi; *Sales Dir:* Javier de Epalza y Aranzadi
Subject: Law
Founded: 1929
ISBN Publisher's Prefix: 84-7016

Editorial **Argos** Vergara SA+*, Aragón 390, Barcelona 13 Tel: (93) 2322211 Cable Add: Leargos Telex: 50464 Argos E
President: Emilio González
Subjects: Fiction, Non-fiction, Reference
ISBN Publisher's Prefix: 84-7178

Editorial **Ariel** SA+, Córcega 270 – 4°, Barcelona 8 Tel: (93) 2186400 Telex: 98255 Sxbl E
General Manager: Miguel García Piriz; *Publisher, Foreign Rights:* Marcelo Covian
Associate Company: Editorial Seix Barral SA (qv)
Subjects: General and Social Sciences, Psychology, Philosophy, Economics, History, Literature, Texts in Catalan, Geography, University Textbooks
Founded: 1941
Miscellaneous: Firm is a member of the Planeta Group (see Editorial Planeta SA)
ISBN Publisher's Prefix: 84-344

Ediciones **Artes** Graficas Cobas SA, see Cobas

Asesoría Técnica de Ediciones SA+*, Ronda General Mitre 90, Barcelona 21 Tel: (93) 2479133/2477066
Man Dir, Editorial: José Dalmau Salvia; *Sales:* Antonio Dalmau Salvia; *Production:* José Luis Arribas; *Rights & Permissions:* Carmen de Eulate Echagüe
Subsidiary Company: Libroexpress

Subjects: Fiction, Anthropology, Computers, Communications, Information Science, Science Fiction, Classics, Microbiology
ISBN Publisher's Prefix: 84-7442

Asociación para el Progresso de la Dirección (APD)*, Montalban 3, Madrid 14 Tel: (91) 2325487
Dir of Publications: Vidal Pérez Herrero
Subject: Business Administration
ISBN Publisher's Prefix: 84-7019

Asuri de Ediciones SA, Apdo 1312, 48001 Bilbao (Located at: Calle Nervión 3 – 4°, Bilbao) Tel: (94) 4244773
Man Dir: Carlos Lopez-Linares Perez de Heredia; *Sales:* Juan Jose de Arteagabeitia Apodaca; *Production:* Luis Santa Coloma Gutierrez
Subsidiary Company: Asuri Mexicana SA, Ave Universidades 757, México 01090, Mexico
Branch Offs: Barcelona, Bilbao, Gijon, Las Palmas de Gran Canaria, Madrid, Malaga, Seville, Valencia, Valladolid, Vigo, Zaragoza
Subjects: Dictionaries, Encyclopaedias, Art, Children's
Founded: 1960
ISBN Publisher's Prefix: 84-7539

Sociedad de Educación **Atenas** SA*, Mayor 81, 28013 Madrid Tel: (91) 2480127
Publicity Manager: Feliciano Villa
Subjects: Religion, Education, Psychology, Biography
ISBN Publisher's Prefix: 84-7020

Ediciones **Atrium** SA+, Calle Muntaner 483 ático 4°, 08021 Barcelona Tel: (93) 2127154 Telex: 98410 Wfe E
Man Dir: Francisco Asensio Cerver
Subjects: Architecture, Interior Decoration
1986: 3 titles *Founded:* 1986
ISBN Publisher's Prefix: 84-7741

Ayalga Ediciones SA*, Apdo 1101, Salinas, Asturias (Located at: Calle Alcalde Luis Treillard 14-16, Salinas, Asturias) Tel: 511299/510599 Cable Add: Ayalga
Man Dir: Ramón Baragaño; *Editorial:* Aquilino Escudero, Agustín Santarúa; *Sales:* Francisco Alzueta; *Publicity:* Astel
Subject: Asturian region
Founded: 1976
ISBN Publisher's Prefix: 84-7411

Editorial **Aymá** SA Editora*, Travessera de Gracia 64, Barcelona 6 Tel: (93) 2000174 Cable Add: Aymol
President: Joan B Cendrós Carbonell
Subjects: General Fiction, Belles Lettres, Poetry, Biography, History, How-to, Music, Art, Philosophy, Religion, Low- and High-priced Paperbacks, Juveniles. In both Castilian and Catalan
Founded: 1952
ISBN Publisher's Prefix: 84-209

Editorial **Ayuso***, San Bernardo 34, Madrid 8
Subject: Social Sciences
ISBN Publisher's Prefix: 84-336

Editorial **Azara** SA+, Calle Zamora 28, 28830 San Fernando de Henares (Madrid) Tel: (91) 6722709/6722618
Man Dir: Angel Delgado Gomez
Associate Company: Didactic SA, Calle Zamora 27, 28830 San Fernando de Henares (Madrid)
Subjects: Textbooks, Educational, Children's, Politics
Founded: 1979

Editorial **Barath** SA+, Blasco de Garay 15, 28015 Madrid Tel: (91) 4496049
Man Dir: Victorino del Pozo; *Sales:* Cinta Barrobes; *Production:* Jorge Viñes
Associate Company: Distribuciones Alfaomega SA, Calle Calvo Asensio 13, 28015 Madrid
Subjects: Astrology, Humanities, Esoteric
Bookshop: Librería Arkano SA (at above address)
1986: 9 titles *1987:* 10 titles *Founded:* 1980
ISBN Publisher's Prefix: 84-85799

Editorial **Barcanova** SA+, Plaza Lesseps 33, 08023 Barcelona Tel: (93) 2172054 Telex: 98634 Vsbn
Dir General: Joan Agut; *Editorial:* Jordi Galofré; *Production:* Enric Canut
Orders to: Grupo Distribuidor Editorial SA, Don Ramón de la Cruz 67, Madrid 1
Parent Company: Grupo Anaya, Josefa Valcárcel 27, 28027 Madrid
Associate Companies: Ediciones Anaya SA (qv for other associates)
Subjects: Educational, University Textbooks, Children's, Catalan Language
1985: 36 titles *1986:* 48 titles *Founded:* 1981
ISBN Publisher's Prefix: 84-7533

Barral Editores SA*, Calabria 235-239, Barcelona 29 Tel: (93) 2175773
Subjects: General Fiction, Belles Lettres, Poetry, Art, Theatre, Paperbacks
Founded: 1964
ISBN Publisher's Prefix: 84-211

Ediciones **Bellaterra** SA*, Felipe de Paz 12, Barcelona 28 Tel: (93) 3390511
Man Dir: Felio Riera Domenech; *Editorial:* Jeannine Rochefort; *Sales:* Angeles Galán Gallego
Subjects: Science & Technology, Social Sciences
Founded: 1972
ISBN Publisher's Prefix: 84-7290

Ediciones **Betis***, Calle Bot 4 bis, Barcelona 2 Tel: (93) 3175844
Man Dir, Editorial, Rights & Permissions: Santiago Subirana; *Sales:* Eugenio Subirana
Subjects: Juveniles, Popular Science, History, Philosophy, Infants
Founded: 1939
ISBN Publisher's Prefix: 84-7160

Biblioteca de Autores Cristianos de la Editorial Católica SA, see Católica

Editorial **Biblioteca Nueva** SL+, Almagro 38, 28010 Madrid Tel: (91) 4100436
Man Dir: José Ruiz-Castillo; *Sales Dir:* Paz Casas Ruiz-Castillo
Subjects: Belles Lettres, Poetry, Biography, History, Psychology
Founded: 1920
ISBN Publisher's Prefix: 84-7030

Editorial **Biblograf** SA, Calle Calabria 108, 08015 Barcelona Tel: (93) 2240000/2241906/2246606 Cable Add: Biblograf Telex: 54155 Cvox E
Man Dir: D Fermin Vargas Lazaro
Parent Company: Grupo Anaya, Josefa Valcárcel 27, 28027 Madrid
Associate Companies: Ediciones Anaya SA (qv for other associates)
Subjects: Dictionaries, Philology
Founded: 1952
ISBN Publisher's Prefix: 84-7153

Editorial **Blume** SA, Calle Milanesat 21-23, Barcelona 17 Tel: (93) 2042300/04/08 Cable Add: Ediblume Telex: 54675 Contbe
Man Dir, Editorial: Siegfried Blume; *Rights & Permissions:* Ursula Fischer
Subjects: Architecture, Art, History, Politics, Ecology, Nature Study, Gardening, Life Sciences, books in Spanish, English and Catalan
Founded: 1965
ISBN Publisher's Prefix: 84-7031

Hermann **Blume** Ediciones+, Calle Rosario 17, 28005 Madrid Tel: (91) 2659200/2659209/2659208 Telex: 41288 Hebl E
Man Dir: Hermann Blume Plaza; *Sales, Publicity, Promotion:* Miguel Angel San José; *Editions Coordinator and Rights:* Marta Bela
Subjects: Architecture & Urban Studies, Alternative Technology, Natural Sciences, Economics, Photography, Crafts, Art and Art Instruction, Plants, Hobbies
Bookshop: At above address
1985: 26 titles *Founded:* 1975
ISBN Publisher's Prefix: 84-7214

Antoni **Bosch** Editor SA+, Manuel Girona 61 baixos, 08034 Barcelona Tel: (93) 2052606
Man Dir: Antoni Bosch-Domenech; *Production, Rights & Permissions:* Marta Lorés-Maragall
Subjects: Economics, Essays, Music, Philosophy, Science
Founded: 1978
ISBN Publisher's Prefix: 84-85855

Bosch Casa Editorial SA, Calle Comte d'Urgell 51 bis, 08011 Barcelona Tel: (93) 2548437/2544629 Fax: (93) 3236736
Man Dir: Agustín Bosch Domenech
Subjects: Law, Science & Technology, Philology, General Literature
1985: 30 titles *1986:* 33 titles *Founded:* 1934
ISBN Publisher's Prefixes: 84-7162, 84-7676

Editorial **Bruño**, Marqués de Mondéjar 32, Madrid 28 Tel: (91) 2460605/7
Man Dir: Ermenter Ars Forner
Subjects: Secondary & Primary Textbooks, Education, Communication
Founded: 1882
ISBN Publisher's Prefix: 84-216

Ediciones **C E D E L**+, Apdo 5326, Barcelona 08008 (Located at: Calle Mallorca 257, Barcelona) Tel: (93) 2156088 Telex: 98355 Baei 018
Man Dir, Rights & Permissions: José Avila
Subjects: Technical, Naturism, Health, Yoga, Agriculture, Biology, Ecology
Founded: 1956
ISBN Publisher's Prefix: 84-352

Silverio **Cañada**, Honesto Batalón 7, Gijon (Asturias) Tel: (985) 355790/357413 Telex: 89736 Edju E
Man Dir, Editorial: Silverio Cañada; *Sales:* Fernando Alvarez Conde; *Production:* Manuel Cárdenas
Orders to: Alto Atocha 7, Gijon
Subjects: Regional Encyclopaedias
Founded: 1970
ISBN Publisher's Prefix: 84-7286

Editorial **Cantabrica** SA+, Plaza del Ensanche 5 – 1° izda, 48009 Bilbao Tel: (94) 4245307
Man Dir: Begoña Grijelmo Mattern
Subjects: Juveniles, Sports, Cooking, Languages, Humour
Founded: 1960
ISBN Publisher's Prefix: 84-221

Luis de **Caralt** Editor SA+, Paseo de Gracia 96, 08008 Barcelona Tel: (93) 2156516 Cable Add: Edinoguer Barcelona Telex: 48148
President: Emilio Ardevol; *Rights & Permissions:* Maruchy Friart
Associate Company: Editorial Noguer SA (qv)
Subjects: General Fiction and Non-fiction, History, Art, Medicine, Geography, Paperbacks
1986: 5 titles *Founded:* 1942
ISBN Publisher's Prefix: 84-217

Casa de Velázquez, Ciudad Universitaria, 28040 Madrid Tel: (91) 2433605
Man Dir: Didier Ozanam; *Editorial:* Jean-Pierre Etienvre
Subjects: Social Sciences, Archaeology, Geography, Aerial prospections
1985: 4 titles *1986:* 8 titles *Founded:* 1928
ISBN Publisher's Prefix: 84-600

Editorial **Casals** SA+, Calle Caspe 79, 08013 Barcelona Tel: (93) 2323713 Telex: 98772 Cllc E ref Casals
Man Dir: Ramón Casals Lamarca; *Rights & Permissions:* Ramón Casals Roca
Branch Offs: 24 in Spain, one in Uruguay, one in Argentina
Subjects: Pre-school Books, Primary Textbooks, Comics, Children's Literature
1985: 44 titles *1986:* 53 titles *Founded:* 1870
ISBN Publisher's Prefix: 84-218

Editorial **Casariego** SA+, Calle Ponzano 69, 28003 Madrid Tel: (91) 4424339/4425178
Man Dir, Production, Rights & Permissions: Rafael Díaz-Casariego; *Editorial, Sales:* Ramón Díaz-Casariego
Subjects: Art, Bibliophily, Facsimiles
Bookshop: Librería Facsimilia, Calle Cristobal Bordiu 36, 28003 Madrid
Founded: 1959
ISBN Publisher's Prefix: 84-85005

Editorial **Castalia***, Zurbano 39, Madrid 10 Tel: (91) 4198940/4195857
Man Dir: Amparo Soler; *Sales Dir:* Federico Ibáñez
Subjects: Literature, Criticism, Classics, Philology
Founded: 1941
Miscellaneous: Specializes in editions of the classics
ISBN Publisher's Prefix: 84-7039

Ediciones **Cátedra** SA+*, Josefa Valcárcel 27, 28027 Madrid Tel: (91) 7428111 Telex: 43341 Gsri E
Man Dir: Gustavo Domínguez; *Rights & Permissions:* Louise Ciallella
Orders to: Grupo Editorial SA, Don Ramón de la Cruz 67, Madrid 1
Parent Company: Grupo Anaya (at above address)
Associate Companies: Ediciones Anaya SA (qv for other associates)
Subjects: Literature, Criticism, Humanities, Linguistics, Art
1985: 70 titles *Founded:* 1974
ISBN Publisher's Prefix: 84-376

Biblioteca de Autores Cristianos de la Editorial **Católica** SA+, Apdo 466, 28036 Madrid (Located at: Mateo Inurria 15, Madrid) Tel: (91) 2592800 Cable Add: Edica Telex: 27727
Dir: José Luis Gutiérrez García; *Sales:* Luis Ortiz Pérez; *Publicity:* Bartolomé Parera Galmés
Subjects: Philosophy, Religion, Theology, Liturgy, History
Founded: 1912
ISBN Publisher's Prefixes: 84-720, 84-220

Ediciones **Ceac** SA+, Apdo 926, 08020 Barcelona (Located at: Calle Perú 164, Barcelona) Tel: (93) 3073004 Telex: 50564 Ceac E
Man Dir: Guillermo Menal Alonso; *International Dir, Rights & Permissions:* José L Quiñones Correa; *Technical, Literary Dir:* Albert Vidal García
Subsidiary Companies: Editorial Timun Mas SA (qv); Ediciones Vidorama SA, Castillejos 294-296, 08025 Barcelona
Associate Company: Centro de Estudios Ceac
Branch Offs: Editorial Siluetas, Bartolomé Mitre 3745-49, 1201 Buenos Aires, Argentina; Aconcagua Ediciones y Publicaciones SA, Mexico (qv)
Subjects: Technical, Arts & Crafts, Homecrafts & Domestic Science, Psychology, Educational
1985: 60 titles *1986:* 68 titles *Founded:* 1957
ISBN Publisher's Prefix: 84-329

El **Cid** Editor SAE*, Cardenal Vives y Tutó 43 – 2° 3a, Barcelona 34 Tel: (93) 2045067 Telex: 51130 Fonotx E clave 16-00591
Man Dir, Rights & Permissions: Dr Eduardo Varela-Cid; *Editorial:* Osiris Troiani; *Sales:* Adriana Buguña; *Production:* José Luis Tolosa i Paredes; *Publicity:* Victor Ramos
Parent Company: El Cid Editor SRL, Argentina (qv)
Subsidiary Company: El Cid Editor CA, Apdo 60010, Caracas 1060, Venezuela
Associate Companies (all in Argentina): Ciudad Educativa SAIC, El Cid Distribuidor SA (both at Alsina 500, 1087 Buenos Aires); La Casa de los Papeles, Bolivar 218, 1066 Buenos Aires
Subjects: Fiction, Sociology and Social Work, Juvenile, Economics, Geo-politics, Research Technology, History
Bookshop: Librería del Colegio, Ciudad Educativa SA, Buenos Aires, Argentina
Founded: 1970
ISBN Publisher's Prefix: 84-85745

Editorial **Científico Médica***, Vía Layetana 53, 08003 Barcelona Tel: (93) 3186828 Telex: 59347 E Cmb
Man Dir: Eugeniano Barrera San Martín; *Chief Editor:* Dr Enrique Sierra Ruiz
Subjects: Medicine, Psychology, Veterinary Science, Engineering, Architecture, Technical Subjects
Founded: 1915
ISBN Publisher's Prefix: 84-224

Editorial **Cincel** SA+*, Calle Alberto Aguilera 32, Madrid 15 Tel: (91) 4458862 Cable Add: Cincel Telex: 46497 Kaci E
Man Dir: Carlos Rodriguez Alvarez; *Editorial, Rights, Sales, Publicity:* Francisco Belloso Cruzado
Parent Company: Editorial Kapelusz SA, Argentina (qv)
Subjects: Psychology, Textbooks, Education and educational materials
Bookshop: Librería Cincel (at above address)

Founded: 1971
ISBN Publisher's Prefix: 84-7046

Editorial **Ciudad Nueva***, Andrés Tamayo 4, 28028 Madrid
Parent Company: Città Nuova Editrice, Italy (qv for associate companies)
Subjects: Religion, Evangelism

Editorial **Claret** SA, Calle Roger de Llúria 5, 08010 Barcelona Tel: (93) 3010887
Man Dir: Pere Prat Serra; *Editorial:* Antoni Andrés Soler; *Sales:* Carlos Delgado Martínez; *Production:* Josep Ll Martínez Martínez; *Publicity:* Ernest Puig Rovira
Subjects: Catalan Culture, Religion
Bookshop: At above address
Founded: 1926
ISBN Publisher's Prefix: 84-7263

Ediciones Artes Graficas **Cobas** SA+, Calle Numancia 75, 08029 Barcelona Tel: (93) 3218594 Telex: 51022 Agcz E
Man Dir: Angel Cobas Ros
Subsidiary Company: Ediciones Garza SA (qv)
Subjects: Children's Picture Books
Founded: 1949
ISBN Publisher's Prefix: 84-215

Alberto **Corazón** Editor*, Roble 22, Madrid 20 Tel: (91) 2704378
Man Dir: Alberto Corazón; *Sales Dir:* José Miguel García
Subjects: Literature, History, Philosophy, Poetry, Social Sciences, University Textbooks
Founded: 1969
ISBN Publisher's Prefix: 84-7053

Ediciones **Cristiandad**+*, Huesca 30, Madrid 20 Tel: (91) 4554759
Subjects: Religion, History
ISBN Publisher's Prefix: 84-7057

Editorial **Crítica** SA*, Aragón 385, 08013 Barcelona Tel: (93) 2587000
Man Dir: Gonzalo Pontón
Parent Company: Ediciones Grijalbo SA (qv)
Subjects: Social Sciences, Politics, Current Affairs, Marxism, Philosophy
Founded: 1976
ISBN Publisher's Prefix: 84-7423

Ediciones **Cultura** Hispánica*, Ave de los Reyes Católicos 4, Madrid 3 Tel: (91) 2440600
Publishing Dir: Cesar Olmos
Subjects: Literature, Poetry, Essays, Theatre, Biography, History, Art, Economics, Law, Philology, Social Science
ISBN Publisher's Prefix: 84-7232

Ediciones **Daimon** — Manuel Tamayo+*, Provenza 284, Barcelona 8 Cable Add: Edidaimón Telex: 97648 kyzt 6
Subjects: Art, History, How-to, Reference, Medicine, Cinematography, Photography, Sexology, Philosophy, Science, Psychology, Music
ISBN Publisher's Prefix: 84-231

Ediciones **Danae** SA, now Ediciones Océano-Éxito SA (qv)

Editorial **De Vecchi** SA, Balmes 247, Barcelona 6 Tel: (93) 2171854/2171858 Cable Add: Deveditor Telex: 51042 Deve E
Man Dir: Giovanni De Vecchi
Subjects: How-to and Practical Books generally
Founded: 1967
ISBN Publisher's Prefix: 84-315

Debate SA+, Calle Zurbano 92 – 5°, 28003 Madrid Tel: (91) 4421221/2 Telex: 44678 Debt E
Man Dir: Angel Lucia Aguirre; *Editorial:* Francisco Pabon Torres
Subjects: Children's, Fiction, Adventure, Ecology, Pacifism, Essays, University Textbooks, Large-print books, Encyclopaedias
1987: 250 titles *Founded:* 1977
ISBN Publisher's Prefix: 84-7444

Editorial Revista de **Derecho Privado**, an imprint of EDERSA (qv)

Edicions **Destino** SA+, Consell de Cent 425 – 5° planta, 08009 Barcelona Tel: (93) 2462305
Dir General: Andreu Teixidor de Ventós; *President:* Joan Teixidor
Subjects: General Fiction, Art Books, History, Children's
Bookshop: Librería Ancora y Delfín (qv under Major Booksellers)
Founded: 1942
ISBN Publisher's Prefix: 84-233

Ediciones **Díaz** de Santos SA+, Calle Juan Bravo 3A, 28006 Madrid Tel: (91) 4312482 Telex: 45141 Dsan E ref Ediciones Fax: (91) 2755563
Man Dir: Joaquin Díaz Gomez; *Sales:* Julian Martin
Subjects: Science, Technology, Library and Information Science, Medicine
Bookshop: Díaz de Santos SA – Libreria Cientifico-Tecnica (qv under Major Booksellers)
1985: 10 titles *1986:* 21 titles *Founded:* 1983
ISBN Publisher's Prefix: 84-86251

Centro de **Difusión** del Libro, see Ediciones CEDEL

Dilagro SA*, Editorial-Librería, Comercío 48, 25007 Lérida Tel: (973) 233480/245100
Man Dir: Jorge Marimón
Subjects: Agriculture, History and Customs of the region of Lérida
Bookshop: Librería Ténica (at above address)
ISBN Publisher's Prefix: 84-7234

Dístein Libros, an imprint of Editorial Timun Mas SA (qv)

Editorial **Don Quijote**, Calle Horno de Haza 21, Edificio La Purísima local 9, 18002 Granada Tel: (958) 278789
Man Dir: Manuel Barrera Blasco
Subjects: History, Fiction, Poetry, Theatre, Essays, University Textbooks
1986: 53 titles *Founded:* 1981
ISBN Publisher's Prefix: 84-85933

Editorial **Dossat** SA*, Plaza de Santa Ana 9, Madrid 12 Tel: (91) 4298568 Telex: 42572 Doat
Man Dir: Eugeniano Barrera San Martín
Branch Off: Vía Layetana 53, Barcelona 3
Subjects: Medicine, Engineering, General Scientific, University Textbooks
ISBN Publisher's Prefix: 84-237

Ediciones **Doyma** SA+, Travesera de Gracia 17-21, 08021 Barcelona Tel: (93) 2000711 Telex: 51964 Ink E Fax: (93) 2091136
Man Dir: José Antonio Dotú Roteta; *Book Division Manager:* Germán Covas Sierra; *Editorial Manager, Foreign Rights:* Xavier Mas López; *Editorial Coordinator:* Pilar Aparicio; *Sales, Publicity:* Lorenzo Matas Muñoz, José Latorre Castell
Subsidiary Companies: AP (Americana de Publicaciones), Cerrito 512, Buenos Aires, Argentina; Doyma Argentina SA, Marcelo T Álvear 2181, Buenos Aires, Argentina; Publicaciones Tecnicas Mediterraneo,

Boldos 2369, Santiago, Chile; Publicaciones Americanas de México, Miguel A Laurent 630, México DF, Mexico
Subject: Medicine
1987: 150 titles *Founded:* 1971
ISBN Publisher's Prefix: 84-85285, 84-7592

Ediciones **Druida** SA+*, Diagonal 331, Barcelona 9
Man Dir: Miguel Pelucer Esteban; *Rights & Permissions:* Susana P Esteban
Subject: Children's
Founded: 1982
ISBN Publisher's Prefix: 84-86087

Durvan SA de Ediciones, Colón de Larreátegui 13, 48001 Bilbao Tel: (94) 4230777
Man Dir: Lorenzo Portillo Sisniega
Subjects: Encyclopaedias, Dictionaries
Founded: 1960
ISBN Publisher's Prefix: 84-85001

Editorial **E D A F** SA+, Jorge Juan 30, Madrid 1 Tel: (91) 4358260
President: Luciano Fossati; *Publicity:* Gerardo Fossati Demichelis
Branch Offs: Ediciones Antonio Fossati SACI, Calle Chile 2222, Buenos Aires, Argentina
Subjects: History, Philosophy, Juveniles, Reference, Textbooks, Natural Medicine, Sports
ISBN Publisher's Prefix: 84-7166

E D E R S A (Editoriales de Derecho Reunidas SA)*, Caracas 21, Apdo 4032, Madrid 4 Tel: (91) 4101862/4199623 Cable Add: Revipriv
Man Dir: Antonio Alvarez de Morales
Imprints: Ediciones Pegaso, Editorial Revista de Derecho Privado
Subjects: Biography, History, Philosophy, Social Science, Law, Technical, University Textbooks
Founded: 1900
ISBN Publisher's Prefix: 84-7130

E D H A S A (Editora y Distribuidora Hispano-Americana SA)+, Diagonal 519/521 – 2°, 08029 Barcelona Tel: (93) 2395105
Man Dir: Javier Pérez Díez
Associate Companies: Editorial Sudamericana SA, Argentina (qv); Editorial Hermes SA, Mexico (qv)
Subjects: Fiction, Literature, Historical novels, Essays
ISBN Publisher's Prefix: 84-350

E U N S A (Ediciones Universidad de Navarra SA)+, Apdo 396, 31080 Pamplona (Located at: Plaza de los Sauces, 1 y 2 Barañain, Pamplona) Tel: (948) 256850 Cable Add: EUNSA Pamplona Telex: 37917 Unav E
Man Dir, Sales: Gerardo Izco; *Editorial Dir:* Francisco Salvadó; *Production:* Luis María Echeverría; *Publicity:* Benigno Sáez; *Rights & Permissions:* Eugenia Puyales
Imprint: Biblioteca 'NT' (number of paperback series covering the Arts and Sciences, Current Affairs, Religion and Philosophy etc)
Subjects: Architecture, Business Administration, Economics, Education, History, Journalism, Law, Canon Law, Language and Literature, Medicine, Biology, Engineering, Nursing, Philosophy, Religion, Theology, Bibliography, Librarianship, Encyclopaedias, Periodicals
1985: 61 titles *1986:* 61 titles *Founded:* 1967
ISBN Publisher's Prefix: 84-313

Edebe, Paseo S J Bosco 62, 08017 Barcelona
Associate Company: Editorial Don Bosco SA, Mexico (qv for other associate companies)

Edica SA*, Apdo 466, Madrid 16 (Located at: Calle Mateo Inurria 15, Madrid) Tel: (91) 2592800 Cable Add: Edica Telex: 27727
Dir: Dr José Luis Gutierrez Garcia; *Sales:* Luis Ortiz Pérez; *Publicity:* Bartolomé Parera Galmés
Subjects: Theology, Asceticism, Mysticism, History, Philosophy, Hagiography, Pocket Editions

Edigol Ediciones SA+, Calle Luis Millet 63, Esplugues de Llobregat (Barcelona) Tel: (93) 3726304/3726361 Telex: 98772 Cllc E
Man Dir: Jorge Onrubia; *Sales:* Salvador Tomas
Subjects: Atlases, Wall Maps, Children's and Juvenile Literature
1986: 6 titles *1987:* 21 titles *Founded:* 1976 (as Edigol Ediciones Cartograficas)
ISBN Publisher's Prefix: 84-85406

Edigraf, Editorial Vilcar y Gráficas Hamburg SA, Tamarit 130, 08015 Barcelona Tel: (93) 3255550 Telex: 97146 Edyg E
Man Dir: Francisco Vilar
Subject: Juveniles
ISBN Publisher's Prefix: 84-7066

Editorial **Ediseis** SA*, General Oraá 32, 28006 Madrid Tel: (91) 4112561 Telex: 47088 Edse E
Man Dir: Luis Maria Saiz Martinez
Branch Off: Ediseis SA, Rosellón 55, 08029 Barcelona
Subject: Spanish for foreign students
Bookshop: The English Bookshop, Calaf 52, 08021 Barcelona
Founded: 1981
ISBN Publisher's Prefix: 84-85786

Editora Nacional+*, Calle Torregalindo 10, Madrid 16 Tel: (91) 2508600
Dir: Alberto de la Puente O'Connor
Subjects: Poetry, History, Art, Essays, Literature, Law
Founded: 1937
ISBN Publisher's Prefix: 84-276

Ediciones **Elfos**, Milanesado 21-23 1a, 08017 Barcelona Tel: (93) 2043028 Telex: 54675 contb E
Man Dir: Rita Schnitzer
Subjects: Gardening, Nature Study, Ecology, Gastronomy, Gift books
Founded: 1980
ISBN Publisher's Prefix: 84-85791

Emalsa SA*, Apdo 46033, 28015 Madrid (Located at: Hilarion Eslava 55, Madrid) Tel: (91) 4496883/2444223/2430307 Telex: 43817 Di E
Man Dir: Daniel L Waingart; *Editorial:* José Antonio Tapia; *Production:* José Luis Timón
Parent Company: CBS Inc, New York, NY, USA
Associate Companies: Nueva Editorial Interamericana SA de CV, Mexico (qv); Holt Rinehart & Winston, New York, NY, USA; W B Saunders, Philadelphia, PA, USA
Subjects: Health Sciences, Biology, Physics, Economics, Sociology
Bookshop: At above address
1985: 32 titles *Founded:* 1984
ISBN Publisher's Prefix: 84-7605

Empeño 14*, Plaza Marqués de Camarines 7, Aravaca, 28023 Madrid Tel: (91) 2079386
Man Dir: Rafael Morales; *Sales:* José S Pérez; *Production:* Carlos Saz; *Publicity:* Jacinto Cabetas
Subjects: Technology, Science, Sociology, Fiction, Poetry, English Language, English for Children
1986: 32 titles *Founded:* 1980
ISBN Publisher's Prefix: 84-85823

Ediciones **Encuentro** SA+*, Cedaceros 3 - 2°, 28014 Madrid Tel: (91) 2322606/2322615
Man Dir: José Miguel Oriol; *Editorial, Rights & Permissions:* Carmina Salgado; *Sales:* Miguel Rovira; *Production:* Norberto Moreno
Subjects: Art, Philosophy, History, Economics, Politics, Theology, Children's Educational, Anthropology, Literature, Sociology, Facsimiles
Founded: 1978
ISBN Publisher's Prefix: 84-7490

Erein+*, Ave de Tolosa 107, Edificio Comercial 2 de Lorea, 20009 San Sebastian Tel: (943) 218300/218211
Man Dir, Production, Rights & Permissions: Julen Lizundia Aramaio; *Editorial:* Anjel Lertxundi Esnal; *Sales, Publicity:* Ascensio Ondarzabal Madrazo
Subjects: Children's, Comics, Textbooks
Founded: 1976
ISBN Publisher's Prefix: 84-7568

Editorial **Espasa-Calpe** SA*, Apdo 547, 28049 Madrid (Located at: Carretera de Irún, km 12,200 (variante de Fuencarral)) Tel: (91) 7343800 Cable Add: Espacalpe Telex: 48850 Espac E
Dir General: José Luis Lechosa González; *President:* Ignacio Bayón Mariné
Branch Offs: Espasa-Calpe SA, Roger de Lluria 33, 08007 Barcelona; Espasa-Calpe SA, Alameda Recalde 34, 48009 Bilbao (both in Spain); Espasa-Calpe Argentina SA, Argentina (qv); Espasa-Calpe Mexicana SA, Mexico (qv); Espasa-Calpe Colombiana Ltda, Carrera 17 núm 39 – 35 5°, Apdo 8924, Bogota DE, Colombia
Subjects: General Fiction, Belles Lettres, Biography, History, How-to, Music, Art, Philosophy, Reference, Religion, Juveniles, Paperbacks, Medicine, Psychology, Law, Technical, University Textbooks
Bookshops: Librería Austral, Roger de Lluria 33, 08009 Barcelona; Casa del Libro Espasa-Calpe SA (qv under Major Booksellers)
Founded: 1925
ISBN Publisher's Prefix: 84-239

Editorial **Espaxs** SA+, Calle Rosellón 132, 08036 Barcelona Tel: (93) 2530706 Telex: 50679 Espx E
Subject: Medicine
Bookshops: Librería Espaxs (at above address); Calle Fernando el Católico 57, 50006 Zaragoza; Calle Zaragoza 5, 11003 Cadiz
ISBN Publisher's Prefix: 84-7179

Eumo Editorial+*, Carrer de Miramarges s/n, Vic (Barcelona) Tel: (93) 8860794/8861222
Man Dir: Ricard Torrents; *Production:* Ton Granero
Subjects: Educational, Literature, History, Pedagogy
Founded: 1979
ISBN Publisher's Prefix: 84-7602

Editorial **Everest** SA+, Apdo 339, 24080 León (Located at: Carretera León-Coruña, Km 5 León) Tel: (987) 235904 Cable Add: Everest León Telex: 89916
Man Dir: José Antonio López Martínez; *Publications Dir:* Adrián Larrosa; *Export Dir:* Severino Fernández
Subsidiary Company: Everest Libros SA (at above address)
Subjects: Belles Lettres, History, How-to, Juveniles, Engineering, Technical,

Secondary & Primary Textbooks, Tourist Guides, Paperbacks, Educational Materials
Founded: 1958
ISBN Publisher's Prefix: 84-241

El **Festín** de Esopo, a subsidiary of Edicions dels Quaderns Crema (qv)

Publicaciones **Fher** SA+*, Apdo 362, 48002 Bilbao (Located at: Camilo Villabaso 9, Bilbao) Tel: (94) 4318000 Cable Add: Publifher Telex: 32195
Man Dir: Ignacio Aguirre Aguirre; *Editorial:* Fhernando Amerzqueta; *Production Manager:* Luis Carlos Sánchez
Subject: Juveniles and Children's
Founded: 1983
ISBN Publisher's Prefix: 84-243

Fondo de Cultura Económica+*, Apdo 582, 28080 Madrid (Located at: Vía de los Poblados s/n, Edificio Indubuilding 4-15, 28033 Madrid) Tel: (91) 7632800 Cable Add: Foraca
Man Dir: Miguel Ángel Otero Blazquez
Parent Company: Fondo de Cultura Económica, Mexico (qv)
Subjects: Economics, Sociology, History, Philosophy, Politics, Law, Anthropology, Psychology and Psychoanalysis, Science and Technology, Language, Literary Studies
Bookshop: Librería Mexico, Fernando el Católico 86, 28015 Madrid
1985: 6 titles *Founded:* 1934
ISBN Publisher's Prefix: 84-375

Editorial **Fontamara** SA*, Calle Entenza 116 – 3° 3a, 08015 Barcelona Tel: (93) 3251683
Man Dir, Editorial: Emilio Olcina; *Sales:* Manuel Muñoz; *Production, Rights & Permissions:* Luisa Sañé
Subjects: Fiction, Social and Political Science, Humanities
Founded: 1973
ISBN Publisher's Prefix: 84-7367

Editorial **Fontanella** SA+*, Escorial 50, Barcelona 24 Tel: (93) 2131731
Man Dir: F Vendrell Bayona; *Permissions:* M Company
Subjects: Education, Psychology, Sexology, Philosophy, Biography, Anthropology, Children's, Juveniles
Founded: 1962
ISBN Publisher's Prefix: 84-244

Heraclio **Fournier** SA*, Apdo 94, Vitoria (Located at: Heraclio Fournier 19, Vitoria) Tel: (945) 251100 Cable Add: Fournier Telex: 35510
Subjects: High-quality Illustrated Books (Art, History, Science, General Knowledge)

Fragua Editorial, Apdo 46215, Madrid 15 (Located at: Andres Mellado 64, Madrid) Tel: (91) 4491806
Man Dir: Mariano Muñoz Alonso
Subjects: Linguistics, Philosophy, Communications, Political Science
Bookshop: At above address
Founded: 1971
ISBN Publisher's Prefix: 84-7074

Editorial **Fundamentos**+, Caracas 15, 28010 Madrid Tel: (91) 4199619/4195584
Man Dir: Juan Serraller Ibañez
Subjects: Social Sciences, Psychology, Psychiatry, Sexology, History, Theatre, Literature, Songs, Fiction, Cinema, Chess, Low-priced Paperbacks
1986: 480 titles *Founded:* 1970
ISBN Publisher's Prefix: 84-245

Ediciones **Gaisa** SL, now Mas Ivars Editores SL (qv)

La **Galera** SA Editorial+, Ronda del Guinardó 38, 08025 Barcelona Tel: (93) 3473400
Man Dir: Romà Dòria Forcada
Subjects: Pre-School and Infant Teaching texts, Children's Books, Education
1985: 106 titles *1986:* 90 titles *Founded:* 1963
ISBN Publisher's Prefix: 84-246

Ediciones **Garriga** SA*, París 143, Barcelona 36 Tel: (93) 2306825/2393547
Man Dir: Xavier Garriga Jové
Subjects: Art, Archaeology, Ancient History, Religion, Nautical
Founded: 1957
ISBN Publisher's Prefix: 84-7079

Ediciones **Garza** SA*, Calle Numancia 73 – 3°A, Barcelona 29 Tel: (93) 2393560
Parent Company: Ediciones Artes Graficas Cobas SA (qv)
Subjects: Children's Picture Books

Editorial **Gedisa** SA+, Muntaner 460, entresuelo 1a, 08006 Barcelona Tel: (93) 2016000 Telex: 51130 clave 16-00147
Publisher: Victor Landman; *Editor, Sales Manager:* Laura Landman
Subjects: Psychology, Psychoanalysis, Education, Philosophy, Social and Human Sciences, General Trade, Non-fiction Paperbacks
1985: 22 titles *Founded:* 1977
ISBN Publisher's Prefix: 84-7432

Editorial Gustavo **Gili** SA+, Apdo 35149, 08080 Barcelona (Located at: Rosellón 87-89, 08029 Barcelona) Tel: (93) 3228161 Cable Add: Gusto Barcelona Telex: 97196 Gili E
Man Dir: Gustavo Gili; *Sales:* Rafael Enríquez (Spain), Ramón Pascual (Export); *Production:* Andrés Martínez; *Foreign Rights:* Helma Hartmann
Associate Companies: Ediciones G Gili SA, Argentina (qv); Editorial Gustavo Gili Ltda, Chile (qv); Editora Gustavo Gili Ltda, Diagonal 45, 16B-11, Bogotá, Colombia; Editorial Gustavo Gili de México SA, Mexico (qv)
Branch Off: Alcántara 21, 28006 Madrid Tel: (91) 4011702/4011703
Subjects: Architecture, Art, Design, Communication and Technology in general
Founded: 1902
ISBN Publisher's Prefix: 84-252

Editorial **Gredos** SA+*, Apdo 2076, 28002 Madrid (Located at: Sánchez Pacheco 81, Madrid) Tel: (91) 4157408/4156836/4157412
Man Dirs: Mr Calonge, Mr Escolar, Mr Yebra, Mr Oliveira
Subjects: Philology, Criticism, Classical Literature, Literary History, Dictionaries, Philosophy, Psychology, Economics, History
Founded: 1944
ISBN Publisher's Prefix: 84-249

Ediciones **Grijalbo** SA, Aragón 385, 08013 Barcelona Tel: (93) 2587000 Cable Add: Edigrijalbo Telex: 53940 egri e
President: Juan Grijalbo; *General Manager:* José M Vives
Subsidiary Companies and Branch Offs: Grijalbo Comercial SA, Grijalbo Dargaud SA, Ediciones Junior (all at above address); Editorial Crítica SA (qv); Grijalbo SA, Argentina (qv); Grijalbo Boliviana Ltda, Bolivia (qv); Grijalbo y Cía Ltda, Chile (qv); Distribuidora Exclusiva Grijalbo SA, Colombia; Grijalbo Ecuatoriana Ltda, Ecuador (qv); Editorial Grijalbo SA, Mexico (qv); Distribuidora exclusivo Grijalbo SA, Peru (qv); Grijalbo Puerto Rico Inc, Puerto Rico (qv); Grijalbo Editor, Uruguay (qv); Editorial Grijalbo SA, Venezuela (qv)
Subjects: General Fiction & Non-fiction, Biography, Philosophy, History, Politics, Religion, Psychology, Technology, Art, Social Science, Reference Works
Founded: 1942
ISBN Publisher's Prefix: 84-253

Artes Gráficas **Grijelmo** SA*, Uribitarte 4, 48001 Bilbao Tel: (94) 4239628 Telex: 31209 aggc e
Man Dir, Rights & Permissions: Juan Carlos Grijelmo Mintegni; *Editorial:* Amancio Gerardo Grijelmo Ribechini; *Sales:* Juan Santiago Grijelmo Ribechini
Subsidiary Companies: Asuri de Edicions; Ediciones Deusto SA; IBC — International Book Creation SA (qv)
Branch Offs: Barcelona, Madrid
Subject: Art

Ediciones **Guadarrama**, an imprint of Editorial Labor SA (qv)

Guara Editorial SA*, Calle José Oto 24, Zaragoza 14 Tel: (976) 396480
Man Dir: José-María Pisa Villarroya
Subjects: History, Geography, Ethnology, Art, Law, Literature
Founded: 1977
ISBN Publisher's Prefix: 84-85303

Editorial **Herder** SA+, Provenza 388, 08025 Barcelona Tel: (93) 2577700 Cable Add: Herder Telex: 54120 Hegr E
Man Dir: Antonio Valtl Friedl; *Publicity:* Carlos Rey Codina
Associate Companies: Verlag Herder & Co, Austria (qv); Verlag Herder GmbH & Co KG, Herder und Herder GmbH (both Federal Republic of Germany – qqv); Herder Editrice e Libreria, Italy (qv); Herder AG, Switzerland (qv)
Branch Offs: Hesperia SA Editorial y Librería, Ave Callao 565, Buenos Aires, Argentina; Herder Editorial y Librería, Calle 12, No 6/89, Apdo Aereo 6855, Bogotá, Colombia
Subjects: Philosophy, Theology, Religion, Medicine, Pedagogy, Psychology, Social Science, Reference Works, Economics, Languages, University & Secondary Textbooks, Atlases
Bookshop: Librería Herder (qv under Major Booksellers)
Founded: 1943
ISBN Publisher's Prefix: 84-254

Ediciones **Hiperión** SL+, Salustiano Olózaga 14, 28001 Madrid Tel: (91) 4010234/4013007
Man Dir, Editorial: Jesus Munárriz Peralta; *Sales:* Maite Merodio Benito
Subjects: Poetry, Novels, Essays, History, Philosophy
Bookshop: Librería Hiperión (at above address)
Founded: 1976
ISBN Publisher's Prefix: 84-7517

Editorial **Hispano Europea**+*, Bori y Fontestá 6, Barcelona 21 Tel: (93) 2013709/2018500
Man Dir, Editorial, Publicity: J Prat-Ballester; *Sales:* J Prat-Rosal; *Production:* J Madueño Machado
Subjects: Business Management, Sports, Social Science, Industrial Processes, General Technology, Photography
Founded: 1956
ISBN Publisher's Prefix: 84-255

Hogar del Libro — Nova Terra+*, Calle Bergara 3 - 2°, 08002 Barcelona Tel: (93) 3182700 Telex: 50066 Ogar E
Bookshops: Hogar del Libro SA (qv under Major Booksellers)
Founded: 1945
Miscellaneous: Group of companies comprising one publisher, one major distributor and eight bookshops
ISBN Publisher's Prefix: 84-7279

SPAIN 369

Hrvatska Revija*, Apdo 14030, 08017 Barcelona (Located at: San Juan Bosco 62, Barcelona) Tel: (93) 2037408
Man Dir, Editorial: Vinko Nikolić
Subjects: Politics, History, Literature, Sociology, Memoirs; Periodical — *Hrvatska Revija* (in Croatian)
Founded: 1951
ISBN Publisher's Prefix: 84-449

Ediciones **Hymsa***, Calle Diputación 211, Barcelona 11 Tel: (93) 2541004 Telex: 50482
Man Dir: Xavier Elies; *Editorial:* Josep Sarret; *Sales, Rights & Permissions:* Carlos Elies; *Production:* Jordi Balmaña
Parent Company: El Hogar y La Moda SA (at above address)
Subsidiary Companies: Servicios Editoriales SA, Calle Aribau 20 pral, Barcelona; Publiventa SA, Calle Aribau 28, Barcelona
Associate Companies: Sociedad General de Publicaciones, Carretera Montcada s/n, Polígono Industrial, Barcelona; ASMI SA, Calle Aribau 20 pral, Barcelona
Subjects: Children's, Dictionaries, Books for Women
Bookshop: Librería Hogar y Moda (at above address)
Founded: 1909
ISBN Publisher's Prefix: 84-7183

I B C — International Book Creation SA*, Juan de Ajuriaguerra 10, Bilbao 9 Tel: (94) 4438195
Sales: Victoria Peña; *Publicity & Advertising:* Maria Saturnina Abón
Parent Company: Artes Gráficas Grijelmo SA (qv)
Subjects: Literature, Biography, History, Music, Art, Reference (in luxury and multi-volume editions)
Founded: 1964
ISBN Publisher's Prefix: 84-7113

Publicaciones **I C C E***, Calle Eraso 3, Madrid 28 Tel: (91) 2557200
Man Dir: F Cubells
Subjects: Education, Psychology Tests, History, Religion, Social Sciences
Founded: 1970
ISBN Publisher's Prefix: 84-7278

Ibérico Europea de Ediciones SA*, Serrano 44 – 3°, Madrid 1 Tel: (91) 2253527/2261578/2754492
Subjects: Biography, How-to, Music, Art, Social Science, Business Management
Founded: 1966
ISBN Publisher's Prefix: 84-256

Icaria Editorial SA+*, Calle de la Torre 14, Barcelona 08006 Tel: (93) 2177686
Man Dir: Maria Rodriguez Bayraguet; *Editorial:* Rafael Argulloz; *Production:* Angela Ackermann
Subjects: Literature, Feminism
Founded: 1975
ISBN Publisher's Prefix: 84-7426

Editorial **Incafo** SA*, Castelló 59, Madrid 28001 Tel: (91) 4313460/4313519/4313589 Telex: 42459 Icf E
Man Dir, Editorial: Luis Blas Aritio; *Production:* Javier Echevarri; *Rights & Permissions:* Margarita Méndez de Vigo
Subjects: Natural History, Art, Ecology and Exploration in Spain and South America (including some books in English), Periodical
Book Club: Club del Libro de la Naturaleza
Founded: 1973
ISBN Publisher's Prefix: 84-85389

Editorial **Index** (Tormes SL), Comandante Zorita 13 – 6°, 28020 Madrid Tel: (91) 2349150/2544980
Man Dir: R L Ortueta

Subjects: Science, Technology, Administration
Founded: 1965
ISBN Publisher's Prefix: 84-7087

Instituto de Estudios de Administración Local, Publicaciones*, Santa Engracia 7, Madrid 10
Dir: Gregorio Burgueño Alvarez
Subjects: Public Administration, Urbanism, City Planning, Periodicals
ISBN Publisher's Prefix: 84-7088

Instituto de Estudios Politicos+*, Plaza Marina Española 8, Madrid 13 Tel: (91) 2415000, 2418300/09
Distributor: LESPO, Calle Arriza 16
Subjects: Law, Politics, History, Social Science, Philosophy
Founded: 1939
ISBN Publisher's Prefix: 84-259

Insula, Librería, Ediciones y Publicaciones SA*, Benito Gutiérrez 26, Madrid 8 Tel: (91) 2435415
Man Dir: Enrique Canito Barrera; *Publicity:* A Muñoz Canito
Subjects: Fiction, Poetry, Literary Studies, Criticism, Essays
Bookshop: See under Major Booksellers
Founded: 1944
ISBN Publisher's Prefix: 84-7185

Ediciones **Istmo**+*, Colombia 18, 28016 Madrid Tel: (91) 4574101/4582582
Man Dir: José Antonio Llardent Viciana; *Sales Dir:* Deogracias González; *Publicity Dir:* Leoncio Martín
Subjects: History, Reference, Social Science, Philosophy, Literature, University Texts
Founded: 1969
ISBN Publishers Prefix: 84-7090

Taller Ediciones **J B**, see Taller

Editorial **Jims** SA+*, Calle Regás 7-9, 08006 Barcelona Tel: (93) 2188800 Cable Add: Editojims
Man Dir, Editorial, Publicity: Antonio Jiménez Sánchez; *Sales:* Teresa Jiménez Sayo; *Production:* Luis Jiménez Sayo
Subject: Medicine
Founded: 1956
ISBN Publisher's Prefix: 84-7092

Ediciones **Jover** SA+, San Pedro Mártir 18, 08012 Barcelona Tel: (93) 2185662/2185408/2185216 Cable Add: Edijover
Man Dir: Juan Jover Biosca; *Editorial:* Montserrat Jover López; *Sales, Rights & Permissions:* María Carmen Hurtado; *Production:* Antonio Pérez Sánchez
Subjects: Educational, Scientific
Founded: 1946
ISBN Publisher's Prefix: 84-7093

Ediciones **Jucar**+, Fernandez de los Rios 20 – 2° Pta 1, 28015 Madrid Tel: (91) 4487084 Telex: 89736 Edju E
Man Dir: Silverio Cañada Acebal; *Editorial:* Maria de Calonje; *Production:* Manuel Cárdenas
Orders to: Honesto Batalón 7, Gijon Tel: (985) 355790/357413
Subjects: Poetry, Music, Literature, Politics, Novels
1985: 52 titles *Founded:* 1974
ISBN Publisher's Prefix: 84-334

Editorial **Juventud** SA+, Apdo 3, 08029 Barcelona (Located at: Provenza 101, Barcelona) Tel: (93) 2392000/3212100 Cable Add: Juventud Telex: 59258 Ejut E
Man Dir: Pablo Zendrera
Subsidiary Companies: Editorial Juventud (Distribuidora Tres Américas SAC), Argentina (qv); Editorial Juventud Ltda, Colombia (qv)

Subjects: General, Fiction, Biography, History, How-to, Music, Art, Nautical, Travel, Pocketbooks, Textbooks, Reference, Juveniles, Paperbacks
1985: 224 titles *Founded:* 1923
ISBN Publisher's Prefix: 84-261

Editorial **Kairos** SA+, Numancia 117-121, 08029 Barcelona Tel: (93) 2303746/4105166
Man Dir: Salvador Pániker; *Editorial, Rights & Permissions, Sales:* Agustín Pániker; *Production, Publicity:* Pilar Tomás
Subjects: Philosophy, Religion, Psychology, Reference, General and Social Science
1986: 9 titles *Founded:* 1966
ISBN Publisher's Prefix: 84-7245

L E D A (Las Ediciones de Arte)+, Riera San Miguel 37, 08006 Barcelona Tel: (93) 2379389
Man Dir: Daniel Basilio Bonet
Subjects: Art and Craft techniques, Technical drawing
1985: 10 titles *1986:* 8 titles *Founded:* 1942
ISBN Publisher's Prefix: 84-7095

Editorial **Labor** SA+, Calabria 235-239, 08029 Barcelona Tel: (93) 3220551 Cable Add: Edilabor Telex: 51130 Fonotx E clave 16-00091
Man Dir: Francisco Gracia Guillen
Imprints: Ediciones Guadarrama; Prensa Científica-Investigación y Ciencia
Branch Offs: Editorial Labor Colombiana Ltda, Colombia (qv); Editorial Labor SA, Uruguay
Subjects: Science and Technology, Medicine, Engineering, Encyclopaedias, Dictionaries, Humanities, History, Art, Business Management, Juveniles, University Textbooks
Founded: 1915
ISBN Publisher's Prefixes: 84-335 (Labor), 84-250 (Ediciones Guadarrama), 84-7593 (Prensa Científica-Investigación y Ciencia)

Laertes SA de Ediciones+, Calle Montseny 43 bjos, Barcelona 12 Tel: (93) 2376869
Man Dir, Editorial, Production: Eduardo Suárez Alonso; *Sales, Publicity:* Carmen Miret; *Rights & Permissions:* Eva Mintenig
Subjects: Contemporary Spanish and other Fiction, Children's Adventure Stories, Comics, Homosexual Literature, Travel
Founded: 1975
ISBN Publisher's Prefixes: 84-85346, 84-7584

Lagos SA, see Publicaciones y Ediciones Lagos SA

Editorial **Laia** SA+*, Guitard 43 – 5°, 08014 Barcelona Tel: (93) 3215562
Man Dir: Benito Milla Navarro; *Editorial:* Josep Verdura Tenas; *Sales:* Frederic Pagès; *Production, Rights & Permissions:* Carme Molero; *Publicity:* Mia Masgrau
Orders to: Itaca, SA Distribuciones Editoriales, López de Hoyos 141 – 5°, 28002 Madrid
Subjects: General Non-fiction, Social Sciences, Politics, Literature, Essays, Psychology, Pedagogy
1985: 68 titles *Founded:* 1972
ISBN Publisher's Prefix: 84-7222

LaSal (Edicions de les Dones), Calle València 226, 08007 Barcelona Tel: (93) 3231798
Subjects: Books by, about and for women
Bookshop: At above address
1986: 32 titles *1987:* 40 titles *Founded:* 1978
ISBN Publisher's Prefix: 84-85627

Loguez Ediciones*, Apdo 558, Santa Marta de Tormes (Salamanca) (Located at: Carretera de Madrid 90, Santa Marta de

Tormes, Salamanca) Tel: (923) 200022
Man Dir, Sales, Production: L Rodríguez López; *Editorial, Publicity, Rights & Permissions:* Maribel G Martínez
Subjects: Children's, Education, Sex Education, Theology, Contemporary Literature
Founded: 1978
ISBN Publisher's Prefix: 84-85334

Editorial **Lumen** SA*, Ramón Miquel y Planas 10, 08034 Barcelona Tel: (93) 2043496/2042139 Telex: 93251 Lume E
Man Dir: Esther Tusquets
Subjects: General Fiction, Belles Lettres, Poetry, Essay, Art, Juveniles, Comics, Bridge, Design, Social Science, Paperbacks
Founded: 1939
ISBN Publisher's Prefix: 84-264

McGraw-Hill Interamericana de España SA, Calle Manuel Ferrero 13, 28036 Madrid Tel: (91) 7330340/7336512 Telex: 42710 Fonotx E clave 4200679 Fax: (91) 3152901
Man Dir: Eduardo Jimenez Ferry; *Editorial:* Antonio Garcia-Maroto; *Sales:* Fernando Serrano
Parent Company: McGraw-Hill International Book Co, 1221 Ave of the Americas, New York, NY 10020, USA
Associate Companies: See McGraw-Hill Book Co (UK) Ltd, UK
Subjects: Scientific, Technical, Medicine and Health
Founded: 1973

Editorial **Magisterio** Español SA+*, Calle de Quevedo 1, Madrid 28014 Tel: (91) 4292211 Cable Add: Magisterio Telex: 44259 em e
Executive President: Alfonso Vericat Núñez; *Rights & Permissions:* María del Carmen Núñez Amador
Subjects: Education, Fiction, Essays, Philosophy, Pedagogy
Bookshops: Calle Cervantes 18, Madrid 28014; Ave Meridiana 28-30, Barcelona 08018
Founded: 1866
ISBN Publisher's Prefix: 84-265

Edicions de la **Magrana** SA, Apdo 9487, 08080 Barcelona (Located at: Carrer Repartidor 47, 08023 Barcelona) Tel: (93) 2103696
Man Dir: Carles-Jordi Guardiola; *Production:* Oriol Castanys
Subjects: Catalan Literature and Culture, Fiction, Children's, Social Sciences
1985: 43 titles *1986:* 54 titles *Founded:* 1975
ISBN Publisher's Prefix: 84-7410

Editorial **Marbán***, Joaquin Maria Lopez 72, 28015 Madrid Tel: (91) 2433767/2444673
Man Dir, Editorial: José Marban Gonzalez; *Sales, Production, Publicity:* José M Marban Corral
Subjects: Medicine, Physiology
Founded: 1949
ISBN Publisher's Prefix: 84-7101

Marcombo SA de Boixareu Editores+*, Apdo FD 329, 08007 Barcelona (Located at: Gran Via de les Corts Catalanes 594, Barcelona) Tel: (93) 3180079 Telex: 98560 Boie E
Man Dir: Josep María Boixareu Vilaplana; *Production:* José Costa Ardiaca
Subsidiary Companies: Boixareu Editores SA (at above address); Publicaciones Marcombo SA, Mexico (qv)
Branch Off: Marcombo SA, Plaza de la Villa 1, 28005 Madrid
Subjects: Engineering, Technology, Science, Automation, Architecture and Building, Economics, Accounting, How-to, University and Secondary Textbooks, Electronics, Mathematics
Bookshop: Librería Hispano Americana (qv under Major Booksellers)
1985: 42 titles *Founded:* 1945
ISBN Publisher's Prefix: 84-267

Editorial **Marfil** SA*, Apdo 54, Alcoy (Located at: San Eloy 17, Alcoy)
Tel: (965) 523311/523496 Cable Add: Marfil
Sales: Rafael Ortiz Botí
Subjects: Secondary & Primary Textbooks, Psychology, Education
Founded: 1947
ISBN Publisher's Prefix: 84-268

Editorial **Marín** SA+, Paseo de Gracia 49, 08007 Barcelona Tel: (93) 2157697 Cable Add: Marinedi Telex: 97065 Mlm E
Man Dir and other offices: Manuel Marin Bruna
Subsidiary Company: Artel SA
Branch Offs: Editorial Marin Argentina SRL, Ave Belgrano 3715, 1210 Buenos Aires, Argentina; Editorial Marin SA, Anaxágoras 1400, Colonia Santa Cruz Atoyac, 03310 México DF, Mexico; Marin Puerto Rico Inc, San Rafael 1400, Santurce, PR 00909, Puerto Rico
Subjects: Art Books, Reference, Medicine, Non-fiction, Encyclopaedias, Children's Books
Founded: 1900
ISBN Publisher's Prefix: 84-7102

Ediciones **Marova** SL+*, Cedaceros 3 - 2°, 28014 Madrid Tel: (91) 2322605/2322606
Man Dir: José Miguel Oriol
Subjects: Religion, Psychology, Education
Founded: 1956
ISBN Publisher's Prefix: 84-269

Marsiega Editorial SA, now Editorial Acebo SA (qv)

Ediciones **Martínez** Roca SA+*, Gran Vía 774, 2a y 7a planta, 08013 Barcelona
Tel: (93) 2327711 Telex: 97278 mrrm e
Man Dirs: Francisco Martínez Roca, Manuel Martínez Roca; *Editorial:* Manuel Martínez Alsinet; *Sales:* Fernando Calvo; *Production:* Sergi Puyol; *Rights & Permissions:* Manuel Martínez
Branch Offs: Ediciones Roca SA, General Francisco Murguía 7, Col Hipodromo de la Condesa, México 06170, DF, Mexico; Ediciones Martínez Roca Venezolana SA, Peligro a Pelelojo, Caracas, Venezuela
Subjects: General Fiction & Non-fiction, Science & Technology, Human & Social Sciences, Chess, Occult Sciences, Science Fiction
1985: 77 titles *Founded:* 1965
ISBN Publisher's Prefix: 84-270

Mas Ivars Editores SL*, Gran Vía Marqués del Turia 64, 46005 Valencia
Tel: (96) 3339321/3333976 Cable Add: Mas Ivars
Man Dir: Miguel Mas Ivars
Subjects: Juveniles, Encyclopaedias, Multi-volume Collections
Founded: 1960
ISBN Publisher's Prefix: 84-7077

Masson SA*, Balmes 151, 08008 Barcelona Tel: (93) 2179954 Cable Add: Massonsa Telex: 54327 tmbn
Man Dir: Patrick Martin
Associate Company: Masson Editeur, France (qv)
Subjects: Medicine, Science
ISBN Publisher's Prefix: 84-311

Editorial **Medica y Tecnica** SA*, Ave Meridiana 328 planta 14, Barcelona 27
Tel: (93) 3115361
Man Dir: Emílio Rotellar Lampre; *Production, Publicity:* José María Ripolles Segarra
Subjects: Medicine, Psychology, Behavioural Psychology, Language, Art
Founded: 1977
ISBN Publisher's Prefix: 84-85298

Ediciones **Medici** SA, Platón 26, 08006 Barcelona Tel: (93) 2013807/2010599
Telex: 98095 Omeg E
Man Dirs: Ana Dexeus, Antonio Paricio, Gabriel Paricio
Subjects: Medicine, Dentistry, Health Education (for professionals and students)
Founded: 1983
ISBN Publisher's Prefix: 84-86193

Editorial **Mediterrania** SA, Carrer de Guillem Tell 15-17 entres 1, 08006 Barcelona Tel: (93) 2183458
Man Dir: Eduard Fornés; *Editorial, Rights & Permissions:* Jordi Oliveres; *Sales:* Ferran Cabestany; *Production:* Carles Oliveres; *Publicity:* Abel Nuñez
Subsidiary Company: Distribucions d'Art Surrealista SA (at above address)
Subjects: History, Art, Literature
Bookshop: Llibreria Surrealista, Pl Gala i Salvador Dali 5-7, Figueres (Girona) Tel: (972) 507070
1985: 8 titles *1986:* 18 titles *Founded:* 1980
ISBN Publisher's Prefix: 84-85984

Ediciones **Mensajero**, Apdo 73, 48080 Bilbao (Located at: Sancho de Azpeitia 2, Bilbao) Tel: (94) 4470358 Cable Add: Mensajero Telex: 32182 Mensajero
Man Dir: Luis Manuel de la Encina; *Editorial, Production:* Jesús Leguina; *Sales:* Juan Aguirre; *Publicity:* Alvaro Sánchez
Branch Off: Templarios 12, 08002 Barcelona
Subjects: Social Science, Religion, Philosophy, Education, How-to, Psychology, Juveniles
Founded: 1915
ISBN Publisher's Prefix: 84-271

Editorial **Mezquita** SA, now part of Editorial Alhambra SA (qv)

Las **Mil y Una** Ediciones+*, Calle Escalinata 9, 28013 Madrid Tel: (91) 2480954
Man Dir: Jose Ignacio Cabal Riera; *Editorial:* Fernando Cabal Riera
Subjects: Medicine, Psychology
Founded: 1979
ISBN Publisher's Prefix: 84-85805

Miraguano SA Ediciones+, Calle Hermosilla 104, 28009 Madrid Tel: (91) 4016990
Man Dir: José M Arizcun Perez-Salas; *Editorial Dir:* José J Fuente; *Sales Dir:* Josefa Arteaga Hernandez
Subjects: Literature, Ecology, Alternative Medicine, Acupuncture
Bookshop: Librería Miraguano (at above address)
1987: 80 titles *Founded:* 1979
ISBN Publisher's Prefix: 84-85639

Editorial **Molino**, Calabria 166, 08015 Barcelona Tel: (93) 3253250 Cable Add: Molino Barcelona Telex: 98772 Cllc E ref Editorial Molino
Man Dir: Luis del Molino Mateus; *Sales & Advertising Dir:* Pablo del Molino Sterna; *Permissions:* L A del Molino
Subjects: Juveniles, Popular Paperbacks, Cookery, Children's books, Education
Founded: 1933
ISBN Publisher's Prefix: 84-272

Editorial **Moll** SA+, Apdo 142, 07080 Palma de Mallorca (Located at: Torre del Amor 4, 07001 Palma de Mallorca) Tel:

(971) 724176/724472
Man Dir: Francesc de B Moll
Subjects: Fiction, Literature, Biography, History, Art, Reference Works, Dictionaries, Linguistics, Social Sciences, Secondary & Primary Textbooks, Natural Science
Bookshop: Libros Mallorca, Fortuny 5, 07001 Palma de Mallorca
1985: 37 titles *1986:* 31 titles *Founded:* 1934
ISBN Publisher's Prefix: 84-273

Creaciones **Monar** Editorial, Escorial 26-28, 08024 Barcelona Tel: (93) 2133928 Telex: 99861 Monar E
Subjects: Bibles (children's & juveniles')

Ediciones **Morata** SA+, Mejía Lequerica 12, 28004 Madrid Tel: (91) 4480926 Cable Add: Moratedi Telex: 47891 Fcli Morata
Man Dir: Flora Morata; *Editorial Dir:* Florentina Gómez Morata
Subjects: Psychology, Medicine, Pedagogy, Philosophy, Psychiatry, Sexology, Sociology, Politics, Mathematics, University Textbooks
1985-86: 55 titles *Founded:* 1920
ISBN Publisher's Prefix: 84-7112

Mundi-Prensa Libros SA+, Castelló 37, 28001 Madrid Tel: (91) 4313399 Cable Add: Mundipren Telex: 49370 Mpli E
Man Dir: Pedro Hernández; *Editorial, Publicity:* José María Hernández; *Sales:* Alfonso Hernández
Subjects: Agriculture, Technology, Ecology, Livestock, University & Secondary Textbooks
Bookshops: Librería Mundi-Prensa (qv under Major Booksellers); Librería Agrícola, Fernando VI 2, 28040 Madrid
1985: 30 titles *1986:* 30 titles *Founded:* 1948
ISBN Publisher's Prefix: 84-7114

Editorial La **Muralla** SA, Constancia 33, Madrid 2 Tel: (91) 4161371/4153687/4135907
Man Dir: Lidio Nieto; *Sales Dir:* Miguel Lendínez; *Publicity, Rights & Permissions:* Pilar Jiménez; *Production:* Julio Sánchez
Subjects: Art, Literature, Geography, History, Religion, Technology, Life and Culture, Biology, all in books with slides for visual education, Pre-school, Primary, Secondary and University Textbooks
Founded: 1968
ISBN Publisher's Prefix: 84-7133

Editorial **Musica** Moderna, Antonio Carmona Reverte, Calle Marqués de Cubas 6, 28014 Madrid Tel: (91) 5215593
Editor, Dir: Andrés Carmona Reverte
Subject: Music
Founded: 1935

Biblioteca **'N T'**, an imprint of EUNSA (qv)

Ediciones **Naranco** SA*, Apdo 542, Oviedo (Located at: Asturias 27, Oviedo) Tel: (985) 236537
President: Santiago Rubio Sáinido; *Man Dir:* Graciano García; *Production:* José Antxon F Lupiáñez; *Sales, Publicity:* Emilio García; *Rights & Permissions:* José Antonio A Rodríguez
Subjects: Photo-strip Editions of Don Quixote, Juveniles, Partworks

Narcea SA de Ediciones+, Dr Federico Rubio 9, 28039 Madrid Tel: (91) 2546484
Editorial: A de Miguel; *Sales:* N Nácher; *Production:* P Pazos; *Rights & Permissions:* C Vegas
Subjects: Education, Psychology, Pedagogy, Religion, Juveniles, Textbooks
1985: 50 titles
ISBN Publisher's Prefix: 84-277

Ediciones **Nauta** SA+, Loreto 16, 08029 Barcelona Tel: (93) 2392204 Cable Add: Edinauta Telex: 54495 sele e
Man Dir: José Luis Ruiz de Villa Macho
Subjects: Non-fiction, Art Books, Reference, Atlases
Founded: 1962
ISBN Publisher's Prefix: 84-278

Neguri Editorial SA, Juan de Ajuriaguerro 10, Bilbao 9 Tel: (94) 4233070 Telex: 31861 Ed E
Manager: Elena Grijelmo
Subjects: Atlases, Plans of Spanish Cities, Road Maps
Bookshop: Librería Deusto, Calle O'Donnell 43, Madrid 9
Founded: 1960
ISBN Publisher's Prefix: 84-85085

Editorial **Noguer** SA+, Paseo de Gracia 96, 08008 Barcelona Tel: (93) 2156516 Cable Add: Edinoguer Barcelona Telex: 48148
President: Emilio Ardevol; *Rights & Permissions:* Maruchy Friart
Associate Company: Luis de Caralt Editor SA (qv)
Subjects: General Fiction and Non-fiction, Belles Lettres, Biography, History, Encyclopaedias, Art, Juveniles, Paperbacks
1986: 17 titles *Founded:* 1949
ISBN Publisher's Prefix: 84-279

Editorial **Noray**, Calle San Gervasio de Cassolas 79, 08022 Barcelona Tel: (93) 2111146/2111712
Man Dir: Pablo Zendrera Zariquiey; *Editorial:* Panxo Pi-Suñer Cañellas
Orders to: Editorial Juventud SA, Provenza 101, 08029 Barcelona
Associate Companies: Odyssea Maritime Book Creations Ltd, 10 Norwich St, London EC4A 1BD, UK; Sirpus SA
Subjects: Sailing, Navigation, Computers, Windsurfing
Bookshop: Libreria Maritima Noray (at above address)
1985: 15 titles *Founded:* 1978
ISBN Publisher's Prefix: 84-7486

Ediciones **Norma** SA+*, Sancho Davila 27, 28028 Madrid Tel: (91) 2565013
Man Dir, Editorial, Rights & Permissions: Florencio Valero; *Publicity Manager:* R Perez Alonso
Subjects: Medicine, Health
Founded: 1978
ISBN Publisher's Prefix: 84-7487

Nova Terra, see Hogar del Libro

Ediciones **Océano-Éxito** SA+, Paseo de Gracia 24, 08007 Barcelona Tel: (93) 3174508/3010182 Telex: 51735 Exit E
Man Dir: Jose Lluis Monreal; *Editorial:* Carlos Gispert; *Sales:* Maria Pericas; *Production:* José Gay; *Publicity:* Roman Bayona; *Rights & Permissions:* Marta Bueno
Subsidiary Company: Instituto Gallach de Libreria y Ediciones SL
Associate Companies: Ediciones Centrum Tecnicas y Cientificas SA; Circe Ediciones SA; Ediciones Manfer SA
Subjects: History, Geography, Art, Dictionaries, Encyclopaedias, Educational, Technical and Scientific, Administration, Management, Fiction, Essays
1985: 20 titles *1986:* 24 titles *Founded:* 1950
Miscellaneous: Formerly Ediciones Danae SA
ISBN Publisher's Prefix: 84-7069

Oikos-Tau SA Ediciones, Apdo 5347, 08340 Vilassar de Mar, Barcelona (Located at: Montserrat 12-14, Vilassar de Mar, Barcelona) Tel: (93) 7590791

Man Dir, Editorial: Jordi Garcia-Bosch; *Sales:* Climent Garcia-Bosch; *Production, Rights & Permissions:* Jordi Garcia-Jacas
Subjects: Scientific and Technical, Economics, Marketing and Management, Agriculture, Geography, Education, History, Politics, Psychology, Architecture, Town Planning
Bookshop: El Racó del Llibre de Text, Gran Via 600, 08007 Barcelona
Founded: 1963
ISBN Publisher's Prefix: 84-281

Ediciones **Omega** SA+, Plató 26, 08006 Barcelona Tel: (93) 2013807/2010599 Telex: 98095 Omeg E
Man Dirs: Gabriel Paricio, Antonio Paricio
Subjects: Science & Technology, Photography, Cinema, Agriculture, University textbooks on Biology, Biochemistry, Geology
ISBN Publisher's Prefix: 84-282

Editorial **Orígenes***, Plaza Tuy 4, 28029 Madrid Tel: (91) 2015800
Man Dir: Eugenio Suarez Galbal Guerra; *Production:* Raul García Bravo
Orders to: Plaza de Tuy 4, Madrid 29
Subject: Literature
Founded: 1978
ISBN Publisher's Prefix: 84-85563

Editorial Alfredo **Ortells** SL+*, Sagunto 5, 46009 Valencia Tel: (96) 3471000/3472112
Man Dir: Alfredo Ortells Ferriz
Subjects: Infants and Juvenile, Children's Classics, Popular Knowledge series, Dictionaries, Encyclopaedias
Founded: 1952
ISBN Publisher's Prefix: 84-7189

P L E S A, see Publicaciones y Ediciones Lagos SA

P P C (Promoción Popular Cristiana)+, Apdo 19049, 28016 Madrid (Located at: Enrique Jardiel Poncela 4, Madrid) Tel: (91) 2592300/44586491 Cable Add: Pepece Telex: 45051
President: Lamberto de Echeverria; *Dir:* Salvador Petit Caro; *Manager:* Gonzalo Márquez; *Sales Dir:* Catalina Jaume; *Import/Export:* Isidro Ferreras Arahda; *Production, Publicity, Advertising:* Manuel Sobrado Royo; *Rights & Permissions:* Mary Salas
Subsidiary Company: Editorial Acebo SA (qv)
Subjects: Religion, Philosophy, Textbooks
Bookshops: Librerías PPC (qv under Major Booksellers)
Founded: 1955
ISBN Publisher's Prefix: 84-288

Ediciones **Paidós** Ibérica SA+, Mariano Cubí 92, 08021 Barcelona Tel: (93) 2000122 Telex: 97550 Edpi E
Man Dir: Enrique Folch; *Sales:* Juan León; *Production:* Lluís Tarrasón
Parent Company: Editorial Paidós, Argentina (qv)
Associate Company: Editorial Paidós Mexicana, Guanajuato 202 – local A, Col Roma, 06700 México DF, Mexico
Subjects: Psychology, Psychoanalysis, Pedagogy, Communication, Sociology, Philosophy, Neurology, Physical Education, Linguistics, Aesthetics
1985: 19 titles *Founded:* 1979
ISBN Publisher's Prefix: 84-7509

Editorial **Paraninfo** SA+*, Magallanes 25, 28015 Madrid Tel: (91) 4463350 Telex: 45890 Edpa E
Man Dir: Alfonso Mangada Sanz; *Sales Dirs:* Miguel Mangada Ferber, Manuel Montalbán Beltrán
Subjects: Science & Technology, Data Processing & Computation, Business

Administration, How-to, Secondary & University Textbooks
Bookshops: Librería Paraninfo, Magallanes 25, Madrid 15; Meléndez Valdés 65, Madrid 15
1985: 156 titles *Founded:* 1948
ISBN Publisher's Prefix: 84-283

Parramon Ediciones SA, Apdo 2001, 08013 Barcelona (Located at: Calle Lepanto 264, Barcelona) Tel: (93) 2457002/2453006 Telex: 93211 Paed E
Man Dir: José María Parramón; *Rights & Permissions:* Mercedes Ros; *International:* Ulisses Farreras
Subjects: Art, Photography, Drawing and Painting (Instruction), Languages, Botanical Interest, Reference, Music, Children's, Juveniles
Founded: 1958
ISBN Publisher's Prefix: 84-342

Ediciones **Partenon**, Paseo de la Habana 56, 28036 Madrid Tel: (91) 2505498 Telex: 27307/22034/23261 Coime attn abonado 859
Man Dir: Rafael Torres Gorriz
Subjects: Literature, Language and Philology, Social Science, University Textbooks
Founded: 1969
ISBN Publisher's Prefix: 84-7119

Ediciones **Paulinas**+, Protasio Gómez 11-15, 28027 Madrid Tel: (91) 7425113 Telex: 41872 Epssp E
President: Ricardo Ares Cerqueiro; *Publications Dir:* Francisco Ares Cerqueiro; *Administration:* Antonio Díaz Martínez; *Commercial Dir:* Francisco Anta Ovelar; *Sales:* Aurelio García Martín; *Production:* Estanislao Conde Martínez
Parent Company: Sociedad de San Pablo
Branch Off: Via Layetana 38, 08003 Barcelona Tel: (93) 3101808
Subjects: Religion, Education, Ethics, Biography, Juvenile
Bookshops: Eight in Spain
Founded: 1936
ISBN Publisher's Prefix: 84-285

Editorial **Paz** Montalvo*, Jorge Juan 127, Madrid 9 Tel: (91) 4019722
Man Dir: José Fernando de Paz; *Advertising:* José Luis Fernández; *Publicity:* J L Fernández Boyano
Subjects: Medicine, Ophthalmology, Psychiatry, Paediatrics, Biochemistry and Associated Fields
Founded: 1947
ISBN Publisher's Prefix: 84-7121

Editorial **Pediátrica**+*, Mayor de Gracia 102, 08012 Barcelona Tel: (93) 2174996
Man Dir: Anselmo Garrido
Subject: Medicine
1984: 3 titles *Founded:* 1969
ISBN Publisher's Prefix: 84-7193

Ediciones **Pegaso**, an imprint of EDERSA (qv)

Ediciones **Peninsula**, Provenza 278 – 1° 1a, 08008 Barcelona Tel: (93) 2160062
Man Dir: Ramon Bastardes i Porcel; *Editorial Dir:* Josep M Castellet; *Sales, Publicity:* Joaquim Sabrià; *Rights & Permissions:* Josefina Revilla
Associate Company: Edicions 62 SA (qv)
Subsidiary Company: Distribuciones de Enlace SA, Bruc 49, 08009 Barcelona
Subjects: General (in Castilian)
1985: 19 titles *1986:* 26 titles *Founded:* 1963
ISBN Publisher's Prefix: 84-297

Editorial Augusto E **Pila** Teleña SA+, Paseo de Yeserias 35, 28005 Madrid Tel: (91) 4743494
Man Dir: Augusto E Pila Teleña; *Editorial:* Augusto Pila; *Sales:* Raquel Laviste
Subjects: Physical Education, Sports
Founded: 1979
ISBN Publisher's Prefix: 84-85514

Ediciones **Pirámide** SA+, Josefa Valcárcel 27, 28027 Madrid Tel: (91) 7429111 Telex: 41071 Maeg E
Chairman: Germán Sánchez Ruipérez; *Dir:* Guillermo de Toca; *Rights & Permissions:* Guillermo de Toca, Teresa Escarpenter
Parent Company: Grupo Anaya (at above address)
Associate Companies: Ediciones Anaya SA (qv for other associates)
Subjects: Economics, Business, Science and Technology, Law, Psychology, Information Science, Dictionaries
Founded: 1973
ISBN Publisher's Prefix: 84-368

Editorial **Planeta** SA+, Córcega 273-277, 08008 Barcelona Tel: (93) 2175050/2179050 Cable Add: Ediplan Telex: 93458 Edtp
Chairman: José Manuel Lara Hernández; *General Managers:* José Manuel Lara Bosch, Fernando Lara Bosch; *Sales Manager:* José Miguel García Piriz; *Production Manager:* Manuel Mainer; *Export Manager:* José Manuel Peidró; *Publicity:* José Creuheras; *Rights & Permissions:* Javier Harillo; *Literary Managers:* José Pardo, Rafael Borrás
Members of the Planeta Group: Editorial Ariel SA (qv); Credito Internacional del Libro SA (CILSA), Balmes 155, 08008 Barcelona; Editorial Seix Barral SA (qv); Editorial Planeta Argentina SAIC, Viamonte 1451, Buenos Aires, Argentina; Editorial Planeta Chilena SA, Olivares 1229 – 4°, Santiago, Chile; Planeta Colombiana Editorial SA, Calle 22, 6-27 3° piso Edificio Distral, Bogotá DE, Colombia; Editorial Planeta del Ecuador, Ave Francisco de Orellana, 1811 y 10 de Agosto, Edificio El Cid planta baja, Quito, Ecuador; Difusion Editorial SA, Clavijero, 70 Col Tránsito, 06820 México DF, Mexico; Ediciones Andinas SA, Camino Real, 159 Oficina 600, San Isidro-Lima, Peru; Editorial Planeta Venezolana SA, Calle Madrid-Quinta Toscanella entre New York y Trinidad, Las Mercedes, Caracas 1050, Venezuela
Associate Companies: Planeta/Agostini (Forum y Fascículos Planeta), Aribau 185, 08021 Barcelona; Sudamericana/Planeta SA (Editores), Argentina (qv); Lord Cochrane SA, Ave Providencia 727, Santiago, Chile; Editorial Artemisa SA, Ave Cuauhtemoc 1236 – 4°, Colonia Vertiz Narvarte, Delegacion Benito Juarez, 03600 México DF, Mexico; Editorial Joaquín Mortiz SA, Mexico (qv)
Subjects: General Fiction & Non-fiction
Founded: 1952
ISBN Publisher's Prefix: 84-320

Editorial **Playor**+, Calle Santa Clara 4, 28013 Madrid Tel: (91) 2412804 Telex: 42252 IVSAE Fax: (91) 2410368
Man Dir: Carlos A Montaner; *Manager:* Linda Periut; *Sales:* Maria Angeles Remior; *Production:* Pio E Serrano
Subjects: Secondary & University Textbooks, How-to, Linguistics, Literature, Spanish & Latin-American Studies, Illustrated Juvenile
ISBN Publisher's Prefix: 84-359

Plaza y Janés SA, Virgen de Guadalupe 21-33, Esplugas de Llobregat, Barcelona Tel: (93) 3710200 Telex: 52010 Janés E
Man Dir: Antonio Cambredó; *Sales:* Rafael Soriano; *Editor-in-Chief:* José Moya
Parent Company: Verlagsgruppe Bertelsmann GmbH, Federal Republic of Germany (qv)
Associate Company: Ediciones Orbis SA, Diagonal 652 – 6°A, 08034 Barcelona
Subjects: General Fiction & Non-fiction, Classics, Paperbacks
Founded: 1959
ISBN Publisher's Prefix: 84-01

Ediciones **Poligrafa** SA+*, Balmes 54, 08007 Barcelona Tel: (93) 3019100 Telex: 97041 Edpo E
President: Manuel de Muga; *Sales:* Juan de Muga
Subject: Art Books, with texts in several languages
ISBN Publisher's Prefix: 84-313

Editorial **Popular** SA*, Apdo 14256, Madrid 13 (Located at: Calle Bola 3, Madrid) Tel: (91) 2482788
Man Dir: Antonio Albarran Cano
Subjects: Adult and Popular Education
1985: 60 titles *Founded:* 1972
ISBN Publisher's Prefix: 84-85016

Ediciones José **Porrúa** Turanzas SA*, Cea Bermúdez 10, 28003 Madrid Tel: (91) 2542344/2541466
Man Dir, Editorial: José Porrúa Venero; *Sales, Production, Publicity, Rights & Permissions:* Enrique Porrúa Venero
Subjects: History of Mexico and Latin America, Humanistic Literature and Commentary
Bookshop: Librería José Porrúa Turanzas SA (qv under Major Booksellers)
Founded: 1958
ISBN Publisher's Prefixes: 84-7317, 0-935568

Editorial **Pòrtic** SA+, Ausiàs March 92-98, esc A, 08013 Barcelona Tel: (93) 2458847
Dir: Carme Casas
Subjects: Fiction, Essays, Social Work, Juveniles (in Catalan)
ISBN Publisher's Prefix: 84-7306

Pre-Textos+, Calle Luis Santángel 10 – 1C, 46005 Valencia Tel: (96) 3333226
Man Dir: D Manuel Borrás Arana; *Publicity:* Manuel Ramírez
Subjects: Literature, Essays, Philosophy, Poetry, Music, Hispanic Studies
1985: 12 titles *1986:* 9 titles *Founded:* 1976
ISBN Publisher's Prefix: 84-85081

Prensa Científica – Investigación y Ciencia, an imprint of Editorial Labor SA (qv)

Editorial **Prensa Española***, Padilla 6, Madrid 6 Tel: (91) 4462616
Dir: Rogelio González-Ubeda
Subjects: General Fiction & Non-fiction
Founded: 1905
ISBN Publisher's Prefix: 84-287

Promoción Popular Cristiana, see PPC

Publicaciones Literarias y Deportivas SA (Pulide SA)+, Calle de Aragón 153, 08011 Barcelona Tel: (93) 3232392
Man Dir: Alberto Maurette Curto
Subjects: Hunting, Fishing
1985: 1 title *1986:* 1 title *Founded:* 1954
ISBN Publisher's Prefix: 84-7262

Publicaciones y Ediciones Lagos SA (PLESA)+, Apdo 80, (Pinto) Madrid (Located at: Calle Sestao 1 Pinto, Madrid) Tel: (91) 6911512/6911562
Man Dir: Antonio Roso Morales
Associate Companies: INDESA (Industria de la Encuadernación SA) (at above address); MELSA (Manufacturas

Editoriales Litograficas SA (at above address)
Subjects: Children's, Juveniles, Educational
1985: 27 titles *1986:* 17 titles *Founded:* 1974
ISBN Publisher's Prefix: 84-7374

Pulide SA, see Publicaciones Literarias y Deportivas SA

Edicions dels **Quaderns** Crema+, F Valls i Taberner 8, 08006 Barcelona Tel: (93) 2128766/2123808
Man Dir: Jaume Vallcorba Plana; *Editorial:* Jordi Cornudella
Subsidiary Company: El Festín de Esopo; Sirmio (both at above address)
Subjects: Poetry, Literature, History, Philology, Essays
1985: 15 titles *1986:* 16 titles *Founded:* 1979
ISBN Publisher's Prefix: 84-85704, 84-7727

Ediciones **R O L** SA, San Elias 31-33, 08006 Barcelona Tel: (93) 2008033
Man Dir: Nestor Bereciartu
Subjects: Nursing, Medicine, Sociology, Psychology, Periodicals
Founded: 1977
ISBN Publisher's Prefix: 84-85535

Selecciones del **Reader's Digest** (Iberia) SA*, Calle Telémaco 3, 28027 Madrid Tel: (91) 7420011 Cable Add: Readigest Telex: 27407
Director General: Richard Crosfield; *Editorial, Rights & Permissions:* Joaquín Amado; *Sales:* M Angel Senén; *Production:* John Servizio; *Publicity:* Xavier Muntañola
Parent Company: The Reader's Digest Association Inc, 200 Park Ave, New York, NY 10166, USA
Branch Off: Barcelona
Subjects: Education, Pocket editions, General Interest, Atlases
Founded: 1952
ISBN Publisher's Prefix: 84-7142

Editorial **Reus** SA*, Preciados 23, 28013 Madrid Tel: (91) 2213619/2223054
Dir: D Luis Fernando Montes Pié
Subjects: Law and General Culture
Founded: 1852
ISBN Publisher's Prefix: 84-290

Editorial **Reverté** SA+, Apdo 1237, 08024 Barcelona (Located at: Calle Encarnación 86-88, Barcelona) Tel: (93) 2193452/2134058/2194353 Cable Add: Edirever Telex: 54996 Ervt E
Dir: Felipe Reverté Planells; *Editorial:* Amado J Sala Inglabaga; *Sales:* Ernesto Granada Ribet; *Rights & Permissions:* Martín Sala Reverté
Associate Companies: Editorial Reverté Argentina SA, Ave Angel Gallardo 613, 1405 Buenos Aires, Argentina; Editorial Reverté Colombiana SA, Calle 37, No 22-72 (Barrio La Soledad), Bogotá DE, Colombia; Ediciones Repla SA, General Francisco Murgia 7, 06170 México, DF Mexico; Editorial Reverté Venezolana SA, Venezuela (qv)
Subjects: Engineering, General Science, University & Secondary Textbooks
Founded: 1947
ISBN Publisher's Prefix: 84-291

Revista de Occidente SA, Milán 38, 28043 Madrid Tel: (91) 2000045 Telex: 45746
President: Diego Hidalgo
Associate Company: Alianza Editorial SA (qv)
Subjects: History, Philosophy, Political & Social Science
Founded: 1923
ISBN Publisher's Prefix: 84-292

Ediciones **Rialp** SA+*, Preciados 34, Madrid 13 Tel: (91) 2311004
Subjects: Belles Lettres, Poetry, History, Music, Art, Philosophy, Religion, Textbooks, Engineering, General & Social Science, High-priced Paperbacks
Founded: 1945
ISBN Publisher's Prefix: 84-321

Editorial **Roasa** SL+*, Apdo 2069, 18009 Granada (Located at: Calle Concepción 14) Tel: (958) 227846 Cable Add: Apdo 2069
Man Dir, Sales: Félix J Rodriguez; *Editorial:* Jorge Alonso; *Production:* Manuel Alonso
Subjects: History, Art
Founded: 1982
ISBN Publisher's Prefix: 84-86043

S A R P E, see Sociedad Anonima de Revistas Periodicos y Ediciones

Ediciones **S M**+*, General Tabanera 39, Madrid 25 Tel: (91) 2085145 Telex: 42704 Smce E
Man Dir: Jorge Delkáder; *Editorial:* J M Benlloch, Manuel Barbadillo; *Sales:* Javier Carretero
Orders to: CESMA SA, Aguacate 25, Madrid 25
Subjects: Scholarly, Children's, Essays, Religion
Founded: 1934
ISBN Publisher's Prefix: 84-348

Editorial **Sal Terrae**+, Apdo 77, 39080 Santander (Located at: Guevara 20, Santander) Tel: (942) 212617
Man Dir: Gregorio de Pablos
Subjects: Religion, Philosophy, Psychology, Parapsychology, Essays, Biography, History, Juveniles, Textbooks, Periodicals
Founded: 1919
ISBN Publisher's Prefix: 84-293

Salvat Editores SA+, Mallorca 41-49, 08029 Barcelona Tel: (93) 2303607 Telex: 53132
Man Dir: Juan Salvat; *Dirs:* Alfonso Elizalde, Jesús Mosterín, Luis Soler, Ramón Vilá
Branch Offs: Salvat Editores Argentina SA; Salvat Editores do Brasil Ltda; Salvat Editores Colombiana SA; Salvat Editores Chilena Ltda; Salvat Editores Ecuatoriana SA; Salvat Mexicana de Ediciones SA de CV, Mexico (qv); Salvat Editores de Puerto Rico Inc; Salvat Editores Venezolana SA
Subjects: Reference, History, Art, Music, Literature, Medicine, Science, Technology, Geography, Language Courses, Dictionaries, Paperbacks
1985: 180 titles *Founded:* 1869
ISBN Publisher's Prefix: 84-345

Salvat SA de Ediciones*, Arrieta 25, Pamplona Tel: (948) 248600 Telex: 37739 Saaae e
Subjects: Encyclopaedias, Dictionaries, Art, History
ISBN Publisher's Prefix: 84-7137

Editorial Miguel A **Salvatella** SA, Calle Santo Domingo 5, 08012 Barcelona Tel: (93) 2189026
Subjects: Primary Textbooks, Educational Materials
Founded: 1922
ISBN Publisher's Prefix: 84-7210

Editorial **San Martin** SL, Apdo 97, 28080 Madrid (Located at: Arenal 23, 28013 Madrid) Tel: (91) 2214292/2216897
Man Dir: Jorge Tarazona
Subjects: History, Aviation, Military
Bookshop: Librería San Martin, Puerta del Sol 6, 28013 Madrid
Founded: 1854
ISBN Publisher's Prefix: 84-7140

Ediciones **San Pio X**, Marqués de Mondéjar 32, 28028 Madrid Tel: (91) 2562817
Dir: Eduardo Malvido Miguel
Subjects: Theology, Pedagogy, Psychology, Catechism, Religion
Founded: 1964
ISBN Publisher's Prefix: 84-7221

Santillana SA de Ediciones+*, Calle Elfo 32, 28027 Madrid Tel: (91) 4034000 Telex: 43944 Elfo
President: Jesús de Polanco Gutérrez; *Vice-Presidents:* Francisco Pérez González, Ricardo Díez Hochleitner; *Man Dir:* Emiliano Martinez Rodriguez; *Editorial:* Antonio Ramos Perez; *Sales:* Jose Muñoz Juan; *Production:* Francisco Jerez Vazquez; *Publicity:* Jaime Mascaró Florit; *Rights & Permissions:* Gloria Roldan Perez
Associate Companies: Editorial Santillana, Argentina; Edyca SA, Dominican Republic; Nutesa, Mexico; Santillana del Pacifico SA, Chile; Santillana Publishing Co, USA; Teduca, Venezuela (qv); Tedupe, Peru
Branch Offs: Capitán Segarra 41, Alicante; Aribau 228, 08006 Barcelona; Ave del Ejército 3, Deusto (Vizcaya); Acera del Casino 15, Granada; Julián Romero Brionez 4, Las Palmas; Alonso Quintanilla 3, Oviedo; Placentines 2, Seville; Jacinto Benavente 19, Valencia 5; Polígono BENS parcela S-l-B, La Coruña; Avda José Luis Arrese 1, Local 5, Valladolid; Isabel la Católica 5, Zaragoza (all in Spain)
Subjects: Textbooks, Educational Materials for Kindergarten, Primary and Secondary, Teachers and Educational Specialists
Founded: 1960
ISBN Publisher's Prefix: 84-294

Ediciones **Scriba** SA+, Apdo FD 308, 08007 Barcelona (Located at: Rambla de Catalunya 60 – pral 1a, Barcelona) Tel: (93) 2152089 Telex: 98772 Cllc E (Scriba)
Man Dir: Manuel Martínez Bravo
Subjects: Medicine, Technical, Science, Reference, University Textbooks, Art, Gift Books
Bookshop: Librería Martínez Pérez, Valencia 246, 08007 Barcelona Tel: (93) 2151933
Founded: 1978
ISBN Publisher's Prefix: 84-85835

Secretariado Trinitario+, Filiberto Villalobos 82, 37007 Salamanca Tel: (923) 235602
Man Dir: Nereo Silanes; *Rights & Permissions:* Laurentino Silanes
Subjects: Religion, Theology
Founded: 1967
ISBN Publisher's Prefix: 84-85376

Editorial **Seix Barral** SA, Córcega 270 – 4°, Barcelona 8 Tel: (93) 2186400/2186466 Telex: 98255 Sxbl E
General Managers: Mario Lacruz, Miguel García Píriz; *Editorial:* Pere Gimferrer
Associate Company: Editorial Ariel SA (qv)
Subjects: Fiction from Spanish, Latin-American, German, French, English, Italian, Soviet Russian, North American, Oriental and other literatures; Poetry, Drama, the Classics
Founded: 1945
Miscellaneous: Firm is a member of the Planeta Group (see Editorial Planeta SA)
ISBN Publisher's Prefix: 84-322

Selecciones Editoriales SA*, Rita Bonnat 9, 08029 Barcelona Tel: (93) 2303400 Telex: 54495 Sele e/97013 Elsv e
Dirs: J L Ruiz de Villa, E Tarrero,

374 SPAIN

H Kleinveld
Subjects: General and Educational Reference Works

Ediciones del Serbal SA+, Carrer Guitard 45, 08014 Barcelona Tel: (93) 3223054
Man Dir, Editorial, Production: José María Riaño de Castro; *Sales, Publicity:* Isabel Baños Regel
1985: 16 titles *1986:* 13 titles *Founded:* 1980
ISBN Publisher's Prefixes: 84-85800, 84-7628

Siglo XXI de España Editores SA+, Apdo 48023, 28043 Madrid (Located at: Plaza 5, Madrid) Tel: (93) 7594809/7594918/7594557 Cable Add: Sigloedit
Man Dir, Production: Joaquín García Ballestero; *Sales:* Eduardo Rivas
Subsidiary Companies: Siglo XXI Editores de Colombia Ltda, Colombia (qv); Siglo XXI Editores SA de CV, Mexico (qv)
Subjects: Anthropology, Psychology, Sociology, History, Philosophy, Politics, Literature and Criticism
Bookshop: At above address
Founded: 1967
ISBN Publisher's Prefix: 84-323

Ediciones **Siguemé** SA, Apdo 332, 37080 Salamanca Tel: (923) 218203 Cable Add: Siguemé Salamanca
Man Dir, Editorial: Germán González; *Sales:* Francisco Tejeda; *Production:* Francisco Lansac; *Publicity:* Jorge Sans Vila
Subjects: Philosophy, Religion, Juveniles, Psychology, Social Science, University Textbooks, Cinema, Education
Bookshop: Librería Siguemé (at above address)
1986: 30 titles *Founded:* 1958
ISBN Publisher's Prefix: 84-301

Editorial **Sintes** SA, Apdo 1078, Barcelona Tel: (93) 3182838
Man Dirs, Editorial: Luis Sintes Pros, Jorge Sintes Pros
Orders to: Ronda Universidad 4, Barcelona 7
Subjects: Sports, Technical, Health
Bookshop: Librería Sintes, Ronda Universidad 4, Barcelona
Founded: 1968
ISBN Publisher's Prefix: 84-302

Sociedad Anonima de Revistas Periodicos y Ediciones (SARPE)+*, Pedro Teixeira 8, 28020 Madrid Tel: (91) 4560048 Telex: 46148 Srpe
Man Dir: Alfredo Marron Gomez; *Editorial:* Marisa Perez Bodegas; *Sales:* José Aguilera Morena; *Production:* Andres Salcedo Peña; *Publicity:* Javier Jaen
Subjects: Cooking, Medicine, Homecraft, Plants and Flowers, Knitting and Sewing, History, Armament, Science, Zoology, Astronomy, Art, Music, Cars, Languages, Hobbies, Sports, Spanish Paintings
Founded: 1952
ISBN Publisher's Prefix: 84-7291

Sociedad General Española de Librería SA, Apdo 85, Poligono Industrial de Alcobendas, Madrid (Located at: Ave Valdelaparra 11, Poligono Industrial de Alcobendas, Madrid) Tel: (91) 6511700 Cable Add: Niola Telex: 22092
Dir General: Mr Ortuzar; *Editorial Dir:* Luis Alonso Tejada; *Sales:* Miguel Angel Santos; *Production:* Juan Martinez
Parent Company: Hachette, France (qv)
Branch Offs: Alicante, Barcelona, Bilbao, Burgos, Irun, La Coruña, Las Palmas, Malaga, Murcia, Oviedo, Seville, Valencia
Subjects: Educational (especially languages)
Bookshops: Centro Pedagógico, Calle Marqués de Valdeiglesias 5, 28004 Madrid; Librería Colón, Calle Real 24, 15003 La Coruña; Franco Española, Gran Vía 54, 28013 Madrid; Librería Francesa (SGEL) (qv under Major Booksellers); Internacional Madrid, Centro Comercial Madrid 2 (La Vaguada), Ave Monforte de Lemos s/n, 28029 Madrid; Internacional San Pablo, Calle San Pablo 41C, 41001 Seville; Internacional, Calle Ruzafa 23, 46004 Valencia
Founded: 1914
ISBN Publisher's Prefix: 84-7143

Ramón **Sopena** SA*, Provenza 93-95, 08029 Barcelona Tel: (93) 2303809 Cable Add: Sopenar Telex: 52195 Sopec E
Man Dir: Ramón Sopena Rimblas; *Rights & Permissions:* Domingo Castellar Andreu; *Production:* Antonio Bometon Garcés
Subsidiary Company: Editorial Ramón Sopena Venezolana SA, Venezuela (qv)
Subjects: History, Art, Reference, Juveniles, Paperbacks, General Science, Languages, Dictionaries, Atlases, Children's books
Founded: 1894
ISBN Publisher's Prefix: 84-303

Ediciones **Susaeta** SA*, Calle Campezo s/n, 28022 Madrid Tel: (91) 7472111 Telex: 22148 Ssta e
Sales Dir: Jose Ignacio Susaeta Erburu
Subjects: Juveniles, Children's, Board books
ISBN Publisher's Prefix: 84-305

T E A Ediciones SA+, Apdo 19007, 28036 Madrid (Located at: Calle Fray Bernardino de Sahagún 24, Madrid) Tel: (91) 4588311 Cable Add: Teacegos Telex: 22135
Man Dir: Agustin Cordero Pando; *Sales:* Marina Gonzalez Criado; *Production:* Manuel Ruiz Claro
Parent Company: Tecnicos Especialistas Asociados SA (at above address)
Branch Offs: Calle Brasil 11, 08028 Barcelona; Hurtado de Amézaga 3, 48008 Bilbao; Monte Carmelo 6 – 2°, 41011 Seville
Subject: Psychology
Bookshop: TEA Libros (at above address)
Founded: 1957
ISBN Publisher's Prefix: 84-7174

Taller Ediciones JB*, Apdo 9129, Madrid 28 (Located at: Ambrós 8, Madrid) Tel: (91) 2551266
Man Dir, Permissions: J Betancor; *Sales Dir:* I Izquierdo; *Publicity Dir:* M Padorno
Subjects: General Literature, Fiction, Philosophy, Psychology, Social Sciences, Art, Cinema
Founded: 1972
ISBN Publisher's Prefix: 84-7330

Ediciones **Tárraco***, Apdo 6, 43003 Tarragona (Located at: Conde de Rius 9, Tarragona) Tel: (977) 233806/233813
Man Dir: Francisco Sugrañes Pedrol; *Sales:* Javier Elias Cabrerizo
Parent Company: F Sugrañes Editors SA (at above address)
Subjects: Educational, Classical Literature, Art
1985: 4 titles *Founded:* 1976
ISBN Publisher's Prefix: 84-7320

Taurus Ediciones SA+, Principe de Vergara 81, Madrid 7
Man Dir: Ambrosio Ochoa; *Editorial:* José Maria F Guelbenzu; *Publicity, Promotion:* Angeles Martín; *Rights & Permissions:* Rosa Benavides
Subjects: Philosophy, Political Science, Linguistics and Philology, Literature, History, Biography, Aesthetics, Art History, Music, Cultural Anthropology
Founded: 1956
ISBN Publisher's Prefix: 84-306

Editores **Técnicos Asociados** SA*, Maignón 26, Barcelona 24 Tel: (93) 2144178/2144266
Man Dir: Carlos Palomar; *Sales, Publicity, Advertising:* Juan Cuenca
Subjects: Engineering, Technical, Construction, Computers, Organization, How-to, University Textbooks
Founded: 1963
ISBN Publisher's Prefix: 84-7146

Editorial **Tecnos** SA+*, Josefa Valcárcel 27, 28027 Madrid Tel: (91) 7428111
Man Dir, Editorial: Alejandro Sierra Benayas; *Production:* Mariano Moreno; *Publicity, Rights & Permissions:* José María Castillo; *Sales:* Grupo Distribuidor Editorial SA, D Ramón de la Cruz 67, 28001 Madrid
Parent Company: Grupo Anaya, Ferrer del Río 35, 28028 Madrid
Associate Companies: Ediciones Anaya SA (qv for other associates)
Subjects: Social Sciences, History, Art, Philology, Science and Technology, Psychology, Philosophy, Literature, Law
Founded: 1947
ISBN Publisher's Prefix: 84-309

Editorial **Teide** SA+, Calle Viladomat 291, 08029 Barcelona Tel: (93) 4104507 Cable Add: Editeide
Man Dir, Publicity, Rights & Permissions, Editorial, Sales: Federico Rahola Aguade; *Production:* Christian Rahola Aguade
Subsidiary Company: Editorial Varazen SA, Mexico (qv)
Subjects: University, Secondary & Primary Textbooks, Pedagogy, Art, Educational Materials, Navigation, Dictionaries, Languages, Mathematics, Literature, Geography, History, Philosophy
Founded: 1940
ISBN Publisher's Prefix: 84-307

Editorial **Timun** Mas SA+, Calle Castillejos 294/296 – 1°, 08025 Barcelona Tel: (93) 3477233 Telex: 50564 Ceac E
Dir: Guillermo Menal Alonso; *Man Dir:* Jaime Pintanel; *International Dir:* José L Quiñones Correa
Parent Company: Ediciones Ceac SA (qv)
Associate Companies: Editorial Siluetas, Bartolomé Mitre 3745-49, 1201 Buenos Aires, Argentina; Aconcagua Ediciones y Publicaciones SA, Mexico (qv)
Imprint: Dístein Libros
Subjects: Children's, Juveniles, Teaching Manuals
1986: 275 titles *1987:* 400 titles
ISBN Publisher's Prefix: 84-7176

Ediciones **Toray** SA+, Duero 6, 08031 Barcelona Tel: (93) 3577550 Cable Add: Toray
Dirs: Mariano Torrecilla, Miguel Vilanova; *Rights & Permissions:* Estanislao Peinado
Branch Offs: Príncipe de Vergara 11, 28001 Madrid; Junín 925, 1113 Buenos Aires, Argentina
Subjects: General Fiction, Children's, Juveniles, Medicine, Psychology, University Textbooks
Founded: 1953
ISBN Publisher's Prefix: 84-310

Toray-Masson SA, now Masson SA (qv)

G del **Toro** Editor*, Hortaleza 81, Madrid 4 Tel: (91) 4190486/4199518/4190139
Subjects: Fiction & Non-fiction, Juveniles, Secondary Textbooks
ISBN Publisher's Prefix: 84-312

Ediciones de la **Torre***, Calle Espronceda 20 bajo izquierda, 28003 Madrid

Tel: (91) 4427793
Manager: José María Gutiérrez;
Editorial: María Luisa Calvo
Subjects: Social Sciences, Humanities, General Literature, Children's and Juveniles, Comics, University Textbooks
1985: 12 titles *1986:* 12 titles *Founded:* 1976
ISBN Publisher's Prefixes: 84-85866, 84-85277

Instituto Eduardo **Torroja** de la Construccion y del Cemento*, Apdo 19002, 28080 Madrid (Located at: Serrano Galvache s/n, 28033 Madrid) Tel: (91) 2020440
Subjects: Construction, Engineering, Architecture
ISBN Publisher's Prefix: 84-7292

Trazo Editorial, Apdo 351, 50080 Zaragoza (Located at: Camino de los Molinos 155, 50015 Zaragoza) Tel: (976) 517586
Man Dir: D Francisco Javier de Miguel;
Publicity: D Fernando Royo
Subjects: General, Tourism
1985: 5 titles *Founded:* 1980
ISBN Publisher's Prefix: 84-85821

Tusquets Editores+, Calle Iradier 24 bajos, 08017 Barcelona Tel: (93) 2474170 Telex: 93251 Lume E
Man Dirs: Beatriz de Moura, Antonio López Lamadrid; *Sales:* Josefa Valero; *Production, Rights & Permissions, Publicity:* Miriam Tey
Subjects: Fiction, Literature, Biography, History, Philosophy, Art, Science, Social Sciences, Eroticism, Gastronomy
1985: 45 titles *1986:* 45 titles *Founded:* 1969
ISBN Publisher's Prefix: 84-7223

Editorial **Txertoa**+*, Apdo 767, 20080 San Sebastián (Located at: Plaza Armerias 4, 20011 San Sebastián) Tel: (943) 459757/ 460941
Man Dir: Luis Aberasturi
Subjects: Literature, Biography, Anthropology, Ethnography, Folklore, History and Art of the Basque Region, Geography, Linguistics, Reprints
Founded: 1968
ISBN Publisher's Prefix: 84-7148

U N A L I SL*, Fray Luis Amigó 8, Edificio Zafiro oficina A, Zaragoza 6 Tel: (976) 373267
Man Dir: José María Saiz Navarro
Branch Off: Paseo Castellana 132, Madrid
Subjects: Regional Encyclopaedias, Literature, Religion, Occult, Hairdressing
Founded: 1972
ISBN Publisher's Prefix: 84-85656

Ultramar Editores SA, Mallorca 49, Barcelona 29 Tel: (93) 3212400 Telex: 53132 Saedi E
Man Dir: Emilio Teixidor
Subjects: General Literature, Fiction, Science Fiction, Paperbacks, Juveniles, Biography, Cinema
Founded: 1973
ISBN Publisher's Prefix: 84-7386

Unión Aragonesa del Libro SL, see UNALI SL

Universidad de Granada*, Secretariado de Publicaciones, Hospital Real, Granada Tel: (958) 278400
Dir: D Francisco Rodríguez Martínez;
Deputy Dir: D José Sánchez Rodrigo
Subjects: Literature, History, Law, Art, Sciences, Philosophy, Social Sciences, Philology, Biology, Geology, Botany, Anthropology, Archaeology, Medicine, Geography, Music, General Interest
1984: approx 35 titles
ISBN Publisher's Prefix: 84-338

Universidad de Malaga*, Colonia Santa Inés, Malaga Tel: (952) 301212
Subjects: Sociology, Philosophy, History, Medicine

Ediciones **Universidad de Navarra** SA, see EUNSA

Ediciones **Universidad de Salamanca***, Apdo 325, Salamanca (Located at: Patio de Escuelas 1, Salamanca) Tel: (923) 214030
Man Dir: Eugenio García Zarza
Subjects: Academic
Founded: 1978
ISBN Publisher's Prefix: 84-7481

Ediciones **Urbión** SA+, Ave del Llano Castellano 13, 28034 Madrid Tel: (91) 7293111/7291438/7291638 Telex: 45151 Edur E
President: Rafael García-Arteaga; *General Manager:* Manuel Herranz; *Editorial Dir:* Javier de Juan y Peñalosa
Subjects: Reference, Encyclopaedias, Children's, Religion, Art, Health, Natural History, History, Cinema, Stamps
1985: 57 titles *Founded:* 1975
ISBN Publisher's Prefix: 84-7523

Urmo SA de Ediciones+, Plaza del Ensanche 5 – 1° izda, 48009 Bilbao Tel: (94) 4245307
Chairman: José Angel Grijelmo Ribechini
Subjects: Engineering, General Science, Microcomputers, University Textbooks
Founded: 1963
ISBN Publisher's Prefix: 84-314

Editorial **Vasco** Americana SA (EVA)*, Carretera Nueva de Galdácano 8, 48004 Bilbao
Subject: Children's, Juveniles
ISBN Publisher's Prefix: 84-319

Editorial De **Vecchi**, see De Vecchi

Editorial **Verbo** Divino+, Carretera de Pamplona 41, 31200 Estella, Navarra Tel: (948) 550449 Cable Add: Verbodivino Fax: (948) 554506
Man Dir: Father Tomás Langarica; *Sales Dir:* Martín Esparza; *Advertising, Rights & Permissions:* Angel Beltran
Subjects: Religion, Bibles, Biography, Social Science, Educational Materials
Founded: 1957
ISBN Publisher's Prefix: 84-7151

Veron Editor+, Ronda del General Mitre 163, 08022 Barcelona Tel: (93) 2121599/ 2119300
Man Dir, Sales: Luis Veron Climent; *Editorial, Publicity, Production, Rights & Permissions:* Lluis Verón Jané
Subjects: Fiction, Juvenile, Ancient & Modern Classics
Bookshop: Libreria Scriba, Ronda del General Mitre 100, 08021 Barcelona Tel: (93) 2010096
1985: 10 titles *Founded:* 1965
ISBN Publisher's Prefix: 84-7255

Ediciones **Versal** SA+, Plaza Lesseps 33, 08023 Barcelona Tel: (93) 2172054 Telex: 98634 Vsbn
Dir General: Joan Agut; *Editorial:* Antoni Munné; *Production:* Enric Canut
Orders to: Grupo Distribuidor Editorial SA, Don Ramón de la Cruz 67, Madrid 1
Parent Company: Grupo Anaya, Josefa Valcárcel 27, 28027 Madrid
Associate Companies: Ediciones Anaya SA (qv for other associates)
Subjects: Literature, Non-fiction
1985: 25 titles *1986:* 45 titles *Founded:* 1984
ISBN Publisher's Prefix: 84-86311

Editorial **Vicens-Vives**, Ave de Sarriá 132-136, 08017 Barcelona Tel: (93) 2034400

Telex: 51425 Live E
Man Dirs: Roser Rahola, Pere Vicens
Subjects: General Literature, Belles Lettres, Art, History, Biography, Geography, General Science, Mathematics, Secondary Textbooks, Education
ISBN Publisher's Prefix: 84-316

Ediciones **Vidorama** SA, a subsidiary company of Ediciones Ceac SA (qv)

Editorial Luis **Vives** (Edelvives), Apdo 387, 50080 Zaragoza (Located at: Carretera de Madrid, Km 315 7, Zaragoza) Tel: (976) 344100 Cable Add: Edelvives Telex: 57856 Elv E
Man Dir: Víctor García Arroyo;
Editorial: Francisco Moliner; *Production Dir:* Jesús Agudo
Branch Offs: Barcelona, Bilbao, Madrid, Málaga, Oviedo, Seville, Valencia, Valladolid, Vigo, Zaragoza
Subjects: University, Secondary & Primary Textbooks, Educational Materials
1985: 65 titles *1986:* 95 titles *Founded:* 1932
ISBN Publisher's Prefix: 84-263

Xarait Libros SA, Paseo de San Francisco de Sales 32, 28003 Madrid Tel: (91) 2341567
Man Dir: Miguel Ortiz Martínez
Subjects: Architecture, Art
Bookshops: At above address; Raset 49, Barcelona
1985: 3 titles *1986:* 3 titles *Founded:* 1978
ISBN Publisher's Prefix: 84-85434

Literary Agents

A C E R*, Calle Bolonia 5, 28028 Madrid Tel: (91) 2559943/2461776
Contacts: Marcel Laignoux, Gussie Laignoux

Carmen **Balcells** Agencia Literaria*, Diagonal 580, 08021 Barcelona Tel: (93) 2008565/2008933 Cable Add: Copyright Barcelona Telex: 50459 copy E (Barcelona)
Manager: Carmen Balcells
Branch Off: Brazil (qv)

Bookbank SA, Rafael Calvo 13, 28010 Madrid Tel: (91) 4104979 Telex: 49387 Bkbnk E Fax: (91) 4455334
Contact: Angela González

Cecilio **Cardeñoso***, Juan Güell 74-76, 08028 Barcelona Tel: (93) 3303416

International Editors' Co SA, Rambla de Cataluña 63 – 3° 1a, 08007 Barcelona Tel: (93) 2158812 Cable Add: Lifeplay Telex: 98478 Rght E
Manager: Isabel Monteagudo
Branch Off: Buenos Aires, Argentina (qv)

Ute **Körner de Moya** Literary Agent, Ronda Guinardó 32 – 5° 5a, 08025 Barcelona Tel: (93) 2550414 Telex: 52012 Eum E attn Mrs Ute Körner

Andrés de **Kramer**, Castello 30, 28001 Madrid Tel: (91) 4316305

Agencia Literaria La **Península***, Calle Angel Guimera 3-20, Amer (Gerona) Tel: (972) 431118

Frédérique **Porretta**, Diagonal 440, Barcelona 37 Tel: (93) 2379169
Also: Paris, France (qv)

Julio F **Yañez**, Agencia Literaria, Via Augusta 139 – 6° 2a, 08021 Barcelona Tel: (93) 2007107 Cable Add: Agenliter Telex: 97348 Gnlt E
Dirs: Julio F Yañez, Mrs Mayte Yañez
Specializations: Modern Literature, Documents and Memoirs; Educational:

History, Art, Sociology; Topical Books on Modern Facts; Co-productions
Covering all Spanish- and Portuguese-speaking countries

Book Clubs

Círculo de Lectores SA*, Valencia 344, Barcelona 9 Tel: (93) 2587600 Cable Add: Cilec Telex: 52532/52560
Members: 1,000,000
Owned by: Bertelsmann AG, Federal Republic of Germany (qv)
Founded: 1962

Club del **Libro de la Naturaleza***, Castelló 59, Madrid 1
Owned by: Editorial Incafo SA (qv). The Club is open only to subscribers to the proprietors' periodical *Periplo*
Subjects: (Books published by Incafo at a 20% discount) Natural History, Geography, Ethnology, especially with regard to Spain and Spanish America

Major Booksellers

Librería **Ancora y Delfín**, Diagonal 564, 08021 Barcelona Tel: (93) 2000746
Owned by: Edicions Destino SA (qv)

Librería **Bosch**, Ronda Universidad 11, 08007 Barcelona Tel: (93) 3175308 Cable Add: Boslibri
Manager: José M Bosch

Casa del Libro SA*, Ronda de San Pedro 3, Barcelona 10 Tel: (93) 3182640

Cinc d'Oros — Jaime Farrás Solé*, Diagonal 462, Barcelona 6 Tel: (93) 2170059

D E L S A, see SA de Distribución, Edición y Librerías

Díaz de Santos SA – Libreria Cientifico-Tecnica, Lagasca 95, 28006 Madrid Tel: (91) 4312482 Telex: 45141 Dsan E Fax: (91) 2755563 (Administration: Juan Bravo 3A, 28006 Madrid)
Also: Díaz de Santos SA – Libreria Medica, Maldonado 6, 28006 Madrid Tel: (91) 4312482; Díaz de Santos SA – Libreria Cientifico-Tecnica, Balmes 417/419, 08022 Barcelona Tel: (93) 2128647 Telex: 54656 Dsan E; Diaz de Santos SA – Agropecuaria, Lagasca 38, 28001 Madrid Tel: (91) 4312482
Owned by: Ediciones Díaz de Santos SA (qv)

SA de **Distribución**, Edición y Librerías (DELSA), Serrano 80, Madrid 6 Tel: (91) 4354780
13 branches throughout Spain
DELSA Importadora de Publicaciones SA is also at the above address

Casa del Libro **Espasa-Calpe** SA*, Gran Via 29, 28013 Madrid Tel: (91) 2216657
Also: Colón de Larreátegui 41, 48009 Bilbao Tel: (94) 4232005
Owned by: Editorial Espasa-Calpe SA (qv)

Librería **Francesa** (SGEL), Paseo de Gracia 91, 08008 Barcelona Tel: (93) 2151417
Manager: Josep María Blasi
Also: Muntaner 224, 08021 Barcelona
Owned by: Sociedad General Española de Libreria SA (qv)

Librería **Herder**, Balmes 26, 08007 Barcelona Tel: (93) 3170578 Telex: 54120 Hegr E
Manager: Hermann Nahm
Owned by: Antonio Valtl Friedl (see Editorial Herder SA)

Librería **Hispano Americana***, Gran Via de las Cortes Catalanas 594, 08007 Barcelona Tel: (93) 3175337/3180079
Manager: Josép M Boixareu Vilaplana
Owned by: Marcombo SA de Boixareu Editores (qv)

Hogar del Libro SA*, Calle Bergara 3, Barcelona 2 Tel: (93) 3182700 Telex: 50066 ogar
Manager: Sebastià Fàbregues
Branches: Via Augusta 64, Barcelona 6; Pg Sant Joan 106-108, Barcelona 37; Pg Plaça Major 12, Sabadell (Barcelona); Pg Plaça Major 34, Sabadell (Barcelona); Carretera Barcelona/Sabadell, Baricentro, Local 35, Sabadell (Barcelona); Ave Sarria 40, Barcelona 29
Also Publisher (qv), and major distributor

Insula, Librería, Ediciones y Publicaciones SA*, Benito Gutiérrez 26, Madrid 8 Tel: (91) 2435415
Also Publisher (qv)

L I N E S A, see Librerías del Norte de España SA

H F **Martínez** de Murguía SA, Valverde 27, 28004 Madrid Tel: (91) 5226634
Manager: Francisco Gugel
Universal supplier and distributor of books published in Spain

Miessner Libreros, José Ortega y Gasset 14, 28006 Madrid Tel: (91) 4350978/4350998

Librería **Mundi-Prensa**, Castelló 37, 28001 Madrid Tel: (91) 4313399 Telex: 49370 Mpli E
Man Dir: José María Hernández
Owned by: Mundi-Prensa Libros SA (qv)
Subsidiary Company: Librería Agricola, Fernando VI 2, 28004 Madrid

Librerías del **Norte de España** SA (LINESA)*, Serrano 80, Madrid 6 Tel: (91) 2764810/2764826
Five branches in Spain

Librerías **P P C** (Promoción Popular Cristiana), Enrique Jardiel Poncela 4, 28016 Madrid Tel: (91) 4582335
Also: Librería Pastoral, Velazquez 1, 04002 Almeria; Librería PPC, Canuda 9, 08002 Barcelona Tel: (93) 3172939; Librería Remei, Badal 144, 08028 Barcelona; Librería Amunt, Alloza 118, 12001 Castellon; Librería Promoción, Conde Cardenas 5, 14002 Cordoba; Librería Piedelatorre, Molina la Rios 8, 29015 Malaga; Librería Selecta, San Felipe de Neri 10, 07002 Palma de Mallorca; Librería Concilio, Teniente Coronel Segui 1, 41001 Seville
Owned by: PPC (qv)

Librería **Pássim** SA, Bailén 134, 08009 Barcelona Tel: (93) 2574757 Cable Add: Pássim
Manager: Rosa Pujol
Publishes catalogues of new and out of print books about Spain and Latin America published in Spain. Specializes in export sales to foreign universities and libraries

Librería José **Porrúa** Turanzas SA*, Cea Bermúdez 10, 28003 Madrid Tel: (91) 2542344/2541466
Manager: José Porrúa Venero
Owned by: Ediciones José Porrúa Turanzas SA (qv)

Libreria **Rubiños***, Alcala 98, 28009 Madrid Tel: (91) 2754227

Major Libraries

Archivo General de la **Administracion** Civil del Estado, Paseo de Aguadores 2, Alcalá de Henares, Madrid
General Archives of the Civil Administration of the State
Documents on administration no longer of current relevance

Archivo General de Indias*, Queipo de Llano 3, Seville
Archives of the Indies

Archivo Historico Nacional*, Calle Serrano 115, Madrid Tel: (91) 2617052/2618003
National Historical Archives
Dir: Dr Carmen Crespo Nogueira

Archivo y Biblioteca Capitulares*, Cathedral of Toledo, Toledo Tel: (925) 212423
Archives and Library of the Cathedral Chapter
Dir: Ramón Gonzálvez

Ateneo Barcelonés Biblioteca*, Calle de la Canuda 6, 08002 Barcelona
Library of the Athenaeum of Barcelona

Biblioteca del **Ateneo de Madrid***, Prado 21, Madrid
Library of the Madrid Athenaeum
Librarian: María José Albo Alvarez

Biblioteca '**Bergnes de las Casas**' de la Generalitat de Catalunya, Palau Moja, Portaferrissa 1, 08002 Barcelona Tel: (93) 3021522
Library of the Department of Culture of the Generalitat de Catalunya
Librarian: María Artal

Biblioteca Nacional*, Paseo de Recoletos 20, Madrid 1 Tel: (91) 2756800
Dir: D Hipolito Escolar Sobrino

Biblioteca de **Catalunya** Diputación de Barcelona*, Apdo 1077, 08001 Barcelona (Located at: Calle del Carmen 47, Barcelona) Tel: (93) 3178990 (Director); (93) 3170778 (General)
Library of Cataluña

Biblioteca General del **Consejo** Superior de Investigaciones Científicas, Medinaceli 6, 28014 Madrid Tel: (91) 4292017
Library of the Council for Scientific Research
Librarian: Dolores Corróns

Archivo de la **Corona** de Aragón, Condes de Barcelona 2, 08002 Barcelona Tel: (93) 3150211
Royal Archives of Aragon
Dir: María-Mercedes Costa
Publications: Colección de Documentos Inéditos del Archivo de la Corona de Aragón (from 1847)

Hemeroteca Municipal de Madrid*, Calle Conde Duque 9-11, Madrid 8
Madrid Periodical Library

Biblioteca del **Instituto de Cooperacion** Iberoamericana, Ave Reyes Católicos 4, 28040 Madrid
Library of the Institute of Spanish-American Fellowship

Biblioteca del **Instituto de Cultura** Hispànica, now Biblioteca del Instituto de Cooperacion Iberoamericana (qv)

Biblioteca del **Instituto Nacional** del Libro Español, see Biblioteca 'Bergnes de las Casas'

Biblioteca de **Menéndez Pelayo**, Calle Rubio 6, Santander Tel: (942) 234534
Librarian: Manuel Revuelta Sañudo
Publications include: La Biblioteca de Menéndez Pelayo; Boletín de la Biblioteca

de Menéndez Pelayo (annual); *Estudios de literatura y pensamiento hispánicos* (series)

Biblioteca **Ministerio de Cultura***, Calle San Marcos 40 – 5a planta, Madrid 4
Library of the Ministry of Culture
Librarian: Araceli González Antón

Patrimonio Nacional, Biblioteca del **Palacio Real***, Calle Bailén s/n, 28071 Madrid Tel: (91) 2487404
Library of the Royal Palace
Librarian: Consolación Morales Borrero

Real Biblioteca de San Lorenzo de El Escorial, El Escorial, Madrid Tel: (91) 8903889
Escorial Library
Librarian: Teodoro Alonso Turienzo

Universidad Autónoma de Barcelona, Biblioteca General, Campus Universitario, Bellaterra (Barcelona) Tel: (93) 6920200 Telex: 52040
Dir: Montserrat Lamarca Morell

Biblioteca de la **Universidad Complutense***, Noviciado 3, 28015 Madrid
Librarian: Fernando Huarte

Universidad Pontificia de Salamanca, Biblioteca General, Calle Compañia 1, Salamanca Tel: (923) 218517
Librarian: Dr Enrique Llamas-Martinez

Biblioteca **Universitaria de Barcelona***, Gran Via 585, 08007 Barcelona Tel: (93) 3189947 Telex: 98871 Unb E Fax: (93) 3170689
Librarian: Dolors Lamarca Morell
Publication: Memòria

Library Associations

Asociación Española de Archiveros, Bibliotecarios, Museólogos y Documentalistas*, Paseo de Recoletos 20, Madrid 1
Spanish Association of Archivists, Librarians, Curators and Documentalists
President: David Torra Ferrer
Secretary: Antonio Magariños Compaired
Publications include: Boletín (with bibliography section)

Asociación Nacional de Bibliotecarios, Archiveros, Arqueologos y Documentalistas (Anabad)*, Paseo de Calvo Sotelo 22, Madrid 1 Tel: (91) 2259868
National Association of Librarians, Archivists, Archaeologists and Documentalists
Secretary: Ms C Iníguez Galíndez

Instituto Bibliográfico Hispánico*, Calle de Atocha 106, 28012 Madrid Tel: (91) 2283878
Dir: Vicente Sánchez Muñoz
Hispanic Bibliographical Institute
Publications: Bibliografía Española (monthly); *Bibliografía Española: Suplemento de Publicaciones Periódicas* (annual); *Revistas Españolas con ISSN* (annual)

Library Reference Books and Journals

Book

Biblioteca Hispana (Spanish Library), Consejo Superior de Investigaciones Cientificas, Serrano 117, Madrid

Journals

Boletín (Bulletin), Asociación Española de Archiveros, Bibliotecarios, Museólogos y Documentalistas, Paseo de Recoletos 20, Madrid 1

Informacion Librera (Library Information), Javier Romani Sopena, Pelayo 11 – 4, Barcelona

Revista de Archivos, Bibliotecas y Museos (Review of Archives, Libraries and Museums), Ministerio de Educación y Ciencia, Servicio de Publicaciónes, Ciudad Universitaria, Madrid 3

Revistas españolas con ISSN (Spanish periodicals with ISSN numbers) (annual), Instituto Bibliográfico Hispánico, Calle de Atocha 106, 28012 Madrid

Literary Associations and Societies

Ateneo Cientifico, Literario y Artistico*, Calle del Prado 21, Madrid Tel: (91) 4296251
Scientific, Literary and Artistic Athenaeum
President: César Navarro; *General Secretary:* Eduardo González

Ateneo Cientifico, Literario y Artistico, Calle Cifuentes 25, Mahón, Minorca, Balearic Islands Tel: (971) 360553
Scientific, Literary and Artistic Athenaeum
Secretary: Gabriel Pons Olives
Publication: Revista de Menorca (quarterly)

Spanish **P E N** Club (Cataluña)*, Ateneu Barcelones, Canuda 6 – 5e, Barcelona 2
President: Jordi Sarsanedas; *Secretary:* Xavier Bru de Sala

Real Academia de Buenas Letras de Barcelona, Calle Obispo Cassador 3, 08002 Barcelona
Barcelona Royal Academy of Belles Lettres
Secretary: José Alsina Clota
Publications: Boletín, Memorias

Real Academia de Córdoba, de Ciencias, Bellas Letras y Nobles Artes*, Calle Ambrosio de Morales 9, Córdoba 3
Royal Cordobese Academy of Science, Literature and Fine Arts
Secretary: Manuel Nieto Cumplido
Publications: Boletín (half-yearly), scientific, historical and literary works

Real Academia Sevillana de Buenas Letras*, Plaza del Museo 8, Selville
Seville Royal Academy of Belles Lettres
Secretary: Dr Ildefonso Camacho Baños
Publication: Boletín de Buenas Letras (quarterly)

Sociedad de Ciencias, Letras y Artes*, Dr Chil 25, Las Palmas, Canary Islands
Scientific, Literary and Art Society
Secretary: Nicolas Díaz-Saavedra de Morales
Publication: El Museo Canario (quarterly)

Sociedad General de Autores de España*, Apdo 484, Madrid 4 (Located at: Fernando VI 4, Madrid)
General Society of Spanish Authors
Secretary-General: José María Segovia Galindo

Literary Periodicals

Camp de l'Arpa, Valencia 72, Entlo 4a, Barcelona 15

Destino, Edicions Destino SA, Consell de Cent 425 – 5° planta, 08009 Barcelona

La Estafeta Literaria (The Literary Courier), Editora Nacional, Ave del Generalísimo 29, Madrid 16

Insula, Ediciones y Publicaciones de Insula, Benito Gutiérrez 26, Madrid 8

SPAIN 377

Bibliographical review of sciences and letters

Litoral, Visor-Libros, Calle del Roble 22, Madrid 20
Monthly poetry review

Nuestro Tiempo (Our Time), EUNSA, Apdo 396, 31080 Pamplona

Quaderns Crema, Edicions dels Quaderns Crema, F Valls i Taberner 8, 08006 Barcelona

Razon y Fe, Pablo Aranda 3, Madrid 6
Spanish-American review

Revista de Literatura (Review of Literature), Libreria Cientifico Medinaceli del CSIC, Madrid

Revista de Occidente (Review of the West), Revista de Occidente SA, Milán 38, 28043 Madrid

Revista Literaria Azor, C Borell 128 - 1 2A, Barcelona 15

Serra d'Or, Publicacions de l'Abadia de Montserrat, Abadia de Montserrat, Barcelona

El Urogallo, Matias Montero 24, Madrid 6

Literary Prizes

Ateneo de Sevilla Prize
Established 1969. 3,000,000 pesetas awarded annually for a literary work. The most recent winner was Emilio Romero for *Tres Chicas y un Forastero*. Enquiries to Editorial Planeta SA, Córcega 273-277, 08008 Barcelona

Ateneo de Valladolid Prize*
Since 1950 500,000 pesetas and publication awarded annually for a short novel. Sponsored by the municipal government of Valladolid in collaboration with Ateneo de Valladolid. Enquiries to Ateneo de Valladolid, General Ruiz 1, 47004 Valladolid

Miguel de **Cervantes** Prize
For the work of a writer who has made an outstanding contribution to Spanish culture. 10,000,000 pesetas. Awarded annually. Enquiries to Dirección General del Libro y Bibliotecas, Ministerio de Cultura, Plaza del Rey 1, 28004 Madrid

Duke of Alba Prize*
Established 1905 for original, unpublished works in Spanish. 48,000 pesetas. Awarded once every nine years. Enquiries to Real Academia Española, Felipe IV 4, 28014 Madrid

Espejo de España Prize
Established 1975. 2,000,000 pesetas awarded annually for an essay. The most recent winner was Xavier Rubert de Ventós for *El Laberinto de la Hispanidad*. Enquiries to Editorial Planeta SA, Córcega 273-277, 08008 Barcelona

Manuel **Espinosa** y Cortina Prize*
Established 1891 for the best dramatic work performed for the first time. 4,000 pesetas. Awarded once every five years. Enquiries to Real Academia Española, Felipe IV 4, 28014 Madrid

Fastenrath Prize*
Established 1909 for works of excellence written in the Spanish language. 6,000 pesetas. Awarded annually in rotation for the following categories of writing: poetry; essays, criticism; novel or story; history, biography; drama. Enquiries to Real Academia Española, Felipe IV 4, Madrid 14

SPAIN — SRI LANKA

Hucha de Oro Prize*
For an unpublished short story in Castilian. Annual awards are made in which the three main prizewinners are selected from the previously-chosen 20 winners of the Hucha de Plata prizes (25,000 pesetas and a chest of silver each). The winner of the Hucha de Oro first prize receives 500,000 pesetas and a chest of gold (hucha de oro); the winner of the second prize receives 200,000 pesetas and a miniature chest of gold; the winner of the third prize receives 50,000 pesetas and a miniature chest of gold. Enquiries to Confederacion Española de Cajas de Ahorros (CECA), Calle de Alcala 27, 28014 Madrid

Hucha de Plata Prizes, see Hucha de Oro Prize

Concurso Nacional **'Leer y Escribir'**, see 'Reading and Writing' National Competition

Ramon **Llull** Prize
Established 1981. 2,500,000 pesetas awarded annually to the winner and 500,000 pesetas to the runner-up for a literary work in Catalan. The most recent winner was Valenti Puig for *Somni Delta* and the runner-up was Antonia Vicens for *Terra Seca*. Enquiries to Editorial Planeta SA, Córcega 273-277, 08008 Barcelona

Marques of Cerralbo XVII Prize*
Established 1922 for the best original, unpublished work related to Spanish language and literature. 40,000 pesetas. Awarded once every four years. Enquiries to Real Academia Española, Felipe IV 4, 28014 Madrid

Eugenio **Nadal** Prize
For the best novel. 3,000,000 pesetas. Awarded annually. Enquiries to Ediciones Destino SA, Consell de Cent 425 – 5° planta, 08009 Barcelona

National Prize for Children's Literature
Founded 1978. An annual award of 1,000,000 pesetas is made for the best literary work intended for children or young people, written in any of the official languages of Spain. Awarded in alternate years in each category. Enquiries to Dirección General del Libro y Bibliotecas, Ministerio de Cultura, Plaza del Rey 1, 28004 Madrid

National Prize for Illustration of Children's Literature
An annual award of 1,000,000 pesetas for the best illustrations in a book for children or young people. Awarded in alternate years in each category. Enquiries to Dirección General del Libro y Bibliotecas, Ministerio de Cultura, Plaza del Rey 1, 28004 Madrid

National Prize for Literature
Founded 1984. An annual award of 2,500,000 pesetas for the best book of poetry, fiction or essays published in the previous year in one of the official languages of Spain. Enquiries to Dirección General del Libro y Bibliotecas, Ministerio de Cultura, Plaza del Rey 1, 28004 Madrid

National Prize of Spanish Letters
Founded 1986. An award of 5,000,000 pesetas in recognition of an author, writing in one of the official Spanish languages, for the whole of his work. Enquiries to Dirección General del Libro y Bibliotecas, Ministerio de Cultura, Plaza del Rey 1, 28004 Madrid

Premio Nacional de Ilustracion de Libros Infantiles y Juveniles, see National Prize for Illustration of Children's Literature

Premio Nacional de las Letras Españoles, see National Prize of Spanish Letters

Premio Nacional de Literatura, see National Prize for Literature

Premio Nacional de Literatura Infantil y Juvenil, see National Prize for Children's Literature

Alvarez **Quintero** Prize*
Established 1949 for the best work in two categories alternately: novel or story collection and theatrical works. 5,000 pesetas. Awarded biennially. Enquiries to Real Academia Española, Felipe IV 4, 28014 Madrid

'Reading and Writing' National Competition
Founded 1978. An annual competition for students at COU, BUP or equivalent levels of 'Formacion Profesional'. Prizes are given for literary works, in any of the official languages of Spain, related to an important figure in Spanish literature. Prizewinners are selected from 150 qualifying works. First, second and third prizes are of 55,000, 50,000 and 45,000 pesetas respectively, and further prizes of 25,000 pesetas each may be awarded. A second group of awards is made for students at EGB level for illustrations related to an important figure in Spanish literature. Prizes are of 55,000 pesetas, 50,000 pesetas and 45,000 pesetas and further prizes of 25,000 pesetas each may be awarded. Winners must use the prize money exclusively for the purchase of books. Enquiries to Dirección General del Libro y Bibliotecas, Ministerio de Cultura, Plaza del Rey 1, 28004 Madrid

Rivadeneyra Prizes*
Established 1940 for the best work on Spanish literature and linguistics. Two prizes, of 30,000 pesetas and 20,000 pesetas. Awarded annually. Enquiries to Real Academia Española, Felipe IV 4, 28014 Madrid

Sri Lanka

General Information

Language: Sinhalese and Tamil (also English)
Religion: Buddhist
Population: 14.9 million
Bank Hours: 0900-1330 Monday-Friday
Shop Hours: 0800-1700 Monday-Friday
Currency: 100 cents = 1 Sri Lanka rupee
Export/Import Information: No tariff on books or advertising. Import licence required for most book importation. Exchange controls
Copyright: Berne, Florence, UCC (see International section)

Book Trade Organizations

Booksellers' Association of Sri Lanka, PO Box 244, Colombo 2 Tel: (01) 22675/7
Secretary: W L Mendis

Sri Lanka Book Publishers' Association, 112 S Mahinda Mavatha, Colombo 10
President: Dayawansa Jayakody; *Secretary:* Henry Samaranayake
Publication: Publishing Scene (newsletter)

Standard Book Numbering Agency*, Sri Lanka National Library Services Board, PO Box 1764, Colombo (Located at: Independence Ave, Colombo) Tel: (01) 95200
ISBN Administrator: N Amarasinghe

Book Trade Reference Journal

Sri Lanka National Bibliography, Sri Lanka National Library Services Board, PO Box 1764, Colombo
Text in English, Sinhalese and Tamil

Publishers

Ananda Books Ltd, an imprint of M D Gunasena & Co Ltd (qv)

Architecture & Arts Publications Co*, 75 Ward Pl, Colombo 7
Subjects: Art, Architecture

W E **Bastian** & Co (Private) Ltd, 23 Canal Row, Fort, Colombo 1 Tel: (01) 32752
Dirs: H A Munideva, Mrs K Hewage, N Munideva, Mrs G C Bastian
Subjects: General, Periodicals
Founded: 1904

Ceylon Printers Ltd, No 20 Sir Chittampalam Gardiner Mawatha, Colombo Tel: (01) 34161 Cable Add: Antopress Telex: 21542 Ceypee Ce
Subject: Belles Lettres

Colombo Catholic Press, 2 Gnanartha Pradipaya Mawatha, Colombo 8 Tel: (01) 595984
Dir, Manager: Rev Father Bertram Dabrera
Founded: 1865

M D **Gunasena** & Co Ltd, PO Box 246, Colombo (Located at: 217 Olcott Mawatha, Colombo 11) Tel: (04) 23981/4
Cable Add: Emdeegee Colombo
Telex: 21306 Imprint CE
Subjects: University & School Books on all subjects
Founded: 1913
Miscellaneous: Associated imprints include Ananda Books Ltd, Sirisara Vidyalaya

Lake House Investments Ltd, PO Box 1453, Colombo 2 (Located at: 41 WAD Ramanayake Mawatha, Colombo) Tel: (01) 33271/2/3 Telex: 21266 Lakexpo CE
Chairman: R S Wijewardene; *Dir:* G B S Gomes; *Editorial, Sales, Production, Publicity, Rights & Permissions:* Henry Samaranayake (Tel: 35175)
Subjects: Education, Law, General Fiction, Children's Books, Dictionaries, Medicine (in English and Sinhala)
Founded: 1965

Ministry of Cultural Affairs*, 212 Bauddhaloka Mawatha, Colombo 7 Tel: (01) 85888 Cable Add: Sunlay
Dir, Publications: R L Wimaladharma; *Deputy Dir, Publications:* K G Amaradasa; *Editorial:* Prof D E Hettiaratchi, Prof J D Dheerasekera, D P Ponnamperuma
Subjects: Literature, Religion, Art, Culture
Bookshop: Jayanti Bookshop, 135 Dharmapala Mawatha, Colombo 7
Book Club: Book Club of the Ministry of Cultural Affairs of Sri Lanka (qv)
Founded: 1971

Department of **National Museums**, PO Box 854, Colombo 7 (Located at: Sir Marcus Fernando Mawatha, Colombo) Tel: (01) 94767
Subjects: Sri Lanka's Antiquities, Anthropology, Natural History; Periodical
See also: National Museum Library (under Major Libraries)

Saman & Madara Publishers, 997/26 Sri Jayawardenapura Mawatha, Kotte Tel: 562055
Subjects: Children's, Novels, Literature, General

Sarexpo International Ltd, PO Box 25, Colombo 1 (Located at: 81 Sir Baron Jayatilaka Mawatha, Colombo) Tel: (01) 22675/6/7 Cable Add: Cave Telex: 1241
Man Dir: B J L Fernando; *Dirs:* B J L Fernando, C J S Fernando
Subjects: History, Archaeology, Juveniles, Literature, Law, Management, Medicine, Engineering, Economics, Education, Psychology, Environmental Studies
Bookshop: At above address
Founded: 1876

K V G De **Silva** & Sons (Kandy), 86 D S Senanayake Veediya, Kandy Tel: (08) 3254 Cable Add: Silco Telex: 22141 Minata CE
Man Dir & Permissions: K V N De Silva; *Sales Dir:* Mrs D Dias; *Publicity & Advertising Dir:* Mrs K V N De Silva
Branch Off: 44/9 YMBA Building, Fort Colombo
Subjects: History, Religion, Local Interest
Bookshops: 86 D S Senanayake Veediya, Kandy; 44/9 YMBA Bldg, Fort, Colombo
Founded: 1898

Sirisara Vidyalaya, an imprint of M D Gunasena & Co Ltd (qv)

Sri Lanka National Library Services Board*, PO Box 1764, Colombo (Located at: Independence Ave, Colombo) Tel: (01) 95200
Dir, Secretary: N Amarasinghe
Branch Off: 23 1/5 Dalada Vidiya, Kandy
Subjects: Librarianship, Folk Culture, Literature and Culture
Founded: 1970
ISBN Publisher's Prefix: 955-9011

The **Union** Press*, PO Box 362, Colombo 2 (Located at: 169 Union Pl, Colombo) Tel: (01) 20485/35912 Cable Add: Unionpress
Managing Proprietor: A H Dhas
Founded: 1942

Book Club

Book Club of the **Ministry** of Cultural Affairs of Sri Lanka*, 135 Dharmabala Mawatha, Colombo 7
Owned by: Ministry of Cultural Affairs (qv)

Major Libraries

British Council Libraries*, 47 Alfred House Gardens, Colombo 3 Tel: (01) 81171/587078 Telex: 21766 Bricon Ce
Branch Library: 170 D S Senanayake Veediya, Kandy Tel: (08) 23140

Ceylon Institute of Scientific and Industrial Research Library*, 363 Bauddhaloka Mawatha, Colombo 7
Head of Information Services: Clodagh Nethsingha
Publications: Current Technical Literature (quarterly); *Bibliographical Series* (irregular)

Colombo Public Library System, Sir Marcus Fernando Mawatha, Colombo 7 Tel: (01) 595156/596530/91968
Chief Librarian: M D H Jayawardhana
Publications include: Libraries and People; A Manual for Public Libraries in Sri Lanka; Road to Wisdom; Treasures of Knowledge

National Archives, PO Box 1414, Colombo 7 (Located at: 7 Reid Ave, Colombo) Tel: (01) 94523/596917 Cable Add: Archives

National Library of Sri Lanka*, PO Box 1764, Colombo (Located at: Independence Ave, Colombo) Tel: (01) 95200
Dir: N Amarasinghe

National Museum Library, Department of National Museums, PO Box 854, Colombo 7 (Located at: Sir Marcus Fernando Mawatha, Colombo) Tel: (01) 93314
Librarian: Miss K V S F de Soysa
Publications: Sri Lanka Periodicals Index; Ceylon Periodicals Directory (Annual Supplements); Spolia Zeylanica: Bulletin of the National Museums of Sri Lanka
See also Department of National Museums (Publisher)

University of Peradeniya Library*, PO Box 35, Peradeniya (Located at: University Park, Peradeniya) Tel: (08) 88301 ext 240/242
Librarian: N T S A Senadeera

Library Associations

Sri Lanka Library Association, OPA Center, 275/75 Bauddhaloka Mawatha, Colombo 7 Tel: (01) 589103
Secretary: Wilfred Ranasinghe; *Publications Officer and Editor:* Miss S N Nawana
Publications: Sri Lanka Library Review (biannual); *SLLA News Letter* (quarterly)

Sri Lanka National Library Services Board*, PO Box 1764, Colombo (Located at: Independence Ave, Colombo) Tel: (01) 95200
Dir, Secretary: N Amarasinghe
Publications: Annual Report; Folk Lore News; Library News (quarterly); *Sri Lanka National Bibliography*

Library Reference Journals

Ceylon Periodicals Directory, National Museum Library, Department of National Museums, PO Box 854, Sir Marcus Fernando Mawatha, Colombo 7
Annual supplements

Library News, Sri Lanka National Library Services Board, PO Box 1764, Colombo

Sri Lanka Library Review, Sri Lanka Library Association, OPA Center, 275/75 Bauddhaloka Mawatha, Colombo 7

Sri Lanka Periodicals Index, National Museum Library, Department of National Museums, PO Box 854, Sir Marcus Fernando Mawatha, Colombo 7

Literary Associations and Societies

Afro-Asian Writers' Bureau*, 73 Castle St, Colombo 8
Publication: Call

The **Dickens** Fellowship*, University of Ceylon, Thurston Rd, Colombo
Honorary Secretary: M M Aryrtane

Literary Periodicals

Call, Afro-Asian Writers' Bureau, 73 Castle St, Colombo 8
Editions in English and French

New Ceylon Writing, Macquarie University, School of English and Linguistics, North Ryde, NSW 2113, Australia
Creative and critical writing

Vidyodaya, University of Sri Lanka, Vidyodaya Campus Library, Nugegoda
Journal of the arts, sciences and letters; text in English, Sinhalese and Tamil

Literary Prizes

Literary Prizes for Sinhala Literature*
For the best books published in the previous year in the Sinhala language in the following categories: novels, short stories, poetry, translations, children's literature, scientific literature, drama; also three awards in miscellaneous literary areas and awards for original works in Pali, Sanskrit and Arabic. 5,000 Sri Lanka rupees each, excepting children's literature for which the prize is 2,000 rupees. Awarded annually. Enquiries to Ministry of Cultural Affairs, 212 Bauddhaloka Mawatha, Colombo 7

Don **Pedrick** Memorial Literary Award*
For the best original literary work in Sinhala. 1,000 Sri Lanka rupees. Awarded annually. Enquiries to Don Pedrick Memorial Literary Award Committee, 79 Dharmapala Mawata, Colombo 7

D R **Wijewardene** Memorial Award
An annual award of 20,000 Sri Lanka rupees established in 1984 by the Lake House Bookshop, Colombo, for the best unpublished manuscript of a novel or short story collection in Sinhala. The most recent winner was Swarnalatha Kiriwaththuduwa for *Isuru Soysa*.
Enquiries to Lake House Bookshop, PO Box 244, Colombo 2

Sudan

General Information

Language: Arabic (English also used)
Religion: Islamic (Sunni sect) in north, traditional in south
Population: 18.7 million
Bank Hours: 0830-1200 Saturday-Thursday
Shop Hours: 0800-1300, 1700-2000 Saturday-Thursday
Currency: 100 piastres (1,000 milliemes) = 1 Sudanese pound
Export/Import Information: No tariff on books; some advertising matter may be dutied. Import licences required. Exchange controls; annual foreign exchange budget

Publishers

Al-**Ayam** Press Co Ltd*, PO Box 363, Khartoum (Located at: Aboul Ela Bldgs, United Nations Sq, Khartoum)
Man Dir: Beshir Muhammad Said
Subjects: General Fiction & Non-fiction, Belles Lettres, Poetry, Reference, Magazines, Books in Arabic, Paperbacks
Founded: 1953

Khartoum University Press*, PO Box 321, Khartoum Tel: 80558/81806/81869
Man Dir, General Editor: Ali El-Mak; *Sales Manager:* Abdel Raham Ibrahim; *Editorial, Rights & Permissions:* Jamal

380 SUDAN — SWAZILAND

Abdel Malik, Judy El-Nagar
Subjects: General Fiction and Non-fiction, Belles Lettres, Poetry, Biography, History, Africana, Philosophy, Reference, Religion, Books in Arabic, Paperbacks, Science & Technology, General & Social Science, University & Secondary Textbooks
Bookshop: University of Khartoum Bookshop (qv under Major Booksellers)
Founded: 1968

Major Booksellers

Apaya Bookshop*, PO Box 110, Juba Tel: 2595 Cable Add: Sudchurch
Manager: Lole Kwaje Lole
The Bookshop of the Episcopal Church of Sudan (formerly The Church Bookshop)

Al **Bashir** Bookshop*, PO Box 1118, Khartoum

The **Church** Bookshop, now Apaya Bookshop (qv)

The **Khartoum** Bookshop, PO Box 968, Khartoum Tel: 77594/74425 Cable Add: Newstand Khartoum Telex: 22159 SD
Manager: P N Flanginis
See also The New Bookshop

The **New Bookshop**, PO Box 968, Khartoum Tel: 77594/74425 Cable Add: Newstand Khartoum Telex: 22159 SD
Manager: P N Flanginis
See also The Khartoum Bookshop

The **Sudan** Bookshop Ltd*, PO Box 1610, Khartoum Tel: 74123/76781 Cable Add: Bookshop Khartoum Telex: 22480 sisco km
Man Dir: Joseph A Tadros

University of Khartoum Bookshop*, PO Box 321, Khartoum Tel: 72271
Manager: Dr Khalid El-Mubarak
Owned by: Khartoum University Press (qv)

Major Libraries

Atbara Public Library*, Atbara

British Council Library*, PO Box 1253, Khartoum (Located at: 31 Zubeir Pasha St, Khartoum) Tel: 70159/76683/80269 Telex: 22790 Bckht Sd
Librarian: Ali Hassan Salih

College for Arab and Islamic Studies Library*, PO Box 328, Omdurman

Khartoum Polytechnic Library*, PO Box 407, Khartoum Tel: 78922
Librarian: Mohammad Bakheit

National Records Office Library*, PO Box 1914, Khartoum Tel: 76082
Librarian: Abdel Aziz Gabir Mohamed

University of Cairo*, Khartoum Branch Library, PO Box 1055, Khartoum

University of Khartoum Library*, PO Box 321, Khartoum Tel: 72271

Library Association

Sudan Library Association*, PO Box 1361, Khartoum Tel: 75100 ext 235
Secretary: Mohd Omer Ahmed
Publication: Libraries Journal

Library Reference Journal

Libraries Journal, Sudan Library Association, PO Box 1361, Khartoum
Text in Arabic and English

Suriname

General Information

Language: Dutch. English is widely spoken
Religion: Hindu, Roman Catholic, Islamic, Protestant
Population: 352,000
Bank Hours: 0800-1230 Monday-Friday; 0800-1100 or 1200 Saturday
Shop Hours: Generally 0700-1300, 1600-1800 Monday-Friday; 0700-1300, 1600-1900 Saturday
Currency: 100 cents = 1 Suriname gulden
Export/Import Information: No tariff on books except children's picture books; none on small quantities of advertising matter. Added taxes charged. Import licences liberally granted. Exchange controls
Copyright: Berne

Book Trade Organizations

Standard Book Numbering Agency, Publishers' Association Suriname, PO Box 1841, Paramaribo (Located at: Domineestr 26, Paramaribo) Tel: 72545 Telex: 123 inco sn Fax: 10563
ISBN Administrator: E Hogenboom

Publishers' Association **Suriname**, PO Box 1841, Paramaribo (Located at: Domineestr 26, Paramaribo) Tel: 72545 Telex: 123 inco sn Fax: 10563

Publishers

Apollo's Reklame en Uitgeversburo*, PO Box 574, Paramaribo (Located at: Torenlastr 3, Paramaribo)
ISBN Publisher's Prefix: 99914-908

NV Drukkerij **Eldorado**, PO Box 793, Paramaribo (Located at: Eldoradolaan 1, Paramaribo)
ISBN Publisher's Prefix: 99914-51

Ideoplastos*, PO Box 1474, Paramaribo (Located at: Keizerstr 83, Paramaribo)
ISBN Publisher's Prefix: 99914-902

C **Kersten & Co***, Steenbakkerijstr 27, Paramaribo Tel: 71133 Telex: 142
ISBN Publisher's Prefix: 99914-52

Ministerie van Cultuur Jeugd en Sport*, nk Dr S Redmondstr/Wanicastr, Paramaribo Tel: 79025
ISBN Publisher's Prefix: 99914-10

Mavis A **Noordwijk***, PO Box 2653, Paramaribo (Located at: Regentessestr 3, Paramaribo)
ISBN Publisher's Prefix: 99914-907

Drs F H R **Oedayrajsingh** Varma+, PO Box 9192, Paramaribo
Dir: Dr Ferdinand H R Oedayrajsingh Varma
Head Off: Postbus 70225, 1007 KE Amsterdam, The Netherlands Tel: (020) 628163
Subjects: Local Interest
ISBN Publisher's Prefix: 99914-903

C D **Ooft***, Dr H Benjaminstr 28, Paramaribo Tel: 99139
ISBN Publisher's Prefix: 99914-910

Orchid Press*, PO Box 28, Paramaribo
ISBN Publisher's Prefix: 99914-904

Sint Kinderkrant Suriname*, PO Box 3013, Paramaribo
ISBN Publisher's Prefix: 99914-53

Educatief Uitg **Sorava***, Vestastr 17, Ma Retraite
ISBN Publisher's Prefix: 99914-906

Stichting Wetenschappelijke Informatie+*, Cornelis Jongbauwstr 19, Paramaribo Tel: 75232
Man Dir, Editorial, Production, Publicity: J K Menke; *Sales:* W Boedhoe
Subjects: Development Problems (especially in the Caribbean and Suriname)
Bookshop: SWI Bookshop (at above address)
Founded: 1977

Vaco NV, PO Box 1841, Paramaribo (Located at: Domineestr 26-32, Paramaribo) Tel: 72545 Cable Add: Vaco Telex: 123 inco sn Fax: 10563
Man Dir: E Hogenboom; *Publicity:* F Terborg
Subjects: Local Interest, History, Low-priced Paperbacks, Primary and Secondary Textbooks, Maps
Bookshop: See under Major Booksellers
Founded: 1952

NV Drukkerij Leo **Victor**+*, PO Box 1820, Paramaribo (Located at: Verlengde Gemenelandsweg 18, Paramaribo) Tel: 10122/10186
General Manager: D S Lo-Fo-Sang

Stichting De **Volksboekwinkel***, PO Box 3040, Paramaribo (Located at: Keizerstr 197, Paramaribo)
ISBN Publisher's Prefix: 99914-901

M **Waagmeester-Verkuyl***, PO Box 9166, Paramaribo (Located at: Nickeriestr 22, Paramaribo)
ISBN Publisher's Prefix: 99914-905

Major Booksellers

Vaco NV, PO Box 1841, Paramaribo (Located at: Domineestr 26-32, Paramaribo) Tel: 72545 Telex: 123 inco sn Fax: 10563
Manager: E Hogenboom
Also Publisher (qv)

Major Libraries

Bibliotheek CCS, see Cultural Centre

Library of the **Cultural Centre** Surinam (Bibliotheek CCS), PO Box 1241, Paramaribo (Located at: Gravenstr 112-114, Paramaribo)
Librarian: Mrs C Carrilho-Fazal Alikhan

Swaziland

General Information

Language: siSwari. English used in business
Religion: Christianity
Population: 731,000
Banks close 1100 Saturday
Currency: 100 cents = 1 lilangeni (plural: emalangeni). 1 lilangeni = 1 rand. South African currency is also legal tender
Export/Import Information: Same as South Africa

Publishers

Boleswa, an imprint of Macmillan Boleswa Publishers (Pty) Ltd (qv)

Macmillan Boleswa Publishers (Pty) Ltd, PO Box 1235, Manzini Tel: 84533 Telex: 2221 WD
Man Dir: L A Balarin; *Editorial:* Richard Howat; *Marketing:* Terence Ball; *Production:* Philip Davis; *Publicity:* Charlotte Ewing
Parent Company: Macmillan Publishers Ltd, UK (qv for associate companies)
Subsidiary Companies: Macmillan Swaziland National Publishing Co (at above address); Macmillan Botswana Publishing Co, PO Box 1155, Gaborone, Botswana
Imprint: Boleswa
Branch Off: Matsapa
Subject: Educational
1985: 78 titles *Founded:* 1978
ISBN Publisher's Prefix: 0-333

Major Booksellers

Swaziland News Agency*, PO Box 157, Mbabane

Webster's (Pty) Ltd, PO Box 292, Mbabane Tel: 42560 Telex: 2174 Wd
Manager: Mrs M Armstrong

Major Libraries

Swaziland College of Technology Library, PO Box 69, Mbabane Tel: 42681
Librarian: Mrs N S Zwane

Swaziland National Library Service, PO Box 1461, Mbabane Tel: Swaziland 42633 Telex: 2270 Wd
Dir: B J K Kingsley
Publication: Annual Report of the Director

University of Swaziland Library*, PB, Kwaluseni Tel: 84011 Telex: 2087 WD
Librarian: D O Bampoe

Library Reference Book

Directory of Swaziland Libraries, PB, Kwaluseni
University of Botswana, Lesotho and Swaziland, 1975

Sweden

General Information

Language: Swedish. Danish and Norwegian are usually intelligible to speakers of Swedish. English is common second language
Religion: Lutheran State Church
Population: 8.4 million
Bank Hours: 0930-1500 Monday-Friday; 0930-1800 bank head offices
Shop Hours: 0900-1800 (later Friday) Monday-Friday; 0900-1400 or 1600 Saturday
Currency: 100 öre = 1 Swedish krona (plural: kronor)
Export/Import Information: Member of the European Free Trade Association. No tariff on books, Advertising Tax. VAT on most imported goods. No import licences.
No exchange controls
Copyright: UCC, Berne, Florence (see International section)

Book Trade Organizations

Bokbranschens Finansieringsinstitut AB, Sveavägen 52, S-111 34 Stockholm
Book Trade Finance Institute

Bokbranschens Marknadsinstitut AB, Sveavägen 52, S-111 34 Stockholm Tel: (08) 230225
Book Trade Marketing Institute
Man Dir: Ing-Britt Ekberg

Bokhandelsrådet, c/o Svenska Bokförläggareföreningen, Sveavägen 52, S-111 34, Stockholm
Book Trade Council

Föreningen Svenska Läromedelsproducenter, Holländargatan 27, S-113 59 Stockholm Tel: (08) 242280
The Swedish Association of Publishers and Manufacturers of Educational Material
Man Dir: Lena Westerberg; *Secretary:* Siv Klässon

Kristna Bokförläggareföreningen, Box 1213, S-701 12 Örebro (Located at: Nastagatan 13, Örebro) Tel: (019) 150050
Christian Publishers' Association
Secretariat: Björn-Ingvar Olsson

Nordiska Musikförläggareföreningen*, Box 27327, S-102 54 Stockholm
Music Publishers Association

Standard Book Numbering Agency, see Swedish National ISBN Centre

Svenska Antikvariatföreningen, Box 22549, S-104 22 Stockholm
Swedish Antiquarian Booksellers' Association

Svenska Bokförläggareföreningen, Sveavägen 52, S-111 34 Stockholm Tel: (08) 231800
Swedish Publishers' Association
Secretary: Urban Skeppstedt
Publication: Svensk Bokhandel (jointly with the Swedish Booksellers' Association)

Svenska Bokhandels-Medhjälpare-Föreningen*, Nya Akademibokhandeln, Box 7634, S-103 94 Stockholm Tel: (08) 219740
Swedish Booksellers' Assistants' Association
Contact: Ann Björnander

Svenska Bokhandlareföreningen, Skeppargatan 27, S-114 52 Stockholm Tel: (08) 6630205
Swedish Booksellers' Association
Secretary: Per Nordenson
Publication: Svensk Bokhandel (jointly with the Swedish Publishers' Association)

Svenska Musikförläggareföreningen UPA*, Box 27327, S-102 54 Stockholm Tel: (08) 7838800 Telex: 15591 Stims
Swedish Music Publishers' Association
General Manager: Christian Sylvan

Sveriges B-Bokhandlareförbund*, S-280 10 Sösdala Tel: (0451) 60096
Swedish Association of Smaller Booksellers

Sveriges Författarförbund, Box 5087, S-102 42 Stockholm (Located at: Grev Turegatan 29, Stockholm)
Swedish Writers' Union
Publication: Författaren

Swedish National ISBN Centre, Bibliographical Department, Royal Library, Box 5039, S-102 41 Stockholm Tel: (08) 241040 Telex: 19640 Kbs S
ISBN Administrator: Folke Sandgren

Book Trade Reference Books and Journals

Books

Boksverige, Författare, Förlag, Bokhandel, Bibliotek (The Book in Sweden: Author, Publisher, Bookshop, Library), Albert Bonniers Förlag AB, Box 3159, S-103 63 Stockholm

Svenska Bokförläggareföreningens. Matrikel över dess Medlemmar och Kommissionärer samt Bokhandelns Föreningar och Organisationer (Swedish Publishers' Association. List of Members and Agents, together with Book Trade Associates and Organizations), Swedish Publishers' Association, Sveavägen 52, S-111 34 Stockholm

Journals

Bokrevy (Book Review), Bibliotekstjänst AB, Box 200, S-221 00 Lund

Bokvännen (The Bibliophile), Sällskapet Bokvännera, Ulvsatervagen 18, S-191 43 Sollentuna 3

Svensk Bokförteckning (Swedish National Bibliography), Kungliga Biblioteket (Royal Library, Bibliographical Institute), Box 5039, S-102 41 Stockholm 5
Cumulates into the *Svensk Bokkatalog*

Svensk Bokhandel (Swedish Book Trade), Svenska Bokförläggareföreningen, Sveavägen 52, S-111 34 Stockholm
Jointly with Swedish Booksellers' Association

Svensk Bokkatalog, see Svensk Bokförteckning

Text, Centre for Bibliographical Studies, Uppsala
Bibliographical journal, in English and Swedish

Publishers

A W E/Gebers, an imprint of Norstedts Förlag AB (qv)

Acta Universitatis Gothoburgensis, Box 5096, S-402 22 Gothenburg Tel: (031) 631733 Telex: 20896 Ubgbg S
Man Dir: Paul Hallberg
Parent Company: Göteborgs Universitetsbibliotek (qv under Major Libraries)
Subjects: Scholarly works in the humanities and the social sciences (monograph series)
1985: 16 titles
ISBN Publisher's Prefix: 91-7346

Akademiförlaget, Box 3075, S-400 10 Gothenburg 3 Tel: (031) 179600
Manager: Håkan Berling
Orders to: Esselte Studium AB, S-171 76 Solna Tel: (08) 7343000
Parent Company: Esselte Studium AB (qv)
Subjects: Languages, Medicine, Technical, Economics, Textbooks
Founded: 1835

Akademilitteratur Förlaget AB+*, Box 50050, S-104 05 Stockholm Tel: (08) 155108 Cable Add: stockacademic Telex: 13115 Akademi S
Man Dir: Gunilla Widengren
Orders to: Akademi distribution (at above address)
Parent Company: Academus AB, Box 50016, S-104 05 Stockholm (a student-owned, non-profit-making chain of bookshops)
Subjects: Economics, Aesthetics, Philosophy, Law, Cultural History, Social

Sciences, Linguistics, General
Founded: 1976
ISBN Publisher's Prefix: 91-7410

Alba, Box 10041, S-100 55 Stockholm (Located at: Karlavägen 86, Stockholm) Tel: (08) 600050 Telex: 11620 Bonbook
Man Dir, Editorial: Dr Daniel Hjorth; *Rights & Permissions:* Ann-Mari Torstensson
Parent Company: Albert Bonniers Förlag AB (qv)
Subjects: General Fiction and Non-fiction
Founded: 1977
ISBN Publisher's Prefix: 91-7458

Alfabeta Bokförlag AB+, Bjurholmsplan 22, S-116 63 Stockholm Tel: (08) 7149353/ 7149336 Cable Add: Alfabeta Stockholm Telex: 12442 Fotex S attn Alfabeta
Man Dir, Rights & Permissions: Dag Hernried; *Editorial, Publicity:* Barbro Lagergren; *Sales, Production:* Anna Bengtsson
Subsidiary Company: Förlaget Barrikaden (at above address)
Subjects: Fiction, Non-fiction, Psychology, Travel, Music, Film, Children's, Art
1985: 25 titles *1986:* 30 titles *Founded:* 1976
ISBN Publisher's Prefixes: 91-85328, 91-7712

Allhems Förlag AB, now part of Bokförlaget Atlantis AB (qv)

Allmänna Förlaget*, Box 5227, S-102 45 Stockholm (Located at: Birger Jarlsgatan 18, Stockholm) Tel: (08) 7399500 Cable Add: Libergraph Telex: 12801 S
Man Dir: Hans Janlinder; *Editorial, Sales:* Christer Bunge-Meyer
Orders to: Liber Kundtjänst, S-162 89 Stockholm
Parent Company: Liber AB (qv)
Associate Company: Utbildningsförlaget (qv)
Subjects: Publications for public authorities, including Swedish Government
1985: 800 titles
ISBN Publisher's Prefix: 91-38

Allt om Hobby AB*, Box 42006, S-126 12 Stockholm Tel: (08) 194040
Publisher: Jan Jangö; *Managing Editor:* Freddy Stenbom
Subjects: Model & Prototype Construction
Book Club: Allt om Hobbys Bokklubb
Bookshop: Hobbybokhandeln, Pipersgatan 25, Box 42006, S-126 12 Stockholm
Founded: 1966
ISBN Publisher's Prefix: 91-85496

Almqvist och Wiksell Förlag AB, an imprint of Norstedts Förlag AB (qv)

Almqvist och Wiksell International, Box 638, S-101 28 Stockholm (Located at: Gamla Brogatan 26, Stockholm) Tel: (08) 237990 Cable Add: Almqvistbook Telex: 12430 Almqwik S
Dirs: Hans Molander, Lars-Erik Linder; *Sales Manager:* Bengt Sjöström
Subjects: Scientific & Technical books and periodicals
Miscellaneous: Affiliated to the Esselte Group and publishers to the universities of Stockholm, Uppsala and Lund
ISBN Publisher's Prefix: 91-22

Almqvist och Wiksell Läromedel AB, Box 1342, S-171 26 Solna (Located at: Sundybergsvägen 1, Solna) Tel: (08) 7343300 Cable Add: Aweduc
Man Dir: Maria Curman; *Marketing Dir:* S-E Westerlund; *International Sales:* Staffan Wahlgren
Subjects: Schoolbooks and Educational Aids (all levels), Foreign Languages, Music
Miscellaneous: Firm is one of the companies comprising Esselte Förlag AB (qv)

Apoteksbolaget AB*, Humlegårdsgatan 20, S-105 14 Stockholm Tel: (08) 7839500
Telex: 11553 apobol s
Man Dir: Åke Hallman
Subject: Special Pharmaceutical Textbooks

Förlagsaktiebolaget **Arbetarkultur**, Kungsgatan 84, S-112 27 Stockholm
Tel: (08) 543882
Man Dir: Jan-Erik Olson
Subjects: Fiction, Political Science, Social Sciences
ISBN Publisher's Prefix: 91-7014

AB **Arcanum**+, Box 14116, S-400 12 Gothenburg Tel: (031) 871516
Man Dir: Bo Ramme
Subjects: Homoeopathy, Natural Medicine, Osteopathy and other techniques (mainly as translations from other languages)

Askelin och Hägglund Förlag*, Box 2008, S-103 11 Stockholm (Located at: Köpmangatan 6, Old Town, Stockholm) Tel: (08) 202089 Cable Add: Askhagpublish Stockholm Telex: 12442/ 12443 Fotex S attn Askhagpublish
Chairman: Per A Sjögren; *Man Dirs:* Karl Hägglund, Christina Askelin
Subjects: General Fiction and Non-fiction, Journalism, Restaurant Guides
1985: 25 titles *Founded:* 1981
ISBN Publisher's Prefix: 91-7684

Askild och Kärnekull Förlag AB, now Bokförlaget Legenda AB (qv)

Asplund, an imprint of Bokförlaget Prisma AB (qv)

Bokförlaget **Atlantis** AB+, Sturegatan 24, S-114 36 Stockholm Tel: (08) 7830440
Cable Add: Atlantisbooks
Man Dir: Kjell Peterson; *Dirs:* Lars Falk, Ove Pihl; *Production:* Lennart Rolf; *Rights & Permissions:* Robert Malmkvist
Subjects: Quality Non-fiction, Illustrated Books, Swedish and Foreign Fiction, including Classics, Art Books
1985: 35 titles *Founded:* 1977
ISBN Publisher's Prefix: 91-7486

B B B, an imprint of Bokforlaget Bra Böcker AB (qv)

Förlaget **Barrikaden**, see Alfabeta

Berghs Förlag AB+, Box 45084, S-104 30 Stockholm Tel: (08) 316559 Fax: (08) 327745
Chairman: Anders Öhman; *Man Dir:* Carl Hafström; *Editorial Dir:* Marianne von Baumgarten-Lindberg; *Editor, Rights & Permissions:* Monica Norberg
Orders to: AB Seelig och Co, Box 1308, S-171 25 Solna Tel: (08) 850300
Subjects: Picture Books, Juveniles, Non-fiction, General fiction, Crime
Founded: 1954
ISBN Publisher's Prefix: 91-502

Bernces Förlag AB*, Södergatan 20, S-211 34 Malmö Tel: (040) 77265 Cable Add: Bebolag
Man Dir: Arvid Bernce; *Editorial:* Margaret Bernce
Subjects: General Fiction and Non-fiction, Biography, Cookery, History, Reference, Art, Large Illustrated Books
ISBN Publisher's Prefix: 91-500

Biblioteksförlaget AB, Box 14143, S-104 41 Stockholm (Located at: Storgatan 25, Stockholm) Tel: (08) 653100 Telex: 11785 Unpress S
Man Dir: Stefan Östergren
Parent Company: Bokförlaget Natur och Kultur (qv)
Subjects: Reference, University and Secondary and Primary Textbooks, Atlases, Physics, Mathematics, Children's Books
Founded: 1923
ISBN Publisher's Prefix: 91-542

Bibliotekstjänst AB*, Box 200, S-221 00 Lund (Located at: Tornavägen 9, Lund)
Tel: (046) 140480 Telex: 32200 btjlund s
Subjects: Library Science, Reference, Periodicals, Indexes
Founded: 1951
ISBN Publisher's Prefix: 91-7018

Bonnier Fakta Bokförlag AB*, Box 3159, S-103 63 Stockholm (Located at: Sveavägen 56, Stockholm) Tel: (08) 229120 Cable Add: Bonniers Telex: 14546 Bonbook S
Chief Executive: Ebbe Carlsson; *Editor-in-Chief:* Lennart Grenholm; *Production:* Arne Björkman, Arne Beime, Robert Hedberg; *Publicity:* Catharina Fjellström; *Rights & Permissions:* Arne Björkman
Parent Company: Albert Bonniers Förlag AB (qv)
Subjects: General Non-fiction, Field Guides, Art, Handbooks, Cookery, University Textbooks, Encyclopaedias, Dictionaries, Co-editions
1985: 62 titles *Founded:* 1981
ISBN Publisher's Prefix: 91-34

Albert **Bonniers Förlag** AB+, Box 3159, S-103 63 Stockholm (Located at: Sveavägen 56, Stockholm) Tel: (08) 229120 Cable Add: Bonniers Telex: 11620/ 14546 Bonbook S
Man Dir: Per-Olov Atle; *Editorial Dirs:* Karl O Bonnier, Åke Runnquist, Ebbe Carlsson; *Sales:* Lars Håkanson; *Rights & Permissions:* Charlotte Enderlein
Subsidiary Companies: Alba (qv); Bokförlaget Forum AB (qv); Bonnier Fakta Bokförlag AB (qv); Bonniers Juniorförlag AB (qv); AB Bokförlaget Viva (qv); AB Wahlström och Widstrand (qv) (all Sweden); J W Cappelens Forlag A/S, Norway (qv)
Associate Company: Bonniers Tidskriftsförlag, Torsgatan 21, S-105 44 Stockholm
Subjects: General Fiction and Non-fiction, Medical and Technical, Reference Works, Juvenile, Young Adult, Paperbacks, Periodicals
Book Clubs: Bokklubben Svalan, Bonniers Bokklubb, Underhållningsbokklubben, Stora Romanklubben, part-owner of Månadens Bok
1985: 700 titles *Founded:* 1837
Miscellaneous: Member of Bonnier Group
ISBN Publisher's Prefix: 91-0

Bonniers Juniorförlag AB+*, Box 3159, S-103 63 Stockholm (Located at: Kammakargatan 9A, Stockholm) Tel: (08) 229120 Telex: 11620 Bonbook S
Man Dir, Publisher: Karin Leijon; *Sales:* Bengt Nordin; *Co-Production:* Bonnier Juveniles International; *Production:* Ulla Persson; *Rights & Permissions:* Monica Norberg
Parent Company: Albert Bonniers Förlag AB (qv)
Subjects: Children's Books, Juveniles
Founded: 1979
ISBN Publisher's Prefix: 91-48

Bokförlaget **Bra Böcker** AB+, Södra Vägen, S-263 00 Höganäs Tel: (042) 39000 Cable Add: Bebebooks
Telex: 72643 Bbbooks S Fax: (042) 30504
President: Bengt Revin; *Editorial, Sales, Publicity:* Staffan Wennberg; *Production:* Lars Danielsson; *Rights & Permissions:* Madeleine Ström
Subsidiary Companies: Bokorama; Bra

Bok; Wiken Publishing House
Associate Company: Tre Böcker AB, PO Box 25, SF-02781 Esbo 78
Imprint: BBB
Subjects: General Fiction, History, Geography, Illustrated Books, Encyclopaedias
Book Clubs: Bokklubben Bra Böcker; Bokklubben Bra Lyrik (poetry); Bokklubben Bra Spänning (thrillers); Koko Kansan Kirjakerho Oy (KKK Book Clubs Ltd), Finland (qv) (jointly owned with Gummerus Publishers, Finland – qv)
1985: 96 titles *1986:* 104 titles *Founded:* 1965
ISBN Publisher's Prefixes: 91-7024 (Wiken), 91-7752 (Bra Bok)

Brombergs Bokförlag AB+, Box 45151, S-104 30 Stockholm (Located at: Rådmansgatan 72, Stockholm) Tel: (08) 329050 Telex: 12442 Fotex Bropublish S Fax: (08) 327745
Man Dir, Editorial, Sales, Publicity: Dorotea Bromberg; *Production, Rights & Permissions:* Dr Adam Bromberg, Lena Pallin
Subjects: General Fiction and Non-fiction, Political Science, Popular Science
1985: 36 titles *1986:* 35 titles *Founded:* 1973
ISBN Publisher's Prefix: 91-7608

Förlaget **By och Bygd**, Box 22087, S-104 22 Stockholm Tel: (08) 520955
Man Dir: Åsa-Britt Karlsson
Subjects: Politics, Social Questions

Byggförlaget+, Narvavägen 19, S-114 60 Stockholm Tel: (08) 635100 Telex: 14579 Byggf S
Man Dir: Karl-Erik Synnemar; *Editorial, Publicity, Sales, Rights & Permissions Manager:* Claes Dymling
Subjects: Building, Architecture
1985: 30 titles *1986:* 40 titles *Founded:* 1948
ISBN Publisher's Prefix: 91-85194

Carlsen if AB*, Bredgränd 2, S-111 30 Stockholm Tel: (08) 246880
Man Dir: Arne Mossberg; *Sales:* Bengt Stagman
Parent Company: Semic International AB (qv)
Associate Companies: Semic Forlagene A/S, Denmark (qv); Carlsen Verlag GmbH, Federal Republic of Germany (qv)
Subjects: Children's Picture-books
Founded: 1968
ISBN Publisher's Prefix: 91-510

Bokförlaget **Carmina**, Box 26032, S-750 26 Uppsala Tel: (018) 110805
Man Dir: Jörn Johanson
Subsidiary Companies: Carmina UK Ltd, 44-45 Chancery Lane, London WC2A 1JB, UK; Carmina International, 370 North St, White Plains, NY 10605, USA
Subjects: General Fiction, History, Art, Sciences, Classics, Textbooks
ISBN Publisher's Prefix: 91-7528

Citadell, an imprint of AB Rabén och Sjögren Bokförlag (qv)

René **Coeckelberghs** Bokförlag AB*, Box 45059, S-104 30 Stockholm (Located at: Saltmätargatan 3B, Stockholm) Tel: (08) 248245 Telex: 14277 reco S
Man Dir: René Coeckelberghs
Subjects: Fiction, Non-fiction, Poetry, Facsimile editions
ISBN Publisher's Prefix: 91-7250

Combi International AB, a subsidiary of Förlagshuset Norden AB (qv)

Consilium Publishers+, Sveavägen 61, S-113 59 Stockholm Tel: (08) 312900 Telex: 14800 Infbok S Fax: (08) 313903
Man Dir: Ulf Heimdahl; *Publisher:* Gunilla Lundborg; *Sales:* Lars-Olof Wiksten; *Production:* Ylva Aaberg
Parent Company: Consilium, Box 7587, S-103 93 Stockholm
Imprints: Idéförlaget; Informationsförlaget; Viking Förlag
Subjects: Reference, Encyclopaedias, Cookery, Wine and Beer, Handbooks, Language
Bookshop: At above address
1985: 35 titles *1986:* 30 titles *Founded:* 1979
ISBN Publisher's Prefixes: 91-7890 (Idéförlaget), 91-7736 (Informationsförlaget), 91-7792 (Viking Förlag)

Editions **Corniche**, a subsidiary of Bengt Forsbergs Förlag AB (qv)

Bokförlaget **Corona** AB+, Box 5, S-201 20 Malmo (Located at: Nobelvägen 135, Malmo) Tel: (040) 189480
Publisher: Nils-Åke Janséus; *Dir:* Lars Welinder
Subjects: Juveniles, Textbooks, Education, Fiction, Non-fiction

Tidnings AB **Dagen**, S-105 36 Stockholm (Located at: Gammelgårdsvägen 38, Stora Essingen) Tel: (08) 130340 Cable Add: Dagen Telex: 10888 dagen
Man Dir, Production, Rights & Permissions: Sverre Larsson; *Editorial:* Olof Djurfeldt; *Sales:* Roger Fahlberg; *Publicity Dir:* Rune Flygg; *Advertising Dir:* Gunnar Forsberg
Subsidiary Companies: Förlaget Filadelfia (qv); Normans Förlag AB (qv)
Subjects: Biography, History, Music, Art, Religion, Juveniles, Low-priced Paperbacks, Educational Materials
Bookshop: Gospel Center, Rörstrandsgatan 9, S-113 40 Stockholm
Book Club: Den Kristna Bokringen
Founded: 1945

Dahlia Books, International Publishers and Booksellers, Box 1025, S-751 40 Uppsala Tel: (018) 100525 Cable Add: Dahlia, Uppsala
Subjects: Bibliography, Australian and Pacific history
Founded: 1973
Miscellaneous: Major function of this company is bookselling (antiquarian and new) at above address

Delta Förlags AB*, Box 15123, S-161 15 Bromma Tel: (08) 254781
Man Dir: Sam J Lundwall
Subjects: General Fiction and Non-fiction, Science fiction, High-priced Paperbacks
Book Club: Delta Science Fiction Bok Klubb
Founded: 1973
ISBN Publisher's Prefix: 91-7228

Doxa Bokförlaget AB+, Bredgatan 24B, S-222 21 Lund Tel: (046) 127277 Cable Add: Doxabook Telex: 35546 Doxabok S
Man Dir: Bertil Belfrage; *Editorial:* Pavel Gabriel
Orders to: Box 17, S-570 20 Bodafors
Subjects: Scholarly, Scientific, Art, Textbooks, Paperbacks
Founded: 1974
ISBN Publisher's Prefix: 91-578

E C Print AB+, Gibraltargatan 48, S-412 58 Gothenburg Tel: (031) 31814661 Telex: 21992 Imce S Fax: (031) 814654
Man Dir: Dr Carlos Ezeyza-Alvear; *Production Manager:* Torbjörn Flinck
Subjects: Technical Manuals and Books, Dictionaries
Founded: 1978

Miscellaneous: Also Translation Agency (qv)
ISBN Publisher's Prefix: 91-86236

E F S-förlaget, see Evangeliska Fosterlands-Stiftelsens Förlag

Ehrlingförlagen AB, Box 21133, S-100 31 Stockholm (Located at: Gävlegatan 12A, Stockholm) Tel: (08) 305025 Cable Add: Ehrlingmusik
Man Dir: Staffan Ehrling
Associate Company: Belwin-Mills Nordiska AB
Subsidiary Companies: Thore Ehrling Musik AB, Nils-Georgs Musikförlags AB, Edition Sylvain AB (all at above address)
Subject: Music
Founded: 1952

Elanders Bokförlag AB*, Box 10184, S-434 01 Kungsbacka Tel: (0300) 50000 Cable Add: Printer Telex: 21234 eba s
Man Dir: Per Elander; *Sales Dir, Permissions:* Otto Elander; *Advertising Dir:* Lars Henriksson
Subsidiary Company: Elanders Kommunikation AB
Subjects: General Non-fiction, especially How-to, Hobbies, Hunting and Fishing, Paperbacks
Book Club: Jaktjournalens Bokklubb
Founded: 1912

Elkan och Schildknecht, Emil Carelius AB, Västmannagatan 95, S-113 43 Stockholm Tel: (08) 338463
Man Dir: Bengt Carelius
Subject: Music

Esselte Focus Uppslagsböcker AB+, Box 2120, S-103 13 Stockholm (Located at: Brunnsgränd 4, Stockholm) Tel: (08) 7893400 Telex: 17924 Esvideo S Fax: (08) 210985
Focus International Book Production AB
Man Dir: Kent Borén; *Publisher:* P Jonas Sjögren
Subject: Reference (Encyclopaedias), Yearbooks
Miscellaneous: Firm is one of the companies comprising Esselte Förlag AB (qv)

Esselte Förlag AB, Tryckerigatan 2, S-103 12 Stockholm 2 Tel: (08) 7893300 Telex: 16536 Espub S Fax: (08) 7964905
Man Dir: Göran Ahlberg
Book Club: Månadens Bok
Miscellaneous: Esselte Förlag is the name of the Publishing Division within the Esselte Group. It consists of six independent houses, namely Almqvist och Wiksell Läromedel AB (qv), Esselte Almanacksförlag AB, Esselte Focus Uppslagsböcker AB (qv), Esselte Kartor AB, Esselte Studium AB (qv), Norstedts Förlag AB (qv)

Esselte Herzogs AB*, Box 155, S-131 06 Nacka Tel: (08) 7162680 Cable Add: Herzogs Telex: 12297
Man Dir: Rune Sirvell
Parent Company: Esselte AB, Sturegatan 11, Stockholm
Subjects: Bibles, Hymnals, Religion
Founded: 1862

Esselte Map Service AB, Box 22069, S-104 22 Stockholm (Located at: Garvargatan 9, Stockholm) Tel: (08) 541920 Cable Add: Esseltemap Telex: 12084 Ems S
General Manager: Bo Gramfors; *Marketing Manager:* Annika Stiernstedt
Subsidiary Companies: Esselte Kartor AB; Generalstabens Litografiska Anstalt (both at above address)
Subjects: Atlases, Maps
Founded: 1833

SWEDEN

Esselte Studium AB*, Sundbybergsvägen 1, S-171 76 Solna Tel: (08) 7343000 Cable Add: Esseltestudium Stockholm Telex: 11681 Studium S
Man Dir: Jorma Nyblin
Subsidiary Company: Akademiförlaget (qv)
Subjects: Educational, Secondary Textbooks, Arts, Social Sciences, Natural Sciences, Mathematics, Technical and Scientific, Economics, Medical and Nursing, Dictionaries, Scandinavian University Books, Educational Aids
Miscellaneous: Firm is one of the companies comprising Esselte Förlag AB (qv)
ISBN Publisher's Prefix: 91-24

Evangeliska Fosterlands-Stiftelsens Förlag (EFS-förlaget), Box 110, S-751 03 Uppsala (Located at: Von Bahr Väg 3, Uppsala) Tel: (018) 169800 Cable Add: Stiftelsen Telex: 76265 Evan S
Man Dir: Per-Erik Ragnarsson
Subjects: Theology and Religion, General Fiction and Non-fiction, Poetry, Reference, Juveniles, Young Adult, High-priced Paperbacks
Founded: 1856
ISBN Publisher's Prefix: 91-7080

Fib's Lyrikklubb, an imprint of Bokförlags AB Tiden (qv)

Förlaget Filadelfia, Dagenhuset, S-105 36 Stockholm (Located at: Gammelgårdsvägen 38, Stora Essingen) Tel: (08) 130340 Cable Add: Dagen Telex: 10888 dagen
Man Dir, Editorial, Production, Rights & Permissions: Sverre Larsson; *Sales:* Per Ove Lannerö; *Publicity:* Rune Flygg
Parent Company: Tidnings AB Dagen (qv)
Associate Companies: Den Kristna Bokringen (Book Club); Normans Förlag AB (qv)
Subjects: Christian religious
Founded: 1915
ISBN Publisher's Prefix: 91-536

Bokförlaget **Fingraf** AB+, Box 2039, S-151 02 Södertalje Tel: (0755) 30023
Man Dir: Ossi Nikula; *Editorial:* Eivor Nikula
Associate Company: Fingraf Bookprinters AB (at above address)
Subjects: Humour, Fiction, Medical History
1985: 10 titles *1986:* 12 titles *Founded:* 1979
ISBN Publisher's Prefix: 91-85964

Focus International Book Production AB, see Esselte Focus Uppslagsböcker AB

Författares Bokmaskin*, Svarvargatan 14, S-112 49 Stockholm Tel: (08) 535880
Subjects: General Fiction and Non-fiction, Poetry, Juvenile, Current Controversies

Författarförlaget, Box 5290, S-102 46 Stockholm (Located at: Grev Turegatan 40, S-114 38 Stockholm) Tel: (08) 605352/605353 Telex: 12442 Fotex S attn Forfafor
Man Dir: Margareta Rye
Subjects: General Fiction and Non-fiction, Arts, Children's
1985: 32 titles *1986:* 10 titles *Founded:* 1969
ISBN Publisher's Prefix: 91-7054

Bengt **Forsbergs** Förlag AB, Södra Tullgatan 4, S-211 40 Malmo Tel: (040) 76320 Cable Add: Godbok
Man Dir: Bengt Forsberg; *Sales Dirs:* Jörgen Forsberg, Claës Forsberg, Matts Forsberg
Subsidiary Company: Editions Corniche
Subjects: History, Medicine, Photography, Yearbooks, Illustrated books
Founded: 1944
ISBN Publisher's Prefix: 91-7046

Bokförlaget **Forum** AB+*, Box 14115, S-104 41 Stockholm (Located at: Riddargatan 23A, Stockholm) Cable Add: Bokforum Telex: 16764 Forum S
Man Dir, Rights & Permissions: Bertil Käll; *Marketing:* Jan-Olof Westrell; *Production:* Majbritt Hagdahl
Shipping Address: Samdistribution, Box 449, Malmvägen 80-82, S-191 04 Sollentuna
Parent Company: Albert Bonniers Förlag AB (qv)
Subjects: General Fiction and Non-fiction, Popular History, How-to, Music, Art, High- & Low-priced Paperbacks
Book Club: Part-owner of Månadens Bok
1985: 90 titles *Founded:* 1944
ISBN Publisher's Prefix: 91-37

Bokförlaget **Fröja** AB, Hjärnegatan 10, S-112 29 Stockholm Tel: (08) 521455/118168 Cable Add: Universitypress Telex: 11061 Landlaw S
Man Dir: Eric Frieberg
Subjects: Atlases, Special Maps, Encyclopaedias, Reference Works, Textbooks, Transparencies
Founded: 1973

Gedins Förlag+, Sibyllegatan 43-45, S-114 42 Stockholm Tel: (08) 621551 Cable Add: Gedinbook Telex: 12442 Fotex S attn Gedinbook
Publisher: Per I Gedin; *Editorial, Production:* Eva Gedin; *Rights & Permissions:* Susanne Ulfsäter
Subjects: General Fiction and Non-fiction
Book Club: Part-owner of Månadens Bok
1987: 25 titles *Founded:* 1987
ISBN Publisher's Prefix: 91-7964

AB Carl **Gehrmans** Musikförlag*, Box 6005, S-102 31 Stockholm (Located at: Odengatan 84, Stockholm) Tel: (08) 165200 Cable Add: Musikgehrman
Man Dir: Kettil Skarby
Subject: Music
Founded: 1893
ISBN Publisher's Prefix: 91-7748

Generalstabens Litografiska Anstalt, a subsidiary of Esselte Map Service AB (qv)

Gidlunds Bokförlag, Box 49104, S-100 28 Stockholm (Located at: Sankt Eriksgatan 41, Stockholm) Tel: (08) 130820
Man Dir: Krister Gidlund; *Editorial:* Claes-Göran Jönsson
Subjects: General Fiction, Biography, History, Art, Philosophy, Juveniles, Social Science
Founded: 1984
ISBN Publisher's Prefix: 91-7844

Hagaberg AB+, Angarn, S-186 00 Vallentuna Tel: (0762) 25004 Fax: (0762) 25300
Man Dir: Ingrid Olausson; *Editorial:* Rune Olausson
Subjects: Philosophy, Gardening, Psychology, Theology, English Classics
1987: 11 titles *Founded:* 1983
ISBN Publisher's Prefix: 91-86584

Hallgren och Fallgren Studieförlag AB+, Box 209, S-751 04 Uppsala Tel: (018) 155390
Man Dir, Editorial, Sales, Publicity, Rights & Permissions: Ella Fallgren; *Production:* Karin Hallgren-Pettersson
Subjects: Educational, Languages (especially Swedish), Popular Science, Home Computers, Children's
Founded: 1973
ISBN Publisher's Prefix: 91-7382

Hälsaböcker/Allt om Hälsa AB, Box 1, Torsviksvängen 26, S-181 21 Lidingö Tel: (08) 7652760
Man Dir: Eskil Svensson
Subject: Health

Hammarström och Åberg Bokförlag, Föreningsvägen 33, S-121 63 Johanneshov Tel: (08) 916633/918894
Publishers: Stina Hammarström, Gösta Åberg
Orders to: AB Seelig och Co, Box 1308, S-171 25 Solna
Subjects: Fiction, Non-fiction, Humanities, Women's, Politics, Social & Natural Sciences, Music & Songbooks, Chess, Satirical Comics
1986: 10 titles *1987:* 15 titles *Founded:* 1979
ISBN Publisher's Prefix: 91-7638

Hamrelius och Stenvall Förlag AB, Föreningsgatan 67, S-211 52 Malmo Tel: (040) 127703 Telex: 8305050
Man Dir: Frank Stenvall
Associate Company: Frank Stenvalls Förlag (qv)
Subjects: Popular Management, Travel, Humour
Founded: 1980
ISBN Publisher's Prefix: 91-7658

Hanse Production AB, Tranhusgatan 29, S-621 55 Visby Tel: (0498) 49318
Chief Executive: Thorbjörn Ödin
Subjects: Art, Local history
Founded: 1978
ISBN Publisher's Prefix: 91-85716

Edition Wilhelm **Hansen** Stockholm, see under Nordiska Musikförlaget

Harriers Publishing House, now merged with InterSkrift (qv)

Hemmets Journal AB*, S-212 05 Malmo Telex: 32449 Hemmet S
Parent Company: Gutenberghus Group, Denmark
Associate Companies: Ehapa-Verlag GmbH, Federal Republic of Germany; Gutenberghus Publishing Service A/S, Denmark (qv); Hjemmets Bokforlag A/S, Norway (qv)
Subjects: Juveniles, Fiction, Human Interest
Founded: 1920

Hillelförlaget, Nybrogatan 19, S-114 39 Stockholm Tel: (08) 621078
Man Dir: Anna Rock
Subjects: Judaica, Jewish History, Hebrew Fiction

Lars **Hökerbergs** Bokförlag+, Box 8071, S-104 20 Stockholm (Located at: Fleminggatan 21) Tel: (08) 244360
Man Dir: Jan Hökerberg
Associate Company: ITK Läromedel (qv)
Subjects: General Fiction and Non-fiction, Technical, Textbooks, Educational Materials, Vocational Training by Correspondence
1987: 65 titles *Founded:* 1882
ISBN Publisher's Prefix: 91-7084

I C A-Förlaget AB, Stora Gatan 41, S-721 85 Västerås Tel: (021) 194000 Cable Add: Icaförlaget Telex: 40486 ica s Fax: (021) 194136
Man Dir: Kjell Gustafsson; *Publisher:* Göran Sunehag; *Production:* Stig Osterlund; *Foreign Rights:* Ulla Joneby
Subjects: Cookery, Handicrafts, Hobbies, Gardening, Health, Domestic Animals, Antiques, Periodicals
1986: 46 titles *Founded:* 1944
ISBN Publisher's Prefix: 91-534

I T K Läromedel+, Box 8071, S-104 20 Stockholm (Located at: Fleminggatan 21, Stockholm) Tel: (08) 244350
Man Dir: Jan Hökerberg
Associate Company: Lars Hökerbergs Bokförlag (qv)
Subjects: Science and Technology,

Textbooks
1985: 22 titles *Founded:* 1923
ISBN Publisher's Prefix: 91-7084

Idéförlaget, an imprint of Consilium Publishers (qv)

Informationsförlaget, an imprint of Consilium Publishers (qv)

Ingenjörsförlaget AB+*, Box 27315, S-102 54 Stockholm (Located at: Midskogsgränd 11, Stockholm) Tel: (08) 651700 Cable Add: Ingforlag Telex: 17191 Tecnews S
Man Dir: Håkan Ryden
Subjects: Technical, Natural Science
1985: 16 titles *Founded:* 1970
ISBN Publisher's Prefix: 91-7284

Ingenjörsvetenskapsakademien (I V A), Box 5073, S-102 42 Stockholm (Located at: Grev Turegatan 14, Stockholm) Tel: (08) 7912900 Cable Add: Ivacademi
Royal Swedish Academy of Engineering Sciences
Man Dir: Hans G Forsberg; *Editorial:* Erik Trillkott
Subjects: Science, Technology
ISBN Publisher's Prefix: 91-7082

Interpublishing AB Stenström+, Taptogatan 4, S-115 28 Stockholm
Tel: (08) 6637601/02 Cable Add: Interpublishing
Manager: Bengt Stenström
Subjects: Biography, History, Hobbies, General Science, Reference
Miscellaneous: Previously Interbook Publishing AB
ISBN Publisher's Prefix: 91-86448

InterSkrift/Harriers Publishing House*, Box 205, S-524 00 Herrljunga (Located at: Fabriksgatan 19, Herrljunga) Tel: (0513) 11930 Telex: Startex S 42109
Man Dir: Jörgen Edelgård; *Editorial, Production, Rights & Permissions:* Nils-Erik Karlsson; *Sales:* Lennart Åsberg
Parent Company: Tyndale House Publisher, 336 Gondersen Drive, Wheaton, Illinois 60187, USA
Associate Company: Living Bibles International (at above address)
Subjects: Bibles, Religion, Fiction, Non-fiction, Biography, Juvenile
Book Clubs: Bokmästar'n; Önskeboken
Founded: 1974 (InterSkrift), 1932 (Harriers)
ISBN Publisher's Prefixes: 91-7336 (InterSkrift), 91-7068 (Harriers)

Invandrarförlaget+, Kvarngatan 16, S-502 44 Borås Tel: (033) 136070
Man Dir: Miguel Benito
Parent Company: Immigrant-institutet (at above address)
Subjects: Immigration, Bibliographies, Children's, Immigrant Writers (in 12 languages)
1985: 8 titles *Founded:* 1973
ISBN Publisher's Prefix: 91-85242

Kursverksamhetens Förlag, Magle Lilla Kyrkogata 4, S-223 51 Lund Tel: (046) 148720/148710
Man Dir: Hjördis Lundgren; *Editorial, Production, Rights & Permissions:* Daqmar Hellstam; *Sales, Publicity, Assistant Editor:* Annalisa Mikaelsson
Subjects: Educational material for adults, especially Swedish as a foreign language
Founded: 1971
ISBN Publisher's Prefix: 91-7434

L I C—Förlag, S-171 83 Solna Tel: (08) 7576000 Cable Add: Licentral, Stockholm Telex: 10528 lic s
This is the Publishing Department of L I C, which deals with the supply of hospital and health care equipment
Chief Executive: Björn Bergman; *Editorial, Production:* Lise-Lotte Lundström; *Publishing Manager, Sales, Publicity, Rights & Permissions:* Olle Sundling
Parent Company: L I C (at above address)
Subjects: Educational books and pamphlets relating to health care
Founded: 1977
ISBN Publisher's Prefix: 91-7584

L Ts Förlag AB (Lantbrukarnas Riksförbund och Studieförbundet Vuxenskolan)+, Ynglingsgatan 2-4, S-105 33 Stockholm Tel: (08) 7875200 Cable Add: Lantförbundet Fax: (08) 322085
Man Dir, Editorial: Pär Frank; *Sales Dir:* Roland Börjesson; *Production Manager:* Harry Krieg; *Permissions:* Ewa Mattill
Subjects: Fiction and Illustrated Books on Popular Science, Farming, Gardening, Handicraft, Pattern Books on Embroidery, Weaving and Wood-work, Economics, Social and Cultural History, Politics, Housekeeping, Study Material for Adult Education
1986: 130 titles *Founded:* 1935
ISBN Publisher's Prefix: 96-36

Bokförlaget Robert **Larson** AB, Lotsvägen 6, Näsbypark, S-183 03 Täby Tel: (08) 7328460 Cable Add: Larsonbooks Fax: (08) 7327176
Dirs: Birgitta Larson, Robert Larson, Joakim Larson
Subjects: Non-fiction
Founded: 1971
ISBN Publisher's Prefix: 91-514

Bokförlaget **Legenda** AB, Box 14105, S-104 41 Stockholm (Located at: Riddargatan 23B, Stockholm) Tel: (08) 651905 Cable Add: Legenda Telex: 12475 Legend
Man Dir, Publisher: Lars Grahn; *Editor-in-Chief:* Erik Timen; *Sales:* Jerker Wennhag; *Production:* Stella Åkerstedt; *Rights & Permissions:* Gunilla Canvert
Parent Company: Bokförlaget Natur och Kultur (qv)
Subjects: Fiction & Non-fiction, Memoirs, Modern History, Popular Psychology and Science
Founded: 1969
Miscellaneous: Formerly Askild och Kärnekull Förlag AB
ISBN Publisher's Prefixes: 91-582, 91-7008

Liber AB, Box 3071, S-103 61 Stockholm (Located at: Luntmakargatan 22-24, Stockholm) Tel: (08) 7399000
Man Dir: Birgitta Johansson-Hedberg (Stockholm); *Editorial Managers:* Per Bergknut (Malmo), Kristina Eriksson (Malmo), Johnny Frid (Malmo), Birgitta Rosenberg (Malmo), Barbro Folke (Stockholm), Rolf Ögren (Stockholm), Viveca Serder (Hermods, Malmo)
Orders to: Liber Kundtjänst, S-162 89 Stockholm
Parent Company: Procordia, Box 2278, S-103 17 Stockholm
Subsidiary Companies: Allmänna Förlaget (qv); Liber Distribution; Skrivab; Utbildningsförlaget (qv)
Branch Off: Slottsgatan 24, S-205 10 Malmo Tel: (040) 70650 Cable Add: Libergraph Telex: 33758 Liberm S
Subjects: Educational Textbooks, all levels and subjects, including Vocational, Technology, Business, Management, Economics, Law, Nursing, Education, Psychology, Social Sciences, Correspondence Courses
Book Clubs: Bättre Data, Bättre Ledarskap, Bättre Marknadsföring, Bättre Samhälle, Bättre Skola, Mitt företag
1985: 427 titles *1986:* 355 titles
ISBN Publisher's Prefix: 91-23

Libris Media AB+*, Box 1213, S-701 12 Örebro (Located at: Nastagatan 13, Örebro) Tel: (019) 150050 Telex: 8275061 Libris
Man Dir: Björn-Ingvar Olsson; *Editorial, Production:* Ingegerd Eklof; *Sales, Publicity:* Kenneth Pettersson; *Rights & Permissions:* Helena Rosén
Subjects: General Interest, Theological, Juveniles, Fiction
Book Club: Libris Bookclub
Founded: 1916
ISBN Publisher's Prefix: 91-7194

Lidman Production AB+, Box 5098, S-102 42 Stockholm (Located at: Karlavägen 71, Stockholm) Tel: (08) 6633615
Publisher: Sven Lidman
Subjects: Educational, Encyclopaedias
Founded: 1973

J A **Lindblads** Bokförlag AB, Warfvinges väg 30, S-112 51 Stockholm Tel: (08) 534640 Cable Add: Bookjal
Telex: 8106110 (Wahlströms) Fax: (08) 509761
Man Dir: Johan Landberg; *Chief Executive:* Bertil Wahlström; *Production:* Gert Fransson; *Permissions:* Eva Melin
Shipping Add: c/o B Wahlströms Bokförlag AB, Lövåsvägen 24, S-791 00 Falun
Subsidiary Company: B Wahlströms Bokförlag AB (qv)
Subjects: General Fiction and Non-fiction, Juveniles
Founded: 1894
ISBN Publisher's Prefix: 91-32

Abr **Lundquist** Musikförlag AB*, Katarina Bangatan 17, S-116 25 Stockholm
Tel: (08) 436767
Editorial: Lars-Johan Rundquist, Anna Orvenius
Subject: Music
Founded: 1838

Bokförlaget **Medium** AB*, Box 511, S-162 15 Vällingby Tel: (08) 380340
Man Dir: Bo Pederby
Subject: School Textbooks
ISBN Publisher's Prefix: 91-512

Gustav **Melins** AB*, Box 1376, S-171 27 Solna Tel: (08) 7343400 Cable Add: Grakoswe Telex: 11978
Man Dir: Göran Brämming
Subjects: Bibles, Hymn Books
Founded: 1898

Metodistkyrkans Förlag, see Sanctus

Bokförlaget **Natur och Kultur**, Box 27323, S-102 54 Stockholm (Located at: Banérgatan 37, Stockholm) Tel: (08) 232480 Cable Add: Naturkultur
Man Dir: Lars Almgren; *Editorial Dirs:* Lars Källquist (Textbooks), Lennart Wolff (General Books); *Publicity, Sales:* Lennart Källum (Textbooks), Ini Ljung (General Books); *Rights & Permissions:* Britta Svensson
Subsidiary Companies: Biblioteksförlaget AB (qv); Bokförlaget Legenda AB (qv)
Subjects: General Non-fiction, Biography, History, Psychology, General Science, Secondary & Primary Textbooks, Audiovisual Materials, Children's
1986: 160 titles *Founded:* 1922
ISBN Publisher's Prefix: 91-27

AB **Nautic***, Skeppsbron 3, S-411 21 Gothenburg Tel: (031) 111200/111500 Cable Add: Nautic Telex: 21785 nautic s
Man Dir: Björn Traung
Subjects: Nautical Literature, Sea Charts
Miscellaneous: Agent for International Hydrographic publications
Founded: 1953

Nautiska Förlaget AB+*, Box 6108, S-102
32 Stockholm   Tel: (08) 345493/345682
Cable Add: Namco
The Nautical Publishing Co Ltd
Manager: H Hultkrantz
Subjects: Shipping Publications,
Navigational and Nautical Literature

Bokförlaget **Niloe** AB, Box 45, S-451 15
Uddevalla (Located at: N Drottninggatan
15-17)   Tel: (0522) 10708
Chairman: Olof Ericson
Subjects: Classical Literature, Reference
1987: 200 titles   *Founded:* 1953
ISBN Publisher's Prefix: 91-7102

AB **Nordbok**, Box 7095, S-402 32
Gothenburg (Located at:
Pusterviksgatan 13, Gothenburg)   Tel: (031)
171085   Cable Add: Nordbokab
Telex: 21782 Nordbok S   Fax: (031) 132842
Publisher: Gunnar Stenmar; *Editors:* Jon
van Leuven, Bengt Ason Holm
Subjects: Nature, Leisure Activities, Cars,
Cookery, Tourism, Outdoor Sports,
Hunting and Fishing, Do-it-yourself
1986: 26 titles   *Founded:* 1974

Förlagshuset **Norden** AB+, Box 305,
S-201 23 Malmo   Tel: (040) 934250
General Manager: Sven-Erik Gunnervall
Subsidiary Company: Combi International
AB
Subjects: Reference, Encyclopaedias,
Technical
Founded: 1931

AB **Nordiska Bokhandelns** Förlag, Box
1034, S-171 21 Solna   Tel: (08) 980234
Cable Add: Nordbok
Man Dir: Hans Molander
Parent Company: Esselte Bokhandel Group
(qv under Major Booksellers)
Subject: Medicine
Bookshop: AB Nordiska Bokhandeln (qv
under Major Booksellers)
Founded: 1851
ISBN Publisher's Prefix: 91-516

AB **Nordiska Musikförlaget**/Edition
Wilhelm Hansen Stockholm*, Box 745,
S-101 30 Stockholm (Located at:
Drottninggatan 37, Stockholm)   Tel: (08)
144240   Cable Add: Musicalia   Telex:
11859
Manager: Barbro Rydefalk
Parent Company: Edition Wilhelm Hansen
AS, Denmark (qv)
Associate Companies: Edition Wilhelm
Hansen, Postfach 2684, D-6000 Frankfurt
am Main, Federal Republic of Germany;
Norsk Musikforlag, Postboks 1499, Vika,
N-Oslo 1, Norway; J & W Chester/Edition
Wilhelm Hansen London Ltd, Eagle
Court, London EC1M 5QD, UK
Subject: Music
Bookshop: At above address

Normans Förlag AB*, Dagenhuset,
S-105 36 Stockholm   Tel: (08) 130340
Cable Add: Normanbok
Man Dir: Sverre Larsson
Parent Company: Tidnings AB Dagen (qv)
Associate Company: Förlaget Filadelfia
(qv)
Subject: Religion
ISBN Publisher's Prefix: 91-536

Norstedts Förlag AB, Box 2052, S-103 12
Stockholm 2 (Located at: Tryckerigatan 2,
Stockholm)   Tel: (08) 7893000   Cable Add:
Espub   Telex: 16536 Espub
Man Dir: Lasse Bergström; *Rights &
Permissions:* Agneta Markas
Imprints: AWE/Gebers; Almqvist och
Wiksell Förlag AB
Subjects: General Fiction, Children's, Non-
fiction, Medicine, Law

Book Clubs: Part-owner of Månadens Bok
and Vår Bok AB
Founded: 1823
Miscellaneous: Firm is one of the
companies comprising Esselte Förlag AB
(qv)
ISBN Publisher's Prefix: 91-1

Bokförlaget **Opal** AB, Box 20113, S-161
20 Bromma (Located at: Tegelbergsvägen
31, Bromma)   Tel: (08) 282179
Joint Publishers: Bengt Christell, Valborg
Segerhjelm
Subject: Juveniles
Book Club: Barnens Bokklub (jointly
owned)
Founded: 1973
ISBN Publisher's Prefix: 91-7270

Ordfront tryckeri & förlag AB+*, Box
20133, S-104 60 Stockholm (Located at:
Tjurbergsgatan 27, Stockholm)   Tel: (08)
449390   Cable Add: Ordfront Stockholm
Man Dir: Leif Ericsson; *Editorial, Rights
& Permissions:* Dan Israel
Subjects: Fiction, Home and International
Politics, Social Science, History, Juveniles
1985: 21 titles   *Founded:* 1969
ISBN Publisher's Prefix: 91-7324

Bokförlaget **Plus** AB*, Skt Eriksgatan 48,
S-112 34 Stockholm   Tel: (08) 547408
Man Dir: Bengt Svensson
Subjects: General Fiction and Non-fiction,
Juvenile
Founded: 1976

Bokförlaget **Prisma** AB, Box 7824, S-103
97 Stockholm (Located at: Brunnsgatan 6,
Stockholm)   Tel: (08) 237280   Cable Add:
Prismabok   Telex: 14500 Prisma S
Man Dir: Stig Edling
Parent Company: AB Rabén och Sjögren
Bokförlag (qv)
Imprint: Asplund
Subjects: General Fiction, Quality
Paperbacks, Humour, Politics, Social
Science, Dictionaries, Handbooks,
Reference, University Textbooks, General
Science
Founded: 1963
ISBN Publisher's Prefix: 91-518

Proklama+, Hagagatan 3, S-113 48
Stockholm   Tel: (08) 345760
Man Dir: Karin Holmström
Subject: Christian Books
Book Club: Proklama Pocketbokklubb
Bookshop: Proklama Bok-Café (at above
address)
Founded: 1966
ISBN Publisher's Prefix: 91-7288

Psykologiförlaget AB, Box 461, S-126 04
Hägersten (Located at: Störtloppsvägen
40, Hägersten)   Tel: (08) 970395
Man Dir: Lars Lindquist
Subjects: Psychology, Education
1985: 5 titles   *1986:* 7 titles   *Founded:* 1957
ISBN Publisher's Prefix: 91-7418

R & S Books, an imprint of AB Rabén
och Sjögren Bokförlag (qv)

AB **Rabén och Sjögren** Bokförlag+, Box
45022, S-104 30 Stockholm (Located at:
Tegnérgatan 28, Stockholm)   Tel: (08)
349960   Cable Add: Rosbook Stockholm
Telex: 14905 KF Data
Man Dir: Kjell Bohlund; *Editorial Dirs:*
Marianne Eriksson (Children's), Tommie
Andersson (General Fiction and Non-
fiction); *Foreign Rights:* Ulla Olsson,
Kerstin Öberg
Subsidiary Company: Bokförlaget Prisma
AB (qv)
Imprints: Citadell, R & S Books
Subjects: Children's, General Fiction &
Non-fiction, Practical Handbooks, Nature,
Outdoor Interests, History, Art, Music,

Psychology, Social Science, Economics
Book Club: Barnens Bokklubb (jointly
owned)
Founded: 1942
ISBN Publisher's Prefix: 91-29

Bokförlaget **Rediviva**, Facsimileförlaget*,
Box 15148, S-161 15 Bromma   Tel: (08)
257007
Man Dir: Michael Skrutkowski
Subjects: Reprints generally; also
Bibliography, Topography, Dictionary of
Anonymous and Pseudonymous Swedish
Literature
Founded: 1968
ISBN Publisher's Prefix: 91-7120

Richters Förlag AB+, Ö Förstadsgatan
46, S-205 75 Malmo   Tel: (040) 380600
Telex: 33180 richt S   Fax: (040) 930820
Man Dir, Rights & Permissions: Lars G
Gustafsson; *Editorial:* Gunilla Wall,
Annika Bladh, Sassa Fölsch, Louise
Moëll; *Sales:* Jörgen Hansen; *Production:*
Anders Enquist; *Publicity:* Charlotte
Wiström
Parent Company: Gutenberghus Group,
Denmark
Associate Companies: See Gutenberghus
Publishing Service A/S, Denmark
Subjects: Fiction, Children's and Juveniles,
Handbooks, International Co-productions
Book Clubs: Disney's Ungdomsbokklubb,
Kalle Ankas Bokklubb, Kalle Ankas
Pocket, Kokboksklubben God Mat,
Richters Bokklubb
1985: 30 titles   *1986:* 50 titles   *Founded:*
1942
ISBN Publisher's Prefix: 91-7706

S A M-förlaget*, Box 615, S-551 18
Jönköping   Tel: (036) 119130   Cable
Add: SAM
Man Dir and other offices: Torbjörn
Wetterö
Subjects: Religious
ISBN Publisher's Prefix: 91-7484

Förlaget **Sanctus** (Metodistkyrkans
Förlag), Box 5020, S-102
41 Stockholm (Located at: Sibyllegatan 18,
S-114 42 Stockholm)   Tel:
(08) 670155
The Publishing House of the United
Methodist Church in Sweden
Subjects: Theology and Christian
Devotional

Semic International AB*, Box 74, S-172 22
Sundbyberg (Located at: Landsvägen 57,
Sundbyberg)   Tel: (08) 981140   Cable Add:
semicpress, Stockholm   Telex: 17370
semic s
Man Dir: Carl-Johan Bonnier; *Editorial:*
Agneta Hyllén (books), Ebbe Zetterstad
(magazines); *Rights & Permissions:* Solveig
Asperen (books), Jan-Olof Sohlén
(magazines)
Parent Company: Bonniers
Tidskriftsförlag, Torsgatan 21, S-105 44
Stockholm (member of the Bonnier
Group)
Subsidiary Companies: Semic Forlagene
A/S (qv), A/S Interpresse (qv), Deres
Forlag ApS, A/S Stilmönster (all
Denmark); Kustannus Oy Semic (see
Semic-Book), Finland; Carlsen Verlag
GmbH (qv), Semic Verlag GmbH (both
Federal Republic of Germany); Semic
Juniorpress BV, Netherlands (qv); Semic
nordisk forlag A/S (qv), A/S Stilmönster
(both Norway); Carlsen if AB (qv),
Jultidningsförlaget AB, Nordisk
Bokdistribution KB, Bokförlaget Semic
AB, Semic Merchandising AB, Semic
Press AB, AB Stilmönster (all Sweden)
Subjects: Knitting, Crochet, Weaving,
Cooking, Sports, Comic Magazines, Comic

Albums, Comic Books, Children's Books, Christmas Publications
Book Club: Serie-pocket-klubben
Founded: 1950
ISBN Publisher's Prefix: 91-552

Bokförlaget **Settern** HB+, Drakabygget, S-286 00 Örkelljunga Tel: (0435) 80050/80070
Man Dir: Magdalena Rönneholm; *Sales, Publicity, Advertising Dir:* Jörgen Wahlén; *Rights & Permissions:* Monica Heyum Agency Tel: (08) 7451934
Subjects: General Fiction and Non-fiction, Paperbacks, Nature, Hunting & Fishing, Children's
1985: 28 titles *Founded:* 1974
ISBN Publisher's Prefix: 91-7586

Sjöstrands Förlag, Hässelby Strandväg 22, S-162 39 Vällingby Tel: (08) 383856
Man Dir: Ulla-Britt Sjöstrand
Subjects: General Fiction and Non-fiction, Juveniles, Handbooks, History

Skeab Förlag AB, now Verbum Gothia (qv)

Skolförlaget Gävle AB+, Box 646, S-801 27 Gävle (Located at: Rälsgatan 2, Gävle) Tel: (026) 115335 Cable Add: Skolförlaget Telex: 47152
Man Dir: Gunnar Helsing; *Deputy Man Dir:* Göran Berger; *Editorial:* Christina Söderberg
Subjects: School Textbooks, Swedish and other modern languages, Mathematics, Sex and Social Education
Founded: 1922
ISBN Publisher's Prefix: 91-42

Skriptor Forlag AB, Torstenssonsgatan 2, S-114 56 Stockholm Tel: (08) 6650745
Editors: Monika Holm, Ewa Lannebo
Subjects: Swedish (as a foreign and as a second language)
Founded: 1960
ISBN Publisher's Prefix: 91-7282

Sober Förlags AB, Birger Jarlsgatan 25, S-111 45 Stockholm Tel: (08) 223480
Man Dir: Kjell E Johanson; *Editorial:* Ann-Marie Tjärnkvist
Subjects: Alcohol, Narcotics and Tobacco addiction

Sparfrämjandet Förlagsaktiebolag, Box 16425, S-103 27 Stockholm (Located at: Drottninggatan 29, Stockholm) Tel: (08) 572000 Telex: 11834 saveorg s Fax: (08) 218437
Man Dir: Gunnar Helsing
Subjects: School Textbooks, Handbooks
Founded: 1925
ISBN Publisher's Prefix: 91-7208

Bokförlaget **Spektra** AB, Box 7024, S-300 07 Halmstad 7 Tel: (035) 36030 Cable Add: Comprint
Man Dirs: Åke Hallberg, Solveig Hallberg
Subjects: General Fiction, How-to, Music, Arts & Crafts, Graphic Design, Printing, Reference, General Science
ISBN Publisher's Prefix: 91-7136

Stenströms Bokförlag AB, Linnégatan 98, S-115 23 Stockholm Tel: (08) 627828
Manager: Barbro Stenström
Associate Company: Stenström Interpublishing AB
Subjects: Fiction, Practical Handbooks
Founded: 1982
ISBN Publisher's Prefix: 91-86600

Frank **Stenvalls** Förlag, Föreningsgatan 67, S-211 52 Malmo Tel: (040) 127703 Telex: 8305050
Man Dir: Frank Stenvall
Associate Company: Hamrelius och Stenvall Förlag AB (qv)
Subjects: Railway, Maritime, Aviation, Motoring
Bookshop: Stenvalls (at above address)
1985: 4 titles *1986:* 12 titles *Founded:* 1966
ISBN Publisher's Prefix: 91-7266

Stiftelsen Kursverksamhetens Förlag, see Kursverksamhetens

Studentlitteratur Utbildningshuset AB, Box 141, S-221 00 Lund 1 Tel: (046) 307070 Cable Add: Studlitt Telex: 33345 educate s
Man Dir: Bertil Bratt; *Publishing Dir:* Sven-Åke Lennung; *Rights & Permissions:* Inge Helander; *Production:* Johnny Månsson
Subsidiary Companies: Bratt Institut für Neues Lernen GmbH, Federal Republic of Germany; Chartwell-Bratt (Publishing & Training) Ltd, UK (qqv)
Subjects: School and University Textbooks, covering Data Processing, Technology, Medicine, Social Sciences, Economics, Humanities
Founded: 1963
ISBN Publisher's Prefix: 91-44

Sveriges Exportråd*, Box 5513, S-114 85 Stockholm (Located at: Storgatan 19, Stockholm) Tel: (08) 7838500 Cable Add: Export Stockholm Telex: 19620 export a
Publishing Department of the Swedish Trade Council
Subjects: International Marketing, Customs, Shipping & Export Regulations, Market Reports
Bookshop: At above address
Founded: 1887
ISBN Publisher's Prefix: 91-7548

Sveriges Radios Förlag, S-105 10 Stockholm Tel: (08) 7840000 Cable Add: Broadcast Telex: 10000 srcent s
Man Dir: Gunnar A Olin
Founded: 1934
Miscellaneous: Publishing branch of the Swedish Broadcasting Corporation
ISBN Publisher's Prefix: 91-522

Swedish Employers' Confederation, Publishing Section, S-103 30 Stockholm (Located at: S Blasieholmshamnen 4A, Stockholm) Tel: (08) 7626000 Cable Add: Employers Telex: 19923 Fax: (08) 7626290
Chief Executive: Karin Ohman
Orders to: NFD, Box 5157, S-102 44 Stockholm
Parent Company: Swedish Employers' Confederation (at above address)
Subjects: Labour law and relations, Economics, Work organization, Education
1985: approx 80 titles *Founded:* 1968
ISBN Publisher's Prefix: 91-7152

Teknografiska Institutet AB*, Box 1013, S-171 21 Solna (Located at: Industrivägen 5, Solna) Tel: (08) 834285
Man Dir: Jan Brodén; *Production:* Ingrid Karpebäck
Subject: Technical books
Founded: 1946
ISBN Publisher's Prefix: 91-7172

Bokförlags AB **Tiden**, Box 30184, S-104 25 Stockholm (Located at: Warfvinges Väg 16, Stockholm) Tel: (08) 130130 Telex: 11934 Tidbook S
Man Dir: Lars Hjalmarson; *Managing Editor:* Hans-Erik Arleskar; *Editorial:* Ulla Freidh, Eva-Maria Westberg; *Sales:* Carl Swartz
Imprint: Fib's Lyrikklubb
Subjects: General Fiction and Non-fiction, Juveniles, Politics, History, Social Science, Psychology, Memoirs, Poetry, Illustrated Books, High-priced Paperbacks
Founded: 1912
ISBN Publisher's Prefix: 91-550

Tidnings AB Dagen, see Dagen

AB **Timbro**+, Birger Jarlsgatan 6B, S-114 34 Stockholm Tel: (08) 243770 Fax: (08) 8106217
President: Kjell-Erik Sellin; *Production:* Ulla Reisberg; *Rights & Permissions:* Kristina von Unge
Orders to: Booksellers, Sveavägen 61, S-113 59 Stockholm
Associate Company: Bokförlaget Ratio
Subjects: Non-fiction, Politics, Economics, Social Science
1986: 20 titles *1987:* 21 titles
ISBN Publisher's Prefixes: 91-7566 (Timbro), 91-7568 (Ratio)

Tomas Förlag KB*, Mälarlunden 4, S-152 00 Strängnäs Tel: (0152) 10931
Man Dir: Alrik Hummel-Gumælius
Subject: Fiction
ISBN Publisher's Prefix: 91-85070

Bokförlaget **Trevi** AB, Barnhusgatan 3, S-111 23 Stockholm Tel: (08) 101850/101590 Fax: (08) 241959
Owner: Solveig Nellinge
Subjects: General Fiction & Non-fiction, Biography, How-to, Illustrated Books
Founded: 1971
ISBN Publisher's Prefix: 91-7160

Unicart Kartografisk Produktion AB, now Bokförlaget Fröja AB (qv)

Utbildningsbolaget M M AB+*, Box 145, S-139 00 Värmdö Tel: (0766) 22300
Man Dir: Mats Myrén
Subjects: Management Training, Teaching Aids

Utbildningsförlaget, Box 3071, S-103 61 Stockholm (Located at: Luntmakargatan 22-24, Stockholm) Tel: (08) 7399000 Cable Add: Libergraph Telex: 12801 S Fax: (08) 7399035
Man Dir: Ulf Åkersten; *Editorial:* Karin Dalunde
Orders to: Liber Kundtjänst, S-162 89 Stockholm
Parent Company: Liber AB (qv)
Associate Company: Allmänna Förlaget (qv)
Subjects: Curricula, books and courses for teacher further training
1985: 55 titles *1986:* 50 titles
ISBN Publisher's Prefixes: 91-40, 91-47

Vår Skola Förlag AB+, Torstenssonsgatan 9, S-114 56 Stockholm Tel: (08) 623351/623124
Man Dirs: Gunnel Rådahl, Stig Rådahl
Subjects: School Textbooks & Periodicals, Non-fiction, Juveniles
ISBN Publisher's Prefixes: 91-7396, 91-7700 (Pandemos)

Förlagsaktiebolaget **Västra** Sverige, now Elanders Bokförlag AB (qv)

Verbum Förlag AB, Box 15269, S-104 65 Stockholm (Located at: St Paulsgatan 2, Stockholm) Tel: (08) 7496500
Man Dir: Lars-G Ståhl; *Editorial:* Ruben Baggström
Associate Company: Verbum Gothia (qv)
Subjects: Religion, Theology, Juveniles, Music, Audiovisuals, Textbooks

Verbum Gothia+, Box 11175, S-404 24 Gothenburg (Located at: Södra Hamngatan 45, Gothenburg) Tel: (031) 805140
Publisher: Gunnar Gärdhagen; *Rights & Permissions:* Kerstin Samuelsson
Associate Company: Verbum Förlag AB (qv)
Subjects: Educational Materials, Juveniles, Religion
Founded: 1985

SWEDEN

Viking Förlag, an imprint of Consilium Publishers (qv)

AB Bokförlaget Viva, Box 3159, S-103 63 Stockholm (Located at: Sveavägen 56, Stockholm) Tel: (08) 229120 Cable Add: Bonniers Telex: 11620 Bonbook S
Publisher: Siv Broman
Parent Company: Albert Bonniers Förlag AB (qv)
Subject: Fiction
1985: 28 titles *1986:* 21 titles *Founded:* 1984
ISBN Publisher's Prefix: 91-614

AB Wahlström och Widstrand, Tysta Gatan 10, S-115 24 Stockholm Tel: (08) 6679815 Cable Add: Wahlwid s Telex: 12757
Man Dir: Jonas Modig; *Sales Dir:* Sigvard Olsson; *Rights & Permissions:* Ulla Asplund
Parent Company: Albert Bonniers Förlag AB (qv)
Subjects: General Fiction & Non-fiction, Handbooks, University & Quality Paperbacks
Founded: 1884
ISBN Publisher's Prefix: 91-46

B Wahlströms Bokförlag AB, Warfvinges väg 30, S-112 51 Stockholm Tel: (08) 244600 Cable Add: Wahlbook, Stockholm Telex: 8106110 Fax: (08) 509761
Chief Executive: Bertil Wahlström; *Man Dir:* Johan Landberg; *Production:* Gert Fransson; *Permissions:* Eva Melin
Parent Company: J A Lindblads Bokförlag AB (qv)
Subjects: General Fiction, Juveniles, Low-priced Paperbacks
1986: 350 titles *1987:* 300 titles *Founded:* 1911
ISBN Publisher's Prefix: 91-32

AB Waldia Förlag*, Brogatan 41, Box 35, S-571 00 Nässjö Tel: (038) 016200
Man Dir: Ernst Wallin

Zindermans Förlag*, Box 310, S-401 25 Gothenburg 1 (Located at: Götgatan 13, Gothenburg) Tel: (031) 136890/137832 Cable Add: Zindermans
Man Dir: Sune Stigsjöö
Subjects: General Fiction and Non-fiction, Biography, History, How-to, Psychology, Social & Political Science
Founded: 1960
ISBN Publisher's Prefix: 91-528

Literary Agents

Arlecchino Teaterförlag*, Gränsvägen 14, S-131 41 Nacka Tel: (08) 7181717/8

A/S Bookman, Fiolstr 12, DK-1171 Copenhagen K, Denmark Tel: Copenhagen 145720 Cable Add: Bookman Copenhagen Fax: 451 120007 (Denmark)
This Danish-based company handles rights in Sweden for foreign authors

D Richard **Bowen**, Box 30037, S-200 61 Malmo 30
Contact: D Richard Bowen Tel: (040) 161200/161230

Gösta **Dahl** och Son AB*, Aladdinsvägen 14, S-161 38 Bromma/Stockholm Tel: (08) 256235 Cable Add: Literarius

Mrs Lena I **Gedin**, c/o Lennart Sane Agency, Holländareplan 9, S-292 00 Karlshamn Tel: (0454) 12356

Folmer **Hansen** Teaterförlag AB*, Lundagatan 6, S-171 63 Solna Tel: (08) 834365 Cable Add: Folmerhansen Stockholm
Dir: Gerd Widestedt-Ericsson; *Public Relations:* Marianne Krantz
Specialization: Foreign Plays in Scandinavia, Scandinavian Plays in Scandinavia and Abroad, Children's Plays

Monica **Heyum** Agency, Box 3300, Vendelsö, S-136 03 Haninge Tel: (08) 7451934 Cable Add: Expression Stockholm Telex: 12442 Fotex S attn Expression
Dir: Monica Heyum

Kerstin **Kvint***, Box 17038, S-161 17 Bromma (Located at: Nyodlingsvägen 18, Bromma) Tel: (08) 803417
Handles foreign rights' sales for individual writers and Scandinavian publishers. Co-productions arranged for children's picture books

Lennart **Sane** Agency AB, Holländareplan 9, S-292 00 Karlshamn Tel: (0454) 12356 Cable Add: Saneagency Karlshamn Telex: 8375002 Saneagy Fax: (0454) 14920
Dir: Lennart Sane; *Assistant Dirs:* Elisabeth Sane, Ulf Töregård, Ann-Mari Selander
Founded: 1968

Book Clubs

Allt om Hobbys Bokklubb*, Box 42006, S-126 12 Stockholm Tel: (08) 194040
Owned by: Allt om Hobby AB (qv)

Barnens Bokklubb, Box 45070, S-104 30 Stockholm Tel: (08) 349960
Owned by: AB Rabén och Sjögren Bokförlag (qv), Bokförlaget Opal AB (qv), Astrid Lindgren, Marianne von Baumgarten-Lindberg

Bättre Data, Box 3071, S-103 61 Stockholm Tel: (08) 7399000 Telex: 12801 S
Contact: Kjell Gerdin
Members: 1,000
Owned by: Liber AB (qv)
Subject: Computer technology
Founded: 1983

Bättre Ledarskap, Box 3071, S-103 61 Stockholm Tel: (08) 7399000 Telex: 12801 S
Contact: Per Bergknut
Members: 3,500
Owned by: Liber AB (qv)
Subjects: Management, Business Administration, Economics
Founded: 1977

Bättre Marknadsföring, Box 3071, S-103 61 Stockholm Tel: (08) 7399000 Telex: 12801 S
Contact: Lars Abramson
Members: 1,500
Owned by: Liber AB (qv)
Subject: Marketing
Founded: 1984

Bättre Samhälle, Box 3071, S-103 61 Stockholm Tel: (08) 7399000 Telex: 12801 S
Members: 1,500
Owned by: Liber AB (qv)
Subject: Social Science (book club for social workers)
Founded: 1983

Bättre Skola, Box 3071, S-103 61 Stockholm Tel: (08) 7399000 Telex: 12801 S
Contact: Ingemar Ternbo
Members: 4,000
Owned by: Liber AB (qv)
Subject: Education (book club for teachers)
Founded: 1975 (as Lärarbokklubben)

Bokmästar'n*, Box 205, S-524 00 Herrljunga
Owned by: InterSkrift/Harriers Publishing House (qv)

Bonniers Bokklubb, Sveavägen 56, S-103 63 Stockholm
Owned by: Albert Bonniers Förlag AB (qv)

Bokklubben **Bra Böcker**, Södra Vägen, S-263 00 Höganäs Tel: (042) 39000 Cable Add: BBBooks Telex: 72643
Owned by: Bokförlaget Bra Böcker AB (qv)

Bokklubben **Bra Lyrik**, Södra Vägen, S-263 00 Höganäs Tel: (042) 39000
Specialization: Poetry
Owned by: Bokförlaget Bra Böcker AB (qv)

Bokklubben **Bra Spänning**, Södra Vägen, S-263 00 Höganäs Tel: (042) 39000
Specialization: Thrillers
Owned by: Bokförlaget Bra Böcker AB (qv)

Delta Science Fiction Bok Klubb*, Box 15123, S-161 15 Bromma
Owned by: Delta Förlags AB (qv)

Disney's Ungdomsbokklubb, Ö Förstadsgatan 46, S-205 75 Malmo Tel: (040) 380600 Telex: 33180 richt s Fax: (040) 930820
Owned by: Richters Förlag AB (qv)

Jaktjournalens Bokklubb*, Box 10184, S-434 01 Kungsbacka Tel: (0300) 50000 Cable Add: Printer, Kungsbacka Telex: 21234
Owned by: Elanders Kommunikation AB, a printing company and a subsidiary of Elanders Bokförlag AB (qv)

Kalle Ankas Bokklubb, Ö Förstadsgatan 46, S-205 75 Malmo Tel: (040) 380600 Telex: 33180 richt s Fax: (040) 930820
Owned by: Richters Förlag AB (qv)

Kalle Ankas Pocket, Ö Förstadsgatan 46, S-205 75 Malmo Tel: (040) 380600 Telex: 33180 richt s Fax: (040) 930820
Owned by: Richters Förlag AB (qv)

Kokboksklubben God Mat, Ö Förstadsgatan 46, S-205 75 Malmo Tel: (040) 380600 Telex: 33180 richt s Fax: (040) 930820
Owned by: Richters Förlag AB (qv)

Den **Kristna Bokringen**, Dagenhuset, S-105 36 Stockholm
Members: 10,000
Owned by: Tidnings AB Dagen (qv)
Founded: 1970

Lärarbokklubben, now Bättre Skola (qv)

Libris Bookclub*, Box 1213, S-701 12 Örebro
Owned by: Libris Media AB (qv)

Månadens Bok, Box 2255, S-103 16 Stockholm (Located at: Skeppsbron 20) Tel: (08) 232310
Man Dir: Karin Lejon; *Marketing Manager:* Stefan Björklund
Owned by: Albert Bonniers Förlag AB (qv), Esselte Förlag AB (qv), Bokförlaget Forum AB (qv), Gedins Förlag (qv), Norstedts Förlag AB (qv)

Mitt företag, Box 3071, S-103 61 Stockholm Tel: (08) 7399000 Telex: 12801 S
Owned by: Liber AB (qv)
Subjects: Small businesses

Önskeboken*, Box 205, S-524 00 Herrljunga
Owned by: InterSkrift/Harriers Publishing House (qv)

SWEDEN 389

Proklama Pocketbokklubb, Trantorp, Hållsta, S-635 90 Eskilstuna
Owned by: Proklama (qv)

Reader's Digest AB, Box 25, S-163 93 Spånga (Located at: Skalholtsgatan 2, Spånga) Tel: (08) 7520360 Telex: 11689 Digest S

Richters Bokklubb, Ö Förstadsgatan 46, S-205 75 Malmo Tel: (040) 380600 Telex: 33180 richt s Fax: (040) 930820
Owned by: Richters Förlag AB (qv)

Serie-pocket-klubben*, Box 74, S-172 22 Sundbyberg (Located at: Landsvägen 57, Sundbyberg)
Owned by: Semic International AB (qv)

Stora Romanklubben, Sveavägen 56, S-103 63 Stockholm
Owned by: Albert Bonniers Förlag AB (qv)

Bokklubben **Svalan**, Sveavägen 56, S-103 63 Stockholm Tel: (08) 229120 Telex: Bonbook 11620
Owned by: Albert Bonniers Förlag AB (qv)

Underhållningsbokklubben, Sveavägen 56, S-103 63 Stockholm
Owned by: Albert Bonniers Förlag AB (qv)

Vår Bok AB, Box 2234, S-103 15 Stockholm 5 (Located at: Brunnsgränd 4, Stockholm)
Subjects: Classics, Dictionaries, Encyclopaedias, Detective fiction, Novels
Owned by: Esselte Forlag AB and Norstedts Förlag AB (qqv)

Major Booksellers

Johan **Åkerbloms** Universitetsbokhandel, Box 83, S-901 03 Umeå (Located at: Östra Rådhusgatan 6, Umeå) Tel: (090) 125770
Manager: Bengt Gyllengahm
Also a subscription agency

Almqvist och Wiksell Bokhandel AB*, Box 62, S-101 20 Stockholm (Located at: Gamla Brogatan 26, Stockholm) Tel: (08) 237990
Member of Esselte Bokhandel Group (qv)

Esselte Bokhandel Eckersteins, Box 11903, S-404 39 Gothenburg Tel: (031) 171100 Telex: 21178
Manager: Erik Engström
Member of Esselte Bokhandel Group (qv)

Esselte Bokhandel Group*, Box 62, S-101 20 Stockholm (Located at: Gamla Brogatan 26, Stockholm) Tel: (08) 237990
Group Members: Almqvist och Wiksell Bokhandel AB, Esselte Bokhandel Eckersteins, Esselte Bokhandel Lundequistska, AB Nordiska Bokhandeln (qqv)

AB C E **Fritzes** Kungl Hovbokhandel*, Box 16356, S-103 27 Stockholm (Located at: Regeringsgatan 12, Stockholm) Tel: (08) 238900 Cable Add: Bokfritze Telex: 12387 S Fritzes
Man Dir: Gunnar Siegel
Owned by: AB Priab, S-112 89 Stockholm

AB **Gleerupska** Universitetsbokhandeln, Box 172, S-221 00 Lund Tel: (046) 117260
Manager: Ann Dyster-Aas

Gumperts Universitetsbokhandel AB*, Box 3184, S-400 10 Gothenburg (Located at: Norra Hamngatan 26, Gothenburg) Tel: (031) 171100 Telex: 21178
Manager: Bo Lindgren

Söderbokhandeln **Hansson och Bruce** AB, Götgatan 37, S-116 21 Stockholm Tel: (08) 405432
Manager: T Fredriksson

Esselte Bokhandel **Lundequistska**, Box 610, S-751 25 Uppsala 1 (Located at: Östra Ågatan 31, Uppsala) Tel: (018) 139830 Telex: 76255 Lundeg S
Manager: Hans Molander
Member of Esselte Bokhandel Group (qv)

AB Edvin **Lundgrens** Bokhandel, Södergatan 3, S-211 34 Malmo Tel: (040) 76660 Fax: (040) 8305084
Manager: Ulla Bella Gustafsson

AB **Nordiska Bokhandeln**, Box 7, S-101 20 Stockholm (Located at: Kungsgatan 4, Stockholm) Tel: (08) 227380
Owned by: AB Nordiska Bokhandelns Förlag (qv)
Member of Esselte Bokhandel Group (qv)

AB **Seelig** och Co, Box 1308, S-171 25 Solna Tel: (08) 850300 Cable Add: Seelig Telex: 12081 Fax: (08) 856774
Manager: Jan Rydemalm
Importers, distributors and wholesalers

Wettergrens Bokhandel AB*, Västra Hamngatan 22, S-411 17 Gothenburg Tel: (031) 101060

Major Libraries

Göteborgs Stadsbibliotek*, Box 5404, S-402 29 Gothenburg
City Library and County Library

Göteborgs Universitetsbibliotek, Centralbiblioteket, Box 5096, S-402 22 Gothenburg (Located at: Renströmsgatan 4, Gothenburg) Tel: (031) 631000 Telex: 20896 Ubgbg s
Librarian: Paul Hallberg
Publications: Acta Bibliothecae Universitatis Gothoburgensis (irregular); *New Literature on Women. A Bibliography* (quarterly)

Kungliga Biblioteket, Box 5039, S-102 41 Stockholm 5 Tel: (08) 241040 Telex: 19640 kbs s
The Royal Library — National Library of Sweden
National Librarian: Lars Tynell
Publications include: AKB-micro; Acta Bibliothecae Regiae Stockholmiensis; Kungl Bibliotekets Utställningskatalog; Rapport; Suecana Extranea; Svensk Bokförteckning (Swedish National Bibliography); *Svensk Musikförteckning*

Kungliga Svenska Vetenskapsakademiens Bibliotek, incorporated with Stockholms Universitetsbibliotek (qv)

Lunds Universitetsbibliotek, National Lending Library, Box 3, S-221 00 Lund Tel: (046) 107500 Telex: 32208 Lublund S (Main Library UB1); Tel: (046) 109230 Telex: 33248 Lubbis S (Branch Library UB2)
Dir: Kari Marklund
Publication: Scripta Academica

Malmö Stadsbibliotek, Regementsgatan 3, S-211 42 Malmo Tel: (040) 77810
City Library, County Library and Lending Centre for Southern and Western Sweden
Librarian: Bengt Holmström
Publications: Annual Report; Catalogue of Annual Acquisition (microfiche); *Bibliographies*

Riksarkivet*, Box 12541, S-102 29 Stockholm (Located at: Fyrverkarbacken 13-17, Stockholm)
National Record Office

Royal Institute of Technology Library, S-100 44 Stockholm Tel: (08) 7906000 Telex: 10389

Statistiska Centralbyråns Bibliotek, S-115 81 Stockholm Tel: (08) 7835066 Telex: 15261 Swestat
Library of Statistics Sweden
Chief Librarian: Malkon Lindmark

Stiftelsen Svenska Barnboksinstitutet, Odengatan 61, S-113 22 Stockholm Tel: (08) 332323
Swedish Institute for Children's Books
Dir: Sonja Svensson; *Librarian:* Lena Törnqvist

Stockholms Stadsbibliotek, Box 6502, S-113 83 Stockholm
City Library of Stockholm

Stockholms Universitetsbibliotek, S-106 91 Stockholm
Stockholm University Library
This Library incorporates the Library of the Royal Swedish Academy of Sciences (Kungliga Svenska Vetenskapsakademiens Bibliotek) covering Humanities, Law, Social Sciences, Mathematics and Science

Sveriges Lantbruksuniversitets Bibliotek, Central Library Ultunabiblioteket, S-750 07 Uppsala Tel: (018) 171000 Telex: 76062 Ultbibl S Libraries of the Swedish University of Agricultural Sciences
Dir: Sten F Vedi

University Libraries, see under town names

Uppsala Universitetsbibliotek, Box 510, S-751 20 Uppsala Tel: (018) 183900 Telex: 76076 ubupps s
Librarian: Thomas Tottie
Publications: Acta Bibliothecae R Universitatis Upsaliensis; Scripta Minora Bibliothecae R Universitatis Upsaliensis; Uppsala Universitetsbiblioteks Utställningskataloger

Library Associations

Svenska Arkivsamfundet, c/o Riksarkivet, Box 12541, S-102 29 Stockholm
Swedish Association of Archivists

Svenska Bibliotekariesamfundet, Lunds Universitetsbibliotek, Box 3, S-221 00 Lund Tel: (046) 109212
Swedish Association of University and Research Librarians
Executive Secretary: Kerstin Dahl
Publications: Bibliotekariesamfundet Meddelar; Svenska Bibliotekariesamfundet Rapport

Svenska Folkbibliotekarieförbundet, Box 760, S-131 24 Nacka Tel: (08) 7162880
Union of Swedish Public Librarians
President: Britt Marie Häggström, Uppsala Stadsbibliotek, Box 643, S-751 27 Uppsala

Sveriges Allmänna Biblioteksförening, Box 200, S-221 00 Lund (Located at: Winstrupsgatan 10, Lund)
Swedish Library Association
Acting Secretary: Jan Nyberg
Publication: Biblioteksbladet

Tekniska Litteratursällskapet*, Box 5073, S-102 42 Stockholm
Swedish Society for Technical Documentation
Secretary: Birgitta Levin
Publications: Tidskrift för Dokumentation (four times a year)

Vetenskapliga Bibliotekens Tjänstemannaförening VBT, c/o D I K/ förbundet, Box 760, S-131 24 Nacka Tel: (08) 7162880

Association of Research Library Employees
President: Anders Schmidt,
Universitetsbibliotek, UB1, Box 3, S-221 00 Lund
Publication: DIK-forum

Library Reference Journals

Bibliotekariesamfundet Meddelar (Reports of the Librarians' Association), Svenska Bibliotekariesamfundet, Lunds Universitetsbibliotek, Box 3, S-221 00 Lund

Biblioteket Presenterar Nya Boecker (The Library Presents New Books), Bibliotekstjänst AB, Box 200, S-221 00 Lund

Biblioteksbladet (Library Journal), Sveriges Allmänna Biblioteksförening, Box 200, S-221 00 Lund
Text in Scandinavian languages with summaries in English

DIK-forum, Vetenskapliga Bibliotekens Tjänstemannaförening VBT, c/o D I K-förbundet, Box 36, S-131 06 Nacka

Svenska Bibliotekariesamfundet Rapport (Reports of the Librarians' Association), Svenska Bibliotekariesamfundet, Lunds Universitetsbibliotek, Box 3, S-221 00 Lund

Tidskrift för Dokumentation (Scandinavian Documentation Journal), Tekniska Litteratursällskapet, Box 5073, S-102 42 Stockholm
Text in Swedish, with summaries and occasional articles in English

Literary Associations and Societies

Kungl Vitterhets Historie och Antikvitets Akademien*, Villagatan 3, S-114 32 Stockholm
Royal Academy of Letters, History and Antiquities
Secretary: Prof Bertil Molde
Publications: Fornvännen (journal), *Handlingar* (memoirs), *Arkiv* (archives), *Årsbok* (Yearbook), *Monografier* (monographs)

Litteraturfrämjandet, Bellmansgatan 30, S-116 47 Stockholm Tel: (08) 449175
Foundation for Promotion of Literature

Svenska Pennklubben (Swedish Centre of International **P E N**)*, AB P A Norstedt & Söners Förlag, Tryckerigatan 2, Box 2052, S-103 12 Stockholm 2
President: Dr Thomas von Vegesack;
Secretary: Lars Grahn
International Secretary: Marianne Eyre

Samfundet de Nio, c/o Anders R Öhman, Villagatan 14, S-114 32 Stockholm
Nine Swedish Authors' Society ('The Society of the Nine')
Secretary: Anders R Öhman

Svenska Österbottens Litteraturförening, c/o Sven-Erik Klinkmann, Henriksgatan 7-9 4N, SF-65320 Vasa, Finland
Swedish Österbottens Literary Association
Publication: Horisont

Literary Periodicals

BLM (Bonniers Litteraera Magasin) (Bonniers Literary Magazine), Albert Bonniers Förlag AB, Box 3159, S-103 63 Stockholm

Horisont (Horizon), Svenska Österbottens Litteraturförening, c/o Sven-Erik Klinkmann, Henriksgatan 7-9 4N, SF-65320 Vasa, Finland

Ord och Bild (Word and Picture), Stiftelsen Ord och Bild, Box 15116, S-104 65 Stockholm

Svensk Litteraturtidskrift (Swedish Journal of Literature), Almqvist och Wiksell Förlag AB, Box 2052, S-103 12, Stockholm

Swedish Book Review, Linda Schenck, Mossgatan 5, S-413 21 Gothenburg
Half yearly translators' review, in English, of works written in Swedish, originating from Sweden or Swedish writers in Finland

Swedish Books, now *Swedish Book Review* (qv)

Tulimuld (Scorched Earth) Bernard Kangro, Skördevägen 1, S-222 38 Lund
Literary and cultural magazine of Estonian exiles; text in Estonian

Literary Prizes

Aniarapriset
Aniara Prize, for adult literature in Sweden. Awarded annually. Enquiries to Sveriges Allmänna Biblioteksförening, Winstrupsgatan 10, Box 200, S-221 00 Lund

Ida **Bäckman** Prize, see Swedish Academy Prizes

Bellmans Prize
For poetry. 50,000 Swedish crowns. Awarded annually. This prize cannot be applied for. Enquiries to Swedish Academy, Börshuset, Källargränd 4, S-111 29 Stockholm

Beskow Prize, see Swedish Academy Prizes

Blom Prize, see Swedish Academy Prizes

Dobloug Prize
For outstanding literary work by two Norwegian and two Swedish writers. 40,000 Swedish crowns in each category awarded annually. This award cannot be applied for. Enquiries to Swedish Academy, Börshuset, Källargränd 4, S-111 29 Stockholm, Sweden

Signe **Ekblad-Eldhs** Prize
To famous Swedish writers. Two prizes of 30,000 Swedish crowns awarded annually. This award cannot be applied for.
Enquiries to Swedish Academy, Börshuset, Källargränd 4, S-111 29 Stockholm

Gun and Olof **Engqvist** Prize
Annual award for Swedish Literature and Cultural Journalism. Two prizes of 40,000 Swedish crowns. This award cannot be applied for. Enquiries to Swedish Academy, Börshuset, Källargränd 4, S-111 29 Stockholm

Lydia and Herman **Erikssons** Prize
Awarded every second year to a Swedish writer for a work of prose or poetry. 25,000 Swedish crowns. This prize cannot be applied for. Enquiries to Swedish Academy, Börshuset, Källargränd 4, S-111 29 Stockholm

Karin **Gierows** Prizes, see Swedish Academy Prizes

Grand Prize
For outstanding literary work written in Swedish. 50,000 Swedish crowns. Awarded annually. Enquiries to Litteraturfrämjandet, Bellmansgatan 30, S-116 47 Stockholm

Grand Prize for a Book of Poetry
For the best original collection of new poems written in Swedish by a single author. 25,000 Swedish crowns. Awarded annually. Enquiries to Litteraturfrämjandet, Bellmansgatan 30, S-116 47 Stockholm

Grand Prize for a Novel
For the best novel written in Swedish. 25,000 Swedish crowns. Awarded annually. Enquiries to Litteraturfrämjandet, Bellmansgatan 30, S-116 47 Stockholm

Kalleberger Foundation — The Tekla **Hanssons** and Gösta Ronnströms Prize
Annual award in memory of Tekla Hansson to a Swedish writer for a work of prose or poetry. 15,000 Swedish crowns. This prize cannot be applied for. Enquiries to Swedish Academy, Börshuset, Källargränd 4, S-111 29 Stockholm

Axel **Hirsch** Prize, see Swedish Academy Prizes

Nils **Holgersson** Plaque
The highest award for children's literature in Sweden. Awarded annually. Enquiries to Sveriges Allmänna Biblioteksförening, Winstrupsgatan 10, Box 200, S-221 00 Lund

Kalleberger Foundation, see Hanssons

Kellgrens Prize
For important achievements in any of the fields of the Academy. 50,000 Swedish crowns. Awarded annually. This prize cannot be applied for. Enquiries to Swedish Academy, Börshuset, Källargrand 4, S-111 29 Stockholm

Ilona **Kohrtz** Prize, see Swedish Academy Prizes

The **'Nine'** Prize
For an author of outstanding literary merit, whether established or not, writing in Swedish. 50,000 Swedish crowns. Awarded annually. This prize cannot be applied for. Enquiries to Samfundet de Nio, Villagatan 14, S-114 32 Stockholm

Royal Prize, see Swedish Academy Prizes

Birger **Schöldström** Prize, see Swedish Academy Prizes

Henrik **Schück** Prize, see Swedish Academy Prizes

Swedish Academy Prizes
In addition to those fully listed individually, the Swedish Academy awards the following prizes:
Ida Bäckman Prize (Literature/Journalism: biennial); Beskow Prize (Literary: biennial); Blom Prize (Swedish Language: annual); Karin Gierows Prizes (for (1) Cultural Information: annual; (2) Promotion of Knowledge: annual); Axel Hirsch Prize (Biographic/Historic: biennial); Ilona Kohrtz Prize (Prose/Poetry: annual); Royal Prize (Cultural/Literary: annual); Birger Schöldström Prize (Literary History/Biography: every 4 years); Henrik Schück Prize (Literary History: annual); Swedish Linguistics Prize (annual); Swedish into Foreign Language Translation Prize (annual); Translation into Swedish Prize (annual); Zibet Prize (Literary/Historic referring to reign of Gustav III: irregular); miscellaneous prizes for work in literary or linguistic fields.
These prizes cannot be applied for. Enquiries to The Swedish Academy, Börshuset, Källargränd 4, S-111 29 Stockholm

Swedish into Foreign Language Translation Prize, see Swedish Academy Prizes

Swedish Linguistics Prize, see Swedish Academy Prizes

SWEDEN — SWITZERLAND 391

Translation into Swedish Prize, see Swedish Academy Prizes

Lena **Vendelfelt** Prize
For a literary work, mainly poetry. 25,000 Swedish crowns awarded annually. This prize cannot be applied for. Enquiries to Swedish Academy, Börshuset, Källargränd 4, S-111 29 Stockholm

Zibet Prize, see Swedish Academy Prizes

Anders and Emma **Zorn** Prize
For outstanding literary work. 20,000 Swedish crowns. Awarded annually. This prize cannot be applied for. Enquiries to Swedish Academy, Börshuset, Källargränd 4, S-111 29 Stockholm

Translation Agencies and Associations

E C Print AB, Gibraltargatan 48, S-412 58 Gothenburg Tel: (031) 814661 Telex: 21992 Imce S Fax: (031) 814654
Man Dir: Dr Carlos Ezeyza-Alvear
Technical Manuals, Books and Dictionaries; also Publisher (qv)

Föreningen Auktoriserade Translatorer, c/o Dr Solfrid Söderlind, Rörläggarvägen 17, S-161 46 Bromma Tel: (08) 268620
Swedish Association of Authorized Translators

Språktjänst*, Box 5513, S-114 85 Stockholm (Located at: Artillerigatan 42, Stockholm) Tel: (08) 7838500/7838697 Telex: 15679
Translating and Interpreting Service of the Swedish Trade Council (See Sveriges Exportråd under Publishers)

Swedish-English Literary Translators' Association (SELTA), see UK Translation Agencies and Associations

Switzerland

General Information

Language: 65% German (dialect known as Swiss German or Schwyzerdütsch), 18% French (in southwest), 12% Italian (in Ticino), 1% Romansh (in Graubünden)
Religion: Protestant and Catholic
Population: 6.5 million
Bank Hours: 0800-1230, 1330-1630 Monday-Friday
Shop Hours: 0800-1200, 1330-1830 Monday-Friday; in most cities, closed Monday morning; 0800-1200, 1330-1600 or 1700 Saturday
Currency: 100 centimes = 1 Swiss franc
Export/Import Information: Member of the European Free Trade Association. No tariff on books. Most books exempt from Turnover Tax. Advertising matter usually dutiable, some exempt from Turnover Tax. No import licences required. No exchange controls
Copyright: UCC, Berne, Florence (see International Section)

Book Trade Organizations

A L S I, see Associazione dei Librai della Svizzera Italiana

Association suisse des Editeurs de Langue française, 2 ave Agassiz, CH-1001 Lausanne Tel: (021) 491911 Telex: 455730
Swiss Publishers' Association (French Language)
Secretary General: Robert Junod

Association suisse des Libraires de Langue française, 2 ave Agassiz, CH-1001 Lausanne Tel: (021) 491911 Telex: 455730
Association of Swiss French-language Bookshops
Secretary: Robert Junod

Association suisse romande des Diffuseurs de Livres, 2 ave Agassiz, CH-1001 Lausanne Tel: (021) 491911 Telex: 455730
Association of Book Distributors of French-speaking Switzerland
Secretary: Robert Junod

Associazione dei Librai della Svizzera Italiana (ALSI)*, CH-6901 Lugano Tel: (093) 313180
Association of Italian-speaking Swiss Booksellers
Secretary: Carlangelo Albergoni

Centre Suisse du Livre, see Schweizer Buchzentrum

Centro Svizzero del Libro, see Schweizer Buchzentrum

S B I, see Schweizer Buchwerbung und Information

S E S I, see Societa Editori della Svizzera Italiana

S L E S R, see Société des Libraires et Editeurs de la Suisse romande

Schweizer Buchwerbung und Information (SBI)*, CH-8245 Feuerthalen Tel: (053) 293484
Swiss Book Publicity and Information Service
Dir: Edwin Nigg
Publications: Bücherkatalog des Schweizer Buchhandels; Katalog Bücher-Sommer; Bücher für Sie (an annual publication distributed to every household in German-speaking Switzerland)

Schweizer Buchzentrum*, CH-4614 Hägendorf Tel: (062) 476161 Telex: 981828
Centre Suisse du Livre/Centro Svizzero del Libro/Swiss Book Centre

Schweizer Verband der Musikalienhändler und Verleger, Lic iur B Thoma, Zeughausgasse 9, PO Box, CH-6301 Zug Tel: (042) 219016
Swiss Association of Music Sellers and Publishers (a department of the Sekretariat des Musikhandels (Music Trade Secretariat) at above address)

Schweizerischer Adressbuchverleger-Verband, c/o Mosse Adress AG, PO Box 216, CH-8045 Zurich (Located at: Räffelstr 25, Zurich) Tel: (01) 4637700 Telex: 814133 moag ch Fax: (01) 4616750
Swiss Association of Directory Publishers
President: Dr G Hüber

Schweizerischer Buchhändler- und Verleger-Verband (SBVV), PO Box 9045, CH-8050 Zurich (Located at: Baumackerstr 42, Zurich) Tel: (01) 3125343
Swiss Booksellers' and Publishers' Association (German language)
Secretary: Peter Birchmeier
Publications: Der Schweizer Buchhandel (bi-monthly) (official organ of this association, also its French equivalent SLESR, and its Italian equivalents SESI and ALSI); *Das Schweizer Buch; Adressbuch des Schweizer Buchhandels; Schweizer Bücherverzeichnis*

Schweizerischer Bühnenverleger-Verband*, c/o Edition Kunzelmann GmbH, Grütstr 28, CH-8134 Adliswil
Association of Swiss Publishers for the Stage
President: Albert Kunzelmann

Schweizerischer Schriftsteller-Verband, Postfach, CH-8022 Zurich (Located at: Kirchgasse 25, CH-8001 Zurich) Tel: (01) 473020
Society of Swiss Writers
Secretary: Otto Böni

Societa Editori della Svizzera Italiana (SESI)*, PO Box 2600, CH-6501 Bellinzona (Located at: Viale Portone 4, Bellinzona) Tel: (092) 258555/56 Telex: 846310 Aseg CH Fax: (092) 258595
Association of Publishers for Italian-speaking Switzerland
Dir: Romano Montalbetti

Société des Libraires et Editeurs de la Suisse romande (SLESR), 2 ave Agassiz, CH-1001 Lausanne Tel: (021) 491911 Telex: 455730
Booksellers' and Publishers' Association of French-speaking Switzerland
Secretary General: Robert Junod
Publications: La Librairie suisse (bi-monthly) (official organ of this association, also its German equivalent SBVV, and its Italian equivalents SESI and ALSI)

Standard Book Numbering Agency (French-language), see Agence francophone pour la Numérotation internationale du Livre, France

Standard Book Numbering Agency, Schweizerischer Buchhändler und Verleger-Verband, Postfach, CH-8050 Zurich (Located at: Baumackerstr 42, Zurich) Tel: (01) 312 5343
This is the agency for German-language ISBNs
ISBN Administrator: Ch Aeberli

Verband evangelischer Buchhandlungen und Verlage der Schweiz, PO Box 645, CH-5401 Baden (Located at: Rathausgasse 8, Baden) Tel: (056) 223610
Association of Swiss Protestant Booksellers and Publishers
Dir: Ernst Jucker

Verband schweizerischer Zeitungsagenturen und Büchergrossisten (Union d'Agences suisses de Journaux et Livres en Gros), St Jakobsstr 25, CH-4002 Basle Tel: (061) 455500
Association of Swiss Newspaper Distributors and Book Wholesalers

Vereinigung katholischer Buchhändler und Verleger der Schweiz*, c/o Anton Scherer, Editions Universitaires SA, Pérolles 42, CH-1700 Fribourg Tel: (037) 246812
Association of Swiss Catholic Booksellers and Publishers

Book Trade Reference Books and Journals

Books

Adressbuch des Schweizer Buchhandels, Schweizerischer Buchhändler- und Verleger-Verband (SBVV), PO Box 9045, CH-8050 Zurich
Directory of the Swiss book trade, containing lists of publishers, booksellers, distributors, trade organizations and cross-reference indices

Adressbuch für den deutschsprachigen Buchhandel

SWITZERLAND

This 'Directory for the German-speaking Book Trade' lists all Swiss, Austrian and German publishers. See Book Trade Reference Books, Federal Republic of Germany

Bücher für Sie (Books for You), Schweizer Buchwerbung und Information (SBI), CH-8245 Feuerthalen

Bücherkatalog des Schweizer Buchhandels (Swiss Book Trade Book Catalogue), Schweizer Buchwerbung und Information (SBI), CH-8245 Feuerthalen

Journals

Bibliographie analytique des Bibliographies suisses courantes (Analytical Bibliography of Current Swiss bibliographies), Schweizerische Landesbibliothek (Bibliothèque nationale Suisse), Hallwylstr 15, CH-3003 Berne

Bibliographie des Publications officielles suisses (Bibliography of Swiss Official Publications), Schweizerische Landesbibliothek (Bibliothèque nationale suisse), Hallwylstr 15, CH-3003 Berne

Edition, Stauffacher Verlag AG, Birmensdorfer Str 318, CH-8055 Zurich 3
Book advertiser

Guilde du Livre (Book Guild), 5 rue de l'Ecole Supérieure, CH-1005 Lausanne

La Librairie suisse (The Swiss Bookseller), Société des Libraires et Editeurs de la Suisse romande, 2 ave Agassiz, CH-1001 Lausanne

Librarium, Schweizerische Bibliophilen-Gesellschaft, Zwingliplatz 3, CH-8001 Zurich
Text in German and French

Das Schweizer Buch (The Swiss Book), Schweizerischer Buchhändler- und Verleger-Verband (SBVV), PO Box 9045, CH-8050 Zurich
Bibliographical bulletin

Schweizer Bücherverzeichnis (Index of Swiss Books), Schweizerischer Buchhändler- und Verleger-Verband (SBVV), PO Box 9045, CH-8050 Zurich

Der Schweizer Buchhandel (The Swiss Book Trade), Schweizerischer Buchhändler- und Verleger-Verband (SBVV), PO Box 9045, CH-8050 Zurich

Publishers

Editions **24 heures**, 33 ave de la Gare, CH-1001 Lausanne Tel: (021) 494549 Telex: 455745 Vgh Ch
Man Dir: P Lamunière
Subjects: Belles Lettres, History, Music, Art, Juveniles, Educational Materials, Railways, Automobiles, Aviation, Military, Food, Horses
Founded: 1969

A B C Verlag+, Rüdigerstr 12, Postfach, CH-8021 Zurich Tel: (01) 2078643 Cable Add: ABC Verlag Zurich
Man Dir, Sales Dir: Katja Pfaeffli
Subjects: Graphic Design, Art
1985: 6 titles *1986:* 4 titles *Founded:* 1936
ISBN Publisher's Prefix: 3-85504

A D, an imprint of André Delcourt & Cie (qv)

A L A Verlag, CH-8213 Neunkirch
Man Dir and other offices: Berta Rahm
Subjects: Human Rights, Feminism, Social Science, Biography, History
1987: 3 titles *Founded:* 1968
ISBN Publisher's Prefix: 3-85509

A T Verlag+, Bahnhofstr 39-43, CH-5001 Aarau Tel: (064) 266161 Telex: 981146
Man Dir, Marketing: Alfred Haefeli; *Editorial:* Marcel Pfändler; *Production:* Hans Peter Kammermann; *Sales:* Helga Wiederkehr; *Rights & Permissions:* Franziska Weber
Branch Off: AT-Fachverlag GmbH, Postfach 500180, D-7000 Stuttgart 50, Federal Republic of Germany Tel: (0711) 527041 Telex: 07254879
Subjects: History, Giftbooks, Domestic, Nature, How-to, Local Interest
Founded: 1967
Miscellaneous: This is the book publishing section of the Aargauer Tagblatt (newspaper)
ISBN Publisher's Prefix: 3-85502

Aare-Verlag, see Schweizer Jugend-Verlag

Aargauer Tagblatt, see AT Verlag

Editions **Adversaires**, now known as Editions François Grounauer (qv)

Aesopus Verlag GmbH*, Grellingerstr 95, CH-4052 Basle Tel: (061) 423373 Telex: basel 63689
Man Dir: Nicolaus M Fisch
Branch Off: Greifstr 6, Wiesbaden, Federal Republic of Germany Tel: (06121) 467473 Telex: 04186895 Wgb
Subjects: Health, Sports, Medicine
Miscellaneous: Publish in nine languages

Editions **L'Age d'Homme** — La Cité*, PO Box 67, CH-1000 Lausanne (Located at: 10 Métropole, Lausanne) Tel: (021) 220095
Man Dir: Vladimir Dimitrijevic
Subjects: General Fiction, Belles Lettres, Poetry, Biography, Music, Art, Philosophy, Religion, Psychology, Social Science, Futurism and Esoterica, Slavica, Science Fiction, Cinema, Literary Criticism, Reprints
Bookshops: Librairie la Proue, Escaliers du Marché 17, CH-1000 Lausanne; Librairie Le Rameau d'Or, 19 blvd Georges Favon, CH-1200 Geneva; Librairie Suisse et Européenne, L'Age d'Homme, 5 rue Férou, F-75006 Paris, France
Founded: 1966
ISBN Publisher's Prefix: 2-8251

J H Göhre **Albanus** Verlag*, Hulfteggstr 10, Postfach, CH-8401 Winterthur 1 Tel: (052) 293503
ISBN Publisher's Prefix: 3-85510

Albatros Verlag AG*, Seestr 139, PO Box 140, CH-8706 Feldmeilen Tel: (01) 9232347
Subjects: Illustrated Reference Books, Animals and Plants, Technical, Culture
ISBN Publisher's Prefix: 3-7156

Ammann Verlag AG+, PO Box 163, CH-8032 Zurich (Located at: Cäcilienstr 5, Zurich) Tel: (01) 694350
Man Dir, Editorial: Egon Ammann; *Sales, Marketing:* Veit Heinichen; *Production:* Ernst Bloch; *Rights & Permissions:* Marie-Louise Flammersfeld
Orders to: Ammann Verlag AG, BD Bücherdienst AG, Kornhausstr 23, CH-8840 Einsiedeln; BDK Bücherdienst Köln GmbH, Kölnerstr 248, Postfach 900120, D-5000 Cologne 90, Federal Republic of Germany
Subjects: Literature, Art, Architecture, Science
1986: 25 titles *1987:* 30 titles *Founded:* 1981
ISBN Publisher's Prefix: 3-250

Ansata-Verlag, Paul A Zemp, Rosenstr 24, CH-3800 Interlaken Tel: (036) 221933
Subjects: Esoteric Traditions, Psychology

Antonius-Verlag, Gärtnerstr 7, CH-4500 Solothurn Tel: (065) 223912
Subjects: Psychology, Therapeutics, Pedagogy
ISBN Publisher's Prefix: 3-85520

Arche Verlag AG, Raabe und Vitali, Rämistr 3, CH-8001 Zurich Tel: (01) 2522154 Telex: 815239
Owners: Elisabeth Raabe, Regina Vitali
Subsidiary Company: Luchterhand Literaturverlag GmbH, Federal Republic of Germany (see Hermann Luchterhand Verlag GmbH & Co KG, Federal Republic of Germany)
Associate Company: Sanssouci Verlag (qv)
Subjects: Belles Lettres, Modern Literature
1986: 12 titles *1987:* 22 titles *Founded:* 1944
ISBN Publisher's Prefix: 3-7160

Archimedes Verlag, PO Box 180, CH-8280 Kreuzlingen (Located at: Marktweg 7, Kreuzlingen) Tel: (072) 722672
Subjects: Mathematics, Electronics, Mechanical Engineering; Periodical
ISBN Publisher's Prefix: 3-85525

Verlag für **Architektur***, Limmatquai 18, CH-8024 Zurich Tel: (01) 2521100 Telex: 0045/59477
The Architectural Publishing Company
Man Dir: Franz Ebner; *Rights & Permissions:* Rosemarie Roth
Parent Company: Artemis Verlags AG (qv for associate companies)

Archivio Storico Ticinese*, Via del Bramantino 3, CH-65000 Bellinzona Tel: (092) 256622 Telex: 846266
Man Dir: Virgilio Gilardoni; *Sales, Production:* Libero Casagrande
Parent Company: Edizioni Casagrande SA (qv)
Subjects: History, History of Art, Economics, Essays
1985: 5 titles *Founded:* 1960
ISBN Publisher's Prefix: 88-7714

Editions **Ariston** Verlag*, PO Box 176, CH-1211 Geneva 6 (Located at: 4 rue de la Scie, CH-1207 Geneva) Tel: (022) 861810 Cable Add: Ariston Telex: 27983
Man Dir, Editorial: Dr Heinz Bundschuh; *Sales, Rights & Permissions:* Mrs A Bundschuh, C Chenevard
Subjects: How-to, Psychology, Nature Medicine, Parapsychology, Hypnosis, Yoga, Self-Help, General Fiction
Founded: 1964
Miscellaneous: Formerly Verlag Ramòn F Keller
ISBN Publisher's Prefix: 3-7205

Ars Edition, PO Box 48, CH-6301 Zug
Publicity: I Nauer
Head Office: Ars Edition GmbH, Federal Republic of Germany (qv)

Artemis Verlags AG*, Limmatquai 18, CH-8024 Zurich Tel: (01) 2521100 (Administration)/2522102 (Production, Editorial) Telex: 59477
Man Dir: Franz Ebner; *Rights & Permissions:* Rosemarie Roth
Subsidiary Company: Verlag für Architektur
Associate Companies: Artemis und Winkler Verlag, Druckenmüller Verlag, Winkler-Verlag (qqv in Federal Republic of Germany)
Subjects: Philosophy, Art, Architecture, Encyclopaedias, Ancient/Mediaeval History, Current Events, Biography, Classics, Textbooks, Juvenile, Travel Guides
Founded: 1943
ISBN Publisher's Prefix: 3-7608

Artou, an imprint of Editions Olizane (qv)

Athenaeum Verlag AG*, Via Miravalle 23, CH-6900 Lugano-Massagno Tel: (091) 571536 Cable Add: athenag
Man Dir: J-E Nussbaumer; *Administration:* J Wüst-Wolfensberger; *Editorial:* J Steiner
Branch Off: Buchauslieferung, Schweizer Buchzentrum, Olten
Subjects: General Non-fiction: Art, History, Science, Literature, Biography, Politics
Founded: 1972
ISBN Publisher's Prefix: 3-85532

Atlantis Verlag AG, Museggstr 12, CH-6000 Lucerne 5 Tel: (041) 513721 Telex: 868122 Reic CH
Branch Off: Atlantis-Verlag GmbH & Co KG, Federal Republic of Germany (qv)
Subjects: Pictorial Geography, Art
Founded: 1930
ISBN Publisher's Prefix: 3-7611

Atrium Verlag AG+, Rütistr 4, CH-8030 Zurich Tel: (01) 473035
Subjects: Juveniles, Belles Lettres
Founded: 1936
ISBN Publisher's Prefix: 3-85535

Augustin-Verlag*, Schlatterweg 11, CH-8240 Thayngen Tel: (053) 67131 Telex: 896657 Augu CH
Subjects: Geography, History, Textbooks (especially series of anatomical booklets for schoolchildren)
ISBN Publisher's Prefix: 3-85540

Editions de la **Baconnière** SA, PO Box 185, CH-2017 Boudry-Neuchâtel (Located at: 19 ave du Collège, Boudry-Neuchâtel) Tel: (038) 421004 Cable Add: Baconnière Boudry
Man Dir and all other offices: Marie-Christine Hauser
Orders to: Diffusion Payot (Booksellers), 30 rue des Côtes de Montbenon, CH-1002 Lausanne
Subjects: Belles Lettres, Poetry, Biography, History, Music, Art, Philosophy, Reference, Psychology, Social Science, University Textbooks
1985: 12 titles *1986:* 14 titles *Founded:* 1927
ISBN Publisher's Prefix: 2-8252

H R **Balmer** AG Verlag*, PO Box 1000, CH-6301 Zug (Located at: Neugasse 12, Zug) Tel: (042) 214141 Telex: 868812
Man Dir: Christoph Balmer
Subjects: Local History, Literature, Psychology, Pedagogy
Bookshop: At above address
ISBN Publisher's Prefix: 3-85548

U **Bär** Verlag+, Tödistr 63, CH-8002 Zurich Tel: (01) 2022515
Man Dir: Dr Ulrich Bär; *Permissions:* Marianne Widmer
Subjects: How-to, Art, Reference

Barbare, an imprint of Editions Olizane (qv)

Bargezzi-Verlag AG+*, PO Box 1199, CH-3001 Berne (Located at: Wasserwerkgasse 17, Berne) Tel: (031) 221380 Cable Add: Bargezzi Berne
Man Dir, Editorial, Sales, Publicity, Rights & Permissions: Josef Grübel; *Production:* Werner F Wägli
Subjects: Novels, Religious Literature
Founded: 1948

Basileia Verlag, Missionsstr 21, CH-4003 Basle Tel: (061) 251766
Man Dir: Rudolf Kellenberger
Subjects: Religion, Missionary Work, Third World
ISBN Publisher's Prefix: 3-85555

Basilius Verlag AG*, Güterstr 86, CH-4002 Basle Tel: (061) 228000 Cable Add: Basilius Verlag Telex: 64519
Man Dir: Dr G Haenggi
Subjects: Non-fiction, Juveniles, Art (Paintings), General Science
Founded: 1957
ISBN Publisher's Prefix: 3-85560

Baufachverlag AG, PO Box 6721, CH-8953 Dietikon (Located at: Schöneggstr 102, Dietikon) Tel: (01) 7407677 Telex: 825227 impag
Dir: Willy Kessler
Subject: Building Trade and Architecture (Technical and Specialist Books)
Founded: 1970
ISBN Publisher's Prefix: 3-85565

Benteli Verlag*, PO Box 102, CH-3000 Berne 8 (Located at: Gerechtigkeitsgasse 6, Berne) Tel: (031) 228866 Cable Add: Bag 3000 Berne 8
Man Dir: Ted Schaap (Scapa)
Subjects: General Fiction, Belles Lettres, Poetry, History, Art, Textbooks, Reference
Founded: 1899
ISBN Publisher's Prefix: 3-7165

Benziger AG+*, Bellerivestr 3, CH-8008 Zurich Tel: (01) 2527050 Cable Add: Benzigerag Zurich Telex: 816497
Man Dir: Gerhard Beckmann; *Editorial:* Franz Cavigelli (Fiction and Non-fiction), Dr Brigitta Neumeister-Taroni (Juveniles), Giuliana Broggi Beckmann (Foreign Books); *Rights & Permissions:* Elsbeth Schneiter; *Production:* Tatiana Wagenbach; *Advertising:* Sonja Berger; *Sales Dir:* Lieselotte Meyer
Branch Off: Benziger Verlag, Federal Republic of Germany (qv)
Subjects: General Fiction & Non-fiction, Religion, Juveniles
Founded: 1792
ISBN Publisher's Prefix: 3-545

Bergh und Bergh Verlagsanstalt GmbH, Zugerstr 186, CH-6314 Neuägeri, Zug Tel: (042) 721010/723077 Cable Add: Sebergh CH-6314 Neuägeri Telex: 58378 mpt ch
Man Dir: Dr S E Bergh; *Editorial:* Liselotte Bergh; *Rights & Permissions:* M Zeberli-Ess
Orders to: VVA — Vereinigte Verlagsauslieferung, Postfach 7777, D-4830 Gütersloh 1, Federal Republic of Germany
Associate Company: Bergh Publishing Inc, 276 Fifth Ave, Suite 715, New York, NY 10001, USA
Subjects: General Fiction, Belles Lettres, Mystery Novels, Picture Books, Juveniles
1986: 12 titles *Founded:* 1970

Berichthaus Verlag, Dr Conrad Ulrich, Voltast 43, CH-8044 Zurich Tel: (01) 2526349
Orders to: Orell Füssli Verlag, Postfach, CH-8022 Zurich
Subject: History
ISBN Publisher's Prefix: 3-85572

Berlitz Guides, an imprint of Macmillan SA (qv)

Editions **Beyeler***, Bäumleingasse 9, CH-4001 Basle Tel: (061) 235412
Owner: Ernst Beyeler
Subject: Art
Founded: 1967
ISBN Publisher's Prefix: 3-85575

Verlag **Bibellesebund**+, Römerstr 151, CH-8404 Winterthur Tel: (052) 274801 Scripture Union of Switzerland
Secretary-General: Peter Hoppler; *Man Dir, Sales, Production, Publicity:* Martin Wassmer; *Editorial, Chief Reader, Rights & Permissions:* Wolfgang Steinseifer
Subjects: Christian and Scriptural literature for all ages
Founded: 1930
ISBN Publisher's Prefix: 3-87982

Bibliographisches Institut und FA Brockhaus AG, Postfach, CH-8010 Zurich (Located at: Riedstr 4, CH-8953 Dietikon) Tel: (01) 7412542 Telex: 825240 Bibr CH
Man Dir: Rudolf Hans Fürrer
Parent Company: Bibliographisches Institut und FA Brockhaus AG, Federal Republic of Germany (qv)
Subjects: Philosophy, Linguistics, General Science, Reference Works
Founded: 1967
ISBN Publisher's Prefix: 3-411

Verlag **Bibliophile Drucke** von Josef Stocker AG*, Hasenbergstr 7, CH-8953 Dietikon-Zurich Tel: (01) 7404444
Man Dir: Mr Stocker
Parent Company: Verlag Stocker-Schmid AG (qv)
Associate Company: Urs Graf-Verlag GmbH (qv)
Subjects: Belles Lettres, Poetry, Reference, Historical Manuscript facsimiles
Bookshop: Buchhandlung Stocker-Schmid (at above address)
ISBN Publisher's Prefix: 3-85577

Société **Biblique de Genève**, see La Maison de la Bible

Birkhäuser Verlag AG*, PO Box 133, CH-4010 Basle (Located at: Ringstrasse 39, CH-4106 Therwil-Basle) Tel: (061) 735300 Cable Add: Edita Telex: 63475 Fax: (061) 731427
General Manager: Karl Hauck; *Marketing Manager:* H Jo Pfeiffer; *Editorial Manager:* H P Thür
Parent Company: Springer-Verlag Berlin — Heidelberg — New York — Tokyo GmbH & Co KG, Federal Republic of Germany (qv)
Subsidiary Company: Birkhaeuser Boston Inc, 380 Green St, PO Box 2007, Cambridge, MA 02139, USA
Subjects: Art, Architecture, Engineering, Mathematics, Computers, Natural Science, Pharmacy, Railway Interest, General & Social Science, University Textbooks, Paperbacks, 25 scientific journals
1985: 120 titles *Founded:* 1879
ISBN Publisher's Prefix: 3-7643

Blaukreuz-Verlag Bern, PO Box 1196, Lindenrain 5a, CH-3001 Berne Tel: (031) 235866 Cable Add: Blaukreuzverlag
Man Dir: Eduard Müller
Parent Company: Blaues Kreuz der deutschen Schweiz
Subjects: Belles Lettres, Biography, Religion, Juveniles, Addiction Problems (alcohol, drugs, tobacco), Periodicals
1987: 12 titles *Founded:* 1884
Miscellaneous: Publishes for the Blue Cross health and religious movement. See also Blaukreuz-Verlag Wuppertal, Federal Republic of Germany
ISBN Publisher's Prefix: 3-85580

Les Editions de la Fondation Martin **Bodmer**, PO Box 7, CH-1223 Cologny-Geneva (Located at: 19-21 Route Guignard, Cologny-Geneva) Tel: (022) 362370
Subjects: Philology, Papyrus Editions
ISBN Publisher's Prefix: 3-85682

Bohem Press Kinderbuchverlag+, Lindenstr 32, CH-8008 Zurich Tel: (01) 2527714
Dir: O Bozejovsky v Rawennoff; *Art Dir:* S Zavrel
ISBN Publisher's Prefix: 3-85581

Brain Anatomy Institute, Untere Zollgasse 71, CH-3072 Ostermundigen BE Tel: (031) 319442
Dir, Rights & Permissions: Prof G Pilleri
Subjects: Biology and Behaviour of Marine Animals, Comparative Anatomy, Investigations on Cetacea
Founded: 1969

394 SWITZERLAND

Brunnen-Verlag, Wallstr 6, CH-4002 Basle Tel: (061) 234406 Telex: 912491 Brunnen
Man Dir: Hans-Peter Züblin
Subjects: Religion, Evangelical Literature
Bookshops: Brunnestube, Schmidstr 3, CH-8570 Weinfelden; Buchhandlung Pilgermission, Spalenberg 20, CH-4002 Basle; Buchhandlung Pilgermission, Untere Bahnhofstr 20, CH-9500 Wil; Christliche Buchhandlung, Schmiedgasse 1, CH-6210 Sursee; Christliche Buchhandlung, Herti-Zentrum, CH-6300 Zug; Evangelische Bücherecke, Thundorferstr 39, CH-8500 Frauenfeld; Evangelische Buchhandlung, Haupstr 25, CH-5734 Reinach
Founded: 1921
Miscellaneous: Firm is a branch office of Brunnen-Verlag GmbH, Federal Republic of Germany (qv)
ISBN Publisher's Prefix: 3-7655

Verlag Alfred **Bucheli***, PO Box 146, CH-6301 Zug (Located at: Baarerstr 43, Zug) Tel: (042) 367066 Telex: 868737
Subjects: Car and Motor Cycle Engineering, Flying

Verlag C J **Bücher**, formerly of Lucerne and Munich, now only in Federal Republic of Germany (qv)

Buchhaus AG, see Office du Livre SA

Büchler Grafino AG+, Seftigenstr 310, CH-3084 Wabern-Berne Tel: (031) 548111 Telex: 911934
Man Dir, Rights & Permissions: Dr Rudolf Gysi; *Marketing:* Erich Hirschi
Subjects: Reference, Guidebooks, Local Interest, Art, Educational Materials
1987: 50 titles *Founded:* 1886
ISBN Publisher's Prefix: 3-7170

Hugo **Buchser** SA, 4 Tour de l'Ile, CH-1211 Geneva Tel: (022) 288155 Telex: 429469 hbsa ch Fax: (022) 288258
Man Dir: G M Maillard; *Editor-in-Chief:* Valentin Philibert; *Sales Dir:* Ph Maillard
Subjects: Watches, Jewellery, Technical Trades, Management, Directories, Periodicals
Founded: 1927

Bundesamt für Landestopographie, see Landestopographie

C E E L (Centre Expérimental pour l'Enseignement des Langues)*, 19 rue du Prieure, CH-1202 Geneva Tel: (022) 325893/325612 Telex: 23964 Ceel
Centre for Experimentation and Evaluation of Language Learning Techniques
Man Dir: Nicolas Ferguson
Subject: Language Textbooks
Founded: 1972
ISBN Publisher's Prefix: 2-88047

Cahiers de la Renaissance Vaudoise, PO Box 3414, CH-1002 Lausanne (Located at: Pl Saint-François 5, Lausanne) Tel: (021) 221914
President: Olivier Delacrétaz
Subjects: History, Politics
ISBN Publisher's Prefix: 2-88017

Carta, Lüthi und Ramseier, Haslerstr 21, CH-3008 Berne Tel: (031) 259548 Cable Add: Zeilerag Telex: 32391 (Zeiler AG)
Man Dir, Sales, Rights & Permissions: Heinz Lüthi; *Production:* Ulrich Ramseier
Orders to: Zeiler AG, Gartenstadtstr 5, PO Box 32, Dept Geo-Carta, CH-3098 Köniz-Berne
Subjects: Maps, Atlases
Founded: 1964

Edizioni **Casagrande** SA*, PO Box 1291, CH-6500 Bellinzona (Located at: Via del Bramantino 3, Bellinzona) Tel: (092) 256622 Telex: 846266
Man Dir, Editorial: Libero Casagrande
Subsidiary Companies: Archivio Storico Ticinese (qv); Istituto Editoriale Ticinese (IET) SA (qv); Istituto Grafico Casagrande
Subjects: Literature, Art, Scholarship, History, Art History
Bookshop: Libreria Casagrande, Viale Stazione, CH-6500 Bellinzona
1985: 30 titles *Founded:* 1972
ISBN Publisher's Prefix: 88-7713

Editions Paul **Castella***, CH-1661 Albeuve Tel: (029) 81010
Man Dir & other offices: Paul Castella
Subjects: Literature, Bibliophily, University Textbooks
1985: 5 titles *Founded:* 1963
ISBN Publisher's Prefix: 2-88087

Editions de **Caux**, CH-1824 Caux Tel: (021) 634821
Man Dir, Editorial, Production, Publicity: Chas Piguet
Parent Company: Caux Verlag, Theater und Film AG (qv)
Subjects: Moral Rearmament, Social Sciences, Religion, Theatre, Biographies
Bookshop: Librairie de Caux (at above address)
1985: 1 title *1986:* 1 title *Founded:* 1965
ISBN Publisher's Prefix: 2-88037

Caux Verlag, Theater und Film AG, PO Box 4419, CH-6002 Lucerne Tel: (041) 422213
Subsidiary Company: Editions de Caux (qv)
Subjects: Social Science, Biography, Religion
ISBN Publisher's Prefix: 3-85601

Verlag Bo **Cavefors***, c/o Mandatropa AG, PO Box 5837, CH-8024 Zurich
Man Dir: Bo Cavefors
Subjects: Roman Catholic Theology, General Fiction, Poetry, University Textbooks
ISBN Publisher's Prefix: 3-85593

Cedilivre SA, subsidiary of Editions Foma SA (qv)

Centre Expérimental pour l'Enseignement des Langues, see C E E L

Christiana-Verlag*, CH-8260 Stein am Rhein Tel: (054) 86820/86847 Telex: 76609
Man Dir: Arnold Guillet
Subject: Religion
Founded: 1948
ISBN Publisher's Prefix: 3-7171

Werner **Classen** Verlag, PO Box 683, CH-8027 Zurich (Located at: Splügenstr 10, Zurich) Tel: (01) 2015606 Cable Add: Classenverlag Zurich
Dir: Werner Classen
Subjects: Belles Lettres, Poetry, Music, Juveniles, Psychology, Humour, Technical Paperbacks
Founded: 1945
ISBN Publisher's Prefix: 3-7172

De **Clivo** Press*, Usterstr 126, PO Box, CH-8600 Dübendorf, Zurich Tel: (01) 8201224/8201212 Cable Add: Declivopress Dübendorf Telex: CH 55256 Serco
Proprietor: Dr Walter Amstutz
ISBN Publisher's Prefix: 3-85634

Cosmos-Verlag AG, PO Box 2637, CH-3001 Berne (Located at: Oberer Wehrliweg 5, CH-3074 Muri bei Bern) Tel: (031) 526611 Telex: Cosm 911900
Man Dir: H R Aeberli
Subjects: Tax and Finance Laws, Politics, High-priced Paperbacks, including publications on behalf of the Swiss Institute of Business Management (Schweizerisches Institut für Unternehmungs-führung im Gewerbe)
Founded: 1923
ISBN Publisher's Prefixes: 3-85621, 2-8296

Edizioni Armando **Dadò**, Tipografia Stazione*, Via G A Orelli 29, CH-6600 Locarno Tel: (093) 314802
Man Dir: Armando Dadò
Subjects: Art, History, Literature, Photography, Swiss Italian Costume (all in Italian)

Daphins-Verlag*, Rainweg 2, CH-8704 Herrliberg Tel: (01) 9153639
Man Dir: J Fischlin
Subjects: Belles Lettres, Poetry, Limited Editions
Founded: 1959
ISBN Publisher's Prefix: 3-85631

Editions **Delachaux et Niestlé** SA*, PO Box 44, CH-1000 Lausanne 21 (Located at: 79 route d'Oron, Lausanne) Tel: (021) 333041 Telex: 25822
Man Dir: David Perret; *Sales, Advertising Dir:* Jean-Jacques Lagane; *Permissions:* Yvette Perret
Subsidiary Company: Delachaux Niestlé, Spes, France (qv)
Subjects: Biography, How-to, Philosophy, Reference, Juveniles, Medicine, Pedagogy, Psychology, General & Social Science, Natural Sciences, Educational Materials
Founded: 1860
ISBN Publisher's Prefix: 2-603

Editions André **Delcourt** & Cie+, Rue de la Borde 27, CH-1018 Lausanne Tel: (021) 379772 Telex: 24535 CH Gmdi
Publisher: André Delcourt
Imprints: AD, Delta, Delta et Spes, Spes
Subjects: Architecture, Medicine, Art and Photography, General Literature
1986: 12 titles *Founded:* 1986
ISBN Publisher's Prefix: 2-88161

Delphin Verlag, PO Box 157, CH-8031 Zurich (Located at: Limmatstr 111) Tel: (01) 440733/6 Cable Add: Delphinverlag Zürich Telex: 822791
Man Dir: Oswald Boxer
Parent Company: Delphin Verlag GmbH, Federal Republic of Germany (qv)
Subject: Juveniles, Non-fiction, Paperbacks
Founded: 1962
ISBN Publisher's Prefix: 3-7735

Delta, an imprint of Editions André Delcourt & Cie (qv)

Delta et Spes, an imprint of Editions André Delcourt & Cie (qv)

Desertina Verlag, CH-7180 Disentis Tel: (086) 75441/75442 Cable Add: Desertina Disentis Telex: 856131
Man Dir, Rights & Permissions, Editorial, Production, Publicity: P Condrau; *Sales:* Hans Rechsteiner; *Manager:* Ruedi Henny
Subjects: Reference, Belles Lettres, Art, Children's
Bookshop: Condrau, Disentis
Founded: 1953

Verlag Harri **Deutsch**, Riedstr 2, CH-3600 Thun Tel: (033) 223975
Man Dirs: Harri Deutsch, Dr Anton Reiter
Parent Company: Verlag Harri Deutsch, Federal Republic of Germany (qv)
Subjects: Maths, Physics, Chemistry, Natural Science, Technology, Economics, Dictionaries
ISBN Publisher's Prefix: 3-87144, 3-8171

Diana Verlag AG+*, Rämistr 7, CH-8001 Zurich Tel: (01) 2528850 Telex: 815284 Dian CH
Dir, Publicity Manager: Dagmar Stecher-Konsalik; *Executive:* Rudolf von Siebenthal; *Manager:* Regula Rey-Koller
Parent Company: Hestia-Verlag GmbH, Federal Republic of Germany (qv)
Subject: Belles Lettres, Non-fiction

SWITZERLAND 395

Founded: 1946
ISBN Publisher's Prefix: 3-905414

Didax, an imprint of Editions Foma SA (qv)

Diogenes Verlag AG, Sprecherstr 8, CH-8032 Zurich Tel: (01) 2528111 Cable Add: Diogenesverlag Zurich
Telex: 816383 Fax: (01) 2528407
Man Dirs & Owners: Daniel Keel (Publisher), Rudolf C Bettschart (Administration & Finance); *Editorial:* Winfried Stephan, Doris Brohn, Susanne Schwager; *Media:* Christine Döring; *Sales:* Stefan Fritsch; *Production:* Manfred Neugebauer, Klaus Schröder, Hans Höfliger; *Rights & Permissions:* Marianne Liggenstorfer
Subjects: Fiction, Art, Paperbacks, Pocket Books, Children's Books
Founded: 1953
ISBN Publisher's Prefix: 3-257

Doulos Verlag+*, Villa Meridiana, Titlisstr 14, CH-8032 Zurich (Located at: Kirchenweg 5, Zurich) Tel: (01) 2517560/475565 Cable Add: Doulosverlag Zurich
Telex: 58761 Deag CH
Proprietor, Man Dir: Dr Wolfgang M Metz
Associate Company: Leonis Verlag (qv)
Subjects: Christian Literature
Founded: 1981
ISBN Publisher's Prefix: 3-7158

Drei Eidgenossen Verlag*, Hüegelweg 15, CH-4102 Binningen Tel: (061) 475166
Man Dir: Mr Hosch
Subject: Juveniles
Founded: 1936
ISBN Publisher's Prefix: 3-85643

Droemersche Verlagsanstalt AG*, Stauffacherquai 46, PO Box 670, CH-8021 Zurich Tel: (01) 394214
Subjects: Fiction, Non-fiction, Natural Sciences

Librairie **Droz** SA, PO Box 389, CH-1211 Geneva 12 (Located at: 11 rue Massot, Geneva) Tel: (022) 466666
Man Dir, Rights & Permissions: A Dufour; *Sales Dir:* Miss Gueguen
Subjects: French language publisher of Belles Lettres, Poetry, History, Literature, Reference, Religion, Social Science, University Textbooks
1985: 60 titles *Founded:* 1924
ISBN Publisher's Prefix: 2-600

Henry-Robert **Dufour**, 7 ave du Théâtre, CH-1005 Lausanne Tel: (021) 233062/233070 Telex: 450186 Hrd
Subjects: French language publisher of General Non-fiction, Fine Arts, Technical, Industrial, Belles Lettres, Education

Gottlieb **Duttweiler** Institute for Economic & Social Studies, CH-8803 Rüschlikon-Zurich Tel: (01) 7240020 Cable Add: Green Meadow Telex: 826510 Fax: (01) 4613739
Subjects: Future Studies, Social Science, Economics
Bookshop: Verlagsbuchhandlung GDI (at above address)
Founded: 1963

Dynamis Verlag, PO Box 256, CH-8280 Kreuzlingen (Located at: Brückenstr 22, Kreuzlingen) Tel: (072) 727781 Cable Add: Dynamis
Man Dir: David Tschudi
Subject: Religion
Bookshops: Christliche Buchhandlung, Hauptstr 7, CH-8280 Kreuzlingen Tel: (072) 727781; Christliche Buchhandlung, Bernstr 49, CH-4852 Rothrist Tel: (062) 443225; Dynamis Bücher, Heimstätte SPM, CH-6376 Emmetten Tel: (041) 645588
Founded: 1973

Editions l'**Eau Vive***, PO Box 2574, CH-1211 Geneva 2 (Located at: 10 rue de Fribourg, Geneva) Tel: (022) 329847
Man Dir: Rolande Gloor
Subjects: Religion, Biography
Founded: 1960
ISBN Publisher's Prefix: 2-88035

Ecart Publications, PO Box 253, CH-1211 Geneva 1 (Located at: 6 rue Plantamour, Geneva) Tel: (022) 311400
Man Dirs: John M Armleder, Patrick Lucchini; *Editorial:* John Armleder
Subsidiary Companies: Leathern Wing Scribble Press, The Geneva Pond Bubbles
Associate Companies: Centre d'Art Contemporain, Palais Wilson, CH-1201 Geneva; Marika Malacorda Editions (qv)
Subjects: Art (especially New Trends), Photography, Video, Cinema
Bookshop: Ecart Books, Librairie, 6 rue Plantamour, PO Box 253, CH-1211 Geneva 1
Founded: 1969

Eco-Verlags AG, Langstr 187, Postfach, CH-8021 Zurich Tel: (01) 2428634
Man Dir: Verena Stettler
Imprints: Neue Szene, Literatheke
Subjects: Non-fiction, City Guides, Literature
Founded: 1976
ISBN Publisher's Prefix: 3-85647

Editeurs Associés SA*, 5 rue César-Soulié, PO Box 84, CH-1260 Nyon Tel: (022) 612676 Telex: Buco 22886 Nyon
Man Dir: F Gendreau
Subjects: Fiction, History
Founded: 1966
ISBN Publisher's Prefix: 2-8291

Editions Universitaires SA (Universitätsverlag)*, Pérolles 42, CH-1700 Fribourg Tel: (037) 246812
Man Dir, Publicity: Anton Scherer
Parent Company: Imprimerie et Librairies Saint-Paul SA (at above address)
Associate Companies: Editions Saint-Paul (qv); Editions de la Sarine (at above address)
Subjects: Literature, History, Music, Art, Philosophy, Reference, Religions, Theology, Psychology, Economic and Political Sciences, Secondary and University Textbooks, Medicine, Ethnology, Law
Bookshop: Librairie et Edition de la Suisse Romande
ISBN Publisher's Prefixes: 3-7278 (German books), 2-8271 (French books)

Edito-Service SA*, PO Box 56, CH-1211 Geneva 6 (Located at: 4 chemin des Vergers, Geneva) Tel: (022) 357233 Cable Add: Editoservice Geneva Telex: 23640 Edito Ch
Dir, General Manager: Julian Ormond; *Production:* René Gioria; *Publishing Dir:* Christian Gallimard; *Rights, Sales:* Anne Hauser-de Coulon
Subjects: General Fiction, Belles Lettres, Poetry, Biography, Nature, History, How-to, Music, Art, Religion, Juveniles, Medicine, Psychology, General Science, Educational Materials, Co-editions in all languages

Editions **Eiselé** SA, PO Box 154, CH-1008 Prilly/Lausanne (Located at: 17 route de Cossonay, Prilly/Lausanne) Tel: (021) 256324
Subjects: Arts, Education, Popular Science, Juveniles, Belles Lettres, Textbooks
ISBN Publisher's Prefix: 2-88002

Verlag **Eisenbahn**, Gut Vorhard, CH-5234 Villigen AG Tel: (056) 441595 Cable Add: Verlageisenbahn Villigen
Man Dir: Rose Jeanmaire; *Editorial:* Jeannine dit-Quartier
Parent Company: Verlag Eisenbahn, Wallstr 7, D-7890 Waldshut, Federal Republic of Germany
Subjects: Railways, Tramcars, Ships, Model Railways, Toys of the Past
Bookshop: Railwaybokkshop (at above address)
1985: 5 titles *1986:* 6 titles *Founded:* 1866
Miscellaneous: Company acts as distribution centre for rail publications of every country, world-wide
ISBN Publisher's Prefix: 3-85649

Emmentaler Druck AG, PO Box 2502, CH-3550 Langnau (Located at: Dorfstr 5, Langnau) Tel: (035) 21911
Man Dir, Sales: H R Bodenmann; *Editorial, Publicity:* Markus F Rubli
Subjects: Dialect, Fiction, Photographic, Periodicals
1985: 2 titles *1986:* 6 titles *Founded:* 1845
ISBN Publisher's Prefix: 3-85654

Erker-Galerie AG*, Franz Larese und Jürg Janett, Gallustr 32, CH-9000 St Gallen Tel: (071) 227979/233607
Subject: Modern Art, Literature
Founded: 1964

Edition **Erpf** by Neptun+, PO Box 1383, CH-3001 Berne Tel: (037) 711385 Cable Add: bucherpf
Man Dir: Hans Erpf
Subjects: Contemporary Literature, Caricature and Cartoons, Current Topics, Monographs, Bernese themes
Founded: 1979
ISBN Publisher's Prefix: 3-256

Espaces Photographiques, an imprint of Editions Olizane (qv)

Eulenburg Edition GmbH, now Edition Kunzelmann GmbH (qv)

Europa Verlag AG, Rämistr 5, CH-8001 Zurich Tel: (01) 471629 Cable Add: Europaverlag Zurich Telex: 816534 fere ch
Man Dir: Emmie Oprecht
Associate Company: Verlag Oprecht, Zurich (Theatrical)
Subjects: History, Politics, Philosophy, Art, Belles Lettres
Founded: 1933
Miscellaneous: Distributor for UNESCO, Paris
ISBN Publisher's Prefix: 3-85665

Europabuch AG, see Bergh (Edition Sven Erik Bergh im Europabuch AG)

Evangelischer Schriften Verlag Schwengeler, see Schwengeler (Switzerland) and Telos (Federal Republic of Germany)

Farb-Dia-Archiv Edmond Van Hoorick, see Verlag Van Hoorick

Editions Pierre Marcel **Favre***, PO Box 3569, CH-1002 Lausanne (Located at: rue de Bourg 29, Lausanne) Tel: (021) 221717 Cable Add: Favrepublisa Lausanne Telex: Fav 24073
Man Dir: P M Favre
Subjects: Current Affairs, Politics, Sport, Ecology, Illustrated Editions, Belles Lettres, Fiction
1985: 200 titles *1986:* 250 titles *Founded:* 1975
ISBN Publisher's Prefix: 2-8289

Editions François **Feij**, pl de l'Eglise, CH-1166 Perroy Tel: (021) 8254675

J **Fischlin**, see Daphins-Verlag

SWITZERLAND

Maurice et Pierre **Foetisch** SA, PO Box 2793, CH-1002 Lausanne (Located at: 6 rue de Bourg, CH-1002 Lausanne) Tel: (021) 239444/5 Telex: 24227
Man Dir and other offices: Jean-Claude Foetisch
Associate Company: Disco SA
Subjects: Music, Records, Pianos, TV, Educational, Textbooks (especially ASSIMIL Language Teaching Courses)
Founded: 1947

Editions **Foma** SA*, Ave de Longemalle 5, PO Box 226, CH-1020 Renens-Lausanne Tel: (021) 351361 Telex: CH-Cedil 25416
Man Dir, Editorial: J-L Peverelli; *Sales:* M Sculati; *Publicity:* Ann-Mari Mingard; *Rights & Permissions:* F Buhler
Subsidiary Companies: 5 Continents, Cedilivre SA
Imprints: Foma, Didax, Cedilivre
Subjects: Cinema, Photography, Psychology, Secondary and Primary Textbooks, Yoga, General Literature
Bookshop: Didax
Founded: 1948
ISBN Publisher's Prefix: 2-88003

Fortuna Finanz-Verlag AG+, Postfach 52, CH-8123 Ebmatingen/ZH Tel: (01) 9803622
Man Dir: F Borner
Subject: Finance
Founded: 1953
ISBN Publisher's Prefix: 3-85684

Foto und Schmalfilm-Verlag (Gemsberg-Verlag), PO Box 778, CH-8401 Winterthur (Located at: Garnmarkt 10, Winterthur) Tel: (052) 857171 Cable Add: Gemsberg-Verlag Telex: 896417
Production: Pius Schwager
Parent Company: Ziegler Druck- und Verlags-AG (Proprietors)
Subjects: Photography, Film, Video
Founded: 1950
ISBN Publisher's Prefix: 3-85701

Francke Verlag, PO Box 1445, CH-3001 Berne (Located at: Neuengasse 43, Berne) Tel: (031) 221715 Cable Add: Frankeverlag Bern
Man Dir: Dr Carl L Lang
Subjects: Germanic, Romance and English Language Studies, History, Philology, Philosophy, Psychology, Reference, Periodicals
Bookshop: Buchhandlung A Francke AG (qv under Major Booksellers)
Founded: 1831
ISBN Publisher's Prefix: 3-317

Fretz Verlag+*, Mühlebachstr 54, Postfach, CH-8021 Zurich Tel: (01) 2521449 Telex: 58897 frez
Publicity Manager: Walter Köpfli
Subjects: Fine and Applied Arts, Illustrated Books, Fiction
Founded: 1860
ISBN Publisher's Prefix: 3-85692

Fretz und Wasmuth Verlag AG*, Bellerivestr 5, CH-8008 Zurich Tel: (01) 323585
Subjects: Archaeology, Architecture, Civil Engineering, Fine & Applied Arts, Illustrated Books
Founded: 1927
ISBN Publisher's Prefix: 3-7180

Frobenius AG, Spalenring 31, CH-4012 Basle Tel: (061) 437610
Publicity: Otto Rymann
Subjects: History, Law, Literature (especially local)
ISBN Publisher's Prefix: 3-85695

Orell **Füssli** Verlag, see Orell

G S Verlag Basle, PO Box 326, CH-4003 Basle (Located at: Petersgraben 29, CH-4003 Basle) Tel: (061) 253514
Man Dir: Dr B Trachsler
Branch Offs: Scheuermattweg 4, CH-3000 Berne 23 Tel: (031) 450777; PO Box 16, CH-8703 Erlenbach Tel: (01) 9105313
Subjects: General Fiction, Belles Lettres, Biography, History, Music, Art, Juveniles, Low-Priced Paperbacks
Founded: 1889
ISBN Publisher's Prefix: 3-7185

Rudolf **Geering** Verlag, a subsidiary of Philosophisch-Anthroposophischer Verlag am Goetheanum

Gemsberg-Verlag, see Foto und Schmalfilm-Verlag

Genfer Bibelgesellschaft, see Maison de la Bible

Pierre **Genillard** Editeur, 9 ch de Primerose, CH-1007 Lausanne Tel: (021) 264632
Subjects: Religion, Philosophy, Psychology, Naturism, Esotericism, Rosicrucian Thought
Founded: 1949
ISBN Publisher's Prefix: 2-88005

Georg et Cie SA*, Librairies-Editeurs, 21 rue de la Corraterie, CH-1211 Geneva 11 Tel: (022) 216633 Telex: 423985
Man Dir: Jacques Matile
Subjects: Medical Science, Administration, Law, Secondary & Primary Textbooks, Religion, Philosophy, Psychology, Economics, Statistics, Social & Natural Sciences, Politics, Military Subjects, Languages, Literature, Geography, Ethnology, Travel, History
Bookshop: See under Major Booksellers
Founded: 1857
ISBN Publisher's Prefix: 2-8257

Georgi Publishing Company/Editions Georgi+, CH-1813 Saint-Saphorin Tel: (021) 529508 Cable Add: Georgedi S Saphorin Lavaux
Owner/President: Heinz Georgi
Subjects: Scientific and technical books and journals in Computer Science, Civil Engineering, Electrical Engineering and Electronics, Mechanical Engineering, Metallurgy (publications in English, French or German, or a combination of languages)
Founded: 1975
ISBN Publisher's Prefix: 2-604

Globi Verlag AG*, Eichstr 23, CH-8045 Zurich Tel: (01) 4634135 Cable Add: Globiverlag Zurich Telex: 813282
Man Dir: Emil Herzog
Subjects: Juveniles (especially illustrated books), Comics
Founded: 1944
ISBN Publisher's Prefix: 3-85703

Victor **Goldschmidt** Verlagsbuchhandlung, Mostackerstr 17, CH-4051 Basle Tel: (061) 236565
Subjects: German-Judaica, Hebraica
Founded: 1902
ISBN Publisher's Prefix: 3-85705

André et Pierre **Gonin**, Editions d'Art, 2 rue Etraz, CH-1003 Lausanne Tel: (021) 226492/229996
Subject: Art
Founded: 1941
ISBN Publisher's Prefix: 2-88016

Gotthelf-Verlag, Badenerstr 69, CH-8026 Zurich Tel: (01) 2428155 Cable Add: Comelivres Telex: 912491 cub
Man Dir: Max Hirt
Associate Company: CVB Buch und Druck (at above address)
Subjects: Religion, Juveniles
1985: 4 titles *1986:* 6 titles *Founded:* 1928
ISBN Publisher's Prefix: 3-85706

Grafino-Verlag, Grafische Betriebe AG*, PO Box 2741, CH-3001 Berne (Located at: Maulbeerstr 10, Berne) Tel: (031) 252911 Telex: 32255
Man Dir: Markus Rubli
Subjects: Specialist Agricultural Texts, Swiss and Berne Regional Interest, General Non-fiction
Founded: 1919
Miscellaneous: Book publishing branch of Grafino Grafische Betriebe AG (Grafino Printing House), formerly Verbandsdruckerei-Betadruck
ISBN Publisher's Prefix: 3-7280

Editions du **Grand-Pont**, Jean-Pierre Laubscher, 2 pl Bel-Air, CH-1003 Lausanne Tel: (021) 223222
Founded: 1971
ISBN Publisher's Prefix: 2-88148

Editions du **Griffon***, PO Box 536, CH-2000 Neuchâtel (Located at: 17 Faubourg du Lac, Neuchâtel) Tel: (038) 252204
Chairman: Dr Marcel Joray
Subject: Modern Art (especially sculpture and the plastic arts generally)
Founded: 1944
ISBN Publisher's Prefix: 2-88006

Editions François **Grounauer***, 1 rue du Belvédère, CH-1203 Geneva 1 Tel: (022) 447948
Subjects: History, Politics, Social Sciences
Founded: 1972
Miscellaneous: Formerly known as Editions Adversaires
ISBN Publisher's Prefix: 2-88076

Th **Gut** & Co Verlag*, Seestr 86, CH-8712 Stäfa Tel: (01) 9281101 Telex: 875668
Publicity: Ulrich Gut
Subjects: Swiss and Regional History and Culture, Politics
ISBN Publisher's Prefix: 3-85717

Gute Schriften Verein, see GS Verlag

Sumus Verlag Jutta **Gütermann**, see Sumus

Habegger Verlag, Gutenbergstr 1, CH-4552 Derendingen-Solothurn Tel: (065) 411151 Telex: 934744
Chief Executive: Hans Ulrich Habegger; *Dir:* Paul Meier; *Production Manager:* Felix Luterbacher; *Editorial Dir:* Dr Elisabeth Kully; *Marketing:* Josef Baumgartner; *Sales:* Annelis Dzélalija
Subjects: Sports, Fitness, Sports Medicine, Photography and Films, Poetry and Fiction in Dialect, Children's, Archaeology
Founded: 1900
ISBN Publisher's Prefix: 3-85723

Haffmans Verlag AG, Postfach, CH-8057 Zurich (Located at: Hubenstr 19, Zurich) Tel: (01) 414133 Cable Add: Haffmans Verlag
Man Dirs: Gerd Haffmans (Publisher), Urs Jakob (Finance, Production); *Editorial:* Thomas Bodmer; *Sales:* Peter Haag; *Production Assistant:* Susanne Haffmans; *Media:* Monica Iseli; *Rights & Permissions:* Elisabeth Mühlemann
Subjects: Fiction, Contemporary German and Translated Literature, Classics, Children's, Cartoons, Literary Periodical
1986: 33 titles *1987:* 46 titles *Founded:* 1982
ISBN Publisher's Prefix: 3-251

Berchtold **Haller** Verlag*, PO Box 15, CH-3000 Berne 7 (Located at: Nägeligasse 9, Berne) Tel: (031) 222583 Cable Add: BEG Berne

General Manager: Alfred Gyger; *Sales Manager:* Peter Schranz
Subjects: Religion, Juveniles
1985: 4 titles *Founded:* 1848
ISBN Publisher's Prefix: 3-85570

Hallwag Verlag AG, Nordring 4, CH-3001 Berne Tel: (031) 423131 Cable Add: Hallwag Berne Telex: 912661 Hawa CH
President: Otto Erich Wagner; *Editorial, Permissions:* Dr K Weibel; *Sales:* Jürg Burri
Branch Off: Hallwag Verlagsgesellschaft mbH, Federal Republic of Germany (qv)
Subjects: General Non-fiction, Travel, History, How-to, Art, Culinary Arts, Horses, General Science, Maps
Founded: 1912
ISBN Publisher's Prefix: 3-444

Harwood Academic Publishers GmbH, Poststr 22, CH-7000 Chur
Dir: Martin B Gordon; *Executive Vice-President:* Patricia J Bardi; *Editorial Dir:* Philip Manor; *Marketing Dir:* John A Lewis; *Rights & Permissions:* Joan Neville
Associate Company: Gordon and Breach Science Publishers Ltd, UK (qv)
Branch Off: (USA Editorial) Harwood Academic Publishers, PO Box 786, Cooper Station, New York, NY 10276, USA
Subjects: Social Sciences, Chemistry, Physics, Engineering, Business and Economics, Music, Life Sciences, Mathematics, Earth Sciences, Computer Science, Periodicals
Founded: 1978
ISBN Publisher's Prefix: 3-7186

Paul **Haupt** Bern, Falkenplatz 14, CH-3001 Berne Tel: (031) 232425 Cable Add: Hauptbern Telex: 912906 haupt ch
Man Dir: Dr Max Haupt; *Production:* Erich Hauri; *Sales, Publicity, Advertising:* Matthias Haupt; *Permissions:* Annemarie Streit
Subjects: Business Economics, General and Social Science, University, Secondary and Primary Textbooks, Pedagogy, Handicrafts, How-to, Music, Art, Educational Materials
Bookshops: Falkenpl 14, Berne; Spitalgasse 26, Berne; Höheweg 11, Interlaken
1986: 20 titles *Founded:* 1906
ISBN Publisher's Prefix: 3-258

Das **Haus** der Bibel, see Maison de la Bible

Heilpädagogisches Institut der Universität Freiburg, Petrus-Kanisius-Gasse 21, CH-1700 Fribourg Tel: (037) 219740
Therapeutic Pedagogy Institute of Fribourg University
Editor: Prof Dr Urs Haeberlin
Subjects: Special Education, Diagnostic Therapy

Helbing und Lichtenhahn Verlag AG, Freie Str 82, CH-4051 Basle Tel: (061) 231116
Dir: Hans Christof Sauerländer; *Procuring Editor:* Hans Durrer
Associate Company: Sauerländer AG (qv)
Subjects: History, Law, Textbooks
Founded: 1822
ISBN Publisher's Prefix: 3-7190

Arts Graphiques **Héliographia** SA*, PO Box 1060, CH-1001 Lausanne (Located at: 2 ave de Tivoli, Lausanne) Tel: (021) 204151 Telex: 24060
Man Dir: Philippe Luquiens

Verlag **Helvetica Chimica** Acta, Postfach, CH-4002 Basle Tel: (061) 376652
President: Dr G Ohloff; *Editor:* Prof E Heilbronner; *Publicity:* Mrs R Stockbauer
Parent Company: Schweizerische Chemische Gesellschaft (at above address)
Subject: Chemistry
ISBN Publisher's Prefix: 3-85727

Herder AG*, Malzgasse 18, CH-4002 Basle 21 Tel: (061) 230818 Telex: 64358
Associate Companies: Verlag Herder GmbH & Co KG, Verlag A G Ploetz GmbH & Co KG, Herder und Herder GmbH (all in Federal Republic of Germany, qqv); Verlag Herder & Co, Austria (qv); Herder Editrice e Libreria, Italy (qv); Editorial Herder SA, Spain (qv)
ISBN Publisher's Prefix: 3-906371

Dr C J **Hogrefe**, see Verlag für Psychologie

Verlag Van **Hoorick**+*, Farb-Dia-Archiv Edmond Van Hoorick, Postfach, CH-8805 Richterswil/ZH Tel: (01) 7846214
Manager: Edmond Van Hoorick
Subjects: Juvenile Picture Books, Meditation Practice, Picture Books of Switzerland, Germany, the Caribbean

Hans **Huber** AG, Medical Publisher and Bookseller, Länggass-Str 76, Postfach, CH-3000 Berne 9 Tel: (031) 242533 Cable Add: Huberverlag Bern Telex: 32516
Board Dir: Max Pauli; *Board Delegate:* Dr C J Hogrefe; *Sales:* Felix Grünig; *Advertising:* Peter Köhli
Subjects: Medicine, Psychology, Pedagogy
Bookshops: See under Major Booksellers
Founded: 1927
ISBN Publisher's Prefix: 3-456

Verlag **Huber & Co AG**, Postfach, CH-8500 Frauenfeld Tel: (054) 271111 Telex: 896383
Man Dir, Publisher: Urs Luedi; *Production:* Peter Guarisco; *Rights & Permissions:* Urs Rueetschi
Subjects: History, Politics, Folklore, Linguistics, Art, Forestry, Agriculture, Thurgau Canton Interest
Bookshop: Buchhandlung Huber & Co AG, Freiestr 8, CH-8500 Frauenfeld
Founded: 1809
ISBN Publisher's Prefix: 3-7193

Hüthig und Wepf Verlag*, Eisengasse 5, CH-4001 Basle Tel: (061) 257574 Cable Add: Wepfco Telex: 0045-62027
Associate Companies: Verlag Wepf & Co AG (qv); Dr Alfred Hüthig Verlag GmbH, Federal Republic of Germany (qv)
Subsidiary Company: Hüthig & Wepf Verlag, Room 213, 611 Broadway, New York, NY 10012, USA
Branch Off: Hüthig und Wepf, im Weiher 10, D-6900 Heidelberg, Federal Republic of Germany
Subjects: Macromolecular Chemistry and Related Subjects, Periodicals
ISBN Publisher's Prefix: 3-85739

I N F E L (Informationsstelle für Elektrizitätsanwendung)*, PO Box 7340, CH-8023 Zurich (Located at: Bahnhofplatz 9, Zurich) Tel: (01) 2110355
Subject: Electrical Engineering
ISBN Publisher's Prefix: 3-85651

Editions **Ides et Calendes** SA+, Evole 19, CH-2001 Neuchâtel Tel: (038) 253861 Cable Add: Idecal
Man Dir: André Rosselet; *Administration Chief:* Alain Bouret
Subjects: Art, Belles Lettres, Law, University Textbooks
Founded: 1941
ISBN Publisher's Prefix: 2-8258

Imba Verlag, PO Box 1052, CH-1701 Fribourg (Located at: 3 ave de Beauregard, Fribourg) Tel: (037) 241341 Cable Add: Kanisiuswerk Fribourg
Man Dir: Martin Stieger; *Production Manager:* Peter Ledergerber
Associate Company: Kanisius Verlag (qv)
Subjects: Social Science, Religion
ISBN Publisher's Prefix: 3-85740

SWITZERLAND 397

Impressum Verlag AG*, Schöneggstr 102, CH-8153 Dietikon Tel: (01) 7407673
ISBN Publisher's Prefix: 3-7200

Verlag **Industrielle Organisation**, Zürichbergstr 18, Postfach, CH-8028 Zurich Tel: (01) 470800
Man Dir, Publicity: Dr Roland H Scheuchzer; *Sales, Advertising Dir:* Gerhard Labitzke
Subjects: Management and Organization, Personnel Studies, Problem-Solving Activities, Product Planning, Marketing, Periodical
1986: 12 titles
ISBN Publisher's Prefix: 3-85743

Informationsstelle für Elektrizitätsanwendung, see INFEL

Institut Universitaire de Hautes Etudes Internationales, PO Box 36, CH-1211 Geneva 21 (Located at: 132 rue de Lausanne, Geneva) Tel: (022) 311730
The Graduate Institute of International Studies
Subjects: Politics, International Law, History, Economics

Inter Documentation Co AG, Poststr 14, CH-6300 Zug Tel: (042) 214974 Cable Add: Indoco Zug Telex: 78819 Zugal
President: Dr L Vieli; *Publicity:* John A Traksel
Subsidiary Company: Inter Documentation Co BV, Hoge Woerd 151-153, 2311 HK Leiden, Netherlands
Subjects: Microfiche/microfilm editions of rare scholarly publications, especially in connection with Slavic and Oriental studies, African, Latin American, Middle Eastern and Jewish Studies, Development Plans, History, Musicology, Anthropology, Natural Sciences, Art, Social Sciences, Religion, Language, Political Science, Human Rights, Law
Founded: 1957
ISBN Publisher's Prefix: 3-3300

Interavia SA, 86 ave Louis Casaï, CH-1216 Cointrin, Geneva Tel: (022) 980505 Telex: 211122 itav ch Fax: (022) 983138
Dirs: K Regelin, J Parvex, R H Gasser
Parent Company: Jane's Publishing Company Ltd, UK (qv)
Subjects: Aerospace and Defence (directories and periodicals)
Founded: 1933
ISBN Publisher's Prefix: 3-85749

Edition **Interfrom**, PO Box 5005, CH-8022 Zurich (Located at: Scheideggstr 78) Tel: (01) 2020900
Publisher: Leo V Fromm; *Executive Vice-President:* Annette Harms-Hunold; *Sales Manager:* Annegret Busch; *Public Relations:* Ursula Malzahn
Associate Companies: Verlag A Fromm GmbH & Co, Federal Republic of Germany (qv); Fromm International Publishing Corp, 560 Lexington Ave, New York, NY 10022, USA
Subjects: Politics, Economics, Culture and Education, Society, Nature and the Environment, Periodicals
ISBN Publisher's Prefix: 3-7201

Iris Verlag AG*, CH-3177 Laupen Tel: (031) 947744
ISBN Publisher's Prefix: 3-85751

Istituto Editoriale Ticinese (IET) SA*, Via del Bramantino 3, CH-6500 Bellinzona Tel: (092) 256624 Telex: 846266
Man Dir: Libero Casagrande
Parent Company: Edizioni Casagrande SA (qv)
Subjects: Fiction, Poetry, Essays
1985: 6 titles *Founded:* 1900
ISBN Publisher's Prefix: 88-7713

R **Jeanmaire** & Co, see Verlag Eisenbahn

Johannes Verlag, Arnold Böcklinstr 42, CH-4051 Basle
Chairman: Dr Hans Urs von Balthasar
Orders to: Paulinus-Verlag, Postfach 30 40, Fleischstr 62-65, D-5500 Trier, Federal Republic of Germany
Subjects: Philosophy, Religion, Spirituality
Founded: 1947
ISBN Publisher's Prefix: 3-265

Juris Druck & Verlag AG, PO Box 816, CH-8039 Zurich (Located at: Basteipl 5, Zurich) Tel: (01) 2117727
Man Dir: Markus Christen
Subjects: History, Art, Philosophy, Religion, Medicine, Law, Psychology, Engineering, General & Social Science
Bookshop: Juris Druck & Verlag AG (at above address)
Founded: 1945
ISBN Publisher's Prefix: 3-260

K B V, see Kinderbuchverlag KBV Luzern AG

Kanisius Verlag, 3 ave du Beauregard, CH-1701 Fribourg Tel: (037) 241341 Cable Add: Kanisiuswerk Fribourg
Man Dir, Publicity: Martin Stieger; *Production Manager:* Peter Ledergerber
Associate Company: Imba Verlag (qv)
Subject: Religion
Founded: 1898
ISBN Publisher's Prefix: 3-85764

S **Karger** AG, Medical and Scientific Publishers+, Allschwilerstr 10, Postfach, CH-4009 Basle Tel: (061) 390880 Cable Add: Kargermed Basle Telex: CH 962652
Man Dir: Dr Thomas Karger; *Publicity:* H Blattner
Subsidiary Companies: Karger Libri AG (bookshop and subscriptions), Petersgraben 31, Postfach, CH-4009 Basle; S Karger GmbH, Federal Republic of Germany (qv); Katakura Libri Inc (bookshop and subscriptions), 36-9 Hongo 3-chome, Bunkyo-ku, Tokyo 113, Japan
Imprints: S Karger (Basle, London, Munich, New Delhi, New York, Paris, Singapore, Sydney, Tokyo)
Subjects: Reference, Medicine, Psychology, University Textbooks, Medical and Scientific Periodicals
Bookshop: Karger Libri AG, Petersgraben 31, Postfach, CH-4009 Basle
Founded: 1890
Miscellaneous: S Karger Literary Agency in North America: S Karger Publishers Inc, 79 Fifth Ave, New York, NY 10003, USA
ISBN Publisher's Prefix: 3-8055

Verlag Ramòn F **Keller**, now Editions Ariston Verlag (qv)

Verlag Walter **Keller**, Lehmenweg 5, CH-4143 Dornach Tel: (061) 722755
Man Dir: Walter Keller
Subjects: Picture Books, Juvenile, Art, Geometry
Founded: 1969

Kinderbuchverlag KBV Luzern AG+, Postfach, CH-6000 Lucerne 6 (Located at: Grendelstr 15, CH-6004 Lucerne) Tel: (041) 516861 Telex: 868238 kibu ch
Man Dir: Jürgen Braunschweiger; *Editorial and Foreign Rights Dir:* Heidrun Diltz; *Sales, Administration, Publicity:* Sauerländer AG (qv)
Associate Company: Sauerländer AG (qv)
Subjects: Juvenile Fiction and Non-fiction, Nature, Animals (with photographic illustrations)
Founded: 1979
ISBN Publisher's Prefix: 3-276

Kindler Verlag AG*, Nelkenstr 20, CH-8006 Zurich Tel: (01) 3633007 Cable Add: Kindlerverlag Zurich Telex: 045 57608
Publishers: Helmut Kindler, Nina Kindler
Subjects: Encyclopaedias, Psychology, Anthropology

Editions **Kister** SA*, 33 quai Wilson, CH-1211 Geneva 21 Tel: (022) 315000
Subjects: General Non-fiction, Mathematics, Physics, Music, Games and Sports, Reference Books
ISBN Publisher's Prefix: 3-463

Verlag **Klett und Balmer** & Co, PO Box 4464, CH-6304 Zug (Located at: Chamerstr 12a, Zug) Tel: (042) 214131/32
Man Dirs: Chr Balmer, Michael Klett, Roland Klett, Dr Thomas Klett; *Editorial, Sales, Publicity, Production, Rights & Permissions:* H Egli
Associate Companies: Dialog Verlags AG, CH-3084 Wabern; Ernst Klett Verlag, Federal Republic of Germany (qv)
Subjects: School Textbooks, Teachers' Training, Educational Politics in Switzerland, Adult Education, Science, Philosophy
1985: 14 titles *Founded:* 1967
ISBN Publisher's Prefix: 3-264

Kobersche Verlagsbuchhandlung AG, PO Box 2481, CH-3001 Berne (Located at: Nordring Dammweg 9, Berne) Tel: (031) 406393
Man Dir, Sales, Publicity: Harald F Blum
Subjects: Religious/Philosophical (especially the teaching texts of Bô Yin Râ)
Founded: 1926
ISBN Publisher's Prefix: 3-85767

Kolumbus-Verlag, Muhlebuhl 10, CH-5737 Menziken Tel: (064) 711370 Cable Add: Vdb Menziken
Man Dir: Dr G van den Bergh
Subjects: Linguistics, Philosophy, School Textbooks (languages)

Galerie **Kornfeld** & Co, Laupenstr 41, CH-3008 Berne Tel: (031) 254673 Cable Add: Artus
Proprietor: Eberhard W Kornfeld
Subjects: Fine Arts (15th-20th centuries); 19th-20th Century Illustrated Books
Founded: 1864
ISBN Publisher's Prefix: 3-85773

Kossodo Verlag AG*, 27a chemin des Hutins, CH-1247 Anières/Geneva Tel: (022) 512247/511156
Dir: Martha Düssel
Subjects: Art Books, De Luxe Limited Editions
Founded: 1956
ISBN Publisher's Prefix: 3-7208

Verlag Karl **Krämer** & Co, Mainaustr 12, CH-8008 Zurich Tel: (01) 2528454
Man Dir: Karl H Kramer
Associate Company: Karl Krämer Verlag GmbH und Co, Federal Republic of Germany (qv)
Subject: Architecture
ISBN Publisher's Prefix: 3-85774

Verlag René **Kramer** AG+*, PO Box 170, CH-6906 Lugano 6 (Located at: Via del Tiglio 33, Lugano) Tel: (091) 518941 Cable Add: Edikramer
Man Dir, Publicity: René Kramer
Subjects: Cookery, International Co-productions
Founded: 1962

Verlag und Druckerei G **Krebs** AG, St Alban-Vorstadt 56, Postfach, CH-4006 Basle Tel: (061) 239723
Dirs: Franz Käser, Willy Kohler; *Manager:* André Horisberger
Orders to: Gesellschaft für Volkskunde (at above address)
Imprint: Schweizerischen Gesellschaft für Volkskunde (Swiss Folklore Society)
Subjects: Folklore Studies, Swiss Handicrafts, Song Books, Periodicals
Founded: 1897
ISBN Publisher's Prefix: 3-85775

Kümmerly und Frey (Geographischer Verlag)*, Hallerstr 6-10, CH-3001 Berne Tel: (031) 235111 Cable Add: Kümmerlyfrey Telex: 32860
Man Dir: W Frey; *Dirs:* Dr B Peters-Kümmerly, Toni Kaufmann, E Zweidler
Associate Companies: J Fink-Kümmerly und Frey Verlag GmbH, Federal Republic of Germany (qv); Kümmerley und Frey Verlags GmbH, Austria (qv)
Subjects: Geography, Maps, Topography, Photobooks
Founded: 1852
ISBN Publisher's Prefix: 3-259

Imprimerie Albert **Kündig** SA*, 49 chemin de l'Etang, CH-1219 Chatelaine/Geneva Tel: (022) 966013
Manager: Georges Naef
Founded: 1923

Edition **Kunzelmann** GmbH*, Grütstr 28, CH-8134 Adliswil-Zürich Tel: (01) 7103681
Subjects: Music and Musicians, Instrumental Sheet Music
Founded: 1945
Miscellaneous: Formerly Eulenburg Edition GmbH
ISBN Publisher's Prefix: 3-85662

L W Edition, an imprint of Editions Luce Wilquin (qv)

L W Promotion, an imprint of Editions Luce Wilquin (qv)

Labor et Fides SA+, 1 rue Beauregard, CH-1204 Geneva Tel: (022) 291134/291133
Chairman: Jean-Marc Chappuis; *Literary Dir:* Serge Molla; *Administrative Dir:* Paulette Reymond
Subjects: Theology, Religion, Ethics, General Subjects
1985-86: 37 titles *Founded:* 1924
ISBN Publisher's Prefix: 2-8309

Bundesamt für **Landestopographie**, Seftigenstr 264, CH-3084 Wabern Tel: (031) 549111 Telex: 912860 topoch
Subject: Maps of Switzerland

Herbert **Lang** & Cie AG, PO Box 82, CH-3000 Berne 7 (Located at: Münzgraben 2, CH-3011 Berne) Tel: (031) 228871 Cable Add: Librilang Telex: 912867 lang ch
President: Christoph H Lang
Subject: Science
Bookshop: At above address
Founded: 1813 (re-formed 1921)
Miscellaneous: Agents for libraries throughout the world
ISBN Publisher's Prefix: 3-261

Verlag Peter **Lang** AG, PO Box 277, CH-3000 Berne 15 (Located at: Jupiterstr 15, CH-3015 Berne) Tel: (031) 321122 Telex: 32420 verl ch
Man Dir, Rights & Permissions: Peter Lang; *Editorial:* Gisela Quast; *Sales:* Reinold Brunner; *Production:* Françoise Santschy, Michel Droz, Heidi Anabühl; *Publicity:* René Knöpfel
Subsidiary Companies: Verlag Peter Lang GmbH, Federal Republic of Germany (qv); Peter Lang Inc, 62 West 45th St, New York, NY 10036, USA
Subjects: Art, Business, Economics, Education, Encyclopaedias, History, Language, Law, Literature, Philosophy,

Psychology, Religion, Social Sciences, Reprints
1985: 900 titles *1986:* 1,000 titles
Founded: 1977
ISBN Publisher's Prefix: 3-261

Langenscheidt AG*, PO Box 326, CH-8021 Zurich (Located at: Löwenstr 19, Zurich) Tel: (01) 2115000
Parent Company: Langenscheidt KG, Federal Republic of Germany (qv)
Subjects: Linguistics, Languages
ISBN Publisher's Prefix: 3-269

Franz **Larese** und Jürg Janett, see Erker-Galerie AG

Larousse (Suisse) SA*, PO Box 502, CH-1211 Geneva 6 Tel: (022) 369140
Man Dir: Jean-Claude Viatte
Parent Company: Librairie Larousse, France (qv for associate companies)
Subjects: Reference Works, Dictionaries, School Books
ISBN Publisher's Prefix: 2-8276

Lenos Verlag, Wallstr 9, CH-4051 Basle Tel: (061) 231333
Programme Dir, Reader, Publicity: Heidi Sommerer; *Sales:* Tom Forrer
Subjects: Swiss and Arabic Fiction, Non-fiction, Politics, Society, Media
Founded: 1970
ISBN Publisher's Prefix: 3-85787

Leobuchhandlung, Verlag der Quellen-Bändchen, Gallusstr 20, CH-9001 St Gallen Tel: (071) 222917 Telex: 77452 Leo ch
Man Dir: Eugen Hettinger
Bookshop: Leobuchhandlung (qv under Major Booksellers)
Founded: 1918
ISBN Publisher's Prefix: 3-85788

Leonis Verlag+*, Villa Meridiana, Titlisstr 14, CH-8032 Zurich
Sales and distribution: PO Box 952, CH-8034 Zurich (Located at: Kirchenweg 5) Tel: (01) 2517560/475565 Cable Add: Leonisverlag Zurich Telex: 58761 Deag CH
Owner & Man Dir: Dr Wolfgang M Metz
Associate Company: Doulos Verlag (qv)
Subjects: Biography, Politics, Social Science, Paperbacks, Travel Books
Founded: 1976
ISBN Publisher's Prefix: 3-721

Edition **Leu**, PO Box 1704, CH-8048 Zurich (Located at: Schöneggstr 26, CH-8953 Dietikon-Zürich) Tel: (01) 7411043
Man Dir, Production, Publicity: Al' Leu; *Editorial:* Daniel Bamert, Eveline Scherer
Subjects: Art, Literature, Graphics, Science
1986: 2 titles *1987:* 2 titles *Founded:* 1977
ISBN Publisher's Prefix: 3-85667

Lia Rumantscha (Ligia Romontscha)*, Via da la Plessur 47, CH-7000 Cuoira/Cuera Tel: (081) 224422/224448
Dir: Dr Bernard Cathomas
Subjects: Books in the Romansh language of Switzerland; Dictionaries, grammar, linguistics, background and history of Romansh; Biography, Belles Lettres, Poetry, Music and Songs, Religion, Periodicals
Miscellaneous: Company also gives financial support to other publications in Romansh in the Romansh-speaking area

Limmat Verlag Genossenschaft+*, Quellenstr 25, Postfach, CH-8031 Zurich Tel: (01) 440833
Publicity: Jürg Zimmerli
Subjects: Socialism, Socio-Political Studies, Feminist Juvenile, Fiction, Art

Literatheke, an imprint of Eco-Verlags AG (qv)

E **Löpfe-Benz** AG Rorschach, Graphische Anstalt und Verlag, Pestalozzistr 5, CH-9400 Rorschach Tel: (071) 414341 Graphical Institute and Publisher
Dirs: Emil Enderle, Dieter Mildenberger; *Editorial:* Werner Meier; *Sales:* Peter Kruijsen; *Advertising:* Hans Schöbi, Peter Bick, Walter Vochezer
Subsidiary Company: Nebelspalter Verlag (qv)
Subjects: Topical Works, Humour, Satire, Juvenile, Poetry, History, Periodical
Founded: 1875
ISBN Publisher's Prefix: 3-85819

The **Lutry** Press, an imprint of Marix Evans & Chilvers SA (qv)

Hans-Rudolf **Lutz***, Lessingstr 11, CH-8002 Zurich Tel: (01) 2017672
Man Dir: H-R Lutz
Subjects: Art, Visual Communication
1985: 1 title *1986:* 3 titles *Founded:* 1966

Macmillan SA*, ave d'Ouchy 61, CH-1000 Lausanne 6 Tel: (021) 277561 Cable Add: Berledit Lausanne Telex: 25492 Berle CH Fax: (021) 261257
Man Dir: Marshall D Mascott; *Editorial:* Konrad Fuchs; *Marketing Dir:* J Nigel Cave; *Production Manager:* Jean-Paul Minder
Parent Company: Macmillan Inc, 866 Third Ave, New York, NY 10022, USA
Imprint: Berlitz Guides
Subjects: Travel, Tourism, Language Teaching, Dictionaries, Leisure
Founded: 1970

La **Maison** de la Bible, Société Biblique de Genève, PO Box 477, CH-1211 Geneva 3 (Located at: 11 rue de Rive, Geneva) Tel: (022) 285259 Cable Add: Bibles-Genève
Subjects: Scriptures (in many languages), Biblical Studies, Biography, Juvenile
Bookshop: La Maison de la Bible (at above address)
Founded: 1917
Miscellaneous: Also known by German name, Das Haus der Bibel (Genfer Bibelgesellschaft)
ISBN Publisher's Prefix: 2-8260

Marika **Malacorda** Editions, 1 rue de l'Évêché, CH-1204 Geneva Tel: (022) 286450
Dir: Marika Malacorda
Orders to: Ecart Publications, PO Box 253, CH-1211 Geneva 1 Tel: (022) 457395/288803/313473
Associate Company: Ecart Publications (qv)
Founded: 1976

Manesse Verlag, Badergasse 9, CH-8001 Zurich Tel: (01) 2525707 Fax: (01) 695347
Man Dir: Franz Cavigelli
Parent Company: Deutsche Verlags-Anstalt GmbH (DVA), Federal Republic of Germany (qv)
Subjects: World Classics, Classical Literature, Far East, Historiography, Essays
1985: 18 titles *1986:* 15 titles *Founded:* 1944
ISBN Publisher's Prefix: 3-7175

Librairie-Editions J **Marguerat**+*, 2 pl St François, CH-1002 Lausanne 2 Tel: (021) 237717
Dir: Jean Marguerat
Subjects: Belles Lettres, History, Travel, Music, Geography, Ethnology
Founded: 1940
ISBN Publisher's Prefix: 2-88008

Marix Evans & Chilvers SA*, CH-1099 Corcelles-le-Jorat, Vaud Tel: (021) 932424
President, Editorial: Timothy R Chilvers; *Sales Dir:* Martin F Marix Evans

Imprint: The Lutry Press
Subjects: General, Music, Sport, Transport, Fiction, Biography, Co-editions
Founded: 1981

Marva+, PO Box 254, CH-1211 Geneva 26 (Located at: Port Franc de Geneve, Geneva) Tel: (022) 925671 Cable Add: Marva Geneva 26
Publishers: Hennecke Kardel, Dietrich Bronder
Subject: Modern History (especially European and Nazi-related)

Les Editions la **Matze**, Postfach, CH-1950 Sion (Located at: 1 rue du Mont, Sion) Tel: (027) 231652
Man Dir, Sales: Guy Gessler
Subjects: General Fiction, Military and General History, Archaeology, Swiss Painters series
Founded: 1975

Médecine et Hygiène, PO Box 229, CH-1211 Geneva 4 (Located at: 78 ave de la Roseraie, Geneva) Tel: (022) 469355
Man Dir, Sales: P Y Balavoine; *Publicity, Advertising Dir:* G Antonietti
Subjects: Medicine, Psychology, General Science, University Textbooks, Specialized Medical and other Periodicals
Founded: 1943

Medlevant AG+, PO Box 3128, CH-6901 Lugano (Located at: Corso Elvezia 4, CH-6900 Lugano) Tel: (091) 236452/236453 Telex: 841295 Mdlv Ch Fax: (091) 236478
Man Dir, Editorial: Moujir M Omari; *Sales:* Mohamed Idriss; *Rights & Permissions:* Sybille Macdonald
Subjects: Children's, Educational, Scientific
1985: 11 titles *Founded:* 1983
ISBN Publisher's Prefix: 88-7674

Peter **Meili** & Co*, Fronwagpl 13, CH-8200 Schaffhausen Tel: (053) 54144/5 Telex: 76777 meibuch
Subjects: History, Literature about the Schaffhausen area, Dialect Stories, Politics
Bookshop: Buchhandlung Meili & Co (qv under Major Booksellers)
Founded: 1838
ISBN Publisher's Prefix: 3-85805

Christoph **Merian** Verlag, St Alban-Vorstadt 5, CH-4002 Basle Tel: (061) 221288
Chief Executive: Dr Cyrill Häring; *Editorial:* Dr Rudolf Suter; *Sales:* Sonja Müller
Subjects: Basle and Area
1985: 5 titles *1986:* 7 titles *Founded:* 1976
ISBN Publisher's Prefix: 3-85616

Editions H **Messeiller** SA, 11 rue St Nicolas, CH-2006 Neuchâtel Tel: (038) 251296
Dir: C-H Messeiller
Subjects: Textbooks, Education, Art, Belles Lettres, Religion, Psychology, Law, Administration
1986-87: 11 titles *Founded:* 1887
ISBN Publisher's Prefix: 2-8261

Editions **Minkoff**, 8 rue Eynard, CH-1211 Geneva 12 Tel: (022) 204660
Dirs: Youval Minkoff, Sylvie Minkoff
Subjects: Music and Musicology, Theatre, Art, History of the Second International
Founded: 1972
ISBN Publisher's Prefix: 2-8266

Moderne Industrie AG*, Dörflistr 73, CH-8050 Zurich Tel: (01) 3118140 Telex: 57547
Subjects: Technical, Data Processing, Personnel, Marketing, Sales
ISBN Publisher's Prefix: 3-478

Editions Mon Village SA, CH-1099 Vulliens, Vaud Tel: (021) 931363
Man Dir, Sales, Production, Publicity, Rights & Permissions: Albert-Louis Chappuis; *Editorial:* André Plomb
Subjects: Fiction
Book Club: Club Mon Village SA
Founded: 1955

Mondo SA (Editions-Verlag-Edizioni), 20 ave de Corsier, CH-1800 Vevey Tel: (021) 9228021 Telex: 452100 Spn Ch Fax: (021) 9217206
Dir: Arslan Alamir

Verlag Rudolf **Mühlemann***, Haus Z Wolfau, CH-8570 Weinfelden Tel: (072) 225353/4
Founded: 1949
ISBN Publisher's Prefix: 3-85809

Albert **Müller** Verlag AG+, PO Box 150, CH-8803 Rüschlikon/Zurich (Located at: Bahnhofstr 69, Rüschlikon-Zurich) Tel: (01) 7241760 Cable Add: Müllerverlag Rüschlikon Telex: 56320 amv ch
Man Dir, Production: Rolf Kleinschnittger; *Publisher, Rights & Permissions:* Dr Bernhard Recher; *Editorial:* Norbert Wengerck; *Publicity:* Mr Voellmy
Subjects: Domestic animals, Juvenile Fiction, How-to, Music, Reference, Sports, Recreation, Cookery, Wines, Self-Help, Health, Yoga, Homecrafts, American Indian subjects
1985: 25 titles *Founded:* 1938
ISBN Publisher's Prefix: 3-275

N Z N-Buchverlag AG+, Hirschengraben 66, CH-8001 Zurich Tel: (01) 474951
President: Dr Jakob Weibel
Subjects: Art, Religion, Architecture, History
Founded: 1972
ISBN Publisher's Prefix: 3-85827

Les Editions **Nagel** SA, 7-5 bis rue de l'Orangerie, CH-1211 Geneva 7 Tel: (022) 341730/9 Cable Add: Nageledit Geneva Telex: 427993 txc ch
Man Dir: Louis Nagel
Subjects: Philosophy, Politics, Archaeology, Art, Travel Guides, *Who's Who in Switzerland*
Founded: 1928
ISBN Publisher's Prefix: 2-8263

Natura-Verlag*, Pfeffingerweg 1, CH-4144 Arlesheim Tel: (061) 717111
Subjects: Nature Cure, Philosophy, Therapeutic Pedagogy texts
ISBN Publisher's Prefix: 3-85817

Nebelspalter Verlag, CH-9400 Rorschach Tel: (071) 414341
Dirs: E Enderle, D Mildenberger
Parent Company: E Löpfe-Benz AG (qv)
Subjects: Humour, Satire, Cartoons, Periodical
ISBN Publisher's Prefix: 3-85819

Neptun-Verlag*, PO Box 307, CH-8280 Kreuzlingen 1 Tel: (072) 727262 Telex: 882221 nept ch
Manager: Herbert Berchtold
Subjects: Contemporary History, Travel
Founded: 1946
ISBN Publisher's Prefix: 3-85820

Verlag **Neue Stadt***, Seestr 426, CH-8032 Zurich Tel: (01) 4826011
Dir: Hans Jutz
Parent Company: Città Nuova Editrice, Italy (qv for associate companies)

Neue Szene, an imprint of Eco-Verlags AG (qv)

Neue Zürcher Zeitung AG Buchverlag+*, Postfach, CH-8021 Zurich (Located at: Mühlebachstr 54, Zurich) Tel: (01) 2581505 Telex: 52137 nzz ch
Publicity Manager: Walter Köpfli
Subject: Textbooks, Illustrated Books
Miscellaneous: Book publishing division of Zurich daily newspaper
ISBN Publisher's Prefix: 3-85823

Neufeld-Verlag und Galerie*, PO Box, CH-9434 Au/SG Tel: (071) 712977 Cable Add: neufeld
Man Dir: K G Löpfe; *Editorial and other offices:* Ivo Löpfe
Orders to: Neufeld-Verlag und Galerie, Austria (qv)
Parent Company: Löpfe KG, A-6890 Lustenau, Austria
Associate Company: Neufeld-Verlag und Galerie, Austria (qv)
Branch Off: Nordstr 227, CH-8037 Zurich
Subject: Art
Founded: 1962

Verlag Arthur **Niggli** AG, CH-9052 Niederteufen AR Tel: (071) 331772 Cable Add: Niggliverlag, Niederteufen Appenzell
Man Dir: Arthur Niggli
Shipping Add: c/o Danzas und Co, St Gallen
Subsidiary Company: Gallery Ida Niggli Ltd, CH-9052 Niederteufen
Subjects: Visual Arts, Architecture, Fine Arts, Periodical
Bookshops: Buchhandlung Niggli, CH-9100 Herisau; Buchhandlung Niggli, CH-9052 Niederteufen
Founded: 1950
ISBN Publisher's Prefix: 3-7212

Nord-Süd Verlag*, PO Box 199, CH-8617 Mönchaltorf Tel: (01) 9351335 Cable Add: nordsued Telex: 875894 nsv ch
Editorial: Brigitte Sidjanski-Hanhart; *Dir, Sales, Production, Publicity, Rights & Permissions:* Davy Sidjanski
Subject: Children's Picture Books
Founded: 1961
ISBN Publisher's Prefix: 3-85825

Novalis Verlag AG*, Hohlenbaumstr 19, CH-8200 Schaffhausen Tel: (053) 41245 Cable Add: Novalis Schaffhausen
Subjects: Arts, Social Sciences, Educational
ISBN Publisher's Prefix: 3-7214

Oesch Verlag AG, Klausstr 10, CH-8008 Zurich Tel: (01) 2511317 Cable Add: Oesch Telex: 816414
Dir: Martin Brugger; *Sales:* Andreas Grob; *Publicity:* Martin Haslinger; *Rights & Permissions:* Margrit Wacker
Subjects: How-to, Philosophy, Religion, Psychology, Management
Founded: 1935
ISBN Publisher's Prefix: 3-85833

L'**Oeuvre Gravée***, PO Box 205, CH-3000 Berne 8 (Located at: Münstergasse 36, CH-3011 Berne) Tel: (031) 225071 Cable Add: Schindlerart
Editorial, Publicity: Werner Schindler

Office du Livre SA (Buchhaus AG)*, PO Box 1061, CH-1701 Fribourg (Located at: 101 route de Villars, Fribourg) Tel: (037) 240744 Cable Add: Livreoffice Telex: 942291 Olf CH
Man Dir: Jean Hirschen; *Sales Manager:* Pierre Engel
Subjects: Art, Architecture, Asian Studies, Arts and Crafts, Golf
Founded: 1947
ISBN Publisher's Prefixes: 3-7215, 2-8264

Editions **Olizane**+, 11 rue des Vieux-Grenadiers, CH-1205 Geneva Tel: (022) 285252 Telex: 427460 Artu CH
Man Dir: Olivier Lombard
Imprints: Barbare, Collection Artou, Espaces Photographiques, Guides Artou
Subjects: Travel, Orientalism, Photography
1985: 5 titles *1986:* 7 titles *Founded:* 1981
ISBN Publisher's Prefix: 2-88086

Edition **Olms** AG+, Basteiplatz 5, Postfach, CH-8039 Zurich
Man Dir and other offices: Manfred Olms
Subjects: Art, Myth and Legend, Magic, Helvetica, Humour, Comics, Chess, Toy Catalogues, Rock Music
Founded: 1977
ISBN Publisher's Prefix: 3-283

Inigo von **Oppersdorff** Publishing House for Bibliophile Editions+, Klusweg 37, CH-8032 Zurich 7 Tel: (01) 551140 Telex: 811050 tkk ch
Man Dir: Emmanuel von Oppersdorff; *Executive Dir:* Thomas Imboden
Subjects: Belles Lettres, Poetry, History, Music, Art, Religion
Founded: 1966
ISBN Publisher's Prefix: 3-85834

Orell Füssli Verlag+, Postfach, CH-8022 Zurich (Located at: Nüschelerstr 22, Zurich) Tel: (01) 2113630 Cable Add: Orellverlag Zurich Telex: 813021 orla ch
Man Dir: Dr Ernst Grab; *Editorial:* Armin Ochs; *Sales, Marketing:* Harry Heusser; *Rights & Permissions:* Brigitte Frey
Parent Company: Orell Füssli Graphische Betriebe AG, Dietzingerstr 3, CH-8036 Zurich
Subsidiary Company: Orell Füssli und Parabel Verlag GmbH, Federal Republic of Germany (qv)
Imprint: Eugen Rentsch Verlag AG
Subjects: Economics, Biography, History, Geography, How-to, Art, Children's, Juveniles, Educational Materials, Railways and Transportation, Photographic Picture Books
Bookshop: Orell Füssli (qv under Major Booksellers)
Founded: 1519
ISBN Publisher's Prefixes: 3-280, 3-7249

Verlag **Organisator** AG, Löwenstr 16, CH-8021 Zurich Tel: (01) 2118155 Cable Add: orga/ch Telex: 813834 Fax: (01) 2112192
Man Dir, Editorial: Dr V Bataillard; *Sales, Publicity, Production:* Bruno Waldburger
Subjects: Swiss Law and Taxes, International Taxes, Industrial Management, Periodical
Bookshops: Basle, Lucerne, St Gallen, Schaffhausen, Winterthur, Zurich and others throughout Switzerland
Founded: 1919
ISBN Publisher's Prefix: 3-7220

Origo-Verlag+, Rathausgasse 30, CH-3011 Berne Tel: (031) 224480 Cable Add: Wildbuch
Proprietor, Man Dir: Alexander Wild
Associate Company: Verlag Alexander Wild (qv)
Subjects: Philosophy and Religion of East and West
Founded: 1947
ISBN Publisher's Prefix: 3-282

Orte-Verlag, PO Box 2028, CH-8033 Zurich (Located at: Ekkehardstr 14) Tel: (01) 3630234
Man Dir: Werner Bucher; *Publicity:* Ruth Good-Ramp
Subjects: Poetry, Belles Lettres

Ostschweiz Druck und Verlag*, Oberer Graben 8, CH-9001 Sankt Gallen Tel: (071) 208585 Telex: 77393
Man Dir, Sales: Dr Emil Dähler
Subjects: Belles Lettres, Poetry, History, Music, Art, Social Science
Founded: 1892
ISBN Publisher's Prefix: 3-85837

Ott Verlag AG Thun+, Länggasse 57, CH-3600 Thun 7 Tel: (033) 221622 Cable Add: Ottpubl Thun Telex: 921299 Fax: (033) 222006
Man Dir: Walter Knecht; *Publicity & Advertising:* Hans M Ott
Subsidiary Companies: Verlags und Versandbuchhandlung Thun AG, Thun; Translegal AG
Subjects: General Non-fiction, Lexicons, Earth Sciences, Military, Sports, Industry and Commerce
Founded: 1923
ISBN Publisher's Prefix: 3-7225

Editions du **Panorama**, PO Box 38, CH-2500 Bienne 3 Tel: (032) 236284
Man Dir: Paul Thierrin
Subjects: General Fiction, Commerce, Secondary Textbooks, Languages, Belles Lettres
1985: 5 titles *1986:* 6 titles *Founded:* 1951
ISBN Publisher's Prefix: 2-88019

Paulusverlag, see Editions Saint-Paul

Librairie **Payot** SA+, Departement des Editions, PO Box 3212, CH-1002 Lausanne (Located at: 4 pl Pépinet, CH-1003 Lausanne) Tel: (021) 203331 Cable Add: Payotco Telex: 24961
Manager: Jacques Scherrer
Subjects: Belles Lettres, Poetry, History, Music, Art, General and Natural Sciences, Philosophy, Psychology, Law, Commerce, Regional, University, Secondary & Primary Textbooks, Transport, Agriculture, Domestic, Sport
Bookshops: See under Major Booksellers
Founded: 1875
ISBN Publisher's Prefix: 2-601

Pedrazzini Tipografia*, Via B Varenna 7, CH-6600 Locarno Tel: (093) 317734/317735
Man Dir and other offices: Carlo Pedrazzini
Subjects: Scholastic, Historical, Church Historical, Literary, Printing and Book Production, Periodical
Founded: 1880

Pendo-Verlag, Wolfbachstr 9, CH-8032 Zurich Tel: (01) 693737
Dirs: Gladys Weigner, Bernhard Moosbrugger
Subjects: Travel, Religion, Literature and Poetry, International Co-operation
ISBN Publisher's Prefix: 3-85842

Pharos-Verlag, Hansrudolf Schwabe AG*, PO Box 68, CH-4011 Basle (Located at: Therwilerstr 5, CH-4011 Basle) Tel: (061) 541021
Man Dir: Hansrudolf Schwabe; *Advertising Dir:* Myrte Schwabe
Subjects: Juveniles, Railway Interest, Wines
Bookshop: Buchhandlung Münsterberg, Münsterberg 13, CH-4011 Basle
Founded: 1958
ISBN Publisher's Prefix: 3-7230

Philosophisch-Anthroposophischer Verlag am Goetheanum, Huegelweg 59, CH-4143 Dornach Tel: (061) 721116
Subsidiary Company: Rudolf Geering Verlag (at above address)
Subjects: Philosophy, Anthroposophy, Natural Sciences, Art, Literature, Medicine (all especially in connection with the thoughts of Rudolf Steiner)
Founded: 1908
ISBN Publisher's Prefix: 3-7235

Phoenix Verlag AG, subsidiary of Scherz Verlag AG (qv)

Editions **Pierrot** SA+*, 51 ave de Rumine, CH-1005 Lausanne Tel: (021) 231447 Telex: pclep 25404 ch
Dir: Ghislaine Vautier
Orders to: Éditions Pierrot, PO Box 3513, CH-1002 Lausanne
Subjects: Literature, Juveniles, Periodical (Children's)
Founded: 1966

R **Piper** & Co Verlag GmbH*, Alte Landstr 67, CH-8700 Küsnacht Tel: (01) 9104044
Parent Company: R Piper GmbH & Co KG Verlag, Federal Republic of Germany (qv)
Subjects: Belles Lettres, Juveniles, Politics, Social Science, Psychology, Education, Natural Sciences
ISBN Publisher's Prefix: 3-7236

Francesco **Pirella** Editore+*, Via Casaregis 51/3, CH-16129 Geneva Tel: (010) 363628
Man Dir: Francesco Pirella
Orders to: Libraria Ligure di Baccanella, Corso Sardegna 77/4, CH-16142 Geneva
Subjects: Essays, Fiction, Art, Poetry, History, Local Interest
1985: 11 titles *Founded:* 1972
ISBN Publisher's Prefix: 88-85514

Populaires*, Ave Tivoli 2, Lausanne Tel: (021) 204141
Man Dir, Publicity: Jean Studemann

Presses Centrales Lausanne SA*, 7 rue de Genève, CH-1003 Lausanne Tel: (021) 205901
Dir: Daniel Kaufmann
Subject: Art

Presses Polytechniques Romandes+, EPFL-Ecublens, Centre Midi, CH-1015 Lausanne Tel: (021) 472130 Telex: 450456 Epfvd CH attn PPR
President: Jacques Neirynck; *Man Dir:* Claire-Lise Delacrausaz; *Editorial, Rights & Permissions:* Marianne Aiassa; *Production:* Pascale Deppierraz; *Sales:* Florence Bersier; *Promotion, Secretary-General:* Olivier Babel
Subjects: University Textbooks, Reference Works, Popular Science and Technology
1985: 25 titles *1986:* 18 titles *Founded:* 1980
ISBN Publisher's Prefix: 2-88074

Verlag **Pro Juventute***, Seefeldstr 8, Postfach, CH-8008 Zurich Tel: (01) 2517244
Orders to: Above address for German editions; Pro Juventute, Secrétariat-romand, Galeries St-François B, CH-1003 Lausanne, for French and Italian editions
Subjects: Children's Books, Children's Education and Welfare (texts in German, French and Italian)

Editions **Pro Schola**, 29 rue des Terreaux, CH-1000 Lausanne 9 Tel: (021) 236655 Cable Add: Dirbenedict Telex: 24357 bbav ch
Man Dir: Dr Jean J Bénédict
Orders to: PO Box 300, CH-1000 Lausanne 9
Subjects: Languages (textbooks, reference; especially, language teaching by the 'Bénédict Direct Progressive Method')
Founded: 1928
ISBN Publisher's Prefix: 2-88009

Verlag für **Psychologie**, Dr C J Hogrefe*, Zeltweg 6, CH-8032 Zurich
Head Off: Verlag für Psychologie, Göttingen, Federal Republic of Germany (qv)
Subjects: Psychology

Psychosophische Gesellschaft*, PO Box 204, CH-8021 Zurich
Subjects: Psychology, Philosophy, Theology, Pedagogy, Mysticism and Magic

R A Verlag*, PO Box 120, CH-8640 Rapperswil
Subjects: Art, Education

Rabe Verlag Zurich*, Oberdorfstr 23, CH-8001 Zurich Tel: (01) 478540 Cable Add: Rabeverlag Zurich
Warehouse: CH-8608 Bubikon Zurich Tel: (055) 382383
Man Dir, Sales: Dr J Kanitz; *Editorial, Rights & Permissions:* Dr Elsa Kanitz; *Production:* Dr P Portmann
Subject: Art
Founded: 1962
ISBN Publisher's Prefix: 3-85852

Raeber Bücher AG*, Frankenstr 9, CH-6002 Lucerne Tel: (041) 230727 Telex: 72381
Man Dir: B L Raeber
Imprint: Edition Raeber
Subjects: General Fiction, Belles Lettres, Poetry, History, Music, Art, Juveniles, Secondary Textbooks, Religion
Bookshops: Raeber Buchhandlung (at above address); Taschenbuchladen Kornmärt, Kornmarktgasse 7, Lucerne
Founded: 1825
ISBN Publisher's Prefix: 3-7239

Verlag für **Recht und Gesellschaft** AG, PO Box 646, CH-4010 Basle (Located at: Wallstr 14, Basle) Tel: (061) 231775 Cable Add: Reges Verlag
Man Dir: Christian Fridli
Associate Company: Sciamed Verlag AG (at above address)
Subject: Law, Taxation
Founded: 1933
ISBN Publisher's Prefix: 3-7242

Recom, an imprint of Reinhardt Communications (qv)

Regenbogen-Verlag, PO Box 240, CH-8025 Zurich Tel: (01) 475860
General Manager: Theo Ruff
Orders to: Prolit Buchvertrieb GmbH, Siemensstr 18a, D-6300 Giessen, Federal Republic of Germany Tel: (0641) 77053
Subjects: Travel Guides, Art Books, Swiss Literature
ISBN Publisher's Prefix: 3-85862

Reich Verlag AG+, Museggstr 12, CH-6000 Lucerne 5 Tel: (041) 513721 Telex: 868122 reic ch
Man Dir: Alfons Wüest
Imprint: Terra Magica
Subject: Photographic Picture Books
Founded: 1974
ISBN Publisher's Prefix: 3-7243

Verlag Friedrich **Reinhardt** AG, Missionstr 36, CH-4012 Basle Tel: (061) 253390 Cable Add: Freinhardt Basle
Man Dir, Rights & Permissions: Dr Ernst Reinhardt
Subsidiary Companies: Eular Verlag; Reinhardt Communications (qv)
Subjects: General Fiction, Belles Lettres, Biography, History, How-to, Religion, Juveniles, Nature
1986: 13 titles *1987:* 13 titles *Founded:* 1900
ISBN Publisher's Prefix: 3-7245

Reinhardt Communications*, Missionstr 36, CH-4012 Basle Tel: (061) 251960/251926 Telex: 63755 rein ch
Man Dir, Sales, Production, Publicity: Alex Sprecher
Parent Company: Verlag Friedrich Reinhardt AG (qv)
Imprint: Recom
Subjects: Medical
Founded: 1971-1985

Eugen **Rentsch** Verlag AG, an imprint of Orell Füssli Verlag (qv)

SWITZERLAND

Rex-Verlag, PO Box 161, CH-6000 Lucerne 5 (Located at: St Karliquai 12, Lucerne) Tel: (041) 514914
Man Dir: Rosa Wicki
Subjects: Belles Lettres, Education, Guides to Conduct, Juveniles, Catholicism
Bookshop: Rex Buchladen (at above address)
Founded: 1931
ISBN Publisher's Prefix: 3-7252

Edizioni Raimondo **Rezzonico***, Via Luini, CH-6600 Locarno

Rocom, now Recom (qv)

Rodana Verlag, see Schweizer Spiegel Verlag AG

Hans **Rohr**, Buchhandlung und Antiquariat zum Oberdorf AG*, Oberdorfstr 5, CH-8024 Zurich 1 Tel: (01) 2513636 Telex: 56385
Man Dir: Hans R Rohr
Subjects: Tourist Interest, Swiss History, Swiss Dialect, Classical Antiquity, Films and the Cinema
Bookshops: Buchhandlung Hans Rohr (qv under Major Booksellers)
Founded: 1921
ISBN Publisher's Prefix: 3-85865

Roth et Sauter SA*, Les Eterpy, CH-1026 Denges Tel: (021) 717561 Telex: 458179 rsd ch
Man Dirs: Michel Logoz, Pierre Sauter
Imprints include: Editions du Verseau
Subjects: Art, Belles Lettres, General
Founded: 1890

Rotten-Verlags AG*, Terbinerstr 2, CH-3930 Visp Tel: (028) 462252

Rütten und Loening Verlag GmbH, a subsidiary of Scherz Verlag AG (qv)

Verlag **S O I** (Schweizerisches Ost-Institut)*, Jubiläumsstr 41, CH-3000 Berne 6 Tel: (031) 431212 Cable Add: Schweizost Telex: 32728
Man Dir: Peter Sager; *Sales Manager:* Peter Burgunder; *Production Manager:* Peter Dolder
Subjects: History, Politics, Social Science (especially with respect to the Eastern Bloc countries)
Bookshop: Buchhandlung SOI (at above address)
Founded: 1958
ISBN Publisher's Prefix: 3-85913

Editions **Saint-Paul**, Pérolles 42, CH-1700 Fribourg Tel: (037) 246812
Dir: Anton Scherer
Parent Company: Imprimerie et Librairies Saint-Paul SA (at above address)
Associate Companies: Editions de la Sarine (at above address); Editions Universitaires SA (qv)
Subjects: Philosophy, Religion, Educational
Bookshops: Librairie Saint-Paul, Pérolles 38, CH-1700 Fribourg; Librairie du Vieux Comté, rue de Vevey, CH-1630 Bulle
Founded: 1873
Miscellaneous: Company is also known as Paulusverlag

Sanssouci Verlag, Rämistr 3, CH-8001 Zurich Tel: (01) 2522154 Telex: 815239
Owners: Elisabeth Raabe, Regina Vitali
Associate Company: Arche Verlag AG, Raabe und Vitali (qv)
Subjects: General Fiction, Large Print Fiction, Humour
1986: 19 titles *1987:* 3 titles
ISBN Publisher's Prefix: 3-7254

Sauerländer AG, PO Box 570, CH-5001 Aarau (Located at: Laurenzenvorstadt 89, Aarau) Tel: (064) 221264 Telex: 981195 sag ch
Publisher and Man Dir: Hans Christof Sauerländer; *Editorial:* Rolf Inhauser, Hanspeter Fuhrer, Martin Röthlisberger; *Sales:* Josef Kälin; *Publicity:* Johannes Hauenstein; *Rights & Permissions:* Ula Werren
Subsidiary Companies: Sauerländer GmbH, Münzgasse 1, A-5020 Salzburg, Austria; Verlag Sauerländer GmbH, Federal Republic of Germany (qv)
Associate Companies: SABE Verlagsinstitut für Lehrmittel, CH-8001 Zurich; Kinderbuchverlag KBV Luzern AG (qv); Helbing und Lichtenhahn Verlag AG (qv)
Subjects: Juvenile, Belles Lettres, Poetry, Biography, History, Medicine, Natural & Social Sciences, University, Secondary & Primary Textbooks, Educational Materials, Periodicals
Founded: 1807
ISBN Publisher's Prefix: 3-7941

Scherz Verlag AG, Marktgasse 25, CH-3000 Berne 7 Tel: (031) 226836 Cable Add: Scherzedit Telex: 32552 sche ch Fax: (031) 210375
Chairman, Man Dir: Rudolf Streit-Scherz; *Sales Dirs:* Wolfgang Radaj, Alfred Vallotton; *Editorial Department:* Ursula Ibler, Jürgen Lütge, Gert Woerner; *Rights & Permissions:* Ursula Griessel
Subsidiary Companies: Otto Wilhelm Barth-Verlag KG, Federal Republic of Germany (qv); Phoenix Verlag AG, Rütten und Loening Verlag GmbH, Taschenbuch Verlag Spectrum (all Switzerland)
Branch Offs: Scherz Verlag GmbH, Federal Republic of Germany (qv); Scherz Verlag, c/o Lechner & Sohn, A-1232 Vienna, Heizwerkstr 5, Austria
Subjects: General Fiction & Non-fiction, Biography, History, Psychology, Parapsychology, Philosophy; Paperback series of Crime Thrillers
Bookshop: Buchhandlung Scherz AG (qv under Major Booksellers)
1986: 125 titles *Founded:* 1939
Miscellaneous: Company is also associated with the Litpress Literary Agency (qv)
ISBN Publisher's Prefix: 3-502

Schläpfer & Co AG, CH-9100 Herisau 1 Tel: (071) 513131 Telex: 77147 Fax: (071) 521422
Man Dir: P Schläpfer
Branch Off: CH-9043 Trogen
Subjects: Domestic, Children's
Founded: 1974
ISBN Publisher's Prefix: 3-85882

Verlag fur **Schöne Wissenschaften**, Unterer Zielweg 36, Postfach, CH-4143 Dornach 2 Tel: (061) 723911
Belles Lettres Publishing Co — Albert Steffen Foundation
Chief Executive: Dr Heinz Matile
Subjects: Works of Albert Steffen (poetry, art, anthroposophy, cultural history, philosophy, pedagogy, therapeutics, literary criticism)
Founded: 1928
ISBN Publisher's Prefix: 3-85889

Hermann **Schroedel** Verlag AG*, Hardstr 95, CH-4020 Basle Tel: (061) 423330
Associate Company: Hermann Schroedel Verlag KG, Federal Republic of Germany (qv)
Subjects: Artistic Picture Books for Nursery Children and Adults, Bibliophile Volumes, Facsimiles and Graphics
ISBN Publisher's Prefix: 3-285

Schubi Interdidac AG+, Mattenbachstr 2, CH-8400 Winterthur Tel: (052) 297221 Telex: 896261 Subi Ch
Man Dir: E R Benz; *Sales, Publicity:* G K Schäfer; *Production:* K Huesmann
Subject: Educational

Schulthess Polygraphischer Verlag AG, Zwingliplatz 2, CH-8022 Zurich Tel: (01) 2519336 Cable Add: Buchschulthess Telex: 56736
Man Dir, Advertising, Permissions: Dr Charlotte Homburger
Subjects: Law, Commerce, Social Science, University Textbooks, Schoolbooks, Periodical
Founded: 1791
Miscellaneous: Firm has incorporated the former Leemann AG Druckerei/Verlag since 1978
ISBN Publisher's Prefix: 3-7255

Hansrudolf **Schwabe AG**, see Pharos-Verlag

Schwabe & Co AG, Steinentorstr 13, CH-4000 Basle 10 Tel: (061) 235523 Cable Add: Schwabeco Basel
Man Dirs: Dr Christian Overstolz, Josef A Niederberger, Marc Götz
Subjects: Medicine, Pharmaceutics, History of Art and Civilization, Philosophy, Psychology, University and Secondary Textbooks
1985: 14 titles *1986:* 14 titles *Founded:* 1488
ISBN Publisher's Prefix: 3-7965

Aare-Verlag/**Schweizer Jugend-Verlag**+*, Werkhofstr 23, CH-4502 Solothurn Tel: (065) 229458
Publishing Manager: Felix Furrer
Orders to: Karlheinz Biersack GmbH, Reichenaustr 202, D-7750 Konstanz, Federal Republic of Germany
Subjects: Reference, Juveniles, Primary Textbooks, Educational Materials
Miscellaneous: Aare-Verlag and Schweizer Jugend-Verlag are divisions of the one company, and are under the same management
ISBN Publisher's Prefix: 3-7260

Schweizer Spiegel Verlag AG & Rodana Verlag, PO Box 373, CH-8024 Zurich 1 (Located at: Rämistr 18, Zurich) Tel: (01) 472195
Dir: Dr P Huggler
Subjects: Poetry, Art, Philosophy, Juveniles, Psychology, Social Science, History
Founded: 1925
ISBN Publisher's Prefixes: 3-85900 (Schweizer Spiegel), 3-85863 (Rodana)

Schweizer Verlagshaus AG+, Klausstr 10, CH-8008 Zurich Tel: (01) 2519134 Cable Add: svzuerich Telex: 816414
Dirs: Dr Armin Meyer, Martin Brugger; *Editorial, Rights & Permissions:* Margrit Wacker; *Sales:* Andreas Grob; *Publicity:* Martin Haslinger
Subjects: General Fiction, Biography, Music, History, General Science
Book Club: Affiliated with NSB Buch- und Phonoclub
Founded: 1907
ISBN Publisher's Prefix: 3-7263

Schweizerische Stiftung für Alpine Forschungen, Binzstr 23, CH-8045 Zurich Tel: (01) 4610147
Swiss Foundation for Alpine Research
Subject: Alpine Research

Schweizerische Zentralstelle für Stahlbau, Seefeldstr 25, CH-8034 Zurich Tel: (01) 478980
Swiss Institute of Steel Construction
Man Dir: Urs Wyss

Schweizerischen Gesellschaft für Volkskunde, an imprint of Verlag und Druckerei G Krebs AG (qv)

Verlag der **Schweizerischen Schallplattenmission**, member of the Telos group (qv in Federal Republic of Germany), publishing evangelical paperbacks

Schweizerisches Jugendschriftenwerk*, PO Box 8022, CH-8008 Zurich (Located at: Seehofstr 15, Zurich) Tel: (01) 2517244
Subjects: Literature for Juveniles (in German, French, Italian, Romansh)
Founded: 1931
ISBN Publisher's Prefix: 3-7269

Verlag **Schweizerisches katholisches Bibelwerk**, Biblisches Institut, Université Misericorde, CH-1700 Fribourg
Dir: Othmar Keel
Subject: Roman Catholic literature on biblical subjects
Miscellaneous: Company is a member of AMB (qv under Federal Republic of Germany)
ISBN Publisher's Prefix: 3-7203

Schweizerisches Ost-Institut, see Verlag SOI

Schwengeler-Verlag*, PO Box 119, CH-9442 Berneck SG (Located at: am Rosenberg, Berneck) Tel: (071) 724358
Man Dir, Editorial, Rights & Permissions: Bruno Schwengeler; *Sales:* Harry Graf; *Production, Publicity:* Walter Nitsche
Subjects: Christian Literature, Science
Bookshop: TELOS-Buchhandlung, Oberer Graben 12, CH-8400 Winterthur
Founded: 1968
Miscellaneous: Member of the Telos group (qv in Federal Republic of Germany), publishing evangelical paperbacks
ISBN Publisher's Prefix: 3-8566

Schwitter Publishing Inc/Schwitter Verlag AG+, PO Box 636, CH-8065 Zurich (Located at: Talackerstr 9, Glattbrugg) Tel: (01) 8101166/(057) 332555 (Editorial) Telex: 828078 sint ch
Man Dir: Fridolin P Schwitter; *Editorial Dir:* Norma Schwitter
Subjects: Reference Works and Encyclopaedias, Science and Technology, Medicine, Countries and Peoples, Natural History, Art, Juveniles
Founded: 1959
ISBN Publisher's Prefix: 3-284

Sciamed Verlag AG, an associate company of Verlag für Recht und Gesellschaft AG (qv)

Editions **Scriptar** SA, PO Box 870, CH-1001 Lausanne (Located at: 23 ave de la Gare, Lausanne) Tel: (021) 202351 Cable Add: Orlog Telex: Green 225587
Publicity Manager: H Marquis
Subjects: Watches and Jewellery, Gems
Founded: 1946
ISBN Publisher's Prefix: 2-88012

Edition **Seefeld**+, Minervastr 33, CH-8032 Zurich Tel: (01) 2524717/2524441 Telex: 58617 seef ch
Dirs: Claudio de Polo, Charles Whitehouse
Subjects: Facsimile reprints of old manuscripts, maps, drawings; Limited editions
Bookshop: Galerie Edition Seefeld (at above address)
Founded: 1976

Sinwel-Buchhandlung Verlag, Lorrainestr 10, CH-3000 Berne 11 Tel: (031) 425205 Telex: 911469
Subjects: Belles Lettres, Technical, Leisure Activities
ISBN Publisher's Prefix: 3-85911

Editions D'Art Albert **Skira** SA*, 89 route de Chêne, CH-1208 Geneva Tel: (022) 495533 Cable Add: Edart Geneva
Man Dir, Editorial: Mrs R Skira; *Sales, Production, Publicity:* Jean-Michel Skira
Subjects: Art, Art History, Art Reference, Low- & High-priced Paperbacks, Educational Materials
Founded: 1928
ISBN Publisher's Prefix: 2-605

Slatkine Reprints, PO Box 765, CH-1211 Geneva 3 (Located at: 5 rue des Chaudronniers, Geneva) Tel: (022) 762551 Telex: 419346
Man Dir: Michel E Slatkine

Société Biblique de Genève, see La Maison de la Bible

Taschenbuch Verlag **Spectrum**, a subsidiary of Scherz Verlag AG (qv)

Speer-Verlag, R Römer, Hofstr 134, CH-8044 Zurich Tel: (01) 2511203 Cable Add: Sperverlag
Man Dir: R Römer
Subjects: General Fiction, Belles Lettres, Philosophy, Juveniles, Poetry
Founded: 1944
ISBN Publisher's Prefix: 3-85916

Spes, an imprint of Editions André Delcourt & Cie (qv)

Sphinx Medien, Nadelberg 47, CH-4003 Basle Tel: (061) 258583 Telex: 965244
Dir: Dieter A Hagenbach
Subjects: Fantasy, Magic, Tarot, Gypsy Lore, Philosophy, Psychology, Religion, Art, Shamanism, New Age, Alternative Lifestyles
Bookshops: Buchhandlung Sphinx, Nadelberg 47 and Spalenberg 38, CH-4003 Basle Tel: (061) 259292
1986: 20 titles *1987:* 30 titles *Founded:* 1975
ISBN Publisher's Prefix: 3-85914

Verlag **Stämpfli** & Cie AG, PO Box 2728, CH-3001 Berne (Located at: Haller-Str 7-9, Berne) Tel: (031) 232323 Cable Add: Buchstämpfli Bern Telex: 911987
Man Dir, Rights & Permissions: Dr Jakob Stämpfli; *Sales & Advertising Dir:* K Zeller
Subjects: Jurisprudence, Political Science, Economics, History, Social Science, University Textbooks, Swiss Law
1985: 43 titles *1986:* 44 titles *Founded:* 1799
ISBN Publisher's Prefix: 3-7272

Rudolf **Steiner** Verlag, Haus Duldeck, PO Box 135, CH-4143 Dornach Tel: (061) 722240/722511
Man Dir, Editorial: Benedikt Marzahn; *Publicity, Sales:* Sabine Scherrer; *Production:* B Marzahn, Carlo Frigeri; *Rights & Permissions:* Administrators of the Rudolf Steiner Literary Estate
Subsidiary Company: Editrice Antroposofica SRL, Italy (qv)
Subjects: Anthroposophy: complete works of Rudolf Steiner
Bookshop: At above address
1986: 43 titles *Founded:* 1956
ISBN Publisher's Prefix: 3-7274

Stephanus Edition Verlags AG+, PO Box 721, CH-8280 Kreuzlingen
Man Dir: Hans Braun
Subsidiary Company: Stephanus Edition Verlags GmbH, Federal Republic of Germany (qv)
Subjects: Juvenile Religious, Christian, Anti-Communist
Founded: 1978
ISBN Publisher's Prefix: 3-921213

Verlag **Stocker-Schmid** AG*, PO Box 66, CH-8953 Dietikon-Zurich (Located at: Hasenbergstr 7, Dietikon-Zurich) Tel: (01) 7404444
Man Dir: Mr Stocker
Subsidiary Companies: Verlag Bibliophile Drucke von Josef Stocker AG (qv); Urs Graf-Verlag GmbH (qv)
Bookshop: Buchhandlung Stocker-Schmid (at above address)
Subjects: Modern and Historical Weapons and Equipment of the Swiss Army, Swiss Interest (especially bibliophile editions, facsimiles of incunabula, old maps, manuscripts)
ISBN Publisher's Prefix: 3-7276

Stroemfeld Verlag AG+, PO Box 79, CH-4007 Basle (Located at: Oetlingerstr 19, CH-4057 Basle) Tel: (061) 324180
Man Dir: J Osolin
Associate Company: Verlag Roter Stern, Federal Republic of Germany (qv)
Founded: 1979
ISBN Publisher's Prefix: 3-87877

Strom-Verlag*, Staffelhof 21, CH-8055 Zurich 3 Tel: (01) 4637415
Man Dir: Ernst Kobelt
Subjects: General Fiction, Art, Philosophy, High-priced Paperbacks, Psychology, Social Science, Poetry
ISBN Publisher's Prefix: 3-85921

Sumus Verlag Jutta Gütermann*, Güstr 6, CH-8700 Küsnacht Tel: (01) 9106184/9230259 Cable Add: Sumus
Editorial: Jutta Gütermann
Subject: Belles Lettres in Large Print, Swiss Literature
Founded: 1976
ISBN Publisher's Prefix: 3-85926

T V F, an imprint of Trachsel Verlag (qv)

Terra Magica, an imprint of Reich Verlag AG (qv)

Theologischer Verlag AG, Postfach, Räffelstr 20, CH-8045 Zurich Tel: (01) 4617710 Telex: 813880 tuz ch
Dir, Editorial: Werner Blum; *Rights & Permissions:* Werner Blum, R Jost; *Publicity:* R Jost
Subjects: Religion, Theology (emphasizing scriptural knowledge and reformation history)
Bookshops: Theologische Buchhandlung (at above address); Nova Buchhandlung, Nansenstr 4, Zurich; Freiestr 5, Uster; Bahnhofstr 12, Wetzikon
Founded: 1934
ISBN Publisher's Prefix: 3-290

Theseus Verlag AG, Im Eigeli 6a, CH-8700 Küsnacht Tel: (01) 9109294
Subject: Eastern Religions

Verlags und Versandbuchhandlung **Thun** AG, a subsidiary of Ott Verlag AG Thun (qv)

Tipografia Stazionne, see Edizioni Armando Dadò

Trachsel Verlag+, CH-3714 Frutigen Tel: (033) 711407
Man Dir: Ernst Trachsel-Pauli; *Editorial, Production, Rights & Permissions, Sales, Publicity:* Ernst Trachsel
Imprint: TVF
Subject: Christianity
Bookshop: At above address
1985: 5 titles *1986:* 3 titles *Founded:* 1946
ISBN Publisher's Prefix: 3-7271

Trans Tech Publications SA*, Trans Tech House, PO Box 10, CH-4711 Aedermannsdorf Tel: (062) 741379
Dir: Dr F H Wohlbier
Subjects: Materials Science, Technology for Heavy Industry, Environmental Sciences, Energy Physics and Technology, Solid State Physics

Nuova Edizioni **Trelingue** SA*, Via Mercoli 8, CH-6900 Lugano
Subjects: Geography, Economics, Law, History

Tribune Editions*, PO Box 434, CH-1211 Geneva 11 Tel: (022) 212121 Telex: 23381 trib ch
Man Dir, Rights & Permissions: Henri Heizmann
Parent Company: SA de la Tribune de Genève
Subjects: Current Affairs, History, Documentaries, Health, Television, Illustrated Books, Juveniles, Art, Comics, Gastronomy
Founded: 1977

Editions du **Tricorne**+, PO Box 229, CH-1211 Geneva 4 Tel: (022) 469355/ 841480 Telex: 421859
Man Dir: Serge Kaplun
Subjects: Art, Psychology, Religion, Tapestry, Circus, Puppetry, Mathematics, Poetry, Local Interest, Catalogues
1986: 7 titles *1987:* 7 titles *Founded:* 1976
ISBN Publisher's Prefix: 2-8293

Editions des **Trois Collines***, 1 rue de la Cité, PO Box 470, CH-1211 Geneva Tel: (022) 561309
Dir: François Lachenal
Subjects: Art, Politics, Belles Lettres, Philosophy, Psychology
Founded: 1936

U Bär Verlag, see Bär

Union Helvetia Fachbuchverlag*, PO Box 4870, CH-6002 Lucerne (Located at: Adligenswilerstr 22, Lucerne) Tel: (041) 515454 Telex: 868397 uhel
Subjects: Hotel-keeping and Catering (including foreign language instruction), Gastronomy, Bar-tending
Bookshops: Adligenswilerstr 22, Lucerne; Freigutstr 10, Zurich; 16 ave des Acacias, Lausanne
Miscellaneous: Publishing branch of the Schweizerischer Zentralverband der Hotel- und Restaurant-Angestellten (Swiss Industrial Union of Hotel and Restaurant Employees)

Unionsverlag+, Zollikerstr 138, CH-8008 Zurich Tel: (01) 557282
Man Dir: Lucien Leitess; *Editorial:* Bernd Zocher
Subjects: Non-fiction, Swiss, Third World and International Literature
Founded: 1978
ISBN Publisher's Prefix: 3-293

Universitätsverlag, see Editions Universitaires SA

Uranium Verlag*, PO Box 42, CH-6317 Oberwil Tel: (042) 217744 Telex: Topaz 58280
Man Dir, Sales: L Young; *Editorial:* Mrs Young
Branch Off: Atzelbergstr 22, D-6000 Frankfurt am Main
Subjects: Children's Books (picture books and non-fiction)
Founded: 1976
ISBN Publisher's Prefix: 3-294

Urs Graf-Verlag GmbH*, Hasenbergstr 7, CH-8953 Dietikon Tel: (01) 7404444
Man Dir: Mr Stocker
Parent Company: Verlag Stocker-Schmid AG (qv)
Associate Company: Verlag Bibliophile Drucke von Josef Stocker AG (qv)
Subjects: University Textbooks, Facsimile Editions of Maps and Manuscripts
ISBN Publisher's Prefix: 3-85951

V C H-Verlags AG, Hardstr 10, Postfach, CH-4020 Basle Tel: (061) 220606 Telex: 965372 Vch Bs
Parent Company: VCH Verlagsgesellschaft mbH, Federal Republic of Germany (qv)

Verlag **Verbandsdruckerei-Betadruck**, now Grafino-Verlag, Grafische Betriebe AG (qv)

Verkehrshaus der Schweiz*, Lidostr 3-7, CH-6006 Lucerne
Subjects: Transport, Traffic, Communications, Tourism, Planetarium, Cosmorama
ISBN Publisher's Prefix: 3-85954

Editions du **Verseau**, an imprint of Roth et Sauter SA (qv)

Verlag Alfred **Vetter***, Schifflaende 22, CH-8001 Zurich
ISBN Publisher's Prefix: 3-85956

Viktoria-Verlag Fritz Marti AG*, Obere Zollgasse 69e, CH-3072 Ostermundigen Tel: (031) 514283
Subjects: Belles Lettres, Books on Berne, Dialect Texts, Humour
ISBN Publisher's Prefix: 3-85958

Vogt-Schild AG Druck & Verlag*, Dornacherstr 39, CH-4501 Solothurn Tel: (065) 247247 Telex: 934646
Dir: Dr Markus H Haefely; *Marketing:* Hans Rölli
Subjects: Road Transport, Chemistry, Pharmacy, Plastics, Environment, Hospital, Medical, Horology, Electronics, Building
Founded: 1906
ISBN Publisher's Prefix: 3-85962

Editions de la **Voie de l'Art**, see VDA

Verlag Die **Waage**+*, Dorfstr 90, CH-8802 Kilchberg, Zurich Tel: (01) 7155569
Publisher and all offices: Felix M Wiesner
Subjects: Chinese Fiction and Folktales in translation; Non-fiction, Belles Lettres, Poetry from other countries; Paperback series
1985: 4 titles *Founded:* 1951
ISBN Publisher's Prefix: 3-85966

Walter-Verlag AG, Amthausquai 21, CH-4600 Olten Tel: (062) 341188 Cable Add: Walterverlag Olten Telex: 981690
Man Dir: Guido Elber; *Editorial:* Dr F J Metzinger, K Hetzar; *Sales:* C Götz; *Publicity:* K Wagner; *Rights & Permissions:* E Straumann
Subsidiary Company: Walter-Verlag GmbH Freiburg, Federal Republic of Germany (qv)
Subjects: Literature, Cultural History, Travel Guides, Psychology, Religion, Picture Books
Founded: 1916
ISBN Publisher's Prefix: 3-530

Weber SA d'Editions, PO Box 2296, CH-1211 Geneva 2 (Located at: 13 rue de Monthoux, Geneva) Tel: (022) 326450/59 Cable Add: Livrart, Geneva
Man Dir: Marcel Weber; *All other offices:* Marcel and Hilde Weber
Subjects: Art, Architecture, Photography, Bibliophily, Practical Living
Founded: 1951
ISBN Publisher's Prefix: 3-295

Weltrundschau Verlag AG*, PO Box 427, CH-6340 Baar (Located at: Oberneuhofstr 1, Baar) Tel: (042) 315431 Cable Add: Worldreview Telex: 865309
Man Dir: G Braun; *Editorial:* E Gysling; *Rights & Permissions:* Jeunesse Verlagsanstalt, Kirchstr 1, FL-9490 Vaduz, Liechtenstein
Founded: 1959

Verlag **Wepf** & Co AG*, Eisengasse 5, CH-4001 Basle Tel: (061) 257574 Cable Add: Wepfco Basle Telex: 62027
Dir: Robert Wepf
Associate Company: Hüthig und Wepf Verlag (qv)

Subjects: Geology, Mineralogy, Natural Sciences, Helvetica
Bookshops: See under Major Booksellers
Founded: 1902
ISBN Publisher's Prefix: 3-85977

Werner Druck AG*, Kanonengasse 32, CH-4001 Basle Tel: (061) 220690
President & Co-Dir: Dr H G Hinderling; *Co-Dir:* N Werner
Subjects: Fine & Applied Arts, Illustrated Books
Founded: 1862
ISBN Publisher's Prefix: 3-85979

Buchverlag der Druckerei **Wetzikon** AG*, CH-8620 Wetzikon Tel: (01) 9333111 Telex: 875547
Subjects: Nature Protection, Belles Lettres
ISBN Publisher's Prefix: 3-85981

Verlag Alexander **Wild**+, Rathausgasse 30, CH-3011 Berne Tel: (031) 224480 Cable Add: Wildbuch
Man Dir/Owner: Alexander Wild
Associate Company: Origo-Verlag (qv)
Subjects: Academic Publications
ISBN Publisher's Prefix: 3-7284

Editions Luce **Wilquin**+, CH-1099 Lausanne Tel: (021) 932800
Publisher: Mrs Luce Wilquin
Imprints: LW Editions, LW Promotion
Subject: General Literature
1987: 4 titles *Founded:* 1987
ISBN Publisher's Prefix: 2-88253

Verlag der **Wolfsbergdrucke** (J E Wolfensberger AG), Bederstr 109, CH-8059 Zurich Tel: (01) 2012777 Telex: 58937
Dir: Ulla Wolfensberger
Subjects: Fine & Applied Arts, Illustrated Books, Juveniles
Founded: 1905
ISBN Publisher's Prefix: 3-85987

Wyss Verlag AG Bern, Effingerstr 17, CH-3008 Berne Tel: (031) 253715
Dir: Christoph Wyss
Subjects: History, Jurisprudence, Art
Founded: 1849
ISBN Publisher's Prefix: 3-7285

Genossenschaft **Z-Verlag***, PO Box 6, CH-4020 Basle (Located at: Adlerstr 7, Basle) Tel: (061) 425765
Subjects: Workers' Movement, Politics, Third World

Zbinden Druck und Verlag AG*, St Alban-Vorstadt 16, CH-4006 Basle Tel: (061) 232105
Man Dir: Kurt Krause
Subjects: Belles Lettres, Poetry, Biography, Educational, Anthroposophical Literature
ISBN Publisher's Prefix: 3-85989

Paul A **Zemp**, see Ansata Verlag

Zodiaque, La Pierre-qui-Vire, c/o Weber SA d'Editions, PO Box 2296, CH-1211 Geneva 2 (Located at: 13 rue de Monthoux, Geneva) Tel: (022) 326450 Cable Add: Livrart
Subjects: Collected Editions

Editions **Zoé***, 28 ave Cardinal-Mermillod, CH-1227 Carouge-Genève Tel: (022) 420578
Man Dir: Marlyse Pietri-Bachmann
Subjects: Social Science, History, Literature, Translations
Founded: 1975

Buchverlag **Zollikofer** AG*, Fürstenlandstr 122, PO Box 805, CH-9001 St Gallen Tel: (071) 292222 Telex: 77537
Parent Company: Zollikofer AG, Druckerei und Verlag, St Gallen
Subjects: Art, Educational, Popular Medicine, Travel Guides, Periodicals

Founded: 1789
ISBN Publisher's Prefix: 3-85993

Zumstein & Cie*, Zeughausgasse 24, CH-3011 Berne
Parent Company: Hertsch & Co
Subject: Philately
ISBN Publisher's Prefix: 3-85994

Adolf **Zwimpfer***, CH-8954 Geroldswil ZH
Associate Companies: Bayerische Verlagsanstalt Bamberg (BVB), Sankt Otto Verlag GmbH, both Federal Republic of Germany (qqv); Morawa & Co, Austria (qv)

Zytglogge Verlag+, PO Box 13, CH-3073 Gümligen (Located at: Eigerweg 16, Gümligen) Tel: (031) 522030
Programme Dir: Hugo Ramseyer; *Sales Dir:* Rolf Attenhofer; *Reader:* Willi Schmid; *Publicity:* Esther Neidhart
Subjects: Belles Lettres, Pedagogy, Theatre, Art, Politics, History, Literature, Children's
Founded: 1965
ISBN Publisher's Prefix: 3-7296

Literary Agents

Dieter **Breitsohl** AG, PO Box 245, CH-8034 Zurich (Located at: Heimatstr 25, Zurich) Tel: (01) 557818
Man Dir: Dieter Breitsohl; *Dir:* Dr Jutta Motz
Specialization: Non-fiction, especially psychology, theology, medicine; illustrators for children's books
Founded: 1983

Ferenczy Verlag AG, Rämistr 5, CH-8024 Zurich Tel: (01) 2516054 Cable Add: Ferenczyverlag Zurich Telex: 816534 fere ch

Paul und Peter **Fritz** AG Literary Agency, Postfach, CH-8032 Zurich (Located at: Jupiterstr 1, CH-8032 Zurich) Tel: (01) 534140 Telex: 817246 book ch
Man Dirs: Paul Fritz, Peter S Fritz
Founded: 1962
Specialization: Representation of American and English authors, agents and publishers in German-language areas

Gesellschaft für Verlagswerte GmbH*, PO Box 163, CH-8280 Kreuzlingen
Manager: Otto Sprenger

Liepman AG, Maienburgweg 23, CH-8044 Zurich Tel: (01) 477660 Cable Add: Litagent Telex: Litag 56739
Dirs: Ruth Liepman, Eva Koralnik, Ruth Weibel

Linder AG Literary Agency, now Paul und Peter Fritz AG Literary Agency (qv)

Litpress, Rudolf Streit & Co, Amtshausgässchen 3, CH-3011 Berne Tel: (031) 226831
Associated with Scherz Verlag AG (qv)
Dir: Ursula Griessel

N P A (Neue Presse Agentur), Haldenstr 5, Haus am Herterberg, CH-8500 Frauenfeld-Herten Tel: (054) 214374
Contact: René Marti
Specialization: Serialization in newspapers and magazines, especially women's and educational interest, fiction, exclusives

Niedieck Linder AG, Holzgasse 6, CH-8039 Zurich Tel: (01) 2021450 Telex: 56096 nck ch
General Manager: Gerda Niedieck
Founded: 1975
Specialization: Representation of German-language authors (including major authors' estates) on a world-wide basis and of Agenzia Letteraria Internazionale for German-speaking countries

Book Clubs

Büchergilde **Gutenberg***, Kanzleistr 126, CH-8021 Zurich
Owned by: Büchergilde Gutenberg Verlagsgesellschaft mbH, Federal Republic of Germany (qv)

Club **Mon Village** SA, CH-1099 Vulliens, Vaud Tel: (021) 931363
Owned by: Editions Mon Village SA (qv)
Subjects: Novels on rural life

N S B Buch- und Phonoclub*, Schweizer Verlagshaus AG, Klausstr 10, CH-8008 Zurich
Managers: Walter Meyer, Dr Armin Meyer
Affiliated with Schweizer Verlagshaus AG (qv)

Punktum*, CH-8625 Gossau Tel: (01) 9352301
Owned by: Rada Matija AG, Postfach, CH-8625 Gossau
This club deals exclusively with children's books, intended as gifts

Major Booksellers

Librairie **Barblan et Saladin***, 10 rue de Romont, CH-1701 Fribourg

Buchhandlung zum **Elsässer** AG, Postfach, CH-8022 Zurich (Located at: Limmatquai 18, CH-8001 Zurich) Tel: (01) 470847 Telex: 57268
Manager: Mrs Cornelia Schweizer

Fehr'sche Buchhandlung AG*, Schmiedgasse 16, CH-9001 St Gallen Tel: (071) 221152
Manager: B Brun

Buchhandlung A **Francke** AG, Neuengasse 43, Von Werdt-Passage, CH-3001 Berne Tel: (031) 221715 Cable Add: Franckebuch Bern Telex: 911822
Manager: Christian Lang
Owned by: Francke Verlag (qv)

Georg et Cie SA*, Librairie de l'Université, 21 rue de la Corraterie, CH-1211 Geneva 11 Tel: (022) 216633 Telex: 423985
Manager: Jacques Matile
Also Publisher (qv)

Gretener & Co, see Buchhandlung Stäheli

Hans **Huber**, Marktgasse 59, CH-3000 Berne 9 Tel: (031) 211414
General literature, medicine and psychology at above address
Also: Zeltweg 6, CH-8032 Zurich Tel: (01) 2523360 (Medicine, Psychology, Science)
Also Publisher (qv)

Leobuchhandlung, Gallusstr 20, CH-9001 St Gallen Tel: (071) 222917
Owned by: Leobuchhandlung, Verlag der Quellen-Bändchen (qv)

Buchhandlung **Meili** & Co*, Fronwagpl 13, CH-8200 Schaffhausen Telex: 76777 Meibuch
Owned by: Peter Meili & Co (qv)

Orell Füssli, Pelikanstr 10, CH-8022 Zurich 1 Tel: (01) 2118011
Manager: Walter Fehr
Also Publisher (qv)

Librairie **Payot** SA, PO Box 3212, CH-1003 Lausanne (Located at: 1 rue de Bourg, Lausanne) Tel: (021) 203331 Telex: 24961
Also: 4 pl Pépinet, CH-1003 Lausanne; Tel: (021) 203331 Telex: 24961 for both shops; 107 Freiestr, CH-4000 Basle 10; 16 Bundesgasse, CH-3001 Berne; 6 rue Grenus, PO Box 381, CH-1211 Geneva 11; 42 ave du Casino, CH-1820 Montreux; 8a rue du Bassin, CH-2000 Neuchâtel; ave du Midi 14, CH-1950 Sion; rue d'Italie 51, CH-1800 Vevey; 9 Bahnhofstr, CH-8001 Zurich
Also Publisher (qv)
Wholesale Supplier: Diffusion Payot SA, 30 rue des Côtes de Montbenon, CH-1003 Lausanne Tel: (021) 205221 Telex: 24953

Buchhandlung Hans **Rohr***, Oberdorfstr 5, CH-8024 Zurich
Antiquarian and General
Branch: Torgasse 4, CH-8024 Zurich
Also: Filmbuchhandlung Hans Rohr, Oberdorfstr 3, CH-8024 Zurich (Film/Cinema)
Owned by: Hans Rohr AG (qv)

Buchhandlung Dr A **Scheidegger***, Obere Bahnhofstr 10A, CH-8910 Affoltern Tel: (01) 7615234 Telex: 59256

Buchhandlung **Scherz** AG, Marktgasse 25, CH-3011 Berne Tel: (031) 226837
Owned by: Scherz Verlag AG (qv)

Buchhandlung **Stäheli***, Bahnhofstr 70, CH-8021 Zurich Tel: (01) 2117362 Telex: 813771 stae ch
Manager: Claus Gretener
Owned by: Gretener & Co (at above address)

Wepf & Co AG, Eisengasse 5, Postfach, CH-4001 Basle Tel: (061) 256377 Cable Add: Wepfco Basle Telex: 965532
Dir: H U Herrmann
Also: Marktgasse 42, CH-4310 Rheinfelden; PO Box 1948, Obere Schanzstr 18, D-7858 Weil am Rhein, Federal Republic of Germany; BP 165, F-68305 Saint-Louis Cédex, France
Bookseller and Antiquarian Bookshop; also Publisher (qv)

Major Libraries

Archives fédérales*, 24 rue des Archives, CH-3003 Berne Tel: (031) 618989
Swiss Federal Archives

Bibliothèque cantonale et universitaire (Kantons- und Universitätsbibliothek)*, 16 rue St-Michel, CH-1701 Fribourg

Bibliothèque cantonale et universitaire de Lausanne, 6 Pl de la Riponne, CH-1005 Lausanne Tel: (021) 228831
The above is the address of the cantonal collection. The University collection is at Dorigny, CH-1015 Lausanne Tel: (021) 461111 Telex: 454014 Lauc Ch
Dir: Hubert Villard

Bibliothèque de la Ville, now Bibliothèque publique et universitaire de Neuchâtel (qv)

Bibliothèque Nationale Suisse, see Schweizerische Landesbibliothek

Bibliothèque publique et universitaire de Genève, Promenade des Bastions, CH-1211 Geneva 4 Tel: (022) 208266
Dir: Gustave Möckli
Publication: Compte rendu (annual)

Bibliothèque publique et universitaire de Neuchâtel, 3 place Numa-Droz, CH-2000 Neuchâtel Tel: (038) 251358
Librarian: Jacques Rychner
Publication: Ville de Neuchâtel: Bibliothèques et Musées (annual)

Fondation Martin **Bodmer**, Bibliotheca Bodmeriana*, PO Box 7, CH-1223 Cologny/Geneva Tel: (022) 362370
Dir: Dr Hans E Braun

Bureau International du Travail, see International Labour Office Library

E T H Bibliothek (Eidgenössische Technische Hochschule Bibliothek), Rämistr 101, CH-8092 Zurich Tel: (01) 2562135 Telex: 817178 Bibl Ch
Library of the Swiss Federal Institute of Technology

International Labour Office, Central Library and Documentation Branch, 4 rte des Morillons, CH-1211 Geneva 22 Tel: (022) 998675/996111 Cable Add: Interlab Genève Telex: 22271 bit ch
Manager: K Wild
Publications include: International Labour Documentation (monthly), *ILO Thesaurus: Labour, Employment and Training Terminology* (in English, French and Spanish); *Labordoc* (data base)

Schweizerische Landesbibliothek (Bibliothèque Nationale Suisse)*, Hallwylstr 15, CH-3003 Berne Tel: Secretary (031) 618911; Lending Department (031) 618979 Telex: 32526 slbbe ch
Swiss National Library
Dir: Dr Franz Georg Maier

Schweizerisches Wirtschaftsarchiv (Archives Économiques Suisses), Postfach, CH-4003 Basle
Swiss Economic Archives
Librarian: Dr H U Sulser
Founded: 1910

Stadt- und Universitätsbibliothek, Postfach 58, CH-3000 Berne 7 (Located at: Münstergasse 61, Berne) Tel: (031) 225519

Stiftsbibliothek*, Klosterhof 6, CH-9000 St Gallen Tel: (071) 225719 (library of former Benedictine abbey of St Gall)

United Nations Library*, Palais des Nations, Geneva

Öffentliche Bibliothek der **Universität Basel**, Schönbeinstr 18/20, CH-4056 Basle Tel: (061) 252250
Public Library of Basle University
Dir: F Groebli

Zentralbibliothek Zürich, Kantons-, Stadt- und Universitätsbibliothek, Zähringerpl 6, Postfach, CH-8025 Zurich Tel: (01) 477272 Telex: 816507 zbzh ch
Librarian: Dr Hermann Köstler

Library Associations

Association des Bibliothécaires Suisses (Vereinigung Schweizerischer Bibliothekare)*, Bibliothèque Nationale Suisse, Hallwylstr 15, CH-3003 Berne Tel: (031) 618911
Association of Swiss Librarians
Secretary: W Treichler
Publication: Arbido (jointly with Swiss Association for Documentation and Swiss Association of Archivists) (eight times a year)

Kantonale Kommission für Gemeinde- und Schulbibliotheken, Zurich*, PO Box 474, CH-8610 Uster 1 Tel: (01) 9413725
Cantonal Commission for Municipal and School Libraries
President: Prof Dr Egon Wilhelm
Publications include: Treffpunkt Bibliothek (quarterly review)

Schweizer Bibliotheksdienst, Zähringerstr 21, CH-3012 Berne Tel: (031) 238266
Swiss Library Service

Vereinigung Schweizerischer Archivare, Bundesarchiv, Archivstr 24, CH-3003 Berne Tel: (031) 618988
Association of Swiss Archivists
Secretary: Dr Bernard Truffer, Archives cantonales, CH-1950 Sion
Publication: Arbido
Founded: 1922

Vereinigung Schweizerischer Bibliothekare, see Association des Bibliothécaires Suisses

Library Reference Journals

Arbido, Association des Bibliothécaires Suisses (Vereinigung Schweizerischer Bibliothekare), Bibliothèque Nationale Suisse, Hallwylstr 15, CH-3003 Berne
Jointly with Swiss Association for Documentation and Swiss Association of Archivists

Literary Associations and Societies

Gesellschaft für deutsche Sprache und Literatur in Zürich, Deutsches Seminar der Universität Zürich, Rämistr 74-76, CH-8001 Zurich Tel: (01) 2572561
Society for German Language and Literature in Zurich
Secretary: J Etzensperger

Thomas **Mann** Gesellschaft, c/o Europa-Verlag, Rämistr 5, CH-8001 Zurich Tel: (01) 471629
President: Z Vakant

Swiss-German **P E N Club Centre**, PO Box 1383, CH-3001 Berne
President: Dr Ernst Reinhardt; *Secretary:* Hans Erpf

P E N Club de Suisse romande, 4 rue Mont de Sion, CH-1206 Geneva Tel: (022) 462749
P E N Club for French-speaking Switzerland
President: Jean-Pierre Moulin; *Secretary:* Juliette Monnin-Hornung
Publication: PEN Club romand Newsletter (twice yearly)

P E N Internazionale — Centro della Svizzera Italiana e Romancia*, PO Box 2126, CH-6901 Lugano 1 Tel: (091) 525617
President: Grytzko Mascioni; *Secretary:* Attilia F Venturini

Schweizerische Bibliophilen-Gesellschaft, c/o Dr C Ulrich, Voltastr 43, CH-8044 Zurich
Swiss Society of Bibliophiles
President: Dr Conrad Ulrich
Publications include: Librarium, published three times a year since 1958

Schweizerischer Bund für Jugendliteratur, Herzogstr 5, CH-3014 Berne Tel: (031) 418116
Swiss Federation for Literature for Young People

Literary Periodicals

Cenobio, Dr Pier-Riccardo Frigeri, PO Box 6655, CH-6901 Lugano
Text in French and Italian

drehpunkt, PO Box 794, CH-4002 Basle

Etudes de Lettres (Literary Studies), Université de Lausanne, Faculté des Lettres, Lausanne

Naos, Edition Leu, PO Box 1704, CH-8048 Zurich
Magazine for contemporary literature

Niemo Press, Emil Rahm, CH-8215 Hallau
Journalism and literature; text in German

Orte, Orte-Verlag, PO Box 2028, CH-8033 Zurich

Poesie, Postfach, CH-4001 Basle

Revue de Belles-Lettres, Société de Belles-Lettres de Lausanne, 4 Plainpalais, PO Box 216, CH-1211 Geneva

Schweizer Monatshefte (Swiss Monthly Magazine), Gesellschaft Schweizer Monatshefte, PO Box 86, CH-8034 Zurich

Literary Prizes

Young People's Book Prize
For an outstanding book or the collected works of a writer or illustrator in the field of juvenile literature. 4,000 Swiss francs. Awarded annually. 1986 award to Sita Jucker for her collected works. Enquiries to Swiss Teachers Association, Ringstr 54, CH-8057 Zurich

City of **Zurich** Literary Prize*
Founded in 1930 by the City of Zurich to reward an author for his or her whole literary work. 40,000 Swiss francs now awarded at irregular intervals. No applications or nominations accepted. Enquiries to Präsidialabteilung der Stadt Zurich, Postfach, CH-8022 Zurich

Translation Agencies and Associations

Association suisse des Traducteurs et Interprètes (ASTI)*, PO Box 4123, CH-4002 Basle Tel: (061) 765335
Swiss Association of Translators and Interpreters

Schweizerischer Ubersetzer- und Dolmetscherverband*, PO Box 4123, CH-4002 Basle Tel: (061) 765335
Swiss Translators' and Interpreters' Association

Syria

General Information

Language: Arabic. French and English are widely spoken in business and official circles
Religion: Islamic (Sunni sect)
Population: 8.9 million
Bank Hours: 0800-1400 Saturday-Thursday
Shop Hours: Vary greatly. Closed Friday. Generally long lunch closing
Currency: 100 piastres = 1 Syrian pound
Export/Import Information: No tariffs on books except children's picture books, with additional taxes; most advertising matter is dutied. State organization for control and execution of publicity and advertising within Syria is Arab Advertising Organization, Damascus. The General

Advertising Institute, PO Box 2842, must get samples of commercial advertising and promotional materials before distribution permitted. Import licence must be submitted to Commercial Bank of Syria in order to obtain exchange licence
Copyright: No copyright conventions signed

Publishers

Arab Advertising Organization*, 28 Moutanabbi St, PO Box 2842 & 3034, Damascus Tel: 225219/225220/1 Cable Add: Golan Damascus Telex: Golan 411923 Sy
Dir-General: Haitham Basheer
Imprint: Golan
Branch Offs: Aleppo, Dar'a, Deir-Ez-Zor, Hama, Homs, Lattakia, Tartous
Subject: Directories
Founded: 1963

Bureau des Documentations Syriennes et Arabes, an associated imprint of Office Arabe de Presse et de Documentation (qv)

Damascus University Press*, Damascus
Subjects: Education, History, Geography, Engineering, Medicine, Law, Sociology, School Textbooks

Golan, an imprint of Arab Advertising Organization (qv)

Institut français d'Etudes arabes de Damas, BP 344, Damascus Tel: 330214/ 331962
Man Dir: Gilbert Delanoue; *Editorial:* Christian Velud
Orders to: Librairie d'Amérique et d'Orient (A Maisonneuve), 11 rue St-Sulpice, F-75006 Paris, France
Parent Body: Ministère des Relations Extérieures, Paris
Subjects: Islamic mediaeval history, Literature (in Arabic), Art & Architecture, Periodicals
1985-86: 2 titles

Nour E-Sham Book Centre+, PO Box 249, Damascus Tel: 454615/217811/454683 Telex: 412432 Nosham
Branch Offs: Aleppo, Homs
Subjects: Language, History, Islam, Children's
Bookshop: Mousalam Barwdist, Hejaz, Damascus
1985: 12 titles *1986:* 23 titles *Founded:* 1983

Office Arabe de Presse et de Documentation, 67 pl Chahbandar, PO Box 3550, Damascus Tel: 459166 Telex: 411613 Ofa Sy
President: Samir A Darwich
Subjects: Economics, Politics, Syria and the Arab World, Periodicals
Imprints: Associated imprints include Bureau des Documentations Syriennes et Arabes
Founded: 1964

Syrian Documentation Papers*, PO Box 2712, Damascus
Dir-General: Louis Farès
Subjects: Reference, Directories, Politics, Economics, Sociology, Law
Founded: 1968

al-Tawjih Press*, Palestine St, PO Box 3320, Damascus
Subject: Literature

Major Booksellers

Avicenne Librairie Internationale*, Tajhiz St, PO Box 2456 Tel: 212911 Telex: Ortexo 419120 SY
Manager: Jean-Pierre Dummar

Dar **Dimashk** (Adib Tunbakji) Bookshop*, Port Said St Tel: 111048

Dar Al-**Fikr** (Salem & Zu'bi) Bookshop*, Saadalah Al-Jabiri St, PO Box 962 Tel: 211041/211166 Cable Add: Fikr Telex: Fkr 411745 Sy

Dakr Abdul **Wahab***, Port Said St Tel: 115486

Major Libraries

Damascus University Library*, Damascus
Publication: Bibliography of the Middle East

Dar al-Kutub al-Wataniah (National Library)*, Homs

Al **Maktabah** Al Wataniah (National Library)*, Bab El-Faradj, Aleppo

National Library of Latakia*, Latakia

Al **Zahiriah** (National Library)*, Bab el Barid, Damascus

Library Reference Journal

Damascus University Library Review, Damascus University Library, Damascus

Literary Periodical

Al-Mawgif Al-Adabi, Ittihad al-Kuttab al-Arab, Shari Murshid Khatir, Damascus

Taiwan

General Information

Language: Chinese: a single written language is used by speakers of several diverse spoken dialects. The most important spoken form is Mandarin, known in Taiwan as *Kuo-Yü* (= national tongue). Other important spoken forms in Taiwan are Amoy-Swatow (also called Taiwanese) and Hakka
Religion: Predominantly Buddhist, Taoist, Christian
Population: 19 million
Bank Hours: 0900-1530 Monday-Friday; 0900-1200 Saturday
Shop Hours: 1000-2130 Monday-Saturday
Currency: 100 cents = 1 new Taiwan dollar
Export/Import Information: No tariffs on books and advertising. Import licences required; exchange available when licence presented at authorized bank. Publications approved for import will not violate the Republic of China's basic national policy, undermine public morality or contravene special regulations
Copyright: No copyright conventions signed. Copyright is protected by the Copyright Law. Companies and individuals, including foreigners, can register their works with the Ministry of the Interior for protection. An amendment broadening the scope of the Republic of China's Copyright Law was passed 28 June 1985 by the Legislative Yuan and put into effect on 12 July 1985. The amendment, aimed at curbing pirating activities, sharply increases the maximum penalty for copyright infringement by raising the maximum

sentence for violating copyrights from three to five years and the maximum fine from US$75 to US$11,250, and brings computer software and video tapes under the scope of the law. Publications printed in Taiwan must acquire approval from the copyright holder before export

Book Trade Reference Books and Journals

Books

Books on China 1980: A Cumulative List with Descriptions of Original and Reprinted Western-Language Titles Available from Taiwan, Chinese Materials Center Inc, PO Box 22048, Taipei

Chung-hua min-kuo ch'u-pan t'u-shu mu-lu wu-nien hul-pien pen ti-ssu chi (National Bibliography of the Republic of China), National Central Library, 20 Chungshan S Rd, Taipei 10040

Journals

Chinese National Bibliography, National Central Library, 20 Chungshan S Rd, Taipei 10040
Text in Chinese and English

Shu mo chi kan, Student Book Co Ltd, 298 Roosevelt Rd, 3rd Section, Taipei
Quarterly bibliography, text in Chinese

Publishers

Business Publications Ltd*, PO Box 58432, Taipei (Located at: Hui Feng Bldg 3rd/4th Floor, No 20 Lane 14 Chi Lin Rd, Taipei) Tel: (02) 5216457/5218784 Cable Add: Andypandy Telex: 21032 Andy
Man Dir: Michelle Yang; *Editorial:* Nigel White; *Sales, Publicity:* Hellen Tsai; *Production:* Dawn Chen; *Rights & Permissions:* Mark Van Roo
Associate Companies: Andy Pandy Ltd (Hui Feng Bldg 3rd Floor); Business English Center (4th Floor)
Subjects: International Business, Business English Textbooks, Business Dictionary (English/Chinese), Periodical
Bookshop: At above address
Founded: 1978

Cheng Chung Book Co*, 20 Hengyang Rd, Taipei
Subjects: Academic

Ch'eng Wen Publishing Company, c/o CMC Taipei Liaison Office, PO Box 22605, Taipei 100 Tel: (02) 7415432 Cable Add: Chewenpb Taipei Telex: 13542 Cwnsb
Chief Executive: Larry C Huang
Subjects: Scholarly, General Interest (in Chinese and English)
Founded: 1964

Chinese Materials Center, Taipei Liaison Office, PO Box 22048, Taipei 10099 Tel: (02) 7529244 Cable Add: Taient Taipei Telex: 13259 Hanroc
President: Robert L Irick
Parent Company: Chinese Materials Center, PO Box 73075, Kowloon Central Post Office, Kowloon, Hong Kong
Associate Companies: Taiwan Enterprise Co Ltd (at above main address); Chinese Materials Center Publications, 633 Post St, Suite 251, San Francisco, CA 94109-8299, USA
Subjects: China, Asia, Scholarly, General
Bookshop: See under Major Booksellers
1985: 3 titles *1986:* 3 titles *Founded:* 1964
ISBN Publisher's Prefix: 0-89644

Chung Hwa Book Co Ltd, 94 Chungking S Rd, Section 1, Taipei 100 Tel: (02) 3117365/3117344/3113541 Cable Add: 2821 Taipei
Man Dir: D S Hsiung; *Sales Dir:* W M Wang; *Publicity Dir:* Mrs S M Sun
Subjects: General Fiction, Belles Lettres, Poetry, Biography, History, How-to, Music, Art, Philosophy, Reference, Religion, Juveniles, Low- & High-priced Paperbacks, Medicine, Psychology, Engineering, General & Social Science, University, Secondary & Primary Textbooks, Educational Materials
Founded: 1911

Far East Book Co, 66-1 (10th Floor) Chungking S Rd, Section 1, Taipei Tel: (02) 3118740 Cable Add: 1418 Taipei
Manager: Jonathan Riverbank
Subjects: Art, Education, History, Physics, Dictionaries, Shakespeare in translation, Tang Poems, Textbooks

Fu-Hsing Book Co*, 44 Huai Ning St, Taipei
Subject: Textbooks

Great China Book Corporation*, 66 Chungking S Rd, Section 1, Taipei
Subject: Textbooks

Hua Kuo Publishing Co*, 218 King San St, Ho-Ping East Rd, Taipei
Publisher: T F Wang; *Publicity Manager:* Y M Yeh
Founded: 1950

San Min Book Co Ltd, 61 Chung Ching S Rd, Section 1, Taipei
Publicity Manager: Cheng-Chiang Liu
Subjects: History, Philosophy, Sociology, Literary

World Book Co*, 99 Chungking S Rd, Section 1, Taipei Tel: (02) 3111616
General Manager: Tsung Mou Shaw
Subjects: Chinese Classics, Novels, Reference & Textbooks for High School, College & University
Founded: 1921

Yee Wen Publishing Co Ltd+*, PO Box 969, Taipei 100 (Located at: 81 Kuang Min St, Pan Chiao) Tel: (02) 9616321
Chief Executive: I-Ping Yen; *Executive Manager:* Tsu-Ken Yao
Branch Off: 21 Vista Court, South San Francisco, CA 94080, USA
Subjects: Chinese Art & History, Archaeology, Oracle Bone Studies, Ancient Chinese Language & Culture, Religion, Philosophy
Bookshop: At above address
1985: 4 titles *1986:* 20 titles *Founded:* 1953
ISBN Publisher's Prefix: 0-88691

Major Booksellers

Chinese Materials Center, c/o CMC Taipei Liaison Office, PO Box 22048, Taipei 10099 Tel: (02) 7529244 Cable Add: Taient Taipei Telex: 13259 Hanroc
International distributor and publisher (qv)
President: Robert L Irick; *Manager:* Ong Hsun-p'ing

H C Ling Book Store & Co Ltd*, PO Box 322, Taipei 100

Literature House Ltd*, 6th Floor, 192 Ho-Ping East Rd, Section 1, Taipei Tel: (02) 3923191
Manager: Julia Lee
Owned by: Mei Ya Publications Inc (qv) Importer

Mei Ya Publications Inc (Sueling, Inc)*, PO Box 22555, Taipei Tel: (02) 3923191
Manager: Julia Lee
Specialize in College and University textbook reprints (all copyrighted)

The **National Book** Co*, 84-5 Section 3, Sing Sung S Rd, Taipei 107 Tel: (02) 3210698 Cable Add: Natlbk Taipei
Manager: J K Chen

Southeast Book Co*, 105 Po Ali Rd, Taipei

Taipei Publications Trading Co*, PO Box 59326, Taipei
Manager: Y C Huang

Win Join Book Co Ltd, 105 Ho-Ping East Rd, Section 1, Taipei Tel: (02) 3934063/3419646 Telex: 26985 Jetwin
Manager: Mrs M C Tasy Lin

Major Libraries

Bureau of International Exchange of Publications, National Central Library, 20 Chungshan S Rd, Taipei 10040 Tel: (02) 3619132 Fax: (02) 3619144

Fu Ssu-Nien Library Institute of History and Philology, Academia Sinica, Taipei 115

Kuomintang Central Committee Library*, Taipei

National Central Library*, 20 Chungshan S Rd, Taipei 10040 Tel: (02) 3113981 (Office of the Director); 3147322 (Reference Section); 3813215 (Resource and Information Centre for Chinese Studies)
Director: Dr Chen-ku Wang
Publications include: National Union List of Chinese Periodicals of the Republic of China; Union Catalog of Books in the Republic of China; National Bibliography of the Republic of China; Yearbook of Libraries in the Republic of China

National War College Library*, Yangmingshan, Taipei

Taipei Municipal Library*, Hsin I Rd, Section 4, Taipei

Taiwan Branch Library, National Central Library*, 1 Hsinshen S Rd, Section 1, Taipei 106
Librarian: Henry H S Jeng

Library Association

Library Association of China, c/o National Central Library, 20 Chungshan S Rd, Taipei 10040 Tel: (02) 3619132
Executive Dir: Teresa Wang Chang
Publications: Library Association of China Newsletter (bi-monthly in Chinese); *Bulletin of the Library Association of China* (annually in Chinese)

Library Reference Books and Journals

Books

Chung-hua min-kuo t'u-shu-kuan nien-chien (Yearbook of Libraries in the Republic of China), National Central Library, 20 Chungshan S Rd, Taipei 10040

Chung-hua min-kuo t'u-shu lien-ho mu-lu (Union Catalog of Books in the Republic of China), National Central Library, 20 Chungshan S Rd, Taipei 10040

Tseng-pu hsiu-ting Chung-hua min-kuo Chung-wen ch'i-k'an lien-ho mu-lu (National Union List of Chinese Periodicals of the Republic of China), National Central Library, 20 Chungshan S Rd, Taipei 10040

Journals

Chung-kuo t'u-shu-kuan hsueh-hui hui-pao (Bulletin of the Library Association of China), National Central Library, 20 Chungshan S Rd, Taipei 10040

Journal of Library and Information Science, National Taiwan Normal University, Department of Social Education, Taipei

Literary Associations and Societies

China National Association of Literature and the Arts*, No 4, Lane 22, Ningpo St West, Taipei

National Council of Ethnographic Arts and Literature of China*, 11 Terrace 5, Lane 5, Section 3, Jan-Ai Rd, Taipei

The **Taipei** Chinese **P E N** Centre, 5th Floor — No 33, Lane 180, Kwang Fu S Rd, Taipei 105 Cable Add: Taipenclub
President: Nancy C Ing; *Secretary:* Prof Kwang-chung Yu
Publication: The Chinese PEN (quarterly, text in English)

Literary Periodicals

The Chinese PEN (quarterly), The Taipei Chinese Center, International PEN, 5th Floor — No 33, Lane 180, Kwang Fu S Rd, Taipei 105
Text in English

Counter Attack, National Institute for Compilation and Translation, 247 Chou-Shan Rd, Taipei

Tamkang Review, Tamkang College, Graduate Institute of Western Languages and Literature, King-Hua St, Taipei
Journal mainly devoted to comparative studies between Chinese and foreign literatures, text in English

Yeh ko (Evensongs), Tamkang College, English Department Evening School, Evensongs Association, No 5, Lane 199, King-hua St, Taipei
Text in Chinese or English

Translation Agencies and Associations

National Institute for Compilation and Translation*, 247 Chou-Shan Rd, Taipei
Dir: Dr Hsien-Chu Hsiung
Publication: Counter Attack

Tanzania

General Information

Language: Swahili is official language. English is widely used
Religion: About 30% Islamic, 25% Christian (mostly Roman Catholic); rest follow traditional beliefs
Population: 17.9 million

Bank Hours: Mainland Tanzania: 0900-1200 Monday-Friday; 0900-1100 Saturday. Zanzibar: 0830-1130 Monday-Friday; 0830-1000 Saturday
Shop Hours: 0800-1200, 1400-1715 or 1800 Monday-Saturday
Currency: 100 cents = 1 Tanzania shilling
Export/Import Information: No tariff on books or advertising matter. Import licence and exchange controls
Copyright: Florence (see International section)

Book Trade Organization

Standard Book Numbering Agency, Tanzania Library Service, PO Box 9283, Dar es Salaam
ISBN Administrator: T E Mlaki

Book Trade Reference Journals

Government and Tanu Publications List, Government Publications Agency, PO Box 1801, Dar es Salaam

Tanzania National Bibliography, Tanzania Library Service, PO Box 9283, Dar es Salaam
The national bibliography, published annually since 1969

Publishers

Africa Inland Church Literature Department, see Inland Publishers

Central Tanganyika Press+, PO Box 1129, Dodoma Tel: (061) 22140
Manager: Frances M Weir
Subject: Religion
1985: 14 titles *1986:* 7 titles *Founded:* 1954
ISBN Publisher's Prefix: 9976-66

Dar es Salaam University Press, PO Box 35182, Dar es Salaam Tel: (051) 49192 exts 2643-6, 2679 Cable Add: University Dar es Salaam
Director: D K Tungaraza
Subjects: University & School Textbooks, Academic Monographs

Eastern Africa Publications Ltd*, PO Box 1002, Arusha Tel: (057) 7513 Cable Add: Eapl Arusha Telex: 42121 Concentre
General Manager: Cleveland Nkata
Editorial: A Saiwaad; *Sales, Marketing, Publicity:* J J Mwijage; *Production:* S M S Poyowela
Parent Company: Tanzania Karatasi Associated Industries, PO Box 2418, Dar es Salaam
Branch Off: PO Box 1408, Dar es Salaam
Subjects: General Non-fiction, Poetry, Biography, History, Geography, Science, Politics, Africana, Primary & Secondary Schools Reference Books in both Kiswahili and English
Founded: 1979

Government Printer*, Government Publications Agency, PO Box 2483, Dar es Salaam

Inland Publishers, PO Box 125, Mwanza Tel: (068) 40064
Dir: Rev S M Magesa
Subjects: General Non-fiction, Religion, Books in Kiswahili and English, Paperbacks
Miscellaneous: A publishing division of Africa Inland Church Literature Department (at above address)

Ndanda Mission Press, Ndanda PO Box 1004, Ndanda via Mtwara
Subjects: Religion, Medical, Social

Oxford University Press, Maktaba Rd, PO Box 5299, Dar es Salaam Tel: (051) 29209 Cable Add: Oxonian
Manager: Lucius M Thonya
Subjects: General Non-fiction, Literature, Poetry, Biography, History, Africana, Reference, Books in Kiswahili, General & Social Science, Secondary & Primary Textbooks
Founded: 1969
Miscellaneous: Firm is a branch of Oxford University Press, East and Central Africa, Kenya (qv)

Pan-African Publishing Co Ltd, 11 Nkrumah St, PO Box 4212, Dar es Salaam Tel: (051) 22380
Man Dir: M W Kanyama Chiume
Subjects: Fiction, Science, Politics, History, General
Bookshop: Pan-African Bookshop, PO Box 5068, Tanga
Founded: 1977

Tanzania Library Services Board*, PO Box 9283, Dar es Salaam Tel: (051) 26121 Cable Add: Tanlis
Dir: E E Kaungamno
Founded: 1963
ISBN Publisher's Prefix: 9976-65

Tanzania Mission Press, see T M P Book Department

Tanzania Publishing House, 47 Samora Ave, PO Box 2138, Dar es Salaam Tel: (051) 32164 Cable Add: Publish Dar es Salaam
General Manager: Walter Bgoya; *Sales Manager:* K Kasaka
Subjects: General Fiction & Non-fiction, Belles Lettres, Poetry, Biography, History, Africana, Philosophy, Juveniles, Paperbacks, Social Science, University & Secondary Textbooks (in Kiswahili and English)
Founded: 1966

Major Booksellers

The **Cathedral** Bookshop*, Mansfield St, PO Box 2381, Dar es Salaam Tel: (051) 22873

The **Dar es Salaam Bookshop**, Indra Gandi St, PO Box 9030, Dar es Salaam Tel: (051) 23416
Manager: E Charokiwa

Dar es Salaam University Bookshop*, PO Box 35090, Dar es Salaam Tel: (051) 48300/49192 exts 2388-90
Manager: Miss C G Barabojik

Inland Bookshop, PO Box 1402, Mwanza Tel: (068) 2132
Branches in Bariadi, Bunda, Geita, Kahama, Magu, Masua, Musoma, Nansio, Sengerema, Shinyanga
Distribution Manager: S D Nungwana
Owned by: Africa Inland Church Literature Department

International Bookshop*, PO Box 21341, Dar es Salaam Tel: (051) 21930/28941 Cable Add: Safina, Dar es Salaam Telex: 41334 Intpub Tz
Dir: Murtaza Alidina
Wholesale, Distribution: International Publishers Agencies Ltd (at above address)
Retail Outlets: International Bookshop (at above address); Les Nouvelles, Kilimanjaro Hotel, Dar es Salaam

The **Standard** Bookshop*, Independence Ave, PO Box 1278, Dar es Salaam Tel: (051) 23126

Tanzania Elimu Supplies Ltd*, Textbook Division, Port Area, Kurasini, PO Box 20873, Dar es Salaam Tel: (051) 25481 Cable Add: Elisup Telex: 41349

Tanzania Mission Press, see T M P Book Department

Major Libraries

American Center Library, US Information Service*, PO Box 9170, Dar es Salaam Tel: (051) 26611
Library Dir: G K Nagri

British Council Library, Samora Ave, Ohio St, PO Box 9100, Dar es Salaam Tel: (051) 22726

Institute of Development Management Library, PO Box 4, Mzumbe, Morogoro Tel: (056) 4380 ext 262 Telex: idm morogoro
Chief Librarian: Andrew S Sefu

Kibaha Public Library, PO Box 30063, Kibaha Tel: 2101 ext 176

Kivukoni College Library, PO Box 9193, Dar es Salaam Tel: (051) 29215
Librarian: George M Gwahemba

Makumira Lutheran Theological College Library, PO Box 55, Usa River
Librarians: N Mbise, R A Ries

Marangu College of National Education Library*, PO Box 3080, Moshi Tel: 16 Marangu
Librarian: Joachim Mkumbara

The **Medical** Library*, Faculty of Medicine, Muhimbili Medical Centre, PO Box 65012, Dar es Salaam Tel: (051) 26211/27081 Cable Add: Muhimbili Dar es Salaam
Chief Librarian: D W K Mwapwele
Publications include: Health Information in Tanzania

Moshi Public Library, PO Box 863, Moshi Tel: (051) 2432
Librarian: Alfred Zacharia Mwasha

Mwanza Regional Library*, PO Box 1363, Mwanza Tel: (068) 2314
Librarian: Fabian M Kadamah

National Archives of Tanzania*, India St, PO Box 2006, Dar es Salaam Tel: (051) 23954

Sokoine University of Agriculture Library, PO Box 3022, Morogoro Tel: (056) 3511 Cable Add: Uniagric Morogoro Telex: 55308 Univmo Tz
Librarian: S S Mbwana
Publications: Library Accessions List (quarterly); *Annual Record of Research*; *The Green Revolution: A Bibliography*

Tanzania Library Service*, PO Box 9283, Dar es Salaam Tel: (051) 26121 Telex: Tanlis
Publications: Tanzania National Bibliography; *Directory of Libraries, Museums and Archives in Tanzania* (1979)

University of Dar es Salaam Library, PO Box 35092, Dar es Salaam Tel: (051) 48235
Dir: Mrs O C Mascarenhas

Zanzibar Government Archives*, PO Box 116, Zanzibar

Library Association

Tanzania Library Association, PO Box 2645, Dar es Salaam Tel: (051) 26121
Secretary: Miss M Ngaiza

Publications: Someni (journal); *Matukio* (TLA newsletter)

Library Reference Books and Journals

Book

Directory of Libraries, Museums and Archives in Tanzania (1979), Tanzania Library Service, PO Box 9283, Dar es Salaam

Journals

Matukio, Tanzania Library Association, PO Box 2645, Dar es Salaam

Someni, Tanzania Library Association, PO Box 2645, Dar es Salaam
Text in English

Literary Periodical

Umma, Eastern Africa Publications Ltd, PO Box 1002, Arusha
Biannual literary magazine published under the auspices of the Department of Literature, University of Dar es Salaam

Thailand

General Information

Language: Thai is official language. English is widely used in government and commercial circles. There are sizeable populations of Chinese, Malay and Khmer speakers
Religion: Theravada Buddhist
Population: 47.1 million
Bank Hours: 0830-1530 Monday-Friday
Shop Hours: Vary. Those catering for tourists generally open 0830-1800 or later
Currency: 100 satangs = 1 baht
Export/Import Information: No tariff on books but Standard Profit Tax and Business Tax apply (also a Municipal Tax of percentage of Business Tax). Advertising subject to same taxes and ad val percentage of import duty. No import licences for books, but special permit required by importer for orders over a certain sum. Certificate of payment (from Exchange Control Authority) required
Copyright: Berne, Florence (see International section)

Book Trade Organizations

Publishers' and Booksellers' Association of Thailand*, 108 Sukhumvit Soi 53, Bangkok Tel: (02) 112447
President and Secretary: M L M Jumsai, Chalermnit Press, 1-2 Erawan Arcade, Bangkok Tel: (02) 528759

Standard Book Numbering Agency*, The National Library of Thailand, Samsen Rd, Bangkok 10300 Tel: (02) 2815449 Telex: 84189 Natlib Th
ISBN Administrator: Mrs Suwakhon Phadung-Ath

Publishers

Aksorn Charerntat, 142 Praengsanpasart, Tanao Rd, Bangkok Tel: (02) 2212371
Subjects: Textbooks, Industry, Arts, Maps, Literature, Mathematics, Education, Physics, Linguistics, Children's Books

Aksorn Charoen Tasna Ltd*, 195 Bamrung Muang Rd, Bangkok
Subject: Textbooks

Bandarnsarn*, 136-138 Nakorn Sawan Rd, Bangkok Tel: (02) 2825511
Subject: Thai books

Banmai*, 1 Soi Prasanmit, Sukhumvit, Bangkok

Barnakarn*, 236 Nakern Kashem, Bangkok Tel: (02) 227796
Subject: Thai books

Barnakieh Trading*, 34 Nakorn Sawan Rd, Bangkok Tel: (02) 825520
Subject: Thai books

Barnasilpa*, 1 Soi Praengsanpasart, Asdang Rd, Bangkok Tel: (02) 220060
Subject: Thai books

Chalermnit Press*, 108 Sukhumvit 53, Bangkok 10110 Tel: (02) 2528759
Managers: M L M Jumsai, Mrs Jumsai
Subjects: Books on Thailand, Pocket books and Children's books in English, French & German, Magazines, Dictionaries
Bookshop: Chalermnit Bookshop (qv under Major Booksellers)
Founded: 1957

Chiangmai Book Centre*, 2 Kochasam Rd, Suriya Cinema, Chiangmai
Bookshop: At above address

Office of **Christian** Education and Literature, an imprint of Suriyaban Publishers (qv)

Dhammabucha*, 5/1-2 Asdang Rd, Bangkok Tel: (02) 2242012
Subject: Thai books on Buddhism

Duang Kamol*, 244-246 Siam Sq Soi 2, Patumwan, Bangkok Tel: (02) 2516335
Subjects: English, French and Thai books

Foreign Relations Publishing House*, 20 Rajprasong Trade Centre, Bangkok 10500 Tel: (02) 2510630/3916456
President: M L Manich Jumsai, CBE
Subjects: Translation and publication of German Works (in collaboration with Publishers' and Booksellers' Association of Thailand (qv) and Deutscher Verein des Buchhandels)
Founded: 1980

Graphic Art Publishing*, 204/12-13 Surawongse Rd, Bangkok 10500 Tel: (02) 2330302 Telex: 20657 Graphic Th
Chief Executive: Mrs Angkana Sajjaraktrakul; *Export Manager:* H J Weber
Subsidiary Company: Pandora Publishing (at above address)
Subjects: Thai-Language Text Books (Chemistry, Physics, Mathematics, Biology, Electronics, English, Thai), Science Fiction, Photography
Book Club: Science Fiction Magazine Club
Bookshop: At above address
Founded: 1972

Hor Samut Klang*, 5 Soi Praeng Sanpasart, Asdang Rd, Bangkok Tel: (02) 219751
Subject: Thai books

Klang Vidhya*, 724 Wang Burapa, Bangkok 10200 Tel: (02) 224546/2219331
Manager: Prachark Chaovanabutvilai
Subject: Thai books
Bookshop: At above address

Languages School*, Wat Phra Singha, Chiangmai

Narongsarn*, 647/14 Charernrat Rd, (Big Circle), Dhonburi, Bangkok Tel: (02) 4668895

Nibondh*, 40-42 New Rd, Bangkok Tel: (02) 212611
Subjects: English and Thai books
Bookshops: See under Major Booksellers

Niyom Vidhya*, 192 Bamrungmuang Rd, Bangkok Tel: (02) 2217661
Subject: Thai Technical Textbooks

Norn*, 1/1 Boonsiri, Sukhumvit Rd, Paknam Tel: 90130
Subject: Thai books

Odeon Store LP*, 862 Wang Burapa, Bangkok Tel: (02) 2210742/2216567 Cable Add: Odeonstore
Man Dir: Vichai Praepanich
Branch Off: Siam Sq soi 1, Bangkok
Subjects: Textbooks, Non-fiction, Paperbacks
Founded: 1947

Pikkhanet*, 99 Praeng Sanpasart, Tanao Rd, Bangkok Tel: (02) 222850
Subject: Thai pocket books

Pittayakarn*, 226 Nakorn Kashem, Bangkok Tel: (02) 221501
Subject: Thai books

Pra Cha Chang & Co Ltd*, 816/3 Talad Noi, New Rd, Bangkok
Subject: Academic

Praepittaya Ltd*, 716-718 Burapa Palace, PO Box 914, Bangkok Tel: (02) 2214283/2211286
Manager: Chitt Praepanich
Subjects: Fiction, Juveniles
Bookshop: See under Major Booksellers

Praphansarn Book Centre*, 236/6-7 Beside Lido Theatre, Siam Square Soi 2, Rama I Rd, Bangkok Tel: (02) 2512342
Man Dir: Suphol Taechatada

Prasarnmitr*, 3382 New Petburi Rd, Bangkok Tel: (02) 3181856
Subject: Textbooks

Progress*, 882 Wang Burapa, Bangkok Tel: (02) 226541
Subject: Thai books, English occasionally

Religious Revival Organization*, 176 Sukhumvit, Santikam Soi 1, T Samrong North, Samutprakarn

Ruamsarn (1977) Co Ltd*, Part, 1091/86-87 New Phetburi Rd, Bangkok Tel: (02) 2531489
Man Dir: Bumrung Tawewatanasarn; *Sales Dir:* Nongyao Tawewatanasarn; *Publicity Dir:* Piya Tawewatanasarn; *Advertising Dir:* Piti Tawewatanasarn
Subsidiary Company: Bumrungsarn Ltd, Part, 864 Burapa Palace, Bangkok 2
Subjects: General Fiction, Belles Lettres, Poetry, Biography, History, How-to, Music, Art, Philosophy, Reference, Religion, Low-priced Paperbacks, General Science, University & Secondary Textbooks
Bookshops: See under Major Booksellers; Dheerasarn Ltd (qv under Major Booksellers)
Founded: 1951

Rungvit Sawarn-Apichon*, Chiengmai Book Centre, 2 Kochasarn Rd, opposite Suriya Cinema, Chiengmai

Sangna Vuddhichai Saranonda*, Prabhasarn, 130 Nakornsauran Rd, Bangkok

Sayam Paritat*, 14-6 Nakorn Lane, Taprachand, Maharat Rd, Bangkok Tel:

(02) 219108
Subject: Thai books

Sermwit Barnakarn*, 222 Nakorn Kashem, Bangkok Tel: (02) 214541
Subject: Thai books

Sinpattana*, 74 Pra Atit Rd, Bangkok Tel: (02) 824357/816917
Subject: Thai books

Social Science Association Press*, 2 Chula Soi, Phya Thai Rd, Bangkok
Manager & Editor: Sulak Sivaraksa
Subject: Textbooks
Founded: 1961

Sommai Press*, 90-18 Ekkachai Rd, Bangkok Tel: (02) 4152007
Subject: Thai books

Suksapan Panit (Business Organization of Teachers Council of Thailand)*, Mansion 9, Rajadamnern Ave, Bangkok 10200 Tel: (02) 816543/815044 Telex: 72031 Suksapa Th
Dir: Kamthon Sathirakul
Subjects: Juveniles, Textbooks, Dictionaries
Founded: 1950

Suksit Siam Co Ltd*, 1715 Rama IV Rd, Samyan, Bangkok 10500 Tel: (02) 511630
Publicity: Mrs Nilchawee Sivaraksa
Subjects: Mainly Thai books on Social Science & Politics
Bookshop: See under Major Booksellers

Suriyaban Publishers*, 14 Pramuan Rd, Bangkok 10500 Tel: (02) 2347991 Cable Add: CCT Office
Man Dir and all other offices: Pisnu Arkkapin
Parent Company: Department of Christian Education and Literature, Church of Christ in Thailand, at above address
Imprint: Office of Christian Education and Literature
Subjects: Religion, Children's Books, Short Stories, Buddhism, Thai Culture
Bookshops: The Christian Bookstore, Suriyaban Bookstore (qqv under Major Booksellers)
Founded: 1953

Sutpaisarn*, 638 Somdet Chaopaya Rd, Bangkok Tel: (02) 664392
Subject: Thai books on Law

Thai Watana Panich*, 599 Maitrijit Rd, Bangkok Tel: (02) 210111
Subject: School books in Thai (occasionally English)

Tong-In Sunsawat*, Wat Prasing, Chiengmai
Subject: English books

Vadhana Panich*, 216-220 Bumrungmuang Rd, Bangkok
Subject: School Textbooks

Viratham*, 141 St Louis Soi 2, Sathorn Tai Rd, Bangkok Tel: (02) 866848
Subjects: English, French and English-Thai books

Wacharin Publishing Co Ltd, 350-352 Prasumen Rd, Bangkok Tel: (02) 2812197/2812205

Wattana Panich*, 216-220 Bumrungmuang Rd, Bangkok
Subjects: Textbooks, Fiction, Maps

White Lotus Co Ltd, 16 Soi 47 Sukhumvit Rd, PO Box 1141, Bangkok Tel: (02) 2587217/2587219 Telex: 82094 Ande Th
Chief Executive: D Ande
Subjects: Scholarly (South-East Asia)
Bookshop: See under Major Booksellers
1986: 3 titles *Founded:* 1972

Book Club

Science Fiction Magazine Club*, 204/12-13 Surawongse Rd, Bangkok 10500 Tel: (02) 2330302/2356931 Telex: 20657 Graphic Th
Owned by: Graphic Art Publishing (qv)

Major Booksellers

Asia Books Co Ltd*, 6/1 Soi Chidlom, Ploenchit Rd, Bangkok 10500 Tel: (02) 2526400/2520064/2516008 Cable Add: Asiabooks Telex: TH81043 TH87202 Asiabooks
Showroom: 221 Sukhumvit Rd, between Soi 15 and 17, Bangkok 10110 Tel: (02) 2527277/2501822
Man Dir: Vinai Suttharoj; *General Manager:* Miss Somporn Suttharoj
Also publishers' agent, distributor and retailer of English books

Bangkok Central Book Depot*, Sikak Phya Sri, Bangkok

Central Department Store, 306 Silom Rd, Bangkok Tel: (02) 2336930/2354430/2355400 Telex: Cetrac TH82768 Cable Add: Cetrac Bangkok
Manager: Mrs Ratana Norabhanlobh
Branches (all Bangkok): 677-681 Wang Burapha; 1027 Chidlom, Ploenchit Rd; 1691 Phaholyothin Rd, Bangkhen; 37 Lardya Rd; 708 Mahachai Rd, Chakrapetr

Chalermnit Bookshop*, 108 Sukhumvit 53, Bangkok 10110 Tel: (02) 3916456
Owned by: Chalermnit Press (qv)
Also importers

Christian Bookstore*, 14 Pramuan Rd, Bangkok
Manager: Charu Panichkul
Owned by: Suriyaban Publishers (qv)

Dheerasarn Ltd*, Part, 326-8 Siam Sq, Bangkok 10500
Also: Tawesarn 89/51 Near President Theatre, Bangkok 10500

International Book Distributors Co Ltd*, 1035-4 Pleonchit Shopping Centre, Pleonchit Rd, PO Box 5-59, Bangkok

Klang Vidhya*, 724 Wang Burapa, Bangkok
Also: 3931/26-29 Chumpol Rd, Nakorn Rajsima; 197/2 Srichan Rd, Tambon Wat Mai, Chantaburi

Nibondh (Gaysorn)*, 975/4 Gaysorn Rd, Bangkok
English books at the above address
English, Thai books and magazines at Nibondh (Sikak), 40-42 New Rd, Bangkok

Praepittaya Ltd*, 716-718 Burapa Palace, PO Box 914, Bangkok
Also importer, wholesaler and Publisher (qv)

Ruamsarn (1977) Co Ltd, 1091/86-7 City Sq, New Petchburee Rd, Bangkok Tel: (02) 210400/531489
Manager: Piya Taweewatanasarn

Suksit Siam Co Ltd*, 1715 Rama IV Rd, Samyan, Bangkok 10500 Tel: (02) 511630
Also importers and library suppliers

Suriwongs Book Centre, Sri Don Chai Rd, Chiengmai 50000 Tel: (053) 252052
Manager: Miss J Jittidecharaks

Suriyaban Bookstore*, 124/1 Silom Rd, Bangkok 10500 Tel: (02) 2356200
Manager: Surapon Byboribankul
Owned by: Suriyaban Publishers (qv)

White Lotus Co Ltd, 16 Soi 47 Sukhumvit, PO Box 1141, Bangkok Tel: (02) 2587217/2587219 Telex: 82094 Ande Th
Also Publisher (qv)

Major Libraries

Academic Resource Center, Chulalongkorn University*, Phya Thai Rd, Bangkok 10500
Director: Mrs Knid Tantavirat
Includes Central Library, Thailand Information Center and Audiovisual Unit
Publications: Academic Resources Journal; Union Catalog of Chulalongkorn University Libraries; Union List of Serials in Thailand (automated)

British Council Library, 428 Rama I Rd, 2 Siam Sq, Bangkok 10500 Tel: (02) 2526136
Librarian: Mrs Pongpan Ratanapoosit

Main Library, **Kasetsart University**, Bangkok 10900 Tel: (02) 5792539
Librarian: Mrs Piboonsin Watanapongse

National Archives Division*, Fine Arts Department, Samsen Rd, Bangkok 10300

The **National Library** of Thailand*, Samsen Rd, Bangkok 10300 Tel: (02) 2815449/2810263 Telex: 84189 Natlib Th
Director: Mrs Kullasap Gesmankit

Siriraj Medical Library, Library Division*, Mahidol University, Siriraj Hospital, Bangkok 10700
Director: Miss Uthai Dhutiyabhodhi

Srinakharinwirot University Central Library*, Sukhumvit 23, Bangkok 10110

Thai National Documentation Centre (TNDC), 196 Phahonyothin Rd, Bangkhen, Bangkok 10900 Tel: (02) 5791121 Cable Add: Tistr Bangkok
Director: Mrs Nongphanga Chitrakorn
Publications: List of Scientific and Technical Literature Relating to Thailand; TISTR Bibliographical Series; Scientific Serials in Thai Libraries; Thai Abstracts; Abstracts of TISTR Technical Reports

Thammasat University Libraries, 2 Prachand Rd, Bangkok 10200 Tel: (02) 2215886
Librarian: Dr Pensri Kueysuwan
Publications include: Dom Thad (journal); *Bibliography of the Ministry of Commerce's Publications in the University Libraries; Bibliography of Books in Thammasat University Libraries; Thai Royal Gazette Index; Biography Index; Abstracts of Periodical Articles in the Field of Library Science; First Steps of Library Automation*

Library Association

Thai Library Association*, 273/275 Viphavadee Rangsit Rd, Phayathai, Bangkok 10400 Tel: (02) 2712084
Secretary: Miss Karnmanee Suckcharoen
Publication: Bulletin (4 a year)

Library Reference Books and Journals

Books

An Annotated Bibliography of Librarianship in Thailand, Department of Library Science, Chulalongkorn University, Faculty of Arts, Phya Thai Rd, Bangkok 10500

List of Scientific Libraries in Thailand, Thai National Documentation Centre, 196 Phahonyothin Rd, Bangkhen, Bangkok 9

Journal

Bulletin, Thai Library Association, 273/275 Viphavadee Rangsit Rd, Phayathai, Bangkok 10400

Literary Associations and Societies

Thailand **P E N** Centre*, 2 Pichai Rd, Dusit, Bangkok 3
President: Miss Nilawan Pintong; *Secretary:* Mrs Chamaiporn Saengkrachang

The **Siam** Society*, PO Box 65, Bangkok (Located at: 131 Soi Asoke, Sukhumvit 21, Bangkok) Tel: (02) 2583491/2583494
President: M R Patanachai Jayant;
Honorary Secretary: Mrs Virginia M Di Crocco
Publications: Journal of the Siam Society (annual); *Natural History Bulletin of the Siam Society* (annual)
Miscellaneous: Formerly The Thailand Society. Founded 1904. Under Royal Patronage. For promotion of Thai and South East Asian art, science and literature

Literary Prizes

Bangkok Bank Foundation Prize*
For prose or poetry in Thai concerning history, art, culture, religion, social affairs, philosophy or new creative ideas. 50,000 baht each for prose and poetry. Awarded annually. Enquiries to Secretary, Bangkok Bank Foundation, Suapa Rd, PO Box 95, Bangkok

Togo

General Information

Language: French is official language
Religion: About 25% Christian (mostly Roman Catholic), 8% Islamic; rest follow traditional beliefs
Population: 3 million
Bank Hours: 0730-1130, 1430-1600 Monday-Friday
Shop Hours: 0800-1200, 1430 or 1500-1730 or 1800 Monday-Friday; 0730-1230 Saturday
Currency: CFA franc
Export/Import Information: No tariff on books; advertising catalogues dutied. Additional taxes: Tax Forfaitaire, Statistical Tax, and Customs Stamp Tax of percentage of duties and added taxes. Small Wharfage Tax. Import licence required for goods from non-franc zones above a certain value; from franc zone, need authorization of Togolese Government Office. Exchange controls on non-franc zone.
Copyright: Berne (see International section)

Publishers

Editions **Akpagnon***, BP 3531, Lomé
Man Dir: Yves-Emmanuel Dogbé
Orders to: Other than Benelux, Canada: L'Harmattan, 7 rue de l'Ecole Polytechnique, 75005 Paris, France; Presence Africaine, 25 bis, rue des Ecoles, 75005 Paris, France; Benelux: Nord-Sud Diffusion, 74 rue Lesbroussart, B-1050 Brussels; Canada: C M D Claude M Diffusion Ltée, 1544 rue Villeray, Montreal H2E 1H1, Canada
Subject: General literature

Founded: 1979
ISBN Publisher's Prefix: 2-86427

Ecole Professionelle de la Mission Catholique*, BP 341, Lomé
Subjects: Religion, Secondary & Primary Textbooks

Editogo, BP 891, Lomé Tel: 213718/216106
Man Dir: Kokou Amedegnato
Subjects: General and Educational
Founded: 1962

Maison d'Edition de la Librairie-Imprimerie **Evangélique** du Togo*, BP 378, Lomé Tel: 212967/213228
Dir General: F K Agbobli; *Editorial:* W Y Aladji, J C van de Werk
Imprint: Editions Haho
Bookshop: Librairie Evangélique (qv under Major Booksellers)

Editions **Haho**, an imprint of Maison d'Edition de la Librairie-Imprimerie Evangélique du Togo (qv)

Les **Nouvelles Editions Africaines** (NEA), BP 4862, Lomé (Located at: 239 blvd du 13 Janvier, Lomé) Tel: 216761 Telex: 5393
Dir: Kokou Aithnard
Parent Company: Les Nouvelles Editions Africaines, Senegal (qv)
Associate Company: Les Nouvelles Editions Africaines, Ivory Coast (qv)
Subjects: General Fiction & Non-fiction, Belles Lettres, Poetry, Biography, History, Africana, Philosophy, Religion, Juveniles, Paperbacks, Psychology, General & Social Science, University & Secondary Textbooks
Bookshop: See under Major Booksellers
Founded: 1979
ISBN Publisher's Prefix: 2-7236

Book Club

Academic Book Club*, BP 3024, Lomé
Manager: R N Onuoha

Major Booksellers

Librarie du **Bon Pasteur***, rue du Commerce, BP 1164, Lomé Tel: 213279
Also at rue de l'Eglise Tel: 213628

Librairie **Centrale**, BP 1164, Lomé Tel: 213424

Cercle Africain du Livre, 6 rue du Commerce, BP 4827, Lomé Tel: 216586

Librairie Imprimerie **Evangélique**, 1 rue du Commerce, BP 378, Lomé Tel: 212967/213228 Telex: 5300 Public TO
Dir: Kokou Wolali Amabley

Librairie **Moderne**, BP 777, Lomé Tel: 214870

Librairie/Editions **Nouvelles Editions Africaines**, BP 4862, Lomé Tel: 216761
Owned by: Les Nouvelles Editions Africaines (NEA) (qv)

Librairie **No Pa To***, BP 1277, Lomé

S A C O M E R (Société Africaine du Commerce), BP 4922, Lomé Tel: 215737

Nouvelle Librairie **Togolaise***, BP 2096, Lomé

Librairie **Walter***, 62 ave du 24 Janvier, BP 397, Lomé

Major Libraries

American Cultural Center Library*, BP 852, Lomé

Bibliothèque nationale*, BP 1002, Lomé
Tel: 216367
Dir: Kanaoua Bekoutare

Centre culturel français, Bibliothèque, BP 2090, Lomé Tel: 210232
Librarian: Mr Marchive

Bibliothèque de l'**Ecole** normale supérieure*, Atakpamé

Bibliothèque de l'**Université du Benin**, BP 1515, Lomé Tel: 214843

Library Associations

A T O D B A M, see Association togolaise pour la Documentation, les Bibliothèques, Archives et Musées

Association togolaise pour la Documentation, les Bibliothèques, Archives et Musées (ATODBAM)*, 9 rue Domlan-Bè, Lomé
Secretary: Komlan Fafamé Afanou

Association togolaise pour le Développement de la Documentation, des Bibliothèques, Archives et Musées*, c/o Bibliothèque de l'Université du Bénin, BP 1515, Lomé Tel: 214843
Secretary: E E Amah

Trinidad and Tobago

General Information

Language: English
Religion: Roman Catholic and Anglican
Population: 1.06 million
Bank Hours: 0800-1400 Monday-Thursday; 0800-1200, 1500-1700 Friday
Shop Hours: 0800-1630 Monday-Friday; 0800-1200 Saturday
Currency: 100 cents = 1 Trinidad and Tobago dollar
Export/Import Information: No tariff on books; duty and postal fee on advertising matter. No import licence required for books; no obscene literature permitted. Exchange controls

Book Trade Organization

Booksellers' Association of Trinidad and Tobago, PO Box 531, 22 Abercromby St, Port of Spain
Secretary: Terry Cassim

Book Trade Reference Books and Journals

Books

Directory of Printers and Booksellers in Trinidad and Tobago, The Main Library, The University of the West Indies, St Augustine

Journals

Trinidad and Tobago and West Indian Bibliography, Central Library of Trinidad and Tobago,
West Indian Reference Section, 20 Queens Park East, Port of Spain

Trinidad & Tobago National Bibliography, Central Library of Trinidad and Tobago, PO Box 547, Port of Spain and The Main Library, The University of the West Indies, St Augustine

Publishers

Charran Educational Publishers+*, 58 Western Main Rd, St James Tel: 6253694/6223832 Telex: 3000 Postlx Wg
Dirs: Reginald Charran, Betty Charran; *Sales:* Terry R Ram
Subjects: Textbooks, Children's Books
Bookshops: Charran's Bookshop (1978) Ltd, Muir Marshall Ltd (qqv under Major Booksellers)

Columbus Publishers Ltd, 64 Independence Sq, PO Box 140, Port of Spain Tel: 6253695
Dir: H M Hoadley
Subjects: General, Books for Students
Founded: 1969
ISBN Publisher's Prefix: 0-85643

Longman Caribbean Ltd, Boundary Rd, San Juan
Parent Company: Longman Group UK Ltd, UK (qv)
Subject: General

Trinidad Publishing Co*, 22-26 St Vincent St, Port of Spain
Subjects: Law, Political Economy

Major Booksellers

Abercromby Bookshop, 22 Abercromby St, Port of Spain Tel: 6237752 Cable Add: Cassia, Port of Spain
Proprietor: Philip Smith

Asgar Ali Book Centre*, 90 Duke St, Port of Spain

Campus Corner Ltd, 72 Pembroke St, Port of Spain Tel: 6231678
Manager: Hilton S Young

Cassia House Bookshop, Corner Pembroke and Oxford Sts, Port of Spain Tel: 6235156 Cable Add: Cassia, Port of Spain
Manager: P Smith

Charran's Bookshop (1978) Ltd*, 58 Western Main Rd, St James
Manager: Betty Charran
Owned by: Charran Educational Publishers (qv)

Cosmic Book Services Ltd, Westmall, Westmoorings Tel: 6334318
Executive Dir: Lionel St Aubyn

Hobby Centre*, 86 Frederick St, Port of Spain

Victor **Manhin** Ltd, 49 High St, San Fernando

Muir **Marshall** Ltd*, 64 Independence Square, Port of Spain
Owned by: Charran Educational Publishers (qv)

Metropolitan Book Suppliers Ltd, 16 Plaza of Golden Doors, 6 Frederick St, Port of Spain
Manager: Terry Cassim

J C **Sealy**, The Book Shop, 22 Queen's Park West, Port of Spain Tel: 6284575

Stephens and Johnsons Book Department*, PO Box 497, 8-10 Frederick St, Port of Spain Tel: 6234141/6232171 Cable Add: Stepjohn, Port of Spain Telex: 3485 Sterol Wg
Manager: Harris Rampersad
Owned by: Stephens & Ross Ltd (at above address)

Major Libraries

Carnegie Free Library*, Harris Promenade, San Fernando Tel: 6523228
Librarian: Lois Barrow

National Archives*, The Government Archivist, PO Box 763, 105 St Vincent St, Port of Spain

Central Library of **Trinidad and Tobago***, PO Box 547, Port of Spain Tel: 6234844/6236137 Cable Add: Centralib Trinidad
County-type Library Department of the Government
Dir: Mrs Angela Bernard
Publication: Trinidad & Tobago National Bibliography, published jointly with the library of the University of the West Indies, St Augustine

Trinidad Public Library*, Knox St, Port of Spain

Main Library, The **University of the West Indies**, St Augustine Tel: 6631439 Cable Add: Stomata, Port of Spain Telex: 24520 Uwi-Wg
Librarian: Dr Alma Jordan
Publications include: Bibliographic Series; Report on the Libraries (annual); *Directory of Printers and Booksellers in Trinidad and Tobago; Trinidad and Tobago National Bibliography* (quarterly)

West Indian Reference Collection*, Central Library of Trinidad and Tobago, 81 Belmont Circular Rd, Belmont Tel: 6241488/6243409

Library Association

Library Association of **Trinidad and Tobago***, PO Box 1275, Port of Spain
Secretary: Ernesta Greeninge
Publication: Blatt (Bulletin of the Library Association of Trinidad and Tobago) (annual)

Library Reference Journal

Blatt, Library Association of Trinidad and Tobago, c/o PO Box 1275, Port of Spain
Bulletin of the Library Association of Trinidad and Tobago

Tunisia

General Information

Language: Arabic. French is used in commerce
Religion: Islamic (Sunni sect)
Population: 7 million
Bank Hours: Winter: 0800/1100, 1400-1600 Monday-Thursday; 0800-1100, 1300-1500 Friday; Summer: 0730-1100 Monday-Friday
Shop Hours: Generally 0800-1200, 1500-1800 Monday-Saturday
Currency: 1,000 millimes = 1 Tunisian dinar
Export/Import Information: Tunisia has preferential tariffs and EEC agreement but most books are dutied. Advertising matter free. Customs Formalities Tax per 1,000 kg or less gross weight, with minimum rate. Consumption Tax on duty and tax paid for books and for advertising matter. Advertising matter subject to Production Tax of percentage of duty and tax paid. Imports liberalized but in practice licences granted dependent on foreign exchange position
Copyright: UCC, Berne (see International section)

Book Trade Organizations

Agence Tunisienne de l'ISBN*, Bibliothèque Nationale Service des publications et du dépôt légal, 20 Souk El Attarine, Tunis Tel: (01) 245338/256921/249902
ISBN Administrator: Miss Samia Bedoui

Standard Book Numbering Agency, see Agence Tunisienne de l'ISBN

Book Trade Reference Books

Bibliographie nationale de la Tunisie (Tunisian National Bibliography), Bibliothèque nationale, 20 Souk-el-Attarine, Tunis

Répertoire des Unités de Documentation en Tunisia, Bibliothèque nationale, 20 Souk-el-Attarine, Tunis

Publishers

Editions **Bouslama**+*, 53 rue Nahas Pacha, Tunis 1 Tel: (01) 243745/243100/243323 Cable Add: Editions Bouslama
Man Dir, Rights & Permissions: Ali Bouslama; *Sales:* Hichem Bouslama; *Production:* Riadh Bouslama; *Publicity:* Hatem Bouslama
Branch Off: 15 bis rue Lamine el Abassi, Tunis
Subjects: History (French and Arabic languages), Children's
Bookshops: See under Major Booksellers
Founded: 1960

Ceres Productions*, BP 56 Tunis Belvedere, Tunis Tel: (01) 282033 LG Cable Add: Cerepro Telex: Ceresp 14363 TN
Man Dir: Mohamed Ben Smail; *Editorial:* Noureddine Ben Khader
Orders to: Demeter, 11A Montplaisir, Tunis Tel: (01) 283579/893083
Subsidiary Company: Demeter (address as above)

Dar Arabia Lil Kitab*, 4 rue 7101 Al Manar 2, BP 1104, Tunis Tel: (01) 236025 Telex: 14966 Kitab
Man Dir: Mahdi Ben Youssef
Parent Company: Dar Arabia Lil Kitab, ave Ghouma Mahmoudi, BP 3185, Tripoli, Libya Tel: (021) 47287 Telex: 20003 Kitab
Subjects: General Literature, Biography, Bibliography, Linguistics, Pedagogy, Religion, History, Economics, Children's Books, Dictionaries
1985: 131 titles *Founded:* 1975

Dar El Amal SA, d'Edition de Diffusion de Presse et de Publicité*, rue 2 Mars 1934, Tunis Tel: (01) 264899 Telex: 12163 Tn
Man Dir: S Zoghlami; *Editorial, Production, Rights & Permissions:* N Tabka
Subjects: Economic and Social Politics
Founded: 1976

En-Najah*, Editions Hedi Ben Abdelgheni, 11 ave de France, Tunis Tel: (01) 246886
Bookshops: At above address and 6 rue Ali Belhaouane, Sousse

TUNISIA — TURKEY

Faculté des Lettres et Sciences Humaines de Tunis*, Service des Publications, 94 blvd du 9 Avril 1938, BP 1128, Tunis Tel: (01) 264417
Secretary: M Maouia
Subjects: History, Africana, Philosophy, Paperbacks, Social Science, University Textbooks

Government Printer (Imprimerie Officielle de la République Tunisienne – IORT), ave Farhat Hached, 2040 Rades, Tunis Tel: (01) 299914/299224 Telex: 14939 TN
Publications include: Journal Officiel de la République Tunisienne

I O R T (Imprimerie Officielle de la République Tunisienne), see Government Printer

Maison Tunisienne d'Edition+*, 36 rue Bab El Khadra, Tunis Tel: (01) 343312/344565/345333 Telex: Mac 12032
Man Dir: Abdelaziz Achouri
Subjects: General Fiction & Non-fiction, Belles Lettres, Poetry, Biography, History, Africana, Philosophy, Reference, Religion, Juveniles, Paperbacks, Social Science, University & Secondary Textbooks, Law, Medicine, Literature, Sciences
Founded: 1966

Imprimerie/Librairie Al **Manar***, BP 121, Tunis Tel: (01) 243224/260641 Cable Add: Manar Telex: 14894
Man Dir: Mohamed Habib El M'Hamdi
Subsidiary Company: Librairie Al Manar, 12 rue du Tribunal, Tunis
Subjects: History, Africana, Religion, Arabic Language, Islam

Société nationale d'Edition et de Diffusion*, 5 ave de Carthage, BP 440, Tunis Tel: (01) 255000 Cable Add: Studiffusion
Bookshop: See under Major Booksellers

Sud Editions, 3 ave Louis Braille, Tunis 1002 Tel: (01) 785179 Telex: 12363 TN
Man Dir: M Masmoudi
Subjects: Art, Art History, Arab Literature
Founded: 1976
ISBN Publisher's Prefix: 2-86444

Major Booksellers

Editions **Bouslama***, 15 ave de France, Tunis Tel: (01) 240100/240056
Also: 53 rue Nahas Pacha, 7 rue Amilcar (both in Tunis)
Also Publisher (qv)

La **Caravelle** Librairie*, 8 ave H Bourguiba, Sfex

Librairie **En-Najah***, Siège Social, 11 ave de France, Tunis Tel: (01) 246886
Branch: 6 rue Ali Belhaouane, Sousse Tel: (03) 21282

Librairie Al **Manar***, 60 ave Bab Djedid, BP 121, Tunis Tel: (01) 243224

Société Librairie nouvelle*, 15 ave de France, Bizerte

Société nationale d'Edition et de Diffusion*, 5 ave de Carthage, BP 440, Tunis Tel: (01) 255000
Also Publisher (qv)

Major Libraries

Archives nationales*, Présedence de la République, Pl du Gouvernement, Tunis

Bibliothèque nationale, 20 Souk-el-Attarine, BP 42, Tunis Tel: (01) 245338
Librarian: M Azzedine Bachaouch
Publications: Bibliographie nationale: Publications officielles et non officielles; Informations bibliographiques; Fahras al-Makhtûtât (catalogue des manuscrits); Répertoire des Unités de Documentation en Tunisie; Bibliographie Nationale: Publications en série; Bibliographies Spécialisées (Thémes tunisiens notamment); Bulletin Arabe des Publications (jointly published with ALECSO)

British Council Library, c/o British Embassy, 5 pl de la Victoire, Tunis Tel: (01) 259053/341477

Ecole nationale d'Administration Bibliothèque, 24 ave Docteur Calmette, Mutuelleville, Tunis 1060 Tel: (01) 288300/288167/288435 Telex: Ena 13198
Librarian: Mohamed Hedi Talbi
Publications: Servir (semi-annual)

Bibliothèque de la **Faculté de Droit** et des Sciences Politiques et Economiques de Tunis, Campus Universitaire, Belvédère, Tunis Tel: (01) 262315
Chief Librarian: Taoufik Lamari
Publications: Liste des Thèses et Mémoires déposés à la Faculté (half-yearly); *Liste des Nouvelles Acquisitions* (quarterly); Liste des Publications du CERP de la Faculté

Bibliothèque de la **Faculté des Lettres** et Sciences Humaines, 94 blvd du 9 Avril 1938, Tunis Tel: (01) 266503
Chief Librarian: M Abdeljaoued
Publications include: Repertoire de la Presse et des Publications Periodiques Tunisiennes

Bibliothèque de la **Faculté des Sciences** de Tunis*, Campus Universitaire El Menzeh, Tunis Tel: (01) 264577

Bibliothèque de l'**Institut** supérieur d'Education et de Formation continue*, 43 rue de la Liberté, Le Bardo Tel: 261092
Librarian: Mohamed Abdeljaoued

Direction de la **Lecture Publique***, 36 rue Chadli Kallala, Tunis 1002 Tel: (01) 782522/780664
Librarian: Abdelbaki Bedoui
Branches throughout the country

Library Association

Association tunisienne de Documentalistes, Bibliothécaires et Archivistes*, BP 575, Tunis
Tunisian Association of Record-Keepers, Librarians and Archivists
President: Mohamed Abdeljaoued
Publications: Bulletin ATD (4 a year); *RASSID*

Library Reference Journal

Bulletin, Association tunisienne des Documentalistes, Bibliothécaires et Archivistes, BP 575, Tunis

Literary Associations and Societies

Institut des Belles Lettres arabes, 12 rue Jamâa el Haoua, 1008 Tunis Bab Menara Tel: (01) 260133
Institute of Arab Belles Lettres
Publication: Revue IBLA (biannual study of cultural problems in the Arab-Moslem world)

Union des Ecrivains tunisiens*, 20 ave de Paris, Tunis Tel: (01) 257591
Tunisian Writers' Union

Turkey

General Information

Language: Turkish (English spoken by many)
Religion: Predominantly Islamic
Population: 52 million
Bank Hours: 0830-1200, 1330-1800 Monday-Friday
Shop Hours: 0900-1200, 1330-1900 Monday-Saturday
Currency: 100 kurus = 1 Turkish lira (or pound)
Export/Import Information: No tariffs on books and advertising matter. Books on liberalized list, so import licences are granted freely, but textbooks must be imported with permission of Ministry of Education. Exchange controls
Copyright: Berne, Florence (see International section)

Book Trade Organization

Türk Editörler Dernegi*, Ankara Cad 60, Istanbul
Turkish Publishers' Association

Book Trade Reference Journal

Turkiye Bibliyografyasi (Turkish National Bibliography), National Library, Bibliographical Institute, Kumrular Sokak 3, Kizilay

Publishers

A B C Yayinevi*, PO Box 539, Karaköy, Istanbul (Located at: Tünel Meydanı, Seferoğlu Han, Beyoğlu, Istanbul) Tel: (01) 444242/442581 Cable Add: Abckit, Istanbul
Man Dir: Artun Altıparmak; *Editorial:* Önder Renkliyıldırım; *Sales:* K Karakush; *Production:* Hasan Günaydın; *Publicity:* Ferit Gürsu; *Rights & Permissions:* Necip Inselel
Subjects: Foreign Language Courses, Dictionaries, Reference, Electronics
Founded: 1977

Arkın Kitabevi*, Ankara Cad 60, Istanbul Tel: (01) 750734/750600/1 Cable Add: Birarkinlar Istanbul
Man Dir, Rights & Permissions: Ramazan Gökalp Arkın;
Branch Off: Arkın Ofset Basimevi, Merter Sitesi Buberoğlu Sokak No 5, Bayrampasa, Istanbul
Subjects: Juveniles, Maps, Educational Materials, Reference, General Science, Secondary & Primary Textbooks
Bookshop: Arkın Kitabevi, Ankara Cad 60, Istanbul
Founded: 1957

Dergâh Yayinlari AS, see Kara

Dogan Kardes Matbaacilik SAS*, Türbedar Sok 22, Istanbul
Subjects: Juveniles, Educational Materials, Weekly Magazines

Dost Yayınları, Tünel Pasaji, B/blok 9-210, Beyoğlu, Istanbul Tel: 1453141
Director: Salim Şengil; *Marketing Manager:* Aslı Sengil Cansever
Subject: Turkish Art
Founded: 1947

Elif Kitabevi, Sahaflar Çarsisi 4, Beyazit, Istanbul Tel: (01) 5222096
Man Dir: Arslan Kaynardag; *Sales Dir:* Gani Yener
Subjects: Belles Lettres, Poetry, History, Music, Art, Philosophy, Social Science
Bookshop: Sahaflar Çarsisi 4, Beyazit, Istanbul
Founded: 1957
Miscellaneous: Firm distributes Turkish publications. Associated imprints include Elif Yayinlari

Gelisim Publishing*, Levent, Istanbul Tel: (01) 692420/682208 Cable Add: Gelbay Telex: 22270 Geby Tr
Chairman and Man Dir: Ercan Arikli
Associate Company: Süreli Yayınlar AS (Periodical Press Inc), Levent, Istanbul Tel: 692420
Subjects: Encyclopaedias, Reference, Non-fiction, Magazines

Hürriyet Yayinlari (Hür Yayin)*, Cemal Nadir Sokak 7, Cağaloğlu, 1183 Istanbul Tel: (01) 222038/271502 Telex: 22276 HA Tr, 22277 HA Tr
Dir: Ali Z Oraloglu
Parent Company: Hürriyet Holding
Subjects: Fiction, History, Classics, Poetry, TV Series, Yearbooks, General Reference

Inkilâp Kitabevi Yayin Sanayii ve Ticaret AS+, Ankara Cad 95, Sirkeci, Istanbul Tel: (01) 5222851/5268641
Man Dirs: Nazar Fikri, Julia Fikri, Errol Fikri
Parent Companies: Anka Offset AS, Teknografik Matbaacilik AS (at above address)
Branch Off: Yeni Zaman Kitabevi, Ankara Cad 155, Sirkeci, Istanbul (correspondence to Inkilâp)
Subjects: General Fiction & Non-fiction, Cartography, Politics, Juveniles, Technical, Domestic
1985: 200 titles *Founded:* 1935

Ismail **Kara**/Dergâh Yayinlari AS Müessese Müdürü*, PO Box 1240, Sirkeci, Istanbul (Located at: Nuruosmaniye Cad 3/1, Cağaloğlu, Istanbul) Tel: (01) 5265370
Man Dir: Ezel Erverdi; *Editorial:* Mustafa Kutlu; *Sales:* Fatih Gokdag; *Production:* Ahmet Debbagoglu; *Publicity:* Mustafa Modanlioglu
Subsidiary Companies: Dergâh kitapcilk AS, Ankara Cad 85 Cağaloğlu, Istanbul; Emek matbaacilik ve ilancilik Ltd sti; Derya Dagitim AS, Babiali Cad 52 Cağaloğlu, Istanbul
Subjects: Encyclopaedias, Islamic Classics, History, Books of 'Hareket', Modern Turkish Philosophy, Modern Turkish Policy, Culture, Islamic Thought, Western Thought, Education, Turkish Literature
Book Clubs: Dergâh kitabevi, Istanbul; Dergâh kitabevi, Erzurum
Bookshop: Dergâh kitabevi, Istanbul
Founded: 1977

Altin **Kitaplar** Publishing Co*, Altin Kitaplar, Celal Ferdi Gokcay Sok, Nebioğlu Han, Cağaloğlu, Istanbul Tel: (01) 224045/268012
Publishers: Fethi Ul, Dr Turhan Bozkurt; *Editorial:* H Mursit Ul; *Sales:* Ugur Gergin; *Production:* Ferhan Filiztekin
Associate Company: Petek Yayincilik ve Ticaret AS, Celal Ferdi Gokcay Sok, Nebioglu Han, Cağaloğlu, Istanbul

Subjects: Fiction, Non-fiction, Memoirs, Textbooks, Children's Books, Classics, History, Crime, Holy Koran, Geographical Atlases
Bookshop: At above address
Founded: 1959

Redhouse Press+, PK 142, 34432 Sirkeci, Istanbul Tel: (01) 5278100/5221498 Telex: 23554 Peettr
Man Dir: William Edmonds; *Editors:* Ann Edmonds, Richard Blakney, Fatih Erdoğan (Children's)
Subjects: Turkish-English Dictionaries, Guidebooks in English, Educational, General, Children's
Bookshop: Redhouse Kitabevi (qv under Major Booksellers)
1986: 10 titles *Founded:* 1822

Remzi Kitabevi*, Selvilimescit Sokak 8, Cağaloğlu, Istanbul Tel: (01) 220583/ 227248 Cable Add: Remzi Kitabevi Istanbul
Man Dir: Erol Erduran
Subsidiary Company: Evrim Matbaacılık Ltd, Sirketi Cağaloğlu, Istanbul
Subjects: General Fiction, Biography, History, Philosophy, Reference, Low-priced Paperbacks, Medicine, Psychology, General & Social Science, Secondary & Primary Textbooks, Educational Books, Children's Encyclopaedias
Bookshop: Ankara Cad 93, Istanbul
Founded: 1931

Sander Yayınları*, Kıragı Sok 78, Osmanbey, Istanbul Tel: (01) 408475/ 483209
Man Dir, Production, Rights & Permissions: Necdet Sander; *Editorial:* Nuran Ücok; *Sales:* Fikret Sander; *Publicity:* Allegra Mitrani
Parent Company: Sander Kitabevi
Subjects: Literature, Fiction, Poetry, Essays, Political History, Sport, Education, Tourist Guides (of Turkey)
Bookshops: Sander Kitabevi (qv under Major Booksellers)

Literary Agents

Hür Yayin ve Ticaret*, Cemai Nadir Sokak 7, Cağaloğlu, Istanbul Tel: (01) 222038/262000 Cable Add: PK 1183 Istanbul

Nurcihan **Kesim** Literary Agency, PO Box 868, Sirkeci, Istanbul Tel: (01) 5285800/ 5285394 Telex: 22418 Nek Tr
Also: Nuruosmaniye Cad 8, Cağaloğlu, Istanbul
Man Dir: Nurcihan Kesim; *Sales:* Ertugrul Kesim; *Rights & Permissions:* Oya Alpar
Specialization: Fiction, Non-fiction, Art Works, Serials, Encyclopaedias

O N K Agency Ltd, Ankara Caddesi 40, Sirkeci, Istanbul
Dir: Osman N Karaca
Specialization: Books, Serials, Comics & Cartoons, Plays, TV Programmes

Book Club

Dergâh kitabevi*, PO Box 1240, Sirkeci, Istanbul
Owned by: Ismail Kara (qv)

Major Booksellers

A B C Kitabevi*, Tünel Meydanı 1, Beyoğlu, Istanbul
Owned by: Gençlik Kitabevi (qv)

Bilgi Yayinevi*, Tuna Cad, Kizilay, Ankara

Gençlik Kitabevi*, Muvakkithane Cad, 35 Kadiköy, Istanbul Tel: (01) 3363017/ 3370734
Also: Gençlik Kitabevi Kırtasiye AS, Mühürdar Cad, 68 Kadıköy, Istanbul Tel: (01) 3379605
Man Dir: Celal Güner; *Sales Dirs:* Meral Güner, Ozan Güner, Olcayto Güner
Parent Company: Gençlik Kitabevi AS, Mühürdar Cad, 68 Kadıköy, Istanbul
Subsidiary Company: ABC Kitabevi (qv)

Hakki Bigeç*, Baskeny Yayinevi, Izmir Cad 55/22, Ankara

Haset Kitabevi AS*, Istiklal cad 469, Beyoğlu, Istanbul Tel: (01) 448460/ 449471 Telex: 24446 Hst Tr
Manager: Erol Aydın
Branches at Cumhuriyet Bulvari 143/G, Izmir; Ziya Gökalp cad 14/E, Yenisehir, Ankara
Formerly Hachette Kitabevi (Librairie Hachette-Succursale de la Turquie)

Nejat Yalki Kitabevi*, Valikonagi Cad, Nisantasi, Istanbul

Orhan Özsisman*, Datiç AS, 452 Sokak, No 7, Konak, Izmir Tel: (051) 138786/ 132838/149595

Redhouse Kitabevi, Rizapasa Yokusu 48, Sultanhamam, Istanbul Tel: (01) 5223905
Manager: James Sowerwine
Owned by: Redhouse Press (qv)

Sander Kitabevi, Necdet Sander*, Halaskârgazi Cad 275-277, Osmanbey, Istanbul Tel: (01) 483209/463075
Also: Istiklal Cad 178, Beyoglu, Istanbul Tel: (01) 440134
Manager: Necdet Sander
Parent Company of Sander Yayinlari (qv)

Major Libraries

Ankara University Library*, Ankara

The **Beyazit** State Library*, Imaret Sokak No 18, Beyazit, Istanbul Tel: (01) 223167
Librarian: Hasan Duman

Bogaziçi University Library*, Bebek, 80815, Istanbul Tel: (01) 631500
Dir: Ender Altug

The **Grand National Assembly** of Turkey, Library and Documentation Center (TBMM Kütüphane ve Dokümantasyon Merkezi), Ankara Tel: (041) 251352 Telex: 43627 Fax: 187601
Dir: Hilmi Celik

Il **Halk Kütüphanesi***, Balikesir Provincial Public Library, formerly the Vatan Library

Istanbul Üniversitesi Merkez Kütüphanesi*, Besim Ömer Pasa Cad 15, Beyazit, Istanbul Tel: (01) 222180
Istanbul University Central Library

Izmir General Library*, Millî Kütüphane Cad 39, Izmir

Middle East Technical University Library, Ankara Tel: (041) 237100 Telex: 42761
Librarian: Dr O Tekin Aybas

Millet Library*, Fatih, Istanbul

Millî Kütüphane*, Kumrular Sokak 3, Kızılay, Ankara
National Library
Dir: Dr Müjgan Cunbur
Publications include: Turkiye Bibliyografyasi

Library of the **Mineral Research and Exploration Institute***, Ismet Inönü Bulvari, Ankara Tel: (041) 234255
Librarian: Sevim Özertan;

Publication: Selected list of New Publications in *MTA News* (bi/annual)

Selimiye Library*, Edirne

Süleymaniye Kütüphanesi Müdürlügü*, Suleymaniye Mahallesi, Ayse Kadin Sokak 30, 35 Beyazit, Istanbul Tel: (01) 206460
Library of the Süleymaniye
Librarian: Muammer Ülker
Publications include: Nail Bayraktar (Catalogue of the important Arabic manuscripts in Bağdatlı Vehbi Efendi Library), Istanbul, 1984; *The Union Catalogue Islamic Medical Manuscripts in Turkish Library*, Istanbul, 1984; *Türkiye Yazmaları Toplu Kataloğu (TÜYATOK)* (The Union Catalogue of Manuscripts in Turkey)

Technical University Library*, Istanbul Teknik Üniversitesi, Merkez Kitaplıgı, Istanbul

Türdok (Turkish Scientific and Technical Documentation Centre)*, Atatürk Bulvari 221, Kavaklidere, Ankara Tel: (041) 262770 Cable Add: Tübitak, Ankara Telex: 43186 Btak Tr

Vatan Library, see Il Halk Kütüphanesi

Library Association

Türk Kütüphaneciler Dernegi, Elgün Sokağı 8/8, 06440, Yenisehir, Ankara Tel: (041) 2301325
Turkish Librarians' Association
Secretary: Aydin Kuran
Publication: Türk Kütuiphaneciligi (4 a year)

Library Reference Journal

Bülten (Bulletin), Türk Kütüphaneciler Dernegi, Elgün Sokağı 8/8, 06440, Yenisehir, Ankara

Literary Associations and Societies

P E N Yazarlar Dernegi*, Operatör Raifbey Sok 48/6, Sisli, Istanbul
PEN — Turkish Centre
President: Prof Tahsin Yücel

Turkish Language Society*, Ataturk Bulvari 217, Ankara

Literary Periodicals

Orta Dogu (Middle East), Celal Tevfik Karasapan, Tunali Hilmi Cad 121-5, Kavaklidere, Ankara

Varlik (Existence), Varlik Yayinevi, Cagaloglu Yokusu, Ankara Cad, Istanbul

Literary Prizes

Award for Literature and Scientific Publications*
To encourage the use of the Turkish language. Five prizes of 40,000 Turkish liras each for literature and one prize of 40,000 liras for scientific publication. Awarded annually. Enquiries to Turkish Language Society, Ataturk Bulvari 217, Ankara

Sait Faik Prize*
For the best short story. 5,000 Turkish liras. Awarded annually. Enquiries to Darussafaka Association, Halaskargazl Cad 231, Istanbul

Orhan **Kemal** Award*
To encourage publication of novels which reflect the views of Orhan Kemal. Awarded annually. Enquiries to Orhan Kemal Family and Associates, c/o Turkish Language Society, Ataturk Bulvari 217, Ankara

Fikret **Madarali** Prize*
For the best novel. Three prizes of 10,000, 5,000 and 3,000 Turkish liras. Awarded annually. Enquiries to Fikret Madarali Family and Associates, c/o Turkish Language Society, Ataturk Bulvari 217, Ankara

Uganda

General Information

Language: English is official language. Swahili is widely spoken in commercial centres
Religion: About 30% Christian, 5% Islamic; rest follow traditional beliefs
Population: 13.2 million
Bank Hours: 0830-1230 Monday-Friday; 0800-1100 Saturday
Shop Hours: 0800-1230, 1400-1630 or longer Monday-Friday; 0800-1230 Saturday
Currency: 100 cents = 1 Uganda shilling
Export/Import Information: No tariff on books or advertising matter but subject to sales tax. Import licence and exchange controls (granted automatically with import licence)

Book Trade Reference Journal

The Uganda Journal, PO Box 4980, Mapala
Published by the Uganda Society; includes annual bibliography of books published in or about Uganda

Publishers

Centenary Publishing House Ltd+*, PO Box 2776, Kampala Tel: (041) 41599
Man Dir, Editorial, Production, Rights & Permissions: Rev Sam Kakiza; *Sales, Publicity:* V Kagga-Senyonga
Parent Organization: Church of Uganda, PO Box 14123, Kampala
Subjects: Religious, Educational, Children's, General
Founded: 1977

Government Printer*, PO Box 33, Entebbe Cable Add: Printer Entebbe Telex: 61336 Print Uga

Longman Uganda Ltd*, PO Box 3409, Kampala Tel: (041) 42940 Cable Add: Longman Kampala
Manager: M K L Mutyaba
Parent Company: Longman Group UK Ltd, UK (qv)
Subjects: Biography, History, Africana, Juveniles, Books in Luganda & other Ugandan Languages, General Science, Secondary & Primary Textbooks
Founded: 1965

Saint Paul Publications*, PO Box 4392, Kampala Tel: (041) 256346
Dir: Teresa Marcazzan; *Editor:* David Glenday

Subjects: Religious and Moral Formation
Bookshop: Saint Paul Book Centre (qv under Major Booksellers)
Founded: 1979

Uganda Publishing House*, MOF House, 37-39 Fifth St, Industrial Area, PO Box 2923, Kampala Tel: (041) 59601/42362/ 34024
Man Dir: Laban O Erapu
Parent Company: Milton Obote Foundation, PO Box 4615, Kampala
Associate Company: Uganda School Supply Ltd, PO Box 20180, Kampala
Subjects: General Fiction & Non-fiction, Belles Lettres, Poetry, Biography, History, Africana, Reference, Juveniles, General & Social Science, Secondary & Primary Textbooks
Founded: 1966

Major Booksellers

E S A Bookshop*, PO Box 2515, Kampala

Makerere University Bookshop*, PO Box 7062, Kampala

Saint Paul Book Centre*, PO Box 4392, Kampala Tel: (041) 256346

Uganda Bookshop, Colville St, PO Box 7145, Kampala Tel: (041) 243756 Cable Add: Bookshop

Major Libraries

Albert **Cook** Library*, Makerere University, Makerere Medical School, PO Box 7072, Kampala Tel: (041) 58731 Cable Add: Makunika Kampala
Medical Librarian: Leonard Ssennyonjo
Publications: East African Medical Bibliography (bi-monthly); *Bulletin and Accession List* (monthly) *Annual Report*

United States Information Service Library*, PO Box 7186, Kampala Tel: (041) 33231

Kabarole Public Library, PO Box 28, Fort Portal Tel: (0493) 2255
Principal Librarian: B N Bagenda

Makerere Institute of Social Research Library, PO Box 16022, Kampala Tel: (041) 254582
Librarian: Mr Kawesa

Makerere University Library*, PO Box 16002, Kampala Tel: (041) 31041
Librarian: James Mugasha
Publication: Library Bulletin (quarterly)

National Institute of Education Library*, Makerere University, PO Box 7062, Kampala
Publication: Journal

Public Libraries Board*, Buganda Rd, PO Box 4262, Kampala Tel: (041) 254661 Cable Add: Library, Kampala
Dir: P K Birungi
Publications: Annual Report, Accessions List (quarterly), *Newsletter* (twice a year) and occasional publications

Uganda Polytechnic Library, PO Box 1991, Kampala Tel: (041) 65211 ext 37 Cable Add: Technical
Chief Librarian: R Nganwa

Library Associations

Uganda Library Association*, PO Box 5894, Kampala Tel: (041) 65001 ext 4
Executive Secretary: L M Ssengero
Publication: Ugandan Libraries

Uganda Schools Library Association*, PO Box 7014, Kampala
Executive Secretary: J W Nabembezi
Publication: Newsletter (quarterly)

Library Reference Journals

Journal of Ugandan Libraries, (biannual), East African School of Librarianship, Makerere University, PO Box 7062, Kampala

Newsletter, Uganda Library Association, PO Box 7014, Kampala

Uganda Libraries, Uganda Library Association, PO Box 5894, Kampala

Literary Periodical

Dhana, Kenya Literature Bureau, PO Box 1317, Kampala (or PO Box 30022, Nairobi)
Biannual literary magazine published on behalf of the Department of Literature at Makerere University

Union of Soviet Socialist Republics

General Information

Language: Russian is the official language. Large number of other languages spoken including Ukrainian, Byelorussian, several Turkic languages, Armenian, Georgian, Lithuanian and Moldavian. English is the commonest foreign language known
Religion: About 25% Christian (mainly Russian Orthodox), 12% Islamic (in the southwest), 2 million Jewish, 12 million Buddhist; rest atheist
Population: 265 million
Bank Hours: 0900-1600 Monday-Friday
Shop Hours: 0800-1900 Monday; 0800-2100 Tuesday-Saturday
Currency: 100 kopeks = 1 rouble
Export/Import Information: Foreign trade is state monopoly and duties and licences only the concern of the corporation Mezhdunarodnaya Kniga, Smolenskaya Sennaya 32-34, Moscow G-200. The State Bank of USSR or its subsidiary, USSR Bank for Foreign Trade, is only organization handling foreign currency matters
Copyright: UCC (see International section)

Book Trade Organizations

Gosudarstvenny komitet SSSR po delam izdatelstv, poligrafii i knizhnoi torgovli*, Petrovka ul 26, Moscow K-51
The USSR State Committee for Publishing, Printing and the Book Trade
Chairman: B I Stukalin

Publishing Council of the Academy of Sciences of the USSR*, Leninsky prospekt 13, Moscow

Standard Book Numbering Agency*, Bibliografičeskij Institut SSSR, Kremlevskaja nab 1-9, 119816 Moscow G-19
ISBN Administrator: Ju I Fartunin

U S S R Writers' Union*, Vorovskogo ul 52, Moscow
First Secretary of the Board: Georgy Markov
Publications: Voprosy Literatury (jointly with the Institute of World Literature of the USSR Academy of Sciences); *Novy Mir; Znamya; Druzhba Narodov; Voprosy Literatury; Yunost; Literaturnoye Obozreniye; Literaturnaya Utchyoba; Detskaya Literatura; Shagi* (anthology); *Sovetskaya Literatura* (in foreign languages); *Proizvedeniya i Mneniya* (in French); *Teatr; Sovetskaya Rodina; Zvezda; Kostyor; Literaturnaya Gazeta*

Vsesoyuznaya Knichnaya Palata*, Kremlevskaya naberezhnaya 1-9, Moscow
All-Soviet Book Chamber
Publications: Knizhnava Letopis'
All books and publications are registered and described

Book Trade Reference Books and Journals

Books

Knizhnaya Moskva: Putevoditel'- Spravochnik (Books in Moscow: A Guide and Handbook), 'Reklama', Moscow

Spravochnik Normativnykh Materialov dlya Rabotnikov Knizhnoi Torgovli (Handbook of Rules and Precedents for Book Trade Workers), Izdatelstvo 'Kniga', Nezhdanovoi ul 8-10, Moscow K-9

Journals

Ezhegodnik Knigi SSSR (USSR National Bibliography), Izdatelstvo 'Kniga', Nezhdanovoi ul 8-10, Moscow K-9

Index to Forthcoming Russian Books, Scientific Information Consultants Ltd, 661 Finchley Rd, London W2 2HN, UK
English translation of bibliographic entries from *Novve Knigi*

Knizhnaya Letopis' (Book Chronicle), Vsesoyuznaya Knichnaya Palata, Kremlevskaya naberezhnaya 1-9, Moscow
Weekly bulletin

Knizhnaya Letopis' — Dopolnitel'nyi Vypusk, Vsesoyuznaya Knichnaya Palata, Kremlevskaya naberezhnaya 1-9, Moscow
Monthly supplement to *Knizhnaya Letopis'*, quoting 'restricted' publications, small imprints, 'not-for-sale' or institutional items

Knizhnaya Torgovlya (Book Trade), Mezhdunarodnaya Kniga, Smolenskaya sennaya pl 32-34, Moscow G-200

Knizhnoe Obozrenie (Book Reviews), USSR Library Council, The Lenin State Library of the USSR, Prospect Kalinina 3, Moscow 101000

Letopis' Pechati BSSR (Byelorussian National Bibliography), Godudarstvennaya Biblioteka BSSR im V I Lenina, Knizhnaya Palata BSSR, Minsk

Letopis' Periodicheskikh i Prodolzhaiushchikhsya Izdanii (Periodicals and Continuations), Mezhdunarodnaya Kniga, Smolenskaya sennaya pl 32-34, Moscow G-200

Novye Knigi (New Books), Mezhdunarodnaya Kniga, Smolenskaya sennaya pl 32-34, Moscow G-200
Announcements of forthcoming books

Sakmatsvilo Literaturis Moambe (Bulletin of Children's Literature), Izdatelstvo Nakaduli, Mardzhanishvili ul 5, Tbilisi 380029

Sovetskaya Bibliografia (Soviet Bibliography), USSR Library Council, The Lenin State Library of the USSR, Prospect Kalinina 3, Moscow 101000

Ukrainska Knyha (Ukrainian Books), Association of Book Lovers, Kyiw Publishing, 4800 North 12th St, Philadelphia, PA 19141, USA
Text in Ukrainian

Publishers

A P N, see Novosti

Atomizdat*, Zhdanova ul 5, 103031 Moscow K-31 Tel: (095) 2942228/2959993
Publishing House for Atomic Literature
Dir: V A Kulyamin
Subjects: Nuclear Science and Technology (peaceful use of nuclear energy)
Founded: 1963

Aurora Art Publishers, Nevsky prospekt 7/9, 191065 Leningrad Tel: 3123753 Cable Add: Exportizdat Aurora Leningrad Telex: 121562
President, Rights & Permissions: Boris Kutkov; *Editor-in-Chief:* Vladimir Gusev; *Production:* Faina Timofeyeva
Subject: Art
Founded: 1969
Miscellaneous: Publishes in foreign languages

Detskaya Entsiklopediya*, Bakuninskaja ul 55, Moscow 107042 Tel: (095) 2695276
Children's Encyclopaedia
Subjects: Literature, Poetry, Historical & Biographical Novels, Science Fiction
Founded: 1933

Izdatelstvo **Detskaya Literatura**, Malyi Cherkaskii pereulok 1, Moscow
Children's Literature Publishing House
Dir: Mrs Tamara M Shatunova
Subject: Juveniles

Znak Pochyota Order **Dosaaf** Publishing House*, Novo-Ryazanskaya 26, Moscow 107066 Tel: (095) 2676545
Voluntary Society for the Promotion of the Army, Air Force and Navy
Subject: Military
Founded: 1951

Izdatelstvo '**Ekonomika**'*, Berezhkovskaya naberezhnaya 6, Moscow 121864 Tel: (095) 2404877
Economics Publishing House
Dir: I D Trotsenko
Subjects: Economics, Management, Commerce, Industry, Agriculture, Catering, Textbooks
Founded: 1963

Izdatelstvo **Energoizdat***, Shluzovaya naberezhnaya 10, Moscow 113114
Energy Publishing House
Dir: S P Rozanov; *Editor-in-Chief:* V Sidorov
Subjects: Scientific and technical literature on Power Engineering, Thermal, Hydro and Electrical Engineering, Automatic and Computer Science, Nuclear Power Engineering/Safety/Physics
Founded: 1931

Izdatelstvo **Finansy**, now Finansy i Statistika Publishing House USSR (qv)

Finansy i Statistika Publishing House USSR*, Chernyshevskogo ul 7, Moscow 101000 Tel: (095) 2234822
Finance and Statistics Publishing House

418 UNION OF SOVIET SOCIALIST REPUBLICS

Dir: V I Vinogradov
Subjects: Banking, Taxation, Accounts, Statistics, Computers, Demography
Founded: 1924

Izdatelstvo **'Fizkultura i Sport'***, Kalyaevskaya ul 27, Moscow 101421 Tel: (095) 2582690
Physical Culture & Sport Publishing House
Dir: Vasili A Zhiltsov
Subjects: Physical Culture, Sport
Founded: 1923

Gidrometeorizdat*, 2 Vasilyevsky Ostrov 23, Leningrad 199053 Tel: 2271531
Subjects: Meteorology, Hydrology, Atmosphere, Geology, Oceanology
Founded: 1936

Izdatelstvo **Iskusstvo***, Tsvetnov bul'var' 25, Moscow K-51 Tel: (095) 2940775
Publishing House for Art Literature
Dir: E Y Savostianov
Branch Off: Leningrad
Subjects: Fine Arts, Music, Theatre
Founded: 1938 (as Izogiz & Iskusstvo)

Izvestiya Publishing House*, Pushkinskaya pl 5, Moscow K-6
Dir: Y I Balanenko
Subjects: Izvestiya, Official Publications of USSR and RSFSR Supreme Soviets

Izdatelstvo **'Khimiya'***, Strominka ul 23, Block 4, Moscow B-76 Tel: (095) 2682976
Publishing House for Chemistry
Dir: Ya S Mashkevich
Subject: Chemistry
Founded: 1963

Izdatelstvo **'Khudozhestvennaya Literatura'**, Novo-Basmannaya ul 19, Moscow B-78 Tel: (095) 2618865
Publishing House for Fiction & Poetry
Dir: G A Andjaparidze
Subjects: Fiction, Literature
Founded: 1930 (as The State Publishers of Fiction)

Izdatelstvo **'Kniga'***, Nezhdanovoi ul 8-10, Moscow K-9 Tel: (095) 2298269
Dir: V F Kravchenko
Subjects: Bibliography, Printing, Publishing, Graphic Arts, Book Trade, Bibliology, Bibliophilism, Librarianship, Miniature and Facsimile Editions
Founded: 1963

Izdatelstvo **'Kolos'***, Sadovaya-Spasskaya ul 18, Moscow I-139 Tel: (095) 2955824
Dir: I P Khramkov
Subjects: Agriculture, Veterinary Science
Founded: 1963

Izdatelstvo **'Legkaya i Pishchevaya** Promyshlennost'***, I Kadashevskii pereulok 12, Moscow 113035 Tel: (095) 2330848
Food and Light Industry Publishing House
Dir: N N Zazin; *Editor-in-Chief:* T G Gromova
Subjects: Light Industries (textiles, leather, glass), Food Industry, Fishing Industry
Founded: 1932

Izdatelstvo **'Lenizdat'***, Fontanka 59, Leningrad D-23 Tel: 2155821
Leningrad Publishing House
Subjects: Politics, Technical, Agriculture, Fiction, Juveniles, Art, Popular Science, Folklore
Founded: 1963

Izdatelstvo **'Lesnaya Promyshlennost'***, Kirova ul 40a, Moscow 101000 Tel: (095) 2287860
Forest Industry Publishing House
Dir: B S Oreshkin
Subjects: Forestry, Wood & Paper Products, Logging, Woodworking, Dendrochemistry, Nature Conservation
Founded: 1963

Izdatelstvo **'Malysh'***, Butyrskii val 68, Moscow A-55 Tel: (095) 2512242
Children's World Publishing House
Dir: I N Boronetsky
Subject: Pre-school Publications

Izdatelstvo **'Mashinostroenie'**, Stromynsky pereulok 4, Moscow 107076 Tel: (095) 2683858
Publishing House for Mechanical Engineering
Dir: A V Astakhov
Subject: Mechanical Engineering
Founded: 1931

Izdatelstvo **'Meditsina'***, Petroverigskii pereulok 6-8, Moscow K-142 Tel: (095) 2948785
Publishing House for Medicine
Dir: V I Maevsky
Subjects: Medicine, Health, Sciences
Founded: 1918

Izdatelstvo **'Metallurgiya'***, 2-oi Obydenskii pereulok 14, Moscow G-34, 119034 Tel: (095) 2025532
Publishing House for Metallurgy
Dir: M A Kovalevskiy
Subject: Metallurgy
Founded: 1939

Izdatelstvo **'Mezhdunarodnye Otnosheniya'***, Kuznetskii most 24, 103031 Moscow K-31 Tel: (095) 2945796
International Relations Publishing House
Dir: S P Emelyanikov
Subjects: International Information, Translations for UN Textbooks

Leidykla **'Mintis'***, Sierakausko 15, Vilnius Tel: 632943
Dir: Algimantas Garliauskas
Subjects: Politics, Law, Philosophy, Tourism, Sport Directories, Economics, History, Hobbies, Social Sciences, Textbooks, Juveniles, Periodicals
Founded: 1949

Izdatelstvo **Mir**, 2 Pervy Rizhskii pereulok, Moscow I-110 Tel: (095) 2861783 Telex: 411466 MIR SU
Dir: Dr V P Kartsev; *Editor-in-Chief:* Dr G B Kurganov
Orders to: Mezhdunarodnaya Kniga, Moscow
Subject: Translations from and into Russian of technical and scientific works
1985: 473 titles *Founded:* 1946

Izdatelstvo **Molodaya Gvardia**, Sushchevskaya ul 21, Moscow 101503 Tel: (095) 9720546
Young Guard Publishing House of the Young Communist League Central Committee
General Dir: Valentin Yurkin
Subjects: Political Science, Social Science, History, Biography, Art, Sport, Poetry, Modern World Literature
Founded: 1922

Izdatelstvo **'Moskovskii Rabochiy'***, Christoprudny bul'var' 8, Moscow 103012 Tel: (095) 2210735
Moscow Worker Publishing House
Dir: N H Eselyek
Subjects: General Fiction & Non-fiction
Founded: 1922

Izdatelstvo **Moskovskogo Universiteta***, Hertzena ul 5-7, Moscow K-9 Tel: (095) 2295091
Moscow University Press
Dir: Dr A K Avelitchev; *Rights & Permissions:* VAAP, Bolshaya Bronnaya 6a, Moscow
Subject: Sciences
Founded: 1926

Izdatelstvo **'Muzyka'***, Neglinnaja ul 14, Moscow 103045 Tel: (095) 2230497

Music Publishing House
Publicity Manager: L Sidelnikov
Subjects: Music, Scores

Izdatelstvo **Mysl'***, Leninsky prospekt 15, Moscow V-71 Tel: (095) 2324248
Thought Publishing House
Dir: A P Porivaev
Subjects: Science, Economics, Geography, Philosophy, History
Founded: 1963

Izdatelstvo **'Nauka'**, Profsojuznaja ul 90, Moscow V-485 Tel: (095) 3347151
Science Publishing House
Dir: S Chybyryayev
Subjects: Natural and Humanitarian Sciences, Physics and Mathematics, Textbooks, Oriental Studies, Foreign-language books, Periodicals
Founded: 1727
Miscellaneous: There are six self-supporting branches of Nauka in Moscow and two divisions in Novosibirsk and Leningrad

Izdatelstvo **'Nedra'***, Tret'yakovskii pereulok 1-19, Moscow K-12 Tel: (095) 2231735
Natural Resources Publishing House
Dir: M S Lvov
Subjects: Meteorology, Geology, Energy
Founded: 1963

Agentstvo Pechati **'Novosti'** (APN)+*, Bolshaya Pochtovaya ul 7, Moscow 107082 Tel: (095) 2655008/2692754 Telex: 411101
Novosti Press Agency Publishing House
Dir: A V Pushkov; *Editorial:* Yu S Fantalov; *Sales, Publicity:* S G Mishchenko; *Production:* V N Katkova
Subjects: History, Philosophy, Social Science, Politics, Economics, International Affairs, General Informative Books, Low- & High-priced Paperbacks
Founded: 1964

Pedagogika*, Lefortovsky pereulok 8, Moscow 107066 Tel: (095) 2611282
Dir: Mr Razumny
Subjects: Science, Education, Reference, Pedagogics
Founded: 1969

Izdatelstvo **'Pishchevaya Promyshlennost'**, now incorporated in Izdatelsvo Legkaya i Pishchevaya Promyshlennost (qv)

Planeta Publishers*, Petrovka 8/11, Moscow 103031 Tel: (095) 2230470
Subjects: Guidebooks, Illustrated books
Founded: 1969

Politizdat*, Myusskaya pl 7, Moscow D-47 Tel: (095) 2531897
Publishing House for Political Literature
Dir: H B Tropkin
Subjects: Political Literature, History
Founded: 1931

Pravda Publishing House*, Pravdy ul 24, Moscow
Dir: B A Feldman

Profizdat, Kirova ul 13, Moscow 101000 Tel: (095) 9245740
Publishing House for All-Union Central Council of Trade Unions
Dir: Alexei N Zakharikov
Subjects: Economics, Sociology, Psychology of Work, Trade Union Movement, Literature, Fiction, Prose
Founded: 1930

Progress Publishers, Zubovsky bul'var' 17, Moscow 119847 Tel: (095) 2469032 Telex: 411800 Kegl
Dir: Volf Nikolayevich Sedykh; *Editor-in-Chief:* Aleksandr Konstantinovich Avelichev; *Production:* Mikhail Pavlovich Kryakovkin

UNION OF SOVIET SOCIALIST REPUBLICS 419

Subjects: Scientific Socialism, Marxism-Leninism, Philosophy, Political Economy, International Relations, International Communist and Workers Movement, History, Sociology, Law, Biographies, Memoirs, Essays, Linguistics, Russian Translations of Fiction, Social and Political Literature
Founded: 1931

Izdatelstvo **'Prosveshchenie'***, 3-ii proezd Marinoi Roshchi 41, Moscow 129110 Tel: (095) 2891405
Dir: D D Zuev
Subjects: Education, Textbooks
Founded: 1963

Izdatelstvo **'Radio i Svyaz'***, Chistoprudnyi bul'var' 2, Moscow 101000 Tel: (095) 2585351/2944807
Communications Publishing House
Dir: N Zabolotsky
Subjects: Communications (postal, telegraphic and wireless, television, Hi-Fi equipment), Philately, Radio Engineering, Electronics, Cybernetics, Computer Engineering, Radio Communications

Raduga Publishers, Zubovsky bul'var' 17, Moscow 119859
Dir: Sergei P Emelianikov

Russky Yazyk*, Pushkinskaya ul 23, Moscow 103009 Tel: (095) 2291079
Russian Language Publishers
Dir: V I Nasarov
Subjects: Textbooks, Reference, Dictionaries
Founded: 1974

Izdatelstvo **'Sovetskaya Entsiklopediya'**, Pokrovskii bul'var' 8, Moscow 109817 Tel: (095) 2973562/2977483
Soviet Encyclopaedia Publishing House
Chairman of Editorial Council:
A Prokhorov
Subjects: General, specialized and technical encyclopaedias and encyclopaedic reference
Founded: 1925

Izdatelstvo **'Sovetskaya Rossiya'***, Suapnova Proezd 13-15, Moscow K-12 Tel: (095) 2213913
Soviet Russia Publishing House
Dir: E A Petrov
Subjects: Popular and Social Sciences, Children's, Political Propaganda, Art, Periodicals
Founded: 1957

Izdatelstvo **'Sovetskii Khudozhnik'***, Chernyahovskogo ul 4a, Moscow 125319 Tel: (095) 1512502
Soviet Artist Publishing House
Dir: V Goryainov
Subject: Art, Reference
Founded: 1969

Izdatelstvo **'Sovetskii Kompozitor'**, 14-12 Sadovaya-Triumfalnaya St, Moscow 103006 Tel: (095) 2092384
Soviet Composer Publishing House
Dir: M Y Kunin
Subject: Music (Reference, Bibliographies, Composers)
Bookshop: Magazin-Salon Sovetskaya Muzyka (at above address)
Founded: 1967

Izdatelstvo **Sovetskii Pisatel***, ul Vorovskovo 11, 121069 Moscow 69 Tel: (095) 2025051
USSR Writer's Union Publishing House
Dir: V N Eramenko
Subjects: Belles Lettres, Art History, Literary History, Poetry, Literary Criticism, Literary Translations
Founded: 1935
Miscellaneous: Publishes monthly magazine *Soviet Motherland* in Yiddish

Izdatelstvo **'Sovetskoe Radio'**, now Izdatelstvo Radio i Svyaz (qv)

Sovremennik Publishers*, Yartsevskaya 4, Moscow 121351 Tel: (095) 1409205
Subjects: Fiction, Literary Criticism, Drama
Founded: 1970

Znak Pochyota Order Izdatelstvo **Standartov***, Novopresnensky pereulok 3, Moscow 123022 Tel: (095) 2520348
Subject: Official Standards
Founded: 1926

Statistika, now Finansy i Statistika Publishing House USSR (qv)

Stroyizdat Publishing House, Kalyayevskaya 23a, Moscow 101442 Tel: (095) 2516967
Subjects: Building Sciences, Machinery, Urban Development, Architecture, Geology, Hydrogeology
Founded: 1932

Izdatelstvo **'Sudostroenie'**+, Gogolya ul 8, Leningrad 191065 Tel: 3124479
Publishing House for Shipbuilding
Man Dir: A A Andreev; *Editor-in-Chief:* A L Mitrofanov; *Production:* U V Rodionov; *Rights & Permissions:* A S Albov
Subjects: Shipbuilding, Ship Repairing, Ship Installations Equipment and Devices, Navigation, Offshore Engineering, University and Secondary Textbooks on these subjects
Bookshop: 'Sudostroenie', 40 Sadovuja St, Leningrad
Founded: 1940

Izdatelstvo **Svyaz**, now Izdatelstvo Radio i Svyaz (qv)

Izdatelstvo **'Transport'***, Basmannyi Tupik 6a, Moscow 107174 Tel: (095) 2626773
Dir: V P Titov
Subjects: Railway, Automobile, Air, Sea and Naval Transport
Founded: 1923

Vsesoyuznoe Obyedineniye **'Vneshtorgizdat'***, Fadyeev ul 1, Moscow 107207 Tel: (095) 411238 Telex: 7238 VTI SU
Foreign Trade Publishing House
President: Sergey P Emelyanikov; *Editorial:* Boris V Lensky; *Sales:* Leonid G Koftov; *Production:* Anatoly D Sorokin
Subject: Foreign Trade
Founded: 1925
Miscellaneous: Publish Catalogues, Prospectuses and Advertising Material in Russian and Foreign Languages on Soviet exports. Execute orders of foreign organizations for translation and publishing in Russian of maintenance and other documents

Voyenizdat*, Upravleniye Voyennogo Izdateltsva, Moscow K-160 Tel: (095) 1950154
Chief: A I Kopytin
Subjects: Military aspects of politics, history; Military Fiction, memoirs

Izdatelstvo **'Vysshaya Shkola'**, Neglinnaya ul 29/14, Moscow Tel: (095) 2000456
Higher School Publishing House
Dir: M V Kiselev
Subject: Textbooks (Secondary & Vocational Education)
Founded: 1959

Izdatelstvo **'Yuridicheskaya Literatura'***, Kachalov ul 14, Moscow 121069 Tel: (095) 2028384
Law Literature Publishing House
Dir: S A Chibiryaev
Subject: Law
Founded: 1917

Znanie*, Novaya ploshchad 3-4, Moscow K-12 Tel: (095) 2271531
Knowledge Publishing House
Dir: V Belyakov
Subjects: General Science, Education, Culture, Politics
Founded: 1951

Literary Agents

V A A P, see entry below

Vsesoyuznoe agentstvo po avtorskim pravam (VAAP)*, Bolshaya Bronnaya ul 6a, Moscow 103670 Tel: (095) 2034599
Cable Add: Moscow Avtor Telex: 411327 Avtor SU
Copyright Agency of the USSR
Contact: B Pankin, Chairman; or M Shisigin, Vice-Chairman

Major Booksellers

Mezhdunarodnaya Kniga*, Smolenskaya sennaya pl 32-34, Moscow G-200 Tel: (095) 2441022 Cable Add: Mezhkniga Moscow Telex: 160
The sole organization in the USSR through which foreign purchasers can obtain books. The leading agent for distribution of USSR books and periodicals abroad is Les Livres Etrangers SA, 10 rue Armand-Moisant, F-75737 Paris cedex 15, France Tel: (01) 7342727/5665680; retail bookshop Maison du Livre Etranger ('Dom Knigi'), 9 rue de l'Eperon, F-75006 Paris, France Tel: (01) 3261060

Major Libraries

Fundamental Library of the **Academy of Medical Sciences***, Baltiyskaya ul 8, Moscow

Biblioteka **Akademii Nauk SSSR***, Birzhevaya liniya 1, Leningrad V-164 Tel: Director's Office 183592 and 184091; Information and Bibliographical Department 183991
Library of the Academy of Sciences of the USSR

Gosudarstvennaya publichnaya nauchno-tekhnicheskaya biblioteka Sibirskogo otdeleniya **Akademii Nauk SSSR***, Voskhod ul 15, 630200 Novosibirsk Tel: Director 661860; Reference and Bibliography Department 661991; Reader Registration 668071
State Public Scientific and Technical Library of the Siberian Department of the Academy of Sciences of the USSR

Institut nauchnoy informatsii po obschestvennym naukam **Akademii Nauk SSSR***, Krasikova ul 28/45, 117418 Moscow V-418 Tel: (095) 1288930
Institute of Scientific Information in the Social Sciences of the Academy of Sciences of the USSR

Tsentral'naya nauchnaya biblioteka **Akademii Nauk USSR***, Vladimirskaya ul 62, 252601 Kiev 601 Tel: Director 243126; Reference/Bibliography Section 213231
Central Scientific Library of the Academy of Sciences of the Ukrainian SSR

All-Union Patent and Technical Library*, Berezhkovskaya naberezhnaya 24, Moscow

Central State **Archives of Early Russian** Historical Records*, Bolshaya Pirogovskaya ul 17, Moscow

Central State **Archives of the October Revolution** and Higher State Bodies*, Bolshaya Pirogovskaya ul 17, Moscow

UNION OF SOVIET SOCIALIST REPUBLICS

Central State **Archives of the RSFSR***, Berezhkovskaya naberezhnaya 26, Moscow

Central State Historical **Archives of the USSR***, Naberezhnaya Krasnogo Flota 4, Leningrad

Central State Literature and Art **Archives of the USSR***, Leningradskoe chausee 50, Moscow
Dir: N B Volkova

Azerbaidzhanskaya gosudarstvennaya respublikanskaya biblioteka im M F Akhundova*, Tsentr ul Khagani 29, 37061 Baku Tel: 936801; Reference and Bibliography Department 936004
M F Akhundov State Republic Library of Azerbaizhan

Nauchnaya biblioteka im M **Gor'kogo Leningradskogo** gosudarstvennogo universiteta im A A Zhdanova, Universitetskaya naberezhnaya 7-9, Leningrad 199034 Tel: Director 2-182741; Reference and Information Department 2-189555
M Gor'kii Scientific Library of the A A Zhadanov State University of Leningrad
Dir: E P Miliutina

Nauchnaya biblioteka im A M **Gor'kogo Moskovskogo** gos universiteta im M V Lomonosova*, Marx prospekt 20, Moscow K-9 Tel: Director's Office (095) 2036525; Service Department (095) 2033751
A M Gor'kii Scientific Library of The Lomonosov State University of Moscow

Vsesoyuznaya **Gosudarstvennaya ordena Trudovogo Krasnogo Znameni biblioteka** inostrannoi literatury*, Ulyanovskaya 1, Moscow 109240 Tel: (095) 2972839
All-Union State Library of Foreign Literature

Gosudarstvennaya publichnaya istoricheskaya biblioteka RSFSR*, 101839 Moscow, Bogdana Khmel'nitskogo ul, Starosadskii per d 9 Tel: Director 2956514; Information 2280582
State Public Historical Library of the RSFSR

Gosudarstvennaya publichnaya nauchno-tekhnicheskaya biblioteka SSSR*, Kuznetskii most 12, Moscow K-31 Tel: Director (095) K59288; Reference-Bibliography (095) B87379
State Public Scientific and Technical Library of the USSR

Gosudarstvennaya ordena Lenina biblioteka SSSR imeni V I **Lenina***, Prospect Kalinina 3, Moscow 101000 Tel: (095) 2024056 Telex: 7167 wgbibl su
V I Lenin State Library of the USSR
Secretary: G A Semenova

Gosudarstvennaya Respublikanskaya biblioteka Gruzinskoi SSR im K **Marksa***, Ketskhoveli ul 5, Tbilisi 380007 Tel: Director's Office 931233/999286
State Republican Karl Marx Library of the Georgian SSR

Gosudarstvennaya biblioteka UzSSR im Alishera **Navoi**, Alleya paradov 5, Tashkent 700000 Tel: 394036/394341/394440/394450
Alisher Navoi State Public Library of the Uzbek SSR

Gosudarstvennaya publichnaya biblioteka im M E **Saltykova-Schedrina***, Sadovaya ul 18, Leningrad D-69 Tel: 152856
M E Saltykov-Shchedrina State Public Library

Tartu Riikliku Ulikooli Teaduslik Raamatükogu, Struve ul 1, 202400 Tartu, Estonian SSR Tel: Tartu 34121/286 Telex: 208010 Nauka
Scientific Library of Tartu State University
Librarian: Laine Peep
Publications: Publicationes bibliothecae universitatis litterarum Tartuensis; Raamat-aeg-restaureerimine; Teadusliku Raamatukogu töid (serials); *Eksliibris TRÜ Teaduslikus Raamatukogus; Tartu Riiklik Ülikool. Bibliograafia*

The Scientific Library of the **Vilnius** Vincas Kapsukas State University, Universiteto gatve 3, 232633 Vilnius Tel: 610616/611076 Telex: 261128 Vaiva
Librarian: B Butkevičiene

Library Associations

Council on Libraries of the **Academy** of Sciences of the USSR*, Prospect Leninsky 14, Moscow
Academy Chairman: P N Fedoseev

U S S R Library Council*, The Lenin State Library of the USSR, Prospect Kalinina 3, Moscow 101000 Tel: (095) 2024656/2228551 Telex: 7167 wgbibl su
President: Professor N M Sikorsky;
Executive Secretary: G A Semenova
Publications: Bibliotekar (Librarian); *Sovetskoje bibliotekovedonie* (Formerly: *Biblioteki SSSR*) (Soviet Library Science); *Nauchnye i tekhnicheskie biblioteki SSSR* (Scientific and Technical Libraries of the USSR); *Nauchnaya i tekhnicheskaya informatsiya* (Scientific and Technical Information) *Seriya I: Organizatsiya i metodika informatsionnoi raboty* (Organization and Methodology of Information Work) *Seriya 2: Informatsionnye processy i systemy* (Information Processes and Systems); *Sovetskaya Bibliografia* (Soviet Bibliography); *Bibliotekovedenie i bibliografiya za rubezhom* (Librarianship and Bibliography Abroad); *Kniga Issledovaniya i materialy* (Book Studies and Materials); *V mire knig* (In the World of Books); *Knizhnoe obozrenie* (Book Reviews); *Informatika* (Information Science) *Bibliotekovedenie i Bibliografovedenie Bibliograficheskaya informatsiya (a) Sovetskaya literatura (b) Inostrannaya literatura* (Library Science and Theory of Bibliography, Bibliographic Information (a) Soviet Literature (b) Foreign Literature); *Bibliotekovedenie i Bibliografovedenie (a) Nauchnyi Referativnyi Sbornik (b) Obzornaya informatsiya (c) Express-informatsiya* (Library Science and Theory of Bibliography (a) Abstracts Collection (b) Survey Information (c) Express-Information)

Library Reference Books and Journals

Books

Bibliotekovedenie i bibliografiya za rubezhom (Librarianship and Bibliography Abroad), USSR Library Council, The Lenin State Library of the USSR, Prospect Kalinina 3, Moscow 101000

Bibliotekovedenie i Bibliografovedenie, Bibliograficheskaya informatsiya (Library Science and Theory of Bibliography, Bibliographic Information), USSR Library Council, The Lenin State Library of the USSR, Prospect Kalinina 3, Moscow 101000

Nauchnye i tekhnicheskie biblioteki SSSR (Scientific and Technical Libraries of the USSR), USSR Library Council, The Lenin State Library of the USSR, Prospect Kalinina 3, Moscow 101000

Journals

Bibliotekar (The Librarian), USSR Library Council, The Lenin State Library of the USSR, Prospect Kalinina 3, Moscow 101000

Sovetskoje bibliotekovedenie (Soviet Library Science), USSR Library Council, The Lenin State Library of the USSR, Prospect Kalinina 3, Moscow 101000

Literary Periodicals

Culture and Life, Union of Soviet Societies for Friendship and Cultural Relations with Foreign Countries, proezd Sapunova 13-15, Moscow-Centre
Text in English, French, German, Russian and Spanish

Litaratura i Mastatstva (Literature and Art), Ministerstva Kul'tury i Sayuz Pismennikaw BSSR, Zakharava ul 19, Minsk

Literaturnaya Gazeta (Literary Newspaper), USSR Writers' Union, Vorovskogo ul 52, Moscow

Literaturnaya Rossiya (Literary Russia), USSR Writers' Union, Vorovskogo ul 52, Moscow

Molodaya Gvardiya (The Young Guards), Vsesoyuznyi Leninskii Kommunisticheskii Soyuz Molodozhi, Tsentral'nyi Komitet, Sushchevskaya ul 21, Moscow A-55

Moskva, Arbart 20, Moscow
Literary magazine

Neva, USSR Writers' Union, Vorovskogo ul 52, Moscow

Novyi Mir (New World), USSR Writers' Union, Vorovskogo ul 52, Moscow
Literary, artistic and socio-political journal

Radyans'ke Literaturoznavstvo (Soviet Literary Studies), Akademiya Nauk Ukrayinskoyi SSR, Instytut Literatury im T H Shevchenka ta Spilka Pys'mennykiv Ukrayiny, Kirova 4, Kiev

Russian Literature, North-Holland Publishing Co, PO Box 211, Amsterdam, Netherlands

Russian Literature Triquarterly, Ardis Publishers, 2901 Heatherway, Ann Arbor, MI 48104, USA

Russkaya Literatura (Russian Literature), Nauka (Science Publishing House), Podsosenskii pereulok 21, Moscow K-62
Journal of the Institute of Russian Literature of the USSR

Soviet Literature, USSR Writers' Union, Vorovskogo ul 52, Moscow
Editions in English, German, Polish, Spanish, Japanese and Czech

V Mire Knig (In the World of Books), USSR Library Council, The Lenin State Library of the USSR, Prospect Kalinina 3, Moscow 101000

Voprosy Literatury (Questions of Literature), USSR Writers' Union, Vorovskogo ul 52, Moscow

United Arab Emirates

General Information

Language: Arabic (English used in business)
Religion: Islamic
Population: 1.04 million
Bank Hours: 0800-1200 Saturday-Thursday (1100 Thursday in Abu Dhabi)
Shop Hours: Abu Dhabi: Summer: 0800-1300, 1600-dusk Saturday-Thursday; Winter: 0800-1300, 1530-1900 Saturday-Thursday. Northern Emirates: Summer: 0900-1300, 1630-2000 or 2100 Saturday-Thursday; Winter: 0900-1300, 1600-2000 or 2100 Saturday-Thursday
Currency: 100 fils = 1 UAE dirham
Export/Import Information: No tariff on books or advertising matter, except duty on imports in Dubai and ad valorem rates in Ras al Khaimah and Sharjah. No import licence required except for obscene publications in Dubai

Publishers

All Prints Distributors and Publishers*, Hamdan St, PO Box 857, Abu Dhabi
Telex: 22844 EM
Partners: Miss Bushra Khayat, Hassan S Khayat

Major Booksellers

Tahseen S **Khayat***, PO Box 857, Abu Dhabi   Tel: (02) 41853
Also: Tahseen S Khayat, Lebanon (qv)

Major Libraries

Centre for Documentation and Research*, Old Palace, PO Box 2380, Abu Dhabi
Dir: Mohammad Morsi Abdullah PhD
Publication: Documents of UAE (annual)

National Library, PO Box 2380, Abu Dhabi   Tel: (02) 215300   Telex: 22414 Culcen Em
Librarian: Hishmat M A Kasem

United Kingdom

General Information

Language: English; Welsh in most of Wales (where it is used alongside English for official purposes). About 80,000 speak Scots Gaelic (in Highlands and Islands of Scotland). Irish is used in parts of Northern Ireland
Religion: Protestant officially. Numerous other religions have significant numbers of adherents
Population: 56.8 million
Bank Hours: 0930-1530 Monday-Friday. Some banks open for personal customers 0930-1200 Saturday
Shop Hours: Generally 0900-1730 Monday-Saturday. Early closing one day a week usually
Currency: 100 pence = 1 pound sterling
Export/Import Information: Member of the European Economic Community. No tariffs on books; advertising matter dutiable over a certain weight. No import licences required; nominal exchange controls. Advertising in UK is regulated by statutes and voluntary codes; for information contact The Advertising Standards Authority Ltd, Brook House, Torrington Pl, London WC1
Copyright: UCC, Berne, Florence (see International section)

Book Trade Organizations

Antiquarian Booksellers' Association, Suite 2, 26 Charing Cross Rd, London WC2H 0DG   Tel: (01) 379 3041
Secretary: Jacqueline White

Association of Authors' Agents, 13 Jubilee Pl, London SW3 3TE   Tel: (01) 352 4311
President: Tessa Sayle
Secretary: Linda Shaughnessy

Association of British Directory Publishers*, 154 High St, Beckenham, Kent BR3 1EA
Tel: (01) 650 7745
Chairman: K S Aukstolis
Hon Secretary: C A Henderson

Association of Learned & Professional Society Publishers, A I P Henton, Sentosa, Hill Rd, Fairlight, East Sussex TN35 4AE   Tel: Hastings 812354 (STD code 0424)

Association of Little Presses, 89A Petherton Rd, London N5 2QT   Tel: (01) 226 2657
Co-ordinator: Bob Cobbing

Association of Mail Order Publishers*, 1 New Burlington St, London W1X 1FD
Tel: (01) 437 0706
Dir: D R Vickers

Association of Publishers' Educational Representatives
Secretary: Fred Mellor, 12 Gregory Pl, South Park, Lytham St Anne's, Lancashire FY8 4SB   Tel: Lytham 736275 (STD code 0253)

Authors' Licensing & Collecting Society, 7 Ridgmount St, London WC1E 7AE   Tel: (01) 255 2034
Secretary-General: Janet Hurrell

B A S H, part of Booksellers Association of Great Britain and Ireland (qv)

B O D, see Booksellers' Order Distribution

The **Book Development** Council, 19 Bedford Sq, London WC1B 3HJ   Tel: (01) 580 6321   Cable Add: Publasoc London WC1 Telex: 267160 Pubass G
Chairman: Julian Rea
International Division of the Publishers Association

The **Book Marketing** Council*, 19 Bedford Sq, London WC1B 3HJ   Tel: (01) 580 6321   Cable Add: Publasoc London WC1 Telex: 267160 Pubass G   Fax: (01) 636 5375
Chairman: Stan Remington; *Director:* Maggie van Reenen
A division of the Publishers Association, working to promote and expand sales of books in the UK market
Publications include: Book Marketing News

Book Publishers' Representatives' Association
Honorary Secretary: Bob Davis, 3 Carolina Way, Tiptree, Essex CO5 0DW   Tel: Tiptree 816710 (STD code 0621)
Publication: Book Publishers' Representatives' Association Handbook

Book Tokens Ltd*, 152 Buckingham Palace Rd, London SW1W 9TZ   Tel: (01) 730 9258
Secretary: J S Crowe

The **Book Trade** Benevolent Society*, Dillon Lodge, The Booksellers Retreat, Kings Langley, Hertfordshire WD4 8LT
Tel: Kings Langley 63128 (STD code 092 77)
Secretary: Ann Brown

Book Trust, Book House, 45 East Hill, Wandsworth, London SW18 2QZ   Tel: (01) 870 9055
Chief Executive: Martyn Goff, OBE
Branch: 15A Lynedoch St, Glasgow G3 6EF   Tel: (041) 332 0391
Libraries: Reference library of current British children's books. Book information service
Publications: Booknews; Children's Books of the Year; The Authors and Illustrators List; Guide to Literary Prizes, Grants and Awards; annotated book lists on specialist topics

Booksellers Association of Great Britain and Ireland, 154 Buckingham Palace Rd, London SW1W 9TZ   Tel: (01) 730 8214
The Irish Branch is at Book House Ireland, 65 Middle Abbey St, Dublin 1, Republic of Ireland (qv)
Dir: Tim Godfray
Publications: Directory of Members; Lists of Specialist Booksellers; Directory of Book Publishers and Wholesalers; Trade Reference Book; Charter Group Economic Survey, and other publications relating to the bookselling trade

Booksellers Clearing House*, 152 Buckingham Palace Rd, London SW1W 9TZ   Tel: (01) 730 9258
Man Dir: W A Barnes

Booksellers' Order Distribution Ltd (BOD), 49 Victoria Rd, Aldershot, Hampshire GU11 1SJ   Tel: Aldershot 20697 (STD code 0252)
Man Dir and Secretary: Robin Young

British Copyright Council*, 29-33 Berners St, London W1P 4AA   Tel: (01) 580 5544

British Guild of Travel Writers, 28 Oakfield Rd, London N3 2HT   Tel: (01) 346 3772
Secretary: Robin Mead

British Printing Industries Federation, 11 Bedford Row, London WC1R 4DX   Tel: (01) 242 6904
Secretary: David Burch
Publications: Introduction to Printing Technology; ASPIF; Printing Industries (monthly); *Printers Yearbook; UK Periodical Printers; UK Book Printers 1987*

C I C I, see Confederation of Information Communication Industries

Children's Book Circle, c/o Macmillan Publishers Ltd, 4 Little Essex St, London WC2R 3LF   Tel: (01) 836 6633
Chairperson: Lynnet Wilson

Children's Book Foundation, Book House, 45 East Hill, Wandsworth, London SW18 2QZ   Tel: (01) 870 9055
A division of Book Trust (qv) handling activities related to the under-16s
Dir: Eunice McMullen

Children's Writers' Group, The Society of Authors, 84 Drayton Gardens, London SW10 9SB   Tel: (01) 373 6642
Secretary: Diana Shine

Confederation of Information Communication Industries, 19 Bedford Sq, London WC1B 3HJ Tel: (01) 580 6321
Manager: Linda Gough
Operates CICInet, containing reference databases

Copyright Licensing Agency, 33/34 Alfred Pl, London WC1 Tel: (01) 580 9729

Crime Writers' Association, PO Box 172, Tring, Hertfordshire HP23 5LP
Secretary: Anthea Fraser

Cyngor Llyfrau Cymraeg, see Welsh Books Council

Educational Publishers Council, 19 Bedford Sq, London WC1B 3HJ Tel: (01) 580 6321 Cable Add: Publasoc, London WC1 Telex: 267160 Pubass G Fax: (01) 636 5375
Dir: John R M Davies
School Books Division of The Publishers Association

Educational Writers' Group, 84 Drayton Gardens, London SW10 9SB Tel: (01) 373 6642
Secretary: Gordon Fielden
Publication: Guidelines for Educational Writers

English Language Book Society (ELBS), The British Council, 65 Davies St, London W1Y 2AA Tel: (01) 499 8011 Telex: 8952201 Bricon G Fax: (01) 493 5035
Dir: Colin Stevenson

Federation of Children's Book Groups, c/o 13 Yewdale, 196 Harborne Park Rd, Harborne, Birmingham B17 0BP Tel: (021) 426 5148
Secretary: Jan Wilde

I B I S, see International Book Information Services

Independent Publishers Guild
Secretary: Rosemary Pettit, 147-149 Gloucester Terrace, London W2 6DX Tel: (01) 723 7328

International Book Information Services, Waterside, Lowbell Lane, London Colney, St Albans, Hertfordshire AL2 1DX Tel: St Albans 25209 (STD code 0727) Telex: 261721 Fax: (0727) 26461
Marketing Dir: John Beale
See also Publishers' Information Card Services

Music Publishers Association, 7th Floor, Kingsway House, 103 Kingsway, London WC2B 6QX Tel: (01) 831 7591
Secretary: P J Dadswell

National Federation of Retail Newsagents, Yeoman House, Sekforde St, London EC1R 0HD Tel: (01) 253 4225
Chief Executive: K E J Peters

National Union of Journalists, (Book Branch), 314 Gray's Inn Rd, London WC1X 8DP Tel: (01) 837 8143
Chairman: Mike Hauser (Tel: (01) 686 8222)

Orders Clearing, IBIS Information Services Ltd, Waterside, Lowbell Lane, London Colney, St Albans, Hertfordshire AL2 1DX Tel: St Albans 25209 (STD code 0727) Telex: 261721
Dir: M W Whitmarsh

P I C S, see Publishers' Information Card Services

Public Lending Right Office, Bayheath House, Prince Regent St, Stockton-on-Tees, Cleveland TS18 1DF Tel: Stockton-on-Tees 604699 (STD code 0642)
Registrar: John W Sumsion

Publishers Association, 19 Bedford Sq, London WC1B 3HJ Tel: (01) 580 6321 Cable Add: Publasoc London WC1 Telex: 21792 ref 2527
Chief Executive: C Bradley

Publishers' Information Card Services, IBIS Ltd, Waterside, Lowbell Lane, London Colney, St Albans, Hertfordshire AL2 1DX Tel: St Albans 25209 (STD code 0727) Telex: 251721 Fax: (0727) 26461
Man Dir: David Clark; *Marketing Dir:* John Beale
Direct mail promotion for publishers. See also International Book Information Services

Publishers' Licensing Society, 19 Bedford Sq, London WC1B 3HJ Tel: (01) 580 6321 Cable Add: Publasoc London WC1 Telex: 21792 ref 2527
Secretary: Peter Phelan

Publishers' Overseas Circle, c/o Helena Svojsikova, Macmillan Publishers Ltd, Houndmills, Basingstoke, Hampshire RG21 2XS Tel: Basingstoke 29242 (STD code 0256)

Publishers Publicity Circle, c/o Christina Thomas, 48 Crabtree Lane, London SW6 6LW
Publications: Directory of members

Retail Book, Stationery and Allied Trades Employees' Association, 8-9 Commercial Rd, Swindon, Wiltshire SN1 5RB Tel: Swindon 615811 (STD code 0793)
General Secretary: D A Williamson

School Bookshop Association, 1 Effingham Rd, Lee, London SE12 8NZ Tel: (01) 852 4953
Director: Richard Hill
Publications: Books for Keeps (bi-monthly); *How to Set up and Run a School Bookshop*

Scottish Book Marketing Group, 25a South West Thistle St Lane, Edinburgh EH2 1EW Tel: (031) 225 5795

Scottish Publishers' Association, 25a South West Thistle St Lane, Edinburgh EH2 1EW Tel: (031) 225 5795
Dir: Lorraine Fannin; *Chairman:* Bill Henderson; *Vice-Chairman:* Stephanie Wolfe-Murray; *Publicist:* Alison Harley
Publication: New Books from Scottish Publishers (twice a year)

Scottish Publishing & Book Society, c/o Department of Publishing, Napier College, Colinton Rd, Edinburgh EH10 5DT Tel: (031) 447 7070 ext 2228
Secretary: Alistair McCleery

Small Press Group of Britain, BM BOZO, London WC1N 3XX Tel: (0234) 211606
Secretary: Cecilia Boggis
Group set up to promote the status of committed small presses in the UK

Society of Authors, 84 Drayton Gardens, London SW10 9SB Tel: (01) 373 6642
General Secretary: Mark Le Fanu
Publication: The Author (quarterly)

The **Society of Indexers**
Secretary: Mrs C Troughton, 16 Green Rd, Birchington, Kent CT7 9JZ Tel: Thanet 41115 (STD code 0843)
Publications: The Indexer; Microindexer

Society of Picture Researchers and Editors, BM Box 259, London WC1N 3XX Tel: (01) 405 5011   Freelance register: (01) 539 5927

Society of Young Publishers, 12 Dyott St, London WC1A 1DF
Chairman: Alexandra Howell, Hodder & Stoughton Ltd, 47 Bedford Sq, London WC1B 3DP Tel: (01) 636 9851
Publication: SYP Inprint (monthly)

Standard Book Numbering Agency Ltd, 12 Dyott St, London WC1A 1DF Tel: (01) 836 8911
Parent Company: J Whitaker & Sons Ltd (qv)
Secretary: Lars Andreasen
Publication: International Standard Book Numbering

U K National Serials Data Centre*, British Library, 2 Sheraton St, London W1V 4BH Tel: (01) 636 1544 ext 346 Telex: 21462 Blref G
Allocates International Standard Serial Numbers (ISSN) to serials published in UK

Welsh Books Council (Cyngor Llyfrau Cymraeg), Castell Brychan, Aberystwyth, Dyfed SY23 2JB Tel: Aberystwyth 4151 (STD code 0970)
Director: Gwerfyl Pierce Jones

Welsh Publishers' Union (Undeb Cyhoeddwyr Cymru), c/o Welsh Books Council, Castell Brychan, Aberystwyth, Dyfed SY23 2JB Tel: Aberystwyth 4151 (STD code 0970)

Women in Publishing, c/o J Whitaker Ltd, 12 Dyott St, London WC1A 1DF
Membership Secretary: Val Stevenson, 96 Mansfield Rd, London NW3 2HX Tel: (01) 485 5002

Writers' Guild of Great Britain, 430 Edgware Rd, London W2 1EH Tel: (01) 723 8074
General Secretary: Walter J Jeffrey

Book Trade Reference Books and Journals

Books

The Authors and Illustrators List, Book Trust, Book House, 45 East Hill, Wandsworth, London SW18 2QZ
Listing around 200 authors, illustrators and poets; compiled by Centre for Children's Books

The Book Report, Euromonitor Publications Ltd, 87-88 Turnmill St, London EC1M 5QU
Annual appraisal of the UK book market

Book Publishing, Jordan & Sons Ltd, PO Box 260, Bristol BS99 7DX

Britain's Book Publishing Industry, Jordan & Sons (Surveys) Ltd, Jordan House, 47 Brunswick Pl, London N1 6EE

British Books in Print (annual), J Whitaker & Sons Ltd, 12 Dyott St, London WC1A 1DF (also monthly on microfiche)

The British Library General Catalogue of Printed Books, K G Saur Ltd, Shropshire House, 2-10 Capper St, London WC1E 6JA
360 volumes to 1975; supplement 1976-82; supplement 1982-85; supplement to 1975 (6 vols)

British Official Publications, Pergamon Press Ltd, Headington Hill Hall, Oxford OX3 0BW

British Paperbacks in Print (annual), J Whitaker & Sons Ltd, 12 Dyott St, London WC1A 1DF

British National Bibliography, British Library, Bibliographic Services, 2 Sheraton St, London W1V 4BH

Cassell & The Publishers Association Directory of Publishing in Great Britain, the Commonwealth, Ireland, Pakistan and South Africa, Cassell PLC, Artillery House, Artillery Row, Westminster, London SW1P 1RT

Children's Books in Print, J Whitaker & Sons, 12 Dyott St, London WC1A 1DF

Current British Directories, CBD Research Ltd, 154 High St, Beckenham, Kent BR3 1EA
A guide to the directories published in the UK and the Republic of Ireland

Dealers in Books: a Directory of Dealers in Secondhand and Antiquarian Books in the British Isles, Europa Publications Ltd, 18 Bedford Sq, London WC1B 3JN

Directory of Book Publishers and Wholesalers, Booksellers Association of Great Britain and Ireland, 154 Buckingham Palace Rd, London SW1W 9TZ

Directory of Specialist Bookdealers in the UK Handling Mainly New Books, 31 Rowliff Rd, High Wycombe, Buckinghamshire

Guide to Literary Prizes, Grants and Awards, Book Trust, Book House, 45 East Hill, Wandsworth, London SW18 2QZ

Junior Fiction Index, Holmes McDougall Bookselling, Sandy Lane, North Gosforth, Newcastle upon Tyne NE3 5HH
Published by Association of Assistant Librarians

Picture Research Handbook, Samuel Smiles House, 11 Granville Park, London SE13 7DY

The Prelims to BBIP, J Whitaker & Sons Ltd, 12 Dyott St, London WC1A 1DF

Printing Trades Directory, Benn Business Information Services, Union House, Eridge Rd, Tunbridge Wells, Kent TN4 8HF

Private Press Books, Private Libraries Association, Ravelston, South View Rd, Pinner, Middlesex

The Publisher's Freelance Directory, Elvendon Press, The Old Surgery, High St, Goring-on-Thames, Reading, Berkshire RG8 9AW
Listing book trade freelances (categories: editorial, illustration, design & production, marketing & sales)

Publishers in the United Kingdom and their Addresses (annual), J Whitaker & Sons Ltd, 12 Dyott St, London WC1A 1DF

The Publishing & Bookselling Directory, Hamilton House Publishing, 17 Staveley Way, Brixworth Industrial Park, Brixworth, Northampton NN6 9EU

Readers' Guide to Fiction Authors, Centre for Library and Information Management, Loughborough University, Loughborough, Leicestershire LE11 3TU

Trade Reference Book, Booksellers Association of Great Britain and Ireland, 154 Buckingham Palace Rd, London SW1W 9TZ

Whitaker's Cumulative Book List (annual and quarterly), J Whitaker & Sons Ltd, 12 Dyott St, London WC1A 1DF

Writer's and Artist's Yearbook (annual), A & C Black (Publishers) Ltd, 35 Bedford Row, London WC1R 4JH

Journals

The Author, Society of Authors, 84 Drayton Gardens, London SW10 9SB

Book Marketing News, The Book Marketing Council, 19 Bedford Sq, London WC1B 3HJ

Booknews, Book Trust, Book House, East Hill, London SW18 2QZ

Book Publishers' Representatives' Association Handbook, Booksellers Association Service House, 154 Buckingham Palace Rd, London SW1W 9TZ

Books for Keeps, School Bookshop Association, 1 Effingham Rd, Lee, London SE12 8NZ

Books in Scotland, The Ramsay Head Press, 15 Gloucester Pl, Edinburgh EH3 6EE

Books of the Month and Books To Come, J Whitaker & Sons Ltd, 12 Dyott St, London WC1A 1DF

The Bookseller (weekly), J Whitaker & Sons Ltd, 12 Dyott St, London WC1A 1DF

Bookselling News, Booksellers Association of Great Britain and Ireland, 154 Buckingham Palace Rd, London SW1W 9TZ

British Book News, British Council, 65 Davies St, London W1Y 2AA
Monthly survey of British books

British Book Design and Production, Book Trust, Book House, East Hill, London SW18

Children's Books of the Year, Book Trust, Book House, East Hill, London SW18

Clique, Stoate & Bishop Printers, St James Sq, Cheltenham, Gloucestershire
The antiquarian booksellers' medium

The Indexer, c/o Hazel K Bell, 139 The Ryde, Hatfield, Hertfordshire AL9 5DP
Journal of British, Australian and American Societies of Indexers

List of Members, Booksellers Association of Great Britain and Ireland, 154 Buckingham Palace Rd, London SW1W 9TZ

Llais Llyfrau, Cyngor Llyfrau Cymraeg, Castell Brychan, Aberystwyth, Dyfed SY23 2JB
List of all books published in Welsh during previous six months and list of books to be published

New Books from Scottish Publishers (twice a year), Scottish Publishers' Association, 25a South West Thistle St Lane, Edinburgh EH2 1EW

Publisher, Macro Publishing, 41b High St, Hoddesdon, Hertfordshire

Publishing News, 43 Museum St, London WC1A 1LY

School Bookshop News, now *Books for Keeps* (qv)

UK Book Printers 1987, British Printing Industries Federation, 11 Bedford Row, London WC1R 4DX

UK Periodical Printers, British Printing Industries Federation, 11 Bedford Row, London WC1R 4DX

Whitaker's Books of the Month and Books to Come (monthly), J Whitaker & Sons Ltd, 12 Dyott St, London WC1A 1DF

Whitaker's Classified Monthly Book List, J Whitaker & Sons Ltd, 12 Dyott St, London WC1A 1DF

Publishers

No **1** Publishing Co Ltd, 64 Pentonville Rd, London N1 Tel: (01) 837 6301 Cable Add: Dons Bar Telex: 946240 Ramb
Man Dir: D Murray; *Editorial:* R Hind
Associate Company: Ramboro Enterprises Ltd (qv)
Subjects: Children's, Dictionaries, Cookery, Reprints
Founded: 1960

A A Publishing, an imprint of the Automobile Association (qv)

A D I S Press Ltd*, Suite 15c, Manchester International Office Centre, Styal Rd, Wythenshawe, Manchester M22 5WL Tel: (061) 436 6428 Telex: 667155 Fax: (061) 437 9551
Chief Editorial Office: ADIS Press Ltd, New Zealand (qv)
Associate Companies: ADIS Press Australasia Pty Ltd, Australia (qv); ADIS Press Publications Ltd, Hong Kong (qv); ADIS Press International Inc, Suite B30, Oxford Court Business Center, Middleton blvd and North Buckstown Dr, Langhorne, PA 19047, USA

A P Books/A P Information Services Ltd, 33 Ashbourne Ave, London NW11 0DU Tel: (01) 458 1607
Chief Executive: Alan Philipp
Imprint: Oliver's Guides
Subjects: Trade Directories & Membership Lists
1987: 14 titles *Founded:* 1969
ISBN Publisher's Prefixes: 0-906285, 0-906247

Abacus, an imprint of Sphere Books Ltd (qv)

Abacus Press+*, Abacus House, Speldhurst Rd, Tunbridge Wells, Kent TN4 0HU Tel: Tunbridge Wells 29783/27237 (STD code 0892) Cable Add: Abacus Tunbridgewells Telex: 957137 Abacus G
Man Dir, Publisher: N A Jaysekera; *Editorial, Publicity:* Mark Bicknell; *Rights & Permissions:* Mrs A F Field
Associate Companies: Abacus-Kent Ltd; Abacus Distribution Services; International Scholarly Book Services
Subjects: Medicine, Science, Technology, Engineering, Mathematics, Computer Sciences, Earth Sciences, Agriculture, Environmental Sciences, Energy Conservation, Bioengineering, Business, Management
Founded: 1970
ISBN Publisher's Prefix: 0-85626

Abelard-Schuman Ltd, now incorporated in Blackie & Son Ltd (qv)

Aberdeen University Press Ltd, see Pergamon Press Ltd

Absolute Press+, 14 Widcombe Crescent, Bath, Avon BA2 6AH Tel: Bath 316013 (STD code 0225) Telex: 449212 Lantel G ref 264 Fax: (0225) 69845
Chief Executive, Editorial, Production, Rights & Permissions: J Croft; *Sales:* J Richards; *Publicity:* P Borton
Subjects: Food & Wine
1985: 10 titles *1986:* 7 titles *Founded:* 1981

Abson Books, Abson, Wick, Bristol BS15 5TT Tel: Abson 2446 (STD code 027 582)
Partners: Anthea Bickerton, Pat McCormack
Subjects: Slang (American/Rhyming/Cockney) and Idioms (Scottish/Irish/Australian/Yiddish), Literary quiz & puzzle books, West Region, Toponyms
ISBN Publisher's Prefix: 0-902920

Academic and University Publishers Group, 1 Gower St, London WC1E 6HA Tel: (01) 580 3994 Telex: 262284 Monref G ref 3407
General Manager: Donald Deeks
Orders to: Biblios Publishers' Distribution Services Ltd, Glenside Industrial Estate, Star Rd, Partridge Green, Horsham, West Sussex RH13 8LD Tel: Partridge Green 710971 (STD code 0403)
Subjects: Belles Lettres, Poetry, Biography, History, Music, Art, Philosophy, Reference, Religion, Paperbacks, Medicine, Psychology, General & Social Science, Photography
Founded: 1965
Miscellaneous: Group includes Bergin & Garvey Publishers Inc, University of British Columbia Press, Duke University Press, University of Hawaii Press, Louisiana State University Press, University of Nebraska Press, University of North Carolina Press, Northeastern University Press, Northern Illinois University Press, Ohio University Press, Pennsylvania State University Press, University of Pennsylvania Press, University of Tokyo Press, University of Wisconsin Press

Academic Press, an imprint of Harcourt Brace Jovanovitch Ltd (qv)

Academic Publications*, Highfield, Dane Hill, Haywards Heath, West Sussex RH17 7EX Tel: Dane Hill 790214 (STD code 0825) Cable Add: Copen Telex: 95246 (Copen G)
Man Dir: F Frogley
Subjects: University Textbooks, Technical & Scientific, Medical, Philosophy, General Literature
Founded: 1974
ISBN Publisher's Prefix: 0-900307

Academy Editions+, 42 Leinster Gardens, London W2 3AN Tel: (01) 402 2141 Telex: 896928
Man Dir: Dr Andreas C Papadakis; *Sales Manager:* Sheila de Vallee; *Rights & Permissions, Publicity:* Margot Schwass
Trade Addresses: 7 Holland St, London W8 Tel: (01) 937 6996; J M Dent & Sons (Distribution) Ltd, Dunhams Lane, Letchworth, Hertfordshire SG6 1LF Tel: Letchworth 686241 (STD code 0462)
Parent Company: Academy Group Ltd, 42 Leinster Gardens, London W2 3AN
Subsidiary Companies: Academy Editions, France (qv); Architectural Design, Academy Design Services, both at 42 Leinster Gardens, London W2 3AN
Imprint: Alec Tiranti (firm also publishes *Architectural Design, Architectural Monographs* and *Art and Design*)
Subjects: Architecture, Fine & Applied Arts, Photography, Fashion, Graphics, Music, Objets d'Art, Painting, Interior Design, Periodicals
Bookshops: Academy Bookshop & London Art Bookshop, 7/8 Holland St, London W8 Tel: (01) 937 6996; The Art Shop, Royal College of Art, Kensington Gore, London SW7
1987: 30 titles *Founded:* 1967
ISBN Publisher's Prefixes: 0-85670, 0-85458, 0-902620

Acorn, an imprint of Jay books (qv)

Acorn Editions, an imprint of James Clarke & Co Ltd (qv)

Actinic Press Ltd, 311 Worcester Rd, Malvern, Worcestershire WR14 1AN Tel: Malvern 65045 (STD code 068 45)
Man Dir: Leslie Smith
Subjects: Chiropody, Medical
Founded: 1926
ISBN Publisher's Prefix: 0-900024

Adamantine Press Ltd, 3 Henrietta St, London WC2E 8LU Tel: (01) 240 0856 Fax: (01) 379 0609
Man Dir: Danny Maher; *Marketing Dir:* Michael Geelan; *Production:* James Mealings; *Publicity:* Alice Taylor; *Rights & Permissions:* Pam Mullan
Subjects: Social Sciences, Humanities, Library & Information Sciences
1985: 10 titles *Founded:* 1984
ISBN Publisher's Prefix: 0-7449

Addison-Wesley Publishers Ltd+, Finchampstead Rd, Wokingham, Berkshire RG11 2NZ Tel: Wokingham 794000 (STD code 0734) Telex: 846136 Fax: 0734 794035
Man Dir: Peter Hoenigsberg; *Sales and Marketing Dir:* Rod Bristow; *Production Dir:* Paul Vinson; *Editor in Chief:* Sarah Mallen; *Senior Executive Editor:* Dr Simon Plumtree
Parent Company: Addison-Wesley Publishing Co Inc, Reading, MA 06187, USA
Associate Companies: Addison-Wesley Publishers (Pty) Ltd, Australia (qv); Addison-Wesley Publishers (Canada) Ltd, 26 Prince Andrew Pl, Don Mills, Ontario, Canada; Addison-Wesley Publishers Japan Ltd, Japan (qv); Addison-Wesley Publishing Group, Netherlands (qv); Addison-Wesley (S) Pte Ltd, Republic of Singapore (qv); Benjamin/Cummings Inc, UK (qv); Benjamin/Cummings Publishing Co Inc, 2727 Sand Hill Rd, Menlo Park, CA 94025, USA; Fondo Educativo Interamericano, Brazil, Chile; Fondo Educativo Interamericano, Colombia (qv); Fondo Educativo Interamericano de Mexico SA, Mexico (qv); Fondo Educativo Interamericano, Puerto Rico (qv); Fondo Educativo Interamericano, Venezuela (qv)
Subjects: Reference, Business, Textbooks, Medicine, Trade and Educational Computing, Academic
Founded: 1942
ISBN Publisher's Prefix: 0-201

Adlib Paperbacks, an imprint of André Deutsch Ltd (qv)

Admiral, an imprint of Multimedia Books Ltd (qv)

Alex **Aiken**+, 48 Merrycrest Ave, Giffnock, Glasgow G46 6BJ Tel: (041) 637 2438
Principal: Alex Aiken
Subjects: Military and Naval History, Biography, Natural Sciences
Founded: 1971
ISBN Publisher's Prefix: 0-9502134

Airlife Publishing Ltd+,7 St John's Hill, Shrewsbury, Salop SY1 1JE Tel: Shrewsbury 235651 (STD code 0743)
Man Dir, Rights & Permissions: A D R Simpson
Subjects: Aviation, Transport, Military, Sports & Outdoor Activities
Founded: 1976
ISBN Publisher's Prefixes: 0-9504543, 0-906393, 1-85310

Akira Press Ltd+, 307 Bethnal Green Rd, London E2 6AH Tel: (01) 729 2623
Man Dir, Editor: Desmond Johnson; *Marketing and Publicity Dir:* Erica Hines
Orders to: PO Box 409, London E2 7EU Tel: (01) 729 2623
Subjects: Fiction, Poetry, General
1985: 23 titles *Founded:* 1983
ISBN Publisher's Prefix: 0-947638

Akros Publications, 18 Warrender Park Terrace, Edinburgh EH9 1EF Tel: (031) 229 3680
Man Dir, Editorial, Production, Publicity,

Rights & Permissions: Duncan Glen; *Sales:* Margaret Glen
Subjects: Scottish Poetry and Literary Criticism
Founded: 1965

Aladdin Books Ltd, 70 Old Compton St, London W1V 5PA Tel: (01) 734 5186 Telex: 21115
Man Dir: Charles Nicholas; *Art Dir:* David West; *Sales Dir:* Lynn Lockett
Subjects: Juveniles, Co-editions
Founded: 1980

Albyn Press Ltd, Whittingehame House, Haddington, Lothian, Scotland
Man Dir: Charles Skilton; *Publicity Manager:* Leonard Holdsworth
Parent Company: Charles Skilton Ltd (qv)
Branch Off: 2 Caversham St, London SW3 Tel: (01) 351 4995
Subjects: Scottish, General
ISBN Publisher's Prefix: 0-284

Alden & Mowbray Ltd, see A R Mowbray & Co Ltd

Aldwych Press+, 3 Henrietta St, London WC2E 8LU Tel: (01) 240 0856 Fax: (01) 379 0609
Man Dir, Marketing Dir, Rights & Permissions: Danny Maher
Subjects: Academic, Library Science, Sociology, Economics, Politics, European Studies, Reference, Philosophy, Military Studies, Law
Founded: 1979
ISBN Publisher's Prefix: 0-86172

The **Alison** Press, a subsidiary of Martin Secker & Warburg Ltd (qv)

Ian **Allan** Ltd+, Coombelands House, Addlestone, Weybridge, Surrey KT15 1HY Tel: Weybridge 58511 (STD code 0932) Cable Add: Ianallanshepp Telex: 929806 Iallan G
Chairman: I Allan; *Man Dir:* D I Allan; *Sales Dir:* J Sherrington; *Editorial:* M Harris (Magazines), S Forty (Books); *Production:* N Lerwill; *Publicity:* Peter Waller; *Rights & Permissions:* S Forty
Parent Company: Ian Allan (Group) Ltd
Associate Companies: A Lewis (Masonic Publishers) Ltd; Locomotive Publishing Co Ltd; Modern Transport Publishing Co Ltd; Railway Publications Ltd; Railway World Ltd; Town & County Books Ltd (qv)
Imprints: A Lewis, Malaga, Modern Transport
Subjects: Railways, Road Transport, Aviation, Military, Naval, Photographic Landscape, Masonic
Founded: 1945
ISBN Publisher's Prefix: 0-7110

Philip **Allan** Publishers Ltd, Market Pl, Deddington, Oxford OX5 4SE Tel: Deddington 38652 (STD code 0869) Cable Add: Allanbooks Oxford Telex: 83147 Viaor G Fax: (0865) 726753
Man Dir, Rights, Sales: Philip Allan; *Editorial:* Philip Cross; *Production:* Helen Ramsay
Subjects: Academic books in Economics, Politics, Accountancy, Finance, Business Studies
1987: 14 titles *1988:* 25 titles *Founded:* 1973
ISBN Publisher's Prefix: 0-86003

R L **Allan** & Son (Publishers) Ltd, see Pickering & Inglis Ltd

J A **Allen** & Co Ltd, 1 Lower Grosvenor Pl, London SW1W 0EL Tel: (01) 834 5606 Cable Add: Allenbooks London SW1 Telex: 28905/3810 Fax: (01) 831 9489
Chairman, Man Dir: J A Allen; *Sales Dir:*

UNITED KINGDOM 425

Mrs C Burt; *Publicity & Advertising:* Mrs E Martyn; *Production:* W Ireson; *Rights & Permissions:* J Grant
Subsidiary Companies: The Caduceus Press, Sporting Book Services (both at above address)
Branch Off: (Trade Counter) The Airfield, Norwich Rd, Mendlesham, Suffolk
Imprint: Thoroughbred Press
Subject: Horsemanship, Horses & Horse Sports
Bookshop: The Horseman's Bookshop, 1 Lower Grosvenor Pl, London SW1
1985: 10 titles *1986:* 12 titles *Founded:* 1926
ISBN Publisher's Prefix: 0-85131

W H Allen & Co PLC+, 44 Hill St, London W1X 8LB Tel: (01) 493 6777 Telex: 28117 Fax: (01) 493 8002
Chairman, Man Dir: Bob Tanner; *Sales Dir:* Ray Mudie; *Rights Manager:* Yvonne Weaver; *Editorial Dirs:* Mike Bailey, Pat Hornsey (Illustrated Books), Robert Postema (Business & Technical), Clive Allison (Allison & Busby); *Production Dir:* Mark Pickard; *Virgin Books:* Cat Ledger
Parent Company (65%): Virgin Vision Ltd, 95-99 Ladbrooke Grove, London W11 1PG. Ultimate parent company Virgin Group PLC
Imprints: Allison & Busby, Comet, Crescent, Mercury, Planet, Star, Target, Virgin
Subjects: Fiction, Non-fiction, Biography, Juveniles, Paperbacks, Cookery, Horror, Humour
Founded: 1780
ISBN Publisher's Prefixes: 0-491 (W H Allen, Crescent), 0-86379 (Comet), 1-85227 (Planet), 0-352 (Star), 0-426 (Target), 0-86369 (Virgin), 0-85031 (Allison & Busby), 1-85251 (Mercury)

Allen & Unwin, an imprint of Unwin Hyman Ltd (qv)

Allen Lane, now Viking (qv)

Allen Lane The Penguin Press, an imprint of Viking (qv)

Allenson, an imprint of James Clarke & Co Ltd (qv)

Almond Press, an imprint of Sheffield Academic Press Ltd (qv)

Allison & Busby, an imprint of W H Allen & Co PLC (qv)

Alphabet & Image Ltd, see Alphabooks

Alphabooks Ltd+, Alpha House, South St, Sherborne, Dorset DT9 3LU Tel: Sherborne 814944 (STD code 0935) Telex: 46534 Alphab G
Man Dir, Production: A E Birks-Hay; *Editorial:* M L Birks-Hay
Subjects: Illustrated Books on Crafts, Fine Arts, Architecture, Horticulture, Archaeology, History, Bee-keeping
Founded: 1972
Miscellaneous: An imprint of A & C Black (Publishers) Ltd (qv)
ISBN Publisher's Prefixes: 0-906670, 0-9506171

Amanuensis Books Ltd, PO Box 23, Didcot, Oxfordshire OX11 9HN Tel: Didcot 850307 (STD code 0235)
Man Dirs: Loraine P Fergusson, Kim P Richardson
Subjects: Illustrated Adult Non-fiction, Children's Non-fiction
Founded: 1986
ISBN Publisher's Prefix: 0-85376

Amber Lane Press Ltd, 9 Middle Way, Summertown, Oxford OX2 7LH Tel: Oxford 510545 (STD code 0865)
Chief Executive, Editorial, Sales, Production, Publicity, Rights & Permissions: Judith Scott
Subjects: Play Scripts, Drama Criticism, Biographies
1985: 7 titles *1986:* 10 titles *Founded:* 1978
ISBN Publisher's Prefix: 0-906399

American University Publishers Group Ltd, now Academic and University Publishers Group (qv)

Amsco Publications, an imprint of Omnibus Press (qv)

Anchor, an imprint of Doubleday & Co Inc (qv)

Andersen Press Ltd+, Brookmount House, 62-65 Chandos Pl, Covent Garden, London WC2N 4NW Tel: (01) 240 8162/(01) 240 3411 Cable Add: Literarius London W1 Telex: 261212
Man Dir, Rights & Permissions: Klaus Flugge; *Sales:* Mike Dugdale (home), Gordon Bryant (export); *Publicity:* Sarah Stott; *Editorial:* Audrey Adams
Orders to: Tiptree Book Services Ltd, Church Rd, Tiptree, Colchester, Essex CO5 0SR Tel: Tiptree 816362 (STD code 0621) Telex: 99487
Associate Company: Century Hutchinson Ltd (qv)
Subjects: Children's Books
1985: 33 titles *Founded:* 1976
ISBN Publisher's Prefixes: 0-905478, 0-86264

Anglo-German Foundation, 17 Bloomsbury Sq, London WC1A 2LP Tel: (01) 404 3137
Secretary-General: Barbara Beck; *Publications Manager:* Philippa Sweeney
Subjects: Socio-economic, Educational
1985: 3 titles *1986:* 5 titles *Founded:* 1973
ISBN Publisher's Prefix: 0-905492

Angus & Robertson (UK)+, 16 Golden Sq, London W1R 4BN Tel: (01) 437 9602 Cable Add: Ausboko W1 Telex: 897284 Arpub G Fax: (01) 434 2080
Man Dir: Barry Winkleman; *Publicity Manager:* Helen Priday; *Rights & Permissions:* Dorothy Henning
Orders to: Bartholomew Sales & Distribution Services, 12 Duncan St, Edinburgh EH9 1TA Tel: (031) 667 9341
Associate Company: Angus & Robertson Publishers, Australia (qv)
Subjects: Art & Photography, Biography, Children's, Cinema, Theatre, Music, Cookery, Nutrition, Fiction, Gardening, Botany, Health, Humour, International Affairs & Politics, Languages, Literature, Natural History, Poetry, Sports
Founded: 1884
Miscellaneous: Angus & Robertson (UK) is a division of Times Books Ltd (qv)
ISBN Publisher's Prefix: 0-207

Angus Hudson Ltd+*, Greater London House, Hampstead Rd, London NW1 7QX Tel: (01) 377 4741 Telex: 885233 Macdon G
Man Dir: Angus Hudson; *Production:* Martin Bailey
Parent Company: Maxwell Communication Corporation plc (qv)
Subjects: Religious and Quality Children's Books in international co-productions
1986: 37 titles *Founded:* 1976

Ann Arbor, an imprint of Butterworth & Co (Publishers) Ltd (qv)

Antique Collectors' Club*, 5 Church St, Woodbridge, Suffolk Tel: Woodbridge 5501 (STD code 039 43) Telex: 987271 Antbok G
Man Dir, Editorial: John Steel; *Production, American Sales:* Diana Steel; *Sales Manager:* David Inman
Imprints: Baron Publishing Ltd, Chancery House Publishing Ltd, Oriental Textile Press Ltd
Subjects: Fine Art Reference, Antiques, Gardening, Architecture
1985: 10 titles *Founded:* 1966
ISBN Publisher's Prefixes: 0-902028, 0-907462, 1-85149

Anvil Press Poetry Ltd*, 69 King George St, London SE10 8PX Tel: (01) 858 2946
Editors: Peter Jay, Julia Sterland
Orders to: J M Dent & Sons (Distribution) Ltd, Dunhams Lane, Letchworth, Hertfordshire SG6 1LF Tel: Letchworth 686241 (STD code 0462)
Subject: Poetry
1985: 14 titles *Founded:* 1968
ISBN Publisher's Prefix: 0-85646

Apollo, an imprint of Salamander Books Ltd (qv)

The **Apple** Press+*, 293 Gray's Inn Rd, London WC1X 8QF Tel: (01) 837 9604 Telex: 261396 Atlas G
Dirs: Warren Bertram, Ashley Bertram
Subjects: General Leisure, Domestic, Art
Founded: 1984
ISBN Publisher's Prefix: 1-185076

Appleford Publishing Group+, Appleford, Abingdon, Oxfordshire OX14 4PB Tel: Abingdon 848319 (STD code 0235)
Chief Executive, Editorial, Rights & Permissions: G E Duffield; *Production:* E Collie
Associate Companies: Marcham Books (qv), News Today and News Extra Magazines (both at above address); Sutton Courtenay Press (c/o above address)
Imprints: G E Duffield, Marcham, Sutton Courtenay
Subjects: Modern History, Religion, Social, Literary, Reference, Periodicals
Bookshop: Appleford Bookroom (at above address)
Founded: 1963

The **Appletree** Press Ltd+, 7 James St South, Belfast BT2 8DL Tel: Belfast 243074/Belfast 246756 (STD code 0232) Telex: 265871 Monref G ref Atp 001
Man Dir, Rights & Permissions: J D Murphy; *Editorial:* D Marshall, Janet Seaton; *Sales:* D Pritchard; *Publicity:* Lorna Stevens
Subjects: Social Studies, Literary Criticism, History, Music, Art, Juveniles, Low- & High-priced Paperbacks, Photography, Fishing, Guide Books, Reference, Folklore, Cookery, Books of Irish Interest
1985: 18 titles *Founded:* 1974
ISBN Publisher's Prefixes: 0-904651, 0-86281

Applied Science Publishers Ltd, see Elsevier Applied Science Publishers

Aquarian Press Ltd+, Denington Estate, Wellingborough, Northamptonshire NN8 2RQ Tel: Wellingborough 76031 (STD code 0933) Cable Add: Thorgroup Wellingborough Telex: 311072 Thopub G Fax: (0933) 72800
Man Dir: David Young; *Production Dir:* David Palmer; *Editorial Dir:* Michael Cox; *Marketing, Sales Dir:* Julian Rivers; *Group Sales Manager:* John Marsh; *Export Sales Manager:* Ray Potts; *Rights & Permissions:* Marjorie Nelson; *Publicity Manager:* Judith Smallwood; *Marketing Manager:* Vivienne Wordley
Parent Company: Thorsons Publishing Group Ltd (qv for associate companies)
Subjects: Esoteric, Philosophy, Parapsychology & the Paranormal, Tarot

426 UNITED KINGDOM

& Divination, Character Analysis Techniques, Oriental Religion & Philosophies, Folklore & Mythology, Astrology, Magic & Occultism, Western Mystery Tradition
1986: 56 titles *1987:* 61 titles *Founded:* 1953
ISBN Publisher's Prefixes: 0-85030, 1-85274

Aquila Publishing (UK) Ltd, PO Box 418, Leek, Staffordshire ST13 8UX Tel: Leek 387368 (STD code 0538) Telex: 8954958 Sharet G
Chairman, Man Dir, Editorial Dir: J C R Green; *Senior Editor:* Roger Elkin; *Production:* R J Plant; *Sales, Trade:* Anne Green; *Publicity:* Liz Townshend
Imprints: Aquila, Critical Studies, Aquila Fiction, Aquila Guides, Aquila Pamphlet Poetry, Aquila/The Phaethon Press, Aquila Poetry, Aquila/The Wayzgoose Press, Iolaire Selection, Moorland Mini-Books
Subjects: Poetry, Short Stories, Fiction, Literary & General Biographies, Critical Studies & Essays, Business Guides, Translations
Founded: 1968
ISBN Publisher's Prefixes: 0-903226, 0-7275

Arcady Books Ltd+, 2 Woodlands Rd, Ashurst, Southampton SO4 2AD Tel: Ashurst 2601 (STD code 042 129)
Man Dir, Sales: Michael Edwards; *Editorial Dir, Production, Publicity, Rights & Permissions:* Anne-Marie Edwards
Subjects: Literature, Outdoor Activities, The New Forest, General Non-fiction
Founded: 1981
ISBN Publisher's Prefix: 0-907753

Architectural Press Ltd+, 33 Bowling Green Lane, London EC1R 0DA Tel: (01) 837 6123 Telex: 299049 Utpres G Fax: (01) 278 4003
Man Dir: Colin Whurr; *Publishing Dir:* Maritz Vandenberg; *Sales and Marketing Manager:* Kasia Paveliev; *Publicity and Promotions Executive:* Sarah Vicary; *Production Manager:* Nigel Ferguson; *Rights & Permissions:* Nicola Hamilton
Parent Company: United Trade Press (Holdings) Ltd. Ultimate parent company Maxwell Communication Corporation plc (qv)
Subsidiary Company: Telecommunications Press
Subjects: Architecture, Telecommunications
Founded: 1895
ISBN Publisher's Prefixes: 0-85139 (Architectural Press), 0-907401 (Telecommunications Press)

Arena Books, an imprint of Arrow Books Ltd (qv)

Argus Books Ltd, Wolsey House, Wolsey Rd, Hemel Hempstead, Hertfordshire HP2 4SS Tel: Hemel Hempstead 41221 (STD code 0442)
Publisher: Rab Macwilliam; *Sales and Marketing Manager:* Iain J Paterson
Parent Company: Argus Press Group
Subjects: Hobbies, Modelling, Crafts, Woodworking, Information Technology, Winemaking & Brewing
1985: 25 titles *1986:* 40 titles
ISBN Publisher's Prefixes: 0-85242, 0-85344, 0-9008

Argus Communications Ltd, DLM House, Edinburgh Way, Harlow, Essex CM20 2HL Tel: Harlow 39441 (STD code 0279) Telex: 817086 Fax: (0279) 20104
Man Dir: Richard De Rosa; *Book Publicity Manager:* Sue Pryor
Imprint: Attica Publications
Subjects: Religion, Character Publishing, Humour, Children's
1985: 6 titles *Founded:* 1985
ISBN Publisher's Prefixes: 0-913592, 0-89505, 1-85176, 0-784

Argus Specialist Publications Ltd*, 1 Golden Sq, London W1R 3AB Tel: (01) 437 0626 Telex: 8811896
Man Dir: Peter Welham
Subjects: Scale Modelling, Hobbies, Crafts & Leisure Interests, Computing, Electronics, Video
ISBN Publisher's Prefixes: 0-85076, 0-85242, 0-85344

Ariel, paperback imprint of BBC Books (qv)

Aris & Phillips Ltd, Teddington House, Warminster, Wiltshire BA12 8PQ Tel: Warminster 213409 (STD code 0985)
Man Dir: Adrian Phillips; *Editorial:* John Aris, Philip Mudd; *Sales, Publicity:* Janet Davis; *Rights & Permissions:* Lucinda Phillips; *Production:* Philip Mudd
Orders to: La Haule Books Ltd, West Lodge, La Haule, Saint Aubin, Jersey, Channel Islands Tel: 44957
Associate Companies: La Haule Books Ltd, West Lodge, La Haule, Saint Aubin, Jersey, Channel Islands; Serindia Publications, 10 Parkfields, Putney, London SW15
Subjects: Ancient History, Oriental, Classical, Middle East, Archaeology, Egyptology, Spanish, Portuguese
1985: 10 titles *1986:* 18 titles *Founded:* 1972
ISBN Publisher's Prefix: 0-85668

Arlington Books (Publishers) Ltd, Kingsbury House, 15-17 King St, London SW1Y 6QU Tel: (01) 930 0097 Telex: 896616 Sendit G
Chairman, Man Dir: Desmond Elliott; *Marketing Manager:* Hazel Hutchison; *Production and Editorial:* Penny Smart; *Publicity and Rights:* Margaret Halton
Trade Dept: Biblios Ltd, Glenside Industrial Estate, Partridge Green, Horsham, West Sussex Tel: Horsham 710971 (STD code 0403)
Imprint: Columbine House
Subjects: General Fiction & Non-fiction, Health
Founded: 1960
ISBN Publisher's Prefix: 0-85140

Armada Books, an imprint of William Collins PLC (qv)

Arms & Armour Press Ltd+, Artillery House, Artillery Row, London SW1P 1RT Tel: (01) 222 7676 Cable Add: Cassellpub London SW1 Telex: 9413701 Caspub G Fax: (01) 799 1514
Chairman, Man Dir: Philip Sturrock; *Editorial Dir:* Roderick Dymott; *Production:* Alan Smith; *Sales Dir:* Stephen Lustig
Orders to: Blandford Publishing Ltd, Link House, West St, Poole, Dorset BH15 1LL Tel: Poole 670581 (STD code 0202) Telex: 418304 Linkho G
Parent Company: Blandford Publishing Ltd (qv). Ultimate parent company Cassell PLC (qv)
Subjects: Aviation, Crafts & Hobbies, Military & War, Nautical, Politics & World Affairs, Transport
1986: 60 titles *1987:* 50 titles *Founded:* 1966
ISBN Publisher's Prefix: 0-85368

Edward **Arnold**, 41 Bedford Sq, London WC1B 3DQ Tel: (01) 637 7161 Cable Add: Scholarly London W1 Telex: 265806 Edward G

A division of Hodder & Stoughton Ltd (qv)
Man Dir: Richard Morris; *Sales and Marketing Dir:* John Wallace; *Production:* C W Davies; *Educational Marketing Dir:* Michael Soper; *Foreign Rights:* John Wallace; *Permissions:* Angela Anderson
Subsidiary Company: Lloyd-Luke (Medical Books) Ltd (qv)
Associate Company: Arnold Publishers (India) Pvt Ltd, India (qv)
Branch Off: 3 East Read St, Baltimore, MD 21202, USA
Subjects: Humanities, Science, Engineering, Medicine, Nursing, University, Secondary and Primary Textbooks, Technical, Education, English Language Teaching, Journals, Computer Software
Founded: 1890
Miscellaneous: Edward Arnold is the educational, academic and medical division of Hodder & Stoughton Ltd (qv)
ISBN Publisher's Prefix: 0-7131

E J **Arnold** & Son Ltd, Parkside Lane, Dewsbury Rd, Leeds LS11 5TD Tel: Leeds 772112 (STD code 0532) Cable Add: Arnold Leeds Telex: 556347
Man Dir: C Bundy; *Publishing Dir:* S E Sharp; *Sales and Marketing Dir:* G R Newton; *Export Dir:* M S S Breene
Parent Company: Hollis PLC, Athene House, 66-73 Shoe Lane, London, EC4P 4AB. Ultimate parent company Pergamon Press (qv)
Imprint: Arnold-Wheaton
Subjects: Primary and Secondary Educational, Educational Material
1985: 71 titles *1986:* 111 titles
Founded: 1863
Miscellaneous: E J Arnold & Son Ltd now incorporates E S A Creative Learning Ltd
ISBN Publisher's Prefixes: 0-560, 0-08

Arnold-Wheaton, publishing imprint of merger of E J Arnold & Son Ltd (qv) and A Wheaton & Co Ltd

Arrow Books Ltd+, Brookmount House, 62-65 Chandos Pl, London WC2N 4NW Tel: (01) 240 3411 Cable Add: Literatus Telex: 261212
Man Dir: Conrad Goulden; *Sales Dir:* Mike Hodge; *Editorial:* Peter Lavery, Alison Berry, Jane Wood
Orders to: Tiptree Book Services Ltd, Church Rd, Tiptree, Colchester, Essex CO5 0SR Tel: Tiptree 816362 (STD code 0621)
Imprints: Arena Books, Beaver Books, Legend, Mysterious Press
Subjects: Paperbacks: Adult, Children's, Fiction, Non-fiction, Health, Crime, Science Fiction
Founded: 1948
Miscellaneous: Arrow Books Ltd is a division of Century Hutchinson Ltd
ISBN Publisher's Prefix: 0-09

Art Guide Publications, an imprint of A & C Black (Publishers) Ltd (qv)

Art Heritage, an imprint of Scorpion Publications Ltd (qv)

The **Art Trade** Press Ltd, 9 Brockhampton Rd, Havant, Hampshire PO9 1NU Tel: Havant 484943 (STD code 0705)
Editorial, Sales, Production, Publicity, Rights & Permissions: J M Curley
Subjects: Art, Reference (*Who's Who in Art*)
Founded: 1907
ISBN Publisher's Prefix: 0-900083

Artech House+, 28 Eaton Row, London SW1W 0JA Tel: (01) 235 9180 Telex: 885744 Fax: (01) 235 7841
Gibson

Chief Executive: William M Bazzy; *Editorial, Production, Rights & Permissions:* Daniel Brown; *Sales, Publicity:* Jonathan Hopkins
Parent Company: Artech House Inc, 685 Canton St, Norwood, MA 02062, USA
Associate Company: Horizon House (at above addresses)
Subjects: Electronic, Engineering
1985: 24 titles *1986:* 27 titles *Founded:* 1970
ISBN Publisher's Prefix: 0-89006

Artemis Press Ltd, an imprint of Vision Press Ltd (qv)

Artists House, an imprint of Mitchell Beazley International Ltd (qv)

Artwork Publishing, PO Box 333, Maldon, Essex CM9 6EY Tel: Maldon 59878 (STD code 0621) Telex: 99489 Permal G
Chief Executive: Colin Campbell; *Marketing, Publicity:* Anne Dolamore; *Sales:* David Harris
Subject: Art
1986: 12 titles *1987:* 12 titles *Founded:* 1985
ISBN Publisher's Prefix: 1-85257

Ashford Press Publishing, 1 Church Rd, Shedfield, Hampshire SO3 2HU Tel: Wickham 834265 (STD code 0329) Telex: 261412 Bound G Fax: (01) 935 0665
Chief Executive, Rights & Permissions: Jane Tatam; *Editorial:* Lindsey Charles; *Sales, Publicity:* Jane Foster
Parent Company: Martins Printing Group Ltd, 94 Wigmore St, London W1H 0BR
Associate Company: Europa Publications Ltd (qv)
Subjects: General Non-fiction, Sport, Field Sports, Nautical, Education, Business
1985: 20 titles *1986:* 70 titles *Founded:* 1984

Ashgrove Press Ltd+, 19 Circus Pl, Bath, Avon BA1 2PW Tel: Bath 25539 (STD code 0225)
Man Dir, Production Manager, Editorial, Rights & Permissions: Robin Campbell; *Sales, Publicity, Man Editor:* Sue Jones
Subjects: Countryside, Health, Healing & Diet, Philosophy, Psychology, Regional & Local
1985: 13 titles *1986:* 9 titles *Founded:* 1979
ISBN Publisher's Prefix: 0-906798

Ashmolean Museum Publications, Ashmolean Museum, Beaumont St, Oxford OX1 2PH Tel: Oxford 278010 (STD code 0865)
Publications Officer: R I H Charlton
Subjects: European & Oriental Art, Archaeology & History, Numismatics, Classical Studies, Egyptology
1985: 10 titles *1986:* 12 titles
ISBN Publisher's Prefixes: 0-900090, 0-907849

Aslan, an imprint of Lion Publishing PLC (qv)

Aslib, The Association for Information Management, Information House, 26-27 Boswell St, London WC1N 3JZ Tel: (01) 430 2671 Telex: 23667 Fax: (01) 430 0514
Chief Executive: Dr Dennis Lewis; *Editorial:* Judith Severne; *Sales, Production, Publicity, Rights & Permissions:* Deborah Auty
Subjects: Information Management/Librarianship, Information Technology, Online, Bibliography, Thesauri, Translations, Directories & Sourcebooks
Founded: 1924
Miscellaneous: See also entry under Library Associations
ISBN Publisher's Prefix: 0-85142

Associated Book Publishers (UK) Ltd, 11 New Fetter Lane, London EC4P 4EE Tel: (01) 583 9855 Cable Add: Elegiacs London EC4P 4EE Telex: 263398 Fax: (01) 583 0701

Associated Business Press+, 76 Shoe Lane, London EC4A 3JB Tel: (01) 583 8888 Telex: 884148 Fax: (01) 583 0005
Man Dir: Peter Cooper
Parent Company: AGB Research PLC, 76 Shoe Lane, London EC4A 3JB
Subjects: Business, Management
Miscellaneous: Associated Business Press is the publishing imprint of Associated Business Programmes Ltd
ISBN Publisher's Prefix: 0-85227

Associated University Presses, an imprint of Golden Cockerel Press Ltd (qv)

Association for Science Education, College Lane, Hatfield, Hertfordshire AL10 9AA Tel: Hatfield 67411 (STD code 070 72)
General Secretary: B G Atwood; *Publications Manager:* Miss J R Hanrott
Subjects: Science Education
ISBN Publisher's Prefix: 0-86357

Association for Scottish Literary Studies, c/o Department of English, University of Aberdeen, Aberdeen AB9 2UB Tel: Aberdeen 272634 (STD code 0224)
Chief Executives: Dr David Hewitt, Dr D S Robb; *Editorial:* Dr D S Mack, Dr Felicity Riddy; *Sales:* Mrs A M Robertson
Subject: Scottish Literature
1985: 6 titles *1986:* 8 titles *Founded:* 1970
ISBN Publisher's Prefix: 0-948877

Athene Publishing Co, an imprint of Thorsons Publishing Group Ltd (qv)

The **Athlone** Press Ltd, 44 Bedford Row, London WC1R 4LY Tel: (01) 405 9836/7 Telex: 261507 ref 1334
Man Dir, Editorial: Brian Southam; *Production, Publicity:* Peter Danckwerts; *Rights & Permissions:* Doris Southam
Warehouse: J M Dent & Sons (Distribution) Ltd, Dunhams Lane, Letchworth, Hertfordshire SG6 1LF Tel: Letchworth 686241 (STD code 0462)
Subjects: Architecture, Archaeology, Classical Studies, Economics, History, Music, Art, Philosophy, General & Social Science, University Textbooks, Japanese and South East Asian Studies
1985: 30 titles *Founded:* 1949
ISBN Publisher's Prefix: 0-485

Atlantic, an imprint of Ramboro Enterprises Ltd (qv)

Atlantic Large Print, an imprint of Chivers Press Publishers (qv)

Attica Publications, an imprint of Argus Communications Ltd (qv)

Augener, an imprint of Stainer & Bell Ltd (qv)

Aurum Press Ltd+, 33 Museum St, London WC1A 1LD Tel: (01) 631 4596 Telex: 299557 Aurum G Fax: (01) 580 2469
Man Dir: Timothy Chadwick; *Publishing Dir:* Michael Alcock; *Managing Editor:* Angela Dyer; *Sales Dir:* Barrie Knight; *Rights:* Rosemary Cameron; *Art Dir:* Alison Rivett
Subjects: Large Format, Illustrated, General
1985: 30 titles *Founded:* 1977
ISBN Publisher's Prefix: 0-948149

Autobooks, Howard Rd, Eaton Socon, Huntingdon, Cambridgeshire PE19 3EZ Tel: Huntingdon 212666 (STD code 0480)
Dir: Charles Black; *Customer Relations Manager:* Rosemary Shepherd
Subject: Car Workshop Manuals (Do-it-Yourself)
Founded: 1958
ISBN Publisher's Prefixes: 0-85146, 0-85147, 0-7136

Autocourse, an imprint of Hazelton Publishing (qv)

Automobile Association, Fanum House, Basingstoke, Hampshire RG21 2EA Tel: Basingstoke 20123 (STD code 0256) Telex: AA Bas 858538 G Fax: (0256) 493389
Sales: Brian Stelling; *Service Dir, Publishing:* Peter Tyer
Imprint: AA Publishing
Subjects: Tourist Guides, Guidebooks, Maps, Atlases, Leisure, Travel
ISBN Publisher's Prefix: 0-86145

Avebury, an imprint of Gower Publishing Co Ltd (qv)

Avon-Anglia Publications & Services, Annesley House, 21 Southside, Weston-super-Mare, Avon BS23 2QU Tel: Weston-super-Mare 31616 (STD code 0934)
Chief Executive: Geoffrey Body
Imprints: Avon-Anglia, Kingsmead Press
Subjects: Transport, History, Countryside, Art, General
Book Club: Transport Publications Service (at above address)
1986: 10 titles *Founded:* 1976
ISBN Publisher's Prefixes: 0-905466 (Avon-Anglia), 0-901571, 0-906230, 1-85026 (all Kingsmead Press)

Award Publications Ltd, Spring House, Spring Place, London NW5 3BH Tel: (01) 485 7747 Telex: 296452 Award G Fax: (01) 267 2140
Man Dir: R Wilkinson; *Production Manager:* Deborah Wadsworth
Subjects: Children's
Founded: 1955

B B C Books+, Woodlands, 80 Wood Lane, London W12 0TT Tel: (01) 576 0202 Cable Add: Broadcasts London Telex: 934678 Bbcent G
Head of Book Publishing: Nicholas Chapman; *Book Sales Manager:* John Allgrove; *Production Manager:* Brian Dickson; *Marketing, Publicity:* Suzanna Zsohar
Orders to: 144/152 Bermondsey St, London SE1 3TH Tel: (01) 407 6961
Imprint: Ariel (paperback)
Subjects: General Fiction, History, How-to, Music, Art, Reference, Religion, Juveniles, Low- & High-priced Paperbacks, Medicine, Engineering, General & Social Science, Secondary Textbooks, Adult Education
Bookshops: 35 Marylebone High St, London W1M 4AA; Broadcasting House, Portland P1, London W1A 1AA; BBC Television Centre, Wood Lane, London W12 7RJ
Founded: 1925
Miscellaneous: Firm is a division of BBC Enterprises Ltd
ISBN Publisher's Prefix: 0-563

B F B S, an imprint of Bible Society (qv)

B F I Publishing+, British Film Institute, 21-28 Stephen St, London W1P 1PL Tel: (01) 255 1444 Cable Add: Brifilinst London W1 Telex: 27624
Head of Publishing: Geoffrey Nowell-Smith; *Editorial:* David Wilson; *Sales, Publicity:* Diana Watt; *Production:* John Smoker; *Rights & Permissions:* Roma Gibson

Orders to: J M Dent & Sons (Distribution) Ltd, Dunhams Lane, Letchworth, Hertfordshire SG6 1LF Tel: Letchworth 686241 (STD code 0462)
Subjects: Film, Television, Academic, General
1985: 8 titles *1986:* 6 titles *Founded:* 1980
ISBN Publisher's Prefix: 0-85170

B I M H Publications+, British Institute of Mental Handicap, Foley Industrial Park, Stourport Rd, Kidderminster, Worcestershire DY11 7QG Tel: Kidderminster 824933 (STD code 0562)
Editorial Dir: Mrs S J Newbould; *Assistant Editor, Advertisement Manager:* Anne Whelpton
Subjects: Mental Handicap, Physical Handicap, Psychiatry, Psychology, Nursing, Education, Social Work, Periodicals
1986: 2 titles *1987:* 3 titles *Founded:* 1971
ISBN Publisher's Prefix: 0-906054

B L A Publishing Ltd, T R House, Christopher Rd, East Grinstead, Sussex RH19 3BT Tel: East Grinstead 313844 (STD code 0342) Telex: 94011210 Blap G
Man Dir: John Bush; *Editorial Dir:* Martin Marix Evans; *Sales Dir:* John Turner
Parent Company: Ling Kee (UK) Ltd (qv for other group members)
Subjects: Non-fiction (Trade & Educational). Specialist packagers

B P C C, see Maxwell Communication Corporation plc

B P S Books+, St Andrews House, 48 Princess Rd East, Leicester LE1 7DR Tel: Leicester 549568 (STD code 0533) Telex: 341401 Jjint G
The British Psychological Society
Publications Manager, Sales, Rights & Permissions: Ms J Collins; *Editorial, Publicity:* C Feeney
Parent Company: The British Psychological Society (at above address)
Subjects: Psychology, Management
1985: 6 titles *1986:* 8 titles *Founded:* 1981
ISBN Publisher's Prefix: 0-901715

B P T, an imprint of Bahá'í Publishing Trust (qv)

B S C Books Ltd+, 18 New Concordia Wharf, Mill St, London SE1 2BB
Man Dir: Bill Smith; *Sales:* Tim Finch
Imprint: Bibliophile Books
Bookshops: Booksmith chain
Miscellaneous: Also remainder dealer and a wholesaler
ISBN Publisher's Prefix: 0-900123

Bernard **Babani** (Publishing) Ltd, The Grampians, Shepherds Bush Rd, London W6 7NF Tel: (01) 603 2581, (01) 603 7296 Cable Add: Radiobooks London W6 (Formerly Babani Press and Bernards (Publishers) Ltd)
Man Dir, Editorial: M H Babani; *Sales, Rights & Permissions:* S Babani; *Production, Publicity:* P Pragnell
Associate Companies: Babani Press; Bernards (Publishers) Ltd
Subjects: Low-priced Paperbacks, Radio Electronics, Computing
Founded: 1977 (Babani Press 1971, Bernards Publishers 1942)
ISBN Publisher's Prefixes: 0-85934, 0-900162

Bachman & Turner, 9 Cork St, London W1X 1PD Tel: (01) 439 3806
Editorial: Marta Bachman; *Rights & Permissions:* Mike Green
Subjects: General Fiction, Biography, History, Art, Philosophy, Popular Interest
1985: 3 titles *1986:* 5 titles *Founded:* 1972
ISBN Publisher's Prefix: 0-85974

Badger Books, an imprint of Studio Publications (Ipswich) Ltd (qv)

Samuel **Bagster**, an imprint of Marshall, Morgan & Scott Publications Ltd (qv)

Bahá'í Publishing Trust, 6 Mount Pleasant, Oakham, Leicester LE15 6HU Tel: Oakham 2780 (STD code 0572) Cable Add: Baha'i Trust Oakham Telex: 342163 Insure G
General Manager: Gordon James Kerr
Imprints: BPT, Nightingale Books
Subjects: Religion, Philosophy, Contemporary Social & Political, Children's Books, Educational
Book Club: Bahá'í Book Club
1986: 14 titles *1987:* 15 titles *Founded:* 1937
ISBN Publisher's Prefix: 0-900125

Bailey Bros & Swinfen Ltd, Warner House, Folkestone, Kent CT19 6PH Tel: Folkestone 56501 (STD code 0303) Cable Add: Forenbuks Telex: 96328 Fax: (0303) 43162
Man Dir: J R Bailey
Subsidiary Companies: Bailey Book Distribution Ltd; Bailey & Swinfen Exports Ltd; Bailey Subscription Agents Ltd; Bailey Subscription Management Service; Shelwing Ltd
Imprint: Hour-Glass Press
Subjects: General Fiction, History, How-to, Reference, Engineering, Languages
Book Clubs: Bailey's German, French, Italian & Spanish Book Clubs
Founded: 1929
ISBN Publisher's Prefix: 0-561

Baillière Tindall, 24-28 Oval Rd, London NN1 7DX Tel: (01) 267 4466 Telex: 25775 Acples G
Man Dir: Joan Fujimoto; *Publishing Dir:* David S B Inglis; *Sales, Marketing Dir:* D Duff; *Sales Manager:* Colin Lill; *Marketing Manager:* Jane Lawrence
Parent Company: Harcourt Brace Jovanovich Inc, Orlando, FL 32887, USA
Subjects: Medical, Veterinary, Nursing, Pharmaceutical
Founded: 1826
Miscellaneous: Baillière Tindall is an imprint of Harcourt Brace Jovanovich, UK (qv)
ISBN Publisher's Prefix: 0-7020

Howard **Baker** Press Ltd, 27A Arterberry Rd, London SW20 Tel: (01) 947 5482 Cable Add: Bakerbook London
Man Dir: W Howard Baker
Imprint: Greyfriars Press
Subjects: Fiction, Non-fiction, Political Science, Poetry, Autobiography, Biography, Reference, Specialist Facsimile Editions, Maps
Book Club: Greyfriars Book Club
ISBN Publisher's Prefix: 0-7030

John **Baker** (Publishers) Ltd, an imprint of A & C Black (Publishers) Ltd (qv)

Bankers Books Ltd+, 10 Lombard St, London EC3V 9AS Tel: (01) 623 3531 Telex: 265871 Monref G ref SQQ085 Fax: (01) 929 4301
Chief Executive: Eric Glover; *Editorial:* Alan Miller; *Sales, Production, Publicity, Rights & Permissions:* Alexander Moffatt
Orders to: Publications Sales, The Chartered Institute of Bankers, Emmanuel House, Burgate Lane, Canterbury, Kent CT1 2XJ
Parent Company: The Chartered Institute of Bankers (at above main address)
Imprint: Chartered Institute of Bankers (CIB) Publications
Branch Off: 17 Salters Hall Court, London EC4N 5AP
Subjects: Banking, Finance, Management, Banking Law, International Trade
Bookshop: Bankers Books Bookshop, 17 St Swithins Lane, London EC4N 8AL
1985: 7 titles *1986:* 4 titles *Founded:* 1987 (as Bankers Books Ltd)
ISBN Publisher's Prefix: 0-85297

The **Banner** of Truth Trust+, 3 Murrayfield Rd, Edinburgh EH12 6EL Tel: (031) 337 7310
Chief Executive: Mervyn T Barter; *Editorial:* Rev Iain H Murray; *Sales, Production:* Humphrey V Mildred
Branch Off: PO Box 621, Carlisle, Pennsylvania 17013, USA
Subject: Christian Faith
1985: 22 titles *Founded:* 1957
ISBN Publisher's Prefix: 0-85151

Bantam Books, an imprint of Transworld Publishers (Corgi & Bantam Books) Ltd (qv)

Bantam Press, an imprint of Transworld Publishers (Corgi & Bantam Books) Ltd (qv)

Barebones Books, a subsidiary of Picton Publishing (Chippenham) Ltd (qv)

Arthur **Barker** Ltd, 91 Clapham High St, London SW4 7TA Tel: (01) 622 9933 Cable Add: Nicobar London SW4 7TA Telex: 918066 Fax: (01) 627 3361
Chief Executive: Lord Weidenfeld; *Deputy Chairman:* Mark Collins; *Sales Dir:* T Collins; *Rights & Permissions:* Miss B J Maclennan
Parent Company: Weidenfeld (Publishers) Ltd (qv)
Subjects: Biography, How-to, Reference, Humour, Crime, Sport
Founded: 1931
ISBN Publisher's Prefix: 0-213

Baron Publishing Ltd, an imprint of Antique Collectors' Club (qv)

Barracuda Books Ltd*, Meadows House, Well St, Buckingham MK18 1EW Tel: Buckingham 814441 (STD code 0280)
Editorial Offices: Radclive Hall, Radclive, Buckingham
Chief Executive and Publisher: Clive Birch; *Marketing:* Vicki Philip; *Sales:* Dorothy Shaw; *Publicity:* Sue Halliday
Associate Company: Quotes Ltd (at above main address)
Imprint: Sporting and Leisure Press
Subjects: Local History, Sport, Railway & Military History, Natural History
1985: 20 titles *Founded:* 1974
ISBN Publisher's Prefix: 0-86023

Barrie & Jenkins Ltd, an imprint of Century Hutchinson Publishing Ltd (qv)

Barry Rose, an imprint of Kluwer Publishing Ltd (qv)

John **Bartholomew & Son** Ltd+, 12 Duncan St, Edinburgh EH9 1TA Tel: (031) 667 9341 Cable Add: Bartholomew Edinburgh Telex: 728134 Barts G Fax: (031) 662 4282
Man Dir: D A Ross Stewart; *Editorial:* Robin Orr; *Marketing, Rights & Permissions:* M J Chittleburgh; *Production:* J V Henderson; *Publishing:* C B Kirkwood; *Publicity:* Helen Priday; *Trade Sales:* R Tucker
Parent Company: News International UK
Subsidiary Companies: T & T Clark Ltd (qv), Map Marketing Ltd
Imprint: Geographia Ltd (qv)
Subjects: Maps, Atlases, Leisure Books
Founded: 1826
ISBN Publisher's Prefixes: 0-7028, 0-85152

Basic Books, see Harper & Row Ltd

The **Basilisk** Press Ltd, 10 Adamson Rd, London NW3 3HR Tel: (01) 722 2142
Man Dir: Charlene B Garry
Subjects: Literature, Architecture, Landscape Gardening, Natural History
Founded: 1973

Baton Transport, Lynden House, 57 High St, Tunbridge Wells, Kent TN1 1XU Tel: Tunbridge Wells 34840 (STD code 0892) Telex: 262508 Message
Chief Executive: Anthony Powell; *Production:* Ray Green; *Publicity, Sales:* Edna Burton
Branch Off: 1 Russell Chambers, Covent Garden, London WC2E 8AA Tel: (01) 240 9849
Subject: Transport (mainly Railway)
1985: 25 titles *Founded:* 1985
ISBN Publisher's Prefix: 0-85936

B T **Batsford** Ltd+, 4 Fitzhardinge St, London W1H 0AH Tel: (01) 486 8484 Cable Add: Batsfordia London W1 Telex: 943763 Crocom G ref Bat
Man Dir: Peter Kemmis Betty; *Editorial Dir:* Timothy Auger; *Sales Dir:* Robert Beard; *Publicity Manager:* Veronique Mott; *Production Dir:* Roger Huggins
Subsidiary Company: Dryad Press Ltd (qv)
Associate Company: B A Seaby Ltd
Subjects: History, Music, Art & Craft, Psychology, Social Work, Sociology, Topography, Lace, Embroidery, Hobbies, Cookery, Costumes, Chess, Archaeology, Architecture, Careers, Horticulture, Linguistics, Politics, Travel, Education, School Books, Film, Sport, Agricultural Sciences, Classical Studies
Founded: 1843
ISBN Publisher's Prefix: 0-7134

Beacon Publications PLC, now incorporated in Matrix Publishing Group Ltd (qv)

Beaumont, see Gower Publishing Co Ltd (qv)

Beaver Books, an imprint of Arrow Books Ltd (qv)

Becknell Books, PO Box 21, King's Lynn, Norfolk PE30 2QP Tel: King's Lynn 761328 (STD code 0553)
Editorial, Production, Rights & Permissions: J Beckett; *Sales:* P R Hemnell; *Publicity:* S J Hemnell
Associate Company: Railmac Publications, PO Box 290, Elizabeth, South Australia 5112
Subject: Transport (Railways and Buses)
1985: 6 titles *Founded:* 1980
ISBN Publisher's Prefix: 0-907087

Bedford Editions Ltd, 52 Bedford Row, London WC1R 4LR Tel: (01) 242 6693 Cable Add: Salamander London WC1 Telex: 261113 Fax: (01) 404 4926
Chairman: J Proost; *Man Dir:* Malcolm H Little; *Production Dir:* Philip Hughes; *Editorial Dirs:* Ray Bonds, Philip de Ste Croix; *Sales Dir:* Keith Allen-Jones; *Rights & Permissions:* Moira McCann
Parent Company: Henri Proost & Cie, Belgium (qv)
Associate Company: Salamander Books Ltd (qv)
Subjects: Packager and repackager of illustrated general interest books
1987: 15 titles *Founded:* 1986

Bedford Square Press of the National Council for Voluntary Organizations+, 26 Bedford Sq, London WC1B 3HU Tel: (01) 636 4066
Chief Executive: Jonathan Croall; *Sales and Promotion Manager:* Victor Dawnay
Orders to: Harper & Row Distributors Ltd, Estover Rd, Plymouth, Devon PL6 7PZ Tel: Plymouth 705251 (STD code 0752)
Subjects: Social Policy, Social Administration, Social Services & Welfare, Reference, Guides & Handbooks for Voluntary Organizations
Founded: 1919 (NCVO), 1969 (BSP)
Miscellaneous: Bedford Square Press also publishes for or in association with other organizations
ISBN Publisher's Prefix: 0-7199

Bedford Way, an imprint of the Institute of Education, University of London (qv)

Beehive, an imprint of Macdonald & Co (Publishers) Ltd (qv)

Belitha Press Ltd+, 31 Newington Green, London N16 9PU Tel: (01) 241 5566 Telex: 8950511 Oneone G ref 32159001
Man Dir: Martin Pick; *Production:* Richard Hayes; *Rights:* Patricia Borlenghi
Subjects: Children's (full colour co-publications), General, Asia
1985: 42 titles *1986:* 55 titles *Founded:* 1980

Bell & Hyman, an imprint of Unwin Hyman Ltd (qv)

Bellew Publishing Co Ltd*, Nightingale Centre, 8 Balham Hill, London SW12 9DS Tel: (01) 673 5611 Telex: 8951182 Gecoms G
Chief Executive: Ib Bellew
Orders to: Harper & Row Distributors, Estover Rd, Plymouth, Devon PL6 7PZ Tel: Plymouth 705251 (STD code 0752)
Subjects: General, Design, Art, Craft. Also international packagers
1985: 5 titles *Founded:* 1983
ISBN Publisher's Prefix: 0-947792

Belton Books, an imprint of Stainer & Bell Ltd (qv)

Benjamin/Cummings Inc, Finchampstead Rd, Wokingham, Berkshire RG11 2NZ Tel: Wokingham 794000 (STD code 0734) Telex: 846136 Fax: (0734) 794035
Man Dir: Peter Hoenigsberg; *Rights & Permissions:* Alison Lobdell (USA)
Parent Company: Benjamin/Cummings Publishing Co Inc (see Addison-Wesley Publishers Ltd, UK)
Associate Company: Addison-Wesley Publishers Ltd, UK (qv)
Subjects: Reference, Science, Technology, University Textbooks
Founded: 1960
ISBN Publisher's Prefix: 0-8053

Ernest **Benn** Ltd, an imprint of A & C Black (Publishers) Ltd (qv)

Berg Publishers Ltd, Market House, Market Pl, Deddington, Oxfordshire OX5 4SW Tel: Deddington 38087 (STD code 0869) Telex: 312440 Pbsspa G
Chief Executive, Rights & Permissions: Marion Berghahn; *Editorial, Production:* Juliet Standing; *Publicity:* Sue Miller; *Sales:* Norman Drake
Imprint: Oswald Wolff Books
Subjects: History, Sociology, Economics, Politics, International Relations, Peace Studies, Philosophy, Literature, Theatre & Media, Women's Studies, Social Anthropology, Reference, Accountancy
1986: 20 titles *1987:* 60 titles *Founded:* 1981
ISBN Publisher's Prefixes: 0-907582, 0-85496

Bernards (Publishers) Ltd, see Bernard Babani (Publishing) Ltd

Better Books*, 15A Chelsea Rd, Lower Weston, Bath, Avon BA1 3DU Tel: Bath 28010 (STD code 0225)
Proprietor: H Welchman; *Publicity Manager:* Pip Mason
Subject: Special Needs
1985: 22 titles *Founded:* 1974
ISBN Publisher's Prefix: 0-904700

Bible Society*, Bible House, Stonehill Green, Westlea, Swindon SN5 7DG Telex: 44283
Executive Dir: R Worthing-Davies; *Publishing Dir:* D Napier; *Marketing:* R L Russell; *Sales:* M A Warwick; *Orders:* R Brock; *Production:* R Heath; *Rights & Permissions:* Miss J M Henderson; *Editorial:* Miss S Mills
Imprints include: BFBS
Subjects: Bibles, Testaments, Bible Books, Bible Study, Christian Resource and Educational Materials (in English and many foreign languages)
1985: 38 titles *Founded:* 1804
ISBN Publisher's Prefix: 0-564

Bibliagora+, PO Box 77, Feltham, Middlesex TW14 8JF Tel: (01) 898 1234 Telex: 935918 Bridge G
Man Dir: D Rex-Taylor; *Editorial:* Sev Hepton; *Sales:* Miss E Taylor; *Production:* D Atkins; *Publicity:* A Cutting; *Rights & Permissions:* K Gee
Subsidiary Companies: Lineage Research Unit, Out-of-Print Tracing Unit (both at above address)
Imprint: St George & Dragon Press
Subjects: Indoor Games, Philosophy, Contract Bridge
Book Club: Bridge Book Club
Founded: 1973
Miscellaneous: Firm is also mail-order international bookseller: Bibliagora (Books old & new), at main company address
ISBN Publisher's Prefix: 0-906031

Bibliophile Books, an imprint of BSC Books Ltd (qv)

Clive **Bingley** Ltd, 7 Ridgmount St, London WC1E 7AE Tel: (01) 636 7543 Telex: 21897 Laldn G
Warehouse: Distribution & Management Services Ltd, Sheldon Way, Larkfield, Maidstone, Kent ME20 6SE Tel: Maidstone 882000 (STD code 0622) Telex: 965514
Man Dir: Charles Ellis; *Editorial Consultant:* Clive Bingley; *Sales Manager:* Beverly Brentnall; *Publicity Manager:* Ann Harrold
Parent Company: Library Association Publishing (at above main address)
Subjects: Library Science, Textbooks, Reference, Directories, Bibliographies
Founded: 1965
ISBN Publisher's Prefix: 0-85157

Birmingham Museums and Art Gallery Publications Unit, Chamberlain Sq, Birmingham B3 3DH Tel: (021) 235 4051
Subjects: Fine & Applied Arts, Archaeology, Local History
ISBN Publisher's Prefix: 0-7093

Bishopsgate Press Ltd, 37 Union St, London SE1 1SE Tel: (01) 403 6544
Chief Executive: Ian Straker; *Editorial, Sales, Production, Publicity, Rights & Permissions:* Austen Smith
Subsidiary Company: Whitstable Litho Ltd, Milstrood Rd, Whitstable, Kent CT5 3PP
Subjects: Crafts, Biography, Gardening, Finance, Cinema, Religion
1985: 10 titles *1986:* 12 titles *Founded:* 1800

Bison Books Ltd+, 176 Old Brompton Rd, London SW5 0BA Tel: (01) 370 3097 Telex: 888014 Bison G Fax: (01) 244 7139
Director: Sydney L Mayer
Head Off: 15 Sherwood Pl, Greenwich, CT 06830, USA

Subjects: Military and Modern History, Animals, Cookery, Transport, Sport, Modelling
Founded: 1975

A & C Black (Publishers) Ltd, 35 Bedford Row, London WC1R 4JH Tel: (01) 242 0946 Cable Add: Biblos London WC1 Telex: 32524 Acblac Fax: (01) 831 8478
Man Dirs: Charles Black, David Gadsby; *Sales Dir:* Paul White; *Production Dir:* Leonard Brown; *Rights Dir:* Paul Langridge; *Children's Dir:* Jill Coleman; *Distribution Dir:* Terry Rouelett; *Publicity:* Jane Thorne
Orders to: Howard Rd, Eaton Socon, Huntingdon, Cambridgeshire PE19 3EZ Tel: Huntingdon 212666 (STD code 0480)
Imprints: Alphabooks (qv), Art Guide Publications, John Baker (Publishers) Ltd, Ernest Benn Ltd, EP Publishing, F Lewis (Publishers) Ltd, Nautical Publishing Co Ltd
Subjects: Children's, Educational, Music, Arts & Crafts, Hobbies, History, Natural History, Reference, Sport, Theatre, Travel (*Blue Guides*)
Founded: 1807
ISBN Publisher's Prefixes: 0-7136 (A & C Black), 0-212 (Baker), 0-510 (Ernest Benn), 0-7158 (EP), 0-85317 (Lewis), 0-333, 0-85177 (Nautical)

Black Dagger Crime, an imprint of Firecrest Publishing Ltd (qv)

Black Pig Editions Ltd, see Justin Knowles Publishing Group

Black Swan, an imprint of Transworld Publishers (Corgi & Bantam Books) Ltd (qv)

Blacker Calmann Cooper Ltd, see John Calmann & King Ltd

Blackie & Son Ltd+, Bishopbriggs, Glasgow G64 2NZ Tel: (041) 772 2311 Telex: 777283 Blacki G
Man Dir: R Michael Miller; *Editorial:* A D Mitchell, Martin West (Children's); Dr A G MacKintosh (Academic); *Sales Managers:* A D Mitchell (Children's), Drew Stuart (Educational), Kenneth Allan (Academic); *Publicity:* Kate Cinamon (Children's), Drew Stuart (Educational), Kenneth Allan (Academic); *Rights:* Liz Allen (Children's)
Orders to: J M Dent & Sons (Distribution) Ltd, Dunhams Lane, Letchworth, Hertfordshire SG6 1LF Tel: Letchworth 686241 (STD code 0462)
Subsidiary Companies: Abelard-Schuman Ltd; International Textbook Co Ltd (qv); Leonard Hill (qv); Surrey University Press (qv)
Imprint: North-South Books
Branch Off: 7 Leicester Pl, London WC2H 7BP Tel: (01) 734 7521
Subjects: School Textbooks, Reference, Children's, Scientific & Engineering, General & Social Science, Quality Paperbacks
Founded: 1809
ISBN Publisher's Prefix: 0-216

Blackstaff Press Ltd, 3 Galway Park, Dundonald, Belfast BT16 0AN Tel: Dundonald 7161 (STD code 023 18)
Man Dir: Anne Tannahill; *Chairman:* Michael Burns; *Publicity & Advertising:* Michael Burns, Anne Tannahill; *Editorial:* Kerry Campbell; *Sales:* Sally Kelso; *Production:* Wendy Dunbar
Orders to: (except Ireland and USA) George Philip Services Ltd, Arndale Rd, Lineside Industrial Estate, Littlehampton, West Sussex BN17 7EN; (USA) Longwood Publishing Group, 27 South Main St, Wolfeboro, NH 03894, USA; (Ireland) Blackstaff Press Ltd (at above main address)
Subjects: General Fiction, Poetry, Drama, Biography, Local History, History, Reference, Paperbacks, General & Social Science, Art, Natural History, Folklore, Politics, Humour
1985: 21 titles *1986:* 22 titles *Founded:* 1971
ISBN Publisher's Prefix: 0-85640

Basil **Blackwell** Ltd, 108 Cowley Rd, Oxford OX4 1JF Tel: Oxford 792792 (STD code 0865) Cable Add: Books Oxford Telex: 83118 Fax: (0865) 791438
Man Dir: David Martin; *Editorial Dirs:* John Davey, James Nash, René Olivieri; *Marketing:* Janet Joyce; *Publicity:* Paul Clifford; *Production:* Ray Addicott; *Rights & Permissions:* Stella Welford
Allied Companies: Blackwell Scientific Publications Ltd (qv); Polity Press
Subsidiary Companies: Blackwell Press Ltd; Blackwell Raintree Ltd; Marston Book Services Ltd, Oxford; Shakespeare Head Press
Imprints: Basil Blackwell, Blackwell Reference
Subjects: Economics and Industrial Relations, History, Philosophy, Politics, Languages, Linguistics, History, Geography, Children's Books, Reference, Religion, Academic Paperbacks, Law, Business, Literature, Psychology, Feminism, Sociology, Primary and Secondary Textbooks, Journals
1985-86: 340 titles *Founded:* 1922
Miscellaneous: Member of the Blackwell Group (see B H Blackwell Ltd under Major Booksellers)
ISBN Publisher's Prefixes: 0-631, 0-85520

Blackwell Scientific Publications Ltd+, Osney Mead, Oxford OX2 0EL Tel: Oxford 240201 (STD code 0865) Cable Add: Research Oxford Telex: 83355
Chairman: Per Saugman; *Man Dir:* Robert Campbell; *Marketing Dir:* Jon Conibear; *Production Dir:* John Robson; *Journals Dir:* Keith Bowker
Allied Companies: Basil Blackwell Ltd (qv); Oxford Illustrators Ltd, Aristotle Lane, Oxford
Subsidiary Companies: Blackwell Scientific Publications (Australia) Pty Ltd, Australia (qv); Munksgaard, International Booksellers & Publishers Ltd, Denmark (qv); Boekhandel Kooyker, Netherlands; Blackwell Videotec Ltd, UK; Blackwell Scientific Publications Inc, 52 Beacon St, Boston, MA 02108, USA; 667 Lytton Ave, Palo Alto, CA 94301, USA
Branch Offs: 8 John St, London WC1N 2ES; 23 Ainslie Place, Edinburgh; also above Australian and US subsidiary company offices
Subjects: Medicine, Dentistry, Nursing, Veterinary Medicine, Chemistry, Life & Earth Sciences, Computer Science, Professional & Technical
1986: 147 titles *Founded:* 1939
ISBN Publisher's Prefix: 0-632

Blaketon Hall Ltd*, 7 South St, Exeter, Devon Tel: Exeter 217652 (STD code 0392) Cable Add: Blaketon-Hall Ashburton
Man Dir: John Shillingford; *Dir:* Pat Shillingford; *Trade Manager:* Derek Warner
Warehouse: Unit 1, Devon Units, Budlake Rd, Marsh Barton, Devon Tel: Exeter 210602 (STD code 0392)
Subjects: Non-fiction, Practical, How-to, Pets, Hobbies, Handicrafts
Founded: 1976
Miscellaneous: Also remainder dealer
ISBN Publisher's Prefix: 0-907

Blandford Press, an imprint of Blandford Publishing Ltd (qv)

Blandford Publishing Ltd, Artillery House, Artillery Row, London SW1P 1RT Tel: (01) 222 7676 Cable Add: Cassellpub London SW1P 1RT Telex: 9413701 Caspub G Fax: (01) 799 1514
Chairman, Man Dir: Philip Sturrock; *Editorial Dir:* Clare Howell; *Sales Dir:* Stephen Lustig; *Sales Managers:* Jonathan King (UK), John Mills (Export); *Production Dir:* Alan Smith; *Manager (Javelin Paperbacks):* Colin Gower; *Rights and Special Sales:* Chris White
Orders to: Blandford Publishing Ltd, Link House, West St, Poole, Dorset BH15 1LL Tel: Poole 670581 (STD code 0202) Telex: 418304 Linkho G
Parent Company: Cassell PLC (qv)
Imprints: Arms & Armour (qv), Blandford Press, Javelin Paperbacks, New Orchard Editions
Subjects: Military, Gardening, Natural History, Art & Craft, Humour
1986: 240 titles *1987:* 190 titles *Founded:* 1919
ISBN Publisher's Prefixes: 0-7137 (Blandford, Javelin), 1-85079 (New Orchard)

Anthony **Blond**, an imprint of Quartet Books Ltd (qv)

Bloodaxe Books Ltd+, PO Box 1SN, Newcastle upon Tyne NE99 1SN Tel: Tyneside 2325988 (STD code 091)
Chairman: Simon Thirsk; *Man Dir, Editorial:* Neil Astley
Orders to: J M Dent & Sons (Distribution) Ltd, Dunhams Lane, Letchworth, Hertfordshire SG6 1LF Tel: Letchworth 686241 (STD code 0462)
Subjects: Poetry (English language and in translation), Fiction, Drama, Literary Criticism, Photography
1985: 9 titles *1986:* 23 titles *Founded:* 1978
ISBN Publisher's Prefixes: 0-906427, 1-85224

Bloomsbury Publishing Ltd+, 2 Soho Sq, London W1V 5DE Tel: (01) 494 2111 Telex: 262964 attn Bloomsbury Fax: (01) 785 9816
Chairman: Nigel Newton; *Editorial Dirs:* Liz Calder, David Reynolds, Kathy Rooney; *Sales, Marketing Dirs:* Lucy Juckes, Alan Wherry; *Production Dir:* Roger Yelland; *Publicity Dir:* Caroline Michel
Orders to: DMS, 3 Sheldon Way, Larkfield, Maidstone, Kent ME20 6SE
Subjects: Fiction, Biography, Politics, Current Affairs, Non-fiction, Reference
Founded: 1986
ISBN Publisher's Prefix: 0-7475

Bobcat Books, an imprint of Omnibus Press (qv)

The **Bodley Head** Ltd+, 32 Bedford Sq, London WC1B 3EL Tel: (01) 631 4434 Cable Add: Bodleian London WC2 Telex: 299080 Fax: (01) 255 1620
Publishing Dir: Chris Holifield; *Editorial Dir:* Caroline Upcher; *Editorial (Children's):* Margaret Clark; *Home Sales:* Charles Turner; *Overseas Sales:* Quentin Hockliffe; *Press Officer:* Suzy Jenrey; *Publicity Manager:* Cathy Fulton; *Production:* Tim Chester; *Rights & Permissions:* Gaye Poulton (Adult), Jill Taylor (Children's)
Subjects: General Fiction, Poetry, Biography, History, Juveniles
Founded: 1887

Miscellaneous: Firm is a member of the Chatto, Bodley Head & Jonathan Cape Ltd Group (qv)
ISBN Publisher's Prefix: 0-370

The **Book Guild** Ltd, Temple House, 25 High St, Lewes, East Sussex BN7 2LU Tel: Lewes 472534 (STD code 0273)
Man Dir: Gerald Konyn; *Production:* Douglas Quiggan; *Editorial, Rights & Permissions:* Carol Biss; *Publicity:* Rebecca Harkin
Orders to: Biblios Publishers' Distribution Services Ltd, Glenside Industrial Estate, Star Rd, Partridge Green, Horsham, West Sussex RH13 8LD Tel: Partridge Green 710971 (STD code 0403)
Imprints: Seagull Books, Temple House Books
Subjects: Fiction, Biography, Travel, War, Adventure, Juvenile
Founded: 1981
ISBN Publisher's Prefix: 0-86332

Book Sales Ltd, see Omnibus Press

Bookmarks Publications+, 265 Seven Sisters Rd, Finsbury Park, London N4 2DE Tel: (01) 802 6145
Editorial, Production: Peter Marsden; *Publicity:* Einde O'Callaghan; *Rights:* Charlie Hore; *Sales:* Jane Butterworth
Subjects: Politics, Economics, Socialism, Labour, History
Bookshop: At above address
1986: 10 titles *1987:* 12 titles *Founded:* 1979
Miscellaneous: Publish for the Socialist Workers Party (GB)
ISBN Publisher's Prefixes: 0-906224 (Bookmarks), 0-905998 (SWP)

Book Sales Ltd, an associate company of Omnibus Press (qv)

Bookward Ltd, 10 Mandeville Rd, Aylesbury, Buckinghamshire HP21 8AA Tel: Aylesbury 435418 (STD code 0296)
Chairman: R Fenn; *Man Dir:* J Goodchild
Orders to: J M Dent & Sons (Distribution) Ltd, Dunhams Lane, Letchworth, Hertfordshire SG6 1LF Tel: Letchworth 686241 (STD code 0462)
Parent Company: Bookward Ltd, Express Works, Church St, Irthlingborough, Northamptonshire NN9 5SE
Subjects: Fiction & Non-fiction (children's & adult), Diet, Handcraft
1985: 48 titles *Founded:* 1983
ISBN Publisher's Prefix: 0-86391

Boosey & Hawkes Music Publishers Ltd, 295 Regent St, London W1R 8JH Tel: (01) 580 2060 Cable Add: Sonorous London W1 Telex: 8954613 Boosey G
Man Dir: R Antony Fell
Subjects: Music, Secondary & Primary Music Textbooks
ISBN Publisher's Prefix: 0-85162

David **Booth** (Publishing) Ltd, 8 Cranedown, Lewes, East Sussex BN7 3NA Tel: Lewes 472039 (STD code 0273) Telex: 878236 DBP G
Chief Executive, Editorial: David Booth; *Marketing Dir, Rights & Permissions:* Sonia Birch
Subject: Children's Books (picture, novelty, pop-up, leisure) international co-edition packager
1986: 20 titles *Founded:* 1981

Bowker & Bertram Ltd (Marine Publishers), Whitewalls, Harbour Way, Old Bosham, Chichester, West Sussex PO18 8QH
Subjects: Marine (literary and technical)
1986: 7 titles

Bowker-Saur Ltd, Borough Green, Sevenoaks, Kent TN15 8PH Tel: Sevenoaks 884567 (STD code 0732) Telex: 95678 Fax: (0732) 884079
Chief Executive: Klaus G Saur; *General Manager:* Shane O'Neill; *Marketing Dir:* Phillip Woods: *Sales:* John Husdon (Books), Noel McPherson (CD-ROM); *Production Manager:* R Gee; *Publicity Manager:* Gary Palmer; *Rights & Permissions:* Roger Hedley-Jones
Parent Company: Butterworth & Co (Publishers) Ltd (qv). Ultimate parent company Reed International PLC, Reed House, 83 Piccadilly, London W1A 1EJ
Imprints: R R Bowker (UK), K G Saur Ltd, Hans Zell
Branch Offs: Shropshire House, 2-10 Capper St, London WC1E 6JA, UK Tel: (01) 637 1571 Fax: (01) 580 4089; Heilmannstr 16, D-8000 Munich 71, Federal Republic of Germany Tel: Munich 791040 Fax: (Munich) 7910499
Subjects: Bibliographic Reference Books & Directories, Professional, Reference, Literary, Music, Biographies, CD-ROM
Founded: 1988
ISBN Publisher's Prefixes: 0-85935, 0-8352 (both Bowker), 0-86291 (Saur), 0-905450 (Hans Zell)

R R **Bowker** (UK), an imprint of Bowker-Saur Ltd (qv)

Boxtree Ltd+, 36 Tavistock St, Covent Garden, London WC2E 7PB Tel: (01) 379 4666 Telex: 263250 Bxt Fax: (01) 349 0049
Man Dir, Editorial: Sarah Mahaffy; *Sales, Finance:* Chris Conolly-Smith; *Publicity:* Nina Martyn
Orders to: W H Smith Distributors, St Johns House, East St, Leicester, Leicestershire LE1 6NE
Parent Company: TVS
Subjects: TV Tie-ins, Non-fiction, Children's
1987: approx 20 titles *Founded:* 1986
ISBN Publisher's Prefix: 1-85283

Marion **Boyars** Publishers Ltd, 24 Lacy Rd, London SW15 1NL Tel: (01) 788 9522
Man Dir, Editorial, Rights & Permissions: Marion Boyars; *Editorial:* Arthur Boyars, Ken Hollings, Stephanie Lewis; *Sales:* S Brockbank; *Publicity:* Ken Hollings
Associate Company: Marion Boyars Publishers Inc, 26 East 33rd St, New York, NY 10016, USA Tel: (212) 213 0167
Subjects: General Fiction, Belles Lettres, Poetry, Literary Criticism, Plays, Music, Dance, Philosophy, Sociology, Psychology
Series: Open Forum, Ideas in Progress, Signature, Critical Appraisals
Founded: 1975
ISBN Publisher's Prefix: 0-7145

Boydell & Brewer Ltd+, PO Box 9, Woodbridge, Suffolk IP12 3DF Tel: Shottisham 411320 (STD code 0394) Telex: 987343 Boydel G
Chairman: R W Barber
Imprints: Boydell Press, D S Brewer
Subjects: Mediaeval and Renaissance Literature and History, General Non-fiction, Country
ISBN Publisher's Prefixes: 0-85115 (Boydell), 0-85991 (Brewer)

Bracken Books, reprint imprint of Bestseller Publications Ltd (qv under Remainder Dealers)

Bradt Publications, 41 Nortoft Rd, Chalfont St Peter, Buckinghamshire SL9 0LA Tel: Chalfont St Giles 3478 (STD code 024 07) Telex: 849021 Fran G
Man Dir, Editorial, Rights: Hilary Bradt; *Manager:* Janet Mears
Subjects: Trekking, Backpacking, Travel
1986: 4 titles *1987:* 7 titles *Founded:* 1975
ISBN Publisher's Prefix: 0-946983

Brassey's Defence Publishers Ltd, see Pergamon Press Ltd

Breslich & Foss+, Golden House, 28-31 Great Pulteney St, London W1R 3DD Tel: (01) 734 0706 Telex: 264188 Bresl G
Man Dir: Paula G Breslich
Orders to: André Deutsch Ltd, 105 Great Russell St, London WC1B 3LJ
Subjects: Health, Sports
Founded: 1983
ISBN Publisher's Prefix: 1-85004

D S **Brewer**, see Boydell & Brewer Ltd

Brilliance Books+*, 14 Clerkenwell Green, London EC1R ODP Tel: (01) 250 0730
Editorial: Tenebris Light, Roy Trevelion; *Sales, Rights & Permissions:* Tenebris Light; *Production:* Roy Trevelion; *Publicity:* Janice Cal
Imprints: Jet, Plain Edition
Subjects: New fiction and reprints by homosexual and lesbian authors (only)
Founded: 1982
ISBN Publisher's Prefix: 0-946189

Brimax Books Ltd, 4-5 Studlands Park Industrial Estate, Exning Rd, Newmarket, Suffolk CB8 7AU Tel: Newmarket 664611 (STD code 0638) Cable Add: Brimax Newmarket Telex: 817625 Brimax G
Man Dir, Sales Dir: Patricia Gillette; *Editorial:* Trevor Weston; *Rights & Permissions:* Brimax Rights Ltd (at above address)
Subjects: General Children's Books, Activity Books, Cloth Books
ISBN Publisher's Prefixes: 0-900195, 0-904494, 0-86112

Bristol Classical Press, Department of Classics, University of Bristol, Bristol BS8 1RJ Tel: Bristol 214187 (STD code 0272)
Chief Executives: J H Betts, T A G Foss; *Editorial:* J H Betts, K Richardson; *Sales:* E Flood; *Production, Publicity, Rights:* K Richardson
Subjects: Classics, Archaeology, English Literature, Classical Studies, Education, Philosophy
1986: 20 titles *Founded:* 1977
ISBN Publisher's Prefixes: 0-906515, 0-86292

The **British Academy**, 20-21 Cornwall Terrace, Regent's Park, London NW1 4QP Tel: (01) 487 5966 Cable Add: Britacademy, London NW1 Telex: 263194
Publications Officer: James Rivington; *Rights & Permissions:* Rachel Ollerearnshaw
Subjects: Archaeology, Art, History, Latin, Music, Numismatics, Philosophy
1985: 4 titles *1986:* 14 titles *Founded:* 1902
ISBN Publisher's Prefix: 0-85672

British & Foreign Bible Society, see Bible Society

The **British Council**, Design, Production and Publishing Department*, 65 Davies St, London W1Y 2AA Tel: (01) 499 8011 Telex: 8952201 Bricon G
Headquarters: 10 Spring Gardens, London SW1A 2BN Tel: (01) 930 8466
Director: Helen Meixner; *Sales Manager:* Frances Nichols
Subjects: Those related to the promotion of a wider knowledge of Britain and the English language abroad and developing closer cultural relations with other countries.

Among book and journal titles published or co-published are *British Book News*, *Media in Education and Development*, *English Language Teaching Journal*, *ELT Documents*, *Language Teaching*, *British Writers*, *How to Live in Britain*, *The British Council Collection 1938-84*, *TV English*, *Video English*
1985: 6 titles (by Council), 13 titles (co-publications) *Founded:* 1934
ISBN Publisher's Prefix: 0-86355

British Film Institute, see BFI Publishing

British Horse Society, British Equestrian Centre, Stoneleigh, Kenilworth, Warwickshire CV8 2LR Tel: Coventry 52241 (STD code 0203) Cable Add: Brithorse, Kenilworth
Director: Col N F Grove-White; *Secretary:* C C Smith; *Public Relations Officer:* Ceri Burgum
Subjects: Equestrian Reference Books
ISBN Publisher's Prefix: 0-900226

British Library, Bibliographic Services, 2 Sheraton St, London W1V 4BH Tel: (01) 323 7077 Telex: 21462
Subjects: Bibliographies, Indexes, Cataloguing and Bibliographical Aids
Founded: 1973
Miscellaneous: See also entry under Major Libraries
ISBN Publisher's Prefix: 0-7123 (previously 0-900220)

British Library, Document Supply Centre Publications Marketing, Boston Spa, Wetherby, West Yorkshire LS23 7BQ Tel: Wetherby 843434 (STD code 0937) Telex: 557381
Dir-General: M B Line; *Dir:* David Russon; *Head of Publications and Publicity Support Services:* Peter Haigh
Parent Body: The British Library, Sheraton St, London W1V 4BH
Subjects: Bibliographical
1985: 6 titles *Founded:* 1973
Miscellaneous: See also entry under Major Libraries
ISBN Publisher's Prefix: 0-7123

British Library Publications+, Humanities and Social Sciences, Great Russell St, London WC1B 3DG Tel: (01) 323 7535 Telex: 21462
Chief Executive: Jane Carr; *Editorial, Rights:* David Way; *Sales, Promotion:* Colin Wight; *Marketing, Special Projects:* Judith Major
Orders to: (UK) Publications Sales Unit, The British Library, Boston Spa, Wetherby, West Yorkshire LS23 7BQ; (USA and Canada) Longwood Publishing Group Inc, 51 Washington St, Dover, NH 03820, USA
Parent Body: The British Library, Sheraton St, London W1V 4BH
Subjects: Arts (Western & Oriental), History, Bibliography, Reference
Founded: 1979
Miscellaneous: See also entry under Major Libraries
ISBN Publisher's Prefix: 0-7123

British Medical Association+, BMA House, Tavistock Sq, London WC1H 9JR Tel: (01) 387 4499 Cable Add: Aitiology Westcent London Telex: 265929
Publishing Dir: Anthony J Smith; *Editor:* Dr S P Lock; *Sales, Marketing:* M Long; *Publishing Manager:* D A Parrott; *Rights & Permissions:* Neil Poppmacher
Subsidiary Company: Professional & Scientific Publications (at above address)
Imprint: British Medical Journal
Subject: Medical
Founded: 1857
ISBN Publisher's Prefix: 0-7279

British Museum (Natural History)+, Cromwell Rd, London SW7 5BD Tel: (01) 589 6323 Cable Add: Nathismus Southkens London Telex: 929437 Nmpubs G
Head of Publications: Clive Reynard; *Editorial:* Chris Owen, Myra Givans; *Sales:* R Cowles; *Production:* Eric Dent; *Publicity Rights & Permissions:* Susan Daniels
Subjects: Natural History, Scientific, Popular, Periodicals
Bookshops: Museum Bookshop (address as above); Museum Bookshop at Zoological Museum, Tring, Herts; Geological Museum at Exhibition Rd, London SW7
1985: 36 titles *1986:* 46 titles *Founded:* 1963
ISBN Publisher's Prefix: 0-565

British Museum Publications Ltd+, 46 Bloomsbury St, London WC1B 3QQ Tel: (01) 323 1234 Telex: 28592 Bmpubs G
Man Dir: Hugh Campbell; *Publishing Manager:* Celia Clear; *Production:* Julie Young; *Rights & Permissions:* Sarah Watkins; *Promotion:* Shona Getty
Orders to: Thames & Hudson Ltd, 44 Clockhouse Rd, Farnborough, Hampshire
Imprint: British Museum Publications
Subjects: Art, Archaeology, Oriental, Numismatics, Ethnography, Children, General Guides to British Museum
Bookshop: British Museum Shop, Great Russell St, London WC1
1985: 31 titles *1986:* 32 titles *Founded:* 1973
ISBN Publisher's Prefix: 0-7141

The **British Psychological** Society, see B P S Books

British Tourist Authority, Thames Tower, Black's Rd, Hammersmith, London W6 9EL Tel: (01) 846 9000 Cable Add: Tagbandi Ldn Bta Telex: 21231 Btaadm B
Chief Executive: Michael Medlicott; *Editorial:* Cyril Palmer; *Sales:* Stephen Mesquita
Orders to: 4 Bromells Rd, London SW4 0BJ
Subject: Travel to Britain
Founded: 1969
ISBN Publisher's Prefix: 0-7095

Broadcast Books, an imprint of Element Books Ltd (qv)

James **Brodie** Ltd*, 15 Springfield Pl, Lansdown, Bath, Avon BA1 5RA Tel: Bath 317706 (STD code 0225)
Man Dir: Corinne Wimpress; *Sales Dir:* Jeremy D Wimpress
Subjects: Primary & Secondary Education, Classical Translations (*Brodie's* and *Kelly's Keys*), *Notes on Chosen Texts* series (produced by Brodie and generally published by Pan Books Ltd (qv))
Founded: 1906 (incorporated 1926)
ISBN Publisher's Prefix: 0-7142

Brodies Notes, an imprint of Pan Books Ltd (qv)

Broomsleigh Press, an imprint of Fudge & Co Ltd (qv)

Trevor **Brown** Associates, Suite 7B, 26 Charing Cross Rd, London WC2H 0LN Tel: (01) 240 8744 Cable Add: Unibooks London WC2 Telex: 24224 ref 3544
Dirs: J Trevor Brown, J G Goellner (USA); *Sales:* Anna Simpson-Muellner
Miscellaneous: Firm is the London office of Cornell University Press (qv), Indiana University Press, The Johns Hopkins University Press (qv), University Press of New England, University of Texas Press, University of Toronto Press, University of Washington Press

Brown, Son & Ferguson, Ltd, 4/10 Darnley St, Glasgow G41 2SD Tel: (041) 429 1234 Cable Add: Skipper Glasgow
Chief Executive, Editorial, Production: T Nigel Brown; *Sales, Publicity:* J A Kyle; *Rights & Permissions:* L Ingram-Brown
Subsidiary Company: James Gowans Ltd (at above address)
Subjects: Nautical, Scottish Plays
Founded: 1858
ISBN Publisher's Prefix: 0-85174

Brown Wells & Jacobs Ltd+, 2 Vermont Rd, London SE19 3SR Tel: (01) 653 7670 Telex: 21685 Fotogr G Fax: (01) 653 7670
Chief Executive: Graham Brown
Associate Company: Alias Design (at above address)
Subjects: Children's — Pre-school, Novelty & Non-fiction, Adult Novelty & Crafts (Packagers)
Founded: 1982

Buchan & Enright Publishers Ltd+, 53 Fleet St, London EC4Y 1BE Tel: (01) 353 4401
Chief Executives, Editorial: J W H de l'A Buchan, Dominique Enright; *Sales:* Michael Hills; *Rights & Permissions:* Kathleen Nathan
Orders to: Fountain Press Ltd, 45 The Broadway, Tolworth, Surrey KT6 7DW Tel: (01) 390 7768
Subjects: Biography, Autobiography, Military History, Humour, Field Sports
1986: 23 titles *Founded:* 1981
ISBN Publisher's Prefix: 0-907675

Burke Publishing Co Ltd+, Pegasus House, 116-120 Golden Lane, London EC1Y 0TL Tel: (01) 253 2145 Cable Add: Burkebooks London EC1 Telex: 27931 Burke G
Chairman, Export Sales: H Starke; *Man Dir, Editorial, Rights & Permissions:* Miss N Galinski
Orders to: 14 Beccles Rd, Loddon, Norwich, Norfolk NR14 6JD
Subsidiary Company: Harold Starke Ltd (qv)
Imprint: Pre-School Publishing
Branch Offs: Burke Publishing (Canada) Ltd, 20 Queen St West, Suite 3000, Box 30, Toronto, Ontario, Canada M5H 1V5; Burke Publishing Co Inc, 333 State St, PO Box 1740, Bridgeport, Connecticut 06601, USA
Subjects: Juveniles, Secondary & Primary Textbooks, Educational Materials
Founded: 1934
ISBN Publisher's Prefix: 0-222

Burns & Oates Ltd+, Wellwood, North Farm Rd, Tunbridge Wells, Kent TN2 3DR Tel: Tunbridge Wells 510850 (STD code 0892) Telex: 957258
Man Dir, Sales: Charlotte de la Bedoyere; *Editorial, Rights & Permissions:* John Bright-Holmes; *Production:* Jennifer Steel; *Publicity:* Ruth Saunders
Associate Company: Search Press Ltd (qv)
Subjects: Philosophy, History, Religion & Theology, Moral Education, Literary
Founded: 1847
ISBN Publisher's Prefix: 0-86012

Butterworth & Co (Publishers) Ltd, Borough Green, Sevenoaks, Kent TN15 8PH Tel: Borough Green 884567 (STD code 0732) Cable Add: Butterwort Sevenoaks Kent TN15 8PH Telex: 95678 Fax: (0732) 884079
The above is the address of the Head Office. The Scientific, Technical and Medical Book Publishing Divisions and the Journals Publishing Division are at Westbury House, Bury St, Guildford, Surrey GU2 5AW Tel: Guildford 31261

(STD code 0483) Telex: 859556 Fax: (0483) 301563. The Legal Publishing Division is at 88 Kingsway, London WC2 6AB Tel: (01) 405 6900 Cable Add: Butterwort London WC2 Fax: (01) 405 1332
Chairman: W Gordon Graham; *Chief Executive:* Neville Cusworth; *Dirs:* David Summers (Law), G Burn (Scientific Technical and Medical), Derek Day (Finance & Services); *Production:* W Robin Smeeton (Law), J Carruthers (Scientific, Technical and Medical); *Publicity:* Christopher Marshall; *Rights & Permissions:* R J Hedley-Jones (UK), Betty Cottrell (Foreign Rights); *International Sales:* J C Hudson, P W Woods (Bowker)
Parent Company: Reed Publishing UK, Quadrant House, The Quadrant, Sutton, Surrey SM2 5AS. Ultimate parent company Reed International PLC, Reed House, 83 Piccadilly, London W1A 1EJ
Subsidiary Companies: Bowker-Saur Ltd, Professional Books Ltd (qqv, both UK); Butterworths Pty Ltd, Australia (qv); Butterworths (a division of Reed Inc), 2265 Midland Ave, Scarborough, Ontario M1P 4S1, Canada; Butterworths of New Zealand Ltd, New Zealand (qv); Butterworth & Co (Asia) Pte Ltd, Republic of Singapore (qv); Butterworth (STM Publishers), 80 Montvale Ave, Stoneham, MA 02180, USA; Butterworths (Legal Publishers), 1501 ME 40th Suite 205, Redmond, WA 98052, USA; 80 Montvale Ave, Stoneham, MA 20180, USA; 1321 Rutherford Lane, Suite 180, Austin, TX 78753-6798, USA; D & S Publishers, PO Box 5105, Calumet, Clearwater, FL 33518, USA, 289 E 5th St, St Paul, MN 55101, USA
Imprints: Ann Arbor, Focal Press, HFL, Malayan Law Journal (Pte) Ltd (Malaysia and Republic of Singapore, qqv), Scientechnica, Westbury House, John Wright
Bookshop: 9-12 Bell Yard, Temple Bar, London WC2
Subjects: Law, Medicine, Engineering, Technology, Science, Social Science, Business Studies, Photography, Reference
1986: approx 400 titles *Founded:* before 1905
ISBN Publisher's Prefixes: 0-406/7/8/9, 0-592 (all Butterworth), 0-86103, 0-902852 (both Westbury House), 0-240 (Focal), 0-250 (Ann Arbor), 0-372 (HFL), 0-85608 (Scientechnica), 0-7236 (John Wright)

Buzby Books Ltd, an imprint of Severn House Publishers Ltd (qv)

Bwrdd Croeso Cymru, see Wales Tourist Board

C B D Research Ltd, 15 Wickham Rd, Beckenham, Kent BR3 2JS Tel: (01) 650 7745
Man Dir: G P Henderson
Subject: Reference
1986: 3 titles *Founded:* 1961
ISBN Publisher's Prefix: 0-900246

C E E P I Ltd (Caxton and English Educational Programmes International Ltd)+*, Maxwell House, 74 Worship St, London EC2A 2EN Tel: (01) 377 4850 Cable Add: Interknow London EC2 Telex: 886048 Bpcc
Joint Man Dirs: John Emler, Edward Hornett
Subjects: Encyclopaedias, Education, Yearbooks, History, Reference, Dictionaries
Miscellaneous: Firm is a member company of Maxwell Communication Corporation plc (qv)
ISBN Publisher's Prefix: 0-907305

C E T, an imprint of Council for Educational Technology (qv)

C I B, see Chartered Institute of Bankers Publications

C O I C, see Manpower Services Commission Careers and Occupational Information Centre

C R E, an imprint of Commission for Racial Equality (qv)

Cadogan Books Ltd+, 16 Lower Marsh, London SE1 7RJ Tel: (01) 261 0621 Telex: 917706 Metbul G Fax: (01) 928 6539
Chairman: F Rice-Oxley; *Man Dir:* P Levey; *Senior Editor:* Rachel Fielding
Subjects: Travel, Motoring
1986: 13 titles *Founded:* 1971
ISBN Publisher's Prefixes: 0-946313, 0-947754

John **Calder** (Publishers) Ltd, 18 Brewer St, London W1R 4AS Tel: (01) 734 3786 Cable Add: Bookdom London
Man, Publishing Dir: John Calder; *Promotion, Sales, Rights & Permissions:* Susan Herbert
Subjects: Modern Literature, Classics, Belles Lettres, Poetry, Biography, History, Music, Opera, Philosophy, Reference, Trade Paperbacks, Psychology, Social Science, Politics, Current Affairs
Founded: 1950
ISBN Publisher's Prefix: 0-7145

Caliban Books, 17 South Hill Park Gardens, Hampstead, London NW3 2TX Tel: (01) 435 0222
Man Dir: Peter Razzell
Orders to: Biblios Publishers' Distribution Services Ltd, Glenside Industrial Estate, Star Rd, Partridge Green, Horsham, West Sussex RH13 8LD Tel: Partridge Green 710971 (STD code 0403)
Subjects: Social History, Historical Autobiography, History of Exploration, Psychotherapy
1986: 60 titles *Founded:* 1977
ISBN Publisher's Prefixes: 0-904573, 1-85066

California University Press, see University Presses of California, Columbia and Princeton

John **Calmann & King** Ltd+, 71 Great Russell St, London WC1B 3BN Tel: (01) 831 6351 Telex: 298246 Owls G
Joint Man Dirs: Marianne Calmann, Laurence King; *Editorial:* Elisabeth Ingles
Founded: 1976
Miscellaneous: Designers and producers of high quality illustrated books, and specialists in international co-editions

Cambridge Information and Research Services Ltd*, PO Box 147, Grosvenor House, High St, Newmarket CB8 9AL Tel: Newmarket 663030 (STD code 0638)
Man Dir: Andrew R Buckley; *Marketing Dir:* Patrick A Wynne-Jones
Subsidiary Companies: Energy Publications; Enterprise Publications (both at above address)
Subjects: Directories & Reference, Energy Management, Engineering, Business Studies, Social Science
Founded: 1975
ISBN Publisher's Prefix: 0-905332

Cambridge University Press+, The Edinburgh Bldg, Shaftesbury Rd, Cambridge CB2 2RU Cable Add: Unipress, Cambridge Tel: Cambridge 312393 (STD code 0223) Telex: 817256 Fax: (0223) 315052
Chief Executive: G A Cass; *Deputy Chief Executive:* P E V Allin; *Man Dir (Publishing Division):* A K Wilson; *Press Editorial Dir:* R J Mynott; *Editorial Dirs:* R Davidson, A B du Plessis, M Y Holdsworth, S Mitton; *Marketing Dir:* D A Knight; *Sales Dir:* Nicholas Reckert, Dennis Stanton; *Publicity Dir:* Peter Langworth; *Production Dir:* H McIlwrick; *Rights & Permissions:* Julie McNair
Branch Offs: Cambridge University Press, Australia (qv); Cambridge University Press (American Branch), 32 East 57th St, New York, NY 10022, USA, and 510 North Ave, New Rochelle, NY 10801, USA
Subjects: Agriculture, Anglo-Saxon, Anthropology, Archaeology, Architecture, Area Studies, Art, Astronomy, Bibliography, Biography, Biological Sciences, Chemistry, Classical Studies, Computer Science, Drama, Earth Sciences, Economics, Education (primary, secondary, tertiary and further education, juvenile information books), Engineering, English Language Teaching, Environmental Sciences, Geography, History, Languages, Law, Linguistics, Literature, Materials Science, Mathematics, Medicine, Music, Philosophy, Physical Sciences, Politics, Psychology, Sociology, Reference, Theology, Journals, Bibles and Prayer Books, Examination Papers
1985: 920 titles *1986:* 1095 titles *Founded:* 1534
ISBN Publisher's Prefix: 0-521

Camden Press Ltd, 43 Camden Passage, London N1 8EB Tel: (01) 226 2061, (01) 354 3186 Telex: 267373
Chief Executive, Editorial, Production: Sian Williams; *Sales:* Siobhan Doyle; *Publicity:* Adrianne Blue; *Rights & Permissions:* Elizabeth Long
Subjects: Art, Fiction, Health, Biography, Graphic Guides (all by women authors)
1986: 11 titles *Founded:* 1986
ISBN Publisher's Prefix: 0-948491

Canongate Publishing Ltd+, 17 Jeffrey St, Edinburgh EH1 1DR Tel: (031) 556 0023/1954
Man Dir, Editorial: Stephanie Wolfe Murray; *Rights, Permissions & Publicity:* Andrew Young; *Production:* Neville Moir
Associate Companies: Equinox (Oxford) Ltd, Phaidon Press Ltd (qqv)
Subjects: General Fiction, Poetry, Biography, History, Art, Current Affairs, Juveniles, Cookery
Founded: 1973
ISBN Publisher's Prefixes: 0-86241, 0-903937 (Canongate), 0-900025 (Southside), 0-905470 (Q Press)

The **Canterbury** Press Norwich, see Hymns Ancient & Modern

Jonathan **Cape Ltd**+, 32 Bedford Sq, London WC1B 3EL Tel: (01) 636 3344 Cable Add: Capajon London WC1 Telex: 299080
Orders to: CVBC Services Ltd, Alma Park Industrial Estate, Grantham, Lincolnshire Tel: Grantham 67421 (STD code 0476)
Chairman: Tom Maschler; *Man Dir:* Graham C Greene; *Editorial Dir:* Frances Coady; *Sales:* Quentin Hockliffe (Export), Charles Turner (Home); *Production Dir:* Tim Chester; *Publicity Dir:* Polly Samson; *Rights & Permissions:* Gaye Poulton; *Design Dir:* Ian Craig; *Children's Books:* Valerie Kettley
Subjects: General Fiction, Belles Lettres, Literary Criticism, Drama, Humour, Poetry, Biography, History, Military History, Politics, International Affairs, Anthropology, Natural History, Science, Art, Philosophy, Juveniles, High-priced Paperbacks, Social Science, Travel and Topography, Food and Drink

Founded: 1921
Miscellaneous: Firm is a member of the Chatto, Bodley Head & Jonathan Cape Ltd Group (qv)
ISBN Publisher's Prefix: 0-224

Carcanet Press Ltd*, 208 Corn Exchange Bldgs, Manchester M4 3BQ   Tel: (061) 834 8730
Man Dir: Michael Schmidt
Imprint: Fyfield Books
Subjects: Fiction, Lives & Letters, Poetry
Founded: 1969
ISBN Publisher's Prefixes: 0-85635, 0-902145

Cardinal, an imprint of Sphere Books Ltd (qv)

Careers Consultants Ltd, an imprint of The Trotman Group (qv)

Careers Research and Advisory Centre Ltd, distributed by Hobsons Publishing PLC (qv)

Carousel, an imprint of Corgi Books Ltd (qv)

Frank **Cass** & Co Ltd, Gainsborough House, 11 Gainsborough Rd, London E11 1RS   Tel: (01) 530 4226   Cable Add: Simfay London   Telex: 897719
Man Dir: Frank Cass; *Editorial:* Margaret Goodare; *Production:* John Smith; *Publicity:* Hayley Osen, Elizabeth Lye; *Trade Manager:* Richard Norris
Orders to: Harper & Row Ltd, Estover Rd, Plymouth, Devon PL6 7PZ   Tel: Plymouth 705251 (STD code 0752)
Associate Companies: The Woburn Press (qv); Vallentine Mitchell & Co Ltd (qv)
Subjects: Third World Studies, Economics, Economic History, Social History, Politics, History, Africana, Middle East Studies, Strategic Studies, Law
Bookshop: Frank Cass (Books) Ltd, 10 Woburn Walk, London WC1
Founded: 1957
ISBN Publisher's Prefix: 0-7146

Cassell PLC+, Artillery House, Artillery Row, London SW1P 1RT   Tel: (01) 222 7676   Cable Add: Cassellpub London   Telex: 9413701 Caspub G   Fax: (01) 799 1514
Orders to: (For Cassell, Cassell Educational, Geoffrey Chapman, Robert Royce, Tycooly) J M Dent & Sons (Distribution) Ltd, Dunhams Lane, Letchworth, Hertfordshire SG6 1LF   Tel: Letchworth 686241 (STD code 0462)   Telex: 825751 Jmdent G; (For Arms & Armour Press, Blandford Press, Javelin, New Orchard Editions, Studio Vista) Blandford Publishing Ltd, Link House, West St, Poole, Dorset BH15 1LL   Tel: Poole 670581 (STD code 0202)
Chairman, Man Dir: Philip Sturrock; *Editorial Dirs:* Stephen Butcher, Clare Howell; *Sales Dir:* Stephen Lustig; *Sales Managers:* Jonathan King (UK), John Mills (Export)
Subsidiary Companies: Blandford Publishing Ltd (qv); Cassell Educational Ltd; Cassell Publishers Ltd
Imprints: Geoffrey Chapman, Robert Royce, Studio Vista, Tycooly
Subjects: General, Reference, Religion, Gardening, Educational (primary, secondary, tertiary), Military, Arts & Crafts, Academic, Business, ELT
1987: 150 titles   *Founded:* 1848
ISBN Publisher's Prefixes: 0-304 (Cassell), 0-225 (Geoffrey Chapman), 0-947728 (Robert Royce), 0-289 (Studio Vista), 1-85148 (Tycooly)

Castle House Publications Ltd, Castle House, 28-30 Church Rd, Tunbridge Wells, Kent TN1 1JP   Tel: Tunbridge Wells 39606 (STD code 0892)
Man Dir: Donald Reinders
Subject: Medical
1985: 14 titles   *1986:* 16 titles   *Founded:* 1973
ISBN Publisher's Prefix: 0-7194

Cathay, an imprint of Octopus Books Ltd (qv)

Catholic Institute for International Relations, 22 Coleman Fields, London N1 7AF   Tel: (01) 354 0883   Telex: 21118 Ciir G
General Secretary: Ian Linden; *Editor:* Francis McDonagh; *Publications Marketing Officer:* Tony Simpson
Subjects: Theology, Politics, Economics, Development
1985: 20 titles   *1986:* 25 titles   *Founded:* 1940
ISBN Publisher's Prefixes: 0-904393, 0-946848

Catholic Truth Society*, 38-40 Eccleston Sq, London SW1V 1PD   Tel: (01) 834 4392   Cable Add: Apostolic London   Telex: 295542 Pavis G
General Secretary: David Murphy; *Editorial:* Brendan Walsh
Subject: Religion
Bookshop: 25 Ashley Pl, London SW1P 1LT
1985: 31 titles   *Founded:* 1884
Miscellaneous: Publishers to the Holy See
ISBN Publisher's Prefix: 0-85183

Causeway Press Ltd, PO Box 13, 48 Southport Rd, Ormskirk, Lancashire L39 5HP   Tel: Ormskirk 76048/77360 (STD code 0695)   Telex: 628781 Obs
Editorial, Publicity, Rights & Permissions: Michael Haralambos; *Sales, Production:* Ian Lyster
Subsidiary Company: Book Production Management Services, 121 Noel Gate, Aughton, Ormskirk, Lancashire L39 5EF
Imprint: Causeway Books
Subject: Educational
1985: 9 titles   *1986:* 6 titles   *Founded:* 1982
ISBN Publisher's Prefix: 0-946183

Paul **Cave** Publications Ltd*, 74 Bedford Pl, Southampton SO1 2DF   Tel: Southampton 333457 (STD code 0703), Southampton 223591
Man Dir: Paul Cave; *Sales:* Joan Cave
Subjects: Local History, Illustrated Guides, Magazines
Bookshop: At above address
1985: 5 titles   *Founded:* 1960
ISBN Publisher's Prefix: 0-86146

Caxton and English Educational Programmes International Ltd, see CEEPI Ltd

Cedar Books, an imprint of William Heinemann Ltd (qv)

Cement & Concrete Association*, Wexham Springs, Slough SL3 6PL   Tel: Fulmer 2727 (STD code 028 16)   Telex: 848352
Head of Publications: Miss E G Bond
Subjects: Engineering, Concrete, Cement
1985: 5 titles
ISBN Publisher's Prefix: 0-7210

Centaur Press Ltd, Fontwell, Arundel, West Sussex BN18 0TA   Tel: Eastergate 3302 (STD code 024 368)
Man Dir: T J L Wynne-Tyson
Subsidiary Company: The Linden Press (at above address); there is no connection with the Simon & Schuster imprint of the same name
Subjects: General, Biography, Philosophy, Social Science, Textbooks, Environment
Bookshop: Keele's (at above address)
Founded: 1954
ISBN Publisher's Prefixes: 0-900000 (Centaur), 0-900001 (Linden Press)

Century, an imprint of Century Hutchinson Publishing Ltd (qv)

Century Hutchinson Ltd, Brookmount House, 62-65 Chandos Pl, Covent Garden, London WC2N 4NW   Tel: (01) 240 3411   Cable Add: Literatus London W1   Telex: 261212 Litldn G   Fax: (01) 836 1409
Chairman: Christopher Bland; *Man Dir:* Anthony Cheetham
Century Hutchinson Ltd operates three UK publishing divisions:
General: Century Hutchinson Publishing Ltd (qv);
Paperbacks: Arrow Books Ltd (qv), Arena Books, Beaver Books
Specialist: Hutchinson Education (qv)
Associate Companies: Andersen Press Ltd (qv), Century Benham Ltd (both UK); Century Hutchinson Australia Pty Ltd, Australia (qv); Century Hutchinson NZ Ltd, New Zealand (qv); Century Hutchinson SA Pty Ltd, Republic of South Africa (qv)

Century Hutchinson Publishing Ltd, Brookmount House, 62-65 Chandos Pl, Covent Garden, London WC2N 4NW   Tel: (01) 240 3411   Cable Add: Literatus London W1   Telex: 261212
Man Dir: Anthony Cheetham; *Publishing Dirs:* Rosemary Cheetham (Century fiction), Gail Rebuck (Non-fiction), Richard Cohen (Hutchinson), Roddy Bloomfield (Stanley Paul, Popular Dogs); *Sales Dir:* Dallas Manderson; *Production Dir:* David Edwards; *Publicity Dir:* Susan Lamb; *Rights & Permissions Managers:* Susan Wakeford, Heather Schiller
Orders to: Tiptree Book Services Ltd, Church Rd, Tiptree, Colchester, Essex CO5 0SR   Tel: Tiptree 816362 (STD code 0621)
Imprints: Barrie & Jenkins Ltd, Hutchinson Business Books, Century, Century Paperbacks, Hutchinson, Hutchinson Children's Books Ltd, Frederick Muller, Stanley Paul & Co Ltd, Popular Dogs Publishing Co Ltd, Rider & Co
Subjects: General Fiction, Non-fiction, Crime, Biography, Memoirs, Travel, Reference, Children's, Eastern Philosophy & Mysticism, Sports & Hobbies, Poetry, Humour, Graphics, Fashion
Founded: 1985 (Century 1982, Hutchinson 1887)
Miscellaneous: Century Hutchinson Publishing Ltd is a division of Century Hutchinson Ltd (qv)
ISBN Publisher's Prefixes: 0-7126 (Century), 0-09 (Hutchinson)

Chadwyck-Healey Ltd, Cambridge Pl, Cambridge CB2 1NR   Tel: Cambridge 311479 (STD code 0223)   Telex: 265871 Monref G ref 83
Man Dir: Alastair Everitt; *Dirs:* Sir Charles Chadwyck-Healey, Lady Chadwyck-Healey, P J Miller; *Associate Dirs:* M Bacon (Customer Services), A Moss (Editorial); *Group Promotions Manager:* John Russell
Associate Companies: Chadwyck-Healey France, 3 rue de Marivaux, 75002 Paris, France; Chadwyck-Healey Inc, 1021 Prince St, Alexandria, VA 22314, USA
Subjects: Reference, Government Documents, Art & Architecture, Economics, Statistics, History, American History & Studies, Literary History, Bibliographies & Catalogues, Radio and TV
ISBN Publisher's Prefix: 0-85964

W & R **Chambers** Ltd+, 43-45 Annandale St, Edinburgh EH7 4AZ Tel: (031) 557 4571 Cable Add: Chambers Edinburgh Telex: 727967 G Fax: (031) 556 2708
Chairman: A S Chambers; *Man Dir:* W G Henderson; *Editorial Dir:* R S R Mair
Subjects: General, Reference, Educational Textbooks, Scottish Interest
1985: 9 titles *1986:* 23 titles *Founded:* 1820
ISBN Publisher's Prefix: 0-550

Chancellor, an imprint of Octopus Books Ltd (qv)

Chancerel Publishers Ltd, 40 Tavistock St, London WC2E 7PB Tel: (01) 240 2811 Telex: 265871 ref Sjj 130
Man Dir: W D B Prowse
Associate Companies: Chancerel Editions SA, France (qv); Twinburn Ltd, London
Subjects: Educational (Geography, Modern Languages, English as a Foreign Language, Computers), Adult Self-study Languages, Business, Travel
Founded: 1976
ISBN Publisher's Prefix: 0-905703

Chancery House Publishing Ltd, an imprint of Antique Collectors' Club (qv)

Geoffrey **Chapman**, an imprint of Cassell PLC (qv)

Chapman & Hall Ltd, 11 New Fetter Lane, London EC4P 4EE Tel: (01) 583 9855 Cable Add: Elegiacs London EC4 Telex: 263398 Abplong Fax: (01) 583 0701
Man Dir: Paul Gardner; *Publisher:* Phillip Read
Orders to: Routledge, Chapman & Hall Ltd, North Way, Andover, Hampshire SP10 5BE Tel: Andover 332424 (STD code 0264) Telex: 47214 Fax: (0264) 64418
Parent Company: Thomson Information Services Ltd (qv). Ultimate parent company International Thomson Organisation Ltd, 20 Queen St West, Box 45, Suite 2206, Toronto, Ontario M5H 3R3, Canada
Imprints: E & F N Spon Ltd (qv), Van Nostrand Reinhold (International) Co Ltd (qv)
Subjects: Science, Technology, Medicine
1986: 96 titles *Founded:* 1830
ISBN Publisher's Prefix: 0-412

Charnwood Library Series, see F A Thorpe (Publishing) Ltd

Chartered Institute of Bankers (CIB) Publications, an imprint of Bankers Books Ltd (qv)

The **Chartered Institute of Building**, Englemere, Kings Ride, Ascot, Berkshire SL5 8BJ Tel: Ascot 23355 (STD code 0990)
Chief Executive: Dr J Hooper; *Editorial, Production, Rights & Permissions:* P A Harlow; *Sales:* K Banbury
Subject: Construction Management
ISBN Publisher's Prefix: 0-906600

Chartwell-Bratt (Publishing & Training) Ltd+, Old Orchard, Bickley Rd, Bromley, Kent BR1 2NE Tel: (01) 467 1956 Telex: 265871 Monref G ref 84 Fax: (01) 467 1754
Man Dir: K J Munro; *Publishing Coordinator:* Philip Yorke
Parent Company: Studentlitteratur Utbildningshuset AB, Sweden (qv)
Imprint: Studentlitteratur
Subjects: Computer Science, Management, Natural Sciences, Behavioural Science
Founded: 1980
ISBN Publisher's Prefix: 0-86238

Chatto & Windus Ltd/The Hogarth Press+, 30 Bedford Sq, London WC1B 3RP Tel: (01) 631 4434 Cable Add: Chaboca London WC1 Telex: 299080
Chairman: John Charlton; *Man Dir, Publishing Dir:* Carmen Callil; *Senior Editorial Dir:* Rupert Lancaster; *Sales:* Charles Turner (Home), Quentin Hockliffe (Export); *Publicity Dir & Advertising:* Nicole Paulissen
Orders to: 9 Bow St, London WC2E 7AL Tel: (01) 379 6637
Subjects: Fiction, Biography & Memoirs, Poetry, History, Literary Criticism, Cartoons, Philosophy, Illustrated Books, Travel, Psychology & Psychoanalysis, Music, Social Sciences, Crime, Humour, Belles Lettres, Trade Paperbacks
1987: 105 titles *Founded:* 1855 (Chatto & Windus), 1917 (The Hogarth Press)
Miscellaneous: Firm is a member of the Chatto, Bodley Head & Jonathan Cape Ltd Group (qv)
ISBN Publisher's Prefixes: 0-7011 (Chatto), 0-7012 (Hogarth)

Chatto, Bodley Head & Jonathan Cape Ltd+, 9 Bow St, London WC2 7AL Tel: (01) 379 6637 Cable Add: Chaboca London Telex: 299080
Group Members: Chatto & Windus Ltd/The Hogarth Press, Jonathan Cape Ltd, The Bodley Head Ltd (qqv)
Parent Company: Random House Inc, 201 East 50th St, New York, NY 10022, USA
Subsidiary Company: Triad Paperbacks (handled by Grafton Books (qv))

The **Chemical Society**, see The Royal Society of Chemistry

Child's Play (International) Ltd+, Ashworth Rd, Bridgemead, Swindon, Wiltshire SN5 7YD Tel: Swindon 616286 (STD code 0793) Telex: 449391
Man Dir: Michael Twinn; *UK Sales:* Rosemary Mills; *Publicity:* Diane Mundy; *Marketing Manager:* Neil Burden
Subsidiary Company: Child's Play Inc, Chicago, USA
Subject: Juveniles (pre- and primary school ages)
1985: 34 titles *1986:* 36 titles *Founded:* 1972
ISBN Publisher's Prefix: 0-85953

Chivers Press Publishers, Windsor Bridge Rd, Bath, Avon BA2 3AX Tel: Bath 335336 (STD code 0225) Telex: 444633 Fax: (0225) 310771
Man Dir: Roger Lewis; *Publishing Dir:* Julian Batson; *Rights Manager:* Nicole Kirkman; *Production Manager:* Lesley Barnes
Parent Company: The Gieves Group PLC, 1 Savile Row, London W1X 2JR
Associate Companies: Chivers Book Sales Ltd, 93-100 Locksbrook Rd, Bath BA1 3HB; Firecrest Publishing Ltd (qv); Lythway Press Ltd (qv)
Imprints: Atlantic Large Print, New Portway Large Print, Windsor Large Print, New Portway Facsimile Reprints, Chivers Audio Books
Subjects: Romance, Thrillers, Mysteries, Western, General Fiction, Non-fiction (including Biography & Memoirs)
Founded: 1979
ISBN Publisher's Prefixes: 0-85995, 0-85997, 0-86220, 0-85119, 0-7451

The **Christian Community** Press, see Floris Books

Christian Journals, an imprint of Marshall, Morgan & Scott Publications Ltd (qv)

Church House Publishing, Church House, Great Smith St, London SW1P 3NZ Tel: (01) 222 9011 Telex: 916010
Publishing Manager: Robin Brookes; *Production:* F W J Burford; *Publicity:* Antonia Coleman
Trade Orders to: J M Dent & Sons (Distribution) Ltd, Dunhams Lane, Letchworth, Hertfordshire SG6 1LF Tel: Letchworth 686241 (STD code 0462)
Parent Company: Central Board of Finance of the Church of England (at above London address)
Subjects: Publications for the Boards and Councils of the Church of England, Synod Reports, Christian Education
Bookshop: Church House Bookshop, 31 Great Smith St, London SW1P 3BN
1987: 30 titles
ISBN Publisher's Prefix: 0-7151

Church Society, Whitefield House, 186 Kennington Park Rd, London SE11 4BT Tel: (01) 582 0132
Publishing Secretary: M J W Barker
Imprints: Churchman, Cross Way
Subjects: Religious, Church History, Hymn Books
ISBN Publisher's Prefix: 0-85190

Churchill Livingstone+, Robert Stevenson House, 1-3 Baxter's Pl, Leith Walk, Edinburgh EH1 3AF Tel: (031) 556 2424 Cable Add: Churchliv Telex: 727511 Longman G (Edin) Fax: (031) 558 1278
Man Dir: R G B Duncan; *Editorial:* A T Stevenson; *Sales, Publicity & Advertising:* P Shepherd; *Marketing:* Gerard Dummett; *Production:* C Cameron; *Rights & Permissions:* Irene Harper
Orders to: Longman Group Ltd, Trade Dept, Pinnacles, Harlow, Essex Tel: Harlow 29655 (STD code 0279)
Branch Offs: 5 Bentinck St, London W1M 5RN Tel: (01) 935 0121; Churchill Livingstone, Longman Cheshire Pty Ltd, Longman Cheshire House, Kings Garden, 91-97 Coventry St, Melbourne, Victoria 3205, Australia Telex: 33501 Lans AA; Churchill Livingstone Inc, 1560 Broadway, New York, NY 10036, USA Tel: (212) 819 5400
Subjects: Medicine, Dentistry, Nursing, Paramedical
Founded: 1863
Miscellaneous: Firm is a division of Longman Group Ltd (qv)
ISBN Publisher's Prefix: 0-443

Churchman, an imprint of Church Society (qv)

Cicerone Press+, 2 Police Sq, Milnthorpe, Cumbria LA7 7PY Tel: Milnthorpe 2069 (STD code 044 82)
Man Dir, Sales, Rights & Permissions: Mrs D Unsworth; *Editorial, Publicity:* W Unsworth; *Production:* R B Evans
Subjects: Outdoor, Guidebooks, Northern Britain, Cookery, Natural History
1985: 10 titles *Founded:* 1969
ISBN Publisher's Prefixes: 0-902363, 1-85284

City Financial, an imprint of Kluwer Publishing Ltd (qv)

Robin **Clark** Ltd, 27-29 Goodge St, London W1P 1FD Tel: (01) 636 3992 Telex: 919034
Chairman: Naim Attallah; *Marketing Dir:* D Elliott; *Production Dir:* G Grant; *Editorial:* Jeremy Beale; *Publicity:* Anna Groundwater
Associate Company: Quartet Books Ltd (qv)
Subjects: Fiction, Biography, Social History, Humour, Reprints
Founded: 1976

Miscellaneous: Firm is a member of the Namara Group, Namara House, 45-46 Poland St, London W1
ISBN Publisher's Prefix: 0-86072

T & T Clark Ltd, 59 George St, Edinburgh EH2 2LQ Tel: (031) 225 4703 Cable Add: Dictionary Edinburgh Telex: 728134
Man Dir: T G Ramsay D Clark; *Editorial, Production, Rights & Permissions:* Dr Geoffrey Green; *Publicity, Sales:* Elizabeth Miller
Parent Company: John Bartholomew & Son Ltd (qv)
Subjects: Theology, Law, Philosophy, History
Founded: 1821
ISBN Publisher's Prefix: 0-567

Anthony **Clarke** Books, 16 Garden Court, Wheathampstead, Hertfordshire AL4 8RF Tel: Wheathampstead 2460 (STD code 058 283) Cable Add: Clarkbook St Albans
Proprietor: Anthony Clarke
Subject: Religion
Bookshop: All Saints Bookshop, All Saints, London Colney, St Albans, Hertfordshire AL2 1AF
Founded: 1970
ISBN Publisher's Prefix: 0-85650

James **Clarke** & Co Ltd+, 50-52 Kingston St, Cambridge CB1 2NT Tel: Cambridge 350865 (STD code 0223) Telex: 817114 Fax: (0223) 66951
Man Dir: A C Brink; *Editorial Manager:* Linda Yeatman; *Sales Manager:* Keith Robinson; *Production:* Patricia Rowland; *Publicity Manager:* Kerry Harvey-Piper
Imprints: Acorn Editions, Allenson, Patrick Hardy Books, Lutterworth Press (qv)
Subjects: Religion, Reference, Academic
1986: 3 titles *Founded:* 1859
ISBN Publisher's Prefix: 0-227

E W **Classey**, PO Box 93, Faringdon, Oxfordshire SN7 7DR Tel: Uffington 399 (STD code 036 782)
Publisher: E W Classey
Subject: Entomology
ISBN Publisher's Prefixes: 0-900848, 0-86096

Classic Thrillers, an imprint of J M Dent & Sons Ltd (qv)

Clematis Press Ltd, 18 Old Church St, London SW3 5DQ Tel: (01) 352 8755 Cable Add: Clematis London SW3
Man Dir: Mrs Clara Waters
Trade Counter: Jay Distribution Ltd, 1-3 Winton Close, Letchworth, Hertfordshire SG6 1BA
Subjects: Co-productions: Art, Sport, Cookery
Founded: 1950
ISBN Publisher's Prefix: 0-568

Clio Press Ltd+, 55 St Thomas' St, Oxford OX1 1JG Tel: Oxford 250333 (STD code 0865) Telex: 83130 Fax: (0865) 790358
Man Dir: John Durrant; *Editorial Dir:* Anthony Sloggett; *Marketing Dir:* Lyndsay Williams
Parent Company: ABC-Clio Information Services, 2040 APS, Santa Barbara, CA 93103, USA
Subsidiary Companies: Clio Distribution Services (at above address); Isis Audio Books; Isis Large Print, Windrush Large Print Children's Books (qqv)
Subjects: History, Politics, International Relations, Art, Bibliographies, General Fiction & Non-fiction, Large Print, Audio
1985: 14 titles *1986:* 34 titles *Founded:* 1971
ISBN Publisher's Prefixes: 0-903450, 1-85109, 1-85089

William **Clowes** (Publishers) Ltd, now Hymns Ancient & Modern (qv)

Cochuideachd Leabhreachean Gàidhlig, an imprint of Volturna Press (qv)

Collet's Holdings Ltd, Denington Estate, Wellingborough, Northamptonshire NN8 2QT Tel: Wellingborough 224351 (STD code 0933) Cable Add: Colholdin Wellingborough Telex: 311165 Chacom G Colholdin
Man Dir: Eva Skelley; *Advertising:* Elizabeth Cook
Subjects: Music, Art (History), Textbooks, Reference (Modern Language, Audiovisual), General & Social Science, Low- & High-priced Paperbacks
Bookshops: Collet's International Bookshop, 129-131 Charing Cross Rd, London WC2; Collet's Penguin Bookshop, 64-66 Charing Cross Rd, London WC2; Collet's Chinese Bookshop, 40 Great Russell St, London WC1
Founded: 1934
Miscellaneous: Specialists in Russian language teaching materials, Soviet & Eastern European Publications
ISBN Publisher's Prefix: 0-569

Colley-Moore International Publishers & Literary Agent+, 14 Lyon Sq, Tilehurst, Reading, Berkshire RG3 4DD Tel: Reading 417748 (STD code 0734) Cable Add: Lyon Square Reading
Chief Executive, Rights & Permissions: Steve Colley-Moore; *Editorial:* Vicky Stanmore; *Sales:* Steve Colley-Moore, Chrys McMasters; *Production:* Stanley Springer; *Publicity:* Brigitte Blaurock
Subsidiary Company: Colley-Moore Literary Agency (qv)
Associate Company: Blowit International Services (at above address)
Subjects: Fiction & Non-fiction, Children's Juvenile/Young Adults Education, Poetry, Plays
1987: approx 8 titles *Founded:* 1986

Rex **Collings** Ltd, 38 Kings St, London WC2E 8JS Tel: (01) 836 8634 Telex: 337340
Man Dir: Rex Collings
Subjects: General, Poetry, Juveniles, Africana, Biography, Drama, Reference
Founded: 1969
ISBN Publisher's Prefixes: 0-86036, 0-901720

William **Collins** PLC, 8 Grafton St, London W1X 3LA Tel: (01) 493 7070 Cable Add: Herakles London W1X Telex: 25611 Colins G Fax: (01) 493 3061
Chairman: F I Chapman; *Vice Chairman:* G Craig; *Man Dir, Publishing:* J Clement; *Divisional Dirs:* E Bell (General), S Warshaw (Education & Reference), Alan Smith (Special Interests), T Palmer (Children's), J Lloyd (Grafton Books); *Rights and Contracts Dir:* Juliet Annan
Orders to: PO Box, Glasgow G4 0NB Tel: (041) 772 3200 Telex: 778107 Fax: (041) 772 3200 ext 3119
Subsidiary Companies: Cobuild Ltd; Adlard Coles Ltd; Dinosaur Publications Ltd (qv); Grafton Books (qv); Multiple Sound Distributors Ltd
Overseas Subsidiary Companies: William Collins Pty Ltd, Australia (qv); Wm Collins Sons & Co (Canada) Ltd, 100 Lesmill Rd, Don Mills, Ontario, Canada; Wm Collins Publishers Ltd, New Zealand (qv); Collins Publishers (SA) (Pty) Ltd, Republic of South Africa (qv); Collins Inc, 50 Osgood Pl, San Francisco, CA 94133, USA
Associate Company: Harper & Row Inc, 10 East 53rd St, New York, NY 10022, USA
Imprints include: Collins — Armada Books, Collins Caedmon, Collins Harvill (qv), Collins Willow, The Crime Club, Gem; Fontana — Dinosaur, Dragon Books, Flamingo, Fontana Press, Fount, Lions, Picture Lions; Triad
Subjects: General Fiction & Non-fiction, Belles Lettres, Biography, History, How-to, Art, Archaeology, Philosophy, Reference, Religion, Bibles, Low- & High-priced Paperbacks, Secondary & Primary Textbooks, Educational Materials, Juveniles, Military, Sports, Travel, ELT, Home & Leisure, Natural History
Bookshops: Claude Gill Books Ltd, Hatchards Ltd (qqv under Major Booksellers); The Ancient House Bookshop, Ipswich, Suffolk; Stanley Botes Ltd, 8 Grafton St, London W1X 3LA
Founded: 1819
Miscellaneous: Collilns-Longman Atlases, Westerhill Rd, Bishopbriggs, Glasgow G64 2QT distributes atlases for Wm Collins and the Longman Group
ISBN Publisher's Prefixes: 0-00 (Collins and Collins Harvill), 0-061 (Fontana)

Collins Harvill+, 8 Grafton St, London W1X 3LA Tel: (01) 493 7070 Cable Add: Herakles London W1X Telex: 25611 Colins G
Publisher: Christopher MacLehose
Miscellaneous: An imprint of William Collins PLC (qv)

Collins Willow, an imprint of William Collins PLC (qv)

Colombus Books Ltd+, 19-23 Ludgate Hill, London EC4M 7PD Tel: (01) 248 6444 Telex: 28673 Consol G Fax: (01) 248 3357
Chairman: Eric Dobby; *Man Dir:* Medwyn Hughes; *Editorial Dir:* Gill Rowley; *Sales Dirs:* David Collins, Catherine Parson (Export); *Promotion, Publicity Manager:* Nathalie Vilemur; *Rights Dir:* Diane Spivey
Parent Company: Stancroft Trust Ltd (at above address)
Subjects: Popular
1985: 130 titles *1986:* 140 titles *Founded:* 1980
ISBN Publisher's Prefix: 0-86287

Colour Library Books Ltd*, 86 Epsom Rd, Guildford, Surrey GU1 2BX Tel: Guildford 579191 (STD code 0483) Telex: 859182
Man Dir: Barry Austin; *Editorial:* David Gibbon; *Sales, Rights, Promotions:* George Sprankling; *Production:* Ted Smart, Gerald Hughes
Subjects: Cookery, Travel, Nature, Art, Animals, Photographic, Beauty, Erotic
Founded: 1959
ISBN Publisher's Prefixes: 0-906558, 0-86283

Columbia University Press, see University Presses of California, Columbia and Princeton

Columbine House, an imprint of Arlington Books (Publishers) Ltd (qv)

Comedia, see Routledge

Comet, an imprint of W H Allen & Co Ltd (qv)

Commission for Racial Equality, Elliot House, 10-12 Allington St, London SW1 Tel: (01) 828 7022
Chief Executive: Sir Peter Newsam; *Editorial, Sales, Production, Publicity, Rights & Permissions:* Lionel Morrison
Imprint: C R E
Branch Offs: Manchester, Leeds, Birmingham, Leicester
Subject: Race & Community Relations
1986: 23 titles *Founded:* 1976
ISBN Publisher's Prefix: 0-907920

Common Ground, an imprint of Longman Group Ltd (qv)

Computational Mechanics Publications+, Ashurst Lodge, Ashurst, Southampton, Hampshire SO4 2AA Tel: Ashurst 3223 (STD code 042 129) Telex: 47388 Compmech Fax: (042 129) 2853
Chief Executive: Dr C Brebbia; *Man Dir, Publicity, Rights & Permissions:* L Sucharov; *Editorial, Production:* Mrs P Hicks; *Sales:* Mrs V Orchard
Subject: Engineering
1985: 9 titles *Founded:* 1976
ISBN Publisher's Prefix: 0-905451

Concertina Publications Ltd*, 19 Broad Court, Covent Garden, London WC2B 5QN Tel: (01) 836 1758, (01) 836 2929 Telex: 268614 Concet G
Man Dir: Jill Dean
Subjects: Illustrated Non-fiction, Reference, Wallcharts

Concorde Paperbacks, an imprint of Ward Lock Ltd (qv)

Condor Books, an imprint of Souvenir Press Ltd (qv)

Connoisseur Carbooks, see Motor Racing Publications Ltd

Conran Octopus Ltd+, 37 Shelton St, London WC2H 9HN Tel: (01) 240 6961 Telex: 296249
Man Dir: Alison Cathie; *Marketing Dir:* Piers Russell-Cobb; *Publishing Manager:* Miss Tristram Holland
Parent Companies: Storehouse PLC, 196 Tottenham Court Rd, London W1P 9LD and Octopus Publishing Group PLC, 59 Grosvenor St, London W1X 9DA
Subjects: Art & Architecture, Design, Children's, Cinema & Photography, Cookery & Wine, Crafts & Hobbies, Do-it-Yourself, Gardening, Home Management, Medicine & Health
1985: approx 20 titles *Founded:* 1984
ISBN Publisher's Prefix: 0-85029

Conservative Political Centre, 32 Smith Sq, London SW1P 3HH Tel: (01) 222 9000 Cable Add: Constitute, London, SW1P 3HH
Director: David Knapp
Subjects: Reference Books, Politics, Political Economy, Sociology, Questions of the Day
ISBN Publisher's Prefix: 0-85070

Constable & Co Ltd+, 10 Orange St, London WC2H 7EG Tel: (01) 930 0801 Cable Add: Dhagoba London WC2H 7EG
Man Dir: B K Glazebrook; *Editorial Dir:* Robin Baird-Smith; *Sales:* Paul Marks; *Production:* Richard Tomkins; *Publicity:* Yvette Evans-Foster; *Rights & Permissions:* Christine Senior
Orders to: Tiptree Book Services Ltd, Church Rd, Tiptree, Colchester, Essex CO5 0SR Tel: Tiptree 816362 (STD code 0621) Cable Add: Literarius Tiptree Telex: 99487
Subjects: General Fiction, Literature, Antiques, Art, Biography, Memoirs, History, Politics, Food, Travel & Guidebooks, Gardening, Social Sciences, Natural History, General Science, Psychology & Psychiatry, Counselling, Social Work, Photography, Reference
Founded: 1896
ISBN Publisher's Prefix: 0-09

Conway Maritime Press Ltd, 24 Bride Lane, Fleet St, London EC4Y 8DR Tel: (01) 583 2412 Telex: 8814206 Popper G
Man Dir: W R Blackmore; *Editorial Dir:* Robert Gardiner; *Rights:* Jane Weeks
Orders to: Marston Book Services Ltd, PO Box 87, Oxford OX4 1LB Tel: Oxford 791155/791179 (STD code 0865)
Associate Companies: Paul Popper Ltd, 24 Bride Lane, Fleet St, London EC4Y 8DR; Putnam & Co Ltd
Imprint: Putnam Aeronautical Books
Subjects: Naval, Maritime, Sailing, Aeronautics
Founded: 1968
ISBN Publisher's Prefix: 0-85177

Leo **Cooper**, an imprint of William Heinemann Ltd (qv)

Trewin **Copplestone** Books, now Sceptre Books Ltd (qv)

Cordee, an imprint of Diadem Books (qv)

Corgi, an imprint of Transworld Publishers (Corgi & Bantam Books) Ltd (qv)

Cornell University Press, c/o Trevor Brown Associates, Suite 7B, 26 Charing Cross Rd, London WC2H 0LN Tel; (01) 240 8774 Cable Add: Unibooks London WC2 Telex: 24224 ref 3545
Dir: J Trevor Brown; *Sales Manager:* Anna Simpson-Muellner
Parent Company: Cornell University Press, 124 Roberts Pl, Ithaca, NY 14850, USA
Subjects: Academic (all disciplines)
ISBN Publisher's Prefix: 0-8014

Cornerstone Books, 55 St Thomas' St, Oxford OX1 1JG Tel: Oxford 250333 (STD code 0865) Telex: 83130
Man Dir: John Durrant; *Marketing Dir:* Lyndsay Williams; *Sales Development Manager:* Jill Fieldgate; *Editorial Dir:* Tony Sloggett; *Promotions Manager:* Chas Walton
Parent Company: ABC-CLIO, 2040 Alameda Padre Serra, PO Box 4397, Santa Barbara, CA 93140-4397, USA
Associate Company: ISIS Large Print Books, 2040 Alameda Padre Serra, PO Box 4397, Santa Barbara, CA 93140-4397, USA
Subjects: Fiction
1986: 24 titles *Founded:* 1987
ISBN Publisher's Prefix: 1-55736

Cornwall Books, an imprint of Golden Cockerel Press Ltd (qv)

Coronet, an imprint of Hodder & Stoughton Ltd (qv)

D J **Costello** (Publishers) Ltd+, 43 High St, Tunbridge Wells, Kent TN1 1XL Tel: Tunbridge Wells 45355 (STD code 0892) Telex: 957565 Cbja G Fax: (0892) 34905
Man Dir: David Costello; *Editorial:* Anne Cree; *Sales:* Richard Sams; *Publicity:* Rosemary Costello
Associate Companies: Weald UK Ltd, Weald Europe Book Marketing Consultants (at above address)
Subjects: Modern & Social History, Special Education, Nursing, Antiques, Craft
1985: 8 titles *Founded:* 1975
ISBN Publisher's Prefix: 0-7104

Cotman House, an imprint of Jarrold Colour Publications (qv)

Cotmancolor, an imprint of Jarrold Colour Publications (qv)

Council for British Archaeology, 112 Kennington Rd, London SE11 6RE Tel: (01) 582 0494
Chief Executive: Dr Henry F Cleere; *Managing Editor, Sales:* Marie Puttick
Subjects: Archaeology (British, some European)
Founded: 1944
ISBN Publisher's Prefixes: 0-900312, 0-906780

Council for Educational Technology, 3 Devonshire St, London W1N 2BA Tel: (01) 636 4186
Dir: Richard Fothergill; *Publications Officer:* Crispin Williams
Imprint: C E T
Subjects: Educational Technology, Microelectronics & Computing, Teacher Education, Copyright, Open Learning, Resource Organization, Educational Costing, Information Technology, Technical Developments
1986: 10 titles *Founded:* 1973
ISBN Publisher's Prefix: 0-86184

Counterpoint, an imprint of Unwin Hyman Ltd (qv)

Countryside Books, 3 Catherine Rd, Newbury, Berkshire RG14 7NA Tel: Newbury 43816 (STD code 0635)
Man Dir, Editorial, Sales, Production: Nicholas Battle; *Publicity, Rights & Permissions:* Suzanne Battle
Subsidiary Company: Local Heritage Books (at above address)
Subjects: Local History, Travel
1986: 18 titles *Founded:* 1976
ISBN Publisher's Prefix: 0-905392

The **Crafts** Council, 12 Waterloo Pl, London SW1Y 4AU Tel: (01) 930 4811
Subject: Crafts
Bookshop: Crafts Council Gallery, 12 Waterloo Pl, London SW1Y 4AU
Founded: 1971
Miscellaneous: Government-financed body promoting Britain's artist craftsmen
ISBN Publisher's Prefix: 0-903798

Crane Russak, an imprint of Taylor & Francis Ltd (qv)

Crescent, an imprint of W H Allen & Co Ltd (qv)

The **Crime** Club, an imprint of William Collins PLC (qv)

Paul H **Crompton** Ltd+*, 638 Fulham Rd, London SW6 Tel: (01) 736 2551
Publicity: Paul Crompton; *Sales:* Sean Dervan, Janet Gleeson
Subjects: Oriental Martial Arts, Health Foods, Zen, Survival, Periodical
Founded: 1968

Croner Publications Ltd, Croner House, 173 Kingston Rd, New Malden, Surrey KT3 3SS Tel: (01) 942 8966 Telex: 267778 Fax: (01) 949 8763
Man Dir: P A Sefton
Subjects: Loose-leaf information: Employment Law, Health & Safety, Export & Import, Transportation, Taxation, Business Law & Management, School Management, Catering, Health Care
1986-87: 16 titles *Founded:* 1941
Miscellaneous: Firm is member of Wolters Kluwer NV, Netherlands (qv for associate companies)
ISBN Publisher's Prefix: 0-900319

Croom Helm Ltd, see Routledge

Cross Way, an imprint of Church Society (qv)

The **Crowood Press**+, Crowood House, Ramsbury, Marlborough, Wiltshire SN8 2HE Tel: Marlborough 20320 (STD code 0672) Telex: 449703 Telser G
Publisher: John F Dennis; *Editorial Dir:* Ken Hathaway; *Production Dir:* Rob Henderson; *Sales:* Sarah Somers
Subjects: Sport, Equestrian, Mountaineering, Fishing, Gardening, Cookery, Leisure
1985: 30 titles *1986:* 45 titles *Founded:* 1982
ISBN Publisher's Prefix: 1-85223

Crucible, an imprint of Thorsons Publishing Group Ltd (qv)

Current Law Publishers Ltd, an imprint of Sweet & Maxwell Ltd (qv)

James **Currey** Ltd, 54b Thornhill Sq, Islington, London N1 1BE Tel: (01) 609 9026 Telex: 262433 ref W6327
Man Dir: James Currey; *Publicity, Rights & Permissions:* Clare Currey; *Sales, Marketing:* Keith Sambrook; *Editorial, Production:* Ingrid Crewdson
Orders to: J M Dent & Sons (Distribution) Ltd, Dunhams Lane, Letchworth, Hertfordshire SG6 1LF
Subjects: African, Caribbean, Third World Studies
1985: 10 titles *1986:* 12 titles *Founded:* 1985
ISBN Publisher's Prefix: 0-85255

Curzon Press Ltd+, 42 Gray's Inn Rd, London WC1 Tel: (01) 242 8310 Cable Add: Libri London WC1
Man Dir: J F Standish
Subjects: Oriental and African Studies
1986: 15 titles *Founded:* 1970
ISBN Publisher's Prefix: 0-7007

D P Publications Ltd, 12 Romsey Rd, Eastleigh, Hampshire SO5 4AL Tel: Eastleigh 617353 (STD code 0703)
Subjects: Finance, Law, Accountancy, Quantitative Techniques, Management, Data Processing, Computer Science, Management Information Systems, Auditing, Costing, Programming, Computer Studies, Economics, Marketing, Statistics, Personnel Management, Mathematics, Study & Revision Manuals
1987: 40 titles
ISBN Publisher's Prefix: 0-905435

Dalesman Publishing Co Ltd, Clapham, Lancaster LA2 8EB Tel: Clapham 225 (STD code 046 85)
Man Dir: D Bullock; *Editorial:* W R Mitchell; *Sales:* A N Jefferies; *Production:* D A W Joy
Subject: Northern England
1986: 19 titles *Founded:* 1939
ISBN Publisher's Prefix: 0-85206

Terence **Dalton** Ltd*, Water St, Lavenham, Sudbury, Suffolk Tel: Lavenham 247572 (STD code 0787)
Man Dir, Production, Rights & Permissions: T R Dalton; *Editorial:* R W Malster; *Sales, Publicity:* Mrs E H Whitehair
Associate Company: The Lavenham Press Ltd (at above address)
Imprints: Eastland Press, Mallard Reprints
Subjects: Maritime & Aeronautical History, East Anglian History & Interest
Founded: 1967
ISBN Publisher's Prefixes: 0-900963, 0-86138, 0-903214, 0-904623

Dance Books Ltd+, 9 Cecil Court, St Martin's Lane, London WC2N 4EZ Tel: (01) 836 2314
Man Dir, Production, Rights & Permissions: David Leonard; *Editorial, Publicity:* Richard Holland; *Sales:* John O'Brien
Subject: Dance and Human Movement
Founded: 1961
ISBN Publisher's Prefixes: 0-903102, 1-85273

The C W **Daniel** Co Ltd+, 1 Church Path, Saffron Walden, Essex CB10 1JP Tel: Saffron Walden 21909 (STD code 0799)
Man Dir: Ian Miller; *Editorial, Rights & Permissions:* Jane Miller; *Sales:* Gill Banks; *Production:* Willie Nilly; *Publicity:* Genevieve Miller
Subsidiary Companies: Health Science Press (qv); Neville Spearman Publishers
Subjects: Natural Healing, Homoeopathy, Falconry, Occult, Mysticism
Founded: 1902
ISBN Publisher's Prefix: 0-85207

Darf Publishers Ltd, 50 Hans Crescent, London SW1X 0NA Tel: (01) 581 1805 Telex: 893717 Kbc G Fax: (01) 581 8988
Chief Executive: M B Fergiani; *Editorial:* Usama Al Fergiani; *Sales:* W Ben Issa; *Production:* Dr A Mayer; *Publicity:* Gussan Al Fergiani; *Rights & Permissions:* Mrs K Burshan
Parent Company: Dar Al Fergiani, PO Box 132, Tripoli, Libya
Subsidiary Company: Dar Al Fergiani, PO Box 2382, Cairo, Egypt
Subjects: History, Travel, Language, Islam, Archaeology
1985: 46 titles *1986:* 40 titles *Founded:* 1983
ISBN Publisher's Prefix: 1-85077

Darton, Longman & Todd Ltd, 89 Lillie Rd, London SW6 1UD Tel: (01) 385 2341 Cable Add: Librabook London SW6 1UD
Man Dir: R Chopping; *Dirs:* Leslie Kay, Ms Lesley Riddle; *Publishing Consultant:* J M Todd; *Publicity & Advertising:* M Percy; *Rights & Permissions:* Ms M Reeve
Subjects: History, Philosophy, Reference, Religion, Bibles, Quality Paperbacks, Medicine, Psychology
1986: 36 titles *1987:* 44 titles *Founded:* 1959
ISBN Publisher's Prefix: 0-232

Darwen Finlayson Ltd+*, Shopwyke Hall, Chichester, West Sussex PO20 6BQ Tel: Chichester 787636 (STD code 0243)
Chairman & Man Dir: Philip Harris; *Editorial Director:* Noel H Osborne
Parent Company: Phillimore & Co Ltd (qv)
Subjects: Local History, Architectural History, Archaeology, Genealogy
ISBN Publisher's Prefix: 0-85033

Datapack Books, an imprint of E J Morten (Publishers) (qv)

David & Charles+, Brunel House, Forde Rd, Newton Abbot, Devon TQ12 4PU Tel: Newton Abbot 61121 (STD code 0626) Cable Add: Books Nabbot Telex: 42904 Books G Fax: (0626) 64463
Chairman: David St John Thomas; *Marketing Dir:* Gareth St John Thomas; *Rights Dir:* Nigel Hollis; *Editorial Dir:* Michael de Luca; *Sales Dir:* Alun Williams; *Production Dir:* Edward Allhusen
Parent Company: David & Charles (Holdings) Ltd
Subjects: Antiques, Architecture, Cookery, Countryside, Crafts, Fine Art, Gardening, Home DIY, Maritime, Military, Music, Natural History, Photography, Railways, Sport, Travel
Bookshop: David & Charles Bookshop, 36 Chiltern St, London W1M 1PM
Book Club: Readers Union Ltd
Founded: 1960
ISBN Publisher's Prefix: 0-7153

Davis-Poynter Ltd, now integrated in William Collins PLC (qv)

Dawson Publishing*, Cannon House, Folkestone, Kent CT19 5EE Tel: Folkestone 57421 (STD code 0303) Cable Add: Dawbooks Folkestone Telex: 96392
Man Dir: D A Brewer; *Publishing:* Gerald Dorman
Subjects: Music, Art, Geography, University Textbooks, Biography, History, Reference, Medicine, General & Social Science, Cartography
Bookshops: Dawson Book Service, 10-14 Macklin St, London WC2B 5NG; Cannon House, Folkestone, Kent CT19 5EE (both UK); Dawson-France SA, BP 40, F-91121 Palaiseau, France (all three general sales); Deighton, Bell & Co and Frank Hammond, both at 13 Trinity St, Cambridge CB2 1TD (antiquarian sales); Stevens and Brown Ltd, Ardon House, Mill Lane, Godalming, Surrey GU7 1HA
Founded: 1809
ISBN Publisher's Prefix: 0-7129

Deans International Publishing, an imprint of Hamlyn Publishing (qv)

Debrett's Peerage Ltd, 73-77 Britannia Rd, London SW6 2JR Tel: (01) 736 6524 Telex: 24224 Monref G
Man Dir: Robert Jarman; *Editorial:* Charles Kidd, David Williamson
Subjects: Art, Design, History, Sport, Humour, Etiquette, British Royal Family and Peerage
Founded: 1769
ISBN Publisher's Prefix: 0-905649

Delightful Books, an imprint of Ramboro Enterprises Ltd (qv)

Deloitte Haskins & Sells, Melrose House, 42 Dingwall Rd, Croydon, Surrey CR0 2EN Tel: (01) 681 5242 Telex: 8812651 Dhs Cdn
The above is the head office; the editorial office is at Hillgate House, 26 Old Bailey, London EC4M 7PL Tel: (01) 248 3913 Telex: 8955899 Fax: (01) 236 2367
Partner: Gareth Stainer; *Editorial, Rights & Permissions:* Robert McKee; *Sales:* Pandemic Ltd (Tel: (01) 278 0333); *Production:* Gerald Smith; *Publicity:* Hadfield Associates (Tel: (01) 435 0192)
Imprint: Farringdon
Subjects: Business, Finance, Management, Computing
1985: 25 titles *Founded:* 1984
ISBN Publisher's Prefix: 0-86349

Denholm House Press, see National Christian Education Council

Dennis Publishing Ltd+, 14 Rathbone Place, London W1P 1DE Tel: (01) 631 1433 Cable Add: Dennis Publishing, London Telex: 8954139 Bunch G
Man Dir: Stephen England; *Production:* Sonia Hunt
Subsidiary Company: Dennis Oneshots Ltd
Subjects: Film, TV, Biography, Leisure, General Interest, Microcomputers, Hi-Fi
Founded: 1974

J M **Dent** & Sons Ltd, 91 Clapham High St, London SW4 7TA Tel: (01) 622 9933 Cable Add: Nicobar London SW4 7TA Telex: 918066 Fax: (01) 627 3361
Chairman, Chief Executive: Lord Weidenfeld; *Man Dir:* Peter Shellard; *Editorial:* Malcolm Gerratt, Jocelyn Burton (General), Vanessa Hamilton (Juvenile), Judy Tagg (Everyman); *Sales Dir:* Ted Collins; *Rights Dir:* Bud MacLennan; *Rights (Juvenile):* Amanda Rees
Orders to: J M Dent & Sons (Distribution) Ltd, Dunhams Lane, Letchworth Hertfordshire SG6 1LF Tel: Letchworth 686241 (STD code 0462)
Parent Company: Weidenfeld (Publishers) Ltd (qv)
Subsidiary Company: J M Dent Pty Ltd, Australia (qv)
Associate Company: J M Dent (Distribution) Ltd
Imprints: Everyman Fiction, Everyman's Library, Everyman's Reference Library, Everyman's University Library, Classic Thrillers, Malaby Press
Subjects: Belles Lettres, Biography,

History, Natural History, Music, Reference, Juveniles, Paperbacks, University Textbooks, Regional, Topography, Archaeology, Cookery, Gardening, Popular Science, Sport, Photography, Military History, Literary Fiction
Founded: 1888
Miscellaneous: Publishers of *Everyman's Encyclopaedia*
ISBN Publisher's Prefix: 0-460

Design Council Books+, The Design Council, 28 Haymarket, London SW1Y 4SU Tel: (01) 839 8000 Telex: 8812963
Publisher: Roy Dodd; *Manager:* Terry Bishop; *Sales:* Bill Garrett; *Publicity, Rights:* Susan Smith
Parent Company: The Design Council (at above address)
Subjects: Design Education, Engineering Design, Design Management, Design History
Bookshops: The Design Centre Bookshop and The Design Centre Bookshop Mail Order (at above address)
Founded: 1974
ISBN Publisher's Prefix: 0-85072

André **Deutsch** Ltd, 105-106 Great Russell St, London WC1B 3LJ Tel: (01) 580 2746 Cable Add: Adlib, London WC1 Telex: 261026 Adlib G Fax: (01) 631 3253
Joint Chairmen and Man Dirs: André Deutsch, Tom Rosenthal; *Editorial Dir:* Diana Athill; *Production Dir:* Jeff Sains; *Publicity Dir, Advertising:* Nicky Mayhew; *Rights & Permissions Dir:* Caroline Knox; *Sales Dir:* Anselm Robinson
Imprint: Adlib Paperbacks
Subjects: General Fiction, Belles Lettres, Poetry, Biography, History, Music, Art, Philosophy, Reference, Juveniles, Humour, Politics, Current Events, Travel, Cookery, Photography
Founded: 1951
ISBN Publisher's Prefix: 0-233

Diadem Books†, 3a De Montfort St, Leicester LE1 7HD Tel: Leicester 543579 (STD code 0533) Telex: 341401 Jjint G
Chief Executive, Rights & Permissions: Ken Vickers; *Editorial:* Ken Wilson; *Sales:* Mike Johnson
Imprint: Cordee
Subjects: Mountain Sports, Outdoor Recreation, Travel
1985: 6 titles *1986:* 8 titles *Founded:* 1973
ISBN Publisher's Prefixes: 0-906371 (Diadem), 0-904405 (Cordee)

Diagram Visual Information Ltd+, 195 Kentish Town Rd, London NW5 Tel: (01) 482 3633 Telex: 21120 ref 2978
Dir: Bruce Robertson
Subjects: Reference, Juveniles, Sport, Leisure Activities, Popular Health, Palaeontology, Art

Dial, an imprint of Doubleday & Co Inc (qv)

Keith **Dickson**, an imprint of Dickson Price Publishers Ltd (qv)

Dickson Price Publishers Ltd, Hawthorn House, Bowdell Lane, Brookland, Kent TN29 9RW Tel: Brookland 626 (STD code 067 94)
Man Dir, Editorial, Rights & Permissions: K E Dickson; *Production:* D S Wanstall
Imprints: Keith Dickson, Norman Price, Quartermaine House, Huddlesford
Subjects: Electronics, Computing, Field Sports
Founded: 1980
ISBN Publisher's Prefixes: 0-907266, 0-85380

Dinosaur Publications Ltd+*, 8 Grafton St, London W1X 3LA Tel: (01) 493 7070 Cable Add: Herakles London Telex: 25611
Publishing Dir: Rosemary Sandberg; *Consultant Editor:* Althea Braithwaite
Parent Company: William Collins PLC (qv)
Subjects: Juveniles, Educational Materials, Sponsored Books
Founded: 1968
ISBN Publisher's Prefix: 0-85122

Director Books, an imprint of Fitzwilliam Publishing (qv)

Discoverers, an imprint of Moonlight Publishing Ltd (qv)

Dennis **Dobson** (Dobson Books Ltd)*, Brancepeth Castle, Durham DH7 8DF Tel: (0385) 780628
Man Dir: Margaret Dobson
Subjects: General Fiction, Belles Lettres, Poetry, Biography, History, Music, Art, Theatre, Juveniles, General & Social Science, Economics, Political Science
ISBN Publisher's Prefix: 0-234

Dod's Parliamentary Companion Ltd*, Elm Cottage, Chilsham Lane, Herstmonceux, Hailsham, East Sussex BN27 4QQ Tel: Herstmonceux 832250 (STD code 0323)
Editor: J B Smith
Subject: Parliamentary Reference (UK and European)
Founded: 1832
ISBN Publisher's Prefix: 0-905702

Dolphin, an imprint of Doubleday & Co Inc (qv)

John **Donald** Publishers Ltd, 138 Stephen St, Edinburgh EH3 5AA
Publishing Dir: J B Tuckwell; *Sales Dir:* J G Angus; *Production Dir:* D L Morrison
Subjects: Academic, Scottish, Sport
1985: 25 titles *Founded:* 1973
ISBN Publisher's Prefix: 0-85976

Dorling Kindersley Ltd+, 9 Henrietta St, Covent Garden, London WC2E 8PS Tel: (01) 836 5411 Telex: 8954527 Deekay G Fax: (01) 836 7570
Man Dirs: Christopher Dorling, Peter Kindersley; *Sales and Marketing Dir:* Mike Strong; *Foreign Sales:* Caroline Oakes, Ruth Sandys; *Editorial:* Christopher Davis; *Design:* Stuart Jackman; *Production:* Lorraine Baird
Orders to: Victor Gollancz Ltd, 14 Henrietta St, Covent Garden, London WC2 Tel: (01) 836 2006
Subjects: Illustrated Reference Books for the International Market on Photography, Gardening, Cookery, Crafts, Family Health, Child Care, History, Computing, Sport, DIY, Leisure
Founded: 1974
ISBN Publisher's Prefix: 0-86318

Doubleday & Co Inc+, 100 Wigmore St, London W1H 9DR Tel: (01) 935 1269 Telex: 264676
Editorial, Rights & Permissions: Marianne Velmans
Orders to: PBD Ltd, St Leonard's House, West Malling, Kent ME19 6PE Tel: West Malling 841149 (STD code 0732)
Parent Company: Doubleday & Co, Inc, 245 Park Ave, New York, NY 10167, USA. Ultimate parent company Verlagsgruppe Bertelsmann GmbH, Federal Republic of Germany (qv)
Associate Company: Doubleday Canada Ltd, 105 Bond St, Toronto 2, Ontario, Canada
Imprints: Anchor, Dial, Dolphin, Image
Subjects: General
Book Clubs: Book Club Associates
Founded: 1897
ISBN Publisher's Prefix: 0-385

UNITED KINGDOM 439

Downlander Publishing, 88 Oxendean Gardens, Lower Willingdon, Eastbourne, East Sussex BN22 0RS Tel: Eastbourne 505814 (STD code 0323)
Directing Editor: Derek Bourne-Jones; *Deputy Editor:* Hilary Bourne-Jones
Associate Company: Gardiner Graphics Ltd, Commercial Rd, Eastbourne, East Sussex
Subject: Poetry (including *The Long Man* series)
1985: 6 titles *1986:* 7 titles *Founded:* 1978
ISBN Publisher's Prefix: 0-906369

Down Memory Lane, an imprint of Milestone Publications (qv)

Dragon Books, an imprint of William Collins PLC (qv)

Dragon's World Ltd, High St, Limpsfield, Surrey RH8 0DY Tel: Oxted 715044 (STD code 0883) Telex: 95631 Dragon G Fax: (0883) 716032
Dir, Publisher, Sales, Rights & Permissions: H A Schaafsma; *Production:* 19 Hereford Sq, London SW7 4TS (Tel: (01) 244 8441)
Orders to: J M Dent & Sons (Distribution) Ltd, Dunhams Lane, Letchworth, Hertfordshire SG6 1LF Tel: Letchworth 686241 (STD code 0462)
Imprint: Paper Tiger Books
Subjects: Illustrated Science Fiction, Fable, Fantasy, Art, Children's, Natural History, How-to
Founded: 1976
ISBN Publisher's Prefixes: 0-905895, 0-185028

Richard **Drew** Publishing Ltd+, 6 Clairmont Gardens, Glasgow G3 7LW Tel: (041) 333 9341 Telex: 777308
Rights & Trade Enquiries: Richard Drew
Subjects: Leisure, General Interest, Fiction, Humour, Sport, Languages, Children's
1985: 45 titles
ISBN Publisher's Prefixes: 0-86267, 0-904002

Dryad Press Ltd+, 8 Cavendish Sq, London W1M 0AJ Tel: (01) 631 3707 Cable Add: Batsfordia London W1
Man Dir: William Waller; *Editorial Dir:* Ruth Taylor; *Publicity Controller:* Deborah Gainsford; *Production Dir:* Roger Huggins; *Sales Manager:* Stephen Mobsby
Parent Company: B T Batsford Ltd (qv)
Subjects: Art, Crafts, Hobbies, Education, Textbooks, Conservation
1985: 25 titles *1986:* 40 titles *Founded:* 1983
ISBN Publisher's Prefix: 0-8521

Gerald **Duckworth** & Co Ltd+, The Old Piano Factory, 43 Gloucester Crescent, London NW1 7DY Tel: (01) 485 3484 Cable Add: Platypus London NW1
Man Dir: Colin Haycraft; *Sales Dir:* David Lines; *Publicity, Advertising, Rights & Permissions:* Colin Haycraft
Subjects: Fiction, General, Academic, Computer Software
Founded: 1898
ISBN Publisher's Prefix: 0-7156

G E **Duffield**, an imprint of Appleford Publishing Group (qv)

Duke University Press, see Academic and University Publishers Group

Dun & Bradstreet Ltd, PO Box 17, 26-32 Clifton St, London EC2P 2LY Tel: (01) 377 4377 Cable Add: Dunbrad London Telex: 886697
Man Dir: K H Williams; *Editorial, Production:* J Hemmings; *Sales:* S Dunn; *Publicity:* A Priestley
Parent Company: Dun & Bradstreet

Corporation, 299 Park Ave, New York, NY 10017, USA
Branch Offs: Birmingham, Glasgow, Leeds, Manchester, Newcastle, Nottingham, Romford, Southampton, Sutton
Subjects: Business Information, Marketing Guides
Founded: 1919
ISBN Publisher's Prefix: 0-900625

Martin **Dunitz** Ltd+*, 154 Camden High St, London NW1 0NE Tel: (01) 482 2202 Telex: 296307 Dunbks
Man Dir, Sales, Rights & Permissions: Martin Dunitz; *Editorial:* Mary Banks, Sally Jones; *Production:* Peter Lord; *Publicity:* Clare Tizard
Orders to: Bookpoint Ltd, 39 Milton Trading Estate, Abingdon, Oxfordshire OX14 4TD Tel: Abingdon 835001 (STD code 0235)
Subjects: Medical, Nursing, Dental, Popular Health & Diet
1985: 10 titles *1986:* 14 titles *Founded:* 1978
ISBN Publisher's Prefix: 0-906348

The **Dunrod** Press, 8 Brown's Rd, Newtownabbey, Belfast BT36 8RN Tel: Glengormley 2362 (STD code 023 13)
General Manager: Ken Lindsay; *Editorial, Rights & Permissions:* Robert Witherspoon; *Sales:* Hugh Hall; *Production:* James Crawford; *Publicity:* John Graham
Associate Company: The Dunrod Press (Ireland), Dublin, Republic of Ireland
Subjects: History, Current Affairs, General
1985: 4 titles *1986:* 3 titles *Founded:* 1979
ISBN Publisher's Prefix: 0-86202

Dyllansow Truran, Trewolsta, Trewirgie, Redruth, Kernow, Cornwall TR15 2TB Tel: Redruth 216796 (STD code 0209)
Chief Executive, Editorial, Rights & Permissions: Len Truran; *Sales:* Joan Truran
Imprint: Truran
Subjects: Cornish Culture (all aspects), General Celtic
1985: 26 titles *Founded:* 1981
ISBN Publisher's Prefixes: 0-907566, 0-9506431, 1-85022

E I T B Publications+, 54 Clarendon Rd, Watford, Hertfordshire WD1 1LB Tel: Watford 38441 (STD code 0923) Fax: (0923) 43025
Dir: W G Friggens; *Publishing, Marketing Manager:* Mrs M J Walsham
Orders to: (UK) PO Box 75, Stockport, Cheshire SK4 1PH Tel: (061) 480 5285; (Overseas) at above main address
Subject: Engineering training
1985: 50 titles *1986:* 50 titles *Founded:* 1965
ISBN Publisher's Prefix: 0-85083

E P Publishing Ltd, an imprint of A & C Black (Publishers) Ltd (qv)

E S A Creative Learning Ltd, now part of E J Arnold & Son Ltd (qv)

E S C Publishing Ltd, Mill St, Oxford OX2 0JU Tel: Oxford 249248 (STD code 0865) Telex: 83147 Viaor G Fax: (0865) 726753
Dir: Nicholas Gingell; *Publicity Manager:* Jane Youens
Subjects: Intellectual Property (Copyright, Patents and Trademarks) and Competition Law, Taxation, International Law, Industrial Relations, Banking Law
1986: 6 titles *1987:* 6 titles *Founded:* 1978
ISBN Publisher's Prefix: 0-906214

E S M (Educational Software for Microcomputers), an imprint of Living & Learning (Cambridge) Ltd (qv)

East-West Publications (UK) Ltd, Newton Works, 27/29 Macklin St, London WC2B 5LX Tel: (01) 831 6767
Chairman: L W Carp; *Man Dir:* B G Thompson
Associate Company: Elron Press Ltd (qv)
Imprint: Gallery Children's Books
Subjects: Far & Middle East Culture & Religion, Children's & Adults Reference Books, Children's Books, Children's Music, Music
ISBN Publisher's Prefix: 0-85692

Eastland Press, an imprint of Terence Dalton Ltd (qv)

Ebury Press, Colquhoun House, 27/37 Broadwick St, London W1V 1FR Tel: (01) 439 7144 Cable Add: Shanmag London W1 Telex: 263879 Fax: (01) 439 0062
Man Dir: Terry Mansfield; *Editorial Dir:* Yvonne McFarlane; *Publisher:* Charles Merullo; *UK Sales Manager:* Mike Beattie; *Rights:* Sheila Christie; *Publicity:* Ondine Upton
Orders to: WHS Distributors, St John's House, East St, Leicester LE1 6NE
Parent Company: National Magazine Co Ltd, 72 Broadwick St, London W1V 2BP
Subjects: General Non-fiction, Reference
ISBN Publisher's Prefix: 0-85223

The **Economist**, 25 St James's St, London SW1A 1HG Tel: (01) 839 7000 Cable Add: Mistecon Ldn Telex: 919555
Man Dir: David Gordon; *Rights & Permissions:* David McGill
Subsidiary Companies: Economist Publications Ltd (UK); The Economist Newspaper Inc, 10 Rockefeller Plaza, NY 10020, USA
Branch Off: 10 Rockefeller Plaza, New York, NY 10020, USA
Subjects: Economic Reference Books, Diaries, Educational Materials, Newsletters
Founded: 1843
ISBN Publisher's Prefix: 0-85058

Eddison Sadd Editions Ltd+, 2 Kendall Pl, London W1H 3AH Tel: (01) 486 3621 Telex: 265871 Monref G ref WXX019
Dirs: Ian N Jackson, Nicholas J Eddison, Graham D Sadd, Ros Edwards
Parent Company: Eddison Sadd & Partners Ltd, 2 Kendall Pl, London W1H 3AH
Subsidiary Company: The London Software Studio — Computer Software Publishers, 2 Kendall Pl, London W1H 3AH
Subjects: Illustrated Non-fiction (packagers for the international co-edition market)
1985: 4 titles *1986:* 6 titles *Founded:* 1982

Edinburgh University Press+*, 22 George Sq, Edinburgh EH8 9LF Tel: (031) 667 1011 Cable Add: Edinpress Telex: 727442
Man Dir, Rights & Permissions: A R Turnbull; *Assistant Secretary & Production Manager:* J McI Davidson
Subjects: Belles Lettres, Poetry, Biography, History, Music, Art, Philosophy, Religion, Textbooks, Reference, Medicine, Psychology, General & Social Science
Founded: 1948
ISBN Publisher's Prefix: 0-85224

Edinburgh University Student Publications Board*, 48 Pleasance, Edinburgh EH8 9TJ Tel: (031) 558 1117
Administration: Mary Gibson; *Sales, Publicity, Rights & Permissions:* Pamela Smith; *Production:* Neville Moir
Imprint: Polygon Books
Subjects: Politics, Sociology, Fiction, Poetry, History, all with special regard to Scotland
ISBN Publisher's Prefix: 0-948275

Educational Explorers, 11 Crown St, Reading, Berkshire RG1 2TQ Tel: Reading 873103 (STD code 0734)
Chairman: Dr Caleb Gattegno; *Man Dir:* M J Hollyfield
Parent Company: Educational Solutions (UK) Ltd of Reading
Associate Companies: Cuisenaire Co, Educational Explorers Film Co (both at above address); Educational Solutions Inc, 95 University Pl, New York, NY 10003-4555, USA
Subjects: Primary & Secondary Textbooks and Teachers Guides, Mathematics, Reading, Foreign Languages, Educational Psychology
ISBN Publisher's Prefix: 0-85225

Educational Productions Ltd, see E P Publishing Ltd

Egmont, an imprint of World International Publishing Ltd (qv)

Element Books Ltd+, Grosvenor Court, 22 Parson's Pool, Shaftesbury, Dorset Tel: Shaftesbury 51448 (STD code 0747)
Man Dir, Editorial Dir: Michael Mann; *Production Dir, Rights & Permissions:* Annie Walton; *Broadcast Books Publisher:* Laura Sanderson; *Sales Manager:* Michael Froomberg; *Promotions Manager:* Alison Webb
Subsidiary Company: Broadcast Books Ltd (at above address)
Imprints: Broadcast Books, Nadder Books
Subjects: Philosophy, Mysticism, Religion, Psychology, Astrology, Complementary Medicine, Biography, Humour, General Non-fiction, Vocational Training, Music
1985: 13 titles *1986:* 20 titles *Founded:* 1978
ISBN Publisher's Prefixes: 0-906540, 1-85230

Edward **Elgar** Publishing Ltd+, Middleton House, Upleadon, Gloucestershire GL18 1EQ Tel: Newent 820595 (STD code 0531) Telex: 858001 Gower G
Man Dir, Publisher, Rights & Permissions: Edward Elgar; *Marketing Dir:* Christopher Simpson; *Production:* Melissa Tulley; *Publicity:* Tim Naylor
Orders to: Wildwood House Ltd, Gower House, Croft Rd, Aldershot, Hampshire GU11 3HR
Parent Company: Gower Publishing Co Ltd (qv)
Subjects: Economics, Political Science, Sociology, Textbooks, Reference & Research
1987-88: 35 titles *Founded:* 1986
ISBN Publisher's Prefix: 1-85278

Elliot Right Way Books+, Kingswood Bldgs, Lower Kingswood, Tadworth, Surrey KT20 6TD Tel: Mogador 832202 (STD code 0737)
Sales Dir: A Clive Elliot; *Production, Publicity Dir:* Malcolm G Elliot
Imprints: Paperfronts, Right Way Books
Subjects: How-to, Reference, Juveniles, Low-priced Paperbacks, Sport, Technical, Education
1986: 12 titles *1987:* 11 titles *Founded:* 1945
ISBN Publisher's Prefix: 0-7160

Aidan **Ellis** Publishing Ltd, Cobb House, Nuffield, Henley-on-Thames, Oxfordshire RG9 5RT Tel: Nettlebed 641496 (STD code 0491) Telex: 825751 J M Dent G
Man Dir: Aidan Ellis
Orders to: J M Dent & Sons (Distribution) Ltd, Dunhams Lane, Letchworth Hertfordshire SG6 1LF Tel: Letchworth 686241 (STD code 0462)
Subjects: Fiction, General, Art, Belles Lettres

UNITED KINGDOM 441

1985: 10 titles *1986:* 12 titles *Founded:* 1971
ISBN Publisher's Prefix: 0-85628

Elm Publications, Seaton House, Kings Ripton, Cambridgeshire PE17 2NJ Tel: Kings Ripton 238 (STD code 048 73)
Man Dir: Sheila Ritchie; *Editorial, Rights & Permissions:* Michael Ryan; *Sales, Publicity:* Sheila Hillyer; *Production:* Eileen Morgan
Subjects: Management, Business & Professional Studies, Educational, Library Reference, Periodicals
1987: 16 titles *1988:* 28 titles *Founded:* 1977
ISBN Publisher's Prefix: 0-946139

Elm Tree Books Ltd, see Hamish Hamilton Ltd

Elron Press Ltd, Newton Works, 27-29 Macklin St, London WC2B 5LX Tel: (01) 831 6767
Dirs: B G Thompson (USA), L W Carp (Dutch)
Parent Company: East-West Holdings Ltd (at above address)
Associate Company: East-West Publications (UK) Ltd (qv)
Subjects: General Non-fiction, Illustrated Adult Reference, Children's Books
Miscellaneous: Provides editorial, design and production services for other publishers
ISBN Publisher's Prefix: 0-904499

Elsevier Applied Science Publishers+, Crown House, Linton Rd, Barking, Essex IG11 8JU Tel: (01) 594 7272 Cable Add: Elsbark Barking Telex: 896950 Fax: (01) 594 5942
Man Dir: Hans Gieskes; *Publishers, Rights & Permissions:* Robert A Lomax, Norman Pasking; *Production:* Alan Chesterton; *UK Sales:* J. Kumar Patel; *Marketing Manager:* Andrew Cullum
Parent Company: Elsevier Science Publishers BV, Netherlands (qv)
Subjects: Agriculture, Architectural Science, Building, Civil Engineering, Bakery, Materials Science, Chemistry, Chemical Engineering, Biotechnology, Biosciences, Medical Sciences, Mechanical Engineering, Environmental Science, Food Technology, Petroleum Technology, Plastics & Rubber, Dictionaries, Periodicals
1986: 90 titles *Founded:* 1971
ISBN Publisher's Prefix: 0-85334

Elvendon Press+, The Old Surgery, High St, Goring-on-Thames, Reading, Berkshire RG8 9AW Tel: Goring-on-Thames 873003 (STD code 0491) Telex: 849021 Fran G
Man Dir: Ray Hurst; *Editorial, Sales, Production, Publicity:* Bernice Hurst; *Rights & Permissions:* Elisabeth Wilson
Subjects: General Non-fiction, Nutrition, Cookery, Handbooks, Business, Current Affairs
Founded: 1978
ISBN Publisher's Prefix: 0-906552

Encyclopaedia Britannica International Ltd, Carew House, Station Approach, Wallington, Surrey SM6 0DA Tel: (01) 669 4355 Telex: 23866 Fax: (01) 773 3631
Man Dir: Joe D Adams; *Advertising Manager:* M Cranch; *Production, Publicity, Rights & Permissions:* Robin Sales
Parent Company: Encyclopaedia Britannica Inc, Britannica Centre, 310 South Michigan Ave, Chicago, Ill 60604, USA
Associate Companies: Encyclopaedia Britannica (Australia) Inc, Australia (qv); Encyclopaedia Britannica Publications Ltd, 175 Holiday Inn Dr, Cambridge, Ontario N3C 3N4, Canada; Encyclopaedia Britannica, Federal Republic of Germany (qv); Korea Britannica Corporation, Republic of Korea (qv); Merriam-Webster Inc, 47 Federal St, Springfield, Mass 01101, USA
Subject: Reference
ISBN Publisher's Prefix: 0-85229

Energy Publications, see Cambridge Information and Research Services Ltd

Epworth Press, Room 195, 1 Central Bldgs, Westminster, London SW1H 9NR Tel: (01) 222 8010 ext 234
Editorial, Rights & Permissions: Rev John Stacey; *Sales:* SCM Press Ltd (qv); *Publicity:* Irena Czerniawska, SCM Press Ltd (qv)
Orders to: SCM Press Ltd, 26-30 Tottenham Rd, London N1 4BZ
Parent Body: The Methodist Conference
Subjects: Biblical, Theology
1987: 12 titles
ISBN Publisher's Prefix: 0-7162

Equation, Denington Estate, Wellingborough, Northamptonshire NN8 2RQ Tel: Wellingborough 76031 (STD code 0933) Cable Add: Thorgroup Wellingborough Telex: 311072 Thopub G Fax: (0933) 72800
Man Dir: David Young; *Production Dir:* David Palmer; *Editorial Dir:* Michael Cox; *Marketing and Sales Dir:* Julian Rivers; *Sales Managers:* John Marsh (Group), Ray Potts (Export); *Rights & Permissions:* Marjorie Nelson; *Publicity Manager:* Judith Smallwood; *Marketing Manager:* Vivienne Wordley
Parent Company: Thorsons Publishing Group Ltd (qv)
Subjects: Antiques & Collecting, Biography & Autobiography, Cinema & Video, Cookery, Crime, Crafts & Hobbies, Fashion & Costume, Gardening, Health & Beauty, Humour, Literature, Music, Natural History, Sports, Theatre, Travel
1987: 9 titles *Founded:* 1987
ISBN Publisher's Prefix: 1-85336

Equinox (Oxford) Ltd, Littlegate House, St Ebbe's St, Oxford OX1 1SQ Tel: Oxford 251499 (STD code 0865) Telex: 83308 Fax: (0865) 251959
Chairman: George Riches; *Man Dir:* Ben Lenthall; *Editorial Dirs:* Graham Bateman, Lawrence Clarke; *Marketing Dir:* David Halford; *Production Dir:* Clive Sparling
Parent Company: Musterlin Group PLC (at above address)
Associate Companies: Canongate Publishing Ltd, Phaidon Press Ltd (qqv)
Subjects: Colour-illustrated series and multi-volume encyclopaedias for the co-editions market or publication under licence

Lawrence **Erlbaum** Associates Ltd*, 27 Palmeira Mansions, Church Rd, Hove, East Sussex BN3 2FA
Man Dir: M F Forster; *Dir:* L Erlbaum; *Managing Editor:* R Perry; *Publicity:* A Browne
Orders to: International Book Distributors Ltd, 66 Wood Lane End, Hemel Hempstead, Hertfordshire HP2 4RG Tel: Hemel Hempstead 58531 (STD code 0442)
Associate Company: Lawrence Erlbaum Associates Inc, 365 Broadway, Hillsdale, NJ 07642, USA
Subjects: Behavioural Science and Related Disciplines
Founded: (UK) 1980
ISBN Publisher's Prefixes: 0-89859, 0-86377

Escape, an imprint of Titan Books Ltd (qv)

Eurobook Ltd+*, 49 Uxbridge Rd, London W5 5SA Tel: (01) 840 4411 Cable Add: Beurok London W5 Telex: 934610
Man Dir, Rights & Permissions: Peter S Lowe; *Editor:* Ruth Spriggs; *Sales, Publicity & Advertising:* Kim P Richardson; *Production:* Jayne Ferdinand
Imprint: Peter Lowe
Subjects: Adult Non-fiction and Juvenile Fiction & Non-fiction (international co-productions)
Founded: 1968
ISBN Publisher's Prefix: 0-85654

Eurobooks, an imprint of Evangelical Press and Services Ltd (qv)

Euromonitor Publications Ltd+, 87-88 Turnmill St, London EC1M 5QU Tel: (01) 251 8024 Telex: 21120 Monref G 2281
Man Dir, Editorial: Robert Senior; *Marketing Dir:* Trevor Fenwick
Subjects: Business Information, Marketing, Statistical Reference, Trade Directories & Yearbooks
1986: 150 titles *Founded:* 1972
ISBN Publisher's Prefixes: 0-903706, 0-86338

Europa Publications Ltd, 18 Bedford Sq, London WC1B 3JN Tel: (01) 580 8236 Cable Add: Europub London WC1 Telex: 21540
Chairman: C H Martin, OBE; *Man Dir:* P A McGinley; *Editorial:* Alan Oliver; *Business Manager:* J P Desmond; *Sales, Publicity & Advertising:* Peter Jackson
Associate Company: Ashford Press Publishing (qv)
Subjects: Reference, History, International Affairs
1987: 11 titles *Founded:* 1928
ISBN Publisher's Prefix: 0-905118

European Schoolbooks Ltd*, Croft St, Cheltenham, Gloucestershire GL53 0HX Tel: Cheltenham 45252 (STD code 0242) Cable Add: Eurobooks, Cheltenham
Man Dir: F A Preiss; *Sales Manager:* D Young
Imprint: European Schoolbooks Publishing Ltd
Subjects: Educational, Modern Languages
ISBN Publisher's Prefix: 0-85048

Eurospan Ltd, 3 Henrietta St, London WC2E 8LU Tel: (01) 240 0856 Cable Add: Eurospan London Fax: (01) 379 0609
Chairman: Peter Geelan; *Man Dir:* Danny Maher; *Marketing Dir:* Michael Geelan
Subjects: Social Sciences, Library Science, Humanities, Reference
Founded: 1964
Miscellaneous: Group includes AMS Press, American Library Association, American Society for Information Science, Auburn House Publishing Co, Brunner/Mazel Inc, Da Capo Press, Eden Press, Fordham University Press, Greenwood Press, Harlan Davidson, Haworth Press, Hamilton Press, Harrington Park Press, Human Sciences Press, JAI Press, Jason Aronson, Kent State University Press, Knowledge Industry Publications, Lynne Rienner Publishers, Madison Books, Mayfield Publishing Co, Meckler Publishing Co, Neal-Schuman Publishing Inc, Oelgeschlager Gunn & Hain Inc Publishers, Ohio State University Press, Porcupine Press, Praeger Publishers, The Psychohistory Press, Quorum Books, Rutgers University Press, Scott-Foresman & Co, M E Sharpe Inc Publishers, Smithsonian Institution Press, South-Western Publishing Co, Teachers' College Press, Thomas Register of American Manufacturers, University of Alabama Press, University of Arizona Press, University of Georgia Press, University Press of Kansas, University of

Massachusetts, University of Mississippi Press, University of Oklahoma, University of Utah Press, University Press of America, Wordware Publishing

Evangelical Press and Services Ltd, 16-18 High St, Welwyn, Hertfordshire AL6 9EQ Tel: Welwyn 7025 (STD code 043 871) Telex: 826542
General Manager: J H Rubens
Subsidiary Company: Welwyn Books Ltd
Imprints: Ediciones Peregrino, Eurobooks
Subjects: Christian Books
Founded: 1967
ISBN Publisher's Prefix: 0-85234

Evans Brothers Ltd, 2A Portman Mansions, Chiltern St, London W1M 1LE Tel: (01) 935 7160 Cable Add: Byronitic London W1 Telex: 8811713 Evbook G
Chairman: L J Browning; *Man Dir:* S T Pawley; *Dirs:* F J Austin; *Rights & Permissions:* Margaret Hayden
Associate Company: Evans Brothers (Nigeria Publishers) Ltd, Nigeria (qv)
Subsidiary Company: Evans Brothers (Africa) Ltd (at above London address)
Subjects: English as a second language, Pre-school, Primary & Secondary Textbooks, Teacher Training for Africa
Founded: 1905
ISBN Publisher's Prefix: 0-237

Everyman Fiction, an imprint of J M Dent & Sons Ltd (qv)

Everyman's Library, Reference Library and University Library, imprints of J M Dent & Sons Ltd (qv)

Exley Publications Ltd+, 16 Chalk Hill, Watford, Hertfordshire WD1 4BN Tel: Watford 50505 (STD code 0923) Telex: 261234 ref H/5753L
Man Dir: Richard Exley; *Editorial Dir:* Helen Exley
Subjects: Anthologies, Humour, Gift Books, General Trade Books
1987: 15 titles *Founded:* 1976
ISBN Publisher's Prefixes: 0-905521, 1-85015

Express Logic Ltd, PO Box 6, Hereford HR4 0UN Tel: Hereford 274516 (STD code 0432)
Man Dir: C B Tannatt Nash; *Sales, Production Manager:* Mrs M R Bishop
Parent Company: Business Management Promotions Ltd
Subjects: General Literature
Founded: 1970
ISBN Publisher's Prefix: 0-904464

Eyre & Spottiswoode (Publishers) Ltd, North Way, Andover, Hampshire SP10 5BE Tel: Andover 332424 (STD code 0264) Cable Add: APT Andover Telex: Abpand G 47214 Fax: (0264) 64418
Chairman: David Blunt; *Man Dir:* Austin Holder; *Marketing Dir:* John Potter
Parent Company: Octopus Publishing Group PLC, Michelin House, 81 Fulham Rd, London SW3 6RB. Ultimate parent company Reed International PLC, Reed House, 83 Piccadilly, London W1A 1EJ
Subjects: Bibles, Book of Common Prayer, Summa Theologiae, Religion
Founded: 1769
ISBN Publisher's Prefix: 0-413

Eyre Methuen Ltd, now Methuen London Ltd (qv)

Faber & Faber Ltd, 3 Queen Sq, London WC1N 3AU Tel: (01) 278 6881 Cable Add: Fabbaf London WC1 Telex: 299633 Faber G
Man Dir: Matthew Evans; *Sales & Marketing Dir:* Martin Cowell; *Publicity, Promotions:* Joanna Mackle; *Senior Rights Manager:* Virginia Bonham Carter
Branch Off: Faber & Faber Inc, 39 Thompson St, Winchester, MA 01890, USA
Subjects: General Fiction, Belles Lettres, Poetry, Biography, History, How-to, Music, Art, Philosophy, Religion, Juveniles, Paperbacks, Medicine, Psychology, Social Science, University & Secondary Textbooks
Founded: 1929
ISBN Publisher's Prefix: 0-571

Facts on File Publications Ltd+, Collins St, Oxford OX4 1XJ Tel: Oxford 728349 (STD code 0865) Telex: 83147 Fax: (0865) 726753
Chief Executive, Sales: Alan Goodworth; *Editorial:* John Thornton; *Production:* Olivia McKean; *Publicity:* Charlotte Baker; *Rights & Permissions:* Paula Litzky
Orders to: Bookpoint Ltd, 39 Milton Trading Estate, Abingdon, Oxfordshire OX14 4TD
Parent Company: Facts on File Inc, 460 Park Ave South, New York, NY 10016, USA
Associate Company: CCH Editions Ltd, Telford Rd, Bicester, Oxfordshire
Subjects: Reference, Business, History, Culture, Natural History, Medical, Military, The Arts, Maps & Atlases, Music, Sport, General Interest
1985: 80 titles *1986:* 75 titles *Founded:* 1984
ISBN Publisher's Prefixes: 0-948894, 0-8160, 0-87196

Falcon Books, an imprint of Kingsway Publications (qv)

Falmer Press, an imprint of Taylor & Francis Ltd (qv)

Family Law, an imprint of Jordan & Sons Ltd (qv)

Farming Press, Fenton House, Wharfedale Rd, Ipswich, Suffolk IP1 4LG Tel: Ipswich 43011 (STD code 0473) Telex: 987703 Chacom G
Chairman: D Barton; *Books Manager:* R G Smith
Parent Company: Farming Press Group. Ultimate holding company United Newspapers, 23-27 Tudor St, London EC4Y 0HR
Subjects: Agriculture, Animal Care, Countryside Humour
1985: 5 titles *1986:* 6 titles
ISBN Publisher's Prefix: 0-85236

Farringdon, an imprint of Deloitte Haskins & Sells (qv)

Fernhurst Books, 53 High St, Steyning, West Sussex Tel: Steyning 816015 (STD code 0903)
Chief Executive: Tim Davison
Orders to: George Philip Services, Arndale Rd, Wick, Littlehampton, West Sussex
Subject: Sport
1985: 5 titles *1986:* 9 titles *Founded:* 1972
ISBN Publisher's Prefix: 0-906754

Sadie **Fields** Productions Ltd+, 8 Pembridge Studios, 27A Pembridge Villas, London W11 3EP Tel: (01) 221 3355 Telex: 262284 ref 1255 Fax: (01) 229 9651
Dirs: Sheri Safran, David Fielder
Subjects: Novelty, Pop-up, board and picture books for children, age 0-12 years (international co-productions)
1985: 28 titles *1986:* 27 titles *Founded:* 1983

Filmscan/Lingual House, Linguaphone Institute Ltd, Beavor Lane, London W6 9AR Tel: (01) 748 4546 Telex: 266181 Lingua G
Chairman: Timothy Sherwen; *Group Man Dir:* Douglas Davidson; *Publishing Manager:* Brenda Satriawan; *Market Development Manager:* David Phillips
Subsidiary Company: Filmscan Japan Ltd, Dorumi Yoyogi 1107, 1-57-2 Yoyogi, Shibuya-ku, Tokyo, Japan
Subject: Language Teaching Materials
1987-88: 50 titles *Founded:* 1982
ISBN Publisher's Prefix: 0-86270

The **Financial Times** Business Information Ltd*, Greystroke Pl, Fetter Lane, London EC4A 1ND Tel: (01) 405 6969 Telex: 883694 Icldn G
Man Dir: John McLachlan; *Marketing Manager:* John Greig; *Diary Dir:* John Suffolk
Subjects: Investment and Financial Planning Guides, Specialized Banking Studies, Business Periodicals
ISBN Publisher's Prefix: 0-902101

Financial Training Publications Ltd, Holland House, 140-144 Freston Road, London W10 6TR Tel: (01) 229 9531 Fax: (01) 727 9964
Man Dir: Alistair MacQueen; *Editorial Dir:* Heather Saward; *Marketing, Sales:* Jonathan Harris
Subjects: Law, Accountancy, Banking, Marketing
1986: 100 titles *Founded:* 1976
Miscellaneous: Firm is a member of Wolters Kluwer NV, Netherlands (qv for associate companies)
ISBN Publisher's Prefixes: 0-906322, 1-85185

The **Findhorn** Press, The Park, Findhorn, Forres, Morayshire IV36 0TZ Tel: Findhorn 30582 (STD code 0309)
Editorial, Rights & Permissions: Sandra Kramer; *Sales, Promotion:* Rosemary Turnbull
Parent Company: Findhorn Foundation (at above address)
Subjects: Spiritual, Biography, Fiction, Conservation, Life styles, Personal Growth, Gardening, Cookery, Philosophy, New Age, Ecology
Bookshop: Phoenix Bookshop (at above address)
1986: 2 titles *1987:* 1 title *Founded:* 1965
ISBN Publisher's Prefixes: 0-905249, 0-906191

Firecrest Publishing Ltd, Windsor Bridge Rd, Bath, Avon BA2 3AX Tel: Bath 335336 (STD code 0225) Telex: 444633 Fax: (0225) 310771
Man Dir: Roger Lewis; *Publishing Dir:* Julian Batson; *Rights Manager:* Nicole Kirkman; *Production Manager:* Lesley Barnes
Parent Company: The Gieves Group PLC, 1 Savile Row, London W1X 2JR
Associate Companies: Chivers Book Sales Ltd, 93-100 Locksbrook Rd, Bath BA1 3HB; Chivers Press Publishers (qv); Lythway Press Ltd (qv)
Imprints: Gunsmoke Westerns, Black Dagger Crime, Firecrest Books, Swift Children's Books
Subjects: Romances, Thrillers, Mysteries, Westerns, General Fiction, Non-fiction, Children's Fiction
Founded: 1977
ISBN Publisher's Prefixes: 0-85997, 0-86220

Fishing News Books Ltd+, 1 Long Garden Walk, Farnham, Surrey GU9 7HX Tel: Farnham 726868 (STD code 0252) Telex: 859500 Sharet G (F/077)
Editorial, Production: W E Redman; *Sales, Publicity, Rights & Permissions:* Vivien M Heighway
Subjects: Commercial Fisheries, Aquaculture, Marine Engineering, Scientific Angling
1985: 4 titles *1986:* 5 titles *Founded:* 1953
ISBN Publisher's Prefix: 0-85238

The **Fitzjames** Press, an imprint of Motor Racing Publications Ltd (qv)

Fitzwilliam Publishing+, Fitzwilliam House, 32 Trumpington St, Cambridge CB2 1QY   Tel: Cambridge 66733 (STD code 0223)   Telex: 818454 Wfpubl G
Man Dir: Martin Woodhead; *Marketing Dir:* Martin Redfern; *Production Manager:* Sally Knowles; *Promotions, Foreign Rights Manager:* Mary-Lou Nash
Parent Company: Woodhead-Faulkner (Publishers) Ltd (qv)
Associate Company: ICSA Publishing (at above address)
Imprint: Director Books
Subjects: Management, Business, Finance
1987-88: approx 10 titles   *Founded:* 1987

Flamingo, a paperback imprint of Fontana Books, see William Collins PLC

Floris Books+, 21 Napier Rd, Edinburgh EH10 5AZ   Tel: (031) 337 2372
Editorial: Michael Jones; *Sales, Production, Publicity, Rights & Permissions:* Christian Maclean
Subsidiary Company: The Christian Community Press
Subjects: Religion, Children's Books, General
1986: 20 titles   *Founded:* 1976
ISBN Publisher's Prefixes: 0-903540 and 0-86315 (Floris), 0-900285 (Christian Community Press)

Focal Press, an imprint of Butterworth & Co (Publishers) Ltd (qv)

The **Folio** Society Ltd, see Book Clubs

Fonndery Press, an imprint of Methodist Publishing House (qv)

Fontana Books, an imprint of William Collins PLC (qv)

Forbes Publications Ltd+, 120 Bayswater Rd, London W2 3JH   Tel: (01) 229 9322
Dirs: Rosemary Crellin, Joan Forbes, Colin Forbes
Subjects: Secondary, University, Commercial & Technical Education, Educational & Scientific, Reference Books, Home Economics, Nutrition, Health Education, Personal and Social Education, Consumer Studies, New Technology
ISBN Publisher's Prefix: 0-901762

Fortune Press, see Charles Skilton Ltd

G T **Foulis** & Co Ltd+, Sparkford, Nr Yeovil, Somerset BA22 7JJ   Tel: North Cadbury 40635 (STD code 0963)   Telex: 46212   Fax: (0963) 40825
Chairman: John H Haynes; *Man Dir:* Jim Scott; *Managing Editorial Dir:* Rod Grainger; *Sales Dir:* Andy Lynch; *Production Dir:* Roger Stagg
Parent Company: Haynes Publishing Group PLC (qv for associate companies)
Subjects: Motoring History, Biographies (car and motorcycle), Motor Sport, Touring, Speedway, Motorcycle Histories, Automobile Engineering
1987: 52 titles   *Founded:* 1928
ISBN Publisher's Prefixes: 0-85429, 0-85614

W **Foulsham** & Co Ltd+*, Yeovil Rd, Slough SL1 4JH   Tel: Slough 26769 (STD code 0753), Slough 30956; Trade Enquiries: Slough 38637   Cable Add: Bariebooks Slough   Telex: 849041 Sharet G
Executive Chairman: R S Belasco; *Man Dir:* B A R Belasco; *Dir Finance, Rights & Permissions:* Graham M Kitchen; *Sales Dir:* Brian Inns; *Production Manager:* Roy Mantel
Subjects: General Non-fiction, Technical, Educational, Computing
Founded: 1819
ISBN Publisher's Prefix: 0-572

The **Foundational** Book Co Ltd, PO Box 659, London SW3 6SJ   Tel: (01) 584 1053
Man Dir: Peggy M Brook
Subject: Spiritual Science
Founded: 1946
ISBN Publisher's Prefix: 0-85241

Fount Paperbacks, an imprint of William Collins PLC (qv)

Fountain Press+*, 45 The Broadway, Tolworth, Surrey KT6 7DW   Tel: (01) 390 7768   Telex: 923753 Monref G 4107
Man Dir: H M Ricketts; *Sales Manager:* G Smith
Subjects: Photography, Graphic Design & Illustration, Painting, Drawing, Crafts, Hobbies, Military History, Children's
Founded: 1923
ISBN Publisher's Prefix: 0-86343

Fourmat Publishing+, 27 St Albans Pl, Islington Green, London N1 0NX   Tel: (01) 226 7497   Fax: (01) 359 3031
Chief Executive: Pauline Callow; *Sales:* Gilmour Drummond
Subjects: Law, Management, Finance
1986: 10 titles   *Founded:* 1979
ISBN Publisher's Prefixes: 1-85190, 0-906840

Fourth Estate Ltd+, Classic House, 113 Westbourne Grove, London W2 4UP   Tel: (01) 727 8993   Cable Add: Donleos London   Telex: 299240 Donleo G
Man Dir, Sales, Rights & Permissions: Victoria Barnsley; *Editorial:* Michael Mason, Giles O'Bryen; *Production, Publicity:* Jane Charteris
Subjects: Art, Current Affairs, Fiction, Guidebooks, Literature, Popular Culture, Women's Studies
Founded: 1984
ISBN Publisher's Prefix: 0-947795

L N **Fowler** & Co Ltd, 1201-03 High Rd, Chadwell Heath, Romford, Essex RM6 4DH   Tel: (01) 597 2491
Man Dir, Editorial, Production: W D Nagle; *Sales:* C J Nagle
Subjects: Astrology, Alternative Healing
Bookshop: Fowler's New Age Bookshop (at above address)
Founded: 1880
ISBN Publisher's Prefix: 0-85243

Foxbury Press, an imprint of Saint Paul's Bibliographies (qv)

W & G **Foyle** Ltd & John Gifford Ltd*, 113-119 Charing Cross Rd, London WC2H 0EB   Tel: (01) 437 0216   Cable Add: Foylibra London WC2
Chairman & Man Dir: Christina Foyle; *Man Dir:* (John Gifford Ltd): C Batty
Subjects: Crafts, Antiques, Reference, Gardening, Natural History
Bookshop: W & G Foyle (at above address)
Founded: 1904
Miscellaneous: Firm is owned by W & G Foyle Ltd
ISBN Publisher's Prefixes: 0-7071 (Foyle), 0-7072 (Gifford)

Framework Press Educational Publishers Ltd, St Leonard's House, St Leonardgate, Lancaster LA1 1NN   Tel: Lancaster 39602 (STD code 0524)
Chief Executive: Mrs Bren Abercrombie; *Editorial:* David Green, Bren Abercrombie; *Sales:* Pamela Kitching; *Production:* Janet Day; *Publicity:* David Green; *Rights & Permissions:* Mary Ayres
Subject: Education
1985: 7 titles   *1986:* 5 titles   *Founded:* 1983
ISBN Publisher's Prefix: 1-85008

Gordon **Fraser** Gallery Ltd+, 15 Duncan Terrace, London N1 8BZ   Tel: 01-833 8286   Telex: 25848 Fraser G   Fax: (01) 833 8395

UNITED KINGDOM 443

Dirs: Ian G Fraser, Margaret A F Moss, Adrian Atkinson, Alan A F Macpherson; *General Manager:* Peter Guy; *Marketing:* Alison Browne; *Editorial:* Neelam Sharma
Orders to: Eastcotts Rd, Bedford MK42 0JX
Subjects: Art, Biography, Photography, Graphic Arts & Design, Quality Paperbacks
Founded: 1936
ISBN Publisher's Prefixes: 0-900406, 0-86092

Free Association Books+, 26 Freegrove Rd, London N7 9RQ   Tel: (01) 609 5646
Chief Executive, Editorial: Robert M Young; *Sales, Publicity:* David Musson; *Production:* David Williams; *Rights & Permissions:* Cathy Miller
Orders to: Turnaround Distribution, 27 Horsell Rd, London N7 1XL
Subjects: Psychoanalysis, Psychology, History, Science & Technology, Periodicals
1985: 12 titles   *1986:* 16 titles   *Founded:* 1984
ISBN Publisher's Prefixes: 0-946960, 1-85343

W H **Freeman** & Co Ltd, 20 Beaumont St, Oxford OX1 2NQ   Tel: Oxford 726975 (STD code 0865)   Telex: 83677
Man Dir: Graham Voaden; *Dirs:* Gerard Piel, Linda Chaput, John MacFarlane
Orders to: Marston Book Services, PO Box 87, Oxford OX4 1LB
Parent Company: W H Freeman & Co, 41 Madison Ave, New York, NY 10017, USA. Ultimate holding company Scientific American, 415 Madison Ave, New York, NY 10014, USA
Subjects: University Textbooks & Monographs in Pure & Applied Science
1985: 40 titles   *Founded:* 1959
ISBN Publisher's Prefix: 0-7167

Samuel **French** Ltd, 52 Fitzroy St, London W1P 6JR   Tel: (01) 387 9373
Chairman: Abbott van Nostrand; *Man Dir:* John Laurence Hughes; *Dirs:* John Bedding, P J Stalworth
Associate Companies: Samuel French (Canada) Ltd, 80 Richmond St East, Toronto, Canada; Samuel French Inc, 45 West 25th St, New York, NY 10010 and 7623 Sunset Blvd, Hollywood, CA 90046, USA
Subjects: Drama, Reference (Theatre)
Bookshop: French's Theatre Bookshop (at above London address)
Founded: 1830
ISBN Publisher's Prefix: 0-573

The **Fruitmarket Gallery**, 29 Market St, Edinburgh EH1 1DF   Tel: (031) 225 2383
Dir, Editorial, Production, Rights & Permissions: Mark Francis; *Sales, Publicity:* Donald Busby
Subject: Contemporary Art
Bookshop: At above address
1985: 5 titles   *1986:* 7 titles   *Founded:* 1984
ISBN Publisher's Prefix: 0-947912

Fudge & Co Ltd+, 2 Caversham St, London SW3   Tel: (01) 351 4995
Man Dir: Charles Skilton
Parent Company: Charles Skilton Ltd (qv for associate companies)
Imprints: Research Publishing Co, Broomsleigh Press, Skilton & Shaw
Subjects: Fiction, Biography, History, Spirituality, Juvenile, Poetry, Art, General
ISBN Publisher's Prefix: 0-7050

David **Fulton** Publishers Ltd+, 14 Chalton Dr, London N2 0QW   Tel: (01) 455 0337
Dir: David Fulton
Orders to: John Wiley & Sons Ltd Publishers, 1 Oldlands Way, Bognor Regis, West Sussex PO22 9SA

Subjects: Architecture, Education, Psychiatry, Psychology, Geography, Computer Science
1987: 3 titles *Founded:* 1987
ISBN Publisher's Prefix: 1-85346

Fun Packs, an imprint of Studio Publications (Ipswich) Ltd (qv)

Futura, an imprint of Macdonald & Co (Publishers) Ltd (qv)

Fyfield Books, an imprint of Carcanet Press Ltd (qv)

G M P Publishers, PO Box 247, London N15 6RW Tel: (01) 800 5861
Editorial: David Fernbach, Richard Dipple, Aubrey Walter; *Sales:* Jim Sprague; *Production:* Aubrey Walter; *Rights & Permissions:* Richard Dipple
Imprints: Gay Artists Series, Gay Men's Press, Gay Modern Classics, Heretic Books
Subjects: Fiction & Non-fiction (for homosexuals), Politics of Survival
Book Club: The Gay Bookclub
1985: 25 titles *1986:* 25 titles *Founded:* 1979
ISBN Publisher's Prefixes: 0-907040, 0-85449 (Gay Men's Press, Classics, Artists), 0-946097 (Heretic)

G P C Books, an imprint of University of Wales Press (qv)

Gaberbocchus Press Ltd, all correspondence to de Harmonie Publishers (Gaberbocchus Books), Singel 390, 1016 AJ Amsterdam, Netherlands

Gallery Children's Books, an imprint of East-West Publications (UK) Ltd (qv)

Galliard, an imprint of Stainer & Bell Ltd (qv)

Garland Publications Ltd, see Motor Racing Publications Ltd

Gateway Books+, 19 Circus Pl, Bath, Avon BA1 2PW Tel: Bath 332443 (STD code 0225)
Chief Executive, Editorial, Production: Alick Bartholomew; *Sales, Publicity:* Pauline Waterson; *Rights & Permissions:* Mari Franklin
Subsidiary Company: Ashgrove-Gateway Distribution (at above address)
Subjects: Medical, Philosophy, Politics & World Affairs, Psychology, Sociology & Anthropology
1985: 8 titles *1986:* 13 titles *Founded:* 1982
ISBN Publisher's Prefix: 0-946551

Gay Artists Series, an imprint of GMP Publishers (qv)

Gay Men's Press, an imprint of GMP Publishers (qv)

Gay Modern Classics, an imprint of GMP Publishers (qv)

Gee & Co, an imprint of Van Nostrand Reinhold (UK) Co Ltd (qv)

Gem, an imprint of William Collins PLC (qv)

Genesis Publications Ltd, Lynwood House, 51 Lynwood, Guildford, Surrey GU2 5NY Tel: Guildford 37431 (STD code 0483)
Man Dir: Brian Roylance
Subsidiary Company: Pageminster Press (at above address)
Subjects: Art, Autobiography, Botany, History, Poetry, Natural History, English Literature, Limited Editions

Gentry Books Ltd, now part of Haynes Publishing Group PLC (qv)

Geo Abstracts Ltd+, Regency House, 34 Duke St, Norwich NR3 3AP Tel: Norwich 626327 (STD code 0603) Telex: 975247 Chacom G
Man Dir, Rights & Permissions: Drs J Grijpma; *Editorial:* I B Woods, L Martin; *Sales:* I B Woods, B Yorke; *Publicity:* I B Woods, C Wilson
Parent Company: Geo Abstracts Ltd (at above address). Ultimate parent company Elsevier Science Publishers BV, Netherlands (qv)
Imprint: Geo Books
Subjects: Geography, Earth Sciences, Planning, Archaeology
1987: 20 titles *Founded:* 1977
ISBN Publisher's Prefixes: 0-86094, 0-902246

Geographia Ltd+*, 105-7 Bath Rd, Cheltenham, Gloucestershire GL53 7LE Tel: Cheltenham 512748 (STD code 0242)
Chief Cartographer: Chris Moore
Orders to: Bartholomew Sales & Distribution Services, 12 Duncan St, Edinburgh EH9 1TA Tel: (031) 667 7067 Telex: 728134 Barts G
Subjects: Maps, Atlases, Guide Books
Bookshop: 58 Ludgate Hill, London EC4M 7HX Tel: (01) 248 3554
Miscellaneous: Geographia Ltd is an imprint of John Bartholomew & Son Ltd (qv)
ISBN Publisher's Prefix: 0-09

The **Geographical** Association, 343 Fulwood Rd, Sheffield S10 3BP Tel: Sheffield 670666 (STD code 0742)
Honorary Secretary, Publications and Communications: Peter Fox; *All other offices:* Noreen Pleavin
Subjects: Geography, Geography Teaching
1985-86: 8 titles *Founded:* 1901
ISBN Publisher's Prefix: 0-54000

Stanley **Gibbons** Publications Ltd, 5 Parkside, Christchurch Rd, Ringwood, Hampshire BH24 3SH Tel: Ringwood 2363 (STD code 042 54) Telex: 41271 Sgppub G Fax: (042 54) 70247
Man Dir: S Zimmerman; *Editor:* D Aggersberg; *Production Dir:* J Curle; *Publicity Manager:* H Jefferies
Orders to: Unit 5, Parkside, Christchurch Rd, Ringwood, Hampshire BH24 3SH Tel: Ringwood 2363 (STD code 042 54) Telex: 41271 Sgppub G
Parent Company: Stanley Gibbons International Ltd, 399 Strand, London WC2R 0LX
Subjects: Philately, Postcards, Banknotes
Founded: 1856
ISBN Publisher's Prefix: 0-85259

John **Gifford** Ltd, see W & G Foyle Ltd

Ginn & Co Ltd+, Prebendal House, Parson's Fee, Aylesbury, Buckinghamshire HP20 2QZ Tel: Aylesbury 88411 (STD code 0296) Telex: 83535 Ginn G Fax: (0296) 25487
Warehouse: Unit 1, Block H, Long Eaton Industrial Estate, Acton Grove, Long Eaton, Nottingham NG10 1GG
Man Dir: W Shepherd; *Editorial Dir:* O J Norris; *Marketing Dir:* E F Keartland; *Sales Dir:* N G Hall; *Production Dir:* D Miller; *Publicity Manager:* R T Tadman
Parent Company: Octopus Publishing Group PLC
Subject: Primary Textbooks
Founded: 1862 (USA), 1920 (London)
ISBN Publisher's Prefix: 0-602

Mary **Glasgow** Publications Ltd+, Avenue House, 131-133 Holland Park Ave, London W11 4UT Tel: (01) 603 4688 Telex: 311890 Mgpubs Fax: (01) 602 5197
Man Dir: Alfred Waller; *Publishing Dir:* Leslie Upton; *UK Educational Sales Manager:* Ron Gellert-Binnie; *Production Dir:* Bill Antrobus; *Publicity Manager:* Annie Scothern; *Rights & Permissions Manager:* Esther Heasman
Orders to: Brookhampton Lane, Kineton, Warwick CV35 0JB
Subsidiary Companies: Paradigm Publishing Ltd (qv); Sound Communication (Publishers) Ltd, Dewsbury, West Yorkshire WF13 1HF
Subjects: Educational Magazines and Audiovisual Materials in EFL, Modern Languages, Humanities
1985: 8 titles *1986:* 14 titles *Founded:* 1957
Miscellaneous: Firm is a member of Wolters Kluwer NV, Netherlands (qv for associate companies)
ISBN Publisher's Prefixes: 0-900400, 0-905999, 0-86158

Glaven, an imprint of Jarrold Colour Publications (qv)

The **Gleniffer** Press, 11 Low Rd, Castlehead, Paisley, Renfrewshire PA2 6AQ Tel: (041) 889 9579
Man Dir: Ian Macdonald
Subjects: General Fiction and Non-fiction, Specialists in Miniature Books, Limited Editions
1985: 3 titles *Founded:* 1968
ISBN Publisher's Prefixes: 0-9502177, 0-906005

Gold Eagle, an imprint of Mills & Boon Ltd (qv)

Golden Cockerel Press Ltd+, 25 Sicilian Ave, London WC1A 2QH Tel: (01) 405 7979 Telex: 23565
Man Dir: Thomas Yoseloff (USA); *Dir:* Sarah Manson
Orders to: J M Dent & Sons (Distribution) Ltd, Dunhams Lane, Letchworth, Hertfordshire SG6 1LF Tel: Letchworth 686241 (STD code 0462)
Associate Company: Associated University Presses Inc, 440 Forsgate Dr, Cranbury, NJ 08512, USA
Imprints: Associated University Presses, Cornwall Books
Subjects: Literary Criticism, Literature, Drama, Film, Music, Art & Architecture, Theology, Philosophy, Judaica, History, Politics, Sociology
Bookshop: Golden Cockerel Bookshop, 25 Sicilian Ave, London WC1A 2QH
1987: approx 80 titles *Founded:* 1979

Golden Handshake, an imprint of Jay Landesman Ltd (qv)

Golden Pleasure Books, an imprint of The Hamlyn Publishing Group Ltd (qv)

Victor **Gollancz** Ltd+, 14 Henrietta St, Covent Garden, London WC2E 8QJ Tel: (01) 836 2006, (01) 836 2515 Cable Add: Vigollan London WC2 Telex: 265033 Fax: (01) 379 0934
Man Dir: Stephen Bray; *Sales Dir:* Kate Pocock; *Publicity:* Adrienne Maguire; *Rights & Permissions:* Jane Blackstock
Subjects: General Fiction, Belles Lettres, Biography, History, Music, Art, Architecture, Philosophy, Juveniles, Travel, Mountaineering
Founded: 1928
ISBN Publisher's Prefix: 0-575

Gomer Press (J D Lewis & Sons Ltd), Llandysul, Dyfed SA44 4BQ Tel: Llandysul 2371 (STD code 055 932) Cable Add: Gomerian Llandysul
Man Dir: J H Lewis; *Editorial, Rights & Permissions:* John Lewis; *Sales, Publicity:* John H Lewis; *Production:* J Huw Lewis
Parent Company: J D Lewis & Sons Ltd
Subjects: Welsh Language Publications,

Books on Wales
Bookshop: Gomerian Press, Llandysul, Dyfed
Founded: 1892
ISBN Publisher's Prefix: 0-86383

Gondola Books, an imprint of The Hamlyn Publishing Group Ltd (qv)

Gordon and Breach Science Publishers Ltd+, 1 Bedford St, London WC2E 9PP Tel: (01) 836 5125 Cable Add: Sciencepub, London WC2 Telex: 23258 Scipub G Fax: (01) 379 0800
Dirs: Martin B Gordon (USA), J A Levene; *Editorial:* John Gillman; *Marketing:* Alison Gridley; *Production:* John Ormiston
Orders to: (Books) Gordon and Breach Science Publishers Inc, 50 West 23 St, New York, NY 10010, USA; (Journals) STBS Ltd, 1 Bedford St, London WC2E 9PP
Parent Company: Gordon and Breach Science Publishers Inc (at US address)
Associate Companies: Harwood Academic Publishers GmbH, Switzerland (qv) and 50 West 23rd St, New York, NY 10010, USA
Subjects: Arts & Humanities, Agriculture & Nutrition, Biology, Psychology, Astronomy and Astrophysics, Nuclear Engineering, Chemistry & Chemical Technology, Civil Engineering, Computers, Systems & Control Engineering, Earth & Planetary Sciences, Economics, Electronics & Electrical Engineering, Life Sciences & Medicine, Management Science & Business, Mathematics & Statistics, Mechanical Engineering, Metallurgy & Materials Science, Music, Dance, Physics, Social Sciences, Space Science & Technology, Learned Journals
ISBN Publisher's Prefixes: 0-677, 2-88124, 3-7186

Gower Medical Publishing, Middlesex House, 34-42 Cleveland St, London W1P 5FB Tel: (01) 631 1888 Telex: 21736 Fax: (01) 631 3594
Man Dir: David S B Inglis; *Publishing Dir and Rights & Permissions:* Fiona Foley
Subjects: Medical, Veterinary
Miscellaneous: Gower Medical Publishing is a division of J B Lippincott Co (see Harper & Row Ltd)
ISBN Publisher's Prefix: 0-397 (backlist 0-906923)

Gower Press, a former imprint of Gower Publishing Co Ltd (qv)

Gower Publishing Co Ltd+, Gower House, Croft Rd, Aldershot, Hampshire GU11 3HR Tel: Aldershot 331551 (STD code 0252) Telex: 858001 Gower G
Man Dir, Sales, Rights & Permissions: N Farrow; *Marketing Dir:* C Simpson; *UK Trade Sales Manager:* Rathan Sippy; *Publicity Manager:* Tim Naylor; *Customer Service Manager:* Keith Dibble; *Production Manager:* C Barber; *Editorial:* Malcolm Stern (Business & Management), John Irwin (Academic & Professional)
Subsidiary Companies: Edward Elgar Publishing Ltd (qv); Gower/TFI (at above address); Technical Press Ltd (qv); Wildwood House Ltd (qv)
Imprints: Gower, Avebury, Maurice Temple Smith, Scolar Press
Subjects: Business & Management, Social Science, Art & Humanities, Computers, Technical, Library Science
Founded: 1967
ISBN Publisher's Prefixes: 0-566 (Gower Publishing, Avebury), 0-85967 (Scolar Press), 0-7161 (Gower Press), 0-86127 (Avebury pre-1985), 0-946065 (Beaumont), 0-905897 (Input Two-Nine), 0-901232 (Mullard), 0-347 (Saxon House pre-1976), 0-85117 (Maurice Temple Smith), 0-904655 (Wilton), 1-85278 (Edward Elgar)

Grafton Books+, 8 Grafton St, London W1X 3LA Tel: (01) 493 7070 Cable Add: Herakles London W1X Telex: 25611 Colins G Fax: (01) 493 7070 ext 4440
Man Dir: J Lloyd; *Sales Dir:* John Sexton (Paperback); *Production Dir:* Malcolm Lee; *Editorial Dirs:* John Boothe (Hardback), Nick Austin (Paperback)
Orders to: Westerhill Distribution Services Ltd, PO Box, Glasgow G4 0NB Tel: (041) 772 3200
Parent Company: William Collins PLC (qv)
Subsidiary Companies: Grafton Paperbacks; Grafton Trade Books Ltd; Paladin Books (all UK)
Subjects: Fiction, Leisure & Hobbies, Biography, History, Non-fiction, Music, Art, Low- & High-priced Paperbacks
Miscellaneous: Grafton Books formerly traded under the name of Granada Publishing Ltd
ISBN Publisher's Prefixes: 0-236, 0-246 (Grafton Hardback Books), 0-586 (Paladin Books)

Frank **Graham***, 6 Queen's Terrace, Newcastle upon Tyne NE2 2PL Tel: Newcastle upon Tyne 2813067 (STD code 091)
Subject: Local History
Founded: 1960
ISBN Publisher's Prefix: 0-85983

Graham & Trotman Ltd+, Sterling House, 66 Wilton Rd, London SW1V 1DE Tel: (01) 821 1123 Cable Add: Infobooks London Telex: 298878 Gramco G Fax: (01) 630 5229
Man Dir, Rights & Permissions: A Graham; *Editorial:* G Bricault, J Carr, A Lintott, A Valenzuela; *Sales:* R Utley; *Marketing Dir:* S Willcox; *Production:* D Blakeley; *Marketing:* T Connors, E Matthews, G Steddy
Subjects: Business Reference, Business Management, Business Law, Earth Sciences, Oil & Gas Technology, Environmental Sciences, Engineering
1987: 60 titles *Founded:* 1974
Miscellaneous: Firm is a member of the Kluwer Group, Netherlands (qv)
ISBN Publisher's Prefix: 0-86010

Granada Publishing Ltd, now Grafton Books (qv)

Grant McIntyre Ltd, see under McIntyre

W **Green & Son** Ltd, 2 St Giles St, Edinburgh EH1 1PU Tel: (031) 225 4879
Subject: Scots Law
Parent Company: Thomson Information Services Ltd (qv). Ultimate parent company International Thomson Organisation Ltd, 20 Queen St West, Box 45, Suite 2206, Toronto, Ontario M5H 3R3, Canada
ISBN Publisher's Prefix: 0-414

Greenhill Books/Lionel Leventhal Ltd, 3 Barham Ave, Elstree, Hertfordshire Tel: (01) 953 2312 Telex: Lundhumpub 8952387
Chief Executive: Lionel Leventhal
Orders to: SPA Books Ltd, Business & Technology Centre, Bessemer Dr, Stevenage, Hertfordshire SG1 2DX
Parent Company: Lionel Leventhal Ltd (at above main address)
Subjects: Napoleonic, Military, Science Fiction & Fantasy, Crime Classics, Vintage Aviation, Bibliographies
1984: 4 titles *1985:* 10 titles *Founded:* 1984
ISBN Publisher's Prefix: 0-947898

Gresham Books, The Gresham Press, PO Box 61, Henley-on-Thames, Oxfordshire RG9 3LQ Tel: Wargrave 3789 (STD code 073522)
Chief Executive: Mrs M V Green
Parent Company: Gift Book Promotions Ltd, 94 Wigmore St, London W1H 0BR
Subjects: Music, Hobbies, Leisure, Facsimile Reproductions of Rare Books, Art, Crafts, Hymn Books
Founded: 1979
ISBN Publisher's Prefixes: 0-905418, 0-946095

Charles **Griffin** & Co Ltd, 16 Pembridge Rd, London W11 3HL Tel: (01) 229 1825
Man Dir, Rights & Permissions: Clive Bingley; *Sales, Publicity & Advertising Manager:* Lionel Leventhal; *Editorial:* James Griffin (30 Disraeli Crescent, High Wycombe, Buckinghamshire HP13 5EJ Tel: High Wycombe 36341 (STD code 0494))
Parent Company: Book Publishing Development PLC (at above address)
Subjects: University & Secondary Textbooks especially Statistics, Engineering, General & Social Science
1985: 3 titles *1986:* 4 titles *Founded:* 1820
ISBN Publisher's Prefix: 0-85264

Grisewood & Dempsey Ltd+, Elsley House, 24-30 Great Titchfield St, London W1P 7AD Tel: (01) 631 0878 Cable Add: Greatbooks, London Telex: 27725 Gridem
Chairman, Man Dir: D Grisewood; *Sales and Marketing Dir:* David Kewley; *Editorial:* J Olliver; *Publicity Manager:* Elinor Malcolm
Imprint: Kingfisher Books (qv)
Subjects: Children's Colour Information Books, Adult Reference
Founded: 1973

Grosvenor Books+, 54 Lyford Rd, London SW18 3JJ Tel: (01) 870 2124
Man Dir, Rights & Permissions: J H V Nowell; *Sales Dir:* D W Locke; *Production Manager:* B Cummock
Parent Company: The Good Road Ltd, 12 Palace St, London SW1E 5JF
Subjects: Contemporary Issues, Religion, Biography, Children's Books
1985: 8 titles *Founded:* 1964
ISBN Publisher's Prefixes: 0-901269, 1-85239

Grub Street, Golden House, 28-31 Great Pulteney St, London W1R 3DD Tel: (01) 437 6114, (01) 437 6121 Telex: 931770 Wibu G
Chief Executives: John Davies, Roger Hammond; *Sales:* Chris Lloyd; *Publicity:* Suzanne Peacock; *Rights & Permissions:* John Davies
Orders to: Chris Lloyd, PO Box 327, Poole, Dorset BH15 2RG Tel: Poole 681776 (STD code 0202)
Subjects: Cookery, Humour, History, Military History
1986: 4 titles *1987:* 6 titles *Founded:* 1986
ISBN Publisher's Prefix: 0-948817

Guild Publishing*, 87 Newman St, London W1P 4EN Tel: (01) 637 0341 Cable Add: Booklub Telex: 24359 Bcalon
Subjects: Archaeology, Cookery, History, Classic Reprints, Humour, Leisure, Natural History
Miscellaneous: Imprint of Book Club Associates (qv under Book Clubs)

Guinness Publishing Ltd, 33 London Rd, Enfield, Middlesex EN2 6DJ Tel: (01) 367 4567 Cable Add: Mostest Enfield Telex: 23573 Gbrldn Fax: (01) 367 5912
Man Dir: D F Hoy; *Editorial Dir:* Donald Sommerville; *Sales Dir:* F Buxton; *Marketing Dir:* Christopher Groves

Parent Company: Guinness PLC, 39 Portman Sq, London W1
Subject: Reference
Founded: 1954
ISBN Publisher's Prefixes: 0-900424, 0-85112

Gunsmoke Westerns, an imprint of Firecrest Publishing Ltd (qv)

Gwasg Prifysgol Cymru, an imprint of University of Wales Press (qv)

Gwasg y Dref Wen+, 28 Church Rd, Whitchurch, Cardiff CF4 2EA Tel: Cardiff 617860 (STD code 0222)
Man Dir, Production, Editorial, Rights & Permissions: Roger Boore; *Publicity, Sales:* Anne Boore
Subjects: Welsh-language books for Children and Schools (Fiction & Non-fiction) including Welsh Children's Encyclopaedia, Picture Dictionary
Founded: 1970
ISBN Publisher's Prefix: 0-946962

H E B, an imprint of Heinemann Educational Books Ltd (qv)

H F L, an imprint of Butterworth & Co (Publishers) Ltd (qv)

H M S O, see Her Majesty's Stationery Office

Michael **Haag** Ltd, PO Box 369, London NW3 4ER Tel: (01) 794 2647
Man Dir: M Haag
Orders to: Biblios Publishers' Distribution Services Ltd, Glenside Industrial Estate, Star Rd, Partridge Green, Horsham, West Sussex RH13 8LD Tel: Partridge Green 710971 (STD code 0403)
Subjects: Travel, General
1986-87: 20 titles *Founded:* 1979
ISBN Publisher's Prefix: 0-902743

Peter **Haddock** Ltd, Pinfold Lane, Bridlington, North Humberside YO16 5BT Tel: Bridlington 678121 (STD code 0262)
Cable Add: Bridbooks Telex: 52180 Fax: (0262) 400043
Man Dir: Peter Haddock; *Sales:* David Haddock; *Production:* Pat Hornby
Subjects: Low-priced Children's Painting, Activity and Story Books
1985: 25 titles *1986:* 30 titles *Founded:* 1952
ISBN Publisher's Prefix: 0-7105

Peter **Halban** Publishers Ltd, 42 South Molton St, London W1Y 1HB Tel: (01) 491 1582
Man Dirs: Peter Halban, Martine Halban
Orders to: Octopus Distribution Services Ltd, Sanders Lodge Estate, Rushden, Northamptonshire NN10 9R2 Tel: Rushden 58521 (STD code 0933)
Subjects: Fiction, Biography, History, Art, Middle East
1987: 8 titles *Founded:* 1986
ISBN Publisher's Prefix: 1-870015

Robert **Hale** Ltd+, Clerkenwell House, 45-47 Clerkenwell Green, London EC1R 0HT Tel: (01) 251 2661 Cable Add: Barabbas London EC1 Telex: 23353 Nurbks G
Warehouse: 4 Vestry Rd, Vestry Estate, Sevenoaks, Kent
Man Dir: John Hale; *Marketing Dir:* Martin Kendall; *Production Dir:* Eric Restall; *Editorial Dir:* Carmel Elwell (Non-fiction); *Rights & Permissions Dir:* Betty Weston; *Publicity:* Sally Randall
Subjects: General Fiction, Belles Lettres, Poetry, Biography, History, How-to, Topography, Music, Art, Sport, Philosophy, Reference, Cookery, Women's Subjects, Low- & High-priced Paperbacks
1985: 425 titles *Founded:* 1936

ISBN Publisher's Prefix: 0-7090 (formerly 0-7091)

The **Hambledon Press**+, 102 Gloucester Ave, London NW1 8HX Tel: (01) 586 0817
Chief Executive: Martin Sheppard
Branch Off: 309 Greenbrier Ave, Ronleverte, West Virginia 24970, USA
Subjects: Academic History (English, European & American), Literature
1985: 15 titles *1986:* 15 titles *Founded:* 1980
ISBN Publisher's Prefixes: 0-907628, 1-85285

Hamish **Hamilton** Ltd, 27 Wright's Lane, London W8 5TZ Tel: (01) 938 3388 Telex: 917181/2 Fax: (01) 937 8704
President: Hamish Hamilton; *Man Dir:* Christopher Sinclair-Stevenson; *Editorial Dir:* Penelope Hoare; *Head of Children's Books:* Jane Nissen; *Head of Elm Tree Books:* Caroline Taggart; *Sales Dir:* Nigel Sisson; *Export Sales:* John Lyon; *Production Dir:* Laurence Byrne; *Publicity Dir:* Helen Ellis; *Rights & Permissions Dir:* Susannah Porter
Parent Company: Penguin Books Ltd (qv)
Subsidiary Companies: Hamish Hamilton Children's Books Ltd; Elm Tree Books Ltd
Subjects: General Fiction, Biography, History, Music, Art, Juveniles
Founded: 1931
ISBN Publisher's Prefix: 0-241

Hamilton House Publishing*, 17 Staveley Way, Brixworth Industrial Park, Northampton NN6 9EU Tel: Northampton 881889 (STD code 0604)
Chief Executive, Production, Publicity, Rights & Permissions: Tony Attwood; *Editorial:* Sue Hesse; *Sales:* Andrew Baskott, Stephen Mister
Associate Companies: Paperbacks By Post; Hamilton House Mailings; School Mailing Service (all at above address)
Branch Off: Hamilton House, Groom Lane, Creaton, Northampton NN6 8NS
Subjects: Trade Directories, Careers. Also packagers specializing in TV and radio tie-ins
Founded: 1979
ISBN Publisher's Prefix: 0-906888

Hamlyn Publishing, Michelin House, 81 Fulham Rd, London SW3 6RB Tel: (01) 581 9393 Cable Add: Octobooks Telex: 920191 Fax: (01) 589 8419
Orders to: Octopus Distribution Services Ltd, PO Box 5, Rushden, Northamptonshire NN10 9YX Tel: Rushden 58521 (STD code 0933)
Chairman: Paul Hamlyn; *Chief Executive:* Ian Irvine; *Man Dir:* David Blunt; *Publishing Dir:* Paul Richardson; *Sales and Marketing Dir:* Barry Jafrato; *Export Sales:* Gunner Lie; *Production:* Derek Freeman; *Publicity Manager:* Patricia Pover
Parent Company: Octopus Publishing Group PLC. Ultimate parent company Reed International PLC, Reed House, 83 Piccadilly, London W1A 1EJ
Imprints: Deans International Publishing, Gondola Books, Newnes Books, Rainbow Books, Spring Books
Subjects: General Non-fiction, Cookery, History, How-to, Music, Arts, Crafts, Antiques, Cinema, Sports, Reference, Juveniles, Trade Paperbacks, Travel, Gardening, Natural History, Motoring, Militaria
Founded: 1947
ISBN Publisher's Prefix: 0-600

Heinrich **Hanau** Publications Ltd+*, PO Box 2JG, London W1A 2JG (Located at: 59 Old Compton St, London W1V 5PN)
Tel: (01) 734 4353
Man Dir: John Hanau
Subjects: International Co-publications
ISBN Publisher's Prefix: 0-902826

Handbag Books, an imprint of Kenneth Mason Publications Ltd (qv)

The **Handsel** Press+, 33 Montgomery St, Edinburgh EH7 5JX Tel: (031) 556 2796
Man Dir, Editorial, Rights & Permissions: Douglas Grant; *Publicity:* Kate Blackadder
Subject: Theology
1985: 5 titles *1986:* 11 titles *Founded:* 1976
Miscellaneous: Associated with The Scottish Academic Press (qv)
ISBN Publisher's Prefix: 0-905312

Harcourt Brace Jovanovich Ltd, 24-28 Oval Rd, London NW1 7DX Tel: (01) 267 4466 Cable Add: Harbrex London NW1 Telex: 25775
Shipping Add: Customer Services, High St, Foots Cray, Sidcup, Kent DA14 5BR
Man Dir: Joan Fujimoto; *Sales Dir:* D Duff; *Production Dir:* M Ewins; *Editorial Dir:* C Guettler; *Marketing Manager:* J Lawrence
Parent Company: The Harcourt Brace Jovanovich Inc, The Harcourt Brace Jovanovich Bldg, Orlando, FL 32887, USA
Subsidiary Companies: Grune and Stratton Ltd; Johnson Reprint Co Ltd
Associate Companies: Harcourt Brace Jovanovich Group (Australia) Pty Ltd, Australia (qv); Academic Press do Brasil Editôra Ltda, Rua des Armando, Fairbanks 314, Butanta 05501, São Paulo, Brazil; Academic Press Canada, 55 Barber Greene Rd, Don Mills, Ontario M3C 2A1, Canada; H B J Japan Inc, Chibancho Central Bldg 22-1, Ichibancho, Chiyoda-ku, Tokyo, Japan; Grune & Stratton Inc and Johnson Reprint Corporation, USA
Imprints: Academic Press, Ballière Tindall (qv), Holt, Rinehart & Winston (qv), WB Saunders (qv)
Subjects: Reference, Scientific, Technical, Medicine, Psychology, Social Science, University Textbooks, Educational Materials
ISBN Publisher's Prefixes: 0-12 (Academic Press), 0-15 (Harcourt Brace Jovanovich), 0-8089 (Grune & Stratton), 0-384 (Johnson Reprint)

Patrick **Hardy** Books, an imprint of James Clarke & Co Ltd (qv)

Harlequin, an imprint of Mills & Boon Ltd (qv)

Harper & Row Ltd, Middlesex House, 34-42 Cleveland St, London W1P 5FB Tel: (01) 631 1888 Telex: 21736 Fax: (01) 631 3594
Man Dir: David S B Inglis; *Marketing Dir:* Hugo Poelvoorde; *Rights & Permissions:* New York Office
Orders to: Harper & Row Distributors, Estover Rd, Plymouth, Devon PL6 7PZ Tel: Plymouth 705251 (STD code 0752) Telex: 45635
Parent Company: Harper & Row Inc, 10 East 53rd St, New York, NY 10022, USA
Subsidiary Companies: Ballinger Publishing Co; Basic Books, 10 East 53rd St, New York, NY 10022, USA; Russell Sage Foundation; Canfield Press; T Y Crowell, 10 East 53rd St, New York, NY 10022, USA; J B Lippincott Co, East Washington Sq, Philadelphia, PA 19105, USA
Associate Companies: Harper & Row (Australasia) Pty Ltd, Australia (qv); Editora Harper & Row do Brasil Ltda, Brazil (qv); Harper & Row Latinoamericana-Harla, SA de CV, Mexico (qv); Harper & Row Publishers, Asia, Pte

Ltd, Republic of Singapore (qv)
Subjects: Academic, Professional, Medical, General
ISBN Publisher's Prefix: 0-06

Harrap Ltd+, 19-23 Ludgate Hill, London EC4M 7PD Tel: (01) 248 6444 Cable Add: Harrapbook London EC4 Telex: 28673 Consol G
Chairman: N W Berry; *Man Dir:* E Dobby; *Editorial Dirs:* Derek Johns (General), Jean-Luc Barbanneau (Dictionaries); *Marketing Dir:* Medwyn Hughes; *Sales Dir:* David Collins; *Rights & Permissions Dir:* D Spivey; *Publicity:* Nathalie Villemur; *Production Managers:* Tim Pearce (General), John Holmes (Dictionaries)
Subsidiary Companies: Harrap France Sàrl, 177 rue St Honoré, F-75001 Paris; Harrap Overseas Ltd, Lord Cartanche House, 66-68 Esplanade, St Helier, Jersey, Channel Islands
Subjects: English as a foreign language, Dictionaries, General
1987: 60 titles *Founded:* 1901
ISBN Publisher's Prefix: 0-245

Harrow House Editions, an imprint of Sceptre Books (qv)

Harvard University Press, 126 Buckingham Palace Rd, London SW1W 9SA Tel: (01) 730 9208 Cable Add: Chibooks Telex: 23933 Chibooks Ldn
General Manager: Neville Gosling; *Publicity Manager:* Ann Sexsmith
Orders to: International Book Distributors Ltd, 66 Wood Lane End, Hemel Hempstead, Hertfordshire HP2 4RG Tel: Hemel Hempstead 58531 (STD code 0442)
Associate Companies: The University of Chicago Press, The MIT Press (qqv)
Subjects: Biography, History, Music, Art, Philosophy, Reference, Paperbacks, Medicine, Psychology, Literature, General & Social Science, Education
Founded: 1913
Miscellaneous: Branch of Harvard University Press, Cambridge, MA, USA
ISBN Publisher's Prefix: 0-674

The **Harvester** Press Ltd, 16 Ship St, Brighton, East Sussex BN1 1AD Tel: Brighton 723031 (STD code 0273) Cable Add: Harvester Brighton Telex: 877101 Olship
Chairman: John Spiers; *Sales, Marketing:* Jean Greetham; *Production:* Beth Humphries
Imprint: Wheatsheaf Books Ltd (qv)
Subjects: History, Politics, Economics, Sociology, Women's Studies, Philosophy, Psychology, Reference, Literature, Fiction
1986: 110 titles *Founded:* 1970
ISBN Publisher's Prefixes: 0-7108, 0-7450, 0-85527

Harvill Press Ltd, now Collins Harvill (qv)

J H Haynes & Co Ltd+, Sparkford, Nr Yeovil, Somerset BA22 7JJ Tel: North Cadbury 40635 (STD code 0963) Telex: 46212 Fax: (0963) 40825
J H Haynes & Co Ltd trades as Haynes Publishing Group
Chairman: John H Haynes; *Man Dir:* Jim Scott; *Executive Editorial Dir, Public Relations, Rights & Permissions:* Jeff Clew; *Editorial Dirs:* Peter Ward, Rod Grainger; *Sales Dir:* Andy Lynch; *Production Dir:* Roger Stagg; *Marketing Manager:* Murray Corfield
Parent Company: Haynes Publishing Group PLC (qv for associate companies)
Subjects: Car and Motorcycle owners workshop manuals/handbooks/servicing guides/paperbacks
1986-87: 159 titles
ISBN Publisher's Prefixes: 1-85010, 0-85696, 0-900550

Haynes Publishing Group PLC, Sparkford, Nr Yeovil, Somerset BA22 7JJ Tel: North Cadbury 40635 (STD code 0963) Telex: 46212 Fax: (0963) 40825
Chairman, Chief Executive: John H Haynes
Subsidiary Companies: J H Haynes & Co Ltd (trading as Haynes Publishing Group), G T Foulis & Co Ltd, Oxford Illustrated Press Ltd (qqv); Gentry Books Ltd; J H Haynes (Overseas) Ltd (at above address); Oxford Publishing Company; Haynes Publications Inc, Newbury Park, CA 91320, USA
Founded: 1960

Hazelton Publishing+, 3 Richmond Hill, Richmond, Surrey TW10 6RE Tel: (01) 948 5151 Telex: 946153 Fax: (01) 948 4111
Chief Executive, Sales: Richard F Poulter; *Editorial, Rights & Permissions:* Elizabeth Le Breton; *Production:* Jane Doyle; *Publicity:* Jane Payton
Parent Company: Hazleton Securities Ltd (at above address)
Imprints: Autocourse, Motocourse, Rallycourse
Subjects: Motor Racing, Motor Cycle Road Racing, Rallying, Sailing
1985: 11 titles *1986:* 10 titles *Founded:* 1975
ISBN Publisher's Prefix: 0-905138

Headline Book Publishing PLC+, Headline House, 79 Great Titchfield St, London W1P 7FN Tel: (01) 631 1687 Telex: 268326 Headln G Fax: (01) 631 1958
Man Dir: Tim Hely-Hutchinson; *Editorial Dir, Rights & Permissions:* Susan Fletcher; *Sales and Publicity Dir:* Sian Thomas; *Production Dir:* Susan Beavan
Orders to: (UK) Bookpoint Ltd, 39 Milton Trading Estate, Abingdon, Oxfordshire OX14 4TD Tel: Abingdon 835001 (STD code 0235) Telex: 837091 Fax: (0235) 832068; (Export) Headline House, 79 Great Titchfield St, London W1P 7FN
Imprints: Headline Fiction, Headline Non Fiction, Headline Paperbacks
Subjects: General Fiction & Non-fiction
Founded: 1986
ISBN Publisher's Prefix: 0-7472

Health Science Press (C W Daniel) Ltd+, 1 Church Path, Saffron Walden, Essex CB10 1JP Tel: Saffron Walden 21909 (STD code 0799)
Dirs: Ian Miller, Jane Miller
Parent Company: The C W Daniel Co Ltd (at above address)
Subjects: Homoeopathy, Acupuncture, Radionics, Radiesthesia, Nature Cure, Biochemistry, Diet and Health
ISBN Publisher's Prefix: 0-85032

Heatherbank Press, 163 Mugdock Rd, Milngavie, Glasgow G62 6BR Tel: (041) 956 2687, (041) 956 5923
Editorial: Sally Kuensberg; *Sales, Marketing & Public Relations:* Rosemary Harvey
Subjects: Local History (Glasgow and Scotland), Biography, Community Publishing, History of Social Welfare
Founded: 1974
ISBN Publisher's Prefix: 0-905192

Heinemann Educational Books Ltd, Halley Court, Jordan Hill, Oxford OX2 8EJ
Chairman: Nicolas Thompson; *Man Dir:* David Fothergill; *Publishing Man Dirs:* Bob Osborne (HEB Schools), Mike Esplen (HEB International); *Maths & Science Dir:* Stephen Ashton; *Production Dir:* Richard Gale; *Sales:* Paul Berry
Orders to: Octopus Distribution Services Ltd, Sanders Lodge Estate, Rushden, Northamptonshire NN10 9R2 Tel: Rushden 58521 (STD code 0933) Telex: 31533 Fax: (0933) 50284
Parent Company: Octopus Publishing Group PLC. Ultimate parent company Reed International PLC, Reed House, 83 Piccadilly, London W1A 1EJ
Imprint: HEB
Subjects: Educational
Founded: 1961
ISBN Publisher's Prefix: 0-435

The **Heinemann Group** of Publishers Ltd, Michelin House, 81 Fulham Rd, London SW3 6RB Tel: (01) 581 9393 Cable Add: Octobooks Telex: 920191 Fax: (01) 589 8419
This is the holding company of the Heinemann publishing companies
Parent Company: Octopus Publishing Group PLC (at above address). Ultimate parent company Reed International PLC, Reed House, 83 Piccadilly, London W1A 1EJ
Subsidiary Companies: Ginn & Co Ltd (qv), Heinemann Educational Books Ltd (qv), William Heinemann Ltd (qv), Heinemann Professional Publishing (qv), Martin Secker & Warburg Ltd (qv) (all UK); Heinemann Publishers Australia Pty Ltd, Australia (qv); Heinemann Educational Books (Caribbean) Ltd, Jamaica (qv); Heinemann Publishers (New Zealand) Ltd, New Zealand (qv); Heinemann Educational Books (Asia) Ltd, Republic of Singapore (qv); Heinemann Publishers Southern Africa Pty Ltd, Republic of South Africa (qv); Heinemann Educational Books Inc, 70 Court St, Portsmouth, NH 03801, USA
Associate Companies: Heinemann Kenya Ltd, Kenya (qv); Heinemann Educational Books (Nigeria) Ltd, Nigeria (qv); Zimbabwe Educational Books, Zimbabwe (qv)

Heinemann/Kingswood, an imprint of William Heinemann Ltd (qv)

William **Heinemann** Ltd+, Michelin House, 81 Fulham Rd, London SW3 6RB Tel: (01) 581 9393 Cable Add: Octobooks Telex: 920191 Fax: (01) 589 8419
Chairman: Paul Hamlyn; *Chief Executive:* Ian Irvine; *Publishers:* Helen Fraser (Fiction & General), Ingrid Selberg (Children's); *Business & Technical:* Doug Fox; *Heinemann/Kingswood:* Derek Wyatt; *Sales:* Tim Whale; *Publicity:* Piers Russell-Cobb; *Rights & Permissions:* Felicity Rubinstein
Orders to: Octopus Distribution Services Ltd, PO Box 5, Rushden, Northamptonshire NN10 9YX Tel: Rushden 58521 (STD code 0933)
Parent Company: Octopus Publishing Group PLC. Ultimate parent company Reed International PLC, Reed House, 83 Piccadilly, London W1A 1EJ
Imprints: Cedar Books, Leo Cooper, Kingswood/Heinemann, Loeb Classical Library, Heinemann/Octopus
Subjects: Fiction, General
Founded: 1890
ISBN Publisher's Prefixes: 0-434 (William Heinemann Ltd), 0-85052 (Leo Cooper)

William **Heinemann Medical** Books Ltd+, Halley Court, Jordan Hill, Oxford OX2 8EJ

Chairman: Nicolas Thompson; *Editorial Dir:* Dr Richard Barling; *Sales Executive:* Sarah Ghidouche; *Production Manager:* Chris Jarvis
Parent Company: Heinemann Professional Publishing (qv)
Subjects: Medicine, Dentistry, Nursing, Medical Technology
1986: 35 titles *Founded:* 1917
ISBN Publisher's Prefix: 0-433

Heinemann/Newnes, an imprint of Heinemann Professional Publishing (qv)

Heinemann Newtech, an imprint of Heinemann Professional Publishing (qv)

Heinemann/Octopus, an imprint of William Heinemann Ltd and Octopus Books Ltd (qqv)

Heinemann Professional Publishing, Halley Court, Jordan Hill, Oxford OX2 8EJ
Chairman: Nicholas Thompson; *Man Dir:* Douglas Fox; *Editorial Dir (Medical):* Dr Richard Barling; *Publishers:* Kathryn Grant (Business), Bridget Buckley, Peter Dixon (both Technical); *Sales Manager:* Tom McGorry; *Marketing Manager:* Edward Gross; *Rights & Permissions:* Sarah Ghidouche
Orders to: Octopus Distribution Services Ltd, PO Box 5, Rushden, Northamptonshire NN10 9YX Tel: Rushden 58521 (STD code 0933)
Parent Company: Octopus Publishing Group PLC. Ultimate parent company Reed International PLC, Reed House, 83 Piccadilly, London W1A 1EJ
Imprints: Heinemann Medical, Heinemann/Newnes, Heinemann Newtech, Made Simple
Subjects: Business & Management, Vocational, Computing, Technical, Medical
Founded: 1987
ISBN Publisher's Prefix: 0-434

Helicon Press, Knight St, Sawbridgeworth, Hertfordshire CM21 9AX Tel: Bishop's Stortford 722318 (STD code 0279)
Man Dir, Editorial: Candida Tobin; *Sales, Production, Publicity, Rights & Permissions:* Christopher Dell
Imprint: Tobin Music Books
Founded: 1973
ISBN Publisher's Prefix: 0-905684

Christopher Helm (Publishers) Ltd+, Imperial House, 21-25 North St, Bromley, Kent BR1 1SD Tel: (01) 466 6622 Telex: 265833 Chrish G
Chief Executive, Rights & Permissions: Christopher Helm; *Joint Man Dirs:* Jo Hemmings, Amanda Halstead; *Editorial:* Jo Hemmings; *Sales:* Amanda Halstead; *Production Dir:* Melanie Crook; *Publicity Manager:* Robert Kirk
Subjects: Ornithology, Natural History, Gardening, Travel, General Non-fiction
1986: 35 titles *Founded:* 1980
ISBN Publisher's Prefix: 0-7470

Hendon Publishing Co Ltd, Hendon Mill, Nelson, Lancashire BB9 8AD Tel: Nelson 63129 (STD code 0282)
Chief Executive, Sales: Henry Nelson; *Editorial:* Dorothy Nelson; *Production:* Jean Marsden; *Publicity, Rights & Permissions:* Jennifer Hartshorn
Parent Company: Hendon Mill Co Ltd (at above address)
Subjects: Local History, Social History, Guide Books, Cookery
1985: 6 titles *Founded:* 1971
ISBN Publisher's Prefix: 0-86067

Ian **Henry** Publications Ltd+, 20 Park Dr, Romford, Essex RM1 4LH Tel: Romford 49119 (STD code 0708)
Man Dir: Ian Wilkes
Orders to: J M Dent & Sons (Distribution) Ltd, Dunhams Lane, Letchworth, Hertfordshire SG6 1LF Tel: Letchworth 686241 (STD code 0462) Telex: 825751
Subjects: History, Fiction Reprints, Automobile Engineering, Medical, Costume, Local History
1986: 18 titles *Founded:* 1975
ISBN Publisher's Prefix: 0-86025

Her Majesty's Stationery Office, St Crispin's House, Duke St, Norwich NR3 1PD Tel: Norwich 622211 (STD code 0603) Telex: 97301 Hemstonery
Director of Publishing: Chris Penn; *Sales Manager:* Duncan Menzies-Kitchin; *Publicity Manager:* Philip Glover
Head Office: Sovereign House, Botolph St, Norwich NR3 1DN Tel: Norwich 622211 (STD code 0603)
London Office: Publications Centre, 51 Nine Elms Lane, London SW8 5DR Tel: (01) 211 5656 Cable Add: Hemstonery London Telex: 297138
Subjects: General Non-fiction, Government Publications
Bookshops: 49 High Holborn, London WC1V 6HB (counter sales); PO Box 276, London SW8 5DT (trade & mail orders); 71 Lothian Rd, Edinburgh EH3 9AZ; 258 Broad St, Birmingham B1 2HE; Southey House, Wine St, Bristol BS1 2BQ; 80 Chichester St, Belfast BT1 4JY; 9-21 Princess St, Manchester M60 8AS
ISBN Publisher's Prefixes: 0-10, 0-11, 0-337

The **Herbert** Press Ltd+, 46 Northchurch Rd, London N1 4EJ Tel: (01) 254 4379 Telex: 8952022 Ctytel G
Man Dir: David Herbert
Orders to: A & C Black, Howard Rd, Eaton Socon, Huntingdon, Cambridgeshire PE19 3EZ Tel: Huntingdon 212666 (STD code 0480)
Subjects: Art, Design, Crafts, Literature, Biography, Theatre, Photography, Archaeology, Natural History, General Non-fiction
1986: 10 titles *1987:* 9 titles *Founded:* 1975
ISBN Publisher's Prefix: 0-906969

Heretic Books, an imprint of G M P Publishers (qv)

Heterodox+, Suite 20, 3 Abbey Orchard St, Westminster, London SW1P 2JJ Tel: (01) 222 8866
Publisher: Graham Lea; *Rights & Permissions:* Valerie Ripley Tel: (01) 580 5522
Subject: General Non-fiction
1986: 2 titles *Founded:* 1986
ISBN Publisher's Prefix: 1-85173

Heyden & Son Ltd, Spectrum House, Hillview Gardens, London NW4 2JQ Tel: (01) 203 5171 Cable Add: Heyspectra London Telex: 28303 Heyldn G Fax: (01) 203 1027
Man Dir: K G Heyden
Subsidiary Company: Heyden & Son GmbH, Devesburgstrasse 6, 4440 Rheine, Federal Republic of Germany
Subjects: Technical & Scientific
ISBN Publisher's Prefix: 0-85501

Adam **Hilger** Ltd+*, Techno House, Redcliffe Way, Bristol BS1 6NX Tel: Bristol 276693 (STD code 0272) Telex: 449149
Chairman: A Pearce; *Editorial Dir:* David Kingham; *Marketing:* Anthony Gresford
Parent Company: IOP Publishing Ltd (qv)
Branch Off: PO Box 230, Accord, MA 02018, USA Tel: 617 749 2966
Subjects: Mathematics, Computer Science, Electronics, Energy, Earth and Environmental Sciences, Astronomy, Physics, Technology, Optics/Colour Science, Analytical and Applied Chemistry, Plastics, Medical Physics, General Science, History of Science
Founded: 1967
ISBN Publisher's Prefix: 0-85274

Leonard **Hill**, see Leonard

Hilmarton Manor Press, Calne, Wiltshire SN11 8SB Tel: Calne 208 (STD code 0249 76)
Man Dir: C Baile de Laperriere
Subjects: Art & Antiques reference, Photographic
1986: 15 titles *1987:* 15 titles *Founded:* 1969
ISBN Publisher's Prefix: 0-904722

Hippo Books, an imprint of Scholastic Publications Ltd (qv)

Hobsons Publishing PLC, Bateman St, Cambridge CB2 1LZ Tel: Cambridge 354551 (STD code 0223) Telex: 81546
Man Dir: Adrian Bridgewater; *Sales:* Alison Cornell
Subjects: Education (Careers & Jobs), Science, Technology, Microelectronics
Miscellaneous: Publishers under licence for the Careers Research and Advisory Centre Ltd
ISBN Publisher's Prefix: 0-86021

Hodder & Stoughton Ltd+, Mill Rd, PO Box 700, Dunton Green, Sevenoaks, Kent TN13 2YA Tel: Sevenoaks 450111 (STD code 0732) Cable Add: Expositor Sevenoaks Telex: 95122 Fax: (01) 631 5248
London Off: 47 Bedford Sq, London WC1B 3DP Tel: (01) 636 9851 Telex: 885887 Fax: (01) 631 5248
Chairman, Chief Executive: Philip Attenborough; *Editorial Dir:* Ion Trewin; *Sales (Hardback):* W J Bailey (Export), J B McEwen (Home); *Sales (Paperback):* C Davis (Home), C Nettleton (Export); *Publicity:* A Hammond; *Production:* J A G Wilson (General/Paperback), C W Davies (Educational); *Rights & Permissions:* Andrew Stuck, Margot Edwards (Children's)
Company is organized in divisions with the following divisional managing directors:
Hodder & Stoughton: Eric Major
Edward Arnold (qv), the educational, academic and medical division of Hodder & Stoughton Ltd: Richard Morris
Hodder & Stoughton Paperbacks: Adrian Bourne
Hodder & Stoughton Children's Books: David Grant
Parent Company: Hodder & Stoughton Holdings Ltd
Subsidiary Companies (UK): Hodder & Stoughton Dunton Green Ltd, Hodder & Stoughton Storage Ltd, Hodder & Stoughton Overseas Ltd, The Lancet Ltd, The New English Library Ltd (qv)
Subsidiary Companies (outside UK): Hodder & Stoughton (Australia) Pty Ltd, Australia (qv); Hodder & Stoughton Canada Ltd, 345 Nugget Ave, Unit 15, Agincourt, Ontario M1S 4J4, Canada; Hodder & Stoughton Ltd, New Zealand (qv); Hodder & Stoughton (Pty) Ltd, PO Box 548, Bergvlei, Sandton 2012, Republic of South Africa; Hodder & Stoughton Inc, Perkins Coic, US Baucorp Tower, Suite 2500, 111 South West Fifth Ave, Portland OR 97204, USA

Associate Companies: Hodder Dargaud Ltd, UK; Southern Book Publishers (Pty) Ltd, Republic of South Africa (qv)
Imprints include: Coronet, Knight, Sceptre, Teach Yourself Books, Unibooks
Subjects: General Fiction, Religion and Theology, Educational, Children's (Fiction & Non-fiction), Medical, Dictionaries, Guidebooks, Travel, Sports & Games, Co-editions (Reader's Digest and Consumers' Association)
Founded: 1868
ISBN Publisher's Prefix: 0-340

The **Hogarth** Press, see Chatto & Windus Ltd/The Hogarth Press

The **Holland** Press, now New Holland Publishing (qv)

Holmes McDougall Ltd+, Allander House, 137-141 Leith Walk, Edinburgh EH6 8NS Tel: (031) 554 9444 Cable Add: Educational Telex: 727508
Man Dir: F J Baillie; *Editorial Dir:* E Ketley; *Export Manager, Rights & Permissions:* R B Shepherd
Subsidiary Companies: Holmes McDougall Bookselling; Minerva Posters; Scottish Field; Climber; Scottish Farmer; The Great Outdoors
Subjects: Secondary & Primary Textbooks
Founded: 1870
ISBN Publisher's Prefix: 0-7157

Holt, Rinehart & Winston, 24-28 Oval Rd, London NW1 7DX Tel: (01) 267 4466 Telex: 25775 Acpres G
Publishing Dir: David S B Inglis; *Sales, Marketing Dir:* D Duff; *Sales Manager:* Colin Lill; *Marketing Manager:* Jane Lawrence
Parent Company: Harcourt Brace Jovanovich Inc, Orlando, FL 32887, USA
Subjects: Economics & Business, Education & Psychology, Engineering & Computer Science, Foreign Languages, Humanities, Mathematics
Miscellaneous: Holt, Rinehart & Winston is an imprint of Harcourt Brace Jovanovich, UK (qv)
ISBN Publisher's Prefix: 0-03

Home Health Education Service, Stanborough Press, Alma Park, Grantham, Lincs Tel: Grantham 591800 (STD code 0476)
Man Dir: William Kitchen
Subjects: Secondary & Primary Education, Religion, Medical, Juveniles
ISBN Publisher's Prefix: 0-900703

Horseman's Handbooks, an imprint of Ward Lock Ltd (qv)

Ellis **Horwood** Ltd+*, Market Cross House, Cooper St, Chichester, West Sussex PO19 1EB Tel: Chicester 789942 (STD code 0243) Cable Add: Horwood Chichester Telex: 86402 Horwood
Editorial: Ellis Horwood MBE, Michael Horwood; *Production:* Clive Horwood, Sue Horwood; *Art & Design:* James Gillison; *Publicity:* Sue Horwood; *Marketing, Sales, Rights & Permissions:* Felicity Horwood
Orders to: John Wiley & Sons Ltd, Baffins Lane, Chichester, West Sussex; (Food Science and Biomedicine) VCH, Postfach 1260-1280, D-6940 Weinheim, Federal Republic of Germany
Subjects: Advanced Scientific Technology, Environmental Science, Engineering, Geology, Food Science, Water Science, Computer Science, School Level Computing, Mathematics, Chemistry, Medical & Biomedical, Sociology, Marine Science, Metallurgy
1986: 500 titles *Founded:* 1973
ISBN Publisher's Prefixes: 0-85312, 0-7458

Roger **Houghton** Ltd+*, Aldine House, 33 Welbeck St, London W1M 8LX Tel: (01) 486 7233 Cable Add: Malaby London W1 Telex: 8954130
Man Dir: Roger Houghton; *Editor:* Valerie Hudson; *Other personnel:* As for J M Dent & Sons Ltd (qv)
Orders to: J M Dent & Sons (Distribution) Ltd, Dunhams Lane, Letchworth, Hertfordshire SG6 1LF Tel: Letchworth 6241 (STD code 046 26)
1986: 8 titles *Founded:* 1985

Hour-Glass Press, an imprint of Bailey Brothers & Swinfen Co Ltd (qv)

How & Why Books, imprint of Transworld Publishers Ltd (qv)

Huddlesford, an imprint of Dickson Price Publishers Ltd (qv)

Angus **Hudson**, see Angus

Hugo's Language Books Ltd, 104 Judd St, London WC1H 9NF Tel: (01) 278 6136, (01) 837 0486 Telex: 8951182 Gecoms
Dirs: Mrs V Lock, Mrs J Lock, Mrs M Bolt, R J Batchelor-Smith, Peter G Lock; *Sales, Publicity, Rights & Permissions:* Peter G Lock; *Editorial:* Robin Batchelor-Smith
Subjects: How-to, Reference, Secondary Textbooks, Courses on cassette, Foreign Languages & EFL
Founded: 1875
ISBN Publisher's Prefix: 0-85285

Hulton Educational Publications Ltd, see Stanley Thornes & Hulton (Publishers) Ltd

Human Horizons Series, an imprint of Souvenir Press Ltd (qv)

C **Hurst** & Co (Publishers) Ltd+, 38 King St, London WC2E 8JT Tel: (01) 240 2666
Shipping Add: J M Dent & Sons Ltd, Dunhams Lane, Letchworth, Hertfordshire SG6 1LF
Man Dir: Christopher Hurst; *Rights & Permissions:* Michael Dwyer
Subjects: Area Studies (Contemporary History, Politics, Religion, Economic Development)
Founded: 1968
ISBN Publisher's Prefixes: 0-905838, 0-903983, 1-850650

Hutchinson, an imprint of Century Hutchinson Publishing Ltd (qv)

Hutchinson Books Ltd, now incorporated in Century Hutchinson Publishing Ltd (qv)

Hutchinson Business Books+, Brookmount House, 62-65 Chandos Pl, Covent Garden, London WC2N 4NW Tel: (01) 240 3411 Cable Add: Literatus Telex: 261212
Publisher: Victoria Huxley; *Marketing:* Mike Dugdale; *Publicity:* Susan Lamb; *Rights & Permissions:* Susan Wakeford
Orders to (trade): Tiptree Book Services Ltd, Church Rd, Tiptree, Colchester, Essex CO5 0SR Tel: Tiptree 816362 (STD code 0621)
Subjects: Management, Advertising, Marketing, Finance and Accounting, Personnel, Computers, Business Law, Small Business, Self Improvement, Business Biographies, Company Stories
1985: 10 titles
Miscellaneous: Hutchinson Business Books is an imprint of Century Hutchinson General Publishing Ltd (qv)
ISBN Publisher's Prefixes: 0-220 (for pre-1979 publications), 0-09 (for 1979 onwards)

Hutchinson Children's Books Ltd, an imprint of Century Hutchinson Publishing Ltd (qv)

Hutchinson Education+, Brookmount House, 62-65 Chandos Pl, Covent Garden, London WC2N 4NW Tel: (01) 240 3411 Cable Add: Literarius London W1 Telex: 261212
Man Dir: Mark Cohen; *Academic Books Dir:* Claire L'Enfant; *Technical Books Dir:* Brian Carvell; *Schoolbooks Dirs:* Pat Rowlinson, Helen Hancock; *Sales:* Dan Levey; *Export:* Gordon Bryant
Orders to: Tiptree Book Services Ltd, Church Rd, Tiptree, Colchester, Essex CO5 0SR Tel: Tiptree 816362 (STD code 0621)
Imprints: Hutchinson Technical Books, Hutchinson University Library
Subjects: School Books, Technical, Vocational, Academic
Miscellaneous: Hutchinson Education is a division of Century Hutchinson Ltd (qv)

The **Hutchinson Publishing Group** Ltd, now incorporated in Century Hutchinson Ltd (qv)

Hutchinson Technical Books, an imprint of Hutchinson Education (qv)

Hutchinson University Library, an imprint of Hutchinson Education (qv)

Hylton Lacy Publishers, an imprint of Profile Books Ltd (qv)

Hymns Ancient & Modern, St Mary's Works, St Mary's Plain, Norwich, Norfolk NR3 3BH Tel: Norwich 612914/616563 (STD code 0603)
Publisher: Gordon Knights
Associate Company: The Canterbury Press Norwich (at above address)
Subjects: Hymn Books, Prayer Books, General Religion
ISBN Publisher's Prefixes: 0-907547, 1-85311

I C Magazines Ltd, see International Communications

I C S A Publishing Ltd, a subsidiary company of Woodhead-Faulkner (Publishers) Ltd (qv)

I O P Publishing Ltd, Techno House, Redcliffe Way, Bristol BS1 6NX Tel: Bristol 297481 (STD code 0272) Telex: 449149 Fax: 0272 294318
Man Dir: Anthony Pearce; *Editorial Dirs:* David Kingham (Books), Dr Kurt Paulus (Journals); *Marketing:* Anthony Gresford (Books), Iain Loe (Journals)
Orders to: 7 Great Western Way, Bristol BS1 6HE Tel: Bristol 292151 (STD code 0272)
Subsidiary Company: Adam Hilger Ltd (qv)
Subjects: Physics, General Science, Medicine, Veterinary, Dentistry
Founded: 1874
ISBN Publisher's Prefixes: 0-85498, 0-85274

I R L Press+, PO Box 1, Eynsham, Oxford OX8 1JJ Tel: Oxford 882283 (STD code 0865) Telex: 83147 Irl Fax: (0865) 882890
Chief Executive: T R Otley; *Editorial, Production, Rights & Permissions:* E M Coast; *Sales, Publicity:* J C Bradley
Associate Company: Information Printing Ltd, Southfield Rd, Eynsham, Oxford OX8 1JJ
Branch Off: I R L Press Inc, PO Box Q, McLean, VA 22101-0850, USA
Subjects: Biomedical Sciences, Technical
1986: 30 titles *1987:* approx 30 titles
Founded: 1965 (as IRL)
ISBN Publisher's Prefixes: 0-904147, 0-947946, 1-85221

I T Publications, an imprint of Intermediate Technology Publications Ltd (qv)

450 UNITED KINGDOM

I T V Books, an imprint of Independent Television Books Ltd (qv)

Image, an imprint of Doubleday & Co Inc (qv)

Immel Publishing, Ely House, 37 Dover St, London W1X 3RB Tel: (01) 409 1343/ (01) 491 1799 Telex: 296582 Eltoup G Fax: (01) 409 1525
Man Dir: Anne Higgins
Subjects: Marine Biology, Middle East
1986: 8 titles
ISBN Publisher's Prefix: 0-907151

Independent Television Books Ltd, 247 Tottenham Court Rd, London W1P 0AU Tel: (01) 323 3222 Telex: 27813, 24643
Chairman: Alwyn Wise; *Editorial:* Colin Shelbourn; *Publicity:* Nigel Cole
Parent Company: Independent Television Publications Ltd (at above address)
Imprint: ITV Books
Subjects: TV Tie-ins, Humour, Reference, Children's Annuals & Paperbacks, Women's Interest, General

The Initial Teaching Alphabet Foundation*, 9 Brindle Close, Bamber Bridge, Preston, Lancs PR5 6ZN Tel: Preston 36963 (STD code 0772)
Secretary: J Bromley
Subject: Primary Education
ISBN Publisher's Prefix: 0-254

Institute of Development Studies, University of Sussex, Brighton BN1 9RE Tel: Brighton 606261 (STD code 0273) Cable Add: Development Brighton Telex: 877997 Idsbtn G
Secretary: B Claxton; *Editorial Assistant, Production, Publicity, Rights & Permissions:* Ms A Segrave; *Sales:* Mrs B Osborn, Mrs B Ferrier
Subjects: Development Studies
1985: 12 titles *Founded:* 1966
ISBN Publisher's Prefix: 0-903354

Institute of Education, University of London+, 20 Bedford Way, London WC1H 0A1 Tel: (01) 636 1500
Dir: Professor Denis Lawton; *Information and Publications Officer:* Denis Baylis
Imprint: Bedford Way
Subject: Educational Studies
1985: 8 titles *1986:* 10 titles *Founded:* 1902
ISBN Publisher's Prefix: 0-85473

Institute of Personnel Management, IPM House, Camp Rd, London SW19 4UW Tel: (01) 946 9100 Telex: 87476
Editorial: Tracey Smith
Orders to: IPM Distribution, George Philip Services Ltd, PO Box 1, Littlehampton, West Sussex BN17 7EN
Subjects: Management, Personnel Management
1985: 15 titles *1986:* 17 titles
ISBN Publisher's Prefix: 0-85292

Institute of Physics, see IOP

Institute of Pyramidology, 31 Station Rd, Harpenden, Hertfordshire AL5 4XB Tel: Harpenden 64510 (STD code 058 27)
Vice President: James Rutherford
Associate Company: Top Stone Books (qv)
Subject: Pyramidology
Founded: 1940
ISBN Publisher's Prefix: 0-903402

Institution of Chemical Engineers, George E Davis Bldg, 165-171 Railway Terrace, Rugby, Warwickshire CV21 3HQ Tel: Rugby 78214 (STD code 0788) Telex: 311780 Fax: (0788) 60833
General Secretary: Dr T J Evans
Subject: Chemical Engineering
Founded: 1922
ISBN Publisher's Prefix: 0-85295

The **Institution of Civil** Engineers (Publications Division), see Thomas Telford Ltd

Institution of Electrical Engineers+, Publishing Dept, PO Box 8, Southgate House, Stevenage, Hertfordshire SG1 1HQ Tel: Stevenage 313311 (STD code 0438) Telex: 825578 Ieestv G Fax: (0438) 313485
Publishing Dir: R Montrose; *Publishing Manager:* Dr Katie Petty-Saphon; *Marketing:* Owen Byatt; *Rights & Permissions:* John St Aubyn
Orders to: Publication Sales Dept, Institution of Electrical Engineers, PO Box 26, Hitchin, Hertfordshire SG5 1SA Tel: Hitchin 53331 (STD code 0462) Telex: 825962
Head Off & Bookshop: Savoy Pl, London WC2R 0BL
Subjects: Electrical & Electronic Engineering, Power, Control Science, Telecommunications, Computer Technology, IEE Conference Publication, Colloquium Digests, Technical Regulations, Vacation Schools, Periodicals
1987: 23 titles *Founded:* 1871
ISBN Publisher's Prefixes: 0-85296, 0-906048, 0-86341

Institution of Mechanical Engineers, see Mechanical Engineering Publications Ltd

Inter-Varsity Press, 38 De Montfort St, Leicester LE1 7GP Tel: Leicester 551700 (STD code 0533)
Publishing Dir: F R Entwistle; *Editorial:* D R W Wood; *Commercial Dir:* P S Rusted; *Production:* M R Sims
Orders to: IVP, Norton St, Nottingham NG7 3HR Tel: Nottingham 781054 (STD code 0602)
Parent Company: UCCF
Subject: Religion
Bookshops: UCCF Bookcentre, Norton St, Nottingham
Founded: 1928
ISBN Publisher's Prefixes: 0-85110, 0-85111

Intermediate Technology Publications Ltd+, 9 King St, London WC2E 8HW Tel: (01) 836 9434 Cable Add: Itdev Telex: 268312 Westcom G Intech
Chief Executive, Editorial, Production: Neal Burton; *Sales, Publicity, Rights & Permissions:* Veronica Hunt
Orders to: Unit 25, Longmead Industrial Estate, Shaftesbury, Dorset SP7 8PL
Parent Company: Intermediate Technology Development Group, Myson House, Railway Terrace, Rugby, Warwickshire CV21
Imprint: I T Publications
Subjects: Technology and Industries appropriate to Developing Countries (emphasis on low-cost, small-scale technology)
Bookshop: Intermediate Technology Bookshop (at above main address)
1986: 27 titles *Founded:* 1973
ISBN Publisher's Prefixes: 0-903031, 0-946688

International Bible Reading Association, see National Christian Education Council

International Biographical Centre, an imprint of Melrose Press Ltd (qv)

International Communications, PO Box 261, London WC2B 5BN (Located at: Carlton House, 69 Gt Queen St, London WC2B 5BN) Tel: (01) 404 4333 Cable Add: Machrak London WC2 Telex: 8811757 Araby G Fax: (01) 404 5336
Chairman & Man Dir: Ahmed Afif Ben Yedder; *Editorial, Rights & Permissions:* Emena Ben Yedder; *Sales:* Mike Cooper;
Publicity: Jean Tomlinson
Subsidiary Company: Ediafric — La Documentation Africaine, 10 rue Vineuse, F-75116 Paris, France
Associate Company: IC Publications Ltd, Suite 1121, 122 East 42nd St, New York, NY 10168, USA
Subjects: Africa and the Middle East (economic monographs, yearbooks and travel guides)
Founded: 1974
ISBN Publisher's Prefix: 0-905268

International Institute for Strategic Studies+, 23 Tavistock St, London WC2E 7NQ Tel: (01) 379 7676 Cable Add: Strategy London Telex: 265871 Monref G, Mag 90073
Dir: François Heisbourg; *Deputy Dir, Rights & Permissions:* Col J P Cross; *Publications Manager:* R J Wheelwright
Orders to: Marketing Services Dept, Jane's Publishing Co Ltd, 238 City Rd, London EC1V 2PU
Subjects: Strategic Studies, International Affairs, Military
1985: 13 titles *1986:* 15 titles *Founded:* 1958
ISBN Publisher's Prefix: 0-86079

International Textbook Co Ltd, Bishopbriggs, Glasgow G64 2NZ Tel: (041) 772 2311 Cable Add: Blackie Glasgow Telex: 777283
London Off: 7 Leicester Pl, London WC2H 7BP Tel: (01) 734 7521
Dir: Dr Graeme MacKintosh; *Sales Manager:* Kenneth J Allan
Orders to: J M Dent & Sons (Distribution) Ltd, Dunhams Lane, Letchworth, Hertfordshire SG6 1LF Tel: Letchworth 686241 (STD code 0462)
Parent Company: Blackie & Son Ltd (qv)
Associate Companies: Leonard Hill Ltd (qv); Surrey University Press (qv)
Subjects: Chemistry, Physics, Mathematics, Business Studies, Hotel and Catering
Founded: 1902
ISBN Publisher's Prefix: 0-7002

Invader Ltd+, 10 Eastgate Sq, Chichester, West Sussex PO19 1JH Tel: Chichester 783587 (STD code 0243) Telex: 946240 Cweasy ref 19018865
Chief Executive: C L Goldsmid
Subsidiary Company: Autumn Publishing Ltd; Zuidnerderlandse Uitgeverij NV, Belgium (qv)
Subject: Children's
1986: 15 titles *Founded:* 1985
ISBN Publisher's Prefix: 1-85129

Iolaire Selection, an imprint of Aquila Publishing (UK) Ltd (qv)

Isis Large Print+, 55 St Thomas' St, Oxford OX1 1JG Tel: Oxford 250333 (STD code 0865) Telex: 83130
Man Dir: John Durrant; *Marketing Dir:* Lyndsay Williams; *Sales Development Manager:* Jill Fieldgate; *Editorial Dir:* Tony Sloggett; *Promotions Manager:* Chas Walton
Parent Company: Clio Press Ltd (qv)
Associate Company: Isis Large Print Books, 2040 Alameda Padre Serra, PO Box 4397, Santa Barbara, CA 93140-4397, USA
Subjects: Non-fiction, Fiction, Reference
1985: 60 titles *Founded:* 1984
ISBN Publisher's Prefix: 1-85089

The **Islamic Foundation**, 223 London Rd, Leicester LE2 1ZE Tel: Leicester 700725 (STD code 0533) Cable Add: Islamfound Leicester UK Telex: 341539 Islamf G
Director General, Editorial: Dr M M Ahsan; *Sales, Production, Publicity:* T A Dale

Orders to: The Islamic Foundation Publications Unit, Unit 9, The Old Dunlop Factory, 62 Evington Valley Rd, Leicester Tel: Leicester 734860 (STD code 0533)
Subjects: Islamic Topics
1985: 14 titles *1986:* 7 titles *Founded:* 1973

J K Publishers*, 23 Denne Rd, Horsham, West Sussex RH12 1JF Tel: Horsham 50726 (STD code 0403)
Man Dir: Mrs Z Rustom; *Editorial, Sales, Production, Publicity:* J Knight
Subjects: Social Sciences, Science, Technology, Medicine, Art, Yoga, Indian Philosophy, Astrology, Palmistry, Geology & Mining, Agriculture, Fisheries, Zoology, Biology, Botany, Oceanography
Founded: 1977
ISBN Publisher's Prefixes: 0-86249, 0-906216, 0-906654

J N M Publications, Winster, Matlock, Derbyshire DE4 2DQ Tel: Winster 454 (STD code 062 988)
Man Dir: John N Merrill
Subjects: Guides (Walking & History)
1985: 15 titles *1986:* 20 titles *Founded:* 1982
ISBN Publisher's Prefix: 0-907496

J S O T Press, an imprint of Sheffield Academic Press Ltd (qv)

Arthur **James** Ltd, 1 Cranbourne Rd, London N10 2BT Tel: (01) 883 1831/2201/8307 Fax: (01) 883 8307
Man Dir: D M Duncan
Subjects: Religion, Psychology
Founded: 1935
ISBN Publisher's Prefix: 0-85305

Jane's Publishing Company Ltd, 238 City Rd, London EC1V 2PU Tel: (01) 251 9281 Telex: 894689 Fax: (01) 251 8900
Man Dir: Michael Goldsmith; *Commercial Dir:* John Stoddart; *European Sales Manager:* George Rainey; *Sales Dir:* Jeremy Gambrill; *Editorial Dirs:* Ken Harris, Bob Hutchinson; *Marketing Manager:* Mike Foster; *Production Manager:* David Moyes
Parent Company: Thomson Information Services Ltd (qv). Ultimate parent company International Thomson Organisation Ltd, 20 Queen St West, Box 45, Suite 2206, Toronto, Ontario M5H 3R3, Canada
Subsidiary Companies: Interavia SA, Switzerland (qv); Jane's Publishing Inc, 4th Floor 115, 5th Ave, New York, NY 10003, USA
Subjects: Naval, Military, Aviation, Transport Reference
Founded: 1979
ISBN Publisher's Prefix: 0-7106

Jarrold Colour Publications, Barrack St, Norwich NR3 1TR Tel: Norwich 660211 (STD code 0603) Cable Add: Jarrolds Telex: 97497
Man Dir, Rights & Permissions: Antony Jarrold; *Sales Manager:* T A Thompson
Imprints: Cotman House, White Horse Books, Cotmancolor, Glaven, Walsingham
Subjects: Topography, Travel, Natural History, Gardening, Hobbies
Bookshop: Jarrold Colour Publications, Barrack St, Norwich NR3 1TR
Founded: 1770
ISBN Publisher's Prefixes: 0-85306, 0-7117

Javelin Paperbacks, an imprint of Blandford Publishing Ltd (qv)

Jay books+, Woodside, Hadlow Park, Hadlow, Tonbridge, Kent TN11 0HZ Tel: Tonbridge 851438 (STD code 0732) Telex: 8955941 Ymeng G
Publisher: Ken Jackson
Imprint: Acorn
Subjects: Christian Communication, Media, Communications, Technology
1985: 2 titles *1986:* 5 titles *Founded:* 1985
ISBN Publisher's Prefixes: 0-9510086, 1-870404

Jet, an imprint of Brilliance Books (qv)

Jewish Chronicle Publications, 25 Furnival St, London EC4A 1JT Tel: (01) 405 9252 Telex: 28452
Chief Executive: M Weinberg
Parent Company: Jewish Chronicle Ltd (at above address)
Subjects: Judaism (all aspects)
Bookshop: At above address
1987: 15 titles

The **Johns Hopkins** University Press, c/o Trevor Brown Associates, Suite 7B, 26 Charing Cross Rd, London WC2H 0LN Tel: (01) 240 8774 Cable Add: Unibooks London WC2 Telex: 24224 ref 3545
Dir: J Trevor Brown; *Sales Manager:* Anna Simpson-Muellner (Export)
Parent Company: The Johns Hopkins University Press, 701 West 40th St, Suite 275, Baltimore, MD 21211, USA
Subjects: Literature, Humanities, Social Sciences, Sciences
ISBN Publisher's Prefix: 0-8018

Johnson Publications Ltd+*, 130 Wigmore St, London W1H 0AT Tel: (01) 486 6757 Telex: 817133
Dirs: M A Murray-Pearce, Z M Pauncefort
Orders to: Spring Court, Abbots Rd, Abbots Langley, Hertfordshire WD5 0BJ
Subjects: Medicine, History, Archaeology, Biography, Memoirs, Politics, Political Economy, Sociology, Questions of the Day, Travel & Adventure, Perfumery, Directories & Guidebooks, General Literature
ISBN Publisher's Prefix: 0-85307

Johnson Reprint Co Ltd, see Academic Press Inc (London) Ltd

Johnston & Bacon, an imprint of Cassell PLC (qv)

Johnston Green Publishing (UK) Ltd, now Aquila Publishing (UK) Ltd (qv)

Jordan & Sons Ltd, 21 St Thomas St, Bristol BS1 6JS Tel: Bristol 230600 (STD code 0272) Telex: 449119 Fax: (0272) 230063
Man Dir: Michael Whitwell; *Editorial and Sales Dir:* Patrick Lockstone; *Publishing Executive:* Stephen Roberts; *Marketing Dir:* Andrew Kampe
Subsidiary Company: Oswalds of Edinburgh Ltd, 24 Castle St, Edinburgh EH2 3HT Tel: (031) 225 7308 Telex: 72428
Imprints: Rose-Jordan, Family Law
London Off: Jordan House, 47 Brunswick Pl, London N1 6EE Tel: (01) 253 3030 Telex: 261010
Branch Offs: 3 Victoria St, Liverpool L2 5QF Tel: (051) 236 3631; 44 Whitchurch Rd, Cardiff CF4 3UQ Tel: Cardiff 371901 (STD code 0222)
Subjects: Legal & Parliamentary, Commercial, Business & Professional, Family Law Journals, Secondary, University, Commercial & Technical Education
Founded: 1863
ISBN Publisher's Prefixes: 0-85308 (Jordan), 0-907313 (Rose-Jordan)

Michael **Joseph** Ltd+, 27 Wright's Lane, London W8 5TZ Tel: (01) 937 7255 Telex: 917181 Fax: (01) 937 8704
Man Dir: Alan Brooke; *Export Sales Dir:* John Lyon; *Rights & Permissions:* Ruth Salazar
Parent Company: Penguin Books Ltd (qv)

Imprints: Mermaid, Pavilion Books, Pelham Books (qv)
Subjects: General, Fiction, Biography, History, How-to, Reference, Young Adult, Quality Paperbacks, Music
Founded: 1936
ISBN Publisher's Prefixes: 0-7181, 0-7207, 1-85145

The **Journeyman** Press Ltd+, 97 Ferme Park Rd, Crouch End, London N8 9SA Tel: (01) 348 9261 Telex: 265871 Monref G (quote 72:Mag 30663) Fax: (0903) 730012
Man Dir: Peter Sinclair; *Sales, Publicity:* Ian Sewell
Orders to: George Philip Services Ltd, Arndale Rd, Lineside Industrial Estate, Littlehampton, West Sussex BN17 7EN Tel: Worthing 717453 (STD code 0903)
Branch Off: Suite 807, 1170 Broadway, NY 10001, USA
Subjects: Politics, Social History, Fiction, Biography, Art, Poetry, Drama
1985: 6 titles *1986:* 2 titles *Founded:* 1975
ISBN Publisher's Prefixes: 0-904526, 1-85172

K P I, 11 New Fetter Lane, London EC4P 4EE Tel: (01) 583 9855
Man Dir: Peter Hopkins; *Marketing, Sales, Distribution:* Routledge (qv)
Associate Company: Routledge (qv)
ISBN Publisher's Prefix: 0-7103

Kahn & Averill*, 9 Harrington Rd, London SW7 3ES Tel: (01) 743 3278
Man Dir: M Kahn
Orders to: 21 Pennard Mansions, Goldhawk Rd, London W12 8DL
Subjects: General Non-fiction (with emphasis on music)
Founded: 1947
ISBN Publisher's Prefix: 0-900707

Kaye & Ward Ltd, now part of William Heinemann Ltd (qv)

Kelly's Directories, Windsor Court, East Grinstead House, East Grinstead, West Sussex RH19 1XB Tel: East Grinstead 26972 (STD code 0342) Telex: 95127 Infser G
Publishing Dir: D Lammin
Parent Company: Information Services Ltd (at above address), a division of Business Press International, Quadrant House, The Quadrant, Sutton, Surrey SM2 5AS
Subject: Directories (business, export, industry)
Founded: 1799
ISBN Publisher's Prefix: 0-610

Kemps Group (Printers & Publishers) Ltd+, Westbury House, 701-705 Warwick Rd, Solihull, West Midlands B91 3DA Tel: (021) 704 9200 Telex: 848314 Chacom G Fax: (021) 704 3791
Branch Off: 1-5 Bath St, London EC1V 9QA Tel: (01) 253 4761
Subjects: Trade Directories and Yearbooks, Chamber of Commerce Publications (annual), Specialised Business-to-Business Publications
Founded: 1912
ISBN Publisher's Prefix: 0-86259

Kershaw Publishing Co Ltd, 7 Bury Pl, London WC1A 2LA Tel: (01) 430 2460 Cable Add: Eurospan London WC2
Man Dir: Peter K Taylor; *Sales, Publicity, Advertising, Rights & Permissions:* Janet Buttery
Branch Off: Bolholt, Walshaw Rd, Bury, Lancs
Subjects: Mathematics, Social Sciences, Scholarly Reprints, Philosophy
1985: 6 titles *1986:* 8 titles *Founded:* 1969
ISBN Publisher's Prefix: 0-901665

Kestrel Books, an imprint of Penguin Books Ltd (qv)

Keswick, an imprint of Marshall Morgan & Scott (Publications) Ltd (qv)

William **Kimber** & Co Ltd, 100 Jermyn St, London SW1Y 6EE Tel: (01) 930 0446
Man Dir, Editor: William Kimber; *Rights & Permissions:* Amy Myers; *Production:* O J Colman; *Publicity Manager:* Betty Crockett
Subjects: Biography, History, General, Fiction, Current Affairs, Travel, Memoirs, Naval, Military, Aviation
Founded: 1950
ISBN Publisher's Prefix: 0-7183

William **Kimberley** Ltd+, 4 Church Close, London N20 0JU Tel: (01) 368 4121 Telex: 8813271 Gecoms G Fax: (01) 318 1439
Chief Executive, Editorial, Production, Publicity, Rights & Permissions: William Kimberley; *Sales:* Soheila Kimberley
Subjects: Automotive, Motor Racing, Children's Books
1985: 6 titles *1986:* 6 titles *Founded:* 1982
ISBN Publisher's Prefix: 0-946132

Kingfisher Books Ltd+, Elsley House, 24-30 Great Titchfield St, London W1P 7AD Tel: (01) 631 0878 Cable Add: Greatbooks London Telex: 27725 Gridem G Fax: (01) 323 4694
Man Dir: D Grisewood
Subjects: Children's, General Non-fiction
Founded: 1977
Miscellaneous: Publishing imprint of Grisewood & Dempsey Ltd (qv)
ISBN Publisher's Prefix: 0-86272

Kingsmead Press, an imprint of Avon–Anglia Publications & Services (qv)

Kingsway Publications Ltd, Lottbridge Drove, Eastbourne, East Sussex BN23 6NT Tel: Eastbourne 410930 (STD code 0323)
Chairman: Gilbert W Kirby; *Man Dir:* Geoff P Ridsdale; *Editorial Dir:* Richard Herkes; *Sales and Marketing Dir:* Neil Martin; *Production Dir:* David Nickalls
Imprints: Falcon Books, Kingsway Publications
Subjects: Religion, High- & Low-priced Paperbacks
1985: 56 titles *Founded:* 1977 (merger of Coverdale House Publishers Ltd and Victory Press)
ISBN Publisher's Prefixes: 0-86065 (Kingsway), 0-902088 and 0-85476 (titles formerly published as Coverdale and Victory respectively)

Kingswood Press, now Heinemann/Kingswood

Kluwer Publishing Ltd, 1 Harlequin Ave, Great West Rd, Brentford, Middlesex TW8 9EW Tel: (01) 568 6441
Man Dir, Editorial, Rights & Permissions: Colin Ancliffe; *Marketing:* Richard Heslop; *Production:* Peter Phillips
Parent Company: Kluwer Group, Netherlands (qv)
Imprints: Barry Rose, Kluwer Conferences, Kluwer Law, Kluwer Professional, City Financial, Questmere, SBIM
Subjects: Business, Management, Law, Taxation, Insurance, Finance, Health & Safety, Dentistry, Medicine, Farming, Security, Video, Pensions
1986: 25 titles *Founded:* 1972
Miscellaneous: Firm was created by Kluwer BV, Netherlands (qv) and George G Harrap & Co (qv)

Knight, an imprint of Hodder & Stoughton Ltd (qv)

Charles **Knight** Ltd, an imprint of Ernest Benn Ltd

Justin **Knowles** Publishing Group+, 9 Colleton Crescent, Exeter, Devon EX2 4BY Tel: Exeter 55467 (STD code 0392) Telex: 42833 Jkpub G Fax: (0392) 211652
Man Dir: Justin Knowles; *Managing Editor:* Lydia Darbyshire; *Production Controller:* Cath Pettyfer
Associate Companies: Black Pig Editions Ltd; Three Duck Editions Ltd (Disney licencee)
Subjects: Collectibles, Memorabilia, Disneyana, Film, Gardening, Dolls (all as international co-editions)
1985-86: 18 titles *1986-87:* 20 titles
Founded: 1983

Kogan Page Ltd+, 120 Pentonville Rd, London N1 9JN Tel: (01) 278 0433 Telex: 263088 Kogan G
Man Dir: Philip Kogan; *Publishing Dir:* Pauline Goodwin; *Sales & Marketing Dir:* Tom Davy; *Production Dir:* Peter Chadwick; *Publicity Manager:* Jenny Ertle
Imprint: North Oxford Academic
Subjects: New Technology & Science, Energy, Business & Management, Personnel, Training & Industrial Relations, Transport, Marketing, Commodities, Education & Educational Technology, Careers, Conservation, EEC/Unesco Publications
1985: 140 titles *Founded:* 1968
ISBN Publisher's Prefixes: 0-85038, 1-85091

L D A (Learning Development Aids), an imprint of Living and Learning (Cambridge) Ltd (qv)

L T P, an imprint of Language Teaching Publications (qv)

Ladybird Books Ltd, Beeches Rd, Loughborough, Leicestershire LE11 2NQ Tel: Loughborough 268021 (STD code 0509) Cable Add: Ladybird, Loughborough Telex: 341347 Fax: 0509 234672
Man Dir: M P Kelley; *Editorial Dir:* Michael Gabb; *Sales & Marketing Dir:* B Cotton; *Art Dir:* R Smith; *Production Dir:* Michael Banks; *Sales Managers:* G Duncan (UK), R Webster (Export); *Publicity:* Mary Hagger
Parent Company: Longman Group UK Ltd (qv)
Subjects: Children's Books, Educational (Infants, Primary, Secondary), Educational Materials
Founded: 1924
Miscellaneous: Formerly Wills & Hepworth Ltd
ISBN Publisher's Prefix: 0-7214

Lakeland, an imprint of Marshall Pickering (qv)

Lamp Press, an imprint of Pickering & Inglis Ltd (qv)

Jay **Landesman**, 8 Duncan Terrace, London N1 8BZ Tel: (01) 837 7290
Man Dir: Jay Landesman; *Editorial:* Cosmo Landesman, Julie Burchill; *Sales:* Stan Stunning; *Production:* Andrew Sanders; *Publicity, Rights:* Ingrid Danckwerts
Imprints: Golden Handshake, Polytantric Press
Subjects: Popular Culture, Social History, Satire, Bibliography, Biography
Founded: 1977
ISBN Publisher's Prefix: 0-905150

Landmark Books, 55 St Thomas' Street, Oxford OX1 1JG Tel: Oxford 250333 (STD code 0865) Telex: 83130
Man Dir: John Durrant; *Marketing Dir:* Lyndsay Williams; *Sales Development Manager:* Jill Fieldgate; *Editorial Dir:* Tony Sloggett; *Promotions Manager:* Chas Walton
Parent Company: ABC-CLIO, 2040 Alameda Padre Serra, PO Box 4397, Santa Barbara, CA 93140-4397, USA
Associate Company: ISIS Large Print Books, 2040 Alameda Padre Serra, PO Box 4397, Santa Barbara, CA 93140-4397, USA
Subjects: Fiction, Non-fiction
1986: 20 titles *Founded:* 1987
ISBN Publisher's Prefix: 1-55736

Allen **Lane**, see Allen

Lang Syne Publishers Ltd, 1 Tenth St, Newtongrange, Dalkeith, Midlothian Tel: (031) 663 4571
Man Dir: Kenneth W Laird
Subjects: Scottish & English Local Histories, Supernatural, Occult, Placename Origins, Engravings, Humour, Sport
1986: 24 titles *1987:* 12 titles *Founded:* 1975
ISBN Publisher's Prefix: 0-946264

Langham Press, an imprint of Octopus Books Ltd (qv)

Language Teaching Publications+, 35 Church Rd, Hove, East Sussex BN3 2BE Tel: Brighton 736344 (STD code 0273) Telex: 87250 Ell
Man Dirs: Michael Lewis, Jimmie Hill
Imprint: LTP
Subject: English language teaching
1986: 6 titles *1987:* 6 titles *Founded:* 1978
ISBN Publisher's Prefix: 0-906717

Lansdowne-Rigby International, now Merehurst Ltd (qv)

Roger **Lascelles**, 47 York Rd, Brentford, Middlesex TW8 0QP Tel: (01) 847 0935
Publisher: Roger Lascelles
Subjects: Travel Guides, Maps, Town Plans
1987: approx 20 titles *Founded:* 1975
ISBN Publisher's Prefix: 0-903909

Lawrence & Wishart, 39 Museum St, London WC1 Tel: (01) 405 0103 Cable Add: Interbook London WC1
Man Dir: J Skelley
Subjects: Biography, History, Philosophy, Politics, Economics
Founded: 1936
ISBN Publisher's Prefix: 0-85315

Legend, an imprint of Arrow Books Ltd (qv)

Leicester University Press+, Fielding Johnson Bldg, University of Leicester, University Rd, Leicester LE1 7RH Tel: Leicester 523334/523333 (STD code 0533) Telex: 341198
Secretary to the Press: P L Boulton
Subjects: Archaeology, History, Literature, International Relations, Politics, Defence Studies
1986: 15 titles *Founded:* 1951
ISBN Publisher's Prefix: 0-7185

Lennard Publishing, 92 Hastings St, Luton, Bedfordshire LU1 5BH Tel: Luton 404333 (STD code 0582) Fax: (0582) 27748
A division of Lennard Books Ltd
Man Dir: Adrian Stephenson; *Editorial:* Mark Booth, Roderick Brown; *Promotion, Sales, Subsidiary Rights:* Claire Sawford
Subjects: Biography, Business, Food & Wine, Gardening, Health, Heritage, Reference, Travel
Founded: 1987

Leonard Hill, Wester Cleddens Rd, Bishopbriggs, Glasgow G64 2NZ Tel: (041) 772 2311 Cable Add: Blacki G Telex: 777283

London Off: 7 Leicester Pl, London WC2H 7BP Tel: (01) 734 7521
Dir: Dr Graeme MacKintosh; *Sales Manager:* Kenneth J Allan
Orders to: J M Dent & Sons (Distribution) Ltd, Dunhams Lane, Letchworth, Hertfordshire SG6 1LF Tel: Letchworth 686241 (STD code 0462)
Parent Co: Blackie & Son Ltd (qv)
Associate Companies: International Textbook Co Ltd, Surrey University Press (qqv)
Subjects: Reference, Food Technology, Industrial Chemistry, Agriculture
ISBN Publisher's Prefix: 0-249

Leopard, an imprint of Scripture Union (qv)

Charles **Letts** & Co Ltd+, Diary House, Borough Rd, London SE1 1DW Tel: (01) 407 8891 Cable Add: Diarists London Telex: 884498
Chairman: A A Letts; *Marketing Dir:* P P Reynolds; *Sales Manager:* P J Matthews
Subjects: Education, General Non-fiction
Founded: 1796
ISBN Publisher's Prefix: 0-85097

Lionel **Leventhal** Ltd see Greenhill Books/Lionel Leventhal Ltd

A **Lewis**, an imprint of Ian Allan Ltd (qv)

F **Lewis** Publishers Ltd, an imprint of A & C Black (Publishers) Ltd (qv)

H K **Lewis** & Co Ltd, 136 Gower St, London WC1E 6BS Tel: (01) 387 4282 Cable Add: Publicavit, London WC1E 6BS
Subjects: Technical & Scientific, Medical
ISBN Publisher's Prefix: 0-7186

J D **Lewis** & Sons Ltd, see Gomer Press

John **Libbey** & Co Ltd, 80-84 Bondway, London SW8 1SF Tel: (01) 582 5266 Telex: 94013503 John
Man Dir: John Libbey; *Editorial Dir:* Eldred Smith-Gordon
Subsidiary Company: John Libbey Eurotext Ltd, 6 rue Blanche, Montrouge, F-92120 France
Subjects: Medical
1985: 23 titles *1986:* 35 titles *Founded:* 1979
ISBN Publisher's Prefix: 0-86196

Library and Information Statistics Unit, Loughborough University, Loughborough, Leicestershire LE11 3TU Tel: Loughborough 223071 (STD code 0509) Cable Add: Technology Loughborough Telex: 34319 Fax: (0509) 231983
Dir: Dr P H Mann
Subject: Library and Information Statistics
1986: 11 titles *Founded:* 1987
Miscellaneous: Previously Library Management Research Unit (1969-79) and Centre for Library and Information Management (1979-87)
ISBN Publisher's Prefix: 0-948848

Library Association Publishing, 7 Ridgmount St, London WC1E 7AE Tel: (01) 636 7543 Telex: 21897 Laldn G
Man Dir: Charles Ellis; *Sales Office Manager:* Beverly Brentnall; *Publicity:* Ann Harrold
Warehouse: Distribution & Management Services Ltd, Sheldon Way, Larkfield, Maidstone, Kent ME20 6SE Tel: Maidstone 882000 (STD code 0622) Telex: 965514
Associate Company: Clive Bingley Ltd (qv)
Branch Off: 9 Station Rd, St Ives, Huntingdon, Cambridgeshire
Subjects: Bibliographies, Library Science, Directories, Catalogues, Indexes, Serials
Founded: 1981
ISBN Publisher's Prefix: 0-85365

Life Changing Books, an imprint of Marshall, Morgan & Scott Publications Ltd (qv)

Frances **Lincoln** Ltd+, Apollo Works, 5 Charlton Kings Rd, London NW5 2SB Tel: (01) 482 3302 Telex: 21376 Fax: (01) 485 0490
Man Dir: Frances Lincoln; *Sales:* Nicholas Kennedy
Associate Company: Frances Lincoln Publishers Ltd
Subjects: Art, Archaeology, Architecture, Interior Design, DIY, Cookery, Gardening, Natural History, Health, Childcare, Photography, Computers, Children's Books (packagers of high-quality illustrated books for international co-editions)
1987: 14 titles *Founded:* 1978
ISBN Publisher's Prefix: 0-906459

Linden Press, see Centaur Press Ltd

Lines, an imprint of Macdonald Publishers (Edinburgh) (qv)

Linford Mystery Library Series, see F A Thorpe (Publishing) Ltd

Linford Romance Library Series, see F A Thorpe (Publishing) Ltd

Linford Western Library Series, see F A Thorpe (Publishing) Ltd

Ling Kee (UK) Ltd, 47 Marylebone Lane, London W1M 6AX Tel: (01) 486 3271 Telex: 266231 Wleco
Chief Operating Officer: A Montague Alfred
UK Group Members: BLA Publishing Ltd, Thames Head, Ward Lock Educational Co Ltd (qqv)
Miscellaneous: Firm is a member of the Ling Kee Group, Hong Kong (qv)

Link House Books, now Blandford Publishing Ltd (qv)

Lion Publishing PLC, Icknield Way, Tring, Hertfordshire HP23 4LE Tel: Tring 5151 (STD code 044 282) Telex: 825850 Lion G Fax: (044 282) 7251
Man Dir: David Vesey; *Editorial:* Pat Alexander; *Rights, International Sales:* Tony Wales, Alan Butler, Rosemary North, Colin Nutt; *Marketing Manager:* Mark Beedell; *Publicity Manager:* Philip Henderson
Subsidiary Company: Lion Publishing Corporation (at above address and Michigan, USA)
Associate Company: Albatross Books, Australia (qv)
Imprint: Aslan
Subjects: Religion, Reference, Children, Educational Materials, Paperback Fiction & Non-fiction
1987: 65 titles *Founded:* 1972
ISBN Publisher's Prefixes: 0-85648, 0-7459

Lions, an imprint of William Collins PLC (qv)

Litor Publishers, 45 Grand Parade, Brighton, East Sussex BN2 2QA Tel: Brighton 603254 (STD code 0273) Telex: 87369
Dir: Bengt Christiansen
Subject: Children's Books
ISBN Publisher's Prefix: 0-85322

Little Stephen, an imprint of Mencap Publications (qv)

Liveright, an imprint of W W Norton & Co Ltd (qv)

Liverpool University Press, PO Box 147, Liverpool L69 3BX Tel: (051) 709 6022 ext 2429/2512 Cable Add: Cormorant Telex: 627095 Fax: (051) 708 6502

Man Dir, Sales & Promotion: R J C Bloxsidge
Orders to: IOP Publishing Ltd, 7 Great Western Way, Bristol BS1 6HE Tel: Bristol 292151 (STD code 0272)
Subjects: Architecture, Archaeology, Oriental Studies, Economics, Education, Philosophy, General & Social Science, Medicine, Politics, History, Literature, Environmental Sciences, University Textbooks, Veterinary Science
Founded: 1899
ISBN Publisher's Prefix: 0-85323

Livewire, an imprint of The Women's Press Ltd (qv)

Living & Learning (Cambridge) Ltd, Duke St, Wisbech, Cambridgeshire PE13 2AE Tel: Wisbech 63441 (STD code 0945)
Man Dir, Sales, Publicity, Rights & Permissions: Simon J Lyne; *Editorial:* Dennis B Blackmore; *Production:* Paul Beresford
Imprints: ESM (Educational Software for Microcomputers), LDA (Learning Development Aids)
Subjects: Primary Education, Educational books and materials for children with learning difficulties, Educational software for microcomputers
Founded: 1973
ISBN Publisher's Prefix: 0-905114

Lloyd-Luke (Medical Books) Ltd, 41 Bedford Sq, London WC1B 3DQ Tel: (01) 637 7161 Telex: 265806 Edward G
Chairman, Man Dir: Anthony Hamilton; *Editorial Dir:* Paul J Price
Parent Company: Edward Arnold (Publishers) Ltd
Subjects: Medical
Founded: 1951
ISBN Publisher's Prefix: 0-85324

Lloyd's of London Press Ltd, Sheepen Pl, Colchester, Essex CO3 3LP Tel: Colchester 772277 (STD code 0206) Cable Add: Lloydslist London EC3 Telex: 987321 Lloyds G Fax: (0206) 46273
Chief Executive: C W Welch; *Marketing Services Manager:* Guy Hewitt; *Production:* Ted Martin; *Press Officer:* Nedda Bradbury
Parent Company: Corporation of Lloyd's, Lime St, London EC3
Subsidiary Companies: Lloyd's of London Press Ltd, Deichstrasse 41, Postfach 112347, D-2000 Hamburg 11, Federal Republic of Germany; Lloyd's of London Press (Far East) Ltd, 903 Chung Nam Bldg, 1 Lockhart Rd, Hong Kong; Lloyd's of London Press Inc, Suite 523, 611 Broadway, New York, NY 10012, USA
Associate Company: Lloyd's Maritime Information Services, Dunster House, 17-20 Mark Lane, London EC3R 7AP
Subjects: Maritime, Law
1985: 26 titles *1986:* 33 titles *Founded:* 1973
ISBN Publisher's Prefix: 1-85044

Local Heritage Books, a subsidiary company of Countryside Books (qv)

Lochee Publications Ltd, Oak Villa, New Alyth, Perthshire, Scotland PH11 8NN Tel: Alyth 2154 (STD code 082 83)
Chief Executive, Editorial, Rights & Permissions: Prof Rex William Last; *Sales, Production, Publicity:* Oksana Susanna Last
Imprint: LocheeSoft
Subjects: Educational, Language & Literature, Scottish Local History, Philosophy
1985: 7 titles *1986:* 11 titles *Founded:* 1983
ISBN Publisher's Prefixes: 0-947584, 1-807139

LocheeSoft, an imprint of Lochee Publications Ltd (qv)

Locomotion Papers, an imprint of Oakwood Press (qv)

Locomotive Publishing Co Ltd, an associate company of Ian Allan Ltd (qv)

Lodenek Press Ltd, 17 Duke St, Padstow, Cornwall   Tel: Padstow 532282 (STD code 0841)
Man Dir, Sales, Production, Rights & Permissions: D R Rawe; *Editorial:* H J Ingrey
Associate Company: Truran Publications, Trewolsta, Trewirgie Hill, Redruth, Cornwall
Subjects: Cornish, West Country and Celtic Books
Bookshop: 17 Duke St, Padstow
Founded: 1970
ISBN Publisher's Prefixes: 0-902899, 0-946143

Loeb Classical Library, an imprint of William Heinemann Ltd (qv)

Y Lolfa Cyf, Hen Swyddfa'r Heddlu, Talybont, Ceredigion, Dyfed SY24 5HE   Tel: Talybont 304 (STD code 097 086)
Man Dir, Production: Robat Gruffudd; *Editorial:* Rhiannon Ifans; *Marketing Manager, Publicity, Rights & Permissions:* Meinir Vittle
Imprint: Lol
Subjects: Welsh-language Fiction and Non-fiction, Welsh-language Instruction, Welsh Politics (in English)
1985: 17 titles   *1986:* 30 titles   *Founded:* 1965
ISBN Publisher's Prefix: 0-86243

London Editions, an imprint of World International Publishing Ltd (qv)

London Magazine Editions, 30 Thurloe Pl, London SW7   Tel: (01) 589 0618
Man Dir, Sales Dir, Rights & Permissions: Alan Ross
Orders to: Biblios Publishers' Distribution Services Ltd, Glenside Industrial Estate, Star Rd, Partridge Green, Horsham, West Sussex RH13 8LD   Tel: Partridge Green 710971 (STD code 0403)
Subsidiary: 'London Magazine' (a monthly review of the contemporary arts)
Subjects: General Fiction, Belles Lettres, Poetry, Biography, Memoirs
Founded: 1954

Longman Group UK Ltd+, Longman House, Burnt Mill, Harlow, Essex CM20 2JE   Tel: Harlow 26721 (STD code 0279)   Cable Add: Longman Harlow   Telex: 81259   Fax: (0279) 31059
Chief Executive: T J Rix; *Group Sales Dir:* J Osborne; *Sales and Marketing Dir:* D Crane; *Foreign Rights:* Lynette Owen; *Permissions:* David Lea
Parent Company: Longman Holdings Ltd (at above address). Ultimate parent company Pearson PLC, Millbank Tower, Millbank, London SW1P 4QZ
Fellow Subsidiary Companies: Crown Eagle Communications Ltd, Ladybird Books Ltd (qv), Longman Cartermill Ltd, Pitman Publishing Ltd (qv), UK Tax Congress Ltd (all UK); Longman Cheshire Pty Ltd (qv), Longman Professional Publishing Pty Ltd (both Australia); Longman Botswana (Pty) Ltd, Botswana (qv); Copp Clark Pitman Ltd, Canada; Longman France SA, 24 rue Lafayette, F-75009, Paris, France; Longman Hellas Publishing SA, Greece; Longman Group (Far East) Ltd, Hong Kong (qv); Longman Italia SRL, via Felice, Casati 20, Milan, Italy; Longman Jamaica Ltd, Jamaica (qv); Longman Penguin Japan Co Ltd, Yamaguchi Bldg, 2-12-9 Kanda Jimbocho, Chiyodu-ku, Tokyo 101, Japan; Longman Kenya Ltd, Kenya (qv); Longman Lesotho (Pty) Ltd, Lesotho (qv); Longman Malaysia Sdn Bhd (qv), Pitman Malaysia Sdn Bhd (both Malaysia); Longman Paul Ltd, Pitman Publishing NZ Ltd (qv) (both New Zealand); Longman Singapore (Pte) Ltd, Republic of Singapore (qv); Longman España SA, San Nicolas 15, 28013 Madrid, Spain; Longman Swaziland (Pty) Ltd, PO Box 1508, Manzini, Swaziland; Longman Tanzania Ltd, Tanzania (qv); Longman Caribbean Ltd, Trinidad (qv); Longman Uganda Ltd, Uganda (qv); Longman Group USA Inc, 520 North Dearborn St, Chicago, IL 60610, USA; Longman Zimbabwe (Pvt) Ltd, Zimbabwe (qv)
Associate Companies: The Egyptian International Publishing Co-Longman, 10A Hussein Wassef, Midan Missaha, Dokki-Giza, Egypt; Armand Colin Longman SA, 103 blvd Saint-Michel, F-75240, Paris, France; Langenscheidt-Longman GmbH, Federal Republic of Germany (qv); B I Churchill Livingstone Pvt Ltd (54 Janpath, New Delhi 100001), Orient Longman Ltd (qv) (both India); Wolters-Noordhoff-Longman BV, Netherlands (qv); Longman Nigeria Ltd, Nigeria (qv); Maskew Miller Longman Pty Ltd (50% owned), Republic of South Africa (qv)
Imprints: Churchill Livingstone (qv), Common Ground, Longman Professional, Longman Scientific & Technical, Meriam Webster, Oliver & Boyd (qv), Pitman (qv), Polytech, Sybex
Branch Offs: 5 Bentinck St, London W1M 5RN; Robert Stevenson House, Baxter's Pl, Leith Walk, Edinburgh   Tel: (031) 556 2424; 21-27 Lamb's Conduit St, London WC1N 3NJ   Tel: (01) 242 2548; Westgate House, The High, Harlow CM20 1NE   Tel: Harlow 442601 (STD code 0279)
Subjects: Agriculture, Archaeology, Atlases & Maps, Aviation, Biography & Autobiography, Business & Tax, History, Children's Books, Dictionaries, Sociology, Economics, Education, Sciences, Geography, Travel, Educational Books, Engineering, Law, Linguistics & Languages, Literature, Mathematics, Medicine & Health, Music, Natural History, Philosophy, Poetry, Politics, Psychology, Reference, Anthropology, Accountancy, Veterinary, Zoology, Study Guides (joint publishers of *York Notes*). Electronic media: database services
Founded: 1724
ISBN Publisher's Prefixes: 0-582 (Longman), 0-85120, 0-85121 (both Longman Professional), 0-7056 (Common Ground), 0-85505 (Polytech), 0-87779 (Meriam Webster), 0-89588 (Sybex)

Louisiana State University Press, see Academic and University Publishers Group

Peter **Lowe**, an imprint of Eurobook Limited (qv)

Robson **Lowe** Ltd+*, 47 Duke St, St James's, London SW1Y 6QX   Tel: (01) 839 4034   Cable Add: Stamps London SW1   Telex: 8950974
Group Man Dir: Charles Leonard; *Publicity & Advertising:* Peter Collins, Louise Burman
Parent Company: Christies International Group
Branch Offs: The Auction House, 39 Poole Hill, Bournemouth, Dorset BH2 5PX; Robson Lowe International, Via Dell'Orso 7a, 20121 Milan, Italy
Subjects: Philately, Postal History
Founded: 1920
ISBN Publisher's Prefix: 0-85397

Lucis Press Ltd, Suite 54, 3 Whitehall Court, London SW1A 2EF   Tel: (01) 839 4512
Dirs: Mary Bailey (USA), J J G Bourne, Janet E Nation, S I W Nation
Associate Company: The Lucis Publishing Co, 113 University Pl, 11th Floor, New York, NY 10003, USA
Subjects: Educational, Religious, Sociology, Questions of the Day, Philosophy, Esoteric, Astrology
ISBN Publisher's Prefix: 0-85330

Lund Humphries Publishers Ltd, 16 Pembridge Rd, London W11 3HL   Tel: (01) 229 1825   Telex: 8952387 ref Lundhumpub
Orders to: IOP Publishing Ltd, 7 Great Western Way, Bristol BS1 6HE
Parent Company: Book Publishing Development PLC (at above main address)
Subjects: Art, Architecture, Graphic Arts, Arabic Language
1986: 15 titles
ISBN Publisher's Prefix: 0-85331

Lutterworth Press+, 50-52 Kingston St, Cambridge CB1 2NT   Tel: Cambridge 350865 (STD code 0223)   Telex: 817114
Man Dir: Adrian Brink; *Editorial, Rights Manager:* Linda Yeatman; *Sales Manager:* Keith Robinson; *Production Manager:* Patricia Rowland; *Publicity Manager:* Kerry Harvey-Piper
Subjects: Biography, History, How-to, Music, Reference, Religion, Juveniles, Paperbacks, Antiques, Architecture, Gardening, Leisure and Craft, Chess, Travel, Arts
1985: 32 titles   *1986:* 23 titles   *Founded:* 1799
Miscellaneous: An imprint of James Clarke & Co Ltd (qv)
ISBN Publisher's Prefix: 0-7188

Luxor Press Ltd, see Charles Skilton Ltd

Lyle Publications Ltd, Glenmayne, Galashiels, Selkirkshire TD1 3NR   Tel: Galashiels 2005 (STD code 0896)
Dirs: T Curtis, Annette Curtis
Subjects: Antiques, Price Guides, Art Reference
ISBN Publisher's Prefix: 0-86248

Lythway Press Ltd, Windsor Bridge Rd, Bath, Avon BA2 3AX   Tel: Bath 335336 (STD code 0225)   Telex: 444633   Fax: (0225) 310771
Man Dir: Roger Lewis; *Publishing Dir:* Julian Batson; *Rights Manager:* Nicole Kirkman; *Production Manager:* Lesley Barnes
Parent Company: The Gieves Group PLC, 1 Savile Row, London W1X 2JR
Associate Companies: Chivers Book Sales Ltd, 93-100 Locksbrook Rd, Bath BA1 3HB; Chivers Press Publishers (qv); Firecrest Publishing Ltd (qv)
Imprints: Lythway Large Print, Lythway Children's Large Print
Subjects: Romance, Thrillers, Mystery, Westerns, General Fiction & Non-fiction, Children's Fiction
Founded: 1972
ISBN Publisher's Prefixes: 0-85046, 0-85119, 0-7451

M C B University Press Ltd, 62 Toller Lane, Bradford, West Yorkshire BD8 9BY   Tel: Bradford 499821 (STD code 0274)   Telex: 51317 Mcbuni G   Fax: (0274) 547143
Man Dir: Professor Gordon Wills; *Sales:* Christine Hudson; *Production, Rights & Permissions:* Cathy Mostyn; *Publicity:*

Sarah Carte
Branch Off: PO Box 10812, Birmingham, Alabama 35201, USA
Subjects: Professional, Management
Founded: 1969
ISBN Publisher's Prefixes: 0-86176, 0-95440

M E P, an imprint of Mechanical Engineering Publications Ltd (qv)

M G P, Mary Glasgow Publications, see under Glasgow

M I N D (National Association for Mental Health), 22 Harley St, London W1N 2ED Tel: (01) 637 0741
Dir: Christopher Heginbotham
Orders to: MIND Publications Mail Order Service, 4th Floor, 24-32 Stephenson Way, London NW1 2HD
Subjects: Mental Health/Illness
1985: 8 titles *1986:* 10 titles *Founded:* 1946
ISBN Publisher's Prefix: 0-900557

The **M I T** Press, 126 Buckingham Palace Rd, London SW1W 9SA Tel: (01) 730 9208 Cable Add: Chibooks Telex: 23933 Chibooks Ldn
General Manager: Neville Gosling; *Publicity Manager:* Ann Sexsmith
Orders to: IBD Ltd, 66 Wood Lane End, Hemel Hempstead, Hertfordshire Tel: Hemel Hempstead 58531 (STD code 0442)
Associate Companies: University of Chicago Press, Harvard University Press (qqv)
Subjects: Biography, History, Music, Art, Philosophy, Reference, Paperbacks, Architecture, Medicine, Psychology, Engineering, General & Social Science, Education, Linguistics, Computer Science
Founded: 1932
Miscellaneous: Branch of MIT Press, Cambridge, MA, USA
ISBN Publisher's Prefix: 0-262

M R P, see Motor Racing Publications Ltd

M T P Press Ltd+, Falcon House, Queen Sq, Lancaster LA1 1RN Tel: Lancaster 68765 (STD code 0524) Telex: 65212 Fax: (0524) 63232
Editorial Dir: Dr P Clarke; *Sales Dir, Rights & Permissions:* C K Timms; *Sales Manager:* T Witcher; *Editor:* Dr J Brewis; *Production Manager:* V Moran; *Promotions Manager:* P Fawley
Parent Company: Kluwer Group, Netherlands (qv)
Subject: Medicine
1985: 75 titles *1986:* 53 titles *Founded:* 1969
ISBN Publisher's Prefixes: 0-85200, 0-7462

M W H London Publishers*, 233 Seven Sisters Rd, London N4 2DA Tel: (01) 272 5170 Cable Add: Muslimdar London N4 Telex: 8812176 Muslim G
Man Dir: Ashur A Shamis
Associate Company: Muslim Information Services, UK
Subjects: Islamic and Arabic Studies
Bookshop: At above address
Founded: 1970
Miscellaneous: Formerly Muslim Welfare House
ISBN Publisher's Prefix: 0-906194

McCrimmon Publishing Co Ltd+, 10-12 High St, Great Wakering, Southend-on-Sea, Essex SS3 0EQ Tel: Southend-on-Sea 218956 (STD code 0702)
Dirs: Donald McCrimmon, Joan McCrimmon, Sylvia McDonald
Associate Companies: Celebration Records; Rainbow Books; Ecuvision
Subjects: Religion, Primary & Secondary Textbooks, Educational Materials, Music, Prayer Books, Liturgy, Hymn Books

Founded: 1968
ISBN Publisher's Prefix: 0-85597

Macdonald 3/4/5, an imprint of Macdonald & Co (Publishers) Ltd (qv)

Macdonald & Co (Publishers) Ltd+, 3rd Floor, Greater London House, Hampstead Rd, London NW1 7QX Tel: (01) 377 4600 Cable Add: Macdon G Telex: 885233 Macdon G Fax: (01) 387 9286
Man Dir: Kevin Maxwell; *Deputy Man Dir:* Ken Pickett; *Marketing & Sales Dir:* Terry Melia; *Export Sales Dir:* David Parrish; *Editorial:* Richard Evans (Futura Non-fiction, Fiction & Paperback), Alan Samson (Queen Anne Press), Mary Tapissier (Macdonald Children's, Purnell Books, Beehive), Sarah Snape (Mac/Orbis Illustrated Books); *Production:* John Moulder; *Publicity Dir:* Penelope McNeile; *Rights & Permissions:* Roberta Bailey (Children's Optima), Ian McLellan (Adult Illustrated/Orbis), Nann du Sautoy (Futura, Queen Anne Press)
Orders to: Purnell Book Centre, Paulton, Bristol BS18 5LQ Tel: Midsomer Norton 413301 (STD code 0761)
Parent Company: Maxwell Communication Corporation plc (qv)
Associate Companies: Macdonald Publishers (NZ) Ltd, New Zealand; Macdonald Purnell (Pty) Ltd, Republic of South Africa (qv)
Imprints: Beehive, Futura, Macdonald Educational, Macdonald Queen Anne Press, Orbis, Orbit, Playfair, Purnell Books, Troubadour
Subjects: General Fiction and Non-fiction, Children's, Sport, Educational, Adult Illustrated
1986: approx 600 titles *Founded:* 1981 (previously Macdonald Educational, Macdonald & Jane's and Futura Publications (all founded 1973), and Macdonald/Futura (founded 1980))
ISBN Publisher's Prefixes: 0-356 (Macdonald, Macdonald Educational, Queen Anne Press), 0-7088, 0-86007 (Futura), 0-361 (Purnell), 0-7107 (Troubadour)

Macdonald & Evans Ltd, an imprint of Pitman Publishing Ltd (qv)

Macdonald Edinburgh, an imprint of Macdonald Publishers (Edinburgh) (qv)

Macdonald Educational, an imprint of Macdonald & Co (Publishers) Ltd (qv)

Macdonald Guidelines, an imprint of Macdonald & Co (Publishers) Ltd (qv)

Macdonald Publishers (Edinburgh), Edgefield Rd, Loanhead, Midlothian EH20 9SY Tel: (031) 440 0246
Man Dir, Publishing Manager: Ian McNee; *Rights & Permissions, Publicity:* Mrs M Laing; *Sales:* Yvonne Burt
Imprints: Macdonald Edinburgh, Lines
Subjects: Biography, Criticism, Fiction, General Non-fiction, Children's Books, Poetry, Guides
ISBN Publisher's Prefixes: 0-904265, 0-86334

Macdonald Queen Anne Press, an imprint of Macdonald & Co (Publishers) Ltd (qv)

Macdonald Starters, an imprint of Macdonald & Co (Publishers) Ltd (qv)

McGraw-Hill Book Co (UK) Ltd, Shoppenhangers Rd, Maidenhead, Berkshire SL6 2QL Tel: Maidenhead 23431 (STD code 0628) Cable Add: McGrawHill Telex: 848484 Fax: (0628) 35895
Man Dir: Stephen White; *Sales Dirs:* Steve Sidaway (UK), Donald Paul (Export);

UNITED KINGDOM 455

Dirs: Jeremy Dicks (College/University), John Watson (Vocational Education), Roland Elgey (Business & Professional)
Parent Company: McGraw-Hill Inc, 1221 Ave of the Americas, New York, NY 10020, USA
Associate Companies: McGraw-Hill Book Co Australia Pty Ltd, Australia (qv); Editora McGraw-Hill do Brasil Ltda, Brazil (qv); McGraw-Hill Ryerson Ltd, Canada; Editorial McGraw-Hill Latinoamericana SA, Colombia (qv); MEDSI, McGraw-Hill Inc, France (qqv); McGraw-Hill Book Co GmbH, Federal Republic of Germany (qv); Tata McGraw-Hill Publishing Co Ltd, India (qv); McGraw-Hill Book Co Japan Ltd, Japan (qv); Libros McGraw-Hill de Mexico SA de CV, Mexico (qv); McGraw-Hill Book Co, New Zealand Ltd, New Zealand (qv); Editorial McGraw-Hill Latinoamericana SA, Panama (qv); Editora McGraw-Hill de Portugal Lda, Portugal (qv); Editorial McGraw-Hill Latinoamericana SA, Puerto Rico (qv); McGraw-Hill International Book Co, Republic of Singapore (qv); McGraw-Hill Interamericana de España SA, Spain (qv)
Subjects: Reference, Medicine, Psychology, Engineering, Computing, General & Social Science, University, Secondary Textbooks, Educational Materials, Gregg Shorthand, Further Education, Management, Computing
Founded: 1899
ISBN Publisher's Prefix: 0-07

Grant **McIntyre** Ltd, now incorporated in Basil Blackwell Publisher Ltd (qv)

Macmillan Children's Books, 4 Little Essex St, London WC2R 3LF Tel: (01) 836 6633 Cable Add: Publish London WC2 Telex: 262024 Fax: (01) 379 4204
Publishing Dir: Michael Wace; *Rights:* Sharon Alpe
Subjects: Picture books, Fiction, Non-fiction, Pop-up, Novelty, Paperbacks
1987: 90 titles
Miscellaneous: A Division of Macmillan Publishers Ltd (qv)

Macmillan Education Ltd, Houndmills, Basingstoke, Hampshire RG21 2XS Tel: Basingstoke 29242 (STD code 0256) Cable Add: Publish Basingstoke Telex: 858493 Fax: (0256) 479476
Chairman: A Soar; *Man Dir:* J E Jackman; *Publishing Dirs:* R S Balkwill (Primary & Secondary Schools Educational Media), P I Murby (College), D J Mortimer (Intek, Packaged Technical Training); *Marketing Dir:* P Bruce-Gardyne; *Rights Manager:* L M Albin
Parent Company: Macmillan Publishers Ltd (qv)
Subjects: Primary, Secondary, College & University Textbooks, Educational Materials & Software
ISBN Publisher's Prefix: 0-333

Macmillan London Ltd+, 4 Little Essex St, London WC2R 3LF Tel: (01) 836 6633 Cable Add: Publish London WC2 Telex: 262024 Fax: (01) 379 4204
Chairman: N Byam Shaw; *Man Dir, Publisher:* Philippa Harrison; *Publishing Dirs:* Kyle Cathie (Papermac), Adam Sisman (Non-fiction), James Hale (Fiction), Michael Wace (Children's Books), Hilary Hale (Crime); *Rights & Permissions Dir:* Mary Pachnos; *Sales Dir:* David Rivers; *Marketing, Publicity Dir:* Martin Neild; *Production Manager:* Tracie Florance
Parent Company: Macmillan Publishers Ltd (qv)
Imprint: Papermac
Subjects: General Fiction, Poetry,

Biography, History, Military History, Natural History, Cookery, Suspense, Art, Reference, Juveniles, High-priced Paperbacks
ISBN Publisher's Prefix: 0-333

The Macmillan Press Ltd+, Houndmills, Basingstoke, Hampshire RG21 2XS Tel: Basingstoke 29242 (STD code 0256) Telex: 858493 Fax: (0256) 479476
Chairman: A Soar; *Man Dir:* C Paterson; *Marketing Dir:* A Gordon; *Dirs:* J Ashby (Reference & Trade), H Holt (Science, Medicine & Journals); *Publishing Dir:* T M Farmiloe; *Rights Manager:* N Piggott
Parent Company: Macmillan Publishers Ltd (qv)
Subjects: Science, Technology, Medicine, Humanities, Social Sciences, Computers, Music
ISBN Publisher's Prefix: 0-333

Macmillan Publishers Ltd, 4 Little Essex St, London WC2R 3LF Tel: (01) 836 6633 Cable Add: Publish London WC2 Telex: 262024 Fax: (01) 379 4204
Firm is a holding company
Chairman: Earl of Stockton; *Man Dir:* N G Byam Shaw
Orders to: Macmillan Distribution Ltd, Houndmills, Basingstoke, Hampshire RG21 2XS Tel: Basingstoke 29242 (STD code 0256)
Parent Company: Macmillan Ltd
Subsidiaries in the UK: BASW Macmillan Ltd (50% owned); Grove's Dictionaries of Music Ltd; Hospital and Social Service Publications Ltd; Macmillan Education Ltd (qv); Macmillan Magazines Ltd (at above address); Macmillan London Ltd (qv); The Macmillan Press Ltd (qv); Macmillan Children's Books Ltd (qv); Macmillan Publishers (UK) Ltd; Macmillan Publishers (Overseas) Ltd; Macmillan Publishers Group Administration Ltd; Macmillan Accounts and Administration Ltd; Macmillan Distribution Ltd; Macmillan Information Systems Ltd; Globe Book Services Ltd; Macmillan Reference Publications Ltd; Macmillan Journals Ltd; Macmillan Production Ltd; Macmillan Film Productions Ltd; Southtek Ltd; Macmillan Intek Ltd; Modern English Publications Ltd; Pan Books (Holdings) Ltd; Pan Books Ltd (qv); Sidgwick & Jackson Ltd (qv); Stockton Press Ltd
Subsidiaries outside the UK: Artists of Australia, The Macmillan Co of Australia Pty Ltd (qv), Mary Martin Bookshop Pty Ltd (all Australia); Macmillan Publishers (China) Ltd, Macmillan Publishers (HK) Ltd (qv), Peninsula Production & Distribution Ltd (all Hong Kong); Macmillan Language House Co Ltd, Macmillan Shuppan KK, Nature Japan Inc (all Japan); Macmillan Kenya (Publishers) Ltd, Kenya; Macmillan Publishers (M) Sdn Bhd, Malaysia (qv); Editorial Macmillan de México SA de CV, Mexico; The Macmillan Co of New Zealand Ltd, Mary Martin Bookshop (NZ) Ltd (both New Zealand); Macmillan South East Asia Private Ltd, Singapore (qv); Macmillan Boleswa Publishers (Pty) Ltd (qv), Macmillan Swaziland National Publishing Company Ltd (both Swaziland); Grove's Dictionaries of Music Inc, Nature America Inc, St Martin's Enterprises Inc, St Martin's Press Inc (all USA); Macmillan (Publishers) Zimbabwe (Private) Ltd, Zimbabwe
Associate Companies: Macmillan India Ltd, India (qv); Gill & Macmillan Ltd, Republic of Ireland (qv); Macmillan Nigeria Publishers Ltd, The Northern Nigerian Publishing Co Ltd (both Nigeria – qqv); The College Press (Pvt) Ltd, Zimbabwe (qv)
Branch Office outside the UK: PO Box 10722, Off Link Rd, Accra, Ghana

Julia **MacRae** Books+, Walker House, 87 Vauxhall Walk, London SE11 5DJ Tel: (01) 387 2000 Telex: 8955572 Fax: (01) 387 4221
A division of Walker Books Ltd (qv)
Man Dir: Julia MacRae; *Sales Dir:* George Taylor; *Rights & Permissions:* Linda Summers; *Production Dir:* Rita Ireland; *Publicity:* Linda Banner
Subjects: Juveniles, Picture Books, Music, General
1985: 40 titles *Founded:* 1979
ISBN Publisher's Prefix: 0-86203

Made Simple, an imprint of Heinemann Professional Publishing (qv)

Magna Print Books, Magna House, Long Preston, Skipton, North Yorkshire Tel: Long Preston 225/526 (STD code 072 94) Fax: (072 94) 683
Man Dir: Derek Cressey; *Production:* John Cressey; *Sales:* Margaret Cressey
Parent Company: The Senior Service Corporation Inc, USA
Imprint: Magna Large Print Series
Subjects: Fiction & Non-fiction (in Large Print)
1985: 103 titles *1986:* 110 titles *Founded:* 1973
ISBN Publisher's Prefixes: 0-86009, 1-85057

Magnet, an imprint of Methuen Children's Books Ltd (qv)

Mainstream Publishing Co (Edinburgh) Ltd, 7 Albany St, Edinburgh EH1 3UG Tel: (031) 557 2959 Telex: 265871 Monref G ref Mnu 377
Dirs: Bill Campbell, Peter Mackenzie; *Publicity:* Bill Campbell; *Sales:* Peter Mackenzie, Raymond Cowie; *Rights & Permissions:* Peter Mackenzie, Bill Campbell
Subjects: Literature, History, Current Affairs, Politics, Biography, Sport, Alternative Medicine
1985: 28 titles *Founded:* 1978
ISBN Publisher's Prefixes: 0-906391, 1-85158

Malaby Press, an imprint of J M Dent & Sons Ltd (qv)

Malaga, an imprint of Ian Allan Ltd (qv)

Mallard Reprints, an imprint of Terence Dalton Ltd (qv)

Management Update Ltd+, 99a Underdale Rd, Shrewsbury, Shropshire SY2 5EE Tel: Shrewsbury 232556 (STD code 0743)
Chief Executive: Hano Johannsen
Subjects: Business & Management
1985: 6 titles *1986:* 6 titles *Founded:* 1983
ISBN Publisher's Prefix: 0-946679

Manchester University Press+*, Oxford Rd, Manchester M13 9PL Tel: (061) 273 5539 Telex: 668932 Mchrul G Fax: (061) 274 3346
Publisher: J M N Spencer; *Editorial:* Ray Offord; *Trade:* C Bowers; *Production:* Max Netileton; *Rights & Permissions:* Ms J G Griffiths; *Publicity:* C J Annabel
Associate Company: Longwood Press, 27 South Main St, Wolfeboro, NH 03894-2069, USA
Subjects: English Language and Literature, Modern Languages, History, Philosophy, Religion, Medicine, Psychology, Engineering, Mathematics, General & Social Science, Economics, Geography, Education, Educational Software, University Textbooks
Founded: 1912
ISBN Publisher's Prefix: 0-7190

Mandala, an imprint of Unwin Hyman Ltd (qv)

Manpower Services Commission Careers and Occupational Information Centre (COIC), Room W1103, Moorfoot, Sheffield S1 4PQ Tel: Sheffield 704563 (STD code 0742)
Manager: Mel Dean; *Editorial, Production, Rights & Permissions:* Michael Burgoyne; *Sales, Publicity:* David Holding
Subjects: Careers, Life & Social Skills teaching
1987-88: approx 75 titles *Founded:* 1974
ISBN Publisher's Prefix: 0-86110

Mansell Publishing Ltd+, 6 All Saints St, London N1 9RL Tel: (01) 837 6676 Telex: 28604 ref 1647
Man Dir: John E Duncan; *Editorial:* Colin Hutchens, Veronica Higgs, Peter Harrison, Penelope Beck; *Marketing Dir:* June S Eaton; *Promotion:* Catherine Johnston; *Production:* Patrick Holloway
Parent Company: The H W Wilson Co, 950 University Ave, Bronx, New York, NY 10452, USA
Subjects: Bibliographies, Reference, Third World, Islamic, Urban Planning, Labour & Social Law
Founded: 1966
ISBN Publisher's Prefix: 0-7201

Manxman Publications, an imprint of Shearwater Press Ltd, Isle of Man (qv)

Marcham Books, Appleford, Abingdon, Oxfordshire OX14 4PB Tel: Abingdon 848319 (STD code 0235)
Chief Executive, Editorial, Rights & Permissions: G E Duffield; *Sales, Publicity:* G Elwes; *Production:* E Collie
Associate Companies: Appleford Printers, Appleford Bookroom, E Collie Associates
Branch Off: Isle of Man
Subjects: Religion, History, Sociology, Children, Africa, Reference, Law, Music
Founded: 1963

Maritime Books+, Lodge Hill, Liskeard, Cornwall PL14 4EL Tel: Liskeard 43663 (STD code 0579) Telex: 45668
Chief Executive: M Critchley; *Sales:* I Lander
Subjects: Naval Current Affairs & History
1986: 5 titles *Founded:* 1980
ISBN Publisher's Prefix: 0-907771

Market House Books Ltd+, Market House, Market Sq, Aylesbury, Buckinghamshire HP20 1TN Tel: Aylesbury 84911 (STD code 0296)
Chairman: A Isaacs; *Dir and Production:* J Daintith
Subject: Packagers of Reference books
Founded: 1969

Marshall Cavendish Books Ltd, 58 Old Compton St, London W1V 5PA Tel: (01) 734 6710 Cable Add: Marcav London W1 Telex: 23880
Chief Executive: Clive Greaves; *Man Dir:* Edward Glover
Parent Company: Marshall Cavendish Ltd (at above address)
Associate Companies: Marshall Cavendish Partworks Ltd, Marshall Cavendish Children's Books Ltd (both at above address); Times Books International, Republic of Singapore (qv); Marshall Cavendish Schools & Library Division, 142 West Merrick Rd, Freeport, NY 11520, USA
Subjects: Partworks, Reference, General Mass Market
Founded: 1968

Marshall Editions Ltd+*, 170 Piccadilly, London W1V 9DD Tel: (01) 629 0079 Cable Add: Marsheds Telex: 22847

UNITED KINGDOM 457

Marsh G
Man Dir & Editorial: Bruce Marshall; *Dirs:* John Bigg, Candy Lee; *Sales:* Barbara Anderson; *Production:* Barry Baker
Subjects: Highly-illustrated Non-fiction including Cookery, Wine, Sailing, Travel, Wild Life, Photography, Interior Design, Home-making, Medicine, Science, Technology, Health & Fitness, Knitting, Embroidery, Gardening, History. Also book packagers
1985: 14 titles *1986:* 12 titles *Founded:* 1977

Marshall, Morgan & Scott Publications Ltd+, 3 Beggarwood Lane, Basingstoke, Hampshire Tel: Basingstoke 59211 (STD code 0256) Cable Add: Grapho Basingstoke Telex: 858669 Marpic G
Man Dir: John Hunt; *Editorial:* Debbie Thorpe; *Production:* Tim Sanders; *Sales, Marketing:* John Robertson
Parent Company: Marshall Pickering Holdings Ltd (UK) — see Marshall Pickering entry — a subsidiary of Zondervan Corporation Inc, Grand Rapids, USA
Associate Company: Pickering & Inglis Ltd (qv)
Imprints include: Samuel Bagster, Christian Journals, Keswick, Life Changing Books, Oliphants
Subjects: Christian
Founded: 1859
ISBN Publisher's Prefix: 0-551

Marshall Pickering, 3 Beggarwood Lane, Basingstoke, Hampshire RG23 7LP Tel: Basingstoke 59211 (STD code 0256) Cable Add: Grapho Basingstoke Telex: 858669 Marpic G Fax: (0256) 758247
Man Dir: John Hunt; *Publisher:* Debbie Thorpe; *Editors:* Christine Whitell, Sian Lloyd-Jones, Rebecca Winter; *Sales:* John Robertson; *Production:* Tim Sanders, Adam Phillips; *Publicity:* Giles Semper; *Rights & Permissions:* Joan Prebble
Parent Company: The Zondervan Corporation Inc, 1415 Lake Dr SE, Grand Rapids, MI 49506, USA
Subsidiary Companies: Marshall Morgan & Scott Publications Ltd, Pickering & Inglis Ltd (qqv)
Imprints: Marshalls, Lakeland
Subjects: Religion, Scriptures
1985: 110 titles *1986:* 123 titles *Founded:* 1794
ISBN Publisher's Prefixes: 0-551, 0-720

Marshalls, an imprint of Marshall Pickering (qv)

Marsland Press, an imprint of Volturna Press (qv)

Martin Books, an imprint of Woodhead-Faulkner (Publishers) Ltd (qv)

Masks, an imprint of Serpent's Tail Ltd (qv)

Kenneth **Mason** Publications Ltd+, The Old Harbourmaster's, 8 North St, Emsworth, Hampshire PO10 7DD Tel: Emsworth 377977 (STD code 0243)
Man Dir: Kenneth Mason
Orders to: J M Dent & Sons (Distribution) Ltd, Dunhams Lane, Letchworth, Hertfordshire SG6 1LF Tel: Letchworth 686241 (STD code 0462)
Imprint: Handbag Books
Branch Off: 260 West 39th St, New York, NY 10018, USA
Subjects: Nautical, Leisure Activities, Patents, Slimming Paperbacks
1985: 5 titles *Founded:* 1958
ISBN Publisher's Prefix: 0-85937

Matrix Publishing Group Ltd, York House, Newton Close, Park Farm, Wellingborough, Northamptonshire NN8 3UW Tel: Wellingborough 673977 (STD code 0933) Telex: 312242 Midtlx G
Man Dir: David J Smith; *Dirs:* M J McWhinnie, T A Jones
Subjects: Business, Leisure
Founded: 1987
Miscellaneous: Incorporates Beacon Publications PLC
ISBN Publisher's Prefix: 0-906358

Maxwell Communication Corporation plc, PO Box 283, 33 Holborn, London EC1N 2NE Tel: (01) 822 2345 Telex: 888804 Brito Fax: (01) 353 3398
Formerly British Printing & Communication Corporation PLC
Parent Company (75%): Pergamon Holding Foundation (incorporated in Liechtenstein)
Divisions include:
Pergamon Press plc, with the following members: Angus Hudson Ltd (qv), CEEPI Ltd (Caxton and English Educational Programmes International Ltd) (qv), Macdonald & Co (Publishers) Ltd (qv) (incorporating Purnell Publishers Ltd, Orbis Book Publishing Corporation Ltd, Purnell Book Centre), Pergamon Journals Ltd, Wheaton, Publishers Ltd, United Trade Press
BPCC plc
British Newspaper Printing Corporation plc
Maxwell Communication Corporation (USA)
See also Pergamon Press
Overseas Subsidiaries include: Cedibra Editora Brasileira Ltda, Brazil (qv); Delphin Verlag GmbH, Federal Republic of Germany (qv); International Learning Systems (Japan) Ltd; Macdonald Purnell (Pty) Ltd, Republic of South Africa (qv); K G Bertmarks Förlag AB, Sweden
Associate Companies include: Usborne Publishing Ltd, UK (qv)
Subjects: Co-editions, Encyclopaedias, General Fiction, Heritage, Travel, Biography, Illustrated, Children's, Educational, History, How-to, Music, Art, Philosophy, Reference, Paperbacks, Journals

Mayhew-McCrimmon Ltd, now McCrimmon Publishing Co Ltd (qv)

Meadowfield Press Ltd, ISA Bldg, Dale Rd Industrial Estate, Shildon, Co Durham DL4 2QZ Tel: Morpeth 55860 (STD code 0670), Bishop Auckland 773065 (STD code 0388)
Man Dir: J Gordon Cook
Associate Company: Merrow Publishing Co Ltd (qv)
Subjects: Technical, Scientific, Academic

Mechanical Engineering Publications Ltd+, PO Box 24, Northgate Ave, Bury St Edmunds, Suffolk IP32 6BW Tel: Bury St Edmunds 63277 (STD code 0284) Telex: 817376 Fax: (0284) 704006
Publications Dir: Patrick Daley; *Editorial, Rights & Permissions:* Fred Whiteley; *Sales, Publicity:* Peter Williams; *Production:* Beryl Elliott
Parent Company: Institution of Mechanical Engineers
Imprint: MEP
Subjects: Mechanical Engineering and allied subjects
Founded: 1974
ISBN Publisher's Prefix: 0-85298

The **Medici** Society Ltd*, 34-42 Pentonville Rd, London N1 9HG Tel: (01) 837 7099 Cable Add: Medici N1
Man Dir: J Gurney

Subjects: Art, Juveniles
Bookshops: The Medici Galleries, 7 Grafton St, London W1X 3LA; 26 Thurloe St, London SW7 2LT; 63 Bold St, Liverpool L1 4HP
1986: 7 titles *Founded:* 1908
ISBN Publisher's Prefix: 0-85503

Melrose Press Ltd+, 3 Regal Lane, Soham, Ely, Cambridgeshire CB7 5BA Tel: Ely 721091 (STD code 0353) Cable Add: Melrospres Ely Telex: 81584
Chairman: Dr Ernest Kay; *Chief Executive:* Richard Kay; *Sales, Publicity, Rights:* Roger W G Curtis; *Editorial, Production:* Nicholas S Law
Imprint: International Biographical Centre
Subject: Reference
1985: 8 titles *1986:* 6 titles *Founded:* 1969
ISBN Publisher's Prefix: 0-900332

Mencap Publications, Mencap National Centre, 123 Golden Lane, London EC1Y 0RT Tel: (01) 253 9433
Man Dir: Sir Brian Rix CBE; *Group Dir Marketing, Communications:* Alan Leighton
Parent Company: Royal Society for Mentally Handicapped Children and Adults (at above address)
Imprint: Little Stephen
Subject: Mental Handicap
Bookshop: The Bookshop (at above address)
Founded: 1971
ISBN Publisher's Prefix: 0-855

Mercat Press, 53-59 South Bridge, Edinburgh EH1 1YS Tel: (031) 556 6743 Cable Add: Bookman Edinburgh
Joint Man Dirs: James Thin, Ainslie Thin, Andrew Thin
Parent Company: James Thin Ltd (at above address)
Subsidiary Company: Melven Press (at above address)
Associate Company: Melven Bookshop Ltd, 60 Fountainhall Rd, Edinburgh EH9 2LP
Subjects: Scottish
Bookshops: James Thin Ltd (see under Major Booksellers); Melven: The Centre, Aviemore; 29 Union St, Inverness; Eldon Bldgs, Blackett St, Newcastle upon Tyne; 176 High St, Perth
Founded: 1970
ISBN Publisher's Prefixes: 0-901824 (Mercat), 0-906664, 0-950588 (both Melven)

Mercury, an imprint of W H Allen & Co PLC (qv)

Merehurst Ltd+, 5 Great James St, London WC1N 3DA Tel: (01) 242 5969 Telex: 296616 Mhurst G Fax: (01) 405 1129
General Manager: Carole Saunders; *Publishing Manager, Production:* Amelia Thorpe; *Sales:* Stuart Binns; *Publicity:* Anne Hay; *Rights & Permissions:* Glynis Watts
Subjects: Natural History, Cookery, Crafts & Hobbies, Travel, Pet Care & Aviculture, Horses & Equitation, Horticulture
1985: 7 titles *1986:* 16 titles *Founded:* 1979
ISBN Publisher's Prefix: 0-948075

Meresborough Books, 17 Station Rd, Rainham, Gillingham, Kent ME8 7RS Tel: Medway 388812 (STD code 0634)
Proprietors: Hamish and Barbara Mackay-Miller
Subsidiary Company: Bygone Kent, 5 Meresborough Cotts, Meresborough, Gillingham, Kent ME8 8PP
Imprints: Bygone Kent, Meresborough Books

UNITED KINGDOM

Subjects: Kent Local History
Bookshop: Rainham Bookshop, 17 Station Rd, Rainham, Gillingham, Kent ME8 7RS
1985: 12 titles *1986:* 4 titles *Founded:* 1977
ISBN Publisher's Prefixes: 0-905270, 0-948193

Meriam Webster, an imprint of Longman Group UK Ltd (qv)

Merlin Books Ltd, 40 East St, Braunton, Devon EX33 2EA Tel: Braunton 816430 (STD code 0271)
Chief Executive: Derek Stockwell; *Editorial:* E A Edwards; *Sales:* Jill Candy; *Production:* Pam Stevens; *Publicity, Rights & Permissions:* B M Stockwell
Subjects: Biography, Autobiography, Non-fiction, General, Children's, Fiction, Poetry
Founded: 1981
ISBN Publisher's Prefix: 0-86303

The **Merlin Press** Ltd+, 3 Manchester Rd, London E14 9BD Tel: (01) 987 7959
Man Dir: Martin Eve
Imprint: Seafarer Books
Subjects: History, Economics, Philosophy, Political & Social Science
Founded: 1956
ISBN Publisher's Prefix: 0-85036

Mermaid, an imprint of Michael Joseph Ltd (qv)

Merrill Publishing International, Holywell House, Osney Mead, Oxford OX2 0ES Tel: Oxford 791497/791378 (STD code 0865)
Sales, Advertising, Publicity: Michael Brightmore; *Rights & Permissions:* Parent Company
Parent Company: Charles E Merrill Publishing Co, 1300 Alum Creek Drive, Columbus, OH 43216, USA
Subjects: Education, Educational Psychology, Special Education, Electronic & Mechanical Technology, Social Sciences, Business & Management, Science, Communication, Speech Pathology
1985: 80 titles *1986:* 70 titles *Founded:* 1842
ISBN Publisher's Prefix: 0-675

The **Merrion** Press, 16 Groveway, London SW9 0AR Tel: (01) 735 7791, (01) 733 5173
Dir: Susan Shaw
Subjects: Finely produced books on English Literature, Printing, Calligraphy, Fine Arts
ISBN Publisher's Prefix: 0-903560

Merrow Publishing Co Ltd, ISA Bldg, Dale Rd Industrial Estate, Shildon, Co Durham DL4 2QZ Tel: Morpeth 55860 (STD code 0670), Bishop Auckland 773065 (STD code 0388)
Man Dir: J Gordon Cook
Associate Company: Meadowfield Press Ltd (qv)
Subjects: Technical, Scientific, Academic
ISBN Publisher's Prefixes: 0-900541, 0-904095

Metal Bulletin Books Ltd+, Park House, Park Terrace, Worcester Park, Surrey KT4 7HY Tel: (01) 330 4311 Cable Add: Metalbul Worcester Park Telex: 21383 Metbul G Fax: (01) 337 8943
The above is the head office, the UK editorial office is at 16 Lower Marsh, London SE1 7RJ
Man Dir: T J Tarring; *Sales, Marketing Dir:* B R Orbell; *Editorial Dir:* R P Cordero
Branch Off: 220 Fifth Ave, New York, NY 10001, USA
Subjects: Steel, Scrap and Metal Industries, Industrial Minerals, Soft Commodities, Investment
Founded: 1937

Methodist Publishing House, Wellington Rd, Wimbledon, London SW19 8EU Tel: (01) 947 5256/9 Cable Add: Metodico, London SW19 8EU
General Manager: Brian Thornton
Imprint: Fonndery Press
Subjects: Ecumenical, Methodist Hymn & Service Books
Founded: 1733
ISBN Publisher's Prefixes: 0-7150, 0-7162, 0-7192, 0-901027, 0-946550

Methuen & Co Ltd, see Routledge

Methuen Children's Books+, Michelin House, 81 Fulham Rd, London SW3 6RB Tel: (01) 581 9393 Cable Add: Octobooks Telex: 920191 Fax: (01) 589 8419
Chairman: David Blunt; *Sales, Publicity:* John Potter; *Production:* Peter Kilborn
Parent Company: Octopus Publishing Group PLC (at above address). Ultimate parent company Reed International PLC, Reed House, 83 Piccadilly, London W1A 1EJ
Imprint: Magnet
Subjects: Juveniles, Fiction & Non-fiction
ISBN Publisher's Prefix: 0-416

Methuen London+, Michelin House, 81 Fulham Rd, London SW3 6RB Tel: (01) 581 9393 Cable Add: Octobooks Telex: 920191 Fax: (01) 589 8419
Chairman: David Blunt; *Man Dir:* Geoffrey Strachan; *Editorial:* Ann Mansbridge, Nicholas Hern, Elsbeth Lindner; *Marketing Dir:* John Potter; *Rights & Permissions:* Fiona Kennedy
Parent Company: Octopus Publishing Group PLC (at above address). Ultimate parent company Reed International PLC, Reed House, 83 Piccadilly, London W1A 1EJ
Subjects: General Fiction, Belles Lettres, Poetry, Biography, History, Low- & High-priced Paperbacks, Current & Social Affairs, Plays, Humour, Film
ISBN Publisher's Prefix: 0-413

Michelin Tyre PLC, Tourism Dept, Maps & Guides Division, Davy House, Lyon Rd, Harrow, Middlesex HA1 2DQ Tel: (01) 861 2121 Cable Add: Pneumicilin London Telex: 919071 Pneumicilin Fax: 01-863 0680
Production: Derek Brown; *Sales Manager:* James Addison
Associate Company: Michelin et Cie (Services de Tourisme), France (qv)
Subjects: Guides (Tourist, Hotel & Restaurant), Maps
ISBN Publisher's Prefixes: 0-206, 0-392

Midland Counties Publications (Aerophile) Ltd, 24 The Hollow, Earl Shilton, Leicester LE9 7NA Tel: Earl Shilton 47256 (STD code 0455)
Dirs: N P Lewis, C J Salter
Warehouse: 3 Land Society Lane, Earl Shilton, Leicester LE9 7LT Tel: Earl Shilton 47091 (STD code 0455)
Subjects: Aviation, Local Interest
Bookshop: At warehouse address
1985: 10 titles *Founded:* 1975
ISBN Publisher's Prefix: 0-904597

Milestone Publications+, 62 Murray Rd, Horndean, Hampshire PO8 9JL Tel: Horndean 597440 (STD code 0705)
Man Dir, Editorial, Production, Publicity, Rights & Permissions: N J Pine; *Sales:* Tim Harland
Parent Company: Goss & Crested China Ltd (at above address)
Imprint: Down Memory Lane
Subjects: Military, Local History, Humour, Heraldic China

1985: 15 titles *1986:* 16 titles *Founded:* 1970
ISBN Publisher's Prefixes: 0-903852, 1-85265

Harvey **Miller** Publishers+, 20 Marryat Rd, London SW19 5BD Tel: (01) 946 4426
Publishers: Mrs Elly Miller, Harvey Miller
Orders to: (Medical Atlases) OUP Distribution Services, Saxon Way West, Corby, Northamptonshire NN18 9ES Tel: Corby 741519 (STD code 0536); (History of Art publications) Biblios, Glenside Industrial Estate, Partridge Green, West Sussex Tel: Horsham 710971 (STD code 0403)
Subjects: History of Art, Medical Atlases
ISBN Publisher's Prefixes: 0-19 (Medical Atlases), 0-905203 (History of Art)

Mills & Boon Ltd, Eton House, 18-24 Paradise Rd, Richmond, Surrey TW9 1SR Tel: (01) 948 0444 Cable Add: Millsator Richmond Surrey Telex: 24420 Milbon G Fax: (01) 940 5899
Chairman: John Boon; *Man Dir:* Robert Williams; *Editorial:* Alan Boon, Frances Whitehead, Linda Fildew, Judith Murdoch; *Sales, Marketing:* Ron Hedley (Hardbacks/Export), Sue Lomax (Export), Gerry Howe (Paperbacks, UK), Heather Walton (Marketing), Nancy Peters (Mail Order); *Production:* Michael Saraceno; *Rights & Permissions:* Deborah Burgess
Orders to: Distribution & Management Services, Sheldon Way, Larkfield, Kent
Parent Company: Harlequin Enterprises Ltd, 225 Duncan Mill Rd, Don Mills, Ontario, Canada M3B 3K9
Imprints: Mills & Boon, Gold Eagle, Harlequin, Silhouette, Worldwide
Subjects: Romantic Fiction, Action/Adventure
Founded: 1908
ISBN Publisher's Prefixes: 0-263 (Mills & Boon), 0-373 (Silhouette, Harlequin, Worldwide, Gold Eagle)

Minimax Books Ltd, Broadgate House, Langtoft Fen, Langtoft, Peterborough PE6 9QB Tel: Market Deeping 347609 (STD code 0778) Telex: 32376 Angtel
Man Dir, Editorial: Lynn Green; *Production:* Bob Lavender; *Publicity, Rights & Permissions:* Lynn Green, Bob Lavender
Subjects: Local Interest, Children's, Autobiographical, General
Founded: 1979
ISBN Publisher's Prefix: 0-906

Mirror Publications Ltd, Athene House, 66-73 Shoe Lane, London EC4P 4AB Tel: (01) 377 4783
Man Dir: Anthony Finn; *Managing Editor:* Alison Mackonochie; *Sales:* Terry Ventham, Odhams Distribution Tel: (01) 831 1707
Parent Company: Mirror Group Holdings Ltd
Subjects: General Non-fiction, Specialist Horse Racing, Crosswords & Puzzles
1986: 14 titles
ISBN Publisher's Prefix: 0-85939

Mitchell Beazley International Ltd, Artists House, 14-15 Manette St, London W1V 5LB Tel: (01) 439 7211 Telex: 24892 MB Book G Fax: (01) 734 0389
Man Dir: Duncan Baird; *Editorial Dir:* Jack Tresidder; *Sales Dirs:* Malcolm Saunders (International), David Hight (UK); *Production:* Peter Phillips; *Publicity:* Lis Rolls
Orders to: (UK trade only) WHS Distributors, St John's House, East St, Leicester LE1 6NE Tel: Leicester 551196 (STD code 0533)

Parent Company: Octopus Publishing Group PLC. Ultimate parent company Reed International PLC, Reed House, 83 Piccadilly, London W1A 1EJ
Subsidiary Company: Millers Publications, Sissinghurst Court, Sissinghurst, Cranbrook, Kent TN17 2JA
Imprint: Artists House
Subjects: Wine, Travel, Gardening, Interiors, Antiques, Popular Reference
1985: 19 titles *1986:* 20 titles *Founded:* 1969
ISBN Publisher's Prefixes: 0-85533 (Mitchell Beazley), 0-86134 (Artists House)

Model & Allied Publications Ltd, now Argus Specialist Publications Ltd (qv)

Modern English Publications Ltd+*, PO Box 129, Oxford OX2 8JU Tel: Oxford 247484 (STD code 0865) Telex: 83147 Viaor
Managing Editor: Susan Holden
Orders to: Edward Arnold, Woodlands Park Ave, Woodlands Park, Maidenhead, Berkshire SL6 5BS Telex: 847918 Arnold G
Imprint: Roundabout
Subject: Language Teaching
Founded: 1976
ISBN Publisher's Prefix: 0-906149

Modern Transport, an imprint of Ian Allan Ltd (qv)

The **Molendinar** Press, now Richard Drew Publishing Ltd (qv)

Moonlight Publishing Ltd, 131c Kensington Church St, London W8 7LP Tel: (01) 229 9275
Dirs: Christine Baker, Robin Baker, P Stanley-Baker
Orders to: (Pocket Puffins) Penguin Books Ltd, Bath Rd, Harmondsworth, West Drayton, Middlesex UB7 0DA Tel: (01) 759 1984; (Discoverers and Pocket Worlds) Ragged Bears Ltd, Ragged Appleshaw, Andover, Hampshire SP11 3HX Tel: Andover 772269 (STD code 0264)
Imprints: Pocket Puffins, Discoverers, Pocket Worlds

Moorland Mini-Books, an imprint of Aquila Publishing (UK) Ltd (qv)

Moorland Publishing Company Ltd+, Moorfarm Rd, Ashbourne, Derbyshire DE6 1HD Tel: Ashbourne 44486 (STD code 0335) Telex: 377106 Chacom Mpc G
Editorial Dir, Production: Dr J A Robey; *Publicity, Sales, Rights & Permissions:* L Porter
Subjects: History, Geography, General Non-fiction, Railways, Natural History, Collecting, Sport, Countryside, Guides, Travel
1986: 19 titles *Founded:* 1972
ISBN Publisher's Prefixes: 0-903485, 0-086190

Morgan-Grampian Book Publishing Co Ltd, 30 Calderwood St, Woolwich, London SE18 6QH Tel: (01) 855 7777 Cable Add: Industpress London Telex: 896238
Publisher: Tony Morse; *Editor:* Phil Brown; *Marketing:* Glen Wilders; *Production:* Mike Biddle
Subjects: Reference, Directories
Founded: 1975
ISBN Publisher's Prefix: 0-86213

E J Morten (Publishers), 6 Warburton St, Didsbury, Manchester M20 0RA Tel: (061) 445 7629
Man Dir, Rights & Permissions: Eric Morten; *Sales, Publicity:* Martyn Pardoe
Parent Company: E J Morten (Booksellers) Ltd, 2-10 Warburton St, Didsbury, Manchester M20 0RA

Imprints: Datapack Books, Pride Publications
Subjects: Local History
Bookshop: At above main address
Founded: 1969
ISBN Publisher's Prefix: 0-85972

Motocourse, an imprint of Hazelton Publishing (qv)

Motor Racing Publications Ltd+, Unit 6, The Pilton Estate, 46 Pitlake, Croydon CR0 3RY Tel: (01) 681 3363
Man Dir, Publicity, Rights & Permissions: John Blunsden; *Editorial:* John Plummer; *Sales, Production:* Jim Starr
Associate Company: Garland Publications Ltd (at above address) Tel: (01) 681 2255
Imprints: MRP, The Fitzjames Press
Branch Off: (Man Dir) 56 Fitzjames Ave, Croydon CR0 5DD
Subjects: Motor Racing and Rallying, Racing Car Design, Motoring History including Cars, Trucks and Motorcycles
1986: 12 titles *Founded:* 1948
ISBN Publisher's Prefixes: 0-900549, 0-947981 (MRP), 0-948358 (Fitzjames Press)

A R **Mowbray** & Co Ltd+, St Thomas House, Becket St, Oxford OX1 1SJ Tel: Oxford 242507 (STD code 0865)
Chief Executive: Denis D Edwards; *Man Dir:* K B Baker; *Sales:* Eva Jesse; *Publicity:* Jackie Edwards; *Production:* Rosie Collyer
Subjects: Christian Religion
Bookshops: 28 Margaret St, Oxford Circus, London W1N 7LB; 14 King's Parade, Cambridge CB2 1SR; St Martins, The Bull Ring, Birmingham B5 5BB
1985: 43 titles *1986:* 41 titles *Founded:* 1858
ISBN Publisher's Prefix: 0-264

Frederick **Muller**, an imprint of Century Hutchinson Publishing Ltd (qv)

Multilingual Matters Ltd+, Bank House, 8A Hill Rd, Clevedon, Bristol, Avon BS21 7HH Tel: Bristol 876519 (STD code 0272) Fax: (0272) 343096
Chief Executive, Sales, Production, Publicity: Mike Grover; *Editorial, Rights & Permissions:* Marjukka Grover
Orders to: Element Books Ltd, Longmead, Shaftesbury, Dorset SP7 8PL
Branch Off: c/o Taylor & Francis, 242 Cherry St, Philadelphia, PA 29106-1906, USA
Subjects: Linguistics, Education, Psychology, Sociology
1985: 8 titles *1986:* 5 titles *Founded:* 1982
ISBN Publisher's Prefix: 0-905028

Multimedia Books Ltd, 32-34 Gordon House Rd, London NW5 1LP Tel: (01) 482 4248 Telex: 295941 Atid G Fax: (01) 482 4203
Man Dir: Arnon Orbach
Imprint: Admiral
Subjects: Packagers of popular illustrated books
1986: 26 titles *Founded:* 1986

Munch Bunch Books, an imprint of Studio Publications (Ipswich) Ltd (qv)

Donald **Murray** (Ramboro Books), 64 Pentonville Rd, London N1 9HD Tel: (01) 837 6301 Telex: 946240 Ramb
Subjects: Children's Books, Dictionaries, Art, Cookery
Miscellaneous: Also Remainder Dealers

John **Murray** (Publishers) Ltd, 50 Albemarle St, London W1X 4BD Tel: (01) 493 4361 Cable Add: Guidebook London W1 Telex: 21312 Murray G Fax: (01) 499 1792

Chairman, General Books Marketing Dir: John R Murray; *Man Dir:* Nick Perren; *General Books Publisher:* Grant McIntyre; *Educational Books Publisher:* Keith Nettle; *Educational Marketing Dir:* Judith Reinhold; *Sales Manager:* John Harbour; *General Marketing, Production Manager:* Lorraine Abraham; *Rights & Permissions Manager:* Sarah Fulford
Orders to: 65 Clerkenwell Rd, London EC1R 5BQ Tel: (01) 405 1627/8
Subjects: General & Educational: Art & Architecture, Biography, Travel & Exploration, Fiction, Craft & Practical, Flying & Nautical, Popular Science, Secondary, College, Adult Education/Self-study. *Easy Readers, Success Studybooks* series
1986: 70 titles *Founded:* 1768
ISBN Publisher's Prefix: 0-7195

Music Sales Ltd, see Omnibus Press

Muslim Welfare House, see M W H London Publishers

Mysterious Press, an imprint of Arrow Books Ltd (qv)

N C C Publications+*, The National Computing Centre Ltd, Oxford Rd, Manchester M1 7ED Tel: (061) 228 6333 Telex: 668962
Manager: G E Hall; *Publicity:* John Wiley & Sons Ltd (qv)
Orders to: John Wiley & Sons Ltd, Distribution Centre, Shripney Rd, Bognor Regis, West Sussex PO22 9SA Tel: Bognor Regis 829121 (STD code 0243)
Subjects: Computing and allied subjects
1985: 180 titles *Founded:* 1971
ISBN Publisher's Prefix: 0-85012

N E L, an imprint of The New English Library Ltd (qv)

The **N F E R-Nelson** Publishing Co Ltd, Darville House, 2 Oxford Rd East, Windsor, Berkshire SL4 1DF Tel: Windsor 858961 (STD code 0753) Telex: 937400 Onecom G ref 24966001 Fax: (0753) 856830
Man Dir: Michael Thompson; *Publishing Dir:* Timothy Cornford; *Marketing Dir:* Michael Jackson
Associate Company: Thomas Nelson & Sons Ltd (qv)
Subjects: Education, Special Education, Social Sciences, Psychology, Educational Materials
Founded: 1981
Miscellaneous: A joint venture of the National Foundation for Educational Research in England and Wales and Thomas Nelson & Sons Ltd, educational publishers
ISBN Publisher's Prefixes: 0-85633, 0-901225

Nadder Books, an imprint of Element Books Ltd (qv)

National Christian Education Council, Robert Denholm House, Nutfield, Redhill, Surrey RH1 4HW Tel: Nutfield Ridge 822411 (STD code 0737)
Sales Manager: Eric A Thorn
Subjects: Primary, Secondary, Education, Religion, Maps & Atlases, Music, Bible Reading Guides, Pictures, Drama
Subsidiary Companies: Denholm House Press, International Bible Reading Association, Shaw Picture Co
1985: 12 titles *1986:* 12 titles
ISBN Publisher's Prefixes: 0-7197 (National Christian Council), 0-85213 (Denholm House)

National Computing Centre, see NCC

National Council for Civil Liberties*, 21 Tabard St, London SE1 4LA Tel: (01) 403 3888
Publications Officer: John Myers
Subjects: Rights and Civil Liberties, Guides to the Law
1985: 10 titles *Founded:* 1934
ISBN Publisher's Prefixes: 0-901108, 0-946088

National Council for Voluntary Organizations, see Bedford Square Press

National Extension College+, 18 Brooklands Ave, Cambridge CB2 2HN Tel: Cambridge 316644 (STD code 0223)
Executive Dir: Ros Morpeth; *Publishing Dir:* Tim Burton; *Marketing Dir:* Pat Gouldstone
Subject: Educational courses for distance education and self-instruction, English as a Second Language, Computing, Adult Basic Education, Business, Health, Training
1985-86: 35 titles *Founded:* 1963
ISBN Publisher's Prefix: 0-86082

National Foundation for Educational Research in England & Wales, see NFER

National Magazine Co Ltd, see Ebury Press

National Marriage Guidance Council, Herbert Gray College, Little Church St, Rugby, Warwickshire CV21 3AP Tel: Rugby 73241 (STD code 0788)
Dir: David French
Subjects: Marriage & Family Relationships, Counselling
Bookshop: At above address
1985: 11 titles *Founded:* 1947
ISBN Publisher's Prefix: 0-85351

National Portrait Gallery (Publications Dept), 2 St Martin's Place, London WC2H 0HE Tel: (01) 930 1552
Head of Publications: John Adamson; *Publications Manager:* Roger Sheppard; *Editorial, Production:* Gillian Forrester; *Rights & Permissions:* Judith Prendergast
Subjects: Art (particularly portraits in the Gallery), Reference
Founded: 1976 (book publishing division)
ISBN Publisher's Prefix: 0-904017

National Youth Bureau, 17-23 Albion St, Leicester LE1 6GD Tel: Leicester 471200 (STD code 0533)
Dir: David C Howie; *Editorial, Sales, Publicity, Rights & Permissions:* Ric Rogers; *Production:* Clive Thomas
Subjects: Young People, Youth & Community Work, Counselling
1985: 13 titles *1986:* 11 titles *Founded:* 1973
ISBN Publisher's Prefix: 0-86155

Natural History Museum, see British Museum (National History)

Nautical Publishing Co Ltd, an imprint of A & C Black (Publishers) Ltd (qv)

Thomas **Nelson** & Sons Ltd, Nelson House, Mayfield Rd, Walton-on-Thames, Surrey KT12 5PL Tel: Walton-on-Thames 246133 (STD code 0932) Cable Add: Thonelson Walton-on-Thames Telex: 929365 Nelson G
Man Dir: Michael Thompson; *Production Dir:* Malcolm Givans; *Rights & Permissions:* Allan Ramsay
Parent Company: Thomas Nelson Companies, 1120 Birchmount Rd, Scarborough, Ontario, Canada M1K 5G4
Associate Company: The NFER-Nelson Publishing Co Ltd (qv)
Subjects: Primary & Secondary Educational Materials, English Language Teaching, Books for Caribbean/Africa/South East Asia

Founded: 1798
ISBN Publisher's Prefix: 0-17

New Cavendish Books+, 23 Craven Hill, London W2 Tel: (01) 262 7905
Publisher: Allan Levy
Subjects: Toys (history & collection), Mechanical Antiquities, Models, 19th and 20th Century Art and Technology
Founded: 1973

New City, London, 57 Twyford Ave, London W3 9PZ Tel: (01) 992 7666
Chairman, Editorial: D Bregant; *Sales, Production, Publicity, Rights & Permissions:* R van Geffen
Parent Company: Città Nuova Editrice, Italy (qv for associate companies)
Subjects: Christian Concerns, Spirituality, Witness, Ecumenism
1985: 2 titles *Founded:* 1958
ISBN Publisher's Prefix: 0-904287

The **New English Library** Ltd+, 47 Bedford Sq, London WC1B 3DP Tel: (01) 323 4881 Cable Add: Nelpublish Telex: 885887 Fax: (01) 631 5248
Sales Dirs: J McEwen (Hardcover), Adrian Bourne, Colin Davis (Paperback); *Publicity:* Brian Levy (Hardback), Morven Knowles (Paperback); *Rights & Permissions:* Nikki Kennedy
Orders to: Hodder & Stoughton Ltd, Mill Rd, Dunton Green, Sevenoaks, Kent TN13 2XX Tel: Sevenoaks 450111 (STD code 0732)
Parent Company: Hodder & Stoughton Holdings Ltd
Imprint: NEL
Subjects: General Fiction & Non-fiction, Science Fiction, Biography, Paperbacks
Founded: 1957
ISBN Publisher's Prefix: 0-450

New Holland Publishing+, 37 Connaught St, London W2 2AZ Tel: (01) 262 6184
Man Dir: J C Beaufoy
Subjects: Natural History, Cookery, Home Design, Craft
Founded: 1956
ISBN Publisher's Prefixes: 1-85368 (New Holland), 0-900470, 0-946323 (both Holland Press)

New Leaf Publishing Ltd+, BCM – New Leaf, London WC1N 3XX Tel: (01) 435 3056, (01) 328 0917 Telex: 261507 ref 3228
Man Dirs: Michael Wright, Terry Jones
Orders to: Patrick Stephens Ltd, Denington Estate, Wellingborough, Northamptonshire NN8 2RQ Tel: Wellingborough 72700 (STD code 0933)
Associate Company: New Leaf Books Ltd (packager, at above London address)
Subjects: Photography, Design
Founded: 1982
ISBN Publisher's Prefix: 0-907916

New Left Books, now Verso (qv)

New Orchard Editions, an imprint of Blandford Publishing Ltd (qv)

New Park Publications Ltd, 21-25 Beehive Pl, Brixton Rd, London SW9 7QR Tel: (01) 274 6885
Sales Manager: Norman Harding
Subjects: Politics, History, Marxism, Biography, Philosophy
Bookshops: Paperbacks Centre, 28 Charlotte St, London W1P 1HP; 10-12 Atlantic Rd, London SW9; 389 Green St, London E13; Hope St Book Centre, 321 Hope St, Glasgow G2 3PT
Founded: 1951
ISBN Publisher's Prefixes: 0-902030, 0-86151

New Portway Facsimile Reprints, an imprint of Chivers Press Publishers (qv)

New University Education, an imprint of Clive Bingley Ltd (qv)

Newnes Books, an imprint of Hamlyn Publishing (qv)

The **Newpoint** Publishing Co Ltd, Newpoint House, St James' Lane, London N10 3RD Tel: (01) 444 7281 Telex: 265544 Newpnt G Fax: (01) 444 5825
Chairman: R H Begley; *Vice-Chairman:* A N Felix; *Dirs:* A B Baldry, W Mager
Subjects: Careers, Employment, Personnel, Industrial Relations, Communications & Information Technology
Founded: 1971
ISBN Publisher's Prefix: 0-86263

Robert **Nicholson** Publications Ltd, 16 Golden Sq, London W1R 4BN Tel: (01) 437 2488 Telex: 897284 Arpub G Fax: (01) 434 2080
The above is the marketing and editorial office; the sales and distribution office is at Bartholomew Sales and Distribution Services, 12 Duncan St, Edinburgh EH9 1TA
Man Dir: Barry Winkleman; *Publicity Manager:* Helen Priday; *Managing Editor:* Louise Cavanagh
Subjects: Maps, Guides, Atlases
Miscellaneous: Robert Nicholson Publications Ltd is a division of Times Books Ltd (qv)
ISBN Publisher's Prefix: 0-905522

Nightingale Books, an imprint of Bahá'í Publishing Trust (qv)

Nile & Mackenzie Ltd*, 13 John Prince's St, London W1M 9HB Tel: (01) 493 0351 Cable Add: Nilemac Telex: 24168
Man Dir: D S Sehbai; *Rights & Permissions:* Linda Bowen
Subjects: Reference, Juveniles, Educational Materials
Founded: 1974

James **Nisbet** & Co Ltd*, 78 Tilehouse St, Hitchin, Hertfordshire SG5 2DY Tel: Hitchin 38331 (STD code 0462)
Chairman: E M Mackenzie-Wood
Subjects: Secondary & Primary Textbooks, Education
Founded: 1810
ISBN Publisher's Prefix: 0-7202

Nonesuch Press Ltd, a subsidiary company of Reinhardt Books Ltd (qv)

Norfolk Press*, 82 Hurlingham Court, Ranelagh Gdns, London SW6 3UR Tel: (01) 736 0189
Man Dir: Raymond Holdsworth
Orders to: BHS Books, 40 Chapel St, Woodbridge, Suffolk IP12 4NF Tel: Woodbridge 7090 (STD code 039 43)
Imprint: Ranelagh Editions
Subjects: Religion, Philosophy, History, Literature, Outdoor Life
Founded: 1969
ISBN Publisher's Prefix: 0-85211

North Oxford Academic, an imprint of Kogan Page Ltd (qv)

North-South Books, an imprint of Blackie & Son Ltd (qv)

Northcote House Publishers Ltd+, Harper & Row House, Estover Rd, Plymouth, Devon PL6 7PZ Tel: Plymouth 705251 (STD code 0752) Telex: 45635 Hardis G Fax: (0752) 777603
Editorial Dir: Roger Ferneyhough; *Marketing Dir:* Brian Hulme; *Publicity:* Jill Marks; *Rights & Permissions:* Barbara Massam
Subjects: Business, Travel, Expatriate

Guides, Dance, How-to, International Reference, Banking & Finance, Textbooks
Founded: 1985
ISBN Publisher's Prefix: 0-7463

Northeastern University Press, see Academic and University Publishers Group

Northern Illinois University Press, see Academic and University Publishers Group

W W Norton & Co Ltd, 37 Great Russell St, London WC1B 3NU Tel: (01) 323 1579 Cable Add: Gavia London WC1 Telex: 946240 Cweasy G ref 19020793
Man Dir: R A Cameron; *Sales:* David Harrison; *Publicity:* Carey Galletti
Orders to: John Wiley & Sons Ltd, Distribution Centre, 1 Oldlands Way, Bognor Regis, Sussex PO22 9SA
Associate Company: New Directions (at above address)
Imprint: Liveright
Subjects: History, Biography, Politics, Nautical, Economics, Music, Psychology, English & American Literature, Life Sciences
1986: 52 titles *Founded:* 1980
ISBN Publisher's Prefix: 0-393

Nova Hrvatska Ltd, 30 Fleet St, London EC4Y 1AJ Tel: (01) 947 0498 Telex: 8811204 Nova G
Man Dir: J Kusan; *Sales Dir:* G Saganic
Subjects: Secondary Textbooks, Educational Materials, Memoirs (all jointly published with Hrvatska Revija of Munich and Barcelona), *Hrvatska Revija* (quarterly literary review), *Nova Hrvatska* (fortnightly current affairs magazine)
Founded: 1959

Novello & Co Ltd, Borough Green, Sevenoaks, Kent TN15 8DT Tel: Borough Green 883261 (STD code 0732) Cable Add: Novellos Sevenoaks Telex: 95583
Man Dir: G Rizza; *Sales, Publicity & Advertising Manager:* M West-Eacott; *Rights & Permissions:* S W Freeman
Subject: Music

Nutshell Press, a subsidiary of Picton Publishing (Chippenham) Ltd (qv)

Oak Publications, an imprint of Omnibus Press (qv)

Oakwood Press, PO Box 122, Headington, Oxford OX3 8LU Tel: Wheatley 4080 (STD code 086 77)
Man Dir: Mrs J Kennedy
Imprints: Oakwood Library of Railway History, Locomotion Papers
Subjects: Transport History
Founded: 1934
ISBN Publisher's Prefix: 0-85361

Oasis Books, 12 Stevenage Rd, London SW6 6ES Tel: (01) 736 5059
Man Dir: Ian Robinson
Subjects: General Fiction, Poetry, Literature, Translations, Periodical
Founded: 1969
ISBN Publisher's Prefix: 0-903375

The **Octagon** Press Ltd, PO Box 227, London N6 4EW Tel: Langton 2045 (STD code 089 286) Telex: 8950511 G (One One) 25662001
Man Dir: George Schrager; *Publicity:* Robert Gates
Subjects: Philosophy, Religion, Psychology, Sociology, Anthropology
ISBN Publisher's Prefixes: 0-900860, 0-863040

Octopus Books Ltd, Michelin House, 81 Fulham Rd, London SW3 6RB Tel: (01) 581 9393 Cable Add: Octobooks Telex: 920191 Fax: (01) 589 8419
Chairman: Paul Hamlyn; *Chief Executive:* Ian Irvine; *Man Dir:* David Blunt; *Editorial:* Paul Richardson; *Sales and Marketing Dir:* Barry Jafrato; *Production:* Derek Freeman
Orders to: Octopus Distribution Services Ltd, PO Box 5, Rushden, Northamptonshire NN10 9YX Tel: Rushden 58521 (STD code 0933)
Parent Company: Octopus Publishing Group PLC (at above address). Ultimate parent company Reed International PLC, Reed House, 83 Piccadilly, London W1A 1EJ
Imprints: Cathay, Chancellor, Heinemann/Octopus, Langham Press, Parent & Child, Peerage, Playtime Press, Sundial, Travellers Press, Treasure Press
Branch Offs: Octopus Pty Ltd, 21st Floor, National Mutual Bldg, 44 Market St, NSW 2000, Australia; Octopus Books Inc, 1 Madison Ave, 25th Floor, New York, NY 10010, USA
Subjects: Children's Classics, Cookery, Handicrafts, Gardening, Natural History, Militaria, Transport, Entertainment, Art, Antiques, Adult & Children's Fiction
Bookshop: Bookwise Service Ltd (qv under Major Booksellers)
Founded: 1971
ISBN Publisher's Prefixes: 0-7064 (Octopus), 0-86178, 0-904644 (both Cathay), 0-907486, 1-85152 (both Chancellor), 0-905712 (Heinemann/Octopus), 0-86362 (Langham), 1-85270 (Parent & Child), 0-907408, 1-85052 (both Peerage), 1-85001 (Playtime), 0-86273, 0-904230, 0-906320 (all Sundial), 1-85150 (Travellers), 0-907407, 0-907812, 1-85051 (all Treasure)

Odhams Books, an imprint of Hamlyn Publishing Group Ltd (qv)

Ohio University Press, see Academic and University Publishers Group

The **Oleander** Press, 17 Stansgate Ave, Cambridge CB2 2QZ Tel: Cambridge 244688 (STD code 0223)
Office for USA & Canada: 210 Fifth Ave, New York, NY 10010, USA
Subjects: Middle East & Far East, Cambridge and Cambridgeshire, Arabia, Language & Literature, Libya, Poetry, Drama, Travel, Reference
Founded: 1960
ISBN Publisher's Prefixes: 0-900891, 0-902675, 0-906672

Oliphants, an imprint of Marshall, Morgan & Scott Publications Ltd (qv)

Oliver & Boyd, Robert Stevenson House, 1/3 Baxter's Pl, Edinburgh EH1 3ZB Tel: (031) 556 2424 Cable Add: Almanac Edinburgh Telex: 727511 Fax: (031) 558 1278
Man Dir: Roger Watson; *General Manager:* A A Dunnett; *Man Editor:* A Paulin; *Sales Manager & Publicity:* Rhys Edwards
Subjects: Secondary & Primary Textbooks, Educational Materials
Miscellaneous: Firm is a division of Longman Group Ltd (qv)
ISBN Publisher's Prefix: 0-05

Oliver's Guides, an imprint of A P Books/A P Financial Registers Ltd (qv)

Michael **O'Mara** Books Ltd+, 20 Queen Anne St, London W1N 9FB Tel: (01) 631 5098 Telex: 263616 Printb G Fax: (01) 580 4909
Chief Executive: Michael O'Mara; *Man Dir:* Lesley O'Mara; *Managing Editor:* Sarah Coombe
Orders to: Macmillan Distribution Ltd, Houndmills, Basingstoke, Hampshire RG21 2XS Tel: Basingstoke 29242 (STD code 0256)
Subjects: Illustrated Non-fiction, Fiction, Biography, History, Humour
1985: 4 titles *1986:* 16 titles *Founded:* 1985
ISBN Publisher's Prefix: 0-948397

Omnibus Press+, 8-9 Frith St, London W1V 5TZ Tel: (01) 434 0066 Telex: 21892 Fax: (01) 439 2848
Man Dir: Robert Wise; *Dirs:* Malcolm Grabham, Frank Johnson; *Editorial:* Chris Charlesworth; *Sales Manager:* Frank Warren; *Rights & Permissions:* Andrew King; *Production:* Robert Sampson
Orders to: Book Sales Ltd, Newmarket Rd, Bury St Edmunds, Suffolk IP33 3YB
Parent Company: Music Sales Ltd (at above London address)
Imprints: Amsco Publications, Bobcat Books, Oak Publications, Wise Publications
Branch Offs: Music Sales Pty Ltd, PO Box 3304, Sydney, NSW 2001, Australia; Music Sales Corporation, 24 East 22nd St, New York, NY 10010, USA
Subjects: Rock & Popular Music (biographies, picture books, songbooks, tutors)
1985: 40 titles (Omnibus and Bobcat)
1986: 50 titles (Omnibus and Bobcat)
Founded: 1979
ISBN Publisher's Prefixes: 0-7119, 0-86001

Online Publications*, Pinner Green House, Ash Hill Dr, Pinner, Middlesex HA5 2AE Tel: (01) 868 4466 Telex: 923498 Online G Fax: (01) 868 9933
Man Dir: Richard Elliot-Green; *Publications Dir:* Rollo Turner; *Publications Manager:* Sybil Richardson
Associate Company: Online International Ltd (at above address)
Subjects: Communications, Computer Applications, Information Technology, Biotechnology
1985: 27 titles *1986:* 29 titles *Founded:* 1970
ISBN Publisher's Prefixes: 0-903796, 0-86353

Open Books Publishing Ltd, Beaumont House, Wells, Somerset BA5 2LD Tel: Wells 77276 (STD code 0749)
Man Dir: Patrick Taylor
Subjects: Social Sciences, General Non-fiction
Founded: 1974
ISBN Publisher's Prefix: 0-7291

Open University Educational Enterprises Ltd+, 12 Cofferidge Close, Stony Stratford, Milton Keynes MK11 1BY Tel: Milton Keynes 566744 (STD code 0908) Telex: 826147
Man Dir: P S Wright; *Publisher* (Open University Press): John Skelton; *Sales Manager:* Corinne Pick; *Production Manager:* Sue Hadden; *Promotion Manager:* Lindsay Thomas; *Rights Executive:* Barbara Martin
Imprint: Open University Press
Subjects: Arts, Education, Mathematics, Science, Social Science, Technology, Adult Education
1985: 160 titles *1986:* 200 titles *Founded:* 1977
ISBN Publisher's Prefix: 0-335

Open University Press, an imprint of Open University Educational Enterprises Ltd (qv)

Orbis, an imprint of Macdonald & Co (Publishers) Ltd (qv)

Orbit, an imprint of Macdonald & Co (Publishers) Ltd (qv)

Orchard Books+, 10 Golden Sq, London W1R 3AF Tel: (01) 734 8738 Cable Add: Frawatts London W1 Telex: 262655 Groluk G Fax: (01) 439 1440
Man Dir: Judith Elliott; *Sales Dir:* George Taylor; *Rights & Permissions:* Katharine Thompson; *Editorial:* Rosemary Davies, Lucy Coats; *Production Dir:* Rita Ireland; *Promotion Manager:* Linda Banner
Orders to: Bookpoint Ltd, 39 Milton Trading Estate, Abingdon, Oxfordshire OX14 4TD
Parent Company: Franklin Watts Inc, 387 Park Ave South, New York, NY 10016, USA. Ultimate parent company The House of Grolier Ltd (at above US address)
Associate Companies: Franklin Watts Ltd UK (qv); Orchard Books Australia, 14 Mars Rd, Lane Cove, NSW 2066, Australia; Orchard Books Canada, 20 Torbay Rd, Markham, Ontario 23P 1G6, Canada; Orchard Books New York, 387 Park Ave South, NY 10016, USA
Subjects: Juveniles, Picture Books, Fiction, Novelty
1986: 8 titles *Founded:* 1986
ISBN Publisher's Prefix: 1-85213

Ordnance Survey, British Government Map Publishers, Romsey Rd, Maybush, Southampton SO9 4DH Tel: Southampton 792000 (STD code 0703) Cable Add: Ordsurvey, Southampton Telex: 477843 Ordsvy G Fax: (0703) 792404
Marketing: D Toft; *Publishing Manager:* J Page (Tel: Southampton 792305 (STD code 0703))
Subjects: Maps, Atlases, Books

Oriel Press, see Routledge

Oriental Textile Press Ltd, an imprint of Antique Collectors' Club (qv)

Osprey Publishing Ltd+, 27a Floral St, London WC2E 9DP Tel: (01) 836 7863 Cable Add: Philip London WC2 Telex: 21667
Man Dir: M A Bovill; *Export Sales Manager:* Julian Clayton; *Marketing Manager:* Alan Greene
Associate Company: George Philip & Son Ltd (qv)
Subjects: Militaria, Motoring, Aviation
ISBN Publisher's Prefix: 0-85045

Overseas Publications Interchange Ltd*, 8 Queen Anne's Gardens, London W4 1TU Tel: (01) 747 0844
Man Dir: S N Mibradovich; *Editor:* N E Karsov
Subjects: Books in Russian and East European languages (especially Soviet dissident literature and books by Western scholars)

Peter **Owen** Ltd, 73 Kenway Rd, London SW5 0RE Tel: (01) 373 5628, (01) 370 6093
Man Dir, Sales & Advertising, Rights & Permissions: Peter Owen; *Publicity:* Antonia Owen
Subjects: General Fiction, Belles Lettres, Biography, Music, Art, Sociology
Founded: 1950
ISBN Publisher's Prefix: 0-7206

Oxfam, 274 Banbury Rd, Oxford OX2 7DZ Tel: Oxford 56777 (STD code 0865) Cable Add: Oxfam Oxford Telex: 83610
Dir: Frank Judd; *Publications Officer:* Jill Bidie; *Publicity Manager:* Toby Milner
Subjects: Poverty, Third World Development and Health Care, and Appropriate Technology, Country briefs
1987: 45 titles *Founded:* 1942
ISBN Publisher's Prefix: 0-85598

Oxford Illustrated Press Ltd+, Sparkford, Nr Yeovil, Somerset BA22 7JJ Tel: North Cadbury 40635 (STD code 0963) Telex: 46212 Fax: (0963) 40825
Editorial Office: The Gables, Newington, Oxford OX9 8AH Tel: Oxford 890026 (STD code 0865)
Chairman: John H Haynes; *Man Dir:* Jim Scott; *Editorial Dir:* Jane Marshall; *Sales Dir:* Andy Lynch; *Production Dir:* Roger Stagg
Parent Company: Haynes Publishing Group PLC (qv for associate companies)
Subjects: Illustrated Leisure, Travel Guides, Sport, Transport, Art, Gardening, Cookery
1987: 12 titles
ISBN Publisher's Prefixes: 0-902280, 0-946609

Oxford Microform Publications Ltd*, Headington Hill Hall, Oxford OX3 0BW Tel: Oxford 64881 (STD code 0865) Telex: 83177
Chairman: I R Maxwell; *Dirs:* P Ashby, T Sloggett
Parent Company: Pergamon Books Ltd (see Pergamon Press)
Subjects: Scholarly & Scientific Journals, Research, Collections, Serial Publications in Economics, Colour Microfiche in Art, Science, Humanities, Bibliography
ISBN Publisher's Prefix: 0-08

Oxford Railway Publishing Co Ltd*, Link House, West St, Poole, Dorset BH15 1LL Tel: Poole 671171 (STD code 0202) Cable Add: Blandpress Poole Telex: 418304
Chairman, Chief Executive: R B Erven; *Sales Dir:* C P Lloyd; *Production Dir:* G L Charters
Parent Company: Link House Publications PLC (at above address)
Subjects: Railways and Transport
Bookshops: The Railway Book Centre, 8 The Roundway, Headington, Oxford; The Railway Book & Model Centre, 302 Holdenhurst Rd, Bournemouth
ISBN Publisher's Prefixes: 0-902888, 0-86093

Oxford University Press+, Walton St, Oxford OX2 6DP Tel: Oxford 56767 (STD code 0865) Cable Add: Clarendon Press Oxford Telex: (Clarpress) 837330 Fax: (0865) 56646
Secretary to the Delegates and Chief Executive: G B Richardson; *Publishing Chairman:* R A Denniston; *International Division Dir:* R Boning
Publishing Divisions:
Academic: *Man Dir:* R D P Charkin; *Sales, Marketing:* S W H Wratten, George Taylor (UK); *Production, Design:* B Townsend; *Rights & Permissions:* A Mulgan
Educational: *Man Dir:* P R Mothersole; *Sales, Marketing:* M D C Cuss; *Production:* G D Tombs
Oxford English (English Language Teaching): *Man Dir:* G Lewis; *Sales, Marketing:* D Stewart; *Production:* M A Price
Orders to: OUP Distribution Services, Saxon Way West, Corby, Northamptonshire NN18 9ES Tel: Corby 741519 (STD code 0536)
Associate Companies: Cornelsen and Oxford University Press GmbH, Federal Republic of Germany (qv); University Press Ltd, Nigeria (qv)
Branch Offs: Oxford University Press, Australia (qv); Oxford University Press, 70 Wynford Dr, Don Mills, Toronto, Ontario M3C 1J9, Canada; Oxford University Press, Hong Kong (qv); Oxford University Press, India (qv); Oxford University Press, P T Pustaka Ilmu, Jalan Kebong Kacang XII/23, Jakarta Pusat, Indonesia; Oxford University Press KK, Japan (qv); Oxford University Press East and Central Africa, Kenya (qv); Oxford University Press, Malaysia (qv); Oxford University Press, New Zealand (qv); Oxford University Press, (Pakistan Branch), Pakistan (qv); Oxford University Press Pte Ltd, Republic of Singapore (qv); Oxford University Press Southern Africa, Republic of South Africa (qv); Oxford University Press, Tanzania (qv); Oxford University Press, 200 Madison Ave, New York, NY 10016, USA; Oxford University Press East Africa, Zimbabwe (qv)
Subjects: Belles Lettres, Poetry, Biography, History, English Language Teaching, Music, Art, Classics, Language, Law, Philosophy, Reference, Bibles, Religion, Juveniles, Paperbacks, Medicine, Politics & International Affairs, Economics, Strategic Studies, Psychology, Mathematics, Science, Engineering, Social Science, Atlases, University, Secondary & Primary Textbooks, Educational Materials, Journals, Software
Founded: 1478
ISBN Publisher's Prefix: 0-19

P B I Publications*, Britannica House, Waltham Cross, Hertfordshire EN8 7DY Tel: Waltham Cross 23691 (STD code 0992) Cable Add: Panbritan Waltham Cross Telex: 23957 Fax: (0992) 26452
Man Dir: Dr D G Hessayon; *Sales Dir:* J N Adkins
Subjects: Horticulture, How-to
ISBN Publisher's Prefix: 0-903505

Packard Publishing Ltd+, 16 Lynch Down, Funtington, Chichester, West Sussex PO18 9LR Tel: Bosham 575621 (STD code 0243)
Man Dir: Michael Packard
Subjects: Biology, Conservation, Landscape Architecture, Planning, Education, Arabic Dictionaries, Music, Biography
1987: 10 titles *Founded:* 1977
ISBN Publisher's Prefixes: 0-906527, 0-948690, 1-85341

Pagoda Books+, 79 Great Titchfield St, London W1P 7FN Tel: (01) 637 0890 Telex: 23539 Vision G
Editorial Dir: Susan Pinkus; *Sales Dir:* David Alexander
Orders to: Bookpoint, Milton Trading Estate, Abingdon, Berkshire
Parent Company: Vision Resource International Ltd (at above address)
Subjects: Photography, Health, Childcare, Wildlife, Almanacs, Illustrated Classics & Opera Libretti, Juvenile, Cuisine, Gardening
Founded: 1983

Paintaway, an imprint of Ramboro Enterprises Ltd (qv)

Paladin Books, see Grafton Books

Pan Books Ltd+, Cavaye Pl, London SW10 9PG Tel: (01) 373 6070 Cable Add: Pandition London Telex: 917466 Fax: (01) 370 0746
Orders to: Houndmills, Basingstoke, Hampshire Tel: Basingstoke 464481 (STD code 0256) Fax: 0256 460675
Man Dir: Alan Gordon Walker; *Group Sales and Marketing Dir:* Brian Davies; *Publishing Dir:* Ian S Chapman; *Sales:* Billy Adair; *Publicity:* Jacqueline Graham; *Rights & Permissions:* Tess Sacco; *Production:* Chris Gibson
Parent Company: Macmillan Publishers Ltd (qv)
Subsidiary Companies: Pan Books

(Australia) Pty Ltd, Australia (qv); Pan Books New Zealand Ltd, New Zealand
Imprints: Brodies Notes, Pan, Pavanne, Picador, Piccolo, Piper
Subjects: Paperbacks, General Fiction & Non-fiction, Children's
Bookshop: At above address
Founded: 1947
ISBN Publisher's Prefix: 0-330

Paper Tiger Books, an imprint of Dragon's World Ltd (qv)

Paperfronts, an imprint of Elliot Right Way Books (qv)

Papermac, an imprint of Macmillan London Ltd (qv)

Paradigm Publishing Ltd+, Avenue House, 131/133 Holland Park Ave, London W11 4UT Tel: (01) 603 4688 Telex: Mgpubs 311890 Fax: (01) 602 5197
Man Dir: Alfred Waller; *Publisher:* Jeremy Swinfen-Green; *Sales and Marketing Manager, Publicity:* Adam Marshall; *Production Dir:* Bill Antrobus; *Rights Manager:* Esther Heasman
Orders to: Brookhampton Lane, Kineton, Warwickshire CV35 0JB Tel: Kineton 640606 (STD code 0926)
Parent Company: Mary Glasgow Publications Ltd (qv)
Associate Company: Sound Communication (Publishers) Ltd, Dewsbury, West Yorkshire WF13 1HF
Subjects: New Technology, Computer Science, Management & Business
1986: 8 titles *Founded:* 1986
Miscellaneous: Firm is a member of Wolters Kluwer NV, Netherlands (qv)
ISBN Publisher's Prefix: 0-948825

Parent & Child, an imprint of Octopus Books Ltd (qv)

Partridge Press, an imprint of Transworld Publishers (Corgi & Bantam Books) Ltd (qv)

The **Paternoster** Press Ltd, Paternoster House, 3 Mount Radford Crescent, Exeter, Devon EX2 4JW Tel: Exeter 50631 (STD code 0392)
Chairman and Man Dir, Sales, Publicity, Advertising: J H L Mudditt; *Editorial, Rights & Permissions:* P E Cousins
Subjects: History, Philosophy, Religion, Paperbacks
1985: 47 titles *1986:* 20 titles *Founded:* 1935
ISBN Publisher's Prefix: 0-85364

Stanley **Paul** & Co Ltd, an imprint of Century Hutchinson Publishing Ltd (qv)

Pavanne, an imprint of Pan Books Ltd (qv)

Pavilion Books, an imprint of Michael Joseph Ltd (qv)

Peerage, an imprint of Octopus Books Ltd (qv)

Pelham Books Ltd, 27 Wright's Lane, London W8 5TZ Tel: (01) 937 7255 Telex: 917181 Fax: (01) 937 8704
Publisher: Roger Houghton; *Sales Dir:* Nigel Sisson; *Publicity & Advertising:* Sally Partington; *Rights:* Ruth Salazar
Subjects: Sports, Crafts, Biography, How-to, Reference
1986: 50 titles
Miscellaneous: An imprint of Michael Joseph Ltd (qv)
ISBN Publisher's Prefix: 0-7207

Pelican, an imprint of Penguin Books Ltd (qv)

Pemberton Publishing Co Ltd*, 88 Islington High St, London N1 8EN Tel: (01) 226 7251 Cable Add: Ratiopres London N1 4EN
Managing Editor, Rights & Permissions: Nicolas Walter
Parent Company: Rationalist Press Association (at above address)
Subjects: Philosophy, Religion, Low-priced Paperbacks, Psychology, General & Social Science, University Textbooks
Founded: 1960
ISBN Publisher's Prefix: 0-301

Penguin Books Ltd, 27 Wright's Lane, London W8 5TZ Tel: (01) 938 2200 Telex: 917181 Fax: (01) 937 8704
Chief Executive: Peter Mayer; *Man Dir:* Trevor Glover; *Editorial Dirs:* Elizabeth Attenborough, Tim Binding (Children's); *Publishing Dir:* Peter Carson; *Marketing Dir:* Barry Cunningham; *Sales Dirs:* Patrick Hutchinson (UK), Antony Moggach (Export); *Sales and Marketing Dir:* Patrick Wright; *Production Dir:* Jonathan Yglesias; *Rights & Permissions:* Carol Heaton
Warehouse & Accounts: Bath Rd, Harmondsworth, West Drayton, Middlesex UB7 0DA Tel: (01) 759 1984 Cable Add: Penguinook West Drayton Telex: 263130
Subsidiary Companies: Hamish Hamilton Ltd (qv), Michael Joseph Ltd (qv), Penguin Overseas Ltd, Sphere Books Ltd (qv), Frederick Warne & Co Ltd (qv), TBL Book Service Ltd (all UK)
Imprints: Viking (formerly Allen Lane) (qv), Viking Kestrel (qv) (both hardcover); others include Pelican Books, Peregrine Books, Puffin Books, Rainbird
Book Clubs: Puffin School Book Clubs
Subjects: Low- & High-priced Paperbacks (General Fiction, General Non-fiction, Juveniles, Technical, Educational)
Bookshops: Penguin Bookshops at: 10 The Market, Covent Garden, London WC2; 157 Kings Rd, London SW10; 2 Plaza House, 191 Camden High St, London NW1; Liberty's, Regent St, London WC1; 27 White Lion Walk, Guildford; Bridlesmith Gate, Nottingham; 44 Cathedral Sq, Peterborough; Coppergate, York
Puffin Bookshop at 1 The Market, Covent Garden, London WC2
1986: 730 titles *Founded:* 1935
ISBN Publisher's Prefixes: 0-14 (Penguin), 0-902935 (Rainbird), 0-670 (Viking, Viking Kestrel)

Penguin Publishing Co Ltd, Bath Rd, Harmondsworth, West Drayton, Middlesex UB7 0DA Tel: (01) 759 1984 Cable Add: Penguinook West Drayton Telex: 263130
Chief Executive: Peter Mayer; *UK Group Man Dir:* Trevor Glover; *Dirs:* Peter Carson (Publishing), Morton Mint (President, Penguin Canada), John Rolfe (Publishing Operations), John Webster (Group Finance), Patrick Wright (Group Sales & Marketing)
This is the holding company for Penguin Books Ltd, UK (qv); Penguin Books Australia Ltd, Australia (qv); Penguin Books Canada Ltd, 2801 John St, Markham, Ontario L3R 1B4, Canada; Penguin Books New Zealand Ltd, New Zealand (qv); New American Library, 32nd Floor, 1663 Broadway, New York, NY, USA; Viking Penguin Inc, 40 West 23 St, New York, NY 10010, USA
Ultimate parent company is Pearson PLC, Millbank Tower, Millbank, London SW1P 4QZ

Pennsylvania State University Press, see Academic and University Publishers Group

The **Pentland** Press Ltd, Kippielaw, By Haddington, East Lothian EH41 4PY Tel: East Linton 860421 (STD code 0620)
Man Dir: Douglas B Law
Subjects: History, Poetry, Novels, Biography, Autobiography, General
1985: 12 titles *Founded:* 1981
ISBN Publisher's Prefix: 0-946270

Peregrine Books, an imprint of Penguin Books Ltd (qv)

Ediciones **Peregrino**, an imprint of Evangelical Press and Services Ltd (qv)

Peter **Peregrinus** Ltd, see Peter

Pergamon Press+, Headington Hill Hall, Oxford OX3 0BW Tel: Oxford 64881 (STD code 0865) Cable Add: Pergapress Oxford Telex: 83177 Fax: (0865) 60285
Chairman & Publisher: Robert Maxwell; *Deputy Publisher:* Kevin Maxwell
Pergamon Books Ltd: *Man Dirs:* W A Snyder, A J Steel; *Production Dir:* B Martell; *Sales Dir:* K Smith; *Editorial, Marketing:* B Barrett; *Rights & Permissions:* Anna Moon
Pergamon Journals Ltd: *Man Dir:* G F Richards; *Marketing Dir:* D Sar; *Rights & Permissions:* Anna Moon
Associate and Subsidiary Companies include: The Aberdeen University Press Ltd, E J Arnold & Son Ltd (qv), Brassey's Defence Publishers, Maxwell Communication Corporation plc (qv), Bumpus Haldane & Maxwell Ltd, Hollis Brothers & ESA PLC, Mirrorsoft Ltd, Mirrorvision, Mirror Group Newspapers, Mirror Publications Ltd, Oxford Microform Publications Ltd (qv), Pergamon Compact Solution, Pergamon Infotech Ltd, Pergamon Orbit Infoline Ltd, Pergamon Technical Services International, Waterlow Publishers Ltd (qv) (all UK); Pergamon Press (Australia) Pty Ltd, Australia (qv); Pergamon Press Canada Ltd, Toronto, Canada; Pergamon Press China, Beijing, People's Republic of China; Pergamon Press France, Paris, France; Pergamon Press GmbH, Kronberg, Federal Republic of Germany; Pergamon Press Japan, Tokyo, Japan; Pergamon Press Inc, Elmsford, New York, USA
Imprints include: Religious and Moral Education Press (qv)
Subjects: Life Sciences & Medicine, Veterinary Sciences, Physical Sciences, Engineering, Psychology, Social & Behavioural Sciences and Liberal Arts, Education, Business Management, Law, Religion, Biography, History, General Science, Open Learning, Scientific, Technical and Professional Journals & Books, Major Reference Works, School & University Textbooks, Educational Materials, Computer Software
1985: 350 titles *1986:* 400 titles *Founded:* 1949
ISBN Publisher's Prefix: 0-08

Peter **Peregrinus** Ltd, an imprint of The Institution of Electrical Engineers (qv)

Phaidon Press Ltd+, Littlegate House, St Ebbe's St, Oxford OX1 1SQ Tel: Oxford 246681 (STD code 0865) Cable Add: Phaidon Oxford Telex: 83308 Fax: (0865) 251959
Chairman: George Riches; *Man Dir:* Derek Phillips; *Dir:* Simon Haviland; *Production Dir:* Alan Peebles; *Marketing Dir:* Geoff Cowen; *Publicity Manager:* Sally Dunsmore; *International Rights, Licences:* Betty Lin; *Editorial Dir:* Roger Sears; *Distribution Dir:* Ian Moncur
Orders to: Unit B, Ridgeway Trading Estate, Iver, Buckinghamshire Tel: Iver 654747 (STD code 0753) Telex: 846440

Parent Company: Musterlin Group PLC (at above main address)
Subsidiary Company: Phaidon-Christie's Ltd (at above main address)
Associate Companies: Canongate Publishing Ltd, Equinox (Oxford) Ltd (qqv)
Subjects: Art, Art History, Applied and Performing Arts, Cultural Travel Guides, Fine Art Photography, Practical Arts, Architecture
Book Club: Artists Book Club Ltd
1985: 30 titles *Founded:* 1923
ISBN Publisher's Prefix: 0-7148

George **Philip & Son** Ltd, 27a Floral St, London WC2E 9DP Tel: (01) 836 7863/1915 Telex: 21667
Orders to: George Philip Services Ltd, Lineside Industrial Estate, Littlehampton, West Sussex
Man Dir, Rights & Permissions: M A Bovill; **International Sales Dir:** John Bennett; **Editorial Dir:** John Gaisford; **Production Dir:** Roger Bonnett; **Sales, Marketing Manager:** Alan Greene
Associate Companies: E Stanford Ltd; Stanford Maritime Ltd (qv); Osprey Publishing Ltd (qv)
Subjects: Atlases and Maps, Textbooks, Educational Materials, Maritime, Militaria, Motoring, General
Founded: 1834
ISBN Publisher's Prefix: 0-540

Philip & Tacey Ltd, see Philograph Publications Ltd

Phillimore & Co Ltd, Shopwyke Hall, Chichester, West Sussex PO2O 6BQ Tel: Chichester 787636 (STD code 0243) Cable Add: Phillimore Chichester
Honorary President: Lord Darwen; **Chairman & Man Dir:** Philip Harris; **Editorial Dir:** Noel H Osborne
Subsidiary Company: Darwen Finlayson Ltd (qv)
Subjects: Local History, Historical Biography, Architectural History, Archaeology, Genealogy, Heraldry, Family History
Bookshop: The Phillimore Bookshop, Shopwyke Hall, Chichester
Founded: 1875 (incorporated: 1897)
ISBN Publisher's Prefixes: 0-900592, 0-85033

Phoebe **Phillips** Editions+, 6 Berners Mews, London W1P 3DG Tel: (01) 637 7933, (01) 637 1673 Telex: 912881 G Attn PPE Fax: (01) 637 7933
Man Dir: Phoebe Phillips; **Editorial Dir:** Tessa Clark
Subjects: Fine & Decorative Arts, Mediaeval History, Cookery, Needlework, Gardening, Health
1985: 7 titles *1986:* 11 titles *Founded:* 1982
ISBN Publisher's Prefix: 1-870050

Philograph Publications Ltd, North Way, Andover, Hampshire SP10 5BA Tel: Andover 332171 (STD code 0264) Telex: 47496 Fax: (0264) 332226
Man Dir: Jon Tacey
Associate Company: Philip & Tacey Ltd (at above address)
Subjects: Primary Education, Teaching Aids
ISBN Publisher's Prefix: 0-85370

Phoenix Publishing Associates Ltd+, 14 Vernon Rd, Bushey, Hertfordshire WD2 2JL Tel: Watford 32109 (STD code 0923) Telex: 923574 Alacol G
Man Dir: Gordon Rae
Subjects: Travel, Leisure, Degree Guides, General
Founded: 1984
ISBN Publisher's Prefix: 0-9465

Piatkus Books, 5 Windmill St, London W1P 1HF Tel: (01) 631 0710 Telex: 266082
Man Dir: Judy Piatkus; **Editorial Dir:** Gill Cormode; **Sales & Publicity Dir:** Philip Cotterell
Orders to: George Philip Services Ltd, PO Box 1, Littlehampton, West Sussex BN17 7EN Tel: Littlehampton 717453 (STD code 0903)
Parent Company: Judy Piatkus (Publishers) Ltd (address as above)
Subjects: Fiction, Cookery, Leisure, Biography, Humour, Giftbooks, Health, Practical
1986: 95 titles *Founded:* 1979
ISBN Publisher's Prefix: 0-86188

Picador, an imprint of Pan Books Ltd (qv)

Piccadilly Press*, 5 Canfield Pl, London NW6 3BT Tel: (01) 625 9582 Telex: 295441
Man Dir, Editorial, Publicity: Brenda Gardner; **Production, Rights & Permissions:** Lee Frank; **Sales:** c/o André Deutsch Ltd, 105-106 Great Russell St, London WC1B 3LJ Tel: (01) 580 2746
Orders to: Westerhill Distribution Services, c/o William Collins PLC, PO Box, Glasgow G4 0NB Tel: (041) 772 3200 Telex: 778107
Subjects: Children's (hardback)
Founded: 1983
ISBN Publisher's Prefix: 0-946826

Piccolo, an imprint of Pan Books Ltd (qv)

Pickering & Inglis Ltd, 3 Beggarwood Lane, Basingstoke, Hampshire RG23 7LP Tel: Basingstoke 59211 (STD code 0256) Cable Add: Grapho Basingstoke Telex: 858669 Marpic G
Production Manager: Tim Sanders; **Editorial:** Debbie Thorpe; **Marketing, Sales Manager:** John Robertson
Parent Company: Marshall Pickering Holdings Ltd (UK) — see Marshall Pickering entry — a subsidiary of Zondervan Corporation Inc, Grand Rapids, USA
Subsidiary Companies: R L Allan & Son (Publishers) Ltd; A McLay & Co Ltd, St Fagans Rd, Fairwater, Cardiff CF5 3XB (Printers)
Associate Company: Marshall Morgan & Scott Publications Ltd (qv)
Imprints: Lamp Press, Pickering Paperbacks, Prisca
Subjects: Religion, Juveniles
Founded: 1870
ISBN Publisher's Prefix: 0-7208

Picton Publishing (Chippenham) Ltd+*, 1 Frome Rd, Beckington, Nr Bath, Somerset BA3 6SN Tel: Frome 830996 (STD code 0373) Fax: (0249) 443024
Chief Executive, Editorial, Sales, Publicity, Rights & Permissions: D B Picton-Phillips; **Production:** A P Hayter
Subsidiary Companies: Barebones Books (basic scholastic), The Military Chest (magazine), Nutshell Press (RAF series)
Subjects: Philately, Thematic, Theatre, Military
Bookshops: The Military Chest, Goose St, Beckington, Nr Bath, Somerset; 1 Cane Cnr, Frome Rd, Beckington, Nr Bath, Somerset
Founded: 1972
ISBN Publisher's Prefix: 0-902633

Picture Lions, an imprint of William Collins PLC (qv)

Frances **Pinter** Ltd+, 25 Floral St, Covent Garden, London WC2E 9DS Tel: (01) 240 9233 Telex: 912881 Attn Pin
Chief Executive: Frances Pinter; **Editorial Dir:** Iain Stevenson; **Sales Dir:** Pamela Fulton
Orders to: Marston Book Services Ltd, PO Box 87, Oxford OX4 1LB Tel: Oxford 791179/791155 (STD code 0865)
Subjects: International Relations, Politics, Political Economy, New Technology, Linguistics, Management, Communications Studies, Development Studies, Environmental Issues, Geography
Founded: 1973
ISBN Publisher's Prefixes: 0-903804, 0-86187

Piper, an imprint of Pan Books Ltd (qv)

Pitkin Pictorials Ltd, North Way, Andover, Hampshire SP10 5BE Tel: Andover 332424 (STD code 0264) Cable Add: APT Andover Telex: Abpand G 47214 Fax: 0264 64418
Subjects: Architectural History, and Guides for the Tourist Industry
ISBN Publisher's Prefix: 0-85372

Pitman Publishing Ltd+, 128 Long Acre, London WC2E 9AN Tel: (01) 379 7383 Cable Add: Ipandsons London WC2 Telex: 261367
Chairman: Robert Duncan; **Man Dir:** Ian Pringle; **Sales and Marketing Dir:** Anselm Robinson; **Sales Manager:** James Pitman; **International Marketing Manager:** Alick Kitchin; **Production:** Barry Finch; **Publicity Manager:** Clare Gallagher; **Rights & Permissions:** Brenda Gvozdanovic
Orders to: Pitman Publishing Ltd, Slaidburn Crescent, Southport, Merseyside PR9 9YF
Holding Company: Longman Group UK Ltd (qv). Ultimate parent company Pearson PLC
Imprint: Macdonald & Evans Ltd
Subjects: Business Education, Professional/Reference, Business/Management, Secretarial/Commercial Studies, Computing, Information Technology
ISBN Publisher's Prefixes: 0-272, 0-273, 0-7121

Plain Edition, an imprint of Brilliance Books (qv)

Planet, an imprint of W H Allen & Co Ltd (qv)

Playfair, an imprint of Macdonald & Co (Publishers) Ltd (qv)

Playtime Press, an imprint of Octopus Books Ltd (qv)

Plexus Publishing Ltd, 30 Craven St, London WC2N 5NT Tel: (01) 839 1315 Telex: 947157 Plexus G
Sales, Production: Terence Porter; **Editorial, Rights & Permissions:** Sandra Wake; **Publicity:** Sandra Wake, Helen Mott, Eveline van Roxy
Orders to: J M Dent & Sons (Distribution) Ltd, Dunhams Lane, Letchworth, Hertfordshire SG6 1LF Tel: Letchworth 686241 (STD code 0462)
Subjects: Illustrated Books on Film, Rock, Folk, Biography, Popular Culture and Art
1985: 12 titles *1986:* 8 titles *Founded:* 1973
ISBN Publisher's Prefix: 0-85965

Plough Publishing House+, Darvell, Robertsbridge, East Sussex TN32 5DR Tel: Robertsbridge 880626 (STD code 0580) Telex: 957493 Coplay G
Man Dir, Rights & Permissions: Delf Fransham; **Sales, Publicity & Advertising Dir:** Lenore Barton
Subjects: Radical Christian Discipleship, Anabaptist History, Juveniles
Founded: 1937
Miscellaneous: Firm is the publishing house

of the Hutterian Brethren
ISBN Publisher's Prefix: 0-87486

Pluto Publishing Ltd+, 11-12 Northdown St, London N1 9BN Tel: (01) 837 3322 Telex: 265628 Fax: (01) 278 1677
Man Dir: Roger van Zwanenberg; *Editorial:* Anne Beech; *Marketing:* Norman Drake
Parent Company: Zwan Publications Ltd (qv)
Associate Company: Pluto Press Australia, Australia (qv)
Imprint: Pluto Press
Subjects: Current Affairs, Politics, Social Sciences, Soviet Studies, Popular Culture, Biography, History
1986: 58 titles *Founded:* 1971
ISBN Publisher's Prefixes: 0-902818, 0-904383, 0-86104

Pocket Classics, an imprint of Alan Sutton Publishing Ltd (qv)

Pocket Puffins, an imprint of Moonlight Publishing Ltd (qv)

Pocket Worlds, an imprint of Moonlight Publishing Ltd (qv)

Poetry Wales Press*, Green Hollows Cottage, Craig-yr-Eos Rd, Ogmore-By-Sea, Mid Glamorgan CF30 0PG Tel: Bridgend 880649 (STD code 0656)
Chief Executive, Editorial: Cary Archard; *Sales, Production, Publicity, Rights & Permissions:* Mike Felton
Subjects: Poetry, Biography, Short Stories, Literary Criticism & Writings
1985: 12 titles *Founded:* 1981
ISBN Publisher's Prefix: 0-907476

Police Review Publishing Ltd, an imprint of Sweet & Maxwell Ltd (qv)

Policy Studies Institute, 100 Park Village East, London NW1 3SR Tel: (01) 387 2171
Dir: W W Daniel; *Sales, Publicity:* Nicholas Evans; *Sales Representation:* Frances Pinter Ltd (qv); *Secretary:* Eileen Reid
Orders to: Marston Book Services Ltd, PO Box 87, Oxford OX4 1LB Tel: Oxford 724041 (STD code 0865)
Subjects: Politics, Economics, Education & Training, Social Policy, Public Administration, European Studies, Industrial Policy & Technology, Labour Relations, Employment, Energy, Transport, Arts
1986: 23 titles *1987:* 28 titles
ISBN Publisher's Prefix: 0-85374

Polity Press, an associate company of Basil Blackwell Ltd (qv)

Polybooks Ltd, see Charles Skilton Ltd

Polygon Books, an imprint of Edinburgh University Student Publications Board (qv)

Polytantric Press, an imprint of Jay Landesman Ltd (qv)

Polytech, an imprint of Longman Group Ltd (qv)

Pond Press, 7 Beasleys Ait, Sunbury-on-Thames, Middlesex TW16 6AS Tel: Sunbury-on-Thames 80091 (STD code 093 27)
Subjects: Reference Books, Directories & Guidebooks, Sports, Games & Pastimes
ISBN Publisher's Prefix: 0-85375

Popular Dogs Publishing Co Ltd, an imprint of Century Hutchinson Publishing Ltd (qv)

H Pordes*, 529b Finchley Rd, London NW3 7BH Tel: (01) 435 9878/9
Subjects: History, Reference

Founded: 1947
Book Club: The Jewish Book Club (R Pordes)
Miscellaneous: Also remainder dealer
ISBN Publisher's Prefix: 0-85376

T & A D Poyser Ltd, Town Head House, Calton, Waterhouses, Stoke-on-Trent, Staffordshire ST10 3JX Tel: Waterhouses 366 (STD code 053 86)
Man Dir: Trevor Poyser; *Sales, Foreign Rights:* Dorothy Poyser
Subjects: Ornithology, Aviation
Founded: 1972
ISBN Publisher's Prefix: 0-85661

Praeger Publishers, see Eurospan Ltd

Pre-School Publishing Co, an imprint of Burke Publishing Co Ltd (qv)

Prentice-Hall (Simon & Schuster International Group)+, 66 Wood Lane End, Hemel Hempstead, Hertfordshire HP2 4RG Tel: Hemel Hempstead 231555 (STD code 0442) Cable Add: Prenhall Hemel Telex: 82445 Fax: (0442) 221485
President: Henry Hirschberg; *Vice-President, Sales Dir:* Charles Gibbes (UK, Europe, Middle East, Africa); *Assistant Vice President:* Henry Reece; *Sales Managers:* Tony Murray (Eastern Europe), Jill Jones (UK), Carolyn Dougherty (Special Sales), Cathy Peck (Medical & Nursing), Debbie Zaharakis (ELT); *Rights & Permissions:* Tony Murray; *Editorial:* Glen Murray (Executive Editor, Professional & Reference), Maggie McDougall (Business), Cathy Peck (Nursing), David Haines (ELT), Helen Martin (Computer Science), Andrew Binnie (Engineering); *Production Dir:* Ron Decent; *Marketing Services Manager:* Nicholas Waller
Parent Company: Gulf & Western Inc, USA
Associate Companies: Prentice-Hall of Australia Pty Ltd, Australia (qv); Prentice-Hall of Canada Ltd, 1870 Birchmount Rd, Scarborough, Ontario, Canada; Prentice-Hall of India Pvt Ltd, India (qv); Prentice-Hall of Japan Inc, Japan (qv); Prentice Hall Hispanoamericana, Mexico; Simon & Schuster (Asia) Pte Ltd, Republic of Singapore (qv); International Book Distributors Ltd, UK; Allyn & Bacon, USA; Appleton & Lange, USA; Institute for Business Planning Inc, IBP Plaza, 320 Hudson Terrace, Englewood Cliffs, NJ 07632, USA; Yourdon, USA
Subjects: History, Music, Art, Philosophy, Religion, Medicine, Psychology, University Science and Technology (University textbooks and postgraduate material), Sociology, Education, Business, Economics, English, English as a Second Language, Political Science, Speech, Drama, Trade Books
Founded: 1913
ISBN Publisher's Prefix: 0-13 (Prentice-Hall)

Norman **Price**, an imprint of Dickson Price Publishers Ltd (qv)

Pride Publications, an imprint of E J Morten (Publishers) (qv)

Princeton University Press, see University Presses of California, Columbia and Princeton

Priory Press Ltd, see Wayland (Publishers) Ltd

Prisca, an imprint of Pickering & Inglis Ltd (qv)

Prism Press Book Publishers Ltd+, 2 South St, Bridport, Dorset DT6 3NQ Tel: Bridport 27022 (STD code 0308) Telex:

265871 Monref G ref 84: Mnu 247
Dirs: Julian King, Colin Spooner
Subjects: Alternative Technology, Self-Sufficiency, Philosophy, Politics, Literature, Cookery, Wine and Beermaking, Computing, Alternative Medicine, The Occult, Building, Pacifism, Ecology
1985: 8 titles *1986:* 14 titles *Founded:* 1974
ISBN Publisher's Prefixes: 0-904727, 0-907061, 1-85327

Professional Books Ltd, 46 Milton Trading Estate, Abingdon, Oxfordshire OX14 4SY Tel: Abingdon 861234 (STD code 0235) Telex: 265871 Monref G (ref Prf 001) Fax: (0235) 861601
Parent Company: Butterworth & Co (Publishers) Ltd (qv)
Subjects: Law, Accountancy, Reference
1987: 15 titles *Founded:* 1965
ISBN Publisher's Prefix: 0-86205

Profile Books Ltd*, Unit 1, Pontiac Works, Fernbank Rd, Ascot, Berkshire SL5 8JH Tel: Winkfield Row 884222 (STD code 0344)
Dirs: J H W Lacy, P E Butler; *Mail Order:* Mrs S Rogers
Imprints: Profile Publications, Hylton Lacy Publishers
Subjects: Aircraft, AFVs, Warships, Small Arms, Locomotives, Textbooks (*Writers and their Work* series), Periodicals

Projecta (UK) Ltd+, PO Box 15, Royston, Hertfordshire SG8 5NQ Tel: Royston 47003 (STD code 0763) Telex: 8812703 Lonsec G
Man Dir: C J Gravatt
Subject: English as a Foreign Language (for schools/home study)
Founded: 1980

Psychic Press Ltd, 20 Earlham St, London WC2H 9LW Tel: (01) 240 3032
Man Dir: Tony Ortzen; *Advertising Dir:* Ronald Baker
Subjects: Spiritualism, Mediumship, Paranormal, Spirit Healing
Bookshop: Psychic News Bookshop (at above address)
Founded: 1932
ISBN Publisher's Prefix: 0-85384

Puffin Books, an imprint of Penguin Books Ltd (qv)

Purnell Books, an imprint of Macdonald & Co (Publishers) Ltd (qv)

Putnam Aeronautical Books, an imprint of Conway Maritime Press Ltd (qv)

Pyramid, an imprint of Salamander Books Ltd (qv)

Q Press Ltd, see Canongate Publishing Ltd

Quaker Home Service, Friends House, Euston Rd, London NW1 2BJ Tel: (01) 387 3601
General Secretary: Jo Farrow; *Assistant General Secretary:* Clifford E Barnard
Orders to: Friends Book Centre (at above address)
Subjects: Religious, Social and Historical Topics with a Quaker content
Bookshop: Friends Book Centre (at above address)
1985-86: 35 titles *Founded:* 1882
ISBN Publisher's Prefix: 0-85245

Quartermaine House, an imprint of Dickson Price Publishers Ltd (qv)

Quartet Books Ltd, 27-29 Goodge St, London W1P 1FD Tel: (01) 636 3992, (01) 636 0968 Telex: 919034
Chairman: Naim Attallah; *Rights, Sales Dir:* David Elliott; *Production Dir:* Gary Grant; *Publicity Manager:* Anna

UNITED KINGDOM

Groundwater
Subsidiary Companies: Quartet Crime (at above address), Namara Publications, Namara House, 45-46 Poland St, London W1; Quartet Books Australia Pty Ltd, Australia (qv)
Associate Company: Robin Clark Ltd (qv)
Imprints: Anthony Blond, Quartet Or Books
Subjects: Fiction, Biography, Memoirs, Music, History, Philosophy, Politics, Social Science, Trade Paperbacks, Psychology, The Arab World, Sexual Politics, Photography, Crime
Bookshop: The Quartet Bookshop, Namara House, 45-46 Poland St, London W1
Founded: 1972
Miscellaneous: Firm is a member of the Namara Group, 45 Poland St, London W1V 4AU
ISBN Publisher's Prefix: 0-7043

Quarto Publishing PLC, The Old Brewery, 6 Blundell St, London N7 9BH Tel: (01) 609 2222 Telex: 298844
Man Dir, Rights & Permissions: Laurence F Orbach; *Publishing Dir:* Christopher Collier; *Art Dir:* Alastair Campbell; *Publicity:* Paul Anness
Parent Company: Quarto Inc, 20 West 20th St, New York, NY 10011, USA
Subsidiary Companies: QDOS Design Ltd, Quintet Publishing Ltd (qv)
Subjects: International Co-editions
1986: 30 titles *Founded:* 1978

Queen Anne Press Ltd, an imprint of Macdonald & Co (Publishers) Ltd (qv)

Quentin Press Ltd*, 10 Brook St, Wivenhoe, nr Colchester, Essex CO7 9DS Tel: Wivenhoe 5433 (STD code 020 622) Telex: 988805 Patem G, Markit 987562 Cochac
Man Dir: Mark Paterson
Subjects: High-class Illustrated Books
Founded: 1978
Miscellaneous: Packagers of books for other publishers

Questmere, an imprint of Kluwer Publishing Ltd (qv)

Quiller Press Ltd, 50 Albemarle St, London W1X 4HE Tel: (01) 499 6529, (01) 499 1825 Telex: 21120
Man Dir, Editorial: J J Greenwood; *Rights & Permissions:* Ms A E Carlile; *Publicity:* Hugo Frost
Orders to: WHS Distributors, St John's House, East St, Leicester LE1 6NE Tel: Leicester 551196 (STD code 0533) Telex: 341415
Subjects: General Non-fiction, Sponsored books
1985: 15 titles *1986:* 14 titles *Founded:* 1981
ISBN Publisher's Prefix: 0-907621

Quintet Publishing Ltd, The Old Brewery, 6 Blundell St, London N7 9BH Tel: (01) 609 2222 Telex: 298844
Man Dir, Rights & Permissions: Laurence F Orbach; *Art Dir:* Robert Morley; *Publicity:* Nick Law
Parent Company: Quarto Publishing PLC (qv)
Subjects: International Co-editions, Popular Health, Military, Art & Craft, Food & Drink, Transport
1986: 24 titles *Founded:* 1984

Quorum Press, an associate company of The Saint Andrew Press (qv)

R A C Motoring Services Ltd, PO Box 100, RAC House, Lansdowne Rd, Croydon CR9 2JA Tel: (01) 686 2525 Telex: 893551
Publications Manager: T G Platt
Orders to: Biblios Publishers' Distribution Services Ltd, Glenside Industrial Estate, Star Rd, Partridge Green, Horsham, West Sussex RH13 8LD Tel: Partridge Green 710971 (STD code 0403)
Parent Company: The Automobile Proprietary Ltd, 89 Pall Mall, London SW1Y 5HS
Subject: Guidebooks
1987: 12 titles *Founded:* 1904
ISBN Publisher's Prefixes: 0-86211, 0-902628

R I B A Publications Ltd+, Finsbury Mission, Moreland St, London EC1V 8VB Tel: (01) 251 0791 Telex: 8813271 Gecoms G
Man Dir: Nicholas Jones; *Production Dir:* M Stribbling; *Editor:* Alaine Hamilton; *Promotion Manager:* James Neal
Parent Company: Royal Institute of British Architects
Associate Company: RIBA Services Ltd
Subjects: Architecture and Design
Bookshop: RIBA Bookshop, 66 Portland Place, London W1N 4AD
Founded: 1967
ISBN Publisher's Prefixes: 0-900630, 0-947877

Railway Publications Ltd, an associate company of Ian Allan Ltd (qv)

Rainbird, an imprint of Penguin Books Ltd (qv)

Rainbow Books, an imprint of The Hamlyn Publishing Group Ltd (qv)

Rallycourse, an imprint of Hazelton Publishing (qv)

Ramboro Enterprises Ltd, 64 Pentonville Rd, London N1 9HD Tel: (01) 837 6301 Cable Add: Donsbar London Telex: 946240 Ramb Fax: (01) 833 0101
Man Dir, Sales: Donald Murray; *Rights & Permissions:* R Hind
Associate Company: No 1 Publishing Co Ltd
Imprints: Atlantic, Delightful Books, Paintaway, Ramboro, University, Varsity
Subjects: Children's Books, Art, Cookery, Dictionaries
Founded: 1960
Miscellaneous: Also remainder dealer

The **Ramsay** Head Press+, 15 Gloucester Pl, Edinburgh EH3 6EE Tel: (031) 225 5646
Editorial Dir: C K Wilson
Subjects: Biography, Literature, Poetry, Art, Architecture, History, Fiction, Reference, New Assessments series (critical studies of outstanding figures in literature and arts)
Founded: 1971
ISBN Publisher's Prefix: 0-902859

Ranelagh Editions, an imprint of Norfolk Press (qv)

Rationalist Press Association, see Pemberton Publishing Co Ltd

Ravette Ltd+, 3 Glenside Estate, Star Rd, Partridge Green, Horsham, Sussex RH13 8RA Tel: Partridge Green 710392 (STD code 0403) Telex: 897506 Dawson G
Chief Executive, Editorial, Rights & Permissions: R D Read; *Publicity:* Janet Cox; *Production:* Jeff Childs; *Sales:* Margaret Lamb
Parent Company: Gordon & Gotch Holdings PLC, New Gotch House, 32-38 Scrutton St, London EC2A 4SS
Subjects: Humour, Children's, Travel, General Non-fiction
Book Club: I-Spy Club
Founded: 1980

ISBN Publisher's Prefixes: 0-906710, 0-948456

The **Reader's Digest** Association Ltd, 25 Berkeley Sq, London W1X 6AB Tel: (01) 629 8144 Cable Add: Readigest London W1 Telex: 264631 Fax: (01) 236 5956
Subjects: Fiction, English Dictionaries, Reference, Maps & Atlases, Nature, Travel, Encyclopaedias, Guidebooks, Cookery, Gardening, DIY
ISBN Publisher's Prefix: 0-276

Redcliffe Press Ltd+, 49 Park St, Bristol BS1 5NT Tel: Bristol 290158 (STD code 0272)
Dir: John Sansom; *Editorial, Production, Sales:* Sarah Barnes; *Rights & Permissions:* Angela Sansom
Imprints include: White Tree Books
Subjects: Local Interest, Architecture, Cricket, Literature, Poetry, Photography, Cookery
1986: 20 titles *1987:* 20 titles *Founded:* 1976
ISBN Publisher's Prefixes: 0-905459, 0-943265

Thomas **Reed** Publications Ltd, 80 Coombe Rd, New Malden, Surrey KT3 4QS Tel: (01) 949 7033 Telex: 883526 Fax: (01) 949 0530
Man Dir: K Allan Brunton-Reed; *Editorial Dir, Rights & Permissions:* Jean Fowler
Parent Company: Thomas Reed Ltd, Double Century House, High Street West, Sunderland, Tyne & Wear
Associate Companies: Thomas Reed Industrial Press Ltd (Surrey address); Thomas Reed Printers Ltd (Sunderland address)
Imprint: Reed's
Subjects: Marine Engineering, Naval Architecture, Navigation, Seamanship, Yachting, Tourist Guides, *Footloose* series
1986: 5 titles *Founded:* 1782
ISBN Publisher's Prefixes: 0-900335, 0-947637

Reinhardt Books Ltd, 27 Wright's Lane, London W8 5TZ Tel: (01) 938 2200
Chairman, Man Dir: Max Reinhardt; *Dirs:* Joan Reinhardt, John Hews
Subsidiary Company: Nonesuch Press Ltd
Subjects: General
Founded: 1987

Religious and Moral Education Press, Hennock Rd, Exeter, Devon EX2 8RP Tel: Exeter 74121 (STD code 0392) Telex: 42749 Fax: (0392) 217170
Publisher: Simon Goodenough; *Man Editor:* Mary Mears; *Sales Manager:* Drummond Johnstone; *Design, Production Manager:* Andy Jones
Orders to: Purnell Book Centre, Paulton, Bristol BS18 5LQ Tel: Midsomer Norton 413301 (STD code 0761) Telex: 44713 Purnel G
Subjects: Religious, moral, personal and social education for schools and trade
Founded: 1921
Miscellaneous: Religious and Moral Education Press is an imprint of Wheaton Publishers Ltd, a division of Maxwell Communication Corporation plc
ISBN Publisher's Prefix: 0-08

Remus Products, an imprint of World International Publishing Ltd (qv)

Research Publishing Co, an imprint of Fudge & Co Ltd (qv)

J **Richardson** & Co (Publishers) Oxford, 50 Marsh Lane, Marston, Oxford OX3 0NQ Tel: Oxford 63828/771285 (STD code 0865)
Chief Executive: J Richardson; *Sales:* Ms S King
Subsidiary Company: J Richardson & Co

(Book Distributors) (at above address)
Subjects: Latin, Music, Poetry, Philosophy, Campanology, Fiction, Esoteric
Bookshop: At above address
Founded: 1986
ISBN Publisher's Prefix: 0-904233

Rider & Co, an imprint of Century Hutchinson Publishing Ltd (qv)

Rigby International & Lansdowne International Pty Ltd, now Merehurst Ltd (qv)

Right Way Books, an imprint of Elliot Right Way Books (qv)

Rivers Press, an imprint of Writers and Readers Publishing Co-operative (qv)

Robinson Publishing+, 11 Shepherd House, Shepherd St, London W1Y 7LD Tel: (01) 493 1064 Telex: 28905 Monref G ref 778
Chief Executive: Nicholas Robinson; *Publicity:* Annabel Edwards
Orders to: Gollancz Services Ltd, 14 Eldon Way, Lineside Estate, Littlehampton, West Sussex BN17 7HE
Subjects: Fiction, General, Science Fiction & Fantasy, Crime, Country Interest
1985: 11 titles *1986:* 12 titles *Founded:* 1983
ISBN Publisher's Prefix: 0-948164

Robson Books Ltd+, Bolsover House, 5-6 Clipstone St, London W1P 7EB Tel: (01) 637 5937, (01) 323 1223 Cable Add: Robsobook London W1 Fax: (01) 636 0798
Man Dir: Jeremy Robson; *Sales Manager:* Carole Robson; *Editor:* Susan Rea; *Publicity Manager:* Cheryll Roberts; *Production Manager:* David Dick
Subjects: General, Biography, Music, Humour
1985: 54 titles *Founded:* 1973
ISBN Publisher's Prefixes: 0-903895, 0-86051

George **Ronald**, Publisher Ltd, 46 High St, Kidlington, Oxford OX5 2DN Tel: Kidlington 5273 (STD code 086 75) Cable Add: Talisman Oxford Telex: 837646
General Manager: Barney Leith
Subjects: Religion, The Bahá'í Faith, Quality Paperbacks
1985: 12 titles *Founded:* 1947
ISBN Publisher's Prefix: 0-85398

Rose-Jordan, an imprint of Jordan & Sons Ltd (qv)

Roundabout, an imprint of Modern English Publications Ltd (qv)

Routledge+, 11 New Fetter Lane, London EC4P 4EE Tel: (01) 583 9855 Cable Add: Elegiacs London EC4 Telex: 263398
Man Dir: David Croom; *Publishers:* Peter Sowden (Business, Politics, Economics, Geography, Education), Gill Davies (Social & Behavioural Sciences), Janice Price (Humanities), Wendy Morris (Reference); *Sales:* Bob Kelly (Home), Teresa Armstrong (Export); *Marketing:* Elizabeth White, Clare Fletcher; *Production:* David Babb, David McCarthy; *Rights & Permissions:* Alison Barr
Orders to: Routledge, Chapman & Hall Ltd, North Way, Andover, Hampshire SP10 5BE Tel: Andover 62141 (STD code 0264) Cable Add: APT Andover Telex: 47214 Fax: (0264) 64418
Parent Company: Thomson Information Services Ltd (qv). Ultimate parent company International Thomson Organisation Ltd, 20 Queen St West, Box 45, Suite 2206, Toronto, Ontario M5H 3R3, Canada
Associate Company: KPI (qv)

Imprints: Comedia, Oriel Press
Subjects: Archaeology, Biography, History, Literature, Politics, Sociology, Education, Psychology, Linguistics, Business, Economics, Law, Development Studies, Geography, Philosophy, Reference, Classical Studies, Religion, Women's Studies, Film, Media & Communication
Founded: 1988
Miscellaneous: Routledge is a new company representing the publishing interests and activities previously undertaken under the names of Routledge & Kegan Paul Ltd, Methuen & Co Ltd, Tavistock Publications Ltd and Croom Helm Ltd
ISBN Publisher's Prefixes: From 1988: 0-415 (all imprints not elsewhere listed) Backlists (where differ from preceding): 1-85178, 0-906890 (both Comedia), 0-7099, 0-85664 (both Croom Helm), 0-416 (Methuen & Co), 0-85362 (Oriel), 0-422 (Tavistock)

Routledge & Kegan Paul Ltd, see Routledge

Roxby Press Ltd, 126 Victoria Rise, London SW4 0NW Tel: (01) 720 8872 Telex: 291829 Tlx G
Man Dir: Hugh Elwes; *Editorial Dir:* Paddy Seymour; *Foreign Rights Editor:* Anne Hunt
Subjects: Illustrated Co-editions, Non-fiction
1986: 7 titles *Founded:* 1973

The **Royal Society** of Chemistry, Burlington House, London W1V 0BN Tel: (01) 734 9864 Telex: 268001
Chief Executive: Robert Welham; *Editorial:* Dr Phil Gardam; *Sales, Publicity:* Barry Anderson; *Production:* Fytton Rowland; *Rights & Permissions:* Dr Ivor Williams
Orders to: The Distribution Centre, Blackhorse Rd, Letchworth, Hertfordshire SG6 1HN
Associate Company: Turpin Transactions Ltd, Blackhorse Rd, Letchworth, Hertfordshire SG6 1HN
Branch Offs: Russell Sq, London WC1; The University, Nottingham NG7 2RD
Subjects: Chemistry, Chemical Technology
Founded: 1851
ISBN Publisher's Prefixes: 0-85186, 0-85404, 0-901886

Robert **Royce**, an imprint of Cassell PLC (qv)

S & S, an imprint of Simon & Schuster Ltd (qv)

S B I M, an imprint of Kluwer Publishing Ltd (qv)

S C M Press Ltd+, 26-30 Tottenham Rd, London N1 4BZ Tel: (01) 249 7262 Cable Add: Torchpres London N1 Telex: 295068 Theolo G
Man Dir: The Rev John Bowden; *Sales, Publicity:* Irena Czerniawska; *Production:* Mark Hammer; *Rights & Permissions:* Margaret Lydamore
Subjects: Religion, Theology, Religious Education, Ethics
Bookshop: SCM Bookroom (at above address)
Founded: 1929
ISBN Publisher's Prefix: 0-334

S P C K (The Society for Promoting Christian Knowledge)+, Holy Trinity Church, Marylebone Rd, London NW1 4DU Tel: (01) 387 5282 Cable Add: Futurity London NW1
General Secretary: Patrick Gilbert; *Editorial:* Judith Longman; *Sales Manager:*

UNITED KINGDOM 467

Brian Keen; *Promotion:* Cazz Colmer
Subjects: Bible Reference Works & Commentaries, Theology, Worship, Biography & Autobiography
Bookshops: At above address and throughout the UK (37 outlets)
1986: 70 titles *Founded:* 1698
Miscellaneous: Divisions of this Society are Sheldon Press (qv) and Triangle (qv)
ISBN Publisher's Prefix: 0-281

S R H E, At the University of Surrey, Guildford, Surrey GU2 5XH Tel: Guildford 39003 (STD code 0483) Society for Research into Higher Education
Editor: Naomi Roth (at Open University Educational Enterprises Ltd, qv)
Subjects: Higher and Further Education
1986: 6 titles
Miscellaneous: The Society is a registered charity and publishes mainly in cooperation with Open University Press (qv)

S T L Books*, PO Box 48, 1 Sherman Rd, Bromley, Kent BR1 3JH Tel: (01) 290 1090 Cable Add: Mobiliser Bromley Telex: 896706 Ebe G
Sales Manager: Daniel van Belzen
Parent Company: Send the Light Ltd (at above address)
Subjects: Religion, Juveniles, Bibles
Bookshops: Bromley Christian Bookshop, 268-272 High St, Bromley, Kent BR1 1PB; Christian Bookshop, 17 Lordship Lane, London SE22; Bolton Christian Bookshop, 204 St Georges Rd, Bolton, Lancashire; Coventry Christian Bookshop, 21 City Arcade, Coventry CV1 3HX
Founded: 1963
ISBN Publisher's Prefix: 0-903843

Sage Publications Ltd*, 28 Banner St, London EC1Y 8QE Tel: (01) 253 1516 Cable Add: Sagepub London Telex: 296207
Man Dir: David Brooks; *Editorial Dir:* David Hill; *Marketing Dir:* Ian Eastment
Associate Companies: Sage Publications India Private Ltd, India (qv); Sage Publications Inc, 275 South Beverly Dr, Beverly Hills, CA 90212, USA
Subjects: Social Sciences (Sociology, Political Science, Methodology, International Relations, Human Services, Evaluation, Psychology, Communication)
Founded: 1971
ISBN Publisher's Prefix: 0-8039

The **Saint Andrew** Press, 121 George St, Edinburgh EH2 4YN Tel: (031) 225 5722 Cable Add: Free, Edinburgh Telex: 727935 Chscot G
Publishing Manager: Dorothy Mitchell Smith; *Publicity:* Derek Auld
Parent Organization: The Church of Scotland Board of Communication
Associate Company: Quorum Press
Subjects: Religion, Theology, Current Issues, History
1985: 12 titles *1986:* 12 titles
ISBN Publisher's Prefix: 0-7152

Saint George & Dragon Press, an imprint of Bibliagora (qv)

Saint James Press Group*, 5-11 Worship St, London EC2A 2AY Tel: (01) 588 6631 Telex: 884339 Stjpub G
Man Dir: D N Blackwell; *Data Editor:* Annabel B Roney
Parent Company: Reed Telepublishing Ltd
Subjects: Travel Directories & Holiday Guides for the travel industry
1986: 8 titles

Saint James Press Ltd, 3 Percy St, London W1P 9FA Tel: (01) 580 4155
Man Dir: George Walsh; *Editorial Dir:*

James Vinson; *Senior Editors:* D L Kirkpatrick, Colin Naylor, Roland Turner, Thomas Dendak
Branch Off: 425 North Michigan Ave, Chicago 60611, USA
Subject: Reference
Founded: 1968

Saint Paul Publications+, St Paul's House, Middlegreen, Slough SL3 6BT Tel: Slough 20621 (STD code 0753)
Subject: Christian Religion
Related Bookshops: Saint Paul Book Centres at 199 Kensington High St, London W8 6BA; 133 Corporation St, Birmingham B4 6PH; 82 Bold St, Liverpool L1 4HR; 5A-7 Royal Exchange Sq, Glasgow G1 3AH
Founded: 1967
ISBN Publisher's Prefix: 0-85439

Saint Paul's Bibliographies*, 1 Step Terrace, Winchester SO22 5BW Tel: Winchester 64037/60524 (STD code 0962)
Dirs: R S Cross, Mrs M C E Cross, E R Cross, D M Herbert
Parent Company: Foxbury Enterprises Ltd (at above address)
Imprint: Foxbury Press
Subjects: Bibliographies, Reference, Biography, Management
1985: 4 titles
ISBN Publisher's Prefixes: 0-906795 (Saint Paul's), 0-946053 (Foxbury Press)

Salamander Books Ltd, 52 Bedford Row, London WC1R 4LR Tel: (01) 242 6693 Cable Add: Salamander London WC1 Telex: 261113 Fax: (01) 404 4926
Chairman: J Proost; *Man Dir:* Malcolm H Little; *Production Dir:* Philip Hughes; *Editorial Dirs:* Ray Bonds, Philip de Ste Croix; *Sales Dir:* Keith Allen-Jones; *Rights & Permissions:* Moira McCann
Orders to: Hodder & Stoughton Ltd, Mill Rd, Dunton Green, Sevenoaks, Kent TN13 2YA Tel: Sevenoaks 450111 (STD code 0732)
Parent Company: Henri Proost & Cie, Belgium (qv)
Associate Company: Bedford Editions Ltd (qv)
Imprints: Apollo Books, Pyramid Books
Subjects: Illustrated Reference Books: Cookery, Homecrafts, Pets, Health, Sports, Gardening, Beauty, General Interest, Military, Natural History, Music, Hobbies
1985: 30 titles *1986:* 40 titles *Founded:* 1974
ISBN Publisher's Prefix: 0-86101

The **Saltire** Society, Saltire House, 13 Atholl Crescent, Edinburgh EH3 8HA Tel: (031) 228 6621
Imprint: Saltire Classics
Subjects: Scottish Art, Literature, Music
Founded: 1936
ISBN Publisher's Prefix: 0-85411

Salvationist Publishing & Supplies Ltd, 117-121 Judd St, King's Cross, London WC1H 9NN Tel: (01) 387 1656 Cable Add: Savingly, London WC1H 9NN
Rights & Permissions: Col Lawrie Fisher
Associate Company: Campfield Press, St Albans
Subjects: Religion, Music, Juveniles
ISBN Publisher's Prefix: 0-85412

Sampson Low, an imprint of Purnell Books (see Macdonald & Co (Publishers) Ltd)

Sangam Books Ltd*, 57 London Fruit Exchange, Brushfield St, London E1 6EP Tel: (01) 377 6399 Cable Add: Sanbook E1
Chief Executive, Sales, Publicity: A A de Souza; *Editorial:* E Raghavan
Parent Company: Orient Longman Ltd, India (qv)

Subjects: Fiction & Non-fiction, Social Sciences, Scientific Technical, Medical, Children's
Founded: 1981
ISBN Publisher's Prefixes: 0-86125, 0-86131, 0-86132

W B Saunders & Co Ltd, 24-28 Oval Rd, London NW1 7DX Tel: (01) 267 4466 Telex: 25775 Acpres G
Man Dir: Joan Fujimojo; *Publishing Dir:* David S B Inglis; *Sales, Marketing Dir:* D Duff; *Sales Manager:* Colin Lill; *Marketing Manager:* Jane Lawrence
Parent Company: Harcourt Brace Jovanovich Inc, Orlando, FL 32887, USA
Subjects: Medical, Veterinary, Nursing, Pharmaceutical
Founded: 1888
Miscellaneous: W B Saunders is an imprint of Harcourt Brace Jovanovich, UK (qv)
ISBN Publisher's Prefix: 0-7216

K G Saur Ltd, an imprint of Bowker-Saur Ltd (qv)

Scala/Philip Wilson, an imprint of Philip Wilson Publishers (qv)

Sceptre, an imprint of Hodder & Stoughton Ltd (qv)

Sceptre Books, Time & Life Bldg, New Bond St, London W1Y 0AA Tel: (01) 499 4080
Manager, Rights & Permissions: David Owen; *Production:* Hartmut Belling
Parent Company: Time Inc (USA)
Associate Company: Harrow House Editions (at above address)
Subjects: Illustrated Reference Books and Series for the International Co-edition Market
Founded: 1980
ISBN Publisher's Prefix: 0-905663

Schofield & Sims Ltd+, Dogley Mill, Fenay Bridge, Huddersfield, West Yorkshire HD8 0NQ Tel: Huddersfield 607080 (STD code 0484) Cable Add: Schosims Huddersfield Telex: 51458 Comhud G for Schosims
Chairman: John S Nesbitt; *Man Dir:* J Stephen Platts; *Sales Dir:* Jack Brierley
Subjects: Secondary & Primary Textbooks, Educational Materials, Computer Software, Peripheral Hardware
1985: 42 titles *1986:* 34 titles *Founded:* 1901
ISBN Publisher's Prefix: 0-7217

Scholastic Publications Ltd, Marlborough House, Holly Walk, Leamington Spa, Warwickshire CV32 4LS Tel: Southam 3910 (STC code 092816) Telex: 312138 Spls G Fax: (0926) 883331
Man Dir, Marketing Dir: John Cox; *Educational Trade Sales and Publishing Dir:* Gavin Lang; *Editors:* Jackie Andrews (Book Clubs), Dorothy Wood (Hippo Books); *Production:* Doug Brown; *Advertising:* Bob Challinor
Parent Company: Scholastic Inc, 730 Broadway, New York, NY 10003, USA
Imprint: Hippo Books
Branch Off: 10 Earlham St, London WC2H 9RX Tel: (01) 240 5753 Telex: 264604 Sbslon G Fax: (01) 240 6927
Subjects: Primary Education, Juvenile Fiction and Non-fiction, Educational Magazines
Book Clubs: Chip, Criterion, Lucky, Scene, See-Saw
1986: 110 titles *Founded:* 1964
ISBN Publisher's Prefix: 0-590

School of Oriental & African Studies, Malet St, London WC1E 7HP Tel: (01) 637 2388 Cable Add: Soasul London WC1
Publications Officer: M J Daly

Subjects: Oriental and African Language, Literature, History, Religion, Bibliography, Art
1986: 6 titles *Founded:* 1917
ISBN Publisher's Prefix: 0-901877, 0-7286

Science of Life Books, an imprint of Thorsons Publishing Group Ltd (qv)

Science Research Associates Ltd, Newtown Rd, Henley-on-Thames, Oxfordshire RG9 1EW Tel: Henley-on-Thames 575959 (STD code 0491) Cable Add: Srauk G, Henley-on Thames RG9 1EW Telex: 848454
Man Dir, Editorial, Sales, Rights & Permissions: Brian Preston; *Production, Advertising, Publicity:* B H Sheldrake
Parent Company: Science Research Associates Inc, 155 North Wacker Dr, Chicago, Illinois 60606 (Science Research Associates Inc is a subsidiary of IBM)
Associate Companies: Science Research Associates Pty Ltd, Australia (qv); Science Research Associates (Canada) Ltd, 707 Gordon Baker Rd, Willowdale, Ontario, Canada
Subjects: Secondary & Primary Textbooks, Commercial & Technical Education, Vocational Guidance Publications, Educational & Industrial Tests
ISBN Publisher's Prefix: 0-574

Scientechnica, an imprint of Butterworth & Co (Publishers) Ltd (qv)

Scolar Press, an imprint of Gower Publishing Co Ltd (qv)

Scorpion Publishing Ltd, Victoria House, Victoria Rd, Buckhurst Hill, Essex IG9 5ES Tel: (01) 506 0606 Telex: 896988 Scoops G
Joint Man Dir, Editorial: L W Harrow; *Joint Man Dir, Production:* Colin Larkin; *Sales Dir:* Alan Ball; *Publicity, Rights & Permissions:* Sue Pipe
Associate Companies: Scorpion Communications, Scorpion Pica
Imprints: Art Heritage, Scorpion Al-Falak
Subjects: Specialist Islamic Publishers: Art, Architecture, Oriental Rugs, Academia, Business Reference, General Non-fiction
1987: 54 titles *Founded:* 1976
ISBN Publisher's Prefix: 0605906

Scottish Academic Press Ltd+, 33 Montgomery St, Edinburgh EH7 5JX Tel: (031) 556 2796
Man Dir: Douglas Grant; *Dirs:* David Dorward, Alan Rodwell, Robert Walker, Harry Whittaker
Subjects: Scholarly, Scottish interest
1985: 38 titles *1986:* 22 titles *Founded:* 1969
Miscellaneous: Associated with The Handsel Press (qv)
ISBN Publisher's Prefix: 0-7073

Scripture Union+, 130 City Rd, London EC1V 2NJ Tel: (01) 250 1966
Publishing Dir: David Rosser; *Production Manager:* Andrew Lee; *Sales, Marketing Manager:* Alex Morton; *Managing Editor:* John Grayston; *Copyright Permissions:* Jill Harris; *Overseas Rights Adminstrator:* Jan Middleton
Trade and Mail Order: Distribution Centre, 9-11 Clothier Rd, Bristol BS4 5RL Tel: Bristol 719709 (STD code 0272)
Subsidiary Companies: Bible Book Publications; Scripture Union Publishing
Imprints: Leopard, Tiger
Subjects: Music, Religion, Juveniles, Educational Materials
Bookshops: 5 Wigmore St, London W1H 0AD; 77 Bridge St, Manchester M3 2RH; 16 Park St, Croydon CR0 1YE;

3 King Edward St, Leeds LS1 6AX; 3 Suffolk Rd, Cheltenham, Gloucestershire GL50 2AG; 280 St Vincent St, Glasgow G2 5RT; 30 Cow Wynd, Falkirk, Stirlingshire; 21 Rutland Sq, Edinburgh EH1 2BB; 8 Kings Rd, Brighton, East Sussex BN1 1NE; 22 Fisher St, Carlisle, Cumbria CA3 8RH; 14 North Bridge St, Sunderland, Tyne and Wear SR5 1LD; 14 Eton St, Richmond, Surrey TW9 1EE; 13 Lower Hillgate, Stockport, Cheshire SK1 1JQ; 12 Wellington Pl, Belfast BT1 6JB; 38 Ardconnel St, Inverness; 68-70 Princes St, Perth; 165 St George's Way, St John's Centre, Liverpool L1 1NE; 66 Queens Rd, Watford, Hertfordshire; 88A Regent St, Cambridge CB2 1DP; 60 Union Row, Aberdeen AB1 1SA; 7 Heavitree Rd, Exeter EX1 2LD; 30 St Loyer St, Bedford MK40 1EP; 48 Queen St, Derby DE1 3GN; 11 Masons Ave, Wealdstone, Harrow HA3 5AH; 11 Faringdon Rd, Swindon, Wiltshire SN1 5AR
Founded: 1867
ISBN Publisher's Prefixes: 0-85421, 0-86201

Seafarer Books, an imprint of The Merlin Press Ltd (qv)

Seagull Books, an imprint of The Book Guild Ltd (qv)

Search Press Ltd+, Wellwood, North Farm Rd, Tunbridge Wells, Kent TN2 3DR Tel: Tunbridge Wells 510850 (STD code 0892) Telex: 957258
Man Dir, Sales: Charlotte de la Bedoyere; *Editorial, Rights & Permissions:* John Bright-Holmes, *Production:* Jennifer Steel; *Publicity:* Ruth Saunders
Associate Company: Burns & Oates Ltd (qv)
Subjects: Philosophy, Theology, Literature and Literary Criticism, Poetry, History, Biography, Religion, General, Moral Education, Mysticism, Third World, Arts and Crafts, Cookery
Founded: 1962
ISBN Publisher's Prefix: 0-85532

Martin **Secker & Warburg** Ltd+, Michelin House, 81 Fulham Rd, London SW3 6RB Tel: (01) 581 9393 Cable Add: Octobooks Telex: 920191 Fax: (01) 589 8419
Chairman: Paul Hamlyn; *Chief Executive:* Ian Irvine; *Editorial:* David Godwin; *Sales:* Tim Whale; *Publicity Manager:* Serena Davies
Orders to: Octopus Distribution Services Ltd, PO Box 5, Rushden, Northamptonshire NN10 9YX Tel: Rushden 58521 (STD code 0933)
Parent Company: Octopus Publishing Group PLC. Ultimate parent company Reed International PLC, Reed House, 83 Piccadilly, London W1A 1EJ
Subsidiary Company: The Alison Press, 5 Harley Gardens, London SW10 9SW
Subjects: General Fiction, Belles Lettres, Poetry, Biography, History, Military History, Music, Cinema, Art, Philosophy, Reference, Psychology, Social Science, Sport, High-priced Paperbacks, Criticism, Photography, Political Science
1985: 80 titles *1986:* 84 titles *Founded:* 1910
ISBN Publisher's Prefix: 0-436

Serindia Publications, 10 Parkfields, Putney, London SW15 6NH Tel: (01) 788 1966 Telex: 923421
Proprietor: Anthony Aris
Orders to: La Haule Books Ltd, West Lodge, La Haule, Saint Aubin, Jersey, Channel Islands
Associate Company: Aris & Philips Ltd (qv)
Subjects: Oriental Art, Travel, Religion
Founded: 1976
ISBN Publisher's Prefix: 0-906026

Serpent's Tail Ltd+, 27 Montpelier Grove, London NW5 2XD Tel: (01) 485 0674
Editorial: Peter Ayrton; *Sales:* John Hampson
Orders to: J M Dent & Sons (Distribution) Ltd, Dunhams Lane, Letchworth, Hertfordshire SG6 1LF Tel: Letchworth 686241 (STD code 0462)
Imprint: Masks
Subjects: Modern Fiction, Literary Biography & Autobiography
1986: 4 titles *1987:* 11 titles *Founded:* 1986
ISBN Publisher's Prefix: 1-85242

Settle & Bendall (Wigmore), an imprint of Settle Press (qv)

Settle Press, 32 Savile Row, London W1X 1AG Tel: (01) 734 0171
Man Dir, Editorial, Rights & Permissions: D Settle; *Sales, Publicity:* M Carter; *Production:* J Sankey
Parent Company: Wigmore House Publishing Ltd (at above address)
Associate Company: Wigmore Professional (at above address)
Imprints: Settle & Bendall (Wigmore), Wigmore House Publishing
Subjects: Guidebooks, Travel, General, Medical, Fiction, Biography
Founded: 1980
ISBN Publisher's Prefix: 0-907070

Severn House Publishers Ltd+, 40-42 William IV St, London WC2N 4DF Tel: (01) 240 9683 Telex: 295041 Severn G
Chairman: Edwin Buckhalter; *Publishing Dir, Rights & Permissions:* Stephanie Townsend; *Sales Dir:* John Oliver; *Publicity:* Charlotte Philcox
Orders to: Tiptree Book Services Ltd, St Luke's Chase, Tiptree, Colchester, Essex CO5 0SR Tel: Tiptree 816362 (STD code 0621)
Parent Company: Severn House Books (Holdings) Ltd (at above main address)
Subsidiary Company: Severn House Paperbacks Ltd (at above address)
Subjects: Fiction, Thrillers, Romance, War, Historical, Science Fiction, Westerns, Film and TV tie-ins, Juveniles, Natural History, Cookery, Biography, Humour, General Non-fiction
1985: 140 titles *Founded:* 1974
ISBN Publisher's Prefix: 0-7278

Shakespeare Head Press, a subsidiary company of Basil Blackwell Ltd (qv)

Shaw & Sons Ltd, Shaway House, Bell Green Lane, Lower Sydenham, London SE26 5AE Tel: (01) 778 5131
Man Dir: J Willoughby; *Editorial Consultant:* G Morris; *Editorial:* D Hubber; *Sales, Publicity:* W P Elliott; *Rights & Permissions:* A Griffin
Subjects: Legal, Local Government, General
Founded: 1750
ISBN Publisher's Prefix: 0-7219

Sheba Feminist Publishers, 10A Bradbury St, London N16 8JN Tel: (01) 254 1590
Orders to: Airlift Book Co, 14 Baltic St, London EC1
Subjects: Feminist Fiction and Non-fiction, Poetry, Black Women's Writings, Children's
Founded: 1980
ISBN Publisher's Prefix: 0-907179

Sheed & Ward Ltd*, 2 Creechurch Lane, London EC3A 5AQ Tel: (01) 283 6330
Dirs: M T Redfern, K G Darke
Subjects: History, Philosophy, Reference, Religion
Founded: 1926
ISBN Publisher's Prefix: 0-7220

Sheffield Academic Press Ltd, 343 Fulwood Rd, Sheffield S10 3BP Tel: Sheffield 670043/670044 (STD code 0742) Telex: 547216
Dirs: David J A Clines, Dr Philip R Davies; *Editorial:* David Orton; *Sales, Production, Publicity, Rights & Permissions:* Catherine Annabel
Imprint: JSOT Press, Almond Press
Subjects: Academic Biblical Study, Research in Old Testament, New Testament, Intertestamental and Jewish Literature, Folklore, Archaeology, Modern Languages, Drama, Periodicals
1986: 15 titles *Founded:* 1976
ISBN Publisher's Prefixes: 0-905774, 1-85075

Sheldon Press+, SPCK Bldg, Marylebone Rd, London NW1 4DU Tel: (01) 387 5282 Cable Add: Futurity London NW1
General Secretary: P N G Gilbert; *Senior Editor:* Darley Anderson; *Sales Manager:* Brian Keen; *Publicity Manager:* Cazz Colman
Subjects: Biography, Health & Self Help, Popular Medicine, Religion
Miscellaneous: A division of SPCK (qv)
ISBN Publisher's Prefix: 0-85969

Shepheard-Walwyn (Publishers) Ltd+, Suite 34, 26 Charing Cross Rd, London WC2H 0DH Tel: (01) 240 5992 Telex: 261234 H5680D
Man Dir: A R A Werner; *Production Dir:* B K Shaw
Subjects: General Non-fiction
Founded: 1971
ISBN Publisher's Prefix: 0-85683

Shire Publications Ltd, Cromwell House, Church St, Princes Risborough, Aylesbury, Buckinghamshire HP17 9AJ Tel: Princes Risborough 4301 (STD code 084 44)
Man Dir: John W Rotheroe
Subjects: Paperbacks on Antiques, Collecting, Architecture, Social History, Military History, Transport, Archaeology, Hand Craft Industries, Natural History, Ethnography, Egyptology
Founded: 1966
ISBN Publisher's Prefix: 0-85263

Shuckburgh Reynolds Ltd+*, 289 Westbourne Grove, London W11 2QA Tel: (01) 727 9636 Telex: 267009
Editorial Dirs: David Reynolds, Julian Shuckburgh, Anne Furniss; *Production:* Robert Christie; *Design:* David Fordham; *Rights:* Paul Marsh, c/o Anthony Sheil Associates Ltd (qv)
Subjects: Illustrated Non-fiction: History, Biography, Art, Music, Literature, Cinema, Countryside, Astrology, Puzzle Books, Humour
1985: 18 titles *Founded:* 1979

Sidgwick & Jackson Ltd, 1 Tavistock Chambers, Bloomsbury Way, London WC1A 2SG Tel: (01) 242 6081 Cable Add: Watergate Westcent London Telex: 8952953
Chairman: Sir William Rees-Mogg; *Man Dir:* William Armstrong; *Sales Dir:* Nicholas Murphy; *Editorial Dir:* Robert Smith; *Publicity:* George Goodwin; *Rights & Permissions:* Robert Gwyn Palmer
Orders to: Macmillan Distribution Ltd, Houndmills, Basingstoke, Hampshire RG21 2XS Tel: Basingstoke 29242 (STD code 0256) Telex: 858493
Parent Company: Macmillan Publishers Ltd (qv)
Subjects: Archaeology, Biography,

Cookery, Current Affairs, Fiction, Future History, History, Military History, Music, Political Economy, Show Business, Sport, Travel
Founded: 1908
ISBN Publisher's Prefix: 0-283

Sigma Press+, 98A Water Lane, Wilmslow, Cheshire SK9 5BB Tel: Wilmslow 531035 (STD code 0625)
Man Dir, Production: Graham Beech; *Editorial:* Graham Beech, Stella Platts; *Sales, Publicity, Rights & Permissions:* through John Wiley & Sons Ltd (qv) Tel: Chichester 784531 (STD code 0243)
Orders to: (Leisure books): to above main aaddress; (All other books): John Wiley & Sons Ltd, Distribution Centre, Shripney Rd, Bognor Regis, West Sussex PO22 9SA Tel: Bognor Regis 829121 (STD code 0243)
Subjects: Computing, Science, Leisure, Education
Founded: 1978
ISBN Publisher's Prefixes: 0-905104, 1-850580

Silhouette, an imprint of Mills & Boon Ltd (qv)

Silver Link Publishing Ltd, The Coach House, Garstang Rd, St Michaels on Wyre, Lancashire PR3 0TG Tel: St Michaels 271 (STD code 099 58)
Chief Executive, Sales, Publicity: Jayne Harris; *Editorial, Production:* Nigel Harris
Subjects: Transport, Countryside
1985: 10 titles *1986:* 12 titles *Founded:* 1985
ISBN Publisher's Prefix: 0-947971

Simon & Schuster Ltd, West Garden Pl, Kendal St, London W2 2AQ Tel: (01) 724 7577 Telex: 21702 Fax: (01) 402 0639
Chief Executive, Trade Publisher: Clyde Hunter; *Editorial Dirs:* Nicholas Brealey (Non-fiction), Robyn Sisman (Fiction), Denise Johnstone-Burt (Children's); *Trade Sales Dir:* Lionel Foot; *Publicity:* Philippa McEwan; *Rights:* Lesley Toll; *Production:* Anthony Short
Orders to: IBD Ltd, 66 Wood Lane End, Hemel Hempstead, Hertfordshire HP2 4RG
Parent Company: Simon & Schuster Inc, 1230 Ave of the Americas, New York, NY 10020, USA
Associate Company: Simon & Schuster Pty Ltd, 7 Grosvenor Pl, NSW 2100, Australia
Imprint: Sportspages
Subjects: General Non-fiction, Fiction, Sport, Children's, Travel, Audio, Science, Biography, Current Affairs
Founded: 1986
ISBN Publisher's Prefix: 0-671

Charles **Skilton** Ltd, 2 Caversham St, London SW3 Tel: (01) 351 4995
Man Dir: Charles Skilton; *Publicity Manager:* Leonard Holdsworth
Subsidiary Companies: Albyn Press Ltd (qv), Fudge & Co Ltd (qv), Luxor Press Ltd, Tallis Press Ltd, Fortune Press, Polybooks Ltd (all at above address)
Branch Off: Whittingehame House, Haddington, Lothian, Scotland
Subjects: Art, Graphic Arts, Reference, Biography, Antiquarian, Cookery, Sexology, Scottish, Poetry
Founded: 1943
ISBN Publisher's Prefixes: 0-284 (Skilton, Albyn, Luxor, Tallis), 0-85240 (Fortune)

Skilton & Shaw, an imprint of Fudge & Co Ltd (qv)

Thomas **Skinner** Directories, Windsor Court, East Grinstead House, East Grinstead, West Sussex RH19 1XE Tel: East Grinstead 26972 (STD code 0342)
Publishing Dir: W J Irlam
Parent Company: Information Services Ltd (at above address), a division of Reed Publishing, Quadrant House, The Quadrant, Sutton, Surrey SM2 5AS
Subject: Directories
ISBN Publisher's Prefixes: 0-611, 0-900808

Colin **Smythe** Ltd, PO Box 6, Gerrards Cross, Buckinghamshire SL9 8XA Tel: Gerrards Cross 886000 (STD code 0753) Cable Add: Smythebooks Gerrardscross
Man Dir: Colin Smythe
Orders to: Biblios Publishers' Distribution Services Ltd, Glenside Industrial Estate, Star Rd, Partridge Green, Horsham, West Sussex RH13 8LD Tel: Partridge Green 710971 (STD code 0403)
Associate Company: Van Duren Publishers Ltd (qv)
Subjects: Belles Lettres, Poetry, Biography, History, Music, Art, Philosophy, Reference, Religion, Parapsychology, High-priced Paperbacks, English and Anglo-Irish Literature & Criticism, Drama, Folklore
1986: 16 titles *Founded:* 1966
ISBN Publisher's Prefixes: 0-900675, 0-901072, 0-86140

The **Society for Promoting** Christian Knowledge, see SPCK

Society for Research into Higher Education, see SRHE

Soho (The Soho Book Company Ltd)+*, 1-3 Brewer St, London W1R 3FN Tel: (01) 439 0100
Man Dir, Sales, Production: Roc Sandford; *Editorial:* Roc Sandford, Pierre Hodgson; *Publicity, Rights & Permissions:* Bridgette Heathcoat Amory
Subsidiary Company: Soho Computing (at above address)
Subjects: Literature, Philosophy, History, Letters, Biography
1985: 8 titles *Founded:* 1984
ISBN Publisher's Prefix: 0-948166

Soncino Press Ltd+, Flat 3, 15 Estelle Rd, London NW3 Tel: (01) 267 4944
Man Dir: P Bloch
Branch Off: 5 Essex St, New York, NY 10002, USA
Subject: Religion (Jewish)
Founded: 1929
ISBN Publisher's Prefix: 0-900689

Sotheby's Publications, an imprint of Philip Wilson Publishers Ltd (qv)

Southside, see Canongate Publishing Ltd

Souvenir Press Ltd+, 43 Great Russell St, London WC1B 3PA Tel: (01) 580 9307, (01) 637 5711 Cable Add: Publisher London WC1 Telex: 24710
Man Dir, Rights & Permissions: Ernest Hecht; *Sales Dir:* Leslie Cramphorn; *Editorial:* Tessa Harrow; *Production:* Rodney King; *Publicity Manager:* Katrina Webster
Associate Company: Souvenir Press (Australia) Pty Ltd
Subsidiary Companies: Souvenir Press (Educational & Academic) Ltd; Souvenir Press (Films) Ltd; Euro-Features Ltd; Pictorial Presentations Ltd; Pop-Universal Ltd; Condor Books
Imprints: Condor Books, Human Horizons Series, Souvenir Press
Branch Off: 311 Singel, Amsterdam, Netherlands
Subjects: General Fiction, Belles Lettres, Poetry, Biography, History, How-to, Music, Art, Philosophy, Religion, Juveniles, Large-format Paperbacks, Medicine, Psychology, Social Science, Disability and Handicap, Sport

Bookshop: Souvenir Press Bookshop (at above London address)
1985: 58 titles *Founded:* 1952
ISBN Publisher's Prefix: 0-285

Sovereign Books Ltd, see Wayland (Publishers) Ltd

Neville **Spearman** Publishers, see The C W Daniel Co Ltd (qv)

Spellmount Ltd Publishers, 12 Dene Way, Speldhurst, Tunbridge Wells, Kent TN3 0NX Tel: Langton 2860 (STD code 089 286)
Chairman: Brian Austin; *Man Dir:* Ian Morley-Clarke; *Editorial Dirs:* Kathleen Morley-Clarke, John Bright-Holmes, David Burnett James
Subjects: Biographies (classical, jazz & popular musicians, sporting personalities), Militaria, Social History
1986: 10 titles *1987:* 14 titles *Founded:* 1983
ISBN Publisher's Prefix: 0-946771

Sphere Books Ltd+, 27 Wright's Lane, London W8 5TZ Tel: (01) 937 8070 Telex: 917181 Fax: (01) 937 8704
Man Dir: Nick Webb; *Editorial Dirs:* Barbara Boote (Sphere), Mike Petty (Abacus), James Tindall (Reference & Cardinal); *Sales Dir:* John O'Connor; *Production Manager:* Martin Scougal; *Publicity Manager:* Cathy Douglas; *Press Officer:* Diana Holmes
Orders to: Sphere Order Dept, TBL Book Service Ltd, 17-25 Nelson Way, Tuscam Trading Estate, Camberley, Surrey GU15 3EU Tel: Camberley 62144 (STD code 0276)
Parent Company: Penguin Books Ltd (qv)
Imprints include: Abacus, Cardinal
Subjects: General Fiction and Non-fiction, Biography, History, Travel, Music, Reference, Business Management, General & Social Science
Founded: 1967
ISBN Publisher's Prefixes: 0-7221, 0-7474 (both Sphere), 0-349 (Abacus)

Spindlewood+, 70 Lynhurst Ave, Barnstaple, Devon EX31 2HY Tel: Barnstaple 71612 (STD code 0271)
Chief Executive: Michael Holloway; *Editorial:* Anne Holloway, Jo Cox
Subjects: Children's, Education, Fiction, History, Travel
1985: 12 titles *1986:* 8 titles *Founded:* 1980
ISBN Publisher's Prefix: 0-907349

Spokesman Books+, Bertrand Russell House, Gamble St, Nottingham NG7 4ET Tel: Nottingham 708318 (STD code 0602) Cable Add: Russfound
Editorial: Ken Coates; *Sales, Publicity:* Ann Kestenbaum; *Production, Rights & Permissions:* Ken Fleet
Parent Company: Bertrand Russell Peace Foundation Ltd (at above address)
Associate Company: Russell Press Ltd (at above address)
Subjects: International Affairs, Disarmament, Economics, Politics, Industrial Relations, Labour History, Trade Unionism
Founded: 1970
ISBN Publisher's Prefix: 0-85124

E & F N **Spon** Ltd, 11 New Fetter Lane, London EC4P 4EE Tel: (01) 583 9855 Cable Add: Elegiacs London EC5 Telex: 263398 Abplong Fax: (01) 583 0701
Man Dir: Paul Gardner; *Publisher:* Phillip Read; *Marketing:* Kate Morcom; *Production:* Brian West
Parent Company: Thomson Information Services Ltd (qv). Ultimate parent company International Thomson

Organisation Ltd, 20 Queen St West, Box 45, Suite 2206, Toronto, Ontario M5H 3R3, Canada
Subjects: Reference, Engineering, Building, Applied Sciences
Founded: 1834
Miscellaneous: E & F N Spon Ltd is an imprint of Chapman & Hall Ltd (qv)
ISBN Publisher's Prefix: 0-419

Sporting and Leisure Press, an imprint of Barracuda Books Ltd (qv)

The **Sportsman's Press**+, 25 King Charles Walk, London SW19 6JA Tel: (01) 789 0229
Chief Executive: Kenneth Kemp
Orders to: TBL Bookservice Ltd, 14-23 Nelson Way, Tuscam Trading Estate, Camberley, Surrey GU15 3EU Tel: Camberley 62144 (STD code 0276)
Subjects: Horses & Equestrian Sports, Shooting, Sporting Art, Sporting Dogs, Fishing
1985: 4 titles *1986:* 6 titles *Founded:* 1984

Spring Books, an imprint of The Hamlyn Publishing Group (qv)

Springwood Books Ltd, Springwood House, The Avenue, Ascot, Berkshire SL5 7LY Tel: Ascot 24053 (STD code 0990) Telex: 8813271 Gecoms G
Man Dir, Editorial, Rights & Permissions: Christopher Foster; *Publicity, Marketing, Sales:* Linda Skinner; *Production, Administration:* Lesley Morris
Orders to: George Philip Services Ltd, PO Box 1, Littlehampton, West Sussex BN17 7EN Tel: Littlehampton 717453 (STD code 0903)
Subjects: Fiction, Poetry, Biography, Children's Books, History, Finance, Music, Archaeology, Art, Cookery, Sport
Founded: 1976
ISBN Publisher's Prefixes: 0-905947, 0-86254

Stacey International*, 128 Kensington Church St, London W8 4BH Tel: (01) 221 7166 Telex: 298768
Man Dir: Tom Stacey
Subjects: Illustrated Non-fiction, Encyclopaedic, Geography, Islamic and Arab Subjects, World Affairs
1985: 20 titles *Founded:* 1974
ISBN Publisher's Prefix: 0-905743

Stainer & Bell Ltd, PO Box 110, 82 High Rd, London N2 9PW Tel: (01) 444 9135
Man Dir: Bernard A Braley; *Executive Chairman & Editorial Dir:* Allen Percival; *Production:* Carol Wakefield; *Sales, Publicity, Rights & Permissions:* Keith Wakefield
Imprints include: Augener, Belton Books, Galliard, A Weekes, Joseph Williams
Subjects: Music, Education, Religion
Founded: 1907
ISBN Publisher's Prefix: 0-85249

Stam Press Ltd, now incorporated in Stanley Thornes & Hulton (Publishers) Ltd (qv)

Stanford Maritime Ltd, 27a Floral St, London WC2E 9DP Tel: (01) 836 7863/1915 Cable Add: Philip London WC2 Telex: 21667
Man Dir: M A Bovill; *Export Sales Manager:* Julian Clayton; *Editorial Dir, Rights & Permissions:* John Gaisford; *Marketing Manager:* Alan Greene
Orders to: George Philip Services Ltd, Arndale Rd, Lineside Industrial Estate, Littlehampton, West Sussex BN17 7EN Tel: Littlehampton 7453 (STD code 090 64)
Associate Company: George Philip & Son Ltd (qv)
Subjects: Nautical books and charts
Bookshop: At above address
ISBN Publisher's Prefix: 0-540

Star, an imprint of W H Allen & Co Ltd (qv)

Harold **Starke** Ltd, Pegasus House, 116-120 Golden Lane, London EC1Y 0TL Tel: (01) 253 2145 Telex: c/o 27931 Burke G
Editorial, Rights & Permissions: Miss N Galinski; *Export Sales:* H Starke
Orders to: 14 Beccles Rd, Loddon, Norwich, Norfolk NR14 6JD
Parent Company: Burke Publishing Co Ltd (qv)
Subjects: General Non-fiction, Reference, Medical
Founded: 1960
ISBN Publisher's Prefix: 0-287

Rudolf **Steiner** Press, 38 Museum St, London WC1A 1LP Tel: (01) 242 4249
Man Dir: S Gordon
Subjects: Art & Architecture, Philosophy, Education, Religion, Social Sciences, Natural Sciences, Agriculture
Bookshop: At above address
Founded: 1920
ISBN Publisher's Prefix: 0-85440

Patrick **Stephens** Ltd+, Denington Estate, Wellingborough, Northamptonshire NN8 2RQ Tel: Wellingborough 76031 (STD code 0933) Cable Add: Thorgroup Wellingborough Telex: 311072 Thopub G Fax: (0933) 72800
Man Dir: David Young; *Editorial Dir:* Darryl Reach; *Marketing & Sales Dir:* Julian Rivers; *Publicity:* Judith Smallwood; *Rights & Permissions:* Marjorie Nelson; *Marketing Manager:* Vivienne Wordley; *Group Sales Manager:* John Marsh; *Export Sales Manager:* Ray Potts
Parent Company: Thorsons Publishing Group Ltd (qv)
Subjects: Maritime, Military, Model Making, Motoring & Motor Racing, Motorcycling, Aviation, Wargaming, Railways, Collecting, Countryside, History, Biographies, Sport & Fitness
1986: 57 titles *1987:* 57 titles *Founded:* 1961
ISBN Publisher's Prefix: 0-85059

Stevens & Sons Ltd, 11 New Fetter Lane, London EC4P 4EE Tel: (01) 583 9855 Cable Add: Subjicio London EC4 Telex: 263398 Fax: (01) 583 0701
Man Dir: Andrew Prideaux
Orders to: Sweet & Maxwell Ltd, North Way, Andover, Hampshire SP10 5BE Tel: Andover 332424 (STD code 0264)
Parent Company: Thomson Information Services Ltd (qv). Ultimate parent company International Thomson Organisation Ltd, 20 Queen St West, Box 45, Suite 2206, Toronto, Ontario M5H 3R3, Canada
Subjects: Reference books for lawyers and solicitors, Textbooks for law students and law teachers
Founded: 1888
ISBN Publisher's Prefix: 0-420

Stillitron*, 72 New Bond St, London W1Y 0QY Tel: (01) 493 1177 Cable Add: Stillitron, Ldn Telex: 23475
President: Gerald B Stillit
Subject: Modern Languages
Founded: 1964
ISBN Publisher's Prefix: 0-288

Stobart & Son Ltd+, 67-73 Worship St, London EC2A 2EL Tel: (01) 247 0501
Publicity: T Hearnden; *Rights & Permissions:* B J Davies
Subjects: Woodwork, Timber, Forestry, Handicrafts
ISBN Publisher's Prefix: 0-85442

Arthur H **Stockwell** Ltd, Elms Court, Torrs Park, Ilfracombe, Devon EX34 8BA Tel: Ilfracombe 62557 (STD code 0271)
Man Dir, Production, Rights & Permissions: D P Stockwell; *Editorial:* B Nott; *Sales, Publicity:* S Hammond
Subjects: Fiction, Non-fiction, Travel, Biography, Religious, War, Humour, Juvenile, Poetry
Founded: 1898
ISBN Publisher's Prefix: 0-7223

Strange but True, an imprint of Xanadu Publications Ltd (qv)

Student Christian Movement Press, see S C M Press Ltd

Studentlitteratur, an imprint of Chartwell-Bratt (Publishing & Training) Ltd (qv)

Studio Publications (Ipswich) Ltd+, The Drift, Nacton Rd, Ipswich, Suffolk IP1 9QR Tel: Ipswich 270880 (STD code 0473) Telex: 98551 Studio G Fax: (0473) 270113
Man Dir, Sales, Rights & Permissions: Barrie John Henderson; *Publicity, Editorial Manager:* Hazel Jones
Imprints: Badger Books, Fun Packs, Munch Bunch Books
Subject: Children's Books
1985: 21 titles *Founded:* 1975
ISBN Publisher's Prefixes: 0-904584, 0-86215

Studio Vista, an imprint of Cassell PLC (qv)

Sundial, an imprint of Octopus Books Ltd (qv)

Surrey University Press, Bishopbriggs, Glasgow G64 2NZ Tel: (041) 772 2311 Cable Add: Blackie Glasgow Telex: 777283
London Off: 7 Leicester Pl, London WC2H 7BP Tel: (01) 736 7521
Dir: Dr Graeme MacKintosh; *Sales Manager:* Kenneth J Allan
Orders to: J M Dent & Sons (Distribution) Ltd, Dunhams Lane, Letchworth, Hertfordshire SG16 1LF Tel: Letchworth 686241 (STD code 0462)
Parent Company: Blackie & Son Ltd (qv)
Associate Companies: International Textbook Co Ltd, Leonard Hill (qqv)
Subjects: Engineering, Microbiology, Biomedicine, Hotel & Catering Studies
Founded: 1972
ISBN Publisher's Prefix: 0-903384

Surveyors Publications, 12 Great George St, Parliament Sq, London SW1P 3AD Tel: (01) 222 7000 ext 272 Cable Add: Surveyable London SW1 Telex: 915443 Rics G
Chief Executive: Alec Sandison; *Publishing Dir:* Lionel Browne
Orders to: Norden House, Basing View, Basingstoke, Hampshire RG21 2HN
Parent Company: Surveyors Holdings Ltd, 12 Great George St, London SW1P 3AD
Associate Company: RICS Journals Ltd, PO Box 87, 1 Pemberton Row, London EC4P 4HL
Subjects: Property, Surveying and related subjects
Bookshop: The Surveyors Bookshop, 12 Great George St, Parliament Sq, London SW1P 3AD
Founded: 1981

Sussex Video Ltd, associate company of World Microfilms Publications Ltd (qv) producing educational videotapes

Alan **Sutton** Publishing Ltd+, 30 Brunswick Rd, Gloucester GL1 1JJ Tel: Gloucester 419575 (STD code 0452) Telex: 43690
Man Dir: A Sutton; *Managing Editor, Rights & Permissions:* P Clifford
Imprint: Pocket Classics
Subjects: Literature, Topography, History, Biography, Letters & Diaries, Travel, Archaeology
Founded: 1978
ISBN Publisher's Prefixes: 0-86299, 0-904387

Swallow Books+, Swallow House, 11-21 Northdown St, London N1 9BN Tel: (01) 278 2444 Telex: 265628 Swallo G Fax: (01) 278 1677
Chief Executive: Michael Edwards; *Sales, Rights & Permissions:* Michael Rainbird; *Editorial:* Stephen Adamson; *Production:* David Young
Parent Company: Swallow Publishing Ltd (at above address)
Associate Companies: CMP London, Swallow Editions Ltd (both at above address)
Subjects: Illustrated Non-fiction (practical & reference)
1985: 5 titles *1986:* 8 titles *Founded:* 1982

Swallow Editions Ltd, an associate company of Swallow Books (qv)

Sweet & Maxwell Ltd, 11 New Fetter Lane, London EC4P 4EE Tel: (01) 583 9855 Cable Add: Subjicio London EC4 Telex: 263398 Fax: (01) 583 0701
Chairman: C D O Evans; *Man Dir:* Andrew Prideaux
Orders to: Sweet & Maxwell Ltd, North Way, Andover, Hampshire SP10 5BE Tel: Andover 332424 (STD code 0264)
Parent Company: Thomson Information Services Ltd (qv). Ultimate parent company International Thomson Organisation Ltd, 20 Queen St West, Box 45, Suite 2206, Toronto, Ontario M5H 3R3, Canada
Imprints: Current Law Publishers Ltd, Police Review Publishing Co Ltd
Subjects: Law (Reference & University Textbooks), Business
Founded: 1799
ISBN Publisher's Prefix: 0-421

Swift Children's Books, an imprint of Firecrest Publishing Ltd (qv)

Sybex, an imprint of Longman Group UK Ltd (qv)

Synergetic Press Inc*, 24 Old Gloucester St, London WC1 3AL Tel: (01) 405 1851 Telex: 885960 Ecohub G
Chief Executive: Tango Parrish Snyder
Orders to: Element Books Ltd, Unit 25, Longmead, Shaftesbury, Dorset SP7 8PL
Branch Off: 312 Houston St, Fort Worth, TX 76102, USA
Subjects: Biospherics, Theatre, Fiction, Poetry, Management
Founded: 1969
ISBN Publisher's Prefix: 0-907791

Syston Publishing Ltd, an imprint of The Trotman Group (qv)

Tabb House+, 11 Church St, Padstow, Cornwall PL28 8BG Tel: Padstow 532316 (STD code 0841)
Chief Executive: Caroline White
Subjects: Literature, Memoirs, Fiction, Poetry, Natural History, Children's, Practical
1985: 6 titles *1986:* 9 titles *Founded:* 1980
ISBN Publisher's Prefix: 0-907018

Tallis Press Ltd, see Charles Skilton Ltd

Tandem, an imprint of W H Allen & Co Ltd (qv)

The **Tantivy** Press Ltd, 2 Bedford Gardens, London W8 7EH Tel: (01) 727 1958 Cable Add: Tantivy London W8 Telex: 8951098 Tanch G
Man Dir, Rights & Permissions: Peter Cowie
Subject: General Non-fiction
ISBN Publisher's Prefix: 0-900730

Target, an imprint of W H Allen & Co Ltd (qv)

Tarquin Publications, Stradbroke, Diss, Norfolk IP21 5JP Tel: Diss 84218 (STD code 0379)
Chief Executive, Editorial, Rights & Permissions: Gerald Jenkins; *Sales:* Margaret Jenkins
Subject: Children's Mathematical & Art/Craft cut-out books
1985: 8 titles *1986:* 10 titles *Founded:* 1970
ISBN Publisher's Prefix: 0-906212

Tate Gallery Publications, Millbank, London SW1P 4RG Tel: (01) 834 5651 Cable Add: Tategal London
Publications Manager: Iain Bain; *Sales Manager:* Brian Lawler; *Rights & Permissions:* Graham Langton
Retail Shop: Tate Gallery, Millbank, London SW1P 4RG
Subjects: Art books and catalogues
1985: 12 titles *1986:* 19 titles *Founded:* 1931
ISBN Publisher's Prefixes: 0-900874, 0-905005

I B **Tauris** & Co Ltd+, 3 Henrietta St, Covent Garden, London WC2E 8PW Tel: (01) 836 5814 Telex: 261507/3166 Tauris
Chairman, Publisher: I Baghrzade; *Man Dir:* J Lynn-Evans; *Publicity, Promotions:* S Dow; *Sales:* E Hyams
Orders to: Biblios Publishers Distribution Services Ltd, Glenside Industrial Estate, Partridge Green, Horsham, Sussex RH13 8LD
Subjects: History, Politics, Current Affairs, Development & Third World general non-fiction
1987: 30 titles *Founded:* 1983
ISBN Publisher's Prefix: 1-85043

Tavistock Publications Ltd, see Routledge

Taylor & Francis Ltd, 4 John St, London WC1N 2ET Tel: (01) 405 2237 Telex: 858540 Fax: (01) 831 2035
Man Dir: A R Selvey; *Publishing Dir:* M I Dawes; *Marketing Dir:* J Lavender; *Sales Manager:* K R Courtney
Orders to: Rankine Rd, Basingstoke, Hampshire RG24 0PR Tel: Basingstoke 840366 (STD code 0256) Fax: (0256) 479438
Subsidiary Companies: Falmer Press Ltd (at above London address); Taylor & Francis (Printers) Ltd (at above Basingstoke address); Crane, Russak & Co Inc, New York, USA; Taylor & Francis Inc, Philadelphia, PA, USA
Imprints include: Crane Russak, Falmer Press
Subjects: Physics, Medicine, Psychology, Engineering, Education, General Science, International Affairs
Founded: 1798
ISBN Publisher's Prefixes: 0-85066 (Taylor & Francis), 0-905273 (Falmer), 0-8448 (Crane Russak)

Teach Yourself Books, an imprint of Hodder & Stoughton Ltd (qv)

Teacher Publishing Co Ltd*, Derbyshire House, Lower St, Kettering, Northamptonshire NN16 8BB Tel: Kettering 518407 (STD code 0536)
ISBN Publisher's Prefix: 0-900642

Teakfield Ltd, now Gower Publishing Co Ltd (qv)

Technical Press Ltd, Gower House, Croft Rd, Aldershot, Hampshire GU11 3HR Tel: Aldershot 331551 (STD code 0252) Telex: 858001 Gower G
Publisher: John Hindley
Parent Company: Gower Publishing Co Ltd (qv)
Subjects: Engineering, Hairdressing, Chemistry, Metallurgy, Industrial Technology
Founded: 1933
ISBN Publisher's Prefix: 0-291

Telecommunications Press, see Architectural Press Ltd

Telegraph Publications+, The Daily Telegraph PLC, 135 Fleet St, London EC4P 4BL Tel: (01) 353 4242 Telex: 22874
Publications Dir: Christopher Milsome; *Sales Manager:* John Wilson
Parent Company: The Daily Telegraph (at above address)
Subjects: Personal Finance & Business, General Interest, Crosswords, Sport, Travel & Guides, Maps, Cookery & Wine, Gardening, Computing
1986: 45 titles *1987:* 99 titles *Founded:* 1930
ISBN Publisher's Prefix: 0-86367

Thomas **Telford** Ltd, Thomas Telford House, 1 Heron Quay, London E14 9XF Tel: (01) 987 6999 Telex: 298105 Civils G
Head of Publications Division: Graham James
Subjects: Civil and Nuclear Engineering and related fields
Bookshop: Telford International Bookshop, 1-7 Great George St, London SW1P 3AA (also mail order)
1985-86: 20 titles *Founded:* 1972
Miscellaneous: Thomas Telford Ltd is the publishing company of the Institution of Civil Engineers and the British Nuclear Energy Society
ISBN Publisher's Prefixes: 0-901948, 0-7277

Templar Publishing Co Ltd+, 107 High St, Dorking, Surrey RH4 1QA Tel: Dorking 76361 (STD code 0306) Telex: 858535 Templr G Fax: (0306) 889097
Man Dir: Richard Carlisle; *Editorial:* Amanda Wood; *Production:* Co van Woerkom; *Publishing:* Ms Del Tucker
Subjects: Packager of Children's (educational & picture books) and Adult Illustrated Non-fiction
1985: 31 titles *1986:* 42 titles *Founded:* 1981

Temple House Books, an imprint of The Book Guild Ltd (qv)

Maurice **Temple Smith** Ltd, an imprint of Gower Publishing Co Ltd (qv)

Thames & Hudson Ltd+, 30-34 Bloomsbury St, London WC1B 3QP Tel: (01) 636 5488 Cable Add: Thameshuds London WC1 Telex: 25992/3 Fax: (01) 636 4799
Man Dir: Thomas Neurath; *Editorial:* Jamie Camplin; *Sales, Marketing:* Simon Huntley; *Production:* Werner Guttmann; *Publicity:* Ludo Craddock; *Rights & Permissions:* Ian Middleton
Orders to: Thames & Hudson (Distributors) Ltd, 44 Clockhouse Rd, Farnborough, Hampshire GU14 7QZ Tel: Farnborough 541602 (STD code 0252) Fax: (01) 636 4799
Associate Companies: Thames & Hudson (Australia) Pty Ltd, 86 Stanley St, West Melbourne, Victoria 3003, Australia; Thames & Hudson Inc, 500 Fifth Ave,

UNITED KINGDOM 473

New York, NY 10036, USA
Subjects: Art, Architecture, Design, History, Archaeology, Biography, Photography, Topography, Music, Theatre, Literature, Travel
Founded: 1949
ISBN Publisher's Prefix: 0-500

Thames Head+, T R House, Christopher Rd, East Grinstead, Sussex RH19 3BT Tel: East Grinstead 313844 (STD code 0342) Telex: 94011210 Blap G
Publisher: Martin Marix Evans
Parent Company: Ling Kee (UK) Ltd (qv for other group members)
Subjects: Specialist packagers (Trade & Non-fiction)
1986: 5 titles

Third Eye Centre (Glasgow) Ltd+, 350 Sauchiehall St, Glasgow G2 3JD Tel: (041) 332 7521
Dir, Editorial, Production: Christopher Carrell; *Publications Co-ordinator, Rights & Permissions:* Roy O'Neil; *Promotions Assistant:* Janie C Munro
Subjects: Art, Scottish History, Poetry, Drama, Photography, Architecture
Bookshop: Third Eye Centre Bookshop (at above address)
1985: 9 titles *1986:* 3 titles *Founded:* 1975
ISBN Publisher's Prefix: 0-906474

A **Thomas**, an imprint of Thorsons Publishing Group Ltd (qv)

Thomson Information Services Ltd, The Quadrangle, 180 Wardour St, London W1A 4YG Tel: (01) 437 9787 Telex: 261349
TISL Members include: Chapman & Hall Ltd (qv), W Green & Son Ltd (qv), Jane's Publishing Co Ltd (qv), Routledge (qv), E & F N Spon Ltd (qv), Stevens & Sons Ltd (qv), Sweet & Maxwell Ltd (qv)
Parent Company: International Thomson Organisation Ltd, 20 Queen St West, Box 45, Suite 2206, Toronto, Ontario M5H 3R3, Canada

Stanley **Thornes & Hulton** (Publishers) Ltd+, Old Station Dr, Leckhampton, Cheltenham, Gloucestershire GL53 0DN Tel: Cheltenham 584429 (STD code 0242) Telex: 43592
Man Dir: Stanley Thornes; *Deputy Man Dir, Production Dir:* Roy Kendall; *Publishing Dir:* Michael Rigby; *Sales Dir:* Margot van de Weijer
Parent Company: Kluwer Group, Netherlands (qv)
Subjects: Mathematics, Engineering, Business Studies, Modern Languages, English Language Teaching, Sciences, Education, Catering, Home Economics, Beauty Therapy, Hairdressing, Religious Education, Social Sciences, History (Primary & Secondary Education), Geography, Music
Miscellaneous: Incorporating Stam Press Ltd
ISBN Publisher's Prefixes: 0-85950, 0-7175, 0-85973

Thornhill Press, 24 Moorend Rd, Cheltenham, Gloucestershire GL53 0EU Tel: Cheltenham 519137 (STD code 0242)
Proprietor: D Badham-Thornhill
Subjects: Topographical Guides, Sport, General
1986: 4 titles *1987:* 5 titles *Founded:* 1972
ISBN Publisher's Prefixes: 0-904110, 0-946328

Thoroughbred Press, an imprint of J A Allen & Co Ltd (qv)

F A **Thorpe** (Publishing) Ltd, The Green, Bradgate Rd, Anstey, Leicester LE7 7FU Tel: Leicester 364325 (STD code 0533) Telex: 342563 Thorpe G
Man Dir: Dr F A Thorpe, OBE
Subjects: Fiction, Travel, Biography
Miscellaneous: Publishers of Ulverscroft Large Print Books, Charnwood Library Series, Linford Mystery Library Series, Linford Romance Library Series, Linford Western Library Series
ISBN Publisher's Prefixes: 0-85456, 0-7089

Thorsons Publishing Group Ltd+, Denington Estate, Wellingborough, Northamptonshire NN8 2RQ Tel: Wellingborough 76031 (STD code 0933) Cable Add: Thorgroup Wellingborough Telex: 311072 Thopub G Fax: (0933) 72800
Man Dir: David Young; *Production Dir:* David Palmer; *Editorial Dir:* Annie Smith; *Marketing and Sales Dir:* Julian Rivers; *Group Sales Manager:* John Marsh; *Rights & Permissions:* Marjorie Nelson; *Publicity Manager:* Judith Smallwood; *Marketing Manager:* Vivienne Wordley
Subsidiary Companies: Aquarian Press Ltd, Equation, Patrick Stephens Ltd (qqv)
Associate Company: Laser Cassettes Ltd
Imprints: Athene Publishing Co, Crucible, Science of Life Books, A Thomas
Subjects: Natural Health & Healing, Natural Foods, Vegetarian Cookery & Philosophy, Special Diets, Consumer Related Books, Alternative Medicine, Nutrition, Animal Rights, Organic Gardening, Self-Help Themes, Books for Women, Public Speaking, Hypnotism & Hypnotherapy, Practical Psychology, Inspiration, Mind Training, Personal Improvement, Yoga & Related Disciplines, Fitness & Exercise, Social Issues, Management
1985: 164 titles *1986:* 220 titles *Founded:* 1930
ISBN Publisher's Prefixes: 0-7225, 0-85454, 0-909911, 0-85059, 0-85030, 0-85500, 1-85274, 1-85336

Three Duck Editions Ltd, see Justin Knowles Publishing Group

The **Thule** Press, incorporated in The Findhorn Press (qv)

Tiger, an imprint of Scripture Union (qv)

Time-Life Books, Time-Life International, 153 New Bond St, London W1Y 0AA Tel: (01) 499 4080 Cable Add: Timeinc London W1 Telex: 22557
Orders to: Bookpoint Ltd, 39 Milton Trading Estate, Abingdon, Oxfordshire OX14 4TD Tel: Abingdon 835001 (STD code 0235) Telex: 837091 Fax: 0235 832068
European Head Off: Time-Life Books BV, Netherlands (qv)

Times Books Ltd, 16 Golden Sq, London W1R 4BN Tel: (01) 434 3767 Telex: 897284 Fax: (01) 434 2080
Man Dir: B Winkleman; *Senior Editor:* P Middleton; *Publicity Manager:* Helen Priday; *Production Manager:* D Rye
Orders to: Bartholomew Sales & Distribution Services, 12 Duncan St, Edinburgh EH9 1TA Tel: (031) 667 9341
Divisions: Angus & Robertson (UK) (qv), Invincible Press, Robert Nicholson Publications Ltd (qv)
Parent Company: News International PLC, 200 Gray's Inn Rd, London WC1X 8EZ
Subjects: Atlases, General Non-fiction, Reference
ISBN Publisher's Prefix: 0-7230

Alec **Tiranti** Ltd, an imprint of Academy Editions (qv)

Titan Books Ltd+, 58 St Giles High St, London WC2H 8LH Tel: (01) 836 4056
Publisher, Rights & Permissions: Nick Landau; *Editorial:* Bernadette Jaye; *Sales:* Stephen Robson; *Production:* Robert Kelly; *Publicity:* Igor Goldkind
Orders to: Titan Distributors, PO Box 250, London E3 4RT
Parent Company: Titan Distributors, 42-44 Copperfield Rd, London E3 4RT
Associate Company: Forbidden Planet Ltd, 23 Denmark St, London WC2H 8LH
Imprint: Escape
Subjects: Comic Art, Science Fiction, Film & TV Fantasy
Bookshops: Forbidden Planet Ltd, Brighton, London, Milton Keynes; Timeslip Ltd, Newcastle
1985: 20 titles *1986:* 60 titles *Founded:* 1981
ISBN Publisher's Prefixes: 1-85286, 0-907610

Tobin Music Books, an imprint of Helicon Press (qv)

Tolley Publishing Co, an imprint of Ernest Benn Ltd (qv)

Tops'l Books+, 43 Northumberland Pl, Teignmouth, Devon TQ14 8DE Tel: Teignmouth 5436 (STD code 062 67)
Chief Executive: Colin Elliott
Subject: Maritime History
Bookshop: Quayside Bookshop (at above address)
1987: 2 titles *Founded:* 1978
ISBN Publisher's Prefix: 0-906397

Town & County Books Ltd, Coombelands House, Addlestone, Weybridge, Surrey KT15 1NY Tel: Weybridge 58511 (STD code 0932) Telex: 929806 Iallan G
Chief Executive: Ian Allan; *Editorial:* Simon Forty; *Production:* Nick Lerwill; *Publicity:* Peter Waller
Parent Company: Ian Allan Group (at above address)
Associate Companies: Ian Allan Ltd (qv), Lewis Masonic (at above address)
Subjects: British Landscape, History & Architecture, Fashion, Photography
Founded: 1982
ISBN Publisher's Prefix: 0-86364

Transport Publishing Co Ltd, 128 Pikes Lane, Glossop, Derbyshire SK13 8EH Tel: Glossop 61508 (STD code 045 74)
Man Dir: John A Senior; *Sales Manager:* Mark D Senior
Subsidiary Company: Senior Publications (at above address)
Subjects: Transport, Travel, Sport, Local History
1985: 4 titles *1986:* 8 titles *Founded:* 1972
ISBN Publisher's Prefixes: 0-903839, 0-86317

Transworld Publishers (Corgi & Bantam Books) Ltd, 61-63 Uxbridge Rd, Ealing, London W5 5SA Tel: (01) 579 2652 Cable Add: Transcable London W5 Telex: 267974 Fax: (01) 579 5749
Man Dir, Chief Executive: Paul Scherer; *Publishers:* Patrick Janson-Smith (Corgi), Anthony Mott (Bantam Paperbacks), Mark Barty-King (Bantam Press); *Editorial Dir:* Alan Earney (Corgi); *Editorial & Rights Dir:* Ursula Mackenzie (Bantam Press); *International Sales Dir:* John Blake; *Foreign, Subsidiary Rights:* Catherine Eccles; *UK Marketing Dir:* Derek Searle; *Publicity, Promotion Dir:* Wendy Tury; *Production Dir:* Frank Gill; *Art Dir:* Liz Laczynska
Parent Company: Bantam Books Inc, 666 Fifth Ave, New York, NY 10103, USA. Ultimate parent company Verlagsgruppe Bertelsmann GmbH, Federal Republic of Germany (qv)
Associate Companies: Bantam Press, UK; Transworld Publishers (Australia) Pty Ltd, Australia (qv); Bantam Books of Canada Inc, 60 St Clair Ave East, Suite 601,

474 UNITED KINGDOM

Toronto, Canada; Trans-South African Book Distributors (Pty) Ltd, Box 17554, Hillbrow 2038, Johannesburg, Republic of South Africa; Corgi & Bantam Books (NZ) Ltd, Car Moselle & Waipareira Aves, Henderson, Auckland, New Zealand
Imprints include: Bantam, Bantam Press, Black Swan, Corgi, Partridge Press, Young Corgi
Subjects: Mass-market and trade paperbacks in all general fiction and non-fiction areas; hard covers in general and sports/leisure markets
Founded: 1950
ISBN Publisher's Prefixes: 0-0552 (Corgi), 0-553 (Bantam), 0-593 (Bantam Press), 1-85225 (Partridge)

Travellers Press, an imprint of Octopus Books Ltd (qv)

Treasure Press, an imprint of Octopus Books Ltd (qv)

Trefoil Publications Ltd+, 13A St John's Hill, London SW11 1TN Tel: (01) 223 7037 Telex: 295218 Slater G
Dirs: Conway Lloyd Morgan, John Latimer Smith, David Leeming, Richard Herner
Subjects: Art, Fine Arts, Decorative Arts, Design, Architecture, Exhibition Catalogues
Founded: 1981
ISBN Publisher's Prefix: 0-86294

Triad, an imprint of William Collins PLC (qv)

Triangle Books+, Holy Trinity Church, Marylebone Rd, London NW1 4DU Tel: (01) 387 5282 Cable Add: Futurity London NW1
General Secretary: Patrick Gilbert; *Editorial:* Myrtle Powley; *Sales Manager:* Brian Keen; *Promotion:* Cazz Colmer
Subject: Popular Religious Paperbacks
1985: 16 titles
Miscellaneous: A division of SPCK (qv)
ISBN Publisher's Prefix: 0-281

Trigon Press*, 117 Kent House Road, Beckenham, Kent BR3 1JJ Tel: (01) 778 0534
Man Dir, Sales: Roger Sheppard; *Editorial, Production:* Judith Sheppard; *Publicity:* Angela Roberts; *Rights & Permissions:* Pat Palmer
Subsidiary Company: Museum and Gallery Publishing (at above address)
Subjects: Bibliography, Business, Typography, Book Collecting, Publishing, Bookselling
Founded: 1974
ISBN Publisher's Prefix: 0-904929

The **Trotman** Group, 12-14 Hill Rise, Richmond, Surrey TW10 6UA Tel: (01) 940 5668
Chief Executive: Andrew Fiennes Trotman; *Editorial:* Philip Schofield; *Sales:* Graham Wessel; *Production:* Cherry Puddicombe; *Publicity, Rights & Permissions:* Jane O'Reilly
Parent Company: Trotman & Co Ltd (at above address)
Subsidiary Companies: Careers Consultants Ltd; Syston Publishing Co Ltd (both at above address)
Imprints: Careers Consultants Ltd, Syston Publishing Ltd
Subjects: Careers, Education, Music, Home Economics
1986: 20 titles *1987:* 30 titles *Founded:* 1971
ISBN Publisher's Prefix: 0-85660

Troubadour, an imprint of Macdonald & Co (Publishers) Ltd (qv)

Truran, an imprint of Dyllansow Truran (qv)

Tycooly, an imprint of Cassell PLC (qv)

Uffici, an imprint of Clematis Press Ltd (qv)

Ulverscroft Large Print Books Ltd, see F A Thorpe (Publishing) Ltd

Uni Books, an imprint of Volturna Press (qv)

Unibooks, an imprint of Hodder & Stoughton Ltd (qv)

United Writers Publications Ltd+, Ailsa, Castle Gate, Penzance, Cornwall TR20 8BG Tel: Penzance 5954 (STD code 0736)
Man Dir, Editorial: Sydney Sheppard; *Sales:* Malcolm Sheppard; *Production:* Richard J Sheppard; *Publicity:* Giles Harmon; *Rights & Permissions:* Julian Tremayne
Subjects: Biography, Travel, General Fiction, Writers' & Poets' Yearbook
Founded: 1962
ISBN Publisher's Prefixes: 0-901976, 1-85200

University, an imprint of Ramboro Enterprises Ltd (qv)

University College Cardiff Press+*, University College, PO Box 78, Cardiff CF1 1XL Tel: Cardiff 874789 (STD code 0222) Telex: 498635 Ulibcf G
Chairman of Editorial Board: Dr C W L Bevan CBE; *Editorial:* D P M Michael CBE (Secretary); *Sales, Production, Publicity, Rights & Permissions:* Bryan Turnbull
Subjects: Teaching Physics, East Asian Studies, Astronomy, Music, Law and Society, Bee-keeping, Philosophy, Sociology, Economics
Founded: 1978

The **University of Chicago** Press, 126 Buckingham Palace Rd, London SW1W 9SA Tel: (01) 730 9208 Cable Add: Chibooks Telex: 23933 Chibooks Ldn
General Manager: Neville Gosling
Publicity Manager: Ann Sexsmith
Orders to: International Book Distributors Ltd, 66 Wood Lane End, Hemel Hempstead, Hertfordshire HP2 4RG Tel: Hemel Hempstead 58531 (STD code 0442)
Associate Companies: Harvard University Press, The MIT Press (qqv)
Subjects: Biography, History, Music, Art, Philosophy, Reference, Paperbacks, Medicine, Psychology, General & Social Science, Literature, Education
Founded: 1891
Miscellaneous: Branch of The University of Chicago Press, Chicago, Illinois, USA
ISBN Publisher's Prefix: 0-226

University of Hawaii Press, see Academic and University Publishers Group

University of London Press Ltd (now Hodder & Stoughton Educational), see Hodder & Stoughton Ltd

University of Nebraska Press, see Academic and University Publishers Group

University of North Carolina Press, see Academic and University Publishers Group

University of Pennsylvania Press, see Academic and University Publishers Group

University of Queensland Press, 24 Thornhill Sq, London N1 1BQ Tel: (01) 609 1965 Telex: 21879 G attn Wlb
British and European Manager and Rights & Permissions: Elisabeth Wilson
Orders to: J M Dent & Sons (Distribution) Ltd, Dunhams Lane, Letchworth, Hertfordshire SG6 1AL Tel: Letchworth 686241 (STD code 0462)
Head Off: University of Queensland Press, Australia (qv)
Subjects: Fiction, Poetry, Children's, Academic, General
ISBN Publisher's Prefix: 0-7022

University of Tokyo Press, see Academic and University Publishers Group

University of Wales Press+, 6 Gwennyth St, Cathays, Cardiff CF2 4YD Tel: Cardiff 31919 (STD code 0222)
Dir: John Rhys; *Sales:* Richard Houdmont
Imprints: Gwasg Prifysgol Cymru, GPC Books
Subjects: History, Music, Art, Reference, Religion, Science, Humanities, Social Sciences, University, Secondary Textbooks (Welsh & English), Journals, Microfiche
Founded: 1922
ISBN Publisher's Prefixes: 0-7083, 0-900768

University of Wisconsin Press, see Academic and University Publishers Group

University Presses of California, Columbia and Princeton, 15A Epsom Rd, Guildford, Surrey GU1 3JT Tel: Guildford 68364 (STD code 0483)
Manager: Wolfgang Wingerter
Parent Companies: Columbia University Press, New York, USA; Princeton University Press, Princeton, NJ, USA; University of California Press, Berkeley, California, USA
Subjects: Academic Books and Paperbacks in the Humanities, Social and Natural Sciences
ISBN Publisher's Prefixes: 0-520 (California), 0-231 (Columbia), 0-691 (Princeton)

Unwin Hyman Ltd, 15-17 Broadwick St, London W1V 1FP Tel: (01) 439 3126 Telex: 23732 Fax: (01) 734 3884
Man Dir: R P Hyman; *Editorial Dirs:* Mary Butler (Trade), Roger Jones (Academic), Chris Kington (Educational); *Sales Dirs:* N C Britten (Educational & Academic), M H Streatfeild (Trade); *Publicity Manager:* Elizabeth Sich; *Rights & Permissions:* Renate Ogilvie
Orders to: Distribution & Management Services, Sheldon Way, New Hythe Lane, Larkfield, nr Maidstone, Kent ME20 6SE
Subsidiary Companies: Allen & Unwin Australia Pty Ltd, Australia (qv); Allen & Unwin (NZ) Ltd (with the Port Nicholson Press), New Zealand (qv); Allen & Unwin Inc, 8 Winchester Pl, Winchester, MA 01890, USA
Imprints: Allen & Unwin, Bell & Hyman, Counterpoint, Mandala, Unwin Paperbacks
Subjects: Primary & Secondary Education, Collecting, Design, Crafts, How-to, Pepys, Tolkien, Humour, Fantasy, History, Biography, Health, Child Care, Natural History, Religion, Social Sciences, Humanities, Life & Earth Sciences, Engineering, Economics, Business
1985: 400 titles *Founded:* 1838
ISBN Publisher's Prefixes: 0-04, 0-7135

Unwin Paperbacks, an imprint of Unwin Hyman Ltd (qv)

Usborne Publishing Ltd, 20 Garrick St, London WC2E 9BJ Tel: (01) 379 3535 Cable Add: Uspub, London WC2 Telex: 8953598 Uspub G Fax: (01) 836 0705
Man Dir: Peter Usborne; *Production, Rights & Permissions:* David Lowe
Associate Company: Maxwell Communication Corporation plc (qv)
Subjects: Children's Books (Non-fiction)
Founded: 1973
ISBN Publisher's Prefixes: 0-86020, 0-7460

V C H Publishers (UK) Ltd, 8 Wellington Court, Wellington St, Cambridge CB4

1NE Tel: Cambridge 321111 (STD code 0223) Fax: (0223) 313321
Man Dir, Sales, Production, Publicity, Rights & Permissions: Richard Ross; *Editor in Chief:* Dr Hans Ebel
Parent Company: VCH Verlagsgesellschaft GmbH, Federal Republic of Germany (qv)
Associate Companies: VCH Verlags AG, Switzerland (qv); VCH Publishers Inc, New York, USA; Ernst & Sohn, Berlin
Subjects: Science, Technology, Medicine
Founded: 1987

Vallentine, Mitchell & Co Ltd, Gainsborough House, 11 Gainsborough Rd, Leytonstone, London E11 1RS Tel: (01) 530 4226 Cable Add: Valmico London Telex: 897719
Warehouse: Harper & Row Distributors, Estover Rd, Estover, Plymouth PL6 7PZ
Man Dir: Frank Cass; *Editorial:* Margaret Goodare; *Trade:* Richard Norris; *Production:* John Smith; *Publicity:* Elizabeth Lye, Hayley Osen
Associate Companies: Frank Cass & Co Ltd (qv); The Woburn Press (qv)
Subjects: Jewish Studies (Literature, History, Politics, Religion)
Founded: 1950
ISBN Publisher's Prefix: 0-85303

Van Duren Publishers Ltd*, PO Box 1, Gerrards Cross, Buckinghamshire SL9 7AE Tel: Gerrards Cross 886575 (STD code 0753)
Man Dir, Rights & Permissions Dir: Colin P Smythe; *Editorial Dir:* Peter Bander van Duren; *Production Dir:* Leslie L Hayward
Associate Company: Colin Smythe Ltd (qv)
Subjects: Matters concerning Holy See or Catholic Church, Heraldry (Ecclesiastical & Secular), Non-fiction
1986: 5 titles *Founded:* 1973
ISBN Publisher's Prefix: 0-905715

Van Nostrand Reinhold (International) Co Ltd+, Molly Millar's Lane, Wokingham, Berkshire RG11 2PY Tel: Wokingham 789456 (STD code 0734) Telex: 848268 Vnr G Fax: (0734) 776722
Man Dir: Paul Gardner; *Publisher:* Dominic Recaldin; *Marketing Dir:* Peter McKay; *Head of Production:* Gavin McDonald
Parent Company: Thomson Information Services Ltd. Ultimate parent company International Thomson Organisation Ltd, 20 Queen St West, Box 45, Suite 2206, Toronto, Ontario M5H 3R3, Canada
Associate Company: Wadsworth International Group (qv)
Imprint: Gee & Co
Subjects: University & College Textbooks (Accounting and Business, Engineering, Biological Science), Reference, Professional, Vocational, Technical
Miscellaneous: Van Nostrand Reinhold (International) Co Ltd is an imprint of Chapman & Hall Ltd (qv)
ISBN Publisher's Prefixes: 0-442, 0-85258

Variorum, 20 Pembridge Mews, London W11 3EQ Tel: (01) 229 6024
Man Dir: J Wisener; *Managing Editor:* J Smedley
Subjects: History, Architecture, Arts, Reference, Religion, University Textbooks, Archaeology, Economics, Mediaeval and Canon Law
1985: 20 titles *1986:* 20 titles *Founded:* 1969
ISBN Publisher's Prefixes: 0-902089, 0-86078

Varsity, an imprint of Ramboro Enterprises Ltd (qv)

Venton Educational Ltd, The Uffington Press, Unit 3, Strattons Walk, High St, Melksham, Wiltshire SN12 6LA Tel: Melksham 703424 (STD code 0225)
Man Dir, Editorial, Publicity, Rights & Permissions: Colin Venton; *Sales:* Stuart Murray; *Production:* Sally Cuff
Subsidiary Company: Colin Venton Ltd (at above address)
Associate Company: Uffington Books (Mail Order) (at above address)
Imprint: White Horse Library
Subjects: Careers, Maritime, Motoring, Travel, West Country, 'Vet' Books
Founded: 1954
ISBN Publisher's Prefixes: 0-85993 (Venton Educational), 0-85475 (Colin Venton), 0-85966 (White Horse Library)

Ventura Publishing Ltd†+, 11-13 Young St, Kensington, London W8 5EH Tel: (01) 221 6395 Telex: 8953658 Venpub G
Man Dir: Robin Ellis; *Sales, Publicity, Rights & Permissions:* Caroline Bidwell; *Production:* Elizabeth York; *Editorial:* Jackie Fortey, Jill Borthwick
Subjects: High-quality Children's Novelty (including *Where's Spot?* series), Adult Leisure & General Non-fiction (all international co-productions)
Founded: 1977

Verbatim+, PO Box 199, Aylesbury, Buckinghamshire HP20 1TQ Tel: Aylesbury 27314 (STD code 0296)
Man Dir, Editorial: Laurence Urdang; *Sales, Rights & Permissions:* Hazel Hall
Parent Company: Laurence Urdang Inc (at above address)
Associate Company: Laurence Urdang Inc, 4 Laurel Heights, Old Lyme, CT 06371, USA
Subject: Language
Book Club: Verbatim Book Club
Founded: 1974
ISBN Publisher's Prefix: 0-930454

Veritas Foundation Publication Centre, 63 Jeddo Rd, London W12 9EE Tel: (01) 749 4965
Man Dir: W Dluzewski; *Sales:* T Wachowiak
Associate Companies: Figaro Press Ltd, Veritas Foundation Press (both at above address)
Subjects: Poland, Polish Culture, Religion, Education
Bookshop: At above address Tel: (01) 749 4957
Founded: 1948
ISBN Publisher's Prefix: 0-901215

Verso+, 6 Meard St, London W1 Tel: (01) 437 3546
Orders to: International Book Distributors, 66 Wood Lane End, Hemel Hempstead, Hertfordshire HP2 4RG Tel: Hemel Hempstead 58531 (STD code 0442)
Subjects: Philosophy, History, Economics, Aesthetics, Psychology, Sociology, Political Theory, Contemporary Politics, Feminism, Fiction, Literary Criticism
1987: approx 25 titles
ISBN Publisher's Prefixes: 0-902308, 0-86091

Viking, 27 Wright's Lane, London W8 5TZ Tel: (01) 938 2200 Telex: 917181 Fax: (01) 937 8704
Chief Executive: Peter Mayer; *Editorial Dir:* Tony Lacey; *Sales Dir:* Nigel Sisson; *Production:* Joy Harrison; *Marketing Dir:* Clare Harington; *Rights & Permissions:* Carol Heaton
Orders to: Penguin Books, Bath Rd, Harmondsworth, Middlesex UB7 0DA Tel: (01) 759 1984
Parent Company: Penguin Books Ltd (qv)

UNITED KINGDOM 475

Imprint: Allen Lane The Penguin Press
Subjects: Fiction, General Non-fiction, Biography, Travel, Cookery, History, Art, Social Science
Founded: 1969
Miscellaneous: Formerly Allen Lane
ISBN Publisher's Prefix: 0-670

Viking Kestrel, 27 Wright's Lane, London W8 5TZ Tel: (01) 938 2200 Telex: 917181 Fax: (01) 937 8704
Chief Executive: Peter Mayer; *Sales Dir:* Nigel Sisson; *Chief Editor:* Elizabeth Attenborough; *Production:* Joy Harrison; *Marketing:* Julie Bushell; *Rights & Permissions:* Susan Elliott
Orders to: Penguin Books, Bath Rd, Harmondsworth, Middlesex UB7 0DA Tel: (01) 759 1984
Parent Company: Penguin Books Ltd (qv)
Subjects: Children's
Founded: 1969
ISBN Publisher's Prefix: 0-670

Virago Press Ltd+, Centro House, 20-23 Mandela St, London NW1 0HQ Tel: (01) 383 5150 Cable Add: Caterwaul London NW1 Telex: 299080
Chairman: Carmen Callil; *Joint Man Dirs:* Ursula Owen, Harriet Spicer; *Deputy Man Dir:* Ms Lennie Goodings; *Dirs:* Alexandra Pringle, Ruth Petrie; *Rights & Permissions:* Gil McNeil
Orders to: CVBC Services Ltd, 9 Bow St, London WC2E 7AL Tel: (01) 379 6637
Subjects: Fiction, Biography, History, Philosophy, Education, Politics, Social Science & History, Women's Studies, Education, Health, Reference, Feminist Books, Illustrated Large-format Paperbacks
1986: 82 titles *Founded:* 1976
ISBN Publisher's Prefix: 0-86068

Virgin, an imprint of W H Allen & Co PLC (qv)

Virtue & Co Ltd, 25 Breakfield, Coulsdon, Surrey CR3 2UE Tel: (01) 668 4632 Cable Add: Virtutis Croydon Telex: 261507 ref 3393
Man Dir: Michael Virtue; *Sales Dir:* R S Cook; *Publicity Manager:* Mike Baggallay
Branch Offs: London, Dublin
Subjects: Hotel and Catering, Reference, Religion, Educational Materials
Founded: 1819
ISBN Publisher's Prefix: 0-900778

Vision Press Ltd, Fulham Wharf, Townmead Rd, London SW6 2SB Tel: (01) 938 2929 Telex: 914052 Tclond G
Man Dir: Alan Moore
Imprint: Artemis Press
Subjects: Belles Lettres, Music, Art, Educational
Founded: 1947
ISBN Publisher's Prefix: 0-85478

Voltaire Foundation, Taylor Institution, St Giles, Oxford OX1 3NA Tel: Oxford 270250 (STD code 0865) Telex: 83147 Voltaire
Executive Dir: Andrew Brown
Subjects: Modern Languages, History, Philosophy
1985: 16 titles *Founded:* 1971
ISBN Publisher's Prefix: 0-7294

Volturna Press*, 52 Ormonde Rd, Hythe, Kent CT21 6DW Tel: Hythe (Kent) 69465 (STD code 0303)
Proprietor: Dr D M C MacEwan
Imprints: Cochuideachd Leabhreachean Gàidhlig, Marsland Press, Uni Books
Subjects: Religion, Conservation, Biographies, Family Memoirs, Academic; Books in minor languages
1985: 4 titles *Founded:* 1968
ISBN Publisher's Prefix: 0-85606

W I Books Ltd+, 39 Eccleston St, London SW1W 9NT Tel: (01) 730 5162
General Manager: Hilary Wharton
Parent Company: National Federation of Women's Institutes (at above address)
Subjects: Crafts, Home Economics, Cookery, Women's Interests
1985: 19 titles *1986:* 27 titles *Founded:* 1979
ISBN Publisher's Prefix: 0-947990

Wadsworth International Group+, Molly Millars Lane, Wokingham, Berkshire RG11 2PY Tel: Wokingham 789456 (STD code 0734) Telex: 848268 Vnruk G
Man Dir: Paul Gardner; *Marketing Dir:* Peter McKay
Parent Company: International Thomson Organisation Ltd, 20 Queen St West, Box 45, Suite 2206, Toronto, Ontario M5H 3R3, Canada
Associate Company: Van Nostrand Reinhold (UK) Co Ltd (qv)
Head Off: 10 Davis Drive, Belmont, CA 94002, USA Telex: 348383
Subjects: University & College Textbooks, Science, Technology, Professional, Psychology
ISBN Publisher's Prefix: 0-534

John **Waite** Ltd+, Tower House, Ivychurch, Romney Marsh, Kent TN29 0AX Tel: Ivychurch 283 (STD code 067 94) Telex: 896671 Airwav G
Man Dir: John Waite
Orders to: Mercury, 70-72 High St, Malmesbury, Wiltshire Tel: Malmesbury 4332 (STD code 066 62)
Subjects: General Non-fiction
1985: 2 titles *Founded:* 1983
ISBN Publisher's Prefix: 0-946714

Wales Tourist Board*, Sales and Distribution Centre, Davis St, Cardiff CF1 2FU Tel: Cardiff 487387 (STD code 0222) Telex: 497269
Sales & Distribution Manager: Rhys Jones
Subjects: Maps, History, Holiday Accommodation & Travel Guides, Guides & Posters
ISBN Publisher's Prefixes: 0-900784, 1-85013

Walker Books Ltd+, Walker House, 87 Vauxhall Walk, London SE11 5DJ Tel: (01) 387 2000 Telex: 8955572 Fax: (01) 387 4221
Chairman: Sebastian Walker; *Man Dir:* David Ford; *Editorial:* Wendy Boase, David Lloyd; *Production:* Judy Burdsall; *Publicity:* Alan Durant, Patsy Merrick; *Sales (UK):* Claire Lister; *Foreign Rights:* Christine De Poortere; *Export:* Sarah Foster; *Special Markets:* Martina Calefice
Division: Julia MacRae Books (qv)
Imprint: Zebra Books
Subjects: Children's
1985: 130 titles *1986:* 134 titles *Founded:* 1978
ISBN Publisher's Prefix: 0-7445

Walsingham, an imprint of Jarrold Colour Publications (qv)

The **Warburg** Institute (University of London), Woburn Sq, London WC1H 0AB Tel: (01) 580 9663
Secretary: Anita Pollard
Subject: Cultural History
1985: 2 titles *1986:* 4 titles *Founded:* (The Institute) 1921
Miscellaneous: The Institute is a non-commercial organization
ISBN Publisher's Prefix: 0-85481

Ward Lock Educational Co Ltd, 47 Marylebone Lane, London W1M 6AX Tel: (01) 486 3271 Telex: 266231
Chief Operating Officer, Man Dir: Stanley B Malcolm; *Sales, Marketing Dir:* Paul M Thompson; *Production:* Peter Ansell; *Publicity:* Caroline Frost; *Rights & Permissions:* Katie Fowler-Tutt
Parent Company: Ling Kee (UK) Ltd (qv for other group members)
Subjects: Primary, Middle & Secondary Educational, Teaching Manuals
1986: 15 titles
ISBN Publisher's Prefix: 0-7062

Ward Lock Ltd+, 8 Clifford St, London W1X 1RB Tel: (01) 439 3100 Telex: 262364 Warlok G Fax: (01) 439 1582
Warehouse: Ward Lock Ltd (Distribution), PO Box 111, Great Ducie St, Manchester M60 3BL Tel: (061) 834 3110
Chairman, Man Dir: R A Wood; *Publishing Dir:* David Holmes; *Publicity:* Charlotte Wollocombe; *Production:* Fiona McIntosh; *Rights & Co-editions:* Janet Slingsby
Parent Company: Egmont Ltd, 61 Great Ducie St, Manchester M60 3BL. Egmont Ltd is a subsidiary of the Gutenberghus Group, Copenhagen, Denmark
Imprints: Concorde Paperbacks, Horseman's Handbooks
Subjects: Cookery, Gardening, Equestrian, Sailing, Crafts, Yoga, Sports, Hobbies, Pets, Specialist Colour Illustrated International Co-editions, How-to, Children's Information Books, Paperbacks, Reference, Guide Books, Antiques, Collectables, Humour
1986: 70 titles *1987:* 100 titles *Founded:* 1854
ISBN Publisher's Prefix: 0-7063

Frederick **Warne** & Co Ltd+, Penguin Books Ltd, 27 Wright's Lane, London W8 5TZ Tel: (01) 938 2200 Telex: 917181 Fax: (01) 937 8704
Chief Executive: Peter Mayer; *Marketing:* Barry Cunningham; *Production:* Jonathan Yglesias; *Publishing Programme:* Sally Floyer; *Sales:* Nigel Sisson; *Rights:* Susan Elliott
Orders to: Penguin Books Ltd, Bath Rd, Harmondsworth, West Drayton, Middlesex UB7 0DA Tel: (01) 759 1984 Cable Add: Penguinook West Drayton Telex: 263130
Parent Company: Penguin Books Ltd (qv)
Associate Company: Frederick Warne & Co Inc, 40 West 23rd St, New York, NY 10010, USA
Imprint: Warne Gerrard
Subjects: Reference, Juveniles, Natural History, Recreation, Outdoor Activities
1985: 33 titles *Founded:* 1865
ISBN Publisher's Prefix: 0-7232

Waterlow Publishers Ltd, Athene House, 66-73 Shoe Lane, London EC4P 4AB Tel: (01) 377 4838 Fax: (01) 353 1400
Man Dir: K Maxwell
Parent Company: Pergamon Press (qv)
Subjects: Legal, General Business
ISBN Publisher's Prefix: 0-900791

Franklin **Watts** Ltd, 12a Golden Sq, London W1R 4BA Tel: (01) 437 0713 Cable Add: Frawatts London W1 Telex: 262655 Groluk G Fax: (01) 439 1440
Man Dir: David Howgrave-Graham; *Editorial Dir:* Chester Fisher; *Production Dir:* Rita Ireland; *Promotion Manager:* Linda Banner; *Rights & Permissions:* Elizabeth Hamilton
Parent Company: The House of Grolier Ltd, 387 Park Ave South, New York, NY 10016, USA
Subsidiary Company: Franklin Watts Australia, Australia (qv)
Associate Company: Orchard Books (qv)
Subjects: Reference, Non-fiction, Juveniles
Founded: 1969
ISBN Publisher's Prefixes: 0-85166, 0-531, 0-86313

Wayland (Publishers) Ltd+, 61 Western Rd, Hove, East Sussex BN3 1JD Tel: Brighton 722561 (STD code 0273) Cable Add: Bookwright Hove Telex: 878170
Man Dir: John Lewis; *Editorial Dir:* Paul Humphrey; *Production Dir:* Keith Lilley; *Sales Dir:* Peter Hyem
Warehouse: Bailey Distribution Ltd, Warner House, Bowles Well Gardens, Folkestone, Kent CT19 6PH
Subsidiary Companies: Priory Press Ltd, Sovereign Books Ltd
Subjects: Illustrated School Library Books, Biography, Geography, History, Natural History, Science, Arts and Crafts, Transport, Careers, Social Studies
Founded: 1969
Miscellaneous: Firm is a member of Wolters Kluwer NV, Netherlands (qv for associate companies)
ISBN Publisher's Prefixes: 0-85340, 1-85210 (both Wayland), 0-85078 (Wayland/Priory Press)

The **Wayzgoose** Press, now Aquila/The Wayzgoose Press, an imprint of Aquila Publishing (UK) Ltd (qv)

Webb & Bower (Publishers) Ltd+, 9 Colleton Crescent, Exeter, Devon EX2 4BY Tel: 35362 (STD code 0392) Cable Add: Webbower Exeter Telex: 42544 Webbow G Fax: (0392) 211652
Man Dir: Richard Webb; *Editorial Dir:* Delian Bower
Orders to: TBL Bookservice Ltd, 17-23 Nelson Way, Tuscan Trading Estate, Camberley, Surrey
Subjects: General Non-fiction, Illustrated Books
1986: 26 titles *Founded:* 1975
ISBN Publisher's Prefix: 0-86350

Adrian **Webster** Ltd+, 18 Meredyth Rd, London SW13 0DY Tel: (01) 878 6197 Telex: 268141 Metmak G
Man Dir, Sales, Rights & Permissions: Adrian Webster; *Editorial Dir:* Susannah Webster
Associate Companies: The Organiser Co Ltd; Webster's Business Traveller's Guides Ltd, Webster's Wine Price Guide Ltd (both at 5 Praed St, London W2 1NJ)
Subjects: Wine, Travel, Business, Consumer Reference
1987: 14 titles *Founded:* 1983

Webster's Business Traveller's Guides Ltd, an associate company of Adrian Webster Ltd (qv)

Webster's Wine Price Guide Ltd, an associate company of Adrian Webster Ltd (qv)

A **Weekes**, an imprint of Stainer & Bell Ltd (qv)

Weidenfeld & Nicolson, an imprint of Weidenfeld (Publishers) Ltd (qv)

Weidenfeld (Publishers) Ltd, 91 Clapham High St, London SW4 7TA Tel: (01) 622 9933 Cable Add: Nicobar London SW4 7TA Telex: 918066 Fax: (01) 627 3361
Chairman, Chief Executive: Lord Weidenfeld; *Deputy Chairman:* Mark Collins; *Production Dir:* Richard Hussey; *Sales Dir:* Ted Collins; *Publicity Dir:* Rose Scott; *Rights & Permissions Dir:* Bud MacLennan
Subsidiary Companies: Arthur Barker Ltd (qv); J M Dent & Sons Ltd (qv)
Imprints include: Weidenfeld & Nicolson, World University Library
Subjects: General Fiction, Belles Lettres, Poetry, Biography, History, Music, Art,

Philosophy, Reference, Religion, High-priced Paperbacks, Psychology, General & Social Science, University Textbooks
ISBN Publisher's Prefix: 0-297

Westbury House, an imprint of Butterworth & Co (Publishers) Ltd (qv)

A **Wheaton** & Co Ltd, see Arnold-Wheaton

Wheaton Publishers Ltd, see Maxwell Communication Corporation plc

Wheatsheaf Books Ltd, 16 Ship St, Brighton BN1 1AD East Sussex Tel: Brighton 723031 (STD code 0273) Cable Add: Harvester Brighton Telex: 877101 Olship
Editorial Dir: John Spears; *Sales Manager:* Jean Greetham; *Production:* Beth Humphries; *Publicity:* Monique Parris; *Rights & Permissions:* Valerie Evans
Parent Company: The Harvester Press Ltd (qv)
Subjects: Economics, Politics, International Relations, The Human Sciences, Social Sciences, Women's Studies, History
ISBN Publisher's Prefix: 0-7450

J **Whitaker** & Sons Ltd, 12 Dyott St, London WC1A 1DF Tel: (01) 836 8911 Cable Add: Whitmanack London WC1 Fax: (01) 836 2909
Chairman: David Whitaker; *Man Dir:* Sally Whitaker
Subsidiary Companies: The Standard Book Numbering Agency Ltd; Whitaker's Book Listing Services Ltd (both at 12 Dyott St, London)
Subjects: Reference, Bibliography
Founded: 1841
ISBN Publisher's Prefixes: 0-85021 (Whitaker), 0-949999 (Standard Book Numbering Agency)

White Horse Books, an imprint of Jarrold Colour Publications (qv)

White Horse Library, an imprint of Venton Educational Ltd (qv)

White Tree Books, an imprint of Redcliffe Press Ltd (qv)

Whittet Books Ltd, 18 Anley Rd, London W14 0BY Tel: (01) 603 1139 Telex: 826542 G (Whit)
Chief Executive: Annabel Whittet
Parent Company: A Whittet & Co Ltd, The Oil Mills, Weybridge, Surrey KT13 8LD
Subjects: Non-fiction, History, Illustrated, Natural History, Architecture, Countryside
Founded: 1976
ISBN Publisher's Prefix: 0-905483

Wigmore House Publishing, an imprint of Settle Press (qv)

Wildwood House Ltd+, Gower House, Croft Rd, Aldershot, Hampshire GU11 3HR Tel: Aldershot 331551 (STD code 0252) Telex: 858001 Gower G
For personnel see Gower Publishing Co Ltd
Parent Company: Gower Publishing Co Ltd (qv)
Subjects: Non-fiction trade paperbacks & hardbacks, Business & Management, Professional & Campus Paperbacks
Founded: 1973
ISBN Publisher's Prefix: 0-7045

John **Wiley** & Sons Ltd+, Baffins Lane, Chichester, West Sussex PO19 1UD Tel: Chichester 779777 (STD code 0243) Cable Add: Wilebook Chichester Telex: 86290 Wibook G Fax: (0243) 775878
Warehouse: John Wiley & Sons Ltd, Distribution Centre, Southern Cross Trading Estate, Shripney Rd, Bognor Regis, West Sussex PO22 9SA Tel: Bognor Regis 829121 (STD code 0243) Telex: 86111 Wileys G Fax: (0243) 820250
Man Dir: M B Foyle; *Editorial Dir:* Dr John Jarvis; *Publishers:* Ian MacIntosh (Mathematics, Engineering), Dr Ernest Kirkwood (Molecular Sciences), Rosemary Altoft (Computing Science); *Marketing Dir:* J Wilde; *Sales:* S Usansky (UK), R Long (Export); *Production Dir:* Mark Bide; *Publicity:* J D E Lea
Parent Company: John Wiley & Sons Inc, 605 Third Ave, New York, NY 10158, USA
Associate Companies: Jacaranda Wiley Ltd, Australia (qv); John Wiley & Sons Canada Ltd, Canada; Wiley Eastern Ltd, India (qv); John Wiley & Sons (SEA) Pte Ltd, Singapore; Wiley Heyden, UK; Wilson Learning Corporation, USA
Subjects: Chemistry, Physics, Life Sciences, Earth & Environmental Sciences, Mathematics, Statistics, Medicine, Psychology, Engineering, Social Sciences, Business Management Science, Computer Science, Reference, University Textbooks, Educational Material
ISBN Publisher's Prefixes: 0-471 (Wiley), 0-470 (Halsted)

Wilfion Books Publishers+*, 4 Townhead Terrace, Paisley, Renfrewshire PA1 2AX Tel: (041) 889 0950
Dirs: Konrad Hopkins, Ronald van Roekel
Subjects: Poetry, Psychic/Spiritual Phenomena, Translations, Fiction, Biography
1985: 30 titles *1986:* 34 titles *Founded:* 1975

Joseph **Williams**, an imprint of Stainer & Bell Ltd (qv)

Willow, see Collins Willow

Philip **Wilson** Publishers Ltd, 26 Litchfield St, London WC2H 9NJ Tel: (01) 379 7886 Telex: 22158 Filwil
Man Dir: Philip Wilson; *Editorial Dir:* Anne Jackson; *Sales, Publicity Dir:* Juliana Powney; *Production Dir:* Mary Osborne
Subsidiary Company: A Zwemmer Ltd (qv)
Imprints: Scala/Philip Wilson, Sotheby's Publications
Subjects: Art, Antiques, Reference
Founded: 1975
ISBN Publisher's Prefix: 0-85667

Winchmore Publishing Services Ltd*, 40 Triton Sq, London NW1 3HG
Chief Executive: Derek Avery; *Editorial:* Margaret Fagan; *Production:* Brian Rooney
Subsidiary Company: WPS Repro Ltd (at above address)
Associate Company: The Connoisseur Press, Princes Bldg, 22nd Floor, Hong Kong
Subjects: Transport, Military, Sport, Cookery, Gardening, The Arts
Founded: 1967
ISBN Publisher's Prefix: 0-907025

Windrush Large Print Children's Books, 55 St Thomas' St, Oxford OX1 1JG Tel: Oxford 250333 (STD code 0865) Telex: 83130
Man Dir: John Durrant; *Marketing Dir:* Lyndsay Williams; *Sales Development Manager:* Jill Fieldgate; *Editorial Dir:* Tony Sloggett; *Promotions Manager:* Chas Walton
Parent Company: Clio Press Ltd (qv)
Associate Company: ISIS Large Print Books, 2040 Alameda Padre Serra, PO Box 4397, Santa Barbara, CA 93140-4397, USA
Subjects: Fiction, Non-fiction

1986: 12 titles *Founded:* 1986
ISBN Publisher's Prefix: 1-85089

Windsor Large Print, an imprint of Chivers Press Publishers (qv)

Wisdom Publications, 23 Dering St, London W1R 9AA Tel: (01) 499 0925 Telex: 8951859 Basil G Fax: (01) 409 2582
Editorial, Production: Robina Courtin; *Publicity, Sales, Rights & Permissions:* Dr Nicholas Ribush
Subjects: Buddhism, Tibetan Culture, East-West themes
1986: 6 titles *1987:* 20 titles *Founded:* 1976
ISBN Publisher's Prefix: 0-86171

Witherby & Co Ltd, 32 Aylesbury St, London EC1R 0ET Tel: (01) 251 5341
Man Dir: Alan Witherby
Subjects: Insurance & Banking, Oil & Shipping
ISBN Publisher's Prefix: 0-900886

H F & G **Witherby Ltd**, 14 Henrietta St, Covent Garden, London WC2E 8QJ Tel: (01) 836 2006 Fax: (01) 379 0934
Chairman: Antony Witherby; *Man Dir:* David Burnett
Parent Company: Gollancz Holdings Ltd (at above address)
Subjects: Sport, Biography, History, How-to, Secondary & University Textbooks, Reference, Natural Science
ISBN Publisher's Prefix: 0-85493

The **Woburn** Press, Gainsborough House, 11 Gainsborough Rd, Leytonstone, London E11 1RS Tel: (01) 530 4226 Cable Add: Simfay London Telex: 897719
Warehouse: Harper & Row Distributors Ltd, Estover Rd, Estover, Plymouth PL6 7PZ Tel: Plymouth 705251 (STD code 0752)
Man Dir: Frank Cass; *Editorial:* Margaret Goodare; *Trade:* Richard Norris; *Production:* John Smith; *Publicity:* Elizabeth Lye
Associate Companies: Frank Cass & Co Ltd (qv); Vallentine, Mitchell & Co Ltd (qv)
Subjects: Educational Studies
Founded: 1969
ISBN Publisher's Prefix: 0-7130

Wolfe Medical Publications Ltd, Brook House, 2-16 Torrington Pl, London WC1E 7LT Tel: (01) 636 4622 Cable Add: Wolfebooks London WC1 Telex: 8814230 Wmpltd G Fax: (01) 637 3021
Man Dir: Michael Manson; *Deputy Man Dir:* Peter Heilbrunn; *Editorial Dir:* Patrick Daly; *Sales Manager:* Derrick Holman; *Export Manager:* Jim Osergby; *Production Dir:* Colin MacPherson; *Publicity:* Paul Chrystal; *Rights & Permissions:* Pauline Manton
Parent Company: Year Book Medical Publishers Inc, 35 East Wacker Dr, Chicago, IL 60601, USA
Subjects: Medical, Dental, Veterinary, Scientific
1985: 30 titles *1986:* 60 titles *Founded:* 1969
ISBN Publisher's Prefix: 0-7234

Wolfe Publishing Ltd, see Wolfe Medical Publications Ltd

Oswald **Wolff** Books, an imprint of Berg Publishers Ltd (qv)

The **Women's** Press Ltd+, 34 Great Sutton St, London EC1V 0DX Tel: (01) 251 3007 Telex: 919034 Fax: (01) 439 6489
Man Dir, Editorial: Ros de Lanerolle; *Rights & Permissions:* Mary Leaming; *Design:* Suzanne Perkins; *Publicity:* Katy Nicholson; *Sales:* Mary Hemming

Orders to: Harper & Row Distributors Ltd, Estover Rd, Estover, Plymouth PL6 7PZ Tel: Plymouth 705251 (STD code 0752)
Imprint: Livewire
Subjects: Fiction, Literature and Criticism, Art History, Politics, Physical and Mental Health (all women writers)
Book Club: The Women's Press Book Club
1985-86: 50 titles *Founded:* 1977
Miscellaneous: Firm is a member of the Namara Group, 45 Poland St, London W1V 4AU
ISBN Publisher's Prefix: 0-7043

Woodhead-Faulkner (Publishers) Ltd+, Fitzwilliam House, 32 Trumpington St, Cambridge CB2 1QY Tel: Cambridge 66733 (STD code 0223) Cable Add: Woodfaulk Cambridge Telex: 818454 Wfpubl
Man Dir: Martin J Woodhead; *Publisher, Martin Books:* Stephen G York; *Sales:* Martin Redfern; *Publicity:* Mary-Lou Nash
Parent Company: Simon & Schuster International Group, 66 Wood Lane End, Hemel Hempstead, Hertfordshire HP2 4RG
Subsidiary Companies: Fitzwilliam Publishing (qv), ICSA Publishing Ltd
Imprint: Martin Books
Subjects: Business Investment and Finance, Social Welfare and Rehabilitation, Careers, Popular Non-fiction
Founded: 1972
ISBN Publisher's Prefixes: 0-85941 (Woodhead-Faulkner, Martin Books), 0-902197 (ICSA)

World Book — Childcraft International*, World Book House, 77 Mount Ephraim, Tunbridge Wells, Kent TN4 8AZ Tel: Tunbridge Wells 47811 (STD code 0892) Telex: 957324 Wbccbi G
Man Dir: J R Threlfall; *Marketing Dir:* J Lowe
Parent Company: World Book Inc, Merchandise Mart Plaza, Chicago, IL, USA
Subjects: Primary & Secondary Education, English Dictionaries, Reference Books, Juveniles, Encyclopaedias
1986: 7 titles
ISBN Publisher's Prefix: 0-7166

World International Publishing Ltd+*, PO Box 111, Manchester M60 3BL (Located at: Great Ducie St, Manchester M60 3BL) Tel: (061) 834 3110 Cable Add: World Manchester Telex: 668609 Fax: (061) 834 0059
Man Dir: Robin Wood; *Editorial, Licensing:* Mae Broadley; *Marketing Dir:* Don Smith; *Production Dir, Foreign Rights:* David Sheldrake
Parent Company: Egmont Ltd, 61 Great Ducie St, Manchester M60 3BL. Egmont Ltd is a subsidiary of the Gutenberghus Group, Copenhagen, Denmark
Imprints: Cliveden Press, Egmont, World, London Editions, Remus Products
Subjects: Children's Books and Annuals
1985: 437 titles
ISBN Publisher's Prefix: 0-7235

World Microfilms Publications Ltd, 62 Queen's Grove, London NW8 6ER Tel: (01) 586 3092 Cable Add: Microworld
Man Dir: Stephen Albert
Associate Companies: Lecon Arts, Pidgeon Audio Visual, Sussex Tapes Exports, Sussex Video Ltd, Transglobe Slides (all at above address)
Subjects: Research Collections in Microform, Periodical Reprints in Microform, Slide series, Audiovisual
1986: 50 titles *Founded:* 1969

World of Information, 21 Gold St, Saffron Walden, Essex CB10 1EJ Tel: Saffron Walden 21150 (STD code 0799) Cable Add: Jaxpress Cambridge Telex: 817197 Jaxprs G
Publisher: Anthony Axon; *Sales, Publicity:* Michael G Morris
Parent Company: Middle East Review Co Ltd (at above address)
Subjects: Commerce, Economics, Politics, Development
Founded: 1972
ISBN Publisher's Prefix: 0-904439

World of Islam Festival Trust, 33 Thurloc Pl, London SW7 2HQ Tel: (01) 581 3522 Cable Add: Islamtrust London SW7
Dir: Alistair Duncan
Orders to: Scorpion Publishing Ltd, Victoria House, Victoria Rd, Buckhurst Hill, Essex IG9 5ES Telex: 896988 Scoops G
Subjects: Islamic Art, Culture and Civilization
Founded: 1974
ISBN Publisher's Prefix: 0-905035

World University Library, an imprint of Weidenfeld & Nicolson Ltd (qv)

Worldwide, an imprint of Mills & Boon Ltd (qv)

John **Wright**, an imprint of Butterworth & Co (Publishers) Ltd (qv)

Gordon **Wright Publishing** Ltd, 25 Mayfield Rd, Edinburgh EH9 2NQ Tel: (031) 667 1300
Man Dir: Gordon Wright
Subjects: General, Scottish Literature, Non-fiction and Fiction
Founded: 1969
ISBN Publisher's Prefix: 0-903065

Xanadu Publications Ltd+, 5 Uplands Rd, London N8 9NN Tel: (01) 340 8172 Telex: 923753 ref 0365
Publisher: Richard Glyn Jones; *Sales Manager:* John Masters; *Editorial:* Simon Pettifar; *Production Manager:* Elizabeth Gilhooly; *Publicity Manager:* Lynn Kirwen; *Rights & Permissions:* Carol E Hollins
Orders to: Biblios Publishers' Distribution Services Ltd, Glenside Industrial Estate, Star Rd, Partridge Green, Horsham, West Sussex RH13 8LD Tel: Partridge Green 710971 (STD code 0403)
Imprints include: Strange but True
Subjects: General, Travel, Food & Wine, Health & Fitness, Autobiography, Graphics, Science Fiction, Crime & Mystery
1986: 16 titles *Founded:* 1984
ISBN Publisher's Prefix: 0-947761

Yale University Press London+, 13 Bedford Sq, London WC1B 3JF Tel: (01) 580 2693 Cable Add: Yalepress London WC1 Telex: 896075 Yupldn G Fax: (01) 631 3913
Man Dir: John Nicoll; *Head of Marketing:* Henry Fryer; *Publicity:* Ann Geneva; *Rights:* Alison Evans
Orders to: International Book Distributors Ltd, 66 Wood Lane End, Hemel Hempstead, Hertfordshire HP2 4RG Tel: Hemel Hempstead 58531 (STD code 0442) Telex: 82445 Fax: (0442) 212485
Subjects: Scholarly Books, Art
1985-86: 180 titles
Miscellaneous: Firm is the British office of Yale University Press, 302 Temple St, New Haven, CT 06511, USA
ISBN Publisher's Prefix: 0-300

York Notes, jointly published by Longman/York Press

Young Corgi, an imprint of Transworld Publishers (Corgi & Bantam Books) Ltd (qv)

Young Library+*, International Press Centre, 76 Shoe Lane, London EC4A 3JB Tel: (01) 353 0186 Telex: 23862
Chief Executive, Editorial, Sales, Publicity, Rights & Permissions: Roger Cleeve; *Production:* James Collins
Branch Off: 45 Norfolk Sq, Brighton BN1 2PE
Subjects: Children's Schools Library, Non-fiction, Nature, World History, European Social Studies, World Resources, Multi-Cultural
1985: 21 titles *Founded:* 1982
ISBN Publisher's Prefix: 0-946003

Zebra Books, an imprint of Walker Books Ltd (qv)

Zed Books Ltd+*, 57 Caledonian Rd, London N1 9BU Tel: (01) 837 4014 Telex: 912881 Zed
Sales: Farouk Sohawon; *Rights & Permissions:* Paul Westlake; *Editorial Dir:* Robert Molteno; *Publicity:* David Hamilton (Tel: (01) 837 8466)
Branch Off: Biblio Inc, 81 Adams Drive, Totowa, NJ 07512, USA
Subjects: Third World Social Science, Africa, Middle East, Asia, Latin America, Imperialism, Labour, Human Rights, Health, Women's Studies
1985: 50 titles *Founded:* 1976
ISBN Publisher's Prefixes: 0-905762, 0-86232

Hans **Zell**, an imprint of Bowker-Saur Ltd (qv)

Hans **Zell Publishers**, PO Box 56, 52 St Giles, Oxford OX1 3EL Tel: Oxford 511428 (STD code 0865)
The above is the editorial office. For orders and other offices see Bowker-Saur Ltd

Zeno Booksellers & Publishers, 6 Denmark St, London WC2H 8LP Tel: (01) 836 2522
Man Dir: M P Zographos
Subjects: Belles Lettres, Poetry, History, Art, Travel
Bookshop: 6 Denmark St, London WC2H 8LP (specializing in Greek books, Greece, The Balkans, Middle East, Antiquarian and Modern)
Founded: 1944
ISBN Publisher's Prefixes: 0-900834, 0-7228

Zomba Books+, Zomba House, 165/67 High Rd, London NW10 2SG Tel: (01) 459 8899 Telex: 919884 Zomba Fax: (01) 451 3900
General Manager: Dede Millar
Orders to: Biblios, Glenside Industrial Estate, Partridge Green, Horsham, West Sussex RH13 8LD Tel: Horsham 710971 (STD code 0403)
Parent Company: Marlowlynn Ltd (at above main address)
Branch Off: Zomba House, 1348 Lexington Ave, New York, NY 10028, USA
Subjects: Music, Film, Leisure, Entertainment
1986: 10 titles *Founded:* 1982
ISBN Publisher's Prefix: 0-946391

Zwan Publishing Ltd, 11-21 Northdown St, London N1 9BN Tel: (01) 837 3322 Telex: 265628 Fax: (01) 278 1677
Chief Executive, Production: Roger van Zwanenberg; *Editorial:* A N Beech; *Sales, Rights & Permissions:* Norman Drake; *Publicity:* Shirley Dow
Orders to: Harper & Row Ltd, Estover Rd, Plymouth, Devon PL6 7PZ

Subsidiary Company: Pluto Publishing Ltd (qv)
Associate Company: Oxon Publishing Ltd, Market House, Deddington, Oxfordshire
Subject: Social Science
1987: 10 titles *Founded:* 1987
ISBN Publisher's Prefix: 1-85305

A **Zwemmer** Ltd, 26 Litchfield St, London WC2H 9NJ Tel: (01) 379 7886 Cable Add: Zwemmera Lesquare London WC2H 9NJ Telex: 22158 Filwil
Chairman: Desmond Zwemmer; *Man Dir:* Philip Wilson
Parent Company: Philip Wilson Publishers Ltd (qv)
Subjects: Art, Architecture
Bookshops: Zwemmers Bookshop, 24 Litchfield St, London WC2H 9NJ; Zwemmers, 80 Charing Cross Rd, London WC2; OUP Bookshop, 72 Charing Cross Rd, London WC2H 0BE; Zwemmer/OUP Music Bookshop, 26 Litchfield St, London WC2H 9NJ

Remainder Dealers

Artlines (UK) Ltd, PO Box 5, Berkeley, Gloucestershire GL13 9PZ Tel: Dursley 810874 (STD code 0453) Telex: 444659 Wdstk
Man Dir: T Hailwood
Specialization: Art

Atlas Book Sales Ltd*, 293 Gray's Inn Rd, London WC1 Tel: (01) 837 9601 Telex: 261396 Atlas G
Sales: Ashley Bertram, Sarah Foster

B S C Books Ltd, 18 New Concordia Wharf, Mill St, London SE1 2BB Tel: (01) 237 9009
Sales: Tim Finch
Owners of the Booksmith chain of bookshops. Also publisher (qv)

Bestseller Publications Ltd, Princess House, 50 Eastcastle St, London W1N 7AP Tel: (01) 631 5070 Telex: 22303 Webbs G Fax: (01) 631 5070
Also issue reprints under the imprints of Bracken Books, Lamboll House, The Mystic Press, Studio Editions

Blaketon Hall Ltd*, 7 South St, Exeter, Devon Tel: Exeter 217652 (STD code 0392)
Man Dir: John Shillingford; *Dir:* Patricia A Shillingford
Warehouse: Unit 1, Devon Units, Budlake Rd, Marsh Barton, Devon Tel: Exeter 210602 (STD code 0392)
Also publisher (qv)

Roy **Bloom** Ltd, 81 Goswell Rd, London EC1V 7ER Tel: (01) 251 4345 Telex: 94016372 Royb G Fax: (01) 250 1354
Sales: Paul White

Bookmark Wholesale, Alpha House, Scarne Industrial Estate, Launceston, Cornwall PL15 9HT Tel: Launceston 2709 (STD code 0566)
Man Dir: D E Phillips

Bookmart Bargain Books, WHS Distributors, St John's House, East St, Leicester LE1 6NE Tel: Leicester 551196 (STD code 0533)
A division of W H Smith Distributors

Booksmith Wholesale, 18 New Concordia Wharf, Mill St, London SE1 2BB Tel: (01) 237 9009
Dir: Bill Smith; *General Manager:* Tim Finch

Bridge Book Co Ltd*, Unit 4, Goldsworth Park Trading Estate, Woking, Surrey GU21 3BA Tel: Woking 20505 (STD code 048 62) Cable Add: Pembridge Woking Telex: 21697 Drakho G
Remainder paperback book merchants, importers and exporters in bulk

Celerity Book Service*, Sedgwick Park, Horsham, Sussex RH13 6QH Tel: Horsham 58834 (STD code 0403)
Sales: A B Simmons

The **Economists'** Bookshop Ltd, Clare Market, Portugal St, London WC2A 2AB Tel: (01) 405 5531 Cable Add: Econbook London WC2 Telex: 27950 ref 856

Godfrey Cave Books Ltd, 42 Bloomsbury St, London WC1B 3QJ Tel: (01) 636 9177
Man Dir: John Maxwell; *Dir:* Geoffrey Howard

Harvey Sales, Magna Rd, Wigston, Leicester LE8 2ZH Tel: Leicester 785154 (STD code 0533) Telex: 34694 Chamco G
Sales: Vance Harvey, Bob Siwecki
Operates 10 discount bookshops

Donald **Murray** (Ramboro Books), 64 Pentonville Rd, London N1 9HD Tel: (01) 837 6301 Telex: 946240 Ramb Fax: (01) 833 0801
Also publisher (qv)

Omega Books Ltd*, 1 West St, Ware, Hertfordshire SG12 9AB Tel: Ware 68961 (STD code 0920)
London showroom: 14 Greville St, London WC2

H **Pordes** Ltd*, 529b Finchley Rd, London NW3 7BH Tel: (01) 435 9878/9
Also publisher (qv)

Ramboro Enterprises Ltd, 64 Pentonville Rd, London N1 9HD Tel: (01) 837 6301 Telex: 946240 Ramb Fax: (01) 833 0801
Also publisher (qv)

U K Book Bargains Ltd, now Artlines (UK) Ltd (qv)

W J **Williams** & Son (Books) Ltd, Barton under Needwood, Burton-on-Trent, Staffordshire DE13 8BA Tel: Barton under Needwood 2948 (STD code 028 371) Telex: 338534 Mtsgsb G
Chief Executive: Anthony Williams

Literary Agents

Aitken & Stone Ltd, 29 Fernshaw Rd, London SW10 0TG Tel: (01) 351 7561 Cable Add: Litaribus London Telex: 298391
Dirs: Brian Stone, Gillon Aitken

Jacintha **Alexander** Associates, 47 Emperor's Gate, London SW7 Tel: (01) 373 9258
Representing British authors for fiction and non-fiction

Badcock & Rozycki, 12 Flitcroft St, London WC2H 8DJ Tel: (01) 836 0782/7127 Telex: 923995 Junbar G
Chief Executives: June Badcock, Barbara Rozycki
Literary scouts for international publishers

Michael **Bakewell** & Associates Ltd, see MBA Literary Agents Ltd

Blake Friedmann Literary Agency, 37-41 Gower St, London WC1E 6HH Tel: (01) 631 4331 Telex: 27950 ref 3820 Fax: (01) 323 1274
Contacts: Carole Blake, Julian Friedmann
Specialization: Thrillers, Film and TV Development, Fiction and Non-fiction

David **Bolt** Associates, 12 Heath Dr, Send, Surrey GU23 7EP Tel: Woking 21118 (STD code 048 62)

Carew Hunt Associates*, Gothic Lodge, 6 Woodhayes Rd, London SW19 Tel: (01) 946 6038
Contact: Victoria Carew Hunt
Specialization: Antiques, Crime fiction

Carnell Literary Agency, Danescroft, Goose Lane, Little Hallingbury, Hertfordshire CM22 7RG Tel: Harlow 723626 (STD code 0279)
Contact: Pamela Buckmaster
Specialization: Science Fiction, Fantasy

Colley-Moore Literary Agency, 14 Lyon Sq, Tilehurst, Reading, Berkshire RG3 4DD Tel: Reading 417748 (STD code 0734) Cable Add: Lyon Square Reading
Contact: Steve Colley-Moore
Also: publisher (qv)

Curtis Brown, 162-168 Regent St, London W1R 5TB Tel: (01) 437 9700 Cable Add: Browncurt W1 Telex: 261536
Man Dir: Michael Shaw

John **Farquharson** Ltd, 162-168 Regent St, London W1R 5TB Tel: (01) 437 9700 Cable Add: Jofachad London W1 Telex: 261536 Brnspk
Contacts: Vanessa Holt, Vivienne Schuster, Andrew Lownie
Also: 250 West 57th St, New York, NY 10107, USA Tel: (212) 245 1993 Cable Add: Jofachad New York
Contacts: Jane Gelfman, Deborah Schneider

Raymond **Foster**, 8 Yew Tree Grove, Highley, Bridgnorth, Shropshire WV16 6DG Tel: Highley 861330 (STD code 0746)
Specialization: Gardening, Natural History

Blake **Friedmann** Literary Agency, see Blake

Peter **Galliner** Associates, PO Box 312, London NW8 6DE Tel: (01) 722 5217 Telex: 21792 ref 728
Chairman: Peter Galliner
Represent foreign publishers, scouts; specialists in international co-productions

David **Grossman** Literary Agency Ltd, 110-114 Clerkenwell Rd, London EC1M 5SA Tel: (01) 251 5046 Telex: 263404 Bkbiz G

June **Hall** Literary Agency, 19 College Cross, London N1 Tel: (01) 609 5991 Fax: (01) 607 0682

A M **Heath** & Co Ltd*, 79 St Martin's Lane, London WC2N 4AA Tel: (01) 836 4271 Cable Add: Script London WC2 Telex: 27370
Dirs: Mark Hamilton, Michael Thomas, William Hamilton

David **Higham** Associates Ltd*, 5-8 Lower John St, Golden Sq, London W1R 4HA Tel: (01) 437 7888 Cable Add: Highlit London W1 Telex: 28910 Higham G Ldn
Contacts: Bruce Hunter, Jacqueline Korn, Anthony Goff, John Rush, Elizabeth Cree

Intercontinental Literary Agency, foreign rights company of A D Peters & Co Ltd (qv)

Dieter **Klein** Associates, 1 Newburgh St, London W1V 1LH Tel: (01) 734 0880 Telex: 22861 Metmak G

M B A Literary Agents Ltd*, 45 Fitzroy St, London W1P 5HR Tel: (01) 387 2076, (01) 387 4785
Dirs: Diana Tyler, John Richard Parker

Marlu Literary Agency, 26 Stratford Rd, London W8 Tel: (01) 937 5161/6191 Telex: 268141 Metmak G
Contact: Mary Hall Mayer

Marsh & Sheil Ltd, 43 Doughty St, London WC1N 2LF Tel: (01) 405 7473 Cable Add: Novelist London Telex: 94013093 Mars G
Man Dir: Paul Marsh

The Maggie **Noach** Literary Agency, 21 Redan St, London W14 0AB Tel: (01) 602 2451

Andrew **Nurnberg** Associates Ltd, Clerkenwell House, 45-47 Clerkenwell Green, London EC1R 0HT Tel: (01) 251 0321 Cable Add: Nurnbooks London Telex: 23353 Fax: (01) 251 0584
Specialization: Translation Rights

Peterborough Literary Agency, The Daily Telegraph, 181 Marsh Wall, London E14 9SR Tel: (01) 538 5000 Cable Add: Telenews London Telex: 22874 Telesyndic
Executive Manager: Ewan MacNaughton

A D **Peters** & Co Ltd*, 10 Buckingham St, London WC2N 6BU Tel: (01) 839 2556
Man Dir: Michael Sissons
Foreign Rights Company: Intercontinental Literary Agency (at above address)

Laurence **Pollinger** Ltd, 18 Maddox St, London W1R 0EU Tel: (01) 629 9761 Cable Add: Laupoll London W1
Man Dir: Gerald J Pollinger; *Foreign Rights:* Margaret Pepper

Murray **Pollinger**, 4 Garrick St, London WC2E 9BH Tel: (01) 836 6781 Cable Add: Chopper London
Chief Executive: Murray Pollinger
Specialization: Adult and Children's Fiction, Non-fiction (no unsolicited manuscripts)

Shelley **Power** Literary Agency Ltd/INPRA, PO Box 149a, Surbiton, Surrey KT6 5JH Tel: (01) 398 7723/8723 Telex: 265871 Monref G ref 87SQQ256
Contact: Shelley Power

Deborah **Rogers** Ltd, 20 Powis Mews, London W11 1JN Tel: (01) 221 3717 Cable Add: Debrogers London W11 Telex: 25930 Debrog G
Dirs: Deborah Rogers, Patricia White (USA); *Consultant:* Ann Warnford-Davis

Sheri **Safran** Literary Agency Ltd, 8 Pembridge Studios, 27A Pembridge Villas, London W11 3EP Tel: (01) 221 3355 Telex: 262284 ref 1255 Fax: (01) 229 9651
Contact: Sheri Safran
Specialization: Non-fiction only for, by and about women by American and British authors

Tessa **Sayle**, Literary and Dramatic Agents, 11 Jubilee Pl, London SW3 3TE Tel: (01) 352 4311 Cable Add: Bookishly London

Scott **Ferris** Associates, PO Box 317, 15 Gledhow Gardens, London SW5 0AY Tel: (01) 373 2762 Cable Add: Scoff Telex: 8954958 Sharet G
Partners: Rivers Scott, Gloria Ferris
All subjects except poetry and children's

Anthony **Sheil** Associates Ltd, 43 Doughty St, London WC1N 2LF Tel: (01) 405 9351 Cable Add: Novelist London Telex: 946240 Cweasy G ref 19008175
Man Dir: Anthony Sheil; *Foreign Rights:* see Marsh & Sheil Ltd
Also: Wallace & Sheil Agency Inc, 177 East 70th St, New York, NY 10021, USA Tel: (212) 5709090

Solo Syndication & Literary Agency Ltd, 8 Bouverie St, London EC4 8BB Tel: (01) 583 9372 Telex: 858623
Man Dir: Don Short
Specialization: Celebrity/autobiographies

Peter **Tauber** Press Agency, 94 East End Rd, London N3 2SX Tel: (01) 346 4165 Cable Add: Tauberpres London N3
Dirs: Peter Tauber, Robert Tauber
Specialization: Fiction, Non-fiction

Watson, Little Ltd*, Suite 8, 26 Charing Cross Rd, London WC2H 0DG Tel: (01) 836 5880
Dirs: Sheila Watson, Amanda Little

A P **Watt** Ltd, 20 John St, London WC1N 2DL Tel: (01) 405 6774 Cable Add: Longevity London Telex: 297903 Apwatt G
Contacts: Hilary Rubinstein, Caradoc King, Linda Shaughnessy, Rod Hall

Book Clubs

20th Century Classics, see Book Club Associates

Ancient & Medieval History Book Club, see Book Club Associates

Anglers Book Society, see Readers Union Ltd

Arena, see Readers Union Ltd
Arena is a general book club aimed at the modern woman

Artists Book Club Ltd, Littlegate House, St Ebbe's St, Oxford OX1 1SQ Tel: Oxford 243557 (STD code 0865) Telex: 83308
Owned by: Phaidon Press Ltd (qv)
Founded: 1977

Arts Guild, see Book Club Associates

Aviation Book Club, see Book Club Associates

Bahá'í Book Club, 6 Mount Pleasant, Oakham, Leicester LE15 6HU Tel: Oakham 2780 (STD code 0572) Cable Add: Baha'i Trust Oakham Telex: 342163 Insure G
Owned by: Bahá'í Publishing Trust (qv)

Belief the Religious Book Society, see Readers Union Ltd

Birds and Natural History Book Society, see Readers Union Ltd

Book Club Associates, 87-91 Newman St, London W1P 4EN Tel: (01) 637 0341 Cable Add: Booklub Telex: 24359
Chief Executive: Graham Williams; *General Manager (Editorial):* Bing Taylor; *Editor-in-Chief:* John Roberts
Monthly Book Clubs: Ancient & Medieval History Book Club, Book of the Month Club, Children's Book of the Month Club, History Guild, Literary Guild, Military Book Society, Mystery and Thriller Guild, World Books *Bi-Monthly Book Club:* Home Computer Club
Quarterly Book Clubs: Arts Guild, Aviation Book Club, Cookery Book Club, Cricket Book Club, Encounters, English Book Club (France, Federal Republic of Germany and Netherlands), English Library (Sweden), Executive World, On the Road, The Railway Book Club, Readers Choice, World of Nature
Book Series: 20th Century Classics, Kings & Queens of England, Great English Classics, Good Housekeeping Step-by-Step Cookery
Imprint: Guild Publishing (qv under Publishers)
Owned by: W H Smith & Son Ltd (qv) and Doubleday & Co Inc, USA (parent company Bertelsmann AG, Federal Republic of Germany (qv))

Book of the Month Club, see Book Club Associates

Bookmarx Club, 265 Seven Sisters Rd, Finsbury Park, London N4 2DE Tel: (01) 802 6145
Owned by: IS Books Ltd

Books for Children, Park House, Dollar St, Cirencester, Gloucestershire GL7 2AN Tel: Cirencester 67081 (STD code 0285)

The **Bookworm** Club, 20 Trinity St, Cambridge CB2 3NG Tel: Cambridge 358351 (STD code 0223) exts 249, 253
Owned by: W Heffer & Sons Ltd (at above address)
Subject: Paperbacks for 8 to 13-year-olds (children's club in schools)
See also Early Worm Club

Bridge Book Club, PO Box 77, Feltham, Middlesex TW14 8JF Tel: (01) 898 1234
Members: 3,700
Owned by: Bibliagora (qv)
Founded: 1980

Children's Book of the Month Club, see Book Club Associates

Chip Book Club, Scholastic Publications Ltd, Marlborough House, Holly Walk, Leamington Spa, Warwickshire CV32 4LS Tel: Southam 3910 (STD code 092 681)
Subjects: Books for junior and middle levels
Owned by: Scholastic Publications Ltd (qv)

Cookery Book Club, see Book Club Associates

Country Book Society, see Readers Union Ltd

Craft Book Society, see Readers Union Ltd

Craftsman Book Society, see Readers Union Ltd

Cricket Book Club, see Book Club Associates

Criterion Book Club, Scholastic Publications Ltd, Marlborough House, Holly Walk, Leamington Spa, Warwickshire CV32 4LS Tel: Southam 3910 (STD code 092 681)
Owned by: Scholastic Publications Ltd (qv)
Subjects: Books and resource materials for primary teachers

Early Worm Book Club*, 20 Trinity St, Cambridge CB2 3NG Tel: Cambridge 358351 (STD code 0223) ext 249
Owned by: W Heffer & Sons Ltd (at above address)
Subjects: For children up to 7 years of age
See also The Bookworm Club

Encounters, see Book Club Associates

Equestrian Book Society, see Readers Union Ltd

Executive World, see Book Club Associates

Fieldsports Book Society, see Readers Union Ltd

Fledgling, see Puffin School Book Clubs

Flight, see Puffin School Book Clubs

The **Folio** Society Ltd, 202 Great Suffolk St, London SE1 1PR Tel: (01) 407 7411 Cable Add: Folios Fax: (01) 378 6684
Man Dir: S J Gauron; *Sales, Publicity, Advertising, Rights & Permissions:*

S Bradbury
Subsidiary Companies: Folio Press, Folio Fine Editions (both UK); Folio Books Ltd New York, 198 Ave of the Americas, New York, NY 10013, USA
Subjects: General Fiction, Belles Lettres, Poetry, Biography, History
Bookshop: Folio Gallery, 5 Royal Arcade, 28 Old Bond St, London W1
Founded: 1947

French Book Club, Warner House, Folkestone, Kent CT19 6PH
Owned by: Bailey Bros & Swinfen Ltd (qv)

Gardeners Book Society, see Readers Union Ltd

The **Gay** Bookclub, PO Box 247, London N15 6RW Tel: (01) 800 5861
Owned by: G M P Publishers (qv)

German Book Club, Warner House, Folkestone, Kent CT19 6PH
Owned by: Bailey Bros & Swinfen Ltd (qv)

Good Housekeeping Step-by-Step Cookery, see Book Club Associates

Great English Classics, see Book Club Associates

Greyfriars Book Club, 27A Arterberry Rd, London SW20
Owned by: Howard Baker Press Ltd (qv)

History Guild, see Book Club Associates

Home Computer Club, see Book Club Associates

I-Spy Club, 3 Glenside Estate, Star Rd, Partridge Green, Horsham, Sussex RH13 8RA Tel: Partridge Green 710392 (STD code 0403)
Owned by: Ravette Ltd (qv)

Italian Book Club, Warner House, Folkestone, Kent CT19 6PH
Owned by: Bailey Bros & Swinfen Ltd (qv)

Jewish Interest Book Club*, PO Box 105, London NW11 0EW

Kings & Queens of England, see Book Club Associates

The **Leisure Circle** Ltd*, York House, Empire Way, Wembley, Middlesex HA9 0PF Tel: (01) 902 8888
Telex: 8951315
Man Dir: G Janetzky; *Marketing Dir:* C Kirby; *Publishing:* C Goulden (Fiction & Children's), Angus McGeeogh (Non-fiction); *Sales:* M Holloway; *Member Service:* L Grothues
Owned by: Bertelsmann AG (Federal Republic of Germany) (qv)
Subjects: General Fiction, Non-fiction, Biography, History, Children's Books

Literary Guild, see Book Club Associates

Lucky Book Club, Scholastic Publications Ltd, Marlborough House, Holly Walk, Leamington Spa, Warwickshire CV32 4LS Tel: Southam 3910 (STD code 092 681)
Subjects: Books for infants and juniors
Owned by: Scholastic Publications Ltd (qv)

Maritime Book Society, see Readers Union

Military Book Society, see Book Club Associates

Music Book Society, see Readers Union Ltd

Mystery and Thriller Guild, see Book Club Associates

Nationwide Book Service, see Readers Union Ltd

Needlecraft Book Society, see Readers Union Ltd

On the Road, see Book Club Associates

Phoenix Book Society, see Readers Union Ltd

Photographic Book Society, see Readers Union Ltd

The **Poetry** Book Society Ltd, 21 Earls Court Sq, London SW5 9DE Tel: (01) 244 9792
Publications: Bulletin (quarterly); *Poetry Supplement* (annual)
Members: 1,600
Founded: 1954

Post, see Puffin School Book Clubs

Puffin School Book Clubs, Penguin Books Ltd, 27 Wrights Lane, London W8 5TZ Tel: (01) 938 2200
Incorporating Fledgling (for up to 6-year-olds), Flight (for 6 to 9-year-olds) and Post (for 9 to 13-year-olds) book clubs
Manager: Alison Stanley
Owned by: Penguin Books Ltd (qv)

The **Railway** Book Club, see Book Club Associates

Ramblers & Climbers Book Society, see Readers Union Ltd

Readers Choice, see Book Club Associates

Readers Union Ltd, PO Box 6, Newton Abbot, Devon TQ12 2DW Tel: Newton Abbot 69881 (STD code 0626) Cable Add: Books Nabbot Telex: 42904
Chairman: David Thomas; *Marketing Dir:* Nicholas Loasby
Includes: Anglers Book Society, Arena, Belief the Religious Book Society, Birds and Natural History Book Society, Country Book Society, Craft Book Society, Craftsman Book Society, Equestrian Book Society, Fieldsports Book Society, Gardeners Book Society, Maritime Book Society, Music Book Society, Nationwide Book Service, Needlecraft Book Society, Phoenix Book Society, Photographic Book Society, Ramblers & Climbers Book Society
Owned by: David & Charles Publishers plc
Founded: 1937

The **Red House Post**, The Red House, Witney, Oxfordshire OX8 6YQ Tel: Witney 74171 (STD code 0993)
Members: 175,000
Owned by: Red House Books Ltd
Founded: 1979
Subjects: Children's

Scene Book Club, Scholastic Publications Ltd, Marlborough House, Holly Walk, Leamington Spa, Warwickshire CV32 4LS Tel: Southam 3910 (STD code 092 681)
Owned by: Scholastic Publications Ltd (qv)
Subjects: Books for secondary and middle school

See-Saw Book Club, Scholastic Publications Ltd, Marlborough House, Holly Walk, Leamington Spa, Warwickshire CV32 4LS Tel: Southam 3910 (STD code 092 681)
Owned by: Scholastic Publications Ltd (qv)
Subjects: Books for nursery and infants

Spanish Book Club, Warner House, Folkestone, Kent CT19 6PH
Owned by: Bailey Bros & Swinfen Ltd (qv)

Transport Publications Service, Annesley House, 21 Southside, Weston-super-Mare, Avon BS23 2QU Tel: Weston-super-Mare 31616 (STD code 0934)
Owned by: Avon–Anglia Publications & Services (qv)

Verbatim Book Club, PO Box 199, Aylesbury, Buckinghamshire HP20 1TQ Tel: Aylesbury 27314 (STD code 0296)

The **Women's** Press Book Club, 34 Great Sutton St, London EC1V 0DX Tel: (01) 253 0009
Owned by: The Women's Press Ltd (qv)
Founded: 1980
Subjects: Books by and about women, with emphasis on fiction, art, politics, health

World Books, see Book Club Associates

World of Nature, see Book Club Associates

Major Booksellers

Athena Bookshops, Trocadero Shopping Centre, 19 Coventry St, London W1V 7FD Tel: (01) 734 5061
Manager: J Thwaites
Also: 119-121 Oxford St, London W1R 1TF; 72 The High St, King's Lynn, Norfolk PE30 1AY. There are in addition 37 Athena Galleries throughout the UK
Owned by: Pentos Retailing Group Ltd (qv)

Austicks Headrow Bookshop*, 91 The Headrow, Leeds LS1 1HD Tel: Leeds 433099 (STD code 0532)
Manager: John Prime

B H Blackwell Ltd*, 48-51 Broad St, Oxford OX1 3BQ Tel: Oxford 249111 (STD code 0865)

Bookwise Service Ltd, Trade Division, Unit 1, Langham Trading Estate, Catteshall Lane, Godalming, Surrey Tel: Godalming 4152 (STD code 048 68) Telex: 859601
Manager: H G E Tompkins
Owned by: Octopus Publishing Group PLC
Major wholesalers

Bowes & Bowes Books, see Sherratt & Hughes

Burchell & Martin Ltd, 34 Granville St, Birmingham B1 2LJ Tel: (021) 643 1888 Telex: 337001 Fax: (021) 455 8670
Man Dir: Keith Burchell

Claude Gill Books Ltd, 19-23 Oxford St, London W1R 1RF Tel: (01) 437 2654
Also: 213 Piccadilly, London W1V 9LD; 10-12 James St, London W1R 2AQ; 64 Ealing Broadway Centre, The Broadway, London W5 5JY; 47-49 Union St, Bristol BS1 2DU; 115 Queen St, Cardiff CF1 4BH; 9-10 High Ousegate, York YO1 2RZ
Owned by: William Collins PLC (qv)

Dillons The Bookstore, 82 Gower St, London WC1E 6EQ Tel: (01) 636 1577 Telex: 27950 ref 2671
General Manager: Roger Dewar
Owned by: Pentos Retailing Group Ltd (qv)

W & G Foyle Ltd*, 113-119 Charing Cross Rd, London WC2H 0EB Tel: (01) 439 8501 (Mail Order), (01) 437 5660 (Head Office)
Manager: V Stimac

William George's Sons Ltd, 89 Park St, Bristol BS1 5PW Tel: Bristol 276602 (STD code 0272)
Manager: Duncan Dewfall

Claude **Gill**, see Claude

Haigh & Hochland Ltd*, 11 Whitworth St, Manchester 1 Tel: (061) 236 9390; The Precinct Centre, Oxford Rd, Manchester M13 9QA Tel: (061) 273 4156

Hammick's Bookshops & Hammick's Wholesale, Albany Park, Frimley, Camberley, Surrey GU15 2PW Tel: Camberley 686286 (STD code 0276) Fax: (0276) 691230
Chief Executive: Mark Abbott
There are Hammick's Bookshops Ltd at Andover, Basingstoke, Cheltenham, Chichester, Epsom, Farnham, Hammersmith, Harrow, Horsham, Kingston, London, Maidenhead, Sheffield, Southampton, Sutton, Tunbridge Wells, Windsor, Woking
Owned by: John Menzies (Holdings) Ltd (qv)

Hatchards Ltd, 187 Piccadilly, London W1V 9DA Tel: (01) 439 9921 Telex: 8953970
Also: Hatchards within Harvey Nichols, Knightsbridge, London SW1; Hatchards, 150-152 King's Rd, London SW3 3NR; Hatchards, 390 Strand, London WC1; Hatchards at Hanningtons, 53 Market St, Brighton, East Sussex; Hatchards, 12-13 High St, Colchester, Essex; Hatchards, 50 Gordon St, Glasgow; Hatchards, The Ancient House, 25-27 Upper Brook St, Ipswich, Suffolk IP4 1ED Tel: Ipswich 57761 (STD code (0473); Hatchards, Botes Books, 1 Brook St, Kingston-upon-Thames, Surrey Tel: (01) 546 7592; Hatchards, Unit 1, Royal Star Arcade, Maidstone, Kent; Hatchards, 1-3 Lower George St, Richmond, Surrey Tel: (01) 948 7181; Hatchards, 20-22 Murray Pl, Stirling, Scotland; Hatchards, Great Hall, Tunbridge Wells, Kent; Hatchards, The Parade, Watford, Hertfordshire; Hatchards, 97 High St, Winchester, Hampshire Tel: Winchester 840379 (STD code 0962)
Owned by: William Collins PLC (qv)

Heffers Booksellers, 20 Trinity St, Cambridge CB2 3NG Tel: Cambridge 358351 (STD code 0223) Telex: 81298
Also: (all Cambridge) 30 Trinity St (children's books); 13 Trinity St and 31 Downing St (both paperbacks); Grafton Centre (general books)
Owned by: W Heffer & Sons Ltd

Hudsons Bookshops*, 116 New St, Birmingham B2 4JJ Tel: (021) 643 8311
Branches: Birmingham (three), Chichester, Coventry (two), Croydon, Harrogate, Leicester, Liverpool, Loughborough, Newcastle upon Tyne, Nottingham (three), Sheffield, Wolverhampton (two)
Bookstalls: Newcastle upon Tyne, London (three)
Owned by: Pentos Retailing Group Ltd (qv)

John Menzies (Holdings) Ltd*, Villiers House, 40 Strand, London WC2N 5HZ Tel: (01) 930 0033
Manager: D Shaw
Branches throughout the United Kingdom. Also major library supplier

Parker & Son Ltd*, 27 Broad St, Oxford OX2 7LP Tel: Oxford 54156 (STD code 0865)
Man Dir: M S Broadbent

Pentos Retailing Group Ltd, Berwick House, 35 Livery St, Birmingham B3 2PB Tel: (021) 236 6886
Incorporating Athena Bookshops and Athena Galleries, Dillons The Bookstore, Hudsons Bookshops (all UK, qqv); Hodges Figgis & Co Ltd, Republic of Ireland (qv)

Sherratt & Hughes, 1 Trinity St, Cambridge CB2 1SX Tel: Cambridge 355488 (STD code 0223)
Incorporating Bowes & Bowes Books
Manager: E G Taylor
Owned by: W H Smith & Son Ltd (qv)

John **Smith** & Son (Glasgow) Ltd*, 57-61 St Vincent St, Glasgow G2 5TB Tel: (041) 221 7472 Cable Add: Books: Glasgow Telex: 778881 Jssglw G

W H Smith & Son Ltd, Strand House, 7 Holbein Pl, Sloane Sq, London SW1W 8NR Tel: (01) 730 1200
There are 370 retail bookshops and 54 bookstalls throughout the UK, and 44 specialist bookshops principally operating under the name of Sherratt & Hughes (qv). The company is also a major wholesaler

James **Thin**, Bookseller, 53-59 South Bridge, Edinburgh Tel: (031) 556 6743
Managers: James Thin, Ainslie Thin, Andrew Thin
Also: (all Edinburgh) 27-31 Buccleugh St; King's Bldgs, West Main's Rd; The Edinburgh Bookshop, 57 George St; James Thin's Bookshop, Waverley Market

Waterstone & Co Ltd*, 193 High St, Kensington, London W8 Tel: (01) 603 1361
Also: Five other branches in London, one at 34 Grey St, Newcastle, one at Southend, Essex and one at 114 George St, Edinburgh EH2 4LX Tel: (031) 225 3436
(*Manager:* Hazel Broadfoot)

Major Libraries

Belfast Public Library, Central Library, Royal Ave, Belfast BT1 1EA Northern Ireland Tel: Belfast 243233 (STD code 0232) Telex: 747359
Chief Librarian: J N Montgomery

Birmingham Public Libraries*, Central Library, Chamberlain Sq, Birmingham B3 3HQ Tel: (021) 235 4511
Telex: 337655 Fax: (021) 233 4458
Librarian: B H Baumfield
Publication: Bibliography of National Socialist Literature

Bodleian Library, Oxford OX1 3BG Tel: Oxford 277000 (STD code 0865) Telex: 83656
Librarian: D G Vaisey

The **British Library**, Sheraton St, London W1V 4BH Tel: (01) 636 1544 Telex: 21462
See individual entries for details of divisions

British Library Bibliographic Services, 2 Sheraton St, London W1V 4BH Tel: (01) 323 7077 ext 242/284 Telex: 21462
Publications: British National Bibliography; British Catalogue of Music; Books in English (microfiche); *Bibliography of Biography* (microfiche); *Serials in the British Library; Name Authority List* (microfiche)
See also entry under Publishers

British Library Document Supply Centre, Boston Spa, Wetherby, West Yorkshire LS23 7BQ Tel: Boston Spa 843434 (STD code 0937) Telex: 557381 Fax: (0937) 845520
Publications include: Keyword Index to Serial Titles (on microfiche); *Current Serials Received; Interlending and Document Supply; Current Research in Britain; British Reports, Translations and Theses; Current British Journals*
The Document Supply Centre lends only to libraries and organizations, not to individual members of the public
See also entry under Publishers

British Library India Office Library and Records, Orbit House, 197 Blackfriars Rd, London SE1 8NG Tel: (01) 928 9531
Co-Directors: G Shaw (Librarian), M I Moir (Archivist)
Publications include: Catalogue of Persian Manuscripts in the Library of India Office, 1980 (reprint of 1903 edition); *Gandhi and Civil Disobedience: documents in the India Office Records, 1922-1946,* 1980; *A List and Index of Parliamentary Papers relating to India 1908-1947,* 1981; *Catalogue of the Sinhalese Manuscripts in the India Office Library,* 1981; *Catalogue of Urdu books in the India Office Library 1800-1920* (supplementary to James Fuller Blumhardt's catalogue of 1900), 1982; *Guide to the Records of the India Office Military Department,* 1982; *Publications proscribed by the Government of India,* 1985; *Catalogue of Nepali printed books in the India Office Library,* 1985

British Library of Political and Economic Science*, 10 Portugal St, London WC2A 2HD Tel: (01) 405 7686 Telex: 24655 Blpes G
Librarian: C J Hunt
Publication: A London Bibliography of the Social Sciences
Miscellaneous: Not a British Library division

British Library Publications, Great Russell St, London WC1B 3DG Tel: (01) 636 1544
Director-General: M Smethurst
Publications include: British Library Journal (twice yearly); *Catalogue of Additions to the Manuscripts in the British Museum; General Catalogue of Printed Books,* microfiche supplement 1976-82; *Catalogue of the Newspaper Collections in the British Library; Subject Index of Modern Books,* supplements to 1961-70; *Guide to the Department of Oriental Manuscripts and Printed Books*
See also entry under Publishers

British Library, Science Reference and Information Service, 25 Southampton Bldgs, London WC2A 1AW Tel: (01) 323 7460 Telex: 266959
and Aldwych Reading Room, 9 Kean St, Drury Lane, London WC2B 4AT Tel: (01) 323 7288 Telex: 22717
Dir: A Gomersall
List of publications available on request

Cambridge University Library, West Rd, Cambridge CB3 9DR Tel: Cambridge 333000 (STD code 0223) Telex: 81395
Librarian: Dr F W Ratcliffe
List of publications available on request

The **Dean and Chapter** Library, The College, Durham DH1 3EH Tel: (091) 386 2489
Deputy Librarian: R C Norris

Durham University Library, Stockton Rd, Durham DH1 3LY Tel: (091) 374 3018
Telex: 537351 Durlib G
Librarian: Agnes M McAulay

Edinburgh University Library, George Sq, Edinburgh EH8 9LJ Tel: (031) 667 1011
Telex: 727442 Unived G Fax: (031) 667 7938

Guildhall Library*, Aldermanbury, London EC2P 2EJ Tel: (01) 606 3030
Librarian: Melvyn Barnes
Publications: Various, mainly on City of London history (list available), Fine Art catalogues, Facsimiles of graphic materials

India Office Library and Records, see British Library India Office

Leeds University Library, Leeds LS2 9JT Tel: Leeds 431751 (STD code 0532)
Librarian: R P Carr
Publications include: Catalogue of German Literature Printed in the 17th and 18th Centuries; A Catalogue of the Icelandic Collection; Catalogue of the Romany Collection; The Brotherton Collection: its contents described with illustrations of fifty books and manuscripts

Liverpool City Libraries, William Brown St, Liverpool L3 8EW Tel: (051) 207 2147 Telex: 629500
Librarian: N Carrick

Llyfrgell Genedlaethol Cymru (National Library of Wales), Aberystwyth, Dyfed SY23 3BU Tel: Aberystwyth 3816 (STD code 0970) Telex: 35165 Fax: (0970) 615709
Librarian: Brynley F Roberts
Publications include: The National Library of Wales Journal (semi-annual); *Handlist of Manuscripts in the National Library of Wales; Bibliotheca Celtica*

The **Mitchell** Library (Glasgow District Libraries), North St, Glasgow G3 7DN Tel: (041) 221 7030 Telex: 778732 Fax: (041) 248 5027
Librarian: R A Gillespie
Publications include: West of Scotland Census Returns and Old Parochial Registers: a directory of public library holdings in the West of Scotland

National Library of Scotland, George IV Bridge, Edinburgh EH1 1EW Tel: (031) 226 4531 Telex: 72638 Nlsedi G Fax: (031) 668 2363
Map Room: NLS Annexe, 137 Causewayside, Edinburgh EH9 1PH Tel: (031) 667 7848
Librarian: Prof E F D Roberts
Publications include: Bibliography of Scotland (annually); *A Short Title Catalogue of Foreign Books Printed up to 1601, 1970; Current Periodicals in the National Library of Scotland* (six-monthly); *Directory of Scottish Newspapers, 1984*

National Library of Wales, see Llyfrgell Genedlaethol Cymru

Oxford University Taylor Institution Library, St Giles, Oxford OX1 3NA Tel: Oxford 278158 (STD code 0865)

P R O N I (Public Record Office of Northern Ireland), 66 Balmoral Ave, Belfast BT9 6NY

Public Record Office, Ruskin Ave, Kew, Richmond, Surrey TW9 4DU Tel: (01) 876 3444
and Chancery Lane, London WC2A 1LR Tel: (01) 405 0741
National archive for the records of the British courts of law and central departments of state

John **Rylands** University Library of Manchester*, Oxford Rd, Manchester M13 9PP Tel: Main Library Bldg (061) 273 3333; Deansgate Bldg (061) 834 5343 Telex: 668932 Mchrul G
Librarian: M A Pegg
Publication: The Bulletin of the John Rylands University Library of Manchester

School of Oriental and African Studies Library, Malet St, London WC1E 7HP Tel: (01) 637 2388
Librarian: Miss B Burton
Publications include: Library Guide; Library Catalogue (1978-84 supplement on microfiche)

Scottish Record Office, HM General Register House, Edinburgh EH1 3YY Tel: (031) 556 6585

Trinity College Library, Cambridge CB2 1TQ Tel: Cambridge 338488 (STD code 0223)
Librarian: D J McKitterick

University Libraries, see also under names of towns

University of London Library, The Senate House, Malet St, London WC1E 7HU Tel: (01) 636 8000 Telex: 269400 Shul G Fax: (01) 636 0373
Director: V T H Parry

Wellcome Institute for the History of Medicine Library, 183 Euston Rd, London NW1 2BP Tel: (01) 387 4477

City of **Westminster** Libraries, Leisure Services, Westminster City Hall, Victoria St, London SW1E 6QP Tel: (01) 828 8070 Telex: 263305 Fax: (01) 828 3153
Director of Leisure: David Bryant

Library Associations

A R L I S (The Art Libraries Society), c/o Central School of Art & Design Library, Southampton Row, London WC1B 4AP
Secretary: Sue Price
Publications: Art Libraries Journal (quarterly); *ARLIS News-sheet* (six a year); *Directory* (annually)

Aslib, Information House, 26-27 Boswell St, London WC1N 3JZ Tel: (01) 430 2671 Telex: 23667
The Association for Information Management, formerly the Association of Special Libraries and Information Bureaux
Dir: Dr Dennis Lewis
Publications include: Index to Theses with Abstracts (quarterly); *Journal of Documentation* (quarterly); *Aslib Proceedings* (monthly); *Aslib Information* (monthly); *Aslib Book List* (monthly); *Current Awareness Bulletin* (monthly); *Program* (quarterly); *Netlink* (bi-monthly); *The Technical Translation Bulletin* (three times a year); practical guides, reports and directories including the 2-volume *Directory of Information Sources in the UK*
See also entry under Publishers

Association for Information Management, see Aslib

Association of Assistant Librarians
Contact: Mrs Avril E Johnston, Scottish Curriculum Development Service, 74 Southbrae Dr, Glasgow G13 1SU Tel: (041) 954 8287
Publications include: Fiction Index; Song Index; Junior Fiction Index; Which Library School; Sequels; Picture Book Index

Association of British Library and Information Studies Schools (ABLISS)*, c/o K J McGarry, School of Librarianship, Polytechnic of North London, 207-225 Essex Rd, London N1 3PN
Chairman: K J McGarry

Association of British Theological and Philosophical Libraries, Bible Society's Library, c/o University Library, West Rd, Cambridge CB3 9DR
Honorary Secretary: A F Jesson
Publication: Bulletin

Association of London Chief Librarians, *Honorary Secretary:* J Lowry, Greenwich Library, 203 Woolwich Rd, Greenwich, London SE10 0RL Tel: (01) 858 6656
Publication: Directory of London Public Libraries

Association of Scottish Health Sciences Librarians, Ms Sandra Watson, Librarian, Borders Health Board, Thornfield, Selkirk TD7 4DT Tel: Selkirk 20212 (STD code 0750)

Bibliographical Society, British Library (Humanities & Social Sciences), Great Russell St, London WC1B 3DG
Honorary Secretary: Mrs Mirjam Foot
Publications: The Library (quarterly); various books on bibliographical subjects

British and Irish Association of Law Librarians, c/o Harding Law Library, University of Birmingham, PO Box 363, Birmingham B15 2TT
Honorary Secretary: Miss D M Blake
Publication: The Law Librarian

Circle of State Librarians, c/o M J D Willsher, Department of Library Services, British Museum (Natural History), Cromwell Rd, London SW7 5BD Tel: (01) 589 6323 ext 670
Honorary Secretary: M J D Willsher
Publication: State Librarian (3 a year)

Classification Research Group*, *Honorary Secretary:* Dr I C McIlwaine, School of Library, Archive and Information Studies, University College, London WC1

Friends of the National Libraries, c/o The British Library, Great Russell St, London WC1B 3DG Tel: (01) 636 1544 ext 7559
Honorary Secretary: J F Fuggles
Publication: Annual Report

Institute of Information Scientists*, 44 Museum St, London WC1A 1LY Tel: (01) 831 8003/8633
Executive Secretary: Mrs S A Carter; *Honorary Secretary:* Penny Brown
Publications: Journal of Information Science; Inform

Institute of Reprographic Technology*, St Catherines, 186 Denmark Rd, Lowestoft, Suffolk NR32 2EN Tel: Lowestoft 84838 (STD code 0502)
Secretary: Mrs J C Odell
Publication: Reprographics International

International Association of Music Libraries, Archives and Documentation Centres, (UK Branch), c/o Miss A E Smart, The Library, Royal Northern College of Music, 124 Oxford Rd, Manchester M13 9RD Tel: (061) 273 6283 ext 244
General Secretary: Miss A E Smart
Publication: Brio (twice yearly)

Library and Information Services Council*, Office of Arts and Libraries, Great George St, London SW1P 3AL Tel: (01) 233 5588 Telex: 2334982
Secretary: J Stuart
Publications include: Library Information series

Library and Information Services Council (Wales), Education Services Division, Welsh Office, Cathays Park, Cardiff Tel: Cardiff 825111 (STD code 0222) ext 3794
Secretary: Mrs S R Brown

The **Library Association**, 7 Ridgmount St, London WC1E 7AE Tel: (01) 636 7543 Telex: 21897
Chief Executive: George Cunningham
Publications include: Library and Information Science Abstracts, Library Association Record, Current Technology Index, British Humanities Index (all monthly); *Applied Social Sciences Index & Abstracts* (bi-monthly); *Journal of Librarianship, Current Research* (both quarterly); *Year Book* (annually); books and pamphlets on librarianship and bibliography, including *Walford's Guide to Reference Material; Libraries in the United*

Kingdom and the Republic of Ireland: a complete list of public library services and a select list of academic and other library addresses; A Librarian's Handbook; British Library and Information Work 1981-1985 (Vols 1 and 2); The Public Library: its origins, purpose and significance as a social institution; Printed Reference Material

School Library Association, Liden Library, Barrington Close, Liden, Swindon, Wiltshire SN3 6HF Tel: Swindon 617838 (STD code 0793)
Executive Secretary: Valerie Fea
Publications include: The School Librarian (quarterly); also practical guidelines on school library management and annotated book lists

School Library Association in Scotland, Menzieshill High School, Dundee
Secretary: Miss E Scott

Scottish Library Association, Motherwell Business Centre, Coursington Rd, Motherwell ML1 1PW Tel: Motherwell 52526 (STD code 0698)
Executive Secretary: R Craig
Publications include: Scottish Libraries (every two months); Scottish Library Studies Series

Society of Archivists, Suffolk Record Office, County Hall, Ipswich IP4 2JS Tel: Ipswich 55801 ext 4232 (STD code 0473)
Secretary: Ms A J E Arrowsmith
Publication: Journal of the Society of Archivists

The **Society of County Librarians**, Hampshire County Library, 81 North Walls, Winchester, Hampshire SO23 8BY Tel: Winchester 60644 (STD code 0962)
Secretary: J C Beard

Standing Conference of National and University Libraries (SCONUL), 102 Euston St, London NW1 2HA Tel: (01) 387 0317
Executive Secretary: A J Loveday

Welsh Library Association, c/o National Library of Wales, Aberystwyth SY23 3BU Tel: Aberystwyth 3816 (STD code 0970) Telex: 35165
Honorary Secretary: Brynmor Jones
Publications include: A Bibliography of Anglo-Welsh Literature 1900-65; bibliographies, reference books and indexes to periodicals relating to Wales

Library Reference Books and Journals

Books

Aslib Directory, Association for Information Management, 26-27 Boswell St, London WC1N 3JZ

Aslib Membership List, Association for Information Management, 26-27 Boswell St, London WC1N 3JZ

British Archives: A Guide to Archives Resources in the United Kingdom, The Macmillan Press Ltd, Houndmills, Basingstoke, Hampshire RG21 2XS

British Librarianship and Information Work 1981-1985 (Vol 1 General Libraries and the Profession; Vol 2 Special Libraries, Materials and Processes), The Library Association, 7 Ridgmount St, London WC1E 7AE

British Library General Catalogue of Printed Books, see Book Trade Reference Books

Current British Journals, British Library Document Supply Centre, Boston Spa, Wetherby, West Yorkshire LS23 7BQ

Directory of Acquisitions Librarians in the UK and Ireland, c/o Sue Usher, Lanchester Library, Coventry, (Lanchester) Polytechnic, Coventry, Warwickshire

Directory of Information Sources in the UK, Association for Information Management, 26-27 Boswell St, London WC1N 3JZ

Guide to Reference Material, The Library Association, 7 Ridgmount St, London WC1E 7AE

A Librarians's Handbook, The Library Association, 7 Ridgmount St, London WC1E 7AE
Documentary and statistical material

Libraries in Colleges of Further and Higher Education in the United Kingdom, The Library Association, 7 Ridgmount St, London WC1E 7AE

Libraries in the United Kingdom and the Republic of Ireland: a complete list of public library services and a select list of academic and other library addresses, The Library Association, 7 Ridgmount St, London WC1E 7AE

Libraries Yearbook, James Clarke & Co Ltd, 7 All Saints' Passage, Cambridge CB2 3LS

Library Association Year Book, The Library Association, 7 Ridgmount St, London WC1E 7AE

Research Libraries and Collections in the UK: a selective inventory and guide, The Library Association, 7 Ridgmount St, London WC1E 7AE
1978, Clive Bingley publication

The SLG Directory to Children's and School Library Services in the British Isles, c/o Helen Pain, Department of Library and Information Studies, Loughborough University, Loughborough, Leicestershire LE11 3TU

Journals

Archives, British Records Association, Masters Court, Charterhouse, Charterhouse Sq, London EC1

Art Libraries Journal, ARLIS (The Art Libraries Society), c/o Secretary, Ms Lyn Turpin, Learning Resources, Brighton Polytechnic, Faculty of Art and Design, Grand Parade, Brighton BN2 2JY

Aslib Information (monthly), Association for Information Management, 26-27 Boswell St, London WC1N 3JZ

Aslib Book List (monthly), Association for Information Management, 26-27 Boswell St, London WC1N 3JZ

Assistant Librarian, Association of Assistant Librarians, c/o Editor, Alan Taylor, Edinburgh City Library, George V Bridge, Edinburgh

The Bibliotheck, Library Association, Scottish Group, University College & Research Section, c/o Editor, G D Hargreaves, University Library, St Andrews, Fife KY16 9TR
A Scottish journal of bibliography and allied topics

Brio, International Association of Music Libraries (UK Branch), Music Department, Town Hall, Green Lanes, Palmers Green, London N13 4XD

British Library Journal, British Library, Reference Division, Great Russell St, London WC1B 3DG

Information & Library Manager, see *New Library World*

Information Scientist, Institute of Information Scientists, 44 Museum St, London WC1A 1LY

Interlending & Document Supply, British Library, Document Supply Centre, Boston Spa, Wetherby, West Yorkshire LS23 7BQ

Journal of Documentation (quarterly), Association for Information Management, 26-27 Boswell St, London WC1N 3JZ

Journal of Librarianship, The Library Association, 7 Ridgmount St, London WC1E 7AE

Journal of the Society of Archivists, Society of Archivists, c/o Editor, Mrs F Strong, South Cloister, Eton College, Windsor, Berkshire SL4 6DB

The Law Librarian, British and Irish Association of Law Librarians, c/o Harding Law Library, University of Birmingham, PO Box 363, Edgbaston, Birmingham B15 2TT

The Library, Bibliographical Society, British Library (Reference Division), Great Russell St, London WC1B 3DG

Library and Information Science Abstracts, The Library Association, 7 Ridgmount St, London WC1E 7AE

Library Association Record, The Library Association, 7 Ridgmount St, London WC1E 7AE

Library Review, W & R Holmes (Book), 30 Clydeholm Rd, Glasgow G14 0BJ

New Library World (incorporating *Information & Library Manager*), ELM, Seaton House, Kings Ripton, Cambridgeshire PE17 2NJ

Private Library, Private Libraries Association, Ravelston, South View Rd, Pinner, Middlesex

Reference Reviews, c/o Editor, Nick Moore, Brompton Ralph, Taunton, Somerset TA4 2RU
Reviews of current reference materials

Scottish Libraries, Scottish Library Association, c/o M C Head, Department of Librarianship, Robert Gordon's Institute of Technology, St Andrew's St, Aberdeen AB1 1HG

State Librarian, c/o Editor, Christopher Murphy, Energy Library, Room 1020, Department of Energy, Thames House South, Millbank, London SW1P 4QJ

Literary Associations and Societies

Yr **Academi** Gymreig (The Welsh Academy), 3rd Floor, Mount Stuart House, Mount Stuart Sq, The Docks, Cardiff CF1 6DQ Tel: Cardiff 492025 (STD code 0222)
Administrators: Ms Sian Ithel (Welsh Language Section); Mr Kevin Thomas (English Language Section)

Association for Scottish Literary Studies, Department of English, University of Aberdeen, Aberdeen AB9 2UB Tel: Aberdeen 272634 (STD code 0224)
Secretary: Dr D S Robb
Publications include: Scottish Literary Journal, Scottish Literary Journal

Supplement (both twice yearly); *Scottish Language* (annually); an edited work of Scottish literature (annually); *New Writing Scotland* (annually)
See also under Publishers

Association of British Science Writers*, c/o British Association for the Advancement of Science, Fortress House, 23 Savile Row, London W1X 1AB Tel: (01) 734 6010 ext 377
Chairman: Dr Robert Walgate; *Secretary:* Ursula Laver

Authors' Club, 40 Dover St, London W1X 3RB
Secretary: Mrs Huldine Ridgway

Francis **Bacon** Society Inc*, Canonbury Tower, Islington, London N1
Chairman: Noel Fermor
Publications: Baconiana (periodically); *Jottings* (periodically); booklets, pamphlets (list on request)

Books across the Sea, The English-Speaking Union, Dartmouth House, 37 Charles St, London W1X 8AB Tel: (01) 408 0013
Librarian: Jean Huse
Publication: Ambassador Booklist (quarterly)

The **British Science Fiction** Association Ltd, 33 Thornville Rd, Hartlepool, Cleveland TS26 8EW
Membership Secretary: Jo Raine
Publications: Vector (bi-monthly critical journal); *Focus* (semi-annual SF writers' magazine); *Matrix* (bi-monthly newsletter); *Paperback Inferno* (bi-monthly reviews)

The Incorporated **Brontë** Society, The Brontë Parsonage, Haworth, Keighley, West Yorkshire BD22 8DR Tel: Haworth 42323 (STD code 0535)
Honorary Secretary: Mrs E Skirrow
Publication: Brontë Society Transactions (bi-annually)

Bulwer-Lytton Circle, 125 Markyate Rd, Dagenham, Essex RM8 2LB
Founder: E Ford
Publication: Bulwer-Lytton Chronicle

Cambridge Bibliographical Society, University Library, Cambridge CB3 9DR Tel: Cambridge 333000 (STD code 0223)
Honorary Secretary: F R Colliesson
Publications: Transactions (annually); *Monographs* (irregular)

The **Dickens** Fellowship, Dickens House, 48 Doughty St, London WC1N 2LF Tel: (01) 405 2127
Honorary General Secretary: Alan Watts
Publications: The Dickensian (four-monthly); *Mr Dick's Kite* (four-monthly newsletter)

Early English Text Society, St Peter's College, Oxford OX1 2DL
Honorary Dir: Prof John Burrow; *Executive Secretary:* T F Hoad
Publications: Texts (annually)

Edinburgh Bibliographical Society, c/o National Library of Scotland, George IV Bridge, Edinburgh EH1 1EW Tel: (031) 226 4531 ext 2317
Honorary Secretary: I C Cunningham
Publication: Transactions (irregular — for members only)

Edwardian Studies Association, 125 Markyate Rd, Dagenham, Essex
Publication: Edwardian Studies

English Association, The Vicarage, Priory Gardens, London W4 1TT Tel: (01) 995 4236
Secretary: Ruth Fairbanks-Joseph
Publications: English (3 times yearly); *Essays and Studies*; *The Year's Work in English Studies*; *Guide to Degree Courses in English*

Thomas **Hardy** Society Ltd, Park Farm, Tolpuddle, Dorchester, Dorset DT2 7HG Tel: Puddletown 651 (STD code 030 584)
Secretary: Kate N Fowler
Publications: Thomas Hardy and the Modern World, 1974; *Budmouth Essays on Thomas Hardy*, 1976; *Thomas Hardy's Sister Kate*, 1982; *The Thomas Hardy Journal* (3 times yearly)

The Sherlock **Holmes** Society of London, The Old Crown Inn, Lopen, nr South Petherton, Somerset TA13 5JX Tel: South Petherton 40717 (STD code 0460)
Honorary Secretary: Captain W R Michell

Iolaire Arts Association, First of May Bookshop, Candlemaker Row, Edinburgh EH1 2QB
Publication: Iolaire Arts News

Johnson Society of London, Round Chimney, Playden, Rye, East Sussex TN31 7UR Tel: Iden 252 (STD code 079 78)
Honorary Secretary: Miss S B S Pigrome
Publication: The New Rambler (annually; enquiries to the Editor, 10 Beaumont Bldgs, Oxford)

Kipling Society, 18 Northumberland Ave, London WC2N 5BJ
Honorary Secretary: Norman Entract
Publication: The Kipling Journal (quarterly)

Charles **Lamb** Society, 1A Royston Rd, Richmond, Surrey TW10 6LT Tel: (01) 940 3837
Honorary Secretary: Mrs M R Huxstep
Publication: The Charles Lamb Bulletin (quarterly)

Lancashire Authors' Association, Kings Fold, Pope Lane, Penwortham, Preston, Lancashire PR1 9JN Tel: Preston 742236 (STD code 0772)
Honorary General Secretary: J D Cameron MBE
Publications: The Record (quarterly); *Lancashire Authors' Anthology*, 1984; *Lancashire Miscellany*, 1985/6/7 (cassette tapes)

London Writer Circle, Bradfield, Leafy Grove, Keston, Kent 2BR 6AH
Honorary Secretary: Miss M E Harris

The **National Book** League, now Book Trust (qv)

Oxford Bibliographical Society, Bodleian Library, Oxford
Secretary: Dr P Bulloch
Publications: First Series, Vols I-VII, 1923-46; *New Series*, Vol I, 1948- ; *Occasional Publications*, No 1, 1967-

P E N English Centre, 7 Dilke St, Chelsea, London SW3 4JE Tel: (01) 352 6303
President: Michael Holroyd; *Secretary:* Miss Josephine Pullein-Thompson
Publications: The Pen (broadsheet, twice a year); *New Poetry*, *New Fiction* (alternate years, in conjunction with Quartet Books (qv))

P E N Scottish Centre, c/o Scott, 33 Drumsheugh Gardens, Edinburgh EH3 7RN Tel: (031) 225 1038
President: Prof Jeffares; *Secretary:* Laura Fiorentini

The **Poetry** Society, 21 Earls Court Sq, London SW5 9DE Tel: (01) 373 7861
General Secretary: Paul Ralph
Publications: The Poetry Review (quarterly)

Romantic Novelists' Association, 20 First Ave, Amersham, Buckinghamshire HP7 9BJ
Secretary: Dorothy Entwistle

Royal Literary Fund, 144 Temple Chambers, Temple Ave, London EC4Y 0DT Tel: (01) 353 7150
Secretary: Fiona Clark
Publications include: Archives of the Royal Literary Fund 1790-1918 (printed guide and microfilm)

Royal Society of Literature of the United Kingdom, 1 Hyde Park Gardens, London W2 2LT Tel: (01) 723 5104
Secretary: Mrs P M Schute
Publications: Transactions, Report, Special Editions

Shakespearean Authorship Trust*, 11 Old Square, Lincoln's Inn, London WC2A 3TS
Honorary Secretary: Dr D W Thomson Vessey
Publication: The Bard (last published May 1984)

Bernard **Shaw Centre**, 125 Markyate Rd, Dagenham, Essex RM8 2LB
Director: E Ford
Publications: Shaw Centre Series

Bernard **Shaw Society**, 125 Markyate Rd, Dagenham, Essex RM8 2LB
Director: E Ford
Publications: The Shavian, etc

Society for the Study of Mediaeval Languages and Literature,
Treasurer: Dr D G Pattison, Magdalen College, Oxford OX1 4AU
Publications: Medium Aevum; *Medium Aevum Monographs* (new series)

The **Tolkien** Society, 35 Amesbury Crescent, Hove, East Sussex BN3 5RD
Secretary: Anne Haward
Distribution/Publications: Chris Oakey, Membership Secretary, Flat 5, 357 High St, Cheltenham, Gloucestershire GL50 3HT
Publications: Amon Hen (bulletin, approx 6 issues a year); *Mallorn* (journal, once/twice a year)

Jules **Verne** Circle, 125 Markyate Rd, Dagenham, Essex RM8 2LB
Founder: E F J Ford
Publication: Jules Verne Voyages

H G **Wells** Society, Department of Language and Literature, Polytechnic of North London, Prince of Wales Rd, London NW5 3LB Tel: (01) 607 2789
Secretary: C Rolfe
Publications: Newsletter (tri-annual); *The Wellsian* (annual)

Wellsiana — The World of H G Wells, 125 Markyate Rd, Dagenham, Essex RM8 2LB
Publication: Wellsiana

The **Welsh Academy**, see Academi Gymreig

Literary Periodicals

Ambit (quarterly), Priory Gardens, Highgate, London N6

Bananas (quarterly), 60 Elgin Crescent, London W11

Book Buyer's Choice, now incorporated in *Books* (qv)

Book Collector, The Collector Ltd, 90-91 Great Russell St, London WC1B 3PS

Books, Gradegate Ltd, 43 Museum St, London WC1A 1LY
Incorporating *Book Buyer's Choice* and *Books and Bookmen*

Books and Bookmen, now incorporated in *Books* (qv)

Books & Issues, Stephen Trombley, 40 Mildmay Grove, London N1

Critical Quarterly, Manchester University Press, Oxford Rd, Manchester M13 9PL

Encounter, Encounter Ltd, 43-44 Great Windmill St, London W1V 7PA

The Fiction Magazine, 5 Jeffreys St, London NW1 9PS

Good Book Guide, Braithwaite & Taylor Ltd, PO Box 400, Havelock Terrace, London SW8 4AU
Independent book-review magazine published bi-monthly in conjunction with an international mail-order bookselling service

Granta, Granta Publications Ltd, 44A Hobson St, Cambridge CB1 1NL; Penguin Books Ltd, 536 King's Rd, London SW10 0UH

Guide to Literary Prizes, Grants and Awards, Book Trust, 45 East Hill, Wandsworth, London SW18 2QZ

The Literary Review, 51 Beak St, London W1R 3LF

The London Review of Books, 6a Bedford Sq, London WC1

Notes and Queries, Oxford University Press, Walton St, Oxford OX2 6DP
For readers and writers, collectors and librarians

Numbers, 6 Kingston St, Cambridge CB1 2NV
Poetry magazine, published twice a year

PN Review (bi-monthly, formerly *Poetry Nation*), 208 Corn Exchange Bldgs, Manchester M4 3BQ

Phoenix, Phoenix Publications, 60 Abbey House, 2 Victoria St, London SW1
Magazine for writers

The Poetry Catalogue, 11 College St, Winchester, Hampshire SO23 9L2

Poetry Nation, see *PN Review*

Poetry Now, 14 The Leathermarket, London SE1

Poetry Review, Poetry Society, 21 Earls Court Sq, London SW5 9DE

Prospice, Aquila Publishing (UK) Ltd, PO Box 418, Leek, Staffordshire ST13 8UX
Independent literary magazine, published quarterly

Quarto, merged with *The Literary Review* (qv) 1982

Review of English Studies, Oxford University Press, Walton St, Oxford OX2 6DP
Quarterly journal of English literature and the English language

Scottish Language, Association for Scottish Literary Studies, Department of English, University of Aberdeen, Aberdeen AB9 2UB

Scottish Literary Journal, Association for Scottish Literary Studies, Department of English, University of Aberdeen, Aberdeen AB9 2UB

Signal, Nancy Chambers, Lockwood, Station Rd, South Woodchester, Stroud, Gloucestershire GL5 5EQ
Approaches to Children's Books

Taliesin, D Tecwyn Lloyd, Maes-yr-onnen, Maerdy, Corwen, Clwyd LL21 9NX
Quarterly Welsh-language magazine for the arts

Telegram (three times a year), Oasis Books, 12 Stevenage Rd, London SW6 6ES

Times Literary Supplement, Priory House, St Johns Lane, London EC1M 4BX

Words International, Words Publications, Bird-in-Eye, Uckfield, East Sussex

Literary Prizes

Angel Literary Prize
Established in 1982 by the Angel Hotel, Bury St Edmunds, for writers living and working in East Anglia. There are two annual awards — £1,000 for a work of non-fiction and £500 for a work of the imagination. Latest prizewinner (1st prize) Oliver Rackham for *The History of the Countryside* (Dent). Enquiries to Caroline Gough, The Angel Hotel, Bury St Edmunds, Suffolk

Authors' Club First Novel Award
For the most promising first novel published in English in the United Kingdom in the preceding year. Award consists of a silver mounted quill and £200, presented to the author at a dinner. Awarded annually. Enquiries to Mrs Huldine Ridgway, Authors' Club, 40 Dover St, London W1X 3RB

Authors' Club Sir Banister Fletcher Prize Trust
For the most deserving book on architecture or the arts. Awarded annually. The 1986 prize went to Richard Cork for *Art Beyond the Gallery in Early Twentieth Century England*. Enquiries to Mrs Huldine Ridgway, Authors' Club, 40 Dover St, London W1X 3RB

Best Book of the Sea Award*
Established 1971. Sponsored by King George's Fund for Sailors. For a non-fiction book, first published in the United Kingdom during the calendar year, judged to have made the most valuable contribution to the knowledge and enjoyment of those who love the sea. £500 and a medal. Also honourable-mention award of £250 given at the discretion of the judges to a book of special merit which had to be passed over. Enquiries to John Coote, King George's Fund for Sailors, 1 Chesham St, London SW1X 8NF

Besterman Medal
The Library Association awards this medal annually for an outstanding bibliography or guide to the literature first published in the United Kingdom during the preceding year. Recommendations for the award are invited from members of The Library Association. Among criteria for the award are the authority of the work, quality of articles and entries, accessibility of information, scope and coverage, up-to-dateness, and originality. The 1986 medal was awarded to *English Poetry of the Second World War: A Bibliography* by Catherine W Reilly. Enquiries to The Library Association, 7 Ridgmount St, London WC1E 7AE

James Tait **Black** Memorial Prizes
These literary prizes were founded by the late Mrs Janet Coats Black in memory of her husband, a partner in the publishing house of A & C Black Ltd, London. Mrs Black set aside £11,000 to be used for two prizes of whatever income the fund would produce after paying expenses. The prizes, supplemented by the Scottish Arts Council, now amount annually to approximately £1,000 each. One prize is given to the author of the best biography in the English language first published in the United Kingdom during the year and the other to the author of the best work of fiction. The choice is made in the spring for books of the preceding year by the Professor of English Literature at the University of Edinburgh. The 1986 biography award was made to D Felicitas Corrigan for *Helen Waddell* (Victor Gollancz). The award for the best work of fiction was made to Jenny Joseph for *Persephone* (Bloodaxe Books). Enquiries to Department of English Literature, David Hume Tower, George Sq, Edinburgh EH8 9JX

Booker Prize, see International Literary Prizes

British Science Fiction Award
Awarded annually for the best science fiction book published in Britain for the first time in the previous year. In 1987 the award went to Bob Shaw for *The Ragged Astronauts* (Gollancz). Enquiries to Mike Muir (Awards Administrator), 27 Hampton Rd, Worcester Park, Surrey

Carnegie Medal
First awarded 1936. Instituted by The Library Association to commemorate the centenary of Andrew Carnegie's birth in 1835. Annual award for an outstanding book for children written in English and first published during the preceding year in the United Kingdom. Recommendations for the award are made by members of The Library Association. The 1986 Medal was awarded to Berlie Doherty for *Granny was a Buffer Girl* (Methuen). Enquiries to The Library Association, 7 Ridgmount St, London WC1E 7AE

Cartier Diamond Dagger Award
Inaugurated 1986 and sponsored by Cartier in conjunction with the Crime Writers' Association. For outstanding contribution to the genre. Annual award of silver book with diamond dagger plunged into it. Enquiries to Crime Writers' Association, BO Box 172, Tring, Hertfordshire HP23 5LP

Children's Book Award
Founded 1980. Awarded annually by the Federation of Children's Book Groups for the best work of fiction (published in the United Kingdom) chosen by children for children. In 1986 the winners were Janet and Allan Ahlberg for *The Jolly Postman* (Heinemann). Enquiries to Martin G Kromer, 22 Beacon Brow, Bradford, West Yorkshire BD6 3DE

Children's Book of the Year Competition*
Inaugurated in 1985 by the 'Burnley Express' and the National and Provincial Building Society. £250 and an engraved silver bookmark awarded annually to the author of an outstanding work of fiction for children between the ages of 5 and 14. Enquiries to Burnley Express, Bull St, Burnley, Lancashire BB11 1DP

Arthur C **Clarke** Award for Science Fiction
Established in 1986, this annual award is made by the Science Fiction Foundation, in conjunction with the British Science Fiction Association and the International Science Policy Foundation. The prize of £1,000 is for the best science fiction novel published in the United Kingdom. The first winner was Margaret Atwood for *The Handmaid's Tale* (Jonathan Cape). Enquiries to Dr Edward James, Department of History, University of York, Heslington, York YO1 5DD

Constable Fiction Trophy*
Annual award, restructured 1984, for an unpublished work of creative writing by an author living in the north of England. The winner receives the Trophy and £1,000, with a further £1,000 on acceptance for publication by Constable & Co Ltd. A contribution towards the prize is made by the five Regional Arts Associations serving the north. Enquiries to The Literature Department, Northern Arts, 10 Osborne Terrace, Jesmond, Newcastle upon Tyne NE2 1NZ

John **Creasey** Memorial Award
Founded 1973. Annual award of magnifying glass with onyx handle and inscribed plate for best crime novel by a previously unpublished author. Enquiries to Crime Writers' Association, PO Box 172, Tring, Hertfordshire HP23 5LP

Mary **Elgin** Prize, see International Literary Prizes

Emil Award, see Maschler

The Geoffrey **Faber** Memorial Prize, see International Literary Prizes

Eleanor **Farjeon** Award*
The Eleanor Farjeon Award was established in 1965 to commemorate the work of the late children's author. The Children's Book Circle makes an annual award of £500 (minimum) which may be given to a librarian, teacher, author, artist, publisher, reviewer, bookseller or television producer who, in the judgment of the Awards Committee, is considered to have done outstanding work for children's books. Awarded in 1987 to Valerie Bierman. Enquiries to Jill Coleman, A & C Black Ltd, 35 Bedford Row, London WC1R 4JH

Prudence **Farmer** Poetry Prize
Founded 1974. £100 awarded annually for the best poem printed in the 'New Statesman' during the previous year. In 1986 the prize was awarded to Michael Hofmann. No applications or nominations accepted. Enquiries to Literary Editor, Foundation House, Perseverance Works, 38 Kingsland Rd, London E2 8BA

Fawcett Book Prize
Awarded annually for a book contributing to an understanding of woman's position in society today. The 1986 prize, awarded in 1987, was £500 for a work of fiction and was won by Shena Mackay for *Redhill Rococo* (Heinemann). Enquiries to Sandra Shulman, Fawcett Society, 46 Harleyford Rd, London SW11 5AY

Kathleen **Fidler** Award
First awarded in 1982. Annual award of £1,000 and a trophy for an unpublished novel written for 8-12 year-olds. The author may have had previous books published, but this must be the first for this age range. The award is sponsored by Blackie & Son Ltd, who have first option on the winning entry. Enquiries to Book Trust Scotland, 15A Lynedoch St, Glasgow G3 6EF

Authors' Club Sir Bannister **Fletcher** Prize Trust, see under Authors' Club

John **Florio** Prize
Established in 1963 under the auspices of the Italian Institute and the British-Italian Society, and named after John Florio. For the best translation into English of a twentieth-century Italian work of literary merit and general interest, published by a British publisher during the preceding two years. £750. The 1986 prize was awarded to Avril Bardoni for her translation of Leonardo Sciascia's *The Wine-Dark Sea* (Carcanet). Enquiries to Secretary, Translators Association, 84 Drayton Gardens, London SW10 9SB

Gold Dagger Award
Inaugurated 1956, revised 1970. A gilded dagger for the best crime-fiction novel of the year awarded annually by a panel of reviewers. Enquiries to Crime Writers' Association, PO Box 172, Tring, Hertfordshire HP23 5LP

Kate **Greenaway** Medal
First awarded 1955. Offered annually by The Library Association for the most distinguished work in the illustration of children's books first published in the United Kingdom during the preceding year. Recommendations for the award are made by members of The Library Association. The 1986 medal was awarded to Fiona French for *Snow White in New York* (Oxford University Press). Enquiries to The Library Association, 7 Ridgmount St, London WC1E 7AE

Eric **Gregory** Trust Fund Awards
A number of awards are made each year to encourage young poets. Candidates for awards must be British subjects by birth, ordinarily resident in the United Kingdom and under the age of 30 on 31 March in the year of the award. Candidates must submit a published or unpublished volume of belles lettres, poetry or drama-poems. In 1987 awards totalling £20,000 were made to Peter McDonald, Maura Dooley, Stephen Knight, Steve Anthony, Jill Maughan and Paul Munder. Enquiries to Society of Authors, 84 Drayton Gardens, London SW10 9SB

Garavi **Gujarat** Annual Book Award for Racial Harmony*
Two awards — major prize of £1,000 and a children's book prize of £100 — for any book, fiction or non-fiction, which best promotes racial harmony, published in the United Kingdom in year ending 30 June of year of presentation. Enquiries to Ramniklai Solanki, Garavi Gujarat Publications Ltd, Garavi Gujarat House, 1-2 Silex St, London SE1 0DW

Thomas **Hardy** Prize
Founded 1984 and sponsored by the Thomas Hardy Society. A biennial prize of a medal and £200 to the writer or editor of a book making the most valuable contribution to Hardy studies. Enquiries to Dr James Gibson, 4 Gore Mews, Canterbury, Kent CT1 1JB

Hawthornden Prize
Founded in 1919 by Miss Alice Warrender, it is awarded annually to a British subject under 41 for the best work of imaginative literature. It is especially designed to encourage young authors, and the word 'imaginative' is given a broad interpretation. Biographies are not excluded. Books do not have to be submitted for the prize; it is awarded without competition. A panel of judges chooses the winner. Enquiries to The Administrator, Hawthornden Castle, Lasswade, Midlothian, Scotland EH18 1EG

Heinemann Award for Literature
A foundation was established in 1944 through a bequest in the will of the late William Heinemann, eminent British publisher. The Royal Society of Literature administers the annual foundation award which is 'primarily to reward those classes of literature which are less remunerative, namely, poetry, criticism, biography, history, etc' and 'to encourage the production of works of real merit'. The amount of the award is not definitely specified. Submitted works must have been written originally in English and published during the calendar year previous to the year in which the prize is presented. A reading committee decides on the winner, whose name is announced in April or May; the prize is presented at a meeting of the Royal Society of Literature in June or July. The award for 1986 was to Richards Dawkins for *The Blind Watchmaker* (Longman). Enquiries to Royal Society of Literature, 1 Hyde Park Gardens, London W2 2LT

Felicia **Hemans** Prize for Lyrical Poetry
For a lyrical poem by past and present members and students of the University of Liverpool. Books or cash awarded annually. Enquiries to Registrar, University of Liverpool, PO Box 147, Liverpool L69 3BX

Winifred **Holtby** Memorial Prize
Founded in 1966 by Vera Brittain in memory of Winifred Holtby. An annual award for the best regional novel of its year; if no suitable work of fiction can be found the jury may consider works of non-fiction. Submissions by publishers, not by individual authors. Enquiries to Secretary, Royal Society of Literature, 1 Hyde Park Gardens, London W2 2LT

Iolaire Arts Open Poetry Competition
Established 1987. For an unpublished poem written in English. Annual award of £400 which may be divided. Enquiries to Iolaire Arts Association, First of May Bookshop, 43 Candlemaker Row, Edinburgh EH1 2QB

Sir Peter **Kent** Conservation Book Prize
Established in 1987 (European Year of the Environment) by BP Exploration Ltd. The award is in memory of Sir Peter Kent FRS and is for a book on creative conservation of our natural environment. Annual award of £1,500. Enquiries to Book Trust, Book House, 45 East Hill, Wandsworth, London SW18 2QZ

Martin Luther **King** Memorial Prize*
Inaugurated 1968. For a literary work reflecting the ideals to which Dr King devoted his life. It may be given for a novel, work of non-fiction, poetry collection, play, television, radio or film script first published or performed in the United Kingdom during the preceding year. Closing date 15th January. Prize of £100 awarded annually. Enquiries to National Westminster Bank, 7 Fore St, Chard, Somerset TA20 1PJ.
No enquiries answered without stamped and addressed envelope

M I N D Book of the Year Award
Inaugurated in 1981 by MIND and the National Book League in memory of Allen Lane. Awarded annually to the author(s) of the book (fiction or non-fiction) which outstandingly furthers public understanding of the prevention, causes, treatment or experience of mental illness and/or mental handicap. Award is £1,000. The 1986 award was made to Lindsay Knight for *Talking to a Stranger* (Fontana). Enquiries to MIND, 22 Harley St, London W1N 2ED

McColvin Medal
This annual award is given for an outstanding reference book first published in the United Kingdom during the preceding year. Encyclopaedias, dictionaries, biographical dictionaries,

annuals, year-books and directories, handbooks and compendia of data, and atlases are eligible. Recommendations are invited from members of The Library Association who are asked to submit a preliminary list of not more than three titles. The 1986 Medal was awarded to James Ayres for *The Artist's Craft: A History of Tools, Techniques and Materials* (Phaidon). Enquiries to The Library Association, 7 Ridgmount St, London WC1E 7AE

Roger **Machell** Prize
Established in 1986 and sponsored by Hamish Hamilton Ltd for a published work of non-fiction directly concerning any of the performing arts. Annual award of £2,000. The first award was made in 1987 and went to Kurt Gänzl for *The British Musical Theatre* (Macmillan). Enquiries to The Society of Authors, 84 Drayton Gardens, London SW10 9SB

Macmillan Silver Pen Award for Fiction
In 1986 Macmillan Publishing Ltd took over sponsorship of this annual award for an outstanding novel written in English and published in the United Kingdom in the previous year. The prize is £500 and a silver pen and is given on PEN Writers' Day. The 1986 award went to Antonia Byatt for *Still Life*. Enquiries to PEN English Centre, 7 Dilke St, London SW3 4JE

McVitie's Prize for Scottish Writer of the Year
Established 1987 and sponsored by United Biscuits plc. For a work of imaginative writing in English, Scots or Gaelic by an author who is Scottish born or is (or has been) working in Scotland. Annual award of £5,000. The winner in the inaugural year was David Thomson for *Memoirs: Nairn in Darkness and Light* (Century Hutchinson). Enquiries to Michael Kelly Associatese Ltd, 65 Bath St, Glasgow G2 2BX

Arthur **Markham** Memorial Prize
Instituted 1927. For a poem, short story, first chapter of a novel or a one-act play by a manual worker in coal-mining. There are specified themes and strict limits on length. Prizes totalling £200 annually. Enquiries to Registrar and Secretary, The University, Sheffield S10 2TN

Kurt **Maschler** Award
Founded 1982. An annual award in memory of Erich Kästner and Walter Trier for 'a work of imagination in the children's field in which text and illustration are of excellence and so presented that each enhances, yet balances, the other'. The prize is £1,000, the author and illustrator each receiving in addition a sculpted 'Emil'. Books published in the current year in the United Kingdom by a native author and/or artist or someone resident for ten years are eligible. The 1986 award was for *The Jolly Postman* (Heinemann) by Allan Ahlberg/Janet Ahlberg, the 1987 award for *Jack the Treacle Eater* (Macmillan) by Charles Causley, illustrated by Charles Keeping. Enquiries to Book Trust, Book House, 45 East Hill, Wandsworth, London SW18 2QZ

Somerset **Maugham** Award
Founded 1946 by Somerset Maugham to encourage young writers to travel abroad. Given to a promising author of a published work of poetry, fiction, criticism, biography, history, philosophy, belles lettres or travel. Candidates must be British subjects by birth and ordinarily resident in the United Kingdom and under 30. Awards must be used for foreign travel. In 1987 awards totalling £7,500 were made to Stephen Gregory for *The Cormorant*, Janni Howker for *Isaac Campion* and Andrew Motion for *The Lamberts*. Enquiries to Society of Authors, 84 Drayton Gardens, London SW10 9SB

Mother Goose Award
Established 1979 as an annual award for the most exciting newcomer to children's book illustration in the United Kingdom, the competiton is open to all illustrators publishing a first major book tor children. The award takes the form of a bronze goose egg, a scroll and £500 for the winner. The 1987 winner was Patrick Lynch for *Bag of Moonshine* (Collins). Enquiries to Books for Children, Park House, Dollar Street, Cirencester, Gloucestershire GL7 2AN

Netta **Muskett** Award
Established 1960. For an unpublished romantic novel by an author who has not previously had a romantic novel published. A trophy is awarded annually, provided a novel is accepted for publication. If no manuscript is accepted, the award is not made. Enquiries to Hon Secretary, Romantic Novelists' Association, 20 First Ave, Amersham, Buckinghamshire HP7 9BJ

N C R Book Award for Non-Fiction, see International Literary Prizes

National Poetry Competition
Founded in 1978. Awarded annually for a poem written in English by a resident of the United Kingdom or the Republic of Ireland. £2,000 first prize, £1,000 second, £500 third and 15 other smaller prizes. The 1986 winner was Carole Satyamorti. Enquiries to The Poetry Society, 21 Earls Court Sq, London SW5 9DE

The **Nelson Hurst & Marsh** Biography Prize
Established in 1986, this national biography biennial award is sponsored by Nelson Hurst & Marsh. Publishers are invited to submit one biography by a British author. The prize was first awarded by the Authors' Club in 1987 and consisted of a trophy and a cheque for £2,000. The winner was Roland Huntford for *Shackleton* (Hodder & Stoughton). Enquiries to Authors' Club, 40 Dover St, London W1X 3RB

Sir Roger **Newdigate** Prize for English Verse
The Newdigate Prize was established in 1806 by Sir Roger Newdigate who had been a member of Parliament for Oxford University from 1750 to 1780. This foundation was the first one founded solely to award a literary prize. The sum of £1,000 was bequeathed by Sir Roger with the stipulation that £21 of the income should be awarded each year to a member of Oxford University for 'a copy of English verse of fifty lines and no more, in recommendation of the study of the ancient Greek and Roman remains of architecture, sculpture, and painting'. Later, with the consent of the Newdigate heirs, these restrictions were modified. The award, increased to about £150, is now open to undergraduate members of the University of Oxford who have not exceeded four years from their matriculation. It is given for a poem of no more than 300 lines on a given subject; the winner recites part of the poem at commemoration in June. The 1987 prize was awarded jointly to Bruce John Gibson and Michael Felix Suarez, SJ; the subject was 'Memoirs of Tiresias'. Enquiries to Head Clerk, University of Oxford, University Offices, Wellington Sq, Oxford OX1 2JD

George **Orwell** Memorial Fund Prize*
Established in 1982 and given for a project of imaginative writing and non-fiction writing in alternate years on Orwell or in the Orwellian spirit. Applicants must be registered as occasional students at Birkbeck College or University College, London. Application must be before 1 April. £2,000 is awarded annually. Enquiries to Secretary & Clerk to the Governors, Birkbeck College, University of London, Malet St, London WC1E 7HX

The **Other** Award*
Commendation of a number of books a year as 'progressive books of literary merit for children'. Enquiries to 4 Aldebert Terrace, London SW8 1BL

'**Parents**' Magazine Best Book for Babies Award
Founded in 1985. £1,000 annual award to the author of a book for infants (up to age 4). The 1987 winner was Jill Murphy for *Five Minutes Peace* (Walker). Enquiries to Parents Magazine, 14 Victoria House, Leicester Pl, London WC2H 7NB

'**Police Review**' Award
Inaugurated 1986. Presented annually to crime novel best portraying police work and procedure. Enquiries to The Editor, Police Review, 14 St Cross St, London EC1N 8FE

The **Queen's** Gold Medal for Poetry*
Instituted in 1933 by King George V, at the suggestion of the Poet Laureate, John Masefield, this Medal is given for a book of verse, on the recommendation of a committee of eminent men and women of letters headed by the Poet Laureate. The Medal is usually given for a book by a British subject writing in the English language, but an exceptional translation may also be considered. The Medal is not necessarily awarded every year. Last awarded in 1981 to Dennis Joseph Enwright. Enquiries to the Press Secretary to the Queen, Buckingham Palace, London SW1

R N A Major Award
Established 1960. For the best romantic novel (modern or historical) published during the year. Trophy and £2,000 prize awarded annually, open to non-members. The award in 1987 was to Marie Joseph for *A Better World Than This* (Century Hutchinson). Enquiries to Clare Cavendish, Romantic Novelists' Association, 29 Through Duncans, Woodbridge, Suffolk IP12 4EA

Runciman Award
The Anglo-Hellenic League offers, through the generosity of the Onassis Foundation, an annual prize of £1,000 for a literary work wholly or mainly about Greece and named because of Sir Steven Runciman's service to Anglo-Greek relations and his outstanding contribution to English knowledge of Byzantium. The work must be published in its first English edition in the UK and may be of fiction, poetry, drama or non-fiction; it may concern arts or antiquity. Works of a polemically political nature will not qualify. First awarded in 1986 to David Constantine for *Early Greek Travellers and the Hellenic Ideal* (Cambridge University Press). Enquiries to Book Trust, Book House, 45 East Hill, Wandsworth, London SW18 2QZ

Schlegel-Tieck Prize
Established in 1964 under the auspices of the Translators Association, a subsidiary organization of the Society of Authors, to be awarded annually for the best translation published by a British publisher during the previous year. Only translations of German twentieth-century works of literary merit and general interest will be considered. The work should be entered by the publisher and not the individual translator. The 1987 prize of £2,000 was won by Anthea Bell for her translation of Hans Bemmann's *The Stone and the Flute* (Viking). Enquiries to Secretary, The Translators Association, 84 Drayton Gardens, London SW10 9SB

Scott Moncrieff Prize
Established in 1964 under the auspices of the Translators Association of the Society of Authors to be awarded annually for the best translation published by a British publisher during the previous year. Only translations of French twentieth-century works of literary merit and general interest will be considered. The work should be entered by the publisher and not the individual translator. Enquiries to Secretary, Translators Association, 84 Drayton Gardens, London SW10 9SB

Scottish Arts Council Book Awards
A limited number of Awards, value £750 each, are made twice yearly by the Scottish Arts Council to the authors of published books of literary merit written by Scots, by writers resident in Scotland, or on topics of Scottish interest. Most categories of books are eligible for consideration, but specialist, technical and academic books are outside the remit. Books are submitted by the authors' publishers. Enquiries to Literature Department, The Scottish Arts Council, 19 Charlotte Sq, Edinburgh EH2 4DF

Scottish Book of the Year
Founded 1981 by The Saltire Society and The Royal Bank of Scotland. For a book of a literary nature written by an author of Scottish descent or living in Scotland, or a book which deals with the work or life of a Scot or with a Scottish problem, event or situation. The Royal Bank contributes £1,500 to be awarded annually. The 1987 winner was Muriel Spark for *The Stories of Muriel Spark*. Enquiries to The Saltire Society, Saltire House, Atholl Crescent, Edinburgh EH3 8HA

Scottish Writer of the Year, see McVitie's Prize for Scottish Writer of the Year

Signal Poetry Award
Annual award of £100. The 1987 winner was Charles Causley for *Early in the Morning* (Viking Kestrel). Enquiries to Signal, Lockwood, Station Rd, South Woodchester, Stroud, Gloucestershire GL5 5EQ

Silver Dagger Award
Inaugurated 1956, revised 1970. A silvered dagger for the runner-up crime-fiction novel of the year (see Gold Dagger Award). Awarded annually by a panel of reviewers. Enquiries to Crime Writers' Association, PO Box 172, Tring, Hertfordshire HP23 5LP

Silver Pen Awards, see Macmillan Silver Pen Award for Fiction and Time-Life Silver Pen Award for Non-Fiction

Smarties Prize for Children's Books
Founded in 1985 and sponsored by Rowntree Mackintosh. Annual awards totalling £10,000 are given to encourage high standards in books for children of primary school age. Books must be written in English by a citizen of, or an author resident in the United Kingdom, and be published in the United Kingdom. There are three prize-winning categories: books for children of five years and under, books for children aged 6-8, and books for children aged 9-11. Each category winner receives £1,000, and a further £7,000 is awarded to the overall winner chosen from the three. The 1987 overall winner was James Berry for *A Thief in the Village* (Hamish Hamilton). Enquiries to Book Trust, Book House, 45 East Hill, Wandsworth, London SW18 2QZ

W H Smith & Son Literary Award, see International Literary Prizes

W H Smith Illustration Awards
Established 1987 to replace the Francis Williams Book Illustration Awards. This annual competition retains the same emphasis as its quinquennial predecessor in encouraging practising book and magazine illustrators producing work published in the United Kingdom in the ordinary manner and through the usual trade channels (thus excluding work produced for limited editions). In 1987 a prize of £3,000 for overall winner was given to Ralph Steadman for *I, Leonardo* (Jonathan Cape), £1,000 second prize for book illustration went to Justin Todd for *Alice's Adventures in Wonderland* and *Through the Looking Glass* (Victor Gollancz). Five further awards of £500 each were made. Enquiries to National Art Library, Victoria & Albert Museum, South Kensington, London SW7 2RL
or Book Trust, Book House, 45 East Hill, Wandsworth, London SW18 2QZ

W H Smith Young Writers' Competition
Established in 1959 as the Children's Literary Competition, and previously run by the 'Daily Mirror', the competition aims to encourage creativity in written English. Open to all children in the United Kingdom and of British nationality abroad, up to the age of 16 years. Ninety-three awards including cash prizes to schools and children totalling more than £4,500 are made and the award-winning work is published in book form. Enquiries to Public Relations Department, W H Smith & Son Ltd, Strand House, 7 Holbein Pl, London SW1W 8NR

Southern Arts Literature Prize
Founded in 1977 and open to writers resident in Hampshire, West Sussex, Isle of Wight, Berkshire, Oxfordshire, Wiltshire and East Dorset. £1,000 is awarded annually. The 1986 winner was Robert Gittings. Enquiries to The Literature Department, Southern Arts Association, 19 Southgate St, Winchester, Hampshire SO23 9EB

The **Spastics** Society Literary Contest*
The Contest, run in 1987 in conjunction with BBC Woman's Hour, is open to anyone with a disability or experience of disability. Entries should be prose compositions of up to 3000 words (if disabled the entry may be on any topic and if able-bodied it must reflect the experience of disability). Prizes totalling £600 will be awarded in Adult and Junior, fiction and non-fiction, categories and in 1987 the overall winner received the BBC Woman's Hour Award. Enquiries to Nina Heycock, Richard House, 30-32 Mortimer St, London W1N 7RA

The Winifred Mary **Stanford** Prize
Founded in 1978 by Leonard Cutts in memory of his wife. A biennial award of £1,000 is made for a published book, readable by the general public, which has been inspired in some way by the Christian faith and written by an author of 50 years of age or under at the date of publication. The 1986 winner was Tom Davies for *Stained Glass Hours* (New English Library). Enquiries to Juliet Newport, Secretary to the Judges, Hodder & Stoughton Ltd, 47 Bedford Sq, London WC1B 3DP

'Sunday Express' Book of the Year Award*
Founded 1986. To be awarded annually for an outstanding new work of fiction written in English by an author of any nationality and published in the United Kingdom. The first £20,000 award was made in 1988 to Brian Moore for *The Colour of Blood* (Jonathan Cape). No applications or nominations accepted. Enquiries to Graham Lord, Literary Editor, Sunday Express, 121 Fleet St, London EC4P 4JT

T L S/Cheltenham Literature Festival Poetry Competition
For an unpublished poem of not more than 50 lines. Two equal-value sets of prizes are awarded annually to winners selected from a short list, the first set chosen by judges at the Cheltenham Festival of Literature and the second by readers of the shortlisted poems subsequently published in the 'Times Literary Supplement'. The prizes are of £500, £250 and £100 in each case. Enquiries to Poetry Competition, Town Hall, Imperial Square, Cheltenham, Gloucestershire GL50 1QA
or Times Literary Supplement, Priory House, St Johns Lane, London EC1M 4BX

Reginald **Taylor** Prize
Instituted 1932. For the best unpublished essay, not exceeding 7,500 words, on any subject of archaeological, art historical, or antiquarian interest within the period from the Roman era to AD 1830. Prize of £100 awarded annually. Enquiries to Dr Martin Henig, Honorary Editor, Institute of Archaeology, 36 Beaumont St, Oxford OX1 2PG

Dylan **Thomas** Award
Instituted in 1983 in honour of the contribution made to English letters by Dylan Thomas and to encourage writers working in two literary genres in which Dylan Thomas's work is celebrated. £1,000 awarded to a poet or short-story writer. The winner of the 1987 award was Andrew Motion for his collection of poetry *Natural Causes*. Enquiries to The Poetry Society, 21 Earls Court Sq, London SW5 9DE

Time-Life Silver Pen Award for Non-Fiction
In 1986 Time-Life took over sponsorship of this annual award for an outstanding work of non-fiction written in English and published in the United Kingdom in the previous year. The prize is £1,000 and a silver pen and is given on PEN Writers' Day. The 1986 award went to Michael Scannell for *Solzhenitsyn*. Enquiries to PEN English Centre, 7 Dilke St, London SW3 4JE

Tom-Gallon Trust Award
Founded 1943. This prize of £500 is awarded biennially to short-story writers of limited means. Entrants must submit a list of already published fiction, one published or unpublished short story, and a brief statement of their financial position and willingness to devote substantial time to writing fiction as soon as they are

financially able. The 1987 award was made to Lawrence Scott. Enquiries to Society of Authors, 84 Drayton Gardens, London SW10 9SB

Welsh Arts Council Awards to Writers
Since 1968, the Welsh Arts Council has given awards to authors whose books are of exceptional literary merit or which make an important contribution to the literature of Wales. The books must be written in English or Welsh. The prizes are awarded to recognize achievement, to draw attention to writers of promise and to encourage the writing of creative literature in English and Welsh. Up to 10 cash prizes of £1,000 awarded annually.
Enquiries to Welsh Arts Council, Museum Pl, Cardiff CF1 3NX

Wheatley Medal
Instituted 1961. Presented by The Library Association, after consultation with The Society of Indexers, for a book published in the UK during the preceding three years which sets an outstandingly high standard in the quality of its index. The award of the 1986 medal was withheld.
Enquiries to The Library Association, 7 Ridgmount St, London WC1E 7AE

Whitbread Literary Awards
Originally instituted in 1971; in 1985 a Whitbread Book of the Year award and a poetry category were introduced. Annual awards totalling £25,000 are given to acknowledge outstanding books in five categories of literature: novel, first novel, children's novel, biography/autobiography, poetry. From each category one book is selected as the Whitbread Category Winner; each of the five nominations carries an award of £1,250 and goes forward to The Whitbread Book of the Year, for which the award is an additional £18,750. Books must first have been published in the UK or Republic of Ireland between 1 November and 31 October in relevant year, and written by authors who have been domiciled in either place since 1 November 1984. The winners of the 1987 Whitbread Literary Awards were (novel) Ian McEwan for *The Child in Time* (Cape); (first novel) Francis Wyndham for *The Other Garden* (Cape); (children's novel) Geraldine McCaughrean for *A Little Lower than the Angels* (Oxford); (biography) Christopher Nolan for *Under the Eye of the Clock* (Weidenfeld & Nicolson); (poetry) Seamus Heaney for *The Haw Lantern* (Faber). Christopher Nolan was the winner of the 1987 Whitbread Book of the Year prize.
Enquiries to the Booksellers Association of Great Britain and Ireland, 154 Buckingham Palace Rd, London SW1W 9TZ

Francis **Williams Book Illustration Awards**, replaced in 1987 by the W H Smith Illustration Awards (qv)

Griffith John **Williams Memorial Prize** (Gwobr Goffa Griffith John Williams)
Awarded to non-members of the Yr Academi Gymreig for the best literary work in Welsh produced in the previous year. About £200 awarded annually.
Enquiries to Yr Academi Gymreig, 3 Llawr, Tŷ Mount Stuart, Sgwâr Mount Stuart, Y Dociau, Cardiff CF1 6DQ

Wolfson Literary Awards for History and Biography
Founded 1972. Two awards totalling £15,000 are made annually to authors of published historical works of outstanding scholarship and literary quality. In 1986 the awards were made to Professor J H Elliott for *The Count Duke of Olivares —* *A Statesman in the Age of Decline* (Oxford University Press) and Professor Jonathan Israel for *European Jewry in the Age of Mercantialism* (Yale University Press).
Enquiries to The Wolfson Foundation, c/o Paisner & Co (Solicitors), Bouverie House, 154 Fleet St, London EC4A 2DQ

Write A Children's Story Competition
Annual competition open to all previously unpublished writers for a story of not more than 1,000 words which would interest and entertain children. First prize of £250, with two further prizes of £100 and £50 each. Enquiries to The Academy of Children's Writers, 6 Auckland View, High Etherley, Bishop Auckland, Co Durham, DL14 0JQ

Young Observer National Children's Poetry Competition
First awarded in 1986 and sponsored then and in 1987 by the Water Authorities Association, the competition is open to three age groups: 10 years and under, 11-14 years and 15-18 years. There is an additional prize for the best group of poems from any school. Enquiries to Chelsea Bridge House, Queenstown Rd, London SW8 4NN

Translation Agencies and Associations

Alpha Translation*, Church Rate Corner, Malting Lane, Cambridge CB3 9HF Tel: (0223) 357657 Telex BTG84: TXT095 Fax: (0223) 358304
Specialist translators of computing and electronics texts.
Associated Company: Alpha Translation, Zug, Switzerland

I P M C Ltd, 25 Marloes Rd, London W8 6LG Tel: (01) 373 0464, (01) 373 2796 Telex: 267009 Fax: (01) 373 5635
Translation, setting and printing in all commercial languages, including Arabic, Chinese, Japanese. Offices and associates in Germany, Hong Kong, Ireland, Netherlands (qv), USA

Institute of Translation and Interpreting, 318a Finchley Rd, London NW3 5HT Tel: (01) 794 9931 Fax: (01) 935 2105
Secretary: D Castellano
Publication: ITI News (quarterly)

Swedish-English Literary Translators' Association (SELTA)*, 49 Beaumont St, London W1N 1RE Tel: (01) 487 4156
Hon Secretary: Tom Geddes
SELTA aims to promote the publication of Swedish literature in English and to represent the interests of those involved in its translation
Publication: Swedish Book Review (twice a year)

Tek Translation & International Print Ltd*, 11 Uxbridge Rd, London W12 8LH Tel: (01) 749 3211 Telex: 265658 Tek G Fax: (01) 743 0880
Dirs: Bernard Keigher, Argyro Keigher, A E Fernandes
Technical specialists in over 100 languages, including Chinese, Arabic, Japanese, Russian

Translators Association, 84 Drayton Gardens, London SW10 9SB Tel: (01) 373 6642

Upper Volta

see Burkina Faso

Uruguay

General Information

Language: Spanish
Religion: Roman Catholic
Population: 2.9 million
Bank Hours: 1300-1700 Monday-Friday
Shop Hours: 0900-1200, 1400-1900 Monday-Friday; 0900-1230 Saturday
Currency: peso (nuevo peso = $N)
Export/Import Information: Member of the Latin American Free Trade Association. No tariffs on books or single copies catalogues but surcharge on advertising matter. Additional surcharge on all imports, plus VAT CIF, plus Stamp Tax of percentage of total invoice value. No import licences. No exchange controls
Copyright: Berne, Buenos Aires (see International section)

Book Trade Organizations

Asociación de Libreros del Uruguay*, Ave Uruguay 1325, Montevideo
Uruguayan Booksellers' Association

Asociación Uruguaya de Escritores*, Bartolomé Mitre 1260, Montevideo
Uruguayan Writers' Association

Cámara Uruguaya del Libro*, Apdo 2, Montevideo (Located at: Carlos Roxlo 1446 piso 1°, Montevideo) Tel: (02) 411860
Uruguayan Publishers' Association
Secretary: Arnaldo Medone

Book Trade Reference Books

Anuario bibliográfico Uruguayo 1968- (Uruguayan Bibliographical Annual), Biblioteca Nacional del Uruguay, Casilla de Correo 452, Montevideo (Located at: 18 de Julio 1790, Montevideo)

Ribliografía uruguaya (Uruguayan Bibliography), Biblioteca de Poder Legislativo, Palacio Legislativo, Ave Agradiada, Montevideo

Publishers

Editorial **Arca** SRL*, Andes 1118, Montevideo
Man Dir: Alberto Oreggioni
Subjects: General Literature, History, Social Science

Barreiro y Ramos SA, Casilla de Correo 15, Montevideo (Located at: Juan Carlos Gómez 1436, Montevideo) Tel: (02) 950150 Cable Add: Bareiramos
Man Dir: Gaston Barreiro Zorrilla; *Sales Dir:* Raúl Catelli
Subjects: General Literature, Textbooks Reference
Bookshops: See under Major Booksellers
Founded: 1871

URUGUAY 491

Editorial y Librería Juridica Amalio M **Fernández**, 25 de Mayo 477, planta baja, Of 11, Montevideo Tel: (02) 952684
Man Dir: Amalio M Fernández; *Editorial:* Carlos W Deamestoy Perez; *Sales:* Andrés Paz López
Subjects: Law, Sociology
Founded: 1951

Fundación de Cultura Universitaria*, 25 de Mayo 568, 1155 Montevideo Tel: (02) 913385
Man Dir: Luis Carlos Benvenuto; *Editorial Dir:* Carlos Fuques
Branch Off: Guayabo 1860, Montevideo
Subjects: Social Science, Law
Founded: 1968

Grijalbo Editor*, Buenos Aires 280, Montevideo
Parent Company: Ediciones Grijalbo SA, Spain (qv)

Editorial **Medina** SRL*, Gaboto 1521, Montevideo Tel: (02) 44100/45800
Man Dir: Marcos Medina Vidal
Subject: Low-priced Paperbacks
Founded: 1933

A **Monteverde** y Cia SA*, Casilla de Correo 371, Montevideo (Located at: 25 de Mayo 577, Montevideo) Tel: (02) 959019/957543
Man Dir: Héctor Mussini; *Sales Dirs:* Raúl Puyo, Boris Faingola; *Production:* Leandro Mendaro
Subjects: History, Literature, Primary & Secondary Textbooks, Educational Materials
Bookshop: Palacio del Libro (qv under Major Booksellers)
Founded: 1879

Mosca Hnos SA, Ave 18 de Julio 1578, Montevideo Tel: (02) 493141 Cable Add: Moscaher
Man Dir: Miguel Angel Mosca; *Sales Dir:* Raúl Mosca
Subjects: General Literature, Religion, Textbooks
Bookshop: See under Major Booksellers
Founded: 1888

Editorial **Nuestra Tierra***, Cerrito 566, Montevideo Tel: (02) 916217
Man Dir: Daniel Aljanati; *Editorial Dir:* Jaime D Aljanati
Subject: General Literature
Founded: 1968

Ediciones **Papacito***, Andes 1340, Montevideo Tel: (02) 902872
Publicity: Carmelo Porcelli
Bookshop: Librerías Papacito (qv under Major Booksellers)
Subject: Essays

Editorial **Técnica Interamericana** ETI Ltda, Casilla de Correos 357, Montevideo (Located at: Av Italia 2574, Montevideo) Tel: (02) 809848
Manager: Mirta Gaidos

Major Booksellers

Albe Soc Com*, Cerrito 566, Montevideo Tel: (02) 85692

América Latina*, 18 de Julio 2089, Montevideo Tel: (02) 415127
Manager: Ismael Muñoz

Barreiro y Ramos SA, Juan Carlos Gómez 1436, Montevideo Tel: (02) 950150
Branches at: Ave 18 de Julio 941; Minas 1491; Ave General Flores 2426; Ave 8 de Octubre 3728; Ave Agraciada 3945; Ave Rivera 2684; Calle 21 de Setiembre 2753; Arocena 1599 (all in Montevideo); Ave General Artigas 714, Las Piedras
Also Publisher (qv)

Feria del Libro, Ave 18 de Julio 1308, Montevideo Tel: (02) 902070
Manager: Domingo A Maestro

Librería Amalio M **Fernández**, 25 de Mayo 477 planta baja ofic 11, Montevideo Tel: (02) 952684

El **Galeón***, Maldonado 1400, Montevideo
Antiquarian bookseller

Ibana, SA*, Julio Herrera y Obes 1626, Montevideo Tel: (02) 914738
Manager: Tomás J Raphael

Librería Inglesa*, Sarandi 580, Montevideo Tel: (02) 901955

Librería **Linardi** y Risso*, Juan Carlos Gomez 1435, Montevideo Tel: (02) 957129/957328 Cable Add: Linbooks
Managers: Adolfo Linardi, Juan I Risso
Antiquarian bookseller

Mosca Hnos, Ave 18 de Julio 1578, Montevideo Tel: (02) 493141

Palacio del Libro*, Casilla de Correo 371, Montevideo (Located at: 25 de Mayo 577, Montevideo) Tel: (02) 959019/957543
Man Dir: Héctor Mussini

Librerías **Papacito***, 18 de Julio 1409, Montevideo Tel: (02) 902872
Manager: Carmelo Porcelli

Major Libraries

Archivo General de la Nación*, Calle Convención 1474, Montevideo

Biblioteca **Artigas-Washington** (USIS)*, Calle Paraguay 1217, Montevideo Tel: (02) 917423

Biblioteca Nacional del Uruguay*, Casilla de Correo 452, Montevideo (Located at: 18 de Julio 1790, Montevideo) Tel: (02) 45030/496011
Dir: Prof Enrique Fierro
Publications: Anuario Bibliográfico Uruguayo 1968-, *Revista Biblioteca Nacional* 1966-

Centro Nacional de Información y Documentación (CENID)*, Avda Libertador Brig General Lavalleja No 2025, Montevideo
Dir: Lelia Laclau de Buzó
Publications: Anales, Enciclopedia de educación, Legislación escolar

Biblioteca Central y Publicaciones de **Consejo** de Educación Secundaria básica y superior*, Eduardo Acevedo 1419, Montevideo Tel: (02) 44273
Dir: Aída Elcarte de Carrió

Biblioteca **Facultad** de Humanidades y Ciencias*, Universidad de la República, Tristán Narvaja 1674, Montevideo Tel: (02) 491104
Librarian: Susana Gil

Biblioteca del **Instituto Cultural** Anglo-Uruguayo*, San José 1426, Montevideo Tel: (02) 910570/908468/904201
Librarian: Cristina Scaron

Biblioteca del **Museo** Histórico Nacional*, Casa Lavalleja, Zaballa 1469, Montevideo

Biblioteca del **Palacio** Legislativo, see Biblioteca del Poder Legislativo

Biblioteca del **Poder** Legislativo*, Palacio Legislativo, Ave Agraciada, Montevideo Tel: (02) 409111
Library of the Legislative Power
Librarians: Mazzeo Condenanza, Hugo Alberto
Publications include: Anales Parlamentarios (semestrial); *Boletin Bibliografico*

(monthly); *Fichas Analiticas de Articulos de Publicaciones Periodicas* (monthly); *Bibliografía Uruguaya* (irregular)

Biblioteca Municipal 'Dr Joaquín de **Salterain**'*, Palacio Municipal, Ave 18 de Julio, Santiago de Chile

Library Associations

Agrupación Bibliotecológica del Uruguay, Cerro Largo 1666, Montevideo Tel: (02) 405740
Uruguayan Library and Archive Science Association
President: Luis Alberto Musso
Publications include: Bibliografía uruguaya sobre Brasil; Aportes para la historia de la bibliotecología en el Uruguay; Bibliografía y documentación en el Uruguay, La estrella del sur-Indice; Bibliografía bibliográfica y bibliotecologica; Archivos del Uruguay

Asociación de Bibliotecólogos y Afines del Uruguay*, Casilla de Correo 1315, Montevideo (Located at: Dante 2255, Montevideo)
Uruguayan Library Association
President: Martha Ottino Ferraro
Secretary: Claudia Simon
Publication: Actualidades Bibliotecológicas

Library Reference Books and Journals

Books

Bibliografía bibliográfica y bibliotecologica del Uruguay (Bibliography of Bibliography and Library Science in Uruguay), Agrupación Bibliotecológica del Uruguay, Cerro Largo 1666, Montevideo

Bibliografía y documentación en el Uruguay (Bibliography and Documentation in Uruguay), Agrupación Bibliotecológica del Uruguay, Cerro Largo 1666, Montevideo

Journal

Revista de la Biblioteca Nacional (National Library Review), Biblioteca Nacional del Uruguay, Casilla de Correo 452, Montevideo (Located at: 18 de Julio 1790, Montevideo)

Literary Associations and Societies

Academia Nacional de Letras*, Calle 1° de Mayo 1445 (Palacio Taranco), Montevideo
Secretary: Luis Bausero
Publications: Boletín de la Academia Nacional de Letras; Revista Nacional

Centro Urugayo **P E N**, Gral Prim 3145, Montevideo
President: Enrique Estrazulas; *Secretary:* Augus Poet

Literary Prizes

Concurso Literario Municipal (Municipal Literary Competition)*
Three prizes are awarded in each of the following four groups: prose, fiction, essay, and biography and history. Enquiries to Intendencia Municipal de Montevideo (Palacio Municipal), 18 de Julio 1360, Montevideo

Gran Premio Nacional de Literatura*
Founded in 1951 by the Ministry of

492 URUGUAY — VENEZUELA

Education and Culture to encourage and acknowledge the writing of literature. The prize of N$200,000 is for the total work of an author. Awarded every three years. The most recent winner was Juan Carlos Onetti. Enquiries to Ministerio de Educación y Cultura, Sarandi 444, Montevideo

Premio de Remuneraciones Literarias*
Four prizes: poetry; fiction, juveniles or biography; essays; science and technology, sociology, history, education or philosophy. Awarded annually. Enquiries to Ministerio de Educación y Cultura, Sarandi 444, Montevideo

Premio Nacional de Literatura*
For a book in the field of culture. Awarded every two years. Enquiries to Ministerio de Educación y Cultura, Sarandi 444, Montevideo

Vatican City State

General Information

Language: Italian
Religion: Roman Catholic
Population: 728
Currency: Vatican lira = Italian lira. Italian currency is used
Copyright: Berne, UCC (see International section)

Publishers

Biblioteca **Apostolica** Vaticana*, I-00120 Vatican City Tel: 6983302
Man Dir: Leonard E Boyle
Subjects: Philology, Classics, Mediaeval History, Philosophy, Theology, Law, Museum Collections, Classical & Papal Coinage, Manuscript Facsimiles, Exhibition Catalogues

Tipografia Poliglotta Vaticana*, Vatican City
Dir: Very Rev Angelo Vedani
Subjects: Juveniles, Education, Natural & Social Science

Urbaniana University Press, Via Urbano VIII, 16-00120 Vatican City Tel: 6875992 Cable Add: Urbaniana University Vatican City
Chief Executive, Rights & Permissions: Prof Maksimilijan Jezernik; *Sales:* Thomas Thengunpallil; *Production:* Vincenzo Marigliano; *Publicity:* Ruggero Grottanelli
Subsidiary Companies: Tipografia Poliglotta Vaticana (qv); Paideia Editrice, Italy (qv); Armellini, Ingrac
Subjects: Philosophy, Theology, Canon Law, Missiology
Bookshops: Alma Mater, Pontificia University Urbaniana, Rean; Mescat, Libreria Vaticana, The Courier
1986-87: 40 titles *Founded:* 1975

Libreria Editrice **Vaticana**, I-00120 Vatican City Tel: 6983532/6985003 Telex: 5042024 Dirgentel Va
Dir: P D Giustino Farnedi
Subjects: Religion, Philosophy, Literature, Art, Latin Philology, Theology, History, Works of Karol Wojtyla

Bookshop: At above address
Founded: 1926

Major Library

Biblioteca **Apostolica** Vaticana*, I-00120 Vatican City Tel: (06) 6983302
Vatican Apostolic Library

Venezuela

General Information

Language: Spanish
Religion: Roman Catholic
Population: 17 million
Bank Hours: 0830-1130, 1400-1630 Monday-Friday
Shop Hours: 0900-1300, 1500-1900 Monday-Saturday
Currency: 100 centimos = 1 bolívar
Export/Import Information: Member of the Latin American Free Trade Association. No exchange controls
Copyright: UCC, Berne (see International section)

Book Trade Organizations

Cámara Venezolana del Libro*, Apdo 51858, Caracas 1050-A (Located at: Ave Andrés Bello, Centro Andrés Bello, Torre Oeste 11° piso, of 112-0, Caracas) Tel: (02) 7812809
Venezuelan Publishers' Association
Secretary: M Morales C

Standard Book Numbering Agency, Instituto Autonomo Biblioteca Nacional y de Servicios de Bibliotecas, Apdo 80593, Prados del Este, Caracas 1080 (Located at: Calle Soledad Ed Rogi 3° piso, Zona Industrial de la Trinidad) Telex: 24621 Iabn VC
ISBN Administrator: Marcela García Jordán

Book Trade Reference Book

Bibliografía Venezolana (Venezuelan Bibliography), Instituto Autónomo Biblioteca Nacional y de Servicios de Bibliotecas, Apdo 6525, Caracas 1010-A

Publishers

Ernesto **Armitano**, Editor, Apdo 50853, Caracas (Located at: Cuarto Transversal de la Ave Principal de Boleita, Edificio Centro Industrial 2° piso, Sabana Grande, Caracas) Tel: (02) 342565 Cable Add: Armitpress Caracas Venezuela Telex: 23115 Panec V
Man Dir: E Armitano; *Sales Dir:* P Salazar
Subjects: Venezuelan Painters, Arts, Architecture, Entymology, Ecology, Anthropology, History, Guides (some titles also in English, German, French and Italian)
1985-86: 7 titles *Founded:* 1957
ISBN Publisher's Prefix: 980-216

Editorial **Ateneo** de Caracas, Apdo 662, Caracas (Located at: Edificio Ateneo de Caracas 5° piso, Plaza Morelos, Los Caobos) Tel: (02) 5734622 (orders 5754475)
President: María Teresa Castillo; *Editorial Dir, Sales, Production:* Antonio Polo
Subjects: Psychology, Arts, Sciences, Politics, History, Literature, Poetry, Children
Bookshop: Librería Ateneo de Caracas (at above address)
Founded: 1978
ISBN Publisher's Prefix: 980-255

Biblioteca **Ayacucho**, Apdos 14413 y 2122, Caracas 1010 (Located at: Centro Financiero Latino, 12° piso of 1, 2 & 3, Esq Animas a Plaza España, Ave Urdaneta, Caracas) Tel: (02) 5616691/5617287/5617589 Cable Add: Biayacucho
President of Editorial Commission, Editorial, Rights & Permissions: Dr José Ramón Medina; *Production:* Oscar Rodriguez Ortiz; *Sales, Publicity:* Miriam Valdez
Subjects: Latin-America, Classic & Contemporary Literature, Belles Lettres, Politics, History, Art
1986: 115 titles *Founded:* 1975
ISBN Publisher's Prefix: 84-660

Editorial **Biosfera** SRL+, Apdo de Correos 50-634, Caracas 1050-A (Located at: Av Chama, Ota Coral, Colinas de Bello Monte, Caracas 1050-A) Tel: (02) 7528892/7519119/7519320
Man Dir, Editorial, Production: Dr Serafin Mazparrote
Subsidiary Company: Litho-Mundo SA, Urb Guaycay, Calle La Pedrera, Edificio Viamonte PB Las Minas de Baruta, Caracas 1080
Subjects: Textbooks, General Non-fiction, Biology, Mathematics, English, Art, Science, Castilian
Bookshop: Ediciones Amanecer (Librería) Centro Polo (at above main address)
Founded: 1979
ISBN Publisher's Prefix: 980-210

Colegial Bolivariana CA*, Apdo de Correo 70324, Caracas 1071-A (Located at: Ave Diego Cisneros (Principal de Los Ruices), Edificio Co-Bo, Caracas 1071-A) Tel: (02) 2391433 Cable Add: Colegial
Man Dir: Antonio Juzgado A
Subjects: Primary & Secondary Textbooks, Juveniles
Founded: 1961

Distribuciones **E D I M E***, Apdo 51666, Caracas 105 (Located at: San Narciso a San Miguel Ed Eduard PB (Ave Panteón – Av Fuerzas Armadas), Caracas 1010)
Tel: (02) 5624929/5622602
Man Dir: Nils Koehler; *Sales Dir, Publicity & Advertising:* E Mascaraque; *Permissions:* Juan Agero
Subjects: Literature, Biography, History & Art of Venezuela, Low-priced Paperbacks
Founded: 1948

Ediciones de la Biblioteca (EBUC)+*, Departamento de Distribución de Publicaciones, Biblioteca, Apdo 47004, Caracas 1041 (Located at: 1° piso, Edificio de la Biblioteca, Universidad Central de Venezuela, Caracas) Tel: (02) 6626242
Editorial Dir: Marcio S Meléndez
Subjects: Belles Lettres, History, Philosophy, Paperbacks, Medicine, Psychology, Engineering, General & Social Science, Law, University Textbooks
Founded: 1961

Editemas y Dilae SA*, Calle Capitolio, Edificio Indelco, Sótano 1, Bolita Sur, Caracas Tel: (02) 333505/391832
Man Dir: Juan-Ramón Igual
Parent Company: Aguilar SA de Ediciones, Spain (qv)

Fondo Editorial Común SC*, Final de la Ave El Bosque, Edificio Royal Palace, Oficina 401, Plaza Brión-Chacaito, Caracas 1050 Tel: (02) 723714 Cable Add: Editcomun Telex: 21753 Comun VC, 28462 Dirfc VC
President: Alba Illaramendi; *Vice-President:* Carlos Suarez; *Man Dir:* Raul Alvarez; *Director:* Peter Neumann
Subjects: Social Science, Communication, Urban Planning, Law

Fondo Educativo Interamericano CA, Apdo 62361, Caracas 1060-A (Located at: Calle Madariaga, Qta El Lago, Los Chaguaramos, Caracas) Tel: (02) 6612356/ 6618407 Telex: 21901 Fondo VC
President: Juan José Fernandez; *Editorial:* in Bogotá, Colombia (qv)
Parent Company: Addison-Wesley Publishing Co Inc, Reading, MA 01867, USA
Associate Companies: See Addison-Wesley Iberoamericana SA, Mexico
Subjects: Mathematics, Biology, Engineering, Business, Textbooks

Editorial **Grijalbo** SA+*, Ave Los Laboratorios Edificio Ofinca 3a, PB, Los Ruices, Caracas Tel: (02) 316746/316721
Man Dir: Manuel Morales
Parent Company: Ediciones Grijalbo SA, Spain (qv)

Grolier de Venezuela*, Apdo 50930, Caracas (Located at: Edificio Continental, Esq Jabillos, S Grande) Tel: (02) 762659/ 7828609
Man Dir: Gilberto Livay
Associate Companies: See under the Grolier Society of Australia

Editorial **Interamericana de Venezuela** CA*, Apdo 50785, Caracas Tel: (02) 729492/723720
General Manager: Pedro Alvarez

Editorial **Kapelusz** Venezolana SA*, Ave Urdaneta, Animas a Platanal, Edificio Camoruco, Caracas 1011-A Tel: (02) 5629177/5629188 Cable Add: Kapelusz Telex: 24039 Ekave VC
Man Dir: Horacio Perotti Beraldo
Parent Company: Editorial Kapelusz SA, Argentina (qv)
Subject: Secondary & Primary Textbooks
Founded: 1963

Editorial **Labor** de Venezuela SA, Apdo 14054, Caracas (Located at: Ave Andrés Bello, Edificio Garten, Caracas) Tel: (02) 7811398/7815819
Man Dir: Jaime Salgado Palacio

Editorial **Mandorla**, Apdo 76978, Caracas 1070 (Located at: Residencia El Recreo, 1-c, Calle El Recreo con Ave Venezuela) Tel: (02) 714070
Subject: Poetry

Monte Avila Editores CA, Apdo 70712, Caracas 1070 (Located at: Ave Principal de la Castellana con 1a, Transversal-Qta Cristina, Caracas 2003) Tel: (02) 326020/ 330760/332137 Telex: 24220 Conac
Man Dir: Néstor Leal; *Editorial:* Silda Cordoliani; *Rights & Permissions:* Eugenio Montejo; *Sales:* Glenda Sanchez; *Production:* Vittoria Giordano
Subjects: Fiction, Literature, Biography, History, How-to, Art, Philosophy, Medicine, Psychology, General Science, Social Science, University Textbooks
1985: 125 titles *Founded:* 1968
ISBN Publisher's Prefix: 980-01

Editorial **Plata** SA, now in Peru (qv)

Editorial **Reverté** Venezolana SA*, Apdo 14520, Caracas 1011-A (Located at: Pelibro a Pelelojo, Edificio Torre Carabobo, local 2, Candelaria, Caracas) Tel: (02) 5726670
Associate Companies: See Editorial Reverté SA, Spain

Editorial Ramón **Sopena** Venezolana SA*, Alcabala a Puente Anauco, Edificio AN-VI, 1° piso, Caracas Tel: (02) 5729709/ 5728368 *Man Dir:* A García Sánchez
Parent Company: Ramón Sopena SA, Spain (qv)

Teduca, Técnicas Educativas, CA, 4a Ave No 15, Qta Mari-Ana, Altamira, Caracas Tel: (02) 2616937/2617961/2618985/339185
Chairman: Eduardo Robles Piquer; *General Manager:* Enrique de Polanco Soutullo
Associate Company: Santillana SA de Ediciones, Spain (qv)
Subject: Education

Editorial **Tiempo** Nuevo SA*, Apdo 50304, Caracas (Located at: Calle San Antonio, Edificio Hotel Royal, Sabana Grande, Caracas) Tel: (02) 729073
Man Dir: Benito Milla Navarro; *Sales Dir:* Ricardo Lozano
Subject: General Literature
Founded: 1970

Universidad de los Andes, Consejo de Publicaciones, Ave Andrés Bello, Via La Parroquía, Antiguo Central Azucarero, Mérida 5101 Tel: (074) 638814 ext 15
Man Dir: Francisco Puleo; *Sales, Production:* Macario Molina; *Publicity:* Ana Allegue de Pietri; *Rights & Permissions:* Asunta Briceño
Subjects: Technology, Science, Medicine, Pharmacy, Social Science, Juvenile, Regional Literature
1985: 34 titles *1986:* 28 titles *Founded:* 1977
ISBN Publisher's Prefix: 980-221

Ediciones **Vega** SRL, Apdo 51662, Caracas 1050 (Located at: Plaza Las Tres Gracias, Edificio Odeón, Los Chaguaramos, Caracas) Tel: (02) 6622092/6621397 Cable Add: Edivega
Man Dir: Fernando Vega Alonso
Subjects: University Textbooks, Technical
Bookshop: Librería Técnica Vega (qv under Major Booksellers)
Founded: 1965

Major Booksellers

El **Amigo** de Todos*, Madrices a Ibarras, Loc 7, Edificio Bergantín, Caracas Tel: (02) 815580

Librería del **Este**, Apdo 60-337, Caracas 1060-A (Located at: Ave Miranda 52, Edificio Galipán, Caracas 1060-A) Tel: (02) 9511297/9512307/9511705
Manager: Tomas Pericas
Exclusive distributors of World Bank, United Nations, Unesco, OIT publications

Fundacion Kuai-Mare*, Conjunto Residencial Coracrevi, Edificio Táchira, loc 10 y 11, Los Caobos
This is the distribution side of the Instituto Autónomo Bibioteca Nacional y de Servicios de Bibliotecas, specializing in publications by Venezuelan official, cultural and university organizations. There are five other branches

Librería **Lectura***, Centro Comercial Chacaito, local 129, Caracas Tel: (02) 717861

Librería **Cultural** SA*, Apdo 15156, Maracaibo (Located at: Ave 5 de Julio 17-31, Maracaibo) Tel: (061) 525724/ 525531/524382 Cable Add: Licultura
Man Dir: Angel Vela González

Librería **Cultural Venezolana***, Santa Capilla a Mijares 26, Caracas Tel: (02) 813306

Librería **Medica** Paris, Apdo 60681, Caracas 1060-A (Located at: Gran Ave, Edif Medica Paris, Caracas 1060-A) Tel: (02) 7812709 Telex: 21420
Manager: Pierre Paneyko

Librería **Mundial***, Apdo 2400, Caracas 1010 (Located at: Santa Capilla a Mijares 26, Edificio San Mauricio, Interior Planta Baja) Tel: (02) 812630

Organización de Bienestar Estudiantil (OBE)*, Universidad Central de Venezuela, Ciudad Universitaria, Caracas

El **Palacio** del Libro*, Bloque 3, loc 4, El Silencio, Caracas Tel: (02) 452854

Librería **Politécnica Moulines***, Apdo 50738, Caracas 105 (Located at: Calle Villaflor, Sabana Grande, Caracas 105) Tel: (02) 710692/729370

Publicaciones Españolas SA*, Pele el Ojo a Puente Brion, Ave Mexico, Caracas Tel: (02) 5715943/5727302/5725224 Telex: 26286 Pesa Vc

Librería **Selecta***, Apdo 111, Mérida (Located at: Ave 3, 231-23, Mérida) Tel: (074) 23609

Tecni Ciencia Libros SA*, Torre Phelps, Mezz, Central, Plaza Venezuela, Caracas Tel: (02) 552091
Manager: Fanett de Ramirez

Librería Técnica **Vega**, Apdo 3093, Caracas 1010 (Located at: Plaza Tres Gracias, Edificio Odeón, Caracas 1010) Tel: (02) 6622848/6622702 Cable Add: Edivega
Manager: Lucia Ribas
Owned by: Fernando Vega, Ediciones Vega SRL (qv)

Venezuelan Book Service SA, Apdo 47963, Caracas 1041-A Tel: (02) 6618407 Telex: 21901 Fondo VC

Major Libraries

Archivo General de la Nación*, Santa Capilla a Carmelitas 5, Caracas

Biblioteca de la Universidad Catolica 'Andrés **Bello**'*, Apdo 29068, Caracas 1021
Librarian: Dr Carmelo Salvatierra

Biblioteca del Congreso*, Plaza del Capitolio, Caracas

Biblioteca Nacional*, Ave Universidad, Frente al Congreso Nacional, Caracas 1010 Tel: (02) 4832705 Telex: 24621
See also Instituto Autónomo Biblioteca Nacional y de Servicios de Bibliotecas

Servicios Bibliotecarios Generales 'Tulio **Febres Cordero**', Edificio Administrativo de la ULA 2° piso, Ave Tulio Febres Cordero, 5101 Mérida Tel: (074) 526244/ 527244/528244 ext 463/553 Telex: 74173 Cdchula
Acting Director: Lic Maria Chavez de Burgos

Instituto Autónomo Biblioteca Nacional y de Servicios de Bibliotecas*, Apdo 6525, Caracas 1010-A (Located at: Calle París con Caroní, Edificio Macanao, Las Mercedes, Caracas 1060) Tel: (02) 911444
National Library, Public Library Services, Audiovisual Archive of Venezuela

Venezuela (continued)

Publications include: *Anuarios Bibliograficos* (to 1977); *Bibliografía Venezolana* (from 1978); *Catalogo de Publicaciones Oficiales*; *Boletín Bibliotécnico*; *Informe Anual*
See also Fundacion Kuai-Mare (Major Booksellers)

Biblioteca 'Marcel **Roche**' del Instituto Venezolano de Investigaciones Científicas, Apdo 21827, Caracas 1020-A (Located at: Altos de Pipe, Km 11 Carretera Panamericana, Caracas 1020-A) Tel: (02) 5727446 Cable Add: Ivicsas Telex: 21338
Library of the Venezuelan Institute for Scientific Research
Librarian: Hana M de David

Biblioteca Central de la **Universidad Central** de Venezuela*, Ciudad Universitaria, Caracas Tel: (02) 619811

Biblioteca Central de la **Universidad de Zulia***, Apdo 526, Maracaibo (Located at: Grano de Oro, Maracaibo) Tel: (061) 515390
Librarian: Margarita Alvárez
Publication: *Boletín* (biennial)

Library Associations

Colegio de Bibliotecólogos, Archivólogos y Afines del Estado Zulia*, Apdo 1295, Maracaibo
College of Librarians and Archivists of Zulia State
Secretary: Lic Lourdes Crespo
Publications include: *Boletín CBAEZ*; *Directorio de Bibliotecólogos y Archivólogos, Región Zulia*

Colegio de Bibliotecólogos y Archivólogos de Venezuela (Colbav)*, Apdo 6282, Caracas 1010 Tel: (02) 7813245
Venezuelan College of Librarians and Archivists
Executive-Secretary: Lic Bernarda Lozada

Library Reference Books and Journals

Book

Directorio de Bibliotecólogos y Archivólogos, Region Zulia (Directory of Librarians and Archivists of Zulia State), CBAEZ, Apdo 1295, Maracaibo

Journal

Codex, Boletin de la Escuela de Biblioteconomia y Archivos (Bulletin of the School of Librarianship and Archives), Universidad Central de Venezuela, Facultad de Humanidades y Educación, Escuela de Biblioteconomia y Archivos, Ciudad Universitaria, Caracas

Literary Associations and Societies

Asociación de Escritores de Venezuela*, Apdo 429, Caracas (Located at: Velázquez a Miseria 22, Caracas)
Venezuelan Writers' Association
General Secretary: Dr Alberto Silva Alvarez
Publication: *Cuadernos*

Galaxia*, Canje al Apdo 4023, Carmelitas 101, Caracas
Venezuelan Writers' Group
Director-Editor: Modesto Vargas Lopez
Publication: *Galaxia 71*

Centro Venezolano del P E N Internacional, Apdo de Correos 14413, Caracas 1010-A Tel: (02) 5616691/5617589/5617287
President: Dr José Ramón Medina;
Secretary: Oswaldo Trejo
Publications: *Con Textos*; *Colección Plural*

Literary Periodicals

Analítica para una Problemática del Sujeto, Editorial Ateneo de Caracas, Apdo 662, Caracas

Con Textos, Centro Venezolano del PEN Internacional, Apdo de Correos 14413, Caracas 1010-A

Colección Plural, Centro Venezolano del PEN Internacional, Apdo de Correos 14413, Caracas 1010-A

Cuadernos (Notebooks), Asociación de Escritores de Venezuela, Velázquez a Miseria 22, Apdo 429, Caracas

Galaxia 71, Venezuelan Writers' Group, Canje al Apdo 4023, Carmelitas 101, Caracas

Literary Prizes

Municipal Prize for Prose and Poetry*
For the best prose or poetry work published in the Federal District or an unpublished work from any part of Venezuela. 5,000 bolivares. Awarded annually. Enquiries to Caracas Municipal Council of Federal District, Caracas

El **Nacional** Annual Story Award*
For the best story by a Venezuelan or foreign resident in Venezuela. Awarded annually. Enquiries to Edificio El Nacional, Puente Nuevo a Puerto Escondido, Apdo 209, Caracas

National Prize for Literature*
Awarded annually to the best Venezuelan author. 30,000 bolivares. Also includes contestants in narrative prose and essays. Enquiries to Concejo Nacional de la Cultura (CONAC), Apdo 50995, Caracas 105

Socialist Republic of Viet Nam

General Information

Language: Vietnamese. Also French and English
Religion: Taoist predominantly
Population: 52.7 million
Currency: 10 xu = 1 hào; 10 hào = 1 dông
Export/Import Information: None available at present
Copyright: Florence (see International section)

Book Trade Organization

Syndicat des Libraires*, 185 rue Catinat, Hô Chí Minh City
Union of Booksellers

Book Trade Reference Journal

Thu' muc quóc gia Viêt nam (National Bibliography), Thu Viên Quóc Gia Viet Nam, 31 Tràng Thi, Hanoi
Monthly, with annual cumulation

Publishers

Foreign Languages Publishing House*, 46 Tran Hung Dao St, Hanoi
Dir: Huu Ngoc
Subjects: Books and Periodicals from Viet Nam (English, French, Russian, Spanish, Chinese languages)

Giao Duc Publishing House*, 81 Tran Hung Dao, Hanoi
Dir: Nguyen Si Ty
Subjects: Education, School Books
Founded: 1957

Khoa Hoc (Social Sciences) Publishing House*, Hanoi
Subject: Social Science

Lao Dong (Labour) Publishing House*, Hanoi

Nha Xuat Ban Van Hoc (Literature Publishing House)*, 49 Tran Hung Dao, Hanoi
Dir: Nhu Phong
Subject: Literature

Pho Thong (Popularization) Publishing House*, Hanoi

Popular Army Publishing House*, Hanoi
Subject: Military

Scientific Publishing House*, Hanoi
Subject: Scientific

Su Hoc (Historical) Publishing House*, Hanoi
Subjects: Politics, Philosophy, Marxist Classics

Su That (Truth) Publishing House*, 24 Quang Trung St, Hanoi Tel: 52008
(Controlled by the Central Committee of the Communist Party of Viet Nam)
Subjects: Marxist-Leninist Classics, Politics, Philosophy, Social Science
Founded: 1945

Trung-Tam San Xuat Hoc-Lieu*, Tran-binh-Trong 240, Hô Chí Minh City 5
Subjects: Textbooks, Audiovisual, Instruction Materials

Y Hoc Publishing House*, Hanoi
Subject: Medical

Major Booksellers

Xunhasoba*, 32 Hai Ba Trung, Hanoi
Distributor for foreign orders

Major Libraries

The **Archives Service** of the Prime Minister's Office of the Socialist Republic of Viet Nam*, South Viet Nam Branch, 72 Nguyên-Du, Hô Chí Minh City

Municipal Library*, 22 Yersin St, Dalat

National Institute of Administration Library*, 10 Tran Quoc Toan, Hô Chí Minh City

Bibliothèque des **Sciences Générales***, 69 Ly tu Trong, Hô Chí Minh City
Dir: Mrs Trinh-Ngoc-Hanh

Social Sciences Library*, 34 Ly tu Trong, Hô Chí Minh City

Thu Viên Quóc Gia Viet Nam*, 31 Tràng Thi, Hanoi Tel: 52643
National Library of the Socialist Republic of Viet Nam
Librarian: Nguyên Thê Dúc
Publications include: Thu' muc quóc gia Viêt nam (National Bibliography); *Cóng tác Thu' viên-Thu' muc* (Journal of Library and Bibliography)

Library Association

Hôi Thu-Viên Viet Nam*, 8 Le Qui Don, Hô Chí Minh City
Vietnamese Library Association
Secretary: Nguyên Van Thu
Publication: Thu'-Viên Tâp-san (Library Bulletin)

Library Reference Journals

Công tác Thu' viên-Thu' muc (Journal of Library and Bibliography), Thu Viên Quóc Gia Viet Nam, 31 Tràng Thi, Hanoi

Thu'-Viên Tâp-san (Library Bulletin), Hôi Thu-Viên Viet Nam, 8 Le Qui Don, Hô Chí Minh City

Literary Periodical

Van Hoc, c/o Phan Kim Thinh, 449 Bhai Ba Trung, Q3 Hô Chí Minh City

Western Samoa

General Information

Note: No replies were received to questionnaires sent to Western Samoa for this edition of *International Literary Market Place*. The information given in the 1987-88 edition has been repeated here but should be treated with caution.

Language: Samoan, English
Population: 156,000
Bank Hours: 0930-1500 Monday-Friday
Shop Hours: 0800-1200, 1330-1630 Monday-Friday; 0800-1230 Saturday
Currency: 100 sene = 1 tala
Export/Import Information: No tariff on most books, printed advertising generally free but some subject to duty. No import licence or exchange controls

Major Libraries

Avele College Library*, Avele

Nelson Memorial Public Library*, PO Box 598, Apia

People's Democratic Republic of Yemen

General Information

Language: Arabic. English is common second language
Religion: Islamic
Population: 2.5 million
Bank Hours: 0730-1400 Saturday-Wednesday; 0730-1300 Thursday
Shop Hours: 0800-1230, 1500-2100 Saturday-Thursday
Currency: 1,000 fils = 1 South Yemen dinar
Export/Import Information: 14th October Corporation, PO Box 4227, Maalah-Aden has sole right to import and distribute books. Import licences required. Exchange controls

Publishers

Dar Alhamadani, c/o 14th October Corporation for Import, Print Distribution and Information, PO Box 4227, Maalah, Aden

Major Booksellers

14th October Corporation*, PO Box 4227, Maalah-Aden
Sole importer and distributor of books

Major Libraries

Miswat Library*, Aden
(Previously called Lake Library. Administration by Aden Municipality)

National Library (Badeeb Library), Al-Saila Rd, nr National Bank of Yemen, Crater-Aden

Teachers' Club Library*, Aden

Yemen Arab Republic

General Information

Language: Arabic. English and Russian are common foreign languages
Religion: Islamic
Population: 5.8 million
Bank Hours: 0800-1200 (1130 Thursday) Saturday-Thursday
Shop Hours: 0800-1200, 1600-2100 Saturday-Thursday
Currency: 100 fils = 1 Yemeni riyal
Export/Import Information: No tariff on books except on children's picture books. Advertising matter dutied. Defence and Statistical Taxes; Cooperation Tax is percentage of CIF. Small Welfare Tax, Import licence required; no pornography permitted. Exchange control approval readily available, generally

Major Libraries

British Council Library*, PO Box 2157, Sana'a (Located at: Beit Mottahar, Harat Handhal, Sana'a) Tel: (02) 73179 Telex: 2748 Brcoun Ye

Library of the **Great Mosque of Sana'a***, Sana'a

Yugoslavia

General Information

Language: Serbo-Croatian in most of the country; Slovene in Slovenia, Macedonian in Macedonia. In some communities, Albanian, Bulgarian, Hungarian, Italian, Romanian, Turkish. English is commonest foreign language known
Religion: About 40% Eastern Orthodox, 30% Roman Catholic, 10% Islamic
Population: 22.3 million
Bank Hours: 0730-1200 Monday-Friday
Shop Hours: 0800-1200, 1700-2000 Monday-Friday; 0800-1500 Saturday. Some open weekdays continuously and early Sunday morning
Currency: 100 para = 1 new dinar
Export/Import Information: No tariffs on books except on publications of Yugoslav publishers printed abroad. Advertising catalogues for such books dutied, otherwise free; non-Yugoslavian language advertising materials dutied. Special equalization tax, Customs clearance charge and import surcharge when goods are subject to duty. No import licences required. Exchange controls. The basic commercial unit is known as an enterprise but there are no state monopolies
Copyright: Berne, UCC (see Internationsal section)

Book Trade Organizations

Association of Yugoslav Publishers and Booksellers, YU-11000 Belgrade, Kneza Milósa 25/I, Poštanski fah 883 Tel: (011) 642533/642248
Dir: Ognjen Lakićević
Publications: Catalogue of Book Fair in Belgrade; Directory of Members of the Association of Yugoslav Publishers and Booksellers; Publishing Plans of the Publishing Houses in Yugoslavia (annual); *Books Published by Yugoslav Publishers* (annual)

Jugoslovenski bibliografski institut, Agencija za ISBN*, YU-11000 Belgrade, Terazije 26 Tel: (011) 687836
ISBN Administrator: Dr Miloje Rakočević

Standard Book Numbering Agency, see Jugoslovenski bibliografski institut, Agencija za ISBN

Book Trade Reference Journals

Bibliografija domace i strane literature (Bibliography of Native and Foreign

YUGOSLAVIA

Literature), Centralna Biblioteka JNA, Belgrade, Balkanska 53a
Text in Serbo-Croatian

Bibliografija Jugoslavije (Yugoslavia Bibliography), Jugoslovenski bibliografski institut, YU-11000 Belgrade, Terazije 26

Books Published by Yugoslav Publishers, Association of Yugoslav Publishers and Booksellers, YU-11000 Belgrade, Kneza Milósa 25/I, Poštanski fah 883

Directory of Members, Association of Yugoslav Publishers and Booksellers, YU-11000 Belgrade, Kneza Milósa 25/I, Poštanski fah 883

Katalog Medunarodnog Sajma Knjige u Beogradu (Catalogue of the International Book Fair at Belgrade), Association of Yugoslav Publishers and Booksellers, YU-11000 Belgrade, Kneza Milósa 25/I, Poštanski fah 883

Knjiga i svet (The Book and the World), Association of Yugoslav Publishers and Booksellers, YU-11000 Belgrade, Kneza Milósa 25/I, Poštanski fah 883

Publishing Plans of the Publishing Houses in Yugoslavia, Association of Yugoslav Publishers and Booksellers, YU-11000 Belgrade, Kneza Milósa 25/I, Poštanski fah 883

Slovenska Bibliografija (Slovene Bibliography), Državna Založba Slovenije, YU-61000 Ljubljana, Mestni trg 26, Poštanski fah 50-1

Publishers

A L F A — Radna organizacija za izdavačku djelatnost*, YU-41000 Zagreb, Čerinina 9a, Poštanski fah 32 Tel: (041) 217614
Manager: Stjepan Martinović
Subjects: War, History, Popular Science, Fiction

August Cesarec, YU-41000 Zagreb, Prilaz JA 57 Tel: (041) 576615/573505 Telex: 22131 Yu Acesar
Chief Executive: Dragan Milković; *Editor-in-Chief:* Zdravko Židovec; *Sales Manager:* Miroslav Janjušić; *Production Manager:* Bože Čović; *Publicity Manager:* Slavica Borošić
Subjects: Belles Lettres, Politics, Science, Fiction, Critiques
Book Club: Klub Prijatelja Knjige 'August Cesarec'
Bookshop: Salon Knjiga 'August Cesarac', YU 41000 Zagreb, Ilica 112
1985: 60 titles *1986:* 65 titles *Founded:* 1967
ISBN Publisher's Prefix: 86-393

B I G Z, an imprint of Beogradski Izdavačko-Grafički Zavod (qv)

Beogradski Izdavačko-Grafički Zavod*, YU-11000 Belgrade, blvd vojvode Mišića 17, Poštanski fah 340 Tel: (011) 651666 Cable Add: BEOGRAF Telex: 11855 Yu Bigz
Man Dir: Gojko Zečar; *Editorial Dir, Permissions:* Vidosav Stevanović
Imprint: BIGZ
Subjects: Belles Lettres, Poetry, Philosophy, Juveniles, Social Science, University Textbooks, Encyclopaedias, Periodicals
Book Club: Book Lovers' Club
Founded: 1831

Birografika*, YU-24000 Subotica, Put Moše Pjade 72 Tel: (024) 26215 Cable Add: Yu Bigraf 15111
Dir: Andrija inž Bukvić

Borba*, YU-11000 Belgrade, trg Marksa i Engelsa 7, Poštanski fah 629 Tel: (011) 334531/344201
Dir: Novica Dukić

Bratsvo-Jedinstvo*, YU-21000 Novi Sad, Arse Teodorovića 11, Poštanski fah 274 Tel: (021) 28032/28036
Dir: Srboslav Bojović
Subjects: Textbooks in Serbo-Croatian, Belles Lettres

C D D (Centar društvenih djelatnosti Saveza socijalističke omladine Hrvatske)*, YU-41001 Zagreb, Opaticka 10, Poštanski fah 99 Tel: (041) 419026/443809/447/055
General Manager: Josip Čondić; *Publishing Manager:* Petar Strpić
Subjects: Fiction, Marxism, Philosophy, Social Sciences, Political Journalism, Science Journalism, Periodicals

Cankarjeva Založba+*, YU-61001 Ljubljana, Kopitarjeva 2, Poštni predal 201/IV Tel: (061) 323841 Telex: 31821 Yu Cankar
Man Dir: Dr Martin Žnideršič; *Editors:* Janez Stanič, Tone Pavček; *Rights & Permissions:* Dagmar Dolinar; *Import/Export Manager:* Veronika Polaynar
Subsidiary Companies: The International Miniature Book Society (at above address); Cankarjeva Založba, Zagreb, Ilica 26
Subjects: Belles Lettres, Poetry, General Fiction, Biography, History, How-to, Philosophy, Reference, Social Science, Psychology, Dictionaries, Encyclopaedias, Miniature Books
Bookshops: See under Major Booksellers
1985: 77 titles *Founded:* 1945
ISBN Publisher's Prefix: 86-361

Centar za Kulturnu Djelatnost Zagreb (CEKADE)+, 41000 Zagreb, Mihanovićeva 28 Tel: (041) 418646/445115
Chief Executive: Branko Miškić; *Editorial:* Slobodan Šnajder; *Sales:* Katica Brajković; *Publicity:* Sanja Koprivnjak
Orders to: Centar za knjigu, Zagreb, Mihanovićeva 32
Subjects: Theatre, Drama, Political Science, Philosophy, Poetry, Economy
Bookshop: Centar za knjigu (at above address)
Founded: 1968

Dečje Novine, see Niro Dečje Novine

Delta Press*, YU-11000 Belgrade, Draže Pavlovića 14, Poštanski fah 467 Tel: (011) 333969
Dir: Jovan Janićijević
Subjects: Reference Material, Juveniles and Young People, Social Sciences
Founded: 1969

Državna Založba Slovenije, YU-61000 Ljubljana, Mestni trg 26, Poštanski fah 50-1 Tel: (061) 332111 Cable Add: DZS Ljubljana
Man Dir: Uroš Istenič
Subjects: General Fiction, Belles Lettres, Poetry, Biography, History, Music, Art, Philosophy, Reference, General & Social Science, University, Secondary & Primary Textbooks, Educational Materials
Founded: 1945

Edit Niro (Novinska-izdavačka radna organizacija)*, YU-51000 Rijeka, bulevar Marxa i Engelsa 20, Poštanski fah 137-138 Tel: (051) 22516/22443/23817 Telex: 24247
Director: Ennio Machin
Subjects: Books, Papers, Periodicals in Italian
Bookshop: YU-51000 Rijeka, Korzo Narodne Revolucije 37

Forum*, YU-21000 Novi Sad, vojvode Mišića 1, Poštanski fah 200 Tel: (021) 57207 Telex: 14199
Director: Kálmán Petkovics
Subjects: Periodicals, Fiction, Politics in Hungarian and Serbo-Croatian
Bookshop: See under Major Booksellers

Glas*, YU-11000 Belgrade, Vlajkovićeva 8 Tel: (011) 335380
Director: Radojko Mrlješ
Provides complete printing services to other publishers

Globus, YU-41000 Zagreb, Ilica 12, Poštanski pretinac 232 Tel: (041) 423368/423268 Cable Add: Globus Zagreb
Editors: I Sor, B Zadro, A Kralj, B Kovaćević
A Buljan
Parent Company: ČGP Delo, YU-61000 Ljubljana, Titova Cesta 35
Subjects: Politics, History, Sociology, Philosophy, General Fiction, Dictionaries, Art, Women's Literature
Founded: 1948

Izdavačka ustanova **Gradina***, YU-18000 Niš, ul Pobede br 38/I, Poštanski fah 242 Pobede 38/I Tel: (018) 25864
Dir: Dobrivoje Jevtić
Subjects: Belles Lettres, Science, Art, Periodicals
Bookshops: (all at Niš) ul Pobede br 38; Pobede 113; Voždova 74; 12 februar 56a; Obilićev venac 50

Gradjevinska Knjiga*, YU-11000 Belgrade, trg Marksa i Engelsa 8, Poštanski fah 798 Tel: (011) 333565
Man Dir: Milan Višnić; *Sales Dir:* Hilailo Nešović
Subjects: Technical, Engineering & University Textbooks
Bookshops: Gradjevinska Knjiga, Narodnog fronta 14 & bulevar Revolucije 84; Student, 27 marta 78 (all in Belgrade)

Grafički zavod Hrvatske, YU-41000 Zagreb, Preobraženska 4, Poštanski fah 227 Tel: (041) 430411/430300 Cable Add: GZH Zagreb Telex: 21606 Yu Gzh
Man Dir: Milan Zinaić; *Editors:* Mate Maras, Nenad Popović; *Sales:* Milorad Bursać; *rights & Permissions:* Maja Kotur; *Production:* Boro Brekalo
Subjects: Belles Lettres, Art, Tourism, Dictionaries, Handbooks
1985: 27 titles *1986:* 30 titles
Founded: 1874

Grafos*, YU-11000 Belgrade, Simina 9A, Poštanski fah 459 Tel: (011) 623980 Cable Add: Grafos Belgrade
Dir: Vito Marković
Subjects: Lexicography, Rare Publications, Fiction, Science, Juveniles, Periodicals

I C S Izdavačko Informativni Centar Studenata*, YU-11000 Belgrade, Balkanska 4/III Tel: (011) 325854
Dir: Aleksandar Urdarević
Bookshops: Novi Belgrade: Studentski grad, II Blok & Dom kultur Studenski grad, bulevar Avnoja 152a; Belgrade: Fakultet političkih nauka, Jove Ilića 165 & Arhitektonski fakultet, bulevar Revolucije 73

Informator*, Izdavački i Birotehnički Zavod, YU-41001 Zagreb, Masarykova ul 1, Poštanski fah 794 Tel: (041) 442222 Cable Add: Yu Inf Telex: 21264
General Dir: Nikola Šaranović
Subjects: Dictionaries, Law

The **International Miniature Book** Society, see Cankarjeva Založba

Jedinstvo*, YU-38000 Priština, Dom Stampe bb, Poštanski pregradak 81 Tel:

(038) 27549/29090 Cable Add: Jedinstvo Pristina
Director: Milan Śeślija
Subjects: Belles Lettres, Social & Political Science, History, Philosophy, Medicine

Jugoreklam*, YU-61000 Ljubljana, Moše Pijade 5, Poštanski fah 142 Tel: (061) 316075
Dir: Hinko Urbanc
Branch Offs: YU-11000 Belgrade: Nebojšina 2 & Dure Dakovića 88; YU-41000 Zagreb, Petretičev trg 4; YU-63320 Velenje, Celjska 27
Subjects: Juveniles, Economics

Jugoslovenska Revija*, YU-11000 Belgrade, Terazije 31 Tel: (011) 345541 Telex: 12954 Yurew
Dir: Rajko Bobot; *Rights & Permissions:* Milovan Ignjatović
Subjects: Art, Tourism, Periodicals

Izdavački Zavod **Jugoslavenske Akademije** Znanosti i Umjetnosti*, YU-41000 Zagreb, Gundulićeva 24, Poštanski fah 1017 Tel: (041) 449099
Publishing House of the Yugoslav Academy of Sciences and Arts
Man Dir: Josip Hanževački
Subjects: History, Philosophy, Medicine, Technical, General & Political Science, Education
Founded: 1918

Jugoslavenski Leksikografski Zavod*, YU-41000 Zagreb, Strossmayerov trg 4, Poštanski fah 410 Tel: (041) 434177/434227
Director: Dr Ivo Cecić
Subjects: Encyclopaedias, Bibliographies, Dictionaries
Bookshop: Poslovnica, Zagreb, Masarykova 26
Founded: 1951

Jugoslavija*, Izdavački Zavod, YU-11000 Belgrade, Nemanjina 34, Poštanski fah 52 Tel: (011) 643870/643852 Cable Add: Pubzavod Belgrade Telex: 11265
Shipping Add: c/o Transjug-Split, YU-11000 Belgrade, Pop Lukina 12
Dir, Editor-in-Chief: Živislav-Žika Bogdanović
Subjects: Art, Travel Guides, Reference, How-to, General Non-fiction, Juveniles, Science Fiction & Epic Fantasy
Founded: 1948

Izdavački Centar **Komunist***, Belgrade, trg Marksa i Engelsa 11, Poštanski fah 233 Tel: (011) 335061/334189
Dir: David Atlagić
Subjects: Communism, Marxism, Literary Criticism
Bookshop: Klub Citalaca 70, Belgrade, trg Marksa i Engelsa 9

Kršćanska sadašnjost*, YU-41000 Zagreb, Marulićev trg 14, Poštanski fah 02748 Tel: (041) 444102
Subjects: Bible, Liturgy, Theology, Art History, Church History, Fine Arts, Periodicals
Miscellaneous: Company also acts as a press agency

Kultura (Izdavačko Pretprijatie)*, YU-91000 Skopje, bulevar JNA 68A, Poštanski fah 298 Tel: (091) 35361/23437
Cable Add: Kultura
Man Dir: Dušan Crvenkovski
Subjects: Art, Philosophy, Political Science, Economics, Juveniles
Bookshops: See under Major Booksellers
Founded: 1945

Sveučilišna Naklada **Liber**, YU-41000 Zagreb, Savska cesta 16, Poštanski fah 493 Tel: (041) 426910/426904
Editors: Vera C Sain, Nikola Petrak
Subjects: Croatian cultural and scientific heritage, Literature, Linguistics, Literary Science, Foreign Fiction, *Povijesti, Temelji, Znanstveni Radovi* (scientific works), Scientific Textbooks, *Biografije-Monografije* collections
Miscellaneous: Publishing service of Zagreb University

Libertatea*, YU-26000 Pančevo, Žarka Zrenjanina br 7, Poštanski fah 27 Tel: (013) 3401/3351 Cable Add: Libertatea Pančevo
Dir: Todor Gilezan
Subjects: Textbooks, Periodicals, Rare Publications, Reprints, Romanian Language publications

Makedonska Knjiga (Knigoizdatelstvo), YU-91000 Skopje, 11 Oktomvri bb, Poštanski fah 349 Tel: (091) 235524
Cable Add: Makedonska Kniga
Man Dir: Radovan Pavleski
Subjects: General Fiction, Belles Lettres, Art, Juveniles
Bookshops: See under Major Booksellers

Medicinska Knjiga*, YU-11000 Belgrade, Mata Vidakovića 24, Poštanski fah 681 Tel: (011) 458135/458165
Dir: Petar Janković; *Editor-in-Chief:* Mile Medić; *Sales Dir:* Dobrica Mitrović; *Publicity Manager:* Ivan M Stanković
Branch Offs: YU-41000 Zagreb, Belostenćeva 3-5 Tel: (041) 272320; YU-91000 Skopje, Naroden Front 33 Tel: (091) 228930; YU-71000 Sarajevo, Rave Janković 99A Tel: (071) 618370; YU-21000 Novi Sad, Železnička 24 Tel: (021) 52271
Subjects: Medicine, Pharmacy, Stomatology, Textbooks, Popular literature
Bookshops: Belgrade, Niš, Zagreb
Book Club: Klub Čitalaca MK
Founded: 1946

Medicinska Naklada*, YU-41000 Zagreb, Gundulićeva 24 Tel: (041) 420701
Dir: Tomislav Slavica
Subject: Medical

'Minerva'*, YU-24000 Subotica, trg 29 novembra br 3, Poštanski fah 116 Tel: (024) 25701 Cable Add: Minerva Subotica
Dir: Josip Prčić
Subjects: Textbooks, Dictionaries, Scientific and Children's Literature
Bookshops: YU-24000 Subotica: ul oktobra 4; Maksima Gorkog 20; Put M Pijade 25

Misla*, YU-91000 Skopje, Gradski zid, Blok 2, Poštanski fah 460 Tel: (091) 23336 Cable Add: Misla Skopje
Dir: Božin Pavlovski; *Head of Sales:* Vančo Spasovski

Mladinska Knjiga*, YU-61000 Ljubljana, Titova 3, Poštanski fah 36/I Tel: (060) 24851 Telex: 31345 Yu Emka
Director General: Karel Trplan; *Publishing Dir:* Ivan Bizjak; *Editor-in-Chief:* Borut Ingolič; *Sales:* Joze Wagner; *Production:* Marjan Ćerne; *Co-production:* Ciril Treek; *Publicity:* Nace Borštnar
Branch Off: YU-11000 Belgrade, 27 Merte; YU-41000 Zagreb, Ilica 30
Subjects: Children's books, General Fiction, Art, Popular Science, Geography, How-to
Book Club: Svet Knjige
Bookshops: See under Major Booksellers
Founded: 1945

Mladost*, YU-11000 Belgrade, Maršala Tita 2, Poštanski fah 252 Tel: (011) 323390
Dir: Borisav Džuverović
Subjects: Marxist literature, Philosophy, Fiction, Periodical
Founded: 1956

Mladost, Izdavačko knjižarska radna organizacija*, YU-41000 Zagreb, Ilica 30, Poštanski fah 1028 Tel: (041) 440211
Cable Add: Ikape Zagreb Telex: 21263
Man Dir: Branko Juričević; *Import-Export Dir:* Branko Vuković; *Publisher:* Josip Fruk; *Production Manager:* Stipan Medak; *Marketing Manager:* Eduard Osredečki
Subjects: Picture Books, Juveniles, General Fiction, Belles Lettres, Poetry, History, How-to, Music, Art, Philosophy, Reference, General & Social Science, Sports, Hobby Books, Dictionaries
Book Club: Mladost's Book Fans Club
Bookshops: See under Major Booksellers
Founded: 1948

Muzička Naklada*, Zagreb, Nikole Tesle 10/I, Poštanski fah 543
Dir: Albert Trinki
Subject: Music
Founded: 1952

Nakladni Zavod Matice Hrvatske*, YU-41000 Zagreb, ul Matice Hrvatske 2, Poštanski fah 515 Tel: (041) 275522
Man Dir, Rights & Permissions: Bogdan Tomašić; *Editorial:* Zane Tvrtko; *Sales, Publicity:* Milovan Radošević; *Production:* Anto Galic; *Publicity:* Luka Roić
Branch Offs: YU-71000 Sarajevo, M Djudje 10; YU-11000 Belgrade, Tršćanska 5
Subjects: General Fiction, Reference, Art, Literature, Political & General Science, Biography, History, Dictionaries
Bookshops: 41000 Zagreb, Ilica 62, Dure Salaja 3; YU-50000 Dubrovnik, Poljana Paska Miličevića bb; YU-54400 Djakovo, ul Jna 15; YU-47000 Karlovac, Pavleka Miškine 4; YU-54500 Našice, Radićeva 23; YU-51270 Senj, Trg Oslobodjenja 1; YU-79000 Mostar, Braće Brkića 8; YU-51000 Rijeka, Djure Djakovića 20
Founded: 1960

Naprijed*, YU-41000 Zagreb, Palmotićeva 30, Poštanski fah 1029 Tel: (041) 442001/442400/442283 Cable Add: Izdavacko Naprijed Telex: 21449 Yu Ikpnzg
Man Dir: Autun Žvan
Subjects: Philosophy, General Fiction, History, Art, General Science, Psychology, Political & Social Science, Economics

Narodna Biblioteka Srbije*, YU-11000 Belgrade, Skerlićeva 1 Tel: (011) 451242
Dir: Svetislav Durić
Subjects: Bibliography, Reference, History

Narodna Knjiga*, YU-11000 Belgrade, Safarikova 11, Poštanski fah 241 Tel: (011) 328610
Dir: Vidak Perić
Subjects: Politics, Encyclopaedias, Dictionaries, Textbooks, Science, Juveniles, Belles Lettres

Narodne Novine*, YU-41000 Zagreb, Ratkejev prolaz 4, Poštanski fah 557 Tel: (041) 411611/411666
Dir: Ilija Dautović
Subjects: Science, Textbooks, Careers
Bookshops: 21 throughout Yugoslavia

Naša Djeca*, YU-41000 Zagreb, Gajeva 25, Poštanski fah 563 Tel: (041) 447077
Cable Add: Násadjeca
Dir: Petar Butković
Subject: Juveniles

Naša Knjiga*, YU-91000 Skopje, Partizanski odred 17, Poštanski fah 132 Tel: (091) 228066/237014
Dir: Vlado Popovski

YUGOSLAVIA

Subjects: Textbooks, Sociology, Politics, Agriculture, Literature

Naučna Knjiga*, YU-11000 Belgrade, Uzun Mirkova 5, Poštanski fah 690 Tel: (011) 637230 Cable Add: Naučna Knjiga
Man Dir: Dragoslav Joković
Subjects: Reference, Medicine, Engineering, Science, University Textbooks, Educational Materials, Maps, Atlases
Bookshops: 'Znanje', Belgrade, Gračanička br 16; 'Naučna knjiga', Belgrade, Knez Mihailova br 19
Founded: 1947

Nio Pobjeda — Oour Izdavačko-Publicistička Djelatnost*, YU-81000 Titograd, ul Petra Matovića 206 Tel: (081) 34254
Dir: Ljubo Burić; *Publishing Dir:* Mileta Radovanović; *Editors:* Branko Banjević, Djerdj Djokaj, Ratko Vujošević, Vojislav Minić; *Sales, Trade Dir:* Miodrag Raonić
Branch Offs: YU-11080 Zemun, Karadordev trg 7 Tel: (011) 600652; YU-21000 Novi Sad, Šafarikova 15 Tel: (021) 51086; YU-38000 Priština, Miladin Popovića bb Tel: (038) 24062
Subjects: Belles Lettres, Popular and Scientific Literature and Lexicography
Founded: 1962

Niro Dečje Novine, YU-32300 Gornji Milanovac, Tihomira Matijevića 4 Tel: (032) 711527/713967/711248 Telex: 13731 Yu Dngrm
Subjects: Juveniles, Picture-books, Albums, Educational Materials

Nolit Publishing House*, YU-11000 Belgrade, Terazije 27/II, Poštanski fah 369 Tel: (011) 333353 Cable Add: Nolit BGD Telex: 11603 Nolit bgd
Man Dir: Dragoljub Gavaric; *Editorial:* Miloš Stambolić; *Sales:* Branko Nikezić; *Production:* Srboljub Milošević
Subjects: General Fiction, Philosophy, Psychology, Sociology, Agriculture, History, Art, Juveniles
Bookshops: See under Major Booksellers
Founded: 1928

Mip Nota*, YU-19350 Knjaževac, Karadordeva 15/I, Poštanski fah 63 Tel: 84375/84516 Cable Add: Nota-Knjaževac
Dir: Nenad Živković; *Editorial:* Stojanović Ljubomir; *Sales:* Jovanovic Negica; *Production:* Nikolić Alexsandar; *Rights & Permissions:* Simić Dura
Branch Off: YU-11000 Belgrade, Balkanska 9
Subject: Music
Founded: 1970

Nova Knjiga*, Obrenovac, Maršala Tita

Obod*, YU-81250 Cetinje, Njegoševa 3, Poštanski fah 59 Tel: (086) 22020 Cable Add: Obod Cetinje
Dir: Slobodan Koljević
Branch Off: Belgrade, Dobračina 32
Subjects: Belles Lettres, Fiction, Textbooks, Dictionaries
Bookshop: Belgrade, Njegoševa 11

Obzor*, YU-21000 Novi Sad, bulevar 23, Oktobra 31/V, Poštanski fah 267 Tel: (021) 21555 Cable Add: Obzor Novi Sad
Dir: Anna Makanová
Bookshop: Bački Petrovac Bodviš Jan

NIP Oslobodenje*, YU-71000 Sarajevo, Maršala Tita 13, Poštanski fah 663 Tel: (071) 35177/34233 Telex: 41148/41136
Dir: Ivica Lovrić

Otokar Keršovani*, YU-51410 Opatija, Maršala Tita 65, Poštanski fah 13 Tel: (051) 711099/711922 Cable Add: Otokar Keršovani
Man Dir, Editor in Chief: Tomislav Pilepić
Branch Offs: Zagreb, Biankinijeva 11; Rijeka, Slaviše Vajiera-Čiče 3; Belgrade, Zrmanjska 2/a; Niš, Nade Tomić 15; Sarajevo, Mehmed-paše Soholovića 24
Subjects: Fiction, Handbooks, Monographs, Biography & Memoirs, Picture Books
Founded: 1954

Pomurska založba*, YU-69000 Murska Sobota, Lendavska c1 Tel: 6923491 Telex: 35-229 Yu Zgpmsb
Dir: Jože Ternar; *Editor-in-Chief:* Jože Hradil
Subjects: Literature, Fiction, Poetry, Essays (Original and Translations)
Bookshops: Dobra knjiga, 69000 Murska Sobota, Titova c; Knjigarna Ljutomer, YU-69240; Knjigarna Lendava, YU-69220; Knjigarna Gornja Radgona, YU-69250

Izdavačko **Preduzeće Matice Srpske***, YU-21000 Novi Sad, trg Svetozara Markovića 2 Tel: (021) 29777/43040 (director)
Dir: Sava Josić
Subjects: Belles Lettres, Science, Politics, Juveniles, Textbooks, Encyclopaedias, Dictionaries
Bookshops: Belgrade, Studentski trg 5; Backa Palanka, Maršala Tita 40 and others

Izdavačko **Preduzeće Sloboda***, YU-11000 Belgrade, Vojvode Stepe 315 Tel: (011) 462131/461721/462341 Cable Add: Sloboda Belgrade
Dir: Streten Hrkalović
Subjects: Belles Lettres, Juveniles, Reference

Primorski Tisk*, YU-66000 Koper, Muzejski trg 7, Poštanski fah 132 Tel: (066) 23291
Dir: Črtomir Kolenc
Branch Off: Studenski servis, Ljubljana, Borstnikov trg 25
Subject: Fiction
Bookshops: 9 throughout Yugoslavia

Privredni Pregled*, YU-11000 Belgrade, Maršala Birjuzova 3, Poštanski fah 903 Tel: (011) 623399/625662 Cable Add: Privredni Pregled Bgd Telex: 11509 Yu Pp
Dir: Toma Marković
Branch Offs: Zagreb, Moše Pijade 21; Ljubljana, Hala 'Tivoli'; Skopje, Orce Nikolova 79; Sarajevo, Maršala Tita 86
Subject: Production Reference Books

Prosveta, YU-11001 Belgrade, Terazije 16 Tel: (011) 687441 Telex: 11609 Yu
General Dir: Vidosav Stevanović; *Editor-in-Chief:* Milisav Savić; *Export Manager:* Milutin Trifunovic; *Rights & Permissions:* Branka Simić
Subjects: Lexicography, Humanities
Book Club: Prosveta
Bookshops: See under Major Booksellers
Founded: 1945

Prosvetno Delo*, YU-91000 Skopje, Ulica Ivo Lola Ribar, bb, Gradski zid, Blok IV, Poštanski fah 6 Tel: (091) 33675/31398
Man Dir: Mihajlo Korveziroski
Subjects: Reference, Textbooks, Educational Materials, Juveniles
Bookshop: Br 1 Skopje, bulevar Kočo Racin, kula B-20

Prosvjeta*, YU-41000 Zagreb, Berislavićeva 10, Poštanski fah 634 Tel: (041) 445450/444664 Cable Add: Prosvjeta Zagreb
Dir: Branislav Ćelap
Subjects: Journalism, Business Books
Bookshop: Zagreb, trg Bratstva i Jedinstva 5

Prosvjeta (Novinsko-izdavačko i Štamparsko)*, Bjelovar, Vladimira Nazora 25 Tel: 3150 Cable Add: Nišp Prosvjeta Bjelovar
Dir: Branimir Premužić; *Production:* Ivan Ninić
Branch Off: Zagreb, Moše Pijade 31

Prva Književna Komuna*, YU-79000 Mostar, trg 14 februar 3/III Tel: 25798 Cable Add: PKK Mostar
Man Dir: Ico Mutevelić
Subjects: Bibliophile Editions, Tourist Publications
Bookshop: Mostar, ul Stari most 3

Izdavačka Organizacija **Rad***, YU-11000 Belgrade, Moše Pijade 12, Poštanski fah 881 Tel: (011) 330923/339758/338994
Man Dir: Bravislav Milošević; *Sales Dir:* Milovan Vlahović
Subjects: Belles Lettres, Poetry, Biography, Philosophy, Low-priced Paperbacks, Engineering, Social Science, Politics, Economics, University Textbooks
Bookshops: Papirus, Belgrade, Terazije 26; Zagreb, Frankopanska 5, and 20 other bookshops throughout Yugoslavia

Radnička Štampa*, YU-11000 Belgrade, trg Marksa i Engelsa 5, Poštanski fah 995 Tel: (011) 330927 Cable Add: Radnička štampa Belgrade
Dir: Radoslav Roso; *Sales Manager:* Čedo Maleš
Subjects: Social, Political and Economic Sciences, Textbooks, Encyclopaedias

Republički Zavod za Unapredivanje Školstva*, YU-81000 Titograd, Novaka Miloševa 36 Tel: (081) 24168, 24126 (Director)
Republic Bureau for the Advancement of Education
Subjects: Primary and Secondary Textbooks, Education

Rilindja*, YU-38000 Priština, Dom Štampe, Poštanski fah 27 Tel: (038) 23868/28611/28411
Dir: Rexhep Zogaj
Subjects: Textbooks, Belles Lettres (in Albanian), Periodicals

Savez Inženjera i Tehničara Jugoslavije, YU-11000 Belgrade, Kneza Mološa 9, Poštanski fah 187 Tel: (011) 343653/335816/332924 Cable Add: Sitj Beograd
Union of Engineers and Technicians of Yugoslavia
Secretary: Milivoje Todorović
Founded: 1945

Savremena Administracija*, YU-11001 Belgrade, Knez Crnotravska 7-9, Poštanski fah 479 Tel: (011) 668567/667436/661913 Telex: 12233 Yu Sa
Dir: Vojin Morača
Subjects: Literature, Law, Work Study, Economics, Reference
Founded: 1954

Škola za Strane Jezike*, YU-41000 Zagreb, Varšavska 14 Tel: (041) 424535/429213
Publishing Manager: Mirko Hrupelj
Subjects: Language textbooks and teaching materials

'Školska knjiga', YU-41000 Zagreb, Masarykova 28, Poštanski fah 1039 Tel: (041) 420784/429111 Cable Add: Školska knjiga Zagreb
Man Dir: Dr Josip Malić; *Publishing Manager:* Professor Antun Zibar; *Sales Manager:* Milan Samardzija
Subjects: University, Secondary & Primary Textbooks, Educational Materials, History, Music, Art, Philosophy, Reference,

Juveniles, Low- & High-priced Paperbacks, Medicine, Psychology, Engineering, General & Social Science, Belles Lettres, Poetry, Biography, How-to
Bookshops: Knjižara 'Školske knjige', YU-41000 Zagreb, Bogovićeva 1/a; knjižara 'Školska knjiga', YU-41000 Zagreb, Masarykova 28; knjižara 'Studentski trg', YU-11000 Belgrade, Studentski trg 6
Founded: 1950

Sloboda*, YU-11040 Belgrade, Vojvode Stepe 315 Tel: (011) 462131/461721/462341 Cable Add: Sloboda Beograd
Dir: Miroslav Marković
Subjects: Historical Literature, Belles Lettres, Juveniles, Encyclopaedias

Slovo ljubve*, YU-11000 Belgrade, Mutapova 12 Tel: (011) 436360/454987
Dir: Ljubiša Pantić; *Editorial, Production:* Rade Vojvodić; *Sales:* Voja Petrović; *Publicity:* Snežana Dabić
Bookshop: Belgrade, Save Kovačevića 26
Book Club: Klub Čitalaca
Founded: 1971

Službeni List*, YU-11000 Belgrade, Jovana Ristića 1, Poštanski fah 226
Tel: (011) 650155 Telex: 11756 Yu Slist
Dir: Dušan Mašović
Subjects: Službeni List (Official Register) in languages of peoples and nationalities of Yugoslavia; Legal, University Textbooks, Federation Regulations, Periodicals
Bookshops: Belgrade: Prodavnica 1, Brankova 16; Prodavnica 2, 29 Novembra 1a

Socialist Thought and Practice*, YU-11000 Belgrade, Trg Marksa i Engelsa 11 Tel: (011) 622532/622011
Chief Executive: Dr Branko Prnjat; *Editorial:* Novak Strugar; *Sales, Publicity, Rights & Permissions:* Nebojša Kandić
Parent Company: NIRO 'Komunist' (at above address)
Founded: 1975

Sportska Knjiga*, YU-11000 Belgrade, Makedonska 19, Poštanski fah 720
Tel: (011) 325361 Cable Add: Sportska Knjiga
Dir: Dragoslav Bajić; *Editor:* Sava Bjelajac
Subject: Sport
Bookshop: At above address
Founded: 1949

Srpska Književna Zadruga, YU-11000 Belgrade, Maršala Tita 19 Tel: (011) 330305/334977
Subjects: History, Belles Lettres
Bookshop: At above address
Founded: 1892

Stvarnost+*, YU-41000 Zagreb, Frankopanska 11, Poštanski fah 734
Tel: (041) 435752/441227/447815
Man Dir, Editorial: Vladimir Štokalo; *Sales:* Vlado Polić
Subjects: General Fiction, Biography, History, How-to, Music, Art, Philosophy, Reference, Juveniles, High-priced Paperbacks, Medicine, General & Social Science
Book Club: Klub 42
Bookshops: Zagreb: Knjizara Stvarnost, Savska 1; Jlica 163b; Rooseveltov trg 4
Founded: 1952

Svjetlost*, YU-71000 Sarajevo, Petra Preradovića 3, Poštanski fah 129 Tel: (071) 512144/31100 Cable Add: Svjetlost Sarajevo Telex: 41326 Yu Ikpres
Man Dir: Abdulah Jesenković; *Sales Dir:* Rizvanbegović Enver; *Editorial:* Miodrag Bogićević
Branch Offs: Belgrade, Obilićev venac 10; Zagreb, Šubičeva 65
Subjects: Belles Lettres, Reference, Science, Juveniles, Business, Textbooks, Business Directories, Encyclopaedias, Periodicals
Bookshops: See under Major Booksellers

Tehnička Knjiga*, YU-11000 Belgrade, ul 7 jula 26, Poštanski fah 307 Tel: (011) 630227
Man Dir: Branko Nikolić
Subjects: General Science, Electronics, Computing, Engineering, Popular Science

Tehnička Knjiga*, YU-41000 Zagreb, Jurišićeva 10, Poštanski fah 816
Tel: (041) 278172 Cable Add: Tehnoknjiga
Man Dir, Chief Editor: Zvonko Vistrička
Subjects: Science, Technical Engineering, Periodicals
Bookshops: See under Major Booksellers, also Knjižara Tehnička Knjiga, Zagreb, Masarykova 17; Antikvarijat, Zagreb, Gundulićeva 19
Founded: 1947

Tehnika, formerly publishing house of Savez Inženjera i Tehničara Jugoslavije (qv)

Tiskarna Ljudske Pravice*, Kopitarjeva 2, YU-61000 Ljubljana Tel: (061) 323841 Telex: 31177 Ljudne
Subjects: Children's, Juvenile, Periodicals

Turistička Štampa*, YU-11000 Belgrade, Knez Mihajlova 21/II, Poštanski fah 606
Tel: (011) 621080/632322
Man Dir: Nikola Korbutovski; *Editorial:* Ranko Mitrović
Subjects: Art, Tourist Guides, Maps, Periodicals

CZ **Uradni** List SRS, YU-61000 Ljubljana, Kardeljeva 12, PO Box 379/VII Tel: (061) 224323
Chief Executive: Juren Peter; *Editorial:* Polutnik Marko
Subject: Law
1985: 16 titles *1986:* 30 titles *Founded:* 1946
ISBN Publisher's Prefix: 86-7085

Veselin Masleša, YU-71000 Sarajevo, Obala v. Stepe 4, Poštanski fah 237 Tel: (071) 214633 Cable Add: Vesmas Masleša Telex: 41154 Yu Vesmas
Man Dir, Editorial, Rights and Permissions: Alija Velić
Branch Offs: Zagreb, Belgrade, Skopje
Subjects: General Fiction, General & Political Science, Reference, Philosophy, Juveniles
Bookshops: See under Major Booksellers
Founded: 1950

Vesti*, YU-31000 Titovo Užice, 4 jula br 14 Tel: (031) 21262
Dir: Mihajlo Rebić

Vojnoizdavački Zavod*, YU-11002 Belgrade, Svetozara Markovića 70
Tel: (011) 641586
Subject: Military

Vuk Karadžic*, YU-11000 Belgrade, Kraljevića Marka 9, Poštanski fah 762
Tel: (011) 628066/628043/620024 (Director) Cable Add: Vuk Karadžić Belgrade
Man Dir: Slobodan Durić; *Editorial:* Vojin Ančić
Branch Offs: Zagreb, Nikole Tesle 14/III; Sarajevo, Sime Milutinovića 10; Novi Sad, Laze Kostića 22; Svetozarevo, Slavke Durdević bb zgr B-3
Subjects: Encyclopaedias and Reference, Art, Popular Science, History, Criticism, Psychology, Sociology, Philosophy, Children's books, Education, Periodicals
Bookshop: See under Major Booksellers
Founded: 1956
ISBN Publisher's Prefix: 86-307

Založba Obzorja, YU-62000 Maribor, Gosposka 3, Poštanski fah 157 Tel: (062) 28971/21086 Telex: 33255 Yu Zomb
Chief Executive: Franc Filipič; *Manager:* Marjan Žnidarič
Subjects: Professional, Science, Journalism, Literature
ISBN Publisher's Prefix: 86-377

Zavod za Izdavanje Udžbenika*, YU-71000 Sarajevo, Otokara Keršovanija 3, Poštanski fah 262
Tel: (071) 33728
Man Dir: Dr Ljubomir Berberović
Subjects: Education, Textbooks

Zavod za Obrazovanje Kadrova za Administrativne Poslove SR Srbije*, Izdavačko-Stamparska OOUR Stručna Knjiga, YU-11000 Belgrade, ul Lole Ribara 48 Tel: (011) 341332/342512/342514 Cable Add: Stručna knjiga
Dir: Mrs V Brgulan
Subjects: Textbooks, Business, Management

Zavod za Udžbenike i Nastavna Sredstva, YU-11000 Belgrade, Obilićev Venac 5, Poštanski fah 312 Tel: (011) 335337
Dir: Dr Tomislav Bogavac
Subjects: Textbooks, Educational Materials
Bookshop: YU-11000 Belgrade, Kosovska 45

Zavod za Udžbenike i Nastavna Sredstva Sap Kosovo*, YU-38000 Priština, Beogradska 29, Poštanski fah 112
Tel: (038) 24752
Dir: Ramuš Rama
Subjects: Textbooks, Educational Materials
Bookshop: Priština, Lenjinova 66
Founded: 1958

Nakladni Zavod **'Znanje'**, YU-41000 Zagreb, Socijalističke revolucije 17, Pretinac 955 Tel: (041) 411500/411483/411474 Cable Add: Znanje Zagreb
Man Dir: Dragutin Brenčun
Branch Offs: Sarajevo, A Šenoe 14; Belgrade, Bulevar Lenjina 119
Subjects: General Fiction, Popular Science, Agriculture
Bookshops: August Šenoa, Socijalističke revolucije 17; Miroslav Krleža, Trg Republike 17; 'Ivan Goran Kovačić', Martićeva 12; Antikvarijat, Tin Ujević, Zrinjevac 17 (all in Zagreb)
Founded: 1946

Literary Agents

Jugoslovenska Autorska Agencija*, Belgrade, Majke Jevrosime 38 Tel: (011) 325902/323155 Cable Add: Autoragencija
General Manager: Mrs Ljiljana Mladenović
Main activities: Protection of the copyrights of Yugoslav authors in Yugoslavia and abroad and of foreign authors in Yugoslavia; marketing of foreign authors' works in Yugoslavia and acquiring options and authorization for the works of Yugoslav authors

V P A (Vjesnikova Press Agencija)*, YU-41000 Zagreb, Ave bratstva i jedinstva 4 Tel: (041) 515555 Telex: 21121

Book Clubs

Book Lovers' Club*, YU-11000 Belgrade, Kosovska 37
Owned by: Beogradski Izdavačko-Grafički Zavod (qv)

Klub 42*, Zagreb, Rooseveltov trg 4
Owned by: Stvarnost (qv)

500 YUGOSLAVIA

Klub Čitalaca*, Belgrade, Save Kovačevića 26
Owned by: Slovo Ljubve (qv)

Klub Čitalaca MK*, YU-11000 Belgrade, Mata Vidakovića 24 Tel: (011) 458165
Members: 3000
Owned by: Medicinska Knjiga (qv)
Founded: 1981

Klub Prijatelja Knjige 'August Cesarec', YU 41000 Zagreb, Braće Oreški 18
Owned by: August Cesarec (qv)

Mladost's Book Fans Club*, Zagreb, Radićeva 37
Owned by: Mladost, Izdavačko Knjižarska radna organizacija (qv under Publishers)

Prosveta, YU-11000 Belgrade, Andricev venac
Owned by: Prosveta (qv under Publishers)

Svet Knjige*, Ljubljana, Nazorjeva 6
Members: 165,000
Owned by: Mladinska Knjiga (qv)
Founded: 1971

Major Booksellers

Cankarjeva Založba*, YU-61001 Ljubljana, Kopitarjeva 2, Poštni predal 201-IV Tel: (061) 323841 Telex: 31821 Yu Cankar
Branches: Kopitarjeva 2, Trg osvoboditve 7, Titova 15, Miklošičeva 16, Tržaška 59, Zaloska 35 (all in Ljubljana); Trbovlje, 1 junija 27; Vrhnika, Usnjarska stolpič S 15
Importer/exporter, antiquarian bookseller, also Publisher (qv)

Export-Press*, YU-11000 Belgrade, Francuska 27, Poštanski fah 358 Tel: (011) 625363
Importer/exporter (the latter particularly as supplier to various US libraries, and UK and US Slavic departments)

Forum, YU-21000 Novi Sad, Vojvode Mišića 1, Poštanski fah 200 Tel: (021) 57207
Importer/exporter, also Publisher (qv)

Jugoslovenska Knjiga, YU-11000 Belgrade, Trg Republike 5/VIII, Poštanski fah 36 Tel: (011) 621992 Cable Add: Jugoknjiga Beograd Telex: 12466 Yu Jkbdg
Importer and exporter of books, periodicals and newspapers

Kultura*, YU-91000 Skopje, JNA 68a, Poštanski fah 298 Tel: (091) 35361
32 bookshops throughout Yugoslavia
Also Publisher (qv)

Makedonska Knjiga, YU-91000 Skopje, 11 Oktomvri bb, Poštanski fah 349 Tel: (091) 231610
Man Dir: Radovan Pavleski
31 bookshops in Skopje and in all major towns in Macedonia
Owned by: Makedonska Knjiga (Knigoizdatelstvo) (qv)

Mladinska Knjiga*, YU-61000 Ljubljana, Titova 3, Poštanski fah 36/1 Tel: (061) 221233 Telex: 31695 Yu Emka Ex
23 bookshops throughout Yugoslavia
Importer/exporter, also Publisher (qv)

Mladost*, YU-41000 Zagreb, Ilica 30, Poštanski fah 1028 Tel: (041) 440211
Telex: 21263 Yu Mladzg
Branches: 20 in Zagreb, two each in Rijeka and Split, one each in Banja Luka, Belgrade, Dubrovnik, Osijek, Pula, Sarajevo, Zadar
Importer/exporter, also Publisher (qv)

Nolit*, YU-11000 Belgrade, Terazije 27/II, Poštanski fah 369 Tel: (011) 333353
50 bookshops throughout Yugoslavia
Importer/exporter
Owned by: Nolit Publishing House (qv)

Prosveta, YU-11000 Belgrade, Terazije 16/I Tel: (011) 687441 (import)/688331 (export)
Over 50 bookshops throughout Yugoslavia
Importer/exporter, also Publisher (qv)

Svjetlost*, YU-71000 Sarajevo, Radojke Lakić 3 Tel: (071) 38678
42 bookshops throughout Yugoslavia
Importer/exporter, also Publisher (qv)

Tehnička Knjiga*, YU-41000 Zagreb, Jurišićeva 10, Poštanski fah 816 Tel: (041) 278172
General Manager: Zvonimir Vistrička
Owned by: Tehnička Knjiga, Zagreb (qv under Publishers)

Veselin Masleša, YU-71000 Sarajevo, Obala v. Stepe 4 Tel: (071) 214633 Telex: 41154
Also: Sarajevo, Maksima Gorkog 2 & Pavla Goranina 2; Belgrade, Terazije 38.
Over 30 group bookshops throughout Yugoslavia
Importer/exporter, also Publisher (qv)

Vuk Karadžic, YU-11000 Belgrade, Kraljevića Marka 9, Poštanski fah 762 Tel: (011) 628066/628043
Manager: Slobodan Durić
Importer/exporter, also Publisher (qv)

Major Libraries

Arhiv Hrvatske*, YU-41000 Zagreb, Marulićev trg 21
Archives of Croatia
Publications: Archival Review (annual); *Acts of Croatian Parliament*

Arhiv na SR Makedonija*, Skopje, Kej Dimitar Vlahov bb, Poštanski fah 496
Archives of Macedonia

Arhiv SR Slovenije*, YU-61000 Ljubljana, Zvezdarska 1 Tel: (061) 216551
Dir: Ema Umek

Arhiv Srbije*, YU-11000 Belgrade, Karnedžijeva 2
Librarian: Mrs L Mirković
Archives of Serbia

Institute for Scientific and Technical Documentation and Information*, Belgrade, Kataniceva 15
Publication: Yugoslav Research Guide

Jugoslovenski centar za tehničku i naučnu dokumentaciju*, Belgrade, S Penezića-Krcuna 29, Poštanski fah 724
Dir: Aleksić Miodrag
Yugoslav Centre for Technical and Scientific Documentation
Publications: Bulletin of Documentation (24 series abstracts from technical literature); *Informatika* (periodical for theory and practice of documentation and information); *Bibliography on Automatic Data Processing, Scientific and Professional Meetings in Yugoslavia and Foreign Countries; MF-Technique* (journal on applying microfilm)

Univerzitetska biblioteka 'Svetozar **Marković'***, YU-11000 Belgrade, Bulevar revolucije 71 Tel: (011) 342116/341446
University Library 'Svetozar Markovič'
Librarian: Stanija Gligorijević

Nacionalna i Sveučilišna Biblioteka*, YU-41001 Zagreb, Marulićev trg 21, Poštanski fah 550 Tel: (041) 445440 (Director); (041) 446322 (Secretariat, Information Office, other departments)
National and University Library
Dir: Dr Petar Piskač
Publications: Bibliografija knjiga tiskanih u SR Hrvatskoj; Bibliografija rasprava, članaka i knjiženih radova u časopisima SR Hrvatske, Grada za hrvatsku retrospektivnu bibliografiju

Centralna **narodna biblioteka SR Crne Gore***, Cetinje, Njegoševa 100
Central National Library of Montenegro

Narodna biblioteka SR Srbije*, YU-11000 Belgrade, Skerlićeva 1 Tel: (011) 451242
National Library of Serbia

Narodna i univerzitetska biblioteka Bosne i Hercegovine, YU-71000 Sarajevo, Obala 42
National and University Library of Bosnia and Herzegovina

Narodna in univerzitetna knjižnica (Ljubljana), YU-61001 Ljubljana pp 259, Turjaška 1 Tel: (061) 332853 (Central); (061) 332847 (Information) Telex: 32285
National and University Library

Naučna biblioteka, YU-51000 Rijeka, Dolac 1, Poštanski fah 132 Tel: (051) 36911/36129
Research Library
Librarian: Srećko Jelušić

Narodna i univerzitetska biblioteka 'Kliment **Ohridski'***, YU-91000 Skopje, bulevar 'Goce Delčev' br 6, Poštanski fah 566 Tel: (091) 226848
'Kliment Ohridski' National and University Library
Publications: Katalog na staropečateni i retki knigi vo Narodnata i Univerzitetskata Biblioteka 'Kliment Ohridski' — Skopje; Bibliografija KPJ-SKM 1919-1979; Bilten na izdanija od oblasta na samoupravuvanjeto vo Jugoslavija; Makedonska Bibliografija

Biblioteka **Srpske** Akademije Nauka i Umetnosti*, YU-11001 Belgrade, Knez Mihailova 35
Library of the Serbian Academy of Sciences and Arts
Librarian: Mile Žegarac

Library Associations

Društvo bibliotekara Bosne i Hercegovine*, YU-71000 Sarajevo, Obala 42 Tel: (071) 537202
Library Association of Bosnia and Herzegovina
Editor-in-chief: Tatjana Praštalo
Publication: Bibliotekarstvo (yearly)

Društvo bibliotekarjev Slovenije, now Zveza bibliotekarskih društev Slovenije (qv)

Društvo na arhivskite rabotnici i arhivite na SRM*, YU-91000 Skopje
Society of Archivists of Macedonia
Secretary: Krasimira Ilievska
Publication: Makedonski arhivist

Hrvatsko bibliotekarsko društvo, YU-41000 Zagreb Marulićev trg 21
Croatian Library Association
Secretary: Daniela Živković
Publication: Vjesnik bibliotekara Hrvatske (quarterly)

Jugoslovenski bibliografski institut*, YU-11000 Belgrade, Terazije 26 Tel: (011) 687836
Yugoslav Bibliographic Institute
Dir: Miloje Rakočevič
Publishes *Bibliografija Jugoslavije* (Yugoslavia Bibliography) which includes books, pamphlets, music scores and articles

of literary, scientific interest, philology, art and sport

Savez bibliotečkih radnika Srbije*, YU-11000 Belgrade, Skerlićeva 1 Tel: (011) 451242/455488
Union of Library Workers of Serbia
Executive Secretary: Dušica Ristić
Publication: Bibliotekar (bimonthly)

Sojuzna društvata na bibliotečnite rabotnici na Jugoslavija*, YU-91000 Skopje, c/o Narodna i Univerzitetska Biblioteka 'Kliment Ohridski', Goce Delčev 6 Tel: (091) 226846
Union of Librarians' Associations of Yugoslavia
Official titles: Savez društava bibliotečkih radnika Jugoslavije (Serbo-Croatian), Sojuz na društvata na bibliotečnite rabotnici na Yugoslavija (Macedonian), Zveza društev bibliotečnih delavcev Jugoslavije (Slovene)
The headquarters of the League is situated in each of the six republics and two provinces of Yugoslavia in turn and changes every two years
Secretary: Mrs Elena Nikodinovska
Publication: Informativen bilten

Sojuz na društvata na bibliotekarite na SR Makedonija, 'Kliment Ohridski' National and University Library, YU-91000 Skopje, ul 'Goce Delčev' br 6, Poštanski fah 566 Tel: (091) 226846
Union of Librarians' Associations of Macedonia
President: Slobodanka Dueva; *Secretary:* Živka Spasovska
Publication: Bibliotekarska iskra

Zveza bibliotekarskih društev Slovenije, YU-61000 Ljubljana, Turjaška 1 Tel: (061) 332853
Library Association of Slovenia
Executive Secretary: Stanislav Bahor
Publications: Knjižnica (quarterly)

Zveza društev bibliotekarjev Jugoslavije (Slovene), see Sojuz na društvata na bibliotekčnite rabotnici na Jugoslavija

Library Reference Books and Journals

Books

Biblioteke u Jugoslaviji (Libraries in Yugoslavia), Jugoslovenski bibliografski institut, YU-11000 Belgrade, Terazije 26

Biblioteke u SR Srbiji (Libraries in Serbia), Narodna biblioteka Srbije, YU-11000 Belgrade, Skerlićeva 1

Journals

Bibliotekar (The Librarian), Savez bibliotečkih radnika Srbije, YU-11000 Belgrade, Skerlićeva 1

Bibliotekarska iskra, Sojuz na društvata na bibliotekarite na SR Makedonija, 'Kliment Ohridski' National and University Library, YU-91000 Skopje, ul 'Goce Delčev' br 6, Poštanski fah 566

Bibliotekarstvo (Librarianship), Društvo bibliotekara Bosne i Hercegovine, YU-71000 Sarajevo, Obala 42

Knjiga i čitaoci (Books and Readers), Hrvatsko bibliotekarsko društvo, YU-41000 Zagreb, Marulićev trg 21

Knjižnica (The Library), Zveza bibliotekarskih društev Slovenije, YU-61000 Ljubljana, Turjaška 1
Text in Slovenian, summaries in English

Makedonski arhivist (Macedonian Archivist), Društvo na arhivskite rabotnici i arhivite na SRM, YU-91000 Skopje
Text in Macedonian, summaries in French

Viesnik bibliotekara hrvatske (Croatian Librarians' Bulletin), Hrvatsko bibliotekarsko društvo, YU-41000 Zagreb, Marulićev trg 21

Literary Associations and Societies

Društvo na pisatelite na SRM*, YU-91000 Skopje, Maksim Gorki 18 Tel: (091) 236205
Society of Writers of Macedonia
Secretaries: Trajan Petrovski, Rade Siljan

Društvo za srpski jezik i književnost, Belgrade University, Belgrade
Society of Serbian Language and Literature
Secretary: D Pavlović
Publication: Pritozi za knjizevnost, jezik, istorija i folklor

Yugoslav **P E N Club**, Croatian Centre, YU-41000 Zagreb, Vlaska 68a
Secretary: Mirko Mirković

Yugoslav **P E N Club**, Macedonian Centre, YU-91000 Skopje, Maksim Gorki 18
Secretary: Ms Gordana Bosnakovska

Yugoslav **P E N Club**, Serbian Centre, YU-11000 Belgrade, Francuska br 7
Secretary: Dušan Veličković
Publications include: Pismo (quarterly, published jointly with 'Jovan Popovic' Library, Zemun)

Yugoslav **P E N Club**, Slovene Centre, YU-61000 Ljubljana, Tomsićeva 12
Secretary: Elza Jereb

Pedagoško-književni zbor, pedagoško društvo SR Hrvatske *, Zagreb
Pedagogical and Literary Union of Croatia

Sojuz na društvata za makedonski jazik i literatura na SRM Filološki fakultet*, YU-91000 Skopje, bul 'Krste Misirkov' bb
Federation of Societies for Macedonian Language and Literature
Secretary: Vančo Tuševski
Publication: Literaturen zbor (Literary Word)

Literary Periodicals

Bagdala, Knjizevni Klub, Krusevac, Obilićeva 20
Literature, art and culture; text in Serbo-Croatian

Brazde, Narodni Univerzitet, Bijeljina, Vase Pelagica 1
Journal for literature and culture

Bridge, Zagreb, trg Republike 7
Literary review

Delo (The Literary Work), Nolit Publishing House, YU-11000 Belgrade, Terazije 27/II, Poštanski fah 369
Text in Serbo-Croation

Forum, Zagreb 1, Zrinski trg 11
Journal of the Section for Contemporary Literature of the Yugoslav Academy of Sciences and Arts; text in Serbo-Croatian

Izraz, Sarajevo, Radojke Lakio Broj 3-1, Poštanski fah 322
Journal of literary and artistic criticism

Književna kritika (Literary Criticism), Izdavačka Organizacija Rad, YU-11000 Belgrade, Moše Pijade 12

Književne novine (Literary News), Novinsko Izdavačko Preduzeće 'Knjizevne Novine', Belgrade, Francuska 7
Text in Serbo-Croatian

Literaturen zbor, Institute for the Macedonian Language, 'Krste Misirkov', YU-91000 Skopje, Grigor Prličev 5
Journal of the Federation of Societies for Macedonian Language and Literature; text in Macedonian

Lumina, Panciova, Zarka Zrenjanina 7
Literary and cultural review

Macedonian Review, Cultural Life, Skopje, Poštanski fah 85
History, culture, literature, arts

Pismo, YU-11000 Belgrade, Francuska br 7
Quarterly, published jointly with 'Jovan Popovic' Library, Zemun

Pregled naših i stranih knjiga i članaka (Review of Domestic and Foreign Books and Articles), Centralna biblioteka JNA, Belgrade, Balkanska 53a

Razgledi, Maršala Tita Iv Baraka, Skopje, Maršala Tita 4, Poštanski fah 345
Review of literature, art and culture; text in Macedonian

Savremenik, Beogradski Izdavačko-Grafički Zavod, YU-11000 Belgrade, blvd vojode Mišića 17, Poštanski fah 340
Literary monthly; text in Serbo-Croatian

Stremez, Prilep, Joska Jordanovski 2
Journal for literature and culture; text in Macedonian

Stremliena, Jedinstvo, YU-38000 Priština, Dom Štampe bb, Poštanski, pregradak 81
Literary review published every two months

Stvaranje, Cedo Vukovic, Titograd, Marka Miljanova 11A
Journal for literature and culture

Translation Agencies and Associations

Društvo na literaturnite preveduvači na SRM*, YU-91000 Skopje
Society of Literary Translators of Macedonia
Secretary: Taško Širilov

Zaire

General Information

Language: Officially French; Swahili common in east, Lingala in west
Religion: About 25% Roman Catholic; rest follow traditional beliefs
Population: 28.3 million
Bank Hours: 0800-1130 Monday-Friday
Shop Hours: 0800-1200, 1500-1800 Monday-Friday; 0800-1200 Saturday
Currency: 100 makutu (singular likuta) = 1 zaïre; 100 sengi = 1 likuta
Export/Import Information: No tariff but for books not of educational, scientific or cultural use there is a revenue tax; children's picture books and atlases are also taxed. Small quantities of advertising matter free. Statistical Tax on all imports. Goods subject to duty also subject to Turnover Tax of percentage of CIF value + customs + statistical tax. No import licences for books. Exchange controls

ZAIRE

Copyright: Berne, Florence (see International section)

Book Trade Reference Book

Bibliographie nationale (National Bibliography), Bibliothèque nationale, 10 blvd Col Rshatshi, BP 3090, Kinshasa-Gombe

Publishers

Bureau d'Etudes et de Recherches pour la Promotion de la Santé, BP 1800, Kangu-Mayombe (BZ)
Man Dir, Rights & Permissions: Dr J Courtejoie
Subjects: Medicine, Health Education

C E E B A Publications, BP 246, Bandundu Cable Add: CEEBA Bandundu
Man Dir, Editorial: Dr Hermann Hochegger; *Sales:* Cit Mbambi
Parent Company: Anthropos Institut
Subjects: Social Anthropology, Ethnology, Myths, Rituals, Sociology, Linguistics, Arts, Agriculture, History, Religion, Development, Dietetics, Development
1985: 5 titles *1986:* 4 titles *Founded:* 1965

C E L T A (Centre de Linguistique Théorique et Appliquée), BP 1607, Lubumbashi
General Manager: Max Pierre
Parent Organization: Faculté des Lettres, BP 1825, Lubumbashi
Subsidiary Companies: CELTA/Kinshasa, BP 4956, Kinshasa I; Editions Impala (qv)
Subjects: Local Languages, French
Bookshop: BP 1607, Lubumbashi
Founded: 1971

Centre International de Sémiologie*, 109 Ave Pruniers, Zone de Kampemba, BP 1825, Campus de Lubumbashi
Secretary: Dr V Y Mudimbe
Publications: Bulletins on Medical Anthropology, Religious Syncretisms, Culture-contact, Africanisms

Centre Protestant d'Editions et de Diffusion (CEDI)*, 209 ave Kalemie, BP 11398, Kinshasa I Tel: 22202
Man Dir: Makela Lutantu
Subjects: General Fiction, Belles Lettres, Poetry, Biography, Religion, Juveniles, Christian Tracts, Books in Kikongo, Lingala and other Zaïre languages, Paperbacks
Bookshops: CEDI Bookshop (qv under Major Booksellers)
Founded: 1935

Commission de l'Education chrétienne*, BP 3258, Kinshasa-Gombe Tel: 30087 Telex: 203 DIA
Man Dir: Abbé Dibalu Didi; *Editorial, Production:* Abbé Ekofo I Tshibala
Subsidiary Company: Editions Scolaires, BP 3258, Kinshasa-Gombe
Subjects: Educational, Academic, Religion

Faculté de Theologie Catholique de Kinshasa, BP 1534, Kinshasa-Limete Tel: 78476
Dir: Prof Buetubela Balembo; *Editorial:* Prof Atal, Prof Mulago, Prof Mudiji, Prof Nyeme
Subjects: Theology, Philosophy, African Religions
Founded: 1957

Government Printer (Imprimerie du Gouvernement Central)*, BP 3021, Kinshasa-Kalina

Editions Impala, BP 1607, Lubumbashi Tel: 5483

Chief Executive, Rights & Permissions: Ruhama Mukandoli; *Editorial, Sales, Production, Publicity:* Max Pierre
Parent Company: CELTA (qv)
Associate Company: Maison des Langues Vivantes, rue des Pierres 9, B-1000 Brussels, Belgium
Subjects: Language, Linguistics
Bookshops: Librairie St Paul (qv under Major Booksellers); Librairie Les Volcans, Goma Libreza, Bukavu; Maison des Langues Vivantes, Brussels, Belgium
Founded: 1981

Editions **Lokole**, BP 5085 Kinshasa X (Located at: ave Colonel Ebeya no 1082, Kinshasa-Gombe) Tel: 22559
Dir: Bokeme Shane Molobay
Miscellaneous: State organization charged with the promotion of literature in Zaire

Editions du **Mont Noir***, BP 1944, Lubumbashi
Man Dir: V Y Mudimbe; *Sales:* Pierre De-tienne; *Secretary and Publicity:* Mukala Kadima Nzuji
Subjects: General Fiction, Belles Lettres, Poetry, Reference
Founded: 1971

P U Z, an imprint of Presses universitaires du Zaïre et l'Office du Livre (qv)

Les **Presses Africaines***, pl du 27 Octobre, BP 12924, Kinshasa I
Man Dir: Mwamba-di-Mbuyi
Subjects: General Non-fiction, Belles Lettres, Poetry, Paperbacks

Presses universitaires du Zaïre et l'Office du Livre (PUZ), Boul du 30 Juin 4113, BP 1682 Kinshasa I Tel: 30652 Cable Add: PUZ Enseignement Telex: 21394 Bce Es
Man Dir, Rights & Permissions: Mumbanza mwa Bawele; *Editorial:* Kabongo Kabongo; *Sales:* Nsolo Abeyingi; *Production:* Kawumbu Kabemba; *Publicity:* Bisimwa Nabintu
Parent Company: Enseignement Superieur, Universitaire et Recherche Scientifique, BP 1682, Kinshasa-Gombe
Imprint: PUZ
Branch Off: Lubumbashi
Subjects: Belles Lettres, Poetry, Biography, History, Africana, Philosophy, Reference, Religion, Paperbacks, Psychology, Medicine, Science & Technology, Agronomy, Social Science, University Textbooks, Economics, Law, Literature, Education
Bookshops: Librairie des Presses universitaires (qv under Major Booksellers); Librairie Universitaire de l'ISP/Kawanga; Librairie du 'Groupe du Mukuba', Lubumbashi
Founded: 1972

Editions **Saint Paul***, 76 ave du Commerce, BP 8505, Kinshasa Tel: 25544
Dir: Sister Franka Perona
Subjects: General Fiction & Non-fiction, Belles Lettres, Poetry, Religion, Juveniles, Christian Tracts, Paperbacks
Bookshops: See under Major Booksellers

Librairie Les **Volcans***, 22 ave Président Mobuto, BP 400, Goma (Kivu) Tel: 366
Man Dir: Ruhama Mukandoli; *Sales Manager:* Pierre Mangez
Subjects: Reference, Social Science
Bookshop: See under Major Booksellers

Literary Agents

Le **Gai Savoir***, BP 12924, Kinshasa I

Major Booksellers

C E D I Bookshop*, 209 ave Kalemie, BP 11398, Kinshasa I Tel: 22202
Man Dir: Makela Lutantu

Diffusion de la Presse, BP 505, Kisangani

La **Générale des Carrières et des Mines**-Exploitation (Gécamines-Exploitation)*, BP 450, Lubumbashi Telex: 41034
Also: BP 8714, Kinshasa Telex: 21207

Librairie de l'**Institut national** d'Etudes politiques*, BP 2307, Kinshasa Tel: 31649

Okapi Centre de Diffusion*, BP 908, Kinshasa

Librairie des **Presses** universitaires*, BP 1682, Kinshasa I Tel: 24786
Owned by: Presses universitaires du Zaïre et l'Office du Livre (PUZ) (qv)

Procure scolaire*, BP 70, Kananga
Manager: Wilfried Meulemeester

Librairie **Saint Paul***, 76 ave du Commerce, BP 8505, Kinshasa
Also: BP 2447, Lubumbashi
Owned by: Editions Saint Paul (qv)

Librairie **Salutiste***, 249 ave du Plateau, BP 8905, Kinshasa

Librairie **Sarma***, BP 7098, Kinshasa

Librairies **Sodimca***, BP 2700, Kinshasa

Librairie Les **Volcans***, 22 ave Président Mobutu, BP 400, Goma
Owned by: Librairie Les Volcans, Publisher (qv)

Librairie du **Zaïre***, 12 ave des Aviateurs, BP 2100, Kinshasa I Tel: 26748

Major Libraries

Archives nationales du Zaïre*, 42 ave Valcke, BP 3428, Kinshasa

Bibliothèque nationale*, 10 blvd Col Rshatshi, BP 3090, Kinshasa-Gombe Tel: 30834
Publication: Bibliographie nationale

Bibliothèque publique de Kinshasa*, BP 410, Kinshasa Tel: 3070
Librarian: M Mongu

Bibliothèque publique de Kisangani*, 2 ave Bawaboli, BP 1741, Kisangani Tel: 2617

Bibliothèque publique de Lubumbashi*, 827 ave Delvaux, Lubumbashi
Supplies 25 branch libraries

Centre culturel français, Bibliothèques, BP 5236, Kinshasa 10 Tel: 25566

Institut pédagogique national*, Bibliothèque, BP 8815, Kinshasa I Tel: 80573

Institut pour la recherche scientifique en Afrique centrale, Bibliothèque*, Dépêche Spéciale, Bukavu, Kivu Tel: 3080
Chief Librarian: Ruhima Kibuka

Bibliothèque centrale de l'**Université de Kisangani***, BP 2012, Kisangani Tel: 2153
Chief Librarian: Label Kakes Muzila

Bibliothèque centrale, **Université de Kinshasa**, BP 125, Kinshasa XI Tel: 30123 exts 114, 153
Librarian: Prof Dr Kuzenzama
Publication: Chronique des Bibliothèques

Bibliothèque centrale de l'**Université nationale, Campus de Lubumbashi***, BP 2896, Lubumbashi Tel: 4479

Library Association

Association Zaïroise des Archivistes, Bibliothècaires et Documentalistes*, BP 805, Kinshasa XI Tel: 30123/4
Zaire Association of Archivists, Librarians and Documentalists
Executive Secretary: E Kabeba-Bangasa
Publication: Mukanda

Library Reference Books and Journals

Book

Liste des bibliothèques publiques (List of Public Libraries), Ministère de la culture et des arts, Bibliothèque centrale, Kinshasa-Kalina

Journal

Mukanda, Association Zaïroise des Archivistes, Bibliothécaires et Documentalistes, BP 805, Kinshasa XI
Archives, libraries and documentation bulletin

Literary Periodicals

Cahiers de Littérature et de Linguistique appliqué (Journal of Literature and Applied Linguistics), Université nationale du Zaïre, Faculté des Lettres, BP 1825, Campus de Lubumbashi

Dombi (bi-monthly), BP 3498, Kinshasa-Kalina
Congolese review of letters and the arts

Zambia

General Information

Language: English is official language
Religion: About 50% Christian (25% Roman Catholic, 25% Protestant); rest follow traditional beliefs
Population: 5.7 million
Bank Hours: 0815-1245 Monday, Tuesday, Wednesday, Friday; 0815-1200 Thursday; 0815-1100 Saturday
Shop Hours: Generally 0800-1700 Monday-Friday; 0800-1300 Saturday
Currency: 100 ngwee = 1 Zambia kwacha
Export/Import Information: No tariffs on books but all imports subject to sales tax. Single copies of advertising free. Import licence required. Exchange controls
Copyright: UCC (see Internationsal section)

Book Trade Organizations

Booksellers' and Publishers' Association of Zambia, c/o PO Box 320199, Lusaka
Chairman: G B Mwangilwa

Standard Book Numbering Agency, Booksellers' and Publishers' Association of Zambia, c/o PO Box 320199, Lusaka
ISBN Administrator: G B Mwangilwa

Book Trade Reference Book

National Bibliography of Zambia, National Archives of Zambia, PO Box 50010, Lusaka

Publishers

Africa Literature Centre*, PO Box 1319, Kitwe Tel: (02) 84712 Cable Add: Mincen
Man Dir: E C Makunike
Subjects: General, Educational, Religion, Books in Zambian Languages
Bookshop: At above address

Directory Publishers of Zambia Ltd*, PO Box 30963, Lusaka (Located at: First Floor, Eureka House, Freedom Way, Lusaka) Tel: (01) 212650/212653
Man Dir, Rights & Permissions: D E Smith; *Editorial, Publicity, Sales:* Siobhan McDonough
Subjects: Reference, Directories
Founded: 1958

Government Printer*, PO Box 30136, Lusaka

Institute of African Studies, PO Box 30900, Lusaka Tel: (01) 282880/282881 Cable Add: Insas Telex: 44370
Editorial: Dr Chisepo J Mphaisha, Prof Mubanga E Kashoki, Dr S P C Moyo, Dr Gatian Lungu; *All other offices:* Miss M A Sifuniso, University Publications Office of University of Zambia, PO Box 32379, Lusaka
Parent Organization: University of Zambia, PO Box 32379, Lusaka
Branch Off: Ndola Campus of University of Zambia, PO Box 21692, Kitwe
Subjects: Social Research in Africa
Bookshops: University Bookshop (qv under Major Booksellers)
Founded: 1938

Kenneth Kaunda Foundation*, Publishing and Printing Division, Washama Rd, PO Box 32708, Lusaka Tel: (01) 218259/218419/215612 Cable Add: Foundation Lusaka Telex: ZA 40056
Publishing and Printing Dir: M C Kondolo; *Editorial:* H Lombe; *Production:* P Kalwa; *Rights & Permissions:* P A Himwiinga
Subjects: General, Poetry, Biography, History, Agriculture, Children's Books, Educational, Language, Literature, Fiction, Folklore, Drama, Politics, Sociology, Zambia Primary Course
Book Club: Read-a-Book Club
Bookshop: Chishango Rd, PO Box 32666, Lusaka
Founded: 1967

Multimedia Zambia+*, PO Box 320199, Lusaka (Located at: Bishops Rd, Kabulonga) Tel: (01) 253864/215950 Telex: 40630 Zau
Executive Dir: Goodwin Bwalya Mwangilwa
Parent Company: Christian Council of Zambia/Zambia Episcopal Conference
Subjects: Political Biographies, Cookery, Comparative Religion, Educational Textbooks for Juveniles, Fiction, Social Sciences, Historical Communications
Founded: 1971

Temco Publishing Ltd*, No 10 Kabelenga Rd, PO Box 30886, Lusaka Tel: (01) 211883 Cable Add: Longman Telex: ZA 45250
Man Dir, Editorial, Production, Publicity, Rights & Permissions: S V Tembo; *Sales:* S I Tembo Jnr
Subjects: Educational, General
Founded: 1977

Book Club

Read-a-Book Club*, PO Box 32664, Lusaka Tel: (01) 218259/218419/215612
Owned by: Kenneth Kaunda Foundation (qv)

Major Booksellers

The **Bookshelf***, Caravelle House, Buteko Ave, PO Box 977, Ndola Tel: (026) 3438

Christian Bookshop*, PO Box 1206, Kitwe

Christian Council of Zambia*, Farmers House, PO Box 315, Lusaka Tel: (01) 73287

Kingstons (Zambia) Ltd*, PO Box 70139, Ndola
Department store with book department (12 other branches)

Malsa Book Service Ltd*, Cairo Rd, PO Box 1700, Lusaka Tel: (01) 81155

Standard Books Ltd*, PO Box 94, Lusaka

University Bookshop, PO Box 32379, Lusaka Tel: (01) 252576 Cable Add: Unza Bookshop, Lusaka Telex: 44370 Unzalu
Manager: A M Simbeya
Also: PO Box 21692, Kitwe
Owned by: University of Zambia

Zambia Catholic Bookshop, PO Box 71581, Ndola

Major Libraries

Evelyn **Hone** College Library, PO Box 30029, Lusaka Tel: (01) 211557
Librarian: Joyce Masempela

Helen **Kaunda** Memorial Library, Cha Cha Cha Rd, PO Box 90310, Luanshya Tel: (02) 510315
Librarian: Charles Sambondu

Kitwe Public Library, PO Box 20070, Kitwe Tel: (02) 213685

Lusaka Urban District Libraries*, PO Box 31304, Katondo Rd, Lusaka Tel: (01) 217282
District Librarian: E N Kantumoya
Publications: Annual Report; New Additions List (quarterly)

Mindolo Ecumenical Foundation, Hammarskjold Memorial Library, PO Box 21493, Kitwe Tel: (02) 215198/214572/211488/211269 Cable Add: Mincen Kitwe Telex: 52050 Za
Publications: Annual Report; Mindolo Newsletter (twice yearly); various reports of conferences and research programmes

National Archives of Zambia*, PO Box 50010, Lusaka Tel: (01) 214844
Librarian: H K Nyendwa
Publications include: National Bibliography of Zambia; National Archives of Zambia Annual Reports; List of Periodicals in the National Archives of Zambia

National Institute of Public Administration Library*, PO Box 31990, Lusaka Tel: (01) 216124
Librarian: A G Kasonso

Natural Resources Development College Library, PO Box CH 99, Lusaka Tel: (01) 214620

Ndola Public Library, PO Box 70388, Ndola Tel: (026) 610537
Librarian: K Mumba Chisaka

Nkrumah Teachers' College Library*, PO Box 80404, Kabwe Tel: (05) 222047/8
Librarian: Francesca K Ng'Ambi

Northern Technical College Library*, PO Box 250093, Ndola Tel: (026) 86211 ext 18
Librarian: M C Banda

University of Zambia Library, PO Box 32379, Lusaka Tel: (01) 213221 Cable

ZAMBIA — ZIMBABWE

Add: UNZA-Library Telex: 44370 Za
Chief Librarian: H Mwacalimba;
Librarians: H Mwacalimba (Lusaka Campus), M C Lundu (Ndola Campus)
Publications include: Zambiana Gazette; Bulletin

Zambia Institute of Technology Library, PO Box 21993, Kitwe Tel: (02) 212066
Librarian: E M Chitwamali
Publications: Annual Report; ZIT Prospectus (annual)

Zambia Library Service*, Educational Services Centre, PO Box 30802, Lusaka Tel: (01) 254655 Cable Add: Zamlibs
Chief Librarian: M Walubita
Publications include: Bulletin (quarterly); *Directory of Library Centres* (annually); *Buyer's Guide to Library Equipment* (twice a year)

Library Association

Zambia Library Association, c/o Zambia Institute of Mass Media Communications, PO Box 50386, Lusaka
Secretary: Adrian K Pamba
Publications: Zambia Library Association Journal; Zambia Library Association Newsletter

Library Reference Books and Journals

Books

Directory of Libraries in Zambia, Zambia Library Association, PO Box 32839, Lusaka
Provides details on all the major libraries in the country

Directory of Library Centres, Zambia Library Service, PO Box 30802, Lusaka

Journal

Zambia Library Association Journal, PO Box 32839, Lusaka

Literary Associations and Societies

Mphala Creative Society*, c/o International House 5-13, University of Zambia, PO Box 2379, Lusaka
Publication: The Jewel of Africa

Literary Periodical

The Jewel of Africa, Mphala Creative Society, c/o International House 5-13, University of Zambia, PO Box 2379, Lusaka
Literary and cultural quarterly

Zimbabwe

General Information

Language: English and native dialects
Population: 7.36 million
Bank Hours: 0830-1400 Monday, Tuesday, Thursday, Friday; 0830-1200 Wednesday; 0830-1100 Saturday

Shop Hours: 0800 or 0830-1700 Monday-Friday; 0800 or 0830-1200 or 1230 Saturday
Currency: 100 cents = 1 Zimbabwe dollar
Export/Import Information: No tariff on books. Advertising matter in bulk has duty and VAT charged. No import licence required for books or advertising matter
Copyright: Berne (see International section)

Book Trade Organizations

Booksellers' Association of Zimbabwe*, PO Box 3916, Harare (Located at: 4th Floor, Room 418, Southern Life Building, Stanley Ave, Harare) Tel: (10) 708577
Chairman: C K Katsande; *Secretary:* M S Samkange

Standard Book Numbering Agency, National Archives, Private Bag 7729, Causeway, Harare Tel: (10) 792741
ISBN Administrator: Miss R Marunda

Book Trade Reference Book

Zimbabwe National Bibliography, National Archives, Causeway, Private Bag 7729, Harare

Publishers

Africana Book Society (Pty) Ltd*, c/o PO Box 1994, Bulawayo
Parent Company: Books of Zimbabwe Publishing Co (Pvt) Ltd (qv)
Subjects: General Academic, Biography, History, Africana, Hunting, Wildlife, Illustrated & Fine Editions, Reprints
Founded: 1975
ISBN Publisher's Prefix: 0-949973

B & T Directories (Pvt) Ltd*, PO Box 1027, Harare (Located at: Satcoy House, 125 Manica Rd, Harare) Tel: (10) 705199/794839/704088 Telex: 4092 ZW
Subject: Directories

Bold Ads, an imprint of Directories of Zimbabwe (Pvt) Ltd

Books of Zimbabwe Publishing Co (Pvt) Ltd*, 137A Rhodes St, PO Box 1994, Bulawayo Tel: (19) 61135
Rights & Permissions: Joan Hopcroft
Orders to: Books of Zimbabwe Publishing Co, PO Box 1994, Bulawayo
Subsidiary Company: Africana Book Society (Pty) Ltd (qv)
Subjects: Rhodesiana Reprints & New Works, Fine Prints, Antique Maps of Africa, General Fiction and Non-fiction, Biography, History, Colour-plate Fine editions, Education, Visual Aids
Founded: 1968
ISBN Publisher's Prefix: 0-86920

A C **Braby** (Pvt) Ltd, see Directories of Zimbabwe (Pvt) Ltd

The **College** Press (Pvt) Ltd+, PO Box 3041, Harare (Located at: 15 Douglas Rd, Workington, Harare) Tel: (10) 66335 Cable Add: Libris Telex: 2558 Colprs ZW
Man Dir: Benias Mugabe; *Sales Dir:* Engelbert Luphahla; *Publisher:* Margo Bedingfield; *Production:* Augustine Bakure; *International Division, Public Relations:* Sue McMillan
Subsidiary Companies: Galaxie Press (1974) (Pvt) Ltd (qv); Scholastic Books (Pvt) Ltd
Associate Companies: Macmillan Publishers Ltd, UK (qv); Teachers Forum (Pvt) Ltd, Harare
Imprints: Scholastic Books, Ventures

Branch Offs: PO Box 298, Bulawayo; PO Box 963, Mutare; PO Box 1239, Gweru; PO Box 355, Masvingo
Subjects: Educational titles for Zimbabwe and Africa, General Interest titles for Zimbabwe
1987: 56 titles *Founded:* 1968
ISBN Publisher's Prefix: 0-86925

Peter **Dearlove** Publishers*, PO Box UA 106, Harare
Man Dir: Peter Dearlove
Subjects: General Non-fiction, Biography, History, Africana, Paperbacks, Social Science

Directories of Zimbabwe (Pvt) Ltd*, PO Box 1027, Harare (Located at: Satcoy House, 125 Manica Rd, Harare) Tel: (10) 705199/794839/704088 Telex: 4092 ZW
Chief Executive: J van der Walt;
Production Manager: E McGorman; *Sales:* Ms L Travers
Parent Company: Zimbabwe Newspapers (Pvt) Ltd
Subsidiary Companies: B & T Directories (Pvt) Ltd (qv), A C Braby (Pvt) Ltd, Publications (C A) (Pvt) Ltd (qv) (all at above address)
Imprint: Bold Ads
Branch Off: PO Box 1027, Bulawayo
Subjects: Information & Directories on Zimbabwe
Founded: 1950

Directory Publishers (Pvt) Ltd*, PO Box 1595, Bulawayo Tel: (19) 78831 Telex: 3333 ZW
Chief Executive: Bruce Gordon Beale;
Production Dir: Charles Anthony Harris;
Editorial Manager: Sheila Whyte; *Sales Manager:* June Davies; *Rights & Permissions:* Kelly Linder
Subsidiary Company: BCF Ltd (at above address)
Subjects: Reference, Directories, Educational, Telephone Books, Diaries, Maps, Periodicals

Flame Lily, an imprint of The Literature Bureau (qv)

Galaxie Press (Pvt) Ltd*, PO Box 3041, Harare
Parent Company: The College Press (Pvt) Ltd (qv)

Gemini Publishers+, PO Box MP 49, Mount Pleasant, Harare Tel: (10) 701515
Secretary: L E Bacon; *Publicity, Sales:* M A Sullivan
Subjects: Science Fiction, Poetry, Fiction, General Non-fiction
1985: 1 title *1986:* 2 titles

Government Printer*, PO Box 8062, Causeway, Harare

The **Literature Bureau**, Ministry of Education, PO Box 8137, Causeway, Harare Tel: (10) 726929 Cable Add: Litburo
Chief Publications Officer: B C Chitsike;
Senior Editorial Officers: O C Chiromo (Shona), D Ndoda (Acting); *Publications Officer:* P Mpofu
Imprint: Flame Lily
Branch Off: PO Box 555, Bulawayo
Subjects: General Fiction & Non-fiction, Belles Lettres, Poetry, Biography, History, Africana, How-to, Study Guides, Books in Shona, Ndebele and English
Book Clubs: Shona Readers' Book Club, Ndebele Readers' Book Club
Bookshop: See under Major Booksellers
Founded: 1954
Miscellaneous: Formerly Rhodesia Literature Bureau
ISBN Publisher's Prefix: 0-86926

Longman Zimbabwe (Pvt) Ltd, PO Box ST125, Southerton, Harare Tel: (10) 62711 Cable Add: Longman Harare Zimbabwe
Man Dir: S G Mpofu; *General Manager:* D R Mackenzie; *Publishing Manager, Rights & Permissions:* Nda Dlodlo; *National Sales Manager:* Willias Masocha; *Publicity:* Janis Joseph
Parent Company: Longman Group UK Ltd, UK (qv)
Subjects: General Fiction & Non-fiction, Belles Lettres, Poetry, Biography, History, Africana, Juveniles, Books in Shona and Ndebele, Paperbacks, General & Social Science, Secondary & Primary Textbooks
1985-86: 49 titles *Founded:* 1964
ISBN Publisher's Prefix: 0-582

Mambo Press, PO Box 779, Gweru Tel: (154) 4016/3806
Man Dir: Albert Plangger; *Sales Manager:* Joe Huber
Branch Offs: Speke Ave/First St, PB 66002 Kopje, Harare Tel: (10) 705899; Gokomere, PB 921329 Masvingo Tel: (139) 2519
Subjects: General Fiction & Non-fiction, Poetry, Religion, Books in Shona, Ndebele and English, Secondary & Primary Textbooks
Bookshops: See under Major Booksellers
Founded: 1958
ISBN Publisher's Prefix: 0-86922

Oxford University Press*, Rooms 317-20, Roslin House, Baker Ave, PO Box 3892, Harare Tel: (10) 27848 Cable Add: Oxonian
Subjects: General Non-fiction, Belles Lettres, Poetry, Biography, History, Africana, Books in Shona & other Zimbabwean Languages, Secondary Textbooks, Music, Prayer Books
Founded: 1915
ISBN Publisher's Prefix: 0-19

Publications (CA) (Pvt) Ltd*, PO Box 1027, Harare (Located at: Satcoy House, 125 Manica Rd, Harare) Tel: (10) 705199/794839/704088 Telex: 4092 ZW
Subjects: Reference, Annuals, Directories, Educational

Scholastic Books, an imprint of The College Press (Pvt) Ltd (qv)

University of Zimbabwe+, Publications Officer, PO Box MP45, Mount Pleasant, Harare Tel: (10) 303211 ext 1236 Cable Add: University Telex: 4152 ZW
Editor: Prof R S Roberts; *Publications Officer:* Roger Stringer
Subjects: History, Africana, Philosophy, Language, Literature, Reference, Religion, Medicine, Science & Technology, General & Social Science, University Textbooks, Periodical
ISBN Publisher's Prefix: 0-908307

Ventures, an imprint of The College Press (Pvt) Ltd (qv)

Z E B, an imprint of Zimbabwe Publishing House (qv)

Z P H, an imprint of Zimbabwe Publishing House (qv)

Zimbabwe Educational Books, a subsidiary of Zimbabwe Publishing House (qv) and an associate of The Heinemann Group of Publishers Ltd, UK (qv)

Zimbabwe Publishing House*, PO Box BW350, Borrowdale, Harare (Located at: 144 Union Ave, Corner 6th St, Harare) Tel: (10) 790148/790416/790483 Telex: 2502
Man Dir, Publicity: David Martin; *Editorial, Rights & Permissions:* Phyllis Johnson; *Sales:* Tainie Mundondo; *Production:* Christopher Russell
Subsidiary Company: Zimbabwe Educational Books (at above address)
Imprints: ZEB, ZPH
Branch Offs: Bulawayo, Gweru, Masvingo, Mutare
Subjects: Educational, African Writing, Children's, Women's, General
Bookshop: Frontline Bookshop (at above address)
1985: 41 titles *Founded:* 1981
ISBN Publisher's Prefixes: 0-949932, 0-949225 (ZPH), 0-908300 (ZEB)

Book Clubs

Ndebele Readers' Book Club, Box 8137, Causeway, Harare Tel: (10) 726929 Cable Add: Litburo
Sponsored by: The Literature Bureau (qv)
Subject: Ndebele Literature
Members: 375
Founded: 1978

Shona Readers' Book Club, Box 8137, Causeway, Harare Tel: (10) 726929 Cable Add: Litburo
Sponsored by: The Literature Bureau (qv)
Subject: Shona literature
Members: 331
Founded: 1978

Major Booksellers

Adventist Book Centre, 114 Jameson St, PO Box 573, Bulawayo Tel: (19) 61845

Alpha Books*, PO Box 1056, Harare Tel: (10) 722553/790160
Manager: L Craven

Baptist Book Centre, PO Box 831, Gweru (Located at: 5th Street, Mandis Bldg, Gweru) Tel: (154) 4242
Manager: Shayne T Masimira

Belmont Press, PO Box 31, Masvingo Tel: (139) 2633
Managers: D G Hill, G W Hill

Book Centre, PO Box 3799, Harare (Located at: Gordon Ave and First St, Harare) Tel: (10) 790691 Cable Add: Textbook Telex: 4071 Texts ZW

Evans Shepherd, PO Box 36, Harare Tel: (10) 739866
Manager: R A Dunkley

Kingstons Ltd, PO Box 2374, Harare Tel: (10) 700526
Wholesaler, also retailer with 11 branches

The **Literature Bureau**, PO Box 8137, Causeway, Harare (Located at: Electra House, Samora Machel Ave, Harare) Tel: (10) 726929 Cable Add: Litburo
Wholesale and retail distributors, also Publisher (qv)

Mambo Press Bookshop, Speke Ave/First St, PB 66002, Kopje, Harare Tel: (10) 705899
Also: PO Box 779, Gweru
Owned by: Mambo Press (qv)

Matopo Book Centre*, PO Box 554, Bulawayo Tel: (19) 71152
Manager: Agrippa V Masiye

National Books of Zimbabwe*, PO Box 4828, Harare Tel: (10) 703257
(Apex Holdings (Pvt) Ltd trade under the above name)
Also: PO Box 2020, Bulawayo
Chief Executive: A J Henderson
Owned by: Apex Corporation of Zimbabwe

Townsend & Co (Pvt) Ltd*, PO Box 3281, Harare Tel: (10) 724611/726679/727732
Manager: D Evans

Major Libraries

Roger **Bone** Library, Hillside Teachers' College, Cecil Ave, PB 2, Hillside, Bulawayo Tel: (19) 42283

Bulawayo Municipal Libraries*, PO Box 2292, Bulawayo Tel: (19) 70111

Bulawayo Public Library, PO Box 586, Bulawayo Tel: (19) 60966
Librarian: R W Doust
Publications: Triennial Report; Bulawayo Book News: Guide to new books

Harare City Library, PO Box 1087, Harare Tel: (10) 704921
Librarian: Mrs M Ross-Smith

Harare Polytechnic Library, Causeway, PO Box 8074, Harare Tel: (10) 705951
Librarian: Mrs D M Thorpe

Library of Parliament, PO Box 8055, Causeway, Harare Tel: (10) 700181 exts 131/132/252
Librarian: W H C Gurure

National Archives, Private Bag 7729, Causeway, Harare Tel: (10) 792741
Dir: Mrs A S Kamba
Publications include: Zimbabwe National Bibliography; Directory of Zimbabwean Libraries (1981)

National Free Library of Zimbabwe, Twelfth Ave, PO Box 1773, Bulawayo Tel: (19) 62359/69827 Telex: 3128
Librarian: Miss D E Barron
Publication: Shelfmark

Queen Victoria Memorial Library, now Harare City Library (qv)

Turner Memorial Library, Queen's Way Civic Complex, PO Box 48, Mutare Tel: (120) 63412
Librarian: S Kapenzi

University of Zimbabwe Library, PO Box MP45, Mount Pleasant, Harare Tel: (10) 303211 Cable Add: University Telex: 4152 Univ Z Zw
Librarian: S Made

Library Association

Zimbabwe Library Association*, PO Box 3133, Harare
Honorary Secretary: S R Dube
Publication: The Zimbabwean Librarian

Library Reference Books and Journals

Book

Directory of Zimbabwean Libraries, National Archives, Private Bag 7729, Causeway, Harare

Journal

The Zimbabwean Librarian, Zimbabwe Library Association, PO Box 3133, Harare

Literary Associations and Societies

Shona/Ndebele Writers' Association*, PO Box 1988, Bulawayo
Secretary: Mrs J G Sibanda

Writer's Club, PO Box 768, Harare
Secretary: Susan Leggett

Literary Periodicals

Moto, PO Box 779, Gweru
A political, cultural and religious weekly originally published by Mambo Press in 1958, with contributions in English and Shona. It was banned for some years, but publication recommenced in January 1980

Two Tone, PO Box MP79, Mount Pleasant, Harare
Poems published in English, Ndebele and Shona (with English translations)

Literary Prizes

The **Literature Bureau** Annual Literary Award
500 Zimbabwe dollars for the best works in Shona and Ndebele. Most genres, including translations, qualify for entry. Enquiries to The Literature Bureau, PO Box 8137, Causeway, Harare

International Section

Copyright Conventions

The Universal Copyright Convention was sponsored by UNESCO in 1952. It states that 'Each signatory country extends to foreign works covered by UCC the same protection which such country extends to works of its own nationals published within its own borders'.

The Berne Convention is a system of international copyright which is maintained among countries which have become signatories to the International Copyright Union for the Protection of Literary and Artistic Works. This Union plan, which was first agreed upon at Berne, Switzerland, in 1888, has been subject to revisions every 20 years. The basic principle of the agreement is that any work properly copyrighted in its country of origin has protection in every Union country. Any work originating in a non-Union country, if it is simultaneously published in a Union country has the same standing as it would if it had originated in a Union country. Since different countries have different relationships under one or more of the revisions (Paris, 1896; Berlin, 1908; Rome, 1928; Brussels, 1948; and Stockholm, 1968), persons interested in obtaining information, including application of the various provisions to territorial areas, should consult the Bureau de l'union internationale pour la protection des oeuvres littéraires et artistiques, 32 chemin des Colombettes, Geneva, Switzerland.

The Florence Agreement, also known as the 'free flow of books', is a UNESCO-sponsored international agreement aimed at easing the flow of books and other scientific, educational and cultural materials, through the elimination or reduction of tariffs and other barriers.

The Buenos Aires Convention: In most Latin-American countries, compliance with the copyright law of the country of first publication protects the work in other countries of the Buenos Aires Convention, 1910. To secure copyright, each work must carry a notice to the effect that any use of the book or article will not be permitted without the consent of the copyright owner, and that copyright is reserved in English or any other language; for complete safety it is advised to add 'All rights reserved'. A later revision of the Buenos Aires Convention was made at the Washington Conference (Pan-American Copyright Convention) of 1946 which goes into greater detail than the Buenos Aires Convention. This Convention has been ratified by Argentina, Bolivia, Brazil, Chile, Costa Rica, Cuba, Dominican Republic, Ecuador, Guatemala, Haiti, Honduras, Mexico, Nicaragua and Paraguay.

International Organizations

International Book Trade, Literary and Library Organizations

A C U R I L, Box S, University of San Juan, Puerto Rico 00931 Tel: 7640000 ext 3319/7908054
Association of Caribbean University, Research and Institutional Libraries
General Secretary: Oneida R Ortiz
Publications: ACURIL Newsletter; *Proceedings of Annual Conference*; *CARINDEX* (Indexing Committee — English)

A I B D A, c/o IICA-CIDIA, 7170 Turrialba, Costa Rica Tel: 566431/560501 Cable Add: Iica San José Telex: 2144 Iica/8005 Catie
Asociación Interamericana de Bibliotecarios y Documentalistas Agrícolas
Inter-American Association of Agricultural Librarians and Documentalists
Secretary-Treasurer: Ana María Paz de Erickson
Publications include: AIBDA Actualidades (irregular, free to members); *Boletín Informativo, Boletín Técnico* (up to 1979); *Boletín Especial* (these two bulletins sent free to members); *Informe RIBDA*; *Revista AIBDA* (twice a year); *Páginas de Contenido: Ciencias de la Información* (quarterly, free to members); *Diccionario Historio del Libro y de la Biblioteca*; *Guía para Bibliotecas Agrícolas*

Commission des Bibliothèques de l'**A I D B A***, BP 375, Dakar, Senegal Tel: 34139
Association internationale pour le Développement de la Documentation des Bibliothèques et des Archives en Afrique
International Association for the Development of Libraries and Archives in Africa
Secretary-General: E K W Dadzie

A I E S I, see Association internationale des Ecoles des Sciences de l'Information

A L E B C I see Asociación Latinoamericana de Escuelas de Bibliotecología y Ciencia de la Información (ALEBCI)

African Training and Research Centre in Administration for Development, Documentation Centre, see Centre africain de Formation et de Recherche administratives pour le Développement, Centre de Documentation

Arab Regional Branch of the International Council on Archives*, Prof Dr Ezz Eldin Ismail, President, c/o The National Library & The General Egyptian Book Organization, Corniche El-Nil, Ramlat Boulaq, Cairo, Egypt Tel: (02) 762971/765436 Telex: 93932
Secretary-General: M J Abdusalim (Sudan)

Asociación Interamericana de Bibliotecarios y Documentalistas Agrícolas, see AIBDA

Asociación Latinoamericana de Escuelas de Bibliotecología y Ciencia de la Información (ALEBCI), Centro Regional Universitario de Veraguas, Escuela de Bibliotecología, Santiago de Veraguas, Panamá, Panama Tel: 984587/984703
Latin American Association of Schools of Library and Information Science
Executive Secretary: Octavio Castillo Sánchez
Publication: ALEBCI Informa (every three months)

Association des Bibliothèques Internationales*, c/o Library, United Nations, Palais des Nations, CH-1211 Geneva 10, Switzerland
Association of International Libraries
President: Th Dimitrov
Publication: Newsletter

Association for the Promotion of the International Circulation of the Press, Beethovenstr 20, CH-8002 Zurich, Switzerland
Association pour la Promotion de la Diffusion Internationale de la Presse
Vereinigung zur Förderung des internationalen Pressevertriebes
President: Abdallah Lahrizi (Morocco);
Man Dir: Arnold Kaulich

Association internationale de Bibliophilie*, c/o Bibliothèque nationale, 58 rue de Richelieu, F-75084 Paris cedex 02, France
International Association of Bibliophiles
Secretary-General: Antoine Coron
Publication: Le Bulletin du Bibliophile (quarterly)

Association internationale des Critiques littéraires (NGO), see International Association of Literary Critics

Association internationale des Documentalistes et Techniciens de l'Information AID*, 74 rue des Saints-Pères, F-75007 Paris, France
International Association of Documentalists and Information Officers
General Secretary: Dr Jacques Samain
Publication: Bulletin

Association internationale des Ecoles des Sciences de l'Information (AIESI), AUPELF, BP 6128, Montreal, Quebec H3C 3J7, Canada Tel: (514) 3436630 Telex: 05560955
International Association of Information Sciences Schools
Secretary: Roland Ducasse

Association internationale pour le Développement de la Documentation des Bibliothèques et des Archives en Afrique, see AIDBA

Association of Caribbean University, Research and Institutional Libraries, see ACURIL

Association of International Libraries (AIL)*, c/o United Nations Library, CH-1211 Geneva 10, Switzerland Tel: (022) 366011/310211 Telex: 289696
Secretary: O Cerny

Association of Libraries of Judaica and Hebraica in Europe, Bibliothèque de l'Alliance Israelite Universelle, 45 rue La Bruyère, F-75425 Paris cedex 09, France
Chairman: Georges Weill
Publication: Annual newsletter

Bibliographical Society of Australia and New Zealand (BSANZ), 76 Warners Ave, Bondi Beach, NSW 2026, Australia Tel: (02) 301014
Secretary: Rose Smith
Publications: Bulletin (quarterly); *Broadsheet*; occasional publications

C E R L A L C, see Centro Régional para el Fomento del Libro en América Latina y el Caribe

C O M L A, see The Commonwealth Library Association

Centre africain de Formation et de Recherche administratives pour le Développement, Centre de Documentation*, BP 310, Tangier, Morocco Cable Add: Cafrad Tangier Telex:33664
African Training and Research Centre in Administration for Development, Documentation Centre
Chief of Documentation Division: Edward S Asieou
Publications include: Directory of Administrative Information Services in Africa

Centre régional de Promotion du Livre en Afrique (CREPLA)*, BP 1646, Yaoundé, United Republic of Cameroun Tel: (022) 4782/2936
Regional Centre for Book Promotion in Africa (co-sponsored by UNESCO)
Secretary: William Moutchia
Publication: CREPLA Bulletin

Centro Régional para el Fomento del Libro en América Latina y el Caribe (CERLALC), Apdo Aeréo 17438, Bogotá, Colombia (Located at: Calle 70 No 9-52, Bogotá) Tel: (01) 2495141/2554574 Cable Add: Cerlal Telex: 44637 Cerla
Regional Centre for Book Promotion in Latin America and Caribbean
Secretary-General: Peter Lewy; *Dir:* Oscar Delgado Sanchez
Publications include: CERLALC: noticias sobre el Libro (news on books); *Boletín Bibliográfico del CERLALC* (current Latin-American bibliography); *Audiovisuales*; *Directorio Latinoamericano de Editoriales, Distribuidoras y Librerias* (Directory of Latin American Publishers, Distributors and Booksellers)

The **Commonwealth** Library Association (COMLA), PO Box 40, Mandeville, Manchester, Jamaica Tel: 9620703 Cable Add: Comla
Executive Secretary: Joan E Swaby
Publication: COMLA Newsletter (quarterly), published and distributed by the Hon Editor, c/o University of Malta Library, Msida, Malta

Congress of South-East Asian Librarians IV (CONSAL IV)*, Thai Library Association, 273-275 Viphavadee Rangsit Rd, Phayathai, Bangkok 10400, Thailand Tel: (02) 2712084
Chairman: Mrs Maenmas Chavalit
Publications include: Proceedings of Congresses on Regional Co-operation for the Development of National Information Services

Conseil international des Associations de Bibliothèques de Théologie, Kardinal-Frings Str 1-3, Postfach 100690, Cologne 1, Federal Republic of Germany Tel: (0221) 164286221
International Council of Theological Library Associations
Secretary: J A Cervelló-Margalef

E L C E, see Editeurs et libraires catholiques d'Europe

Eastern and Southern Africa Regional Branch of the International Council on Archives (ESARBICA), c/o Kenya National Archives, PO Box 49210, Nairobi, Kenya Tel: (02) 26007/28020/28959 Cable Add: Archives Nairobi
Publication: Journal

Editeurs et libraires catholiques d'Europe (ELCE)*, Lehenstr 31, D-7000 Stuttgart 1, Federal Republic of Germany Tel: (0711) 6402061
Internationale Vereinigung katholischer Verleger und Buchhändler
International Association of Catholic Publishers and Booksellers
Secretary: Wolfgang Grossmann

European Association for the Promotion of Poetry*, Boskantstr 30, B-3200 Kessel-Lo (Leuven), Belgium Tel: (016) 235351
General Secretary: E Van Itterbeek
Publications: π (trimestrial poetry review); *Leuvense cahiers* (European and ACP series)

European Association of Directory Publishers*, chaussée d'Alsemberg 238 Bte 11, B-1180 Brussels, Belgium Tel: (02) 3453257
Association Européene des Editeurs d'Annuaires
Europäischer Adressbuchverleger-Verband
President: M G Delaubier; *Secretary-General:* Jean Lerat

European Parliament Library*, Bâtiment Schumann, Luxembourg, Grand Duchy of Luxembourg
Bibliothèque du Parlement Européen

F I D, see International Federation for Documentation

Fédération internationale des Libraries (FIL), see International Booksellers Federation (IBF)

Fédération internationale des Traducteurs (FIT)*, Heiveldstr 245, B-9110 Gent/Sint-Amandsberg, Belgium
International Federation of Translators
Secretary-General: Dr Rene Haeseryn
Publications include: Newsletter, Conference proceedings

G E L C, see Groupe des Editeurs de livres de la CEE

Groupe des Editeurs de livres de la CEE (GELC), 111 ave du Parc, B-1060 Brussels, Belgium Tel: (02) 5382167
Book Publishers Group of the EEC
President: G J van Roozendaal; *Executive Vice-President:* J J Schellens; *Dir:* B Gerard
The Group consists of the book associations of the Common Market member states and aims at representing jointly the interests of the European Communities for all matters arising from the Treaty of Rome
Founded: 1967

I B B Y, see International Board on Books for Young People

I F L A, see International Federation of Library Associations and Institutions

I S B N, see International Standard Book Number Agency

I S S N, see International Serials Data System

Intergovernmental Copyright Committee, see United Nations Educational, Scientific and Cultural Organization (UNESCO)

International Association for Mass Communication Research, c/o Professor J D Halloran, Centre for Mass Communication Research, University of Leicester, 104 Regent Road, Leicester LE1 7LT, UK Tel: (0533) 523864
Association internationale des études et recherches sur l'information
Administrative Secretary: Peggy Gray
Publications include: Mass Media and Socialization; Mass Media and Man's View of Society; Mass Media and National Cultures; New Structures of International Communication: The Role of Research; Communication and Democracy: Directions in Research; Social Communication and Global Problems

International Association of Agricultural Librarians and Documentalists (IAALD), c/o Jan van der Burg, PUDOC, Jan-Kopshuis, Postbus 4, 6700 AA Wageningen, Netherlands
Association Internationale des Bibliothécaires et Documentalistes Agricoles
Secretary-Treasurer: Jan van der Burg
Publications: Quarterly Bulletin; IAALD News; Primer for Agricultural Libraries; Proceedings of World Congresses
Founded: 1955

International Association of Law Libraries (IALL), c/o The University of Chicago, The Law School Library, 1121 East 60th St, Chicago, IL 60637, USA Tel: (312) 9629599
Association internationale des bibliothèques de droit
President: Adolf Sprudzs; *Secretary:* Timothy Kearley
Publications: International Journal of Legal Information (three times a year); *The IALL Messenger* (irregular)

International Association of Literary Critics, 38 rue du Faubourg St Jacques, F-75014 Paris, France
Association internationale des Critiques littéraires (NGO)
President: Robert André
Publication: Revue (twice a year)

International Association of Metropolitan City Libraries (INTAMEL), Dienst Openbare Bibliotheek 's-Gravenhage, Bilderdijkstr 1-3, 2513 CM The Hague, Netherlands Tel: (070) 469235
Secretary-Treasurer: Wim M Renes

International Association of Music Libraries, Archives and Documentation Centres (IAML)*, c/o Music Library/Hornbake Library, University of Maryland, College Park, MD 20742, USA
Association internationale des bibliothèques, archives et centres de documentation musicaux (AIBM)
Internationale Vereinigung der Musikbibliotheken, Musikarchive und Musikdokumentations zentren (IVMB)
President: Anders Lönn (Musikaliska akademiens bibliotek, Stockholm); *Secretary-General:* Neil Ratliff
Publication: Fontes artis musicae

International Association of Orientalist Librarians, c/o Asian Library, 325 Library, University of Illinois, 1408 West Gregory Drive, Urbana, IL 61801, USA
Secretary-Treasurer: William S Wong
Publication: International Association of Orientalist Librarians Bulletin (half-yearly)

International Association of School Librarianship, PO Box 1486, Kalamazoo, MI 49005, USA Tel: (616) 3831849
Executive Secretary: Ms J Lowrie
Publications: Newsletter of the International Association of School Librarianship (quarterly to members); *Annual Conference Proceedings; People to Contact for Visiting School Libraries/Media Centers; Indicators of Quality*

International Association of Scholarly Publishers (IASP), c/o Edvard Aslaksen, Universitetsforlaget, Postboks 2959, Tøyen, N-0608 Oslo 6, Norway Tel: (02) 276060 Cable Add: Universitypress Oslo Telex: 71896 Ufor
President: Edvard Aslaksen
Publication: IASP Newsletter and Proceedings
Founded: 1972

International Association of Technological University Libraries (IATUL)*, c/o Dr Nancy Fjällbrant, The Library of Chalmers University of Technology, S-412 96 Gothenberg, Sweden Tel: (031) 810100 Telex: 2369 Chalbib
President: Dr Dennis Shaw CBE (Oxford); *Secretary:* Dr Nancy Fjällbrant
Publications: IATUL Proceedings; IATUL Conference Proceedings; IATUL Quarterly (OUP)

International Board on Books for Young People (IBBY), Leonhardsgraben 38a, Postfach, CH-4003 Basle, Switzerland Tel: (061) 253404 Telex: 963669 Kerrch
Dir of Secretariat: Mrs Leena Maissen
Publications: Bookbird (quarterly, joint publication); *Congress Proceedings; International Directory of Children's Literature Specialists* (published by K G Saur Verlag KG, Federal Republic of Germany (qv)); Publications in UNESCO series 'Studies on Books and Reading'; Booklists

International Booksellers Federation (IBF), A-1010 Vienna, Grünangergasse 4, Austria Tel: (0222) 5121535 Cable Add: Buchverein Vienna Att IBF
Fédération internationale des Libraries (FIL)
Internationale Buchhändler-Vereinigung (IBV)
General Secretary: Dr Gerhard Prosser; *President:* Peter Meili
Publications include: The Maintained Price of Books; The Image of the Bookseller; Books and their Prices; Book, Book Trade and Society; What is IBF?; Booksellers International

International Center for the Registration of Serials, see International Serials Data System

International Comparative Literature Association*, Institut de littérature comparée, Université de la Sorbonne-Nouvelle (Paris-III), 17 rue de la Sorbonne, F-75005 Paris, France
Association internationale de littérature comparée
Secretaries-General: José Lambert, Université de Louvain, Louvain, Belgium; Ulrich Weisstein, University of Indiana, Bloomington, IN 47402, USA

Publications: ICLA Bulletin, AILC Information
Founded: 1954

International Confederation of Societies of Authors and Composers*, 11 rue Keppler, F-75116 Paris, France
Confédération internationale des Sociétés d'Auteurs et Compositeurs
Secretary-General: Jean-Alexis Ziegler

International Copyright Union for the Protection of Literary and Artistic Works, now World Intellectual Property Organization (WIPO) (qv)

International Council of Theological Library Associations, see Conseil international des Associations de Bibliothèques de Théologie

International Council on Archives, 60 rue des Francs-Bourgeois, F-75003 Paris, France Tel: (1) 42771130
Conseil international des archives
Executive Secretary: Dr Charles Kecskemeti
Publications: Archivum; ADPA/Archives and Automation; Bulletin of the ICA; Bulletin of the Business Archives Committee; CAD Information, Bulletin of the Commission for Archival Development; Bulletin of the Committee on Conservation and Restoration and the Committee on Archival Reprography; Janus, Bulletin of the Section of Professional Archival Associations

International Federation for Documentation (FID)*, Postbus 90402, 2509 LK, The Hague, Netherlands Tel: (070) 140671
Fédération internationale de documentation
Publications: FID News Bulletin; International Forum on Information and Documentation; R & D Projects in Documentation and Librarianship; FID Directory; Annual Report; Extensions and Corrections to the UDC (annual); Proceedings of Congresses and Seminars, UDC editions in several languages, Studies on Information Science, Manuals, Bibliographies and Directories

International Federation for Information Processing (IFIP)*, c/o A A Verrijn Stuart, Postbus 9512, 2300 RA Leiden, Netherlands

International Federation of Film Archives*, Coudenberg 70, B-1000 Brussels, Belgium Tel: (02) 5111390
Fédération internationale des archives du film (FIAF)
Executive Secretary: Brigitte van der Elst
Publications include: International Index to Film and TV Periodicals (annual); *A Handbook for Film Archives; International Directory to Film and TV Documentation Sources; Bibliography of National Filmographies; The Usage of Computers for Film Cataloguing; Glossary of Filmographic Terms* (English, French, Spanish, German and Russian)

International Federation of Library Associations and Institutions (IFLA), c/o The Royal Library, Postbus 95312, 2509 CH The Hague, Netherlands Tel: (070) 140884 Telex: 34402 Kb
Fédération internationale des associations de bibliothécaires et des bibliothèques
Secretary-General: Paul Nauta
Publications: IFLA Journal, including *IFLA News* (quarterly); *IFLA Annual; IFLA Directory* (biennially); *International Cataloguing* (quarterly); *IFLA's Medium-term Programme 1986-1991; IFLA Publications* (series of monographs, published by K G Saur Verlag KG, Federal Republic of Germany (qv)); *IFLA Professional Reports* (series of reports published by IFLA)

International Federation for Modern Languages and Literatures, Birkbeck College, Malet St, London WC1E 7HX, UK Tel: (01) 580 6622
Secretary-General: Prof D A Wells
Publication: Proceedings of the Triennial Congresses
Founded: 1928

International Fiction Association, Department of German and Russian, University of New Brunswick, Fredericton, New Brunswick E3B 5A3, Canada
Publication: The International Fiction Review (twice a year)

International Group of Scientific, Technical and Medical Publishers (STM), Keizersgracht 462, 1016 GE Amsterdam, Netherlands Tel: (020) 225214 Fax: (020) 381566
Secretary-General: Paul Nijhoff Asser
Publications: STM Newsletter; STM Marketing Studies; STM Copyright Bulletin; STM Innovations Bulletin. Rights — Copyright and Related Rights in the Service of Creativity (joint publication with International Publishers Association (IPA))

International Institute for Children's Literature and Reading Research (UNESCO category C), A-1040 Vienna, Mayerhofgasse 6, Austria Tel: (0222) 650359
Institut International de Littérature pour Enfants et de Recherches sur la Lecture
Dir: Dr Lucia Binder
Publications include: Bookbird (quarterly, joint publication with IBBY); *1001-Buch* (joint publication with Ministry of Education); *PA-Kontakte; Jugend und Buch* (Youth and Books) (co-sponsored with Österreichischer Buchklub der Jugend)

International Institute of Iberoamerican Literature*, 1312 CL, University of Pittsburgh, PA 15260, USA
Secretary-Treasurer: Keith A McDuffie
Publications: Revista Iberoamericana; Memorias

International League of Antiquarian Booksellers (ILAB), c/o Secretary, Konrad Meuschel, Hauptstr 19a, D-5340 Bad Honnef 1, Federal Republic of Germany
President: Hans Bagger (Denmark); *Secretary:* Konrad Meuschel

International Publishers Association (IPA), 3 ave de Miremont, CH-1206 Geneva, Switzerland Tel: (022) 463018 Cable Add: Inpublass Telex: 421883
Secretary-General: J Alexis Koutchoumow
Publications: International Publishers Bulletin; Rights; Freedom to Publish, 1984 (also in French and Spanish); *Index on Censorship; Upon Entering the Electronic Publishing Marketplace* by Dr J Kist. *Rights — Copyright and Related Rights in the Service of Creativity* (joint publication with International Group of Scientific, Technical and Medical Publishers (STM))
Founded: 1896

International Reading Association*, 800 Barksdale Rd, PO Box 8139, Newark, DE 19714, USA Tel: (302) 7311600 Cable Add: Reading Newark Delaware Telex: 5106002813 Reading

International Scientific Film Library (ISFL)*, 31 rue Vautier, B-1040 Brussels, Belgium
Cinémathèque scientifique internationale
Director-Curator: P Bormans
Publications: Catalogue of films deposited; *The Pioneers of the Scientific Cinema* (series)
Founded: 1961

International Serials Data System*, 20 rue Bachaumont, F-75002 Paris, France Tel: (1) 2367381/45089837 Telex: 680047
The International Center for the Registration of Serials, which administers the International Standard Serial Number (ISSN) system, is at the above address

International Standard Book Number Agency*, Staatsbibliothek Preussischer Kulturbesitz, Potsdamerstr 33, Postfach 1407, D-1000 Berlin 30, Federal Republic of Germany Tel: (030) 2661 Telex: 183160 Staab
Dir: Dr Hartmut Walravens
This is the international ISBN office. For national offices and further details please see the ISBN System section of this book
Publications: User's Manual; ISBN Review; International ISBN Publishers' Directory; ISBN System and its Uses (Video film in English, French, German, Spanish; slide-sound show in English, Spanish)

International Study Group of Restorers of Archives, Libraries and Graphic Reproductions, Geschäftsstelle der IADA, Postfach 540, D-3550 Marburg, Federal Republic of Germany Tel: (06421) 25078
Internationale Arbeitsgemeinschaft der Archiv-, Bibliotheks- und Grafikrestauratoren
General Secretary: Ludwig Ritterpusch
Publication: IADA-Mitteilungen in: Maltechnik

International Translations Centre (ITC), Schuttersveld 2, 2611 WE Delft, Netherlands Tel: (015) 142242 Telex: 38104
Dir: Mrs M Risseeuw
The Centre compiles, processes and disseminates information on existing scientific and technical translations from any language source into Western languages
Publication: World Translations Index

Internationale Buchhändler-Vereinigung (IBV), see International Booksellers Federation (IBF)

Internationale Jugendbibliothek (IJB), Schloss Blutenburg, D-8000 Munich 60, Federal Republic of Germany Tel: (089) 8112028
International Youth Library
Dir: Dr Andreas Bode
Publications include: IJB Bulletin; IJB Report; The White Ravens

Internationale Vereinigung katholischer Verleger und Buchhändler, see Editeurs et libraires catholiques d'Europe (ELCE)

Ligue des Bibliothèques Européennes de Recherche (LIBER), c/o Prof Dr Hans-Albrecht Koch, Staats- und Universitätsbibliothek Bremen, Bibliotheksstr, Postfach 330160, D-2800 Bremen 33, Federal Republic of Germany Tel: (0421) 2182601 Telex: 245811 Unibr
League of European Research Libraries
President: Dr Franz Kroller
Publications: LIBER Bulletin, LIBER News Sheet

Library **Luxembourg**, Commission of the European Communities, Bâtiment Jean Monnet, BP 1907, L-2920 Luxembourg, Grand Duchy of Luxembourg Tel: 43011 Telex: 3423/3446 Comeur

Middle East Librarians Association, Room B-2-H-2, Firestone Library, Princeton University, Princeton, NJ 08544, USA Tel: (609) 4523248
Publication: MELA Notes (three times a year)

Nordisk Musikförläggarunion*, c/o Nordiska Musikförläggareföreningen, Box 27327, S-102 54, Stockholm, Sweden
Nordic Music Publishers Union

Nordisk Videnakbeligt Bibliotekarforbund*, c/o Ulla Jensen, IDE Danish Institute of International Exchange of Publications, Amaliegade 38, DK-1256 Copenhagen K, Denmark Tel: (01) 156521
Scandinavian Association of Research Librarians
President: Ulla Jensen
Publications: Monographs, Guides (available from Bibliotekcentralen, Tempovej 5-7, DK 2750 Ballerup, Denmark)

International **P E N**, 38 King St, London WC2E 8JT, UK Tel: (01) 379 7939
A World Association of Writers
General-Secretary: Alexandre Blokh
Publications: PEN International (in English and French, issued with the assistance of UNESCO); various regional bulletins

Bibliothèque du **Parlement** Européen, Luxembourg, see European Parliament Library

The **Penman** Club, 175 Pall Mall, Leigh-on-Sea, Essex SS9 1RE, UK Tel: Southend-on-Sea 74438 (STD Code 0702)
Secretary: Leonard G Stubbs
Literary advice, criticism

Private Libraries Association (PLA), Ravelston, South View Rd, Pinner, Middlesex, UK
An international society of book collectors
Executive Secretary: Frank Broomhead
Publications include: Private Press Books; The Private Library (official journal); *Newsletter*

S T M, see International Group of Scientific, Technical and Medical Publishers

Seminar on the Acquisition of Latin American Library Materials (SALALM), SALALM Secretariat, Memorial Library, University of Wisconsin-Madison, Madison, WI 53706, USA Tel: (608) 2623240
Executive Secretary: Suzanne Hodgman
Publications: Newsletter; Papers; Microfilming Projects Newsletter; Bibliography and Reference Series

Société internationale de Bibliographie classique, 11 ave René Coty, F-75014 Paris, France
General Secretary: Pierre Paul Corsetti Tel: (1) 45843576
Publication: L'Année philologique (Bibliographie de l'antiquité gréco-latine 1924 ss)

Société internationale des Bibliothèques-Musées des Arts du Spectacle (SIBMAS), 1 rue de Sully, F-75004 Paris, France Tel: (1) 42774421
International Society of Libraries and Museums for the Performing Arts
Publication: Bibliothèques et Musées des Arts du Spectacle dans le Monde (from Librairie des Editions du CNRS, see Editions du CNRS, France)

Southeast Asian Regional Branch of the International Council on Archives (SARBICA), c/o National Archives of Malaysia, Jalan Duta, 50568 Kuala Lumpur, Malaysia Tel: (03) 2543244
Chairman: Dra Soemartini (Indonesia)
Publications: Southeast Asian Archives; Southeast Asian Microfilms Newsletter; Masterlist of Southeast Asian Microforms

Standing Conference of African Library Schools (SCALS)*, c/o School of Librarians, Archivists and Documentalists, University of Dakar, BP 2006, Dakar, Senegal
Publication: SCALS Newsletter

Standing Conference of African University Libraries (SCAUL)*, c/o E Bejide Bankole, Editor, African Journal of Academic Librarianship, PO Box 46, Yaba, Lagos, Nigeria
Publication: SCAUL Newsletter

Standing Conference on Library Materials on Africa (SCOLMA), c/o Institute of Commonwealth Studies, 27-28 Russell Sq, London WC1B 5DS, UK Tel: (01) 580 5876
Publication: African Research and Documentation (Subscriptions to Subscriptions Manager, University Library, University of Birmingham, Birmingham B15 2TT, UK)

Union des Editeurs de langue française*, 111 ave du Parc, B-1060 Brussels, Belgium
Union of French-language Publishers
President: V Dimitrijevic; *Dir:* B Gerard

Union of Writers of the African Peoples*, c/o National Association of Writers, PO Box 2738, Accra, Ghana
Union des Ecrivains Negro Africains
Secretary-General: Wole Soyinka, Dept of Literature, University of Ife, Ife-Ife, Nigeria
Objectives include the operation of a writers' publishing co-operative and the encouragement of the use of Swahili as the common language of all black African peoples
Publication: African World Alternatives

United Nations Economic Commission for Africa Library, PO Box 3001, Addis Ababa, Ethiopia Tel: (01) 447200 Cable Add: Eca Telex: 21029
Librarian: Abdel-Rahman M Tahir

West African University Booksellers Association, c/o The General Secretary's Office, University Bookshop, PO Box 1, University of Ghana, Legon, Ghana Tel: 75381 ext 8827
Secretary: S O Cofie

World Intellectual Property Organization (WIPO), 34 chemin des Colombettes, CH-1211 Geneva 20, Switzerland Tel: (022) 999111 Cable Add: Ompi Telex: 22376 Ompi
Organisation mondiale de la Propriété intellectuelle (OMPI)
Director General: Dr Arpad Bogsch
Responsible for the promotion of the protection of intellectual property (industrial property and copyright and neighbouring rights) throughout the world. Administers, among other conventions, the Paris Convention for the Protection of Industrial Property and the Berne Convention for the Protection of Literary and Artistic Works. Its library, specializing in intellectual property, is open to the public
Publications include: Copyright (Le droit d'auteur) (monthly, in English and French); *Industrial Property* (monthly, in English and French); *Les Marques internationales* (monthly, in French); *PCT Gazette* (fortnightly, in English and French)

United Nations Agencies with Publishing Activities

Accord general sur les Tarifs douaniers et le Commerce, see GATT (General Agreement on Tariffs and Trade)

INTERNATIONAL ORGANIZATIONS

Asian Cultural Centre for UNESCO*, 6 Fukuromachi, Shinjuku-ku, Tokyo 162, Japan Tel: (03) 2694435 Cable Add: Asculcentre Tokyo
Executive Dir: Taichi Sasaoka
Asian/Pacific Copublication Programme (ACP) is a joint programme of UNESCO member states in Asia and the Pacific to produce children's books of good quality and in quantity. Publishes *Asian Book Development*
Founded: 1971

Centro Latinoamericano de Demografía (CELADE), Edificio Naciones Unidas, Ave Dag Hammarskjöld, Casilla 91, Santiago, Chile Tel: (02) 2283206 Cable Add: Unations Telex: 240077
Dir: Reynaldo Bajraj
Branch Offs: CELADE Subcentre, Apdo 5249, San José, Costa Rica; ECLAC/CELADE Demography Unit, ECLAC, Port of Spain, Trinidad and Tobago; Demography Unit, ECLAC, Buenos Aires, Argentina
Subjects: Demography, Statistics, Sociology, Periodicals

Food and Agriculture Organization of the United Nations (FAO), Via delle Terme di Caracalla, I-00100 Rome, Italy Tel: (06) 57971 Cable Add: Foodagri Rome Telex: 610181 Fao
Director-General: E Saouma; *Director of Publications:* M de Francisco; *Chief Editor (for copyright and copublication):* K H Richmond; *Chief, Distribution and Sales Section (for advertising and publicity):* C Beauchamp
Subjects: Agriculture, World Food Situation, Economics & Statistics, Fisheries, Forestry & Forest Products, Nutrition, Legislation, Educational Materials
Founded: 1945
A specialized agency of the United Nations, the Food and Agriculture Organization was created in 1945. Since the purpose of FAO is to increase world agricultural production and raise the standard of living, all its publications are directed toward that goal. The FAO titles consist of monographs, periodicals, official records of the work of FAO, yearbooks and annuals — in sum, what the FAO describes as a 'world intelligence service on production, price and trade that covers almost every commodity used to feed, clothe and house people throughout the world'. All FAO publications and documents are also available on microfiche. Unsolicited manuscripts are automatically rejected. Technical articles of no more than 2,500 words on international aspects of the animal industry, forestry, and food and nutrition are occasionally accepted; no payment is made
ISBN Publisher's Prefixes: 92-5 (publications by Headquarters), 92-851 (African Regional Office), 92-852 (Regional Office for Asia and Far East), 92-853 (European Regional Office), 92-854 (Latin American Regional Office), 92-855 (Near East Regional Office)

G A T T (General Agreement on Tariffs and Trade), Centre William Rappard, 154 rue de Lausanne, CH-1211 Geneva 21, Switzerland Tel: (022) 310231 Cable Add: Gatt Geneva Telex: 28787 Gatt
Accord general sur les Tarifs douaniers et le Commerce
Subjects: Economics, International exchanges
1987: 4 titles *Founded:* 1948
ISBN Publisher's Prefix: 92-870

International Atomic Energy Agency (IAEA), Vienna International Centre, A-1400 Vienna, Wagramerstr 5, Postfach 100, Austria Tel: (0222) 2360 Cable Add: Inatom Vienna
Publications Dir: G Githii; *Editorial:* R F Kelleher; *Sales, Publicity:* K Fiala; *Production, Rights & Permissions:* W Dietl
Subjects: Life Sciences, Nuclear Safety and Environmental Protection, Physics, Chemistry, Geology and Raw Materials, Reactors and Nuclear Power, Industrial Applications, Miscellaneous
Founded: 1957
The International Atomic Energy Agency is an international organization within the United Nations family, having the general purpose of seeking 'to accelerate and enlarge the contribution of atomic energy to peace, health and prosperity throughout the world'. The Agency's publications result, almost exclusively, from its own activities; published material is of intense interest only to a relatively small group of scientists and technicians
ISBN Publisher's Prefix: 92-0

International Bureau of Education (IBE), PO Box 199, CH-1211 Geneva 20, Switzerland Tel: (022) 981455 Cable Add: Intereduc Geneve Telex: 22644
Senior Editor: Rodney Stock; *Editorial, Sales, Production, Publicity, Rights & Permissions:* See United Nations Educational, Scientific and Cultural Organization
Orders to: National distributors of UNESCO publications, or UNESCO, 7 pl de Fontenoy, F-75700 Paris, France
Subject: Comparative Education
Founded: 1925
Founded in 1925 as a private organization, the IBE was given new status in 1929 whereby it became the first inter-governmental organization in the field of education. It became an integral part of UNESCO in 1969, and today serves all 159 Member States of the Organization as a centre of comparative education

International Institute for Educational Planning (IIEP), 7-9 rue Eugène-Delacroix, F-75116 Paris, France Tel: (1) 45042822 Cable Add: Eduplan Paris Telex: 620074
Dir: Sylvain Lourié; *Publications Officer:* John Hall
Subjects: Educational Planning (Administration & Management, Methodologies, Manpower & Employment, School Locations, Non-formal, adult and rural Education & Literacy)
1986: 20 titles *1987:* 20 titles *Founded:* 1963
Established by UNESCO, IIEP is an international centre for advanced training and research in educational planning. The Institute's aim is to contribute to the development of education by expanding both knowledge and the supply of competent professionals in the field of educational planning. In this endeavour the Institute cooperates with interested training and research institutions throughout the world. IIEP is financed by UNESCO and by voluntary contributions from individual member states. The programme and budget of the Institute is approved by its own Governing Board
ISBN Publisher's Prefix: 92-803

International Labour Organisation (ILO), International Labour Office, ILO Publications, 4 route des Morillons, CH-1211 Geneva 22, Switzerland Tel: (022) 996111 Cable Add: Interlab Geneva Telex: 22271 Fax: (022) 988685
Director-General: Francis Blanchard; *Chief, Editorial Services:* R S Kirkman; *Chief, Marketing and Rights Services:* I M C S Elsmark
Branch Offs: 96-98 Marsham St, London SW1P 4LY, UK; 1750 New York Ave NW, Suite 330, Washington, DC 20006, USA; 75 Albert St, Fuller Bldg, Suite 202, Ottawa, Ontario K1P 5E7, Canada; Hohenzollernstr 21, D-5300 Bonn 2, Federal Republic of Germany
Subjects: Conditions of Work and Welfare, Cooperatives, Developing Countries & Technical Cooperation, Economics, Income Distribution, Intermediate Technology, Employment and Employment Creation, Holidays & Weekly Rest, Human Rights, Labour, Standards & Administration, Migration of Workers & Popular Questions, Productivity & Management Development & Training, Occupational Safety & Health, Statistics, Social Security, Trade Unions, Unemployment, Vocational Guidance & Training, Wages & Hours of Work, Worker's Education, Women's questions, Audiovisual material, Microfiches, Periodicals
From the creation of the ILO in 1919, publishing has formed an important part of its activities. The publishing work falls into six main categories: international exchange of factual information; analysis of trends in social affairs; issuing the results of ILO research, including comparative studies as a basis for international cooperation in solving economic and social problems; issuing the required reports for the discussions of international labour conferences leading to the adoption of international labour standards; providing government officials, employers and workers with practical information and guidance; and issuing official records.
This substantial publishing programme has over 1,300 titles in print which cover not only studies, monographs, handbooks, training material and periodicals, but also reports on conditions and practices in different countries prepared for the General Conference, regional conferences and meetings for special industries and subjects
ISBN Publisher's Prefix: 92-2

International Maritime Organization (IMO)*, 4 Albert Embankment, London SE1 7SR, UK Tel: (01) 735 7611 Cable Add: Intermar Telex: 044 23588
Subjects: Texts of International Maritime Treaties concluded under its auspices, Maritime Technical Publications
ISBN Publisher's Prefix: 92-801

International Telecommunication Union (ITU)*, pl des Nations, CH-1211 Geneva 20, Switzerland Tel: (022) 995111 Telex: 421000 Uit
Secretary-General: Richard E Butler
The ITU was founded in 1865 as the International Telegraphic Union. It became the International Telecommunication Union in 1934 and a specialized agency of the UN in 1947. Structure: 4 permanent organs — General Secretariat, International Telegraph and Telephone Consultative Committee (CCITT), International Radio Consultative Committee (CCIR) and the International Frequency Registration Board (IFRB). It regulates, plans, coordinates and standardizes international telecommunications
ISBN Publisher's Prefixes: 92-61, 92-71

U N C T A D, see United Nations Conference on Trade and Development

U N E S C O, see United Nations Educational, Scientific and Cultural Organization

U N E S C O Institute for Education (UIE)*, Feldbrunnenstr 58, D-2000 Hamburg 13, Federal Republic of Germany Tel: (040) 447843 Cable Add: Edinst
Dir: Dr Ravindra H Dave
The UIE was created in 1951 with the financial support of UNESCO and a number of member states. It is funded by the Federal Republic of Germany, UNESCO and other donors, and housed in premises provided by the City of Hamburg. It is a research and dissemination centre which has enabled more than 2,000 scholars to participate in international cooperative research projects and has developed a particular interest in lifelong education. Major areas of the current research programme include the relation of lifelong education to national systems of education, to the curriculum, to learning strategies for neo-literates, teacher training and evaluation. Publications include over 120 titles and the quarterly *International Review of Education*, for which there is a concessionary subscription rate for developing countries. In the field of lifelong education and related aspects, it has published over 60 books under the series of UIE Monographs, Case Studies, Advances in Lifelong Education and UIE Studies on Post-literacy and Continuing Education, based on both theoretical and operational research
ISBN Publisher's Prefix: 92-820

United Nations*, Sales Section, Publishing Division, Room DC2-853, New York, NY 10017, USA Tel: (0212) 7548302 Cable Add: Unations Nyk Telex: 62450
Chief of Section: Thomas S Hinds; *Deputy Chief:* Nina K Leneman; *Rights & Permissions:* Vladimir Lubomondrov (New York), Patrice Piguet (Geneva)
European Office: Palais des Nations, Geneva, Switzerland
Chief of Unit: Patrice Piguet
Subjects: Reference, Economics, International Trade, International Law, Social Science
Founded: 1945
Since 1946, United Nations has published more than 4,000 reports, studies, annual surveys, yearbooks, and monthly and quarterly periodicals in addition to the United Nations Official Records. Reflecting the varied work of the Organization, the subjects include international trade, world and regional economic questions, international law, social questions, atomic energy, public administration, and literature concerning the role and activities of the United Nations
ISBN Publisher's Prefix: 92-1

United Nations Conference on Trade and Development (UNCTAD), Palais des Nations, CH-1211 Geneva 10, Switzerland Tel: (022) 346011 Cable Add: Unations Geneva Telex: 289696
Secretary-General: Kenneth K S Dadzie
Subjects: Trade & development
Founded: 1964

United Nations, Economic and Social Commission for Asia and the Pacific Library, United Nations Bldg, Rajadamnern Ave, Bangkok 10200, Thailand Tel: (02) 2829161 ext 1332 Cable Add: Escap Bangkok Telex: 82392/82315 Escap
Chief: N P Cummins
Subjects: Economic and Social Development in Asia and the Pacific Region

United Nations Educational, Scientific and Cultural Organization (UNESCO)*, 7 pl de Fontenoy, F-75700 Paris, France Tel: (1) 45681000 Cable Add: Unesco Paris Telex: 204461/270602
Director-General: Amadou-Mahtar M'Bow; *Director, The Unesco Press:* Mamadou Seck; *Chief, Promotion and Rights Division:* Eduardo Sainz; *Promotion:* Michiko Tanaka; *Sales:* Dieter Kraatz; *Rights & Permissions:* Suzanne Adlung
Orders to: The Unesco Press, Commercial Services (at above address)
Subjects: Education, Science, Social Science, Culture, Communications
Bookshop: Unesco Bookshop (at above address)
1985: 334 titles *1986:* 310 titles *Founded:* 1946
UNESCO now has more than 3,000 titles in print, intended for specialists in the fields of education, science and technology, social sciences, human rights, libraries, documentation and archives, copyright, culture, art, museums and monuments, and communications. Some titles are aimed at a broad public with a view to fostering international intellectual, scientific and cultural exchange. Books are published in the official languages of the Organization: mainly in English, French and Spanish; some titles are also published in Arabic, Russian and Chinese. An increasing number of titles are copublished with commercial publishers under joint imprint. To date, UNESCO books have been translated into more than seventy languages.
UNESCO acts as Standard Book Numbering Agency, administering ISBNs, for UN publications. It also maintains responsibility, within its Copyright Division, for the Intergovernmental Copyright Committee.
UNESCO publishes seven periodicals, including the illustrated monthly review *The Unesco Courier* and *Copyright Bulletin* (quarterly)
ISBN Publisher's Prefix: 92-3

United Nations Research Institute for Social Development (UNRISD), Palais des Nations, CH-1211 Geneva 10, Switzerland Tel: (022) 988400 Cable Add: Unations Geneva Telex: 289696
Dir: Dharam Ghai
Orders to: Reference Center (at above address)
Subjects: Social Development, Food Systems and Society, Popular Participation, Social Processes of Refugee Integration, Improvement of Development Data and of Methods of Analysis and Monitoring
Founded: 1963

United Nations University, Toho Seimei Bldg, 15-1 Shibuya 2-chome, Shibuya-ku, Tokyo 150, Japan Tel: (03) 4992811 Cable Add: Unatuniv Tokyo Telex: 25442 Fax: (03) 4992828
Chief, Academic Publication Services: Amadio A Arboleda
1985-86: 72 titles *Founded:* 1975
Publishes scholarly books and journals in the social sciences, humanities and pure and applied natural sciences related to the University's research into the pressing global problems of human survival, development and welfare
ISBN Publisher's Prefix: 92-808

Universal Postal Union (UPU), CP, CH-3000 Berne 15, Switzerland Tel: (031) 432211 Cable Add: Upu Berne Telex: 912761 Upu Fax: (031) 432210
Director-General: A C Botto de Barros
Founded: 1874
ISBN Publisher's Prefix: 92-62

World Health Organization (WHO), 20 ave Appia, CH-1211 Geneva 27, Switzerland Tel: (022) 912111 Cable Add: Unisante Geneva Telex: 27821
Director-General: Dr H Mahler; *Chief, Distribution & Sales Section:* M J Harriague
Subjects: Public Health, Reference, Medicine, Mental Health, Environmental Health, Social Science, Textbooks
The WHO is a specialized agency of the United Nations with primary responsibility for international health matters and public health. Through this organization the health professions of some 166 countries exchange their knowledge and experience with the aim of making possible the attainment by all citizens of the world by the year 2000 of a level of health that will permit them to lead a socially and economically productive life
Founded: 1948
ISBN Publisher's Prefix: 92-4

World Meteorological Organization (WMO), PO Box 5, CH-1211 Geneva 20, Switzerland
In early 1951, the WMO took over the work of the 78-year-old International Meteorological Organization; later that year, it became a specialized agency of the United Nations. It promotes world-wide cooperation in meteorology and hydrology by establishing a network of observation stations, helps to bring about the development of service centres, sets up systems of rapid exchange of information, standardizes statistics and observations, furthers the application of meteorology to aviation, shipping, water problems, agriculture and other human activities, promotes activities in operational hydrology, furthers close cooperation between meteorological and hydrological services, and encourages research and training in meteorology and hydrology.
The publications of WMO include basic documents, operational publications, official records, WMO guides, annual reports and the *WMO Bulletin*
ISBN Publisher's Prefix: 92-63

Other International Organizations with Publishing Activities

American-Scandinavian Foundation, 127 East 73rd St, New York, NY 10021, USA Telex: 661553 Amscan
President/Publisher: Patricia McFate
Publications: Scandinavian Review (quarterly cultural/literary/political magazine); *Scan* (four times a year membership newsletter)

Association of African Universities, PO Box 5744, Accra-North, Ghana Tel: 665461 ext 610/623 Cable Add: Afuniv Accra Telex: 2284 Adua
Secretary-General: Prof Levy Makany
Subject: Higher Education in Africa
Founded: 1967

C A B International, Wallingford, Oxon OX10 8DE, UK Tel: Wallingford 32111 (STD code 0491) Cable Add: Comag Telex: 847964 Comagg

Director-General: D Mentz; *Editorial:* J R Metcalfe; *Sales, Publicity, Rights & Permissions:* A J Woodcock; *Production:* C P Ogbourne
Subjects: Agriculture, Applied Biology, Forestry, Economics, Rural Sociology, Nutrition, Environmental Medicine
1985: 53 titles *Founded:* 1929
ISBN Publisher's Prefix: 0-85198

Centre international de documentation parlementaire (CIDP), Union interparlementaire, pl du Petit-Saconnex, PO Box 438, CH-1211 Geneva 19, Switzerland Tel: (022) 344150 Telex: 289784

Commonwealth Agricultural Bureaux, now CAB International

Conference of European Churches, 150 route de Ferney, PO Box 66, CH-1211 Geneva 20, Switzerland Tel: (022) 916111 Cable Add: Oikoumene Telex: 23423 Oik
General Secretary: Jean Eugène Fischer
Orders to: (English) The Saint Andrew Press, 121 George St, Edinburgh EH2 4YN, UK; (French) Editions Labor et Fides, 1 rue Beauregard, CH-1204 Geneva, Switzerland; (German) Conference of European Churches, 150 route de Ferney, PO Box 66, CH-1211 Geneva 20, Switzerland
Subjects: Ecumenical Theology, International Relationships
Founded: 1959
ISBN Publisher's Prefix: 2-88070

Council of Europe, Publications Section, F-67006 Strasbourg cedex, France Tel: 88614961 Cable Add: Europa Strasbourg Telex: 870943
Head of Publications: J A Tsimaratos
Subjects: Human Rights, Law, Criminology, Public Health, Sociology, Nature, Consumer Protection, Education, Sport
Founded: 1949
ISBN Publisher's Prefix: 92-871

Institut Panafricain pour le Developpement (IPD)*, Secretariat-General, BP 4056, Douala, United Republic of Cameroun Tel: (042) 1061/4335 Telex: 6048
Editor: J B Adotevi; *Editorial, Sales, Production, Publicity:* A J B Adotevi; *Rights & Permissions:* Alfred Comlam Mondjanagni
Orders (for Europe) to: IPD Bureau de Genève, rue de Varembe 3, Postfach 38, CH-1211 Geneva 20, Switzerland Telex: 27102 Ipd
Subject: Development (in particular rural development)
Founded: 1964

International African Institute*, Lionel Robbins Building, 10 Portugal St, London WC2A 2HD, UK Tel: (01) 831 3068 Cable Add: Afrilac London WC2
Branch Offs: Paris, Nigeria
Subjects: Academic books on Africa, including History, Ethnography, Environmental Studies, Bibliography, *The African Bibliography* (annual), *Africa* (quarterly)
1986: 3 titles *Founded:* 1926
Miscellaneous: 1,500 institutions and individuals are subscribing members and the governing body includes representatives from 50 countries, 30 in Africa
ISBN Publisher's Prefix: 0-85302

International Association of Sound Archives (IASA)*, Helen P Harrison, Media Librarian, Open University Library, Walton Hall, Milton Keynes, Bucks MK7 6AA, UK Tel: (0908) 653530 Telex: 826739
Secretary-General: Helen P Harrison
A non-governmental UNESCO-affiliated organization established to function as a medium for international cooperation between archives which preserve recorded sound documents
Founded: 1969

International Monetary Fund, 700 19th St, NW Washington, DC 20431, USA Tel: (202) 6237430 Cable Add: Interfund Telex: 248331 Imf Ur
Man Dir: M Camdessus; *Chief Editor:* Bahram Nowzad; *Sales, Publicity:* Kenneth R Young; *Rights & Permissions:* Ian S McDonald
Subjects: Economics, International monetary and trade issues, Domestic fiscal and monetary topics, Activities and operations of the International Monetary Fund, Balance of payments and external adjustment problems, International finance, International statistics
Bookshop: Publications Unit (at above address) (including language editions)
1986: 42 titles *Founded:* 1946
Publications include: Annual Report; Annual Report on Exchange Arrangements and Exchange Restrictions; Books and Seminar volumes; Statistical publications; Occasional papers; *IMF Survey* (23 times a year); *Finance and Development* (published jointly with World Bank)
ISBN Publisher's Prefix: 0-939934

International Union for Conservation of Nature and Natural Resources (IUCN)*, ave du Mont-Blanc, CH-1196 Gland, Switzerland Tel: (022) 647181 Cable Add: Iucnature Gland Telex: 22618 Iucn
Director-General: Dr Kenton R Miller
Orders to: Unipub, 10033F King Highway, Lanham, MD 20706, USA (for North America); Green Scientific Book Inc, 610-1-506 Ogura, Saiwai-ku, Kawasaki 211, Japan (for Japan); IUCN Conservation Monitoring Centre, 219C Huntingdon Rd, Cambridge CB3 0DL, UK (for rest of world)
Subjects: Conservation and development, Land and freshwater animals, Marine and coastal ecology and management, National parks and other protected areas, regional conservation, Environmental policy and law papers
Founded: 1948
ISBN Publisher's Prefix: 2-88032

International Union of Geological Sciences (IUGS)*, 'Episodes' Secretariat, Room 177, 601 Booth St, Ottawa, Ontario K1A 0E8, Canada Tel: (613) 9954927 Telex: 0533117 Emar Ott

Union internationale des Sciences Géologiques
Rights & Permissions: Dr A R Berger
Subjects: Earth Sciences, Quarterly *Episodes*
Founded: 1961

League of Arab States, Department of Documentation and Information*, Tahrir Square, Cairo, Egypt Tel: (02) 811960 exts 236, 270, 274 Telex: 92111 Alsun

Organization for Economic Cooperation & Development (OECD), 2 rue André-Pascal, F-75775 Paris cedex 16, France Tel: (1) 45248200 Cable Add: Developeconomie Telex: 620160 Ocde
Orders to: OECD Publications and Information Centres: Simrockstr 4, D-5300 Bonn, Federal Republic of Germany (for Austria, Germany and Switzerland); Landic Akasaka Bldg, 2-3-4 Akasaka Bldg, Tokyo 107, Japan (for Japan); 2001 L St NW, Washington, DC 20036, USA (for USA); OECD Publications Office, at above French address (for rest of world)
Subjects: Economics, Statistics, Environment, Energy, Education, Transportation, Agriculture, Development, Finance, Urban Affairs, Labour, Science and Technology, Tourism, Consumer policy, Social problems
Founded: 1960
ISBN Publisher's Prefix: 92-64

Organization of American States*, Department of Public Information, 19th St and Constitution Ave, NW Washington, DC 20006, USA
Sales & Publicity: Guido E Gárate
There are OAS offices/bookstores in 31 countries outside the USA
Subjects: Development of American Nations (Regional, Social, Historical), Bibliography, Cultural Affairs, Economics, Education, Human Rights, Law, Sciences, Statistics, Periodicals
ISBN Publisher's Prefix: 0-8270

Southeast Asian Ministers of Education Organization (SEAMEO), Regional Language Centre (RELC), 30 Orange Grove Rd, Singapore 1025, Republic of Singapore Tel: 7379044 Cable Add: Relcentre Telex: 55598 Relc
Dir: Earnest Lau
Subjects: Language Teaching and Research, Linguistics, English in multilingual, multicultural situations
1986: 78 titles *Founded:* 1968

World Council of Churches (WCC), 150 route de Ferney, PO Box 66, CH-1211 Geneva 20, Switzerland Tel: (022) 916111 Cable Add: Oikoumene Geneva Telex: 23423 Oik
General Secretary: Dr Emilio Castro; *Director, Publications:* Jan H Kok
Subjects: Ecumenism, Church Unity, Mission and Evangelism, Dialogue with people of other faiths, Social Justice, Human Rights, Development, Racism
Founded: 1948
ISBN Publisher's Prefix: 2-8254

International Bibliography

Books

2Plus2: A Collection of International Writing, Mylabris Press SA, PO Box 171, CH-1018 Lausanne, Switzerland; Mylabris Press Ltd, PO Box 20725, New York, NY 10025, USA
Annual international collection of new works of poetry, fiction, translations, interviews, drama and essays

5001 Hard-to-Find Publishers and Their Addresses, Alan Armstrong & Associates Ltd, 2 Arkwright Rd, Reading, Berkshire RG2 0SQ, UK

The ABC of Copyright, The Unesco Press, 7 pl de Fontenoy, F-75700 Paris, France
Published in Arabic, English, French, Russian, Spanish

ALA World Encyclopedia of Library & Information Services, American Library Association, 50 East Huron St, Chicago, IL 60611, USA

Adressbuch für den deutschsprachigen Buchhandel (Directory of the German-language Book Trade), Buchhändler-Vereinigung GmbH, Adressbuch-Redaktion, Postfach 2404, D-6000 Frankfurt am Main 1, Federal Republic of Germany

The African Book World and Press: A Directory, Hans Zell Publishers, PO Box 56, Oxford OX1 3EL, UK
Information in English and French

African Books in Print, Mansell Publishing Ltd, 6 All Saints St, London N1 9RL, UK

Author's and Writer's Who's Who, see *International Authors and Writers Who's Who*

Bibliographie nationale courante de l'Année . . . des pays d'Afrique d'expression française (National Bibliography for the Year . . . of Francophone African Countries), Ecole de Bibliothécaires, Archivistes, et Documentalistes de Dakar, Université de Dakar, BP 3252, Dakar, Senegal
Annual bibliography covering books and other materials published in Francophone Africa since 1967

Bibliography of German Language Publications, K G Saur Verlag, Pössenbacherstr 2b, Postfach 711009, D-000 Munich 71, Federal Republic of Germany

Bibliography of the Middle East, Damascus University Library, Damascus, Syria
Complete and classified list of all books published in about ten Middle Eastern countries

Bibliothèques et Musées des Arts du Spectacle dans le Monde (Performing Arts Libraries and Museums of the World), Société internationale des Bibliothèques-Musées des Arts du Spectacle, Librairie des Editions du CNRS, 295 rue St Jacques, F-75005 Paris, France

Book-Auction records, Dawson Publishing, Cannon House, Folkestone, Kent CT19 5EE, UK

Book Markets in Western and Eastern Europe (1984), Euromonitor Publications Ltd, 87-88 Turnmill St, London EC1M 5QU, UK

Book Publishers Directory, Gale Research Co, Book Tower, Detroit, MI 48226, USA
USA and Canada

Book Review Index, Gale Research Co, Book Tower, Detroit, MI 48226, USA
Includes listings from outside USA and Canada

Book World Directory of the Arab Countries, Turkey and Iran, Mansell Publishing Ltd, 6 All Saints St, London N1 9RL, UK

Bookdealers in India, Pakistan and Sri Lanka (1977), Sheppard Press, 18 Bedford Sq, London WC1B 3JN, UK

Bookman's Price Index, Gale Research Co, Book Tower, Detroit, MI 48226, USA

Books in Print, R R Bowker Co, 245 West 17th St, New York, NY 10010, USA

The Bowker Annual of Library and Book Trade Information, R R Bowker (UK) Ltd, Borough Green, Sevenoaks, Kent TN15 8PH, UK

British Library General Catalogue of Printed Books, K G Saur, Shropshire House, 2-10 Capper St, London WC1E 6JA, UK
360 volumes to 1975; supplement 1976-82; supplement 1982-85; supplement to 1975 (6 vols)

Cassell & The Publishers Association Directory of Publishing, Cassell PLC, Artillery House, Artillery Row, London SW1P 1RT, UK

Catalogue général des ouvrages parus en langue française (Catalogue of Books Published in the French Language), Cercle de la Librairie, 35 rue Grégoire de Tours, F-75279 Paris cedex 06, France

Contemporary Authors, Gale Research Co, Book Tower, Detroit, MI 48226, USA
Includes listings from outside USA and Canada

Copyright Laws and Treaties of the World, The Unesco Press, 7 pl de Fontenoy, F-75700 Paris, France
Published in English, French and Spanish

Cumulative Book Index, H W Wilson Co, 950 University Ave, New York, NY 10452, USA
World index of English-language books

Current African Directories, CBD Research Ltd, 154 High St, Beckenham, Kent BR3 1EA, UK
Incorporating *African Companies*, a guide to directories published in or concerned with Africa and to sources of information on business enterprises in Africa

Current European Directories, CBD Research Ltd, 154 High St, Beckenham, Kent BR3 1EA, UK
Annotated guide to international, national, city and specialized directories and similar reference works for all countries of Europe

Dictionarium bibliothecarii praticum (ad usum internationalem in XXII linguis) (The Librarian's practical dictionary in 22 languages), Akadémiai Kiadó, H-1363 Budapest, Postafiók 24, Hungary; K G Saur Verlag, Postfach 711009, D-8000 Munich 71, Federal Republic of Germany

Directorio Latinoamericano de Editoriales, Distribuidoras y Librerias (Directory of Latin American Publishers, Distributors and Booksellers), Centro Régional para el Fomento del Libro en América Latina y el Caribe (CERLALC), Apdo Aeréo 17438, Bogotá, Colombia

Directory of Documentation, Libraries and Archives Services in Africa, UNESCO, 7 pl de Fontenoy, F-75700 Paris, France

Directory of Government Printers and Prominent Bookshops in the African Region, United Nations Economic Commission for Africa, PO Box 3001, Addis Ababa, Ethiopia

Directory of Libraries and Documentation Centres in the United Nations System, United Nations, Sales Section, Publishing Division, Room DC2-853, New York, NY 10017, USA

Directory of Special Libraries and Information Centers, Gale Research Co, Book Tower, Detroit, MI 48226, USA
USA and Canada

Ensemble, DTV-Deutscher Taschenbuch Verlag GmbH & Co KG, Postfach 400422, D-8000 Munich 40, Federal Republic of Germany
International literary yearbook, published in English, French and German

European Bookdealers: A Directory of Dealers in Secondhand and Antiquarian Books on the Continent of Europe, Sheppard Press, 18 Bedford Sq, London WC1B 3JN, UK

Foreign Literary Prizes (Romance and Germanic Languages), R R Bowker (UK) Ltd, Borough Green, Sevenoaks, Kent TN15 8PH, UK

Frankfurt Book Fair Catalogue, Ausstellungs- und Messe-GmbH des Deutschen Buchhandels, Kleiner Hirschgraben 10-12, D-6000 Frankfurt am Main 1, Federal Republic of Germany

German Language Books Backlist, Mäander Verlag GmbH, Hundingstr 9, D-8000 Munich 19, Federal Republic of Germany

Guia de Bibliografía Especializada (Guide to Specialist Libraries), Associação Profissional de Bibliotecários do Estado de Rio de Janeiro, Rua Martins Torres 99, Santa Rosa, Niterói, 24000 Rio de Janeiro RJ, Brazil
Covers all Latin America

Guide du Livre Ancien et du Livre d'occasion (Guide to Antiquarian and Second-hand Books), Syndicat du Livre ancien et des Metiers annexes, 14 ave de Friedland, F-75008 Paris, France

Guide technique, Lavoisier Abonnements, 11 rue Lavoisier, F-75384 Paris cedex 08, France
Listing 15,000 international scientific and technical periodicals

IFLA Directory (biennially), International Federation of Library Associations and Institutions, The Royal Library, Postbus 95312, 2509 CH The Hague, Netherlands

IFLA Standards for Public Libraries, K G Saur Verlag, Postfach 711009, D-8000 Munich 71, Federal Republic of Germany

Index translationum, International bibliography of translations, UNESCO, 7 pl de Fontenoy, F-75700 Paris, France

International Authors and Writers Who's Who, Melrose Press Ltd, 3 Regal Lane, Soham, Ely, Cambridgeshire CB7 5BA, UK; Gale Research Co, Book Tower, Detroit, MI 48226, USA

Information on 10,000 of world's leading writers, including index of pseudonyms and literary agents

International Bibliography of Reprints/ Internationales Verzeichnis der Reprints, K G Saur Verlag, Postfach 711009, D-8000 Munich 71, Federal Republic of Germany

International Bibliography of the Book Trade and Librarianship, 1976-79, K G Saur Verlag, Postfach 711009, D-8000 Munich 71, Federal Republic of Germany

International Book Trade Directory, R R Bowker (UK) Ltd, Borough Green, Sevenoaks, Kent TN15 8PH, UK
Listing details of booksellers world-wide

International Books in Print, K G Saur Verlag, Postfach 711009, D-8000 Munich 71, Federal Republic of Germany; K G Saur, Shropshire House, 2-10 Capper St, London WC1E 6JA, UK
Listing titles published in the English language outside the UK and USA

International Directory of Antiquarian Booksellers, International League of Antiquarian Booksellers, Hans Bagger, Rosenkilde og Bagger, Postboks 2184, DK-1017 Copenhagen K, Denmark

International Directory of Children's Literature, George Kurian Reference Books, PO Box 5109, Baldwin Place, NY 10505, USA

International Directory of Children's Literature Specialists, International Board on Books for Young People (IBBY), Leonhardsgraben 38a, Postfach, CH-4003 Basle, Switzerland
Published by K G Saur Verlag, Federal Republic of Germany (qv)

International ISBN Publishers' Directory, IPI, WHS Distribution Services, Wildwood House Ltd, Unit 3, Lower Farnham Rd, Aldershot, Hants GU12 4DY, UK

International Literary Market Place, R R Bowker (UK) Ltd, Borough Green, Sevenoaks, Kent TN15 8PH, UK
Covers the world apart from the North American continent, which is covered by *Literary Market Place*

International Who's Who in Poetry, Melrose Press Ltd, 3 Regal Lane, Soham, Ely, Cambridgeshire CB7 5BA, UK; Gale Research Co, Book Tower, Detroit, MI 48226, USA

Internationales Jahrbuch für Literatur, DTV-Deutscher Taschenbuch Verlag GmbH & Co KG, Postfach 400422, D-8000 Munich 40, Federal Republic of Germany

Irregular Serials and Annuals: An International Directory, R R Bowker (UK) Ltd, Borough Green, Sevenoaks, Kent TN15 8PH, UK

Jahrbuch der Auktionspreise (Yearbook of Auction Prices), Dr Ernst Hauswedell und Co Verlag, Postfach 723, D-7000 Stuttgart 1, Federal Republic of Germany
Book auction prices in Germany, Austria, Switzerland and the Netherlands

Large Type Books in Print, R R Bowker (UK) Ltd, Borough Green, Sevenoaks, Kent TN15 8PH, UK

Literary and Library Prizes, R R Bowker Co, 245 West 17th St, New York, NY 10011, USA; R R Bowker (UK) Ltd, Borough Green, Sevenoaks, Kent TN15 8PH, UK

Literary Market Place, R R Bowker Co, 245 West 17th St, New York, NY 10011, USA; R R Bowker (UK) Ltd, Borough Green, Sevenoaks, Kent TN15 8PH, UK
Covers North American continent — rest of world covered by *International Literary Market Place*

Private Press Books, Private Libraries Association (PLA), Ravelston, South View Rd, Pinner, Middlesex, UK
Annual bibliography of the work of private presses throughout the world

Publishers' International Directory (*Internationales Verlagsadressbuch*), K G Saur Verlag, Postfach 711009, D-8000 Munich 71, Federal Republic of Germany

Publishing in Africa in the Seventies, University of Ife Press, Ile-Ife, Oyo State, Nigeria

Répertoire international des Editeurs et Diffuseurs de Langue française (International List of French-language Publishers and Distributors), Cercle de la Librairie, 35 rue Grégoire de Tours, F-75279 Paris cedex 06, France

Répertoire international des Librairies de Langue française (International List of French-language Bookshops), Cercle de la Librairie, 35 rue Grégoire de Tours, F-75279 Paris cedex 06, France

Rights — Copyright and Related Rights in the Service of Creativity, International Group of Scientific, Technical and Medical Publishers (STM), Keizersgracht 462, 1016 GE Amsterdam, Netherlands; International Publishers Association (IPA), 3 ave de Miremont, CH-1206 Geneva, Switzerland

South Asian Bibliography: A Handbook and Guide, The Harvester Press Ltd, 16 Ship St, Brighton, East Sussex BN1 1AD, UK

South Pacific Bibliography (annual), University of the South Pacific Library, PO Box 1168, Suva, Fiji

Subject Collections in European Libraries, R R Bowker (UK) Ltd, Borough Green, Sevenoaks, Kent TN15 8PH, UK

Subject Guide to Inernational Books in Print, K G Saur Verlag, Postfach 711009, D-8000 Munich 71, Federal Republic of Germany; K G Saur, Shropshire House, 2-10 Capper St, London WC1E 6JA, UK

Ulrich's International Periodicals Directory, R R Bowker (UK) Ltd, Borough Green, Sevenoaks, Kent TN15 8PH, UK

Who Distributes What and Where: An International Directory of Publishers, Imprints, Agents and Distributors, R R Bowker Co, 245 West 17th St, New York, NY 10010, USA; R R Bowker (UK) Ltd, Borough Green, Sevenoaks, Kent TN15 8PH, UK

Who's Who at the Frankfurt Book Fair: An International Publishers' Guide, K G Saur Verlag, Postfach 711009, D-8000 Munich 71, Federal Republic of Germany

Willings Press Guide, Thomas Skinner Directories, Windsor Court, East Grinstead House, East Grinstead, West Sussex RH19 1XE, UK

World Guide to Libraries, K G Saur Verlag, Postfach 711009, D-8000 Munich 71, Federal Republic of Germany

World Guide to Library Schools and Training Courses in Documentation, Clive Bingley Ltd, 7 Ridgmount St, London WC1E 7AE, UK

World Guide to Special Libraries, K G Saur Verlag, Postfach 711009, D-8000 Munich 71, Federal Republic of Germany

World Photography Sources, Directories, 436 East 88th St, New York, NY 10028, USA

The Writers' & Artists' Yearbook, A & C Black (Publishers) Ltd, 35 Bedford Row, London WC1R 4JH, UK

The Writers Directory, Macmillan Publishers Ltd (Journals Division), Brunel Rd, Houndmills Industrial Estate, Basingstoke, Hampshire RG21 2XS, UK

Journals

African Book Publishing Record, K G Saur Verlag, Postfach 711009, D-8000 Munich 71, Federal Republic of Germany
Text occasionally in French

African Books Newsletter, K K Roy (Pvt) Ltd, 55 Gariahat Rd, PO Box 10210, Calcutta 700019, India
Checklist of recent books published in English, arranged according to subject

African Journal of Academic Librarianship, PO Box 46, Yaba, Lagos, Nigeria

African Research and Documentation, Standing Conference on Library Materials on Africa (SCOLMA), c/o Institute of Commonwealth Studies, 27-28 Russell Sq, London WC1B 5DS, UK

L'Afrique littéraire, 2 rue Cretet, F-75009 Paris, France

Asian Book Development, Asian Cultural Centre for UNESCO, 6 Fukuromachi, Shinjuku-ku, Tokyo 162, Japan

Asian Books Newsletter, K K Roy (Pvt) Ltd, 55 Gariahat Rd, PO Box 10210, Calcutta 700019, India
Checklist of recent books published in English, arranged according to subject

Babel (International Journal of Translation), Kultura, H-1389 Budapest 62, Postafiók 149, Hungary

Bibliografía actual de Caribe (Current Caribbean Bibliography) Caribbean Regional Library, University Station, Apdo 21927, San Juan, PR 00931, Puerto Rico

Bibliographie Documentation, Terminologie, UNESCO, Département de la Documentation des Bibliothèques et des Archives, 7 pl de Fontenoy, F-75700 Paris, France
Published in English, French, Russian and Spanish

Bibliography of German-Language Academic Publications (1966-1980), K G Saur Verlag, Postfach 711009, D-8000 Munich 71, Federal Republic of Germany

Bibliography of German-Language Publications (1700-1910 and 1911-1965), K G Saur Verlag, Postfach 711009, D-8000 Munich 71, Federal Republic of Germany

Bibliography of German-Language Publications outside the Booktrade (1966-1980), K G Saur Verlag, Postfach 711009, D-8000 Munich 71, Federal Republic of Germany

Bibliotheca Orientalis, Nederlands Instituut voor Het Nabije Oosten, Postbus 9515, 2300 RA Leiden, Netherlands
International bibliographical and reviewing journal for Near Eastern and Mediterranean Studies, published in English, French and German, bi-monthly

Boletín Bibliográfico del CERLALC, Centro Régional para el Fomento del Libro en América Latina y el Caribe (CERLALC), Calle 70 No 9-52, Apdo Aeréo 17438, Bogotá, Colombia
Current Latin-American bibliography

Bookbird, International Institute for Children's Literature and Reading Research (UNESCO category C), A-1040 Vienna, Mayerhofgasse 6, Austria
Literature for children and young people, news from all over the world, recommendations for translation, quarterly

'The Bookseller' Frankfurt Rights Guide, J Whitaker & Sons Ltd, 12 Dyott St, London WC1A 1DF, UK

Bulletin (quarterly), Bibliographical Society of Australia and New Zealand (BSANZ), c/o Secretary, 76 Warners Ave, Bondi Beach, NSW 2026, Australia

Le Bulletin du Bibliophile, Association internationale de Bibliophilie, c/o Bibliothèque nationale, 58 rue de Richelieu, F-75084 Paris cedex 02, France
Published in English, French and German, quarterly

Bulletin de l'Association internationale des Documentalistes et Techniciens de l'Information, Association internationale des Documentalistes et Techniciens de l'Information AID, 74 rue des Saints-Pères, F-75007 Paris, France

Buying for Libraries (twice a year), 500 Chesham House, 150 Regent St, London W1R 5FA, UK

CERLALC; noticias sobre el Libro (CERLALC; news on books), Centro Régional para el Fomento del Libro en América Latina y el Caribe (CERLALC), Calle 70 No 9-52, Apdo Aeréo 17438, Bogotá, Colombia

CREPLA Bulletin, Centre régional de Promotion du Livre en Afrique (CREPLA), BP 1646, Yaoundé, United Republic of Cameroun

Caribbean Quarterly, Department of Extra-Mural Studies, University of the West Indies, Mona, Kingston 7, Jamaica

Copyright (Le droit d'auteur), World Intellectual Property Organization, 34 chemin des Colombettes, CH-1211 Geneva 20, Switzerland
Published in English and French, monthly

Copyright Bulletin, The Unesco Press, 7 pl de Fontenoy, F-75700 Paris, France
Published in English, French and Spanish, (quarterly)

Le droit d'auteur, see *Copyright*

Fichero Bibliográfico Hispanoamericano, Melcher Ediciones, Apdo 6000, San Juan, PR 00906, Puerto Rico
Monthly review of librarians, booksellers, distributors and publishers

Frankfurt Rights Guide, see *'The Bookseller'*

Germanistik, Internationales Referatenorgan mit bibliographischen Hinweisen (German Language and Literature: International Review Journal with Bibliographical References), Max Niemeyer Verlag, Postfach 2140, D-7400 Tübingen, Federal Republic of Germany

Helikon Vilagirodalmi Figyelo (Helikon Review of World Literature), Akademiai Kiadó, H-1363 Budapest, Postafiók 24, Hungary
Summaries published in French and Russian

Heritage, PO Box 610, Apapa, Lagos, Nigeria
African arts and letters, quarterly

Inter-American Review of Bibliography (Revista Interamericana de Bibliografía), Organization of American States, Department of Public Information, 19th St and Constitution Ave, NW Washington, DC 20006, USA

International Association of Orientalist Librarians Bulletin (half-yearly), International Association of Oriental Librarians, c/o Asian Library, 325 Library, University of Illinois, 1408 West Gregory Drive, Urbana, IL 61801, USA

International Cataloguing, IFLA Committee on Cataloguing, Longman Group UK Ltd, Journals Dept, Fourth Ave, Harlow, Essex CM19 5AA, UK

The International Fiction Review (twice a year), Department of German and Russian, University of New Brunswick, Fredericton, New Brunswick E3B 5A3, Canada

International Library Review (quarterly), Academic Press Inc (London) Ltd, 24-28 Oval Rd, London NW1 7DX, UK

The Journal of Commonwealth Literature, K G Saur Verlag, Postfach 711009, D-8000 Munich 71, Federal Republic of Germany

Jugend und Buch (Youth and Books), International Institute for Children's Literature and Reading Research (UNESCO category C), A-1040 Vienna, Mayerhofgasse 6, Austria
Co-sponsored by Österreichischer Buchklub der Jugend

LIBER Bulletin, Ligue des Bibliothèques Européenes de Recherche (LIBER), c/o Prof Dr Hans-Albrecht Koch, Staats- und Universitätsbibliothek Bremen, Bibliotheksstr, Postfach 330160, D-2800 Bremen 33, Federal Republic of Germany
Published in English and French

Latin American Books Newsletter, K K Roy (Pvt) Ltd, 55 Gariahat Rd, PO Box 10210, Calcutta 700019, India

Library & Information Science Abstracts, The Library Association, 7 Ridgmount St, London WC1E 7AE, UK

Log, A-9020 Klagenfurt, August-Jaksch-Str 15, Austria
International literary magazine

Pacific Islands Books News Letter, K K Roy (Pvt) Ltd, 55 Gariahat Rd, PO Box 10210, Calcutta 700019, India

PEN International, International PEN, 38 King St, London WC2E 8JT, UK
Published in English and French and issued with the assistance of UNESCO

Publishers Weekly, R R Bowker Co, PO Box 1428, Riverton, NJ 08077, USA

Review, Center for Inter-American Relations, 680 Park Ave, New York, NY 10021, USA
Contemporary Latin American literature in English translation

Revista Interamericana de Bibliografía, see *Inter-American Review of Bibliography*

SCALS Newsletter, c/o School of Librarians, Archivists and Documentalists, University of Dakar, BP 2006, Dakar, Senegal
Official publication of the Standing Conference of African Library Schools (SCALS)

SCAUL Newsletter, c/o E Bejide Bankole, Editor, African Journal of Academic Librarianship, PO Box 46, Yaba, Lagos, Nigeria
Official publication of the Standing Conference of African University Libraries (SCAUL)

Scandinavian Public Library Quarterly, A/L Biblioteksentralen, Malerhaugveien 20, N-Oslo 6, Norway

Scandinavian Review, American-Scandinavian Foundation, 127 East 73rd St, New York, NY 10021, USA
Cultural/literary/political magazine, quarterly

Scottish Slavonic Review (twice a year), University of Glasgow, Department of Slavonic Languages and Literatures, Hetherington Bldg, The University, Glasgow G12 8QQ, UK

South Asia Library Notes and Queries, University of Chicago Library, 5801 Ellis Ave, Chicago, IL 60637, USA

South Pacific Periodicals Index, University of the South Pacific Library, PO Box 1168, Suva, Fiji

Southeast Asian Archives, Southeast Asian Regional Branch of the International Council on Archives (SARBICA), c/o National Archives of Malaysia, Jalan Duta, 50568 Kuala Lumpur, Malaysia

Stand Magazine, 179 Wingrove Rd, Newcastle upon Tyne NE4 9DA, UK
New writing, quarterly

Swedish Book Review (twice a year), Linda Schenck, Mossgatan 5, S-413 21 Gothenburg, Sweden (for Scandinavia); Valerie Gustaveson, 260 East José Ave, Claremont, CA 91711, USA (for USA and Canada); St David's University College, Lampeter, SA48 7ED, Wales, UK (for rest of world)

UNESCO Journal of Documentation Science, Librarianship and Archives Administration, The Unesco Press, 7 pl de Fontenoy, F-75700 Paris, France

Ulrich's Quarterly, R R Bowker (UK) Ltd, Borough Green, Sevenoaks, Kent TN15 8PH, UK

World Book News, Euromonitor Publications Ltd, 87-88 Turnmill St, London EC1M 5QU, UK

International Literary Prizes

Alexander Prize
For an essay in English on a historical subject by an author under the age of 30; must be a genuine work of original research, not hitherto published, and not awarded any other prize. Silver medal plus £100, awarded annually. Enquiries to Secretary, Royal Historical Society, University College London, Gower St, London WC1E 6BT, UK

Allen Lane Award, see Lane

American-Scandinavian Foundation Translation Prize
Initiated in 1980 by 'Scandinavian Review' (quarterly magazine of ASF) to bring best of contemporary Scandinavian literature to American readers. There is a prize of US$1,000, either for poetry or fiction, in addition to publication. Awarded annually for the best translation of work by a Danish, Finnish, Icelandic, Norwegian or Swedish author born within the last 100 years. Enquiries to American-Scandinavian Foundation, 127 East 73rd St, New York, NY 10021, USA

Hans Christian **Andersen** Awards
The International Board on Books for Young People (IBBY) makes these awards every two years to a living author and a living illustrator who, through their works, have made distinguished contributions to international children's and young adult literature. (Until 1966 a prize was awarded for a specific book and to an author only.) A jury of ten members, appointed by the Executive Committee of IBBY, makes the decision from selections submitted from member countries all over the world. Awarded in 1986 to Patricia Wrightson (author) and Robert Ingpen (illustrator), both from Australia. Enquiries to IBBY Secretariat, Leonhardsgraben 38a, Postfach, CH-4003 Basle, Switzerland

Arts Council Awards and Bursaries
Full details of the help given to playwrights is available on request. Enquiries to Drama Director, Arts Council of Great Britain, 105 Piccadilly, London W1V 0AU, UK

Arvon Foundation International Poetry Competition
First organized in 1980, since when there have been three further competitions (1982, 1985 and 1987) with 'The Observer', Sotheby's and merchant bankers Duncan Lawrie sponsorship. In 1987 the main prize was £5,000; there were in addition five prizes of £500 each and 10 of £250 each. Entries for the competition must be previously unpublished poems written in English. Enquiries to Arvon Foundation, Kilnhurst, Kilnhurst Rd, Todmorden, Lancashire OL14 6AX, UK

Austrian State Prize for European Literature*
A prize of 200,000 Austrian Schillings and testimonial, established in 1965, are presented by the Austrian Minister of Education to a renowned European author (with the exception of an Austrian national) for the sum of his work. Awarded annually. Enquiries to Bundesministerium für Unterricht und Kunst, A-1014 Vienna, Postfach 65, Sektion IV/Abteilung 43A, Austria

Bennett Award
For a writer of substantial achievement whose work has not received full recognition, or who is at a critical stage of development. US$15,000, biennially. No applications or nominations accepted. Enquiries to The Hudson Review, 684 Park Ave, New York, NY 10021, USA

Benson Medal
Founded 1916 by Dr A C Benson. For a body of meritorious work in poetry, fiction, history, biography or belles lettres. A silver medal given at the discretion of the Council of the Royal Society of Literature. Applications are not invited. Last awarded in 1982 to Dr A L Rowse (UK). Enquiries to Royal Society of Literature of the United Kingdom, 1 Hyde Park Gardens, London W2 2LT, UK

Anton **Bergmann** Prize*
For the author of a historical account or monograph, written in Dutch and relating to a Flemish town or community in Belgium. 60,000 Belgian francs. Awarded every five years for a work appearing in print or (provisionally) in manuscript form, during the period. Foreign authors may also compete, provided work is in Dutch and is published in Belgium or the Netherlands. Winner for 18th period (1980-1985), Hoegaardse Heemkundige Kring. Enquiries to Académie Royale de Belgique, Palais des Académies, 1 rue Ducale, B-1000 Brussels, Belgium

David **Berry** Prize
For an essay in English on any subject dealing with Scottish history within the reigns of James I to James VI inclusive. Monetary prize awarded every three years. Enquiries to Secretary, Royal Historical Society, University College London, Gower St, London WC1E 6BT, UK

Biennial International Art Book Prize
To promote the publication of fine illustrated books on archaeology, fine arts, architecture and applied arts, including photography. Prize consists of silver and bronze medals, free flight and hotel accommodation in Jerusalem during the Jerusalem International Book Fair for the publisher and designer of the winning entry. Prizes are awarded in three categories with the overall winner selected from these three. All entries to be exhibited as a special exhibit of the International Book Fair and to remain in the Israel Museum Library. Next award in 1989. Enquiries to The Public Affairs Department, The Israel Museum, PO Box 1299, Jerusalem 91012, Israel

Boardman Tasker Prize for Mountain Literature
Established in 1983 to commemorate the lives of distinguished mountaineers Peter Boardman and Joe Tasker who died in 1982 on Mount Everest. An annual prize of £1,000 will go to an author of a published work of non-fiction or fiction, written in the English language, initially or in translation, which makes an outstanding contribution to mountain literature. The 1986 prize went to Stephen Venables for *Painted Mountains* (Hodder & Stoughton, UK). Enquiries to Mrs D Boardman, 56 St Michael's Ave, Bramhall, Stockport, Cheshire SK7 2PL, UK

Bologna Book Fair 'Critici in erba' Prize
Award by a jury of nine children, between 6 and 9 years of age, for the best illustrated book among those sent by the publishers exhibiting at the Bologna Children's Book Fair. 1987 award went to *That's my Dad* (Andersen Press, UK). Enquiries to Fiera del Libro per Ragazzi — Ente Autonomo per le Fiere di Bologna, Piazza della Costituzione 6, I-40128 Bologna, Italy

Bologna Book Fair Graphic Prize for Children and Youth
Awarded for typographical, artistic and technical merit or innovation at the Bologna Children's Book Fair, by an international committee of graphic designers appointed by the Fair authorities. The prizes, consisting of golden plates, are awarded to the publishers of the winning works. The graphic prize for the book for children was awarded in 1987 for *The Great Games Book* (A & C Black, UK). The graphic prize for the book for young people was awarded in 1987 for *Découvertes Gallimard* (Editions Gallimard, France). Enquiries to Fiera del Libro per Ragazzi — Ente Autonomo per le Fiere di Bologna, Piazza della Costituzione 6, I-40128 Bologna, Italy

Booker Prize
Instituted in 1969. £15,000 donated by Booker PLC and administered by Book Trust, for any full-length novel, written in English by a citizen of The Commonwealth, the Republic of Ireland, Pakistan or the Republic of South Africa and entered by a United Kingdom publisher. Awarded in 1987 to Penelope Lively for *Moon Tiger* (André Deutsch, UK). Enquiries to Book Trust, Book House, 45 East Hill, Wandsworth, London SW18 2QZ, UK

Bremen Literature Encouragement Prize*
Given by Rudolf-Alexander-Schröder Foundation to young German-speaking poets and writers in order to encourage literature. 7,500 DM awarded annually. Enquiries to Senator für Bildüng Wissenschaft und Kunst, Freie Hansestadt Bremen, D-2800 Bremen 1, Federal Republic of Germany

Bremen Literature Prize
Given by Rudolf-Alexander-Schröder Foundation to German-speaking poets and writers in order to encourage literature. 15,000 DM awarded annually. Enquiries to Senator für Bildüng Wissenschaft und Kunst, Freie Hansestadt Bremen, D-2800 Bremen 1, Federal Republic of Germany

John W **Campbell** Memorial Award
Founded 1973 for the best science-fiction novel in any language. First prize according to funding of sponsoring institution (at present University of Kansas). Enquiries to The Secretary, Prof T A Shippey, School of English, Leeds University, Leeds LS2 9JT, UK

'The Times'/Jonathan **Cape** Young Writers Prize, see 'The Times'

Carducci Prize*
Established 1950. For poetry, monographs and essays on poetry and poets. 1,500,000 lire. Awarded annually. Enquiries to Bologna University, Bologna, Italy

Casa de las Américas Literary Award*
An annual prize of US$3,000 (or equivalent in national currency) is awarded to an author for unpublished work in one or other of the following groups (alternately, each year): (1) novels, plays, 'testimonial' books, essays on artistic and literary themes — Brazilian and French Caribbean (or national language) works; (2) short stories, poetry, essays on historical and social themes, books for children and young people and Anglo-Caribbean (or national language) works. The winning work will be published. Enquiries to Casa de las Américas, Tercera y G, Vedado 4, Havana, Cuba or PO Box, CH-3000 Berne 16, Switzerland

Children's Book Award
Established 1974. Awarded annually for a first or second book (any language) to authors who show unusual promise. In 1987 the winners were Marisabina Russo in younger readers' category for *The Line Up Book* (Greenwillow, USA) and Margaret I Rostkowski in young adult category for *After the Dancing Days* (Harper & Row, USA). Enquiries to International Reading Association, 800 Barksdale Rd, PO Box 8139, Newark, DE 19714, USA

Cholmondeley Award for Poets
Established by the Dowager Marchioness of Cholmondeley in 1965 for 'the benefit and encouragement of poets of any age, sex or nationality'. The non-competitive award is for work generally, *not* for a specific book and submissions are not required. Approximately £4,000 awarded annually. The 1987 award was shared by Wendy Cope, Matthew Sweeney and George Szirtes. Enquiries to Society of Authors, 84 Drayton Gardens, London SW10 9SB, UK

Collins Religious Book Award
Founded 1969 to commemorate the 150th anniversary of the publisher William Collins Sons & Co Ltd. For the book which has made the most distinguished contribution to the relevance of Christianity in the modern world. Open to living citizens of The Commonwealth, the Republic of Ireland and the Republic of South Africa. Prize of £2,000 awarded every two years. Enquiries to Sarah Baird-Smith, William Collins Sons PLC, 8 Grafton St, London W1X 3LA, UK

The **Commonwealth** Poetry Prize Awards*
Instituted in 1972 and organized in partnership with the Commonwealth Foundation. Awarded annually and open to all published Commonwealth (including UK) poets, in any officially recognized Commonwealth national language, if accompanied by English translation. Sponsorship in 1986 by British Airways for the following: (1) best published poet, £6,000; (2) best first-time published poet, £2,000; (3) five regional awards of £1,000 each to poets from Africa, Americas (including Canada and Caribbean), Asia, Australia/Pacific, UK/Europe. Closing date for entries is 30 June. The 1986 £6,000 prize was shared by Niyi Osundare for *The Eye of the Earth* (HEB, Nigeria) and Vikram Seth for *The Golden Gate* (Faber, UK); the £2,000 prize went to Vicki Raymond (Australia) for *Holiday Girls* (Twelvetrees). Enquiries to The Librarian (Poetry Prize), Library & Resource Centre, The Commonwealth Institute, Kensington High Street, London W8 6NQ, UK

Thomas **Cook** Travel and Guide Book Awards*
Two awards: one of £2,000 for the best travel book and one of £1,000 for the best guide book of the year. Books must have been published in the twelve months ending 31 October and be written in English. The 1987 travel book award went to Patrick Leigh Fermor for *Between the Woods and the Water* (Murray, UK); the guide book award was for *Fontana/Hachette Guide to France 1986* (Collins/Fontana, UK). Enquiries to Book Trust, Book House, 45 East Hill, Wandsworth, London SW18 2QZ, UK

Albert **Counson** Prize*
For a scholarly work on romance languages, in relation to or connected with Belgium. Monetary prize. Awarded every five years. Enquiries to Académie royale de Langue et de Littérature françaises, Palais de Académies, 1 rue Ducale, B-1000 Brussels, Belgium

Count of Cartagena Prizes
Established 1929. For unpublished works by Spaniards or Latin-Americans written in Spanish on a theme to be decided for each competition. 90,000 pesetas. Awarded annually. Enquiries to Real Academia Española, Felipe IV 4, Madrid 14, Spain

The Rose Mary **Crawshay** Prizes
Founded 1888. Awarded by the Council of the British Academy to women writers of any nationality for an historical or critical work of value on any subject concerning English literature. Preference is given to works on Byron, Shelley or Keats. One or more prizes awarded annually. Applications are not sought. Enquiries to The Secretary, British Academy, 20-21 Cornwall Terrace, London NW1 4QP, UK

Croom Helm Ancient History Prize
Established 1986. For the manuscript by a writer under 40 of any nationality making the best contribution in English to the understanding of the history of the classical world. Annual award of £500 and publication. Enquiries to Richard Stoneman, Croom Helm Ltd, Provident House, Burrell Row, Beckenham, Kent BR3 1AT, UK

Franz **Cumont** Prize*
For a work by a Belgian or foreign author dealing with the history of religion or science in antiquity, i.e. in the Mediterranean area prior to the time of Mohammed. No application necessary. The prize cannot be divided, except where one or more authors have acted in collaboration. 100,000 Belgian francs. Awarded every three years. Winner for fifth period (1982-1984) J-M Blázques Martines. Enquiries to Académie Royale de Belgique, Palais des Académies, 1 rue Ducale, B-1000 Brussels, Belgium

Cyril and Methodius Prize*
For original research in the field of old Bulgarian literature, linguistics and art. 2,000 leva. Awarded annually. Enquiries to Bulgarian Academy of Sciences, Institute of Literature, blvd Vitosha 39, Sofia C, Bulgaria

Isaac **Deutscher** Memorial Prize
Instituted 1968. For a work published or in typescript in any of the main European languages which contributes to the development of Marxist thought. £100 awarded annually. Enquiries to Isaac Deutscher Memorial Prize, c/o Lloyds Bank PLC, 68 Warwick Sq, London SW1V 2AS, UK

Ernest **Discailles** Prize*
Alternates between the best work on the history of French literature and on contemporary history. Open to (1) Belgians, (2) foreigners who are studying or have studied at the University of Ghent. 60,000 Belgian francs. Awarded every five years. Enquiries to Académie Royale de Belgique, Palais des Académies, 1 rue Ducale, B-1000 Brussels, Belgium

Duff **Cooper** Memorial Prize
First awarded 1956. For a non-fictional literary work published in English or French. The Prize is the interest from a Trust Fund. Awarded annually. The 1986 winner was Alan Crawford for *C R Ashbee: Architect, Designer and Romantic Socialist* (Yale University Press, UK). Enquiries to Lord Norwich, 24 Blomfield Rd, London W9, UK

Mary **Elgin** Prize
Established in 1969 for the encouragement of gifted new writers of fiction published by Hodder & Stoughton. £50 awarded annually. There are no restrictions on age, sex or nationality. No award in 1986. Enquiries to Hodder & Stoughton Ltd, 47 Bedford Square, London WC1B 3DP, UK

Camille **Engelman** Prize*
For the outstanding literary work of the year (published or unpublished) written in French. Monetary prize. Awarded annually. Enquiries to Académie royale de Langue et de Littérature françaises, Palais des Académies, 1 rue Ducale, B-1000 Brussels, Belgium

European Poetry Translation Prize
Founded 1983 and awarded biennially. The prize is for a translation into English of any European work of poetry. The 1987 winner was Ewald Osers for his translation of the German poet Jaroslav Seifert's works. The 1987 prize is of £500. Enquiries to The Poetry Society, 21 Earls Court Sq, London SW5 9DE, UK

Christopher **Ewart-Biggs** Memorial Prize
Established in 1977 to commemorate Christopher Ewart-Biggs, the British Ambassador to Ireland, who was assassinated in Dublin in 1976. This award is made biennially to writings from any nationality where the published work contributes most to peace and understanding in Ireland, closer ties between the peoples of Britain and Ireland, or to cooperation between the partners of the European Community. Entries should be in English or French and the prize is £4,000. Enquiries to Hugo Arnold, 30 Sherwood Court, Bryanston Place, London W1H 5FE, UK

F I T Translation Prizes*
(1) Established in 1970 and sponsored by Carl-Bertil Nathhorst-Stiftelser (Stockholm, Sweden). Awarded every three or four years, for (a) a literary and (b) a non-literary translation which make an outstanding contribution to the improvement of the quality of translation. The 1984 award went (a) to Prof Ryoichi Sato (Japan), and (b) to Krista Schmidt (Austria). (2) Established in 1981 and sponsored to commemorate Astrid Lindgren (Stockholm, Sweden). Awarded every three or four years for a translation promoting a work written for children. The 1984 award went to Patricia Crampton (UK). Enquiries to Fédération internationale des Traducteurs (FIT), Heiveldstr 245, B-9110 Gent/Sint-Amandsberg, Belgium

The Geoffrey **Faber** Memorial Prize
Established in 1963 by Faber & Faber Ltd as a memorial to the founder and first Chairman of the firm, this prize of £500 is

awarded annually. It is given, in alternate years, for a volume of verse and for a volume of prose fiction. It is given to that volume of verse or prose fiction first published originally in the United Kingdom during the two years preceding the year in which the Award is given which is, in the opinion of the judges, of the greatest literary merit. To be eligible for the prize the volume of verse or prose fiction in question must be by a writer who is: (a) not more than forty years old at the date of publication, (b) a citizen of the United Kingdom and Colonies, of any other Commonwealth state, of the Republic of Ireland or of the Republic of South Africa. There are three judges, who are reviewers of poetry or fiction as the case may be, and they are nominated each year by the editors or literary editors of newspapers and magazines which regularly publish such reviews. Faber & Faber invite nominations from such editors and literary editors. No submissions for the prize are to be made. The 1987 prize was awarded to Guy Vanderhaeghe for his volume of short stories *Man Descending* (The Bodley Head, UK). Enquiries to Faber & Faber Ltd, 3 Queen Sq, London WC1N 3AU, UK

Antonio **Feltrinelli** Prize*
Each year the Lincei Academy (the National Italian Academy of Sciences) awards Antonio Feltrinelli prizes for accomplishment in the various branches of sciences, humanities, and literature. These prizes were instituted by an Italian businessman who died in 1942 and bequeathed his fortune to the Academy for the purpose of 'rewarding toil, study, intelligence . . . those men who with greater success distinguished themselves with high achievements in art and science, since they are the true benefactors of their own country as well as of all humanity'. The literature award is granted every five years and the amount varies. Enquiries to Accademia Nazionale dei Lincei, Via della Lungara 10, I-00165 Rome, Italy

French Language Prize
Established 1914 to recognize contributions made to the French language. The prize is in the form of medals. Awarded annually. Enquiries to Académie Française, Institut de France, 23 quai de Conti, F-75006 Paris, France

Rómulo **Gallegos** International Novel Prize*
The prize was established in 1965 by the National Institute of Culture and Fine Arts of the Republic of Venezuela. Originally instituted to mark the 80th anniversary of the birth of the illustrious author Rómulo Gallegos, which was celebrated in August 1964, the first award was made in 1967, the 400th anniversary of the founding of Caracas — birthplace of the novelist. Competition is open to any writer from Latin America, Spain or the Philippines whose novel is written in Spanish and has been published originally in one of the countries of the above designated areas. The amount of the prize is approximately $22,223 and will be granted every five years — the next award to be in 1987. Enquiries to Consejo Nacional de la Cultura, Premio Internacional de Novela 'Rómulo Gallegos', Apdo 50995, Caracas 105, Venezuela or Centro de Estudios Latinoamericanos 'Rómulo Gallegos', Apdo 55667, Caracas 1070A, Venezuela

German Peace Prize
The Peace Prize of the German Book Trade (Friedenspreis des Deutschen Buchhandels) is awarded annually during the Frankfurt Book Fair. The prize is supported by the Börsenverein des Deutschen Buchhandels (organization of the German Book Trade) and is awarded without regard to nationality, race or creed. Prize of 25,000 DM since 1979. Enquiries to Börsenverein des Deutschen Buchhandels eV, Friedenspreisarchiv, Grosser Hirschgraben 17-21, Postfach 100442, D-6000 Frankfurt am Main 1, Federal Republic of Germany

The **German Youth** Book Award
The German Youth Book Award is given by the Federal Ministry for Youth, Family, Woman and Health. The selection of the books and the arrangements for granting the award are in the hands of the Arbeitskreis für Jugendliteratur eV, a body in which the organizations concerned with promoting good books for the young in Germany are represented. The selection is restricted to books published in the German language, primarily books from the Federal Republic of Germany, Austria and Switzerland (translations included). The rules for the award have been altered periodically. The award consists of a total of four prizes, each 10,000 DM, which can be awarded for picture-books, fiction, non-fiction and for appreciation of outstanding achievement. In 1987 the prizes were awarded to David McKee for *Du hast angefangen! Nein, du!*, translated by Rolf Inhauser (Verlag Sauerländer, Switzerland); Achim Bröger for *Oma und ich*, illustrated by Nell Graber (Verlag Nagel & Kimche, Switzerland); Inger Edelfeldt for *Briefe an die Königin der Nacht*, translated by Birgitta Kicherer (Spectrum Verlag, Federal Republic of Germany); Huynh Quang Nhuong for *Mein verlorenes Land*, translated by Helga Pfetsch, illustrated by Jub Mönster (Verlag Sauerländer, Switzerland) and Charlotte Kerner for *Lise, Atomphysikerin* (Verlag Beltz & Gelberg, Federal Republic of Germany) (shared). Enquiries to Arbeitskreis für Jugendliteratur eV, Elisabethstr 15, D-8000 Munich 40, Federal Republic of Germany

Grand Prix de la Francophonie
Established in 1986 by the Government of Canada in collaboration with the Académie Française. The Government of Canada donated C$400,000 as a founding sum with the expectation that other countries, organizations and groups would make further contributions. The prize is to reward the work of a French-speaking writer who has contributed in an outstanding manner to the upholding and exemplification of the French language. The prize can also be for literary or philosophical work which individually or collectively has assured the regeneration of the French language in the fields of science, technology or information. Annual award of 400,000 French francs. Enquiries to Académie Française, Institut de France, 23 quai de Conti, F-75006 Paris, France

Grand Prix des Biennales Internationales de Poésie, see International Grand Prix for Poetry

Grand Prize for the Dissemination of the French Language
For work contributing to the dissemination of the French language. Monetary prize awarded annually. Enquiries to Académie Française, Institut de France, 23 quai de Conti, F-75006 Paris, France

'The **Guardian**' Award for Children's Fiction
Instituted in 1967 and awarded annually. The prize of £500 (subject to revision) is given for an outstanding work of fiction for children by a citizen of The Commonwealth. The 1987 prize was awarded to James Aldridge for *The True Story of Spit MacPhee* (Viking Kestrel, UK). Enquiries to Literary Editor, The Guardian, 119 Farringdon Rd, London EC1R 3ER, UK

'The **Guardian**' Fiction Prize
Instituted in 1965 and awarded annually. The prize of £1,000 is given for a novel published by a citizen of the Commonwealth and is intended to encourage ambitious and original work. The 1987 winner was Peter Benson for *The Levels* (Constable, UK) and a runner-up was nominated: Ian Sinclair for *White Chappell, Scarlet Tracings* (Goldmark Press, UK). Enquiries to Literary Editor, The Guardian, 119 Farringdon Rd, London EC1R 3ER, UK

Wilhelm **Heinse** Medal for Literature in Essay Form
Founded in 1978 and awarded annually. The winner in 1986 was Werner Haftmann. Enquiries to Akademie der Wissenschaften und der Literatur, Geschwister-Schollstr 2, D-6500 Mainz, Federal Republic of Germany

Rafael **Heliodoro Valle** Prize
Founded in 1976 to reward an especially notable writer (in odd-numbered years — in even-numbered years to an historian for research work and synthesis). The candidate must have been born in Latin America, be aged over 50, and the work written in Spanish or Portuguese. 2,000,000 pesos prize. Enquiries to Instituto de Investigaciones Bibliográficas, Centro Cultural, Ciudad Universitaria, Delegación Coyoacán, 04510 México, DF, Mexico

Hemingway Award, see The Ritz Paris Hemingway Award

Hérédia Prize
Monetary award given in alternate years to (1) a Latin American writer for a piece of prose or poetry written in French, (2) the author of a collection of printed sonnets. Enquiries to Académie Française, Institut de France, 23 quai de Conti, F-75006 Paris, France

The Historical Novel Prize in Memory of Georgette **Heyer**
Established in 1977 for previously unpublished outstanding historical novel written in English. The novel should be set pre-1939 and have a minimum length of 40,000 words. Annual award of £2,000 and the guarantee of hardback and paperback publication. No award was made in 1987 as the required standard was not reached. Enquiries to The Bodley Head, 32 Bedford Sq, London WC1B 3EL, UK or Transworld Publishers (Corgi & Bantam Books) Ltd, 61-63 Uxbridge Rd, Ealing, London W5 5SA, UK

David **Higham** Prize for Fiction
Founded 1975. For the best first novel or book of short stories, in the opinion of the judges, written in English by a citizen of The Commonwealth, Republic of Ireland, Pakistan or Republic of South Africa. Prize of £1,000 awarded annually. Awarded in 1987 to Adam Zameenzad for *The Thirteenth House* (Heinemann, UK). Enquiries to Book Trust, Book House, 45 East Hill, Wandsworth, London SW18 2QZ, UK

Clarence L Holte Literary Prize
Founded in 1977. Awarded for published writings of excellence in literature and the humanities making important contributions to the cultural heritage of Africa and the African Diaspora. The prize is biennial. Enquiries to Dr Ronald A Wells, Phelps Stokes Fund, 10 East 87th St, New York, NY 10128, USA

The Hugo Awards*
Established 1953 as Science Fiction Achievement Awards for the best science fiction writing in several categories. Chrome-plated rocket ship model awarded annually. Enquiries to c/o Howard DeVore, 4705 Weddel St, Dearborn Heights, MI 48125, USA

Alice Hunt Bartlett Prize
Established in 1966 and awarded annually. £500 prize for a published collection of poetry, not less than 20 poems or 400 lines. Special consideration is given to younger or newly emerging poets. Closing date for entries each year is 28 February. The 1987 award went to Helen Dunmore for *The Sea Skaters* (Bloodaxe, UK). Enquiries to The Secretary, The Poetry Society, 21 Earls Court Sq, London SW5 9DE, UK

International French Friendship Prize
For poetry written in French by a foreigner. Awarded biennially. Enquiries to Société des Poètes Français, Hôtel de Massa, 38 rue du Faubourg St Jacques, F-75014 Paris, France

International Grand Prize for Poetry
For poetry by a living author. 100,000 Belgian francs awarded biennially. Entries are judged by an international jury of 15 and submissions are not invited. Enquiries to La Maison Internationale de Poésie, 95 ave des Ortolans, B-1170 Brussels, Belgium

International Publications Cultural Award*
Established in 1966. Awarded to books or periodical publications published in a European language in Japan which contribute to raising the level of world culture or to increasing understanding of Japan. The 'Grand Prix' is awarded by the Foreign Minister and special prizes are awarded by the Japan Foundation, the Mainichi Newspaper, the Japan Broadcasting Corporation and the Publishers Association for Cultural Exchange. Enquiries to Secretary, Publishers Association for Cultural Exchange, 1-2-1 Sarugaku-cho, Chiyoda-ku, Tokyo 101, Japan

Irish American Cultural Institute Literary Awards*
Established 1966. For writers in the Irish or English language. Awards total US$10,000 for each language in alternate years. The awards in 1987 were for writers in English. Enquiries to Irish American Cultural Institute, 683 Osceola Ave, St Paul, MN 55105, USA

Irish Poetry Award, see Prize for Poetry in Irish

The Jerusalem Prize
This international prize of $5,000 was established in 1963 and is awarded during the Jerusalem International Book Fair which is held every two years. The award is made to an author or philosopher whose life's work has been devoted to the idea of 'The Freedom of the Individual in Society'. In 1987 the winner was John Coetzee. Enquiries to Zev Birger, Chairman and Managing Director, Jerusalem International Book Fair, 212 Jaffa Rd, PO Box 1241, Jerusalem 91012, Israel

Jewish Chronicle — Harold H Wingate Book Awards, see H H Wingate Prize

Stanislas Julien Prize*
For the best work related to China. Monetary prize. Awarded annually. Enquiries to Academie des Inscriptions et Belles Lettres, 23 quai de Conti, F-75006 Paris, France

Kalinga Prize*
This prize, awarded annually by UNESCO, was established in 1951 by the Kalinga Foundation Trust, for the dual purpose of recognizing outstanding interpretation of science to the general public and of strengthening scientific and cultural links between India and other nations. The recipient of the prize is selected by an international jury and may be anyone who has contributed to the promotion of the public understanding of science and technology. The winner receives a cash prize of £1,000. The award takes its name from an ancient empire of the Indian subcontinent, which was conquered in the third century BC by the Emperor Asoka, who was so appalled by the cost of his conquest in terms of human life and suffering that he swore never to wage war again. Enquiries to UNESCO SC/SER/SCW, 7 pl de Fontenoy, F-75700 Paris, France

Gottfried Keller Prize
Founded in 1921 by Martin Bodmer for Swiss and other writers who have honoured the Swiss spirit. Now biennial prize of 15,000 Swiss francs. Enquiries to Martin-Bodmer-Stiftung, 1 route du Guignard, CH-1223 Cologny-Geneva, Switzerland

Kraszna-Krausz Awards*
Founded in 1985 in an interim form with prize money totalling £5,000, the Awards will ultimately result in substantial prizes benefiting from the generosity of Andor Kraszna-Krausz, founder of Focal Press, who has arranged for the bulk of his estate to pass on to a Trust established to run the Awards. Prizes are given for literature making an outstanding, original or lasting contribution to the art and practice of audiovisual media (published books and articles, original manuscripts and other media — including audiovisual material — may all qualify for consideration as 'literature' in the spirit of acknowledging how new media and print are becoming inseparable). The first award, for books on photography, was made in 1986 and shared by Bernard F Stehle for *Incurably Romantic* (Temple University Press, USA), Lennart Nilsson, Jan Lindberg, Stig Nordfeldt and Kjell Lindquist for *Kroppens Försvar* (Human Body's Defence) (Bonnier Fakta, Sweden), and Ben Maddow for *Let Truth be the Prejudice: W Eugene Smith — His Life and Photographs* (Aperture, USA). Enquiries to John Chittock OBE, Kraszna-Krausz Foundation, 37 Gower St, London WC1E 6HH, UK

Allen Lane Award*
Established in 1985 in memory of the founder of Penguin Books fifty years before. An annual prize of £2,000 is awarded to a Commonwealth author for a first book in the area of literature or history which best exemplifies the spirit of Allen Lane. Paperback publication is guaranteed by Penguin of the book, which must already have been published in hardback by Hamish Hamilton, Michael Joseph or Viking. The 1987 award went to John Hooper for *The Spaniards* (Viking, UK). Enquiries to Penguin Books Ltd, 27 Wrights Lane, London W8 5TZ, UK

Literary Critics' Grand Prize
For the best work of literary criticism or literary history. Established 1959. 3,000 French francs, awarded annually. Awarded in 1986 to Jean Blot for *Gontcharov* (Age d'Homme, Switzerland). Enquiries to Association internationale des Critiques littéraires, 58 rue Claude Bernard, F-75005 Paris, France

John Llewellyn Rhys Memorial Prize
Established in 1941 by the widow of an airman killed on active service who was awarded the Hawthornden Prize posthumously. For a 'memorable work' by a Commonwealth citizen who was under 35 at the time of its publication. Prize of £500 awarded annually for a book published in English in the year of the award. Entries should be received by 31 July of the year of the award. The 1987 prize was awarded to Jeanette Winterson for *The Passion* (Heinemann, UK). Enquiries to Book Trust, Book House, 45 East Hill, Wandsworth, London SW18 2QZ, UK

Enid McLeod Prize
Founded 1981. An annual prize for the book judged to have contributed most to Franco-British understanding. Awarded in 1986 to Piers Paul Read for *The Free Frenchman* (Alison Press/Secker & Warburg, UK). Enquiries to Executive Secretary, The Franco-British Society, Room 636, Linen Hall, 162-168 Regent St, London W1R 5TB, UK

Malaparte Prize*
The prize, worth 3,000,000 lire, was awarded in 1985 to Nadine Gordimer in recognition of her achievement as a novelist. Enquiries to Associazione Amici di Capri, Villa Mura, Via Castello, Capri, Italy

Mandat des Poètes Prize*
Founded in 1950 by Pierre Béarn, to aid a French-language poet of talent, young or old, in time of need. Awarded annually. Enquiries to Pierre Béarn, 60 rue Monsieur-le-Prince, F-75006 Paris, France

Katherine Mansfield Menton Memorial Prize
Instituted 1959. Two prizes awarded for published collections of short stories, one English and one French. 10,000 francs each. Next award probably 1988, the 100th anniversary of Katherine Mansfield's birth. The 1984 English award went to Jane Gardam for *The Pangs of Love* (Hamish Hamilton/Abacus, UK) and the French award to Michel Grisolia for *L'Homme Devant le Square* (J-C Lattès, France). Enquiries to The Secretary, PEN English Centre, 7 Dilke St, London SW3 4JE, UK (Enquiries regarding the French short story to General Secretary, PEN Club français, 6 rue François Miron, F-75004 Paris, France — marked Prix Menton)

Médicis Essay Prize*
Established 1970. For the best essay in French, including translated writing, appearing during the preceding year. Monetary prize. Awarded annually. In 1986 the winner was *Flaubert's Parrot* by Julian Barnes, translated by Jean Guiloineau as *Le Perroquet de Flaubert* (Stock, France). Enquiries to Le Prix Médicis de l'Essai, c/o Francine Mallet, 25 rue Dombasle, F-75015 Paris, France

Médicis Foreign Prize*
For the best foreign novel appearing in French during the preceding year. Monetary prize. Awarded annually. In 1986 the award went to John Hawkes for *Adventures in the*

Skin Trade/Aventures dans le commerce des peaux en Alaska (Le Seuil, France). Enquiries to Le Prix Médicis étranger, c/o Francine Mallet, 25 rue Dombasle, F-75015 Paris, France

Ramón Menéndez Pidal Prize*
For an outstanding work in the fields of Spanish linguistics or Spanish literature. 30,000 pesetas. Awarded biennially. Enquiries to Real Academia Española, Felipe IV 4, 28014 Madrid, Spain

N C R Book Award for Non-Fiction
Established in 1987 and sponsored by NCR Ltd for an outstanding work of non-fiction (other than academic, children's or practical books). Entries must have been written in English by a citizen of The Commonwealth or the Republic of Ireland and have been published in the United Kingdom for the first time in the twelve months preceding the year ending 31 March. The first award, to be administered on behalf of NCR by the Publishers Publicity Circle, is being made in 1988, the winning author receiving £25,000, with £1,500 going to each of the three remaining short-listed authors. Enquiries to The Administrator, NCR Book Award, 206 Marylebone Rd, London NW1 6LY, UK

The Shiva Naipaul Memorial Prize
Founded 1985 and awarded annually. A prize of £1,000 is given to an English-language writer of any nationality under 35 years of age best able to describe a visit to a foreign place or people. The award will not be for travel writing in the conventional sense, but for the most acute and profound observation of cultures and/or scenes (which could be within the writer's native country) evidently alien to the writer. The winning entry will be published in 'The Spectator'. Submissions should not previously have been published and should not be more than 4,000 words. The winner in 1986 was Hilary Mandel. Enquiries to The Spectator, 56 Doughty St, London WC1N 2LL, UK

Neustadt International Prize for Literature
'World Literature Today', an international literary quarterly, established in 1969 a biennial award for distinguished and continuing artistic achievement in the fields of poetry, drama or fiction. A new international jury of twelve is appointed for each successive award by the editor in consultation with the editorial board. Each juror presents one candidate for the prize. A majority (seven) of the jury must be present for the deliberations and the final voting. Representative selections of a candidate's work must be available to the jury in either French or English translation. Announcement of the winner is made in February, and the award is officially presented at The University of Oklahoma, Norman, Oklahoma, every other year. The prize is an award certificate, a replica of an eagle's feather in silver, and US$25,000. 'World Literature Today' dedicates one issue to the recipient. The University of Oklahoma Press will seriously consider the publication of a book by or on the winner. Prize not open to application. Enquiries to World Literature Today, 630 Parrington Oval, Room 110, Norman, OK 73019, USA

Martinus Nijhoff Award for Translators
Established 1953. For translation of literary work into and from Dutch. 15,000 Dutch florins. Awarded annually. Enquiries to Prince Bernhard Foundation, Herengracht 476, 1017 CB Amsterdam, Netherlands

Nobel Prize for Literature
Of all the literary prizes, the Nobel Prize for literature is the highest in value and in honour bestowed. It is one of the five prizes founded by Alfred Bernhard Nobel (1833-1896); the other four awards are for physics, chemistry, physiology or medicine, and peace. By the terms of Nobel's will, the prize for literature is to be given to the person 'who shall have produced in the field of literature the most distinguished work of an idealistic tendency'. It consists of a gold medal, a diploma and a sum of money; the amount in 1987 was over US$330,000. The award is administered by the Swedish Academy in Stockholm and official presentation is made on December 10, the anniversary of Nobel's death. No one may apply for the Nobel Prize; there is no competition. It is awarded to an author usually for his total literary output and not for any single work. Awarded in 1986 to Joseph Brodsky (USSR, now citizen of US). Enquiries to Swedish Academy, Källargränd 4, Börshuset, S-111 29 Stockholm, Sweden

The Noma Award for Publishing in Africa
Established in 1979 by Shoichi Noma, Honorary Chairman of the Japanese publishing company Kodansha Ltd, for African writers whose work in its original form has been published in Africa. The annual award of US$3,000 is given for an outstanding work in any of the following categories (1) scholarly or academic, (2) children's books, (3) literature and creative writing (including fiction, drama or poetry). Awarded in 1986 to Antonio Jacinto (Angola) for *Sobreviver em Tarrafal de Santiago* (Instituto Nacional do Livro e do Disco, Luanda). Enquiries to The African Book Publishing Record, PO Box 56, Oxford OX1 3EL, UK

The Noma Literacy Prize*
Established by the late Shoichi Noma, this is one of four UNESCO prizes for meritorious work in the field of literacy. Annual award of US$5,000. Enquiries to UNESCO, Literacy Division, 7 pl de Fontenoy, F-75700 Paris, France

Nordic Council Literary Prize
Established 1962. To an individual author for a current work of literature in one of the Nordic languages, including Faeroese, Greenlandic and Sami. 125,000 Danish crowns. Awarded annually. No submissions for the prize are to be made. Enquiries to Nordic Council, Swedish Delegation, Box 2082, S-103 12 Stockholm, Sweden

'Observer' Teenage Fiction Prize
Founded 1981 for the best fiction work for teenage readers written by a citizen of The Commonwealth, Republic of Ireland, Pakistan or Republic of South Africa. £600 awarded annually. The winner in 1986 was Margaret Mahy (New Zealand) for *Memory* (Dent, UK). Enquiries to Sue Matthias, Observer Magazine, Chelsea Bridge House, Queenstown Rd, London SW8 4NN, UK

Odd Fellows (Manchester Unity) Social Concern Book Awards
Established 1977. £2,000 awarded annually for a book or pamphlet of not less than 10,000 words in an area of social concern (to be specified each year). Entries must first have appeared in English and been written by citizens of The Commonwealth, Republic of Ireland, Pakistan or Republic of South Africa. Enquiries to Book Trust, Book House, 45 East Hill, Wandsworth, London SW18 2QZ, UK

Pavol Országh-Hviezdoslav Prize
Awarded annually by the Union of Slovak Writers to outstanding translators of Slovak literature abroad during the preceding year. Enquiries to Zväz slovenských spisovateľov, 81508 Bratislava, ul Obrancov mieru 14, Czechoslovakia

Serbian P E N Centre Prizes
First awarded in 1987 for the best book of the year by a foreign author which has been translated into Serbo-Croation for the first time and published in Yugoslavia (provided it has been published in the original language within the last decade). Novels, collections of stories, poems, literary essays or dramas are eligible. The prizes are a medal, a special issue of the journal 'Pismo' devoted to the winning author, and honorary membership of the Serbian PEN Centre. Enquiries to Yugoslav PEN Club, Serbian Centre, YU-11000 Belgrade, Francuska br 7, Yugoslavia

Yugoslav P E N Club Award
For the translation of a book from and into languages spoken or used in Yugoslavia. Monetary prize. Enquiries to Yugoslav PEN Club, Serbian Centre, YU-11000 Belgrade, Francuska br 7, Yugoslavia

Hungarian P E N Club Medal*
For translation of Hungarian literary work into foreign languages. Awarded when merited. Enquireis to Hungarian PEN Club, H-1051 Budapest V, Vörösmarty tér 1, Hungary

Polish P E N Club Prizes*
Founded by Robert Graves for best translations of foreign poetry and prose into Polish, and of Polish literature into foreign languages. Three awards 20,000 zlotys each. Awarded annually. Enquiries to Polish PEN Club, Palac Kultury i Nauki, 00-901 Warsaw, Poland

Leopoldo Panero Prize*
For poetry. 100,000 pesetas. Awarded annually. Enquiries to Instituto de Cooperación Iberoamericana, Ave de los Reyes Católicos 4, Ciudad Universitaria, 28040 Madrid, Spain

Pegasus Prize for Literature
Established in 1977 and sponsored by Mobil Oil Corporation affiliates to encourage the recognition of distinguished works from countries whose literature is rarely translated into English. Usually awarded annually. Prize of approximately US$3,000, a medal, translation into English and publication by the Louisiana State University Press (USA). The 1987 winner was Ismail Marahimin (Indonesia) for *And the War is Over*, translated from Bahasa Indonesia by John McGlynn. Enquiries to Mobil Oil Corporation, 150 East 42nd St, New York, NY 10017-5666, USA

Lorne Pierce Medal
Established 1926. For achievement and conspicuous merit in the field of imaginative or critical literature, in English or French. Medal and C$1,500. Awarded biennially. Enquiries to Royal Society of Canada, 344 Wellington St, Ottawa, Ontario K1A ON4, Canada

Pilgrim Award
Established 1970 and awarded annually by a committee of the Science Fiction Research Association for outstanding contributions made over a period of time to scholarship relating to the study of science fiction and modern fantasy. Enquiries to Science Fiction Research Association Inc, Box 3186, The College of Wooster, Wooster, OH 44691, USA

Planeta Prize
Established 1952. For the best unpublished novel. Open to writers of Spanish-speaking countries. 15,000,000 pesetas, and publication by Planeta. Awarded annually. Enquiries to Editorial Planeta SA, Córcega 273, Barcelona 8, Spain

Pluto Crime Award*
Founded 1985. Awarded every two years for the best new crime novel with a radical political edge written in English. £2,000. The first winner was John Lear for *Death in Leningrad*. Enquiries to Pluto Press, The Works, 105A Torriano Ave, London NW5 2RX, UK

Polish Society of Authors (Zaiks) Prizes
For best translations of Polish literature into foreign languages. Two or three prizes, 100,000 zlotys each. Awarded annually. Enquiries to Stowarzyszenie Autorów Zaiks, ul Hipoteczna 2, 00-092 Warsaw, Poland

Poetry in Irish, see Prize for Poetry in Irish

Prince Pierre de Monaco Prize for Literature
Restricted to French-speaking writers. For the entire literary work of one author. 40,000 French francs awarded annually. No applications accepted. Enquiries to Fondation Prince Pierre de Monaco, 4 rue des Iris, Monte Carlo 98000, Monaco

Prize for Poetry in Irish
Established 1962. To the author of best book of poetry in the Irish language (Gaelic) published in the previous three years. IR£1,000. Next award 1989. Enquiries to Arts Council/An Chomhairle Ealaíon, 70 Merrion Sq, Dublin 2, Republic of Ireland

Regina Medal
Established 1959. For recognition of continued distinguished contributions to children's literature. Silver Medal. Awarded annually. Won in 1987 by Betsy Byars. Enquiries to Catholic Library Association, 461 West Lancaster Ave, Haverford, PA 19041, USA

Lucien de Reinach Prize
Awarded every other year for the best original work written in French in the most recent two years on an overseas subject. Enquiries to Bernard Chenot, Académie des Sciences Morales et Politiques, Institut de France, 23 quai de Conti, F-75006 Paris, France

Felix Restrepo Prize*
For distinguished contributions to philology. 100,000 Colombian pesos and publication of the work. Awarded annually. Enquiries to Academia Colombiana, Apdo Aéreo 13922, Bogotá, Colombia

Alfonso Reyes Prize*
Founded 1973. Awarded by the Federal Government of Mexico to an author of any nationality for his or her literary output on the study of the works of Alfonso Reyes or on Mexico. 200,000 Mexican pesos annually. Enquiries to Sociedad Alfonsina Internacional, Ave Transmisiones 42, Lomas de San Angel Inn, México 01790, DF, Mexico

The **Ritz Paris** Hemingway Award*
Founded 1984 under the patronage of His Majesty Hassanal Bolkiah, the Sultan of Brunei Darussalam. Awarded annually to commemorate the long personal association of Ernest Hemingway with the Hotel Ritz in Paris and to promote worldwide literary excellence. US$50,000 is given for the best novel of the year published in English, and US$100,000 in scholarships and grants to individuals, organizations and institutions that best further the study of the life and works of Ernest Hemingway. Nominations are not accepted from publishers nor may applications for the prize be made. The 1986 winner was Marguerite Duras (France) for *L'Amant*. Enquiries to The Executive Director, The Ritz Paris Hemingway Award, 75 Rockefeller Plaza Suite 1809, New York, NY 10019, USA

Rose of French Poets Prize*
Established 1949. For a foreign poet who has celebrated France in his verse. Medal awarded every two years. Enquiries to Société des Poètes Français, Hôtel de Massa, 38 rue du Faubourg St Jacques, F-75014 Paris, France

Rotterdam International Poetry Prize*
Founded in 1979 to honour a poet who is a political prisoner due to his or her literary work. The award must be effective in some way for the poet or the poet's family. Awarded in 1986 to Irini Ratushinskaya (USSR). Enquiries to Rotterdamse Kunststichting, Poetry International, Westersingel 20, 3014 GP Rotterdam, Netherlands

Salon de l'Enfance et de la Jeunesse Grand Literary Prize*
Founded in 1953 with the object of encouraging authors towards the betterment of children's literature. 4,000 French francs is awarded for an original work in French which has been published in the preceding year and which is intended for children in the 10-12 years age group; the entries are judged mainly by a jury of 10 French children in this group. A further 2,000 French francs may be given for an outstanding work of science fiction. Enquiries to Grand Prix de Littérature du Salon de l'Enfance et de la Jeunesse, 11 rue St-Florentin, F-75008 Paris, France

Science Fiction Achievement Awards, see The Hugo Awards

W H Smith & Son Literary Award
Established 1959. Given to an author from The Commonwealth whose book, written in English and published in the United Kingdom, makes the most outstanding contribution to literature. Award of £4,000 annually. The award for 1987 went to Elizabeth Jennings for her *Collected Poems 1953–1985* (Carcanet). Enquiries to W H Smith & Son Ltd, Strand House, 7 Holbein Place, London SW1W 8NR, UK

'La **Sonrisa** Vertical' Prize
Founded in 1978 in homage to Lopez Barbadillo. Awarded annually for the best erotic novel written in Spanish or another language of the Spanish State. The prize is 500,000 pesetas advance on the work prior to publication, together with an artistic object. The 1986 award went to Josep Bras for *El bajel de las vaginas voraginosas* (Tusquets Editores, Spain). Enquiries to La Sonrisa Vertical, Tusquets Editores, Calle Iradier 24 bajos, Barcelona 08017, Spain

'**Stand Magazine**' International Short Story Competition
Founded in 1983, and now in association with the Harrogate International Festival, to encourage and promote the work of new or unknown short-story writers. Awarded biennially: next competition begins autumn 1988. First prize of £1,000, further prizes totalling £1,000 and runners-up prizes of one-year subscription to magazine. Please send stamped-addressed envelope or international reply coupon. Enquiries to Stand Magazine, 179 Wingrove Rd, Newcastle upon Tyne NE4 9DA, UK

'The **Times** Educational Supplement' Information Book Awards
Instituted 1972. For outstandingly good information books originating in any Commonwealth country. Two awards are offered for a book for children up to the age of 9 and for a book for those aged between 10 and 16, both awards for £500. The judges may award a further £250 to the illustrator of either or both books. Enquiries to Literary Editor, The Times Educational Supplement, Priory House, St John's Lane, London EC1M 4BX, UK

'The **Times**'/**Jonathan Cape** Young Writers Prize*
Founded 1984. A prize of £5,000 and publication is the annual award to a writer under 30 years of age for an exciting and original work of fiction or non-fiction written in English. Enquiries to Jonathan Cape Ltd, 32 Bedford Sq, London WC1B 3EL, UK

The Betty **Trask** Awards
Established in 1983, the Awards are for the benefit of authors under 35 years of age who are Commonwealth citizens and are given for a first novel (published or unpublished) of a romantic or traditional nature. First awarded in 1984 the main prize is £12,500, with additional travel awards of £1,000 each. All winners are required to use the money for a period or periods of foreign travel with a view to increasing their experience and knowledge for future literary benefit. The 1987 main prize was awarded to James Maw for *Hard Luck* (Quartet Books, UK). Enquiries to The Society of Authors, 84 Drayton Gardens, London SW10 9SD, UK

Triennial Prize for Bibliography
The International League of Antiquarian Booksellers (ILAB) awards a prize, every three years, of US$1,000 to the author of the best work, published or unpublished, of learned bibliography, of research into the history of the book or typography, or a book of general interest on the subject. The competition is open, without restriction, but entries must be submitted in a language which is universally read. An already published work is eligible only if it has an imprint bearing a date within the three years preceding the closing date for submission. Enquiries to Dr Frieder Kocher-Benzing, Rathenaustr 21, D-7000 Stuttgart 1, Federal Republic of Germany

H H **Wingate** Prize
Originally instituted in 1977 by the 'Jewish Chronicle' and the Wingate Foundation. Awarded to the book which best stimulates an interest in and awareness of Jewish concern among a wider reading public. Books must be published in English and authors normally resident in Israel, The Commonwealth, Republic of South Africa, Pakistan or the Republic of Ireland are eligible. £3,000 is awarded annually. Enquiries to Book Trust, Book House, 45 East Hill, Wandsworth, London SW18 2QZ, UK

The **World of Books** Prizes
Established in 1988. One prize for poetry and one for prose awarded annually to authors who live in the European Community or who write in one of the languages of the Community members. Enquiries to The World of Books Ltd, Friedrich-Ebert-Str 80, D-6520 Worms, Federal Republic of Germany

Abraham **Woursell** Prize (University of Vienna)*
Instituted 1965. For young creative writers. US$25,000 annually for five years. Enquiries to Selection Committee Chairman, Faculty of Philosophy, University of Vienna, Austria

'Yorkshire Post' Book of the Year Award
Instituted 1964 for the best book published each year in the United Kingdom (although the author need not be British). Translations, reissues and works of a strictly scientific or technical nature are excluded. First prize of £1,000 for Book of the Year in 1986 went to Robert Rhodes James for *Anthony Eden* (Weidenfeld & Nicolson, UK). In addition there are Best First Work awards to new authors; in 1986 the £800 first prize went to John Charmley for *Duff Cooper: the authorised biography* (Weidenfeld & Nicolson, UK). (There are also special annual awards for books selected to advance the popular appreciation of art and of music; in 1986 the awards were of £500 each.) Enquiries to The Organizer, Book of the Year Awards, Yorkshire Post Newspapers Ltd, PO Box 168, Wellington St, Leeds LS1 1RF, UK

'Young Observer' Teenage Fiction Prize, see 'Observer' Teenage Fiction Prize

The ISBN System

Background

The question of the need and feasibility of an international numbering system for books was first discussed at the third International Conference on Book Market Research and Rationalization in the Book Trade held in November 1966 in Berlin. At that time a number of publishers and book distributors in Europe were considering the use of computers in order processing and inventory control and it was evident that a pre-requisite of an efficient machine system was a unique and simple identification number for a published item.
The system which fulfilled this requirement and which became known as the International Standard Book Number (ISBN) System developed out of the book numbering system introduced into the United Kingdom in 1967.
In a report to the British Publishers Association, Professor F G Foster of the London School of Economics stated that there was '. . . a clear need for the introduction into the book trade of standard numbering . . . and substantial benefits would accrue to all parties therefrom'. After further study and deliberation, a detailed plan for standard numbering was produced. At the same time, the Technical Committee Documentation of the International Standards Organization (ISO/TC 46) set up a working party (with the British Standards Institution acting as secretariat) to investigate the possibility of adapting the British system for international use.
A meeting was held in London in 1968 with representatives from Denmark, France, Federal Republic of Germany, Eire, the Netherlands, Norway, the United Kingdom, the United States of America and an observer from UNESCO. Other countries contributed written suggestions and expressions of interest. A report of the meeting was circulated to all countries belonging to the ISO. Comments on this report and subsequent proposals were considered at meetings held in Berlin and Stockholm in 1969.
As a result of these meetings there emerged ISO Recommendation 2108 which sets out the principles and procedure for international standard book numbering. The purpose of the ISO Recommendation is to coordinate and standardize internationally the use of book numbers so that an International Standard Book Number (ISBN) identifies one title or edition of a title from one specific publisher and is unique to that edition.
The ISBN applies in the main to books — for which the system was originally created — but, by extension, it may be used for any item produced by publishers or collected by libraries.

How the International Standard Book Number (ISBN) is Built Up

Every International Standard Book Number (ISBN) consists of ten digits and whenever it is printed it is preceded by the letters ISBN. (Note: In those countries where the Latin alphabet is not used, an abbreviation in the characters of the local alphabet may be used in addition to the Latin letters ISBN.)
The ten-digit number is divided into four parts of variable length, each part when printed being separated by a hyphen or space. (Note: Experience suggests that the hyphen is preferable to the space.)
The four parts are as follows:

Part 1. Group Identifier
This part identifies the national, geographic or other similar grouping of publishers.

Part 2. Publisher's Prefix
This part identifies a particular publisher within a group.

Part 3. Title Identifier
This part identifies a particular title or edition of a title published by a particular publisher.

Part 4. Check Digit
This is a single digit at the end of the ISBN which provides an automatic check on the correctness of the ISBN.

Group identifier
Group identifiers are allocated by the International ISBN Agency and a publisher wishing to participate in the ISBN system must belong to a recognized ISBN group. Groups are determined by national, geographic, language or other pertinent considerations. Experience has shown that groups based on national or geographic considerations are the most satisfactory.
The following group identifiers are in use at present:

0 and 1	Australia, English-speaking Canada, New Zealand, Republic of South Africa, UK, USA, Zimbabwe
2	France, French-speaking Belgium, French-speaking Canada, French-speaking Switzerland
3	Austria, German Democratic Republic, Federal Republic of Germany, German-speaking Switzerland
4	Japan
5	Union of Soviet Socialist Republics
7	People's Republic of China
81	India (also 93)
82	Norway
83	Poland
84	Spain, Spanish-speaking South America (partly)
85	Brazil
86	Yugoslavia
87	Denmark
88	Italy
90	Netherlands, Dutch-speaking Belgium
91	Sweden
92	International Publishers (UNESCO)
93	India (also 81)
950	Argentina
951	Finland
955	Sri Lanka
956	Chile
958	Colombia
960	Greece
962	Hong Kong
963	Hungary
965	Israel
967	Malaysia
968	Mexico (also 970)
969	Pakistan
970	Mexico (also 968)
971	Philippines
972	Portugal
974	Thailand
976	Caribbean Community (CARICOM)
977	Egypt
978	Nigeria

524 THE ISBN SYSTEM

979	Indonesia
980	Venezuela
981	Republic of Singapore (also 9971)
982	South Pacific
9963	Cyprus
9964	Ghana
9966	Kenya
9971	Republic of Singapore (also 981)
9973	Tunisia
9976	Tanzania
9977	Costa Rica
9978	Ecuador
9980	Papua New Guinea
9982	Zambia
9983	Gambia
99913	Andorra
99914	Suriname

Publisher's Prefix
The publisher's prefix designates the publisher of a given book. Publishers with a large output of books are assigned a short publisher's prefix; publishers with a small output of books are assigned a longer publisher's prefix.

Title identifier
The title identifier is assigned to a particular title or edition of a title by the publisher from within the range of numbers assigned to him and which will depend upon the length of his publisher's prefix. Title identifiers are normally assigned by the publisher himself. Publishers who assign their own title identifiers may use them to identify titles in the publishing house throughout the planning stages.

Check digit
The 'check digit' is the last digit in an ISBN and is computed as the result of an elaborate calculation on the other nine digits.
This calculation is performed almost instantaneously by an electronic computing device, and is a means of detecting incorrectly transcribed numbers. The check digit is calculated on a modulus 11 with weights 10-2, using X in lieu of 10 where ten would occur as a check digit.
This means that each of the first nine digits of the ISBN — ie excluding the check digit itself — is multiplied by a number ranging from 10 to 2 and the sum of the products thus obtained, plus the check digit, must be divisible, without remainder, by 11. For example:

	Group Identifier		Publisher's Prefix		
ISBN ..	0	8	4	3	6
Weight ..	10	9	8	7	6
Products ..	0 +	72 +	32 +	21 +	36 +

	Title Number			Check Digit
ISBN ..	1	0	7	2	7
Weight ..	5	4	3	2	
Products ..	5 +	0 +	21 +	4 +	7

Total: 198

As 198 can be divided by 11 without remainder 0 8436 1072 7 is a valid International Standard Book Number.

The number of digits in each part; and how to recognize them in an ISBN
The number of digits in each of the identifying parts 1, 2 and 3 is variable, though the total number of digits contained in these parts is always 9. These nine digits together with the check digit bring the total number of digits in an ISBN to ten.
The number of digits in the group identifier will vary according to the likely output of books in a group. Thus groups with an expected large output will get numbers of one or two digits and publishers with an expected large output will get numbers of two or three digits.
Exceptionally, a one-digit number may be assigned to a publisher but it will be appreciated that the assignment of one-digit publisher identifiers greatly reduces the range of possible identifiers in the group.
For ease of reading, the four parts of the ISBN are divided by spaces or hyphens. These spaces or hyphens, however, are not retained in a computer which depends upon the special distribution of ranges of numbers for the recognition of the parts.

Scope of the ISBN

For the purposes of the ISBN system books and other items to be numbered include:

Printed books and pamphlets

Mixed media publications

Other similar media including educational films/video and transparencies

Books on cassettes

Microcomputer software

Electronic publications

– machine-readable tapes (designed to produce readable printout)

– CD RoM etc

Micro-form publications

Braille publications

Maps

Except:
Ephemeral printed materials such as diaries, calendars, advertising matter and the like

Art prints and art folders without title page and text

Sound recordings

Serial publications

Principles and procedures to be observed by the publisher numbering his own publications

A publisher must ensure that a competent person is responsible for the assignment of ISBN and the application of the pertinent regulations. A publisher will be assigned a publisher identifier (publisher's prefix) by the group agency which will determine the range of title identifiers available to him. The number of title identifiers will depend upon the length of the publisher identifier assigned to him. The publisher should ensure that the group agency has as much information as possible about his back lists of books still available, and present and future publication programmes in order that a suitable publisher identifier can be assigned. A publisher is responsible for assigning title identifiers to the individual items that he publishes.
A publisher may wish to incorporate an existing non classifying identification system into his ISBN allocation. This may be arranged provided that such incorporation does not alter the fundamental characteristics of the ISBN system or reduce the amount of numbers available. For example: the publisher must not incorporate digits other than numerals, nor must he incorporate numbers which cause the resulting ISBN to be longer than or shorter than ten digits, nor must the publisher attempt to build in special meanings or hierarchical order to groups of numbers if by so doing he reduces the amount of available numbers in the range allocated to him.

Non-participating publishers

If by choice or for any other reason, a publisher does not accept responsibility for assigning ISBN to his publications, two alternatives are open to the group agency.
1. The group agency can allocate a block of numbers for miscellaneous publishers and number all titles within that block irrespective of the publisher. In such a case the resulting ISBN will not identify the publisher of a specific title. (It is strongly recommended that this procedure should be reserved for publishers who only publish an occasional title and who are never likely to be in a position to assume the responsibility for numbering themselves).
2. The group agency can assume responsibility for assigning a publisher identifier, a block of ISBN associated with that publisher identifier, assign a number to each publication and inform the publisher before publication of the number assigned. In such a case, if the publisher agrees to do so, the ISBN can be printed in the book. It is expected that such a publisher will eventually assume full responsibility for assigning his own ISBN.

Application of ISBN

General
A separate ISBN must be assigned to every different edition of a book, but NOT to an unchanged impression or unchanged reprint of the same book in the same format and by the same publisher. Price changes do not need new ISBN.

Facsimile reprints
A separate ISBN must be assigned to a facsimile reprint produced by a different publisher.

Books in different formats
A separate ISBN must be assigned to the different formats in which a particular title is published. For example: a hardback edition and a paperback edition each receives a separate ISBN. On the same principle, a microform edition receives a separate ISBN.

Loose-leaf publications
If a publication appears in loose-leaf form an ISBN is allocated to identify an edition at a given time. Individual issues of additions or replacement sheets will likewise be given an ISBN.

Multi-volume works
An ISBN must be assigned to the whole set of volumes of a multi-volume work as well as to each individual volume in the set.

Back stock
A publisher is required to number his back stock and publish the ISBN in his catalogues.
He must also print the ISBN in the first available reprint of an item from his back stock.

Collaborative publications
A publication issued as a coedition or joint imprint with other publishers is assigned an ISBN by the publisher in charge of distribution.

Books sold or distributed by agents
According to the principles of the ISBN system, a particular edition, published by a particular publisher receives only one ISBN and this ISBN must be retained no matter where or by whom the book is distributed or sold.
  A book imported by an exclusive distributor or sole agent from an area not yet in the ISBN system and for which therefore no ISBN has been assigned, may be assigned an ISBN by the exclusive distributor.
  A book imported by an exclusive distributor or sole agent to which a new title-page, bearing the imprint of the exclusive distributor, has been added in place of the title page of the original publisher, is to be given a new ISBN by the exclusive distributor or sole agent. The ISBN of the original publisher is also to be given as a related ISBN.
  A book imported by several distributors from an area not yet in the ISBN system and for which, therefore, no ISBN has been assigned, may be assigned an ISBN by the group agency responsible for those distributors.

Publishers with more than one place of publication
A publisher operating in a number of places which are listed together in the imprint of a book will assign only one ISBN to the book. A publisher operating separate and distinct offices or branches in different places may have a publisher identifier for each office or branch. Nevertheless, each book published is to be assigned only one ISBN, the assignment being made by the office or branch responsible for publication.

Register of ISBN's
Every publisher must keep a register of ISBNs that have been assigned to published and forthcoming books. The register is to be kept in numerical sequence giving ISBN, author, title and edition (where appropriate).

ISBN not to be re-used under any circumstances
An ISBN once allocated must not under any circumstances be re-used. This is of the utmost importance to avoid confusion. It is recognized that, owing to clerical errors, numbers will be incorrectly assigned. If this happens, the number must be deleted from the list of usable numbers and must not be assigned to another title. Every publisher will have sufficient numbers in his range for the loss of these numbers to be insignificant. Publishers should advise the group agency of the numbers thus deleted and of the titles to which they were erroneously assigned.

Guidelines for ISBN assignment to software

An ISBN is used to identify a specific software product. If there is more than one version (perhaps versions adapted for different machines, carrier media or language version), each version must have a different ISBN. When a software product is updated, revised or otherwise amended and the changes are sufficiently substantial for the product to be called a new edition (and thus probably the subject of a new launch, or marketing push) then a new ISBN must be allocated. A relaunch of an existing product, even in new packaging, where there is no basic difference in the performance of the new and the old product, does NOT justify a new ISBN, and the original ISBN must not be used.
When software is accompanied by a manual, useful only as an adjunct to the software, and the software needs the manual before it can be operated, and the two items are always sold as a package, one ISBN must be used to cover both items. When two or more items in a software package (as above) can be used separately, or are sold separately as well as together, then
  (i) the package as a whole must have an ISBN
  (ii) each item in the package must have its own ISBN.
ISBNs should be allocated to a software product independent of its physical form, eg if software is only available from a remote database from whence it is downloaded to the customer.
As well as identifying the product itself, an ISBN identifies the publisher or manufacturer; it should not be used to identify a distributor or wholesaler.

Printing of the ISBN

General
The ISBN must appear on the item itself. This is essential for the efficient running of the system.

Printing of ISBN on books
In the case of books, the ISBN must appear whenever possible: On the reverse of the title-page, or, if this is not possible, on the base of the title-page, or, if this too is not possible, at some other conspicuous location in the book. On the base of the spine.
On the back of the cover in 9-point type or larger.
On the back of the dust-jacket, and on the back of any other protective case or wrapper.
The ISBN should always be printed in type large enough to be easily legible (ie not smaller than 9 point).

Printing of ISBN on books in machine readable coding
In the last few years there has been much work done on machine-readable representations of the ISBN. Many books now carry ISBNs in OCR (Optical Character Recognition) form. The rapid, worldwide extension of bar code scanning has brought into prominence the agreement reached between the International Article Numbering Association (EAN) and the International ISBN Agency, which allows the ISBN to be translated into an EAN bar code.
All EAN bar codes start with a national identifier **except** those on books and periodicals. The agreement replaces the usual national identifier with a special 'Bookland' identifier represented by the digits 978 for books and 977 for periodicals. The 978 Bookland/EAN prefix is followed by the first nine digits of the ISBN. The check digit of the ISBN is dropped and replaced by a check digit calculated according to the EAN rules.

Optional 5 digit add-on code
There is an optional 5 digit add-on code which can be used for additional information. In the publishing industry it can be used for price information which may have the following formats:
a) Five digit bar code indicating the price with human readable numbers above the bar code or
b) Five digit bar code indicating the price with no human readable numbers.

Administration of the ISBN System

General
The administration of the ISBN system is carried on at three levels. These are the international, group and publisher levels.

International administration
The international administration of the system is in the hands of the International Standard Book Number Agency which has an Advisory Panel representing the ISO and the publishing and library world. The address of the Interntional Agency is:

  The International Standard Book Number Agency,
  Staatsbibliothek Preussischer Kulturbesitz,
  Potsdamer Str 33, Postfach 1407,
  D-1000 Berlin 30,
  Federal Republic of Germany

The principal functions of the International Agency are:

To supervise the use of the system

To approve the definition and structure of groups

To allocate identifiers to groups

To advise groups on the setting up and functioning of group agencies

To advise group agencies on the allocation of publisher identifiers

To promote the world-wide use of the system

In addition, the International Agency also offers the following services. It will:

Provide a group agency with lists of ISBNs (with computer-generated check digits) for the use of publishers in the group.

Provide international registers of publishers, prefixes and publishers' names.

Provide from information supplied by group agencies a computer printout of lists of publishers' prefixes, names and locations.

Provide from information supplied by group agencies a computer printout of invalid or duplicate ISBNs.

Group administration
Groups are administered by Group Agencies. Within the group there may be several national agencies, eg group 0/1 has separate agencies in USA, United Kingdom, Canada, Australia etc, with the main agency for the whole group in the UK.

The functions of a group agency are:

To manage and administer the affairs of the group.

To handle relations with the International ISBN Agency on behalf of all the publishers in the group.

To decide, in consultation with trade organizations and publishers, the publisher identifier ranges required.

To allocate publishers' prefixes to publishers eligible to join the group and to maintain a register of publishers and their prefixes.

To decide, in consultation with trade organizations and publishers, which publishers shall assign numbers to their own titles and which publishers shall have numbers assigned to their titles by the group agency.

To provide technical advice and assistance to the publishers and to ensure that standards and approved procedures are observed in the group.

To make available a manual of instruction for publishers.

To make available computer printouts of ISBNs to publishers numbering their own books with check digits already calculated. (Such printouts may be obtained from the International Agency on request.)

To validate all ISBNs assigned by publishers numbering their own books and keep a register of them.

To inform publishers of any invalid or duplicate ISBNs assigned by them.

To assign numbers to all publications from those publishers who do not assign their own ISBNs and advise the publishers concerned of ISBNs assigned upon request.

To achieve, thereby, total numbering in the group.

To arrange with book listing and bibliographic agencies for the publication of ISBNs with the titles to which they refer.

To arrange with publishers for the numbering of their back lists and for the publication of these in appropriate trade lists and bibliographies.

To maintain liaison with all elements of the book trade and introduce new publishers to the system.

To assist the trade in the use of the ISBN in computer systems.

The national agencies are:

Andorra
Daniela Sirès, Andorran Standard Book Numbering Agency, National Library of Andorra, Prada Casadet, Andorra la Vella

Argentina
José E Encinas, Cámara Argentina del Libro, Ave Belgrano 1580 – 6° piso, 1093 Buenos Aires

Australia
Senior Librarian, Standard Numbering, National Library of Australia, Canberra, ACT 2600

Austria
H Walter Ess, Hauptverband des Österreichischen Buchhandels, A-1010 Vienna 1, Grünangergasse 4

Belgium (Dutch-speaking)
Netherlands agency

Belgium (French-speaking)
French agency

Brazil
Mrs Selma Mendes Fontes Sodré, Agência Brasileira do ISBN, Biblioteca Nacional, Ave Rio Branco 219/39 – 3° andar, 20042 Rio de Janeiro, RJ

Canada (English-speaking)
Paul McCormick, National Library of Canada, 395 Wellington St, Ottawa, Ontario K1A ON4

Canada (French-speaking)
Ms C Bilodeau, ISBN/BNQ. Bureau du dépôt légal, Bibliothèque nationale du Québec, 1700 rue St-Denis, Montreal, Québec H2X 3K6

Caribbean Community
Carol Collins, Regional ISBN Agency (CARICOM) Caribbean Community Secretariat, PO Box 10827, Georgetown, Guyana

Chile
Héctor Velis Meza, Cámara Chilena del Libro AG, Casilla 13526, Santiago

People's Republic of China
Mrs Sha Hongye, China ISBN Agency, The Press and Publication Administration of the People's Republic of China, 85 Dongsi Nan Dajie, Beijing

Colombia
Juan Luis Mejia Arango, Cámara Colombiana de la Industria Editorial, Apdo Aéreo 8998, Bogatá

Costa Rica
Efrain Picado, Director-General, Biblioteca Nacional, Apdo 10-008, San José

Cyprus
Savvas L Petrides, c/o Cyprus Centre for Registration of Books & Serials, Ministry of Education Cultural Service, Nicosia

Denmark
Morten Garde, Danish ISBN Agency, Bibliotekscentralen, Tempovej 7-11, DK-2750 Ballerup

Ecuador
Luis Aulestia Buttinoni, President, Cámara Ecuatoriana del Libro, Núcleo de Pichincha, Casilla No 3329, Quito

Egypt
Dr Ezz El Dine Ismail, General Egyptian Book Organization, Corniche el Nil, Boulac, Cairo

Finland
Dr Thea Aulo, Standard Book Numbering Agency, Bibliographic Dept, Helsinki University Library, PL 312, SF-00171 Helsinki

France
Nathalie Bréaud, Agence francophone pour la Numérotation internationale du Livre (AFNIL-ISBN), Cercle de la Librairie, 35 rue Grégoire de Tours, F-75279 Paris cedex 06

Gambia
Sally N'Jie, National Library, PO Box 552, Banjul

German Democratic Republic
Klaus-Dieter Wilke, Deutsche Bücherei Erwerbung ISBN-Agentur der DDR, Deutscher Pl 1, DDR-7010 Leipzig

Federal Republic of Germany
Wilfried H Schinzel, Buchhändler-Vereinigung GmbH, Postfach 2404, D-6000 Frankfurt am Main 1

Ghana
Christina D T Kwei, Ghana Library Board, Research Library on African Affairs, PO Box 2970, Accra

Greece
Ms A L Martin-Papazoglou, Information and Library Services Books' Distribution Organization, Doxapatri 18, GR-11473 Athens

Hong Kong
Edward W S Tse, Books Registration Office, MSB, 2201 Park-in Commercial Centre, Dundas St, Mongkok, Kowloon

Hungary
Dr Susánszky Zoltánné, Országos Széchényi Könyvtár Magyar ISBN Iroda, H-1827 Budapest, Pollack Mihálytér 10.

India
Vijai Govind, National Agency for ISBN, Raja Rammohun Roy National Educational Resources Centre, Ministry of Human Resources Development, 1-W-3 Curzon Road Barracks, Kasturba Gandhi Marg, New Delhi 110001

Indonesia
Drs Nurhadi, Indonesian ISBN Agency, Perpustakaan Nasional, Department of Education and Culture, PO Box 3624, Jakarta 10002

International Publishers (UNESCO)
C Nair, Unesco, Division for Book Promotion, Audio-visual Archives and International Exchanges, 7 pl de Fontenoy, F-75700 Paris, France

THE ISBN SYSTEM

Israel
Gad Rosenblatt, Israel ISBN Group Agency, c/o Centre for Public Libraries, PO Box 242, Jerusalem 91002

Italy
Michele Costa, Agenzia per l'Area di Lingua Italiana ISBN, Editrice Bibliografica SRL, Viale Vittorio Veneto 24, I-20124 Milan

Japan
Naotoshi Matsudaira, Japan ISBN Agency, Japan Publishers Bldg, 6 Fukuro-machi, Shinjuku-ku, Tokyo 162

Kenya
Francis C Ochola, Kenya National Library Service, PO Box 30573, Nairobi

Malaysia
Mrs Primalani Kukanesan, c/o National Library of Malaysia, Acquisition Division, 4th & 5th Floors, Wisma SYS, Jalan Raja Laut, 50572 Kuala Lumpur

Mexico
Isabel Fuentes Villalobos, Agencia Nacional ISBN, Dirección General del Derecho de Autor, Centro Nacional de Información del Derecho de Autor, Mariano-Escobedo 438 – 3° piso, Col Verónica Anzures, 11590 México, DF

Netherlands
Dick Denteneer, Bureau ISBN, Centraal Boekhuis, Postbus 125, 4100 AC Culemborg

New Zealand
Ms K S Williams, National Library of New Zealand, Private Bag, Wellington 1

Nigeria
The Director, National Library of Nigeria, 4 Wesley St, PMB 12626, Lagos

Norway
Tove Jareld, Norsk Boknummerkontor, Universitetsbiblioteket i Oslo, Drammensvegen 42, N-0255 Oslo 2

Pakistan
Abdul Hafeez Akhtar, Government of Pakistan, Department of Libraries (Ministry of Education), House No 555, Street 83, Islamabad

Papua New Guinea
Fraiser McConnell, National Library Service, PO Box 5770, Boroko

Philippines
Lily Orbase, The National Library of the Philippines, TM Kalaw St, Manila

Poland
Mrs Halina Wylezinska, Bioru Miedzynarodowego Numeru Ksiazki, ul Mazowiecka 9, 00-052 Warsaw

Portugal
Isabel Carvalho, Associação Portuguesa dos Editores e Livreiros, Largo de Anduluz 16 – 1° Esq°, 1000 Lisbon

Republic of Singapore
Mrs Ting Meng Hong & Miss Tok Sok Hoon, National Library, Stamford Rd, Singapore 0617

Republic of South Africa
Miss B C Keilermann, State Library, PO Box 397, Pretoria 0001

South Pacific
Mrs Esther Williams, Regional ISBN Agency, Pacific Information Centre, The University of the South Pacific Library, PO Box 1168, Suva, Fiji

Spain
Rafael Martinez Ales, Agencia Española del ISBN, Instituto Nacional del Libro Español, Calle Santiago Rusiñol 8, Madrid 3

Sri Lanka
N Amarasinghe, Sri Lanka National Library Services Board, PO Box 1764, Independence Ave, Colombo

Suriname
E Hogenboom, Standard Book Numbering Agency, Suriname Publishers' Association, Domineestr 26, Paramaribo

Sweden
Folke Sandgren, Swedish National ISBN Centre, Bibliographical Department, Royal Library, Box 5039, S-102 41 Stockholm

Switzerland (French-speaking)
French agency

Switzerland German-speaking)
Ch Aeberli, Schweizerischer Buchhändler und Verleger-Verband, Postfach, CH-8050 Zurich

Tanzania
T E Mlaki, Tanzania Library Service, PO Box 9283, Dar es Salaam

Thailand
Mrs Suwakhon Phadung-Ath, National Library, Samsen Rd, Tawasurkree, Bangkok 10300

Tunisia
Miss Samia Bedoui, Agency Tunisienne de l'ISBN, Bibliothèque nationale Service des publications et du dépôt légal, 20 Souk El Attarine, Tunis

Union of Soviet Socialist Republics
G G Rodin, Bibliograficeskij Institut SSSR, Kremlevskaja nab 1/9, 119816 Moscow G-19

UK
Lars Andreasen, Standard Book Numbering Agency Ltd, 12 Dyott St, London WC1A 1DF

United Nations, see *International Publishers*

USA
Emery Koltay, Standard Book Numbering Agency, The R R Bowker Co, 245 West 17th St, New York, NY 10011

Venezuela
Marcela García Jordán, IABN Dirección de Servicios Técnicos Bibliotecarios, Apdo 80593, Prados del Este, Caracas 1080

Yugoslavia
Miloje Rakočević, Jugoslovenski bibliografski institut, Agencija za ISBN, YU-11000 Belgrade, Terazije 26

Zambia
G G Mwangilwa, Booksellers' and Publishers' Association of Zambia, PO Box 320199, Lusaka

Zimbabwe
Miss R Marunda, National Archives of Zimbabwe, Private Bag 7729, Causeway, Harare

ISBN and ISSN

In addition to the International Standard Book Number System, a complementary numbering system for serial publications has also been established.
A serial is defined as any publication issued in successive parts, usually bearing numerical or chronological designations and intended to be continued indefinitely. Serials include periodicals, yearbooks and monographic series.
The International Standard Serial Number System (ISSN) is administered by the International Centre for the Registration of Serials (ISDS), whose address is:

International Serial Data System,
International Centre,
20 rue Bachaumont, F-75002 Paris,
France

Publishers of serials should apply to the International Serials Data System or to their National Serials Data Centre, if there is one, for ISSNs for their serial publications. Certain publications, such as yearbooks, annuals, monographic series, etc, should be assigned an ISSN for the serial title (which will remain the same for all the parts or individual volumes of the serial) and an ISBN for each individual volume.
Both ISSN and ISBN where they are assigned must be given on the publication and clearly identified.

(The preceding information is mainly from the ISBN *Users' Manual*, compiled by the International ISBN Agency, Staatsbibliothek Preussischer Kulturbesitz, Berlin, Federal Republic of Germany.)

Book Trade Calendar

DATE	EVENT	CONTACT
1988		
January 9–14	American Library Association: Midwinter Conference. San Antonio, Texas, USA	American Library Association, 50 East Huron St, Chicago, IL 60611, USA *Tel:* (312) 944 6780
January 25–30	3rd Enugu International Book and Library Fair. Enugu, Nigeria	Fair Director, Anambra State Library Board, Market Rd, PMB 01026, Enugu, Nigeria *Tel:* (042) 336644/334103
January 27–February 9	20th Cairo International Book Fair. Cairo, Egypt	General Egyptian Book Organization, Corniche El Nil, Boulac, Cairo, Egypt *Tel:* (02) 775649
February 2–5	12th Ife Book Fair. Ile-Ife, Nigeria	University Bookshop, Obafemi Awolowo University, Ile-Ife, Nigeria *Tel:* (038) 2291
February 2–6	Didacta '88. Basle, Switzerland	Worlddidac, Bollwerk 21, Postfach 2550, CH- 3001 Berne 1, Switzerland *Tel:* (031) 227682
February 5–15	8th World Book Fair. New Delhi, India	Deputy Director (Exhibition), National Book Trust, A-5 Green Park, New Delhi 110016, India *Tel:* (011) 664020/664667
February 20–28	7th Bookfair Manila. Manila, Philippines	Exhibitions Director, Philcite, Cultural Center Complex, Roxas Blvd, PO Box 598, Manila, Philippines *Tel:* 8323411/8332023/8320304
March 3	New Zealand Publishers' Association: Annual General Meeting. New Zealand	Book Publishers Association of New Zealand Inc, PO Box 44-146, Point Chevalier, Auckland 2, New Zealand *Tel:* (09) 892533
March 5–13	Brussels International Book Fair. Brussels, Belgium	International Book Fair, 111 ave du Parc, B- 1060 Brussels, Belgium. *Tel:* (02) 5389293
March 6–11	1988 Writers' Week Adelaide Festival of Arts. Adelaide, Australia	Writers' Week Committee, Adelaide Festival, Adelaide Festival Centre, King William Rd, Adelaide, SA 5000, Australia *Tel:* (08) 2168600
March 7–10	Christian Booksellers Convention. Blackpool, UK	Christian Booksellers Convention Ltd, 5 Crown Close, London E3 2JQ, UK *Tel:* (01) 981 1692
March 10–12	European Christian Publishers Conference. Blackpool, UK	Angus Hudson, European Christian Publishers Conference Ltd, Greater London House, Hampstead Rd, London NW1 7QX, UK *Tel:* (01) 377 4741
March 13–19	Leipzig International Book Fair (at Leipzig Spring Fair). Leipzig, German Democratic Republic	Buchexport, Leninstr 16, DDR-7010 Leipzig, German Democratic Republic *Tel:* (041) 71370

DATE	EVENT	CONTACT
1988 (Cont'd)		
March 18–20	Independent Publishers Guild: Spring Conference. Exeter, Devon, UK	Ms R Pettitt, 147-149 Gloucester Terrace, London W2 6DX, UK *Tel:* (01) 723 7328
March 23–24	London International Book Print Fair. London, UK	London International Book Print Fair, The PAMS Group, St Ives House, Faringdon Ave, Harold Hill, Romford, Essex RM3 8XL, UK *Tel:* (04023) 40059
March 28–30	London International Book Fair. London, UK	Fair Manager, London International Book Fair, ITF, Oriel House, 26 The Quadrant, Richmond-upon-Thames, Surrey TW9 1DL, UK *Tel:* (01) 940 6065
April 2	International Children's Book Day. (1988 Sponsor: Australia)	IBBY Secretariat, Leonhardsgraben 38a, Postfach, CH-4003 Basle, Switzerland *Tel:* (061) 253404
April 6–9	PEN International Conference. Cambridge, UK	International PEN, 38 King St, London WC2E 8JT, UK *Tel:* (01) 379 7939
April 7–10	25th Children's Book Fair and 21st Exhibition for Illustrators. Bologna, Italy	Managing Director, Ente Autonomo per le Fiere di Bologna, Piazza della Costituzione 6, I-40128 Bologna, Italy *Tel:* (051) 282111
April 7–25	14th Buenos Aires International Book Fair. Buenos Aires, Argentina	Executive Committee, International Book Fair, Ave Cordoba 744 – PB, 1054 Buenos Aires, Argentina *Tel:* (01) 3922255/3922165
April 14–20	Salon du Livre (Professional – 17–20 April). Paris, France	Jean-Pierre Jouet, OIP, 62 rue de Miromesnil, F-75008 Paris, France *Telex:* 660259 F
April 17–23	National Library Week. USA	American Library Association, 50 East Huron St, Chicago. IL 60611, USA *Tel:* (312) 944 6780
April 19–22	ASLIB 60th Annual Conference. Nottingham, UK	Conference Secretary, ASLIB, 26–27 Boswell St, London WC1N 3JZ, UK *Tel:* (01) 430 2671
April 19–24	Quebec International Book Fair. Quebec, Canada	Lorenzo Michaud, Quebec International Book Fair, pl Belle-Cour, 2590 blvd Laurier, Chambre 760, Sainte-Foy, Quebec G1V 4M6, Canada *Tel:* (418) 658 1974
April 21	The Publishers Association: Annual General Meeting. London, UK	The Publishers Association, 19 Bedford Sq, London WC1B 3HJ, UK *Tel:* (01) 580 6321
May 1–6	International Reading Association: 33rd Annual Convention. Toronto, Canada	Director of Conferences, International Reading Association, 800 Barksdale Rd, PO Box 8139 Newark, DE 19711, USA *Tel:* (302) 731 1600
May 4–8	The Booksellers Association of Great Britain & Ireland: Annual Conference and Trade Exhibition. Bournemouth, Dorset, UK	Laverne Moseley, Booksellers Association Service House Ltd, 154 Buckingham Palace Rd, London SW1W 9TZ, UK *Tel:* (01) 730 8214

530 BOOK TRADE CALENDAR

DATE	EVENT	CONTACT
1988 (Cont'd)		
May 16–19	IBF General Assembly. Stein am Rhein, Chlosterhof, Switzerland	President Peter Meili, Fronwagplatz 13, CH-8200 Schaffhausen, Switzerland *Tel:* (053) 54144
May 18–23	33rd International Book Fair. Warsaw, Poland	Ars Polona, Secretariat of International Book Fair, PO Box 1001, 00-950 Warsaw, Poland *Tel:* (022) 178641
May 22–28	32nd IBF Congress of Young Booksellers. Barcelona, Spain	M A Fabregues, Gremi de Llibreters de Barcelona i Catalunya, Mallorca 272–276 1 apl, Barcelona, Spain *Tel:* (93) 2154254
May 28–31	American Booksellers Association: Annual Convention. Anaheim, California, USA	Director, Meetings & Conventions, American Booksellers Association, 137 West 25th St, New York, NY 10001, USA *Tel:* (212) 463 8450
May 28– June 11	Feminist Book Fortnight '88. UK	Carole Spedding, 7 Loddon House, Church St, London NW8 8PX, UK *Tel:* (01) 402 8159
June 1–3	4th International Conference on Scholarly Publishing. Helsinki, Finland	Dr Hanna Heikkila, Federation of Finnish Scientific Societies, Mariankatu 5, 00170 Helsinki, Finland *Tel:* (90) 652572
June 2–7	18th Sofia International Book Fair. Sofia, Bulgaria	International Book Fair, Department for Exhibitions & Fairs, 11 Slaveikov Sq, 1000 Sofia, Bulgaria *Tel:* 879111
June 8–13	International Association of Literary Critics: XIII Congress. Toruń, Poland	Association international des critiques littéraires, 38 rue de Faubourg St-Jacques, F-75014 Paris, France *Tel:* (1) 43541866
June 10–14	Union internationale des Industries graphiques de reproduction: 42nd International Congress. Monte Carlo, Monaco	Francis Ducos, Chambre Syndicale nationale des Industries graphiques de reproduction, 7 rue de Villersexel, F-75007 Paris, France *Tel:* (1) 45494669
June 12–17	International Publishers Association Congress. London, UK	Conference Associates IPA, 27A Medway St, London SW1P 2BD, UK *Tel:* (01) 222 9493
June 14–21	3rd International Feminist Book Fair. Montreal, Canada	Carole Spedding, 7 Loddon House, Church St, London NW8 8PX, UK *Tel:* (01) 402 8159
June 16–20	CLA Annual Conference. Halifax, Nova Scotia, Canada	Canadian Library Association, 200 Elgin St, Suite 602, Ottawa, Ontario K2P 1L5, Canada *Tel:* (613) 232 9625
June 21–23	29th London Antiquarian Book Fair. London, UK	Antiquarian Booksellers Association, Suite 2, 26 Charing Cross Rd, London WC2H 0DG, UK *Tel:* (01) 379 3041
July 5–8	International Reading Association: 12th World Congress. Gold Coast, Australia	Director of Conferences, International Reading Association, 800 Barksdale Rd, PO Box 8139, Newark, DE 19711, USA *Tel:* (302) 731 1600

DATE	EVENT	CONTACT
1988 (Cont'd)		
July 9–14	American Library Association: Annual Conference. New Orleans, Louisiana, USA	American Library Association, 50 East Huron St, Chicago, IL 60611, USA *Tel:* (312) 944 6780
July 23–26	New Zealand Booksellers 67th Annual Conference. Christchurch, New Zealand	Booksellers Association of New Zealand (Inc), PO Box 11-377, Wellington, New Zealand *Tel:* (04) 728678
July 23–26	Book Publishers Association of New Zealand: Joint Book Trade Conference and Exhibition. New Zealand	Book Publishers Association of New Zealand Inc, PO Box 44-146, Point Chevalier, Auckland 2, New Zealand *Tel:* (09) 892533
August 13–19	40th Writers' Summer School. Swanwick, Derbyshire, UK	The Secretary, Writers' Summer School, The Red House, Mardens Hill, Crowborough, Sussex TN6 1XN, UK *Tel:* (08926) 3943
August 18–28	São Paulo X Biennial Book Fair. São Paulo, Brazil	São Paulo X Bienal Internacional do Livro, Av Ipiranga 1267–10° andar, 01039 São Paulo 2 SP, Brazil *Tel:* (011) 2297855
August 28– September 1	Federation Internationale de Documentation (FID): 44th Conference and Congress. Helsinki, Finland	Finnish Society for Information Services, 44th FID Congress and Conference, Local Organizing Committee, PO Box 1025, SF-00101 Helsinki, Finland *Tel:* (90) 6091490
August 28– September 3	PEN 52nd International Congress. Seoul, Republic of Korea	International PEN, 38 King St, London WC2E 8JT, UK *Tel:* (01) 379 7939
August 30– September 3	IFLA Annual Conference. Sydney, Australia	IFLA, c/o The Royal Library, Postbus 95312, 2509 CH The Hague, Netherlands *Tel:* (070) 140884
August (end)	Annual General Meetings of: South African Publishers Association Associated Booksellers of Southern Africa Overseas Publishers Representatives Book Trade Association. Durban, Republic of South Africa	Associated Booksellers of Southern Africa Ltd, PO Box 326, Howard Place 7450, Republic of South Africa *Tel:* (021) 538907
September 1–7	Beijing International Book Fair '88. Beijing, People's Republic of China	China National Publications Import and Export Corporation, PO Box 88, Beijing, People's Republic of China China Business Enterprises Inc, 109 East 15th St, New York, NY 10003, USA *Tel:* (212) 682 1511
September 4–10	Distripress Annual Congress. Toronto, Canada	Distripress, Beethovenstr 20, CH-8002 Zurich, Switzerland *Tel:* (01) 2024121
September 11–18	International League of Antiquarian Booksellers: Congress and Book Fair. (29th Congress – 11-14 September; 12th Book Fair – 15-18 September) Paris, France	Syndicat National de la Librairie Ancienne et Moderne, 4 rue Gît-le-Coeur, F-75006 Paris, France *Tel:* (1) 43294638

532 BOOK TRADE CALENDAR

DATE	EVENT	CONTACT
1988 (Cont'd)		
September 13–24	British Book Design and Production Exhibition 1988. London, UK	BPIF (Book Exhibition), 11 Bedford Row, London WC1R 4DX, UK *Tel:* (01) 242 6904
September 21–24	International Association of Bibliophiles: Annual Conference. Manchester, UK	Association Internationale de Bibliophile, c/o Biliothèque nationale, 58 rue Richelieu, F-75084 Paris cedex 02, France
September 26–30	International Board on Books for Young People: 21st Biennial Congress. Oslo, Norway	IBBY Secretariat, Leonhardsgraben 38a, Postfach, CH-4003 Basle, Switzerland *Tel:* (061) 253404
September 27– October 2	International Book Fair – Liber '88. Barcelona, Spain	Directora de Liber, Federación de Gremios de Editores de España, Juan Ramon Jimenez 45, 28036 Madrid, Spain *Tel:* (91) 4574404
October 4–5	Frankfurt Book Production Fair. Frankfurt am Main, Federal Republic of Germany	Frankfurt Book Production Fair, The PAMS Group, St Ives House, Faringdon Ave, Harold Hill, Romford, Essex RM3 8XL, UK *Tel:* (04023) 40059
October 5–10	40th Frankfurt Book Fair. Frankfurt am Main, Federal Republic of Germany	Ronald Weber, Ausstellungs- und Messe-GmbH des Börsenvereins des deutschen Buchhandels, Postfach 100442, D-6000 Frankfurt am Main 1, Federal Republic of Germany *Tel:* (069) 2102218 ext 221
October 8–15	Children's Book Week. UK	Administrator, Children's Book Week, Book Trust, Book House, 45 East Hill, Wandsworth, London SW18 2QZ, UK *Tel:* (01) 874 6361
October 25–31	33rd Belgrade International Book Fair. Belgrade, Yugoslavia	Association of Yugoslav Publishers and Booksellers, YU-11000 Belgrade, Kneza Milósa 25, Yugoslavia *Tel:* (011) 642248/642533
October 30– November 2	Book Manufacturers' Institute: Annual Conference. Laguna Niguel, California, USA	Book Manufacturers' Institute Inc, 111 Prospect St, Stamford, CT 06901, USA *Tel:* (203) 324 9670
November 2–11	14th Arabic Book Exhibition. Kuwait	Kuwait International Fair, PO Box 656, Safat Kuwait, 13007 Kuwait *Tel:* 5387100
November 4–7	UK Library Association Annual Conference and Exhibition. Blackpool, Lancashire, UK	Annual Conference Administrator, The Library Association, 7 Ridgmount St, London WC1E 7AE, UK *Tel:* (01) 636 7543
November 4– December 4	Jewish Book Month. USA	The Jewish Book Council of the National Jewish Welfare Board, 15 East 26th St, New York, NY 10010, USA *Tel:* (212) 532 4949 ext 297
November 14–20	National Children's Book Week. USA	The Children's Book Council, 67 Irving Pl, New York, NY 10003, USA *Tel:* (212) 254 2666
November 23– December 6	5th Cairo International Children's Book Fair. Cairo, Egypt	Cairo International Children's Book Fair, General Egyptian Book Organization, Corniche El Nil, Boulac, Cairo, Egypt *Tel:* (02) 775649

DATE	EVENT	CONTACT
1988 (Cont'd)		
December 4–11	Colombo Children's Book Fair. Colombo, Sri Lanka	Colombo Children's Book Fair, K V G de Silva & Sons (Colombo) Ltd, 415 Galle Rd, Colombo 4, Sri Lanka *Tel:* (01) 84146
December 6–8	International Online Information Meeting. London, UK	Learned Information Ltd, Woodside Hinksey Hill, Oxford OX1 5AU, UK *Tel:* (0865) 730275
December 27–30	Modern Language Association of America: Annual Convention. New Orleans, Louisiana, USA	MLA, Modern Language Association of America, 10 Astor Pl, New York, NY 10003, USA *Tel:* (212) 475 9500
1989		
January 7–12	American Library Association: Midwinter Conference. Washington, DC, USA	American Library Association, 50 East Huron St, Chicago, IL 60611, USA *Tel:* (312) 944 6780
January 26–February 8	21st Cairo International Book Fair. Cairo, Egypt	General Egyptian Book Organization, Corniche El Nil, Boulac, Cairo, Egypt *Tel:* (02) 775649
January 29–February 2	Saudi Book Fair '89 (in connection with Saudi Education Fair). Riyadh, Saudi Arabia	Saudi Book Fair '89, Overseas Exhibition Services Ltd, 11 Manchester Sq, London W1M 5AB, UK *Tel:* (01) 486 1951
February 15–19	8th Bookfair Manila. Manila, Philippines	Exhibitions Director, Philcite, Cultural Center Complex, Roxas Blvd, PO Box 598, Manila, Philippines *Tel:* 8323411/8332023/8320304
March 6–9	Christian Booksellers Convention. Blackpool, UK	Christian Booksellers Convention Ltd, 5 Crown Close, London E3 2JQ, UK *Tel:* (01) 981 1692
March 12–18	14th Jerusalem International Book Fair. Jerusalem, Israel	Events Co-ordinator, Jerusalem International Book Fair, 12 Sarei Israel St, PO Box 1241, Jerusalem 91012, Israel *Tel:* (02) 380896/382545
March 12–18	Leipzig International Book Fair (at Leipzig Spring Fair). Leipzig, German Democratic Republic	Buchexport, Leninstr 16, DDR-7010 Leipzig, German Democratic Republic *Tel:* (041) 71370
April	PEN International Conference. Maastricht, The Netherlands	International PEN, 38 King St, London WC2E 8JT, UK *Tel:* (01) 379 7939
April 2	International Children's Book Day. (1989 Sponsor: Ghana)	IBBY Secretariat, Leonhardsgraben 38a, Postfach, CH-4003 Basle, Switzerland *Tel:* (061) 253404
April 6–24	15th Buenos Aires International Book Fair. Buenos Aires, Argentina	Executive Committee, International Book Fair, Ave Cordoba 744 – PB, 1054 Buenos Aires, Argentina *Tel:* (01) 3922255/3922165
April 18–23	Quebec International Book Fair. Quebec, Canada	Lorenzo Michaud, Quebec International Book Fair, pl Belle-Cour, 2590 blvd Laurier, Chambre 760, Sainte-Foy, Quebec G1V 4M6, Canada *Tel:* (418) 658 1974

534 BOOK TRADE CALENDAR

DATE	EVENT	CONTACT
1989 (Cont'd)		
April 30–May 4	International Reading Association: 34th Annual Convention. New Orleans, Louisiana, USA	Director of Conferences, International Reading Association, 800 Barksdale Rd, PO Box 8139, Newark, DE 19711, USA *Tel:* (302) 731 1600
May 9–13	Asean Worlddidac Expo 89. Singapore, Republic of Singapore	Worlddidac, Bollwerk 21, Postfach 2550, CH-3001 Berne 1, Switzerland *Tel:* (031) 227682
May 17–22	34th International Book Fair. Warsaw, Poland	Ars Polona, Secretariat of International Book Fair, PO Box 1001, 00-950 Warsaw, Poland *Tel:* (022) 178641
May 31–June 3	8th International Booksellers Congress and IBF General Assembly (in connection with ABA Convention). Washington, DC, USA	Bernard Rath, American Booksellers Association, 137 West 25th St, New York, NY 10001, USA *Tel:* (212) 463 8450
June 3–6	American Booksellers Association: Annual Convention. Washington, DC, USA	Director, Meetings & Conventions, American Booksellers Association, 137 West 25th St, New York, NY 10001, USA *Tel:* (212) 463 8450
June 19–23	UNESCO Intergovernmental Copyright Committee: 8th Session. Paris, France	Copyright Division, UNESCO, 7 pl de Fontenoy, F-75700 Paris, France *Tel:* (1) 45681000
June 22–26	CLA Annual Conference. Edmonton, Alberta, Canada	Canadian Library Association, 200 Elgin St, Suite 602, Ottawa, Ontario K2P 1L5, Canada *Tel:* (613) 232 9625
June 24–29	American Library Association: Annual Conference. Dallas, Texas, USA	American Library Association, 50 East Huron St, Chicago, IL 60611, USA *Tel:* (312) 944 6780
August 12–18	41st Writers' Summer School. Swanwick, Derbyshire, UK	The Secretary, Writers' Summer School, The Red House, Mardens Hill, Crowborough, Sussex TN6 1XN, UK *Tel:* (08926) 3943
August 20–25	IFLA Annual Conference. Paris, France	IFLA, c/o The Royal Library, Postbus 95312, 2509 CH The Hague, Netherlands *Tel:* (070) 140884
August 21–26	5th Zimbabwe International Book Fair and Exhibition. Harare, Zimbabwe	Zimbabwe International Book Fair, African Book Publishing Record, Hans Zell Publishers, PO Box 56, Oxford OX1 3EL, UK *Tel:* (0865) 512934
September	PEN 53rd International Congress. Toronto/Montreal, Canada	International PEN, 38 King St, London WC2E 8JT, UK *Tel:* (01) 379 7939
September 4–7	UK Library Association Annual Conference and Exhibition. Brighton, Sussex, UK	Annual Conference Administrator, The Library Association, 7 Ridgmount St, London WC1E 7AE, UK *Tel:* (01) 636 7543
September 18–23	International Association of Bibliophiles: XVI International Congress. Budapest, Hungary	Association Internationale de Bibliophilie, c/o Bibliothèque nationale, 58 rue Richelieu, F-75084 Paris cedex 02, France

DATE	EVENT	CONTACT
1989 (Cont'd)		
October 1–7	Distripress Annual Congress. Monte Carlo, Monaco	Distripress, Beethovenstr 20, CH-8002 Zurich, Switzerland *Tel:* (01) 2024121
October 11–16	41st Frankfurt Book Fair. Frankfurt am Main, Federal Republic of Germany	Ronald Weber, Ausstellungs- und Messe-GmbH des Börsenvereins des deutschen Buchhandels, Postfach 100442, D-6000 Frankfurt am Main 1, Federal Republic of Germany *Tel:* (069) 2102218 ext 221
October 24–30	34th Belgrade International Book Fair. Belgrade, Yugoslavia	Association of Yugoslav Publishers and Booksellers, YU-11000 Belgrade, Kneza Milósa 25, Yugoslavia *Tel:* (011) 642248/642533
November 13–19	National Children's Book Week. USA	The Children's Book Council, 67 Irving Pl, New York, NY 10003, USA *Tel:* (212) 254 2666
November 23– December 23	Jewish Book Month. USA	The Jewish Book Council of the National Jewish Welfare Board, 15 East 26th St. New York, NY 10010, USA *Tel:* (212) 532 4949 ext 297
December 4–11	Colombo Children's Book Fair. Colombo, Sri Lanka	Colombo Children's Book Fair, K V G de Silva & Sons (Colombo) Ltd, 415 Galle Rd, Colombo 4, Sri Lanka *Tel:* (01) 84146
December 27–30	Modern Language Association of America: Annual Convention. Washington, DC, USA	MLA, Modern Language Association of America, 10 Astor Pl, New York, NY 10003, USA *Tel:* (212) 475 9500
Date unknown at time of going to press	Belfast Academic and Professional Book Fair. Belfast, Northern Ireland	The Publishers Association, 19 Bedford Sq, London WC1B 3HJ, UK *Tel:* (01) 580 6321
Date unknown at time of going to press	Scottish Antiquarian Book Fair. Edinburgh, Scotland	Mrs Grant, 7 Dundas St, Edinburgh EH3 6QG, Scotland *Tel:* (031) 556 9698
1990		
March 4–9	1990 Writers' Week Adelaide Festival of Arts. Adelaide, Australia	Writers' Week Committee, Adelaide Festival, Adelaide Festival Centre, King William Rd, Adelaide, SA 5000, Australia *Tel:* (08) 2168600
March 11–17	Leipzig International Book Fair (at Leipzig Spring Fair). Leipzig, German Democratic Republic	Buchexport, Leninstr 16, DDR-7010 Leipzig, German Democratic Republic *Tel:* (041) 71370
April 2	International Children's Book Day. (1990 Sponsor: Canada)	IBBY Secretariat, Leonhardsgraben 38a, Postfach, CH-4003 Basle, Switzerland *Tel:* (061) 253404
April 24–29	Quebec International Book Fair. Quebec, Canada	Lorenzo Michaud, Quebec International Book Fair, pl Belle-Cour, 2590 blvd Laurier, Chambre 760, Sainte-Foy, Quebec G1V 4M6, Canada *Tel:* (418) 658 1974
May 6–10	International Reading Association: 35th Annual Convention. Atlanta, Georgia, USA	Director of Conferences, International Reading Association, 800 Barksdale Rd, PO Box 8139, Newark, DE 19711, USA *Tel:* (302) 731 1600

536 BOOK TRADE CALENDAR

DATE	EVENT	CONTACT
1990 (Cont'd)		
May 8–12	Worlddidac Expo 90 Basle. Basle, Switzerland	Worlddidac, Bollwerk 21, Postfach 2550, CH- 3001 Berne 1, Switzerland *Tel:* (031) 227682
May 16–21	35th International Book Fair. Warsaw, Poland	Ars Polona, Secretariat of International Book Fair, PO Box 1001, 00-950 Warsaw, Poland *Tel:* (022) 178641
June 2–5	American Booksellers Association: Annual Convention. Las Vegas, Nevada, USA	Director, Meetings & Conventions, American Booksellers Association, 137 West 25th St, New York, NY 10001, USA *Tel:* (212) 463 8450
June 14–18	CLA Annual Conference. Ottawa, Ontario, Canada	Canadian Library Association, 200 Elgin St, Suite 602, Ottawa, Ontario K2P 1L5, Canada *Tel:* (613) 232 9625
August	International Federation for Modern Languages and Literatures: XVIII International Congress. Belgrade, Yugoslavia	Prof Dragan Nedeljković, YU-11000 Belgrade, ul Kneza Milósa 67/IV, Yugoslavia
August 18–24	IFLA Annual Conference. Stockholm, Sweden	IFLA, c/o The Royal Library, Postbus 95312, 2509 CH The Hague, Netherlands *Tel:* (070) 140884
September 1–7	International Board on Books for Young People: 22nd Biennial Congress. Williamsburg, Virginia, USA	IBBY Secretariat, Leonhardsgraben 38a, Postfach, CH-4003 Basle, Switzerland *Tel:* (061) 253404
September 17–20	UK Library Association Annual Conference and Exhibition. Bournemouth, Dorset, UK	Annual Conference Administrator, The Library Association, 7 Ridgmount St, London WC1E 7AE, UK *Tel:* (01) 636 7543
October	42nd Frankfurt Book Fair. Frankfurt am Main, Federal Republic of Germany	Ronald Weber, Ausstellungs- und Messe-GmbH des Börsenvereins des deutschen Buchhandels, Postfach 100442, D-6000 Frankfurt am Main 1, Federal Republic of Germany *Tel:* (069) 2102218 ext 221
November 4–7	Book Manufacturers' Institute: Annual Conference. Castle Harbor, Bermuda	Book Manufacturers' Institute Inc, 111 Prospect St, Stamford, CT 06901, USA *Tel:* (203) 324 9670
November 12–December 12	Jewish Book Month. USA	The Jewish Book Council of the National Jewish Welfare Board, 15 East 26th St, New York, NY 10010, USA *Tel:* (212) 532 4949 ext 297
December 4–11	Colombo Children's Book Fair. Colombo, Sri Lanka	Colombo Children's Book Fair, K V G de Silva & Sons (Colombo) Ltd, 415 Galle Rd, Colombo 4, Sri Lanka *Tel:* (01) 84146
December 27–30	Modern Language Association of America: Annual Convention	MLA, Modern Language Association of America, 10 Astor Pl, New York, NY 10003, USA *Tel:* (212) 475 9500

Index

The order of the index is word by word so that, for example, Alpha Translation comes before Alphabet & Image.
Some words at the beginning of names are ignored when indexing. These include initials and forenames of personal names (so Jonathan Cape Ltd is listed under C) and words which simply mean 'publisher', 'bookseller' or 'company' (so Verlag Peter Lang is listed under L). In the text the first word of a name that is counted when indexing is printed in bold type.
Names that start with numbers are put before A in the index (so Edition No 1 is the first entry in the index, while Les Editions des Deux Coqs d'Or is listed under D).

1, Edition No (France)   97
1, No, Publishing Co Ltd (United Kingdom)   423
3 Arches (Belgium)   36
4 Fevereiro, Livraria (Angola)   2
'8' Nentori Publishing House (Albania)   1
'13 Calle, Librería, El Tecolote' (Guatemala)   185
14th October Corporation (People's Democratic Republic of Yemen)   495
20th Century Classics (United Kingdom)   480
24 heures, Editions (Switzerland)   392
29, Ediciones (Spain)   363
62, Edicions, SA (Spain)   363
70, Edições, Lda (Portugal)   340
707, Klub (Republic of South Africa)   359

'A' Publishing Institute (Israel)   226
A A B I T T I (Associazione Anna Bonanome Interpreti Traduttori Trascrittori Italiani) (Italy)   253
A A Publishing (United Kingdom)   423
A B, The, Book Club (BAB) (Iceland)   194
A B C, Jill Anderson's, Bookshop (New Zealand)   311
A B C, Librarías, SA (Peru)   331
A B C, Librerías, SA (Argentina)   8
A B C, Librerías, SA (Peru)   330
A B C Editions (France)   97
A B C Kitabevi (Turkey)   415
A B C Verlag (Switzerland)   392
A B C Yayinevi (Turkey)   414
A B E F (France)   117
A B G R A (Asociación de Bibliotecarios Graduados de la República Argentina) (Argentina)   9
A B I C (Publishers) (Nigeria)   315
A B M, Librairie-Papeterie (Benin)   47
A B M, Maison d'Edition (Benin)   47
A B P (NZ) Ltd (New Zealand)   307
A C E R (Spain)   375
A C L A (France)   97
A C P O (Colombia)   69
A C R Edition Internationale (France)   97
A C U R I L (International Organizations)   507
A D (Switzerland)   392
A D A Edita Tokyo Co Ltd (Japan)   256
A D A C Verlag GmbH (Federal Republic of Germany)   130
A D B S (France)   117
A D I S Health Science Press (Australia)   10
A D I S Press Australasia Pty Ltd (Australia)   10
A D I S Press Ltd (New Zealand)   308
A D I S Press Ltd (United Kingdom)   423
A D I S Press Publications Ltd (Hong Kong)   187
A D L A F (Federal Republic of Germany)   130
A E D O S, Editorial, SA (Spain)   363
A E I (Portugal)   340
A E I (Portugal)   343
A E Press (Australia)   10
A F E R (African Ecclesial Review) (Kenya)   267
A G A V (Arbeitsgemeinschaft alternativer Autoren und Verlage) (Federal Republic of Germany)   128
A G I R (Artes Graficas Industrias Reunidas SA) (Brazil)   50
A G P O L (Przedsiebiorstwo Reklamy i Wydawnictw Handlu Zagranicznego) (Poland)   334
A I B D A (International Organizations)   507
A I D B A, Commission des Bibliothèques de l' (International Organizations)   507

A I E S I (International Organizations)   507
A K O Literature Prize (Netherlands)   306
A L A Verlag (Switzerland)   392
A L E B C I (International Organizations)   507
A L F A (Netherlands)   293
A L F A — Radna organizacija za izdavačku djelatnost (Yugoslavia)   496
A L S I (Switzerland)   391
A M B (Arbeitsgemeinschaft mitteleuropäischer Bibelwerke) (Federal Republic of Germany)   130
A M P (France)   117
A M P SA (France)   97
A M Z Editrice SpA (Italy)   233
A N B A D S (Senegal)   349
A N I T I (Associazione Nazionale Italiana Traduttori ed Interpreti) (Italy)   253
A O (Netherlands)   293
A P A (Academic Publishers Associated) (Netherlands)   293
A P Books/A P Information Services Ltd (United Kingdom)   423
A P C O L (Australia)   10
A P E, Edizioni, SpA (Italy)   233
A P E, Bologna (Italy)   233
A P N (Union of Soviet Socialist Republics)   417
A R E S, Edizioni (Italy)   233
A R L I S (The Art Libraries Society) (United Kingdom)   483
A S Prakashan (India)   196
A S Prakashan (India)   212
A Sp B (Federal Republic of Germany)   176
A T C (France)   96
A T L F (France)   121
A T O D B A M (Togo)   412
A T Verlag (Switzerland)   392
A U Press & Publications (India) Ltd   196
A W E/Gebers (Sweden)   381
A Z Editora SA (Argentina)   3
Aadab, Al-, Bookshop (Bahrain)   34
Aadiesh Book Depot (India)   196
Aalborg Universitetsbibliotek (Denmark)   84
Aane-Adab (Pakistan)   325
Aar-Verlag (Federal Republic of Germany)   131
Aare-Verlag (Switzerland)   392
Aarestrup, Emil, Prize (Denmark)   86
Aargauer Tagblatt (Switzerland)   392
Abacacía, Editorial, SRL (Argentina)   3
Abaco, Editorial, de Rodolfo de Palma SRL (Argentina)   3
Abacus (United Kingdom)   423
Abacus Press (United Kingdom)   423
Abadia, Publicacions de l', de Montserrat (Spain)   363
Abakus Schallplatten und Ulmtal Musikverlag Barbara Fietz (Federal Republic of Germany)   131
Abbey's Bookshop (Australia)   20
Abdulghani, Abdulla, & Bros Co (Qatar)   345
Abelard-Schuman Ltd (United Kingdom)   423
Abele, Edizioni Gruppo (Italy)   233
Abeledo, Editorial, Perrot SAE e I (Argentina)   3
Abercromby Bookshop (Trinidad and Tobago)   413
Aberdeen University Press Ltd (United Kingdom)   423
Abete, Edizioni (Italy)   233
Abhinav Publications (India)   196
Abhishek Publications (India)   196
Abiva Publishing House Inc (Philippines)   332
Abril, Editorial, SA (Argentina)   3
Abril SA Cultural e Industrial (Brazil)   50
Absolute Press (United Kingdom)   423
Abson Books (United Kingdom)   423
Abtour, Georges, SA, Librairie-Papeterie (Chad)   65
Acacia Books (Republic of South Africa)   355
Academi, Yr, Gymreig (The Welsh Academy) (United Kingdom)   484
Academia, Biblioteca da, das Ciências de Lisboa (Portugal)   343
Academia (Czechoslovakia)   75
Academia, Edition et Diffusion (Belgium)   36
Academia Amazonense de Letras (Brazil)   59
Academia Argentina de Letras (Argentina)   9
Academia Brasileira de Letras (Brazil)   59
Academia Brasiliense de Letras (Brazil)   59
Academia Cachoeirense de Letras (Brazil)   59
Academia Catarinense de Letras (Brazil)   59
Academia Cearense de Letras (Brazil)   59
Academia de Ciencias de la República de Cuba (Cuba)   74
Academia de Letras (Brazil)   59
Academia de Letras da Bahia (Brazil)   59
Academia de Letras de Piauí (Brazil)   59

Academia de Letras 'Humberto de Campos' (Brazil)   59
Academia de Studii Economice, Biblioteca Centrala (Romania)   347
Academia Feminina Espírito Santense de Letras (Brazil)   59
Academia Matogrossense de Letras (Brazil)   59
Academia Mineira de Letras (Brazil)   59
Academia Nacional de Letras (Uruguay)   491
Academia Nicaragüense de la Lengua (Nicaragua)   314
Academia Paraibana de Letras (Brazil)   59
Academia Paranaense de Letras (Brazil)   59
Academia Paulista de Letras (Brazil)   59
Academia Pernambucana de Letras (Brazil)   59
Academia Publications P Ltd (Malaysia)   278
Academia Riograndense de Letras (Brazil)   59
Academic and University Publishers Group (United Kingdom)   424
Academic Book Club (Togo)   412
Academic Book Club (United Republic of Cameroun)   64
Academic Press, The (India)   196
Academic Press (United Kingdom)   424
Academic Publications (United Kingdom)   424
Academic Publishers (India)   196
Academic Publishers Associated (Netherlands)   293
Academic Resource Center, Chulalongkorn University (Thailand)   411
Academica Lda (Mozambique)   291
Académie des Lettres et des Arts (France)   118
Académie Goncourt (France)   118
Académie Internationale de Tourisme (Monaco)   289
Académie mauricienne de Langue et de Littérature (Mauritius)   283
Académie royale de Langue et de Littérature françaises (Belgium)   45
Académie royale des Sciences, des Lettres et des Beaux-Arts de Belgique (Belgium)   45
Academiei, Editura, Republicii Socialiste România (Romania)   346
Academiei Republicii Socialiste România, Biblioteca (Romania)   347
Academiei Republicii Socialiste România, Biblioteca Filialei Cluj a (Romania)   347
Academon (The Hebrew University Students' Printing and Publishing House) (Israel)   226
Academy, Council on Libraries of the, of Sciences of the USSR (Union of Soviet Socialist Republics)   420
Academy, The, Press (Republic of Ireland)   221
Academy Editions (France)   97
Academy Editions (United Kingdom)   424
Academy Microfilms (Dublin) (Republic of Ireland)   221
Academy of Comparative Philosophy & Religion (India)   196
Academy of Islamic Research & Publications (India)   196
Academy of Medical Sciences, Fundamental Library of the (Union of Soviet Socialist Republics)   419
Academy of Sciences Publishing House (Democratic People's Republic of Korea)   268
Academy of Social Sciences Publishing House (Democratic People's Republic of Korea)   268
Academy of the Hebrew Language (Israel)   226
Academy of Thirteen Prize (France)   118
Academy Press Ltd (Nigeria)   315
Accademia, Libreria all', SNC di Randi Pietro (Italy)   251
Accademia di Scienze, Lettere ed Arti (Italy)   252
Accademia Ligure di Scienze e Lettere (Italy)   252
Accademia (Milano) (Italy)   233
Accademia Naz dei Lincei (Italy)   233
Accademia Nazionale di Scienze, Lettere ed Arti (Italy)   252
Accademia Petrarca di Lettere, Arti e Scienze (Italy)   252
Accademia Virgiliana di Scienze, Lettere ed Arti di Mantova (Italy)   252
Access Books (Australia)   10
Accidentia und Zester Druck- und Verlagsgesellschaft mbH (Federal Republic of Germany)   131
Accion Cultural Popular ACPO — Editorial Andes (Colombia)   69
Acco (Netherlands)   293
Acco SV (Belgium)   36
Accord general sur les Tarifs douaniers et le Commerce (International Organizations)   510
Accordo, Edizioni, SRL (Italy)   233
Acebo, Editorial, SA (Spain)   363

Acervo, Editorial, SL (Spain) 363
Achiasaf Publishing House Ltd (Israel) 226
Achiever (Israel) 226
Ackermanns, F A, Kunstverlag (Federal Republic of Germany) 131
Acme, Editorial, SA (Argentina) 3
Aconcagua Ediciones y Publicaciones SA (Mexico) 283
Acorn (United Kingdom) 424
Acorn Books (Republic of Ireland) 221
Acorn Editions (United Kingdom) 424
Acribia, Editorial, SA (Spain) 363
Acropole, Editions (France) 97
Acrópolis, Librería (Guatemala) 185
Acta Medica Belgica ASBL (Belgium) 36
Acta Universitatis Gothoburgensis (Sweden) 381
Actes, Editions, Sud (France) 97
Actinic Press Ltd (United Kingdom) 424
Action Publications (New Zealand) 308
Actuaquarto (Belgium) 36
Acum Ltd (Society of Authors, Composers and Music Publishers in Israel) (Israel) 231
Adab, Al-, Bookshop (Saudi Arabia) 348
Adam Publishers (Israel) 226
Adamantine Press Ltd (United Kingdom) 424
Adamjee Prize (Pakistan) 327
Adams & Co Ltd (Republic of South Africa) 360
Adda, Mario, Editore SNC (Italy) 233
Addis Ababa University Library (Ethiopia) 91
Addis Ababa University Press (Ethiopia) 91
Addison-Wesley Iberoamericana SA (Mexico) 283
Addison-Wesley Publishers Japan Ltd (Japan) 256
Addison-Wesley Publishers Ltd (United Kingdom) 424
Addison-Wesley Publishers (Pty) Ltd (Australia) 10
Addison-Wesley Publishing Co Inc (Philippines) 332
Addison-Wesley Publishing Group (Netherlands) 293
Addison-Wesley (S) Pte Ltd (Republic of Singapore) 351
Adebara Publishers Ltd (Nigeria) 315
Adelphi Edizioni SpA (Italy) 233
Adeyle Brothers (Bangladesh) 35
Adeylebros & Co (Bangladesh) 34
Adlib Paperbacks (United Kingdom) 424
Administracion, Archivo General de la, Civil del Estado (Spain) 376
Administration Library (Namibia) 291
Administrative College of Papua New Guinea Library (Papua New Guinea) 329
Admiral (United Kingdom) 424
Adressbuchausschuss der Deutschen Wirtschaft (Federal Republic of Germany) 128
Adret, l', éditions (France) 97
Adult, Directorate of, Education (India) 196
Advaita Ashrama (India) 196
Advance Publishing Co Ltd (Ghana) 180
Adventist Book Centre (Zimbabwe) 505
Adversaires, Editions (Switzerland) 392
Adwinsa Publications (Ghana) Ltd (Ghana) 180
Adyar-Verlag (Austria) 26
Aesopus Verlag GmbH (Switzerland) 392
Affiliated East West Press Pvt Ltd (India) 196
Afram Publications (Ghana) Ltd (Ghana) 180
Africa Christian Press (Ghana) 180
Africa Editions (Senegal) 349
Africa Inland Church Literature Department (Tanzania) 409
Africa Literature Centre (Zambia) 503
African Library Association of South Africa (Republic of South Africa) 361
African Training and Research Centre in Administration for Development, Documentation Centre (International Organizations) 507
African Universities Press (Nigeria) 315
Africana Book Society (Pty) Ltd (Zimbabwe) 504
Africana-FEP Publishers Ltd (Nigeria) 315
Africana Publishers (Nig) Ltd (Nigeria) 315
Africasouth Paperbacks (Republic of South Africa) 355
Afrique-Loisirs, Club (Senegal) 349
Afro-Asian Writers, Permanent Bureau of (Egypt) 88
Afro-Asian Writers' Bureau (Sri Lanka) 379
Afrontamento, Ediçoes (Portugal) 340
Agam Kala Prakashan (India) 196
Agathon (Netherlands) 293
Age', 'The, Book of the Year (Australia) 23
Age d'Homme, Editions L', — La Cité (Switzerland) 392
Age d'Homme-Karolinger Verlag GmbH & Co KG (Austria) 26
Agence de Distribution de Presse (Senegal) 349
Agence francophone pour la Numérotation internationale du Livre (AFNIL-ISBN) (France) 96
Agence Tunisienne de l'ISBN (Tunisia) 413
Agência Brasileira do ISBN (Brazil) 49
Agencia Española del ISBN (Spain) 362
Agencja Autorska (Poland) 335
Agencja Autorska (Poland) 337
Agents Editores Ltda (Brazil) 50
Agenzia Letteraria Internazionale SRL (Italy) 251

Agenzia per l'Area di Lingua Italiana ISBN (Italy) 232
Agertofts Forlag (Denmark) 80
Agir, Livraria (Brazil) 57
Agis Verlag GmbH (Federal Republic of Germany) 131
Agnelli, Giacomo, Editore (Italy) 233
Agora-Verlag (Federal Republic of Germany) 131
Agricole Publishing Academy (India) 196
Agricultural Books Publishing House (Democratic People's Republic of Korea) 268
Agricultural Experiment Station Library (Puerto Rico) 345
Agricultural Institute Library (Ethiopia) 91
Agricultural Library (Nigeria) 318
Agricultural Science, Central Library of (Israel) 231
Agriculture University Library (Pakistan) 327
Agropecuaria, Biblioteca, de Colombia (BAC) (Colombia) 71
Agrupación Bibliotecológica del Uruguay (Uruguay) 491
Agrupación para la Integración de la Información Socio-Económica (ABIISE) (Peru) 331
Agudat Harashash (Israel) 226
Aguilar, Editora Nova, SA (Brazil) 50
Aguilar Chilena de Ediciones (Chile) 65
Aguilar SA (Argentina) 3
Aguilar SA (Mexico) 283
Aguilar SA de Ediciones (Spain) 363
Aguirre, Librería (Colombia) 71
Ahd, Al, Al Gadeed Bookstore (Egypt) 89
Ahlwalia Book Depot (India) 196
Ahmadu Bello University Bookshop Ltd (Nigeria) 318
Ahmadu Bello University Library (Nigeria) 319
Ahmadu Bello University Press Ltd (Nigeria) 315
Ahmedabad Publishers' & Booksellers' Association (India) 195
Ahnert, L B, -Verlag (Federal Republic of Germany) 131
Ahora, Publicaciones, C por A (Dominican Republic) 86
Ahram, Al (Egypt) 90
Ahram, Al, Book Club (Egypt) 89
Ahram, Al, Bookshops (Egypt) 89
Ahram, Al, Establishment (Egypt) 88
Aiken, Alex (United Kingdom) 424
Ain Shams University Library (Egypt) 89
Airlife Publishing Ltd (United Kingdom) 424
Airport Bookshop (Republic of Korea) 271
Aitken & Stone Ltd (United Kingdom) 479
Ajanta Books International (India) 212
Ajanta Publications (India) (India) 196
Ajuda, Biblioteca da (Portugal) 343
Akadémiai Kiadó (Hungary) 190
Akademie-Verlag Berlin (German Democratic Republic) 123
Akademiförlaget (Sweden) 381
Akademii Nauk SSSR, Biblioteka (Union of Soviet Socialist Republics) 419
Akademii Nauk SSSR, Gosudarstvennaya publichnaya nauchno-tekhnicheskaya biblioteka Sibirskogo otdeleniya (Union of Soviet Socialist Republics) 419
Akademii Nauk SSSR, Institut nauchnoy informatsii po obschestvennym naukam (Union of Soviet Socialist Republics) 419
Akademii Nauk USSR, Tsentral'nava nauchnaya biblioteka (Union of Soviet Socialist Republics) 419
Akademika (Norway) 320
Akademilitteratur Förlaget AB (Sweden) 381
Akademische Druck- und Verlagsanstalt (Austria) 26
Akademisk Boghandel (Denmark) 84
Akademisk Forlag (Denmark) 80
Akadia, Librería, Editorial (Argentina) 3
Akadoma (Indonesia) 217
Akane Shobo Co Ltd (Japan) 256
Akateeminen Kirjakauppa (Finland) 94
Akateeminen Kustannusliike Oy (Finland) 92
Åkerbloms, Johan, Universitetsbokhandel (Sweden) 389
Akhil Bhartiya Hindi Prakashak Sangh (India) 195
Akhila Bharaliya Sanskrit Parishad (India) 196
Akira Press Ltd (United Kingdom) 424
Akita Shoten Publishing Co Ltd (Japan) 256
Akpagnon, Editions (Togo) 412
Akros Publications (United Kingdom) 424
Akselrad, Michael (Federal Republic of Germany) 131
Aksorn Chareentat (Thailand) 410
Aksorn Charoen Tasna Ltd (Thailand) 410
Akutagawa Prize (Japan) 265
Al Book Co (Pvt) Ltd (India) 213
Al Liamm, Editions (France) 97
Aladdin Books Ltd (United Kingdom) 424
'Alas', Editorial (Spain) 363
Alba (Sweden) 382
Alba Fachverlag GmbH und Co KG (Federal Republic of Germany) 131
Alba Publikation Alf Teloeken GmbH und Co KG (Federal Republic of Germany) 131

Alba SA (Spain) 363
Albah Publishers (Nigeria) 315
Albanus, J H Göhre, Verlag (Switzerland) 392
Albatros (Czechoslovakia) 75
Albatros, Editions (France) 97
Albatros, Editorial, SRL (Argentina) 3
Albatros, Editura (Romania) 346
Albatros Verlag AG (Switzerland) 392
Albatross Books (Australia) 10
Albe Soc Com (Uruguay) 491
Albér, Verlag Karl, GmbH (Federal Republic of Germany) 131
Albert Ier, Bibliothèque royale (Belgium) 44
Albertelli, Ermanno, Editore (Italy) 233
Albin, Editions, Michel Bandes dessinées (France) 97
Albyn Press Ltd (United Kingdom) 424
Alcheh, Librairie Française (Israel) 231
Alden & Mowbray Ltd (United Kingdom) 424
Aldwych Press (United Kingdom) 424
Alekh Prakashan (India) 196
Alemany, Juan Max (Dominican Republic) 86
Alemar-Phoenix Publishing House Inc (Philippines) 332
Alemar's (Philippines) 333
Alemar's Best Sellers Club (Philippines) 333
Alemaya University of Agriculture Library (Ethiopia) 91
Aleph Publishers Ltd (Israel) 226
Alexander, Jacintha, Associates (United Kingdom) 479
Alexander Prize (International Literary Prizes) 517
Alexandria Municipal Library (Egypt) 89
Alfa, Editorial, Argentina SA (Argentina) 3
'Alfa', Wydawnictwa Normalizacyjne (Poland) 335
Alfa — Vydavatel'stvo technickej a ekonomickej literatúry (Czechoslovakia) 75
Alfa y Omega, Editora (Dominican Republic) 86
Alfabeta Bokförlag AB (Sweden) 382
Alfaguara, Ediciones, SA (Spain) 363
Alfani, Libreria, Editrice SRL (Italy) 233
Alfieri Edizioni d'Arte (Italy) 233
Algamiia Almasriia Lilmaktabat Almadrasiia (Egypt) 89
Algemene Vlaamse Boekverkopersbond (Belgium) 35
Algona Publications Pty Ltd (Australia) 10
Alhambra, Editorial, SA (Spain) 363
Ali Publications (Bangladesh) 35
Alianza Editorial Mexicana (Mexico) 284
Alianza Editorial SA (Spain) 364
Alice, The, Literary Award (Australia) 23
Alinari Fratelli SpA Istituto di Edizioni Artistiche (Italy) 233
Alip & Sons Publishing Inc (Philippines) 332
Alison, The, Press (United Kingdom) 424
All India Booksellers' & Publishers' Association (India) 195
All Prints Distributors and Publishers (United Arab Emirates) 421
All-Union Patent and Technical Library (Union of Soviet Socialist Republics) 419
Állami könyvterjesztő vállalat (Hungary) 191
Állami könyvterjesztő vállalat országos antikvár (Hungary) 191
Allan, Ian, Ltd (United Kingdom) 424
Allan, Philip, Publishers Ltd (United Kingdom) 424
Allan, R L, & Son (Publishers) Ltd (United Kingdom) 424
Allara Publishing (Australia) 10
Allen, J A, & Co Ltd (United Kingdom) 424
Allen & Co, W H, PLC (United Kingdom) 425
Allen & Unwin (United Kingdom) 425
Allen & Unwin Australia Pty Ltd (Australia) 11
Allen & Unwin (with the Port Nicholson Press) (New Zealand) 308
Allen Lane (United Kingdom) 425
Allen Lane Award (International Literary Prizes) 517
Allen Lane The Penguin Press (United Kingdom) 425
Allenson (United Kingdom) 425
Allhems Förlag AB (Sweden) 382
Alliance, L', française, Bibliothèque (Senegal) 349
Alliance West African Publishers & Co (Nigeria) 315
Allied Press Ltd (New Zealand) 308
Allied Publishers Private Ltd (India) 196
All'Insegna, Edizioni, del Veltro (Italy) 233
Allison & Busby (United Kingdom) 425
Allmänna Förlaget (Sweden) 382
Allos, Editions (France) 97
Allot, Librairie (Mauritius) 283
Allt om Hobby AB (Sweden) 382
Allt om Hobbys Bokklubb (Sweden) 388
Alma (Denmark) 80
Alma Mater, Librería, Inc (Puerto Rico) 345
Alma'Arif (Indonesia) 217
Almedina, Livraria (Portugal) 340
Almendro, Ediciones El (Spain) 364
Almenna Bókafélagid (Iceland) 193
Almond Press (United Kingdom) 425
Almqvist och Wiksell Bokhandel AB (Sweden) 389
Almqvist och Wiksell Förlag AB (Sweden) 382
Almqvist och Wiksell International (Sweden) 382

INDEX 539

Almqvist och Wiksell Läromedel AB (Sweden) 382
Alonso, Editorial Rodolfo (Argentina) 3
Alpha Books (Zimbabwe) 505
Alpha Literatur Verlag (Federal Republic of Germany) 131
Alpha Translation (United Kingdom) 490
Alphabet & Image Ltd (United Kingdom) 425
Alphabooks Ltd (United Kingdom) 425
Alpina, Editions (France) 97
Alsatia SA (France) 97
Altberliner Verlag (German Democratic Republic) 123
Altea, Ediciones, SA (Spain) 364
Alternative Publishing Co-operative Ltd (Australia) 11
Alternative Verlag GmbH (Federal Republic of Germany) 131
Althoff, Anneliese (Federal Republic of Germany) 131
Altiora NV (Belgium) 36
Alumni Press (Indonesia) 217
Alves, Livraria Francisco, Editora SA (Brazil) 50
Alviella, Goblet d', Prize (Belgium) 46
Am Hasefer (Israel) 226
Am Oved Publishers Ltd (Israel) 226
Amadeus Forlag ApS (Denmark) 80
Amado, Arménio, Editora de Simões, Beirão & Ca Lda (Portugal) 340
Amalthea-Verlag (Austria) 26
Aman, Pustaka, Press Sdn Bhd (Malaysia) 278
Amanuensis Books Ltd (United Kingdom) 425
Amar Prakashan (India) 197
Amarko Book Agency (India) 197
Ambassade, Bibliothèque de l', de France (Niger) 314
Amber Lane Press Ltd (United Kingdom) 425
Ambika Publications (India) 197
Ambo, Uitgeverij, BV (Netherlands) 293
Ambozontany, Editions (Democratic Republic of Madagascar) 276
Ambro Lacus, Buch- und Bildverlag W Kremnitz (Federal Republic of Germany) 131
Ambrosiana, Biblioteca (Italy) 252
Amebo Book Club (Nigeria) 318
América, Librería (Colombia) 71
América, Librería (Nicaragua) 314
América Latina (Uruguay) 491
Américalee, Editorial, SRL (Argentina) 3
American Book Store SA de CV (Mexico) 288
American Books (Argentina) 8
American Bookstore (Greece) 184
American Center Library (India) 214
American Center Library (Jordan) 266
American Center Library, US Information Service (Tanzania) 409
American Cultural Center Library (Burkina Faso) 62
American Cultural Center Library (Togo) 412
American Library (Nepal) 292
American Library Resource Center (Republic of Singapore) 353
American-Scandinavian Foundation (International Organizations) 512
American-Scandinavian Foundation Translation Prize (International Literary Prizes) 517
American University, Libraries of, of Beirut (Lebanon) 273
American University, The, in Cairo Press (Egypt) 88
American University in Cairo Library (Egypt) 89
American University Publishers Group Ltd (United Kingdom) 425
Americana, Editorial (Argentina) 3
Americas, Editora Das, SA Edameris (Brazil) 50
Amerind Publishing Co (P) Ltd (India) 197
Amerind Publishing Co (P) Ltd (India) 216
Amérique, Editions d', et d'Orient, Adrien Maisonneuve (France) 98
Amersfoort, Academische Uitgeverij, VB (Netherlands) 293
Amichai Publishing House (Israel) 226
Amigo, El, de Todos (Venezuela) 493
Amigos del Libro, Ediciones los (Bolivia) 48
Amigos del Libro, Editorial los (Bolivia) 48
Amigos del Libro, Librería los (Bolivia) 48
Amigos do Livro (Portugal) 340
Amikam (Israel) 226
Amina Book Stall (India) 197
Amir Kabir Book Publishing Co (Iran) 220
Amir Publishing Co Ltd (Israel) 226
Amis, Les, de Milosz (France) 118
Amitié, Editions de l' (France) 98
Amitié par le Livre, L' (France) 98
Amitié par le Livre, L' (France) 116
Amman Public Library (Jordan) 266
Ammann Verlag AG (Switzerland) 392
Amorrortu Editores SA (Argentina) 3
Ampersand, The, Press (CI) Ltd (Channel Islands) 65
Amphora, Editions, SA (France) 98
Amsco Publications (United Kingdom) 425
Amsterdam Boek BV (Netherlands) 293
Amsterdam Prizes (Netherlands) 306
Amudha Nilayam Ltd (India) 197

Anabas-Verlag Günter Kämpf KG (Federal Republic of Germany) 131
Anagrama, Editorial (Spain) 364
Anambra State Central Library (Nigeria) 319
Anambra State School Libraries Association (Nigeria) 319
Anand Book Club (India) 212
Anand Paperbacks (India) 197
Ananda Ashram (India) 197
Ananda Books Ltd (Sri Lanka) 378
Anaya, Ediciones, SA (Spain) 364
Anchor (United Kingdom) 425
Ancient & Medieval History Book Club (United Kingdom) 480
Ancora, Editrice (Italy) 233
Ancora, El, Editores Ltda (Colombia) 69
Ancora y Delfín, Librería (Spain) 376
Andaluzas, Editoriales, Unidas SA (Spain) 364
Andersen, Hans Christian, Awards (International Literary Prizes) 517
Andersen, Hans Christian, Prize (Denmark) 86
Andersen, The H C, Prize (Denmark) 86
Andersen Press Ltd (United Kingdom) 425
Andes, Editorial (Colombia) 69
Andhra Pradesh Sahitya Akademi Awards (India) 215
Andreas und Andreas Verlagsbuchhandel (Austria) 26
Andrei, Organização, Editora Ltda (Brazil) 50
Andromeda, Ediciones (Argentina) 3
Ang, K C, Publishing Pte Ltd (Republic of Singapore) 351
Angel Literary Prize (United Kingdom) 486
Angeli, Franco, Libri SRL (Italy) 233
Angelica, Biblioteca (Italy) 252
Angkasa, CV, (Publishers) (Indonesia) 217
Angkatan Sasterawan dan Sasterawani (Asterawani) (Brunei) 60
Anglers Book Society (United Kingdom) 480
Anglo American, The, Bookshop (Egypt) 89
Anglo-Chinese Textbook Publishers Organization Ltd (Hong Kong) 187
Anglo Egyptian, The, Bookshop (Egypt) 89
Anglo-German Foundation (United Kingdom) 425
Anglo-Hellenic Agency (Greece) 184
Angolana, Nova Editorial, SARL (Angola) 2
Angus & Robertson Bookshops (Australia) 20
Angus & Robertson Publishers (Australia) 11
Angus & Robertson (UK) (United Kingdom) 425
Angus & Robertson Writers' Fellowship (Australia) 23
Angus & Robertson Writers for the Young Fellowship (Australia) 23
Angus Hudson Ltd (United Kingdom) 425
Angyra Publishing House, D A Papadimitriou SA (Greece) 182
Aniarapriset (Sweden) 390
Anjuman Taraqqi-e-Urdu Pakistan (Pakistan) 327
Ankara University Library (Turkey) 415
Ankh-Hermes BV (Netherlands) 293
Ankur Publishing House (India) 197
Ann Arbor (United Kingdom) 425
Anowuo Educational Publications (Ghana) 180
Anrich Verlag GmbH (Federal Republic of Germany) 131
Ansata-Verlag (Switzerland) 392
Ansay Pty Ltd (Australia) 11
Ansgar Forlag A/S (Norway) 320
Antara, Pustaka (Indonesia) 217
Antara, Pustaka (Malaysia) 278
Antarkarya, CV (Indonesia) 217
Antenna Edições Técnicas Ltda (Brazil) 50
Anthèse, Edition (France) 98
Anthonian Store Sdn Bhd (Malaysia) 278
Anthonian Store Sdn Bhd (Malaysia) 280
Anthropos, Editions, Sàrl (France) 98
Antígona, Edições (Portugal) 340
Antigruppo Siciliano, Coop Editrice (Italy) 233
Antillana, Editorial (Puerto Rico) 344
Antiquarian Book House (India) 197
Antiquarian Booksellers' Association (United Kingdom) 421
Antiquarian Booksellers' Association of Japan (Japan) 255
Antique Collectors' Club (United Kingdom) 425
Antoine, Librairies (Lebanon) 273
Antoine, SC des Editions Jacques (Belgium) 36
Antonius-Verlag (Switzerland) 392
Antroposofica, Editrice, SRL (Italy) 233
'Antso', Maison d'Edition Protestante (Democratic Republic of Madagascar) 276
Antwerp Bibliophile Society (Belgium) 45
Antwerpse Lloyd NV (Belgium) 36
Anugerah Sastera Negara Prize (Malaysia) 281
Anvil Books Ltd (Republic of Ireland) 221
Anvil Press Poetry Ltd (United Kingdom) 425
Anwari Publications (Bangladesh) 34
Ao Livro Técnico SA (Brazil) 57
Ao Livro Técnico SA Indústria a Comércio (Brazil) 50

Aoki Shoten Co Ltd (Japan) 256
Aowa Press & Publications (Nigeria) 315
Apa Productions (Pte) Ltd (Republic of Singapore) 351
Apáginastantas - Cooperativa de Serviços Culturais (Portugal) 340
Apaya Bookshop (Sudan) 380
Ape, Organizzazione Didattica Editoriale (Italy) 233
Ape, Milan (Italy) 233
Apollo (United Kingdom) 425
Apollo's Reklame en Uitgeversburo (Suriname) 380
Apostolado, Livraria, da Imprensa (Portugal) 340
Apostolica, Biblioteca, Vaticana (Vatican City State) 492
Apostolica Vaticana, Biblioteca (Vatican City State) 492
Apostoliki Diakonia of the Church of Greece (Greece) 182
Apostrof, Forlaget, ApS (Denmark) 80
Apoteksbolaget AB (Sweden) 382
Apple, The, Press (United Kingdom) 425
Appleford Publishing Group (United Kingdom) 425
Appletree, The, Press Ltd (United Kingdom) 425
Applied Science Publishers Ltd (United Kingdom) 425
Aprile, Ruggero (Italy) 233
Aquamarin-Verlag (Federal Republic of Germany) 131
Aquarian Press Ltd (United Kingdom) 425
Aquarius Editora e Distribuidora de Livros Ltda (Brazil) 50
Aquila Publishing (UK) Ltd (United Kingdom) 426
Aquilina, A C, & Co (Malta) 281
Aquilina, A C, & Co (Malta) 282
Arab, Al, Bookshop (Egypt) 89
Arab Advertising Organization (Syria) 407
Arab Archivists Institute (Iraq) 221
Arab Institute for Research and Publishing (Lebanon) 272
Arab Library (Mauritania) 282
Arab Publishing, Al, House (Egypt) 88
Arab Regional Branch of the International Council on Archives (International Organizations) 507
Aramith Uitgevers (Netherlands) 293
Arango, Biblioteca Luis-Angel (Colombia) 71
Aranha, Graca, Prize (Brazil) 59
Arani-Verlag GmbH (Federal Republic of Germany) 131
Aranzadi, Editorial, SA (Spain) 364
Ararat Verlag GmbH (Federal Republic of Germany) 131
Arbalète, L' (France) 98
Arbeiderspers, BV Uitgeverij de (Netherlands) 293
Arbeiterbewegung und Gesellschaftswissenschaft, Verlag (Federal Republic of Germany) 131
Arbeitsgemeinschaft Buchgemeinschaften im Börsenverein des Deutschen Buchhandels (Federal Republic of Germany) 128
Arbeitsgemeinschaft der Archive und Bibliotheken in der evangelischen Kirche (Federal Republic of Germany) 176
Arbeitsgemeinschaft der kirchlichen Büchereiverbände Deutschlands (Federal Republic of Germany) 176
Arbeitsgemeinschaft der Kunstbibliotheken (Federal Republic of Germany) 177
Arbeitsgemeinschaft der Parlaments- und Behördenbibliotheken (Federal Republic of Germany) 177
Arbeitsgemeinschaft der Punktschrift-Drükerein (Federal Republic of Germany) 128
Arbeitsgemeinschaft der Regionalbibliotheken (Federal Republic of Germany) 177
Arbeitsgemeinschaft der Spezialbibliotheken eV (ASpB) (Federal Republic of Germany) 177
Arbeitsgemeinschaft der Vertriebsfachverbände (Federal Republic of Germany) 128
Arbeitsgemeinschaft Deutsche Lateinamerika-Forschung (ADLAF) (Federal Republic of Germany) 131
Arbeitsgemeinschaft für juristisches Bibliotheks- und Dokumentationswesen (Federal Republic of Germany) 177
Arbeitsgemeinschaft für medizinisches Bibliothekswesen (Federal Republic of Germany) 177
Arbeitsgemeinschaft katholischtheologischer Bibliotheken (Federal Republic of Germany) 177
Arbeitsgemeinschaft literarische und Sachbuchverlage (Federal Republic of Germany) 128
Arbeitsgemeinschaft mitteleuropäischer Bibelwerke (Federal Republic of Germany) 131
Arbeitsgemeinschaft rechts- und staatswissenschaftlicher Verleger (Federal Republic of Germany) 128
Arbeitsgemeinschaft von Jugendbuchverlegern in der Bundesrepublik Deutschland eV (Federal Republic of Germany) 129
Arbeitsgemeinschaft wissenschaftliche Literatur eV (Federal Republic of Germany) 129
Arbeitskreis für Deutsche Dichtung eV (Federal Republic of Germany) 178

Arbeitskreis für Jugendliteratur eV (Federal Republic of Germany) 129
Arbeitskreis für Jugendliteratur eV (Federal Republic of Germany) 178
Arbeitswelt, Verlag Die, GmbH (Federal Republic of Germany) 131
Arbetarkultur, Förlagsaktiebolaget (Sweden) 382
Arbó SAC e I (Argentina) 3
Arbol Editorial SA de CV (Mexico) 284
Arca, Editorial, SRL (Uruguay) 490
Arcade-Fonds, Editions, Mercator (Belgium) 36
Arcady Books Ltd (United Kingdom) 426
Arcam, Editions (France) 98
Arcanum, AB (Sweden) 382
Archaeological Survey of India (India) 197
Archbishop Macarios, The Library of the, III Foundation (Cyprus) 74
Archbishopric, Library of the (Cyprus) 74
Arche Verlag AG, Raabe und Vitali (Switzerland) 392
Archer-Burton, The Kitty, Award (Australia) 23
Archief- en Bibliotheekwezen in België (Belgium) 44
Archiginnasio, Biblioteca Comunale dell' (Italy) 252
Archimedes Verlag (Switzerland) 392
Architectural Press Ltd (United Kingdom) 426
Architecture & Arts Publications Co (Sri Lanka) 378
Architektur, Verlag für (Federal Republic of Germany) 131
Architektur, Verlag für (Switzerland) 392
Archivele Statului (Romania) 347
Archives, Central Historical (Bulgaria) 61
Archives, Central, of the People's Republic of Bulgaria (Bulgaria) 61
Archives, Department of (Bahamas) 34
Archives, Direction des Services d', de la Martinique (Martinique) 282
Archives, Inspection des, Musées et Bibliothèques du Mali (Mali) 281
Archives, Public, of Sierra Leone (Sierra Leone) 350
Archives, The Central, for the History of the Jewish People (Israel) 231
Archives de l'Etat (Grand Duchy of Luxembourg) 276
Archives départementales de la Réunion (Réunion) 346
Archives du Sénégal (Senegal) 349
Archives et bibliothèque nationale (Republic of Gabon) 122
Archives fédérales (Switzerland) 405
Archives générales du Royaume (Belgium) 44
Archives nationales (Algeria) 2
Archives nationales (Burkina Faso) 62
Archives nationales, Direction des, Bibliothèque publique et Centre du Documentation (Mauritania) 282
Archives nationales (France) 116
Archives nationales (Niger) 314
Archives nationales (Tunisia) 414
Archives Nationales de Côte d'Ivoire (Ivory Coast) 254
Archives nationales de Madagascar (Democratic Republic of Madagascar) 277
Archives nationales du Benin (Benin) 47
Archives nationales du Cameroun (United Republic of Cameroun) 64
Archives nationales du Zaïre (Zaire) 502
Archives of Early Russian, Central State, Historical Records (Union of Soviet Socialist Republics) 419
Archives of the October Revolution, Central State, and Higher State Bodies (Union of Soviet Socialist Republics) 419
Archives of the RSFSR, Central State (Union of Soviet Socialist Republics) 420
Archives of the USSR, Central State Historical (Union of Soviet Socialist Republics) 420
Archives of the USSR, Central State Literature and Art (Union of Soviet Socialist Republics) 420
Archives Service (Namibia) 291
Archives Service, The, of the Prime Minister's Office of the Socialist Republic of Viet Nam (Socialist Republic of Viet Nam) 494
Archivio Centrale dello Stato (Italy) 252
Archivio Storico, Biblioteca dell', Civico e Biblioteca Trivulziana (Italy) 252
Archivio Storico Ticinese (Switzerland) 392
Archivo General de Centro (Guatemala) 186
Archivo General de Indias (Spain) 376
Archivo General de la Nación (Dominican Republic) 87
Archivo General de la Nación (Mexico) 288
Archivo General de la Nación (Uruguay) 491
Archivo General de la Nación (Venezuela) 493
Archivo General de la Nación del Peru (Peru) 331
Archivo General de Puerto Rico (Puerto Rico) 345
Archivo Histórico de la Provincia Ciudad de la Habana (Cuba) 74
Archivo Historico Nacional (Spain) 376
Archivo Nacional (Mexico) 288
Archivo Nacional (Nicaragua) 314

Archivo Nacional de Colombia, Biblioteca Nacional (Colombia) 71
Archivo Nacional de Historia (Ecuador) 88
Archivo y Biblioteca Capitulares (Spain) 376
Archivos Históricos y Bibliotecas (Mexico) 288
Archiwów Państwowych, Naczelna Dyrekcja (Poland) 338
Archiwum Akt Nowych (Poland) 338
Archiwum Główne Akt Dawnych (Poland) 338
Arciere, Edizioni L', SRL (Italy) 233
Aredit, Publications (France) 98
Arena (United Kingdom) 480
Arena Books (United Kingdom) 426
Arena-Verlag Georg Popp AG & Co (Federal Republic of Germany) 131
Arenabuku Sdn Bhd (Malaysia) 278
Argalia Editore delle Arti Grafiche Editoriali SRL (Italy) 233
Argente, Sentos & Cia Lda (Angola) 2
Argentine National Prize for Literature (Argentina) 9
Argo Press (Australia) 11
Argos, Editorial, Vergara SA (Spain) 364
Argos Press (Federal Republic of Germany) 131
Argosy, Librería (Panama) 328
Argus Books Ltd (United Kingdom) 426
Argus Communications Ltd (United Kingdom) 426
Argus Specialist Publications Ltd (United Kingdom) 426
Arhiv Hrvatske (Yugoslavia) 500
Arhiv na SR Makedonija (Yugoslavia) 500
Arhiv SR Slovenije (Yugoslavia) 500
Arhiv Srbije (Yugoslavia) 500
Århus Kommunes Biblioteker (Denmark) 84
Arica, Librería (Peru) 331
Ariel, Editorial, SA (Spain) 364
Ariel (Mexico) 284
Ariel (United Kingdom) 426
Ariel Publishing House (Israel) 226
Aries Lima (Indonesia) 217
Arinos, Afonso, Prize (Brazil) 59
Aris & Phillips Ltd (United Kingdom) 426
Aristea Editrice SpA (Italy) 234
Ariston, Editions, Verlag (Switzerland) 392
Ark Boeken Publishing House (Netherlands) 294
Arka, Savitri SRL — Edizioni (Italy) 234
Arkady, Wydawnictwo (Poland) 335
Arkana-Verlag (Federal Republic of Germany) 132
Arkel, Uitgeverij Jan van (Netherlands) 294
Arkib Negara Malaysia (Malaysia) 280
Arkın Kitabevi (Turkey) 414
Arkistoyhdistys ry (Finland) 94
Arkivarforeningen (Norway) 324
Arkivforeningen (Denmark) 85
Arlecchino Teaterförlag (Sweden) 388
Arlekin (Greece) 182
Arlen House Ltd (Republic of Ireland) 221
Arlington Books (Publishers) Ltd (United Kingdom) 426
Armada Books (United Kingdom) 426
Armando, Editore Armando, SRL (Italy) 234
Armazens Distribuidores Lta (Mozambique) 291
Armed Forces Library Service (Ghana) 181
Armenia Editore SpA (Italy) 234
Armitano, Ernesto (Venezuela) 492
Armon Publishing House Ltd (Israel) 226
Arms & Armour Press Ltd (United Kingdom) 426
Arnado, Livraria, Lda (Portugal) 340
Arnar og Örlygs, Bókaklúbbur (Iceland) 194
Arnaud Editrice SRL (Italy) 234
Arndt-, Ernst-Moritz-, Universität Universitätsbibliothek (German Democratic Republic) 127
Arnkrone Forlaget A/S (Denmark) 80
Arnold, Edward (United Kingdom) 426
Arnold, Edward, (Australia) Pty Ltd (Australia) 11
Arnold & Son, E J, Ltd (United Kingdom) 426
Arnold Publishers (India) Pvt Ltd (India) 197
Arnold-Wheaton (United Kingdom) 426
Aromolaran Publishing Co Ltd (Nigeria) 315
Arquivo Historico de Moçambique (Mozambique) 291
Arquivo Nacional (Brazil) 58
Arquivo Nacional da Torre do Tombo (Portugal) 343
Arrow (Australia) 20
Arrow (New Zealand) 311
Arrow Books Ltd (United Kingdom) 426
Arrow Co (Israel) 226
Ars Christiana (Poland) 335
Ars Edition (Switzerland) 392
Ars Edition GmbH (Federal Republic of Germany) 132
Ars Polona (Poland) 334
Ars Polona (Poland) 337
Arsan Publishing House Ltd (Israel) 226
Arsenal, Bibliothèque de l' (France) 116

Arsenal, Das, Verlag für Kultur und Politik GmbH (Federal Republic of Germany) 132
Arsenale Editrice SRL (Italy) 234
Arsenides, John, Ekdotis (Greece) 182
Arsip Nasional Republik Indonesia (Indonesia) 219
Art, The, Publisher (Hong Kong) 187
Art Address Verlag Müller GmbH und Co KG (Federal Republic of Germany) 132
Art Calédoniennes, Editions d' (New Caledonia) 307
Art et d'Archéologie, Bibliothèque d', (Fondation Jacques Doucet) (France) 116
Art Guide Publications (United Kingdom) 426
Art Heritage (United Kingdom) 426
Art Trade, The, Press Ltd (United Kingdom) 426
Artbook International (Federal Republic of Germany) 132
Artech House (United Kingdom) 426
Arted (Editions d'Art) (France) 98
Artemis Press Ltd (United Kingdom) 427
Artemis und Winkler Verlag (Federal Republic of Germany) 132
Artemis Verlags AG (Switzerland) 392
Artenova, Editora, Ltda (Brazil) 50
Artes, Ediciones, Graficas Cobas SA (Spain) 364
Artes, Livraria Editora, Medicas Ltda (Brazil) 50
Artexim — Foreign Trade Co (Romania) 347
Arthaud, Editions, SA (France) 98
Artia (Czechoslovakia) 75
Artia (Czechoslovakia) 78
Artibus et Literis (Federal Republic of Germany) 175
Artigas-Washington, Biblioteca, (USIS) (Uruguay) 491
Artis-Historia, SC (Belgium) 36
Artis-Historia, SC (Belgium) 44
Artisjus (Hungary) 191
Artists' and Writers' Guild of South Africa (Republic of South Africa) 361
Artists Book Club Ltd (United Kingdom) 480
Artists House (United Kingdom) 427
Artlines (UK) Ltd (United Kingdom) 479
Artlook Books (Australia) 11
Artou (Switzerland) 392
Arts Council Awards and Bursaries (International Literary Prizes) 517
Arts et Métiers Graphiques (France) 98
Arts Graphiques, Compagnie Française des, SA (France) 98
Arts Guild (United Kingdom) 480
Artwork Publishing (United Kingdom) 427
Artystyczne i Filmowe, Wydawnictwa (Poland) 335
Aruba Boekhandel (Netherland Antilles) 307
Arvon Foundation International Poetry Competition (International Literary Prizes) 517
Asahiya Shoten Ltd (Booksellers) (Japan) 263
Asakura Publishing Co Ltd (Japan) 256
Aschehoug, H, & Co (W Nygaard) A/S (Norway) 320
Aschehoug Dansk Forlag A/S (Denmark) 80
Aschendorffsche Verlagsbuchhandlung (Federal Republic of Germany) 132
Asempa Publishers (Ghana) 180
Asesoría Técnica de Ediciones SA (Spain) 364
Asgar Ali Book Centre (Trinidad and Tobago) 413
Asher, A, & Co, BV (Netherlands) 294
Ashford Press Publishing (United Kingdom) 427
Ashgrove Press Ltd (United Kingdom) 427
Ashish Publishing House (India) 197
Ashmolean Museum Publications (United Kingdom) 427
Ashraf, Shaikh Muhammad (Pakistan) 325
Ashton & Denton Publishing Co (CI) Ltd (Channel Islands) 65
Ashton Scholastic (Australia) 11
Ashton Scholastic Ltd (New Zealand) 308
Asia Afrika (Indonesia) 217
Asia Book Co (Republic of Singapore) 353
Asia Books Co Ltd (Thailand) 411
Asia Pacific Books (New Zealand) 308
Asia Publishing Co (India) 197
Asian Cultural Centre for UNESCO (International Organizations) 511
Asian Educational Services (India) 197
Asian Publishers (India) 197
Asian Trading Corporation (India) 197
Asiathèque, L' (France) 98
Asiatic Society Library (India) 214
Askelin och Hägglund Förlag (Sweden) 382
Askild och Kärnekull Förlag AB (Sweden) 382
Aslan (United Kingdom) 427
Aslib (United Kingdom) 483
Aslib, The Association for Information Management (United Kingdom) 427
Asmara Bookshop (Ethiopia) 91
Asmara Public Library (Ethiopia) 91
Asmara University Library (Ethiopia) 91
Asociación Argentina de Bibliotecas y Centros de Información Cientificos y Tecnicos (Argentina) 9
Asociación Bautista Argentina de Publicaciones (Argentina) 3

Asociación Bibliotecologica Guatemalteca (Guatemala) 186
Asociación Boliviana de Bibliotecarios (ABB) (Bolivia) 48
Asociación Colombiana de Bibliotecarios (Colombia) 71
Asociación Costarricense de Bibliotecarios (Costa Rica) 73
Asociación de Bibliotecarios de El Salvador (El Salvador) 90
Asociación de Bibliotecarios de Instituciones de Enseñanza Superior e Investigación (ABIESI) (Mexico) 289
Asociación de Bibliotecarios del Paraguay (Paraguay) 330
Asociación de Bibliotecarios Graduados del Istmo de Panamá (Panama) 328
Asociación de Bibliotecarios Graduados del Paraguay (Paraguay) 330
Asociación de Bibliotecarios Universitarios del Paraguay (Paraguay) 330
Asociación de Bibliotecarios y Archiveros de Honduras (Honduras) 187
Asociación de Bibliotecas Agricolas (Peru) 331
Asociación de Bibliotecas Universitarias y Especializadas de Nicaragua (Nicaragua) 314
Asociación de Bibliotecólogos y Afines del Uruguay (Uruguay) 491
Asociación de Escritores de Venezuela (Venezuela) 494
Asociación de Escritores y Artistas Españoles (Spain) 362
Asociación de Ex-Alumnos de la Escuela Nacional de Bibliotecarios (Argentina) 9
Asociación de Libreros del Uruguay (Uruguay) 490
Asociación Dominicana de Bibliotecarios (ASODOBI) (Dominican Republic) 87
Asociación Ecuatoriana de Bibliotecarios (AEB) (Ecuador) 88
Asociación Educacionista Argentina (Argentina) 3
Asociación Española de Archiveros, Bibliotecarios, Museólogos y Documentalistas (Spain) 377
Asociación Española de Editores de Musica (AEDEM) (Spain) 362
Asociación General de Archivistas de El Salvador (El Salvador) 90
Asociación Interamericana de Bibliotecarios y Documentalistas Agrícolas (International Organizations) 507
Asociación Latinoamericana de Escuelas de Bibliotecología y Ciencia de la Información (ALEBCI) (International Organizations) 507
Asociación Mexicana de Bibliotecarios AC (AMBAC) (Mexico) 289
Asociación Nacional de Bibliotecarios, Archiveros, Arqueologos y Documentalistas (Anabad) (Spain) 377
Asociación Nacional de Escritores y Artistas (ANEA) (Peru) 330
Asociación Nicaragüense de Bibliotecarios (ASNIBI) (Nicaragua) 314
Asociación Panameña de Bibliotecarios (Panama) 328
Asociación para el Progresso de la Dirección (APD) (Spain) 364
Asociación Peruana de Archiveros (Peru) 331
Asociación Peruana de Bibliotecas (APB) (Peru) 331
Asociación Uruguaya de Escritores (Uruguay) 490
Asociatia Bibliotecarilor din RSR (Romania) 347
Asociation di Biblioteka i Archivo di Korsow (Carbido) (Netherland Antilles) 307
Aspioti-Elka SA (Greece) 182
Asplund (Sweden) 382
Assam Publishers' & Booksellers' Association (India) 195
Assayad, Dar (Lebanon) 272
Assimakopouli (Greece) 182
Assimil, Editions, SA (France) 98
Assimil, Uitgaven Nelis PVBA (Belgium) 36
Assimil-Verlag KG (Federal Republic of Germany) 132
Asso Verlag (Federal Republic of Germany) 132
Associação Brasileira de Bibliotecários (Brazil) 58
Associação Brasileira de Livreiros Antiquarios (Brazil) 49
Associação Brasileira do Livro (Brazil) 49
Associação dos Arquivistas Brasileiros (Brazil) 58
Associação Paulista de Bibliotecários (Brazil) 58
Associação Portuguesa de Bibliotecários, Arquivistas e Documentalistas (Portugal) 344
Associação Portuguesa dos Editores e Livreiros (Portugal) 339
Associação Profissional de Bibliotecários do Estado do Rio de Janeiro (APBERJ) (Brazil) 58
Associação Rio-Grandense de Bibliotecários (Brazil) 58
Associació d'Editors en Llengua Catalana (Spain) 363
Associated Book Publishers (Aust) Ltd (Australia) 11

Associated Book Publishers (NZ) Ltd (New Zealand) 308
Associated Book Publishers (UK) Ltd (United Kingdom) 427
Associated Booksellers of Southern Africa Ltd (Republic of South Africa) 354
Associated Business Press (United Kingdom) 427
Associated Publishers Amsterdam (Netherlands) 294
Associated Publishers Inc (Philippines) 332
Associated Publishing House (India) 197
Associated University Presses (United Kingdom) 427
Association belge de Documentation (Belgium) 45
Association de l'Ecole nationale supérieure de Bibliothécaires (France) 117
Association des Amis du Livre (French Guiana) 122
Association des Archivistes et Bibliothécaires (Belgium) 45
Association des Archivistes français (France) 117
Association des Bibliothécaires, Archivistes, Documentalistes et Muséographes du Cameroun (ABADCAM) (United Republic of Cameroun) 64
Association des Bibliothécaires-Documentalistese de l'Institut d'Etudes sociales de l'Etat (Belgium) 45
Association des Bibliothécaires et Documentalistes Spécialisés (France) 117
Association des Bibliothécaires et du Personnel des Bibliothèques des Ministères de Belgique (Belgium) 45
Association des Bibliothécaires français (France) 117
Association des Bibliothécaires Laotiens (Laos) 272
Association des Bibliothécaires Suisses (Vereinigung Schweizerischer Bibliothekare) (Switzerland) 406
Association des Bibliothèques ecclésiastiques de France (ABEF) (France) 117
Association des Bibliothèques Internationales (International Organizations) 507
Association des Diplômes de l'Ecole de Bibliothécaires-Documentalistes (France) 117
Association des Ecrivains belges de Langue française (Belgium) 45
Association des Editeurs belges (Belgium) 35
Association des Libraires spécialisés pour la Jeunesse (France) 96
Association des Sociétés scientifiques médicales belges (ASBL) (Belgium) 36
Association des Traducteurs Littéraires de France (France) 121
Association for Information Management (United Kingdom) 483
Association for Science Education (United Kingdom) 427
Association for Scottish Literary Studies (United Kingdom) 427
Association for Scottish Literary Studies (United Kingdom) 484
Association for the Promotion of the International Circulation of the Press (International Organizations) 507
Association for the Study of Australian Literature Ltd (Australia) 22
Association française des Documentalistes et Bibliothécaires spécialisés (France) 117
Association internationale de Bibliophilie (International Organizations) 507
Association internationale des Critiques littéraires (NGO) (International Organizations) 507
Association internationale des Documentalistes et Techniciens de l'Information AID (International Organizations) 507
Association internationale des Ecoles des Sciences de l'Information (AIESI) (International Organizations) 507
Association internationale pour le Développement de la Documentation des Bibliothèques et des Archives en Afrique (International Organizations) 507
Association nationale des Bibliothécaires, Archivistes et Documentalistes sénégalais (ANBADS) (Senegal) 349
Association nationale des Bibliothécaires d'Expression française (Belgium) 45
Association nationale des Bibliothécaires Municipaux (France) 117
Association nationale des Poètes et Ecrivains camerounais (APEC) (United Republic of Cameroun) 64
Association of African Universities (International Organizations) 512
Association of Arts and Letters (Greece) 185
Association of Assistant Librarians (United Kingdom) 483
Association of Australian University Presses (Australia) 10
Association of Authors' Agents (United Kingdom) 421
Association of British Directory Publishers (United Kingdom) 421
Association of British Library and Information Studies Schools (ABLISS) (United Kingdom) 483

Association of British Science Writers (United Kingdom) 485
Association of British Theological and Philosophical Libraries (United Kingdom) 483
Association of Caribbean University, Research and Institutional Libraries (International Organizations) 507
Association of Hebrew Writers (Israel) 225
Association of International Libraries (AIL) (International Organizations) 508
Association of Learned & Professional Society Publishers (United Kingdom) 421
Association of Libraries of Judaica and Hebraica in Europe (International Organizations) 508
Association of Little Presses (United Kingdom) 421
Association of London Chief Librarians (United Kingdom) 483
Association of Mail Order Publishers (United Kingdom) 421
Association of Publishers' Educational Representatives (United Kingdom) 421
Association of Registered Archivists of Iran Secretariat (Iran) 220
Association of Scottish Health Sciences Librarians (United Kingdom) 483
Association of Special Libraries of the Philippines (ASLP) (Philippines) 333
Association of Yugoslav Publishers and Booksellers (Yugoslavia) 495
Association pour la Médiathèque Publique (AMP) (France) 117
Association pour le Développement de la Documentation, des Bibliothèques et Archives de la Côte d'Ivoire (ADBACI) (Ivory Coast) 254
Association professionnelle des Bibliothécaires et Documentalistes (APBD) (Belgium) 45
Association suisse des Editeurs de Langue française (Switzerland) 391
Association suisse des Libraires de Langue française (Switzerland) 391
Association suisse des Traducteurs et Interprètes (ASTI) (Switzerland) 406
Association suisse romande des Diffuseurs de Livres (Switzerland) 391
Association togolaise pour la Documentation, les Bibliothèques, Archives et Musées (ATODBAM) (Togo) 412
Association togolaise pour le Développement de la Documentation, des Bibliothèques, Archives et Musées (Togo) 412
Association tunisienne de Documentalistes, Bibliothécaires et Archivistes (Tunisia) 414
Association voltaique pour le Développement des Bibliothèques, des Archives et de la Documentation (AVDBAD) (Burkina Faso) 62
Association Zairoise des Archivistes, Bibliothècaires et Documentalistes (Zaire) 503
Associazione dei Librai della Svizzera Italiana (ALSI) (Switzerland) 391
Associazione Italiana Biblioteche (Italy) 252
Associazione Italiana Editori (Italy) 232
Associazione Librai Antiquari d'Italia (Italy) 232
Associazione Librai Italiani (Italy) 232
Associazione Nazionale Archivistica Italiana (Italy) 252
Astab Books Ltd (Ghana) 181
Astaneh Qods Central Library (Iran) 220
Aster, Editorial (Portugal) 340
Ästhetik und Kommunikation Verlags-GmbH (Federal Republic of Germany) 132
Astir (Greece) 182
Astrea, Editorial, de Alfredo y Ricardo Depalma SRL (Argentina) 3
Astrolabe, L' (France) 98
Astrolabio-Ubaldini, Casa Editrice, Editore (Italy) 234
Asuri de Ediciones SA (Spain) 364
Atanor, Editrice, SRL (Italy) 234
Atbara Public Library (Sudan) 380
Atelier (Egypt) 90
Atelier im Bauernhaus, Verlag (Federal Republic of Germany) 132
Atelier Verlag Andernach (AVA) (Federal Republic of Germany) 132
Atenas, Sociedad de Educación, SA (Spain) 364
Ateneo, Editorial, de Caracas (Venezuela) 492
Ateneo, Editorial El, Pedro García SALEI (Argentina) 3
Ateneo, Edizioni Dell', SpA (Italy) 234
Ateneo, El (Argentina) 8
Ateneo, Librería El (Paraguay) 329
Ateneo Barcelonés Biblioteca (Spain) 376
Ateneo Cientifico, Literario y Artistico (Spain) 377
Ateneo de Madrid, Biblioteca del (Spain) 376
Ateneo de Manila University Libraries (Philippines) 333
Ateneo de Manila University Press (Philippines) 332
Ateneo de Sevilla Prize (Spain) 377
Ateneo de Valladolid Prize (Spain) 377

542 INDEX

Athena Bookshops (United Kingdom) 481
Athenaeum Boekhandel (Netherlands) 304
Athenaeum Verlag AG (Switzerland) 393
Athenäum Verlag GmbH (Federal Republic of Germany) 132
Athene Publishing Co (United Kingdom) 427
Atheneu, Livraria, Ltda (Brazil) 50
Athenon, Ekdotike, SA (Greece) 182
Athens Academy Library (Greece) 185
Athens College Library (Greece) 185
Atheret Publishing House (Israel) 226
Athesia, Verlagsanstalt (Italy) 234
Athlone, The, Press Ltd (United Kingdom) 427
Atica, Editora, SA (Brazil) 51
Atlantic (United Kingdom) 427
Atlantic Large Print (United Kingdom) 427
Atlantica Editrice SARL (Italy) 234
Atlántida, Editorial, SA (Argentina) 3
Atlântida, Livraria Editora, Ltda (Portugal) 340
Atlantis, Bokförlaget, AB (Sweden) 382
Atlantis M Pechlivanides & Co SA (Greece) 182
Atlantis Verlag AG (Switzerland) 393
Atlantis-Verlag GmbH & Co KG (Federal Republic of Germany) 132
Atlas, Editora, SA (Brazil) 51
Atlas, The, Bookshop (Ghana) 181
Atlas Book Sales Ltd (United Kingdom) 479
Atlas-Diagoras (Greece) 182
Atma Ram & Sons (India) 197
Atma Ram & Sons (India) 213
Atomizdat (Union of Soviet Socialist Republics) 417
Atrium, Ediciones, SA (Spain) 364
Atrium (Netherlands) 294
Atrium Verlag AG (Switzerland) 393
Attic Press (Republic of Ireland) 221
Attica Publications (United Kingdom) 427
Attié, Librairie (Burkina Faso) 62
Attila, József, Prize (Hungary) 192
Atual Editora Ltda (Brazil) 51
Au Messager (Central African Republic) 64
Au Ping-Pong, Librairie (French Polynesia) 122
Aubanel SA (France) 98
Aubepine, Editions (France) 98
Aubier-Montaigne, Editions, SA (France) 98
Auckland Public Library (New Zealand) 312
Auckland University Press (New Zealand) 308
Audiffred, François-Joseph, Prize (France) 119
Audivox (Belgium) 36
Audivox (Belgium) 44
Auer, Ludwig, GmbH (Federal Republic of Germany) 132
Aufbau-Verlag Berlin und Weimar (German Democratic Republic) 123
Augener (United Kingdom) 427
August Cesarec (Yugoslavia) 496
Augustin-Verlag (Switzerland) 393
Augustiniennes, Etudes (France) 98
Augustinus, Boekhandel (Netherland Antilles) 307
Augustinus, Edizioni (Italy) 234
Aujourd'hui, Editions d', ('Les Introuvables') (France) 98
Aujourd'hui Prize (France) 119
Aulis Verlag Deubner & Co KG (Federal Republic of Germany) 132
Aurelia Books PVBA (Belgium) 36
Auria, M d', Editore della 'EST — Editoriale Studi e Testi — SNC' (Italy) 234
Aurobindo, Sri, Books Distribution Agency (SABDA) (India) 197
Aurora, Asociación Ediciones La (Argentina) 3
Aurora, Gráfica Editora, Ltda (Brazil) 51
Aurora Art Publishers (Union of Soviet Socialist Republics) 417
Aurora Press (Australia) 11
Aurum Press Ltd (United Kingdom) 427
Aurum Verlag GmbH & Co KG (Federal Republic of Germany) 132
Aussaat-und-Schriftenmissions-Verlag GmbH (Federal Republic of Germany) 132
Aussenhandels-Ausschuss (Federal Republic of Germany) 129
Austicks Headrow Bookshop (United Kingdom) 481
Australasian Educa Press Pty Ltd (AE Press) (Australia) 11
Australasian Publishing Co Pty Ltd (Australia) 11
Australia & New Zealand Book Co Pty Ltd (Australia) 11
Australian Academy of Science (Australia) 11
Australian Advisory Council on Bibliographical Services (AACOBS) (Australia) 21
Australian Archives, NSW Regional Office (Australia) 21
Australian Association for Health Literature and Information Services Inc (Australia) 21
Australian Awards for Young Writers (Australia) 23
Australian Book Publishers' Association (Australia) 10
Australian Booksellers Association Inc (Australia) 10

Australian Broadcasting Corporation (Enterprises) (Australia) 11
Australian Copyright Council (Australia) 10
Australian Council, The, for Educational Research Ltd (Australia) 11
Australian Encyclopaedia Pty Ltd (Australia) 11
Australian Government Publications (Australia) 20
Australian Government Publishing Service (Australia) 11
Australian Institute of Aboriginal Studies (Australia) 11
Australian Institute of Criminology (Australia) 12
Australian Library Promotion Council (Australia) 21
Australian Literature Society (Australia) 22
Australian Literature Society Gold Medal (Australia) 23
Australian Medical Librarians' Group, ACT Branch (Australia) 21
Australian National Gallery (Australia) 12
Australian National University Library (Australia) 21
Australian National University Press (Australia) 12
Australian Natives' Association Literature Award (Australia) 23
Australian Reader's Choice (Australia) 20
Australian School Library Association (Australia) 21
Australian Society of Archivists Inc (Australia) 21
Australian Society of Authors Ltd (Australia) 22
Australian Society of Indexers (Australia) 10
Australian Standard Book Numbering Agency (Australia) 10
Australian Universities Press Pty Ltd (Australia) 12
Australian Writers' Guild Ltd (Australia) 22
Austrian Children's and Young People's Book Prizes (Austria) 33
Austrian State Prize for European Literature (International Literary Prizes) 517
Austrian State Prize for Literature for Children and Young People (Austria) 33
Auteurs, Les, Associés (France) 98
Author Press (Australia) 12
Authors' Club (United Kingdom) 485
Authors' Club First Novel Award (United Kingdom) 486
Authors' Club Sir Banister Fletcher Prize Trust (United Kingdom) 486
Authors' Guild of India (India) 195
Authors' Licensing & Collecting Society (United Kingdom) 421
Autobooks (United Kingdom) 427
Autocourse (United Kingdom) 427
Automobile Association (United Kingdom) 427
Automobilia (Italy) 234
Autonomie, Edizioni delle, SRL (Italy) 234
Autoren, Verlag der, GmbH & Co KG (Federal Republic of Germany) 132
Autoren- und Verlagsgesellschaft, Syndikat (Federal Republic of Germany) 132
Autran, Joseph, Prize (France) 119
'Aux Belles Images', Librairie (Morocco) 290
'Aux Frères Réunis', Librairie (United Republic of Cameroun) 64
Auzou, Editions Philippe (France) 98
Avant-Scène, Editions l' (France) 98
Avante, Editorial, SA (Mexico) 284
'Avante!', Editorial (Portugal) 340
Avebury (United Kingdom) 427
Avele College Library (Western Samoa) 495
Aventura Forlag (Norway) 320
Avery, Thomas, & Sons Ltd (New Zealand) 308
Avery, Thomas, and Sons Ltd (New Zealand) 311
Aviation Book Club (United Kingdom) 480
Avicenne Librairie Internationale (Syria) 407
Avicenum, zdravotnické nakladatelství (Czechoslovakia) 75
Avinash Reference Publications (India) 197
Avon-Anglia Publications & Services (United Kingdom) 427
Award for Achievement (New Zealand) 313
Award for Literature and Scientific Publications (Turkey) 416
Award Publications Ltd (United Kingdom) 427
Awoko (Nigeria) 315
Awqaf, Al- (Iraq) 220
Axel-Juncker Verlag Jacobi KG (Federal Republic of Germany) 132
Axster, Brigitte (Federal Republic of Germany) 175
Ayacucho, Biblioteca (Venezuela) 492
Ayala Museum Library & Iconographic Archives (Philippines) 333
Ayalga Ediciones SA (Spain) 364
Ayam, Al-, Press Co Ltd (Sudan) 379
Aymá, Editorial, SA Editora (Spain) 364
Ayuso, Editorial, Ayuso (Spain) 364
Azara, Editorial, SA (Spain) 364
Azerbaidzhanskaya gosudarstvennaya respublikanskaya biblioteka im M F Akhundova (Union of Soviet Socialist Republics) 420

Azhar, Al-, University Library (Egypt) 89
Azim Publishing House (Pakistan) 325
Azteca, Editorial, SA (Mexico) 284

B & T Directories (Pvt) Ltd (Zimbabwe) 504
B A B (Iceland) 194
B A G Buchhändler-Abrechnungs-Gesellschaft mbH (Federal Republic of Germany) 129
B A S H (United Kingdom) 421
B B B (Sweden) 382
B B C Books (United Kingdom) 427
B C N Z Enterprises (New Zealand) 308
B E (Portugal) 340
B F B S (United Kingdom) 427
B F I Publishing (United Kingdom) 427
B H I (Republic of Ireland) 221
B I G Database Publishing Pvt Ltd (India) 197
B I G Z (Yugoslavia) 496
B I M H Publications (United Kingdom) 428
B K V-Brasilienkunde Verlag GmbH (Federal Republic of Germany) 132
B L A C Publishing House (Republic of South Africa) 355
B L A Publishing Ltd (United Kingdom) 428
B L V Verlagsgesellschaft mbH (Federal Republic of Germany) 132
B O D (United Kingdom) 421
B P B Publications (India) 198
B P C C (United Kingdom) 428
B P S Books (United Kingdom) 428
B P T (United Kingdom) 428
B R G M, Editions (France) 98
B R Publishing Corporation (India) 198
B S C Books Ltd (United Kingdom) 428
B S C Books Ltd (United Kingdom) 33
B S-Verlag Manfred Kerler (Federal Republic of Germany) 133
B V B (Federal Republic of Germany) 133
Baars-Jelgersma, Auteursbureau Greta (Netherlands) 304
Babani, Bernard, (Publishing) Ltd (United Kingdom) 428
Bachem, J P, Verlag GmbH (Federal Republic of Germany) 133
Bachman & Turner (United Kingdom) 428
Bäckman, Ida, Prize (Sweden) 390
Bacon, Francis, Society Inc (United Kingdom) 485
Bacon, S John, Pty Ltd (Australia) 12
Baconnière, Editions de la, SA (Switzerland) 393
Badcock & Rozycki (United Kingdom) 479
Badger Books (United Kingdom) 428
Baedeker, Buchhandlung G D (Federal Republic of Germany) 175
Baedeker, Karl, GmbH (Federal Republic of Germany) 133
Baedekers Autoführer-Verlag GmbH (Federal Republic of Germany) 133
Baekelmans, Lode, Prize (Belgium) 46
Baensch, Hans A (Federal Republic of Germany) 133
Bagchi, K P, & Co (India) 198
Bagster, Samuel (United Kingdom) 428
Bagutta Prize (Italy) 253
Bahá'í Book Club (United Kingdom) 480
Bahá'í Publishing Trust (India) 198
Bahá'í Publishing Trust (United Kingdom) 428
Bahá'í Verlag GmbH (Federal Republic of Germany) 133
Bahá'íes, Maison d'Editions, ASBL (Belgium) 36
Bahamas Anglo American Book Store (Bahamas) 34
Bahamas Book & Bible House (Bahamas) 34
Bahloo Computers (Australia) 12
Bahloo Publishers (Australia) 12
Bahn, Friedrich, Verlag GmbH (Federal Republic of Germany) 133
Bahrain Bookshop (Bahrain) 34
Bahrain Writers and Literators Association (Bahrain) 34
Baifukan Co Ltd (Japan) 256
Baik Rog Publishing Co (Republic of Korea) 269
Bailey Bros & Swinfen Ltd (United Kingdom) 428
Baillière, Editions J-B (France) 98
Baillière Tindall (United Kingdom) 428
Bak Yung Sa (Republic of Korea) 269
Bakalov', Knigoizdatelstvo 'Georgi (Bulgaria) 60
Baker Press, Howard, Ltd (United Kingdom) 428
Baker (Publishers), John, Ltd (United Kingdom) 428
Bakewell, Michael, & Associates Ltd (United Kingdom) 479
Bakker, Bert, BV (Netherlands) 294
Balai, Perum, Pustaka (Indonesia) 217
Balans, Uitgeverij (Netherlands) 294
Balcells, Carmen, Agencia Literaria (Brazil) 57
Balcells, Carmen, Agencia Literaria (Spain) 375
Bale Bandung — Sumur Bandung (Indonesia) 217

Balkan-Press (Federal Republic of Germany) 175
Balkema, A A (Netherlands) 294
Balkema, A A, Publishers (Republic of South Africa) 355
Ball, Jonathan, Publishers (Pty) Ltd (Republic of South Africa) 355
Balland, André (France) 98
Balme Library (Ghana) 181
Balmer, H R, AG Verlag (Switzerland) 393
Banca y Comercio, Editorial, SA (Mexico) 284
Banco, Biblioteca del, Central de la República Argentina (Argentina) 8
Bandarnsarn (Thailand) 410
Bandicoot Books (Australia) 12
Bang, Herman, Memorial Prize (Denmark) 86
Banga Sahitya Bhavan (Bangladesh) 34
Bangalore, The, Printing & Publishing Co Ltd (India) 198
Bangalore Book Bureau (India) 213
Bangkok Bank Foundation Prize (Thailand) 412
Bangkok Central Book Depot (Thailand) 411
Bangladesh Books International Ltd (Bangladesh) 34
Bangladesh Books International Ltd (Bangladesh) 35
Bangladesh Braille Library for the Blind International (Bangladesh) 35
Bangladesh Granthagar Samity (Bangladesh) 35
Bangladesh Institute of Development Studies Library (Bangladesh) 35
Bangladesh Pustak Prokashak o Bikreta Samity (Bangladesh) 34
Bani Mandir (India) 198
Bani Publications (India) 198
Bank of New Zealand Novice Writers' Award (New Zealand) 313
Bank of New Zealand Young Writers' Awards (New Zealand) 313
Bankers Books Ltd (United Kingdom) 428
Banmai (Thailand) 410
Banner, The, of Truth Trust (United Kingdom) 428
Bansal & Co (India) 198
Bantam (Australia) 12
Bantam Books (United Kingdom) 428
Bantam Press (United Kingdom) 428
Baptist Book Centre (Zimbabwe) 505
Bär, U, Verlag (Switzerland) 393
Bar-David Literary Agency (Israel) 230
Bar Ilan University Library (Israel) 231
Bar Ilan University Press (Israel) 226
Bar Urian Publishing House (Israel) 226
Barath, Editorial SA (Spain) 365
Barbare (Switzerland) 393
Barbera, Giunti, Editore (Italy) 234
Barblan et Saladin, Librairie (Switzerland) 405
Barcanova, Editorial, SA (Spain) 365
Bardet, René, Prize (France) 119
Barebones Books (United Kingdom) 428
Bärenreiter-Verlag (Federal Republic of Germany) 133
Bargezzi-Verlag AG (Switzerland) 393
Bari, Editoriale (Italy) 234
Barjes, Edizioni Oreste (Italy) 234
Barker, Arthur, Ltd (United Kingdom) 428
Barlevi (Israel) 226
Barn, Bokklubbens (Norway) 323
Barnakarn (Thailand) 410
Barnakieh Trading (Thailand) 410
Barnasilpa (Thailand) 410
Barnens Bokklubb (Sweden) 388
Baron Publishing Ltd (United Kingdom) 428
Barque & Co (Pakistan) 325
Barr Smith, The, Library (Australia) 21
Barracuda Books Ltd (United Kingdom) 428
Barral Editores SA (Spain) 365
Barrau (New Caledonia) 307
Barre, André, Prize (France) 119
Barreiro y Ramos SA (Uruguay) 490
Barreiro y Ramos SA (Uruguay) 491
Barrie & Jenkins Ltd (United Kingdom) 428
Barrikaden, Förlaget (Sweden) 382
Barry Editorial Com Ind SRL (Argentina) 3
Barry Rose (United Kingdom) 428
Bartels und Wernitz, Verlag, KG (Federal Republic of Germany) 133
Barth, Johann Ambrosius, Verlagsbuchhandlung (German Democratic Republic) 124
Barth, Otto Wilhelm, -Verlag KG (Federal Republic of Germany) 133
Bartholomew & Son, John, Ltd (United Kingdom) 428
Barthou, Alice Louis, Prize (France) 119
Barthou, Louis, Prize (France) 119
Barthou, Max, Prize (France) 119
Barudio und Hess Verlag (Federal Republic of Germany) 133
Baschet et Cie, Editeurs (France) 98
Baseball Magazine-Sha Co Ltd (Japan) 256
Bashir, Al, Bookshop (Sudan) 380
Basic Books (United Kingdom) 428
Básica Editora (Portugal) 340

Basileia Verlag (Switzerland) 393
Basilisk, The, Press Ltd (United Kingdom) 429
Basilius Verlag AG (Switzerland) 393
Basis-Verlag (Federal Republic of Germany) 133
Bassermann'sche, Friedrich, Verlagsbuchhandlung im Falken-Verlag GmbH (Federal Republic of Germany) 133
Bastei-Verlag Gustav H Lübbe (Federal Republic of Germany) 133
Bastian, W E, & Co (Private) Ltd (Sri Lanka) 378
Bastian Prize (Norway) 324
Bastilla, Ediciones La (Argentina) 4
Bastogi (Italy) 234
Bateman, David, Ltd (New Zealand) 308
Baton Transport (United Kingdom) 429
Batsford, B T, Ltd (United Kingdom) 429
Battei, Casa Editrice Luigi (Italy) 234
Battenberg, Ernst, Verlag (Federal Republic of Germany) 133
Bättre Data (Sweden) 388
Bättre Ledarskap (Sweden) 388
Bättre Marknadsföring (Sweden) 388
Bättre Samhälle (Sweden) 388
Bättre Skola (Sweden) 388
Bauer, Hermann, Verlag KG (Federal Republic of Germany) 133
Baufachverlag (Switzerland) 393
Bauverlag GmbH (Federal Republic of Germany) 133
Bauwesen, VEB Verlag für (German Democratic Republic) 124
Baxters Ltd (Bermuda) 47
Bayard-Presse SA, Editions du Centurion (France) 98
Bayerische Staatsbibliothek (Federal Republic of Germany) 176
Bayerische Verlagsanstalt Bamberg (B V B) (Federal Republic of Germany) 133
Bayerischer Schulbuch-Verlag (Federal Republic of Germany) 133
Bayly, A W, & Co Lda (Mozambique) 291
Beacon Publications PLC (United Kingdom) 429
Beattie and Forbes (New Zealand) 311
Beatty, The Chester, Library (Republic of Ireland) 224
Beauchesne, Editions (France) 98
Beaufort, Mme (French Guiana) 122
Beaumont (United Kingdom) 429
Beaux Livres, Les (Monaco) 289
Beaver Books (United Kingdom) 429
Becher, Institut für Literatur Johannes R (German Democratic Republic) 128
Becher, Johannes R, Prize (German Democratic Republic) 128
Bechtle (Federal Republic of Germany) 133
Becht's, H J W, Uitgeversmij BV/Uitgeverij J H de Bussy BV (Netherlands) 294
Beck, Edition Monika (Federal Republic of Germany) 133
Beck, Verlag C H (Federal Republic of Germany) 133
Becknell Books (United Kingdom) 429
Bedford Editions Ltd (United Kingdom) 429
Bedford Square Press of the National Council for Voluntary Organizations (United Kingdom) 429
Bedford Way (United Kingdom) 429
Bedout, Editorial, SA (Colombia) 69
Beehive (United Kingdom) 429
Beernaert Prize (Belgium) 46
Beginners' Prize (German Democratic Republic) 128
Behzad Bookshop (Afghanistan) 1
Behzad Bookstore (Afghanistan) 1
Beijing daxue tushuguan (People's Republic of China) 68
Beijing tushuguan (People's Republic of China) 68
Beirut Arab University, Library of (Lebanon) 273
Beit Lochamei Hagetha'ot (Israel) 226
Bekadidact, Uitgeverij (Netherlands) 294
Belaieff, M P (Federal Republic of Germany) 133
Belfast Public Library (United Kingdom) 482
Belfond, Editions Pierre (France) 99
Belgian Government Prizes for Literature (Ministry of French Culture) (Belgium) 46
Belgian Government Prizes for Literature (Ministry of the Flemish Community) (Belgium) 46
Belgisch Instituut voor Voorlichting en Documentatie (INBEL) (Belgium) 36
Belief the Religious Book Society (United Kingdom) 480
Belin, Editions (France) 99
Belis-Vinck, Boekhandel (Belgium) 44
Belitha Press Ltd (United Kingdom) 429
Belize Book Shop (Anglican Diocese) (Belize) 47
Belize Library Association (Belize) 47
Bell, SA Editorial (Argentina) 4
Bell & Hyman (United Kingdom) 429
Bell Best Sellers (Greece) 182
Bellas Artes, Librería (Mexico) 288
Bellaterra, Ediciones, SA (Spain) 365
Belle, Uitgeverij van, PVBA (Belgium) 36
Belles Lettres, Société d'Edition 'Les, ' (France) 99

Bellew Publishing Co Ltd (United Kingdom) 429
Bellmans Prize (Sweden) 390
Bello, Andrés, Prize (Chile) 66
Bello', Biblioteca de la Universidad Catolica 'Andrés (Venezuela) 493
Bello', Clubs de Lectores 'Andrés (Chile) 66
Bello, Editorial Andrés, /Editorial Juridíca de Chile (Chile) 65
Bello, Librería Andrés (Chile) 66
Belmont Press (Zimbabwe) 505
Belser, Chr, AG für Verlagsgeschäfte und Co KG (Federal Republic of Germany) 134
Belton Books (United Kingdom) 429
Beltz Verlag (Federal Republic of Germany) 134
Ben-Gurion University of the Negev Library (Israel) 231
Ben-Zvi Institute (Israel) 226
Bendel State Library (Nigeria) 319
Benediktinerklosters, Bibliothek des, Melk in Niederösterreich (Austria) 32
Bengali Academy Literary Awards (Bangladesh) 35
Benghazi Public Library (Libya) 275
Benibengor Book Agency (Ghana) 180
Benin University Bookshop (Nigeria) 318
Benin University Library (Nigeria) 319
Benjamin/Cummings Inc (United Kingdom) 429
Benjamins, John, BV (Netherlands) 294
Benn, Ernest, Ltd (United Kingdom) 429
Bennett, G H, & Co Ltd (New Zealand) 311
Bennett Award (International Literary Prizes) 517
Benson Medal (International Literary Prizes) 517
Benteli Verlag (Switzerland) 393
Benton Ross Publishers Ltd (New Zealand) 308
Benziger AG (Switzerland) 393
Benziger Verlag (Federal Republic of Germany) 134
Beogradski Izdavačko-Grafički Zavod (Yugoslavia) 496
Berg International Editeurs (France) 99
Berg Publishers Ltd (United Kingdom) 429
Bergadi Editions (Greece) 182
Bergen offentlige Bibliotek Horda land Fylkesbibliotek (Norway) 323
Bergendal Forlag (Norway) 320
Berger, Centre culturel français Gaston, Bibliothèque (Senegal) 349
Berger, Ferdinand, und Söhne (Austria) 26
Berger-Levrault SA (France) 99
Bergh, Edition Sven Erik (Federal Republic of Germany) 134
Bergh und Bergh Verlagsanstalt GmbH (Switzerland) 393
Berghaus Verlag (Federal Republic of Germany) 134
Berghs Förlag AB (Sweden) 382
Bergland-Buch', Verlag 'Das (Austria) 26
Bergland Verlag (Austria) 26
Bergmann, Anton, Prize (International Literary Prizes) 517
Bergmann, J F (Federal Republic of Germany) 134
'Bergnes de las Casas', Biblioteca, de la Generalitat de Catalunya (Spain) 376
Bergs, H M, Forlag ApS (Denmark) 80
Bergverlag Rudolf Rother GmbH (Federal Republic of Germany) 134
Berhan Bookshop and Stationery (Ethiopia) 91
Berichthaus Verlag, Dr Conrad Ulrich (Switzerland) 393
Berita Publishing Sdn Bhd (Malaysia) 278
Berlin Verlag Arno Spitz (Federal Republic of Germany) 134
Berliner Handpresse Wolfgang Joerg und Erich Schoenig (Federal Republic of Germany) 134
Berliner Stadtbibliothek (German Democratic Republic) 127
Berliner Union GmbH (Federal Republic of Germany) 134
Berliner Verleger- und Buchhändlervereinigung eV (Federal Republic of Germany) 129
Berlitz, Société Internationale des Ecoles, SA (France) 99
Berlitz Guides (Switzerland) 393
Bermuda Archives (Bermuda) 47
Bermuda Book Store Ltd (Bermuda) 47
Bermuda Library (Bermuda) 47
Bermuda Press Ltd (Bermuda) 47
Bermudian Publishing (Bermuda) 47
Bernard, Librería Claudio (El Salvador) 90
Bernard und Graefe Verlag (Federal Republic of Germany) 134
Bernards (Publishers) Ltd (United Kingdom) 429
Bernces Förlag AB (Sweden) 382
Bernhardt, Verlag Alexander (Austria) 27
Bernheim, Bibliothèque, Bibliothèque territoriale de la Nouvelle-Calédonie (New Caledonia) 307
Berry, David, Prize (International Literary Prizes) 517
Bertelsmann AG (Federal Republic of Germany) 134
Bertelsmann de Mexico SA (Mexico) 288
Bertelsmann GmbH, Verlagsgruppe (Federal Republic of Germany) 134

544 INDEX

Bertelsmann Lesering (Federal Republic of Germany) 175
Bertelsmann Lexikothek Verlag GmbH (Federal Republic of Germany) 134
Bertelsmann Verlag, C, GmbH (Federal Republic of Germany) 134
Bertrand, Livraria (Portugal) 343
Bertrand, Livraria, SARL (Portugal) 340
Bertrand-Lacoste, Editions (France) 99
Beskow Prize (Sweden) 390
Best Book of the Sea Award (United Kingdom) 486
Best First Book of Poetry Award (New Zealand) 313
Best First Book of Prose Award (New Zealand) 313
Beste, Det, A/S (Norway) 323
Beste, Verlag Das, GmbH (Federal Republic of Germany) 134
Besterman Medal (United Kingdom) 486
Bestetti, Edizioni d'Arte di Carlo E, & C SAS (Italy) 234
Bestseller Publications Ltd (United Kingdom) 479
Beta, Editora, Ltda (Brazil) 51
Beta, Editorial, SRL (Argentina) 4
Betis, Ediciones (Spain) 365
Beton-Verlag GmbH (Federal Republic of Germany) 134
Better Books (United Kingdom) 429
Better Yourself Books (India) 198
Betz, Annette, Verlag (Austria) 27
Betz, Annette, Verlag (Federal Republic of Germany) 134
Betzel, Elke, Verlag (Federal Republic of Germany) 134
Beuhler's Shoppe (Belize) 47
Beupmun Sa Publishing Co (Republic of Korea) 269
Beuroner Kunstverlag GmbH (Federal Republic of Germany) 134
Beuth Verlag GmbH (Federal Republic of Germany) 134
Beyazit, The, State Library (Turkey) 415
Beyeler, Editions (Switzerland) 393
Beyer, F, Bok-Og Papirhandel A/S (Norway) 323
Bezige, De, Bij (Netherlands) 294
Bhai Santokh Singh Prize (India) 215
Bhaimi Prakashan (India) 198
Bhakti, PT, Centra Baru (Indonesia) 217
Bhaktivedanta Book Trust (India) 198
Bharat-Bharati (India) 198
Bharat Law House (India) 198
Bharati Sahitya Sadan Sales (India) 198
Bharatiya Jnanpith (India) 198
Bharatiya Publishing House (India) 198
Bharatiya Vidya Bhavan (India) 198
Bhratara, PT, Karya Aksara (Indonesia) 217
Bialik, The, Institute (Israel) 226
Bialik Prize for Literature (Israel) 232
Bianchi, Alfredo A, Essay Prize (Argentina) 9
Bianco, Del, Editore (Italy) 234
Bias Editora (Argentina) 4
Bias Editora (Libros Jurídicos) (Argentina) 8
Bibelbesbund, Verlag (Switzerland) 393
Bibelbesbund eV (Federal Republic of Germany) 135
Biblarte Lda (Portugal) 343
Bible, The, Churchmen's Missionary Society (Ethiopia) 91
Bible Society (United Kingdom) 429
Bible Society of South Africa (Republic of South Africa) 355
Bible Society of SWA/Namibia (Namibia) 291
Biblia Impex Pvt Ltd (India) 213
Bibliagora (United Kingdom) 429
Biblical Institute Press (Italy) 234
Bibliofiilien Seura (Finland) 95
Bibliographical Society (United Kingdom) 483
Bibliographical Society of Australia and New Zealand (BSANZ) (Australia) 22
Bibliographical Society of Australia and New Zealand (BSANZ) (International Organizations) 508
Bibliographical Society of Australia and New Zealand (BSANZ) (New Zealand) 312
Bibliographical Society of the Philippines (Philippines) 333
Bibliographisches Institut, VEB, Leipzig (German Democratic Republic) 124
Bibliographisches Institut GmbH (Austria) 27
Bibliographisches Institut und F A Brockhaus AG (Federal Republic of Germany) 135
Bibliographisches Institut und FA Brockhaus AG (Switzerland) 393
Bibliomad (Democratic Republic of Madagascar) 277
Bibliomed — Medizinische Verlagsgesellschaft mbH (Federal Republic of Germany) 135
Bibliophile, Le, (The Book Lover) (Haiti) 187
Bibliophile Books (United Kingdom) 429
Bibliophile Drucke, Verlag, von Josef Stocker AG (Switzerland) 393
Bibliopolis—Edizioni di Filosofia e Scienze SpA (Italy) 234

Biblioteca Central (Mexico) 288
Biblioteca Centrala de Stat a Republicii Socialiste România (Romania) 347
Biblioteca Centrala Universitara (Romania) 347
Biblioteca Centrala Universitara 'Mihail Eminescu' (Romania) 347
Biblioteca de Autores Cristianos de la Editorial Católica SA (Spain) 365
Biblioteca de México (Mexico) 288
Biblioteca del Congreso (Venezuela) 493
Biblioteca Dominicana (Dominican Republic) 87
Biblioteca Ecuatoriana 'Aurelio Espinosa Pólit' (Ecuador) 88
Biblioteca Estadual (Brazil) 58
Biblioteca General de Puerto Rico (General Library) (Puerto Rico) 345
Biblioteca Histórica Cubana y Americana (Cuba) 74
Biblioteca Judeteana Timis (Romania) 347
Biblioteca Municipal (Angola) 2
Biblioteca Municipal (Mozambique) 291
Biblioteca Municipal Central (Portugal) 343
Biblioteca Múnicipal Mário de Andrade (Brazil) 58
Biblioteca Nacional (Argentina) 8
Biblioteca Nacional (Brazil) 58
Biblioteca Nacional (Costa Rica) 73
Biblioteca Nacional (Dominican Republic) 87
Biblioteca Nacional (El Salvador) 90
Biblioteca Nacional (Nicaragua) 314
Biblioteca Nacional (Panama) 328
Biblioteca Nacional (Peru) 331
Biblioteca Nacional (Portugal) 343
Biblioteca Nacional (Spain) 376
Biblioteca Nacional (Venezuela) 493
Biblioteca Nacional de Agricultura (Mexico) 288
Biblioteca Nacional de Antropología e Historia (Mexico) 288
Biblioteca Nacional de Chile de la Dirección de Bibliotecas, Archivos y Museos (Chile) 66
Biblioteca Nacional de Colombia (Colombia) 71
Biblioteca Nacional de Guatemala (National Library) (Guatemala) 186
Biblioteca Nacional de Honduras (Honduras) 187
Biblioteca Nacional de Macau (Macau) 276
Biblioteca Nacional de Maestros (Argentina) 8
Biblioteca Nacional de México (Mexico) 288
Biblioteca Nacional de Moçambique (Mozambique) 291
Biblioteca Nacional del Ecuador (Ecuador) 88
Biblioteca Nacional del Uruguay (Uruguay) 491
Biblioteca Nacional José Martí (Cuba) 74
Biblioteca Nazionale Braidense (Italy) 252
Biblioteca Nazionale Centrale (Italy) 252
Biblioteca Nazionale Centrale Vittorio Emanuele II (Italy) 252
Biblioteca Nazionale Marciana (Italy) 252
Biblioteca Nazionale Vittorio Emanuele III (Italy) 252
Biblioteca Nueva, Editorial, SL (Spain) 365
Biblioteca Popular de Lisboa (Portugal) 343
Biblioteca Publica Central (Argentina) 8
Biblioteca Pública de Braga (Portugal) 344
Biblioteca Pública de Minas Gerais (Brazil) 58
Biblioteca Pública de Ponta Delgada (Portugal) 344
Biblioteca Pública do Estado do Rio de Janeiro (Brazil) 58
Biblioteca Pública e Arquivo Distrital de Évora (Portugal) 344
Biblioteca Pública Municipal do Porto (Portugal) 344
Biblioteca Universitaria (Italy) 252
Biblioteca y Archivo Nacional de Bolivia (Bolivia) 48
Biblioteca y Archivo Nacionales (Paraguay) 330
Bibliotecas Públicas, Dirección de, Municipales (Argentina) 9
Biblioteka Jagiellońska (Poland) 338
Biblioteka Narodowa (Poland) 338
Biblioteka Publiczna m st Warszawy (Poland) 338
Bibliotekarforbundet (Denmark) 85
Bibliotekës Kombëtare, Botim i (Albania) 1
Biblioteksboghandelen ApS (Denmark) 84
Bibliotekscentralen (Denmark) 85
Bibliotekscentralens Forlag (Denmark) 80
Biblioteksförlaget AB (Sweden) 382
Bibliotekstjänst AB (Sweden) 382
Bibliotheca, Verlag, Christiana (Federal Republic of Germany) 175
Bibliotheek CCS (Suriname) 380
Bibliothek für Zeitgeschichte (Federal Republic of Germany) 176
Bibliotheksverband der Deutschen Demokratischen Republik (German Democratic Republic) 127
Bibliothèque cantonale et universitaire de Lausanne (Switzerland) 405
Bibliothèque cantonale et universitaire (Kantons- und Universitätsbibliothek) (Switzerland) 405
Bibliothèque centrale de la Côte d'Ivoire (Ivory Coast) 254
Bibliothèque centrale de Prêt (Réunion) 346
Bibliothèque centrale municipale (Algeria) 2

Bibliothèque de Gouvernement (Grand Duchy of Luxembourg) 276
Bibliothèque de la Ville (Grand Duchy of Luxembourg) 276
Bibliothèque de la Ville (Switzerland) 405
Bibliothèque de l'Université nationale de Côte d'Ivoire (Ivory Coast) 254
Bibliothèque départementale (Réunion) 346
Bibliothèque du petit Séminaire (Haiti) 187
Bibliothèque Franconie (French Guiana) 122
Bibliothèque générale et Archives (Morocco) 290
Bibliothèque générale et Archives du Maroc (Morocco) 290
Bibliothèque Louis Notari (Monaco) 289
Bibliothèque mazarine (France) 117
Bibliothèque municipale (Democratic Republic of Madagascar) 277
Bibliothèque municipale (Ivory Coast) 254
Bibliothèque municipale (Mali) 281
Bibliothèque municipale (Morocco) 290
Bibliothèque municipale (Réunion) 346
Bibliothèque municipale de Besançon (France) 117
Bibliothèque municipale de Constantine (Algeria) 2
Bibliothèque municipale de Grenoble (France) 117
Bibliothèque municipale de la Ville de Lyon (France) 117
Bibliothèque municipale d'Oran (Algeria) 2
Bibliothèque municipale (Meknès) (Morocco) 290
Bibliothèque nationale (Algeria) 2
Bibliothèque nationale (Democratic Republic of Madagascar) 277
Bibliothèque nationale (France) 99
Bibliothèque nationale (France) 117
Bibliothèque nationale (Guinea) 186
Bibliothèque nationale (Ivory Coast) 254
Bibliothèque nationale (Laos) 272
Bibliothèque nationale (Mali) 281
Bibliothèque nationale (Mauritania) 282
Bibliothèque nationale (Togo) 412
Bibliothèque nationale (Tunisia) 414
Bibliothèque nationale (Zaire) 502
Bibliothèque nationale d'Haiti (National Library) (Haiti) 187
Bibliothèque nationale du Benin (Benin) 47
Bibliothèque nationale du Cameroun (United Republic of Cameroun) 64
Bibliothèque nationale du Congo, Direction des Services de Bibliothèques, d'Archives et de Documentation (Popular Republic of Congo) 72
Bibliothèque nationale du Grand-Duché de Luxembourg (Grand Duchy of Luxembourg) 276
Bibliothèque nationale du Liban (Lebanon) 273
Bibliothèque nationale et universitaire de Strasbourg (France) 117
Bibliothèque nationale populaire (Popular Republic of Congo) 72
Bibliothèque Nationale Suisse (Switzerland) 405
Bibliothèque orientale (Lebanon) 273
Bibliothèque paroissiale (Chad) 65
Bibliothèque principale de Bruxelles 1 (Belgium) 44
Bibliothèque publique (Burundi) 63
Bibliothèque publique de Kinshasa (Zaire) 502
Bibliothèque publique de Kisangani (Zaire) 502
Bibliothèque publique de Kitega (Burundi) 63
Bibliothèque publique de Lubumbashi (Zaire) 502
Bibliothèque publique et universitaire de Genève (Switzerland) 405
Bibliothèque publique et universitaire de Neuchâtel (Switzerland) 405
Bibliothèque universitaire (Burkina Faso) 62
Bibliothèque universitaire (Democratic Republic of Madagascar) 277
Bibliothèque Universitaire de Bangui (Central African Republic) 64
Biblique, Société, Française (France) 99
Biblique de Genève, Société (Switzerland) 393
Biblograf, Editorial, SA (Spain) 365
Bidang Bibliografi dan Deposit, Pusat Pembinaan Perpustakaan (Indonesia) 219
Biederstein Verlag (Federal Republic of Germany) 135
Biennial International Art Book Prize (International Literary Prizes) 517
Bierman og Bierman A/S (Denmark) 80
Bigot en Van Rossum, Uitgeverij, BV (Netherlands) 294
Bihar Hindi Granth Akademi (India) 198
Bihar Rajya Pustak Vyayasayee Sangh (India) 195
Bihar State, The, Textbook Publishing Corporation Ltd (India) 198
Bijleveld, Erven J (Netherlands) 294
Bijutsu Shuppan-Sha (Japan) 256
Bilac, Olavo, Prize (Brazil) 59
Bilgi Yayinevi (Turkey) 415
Billeret, Librairie (Chad) 65
Bina Ilmu (Indonesia) 217
Binacipta (Indonesia) 217
Bingley, Clive, Ltd (United Kingdom) 429

Binsfeld, Editions Guy (Grand Duchy of Luxembourg) 275
Bioru Miedzynarodowego Numeru Ksiazki (Poland) 334
Biosfera, Editorial, SRL (Venezuela) 492
Bir Library (Nepal) 292
Birchall, A W, & Sons Pty Ltd (Australia) 20
Birds and Natural History Book Society (United Kingdom) 480
Birkhäuser Verlag AG (Switzerland) 393
Birmingham Museums and Art Gallery Publications Unit (United Kingdom) 429
Birmingham Public Libraries (United Kingdom) 482
Biro, Perpustakaan, Pusat Statistik (Indonesia) 219
Birografika (Yugoslavia) 496
Bishopsgate Press Ltd (United Kingdom) 429
Bison Books Ltd (United Kingdom) 429
Biswakosh (Bangladesh) 34
Bitan (Israel) 226
Bitter, Georg, Verlag (Federal Republic of Germany) 135
Bjarnarsonar, Bókaútgáfa Thórhalls (Iceland) 193
Björk, Bókaútgáfan (Iceland) 193
Björnssonar, Bokaforlag Odds (Iceland) 193
Black, A & C, (Publishers) Ltd (United Kingdom) 430
Black, James Tait, Memorial Prizes (United Kingdom) 486
Black, Stephen, Prize for Drama (Republic of South Africa) 361
Black Academy Press (Nigeria) 315
Black Dagger Crime (United Kingdom) 430
Black Mask Ltd (Ghana) 180
Black Pig Editions Ltd (United Kingdom) 430
Black Swan (United Kingdom) 430
Blacker Calmann Cooper Ltd (United Kingdom) 430
Blackie & Son Ltd (United Kingdom) 430
Blackstaff Press Ltd (United Kingdom) 430
Blackwell, B H, Ltd (United Kingdom) 481
Blackwell, Basil, Ltd (United Kingdom) 430
Blackwell Scientific Publications (Australia) Pty Ltd (Australia) 12
Blackwell Scientific Publications Ltd (United Kingdom) 430
Bladkompaniet A/S (Norway) 320
Blake Friedmann Literary Agency (United Kingdom) 479
Blaketon Hall Ltd (United Kingdom) 430
Blaketon Hall Ltd (United Kingdom) 479
Blanc, Charles, Prize (France) 119
Blanchart, Editions Gérard, & Cie SA (Belgium) 36
Blandford Press (United Kingdom) 430
Blandford Publishing Ltd (United Kingdom) 430
Blanvalet Verlag (Federal Republic of Germany) 135
Bläschke, Josef Gotthard, -Verlag (Austria) 27
Blaukreuz-Verlag Bern (Switzerland) 393
Blaukreuz-Verlag Wuppertal (Federal Republic of Germany) 135
Blazek und Bergmann (Federal Republic of Germany) 175
Bleicher Verlag (Federal Republic of Germany) 135
Blinde, Stiftung Centralbibliothek für (Federal Republic of Germany) 176
Blindenstudienanstalt, Deutsche, eV (Federal Republic of Germany) 135
Bloch Editores SA (Brazil) 51
Blok, H W, Uitgeverij BV (Netherlands) 294
Blok, Nakladatelství (Czechoslovakia) 75
Blom Prize (Sweden) 390
Blond, Anthony (United Kingdom) 430
Blondel La Rougery SA (France) 99
Bloodaxe Books Ltd (United Kingdom) 430
Bloom, Roy, Ltd (United Kingdom) 479
Bloomsbury Publishing Ltd (United Kingdom) 430
Blücher, Editora Edgard, Ltda (Brazil) 51
Bluett & Co Ltd (Republic of Ireland) 221
Blume, Editorial, SA (Spain) 365
Blume Ediciones, Hermann (Spain) 365
Boardman Tasker Prize for Mountain Literature (International Literary Prizes) 517
Bobcat Books (United Kingdom) 430
Bock und Herchen Verlag (Federal Republic of Germany) 135
Bodleian Library (United Kingdom) 482
Bodley Head, The, Ltd (United Kingdom) 430
Bodmer, Fondation Martin, Bibliotheca Bodmeriana (Switzerland) 406
Bodmer, Les Editions de la Fondation Martin (Switzerland) 393
Boeck, Maison d'Edition A de, SA (Belgium) 36
Boek Promotions BV (Netherlands) 294
Boekencentrum BV (Netherlands) 294
Boer, de, Maritiem (Netherlands) 294
Boethius Press Ltd (Republic of Ireland) 221
Bofur (New Zealand) 311
Bogans Forlag A/S (Denmark) 80
Boğaziçi University Library (Turkey) 415
Boggero, B, Editore (Italy) 234

Bohem Press Kinderbuchverlag (Switzerland) 393
Böhlau Verlag GmbH (Austria) 27
Böhlau-Verlag GmbH & Cie (Federal Republic of Germany) 135
Böhlaus, Hermann, Nachfolger (German Democratic Republic) 124
Bohmann Druck und Verlag GmbH & Co KG (Austria) 27
Bohn, Scheltema en Holkema (Netherlands) 294
Boighar (Bangladesh) 34
Bois, Editions Relais du, l'Abbé (France) 99
Boje-Verlag GmbH (Federal Republic of Germany) 135
Bok Og Papiransattes Forening (Norway) 320
Bokas hf (Iceland) 193
Bókavardafélag Islands (Iceland) 194
Bokbranschens Finansieringsinstitut AB (Sweden) 381
Bokbranschens Marknadsinstitut AB (Sweden) 381
Bokhandelsrådet (Sweden) 381
Bokmästar'n (Sweden) 388
Bold Ads (Zimbabwe) 504
Boldt, Harald, Verlag GmbH (Federal Republic of Germany) 135
Boleswa (Swaziland) 381
Bolivar Bookshop (Jamaica) 255
Bolivian Grand Prize for Literature (Bolivia) 49
Bollati Boringhieri Editore SpA (Italy) 234
Bollmann-Bildkarten-Verlag GmbH & Co KG (Federal Republic of Germany) 135
Bologna Book Fair 'Critici in erba' Prize (International Literary Prizes) 517
Bologna Book Fair Graphic Prize for Children and Youth (International Literary Prizes) 517
Bolt, David, Associates (United Kingdom) 479
Bolte, Dr, KG (Federal Republic of Germany) 135
Bombal, María Luisa, Prize (Chile) 66
Bombay Booksellers' and Publishers' Association (India) 195
Bombay University Library (India) 214
Bompiani (Italy) 234
Bon Pasteur, Librarie du (Togo) 412
Bonacci-Libreria Editrice (Italy) 234
Bonanno, Giuseppe, Editore (Italy) 234
Bonanza, Librairie (Mauritius) 283
Bond Alleenverkopers van Nederlandstalige Boeken (BANB) (Belgium) 35
Bone, Roger, Library (Zimbabwe) 505
Bonechi, Casa Editrice (Italy) 235
Bonetti, Pascal, Grand Prize (France) 119
Bongers, Verlag Aurel (Federal Republic of Germany) 135
Bongiovanni, Ditta F, SAS (Italy) 235
Bonn Aktuell GmbH (Federal Republic of Germany) 135
Bonner Buchgemeinde (BBG) (Federal Republic of Germany) 175
Bonnier Fakta Bokförlag AB (Sweden) 382
Bonniers Bokklubb (Sweden) 388
Bonniers Förlag, Albert, AB (Sweden) 382
Bonniers Juniorförlag AB (Sweden) 382
Bonniers Specialmagasiner A/S (Denmark) 80
Bonum, Librería, SACI (Argentina) 4
Boobook Publications (Australia) 12
Book, The, House (Pakistan) 325
Book, The, Trade Group of Western Australia (Australia) 10
Book and Printing Center — Israel Export Institute (Israel) 225
Book Centre, The (Belize) 47
Book Centre, The (Gibraltar) 182
Book Centre (Zimbabwe) 505
Book Club Associates (United Kingdom) 480
Book Collectors' Society of Australia (Australia) 22
Book Development, The, Council (United Kingdom) 421
Book Development Association of the Philippines (BDAP) (Philippines) 331
Book Distributors Sdn Bhd (Malaysia) 278
Book Emporium Singapore (Pte) Ltd (Republic of Singapore) 351
Book Field Centre (India) 198
Book Guild, The, Ltd (United Kingdom) 431
Book House Ireland (Republic of Ireland) 221
Book Lovers Club (India) 212
Book Lovers' Club (Yugoslavia) 499
Book Mark (India) 198
Book Marketing, The, Council (United Kingdom) 421
Book Marketing Council Inc (New Zealand) 307
Book Marketing Ltd (Hong Kong) 187
Book-of-the-Month Club (Australia) 20
Book of the Month Club (New Zealand) 311
Book of the Month Club (United Kingdom) 480
Book of the Month Ltd Finland (Finland) 94
Book Publishers', The, Association of Israel, International Promotion and Literary Rights Department (Israel) 230
Book Publishers' Association of Israel (Israel) 225

Book Publishers Association of New Zealand Inc (New Zealand) 307
Book Publishers' Representatives' Association (United Kingdom) 421
Book Publishing Institute (Afghanistan) 1
Book Representation Co Ltd (Nigeria) 318
Book Sales Ltd (United Kingdom) 431
Book Society of Islamic Republic of Iran (Iran) 220
Book Stop (Republic of Ireland) 224
Book Tokens Ltd (United Kingdom) 421
Book Trade, The, Benevolent Society (United Kingdom) 421
Book Trade Association of South Africa (Republic of South Africa) 354
Book Trust (United Kingdom) 421
BookAustralia (Australia) 20
Bookbank SA (Spain) 375
Booker Prize (International Literary Prizes) 517
Booker Prize (United Kingdom) 486
Booklinks Corporation (India) 198
Bookman, A/S (Denmark) 84
Bookman, A/S (Finland) 94
Bookman, A/S (Iceland) 194
Bookman, A/S (Norway) 322
Bookman, A/S (Sweden) 388
Bookman of the Year Award (Australia) 23
Bookman Publishing House (Philippines) 332
Bookmark Inc (Philippines) 333
Bookmark Wholesale (United Kingdom) 479
Bookmarks Publications (United Kingdom) 431
Bookmart, The (Bermuda) 47
Bookmart Bargain Books (United Kingdom) 479
Bookmarx Club (United Kingdom) 480
BookNewZealand (New Zealand) 311
Bookrama (Pakistan) 326
Books across the Sea (United Kingdom) 485
Books Bargain (India) 212
Books for Children (United Kingdom) 480
Books for Neoliterates Prizes (India) 215
Books of Africa (Pty) Ltd (Republic of South Africa) 355
Books of Zimbabwe Publishing Co (Pvt) Ltd (Zimbabwe) 504
Books-on-Japan-in-English Club (Japan) 263
Books Registration Office MSB (Hong Kong) 187
Booksellers' and Publishers' Association of South India (India) 195
Booksellers' and Publishers' Association of Zambia (Zambia) 503
Booksellers Association of Great Britain and Ireland (United Kingdom) 421
Booksellers Association of Great Britain and Ireland (Irish Branch) (Republic of Ireland) 221
Booksellers' Association of Jamaica (Jamaica) 254
Booksellers' Association of New Zealand (Inc) (New Zealand) 307
Booksellers' Association of Sri Lanka (Sri Lanka) 378
Booksellers' Association of Trinidad and Tobago (Trinidad and Tobago) 412
Booksellers' Association of Zimbabwe (Zimbabwe) 504
Booksellers Clearing House (United Kingdom) 421
Booksellers' Order Distribution Ltd (BOD) (United Kingdom) 421
Bookshelf, The (Zambia) 503
Bookshop, The, Ltd (Kenya) 268
Booksmith Wholesale (United Kingdom) 479
Bookventure (India) 198
Bookward Ltd (United Kingdom) 431
Bookwise International (Australia) 12
Bookwise (Pty) Ltd (Republic of South Africa) 360
Bookwise Service Ltd (United Kingdom) 481
Bookworm, The, Club (United Kingdom) 480
Boolarong Publications (Australia) 12
Boole Library (Republic of Ireland) 224
Boole Press Ltd (Republic of Ireland) 221
Boom-Pers Boeken- en Tijdschriftenuitg BV (Netherlands) 294
Boosey & Hawkes Music Publishers Ltd (United Kingdom) 431
Boosey & Hawkes Sagem (France) 99
Boostan Publishing House (Israel) 226
Booth, David, (Publishing) Ltd (United Kingdom) 431
Bora, Edizioni, SNC di E Brandani & C (Italy) 235
Borba (Yugoslavja) 496
Bordas, Editions (France) 99
Bordas-Dunod, Société, Bruxelles SA (Belgium) 36
Bordas et Fils, Pierre (France) 99
Bordewijk, F, Prize (Netherlands) 306
Bordin Prize (France) 119
Borgarbókasafn Reykjavíkur (Iceland) 194
Borgens Forlag A/S (Denmark) 80
Borla, Edizioni, SRL (Italy) 235
Born NV Uitgeversmaatschappij (Netherlands) 294
Bornemann, Editions (France) 99
Borntraeger, Gebrüder, Verlagsbuchhandlung (Federal Republic of Germany) 135
Borotha-Schoeler, Verlag Dr Gerda (Austria) 27

546 INDEX

Børsens Forlag (Denmark) 80
Börsenverein der Deutschen Buchhändler zu Leipzig (German Democratic Republic) 123
Börsenverein des Deutschen Buchhandels eV (Federal Republic of Germany) 129
Bosch, Antoni, Editor SA (Spain) 365
Bosch, Librería (Spain) 376
Bosch Casa Editorial SA (Spain) 365
Bosch en Keuning (Netherlands) 294
Boscq, Jean-Pierre (France) 116
Bösendahl, C (Federal Republic of Germany) 135
Bosse, Editions (Federal Republic of Germany) 135
Bosse, Gustav, Verlag GmbH & Co KG (Federal Republic of Germany) 135
Botas, Libreria y Ediciones, SA (Mexico) 284
Botella, Ediciones, al Mar (Argentina) 4
Botswana Book Centre (Botswana) 49
Botswana Library Association (Botswana) 49
Botswana National Archives (Botswana) 49
Botswana National Library Service (Botswana) 49
Bottega d'Erasmo (Italy) 235
Boubée, Société Nouvelle Editions N (France) 99
Boukoumanis' Editions (Greece) 182
Bourbon, Librairie (Grand Duchy of Luxembourg) 276
Bourbon, Librairie (Mauritius) 283
Bourcy, Librairie De (Grand Duchy of Luxembourg) 276
Bourdeaux-Capelle SA (Belgium) 37
Bourgois, Christian (France) 99
Bourrelier, Editions Colin (France) 99
Bouscatel, Jean, Foundation Prize (France) 119
Bouslama, Editions (Tunisia) 413
Bouslama, Editions (Tunisia) 414
Boutique, La, Bleue (French Guiana) 122
Bouvier, Universitätsbuchhandlung, GmbH (Federal Republic of Germany) 175
Bouvier-Parviliez, Ernest, Prize (Belgium) 46
Bovolenta (Italy) 235
Bowen, D Richard (Sweden) 388
Bowes & Bowes Books (United Kingdom) 481
Bowker & Bertram Ltd (Marine Publishers) (United Kingdom) 431
Bowker-Saur Ltd (United Kingdom) 431
Bowker (UK), R R (United Kingdom) 431
Boxtree Ltd (United Kingdom) 431
Boyars, Marion, Publishers Ltd (United Kingdom) 431
Boyce, David, Publishing & Associates (Australia) 12
Boydell & Brewer Ltd (United Kingdom) 431
Bra Böcker, Bokförlaget, AB (Sweden) 382
Bra Böcker, Bokklubben (Sweden) 388
Bra Lyrik, Bokklubben (Sweden) 388
Bra Spänning, Bokklubben (Sweden) 388
Braby, A C, (Pvt) Ltd (Zimbabwe) 504
Bracciodieta Editore (Italy) 235
Bracken Books (United Kingdom) 431
Bradt Publications (United Kingdom) 431
Brain Anatomy Institute (Switzerland) 393
Bramante Editrice SpA (Italy) 235
Branding, De, NV (Belgium) 37
Brandon Book Publishers Ltd (Republic of Ireland) 221
Brandstetter, Oscar, Verlag GmbH & Co KG (Federal Republic of Germany) 135
Brash, Graham, Pte Ltd (Republic of Singapore) 351
Brasil, Editora Bertrand, SA (Brazil) 51
Brasil, Editora do, SA (Brazil) 51
Brasil-América, Editora, (EBAL) SA (Brazil) 51
Brasília Editora (J Carvalho Branco & Cia Lda) (Portugal) 340
Brasilia Editora Ltda (Brazil) 51
Brasilienkunde Verlag GmbH (Federal Republic of Germany) 135
Brasiliense, Editora, SA (Brazil) 51
Brasiliense, Livraria, Editora SA (Brazil) 57
Brassey's Defence Publishers Ltd (United Kingdom) 431
Bratislava Town Prize (Czechoslovakia) 79
Bratsvo-Jedinstvo (Yugoslavia) 496
Bratt Institut für Neues Lernen GmbH (Federal Republic of Germany) 135
Braumüller, Wilhelm, Universitätsverlag GmbH (Austria) 27
Braun, Verlag G, GmbH (Federal Republic of Germany) 135
Braun und Schneider, Verlag (Federal Republic of Germany) 135
Bray, The, Bookshop (Republic of Ireland) 224
Bread and Cheese Club (Australia) 22
Breakthroughs (Australia) 12
Bréal (France) 99
Breidenstein, Umschau Verlag, GmbH (Federal Republic of Germany) 136
Breitkopf und Härtel (Federal Republic of Germany) 136
Breitkopf und Härtel, VEB, Musikverlag (German Democratic Republic) 124

Breitschopf, Julius, KG (Federal Republic of Germany) 136
Breitschopf, Verlagsbuchhandlung Julius (Austria) 27
Breitsohl, Dieter, AG (Switzerland) 405
Breiz, Emgleo (France) 99
Breklumer Verlag (Federal Republic of Germany) 136
Bremen Literature Encouragement Prize (International Literary Prizes) 517
Bremen Literature Prize (International Literary Prizes) 517
Brendow-Verlag (Federal Republic of Germany) 136
Brennan, Christopher, Award (Australia) 23
Brenner, Edizioni (Italy) 235
Brenner Prize (Israel) 232
Brenthurst, The, Press (Pty) Ltd (Republic of South Africa) 355
Brepols, Editions, SA (France) 99
Brepols Publishers IGP (Belgium) 37
Bresci Editore (Italy) 235
Bresciane, Edizioni (Italy) 235
Breslich & Foss (United Kingdom) 431
Bretschneider, Dr Giorgio (Italy) 235
Bretschneider, L'Erma di, SRL (Italy) 235
Brewer, D S (United Kingdom) 431
Brice, Beverly A, Publisher (Bahamas) 34
Brick Row Publishing Co Ltd (New Zealand) 308
Bridge Book Club (United Kingdom) 480
Bridge Book Co Ltd (United Kingdom) 479
Bridge Bookshop Ltd (Isle of Man) 225
Brigg Verlag GmbH (Federal Republic of Germany) 136
Bright Careers Institute (India) 198
Brill, E J (Netherlands) 294
Brilliance Books (United Kingdom) 431
Brimax Books Ltd (United Kingdom) 431
Brink, Educational Uitgeverij Ten (Netherlands) 295
Bristol Classical Press (United Kingdom) 431
British & Foreign Bible Society (United Kingdom) 431
British Academy, The (United Kingdom) 431
British and Irish Association of Law Librarians (United Kingdom) 483
British Copyright Council (United Kingdom) 421
British Council, The, Design, Production and Publishing Department (United Kingdom) 421
British Council Educational Resource Centre (Lesotho) 274
British Council Libraries (Sri Lanka) 379
British Council Library (Bangladesh) 35
British Council Library (Colombia) 71
British Council Library (Cyprus) 74
British Council Library (Ethiopia) 91
British Council Library (Ghana) 181
British Council Library (Greece) 185
British Council Library (Hong Kong) 189
British Council Library (India) 214
British Council Library (Indonesia) 219
British Council Library (Jordan) 266
British Council Library (Malawi) 277
British Council Library (Malaysia) 280
British Council Library (Mauritius) 283
British Council Library (Nepal) 292
British Council Library (Pakistan) 327
British Council Library (Sierra Leone) 350
British Council Library (Sudan) 380
British Council Library (Tanzania) 409
British Council Library (Thailand) 411
British Council Library (Tunisia) 414
British Council Library (United Republic of Cameroun) 64
British Council Library (Yemen Arab Republic) 495
British Film Institute (United Kingdom) 432
British Guild of Travel Writers (United Kingdom) 421
British Horse Society (United Kingdom) 432
British Library, The (India) 214
British Library, The (United Kingdom) 482
British Library, Bibliographic Services (United Kingdom) 432
British Library Bibliographic Services (United Kingdom) 482
British Library Document Supply Centre (United Kingdom) 482
British Library, Document Supply Centre Publications Marketing (United Kingdom) 432
British Library India Office Library and Records (United Kingdom) 482
British Library of Political and Economic Science (United Kingdom) 482
British Library Publications (United Kingdom) 432
British Library Publications (United Kingdom) 482
British Library, Science Reference and Information Service (United Kingdom) 482
British Medical Association (United Kingdom) 432
British Museum (Natural History) (United Kingdom) 432
British Museum Publications Ltd (United Kingdom) 432

British Printing Industries Federation (United Kingdom) 421
British Psychological, The, Society (United Kingdom) 432
British Science Fiction, The, Association Ltd (United Kingdom) 485
British Science Fiction Award (United Kingdom) 486
British Tourist Authority (United Kingdom) 432
Brno Literary Prize (Czechoslovakia) 79
Broadcast Books (United Kingdom) 432
Brockhaus, F A, GmbH (Federal Republic of Germany) 136
Brockhaus, R, Verlag (Federal Republic of Germany) 136
Brockhaus, VEB F A, Verlag Leipzig (German Democratic Republic) 124
Brodie, James, Ltd (United Kingdom) 432
Brodie's Notes (Australia) 12
Brodies Notes (United Kingdom) 432
Broele, Vanden, BVBA (Belgium) 37
Broese Kemink BV (Netherlands) 304
Brogeen Books (Republic of Ireland) 221
Brombergs Bokförlag AB (Sweden) 383
Bronfman's Agency Ltd (Israel) 226
Bronfman's Agency Ltd (Israel) 231
Brönner Verlag Breidenstein GmbH (Federal Republic of Germany) 136
Brontë, The Incorporated, Society (United Kingdom) 485
Bronze Swagman Award (Australia) 23
Brookfield Press (New Zealand) 308
Brooks Queensland, William (Australia) 12
Brooks Waterloo (Australia) 12
Broomsleigh Press (United Kingdom) 432
Brophy Educational Books Ltd (Republic of Ireland) 222
Broquette-Gonin Grand Prize (France) 119
Broschek Druck GmbH & Co KG (Federal Republic of Germany) 136
Broschek Verlag (Federal Republic of Germany) 136
Broutta, Michèle, Oeuvres Graphiques Contemporaines (France) 99
Brown, Emanuel (Israel) 231
Brown Associates, Trevor (United Kingdom) 432
Brown, Son & Ferguson, Ltd (United Kingdom) 432
Brown Wells & Jacobs Ltd (United Kingdom) 432
Bruck, Librairie Paul (Grand Duchy of Luxembourg) 276
Bruckmann Kunst, Studio, im Druck GmbH (Federal Republic of Germany) 136
Bruckmann München, Verlag (Federal Republic of Germany) 136
Brug-, De -Djambatan BV (Netherlands) 295
Bruggen, Jochem van, Prys vir Prosa (Republic of South Africa) 361
Bruguera, Editora, do Brasil Ltda (Brazil) 51
Bruguera, Editorial, Argentina SAFIC (Argentina) 4
Bruguera, Editorial, Centroamericana y Panamá SA (Panama) 328
Bruguera, Editorial, Colombiana Ltda (Colombia) 69
Bruguera, Editorial, Mexicana SA (Mexico) 284
Bruna, A W, en Zoon NV (Belgium) 37
Bruna BV (Netherlands) 304
Bruna en Zoon's, A W, Uitgeversmaatschappij BV (Netherlands) 295
Bruna Pockethuis BV (Netherlands) 295
Brunei, The, Press (Brunei) 60
Brunette (Netherlands) 295
Brunnen- Verlag (Switzerland) 394
Brunnen-Verlag GmbH (Federal Republic of Germany) 136
Brunnquell-Verlag der Bibel-und Missions-Stiftung Metzingen (Federal Republic of Germany) 136
Bruño, Asociación Editorial (Peru) 330
Bruño, Editorial (Spain) 365
Bruns, F, Bokhandel (Norway) 323
Bruns, F, Bokhandels Forlag A/S (Norway) 320
Bruylant, Etablissements Emile, SA (Belgium) 37
Bucalo, Edizioni, SMC (Italy) 235
Buch und Verlagsdruckerei AG (Liechtenstein) 275
Buchan & Enright Publishers Ltd (United Kingdom) 432
Buchclub 65 (German Democratic Republic) 127
Buchclub 69 GmbH (Federal Republic of Germany) 175
Bucheli, Verlag Alfred (Switzerland) 394
Bücher, Verlag C J (Switzerland) 394
Bucher, Verlag C J, GmbH (Federal Republic of Germany) 136
Buchet/Chastel, Editions (France) 100
Buchexport — Volkseigener Aussenhandelsbetrieb der Deutschen Demokratischen Republik (German Democratic Republic) 123
Buchhändler-Abrechnungs — Gesellschaft mbH (Federal Republic of Germany) 129
Buchhändler-Vereinigung GmbH (Federal Republic of Germany) 129

INDEX 547

Buchhaus AG (Switzerland) 394
Buchholz, Librería (Colombia) 71
Buchholz, Livraria (Portugal) 343
Büchler Grafino AG (Switzerland) 394
Buchmarkt- und Medien-Forschung, Verlag für (Federal Republic of Germany) 136
Büchner, Georg, Prize (Federal Republic of Germany) 179
Büchse, Verlag, der Pandora GmbH (Federal Republic of Germany) 136
Buchser, Hugo, SA (Switzerland) 394
Buckland Award (New Zealand) 313
Budapesti Müszaki Egyetem Központi Könyvtára (Hungary) 191
Buenos Aires Literary Prizes (Argentina) 9
Buffetti (Italy) 235
Buijten en Schipperheijn BV Drukkerij en Uitg Mij v/h (Netherlands) 295
Bukié, De l'édition, Banané (Mauritius) 282
Bulan, PT, Bintang, Penerbit dan Penyebar Buku-buku (Indonesia) 217
Bulawayo Municipal Libraries (Zimbabwe) 505
Bulawayo Public Library (Zimbabwe) 505
Bulgarian Academy of Sciences, Central Library (Bulgaria) 61
Bulgarian Academy of Sciences, Institute of Literature (Bulgaria) 61
Bulgarian Publishing Award (Bulgaria) 62
Bulgarian Union of Public Libraries (Bulgaria) 61
Bulgarian Writers' Union (Bulgaria) 61
'Bulgarska kniga', Darzhavno sdruzhenie, i petchat (Bulgaria) 60
Bulgarskata Akademia, Izdatelstvo na, na Naukite (Bulgaria) 60
Bulgarskata Komunisticheska Partiya, Izdatelstvo na (Bulgaria) 60
Bulgarski Houdozhnik (Bulgaria) 60
Bulgarski Pissatel (Bulgaria) 60
Bulgarskiya, Izdatelstvo na, Zemedelski Naroden Suyuz (Bulgaria) 60
Bulpin, T V, Publications (Republic of South Africa) 355
Bulwer-Lytton Circle (United Kingdom) 485
Bulzoni Editore SRL (Le Edizioni Universitarie d'Italia) (Italy) 235
Buma Kor, Editions (United Republic of Cameroun) 63
Bumi Restu (Indonesia) 217
Bund-Verlag GmbH (Federal Republic of Germany) 136
Bunda College of Agriculture Library (Malawi) 277
Bundes-Verlag GmbH (Federal Republic of Germany) 136
Bundesamt für Landestopographie (Switzerland) 394
Bundesarbeitsgemeinschaft der katholisch-kirchlichen Büchereiarbeit (Federal Republic of Germany) 177
Bundesarchiv (Federal Republic of Germany) 176
Bundesgremium des Handels mit Büchern, Kunstblättern und Musikalien, Zeitungen und Zeitschriften (Austria) 25
Bundeskanzleramt, Administrative Bibliothek und Österreichische Rechtsdokumentation im (Austria) 32
Bundesstaatliche Studienbibliothek Linz (Austria) 32
Bundesverband der deutschen Versandbuchhändler eV (Federal Republic of Germany) 129
Bundesverband der Dolmetscher und Übersetzer eV (BDÜ) (Federal Republic of Germany) 179
Bundesverband deutscher Autoren eV (Federal Republic of Germany) 178
Bungeishunju Ltd (Japan) 256
Bunny Books (Republic of Singapore) 351
Burchell & Martin Ltd (United Kingdom) 481
Burckhardthaus-Laetare Verlag GmbH (Federal Republic of Germany) 136
Burda, Verlag Aenne, GmbH & Co KG (Federal Republic of Germany) 137
Bureau de Recherches Géologiques et Minières (BRGM) (France) 100
Bureau des Copyrights Français (Japan) 262
Bureau des Documentations Syriennes et Arabes (Syria) 407
Bureau d'Etudes et de Recherches pour la Promotion de la Santé (Zaire) 502
Bureau for Indigenous Languages (Namibia) 291
Bureau International du Travail (Switzerland) 406
Bureau of Ghana Languages (Ghana) 180
Bureau of Ghana Languages (Ghana) 181
Bureau of International Exchange of Publications (Taiwan) 408
Burke Publishing Co Ltd (United Kingdom) 432
Burma Library Association (Burma) 63
Burmese Publishers' Union (Burma) 62
Burns & Oates Ltd (United Kingdom) 432
Burns Philp (NG) Ltd (Papua New Guinea) 329
Büro für Urheberrechte (BfU) (German Democratic Republic) 126

Burundi Literature Center (Burundi) 63
Busche, Kartographischer Verlag, GmbH (Federal Republic of Germany) 137
Busck, Arnold, International Boghandel A/S (Denmark) 84
Busck, Nyt Nordisk Forlag Arnold, A/S (Denmark) 80
Bush Press Communications Ltd (New Zealand) 308
Bushatsky, Livraria e Editora Juridica José, Ltda (Brazil) 51
Business Center for Academic Societies Japan (Japan) 256
Business Information Group (India) 199
Business Publications Ltd (Taiwan) 407
Buske, Helmut, Verlag (Federal Republic of Germany) 137
Busse und Seewald, Verlag, GmbH (Federal Republic of Germany) 137
Bussy, J H de, BV (Netherlands) 295
Bustamente Press Inc (Philippines) 332
Butler, Dorothy, Ltd (New Zealand) 312
Butterbach, Christian (Grand Duchy of Luxembourg) 275
Butterworth & Co (Asia) Pte Ltd (Republic of Singapore) 351
Butterworth & Co (Publishers) Ltd (United Kingdom) 432
Butterworth Publishers (Pty) Ltd (Republic of South Africa) 355
Butterworths of New Zealand Ltd (New Zealand) 308
Butterworths Pty Ltd (Australia) 12
Butzon und Bercker, Verlag, GmbH (Federal Republic of Germany) 137
Buzby Books Ltd (United Kingdom) 433
Bwrdd Croeso Cymru (United Kingdom) 433
By och Bygd, Förlaget (Sweden) 383
Bybelgenootskap (Republic of South Africa) 355
Byggförlaget (Sweden) 383

C A B International (International Organizations) 512
C B D Research Ltd (United Kingdom) 433
C B S Australia Publishing Pty Ltd (New Zealand) 308
C B S Publishing Asia Ltd (Hong Kong) 187
C D D (Centar društvenih djelatnosti Saveza socijalističke omladine Hrvatske) (Yugoslavia) 496
C D E SpA Gruppo Mondadori (Italy) 251
C D L (Central Distribuidora Livreira) Sarl (Portugal) 343
C D P — Julien Prélat SA (France) 100
C D U (France) 100
C E A — Casa Editrice Ambrosiana (Italy) 235
C E A (Collectif des Editeurs Associés) (France) 100
C E D A M (Casa Editrice Dr A Milani) (Italy) 235
C E D E (Centro de Estudios sobre Desarrollo Económico) (Colombia) 69
C E D E L, Ediciones (Spain) 365
C E D I Bookshop (Zaire) 502
C E D I S SRL (Italy) 235
C E D-Samsom (Belgium) 37
C E E B A Publications (Zaire) 502
C E E L (Centre Expérimental pour l'Enseignement des Langues) (Switzerland) 394
C E E P I Ltd (Caxton and English Educational Programmes International Ltd) (United Kingdom) 433
C E E S, Librería (Guatemala) 186
C E F A, Editions, (Centre d'Education à la Famille et à l'Amour) (Belgium) 37
C E L (France) 100
C E L F (France) 96
C E L S E (Compagnie d'Editions Libres, Sociales et Economiques SA) (France) 100
C E L T A (Centre de Linguistique Théorique et Appliquée) (Zaire) 502
C E L U P SRL (Italy) 235
C E M (Italy) 235
C E P A — Centro Editor de Psicologia Aplicada Ltda (Brazil) 51
C E P A D (France) 100
C E P Editions (France) 100
C E P I M, Edizioni (Italy) 235
C E P L (Centre d'Etude et de Promotion de la Lecture) (France) 100
C E R L A L C (International Organizations) 508
C E T (United Kingdom) 433
C E T E M (Casa Editrice Testi Elementari Milano) SRL (Italy) 235
C F E Belgique (Belgium) 37
C F W Publications Ltd (Hong Kong) 188
C I A C O Editeur (Belgium) 37
C I B (United Kingdom) 433
C I C I (United Kingdom) 421
C I E S P A L (Centro Internacional de Estudios Superiores de Comunicación para América Latina) (Ecuador) 87

C I L F (France) 100
C I S – Verlag (Christlich-Islamisches Schriftum) (Federal Republic of Germany) 137
Č K P (Členská knižnica Pravdy) (Czechoslovakia) 77
C L A I M Bookshop (Malawi) 277
C L D (France) 100
C L E, Editions (United Republic of Cameroun) 63
C L E T (Centre de Librairie et d'Editions Techniques) (France) 100
C L É: The Irish Book Publishers' Association (Republic of Ireland) 221
C L E U P — Cooperativa Libraria Editrice dell'Università di Padova (Italy) 235
C L U E B, Editrice (Italy) 235
C L U E D — Cooperativa Libraria Universitaria Editrice Democratica (Italy) 235
C L U P — Cooperativa Libraria Universitaria del Politecnico (Italy) 235
C L U T Editrice (Italy) 235
C M P Reprints (Republic of South Africa) 355
C N A (Republic of South Africa) 355
C N A Literary Award (Republic of South Africa) 361
C N R S, Editions du, (Centre national de la recherche scientifique) (France) 100
C O I C (United Kingdom) 433
C O L I V R O — Comércio e Distribuição de Livros Ltda (Brazil) 57
C O M L A (International Organizations) 508
C P E — Centro Programmazione Editoriale (Italy) 236
C P I (Kenya) 267
C R E (United Kingdom) 433
C R E R (France) 100
C S I R Central Reference and Research Library (Ghana) 181
C S I R O (Commonwealth Scientific and Industrial Research Organization) (Australia) 12
C S I R O (Commonwealtht Scientific and Industrial Research Organization) (Australia) 21
C S S Bookshops, Agency and Publishing Division (Nigeria) 315
C S S (Nigeria) Bookshops Ltd (Nigeria) 318
C U M Books (Pty) Ltd (Republic of South Africa) 355
Caann Verlag GmbH (Federal Republic of Germany) 137
Caballito, Ediciones el, SA (Mexico) 284
Cacoulides, Librairie, (T Cacoulides & Co) (Greece) 184
Cadmo Editore SRL (Italy) 236
Cadogan Books Ltd (United Kingdom) 433
Cahiers d'Art, Editions (France) 100
Cahiers de la Renaissance Vaudoise (Switzerland) 394
Cahiers Fiscaux, Les, Européens Sàrl (France) 100
Cairo University Press (Egypt) 88
Calder, John, (Publishers) Ltd (United Kingdom) 433
Calderini, Edizioni (Italy) 236
Caliban Books (United Kingdom) 433
Calicanto, Editorial (Argentina) 4
California University Press (United Kingdom) 433
Calinescu', Institutul de Istorie si Teorie Literara 'George (Romania) 347
Callenbach, Uitgeverij G F, BV (Netherlands) 295
Callwey, Verlag Georg D W, GmbH & Co (Federal Republic of Germany) 137
Calmann & King, John, Ltd (United Kingdom) 433
Calmann-Lévy, Editions, SA (France) 100
Calvyn-Jubileumboekefonds (Republic of South Africa) 355
Calwer Verlag (Federal Republic of Germany) 137
Cámara Argentina de Publicaciones (Argentina) 3
Cámara Argentina del Libro (Argentina) 3
Cámara Boliviana del Libro (Bolivia) 48
Cámara Brasileira do Livro (Brazil) 49
Cámara Chilena del Libro AG (Chile) 65
Cámara Colombiana de la Industria Editorial (Colombia) 69
Cámara Colombiana del Libro (Colombia) 69
Cámara Ecuatoriana del Libro (Ecuador) 87
Cámara Nacional de Comercio, Sección de Librerías (Mexico) 283
Cámara Nacional de la Industria Editorial (Mexico) 283
Cámara Oficial, Biblioteca de la, de Comercio, Agricultura e Industria del Distrito Nacional (Dominican Republic) 87
Cámara Paraguaya del Libro (Paraguay) 329
Cámara Peruana del Libro (Peru) 330
Cámara Uruguaya del Libro (Uruguay) 490
Cámara Venezolana del Libro (Venezuela) 492
Cambridge Bibliographical Society (United Kingdom) 485
Cambridge Information and Research Services Ltd (United Kingdom) 433
Cambridge University Library (United Kingdom) 482
Cambridge University Press (Australia) 12

Cambridge University Press (United Kingdom) 433
Camden Press Ltd (United Kingdom) 433
Camera dei Deputati Ufficio Stampa e Pubblicazioni (Italy) 236
Camerapix Publishers International Ltd (Kenya) 267
Cameroun Book Centre (United Republic of Cameroun) 64
Caminho, Editorial, SARL (Portugal) 340
Campbell, John W, Memorial Award (International Literary Prizes) 517
Campbell, Killie, Africana Library (Republic of South Africa) 355
Campbell, Roy, Prize for Poetry (Republic of South Africa) 361
Campert, Jan, Prize (Netherlands) 306
Campiello Prize (Italy) 253
Campus, Editora, Ltda (Brazil) 51
Campus Corner Ltd (Trinidad and Tobago) 413
Campus Verlag GmbH (Federal Republic of Germany) 137
Camus', Bibliothèque du Centre culturel 'Albert (Democratic Republic of Madagascar) 277
Cana Publishing House Ltd (Israel) 226
Cañada, Silverio (Spain) 365
Canavaun Books (Republic of Ireland) 222
'Canberra Times', The, and the Commonwealth Bank National Short Story of the Year (Australia) 23
Cangallo, Editorial, SACI (Argentina) 4
Cankarjeva Založba (Yugoslavia) 496
Cankarjeva Založba (Yugoslavia) 500
Canongate Publishing Ltd (United Kingdom) 433
Canova SRL (Italy) 236
Cantabrica, Editorial, SA (Spain) 365
Cantagalli, Edizioni (Italy) 236
Cantecleer, Uitgeverij, BV (Netherlands) 295
Canterbury, The, Press Norwich (United Kingdom) 433
Canterbury Public Library (New Zealand) 312
Canterbury University Library (New Zealand) 312
Cantor, Editio (Federal Republic of Germany) 137
Canuto, Livraria, Ltda (Brazil) 57
Cape, 'The Times'/Jonathan, Young Writers Prize (International Literary Prizes) 517
Cape Catley Ltd (New Zealand) 308
Cape Coast University Bookshop (Ghana) 181
Cape Ltd, Jonathan (United Kingdom) 433
Cape Provincial Library Service (Republic of South Africa) 360
Cape Town City Libraries (Republic of South Africa) 360
Capexil Book Division (India) 195
Capital Book House (India) 199
Capitol Editrice Dischi CEB (Italy) 236
Capitol Publishing House Inc (Philippines) 332
Capone Editore SRL (Italy) 236
Cappelens, J W, Forlag A/S (Norway) 320
Cappelli, Nuova Casa Editrice Licinio, SpA (Italy) 236
Capper Press Ltd (New Zealand) 308
Captan, Wadih M, Bookstores (Liberia) 274
Caraibes, Editions (Haiti) 187
Caralt, Luis de, Editor SA (Spain) 365
Caravelle, La, Librairie (Tunisia) 414
Carcanet Press Ltd (United Kingdom) 434
Cardeñoso, Cecilio (Spain) 375
Cardinal (United Kingdom) 434
Carducci Prize (International Literary Prizes) 517
Careers & Educational Publishers Ltd (Republic of Ireland) 222
Careers Consultants Ltd (United Kingdom) 434
Careers Research and Advisory Centre Ltd (United Kingdom) 434
Carew Hunt Associates (United Kingdom) 479
Caribbean Regional Library (Puerto Rico) 345
Caribbean Universities Press Jamaica Ltd (Jamaica) 254
Caribe, Editora El (Dominican Republic) 86
Caribe Grolier Inc (Dominican Republic) 87
Carinthia, Verlag (Austria) 27
Carit Andersens Forlag A/S (Denmark) 80
Caritas, Librairie (Rwanda) 348
Carl, Verlag Hans, GmbH & Co KG (Federal Republic of Germany) 137
Carlsen if AB (Sweden) 383
Carlsen if International Publishers (Denmark) 80
Carlsen Verlag GmbH (Federal Republic of Germany) 137
Carmina, Bokförlaget (Sweden) 383
Carnegie Free Library (Trinidad and Tobago) 413
Carnegie Library (Mauritius) 283
Carnegie Medal (United Kingdom) 486
Carnell Literary Agency (United Kingdom) 479
Caro y Cuervo, Instituto (Colombia) 69
Carolina, Impresora, C or A (Dominican Republic) 86
Carousel (United Kingdom) 434
Carr, David, Literary Agency (Federal Republic of Germany) 175
Carrara, Casa Musicale Edizioni, SRL (Italy) 236

Carrefour, Librairie (Ivory Coast) 254
Carroccio, Edizioni (Italy) 236
Carroll's (Australia) 12
Carson-Gold, Ronald, Memorial Short Story Competition (Australia) 23
Carta, Lüthi und Ramseier (Switzerland) 394
Carta, The Israel Map and Publishing Co Ltd (Israel) 227
Cartea Românească, Editura (Romania) 346
Cartier Diamond Dagger Award (United Kingdom) 486
Carto BVBA (Belgium) 37
Cartographia (Hungary) 190
Caruana, Francis (Gibraltar) 182
Carvajal SA (Colombia) 69
Carvan Book House (Pakistan) 325
Casa de la Cultura Ecuatoriana, Biblioteca de la (Ecuador) 88
Casa de las Américas (Cuba) 73
Casa de las Américas (Cuba) 74
Casa de las Américas Literary Award (International Literary Prizes) 518
Casa de Velázquez (Spain) 365
Casa del Libro, Librería, H Rajul & Cia Ltda (Colombia) 71
Casa del Libro Editrice (Italy) 236
Casa del Libro SA (Spain) 376
Casagrande, Edizioni, SA (Switzerland) 394
Casalini Libri (Italy) 236
Casalini Libri (Italy) 251
Casals, Editorial, SA (Spain) 365
Casariego, Editorial, SA (Spain) 365
Casavalle, Carlos, Prize (Argentina) 9
Casini, Edistudio di Brunetto (Italy) 236
Cass, Frank, & Co Ltd (United Kingdom) 434
Cassell PLC (United Kingdom) 434
Cassia House Bookshop (Trinidad and Tobago) 413
Castaigne, Librairie, SPRL (Belgium) 44
Castalia, Editorial (Spain) 365
Casteilla, Editions (France) 100
Castella, Editions Paul (Switzerland) 394
Castello-Collane, Il, Tecniche (Italy) 236
Castello di Antonio Careddu, Edizioni (Italy) 236
Casterman, Editions (Belgium) 37
Casterman, Editions (France) 100
Castex, Louis, Prize (France) 119
Castle House Publications Ltd (United Kingdom) 434
Castro e Silva, Livraria (Portugal) 343
Castrum Peregrini Presse (Netherlands) 295
Catalunya, Biblioteca de, Diputación de Barcelona (Spain) 365
Cátedra, Ediciones, SA (Spain) 365
Cátedra, Livraria Editora, Ltda (Brazil) 51
Catenacci, Hercule, Prize (France) 119
Cathasia (France) 100
Cathay (United Kingdom) 434
Cathedral, The, Bookshop (Tanzania) 409
Catholic Bookshop, The, Ltd (Kenya) 268
Catholic Institute for International Relations (United Kingdom) 434
Catholic Library, Central (Republic of Ireland) 224
Catholic Library, Central, Association Inc (Republic of Ireland) 224
Catholic Truth Society (United Kingdom) 434
Católica, Biblioteca de Autores Cristianos de la Editorial, SA (Spain) 366
Causeway Press Ltd (United Kingdom) 434
Caux, Editions de (Switzerland) 394
Caux Verlag, Theater und Film AG (Switzerland) 394
Cavalier Press Pty Ltd (Australia) 12
Cave, Paul, Publications Ltd (United Kingdom) 434
Cavefors, Verlag Bo (Switzerland) 394
Caveman Publications Ltd (New Zealand) 308
Caxton, The, Press (New Zealand) 308
Caxton and English Educational Programmes International Ltd (United Kingdom) 434
Caymi, Editorial (Argentina) 4
Ceac, Ediciones, SA (Spain) 366
Cedar Books (United Kingdom) 434
Cedibra Editora Brasileira Ltda (Brazil) 51
Cedic, Editions (France) 100
Cedilivre SA (Switzerland) 394
Celcius, Editorial, SA (Argentina) 4
Celebrity Educational Publishers (Republic of Singapore) 351
Celerity Book Service (United Kingdom) 479
Celuc Libri (Italy) 236
Cement & Concrete Association (United Kingdom) 434
Cenacolo di Studi Storico, Artistico, Letterari (Italy) 252
Centar za Kulturnu Djelatnost Zagreb (CEKADE) (Yugoslavia) 496
Centaur, De (Netherlands) 295
Centaur Press Ltd (United Kingdom) 434
Centaur Publishers (Pty) Ltd (Republic of South Africa) 355
Centenary Publishing House Ltd (Uganda) 416

Center for Academic Publications Japan (Japan) 256
Centraal Boekhuis BV (Netherlands) 292
Centraal Bureau, Bibliotheek van het, voor de Statistiek (Netherlands) 304
Central Agricultural Library, National Agro-industrial Union (Bulgaria) 61
Central Book Depot (Publishers) (India) 199
Central Bookshop Ltd (Malawi) 277
Central Bureau of Statistics, Economic Library (Ghana) 181
Central de Publicaciones SA (Mexico) 288
Central Department Store (Thailand) 411
Central Hindi Directorate (India) 199
Central Hindi Directorate Awards (India) 215
Central Institute of Indian Languages (India) 199
Central Library (India) 214
Central Medical Library (Bulgaria) 61
Central News Agency (Namibia) 291
Central News Agency Ltd (Republic of South Africa) 355
Central News Agency Ltd (Republic of South Africa) 360
Central Scientific Technical Library (Bulgaria) 61
Central Secretariat Library (India) 214
Central Secretariat Library (Pakistan) 327
Central Statistical, Library of the, Office of Finland (Finland) 94
Central Tanganyika Press (Tanzania) 409
Central Tibetan Secretariat (India) 199
Centrala Editoriala (Romania) 346
Centrale, Librairie (Togo) 412
Centralnej Rady Związków Zawodowych, Instytut Wydawniczy (Poland) 335
Centre, Librairie du (Grand Duchy of Luxembourg) 276
Centre africain de Formation et de Recherche administratives pour le Développement, Centre de Documentation (International Organizations) 508
Centre belge de Traduction (Belgium) 47
Centre Bibliothèque d'Information (Republic of Gabon) 122
Centre culturel américain, Bibliothèque (Ivory Coast) 254
Centre culturel américain, Bibliothèque (Republic of Gabon) 122
Centre culturel américain, Bibliothèque (Senegal) 349
Centre culturel américain, Bibliothèque de Prêt (United Republic of Cameroun) 64
Centre culturel du Burundi (Burundi) 63
Centre culturel français, Bibliothèque du, de Bamako (Mali) 281
Centre culturel français, Bibliothèque (Chad) 65
Centre culturel français, Bibliothèque (Ivory Coast) 254
Centre culturel français, Bibliothèque (Morocco) 290
Centre culturel français, Bibliothèque (Popular Republic of Congo) 72
Centre culturel français, Bibliothèque (Senegal) 349
Centre culturel français, Bibliothèque (Togo) 412
Centre culturel français, Bibliothèque (United Republic of Cameroun) 64
Centre culturel français, Bibliothèqueque (Central African Republic) 64
Centre culturel français, Bibliothèques (Zaire) 502
Centre culturel français de Constantine, Bibliothèque (Algeria) 2
Centre culturel français d'Oran, Bibliothèque (Algeria) 2
Centre culturel français Gaston Berger (Senegal) 349
Centre culturel français St-Exupéry Bibliothèque (Republic of Gabon) 122
Centre de Documentation de l'Autorité du Bassin du Niger (Niger) 314
Centre de Documentation et des Statistiques UNESCO (Chad) 65
Centre de Documentation Universitaire et Société d'Edition d'Enseignement Supérieur Réunis (CDU & SEDES) (France) 100
Centre de Librairie et d'Editions Techniques (France) 100
Centre de Littérature Chrétienne (Benin) 47
Centre de Littérature Evangélique (Republic of Gabon) 122
Centre de Publications Evangeliques (Ivory Coast) 253
Centre de Recherches et de Documentation du Sénégal (CRDS) (Senegal) 349
Centre d'Edition et de Diffusion africaines (Ivory Coast) 254
Centre d'Edition et de Diffusion africaines (CEDA) (Ivory Coast) 253
Centre d'Edition et de Production de Manuels scolaires de l'UNESCO (United Republic of Cameroun) 63
Centre d'Edition et de Production pour l'Enseignement et la Recherche (CEPER) (United Republic of Cameroun) 63
Centre d'Education à la Famille et à l'Amour (Belgium) 37

INDEX 549

Centre d'Enseignement supérieur de Niamey (Niger) 314
Centre d'Etude et de Promotion de la Lecture (France) 100
Centre d'Exportation du Livre Français (France) 96
Centre Djoliba recherche-formation pour le développement, Bibliothèque (Mali) 281
Centre Expérimental pour l'Enseignement des Langues (Switzerland) 394
Centre for Documentation and Research (United Arab Emirates) 421
Centre for Pedagogical Information and Documentation (Bulgaria) 61
Centre for Public Libraries (Israel) 231
Centre for Resource Management (New Zealand) 308
Centre for Scientific and Technical Information of the National Institute for Informatics (Republic of South Africa) 360
Centre français de Documentation (Mali) 281
Centre international de documentation parlementaire (CIDP) (International Organizations) 513
Centre International de Sémiologie (Zaire) 502
Centre international d'Etudes de la Formation religieuse Lumen Vitae ASBL (Belgium) 37
Centre national de Documentation (Morocco) 291
Centre national de Documentation scientifique et technique (Belgium) 45
Centre national de la recherche scientifique (France) 100
Centre national de Recherches 'Primitifs Flamands' ASBL (Belgium) 37
Centre national des Lettres (France) 118
Centre Orstrom de Brazzaville, Bibliothèque (Popular Republic of Congo) 72
Centre Protestant d'Editions et de Diffusion (CEDI) (Zaire) 502
Centre Publications (Australia) 12
Centre régional de Promotion du Livre en Afrique (CREPLA) (International Organizations) 508
Centre Sénégalaise d'Editions et de Diffusion (Senegal) 349
Centre Suisse du Livre (Switzerland) 391
Centro, Biblioteca del, Cultural Costarricense-Norteamericano (Costa Rica) 73
Centro, Fundación, de Investigación y Educación Popular (CINEP) (Colombia) 69
Centro Cultural Bautista (Nicaragua) 314
Centro de Documentacão Científica e Técnica (Portugal) 344
Centro de Documentação e Informação da Câmara dos Deputados (Brazil) 58
Centro de Documentación Bibliotecológica (Argentina) 9
Centro de Estudios Monetarios Latinoamericanos (CEMLA) (Mexico) 284
Centro de Estudios sobre Desarrollo Económico CEDE (Colombia) 71
Centro de Investigação e Documentação (Brazil) 58
Centro Di (Italy) 236
Centro do Livro Brasileiro Lda (Portugal) 340
Centro Documentazione Alpina (Italy) 236
Centro Editor de America Latina SA (Argentina) 4
Centro Editor de Psicologia Aplicada Ltda (Brazil) 51
Centro Editorial Latino Americano Ltda (Brazil) 51
Centro Filosófico-Literario (Colombia) 71
Centro Internazionale del Libro SpA (Italy) 236
Centro Latinoamericano de Demografía (CELADE) (International Organizations) 511
Centro Mexicano de Escritores AC (Mexico) 283
Centro Nacional de Documentación Científica y Tecnológica (Bolivia) 49
Centro Nacional de Documentación e Información Educativa (Bolivia) 49
Centro Nacional de Información, Agencia Nacional I S B N (Mexico) 283
Centro Nacional de Información y Documentación (CENID) (Chile) 66
Centro Nacional de Información y Documentación (CENID) (Uruguay) 491
Centro Regional para el Fomento del Libro en América Latina y el Caribe (CERLALC) (International Organizations) 508
Centro Studi Terzo Mondo (Italy) 236
Centro Svizzero del Libro (Switzerland) 391
Centrul de Lingvistica Istorie Literara si Folclor (Romania) 347
Centrum Informacji Naukowej, Technicznej i Ekonomicznej (Poland) 338
Centrum voor Literatuuronderzoekers (Netherlands) 305
Centurion, Editions du (France) 101
Century (United Kingdom) 434
Century Hutchinson Australia Pty Ltd (Australia) 13
Century Hutchinson Ltd (United Kingdom) 434
Century Hutchinson NZ Ltd (New Zealand) 308
Century Hutchinson Publishing Ltd (United Kingdom) 434

Century Hutchinson SA Pty Ltd (Republic of South Africa) 355
Cepadues Editions (CEPAD) SA (France) 101
Cercle Africain du Livre (Togo) 412
Cercle Belge de la Librairie (Belgium) 36
Cercle d'Art, Editions, SA (France) 101
Cercle de la Librairie, Editions du (France) 101
Cercle de la Librairie (France) 96
Cercle d'Or, Editions le (France) 101
Cerdas (Indonesia) 217
Ceres, Editura (Romania) 346
Ceres Productions (Tunisia) 413
Ceres-Verlag Rudolf-August Oetker KG (Federal Republic of Germany) 137
Cerf, Editions du (France) 101
Certificate of Honour (India) 215
Cervantes, Librería (Ecuador) 87
Cervantes, Librería, — Libroclub de Guatemala (Guatemala) 186
Cervantes, Miguel de, Prize (Spain) 377
České socialistické republiky, Státní knihovna (Czechoslovakia) 78
Českého fondu, Výtvarná služba, výtvarných umělcu, sekce krásné knihy a grafiky (Czechoslovakia) 75
Československý spisovatel (Czechoslovakia) 75
Ceylon Institute of Scientific and Industrial Research Library (Sri Lanka) 379
Ceylon Printers Ltd (Sri Lanka) 378
Chacko, I C, Award (India) 215
Chadwyck-Healey France (France) 101
Chadwyck-Healey Ltd (United Kingdom) 434
Chalantika (Bangladesh) 34
Chalermnit Bookshop (Thailand) 411
Chalermnit Press (Thailand) 410
Chalet, Editions du (France) 101
Challenge (Australia) 13
Challenge Bookshops (Nigeria) 318
Challenge Publications (Nigeria) 315
Chambers, W & R, Ltd (United Kingdom) 435
Chambre syndicale des Editeurs d'Annuaires et de Publications similaires (France) 96
Champ Libre, Editions (France) 101
Champs-Elysées, Librairie des, SA (France) 101
Chanakya Publications (India) 199
Chancellor (United Kingdom) 435
Chancerel Editions SA (France) 101
Chancerel Publishers Ltd (United Kingdom) 435
Chancery House Publishing Ltd (United Kingdom) 435
Chand, S, & Co Ltd (India) 199
Chandigarh Booksellers' Association (India) 195
Changjo Sa (Republic of Korea) 269
Chanlis (Belgium) 37
Chantecler, Editions (Belgium) 37
Chapman, Agence Littéraire Alexandra (France) 116
Chapman, Geoffrey (United Kingdom) 435
Chapman & Hall Ltd (United Kingdom) 435
Charles-Lavauzelle, Editions, SA (France) 101
Charnwood Library Series (United Kingdom) 435
Charotar Publishing House (India) 199
Charran Educational Publishers (Trinidad and Tobago) 413
Charran's Bookshop (1978) Ltd (Trinidad and Tobago) 413
Charte, La, NV (Belgium) 37
Chartered Institute of Bankers (CIB) Publications (United Kingdom) 435
Chartered Institute of Building, The (United Kingdom) 435
Chartwell-Bratt (Publishing & Training) Ltd (United Kingdom) 435
Chat, Editions du, Perché (France) 101
Chatam Sofer Institute (Israel) 227
Chateauneuf-du-Pape Grand Prize (France) 119
Chatto & Windus Ltd/The Hogarth Press (United Kingdom) 435
Chatto, Bodley Head & Jonathan Cape Australia Pty Ltd (Australia) 13
Chatto, Bodley Head & Jonathan Cape Ltd (United Kingdom) 435
Chaukhambha Orientalia (India) 199
Chavée, Honoré, Prize (France) 119
Chemical Society, The (United Kingdom) 435
Chemie, Verlag, GmbH (Federal Republic of Germany) 137
Chemin Facile (United Republic of Cameroun) 63
Chêne, Editions du (France) 101
Cheng Chung Book Co (Taiwan) 407
Ch'eng Wen Publishing Company (Taiwan) 407
Cherche-Midi, Le, Éditeur (France) 101
Cheshire (Australia) 13
Chetana Pvt Ltd (India) 199
Chez Nanon (Seychelles) 350
Chi Rho (Australia) 13
Chiangmai Book Centre (Thailand) 410
Chiendent, Editions du, Sàrl (France) 101
Chikuma Shobo Publishing Co Ltd (Japan) 256

Child Honsha Co Ltd (Japan) 256
Childerset Pty Ltd (Australia) 13
Children Book House (India) 199
Children's, The, Press (Republic of Ireland) 222
Children's and Juvenile Literature Prize (Portugal) 344
Children's Book Award (International Literary Prizes) 518
Children's Book Award (United Kingdom) 486
Children's Book Circle (United Kingdom) 421
Children's Book Council of Australia (Australia) 22
Children's Book Foundation (United Kingdom) 421
Children's Book of the Month Club (United Kingdom) 480
Children's Book of the Year Awards (Australia) 23
Children's Book of the Year Competition (United Kingdom) 486
Children's Book Prize (Norway) 324
Children's Book Trust (India) 199
Children's Bookclubs (Denmark) 84
Children's Writers' Group (United Kingdom) 421
Child's Play (International) Ltd (United Kingdom) 435
China Cultural Corporation (Hong Kong) 188
China Engineering Industry Press (CEIP) (People's Republic of China) 67
China I S B N Agency (People's Republic of China) 67
China International Book Trading Corporation (CIBTC) (Guoji Shudian) (People's Republic of China) 68
China Meteorological Press (People's Republic of China) 67
China National Association of Literature and the Arts (Taiwan) 408
China National Publications Import and Export Corporation (CNPIEC) (People's Republic of China) 67
China National Publishing Industry Trading Corp (People's Republic of China) 67
China National Publishing Industry Trading Corporation (People's Republic of China) 67
China Ocean Press (People's Republic of China) 67
China Social Sciences Publishing House (People's Republic of China) 67
China Society of Library Science (People's Republic of China) 68
China Youth Publishing House (People's Republic of China) 67
Chindwin Book Distributors (Burma) 62
Chinese Language and Literary Society (Republic of Singapore) 354
Chinese Language and Literature Association (Hong Kong) 189
Chinese Materials Center (Taiwan) 407
Chinese Materials Center (Taiwan) 408
Chinese Philatelic Magazine Press (People's Republic of China) 67
Chinese University of Hong Kong Library System (Hong Kong) 189
Chinese University Press, The (Hong Kong) 188
Chip Book Club (United Kingdom) 480
Chiron, Editions (France) 101
Chivers Press Publishers (United Kingdom) 435
Cholmondeley Award for Poets (International Literary Prizes) 518
Chomhairle, An, Leabharlanna (Republic of Ireland) 224
Chongqing Library (People's Republic of China) 68
Chopmen Publishers (Republic of Singapore) 351
Chopmen Publishers (Republic of Singapore) 353
Chopsticks Publications Ltd (Hong Kong) 188
Chotard et Associés, Editeurs (France) 101
Chowkhamba Sanskrit Series Office (India) 199
Choysa Bursaries for Children's Book Writers and Illustrators (New Zealand) 313
Chrissi Penna — Les Editions de la Plume d'Or (Greece) 183
Christian, Office of, Education and Literature (Thailand) 410
Christian, The, Literature Society (India) 199
Christian Book, The, Centre (Papua New Guinea) 329
Christian Book Shop (Bahamas) 34
Christian Booksellers' Association (NZ Chapter) (New Zealand) 307
Christian Bookselling Association of Australia (Australia) 10
Christian Bookshop (Zambia) 503
Christian Bookstore (Thailand) 411
Christian Community, The, Press (United Kingdom) 435
Christian Council of Zambia (Zambia) 503
Christian Journals (United Kingdom) 435
Christian Literature (Belize) 47
Christian Literature Association in Malawi (Malawi) 277
Christian Literature Crusade (Barbados) 35
Christian Publishing Co — CUM Books (Pty) Ltd (Republic of South Africa) 355
Christian Verlag GmbH (Federal Republic of Germany) 137

Christiana-Verlag (Switzerland) 394
Christians, Hans, Druckerei und Verlag (Federal Republic of Germany) 137
Christliche Verlagsanstalt GmbH (Federal Republic of Germany) 137
Christliche Verlagsgessellschaft mbH (Federal Republic of Germany) 137
Christlicher Bildungskreis Verlags GmbH (Federal Republic of Germany) 175
Christliches Verlagshaus GmbH (Federal Republic of Germany) 137
Christophorus-Verlag GmbH (Federal Republic of Germany) 138
Chryssos Typos (Greece) 183
Chugh Publications (India) 199
Chung Hwa Book Co Ltd (Taiwan) 408
Chuo-Tosho Co Ltd (Japan) 256
Chuokoron-Sha Inc (Japan) 256
Chur, Verlag Gisela (Federal Republic of Germany) 138
Church, Hubert, Award (New Zealand) 313
Church, The, Bookshop (Sudan) 380
Church House Publishing (United Kingdom) 435
Church Publishing Trust (Republic of South Africa) 355
Church Society (United Kingdom) 435
Churchill Livingstone (Australia) 13
Churchill Livingstone (United Kingdom) 435
Churchman (United Kingdom) 435
Cia Internacional de Publicaciones SA de CV (Mexico) 288
Ciapanna, Cesco, Editore SpA (Italy) 236
Ciarrapico Editore (Italy) 236
Ciba — Geigy Edizioni (Italy) 236
Cicada Press (New Zealand) 309
Cicero (Netherlands) 295
Cicero International Art GmbH (Federal Republic of Germany) 138
Cicerone Press (United Kingdom) 435
Cid, El, Editor SAE (Spain) 366
Cid, El, Editor SRL (Argentina) 4
Cidade Nova (Portugal) 340
Cidade Nova (Brazil) 51
Ciência e Vida, Publicações, Lda (Portugal) 340
Ciencias Sociales, Editorial de (Cuba) 73
Científica Argentina, Editorial (Argentina) 4
Científica Técnica, Livraria (Brazil) 57
Científico, Editorial, Técnica (Cuba) 73
Científico Médica, Editorial (Spain) 366
Cima, Librería (Ecuador) 88
Cinc d'Oros — Jaime Farrás Solé (Spain) 376
Cincel, Editorial, SA (Spain) 366
Cinque, Edizioni, Lune (Italy) 237
Ciordia, Editorial, SRL (Argentina) 4
Ciranna e Ferrara (Italy) 237
Ciranna — Roma, Editrice (Italy) 237
Circle, The, of Greek Children's Books (Greece) 185
Circle of State Librarians (United Kingdom) 483
Circle of the Greek Children's Book IBBY (Greek Section) Prizes (Greece) 185
Circolo Astrolabio (Italy) 251
Círculo de Lectores SA (Argentina) 8
Círculo de Lectores (Colombia) 71
Círculo de Lectores SA (Spain) 376
Círculo de Leitores (Portugal) 343
Círculo do Livro SA (Brazil) 57
Círculo Mexicano de Lectores (Mexico) 288
Circus Books (Australia) 13
Cisalpino — La Goliardica (Italy) 237
Citadell (Sweden) 383
Città Nuova Editrice (Italy) 237
Cittadèlla Editrice (Italy) 237
City, The, Bookshop (Ethiopia) 91
City Financial (United Kingdom) 435
City Library (Mauritius) 283
Ciudad Educativa, Librería, SA (Antigua Librería del Colegio) (Argentina) 8
Ciudad Nueva (Argentina) 4
Ciudad Nueva (Colombia) 69
Ciudad Nueva, Editorial (Spain) 366
Civilização, Editora, Brasileira SA (Brazil) 51
Civilização, Livraria, (Américo Fraga Lamares & Ca Lda) (Portugal) 340
Claassen-Verlag GmbH (Federal Republic of Germany) 138
Claret, Editorial, SA (Spain) 366
Claretiana, Editorial (Argentina) 4
Claridad, Editorial, SA (Argentina) 4
Clarion Book Club (India) 212
Clark, Robin, Ltd (United Kingdom) 435
Clark, Russell, Award (New Zealand) 313
Clark, T & T, Ltd (United Kingdom) 436
Clarke, Anthony, Books (United Kingdom) 436
Clarke, Arthur C, Award for Science Fiction (United Kingdom) 486
Clarke, James, & Co Ltd (United Kingdom) 436
Clasicos Roxsil (El Salvador) 90

Classen, Werner, Verlag (Switzerland) 394
Classey, E W (United Kingdom) 436
Classic (Pakistan) 325
Classic Thrillers (United Kingdom) 436
Classical Publishing Co (India) 199
Classics Club (India) 212
Classification Research Group (United Kingdom) 483
Classroom Magazine (Australia) 13
Claude Gill Books Ltd (United Kingdom) 481
Claudiana Editrice (Italy) 237
Claudius Verlag GmbH (Federal Republic of Germany) 138
Clausens, J Fr, Forlag (Denmark) 80
Clauwaert, Boekengilde de (Belgium) 44
Clauwaert, De (Belgium) 37
Clé International (France) 101
Clearway (Australia) 13
Cleary, R J (Australia) 13
Clematis Press Ltd (United Kingdom) 436
Clio Press Ltd (United Kingdom) 436
Clivo, De, Press (Switzerland) 394
Clócomhar, An, TTA (Republic of Ireland) 222
Clódhanna Teo (Republic of Ireland) 222
Cloister Book Store Ltd (Barbados) 35
Close Up, Editora, SA (Argentina) 4
Clowes, William, (Publishers) Ltd (United Kingdom) 436
Club, Editorial, de la Prensa (Puerto Rico) 344
Club de Lectores (Argentina) 4
Club de Lectores Extemporaneos (Mexico) 288
Club de Poetas (Argentina) 9
Club dei Bibliofili (Italy) 251
Club des Masques (France) 101
Club du Livre d'Art (France) 116
Club du Livre SA (France) 116
Club Français du Livre (France) 116
Club of Twentieth Century Poetry (Poland) 337
Club of Young Readers (Czechoslovakia) 77
Cobas, Ediciones Artes Graficas, SA (Spain) 366
Cobra, Agentur (Federal Republic of Germany) 175
Coccinella, La, Editrice SRL (Italy) 237
Cocco, Libreria Internazionale Fratelli (Italy) 251
Cochuideachd Leabhreachean Gàidhlig (United Kingdom) 436
Codco Est (Qatar) 345
Codecri, Editora, Ltda (Brazil) 51
Codesria (Senegal) 349
Codices Selecti (Austria) 27
Coeckelberghs, René, Bokförlag AB (Sweden) 383
Cogedi SA (Belgium) 37
Cohen, Mo (Federal Republic of Germany) 175
Coimbra Editora Lda (Portugal) 340
Cole & Yancy (Liberia) 274
Cole & Yancy Bookshop Ltd (Liberia) 274
Cole Publications (Australia) 13
Colediciones, Colombiana de Ediciones SA (Colombia) 69
Colegial Bolivariana CA (Venezuela) 492
Colegio, El, de México AC (Mexico) 284
Colegio, El, SA (Paraguay) 329
Colegio, Librería del, SA (Argentina) 4
Colegio de Bibliotecarios de Chile (Chile) 66
Colegio de Bibliotecarios de la Provincia de Buenos Aires (Argentina) 9
Colegio de Bibliotecólogos, Archivólogos y Afines del Estado Zulia (Venezuela) 494
Colegio de Bibliotecólogos y Archivólogos de Venezuela (Colbav) (Venezuela) 494
Colibrant (Belgium) 37
Colibri, Librairie Le (Mauritius) 283
Colin, Armand, Editeur (France) 101
Collectieve Propaganda van het Nederlandse Boek (CPNB) (Netherlands) 292
Collectif des Editeurs Associés (France) 101
Collectors Club of Franco Maria Ricci (Italy) 251
College, The, Press (Pvt) Ltd (Zimbabwe) 504
College Book House (India) 199
Collège camerounais des Arts, des Sciences et de la Technologie, Bibliothèque (United Republic of Cameroun) 64
College for Arab and Islamic Studies Library (Sudan) 380
Collège Jésus Marie Bibliothèque (Republic of Gabon) 122
College of Agriculture Library, University of Baghdad (Iraq) 220
College of Careers (Pty) Ltd (Republic of South Africa) 355
College of Our Lady of Fatima Library (Liberia) 274
College of the Bahamas Library (Bahamas) 34
Collège rural d'Ambatobe (Democratic Republic of Madagascar) 277
College Tutorial Press (Republic of South Africa) 355
Collet's Holdings Ltd (United Kingdom) 436
Colley-Moore International Publishers & Literary Agent (United Kingdom) 436
Colley-Moore Literary Agency (United Kingdom) 479

Collings, Rex, Ltd (United Kingdom) 436
Collins, Tom, Poetry Prize (Australia) 23
Collins, William, PLC (United Kingdom) 436
Collins, William, Pty Ltd (Australia) 13
Collins, William, Publishers Ltd (New Zealand) 309
Collins Booksellers Pty Ltd (Australia) 21
Collins Dove (Australia) 13
Collins Harvill (United Kingdom) 436
Collins Publishers (SA) (Pty) Ltd (Republic of South Africa) 355
Collins Religious Book Award (International Literary Prizes) 518
Collins Willow (United Kingdom) 436
Colloquium Verlag GmbH (Federal Republic of Germany) 138
Colmegna SA (Argentina) 4
Colombo Catholic Press (Sri Lanka) 378
Colombo Public Library System (Sri Lanka) 379
Colombus Books Ltd (United Kingdom) 436
Colonial, Editora (Dominican Republic) 86
Colonnes, Librairie des (Morocco) 290
Colour Library Books Ltd (United Kingdom) 436
Colporteur Press Pty Ltd (Australia) 13
Columba, Editorial, SA (Argentina) 4
Columba, The, Press (Republic of Ireland) 222
Columbia University Press (United Kingdom) 436
Columbine House (United Kingdom) 436
Columbus Publishers Ltd (Trinidad and Tobago) 413
Columbus Verlag Paul Oestergaard GmbH (Federal Republic of Germany) 138
Comb Books (Kenya) 267
Combi International AB (Sweden) 383
Combo Uitgeversgroep (Netherlands) 295
Comedia (United Kingdom) 436
Comet (United Kingdom) 436
Comisión Paraguaya Documentación e Información (Paraguay) 330
Commemorative Editions Pty Ltd (Australia) 13
Commercial Press (People's Republic of China) 67
Commercial Press Ltd (Hong Kong Branch) (Hong Kong) 188
Commission belge de Bibliographie (Belgium) 45
Commission de l'Education chrétienne (Zaire) 502
Commission des Bibliothèques de l'ASDBAM (Association Senegalaise pour le Développement de la Documentation, des Bibliothèques, des Archives et des Musées) (Senegal) 349
Commission for Racial Equality (United Kingdom) 436
Common Ground (United Kingdom) 437
Commonwealth, The, Library Association (COMLA) (International Organizations) 508
Commonwealth, The, Poetry Prize Awards (International Literary Prizes) 518
Commonwealth Agricultural Bureaux (International Organizations) 513
Commonwealth Government Bookshops (Australia) 21
Communication Foundation for Asia (Philippines) 332
Compagnie d'Editions Libres, Sociales et Economiques (France) 101
Compagnie Européenne de Fournitures et de Services Informatiques (France) 101
Compagnie Européenne de Publication (France) 101
Compañia General de Ediciones SA de CV (Mexico) 284
Compañia Impresora Argentina SA (Argentina) 4
Compass Verlagsgesellschaft Rudolf Hanel und Sohn (Austria) 27
Complexe, Editions, SPRL (Belgium) 37
Compograf Edizioni La Salamandra (Italy) 237
Computational Mechanics Publications (United Kingdom) 437
Comuneros, Editorial (Paraguay) 329
Comuneros, Librería (Paraguay) 329
Comunità, Edizioni di, SpA (Italy) 237
Conamore (Gyldendals underholdningsbogklub) (Denmark) 84
Concept Publishing Co (India) 199
Concepto, Editorial, SA (Mexico) 284
Concertina Publications Ltd (United Kingdom) 437
Conch Magazine Ltd, Publishers (Nigeria) 315
Concord Press Award for Academic Publishing (Nigeria) 319
Concorde Paperbacks (United Kingdom) 437
Concordia Editora Ltda (Brazil) 51
Concurso Literario Municipal (Municipal Literary Competition) (Uruguay) 491
Condor Books (United Kingdom) 437
Confederation of Information Communication Industries (United Kingdom) 422
Conference of European Churches (International Organizations) 513
Confluência, Editorial, Lda (Portugal) 340
Confraria dos Amigos do Livro Ltda (Brazil) 52
Congreso, Biblioteca del, de la Nación (Argentina) 8
Congreso, Biblioteca del, Nacional (Bolivia) 48
Congreso, Biblioteca del, Nacional (Chile) 66

INDEX 551

Congreso de Poesia de Puerto Rico (Puerto Rican Congress of Poetry) (Puerto Rico) 345
Congress of South-East Asian Librarians IV (CONSAL IV) (International Organizations) 508
Congresso de la Unión, Biblioteca del (Mexico) 288
Conjunta, Editorial, SRL (Argentina) 4
Connemara (State Central) Public Library (India) 214
Connoisseur Carbooks (United Kingdom) 437
Conquista, Empresa de Publicações Ltda (Brazil) 52
Conran Octopus Ltd (United Kingdom) 437
Conseil international des Associations de Bibliothèques de Théologie (International Organizations) 508
Consejo, Biblioteca Central y Publicaciones de, de Educación Secundaria básica y superior (Uruguay) 491
Consejo, Biblioteca General del, Superior de Investigaciones Científicas (Spain) 376
Conselho Federal de Biblioteconomia (CFB) (Brazil) 58
Conservative Political Centre (United Kingdom) 437
Conservatorio di Musica, Biblioteca Musicale Governativa del, S Cecilia (Italy) 252
Consilium Publishers (Sweden) 383
Constable & Co Ltd (United Kingdom) 437
Constable Fiction Trophy (United Kingdom) 487
Contabilidad, Ediciones, Moderna SACIC (Argentina) 4
Contables y Administrativas, Ediciones, SA (Mexico) 284
Contact, Uitgeverij, BV (Netherlands) 295
Contact NV (Belgium) 37
Conte, Fratelli, Editore SRL (Italy) 237
Contempora, Editorial, SRL (Argentina) 4
Continental, Cía Editorial, SA (CESCA) (Mexico) 284
Continental SRL Editrice (Italy) 237
Convent van Universiteitsbibliothekarissen in Nederland (Netherlands) 305
Conway Maritime Press Ltd (United Kingdom) 437
Cook, Albert, Library (Uganda) 416
Cook, James, Australian Literary Studies Award (Australia) 23
Cook, Thomas, Travel and Guide Book Awards (International Literary Prizes) 518
Cookery Book Club (United Kingdom) 480
Cooper, Leo (United Kingdom) 437
Cooperativa Libraria Editrice dell'Università di Padova (Italy) 237
Cooperativa Libraria Universitaria Editrice Bologna (Italy) 237
Cooperativa Libraria Universitaria Torinese (Italy) 237
Cooperative das Casas (Mozambique) 291
Coopérative de l'Enseignement Laïc (CEL) SA (France) 101
Coopérative Régionale de l'Enseignement Religieux (CRER) (France) 101
Copernic (France) 102
Copilco, Ediciones, SA (Mexico) 284
Coppée, François, Prize (France) 119
Coppenrath, Verlag F (Federal Republic of Germany) 138
Copplestone, Trewin, Books (United Kingdom) 437
Copress-Verlag (Federal Republic of Germany) 138
Copyright Council of New Zealand Inc (New Zealand) 307
Copyright Licensing Agency (United Kingdom) 422
Copyright Research Institute (Japan) 255
Coquito, Ediciones (Dominican Republic) 87
Corazón, Alberto, Editor (Spain) 366
Cordee (United Kingdom) 437
Cordillera, Editorial, Inc (Puerto Rico) 344
Cordoba Stories Prizes (Colombia) 72
Corgi (Australia) 13
Corgi (United Kingdom) 437
Corian-Verlag Heinrich Wimmer (Federal Republic of Germany) 138
Cork University Press (Republic of Ireland) 222
Cornell University Press (United Kingdom) 437
Cornelsen und Oxford University Press GmbH (Federal Republic of Germany) 138
Cornelsen und Schroedel GmbH & Co Geographische Verlagsgesellschaft KG (Federal Republic of Germany) 138
Cornelsen Verlag GmbH & Co (Federal Republic of Germany) 138
Cornelsen Verlagsgesellschaft mbH & Co KG (Federal Republic of Germany) 138
Cornerstone Books (United Kingdom) 437
Cornfeld, Gaalyah (Israel) 227
Corniche, Editions (Sweden) 383
Cornwall Books (United Kingdom) 437
Corona, Archivo de la, de Aragón (Spain) 376
Corona, Bokförlaget, AB (Sweden) 383
Corona Publishing Co Ltd (Japan) 256
Corona Verlag KG (Federal Republic of Germany) 138
Coronet (Australia) 13

Coronet (United Kingdom) 437
Corporan, Rafael, de los Santos (Dominican Republic) 86
Correa, Viriato, Prize (Brazil) 59
Corregidor, Ediciones, SAICI y E (Argentina) 4
Corti, Librairie José (France) 102
Cortina, Edizioni Libreria, Verona SRL (Italy) 237
Corvina Press (Hungary) 190
Corvus Verlag (Federal Republic of Germany) 138
Cosdel (Singapore) Pte Ltd (Malaysia) 280
Cosmic Book Services Ltd (Trinidad and Tobago) 413
Cosmopolita SRL (Argentina) 4
Cosmos, Edições (Portugal) 341
Cosmos, Editora (Dominican Republic) 86
Cosmos, Librería (Mexico) 288
Cosmos, Publicaciones (Mexico) 284
Cosmos-Verlag AG (Switzerland) 394
Cossio Salinas, Hector, National Biography Prize (Bolivia) 49
Costa, Sá da, Editora (Portugal) 341
Costa e Nolan SpA (Italy) 237
Costa Rica, Editorial (Costa Rica) 72
Costa Rica, Editorial, Literary Prize (Costa Rica) 73
Costello, D J, (Publishers) Ltd (United Kingdom) 437
Cotman House (United Kingdom) 437
Cotmancolor (United Kingdom) 437
Cotta'sche Buchhandlung, Verlag J G (Federal Republic of Germany) 138
Council for British Archaeology (United Kingdom) 437
Council for Educational Technology (United Kingdom) 437
Council of Europe, Publications Section (International Organizations) 513
Council of Libraries (Albania) 1
Counson, Albert, Prize (International Literary Prizes) 518
Count of Cartagena Prizes (International Literary Prizes) 518
Counterpoint (United Kingdom) 437
Country Book Society (United Kingdom) 480
Countryside Books (United Kingdom) 437
Countrywide Books (Republic of South Africa) 355
Courrier du Livre Sàrl (France) 102
Coutinho, Dick, BV (Netherlands) 295
Couto, Editora e Gráfica Miguel, SA (Brazil) 52
Cracow City Literary Prize (Poland) 339
Craft Book Society (United Kingdom) 480
Crafts, The, Council (United Kingdom) 437
Craftsman Book Society (United Kingdom) 480
Cramer, J (Federal Republic of Germany) 138
Crane Russak (United Kingdom) 437
Crawshay, The Rose Mary, Prizes (International Literary Prizes) 518
Crea, Editorial, SA (Argentina) 4
Creadif (Belgium) 37
Creanga, Editure Ion (Romania) 346
Creasey, John, Memorial Award (United Kingdom) 487
Crédit Communal de Belgique SA (Belgium) 37
Cremers (Schoollandkaarten) PVBA (Belgium) 37
Cremonese, Edizioni, SpA (Italy) 237
Crépin-Leblond, Editeurs, et Cie SA (France) 102
Crescent (United Kingdom) 437
Crescent Publishers (Bangladesh) 34
Crescent Publishing Co (India) 199
Crespillo, Editorial, SA (Argentina) 4
Cricket Book Club (United Kingdom) 480
Crime, The, Club (United Kingdom) 437
Crime Writers' Association (United Kingdom) 422
Crisp (Belgium) 37
Cristal, Librerías de (Mexico) 288
Cristiandad, Ediciones (Spain) 366
Criterion Book Club (United Kingdom) 480
Critica, Editorial, SA (Spain) 366
Cromograf SA (Ecuador) 87
Crompton, Paul H, Ltd (United Kingdom) 437
Croner Publications Ltd (United Kingdom) 437
Croom Helm Ancient History Prize (International Literary Prizes) 518
Croom Helm Ltd (United Kingdom) 437
Cross Continent Press Ltd (Nigeria) 315
Cross Way (United Kingdom) 437
Crowood Press, The (United Kingdom) 437
Crucible (United Kingdom) 437
Cubanas, Ediciones (Cuba) 73
Cuello, Casa (Dominican Republic) 87
Cujas, Editions (France) 102
Cultrix, Editora (Brazil) 52
Cultura, Casa de la, Ecuatoriana (Ecuador) 87
Cultura, Ediciones, Hispánica (Spain) 366
Cultura, Librería La (Paraguay) 329
Cultura, Premio Nacional de (Bolivia) 49
Cultura-Maroc (Morocco) 290
Cultura Médica, Editora, Ltda (Brazil) 52
Cultura y Ciencia, Empresa Editoriales de (Cuba) 73
Cultural, Librería, Colombiana (Colombia) 71

Cultural, Librería, Salvadoreña SA de CV (El Salvador) 90
Cultural, Publicaciones, SA (Mexico) 284
Cultural Centre, Library of the, Surinam (Bibliotheek CCS) (Suriname) 380
Cultural Centre of the Philippines Literary Awards (Philippines) 334
Cultural Colombiana Ltda (Colombia) 69
Cultural Panameña, Ediciones Librería, SA (Panama) 328
Cultural Supplies, The, Co (Malaysia) 278
Culturale, La (Italy) 237
Culture and Education Enterprises Ltd (Israel) 227
Culture et Civilisation, Editions (Belgium) 38
Culture Prize (Japan) 265
Cumann Leabharfhoilsitheoirí Éireann (Republic of Ireland) 221
Cumann Leabharlann na h-Éireann (Republic of Ireland) 224
Cumann Leabharlannaithe Scoile (CLS) (Republic of Ireland) 224
Cumont, Franz, Prize (International Literary Prizes) 518
Cura Verlag GmbH (Austria) 27
Curaçaosche Drukkerij en Uitgevers Maatschappij (Netherland Antilles) 306
Curci, Edizioni, SRL (Italy) 237
Curcio, Armando, Editore SpA (Italy) 237
Currawong Press Pty Ltd (Australia) 13
Currency Press Pty Ltd (Australia) 13
Current Books (India) 199
Current Law Publishers Ltd (United Kingdom) 438
Current Technical Literature Co (Pvt) Ltd (India) 213
Currey, James, Ltd (United Kingdom) 438
Curriculum Development Centre (Australia) 13
Curtis Brown (United Kingdom) 479
Curtis Brown (Australia) Pty Ltd (Australia) 20
Curzon Press Ltd (United Kingdom) 438
Cuspide, Distribuidora (Argentina) 8
Cuttington University College Library (Liberia) 274
Cygne, Librairie Le (Mauritius) 283
Cygnet Books (Australia) 13
Cyngor Llyfrau Cymraeg (United Kingdom) 422
Cyprus Booksellers Association (Cyprus) 74
Cyprus Museum, Library of the (Cyprus) 74
Cyril and Methodius National Library (Bulgaria) 61
Cyril and Methodius Prize (International Literary Prizes) 518
'Czytelnik', Spóldzielnia Wydawnicza (Poland) 335

D A F S A (France) 102
D B K — Bookdistribution (Denmark) 79
D B M I S T (France) 117
D C Book Club (India) 212
D C Books (India) 200
D C Press (India) 200
D E B Verlag (das europäische Buch Literaturvertrieb GmbH) (Federal Republic of Germany) 138
D E I, Edizioni, Roma (Italy) 237
D E L S A (Spain) 376
D I F E L - Difusão Editorial Lda (Portugal) 341
D I L I A (Czechoslovakia) 77
D J I (Federal Republic of Germany) 138
D K Agencies (P) Ltd (India) 213
D K F Trust (India) 200
D K Publications (India) 200
D K Publishers' Distributors (India) 213
D M Agence Littéraire (France) 116
D P Publications Ltd (United Kingdom) 438
D S I R (New Zealand) 309
D T V (Federal Republic of Germany) 138
D V A (Federal Republic of Germany) 138
Daan Retief Publishers (Republic of South Africa) 355
Dabbous Stores (Saudi Arabia) 348
Dacca Book Mart (Bangladesh) 35
Dacca University Library (Bangladesh) 35
Dachs-Verlag GmbH (Austria) 27
Dacia, Editura (Romania) 346
Dacosta, Les Editions Roger (France) 102
Dadò, Edizioni Armando, Tipografia Stazione (Switzerland) 394
Dagbreek, Klub- (Republic of South Africa) 359
Dagen, Tidnings AB (Sweden) 383
Dageraad, De, PVBA (Belgium) 38
Dahl, Gösta, och Son AB (Sweden) 388
Dahlia Books, International Publishers and Booksellers (Sweden) 383
Daihak Publishing Co (Republic of Korea) 269
Daiichi Shuppan Co Ltd (Japan) 256
Daily-Bul, Le (Belgium) 38
Daily Times of Nigeria Ltd (Nigeria) 315
Daimon, Ediciones, — Manuel Tamayo (Spain) 366

Dais Literary Agency (Italy) 251
Dale, Van, Lexicografie (Netherlands) 295
Dalesman Publishing Co Ltd (United Kingdom) 438
Dalla Parte, Edizioni, delle Bambine (Italy) 237
Dall'Oglio Editore SRL (Italy) 237
Dalloz, Jurisprudence Générale (France) 102
Dalsum, Albert van, Prize (Netherlands) 306
Dalton, Terence, Ltd (United Kingdom) 438
Daman, Librairie R (Grand Duchy of Luxembourg) 276
Damascus University Library (Syria) 407
Damascus University Press (Syria) 407
Dami Editore SRL (Italy) 237
Damm, N W, Children's Book Prize (Norway) 324
Damm, N W, og Søn A/S (Norway) 321
Damnitz Verlag (Federal Republic of Germany) 138
Dan Kook University Press (Republic of Korea) 269
Danae, Ediciones, SA (Spain) 366
Dance Books Ltd (United Kingdom) 438
Daneshdjou Bookstore (Iran) 220
Dangles, Editions, SA (France) 102
Daniel, The C W, Co Ltd (United Kingdom) 438
Danish Academy Prize for Literature (Denmark) 86
Danish Critics Literary Prize (Denmark) 86
Danish ISBN Agency (Denmark) 79
Danish Prize for Children's Literature (Denmark) 86
Danish Translations Centre (DTC) (Denmark) 86
Danmark, Forlaget, A/S (Denmark) 80
Danmarks Biblioteksforening (Denmark) 85
Danmarks Biblioteksforening Forlag ApS (Denmark) 80
Danmarks Forskningsbiblioteksforening (Denmark) 85
Danmarks Pædagogiske Bibliotek (Denmark) 84
Danmarks Skolebibliotekarforening (Denmark) 85
Danmarks Skolebiblioteksforening (Denmark) 85
Danmarks Statistik Biblioteket (Denmark) 84
Danmarks Tekniske Bibliotek (DTB) (Denmark) 84
D'Anna, Casa Editrice G (Italy) 237
Danov', Darzhavno Izdatelstvo 'Christo G (Bulgaria) 60
Dansk Exlibris Selskab (Denmark) 85
Dansk Forfatterforening (Denmark) 79
Dansk Historisk Haandbogsforlag Ltd (Denmark) 80
Dansk Litteraturselskab, Nyt (Denmark) 85
Dansk Musikbiblioteksforening (Denmark) 85
Dansk Teknisk Litteraturselskab — DTL (Denmark) 85
Danske Antikvarboghandlerforening (Denmark) 79
Danske Boghandleres Kommissionsanstalt (DBK) (Denmark) 79
Danske Boghandlerforening, Den (Denmark) 79
Danske Bogsamleres Klub (Denmark) 84
Danske Forlaeggerforening, Den (Denmark) 79
Danske Sprog-og Litteraturselskab (Denmark) 85
Dante, Libreria, di A M Longo (Italy) 251
Dap-Reinart, Uitgeverij, SV (Belgium) 38
Dap-Reinart Uitgeven (Belgium) 44
Daphins-Verlag (Switzerland) 394
Daphne Diffusion SA (Belgium) 38
Dar al-Kutub al-Wataniah (National Library) (Syria) 407
Dar Alhamadani (People's Democratic Republic of Yemen) 495
Dar Arabia Lil Kitab (Tunisia) 413
Dar El Amal SA, d'Edition de Diffusion de Presse et de Publicité (Tunisia) 413
Dar es Salaam Bookshop, The (Tanzania) 409
Dar es Salaam University Bookshop (Tanzania) 409
Dar es Salaam University Press (Tanzania) 409
Dar-ul-Kutub (Egypt) 89
Dardanos, G, — H Karakatsanis-C Dardanos & Co Ltd — Gutenberg (Greece) 183
Dardelet, Editions, SA (France) 102
Darf Publishers Ltd (United Kingdom) 438
Dargaud Editeur (France) 102
Dario', Librería Recinto 'Ruben (Nicaragua) 314
Darling Downs Institute Press (Australia) 13
Darmstädter Blätter, Verlag, Schwarz und Co (Federal Republic of Germany) 138
Darsan Books Private Ltd (India) 200
Darsan Books Private Ltd (India) 212
Darsan International Bestsellers Book Club (India) 213
Darton, Longman & Todd Ltd (United Kingdom) 438
Darwen Finlayson Ltd (United Kingdom) 438
Das Beste, Verlag (Federal Republic of Germany) 138
Dastane Ramchandra & Co (India) 200
Datapack Books (United Kingdom) 438
Daude, Librairie (Réunion) 346
Dauphin, Editions du (France) 102
Dausien, Werner (Federal Republic of Germany) 138
Dauzat, Albert, Prize (France) 119
Davar (Israel) 227
David & Charles (United Kingdom) 438
David Prize (Cuba) 74
Davidsfonds VZW (Belgium) 38
Davis-Poynter Ltd (United Kingdom) 438
Dawn Books (Hong Kong) 188
Dawood Prize for Literature (Pakistan) 327

Dawson Publishing (United Kingdom) 438
Daystar Press (Publishers) (Nigeria) 315
Daystar Publications (India) 200
Daystar Publications (India) 213
De Boccard Edition-Diffusion (France) 102
De Boeck-Wesmael, Editions, SA (Belgium) 38
De Bono, G, Editore (Italy) 238
De Garve, Uitgeverij (Belgium) 38
De Horstink (Belgium) 38
De Vecchi, Editorial, SA (Spain) 366
De Vecchi, Giovanni, Editore SpA (Italy) 238
Deakin University Press (Australia) 13
Dean and Chapter, The, Library (United Kingdom) 482
Deans International Publishing (United Kingdom) 438
Dearlove, Peter, Publishers (Zimbabwe) 504
Debate SA (Spain) 366
Debresse, Nouvelles Editions (France) 102
Debrett's Peerage Ltd (United Kingdom) 438
Debutantenpreis (German Democratic Republic) 128
Dečje Novine (Yugoslavia) 496
Decker's, R v, Verlag G Schenck GmbH (Federal Republic of Germany) 138
Découverte, La (France) 102
Dedalo, Edizioni, SpA (Italy) 238
Deduce SA (Mexico) 284
Deep & Deep Publications (India) 200
Dehoniane, Edizioni (Italy) 238
Dehoniane, Edizioni, Bologna (EDB) (Italy) 238
Deichmanske Bibliotek (Norway) 323
Dejaie, Maison d'Editions Cl (Belgium) 38
Dekker en Nordemann BV (Netherlands) 304
Dekker en Van de Vegt (Netherlands) 295
Dekker v d Vegt (Netherlands) 304
Delachaux et Niestlé, Editions, SA (Switzerland) 394
Delachaux Niestlé France SA (France) 102
Delacroix, Eve, Prize (France) 119
Delagrave, Librairie, Sàrl (France) 102
Delcourt, Editions André, & Cie (Switzerland) 394
Deldebat de Gonzalva Foundation Prize (France) 119
Delft University Press (Netherlands) 295
Delhi Library Association (India) 214
Delhi Public Library (India) 214
Delhi State Booksellers' and Publishers' Association (India) 195
Delhi University Library System (India) 214
Delightful Books (United Kingdom) 438
Delius, Klasing und Co (Federal Republic of Germany) 139
Dell (Australia) 13
dell'Orso, Edizioni, SAS (Italy) 238
Delmas, Editions J, et Cie (France) 102
Deloitte Haskins & Sells (United Kingdom) 438
Delphin Verlag (Switzerland) 394
Delphin Verlag GmbH (Federal Republic of Germany) 139
Delp'sche Verlagsbuchhandlung (Federal Republic of Germany) 139
Delta, Editions, SA (Belgium) 38
Delta (Switzerland) 394
Delta Books (Pty) Ltd (Republic of South Africa) 355
Delta et Spes (Switzerland) 394
Delta Fiction Award (Nigeria) 319
Delta Förlags AB (Sweden) 383
Delta Press (Yugoslavia) 496
Delta Publications (Nigeria) Ltd (Nigeria) 315
Delta Science Fiction Bok Klubb (Sweden) 388
Deltas (Belgium) 38
Delville, Editions (France) 102
Démuth, Dr rer pol Dr Julius (Federal Republic of Germany) 175
Denayer, Felix, Prize (Belgium) 46
Denholm House Press (United Kingdom) 438
Denis, Firma, & Co PVBA (Belgium) 44
Denis & Co PVBA (Belgium) 38
Dennis Award, C J (Australia) 23
Dennis Prize, C J, for Poetry (Australia) 24
Dennis Publishing Ltd (United Kingdom) 438
Denoël, Editions, Sàrl (France) 102
Dent, J M, & Sons Ltd (United Kingdom) 438
Dent, J M, Pty Ltd (Australia) 13
Denzel-Verlag Auto- und Wanderführer (Austria) 27
Depalma SRL (Argentina) 4
Departamento de Documentación y Bibliotecas (Dominican Republic) 87
Department of National Education Library (Republic of South Africa) 360
Department of National Education Literary Prizes for South African Citizens (Republic of South Africa) 361
Department of Publicity (Nepal) 292
Derecho Privado, Editorial Revista de (Spain) 366
Dergâh kitabevi (Turkey) 415
Dergâh Yayinlari AS (Turkey) 414
Desai Bookshops (Fiji) 91
Desarrollo, Editorial, SA (Peru) 330
Desbordes-Valmore, Marceline, Prize (France) 119

Deschamps, Maison Henri (Haiti) 187
Deschamps, Prix littéraire Henri (Haiti) 187
Desclée de Brouwer SA (France) 102
Desclée, Editeurs (Belgium) 38
Desclée et Cie, Editions (France) 102
Desertina Verlag (Switzerland) 394
Desforges, Librairie (France) 102
Design Council Books (United Kingdom) 439
Desire und Gegenrealismus (Federal Republic of Germany) 139
Dessain et Tolra SA (France) 102
Dessain NV, H (Belgium) 38
Dessain SPRL, H (Belgium) 38
Dessart, Engelbert, Verlag KG (Federal Republic of Germany) 139
Destino, Edicions, SA (Spain) 366
Desvigne, Editions (France) 102
Detskaya Entsiklopediya (Union of Soviet Socialist Republics) 417
Detskaya Literatura, Izdatelstvo (Union of Soviet Socialist Republics) 417
Deubner, Dr Peter, Verlag GmbH (Federal Republic of Germany) 139
Deuticke, Franz, Verlagsges mbH (Austria) 27
Deutsch, André, Ltd (United Kingdom) 439
Deutsch, Verlag für (Federal Republic of Germany) 139
Deutsch, Verlag Harri (Federal Republic of Germany) 139
Deutsch, Verlag Harri (Switzerland) 394
Deutsche Akademie für Sprache und Dichtung (Federal Republic of Germany) 178
Deutsche Bibelgesellschaft (Federal Republic of Germany) 139
Deutsche Bibliothek (Federal Republic of Germany) 176
Deutsche Blindenstudienanstalt eV (Federal Republic of Germany) 139
Deutsche Buch-Gemeinschaft C A Koch's Verlag Nachfolger (Austria) 31
Deutsche Buch-Gemeinschaft C A Koch's Verlag Nachfolger (Federal Republic of Germany) 175
Deutsche Bücherei (German Democratic Republic) 127
Deutsche Bücherei Abteilung Erwerbung ISBN-Agentur der DDR (German Democratic Republic) 123
Deutsche Dante-Gesellschaft eV (Federal Republic of Germany) 178
Deutsche Freidrich-Schiller Stiftung eV (Federal Republic of Germany) 178
Deutsche Gesellschaft für Dokumentation eV (Federal Republic of Germany) 177
Deutsche Jugend-Presse-Agentur KG (Federal Republic of Germany) 139
Deutsche Schiller-Stiftung (German Democratic Republic) 128
Deutsche Schillergesellschaft eV (Federal Republic of Germany) 178
Deutsche Shakespeare-Gesellschaft (German Democratic Republic) 128
Deutsche Shakespeare-Gesellschaft West eV (Federal Republic of Germany) 178
Deutsche Staatsbibliothek (German Democratic Republic) 127
Deutsche Thomas-Mann-Gesellschaft Sitz Lübeck (Federal Republic of Germany) 178
Deutsche Verlags-Anstalt GmbH (DVA) (Federal Republic of Germany) 139
Deutscher, Isaac, Memorial Prize (International Literary Prizes) 518
Deutscher Adressbuch-Verlag für Wirtschaft und Verkehr GmbH (Federal Republic of Germany) 139
Deutscher Apotheker Verlag Dr Roland Schmiedel GmbH und Co (Federal Republic of Germany) 139
Deutscher Autoren Verband eV (Federal Republic of Germany) 129
Deutscher Betriebswirte-Verlag GmbH (Federal Republic of Germany) 139
Deutscher Bibliotheksverband eV (Federal Republic of Germany) 177
Deutscher Bücherbund GmbH & Co (Federal Republic of Germany) 175
Deutscher Buchkreis (Federal Republic of Germany) 175
Deutscher Eichverlag (Federal Republic of Germany) 139
Deutscher Fachschriften-Verlag Braun GmbH & Co KG (Federal Republic of Germany) 139
Deutscher Fachverlag GmbH (Federal Republic of Germany) 139
Deutscher Gemeindeverlag GmbH (Federal Republic of Germany) 139
Deutscher Instituts-Verlag GmbH (Federal Republic of Germany) 139
Deutscher Jugendbuchpreis (Federal Republic of Germany) 179
Deutscher Kunstverlag GmbH (Federal Republic of Germany) 140

INDEX 553

Deutscher Landwirtschaftsverlag, VEB (German Democratic Republic)   124
Deutscher Literatur-Verlag (Federal Republic of Germany)   140
Deutscher Taschenbuch, D T V-, Verlag GmbH & Co KG (Federal Republic of Germany)   140
Deutscher Verband evangelischer Büchereien eV (Federal Republic of Germany)   177
Deutscher Verlag der Wissenschaften, VEB (German Democratic Republic)   124
Deutscher Verlag für Grundstoffindustrie, VEB (German Democratic Republic)   124
Deutscher Verlag für Kunstwissenschaft GmbH (Federal Republic of Germany)   140
Deutscher Verlag für Musik, VEB (German Democratic Republic)   124
Deutscher Wirtschaftsdienst John von Freyend GmbH (Federal Republic of Germany)   140
Deutsches Bibliotheksinstitut (Federal Republic of Germany)   177
Deutsches Bucharchiv München, Institut für Buchwissenschaften (Federal Republic of Germany)   176
Deutsches Jugendinstitut (DJI) (Federal Republic of Germany)   140
Deutsches Jugendschriftenwerk eV (Federal Republic of Germany)   129
Deux Coqs d'Or, Les Editions des (France)   103
Deux Magots Prize (France)   119
Dev Sahitya Kutir (P) Ltd (India)   200
Deves et Chaumet, Librairie (Mali)   281
Devlin, Denis, Memorial Award for Poetry (Republic of Ireland)   225
Dewan, Perpustakaan, Perwakilan Rakjat — RI (Indonesia)   219
Dewan Bahasa dan Pustaka (Malaysia)   278
Dewan Bahasa dan Pustaka (Malaysia)   281
Dezsery Publications Pty Ltd (Australia)   13
Dhammabucha (Thailand)   410
Dhanani's Ltd (Kenya)   268
Dhanpat Rai & Sons (India)   200
Dheerasarn Ltd (Thailand)   411
Di Baio Editore SpA (Italy)   238
Diadem Books (United Kingdom)   439
Diagram Visual Information Ltd (United Kingdom)   439
Dial (United Kingdom)   439
Diálogo, Ediciones (Paraguay)   329
Diamond Comics (P) Ltd (India)   200
Diamond Inc (Japan)   256
Dian Rakyat (Indonesia)   217
Diana, Editorial, SA (Mexico)   284
Diana Verlag AG (Switzerland)   394
Dianus-Trikont Buchverlag GmbH (Federal Republic of Germany)   140
Díaz, Ediciones, de Santos SA (Spain)   366
Díaz de Santos SA – Libreria Cientifico-Tecnica (Spain)   376
Dickens, The Christchurch, Fellowship (New Zealand)   312
Dickens, The Dunedin, Fellowship (New Zealand)   312
Dickens, The, Fellowship (Australia)   22
Dickens, The, Fellowship (France)   118
Dickens, The, Fellowship (Japan)   264
Dickens, The, Fellowship (Netherlands)   305
Dickens, The, Fellowship (Sri Lanka)   379
Dickens, The, Fellowship (United Kingdom)   485
Dickens, The, Fellowship (Argentine Branch) (Argentina)   9
Dickens, The Wellington, Fellowship, Branch 121 (New Zealand)   312
Dickson, Keith (United Kingdom)   439
Dickson Price Publishers Ltd (United Kingdom)   439
Dictionnaire, La Maison du (France)   103
Dictionnaires Le Robert (France)   103
Didactica si Pedagogica, Editura (Romania)   346
Didax (Switzerland)   395
Diderich, Librairie, Sàrl (Grand Duchy of Luxembourg)   276
Diderot, Livre Club (France)   116
Didier Editions, John (France)   103
Didier Erudition, Société Nouvelle (France)   103
Didot-Bottin, Société, SA (France)   103
Diederichs, Eugen, Verlag GmbH & Co KG (Federal Republic of Germany)   140
Diesterweg, Verlag Moritz, /Otto Salle Verlag (Federal Republic of Germany)   140
Dieterich'sche Verlagsbuchhandlung (German Democratic Republic)   124
Dietrich, Maximilian, Verlag (Federal Republic of Germany)   140
Dietz, Verlag J H W, Nachf GmbH (Federal Republic of Germany)   140
Dietz Verlag Berlin (German Democratic Republic)   124
Diffusion de la Presse (Zaire)   502
Difros (Greece)   183

Difusão Editorial SA (DIFEL) (Brazil)   52
Difusión, Centro de, del Libro (Spain)   366
Difusión, Editorial (Bolivia)   48
Difusión, Editorial, SA (Argentina)   4
Difusión, Librería (Bolivia)   48
Diglivro Lda (Distribuidora de Informação Geral) (Portugal)   343
Digma Publications (Republic of South Africa)   355
Dijkstra's Uitgeversmaatschappij, Jacob, BV (Netherlands)   295
Dilagro SA (Spain)   366
Diligentia BV (Netherlands)   295
Diligentia-Uitgeverij (Belgium)   38
Dillons The Bookstore (United Kingdom)   481
Dimashk, Dar, (Adib Tunbakji) Bookshop (Syria)   407
Dimensione Umana (Italy)   238
Din Mohammad, Malik, & Sons (Pakistan)   325
Dini Book Depot (India)   200
Dinosaur Publications Ltd (United Kingdom)   439
Diogenes, Editorial, SA (Mexico)   284
Diogenes Verlag AG (Switzerland)   395
Dipa-Verlag und Druck GmbH & Co (Federal Republic of Germany)   140
Diponegoro, C V, Penerbit (Indonesia)   217
Direcção dos Serviços de Geologia e Minas de Angola Biblioteca (Angola)   2
Dirección de Cultura, Biblioteca de la (Bolivia)   48
Dirección de Estadística y Censo (Panama)   328
Dirección de Publicaciones (Costa Rica)   72
Direction de la Bibliothèque nationale (Guinea)   186
Direction de la Recherche scientifique et technique (Guinea)   186
Direction des Bibliothèques, des Musées et de l'Information Scientifique et Technique (France)   117
Direction Générale de la Banque des Données de l'Etat (Democratic Republic of Madagascar)   277
Director Books (United Kingdom)   439
Directorate of Archives and Libraries (Bangladesh)   35
Directorate of Publications (Republic of South Africa)   354
Directories of Zimbabwe (Pvt) Ltd (Zimbabwe)   504
Directory of Librarians in Malaysia (Malaysia)   281
Directory Publishers of Zambia Ltd (Zambia)   503
Directory Publishers (Pvt) Ltd (Zimbabwe)   504
Discailles, Ernest, Prize (International Literary Prizes)   518
Discoverers (United Kingdom)   439
Disesa (Dominican Republic)   87
Disha Publications (India)   200
Dishoeck, van (Netherlands)   295
Disney Junior Bokklub (Norway)   323
Disney's Ungdomsbokklubb (Sweden)   388
Dissal SA de CV (El Salvador)   90
Distasa (Argentina)   4
Dístein Libros (Spain)   366
Distri Editora-Sociedade Editora Lda (Portugal)   341
Distribución, SA de, Edición y Librerías (DELSA) (Spain)   376
Distribuidora de Libros (Guatemala)   186
Distribuidora Escolar SA (DISESA) (Dominican Republic)   87
Distributors' Centre for Israeli Books Ltd (Israel)   231
Ditmar, van (Netherlands)   295
Diwan, The, Library, Ministry of Education (Iraq)   220
Djambatan, De Brug-, BV (Netherlands)   295
Djambatan, PT, Penerbit NV (Indonesia)   217
Doaba House (India)   200
Döblin, Alfred-, Prize (Federal Republic of Germany)   179
Doblinger, Ludwig, (Bernard Herzmansky) Musikverlag (Austria)   27
Dobloug Prize (Norway)   324
Dobloug Prize (Sweden)   390
Dobson, Dennis, (Dobson Books Ltd) (United Kingdom)   439
Doctrine and Life Book Club (Republic of Ireland)   224
Documentaire Research, Hoofdafdeling, en Informatieverstrekking van de Exportbevorderings- en Voorlichtingsdienst (Netherlands)   304
Documentation et d'Analyses, Société de, Financières (France)   103
Documentation Française, La (France)   103
Documentation Internationale, Bibliothèque de, Contemporaine (France)   117
Documentation Research and Training Centre (India)   214
Dodoni (Greece)   183
Dod's Parliamentary Companion Ltd (United Kingdom)   439
Doepgen, Edition, Verlag (Belgium)   38
Dogan Kardes Matbaacilik SAS (Turkey)   414
Doin Editeurs (France)   103
Dokumentasi dan Informasi Ilmiah, Pusat (Indonesia)   219
Dokumentation Saur, Verlag, KG (Federal Republic of Germany)   140

Dokumentationsstelle für neuere österreichische Literatur (Austria)   32
Dollar Books (Australia)   14
Dolmen, The, Press Ltd (Republic of Ireland)   222
Dolphin (United Kingdom)   439
Dolphin Books (People's Republic of China)   67
Dom Ksiazki (Poland)   338
Dom Quixote, Publicações, Lda (Portugal)   341
Domi, Ekdoseis, AE (Greece)   183
Dominican Books — Distribution Inc (Dominican Republic)   86
Dominican Publications (Republic of Ireland)   222
Domino, The, Press Ltd (Israel)   227
Domowina, VEB, Verlag (German Democratic Republic)   124
Domus Editoriale (Italy)   238
Don Bosco, Ediciones (Mexico)   284
Don Bosco, Editorial y Librería (Bolivia)   48
Don Bosco Verlag der Gesellschaft der Salesianer (Federal Republic of Germany)   140
Don Quijote, Editorial (Spain)   366
Donald, John, Publishers Ltd (United Kingdom)   439
Donald Ducks Bokklubb (Norway)   323
Donauland, Buchgemeinschaft, Kremayr & Scheriau (Austria)   31
Dong Hwa Publishing Co (Republic of Korea)   269
Dongguk University Central Library (Republic of Korea)   271
Donker, Ad, (Pty) Ltd (Republic of South Africa)   355
Donker, Uitgeversmaatschappij Ad, BV (Netherlands)   295
Dopravy, Nakladatelství, a spoju (Czechoslovakia)   75
Dorikos Publishing House (Greece)   183
Dorling Kindersley Ltd (United Kingdom)   439
Dorp Aruba, Van, NV (Netherland Antilles)   306
Dorp-Eddine, Van, NV (Netherland Antilles)   307
Dosaaf, Znak Pochyota Order, Publishing House (Union of Soviet Socialist Republics)   417
Dossat, Editorial, SA (Spain)   366
Dost Yayınları (Turkey)   415
Doubleday (Australia)   14
Doubleday & Co Inc (United Kingdom)   439
Doubleday Australia Pty Ltd, Book Club Division (Australia)   20
Doubleday Book Club (Australia)   20
Doubleday Book Club (New Zealand)   311
Doubleday History Book Club (Australia)   20
Doubleday History Book Club (New Zealand)   311
Doubleday Military Book Club (New Zealand)   311
Doubleday New Zealand Ltd, Book Club Division (New Zealand)   311
Doucet, Bibliothèque littéraire Jacques (France)   117
Douglas, The, Public Library (Isle of Man)   225
Doulos Verlag (Switzerland)   395
Dove Communications Pty Ltd (Australia)   14
Down Memory Lane (United Kingdom)   439
Downlander Publishing (United Kingdom)   439
Doxa Bokförlaget AB (Sweden)   383
Doyma, Ediciones, SA (Spain)   366
Draeger Editeur (France)   103
Dragon Books (United Kingdom)   439
Dragon's World Ltd (United Kingdom)   439
Drammen Folkebibliotek (Norway)   323
Drei Eidgenossen Verlag (Switzerland)   395
Dreisam-Verlag (Federal Republic of Germany)   140
Drejtoria Quëndrore e Përhapjes dhe e Propagandimit të Librit (Albania)   1
Dressler, Cecilie, Verlag (Federal Republic of Germany)   140
Drew, Richard, Publishing Ltd (United Kingdom)   439
Dreyers Forlag A/S (Norway)   321
Driehoek , De, BV (Netherlands)   295
Droemersche Verlagsanstalt AG (Switzerland)   395
Droemersche Verlagsanstalt Th Knaur Nachf (Federal Republic of Germany)   140
Droguet et Ardant (France)   103
Droit et de Jurisprudence, Librairie Générale de (France)   103
Drommedaris (Republic of South Africa)   356
Droste Verlag GmbH (Federal Republic of Germany)   140
Drouot, Librairie, (Ets Robert Drouot) (Benin)   47
Droz, Librairie, SA (Switzerland)   395
Druckenmüller Verlag (Federal Republic of Germany)   141
Druffel-Verlag (Federal Republic of Germany)   141
Druida, Ediciones, SA (Spain)   367
Drukarnia Narodowa (Poland)   335
Drukkerij de Stad NV (Netherland Antilles)   306
Drumlin Verlag GmbH (Federal Republic of Germany)   141
Drummond (Australia)   14
Društvo bibliotekara Bosne i Hercegovine (Yugoslavia)   500
Društvo bibliotekarjev Slovenije (Yugoslavia)   500

554 INDEX

Društvo na arhivskite rabotnici i arhivite na SRM (Yugoslavia)   500
Društvo na literaturnite preveduvači na SRM (Yugoslavia)   501
Društvo na pisatelite na SRM (Yugoslavia)   501
Društvo za srpski jezik i književnost (Yugoslavia)   501
Dryad Press Ltd (United Kingdom)   439
Državna Založba Slovenije (Yugoslavia)   496
Duang Kamol (Thailand)   410
Duas Cidades, Livraria, Ltda (Brazil)   52
Duas Cidades, Livraria, Ltda (Brazil)   57
Dublin Institute for Advanced Studies (Republic of Ireland)   222
Dublin Public Libraries (Republic of Ireland)   224
Duckworth, Gerald, & Co Ltd (United Kingdom)   439
Duculot, Editions J , SA (Belgium)   38
Duculot, Jules, Prize (Belgium)   46
Duden, Konrad, Prize (Federal Republic of Germany)   179
Duff Cooper Memorial Prize (International Literary Prizes)   518
Duffield, G E (United Kingdom)   439
Dufour, Henry-Robert (Switzerland)   395
Duke of Alba Prize (Spain)   377
Duke University Press (United Kingdom)   439
Dülk, Monika, Verlag (Federal Republic of Germany)   141
Dumas-Millier Prize (France)   119
Dumjahn, Horst-Werner, Verlag (Federal Republic of Germany)   141
Dümmlers, Ferd, Verlag (Federal Republic of Germany)   141
DuMont Buchverlag GmbH & Co KG (Federal Republic of Germany)   141
Dun & Bradstreet Ltd (United Kingdom)   439
Duncker und Humblot GmbH (Federal Republic of Germany)   141
Dundrum, The, Bookshop (Republic of Ireland)   224
Dunedin Public Library (New Zealand)   312
Dunia, PT, Pustaka Jaya (Indonesia)   217
Dunitz, Martin, Ltd (United Kingdom)   440
Dunmore Press Ltd (New Zealand)   309
Dunod (France)   103
Dunrod, The, Press (United Kingdom)   440
Dupuch, Etienne, Jnr Publications Ltd (Bahamas)   34
Dupuis, Editions Jean, SA (Belgium)   38
Dupuis, Maison d'Editions J , Fils et Cie SA (France)   103
Durban Municipal Library (Republic of South Africa)   360
Durham University Library (United Kingdom)   482
Durvan SA de Ediciones (Spain)   367
Dustri-Verlag Dr Karl Feistle (Federal Republic of Germany)   141
Dutch Literature Prize (Netherlands)   306
Dutch Prize for the Best Children's Book (Netherlands)   306
Dutch Reformed Church Publishers (Republic of South Africa)   356
Dutens, Alfred, Prize (France)   119
Duttweiler, Gottlieb, Institute for Economic & Social Studies (Switzerland)   395
Duvivier, Charles, Prize (Belgium)   46
'Dvir Bialik' Municipal Central Public Library (Israel)   231
Dvir Publishing House (Israel)   227
Dwarsstap, Uitgeverij (Netherlands)   295
Dyllansow Truran (United Kingdom)   440
Dymock's Pty Ltd (Australia)   21
Dynamis Verlag (Switzerland)   395
Dynasty Books (Republic of Singapore)   351
Dyonon Mifal Hashichpul (Israel)   231

E, Edizioni, — Elle SRL (Italy)   238
E/O, Edizioni (Italy)   238
E A Books (Australia)   14
E A C (France)   103
E A I S (France)   116
E B A L (Brazil)   73
E B C Publishing Pvt Ltd (India)   200
E B E, Edizioni (Italy)   238
E B G Verlags GmbH (Federal Republic of Germany)   175
E C A Bookshop Co-op Society (Ethiopia)   91
E C A (Ediciones Culturales Argentinas) (Argentina)   4
E C I G — Edizioni Culturali Internazionali Genova (Italy)   238
E C I voor Boeken en Grammofoonplaten BV (Netherlands)   295
E C I voor Boeken en Platen BV (Netherlands)   304
E C Print AB (Sweden)   383
E C Print AB (Sweden)   391
E C W Productions Ltd (Nigeria)   315
E D A F , Editorial, SA (Spain)   367

E D A M E X (Mexico)   284
E D B (Italy)   238
E D E R S A (Editoriales de Derecho Reunidas SA) (Spain)   367
E D H A S A (Editora y Distribuidora Hispano-Americana SA) (Spain)   367
E D H I S (France)   103
E D I M E, Distribuciones (Venezuela)   492
E D T/Musica (Italy)   238
E F S-förlaget (Sweden)   383
E I T B Publications (United Kingdom)   440
E L C E (International Organizations)   508
E L D Trust (Republic of South Africa)   356
E M B L A (Norway)   322
E M E S C O Book Club (India)   213
E M I (Italy)   238
E M P (Italy)   238
E O S Verlag, Erzabtei Sankt Ottilien (Federal Republic of Germany)   141
E P A SA (France)   103
E P Book Depot (Ghana)   181
E P L S — A C L A (France)   103
E P O (Belgium)   38
E P Publishing Ltd (United Kingdom)   440
E P U (Brazil)   52
E R B (Czechoslovakia)   78
E R G A SNC di Carla Ottino Merli & C (Edizioni Realizzazioni Grafiche — Artigiana) (Italy)   238
E R I — Edizioni R A I Radiotelevisione Italiana SpA (Italy)   238
E S A Bookshop (Kenya)   268
E S A Bookshop (Uganda)   416
E S A Creative Learning Ltd (United Kingdom)   440
E S C Publishing Ltd (United Kingdom)   440
E S D U C K (Egypt)   88
E S F, Editions, (Editions Sociales Françaises) (France)   103
E S H (English for Speakers of Hebrew) (Israel)   227
E S I (Italy)   238
E S M (Educational Software for Microcomputers) (United Kingdom)   440
E T H Bibliothek (Eidgenössische Technische Hochschule Bibliothek) (Switzerland)   406
E T S F (France)   103
E U D E B A (Editorial Universitaria de Buenos Aires) (Argentina)   4
E U N S A (Ediciones Universidad de Navarra SA) (Spain)   367
Early English Text Society (United Kingdom)   485
Early Worm Book Club (United Kingdom)   480
Eason & Son Ltd (Republic of Ireland)   222
Eason & Son Ltd (Republic of Ireland)   224
East African Directory Co (Kenya)   267
East African Literature Bureau (Kenya)   267
East African Publishing House (Kenya)   267
East and West Centre Pte Ltd (Republic of Singapore)   353
East and West Publishing Co (Pakistan)   325
East Asia Book Co (Hong Kong)   189
East-West Publications Fonds BV (Netherlands)   295
East-West Publications (UK) Ltd (United Kingdom)   440
Eastern Africa Publications Ltd (Tanzania)   409
Eastern and Southern Africa Regional Branch of the International Council on Archives (ESARBICA) (International Organizations)   508
Eastern Book Co (India)   200
Eastern Book Service Corp (Philippines)   333
Eastern Book Service Ltd (Hong Kong)   189
Eastern Book Service Sdn Bhd (Malaysia)   280
Eastern Law House Pvt Ltd (India)   200
Eastern Universities Press (Malaysia)   278
Eastland Press (United Kingdom)   440
Eastview Productions Sdn Bhd (Malaysia)   278
Eau Vive, Editions l' (Switzerland)   395
Ebibi Book Centre (United Republic of Cameroun)   64
Ebury Press (United Kingdom)   440
Ecart Publications (Switzerland)   395
Ecclesia Press (Republic of Ireland)   222
Echeverría, Aquileo J, Prize (Costa Rica)   73
Echeverría', Biblioteca 'José Antonio (Cuba)   74
Echter Würzburg Fränkische Gesellschafts-Druckerei (Federal Republic of Germany)   141
Eck, Frank P van, Publishers (Liechtenstein)   275
Eckersteins, Esselte Bokhandel (Sweden)   389
Eco-Verlags AG (Switzerland)   395
Ecole, Bibliothèqe l', nationale d'administration du Niger (Niger)   314
Ecole, Bibliothèque de l', des Langues orientales (France)   117
Ecole, Bibliothèque de l', normale supérieure (Senegal)   349
Ecole, Bibliothèque de l', normale supérieure (Togo)   412
Ecole, Bibliothèque de l', royale de Médecine (Laos)   272

Ecole, Bibliothèque de l', supérieure des Lettres (Lebanon)   273
Ecole, L', /L'Ecole des Loisirs Sàrl (France)   103
Ecole, Presses de l', Normale Supérieure (France)   103
Ecole des Hautes Etudes en Sciences Sociales, Editions de l' (France)   103
Ecole française d'Athènes (Greece)   183
Ecole Francaise de Rome (Italy)   238
Ecole Mohammedia d'Ingénieurs (Morocco)   291
Ecole nationale d'Administration Bibliothèque (Tunisia)   414
Ecole nationale polytechnique, Bibliothèque (Algeria)   2
Ecole normale primaire et supérieure, Bibliothèque (Central African Republic)   64
Ecole normale supérieure (Mali)   281
Ecole normale supérieure, Bibliothèque (Burundi)   63
Ecole normale supérieure Bibliothèque (Republic of Gabon)   122
Ecole normale supérieure, Bibliothèque (United Republic of Cameroun)   64
Ecole normale supérieure de l'Afrique centrale, Bibliothèque (Popular Republic of Congo)   72
Ecole Professionelle de la Mission Catholique (Togo)   412
Ecoles, Librairie des (Morocco)   290
Ecoma, Editorial, SA (Peru)   330
Econ-Verlag GmbH (Federal Republic of Germany)   141
Econ Verlagsgruppe (Federal Republic of Germany)   141
Economic & Social, The, Research Institute (Republic of Ireland)   222
Economic and Industrial Publications (Pakistan)   325
Economische, Bibliotheek- en Documentatie-centrum van de, Voorlichtingsdienst (Netherlands)   305
Economist, The (United Kingdom)   440
Economists' Bookshop, The, Ltd (United Kingdom)   479
Ecumenical Literature, The, Distribution Trust (Republic of South Africa)   356
Edagricole-Edizioni Agricole (Italy)   238
Edameris (Brazil)   52
Edanim Publishers (Israel)   227
Edart São Paulo Livraria Editora Ltda (Brazil)   52
Eddison Sadd Editions Ltd (United Kingdom)   440
Edebe (Spain)   367
Edekes Bookshop Stores Ltd (Nigeria)   318
Edelcid Libros Científicos (Guatemala)   186
Ediapsa de CV/Librerías de Cristal (Mexico)   288
Edica SA (Spain)   367
Edicient SAIC (Argentina)   5
Ediciones de la Biblioteca (EBUC) (Venezuela)   492
Ediciones Populares (Netherland Antilles)   306
Edicol, Editorial, SA (Mexico)   284
Edigol Ediciones SA (Spain)   367
Edigraf, Editorial Vilcar y Gráficas Hamburg SA (Spain)   367
Edil, Editorial, Inc (Puerto Rico)   344
Edinburgh Bibliographical Society (United Kingdom)   485
Edinburgh University Library (United Kingdom)   482
Edinburgh University Press (United Kingdom)   440
Edinburgh University Student Publications Board (United Kingdom)   440
Ediseis, Editorial, SA (Spain)   367
Edisud (France)   103
Edit Niro (Novinska-izdavačka radna organizacija) (Yugoslavia)   496
Editalia (Edizioni d'Italia) (Italy)   238
Editart, Société, Quatre Chemins (France)   103
F.Jitemas y Dilae (Venezuela)   492
Editeurs Associés SA (Switzerland)   395
Editeurs de Litterature Biblique (Belgium)   38
Editeurs et libraires catholiques d'Europe (ELCE) (International Organizations)   508
Editeurs Réunis, Les (France)   103
Edition No 1 (France)   103
Editions Arabes, Les (Lebanon)   272
Editions de Physique, Les (France)   103
Editions des Archives Contemporaines (France)   104
Editions interuniversitaires (Belgium)   38
Editions Juridiques et Techniques (France)   104
Editions Maritimes et d'Outre-Mer SA (France)   104
Editions Modernes Média (France)   104
Editions Sociales Françaises (France)   104
Editions Sociales-Messidor, Les (France)   104
Editions Techniques et Scientifiques Françaises (France)   104
Editions techniques et scientifiques SPRL (Belgium)   38
Editions Techniques SA (France)   104
Editions universitaires, Les, d'Egypte (Egypt)   88
Editions universitaires SA (Belgium)   38
Editions Universitaires SA (Universitätsverlag) (Switzerland)   395
Edito-Service SA (Switzerland)   395
Editogo (Togo)   412
Editora Cultural Dominicana (Dominican Republic)   86

INDEX 555

Editora Interamericana Ltda (Brazil) 52
Editora Moderna Ltda (Brazil) 52
Editora Nacional, Cía (Brazil) 52
Editora Nacional (Mexico) 285
Editora Nacional (Spain) 367
Editora Pedagógica e Universitaria Ltda (EPU) (Brazil) 52
Editora Política (Cuba) 73
Editora Portuguesa de Livros Técnicos e Científicos Lda (Portugal) 341
Editorama SA (Dominican Republic) 86
Editores Asociados Mexicanos SA (EDAMEX) (Mexico) 285
Editorial and Publishing Services (Ghana) 180
Editorial Consultancy & Agency Services (Nigeria) 318
Editorial Cultural (Puerto Rico) 344
Editorial Interamericana del Ecuador CA (Ecuador) 87
Editorial Interamericana SA (Peru) 331
Editorial Librería Dominicana (Dominican Republic) 86
Editorial Universidad SRL (Argentina) 5
Editorial Universitaria (Honduras) 187
Editorial Universitaria (Panama) 328
Editorial Universitaria Centroamericana (EDUCA) (Costa Rica) 72
Editorial Universitaria de Buenos Aires (Argentina) 5
Editorial Universitaria de la Universidad de El Salvador (El Salvador) 90
Editorialebari (Italy) 238
Editrice Bibliografica SRL (Italy) 238
Editrice Cooperativa (Italy) 238
Editrice Scientifica, L' (Italy) 238
Edizioni del Centro (Italy) 238
Edu'Actief, Educatieve Uitgeverij, BV (Netherlands) 295
Educa International (Netherlands) 295
Educaboek BV (Netherlands) 295
Education et Culture (France) 116
Educational, The, Publishing House Ltd (Hong Kong) 188
Educational Aids Production Co Pte Ltd (Republic of Singapore) 353
Educational Book Centre (Israel) 231
Educational Book Centre Pte Ltd (Republic of Singapore) 353
Educational Books Publishing House (Democratic People's Republic of Korea) 268
Educational Company, The, of Ireland (Republic of Ireland) 222
Educational Enterprise (Nepal) 292
Educational Enterprises (India) 200
Educational Enterprises (Pvt) Ltd (Nepal) 292
Educational Explorers (United Kingdom) 440
Educational Library (Saudi Arabia) 348
Educational Material Aid (Australia) 14
Educational Materials Enterprises SA (Greece) 184
Educational Productions Ltd (United Kingdom) 440
Educational Publications Bureau Pte Ltd (Republic of Singapore) 351
Educational Publishers' Association (India) 195
Educational Publishers Council (United Kingdom) 422
Educational Research Institute (Nigeria) 315
Educational Writers' Group (United Kingdom) 422
Educum Uitgewers Beperk (Republic of South Africa) 356
Edumeds Pty Ltd (Namibia) 291
Eduskunnan Kirjasto (Finland) 94
Edwardian Studies Association (United Kingdom) 485
Effelle, SAS Editrice, di Marino Fabbri (Italy) 238
Effendi Harahap Bookstore (Indonesia) 218
Efstathiadis, P, & Sons SA (Greece) 183
Efstathiadis, P, & Sons SA (Greece) 184
Egans Bookshop (Republic of Ireland) 224
Egerton College Library (Kenya) 268
Eghbal Publishing Organisation (Iran) 220
Egmont (United Kingdom) 440
Egyptian Association for Archives and Librarianship (Egypt) 89
Egyptian Society, The, for the Dissemination of Universal Culture and Knowledge (ESDUCK) (Egypt) 88
Egyptian Society, The, for the Dissemination of Universal Culture and Knowledge (ESDUCK) (Egypt) 89
Egyptian Society, The, for the Dissemination of Universal Culture and Knowledge (ESDUCK) (Egypt) 90
Ehrenwirth Verlag GmbH (Federal Republic of Germany) 141
Ehrlingförlagen AB (Sweden) 383
Eichborn Verlag (Federal Republic of Germany) 141
Eides, J W, Forlag A/S (Norway) 321
Eike-Boekklub (Republic of South Africa) 359
Einaudi, Giulio, Editore SpA (Italy) 238
Eiselé, Editions, SA (Switzerland) 395
Eisenbahn, Verlag (Federal Republic of Germany) 141
Eisenbahn, Verlag (Switzerland) 395

Eisenbahn-Kurier Verlag (Federal Republic of Germany) 141
Ejlers', Christian, Forlag (Denmark) 80
Ekblad-Eldhs, Signe, Prize (Sweden) 390
Eked Publishing House (Israel) 227
Ekenäs Tryckeri AB (Finland) 92
Ekonomiczne, Państwowe Wydawnictwo (Poland) 335
'Ekonomika', Izdatelstvo (Union of Soviet Socialist Republics) 417
Ekstrabøker, Bokklubbens (Norway) 323
El-Am Publishing (Israel) Ltd (Israel) 227
'El Libro del Mes', Club (Argentina) 8
Elanders Bokförlag AB (Sweden) 383
Elder, Anne, Poetry Award (Australia) 24
Eldorado, A Casa do Livro, Ltda (Brazil) 57
Eldorado, NV Drukkerij (Suriname) 380
Electa Editrice (Italy) 239
Elefante, Edizioni dell' (Italy) 239
Eleftheroudakis, G C, Co Ltd (Greece) 184
Eleftheroudakis, G C, SA (Greece) 183
Element Books Ltd (United Kingdom) 440
Eletrônicas Editora, Seleções, Ltda (Brazil) 52
Elfos, Ediciones (Spain) 367
Elgar, Edward, Publishing Ltd (United Kingdom) 440
Elgin, Mary, Prize (International Literary Prizes) 518
Elgin, Mary, Prize (United Kingdom) 487
Elif Kitabevi (Turkey) 415
Elingaard Forlag A/S (Norway) 321
Elizabethan Publishing Co (Nigeria) 316
Elkan och Schildknecht (Sweden) 383
Ell, David, Press Pty Ltd (Australia) 14
Ellenberg Verlag GmbH (Federal Republic of Germany) 141
Ellermann, Verlag Heinrich, GmbH & Co KG (Federal Republic of Germany) 141
Elliot Right Way Books (United Kingdom) 440
Ellipses — Edition Marketing Sàrl (France) 104
Ellis, Aidan, Publishing Ltd (United Kingdom) 440
Ellsyd Press (Australia) 14
Elm Publications (United Kingdom) 441
Elm Tree (Australia) 14
Elm Tree Books Ltd (United Kingdom) 441
Elmar BV (Netherlands) 296
Elo (Portugal) 341
Elpis Verlag GmbH (Federal Republic of Germany) 141
Elron Press Ltd (United Kingdom) 441
Elsässer, Buchhandlung zum, AG (Switzerland) 405
Elsevier (Netherlands) 296
Elsevier Applied Science Publishers (United Kingdom) 441
Elsevier Biomedical Press (Netherlands) 296
Elsevier Boeken BV (Netherlands) 296
Elsevier Librico NV (Belgium) 38
Elsevier Science Publishers BV (Netherlands) 296
Elsevier Science Publishers (Japan) (Japan) 256
Elsevier's Wetenschappelijke Uitgeverij (Netherlands) 296
Elvendon Press (United Kingdom) 441
Elwert, N G, Verlag (Federal Republic of Germany) 141
Elwert und Meurer GmbH, Buchhandlung (Federal Republic of Germany) 175
Elwert und Meurer GmbH (Federal Republic of Germany) 141
Elzenga, Uitgeverij Hans, BV (Netherlands) 296
Emalsa SA (Spain) 367
Emecé, Premio, Annual Prize (Argentina) 9
Emecé Editores SA (Argentina) 5
Emecé Mexicana SA de CV (Mexico) 285
Emil Award (United Kingdom) 487
Eminescu, Editura (Romania) 346
Emmanuel Publishing Services (Ghana) 180
Emmaus (Belgium) 39
Emme Edizioni (Italy) 239
Emmentaler Druck AG (Switzerland) 395
Emmerich, Monika, Amazonen Frauenverlag (Federal Republic of Germany) 141
Emotan Publishing Co (Nigeria) Ltd (Nigeria) 316
Empeño 14 (Spain) 367
Empire International Club (Italy) 252
Empire Shop (Montserrat) 290
Emporium, The (Belize) 47
Empresa Moderna Lda (Mozambique) 291
Empresas Editoriales SA (Mexico) 285
En-Najah, Librairie (Tunisia) 414
En-Najah (Tunisia) 413
Enciclopédia, Editorial, Lda (Portugal) 341
Encounters (United Kingdom) 480
'Encouragement Prize' (Austria) 33
Encuentro, Ediciones, SA (Spain) 367
Encyclopaedia Britannica (Federal Republic of Germany) 141
Encyclopaedia Britannica (Australia) Inc (Australia) 14
Encyclopaedia Britannica International Ltd (United Kingdom) 441
Encyclopaedia Judaica (Israel) 227

Encyclopaedia Universalis France SA (France) 104
Endeavour (New Zealand) 309
Energoizdat, Izdatelstvo (Union of Soviet Socialist Republics) 417
Energy Publications (United Kingdom) 441
Engel, Friedemann von, Verlag (Federal Republic of Germany) 142
Engelbert-Verlag GmbH & Co KG (Federal Republic of Germany) 142
Engelhorn Verlag (Federal Republic of Germany) 142
Engelman, Camille, Prize (International Literary Prizes) 518
Engels, Carl, Musikverlag (Federal Republic of Germany) 142
Englisch, F, Verlag GmbH (Federal Republic of Germany) 142
English Agency, The, (Japan) (Japan) 262
English Association (United Kingdom) 485
English Association (South African Branch) Literary Prize (Republic of South Africa) 362
English Book Club (Netherlands) 304
English Book Store (India) 213
English Bookshop, The (Iceland) 194
English Language Book Society (ELBS) (United Kingdom) 422
Engvist, Gun and Olof, Prize (Sweden) 390
Enke, Ferdinand, Verlag (Federal Republic of Germany) 142
Ennsthaler, Wilhelm (Austria) 27
Enossis Ellenon Bibliothakarion (Greece) 185
Enriquillo, Editora (Dominican Republic) 86
Enschedé en Zonen (Netherlands) 296
Enseignement laïc, Coopérative de l' (France) 104
Ensslin Jugendbuchverlag (Federal Republic of Germany) 142
Ensslin und Laiblin Verlag GmbH & Co KG (Federal Republic of Germany) 142
Entente, Editions (France) 104
Enterprise nationale du Livre (ENAL) (Algeria) 2
Entreprise Moderne d'Edition (France) 104
Enzyklopädie, VEB Verlag, Leipzig (German Democratic Republic) 124
Eötvös Loránd Tudományegyetem Egyetemi Könyvtár (Hungary) 191
Epargne, Les Editions de l' (France) 104
Epi (France) 104
Epoca, Librería (Peru) 331
'Epoka', Wydawnictwo (Poland) 335
Eppinger, Hans P (Federal Republic of Germany) 142
Epworth Press (United Kingdom) 441
Equation (United Kingdom) 441
Equestri, Edizioni, SRL (Italy) 239
Equestrian Book Society (United Kingdom) 480
Equinox (Oxford) Ltd (United Kingdom) 441
Era, Ediciones, SA de CV (Mexico) 285
Era Book Enterprises (India) 200
Era Publications (Australia) 14
Erasme, Editions, (Scriptoria NV) (Belgium) 39
Erd, Verlag Peter, GmbH (Federal Republic of Germany) 142
Erdmann, Edition (Federal Republic of Germany) 142
Erdmann Verlag, Horst, für Internationalen Kulturaustausch (Federal Republic of Germany) 142
Erehwon Publishing House (Philippines) 332
Erein (Spain) 367
Erel PVBA (Belgium) 39
Eremiten-Presse und Verlag GmbH (Federal Republic of Germany) 142
Eres, Edition, Horst Schubert Musikverlag (Federal Republic of Germany) 142
Eresco PT (Indonesia) 217
Erichsens, Chr, Forlag A/S (Denmark) 80
Erikssons, Lydia and Herman, Prize (Sweden) 390
Erina se Boekklub (Republic of South Africa) 359
Erker-Galerie AG (Switzerland) 395
Erlanger Foundation Prize (France) 119
Erlangga (Indonesia) 217
Erlbaum, Lawrence, Associates Ltd (United Kingdom) 441
Erma, L', di Bretschneider SRL (Italy) 239
Ermes, Edi, SRL (Italy) 239
Ernst, Wilhelm, und Sohn Verlag für Architektur und technische Nissenschaft (Federal Republic of Germany) 142
Ernster, Librairie (Grand Duchy of Luxembourg) 276
Erpf, Edition, by Neptun (Switzerland) 395
Erroll Marx Publishers (Republic of South Africa) 356
Erudita Publications (Pty) Ltd (Republic of South Africa) 356
Escape (United Kingdom) 441
Escolar, Livraria, Infante (Portugal) 341
Escorial, Librería (Puerto Rico) 345
Escorts Book Award (India) 215
Escuela Nacional de Biblioteconomía y Archivonomía (Mexico) 289
Esfinge, Editorial, SA (Mexico) 285
Eshkol-Jerusalem (Israel) 227

556 INDEX

Espaces Photographiques (Switzerland) 395
Espacio Editora SA (Argentina) 5
Española, Librería, SCA (Argentina) 8
Espasa-Calpe, Casa del Libro, SA (Spain) 376
Espasa-Calpe, Editorial, SA (Spain) 367
Espasa-Calpe Argentina SA (Argentina) 5
Espasa-Calpe Mexicana SA (Mexico) 285
Espaxs, Editorial, SA (Spain) 367
Espejo de España Prize (Spain) 377
Espinosa, Manuel, y Cortina Prize (Spain) 377
Espiritualista, Editora (Brazil) 52
Esquire (Lebanon) 273
Ess Ess Publications (India) 200
Esselte Bokhandel Group (Sweden) 389
Esselte Focus Uppslagsböcker AB (Sweden) 383
Esselte Förlag AB (Sweden) 383
Esselte Herzogs AB (Sweden) 383
Esselte Map Service AB (Sweden) 383
Esselte Studium AB (Sweden) 384
Est-Ouest, Editions (Belgium) 39
Este, Librería del (Venezuela) 493
Estense, Biblioteca (Italy) 252
Estorff Reference Library (Namibia) 291
Estoup et Roy, Publications, Sàrl (France) 104
Estrada, Angel, y Cía SA (Argentina) 5
Estúdios, Editorial, Cor Sarl (Portugal) 341
Età, Edizioni L', dell'Acquario (Italy) 239
Etairia Ellinon Logotechnon (Greece) 182
Etas Libri (Italy) 239
Etelä-Suomen Kustannus Oy (Finland) 92
Eteria Ellinikon Ekdoseon (Greece) 183
Ethiope Publishing Corporation (Nigeria) 316
Ethiopian Library Association (Ethiopia) 91
Ethiopian Manuscript Microfilm Library (Ethiopia) 91
Etudes Augustiniennes (France) 104
Eugenides Foundation Technical Library (Greece) 185
Eugenio Espejo, Biblioteca Nacional, de la Casa de la Cultura Ecuatoriana Benjamín Carrión (Ecuador) 88
Eulama SA (Federal Republic of Germany) 175
Eulama SRL (Italy) 251
Eulama SRL (Italy) 253
Eulenburg Edition GmbH (Switzerland) 395
Eulenhof-Verlag Ehrhardt Heinold (Federal Republic of Germany) 142
Eulenspiegel Verlag für Satire und Humor (German Democratic Republic) 124
Eulyoo Publishing Co Ltd (Republic of Korea) 269
Eumo Editorial (Spain) 367
Euphorion, Freundeskreis des, Verlags (Federal Republic of Germany) 175
Euphorion Verlag Hans Imhoff (Federal Republic of Germany) 142
Eurasia Publishing House Pvt Ltd (India) 201
Euroamericanas, Ediciones (Mexico) 285
Eurobook Ltd (United Kingdom) 441
Eurobooks (United Kingdom) 441
Euromonitor Publications Ltd (United Kingdom) 441
Europa, Edizioni (Italy) 239
Europa-America, Publicações, Lda (Portugal) 341
Európa Könyvkiadó (Hungary) 190
Europa-Lehrmittel, Verlag, Nourney, Vollmer GmbH & Co (Federal Republic of Germany) 142
Europa Publications Ltd (United Kingdom) 441
Europa Verlag AG (Switzerland) 395
Europa Verlags-GmbH (Austria) 27
Europabuch AG (Switzerland) 395
Europäische Bildungsgemeinschaft Verlags GmbH (Federal Republic of Germany) 175
Europäische Buch, Das (Federal Republic of Germany) 142
Europäische Märchengesellschaft eV (Federal Republic of Germany) 178
Europäische Verlagsanstalt GmbH (Federal Republic of Germany) 142
Europäische Verlagsgemeinschaft 'Ost' (Federal Republic of Germany) 129
Europaring der Buch- und Schallplattenfreunde (Federal Republic of Germany) 175
European Association for the Promotion of Poetry (International Organizations) 508
European Association of Directory Publishers (International Organizations) 508
European Parliament Library (International Organizations) 508
European Poetry Translation Prize (International Literary Prizes) 518
European Press Scientific Publisher (Belgium) 39
European Schoolbooks Ltd (United Kingdom) 441
European University Institute Library (Italy) 252
Europress Editores e Distribuidores de Publicaçoẽs Lda (Portugal) 341
Europrisma-Verlag (Federal Republic of Germany) 142
Eurospan Ltd (United Kingdom) 441
Evangel Publishing House (Kenya) 267
Evangelical Press and Services Ltd (United Kingdom) 442

Evangélique, Librairie (Burkina Faso) 62
Evangélique, Librairie Imprimerie (Togo) 412
Evangélique, Maison d'Edition de la Librairie-Imprimerie, du Togo (Togo) 412
Evangelisch Lutherischen Mission, Verlag der (Federal Republic of Germany) 142
Evangelische Verlagsanstalt GmbH (German Democratic Republic) 124
Evangelischen Gesellschaft, Verlag und Schriftenmission der, für Deutschland GmbH (Federal Republic of Germany) 142
Evangelischer Missionsverlag (Federal Republic of Germany) 142
Evangelischer Presseverband für Bayern eV (Federal Republic of Germany) 142
Evangelischer Pressverband in Österreich (Austria) 27
Evangelischer Schriften Verlag Schwengeler (Switzerland) 395
Evangelisches Verlagswerk GmbH (Federal Republic of Germany) 142
Evangeliska Fosterlands-Stiftelsens Förlag (EFS-förlaget) (Sweden) 384
Evans Brothers Ltd (United Kingdom) 442
Evans Brothers (Nigeria Publishers) Ltd (Nigeria) 316
Evans Shepherd (Zimbabwe) 505
Everest, Editorial, SA (Spain) 367
Everyman Fiction (United Kingdom) 442
Everyman's Library, Reference Library and University Library (United Kingdom) 442
Ewald, Johannes, Prize (Denmark) 86
Ewart-Biggs, Christopher, Memorial Prize (International Literary Prizes) 518
Ewha Womans University Library (Republic of Korea) 271
Ewha Womans University Press (Republic of Korea) 269
Ewing Memorial Library (Pakistan) 327
Ex Libris Forlag A/S (Norway) 321
Excerpta Medica (Netherlands) 296
Exclusive Books (Pty) Ltd (Republic of South Africa) 360
Executive World (United Kingdom) 480
Exley Publications Ltd (United Kingdom) 442
Expansion, L', Scientifique Française (France) 104
Exped-Expansaõ Editorial Ltda (Brazil) 52
Expert Verlag GmbH (Federal Republic of Germany) 142
Export-Press (Yugoslavia) 500
Express Edition GmbH (Federal Republic of Germany) 143
Express Logic Ltd (United Kingdom) 442
Expresso Sarl (Portugal) 343
Extemporaneos, Editorial, SA (Mexico) 285
Extrabuch Verlag in der pädex-Verlags-GmbH (Federal Republic of Germany) 143
Eymundssonar, Bókaverslun Sigfusar (Iceland) 193
Eyre & Spottiswoode (Publishers) Ltd (United Kingdom) 442
Eyre Methuen Ltd (United Kingdom) 442
Eyrolles, Editions (France) 104

F A D L's Forlag A/S (Foreningen af danske Laegestuderendes Forlag) (Denmark) 80
F A E — Fundação de Assistência ao Estudante (Brazil) 52
F A W Alan Marshall Award (Australia) 24
F A W Barbara Ramsden Award (Australia) 24
F A W Christopher Brennan Award (Australia) 24
F A W John Shaw Neilson Poetry Award (Australia) 24
F A W Local History Award (Australia) 24
F A W Regional Branch Awards (Australia) 24
F B V Frauenbuchvertrieb GmbH (Federal Republic of Germany) 175
F E D, Uitgeverij, BV (Netherlands) 296
F E N A M E — Fundação Nacional de Material Escolar (Brazil) 52
F E P International (HK) Ltd (Hong Kong) 188
F E P International Private Ltd (Republic of Singapore) 351
F E P International Sdn Bhd (Malaysia) 278
F F I I G (France) 96
F I D (International Organizations) 508
F I T Translation Prizes (International Literary Prizes) 518
F N A C (France) 116
F T D, Editora, SA (Brazil) 52
Fabbri, Gruppo Editoriale, SpA (Italy) 239
Fabbri, Bompiani, Gruppo Editoriale, Sonzogno, Etas SpA (Italy) 239
Faber, The Geoffrey, Memorial Prize (International Literary Prizes) 518
Faber, The Geoffrey, Memorial Prize (United Kingdom) 487

Faber & Faber Ltd (United Kingdom) 442
Fabril Editora SA (Argentina) 5
Fabritius Forlag A/S (Norway) 321
Fachbuchverlag, VEB (German Democratic Republic) 124
Fackelträger-Verlag GmbH (Federal Republic of Germany) 143
Fackelverlag G Bowitz GmbH (Federal Republic of Germany) 143
Facla, Editura (Romania) 346
Facsimile Uitgaven Nederland BV (FUN) (Netherlands) 296
Facts on File Publications Ltd (United Kingdom) 442
Facultad, Biblioteca, de Humanidades y Ciencias (Uruguay) 491
Facultas Verlag (Austria) 27
Facultatii, Biblioteca, de Medicina din Bucuresti (Romania) 347
Faculté de Droit, Bibliothèque de la, et des Sciences Politiques et Economiques de Tunis (Tunisia) 414
Faculté de Theologie Catholique de Kinshasa (Zaire) 502
Faculté des Lettres, Bibliothèque de la, et Sciences Humaines (Tunisia) 414
Faculté des Lettres et Sciences Humaines de Tunis (Tunisia) 414
Faculté des Sciences, Bibliothèque de la, de Tunis (Tunisia) 414
Faculty of Engineering, Library of the (Lebanon) 273
Faculty of Law, Library of the (Lebanon) 273
Faellesekspeditionen (Denmark) 79
Faenza Editrice SpA (Italy) 239
Fagbamigbe, Olaiya, Ltd (Publishers) (Nigeria) 316
Faglitteratur, Forlaget for, A/S (Denmark) 80
Faik, Sait, Prize (Turkey) 416
Faircape Books (Republic of South Africa) 356
Fajar, Penerbit, Bakti Sdn Bhd (Malaysia) 279
Falcon Books (United Kingdom) 442
Falk-Verlag für Landkarten und Stadtpläne Gerhard Falk GmbH (Federal Republic of Germany) 143
Falken-Verlag GmbH (Federal Republic of Germany) 143
Falkplan/CIB (Netherlands) 296
Falkplan-Suurland BV (Netherlands) 296
Fall, Lycée de Jeunes Filles Ameth, Bibliothèque (Senegal) 349
Fallon, C J (Republic of Ireland) 222
Falmer Press (United Kingdom) 442
Familia, Librería La, SA (Peru) 331
Familia et Patria PVBA (Belgium) 39
Family Bookshop (Qatar) 345
Family Bookshop (Bahrain) WLL (Bahrain) 34
Family Law (United Kingdom) 442
Fantasia Prize (France) 119
Far East Book Co (Republic of Singapore) 353
Far East Book Co (Taiwan) 408
Far East Publications Ltd (Hong Kong) 189
Far Eastern University Library (Philippines) 333
Farairre, Librairie (Morocco) 290
Farandole/Messidor, Editions La (France) 104
Farb-Dia-Archiv Edmond Van Hoorick (Switzerland) 395
Farjeon, Eleanor, Award (United Kingdom) 487
Farmer, Prudence, Poetry Prize (United Kingdom) 487
Farming Press (United Kingdom) 442
Farquharson, John, Ltd (United Kingdom) 479
Farringdon (United Kingdom) 442
Fastenrath Prize (Spain) 377
Fatah, Al-, University, General Administration of Libraries, Printing & Publications (Libya) 274
Fateh, Al-, University, The Central Library (Libya) 275
Fausto, Ediciones Librerías (Argentina) 5
Fausto, Librerías (Argentina) 8
Favorit-Verlag Huntemann und Markus & Co GmbH (Federal Republic of Germany) 143
Favre, Editions Pierre Marcel (Switzerland) 395
Favre, Jules, Prize (France) 119
Fawcett Book Prize (United Kingdom) 487
Faxon Europe BV (Netherlands) 304
Fayard, Librairie Arthème (France) 104
Fazer, Edition (Finland) 92
Febres Cordero', Servicios Bibliotecarios Generales 'Tulio (Venezuela) 493
Federação Brasileira de Associações de Bibliotecários — Comissão Brasileira de Documentação Jurídica (FEBAB/CBDJ) (Brazil) 59
Federação Brasileira de Associações de Bibliotecários (FEBAB) (Brazil) 58
Federación Argentina de Librerías, Papelerías y Actividades Afines (Argentina) 3
Federación de Asociaciones Nacionales de Distribuidores de Ediciones (Spain) 363
Federación de Gremios de Editores de España (Spain) 363
Federal Publications (HK) Ltd (Hong Kong) 188

Federal Publications (S) (Pte) Ltd (Republic of Singapore) 351
Federal Publications Sdn Bhd (Malaysia) 279
Federal Radio Corporation of Nigeria (Nigeria) 319
Federatie van Organisaties van Bibliotheek-, Informatie-, Dokumentatiewezen (FOBID) (Netherlands) 305
Fédération des Associations de Documentalistes et Bibliothécaires de l'Education nationale (France) 117
Fédération française de l'Imprimerie et des Industries Graphiques (France) 96
Fédération française des Syndicats de Libraires (France) 96
Fédération internationale des Librairies (FIL) (International Organizations) 508
Fédération internationale des Traducteurs (FIT) (International Organizations) 508
Fédération Luxembourgeoise des Editeurs de Livres (Grand Duchy of Luxembourg) 275
Fédération luxembourgeoise des Travailleurs du Livre (Grand Duchy of Luxembourg) 275
Federation of Children's Book Groups (United Kingdom) 422
Federation of Indian Library Associations (India) 214
Federation of Indian Publishers (India) 195
Federation of Publishers and Booksellers Associations in India (India) 195
Fédération panhellénique des Editeurs et Libraires (Greece) 182
Federspiel, Librería Universal Carlos (Costa Rica) 73
Feger, Siegfried (Liechtenstein) 275
Fehling, Willy F P, GmbH (Federal Republic of Germany) 143
Fehmers, Frank, Productions (Netherlands) 296
Fehr'sche Buchhandlung AG (Switzerland) 405
Feij, Editions François (Switzerland) 395
Feistle, Dr Karl (Federal Republic of Germany) 143
Felag bokavarda i islenskum rannsoknarbokasofnum (Iceland) 194
Félag Islenzkra Bókaútgefenda (Iceland) 193
Félag Islenzkra Bókaverzlana (Iceland) 193
Feldheim Publishers Ltd (Israel) 227
Fellesbiblioteket for det Kongelige Norske Videnskabers Selskab, Museet og Norges Laererhøgskole (Norway) 323
Fellicelli et Poli, Librairie (Niger) 314
Fellowship of Australian Writers Federal Council (Australia) 22
Fellowship of Australian Writers (NSW) (Australia) 22
Fellowship of Australian Writers, Victorian (Australia) 22
Fellowship of Australian Writers (WA) (Australia) 22
Feltrinelli, Antonio, Prize (International Literary Prizes) 519
Feltrinelli, Giangiacomo, SpA (Italy) 239
Feltrinelli, Libreria (Italy) 251
Femina (Republic of South Africa) 356
Fémina Prize (France) 119
Feminina, Bokklubben (Norway) 323
Feministische Uitgeverij Sara (Netherlands) 296
Femme d'aujourd'hui (France) 104
Femmes, Des (France) 104
Fenice, La, SRL (Italy) 239
Ferenczy Verlag AG (Switzerland) 405
Ferguson, John, Pty Ltd (Australia) 14
Feria Chilena del Libro Ltda (Chile) 66
Feria del Libro (Uruguay) 491
Fernández, Editorial y Librería Juridica Amalio M (Uruguay) 491
Fernández, Librería Amalio M (Uruguay) 491
Fernández Editores SA de CV (Mexico) 285
Fernhurst Books (United Kingdom) 442
Ferozsons (Private) Ltd (Pakistan) 325
Ferozsons (Private) Ltd (Pakistan) 326
Ferro, Edizioni, SpA (Italy) 239
Fersobe, Papelería, Hnos (Dominican Republic) 87
Festín, El, de Esopo (Spain) 368
Festival, The, Awards for Literature (Australia) 24
Feu, Editions du, Nouveau (France) 104
'Feuilles Familiales', Maison d'Edition:, ASBL (Belgium) 39
Fher, Publicaciones, SA (Spain) 368
Fib's Lyrikklubb (Sweden) 384
Fidler, Kathleen, Award (United Kingdom) 487
Fields, Sadie, Productions Ltd (United Kingdom) 442
Fieldsports Book Society (United Kingdom) 480
Fierro', Librería 'Martín (Argentina) 8
Fietkau, Wolfgang, Verlag (Federal Republic of Germany) 143
Fietz, Barbara (Federal Republic of Germany) 143
Figueirinhas, Livraria Editora, Lda (Portugal) 341
Fiji Library Association (FLA) (Fiji) 92
Fikentscher und Co (Federal Republic of Germany) 143
Fikr, Dar Al- (Salem & Zu'bi) Bookshop (Syria) 407
Filadelfia, Förlaget (Sweden) 384
Filipacchi, Editions (France) 104

Filmscan/Lingual House (United Kingdom) 442
Filon, Ekdoseis (Greece) 183
Financial Times, The, Business Information Ltd (United Kingdom) 442
Financial Training Publications Ltd (United Kingdom) 442
Finansy, Izdatelstvo (Union of Soviet Socialist Republics) 417
Finansy i Statistika Publishing House USSR (Union of Soviet Socialist Republics) 417
Findhorn, The, Press (United Kingdom) 442
Fine Arts Press Pty Ltd (Australia) 14
Fingraf, Bokförlaget, AB (Sweden) 384
Fink GmbH, Wilhelm, & Co Verlags KG (Federal Republic of Germany) 143
Fink — Kümmerly und Frey, J, Verlag GmbH (Federal Republic of Germany) 143
Fink Verlag, Emil (Federal Republic of Germany) 143
Finken-Verlag (Federal Republic of Germany) 143
Finlands Svenska Författareförening (Finland) 95
Finot, Jean, Prize (France) 119
Fiorentina, Libreria Editrice, di Vittorio e C SAS (Italy) 239
Firecrest Publishing Ltd (United Kingdom) 442
Firma KLM Private Ltd (Incorporating Firma KL Mukhopadhyay) (India) 201
First Book Prize (Argentina) 9
First, Inc (France) 104
Fischbacher, Librairie, International Art Book Distribution (import-export) (France) 105
Fischer, Verlag für Medizin Dr Ewald (Federal Republic of Germany) 143
Fischer Taschenbuch Verlag GmbH (Federal Republic of Germany) 143
Fischer Verlag, Gustav, GmbH & Co KG (Federal Republic of Germany) 143
Fischer Verlag, Rita G (Federal Republic of Germany) 143
Fischer Verlag, S, GmbH (Federal Republic of Germany) 143
Fischer Verlag, VEB Gustav, Jena (German Democratic Republic) 124
Fischer Verlag und Vertriebs, W, GmbH (Federal Republic of Germany) 143
Fischlin, J (Switzerland) 395
Fisher, H (Israel) 227
Fishing News Books Ltd (United Kingdom) 442
Fitzjames, The, Press (United Kingdom) 443
Fitzpatrick, Percy, Medal (Republic of South Africa) 362
Fitzwilliam Publishing (United Kingdom) 443
Five Lamps Press (Republic of Ireland) 222
Fix, Verlag Johannes (Federal Republic of Germany) 143
'Fizkultura i Sport', Izdatelstvo (Union of Soviet Socialist Republics) 418
Fjolva, Bókaklúbber (Iceland) 194
Fjolvi (Iceland) 193
Flaccovio, Libreria SF (Italy) 251
Flaccovio, S F, Editore (Italy) 239
Flambeau, Editions Le (United Republic of Cameroun) 64
Flame Lily (Zimbabwe) 504
Flamingo (United Kingdom) 443
Flammarion (France) 116
Flammarion et Cie (France) 105
Flat, Paul, Prize (France) 119
Fledgling (United Kingdom) 480
Fleischhauer und Spohn Verlag (Federal Republic of Germany) 143
Flesch Financial Publications (Pty) Ltd (Republic of South Africa) 356
Fletcher, Authors' Club Sir Bannister, Prize Trust (United Kingdom) 487
Fleurus, Editions, SA (France) 105
Fleury, Ernest, Prize (France) 119
Fleuve, Editions, Noir (France) 105
Flight (United Kingdom) 480
Flor, Ediciones de la, SRL (Argentina) 5
Florentz, Verlag V, GmbH (Federal Republic of Germany) 143
Florio, John, Prize (United Kingdom) 487
Floris Books (United Kingdom) 443
Föapátsági Könyvtár (Hungary) 191
Focal Press (United Kingdom) 443
Foch, Marshal, Prize (France) 119
Focus International Book Production AB (Sweden) 384
Focus-Verlag (Federal Republic of Germany) 144
Foetisch, Maurice et Pierre, SA (Switzerland) 396
Fogarty's Bookshop (Republic of South Africa) 360
Fògola Editore in Torino (Italy) 239
Fogtdals Blade A/S (Denmark) 81
Foilseacháin Náisiúnta Tta (Republic of Ireland) 222
Folens and Co Ltd (Republic of Ireland) 222
Folio (Republic of South Africa) 356
Folio, The, Society Ltd (United Kingdom) 443

Folio, The, Society Ltd (United Kingdom) 480
Foma, Editions, SA (Switzerland) 396
Fondo de Cultura Económica (Mexico) 285
Fondo de Cultura Económica (Spain) 368
Fondo Editorial Común SC (Venezuela) 493
Fondo Educativo Interamericana de Mexico SA (Mexico) 285
Fondo Educativo Interamericano (Panama) 328
Fondo Educativo Interamericano (Puerto Rico) 345
Fondo Educativo Interamericano CA (Venezuela) 493
Fondo Educativo Interamericano SA (Colombia) 69
Fonds, Bibliothèque, Quetelet (Belgium) 44
Fonds Mercator SA (Belgium) 39
Fonna Forlag L/L (Norway) 321
Fonndery Press (United Kingdom) 443
Font, Librería (Mexico) 288
Fontamara, Editorial, SA (Spain) 368
Fontana Books (United Kingdom) 443
Fontane, Theodor, Prize (Federal Republic of Germany) 179
Fontanella, Editorial, SA (Spain) 368
Fontein, Uitgeverij De, BV (Netherlands) 296
Fontes Pers (APA) (Netherlands) 296
Food and Agriculture Organization of the United Nations (FAO) (International Organizations) 511
Foras, An, Forbartha (Republic of Ireland) 222
Forbes Publications Ltd (United Kingdom) 443
Förder Prize (German Democratic Republic) 128
Foreign Language Bookshop (Australia) 21
Foreign Language Teaching & Research Press (People's Republic of China) 67
Foreign Languages Press (People's Republic of China) 67
Foreign Languages Publishing House (Democratic People's Republic of Korea) 268
Foreign Relations Publishing House (Thailand) 410
Forening for Boghaandvaerk (Denmark) 79
Forening for Forlagsfolk (Denmark) 79
Foreningen af Medarbejdere ved Danmarks Forskningsbiblioteker (Denmark) 79
Föreningen Auktoriserade Translatorer (Sweden) 391
Föreningen Svenska Läromedelsproducenter (Sweden) 381
Forense-Universitaria, Editora, Ltda (Brazil) 52
Författares Bokmaskin (Sweden) 384
Författarförlaget (Sweden) 384
Förg, Alfred, GmbH & Co KG (Federal Republic of Germany) 144
Foris Publications Holland (Netherlands) 296
Forja Editora Sarl (Portugal) 341
Forkel-Verlag GmbH (Federal Republic of Germany) 144
Forlagid (Iceland) 193
Formar, Editora e Encadernadora, Ltda (Brazil) 52
Format Publishing (United Kingdom) 443
Formgebung, Rat für (Federal Republic of Germany) 144
Forni, Arnaldo, Editore SRL (Italy) 239
Forsamlingsforbundets Forlags AB (Finland) 92
Forsbergs, Bengt, Förlag AB (Sweden) 384
Fortschritt für alle-Verlag (Federal Republic of Germany) 144
Fortuna Finanz-Verlag AG (Switzerland) 396
Fortune Press (United Kingdom) 443
Fortuny, Pascal, Prize (France) 119
Forum, Bokförlaget, AB (Sweden) 384
Forum, Forlaget, A/S (Denmark) 81
Forum (New Zealand) 309
Forum (Yugoslavia) 496
Forum (Yugoslavia) 500
Forum littéraire camerounais (United Republic of Cameroun) 64
Forum Verlag GmbH (Austria) 27
Foster, Raymond (United Kingdom) 479
Föszékesegyházi Könyvtár (Hungary) 191
Foto und Schmalfilm-Verlag (Gemsberg-Verlag) (Switzerland) 396
Fotokinoverlag, VEB (German Democratic Republic) 124
Foucher, Les Editions (France) 105
Foulis, G T, & Co Ltd (United Kingdom) 443
Foulsham, W, & Co Ltd (United Kingdom) 443
Foundation Books (Kenya) 267
Foundation for the Promotion of the Translation of Dutch Literature (Netherlands) 305
Foundational, The, Book Co Ltd (United Kingdom) 443
Fount Paperbacks (United Kingdom) 443
Fountain Press (United Kingdom) 443
Four Courts Press Ltd (Republic of Ireland) 222
Four Winds Press (Australia) 14
Fourah Bay College Bookshop Ltd (Sierra Leone) 350
Fourah Bay College Library (Sierra Leone) 350
Fouraignan Foundation Prize (France) 119
Fournier, Heraclio, SA (Spain) 368
Fourth Dimension Publishing Co Ltd (Nigeria) 316
Fourth Estate Books Ltd (New Zealand) 309

558 INDEX

Fourth Estate Ltd (United Kingdom)   443
Fowler, L N, & Co Ltd (United Kingdom)   443
Foxbury Press (United Kingdom)   443
Foyle, W & G, Ltd (United Kingdom)   481
Foyle, W & G, Ltd & John Gifford Ltd (United Kingdom)   443
Fragua Editorial (Spain)   368
Fralit-F K Albrecht (Federal Republic of Germany)   175
Framework Press Educational Publishers Ltd (United Kingdom)   443
Française, Librairie (Grand Duchy of Luxembourg)   276
France, Librairie de (Burkina Faso)   62
France, Librairie de (Ivory Coast)   254
France, Librairie de (Morocco)   290
France-Caraïbes (France)   105
France Empire, Editions (France)   105
France-Loisirs (France)   105
Francesa, Librería, (SGEL) (Spain)   376
Franciscaines, Les Editions, SA (France)   105
Franciscan Printing Press (Israel)   227
Franciscana, Editorial (Portugal)   341
Francisci, Aldo, Editore (Italy)   239
Francité, Editions de la, (Imprimeries Havaux) (Belgium)   39
Francke , Buchhandlung A, AG (Switzerland)   405
Francke Buchhandlung, Verlag der, GmbH (Federal Republic of Germany)   144
Francke Verlag (Switzerland)   396
Franckh'sche Verlagshandlung W Keller & Co (Federal Republic of Germany)   144
Frank Brothers & Co (Publishers) Pvt Ltd (India)   201
Frank Publishing Ltd (Ghana)   180
Frankfurter Bücher, Verlag (Federal Republic of Germany)   144
Frankfurter Fachverlag Michael Kohl GmbH & Co KG (Federal Republic of Germany)   144
Fränkische Gesellschafts-Druckerei Würzburg/Echter Verlag (Federal Republic of Germany)   144
Franklin', Biblioteca 'Benjamin, (USIS) (Mexico)   288
Franklin, Miles, Award (Australia)   24
Franklin Book Programs Inc (Afghanistan)   1
Frankonius Verlag in Pallottinerdruck und Lahn-Verlag GmbH (Federal Republic of Germany)   144
Franz, Ernst, und Sternberg-Verlag (Federal Republic of Germany)   144
Franzis-Verlag GmbH (Federal Republic of Germany)   144
Fraser, Gordon, Gallery Ltd (United Kingdom)   443
Frassinelli, Edizioni, SRL (Italy)   239
Frau, Verlag für die (German Democratic Republic)   124
Frauenbuchverlag (Federal Republic of Germany)   144
Frauenoffensive, Verlag (Federal Republic of Germany)   144
Frech-Verlag GmbH und Co Druck KG (Federal Republic of Germany)   144
Free Association Books (United Kingdom)   443
Free German Authors' Association (Federal Republic of Germany)   178
Free University Press (Netherlands)   297
Freeman, W H, & Co Ltd (United Kingdom)   443
freies Geistesleben, Verlag (Federal Republic of Germany)   144
Freitas, Livraria, Bastos SA (Brazil)   53
Freitas, Livraria, Bastos SA (Brazil)   58
Fremad (Denmark)   81
French, Samuel, Ltd (United Kingdom)   443
French Book Club (United Kingdom)   481
French Faculty of Medicine, Library of the, Pharmacy and Dentistry (Lebanon)   273
French Language Prize (International Literary Prizes)   519
Fretz und Wasmuth Verlag AG (Switzerland)   396
Fretz Verlag (Switzerland)   396
Freud, Sigmund, Prize (Federal Republic of Germany)   179
Freund Publishing House Ltd (Israel)   227
Freund Publishing House Ltd (Israel)   232
Freytag-Berndt und Artaria, Kartographische Anstalt (Austria)   27
Frías, Universidad Boliviana Tomás, Div de Extensión Universitaria (Bolivia)   48
Fricke, Verlag Dieter, GmbH (Federal Republic of Germany)   144
Friedman, S, Publishing House Ltd (Israel)   227
Friedmann, Blake, Literary Agency (United Kingdom)   479
Friedrich, Erhard, Verlag (Federal Republic of Germany)   144
Friends of Antiquity (Czechoslovakia)   78
Friends of the National Libraries (United Kingdom)   483
Frimodts, J, Forlag (Denmark)   81
Frisia-Verlag GmbH (Federal Republic of Germany)   144

Fritz, Paul und Peter, AG Literary Agency (Switzerland)   405
Fritzes, AB C E, Kungl Hovbokhandel (Sweden)   389
Friundervisningens Forlag (Norway)   321
Frobenius AG (Switzerland)   396
Froebel-Kan Co Ltd (Japan)   256
Fröja, Bokförlaget, AB (Sweden)   384
Fromm, Verlag A, GmbH & Co (Federal Republic of Germany)   144
Frommann, Friedrich, Verlag, Günther Holzboog GmbH & Co (Federal Republic of Germany)   144
Fromme, Georg, und Co (Austria)   27
Frontier Publishing Co (Pakistan)   325
Frossard, Henri (France)   105
Fruitmarket Gallery, The (United Kingdom)   443
Fu-Hsing Book Co (Taiwan)   408
Fu Ssu-Nien Library Institute of History and Philology (Taiwan)   408
Fuchs, Dr Heinrich (Austria)   27
Fudge & Co Ltd (United Kingdom)   443
Fukuinkan Ehon Library (Japan)   263
Fukuinkan Shoten Publishers Inc (Japan)   257
Fulton, David, Publishers Ltd (United Kingdom)   443
Fun Packs (United Kingdom)   444
Fundação Instituto Brasileiro de Geografia e Estatística (IBGE — CDDI/GECOM) (Brazil)   53
Fundação Nacional de Material Escolar (Brazil)   53
Fundación de Cultura Universitaria (Uruguay)   491
Fundacion Kuai-Mare (Venezuela)   493
Fundamentos, Editorial (Spain)   368
Fürstelberger, Hans (Austria)   31
Füssli, Orell, Verlag (Switzerland)   396
Futura, Editorial (Portugal)   341
Futura (United Kingdom)   444
Futuro, Edizioni (Italy)   239
Fuzambo Publishing Co (Japan)   257
Fyfield Books (United Kingdom)   444

G A T T (General Agreement on Tariffs and Trade) (International Organizations)   511
G D Bücherei (Federal Republic of Germany)   144
G D K Publications (India)   201
G E C T I (Gabinete de Especialização e Cooperação Tecnica Internacional L) (Portugal)   341
G E L C (International Organizations)   508
G M P Publishers (United Kingdom)   444
G M T, Forlaget (Denmark)   81
G P A (Gerd Plessl Agentur und Verlags GmbH) (Federal Republic of Germany)   175
G P C Books (United Kingdom)   444
G S Verlag Basle (Switzerland)   396
G T B Siebenstern (Federal Republic of Germany)   144
G W P (Australia)   14
Gaade, Uitgeverij W, BV (Netherlands)   297
Gaba Publications (Kenya)   267
Gabalda, J, et Cie (Librairie Lecoffre) SA (France)   105
Gaber, Franz-J (Federal Republic of Germany)   144
Gaberbocchus Press (Netherlands)   297
Gaberbocchus Press Ltd (United Kingdom)   444
Gabinete de Especialização e Cooperação Tecnica Internacional (Portugal)   341
Gabler, Betriebswirtschaftlicher Verlag Dr Th, GmbH (Federal Republic of Germany)   144
Gad, G E C, Dansk og Udenlandsk Boghandel A/S (Denmark)   84
Gades, Hans, Harbour Pilots Succ A/S (Denmark)   81
Gads, G E C, Forlag (Denmark)   81
Gaggi, Aulo, Editore (Italy)   239
Gai Savoir, Le (Zaire)   502
Gaisa, Ediciones, SL (Spain)   368
Gakken Co Ltd (Japan)   257
Gakujutsu Bunken Fukyu-Kai (Japan)   264
Gakuseisha Publishing Co Ltd (Japan)   257
Galaxia (Venezuela)   494
Galaxie Press (Pvt) Ltd (Zimbabwe)   504
Galeón, El (Uruguay)   491
Galera, La, SA Editorial (Spain)   368
Galería, Librería, Castro Soto (Peru)   331
Galerna, Editorial, SA (Argentina)   5
Galgotia, E D, & Sons (India)   213
Galgotia Booksource (India)   201
Galgotia Publications Pvt Ltd (India)   201
Galilée, Editions (France)   105
Gallegos, Rómulo, International Novel Prize (International Literary Prizes)   519
Gallery, The, Press (Republic of Ireland)   222
Gallery Children's Books (United Kingdom)   444
Galliard (United Kingdom)   444
Gallimard, Editions (France)   105
Gallina, Adriano, Editore (Italy)   239
Galliner, Peter, Associates (United Kingdom)   479
Galve, Impresora, SA (Mexico)   285
Galzerano, Giuseppe, Editore (Italy)   239

Gama, Da, Publishers (Pty) Ltd (Republic of South Africa)   356
Gambia, The, Methodist Bookshop Ltd (The Gambia)   123
Gambia College Library (The Gambia)   123
Gambia National Library (The Gambia)   123
Gamma, Editions (Belgium)   39
Gamma, Editions (France)   105
Gamma (Netherlands)   297
Gammalibri, Editrice (Italy)   240
Gamsberg Publishers (Pty) Ltd (Namibia)   291
Ganesh & Co (India)   201
Gangan (Nigeria)   316
Gangarams Book Bureau (India)   212
Gangemi (Italy)   240
Gangemi Editore e Casa del Libro (Italy)   240
Gans en Rombach Auteursagenter (Netherlands)   304
Gantner, A R, Verlag KG (Liechtenstein)   275
Gantrelle, Joseph, Prize (Belgium)   46
Garcia, R M, Publishing House (Philippines)   332
García SA, Librería y Papelería Casa (Argentina)   5
Gardeners Book Society (United Kingdom)   481
Gardet, Imprimerie Librairie (France)   105
Gardum A/S (Norway)   323
Garigliano, Editrice, SRL (Italy)   240
Garland Publications Ltd (United Kingdom)   444
Garnier, Editions (France)   105
Garriga, Ediciones, Argentinas SA (Argentina)   8
Garriga, Ediciones, SA (Spain)   368
Garza, Ediciones, SA (Spain)   368
Garzanti Editore (Italy)   240
Gateway Books (United Kingdom)   444
Gaurav Publishing House (India)   201
Gauthier-Villars, Société (France)   105
Gautier-Languereau, Les Editions, SA (France)   105
Gay, The, Bookclub (United Kingdom)   481
Gay Artists Series (United Kingdom)   444
Gay Men's Press (United Kingdom)   444
Gay Modern Classics (United Kingdom)   444
Gaya, PT, Favorit Press, Book Division (Indonesia)   217
Gbabeks Publishers Ltd (Nigeria)   316
Gedin, Mrs Lena I (Sweden)   388
Gedins Förlag (Sweden)   384
Gedisa, Editorial, SA (Spain)   368
Gedit Editions SA (Belgium)   39
Gee & Co (United Kingdom)   444
Geering, Rudolf, Verlag (Switzerland)   396
Geest und Portig, Akademische Verlagsgesellschaft, KG (German Democratic Republic)   124
Geeta Prize (India)   215
Geetha Book House (India)   201
Geetha Publishers Sdn Bhd (Malaysia)   279
Gegenrealismus, Verlag für (Federal Republic of Germany)   145
Gegner Prize (France)   119
Gehrmans, AB Carl, Musikförlag (Sweden)   384
Geisenheyner und Crone (Federal Republic of Germany)   175
Gelisim Publishing (Turkey)   415
Gem (United Kingdom)   444
Gemeentebibliotheek Rotterdam (Netherlands)   305
Gemini Publishers (Zimbabwe)   504
Géminis, Editorial, SRL (Argentina)   5
Gemsberg-Verlag (Switzerland)   396
Gençlik Kitabevi (Turkey)   415
General Assembly Library (New Zealand)   312
General Company for Publishing, Advertising and Distribution (Libya)   275
General Egyptian Book Organization (Egypt)   88
General Organization, The, for Government Press Affairs (Egypt)   88
General Press Corporation (Libya)   274
Générale des Carrières et des Mines, La, -Exploitation (Gécamines-Exploitation) (Zaire)   502
Generalstabens Litografiska Anstalt (Sweden)   384
Genesis Publications Ltd (United Kingdom)   444
Genfer Bibelgesellschaft (Switzerland)   396
Genillard, Pierre, Editeur (Switzerland)   396
Genin, Editions M Th (France)   105
Gennadius Library (Greece)   185
Gennep, Van, Ltd (Netherlands)   297
Gensy, Creazioni (Italy)   240
Gente Nueva, Editorial (Cuba)   73
Gentofte Kommunebibliotek (Denmark)   84
Gentry Books Ltd (United Kingdom)   444
Geo Abstracts Ltd (United Kingdom)   444
GeoCenter Verlagsvertrieb GmbH (Federal Republic of Germany)   145
Geodetický a kartografický podnik v Praze NP (Czechoslovakia)   75
Geographia Ltd (United Kingdom)   444
Geographical, The, Association (United Kingdom)   444
Géographie, Bibliothèque de (France)   117
Geological Publishing House (People's Republic of China)   67
Geological Survey Department Library (Botswana)   49

INDEX 559

Geological Survey Department Reference Library (Ghana) 181
Geological Survey of India (India) 201
Geologiczne, Wydawnictwa (Poland) 335
Geoprojects Sàrl (Lebanon) 272
Georg et Cie SA (Switzerland) 396
Georg et Cie SA (Switzerland) 405
George's, William, Sons Ltd (United Kingdom) 481
Georgi, Kunstverlag Dr Rudolf, Woldemar Klein (Federal Republic of Germany) 145
Georgi Publishing Company/Editions Georgi (Switzerland) 396
Gérard, Editions, et Cie SPRL (Belgium) 39
Gerber, Carl, Verlag (Federal Republic of Germany) 145
Gerhardt Verlag (Federal Republic of Germany) 145
Germain, Françoise (France) 116
German Book Club (United Kingdom) 481
German Peace Prize (International Literary Prizes) 519
German Youth, The, Book Award (International Literary Prizes) 519
German Youth Book Award (Federal Republic of Germany) 179
Gerold & Co (Austria) 27
Gerold & Co (Austria) 31
Gerstenberg Verlag (Federal Republic of Germany) 145
Gerth, Musikverlag Klaus (Federal Republic of Germany) 145
Geschichte und Politik, Verlag für (Austria) 27
Gesellschaft für Bibliothekswesen und Dokumentation des Landbaues (GBDL) (Federal Republic of Germany) 177
Gesellschaft für deutsche Sprache und Literatur in Zürich (Switzerland) 406
Gesellschaft für Information und Dokumentation mbH (GID) (Federal Republic of Germany) 177
Gesellschaft für Verlagswerte GmbH (Switzerland) 405
Geuthner, Librairie Orientaliste Paul, SA (France) 105
Ghana Association of Writers (Ghana) 180
Ghana Book Development Council (Ghana) 180
Ghana Book Publishers' Association (Ghana) 180
Ghana Booksellers' Association (Ghana) 180
Ghana Institute of Management and Public Administration, Library and Documentation Centre (Ghana) 181
Ghana Library Association (Ghana) 181
Ghana Library Board (Ghana) 181
Ghana Publishing Corporation (Ghana) 180
Ghana Publishing Corporation, Distribution and Sales Division (Ghana) 181
Ghana Universities Press (Ghana) 180
Ghaqda Bibljotekarji/Library Association (Valletta) (Malta) 282
Gharelu Library Yojna (India) 213
Ghetto Fighters' House Publishers (Israel) 227
Ghigi, Bruno, Editore (Italy) 240
Ghisetti e Corvi Editori SpA (Italy) 240
Ghosh, CM, Publishers Pvt Ltd (India) 201
Ghulam, Sh, Ali & Sons (Pvt) Ltd (Pakistan) 325
Giada, Edizioni (Italy) 240
Giannotta, Editrice, di Sebastiano Pace Giannotta (Italy) 240
Gianotten, Boekhandel, BV (Netherlands) 304
Giao Duc Publishing House (Socialist Republic of Viet Nam) 494
Giappichelli, G, Editore di Giorgio Giappichelli & C SAS (Italy) 240
Gibbons, Stanley, Publications Ltd (United Kingdom) 444
Gibert, Librairie Joseph (France) 116
Gibert Jeune SNC (France) 105
Gibraltar Bookshop (Gibraltar) 182
Gibraltar Garrison Library (Gibraltar) 182
Gibraltar Junior Bookshop (Gibraltar) 182
Gibraltar Library Service (Gibraltar) 182
Gidlunds Bokförlag (Sweden) 384
Gidrometeoroizdat (Union of Soviet Socialist Republics) 418
Gierows, Karin, Prizes (Sweden) 390
Giertsen, Ed B, A/S (Norway) 323
Gieseking, Verlag Ernst und Werner (Federal Republic of Germany) 145
Gifford, John, Ltd (United Kingdom) 444
Gigord, Editions De (France) 105
Gilbert, Girault, SPRL (Belgium) 39
Giles Prize (France) 119
Gili, Ediciones G, SA (Argentina) 5
Gili, Editora Gustavo, do Brasil SA (Brazil) 53
Gili, Editorial Gustavo, de Mexico SA (Mexico) 285
Gili, Editorial Gustavo, Ltda (Chile) 65
Gili, Editorial Gustavo, SA (Spain) 368
Gill, Claude (United Kingdom) 481
Gill & Macmillan Ltd (Republic of Ireland) 222
Gillani, S I (Pakistan) 326
Gilles und Francke Verlag (Federal Republic of Germany) 145

Gimm-Young Press (Republic of Korea) 269
Ginn & Co Ltd (United Kingdom) 444
Ginsberg Univ Boekhandel (Netherlands) 304
Giovanis (Greece) 183
Girardet, W, Buchverlag GmbH (Federal Republic of Germany) 145
Girasole, Mario Lapucci — Edizioni del (Italy) 240
Gisbert y Cía SA (Bolivia) 48
Gisbert y Cia SA (Bolivia) 48
Gitanjali Publishing House (India) 201
Giuffrè, A, Editore SpA (Italy) 240
Giunti Publishing Group (Italy) 240
Gjellerup og Gad Forlagsaktieselskab (Denmark) 81
Glas (Yugoslavia) 496
Glasgow, Mary, Publications Ltd (United Kingdom) 444
Glaven (United Kingdom) 444
Gleerupska, AB, Universitetsbokhandeln (Sweden) 389
Glem, Editorial, SACIF (Argentina) 5
Glen, Esther, Award (New Zealand) 313
Glenat, Editions J, SA (France) 105
Glendale, The, Press Ltd (Republic of Ireland) 222
Gleniffer, The, Press (United Kingdom) 444
Global Editora e Distribuidora Ltda (Brazil) 53
Globetrotter-Verlag (Federal Republic of Germany) 145
Globi Verlag AG (Switzerland) 396
Globo, Editora, Ltda (Brazil) 53
Globo, Livraria do, SA (Brazil) 58
Globus (Yugoslavia) 496
'Globus' Zeitungs-, Druck- und Verlagsanstalt GmbH (Austria) 27
Glock und Lutz Verlag Heroldsberg (Federal Republic of Germany) 145
Glöss, Verlagsgesellschaft R, und Co (Federal Republic of Germany) 145
Glówna Biblioteka Lekarska (Poland) 338
Glówna Politechniki, Biblioteka, Warszawskiej (Poland) 338
Glückauf, Verlag, GmbH (Federal Republic of Germany) 145
Glückler, Hans-Peter, Literary Agency (Federal Republic of Germany) 175
Gmünder, Bruno, Verlag (Federal Republic of Germany) 145
Goddard's Bookshop Ltd (New Zealand) 312
Godfrey Cave Books Ltd (United Kingdom) 479
Goede Boek, BV Uitgeversbedryf Het (Netherlands) 297
Goel Publishing House (India) 201
Goethe Book Dealers Inc (Japan) 263
Goethe-Institut — Deutsche Bibliothek (Belgium) 44
Goethe Prize (Federal Republic of Germany) 179
Golan (Syria) 407
Gold Dagger Award (United Kingdom) 487
Gold Eagle (United Kingdom) 444
Golden Book House (Bangladesh) 35
Golden Cockerel Press Ltd (United Kingdom) 444
Golden Eagle Books Ltd (Republic of Ireland) 222
Golden Handshake (United Kingdom) 444
Golden Pleasure Books (United Kingdom) 444
Golden Press (New Zealand) 309
Golden Press Pty Ltd (Australia) 14
Goldmann, Wilhelm, Verlag GmbH (Federal Republic of Germany) 145
Goldschmidt, Victor, Verlagsbuchhandlung (Switzerland) 396
Goldsmith, The, Press Ltd (Republic of Ireland) 222
Goldstadtverlag (Federal Republic of Germany) 145
Goliardica, Società Editrice La, Pavese SRL (Italy) 240
Gollancz, Victor, Ltd (United Kingdom) 444
Gomer Press (J D Lewis & Sons Ltd) (United Kingdom) 444
Gómez, P A (Dominican Republic) 86
Goncourt, Editorial y Librería (Argentina) 5
Goncourt Prize (France) 120
Gondola Books (United Kingdom) 445
Gondolat Könyvkiadó (Hungary) 190
Gondrom Verlag GmbH & Co Kg (Federal Republic of Germany) 145
Gondu (Burma) 62
Gonin, André et Pierre (Switzerland) 396
Gonski, Buchhandlung Heinrich, GmbH & Co (Federal Republic of Germany) 175
Gonvill, Librerías, SA de CV (Mexico) 288
Good Companions (India) 201
Good Earth Publishing Co (Hong Kong) 188
Good Housekeeping Step-by-Step Cookery (United Kingdom) 481
Goodwill Trading Co Inc (Philippines) 333
Gorachek, V, KG (Federal Republic of Germany) 145
Gorachek, V, KG (Federal Republic of Germany) 179
Gorcum, Van, BV (Netherlands) 297
Gordon and Breach Science Publishers Ltd (United Kingdom) 445
Gordon and Gotch (PNG) Pty Ltd (Papua New Guinea) 329

Gorgas, Biblioteca Bio-Médica del Laboratorio Conmemorativo (Panama) 328
Gor'kogo Leningradskogo, Nauchnaya biblioteka im M, gosudarstvennogo universiteta im A A Zhdanova (Union of Soviet Socialist Republics) 420
Gor'kogo Moskovskogo, Nauchnaya biblioteka im A M, gos universiteta im M V Lomonosova (Union of Soviet Socialist Republics) 420
Gorter, Herman, Prize (Netherlands) 306
Göschl, Alois, & Co (Austria) 27
Gosudarstvennaya ordena Trudovogo Krasnogo Znameni biblioteka, Vsesoyuznaya, inostrannoi literatury (Union of Soviet Socialist Republics) 420
Gosudarstvennaya publichnaya istoricheskaya biblioteka RSFSR (Union of Soviet Socialist Republics) 420
Gosudarstvennaya publichnaya nauchno-tekhnicheskaya biblioteka SSSR (Union of Soviet Socialist Republics) 420
Gosudarstvenny komitet SSSR po delam izdatelstv, poligrafii i knizhnoi torgovli (Union of Soviet Socialist Republics) 417
Göteborgs Stadsbibliotek (Sweden) 389
Göteborgs Universitetsbibliotek (Sweden) 389
Gotthelf-Verlag (Switzerland) 396
Gottmer, Uitgeverij J H, /H J W Becht BV (Netherlands) 297
Gottmer's, BV v/hB, Uitgeversbedrijf (Netherlands) 297
Gouda Quint BV (Netherlands) 297
Government, Directorate of, Publications (India) 201
Government Archives, Cape Archives Depot, Library (Republic of South Africa) 360
Government Archives, Natal Archives Depot, Library (Republic of South Africa) 360
Government Archives, Orange Free State Archives Depot, Library (Republic of South Africa) 360
Government Archives, Transvaal Archives Depot, Library (Republic of South Africa) 360
Government College Library (Pakistan) 327
Government Library (Libya) 275
Government of India Librarians Association (India) 214
Government of Pakistan Department of Libraries (Pakistan) 327
Government Press (Afghanistan) 1
Government Press, The (The Gambia) 123
Government Printer (Botswana) 49
Government Printer (Burundi) 63
Government Printer (Chad) 65
Government Printer (Democratic Republic of Madagascar) 276
Government Printer (Egypt) 88
Government Printer (Ethiopia) 91
Government Printer (Ivory Coast) 253
Government Printer (Kenya) 267
Government Printer (Lesotho) 274
Government Printer (Liberia) 274
Government Printer (Popular Republic of Congo) 72
Government Printer (Republic of South Africa) 356
Government Printer (Somalia) 354
Government Printer (Tanzania) 409
Government Printer, The, (Ghana Publishing Corporation, Printing Division) (Ghana) 181
Government Printer (Uganda) 416
Government Printer (United Republic of Cameroun) 64
Government Printer (Zambia) 503
Government Printer (Zimbabwe) 504
Government Printer (Impressa Nacional de Moçambique) (Mozambique) 291
Government Printer (Imprimerie Centrale d'Afrique) (Central African Republic) 64
Government Printer (Imprimerie Centrale d'Afrique) (Republic of Gabon) 122
Government Printer (Imprimerie du Gouvernement) (Senegal) 349
Government Printer (Imprimerie du Gouvernement Central) (Zaire) 502
Government Printer (Imprimerie Générale du Niger) (Niger) 314
Government Printer (Imprimerie National du Rwanda) (Rwanda) 348
Government Printer, Imprimerie Nationale (Burkina Faso) 62
Government Printer (Imprimerie Nationale) (Malawi) 277
Government Printer (Imprimerie Nationale) (Mali) 281
Government Printer (Imprimerie Nationale) (Mauritania) 282
Government Printer (Imprimerie Nationale) (Mauritius) 282
Government Printer (Imprimerie Officielle) (Morocco) 290
Government Printer (Imprimerie Officielle de la République Tunisienne — IORT) (Tunisia) 414
Government Printer (Office nationale d'edition de presse et d'imprimerie) (Benin) 47

560 INDEX

Government Printing Centre (Finland) 92
Government Printing Office (Jamaica) 254
Government Public Library (Liberia) 274
Government Publications (Pakistan) 325
Government Publishing Awards for the New Zealand Children's Books of the Year (New Zealand) 313
Government Teacher Training College Library (Botswana) 49
Gower Medical Publishing (United Kingdom) 445
Gower Press (United Kingdom) 445
Gower Publishing Co Ltd (United Kingdom) 445
Goyanarte Editor SA (Argentina) 5
Gozo Public Library (Malta) 282
Graaf, De, Publishers (Netherlands) 297
Graal, Edições, Ltda (Brazil) 53
Graal, Ordem do, na Terra (Brazil) 53
Grabert-Verlag (Federal Republic of Germany) 145
Gracklauer, O, Verlag und Bibliographische Agentur (Federal Republic of Germany) 129
Gradina, Izdavačka ustanova (Yugoslavia) 496
Gradiva-Publicações Lda (Portugal) 341
Gradjevinska Knjiga (Yugoslavia) 496
Gräfe und Unzer GmbH (Federal Republic of Germany) 145
Grafica e Arte Bergamo (Italy) 240
Grafički zavod Hrvatske (Yugoslavia) 496
Grafino-Verlag, Grafische Betriebe AG (Switzerland) 396
Grafis Edizioni (Italy) 240
Grafisk Forlag (Denmark) 81
Grafo Edizioni (Italy) 240
Grafos (Yugoslavia) 496
Grafton Books (United Kingdom) 445
Graham, Frank (United Kingdom) 445
Graham & Trotman Ltd (United Kingdom) 445
Grahame Book Co (Australia) 14
Grahames Bookshop (Australia) 21
Gralsbotschaft, Verlag der Stiftung, GmbH (Federal Republic of Germany) 145
Gram Editora (Argentina) 5
Gramedia, PT (Indonesia) 217
Gramedia Bookshop (Indonesia) 218
Gran Colombia, Librería La (Colombia) 71
Gran Premio Nacional de Literatura (Uruguay) 491
Granada Publishing Ltd (United Kingdom) 445
Grancher, Jacques, Editeur (France) 105
Grand, Bibliothèque du, Seminaire de Koumi (Burkina Faso) 62
Grand Franco-Belgian Literary Prize (France) 120
Grand Franco-Belgian LiteraryZ Prize (Belgium) 46
Grand National Assembly, The, of Turkey, Library and Documentation Center (TBMM Kütüphane ve Dokümantasyon Merkezi) (Turkey) 415
Grand-Pont, Editions du (Switzerland) 396
Grand Prix de la Francophonie (International Literary Prizes) 519
Grand Prix des Biennales Internationales de Poésie (International Literary Prizes) 519
Grand Prize (Sweden) 390
Grand Prize for a Book of Poetry (Sweden) 390
Grand Prize for a Novel (Sweden) 390
Grand Prize for Literature (France) 120
Grand Prize for Poetry Criticism (France) 120
Grand Prize for the Dissemination of the French Language (International Literary Prizes) 519
Grand Prize of French Poets (France) 120
Granda, Editorial Juan Carlos (Argentina) 5
Grant McIntyre Ltd (United Kingdom) 445
Graphic Art Publishing (Thailand) 410
Graphik Klub (Federal Republic of Germany) 175
Grass Roots (Australia) 14
Grasset et Fasquelle, Société des Editions (France) 106
Grassin, Jean, Editeur (France) 106
Grasso, Editoriale, SRL (Italy) 240
Gratien, Emilio (French Guiana) 122
Gravesande, The G H 's-, Prize (Netherlands) 306
Great Austrian State Prize (Austria) 33
Great China Book Corporation (Taiwan) 408
Great English Classics (United Kingdom) 481
Great Mosque of Sana'a, Library of the (Yemen Arab Republic) 495
Great Western Press Pty Ltd (Australia) 14
Gredos, Editorial, SA (Spain) 368
Green & Son, W, Ltd (United Kingdom) 445
Greenaway, Kate, Medal (United Kingdom) 487
Greene & Co (Republic of Ireland) 224
Greenhill Books/Lionel Leventhal Ltd (United Kingdom) 445
Greenhouse Publications Pty Ltd (Australia) 14
Greenwood Press (Hong Kong) 188
Gregorian University Press (Italy) 240
Gregoriana, Libreria (Italy) 251
Gregoriana, Libreria Editrice (Italy) 240
Gregory, Eric, Trust Fund Awards (United Kingdom) 487
Gregory Medal (Republic of Ireland) 225

Greifenverlag zu Rudolstadt (German Democratic Republic) 124
Gremese Editore, Ernesto, SRL (Italy) 240
Gremese Editore SRL (Italy) 240
Gremi de Llibreters de Barcelona i Catalunya (Spain) 363
Gremial de Libreros de Guatemala (Guatemala) 185
Grenfell 'Henry Lawson' Festival of Arts Prizes (Australia) 24
Grente, Cardinal, Foundation Prize (France) 120
Gresham Books (United Kingdom) 445
Greshoff, J, Prize (Netherlands) 306
Gretener & Co (Switzerland) 405
Grevas Forlag (Denmark) 81
Greven Verlag Köln GmbH (Federal Republic of Germany) 145
Greyfriars Book Club (United Kingdom) 481
Gribaudi, Piero, Editore (Italy) 240
Griegs, John, Forlag (Norway) 321
Griffin, Charles, & Co Ltd (United Kingdom) 445
Griffioen Paperbacks (Netherlands) 297
Griffon, Editions du (Switzerland) 396
Griggs, T W, & Co (Pty) Ltd (Republic of South Africa) 356
Grijalbo, Distribuidora exclusivo, SA (Peru) 330
Grijalbo, Ediciones, SA (Spain) 368
Grijalbo, Editorial, Ltda (Brazil) 53
Grijalbo, Editorial, SA (Mexico) 285
Grijalbo, Editorial, SA (Venezuela) 493
Grijalbo Boliviana Ltda (Bolivia) 48
Grijalbo Ecuatoriana Ltda (Ecuador) 87
Grijalbo Editor (Uruguay) 491
Grijalbo Puerto Rico Inc (Puerto Rico) 345
Grijalbo SA (Argentina) 5
Grijalbo y Cía Ltda (Chile) 65
Grijelmo, Artes Gráficas, SA (Spain) 368
Grip, PT (Indonesia) 217
Grisewood & Dempsey Ltd (United Kingdom) 445
Grolier, The, Society of Australia Pty Ltd (Australia) 14
Grolier de Venezuela (Venezuela) 493
Grøndahl og Søn Forlag A/S (Norway) 321
Grønlandske Forlag, Det (Denmark) 81
Groos, Julius, Verlag KG (Federal Republic of Germany) 145
Groot, De, Goudriaan (Netherlands) 297
Grosskopf, J W F, Prys vir Drama (Republic of South Africa) 362
Grossman, David, Literary Agency Ltd (United Kingdom) 479
Grossohaus Wegner und Co (Federal Republic of Germany) 175
Grosvenor Books (United Kingdom) 445
Grote Beren (Netherlands) 297
Grote'sche Verlagsbuch-handlung KG (Federal Republic of Germany) 145
Grounauer, Editions François (Switzerland) 396
Ground, Editora, Ltda (Brazil) 53
Groupe des Editeurs de livres de la CEE (GELC) (International Organizations) 508
Groupe Expansion (France) 106
Grub Street (United Kingdom) 445
Gründ, Librairie (France) 106
Grundlagen, Verlag, und Praxis GmbH & Co (Federal Republic of Germany) 145
Grundt, Johan, Tanum A/S (Norway) 323
Grüner, B R, BV (Netherlands) 297
Grünewald, Matthias-, -Verlag (Federal Republic of Germany) 145
Grupo Bibliografico Nacional de la Republica Dominicana (Dominican Republic) 87
Gruyter, Walter de, & Co (Federal Republic of Germany) 145
Guadagni, L'Editrice Scientifica SAS di L G (Italy) 241
Guadalupe, Editora, Ltda (Colombia) 69
Guadalupe, Editorial (Argentina) 5
Guadarrama, Ediciones (Spain) 368
Guanabara, Editora, Koogan SA (Brazil) 53
Guanda (Italy) 241
Guara Editorial SA (Spain) 368
Guardian' Award, 'The, for Children's Fiction (International Literary Prizes) 519
Guardian' Fiction, 'The, Prize (International Literary Prizes) 519
Guazzelli, Livraria Pioneira Editora/Enio Matheus, e Cia Ltd (Brazil) 53
Gudjónssonar, Bókaútgáfa Gudjóns Ó (Iceland) 193
Guénégaud, Librairie, Sàrl (France) 106
Guerra, Tipografia Editrice (Italy) 241
Guhl, Verlag Klaus (Federal Republic of Germany) 146
Guida Editori SpA (Italy) 241
Guidicini e Rosa Editori SNC (Italy) 241
Guild Publishing (United Kingdom) 445
Guildhall Library (United Kingdom) 482

Guillot, Editions d'Art Albert (France) 106
Guinness (Denmark) 81
Guinness Publishing Ltd (United Kingdom) 445
Guitarra Facil (Colombia) 71
Gujarat, Garavi, Annual Book Award for Racial Harmony (United Kingdom) 487
Gujarat State English Language Booksellers' Association (India) 195
Gujarat Textbook, The, Publishers' Association (India) 195
Gujarat Vidyapith Granthalaya (India) 214
Gulf Publishing Ltd (Malta) 281
Gulf Union Co (Kuwait) 272
Gúm, An (Republic of Ireland) 222
Gummeruksen Kirjakauppa (Finland) 94
Gummerus Publishers (Finland) 92
Gumperts Universitetsbokhandel AB (Sweden) 389
Gunasena, M D, & Co Ltd (Sri Lanka) 378
Gundert, D, Verlag (Federal Republic of Germany) 146
Gundolf, Friedrich, Prize for Germanistics abroad (Federal Republic of Germany) 179
Gunsmoke Westerns (United Kingdom) 446
Gunung Agung, PT (Indonesia) 219
Gunung Agung (S) Pte Ltd (Republic of Singapore) 351
Gunung Mulia, Penerbit PT BPK (Indonesia) 218
Gunung Mulia, Toko Buku PT BPK (Indonesia) 219
Guoji Shudian (People's Republic of China) 68
Güse, Verlag August, GmbH (Federal Republic of Germany) 146
Gut, Th, & Co Verlag (Switzerland) 396
Gute Schriften Verein (Switzerland) 396
Gutenberg, Büchergilde (Federal Republic of Germany) 175
Gutenberg, Büchergilde (Switzerland) 405
Gutenberg, Dardanos (Greece) 183
Gutenberg-Gesellschaft (Federal Republic of Germany) 146
Gutenberg-Gesellschaft (Federal Republic of Germany) 178
Gutenberg Verlagsgesellschaft, Büchergilde, mbH (Federal Republic of Germany) 146
Gutenberghus Publishing Service A/S (Denmark) 81
Gütermann, Sumus Verlag Jutta (Switzerland) 396
Gütersloher Verlagshaus Gerd Mohn (Federal Republic of Germany) 146
Guttentag', Premio de Novela 'Erich (Bolivia) 49
Guyana Library Association (Guyana) 186
Guyana Medical Science Library (Guyana) 186
Guyana National Printers Ltd (Guyana) 186
Guyana National Trading Corporation (GNTC) (Guyana) 186
Gwasg Prifysgol Cymru (United Kingdom) 446
Gwasg y Dref Wen (United Kingdom) 446
Gyan Bharati (India) 201
Gyldendal, Søren, Prize (Denmark) 86
Gyldendal Norsk Forlag (Norway) 321
Gyldendals Bogklub (Denmark) 84
Gyldendals Børnebogklub (Denmark) 84
Gyldendalske Boghandel — Nordisk Forlag A/S (Denmark) 81

H & R Academica (Pty) Ltd (Republic of South Africa) 356
H A U M Academic Bookshop (Republic of South Africa) 360
H A U M Booksellers (Republic of South Africa) 360
H A U M-Daan Retief Publishers (Pty) Ltd (Republic of South Africa) 356
H A U M Educational Publishers (Republic of South Africa) 356
H A U M (Hollandsch Afrikaansche Uitgevers Maatschappij) (Republic of South Africa) 356
H E B (United Kingdom) 446
H E S Publishers (Netherlands) 297
H F L (United Kingdom) 446
H K Health Knowledge Publication (Hong Kong) 188
H M S O (United Kingdom) 446
H V A — Edition Schindele (Federal Republic of Germany) 146
Haack, VEB Hermann, Geographisch-Kartographische Anstalt Gotha (German Democratic Republic) 125
Haag, Michael, Ltd (United Kingdom) 446
Haag und Herchen Verlag (Federal Republic of Germany) 146
Haan, de (Netherlands) 297
Haase, P, & Søns Forlag A/S (Denmark) 81
Habegger Verlag (Switzerland) 396
Habelt, Dr Rudolf, GmbH (Federal Republic of Germany) 146
Habib Bank Prize for Literature (Pakistan) 327
Hachette (France) 106
Hachette, Librairie (Egypt) 89

Hachette, Librairie (Popular Republic of Congo) 72
Hachette, Librería, SA (Argentina) 5
Hachette, Librería, SA (Argentina) 8
Hachette, Société congolaise (Popular Republic of Congo) 72
Hachette/Enseignement (Hachette Educational) (France) 106
Hachette Calédonie (New Caledonia) 307
Hachette Export Livre (France) 106
Hachette Guides Bleus (France) 106
Hachette International (Belgium) 39
Hachette-Jeunesse (France) 106
Hachette-Littérature Générale (France) 106
Hachette Pacifique, Librairie, SA (French Polynesia) 122
Hachette Pratique (France) 106
Hadar (Israel) 227
Haddock, Peter, Ltd (United Kingdom) 446
Hädecke, Walter, Verlag (Federal Republic of Germany) 146
Hadiah Sastera Malaysia Prize (Malaysia) 281
Hadow, Lyndal, Short Story Award (Australia) 24
Haere Po No Tahiti (French Polynesia) 122
Haffmans Verlag AG (Switzerland) 396
Hagaberg AB (Sweden) 384
Hagedorn, Hans Hermann (Federal Republic of Germany) 175
Hagemann, Lehrmittelverlag Wilhelm, GmbH (Federal Republic of Germany) 146
Hagen, Ten, BV (Netherlands) 297
Hagerups, H, Forlag (Denmark) 81
Hahn's, Mary, Kochbuchverlag (Federal Republic of Germany) 146
Haho, Editions (Togo) 412
Haigh & Hochland Ltd (United Kingdom) 481
Hain, Verlag Anton (Federal Republic of Germany) 146
Hak Won Publishing Co Ltd (Republic of Korea) 269
Hakibbutz Hameuchad Publishing House Ltd (Israel) 227
Hakki Bigeç (Turkey) 415
Hakkim's Bookshop (Bangladesh) 35
Hakusui-Sha Co Ltd (Japan) 257
Hakuyu-Sha (Japan) 257
Halban, Peter, Publishers Ltd (United Kingdom) 446
Halcyon Publishing Ltd (New Zealand) 309
Hale, Robert, Ltd (United Kingdom) 446
Hali Prize (India) 215
Halk Kütüphanesi, Il (Turkey) 415
Hall, June, Literary Agency (United Kingdom) 479
Haller, Berchtold, Verlag (Switzerland) 396
Hallgren och Fallgren Studieförlag AB (Sweden) 384
Hallwag Verlag AG (Switzerland) 397
Hallwag Verlagsgesellschaft mbH (Federal Republic of Germany) 146
Hälsaböcker/Allt om Hälsa AB (Sweden) 384
Hambledon Press, The (United Kingdom) 446
Hamburger Lesehefte Verlag Iselt & Co Nfl mbH (Federal Republic of Germany) 146
Hamburgische Geschichte, Verein für (Federal Republic of Germany) 178
Hamburgo, Librería, SA (Mexico) 288
Hamdard Foundation (Pakistan) 325
Hameau, Le, Editeur (France) 106
Hamidia Library (Bangladesh) 35
Hamilton, Hamish (Australia) 14
Hamilton, Hamish, Ltd (United Kingdom) 446
Hamilton House Publishing (United Kingdom) 446
Hamlet, Forlaget (Denmark) 81
Hamlyn Publishing (United Kingdom) 446
Hammarström och Åberg Bokförlag (Sweden) 384
Hammer, Peter, Verlag GmbH (Federal Republic of Germany) 146
Hammick's Bookshops & Hammick's Wholesale (United Kingdom) 482
Hamrelius och Stenvall Förlag AB (Sweden) 384
Hamrun, The, Library (Malta) 282
Han Jin Publishing Co (Republic of Korea) 269
Hanau, Heinrich, Publications Ltd (United Kingdom) 446
Handbag Books (United Kingdom) 446
Handsel, The, Press (United Kingdom) 446
Hanguk Seoji Hakhoe (Republic of Korea) 271
Hanguk Tosogwan Hakhoe (Republic of Korea) 271
Hanna, Fred, Ltd (Republic of Ireland) 224
Hans Prakashan (India) 201
Hans Publishers (India) 201
Hansa Verlag Ingwert Paulsen Jnr (Federal Republic of Germany) 146
Hanse Production AB (Sweden) 384
Hansen, Edition Wilhelm, AS (Denmark) 81
Hansen, Edition Wilhelm, Stockholm (Sweden) 384
Hansen, Folmer, Teaterförlag AB (Sweden) 388
Hanser, Carl, Verlag (Federal Republic of Germany) 146
Hänssler-Verlag (Federal Republic of Germany) 146

Hansson och Bruce, Söderbokhandeln, AB (Sweden) 389
Hanssons, Kalleberger Foundation — The Tekla, and Gösta Ronnströms Prize (Sweden) 390
Hanstein, Peter, Verlag GmbH (Federal Republic of Germany) 146
Hanthawaddy Book House (Burma) 62
Hanthawaddy Bookshop (Burma) 62
Harare City Library (Zimbabwe) 505
Harare Polytechnic Library (Zimbabwe) 505
Haraucourt, Edmond, Prize (France) 120
Harbra (Brazil) 53
Harck og Gjellerup Booksellers Ltd (Denmark) 84
Harcourt Brace Jovanovich Group (Australia) Pty Ltd (Australia) 14
Harcourt Brace Jovanovich Group Australia Pty Ltd (New Zealand) 309
Harcourt Brace Jovanovich Ltd (United Kingdom) 446
Hardiman, James, Library (Republic of Ireland) 224
Hardy, Patrick, Books (United Kingdom) 446
Hardy, Thomas, Prize (United Kingdom) 487
Hardy, Thomas, Society Ltd (United Kingdom) 485
Hargreen Publishing Co (Australia) 15
Harjeet & Co (India) 201
Harla SA de CV (Mexico) 285
Harlekin-Presse (Federal Republic of Germany) 147
Harlenic Hellas AE (Greece) 183
Harlequin (United Kingdom) 446
Harmi-Press Publications, Haroula Papadimitriou (Greece) 183
Harmonie, De (Netherlands) 297
Harper & Row, Editora, do Brasil Ltda (Brazil) 53
Harper & Row (Australasia) Pty Ltd (Australia) 15
Harper & Row Latinoamericana-Harla SA de CV (Mexico) 285
Harper & Row Ltd (United Kingdom) 446
Harper & Row, Publishers (Netherlands) 297
Harper & Row Publishers, Asia, Pte Ltd (Republic of Singapore) 351
Harrach Verlag (Federal Republic of Germany) 147
Harrap France SA (France) 106
Harrap Ltd (United Kingdom) 447
Harrassowitz, Otto (Federal Republic of Germany) 175
Harrassowitz, Verlag Otto (Federal Republic of Germany) 147
Harriers Publishing House (Sweden) 384
Harries, Katrine, Award (Republic of South Africa) 362
Harris, Firma (Indonesia) 218
Harrow House Editions (United Kingdom) 447
Hart Mossman & Co Ltd (Nigeria) 318
Harth, VEB, Musik Verlag (German Democratic Republic) 125
Hartmann, Litteraturverlag Karlheinz (Federal Republic of Germany) 147
Harvard, John, Lending Library (Bahamas) 34
Harvard University Press (United Kingdom) 447
Harvester, The, Press Ltd (United Kingdom) 447
Harvey, Denise, & Co (Greece) 183
Harvey Sales (United Kingdom) 479
Harvill Press Ltd (United Kingdom) 447
Harwood Academic Publishers GmbH (Switzerland) 397
Haryana Sahitya Prize (India) 215
Hasanuddin, Library of, University (Indonesia) 219
Hasbach, A L (Austria) 31
Haset Kitabevi AS (Turkey) 415
Hashichpul, Mifal (Israel) 231
Hashim bin Haji Abdullah (Republic of Singapore) 353
Háskólabókasafn (Iceland) 194
Hatchards Ltd (United Kingdom) 482
Hatier, Librairie, SA (France) 106
Hatje, Verlag Gerd (Federal Republic of Germany) 147
Hatta, Perpustakaan Jajasan (Indonesia) 219
Haude und Spener Verlag (Federal Republic of Germany) 147
Haufe, Rudolf, Verlag GmbH & Co KG (Federal Republic of Germany) 147
Haug, Karl F, Verlag GmbH & Co (Federal Republic of Germany) 147
Haupt, Paul, Bern (Switzerland) 397
Hauptverband der graphischen Unternehmungen Österreichs (Austria) 25
Hauptverband des österreichischen Buchhandels (Austria) 25
Haus, Das, der Bibel (Switzerland) 397
Haus, Volksbuchhandlung, des Buches (German Democratic Republic) 127
Hauschild, Verlag H M, GmbH (Federal Republic of Germany) 147
Hauswedell, Dr Ernst, und Co Verlag (Federal Republic of Germany) 147
Hautot, Pierre, SA (France) 106
Havaux, Imprimeries (Belgium) 39

Have, Uitgeverij ten, NV (Netherlands) 297
Havez-Planque, Marie, Prize (France) 120
Hawthorn Books (Republic of Ireland) 223
Hawthornden Prize (United Kingdom) 487
Hayakawa Publishing Inc (Japan) 257
Hayez, Imprimerie, SPRL (Belgium) 39
Hayit Verlag GmbH (Federal Republic of Germany) 147
Haynes & Co, J H, Ltd (United Kingdom) 447
Haynes Publishing Group PLC (United Kingdom) 447
Hazan, Fernand, Editeur SA (France) 106
Hazelton Publishing (United Kingdom) 447
Headline Book Publishing PLC (United Kingdom) 447
Health Science Press (C W Daniel) Ltd (United Kingdom) 447
Heartlines (Australia) 15
Heath, A M, & Co Ltd (United Kingdom) 479
Heatherbank Press (United Kingdom) 447
Heckners Verlag (Federal Republic of Germany) 147
Hedley's Bookshop Ltd (New Zealand) 312
Heenemann, H, Verlagsgesellschaft mbH (Federal Republic of Germany) 147
Heffers Booksellers (United Kingdom) 482
Heibonsha Ltd, Publishers (Japan) 257
Heideland, Boekhandel (Belgium) 44
Heideland NV (Heideland PVBA) (Belgium) 39
Heideland-Orbis (NV M en I) (Belgium) 39
Heidmük-Verlag Günther U Müller (Federal Republic of Germany) 147
Heidrich, Leopold (Austria) 31
Heiliger & Co Ltd (Israel) 231
Heilpädagogisches Institut der Universität Freiburg (Switzerland) 397
Heima er Bezt Book Club (Iceland) 194
Heimskringla (Iceland) 193
Heinemann, Verlag Egon (Federal Republic of Germany) 147
Heinemann/Kingswood (United Kingdom) 447
Heinemann/Newnes (United Kingdom) 448
Heinemann/Octopus (United Kingdom) 448
Heinemann Award for Literature (United Kingdom) 487
Heinemann Educational Australia (Australia) 15
Heinemann Educational Books (Asia) Ltd (Republic of Singapore) 351
Heinemann Educational Books (Caribbean) Ltd (Jamaica) 254
Heinemann Educational Books Ltd (United Kingdom) 447
Heinemann Educational Books (Nigeria) Ltd (Nigeria) 316
Heinemann Group, The, of Publishers Ltd (United Kingdom) 447
Heinemann Kenya Ltd (Kenya) 267
Heinemann Ltd, William (United Kingdom) 447
Heinemann Medical, William, Books Ltd (United Kingdom) 447
Heinemann Newtech (United Kingdom) 448
Heinemann Professional Publishing (United Kingdom) 448
Heinemann Publishers Australia Pty Ltd (Australia) 15
Heinemann Publishers (New Zealand) Ltd (New Zealand) 309
Heinemann Publishers Southern Africa Pty Ltd (Republic of South Africa) 356
Heinold, Ehrhardt (Federal Republic of Germany) 147
Heinrichshofen's Verlag (Federal Republic of Germany) 147
Heinse, Wilhelm, Medal for Literature in Essay Form (International Literary Prizes) 519
Heintz, Verlag Georg (Federal Republic of Germany) 147
Heinzle's, Gebhard, Erben (Austria) 31
Hekla Forlag (Denmark) 81
Helbing und Lichtenhahn Verlag AG (Switzerland) 397
Helgafell, Bókabúdin (Iceland) 194
Helgafell, Bókaútgáfan (Iceland) 193
Helicon Press (United Kingdom) 448
Helikon Kiadó (Hungary) 190
Heliodoro Valle, Rafael, Prize (International Literary Prizes) 519
Héliographia, Arts Graphiques, SA (Switzerland) 397
Helios, Uitgeverij (Belgium) 39
Hellenic Distribution Agency (Cyprus) Ltd (Cyprus) 74
Helm, Christopher, (Publishers) Ltd (United Kingdom) 448
Helmond (Netherlands) 297
Help Bookshop (Lebanon) 273
Helsingin Kaupunginkirjasto — Valtakunnallinen yleisten kirjastojen keskuskirjasto (Finland) 94
Helsingin Yliopiston Kirjasto (Finland) 94
Helsinki Prize (Finland) 95
Helvetica Chimica, Verlag, Acta (Switzerland) 397
Hemans, Felicia, Prize for Lyrical Poetry (United Kingdom) 487
Hemeroteca Municipal de Madrid (Spain) 376
Hemeroteca Nacional de México (Mexico) 288

Hemingway Award (International Literary Prizes) 519
Hemisferio, Editorial, Sur SA (Argentina) 5
Hemkunt Press (India) 201
Hemma, Editions, SPRL (Belgium) 39
Hemmets Journal AB (Sweden) 384
Hemus Editora Ltda (Brazil) 53
'Hemus' Foreign Trade Organization (Bulgaria) 61
Henderson's Book Store (Jamaica) 255
Hendon Publishing Co Ltd (United Kingdom) 448
Hengellinen Laukibeirja (Finland) 92
Henle, G, Verlag (Federal Republic of Germany) 147
Henny's Forlag (Norway) 321
Henry, Ian, Publications Ltd (United Kingdom) 448
Henschelverlag Kunst und Gesellschaft (German Democratic Republic) 125
Henssel Verlag (Federal Republic of Germany) 147
Her Majesty's Stationery Office (United Kingdom) 448
Herbert, The, Press Ltd (United Kingdom) 448
Herbig, F A, Verlagsbuchhandlung (Federal Republic of Germany) 147
Herbita Editrice di Leonardo Palermo (Italy) 241
Herchen (Federal Republic of Germany) 147
Herder, Editorial, SA (Spain) 368
Herder, Librería (Spain) 376
Herder, Verlag, & Co (Austria) 28
Herder, Verlag, GmbH & Co KG (Federal Republic of Germany) 147
Herder & Co (Austria) 31
Herder AG (Switzerland) 397
Herder-Buchgemeinde (Federal Republic of Germany) 175
Herder Editrice e Libreria (Italy) 241
Herder und Herder GmbH (Federal Republic of Germany) 148
Hérédia Prize (International Literary Prizes) 519
Heretic Books (United Kingdom) 448
Heritage Books (Nigeria) 316
Heritage Books (Republic of Ireland) 223
Heritage Publishers (India) 201
Heritage Publishing House (Philippines) 332
Hermann (Editeurs des Sciences et des Arts) SA (France) 106
Hermes, Editions (France) 106
Hermes, Editorial, SA (Mexico) 285
Hermes Edizioni SRL (Italy) 241
Herne, Editions de l' (France) 106
Hernieuwen-Uitgaven PVBA (Belgium) 39
Hernovs Book Club (Denmark) 84
Hernovs Forlag (Denmark) 81
Herold Druck- und Verlagsgesellschaft mbH (Austria) 28
Herold Verlag Brück KG (Federal Republic of Germany) 148
Herrera, Casa (Dominican Republic) 87
Herrera, Febio (Dominican Republic) 87
Herrero, Editorial, SA (Mexico) 285
Hertenstein-Presse (Federal Republic of Germany) 148
Hertoghs, Drukkerij-Uitgeverij (Belgium) 39
Hertzog Prize (Republic of South Africa) 362
Herzmansky, Bernard (Austria) 28
Herzog August Bibliothek (Federal Republic of Germany) 176
Hessische Landes- und Hoch-schulbibliothek Darmstadt (Federal Republic of Germany) 176
Hessischer Verleger- und Buchhändler-Verband eV (Federal Republic of Germany) 129
Hestia Bookstore (Greece) 184
Hestia-Verlag GmbH (Federal Republic of Germany) 148
Heterodox (United Kingdom) 448
Heuff, Uitgeverij, Nieuwkoop (Netherlands) 297
Heureka, Uitgeverij (Netherlands) 297
Heures Claires, Editions d'Art Les, SA (France) 106
Heusden, Gérard Th Van, (APA) (Netherlands) 297
Heyden & Son Ltd (United Kingdom) 448
Heyer, The Historical Novel Prize in Memory of Georgette (International Literary Prizes) 519
Heymanns, Carl, Verlag KG (Federal Republic of Germany) 148
Heyn, Buchhandlung Johannes (Austria) 31
Heyn, Johannes (Austria) 28
Heyne, Wilhelm, Verlag (Federal Republic of Germany) 148
Heyum, Monica, Agency (Sweden) 388
Hichtum, Nienke van, Prize (Netherlands) 306
Hid Íslenzka bókmenntafélag (Iceland) 194
Hidakarya Agung (Indonesia) 218
Hiersemann, Anton, Verlag (Federal Republic of Germany) 148
Higginbothams Ltd (India) 213
High Council of Arts & Literature (Egypt) 90
Higham, David, Associates Ltd (United Kingdom) 479
Higham, David, Prize for Fiction (International Literary Prizes) 519
Higher Educational Books Publishing House (Democratic People's Republic of Korea) 268
Hikarinokuni Ltd (Japan) 257

Hilal, Dar Al, Publishing Institution (Egypt) 88
Hildur, Bókaútgáfan (Iceland) 193
Hilger, Adam, Ltd (United Kingdom) 448
Hilger, Edition E (Austria) 28
Hill, Leonard (United Kingdom) 448
Hill of Content Publishing Co Pty Ltd (Australia) 15
Hillelförlaget (Sweden) 384
Hilmarton Manor Press (United Kingdom) 448
Himachal Publishers' & Booksellers' Association (India) 195
Himalaya Publishing House (India) 201
Himalayan Books (India) 201
Himpunan Masyarakat Pencinta Buku (Indonesia) 218
Hind Pocket Books Private Ltd (India) 201
Hinder und Deelmann, Verlag (Federal Republic of Germany) 148
Hindi Book Centre (India) 213
Hindi Pracharak Sansthan (India) 201
Hindustan Publishing Corporation (India) (India) 201
Hinnenthal, Edition (Federal Republic of Germany) 148
Hinstorff, VEB, Verlag (German Democratic Republic) 125
Hinzelin, Emile, Foundation Prize (France) 120
Hiperión, Ediciones, SL (Spain) 368
Hippo Books (United Kingdom) 448
Hippokrates-Verlag GmbH (Federal Republic of Germany) 148
Hirmer Verlag (Federal Republic of Germany) 148
Hirokawa Publishing Co (Japan) 257
Hirsch, Axel, Prize (Sweden) 390
Hirsch, Carlos, SRL (Argentina) 8
Hirschgraben-Verlag GmbH (Federal Republic of Germany) 148
Hirschsprungs, H, Forlag (Denmark) 81
Hirt, Ferdinand, mbH & Co KG (Austria) 28
Hirzel, S, Verlag (German Democratic Republic) 125
Hirzel, S, Verlag GmbH und Co (Federal Republic of Germany) 148
Hispano Americana, Librería (Spain) 376
Hispano Europea, Editorial (Spain) 368
Hispanoamericana, Librería (Puerto Rico) 345
Hissink, G W, & Co (APA) (Netherlands) 297
Histoire Sociale, Editions d', (EDHIS) (France) 106
Historical Society, The, of Israel (Israel) 227
Historical Society of Afghanistan (Afghanistan) 1
History Guild (United Kingdom) 481
Hjemmenes Forlag A/S (Norway) 321
Hjemmet A/S (Norway) 321
Hjemmets Bokforlag A/S (Norway) 321
Hjemmets Bokklubb (Norway) 323
Hjemmets Kokebokklubb (Norway) 323
Hladbúd hf (Iceland) 193
Hlidskjálf, Bókaútgáfan (Iceland) 193
Hna Lon Hla (Burma) 62
Hobbit Presse (Federal Republic of Germany) 148
Hobby, Editorial (Argentina) 5
Hobby Centre (Trinidad and Tobago) 413
Hobsons Publishing PLC (United Kingdom) 448
Hoch-Verlag (Federal Republic of Germany) 148
Hodder & Stoughton (Australia) Pty Ltd (Australia) 15
Hodder & Stoughton Ltd (New Zealand) 309
Hodder & Stoughton Ltd (United Kingdom) 448
Hodges Figgis & Co Ltd (Republic of Ireland) 224
Hoepli, Casa Editrice Libraria Ulrico, SpA (Italy) 241
Hoepli, Ulrico, Libreria Internazionale (Italy) 251
Hoernle, Volksbuchhandlung Edwin (German Democratic Republic) 127
Hofacker, Ing W, GmbH Verlag (Federal Republic of Germany) 148
Hofbauer, Buchhandlung Karl (Austria) 31
Hoffman, Agence (Federal Republic of Germany) 175
Hoffman, Agence (France) 116
Hoffmann, Dieter, Verlag (Federal Republic of Germany) 148
Hoffmann, Julius, Verlag (Federal Republic of Germany) 148
Hoffmann und Campe Verlag (Federal Republic of Germany) 148
Hofmann, Verlag Karl, GmbH & Co (Federal Republic of Germany) 148
Hofmeister, VEB Friedrich, Musikverlag (German Democratic Republic) 125
Hofmeyr, W A, Prize (Republic of South Africa) 362
Hogar del Libro — Nova Terra (Spain) 368
Hogar del Libro SA (Spain) 376
Hogarth, The, Press (United Kingdom) 449
Hogrefe, Dr C J (Switzerland) 397
Hogrefe, Verlag für Psychologie, Dr C J (Federal Republic of Germany) 149
Hohenloher Druck- und Verlagshaus (Federal Republic of Germany) 149
Hohenrain-Verlag GmbH (Federal Republic of Germany) 149
Hohenstaufen Verlag Schumann KG (Federal Republic of Germany) 149

Hôi Thu-Viên Viet Nam (Socialist Republic of Viet Nam) 495
Hoikusha Publishing Co Ltd (Japan) 257
Hökerbergs, Lars, Bokförlag (Sweden) 384
Hokkaido University Library (Japan) 263
Hokuryukan Co Ltd (Japan) 257
Hokuseido, The, Press (Japan) 257
Holberg Medal (Denmark) 86
Hölder-Pichler-Tempsky, Verlag (Austria) 28
Hole in the Bank Books (New Zealand) 309
Holgersson, Nils, Plaque (Sweden) 390
Holkema, Van, en Warendorf (Netherlands) 297
Hölker, Verlag Wolfgang (Federal Republic of Germany) 149
Holland (Netherlands) 297
Holland, The, Press (United Kingdom) 449
Holland University Press BV (APA) (Netherlands) 297
Hollandia, Uitgeverij, BV (Netherlands) 297
Holle Verlag GmbH (Federal Republic of Germany) 149
Höller und Zwick, Verlags-GmbH (Federal Republic of Germany) 149
Hollinek, Brüder, & Co GmbH (Austria) 28
Holloway, Tienie, Medal (Republic of South Africa) 362
Höllrigl, Eduard (Austria) 31
Holly, Jan, Prize (Czechoslovakia) 79
Hollym Corporation, Publishers (Republic of Korea) 269
Holmes, The Sherlock, Society of London (United Kingdom) 485
Holmes McDougall Ltd (United Kingdom) 449
Holon Literary Prize (Israel) 232
Holp Book Co Ltd (Japan) 257
Holsten Verlag Wolf Schenke KG (Federal Republic of Germany) 149
Holt, Rinehart & Winston (United Kingdom) 449
Holtby, Winifred, Memorial Prize (United Kingdom) 487
Holte, Clarence L, Literary Prize (International Literary Prizes) 520
Holy Land Map Co Ltd (Israel) 227
Holzapfel, Verlag Gebr (Federal Republic of Germany) 149
Holzboog, Gunther, GmbH & Co (Federal Republic of Germany) 149
Holzmann, Hans, Verlag GmbH und Co KG (Federal Republic of Germany) 149
Home Computer Club (United Kingdom) 481
Home Health Education Service (United Kingdom) 449
Home Library Plan (India) 213
Hommes et Techniques, Editions (France) 107
Hone, Evelyn, College Library (Zambia) 503
Hong Kong Book Centre Ltd (Hong Kong) 189
Hong Kong Booksellers' & Stationers' Association (Hong Kong) 187
Hong Kong Cultural Press Ltd (Hong Kong) 188
Hong Kong Educational Publishers Association Ltd (Hong Kong) 187
Hong Kong Junior Chamber of Commerce Libraries (Hong Kong) 189
Hong Kong Library Association (Hong Kong) 189
Hong Kong Polytechnic Library (Hong Kong) 189
Hong Kong Publishers' & Distributors' Association (Hong Kong) 187
Hong Kong Publishing Co Ltd (Hong Kong) 188
Hong Kong University Press (Hong Kong) 188
Hoogenhout, C P, Award (Republic of South Africa) 362
Hoogt, Lucy B and C W van der, Prize (Netherlands) 306
Hoorick, Verlag Van (Switzerland) 397
Hor Samut Klang (Thailand) 410
Horay, Pierre, Editeur (France) 107
Horizon Bookshop Ltd (New Zealand) 312
Horizonte, Editorial (Peru) 330
Horizonte, Livros, Lda (Portugal) 341
Horizontes, Editora, de América (Dominican Republic) 86
Hörnemann, Werner, Verlag (Federal Republic of Germany) 149
Horseman's Handbooks (United Kingdom) 449
Horst-Werner Dumjahn Verlag (Federal Republic of Germany) 149
Horstink, De (Netherlands) 297
Horwitz Grahame Pty Ltd (Australia) 15
Horwood, Ellis, Ltd (United Kingdom) 449
'Horyzonty', Wydawnictwo Harcerskie (Poland) 335
Høst & Søns Forlag (Denmark) 82
Houghton, Roger, Ltd (United Kingdom) 449
Hour-Glass Press (United Kingdom) 449
Hove, M van, DPN (Belgium) 39
Høvring's, Birgitte, Icelandic World Literature (Denmark) 82
How & Why Books (United Kingdom) 449
Howard Book Co (Hong Kong) 189
Hraundragni Book Club (Iceland) 194

Hrvatska Revija (Spain) 369
Hrvatsko bibliotekarsko društvo (Yugoslavia) 500
Hua Kuo Publishing Co (Taiwan) 408
Huber, Hans (Switzerland) 405
Huber & Co AG, Verlag (Switzerland) 397
Huber AG, Hans (Switzerland) 397
Hucha de Oro Prize (Spain) 378
Hucha de Plata Prizes (Spain) 378
Huddlesford (United Kingdom) 449
Hudson, Angus (United Kingdom) 449
Hudsons Bookshops (United Kingdom) 482
Huemul, Editorial, SA (Argentina) 5
Huemul, Librería, SA (Argentina) 5
Huemul, Librería, SA (Argentina) 8
Huet, Busken, Prize (Netherlands) 306
Hugendubel, Heinrich (Federal Republic of Germany) 175
Hugo, The, Awards (International Literary Prizes) 520
Hugo's Language Books Ltd (United Kingdom) 449
Hugues, Clovis, Prize (France) 120
Hulton Educational Publications Ltd (United Kingdom) 449
Human & Rousseau (Pty) Ltd (Republic of South Africa) 356
Human Horizons Series (United Kingdom) 449
Humanitas, Editorial (Argentina) 5
Humanoïdes, Les, Associés (France) 107
Humboldt, Volksbuchhandlung Alexander von (German Democratic Republic) 127
Humboldt-Buchhandlung (German Democratic Republic) 127
Humboldt-Taschenbuchverlag Jacobi KG (Federal Republic of Germany) 149
Humboldt Universität zu Berlin (German Democratic Republic) 127
Hundertmark, Edition (Federal Republic of Germany) 149
Hune, Librairie La (France) 116
Hung Fung Book Co (Hong Kong) 188
Hunt Bartlett, Alice, Prize (International Literary Prizes) 520
Hür Yayin ve Ticaret (Turkey) 415
Hürriyet Yayinlari (Hür Yayin) (Turkey) 415
Hurst, C, & Co (Publishers) Ltd (United Kingdom) 449
Husain, Dr Mahmud, Library (Pakistan) 327
Husum Druck- und Verlagsgesellschaft mbH & Co KG (Federal Republic of Germany) 149
Hutchinson (United Kingdom) 449
Hutchinson Books Ltd (United Kingdom) 449
Hutchinson Business Books (United Kingdom) 449
Hutchinson Children's Books Ltd (United Kingdom) 449
Hutchinson Education (United Kingdom) 449
Hutchinson Group (NZ) Ltd (New Zealand) 309
Hutchinson Group (SA) (Pty) Ltd (Republic of South Africa) 356
Hutchinson Publishing Group, The, Ltd (United Kingdom) 449
Hutchinson Publishing Group (Australia) Ltd (Australia) 15
Hutchinson Technical Books (United Kingdom) 449
Hutchinson University Library (United Kingdom) 449
Hüthig, Dr Alfred, Verlag GmbH (Federal Republic of Germany) 149
Hüthig und Pflaum Verlag GmbH & Co KG (Federal Republic of Germany) 149
Hüthig und Wepf Verlag (Switzerland) 397
Hutten, Ulrich v, Volksbuchhandlung (German Democratic Republic) 127
Huygens, Constantijn, Prize (Netherlands) 306
Hviezdoslavova knižnica (Czechoslovakia) 78
Hwimoon Publishing Co (Republic of Korea) 269
Hyang Mun Publishing Co (Republic of Korea) 269
Hyland House Publishing Pty Ltd (Australia) 15
Hylton Lacy Publishers (United Kingdom) 449
Hymns Ancient & Modern (United Kingdom) 449
Hymsa, Ediciones (Spain) 369
Hyoronsha Publishing Co Ltd (Japan) 257
Hyun Am Publishing Co (Republic of Korea) 269
Hyvän Sanoman Kirjat (Finland) 94

I B A M (Brazil) 53
I B B Y (International Organizations) 508
I B C — International Book Creation SA (Spain) 369
I B D (India) 202
I B E P (Brazil) 53
I B H (India) 202
I B I C T (Brazil) 53
I B I S (United Kingdom) 422
I B I S Information Services Ltd (Australia) 10
I B R A (Ghana) 181
I B R A S A (Instituição Brasileira de Difusão Cultural Ltda) (Brazil) 53
I B R E X — Distribuidora de Livros e Material de Escritório Ltda (Brazil) 58
I C A-Förlaget AB (Sweden) 384
I C C E, Publicaciones (Spain) 369
I C I C (Directory Publishers) Ltd (Nigeria) 316
I C I Writer's Bursary (New Zealand) 313
I C Magazines Ltd (United Kingdom) 449
I C S A Publishing Ltd (United Kingdom) 449
I C S Izdavačko Informativni Centar Studenata (Yugoslavia) 496
I C U, NV, (Informatie en Communicatie Unie NV) (Netherlands) 298
I D E P (Senegal) 349
I D W-Verlag GmbH (Federal Republic of Germany) 149
I E Aust Publications (Australia) 15
I F L A (International Organizations) 508
I G A, Distribuidora Cultural, Bookstore (Guatemala) 186
I G N (Institut Géographique National) (France) 107
I L A (International Literary Agency) (Italy) 251
I L S (Institut für Lernsysteme) GmbH (Federal Republic of Germany) 149
I M S F (Federal Republic of Germany) 149
I N A D E S — Édition (Institut africain pour le développement économique et social) (Ivory Coast) 253
I N A D E S (Institut africain pour le Développement économique et social) Documentation (Ivory Coast) 254
I N B E L (Belgium) 39
I N F E L (Informationsstelle für Elektrizitätsanwendung) (Switzerland) 397
I N I D (Romania) 347
I N S E R M, Editions (France) 107
I O P Publishing Ltd (United Kingdom) 449
I O R T (Imprimerie Officielle de la République Tunisienne) (Tunisia) 414
I P E A (Instituto de Planejamento Econômico e Social) Servicio Editorial (Brazil) 53
I P L (Istituto Propaganda Libraria) (Italy) 232
I P M C International (Netherlands) 306
I P M C Ltd (United Kingdom) 490
I R L Press (United Kingdom) 449
I R R I (Philippines) 332
I S A E C (Brazil) 53
I S B N, Bureau (Netherlands) 292
I S B N (International Organizations) 508
I S P C K (India) 202
I S P-Verlag (Internationale Sozialistische Publikationen) (Federal Republic of Germany) 149
I S S N (International Organizations) 508
I-Spy Club (United Kingdom) 481
I T A U, Edições, (Instituto Tecnico de Alimentação Humana) Lda (Portugal) 341
I T K Läromedel (Sweden) 384
I T Publications (United Kingdom) 449
I T V Books (United Kingdom) 450
I V I O, Stichting (Netherlands) 298
Ibadan University Library (Nigeria) 319
Ibadan University Press (Nigeria) 316
Ibana, SA (Uruguay) 491
Ibérico Europea de Ediciones SA (Spain) 369
Ibero-Americano, Livro, Ltda (Brazil) 53
Ibero-Americano, Livro, Ltda (Brazil) 58
Ibero-Amerikanisches Institut Preussischer Kulturbesitz (Federal Republic of Germany) 176
Ibis (Denmark) 82
Icaria Editorial SA (Spain) 369
Iceland Review (Iceland) 193
Icelandic Cultural Fund, Publishing Department (Iceland) 193
Icelandic Libertarians', The, Book Club (Iceland) 194
Icelandic Libertarians', The, Bookshop (Iceland) 194
Ichtiar Baru — van Hoeve (Indonesia) 218
Icob cv (Netherlands) 298
Icob cv (Netherlands) 304
Icthus, Librería (Bolivia) 48
Idara-e-Faroghe-Undu (Pakistan) 325
Idara Siqafat-e-Islamia (Pakistan) 325
Idarah Fikre Jadeed (India) 202
Idarah-I-Adabiyat-I-Delli (India) 202
Idea Books (Italy) 241
Idea Verlag GmbH (Federal Republic of Germany) 149
Ideal (Malta) 281
Ideal, The, Bookshop (Malta) 282
Idéförlaget (Sweden) 385
Idelson, Casa Editrice Libraria, di G Gnocchi (Italy) 241
Ideoplastos (Suriname) 380
Ides et Calendes, Editions, SA (Switzerland) 397
Idunn (Iceland) 193
Ie-No-Hikari Association (Japan) 257
Ife Book Fair Prizes (Nigeria) 319
Igaku-Shoin Ltd (Japan) 257
Igbo Language Translation Agency (Nigeria) 320

Ikaros Ekdotiki (Greece) 183
Ikatan Penerbit Indonesia (IKAPI) (Indonesia) 216
Ikatan Pustakawan Indonesia (Indonesia) 219
Ikhwan, PD & I (Indonesia) 218
Ikubundo Publishers Co (Japan) 263
Il Cerchio, Edizioni (Italy) 241
Il Cho Kak (Republic of Korea) 269
Il Ji Sa Publishing Co (Republic of Korea) 269
Il Quadrante SRL (Italy) 241
Ila — Palma (Italy) 241
Ilesanmi Press (Educational Publishers) Ltd (Nigeria) 316
Ilidio da Fonseca Matos (Portugal) 343
Illustration, Editions de l' (France) 107
Ilm, Dar el-, Lilmalayin (Lebanon) 272
Ilmi Kitab Khana (Pakistan) 325
Image (United Kingdom) 450
Imba Verlag (Switzerland) 397
Imediex SA (Costa Rica) 72
Imhoff, Hans (Federal Republic of Germany) 149
Immel Publishing (United Kingdom) 450
Impala, Editions (Zaire) 502
Imparudi (Imprimerie et Papeterie du Burundi) (Burundi) 63
Imperial News Agency and Bookshop (Gibraltar) 182
Imprensa Nacional-Casa da Moeda (Portugal) 341
Impressum Verlag AG (Switzerland) 397
Imprimerie, A l', Quotidienne (France) 107
Imprimerie Commerciale et Administrative de Mauritanie (Mauritania) 282
Imprimerie de Kabgayi (Rwanda) 348
In, Uitgeverij J van (Belgium) 39
In den Toren, Uitgeverij (Netherlands) 298
Inba Nilayam (India) 202
Inbal Travel Information (1983) Ltd (Israel) 227
Inca, Promotion Editorial, SA (Peru) 330
Incafo, Editorial, SA (Spain) 369
Independent Publishers Guild (United Kingdom) 422
Independent Television Books Ltd (United Kingdom) 450
Index, Editorial, (Tormes SL) (Spain) 369
Index eV (Federal Republic of Germany) 149
India Book House (India) 213
India Book House Pvt Ltd (India) 202
India Office Library and Records (United Kingdom) 482
Indian Association of Academic Librarians (India) 214
Indian Association of Special Libraries and Information Centres (India) 214
Indian Books Centre (India) 202
Indian Books Centre Oriental Studies Award (India) 215
Indian College Library Association (India) 214
Indian Council for Cultural Relations (India) 202
Indian Council of Agricultural Research (India) 202
Indian Council of Medical Research (India) 202
Indian Council of Social Science Research (ICSSR) (India) 202
Indian Council of World Affairs Library (India) 214
Indian Documentation Service (India) 202
Indian Folklore Society (India) 202
Indian Folklore Society (India) 215
Indian Institute of Advanced Study (India) 202
Indian Institute of Technology Central Library (India) 214
Indian Institute of World Culture (India) 202
Indian Library Association (India) 214
Indian Museum (India) 202
Indian National Academy of Letters Awards (India) 215
Indian National Scientific Documentation Centre (India) 216
Indian Press (Publications) Pvt Ltd (India) 202
Indian Printing and Publishing Co (Fiji) 91
Indian Publications (India) 202
Indian Publishing House (India) 202
Indian Society for Promoting Christian Knowledge (ISPCK) (India) 202
Indira, PT (Indonesia) 218
Indira, PT (Indonesia) 219
Indonesian ISBN Agency (Indonesia) 217
Indrajaya (Indonesia) 218
Industrial Publishing House (Democratic People's Republic of Korea) 268
Industrielle Organisation, Verlag (Switzerland) 397
Industrielle Rettsvern, Styret for det, Bibliotek (Norway) 323
Industry & Trade Publishers (Philippines) 332
Infoboek (Belgium) 39
Infopers (Netherlands) 298
Información, La (Dominican Republic) 86
Information Office for Norwegian Literature Abroad (Norway) 324
Information Processing Association of Israel (Israel) 231
Informations Forlag ApS (Denmark) 82

Informations-Zentrum Buch (Federal Republic of Germany) 129
Informationsförlaget (Sweden) 385
Informationsstelle für Elektrizitätsanwendung (Switzerland) 397
Informator (Yugoslavia) 496
Ingeniero, Librería del (Colombia) 71
Ingenjörsförlaget AB (Sweden) 385
Ingenjörsvetenskapsakademien (I V A) (Sweden) 385
Initial Teaching, The, Alphabet Foundation (United Kingdom) 450
Inkata Press Pty Ltd (Australia) 15
Inkilâp Kitabevi Yayin Sanayii ve Ticaret AS (Turkey) 415
Inland Bookshop (Tanzania) 409
Inland Publishers (Tanzania) 409
Inn-Verlag (Austria) 28
Innkaupasamband Bóksala HF (Iceland) 193
Innocenti, Editrice, SNC (Italy) 241
Innovacion, Editorial, SA (Mexico) 285
Inquérito, Editorial, Lda (Portugal) 342
Insel Verlag (Federal Republic of Germany) 149
Insel-Verlag Anton Kippenberg (German Democratic Republic) 125
Insight Chronicles, The (Republic of Singapore) 351
Insight Guides (Republic of Singapore) 351
Instant, Editions l', Durable (Soprep) (France) 107
Instituçao Brasileira de Difusão Cultural Ltda (Brazil) 53
Institut, Bibliothèque de l', Français d'Archéologie du Proche Orient (Lebanon) 273
Institut, Bibliothèque de l', supérieur d'Education et de Formation continue (Tunisia) 414
Institut, Perpustakaan Pusat, Teknologi Bandung (Indonesia) 219
Institut africain de Développement Economique et de Planification (IDEP), Bibliothèque (Senegal) 349
Institut belge d'Information et de Documentation (INBEL) (Belgium) 39
Institut Culturel Français Bibliothèque (Libya) 275
Institut Dagang Muchtar (Indonesia) 218
Institut Danois des Echanges Internationaux de Publications (IDE) (Denmark) 84
Institut de Bibliothéconomie et des Sciences documentaires (Algeria) 2
Institut de France, Bibliotheque de l' (France) 117
Institut de France (France) 120
Institut de recherche en Sciences humaines (Niger) 314
Institut des Belles Lettres arabes (Tunisia) 414
Institut d'etudes politiques et de l'information, Bibliothèque (Algeria) 2
Institut d'Etudes Slaves (France) 107
Institut fondamental d'Afrique noire, Bibliothèque (Senegal) 349
Institut français de Recherche Scientifique pour le Developpement en Cooperation (French Guiana) 122
Institut français d'Etudes arabes de Damas (Syria) 407
Institut für Lernsysteme (ILS) (Federal Republic of Germany) 149
Institut für Marxistische Studien und Forschungen eV (IMSF) (Federal Republic of Germany) 149
Institut Géographique National (France) 107
Institut Murundi d'Information et de Documentation (IMIDOC) (Burundi) 63
Institut national, Bibliothèque de l', de la recherche scientifique (Rwanda) 348
Institut national, Librairie de l', d'Etudes politiques (Zaire) 502
Institut national agronomique, Bibliothèque (Algeria) 2
Institut national de la Langue française (France) 107
Institut national de la statistique et de la recherche économique (Democratic Republic of Madagascar) 277
Institut national de Recherche Pedagogique (France) 107
Institut national pour la formation et la recherche en éducation (Centre de documentation et d'information pédagogique) (Benin) 47
Institut Panafricain pour le Developpement (IPD) (International Organizations) 513
Institut Pasteur d'Algérie, Bibliothèque (Algeria) 2
Institut pédagogique national (Zaire) 502
Institut polytechnique de Conakry Bibliothèque (Guinea) 186
Institut polytechnique de l'Afrique centrale Bibliothèque (Republic of Gabon) 122
Institut pour la recherche scientifique en Afrique centrale, Bibliothèque (Zaire) 502
Institut royal des Relations internationales (Belgium) 39
Institut royal des Sciences naturelles de Belgique, Bibliothèque (Belgium) 44
Institut scientifique chérifien (Morocco) 291

Institut supérieur des sciences de l'éducation, Bibliothèque (Popular Republic of Congo) 72
Institut Universitaire de Hautes Etudes Internationales (Switzerland) 397
Institute, The, for the Translation of Hebrew Literature (Israel) 225
Institute, The, for the Translation of Hebrew Literature (Israel) 232
Institute for Christian Publishing & Communications Research (India) 202
Institute for Palestine Studies, Publishing and Research Organization (Lebanon) 273
Institute for Publishing Hebrew Books (Israel) 227
Institute for Reformational Studies (Republic of South Africa) 356
Institute for Scientific and Technical Documentation and Information (Yugoslavia) 500
Institute for the Talmudic Encyclopaedia and Complete Israeli Talmud (Israel) 227
Institute for the Translation, The, of Hebrew Literature (Israel) 227
Institute of African Studies (Nigeria) 316
Institute of African Studies (Zambia) 503
Institute of African Studies Library (Ghana) 181
Institute of Arab Research & Studies Library (Egypt) 89
Institute of Development Management Library (Tanzania) 409
Institute of Development Studies (United Kingdom) 450
Institute of Economics Library (Burma) 62
Institute of Education Library (Burma) 62
Institute of Education Library, Kabul University (Afghanistan) 1
Institute of Education, University of London (United Kingdom) 450
Institute of Ethiopian Studies Library (Ethiopia) 91
Institute of Information Scientists (United Kingdom) 483
Institute of Jamaica Publications (Jamaica) 254
Institute of Personnel Management (United Kingdom) 450
Institute of Physics (United Kingdom) 450
Institute of Public Administration (Republic of Ireland) 223
Institute of Public Administration Library (Saudi Arabia) 348
Institute of Pyramidology (United Kingdom) 450
Institute of Reprographic Technology (United Kingdom) 483
Institute of Southeast Asian Studies (Republic of Singapore) 351
Institute of Technology, Rangoon, Library (Burma) 62
Institute of Translation and Interpreting (United Kingdom) 490
Institution of Chemical Engineers (United Kingdom) 450
Institution of Civil, The, Engineers (Publications Division) (United Kingdom) 450
Institution of Electrical Engineers (United Kingdom) 450
Institution of Mechanical Engineers (United Kingdom) 450
Instituto, Biblioteca del, Chileno-Británico de Cultura (Chile) 66
Instituto Anglo-Mexicano de Cultura, Biblioteca del (Mexico) 288
Instituto Autónomo Biblioteca Nacional y de Servicios de Bibliotecas (Venezuela) 493
Instituto Bibliográfico Hispánico (Spain) 377
Instituto Brasileiro de Administraçao Municipal (IBAM) (Brazil) 53
Instituto Brasileiro de Ediçôes Pedagógicas (IBEP) (Brazil) 53
Instituto Brasileiro de Geografia, Fundação, e Estatística (IBGE — CDDI/GECOM) (Brazil) 53
Instituto Brasileiro de Informação em Ciência e Tecnologia (IBICT) (Brazil) 53
Instituto Brasileiro de Informação em Ciência e Tecnologia (IBICT) (Brazil) 54
Instituto Campineiro de Ensino Agrícola (Brazil) 54
Instituto Centro Americano de Administración Pública (ICAP) (Costa Rica) 72
Instituto Cultural, Biblioteca del, Anglo-Uruguayo (Uruguay) 491
Instituto de Bibliografía del Ministerio de Educación de la Provincia de Buenos Aires (Argentina) 9
Instituto de Cooperacion, Biblioteca del, Iberoamericana (Spain) 376
Instituto de Cultura, Biblioteca del, Hispànica (Spain) 376
Instituto de Cultura Puertorriqueña (Puerto Rico) 345
Instituto de Estudios de Administración Local, Publicaciones (Spain) 369
Instituto de Estudios Peruanos (Peru) 330
Instituto de Estudios Politicos (Spain) 369
Instituto de Investigaciones Bibliográficas (Mexico) 289

Instituto de Investigaciones Sociales — Universidad Nacional Autónoma de Mexico (Mexico) 285
Instituto de Literatura (Argentina) 9
Instituto de Literatura, Biblioteca del, y Linguistica (Cuba) 74
Instituto de Planejamento Econômico e Social (Brazil) 54
Instituto de Publicaciones Navales (Argentina) 5
Instituto del Libro (Costa Rica) 72
Instituto Indigenista Interamericano (Mexico) 285
Instituto Interamericano de Cooperación para la Agricultura (IICA) (Costa Rica) 72
Instituto Mexicano del Libro AC (Mexico) 283
Instituto Nacional, Biblioteca del, del Libro Español (Spain) 376
Instituto Nacional, Ediciones, de Cultura (Panama) 328
Instituto Nacional de Antropologia e Historia (Mexico) 285
Instituto Nacional de Bellas Artes (Mexico) 285
Instituto nacional de Geologia (Centro de Documentação) (Mozambique) 291
Instituto Nacional del Libro Español (Spain) 363
Instituto Nacional do Livro (Brazil) 49
Instituto Nacional do Livro e do Disco (Mozambique) 291
Instituto Panamericano de Geografia, Biblioteca del, e Historia (Mexico) 288
Instituto Panamericano de Geografía e Historia (Mexico) 285
Instituto Português da Sociedade Cientifica de Goerres (Portugal) 344
Instituto Português do Livro e da Leitura (Portugal) 339
Instituto Pre-universitario, Biblioteca del, de la Habana (Cuba) 74
Instituto Tecnico de Alimentaçao Humana (Portugal) 342
Instituto Tecnológico, Biblioteca del, y de Estudios Superiores de Monterrey (Mexico) 289
Instituts für Weltwirtschaft, Bibliothek des, — Zentralbibliothek der Wirtschaftswissenschaften (Federal Republic of Germany) 176
Institutul de medicina si farmacie Biblioteca Centrala (Romania) 347
Institutul National de Informare si Documentare (INID) (Romania) 347
Institutului Politehnic, Biblioteca, Bucuresti (Romania) 347
Instytut, Państwowy, Wydawniczy (Poland) 335
Instytut Badań Literackich (Poland) 339
Instytut Bibliograficzny Biblioteki Narodowej (Poland) 338
Insula, Librería, Ediciones y Publicaciones SA (Spain) 369
Insula, Librería, Ediciones y Publicaciones SA (Spain) 376
Intellectual Publishing House (India) 202
Inter American University of Puerto Rico Library (Puerto Rico) 345
Inter Documentation Co AG (Switzerland) 397
Inter-India Publications (India) 202
Inter-Kunst und Buch GmbH (Federal Republic of Germany) 150
Inter Library Resources Centre (India) 214
Inter-Médica, Editorial, SAICI (Argentina) 5
Inter-Varsity Press (United Kingdom) 450
Interacadémica, Librería, SA de CV (Mexico) 288
Interallié Prize (France) 120
Interamericana de Venezuela, Editorial, CA (Venezuela) 493
Interavia SA (Switzerland) 397
Interbac (Australia) 15
Interbankendienst, Uitgaven van, NV (Belgium) 40
Interbooks (Belgium) 40
Interciência, Livraria, Ltda (Brazil) 54
Intercontinental Literary Agency (United Kingdom) 479
InterEditions Paris (France) 107
Interessengemeinschaft österreichischer Autoren (Austria) 25
Interfrom, Edition (Switzerland) 397
Intergéo, CNRS Laboratoire (France) 107
Intergovernmental Copyright Committee (International Organizations) 508
Interkerklike Uitgewerstrust (Republic of South Africa) 356
Intermediate Technology Publications Ltd (United Kingdom) 450
Intermedium (Netherlands) 298
Internationaal Instituut, Bibliotheek van het, voor Sociale Geschiedenis (Netherlands) 305
International African Institute (International Organizations) 513
International Association for Mass Communication Research (International Organizations) 508
International Association of Agricultural Librarians and Documentalists (IAALD) (International Organizations) 508

INDEX 565

International Association of Law Libraries (IALL) (International Organizations) 508
International Association of Literary Critics (International Organizations) 508
International Association of Metropolitan City Libraries (INTAMEL) (International Organizations) 508
International Association of Music Libraries, Archives and Documentation Centres, Australian Branch (Australia) 22
International Association of Music Libraries, Archives and Documentation Centres (IAML) (International Organizations) 508
International Association of Music Libraries, Archives and Documentation Centres, (UK Branch) (United Kingdom) 483
International Association of Music Libraries, New Zealand Branch, Inc (New Zealand) 312
International Association of Orientalist Librarians (International Organizations) 509
International Association of Scholarly Publishers (IASP) (International Organizations) 509
International Association of School Librarianship (International Organizations) 509
International Association of Sound Archives (IASA) (International Organizations) 513
International Atomic Energy Agency (IAEA) (International Organizations) 511
International Bible Reading Association (United Kingdom) 450
International Biographical Centre (United Kingdom) 450
International Board on Books for Young People (IBBY) (International Organizations) 509
International Book Distributors (India) 203
International Book Distributors Co Ltd (Thailand) 411
International Book House Pvt Ltd (India) 213
International Book Information Services (United Kingdom) 422
International Book Promotion (France) 107
International Book Service (Malaysia) 279
International Book Traders (India) 213
International Booksellers Federation (IBF) (International Organizations) 509
International Bookshop (Tanzania) 409
International Bookshop, The (Iceland) 194
International Bureau of Education (IBE) (International Organizations) 511
International Center for the Registration of Serials (International Organizations) 509
International Children's Book Service (Denmark) 84
International Communication Agency Library (Liberia) 274
International Communication Agency Library (Republic of Korea) 271
International Communications (United Kingdom) 450
International Comparative Literature Association (International Organizations) 509
International Confederation of Societies of Authors and Composers (International Organizations) 509
International Copyright Union for the Protection of Literary and Artistic Works (International Organizations) 509
International Council of Theological Library Associations (International Organizations) 509
International Council on Archives (International Organizations) 509
International Documentary, The, Centre of Arab Manuscripts (Lebanon) 273
International Editors' Co (Argentina) 8
International Editors' Co SA (Spain) 375
International Federation for Documentation (FID) (International Organizations) 509
International Federation for Information Processing (IFIP) (International Organizations) 509
International Federation for Modern Languages and Literatures (International Organizations) 509
International Federation of Film Archives (International Organizations) 509
International Federation of Library Associations and Institutions (IFLA) (International Organizations) 509
International Federation of Library Associations and Institutions (IFLA) (Netherlands) 305
International Fiction Association (International Organizations) 509
International French Friendship Prize (International Literary Prizes) 520
International Grand Prize for Poetry (International Literary Prizes) 520
International Group of Scientific, Technical and Medical Publishers (STM) (International Organizations) 509
International Institute for Children's Literature and Reading Research (UNESCO category C) (International Organizations) 509
International Institute for Educational Planning (IIEP) (International Organizations) 511
International Institute for Strategic Studies (United Kingdom) 450
International Institute of Advanced Buddhistic Studies Library (Burma) 62
International Institute of Iberoamerican Literature (International Organizations) 509
International Institute of Tropical Agriculture Library (Nigeria) 319
International Labour Office, Central Library and Documentation Branch (Switzerland) 406
International Labour Organisation (ILO) (International Organizations) 511
International League of Antiquarian Booksellers (ILAB) (International Organizations) 509
International Literatuur Bureau BV (Netherlands) 304
International Maritime Organization (IMO) (International Organizations) 511
International Miniature Book, The, Society (Yugoslavia) 496
International Monetary Fund (International Organizations) 513
International Nursing, The, Foundation of Japan (Japan) 257
International Press, The, Agency (Pty) Ltd (Republic of South Africa) 359
International Progressive Books and Periodicals (Nepal) 292
International Publications Cultural Award (International Literary Prizes) 520
International Publishers Association (IPA) (International Organizations) 509
International Reading Association (International Organizations) 509
International Rice Research Institute (IRRI) (Philippines) 332
International Science Services (Israel) 227
International Scientific Film Library (ISFL) (International Organizations) 509
International Serials Data System (International Organizations) 510
International Society for Educational Information Inc (Japan) 257
International Standard Book Number Agency (International Organizations) 510
International Standards Books and Periodicals (P) Ltd (Nepal) 292
International Study Group of Restorers of Archives, Libraries and Graphic Reproductions (International Organizations) 510
International Telecommunication Union (ITU) (International Organizations) 511
International Textbook Co Ltd (United Kingdom) 450
International Translations Centre (ITC) (International Organizations) 510
International Union for Conservation of Nature and Natural Resources (IUCN) (International Organizations) 513
International Union of Geological Sciences (IUGS) (International Organizations) 513
International Writers Workshop New Zealand (Inc) (New Zealand) 312
Internationale Buchhändler-Vereinigung (IBV) (International Organizations) 510
Internationale Jugendbibliothek (IJB) (International Organizations) 510
Internationale Presse, Import- und Export GmbH (Federal Republic of Germany) 176
Internationale Solidarität, Verlag, Verlagsgesellschaft mbH (Federal Republic of Germany) 150
Internationale Vereinigung der Musikbibliotheken (Federal Republic of Germany) 177
Internationale Vereinigung katholischer Verleger und Buchhändler (International Organizations) 510
Internationales Landkartenhaus, Geo Center GmbH (Federal Republic of Germany) 150
'Interpress', Wydawnictwo (Poland) 335
Interpresse, A/S (Denmark) 82
Interprint (India) 203
Interpublishing AB Stenström (Sweden) 385
Intersistemas SA de CV (Mexico) 286
InterSkrift/Harriers Publishing House (Sweden) 385
Intertrade Publications (India) Pvt Ltd (India) 203
Invader Ltd (United Kingdom) 450
Invandrarförlaget (Sweden) 385
Inversiones Editoriales La Carreta (Colombia) 69
Iolaire Arts Association (United Kingdom) 485
Iolaire Arts Open Poetry Competition (United Kingdom) 487
Iolaire Selection (United Kingdom) 450
Iranian Documentation Centre (IRANDOC) (Iran) 220
Iraq Library Association (Iraq) 221
Iraq Museum, Library of the (Iraq) 220
Iraq Natural History, Library of the, Research Centre and Museum (Iraq) 221
Irini Publishing House — Vassilis G Katsikeas Ltd (Greece) 183
Iris SA (Peru) 330
Iris Verlag AG (Switzerland) 397
Irish Academic Press (Republic of Ireland) 223
Irish Academy of Letters (Republic of Ireland) 225
Irish American Cultural Institute Literary Awards (International Literary Prizes) 520
Irish Books Marketing Group (Republic of Ireland) 221
Irish Educational Publishers' Association (Republic of Ireland) 221
Irish Heritage Series (Republic of Ireland) 223
Irish Management Institute (Republic of Ireland) 223
Irish Poetry Award (International Literary Prizes) 520
Irish Society for Archives (Republic of Ireland) 224
Irish Times, The, Ltd (Republic of Ireland) 223
Irish University Press (Republic of Ireland) 223
Ísafoldar, Bókaverzlun (Iceland) 194
Ísafoldarprentsmidja hf (Iceland) 193
Iselt und Co Nfl mbH (Federal Republic of Germany) 150
Ishiyaku Publishers Inc (Japan) 257
Isis Large Print (United Kingdom) 450
Iskra, Editrice (Italy) 241
'Iskry', Państwowe Wydawnictwo (Poland) 335
Iskusstvo, Izdatelstvo (Union of Soviet Socialist Republics) 418
Isla Negra SA (Chile) 65
Islam, Perpustakaan (Indonesia) 219
Islami Kitab Khana (Pakistan) 325
Islamic Book Centre (Pakistan) 325
Islamic Cultural Bookshop (Bahrain) 34
Islamic Culture, Institute of (Pakistan) 325
Islamic Foundation, The (United Kingdom) 450
Islamic Publications Bureau (Nigeria) 316
Islamic Publications (Private) Ltd (Pakistan) 325
Islamic Research Institute (Pakistan) 325
Islamic Research Institute Library (Pakistan) 327
Islamic University Library (Saudi Arabia) 348
Islamiyah (Indonesia) 218
Island, The, Shop (Bahamas) 34
Island Press (Australia) 15
Íslenzka Bókmenntafélag, Hid (Iceland) 193
Isper Club (Italy) 251
Isper SRL (Italy) 241
Israbook (Israel) 231
Israel, B M, BV (Netherlands) 298
Israel, Nico (Netherlands) 298
Israel Academy, The, of Sciences & Humanities (Israel) 227
Israel Exploration Society (Israel) 227
Israel I S B N Group Agency (Israel) 225
Israel Library Association (Israel) 231
Israel Program for Scientific Translations (Israel) 227
Israel Society of Special Libraries and Information Centres (ISLIC) (Israel) 231
Israel State Archives (Israel) 231
Israel Universities Press (Israel) 228
Israel Yearbook Publications Ltd (Israel) 228
Israeli Music Publications Ltd (Israel) 228
Israeli Prize in Humanities and Social Sciences (Israel) 232
Israeli Prize in Jewish Studies, Hebrew Literature and Education (Israel) 232
Israeli Prize in the Arts (Israel) 232
Istanbul Üniversitesi Merkez Kütüphanesi (Turkey) 415
Istituto Centrale di Statistica (Italy) 241
Istituto Centrale per il Catalogo Unico delle Biblioteche Italiane e per le Informazioni Bibliografiche (Italy) 241
Istituto Centrale per il Catalogo Unico delle Biblioteche Italiane e per le Informazioni Bibliografiche (Italy) 252
Istituto Centrale per la Patologia del Libro (Italy) 252
Istituto della Enciclopedia Italiana (Italy) 241
Istituto della Santa, Casa Editrice (Italy) 241
Istituto Editoriale Ticinese (IET) SA (Switzerland) 397
Istituto Geografico de Agostini SpA (Italy) 241
Istituto Grafologico (Italy) 241
Istituto Idrografico della Marina (Italy) 241
Istituto Lombardo Accademia di Scienze e Lettere (Italy) 253
Istituto Nazionale di Studi Romani (Italy) 241
Istituto Padano, Casa Editrice, di Arti Grafiche (Italy) 242
Istituto per l'Enciclopedia del Friuli Venezia Giulia (Italy) 242
Istituto Poligrafico e Zecca dello Stato (Italy) 242
Istituto Storico Italiano per l'Età Moderna e Contemporanea (Italy) 242
Istmo, Ediciones (Spain) 369
Italian Book Club (United Kingdom) 481
Italscambi, Editrice (Italy) 242
Ittihad, Al, Bookstore (Egypt) 89
Iwanami Shoten (Japan) 258
Iwasaki Publishing Co Ltd (Japan) 258
Izmir General Library (Turkey) 415
Izreel Publishing House Ltd (Israel) 228
Iztaccihuatl, Editorial, SA (Mexico) 286

566 INDEX

Izvestiya Publishing House (Union of Soviet Socialist Republics) 418

J B, Taller Ediciones (Spain) 369
J K Export House (India) 213
J K Publishers (United Kingdom) 451
J N M Publications (United Kingdom) 451
J P L (New Caledonia) 307
J R Editores (Colombia) 69
J R O-Kartografische Verlagsgesellschaft mbH (Federal Republic of Germany) 150
J S O T Press (United Kingdom) 451
J U R I F Belgique (Belgium) 40
Jabatan Penerbitan Universiti Malaya (Malaysia) 279
Jaca, Editoriale, Book (Italy) 242
Jacaranda Wiley Ltd (Australia) 15
Jacaranda Wiley Ltd (New Zealand) 309
Jackson, Gruppo Editoriale, SpA (Italy) 242
Jacobi, Verlag, KG (Federal Republic of Germany) 150
Jaeger und Waldmann (Federal Republic of Germany) 150
Jafet, Nami C, Memorial Library (Lebanon) 273
Jaffe Books (India) 212
Jaffe Publishing Management Service (India) 212
Jager, De, — HAUM (Republic of South Africa) 356
Jaguar, Les Editions du (France) 107
Jahreszeitenverlag (Federal Republic of Germany) 150
J'ai Lu, Editions (France) 107
Jaico Publishing House (India) 203
Jaicos (India) 213
Jain Publishers, B, (P) Ltd (India) 203
Jain Publishing Co (India) 203
Jaipur Publishing House (India) 203
Jaisingh & Mehta Publishers Pvt Ltd (India) 203
Jakobsohn, Verlag Eduard (Federal Republic of Germany) 150
Jaktjournalens Bokklubb (Sweden) 388
Jamaica Archives (Jamaica) 255
Jamaica Library Association (Jamaica) 255
Jamaica Library Service (Jamaica) 255
Jamaica Publishing House Ltd (Jamaica) 254
James, Arthur, Ltd (United Kingdom) 451
Jamjoom & Bros, Mohamed Noor Salah (Saudi Arabia) 348
Jane's Publishing Company Ltd (United Kingdom) 451
Janin, Jules, Prize (France) 120
Janssen, Stern-Verlag, und Co (Federal Republic of Germany) 150
Janssens, J, PVBA (Belgium) 40
Janssens, Toneelfonds J, PVBA (Belgium) 44
Januka Pustak Bhandar (Nepal) 292
Janus, Editrice, SpA (Italy) 242
Japadre, L U, Editore (Italy) 242
Japan Book Importers Association (Japan) 255
Japan Book Publishers Association (Japan) 255
Japan Broadcast Publishing Co Ltd (Japan) 258
Japan Essayists' Club (Japan) 264
Japan Essayists' Club Prize (Japan) 265
Japan Foreign Rights Centre (JFC) (Japan) 263
Japan I S B N Agency (Japan) 255
Japan Poet Club (Japan) 264
Japan Poet Club Prize (Japan) 265
Japan Poets' Association (Japan) 264
Japan Publications Inc (Japan) 258
Japan Publications Trading Co Ltd (Import and Export) (Japan) 263
Japan Scientific Societies Press (Japan) 258
Japan Society of Translators (Japan) 266
Japan Times, The (Japan) 258
Japan Translation Prize for Publisher (Japan) 265
Japan Travel Bureau Inc (Japan) 258
Japan U N I Agency Inc (Japan) 263
Japan Woman Writer Prize (Japan) 265
Japan Women Writers' Literary Prizes (Japan) 265
Jarrold Colour Publications (United Kingdom) 451
Javelin Paperbacks (United Kingdom) 451
Jay books (United Kingdom) 451
Jaya Baya, Yayasan (Indonesia) 218
Jaypee Brothers Medical Publishers (India) 203
Jazirah, Al, Organization for Press, Printing, Publishing (Saudi Arabia) 348
Jean-Charles, A (Martinique) 282
Jean-Christophe Prizes (France) 120
Jeanmaire, R, & Co (Switzerland) 398
Jedinstvo (Yugoslavia) 496
Jeng's Bookshop (The Gambia) 123
Jeongeumsa Publishing Co (Republic of Korea) 270
Jerusalem, The, Prize (International Literary Prizes) 520
Jerusalem City (Public) Library (Israel) 231
Jerusalem Publishing House Ltd (Israel) 228
Jespersen og Pios Forlag (Denmark) 82
Jet (United Kingdom) 451

Jeugd Salamander (Netherlands) 298
Jeune Afrique, Editions (France) 107
Jeune France Prize (France) 120
Jeunesse d'Afrique, Librairie (Burkina Faso) 62
Jewish Chronicle — Harold H Wingate Book Awards (International Literary Prizes) 520
Jewish Chronicle Publications (United Kingdom) 451
Jewish Interest Book Club (United Kingdom) 481
Jewish National and University Library (Israel) 231
Jims, Editorial, SA (Spain) 369
Jing Kung Book Store (Hong Kong) 189
Jing Kung Educational Press (Hong Kong) 188
Jnanada Prakashan (India) 203
Jnanpith, Bharatiya (India) 203
Jnanpith Literary Award (India) 215
Joannides, A, & Co (Cyprus) 74
Joerg, Wolfgang, und Erich Schoenig (Federal Republic of Germany) 150
Johannes Verlag (Switzerland) 398
Johannesburg Public Library (Republic of South Africa) 361
Johannesburgse Boekwinkel (Republic of South Africa) 360
Johns Hopkins, The, University Press (United Kingdom) 451
Johnson Publications Ltd (United Kingdom) 451
Johnson Reprint Co Ltd (United Kingdom) 451
Johnson Society of London (United Kingdom) 485
Johnston & Bacon (United Kingdom) 451
Johnston Green Publishing (UK) Ltd (United Kingdom) 451
Joho Kagaku Gijutsu Kyokai (Japan) 264
Joho Shori Gakkai (Japan) 264
Johore Central Store Sdn Bhd (Malaysia) 280
Joie, La, par les Livres (France) 118
Joint Board, The, of Christian Education of Australia and New Zealand (Australia) 15
Joint Board, The, of Christian Education of Australia and New Zealand (New Zealand) 309
Jonckheere, Tobie, Prize (Belgium) 46
Jonef Publications (Philippines) 332
Jonge Onderzoekers, Stichting De (Netherlands) 298
Jonsson, Snaebjörn, & Co hf (The English Bookshop) (Iceland) 193
Jordan & Sons Ltd (United Kingdom) 451
Jordan Book Centre Co Ltd (Jordan) 266
Jordan Distribution Agency (Jordan) 266
Jordan House for Publication (Jordan) 266
Jordan Library Association (Jordan) 266
Joseph, Michael (Australia) 15
Joseph, Michael, Ltd (United Kingdom) 451
Joshi, Sumnesh, Award (India) 215
Journal des Notaires et des Avocats SA (France) 107
Journeyman, The, Press Ltd (United Kingdom) 451
Jouy Prize (France) 120
'Joven Creacion' Literary Prize (Costa Rica) 73
Jovene, Casa Editrice Dr Eugenio, SpA (Italy) 242
Jover, Ediciones, SA (Spain) 369
József Attila Tudományegyetem Központi Könyvtára (Hungary) 191
Jubilee Library Association (Burma) 63
Jucar, Ediciones (Spain) 369
Judía, Biblioteca Popular (Argentina) 6
Jüdischer Verlag (Federal Republic of Germany) 150
Jugend und Volk Verlag GmbH (Federal Republic of Germany) 150
Jugend und Volk Verlagsgesellschaft mbH (Austria) 28
Jugenddienst-Verlag (Federal Republic of Germany) 150
Jugoreklam (Yugoslavia) 497
Jugoslavenske Akademije, Izdavački Zavod, Znanosti i Umjetnosti (Yugoslavia) 497
Jugoslavenski Leksikografski Zavod (Yugoslavia) 497
Jugoslavija (Yugoslavia) 497
Jugoslovenska Autorska Agencija (Yugoslavia) 499
Jugoslovenska Knjiga (Yugoslavia) 500
Jugoslovenska Revija (Yugoslavia) 497
Jugoslovenski bibliografski institut (Yugoslavia) 500
Jugoslovenski bibliografski institut, Agencija za ISBN (Yugoslavia) 495
Jugoslovenski centar za tehničku i naučnu dokumentaciju (Yugoslavia) 500
Julien, Stanislas, Prize (International Literary Prizes) 520
Julliard, Editions René (France) 107
Juncker, Axel, -Verlag Jacobi KG (Federal Republic of Germany) 150
Jungbrunnen, Verlag (Austria) 28
Junge Welt, Verlag (German Democratic Republic) 125
Jungjohann Verlagsgesellschaft mbH (Federal Republic of Germany) 150
Jungwoo Sa (Republic of Korea) 270
Junimea, Editura (Romania) 346
Junior International (Federal Republic of Germany) 150
Junior Library (Mauritius) 283

Junius Verlag GmbH (Federal Republic of Germany) 150
Junk, Dr W, Publishers (Netherlands) 298
Junpa Kwahak Sa (Republic of Korea) 270
Junta de Educação Religiosa e Publicações da Convenção Batista Brasileira (JUERP) (Brazil) 54
Jurídica, Ediciones y Librería (Argentina) 6
Jurídica, Editorial, de Chile (Chile) 65
Juridica-Verlag GmbH (Austria) 28
Juridiques et Techniques, Editions (France) 107
Jurif (Société d'Etudes Juridiques Internationales et Fiscales) (France) 107
Juris Druck & Verlag AG (Switzerland) 398
Jus, Editorial, SA de CV (Mexico) 286
Jusautor (Bulgaria) 61
Juta & Co Ltd (Republic of South Africa) 356
Juta & Co Ltd (Republic of South Africa) 360
Juventa Verlag GmbH (Federal Republic of Germany) 150
Juventud, Editorial, (Distribuidora Tres Américas SAC) (Argentina) 6
Juventud, Editorial, Ltda (Colombia) 69
Juventud, Editorial, SA (Spain) 369
Juventud, Librería (Bolivia) 48
Juventud, Librería y Editorial (Bolivia) 48
Juventus/Femina Publishers (Republic of South Africa) 356
Jyväskylän Yliopiston Kirjasto (Finland) 94

K A I B (Netherlands) 298
K B S (Netherlands) 298
K B V (Switzerland) 398
K L V (Federal Republic of Germany) 150
K M Č (Czechoslovakia) 78
K M P (Kruh milovníkov poézie) (Czechoslovakia) 78
K P I (Indonesia) 218
K P I (United Kingdom) 451
K T K/Terra Scientific Publishing Co (Japan) 258
Kabarole Public Library (Uganda) 416
Kabel, Ernst, Verlag GmbH (Federal Republic of Germany) 150
Kabete Library (Kenya) 268
Kadmos, Uitgeverij (Netherlands) 298
Kadokawa Shoten (Japan) 258
Kaduna, Library Board of, State (Nigeria) 319
Kaffke, Verlagsgesellschaft Gerhard, mbH (Federal Republic of Germany) 150
Kahn, Lonnie, & Co Ltd (Israel) 231
Kahn & Averill (United Kingdom) 451
Kaibundo Publishing Co Ltd (Japan) 258
Kairali Children's Book Trust (India) 203
Kairali Club (India) 213
Kairali Mudralayam (India) 203
Kairos, Editorial, SA (Spain) 369
Kairyudo Publishing Co (Japan) 258
Kaisei-Sha Publishing Co Ltd (Japan) 258
Kaiser, Chr, Verlag GmbH (Federal Republic of Germany) 150
Kaitaku-Sha (Japan) 258
Kajima Institute Publishing Co Ltd (Japan) 258
Kakaki (Nigeria) 316
Kakoulides, C (Greece) 184
Kalinga Prize (International Literary Prizes) 520
Kalle Ankas Bokklubb (Sweden) 388
Kalle Ankas Pocket (Sweden) 388
Kalleberger Foundation (Sweden) 390
Kaloudis, Gr (Greece) 184
Kalyani Publishers (India) 203
Kam Sung Publishing Co Ltd (Republic of Korea) 270
Kamarad (Czechoslovakia) 78
Kamp, Verlag Ferdinand, GmbH & Co KG (Federal Republic of Germany) 150
Kanda Bookshop (Japan) 263
Kanehara & Co Ltd (Japan) 258
Kangaroo Press Pty Ltd (Australia) 15
Kanisian (Indonesia) 218
Kanisius Verlag (Switzerland) 398
Kano State Library Board (Nigeria) 319
Kantonale Kommission für Gemeinde- und Schulbibliotheken, Zurich (Switzerland) 406
Kantoor Boekhandel Salinja NV KBS (Netherland Antilles) 307
Kaos Edizioni (Italy) 242
Kapelusz, Editorial, Colombiana SA (Colombia) 70
Kapelusz, Editorial, SA (Argentina) 6
Kapelusz, Editorial, Venezolana SA (Venezuela) 493
Kara, Ismail, /Dergâh Yayinlari AS Müessese Müdürü (Turkey) 415
Karachi University Library Science Alumni Association (Pakistan) 327
Karas-Sana Oy (Finland) 92
Karger, S, AG, Medical and Scientific Publishers (Switzerland) 398

INDEX

Karger, S, GmbH Verlag für Medizin und Naturwissenschaften (Federal Republic of Germany)   150
Karilas, Tauno, Prize (Finland)   95
Karisto Oy (Finland)   92
Karl-Marx-Universität (German Democratic Republic)   127
Karl-May-Verlag, Joachim Schmid & Co (Federal Republic of Germany)   150
Karnataka Cooperative Publishing House Ltd (India)   203
Karnataka Publishers' and Booksellers' Association (India)   195
Karni Publishers Ltd (Israel)   228
Karo-Bücher (Federal Republic of Germany)   150
Karthala Editions (France)   107
Kartograficznych, Państwowe Przedsiebiorstwo Wydawnictw (Poland)   335
Kartographischer Verlag Wagner & Co KG (Federal Republic of Germany)   150
Kartographisches Institut Bertelsmann (Federal Republic of Germany)   150
Karunia (Indonesia)   218
Kasetsart University, Main Library, (Thailand)   411
Kash'shaf, Dar al (Lebanon)   273
Kastaniotis Editions (Greece)   183
Katalis PT Bina Mitra Plaosan (Indonesia)   218
Kataria, B D, & Sons (India)   203
Katholieke Bijbelstichting (Netherlands)   298
Katholieke Universiteit Leuven (Belgium)   44
Katholisches Bibelwerk, Verlag, GmbH (Federal Republic of Germany)   150
Katzmann-Verlag KG (Federal Republic of Germany)   150
Kaufmann (Greece)   184
Kaufmann, Verlag Ernst, GmbH (Federal Republic of Germany)   150
Kaunda, Helen, Memorial Library (Zambia)   503
Kaunda, Kenneth, Foundation (Zambia)   503
Kawade Shobo Shinsha (Japan)   258
Kawanku, Yayasan (Indonesia)   218
Kawika (Philippines)   334
Kaye & Ward Ltd (United Kingdom)   451
Kaynar GmbH (Federal Republic of Germany)   151
Kazi Publications (Pakistan)   325
Keats-Shelley Memorial Association (Italy)   253
Kedros (Greece)   183
Keesing — Internationale Drukkerij en Uitgeverij NV (Belgium)   40
Keesing Uitgeversmaatschappij BV (Netherlands)   298
Keigaku Publishing Co Ltd (Japan)   258
Keip, Antiquariat und Verlag, GmbH (Federal Republic of Germany)   151
Keller, Franckh'sche Verlagshandlung, W , & Co (Federal Republic of Germany)   151
Keller, Gottfried, Prize (International Literary Prizes)   520
Keller, Verlag Ramòn F (Switzerland)   398
Keller, Verlag Walter (Switzerland)   398
Kellgrens Prize (Sweden)   390
Kelly Books (Australia)   16
Kelly's Directories (United Kingdom)   451
Kemal, Orhan, Award (Turkey)   416
Kemongsa (Republic of Korea)   270
Kemps Group (Printers & Publishers) Ltd (United Kingdom)   451
Kendriya Hindi Sansthan (India)   203
Kenkyusha Ltd (Japan)   258
Kent, Sir Peter, Conservation Book Prize (United Kingdom)   487
Kentron Ekdoseos Ellinon Syngrafeon (Greece)   185
Kenya Agricultural Research Institute (Kenya)   268
Kenya Booksellers' and Stationers' Association (Kenya)   266
Kenya Library Association (Kenya)   268
Kenya Literature Bureau (Kenya)   267
Kenya National Archives (Kenya)   268
Kenya National Library Service (Kenya)   268
Kenya Polytechnic Library (Kenya)   268
Kenya Publishers' Association (Kenya)   266
Kenya Technical Teachers' College Library (Kenya)   268
Kenyatta, The Jomo, Foundation (Kenya)   267
Kenyatta University Library (Kenya)   268
Képzőművészeti Alap Kiadóvállalata (Hungary)   190
Kerala Publishers & Booksellers Association (India)   195
Kerala Sahitya Akademi (India)   203
Kerala Sahitya Akademi Awards (India)   215
Kerala University, Department of Publications (India)   203
Kern, BV Uitgeverij De (Netherlands)   298
Kernerman Publishing Ltd (Israel)   228
Kerr, The Alfred, Prize for Literary Criticism (Federal Republic of Germany)   179
Kerryman Ltd (Republic of Ireland)   223
Kershaw Publishing Co Ltd (United Kingdom)   451

Kersten & Co, C (Suriname)   380
Kesari Award (India)   216
Kesim, Nurcihan, Literary Agency (Turkey)   415
Kessler Verlag für Sprachmethodik (Federal Republic of Germany)   151
Kestrel Books (United Kingdom)   452
Keswick (United Kingdom)   452
Keswick Book Society (Kenya)   268
Keter Publishing House Jerusalem Ltd (Israel)   228
Keurbiblioteek (Republic of South Africa)   359
Keure, Die, NV (Belgium)   40
Keysersche Buchhandlung (German Democratic Republic)   127
Keysersche Verlagsbuchhandlung GmbH (Federal Republic of Germany)   151
Keystone Paperbacks (Australia)   16
Keystone Picture Books (Australia)   16
Khanna Publishers (India)   203
Khartoum, The, Bookshop (Sudan)   380
Khartoum Polytechnic Library (Sudan)   380
Khartoum University Press (Sudan)   379
Khayat, Tahseen S (Lebanon)   273
Khayat, Tahseen S (United Arab Emirates)   421
Khayat Book and Publishing Co Sàrl (Lebanon)   273
'Khimiya', Izdatelstvo (Union of Soviet Socialist Republics)   418
Khoa Hoc (Social Sciences) Publishing House (Socialist Republic of Viet Nam)   494
'Khudozhestvennaya Literatura', Izdatelstvo (Union of Soviet Socialist Republics)   418
Khyber Bookshop (Pakistan)   326
Khyber Medical College Library (Pakistan)   327
Kibaha Public Library (Tanzania)   409
Kibu-Verlag GmbH (Federal Republic of Germany)   151
Kiefel, Johannes, Verlag (Federal Republic of Germany)   151
Kiehl, Friedrich, Verlag GmbH (Federal Republic of Germany)   151
Kienreich, Jos A (Austria)   31
Kiepenheuer, Gustav, Verlag (German Democratic Republic)   125
Kiepenheuer und Witsch, Verlag (Federal Republic of Germany)   151
Kier, Editorial, SACIFI (Argentina)   6
Kier, Librería (Argentina)   8
Kikuchi Prize (Japan)   265
Kilda Verlag (Federal Republic of Germany)   151
Kimber, William, & Co Ltd (United Kingdom)   452
Kimberley, William, Ltd (United Kingdom)   452
Kinderbuchverlag, Der, Berlin (German Democratic Republic)   125
Kinderbuchverlag KBV Luzern AG (Switzerland)   398
Kinderkeur (Republic of South Africa)   359
Kinderklub (Republic of South Africa)   359
Kinderpers, Die, Van SA (Republic of South Africa)   357
Kindler Verlag AG (Switzerland)   398
Kindler Verlag GmbH (Federal Republic of Germany)   151
King, Martin Luther, Memorial Prize (United Kingdom)   487
King Abdulaziz University Library (Saudi Arabia)   348
King Paul National Foundation Prize (Greece)   185
King Shing Publishing Co (Hong Kong)   188
Kingfisher Books Ltd (United Kingdom)   452
Kings & Queens of England (United Kingdom)   481
Kingsmead Press (United Kingdom)   452
Kingston Bookshop Ltd (Jamaica)   255
Kingston Publishers Ltd (Jamaica)   254
Kingstons Ltd (Zimbabwe)   505
Kingstons (Zambia) Ltd (Zambia)   503
Kingsway Publications Ltd (United Kingdom)   452
Kingsway Stores, Books and Periodicals Department (Ghana)   181
Kingswood Press (United Kingdom)   452
Kinokuniya Co Ltd (Japan)   263
Kinokuniya Co Ltd (Publishing Department) (Japan)   258
Kinta (Indonesia)   218
Kipling Society (United Kingdom)   485
Kirja-ja Paperikauppojen Liitto ry (Finland)   92
Kirja-Otava Oy (Finland)   94
Kirjallisuudentutkijain Seura (Finland)   95
Kirjaneliö, Kustannusliike (Finland)   92
Kirjaston Hoitajien Liitd (Finland)   95
Kirjastonhoitajaliitto — Bibliotekarieförbundet ry (Finland)   94
Kirjastonhoitajat ja informaatikot — Bibliotekarier och informatiker ry (Finland)   95
Kirjastovirkailijat-Biblioteksanstallda ry (Finland)   95
Kirjatoimi omi Suomen Adrenttikirkko (Finland)   93
Kirjayhtymä Oy (Finland)   93
Kiryat Sefer Ltd (Israel)   228
Kishida Prize for Drama (Japan)   265
Kister, Editions, SA (Switzerland)   398
Kitab, Dar Al-, Al-Masri (Egypt)   89

Kitab, Dar Al-, Allubnani (Lebanon)   273
Kitab, Dar El (Morocco)   290
Kitab Ghar (India)   203
Kitabastan (India)   203
Kitabi Dunya (Pakistan)   325
Kitaplar, Altin, Publishing Co (Turkey)   415
Kitwe Public Library (Zambia)   503
Kivukoni College Library (Tanzania)   409
Kivunim Publishing House Ltd (Israel)   228
Kiwi Tales Publications (New Zealand)   309
Klang Vidhya (Thailand)   410
Klang Vidhya (Thailand)   411
Klartext Verlagsgesellschaft mbH (Federal Republic of Germany)   151
Klasing und Co GmbH (Federal Republic of Germany)   151
Klein, Dieter, Associates (United Kingdom)   479
Klein, Kunstverlag Dr Rudolf Georgi, Waldemar (Federal Republic of Germany)   151
Klens-Verlag GmbH (Federal Republic of Germany)   151
Klett, Ernst, Verlag (Federal Republic of Germany)   151
Klett-Cotta Verlag (Federal Republic of Germany)   151
Klett und Balmer, Verlag, & Co (Switzerland)   398
Klima, Librairie R (French Polynesia)   122
Klincksieck, Editions (France)   107
Klinkhardt und Biermann Verlagsbuchhandlung (Federal Republic of Germany)   151
Kloeden, v, KG (Federal Republic of Germany)   151
Klopp, Erika, Verlag GmbH (Federal Republic of Germany)   151
Klostermann, Vittorio, GmbH (Federal Republic of Germany)   151
Klotz, Ehrenfried, Verlag (Federal Republic of Germany)   151
Klub 42 (Yugoslavia)   499
Klub Čitalaca (Yugoslavia)   500
Klub Čitalaca MK (Yugoslavia)   500
Klub čtenářů technické literatury (Czechoslovakia)   78
Klub přátel poezie (Czechoslovakia)   78
Klub Prijatelja Knjige 'August Cesarec' (Yugoslavia)   500
Kluitman, Uitgeverij, Alkmaar BV (Netherlands)   298
Kluwer, NV Uitgeverij (Belgium)   40
Kluwer Algemene Boeken BV (Netherlands)   298
Kluwer Algemene Informatieve Boeken BV (Netherlands)   298
Kluwer Bedrijfswetenschappen (Netherlands)   298
Kluwer Group (Netherlands)   298
Kluwer Law and Taxation Publishers (Netherlands)   299
Kluwer Publishing Ltd (United Kingdom)   452
Kluwer Technische Boeken BV (Netherlands)   299
Kluwerpers (Netherlands)   299
Knapp, Fritz, Verlag GmbH (Federal Republic of Germany)   151
Knapp, Wilhelm, Verlag GmbH (Federal Republic of Germany)   152
Knaur, Droemer, Verlag (Federal Republic of Germany)   152
Knaus, Albrecht, Verlag (Federal Republic of Germany)   152
Knecht, Verlag Josef, -Carolusdruckerei GmbH (Federal Republic of Germany)   152
Knesset Library (Israel)   231
'Kniga', Izdatelstvo (Union of Soviet Socialist Republics)   418
Knight (Australia)   16
Knight, Charles, Ltd (United Kingdom)   452
Knight (United Kingdom)   452
Kniha (Czechoslovakia)   78
Knihovna Národního muzea (Czechoslovakia)   78
Knorr und Hirth Verlag GmbH (Federal Republic of Germany)   152
Knowledge Book House (Burma)   62
Knowledge Printing & Publishing House (Burma)   62
Knowles, Justin, Publishing Group (United Kingdom)   452
Knuf, F, Publishers (Netherlands)   299
Knutseltjie (Republic of South Africa)   359
Ko Mun Sa (Republic of Korea)   270
Københavns Kommunes Biblioteker (Denmark)   84
Københavns Stadsarkiv (Denmark)   84
Kobersche Verlagsbuchhandlung AG (Switzerland)   398
Koch, Verlagsanstalt Alexander, GmbH (Federal Republic of Germany)   152
Koch, Volksbuchhandlung Robert (German Democratic Republic)   127
Koch, Neff und Oetinger & Co (Federal Republic of Germany)   176
Kodansha Disney Children's Book Club (Japan)   263
Kodansha International Ltd (Japan)   259
Kodansha Ltd (Japan)   259
Kodansha Scientific Ltd (Japan)   259

Koehler, K F, Verlag (Federal Republic of Germany)   152
Koehler und Amelang (German Democratic Republic)   125
Koehlers Verlagsgesellschaft (Federal Republic of Germany)   152
Koerner, Verlag Valentin, GmbH (Federal Republic of Germany)   152
Kogan Page Ltd (United Kingdom)   452
Kohlhammer, Verlag W, GmbH (Federal Republic of Germany)   152
Kohl's Technischer Verlag Erwin Kohl GmbH & Co KG (Federal Republic of Germany)   152
Kohrtz, Ilona, Prize (Sweden)   390
Koivu, Rudolf, Prize (Finland)   95
Kok, Uitgeversmaatschappij J H, BV (Netherlands)   299
Kok Agora (Netherlands)   299
Kokbokklubben God Mat (Sweden)   388
Koko Kansan Kirjakerho Oy (KKK Book Clubs Ltd) (Finland)   94
Kokuritsu Kobunshokan (Japan)   263
Kolasanya Publishing Enterprise (Nigeria)   316
Kollaros, I D, & Co Corporation (Greece)   183
'Kolos', Izdatelstvo (Union of Soviet Socialist Republics)   418
Kolumbus-Verlag (Switzerland)   398
Komar (Federal Republic of Germany)   152
Komine Shoten Publishing Co Ltd (Japan)   259
Komitet za Izkoustvo i Koultoura (Bulgaria)   61
Komma, Forlaget, A/S (Denmark)   82
Kommentator, Verlag (Federal Republic of Germany)   152
Kommunale Bibliotekarbeideres Forening (Norway)   324
Komunikacji i Laczności, Wydawnictwa (Poland)   335
Komunist, Izdavački Centar (Yugoslavia)   497
Kongelige Bibliotek, Det (Denmark)   84
Kongelige Danske Videnskabernes Selskab (Denmark)   85
Kongelige Norske Videnskabers Selskab, Det (Norway)   323
Königshausen und Neumann, Verlag (Federal Republic of Germany)   152
Koninklijk Instituut voor Internationale Betrekkingen (Belgium)   40
Koninklijke Academie voor Nederlandse Taal- en Letterkunde (Belgium)   45
Koninklijke Academie voor Wetenschappen, Letteren en Schone Kunsten van België (Belgium)   40
Koninklijke Academie voor Wetenschappen, Letteren en Schone Kunsten van België (Belgium)   45
Koninklijke Bibliotheek (Netherlands)   305
Koninklijke Nederlandse Akademie, Bibliotheek der, van Wetenschappen (Netherlands)   305
Koninklijke Nederlandse Uitgeversbond (Netherlands)   292
Konkani Bhasha Mandal (India)   203
Konkordia Verlag GmbH (Federal Republic of Germany)   152
Konkret, KLV, Literatur Verlag GmbH (Federal Republic of Germany)   152
Konrad, Anton H, Verlag (Federal Republic of Germany)   152
Konsalik Novel Prize (Federal Republic of Germany)   179
Könyvértékesítő Vállalat (Hungary)   191
Könyvtártudományi és módszertani központ (Hungary)   191
Konzepte der Humanwissenschaften (Federal Republic of Germany)   152
Kookaburra Technical Publications Pty Ltd (Australia)   16
Kooy, Maydo, Literary Agency (Netherlands)   304
Kooyker BV (Netherlands)   304
Korea Book Club (Republic of Korea)   271
Korea Britannica Corporation (Republic of Korea)   270
Korea Directory Co (Republic of Korea)   270
Korea Institute of Science and Technology Library (Republic of Korea)   271
Korea Publications Export & Import Corporation (Democratic People's Republic of Korea)   269
Korea Textbook Co Ltd (Republic of Korea)   270
Korea University Library (Republic of Korea)   271
Korea University Press (Republic of Korea)   270
Korean Culture, The, and Arts Foundation (Republic of Korea)   270
Korean Library Association (Republic of Korea)   271
Korean Micro-Library Association (Republic of Korea)   271
Korean Publishers Association (Republic of Korea)   269
Koren Publishers (Israel)   228
Korn, Bergstadtverlag Wilhelm Gottlieb, GmbH (Federal Republic of Germany)   152
Körner de Moya, Ute, Literary Agent (Spain)   375
Kornfeld, Galerie, & Co (Switzerland)   398
Kosei Publishing Co (Japan)   259

Koseisha-Koseikaku Co Ltd (Japan)   259
Kösel-Verlag GmbH & Co (Federal Republic of Germany)   152
Koshal Book Depot (India)   212
Kosi Books (India)   203
Koska, Verlag A F (Austria)   28
Kosmos, Livraria (Brazil)   58
Kosmos, Livraria, Editora (Brazil)   54
Kosmos BV (Netherlands)   299
Kosmos Gesellschaft (Federal Republic of Germany)   175
Kossodo Verlag AG (Switzerland)   398
Kossuth Könyvkiadó (Hungary)   190
Kossuth Lajos Tudományegyetem Egyetemi Könyvtár (Hungary)   191
Kothari Publications (India)   203
Koymantereas (Greece)   183
Közgazdasági és Jogi Könyvkiadó (Hungary)   190
Központi statisztikai hivatal könyvtár és dokumentációs szolgálat (Hungary)   191
Krains, Hubert, Prize (Belgium)   46
Krajowa Agencja Wydawnicza (KAW) (Poland)   335
Kraks Forlag A/S (Denmark)   82
Král', Fraňo, Prize (Czechoslovakia)   79
Kramer, Andrés de (Spain)   375
Krämer, Verlag Karl, & Co (Switzerland)   398
Kramer, Verlag René, AG (Switzerland)   398
Kramer Verlag, Karin (Federal Republic of Germany)   152
Krämer Verlag GmbH, Karl, und Co (Federal Republic of Germany)   152
Kramer Verlagsbuchhandlung, Dr Waldemar (Federal Republic of Germany)   152
Kramers (Netherlands)   299
Kraszna-Krausz Awards (International Literary Prizes)   520
Krausskopf, Vereinigte Fachverlage, Ingenieur Digest GmbH (Federal Republic of Germany)   153
Krebs, Verlag und Druckerei G, AG (Switzerland)   398
Kremayr und Scheriau, Verlag (Austria)   28
Kremnitz, Buch- und Bildverlag W (Federal Republic of Germany)   153
Kreuz Verlag (Federal Republic of Germany)   153
Krieg, Antiquariat Walter, Verlag (Austria)   31
Kriegsarchivs Wien, Bibliothek des (Austria)   32
Kriminalistik Verlag GmbH (Federal Republic of Germany)   153
Krippler-Muller, Publisher (Grand Duchy of Luxembourg)   275
Krishna Brothers (India)   204
Krishna Prakashan Mandir (India)   204
Kristiansand Folkebibliotek (Norway)   323
Kristna Bokförläggareföreningen (Sweden)   381
Kristna Bokringen, Den (Sweden)   388
Kristne Bogklub, Den (Denmark)   84
Kritak uitgeverij (Belgium)   40
Kriterion, Editura (Romania)   346
Kröner, Alfred, Verlag (Federal Republic of Germany)   153
Krščanska sadašnjost (Yugoslavia)   497
Kruger, Wolfgang, Verlag (Federal Republic of Germany)   153
Kruh (Czechoslovakia)   76
Kruh priateľov detskej knihy na Slovensku (Czechoslovakia)   78
'Ksiazka i Wiedza', Wydawnictwo (Poland)   335
Kuala Lumpur Public Library (Malaysia)   280
Kübler und Akselrad Verlag (Federal Republic of Germany)   153
Kubon und Sagner (Federal Republic of Germany)   153
Kugler Publications BV (Netherlands)   299
Kultura (Hungary)   191
Kultura (Yugoslavia)   500
Kultura (Izdavačko Pretprijatie) (Yugoslavia)   497
Kumar, C B, Award (India)   216
Kumm, Wilhelm, Verlag (Federal Republic of Germany)   153
Kümmerley und Frey (Federal Republic of Germany)   153
Kümmerley und Frey Verlags GmbH (Austria)   28
Kümmerly und Frey (Geographischer Verlag) (Switzerland)   398
Kumsong Youth Publishing House (Democratic People's Republic of Korea)   268
Kundalini Research and Publication Trust (India)   204
Kündig, Imprimerie Albert, SA (Switzerland)   398
Kungl Vitterhets Historie och Antikvitets Akademien (Sweden)   390
Kungliga Biblioteket (Sweden)   389
Kungliga Svenska Vetenskapsakademiens Bibliotek (Sweden)   389
Kunkumam Award (India)   216
Kunnskapsforlaget I/S (Norway)   321
Kunst, VEB Verlag der (German Democratic Republic)   125

Kunst und Wissen Erich Bieber OHG (Federal Republic of Germany)   153
Kunst und Wohnen Verlag (Federal Republic of Germany)   153
Kunstwissenschaft, Deutscher Verlag für (Federal Republic of Germany)   153
Kunzelmann, Edition, GmbH (Switzerland)   398
Kuomintang Central Committee Library (Taiwan)   408
Küpper, Verlag Helmut (Federal Republic of Germany)   153
Kurita Bando Literary Agency (Japan)   263
Kurita Shuppan Hanbai Co Ltd (Japan)   263
Kurnia Esa (Indonesia)   218
Kursverksamhetens Förlag (Sweden)   385
Kutab, Dar Al, Al Hadeetha (Egypt)   89
Kutter, Edouard (Grand Duchy of Luxembourg)   276
Kuttippuzha Award (India)   216
Kutub, Dar al, al-Wataniya (Saudi Arabia)   348
Kutub Khana Ishayat-ul-Islam (India)   204
Kuwait Central Library (Kuwait)   272
Kuwait Publishing House (Kuwait)   272
Kuwait University Central Library (Kuwait)   272
Kuwait University Libraries Department (Kuwait)   272
Kvint, Kerstin (Sweden)   388
Kwang Hwa, Sharikat Toko Buku (Brunei)   60
Kwang Hwa Bookstore Pte Ltd (Malaysia)   280
Kwang Jang Press (Republic of Korea)   270
Kwangmyong Printing & Publishing Co Ltd (Republic of Korea)   270
Kwaratech Bookshop (Nigeria)   318
Kwong Hin Bookstore (Hong Kong)   189
Kyi-Pwar-Ye Book House (Burma)   62
Kyo Bun Kwan Inc (Japan)   259
Kyobo Book Centre Co Ltd (Republic of Korea)   271
Kyobo Publishing Inc (Republic of Korea)   270
Kyohaksa Publishing Co Ltd (Republic of Korea)   270
Kyoritsu Shuppan Co Ltd (Japan)   259
Kyoto Sangyo University Library (Japan)   263
Kyriakou, K P, (Books — Stationery) Ltd (Cyprus)   74
Kyrios-Verlag GmbH (Federal Republic of Germany)   153
Kyung Hee University Press (Republic of Korea)   270
Kyung In Munwha Sa (Republic of Korea)   270
Kyungnam University Press (Republic of Korea)   270
Kyungpook National University Central Library (Republic of Korea)   271
Kyushu University Library (Japan)   263

L D A (Learning Development Aids) (United Kingdom)   452
L E D A (Las Ediciones de Arte) (Spain)   369
L E G I S — Legislación Económica Ltda (Colombia)   70
L E R, Livraria (Brazil)   58
L I C E T (France)   107
L I C — Förlag (Sweden)   385
L I N E S A (Spain)   376
L I S A (Livros Irradiantes SA) (Brazil)   54
L I T A (Czechoslovakia)   77
L I T E C, Librairies Techniques SA (France)   107
L I T E C — Livraria Editora Técnica Ltda (Brazil)   58
L K G (Leipziger Kommissions- und Grossbuchhandel) (German Democratic Republic)   127
L N-Verlag Lübeck, Lübecker Nachrichten GmbH (Federal Republic of Germany)   153
L P3 E S (Lembaga Penelitian, Pendidikan Dan Penerangan Ekonomi Dan Sosial) (Indonesia)   218
L T C-Livros Técnicos e Científicos Editora SA (Brazil)   54
L T Editions (France)   107
L T P (United Kingdom)   452
L T r Editora Ltda (Brazil)   54
L Ts Förlag AB (Lantbrukarnas Riksförbund och Studieförbundet Vuxenskolan) (Sweden)   385
L W Edition (Switzerland)   398
L W Promotion (Switzerland)   398
La Casa Verde Editrice SNC (Italy)   242
'La Nación', Premio de, Prize (Argentina)   9
La Paz, Librería (Bolivia)   48
La Porte, Editions (Morocco)   290
'La Prensa', Biblioteca Pública Gratuita de (Argentina)   8
La Rivière en Voorhoeve (Netherlands)   299
La Scala, Edizioni (Italy)   242
La Tartaruga Edizioni (Italy)   242
Lääketieteellinen Keskuskirjasto (Finland)   94
Labbé-Vauquelin Foundation Prize (France)   120
Labor, Editorial, de Venezuela SA (Venezuela)   493
Labor, Editorial, do Brasil SA (Brazil)   54
Labor, Editorial, SA (Spain)   369
Labor et Fides SA (Switzerland)   398

INDEX 569

Labor-Nathan, Editions (Belgium) 40
Labor SA, Editorial, Colombiana Ltda (Colombia) 70
Lacus, Ambro, Buch- und Bildverlag W Kremnitz (Federal Republic of Germany) 153
Lademann Ltd, Publishers (Denmark) 82
Ladybird Books Ltd (United Kingdom) 452
Laertes SA de Ediciones (Spain) 369
Laetare (Federal Republic of Germany) 153
Laetitia, Boekhandel en Uitgeverij (Netherlands) 299
Lafenestre, Georges, Foundation Prize (France) 120
Laffont, Editions Robert (France) 107
Lafite, Verlag Elisabeth (Austria) 28
Lafontaine Prize (France) 120
Laget, Librairie Léonce (France) 108
Lagos City Council Libraries (Nigeria) 319
Lagos SA (Spain) 369
Lagos University Press Ltd (Nigeria) 316
Lahn-Verlag (Federal Republic of Germany) 153
Lahumière, Editions (France) 108
Laia, Editorial, SA (Spain) 369
Lake House Investments Ltd (Sri Lanka) 378
Lakeland (United Kingdom) 452
Lakoul Press (Nepal) 292
Lakshmi Narain Agarwal (India) 204
Lalit Kala Akademi (National Academy of Art) (India) 204
Lalli, Antonio, Editore (Italy) 242
Lalvani Brothers (India) 204
Lamares, Américo Fraga, & Ca Lda (Portugal) 342
Lamarre-Poinat, Editions, SA (France) 108
Lamb, Charles, Society (United Kingdom) 485
Lambert Prize (France) 120
Lambertus Verlag GmbH (Federal Republic of Germany) 153
Lamp Press (United Kingdom) 452
Lampe, Editions, d'Or ASBL (Belgium) 40
Lamuv Verlag GmbH (Federal Republic of Germany) 153
Lamy SA, Editions Juridiques et Techniques (France) 108
Lancashire Authors' Association (United Kingdom) 485
Landbouwhogeschool, Bibliotheek der (Netherlands) 305
Landbouwuniversiteit, Bibliotheek der (Netherlands) 305
Landbuch-Verlag GmbH (Federal Republic of Germany) 153
Landesgremium Kärnten des Handels mit Büchern, Kunstblättern, Musikalien, Zeitungen und Zeitschriften (Austria) 25
Landesgremium Niederösterreich des Handels mit Büchern, Kunstblättern, Musikalien, Zeitungen und Zeitschriften (Austria) 25
Landesgremium Oberösterreich des Handels mit Büchern, Kunstblättern, Musikalien, Zeitungen und Zeitschriften (Austria) 25
Landesgremium Salzburg des Handels mit Büchern, Kunstblättern, Musikalien, Zeitungen und Zeitschriften (Austria) 25
Landesgremium Steiermark des Handels mit Büchern, Kunstblättern, Musikalien, Zeitungen und Zeitschriften (Austria) 26
Landesgremium Tirol des Handels mit Büchern, Kunstblättern, Musikalien, Zeitungen und Zeitschriften (Austria) 26
Landesgremium Vorarlberg des Handels mit Büchern und Musikalien (Austria) 26
Landesgremium Wien des Handels mit Büchern, Kunstblättern, Musikalien, Zeitungen und Zeitschriften (Austria) 26
Landesman, Jay (United Kingdom) 452
Landestopographie, Bundesamt für (Switzerland) 398
Landesverband der Buchhändler und Verleger in Niedersachsen eV (Federal Republic of Germany) 129
Landesverband der Verleger und Buchhändler Bremen-Unterweser eV (Federal Republic of Germany) 129
Landesverband der Verleger und Buchhändler Rheinland-Pfalz eV (Federal Republic of Germany) 129
Landesverband der Verleger und Buchhändler Saar eV (LVBS) (Federal Republic of Germany) 129
Landesverband des werbenden Buch- und Zeitschriftenhandels von Südwestdeutschland eV (Federal Republic of Germany) 129
Landesverlag Buchverlag (Austria) 28
Landi, Luciano, Editore SRL (Italy) 242
Landmark Books (United Kingdom) 452
Landsberger Verlagsanstalt Martin Neumeyer (Federal Republic of Germany) 153
Landsbókasafn Íslands (Iceland) 194
Landwirtschaftliche Zentralbibliothek (German Democratic Republic) 127
Landwirtschaftlicher Staatsverlag (Agricultural Publishing House) (Czechoslovakia) 76
Landy, Livraria D (Brazil) 58
Lane, Allen (United Kingdom) 452
Lane, Allen, Award (International Literary Prizes) 520
Lang, Herbert, & Cie AG (Switzerland) 398

Lang, Verlag Peter, AG (Switzerland) 398
Lang, Verlag Peter, GmbH (Federal Republic of Germany) 153
Lang Syne Publishers Ltd (United Kingdom) 452
Lange, Allert de, BV (Netherlands) 299
Langen-Georg Müller Verlag, Albert (Federal Republic of Germany) 153
Langenhoven, C J, Prize (Republic of South Africa) 362
Langenscheidt AG (Switzerland) 399
Langenscheidt Group, The (Federal Republic of Germany) 153
Langenscheidt-Hachette GmbH (Federal Republic of Germany) 154
Langenscheidt KG (Federal Republic of Germany) 153
Langenscheidt-Longman GmbH (Federal Republic of Germany) 154
Langenscheidt-Verlag GmbH (Austria) 28
Langewiesche, Karl Robert, Nachfolger Hans Koester KG (Federal Republic of Germany) 154
Langewiesche-Brandt, Verlag, KG (Federal Republic of Germany) 154
Langham Press (United Kingdom) 452
Langlois Prize (France) 120
Language Book Centre (Australia) 21
Language Teaching Publications (United Kingdom) 452
Languages School (Thailand) 410
Lanka Booksellers' Association (India) 195
Lannoo, Uitgeverij (Belgium) 40
Lannoo, Uitgeverij (Netherlands) 299
Lanore, Editions Fernand, Sàrl (France) 108
Lanore, LT Editions-J, -H Laurens (France) 108
Lansdowne Editions (Australia) 16
Lansdowne Press (Australia) 16
Lansdowne Press (NZ) Ltd (New Zealand) 309
Lansdowne-Rigby International (United Kingdom) 452
Lanser Forlag A/S (Norway) 321
Lantern Books (Nigeria) 316
Lantern House (Australia) 16
Lao Dong (Labour) Publishing House (Socialist Republic of Viet Nam) 494
Lao-phanit (Laos) 272
Lapautre, Michelle (France) 116
Lappeenrannan Kirjakauppa Oy (Finland) 94
Lapucci, Mario (Italy) 242
Lärarbokklubben (Sweden) 388
Larcier, Maison Ferdinand, SA (Belgium) 40
Larese, Franz, und Jürg Janett (Switzerland) 399
Larousse, Ediciones, Argentina SA (Argentina) 6
Larousse, Ediciones, Colombiana Ltda (Colombia) 70
Larousse, Librairie (France) 108
Larousse (Suisse) SA (Switzerland) 399
Larson, Bokförlaget Robert, AB (Sweden) 385
LaSal (Edicions de les Dones) (Spain) 369
Lascelles, Roger (United Kingdom) 452
Lasie Australia Co Ltd (Australia) 22
Lasser Press Mexicana SA (Mexico) 286
Lasten Keskus Oy (Finland) 93
Lasten parhaat kirjat (Finland) 94
Laterna magica, Verlag, Joachim F Richter (Federal Republic of Germany) 154
Laterza, Giuseppe, e Figli SpA (Italy) 242
Latina SA (Argentina) 6
Latomus — Société d'Études Latines de Bruxelles ASBL (Belgium) 40
Lattès, Editions Jean-Claude (France) 108
Laurens, Editions Henri, Successeurs Sàrl (France) 108
Laurenziana, Biblioteca Medicea (Italy) 252
Laurus, Edizioni, Robuffo (Italy) 242
Lavauzelle, Editions Charles-, SA (France) 108
Lavoro Editoriale, Il (Italy) 242
Lavoro SRL, Edizioni (Italy) 242
Law, The, Book Co Ltd (Australia) 16
Law Books in Hindi Prize (India) 216
Law Books in Hindi Publishers (India) 204
Law Publishers (India) 204
Lawrence & Wishart (United Kingdom) 452
Lawyers' Co-operative Publishing Co (Philippines) Inc (Philippines) 332
Lax, August (Federal Republic of Germany) 154
Le Cri, Edition (Belgium) 40
Le Lettere, Casa Editrice, SRL (Italy) 242
Le Monnier, Casa Editrice Felice (Italy) 242
Le Mouël, Eugène, Foundation Prize (France) 120
Le Prat, Editions Guy (France) 108
League of Arab States, Department of Documentation and Information (International Organizations) 513
Lebanese Library, The, Association (Lebanon) 273
Lebanon Bookshop (Lebanon) 273
Lebovici/Champ Libre, Editions Gérard (France) 108
A l'Ecart, Editions (France) 97
Lechevalier, Editions, Sàrl (France) 108
Lecoffre, Librairie (France) 108
Leconte, Sébastien-Charles, Foundation Prize (France) 120
Lectura, Librería (Venezuela) 493

Lecture Publique, Direction de la (Tunisia) 414
Ledori (Israel) 228
Lee, T H, & Co Ltd (Hong Kong) 188
Leeds University Library (United Kingdom) 483
'Leer y Escribir', Concurso Nacional (Spain) 378
Lee's Book Centre (Bahamas) 34
Lefebvre, Editions Francis (France) 108
Legend (United Kingdom) 452
Legenda, Bokförlaget, AB (Sweden) 385
Legislación Económica Ltda (Colombia) 70
'Legkaya i Pishchevaya', Izdatelstvo, Promyshlennost' (Union of Soviet Socialist Republics) 418
Lehmann, Librería Imprenta y Litografía, SA (Costa Rica) 73
Lehnert & Landrock (Egypt) 89
Leibniz-Volksbuchhandlung (German Democratic Republic) 127
Leicester University Press (United Kingdom) 452
Leiden University Press (Netherlands) 299
Leiftur hf (Iceland) 193
Leins, Verlag Hermann (Federal Republic of Germany) 154
Leipoldt, C Louis, Prys vir Poesie (Republic of South Africa) 362
Leipzig, VEB Edition (German Democratic Republic) 125
Leipziger Kommissions- und Grossbuchhandel (German Democratic Republic) 127
Leisure Circle, The, Ltd (United Kingdom) 481
Leisure Press (Australia) 16
Leitfadenverlag Dieter Sudholt (Federal Republic of Germany) 154
Lekarskich, Państwowy Zakład Wydawnictw (Poland) 335
Lekha Prokashani (Bangladesh) 34
Lello & Cia Lda (Angola) 2
Lello e Cia Lda (Portugal) 342
Lello e Irmão (Portugal) 342
Lelong, Daniel, Editeur (France) 108
Lembeck, Verlag Otto (Federal Republic of Germany) 154
Lemniscaat (Netherlands) 299
Lenclud, Anne, Pierre Lenclud (France) 108
Lenina, Gosudarstvennaya ordena Lenina biblioteka SSSR imeni V I (Union of Soviet Socialist Republics) 420
'Lenizdat', Izdatelstvo (Union of Soviet Socialist Republics) 418
Lennard Publishing (United Kingdom) 452
Lenos Verlag (Switzerland) 399
Lensing, Verlag Lambert, GmbH (Federal Republic of Germany) 154
Lentz, Georg, Verlag (Federal Republic of Germany) 154
Leo, Franz, & Co KG (Austria) 31
Leobuchhandlung (Switzerland) 405
Leobuchhandlung, Verlag der Quellen-Bändchen (Switzerland) 399
Leon Editions (Greece) 183
Leonard Hill (United Kingdom) 452
Leonardo da Vinci, Nova Livraria, Ltda (Brazil) 58
Leong Brothers (Brunei) 60
Leonhardt Literary Agency ApS (Denmark) 84
Leonis Verlag (Switzerland) 399
Leopard (United Kingdom) 453
Leopold, Uitgeverij, BV (Netherlands) 299
Lerner, Ediciones, Ltda (Colombia) 70
Lerner, Librería (Colombia) 71
Leroy, Editions Dominique (France) 108
Lerú, Editorial Victor, SA (Argentina) 6
Leserskring (Republic of South Africa) 359
Leske Verlag und Budrich GmbH (Federal Republic of Germany) 154
'Lesnaya Promyshlennost', Izdatelstvo (Union of Soviet Socialist Republics) 418
Lesoil, Uiteverij Leon, VZW (Belgium) 40
Lesotho Book Centre (Lesotho) 274
Lesotho Library Association (Lesotho) 274
Lesotho National Library Service (Lesotho) 274
Lessing Prize der Freien und Hansestadt Hamburg (Federal Republic of Germany) 179
Letouzey, Société Nouvelle des Editions, et Ané Sàrl (France) 108
Letrán, Librería (Mexico) 288
Lettres Libres, Les (France) 108
Lettres Modernes Minard (France) 108
Letts, Charles, & Co Ltd (United Kingdom) 453
Leu, Edition (Switzerland) 399
Leuchter-Verlag EG (Federal Republic of Germany) 154
Leuven University Press (Belgium) 40
Leven, The Grace, Prize for Poetry (Australia) 24
Leventhal, Lionel, Ltd (United Kingdom) 453
Levi, Editions Liana, Sàrl (France) 108
Levrotto e Bella Libreria Editrice Universitaria SAS (Italy) 243
Lewin-Epstein Ltd (Israel) 228

Lewin-Epstein-Modan, A, Ltd (Israel) 228
Lewis, A (United Kingdom) 453
Lewis, F, Publishers Ltd (United Kingdom) 453
Lewis, H K, & Co Ltd (United Kingdom) 453
Lewis, J D, & Sons Ltd (United Kingdom) 453
Lex Editora SA (Brazil) 54
Lexicon, The, Bookshop (Isle of Man) 225
Lexicon Publishers (Pty) Ltd (Republic of South Africa) 357
Ley, La, SA Editora e Impresora (Argentina) 6
Leykam Buchverlagsges mbH (Austria) 28
Lia Rumantscha (Ligia Romontscha) (Switzerland) 399
Lianoning People's Publishing House (People's Republic of China) 67
Liaoning Library (People's Republic of China) 68
Liaquat Memorial Library (Pakistan) 327
Libbey, John, & Co Ltd (United Kingdom) 453
Liber, Sveučilišna Naklada (Yugoslavia) 497
Liber AB (Sweden) 385
Liber Juris, Editora, Ltda (Brazil) 54
Liber Verlag GmbH (Federal Republic of Germany) 154
Liberian Educational Materials Supply Corporation (Liberia) 274
Liberian Literary & Educational Publications (Liberia) 274
Liberma, Libreria (Italy) 251
Libertatea (Yugoslavia) 497
Liberty Books (Pvt) Ltd (Pakistan) 326
Libra (Netherlands) 299
Libra Books Pty Ltd (Australia) 16
Librairie afrique (Senegal) 349
Librairie Bilingue/The Bilingual Bookshop (United Republic of Cameroun) 64
Librairie centrafricaine (Central African Republic) 64
Librairie clairafrique (Senegal) 349
Librairie Commerciale et Technique (Licet) Sàrl (France) 108
Librairie de Madagascar (Democratic Republic of Madagascar) 277
Librairie du Liban (Lebanon) 273
Librairie du Liban (Lebanon) 273
Librairie encyclopédique, Editions de la (Belgium) 40
Librairie évangélique (Central African Republic) 64
Librairie évangélique (Chad) 65
Librairie Evangélique du Burundi (Burundi) 63
Librairie Générale de Droit et de Jurisprudence (France) 108
Librairie Générale Française SA (France) 108
Librairie luthérienne (Democratic Republic of Madagascar) 277
Librairie mixte Sàrl (Democratic Republic of Madagascar) 277
Librairie nationale (Morocco) 290
Librairie nouvelle de l'Ouest Africain (LINOA) (Senegal) 349
Librairie-Papeterie Moderne (United Republic of Cameroun) 64
Librairie-Papeterie Protestante CEBEC (United Republic of Cameroun) 64
Librairie-Papeterie Universelle (French Guiana) 122
Librairie Populaire (Popular Republic of Congo) 72
Librairie Populaire (United Republic of Cameroun) 64
Librairie populaire de Mali (Mali) 281
Librairie universitaire (Democratic Republic of Madagascar) 277
Librairie universitaire (Rwanda) 348
Librairie Universitaire de la Réunion (Réunion) 346
Librairie universitaire et technique (Senegal) 349
Librairies Techniques SA (France) 108
Libraport (Guinea) 186
Library, School of, and Information Science Library (Japan) 263
Library, The, and Documentation Centre (Saudi Arabia) 348
Library, The, Shop (Republic of Ireland) 224
Library and Information Services Council (United Kingdom) 483
Library and Information Services Council (Wales) (United Kingdom) 483
Library and Information Statistics Unit (United Kingdom) 453
Library Association, The (United Kingdom) 483
Library Association of Australia (Australia) 22
Library Association of Barbados (Barbados) 35
Library Association of China (Taiwan) 408
Library Association of Cuba (Cuba) 74
Library Association of Cyprus (Cyprus) 75
Library Association of Singapore (Republic of Singapore) 354
Library Association of the Democratic People's Republic of Korea (Democratic People's Republic of Korea) 269
Library Association Publishing (United Kingdom) 453
Library Automated Systems, The, Information Exchange (Australia) 22

Library Board, The, of Western Australia (Australia) 21
Library of Parliament (Republic of South Africa) 361
Library of Parliament (Zimbabwe) 505
Library Promotion Bureau (Pakistan) 327
Library Service of Fiji (Fiji) 91
Librería Científica SA (Ecuador) 88
Librería Contemporanea (Puerto Rico) 345
Librería Continental (Colombia) 71
Librería Cultural (Puerto Rico) 345
Librería Cultural Nicaraguense (Nicaragua) 314
Librería Cultural Panameña SA (Panama) 328
Librería Cultural Puertorriqueña Inc (Puerto Rico) 345
Librería Cultural SA (Venezuela) 493
Librería Cultural Venezolana (Venezuela) 493
Librería Española (Ecuador) 88
Librería Inglesa (Uruguay) 491
Librería Internacional (Paraguay) 329
Librería Internacional del Perú (Peru) 331
Librería Nacional Ltda (Colombia) 71
Librería Tecnológica Universitaria (Nicaragua) 314
Librería Tecnológico SA (Mexico) 288
Librería Universal (Guatemala) 186
Librería Universal (Paraguay) 329
Librería Universitaria (Chile) 66
Librería Universitaria (Ecuador) 88
Librería Universitaria (Mexico) 288
Librería Universitaria (Nicaragua) 314
Librería Universitaria de Puerto Rico (Puerto Rico) 345
Librex, Edizioni (Italy) 243
Libris Bookclub (Sweden) 388
Libris Media AB (Sweden) 385
Libro de la Naturaleza, Club del (Spain) 376
Libroclub de Guatemala (Guatemala) 185
Librolandia del Centro SA de CV (Mexico) 288
Libros y Revistas SA de CV (Mexico) 286
Licet (France) 108
Licht og Licht (Denmark) 84
Lichterfelde, Edition (Federal Republic of Germany) 154
Licosa SpA (Italy) 243
Lidador, Editora, Ltda (Brazil) 54
Lidis, Editions, SA (France) 108
Lidman Production AB (Sweden) 385
Lidové nakladatelství (Czechoslovakia) 76
Liebenzeller Mission, Verlag der (Federal Republic of Germany) 154
Liechtenstein Verlag AG (Liechtenstein) 275
Liechtensteinische Landesbibliothek (Liechtenstein) 275
Lied, VEB, der Zeit Musikverlag (German Democratic Republic) 125
Liedl, Agenzia di Rosemary Ann, & Co (Italy) 251
Liepman AG (Switzerland) 405
Lietzow, Edition/Galerie (Federal Republic of Germany) 154
Life Changing Books (United Kingdom) 453
Life Sciences Research Reports (Federal Republic of Germany) 154
Ligue des Bibliothèques Européennes de Recherche (LIBER) (International Organizations) 510
Liguori Editore SRL (Italy) 243
Liguria, Editrice, SNC di Norberto Sabatelli & C (Italy) 243
Lile, Editions Michel de, et Philippe Auzou (France) 108
Lilja, Bókagerdin (Iceland) 193
Lilliput, The, Press Ltd (Republic of Ireland) 223
Lima, Waldyr, Editora (Brazil) 54
Limes Verlag (Federal Republic of Germany) 154
Limmat Verlag Genossenschaft (Switzerland) 399
Limonad, Editora Max, Ltda (Brazil) 54
Limpert Verlag (Federal Republic of Germany) 154
Limusa, Editorial, SA (Mexico) 286
Linardi, Librería, y Risso (Uruguay) 491
Lincoln, Biblioteca (Argentina) 8
Lincoln, Frances, Ltd (United Kingdom) 453
Lincoln Resource Center (Malaysia) 280
Lindblads, J A, Bokförlag AB (Sweden) 385
Linden Press (United Kingdom) 453
Linder AG Literary Agency (Switzerland) 405
Lindhardt og Ringhof (Denmark) 82
Lindon Publishing (New Zealand) 309
Linea Verde (Italy) 243
Lines (United Kingdom) 453
Linford Mystery Library Series (United Kingdom) 453
Linford Romance Library Series (United Kingdom) 453
Linford Western Library Series (United Kingdom) 453
Ling, H C, Book Store & Co Ltd (Taiwan) 408
Ling Kee Group (Hong Kong) 188
Ling Kee Publishing Co Ltd (Hong Kong) 188
Ling Kee (UK) Ltd (United Kingdom) 453
Lingen Verlag (Federal Republic of Germany) 154
Lingenbrink, Barsortiment Georg (Federal Republic of Germany) 176
Link House Books (United Kingdom) 453

Lint, Casa Editrice (Italy) 243
Lion, Editions du (Republic of Gabon) 122
Lion Publishing PLC (United Kingdom) 453
Lions (United Kingdom) 453
Lipi Prakashan (India) 204
Lisciani e Giunti Editori (Italy) 243
Lisieux, Office Central de, SA (France) 108
List, Paul, Verlag (German Democratic Republic) 125
List, Paul, Verlag KG (Federal Republic of Germany) 154
List Verlag und Schroedel, Paul, Schulbuchverlag (Federal Republic of Germany) 154
Listín, Editora, Diario (Dominican Republic) 86
Lit Verlag (Federal Republic of Germany) 154
Litchfield, Jessie, Memorial Award (Australia) 24
Litera Publishing House (Romania) 346
Literackie, Wydawnictwo (Poland) 336
Literamed Publications Nigeria Ltd (Nigeria) 316
Literar-Mechana, Wahrnehmungsgesellschaft für Urheberrechte GmbH (Austria) 26
Literarische Agentur und Verlagsgesellschaft (Liechtenstein) 275
Literarischer Verein in Stuttgart eV (Federal Republic of Germany) 178
Literary Arts Board of the Australia Council (Australia) 10
Literary Arts Board of the Australia Council (Australia) 24
Literary Award (Romania) 348
Literary Critics' Grand Prize (International Literary Prizes) 520
Literary Fund Writing Bursary (New Zealand) 313
Literary Guild, The (Australia) 20
Literary Guild, The (New Zealand) 311
Literary Guild (United Kingdom) 481
Literary Prize (Panama) 328
Literary Prize (Republic of Korea) 272
Literary Prizes for Sinhala Literature (Sri Lanka) 379
Literary Services (Pty) Ltd (Republic of South Africa) 360
Literary Supplies (Jamaica) 255
Literary Translation Prize (Denmark) 86
Literas-Verlag GmbH (Austria) 28
Literatheke (Switzerland) 399
Literature and Art Publishing House (Democratic People's Republic of Korea) 268
Literature Bureau, The (Zimbabwe) 504
Literature Bureau, The (Zimbabwe) 505
Literature Bureau, The, Annual Literary Award (Zimbabwe) 506
Literature House Ltd (Taiwan) 408
Literature Institute (Czechoslovakia) 78
Literature Prize (Democratic Republic of Madagascar) 277
Literature Prize (Federal Republic of Germany) 179
Literature Prize of the Province of Steiermark (Austria) 33
Literaturkreis der Autoren (Austria) 32
Literaturkritikernes Laug (Critics Literary Prize) (Denmark) 86
Lito, Editions (France) 108
Lito Technion Ltda (Colombia) 70
Litoimpresores SA (Mexico) 286
Litolff's, Henry, Verlag (Federal Republic of Germany) 154
Litor Publishers (United Kingdom) 453
Litpress (Switzerland) 405
Littera Scripta Manet (Netherlands) 299
Littérature, Editeurs de, biblique (Belgium) 40
Litteraturfrämjandet (Sweden) 390
Little Flower, The, Co (India) 204
Little Golden Books (Australia) 16
Little Hills Press (Australia) 16
Little Stephen (United Kingdom) 453
Little Swan (India) 204
Liveright (United Kingdom) 453
Liverpool City Libraries (United Kingdom) 483
Liverpool University Press (United Kingdom) 453
Livewire (United Kingdom) 453
Liviana Editrice SpA (Italy) 243
Living & Learning (Cambridge) Ltd (United Kingdom) 453
Living Literary Agency Elfriede Pexa (Italy) 251
Livraria Editora Técnica Ltda (LITEC) (Brazil) 54
Livre de Paris, Le, Hachette (France) 108
Livre de Poche, Le (France) 108
Livre-Service, Librairie (Morocco) 290
Livres de France (Egypt) 89
Livro Científico, Club do (Brazil) 57
Livros, Editora, do Brasil Sarl (Portugal) 342
Livros Irradiantes SA (Brazil) 54
Livros Técnicos, Editora Portuguesa de, e Científicos Lda (Portugal) 342
Llewellyn Rhys, John, Memorial Prize (International Literary Prizes) 520
Lloyd Anversois SA (Antwerpse Lloyd NV) (Belgium) 40

INDEX 571

Lloyd-Luke (Medical Books) Ltd (United Kingdom) 453
Lloyd's of London Press Ltd (United Kingdom) 453
Llull, Ramon, Prize (Spain) 378
Llyfrgell Genedlaethol Cymru (National Library of Wales) (United Kingdom) 483
Lo Faro, Vincenzo, Editore (Italy) 243
Lobato, Monteiro, Prize (Brazil) 59
Local Government Council Library (Somalia) 354
Local Heritage Books (United Kingdom) 453
Local History Award (Australia) 24
Local Publications Ltd (United Kingdom) 453
Lochee Classical Library (United Kingdom) 453
LocheeSoft (United Kingdom) 454
Löcker Verlag (Austria) 28
Lockhart, Joseph, Associates Ltd (New Zealand) 311
Locomotion Papers (United Kingdom) 454
Locomotive Publishing Co Ltd (United Kingdom) 454
Locusta, Editrice La (Italy) 243
Lodenek Press Ltd (United Kingdom) 454
Lodzkie, Wydawnictwo (Poland) 336
Loeb Classical Library (United Kingdom) 454
Loeper, von, Verlag GmbH (Federal Republic of Germany) 154
Loescher Editore SpA (Italy) 243
Loewes Verlag KG (Federal Republic of Germany) 155
Loffredo Editore Napoli SpA (Italy) 243
Lofler, Paul, Foundation Prize (France) 120
Logans University Bookshop (Pty) Ltd (Republic of South Africa) 360
Loghum, Van, Slaterus (Netherlands) 299
Logos Consorcio Editorial SA (Mexico) 286
Logosófica, Editora (Brazil) 54
Loguez Ediciones (Spain) 369
Lohlé, Carlos, SA (Argentina) 6
Løhren, Ulla, Literary Agency (Norway) 323
Lohses Forlag (Denmark) 82
Lok Vangmaya Griha Ltd (India) 204
Lokole, Editions (Zaire) 502
Lolfa, Y, Cyf (United Kingdom) 454
Lombard, Les Editions du, SA (Belgium) 40
London Bookshops Ltd (New Zealand) 312
London Editions (United Kingdom) 454
London Magazine Editions (United Kingdom) 454
London Writer Circle (United Kingdom) 485
Lonely Planet Publications Pty Ltd (Australia) 16
Longanesi & C (Italy) 243
Longman Botswana (Pty) Ltd (Botswana) 49
Longman Caribbean Ltd (Trinidad and Tobago) 413
Longman Cheshire Pty Ltd (Australia) 16
Longman Group (Far East) Ltd (Hong Kong) 188
Longman Group UK Ltd (United Kingdom) 454
Longman Jamaica Ltd (Jamaica) 254
Longman Kenya Ltd (Kenya) 267
Longman Lesotho (Pty) Ltd (Lesotho) 274
Longman Malaysia Sdn Bhd (Malaysia) 279
Longman Nigeria Ltd (Nigeria) 316
Longman Paul Ltd (New Zealand) 309
Longman Penguin Southern Africa (Pty) Ltd (Republic of South Africa) 357
Longman Singapore (Pte) Ltd (Republic of Singapore) 351
Longman Uganda Ltd (Uganda) 416
Longman Zimbabwe (Pvt) Ltd (Zimbabwe) 505
Longo, Angelo, Editore (Italy) 243
Look and Cook Club (Republic of South Africa) 359
Lope de Vega, Librería y Papelería (Dominican Republic) 87
Lopes, Julia, de Ameida Prize (Brazil) 60
Lopes Da Silva, Livraria, -Editora de M Moreira Soares Rocha Lda (Portugal) 342
López Libreros Editores (Argentina) 6
Löpfe-Benz, E, AG Rorschach, Graphische Anstalt und Verlag (Switzerland) 399
Lorber-Verlag (Federal Republic of Germany) 155
Lorch-Verlag GmbH (Federal Republic of Germany) 155
Lord International (India) 204
Losada, Editorial, SA (Argentina) 6
Lothian, Thomas C, Pty Ltd (New Zealand) 309
Lothian Publishing Co Pty Ltd (Australia) 16
Lotu Pasifika Productions (Fiji) 91
Lotus, Uitgeverij, /Editions Lotus (Belgium) 40
Louisiana State University Press (United Kingdom) 454
Lovedale Press (Republic of South Africa) 357
Lowden Publishing Co (Australia) 16
Lowe, Peter (United Kingdom) 454
Lowe, Robson, Ltd (United Kingdom) 454
Löwit, R, GmbH (Federal Republic of Germany) 155
Loyola, Edições, SA (Brazil) 54
Lübbe, Gustav, Verlag GmbH (Federal Republic of Germany) 155
Lubelskie, Wydawnictwo (Poland) 336
Lucarini Editore SRL (Italy) 243

Luchterhand, Hermann, Verlag GmbH & Co KG, Neuwied und Darmstadt (Federal Republic of Germany) 155
Lucis Press Ltd (United Kingdom) 454
Lucky (Australia) 20
Lucky (New Zealand) 311
Lucky Book Club (United Kingdom) 481
Luctor Publishing — Stadler en Sauerbier BV (Netherlands) 299
Ludowa Spóldzielnia Wydawnicza (Poland) 336
Ludwig, W, Verlag (Federal Republic of Germany) 155
Luitingh, Uitgeverij, BV (Netherlands) 299
Lumen, Editions, Vitae ASBL (Belgium) 40
Lumen, Editorial, SA (Spain) 370
'Lumen Christi', Edições (Brazil) 54
Lumiere Biblique (France) 108
Luna, Libreria Internazionale Giuseppe (Italy) 251
Lund Humphries Publishers Ltd (United Kingdom) 454
Lunde Forlag og Bokhandel A/S (Norway) 321
Lundequistska, Esselte Bokhandel (Sweden) 389
Lundgrens, AB Edvin, Bokhandel (Sweden) 389
Lundquist, Abr, Musikförlag AB (Sweden) 385
Lunds Universitetsbibliotek (Sweden) 389
Lusaka Urban District Libraries (Zambia) 503
Lusva Editrice (Italy) 243
Luther Forlag A/S (Norway) 321
Luther-Verlag GmbH (Federal Republic of Germany) 155
Lutheran Publishing House (Australia) 16
Lutherisches Verlagshaus GmbH (Federal Republic of Germany) 155
Lutry, The, Press (Switzerland) 399
Lutterworth Press (United Kingdom) 454
Lutz, Hans-Rudolf (Switzerland) 399
Lutz, Verlag Waldemar (Federal Republic of Germany) 155
Lux Press (Malta) 281
Lux Verbi (Pty) Ltd (Republic of South Africa) 357
Luxembourg, Library, Commission of the European Communities (International Organizations) 510
Luxor Press Ltd (United Kingdom) 454
Luzo-Espanhola, Livraria, Lda (Portugal) 342
Lyche, Harald, & Co A/S (Norway) 321
Lydecken, Arvid, Prize (Finland) 95
Lyle Publications Ltd (United Kingdom) 454
Lyngs Bokhandel A/S (Norway) 323
Lypsa, Industria Editorial (Honduras) 187
Lypsa, Librería (Honduras) 187
Lyra, Carmen, Literary Prize (Costa Rica) 73
Lyra Libri SAS (Italy) 243
Lyrikvaennene, Bokklubbens (Norway) 323
Lythway Press Ltd (United Kingdom) 454

M A B, The, Cookery Book Club (Iceland) 194
M A M (The House of the Cyprus Publications) (Cyprus) 74
M B A Literary Agents Ltd (United Kingdom) 479
M C B University Press Ltd (United Kingdom) 454
M C S Enterprises Inc (Philippines) 332
M D I, Editions, (La Maison des Instituteurs) (France) 108
M E B, Casa Editrice, SRL (Italy) 243
M E/D I Sviluppo (Italy) 243
M E D S I (Japan) 259
M E D S I (Médecine et Sciences Internationales) (France) 109
M E P (United Kingdom) 455
M E R Prize (Republic of South Africa) 362
M en I, NV (Belgium) 40
M F B — Produktion (Phono- und Schriftenmission des Missionswerkes Frohe Botschaft eV) (Federal Republic of Germany) 155
M G P (United Kingdom) 455
M I N D Book of the Year Award (United Kingdom) 487
M I N D (National Association for Mental Health) (United Kingdom) 455
M I T, The, Press (United Kingdom) 455
M O D (United Kingdom) 455
M P H Bookstores (S) Pte Ltd (Republic of Singapore) 353
M P H Distributors Sdn Bhd (Malaysia) 280
M P S A (Republic of South Africa) 357
M P Text Book Corporation (India) 204
M R P (United Kingdom) 455
M T P Press Ltd (United Kingdom) 455
M V G (Federal Republic of Germany) 155
M W H London Publishers (United Kingdom) 455
Ma'alot (Israel) 228
Mäander Verlag GmbH (Federal Republic of Germany) 155
Maaref, Dar Al (Egypt) 88
Maaref, Dar Al-, Liban Sàrl (Lebanon) 273

Ma'arif, Al, Ltd (Iraq) 220
Ma'ariv Book Club (Israel) 230
Ma'ariv Book Guild (Sifriat Ma'ariv) (Israel) 228
Maarten Kluwer's Internationale Uitgeversonderneming NV (Belgium) 40
Maatschappij der Nederlandse Letterkunde (Netherlands) 305
Mabrochi International Co Ltd (Nigeria) 318
Mac Purcell (Lebanon) 273
Macaulay Fellowship (Republic of Ireland) 225
Maccari, Casa Editrice, (C E M) (Italy) 243
Macchi, Ediciones (Argentina) 6
McColvin Medal (United Kingdom) 487
McCrimmon Publishing Co Ltd (United Kingdom) 455
Macdonald & Co (Publishers) Ltd (United Kingdom) 455
Macdonald & Evans Ltd (United Kingdom) 455
Macdonald 3/4/5 (United Kingdom) 455
Macdonald Edinburgh (United Kingdom) 455
Macdonald Educational (United Kingdom) 455
Macdonald Guidelines (United Kingdom) 455
Macdonald Middle East Sàrl (Lebanon) 273
Macdonald Publishers (Edinburgh) (United Kingdom) 455
Macdonald Purnell (Pty) Ltd (Republic of South Africa) 357
Macdonald Queen Anne Press (United Kingdom) 455
Macdonald Starters (United Kingdom) 455
Mace, Jean, Prize (France) 120
McGraw-Hill, Editora, de Portugal Lda (Portugal) 342
McGraw-Hill, Editora, do Brasil Ltda (Brazil) 54
McGraw-Hill, Editorial, Latinoamericana SA (Colombia) 70
McGraw-Hill, Editorial, Latinoamericana SA (Panama) 328
McGraw-Hill, Editorial, Latinoamericana SA (Puerto Rico) 345
McGraw-Hill, Libros, de Mexico SA de CV (Mexico) 286
McGraw-Hill, Tata, Publishing Co Ltd (India) 204
McGraw-Hill Book Co Australia Pty Ltd (Australia) 16
McGraw-Hill Book Co GmbH (Federal Republic of Germany) 155
McGraw-Hill Book Co Japan Ltd (Japan) 259
McGraw-Hill Book Co, New Zealand Ltd (New Zealand) 309
McGraw-Hill Book Co (South Africa) (Pty) Ltd (Republic of South Africa) 357
McGraw-Hill Book Co (UK) Ltd (United Kingdom) 455
McGraw-Hill Inc (France) 109
McGraw-Hill Interamericana de España SA (Spain) 370
McGraw-Hill International Book Co (Republic of Singapore) 352
Machado, Fernando, e Co Ltd (Portugal) 342
Machado de Assis Prize (Brazil) 60
Machbarot Lesifrut (Israel) 228
Machell, Roger, Prize (United Kingdom) 488
Machreq, Darl el-, Sàrl (Lebanon) 273
McIndoe, John, Ltd (New Zealand) 309
McIntyre, Grant, Ltd (United Kingdom) 455
Mackay, Jessie, Award (New Zealand) 313
McKee et Mouche (France) 116
Mackintosh Hall, John, Library (Gibraltar) 182
McLeod, Enid, Prize (International Literary Prizes) 520
Macmillan Boleswa Publishers (Pty) Ltd (Swaziland) 381
Macmillan Children's Books (United Kingdom) 455
Macmillan Co, The, of Australia Pty Ltd (Australia) 16
Macmillan Company, The, of New Zealand Ltd (New Zealand) 309
Macmillan Education Ltd (United Kingdom) 455
Macmillan India Ltd (India) 204
Macmillan London Ltd (United Kingdom) 455
McMillan Memorial Libraty (Kenya) 268
Macmillan Nigeria Publishers Ltd (Nigeria) 317
Macmillan Press, The, Ltd (United Kingdom) 456
Macmillan Publishers (China) Ltd (Hong Kong) 188
Macmillan Publishers Ltd (United Kingdom) 456
Macmillan Publishers (M) Sdn Bhd (Malaysia) 279
Macmillan SA (Switzerland) 399
Macmillan Silver Pen Award for Fiction (United Kingdom) 488
Macmillan South Africa (Publishers) (Pty) Ltd (Republic of South Africa) 357
Macmillan Southeast Asia Pte Ltd (Republic of Singapore) 352
Macondo Ediciones SRL (Argentina) 6
McPhee Gribble Publishers Pty Ltd (Australia) 16
MacRae, Julia, Books (United Kingdom) 456
McRae Russell, The Walter, Award (Australia) 24
McVitie's Prize for Scottish Writer of the Year (United Kingdom) 488

572 INDEX

Madagascar Print & Press Co (Democratic Republic of Madagascar) 276
Madáh (Czechoslovakia) 76
Madarali, Fikret, Prize (Turkey) 416
Made Simple (United Kingdom) 456
Madhyo Pradesh Hindi Granth Academy (India) 204
Madju (Indonesia) 218
Madras Literary Society and Auxiliary of the Royal Asiatic Society (India) 215
Madras Literary Society Library (India) 214
Mafra (Portugal) 342
Magalhães, Livraria, Sarl (Angola) 2
Magasin du Nord A/S (Denmark) 84
Maghreb Livres (Morocco) 290
Maghrebines, Les Editions (Morocco) 290
Magic Bean Shared-Readers (Australia) 16
Magic-Corte, Editora, S/A (Brazil) 54
Magic-Strip SA (Belgium) 40
Magisterio, Editorial, Español SA (Spain) 370
Magistero, Edizioni (Italy) 243
Magna Print Books (United Kingdom) 456
Magnard, Les Editions, Sàrl (France) 109
Magnes, The, Press (Israel) 228
Magnet (United Kingdom) 456
Magnus Edizioni SpA (Italy) 243
Magnus Verlag (Federal Republic of Germany) 155
Magrana, Edicions de la, SA (Spain) 370
Magvető Könyvkiadó (Hungary) 190
Magwe College Library (Burma) 63
Magyar Bibliofil társaság (Hungary) 192
Magyar Irodalomtörténeti Társaság (Hungary) 192
Magyar Írók Szövetsége (Hungary) 190
Magyar Írók Szövetsége (Hungary) 193
Magyar Könyvkiadók és Könyvterjesztők Egyesülése (Hungary) 190
Magyar Könyvtárosok Egyesülete (Hungary) 192
Magyar Központi, Uj, Levéltár (Hungary) 191
Magyar Országos Levéltár (Hungary) 192
Magyar Tudományos Akadémia Irodalomtudományi Intézete (Hungary) 192
Magyar Tudományos Akadémia Könyvtára (Hungary) 192
Mahabir Singh Chiniya Main (Nepal) 292
Mahajan Brothers (India) 204
Maier, Otto, Benelux BV (Netherlands) 299
Maille-Latour-Landry Prize (France) 120
Mainichi Publishing Culture Prize (Japan) 265
Mainstream Publishing Co (Edinburgh) Ltd (United Kingdom) 456
Mairs Geographischer Verlag (Federal Republic of Germany) 155
Mai's Reiseführer Verlag (Federal Republic of Germany) 155
Maison, La, de la Bible (Switzerland) 399
Maison, La, du Livre (Benin) 47
Maison, La, Rustique SA (France) 109
Maison de la Presse, Société congolaise Hachette (Popular Republic of Congo) 72
Maison des Ecrivains (France) 118
Maison des Instituteurs, La (France) 109
Maison des Livres (Ivory Coast) 254
'Maison des Livres', Librairie (Algeria) 2
Maison des Sciences de l'Homme, Editions de la (France) 109
Maison du Dictionnaire, La (France) 109
Maison Tunisienne d'Edition (Tunisia) 414
Maisonneuve, Adrien (France) 109
Maisonneuve et Larose, Editions G P (France) 109
Maisonneuve SA, Editeur (France) 109
Máj (Czechoslovakia) 78
Majerove, Marie, Prize (Czechoslovakia) 79
Majlis Press (Iran) 220
Makedonska Knjiga (Yugoslavia) 500
Makedonska Knjiga (Knigoizdatelstvo) (Yugoslavia) 497
Makerere Institute of Social Research Library (Uganda) 416
Makerere University Bookshop (Uganda) 416
Makerere University Library (Uganda) 416
Maklu Uitgevers NV (Belgium) 40
Makor Publishing Ltd (Israel) 228
Maktaba-i-Danial (Pakistan) 325
Maktaba Jadeed (Pakistan) 325
Maktaba Meri Library (Pakistan) 325
Maktabah, Al, Al Wataniah (National Library) (Syria) 407
Makumira Lutheran Theological College Library (Tanzania) 409
Mál og menning (Iceland) 193
Mal og menning (Iceland) 194
Malabar, Toko Buku (Indonesia) 219
Malaby Press (United Kingdom) 456
Malacorda, Marika, Editions (Switzerland) 399
Malaga (United Kingdom) 456
Malan, H Recht, Prize (Republic of South Africa) 362
Malaparte Prize (International Literary Prizes) 520
Malatestiana, Biblioteca Comunale (Italy) 252
Malawi Book Service (Malawi) 277

Malawi Library Association, The (Malawi) 278
Malawi National Library Service (Malawi) 277
Malaya Books Suppliers Co (Malaysia) 279
Malaya Educational Supplies Sdn Bhd (Malaysia) 279
Malaya Press, The, Sdn Bhd (Malaysia) 279
Malayan Law Journal (Pte) Ltd (Malaysia) 279
Malayan Law Journal (Pte) Ltd (Republic of Singapore) 352
Malaysia Press Sdn Bhd (Republic of Singapore) 352
Malaysian Book Publishers' Association (Malaysia) 278
Malaysian Law Publishers Sdn Bhd (Malaysia) 279
Malheiros, Ricardo, Prize (Portugal) 344
Mali, Editions Imprimeries du (Mali) 281
Malik Din Mohammad & Sons (Pakistan) 325
Malik Sirajuddin & Sons (Pakistan) 325
Malipiero SpA Editore (Italy) 243
Mallard Reprints (United Kingdom) 456
Mallings ApS (Denmark) 82
Mallinson Rendel Publishers Ltd (New Zealand) 309
Malmberg, L C G, BV (Netherlands) 299
Malmö Stadsbibliotek (Sweden) 389
Malpertuis Prize (Belgium) 46
Máls og menningar, Bókabúd (Iceland) 194
Malsa Book Service Ltd (Zambia) 503
'Malysh', Izdatelstvo (Union of Soviet Socialist Republics) 418
Mamadou Traoré Ray Autra (Senegal) 349
Mambo Press (Zimbabwe) 505
Mambo Press Bookshop (Zimbabwe) 505
Mame, Nouvelles Editions (France) 109
Månadens Bok (Sweden) 388
Management Update Ltd (United Kingdom) 456
Manar, Imprimerie/Librairie Al (Tunisia) 414
Manar, Librairie Al (Tunisia) 414
Manchester University Press (United Kingdom) 456
Mandala (United Kingdom) 456
Mandalay University Library (Burma) 63
Mandarino, Editora, Ltda (Brazil) 54
Mandas Sugatdas (Nepal) 292
Mandat des Poètes Prize (International Literary Prizes) 520
Mandorla, Editorial (Venezuela) 493
Manesse Verlag (Switzerland) 399
Manfredi, Umberto (Italy) 243
Manfrini Editori (Italy) 243
Mangold, Paul, Verlag (Austria) 28
Manhattan Press (Singapore) Pte Ltd (Republic of Singapore) 352
Manhin, Victor, Ltd (Trinidad and Tobago) 413
Manila City Library (Philippines) 333
Mann, Gebr, Verlag GmbH & Co (Federal Republic of Germany) 155
Mann, Thomas, Gesellschaft (Switzerland) 406
Mann, Thomas, Prize (Federal Republic of Germany) 179
Mann, Volksbuchhandlung Thomas (German Democratic Republic) 127
Manohar Publications (India) 204
Manoharlal, Munshiram, Publishers Pvt Ltd (India) 204
Manole, Editora, Ltda (Brazil) 55
Manosabdam Books (India) 204
Manpower Services Commission Careers and Occupational Information Centre (COIC) (United Kingdom) 456
Mansell Publishing Ltd (United Kingdom) 456
Mansfield, Katherine, Memorial Award (New Zealand) 313
Mansfield, Katherine, Menton Memorial Prize (International Literary Prizes) 520
Mansk, The, Svenska Publishing Co Ltd (Isle of Man) 225
Mansour, S J (Israel) 228
Manteau (Netherlands) 300
Manteau, Uitgeversmaatschappij A, NV (Belgium) 41
Manual, Editorial El, Moderno SA de CV (Mexico) 286
Manukau Public Libraries (New Zealand) 312
Manxman Publications (United Kingdom) 456
Manz Verlag (Federal Republic of Germany) 155
Manz'sche Verlags- und Universitätsbuchhandlung (Austria) 28
Manz'sche Verlags- und Universitätsbuchhandlung (Austria) 31
Map Studio (Republic of South Africa) 357
Mapa Fiscal Editora Ltda (Brazil) 55
Maqbool Academy (Pakistan) 325
Marabout, Les Nouvelles Editions, SA (Belgium) 41
Marais, Eugène, Prize (Republic of South Africa) 362
Marangu College of National Education Library (Tanzania) 409
Marbán, Editorial (Spain) 370
Marca, Editorial, Ltda (Colombia) 70
Marchal, Joseph-Edmond, Prize (Belgium) 46
Marcham Books (United Kingdom) 456
Marcombo, Publicaciones, SA (Mexico) 286

Marcombo SA de Boixareu Editores (Spain) 370
Marcus, Editions (France) 109
Marcus, Y, & Co Ltd (Israel) 228
Marczell, Tibor (Federal Republic of Germany) 155
Mardaga, Pierre, SA (Belgium) 41
Maredsous ASBL (Belgium) 41
Marfiah (Indonesia) 218
Marfil, Editorial, SA (Spain) 370
Marg Publications (India) 204
Margai, Milton, Teachers' College Library (Sierra Leone) 350
Marguerat, Librairie-Editions J (Switzerland) 399
Marhold, Carl, Verlagsbuchhandlung (Federal Republic of Germany) 155
Marican & Sons (M) Sdn Bhd (Malaysia) 279
Marican Sdn Bhd (Malaysia) 280
Marie-Médiatrice, Editions, ASBL (Belgium) 41
Marietti Scuola, Casa Editrice, SpA (Italy) 244
Marietti SpA, Casa Editrice (Italy) 244
Marietti SpA, Pietro (Italy) 244
Marin, Editorial, SA (Spain) 370
Marino, Aldo, Editore (Italy) 244
Maritim, Edition (Federal Republic of Germany) 155
Maritime Book Society (United Kingdom) 481
Maritime Books (United Kingdom) 456
Maritimes et d'Outre-Mer, Editions, SA (France) 109
Marix Evans & Chilvers SA (Switzerland) 399
Markazi Maktaba Islami (India) 205
Market House Books Ltd (United Kingdom) 456
Markham, Arthur, Memorial Prize (United Kingdom) 488
Marković, Univerzitetska biblioteka 'Svetozar' (Yugoslavia) 500
Marksa, Gosudarstvennaya Respublikanskaya biblioteka Gruzinskoi SSR im K (Union of Soviet Socialist Republics) 420
Marlu Literary Agency (United Kingdom) 480
Maro Verlag (Federal Republic of Germany) 155
Marotta, Alberto, Editore SpA (Italy) 244
Marova, Ediciones, SL (Spain) 370
Marques de Cerralbo XVII Prize (Spain) 378
Marsh & Sheil Ltd (United Kingdom) 480
Marshall, Alan, Award (Australia) 24
Marshall, Muir, Ltd (Trinidad and Tobago) 413
Marshall Cavendish Books Ltd (United Kingdom) 456
Marshall Editions Ltd (United Kingdom) 456
Marshall, Morgan & Scott Publications Ltd (United Kingdom) 457
Marshall Pickering (United Kingdom) 457
Marshalls (United Kingdom) 457
Marsiega Editorial SA (Spain) 370
Marsilio Editori SpA (Italy) 244
Marsland Press (United Kingdom) 457
Martano, Editore (Italy) 244
Martello, Giunti, Editore (Italy) 244
Martin Books (United Kingdom) 457
Martin Educational (Australia) 16
Martínez, Ediciones, Roca SA (Spain) 370
Martínez, H F, de Murguía SA (Spain) 376
Martínez, H F, de Murguía SAC y E (Argentina) 8
Martins, Livraria, Editora SA (Brazil) 55
Martins, Livraria Tavares (Portugal) 342
Martins Forlag A/S (Denmark) 82
Martinucci Pubblicazioni Mediche SAS (Italy) 244
Maruzen Asia (Pte) Ltd (Republic of Singapore) 352
Maruzen Co Ltd (Japan) 259
Maruzen Co Ltd (Japan) 263
Marva (Switzerland) 399
Marwah Publications (India) 205
Marxistische Blätter, Verlag, GmbH (Federal Republic of Germany) 155
Marymar Ediciones SA (Argentina) 6
März Verlag GmbH (Federal Republic of Germany) 155
Marzocco, Editrice Giunti (Italy) 244
Marzorati Editore SRL (Italy) 244
Mas Ivars Editores SL (Spain) 370
Masagung, CV Haji (Indonesia) 218
Masagung Books Pte Ltd (Republic of Singapore) 352
Masagung Books Pte Ltd (Republic of Singapore) 353
Mascareignes, Librairie des (Mauritius) 283
Maschler, Kurt, Award (United Kingdom) 488
'Mashinostroenie', Izdatelstvo (Union of Soviet Socialist Republics) 418
Maskew Miller Longman (Pty) Ltd (Republic of South Africa) 357
Maskew Miller Longman (Pty) Ltd (Republic of South Africa) 360
Masks (United Kingdom) 457
Mason Publications, Kenneth, Ltd (United Kingdom) 457
Masque, Le (France) 109
Mass, Rubin, Ltd (Israel) 228
Mass Culture Publishing House (Democratic People's Republic of Korea) 268
Massada Press Ltd (Israel) 228
Massada Press Ltd (Israel) 231

Massada Publishers Ltd (Israel) 228
Massimo, Editrice, SAS di Crespi Cesare e C (Italy) 244
Massin, Editions Charles, et Cie (France) 109
Masson, Editora, do Brasil Ltda (Brazil) 55
Masson Editeur (France) 109
Masson Editores (Mexico) 286
Masson Italia Editori SpA (Italy) 244
Masson SA (Spain) 370
Mastrogiacomo Editore (Italy) 244
Matica slovenská (Czechoslovakia) 76
Matica slovenská (Czechoslovakia) 78
Matice moravská (Czechoslovakia) 78
Matopo Book Centre (Zimbabwe) 505
Matrix Publishing Group Ltd (United Kingdom) 457
Matthaes, Hugo, Druckerei und Verlag GmbH & Co KG (Federal Republic of Germany) 155
Matthes und Seitz Verlag GmbH (Federal Republic of Germany) 155
Matthias-Estienne (France) 116
Matthias-Grünewald-Verlag (Federal Republic of Germany) 156
Matthiesen Verlag Ingwert Paulsen Jnr (Federal Republic of Germany) 156
Matze, Les Editions la (Switzerland) 399
Mauclert, Librairie, et Cie (Niger) 314
Maudrich, Buchhandlung Wilhelm, für medizinische Wissenschaften (Austria) 31
Maudrich, Verlag Wilhelm (Austria) 28
Maugham, Somerset, Award (United Kingdom) 488
Mauritius Archives (Mauritius) 283
Mauritius Institute Public Library (Mauritius) 283
Mauritius Library Association (Mauritius) 283
Maximilian-Gesellschaft eV (Federal Republic of Germany) 178
Maximilian-Verlag (Federal Republic of Germany) 156
Maximilian-Verlagsgruppe (Federal Republic of Germany) 156
Maxwell Communication Corporation plc (United Kingdom) 457
May, Franca, Edizioni SRL (Italy) 244
May, Karl-, -Verlag (Federal Republic of Germany) 156
Mayela, Librería Editorial Gerardo (Mexico) 288
Mayer, Edition Hansjörg (Federal Republic of Germany) 156
Mayer, Editions (France) 109
Mayer, Ludwig, Ltd (Israel) 231
Mayer'sche, J A, Buchhandlung (Federal Republic of Germany) 156
Mayersche Buchhandlung, J A (Federal Republic of Germany) 176
Mayfair Paperbacks (India) 205
Mayhew-McCrimmon Ltd (United Kingdom) 457
Mayoor Paperbacks (India) 205
Mazarine, Editions (France) 109
Mazenod Book Centre (Lesotho) 274
Mazenod-Editio, Editions, SA (France) 109
Mazenod Institute (Lesotho) 274
Mazzotta, Nuove Edizioni Gabriele, SRL (Italy) 244
Mead & Beckett Publishing (Australia) 17
Meadowfield Press Ltd (United Kingdom) 457
Meca, Editora, Ltda (Brazil) 55
Mechanical Engineering Publications Ltd (United Kingdom) 457
Medea Frauenverlag (Federal Republic of Germany) 156
Médecine, Bibliothèque Interuniversitaire de (France) 117
Médecine et Hygiène (Switzerland) 399
Médecines et Sciences Internationales (France) 109
Mediabank (Republic of Korea) 271
Médiaspaul, Editions (France) 109
Medica, Librería, Paris (Venezuela) 493
Médica, Librería y Editorial La (Argentina) 6
Médica Panamericana, Editorial, SA (Argentina) 6
Medica y Tecnica, Editorial, SA (Spain) 370
Medical, The, Library (Tanzania) 409
Medical Friend Co Ltd (Japan) 259
Medical Media (Italy) 244
Medical Sciences International Ltd (Japan) 259
Medicala, Editura (Romania) 346
Medicea, Edizioni, SRL (Italy) 244
Mediche Italiane, Edizioni, di Giovanni Sartorio (Italy) 244
Medici, Ediciones, SA (Spain) 370
Medici, The, Society Ltd (United Kingdom) 457
Medicina Könyvkiadó (Hungary) 191
Medicinska Knjiga (Yugoslavia) 497
Medicinska Naklada (Yugoslavia) 497
Médicis Essay Prize (International Literary Prizes) 520
Médicis Foreign Prize (International Literary Prizes) 520
Médicis Prize (France) 120
Medico Farmaceutica, Organizzazione Editoriale, SRL (Italy) 244
Medina, Editorial, SRL (Uruguay) 491

Mediolanum Editori Associati SRL (Italy) 244
Mediterranean Publishing Co Ltd (Malta) 281
Mediterranee, Edizioni, SRL (Italy) 244
Mediterrania, Editorial, SA (Spain) 370
'Meditsina', Izdatelstvo (Union of Soviet Socialist Republics) 418
Meditsina i Fizkultura (Bulgaria) 60
Medium, Bokförlaget, AB (Sweden) 385
Medizin, Buchhandlung für (German Democratic Republic) 127
Medizin, Verlag für, Dr Ewald Fischer GmbH (Federal Republic of Germany) 156
Medizinisch-Literarische Verlagsgesellschaft mbH (Federal Republic of Germany) 156
Medlevant AG (Switzerland) 399
Meeking, The Charles, Award (Australia) 24
Meenakshi Prakashan (India) 205
Meera Memorial Award (India) 216
Meerut Publishers' Association (India) 195
Meerwein, Rose M (Federal Republic of Germany) 175
Megalong Books (Australia) 17
Megapress, Verlagsbuchhandlung, Franz-J Gaber und W Poth GbR (Federal Republic of Germany) 156
Megiddo Publishing Co (Israel) 228
Mei Ya Publications Inc (Sueling, Inc) (Taiwan) 408
Meier, Otto, Verlag (Federal Republic of Germany) 155
Meiji Shoin Co Ltd (Japan) 259
Meili, Buchhandlung, & Co (Switzerland) 405
Meili, Peter, & Co (Switzerland) 399
Meinema/Waltman (Netherlands) 300
Meiner, Felix, Verlag GmbH (Federal Republic of Germany) 156
Meisenheim, Verlag Anton Hain, GmbH (Federal Republic of Germany) 156
Meissner, Otto, Verlag (Federal Republic of Germany) 156
Mejía, Librería-Editorial Juan, Baca (Peru) 330
Mejía, Librería Juan, Baca (Peru) 331
Mekise Nirdamin Society (Israel) 231
Melantrich (Czechoslovakia) 76
Melawai, Toko Buku (Indonesia) 219
Melayu, Pustaka, Baru (Malaysia) 279
Melbourne House (Australia) Pty Ltd (Australia) 17
Melbourne University Press (Australia) 17
Melhoramentos, Companhia, de São Paulo (Brazil) 55
Melins, Gustav, AB (Sweden) 385
Melissa Publishing House (Greece) 183
Mella (Dominican Republic) 87
Mellinger, J Ch, Verlag GmbH (Federal Republic of Germany) 156
Melrose Press Ltd (United Kingdom) 457
Melzer GmbH, Verlag Abi (Federal Republic of Germany) 156
Melzer Verlag KG (Federal Republic of Germany) 156
Memorie Domenicane (Italy) 244
Mencap Publications (United Kingdom) 457
Mendes, Odorico, Prize (Brazil) 60
Menéndez, Librería (Panama) 328
Menéndez, Ramón, Pidal Prize (International Literary Prizes) 521
Menéndez Pelayo, Biblioteca de (Spain) 376
Mengès, Société des Editions (France) 109
Menna, Casa Editrice, di Sinisgalli Menna Giuseppina (Italy) 245
Menningarsjóds og Pjódvinafélagsins, Bókaútgáfa (Iceland) 193
Mensajero, Ediciones (Spain) 370
Mensch und Arbeit, Verlag, Robert Pfützner GmbH (Federal Republic of Germany) 156
Mensing's Caminada (Netherland Antilles) 307
Mentor-Verlag Dr Ramdohr KG (Federal Republic of Germany) 156
Menzies, John, (Holdings) Ltd (United Kingdom) 482
Merbabu, Toko Buku (Indonesia) 219
Mercantila, Forlaget, A/S (Denmark) 82
Mercat Press (United Kingdom) 457
Mercatorfonds Arcade (Belgium) 41
Mercatorfonds SA (Belgium) 41
Mercier, The, Bookshop Ltd (Republic of Ireland) 224
Mercier, The, Press Ltd (Republic of Ireland) 223
Merck, Johann Heinrich, Prize (Federal Republic of Germany) 179
Merckx, Editeur Paul F (Belgium) 41
Mercure de France SA (France) 109
Mercurius PVBA (Belgium) 41
Mercury (United Kingdom) 457
Merehurst Ltd (United Kingdom) 457
Meresborough Books (United Kingdom) 457
Mergus Verlag Hans A Baensch (Federal Republic of Germany) 156
Meriam Webster (United Kingdom) 458
Merian, Christoph, Verlag (Switzerland) 399
Meribérica — Editorial e Comercialização de Direitos Lda (Portugal) 342

Meridiane, Editura (Romania) 346
Merkaz Le-Chinuch Torani (Israel) 228
Merlin Books Ltd (United Kingdom) 458
Merlin Library Ltd (Malta) 282
Merlin Press, The, Ltd (United Kingdom) 458
Merlin Verlag Andreas Meyer Verlags GmbH und Co KG (Federal Republic of Germany) 156
Mermaid (United Kingdom) 458
Merrill Publishing International (United Kingdom) 458
Merrion, The, Press (United Kingdom) 458
Merrow Publishing Co Ltd (United Kingdom) 458
Mersch, Verlag Wolf (Federal Republic of Germany) 156
Mertin, Dr Ray-Güde (Federal Republic of Germany) 175
Merve Verlag (Federal Republic of Germany) 156
Messageries du Livre (Grand Duchy of Luxembourg) 276
Messaggero di San Antonio (Italy) 245
Messeiller, Editions H, SA (Switzerland) 399
Messepublikationen, Verlag für (Federal Republic of Germany) 156
Messidor (France) 109
Messinger, Sylvie, Editrice (France) 109
Mestre Jou SA (Brazil) 55
Mestre Jou SA (Brazil) 58
Městská knihovna v Praze (Czechoslovakia) 78
Métailié, Editions A M (France) 110
Metal Bulletin Books Ltd (United Kingdom) 458
'Metallurgiya', Izdatelstvo (Union of Soviet Socialist Republics) 418
Methodist, The, Publishing House and Book Depot (Republic of South Africa) 357
Methodist Book Depot Ltd (Ghana) 181
Methodist Publishing House (United Kingdom) 458
Methuen & Co Ltd (United Kingdom) 458
Methuen Australia Pty Ltd (Australia) 17
Methuen Children's Books (United Kingdom) 458
Methuen LBC Ltd (Australia) 17
Methuen London (United Kingdom) 458
Methuen New Zealand (New Zealand) 309
Metodistkyrkans Förlag (Sweden) 385
Metropolitan Book Suppliers Ltd (Trinidad and Tobago) 413
Metzlersche Verlagsbuchhandlung, J B (Federal Republic of Germany) 156
Metzner, Alfred, Verlag (Federal Republic of Germany) 157
Meulenhoff Educatief BV (Netherlands) 300
Meulenhoff Informatief (Netherlands) 300
Meulenhoff International (Netherlands) 300
Meulenhoff Nederland BV (Netherlands) 300
Mexicanos, Editores, Unidos (Mexico) 288
Mexicanos Unidos, Editores, SA (Mexico) 286
Mezhdunarodnaya Kniga (Union of Soviet Socialist Republics) 419
'Mezhdunarodnaya Otnosheniya', Izdatelstvo (Union of Soviet Socialist Republics) 418
Mezőgazdasági Könyvkiadó Vállalat (Hungary) 191
Mezquita, Editorial, SA (Spain) 370
Michaelmark Books (Israel) 229
Michaud, Narcisse, Prize (France) 120
Michel, Editions Albin (France) 110
Michelin (Département Cartes & Guides) SA (Belgium) 41
Michelin et Cie (Services de Tourisme) (France) 110
Michelin Tyre PLC, Tourism Dept, Maps & Guides Division (United Kingdom) 458
Micolini's, Progress-Verlag Dr, Wtw (Austria) 29
Microshur Ltd (Israel) 229
Microzine (Australia) 17
Middelhauve, Gertraud, Verlag (Federal Republic of Germany) 157
Middle East Book Centre (Egypt) 89
Middle East Librarians Association (International Organizations) 510
Middle East Technical University Library (Turkey) 415
Midland Counties Publications (Aerophile) Ltd (United Kingdom) 458
Miessner Libreros (Spain) 376
Mifalei Tarbut Vehinuch (Israel) 229
Mihalopoulos, John, & Son SA (Greece) 184
Mil y Una, Las, Ediciones (Spain) 370
Miland Publishers (Netherlands) 300
Milano Editore, Nicola (Italy) 245
Milano Libri (Italy) 245
Milella Editore (Italy) 245
Milestone Publications (United Kingdom) 458
Milind Publications Pvt Ltd (India) 205
Militara, Editura (Romania) 347
Militärverlag der DDR (VEB) (German Democratic Republic) 125
Military Book Club (Australia) 20
Military Book Society (United Kingdom) 481
Militz, Wolfgang, und Co KG (Federal Republic of Germany) 157
Miller, Harvey, Publishers (United Kingdom) 458

574 INDEX

Miller, Louis P, Prize (France) 120
Millet Library (Turkey) 415
Milli Kütüphane (Turkey) 415
Millier, Marcelle, Prize (France) 120
Mills & Boon Ltd (United Kingdom) 458
Mills Publications Ltd (New Zealand) 309
Millwood Press Ltd (New Zealand) 310
Mimbar, Toko Buku Pustaka (Indonesia) 219
Min Eum Sa (Republic of Korea) 270
Minard, Lettres Modernes (France) 110
Minard, Librairie (France) 110
Mindolo Ecumenical Foundation, Hammarskjold Memorial Library (Zambia) 503
Mineral Research and Exploration Institute, Library of the (Turkey) 415
Minerva, Editora, Central (Mozambique) 291
Minerva, Editorial (Portugal) 342
Minerva, Editura (Romania) 347
Minerva, Libreria Editrice (Italy) 251
'Minerva' (Yugoslavia) 497
Minerva Associates (Publications) Pvt Ltd (India) 205
Minerva Central (Mozambique) 291
Minerva Italica SpA (Italy) 245
Minerva Publications (Malaysia) 279
Minerva Publikation Saur GmbH (Federal Republic of Germany) 157
Minerva Publishing, The, House (India) 205
Minerva Shobo Co Ltd (Japan) 259
Minerva's Express (Australia) 17
Mines and Geological Department Library (Kenya) 268
Mingus, Uitgeverij, BV (Netherlands) 300
Minimax Books Ltd (United Kingdom) 458
Ministère de l'Education, Bibliothèque centrale du, nationale (Belgium) 44
Ministère de l'Education, Editions du, Nationale (Guinea) 186
Ministerie van Cultuur Jeugd en Sport (Suriname) 380
Ministério das Relações Exteriores, Biblioteca do (Brazil) 58
Ministerio de Cultura, Biblioteca (Spain) 377
Ministerio de Cultura (Cuba) 73
Ministerio de Educacion, Editorial del, 'Jose de Pineda Ibarra' (Guatemala) 185
Ministerio de Educación del Gobierno de El Salvador (El Salvador) 90
Ministerrat der Deutschen Demokratischen Republik, Ministerium für Kultur, Hauptverwaltung Verlage und Buchhandel (German Democratic Republic) 123
Ministerstvo kultury CSR, Odbor knižní kultury (Czechoslovakia) 75
Ministerstwa Obrony Narodowej, Wydawnictwo (Poland) 336
Ministry, Book Club of the, of Cultural Affairs of Sri Lanka (Sri Lanka) 379
Ministry of Agriculture and Livestock Development Library (Kenya) 268
Ministry of Agriculture Library (Malaysia) 280
Ministry of Cultural Affairs (Sri Lanka) 378
Ministry of Culture, Department of Ancient Literature and Culture, (Burma) 63
Ministry of Culture and Information, Book Publishing Department (Afghanistan) 1
Ministry of Defence Publishing House (Israel) 229
Ministry of Education, Department of Educational Publications (Afghanistan) 1
Ministry of Education Library (Afghanistan) 1
Ministry of Education Library (Cyprus) 74
Ministry of Education Library (Egypt) 89
Ministry of Information (Kuwait) 272
Ministry of Information & Broadcasting (India) 205
Ministry of Justice Library (Egypt) 89
Minjungseorim Publishing Co (Republic of Korea) 270
Minkoff, Editions (Switzerland) 399
Minoas (Greece) 183
Minoas (Greece) 185
'Mintis', Leidykla (Union of Soviet Socialist Republics) 418
Minuit, Les Editions de, SA (France) 110
Mir, Izdatelstvo (Union of Soviet Socialist Republics) 418
Mir, S M (Pakistan) 326
Miraguano SA Ediciones (Spain) 370
Mirananda Publishers BV (Netherlands) 300
Miranda, G, & Sons (Philippines) 333
Miroir Sprint Publications (France) 110
Mirror Publications Ltd (United Kingdom) 458
Mirza Book Agency (Pakistan) 326
Mishima, Yukio, Award (Japan) 265
Misla (Yugoslavia) 497
Misr Bookshop (Egypt) 89
Misr Import & Export Co (Egypt) 89
Misrachi, Galeria de Arte, SA (Mexico) 286
Missio aktuell Verlag GmbH (Federal Republic of Germany) 157
Missionaria, Editrice, Italiana (E M I) (Italy) 245

Missionswerkes Frohe Botschaft (Federal Republic of Germany) 157
Misuzu Shobo Publishing Co Ltd (Japan) 259
Miswat Library (People's Democratic Republic of Yemen) 495
Mita Society for Library and Information Science (Japan) 264
Mitchell, The, Library (Glasgow District Libraries) (United Kingdom) 483
Mitchell Beazley International Ltd (United Kingdom) 458
Mitra & Ghosh Publishers Pvt Ltd (India) 205
Mitre, Editorial Librería, SRL (Argentina) 6
Mitt företag (Sweden) 388
Mitteldeutscher Verlag Halle-Leipzig (German Democratic Republic) 125
Mittler, E S, und Sohn GmbH (Federal Republic of Germany) 157
Mizrahi, M, Publishing House (Israel) 229
Mladá fronta (Czechoslovakia) 76
Mladá fronta Award (Czechoslovakia) 79
Mladé letá (Czechoslovakia) 76
Mladé letá Prize (Czechoslovakia) 79
Mladinska Knjiga (Yugoslavia) 497
Mladinska Knjiga (Yugoslavia) 500
Mladost (Yugoslavia) 497
Mladost (Yugoslavia) 500
Mladost, Izdavačko knjižarska radna organizacija (Yugoslavia) 497
Mladost's Book Fans Club (Yugoslavia) 500
Mlodziezowa Agencja Wydawnicza (Poland) 336
Mlodziezowa Agencja Wydawnicza (Poland) 337
Moa Publications Ltd (New Zealand) 310
Moadim (Israel) 230
Mockel, Albert, Grand Prize for Poetry (Belgium) 46
Model & Allied Publications Ltd (United Kingdom) 459
Modern Book Agency Pvt Ltd (India) 205
Modern Book Store (Republic of Singapore) 353
Modern Cairo Bookshop (Egypt) 89
Modern English Publications Ltd (United Kingdom) 459
Modern Poet Prize (Japan) 265
Modern Teaching Aids Pty Ltd (Australia) 17
Modern Transport (United Kingdom) 459
Moderne, Edizioni, SRL (Italy) 245
Moderne, Librairie (Togo) 412
Moderne Industrie, Verlag, AG & Co, Buchverlag (Federal Republic of Germany) 157
Moderne Industrie AG (Switzerland) 399
Moderne Jugende Heute GmbH (Austria) 29
Moderne Verlagsgesellschaft mbH (MVG) (Federal Republic of Germany) 157
Modtryk, Forlaget, AMBA (Denmark) 82
Modulverlag GmbH (Austria) 29
Mofolo-Plomer Prize (Republic of South Africa) 362
Mohammadi Library (Bangladesh) 35
Mohn, Gütersloher Verlagshaus Gerd (Federal Republic of Germany) 157
Mohn, Vereinigte Verlagsauslieferung R, HG (Federal Republic of Germany) 176
Mohr, J C B, (Paul Siebeck) (Federal Republic of Germany) 157
Mohr, Robert (Austria) 31
Molden, Verlag, — S Seewald GmbH (Federal Republic of Germany) 157
Molendinar, The, Press (United Kingdom) 459
Molho's International Bookshop (Greece) 185
Molino, Editorial (Spain) 370
Moll, Editorial, SA (Spain) 370
Mollat, Librairie (France) 116
Molodaya Gvardia, Izdatelstvo (Union of Soviet Socialist Republics) 418
Mon Village, Club, SA (Switzerland) 405
Mon Village, Editions, SA (Switzerland) 400
Monar, Creaciones, Editorial (Spain) 371
Monas Hieroglphica Centro Studi (Italy) 245
Monastery of St-Saviour, Library of the, (Basilian Missionary Order of St-Saviour) (Lebanon) 273
Mönch-Verlag GmbH & Co (Federal Republic of Germany) 157
Mondadori, Arnoldo, Editore SpA (Italy) 245
Mondadori, Edizioni Scolastiche Bruno (Italy) 245
Mondadori Ragazzi (Italy) 245
Mondo, Edizioni del, Giudiziario (Italy) 245
Mondo SA (Editions-Verlag-Edizioni) (Switzerland) 400
Mondria Publishers (Netherlands) 300
Mondrup, Svend, International Literary Agency (Denmark) 84
Monduzzi Editore SpA (Italy) 245
Monfort, Gérard (France) 110
Mongolgosknigotorg (Mongolian People's Republic) 290
Moniteur, Editions du, et de l'Usine Nouvelle (France) 110
Monserrate, Ediciones, Ltda (Colombia) 70
Mont Noir, Editions du (Zaire) 502
Montaigne (New Caledonia) 307

Montchrestien, Editions, SA (France) 110
Monte Avila Editores CA (Venezuela) 493
Montel, Editions Paul (France) 110
Monteverde, A, y Cia SA (Uruguay) 491
Montserrat Public Library (Montserrat) 290
Montyon Prize (France) 120
Moonlight Publishing Ltd (United Kingdom) 459
Moore, S J, Ltd (Kenya) 268
Moorland Mini-Books (United Kingdom) 459
Moorland Publishing Company Ltd (United Kingdom) 459
Moos, Verlag, und Partner KG (Federal Republic of Germany) 157
Mor-Carmi, M C, Ltd (Israel) 229
Móra Ferenc Ifjúsági Könyvkiadó (Hungary) 191
Moraes, Editora, Ltda (Brazil) 55
Moraes Editores SARL (Portugal) 342
Morancé, Editions Albert (France) 110
Morata, Ediciones, SA (Spain) 371
Morawa & Co (Austria) 29
Morcelliana, Editrice, SpA (Italy) 245
Moreau, Editions Alain (France) 110
Morel Editeurs (France) 110
Moreno, Fernando, Poetry Prize (Argentina) 9
Moreshet (Israel) 229
Moressopulos, Editions (Greece) 183
Moretti, Istituto Grafologico Girolamo (Italy) 245
Moretus Plantin, Bibliothèque Universitaire (Belgium) 44
Morgan-Grampian Book Publishing Co Ltd (United Kingdom) 459
Morgen, Buchverlag Der (German Democratic Republic) 125
Morija Sesuto Book Depot (Lesotho) 274
Morikita Shuppan Co Ltd (Japan) 259
Morison Arnold Ltd (Nigeria) 318
Morrigan Book Co (Republic of Ireland) 223
Morsak Verlag (Federal Republic of Germany) 157
Morskie, Wydawnictwo (Poland) 336
Morten, E J, (Publishers) (United Kingdom) 459
Mortensens, Ernst G, Forlag A/S (Norway) 321
Mortiz, Editorial Joaquín, SA (Mexico) 286
Morus-Verlag (Federal Republic of Germany) 157
Mosaik Verlag (Federal Republic of Germany) 157
Mosca Azul Editores SRL (Peru) 330
Mosca Hnos (Uruguay) 491
Mosca Hnos SA (Uruguay) 491
Moshi Public Library (Tanzania) 409
'Moskovskii Rabochiy', Izdatelstvo (Union of Soviet Socialist Republics) 418
Moskovskogo Universiteta, Izdatelstvo (Union of Soviet Socialist Republics) 418
Mossad Harav Kook (Israel) 229
Mosul Museum, Library of the (Iraq) 221
Mosul Public Library (Iraq) 221
Mother Goose Award (United Kingdom) 488
Motilal Banarsidass (India) 205
Motilal Banarsidass (India) 213
Motocourse (United Kingdom) 459
Motor Racing Publications Ltd (United Kingdom) 459
Motorbuch-Verlag (Federal Republic of Germany) 157
Motta, Federico, Editore SpA (Italy) 245
Mouj Prakashan Griha (India) 205
Mount Kenya Bookshop Ltd (Kenya) 268
Mouton de Gruyter (Federal Republic of Germany) 157
Mouton Publishers (Netherlands) 300
Mouvement pour le Couple et la Famille (Belgium) 41
Moving Into Maths Pty Ltd (Australia) 17
Mowbray, A R, & Co Ltd (United Kingdom) 459
Moxon Paperbacks (Ghana) 181
Mphala Creative Society (Zambia) 504
Mr H's Prize (Japan) 265
Mucchi Editore SRL (Italy) 245
Mudra Prakashan (India) 205
Mühlemann, Verlag Rudolf (Switzerland) 400
Muiderkring, De, BV (Netherlands) 300
Mukherjee, A, & Co Pvt Ltd (India) 205
Mukherji Book House (India) 205
Mulder Holland BV (Netherlands) 300
Mulino, Società Editrice Il (Italy) 245
Müller, Albert, Verlag AG (Switzerland) 400
Muller, Frederick (United Kingdom) 459
Müller, Otto, Verlag KG (Austria) 29
Müller, Rudolf, International Booksellers (Netherlands) 304
Müller, Verlag C F (Federal Republic of Germany) 157
Müller, Verlagsgesellschaft Rudolf, GmbH (Federal Republic of Germany) 157
Müller/Herbig, Buchverlag Ullstein Langen- (Federal Republic of Germany) 157
Muller-Groff, Librairie (Grand Duchy of Luxembourg) 276
Müller Juristischer, C F, Verlag GmbH (Federal Republic of Germany) 157

Müller und Kiepenheuer, Verlag (Federal Republic of Germany) 158
Müller und Steinicke Verlag (Federal Republic of Germany) 158
Müller Verlag, Albert Langen-Georg (Federal Republic of Germany) 158
Mullick Bros (Bangladesh) 34
Mullick Bros (Bangladesh) 35
Multatuli Prize (Netherlands) 306
Multieditions Ltd (Greece) 183
Multigrafica Editrice SRL (Italy) 245
Multilingual Matters Ltd (United Kingdom) 459
Multimedia Books Ltd (United Kingdom) 459
Multimedia SRL (Italy) 245
Multimedia Zambia (Zambia) 503
Multiple, Impresora, SA (Mexico) 286
Mun Woon Dang (Republic of Korea) 270
Munch Bunch Books (United Kingdom) 459
Munchner Arbeitsgemeinschaft der Verlagshersteller (Federal Republic of Germany) 129
Mundi, Editorial, SAIC y F (Argentina) 6
Mundi-Prensa, Librería (Spain) 376
Mundi-Prensa Libros SA (Spain) 371
Mundial, Librería (Venezuela) 493
Mundo, Editorial, Técnico SRL (Argentina) 6
Mundus, Österreichische Verlagsgesellschaft mbH (Austria) 29
Municipal Library (Bulgaria) 61
Municipal Library (Cyprus) 74
Municipal Library (Cyprus) 75
Municipal Library (Israel) 231
Municipal Library (Socialist Republic of Viet Nam) 494
Municipal Prize for Prose and Poetry (Venezuela) 494
Munin Verlag GmbH (Federal Republic of Germany) 158
Munksgaard Book & Subscription Service (Denmark) 84
Munksgaard, International Booksellers & Publishers Ltd (Denmark) 82
Muntinga, Uitgeverij Maarten (Netherlands) 300
Muralla, Editorial La, SA (Spain) 371
Murray, Donald, (Ramboro Books) (United Kingdom) 459
Murray, Donald, (Ramboro Books) (United Kingdom) 479
Murray, John, (Publishers) Ltd (United Kingdom) 459
Mursia, Ugo, Editore SpA (Italy) 245
Muscat, Giov, & Co Ltd (Malta) 282
Musée de l'Homme, Bibliothèque du (France) 117
Musée royal de Mariemont, Bibliothèque du (Belgium) 44
Musées Nationaux, Editions de la Réunion des (France) 110
Museo, Biblioteca del, Histórico Nacional (Uruguay) 491
Museo de Zoología, Biblioteca del (Cuba) 74
Museo y Biblioteca Municipal (Ecuador) 88
Museum, Perpustakaan, Nasional, Departemen Pendidikan dan Kebudayaan (Indonesia) 219
Muséum national, Bibliothèque centrale du, d'Histoire naturelle (France) 117
Muséum National, Editions du, d'Histoire naturelle (France) 110
Music Book Society (United Kingdom) 481
Music Publishers Association (United Kingdom) 422
Music Sales Ltd (United Kingdom) 459
Musica, Editorial, Moderna (Spain) 371
Musica Budapest, Editio (Hungary) 191
Musikverleger Union Österreich (Austria) 26
Muskett, Netta, Award (United Kingdom) 488
Muslim Welfare House (United Kingdom) 459
Mustard Seed Christian Publishers (Republic of South Africa) 357
Muster-Schmidt Verlag (Federal Republic of Germany) 158
Müszaki Könyvkiadó (Hungary) 191
Mutiara, PT, Sumber Widya (Indonesia) 218
Mutual Books Inc (Philippines) 332
Muusses (Netherlands) 300
Müvelt Nép Könyvterjesztö Vállalat (Hungary) 191
Muzicala, Editura (Romania) 347
Muzička Naklada (Yugoslavia) 497
Muzyczne, Polskie Wydawnictwo (Poland) 336
'Muzyka', Izdatelstvo (Union of Soviet Socialist Republics) 418
Muzzio, Franco, & C Editore SpA (Italy) 246
Mwanza Regional Library (Tanzania) 409
Myna Press (India) 205
Mysl, Izdatelstvo (Union of Soviet Socialist Republics) 418
Mysterious Press (United Kingdom) 459
Mystery and Thriller Guild (United Kingdom) 481

N B C Medal (Australia) 24
N C C Publications (United Kingdom) 459
N C R Book Award for Non-Fiction (International Literary Prizes) 521
N C R Book Award for Non-Fiction (United Kingdom) 488
N D V (Neue Darmstädter Verlagsanstalt) (Federal Republic of Germany) 158
N E L (United Kingdom) 459
N F E R-Nelson, The, Publishing Co Ltd (United Kingdom) 459
N F F (Nouvelles Feuilles Familiales) (Belgium) 41
N G Kerk Jeugboekhandel (Republic of South Africa) 357
N G Kerkboekhandel Transvaal (Republic of South Africa) 360
N G Kerkboekhandel Transvaal (DRC Publishers) (Republic of South Africa) 357
N G M Communication (Pakistan) 326
N I B, Uitgeverij (Netherlands) 300
N I S H Shtypshkronjave 'Mihal Duri' (Albania) 1
N K I-Forlaget (Norway) 321
N K S-Forlaget (Norway) 321
N O E (France) 110
N P A (Neue Presse Agentur) (Switzerland) 405
N S B Buch- und Phonoclub (Switzerland) 405
N S T (Nová sovietska tvorba) (Czechoslovakia) 78
'N T', Biblioteca (Spain) 371
N Z Listener (New Zealand) 310
N Z N-Buchverlag AG (Switzerland) 400
Nå Forlag A/S (Norway) 322
Nabco Pendidekan Sdn Bhd (Malaysia) 280
Nachrichten-Verlags-GmbH (Federal Republic of Germany) 158
Nacional, Biblioteca, Central de Angola (Angola) 2
Nacional, El, Annual Story Award (Venezuela) 494
Nacionalna i Sveučilišna Biblioteka (Yugoslavia) 500
Nadal, Eugenio, Prize (Spain) 378
Nadder Books (United Kingdom) 459
Nafees Academy (Pakistan) 325
Nagai Shoten Co Ltd (Japan) 259
Nagel (Federal Republic of Germany) 158
Nagel, Les Editions, SA (Switzerland) 400
Nagoya University Library (Japan) 263
Nah Shperndarjes Të Librit (NST) (Albania) 1
Nahda, Dar al-, al Arabia (Egypt) 89
Naim Frasheri (Albania) 1
Naipaul, The Shiva, Memorial Prize (International Literary Prizes) 521
Nakladni Zavod Matice Hrvatske (Yugoslavia) 497
Nalanda Books (India) 205
Nalanda Co Ltd (Mauritius) 283
Namboodiri, K R, Award (India) 216
Námsgagnastofnun (Iceland) 193
Nanjing tushuguan (People's Republic of China) 68
Nankodo Co Ltd (Japan) 259
Nanyang University Library (Republic of Singapore) 353
Nanzando Co Ltd (Japan) 259
Naoki Prize (Japan) 265
Napoleone, Casa Editrice Roberto (Italy) 246
Naprijed (Yugoslavia) 497
Naranco, Ediciones, SA (Spain) 371
Narcea SA de Ediciones (Spain) 371
Nardini Editore — Centro Internazionale del Libro SpA (Italy) 246
narodna biblioteka SR Crne Gore, Centralna (Yugoslavia) 500
Narodna biblioteka SR Srbije (Yugoslavia) 500
Narodna Biblioteka Srbije (Yugoslavia) 497
Narodna i univerzitetska biblioteka Bosne i Hercegovine (Yugoslavia) 500
Narodna in univerzitetna knjižnica (Ljubljana) (Yugoslavia) 500
Narodna Knjiga (Yugoslavia) 497
Narodna Kultura (Bulgaria) 61
Narodna Mladezh (Bulgaria) 61
'Narodna Prosveta', Darzhavno Izdatelstvo (Bulgaria) 61
Narodne Novine (Yugoslavia) 497
Narongsarn (Thailand) 410
Narosa Publishing House (India) 205
Narr, Gunter, Verlag (Federal Republic of Germany) 158
Naša Djeca (Yugoslavia) 497
Naša Kniga (Yugoslavia) 497
Nascimento, Editorial, SA (Chile) 65
Naše vojsko, nakladatelství a distribuce knih NP (Czechoslovakia) 76
Naše vojsko Prizes (Czechoslovakia) 79
Nasional, Perpustakaan (Indonesia) 219
Nasional, Pustaka, Pte Ltd (Republic of Singapore) 352
Nasionale Boekhandel Ltd (Republic of South Africa) 357
Nasionale Boekhandel (SWA) (Pty) Ltd (Namibia) 291

Nasionale Boekwinkels Bpk (Republic of South Africa) 360
Nasou Ltd (Republic of South Africa) 357
Nassau Public Library (Bahamas) 34
'Nasza Ksiegarnia', Instytut Wydawniczy (Poland) 336
Nateev-Printing and Publishing Enterprises Ltd (Israel) 229
Nathan, Fernand (France) 110
Nation, Verlag der (German Democratic Republic) 125
National Academy of Letters (India) 215
National Agency for ISBN (India) 195
National Archives (Egypt) 89
National Archives (Libya) 275
National Archives (New Zealand) 312
National Archives (Republic of Singapore) 353
National Archives (Sri Lanka) 379
National Archives (Trinidad and Tobago) 413
National Archives (Zimbabwe) 505
National Archives Division (Thailand) 411
National Archives of Fiji (Fiji) 91
National Archives of India (India) 214
National Archives of Malawi (Malawi) 277
National Archives of Malaysia (Malaysia) 280
National Archives of Nigeria Library (Nigeria) 319
National Archives of Pakistan (Pakistan) 327
National Archives of Tanzania (Tanzania) 409
National Archives of Zambia (Zambia) 503
National Assembly Library (Egypt) 89
National Assembly Library (Republic of Korea) 271
National Award for Poetry and the Novel (Portugal) 344
National Bank, Library of the (Afghanistan) 1
National Bank of Pakistan Prize for Literature (Pakistan) 328
National Board of Survey, Publications Division (Finland) 93
National Book, The, Co (Taiwan) 408
National Book, The, League (United Kingdom) 485
National Book Agency (P) Ltd (India) 205
National Book Centre of Bangladesh (Bangladesh) 34
National Book Council (Australia) 10
National Book Council Awards (Australia) 24
National Book Council of Pakistan (Pakistan) 324
National Book Development Council of Singapore (Republic of Singapore) 350
National Book Development Council of Singapore Book Awards (Republic of Singapore) 354
National Book Institute Prizes (Brazil) 60
National Book Store (Philippines) 332
National Book Store (Philippines) 333
National Book Trust India (India) 205
National Books of Zimbabwe (Zimbabwe) 505
National Bookshop and Branches (Bahrain) 34
National Bookstore (Liberia) 274
National Central Library (Taiwan) 408
National Centre of Archives (Iraq) 221
National Christian Education Council (United Kingdom) 459
National Computing Centre (United Kingdom) 459
National Council for Civil Liberties (United Kingdom) 460
National Council for Voluntary Organizations (United Kingdom) 460
National Council of Applied Economic Research, Publications Division (India) 205
National Council of Educational Research & Training, Publication Department (India) 205
National Council of Ethnographic Arts and Literature of China (Taiwan) 408
National Diet Library (Japan) 263
National Essay Award (Portugal) 344
National Extension College (United Kingdom) 460
National Federation of Retail Newsagents (Republic of Ireland) 422
National Federation of Retail Newsagents (United Kingdom) 422
National Foundation for Educational Research in England & Wales (United Kingdom) 460
National Free Library of Zimbabwe (Zimbabwe) 505
National Gallery of Ireland (Republic of Ireland) 223
National Grand Prize for Literature (France) 120
National Grand Prize for Poetry (France) 120
National Grand Prize for Translation (France) 121
National House for Publishing, Distributing and Advertising (Iraq) 220
National Information and Documentation Centre (Egypt) 89
National Institute, The, of Development Research and Documentation (Botswana) 49
National Institute for Compilation and Translation (Taiwan) 408
National Institute of Administration Library (Socialist Republic of Viet Nam) 494
National Institute of Education Library (Uganda) 416
National Institute of Public Administration Library (Zambia) 503

576 INDEX

National Institute of Science and Technology, Division of Documentation (Philippines) 333
National Library (Burma) 63
National Library, Central (Republic of Korea) 271
National Library (Guyana) 186
National Library (Iraq) 221
National Library (Libya) 275
National Library (Nepal) 292
National Library (Pakistan) 327
National Library (Qatar) 345
National Library (Republic of Singapore) 353
National Library (Saudi Arabia) 348
National Library, The, Government of India (India) 214
National Library, The, of Iran (Iran) 220
National Library, The, of Thailand (Thailand) 411
National Library, The, of the Philippines (Philippines) 333
National Library (United Arab Emirates) 421
National Library and Archives of Ethiopia (Ethiopia) 91
National Library (Badeeb Library) (People's Democratic Republic of Yemen) 495
National Library for Agricultural Sciences (Indonesia) 219
National Library 'Ivan Vazov' (Bulgaria) 61
National Library of Australia (Australia) 17
National Library of Australia (Australia) 21
National Library of China (People's Republic of China) 68
National Library of Greece (Greece) 185
National Library of Higher Education and Culture (Somalia) 354
National Library of Indonesia (Indonesia) 219
National Library of Ireland (Republic of Ireland) 224
National Library of Ireland Society (Republic of Ireland) 224
National Library of Jamaica (Jamaica) 255
National Library of Latakia (Syria) 407
National Library of Malaysia (Malaysia) 280
National Library of Malta (Malta) 282
National Library of New Zealand (New Zealand) 312
National Library of Nigeria (Nigeria) 319
National Library of Scotland (United Kingdom) 483
National Library of Sri Lanka (Sri Lanka) 379
National Library of Wales (United Kingdom) 483
National Library Service (Barbados) 35
National Library Service (Belize) 47
National Library Service of Papua New Guinea (Papua New Guinea) 329
National Literary Awards (Burma) 63
National Magazine Co Ltd (United Kingdom) 460
National Marriage Guidance Council (United Kingdom) 460
National Minorities Publishing House (People's Republic of China) 67
National Museum (India) 205
National Museum Library (India) 214
National Museum Library (Sri Lanka) 379
National Museums, Department of (Sri Lanka) 378
National Poetry Competition (Republic of Ireland) 225
National Poetry Competition (United Kingdom) 488
National Portrait Gallery (Publications Dept) (United Kingdom) 460
National Prize for Children's Literature (Spain) 378
National Prize for Illustration of Children's Literature (Spain) 378
National Prize for Literature (Chile) 66
National Prize for Literature (Mexico) 289
National Prize for Literature (Spain) 378
National Prize for Literature (Venezuela) 494
National Prize of Spanish Letters (Spain) 378
National Publishing House (India) 205
National Records Office Library (Sudan) 380
National Scientific and Technical Information Center (NSTIC) (Kuwait) 272
National Social Science Documentation Centre (India) 216
National Technological University, Library of the, of Athens (Greece) 185
National Union of Journalists, (Book Branch) (United Kingdom) 422
National University of Lesotho Library (Lesotho) 274
National University of Malaysia Library (Malaysia) 280
National University of Singapore Library (Republic of Singapore) 354
National War College Library (Taiwan) 408
National Youth Bureau (United Kingdom) 460
Nationale, Librairie, (Ministère Education National) (Benin) 47
Nationale Forschungs- und Gedenkstätten der klassischen deutschen Literatur — Zentralbibliothek der deutschen Klassik (German Democratic Republic) 127
Nationwide Book Service (United Kingdom) 481
Natoli and Stefan Literary Agency (Italy) 251
Natoli and Stefan Literary Agency (Italy) 253

Natsionalniya Savet, Izdatelstvo na, na Otetchestveniya Front (Bulgaria) 61
Natur och Kultur, Bokförlaget (Sweden) 385
Natur og Harmoni (Denmark) 82
Natura-Verlag (Switzerland) 400
Natural History Museum (United Kingdom) 460
Natural Resources Development College Library (Zambia) 503
Naučna biblioteka (Yugoslavia) 500
Naučna Knjiga (Yugoslavia) 498
Naufal Group Sàrl (Lebanon) 273
'Nauka', Izdatelstvo (Union of Soviet Socialist Republics) 418
'Nauka i Izkustvo', Darzhavno Izdatelstvo (Bulgaria) 61
Naukowe, Państwowe Wydawnictwo (Poland) 336
Naukowo-Techniczne, Wydawnictwa (Poland) 336
Nauta, Ediciones, SA (Spain) 371
Nautic, AB (Sweden) 385
Nautical Publishing Co Ltd (United Kingdom) 460
Nautiska Förlaget AB (Sweden) 386
Nauwelaerts Edition SA (Belgium) 41
Navajivan Trust (India) 206
Navers, Rasmus (Denmark) 82
Navoi, Gosudarstvennaya biblioteka UzSSR im Alishera (Union of Soviet Socialist Republics) 420
Navrang (India) 206
Navyug Publishers (India) 206
Naya Prokash (India) 206
Ndanda Mission Press (Tanzania) 409
Ndebele Readers' Book Club (Zimbabwe) 505
Ndërmarrja e Botimeve Ushtarake (Albania) 1
Ndërmarrja e Përhapjes së Librit (Albania) 1
Ndola Public Library (Zambia) 503
Near East School, Library of the, of Theology (Lebanon) 273
Nebelspalter Verlag (Switzerland) 400
Nederlands Bibliotheek en Lektuur Centrum (NBLC) (Netherlands) 305
Nederlandsche Boekhandel, Uitgeverij De (Belgium) 41
Nederlandsche Vereniging van Antiquaren (Netherlands) 293
Nederlandsche Vereniging voor Druk- en Boekkunst (Netherlands) 293
Nederlandsche Zondagsschool Vereeniging (Netherlands) 300
Nederlandse Boekenclub (Netherlands) 304
Nederlandse Boekverkopersbond (Netherlands) 293
Nederlandse Lezerskring Boek en Plaat BV (Netherlands) 304
Nederlandse Vereniging van Bibliothekarissen, Documentalisten en literatuuronderzoekers (NVB) (Netherlands) 305
'Nedra', Izdatelstvo (Union of Soviet Socialist Republics) 418
Née, Alfred, Prize (France) 121
Needlecraft Book Society (United Kingdom) 481
Neeraj Publishing House (India) 206
Neeta Prakashan (India) 206
Neff, Paul, Verlag KG (Austria) 29
Negara, Perpustakaan (Indonesia) 219
Nègre, Librairie SA Gaston (Benin) 47
Neguri Editorial SA (Spain) 371
Nehru Memorial Museum and Library (India) 214
Neilson, John Shaw, Poetry Award (Australia) 24
Nejat Yalki Kitabevi (Turkey) 415
Nelissen, Uitgeverij H, BV (Netherlands) 300
Nelles Verlag GmbH (Federal Republic of Germany) 158
Nélod, Gilles, Prize (Belgium) 46
Nelson, Thomas, & Sons Ltd (United Kingdom) 460
Nelson, Thomas, (Nigeria) Ltd (Nigeria) 317
Nelson Australia, Thomas (Australia) 17
Nelson Hurst & Marsh, The, Biography Prize (United Kingdom) 488
Nelson Memorial Public Library (Western Samoa) 495
Nelson Wadsworth (Australia) 17
Nem Chand & Brothers (India) 206
Nepal Academy (Nepal) 292
Nepal-Bharat Sanskritik Kendra Pustakalaya (Nepal) 292
Nepal Booksellers (Nepal) 292
Nepal Library Association (Nepal) 292
Neptun-Verlag (Switzerland) 400
Neruda, Librería e Importadora (El Salvador) 90
Neske, Verlag Günther (Federal Republic of Germany) 158
Nettikadan Corporation (Books Unit) (India) 206
Netzach (Israel) 229
Neue Berlin, Verlag Das (German Democratic Republic) 125
Neue Brehm-Bücherei, Die (German Democratic Republic) 127
Neue Darmstädter Verlagsanstalt (Federal Republic of Germany) 158
Neue Gesellschaft, Verlag, GmbH (Federal Republic of Germany) 158

Neue Kritik, Verlag, KG (Federal Republic of Germany) 158
Neue Mitte, Edition (Austria) 29
Neue Musik, Verlag (German Democratic Republic) 125
Neue Schulmann, Verlag der (Federal Republic of Germany) 158
Neue Stadt, Verlag (Switzerland) 400
Neue Stadt, Verlag, GmbH (Austria) 29
Neue Stadt, Verlag, GmbH (Federal Republic of Germany) 158
Neue Szene (Switzerland) 400
Neue Wirtschafts-Briefe, Verlag, GmbH & Co (Federal Republic of Germany) 158
Neue Zürcher Zeitung AG Buchverlag (Switzerland) 400
Neuer Finken-Verlag (Federal Republic of Germany) 158
Neuer Jugendschriften-Verlag (Federal Republic of Germany) 158
Neuer Weg, Verlag, GmbH (Federal Republic of Germany) 158
Neues Leben, Verlag (German Democratic Republic) 125
Neufeld-Verlag und Galerie (Austria) 29
Neufeld-Verlag und Galerie (Switzerland) 400
Neugebauer, Buchhandlung W (Austria) 31
Neugebauer, Wolfgang, Verlag GmbH (Austria) 29
Neukirchener Verlag des Erziehungvereins GmbH (Federal Republic of Germany) 158
Neumann, Verlag Dr Thomas (Federal Republic of Germany) 158
Neumann-Neudamm, Verlag J, KG (Federal Republic of Germany) 158
Neumann Verlag (German Democratic Republic) 125
Neumeyer, Martin (Federal Republic of Germany) 158
Neureuter, Verlag für Messepublikationen Thomas, KG (Federal Republic of Germany) 158
Neustadt International Prize for Literature (International Literary Prizes) 521
New American Library (Australia) 17
New Aqua, PT, Press/Aries Lima (Indonesia) 218
New Book Centre (India) 206
New Bookshop, The (Sudan) 380
New Cavendish Books (United Kingdom) 460
New City (Philippines) 332
New City, London (United Kingdom) 460
New Countryside Book Club (Poland) 337
New Day Readers Circle (Republic of South Africa) 359
New English Library (Australia) 17
New English Library, The, Ltd (United Kingdom) 460
New Era Publications International ApS (Denmark) 82
New Holland Publishing (United Kingdom) 460
New Horn Press Ltd (Nigeria) 317
New Interlitho SpA (Italy) 246
New Leaf Publishing Ltd (United Kingdom) 460
New Left Books (United Kingdom) 460
New Light Publishers (India) 206
New Orchard Editions (United Kingdom) 460
New Order, The, Book Co (India) 206
New Park Publications Ltd (United Kingdom) 460
New Portway Facsimile Reprints (United Kingdom) 460
New South Wales Booksellers' Association (Australia) 17
New South Wales Premier's Literary Awards (Australia) 24
New South Wales University Press Ltd (Australia) 17
New South Wales Writer's Fellowship (Australia) 24
New University Education (United Kingdom) 460
New Women's Press Ltd (New Zealand) 310
New Writers' Press (Republic of Ireland) 223
New Writers Stipendium for Literature (Austria) 33
New Zealand Authors', The, Fund (New Zealand) 312
New Zealand Book Awards (New Zealand) 313
New Zealand Book Council (New Zealand) 312
New Zealand Book Trade Organization Inc (New Zealand) 307
New Zealand Children's Books of the Year (New Zealand) 313
New Zealand Council for Educational Research (New Zealand) 310
New Zealand Government Printing Office (New Zealand) 310
New Zealand Library Association (New Zealand) 312
New Zealand Literary Fund (New Zealand) 313
New Zealand Maori Artists & Writers Society Inc (New Zealand) 312
New Zealand Women Writers' Society (New Zealand) 313
New Zealand Writers Guild (New Zealand) 313
Newdigate, Sir Roger, Prize for English Verse (United Kingdom) 488
Newman, M (Israel) 229
Newnes Books (United Kingdom) 460

INDEX 577

Newpoint, The, Publishing Co Ltd (United Kingdom) 460
Newrick Associates Ltd (New Zealand) 310
Newservice Ltd (Seychelles) 350
Newspread International (Kenya) 267
Newton Compton Editori SRL (Italy) 246
Nexø, Martin Andersen, Prize (Denmark) 86
Nexus Books (New Zealand) 310
Ney's Libros and Revistas (Honduras) 187
Nga Puna Waihanga (New Zealand) 313
Nha Xuat Ban Van Hoc (Literature Publishing House) (Socialist Republic of Viet Nam) 494
Nibondh (Thailand) 410
Nibondh (Gaysorn) (Thailand) 411
Nicholson, Robert, Publications Ltd (United Kingdom) 460
Nicolaische Verlagsbuchhandlung Beuermann GmbH (Federal Republic of Germany) 158
Nicoli, Umberto, Editore (Italy) 246
Niederösterreichisches Pressehaus, Verlag, mbH (Austria) 29
Niedersächsische Staats- und Universitätsbiliothek Göttingen (Federal Republic of Germany) 176
Niedieck Linder AG (Switzerland) 405
Niedlich, Buchhandlung Wendelin, KG (Federal Republic of Germany) 176
Niemeyer, Max, Verlag (Federal Republic of Germany) 158
Niemeyer, Verlag C W (Federal Republic of Germany) 158
Nieuwe Stad (Netherlands) 300
Nieuwe Wieken (Netherlands) 300
Nigar, Librería y Editorial, SRL (Argentina) 6
Niger (Acada) Bookshop Ltd (Nigeria) 318
Nigeria Educational Research, The, Council (Nigeria) 320
Nigerian Association of Agricultural Librarians and Documentalists (NAALD) (Nigeria) 319
Nigerian Baptist Book Store Ltd (Nigeria) 318
Nigerian Book Development Council (Nigeria) 314
Nigerian Book Development Council Book Prize (Nigeria) 320
Nigerian Book Development Council Literary Prize (Nigeria) 320
Nigerian Book Suppliers Ltd (Nigeria) 318
Nigerian Booksellers' Association (Nigeria) 314
Nigerian I S B N Agency (Nigeria) 314
Nigerian Institute of International Affairs (Nigeria) 317
Nigerian Library Association (Nigeria) 319
Nigerian Publishers' Association (Nigeria) 314
Nigerian Publishers' Services Ltd (Nigeria) 318
Nigerian Trade Review (Nigeria) 317
Nigerian Writers' Club (Nigeria) 319
Niggli, Verlag Arthur, AG (Switzerland) 400
Night Owl Publishers Pty Ltd (Australia) 17
Nightingale Books (United Kingdom) 460
Nihon Bunka Kagakusha Co Ltd (Japan) 259
Nihon Dokubungakkai (Japan) 264
Nihon Eibungakkai (Japan) 264
Nihon Shoten Kumiai Rengokai (Japan) 255
Nihon Toshokan Kyokai (Japan) 264
Nihon Vogue Co Ltd (Japan) 259
Nijgh en Van Ditmar, NV Uitgeverij (Netherlands) 300
Nijhoff, Martinus, /Dr W Junk Publishers (Netherlands) 300
Nijhoff, Martinus, Award for Translators (International Literary Prizes) 521
Nijhoff, Martinus, BV (Netherlands) 304
Nikas (Greece) 183
Nile & Mackenzie Ltd (United Kingdom) 460
Niloe, Bokförlaget, AB (Sweden) 386
Nimaroo Publishers (Australia) 17
'Nine', The, Prize (Sweden) 390
Nio Pobjeda — Oour Izdavačko-Publicistička Djelatnost (Yugoslavia) 498
Niove (Dominican Republic) 87
Nippon Bungaku Kyokai (Japan) 264
Nippon Furansu-go Furansu-bungaku Kai (Japan) 264
Nippon Hikaku Bungakukai (Japan) 264
Nippon Igaku Toshokan Kyokai (Japan) 264
Nippon Nogaku Toshokan Kyogikai (JAALD) (Japan) 264
Nippon Romazikai (Japan) 264
Nippon Rosiya Bungakkai (Japan) 264
Nippon Shuppan Hanbai Inc (Japan) 263
Nippon Toshokan Gakkai (Japan) 264
Nippon Yakugaku Toshokan Kyogikai (Japan) 264
Nirmal Book Agency (India) 206
Niro Dečje Novine (Yugoslavia) 498
Nisbet, James, & Co Ltd (United Kingdom) 460
Nishimura Co Ltd (Japan) 259
Nistri — Lischi Editori (Italy) 246
Nitzanim (Israel) 229
Niugini Press (Australia) 17
Niyom Vidhya (Thailand) 410
Nizet, Librairie A-G, Sàrl (France) 110

Nizza, Agencia de Librerías, SA (Paraguay) 330
Nizza, Ediciones (Paraguay) 329
Njala Educational Services Centre (Sierra Leone) 350
Njala University College Bookshop (Sierra Leone) 350
Njala University College Library (University of Sierra Leone) (Sierra Leone) 350
Njogu Gitene Publications (Kenya) 267
Nkrumah Teachers' College Library (Zambia) 503
Nnamdi Azikiwe Library (Nigeria) 319
No Pa To, Librairie (Togo) 412
Noach, The Maggie, Literary Agency (United Kingdom) 480
Nobel, Livraria (Brazil) 58
Nobel, Livraria, SA Editora (Brazil) 55
Nobel Prize for Literature (International Literary Prizes) 521
Nobèle, F De (France) 110
Noblet Indústria Gráfica e Editora Ltda (Brazil) 55
Noguer, Editorial, SA (Spain) 371
Nok Publishers (Nigeria) Ltd (Nigeria) 317
Nolit (Yugoslavia) 500
Nolit Publishing House (Yugoslavia) 498
Noma Award, The, for Publishing in Africa (International Literary Prizes) 521
Noma Literacy, The, Prize (International Literary Prizes) 521
Noma Prize for Juvenile Novel (Japan) 265
Noma Prize for Literature (Japan) 265
Nomos Verlagsgesellschaft mbH und Co KG (Federal Republic of Germany) 158
Nonesuch Press Ltd (United Kingdom) 460
Noord-Hollandsche, BV, Uitgeversmaatschappij (Netherlands) 300
Noordhoff International Publishing (Netherlands) 300
Noorduijn BV (Netherlands) 300
Noordwijk, Mavis A (Suriname) 380
Noray, Editorial (Spain) 371
Nord, Editrice, SRL (Italy) 246
Nord-Süd Verlag (Switzerland) 400
Nordbok, AB (Sweden) 386
Norddeutscher Verleger- und Buchhändler-Verband eV (Federal Republic of Germany) 129
Norden, Förlagshuset, AB (Sweden) 386
Nordic Council Literary Prize (International Literary Prizes) 521
Nórdica, Editorial, Ltda (Brazil) 55
Nordisk Boghandel A/S (Denmark) 84
Nordisk Musikförläggarunion (International Organizations) 510
Nordisk Videnakbeligt Bibliotekarforbund (International Organizations) 510
Nordiska Bokhandeln, AB (Sweden) 389
Nordiska Bokhandelns, AB, Förlag (Sweden) 386
Nordiska Musikförlaget, AB, /Edition Wilhelm Hansen Stockholm (Sweden) 386
Nordiska Musikförläggareföreningen (Sweden) 381
Nordjyske Landsbibliotek, Det (Denmark) 85
Noregs Boklag L/L (Norway) 322
Norfolk Press (United Kingdom) 460
Norges Landbrukshøgskoles Bibliotek (Norway) 323
Norlis, Olaf, Bokhandel A/S (Norway) 323
Norma, Ediciones, SA (Spain) 371
Norma, Editorial, SA (Colombia) 70
Normalizacyjne, Wydawnictwa (Poland) 336
Normans Förlag AB (Sweden) 386
Norn (Thailand) 410
Norris Press (Isle of Man) 225
Norsk Antikvarbokhandlerforening (Norway) 320
Norsk Bibliotekforening (Norway) 324
Norsk Bokhandler Medhjelper Forening (Norway) 320
Norsk Bokhandlersamband (Norway) 320
Norsk Bokimport A/S (Norway) 323
Norsk Boknummerkontor (Norway) 320
Norsk Dokumentasjonsgruppe (Norway) 324
Norsk Fagbibliotekforening (Norway) 324
Norsk Forleggersamband (Norway) 320
Norsk Kunstforlag A/S (Norway) 322
Norsk Musikkforleggerforening (Norway) 320
Norske Akademi for Sprog og Litteratur (Norway) 324
Norske Bibliotekansattes Landsforbund (Norway) 324
Norske Bokhandlerforening (Norway) 320
Norske Bokklubben, Den, A/S (Norway) 323
Norske Deitidsbibliotekarers Yrkeslag (Norway) 324
Norske Forfatterforening, Den (Norway) 320
Norske Forleggerforening, Den (Norway) 320
Norske Forskningsbibliotekarers Forening (Norway) 324
Norske Samlaget, Det (Norway) 322
Norske Videnskaps-Akademi, Det (Norway) 324
Norstedts Förlag AB (Sweden) 386
Norte, Editorial, SA (Argentina) 6
Norte, Librería (Argentina) 8
Norte de España, Librerías del, SA (LINESA) (Spain) 376
North Holland (Netherlands) 300
North Oxford Academic (United Kingdom) 460
North-South Books (United Kingdom) 460
Northcote House Publishers Ltd (United Kingdom) 460

Northcott Reeves, Publishers (New Zealand) 310
Northeastern University Press (United Kingdom) 461
Northern Illinois University Press (United Kingdom) 461
Northern Nigerian Publishing Co Ltd (Nigeria) 317
Northern Technical College Library (Zambia) 503
Norton, W W, & Co Ltd (United Kingdom) 461
Norwegian Association of Children's and Young People's Authors (Norway) 320
Norwegian Association of Translators (Norway) 324
Norwegian University Press (Norway) 322
Nota, Mip (Yugoslavia) 498
Notre Dame, Librairie (Benin) 47
Notre Dame, Librairie (Chad) 65
Nottbeck, Verlag Wissenschaft und Politik, Berend von (Federal Republic of Germany) 159
Nour E-Sham Book Centre (Syria) 407
Nouveau Cercle Parisien du Livre (France) 116
Nouvel Office d'Edition (France) 110
Nouvelle, Librairie (Republic of Gabon) 122
Nouvelle Agence, La (France) 116
Nouvelle Cité (France) 110
Nouvelle Diffusion SPRL DPI (Belgium) 41
Nouvelles Editions Africaines, Les (Ivory Coast) 253
Nouvelles Editions Africaines, Les (Senegal) 349
Nouvelles Editions Africaines, Les, (NEA) (Togo) 412
Nouvelles Editions Africaines, Librairie/Editions (Togo) 412
Nouvelles Editions Françaises (France) 110
Nouvelles Editions Latines (France) 110
Nouvelles Editions Marabout, Les, SA (Belgium) 41
Nouvelles Editions Rationalistes SA (France) 110
Nouvelles Feuilles Familiales (Belgium) 41
Nova Aguilar, Editora, SA (Brazil) 55
Nova Epoca Editorial Ltda (Brazil) 55
Nova Fronteira, Editora, SA (Brazil) 55
Nova Hrvatska Ltd (United Kingdom) 461
Nova Knjiga (Yugoslavia) 498
Nova Pacifica Publishing Co Ltd (New Zealand) 310
Nova Renascença (Portugal) 342
Nova Terra (Spain) 371
Novalis Verlag AG (Switzerland) 400
Novapres BV (Netherlands) 300
Novaro, Organización Editorial, SA (Mexico) 286
Novel Prize (France) 121
Novel Prize (Republic of Ireland) 225
Novello & Co Ltd (United Kingdom) 461
Novelty Trading Co (Jamaica) 255
Novo Book and Gift Store (Netherland Antilles) 307
'Novosti', Agentstvo Pechati, (APN) (Union of Soviet Socialist Republics) 418
Novus Forlag A/S (Norway) 322
Nüchtern, Verlag Monika (Federal Republic of Germany) 159
Nuestra Tierra, Editorial (Uruguay) 491
Nuestro Tiempo, Editorial, SA (Mexico) 286
Nueva Editorial Interamericana SA de CV (Mexico) 286
Nueva Imagen, Editorial, SA (Mexico) 286
Nueva Nicaragua, Editorial (Nicaragua) 314
Nueva Visión (Argentina) 8
Nueva Visión, Ediciones, SAIC (Argentina) 6
Nuevo, Editorial, Continente (Honduras) 187
Nunes, Livraria (Portugal) 343
Nuova Alfa Editoriale (Italy) 246
Nuova Italia, La, Editrice SpA (Italy) 246
Nuova Vita, Gruppo Editoriale, SpA (Italy) 246
Nuovi Autori, Editrice (Italy) 246
Nuovi Sentieri, Editrice (Italy) 246
Nurnberg, Andrew, Associates Ltd (United Kingdom) 480
Nusa, Penerbit, Indah (Indonesia) 218
Nusser Verlag (Federal Republic of Germany) 159
Nutshell Press (United Kingdom) 461
Nwamife Publishers Ltd (Nigeria) 317
Nwapa, Flora, & Co (Nigeria) 317
Ny Krim, Bokklubben (Norway) 323
Nye Bøker, Bokklubben, (New Book Club) (Norway) 323
Nymphenburger Verlagshandlung GmbH (Federal Republic of Germany) 159
Nyt Nordisk Forlag Arnold Busck A/S (Denmark) 82

O E M F (Italy) 246
O N K Agency Ltd (Turkey) 415
O R S T O M (France) 110
O S (Organizzazioni Speciali SRL) (Italy) 246
Oak Publications (United Kingdom) 461
Oakwood Press (United Kingdom) 461
Oasis Books (United Kingdom) 461
Obafemi Awolow University Press Ltd (Nigeria) 317
Obafemi Awolowo University Library (Nigeria) 319
Obelisk, Nakladatelství (Czechoslovakia) 76
Obelisk-Verlag (Austria) 29

INDEX

Oberbaumverlag (Federal Republic of Germany) 159
Oberösterreichischer Landesverlag (Austria) 29
Obobo Books (Nigeria) 317
Obod (Yugoslavia) 498
O'Brien, The, Press (Republic of Ireland) 223
O'Brien Educational (Republic of Ireland) 223
'Observer' Teenage Fiction Prize (International Literary Prizes) 521
Obunsha Co Ltd (Japan) 260
Obzor, Vydavateľstvo, NP (Czechoslovakia) 76
Obzor (Yugoslavia) 498
Oceania Printers Ltd (Fiji) 91
Océano-Éxito, Ediciones, SA (Spain) 371
Octagon, The, Press Ltd (United Kingdom) 461
Octopus Books Ltd (United Kingdom) 461
Octopus Verlag (Austria) 29
Odana Editions Pty Ltd (Australia) 17
Odd Fellows (Manchester Unity) Social Concern Book Awards (International Literary Prizes) 521
Odense Centralbibliotek (Denmark) 85
Odense Universitetsbibliotek (Denmark) 85
Odense University Press (Denmark) 82
Odeon Book Club (Klub čtenářů) (Czechoslovakia) 78
Odeon, nakladatelství krásné literatury a umění (Czechoslovakia) 76
Odeon Store LP (Thailand) 410
Odhams Books (United Kingdom) 461
O'Donovan, Anne, Pty Ltd (Australia) 17
Odusote Bookstores Ltd (Nigeria) 318
Oedayrajsingh, Drs F H R, Varma (Suriname) 380
Oehlenschläger, Adam Gottlob, Prize (Denmark) 86
Oekumenischer Verlag Dr R-F Edel (Federal Republic of Germany) 159
Oesch Verlag AG (Switzerland) 400
Oestergaard, Paul, GmbH (Federal Republic of Germany) 159
Oetinger, Verlag Friedrich (Federal Republic of Germany) 159
Oetker, August (Federal Republic of Germany) 159
Oeuvre Gravée, L' (Switzerland) 400
Ofer Publishing House (Israel) 229
Offene Worte, Verlag (Federal Republic of Germany) 159
Office Arabe de Presse et de Documentation (Syria) 407
Office Central de Lisieux SA (France) 110
Office de Documentation Bibliographique et de Diffusion (France) 110
Office de la Recherche Scientifique et Technique Outre Mer (France) 110
Office de Promotion de L'Edition Française (France) 96
Office du Livre Malagasy (OLM) (Democratic Republic of Madagascar) 276
Office du Livre SA (Buchhaus AG) (Switzerland) 400
Office international de Librairie (Belgium) 44
Office national des Librairies Populaires (ONLP) (Popular Republic of Congo) 72
Officina Edizioni di Aldo Quinti (Italy) 246
Ofiria, Edizioni (Italy) 246
Ogbalu, F C (Nigeria) 318
O'Gorman Ltd (Republic of Ireland) 224
Ogunsanya Press, Publishers and Bookstores Ltd (Nigeria) 317
Ohio University Press (United Kingdom) 461
Ohmsha Ltd (Japan) 260
Ohridski', Narodna i univerzitetska biblioteka 'Kliment (Yugoslavia) 500
Oifig an tSoláthair (Republic of Ireland) 223
Oikos-Tau SA Ediciones (Spain) 371
Oireachtas Library (Republic of Ireland) 224
Oiseau-Lyre, Editions de l' (Monaco) 289
Ojeda Fierro, Nicolas, e Hijos (Peru) 331
Okapi Centre de Diffusion (Zaire) 502
Oldenbourg, R, Verlag GmbH (Federal Republic of Germany) 159
Oldenbourg, Verlag (Austria) 29
Oleander, The, Press (United Kingdom) 461
Olimpia, Editoriale, SpA (Italy) 246
Oliphants (United Kingdom) 461
Oliver & Boyd (Australia) 17
Oliver & Boyd (United Kingdom) 461
Oliver's Guides (United Kingdom) 461
Olizane, Editions (Switzerland) 400
Olle und Wolter, Verlag, GmbH (Federal Republic of Germany) 159
Olms, Edition, AG (Switzerland) 400
Olms, Georg, Verlag AG (Federal Republic of Germany) 159
Olschki, Casa Editrice Leo S (Italy) 246
Ölschläger, Verlag für Wirtschaftsskripten, Dipl Kfm C, GmbH (Federal Republic of Germany) 159
Ölschläger, Verlag, GmbH (Federal Republic of Germany) 159
Olympia, Nakladatelství (Czechoslovakia) 76
Olympia Press Italia (Italy) 246

Olympio, Livraria José, Editora SA (Brazil) 55
Olzog, Günter, Verlag GmbH (Federal Republic of Germany) 159
O'Mahony & Co Ltd (Republic of Ireland) 224
O'Mara, Michael, Books Ltd (United Kingdom) 461
Omega, Ediciones, SA (Spain) 371
Omega Boek BV (Netherlands) 301
Omega Books Ltd (United Kingdom) 479
Omniboek, Uitgeverij (Netherlands) 301
Omnibus (Australia) 17
Omnibus Books (Australia) 17
Omnibus Press (United Kingdom) 461
Omoleye Publishing Co Ltd (Nigeria) 317
Omun Kak (Republic of Korea) 270
On the Road (United Kingdom) 481
Oncken Verlag KG (Federal Republic of Germany) 159
Ondori Sha Publishers Co Ltd (Japan) 260
O'Neil, Lloyd, Pty Ltd (Australia) 17
Ongaku No Tomo Sha Corporation (Japan) 260
Onibonoje Book Club (Nigeria) 318
Onibonoje Press & Book Industries (Nigeria) Ltd (Nigeria) 317
Online Publications (United Kingdom) 461
Önskeboken (Sweden) 388
Ontwikkeling, Uitgeverij S V (Belgium) 41
Ooft, C D (Suriname) 380
Oosthoek (Netherlands) 301
Opal, Bokförlaget, AB (Sweden) 386
Opdebeek, Uitgeverij (Belgium) 41
Open Books Publishing Ltd (United Kingdom) 461
Open University Educational Enterprises Ltd (United Kingdom) 461
Open University Press (United Kingdom) 461
Openbare Bibliotheek (Netherlands) 305
Openbare Leeszaal en Bibliotheek (Netherland Antilles) 307
Openbare Leeszaal en Boekerij (Netherland Antilles) 307
Operaie, Nuove Edizioni, SRL (Italy) 246
Ophrys, Editions (France) 111
Oppersdorff, Inigo von, Publishing House for Bibliophile Editions (Switzerland) 400
Opus Records and Publishing House (Czechoslovakia) 76
Orac, Verlag (Austria) 29
Orakau House (New Zealand) 310
Orange Free State Provincial Library (Republic of South Africa) 361
Orangerie Galerie und Verlag, Gerhard F Reinz (Federal Republic of Germany) 159
Orante, Editions de l' (France) 111
Orban, Editions Olivier (France) 111
Orbis, Nakladatelství (Czechoslovakia) 76
Orbis (United Kingdom) 461
Orbis en Orion Uitgevers NV (Belgium) 41
Orbit (United Kingdom) 461
Orbit BV (Netherlands) 301
Orchard Books (United Kingdom) 462
Orchid Press (Suriname) 380
Orders Clearing (United Kingdom) 422
Ordfront tryckeri & förlag AB (Sweden) 386
Ordnance Survey (United Kingdom) 462
Orell Füssli (Switzerland) 405
Orell Füssli und Parabel Verlag GmbH (Federal Republic of Germany) 159
Orell Füssli Verlag (Switzerland) 400
Orellana, Librería (Chile) 66
Organisation, Les Editions d' (France) 111
Organisator, Verlag, AG (Switzerland) 400
Organización de Bienestar Estudiantil (OBE) (Venezuela) 493
Organization for African Unity Library (Ethiopia) 91
Organization for Economic Cooperation & Development (OECD) (International Organizations) 513
Organization of American States (International Organizations) 513
Organizzazioni Speciali SRL (Italy) 246
Orhan Özsisman (Turkey) 415
Oriel Press (United Kingdom) 462
Orient Book Club (India) 213
Orient Bookshop (Libya) 275
Orient Longman Ltd (India) 206
Orient Paperbacks (India) 206
Oriental & Religious, The, Publishing Corp Ltd (Pakistan) 325
Oriental Economist, The (Japan) 260
Oriental Press BV (APA) (Netherlands) 301
Oriental Textile Press Ltd (United Kingdom) 462
Orientalia Christiana, Edizioni (Italy) 246
Orientalia Publishers & Booksellers (Pakistan) 326
Orientaliste, Librairie (France) 111
Orientaliste, Uitgeverij, PVBA (Belgium) 41
Oriente, Editorial (Cuba) 73
Orígenes, Editorial (Spain) 371
Origo-Verlag (Switzerland) 400
Orion (Belgium) 41

Orion, Editorial (Mexico) 287
Orion-Heimreiter Verlag (Federal Republic of Germany) 159
Orion Press (Japan) 263
Orissa Sahitya Akademi Award (India) 216
Orisun Editions (Nigeria) 317
Orlanda Frauenverlag (Federal Republic of Germany) 159
Ormeraie, Michel de l' (France) 111
Örn og Örlyguru, Bókaútgáfan, hf (Iceland) 194
Orpan Export (Poland) 338
Országh-Hviezdoslav, Pavol, Prize (International Literary Prizes) 521
Országos Müszaki, Információs Központ és Könyvtár (Hungary) 192
Országos Széchényi Könyvtár (Hungary) 192
Országos Széchényi Könyvtár Magyar ISBN Iroda (Hungary) 190
Orte-Verlag (Switzerland) 400
Ortells, Editorial Alfredo, SL (Spain) 371
Orwell Memorial Fund Prize, George (United Kingdom) 488
Osaka Gakuin University Library (Japan) 263
Osaka Prefectural Nakanoshima Library (Japan) 263
Oscar Press (Greece) 183
Oslobodenje, NIP (Yugoslavia) 498
Osprey Publishing Ltd (United Kingdom) 462
Ossolińskich, Zakład Narodowy im, Wydawnictwo Polskiej Akademii Nauk (Poland) 336
Ossolińskich Biblioteka, Zakład Narodowy im, Polskiej Akademii Nauk (Poland) 338
Österreichische Exlibris-Gesellschaft (Austria) 32
Österreichische Gesellschaft für Dokumentation und Information (Austria) 32
Österreichische Gesellschaft für Literatur (Austria) 32
Österreichische Nationalbibliothek (Austria) 32
Österreichische Verlagsanstalt GmbH (Austria) 29
Österreichischen Akademie der Wissenschaften, Bibliothek der (Austria) 32
österreichischen Akademie der Wissenschaften, Verlag der (Austria) 29
österreichischen Gewerkschaftsbundes, Verlag des, GmbH (Austria) 29
Österreichischen Patentamtes, Bibliothek des (Austria) 32
Österreichischer Agrarverlag, Druck- und Verlags-GmbH (Austria) 29
Österreichischer Buchhändlerverband (Austria) 26
Österreichischer Buchklub der Jugend (Austria) 31
Österreichischer Bundesverlag (Austria) 29
Österreichischer Gewerbeverlag GmbH (Austria) 29
Österreichischer Schriftstellerverband (Austria) 33
Österreichischer Übersetzer- und Dolmetscherverband Universitas (Austria) 33
Österreichischer Verlegerverband (Austria) 26
Österreichisches Institut für Bibliotheksforschung, Dokumentations- und Informationswesen (Austria) 32
Österreichisches Katholisches Bibelwerk (Austria) 29
Österreichisches Staatsarchiv (Austria) 32
Osterrieth, Verlag (Federal Republic of Germany) 159
Ostrowiak, Rebecca, School of Reading (Republic of South Africa) 357
Ostschweiz Druck und Verlag (Switzerland) 400
Osveta (Czechoslovakia) 76
Otago Heritage Books (New Zealand) 310
Otava Kustannusosakeyhtiö (Finland) 93
Otechestvenija, Izdatelstvo na, Front (Bulgaria) 61
Other, The, Award (United Kingdom) 488
Otokar Keršovani (Yugoslavia) 498
Otpaz (Israel) 229
Otsuki Shoten Publishers (Japan) 260
Ott Verlag AG Thun (Switzerland) 401
Otter Books (Republic of South Africa) 357
Otzar Hamoreh (Israel) 229
Oude, De, Linden NV (Belgium) 41
Oudiovista Productions (Pty) Ltd (Republic of South Africa) 357
Oulun Yliopiston Kirjasto (Finland) 94
Outback Press Pty Ltd (Australia) 17
Outlines (Republic of South Africa) 357
Outrigger Publishers & Rimu Publishing Co Ltd (New Zealand) 310
Ouvrières, Les Editions, SA (France) 111
Oveja, Editorial La, Negra Ltda (Colombia) 70
Overseas Publications Interchange Ltd (United Kingdom) 462
Overseas Publishers' Representatives Association of Southern Africa (Republic of South Africa) 354
Owen, Peter, Ltd (United Kingdom) 462
Oxfam (United Kingdom) 462
Oxford & I B H Publishing Co Pvt Ltd (India) 206
Oxford Bibliographical Society (United Kingdom) 485
Oxford Book & Stationery Co (India) 213
Oxford Illustrated Press Ltd (United Kingdom) 462
Oxford Microform Publications Ltd (United Kingdom) 462

INDEX 579

Oxford Railway Publishing Co Ltd (United Kingdom) 462
Oxford University Press (Australia) 17
Oxford University Press (Hong Kong) 189
Oxford University Press (India) 206
Oxford University Press (Kenya) 267
Oxford University Press (Malaysia) 279
Oxford University Press (New Zealand) 310
Oxford University Press (Tanzania) 409
Oxford University Press (United Kingdom) 462
Oxford University Press (Zimbabwe) 505
Oxford University Press KK (Japan) 260
Oxford University Press (Pakistan Branch) (Pakistan) 326
Oxford University Press Pte Ltd (Republic of Singapore) 352
Oxford University Press Southern Africa (Republic of South Africa) 357
Oxford University Taylor Institution Library (United Kingdom) 483
Oxonian Press (P) Ltd (India) 206
Oya Soichi Non-fiction Prize (Japan) 265

P A C, Editions, (Presse-Auto-Conseil) (France) 111
P A T C O (Indonesia) 218
P B I Publications (United Kingdom) 462
P E A — Produzioni Editoriale Aprile (Italy) 246
P E G Ltd (Malta) 281
P E N, All-India, Centre (India) 215
P E N, Bulgarian, Centre (Bulgaria) 61
P E N, Centre de, de Côte d'Ivoire (Ivory Coast) 254
P E N, Centro del, Internacional (Peru) 331
P E N, Centro Urugayo (Uruguay) 491
P E N, Centro Venezolano del, Internacional (Venezuela) 494
P E N, Chilean, Centre (Chile) 66
P E N, China, Centre (People's Republic of China) 68
P E N, Chinese Shanghai, Centre (People's Republic of China) 68
P E N, Cyprus (Cyprus) 75
P E N, Czechoslovakian, Centre (Czechoslovakia) 78
P E N, Dacca Centre for International (Bangladesh) 35
P E N, Danish, Centre (Denmark) 85
P E N, Egyptian, Centre (Egypt) 90
P E N, Finnish, Center (Finland) 95
P E N, Friesian, Centre (Netherlands) 305
P E N, Guangzhou Chinese, Centre (People's Republic of China) 68
P E N, Hong Kong Chinese, Centre (Hong Kong) 189
P E N, Hong Kong English, Centre (Hong Kong) 190
P E N, International (International Organizations) 510
P E N, International, Centre (Iceland) 194
P E N, International, Centre (Philippines) 334
P E N, International, (Melbourne Centre) (Australia) 22
P E N, International, (Sydney Centre) (Australia) 23
P E N, Irish (Republic of Ireland) 225
P E N, Israeli, Centre (Israel) 232
P E N, Japan, Club (Japan) 265
P E N, Korean, Centre (Republic of Korea) 272
P E N, Lebanese, Club (Lebanon) 274
P E N, Mexican, Centre (Mexico) 289
P E N, Netherlands Centre of the International (Netherlands) 306
P E N, Nicaraguan, Centre (Nicaragua) 314
P E N, Norwegian, Centre (Norway) 324
P E N, Polish, Centre (Poland) 339
P E N, Portuguese, Centre (Portugal) 344
P E N, San Miguel, Centre (Mexico) 289
P E N, Spanish, Club (Cataluña) (Spain) 377
P E N, Svenska Pennklubben (Swedish Centre of International,) (Sweden) 390
P E N, Thailand, Centre (Thailand) 412
P E N, The Taipei Chinese, Centre (Taiwan) 408
P E N Centre (Greece) 185
P E N Centre (Indonesia) 219
P E N Centre, Romanian (Romania) 347
P E N Centre Prizes, Serbian (International Literary Prizes) 521
P E N Club (Jamaica) 255
P E N Club (Monaco) 289
P E N Club, Magyar (Hungary) 192
P E N-Club, Österreichischer (Austria) 33
P E N Club (Republic of South Africa) 361
P E N Club, Yugoslav, Croatian Centre (Yugoslavia) 501
P E N Club, Yugoslav, Macedonian Centre (Yugoslavia) 501
P E N Club, Yugoslav, Serbian Centre (Yugoslavia) 501
P E N Club, Yugoslav, Slovene Centre (Yugoslavia) 501
P E N Club Award, Yugoslav (International Literary Prizes) 521

P E N Club, Belgian French-Speaking Centre, International (Belgium) 45
P E N Club Centre, Swiss-German (Switzerland) 406
P E N Club de Bolivia (Centro Internacional de Escritores) (Bolivia) 49
P E N Club de Puerto Rico (Puerto Rico) 345
P E N Club de Suisse romande (Switzerland) 406
P E N Club del Paraguay (Paraguay) 330
P E N Club du Senegal (Senegal) 350
P E N Club, Flemish-Speaking Centre, International (Belgium) 45
P E N Club français (France) 118
P E N Club International de Argentina (Argentina) 9
P E N Club Liechtenstein (Liechtenstein) 275
P E N Club Medal, Hungarian (International Literary Prizes) 521
P E N Club Prizes, Polish (International Literary Prizes) 521
P E N Clube do Brasil (Associação Universal de Escritores) (Brazil) 59
P E N English Centre (United Kingdom) 485
P E N Internacional de Escritores de Colombia (Colombia) 71
P E N International Centre (Italy) 253
P E N International New Zealand Centre (New Zealand) 313
P E N Internazionale — Centro della Svizzera Italiana e Romancia (Switzerland) 406
P E N Scottish Centre (United Kingdom) 485
P E N Yazarlar Derneği (Turkey) 416
P E N Zentrum Bundesrepublik Deutschland (Federal Republic of Germany) 178
P E N Zentrum Deutsche Demokratische Republik (German Democratic Republic) 128
P G Publishing Pte Ltd (Republic of Singapore) 352
P I A G (Federal Republic of Germany) 159
P I C S (United Kingdom) 422
P L E S A (Spain) 371
P O F (France) 111
P P C, Librerías, (Promoción Popular Cristiana) (Spain) 376
P P C Ltd (Barbados) 35
P P C (Promoción Popular Cristiana) (Spain) 371
P P H (Pakistan) 326
P R O N I (Public Record Office of Northern Ireland) (United Kingdom) 483
P R Verlag Wiesbaden, H G Schwieger (Federal Republic of Germany) 159
P U F (France) 111
P U F, Librairie générale des (France) 116
P U L (France) 111
P U Z (Zaire) 502
P W E (Państwowe Wydawnictwo Ekonomiczne) (Poland) 336
P W N (Państwowe Wydawnictwo Naukowe) (Poland) 336
P Y C Edition (France) 111
Pacific Book Centre (S) Pte Ltd (Republic of Singapore) 353
Pacific Publications (Australia) Pty Ltd (Australia) 17
Pacific Publishers (New Zealand) 310
Pacifica Ltd (Japan) 260
Pacifique, Les Editions du (France) 111
Pacifique, Les Editions du (Republic of Singapore) 352
Pacifique, Société Nouvelle des Editions du (French Polynesia) 122
Packard Publishing Ltd (United Kingdom) 462
Päd extra buchverlag in der pädex Verlags GmbH (Federal Republic of Germany) 160
Pädagogischer Verlag Schwann/Bagel GmbH (Federal Republic of Germany) 160
Padilla, Editorial (Dominican Republic) 86
Padilla, Editorial (Dominican Republic) 87
Paedagogiki Academia, Library of the, (College of Education) (Cyprus) 75
Paes Barreto, Rómulo (Brazil) 57
Pagan Publishing House (Burma) 62
Pagoda Books (United Kingdom) 462
Pahl-Rugenstein Verlag GmbH (Federal Republic of Germany) 160
Paico Publishing House (India) 207
Paideia Editrice (Italy) 246
Paidós, Ediciones, Ibérica SA (Spain) 371
Paidós, Editorial, SAICF (Argentina) 6
Paintaway (United Kingdom) 462
Pak American Commercial Ltd (Pakistan) 326
Pak Book Corporation (Pakistan) 326
Pak Kitab Ghar (Bangladesh) 34
Pak Publishers (Pakistan) 326
Pakistan Board for Advancement of Literature (Pakistan) 327
Pakistan Board for Advancement of Literature Awards (Pakistan) 328
Pakistan Forest Institute, Central Forest Library (Pakistan) 327

Pakistan Institute of Nuclear Science & Technology Library (Pakistan) 327
Pakistan Law Times Publications (Pakistan) 326
Pakistan Library Association (Pakistan) 327
Pakistan Publications (Pakistan) 326
Pakistan Publishers' and Booksellers' Association (Pakistan) 324
Pakistan Publishing House (Pakistan) 326
Pakistan Scientific and Technological Information Centre (PASTIC) (Pakistan) 327
Pakistan Writers' Guild (Pakistan) 327
Pakpassak Kanphin (Laos) 272
Pal Singh, M/s Bishan Singh Mahendra (India) 207
Palacio, Biblioteca del, Legislativo (Uruguay) 491
Palácio, Biblioteca do, Nacional de Mafra (Portugal) 344
Palacio, El, del Libro (Venezuela) 493
Palacio, Patrimonio Nacional, Biblioteca del, Real (Spain) 371
Palacio del Libro (Uruguay) 491
Paladin Books (United Kingdom) 462
Paladin Verlag GmbH (Federal Republic of Germany) 160
Palanca, Don Carlos, Memorial Awards for Literature Contest (Philippines) 334
Palatina Editrice (Italy) 246
Pallas, Vydavatel'stvo SFVU (Czechoslovakia) 76
Pallas Editora e Distribuidora Ltda (Brazil) 55
'Pallottinum' Wydawnictwo Stowarzyszenia Apostolstwa Katolickiego (Poland) 336
Palme, Suzanne, Literary Agency (Norway) 323
Palmer Prizes (Australia) 25
Palmerston North Public Library (New Zealand) 312
Palombi, Fratelli, SRL (Italy) 246
Paludans, Jörgen, Forlag ApS (Denmark) 82
Palumbo, G B, & C Editore SpA (Italy) 246
Památník národního písemnictví, Strahovská knihovna (Czechoslovakia) 78
Pamplona and its Culture Prize (Colombia) 72
Pan African Institute for Development (United Republic of Cameroun) 64
Pan-African Publishing Co Ltd (Tanzania) 409
Pan Books (Australia) Pty Ltd (Australia) 18
Pan Books Ltd (United Kingdom) 462
Pan Horizons (Australia) 18
Pan Korea Book Corporation (Republic of Korea) 270
Pan Library ('Circle of the Friends of Progress') (Greece) 185
Pan Malayan Publishing Co Sdn Bhd (Malaysia) 279
Pan Pacific Book Distributors (S) Pte Ltd (Republic of Singapore) 352
Pancaldi, Libreria Commissionaria Internazionale di Raffaele (Italy) 251
Panchasheel Prakashan (India) 207
Pandora Pockets (Netherlands) 301
Panero, Leopoldo, Prize (International Literary Prizes) 521
Panhellenic Federation of Publishers and Booksellers (PFPB) (Greece) 182
Panini, Edizioni, SpA (Italy) 246
Panjab University Publication Bureau (India) 207
Pankaj Publications International (India) 207
Panmun Book Co Ltd (Republic of Korea) 270
Panmun Book Co Ltd (Republic of Korea) 271
Pannedille, Ediciones (Argentina) 6
Panorama, Editions du (Switzerland) 401
Panorama, Nakladatelství a vydavatelství (Czechoslovakia) 76
Panorama Books (Australia) 18
Pantelides, John (Greece) 185
Panther Publishing (Malaysia) 279
Panton (Czechoslovakia) 76
Paoline, Edizioni, SRL (Italy) 246
Papachrysanthou Chryss SA (Greece) 184
Papacito, Ediciones (Uruguay) 491
Papacito, Librerías (Uruguay) 491
Papadimitriou, D A (Greece) 184
Papadimitriou, Haroula (Greece) 184
Papadopoulos, Kyr I, E E (Greece) 184
Papaioannou (Greece) 184
Papazissis Publishers SA (Greece) 184
Paper Tiger Books (United Kingdom) 463
Paperback Centre (Republic of Ireland) 224
Paperfronts (United Kingdom) 463
Papermac (United Kingdom) 463
Papeterie Centrale (Central African Republic) 64
Papilio Print (Federal Republic of Germany) 160
Papua New Guinea Book Depot (Papua New Guinea) 329
Papua New Guinea Library Association (Papua New Guinea) 329
Papusa Ltda (Colombia) 70
Papyros Press (Greece) 184
'Papyrus' (Central African Republic) 64
Papyrus (Israel) 229
Paradigm Publishing Ltd (United Kingdom) 463

580 INDEX

Paradise Book Stall (Pakistan) 326
Parallelo 38, Edizioni (Italy) 247
Paramount Books (Pvt) Ltd (Pakistan) 327
Paraninfo, Editorial, SA (Spain) 371
Paravia, G B, & C SpA (Italy) 247
Pardo, Casa, SAC (Argentina) 6
Pardo, Librería General de Tomas, SRL (Argentina) 8
Parent & Child (United Kingdom) 463
'Parents' Magazine Best Book for Babies Award (United Kingdom) 488
Parera, Librería (Chile) 66
Parey, Verlag Paul (Federal Republic of Germany) 160
Parhélie, Editions du (France) 111
Parimal Prakashan (India) 207
Paris-Caraïbes (France) 111
Paris Grand Prize for Literature (France) 121
Paris Prize (France) 121
Parkash Brothers (India) 207
Parker & Son Ltd (United Kingdom) 482
Parkland Verlag GmbH (Federal Republic of Germany) 160
Parlement, Bibliothèque du (Belgium) 44
Parlement, Bibliothèque du, Européen (International Organizations) 510
Parliament Library (Greece) 185
Parliament Library, No 1 (Ketab-Khaneh Majles-e Showraye Eslami, no 1) (Iran) 220
Parliament Library, No 2 (Ketab-Khaneh Majles-e Showraye Eslami, no 2) (Iran) 220
Parma (Brazil) 55
Parramon Ediciones SA (Spain) 372
Parry's Book Center (Sri Abdul Wahab Sdn Bhd) (Malaysia) 280
Parsifal Publishing Co (Belgium) 41
Parsons, Roy (New Zealand) 312
Partenon, Ediciones (Spain) 372
Partizdat (Bulgaria) 61
Partridge Press (United Kingdom) 463
Passano editor (Mexico) 288
Passavia, Verlag (Federal Republic of Germany) 160
Passavia Universitätsverlag und -Druck GmbH (Federal Republic of Germany) 160
Passigli Editori di A Passigli & C SAS (Italy) 247
Pássim, Librería, SA (Spain) 376
Patakis Publications (Greece) 184
Paternoster, The, Press Ltd (United Kingdom) 463
Path Publishers (India) 207
Patio, Galerie, Verlag (Federal Republic of Germany) 160
Patmos, Uitgeverij (Belgium) 41
Patmos Verlag GmbH (Federal Republic of Germany) 160
Patria, Editorial, SA de CV (Mexico) 287
Patria, Librería (Mexico) 288
Patria, Libreria, SA (Mexico) 287
Patria Grande, Editora (Argentina) 6
Pàtron, Libreria Internazionale (Italy) 251
Pàtron Editore SRL (Italy) 247
Pattloch, Paul, im Weltbild Verlag GmbH (Federal Republic of Germany) 160
Patwa (Embakasi) Ltd (Kenya) 268
Paul, M P, Award (India) 216
Paul, M P, Prize (India) 216
Paul, Stanley, & Co Ltd (United Kingdom) 463
Paulinas, Ediciones (Argentina) 7
Paulinas, Ediciones (Chile) 65
Paulinas, Ediciones (Colombia) 70
Paulinas, Ediciones (Spain) 372
Paulinas, Ediciones, SA (Mexico) 287
Paulinas, Edições (Brazil) 55
Paulinus Verlag (Federal Republic of Germany) 160
Paulsen, Ingwert, Jnr (Federal Republic of Germany) 160
Paulusverlag (Switzerland) 401
Pause, Firmin (Réunion) 346
Pauvert, Jean-Jacques, Editeur (France) 111
Pavanne (Australia) 18
Pavanne (United Kingdom) 463
Pavilion (Australia) 18
Pavilion Books (United Kingdom) 463
Pawel Pan Presse (Federal Republic of Germany) 160
Pawlak, Manfred, Grossantiquariat und Verlagsgesellschaft mbH (Federal Republic of Germany) 160
Pax, Instytut Wydawniczy (Poland) 336
Pax, Livraria Editora, Lda (Portugal) 342
Pax-Chile, Librería y Editorial, Ltda (Chile) 66
Pax Forlag A/S (Norway) 322
Payot, Editions (France) 111
Payot, Librairie, SA (Switzerland) 401
Payot, Librairie, SA (Switzerland) 405
Paz, Editorial, Montalvo (Spain) 372
Paz e Terra, Editora (Brazil) 55
Peace and Socialism International Publishers (Czechoslovakia) 76

Pearl Publishers (India) 207
Pédagogie Moderne (France) 111
Pedagogika (Union of Soviet Socialist Republics) 418
Pedagogisk Forlag A/S (Norway) 322
Pedagoško-književni zbor, pedagoško društvo SR Hrvatske (Yugoslavia) 501
Pedersen, Agentur für wissenschaftliche Literatur Ulf, GmbH (Federal Republic of Germany) 160
Pediátrica, Editorial (Spain) 372
Pédone, Editions (France) 111
Pedrazzini Tipografia (Switzerland) 401
Pedrick, Don, Memorial Literary Award (Sri Lanka) 379
Peerage (United Kingdom) 463
Peeters Publishers (Belgium) 41
Pegaso, Ediciones (Spain) 372
Pegasus Prize for Literature (International Literary Prizes) 521
Pehuén Editores Ltda (Chile) 65
Peiffer, Librairie Armand (Grand Duchy of Luxembourg) 276
Peisa, Ediciones, (Promoción Editorial Inca SA) (Peru) 330
Pelajar (Indonesia) 218
Pelham (Australia) 18
Pelham Books Ltd (United Kingdom) 463
Peli, Alexander, Ltd (Israel) 229
Pelican (Australia) 18
Pelican (United Kingdom) 463
Pelita Masa (Indonesia) 218
Pelled, Dahlia, Publishers Ltd (Israel) 229
Pellegrini, Luigi, Editore (Italy) 247
Pembangunan (Indonesia) 218
Pemberton Publishing Co Ltd (United Kingdom) 463
Pembimbing, PT, Masa (Indonesia) 219
Pembimbing Masa (Indonesia) 218
Pembinaan, Pusat, Perpustakaan, Departemen P dan K Bidang, Bibliografi dan Deposit (Indonesia) 219
Peña, A, Lillo SA (Argentina) 7
Pendo-Verlag (Switzerland) 401
Pendragon Verlag (Federal Republic of Germany) 160
Penguin Books Australia Ltd (Australia) 18
Penguin Books Ltd (United Kingdom) 463
Penguin Books (NZ) Ltd (New Zealand) 310
Penguin Publishing Co Ltd (United Kingdom) 463
Península, Agencia Literaria La (Spain) 375
Peninsula, Ediciones (Spain) 372
Peninsula Press (Republic of Ireland) 223
Penman, The, Club (International Organizations) 510
Pennsylvania State University Press (United Kingdom) 463
Pensamento, Editora (Brazil) 56
Pensiero, Il, Scientifico Editore SRL (Italy) 247
Pentacle Press (Australia) 18
Pentecost (New Caledonia) 307
Pentland, The, Press Ltd (United Kingdom) 463
Pentos Retailing Group Ltd (United Kingdom) 482
People's Grand Study Centre (Democratic People's Republic of Korea) 269
People's Literature Publishing House (People's Republic of China) 67
People's Medical Publishing House (PMPH) (People's Republic of China) 67
People's Publishing Co Ltd (Nigeria) 317
People's Publishing House (Pakistan) 326
People's Publishing House (P) Ltd (India) 207
People's Sports Publishing House (People's Republic of China) 68
Père Castor (France) 111
Peregrine Books (United Kingdom) 463
Peregrino, Ediciones (United Kingdom) 463
Peregrinus, Peter, Ltd (United Kingdom) 463
Pereira, Parceria A M, Lda (Portugal) 342
Peretz, Y L, Publishing Co (Israel) 229
Perfecting Press (Hong Kong) 189
Pergamini Editions (Greece) 184
Pergamon Press (United Kingdom) 463
Pergamon Press (Australia) Pty Ltd (Australia) 18
Periféria, Ediciones, SRL (Argentina) 7
Perimed Fachbuch-Verlagsgesellschaft mbH (Federal Republic of Germany) 160
Perlinger-Verlag GmbH (Austria) 29
Perpétuo, Editorial, Socorro (Portugal) 342
Perpustakaan Dewan Bahasa, , dan Pustaka Brunei, Kementerian Kebudayaan, Belia dan Sukan (Brunei) 60
Perpustakaan Negeri Sabah (Malaysia) 280
Perrin, Librairie Académique (France) 111
Persatuan Pengimpot-Pengimpot Buku Malaysia (Malaysia) 278
Persatuan Penjual-Penjual Buku Malaysia (Malaysia) 278
Persatuan Perpustakaan Kebangsaan Negara Brunei Darussalam (Brunei) 60
Persatuan Perpustakaan Malaysia (Malaysia) 281
Perskor Books (Pty) Ltd (Republic of South Africa) 357

Perskor Bookshop (Republic of South Africa) 360
Perskor Prize for Light Reading (Republic of South Africa) 362
Perskor Prize for Literature (Republic of South Africa) 362
Perskor Prize for Youth Literature (Republic of South Africa) 362
Personal Computer News Library (Australia) 18
Perspectiva, Editora (Brazil) 56
Perspectivas e Realidades (Portugal) 342
Pestalozzi-Verlag graphische Gesellschaft mbH (Federal Republic of Germany) 160
Peter, Verlag J P, Gebr Holstein GmbH & Co KG (Federal Republic of Germany) 160
Peter Peregrinus Ltd (United Kingdom) 463
Peterborough Literary Agency (United Kingdom) 480
Peters, A D, & Co Ltd (United Kingdom) 480
Peters, VEB Edition, Musikverlag (German Democratic Republic) 125
Peters Musikverlag, C F, GmbH & Co KG (Federal Republic of Germany) 160
Peters Verlag, Dr Hans (Federal Republic of Germany) 160
Petersen, Hans Heinrich, Buchimport GmbH (Federal Republic of Germany) 176
Petiwala Corporation (Pakistan) 327
Pevsner Public Library (Israel) 231
Pfanneberg, Fachbuchverlag Dr, & Co (Federal Republic of Germany) 160
Pfeiffer, Verlag J (Federal Republic of Germany) 161
Pflaum, Richard, Verlag KG (Federal Republic of Germany) 161
Pfriemer, Udo, Verlag GmbH (Federal Republic of Germany) 161
Pfützner, Robert, GmbH (Federal Republic of Germany) 161
Phaidon Press Ltd (United Kingdom) 463
Phaneromeni, Library of (Cyprus) 75
Pharmacie, Bibliothèque Interuniversitaire de (France) 117
Pharos-Verlag, Hansrudolf Schwabe AG (Switzerland) 401
Phébus, Editions (France) 111
Philip, David, Publisher (Pty) Ltd (Republic of South Africa) 358
Philip & Son, George, Ltd (United Kingdom) 464
Philip & Tacey Ltd (United Kingdom) 464
Philippine Book Co (Philippines) 332
Philippine Book Co (Philippines) 333
Philippine Book Dealers' Association (Philippines) 331
Philippine Education Co Inc (Philippines) 332
Philippine Education Co Inc (Philippines) 333
Philippine Educational Publishers' Association (Philippines) 331
Philippine Library Association (Philippines) 333
Philippine Normal College Library & Library Science Departments (Philippines) 333
Philips Fachbücher, Dr Alfred Hüthig Verlag GmbH (Federal Republic of Germany) 161
Phillimore & Co Ltd (United Kingdom) 464
Phillips, Phoebe, Editions (United Kingdom) 464
Philo Press-Van Heusden-Hissink & Co CV (APA) (Netherlands) 301
Philograph Publications Ltd (United Kingdom) 464
Philosophia Verlag GmbH (Federal Republic of Germany) 161
Philosophisch-Anthroposophischer Verlag am Goetheanum (Switzerland) 401
Pho Thong (Popularization) Publishing House (Socialist Republic of Viet Nam) 494
Phoenix Book Society (United Kingdom) 481
Phoenix Publishing Associates Ltd (United Kingdom) 464
Phoenix Publishing House Inc (Philippines) 332
Phoenix Verlag AG (Switzerland) 401
Photographia Book Club (Greece) 184
Photographic Book Society (United Kingdom) 481
Physica-Verlag GmbH & Co (Federal Republic of Germany) 161
Physik-Verlag GmbH (Federal Republic of Germany) 161
Piatkus Books (United Kingdom) 464
Picador (Australia) 18
Picador (United Kingdom) 464
Picard, Editions A et J, SA (France) 111
Piccadilly Press (United Kingdom) 464
Piccin Nuova Libraria SpA (Italy) 247
Piccoli, Cartiere Binda de Medici SpA Divisione Editoriale (Italy) 247
Piccolo (Australia) 18
Piccolo (United Kingdom) 464
Pickering & Inglis Ltd (United Kingdom) 464
Picollec, Editions Jean (France) 111
Picton Publishing (Chippenham) Ltd (United Kingdom) 464
Picture Lions (United Kingdom) 464
Piedra Santa (Guatemala) 185

Piedra Santa (Guatemala) 186
Piemme, Edizioni, di Pietro Marietti SpA (Italy) 247
Pierce, Lorne, Medal (International Literary Prizes) 521
Pierron, Editions (France) 111
Pierrot, Editions, SA (Switzerland) 401
Pietra, La (Italy) 247
Pikkhanet (Thailand) 410
Pila, Editorial Augusto E, Teleña SA (Spain) 372
Pilgrim Award (International Literary Prizes) 521
Pilgrim Books Ltd (Nigeria) 317
Pilgrim Publishers (India) 207
Pilgrims Booksellers (Pty) (Republic of South Africa) 360
Pilgrims South Press Ltd (New Zealand) 310
Pilotta, La, Editrice Coop RL (Italy) 247
Pimodan, De, Foundation Prize (France) 121
Pinchgut Press (Australia) 18
Pineda Libros (Chile) 65
Pinguin-Verlag, Pawlowski KG (Austria) 29
Pinter, Frances, Ltd (United Kingdom) 464
Pioneer Design Studio Pty Ltd (Australia) 18
Piper, R, & Co Verlag GmbH (Switzerland) 401
Piper, R, GmbH & Co KG, Verlag (Federal Republic of Germany) 161
Piper (United Kingdom) 464
Pirámide, Ediciones, SA (Spain) 372
Pirella, Francesco, Editore (Switzerland) 401
Pirola (Italy) 247
'Pishchevaya Promyshlennost', Izdatelstvo (Union of Soviet Socialist Republics) 418
Pitagora SNC (Italy) 247
Pitambar Publishing Co (India) 207
Pitkin Pictorials Ltd (United Kingdom) 464
Pitman Publishing (Australia) 18
Pitman Publishing Ltd (United Kingdom) 464
Pitman Publishing NZ Ltd (New Zealand) 310
Pitou, Charles, Foundation Prize (France) 121
Pittayakarn (Thailand) 410
Pizzi, Amilcare, SpA (Italy) 247
Plain Edition (United Kingdom) 464
Plambeck & Co, Druck und Verlag GmbH (Federal Republic of Germany) 161
Planet (United Kingdom) 464
Planeta, Editorial, SA (Spain) 372
Planeta, Grupo Editorial (Mexico) 287
Planeta Prize (International Literary Prizes) 522
Planeta Publishers (Union of Soviet Socialist Republics) 418
Planning Commission Library (Pakistan) 327
Plantin-Moretus, Museum (Belgium) 44
Plantyn, Uitgeverij (Belgium) 41
Plata, Editorial, SA (Peru) 330
Plata, Editorial, SA (Venezuela) 493
Platano Editora SARL (Portugal) 342
Play to Learn (Australia) 18
Playfair (United Kingdom) 464
Playor, Editorial (Spain) 372
Playtime Press (United Kingdom) 464
Playwrights, The, Association of New Zealand (Inc) (New Zealand) 313
Plaza y Janés, Editorial Argentina, SA (Argentina) 7
Plaza y Janés SA (Spain) 372
Pleamar, Editorial (Argentina) 7
Plessl, Gerd, Agentur (Federal Republic of Germany) 175
Plexus Publishing Ltd (United Kingdom) 464
Ploegsma, Uitgeverij (Netherlands) 301
Ploetz, Verlag A G, GmbH & Co KG (Federal Republic of Germany) 161
Plon, Librairie, SA (France) 111
Plough Publishing House (United Kingdom) 464
Pluma, Editorial, Ltda (Colombia) 70
Pluriel (France) 111
Plus, Bokförlaget, AB (Sweden) 386
Plus Ultra, Editorial, SAI & C (Argentina) 7
Pluto Crime Award (International Literary Prizes) 522
Pluto Press Australia (Australia) 18
Pluto Publishing Ltd (United Kingdom) 465
Po Chin Chai Co Ltd (Republic of Korea) 270
Pock, Max, Universitätsbuchhandlung (Austria) 31
Pocket, Presses (France) 111
Pocket Classics (United Kingdom) 465
Pocket Puffins (United Kingdom) 465
Pocket Worlds (United Kingdom) 465
Poder, Biblioteca del, Legislativo (Uruguay) 491
Podzun-Pallas Verlag GmbH (Federal Republic of Germany) 161
Poeschel, C E, Verlag (Federal Republic of Germany) 161
Poètes Présents (France) 116
Poetry, The, Book Society Ltd (United Kingdom) 481
Poetry, The, Society (United Kingdom) 485
Poetry Australia (South Head Press) (Australia) 18
Poetry in Irish (International Literary Prizes) 522
Poetry Society of Australia (Australia) 23
Poetry Wales Press (United Kingdom) 465

Pohjalainen Kirjakauppa Oy (Finland) 94
Pohl Druckerei und Verlagsanstalt Otto Pohl (Federal Republic of Germany) 161
Poincaré, Raymond, Prize (France) 121
Point d'Interrogation, Librairie du (Senegal) 349
'Pojezierze', Wydawnictwo Stowarzyszenia Spoleczno-Kulturalnego (Poland) 336
Polak, Emil, Prize (Belgium) 46
Polak en Van Gennep Uitg Mij BV (Netherlands) 301
Polding, The, Press (Australia) 18
'Police Review' Award (United Kingdom) 488
Police Review Publishing Ltd (United Kingdom) 465
Policy Studies Institute (United Kingdom) 465
Poligrafa, Ediciones, SA (Spain) 372
Poligraficheskata Promishlenost i Kulturnite Instituti, Sekciya na Bibliotechnite Rabotnitsi pri Centralniya Komitet na Profesionalniya Sŭyuz na Rabotnitsite ot (Bulgaria) 61
Polish Academy of Sciences, Scientific Information Centre (Poland) 338
Polish Ministry of National Defence Prize (Poland) 339
Polish Prime Minister Award for Literature for Children and Youth (Poland) 339
Polish Scientific Publishers (Poland) 336
Polish Society of Authors (Zaiks) Prizes (International Literary Prizes) 522
Polish Union of Socialist Youth Prose Award (Poland) 339
Politécnica Moulines, Librería (Venezuela) 493
Politica, Editura (Romania) 347
Political and Social History, Library of (Indonesia) 219
Politikens Forlag A/S (Denmark) 82
Politizdat (Union of Soviet Socialist Republics) 418
Polity Press (United Kingdom) 465
polizeiliches Fachschrifttum, Verlag für (Federal Republic of Germany) 161
Polla, Studio Bibliografico Adelmo (Italy) 247
Pollinger, Laurence, Ltd (United Kingdom) 480
Pollinger, Murray (United Kingdom) 480
Polskie Towarzystwo Wydawców Ksiazek (Poland) 334
Polybooks Ltd (United Kingdom) 465
Polyglott-Verlag Dr Bolte KG (Federal Republic of Germany) 161
Polygon Books (United Kingdom) 465
Polygraph Verlag GmbH (Federal Republic of Germany) 161
Polytantric Press (United Kingdom) 465
Polytech (United Kingdom) 465
Polyteknisk Boghandel og Forlag (Denmark) 84
Pomaire, Editorial, Ltda (Chile) 65
Pompidou, Editions du Centre Georges (France) 111
Pomurska založba (Yugoslavia) 498
Pond Press (United Kingdom) 465
Pontificia, Biblioteca Central de la, Universidad Católica del Perú (Peru) 331
Pontificia, Editrice, Università Gregoriana (Italy) 247
Pontificio, Editrice, Istituto Biblico (Italy) 247
Pontoppidan, Henrik, Memorial Prize (Denmark) 86
Pool Editorial Ltda (Brazil) 56
Poolbeg Press Ltd (Republic of Ireland) 223
Poona Booksellers' & Publishers' Association (India) 195
Poplar Publishing Co Ltd (Japan) 260
Popp, Edition Georg, GmbH & Co (Federal Republic of Germany) 161
Populaires (Switzerland) 401
Popular, Editorial, SA (Spain) 372
Popular, Libreria Editorial (Bolivia) 48
Popular Army Publishing House (Socialist Republic of Viet Nam) 494
Popular Book Depot (India) 213
Popular Book Store (Philippines) 333
Popular Dogs Publishing Co Ltd (United Kingdom) 465
Popular Prakashan Pvt Ltd (India) 207
Popular Publications (Malawi) 277
Popular Science Prize (Denmark) 86
Pordes, H (United Kingdom) 465
Pordes, H, Ltd (United Kingdom) 479
Porgès, Hélène, Prize (France) 121
Porretta, Frédérique (France) 116
Porretta, Frédérique (Spain) 375
Porrúa, Ediciones José, Turanzas SA (Spain) 372
Porrúa, Editorial, SA (Mexico) 287
Porrúa, Librería de, Hnos y Cía (Mexico) 288
Porrúa, Librería José, Turanzas SA (Spain) 376
Port Nicholson Press Ltd (New Zealand) 310
Pòrtic, Editorial, SA (Spain) 372
Portico, Editorial (Portugal) 342
Porto Editora Lda (Portugal) 342
Portugal, Livraria, Dias e Andrade Lda (Portugal) 343
Possev-Verlag V Gorachek KG (Federal Republic of Germany) 161
Post (United Kingdom) 481
Postmarket (Australia) 20
Poth, W, GbR (Federal Republic of Germany) 161

Power, Shelley, Literary Agency Ltd/INPRA (United Kingdom) 480
Powszechna Ksiegarnia Wysylkowa (Poland) 338
Poyser, T A & D, Ltd (United Kingdom) 465
Poznańskie, Wydawnictwo (Poland) 336
Pozza, Casa Editrice Neri (Italy) 247
Pozzi, Edizioni Luigi, SRL (Italy) 247
Pra Cha Chang & Co Ltd (Thailand) 410
Prabhat Prakashan (India) 207
'Práca', Vydavatel'stvo ROH (Czechoslovakia) 76
'Práca' (Czechoslovakia) 76
Pracharak Book Club (India) 213
Prachi Prakashan (India) 207
Prachner, Georg, KG (Austria) 29
Prachner, Georg, KG (Austria) 32
Pradnya Paramita (Indonesia) 218
Pradnya Paramita (Indonesia) 219
Praeger Publishers (United Kingdom) 465
Praepittaya Ltd (Thailand) 410
Praepittaya Ltd (Thailand) 411
Praesentverlag Heinz Peter (Federal Republic of Germany) 161
Prague Literary Prize (Czechoslovakia) 79
Prakash Prakashan (India) 207
Prakasham Publications (India) 207
Praphansarn Book Centre (Thailand) 410
Prasarnmitr (Thailand) 410
Präsenz-Verlag der Jesus-Bruderschaft (Federal Republic of Germany) 161
Pratiche Editrice (Italy) 247
Pravda, Nakladatelstvo (Czechoslovakia) 76
Pravda Publishing House (Union of Soviet Socialist Republics) 418
Prawnicze, Wydawnictwo (Poland) 337
Prayer Books (India) 207
Pre-Ecole (Belgium) 41
Pre-School Publishing Co (United Kingdom) 465
Pre-Textos (Spain) 372
Preduzeće Matice Srpske, Izdavačko (Yugoslavia) 498
Preduzeće Sloboda, Izdavačko (Yugoslavia) 498
Preescolar, Ediciones, SA (Argentina) 7
Prélat, Julian (France) 111
Preller, Gustav, Prize (Republic of South Africa) 362
Premier Book House (Pakistan) 326
Premio de Remuneraciones Literarias (Uruguay) 492
Premio Nacional de Ilustracion de Libros Infantiles y Juveniles (Spain) 378
Premio Nacional de las Letras Españolas (Spain) 378
Premio Nacional de Literatura (Spain) 378
Premio Nacional de Literatura (Uruguay) 492
Premio Nacional de Literatura Infantil y Juvenil (Spain) 378
Prensa Científica – Investigación y Ciencia (Spain) 372
Prensa Española, Editorial (Spain) 372
Prensa Médica, La, Mexicana (Mexico) 287
Prentice, Jeffrey B, Literary Agent (Australia) 20
Prentice-Hall of Australia Pty Ltd (Australia) 18
Prentice-Hall of India Pvt Ltd (India) 207
Prentice-Hall of Japan Inc (Japan) 260
Prentice-Hall (Simon & Schuster International Group) (United Kingdom) 465
Presbiteriana, Casa Editora (Brazil) 56
Presbyterian Book Depot and Printing Press Ltd (PRESBOOK) (United Republic of Cameroun) 64
Presbyterian Book Depot Ltd (Ghana) 181
Preschool (Belgium) 41
Presença, Editorial (Portugal) 342
Présence Africaine, Société Nouvelle (France) 111
Presencia, Editorial, Ltda (Colombia) 70
President Boekklub (Republic of South Africa) 360
President's Award for Pride of Performance (Pakistan) 328
Press Agency (Kuwait) 272
Press Department, Library of the (Afghanistan) 1
Presse, Verlag, Informations Agentur GmbH (PIAG) (Federal Republic of Germany) 161
Presse-Auto-Conseil (France) 112
Presse-Grosso (Federal Republic of Germany) 129
Presses, Les, Africaines (Burkina Faso) 62
Presses, Librairie des, universitaires (Zaire) 502
Presses Africaines, Les (Zaire) 502
Presses agronomiques de Gembloux ASBL (Belgium) 41
Presses Centrales Lausanne SA (Switzerland) 401
Presses de la Cité, Les (France) 112
Presses de la Fondation Nationale des Sciences Politiques (France) 112
Presses de la Renaissance (France) 112
Presses d'Ile-de-France, Les, Sàrl (France) 112
Presses Polytechniques Romandes (Switzerland) 401
Presses universitaires de Bruxelles, Librairie des (Belgium) 44
Presses universitaires de Bruxelles ASBL (Belgium) 41
Presses Universitaires de France (PUF) (France) 112
Presses Universitaires de Grenoble (France) 112
Presses universitaires de Liège ASBL (Belgium) 41

582 INDEX

Presses Universitaires de Lille (PUL) (France) 112
Presses Universitaires de Lyon (France) 112
Presses Universitaires de Namur (Belgium) 41
Presses Universitaires de Nancy (France) 112
Presses universitaires du Zaïre et l'Office du Livre (PUZ) (Zaire) 502
Pressler, Guido, Verlag (Federal Republic of Germany) 162
Prestel Verlag (Federal Republic of Germany) 162
Prestige Booksellers (Kenya) 268
Preston Corporation Sdn Bhd (Malaysia) 279
Pretoria Boekhandel (Pty) Ltd (Republic of South Africa) 358
Pretoria Public Library (Republic of South Africa) 361
Preussler, Helmut, Verlag (Federal Republic of Germany) 162
Price, Norman (United Kingdom) 465
Price Milburn & Co Ltd (New Zealand) 310
Pride Publications (United Kingdom) 465
Primary Education (Australia) 18
Primavera, Edizioni, SRL (Italy) 247
Primor, Editora, Ltda (Brazil) 56
Primor, Gráfica Editora, Ltda (Brazil) 56
Primorski Tisk (Yugoslavia) 498
Prince Pierre de Monaco Prize for Literature (International Literary Prizes) 522
Princeton University Press (United Kingdom) 465
Principato (Italy) 247
Pringle, Thomas, Awards (Republic of South Africa) 362
Prins (Belgium) 41
Prins en Prins (Netherlands) 304
Printox (India) 207
Priory Press Ltd (United Kingdom) 465
Príroda, vydavateľstvo kníh a časopisov (Czechoslovakia) 76
Prisca (United Kingdom) 465
Prism Books (Poetry Society of Australia) (Australia) 18
Prism Press Book Publishers Ltd (United Kingdom) 465
Prisma, Bokförlaget, AB (Sweden) 386
Prisma Verlag GmbH (Federal Republic of Germany) 162
Prisma-Verlag Zenner und Gürchott (German Democratic Republic) 125
Prithviraj Memorial Award (India) 216
Priuli e Verlucca, Editori (Italy) 247
Privat, Editions Edouard, SA (France) 112
Private Libraries Association (PLA) (International Organizations) 510
Privredni Pregled (Yugoslavia) 498
Prix Littéraire Mobil (Ivory Coast) 254
Prize for Poetry in Irish (International Literary Prizes) 522
Prize for Poetry in Irish (Republic of Ireland) 225
Prizes for Manuscripts for Juveniles (Pakistan) 328
Pro Civitate (Belgium) 41
Pro Juventute, Verlag (Switzerland) 401
Pro Media Literaturvertrieb GmbH (Federal Republic of Germany) 176
Pro Musica Verlag (German Democratic Republic) 125
Pro Rege Press Ltd (Republic of South Africa) 358
Pro Schola, Editions (Switzerland) 401
Procultura SA (Colombia) 70
Procura, SA (Belgium) 41
Procure scolaire (Zaire) 502
Prodim SPRL (Belgium) 42
Production et Diffusion medico-techniques SPRL (Belgium) 42
Professional Books Ltd (United Kingdom) 465
Professional Publications (New Zealand) 310
Profil, Nakladatelství (Czechoslovakia) 76
Profile Books Ltd (United Kingdom) 465
Profizdat, Izdatelstvo (Bulgaria) 61
Profizdat (Union of Soviet Socialist Republics) 418
Progrès, Editions le (Egypt) 89
Progreso, Editorial, SA (Mexico) 287
Progress (Thailand) 410
Progress Press (Malta) 281
Progress Publishers (Union of Soviet Socialist Republics) 418
Progressive Corporation Pvt Ltd (India) 207
Projecta (UK) Ltd (United Kingdom) 465
Proklama (Sweden) 386
Proklama Pocketbokklubb (Sweden) 389
Prol (Brazil) 56
Prolam SRL (Ediciones Economia y Empresa) (Argentina) 7
Promilla and Co (India) 207
Promoboek (Netherlands) 301
Promoción Popular Cristiana (Spain) 372
Promoculture, Librairie (Grand Duchy of Luxembourg) 276
Promotion Littéraire (France) 116
Proost, Henri, & Cie (Belgium) 42
Propia (Bolivia) 48

Pröpster, Albert (Federal Republic of Germany) 162
Propyläen Verlag (Federal Republic of Germany) 162
Prose Poétique Prize (France) 121
'Prosveshchenie', Izdatelstvo (Union of Soviet Socialist Republics) 419
Prosveta (Yugoslavia) 498
Prosveta (Yugoslavia) 500
Prosvetno Delo (Yugoslavia) 498
Prosvjeta (Yugoslavia) 498
Prosvjeta (Novinsko-izdavačko i Štamparsko) (Yugoslavia) 498
Protestante, Librairie (Benin) 47
Protestantse Stichting tot Bevordering van het Bibliotheekwezen en de Lectuurvoorlichting in Nederland (Netherlands) 305
Proton Editora Ltda (Brazil) 56
Provence, Librairie de (France) 116
Provincial Book Depot (Bangladesh) 35
Provincial Library (Bangladesh) 35
Prugg Verlag (Austria) 30
Prva Književna Komuna (Yugoslavia) 498
Psaropoulos, M, & Co EE (Greece) 184
Psyche, Bookclub (Japan) 263
Psychic Press Ltd (United Kingdom) 465
Psychologie, Verlag für, Dr C J Hogrefe (Federal Republic of Germany) 162
Psychologie, Verlag für, Dr C J Hogrefe (Switzerland) 401
Psychosophische Gesellschaft (Switzerland) 401
Psykologiförlaget AB (Sweden) 386
Publi-Union (France) 112
Public Lending Right Office (United Kingdom) 422
Public Lending Right Scheme (Australia) 10
Public Lending Right Scheme (Australia) 22
Public Libraries Board (Uganda) 416
Public Library (Afghanistan) 1
Public Library (Barbados) 35
Public Library, Central, Dacca (Bangladesh) 35
Public Library (Jordan) 266
Public Organization, The, for Books and Scientific Appliances (Egypt) 88
Public Organization, The, for Books and Scientific Appliances (Egypt) 89
Public Record Office (United Kingdom) 483
Public Record Office of Ireland (Republic of Ireland) 224
Publicaciones Cultural SA de CV (Mexico) 287
Publicaciones Españolas SA (Venezuela) 493
Publicaciones Literarias y Deportivas SA (Pulide SA) (Spain) 372
Publicaciones Marcombo SA (Mexico) 287
Publicaciones y Ediciones Lagos SA (PLESA) (Spain) 372
Publicações Científicas, Editora de, Ltda (Brazil) 56
Publication Board of Assam (India) 207
Publications & Information Directorate (India) 207
Publications Appeal Board (Republic of South Africa) 354
Publications (CA) (Pvt) Ltd (Zimbabwe) 505
Publications de l'Ecole Moderne Française (PEMF) (France) 116
Publications Filmées d'Art et d'Histoire (France) 112
Publications Orientalistes de France (POF) (France) 112
Publiexport SA (Spain) 363
Publishers' & Booksellers' Association of Andhra Pradesh (India) 195
Publishers' and Booksellers' Association of Bengal (India) 195
Publishers' and Booksellers' Association of Thailand (Thailand) 410
Publishers' and Booksellers' Guild (India) 195
Publishers Association (United Kingdom) 422
Publishers' Association for Cultural Exchange (Japan) 255
Publishers Association of China (People's Republic of China) 67
Publishers' Association of South India (India) 195
Publisher's Bookshop (Poland) 338
Publisher's Club (Poland) 337
Publishers' Enterprises Group (PEG) Ltd (Malta) 281
Publishers Group South West (Ireland) (Republic of Ireland) 223
Publishers' Information Card Services (United Kingdom) 422
Publishers International (Pakistan) 326
Publishers' Licensing Society (United Kingdom) 422
Publishers' Overseas Circle (United Kingdom) 422
Publishers' Promotional Fund Inc (New Zealand) 307
Publishers Publicity Circle (United Kingdom) 422
Publishers United Ltd (Pakistan) 326
Publishing Council of the Academy of Sciences of the USSR (Union of Soviet Socialist Republics) 417
Publishing House, The, of Law (People's Republic of China) 68
Publitoria (Pty) Ltd (Republic of South Africa) 358

Pucci, Christa (Italy) 251
Pudoc, Centre for Agricultural Publishing and Documentation (Netherlands) 301
Puffin (Australia) 18
Puffin Books (United Kingdom) 465
Puffin School Book Clubs (United Kingdom) 481
Pula Press (Republic of South Africa) 358
Pulide SA (Spain) 373
Punjab Public Library (Pakistan) 327
Punjab State University Textbook Board (India) 208
Punjab Textbook Board (Pakistan) 327
Punjab University Library (Pakistan) 327
Punjabi Pustak Bhandar (India) 208
Punktum (Switzerland) 405
Punnoose, K P, Communications Co (India) 208
Purnell Books (United Kingdom) 465
Pushtu Toulana, Afghan Academy (Afghanistan) 1
Pustet, Anton (Federal Republic of Germany) 162
Pustet, Universitätsverlag Anton (Austria) 30
Pustet, Verlag Friedrich (Federal Republic of Germany) 162
Puthigar Ltd (Bangladesh) 35
Putnam Aeronautical Books (United Kingdom) 465
Pygmalion, Editions, — Gérard Watelet (France) 112
Pyramid (United Kingdom) 465

Q Press Ltd (United Kingdom) 465
Qaumi Kutab Khana (Pakistan) 326
Qinghua daxue tushuguan (People's Republic of China) 68
Quaderns, Edicions dels, Crema (Spain) 373
Quaid-i-Azam University (Pakistan) 326
Quaker Home Service (United Kingdom) 465
Quartermaine House (United Kingdom) 465
Quartet Books Ltd (United Kingdom) 465
Quartier-Latin (Monaco) 289
Quarto Publishing PLC (United Kingdom) 466
Quasar, Edizioni, di Severino Tognon (Italy) 247
Quatre Bornes Book Centre (Mauritius) 283
Quatre Chemins, Société (France) 112
Quatro Elementos Editores (Portugal) 342
Quattro Venti, Edizioni (Italy) 248
Queen Anne Press Ltd (United Kingdom) 466
Queen Victoria Memorial Library (Zimbabwe) 505
Queen's, The, Gold Medal for Poetry (United Kingdom) 488
Queensland Book Depot (Australia) 21
Queensway Bookshop and Stores Ltd (Ghana) 181
Quell-Verlag (Federal Republic of Germany) 162
Quelle Press (Federal Republic of Germany) 175
Quelle und Meyer Verlag GmbH & Co (Federal Republic of Germany) 162
Quentin Press Ltd (United Kingdom) 466
Querido's, Em, Uitgeverij BV (Netherlands) 301
Queriniana, Editrice (Italy) 248
Questmere (United Kingdom) 466
Quiller Press Ltd (United Kingdom) 466
Quintero, Alvarez, Prize (Spain) 378
Quintet Publishing Ltd (United Kingdom) 466
Quinti, Aldo (Italy) 248
Quisqueyana, Editora Colegial, SA (Dominican Republic) 86
Quisqueyana, Editora Colegial, SA (Dominican Republic) 87
Quorum Press (United Kingdom) 466
Qvist, Erik, Bokhandel A/S (Norway) 323

'R', Editions, Société Civile Typo, Graphique et Littéraire (France) 112
R & S Books (Sweden) 386
R A C Motoring Services Ltd (United Kingdom) 466
R A I, Edizioni, Radiotelevisione Italiana SpA (Italy) 248
R A M Editores (Colombia) 70
R A Verlag (Switzerland) 401
R C S Rizzoli Libri SpA (Italy) 248
R E C T A Foldex (France) 112
R E M I (France) 112
R I B A Publications Ltd (United Kingdom) 466
R K W (Federal Republic of Germany) 162
R N A Major Award (United Kingdom) 488
R O L, Ediciones, SA (Spain) 373
R P L A Pty Ltd (Australia) 18
R S W (Robotnicza Spółdzielnia Wydawnicza) 'Prasa-Ksiazka-Ruch' (Poland) 334
R S W (Robotnicza Spółdzielnia Wydawnicza) 'Prasa-Ksiazka-Ruch' (Poland) 337
R T L (Radio Télé Luxembourg)/Poésie 1 Prize (France) 121
R V (Federal Republic of Germany) 162
Raamatun Tietokirja (Finland) 93

INDEX 583

Raasveld, Julien C (Belgium) 44
Rabaul Newsagency (Papua New Guinea) 329
Rabe, Musikverlag Gerhard, GmbH (Federal Republic of Germany) 162
Rabe Verlag Zurich (Switzerland) 401
Rabén och Sjögren, AB, Bokförlag (Sweden) 386
Rache, André De (Belgium) 42
Rad, Izdavačka Organizacija (Yugoslavia) 498
Radha Krishna Prakashan (India) 208
Radha Soami Satsang Beas (India) 208
Radia i Telewizji, Wydawnictwo (Poland) 337
Radiant Publishers (India) 208
Radical Book Club (India) 213
Radio, Société des Editions (France) 112
'Radio i Svyaz', Izdatelstvo (Union of Soviet Socialist Republics) 419
Radius-Verlag GmbH (Federal Republic of Germany) 162
Radnička Štampa (Yugoslavia) 498
Raduga Publishers (Union of Soviet Socialist Republics) 419
Raeber Bücher AG (Switzerland) 401
Raed, Dar Al, Al Lubnani (Lebanon) 273
Rageot, G-T (France) 112
Raghav, Ranghey, Award (India) 216
Rahman Brothers (Bangladesh) 34
Railway, The, Book Club (United Kingdom) 481
Railway Publications Ltd (United Kingdom) 466
Railway Publishing House (Democratic People's Republic of Korea) 268
Rainbird (United Kingdom) 466
Rainbow Books (United Kingdom) 466
Rainbow Pocketboeken (Netherlands) 301
Rainer Verlag GmbH (Federal Republic of Germany) 162
Rajasthan Hindi Granth Academy (India) 208
Rajasthan Pustak Vyavasayee Sangh (India) 195
Rajasthan Sahitya Akademi Awards (India) 216
Rajesh Publications (India) 208
Rajhans Prakashan Mandir (India) 208
Rajkamal Prakashan Pvt Ltd (India) 208
Rajneesh Foundation (India) 208
Rajpal & Sons (India) 208
Rakennuskirja Oy (Finland) 93
Rallycourse (United Kingdom) 466
Ram Prasad & Sons (India) 208
Ramakrishna, Sri, Math (India) 208
Ramblers & Climbers Book Society (United Kingdom) 481
Ramboro Enterprises Ltd (United Kingdom) 466
Ramboro Enterprises Ltd (United Kingdom) 479
Ramdohr, Dr, KG (Federal Republic of Germany) 162
Ramdor Publishing Co Ltd (Israel) 229
Ramos, Edições António (Portugal) 342
Ramsay, Editions (France) 112
Ramsay, The, Head Press (United Kingdom) 466
Ramsden, Barbara, Award (Australia) 25
Ramsey Library (Isle of Man) 225
Randi Pietro (Italy) 251
Randow, Dokument und Analyse Verlag Bogislaw von (Federal Republic of Germany) 162
Ranelagh Editions (United Kingdom) 466
'Rast Gufter' Press (Pakistan) 326
Rastogi Publications (India) 208
Rational Bookshops (Nigeria) (Nigeria) 318
Rationalisierungs-Kuratorium der Deutschen Wirtschaft eV (RKW) (Federal Republic of Germany) 162
Rationalist Press Association (United Kingdom) 466
Ratna Pustak Bhandar (Nepal) 292
Ratnabharati (India) 208
Rau, Walter, Verlag (Federal Republic of Germany) 162
Rauch, Karl, Verlag KG (Federal Republic of Germany) 162
Rauhen Hauses, Agentur des, Hamburg GmbH (Federal Republic of Germany) 162
Rauriser Encouragement Award (Austria) 33
Rauriser Literature Prize (Austria) 33
Rautenberg, Gerhard, Druckerei und Verlag GmbH & Co KG (Federal Republic of Germany) 162
Rav Kook Institute (Israel) 229
Ravan Press (Pty) Ltd (Republic of South Africa) 358
Ravenna Presse (Federal Republic of Germany) 162
Ravensburger Buchverlag Otto Maier GmbH (Federal Republic of Germany) 162
Ravenstein Verlag GmbH (Federal Republic of Germany) 162
Ravette Ltd (United Kingdom) 466
Rayas, G (Greece) 184
Razon, Editora La (Dominican Republic) 86
Read-a-Book Club (Zambia) 503
Readers' Book Shop (Jamaica) 255
Readers Choice (United Kingdom) 481
Readers Club of Svoboda (Czechoslovakia) 78
Reader's Digest, Selecciones del, (Iberia) SA (Spain) 373

Reader's Digest, Sélection du, SA (France) 112
Reader's Digest, The, Association Ltd (United Kingdom) 466
Reader's Digest, The, of Japan Ltd (Japan) 260
Reader's Digest AB (Sweden) 389
Reader's Digest Condensed Books (Australia) 20
Reader's Digest SA (Belgium) 42
Reader's Digest Services Pty Ltd (Australia) 18
Reader's Digest South Africa (Republic of South Africa) 358
Readers Union Ltd (United Kingdom) 481
'Reading and Writing' National Competition (Spain) 378
Readucate (Pty) Ltd (Republic of South Africa) 358
Real Academia de Buenas Letras de Barcelona (Spain) 377
Real Academia de Córdoba, de Ciencias, Bellas Letras y Nobles Artes (Spain) 377
Real Academia Sevillana de Buenas Letras (Spain) 377
Real Biblioteca de San Lorenzo de El Escorial (Spain) 377
Real-Life Education (Australia) 18
Réalisations pour l'Enseignement Multilingue International (REMI) (France) 113
Realizações Artis Lda (Portugal) 342
Recalde, Librería (Nicaragua) 314
Recht und Gesellschaft, Verlag für, AG (Switzerland) 401
Recht und Wirtschaft, Verlag, GmbH (Federal Republic of Germany) 163
Reclam, Philipp, Jun Verlag GmbH (Federal Republic of Germany) 163
Reclam, Verlag Philipp, Jnr (German Democratic Republic) 125
'Recognition Prize' (Austria) 33
Recom (Switzerland) 401
Record, Distribuidora, de Serviços de Imprensa SA (Brazil) 56
Red/Studio Redazionale SRL (Italy) 248
Red House Post, The (United Kingdom) 481
Redcliffe Press Ltd (United Kingdom) 466
Redhouse Kitabevi (Turkey) 415
Redhouse Press (Turkey) 415
Rediviva, Bokförlaget, Facsimileförlaget (Sweden) 386
Reed, A H & A W, Ltd (New Zealand) 310
Reed, Thomas, Publications Ltd (United Kingdom) 466
Reed Books Pty Ltd (Australia) 18
Reed Methuen Publishers Ltd (New Zealand) 310
Reforma, Editorial y Librería La (Puerto Rico) 345
Regain, Editions (Monaco) 289
Regal Publishing Co (Philippines) 332
Regenbogen-Verlag (Switzerland) 401
Regina Medal (International Literary Prizes) 522
Regio Verlag (Federal Republic of Germany) 163
Regional ISBN Agency (Fiji) 91
Regional ISBN Agency (CARICOM) (Guyana) 186
Regional Library for the North (Malawi) 277
Regional Library for the South (Malawi) 277
Regional Literature Awards (Pakistan) 328
Regra, A, do Jogo (Portugal) 342
Reich Verlag AG (Switzerland) 401
Reichert, Dr Ludwig, Verlag (Federal Republic of Germany) 163
Reichl, Otto, Verlag (Federal Republic of Germany) 163
Reichmann, Livraria Científica Ernesto, Ltda (Brazil) 58
Reidel, D, Publishing Co (Netherlands) 301
Reim, Verlag Knut (Federal Republic of Germany) 163
Reimer, Dietrich, Verlag (Federal Republic of Germany) 163
Reinach, Lucien de, Prize (International Literary Prizes) 522
Reinart Uitgaven (Belgium) 42
Reinhardt, Ernst, GmbH & Co Verlag (Federal Republic of Germany) 163
Reinhardt AG, Verlag Friedrich (Switzerland) 401
Reinhardt Books Ltd (United Kingdom) 466
Reinhardt Communications (Switzerland) 401
Reise- und Verkehrsverlag GmbH (RV) (Federal Republic of Germany) 163
Reiter, Elisabeth (Austria) 31
Reitzel, C A, A/S (Denmark) 83
Reitzel, C A, A/S (Denmark) 84
Reitzels, Hans, Forlag A/S (Denmark) 83
Rekha Prakashan (India) 208
Reliance Publishing House (India) 208
Religious and Moral Education Press (United Kingdom) 466
Religious Life Review Book Club (Republic of Ireland) 224
Religious Revival Organization (Thailand) 410
Remaja Karya (Indonesia) 218
Rembrandt Verlag GmbH (Federal Republic of Germany) 163
Remus Products (United Kingdom) 466

Remzi Kitabevi (Turkey) 415
Renacimiento, Librería, SA de CV (El Salvador) 90
Renaissance, La, du Livre SA (Belgium) 42
Renaitour, J-M, Prize (France) 121
Renard, Fondation André (Belgium) 42
Renaudot, Théophraste, Prize (France) 121
René, Les Editions Albert (France) 113
Renner, Verlag Klaus G (Federal Republic of Germany) 163
Rent-a-Lesson (Australia) 18
Rentrop, Verlag Norman (Federal Republic of Germany) 163
Rentsch, Eugen, Verlag AG (Switzerland) 401
Representaciones y Servicios de Ingeniería SA (Mexico) 287
Representative Church Body Library (Republic of Ireland) 224
Republički Zavod za Unapredivanje Školstva (Yugoslavia) 498
Research Library on African Affairs (Ghana) 181
Research Publishing Co (United Kingdom) 466
Researchco (India) 208
Resenha, Editora, Tributaria Ltda (Brazil) 56
Residenz Verlag (Austria) 30
Restrepo, Felix, Prize (International Literary Prizes) 522
Retail Book, Stationery and Allied Trades Employees' Association (United Kingdom) 422
Reus, Editorial, SA (Spain) 373
Revelation Awards (Poetry and Prose) (Portugal) 344
Reverté, Editora, Ltda (Brazil) 56
Reverté, Editorial, SA (Spain) 373
Reverté, Editorial, Venezolana SA (Venezuela) 493
Review Publications Pty Ltd (Australia) 18
Revista, Editora, dos Tribunais Ltda (Brazil) 56
Revista de Occidente SA (Spain) 373
Revue, La, nouvelle ASBL (Belgium) 42
Rex Book Store (Malaysia) 280
Rex Bookstore (Brunei) 60
Rex-Verlag (Switzerland) 402
Reyes, Alfonso, Prize (International Literary Prizes) 522
Reyes, Librería Universitaria Jose T (Honduras) 187
Reynaud, Jean, Prize (France) 121
Rezzonico, Edizioni Raimondo (Switzerland) 402
Rheingauer Verlagsgesellschaft mbH (Federal Republic of Germany) 163
Rheinland-Palatinate Prize (Federal Republic of Germany) 179
Rheinland-Verlag GmbH (Federal Republic of Germany) 163
Rhodos, International Science and Art Publishers (Denmark) 83
Rialp, Ediciones, SA (Spain) 373
Riccardiana, Biblioteca (Italy) 252
Ricci, Franco Maria, Editore (Italy) 248
Ricci, Librerie (Italy) 251
Ricciardi, Riccardo, Editore SpA (Italy) 248
Riccio, Edizioni del, SAS di G Bernardi (Italy) 248
Richards, Ray, Publisher (New Zealand) 310
Richards Literary Agency (New Zealand) 311
Richardson, J, & Co (Publishers) Oxford (United Kingdom) 466
Richters Bokklubb (Sweden) 389
Richters Förlag AB (Sweden) 386
Ricordi, G e C, SpA (Italy) 248
Ricordi Americana SAEC (Argentina) 7
Rideel, Editora, Ltda (Brazil) 56
Rider & Co (United Kingdom) 467
Riederer, Dr, Verlag GmbH (Federal Republic of Germany) 163
Rigby Education (Australia) 18
Rigby International & Lansdowne International Pty Ltd (United Kingdom) 467
Rigby Publishers (Australia) 19
Rigby School Centre (Australia) 21
Right Way Books (United Kingdom) 467
Rigsarkivet (Denmark) 85
Rijksmuseum Meermanno-Westreenianum/Museum van het Boek (Netherlands) 305
Rijksuniversitair Centrum, Bibliotheek (Belgium) 44
Rijksuniversiteit, Bibliotheek der (Netherlands) 305
Rijksuniversiteit te Gent, Bibliotheek van de (Belgium) 44
Rijksuniversiteit te Groningen, Bibliotheek der (Netherlands) 305
Rijksuniversiteit te Leiden, Bibliotheek der (Netherlands) 305
Ríkisútgáfa Námsbóka (Iceland) 194
Riksarkivet (Norway) 323
Riksarkivet (Sweden) 389
Riksbibliotektjenesten (Norway) 324
Rilindja (Yugoslavia) 498
Rimbaud Verlagsgesellschaft mbH (Federal Republic of Germany) 163
Rimu Publishing Co Ltd (New Zealand) 311

Ringier-Verlag GmbH (Federal Republic of Germany) 163
Rio, Editora, Gráfica (Brazil) 56
Ripostes, Edizioni (Italy) 248
Risosha Ltd (Japan) 260
Ristin Voitto ry (Finland) 93
Rithöfundasamband Islands (Iceland) 193
Ritter Verlag (Austria) 30
Ritz Paris, The, Hemingway Award (International Literary Prizes) 522
Ritzau KG Verlag Zeit und Eisenbahn (Federal Republic of Germany) 163
Riuniti, Editori (Italy) 248
Rivadeneyra Prizes (Spain) 378
Rivers Press (United Kingdom) 467
Rivière, Yves (France) 113
Riyadh Modern Bookshop (Saudi Arabia) 348
Rizzoli, Libreria, della Rizzoli Editore SpA (Italy) 251
Rizzoli Editore SpA (Italy) 248
Rizzoli Editore SpA (Italy) 251
Roasa, Editorial, SL (Spain) 373
Roberge Prizes (France) 121
Robert, Dictionnaire Le (France) 113
Robert, Editions E, L'Ecole et la Famille (France) 113
Roberts Stationery Ltd (Barbados) 35
Robin Books (Australia) 19
Robinson, J, & Co (Israel) 231
Robinson Publishing (United Kingdom) 467
Robinson Verlag (Federal Republic of Germany) 163
Robson Books Ltd (United Kingdom) 467
Rocha, M Moreira Soares, Lda (Portugal) 343
Roche, Biblioteca 'Marcel,' del Instituto Venezolano de Investigaciones Científicas (Venezuela) 494
Rocher, Les Editions du (Monaco) 289
Rocheron, Albéric, Foundation Prize (France) 121
Rocom (Switzerland) 402
Rodana Verlag (Switzerland) 402
Röderberg-Verlag GmbH (Federal Republic of Germany) 163
Rodopi, Editions, BV (Netherlands) 301
Rodriguez, Librería, SA (Argentina) 7
Rodriguez, Librería, SA (Argentina) 8
Roerdomp, De (Belgium) 42
Rogan-Pikarski Literary Agency (Israel) 230
Rogate, Libreria Editrice (Italy) 248
Rogers, Deborah, Ltd (United Kingdom) 480
Rogner und Bernhard GmbH & Co Verlags KG (Federal Republic of Germany) 163
Rohan, Duchess of, Foundation Prize (France) 121
Rohr, Buchhandlung Hans (Switzerland) 405
Rohr, Hans, Buchhandlung und Antiquariat zum Oberdorf AG (Switzerland) 402
Roitman, Lev, Verlag (Federal Republic of Germany) 163
Rojas, Pablo, Paz Prize (Argentina) 9
Rojas, Ricardo, Prize (Argentina) 9
Rökkur, bókaútgáfan (Iceland) 194
Roli Books International (India) 208
Rolim, Edições, Lda (Portugal) 343
Rolnicze i Leśne, Państwowe Wydawnictwo (Poland) 337
Romankeur (Republic of South Africa) 360
Romano, Dott Prof Tommaso (Italy) 248
Romantic Novelists' Association (United Kingdom) 485
Rombach & Partners (Netherlands) 304
Rombach Verlagshaus KG (Federal Republic of Germany) 163
Rombaldi, Editions, SA (France) 113
Romiosyni (Greece) 184
Ronald, George, Publisher Ltd (United Kingdom) 467
Rooney Prize (Republic of Ireland) 225
Roorkee Press (India) 208
Rosa, Editora Ana (Brazil) 56
Rosa, Editorial La (Colombia) 70
Rosda (Indonesia) 218
Rose-Jordan (United Kingdom) 467
Rose of French Poets Prize (International Literary Prizes) 522
Rose-Verlag und Edition Rose-Verlag (Federal Republic of Germany) 164
Rosenberg e Sellier Editori in Torino (Italy) 248
Rosenberg e Sellier SpA (Italy) 251
Rosenheimer Verlagshaus Alfred Förg GmbH & Co KG (Federal Republic of Germany) 164
Rosenkilde og Bagger (Denmark) 83
Rosenwald, Guide (France) 113
Rosinante (Denmark) 83
Roskilde University Library (Denmark) 85
Ross, Benton, Publishers Ltd (New Zealand) 311
Ross, Librería (Argentina) 8
Rossel, Victor, Prize (Belgium) 46
Rossel Edition SA (Belgium) 42
Rostock, Wilhelm-Pieck-Universität, Universitätsbibliothek (German Democratic Republic) 127
Rostrum Publishing (Netherlands) 301

Rotbuch Verlag GmbH (Federal Republic of Germany) 164
Roter Morgen, Verlag (Federal Republic of Germany) 164
Roter Stern, Verlag (Federal Republic of Germany) 164
Röth, Erich, -Verlag, Kassel (Federal Republic of Germany) 164
Roth et Sauter SA (Switzerland) 402
Rother, Bergverlag Rudolf (Federal Republic of Germany) 164
Rotten-Verlags AG (Switzerland) 402
Rotterdam International Poetry Prize (International Literary Prizes) 522
Rotterdam University Press (Netherlands) 301
Roucoules Foundation Grand Prize for Poetry (France) 121
Roudil, Editions (France) 113
Rouff, Editions, SA (France) 113
Rouge et Or, G P (France) 113
Rougery, La (France) 113
Roundabout (United Kingdom) 467
Routledge (United Kingdom) 467
Routledge & Kegan Paul Ltd (United Kingdom) 467
Rowohlt Taschenbuch Verlag GmbH (Federal Republic of Germany) 164
Roxby Press Ltd (United Kingdom) 467
Roy, K K, (Pvt) Ltd (India) 208
Roy, Publications (France) 113
Royal Afghanistan Press Department (Afghanistan) 1
Royal Book Co (Pakistan) 326
Royal Book Co (Pakistan) 327
Royal College of Surgeons in Ireland Library (Republic of Ireland) 224
Royal Dublin Society (Republic of Ireland) 223
Royal Dublin Society Library (Republic of Ireland) 224
Royal Gazette Ltd (Bermuda) 47
Royal Institute of Technology Library (Sweden) 389
Royal Literary Fund (United Kingdom) 485
Royal Palace, Library of the (Afghanistan) 1
Royal Prize (Sweden) 390
Royal Society, The, of Chemistry (United Kingdom) 467
Royal Society of Literature of the United Kingdom (United Kingdom) 485
Royal Society of South Africa Library (Republic of South Africa) 361
Royce, Robert (United Kingdom) 467
Ruamsarn (1977) Co Ltd (Thailand) 410
Ruamsarn (1977) Co Ltd (Thailand) 411
Rubber Research Institute of Malaysia Library (Malaysia) 280
Rubbettino Editore (Italy) 248
Rubiños, Libreria (Spain) 376
Rubinstein, E (Israel) 229
Ruhland Verlag (Federal Republic of Germany) 164
Rump, Peter, Verlag (Federal Republic of Germany) 164
Runa Press (Republic of Ireland) 223
Runaway (Australia) 19
Runciman Award (United Kingdom) 488
Rune Forlag (Norway) 322
Rungvit Sawarn-Apichon (Thailand) 410
Rupa & Co (India) 208
Rupa & Co (India) 213
Rural, The, Library (Isle of Man) 225
Rusconi Libri SpA (Italy) 248
Russky Yazyk (Union of Soviet Socialist Republics) 419
Rustem, K, & Bro (Cyprus) 74
Rütten und Loening, Verlag, Berlin (German Democratic Republic) 126
Rütten und Loening Verlag GmbH (Switzerland) 402
Ruy, Editorial, Diaz SAEIC (Argentina) 7
Ruže, Nakladatelství (Czechoslovakia) 77
Rwandaises, Editions (Rwanda) 348
Ryborsch, VWK, GmbH (Federal Republic of Germany) 164
Rylands, John, University Library of Manchester (United Kingdom) 483
Ryman New Writers Awards (Republic of Ireland) 225
Ryosho-Fukyu-Kai Co Ltd (Japan) 260

S & S (United Kingdom) 467
S A C O M E R (Société Africaine du Commerce) (Togo) 412
S A Cultural Holdings (Pty) Ltd (Republic of South Africa) 358
S A D E, Medalla de Oro de la, (Sociedad Argentina de Escritores) (Argentina) 9
S A D E (Sociedad Argentina de Escritores) (Argentina) 3
S A G E P (Italy) 248

S A I E Editrice SRL (Italy) 248
S A Kultuurbeleggings (Republic of South Africa) 358
S A M-förlaget (Sweden) 386
S A R P E (Spain) 373
S A S S-Verlagsgesellschaft mbH und Co KG (Federal Republic of Germany) 164
S B D Enterprises (India) 208
S B I (Switzerland) 391
S B I M (United Kingdom) 467
S C M Press Ltd (United Kingdom) 467
S D X (Shenghuo-Dushu-Xinzhi) Joint Publishing Co (People's Republic of China) 68
S E C A Codes Rousseau (France) 113
S E C F Editions Radio (France) 113
S E D E S (France) 113
S E I (Società Editrice Internationale) (Italy) 248
S E L E C (France) 96
S E L F (France) 118
S E N H A, Société d'Exploitation des Nouveaux Humanoïdes Associés (France) 113
S E S I (Switzerland) 391
S I A D Edizioni SRL (Italy) 248
S I M E P SA (France) 113
S I P C (New Zealand) 311
S L A M (France) 96
S L C F (France) 96
S L E S R (Switzerland) 391
S L L R (France) 96
S L U T (France) 96
S M, Ediciones (Spain) 373
S M D Educatieve Uitgevers (Spruyt, Van Mantgem en De Does) (Netherlands) 301
S M E R Diffusion (Morocco) 290
S N A C (France) 118
S N L (France) 113
S N T L — Nakladatelství technické literatury (Czechoslovakia) 77
S N-Verlag, Salzburger Nachrichten Verlags GmbH & Co KG (Austria) 30
S O I, Verlag, (Schweizerisches Ost-Institut) (Switzerland) 402
S O S, Editions, (Editions du Secours Catholique) (France) 113
S P C K (The Society for Promoting Christian Knowledge) (United Kingdom) 467
S P E L D (France) 113
S P K K (Spoločnosť priateľov krásnych kníh) (Czechoslovakia) 78
S R H E (United Kingdom) 467
S T L Books (United Kingdom) 467
S T M (International Organizations) 510
S T P Distributors Sdn Bhd (Republic of Singapore) 353
S U D (France) 113
S U D E L (Société Universitaire d'Editions et de Librairie) (France) 113
S U N, Uitgeverij (Netherlands) 301
S Z O T Prizes (Hungary) 192
Sá, Livraria, da Costa (Portugal) 343
Sá da Costa Editora (Portugal) 343
Saarbrücker Druckerei, S D V, und Verlag GmbH (Federal Republic of Germany) 164
Saatkorn-Verlag GmbH (Federal Republic of Germany) 164
Sabah State Library (Malaysia) 280
Sabatelli, Norberto, & C (Italy) 248
Sabe U (Burma) 62
Sable (Republic of South Africa) 358
Sacem (Société des Auteurs Compositeurs et Editeurs de Musique) (France) 96
Sachs, Nelly, Prize (Federal Republic of Germany) 179
Sächsische Landesbibliothek (German Democratic Republic) 127
Sadan Publishing House Ltd (Israel) 229
Sadoveanu', Biblioteca Municipala 'Mihail (Romania) 347
Saeed, H M, Co (Pakistan) 326
Saera Shobo (Librairie Çà et Là) (Japan) 260
Saffier, Klub (Republic of South Africa) 360
Safran, Sheri, Literary Agency Ltd (United Kingdom) 480
Saga Publishing Co (Iceland) 194
Sage Publications India Pvt Ltd (India) 209
Sage Publications Ltd (United Kingdom) 467
Saggiatore, Il, SpA (Italy) 248
Sagittaire, Les Editions du (France) 113
Sagner, Verlag Otto (Federal Republic of Germany) 164
Sahal, Kanhaiyalal, Award (India) 216
Sahayogi Prakashan (Nepal) 292
Sahitya Akademi (India) 209
Sahitya Akademi (India) 215
Sahitya Akademi Awards (India) 216
Sahitya Akademi Library (India) 214
Sahitya Bhawan Pvt Ltd (India) 209

INDEX 585

Sahitya Pravarthaka Benefit Fund Awards (India)   216
Sahitya Pravarthaka Co-operative Society Ltd (India)   209
Sahitya Samsad (India)   209
Saint-André, Publications de (Belgium)   42
Saint Andrew, The, Press (United Kingdom)   467
Saint-Cricq-Theis Prize (France)   121
Saint-Exupery, Centre culturel, Bibliothèque (Mauritania)   282
Saint-Genois Prize (Belgium)   46
Saint George & Dragon Press (United Kingdom)   467
Saint George Books (Australia)   19
Saint-Germain-des-Prés, Editions, SA (France)   113
Saint James Press Group (United Kingdom)   467
Saint James Press Ltd (United Kingdom)   467
Saint-Joseph (Republic of Gabon)   122
Saint Louis, Publications des Facultés universitaires (Belgium)   42
Saint Louis de Gonzague, Bibliothèque (Haiti)   187
Saint Michael's Mission (Lesotho)   274
Saint-Paul, Editions (Switzerland)   402
Saint-Paul, Editions (Zaire)   502
Saint-Paul, Editions, SA (France)   113
Saint-Paul, Imprimerie, SA (Grand Duchy of Luxembourg)   276
Saint Paul, Librairie (Burundi)   63
Saint Paul, Librairie (United Republic of Cameroun)   64
Saint Paul, Librairie (Zaire)   502
Saint Paul, Librairie/Imprimerie (United Republic of Cameroun)   64
Saint Paul Book Centre (Uganda)   416
Saint Paul Publications (India)   209
Saint Paul Publications (Uganda)   416
Saint Paul Publications (United Kingdom)   468
Saint Paul's Bibliographies (United Kingdom)   468
St Paul's Bookshop (Isle of Man)   225
Sainte-Dévote (Monaco)   289
Sainte-Geneviève, Bibliothèque (France)   117
Saintour Prize (France)   121
Sajha Prakashan, Co-operative Publishing Organization (Nepal)   292
Sal Terrae, Editorial (Spain)   373
Saladdine Publications & Distributors Inc (Egypt)   89
Salama Publications Ltd (Kenya)   267
Salamander Books Ltd (United Kingdom)   468
Salamander Paperbacks (Netherlands)   301
Salamandra, La (Italy)   249
Salas, Boekhandel, NV (Netherland Antilles)   307
Salerno Editrice SRL (Italy)   249
Salesianas, Edições (Portugal)   343
Salle, Otto, Verlag (Federal Republic of Germany)   164
Salon de l'Enfance et de la Jeunesse Grand Literary Prize (International Literary Prizes)   522
Salterain', Biblioteca Municipal 'Dr Joaquín de (Uruguay)   491
Saltire, The, Society (United Kingdom)   468
Saltykova-Schedrina, Gosudarstvennaya publichnaya biblioteka im M E (Union of Soviet Socialist Republics)   420
Salutiste, Librairie (Zaire)   502
Salvadoreña, Distribuidora, de Revistas y Libros SA de CV (El Salvador)   90
Salvat Editores SA (Spain)   373
Salvat Mexicana de Ediciones SA de CV (Mexico)   287
Salvat SA de Ediciones (Spain)   373
Salvatella, Editorial Miguel A, SA (Spain)   373
Salvationist Publishing & Supplies Ltd (United Kingdom)   468
Salvator, Editions, Sàrl (France)   113
Salvator Verlag GmbH (Federal Republic of Germany)   164
Salzburger Druckerei, Verlag der (Austria)   30
Salzer, Eugen, -Verlag GmbH & Co KG (Federal Republic of Germany)   164
Sam Joong Dang Publishing Co (Republic of Korea)   270
Sam-seong Publishing Co Ltd (Republic of Korea)   270
Saman & Madara Publishers (Sri Lanka)   379
Samater's Bookshop (Somalia)   354
Samfund til Udgivelse af Gammel Nordisk Litteratur (Denmark)   85
Samfundet de Nio (Sweden)   390
Samfundslitteratur (Denmark)   83
Samlerens Bogklub (Denmark)   84
Samlerens Forlag A/S (Denmark)   83
Sammenslutningem af Danmarks Forskningsbiblioteker (Denmark)   85
Sammler, Verlag für (Austria)   30
Sammlung Luchterhand (Federal Republic of Germany)   164
'Samopomoc Chlopska', Wydawnictwo Spóldzielcze CZSR (Poland)   337
Samouhos, A, Bookstore (Greece)   185
Sampson Low (United Kingdom)   468

Samsom (CED) (Belgium)   42
Samsom Stafleu (Netherlands)   301
Samsom Uitgeverij BV (Netherlands)   301
Samwha Publishing Co (Republic of Korea)   270
San Bonaventura, Collegio, di Grottaferrata (Italy)   249
San José, Editorial (Nicaragua)   314
San Martin, Editorial, SL (Spain)   373
San Min Book Co Ltd (Taiwan)   408
San Pablo, Librería (Chile)   66
San Pablo, Librería (Colombia)   71
San Pio X, Ediciones (Spain)   373
Sanchi Prakashan (India)   209
Sanctus, Förlaget, (Metodistkyrkans Förlag) (Sweden)   386
Sand et Tchou, Editions, SA (France)   113
Sandberg, Erik, A/S (Norway)   322
Sander Kitabevi, Necdet Sander (Turkey)   415
Sander Yayınları (Turkey)   415
Sanderus PVBA (Belgium)   42
Sändig Reprint Verlag Hans R Wohlwend (Liechtenstein)   275
Sane, Lennart, Agency AB (Sweden)   388
Sang-e-Meel Publications (Pakistan)   326
Sangam Books (India)   209
Sangam Books Ltd (United Kingdom)   468
Sangam Sarada Printing Press (Fiji)   91
Sangna Vuddhichai Saranonda (Thailand)   410
Sangster's Book Stores Ltd (Jamaica)   255
Sanguily', Biblioteca 'Manuel (Cuba)   74
Sangyo-Tosho Publishing Co Ltd (Japan)   260
Sankei, The, Award for Children's Books and Publications (Japan)   265
Sankei Shuppan Co (Japan)   260
Sanket Library Yojna (India)   213
Sankore, Librairie Editions PFD (Senegal)   349
Sankt-Benno Verlag GmbH (German Democratic Republic)   126
Sankt Gabriel, Verlag (Austria)   30
Sankt-Johannis-Druckerei, Verlag der, C Schweickhardt (Federal Republic of Germany)   164
Sankt Otto Verlag GmbH (Federal Republic of Germany)   164
Sankt Peter, Verlag (Austria)   30
Sanseido Co Ltd (Japan)   260
Sanskrit Pustak Bhandar (India)   209
Sanskriti (India)   209
Sansoni Editore Nuova (Italy)   249
Sanssouci Verlag (Switzerland)   402
Sansthan, Rashtriya Sanskrit (India)   209
Sansyusya Publishing Co Ltd (Japan)   260
Santa Fe, Librería (Argentina)   8
Santiago, Editorial, Rueda SRL (Argentina)   7
Santillana SA de Ediciones (Spain)   373
Santo Domingo, Biblioteca Municipal de (Dominican Republic)   87
Sanyo Shuppan Boeki Co Inc (Japan)   260
São Paulo Editora (Brazil)   56
Sapere 2000 SRL (Italy)   249
Sapienza's Library (Malta)   282
Sapphire Books Pty Ltd (Australia)   19
Sappl, Paul, Schulbuch- und Lehrmittelverlag (Austria)   30
Sara, Feministische Uitgeverij (Netherlands)   301
Saraiva SA, Livreiros Editores (Brazil)   56
Saraswat Library (India)   209
Sarawak State Library (Malaysia)   280
Sardegna Cinque (Italy)   251
Sardini, Fausto, Editrice (Italy)   249
Sarexpo International Ltd (Sri Lanka)   379
Sari Agung, Toko Buku (Indonesia)   219
Sarita Prakashan (India)   209
Sarkar, M C, & Sons (P) Ltd (India)   209
Sarma, Librairie (Zaire)   502
Sarment, Editions Le (France)   113
Sarmiento, Librería (Argentina)   8
Sarmiento Prize (Argentina)   9
Sarpay Beikman Best Manuscripts Awards (Burma)   63
Sarpay Beikman Board (Burma)   62
Sarpay Beikman Book Club (Burma)   62
Sarpay Beikman Bookshop (Burma)   62
Sarpay Lawka (Burma)   62
Sartorio, Giovanni (Italy)   249
Sarvier — Editora de Livros Medicos Ltda (Brazil)   56
Sasavona Publishers & Booksellers (Republic of South Africa)   358
Sassafras Verlag (Federal Republic of Germany)   164
Sasta Sahitya Mandal (India)   209
Sastra Hudaya (Indonesia)   218
Satguru, Sri, Publications (India)   209
Satire Verlag GmbH (Federal Republic of Germany)   164
Satya Press (India)   209
Saud, Iman M Ben, Islamic University, Deanery Libraries (Saudi Arabia)   349
Saudi Library (Saudi Arabia)   349
Saudi Publishing and Distributing House (Saudi Arabia)   348

Sauer, I H, Verlag GmbH (Federal Republic of Germany)   164
Sauerländer, Verlag, GmbH (Federal Republic of Germany)   164
Sauerländer AG (Switzerland)   402
Sauerländer's, J D, Verlag (Federal Republic of Germany)   165
Saunders, W B, & Co Ltd (United Kingdom)   468
Saur, K G, Editeur (France)   113
Saur, K G, Ltd (United Kingdom)   468
Saur, K G, Verlag GmbH & Co KG (Federal Republic of Germany)   165
Sauramps, Librairie (France)   116
Sauret, Editions André, SA (Monaco)   289
Savez bibliotečkih radnika Srbije (Yugoslavia)   501
Savez Inženjera i Tehničara Jugoslavije (Yugoslavia)   498
Savitri SRL (Italy)   249
Savremena Administracija (Yugoslavia)   498
Sawan Kirpal Publications (India)   209
Sayam Paritat (Thailand)   410
Sayle, Tessa, Literary and Dramatic Agents (United Kingdom)   480
Sayrols, Publicaciones, SA de CV (Mexico)   287
Scala/Philip Wilson (United Kingdom)   468
Scala Istituto Fotografico Editoriale (Italy)   249
Scam (Société Civile des Auteurs Multimédias) (France)   118
Scandinavia Publishing House (Denmark)   83
Scarabée, Amis du (France)   116
Scarabée, Editions du (France)   113
Scarabée d'Or (France)   113
Scene Book Club (United Kingdom)   481
Sceptre (Australia)   19
Sceptre (United Kingdom)   468
Sceptre Books (United Kingdom)   468
Schäfer, Karl A, Buch-und Offsetdruckerei-Goldstadtverlag (Federal Republic of Germany)   165
Schaffstein, Hermann, Verlag (Federal Republic of Germany)   165
Schaik, J L van, (Pty) Ltd (Republic of South Africa)   358
Schaik's, Van, Bookstore (Pty) Ltd (Republic of South Africa)   360
Schangrila, Edition (Federal Republic of Germany)   165
Schapire Editor SRL (Argentina)   7
Schattauer, F K, Verlag GmbH (Federal Republic of Germany)   165
Schaubroeck PVBA (Belgium)   42
Schauenburg, Moritz, Verlag GmbH und Co KG (Federal Republic of Germany)   165
Scheepers Prize (Republic of South Africa)   362
Scheffler, Verlag Heinrich (Federal Republic of Germany)   165
Scheidegger, Buchhandlung Dr A (Switzerland)   405
Scheltema Holkema Vermeulen BV (Netherlands)   304
Schenck, G (Federal Republic of Germany)   165
Schendl, Dr A, GmbH und Co KG (Austria)   30
Scherpe Verlag (Federal Republic of Germany)   165
Scherz, Buchhandlung, AG (Switzerland)   405
Scherz Verlag AG (Switzerland)   402
Scherz Verlag GmbH (Federal Republic of Germany)   165
Scheuerer, Gertrud E, Verlag (Federal Republic of Germany)   165
Schibsteds, Chr, Forlag (Norway)   322
Schiele und Schön, Fachverlag, GmbH (Federal Republic of Germany)   165
Schildts, Holger, Förlagsaktiebolag (Finland)   93
Schiller Prize (Federal Republic of Germany)   179
Schilling, Kurt (Federal Republic of Germany)   165
Schillinger, Verlag Karl, KG (Federal Republic of Germany)   165
Schindele, G, Verlag (Federal Republic of Germany)   165
Schindler, Mrs Karin, — Dr J E Bloch Literary Agency (Brazil)   57
Schirmer/Mosel Verlag GmbH (Federal Republic of Germany)   165
Schläpfer & Co AG (Switzerland)   402
Schlegel-Tieck Prize (United Kingdom)   489
Schlender, Verlag Bert (Federal Republic of Germany)   165
Schlueck, Thomas (Federal Republic of Germany)   175
Schmid, Joachim, & Co (Federal Republic of Germany)   165
Schmidt, Erich, Verlag GmbH (Federal Republic of Germany)   165
Schmidt, Verlag Dr Otto, KG (Federal Republic of Germany)   165
Schmidt-Römhild, Max, Verlag (Federal Republic of Germany)   165
Schmidt-Römhild, Verlag für polizeiliches Fachschrifttum Georg (Federal Republic of Germany)   165

Schmiedel, Dr Roland (Federal Republic of Germany) 165
Schmitz, Wilhelm, Verlag (Federal Republic of Germany) 165
Schmücking, Galerie, Verlag (Federal Republic of Germany) 165
Schneekluth, Franz, Verlag (Federal Republic of Germany) 165
Schneider, Musikantiquariat und Verlag Dr Hans (Federal Republic of Germany) 166
Schneider GmbH, Verlag Lambert (Federal Republic of Germany) 166
Schneider Verlag, Rudolf (Federal Republic of Germany) 166
Schneider Verlag GmbH, Franz, Schneider Verlag GmbH (Federal Republic of Germany) 166
Schnell und Steiner, Verlag, GmbH und Co (Federal Republic of Germany) 166
Schocken Publishing House Ltd (Israel) 229
Schoelcher, Bibliothèque Victor (Martinique) 282
Schoenbergske, Det, Forlag A/S (Denmark) 83
Schofield & Sims Ltd (United Kingdom) 468
Scholastic (Australia) 19
Scholastic Books (Zimbabwe) 505
Scholastic Publications Ltd (United Kingdom) 468
Scholastic Publishers (Republic of South Africa) 358
Schöldström, Birger, Prize (Sweden) 390
Schönbrunn-Verlag GmbH (Austria) 30
Schöne Wissenschaften, Verlag fur (Switzerland) 402
Schönen Bücher, Verlag die (Federal Republic of Germany) 166
Schöner, Verlag Hans (Federal Republic of Germany) 166
Schöningh, Ferdinand, Verlag (Federal Republic of Germany) 166
School Bookshop Association (United Kingdom) 422
School Library Association (United Kingdom) 484
School Library Association in Scotland (United Kingdom) 484
School of Administration Library (Ghana) 181
School of Oriental & African Studies (United Kingdom) 468
School of Oriental and African Studies Library (United Kingdom) 483
School Supplies Ltd (New Zealand) 312
Schoolpers (Netherlands) 301
Schott Frères Sàrl (France) 113
Schott Frères SPRL (Éditeurs de Musique) (Belgium) 42
Schott's, B, Söhne, Musikverlag (Federal Republic of Germany) 166
Schreiber, Verlag J F, GmbH (Federal Republic of Germany) 166
Schreiner, Olive, Prize for English Literature (Republic of South Africa) 362
Schriftenmission, Verlag und, der Ev Ges für Deutschland GmbH* (Federal Republic of Germany) 166
Schroedel, Hermann, Verlag AG (Switzerland) 402
Schroedel Schulbuchverlag GmbH (Federal Republic of Germany) 166
Schroeder, Kurt, Verlag (Federal Republic of Germany) 166
Schroeder, Marion von, Verlag GmbH (Federal Republic of Germany) 166
Schroll, Anton, & Co (Austria) 30
Schroll, Anton, & Co GmbH (Federal Republic of Germany) 166
Schroll, Ferdinand (Federal Republic of Germany) 166
Schubi Interdidac AG (Switzerland) 402
Schück, Henrik, Prize (Sweden) 390
Schule und Elternhaus, Verlag (Federal Republic of Germany) 166
Schuler Verlagsgesellschaft mbH (Federal Republic of Germany) 166
Schulfernsehen, v g s — Verlagsgesellschaft, mbH & Co KG (Federal Republic of Germany) 166
Schulte, Verlag, und Gerth GmbH & Co KG (Federal Republic of Germany) 166
Schulthess Polygraphischer Verlag AG (Switzerland) 402
Schultz, A/S J H, Forlag (Denmark) 83
Schulz, Verlag R S (Federal Republic of Germany) 166
Schumann, Hohenstaufen Verlag, KG (Federal Republic of Germany) 166
Schünemann, Carl Ed, KG (Federal Republic of Germany) 166
Schütz, Verlag K W (Federal Republic of Germany) 166
Schuyt en Co CV (Netherlands) 301
Schwabe & Co AG (Switzerland) 402
Schwabe AG, Hansrudolf (Switzerland) 402
Schwabenverlag AG (Federal Republic of Germany) 166
Schwaneberger Verlag GmbH (Federal Republic of Germany) 167

Schwann, Edition (Federal Republic of Germany) 167
Schwann/Bagel, Pädagogischer Verlag, GmbH (Federal Republic of Germany) 167
Schwartz, Otto, & Co (Federal Republic of Germany) 167
Schwartz, Uitgeverij Gary (Netherlands) 301
Schwartz Publishing (Victoria) Pty Ltd (Australia) 19
Schwarz, Verlag, GmbH (Federal Republic of Germany) 167
Schwarze, Dr Wolfgang, Verlag (Federal Republic of Germany) 167
Schweickhardt, Verlag der Sankt-Johannis-Druckerei C (Federal Republic of Germany) 167
Schweitzer, J, Verlag (Federal Republic of Germany) 167
Schweizer Bibliotheksdienst (Switzerland) 406
Schweizer Buchwerbung und Information (SBI) (Switzerland) 391
Schweizer Buchzentrum (Switzerland) 391
Schweizer Jugend-Verlag, Aare-Verlag/ (Switzerland) 402
Schweizer Spiegel Verlag AG & Rodana Verlag (Switzerland) 402
Schweizer Verband der Musikalienhändler und Verleger (Switzerland) 391
Schweizer Verlagshaus AG (Switzerland) 402
Schweizerbart'sche Verlagsbuchhandlung, E (Federal Republic of Germany) 167
Schweizerische Bibliophilen-Gesellschaft (Switzerland) 406
Schweizerische Landesbibliothek (Bibliothèque Nationale Suisse) (Switzerland) 406
Schweizerische Stiftung für Alpine Forschungen (Switzerland) 402
Schweizerische Zentralstelle für Stahlbau (Switzerland) 402
Schweizerischen Gesellschaft für Volkskunde (Switzerland) 402
Schweizerischen Schallplattenmission, Verlag der (Switzerland) 402
Schweizerischer Adressbuchverleger-Verband (Switzerland) 391
Schweizerischer Buchhändler- und Verleger-Verband (SBVV) (Switzerland) 391
Schweizerischer Bühnenverleger-Verband (Switzerland) 391
Schweizerischer Bund für Jugendliteratur (Switzerland) 406
Schweizerischer Schriftsteller-Verband (Switzerland) 391
Schweizerischer Ubersetzer- und Dolmetscherverband (Switzerland) 406
Schweizerisches Jugendschriftenwerk (Switzerland) 403
Schweizerisches katholisches Bibelwerk, Verlag (Switzerland) 403
Schweizerisches Ost-Institut (Switzerland) 403
Schweizerisches Wirtschaftsarchiv (Archives Économiques Suisses) (Switzerland) 406
Schwengeler-Verlag (Switzerland) 403
Schwiger, H G (Federal Republic of Germany) 167
Schwinghammer, Verlag Junge Gemeinde E, KG (Federal Republic of Germany) 167
Schwitter Publishing Inc/Schwitter Verlag AG (Switzerland) 403
Scialtiel, Bureau littéraire international Marguerite (France) 116
Sciamed Verlag AG (Switzerland) 403
Sciascia, Salvatore (Italy) 249
Science, The, Press (Pty) Ltd (Republic of South Africa) 358
Science and Encyclopaedia Publishing House (Democratic People's Republic of Korea) 268
Science Fiction Achievement Awards (International Literary Prizes) 522
Science Fiction Magazine Club (Thailand) 411
Science Information Publishing Centre (SIPC) (New Zealand) 311
Science of Life Books (United Kingdom) 468
Science Press (People's Republic of China) 68
Science Publications Centre (Republic of Korea) 271
Science Research Associates Ltd (United Kingdom) 468
Science Research Associates Pty Ltd (Australia) 19
Sciences et Lettres, Editions (Belgium) 42
Sciences Générales, Bibliothèque des (Socialist Republic of Viet Nam) 495
Scientechnica (United Kingdom) 468
Scientia Verlag und Antiquariat Kurt Schilling (Federal Republic of Germany) 167
Scientific and Cultural Publications Center (Iran) 220
Scientific Book Agency (India) 209
Scientific Clearinghouse and Documentation Services Division (Philippines) 333
Scientific Documentation Centre (Iraq) 221
Scientific Publishers (India) 209
Scientific Publishing House (Socialist Republic of Viet Nam) 494
Scientific Translations International Ltd (Israel) 232

Scientifica Cortina, Libreria (Italy) 249
Scientifiche Italiane, Edizioni (Italy) 249
Scientology Publications Organization ApS (Denmark) 83
Scode, Casa Editrice, SpA (Italy) 249
Scolar Press (United Kingdom) 468
Scolavox (France) 113
Scorpion Publishing Ltd (United Kingdom) 468
Scott Ferris Associates (United Kingdom) 480
Scott Moncrieff Prize (United Kingdom) 489
Scottish Academic Press Ltd (United Kingdom) 468
Scottish Arts Council Book Awards (United Kingdom) 489
Scottish Book Marketing Group (United Kingdom) 422
Scottish Book of the Year (United Kingdom) 489
Scottish Library Association (United Kingdom) 484
Scottish Publishers' Association (United Kingdom) 422
Scottish Publishing & Book Society (United Kingdom) 422
Scottish Record Office (United Kingdom) 483
Scottish Writer of the Year (United Kingdom) 489
Scriba, Ediciones, SA (Spain) 373
Scriptar, Editions, SA (Switzerland) 403
Scriptor Verlag GmbH (Federal Republic of Germany) 167
Scripts Publications (Australia) 19
Scripture in Church Book Club (Republic of Ireland) 224
Scripture Union (United Kingdom) 468
'Scrisul Românesc', Editura (Romania) 347
Scuola, Editrice La, SpA (Italy) 249
Scuola Vita (Italy) 249
Se Kwang Music Publishing Co (Republic of Korea) 270
Seafarer Books (United Kingdom) 469
Seagull Books (United Kingdom) 469
Sealy, J C (Trinidad and Tobago) 413
Search Press Ltd (United Kingdom) 469
Secker & Warburg, Martin, Ltd (United Kingdom) 469
Second Back Row Press Pty Ltd (Australia) 19
Secours, Editions du, Catholique (France) 113
Secretaría de Estado de Relaciones Exteriores, Biblioteca de la (Dominican Republic) 87
Secretariado Trinitario (Spain) 373
Século, Editorial o (Portugal) 343
Sécuritas, La Société, SA (France) 113
Sedco Publishing Ltd (Ghana) 181
Seditas (Société d'Editions et de Diffusion Tambourinaire-Sofradel) (France) 113
See-Saw Book Club (United Kingdom) 481
Seeber, Libreria Internazionale (Italy) 252
Seefeld, Edition (Switzerland) 403
Seelig, AB, och Co (Sweden) 389
Seemann, E A, Verlag (Federal Republic of Germany) 167
Seemann, VEB E A, Buch- und Kunstverlag (German Democratic Republic) 126
Seemant Prakashan (India) 209
Seewald, S (Federal Republic of Germany) 167
Seewald Verlag GmbH & Co (Federal Republic of Germany) 167
Seghers, Les Editions, SA (France) 114
Seibt Verlag (Federal Republic of Germany) 167
Seibu Time Co Ltd (Japan) 260
Seibundo Shinkosha Publishing Co Ltd (Japan) 260
Seiwa Shoten Co Ltd (Japan) 261
Seix Barral, Editorial, SA (Spain) 373
Seix Barral (Mexico) 287
Seizando-Shoten Publishing Co Ltd (Japan) 261
Seizoenen, De, PVBA (Belgium) 42
Sejong Daewang Kinyom Saophoe (Republic of Korea) 270
Sekai Bunka Publishing Inc (Japan) 261
Selangor Public Library (Malaysia) 280
Selcon SAEC & I (Selección Contable) (Argentina) 7
Selecciones, Librería (Ecuador) 88
Selecciones, Librería, SRL (Bolivia) 48
Selecciones Editoriales SA (Spain) 373
Selecciones SA Comercial (Paraguay) 330
Seleções Elêtronicas Editora Ltda (Brazil) 56
Select Books Pte Ltd (Republic of Singapore) 352
Select Books Pte Ltd (Republic of Singapore) 353
Selecta, Librería (Venezuela) 493
Sélection, Editions, J Jacobs SA (France) 114
Selimiye Library (Turkey) 416
Selina Publishers (India) 209
Sella, Shalom (Israel) 230
Sellerio Editore (Italy) 249
Sellevolds Bokhandel A/S (Norway) 323
Sellier Verlag GmbH (Federal Republic of Germany) 167
Sembrador, Editorial El (Chile) 65
Sembrador, Librería El (Chile) 66
Semences, Editions, Africaines (United Republic of Cameroun) 64
Semic-Book (Finland) 93

Semic Forlagene A/S (Denmark) 83
Semic International AB (Sweden) 386
Semic Juniorpress BV (Netherlands) 302
Semic nordisk forlag A/S (Norway) 322
Seminar on the Acquisition of Latin American Library Materials (SALALM) (International Organizations) 510
Seminario, Librería del (Colombia) 71
Seminario de Integración Social Guatemalteca (Guatemala) 185
Sendler Verlag (Federal Republic of Germany) 167
Senmon Toshokan Kyogikai (SENTOKYO) (Japan) 264
Senouhy Publishers (Egypt) 89
Sentis, Santiago, Melendo (Argentina) 7
Sentral Bokhandel A/S (Norway) 320
Sentral Bokhandel A/S (Norway) 323
Seoul Computer Press (Republic of Korea) 270
Seoul International Publishing House (Republic of Korea) 271
Seoul National University Library (Republic of Korea) 271
Seoul National University Press (Republic of Korea) 271
Septième, La, Aurore (France) 114
Septimus Editions (France) 114
Septuaginta BV Uitgeverij (Netherlands) 302
Serbal, Ediciones del, SA (Spain) 374
Serie-pocket-klubben (Sweden) 389
Serindia Publications (United Kingdom) 469
Sermwit Barnakarn (Thailand) 411
Serpent's Tail Ltd (United Kingdom) 469
Servei del Llibre de la Generalitat de Catalunya (Spain) 363
Service, Bibliothèque du, geologique du Rwanda (Rwanda) 348
Service de la Documentation de la publication, d'information scientifique et technique (Benin) 47
Service SA, Editions (Belgium) 42
Service Technique pour l'Education (France) 114
Services, Direction générale des, de Bibliothèques, Archives et Documentation (Popular Republic of Congo) 72
Services interbancaires SA (Belgium) 42
Servicio Continental de Publicaciones (Panama) 328
Servicio de Lewis (Panama) 328
Servire BV Uitgevers (Netherlands) 302
Servire BV Uitgevers (Netherlands) 304
Setberg (Iceland) 194
Seto Publishing Ltd (New Zealand) 311
Settern, Bokförlaget, HB (Sweden) 387
Settle & Bendall (Wigmore) (United Kingdom) 469
Settle Press (United Kingdom) 469
Seuil, Editions du (France) 114
Seung mun Book Co (Republic of Korea) 271
Seven Seas Publishers (German Democratic Republic) 126
Sevenseas Publishing Pty Ltd (New Zealand) 311
Severin Presse (Austria) 30
Severn House Publishers Ltd (United Kingdom) 469
Severočeské nakladatelství (Czechoslovakia) 77
Shadeed's Educational & General Supplies Ltd (Jamaica) 255
Shakai Shiso-Sha (Japan) 261
Shaker, Ahmed, Al Ansary (Egypt) 89
Shakespeare Head Press (Australia) 19
Shakespeare Head Press (United Kingdom) 469
Shakespearean Authorship Trust (United Kingdom) 485
Shakti Books (India) 209
Shanghai Book Co Ltd (Hong Kong) 189
Shanghai Book Co Pte Ltd (Republic of Singapore) 353
Shanghai Educational Publishing House (People's Republic of China) 68
Shanghai Scientific & Technical Publishers (People's Republic of China) 68
Shanghai Scientific & Technological Literature Publishing House (People's Republic of China) 68
Shanghai tushuguan (People's Republic of China) 68
Sharbain's Bookshop (Israel) 231
Sharbain's Bookshop (Jordan) 266
Sharda Prakashan (India) 209
Shaw, Pat, Associates (Norway) 323
Shaw & Sons Ltd (United Kingdom) 469
Shaw Centre, Bernard (United Kingdom) 485
Shaw Society, Bernard (United Kingdom) 485
Shazar Prize (Israel) 232
Shearwater Press Ltd (Isle of Man) 225
Sheba Feminist Publishers (United Kingdom) 469
Sheed & Ward Ltd (United Kingdom) 469
Sheffield Academic Press Ltd (United Kingdom) 469
Sheil, Anthony, Associates Ltd (United Kingdom) 480
Sheldon Press (United Kingdom) 469
Shepheard-Walwyn (Publishers) Ltd (United Kingdom) 469
Sherratt & Hughes (United Kingdom) 482
Sheth, R R, & Co (India) 209

Sheth, R R, & Co (India) 213
Shikmona Publishing Co Ltd (Israel) 229
Shiko-Sha Co Ltd (Japan) 261
Shiksha Bharati (India) 210
Shin Jin Gak (Republic of Korea) 271
Shincho Gakugei-Sho (Japan) 265
Shincho-Sha Co Ltd (Japan) 261
Shindan to Chiryo Co Ltd (Japan) 261
Shing Lee Book Store (Republic of Singapore) 352
Shinkenchiku-Sha Co Ltd (Japan) 261
Shire Publications Ltd (United Kingdom) 469
Shishu Sahitya Samsad Pvt Ltd (India) 210
Shkencore e Universitetit Shtetëror të Tiranës, Biblioteka (Albania) 1
Shkodër Public Library (Albania) 1
Shmulik (Israel) 229
Shogakukan Inc (Japan) 261
Shogakukan Literary Prize (Japan) 265
Shokabo Publishing Co Ltd (Japan) 261
Shokokusha Publishing Co Ltd (Japan) 261
Shona/Ndebele Writers' Association (Zimbabwe) 505
Shona Readers' Book Club (Zimbabwe) 505
Shorouk, Dar El (Egypt) 89
Short Story Prize (France) 121
Shortland Educational Publications (New Zealand) 311
Shree Mahavir Book Depot (Publishers) (India) 210
Shree Saraswati Sadan (India) 210
Shri Ram Centre for Industrial Relations and Human Resources (India) 210
Shuckburgh Reynolds Ltd (United Kingdom) 469
Shueisha Publishing Co Ltd (Japan) 261
Shufu-to-Seikatsu Sha Ltd (Japan) 261
Shufunotomo Co Ltd (Japan) 261
Shumawa Book House (Burma) 62
Shumawa Publishing House (Burma) 62
Shuppan News Co Ltd (Japan) 261
Shuter & Shooter (Pty) (Republic of South Africa) 362
Shuter & Shooter (Pty) Ltd (Republic of South Africa) 358
Shwepyidan Printing & Publishing House (Burma) 62
Si-sa-yong-o-sa Publishers Inc (Republic of Korea) 271
Siam, The, Society (Thailand) 412
Siamandas (Greece) 184
Sibelius-Akatemian Kirjasto (Finland) 94
Sideris, J, OE Ekdoseis (Greece) 184
Sidgwick & Jackson Ltd (United Kingdom) 469
Sidhawat Award (India) 216
Siebeck, Paul (Federal Republic of Germany) 167
Siebert und Engelbert Dessart Verlag GmbH (Federal Republic of Germany) 167
Siebert Verlag GmbH (Federal Republic of Germany) 167
Siegler, J (Federal Republic of Germany) 167
Siemens AG — ZVW 5, Verlag (Federal Republic of Germany) 167
Siemens-Penuntun Berencana (Indonesia) 218
Sierra Leone, The, Diocesan Bookshops Ltd (Sierra Leone) 350
Sierra Leone Library Association (Sierra Leone) 350
Sierra Leone Library Board (Sierra Leone) 350
Sierra Leone University Press (Sierra Leone) 350
Sifriat Poalim Ltd (Israel) 229
Sifriat Poalim Ltd (Israel) 231
Sigla, Editrice, Tre SNC (Italy) 249
Siglo XX, Ediciones, SAC & I (Argentina) 7
Siglo XXI de España Editores SA (Spain) 374
Siglo XXI Editores de Colombia Ltda (Colombia) 70
Siglo XXI Editores SA de CV (Mexico) 287
Sigma Press (United Kingdom) 470
Sigmar, Editorial, SACI (Argentina) 7
Signal Poetry Award (United Kingdom) 489
Signal-Verlag Hans Frevert (Federal Republic of Germany) 167
Signorelli, Angelo, Editore SNC (Italy) 249
Sigueme, Ediciones, SA (Spain) 374
Sijthoff's, A W, Uitgeversmaatschappij BV (Netherlands) 302
Sikkel, Uitgeverij De, NV (Belgium) 42
Silhouette (United Kingdom) 470
Silliman University Library (Philippines) 333
Silmore, The Mary, Award (Australia) 25
Siloé, Editions, Sàrl (France) 114
Silva, K V G De, & Sons (Kandy) (Sri Lanka) 379
Silvaire, Editions André, Sàrl (France) 114
Silvana Editoriale SpA (Italy) 249
Silver Dagger Award (United Kingdom) 489
Silver Link Publishing Ltd (United Kingdom) 470
Silver Pen Awards (United Kingdom) 489
Silvio Romero Prize (Brazil) 60
Simon, Verlag Ludwig (Federal Republic of Germany) 167
Simon & Schuster (Asia) Pte Ltd (Republic of Singapore) 352
Simon & Schuster Ltd (United Kingdom) 470
Simon Stevin NV (Belgium) 42

Simon und Magiera, Verlag, KG (Federal Republic of Germany) 167
Simson, Samuel, Ltd (Israel) 229
Simul, The, Press Inc (Japan) 261
Sinag-Tala Publishers Inc (Philippines) 332
Sinai Publishing Co (Israel) 229
Sind University Central Library (Pakistan) 327
Sindbad (France) 114
Sindhi Adabi Board (Pakistan) 327
Sindicato Nacional dos Editores de Livros (SNEL) (Brazil) 49
Singapore Book Emporium (Republic of Singapore) 352
Singapore Book Publishers' Association (Republic of Singapore) 353
Singapore Booksellers' Association (Republic of Singapore) 350
Singapore University Press Pte Ltd (Republic of Singapore) 352
Singu Munwha Sa (Republic of Korea) 271
Sinite Parvulos VBVB (Belgium) 42
Sino-Malay Publishing Co (Malaysia) 279
Sinodal, Editora (Brazil) 56
Sinodalno Izdatelstvo (Bulgaria) 61
Sinolingua (People's Republic of China) 68
Sinpattana (Thailand) 411
Sint Kinderkrant Suriname (Suriname) 380
Sintal (Belgium) 42
Sintes, Editorial, SA (Spain) 374
Sinwel-Buchhandlung Verlag (Switzerland) 403
Sir Robert Ho Tung, Biblioteca (Macau) 276
Sirajuddin, Malik, & Sons (Pakistan) 326
Sirey, Editions (France) 114
Siriraj Medical Library, Library Division (Thailand) 411
Sirisara Vidyalaya (Sri Lanka) 379
Sirkis, R, Publishers Ltd (Israel) 229
Sistem, Pustaka, Palajaran Sdn Bhd (Malaysia) 279
Sistema Bibliotecario (Honduras) 187
Sitti, A B, Syamsiyah (Indonesia) 218
Sjöstrands Förlag (Sweden) 387
Skandinavia Verlag (Federal Republic of Germany) 175
Skarabee, Uitgeverij, BV (Netherlands) 302
Skarv Publications ApS (Denmark) 83
Skattekartoteket, A/S (Denmark) 83
Skeab Förlag AB (Sweden) 387
Sketch Press Ltd (Nigeria) 317
Skilton, Charles, Ltd (United Kingdom) 470
Skilton & Shaw (United Kingdom) 470
Skinner, Thomas, Directories (United Kingdom) 470
Skira, Editions D'Art Albert, SA (Switzerland) 403
Skjaldborg, Bókaútgáfan, sf (Iceland) 194
'Skladnica Ksiegarska', Państwowe, Przedsiebiorstwo (Poland) 338
Škola za Strane Jezike (Yugoslavia) 498
Skolebokforlaget I/S Undervisningslitteratur (Norway) 322
Skolförlaget Gävle AB (Sweden) 387
'Školska knjiga' (Yugoslavia) 498
Skriptor Forlag AB (Sweden) 387
Skuggsjá bókaforlag (Iceland) 194
Skyline Publishing House (India) 210
'Slask', Wydawnictwo (Poland) 337
Ślaska, Biblioteka (Poland) 338
Slatkine Reprints (Switzerland) 403
Slezak, Verlag Josef Otto (Austria) 30
Sloboda (Yugoslavia) 499
Slovart Co Ltd (Czechoslovakia) 78
Slovenská kartografia NP (Czechoslovakia) 77
Slovenská knižničná RADA (Czechoslovakia) 78
Slovenská technická knižnica (Czechoslovakia) 78
Slovenské pedagogické nakladateľstvo (Czechoslovakia) 77
Slovenské ústredie knižnej kultúry (Czechoslovakia) 75
Slovenskej akadémie, Ustredná knižnica, vied (Czechoslovakia) 78
Slovenskej akadémie vied, Vydavateľstvo (Czechoslovakia) 78
Slovenský spisovateľ (Czechoslovakia) 77
Slovenský spisovateľ Prize (Czechoslovakia) 79
Slovo ljubve (Yugoslavia) 499
Službeni List (Yugoslavia) 499
Small Press Group of Britain (United Kingdom) 422
Smart & Mookerdum (Burma) 62
Smarties Prize for Children's Books (United Kingdom) 489
Smeets Illustrated Projects (Netherlands) 302
Smena (Czechoslovakia) 77
Smena Prize (Czechoslovakia) 79
Smith, John, & Son (Glasgow) Ltd (United Kingdom) 470
Smith, Lawrence, Literary Agency (1938) (Argentina) 8
Smith, Pauline, Prize for Prose (Republic of South Africa) 362

588 INDEX

Smith & Son, W H, Literary Award (United Kingdom) 489
Smith & Son, W H, Literary Awardn (International Literary Prizes) 522
Smith & Son, W H, Ltd (United Kingdom) 482
Smith Illustration, W H, Awards (United Kingdom) 489
Smith Young Writers', W H, Competition (United Kingdom) 489
Smriti Prakashan (India) 210
Smythe, Colin, Ltd (United Kingdom) 470
Snaefell, Bókaútgáfan (Iceland) 194
Snoeck-Ducaju en Zoon NV (Belgium) 42
Snøfugl Forlag (Norway) 322
Sober Förlags AB (Sweden) 387
Sobrier-Arnould Prize (France) 121
Social Science Association Press (Thailand) 411
Social Sciences Library (Socialist Republic of Viet Nam) 495
Socialist Thought and Practice (Yugoslavia) 499
Sociedad Anonima de Revistas Periodicos y Ediciones (SARPE) (Spain) 374
Sociedad Cientifica, Biblioteca de la, del Paraguay (Paraguay) 330
Sociedad de Bibliófilos Chilenos (Chile) 66
Sociedad de Bibliotecarios de Puerto Rico (Puerto Rico) 345
Sociedad de Ciencias, Letras y Artes (Spain) 377
Sociedad Editorial — Dominicana SA (Dominican Republic) 86
Sociedad General de Autores de España (Spain) 377
Sociedad General de Autores de la Argentina (Argentina) 3
Sociedad General Española de Librería SA (Spain) 374
Sociedad Puertorriqueña de Escritores (Puerto Rico) 344
Sociedade Brasileira, Biblioteca da, de Cultura Inglesa (Brazil) 58
Società Dante Alighieri (Italy) 253
Società Dantesca Italiana (Italy) 253
Societa Editori della Svizzera Italiana (SESI) (Switzerland) 391
Società Italiana di Documentazionen e d'Informazione (Italy) 252
Società Storica Catanese (Italy) 249
Societäts-Verlag (Federal Republic of Germany) 167
Société Africaine d'Edition (Senegal) 349
Société belge des Auteurs, Compositeurs et Editeurs (SABAM) (Belgium) 45
Société Biblique de Genève (Switzerland) 403
Société de Langue et de Littérature wallonnes ASBL (Belgium) 45
Société de Presse et d'Edition de Madagascar (Democratic Republic of Madagascar) 276
Société d'Edition d'Afrique Nouvelle (Senegal) 349
Société d'Edition d'Enseignement Supérieur (France) 114
Société d'Editions Scientifiques, Dimedia (France) 114
Société des Gens de Lettres (France) 118
Société des Libraires et Editeurs de la Suisse romande (SLESR) (Switzerland) 391
Société des Poètes Français (France) 118
Société d'Etudes dantesques (France) 118
Société d'Etudes Juridiques Internationales et Fiscales (France) 114
Société d'Exploitation des Nouveaux Humanoïdes Associés (France) 114
Société d'Exploitation et de Diffusion des Codes Rousseau (France) 114
Société d'Histoire littéraire de la France (France) 118
Société d'Information médicale. et d'enseignement post-universitaire (France) 114
Société du Nouveau Littré (France) 114
Société du Vieux Montmartre (France) 118
Société Française des Imprimeries Administratives Centrales (France) 114
Société Française des Traducteurs (France) 121
Société internationale de Bibliographie classique (International Organizations) 510
Société internationale des Bibliothèques-Musées des Arts du Spectacle (SIBMAS) (International Organizations) 510
Société Kenkoson d'Etudes Africaines (United Republic of Cameroun) 64
Société Librairie nouvelle (Tunisia) 414
Société Malgache d'Edition (Democratic Republic of Madagascar) 276
Société Malgache d'Edition (Democratic Republic of Madagascar) 277
Société nationale d'Edition et de Diffusion (Tunisia) 414
Société nationale d'Edition et de Diffusion (SNED) (Algeria) 2
Société Nouvelle de l'Imprimerie Centrale (Democratic Republic of Madagascar) 276

Société royale des Bibliophiles et Iconophiles de Belgique (Belgium) 45
Société Universitaire d'Editions et de Librairie (France) 114
Society for Promoting, The, Christian Knowledge (United Kingdom) 470
Society for Research into Higher Education (United Kingdom) 470
Society for the Promotion and Improvement of Libraries (Pakistan) 327
Society for the Promotion of Japanese Literature (Japan) 265
Society for the Study of Mediaeval Languages and Literature (United Kingdom) 485
Society of Archivists (United Kingdom) 484
Society of Arts, Literature and Welfare (Bangladesh) 35
Society of Authors (United Kingdom) 422
Society of County Librarians, The (United Kingdom) 484
Society of Editors (Victoria) (Australia) 10
Society of Indexers, The (United Kingdom) 422
Society of Picture Researchers and Editors (United Kingdom) 422
Society of Women Writers (Australia) (Australia) 23
Society of Young Publishers (United Kingdom) 422
Sodalitas, Libraria Editoriale, SAS (Italy) 249
Sodel (Editeur) SA (France) 114
Söderström et Co Förlagsaktiebolag (Finland) 93
Sodexport (France) 116
Sodimca, Librairies (Zaire) 502
Soethoudt & Co NV (Belgium) 42
Sofia City and District State Archives (Bulgaria) 61
Sofia Press Agency (Bulgaria) 61
Sofiac (Société Française des Imprimeries Administratives Centrales) (France) 114
Sofiiski Universitet 'Kliment Ohridsky' Biblioteka (Bulgaria) 61
Sofradel-Seditas (France) 114
Sofradif Editions Philippe Auzou (France) 114
Sogalivre, Librairie (Republic of Gabon) 122
Sogang University Press (Republic of Korea) 271
Sogapresse (Republic of Gabon) 122
Sogensha Publishing Co Ltd (Japan) 261
Soho (The Soho Book Company Ltd) (United Kingdom) 470
Sojuz na društvata na bibliotekarite na SR Makedonija (Yugoslavia) 501
Sojuz na društvata za makedonski jazik i literatura na SRM Filološki fakultet (Yugoslavia) 501
Sojuzna društvata na bibliotečnite rabotnici na Jugoslavija (Yugoslavia) 501
Sokoine University of Agriculture Library (Tanzania) 409
Solar (France) 114
Sole, Edizioni del, 24 Ore (Italy) 249
Soledi (Imprimeur-Editeur) SA (Belgium) 42
Soleil, Editions du (Haiti) 187
Solidaridad Publishing House (Philippines) 333
Solo Syndication & Literary Agency Ltd (United Kingdom) 480
Solum Forlag A/S (Norway) 322
Somaiya Publications Pvt Ltd (India) 210
Somalia d'Oggi (Somalia) 354
Somec-Rwanda (Rwanda) 348
Sommai Press (Thailand) 411
Sommer og Sörensen Forlag ApS (Denmark) 83
Somogy, Editions d'Art Aimery (France) 114
Sonapal (Benin) 47
Soncino Press Ltd (United Kingdom) 470
Sondagskool Boekhandel (Republic of South Africa) 358
Sonnenweg-Verlag (Federal Republic of Germany) 167
Sonneville Press (Uitgeverij) VTW (Belgium) 42
Sonrisa, 'La, Vertical' Prize (International Literary Prizes) 522
Sonzogno (Italy) 249
Sopena, Editorial, Argentina SACI e I (Argentina) 7
Sopena, Ramón, SA (Spain) 374
Sopena Venezolana, Editorial Ramón, SA (Venezuela) 493
Soprep (France) 118
Sorava, Educatief Uitg (Suriname) 380
Sorbonne, Bibliothèque de la (France) 117
Sorgente, La, SRL (Italy) 249
Sorrett (Australia) 19
Sotheby's Publications (United Kingdom) 470
Soulanges, Editions Louis, 'Le Livrer Ouvert' (France) 114
Source, Les Editions de la, Sàrl (France) 114
Sousa, Luisa Claudio de, Prize (Brazil) 60
Sousa e Almeida, Livraria, Lda (Portugal) 343
South African Academy of Science and Arts Prizes (Republic of South Africa) 362
South African Institute for Librarianship and Information Science (Republic of South Africa) 361

South African Institute for Librarianship and Information Science (South West Africa/Namibia Branh) (Namibia) 291
South African Library (Republic of South Africa) 361
South African Publishers' Association (Republic of South Africa) 354
South Asian Publishers Pvt Ltd (India) 210
South Australian Government Festival Awards for Literature (Australia) 25
South China Morning Post Ltd (Hong Kong) 189
South Head Press (Poetry Australia) (Australia) 19
South Pacific Commission Library (New Caledonia) 307
Southeast Asian Ministers of Education Organization (SEAMEO) (International Organizations) 513
Southeast Asian Ministers of Education Organization (SEAMEO), Regional Language Centre (RELC) (Republic of Singapore) 353
Southeast Asian Regional Branch of the International Council on Archives (SARBICA) (International Organizations) 510
Southeast Book Co (Taiwan) 408
Southern Arts Literature Prize (United Kingdom) 489
Southern Book Publishers (Pty) Ltd (Republic of South Africa) 358
Southern Press Ltd (New Zealand) 311
Southside (United Kingdom) 470
Souvenir Press Ltd (United Kingdom) 470
Sovereign Books Ltd (United Kingdom) 470
'Sovetskaya Entsiklopediya', Izdatelstvo (Union of Soviet Socialist Republics) 419
'Sovetskaya Rossiya', Izdatelstvo (Union of Soviet Socialist Republics) 419
'Sovetskii Khudozhnik', Izdatelstvo (Union of Soviet Socialist Republics) 419
'Sovetskii Kompozitor', Izdatelstvo (Union of Soviet Socialist Republics) 419
Sovetskii Pisatel, Izdatelstvo (Union of Soviet Socialist Republics) 419
'Sovetskoe Radio', Izdatelstvo (Union of Soviet Socialist Republics) 419
Soviet Land Nehru Awards (India) 216
Sovremennik Publishers (Union of Soviet Socialist Republics) 419
Spangenberg (Federal Republic of Germany) 167
Spanish Book Center (Spain) 363
Spanish Book Club (United Kingdom) 481
Spanos, Costas (Greece) 184
Sparfrämjandet Förlagsaktiebolag (Sweden) 387
Spastics, The, Society Literary Contest (United Kingdom) 489
Spearhead (Kenya) 267
Spearman, Neville, Publishers (United Kingdom) 470
Spectrum, Het, (IUM NV) (Belgium) 42
Spectrum, Taschenbuch Verlag (Switzerland) 403
Spectrum, Uitgeverij Het, BV (Netherlands) 302
Spectrum Books Ltd (Nigeria) 317
Spectrum Publications (India) 210
Spectrum Publications Pty Ltd (Australia) 19
Spectrum Verlag Stuttgart GmbH (Federal Republic of Germany) 167
Spee Buchverlag GmbH (Federal Republic of Germany) 167
Speer-Verlag (Switzerland) 403
Spektra, Bokförlaget, AB (Sweden) 387
Speld (Société de promotion à l'étranger du livre de droit, science économiques, sociales et humaines) (France) 96
Spellmount Ltd Publishers (United Kingdom) 470
Spemann, W, Verlag (Federal Republic of Germany) 168
Sperling e Kupfer, Libreria Internazionale (Italy) 252
Sperling e Kupfer Editori SpA (Italy) 249
Spes (Switzerland) 403
Sphere (Australia) 19
Sphere Books Ltd (United Kingdom) 470
Sphinx, Le, SA (Belgium) 42
Sphinx, The (Egypt) 89
Sphinx Medien (Switzerland) 403
Spiegelserie Boekenclub (Netherlands) 304
Spies, Musikverlag Fritz, GmbH (Federal Republic of Germany) 168
Spiess, Verlag Volker (Federal Republic of Germany) 168
Spindlewood (United Kingdom) 470
Spirali Edizioni (Italy) 249
Spitz, Arno (Federal Republic of Germany) 168
Splichal SA (Belgium) 42
Spokesman Books (United Kingdom) 470
Společnost přátel knihy pro mládež (Czechoslovakia) 78
Společnost pro Československou literaturu, Index-, v zahraničí (Czechoslovakia) 78
Společnost pro krásné písmo a typografii (Czechoslovakia) 75
Spolek Českých bibliofilu (Czechoslovakia) 78
Spon, E & F N, Ltd (United Kingdom) 470

INDEX 589

Sponholtz, Adolf, Verlag (Federal Republic of Germany) 168
Sport (Czechoslovakia) 77
Sport i Turystyka, Wydawnictwo (Poland) 337
Sport-Turism, Editura (Romania) 347
Sporting and Leisure Press (United Kingdom) 471
Sportska Knjiga (Yugoslavia) 499
Sportsman's Press, The (United Kingdom) 471
Sportverlag (German Democratic Republic) 126
Sprachmethodik, Verlag für (Federal Republic of Germany) 168
Språktjänst (Sweden) 391
Spring Books (United Kingdom) 471
Springer Books (India) Pvt Ltd (India) 210
Springer-Verlag Berlin — Heidelberg — New York — Tokyo GmbH & Co KG (Federal Republic of Germany) 168
Springer-Verlag KG (Austria) 30
Springwood Books Ltd (United Kingdom) 471
Spruyt, van Mantgem en de Does BV (Netherlands) 302
Square One Books (New Zealand) 311
Sreberk, J (Israel) 230
Sree Rama Publishers (India) 210
Sri Jaya, Pustaka, Sdn Bhd (Malaysia) 279
Sri Lanka Book Publishers' Association (Sri Lanka) 378
Sri Lanka Library Association (Sri Lanka) 379
Sri Lanka National Library Services Board (Sri Lanka) 379
Sri Lanka National Library Services Board (Sri Lanka) 379
Srinakharinwirot University Central Library (Thailand) 411
Srpska Književna Zadruga (Yugoslavia) 499
Srpske, Biblioteka, Akademije Nauka i Umetnosti (Yugoslavia) 500
Staackmann, L, Verlag KG (Federal Republic of Germany) 168
Staatlich genehmigte Literarische Verwertungsgesellschaft (LVG) Reg Gen mbH (Austria) 26
Staats- und Universitätsbibliothek (Federal Republic of Germany) 176
Staatsarchiv, Zentrales (German Democratic Republic) 127
Staatsbibliothek Bamberg (Federal Republic of Germany) 176
Staatsbibliothek Preussischer Kulturbesitz (Federal Republic of Germany) 176
Staatsdrukkerij en Uitgeverijbedrijf (Netherlands) 302
Staatsverlag der Deutschen Demokratischen Republik (German Democratic Republic) 126
Stabenfeldt A/S (Norway) 322
Stacey International (United Kingdom) 471
Stadsbibliotheek (Belgium) 44
Stadt- und Bezirksbibliothek Leipzig (German Democratic Republic) 127
Stadt- und Universitätsbibliothek (Federal Republic of Germany) 176
Stadt- und Universitätsbibliothek (Switzerland) 406
Städte-Verlag, E v Wagner und J Mitterhuber (Federal Republic of Germany) 168
Stafleu's Wetenschappelijke Uitgeversmaatschappij BV (Netherlands) 302
Stäheli, Buchhandlung (Switzerland) 405
Stähle und Friedel Verlagsgesellschaft mbH und Co (Federal Republic of Germany) 168
Stahleisen, Verlag, mbH (Federal Republic of Germany) 168
Stainer & Bell Ltd (United Kingdom) 471
Stam/Robijns (Netherlands) 302
Stam Press Ltd (United Kingdom) 471
Stam Technische Boeken (Netherlands) 302
Stamford College Publishers (Republic of Singapore) 353
Stampa Alternativa Editrice (Italy) 249
Stämpfli, Verlag, & Cie AG (Switzerland) 403
'Stand Magazine' International Short Story Competition (International Literary Prizes) 522
Standaard Uitgeverij (Scriptoria NV) (Belgium) 42
Standard, The, Book Depot (India) 210
Standard, The, Bookshop (Tanzania) 409
Standard Book Numbering Agency (Argentina) 3
Standard Book Numbering Agency (Australia) 10
Standard Book Numbering Agency (Austria) 26
Standard Book Numbering Agency (Belgium) 36
Standard Book Numbering Agency (Brazil) 49
Standard Book Numbering Agency (Chile) 65
Standard Book Numbering Agency (Colombia) 69
Standard Book Numbering Agency (Costa Rica) 72
Standard Book Numbering Agency (Cyprus) 74
Standard Book Numbering Agency (Denmark) 79
Standard Book Numbering Agency (Ecuador) 87
Standard Book Numbering Agency (Egypt) 88
Standard Book Numbering Agency (Federal Republic of Germany) 129
Standard Book Numbering Agency (Fiji) 91

Standard Book Numbering Agency (Finland) 92
Standard Book Numbering Agency (France) 96
Standard Book Numbering Agency (German Democratic Republic) 123
Standard Book Numbering Agency (Ghana) 180
Standard Book Numbering Agency (Greece) 182
Standard Book Numbering Agency (Guyana) 186
Standard Book Numbering Agency (Hong Kong) 187
Standard Book Numbering Agency (Hungary) 190
Standard Book Numbering Agency (India) 195
Standard Book Numbering Agency (Israel) 225
Standard Book Numbering Agency (Italy) 232
Standard Book Numbering Agency (Japan) 255
Standard Book Numbering Agency (Kenya) 267
Standard Book Numbering Agency (Malaysia) 278
Standard Book Numbering Agency (Mexico) 283
Standard Book Numbering Agency (Netherlands) 293
Standard Book Numbering Agency (New Zealand) 307
Standard Book Numbering Agency (Nigeria) 314
Standard Book Numbering Agency (Norway) 320
Standard Book Numbering Agency (Pakistan) 324
Standard Book Numbering Agency (Papua New Guinea) 329
Standard Book Numbering Agency (People's Republic of China) 67
Standard Book Numbering Agency (Philippines) 332
Standard Book Numbering Agency (Poland) 334
Standard Book Numbering Agency (Portugal) 339
Standard Book Numbering Agency (Republic of Singapore) 350
Standard Book Numbering Agency (Republic of South Africa) 354
Standard Book Numbering Agency (Spain) 363
Standard Book Numbering Agency (Sri Lanka) 378
Standard Book Numbering Agency (Suriname) 380
Standard Book Numbering Agency (Sweden) 381
Standard Book Numbering Agency (Switzerland) 391
Standard Book Numbering Agency (Tanzania) 409
Standard Book Numbering Agency (Thailand) 410
Standard Book Numbering Agency (The Gambia) 123
Standard Book Numbering Agency (Tunisia) 413
Standard Book Numbering Agency (Union of Soviet Socialist Republics) 417
Standard Book Numbering Agency (Venezuela) 492
Standard Book Numbering Agency (Yugoslavia) 495
Standard Book Numbering Agency (Zambia) 503
Standard Book Numbering Agency (Zimbabwe) 504
Standard Book Numbering Agency Ltd (United Kingdom) 422
Standard Books Ltd (Zambia) 503
Standartov, Znak Pochyota Order Izdatelstvo (Union of Soviet Socialist Republics) 419
Standing Conference of African Library Schools (SCALS) (International Organizations) 510
Standing Conference of African University Libraries (SCAUL) (International Organizations) 510
Standing Conference of National and University Libraries (SCONUL) (United Kingdom) 484
Standing Conference on Library Materials on Africa (SCOLMA) (International Organizations) 510
Stanford, The Winifred Mary, Prize (United Kingdom) 489
Stanford Maritime Ltd (United Kingdom) 471
Stapp Verlag Wolfgang Stapp (Federal Republic of Germany) 168
Star (Australia) 20
Star, Pustaka (Indonesia) 218
Star, The, Press (Brunei) 60
Star (United Kingdom) 471
Star Book Bank (India) 213
Star Publications (Pvt) Ltd (India) 210
Star Publications (Pvt) Ltd (India) 213
Star Schools (Republic of South Africa) 358
Starczewski, Hanns-Joachim, Verlag/Künstlerhof-Galerie (Federal Republic of Germany) 168
Starke, Harold, Ltd (United Kingdom) 471
State Archives (Mongolian People's Republic) 290
State Book Trading Office (Mongolian People's Republic) 290
State Central Library (Democratic People's Republic of Korea) 269
State Central Library (India) 214
State Institute of Languages (India) 210
State Librarians' Council (Australia) 22
State Library (Burma) 63
State Library (Republic of South Africa) 361
State Library of New South Wales, The (Australia) 21
State Library of Queensland (Australia) 21
State Library of South Australia (Australia) 21
State Library of Tasmania (Australia) 21
State Library of Victoria (Australia) 21
State Library Service of Western Australia (Australia) 21
State of Victoria Short Story Awards (Australia) 25
State Press (Mongolian People's Republic) 290
State Prize for Children's and Youth Literature (Netherlands) 306

State Prize for Literature, the P C Hooft Prize (Netherlands) 306
State Prizes for Literature (Finland) 95
State Stipendium for Literature (Austria) 33
Stationery & Educational Book Centre Ltd (Jamaica) 255
Stationery Office (Oifig an tSolathair) (Republic of Ireland) 223
Statisticke a evidencni vydavatelství tiskopisu (Czechoslovakia) 77
Statistics Library (Finland) 94
Statistika (Union of Soviet Socialist Republics) 419
Statistisk Sentralbyras Bibliotek (Norway) 323
Statistiska Centralbyråns Bibliotek (Sweden) 389
Statisztikai Kiadó Vállalat (Hungary) 191
Státní pedagogické nakladatelství (Czechoslovakia) 77
Státní technická knihovna (Czechoslovakia) 78
Státní vědecká knihovna (Czechoslovakia) 78
Státní vědecká knihovna odbor technické literatury (Czechoslovakia) 78
Státní zemědělské nakladatelství (Czechoslovakia) 77
Statsbiblioteket (Denmark) 85
Statystycznych i Drukarni, Zarzad Wydawnictw (Poland) 337
Stauda, Johannes, Verlag (Federal Republic of Germany) 168
Stavanger Bibliotek (Norway) 323
Steamships Trading Co (Papua New Guinea) 329
Steensballes, P F, Forlag (Norway) 322
Steenuil, De (Netherlands) 302
Steiger Verlag (Austria) 30
Steimatzky Ltd (Israel) 230
Steimatzky Ltd (Israel) 231
Steiner, Franz, Verlag Wiesbaden GmbH (Federal Republic of Germany) 168
Steiner, Rudolf, Press (United Kingdom) 471
Steiner, Rudolf, Verlag (Switzerland) 403
Steinheim Verlag und Vertrieb GmbH (Federal Republic of Germany) 168
Steinkopf, J F, Verlag GmbH (Federal Republic of Germany) 168
Steinkopff, Dr Dietrich, Verlag (Federal Republic of Germany) 168
Steintor Verlag, Rudolf Jüdes (Federal Republic of Germany) 168
Stella, Editorial (Argentina) 7
Stelle, Gruppo Editoriale Le, SpA (Italy) 249
Stenströms Bokförlag AB (Sweden) 387
Stenvalls, Frank, Förlag (Sweden) 387
Stenvert, Educational Publishers M, en Zoon BV (Netherlands) 302
Step Ahead (New Zealand) 311
Stephanus Edition Verlags AG (Switzerland) 403
Stephanus Edition Verlags GmbH (Federal Republic of Germany) 168
Stephens, Patrick, Ltd (United Kingdom) 471
Stephens and Johnsons Book Department (Trinidad and Tobago) 413
Stephenson, Carl, Verlag GmbH & Co (Federal Republic of Germany) 168
Steppe (Belgium) 42
Sterling Publishers Pvt Ltd (India) 210
Stern-Verlag Janssen & Co (Federal Republic of Germany) 168
Stern-Verlag Janssen & Co (Federal Republic of Germany) 176
Sternberg-Verlag (Federal Republic of Germany) 169
Stevens & Son Ltd (United Kingdom) 471
Steyler Verlag (Federal Republic of Germany) 169
Stichting Bibliotheek en Documentatieacademies (Netherlands) 305
Stichting Speurwerk betreffende het Boek (Netherlands) 293
Stichting Wetenschappelijke Informatie (Suriname) 380
Stiehm, Lothar, Verlag GmbH (Federal Republic of Germany) 169
Stiftelsen Kursverksamhetens Förlag (Sweden) 387
Stiftelsen Svenska Barnboksinstitutet (Sweden) 389
Stifter, Adalbert, -Gesellschaft (Austria) 33
Stifter, Adalbert, Verein eV (Federal Republic of Germany) 178
Stiftsbibliothek (Switzerland) 406
Stiintifică si Enciclopedică, Editura (Romania) 347
Stillitron (United Kingdom) 471
Stobart & Son Ltd (United Kingdom) 471
Stock, Editions (France) 114
Stocker, Leopold, Verlag (Austria) 30
Stocker-Schmid, Verlag, AG (Switzerland) 403
Stockholms Stadsbibliotek (Sweden) 389
Stockholms Universitetsbibliothek (Sweden) 389
Stockwell, Arthur H, Ltd (United Kingdom) 471
Stofnun Árna Magnússonar á Íslandi (Iceland) 194
Stollfuss Verlag Bonn GmbH & Co KG (Federal Republic of Germany) 169
Stone, Walter, Memorial Award (Australia) 25
Stora Romanklubben (Sweden) 389
Storia, Edizioni di, e Letteratura (Italy) 249

Story-Scientia, E, (NV M en I) (Belgium) 43
Story-Scientia, J, PVBA (Belgium) 44
Stowarzyszenie Autorów Zaiks (Poland) 334
Stowarzyszenie Bibliotekarzy Polskich (Poland) 338
Stowarzyszenie Ksiegarzy Polskich (Poland) 334
Stowarzyszenie Tlumaczy Polskich (Poland) 339
Strache, Verlag Dr Wolf, GmbH & Co KG (Federal Republic of Germany) 169
Strandbergs Forlag (Denmark) 83
Strange but True (United Kingdom) 471
Strassova, Greta (France) 116
Středočeské nakladatelství knihkupectví (Czechoslovakia) 77
Strega Award (Italy) 253
Strengholt's, A J G, Boeken, Anno 1928, BV (Netherlands) 302
Stroemfeld Verlag AG (Switzerland) 403
Strom-Verlag (Switzerland) 403
Stroyizdat Publishing House (Union of Soviet Socialist Republics) 419
Struik Publishers (Republic of South Africa) 358
Struik-Winchester (Republic of South Africa) 358
Stuart, Donald, Short Story Award (Australia) 25
Student Christian Movement Press (United Kingdom) 471
Studentlitteratur (United Kingdom) 471
Studentlitteratur Utbildningshuset AB (Sweden) 387
Students', The, Book Co (India) 210
Studia, Editions, SA (France) 114
Studia Croatica (Argentina) 7
Studio, Librería, SA (Mexico) 288
Studio Publications (Ipswich) Ltd (United Kingdom) 471
Studio Vista (United Kingdom) 471
Studium, Edizioni, SpA (Italy) 250
Studium, Librería, SA (Peru) 330
Studium, Librería, SA (Peru) 331
Studium, Verlag für das, der Arbeiterbewegung GmbH (Federal Republic of Germany) 169
Stürtz Verlag (Federal Republic of Germany) 169
Stvarnost (Yugoslavia) 499
Styria, Buchhandlung (Austria) 32
Styria, Verlag (Austria) 30
Su Hoc (Historical) Publishing House (Socialist Republic of Viet Nam) 494
Su Librería (Ecuador) 88
Su That (Truth) Publishing House (Socialist Republic of Viet Nam) 494
Subodh Pocket Books (India) 211
Success Education (Australia) 19
Success Publications (Kenya) 267
Sud Editions (Tunisia) 414
Sudamericana, Editorial, SA (Argentina) 7
Sudamericana/Planeta SA (Editores) (Argentina) 7
Sudan, The, Bookshop Ltd (Sudan) 380
Sudan Library Association (Sudan) 380
Südbuch Vertriebsgesellschaft mbH (Federal Republic of Germany) 169
Süddeutsche Verlagsgesellschaft Ulm (Federal Republic of Germany) 169
Süddeutscher Verlag Buchverlag (Federal Republic of Germany) 169
Sudha Publications Pvt Ltd (India) 211
Sudhindra Award (India) 216
'Sudostroenie', Izdatelstvo (Union of Soviet Socialist Republics) 419
Sudri, Bókaútgáfan (Iceland) 194
Südwest Verlag GmbH und Co KG (Federal Republic of Germany) 169
Suenson, Finn, Forlag (Denmark) 83
Sugar and Snails Press Co-op Ltd (Australia) 19
Sugarco Edizioni SRL (Italy) 250
Suhrkamp Verlag (Federal Republic of Germany) 169
Suksapan Panit (Business Organization of Teachers Council of Thailand) (Thailand) 411
Suksit Siam Co Ltd (Thailand) 411
Süleymaniye Kütüphanesi Müdürlügü (Turkey) 416
Sulina, Livraria (Brazil) 58
Sulina, Livraria, Editora (Brazil) 56
Sultan Chand & Sons (India) 211
Sultan's Library (Cyprus) 75
Suman Prakashan Pvt Ltd (India) 211
Sumatera (Indonesia) 218
Sumur Bandung (Indonesia) 218
Sumus Verlag Jutta Gütermann (Switzerland) 403
Sun Books Pty Ltd (Australia) 19
Sun Papermac (Australia) 19
Sun Ya Publications (HK) Ltd (Hong Kong) 189
Sun Yat-Sen Library (Hong Kong) 189
'Sunday Express' Book of the Year Award (United Kingdom) 489
Sundems, H, Bokhandel A/S (Norway) 323
Sundial (United Kingdom) 471
Sung Eum Kak Seoul (Republic of Korea) 271
Suomalainen Kirjakauppa Oy (Finland) 94
Suomalainen Tiedeakatemia (Finland) 95
Suomalaisen Kirjallisuuden Seura (Finland) 93

Suomalaisen Kirjallisuuden Seura (Finland) 95
Suomen Antikvariaattiyhdistys-Finska Antikvariatföreningen (Finland) 92
Suomen Arvostelijain Liitto (Finland) 95
Suomen Kirjailijaliitto (Finland) 92
Suomen Kirjallisuuspalvelun Seura (Finland) 95
Suomen Kirjastoseura (Finland) 95
Suomen Kustannusyhdistys (Finland) 92
Suomen Nuorisokirjailijat ry (Finland) 95
Suomen Nuortenkirjaneuvosto (Finland) 92
Suomen Tieteellinen Kirjastoseura (Finland) 95
Supraphon (Czechoslovakia) 77
Sur, Editorial, SA (Argentina) 7
Sur Prize (India) 216
Suriname, Publishers' Association (Suriname) 380
Suriwongs Book Centre (Thailand) 411
Suriyaban Bookstore (Thailand) 411
Suriyaban Publishers (Thailand) 411
Surjeet Book Depot (Regd) (India) 211
Surjeet Book Depot (Regd) (India) 212
Surrey University Press (United Kingdom) 471
Surveyors Publications (United Kingdom) 471
Susaeta, Ediciones, SA (Spain) 374
Sussex Video Ltd (United Kingdom) 471
Sutpaisarn (Thailand) 411
Sutton, Alan, Publishing Ltd (United Kingdom) 472
Suuri Suomalainen Kirjakerho Oy (Finland) 94
Suva Book Shop (Fiji) 91
Suva City Library (Fiji) 91
Svalan, Bokklubben (Sweden) 389
Svart á hvítu (Iceland) 194
Svart á hvítu Bókafélag (Iceland) 194
Svaz československých spisovatelu (Czechoslovakia) 75
Svaz českých spisovatelu (Czechoslovakia) 75
Svenska Antikvariatföreningen (Sweden) 381
Svenska Arkivsamfundet (Sweden) 389
Svenska Bibliotekariesamfundet (Sweden) 389
Svenska Bokförläggareföreningen (Sweden) 381
Svenska Bokhandels-Medhjälpare-Föreningen (Sweden) 381
Svenska Bokhandlareföreningen (Sweden) 381
Svenska Folkbibliotekarieförbundet (Sweden) 389
Svenska Litteratursällskapet i Finland (Finland) 95
Svenska Musikförläggareföreningen UPA (Sweden) 381
Svenska Österbottens Litteraturförening (Finland) 95
Svenska Österbottens Litteraturförening (Sweden) 390
Svepomoc (Czechoslovakia) 77
Sveriges Allmänna Biblioteksförening (Sweden) 389
Sveriges B-Bokhandlareförbund (Sweden) 381
Sveriges Exportråd (Sweden) 387
Sveriges Författarförbund (Sweden) 381
Sveriges Lantbruksuniversitets Bibliotek (Sweden) 389
Sveriges Radios Förlag (Sweden) 387
Svet Knjige (Yugoslavia) 500
Svjetlost (Yugoslavia) 499
Svjetlost (Yugoslavia) 500
Svoboda (Czechoslovakia) 77
Svyaz, Izdatelstvo (Union of Soviet Socialist Republics) 419
Swallow Books (United Kingdom) 472
Swallow Editions Ltd (United Kingdom) 472
Swami, Sree Padmanabha, Prize (India) 216
Swan, Anni, Medal (Finland) 95
Swan (India) 211
Swaziland College of Technology Library (Swaziland) 381
Swaziland National Library Service (Swaziland) 381
Swaziland News Agency (Swaziland) 381
Swedish Academy Prizes (Sweden) 390
Swedish Employers' Confederation, Publishing Section (Sweden) 387
Swedish-English Literary Translators' Association (SELTA) (Sweden) 391
Swedish-English Literary Translators' Association (SELTA) (United Kingdom) 490
Swedish into Foreign Language Translation Prize (Sweden) 390
Swedish Linguistics Prize (Sweden) 390
Swedish National ISBN Centre (Sweden) 381
Sweet & Maxwell Ltd (United Kingdom) 472
Sweet & Maxwell (NZ) Ltd (New Zealand) 311
Swets en Zeitlinger BV (Netherlands) 302
Świetego Wojciecha, Ksiegarnia (Poland) 337
Swift Children's Books (United Kingdom) 472
Swindon Book Co (Hong Kong) 189
Swiss Mission Publications (Republic of South Africa) 358
Syarikat Cultural Supplies Sdn Bhd (Malaysia) 279
Syarikat Dian Sdn Bhd (Malaysia) 279
Syarikat United Book Sdn Bhd (Malaysia) 279
Sybex (United Kingdom) 472
Sybex Verlag GmbH (Federal Republic of Germany) 169
Sydney University Press (Australia) 19
Syllogos Ekdoton Bibliopolon Athinon (Greece) 182

Symposion-Verlag, J Siegler (Federal Republic of Germany) 169
Syndicat de la Librairie ancienne et du Commerce de l'Estampe en Suisse (Vereinigung der Buchantiquare und Kupferstichhändler der Schweiz) (Liechtenstein) 275
Syndicat des Conseils littéraires français (France) 96
Syndicat des Critiques littéraires (France) 118
Syndicat des Ecrivains de Langue Française (France) 118
Syndicat des Libraires (Socialist Republic of Viet Nam) 494
Syndicat des Libraires Classiques de France (France) 96
Syndicat des Libraires de Littérature Religieuse (France) 96
Syndicat des Libraires Universitaires et Techniques (France) 96
Syndicat des Libraries du Maroc (Morocco) 290
Syndicat national de la Librairie Ancienne et Moderne (SLAM) (France) 96
Syndicat national de l'Edition (France) 96
Syndicat National des Auteurs et Compositeurs (France) 118
Syndicat national des Importateurs et Exportateurs de Livres (France) 96
Syndicat professionel Annuaire, Télématique et Communication (ATC) (France) 96
Syndikat Autoren- und Verlagsgesellschaft (Federal Republic of Germany) 169
Synergetic Press Inc (United Kingdom) 472
Syokabo Publishing Co Ltd (Japan) 261
Syrian Documentation Papers (Syria) 407
Syrian Patriarchal Seminary, Library of the (Lebanon) 273
Syston Publishing Ltd (United Kingdom) 472
Szabó, Fövárosi, Ervin Könyvtár (Hungary) 192
Szépirodalmi Kiadó (Hungary) 191
Szkolne i Pedagogiczne, Wydawnictwa (Poland) 337

T E A Ediciones SA (Spain) 374
T E A (Tipográfica Editora Argentina) (Argentina) 7
T E B R O C (Tehran Book Processing Centre) (Iran) 220
T H E Foundation (Australia) 19
T L S/Cheltenham Literature Festival Poetry Competition (United Kingdom) 489
T R- Verlagsunion GmbH (Federal Republic of Germany) 169
T Ü V, Verlag, Rheinland GmbH, Sicherheitstechnik, Energie und Umweltschutz (Federal Republic of Germany) 169
T V F (Switzerland) 403
T V N Z Enterprises (New Zealand) 311
T V N Z Publishing (New Zealand) 311
Tabajara, Edições (Brazil) 56
Tabb House (United Kingdom) 472
Table, Les Editions de la, Ronde (France) 114
Tafe Educational Books (Australia) 19
Tafelberg Publishers Ltd (Republic of South Africa) 358
Tagore Award (India) 216
Tai Kuen Book Store (Hong Kong) 189
Taipei Municipal Library (Taiwan) 408
Taipei Publications Trading Co (Taiwan) 408
Taishukan Publishing Co Ltd (Japan) 261
Taiwan Branch Library, National Central Library (Taiwan) 408
Taizé, Les Presses de (France) 114
Taj Co Ltd (Pakistan) 326
Tájékoztatási Tudományos, MTESZ, Tanács (Hungary) 192
Takahashi Shoten Co Ltd (Japan) 261
Takariva, Imprimerie (Democratic Republic of Madagascar) 276
Tallandier, Editions (France) 114
Taller Ediciones JB (Spain) 374
Tallis Press Ltd (United Kingdom) 472
Talmudic Encyclopaedia Publications (Israel) 230
Tamayo, Franz, Prize (Bolivia) 49
Tamgu Dang Publishing Co (Republic of Korea) 271
Tamil Puthakalayam (India) 211
Tammi Kustannusosakeyhtiö (Finland) 93
Tampere Prize (Finland) 95
Tampereen Kirjakauppa Oy (Finland) 94
Tampereen Yliopiston Kirjasto (Finland) 94
Tana Press and Flora Nwapa & Co (Nigeria) 317
Táncsics Szakszervezeti Kiadó (Hungary) 191
Tandem (United Kingdom) 472
Tanizaki Junichiro Prize (Japan) 265
Tankönyvkiadó Vállalat (Hungary) 191
Tankosha Publishing Co Ltd (Japan) 261
Tano A/S Forlaget (Norway) 322
Tansy Books (Republic of Ireland) 223

INDEX 591

Tantivy, The, Press Ltd (United Kingdom)   472
Tanum-Karl Johan A/S (Norway)   323
Tanum-Norli Forlaget A/S (Norway)   322
Tanzania Elimu Supplies Ltd (Tanzania)   409
Tanzania Library Association (Tanzania)   409
Tanzania Library Service (Tanzania)   409
Tanzania Library Services Board (Tanzania)   409
Tanzania Mission Press (Tanzania)   409
Tanzania Publishing House (Tanzania)   409
Tapir (Norway)   323
Tara Press (Fiji)   91
Taraporevala (DB) Sons & Co Pvt Ltd (India)   211
Taraporevala Publishing Industries Pvt Ltd (India)   211
Tarate (Indonesia)   218
Tarbut Vehinuch (Israel)   230
Tardy, Editions, SA (France)   114
Target (United Kingdom)   472
Target Publishers (Edms) Bpk (Republic of South Africa)   359
Taride, Editions, Sàrl (France)   114
Tarquin Publications (United Kingdom)   472
Tárraco, Ediciones (Spain)   374
Tartu Riikliku Ulikooli Teaduslik Raamatükogu (Union of Soviet Socialist Republics)   420
Tasmanian Booksellers' Association (Australia)   10
Tassier, Suzanne, Prize (Belgium)   46
Tata McGraw-Hill Publishing Co Ltd (India)   211
Tate Gallery Publications (United Kingdom)   472
Tatran (Czechoslovakia)   77
Tauber, Peter, Press Agency (United Kingdom)   480
Tauris, I B, & Co Ltd (United Kingdom)   472
Taurus (Republic of South Africa)   359
Taurus Ediciones SA (Spain)   374
Tavistock Publications Ltd (United Kingdom)   472
Tawjih, al-, Press (Syria)   407
Taxation (Pakistan)   326
Taylor, Alister, Publishers (New Zealand)   311
Taylor, Reginald, Prize (United Kingdom)   489
Taylor & Francis Ltd (United Kingdom)   472
Taylorix Fachverlag Stiegler und Co (Federal Republic of Germany)   169
Tcherikover Publishers Ltd (Israel)   230
Tchernichowsky Prize (Israel)   232
Tchou, Société d'Exploitation de, Editeur Sàrl (France)   115
Teach Yourself (Australia)   19
Teach Yourself Books (United Kingdom)   472
Teacher Publishing Co Ltd (United Kingdom)   472
Teachers' Book Centre Ltd (Jamaica)   255
Teachers Bookshelf (Australia)   20
Teachers' Bookshelf (New Zealand)   311
Teachers' Club Library (People's Democratic Republic of Yemen)   495
Teachers' Union (Israel)   230
Teakfield Ltd (United Kingdom)   472
Technica (Bulgaria)   61
Technical Chamber, Library of the, of Greece (Greece)   185
Technical Chamber of Greece (Greece)   184
Technical High School Library (Namibia)   291
Technical Institutes, Central Library of the Higher (Bulgaria)   61
Technical Press Ltd (United Kingdom)   472
Technical University, The, Library of Norway (Norway)   323
Technical University Library (Turkey)   416
Techniek, De (Belgium)   43
Technik, VEB Verlag (German Democratic Republic)   126
Technik Tabellen Verlag Fikentscher und Co (Federal Republic of Germany)   169
Technion — Israel Institute of Technology Libraries (Israel)   231
Technip, Société des Éditions (France)   115
Technique et Documentation (Librairie Lavoisier) (France)   115
Technique et Vulgarisation SA (France)   115
Techniques de l'Ingénieur Sàrl (France)   115
Technitrain (Pty) Ltd (Republic of South Africa)   359
Technology, Faculty of, Library (Ethiopia)   91
Tecni Ciencia Libros SA (Venezuela)   493
Técnica Interamericana, Editorial, ETI Ltda (Uruguay)   491
Tecniche Nuove SRL (Italy)   250
Técnicos Asociados, Editores, SA (Spain)   374
Técnicos e Científicos, Livros, Editora SA (Brazil)   56
Tecnoprint, Editora, Ltda (Brazil)   57
Tecnos, Editorial, SA (Spain)   374
Tecolote, El (Guatemala)   186
Teduca, Técnicas Educativas, CA (Venezuela)   493
Teenage (Australia)   20
Teenage (New Zealand)   311
Tegopoulos (Greece)   184
Tehnica, Editura (Romania)   347
Tehnička Knjiga (Yugoslavia)   499
Tehnička Knjiga (Yugoslavia)   500
Tehnika (Yugoslavia)   499

Teide, Editorial, SA (Spain)   374
Teikoku-Shoin Co Ltd (Japan)   261
Teirlinck, Auguste, Prize (Belgium)   46
Teissonnière, Paul, Prize (France)   121
Teixeira, A M, e Cia (Filhos) Lda (Livraria Classica Editora) (Portugal)   343
Tejerina, Alfonso, Ltda (Bolivia)   48
Tek Translation & International Print Ltd (United Kingdom)   490
Teknillisen Korkeakoulun Kirjasto (Finland)   94
Teknisk Forlag A/S (Denmark)   83
Tekniska Litteratursällskapet (Sweden)   389
Teknografiska Institutet AB (Sweden)   387
Teknologisk Forlag (Norway)   322
Teknologisk Instituts Forlag (Denmark)   83
Tel Aviv University Library (Israel)   231
Tel Aviv University, Publications Sales Division (Israel)   230
Telecommunications Press (United Kingdom)   472
Telegraph Publications (United Kingdom)   472
Telex-Verlag Jaeger und Waldmann GmbH (Federal Republic of Germany)   169
Telford, Thomas, Ltd (United Kingdom)   472
Tella, Instituto Torcuato di (Argentina)   7
Teloeken, Alf, Verlag KG (Federal Republic of Germany)   169
Telos series of Paperbacks (Federal Republic of Germany)   169
Temco Publishing Ltd (Zambia)   503
Temis, Editorial, SA (Colombia)   70
Temis, Librería, Ltda (Colombia)   71
Tempel, BVBA Uitgeverij De (Belgium)   43
Templar Publishing Co Ltd (United Kingdom)   472
Temple House Books (United Kingdom)   472
Temple Smith, Maurice, Ltd (United Kingdom)   472
Temps, Editions, Futurs Sàrl (France)   115
Tende Verlag GmbH (Federal Republic of Germany)   169
Tenderini, Mirella Vescovi (Italy)   251
Tenri Central Library (Japan)   263
Téqui, Librairie Pierre, et Editions Téqui (France)   115
Tercer, Ediciones, Mundo Ltda (Colombia)   70
Tercer, Librería, Mundo (Colombia)   71
Teresianum, Edizioni del (Italy)   250
Terra Magica (Switzerland)   403
Terra Sancta Arts (Israel)   230
Tertulia, Librería La (Puerto Rico)   345
Testi, Casa Editrice, Elementari Milano SRL (Italy)   250
Tests, Editions (France)   115
Teti, Nicola, e C Editore SRL (Italy)   250
Teubner, B G, GmbH (Federal Republic of Germany)   170
Teubner, BSB B G, Verlagsgesellschaft (German Democratic Republic)   126
Text Book Centre Ltd (Kenya)   267
Text Book Centre Ltd (Kenya)   268
Text Books Malaysia Sdn Bhd (Malaysia)   279
Text und Kritik, Edition, GmbH (Federal Republic of Germany)   170
Textbook Publishers' Association of Japan (Kyokasho Kyokai) (Japan)   255
Texto Editora (Portugal)   343
Thacker & Co Ltd (India)   211
Thai Library Association (Thailand)   411
Thai National Documentation Centre (TNDC) (Thailand)   411
Thai Watana Panich (Thailand)   411
Thames & Hudson Ltd (United Kingdom)   472
Thames Head (United Kingdom)   473
Thammasat University Libraries (Thailand)   411
Thaning og Appels Forlag (Denmark)   83
Theatrum Orbis Terrarum (Netherlands)   302
Theegarten-Schlotterer, Corry (Federal Republic of Germany)   170
Theiss, Konrad, Verlag GmbH (Federal Republic of Germany)   170
Thekes, Librería (Puerto Rico)   345
Theodor (Haiti)   187
Theologischer Verlag AG (Switzerland)   403
Theoria, Ediciones, SRL (Argentina)   7
Theosophical Publishing, The, House (India)   211
Thesen Verlag Vowinckel und Co (Federal Republic of Germany)   170
Theseus Verlag AG (Switzerland)   403
Thiele und Schwarz Verlagshaus GmbH (Federal Republic of Germany)   170
Thielen, Verlag-Buchhandlung Joseph (Grand Duchy of Luxembourg)   276
Thieme, BV Uitgeverij en Boekhandel W J, & Cie (Netherlands)   302
Thieme, Georg, Verlag (Federal Republic of Germany)   170
Thieme, VEB Georg, Leipzig (German Democratic Republic)   126

Thiemig, Karl, AG München (Federal Republic of Germany)   170
Thienemanns, K, Verlag (Federal Republic of Germany)   170
Thiers Prize (France)   121
Thin, James, Bookseller (United Kingdom)   482
Third Eye Centre (Glasgow) Ltd (United Kingdom)   473
Third World First Publications (Nigeria)   317
Thjódsaga, Bókaútgáfan (Iceland)   194
Thjodskjalasafn (National Archives) (Iceland)   194
Tholenaar, Jan, Verlag GmbH, G D Bücherei (Federal Republic of Germany)   170
Thomas, A (United Kingdom)   473
Thomas, Dylan, Award (United Kingdom)   489
Thomas, Herb, Award (Australia)   25
Thomasons, Joseph, & Co (India)   211
Thomson Information Services Ltd (United Kingdom)   473
Thomson Press (India) Ltd (India)   211
Thomson Publications SA (Pty) Ltd (Republic of South Africa)   359
Thone, Imprimerie Georges, SA (Belgium)   43
Thorbecke, Jan, Verlag GmbH & Co (Federal Republic of Germany)   170
Thornes & Hulton, Stanley, (Aust) Pty Ltd (AE Press) (Australia)   19
Thornes & Hulton, Stanley, (Publishers) Ltd (United Kingdom)   473
Thornhill Press (United Kingdom)   473
Thoroughbred Press (United Kingdom)   473
Thorpe, D W, Pty Ltd (Australia)   19
Thorpe, F A, (Publishing) Ltd (United Kingdom)   473
Thorsons Publishing Group Ltd (United Kingdom)   473
Three Duch Editions Ltd (United Kingdom)   473
Three Hierarchs, Library of the (Greece)   185
Thu Viên Quóc Gia Viet Nam (Socialist Republic of Viet Nam)   495
Thudhammawaddy Press (Burma)   62
Thule, Dott Prof Tommaso Romano — Edizioni (Italy)   250
Thule, Edi, Club (Italy)   251
Thule, The, Press (United Kingdom)   473
Thun , Verlags und Versandbuchhandlung, AG (Switzerland)   403
Thwe Thauk (Burma)   62
Thyrus, Edizioni, SRL (Italy)   250
Tibetan, Central, Secretariat (India)   211
Tiden, Bokförlags AB (Sweden)   387
Tiden Norsk Forlag (Norway)   322
Tiderne Skifter (Denmark)   83
Tidnings AB Dagen (Sweden)   387
Tiempo, Editorial, Nuevo SA (Venezuela)   493
Tiempo Contemporaneo, Editorial (Argentina)   7
Tiers Monde, Librairie du (Algeria)   2
Tieteellisen Informoinnin Neuvosto (Finland)   95
Tieteellisten Kirjastojen Virkailijat — Vetenskapliga Bibliotekens Tjänstemannaförening ry (Finland)   95
Tietoteos Publishing Co (Finland)   93
Tiger (United Kingdom)   473
Tijdstroom, Uitgeversmaatschappij de, BV (Netherlands)   302
Tilgher-Genova SAS (Italy)   250
Timbro, AB (Sweden)   387
Time-Life Books (United Kingdom)   473
Time-Life Books BV (Netherlands)   302
Time-Life International de México SA (Mexico)   287
Time-Life Silver Pen Award for Non-Fiction (United Kingdom)   489
Times'/Jonathan Cape, 'The, Young Writers Prize (International Literary Prizes)   522
Times Book Centre (Hong Kong)   189
Times Book Club (Nigeria)   318
Times Books International (Malaysia)   279
Times Books International (Republic of Singapore)   353
Times Books Ltd (United Kingdom)   473
Times Bookshop Ltd (Malawi)   277
Times Distributors Sdn Bhd (Malaysia)   280
Times Editions/Les Editions du Pacifique (Republic of Singapore)   353
Times Educational Co Ltd (Hong Kong)   189
Times Educational Co Sdn Bhd (Malaysia)   279
Times Educational Supplement', 'The, Information Book Awards (International Literary Prizes)   522
Times Stores Ltd (Jamaica)   255
Times The Bookshop (Republic of Singapore)   353
Timmins Publishers (Pty) Ltd (Republic of South Africa)   359
Timun, Editorial, Mas SA (Spain)   374
Tintamas Indonesia PT (Indonesia)   218
Tipografia Nacional (Netherland Antilles)   306
Tipografia Poliglotta Vaticana (Vatican City State)   492
Tipografia Stazionne (Switzerland)   403
Tips für Trips (Federal Republic of Germany)   170
Tiranti, Alec, Ltd (United Kingdom)   473
Tirona, Ramona S, Memorial Library (Philippines)   333
Tirrenia, Editrice, Stampatori SAS (Italy)   250

Tiskarna Ljudske Pravice (Yugoslavia) 499
Tisserand, Lucien, Prize (France) 121
Tiszáninneni Református Egyházkerület Nagykönyvtára (Hungary) 192
Titan Books Ltd (United Kingdom) 473
Titania-Verlag Ferdinand Schroll (Federal Republic of Germany) 170
Tjeenk Willink, H D , BV (Netherlands) 302
Tjeenk Willink, W E J, BV (Netherlands) 302
Tobin Music Books (United Kingdom) 473
Todariana Editrice (Italy) 250
Today & Tomorrow's Printers & Publishers (India) 211
Toeche-Mittler, S, Verlag (Federal Republic of Germany) 170
Togolaise, Nouvelle Librairie (Togo) 412
Tohoku University Library (Japan) 263
Toison, Libris, d'Or SA (Belgium) 44
Tokai University Press (Japan) 261
Tokuma-Shoten (Japan) 262
Tokyo Kagaku Dozin Co Ltd (Japan) 262
Tokyo Metropolitan Central Library (Japan) 263
Tokyo News Service Ltd (Japan) 262
Tokyo Shoseki Co Ltd (Japan) 262
Tokyo Shuppan Hanbai Co Ltd (Distributors) (Japan) 263
Tokyo Sogensha Co Ltd (Japan) 262
Tokyo Tosho Co Ltd (Japan) 262
Tolkien, The, Society (United Kingdom) 485
Tolley Publishing Co (United Kingdom) 473
Tom-Gallon Trust Award (United Kingdom) 489
Tomas Förlag KB (Sweden) 387
Tomus Verlag GmbH (Federal Republic of Germany) 170
Tong-In Sunsawat (Thailand) 411
Tonger, P J, Musikverlag GmbH & Co (Federal Republic of Germany) 170
Toonder, Marten, Award (Republic of Ireland) 225
Toorts, Uitgeverij De (Netherlands) 302
Topelius Prize (Finland) 95
Topos Verlag AG (Liechtenstein) 275
Toppan Co Ltd (Japan) 262
Toppan Co (S) Pte Ltd (Republic of Singapore) 353
Tops'l Books (United Kingdom) 473
Toray, Ediciones, SA (Spain) 374
Toray-Masson SA (Spain) 374
Toro, G del, Editor (Spain) 374
Torpis Publishing Co (Republic of South Africa) 362
Torre, Ediciones de la (Spain) 374
Torre, Edizioni della (Italy) 250
Torres, João Romano, & Cia Lda (Portugal) 343
Torroja, Instituto Eduardo, de la Construccion y del Cemento (Spain) 375
Toucan Press (Channel Islands) 65
Toulon (Belgium) 43
Tourist, VEB, Verlag (German Democratic Republic) 126
Touropa-Urlaubsberater (Federal Republic of Germany) 170
'Tout pour l'Ecole', Librairie (Democratic Republic of Madagascar) 277
Towarzystwo Literackie im Adama Mickiewicza (Poland) 339
Towarzystwo Przyjaciól Ksiazki (Poland) 339
Towarzystwo Przyjaciól Ksiazki (TPK) (Poland) 337
Towarzystwo Przyjaciól Nauk w Przemyślu (Poland) 339
Town & County Books Ltd (United Kingdom) 473
Townsend & Co (Pvt) Ltd (Zimbabwe) 505
Townsville Foundation for Australian Literary Studies Award (Australia) 25
Toyo, The, Bunko (Japan) 264
Toyo Keizai Shinposha Ltd (The Oriental Economist) (Japan) 262
Trachsel Verlag (Switzerland) 403
Tradicion, Editorial, SA (Mexico) 287
Trakl, Georg, Prize (Austria) 33
Traklin Ltd (Israel) 230
Trano Printy Loterana (Democratic Republic of Madagascar) 277
Trano Printy Loterana-Trano Printy Fiangonana Loterana Malagasy (TPFLM)-(Imprimerie Luthérienne) (Democratic Republic of Madagascar) 276
Trans Tech Publications SA (Switzerland) 403
Transafrica Press (Kenya) 267
Transcom — General Translation and Communication Co Ltd (France) 121
Transédition (France) 115
Translation into Swedish Prize (Sweden) 391
Translation Prize (Norway) 324
Translation Prize (Republic of South Africa) 362
Translatørforeningen (Denmark) 86
Translators Association (United Kingdom) 490
'Transport', Izdatelstvo (Union of Soviet Socialist Republics) 419
Transport Library (Republic of Korea) 271

Transport Publications Service (United Kingdom) 481
Transport Publishing Co Ltd (United Kingdom) 473
Transpress, VEB Verlag für Verkehrswesen (German Democratic Republic) 126
Transvaal Provincial Library and Museum Service (Republic of South Africa) 361
Transworld Publishers (Australia) Pty Ltd (Australia) 19
Transworld Publishers (Corgi & Bantam Books) Ltd (United Kingdom) 473
Trask, The Betty, Awards (International Literary Prizes) 522
Trauner, Rudolf, Verlag (Austria) 30
Trautvetter und Fischer Nachf (Federal Republic of Germany) 170
Travancore Law House (India) 211
Travel Publishing Asia Ltd (Hong Kong) 189
Travellers Press (United Kingdom) 474
Travintal Ltd (Greece) 184
Trazo Editorial (Spain) 375
Tre Böcker, Bokklubben (Finland) 94
Treasure Press (United Kingdom) 474
Treffer-Boekklub (Republic of South Africa) 360
Treffer-Uitgewers (Edms) Ltd (Republic of South Africa) 359
Trèfle, Librairie du (Mauritius) 283
Trefoil Publications Ltd (United Kingdom) 474
Trejos, Librería, SA (Costa Rica) 73
Trelingue, Nuova Edizioni, SA (Switzerland) 403
Tres Américas, Distribuidora, Libros SAC (Argentina) 8
Tres Tiempos, Ediciones, SRL (Argentina) 8
Trèves, Editions (Federal Republic of Germany) 170
Trevi, Bokförlaget, AB (Sweden) 387
Trévise, Editions de, BFB (France) 115
Trevisini, Casa Editrice Luigi (Italy) 250
Trevo, Publicações, Lda (Portugal) 343
Tria Phylla Editions (Greece) 184
Triad (United Kingdom) 474
Triangle Books (United Kingdom) 474
Triangulo, Livraria, Editora SA (Brazil) 58
Tribhuvan, Central Library,, University (Nepal) 292
Tribune Editions (Switzerland) 404
Tribüne Verlag und Druckereien des FDGB (German Democratic Republic) 126
Tricorne, Editions du (Switzerland) 404
Triennial Prize for Bibliography (International Literary Prizes) 522
Trigon Press (United Kingdom) 474
Trikont-Dianus (Federal Republic of Germany) 170
Trillas, Editorial, SA (Mexico) 287
Trimurti Publications Pvt Ltd (India) 211
Trinidad and Tobago, Central Library of (Trinidad and Tobago) 413
Trinidad and Tobago, Library Association of (Trinidad and Tobago) 413
Trinidad Public Library (Trinidad and Tobago) 413
Trinidad Publishing Co (Trinidad and Tobago) 413
Trinity College Library (Republic of Ireland) 224
Trinity College Library (United Kingdom) 483
Tripathi, N M, Pvt Ltd (India) 211
Tripathi, N M, Pvt Ltd (India) 213
Tripode, Edizioni Il, SRL (Italy) 250
Tripoli Public Library (Libya) 275
Triton Pers (Netherlands) 302
Trobisch, Editions, GmbH (Federal Republic of Germany) 170
Trois Arches (Belgium) 43
Trois Collines, Editions des (Switzerland) 404
Trois Fleuves, Editions des (Senegal) 349
Tropen, CV Toko Buku (Indonesia) 219
Troquel, Editorial, SA (Argentina) 8
Troubadour (United Kingdom) 474
Trotman, The, Group (United Kingdom) 474
Trubert, Maurice, Prize (France) 121
Trung-Tam San Xuat Hoc-Lieu (Socialist Republic of Viet Nam) 494
Truran (United Kingdom) 474
Tryma Book Shop (Bahamas) 34
Tsakalos Prize (Greece) 185
Tübinger Vereinigung für Volkskunde eV (Federal Republic of Germany) 170
Tuduv Verlagsgesellschaft mbH (Federal Republic of Germany) 170
Tun Razak Library (Malaysia) 280
Tun Seri, Library, Lanang, Universiti Kebangsaan Malaysia (Malaysia) 280
Tuncho, Librería, Granados G (Guatemala) 186
Türdok (Turkish Scientific and Technical Documentation Centre) (Turkey) 416
Turistička Štampa (Yugoslavia) 499
Türk Editörler Dernegi (Turkey) 414
Türk Kütüphaneciler Dernegi (Turkey) 416
Turkish Language Society (Turkey) 416
Turkish Public Library (Cyprus) 75
Turm-Verlag (Federal Republic of Germany) 170

Turmberg-Verlag (Musikverlag Klaus Gerth) (Federal Republic of Germany) 171
Turnbull, Alexander, Library (New Zealand) 312
Turner Ediciones (Argentina) 8
Turner Memorial Library (Zimbabwe) 505
Turoe Press Ltd (Republic of Ireland) 223
Turton & Armstrong Publishers Pty Ltd (Australia) 19
Turun Kansallinen Kirjakauppa Oy (Finland) 94
Turun Yliopiston Kirjasto (Finland) 94
Tusch, Edition (Austria) 30
Tusquets Editores (Spain) 375
Tuttle, Charles E, Co Inc (Japan) 262
Tuttle-Mori Agency Inc (Japan) 263
Tüv Rheinland, Verlag, GmbH (Federal Republic of Germany) 171
Twistaplot (Australia) 19
Txertoa, Editorial (Spain) 375
Tycooly (United Kingdom) 474
Tygre, Editions (Martinique) 282
Typos (Greece) 184
Tyrolia (Austria) 32
Tyrolia, Verlagsanstalt (Austria) 30

U B S Publishers' Distributors Ltd (India) 213
U Bär Verlag (Switzerland) 404
U C A, Librería (El Salvador) 90
U C A Editores (El Salvador) 90
U C A Editores Literary Prize (El Salvador) 90
U C C S A, The, Publications Department (Republic of South Africa) 359
U D E F Export (France) 96
U G A, Editions, (Uitgeverij) (Belgium) 43
U G E 10/18 (France) 115
U K B (Samenwerkingsverband van de Universiteitsbibliotheken, de Koninklijke Bibliotheek en de Bibliotheek van de Koninklijke Nederlandse Akademie van Wetenschappen) (Netherlands) 305
U K Book Bargains Ltd (United Kingdom) 479
U K National Serials Data Centre (United Kingdom) 422
U N A C Tokyo (Japan) 262
U N A L I SL (Spain) 375
U N C T A D (International Organizations) 511
U N E A C Prize (Cuba) 74
U N E S C O (International Organizations) 512
U N E S C O Institute for Education (UIE) (International Organizations) 512
U O P C (Belgium) 43
U O P C (Belgium) 44
U P Indonesia (Indonesia) 218
U S L F (France) 96
U S S R Library Council (Union of Soviet Socialist Republics) 420
U S S R Writers' Union (Union of Soviet Socialist Republics) 417
U T B (Federal Republic of Germany) 171
U T E T (Unione Tipografico-Editrice Torinese) (Italy) 250
Ubulibri (Italy) 250
Ueberreuter, Verlag Carl (Austria) 30
Uffici (United Kingdom) 474
Uganda Bookshop (Uganda) 416
Uganda Library Association (Uganda) 416
Uganda Polytechnic Library (Uganda) 416
Uganda Publishing House (Uganda) 416
Uganda Schools Library Association (Uganda) 417
Uglan (Iceland) 194
Uhl, Verlag Dr Alfons (Federal Republic of Germany) 171
Ulisseia, Editora, Lda (Portugal) 343
Ullstein, Verlag, GmbH (Federal Republic of Germany) 171
Ullstein Langen-Müller/Herbig, Buchverlage (Federal Republic of Germany) 171
Ulmer, Verlag Eugen, GmbH & Co (Federal Republic of Germany) 171
Ultima Hora (Dominican Republic) 87
Ultramar Editores SA (Spain) 375
Ulverscroft Large Print Books Ltd (United Kingdom) 474
Umbra, Editoriale, SNC di Carnevali e Zanello (Italy) 250
Umbria Editrice (Italy) 250
Umschau Verlag Breidenstein GmbH (Federal Republic of Germany) 171
Underhållningsbokklubben (Sweden) 389
Undervisningslitteratur, I/S (Norway) 322
Ungarischer Kultureller und Sozialer Fonds eV in der BRD (Federal Republic of Germany) 171
Uni Books (United Kingdom) 474
Uni-Taschenbücher (UTB) GmbH (Federal Republic of Germany) 171
Uni-Text Book Company (Malaysia) 280

INDEX 593

Uniandes, Librería (Colombia) 71
União dos Escritores Angolanos (Angola) 2
Unibooks (United Kingdom) 4
Unicart Kartografisk Produktion AB (Sweden) 387
Unicopli, Edizioni, Scrl (Italy) 250
Unicorn Books Ltd (Hong Kong) 189
Unieboek BV (Netherlands) 302
Uniepers BV (Netherlands) 302
Unilit Publishing Co (Ghana) 181
Unión, Ediciones (Cuba) 73
Unión, Editorial (Nicaragua) 314
Union, The, Press (Sri Lanka) 379
Unión Aragonesa del Libro SL (Spain) 375
Union Book Clubs (Denmark) 84
Unión de Escritores y Artistas de Cuba (Cuba) 73
Union des Ecrivains algériens (Algeria) 2
Union des Ecrivains tunisiens (Tunisia) 414
Union des Editeurs de langue française (International Organizations) 510
Union des Editeurs de Langue française (UELF) (Belgium) 36
Union des Editeurs Français en Sciences Humaines (France) 96
Union et Orientation de Presse et de Culture (UOPC) SA (Belgium) 43
Union Helvetia Fachbuchverlag (Switzerland) 404
Union of Writers and Artists of Albania (Albania) 1
Union of Writers of the African Peoples (International Organizations) 510
Union Press Ltd (Hong Kong) 189
Union Syndicale des Libraires de France (France) 96
Union Verlag Berlin VOB (German Democratic Republic) 126
Union Verlag Stuttgart (Federal Republic of Germany) 171
Unionsverlag (Switzerland) 404
Unistad VZW (Belgium) 43
Unitas Forlag (Denmark) 83
United Africa Press Ltd (Kenya) 267
United Bank Prize for Literature (Pakistan) 328
United Book Distributors (Pty) Ltd (Republic of South Africa) 360
United Book Traders (India) 213
United Bookshop & Stationers Ltd (Bahamas) 34
United Christian Council Literature Bureau (Sierra Leone) 350
United Congregational, The, Church of South Africa Publications Department (Republic of South Africa) 359
United Nations (International Organizations) 512
United Nations Conference on Trade and Development (UNCTAD) (International Organizations) 512
United Nations Depository Library (Republic of Korea) 271
United Nations, Economic and Social Commission for Asia and the Pacific Library (International Organizations) 512
United Nations Economic Commission for Africa Library (Ethiopia) 91
United Nations Economic Commission for Africa Library (International Organizations) 510
United Nations Educational, Scientific and Cultural Organization (UNESCO) (International Organizations) 512
United Nations Library (Switzerland) 406
United Nations Research Institute for Social Development (UNRISD) (International Organizations) 512
United Nations University (International Organizations) 512
United Protestant Publishers (Pty) Ltd (Republic of South Africa) 359
United Publishers (India) 213
United Publishers Services Ltd (Japan) 263
United Publishers Services (M) Sdn Bhd (Malaysia) 280
United States Book Association (Australia) 10
United States Information Agency Library (Democratic Republic of Madagascar) 277
United States Information Service Library (Sierra Leone) 350
United States Information Service Library (Uganda) 416
United Writers Publications Ltd (United Kingdom) 474
Uniting Church Press (Australia) 19
Unity Books Ltd (New Zealand) 312
Uniunea Scriitorilor din Republica Socialistă România (Romania) 346
Univers, Editura (Romania) 347
Universa PVBA (Belgium) 43
Universal, La, SRL (Bolivia) 48
Universal Book Distributors (India) 213
Universal Book Shop (India) 214
Universal Business Directories Pty Ltd (Australia) 19
Universal Distributors Ltd (Nigeria) 318
Universal Edition AG (Austria) 30
Universal Library (Israel) 231

Universal Librería, Imprenta y Fotolitografia (Carlos Federspiel & Co) SA (Costa Rica) 73
Universal Postal Union (UPU) (International Organizations) 512
Universal Press Pty Ltd (Australia) 19
Universal Publications Agency Ltd (Republic of Korea) 271
Universidad', Librería 'La, Nicolas Ojeda Fierro e Hijos SRL Ltda (Peru) 331
Universidad Autónoma, Biblioteca de la, de Santo Domingo (Dominican Republic) 87
Universidad Autónoma de Barcelona, Biblioteca General (Spain) 377
Universidad Autónoma de Santo Domingo, Ciudad Universitaria (Dominican Republic) 87
Universidad Boliviana, Biblioteca Universitaria, Departamento de Bibliotecas, Tomás Frías (Bolivia) 48
Universidad Católica, Fondo Editorial de la (Peru) 330
Universidad Católica, Pontificia, de Ecuador (Ecuador) 87
Universidad Católica de Chile, Ediciones (Chile) 66
Universidad Católica de Chile, Sistema de Bibliotecas de la Pontificia (Chile) 66
Universidad Católica de Valparaíso, Biblioteca de la (Chile) 66
Universidad Católica Madre y Maestra (Dominican Republic) 87
Universidad Central, Biblioteca Central de la, de Venezuela (Venezuela) 494
Universidad Central, Biblioteca General de la, de las Villas (Cuba) 74
Universidad Central de Ecuador, Biblioteca de la (Ecuador) 88
Universidad Central de la Villas, Carretera de Camajuani (Cuba) 73
Universidad Central del Ecuador, Dpto de Publicaciones (Ecuador) 87
Universidad Centroamericana, Biblioteca de la, José Simeón Cañas (El Salvador) 90
Universidad Complutense, Biblioteca de la (Spain) 377
Universidad de Antioquia, Departamento de Bibliotecas (Colombia) 71
Universidad de Antioquia, Departamento de Publicaciones (Colombia) 70
Universidad de Buenos Aires, Biblioteca de la (Argentina) 8
Universidad de Chile, Biblioteca Central de la (Chile) 66
Universidad de Concepción Direccion de Bibliotecas (Chile) 66
Universidad de Costa Rica, Biblioteca de la (Costa Rica) 73
Universidad de Costa Rica, Editorial de la (Costa Rica) 73
Universidad de El Salvador, Biblioteca Central de la (El Salvador) 90
Universidad de Granada (Spain) 375
Universidad de Guayaquil, Biblioteca General, (Ecuador) 88
Universidad de Guayaquil, Dpto de Publicaciones (Ecuador) 87
Universidad de la Habana (Cuba) 73
Universidad de la Habana, Direccion de Informacion Cientifica (Cuba) 74
Universidad de los Andes, Biblioteca General, Desarrollo de Colecciones (Colombia) 71
Universidad de los Andes, Centro de Estudios sobre Desarrollo Económico (CEDE) (Colombia) 71
Universidad de los Andes, Consejo de Publicaciones (Venezuela) 493
Universidad de Malaga (Spain) 375
Universidad de Navarra, Ediciones, SA (Spain) 375
Universidad de Oriente, Biblioteca Central de la (Cuba) 74
Universidad de Panama, Biblioteca Interamericana Simón Bolívar (Panama) 328
Universidad de Salamanca, Ediciones (Spain) 375
Universidad de San Carlos, Biblioteca Central de la (Guatemala) 186
Universidad de San Carlos de Guatemala, Editorial Universitaria (Guatemala) 185
Universidad de Zulia, Biblioteca Central de la (Venezuela) 494
Universidad del Salvador, Biblioteca Central, (Argentina) 8
Universidad Estatal, Editorial, a Distancia (EUNED) (Costa Rica) 73
Universidad Iberoamericana, Biblioteca de la (Mexico) 289
Universidad Mayor de San Andrés, Biblioteca Central de la (Bolivia) 48
Universidad Mayor de San Andres, Editorial Universitaria (Bolivia) 48
Universidad Mayor de San Francisco Xavier, Biblioteca Central de la (Bolivia) 48

Universidad Nacional, Biblioteca Central del, de Nicaragua (Nicaragua) 314
Universidad Nacional Autónoma de México (Mexico) 288
Universidad Nacional de Colombia, Biblioteca Central (Colombia) 71
Universidad Nacional de Córdoba, Biblioteca Mayor de la (Argentina) 8
Universidad Nacional de Cuzeco, Biblioteca Central de la (Peru) 331
Universidad Nacional de La Plata, Biblioteca Pública de la (Argentina) 8
Universidad Nacional de Nicaragua, Librería y Editorial (Nicaragua) 314
Universidad Nacional de San Agustín, Biblioteca Central de la (Peru) 331
Universidad Nacional Mayor de San Marcos, Biblioteca Central de la (Peru) 331
Universidad Nacional Mayor de San Marcos, Librería de la (Peru) 331
Universidad Nacional Mayor de San Marcos (Peru) 330
Universidad Pontificia de Salamanca, Biblioteca General (Spain) 377
Universidade de Brasília, Clube do Livro da (Brazil) 57
Universidade de Brasília, Editora (Brazil) 57
Universidade de Brasília, Biblioteca Central (Brazil) 58
Universidade de Coimbra, Biblioteca Geral da (Portugal) 344
Universidade de Luanda Biblioteca (Angola) 2
Universidade de São Paulo, Editora da (Brazil) 57
Universidade de São Paulo, Sistema de Bibliotecas da, (SIBI) (Brazil) 58
Universidade Eduardo Mondlane, Bibliotecas da (Mozambique) 291
Universidade Federal do Paraná, Biblioteca Central da (Brazil) 58
Universidade Federal do Rio de Janeiro, Centro de Ciências da Saude da (Brazil) 58
Universidade Federal do Rio Grande do Sul (UFRGS), Biblioteca Central (Brazil) 58
Università degli Studi di Firenze, Biblioteca della Facolta di Lettere e Filosofia (Italy) 252
Universita Nazionale, Biblioteca dell', della Somalia (Somalia) 354
Universitaire centrale, Bibliothèque (Benin) 47
Universitaire Pers Leuven (Belgium) 43
Universitaires, Editions (France) 115
universitaires, Editions, SA (Belgium) 43
Universitaires, Presses, de Bruxelles, de Liège, de Namur (Belgium) 43
Universitaires, Presses, de France, de Grenoble, de Lille, de Lyon, de Nancy (France) 115
universitaires, Publications des Facultés, Saint Louis (Belgium) 43
Universitaria, Editorial (Chile) 66
Universitaria, Editrice (Italy) 250
Universitaria, Librería, de la Universidad de El Salvador (El Salvador) 90
Universitaria Centroamericana, Editorial, (EDUCA) (Costa Rica) 73
Universitaria de Barcelona, Biblioteca (Spain) 377
Universitária de Direito, Livraria e Editora, Ltda (Brazil) 57
Universitaria 'José Antonio Arze', Biblioteca Central (Bolivia) 48
Universitarias, Ediciones, de Valparaíso (Chile) 66
Universitaire Pers Leiden (Netherlands) 303
Universitas Books (Pty) Ltd (Republic of South Africa) 360
Universitas Verlag (Federal Republic of Germany) 171
Universität Basel, Öffentliche Bibliothek der (Switzerland) 406
Universitäts- und Landesbibliothek Sachsen-Anhalt (German Democratic Republic) 127
Universitäts- und Stadtbibliothek (Federal Republic of Germany) 176
Universitätsbibliothek (Federal Republic of Germany) 176
Universitätsbibliothek (German Democratic Republic) 127
Universitätsbibliothek/Technische Zentralbibliothek der DDR, Technische Universität Dresden (German Democratic Republic) 127
Universitätsbibliothek der Eberhard-Karls-Universität (Federal Republic of Germany) 176
Universitätsbibliothek Erlangen-Nürnberg (Federal Republic of Germany) 176
Universitätsbibliothek Graz (Austria) 32
Universitätsbibliothek Heidelberg (Federal Republic of Germany) 176
Universitätsbibliothek Innsbruck (Austria) 32
Universitätsbibliothek Wien (Austria) 32
Universitätsbuchhandlung (German Democratic Republic) 127
Universitätsverlag (Switzerland) 404
Université, Editions de l', de Bruxelles (Belgium) 43

Université, Librairie de l' (France) 116
Université Al Quarawiyin, Bibliothèque de l' (Morocco) 291
Université Ben Youssef, Bibliothèque de l' (Morocco) 291
Université Catholique de Louvain, Bibliothèque centrale de l' (Belgium) 44
Université d'Abidjan (Ivory Coast) 254
Université d'Alger, Bibliothèque universitaire, (Algeria) 2
Université de Constantine, Bibliothèque de l' (Algeria) 2
Université de Dakar, Bibliothèque (Senegal) 349
Université de Kinshasa, Bibliothèque centrale, (Zaire) 502
Université de Kisangani, Bibliothèque centrale de l' (Zaire) 502
Université de la Réunion, Bibliothèque Universitaire (Réunion) 346
Université de Liège, Bibliothèque générale de l' (Belgium) 44
Université de Niamey, Bibliothèque de l' (Niger) 314
Université de Strasbourg, Bibliothèque de l' (France) 117
Université de Yaoundé, Bibliothèque (United Republic of Cameroun) 64
Université d'Oran, Bibliothèque (Algeria) 2
Université du Benin, Bibliothèque de l' (Togo) 412
Université du Burundi, Bibliothèque de l' (Burundi) 63
Université du Tchad, Bibliothèque de l' (Chad) 65
Université Jean-Bédel Bokassa, Bibliothèque de l' (Central African Republic) 64
Université libre de Bruxelles, Bibliothèques de l' (Belgium) 44
Université Marien Ngouabi, Bibliothèque universitaire, (Popular Republic of Congo) 72
Université Mohammed V, Bibliothèque de l' (Morocco) 291
Université nationale, Campus de Lubumbashi, Bibliothèque centrale de l' (Zaire) 502
Université nationale de Côte d'Ivoire (Ivory Coast) 254
Université Nationale du Rwanda, Bibliothèque de l' (Rwanda) 348
Université Omar Bongo, Bibliothèque de l' (Republic of Gabon) 122
Universiteit Antwerpen Bibliotheken (Belgium) 44
Universiteits-Bibliotheek, Universiteit van de Nederlandse Antillen (Netherland Antilles) 307
Universiteitsbibliotheek (Netherlands) 305
Universités de Paris, Bibliothèques des (France) 117
Universitetsbibliotek, Odense (Denmark) 85
Universitetsbiblioteket 1 (Denmark) 85
Universitetsbiblioteket 2: Danmarks natur- og laagevidenskabelige Bibliotek (Denmark) 85
Universitetsbiblioteket i Bergen (Norway) 323
Universitetsbiblioteket i Oslo (Norway) 323
Universitetsbiblioteket i Trondheim (Norway) 323
Universitetsbogladen (Panumbogladen/Naturfagsbogladen) (Denmark) 84
Universitetsbokhandeln (Norway) 323
Universitetsforlaget (Norway) 322
Universiti Kebangsaan (Malaysia) 280
Universiti Teknologi Malaysia Library (Malaysia) 280
Universities Administration Office (Burma) 62
Universities' Central Library (Burma) 63
University (United Kingdom) 474
University Book Agency (Pakistan) 326
University Book Shop (Auckland) Ltd (New Zealand) 312
University Book Shop (Canterbury) Ltd (New Zealand) 312
University Book Shop Inc (Papua New Guinea) 329
University Book Shop (Otago) Ltd (New Zealand) 312
University Book Store (Hong Kong) 189
University Book Store (Republic of Singapore) 353
University Booksellers Association of Nigeria (Nigeria) 315
University Bookshop (Ghana) 181
University Bookshop (Zambia) 503
University Bookshop Ltd (Nigeria) 318
University Bookshop (Nigeria) Ltd (Nigeria) 318
University Bookstore (Liberia) 274
University Co-operative Bookshop Ltd (Australia) 21
University College Cardiff Press (United Kingdom) 474
University College Cork, Boole Library (Republic of Ireland) 224
University College Dublin Library (Republic of Ireland) 224
University College Galway, James Hardiman Library (Republic of Ireland) 224
University Karlovy, Knihovny fakult a ústavu (Czechoslovakia) 78
University Libraries (Finland) 94
University Libraries (Japan) 264
University Libraries (Romania) 347

University Libraries (Saudi Arabia) 349
University Libraries (Sweden) 389
University Libraries (United Kingdom) 483
University Library (Afghanistan) 1
University Library (Honduras) 187
University Library (Iceland) 194
University Library, Universiti Sains Malaysia (Malaysia) 280
University of Agriculture Library (Pakistan) 327
University of Agriculture Malaysia Library (Malaysia) 280
University of Ain Shams Library (Egypt) 89
University of Alexandria Library (Egypt) 89
University of Auckland Library (New Zealand) 312
University of Baghdad, Central Library of the (Iraq) 221
University of Baluchistan Library (Pakistan) 327
University of Botswana Library (Botswana) 49
University of Cairo (Sudan) 380
University of Cairo Library (Egypt) 89
University of Canterbury Publications Committee (New Zealand) 311
University of Cape Coast Library (Ghana) 181
University of Cape Town Libraries (Republic of South Africa) 361
University of Chicago, The, Press (United Kingdom) 474
University of Dar es Salaam Library (Tanzania) 409
University of Engineering and Technology Library (Pakistan) 327
University of Ferdowsi Library (Iran) 220
University of Garyounis Library (Libya) 275
University of Ghana Library (Ghana) 181
University of Haifa Library (Israel) 231
University of Hawaii Press (United Kingdom) 474
University of Hong Kong Libraries (Hong Kong) 189
University of Ife Press (Nigeria) 318
University of Isfahan Library (Iran) 220
University of Jordan Bookshop (Jordan) 266
University of Jordan Library (Jordan) 266
University of Kabul Bookstores (Afghanistan) 1
University of Karachi Library (Pakistan) 327
University of Khartoum Bookshop (Sudan) 380
University of Khartoum Library (Sudan) 380
University of Lagos Bookshop (Nigeria) 318
University of Lagos Library (Nigeria) 319
University of Liberia Libraries (Liberia) 274
University of Libya Library (Libya) 275
University of London Library (United Kingdom) 483
University of London Press Ltd (United Kingdom) 474
University of Loránd Eötvös Central Library (Hungary) 192
University of Malawi Libraries (Malawi) 277
University of Malawi, Polytechnic Library (Malawi) 277
University of Malaya Co-operative Bookshop Ltd (Malaysia) 280
University of Malaya, Department of Publications (Malaysia) 280
University of Malaya Library (Malaysia) 280
University of Malta, The, Publications Section (Malta) 282
University of Malta Library (Malta) 282
University of Manila Central Library (Philippines) 333
University of Mauritius Library (Mauritius) 283
University of Melbourne Library (Australia) 21
University of Nairobi Bookshop (Kenya) 268
University of Nairobi Libraries (Kenya) 268
University of Natal Press (Republic of South Africa) 359
University of Nebraska Press (United Kingdom) 474
University of New South Wales (Australia) 19
University of New South Wales Library (Australia) 21
University of Nigeria Bookshop Ltd (Nigeria) 318
University of Nigeria Library (Nigeria) 319
University of North Carolina Press (United Kingdom) 474
University of Otago Library (New Zealand) 312
University of Otago Press (New Zealand) 311
University of Papua New Guinea Library (Papua New Guinea) 329
University of Pennsylvania Press (United Kingdom) 474
University of Peradeniya Library (Sri Lanka) 379
University of Peshawar Library (Pakistan) 327
University of Pretoria, Library Services (Republic of South Africa) 361
University of Puerto Rico, General Library, Mayaguez Campus (Puerto Rico) 345
University of Puerto Rico, General Library, Rio Piedras Campus (Puerto Rico) 345
University of Puerto Rico, Medical Sciences Campus Library (Puerto Rico) 345
University of Puerto Rico Press (EDUPR) (Puerto Rico) 345
University of Queensland Library (Australia) 21
University of Queensland Press (Australia) 19
University of Queensland Press (United Kingdom) 474
University of Rajshahi Library (Bangladesh) 35

University of Salonika, Library of the (Greece) 185
University of San Carlos Library System (Philippines) 333
University of Santo Tomas Library (Philippines) 333
University of Science and Technology Library (Ghana) 181
University of Sierra Leone (Sierra Leone) 350
University of Sofia Library (Bulgaria) 61
University of South Africa (Republic of South Africa) 359
University of South Africa Library (Republic of South Africa) 361
University of Swaziland Library (Swaziland) 381
University of Sydney Library (Australia) 21
University of Tabriz, Central Library, (Iran) 220
University of Technology Malaysia Library (Malaysia) 280
University of Tehran, Central Library and Documentation Centre of (Iran) 220
University of Tehran Publication & Printing Organization (Iran) 220
University of the East Library (Philippines) 333
University of the Philippines Library (Philippines) 333
University of the Philippines Press (Philippines) 333
University of the South Pacific Library (Fiji) 91
University of the West Indies (Barbados) 35
University of the West Indies, Main Library, The (Trinidad and Tobago) 413
University of the West Indies Library (Jamaica) 255
University of the West Indies Publishers Association (Jamaica) 254
University of the Witwatersrand Library (Republic of South Africa) 361
University of Tokyo Library (Japan) 264
University of Tokyo Press (Japan) 262
University of Tokyo Press (United Kingdom) 474
University of Trondheim, The, Norwegian Institute of Technology (Norway) 323
University of Wales Press (United Kingdom) 474
University of Western Australia Library (Australia) 21
University of Western Australia Press (Australia) 20
University of Wisconsin Press (United Kingdom) 474
University of Zambia Library (Zambia) 503
University of Zimbabwe (Zimbabwe) 505
University of Zimbabwe Library (Zimbabwe) 505
University Press, The, of Ireland (Republic of Ireland) 223
University Press Ltd (Bangladesh) 34
University Press Ltd (Nigeria) 318
University Presses of California, Columbia and Princeton (United Kingdom) 474
University Publishers (India) 211
University Publishers & Booksellers (Pty) Ltd (Republic of South Africa) 359
University Publishing Co (Israel) 230
University Publishing Co (Nigeria) 318
University Publishing Co (Philippines) 333
Universo, Editorial, SA (Peru) 331
Universo, Editorial, SA de CV (Mexico) 288
Universo, Premio (Peru) 331
Universo, Società Editrice (Italy) 250
Univerzitná knižnica (Czechoslovakia) 78
Uniwersytecka, Biblioteka (Poland) 338
Uniwersytecka w Warszawie, Biblioteka (Poland) 338
Uniwersytecka we Wrocławiu, Biblioteka (Poland) 338
Uniwersytetu Mikołaja Kopernika, Biblioteka (Poland) 338
Unwin Hyman Ltd (United Kingdom) 474
Unwin Paperbacks (United Kingdom) 474
Uomini, Edizioni, Nuovi (Italy) 250
Upkar Prakashan (India) 211
Upper India, The, Publishing House Pvt Ltd (India) 211
Uppsala Universitetsbibliotek (Sweden) 389
Urachhaus, Verlag, Johannes M Mayer GmbH (Federal Republic of Germany) 171
Uradni, CZ, List SRS (Yugoslavia) 499
Uraki, Toshiichi (Japan) 262
Urania-Verlag (für populärwissen-schaftliche Literatur) (German Democratic Republic) 126
Uranium Verlag (Switzerland) 404
Urban Council Public Libraries (Hong Kong) 189
Urban und Schwarzenberg GmbH (Austria) 30
Urban und Schwarzenberg GmbH (Austria) 32
Urban und Schwarzenberg GmbH, Verlag für Medizin (Federal Republic of Germany) 171
Urbaniana University Press (Vatican City State) 492
Urbión, Ediciones, SA (Spain) 375
Urdu Academy Sind (Pakistan) 326
Urdu Akademy Awards (India) 216
Ure Smith (Australia) 20
Urmo SA de Ediciones (Spain) 375
Urs Graf-Verlag GmbH (Switzerland) 404
Usborne Publishing Ltd (United Kingdom) 474
Usine Nouvelle, Editions de l' (France) 115
Ústřední knihovnická rada ČSR (Czechoslovakia) 78
Utbildningsbolaget M M AB (Sweden) 387

INDEX

Utbildningsförlaget (Sweden) 387
Utley, Christa-Jo (Republic of Ireland) 223
Utusan Publications and Distributors Sdn Bhd (Malaysia) 280
Uudet Kirjat (Finland) 94
Uusi Kirjakerho Oy (Finland) 94
Uusi Tie, Kustannus Oy (Finland) 93
Uzima Press Ltd (Kenya) 267

V A A P (Union of Soviet Socialist Republics) 419
V A M, Stichting (Netherlands) 303
V C H Publishers (UK) Ltd (United Kingdom) 474
V C H-Verlags AG (Switzerland) 404
V C H Verlagsgesellschaft mbH (Federal Republic of Germany) 171
V C L (Netherlands) 304
V C T A Publishing Pty Ltd (Australia) 20
V D D, Berufsverband Dokumentation, Information, Kommunikation eV (Federal Republic of Germany) 177
V D E-Verlag GmbH (Verband Deutscher Elektrotechniker) (Federal Republic of Germany) 171
V D I-Verlag GmbH (Verlag des Vereins Deutscher Ingenieure) (Federal Republic of Germany) 171
V-Dia-Verlag GmbH (Federal Republic of Germany) 172
V E D A, Vydavatel'stvo Slovenskej akadémie vied (Czechoslovakia) 77
V F M (Federal Republic of Germany) 172
v g s — Verlagsgesellschaft mbH & Co KG (Federal Republic of Germany) 172
V M B (Federal Republic of Germany) 172
V N U Business Press Group BV (Netherlands) 303
V N U Business Publications BV (Netherlands) 303
V N U — Verenigde Nederlandse Uitgeversbedrijven BV (Netherlands) 303
V P A (Vjesnikova Press Agencija) (Yugoslavia) 499
V S A (Verlag für das Studium der Arbeiterbewegung GmbH) (Federal Republic of Germany) 172
V U Boekhandel/Uitgeverij BV (Netherlands) 303
V V A (Vereinigte Verlagsauslieferung GmbH) (Federal Republic of Germany) 176
V W G Ö (Austria) 31
V W K (Verlag für Wirtschafts-und-Kartographie Publikationen) Ryborsch GmbH (Federal Republic of Germany) 172
Vaad Hayeshivot Be'eretz Israel (Israel) 230
Vaco NV (Suriname) 380
Vademecum de Pharmacie (Belgium) 43
Vadhana Panich (Thailand) 411
Vagabond (Australia) 20
Vahlen, Franz, GmbH (Federal Republic of Germany) 172
Vaillant/Miroir, Les Editions, Sprint Publications (France) 115
Vaillant-Carmanne, Imprimeur — Editeur, SA (Belgium) 43
Vakils Feffer & Simons Ltd (India) 211
Valabrègue, Antony, Prize (France) 121
Vale, The Helen, Foundation (Australia) 20
Valencia, Carlos, Editores SA (Colombia) 70
Valiant Publishers (Pty) Ltd (Republic of South Africa) 359
Vallardi Industrie Grafiche (Italy) 250
Vallecchi Editore SpA (Italy) 250
Vallentine, Mitchell & Co Ltd (United Kingdom) 475
Valmartina Editore SRL (Italy) 250
Valtionarkisto (Finland) 94
Van de Velde, Editions (France) 115
Van de Velde, Editions Francis (France) 115
Van Duren Publishers Ltd (United Kingdom) 475
Van Leer, The, Jerusalem Institute (Israel) 230
Van Nostrand Reinhold (International) Co Ltd (United Kingdom) 475
Vandenhoeck und Ruprecht (Federal Republic of Germany) 172
Vander Publishing (Belgium) 43
Vanderlinden, Librairie, SA (Belgium) 43
Vanderlinden, Librairie, SA (Belgium) 44
Vani Prakashan (India) 211
Vanmelle, L, (Drukkerij) NV (Belgium) 43
Vannini, Società Editrice (Italy) 250
Vår Bok AB (Sweden) 389
Vår Skola Förlag AB (Sweden) 387
Varazen, Editorial, SA (Mexico) 288
Vardikos, D & J (Greece) 184
Vargas, Fundação Getúlio (Brazil) 57
Variorum (United Kingdom) 475
Varsity (United Kingdom) 475
Varsity Book Club (Nigeria) 318
Varsity Industrial Press (Nigeria) 318
Vasco, Editorial, Americana SA (EVA) (Spain) 375
Vasiliou, J, Bibliopoleion (Greece) 184

Vassallo, A, and Sons Ltd (Malta) 282
Västra, Förlagsaktiebolaget, Sverige (Sweden) 387
Vatan Library (Turkey) 416
Vaticana, Libreria Editrice (Vatican City State) 492
Vavrín (Czechoslovakia) 78
Vecchi, Editora, SA (Brazil) 57
Vecchi, Editorial De (Spain) 375
Vecchi, Giovanni De, Editore SpA (Italy) 250
Veen/Reflex & Uitgeverij L J Veen, Uitgeverij, BV (Netherlands) 303
Vega, Ediciones, SRL (Venezuela) 493
Vega, Librería Técnica (Venezuela) 493
Velhagen und Klasing GmbH & Co (Federal Republic of Germany) 172
Vendelfelt, Lena, Prize (Sweden) 391
Venezuelan Book Service SA (Venezuela) 493
Venton Educational Ltd (United Kingdom) 475
Ventura Publishing Ltd (United Kingdom) 475
Ventures (Zimbabwe) 505
Venus Press & Book Depot (India) 211
Vera-Reyes Inc (Philippines) 333
Verband bayerischer Verlage und Buchhandlungen eV (Federal Republic of Germany) 129
Verband der Antiquare Österreichs (Austria) 26
Verband der Bibliotheken des Landes Nordrhein-Westfalen eV (Federal Republic of Germany) 177
Verband der österreichischen Zeitungs- und Zeitschriften-Grossisten und der Werbenden Zeitschriftenhändler (Austria) 26
Verband der Schulbuchverlage eV (Federal Republic of Germany) 129
Verband der Verlage und Buchhandlungen in Baden-Württemberg eV (Federal Republic of Germany) 129
Verband der Verlage und Buchhandlungen in Nordrhein-Westfalen eV (Federal Republic of Germany) 129
Verband der wissenschaftlichen Gesellschaften Österreichs (VWGÖ) (Austria) 31
Verband deutscher Adressbuchverleger eV (Federal Republic of Germany) 129
Verband deutscher Antiquare eV (Federal Republic of Germany) 129
Verband deutscher Bahnhofsbuchhändler (Federal Republic of Germany) 129
Verband Deutscher Buch-, Zeitungs- und Zeitschriften-Grossisten eV (Federal Republic of Germany) 129
Verband deutscher Bühnenverleger eV (Federal Republic of Germany) 129
Verband deutscher Schriftsteller (Federal Republic of Germany) 129
Verband deutscher Schulbuchhändler eV (Federal Republic of Germany) 129
Verband deutscher Werkbibliotheken eV (Federal Republic of Germany) 177
Verband deutschsprachiger Übersetzer literarischer und wissenschaftlicher Werke eV (VDU) (Federal Republic of Germany) 179
Verband evangelischer Buchhandlungen und Verlage der Schweiz (Switzerland) 391
Verband katholischer Verleger und Buchhändler eV (Federal Republic of Germany) 130
Verband norddeutscher Buch- und Zeitschriftenhändler eV (Federal Republic of Germany) 130
Verband österreichischer Archivare (Austria) 32
Verband österreichischer Kommissionäre, Grossobuchhändler und Auslieferer (Austria) 26
Verband österreichischer Volksbüchereien und Volksbibliothekare (Austria) 32
Verband schweizerischer Zeitungsagenturen und Büchergrossisten (Union d'Agences suisses de Journaux et Livres en Gros) (Switzerland) 391
Verbandsdruckerei-Betadruck, Verlag (Switzerland) 404
Verbatim (United Kingdom) 475
Verbatim Book Club (United Kingdom) 481
Verbo, Editora, Ltda (Brazil) 57
Verbo, Editorial, Divino (Spain) 375
Verbo, Editorial, SA (Portugal) 343
Verbum Förlag AB (Sweden) 387
Verbum Gothia (Sweden) 387
Verdade e Vida, Livraria, Editora (Portugal) 343
Verden, Bokenes (Norway) 323
Vereeniging der Antwerpsche Bibliophielen (Belgium) 45
Vereeniging ter bevordering van de belangen des Boekhandels (Netherlands) 293
Vereeniging tot Verspreiding der H Schrift (Netherlands) 303
Verein Angehörige des mittleren und nichtdiplomierten Bibliotheksdienstes eV (Federal Republic of Germany) 177
Verein der Bibliothekare an öffentlichen Bibliotheken eV (Federal Republic of Germany) 177
Verein der Diplom-Bibliothekare an wissenschaftlichen Bibliotheken eV (Federal Republic of Germany) 177
Verein deutscher Archivare (VdA) (Federal Republic of Germany) 177
Verein deutscher Bibliothekare eV (Federal Republic of Germany) 177

Verein Deutscher Dokumentare eV (Federal Republic of Germany) 177
Verein für Verkehrsordnung im Buchhandel eV (Federal Republic of Germany) 130
Vereinigung des katholischen Buchhandels in Österreich (Austria) 26
Vereinigung evangelischer Buchhändler (Federal Republic of Germany) 130
Vereinigung katholischer Buchhändler und Verleger der Schweiz (Switzerland) 391
Vereinigung österreichischer Bibliothekare (Austria) 32
Vereinigung Schweizerischer Archivare (Switzerland) 406
Vereinigung Schweizerischer Bibliothekare (Switzerland) 406
Vereinigung selbständiger Verlagsvertreter (Federal Republic of Germany) 130
Vereniging ter Bevordering van het Vlaamse Boekwezen (Belgium) 36
Vereniging van Archivarissen in Nederland (Netherlands) 305
Vereniging van de belgische medische wetenschappelijke genootschappen VZW (Belgium) 43
Vereniging van Religieus-Wetenschappelijke Bibliothecarissen (Belgium) 45
Vereniging van Uitgevers van Nederlandstalige Boeken (Belgium) 36
Vereniging van Uitgeversvertegen-woordigers (Netherlands) 293
Vereniging voor het Theologisch Bibliothecariaat (Netherlands) 305
Vergara, Javier, Editor SA (Argentina) 8
Vergara y Vergara, José Ma, Prize (Colombia) 72
Vergeures, Editions de (France) 115
Veríssimo, José, Prize (Brazil) 60
Veritas, Buchhandlung (Austria) 32
Veritas & Co Ltd (Republic of Ireland) 224
Veritas Foundation Publication Centre (United Kingdom) 475
Veritas Publications (Republic of Ireland) 223
Veritas-Verlag (Austria) 31
Verkehrshaus der Schweiz (Switzerland) 404
Verlag für Deutsch (Federal Republic of Germany) 172
Verlain, Valentine Abraham, Prize (France) 121
Verlaine Prize (France) 121
Verlegervereinigung Rechtsinformatik eV (Federal Republic of Germany) 130
Verne, Jules, Circle (United Kingdom) 485
'Verold', Particip (Iceland) 194
Veron Editor (Spain) 375
Verrycken, Editions (Belgium) 43
Versal, Ediciones, SA (Spain) 375
Verseau, Editions du (Switzerland) 404
Versluys' Uitgeverij BV (Netherlands) 303
Verso (United Kingdom) 475
Vertente Editora Ltda (Brazil) 57
Vértice Ltda (Colombia) 71
Vertiges (France) 115
Vertiges Bulles (France) 115
Vervuert, Klaus Dieter, Buchhandel und Verlag (Federal Republic of Germany) 172
Verwertungsgesellschaft Wort (Federal Republic of Germany) 130
Vesaas, Tarjei, Debutant Prize (Norway) 324
Veselin Masleša (Yugoslavia) 499
Veselin Masleša (Yugoslavia) 500
Vesti (Yugoslavia) 499
Vetenskapliga Bibliotekens Tjänstemannaförening VBT (Sweden) 389
Vetter, Verlag Alfred (Switzerland) 404
Veyrier (France) 115
Via Afrika Book Store (Republic of South Africa) 360
Via Afrika Ltd (Republic of South Africa) 359
Viareggio Prizes (Italy) 253
Vicens-Vives, Editorial (Spain) 375
Victor, NV Drukkerij Leo (Suriname) 380
Victoria Public Library (United Republic of Cameroun) 64
Victoria University Press (New Zealand) 311
Victorian Fellowship of Australian Writers (Australia) 23
Victorian Premier's Literary Awards (Australia) 25
Videnskabers Selskab Biblioteket (Norway) 323
Vidhi Sahitya Prakashan (India) 211
Vidorama, Ediciones, SA (Spain) 375
Vidyapuri (India) 211
Vidyarthi Mithram Book Depot (India) 214
Vidyarthi Mithram Novel Club (India) 213
Vidyarthi Mithram Press (India) 212
Vie, Les Editions, ouvrière ASBL (Belgium) 43
Vienna International Centre Library (Austria) 32
Vienna Prize, City of (Austria) 33
Vienna Prize for Books, City of, for Children and Young People (Austria) 33
Viergang, De (Netherlands) 303

596 INDEX

Vieweg & Sohn, Friedr, Verlagsgesellschaft mbH (Federal Republic of Germany) 172
Vigília, Editora, Ltda (Brazil) 57
Vigot, Editions, Frères (France) 115
Vijverberg Prize (Netherlands) 306
Vikas Publishing House Pvt Ltd (India) 212
Viking (Australia) 20
Viking (United Kingdom) 475
Viking Förlag (Sweden) 388
Viking Kestrel (Australia) 20
Viking Kestrel (United Kingdom) 475
Viking O'Neil (Australia) 20
Viking Sevenseas Ltd (New Zealand) 311
Viktoria-Verlag Fritz Marti AG (Switzerland) 404
Villaurrutia, Xavier, Prize (Mexico) 289
Ville de Paris, Service des Travaux Historiques de la, et Bibliothèque historique de la Ville de Paris (France) 117
Villepastour, Librairie (Ivory Coast) 254
Vilnius, The Scientific Library of the, Vincas Kapsukas State University (Union of Soviet Socialist Republics) 420
Vilo, Editions, SA (France) 115
Vincentz, Curt R, Verlag (Federal Republic of Germany) 172
Vindrose, Forlaget, A/S (Denmark) 83
Vintens Forlag Ltd (Denmark) 83
Vipopremo Agencies (Kenya) 268
Virago Press Ltd (United Kingdom) 475
Viratham (Thailand) 411
Virdi, Major Tek Singh, Literary Prizes (India) 216
Virenque, Claire, Prize (France) 121
Virgin (United Kingdom) 475
Virtue & Co Ltd (United Kingdom) 475
Visa Books (Australia) 20
Visão, Editora, Ltda (Brazil) 57
Visel, Edition Curt (Federal Republic of Germany) 172
Visentini, Olga, Prize (Italy) 253
Vishal Publications (India) 212
Vision Books Pvt Ltd (India) 212
Vision Press Ltd (United Kingdom) 475
Visscher, Albert de, Editeur (Belgium) 43
Vita e Pensiero (Italy) 250
Viva, AB Bokförlaget (Sweden) 388
Vives, Editorial Luis, (Edelvives) (Spain) 375
Vivliofilia (Greece) 184
Vlaams Ekonomisch Verbond VZW (Belgium) 43
Vlaamse Bibliotheek Centrale (VzW)/VBC (Belgium) 44
Vlaamse Bijbelstichting (Belgium) 43
Vlaamse Toeristenbond — Vlaamse Automobilistenbond (Belgium) 43
Vlaamse Vereniging voor Bibliotheek-, Archief en Documentatiewezen (VVBAD) (Belgium) 45
Vlasis, Frères (Greece) 184
'Vneshtorgizdat', Vsesoyuznoe Obyedineniye (Union of Soviet Socialist Republics) 419
Voce della Bibbia (Italy) 250
Voenno Izdatelstvo (Bulgaria) 61
Vogel-Verlag KG (Federal Republic of Germany) 172
Vogt-Schild AG Druck & Verlag (Switzerland) 404
Voie de l'Art, Editions de la (Switzerland) 404
Vojnoizdavački Zavod (Yugoslavia) 499
Volcans, Librairie Les (Zaire) 502
Volk, Boekhandel Het (Belgium) 44
Volk, Drukkerij Het, NV (Belgium) 43
Volk und Gesundheit, VEB Verlag (German Democratic Republic) 126
Volk und Welt, Verlag, (Verlag für internationale Literatur) (German Democratic Republic) 126
Volk und Wissen Volkseigener Verlag Berlin (German Democratic Republic) 126
Volksboekwinkel, Stichting De (Suriname) 380
Volkseigene Verlage für Medizin und Biologie (German Democratic Republic) 126
Vollmer, Emil, Verlag (Federal Republic of Germany) 172
Vollmer/Löwit Verlagsgruppe (Federal Republic of Germany) 172
Volney Prize (France) 121
Volturna Press (United Kingdom) 475
Voluntad Editores Ltda y Cía SCA (Colombia) 71
Voluntary Health Association of India (India) 212
Voorhoeve, J N (Netherlands) 303
Vora & Co Publishers Pvt Ltd (India) 212
Vorarlberger Verlagsanstalt GmbH (Austria) 31
Voss, Johann Heinrich, Translation Prize (Federal Republic of Germany) 179
Vowinckel, Kurt, Verlag (Federal Republic of Germany) 172
Vowinckel, Thesen Verlag, und Co (Federal Republic of Germany) 172
Voyenizdat (Union of Soviet Socialist Republics) 419
Vozes Editora Ltda (Brazil) 57
Vries, BV Algemene Boekhandel en Antiquariaat H De, Boeken (Netherlands) 304
Vries, C De, Brouwers PVBA (Belgium) 43
Vrin, Librairie Philosophique J (France) 115
Vroente, De (Belgium) 43
Vsesoyuznaya Knizhnaya Palata (Union of Soviet Socialist Republics) 417
Vsesoyuznoe agenstvo po avtorskim pravam (VAAP) (Union of Soviet Socialist Republics) 419
Vuibert, Librairie, SA (France) 115
Vuk Karadžic (Yugoslavia) 499
Vuk Karadžic (Yugoslavia) 500
Vulkan (Denmark) 83
Východoslovenské vydavateľstvo NP (Czechoslovakia) 77
Vyncke, PVBA Imprimerie-Editions (Belgium) 43
Vyšehrad (Czechoslovakia) 77
'Vysshaya Shkola', Izdatelstvo (Union of Soviet Socialist Republics) 419

W I Books Ltd (United Kingdom) 476
W R S-Verlag (Wirtschaft, Recht und Steuern) GmbH & Co (Federal Republic of Germany) 172
Waage, Verlag Die (Switzerland) 404
Waagmeester-Verkuyl, M (Suriname) 380
Wacharin Publishing Co Ltd (Thailand) 411
Wachholtz, Karl, Verlag (Federal Republic of Germany) 172
Wadsworth International (Australia) 20
Wadsworth International Group (United Kingdom) 476
Wagenbach, Verlag Klaus, GmbH (Federal Republic of Germany) 172
Wagner, Kartographischer Verlag, & Co KG (Federal Republic of Germany) 172
Wagner, Universitätsverlag, GmbH (Austria) 31
Wagner'sche Universitätsbuchhandlung (Austria) 32
Wahab, Dakr Abdul (Syria) 407
Wahbah, Ali, Bookshop (Saudi Arabia) 348
Wahle, Eugène (Belgium) 43
Wahlström och Widstrand, AB (Sweden) 388
Wahlströms, B, Bokförlag AB (Sweden) 388
Waite, John, Ltd (United Kingdom) 476
Waiwen Shudian (People's Republic of China) 68
Walburg, De, Pers (Netherlands) 303
Waldia, AB, Förlag (Sweden) 388
Wales Tourist Board (United Kingdom) 476
Walker Books Ltd (United Kingdom) 476
Walraven, Uitgeverij Van, BV (Netherlands) 303
Walsingham (United Kingdom) 476
Walt, J P van der, en Seun (Pty) Ltd (Republic of South Africa) 359
Walt Disney, Clube (Portugal) 343
Walt Disney Wonderful World of Reading (Denmark) 84
Walter, Librairie (Togo) 412
Walter-Verlag AG (Switzerland) 404
Walter-Verlag GmbH Freiburg (Federal Republic of Germany) 172
Waltman, Uitgeverij (Netherlands) 303
Wandel Cruse, Elise (France) 116
Wandels Forlag A/S (Denmark) 83
Wanyee Bookshop Ltd (Kenya) 268
Warana Writers' Awards (Australia) 25
Warburg, The, Institute (United Kingdom) 476
Ward Lock Educational Co Ltd (United Kingdom) 476
Ward Lock Ltd (United Kingdom) 476
Ward River Press (Republic of Ireland) 224
Warga (Indonesia) 218
Warne, Frederick (Australia) 20
Warne, Frederick, & Co Ltd (United Kingdom) 476
Warsaw City Prize (Poland) 339
Warsaw City Prize for Young Poets (Poland) 339
Was Is Press (Australia) 20
Waseda University Library (Japan) 264
Wasmuth, Ernst, Verlag GmbH & Co (Federal Republic of Germany) 173
Watelet, Gerard (France) 115
Waterkant-Uitgewers (Edms) Bpk (Republic of South Africa) 359
Waterlow Publishers Ltd (United Kingdom) 476
Waterstone & Co Ltd (United Kingdom) 482
Waterville Publishing House (Ghana) 181
'Watra', Wydawnictwo Kultura Zycia Codziennego (Poland) 337
Watson, Little Ltd (United Kingdom) 480
Watt, A P, Ltd (United Kingdom) 480
Wattana Panich (Thailand) 411
Wattie Book of the Year Award (New Zealand) 313
Watts, Franklin, Australia (Australia) 20
Watts, Franklin, Ltd (United Kingdom) 476
Wayfarer Book Store Ltd (Barbados) 35
Wayland (Publishers) Ltd (United Kingdom) 476
Wayzgoose, The, Press (United Kingdom) 476
Weatherhill, John, Inc (Japan) 262
Webb & Bower (Publishers) Ltd (United Kingdom) 476

Weber, Editions et Librairie (France) 115
Weber SA d'Editions (Switzerland) 404
Webster, Adrian, Ltd (United Kingdom) 476
Webster's Business Traveller's Guides Ltd (United Kingdom) 476
Webster's (Pty) Ltd (Swaziland) 381
Webster's Wine Price Guide Ltd (United Kingdom) 476
Weekes, A (United Kingdom) 476
Wehr und Wissen Verlagsgesellschaft mbH (Federal Republic of Germany) 173
Weichert, A, Verlag (Federal Republic of Germany) 173
Weickhardt, Con, Award (Australia) 25
Weickhardt, Patricia, Award (Australia) 25
Weidenfeld & Nicolson (United Kingdom) 476
Weidenfeld (Publishers) Ltd (United Kingdom) 476
Weidlich, Wolfgang, Verlag (Federal Republic of Germany) 173
Weidmannsche Verlagsbuchhandlung (Federal Republic of Germany) 173
Weilburg-Verlag (Austria) 31
Weilin ja Göös, Amer-yhtymä Oy (Finland) 93
Weill, Galerie Lucie (France) 115
Weill Publishers (Israel) 230
Weinert, Erich-, -Buchhandlung (German Democratic Republic) 127
Weinmann, Verlag (Federal Republic of Germany) 173
Weis, Rupertusbuchhandlung Augustin, und Söhne KG (Austria) 32
Weismann Verlag-Frauenbuchverlag GmbH (Federal Republic of Germany) 173
Weiss, Gebrüder, Verlag (Federal Republic of Germany) 173
Weiss, J J, Prize (France) 121
Weitbrecht, Edition (Federal Republic of Germany) 173
Weizmann, The, Science Press of Israel (Israel) 230
Weizmann Institute of Science Libraries (Israel) 231
Weka, Editions (France) 116
Weldon Hardie Pty Ltd (Australia) 20
Weldons (Australia) 20
Wellcome Institute for the History of Medicine Library (United Kingdom) 483
Wellington Public Library (New Zealand) 312
Wells, H G, Society (United Kingdom) 485
Wellsiana — The World of H G Wells (United Kingdom) 485
Welsermühl, Verlag (Austria) 31
Welsermühl, Verlag (Federal Republic of Germany) 173
Welsh Academy, The (United Kingdom) 485
Welsh Arts Council Awards to Writers (United Kingdom) 490
Welsh Books Council (Cyngor Llyfrau Cymraeg) (United Kingdom) 422
Welsh Library Association (United Kingdom) 484
Welsh Publishers' Union (Undeb Cyhoeddwyr Cymru) (United Kingdom) 422
Welt im Heim Morawa & Co (Austria) 31
Weltforum Verlag GmbH (Federal Republic of Germany) 173
Weltkreis-Verlags-GmbH (Federal Republic of Germany) 173
Weltrundschau Verlag AG (Switzerland) 404
Welz, Verlag Galerie, Salzburg (Austria) 31
'Wema', Wydawnictwa Przemyslu Maszynowego (Poland) 337
Wenschow, Karl, GmbH (Federal Republic of Germany) 173
Wepf, Verlag, & Co AG (Switzerland) 404
Wepf & Co AG (Switzerland) 405
Wereldbibliotheek BV (Netherlands) 303
Wereldbibliotheek NV (Belgium) 43
Wereldschool (Netherlands) 303
Wereldvenster, het (Netherlands) 303
Werner Druck AG (Switzerland) 404
Werner Söderström Osakeyhtiö (WSOY) (Finland) 93
Werner Söderström Osakeyhtiö (WSOY) (Finland) 94
Werner Verlag GmbH (Federal Republic of Germany) 173
Wesmael-Charlier, Maison d'Editions Ad, SA (Belgium) 43
West, John, Publications Ltd (Nigeria) 318
West African Book Publishers Ltd (Nigeria) 318
West African University Booksellers Association (International Organizations) 510
West-Friesland, Uit-Mij (Netherlands) 303
West-Friesland/Boekproject-ontwikkeling, Drukkerij (Netherlands) 303
West-Friesland Literary Prize (Netherlands) 306
West Indian Reference Collection (Trinidad and Tobago) 413
West-Pak Publishing Co (Pvt) Ltd (Pakistan) 326
Westbooks Pty Ltd (Australia) 20
Westbury House (United Kingdom) 477

INDEX 597

Westdeutscher Verlag GmbH (Federal Republic of Germany) 173
Westermann Schulbuchverlag GmbH (Federal Republic of Germany) 173
Westermann Verlag, Georg, GmbH (Federal Republic of Germany) 173
Western Australian Booksellers' Association (Australia) 10
Western Regional Library (Fiji) 92
Westers, Uitgeverij (Netherlands) 303
Westminster, City of, Libraries (United Kingdom) 483
Wettergrens Bokhandel AB (Sweden) 389
Wetzikon , Buchverlag der Druckerei, AG (Switzerland) 404
Wever, Uitgeverij T, BV (Netherlands) 303
Wewel, Erich, Verlag (Federal Republic of Germany) 173
Wheatley Medal (United Kingdom) 490
Wheaton & Co, A, Ltd (United Kingdom) 477
Wheaton Publishers Ltd (United Kingdom) 477
Wheatsheaf Books Ltd (United Kingdom) 477
Wheeler, A H, & Co (P) Ltd (India) 212
Whitaker, J, & Sons Ltd (United Kingdom) 477
Whitbread Literary Awards (Republic of Ireland) 225
Whitbread Literary Awards (United Kingdom) 490
Whitcoulls Ltd (New Zealand) 312
Whitcoulls Publishers (New Zealand) 311
White, Patrick, Literary Award (Australia) 25
White Horse Books (United Kingdom) 477
White Horse Library (United Kingdom) 477
White Lotus Co Ltd (Thailand) 411
White Tree Books (United Kingdom) 477
Whitman (New Zealand) 311
Whittet Books Ltd (United Kingdom) 477
Who's Who of Southern Africa (Republic of South Africa) 359
Who's Who — the International Red Series Verlag GmbH (Federal Republic of Germany) 173
Wiart, Carton de, Prize (Belgium) 46
Wichmann, Herbert, Verlag GmbH (Federal Republic of Germany) 173
Widjaja (Indonesia) 218
'Wiedza Powszechna' Państwowe Wydawnictwo (Poland) 337
Wiener Dom-Verlag (Austria) 31
Wiener Goethe-Verein (Austria) 33
Wiener Stadt- und Landesarchiv (Austria) 32
Wiener Stadt- und Landesbibliothek (Austria) 32
Wiener Urtext Edition-Musikverlag GmbH & Co KG (Austria) 31
Wigmore House Publishing (United Kingdom) 477
Wijewardene, D R, Memorial Award (Sri Lanka) 379
Wilco Publishing House (India) 212
Wild, Verlag Alexander (Switzerland) 404
Wild & Woolley Pty Ltd (Australia) 20
Wildfire (Australia) 20
Wildgans, Anton, -Gesellschaft (Austria) 33
Wildgans, Anton, Prize of Austrian Industry (Austria) 33
Wildwood House Ltd (United Kingdom) 477
Wiley, John (Australia) 20
Wiley, John, & Sons Ltd (United Kingdom) 477
Wiley Eastern Ltd (India) 212
Wilfion Books Publishers (United Kingdom) 477
Wilke Literary Award (Australia) 25
Williams, Joseph (United Kingdom) 477
Williams, W J, & Son (Books) Ltd (United Kingdom) 479
Williams & Wilkins, and Associates Pty Ltd (Australia) 20
Williams Book Illustration Awards, Francis (United Kingdom) 490
Williams Memorial Prize, Griffith John, (Gwobr Goffa Griffith John Williams) (United Kingdom) 490
Willow (United Kingdom) 477
Wilquin, Editions Luce (Switzerland) 404
Wilson, Philip, Publishers Ltd (United Kingdom) 477
Wilson & Horton Ltd (New Zealand) 311
Win Join Book Co Ltd (Taiwan) 408
Winchmore Publishing Services Ltd (United Kingdom) 477
Windhoek Public Library (Namibia) 291
Windrush Large Print Children's Books (United Kingdom) 477
Windsor Large Print (United Kingdom) 477
Windswept (Australia) 20
Wingate, H H, Prize (International Literary Prizes) 522
Winkler (Belgium) 44
Winkler Prins (Netherlands) 303
Winkler-Verlag (Federal Republic of Germany) 173
Winter, Carl, Universitätsverlag GmbH (Federal Republic of Germany) 174
Winthers Forlag ApS (Denmark) 84
Wirtschaft, Verlag Die (German Democratic Republic) 126

Wirtschaft, Recht, Steuern (Federal Republic of Germany) 174
Wirtschaft und Recht, Fachbuchhandlung für (Austria) 32
Wirtschafts- und Kartographie, Verlag für, -Publikationen, Ryborsch (Federal Republic of Germany) 174
Wirtschaftsskripten, Verlag für (Federal Republic of Germany) 174
Wirtschaftsverlag (Federal Republic of Germany) 174
Wisdom Publications (United Kingdom) 477
Wison Verlag GmbH (Federal Republic of Germany) 174
Wissen Verlag GmbH (Federal Republic of Germany) 174
Wissenschaft und Politik, Verlag (Federal Republic of Germany) 174
Wissenschaft, Wirtschaft und Technik, Verlag für, GmbH und Co KG (Federal Republic of Germany) 174
Wissenschaftliche Buchgesellschaft (Federal Republic of Germany) 174
Wissenschaftliche Buchgesellschaft (Federal Republic of Germany) 175
Wissenschaftliche Verlagsgesellschaft mbH (Federal Republic of Germany) 174
Wissenschaftlicher Autoren Verlag (Federal Republic of Germany) 174
Wit, De, Stores NV (Netherland Antilles) 307
Witherby & Co Ltd (United Kingdom) 477
Witherby Ltd, H F & G (United Kingdom) 477
Witman Publishing Co (HK) Ltd (Hong Kong) 189
Witte Raven (Netherlands) 303
Wittig, Friedrich, Verlag (Federal Republic of Germany) 174
Wittwer, Buchhandlung Konrad, GmbH (Federal Republic of Germany) 176
Wittwer, Verlag Konrad, GmbH (Federal Republic of Germany) 174
Witwatersrand University Press (Republic of South Africa) 359
Wizware (Australia) 20
Wkallat Matbouat (Kuwait) 272
Wobbledagger (Australia) 20
Woburn, The, Press (United Kingdom) 477
Wøldike, Forlaget, K/S (Denmark) 84
Wolfe Medical Publications Ltd (United Kingdom) 477
Wolfe Publishing Ltd (United Kingdom) 477
Wolff, Oswald, Books (United Kingdom) 477
Wolfhound Press (Republic of Ireland) 224
Wolfrum, Kunstverlag (Austria) 31
Wolfrum, Kunstverlag (Austria) 32
Wolfsbergdrucke, Verlag der, (J E Wolfensberger AG) (Switzerland) 404
Wolfson Literary Awards for History and Biography (United Kingdom) 490
Wolmar, Valentine de, Prize (France) 121
Wolters Kluwer NV (Netherlands) 303
Wolters Leuven, J B, NV (Belgium) 44
Wolters-Noordhoff BV (Netherlands) 303
Wolters-Noordhoff-Longman BV (Netherlands) 303
Wolters Samsom België NV (Belgium) 44
Wombat (Australia) 20
Women in Publishing (United Kingdom) 422
Women Writers' Association (Japan) 255
Women's, The, Press (Republic of Ireland) 224
Women's, The, Press Book Club (United Kingdom) 481
Women's, The, Press Ltd (United Kingdom) 477
Women's Literary Society (Greece) 185
Women's Literary Society Prizes (Greece) 185
Women's Movement Children's Literature Co-op Ltd (Australia) 20
Won Yit, The, Book Co (Hong Kong) 189
Woodhead-Faulkner (Publishers) Ltd (United Kingdom) 478
Workers' Party of Korea Publishing House (Democratic People's Republic of Korea) 269
World Book, The, Co (Pte) Ltd (Republic of Singapore) 353
World Book, The, Company (Macau) 276
World Book — Childcraft International (United Kingdom) 478
World Book Co (Taiwan) 408
World Books (United Kingdom) 481
World Council of Churches (WCC) (International Organizations) 513
World Health Organization (WHO) (International Organizations) 512
World Homoeopathic Links (India) 212
World Intellectual Property Organization (WIPO) (International Organizations) 510
World International Publishing Ltd (United Kingdom) 478
World Meteorological Organization (WMO) (International Organizations) 512

World Microfilms Publications Ltd (United Kingdom) 478
World of Books, The, Ltd (Federal Republic of Germany) 174
World of Books, The, Prizes (International Literary Prizes) 522
World of Information (United Kingdom) 478
World of Islam Festival Trust (United Kingdom) 478
World of Nature (United Kingdom) 481
World Press, The, Pvt Ltd (India) 212
World Scientific Publishing Co Pte Ltd (Republic of Singapore) 353
World University Library (United Kingdom) 478
Worldwide (United Kingdom) 478
Wort und Welt Verlag (Austria) 31
Woursell, Abraham, Prize (University of Vienna) (International Literary Prizes) 523
Wright, Ellen (France) 116
Wright, John (United Kingdom) 478
Wright Publishing, Gordon, Ltd (United Kingdom) 478
Write A Children's Story Competition (United Kingdom) 490
Writers', The, Group (Malawi) 278
Writer's Club (Zimbabwe) 505
Writers' Guild of Great Britain (United Kingdom) 422
Writers' Publishing House (People's Republic of China) 68
Writers' Union Prize (Romania) 348
Writers Workshop (India) 212
'Wspólna Sprawa', Wydawniczo Oświatowa Spółdzielnia Inwalidów (Poland) 337
Wspólpraca, Wydawnictwo TPPR ', ' (Poland) 337
Wunderlich, Rainer, Verlag Hermann Leins (Federal Republic of Germany) 174
Würdigungspreis für Kinder- und Jugendliteratur (Austria) 33
Württembergische Bibliotheksgesellschaft (Federal Republic of Germany) 177
Württembergische Landesbibliothek (Federal Republic of Germany) 176
Würzburg, Echter, Fränkische Gesellschaftsdruckerei und Verlag GmbH (Federal Republic of Germany) 174
Wyss Verlag AG Bern (Switzerland) 404

Xanadu Publications Ltd (United Kingdom) 478
Xarait Libros SA (Spain) 375
Xenos Verlagsgesellschaft mbH (Federal Republic of Germany) 174
Xinhua Publishing House (People's Republic of China) 68
Xunhasoba (Socialist Republic of Viet Nam) 494

Y Hoc Publishing House (Socialist Republic of Viet Nam) 494
Y M C A-Press (France) 116
Yachdav, United Publishers Co Ltd (Israel) 230
Yad Eliahu Chitov (Israel) 230
Yad Vashem — the Holocaust Martyrs' and Heroes' Remembrance Authority (Israel) 230
Yale University Press London (United Kingdom) 478
Yama-Kei (Publishers) Co Ltd (Japan) 262
Yamami, The, Agency (Japan) 263
Yamamoto, Shugoro, Award (Japan) 265
Yañez, Julio F, Agencia Literaria (Spain) 375
Yarmouk University Bookstore (Jordan) 266
Yarmouk University Library (Jordan) 266
Yasaguna, C V (Indonesia) 218
Yavneh Ltd (Israel) 230
Yediot Ahronoth Enterprises (Book Dept) (Israel) 230
Yee Wen Publishing Co Ltd (Taiwan) 408
Yeshurun (Israel) 230
Yesod (Israel) 230
Yiannakis, Iakovou (Cyprus) 74
Yliopistokirjakauppa Oy (Finland) 94
Yoga Life (India) 212
Yohan Publications Inc (Japan) 262
Yohan (Western Publications Distribution Agency) (Japan) 263
Yokendo Ltd (Japan) 262
Yomiuri Literature Prize (Japan) 265
Yonsei University Library (Republic of Korea) 271
Yonsei University Press (Republic of Korea) 271
York Notes (United Kingdom) 478
'Yorkshire Post' Book of the Year Award (International Literary Prizes) 523
Yoshikawa Prizes (Japan) 266
Young Corgi (United Kingdom) 478
Young Library (United Kingdom) 478

598 INDEX

Young Observer National Children's Poetry Competition (United Kingdom) 490
'Young Observer' Teenage Fiction Prize (International Literary Prizes) 523
Young People's Book Club (Republic of South Africa) 360
Young People's Book Prize (Switzerland) 406
Young Writers' Incentive Awards (New Zealand) 313
Youth Publishing House (People's Republic of China) 68
Yritystieto Oy — Foretagsdata AB (Finland) 94
Yrkeskopplæring I/S (Norway) 322
Yugaku-sha Ltd (Japan) 262
Yuhikaku Publishing Co Ltd (Japan) 262
Yundum College Library (The Gambia) 123
Yunnan Provincial Library (People's Republic of China) 68
'Yuridicheskaya Literatura', Izdatelstvo (Union of Soviet Socialist Republics) 419
Yushodo Co Ltd (Japan) 262
Yuval (Israel) 230
Yvert et Tellier, Editions Philateliques (France) 116

Z A Reprints (German Democratic Republic) 126
Z E B (Zimbabwe) 505
Z O E (Greece) 184
Z P H (Zimbabwe) 505
Z V W 5 (Federal Republic of Germany) 174
Z-Verlag, Genossenschaft (Switzerland) 404
Zabern, Verlag Philipp von (Federal Republic of Germany) 174
Zahar Editores (Brazil) 57
Zahiriah, Al, (National Library) (Syria) 407
Zaïre, Librairie du (Zaire) 502
Zak, S, & Co (Israel) 230
Zalman Shazar, The, Centre (Israel) 230
Založba Obzorja (Yugoslavia) 499
Zambia Catholic Bookshop (Zambia) 503
Zambia Institute of Technology Library (Zambia) 504
Zambia Library Association (Zambia) 504
Zambia Library Service (Zambia) 504
Zambon, Dr (Federal Republic of Germany) 174
Zanibon, G, Edizioni Musicali (Italy) 251
Zanichelli, Nicola, SpA (Italy) 251
Zanzibar Government Archives (Tanzania) 409
Západočeské nakladatelství (Czechoslovakia) 77
Zara, Edizioni (Italy) 251
Zaruski, Mariusz, Literary Prize (Poland) 339
Zavalía, Victor P de, SA (Argentina) 8
Zavod za Izdavanje Udžbenika (Yugoslavia) 499

Zavod za Obrazovanje Kadrova za Administrativne Poslove SR Srbije (Yugoslavia) 499
Zavod za Udžbenike i Nastavna Sredstva (Yugoslavia) 499
Zavod za Udžbenike i Nastavna Sredstva Sap Kosovo (Yugoslavia) 499
Zbinden Druck und Verlag AG (Switzerland) 404
Zebra Books (United Kingdom) 478
Zebra Books for Children (India) 212
Zechner und Hüthig Verlag GmbH (Federal Republic of Germany) 174
Zed Books Ltd (United Kingdom) 478
Zeit, Verlag, im Bild (German Democratic Republic) 126
Zelkowitz (Israel) 230
Zell, Hans (United Kingdom) 478
Zell Publishers, Hans (United Kingdom) 478
Zemizdat, Darzhavno Izdatelstvo (Bulgaria) 61
Zemp, Paul A (Switzerland) 404
Zeno Booksellers & Publishers (United Kingdom) 478
Zentralantiquariat der DDR — Reprintabteilung (ZA Reprints) (German Democratic Republic) 126
Zentralbibliothek der deutschen Klassik (German Democratic Republic) 127
Zentralbibliothek Zürich (Switzerland) 406
Zentralgesellschaft für buchgewerbliche und graphische Betriebe (Austria) 32
Zentralinstitut für Information und Dokumentation der Deutschen Demokratischen Republik (German Democratic Republic) 127
Zentralstelle für maschinelle Dokumentation (Federal Republic of Germany) 177
Zerling, Verlag C (Federal Republic of Germany) 174
Zero Verlag (Federal Republic of Germany) 174
Zester Druck- und Verlagsgesellschaft mbH (Federal Republic of Germany) 174
Zettner, Verlag Andreas, KG (Federal Republic of Germany) 174
Zhejiang tushuguan (People's Republic of China) 68
Zhong-guo guo jia tushuguan (People's Republic of China) 68
Zhong-guo ke xue yuan tushuguan (People's Republic of China) 68
Zhong Hua Book Co (People's Republic of China) 68
Zhongshan Library of Guangdong Province (People's Republic of China) 68
Zibet Prize (Sweden) 391
Ziemsen, A, Verlag (German Democratic Republic) 126
Zig-Zag, Empresa Editora, SA (Chile) 66
Zimbabwe Educational Books (Zimbabwe) 505
Zimbabwe Library Association (Zimbabwe) 505
Zimbabwe Publishing House (Zimbabwe) 505

Zimmer, Verlag Wolfgang (Federal Republic of Germany) 174
Zindermans Förlag (Sweden) 388
Zip Editora Ltda (Brazil) 57
Zjednoczenie Przedsiebiorstw Wydawniczych Naczelny Zarzad Wydawnictw (Poland) 334
Zmora Bitan-Publishing House (Israel) 230
'Znak', Spoleczny Instytut Wydawniczy (Poland) 337
Znanie (Union of Soviet Socialist Republics) 419
'Znanje', Nakladni Zavod (Yugoslavia) 499
Zodiaque (France) 116
Zodiaque, La Pierre-qui-Vire (Switzerland) 404
Zoé, Editions (Switzerland) 404
Zolindakis, Har (Greece) 184
Zollikofer, Buchverlag, AG (Switzerland) 404
Zomba Books (United Kingdom) 478
Zomer en Keuning Boeken BV (Netherlands) 303
Zorn, Anders and Emma, Prize (Sweden) 391
Zoshindo Juken-Kenkyusha (Japan) 262
Zrinyi Katonai Kiadó (Hungary) 191
Zrzeszenie Ksiegarstwa (Poland) 338
Zsolnay, Paul, Verlag GmbH (Austria) 31
Zsolnay, Paul, Verlag GmbH (Federal Republic of Germany) 174
Zuckmayer, Carl, Gesellschaft eV (Federal Republic of Germany) 178
Zuckmayer, Carl, Medal (Federal Republic of Germany) 179
Zuid Boekprodukties BV (Netherlands) 304
Zuidnederlandse Uitgeverij NV (Belgium) 44
Zumstein & Cie (Switzerland) 405
Zurich, City of, Literary Prize (Switzerland) 406
Zväz slovenských knihovníkov a informatikov (Czechoslovakia) 78
Zväz slovenských spisovateľov (Czechoslovakia) 75
Zväz slovenských spisovateľov Prize (Czechoslovakia) 79
Zveza bibliotekarskih društev Slovenije (Yugoslavia) 501
Zveza društev bibliotekarjev Jugoslavije (Slovene) (Yugoslavia) 501
Zwan Publishing Ltd (United Kingdom) 478
Zwarte Beertjes (Netherlands) 304
Zweipunkt Verlag KG (Federal Republic of Germany) 174
Zwemmer, A, Ltd (United Kingdom) 479
Zwiazek Literatów Poliskich (Poland) 334
Zwijsen, Uitgeverij, BV (Netherlands) 304
Zwimpfer, Adolf (Switzerland) 405
'Zycie Literackie' Prize (Poland) 339
Zytglogge Verlag (Switzerland) 405

1. Ref.
2. Stacks

JUN 10 1988